W9-BXX-609

Cruden's Compact Concordance

CLASSIC COMPACT SERIES

Cruden's Compact Concordance
Nave's Compact Topical Bible
Zondervan's Compact Bible Dictionary

Cruden's Compact Concordance

GRAND RAPIDS, MICHIGAN 49530

ZONDERVAN™

CRUDEN'S COMPACT CONCORDANCE

To make the book more valuable to Bible students, bold face key words appear at the top of each page of the Concordance, making it easy to find key word desired.

ISBN 0-310-48971-7

Requests for information should be addressed to:

Zondervan, *Grand Rapids, Michigan 49530*

Printed in the United States of America

01 02 03 04 05 /DC/ 10 9 8 7 6 5 4

Cruden's
Compact
Concordance

CRUDEN'S COMPACT CONCORDANCE

Based on the Famous Work of Alexander Cruden

as Edited by John Eadie

A

AARON.
Luke 1:5 wife of daughters of A.
Acts 7:40 saying to A. make gods
Heb. 5:4 called of God, as was A.
7:11 not called after order of A.
9:4 A's rod that budded

AARONITES. 1 *Chr.*12:27; 27:17
ABADDON. *Rev.* 9:11
ABAGTHA. *Est.* 1:10
ABANA. 2 *K.* 5:12

ABASE.
Job 40:11 Behold proud, and *a.*
Is. 31:4 lion will not *a.* himself
Eze. 21:26 and *a.* him that is high
Dan. 4:37 in pride is able to *a.*

ABASED.
Mat. 23:12 exalt, shall be *a.*
Luke 14:11; 18:14
Phil. 4:12 I know how to be *a.*

ABASING.
2 *Cor.* 11:7 offence in *a.* myself

ABBA.
Mark 14:36 *a.* Father, all things
Rom. 8:15 we cry, *a.* Father
Gal. 4:6 crying *a.* Father

ABDA. 1 *K.* 4:6 ; *Neh.* 11:17
ABDI. 2 *Chr.* 29:12 ; *Ezr.* 10:26
ABDIEL. 1 *Chr.* 5:15
ABDON. *Jud.* 12:13 ; 2 *Chr.* 34:20
ABED-NEGO. *Dan.*1:7;2:49; 3:23

ABEL, person, *or* place.
1 *Sam.* 6:18 stone of A. they set
2 *Sam.* 20:18 ask counsel at A.
Mat. 23:35 blood of A. *Luke* 11:51
Heb. 11:4 by faith A. offered

12:24 things than blood of A.
ABEL-BETH-MAACHAH. 1 *K.* 15:20 ; 2 *K.* 15:29
ABEL-MAIM. 2 *Chr.* 16:4
ABEL-MEHOLAH. *Jud.* 7:22 ; 1 *K.* 19:16
ABEL-MIZRAIM. *Gen.* 50:11

ABHOR.
Lev. 26:11 soul shall not *a.* you
15 your soul *a.* my judgments
30 my soul shall *a.* you
44 nor will I *a.* them
Deut. 7:26 shalt utterly *a.* it
23:7 not *a.* Edomite, Egyptian
1 *Sam.* 27:12 his people to *a.* him
Job 9:31 clothes shall *a.* me
30:10 they *a.* me, they flee far
42:6 I *a.* myself and repent in
Ps. 5:6 Lord will *a.* bloody man
119:163 I hate and *a.* lying
Prov. 24:24 nations shall *a.* him
Jer. 14:21 do not *a.* us
Amos 5:10 they *a.* him
6:8 I *a.* the excellency of Jacob
Mic. 3:9 ye that *a.* judgment
Rom. 12:9 *a.* that which is evil

ABHORRED.
Ex. 5:21 made savor to be *a.*
Lev. 20:23 therefore I *a.* them
26:43 their soul *a.* my statutes
Deut. 32:19 saw it, he *a.* them
1 *Sam.* 2:17 men *a.* the offering
2 *Sam.* 16:21 art *a.* of thy father
Job 19:19 inward friends *a.* me
Ps. 22:24 nor *a.* affliction
78:59 he greatly *a.* Israel
89:38 thou hast cast off and *a.*
106:40 that he *a.* inherit.
Prov. 22:14 *a.* of the Lord
Lam. 2:7 hath *a.* his sanctuary
Ezek. 16:25 beauty to *a.* me
Zec. 11:8 their soul also *a.* me

ABHORREST.
Is. 7:16 thou *a.* shall be forsa.
Rom. 2:22 thou that *a.* idols

ABHORRETH.
Job 33:20 so life *a.* bread
Ps. 10:3 whom the Lord *a.*
36:4 mischief on bed, he *a.* not
107:18 their soul *a.* meat
Is. 49:7 to him whom nation *a.*

ABHORRING.
Is. 66:24 an *a.* to all flesh

ABIAH.
1 *Sam.* 8:2 sec. son was A.
1 *Chr.* 2:24 A. Hezron's wife
7:8 son of Becher, A.
3:10 son of R. was A. *Mat.* 1:7

ABI-ALBON. 2 *Sam.* 23:31

ABIATHAR.
1 *Sam.* 22:20 A. escaped and fled
23:6 when A. son of Ahimelech
9 David said to A. bring, 30:7
2 *Sam.* 8:17 Zadok and A. 20:25 ; 1 *K.* 4:4
1 *K.* 2:22 king. for him and A.
27 so Solomon thrust out A.
Mark 2:26 in days of A.

ABIB.
Ex. 13:4 out in A. 34:18
23:15 unleav. bread in **month** A. 34:18 ; *Deut.* 16:1

ABIDAN.
Num. 1:11 A. son of Gid. 2:22
7:60 A. of Benjamin offered, 65

ABIDE.
Gen. 22:5 *a.* you here with
Ex. 16:29 *a.* every man in
Lev. 8:35 *a.* at door of tabernacle
1 *Sam.* 5:7 ark shall not *a.* with
22:23 *a.* thou with me, fear not
2 *Sam.* 16:18 with him will I *a.*
Job 24:13 nor *a.* in paths of light

Ps. 15:1 shall *a.* in tabernacle?
  61:4 I will *a.* in thy tabernacle

  7 he shall *a.* before God
Ps. 91:1 shall *a.* under the shadow
Prov. 7:11 her feet *a.* not in
  19:23 shall *a.* satisfied
Ec. 8:15 shall *a.* of his labor
Jer. 10:10 not *a.* his indigna.
  49:18 no man *a.* there, 33 ; 50:40
Joel 2:11 terrible, who can *a.* it ?
Mic. 5:4 they shall *a.* for now
Nah. 1:6 can *a.* in his anger ?
Mal. 3:2 whom may *a.* day of
Mat. 10:11 there *a. Mark* 6:10;
   Luke 9:4
Luke 19:5 I must *a.* at thy house
  24:29 *a.* with us
John 12:46 not *a.* in darkness
  14:16 Comforter that he may *a.*
  15:4 *a.* in me, except ye *a.* 7
  6 if a man *a.* not in me
  10 *a.* in my love, *a.* in his love
Acts 27:31 these *a.* in ship
1 *Cor.* 3:14 if any man's work *a.*
  7:8 good if they *a.* even as I
  20 let every man *a.* in same
  40 happier if she so *a.*
Phil. 1:24 to *a.* in the flesh
1 *John* 2:24 let that *a.* in you
  27 ye shall *a.* ; 28 children *a.*

2 *Sam.* 16:3 he *a.* at Jerus.
Ps. 49:12 man in honor, *a.* not
  55:19 even he that *a.* of old
  119:90 earth, and it *a.*
  125:1 Zion, which *a.* ever
Prov. 15:31 *a.* among the wise
Ec. 1:4 the earth *a.* for ever
John 3.36 wrath of God *a* on
  8:35 servant *a.* not, son *a.*
  12:34 heard that Christ *a.*
  15:5 he that *a.* in me bringeth
1 *Cor.* 13:13 now *a.* faith, hope
2 *Tim.* 2:13 yet he *a.* faithful
Heb. 7:3 Melchizedek *a.* a priest
1 *Pet.* 1:23 word of God which *a.*
1 *John* 2:6 he *a.* in him ought
  10 loveth his brother *a.* in
  14 the word of God *a.* in you
  17 doeth will of God *a.* for ever
  27 the anointing *a.* in you
  3:6 whosoever *a.* in him
  3:14 loveth not brother *a.* in
  24 we know that he *a.* in us
2 *John* 9 whoso *a.* not in the

ABIDING.
1 *Sam.* 26:19 from *a.* in inherit.
1 *Chr.* 29:15 here is done *a.*
Luke 2:8 shepherds *a.* in the field
John 5:38 his word *a.* in you
1 *John* 3:15 mur. hath eter. life *a.*

ABIEZER.
Jos. 17:2 for children of A.
Jud. 6:34 and A. was gathered
  8:2 better than the vintage of A.
2 *Sam.* 23:27 A. one of David's
ABI-EZRITE. *Jud.* 6:11

ABIGAIL.
1 *Sam.* 25:3 Nabal's wife A.
  27:3 dwelt at Gath with Ahi
  and A. 30:5 ; 2 *Sam.* 2:2
1 *Chr.* 2:16 sists. Zeruiah and A.

ABIHAIL.
2 *Chr.* 11:18 Rehoboam took A.
Est. 2:15 daughter of A. 9:29

ABIHU.
Ex. 6:23 Aaron's sons Nadab and
  A. 28:1 ; *Lev.* 10:1 ; *Num.* 3:2;
  26:60 ; 1 *Chr.* 6:3 ; 24:1
  24:1 come up A. ; 9 A. went up
Num. 3:4 A. died bef. Lord, 26:61

ABIJAH, ABIJAM.
1 *K.* 14:1 A. son of Jero.
  31 A. son of Reho. 15:1, 7

1 *Chr.* 24:10 eighth lot came to A.
2 *Chr.* 29:1 mother's name A.

ABILITY.
Ezr. 2:69 gave after their *a.*
Neh. 5:8 after our *a.* redeemed
Dan. 1:4 had *a.* to stand in pal.
Mat. 25:15 each accord. to his *a.*
Acts 11:29 according to *a.* to send
1 *Pet.* 4:11 as of the *a.* God giv.

ABIMELECH.
Gen. 20:2 A. king of Gerar sent
  21:22 A. and Phichol spake
  26:1 Isaac went unto A.
  16 A. said unto Isaac, go
Jud. 8:31 Gideon's con. bare A.
2 *Sam.* 11:21 smote A. son of Jer.
1 *Chr.* 18:16 Zadok and A.

ABINADAB.
1 *Sam.* 7:1 into the house of A.
  16:8 Jesse called A. made him
2 *Sam.* 6:3 out of house of A.
   1 *Chr.* 13:7
1 *K.* 4:11 A. had Sol. daughter
ABINOAM. *See* BARAK.

ABIRAM.
Num. 16:1 Dathan and A. 26:9
  · 12 sent to call Dath. and A.
Deut. 11:6 did to Dathan and A.
1 *K.* 16:34 laid founda. in A.
Ps. 106:17 company of A.

ABISHAG. 1 *K.* 1:15 ; 2:22

ABISHAI.
1 *Sam.* 26:6 A. said, I will go
2 *Sam.* 2:18 three sons, Joab, A.
  and Asahel, 1 *Chr.* 2:16
  23:18 A. was chief, 1 *Chr.* 11:20
1 *Chr.* 18:12 A. slew of Edomites
ABIUD. *Mat.* 1:13

ADJECTS.
Ps. 35:15 the *a.* gathered

ABLE.
Ex. 18:21 provide *a.* men
Num. 1:3 *a.* to go to war, 26:2
  13:30 well *a.* to overcome it
Deut. 16:17 man give as he is *a.*

Jos. 23:9 man been *a.* to stand
1 *Sam.* 6:20 who *a.* to stand
1 *K.* 3:9 who is *a.* to judge
2 *Chr* 2:6 who is *a.* to build
  20:6 none is *a.* to withstand thee
  25:9 Lord is *a.* to give
Job 41:10 who *a.* to stand
Prov. 27:4 who *a.* to stand bef.
Dan. 3:17 our God is *a.* to deliv.
  6:20 God is *a.* to deliver from
Mat. 3:9 God is *a.* of these stones
  to raise up, *Luke* 3:8
  9:28 believe ye I am *a.* to do
  19:12 he that is *a.* to receive it
  20:22 are ye *a.* to drink
  22:46 no man was *a.* to answer
Mark 4:33 as they were *a.* to hear
John 10:29 no man is *a.* to pluck
Acts 15:10 yoke fathers nor we *a.*
  20:32 word of grace, *a.* to build
Rom. 4:21 he was *a.* to perform
  11:23 for God is *a.* to graff them
  14:4 God is *a.* to make him
  15:14 ye are *a.* also to admonish
1 *Cor.* 3:2 ye were not *a.* nor yet
  10:13 above that ye are *a.*
2 *Cor.* 3:6 made us *a.* ministers of
  9:8 God is *a.* to make all grace
Eph. 3:20 that is *a.* to do
Phil. 3:21 he is *a.* to subdue all
2 *Tim.* 1:12 he is *a.* to keep that I
  3:7 nevera.to come to the know.
  15 scriptures *a.* to make wise.
Heb. 2:18 he is *a.* to succor them
  5:7 to him that was *a.* to save
  7:25 is *a.* to save to uttermost
  11:19 that God was *a.* to raise
Jam. 1:21 which is *a.* to save
  3:2 *a.* to bridle the whole body

  4:12 one lawgiver *a.* to save and
Jude 24 to him that is *a.* to keep
Rev. 5:3 no man was *a.* to open
  13:4 who is *a.* to make war with
  15:18 no man was *a.* to enter

Be ABLE.
Jos. 1:5 any man be *a.* to stand
Deut. 7:24 no man *be a.* to, 11:25
2 *Chr.* 32:14 should *be a.* to profit
Is. 47:12 thou shalt *be a.* to profit
Eze. 33:12 righteous *be a.* to live
Luke 14:31 he *be a.* with 10,000
Rom. 8:39 *be a.* to separate us
1 *Cor.* 10:13 may *be a.* to bear
Eph. 3:18 *be a.* to comprehend
  6:11 that ye may *be a.* to stand
  16 ye shall *be a.* to quench
2 *Tim.* 3:2 who shall *be a.* to t.
Tit. 1:9 may *be a.* by sound
2 *Pet.* 1:15 *be a.* after my decease
Rev. 6:17 who shall *be a.* to stand

Not be ABLE.
2 *K.* 18:29 *n. be a.* to de. *Is.* 36:14
Ps. 36:12 shall *not be a.* to rise
Ec. 8:17 yet *not be a.* to find it
Is. 47:11 shall *not be a.* to put
Jer. 11:11 to escape ; 49:10 to hide
Ezek. 7:19 gold shall *not be a.* to
Luke 13:24 seek, *n. be a.* ; 21:15 to

Not ABLE.
Num. 13:31 we be *not a.* to go up
  14:16 Lord was *n. a. Deut.* 9:28
Ezr. 10:13 we are *not a.* to stand
Neh. 4:10 we are *not a.* to build
Ps. 18:38 wounded *not a.* to rise
  21:11 are *not a.* to perform
  40:12 I am *not a.* to look up
Amos 7:10 land is *not a.* to bear
Luke 12:26 *not a.* to do that is l.
  14:29 laid found. and *not a.* to
John 21:6 *not a.* to draw for the f.
Acts 6:10 *not a.* to resist the w.

ABNER.
1 *Sam.* 14:51 Ner father of A.
  17:55 said to A. whose son ?
  26:7 but A. and the people lay
  14 cried answer thou not A.
2 *Sam.* 2:14 A. said, let your men
  3:25 A. the s. of Ner. 30,32,33,37
  4:1 Saul's son heard A. was d.
  12 Ish-bosheth in A. sepul.
1 *K.* 2:5 what Joab did to A.
1 *Chr.* 26:28 all that A. dedicated
  27:21 Jaasiel son of A. rul. of B.

ABOARD.
Acts 21:2 went *a.* and set forth

ABODE, Substantive.
2 *K.* 19:27 I know thy *a. Is.* 37:28
John 14:23 come and make our *a.*

ABODE, Verb.
Gen. 29:14 Jacob *a.* with him
  49:24 but his bow *a.* in strength
Ex. 24:16 glory of God *a.* on Si.
Num. 9:17 cloud *a.* 18
  20 they *a.* in their tents, 22
  11:35 the people *a.* at Hazeroth
Num. 20:1 the p. *a. Jud.* 11:17
  22:8 princes of Moab, *a.* with B.
Deut. 1:46 so ye *a.* in Kadesh
  3:29 we *a.* in the valley
  9:9 I *a.* in the mount
Jos. 5:8 they *a.* in their places
  8:9 they *a.* between Bethel
Jud. 5:17 Gilead *a.* beyond Jor.
  Asher *a.* in his breaches
  19:4 Levite *a.* with him 3 days
  20:47 and *a.* in the rock Rim.
1 *Sam.* 1:23 the woman *a.* and g.
  7:2 while the ark *a.* in Kirjath
  13:16 Saul and Jona. *a.* in Gib.
  22:6 Saul *a.* ; 23:14,Dav.*a.*25;26:3
  23:18 *a.* in wood; 2 *Sam.*1:1 Zik.
2 *Sam.* 14:12 Uriah *a.* in Jerusa.
  15:8 vowed while I *a.* at
1 *K.* 17:19 *a.* loft where he *a.*

Jer. 38:28 Jeremiah *a.* in the ct.
Mat. 17:22 while they *a.* in Gal.
Luke 1:56 Mary *a.* with her a.
  8:27 nor *a.* in any house, but
John 1:32 Spirit and it *a.* on him
  39 they came and *a.* with him
  7:9 he *a.* in Galilee
  8:44 murderer and *a.* not in t.
  11:6 he *a.* two days still
Acts 1:13 room where *a.* Peter
  14:3 long time *a.* they speaking
  18:3 Paul *a.* with them and w.
  21:7 came and *a.* with brethren
  8 house of Philip and *a.* with
Gal. 1:18 and *a.* with Peter

ABODE there, *or* **there ABODE.**
Jud. 21:2 people *a. there* till e.
Ezr. 8:15 *there a.* we in tents
John 4:40 Jesus *a. there* two d.
  10:40 John bapt. and *there a.*
Acts 14:28 *there* they *a.* long t.
  17:14 Silas and Tim. *a. there*

ABODEST.
Jud. 5:16 why *a.* among the sh.

ABOLISH.
Is. 2:18 idols he shall utterly *a.*

ABOLISHED.
Is. 51:6 right shall not be *a.*
Ezek. 6:6 your works may be *a.*
2 *Cor.* 3:13 that which is *a.*
Eph. 2:15 having *a.* in his flesh
2 *Tim.* 1:10 C. who hath *a.* death

ABOMINABLE.
Lev. 7:21 touch any *a.* thing
  11:43 make yourselves *a.* with
  18:30 commit not these *a.* cus.
  19:7 on the third day, it is *a.*
  20:25 make souls *a.* by beast
Deut. 14:3 eat any *a.* thing
1 *Chr.* 21:6 king's word was *a.* to
2 *Chr.* 15:8 Asa put away *a.* idols
Job. 15:16 much more *a.* is man
Ps. 14:1 have done *a.* works
  53:1 have done *a.* iniquity
Is. 14:19 like an *a.* branch
  65:4 broth of *a.* things is in
Jer. 16:18 carcasses of their *a.*
  44:4 this *a.* thing I hate
Ezek. 4:14 came *a.* flesh into my
  8:10 and behold *a.* beasts
  16:52 sins committed more *a.*
Mic. 6:10 scant measure that is *a.*
Nah. 3:6 I will cast *a.* filth on
Tit. 1:16 deny him being *a.*
1 *Pet.* 4:3 walked in *a.* idolatries
Rev. 21:8 unbelieving and the *a.*

ABOMINABLY.
1 *K.* 21:26 Ahab did very *a.*

ABOMINATION.
Gen. 43:32 is an *a.* to Egyptians
  46:34 shepherds is *a.* to Egyp.
Ex. 8:26 sacrifice the *a.* of Egyp.
Lev. 7:18 be an *a.* to you, 12, 20, 23
  11:10 be an *a.* to you, 12, 20, 23
  18:22 womankind it is *a.* 20:13
Deut. 7:25 it is *a.* to the Ld. 17:1
  26 bring an *a.* into thy house
  12:31 every *a.* they have done
  13:14 such *a.* is wrought, 17:4
  18:12 that do these are *a.* 22:5
  23:18 these are an *a.* to God
  24:4 is an *a.* before the Lord
  25:16 that do unright. are *a.*
  27:15 that maketh *a.* to Lord
1 *K.* 11:5 Milcom the *a.* of Am.
  7 Chemosh the *a.* of Moab
2 *K.* 23:13 Ashtoreth *a.* of Zid.
Ps. 88:8 thou hast made me an *a.*
Prov. 3:32 froward is an *a.*
  6:16 seven things are an *a.*
  8:17 wickedness is an *a.*
  11:1 a false balance is *a.* to Lord
  20 froward heart are *a.*
  12:22 lying lips are *a.* to

  13:19 *a.* to fools to depart
Prov. 15:8 sacrifi. of w. is *a.* 21:27
  9 of the wicked is an *a.*
  26 of wicked are *a.* to L.
  16:5 one proud in heart is *a.*
  12 *a.* to kings to commit
  17:15 both are an *a.* to the Lord
  20:10 both of them are alike *a.*
  23 weights are an *a.* to Lord
  24:9 the scorner is an *a.* to men
  28:9 even his prayer shall be *a.*
  29:27 unjust man is *a.* to just,
  upright in the way *a.* to
Is. 1:13 incense is an *a.* to me
  41:24 an *a.* is he that
  44:19 residue thereof an *a. ?*
  66:17 eating swine's flesh an *a.*
Jer. 2:7 my heritage an *a.*
  6:15 they committed *a.* 8:12
  32:35 that they should do this *a.*
Ezek. 16:50 and committed *a.*
  18:12 to idols and committed *a.*
  22:11 *a.* with neighbor's wife
  33:26 and ye work *a.*
Dan. 11:31 *a.* that maketh
  12:11 *a.* that maketh desolate
Mal. 2:11 an *a.* is committed
Mat. 24:15 *a.* of desol. *Mar.* 13:14
Luke 16:15 is *a.* with God
Rev. 21:27 enter that worketh *a.*

ABOMINATIONS.
Deut. 18:9 not learn to do after *a.*
  32:16 with *a.* provoked they him
1 *K.* 14:24 did all *a.* of nations
2 *K.* 21:2 *a.* of heathen, 2 *Chr.*
  33:2.
  23:24 *a.* Jos. put away, 2 *Chr.*
  34:2
2 *Chr.* 36:8 Jehoiakim and his *a.*
  14 transgressed after all *a.*
Prov. 26:25 seven *a.* in his heart
Jer. 44:22 L. could not bear for *a.*
Ezek. 6:11 alas for all the evil *a.*
  8:6 shalt see greater *a.* 13, 15
  9 wicked *a.* that they do here
  17 light thing to commit *a.*
  9:4 that sigh and cry for the *a.*
  11:18 take away all *a.* thereof
  14:6 your faces from your *a.*
  16:2 Jerusa. to know her *a.*
  18:24 when righteous doth *a.*
  20:4 the *a.* of their fathers
  7 cast ye away *a.* of eyes
  22:2 show her all her *a.*
  36:31 loathe yourselves for *a.*
  44:6 O Israel, let it suffice of *a.*
Dan. 9:27 overspreading of *a.*
Zec. 9:7 *a.* from between
Rev. 17:4 golden cup full of *a.*
  5 harlots and *a.* of earth

Their ABOMINATIONS.
Deut. 20:18 not after *t. a.*
Ezr. 9:11 *t. a.* which have
Is. 66:3 delighteth in *their a.*
Jer. 7:30 set *t. a.* in the, 32:34
Ezek. 11:21 walketh after *t. a.*
  12:16 declare all *t. a.*
  16:47 done after *t. a.*
  23:36 declare to them *t. a.*
  33:29 desolate because of *t. a.*
  43:8 holy name by *t. a.*
  44:13 bear their shame and *t. a.*
Hos. 9:10 *t. a.* were as they loved

These ABOMINATIONS.
Lev. 18:26 not com. any of *t. a.*
Deut. 18:12 bec. of *t. a.* L. doth
2 *K.* 21:11 hath done *t. a.*
Ezr. 9:14 with people of *t. a.*
Jer. 7:10 to do all *these a.*
Ezek. 18:13 done *t. a.* shall

Thine ABOMINATIONS.
Jer. 4:1 wilt put away *thine a.*
  13:27 I have seen *t. a.* on hills
Ezek. 5:9 not because of *t. a.*
  11 my sanctuary with *t. a.*

  7:3 recompense all *t. a.* 4, 8, 9
  16:36 the idols of *thine a.*
  43 lewdness above all *t. a.*
  51 multiplied *t. a.* more
  58 hast borne *t. a.* saith

ABOVE.
Deut. 28:13 shalt be *a.* only
Jos. 3:13 that came from *a.* 16
2 *Sam.* 22:17 sent from *a. Ps.* 18:16
John 8:23 I am from *a.* ye of
  19:11 were given from *a.*
Col. 3:1 seek things which are *a.*
  2 set your affection on things *a.*

ABOVE all.
John 3:31 from heaven is *a. all*
Eph. 3:20 *a. all* that we ask
  4:6 one God *a. all*
Col. 3:14 *a. all* these put on
2 *Thes.* 2:4 exalteth *a. all* called
Jam. 5:12 *a. all* things, swear not
1 *Pet.* 4:8 *a. all* things have ch.

ABOVE *all* GODS. *See* GODS.
ABOVE *heaven.* *See* HEAVEN.
Stood ABOVE. *See* STOOD.

ABOUND.
Prov. 28:20 faithful *a.* with
Mat. 24:12 iniquity shall *a.*
Rom. 5:20 the offence might *a.*
  6:1 in sin, that grace may *a. ?*
  15:13 that ye may *a.* in hope
2 *Cor.* 1:5 as sufferings *a.* so
  8:7 as ye *a.* in every thing, see
  9:8 make all grace *a.* to you
Phil. 1:9 love may *a.* more
  4:12 I know how to *a.* both to *a.*
  17 may *a.* to your account
  18 I have all and *a.* I am full
1 *Thes.* 3:12 make you to *a.* in love
  4:1 would *a.* more and more
2 *Pet.* 1:8 things be in you *a.* and

ABOUNDED, ETH, ING.
Prov. 8:24 no fount. *a.* with
  29:22 furious man *a.* in
Rom. 3:7 of God hath more *a.*
  5:15 grace by J. C. hath *a.* to
  20 sin *a.* grace did more *a.*
1 *Cor.* 15:58 always *a.* in the
2 *Cor.* 8:2 poverty *a.* to riches
Eph. 1:8 he hath *a.* toward
Col. 2:7 *a.* therein with thanksg.
2 *Thes.* 1:3 charity to ea. other *a.*

ABOUT.
John 7:19 go yet *a.* to kill me ?
See GONE, ROUND, STOOD, TIME,
  WENT.

ABRAHAM *with father.*
Gen. 26:3 the oath to A. thy *f*
  24 God of A. thy *f.* 28:13
  32:9 G. of *f.* A. and God of
Jos. 24:3 took *f.* A. from
Is. 51:2 look to A. your *f.*
Mat. 3:9 A. to our *f., Luke* 3:8
Luke 1:73 he sware to *f.* A.
  16:24 *f.* A. have mercy on me
  30 nay, *f.* A. but if one from
John 8:39 A. is our *f.*
  53 greater than *f.* A. ?
  56 *f.* A. rejoiced to see
Acts 7:2 appeared to *f.* A.
Rom. 4:1 that A. our *f.* hath
  12 in the steps of faith of *f.* A.
  16 of A. who is *f.* of us all
Jam. 2:21 A. our *f.* justified **by**

ABRAHAM *joined with* **seed.**
2 *Chr.* 20:7 gavest it to *seed* of A.
Ps. 105:6 O ye *s.* of A. his
Is. 41:8 thou Israel, the *s.* of A.
Jer. 33:26 rulers over *s.* of A.
Luke 1:55 spake to A. and his *s.*
John 8:33 A.'s *s.* never in bond.
  37 A. *s.* but ye seek to kill me
Rom. 4:13 promise not to A. or *s.*
  9:7 they are the *seed* of A.
  11:1 of the *s.* of A. 2. *Cor.* 11:22
Gal. 3:16 to A. and *s.* prom.

3:29 then A. s. and heirs
Heb. 2:16 on him the s. of A.

ABROAD.

Ex. 12:46 aught of flesh a.
Lev. 18:9 born at home or a.
Jud. 12:9 daughters from a.
2 K. 4:3 borrow thee vessels a.
2 Chr. 31:5 as com. came a.
Job 15:23 wandereth a. for bread
Ps. 41:6 he goeth a. telleth it
Prov. 5:16 be dispersed a.
Is. 44:24 spreadeth a. the earth
Jer. 6:11 on children a.
Lam. 1:20 a. the sword
Mark 1:45 blaze a. the matter
4:22 it should come a.
Luke 1:65 sayings were noised a.
2:17 a. the saying about
Acts 2:6 noised a. the multitude
Rom. 5:5 love of God shed a. in
16:19 your obedience is come a.
See CAST, SPREAD, STAND, SCAT-
TER, WENT.

ABSENCE.

Luke 22:6 betray him in a. of
Phil. 2:12 much more in my a.

ABSENT.

Gen. 31:49 we are a. one from
1 Cor 5:3 verily as a. in body
2 Cor. 5:6 at home in body are a.
8 willing to be a. from body
9 present or a. accepted
10:1 being a. am bold
11 by letters when a. such
13:2 being a. now I write, 10
Phil. 1:27 I come, or else a.
Col. 2:5 I be a. in the flesh

ABSTAIN.

Acts 15:20 a. from pollutions
29 that ye a. from meats
1 Thes. 4:3 a. from fornication
1 Thes. 5:22 a. from all appear.
1 Tim. 4:3 com. to a. from meats
1 Pet. 2:11 a. from fleshly lusts

ABSTINENCE.

Acts 27:21 after long a. Paul stood

ABUNDANCE.

Deut. 33:19 suck of the a. of the
1 Sam. 1:16 out of a. of my
1 K. 18:41 sound of a. of rain
2 Chr. 9:9 spices great a.
Job 22:11 a. waters cover, 38:34
Ps. 72:7 shall be a. of peace
Ec. 5:10 that loveth a. with
12 a. of the rich not suffer
Is. 15:7 the a. they have gotten
47:9 a. of thy enchantments
60:5 the a. of the sea
66:11 with the a. of her glory
Jer. 33:6 reveal a. of peace
Ezek. 16:49 a. of idleness was
Zec. 14:14 apparel in great a.
Mat. 12:34 a. of heart, Luke 6:45
13:12 have more a. 25:29
Mark 12:44 of their a. Luke 21:4
Rom. 5:17 receive a. of grace
2 Cor. 8:2 a. of their joy
14 your a. a supply, their a.
12:7 a. of the revelations
Rev. 18.3 thro' a. of delicacies

In ABUNDANCE.

Ps. 37:11 delight in a. of peace
52:7 in the a. of his riches
Luke 12:15 consisteth not in a.
2 Cor. 8:20 blame us in this a.

ABUNDANT.

Ex. 34:6 God a. in goodness
Is. 56:12 this day and more a.
1 Cor. 12:23 bestow more a. hon.
24 more a. honor to that part
2 Cor. 4:15 a. grace might
7:15 inward affection is more a.
9:12 the administration is a.
11:23 labors more a. in stripes
Phil. 1:26 rejoicing be more a.

---

1 Tim. 1:14 was exceeding a.
1 Pet. 1:3 his a. mercy

ABUNDANTLY.

Gen. 1:20 waters bring forth a. 21
8:17 that they may breed a.
9:7 multiply, bring forth a.
Ex. 1:7 Israel increased a.
Num. 20:11 water came out a.
1 Chr. 22:5 so David prepared a.
8 thou hast shed blood a.
Job 12:6 whose hand G. bring a.
36:28 distil upon man a.
Ps. 36:8 a. satisfied with fatness
65:10 thou waterest the ridges a.
132:15 I will a. bless her
145:7 shall a. utter the memory
Cant. 5:1 yea drink a. O beloved
Is. 15:3 shall howl, weeping a.
35:2 blossom a. and rejoice
55:7 for he will a. pardon
John 10:10 have life more a.
1 Cor. 15:10 I labored more a.
2 Cor. 1:12 and more a. to you
2:4 love I have more a. to you
10:15 according to our rule a.
12:15 though the more a. I love
Eph. 3:20 able to do exceeding a.
1 Thes. 2:17 more a. to see your
Tit. 3:6 he shed a. through
Heb. 6:17 God willing more a. to
2 Pet. 1:11 be ministered a.

ABUSE, ED.

Jud. 19:25 a. her all the night
1 Sam. 31:4 lest uncircum. a. me
1 Chr. 10:4
1 Cor. 9:18 I a. not my power

ABUSERS, ING.

1 Cor. 6:9 nor a. of themselves
71:31 use this world as not a. it

ACCEPT.

Deut. 33:11 and a. the work
1 Sam. 26:19 him a. an offering
2 Sam. 24:23 the L. thy God a.
Job. 13:8 will ye a. his person ?
10 if ye do secretly a. persons
32:21 not a. any man's per.
42:8 shall pray, him will I a.
Ps. 20:3 and a. thy burnt-sac.
82:2 a. the persons of the wick.
119:108 a. freewill-offerings
Prov. 18:5 not good to a. the
Jer. 14:10 Lord doth not a. them
12 not a. them, Amos 5:22
Ezek. 20:40 there will I a. them
41 will a. you with sweet savor
43:27 and I will a. you, saith L.
Mal. 1:8 pleased, or a. thy
10 nor will I a. an offering
13 should I a. this of your h.?
Acts 24:3 we a. it always and

ACCEPTABLE.

Deut. 33:24 be a. to his brethren
Ps. 19:14 med. of my heart be a.
69:13 my prayer is in an a. time
Prov. 10:32 know what is a.
21:3 to do justice is more a.
Ec. 12:10 sought a. words
Is. 49:8 in an a time have I
58:5 call this an a. day
61:2 to proclaim the a. yr. of L.
Jer. 6:20 burnt-offerings are n. a.
Dan. 4:27 let my counsel be a.
Luke 4:19 to preach the a. year
Rom. 12:1 holy, a. to God
2 that good and a. will of God
14:18 is a. to God and approved
15:16 of Gentiles might be a.
Eph. 5:10 proving what is a unto
Phil. 4:18 sac. a. well-pleasing
1 Tim. 2:3 a. in the sight of God
5:4 good and a. before God
1 Pet. 2:5 sacrifices a. to God
20 this is a. with God

ACCEPTABLY.

Heb. 12:28 we may serve God a.

ACCEPTANCE.

Is. 60:7 with a. on mine altar

ACCEPTATION.

1 Tim. 1:15 worthy of all a. 4:9

ACCEPTED.

Gen. 4:7 shalt thou not be a.
19:21 I have a. thee concerning
Ex. 28:38 may be a. before
Lev. 1:4 offering shall be a. 22:27
7:18 not be a. 19:7 ; 22:23, 25
10:19 should it have been a. in
22:21 offering perfect, to be a.
1 Sam. 18:5 he was a. in the sight
25:35 see I have a. thy person
Est. 10:3 a. of his brethren
Job 42:9 the Lord also a. Job
Is. 56:7 their sacrifice shall be a.
Jer. 37:20 let supplication be a.
42:2 let our supplication be a.
Luke 4:24 no prophet is a. in his
Acts 10:35 righteousness is a.
Rom. 15:31 service may be a.
2 Cor. 5:9 or pres. we may be a.
6:2 in a time a. now is a. time
8:12 a. according to that a man
17 indeed he a. the exhortation
11:4 gospel which ye have not a.
Eph. 1:6 us a. in the Beloved

ACCEPTEST.

Luke 20:21 neither a. thou

ACCEPTETH.

Job 34:19 a. not persons of prin.
Ec. 9:7 for God now a. thy works
Hos. 8:13 Lord a. them not
Gal. 2:6 God a. no man's person

ACCEPTING. See DELIVERANCE

ACCESS.

Rom. 5:2 also we have a.
Eph. 2:18 have a. to the Father
3:12 boldness and a. by faith

ACCHO. Jud. 1:31
ACCOMPANY. See SALVATION.

ACCOMPANIED.

Acts 10:23 breth. from Joppa a.
11:12 these six brethren a. me
20:4 Sopater a. Paul into Asia
38 and they a. him to the ship

ACCOMPANYING. See ARK
of God.

ACCOMPLISH.

Job 14:6 shall a. as hireling
Ps. 64:6 they a. a diligent
Is. 55:11 it shall a. that I please
Jer. 44:25 surely a. your vows
Ezek. 6:12 will I a. my fury
7:8 will I a. mine anger on thee
13:15 a. my wrath on the wall
20:8 fury to a. my anger, 21
Dan. 9:2 he would a. 70 years
Luke 9:31 should a. at Jerusalem

ACCOMPLISHED.

Est. 2:12 da. of puri. a. Luke 2:22
Job 15:32 shall be a. before
Prov. 13:19 desire a. is sweet
Is. 40:2 her warfare is a.
Jer. 25:12 70 years are a. 29:10
39:16 my words shall be a.
Lam. 4:11 Lord hath a. his fury
22 punish. of thine iniq. is a.
Ezek. 5:13 shall mine anger be a.
Dan. 11:36 indignation be a.
12:7 a. to scatter the power
Luke 1:23 his ministration a.
2:6 the days were a. that she
21 when eight days were a.
12:50 am I straitened till it be a.
18:31 concerning Son shall be a.
22:37 must yet be a. in me

John 19:28 things were now a.
Acts 21:5 had a. those days
1 Pet. 5:9 same afflictions are a.

ACCOMPLISHING. See SER-
VICE.

ACCOMPLISHMENT.
Acts 21:26 *a.* of days of purifica.

ACCORD.
Lev. 25:5 groweth of its own *a.*
Acts 1:14 with one *a.* in prayer
  2:1 all with one *a.* in one place
  46 daily with one *a.* in temple
  4:24 voice to God with one *a.*
  5:12 one *a.* in Solomon's porch
  7:57 upon Stephen with one *a.*
  8:6 with one *a.* gave heed
  12:10 opened of his own *a.*
  20 but they came with one *a.*
  15:25 assembled with one *a.*
  18:12 with one *a.* made insur.
  19:29 one *a.* into the theatre
2 Cor. 8:17 forward of his own *a.*
Phil. 2:2 of one *a.* of one mind

ACCORDING.
Ps. 7:8 judge *a.* to my righteous.
  17 praise *a.* to his righteous.
  25:7 *a.* to thy mercy remember,
    51:1; 106:45; 109:26; 119:124
  28:4 give them *a.* to their deeds
  33:22 *a.* as we hope in thee
  35:24 judge *a.* to thy right.
  48:10 *a.* to thy name, so
  62:12 to every man *a.* to his
    work, *Prov.* 24:12, 29
  79:11 *a.* to greatness of
  90:11 *a.* to thy fear, so is
  103:10 rewarded us *a.* to iniq.
  119:25 *a.* to thy word.28,41,58,65,
    76, 107, 116, 154, 169, 170
  159 *a.* to thy kindness, *Is.* 63:7
  150:2 praise him *a.* to his
Is. 8:20 speak not *a.* to this

ACCORDING *to all.* See ALL.

ACCORDING to that.
2 Cor. 8:12 *a.* to that a man hath

ACCORDINGLY. See REPAY.

ACCOUNT, Substantive.
Job 33:13 giveth not *a.* of his
Ps. 144:3 son of man that thou
  makest *a.* of him
Ec. 7:27 to find the *a.*
Dan. 6:2 princes might give *a.*
Mat. 12:36 give *a.* thereof
  18:23 take *a.* of his servants
Luke 16:2 an *a.* of stewardship
Acts 19:40 give an *a.* of this
Rom. 14:12 give *a.* of himself
Phil. 4:17 abound to your *a.*
Phile. 18 put that on mine *a.*
Heb. 13:17 that must give *a.*
2 Pet. 4:5 *a.* to him that judgeth

ACCOUNT, ED, ING.
1 K. 1:21 shall be *a.* offenders
  10:21 silver noth. *a.* 2 *Chr.*9:20
Ps. 22:30 *a.* for a genera'ion
Is. 2:22 is he to be *a.* of?
Mark 10:42 *a.* to rule over
Luke 20:35 be *a.* worthy
  22:24 should be *a.* greatest
Rom. 8:36 we are *a.* as sheep
Gal. 3:6 *a.* to him for right.
Heb. 11:19 *a.* that God was able
2 Pet. 3:15 *a.* that the long-suff.

ACCURSED.
Deut. 21:23 hanged is *a.* of G.
Jos. 6:17 shall be *a.* it and
  18 keep from *a.* thing
  7:1 trespass in the *a.* thing
  11 taken of the *a.* thing
  12 because they were *a.*
    destroy the *a.* from
  13 there is an *a.* thing in
  15 that is taken with *a.* thing
  22:20 trespass in *a.* thing
1 Chr. 2:7 transgressed in thing *a.*
Is. 65:20 100 years old shall be *a.*
Rom. 9:3 could wish myself *a.*
1 Cor. 12:3 spirit calleth Jesus *a.*

Gal. 1:8 gospel, let him be *a.* 9

ACCUSATION.
Ezr. 4:6 an *a.* against Judah-
*Mat.*27:37 head his *a.* *Mark* 15:26
Luke 6:7 find an *a.* against
  19:8 any thing by false *a.*
John 18:29 what *a.* bring ye
Acts 25:18 they brought no *a.*
1 Tim. 5:19 receive not an *a.*
2 Pet. 2:11 bring not *a* railing *a.*
Jude 9 durst not bring a railg. *a.*

ACCUSE.
Prov. 30:10 *a.* not a servant to
Mat. 12:10 might *a.* him; *Mar.*
  3:2; *Luke* 11:54
Luke 3:14 nor *a.* any falsely
  23:2 and they began to *a.* him.
  14 things whereof ye *a.* him
John 5:45 that I will *a.* you to F.
  8:6 might have to *a.* him
Acts 24:2 Tertullus began to *a.*
  8 all things whereof we *a.*
  13 prove whereof they *a.* me
  25:5 with me, and *a.* this man
  11 if none, whereof these *a.* me
  28:19 aught to *a.* my nation
1 Pet. 3:16 falsely *a.* your good

ACCUSED.
Dan. 3:8 Chaldeans *a.* the Jews
  6:24 them which had *a.* Daniel
Mat. 27:12 *a.* answered nothing
Mark 15:3 priests *a.* *Luke* 23:10
Luke 16:1 *a.* that he had wasted
Acts 22:30 certainty wherefore *a.*
  23:28 cause whereof they *a.* him
  29 perceived to be *a.* of qu.
  25:16 before he which is *a.* have
  26:2 things whereof I am *a.*
  7 for which hope's sake I am *a.*
Tit. 1:6 not *a.* of riot, or unruly
Rev. 12:10 who *a.* them before

ACCUSER. See CAST *down.*

ACCUSERS.
John 8:10 those thine *a.*
Acts 23:30 com. to his *a.* also
  35 when thine *a.* are come
  24:8 commanding his *a.* to come
  25:16 he have the *a.* face to face
  18 against whom,when *a.*stood
2 Tim. 3:3 affection, false *a.*
Tit. 2:3 not false *a.* not given to

ACCUSETH, ING.
John 5:45 there is one that *a.* you
Rom. 2:15 thoughts *a.* or exc.

ACCUSTOMED. See DO EVIL.

ACELDAMA. See FIELD.

ACHAIA.
Acts 18:12 Gallio was dep. of A.
  27 Apollos to pass into A.
Rom. 15:26 them of A. to make
  16:5 Epenetus, first-fruits of A.
1 Cor. 16:15 Steph., first-fr. of A.
2 Cor. 9:2 A. ready a year ago
  11:10 in the regions of A
1 Thes. 1:7 ensamples to all in A.
  8 sounded not only in A.

ACHAICUS. *1 Cor.* 16:17

ACHAN, *or* ACHAR. *Jos.* **7.**
  22:20; 1 *Chr.* 2:7

ACHIM. *Mat.* 1:14

ACHISH.
1 Sam. 21:10 David fled to A. **27:2**
  12 David was sore afraid of A.
  27:6 A. gave him Ziklag
  29:2 in the rereward with A.
1 Kings 2:40 went to Gath to A.

ACHMETHA. *Ezr.* 6:2

ACHOR.
Jos. 7:26 valley of A. to this
Is. 65:10 valley of A. place for
Hos. 2:15 A. for a door of hope

ACHSAH. *Jos.* 15:16 ; *Jud.* 1:12

ACHSHAPH.
Jos. 11:1 sent to the king of A.
  12:20 king of A. one, 19:25

ACHZIB. *Jos.* 19:29 ; *Mic.* 1:14

ACKNOWLEDGE, ED.
Deut. 21:17 *a.* son of hated
  33:9 nor did he *a.* his brethren
Ps. 32:5 I *a.* my sin; 51:3 *a.* trans.
Prov. 3:6 in all thy ways *a.* him
Is. 33:13 are near, *a.* my might
  61:9 all that see shall *a.* them
  63:16 Father, tho' Israel *a.* us
Jer. 3:13 only *a.* thine iniquity
  14:20 we *a.* our wickedness
Dan. 11:39 god, he shall *a.*
Hos. 5:15 they *a.* their offence
1 Cor. 14:37 let him *a.* the things
  16:18 therefore *a.* ye them that
2 Cor. 1:13 *a.* and I trust shall *a.*
  14 you have *a.* us in part

ACKNOWLEDGING, ETH.
2 Tim. 2:25 repentance to the *a.*
Tit. 1:1 to the *a.* the truth which
Philem. 6 by the *a.* every good
1 John 2:23 he that *a.* the Son

ACKNOWLEDGMENT.
Col. 2:2 to the *a.* of the mystery

ACQUAINT, ED, ING.
Job 22:21 *a.* thyself with him
Ps. 139:3 *a.* with all my ways
Ec. 2:3 *a.* my heart with
Is. 53:3 sorrows, and *a.* with

ACQUAINTANCE.
2 K. 12:5 every man of his *a.*
  7 no more money of your *a.*
Job 19:13 mine *a.* are estranged
  42:11 all that had been of his *a.*
Ps. 31:11 a reproach to mine *a.*
  55:13 mine equal, and mine *a.*
  88:8 hast put away mine *a.* far
  18 and my *a.* into darkness
Luke 2:44 sought among their *a.*
  23:49 all his *a.* stood afar off
Acts 24:23 forbid none of his *a.* to

ACQUIT.
Job 10:14 not *a.* me from mine
Nah. 1:3 L. not at all *a.* wicked

ACRE, S.
1 Sam. 14:14 half an *a.* of land
Is. 5:10 ten *a.* of vineyard

ACT.
Is. 28:21 his *a.* his strange *a.*
  59:6 and the *a.* of violence
John 8:4 adultery, in the very *a.*

ACTS.
Deut. 11:7 seen the great *a.* of
Jud. 5:11 the righteous *a.*
1 Sam. 12:7 all righteous *a.*
2 Sam. 23:20 Benaiah who had
  done many *a.* 1 *Chr.* 11:22
1 K. 10:6 true report of thy *a.*
  11:41 the *a.* of Solomon,2 *Chr.*9:5
2 K. 10:34 the *a.* of Jehu
  23:28 the *a.* of Josiah
1 Chr. 29:29 the *a.* of David
2 Chr. 16:11 the *a.* of Asa
  20:34 the *a.* of Jehoshaphat
  32:32 *a.* of Hezekiah, 2 *K.* 20:20
Est. 10:2 all the *a.* of his power
Ps. 103:7 his *a.* to the children
  106:2 can utter the mighty *a.*
  145:4 declare thy mighty *a.* 6:12
  150:2 praise him for mighty *a.*

ACTIONS.
1 Sam. 2:3 by L. *a.* are weighed

ACTIVITY.
Gen. 47:6 knowest any man of *a.*

ADAM.
Gen. 2:20 A. gave names to all
  5:2 and called their name A.
Deut. 32:8 separated sons of A.
Job 31:33 transgressions as A.
Rom. 5:14 death reigned from A.

1 *Cor.* 15:22 for as in A. all die
   45 first man A. the last A.
1 *Tim.* 2:13 A. was first formed
   14 and A. was not deceived
Jude 14 Enoch the 7th from A.
ADAM. *Jos.* 3:16 the city A.

ADAMANT.
Ezek. 3:9 as an *a.* have I made
Zec. 7:12 heart as an *a.* stone

ADAR.
Ezr. 6:15 finished on 3d day of A.
Est. 3:7 twelfth month A.
   13 day of month A. 8:12; 9:1,17
   9:15 gathered on 14th day of A.

ADD.
Gen. 30:24 L. shall *a.* to me
Deut. 4:2 not *a.* to, 12:32
   29:19 to *a.* drunkenness
2 *K.* 20:6 I *a.* 15 years, *Is.* 38:5
1 *Chr.* 22:14 mayest *a.* thereto
2 *Chr.* 28:13 to *a.* more to sins
Ps. 69:27 *a.* iniquity to iniquity
Prov. 3:2 long life shall they *a.*
   30:6 *a.* thou not to my words
Is. 29:1 *a.* ye year to year
   30:1 may *a.* sin to sin
*Mat.*6:27 can *a.*one cub.,*Lu.*12:25
Phil. 1:16 supposing to *a.* afflict.
2 *Pet.* 1:5 *a.* to your faith virtue
Rev. 22:18 G. shall *a.* to him

ADDED.
Deut. 5:22 and he *a.* no more
1 *Sam.* 12:19 *a.* to all our sins
Jer. 36:32 there were *a.* besides
   45:3 Lord hath *a.* grief
Dan. 4:36 majesty was *a.* to me
Mat. 6:33 shall be *a.* to you
Luke 3:20 Herod *a.* yet this
   19:11 he *a.* and spake a parable
Acts 2:41 were *a.* 3,000 souls
   47 *a.* to the church daily such
   5:14 believers were the more *a.*
   11:24 people was *a.* to the L.
Gal. 2:6 *a.* nothing to me.
   3:19 the law was *a.* because of

ADDER.
Gen. 49:17 Dan shall be an *a.*
Ps. 58:4 the deaf *a.* that stops
   91:13 thou shalt tread on the *a.*
   140:3 *a.'s* poison is under
Prov. 23:32 stingeth like an *a.*

ADDETH.
Job 34:37 he *a.* rebellion
Prov. 10:22 he *a.* no sorrow
   16:23 wise *a.* learning
Gal. 3:15 disannulleth or *a.*

ADDICTED.
1 *Cor.* 16:15 *a.* themselves

ADJURE, ED.
Jos. 6:26 Joshua *a.* them
1 *Sam.* 14:24 Saul had *a.*
1 *K.* 22:16 how many times shall
   I *a.* thee, 2 *Chr.* 18:15
Mat. 26:63 I *a.* thee by the living
Mark 5:7 I *a.* thee by God
Acts 19:13 we *a.* you by Jesus

ADMAH.
Gen. 14:2 Shinab king of A.
Deut. 29:23 the overthrow of A.
Hos. 11:8 make thee as A.

ADMINISTERED.
2 *Cor.* 8:19 *a.* by us to the glory
   20 this abundance which is *a.*

ADMINISTRATION, S.
1 *Cor.* 12:5 differences of *a.*
2 *Cor.* 9:12 *a.* of this service

ADMIRATION.
Jude 16 men's persons in *a.*
Rev. 17:6 wondered with great *a.*

ADMIRED.
2 *Thes.* 1:10 to be *a.* in all

ADMONISH, ED.
Ec. 4:13 will no more be *a.*
   12:12 by these, my son, be *a.*
Jer. 42:19 certainly I have *a.*
Acts 27:9 Paul *a.* them
Rom. 15:14 to *a.* one another
Col. 3:16 *a.* one another
1 *Thes.* 5:12 over you and *a.* you
2 *Thes.* 3:15 *a.* him as a brother
Heb. 8:5 as Moses was *a.* of God

ADMONITION.
1 *Cor.*10:11 are written for our *a.*
Eph. 6:4 bring them up in the *a.*
Tit. 3:10 after first and second *a.*

ADO.
Mark 5:39 why make ye this *a.*
ADONI-BEZEK. *Jud.* 1:5

ADONIJAH.
2 *Sam.* 3:4 A. son of Haggith
1 *K.* 1:5 A. exalted himself
   25 God save king A.
   2:21 let Abishag be given to A.
2 *Chron.*17:8 sent Lev.to teach A.
Neh. 10:16 the people sealed, A.
ADONIKAM. *Ezr.*2:13; *Neh.*7:18

ADOPTION.
*Rom.*8:15 received the spirit of *a.*
   23 waiting for the *a.*
   9:4 to whom pertaineth the *a.*
Gal. 4:5 receive the *a.* of sons
Eph. 1:5 predestinated us to *a.*

ADORN, ED, ETH, ING.
Is. 61:10 as a bride *a.* herself
Jer. 31:4 again *a.* with tabrets
Luke 21:5 temple *a.* with goodly
1 *Tim.* 2:9 women *a.* in modest
Tit. 2:10 *a.* the doctrine of God
1*Pet.*3:3 whose *a.* not outward *a.*
   5 women *a.* themselves
Rev. 21:2 prepared as a bride *a.*

ADRAMMELECH.
2 *K.* 17:31 burnt children to A.
   19:37 A. and Sharezer, *Is.* 37:38
ADRAMYTTIUM. *Acts* 27:2
ADRIA. *Acts* 27:27

ADULLAM.
1 *Sam.* 22:1 cave A. 1 *Chr.* 11:15
2 *Sam.* 23:13 came to David to A.
Mic. 1:15 he shall come to A.

ADULTERER, S.
Lev. 20:10 *a.* put to death
Job 24:15 the eye of *a.* waiteth
Ps. 50:18 partaker with *a.*
Is. 57:3 seed of *a.* and the whore
Jer. 9:2 for they be all *a.*
   23:10 the land is full of *a.*
Hos. 7:4 all *a.* as an oven
Mal. 3:5 witness against the *a.*
Luke 18:11 I am not as others, *a.*
1 *Cor.* 6:9 neither *a.* shall inherit
Heb. 13:4 *a.* God will judge
Jam. 4:4 ye *a.* know ye not that

ADULTERESS, ES.
Lev. 20:10 the *a.* put to death
Prov. 6:26 the *a.* will hunt
Ezek. 23:45 judge them as *a.*
Hos. 3:1 a woman yet an *a.*
Rom. 7:3 no *a.* though married

ADULTEROUS.
Prov. 30:20 the way of *a.* wom.
Mat. 12:39 an *a.* generation, 16:4
Mark 8:38 ashamed in this *a.*

ADULTERY, IES.
Ex. 20:14 thou shalt not com. *a.*
   Deut. 5:18 ; *Mat.* 5:27 ; 19:18 ;
   Rom. 13:9
Prov. 6:32 commits *a.* lacketh
*Jer.*3:8 backsliding Israel com.*a.*
   9 committed *a.* with stones
   5:7 then they committed *a.*
   7:9 will ye steal and commit *a.*

   13:27 I have seen thine *a.*
   23:14 they commit *a.* and walk
   29:23 they committed *a.*
Ezek. 16:32 a wife that com. *a.*
   23:37 with their idols com. *a.*
   43 said I to her old in *a.*
Hos. 2:2 *a.* between her breasts
   4:2 committing *a.* they break
   13 spouses shall commit *a.*
Hos. 4:14 punish when com. *a.*
Mat. 5:28 *a.* in his heart
   32 marry her divorced committeth *a.* 19:9 ; *Luke* 16:18
   15:19 heart proceed *a. Mark*
   7:21
Mark 10:11 his wife and marry
   another com. *a. Luke* 16:18
   19 not com.*a.Lu.*18:20;*Jas.*2:11
John 8:3 woman taken in *a.* 4
Rom. 2:22 should not commit *a.*
Gal. 5:19 flesh manifest *a.*
2 *Pet.* 2:14 having eyes full of *a.*
Rev. 2:22 cast them that com. *a.*

ADVANTAGE, ED, ETH.
Job 35:3 what *a.* will it be
Luke 9:25 a man *a.* if he gain
Rom. 3:1 what *a.* then hath Jew
1 *Cor.* 15:32 what *a.* if the dead
2 *Cor.* 2:11 Satan get an *a.* of us
Jude 16 admiration because of *a.*

ADVENTURE, ED.
Deut. 28:56 not *a.* to set the sole
Jud. 9:17 father *a.* his life far
Acts 19:31 not *a.* into the theatre

ADVERSARY.
Ex. 23:22 be an *a.* to thine
Num. 22:22 angel *a.* against Bal.
1 *Sam.* 1:6 her *a.* provoked her
   29:4 lest in battle he be an *a.*
1 *K.* 5:4 there is neither *a.* nor
   11:14 an *a.* to Solomon, 23
   25 was an *a.* to Israel
Est. 7:6 *a.* is wicked Haman
Job 31:35 *a.* had written a book
Ps. 74:10 shall *a.* reproach
Is. 50:8 who is mine *a.* let him
Lam. 1:10 the *a.* hath spread out
   2:4 with his right hand as an *a.*
   4:12 *a.* have entered the gates
Amos 3:11 *a.* be round about
Mat. 5:25 *a.* quickly lest *a.* deliv.
Luke 12:58 goest with thine *a.*
   18:3 avenge me of mine *a.*
1 *Tim.* 5:14 give no occas. to *a.*
1 *Pet.* 5:8 your *a.* the devil

ADVERSARIES.
Deut. 32:27 *a.* behave strangely
   43 render vengeance to his *a.*
Jos. 5:13 for us, or for our *a. ?*
1 *Sam.* 2:10 *a.* of L. shall be
Ezr. 4:1 *a.* of Judah heard
Neh. 4:11 *a.* said, they shall not
Ps. 38:20 evil for good are my *a.*
   69:19 mine *a.* are all before thee
   71:13 that are *a.* to my soul
   81:14 my hand against their *a.*
   89:42 the right hand of his *a.*
   109:4 for my love they are *a.*
   20 be the reward of my *a.*
   29 *a.* be clothed with shame
Is. 1:24 I will ease me of my *a.*
   9:11 shall set up the *a.* of Rezin
   11:13 *a.*of Judah shall be cut off
   59:18 he will repay fury to his *a.*
   63:18 our *a.* have trodden down
   64:2 name known to thine *a.*
Jer. 30:16 *a.* shall go into cap.
   46:10 may avenge him of his *a.*
   50:7 their *a.* said, we offend not
Lam. 1:5 her *a.* are the chief
   7 *a.* saw her, and did mock
   17 his *a.* should be round abt.
   2:17 set up the horn of thine *a.*
Mic. 5:9 hand lifted up on *a.*
Nah. 1:2 vengeance on his *a.*
Luke 13:17 *a.* were ashamed

21:15 your *a*. not able to gainsay
1 *Cor.* 16:9 and there are many *a*.
Phil. 1:28 nothing terrified by *a*.
Heb. 10:27 shall devour the *a*.

ADVERSITY, IES.
1 *Sam.* 10:19 saved you of all *a*.
2 **Sam.** 4:9 my soul out of all *a*.
2 *Chr.* 15:6 vex them with all *a*.
Ps. 10:6 I shall never be in *a*.
31:7 known my soul in *a*.
35:15 in my *a*. they rejoiced
94:13 rest from the days of *a*.
Prov. 17:17 brother born for *a*.
24:10 if thou faint in day of *a*.
Ec. 7:14 day of *a*. consider
Is. 30:20 tho' L. give bread of *a*.
Heb. 3:3 remem. them suffer *a*.

ADVERTISE.
Num. 24:14 I will *a*. thee
Ruth 4:4 I thought to *a*. thee

ADVICE.
Jud. 20:7 your *a*. and counsel
1 *Sam.* 25:33 blessed be thy *a*.
2 *Sam.* 19:43 our *a*. not be first
2 *Chr.* 10:14 after *a*. of young
Prov. 20:18 good *a*. make war
2 *Cor.* 8:10 herein I give my *a*.

ADVISE, ED.
2 *Sam.* 24:13 *a*. and see,1 *Chr.* 21:12
1 *K.* 12:6 how do ye *a*. that I
Prov. 13:10 well *a*. is wisdom
Acts 27:12 more part *a*. to depart
ADVISEMENT. 1 *Chr.* 12:19

ADVOCATE.
1 *John* 2:1 have an *a*. with the

AFAR, AFAR OFF.
Gen. 37:18 saw Joseph *a*. *off*.
Ex. 24:1 worship ye *a*. *off*.
Ezr. 3:13 noise was heard *a*. *off*.
Neh. 12:43 Jeru. heard *a*. *off*.
Job 36:3 my knowledge from *a*.
25 man may behold it *a*. *off*.
39:29 her eyes behold *a*. *off*.
Ps. 65:5 are *a*. *off* on the sea
139:6 proud he knoweth *a*. *off*.
139:2 my thoughts *a*. *off*.
Prov. 31:14 bringeth food from *a*.
Is. 23:7 shall carry her *a*. *off*.
66:19 escape to the isles *a*. *off*.
Jer. 23:23 am I not a God *a*. *off*.
30:10 save thee from *a*. 46:27
31:10 declare in isles *a*. *off*.
51:50 remember the Lord *a*. *off*.
Mic. 4:3 strong nations *a*. *off*.
Mat. 26:58 Peter followed *a*. *off*.
Mark 14:54 ; *Luke* 22:54
27:55 wom.behold *a*.*off*,*Ma*.15:40
Mark 5:6 he saw Jesus *a*. *off*.
Luke 16:23 seeth Abraham *a*. *off*.
Acts 2:39 promise is to all *a*. *off*.
Eph. 2:17 peace to you *a*. *off*.
Heb. 11:13 seen promises *a*. *off*.
2 *Pet.* 1:9 and cannot see *a*. *off*.
See FAR, STAND, STOOD.

AFFAIRS.
Ps. 112:5 guide *a*. with discr.
Eph. 6:21 ye may know my *a*.
22 that ye might know our *a*.
Phil. 1:27 I may hear of your *a*.
2 *Tim.* 2:4 entangleth with *a*.

AFFECT, ED, ETH.
Lam. 3:51 eye *a*. my heart
Acts 14:2 their minds evil *a*.
Gal. 4:17 zealously *a*. you
18 good to be zealously *a*.

AFFECTION.
1 *Chr.* 29:3 *a*. to house of God
Rom. 1:31 without natural *a*. 2
Tim. 3:3
2 *Cor.* 7:15 his inward *a*. is more
Col. 3:2 your *a*. on things above
5 mortify inordinate *a*.

AFFECTIONS.
Rom. 1:26 G. gave up to vile *a*.

Gal. 5:24 crucified flesh with *a*.

AFFECTIONATELY.
1 *Thes.* 2:8 *a*. desirous of you

AFFECTIONED.
Rom. 12:10 kindly *a*. one to

AFFINITY.
Ezr. 9:14 join in *a*. with

AFFIRM.
Rom. 3:8 and as some *a*. we **say**
1 *Tim.* 1:7 nor whereof they *a*.
Tit. 3:8 things *a*. constantly

AFFIRMED.
Luke 22:59 hour after another *a*.
Acts 12:15 Rhoda constantly *a*.
25:19 whom Paul *a*. alive

AFFLICT.
Gen. 15:13 shall *a*. them 400 yrs.
31:50 if thou *a*. my daughters
Ex. 1:11 taskmasters to *a*.
22:22 shall not *a*. any widow
Lev. 16:29 shall *a*. your souls, 31 ;
23:27. 32 ; *Num.* 29:7
Num. 24:24 ships shall *a*. Ashur
Jud. 16:19 *a* him, his **strength**
2 *Sam.* 7:10 ch'n of wickedness *a*.
1 *K.* 11:39 *a*. seed of David
2 *Chr.* 6:26 turn when thou dost *a*.
1 *K.* 8:35.
Ezr. 8:21 *a*. ours. before God
Job 37:23 Almighty, he not *a*.
Ps. 44:2 thou didst *a*. the peo.
55:19 God shall hear and *a*.
89:22 son of wickedness *a*.
94:5 they *a*. thy heritage
143:12 all that *a*. my soul
Is. 9:1 grievously *a*. her
51:23 them that *a*. thee
58:5 for a man to *a*. his soul
64:12 wilt thou *a*. us very sore?
Jer. 31:28 as I watched to *a*.
Lam. 3:33 Lord not *a*. willingly
Amos 5:12 they *a*. the just, they
Nah. 1:12 I will *a*. thee no more
Zep. 3:19 I will undo all that *a*.

AFFLICTED.
Ex. 1:12 more *a*. more grew
2 *Sam.* 22:28 *a*. people wilt save
1 *K.* 2:26 *a*. in all father was *a*.
Job 6 14 to *a*. pity should be
30:11 loosed cord, and *a*. me
34:28 heareth cry of the *a*.
Ps. 18:27 save the *a*. people
22:24 abhorred affliction of *a*.
25:16 I am desolate and *a*.
82:3 do justice to the *a*.
88:7 hast *a*. me with waves
15 I am *a*. and ready to die
90:15 wherein thou hast *a*. us
107:17 fools because of iniq. *a*.
116:10 I was greatly *a*.
119:67 before I was *a*.
71 good that I have been *a*.
75 in faithfulness hast *a*. me
107 am *a*. very much, quicken
128:1 have *a*. me from youth, 2
140:12 L. maintain cause of *a*.
Prov. 15:15 days of the *a*. are evil
22:22 neither oppress *a*. in gate
26:28 lying tongue hateth *a*.
31:5 lest pervert judgment of *a*.
Is. 9:1 lightly *a*. the land
49:13 L. have mercy on his *a*.
51:21 hear now this, thou *a*.
53:4 smitten of God and *a*.
7 and was *a*. yet he opened not
54:11 O thou *a*. tossed with
58:3 have we *a*. our souls
10 if thou satisfy the *a*. soul
60:14 sons of them that *a*. thee
63:9 their affliction he was *a*.
Lam. 1:12 sorrow wherew. L. *a*,
Mic. 4:6 gather her that I have *a*.
Nah. 1:12 *a*. afflict no more
Zep. 3:12 leave an *a*. people
Mat. 24:9 deliver you up to be *a*.

---

2 *Cor.* 1:6 whether we be *a*. it is
1 *Tim.* 5:10 if she relieved the *a*.
Heb. 11:37 being destitute, *a*.
Jam. 4:9 *a*. and mourn and weep
5:13 is any among you *a*. ? let

AFFLICTION.
Gen. 41:52 fruitful in land of *a*.
Ex. 3:17 *a*. of my p. *Acts* 7:34
3:17 out of the *a*. of Egypt
Deut. 16:3 shalt eat bread of *a*.
1 *K.* 22:27 ; 2 *Chr.* 18:26
26:7 L. heard and looked on *a*.
2 *Sam.* 16:12 L. look on my *a*.
2 *K.* 14:26 Lord saw *a*. of Israel
2 *Chr.* 20:9 cry in *a*. wilt hear
33:12 Manasseh was in *a*.
Neh. 1:3 remnant are in great *a*.
Job 5:6 *a*. cometh not forth
10:15 confusion see mine *a*.
30:16 days of *a*. have taken hold
27 the days of *a*. prevented me
36:8 holden in cords of *a*.
15 delivereth poor in his *a*.
21 chosen rather than *a*.
Ps. 25:18 my *a*. and pain
44:24 and forgettest our *a*.
66:11 laidst *a*. upon our loins
88:9 mourneth by reason of *a*.
106:44 regarded their *a*. when
107:10 bound in *a*. and iron
39 low through *a*. and sorrow
41 setteth poor on high from *a*.
119:50 comfort in my *a*.
92 perished in mine *a*.
153 mine *a*. deliver me
Is. 30:20 L. give water of *a*.
48:10 chosen in furnace of *a*.
63:9 their *a*. he was afflicted
Jer. 16:19 refuge in days of *a*.
30:15 criest thou for thine *a*.
Lam. 1:7 Jerusa. remem'd in *a*.
3:1 that hath seen *a*. by the rod
19 remembering my *a*. and
Hos. 5:15 in *a*. seek me early
Amos 6:6 grieved for *a*. of Jos.
Nah. 1:9 *a*. not rise second time
Zec. 1:15 helped forward the *a*.
10:11 pass thro' sea with *a*.
Mark 4:17 *a*. ariseth
13:19 shall be *a*. such
Acts 7:11 a dearth and great *a*.
2 *Cor.* 2:4 out of much *a*. I wrote
4:17 light *a*. which is but for
8:2 in a great trial of *a*.
Phil. 1:16 to add *a*. to my
4:14 communicate with in *a*.
1 *Thes.* 1:6 word in much *a*.
3:7 comforted in all our *a*.
Heb. 11:25 rather to suffer *a*.
Jam. 1:27 to visit fatherless in *a*.
5:10 an example of suffering *a*.

AFFLICTIONS.
Ps. 34:19 the *a*. of righteous
132:1 rememb. David and his *a*.
Acts 7:10 deliver out of all his *a*.
20:23 bonds and *a*. abide me
6:4 approving in *a*.
Col. 1:24 behind of *a*. of Christ
1 *Thes.* 3:3 be moved by these *a*.
2 *Tim.* 1:8 of the *a*. of the gospel
3:11 *a*. which came at Antioch
4:5 watch in all, endure *a*.
Heb. 10:32 great fight of *a*.
33 made a gazing-stock by *a*.
1 *Pet.* 5:9 *a*. accomplished in

AFFRIGHT, ED.
Job 18:20 that went before *a*.
39:22 mocketh at fear and not *a*.
Is. 21:4 fearfulness *a*. me
Mark 16:5 were *a*. *Luke* 24:37
6 be not *a*. ye seek Jesus
Rev. 11:13 remnant *a*. gave glo.

AFOOT.
Mark 6:33 many ran *a*. thither
Acts 20:13 Paul minding to go *a*.

AFORETIME.

Jer. 30:20 their children as *a*
Dan. 6:10 he prayed as he did *a.*
Rom. 15:4 things were written *a.*

AFRAID.

Ex. 34:30 were *a.* to come nigh
Lev. 26:6 none make *a. Job* 11:19
Num. 12:8 why not *a.* to speak
1 *Sam.* 4:7 Philistines were *a.*
    18:29 yet more *a.* of David
2 *Sam.* 1:14 not *a.* to destroy
    22:5 ungodly men made me *a.*
        Ps. 18:4
Neh. 6:9 all made us *a.*
Job 9:28 *a.* of all my sorrows
    11:19 none make thee *a.*
    13:11 excellency make you *a.*
    21 not thy dread make me *a.*
    15:24 anguish make him *a.*
    18:11 terrors make him *a.*
    21:6 when I remember, I am *a.*
    23:15 consider, I am *a.* of him
    33:7 terror not make thee *a.*
    41:25 raiseth hims. mighty *a.*
Ps. 50:3 what time I am *a.*
    65:8 dwell are *a.* at thy tokens
    77:16 saw thee and were *a.*
    83:15 *a.* with thy storm
    119:120 *a.* of thy judgments
Is. 17:2 none make them *a. Ezek.*
    34:28; *Mic.* 4:4; *Zep.* 3:13.
    33:14 sinners in Zion are *a.*
    41:5 ends of the earth were *a.*
Jer. 30:10 none make him *a.*
Ezek. 39:26 none made them *a.*
        Nah. 2:11.
Dan. 4:5 dream made me *a.*
Jon. 1:5 mariners were *a.* 10
Mark 5·15 in right mind were *a.*
    Luke 8:35
    9:32 and were *a.* to ask him
    10:32 as they followed were *a.*
    16:8 said any thing, were *a.*
Luke 8:25 being *a.* wondered
Acts 9:26 were all *a.* of Saul
    22:9 saw the light and were *a.*
Gal. 4:11 I am *a.* of you lest
1 *Pet.* 3:6 not *a.* with amazem.
2 *Pet.* 2:10 *a.* to speak evil of dig.

Be AFRAID.

Deut. 1:29 nei. be *a.* of them, 31:6
2 *Sam.* 22:46 be *a.* out of close
        Ps. 18:45
Job 5:21 nor be *a.* of destruction
    19:29 be ye *a.* of the sword, for
Ps. 27:1 of whom shall I be *a.?*
Is. 8:12 nor fear nor be *a.* 44:8
    19:17 shall *be a.* in himself
    51:12 shouldest be *a.* of a man
Rom. 13:4 if thou do evil, be *a.*

Not be AFRAID.

Deut. 1:17 not be *a.* of face
    7:18 shall *not* be *a.* of, 18:22
Ps. 3:6 *not* be *a.* of ten thous.
    56:11 *not* be *a.* what man can do
    91:5 *not* be *a.* for terror by night
Ps. 112:7 *not* be *a.* of evil tidings
    8 estab'd, he shall *not* be *a.*
Prov. 3:24 liest down *not* be *a.*
Is. 12:2 trust and *not* be *a.*
    31:4 *not* be *a.* of their voice
Amos 3:6 blown, people *not* be *a.*
Rom. 13:3 *not* be *a.* of the power

Be not AFRAID.

Deut. 20:1 be *not a.* of them, *Jos.*
    11:6; *Neh.* 4:14; *Jer.* 10:5;
    Ezek. 2:6; *Luke* 12:4
1 *Sam.* 28:13 be *not a.* what saw.
Ps. 49:16 be *not a.* when one is
Prov. 3:25 be *not a.* of sudden
Is. 40:9 up thy voice, be *not a.*
Jer. 1:8 be *not a.* of their faces
Mat. 17:7 it is I, be *not a. Mark*
    6:50; *John* 6:20
    17:7 Jesus said, Arise, be *not a.*
    28:10 be *not a.* go tell brethren

Mark 5:36 ruler, be *not a.* only
Acts 18:9 be *not a.* but speak
1 *Pet.* 3:14 be *not a.* of their

Sore AFRAID.

Num. 22:3 Moab *s.* *a.* of people
Jos. 9:24 *s. a.* of our lives
1 *Sam.* 17:24 from Goliah *s. a.*
    28:20 Saul fell along *sore a.*
    31:4 armor-bearer *s. a.* 1 *Chr.*10:4
Mark 9:6 for they were *sore a.*
Luke 2:9 and they were *sore a.*

Was AFRAID.

Gen. 3:10 thy voice and *w. a.*
Ex. 3:6 Moses *w. a.* to look
Deut. 9:19 I *was a.* of the anger
1 *Sam.* 18:12 *was a.* of David, 15
    28:5 saw Philistines, he *was a.*
2 *Sam.* 6:9 David *was a.* of the L.
        1 *Chr.* 13:12
Job 3:25 that I *was a.* is come
    32:6 I *was a.* and durst not
Dan. 8:17 *was a.* and fell
Hab. 3:2 thy speech and *was a.*
Mal. 2:5 feared me and *was a.*
Mat. 2:22 *was a.* to go thither
    14:30 saw wind boisterous, *w.a.*
    25:25 *was a.* and hid thy talent
John 19:8 *was* the more *a.*
Acts 10:4 Corn. looked, he *w.a.*

AFRESH.

Heb. 6:6 crucify Son of God *a.*

AFTER.

Jos. 10:14 no day like that *a.* it

AFTER that.

Luke 12:4 *a. t.* have no more that
1 *Cor.* 15:6 *a. t.* was seen of 500

AFTERNOON.

Jud. 19:8 they tarried till *a.*

AFTERWARD, S.

Ps. 73:24 *a.* receive me to glory
Prov. 29:11 keepeth it in till *a.*
John 13:36 shalt follow me *a.*
1 *Cor.* 15:23 *a.* that are Christ's
Heb. 12:11 *a.* yieldeth fruit

AGABUS. *Acts* 11:28; 21:10

AGAG.

Num. 24:7 be higher than A.
1 *Sam.* 15:9 the people spared A.
    33 Samuel hewed A. in pieces

AGAGITE. *See* HAMAN.

AGAINST.

Gen. 16:12 hand will be *a.* every
Mat. 10:35 man *a.* his f. *Lu.*12:53
    12:30 he not with me, is *a.* me
Luke 2:34 for a sign spoken *a.*
    14:31 cometh *a.* him with 20,000
Acts 19:36 cannot be spoken *a.*
    28:22 sect everywh. spoken *a.*

See ANOTHER, GOD, JERUSALEM,
    ISRAEL, LORD, OVER.

AGAR. *Gal.* 4:24, 25

AGATE, S.

Ex. 28:19 third row, an *a.* 39:12
Is. 54:12 thy windows of *a.*
Ezek. 27:16 Syria occup. with *a.*

AGE.

Gen. 47:28 *a.* of Jacob 147 years
    48:10 eyes of Israel dim for *a.*
Num. 8:25 *a.* of fifty cease
1 *Sam.* 2:33 flower of their *a.*
1 *K.* 14:4 set by reason of *a.*
2 *Chr.* 36:17 that stooped for *a.*
Job 5:26 come to grave in a full *a.*
    8:8 inquire of the former *a.*
    11:17 thy *a* clearer than
Ps. 39:5 my *a.* is as nothing
Is. 38:12 my *a.* is departed
Zec. 8:4 with his staff for *a.*
Mark 5:42 *a.* of 12 years, *Lu.*8:42
Luke 2:36 Anna of a great *a.*
    3:23 Jesus about 30 years of *a.*
John 9:21 he is of *a.* ask him, 23

1 *Cor.* 7:36 pass flower of *a.*
Heb. 5:14 strong meat to full *a.*

See OLD, STRICKEN.

AGES.

Eph. 2:7 *a.* to come he might
    3:5 other *a.* not made known
    21 in church through all *a.*
Col. 1:26 mystery hid from *a.*

AGED.

2 *Sam.* 19:32 Barzillai very *a.*
Job 12:20 the understanding of *a.*
    15:10 grey-headed and very *a.*
    29:8 the *a.* arose and stood up
    32:9 do the *a.* understand
Jer. 6:11 *a.* with him full of days
Tit. 2:2 that the *a.* men be sober
    3 the *a.* women be in behavior
Phile. 9 such a one as Paul the *a.*

AGO.

1 *Sam.* 9:20 asses lost 3 days *a.*
1 *K.* 19:25 long *a. Is.* 37:26
Ezr. 5:11 builded many years *a.*
Mat. 11:21 long *a. Luke* 10:13
Mark 9:21 how long *a.* since this
Acts 10:30 four days *a.* I was
    15:7 a good while *a.*
2 *Cor.* 8:10 be forward a year *a.*
    9:2 Achaia was ready a year *a.*
    12:2 above fourteen years *a.*

AGONE.

1 *Sam.* 30:13 three days *a.* I fell

AGONY.

Luke 22:44 in an *a.* he prayed

AGREE, ED, ETH.

Amos 3:3 walk except they be *a.*
Mat. 5:25 *a.* with adversary
    18:19 if two shall *a.* on earth
    20:2 had *a.* with laborers
    13 not *a.* with me for a penny?
Mark 14:56 witness *a.* not, 59
    70 Galilean, and thy speech *a.*
Luke 5:36 out of new, *a.* not
John 9:22 Jews had *a.* already
Acts 5:9 ye have *a.* to tempt
    40 and to him they *a.* and
    15:15 to this *a.* words of proph.
    23:20 Jews have *a.* to desire
    28:25 *a.* not among themselves
1 *John* 5:8 blood, these *a.* in one
Rev. 17:17 *a.* to give their kingd.

AGREEMENT.

2 *K.* 18:31 *a.* by a pres. *Is.* 36:16
Is. 28:15 with hell are we at *a.*
    18 *a.* with hell shall not stand
Dan. 11:6 of north. to make *a.*
2 *Cor.* 6:16 what *a.* hath the

AGRIPPA.

Acts. 25:13 A. and Bernice came
    22 A. said, I would also hear
    26:7 which hope's sake, king A.
    28 A. said, almost thou per.

AGROUND.

Acts 27:41 they ran the ship *a.*

AGUE.

Lev. 26:16 appoint burning *a.*

AGUR. *Prov.* 30:1

AH.

Ps. 35:25 *a.* so would we have it
Is. 1:4 *a.* sinful nation. a people
    24 *a.* I will ease me of
Jer. 1:6 *a.* Lord God, I cannot
    4:10 *a.* Lord thou hast
    22:18 *a.* brother, *a.* sister, *a.* L.
    32:17 *a.* Lord, thou made
    34:5 lament thee, saying *a.* L.
Ezek. 9:8 *a.* Lord, wilt thou
Mark 15:29 *a.* thou that

AHA.

Ps. 35:21 *a.* our eye hath seen
    40:15 that say unto me *a.*
    70:3 turned back that say *a. a.*
Is. 44:16 *a.* I am warm, I have

Ezek. 25:3 said*st a.* against sanc.
26:2 Tyrus said, *a.* she is brok.
36:2 *a.* the ancient places

AHAB.

1 *K.* 16:30, 33; 18:6, 9, 42, 46;
20:13; 21:4, 21, 25, 29; 22:20
2 *K.* 1:1; 3:5; 8:18, 27; 9:7, 8, 25;
10:11; 21:3, 13
2 *Chr.* 21:13 whored. of ho. of A.
Jer. 29:21 saith the Lord of A.
22 the L. make thee like A.
Mic. 6:16 works of house of A.

AHASUERUS.

Ezr. 4:6 reign of A. wrote
Est. 1:1 is A. which reigned
Dan. 9:1 of Darius, son of A.

AHAVAH. *Ezr.* 8:15, 21, 31

AHAZ.

2 *K.* 16:2 A. was 20 years
1 *Chr.* 8:35 Mic. Pithon, A. 9:41
2 *Chr.* 28:19 Judah low, bec. of A.
Is. 1:1 the vision in days of A.
Hos. 1:1; *Mic.* 1:1.
7:3 go forth to meet A. 10

AHAZIAH.

1 *K.* 22:40 A. his son, 2 *K.* 8:24
K. 1:2 A. fell through
8:29 A. king of Judah, went
10:13 the brethren of A.
2 *Chr.* 20:35 Jehosh. join with A.
22:7 destruction of A. was of

AHIAH. 1 *Sam.* 14:3; 1 *K.* 4:3

AHIJAH.

1 *K.* 11:29; 12:15; 14:2, 4, 6
15:27 Baasha, son of A.
1 *Chr.* 2:25 sons of Jerahmeel, A.

AHIKAM.

2 *K.* 22:12 Josiah commanded A.
to inquire, 2 *Chr.* 34:20
25:22 Gedaliah the son of A.
Jer. 26:24 hand of A. was with
40:6 Gedaliah the son of A.

See GEDALIAH.

AHIMAAZ.

1 *Sam.* 14:50 the daughter of A.
2 *Sam.* 17:17 Jonathan and A.
18:27 is like the running of A.
1 *K.* 4:15 A. in Naphtali
1 *Chr.* 6:8 and Zadok begat A.

AHIMAN.

Num. 13:22 A. of the children
Jud. 1:10 Judah slew A.
1 *Chr.* 9:17 and the porters, A.

AHIMELECH.

1 *Sam.* 21:1 A. was afraid at the
22:9 son of Jesse coming to A.
16 thou shalt surely die A.
26:6 David said to A. who
2 *Sam.* 8:17 Zadok and A. 1 *Chr.*
18:16
1 *Chr.* 24:3 A. of the sons of, 6, 31

AHINOAM. 1 *Sam.* 14:50; 25:43
AHIO. 2 *Sam.* 6:3; 1 *Chr.* 13:7
AHISAMACH. *Ex.* 35:34

AHITHOPHEL.

2 *Sam.* 15:12 Absalom sent for A.
16:15 came to Jerusal. and A.
23 counsel of A. was as if a
17:7 counsel of A. is not good
15 thus did A. counsel, 23
1 *Chr.* 27:33 A. was the king's

AHITUB.

1 *Sam.* 22:12 thou son of A.
2 *Sam.* 8:17 Zadok the son of A.
1 *Chr.* 18:16

AHOLAH, AHOLIBAH.

Ezek. 23:4 Sama. is A. Jerus. A.
36 wilt thou judge A. and A.?

AHOLIAB. *Ex.* 36:1
AHOLIBAMAH. *Gen.* 36:2, 5

AI, *or* HAI.

Gen. 13:3 betw. Beth-el and A.

Jos. 7:4 before the men of A.
8:1 up to A. 10:2 greater than A.
Ezr. 2:28 the men of Beth-el and
A. *Neh.* 7:32
Jer. 49.3 howl, O Heshbon, for A.

AIATH. *Is.* 10:28

AILED, ETH.

Gen. 21:17 what *a.* thee, Hagar ?
Jud. 18:23 Micah, what *a.* thee ?
1 *Sam.* 11:5 what *a.* the people
2 *Sam.* 14:5 the king said unto
her, what *a.* thee ? 2 *K.* 6:28
Ps. 114:5 what *a.* thee, O sea
Is. 22:1 what *a*) thee now that

AIR.

2 *Sam.* 21:10 birds of the *a.*
Job 41:16 no *a.* can come bet.
Prov. 30:19 an eagle in the *a.*
Ec. 10:20 bird of the *a.* carry
Mat. 8:20 birds of *a.* have nests
13:32 birds of the *a.* lodge in the
Mark 4:32; *Luke* 9:58
Acts 22:23 threw dust into the *a.*
1 *Cor.* 9:26 one that beateth *a.*
14:9 ye shall speak into the *a.*
Eph. 2:2 prince of power of the *a.*
1 *Thes.* 4:17 meet the L. in the *a.*
Rev. 9:2 sun and *a.* were dark
16:17 poured out vial into the *a.*

See FOWLS.

AJALON. *Jos.* 10:12

ALARM.

Num. 10:5 when ye blow an *a.* 6
7 blow, but not sound an *a.*
9 if ye go to war, blow an *a.*
2 *Chr.* 13:12 trumpets to cry an *a.*
Jer. 4:19 O my soul, *a.* of war
49:21 will cause an *a.* of war
Joel 2:1 an *a.* in my holy mount.
Zep. 1:16 *a.* against fenced cities

ALAS.

Num. 24:23 *a.* who shall live
Jud. 6:22 *a.* I have seen an angel
11:35 *a.* daughter thou hast
1 *K.* 13:30 *a.* my brother
2 *K.* 6:5 *a.* master, for it was
15 *a.* master, how shall we do?
Ezek. 6:11 stamp with foot, say *a.*
Joel 1:15 *a.* for the day of the L.
Amos 5:16 say in highways, *a. a.*
Rev. 18:10 *a. a.* that great, 16,19

ALBEIT.

Eze. 13:7 L. saith, *a.* I have not
Phile. 19 *a.* I say not, how thou

ALEXANDER.

Mark 15:21 Simon, father of A.
Acts 4:6 Annas, Caiaphas, A.
19:33 they drew A. out of the
1 *Tim.* 1:20 Hymeneus and A.
2 *Tim.* 4:14 A. the coppersmith

ALEXANDRIA, ANS.

Acts 6:9 of the Libertines and A.
18:24 nam. Apollos, born at A.
27:6 centurion found ship of A.

ALIEN, S.

Ex. 18:3 been *a.* in a strange
Deut. 14:21 mayest sell to an *a.*
Job 19:15 am an *a.* in their sight
Ps. 69:8 *a.* to my mother's child.
Is. 61:5 of *a.* your ploughmen
Lam. 5:2 our houses turned to *a.*
Eph. 2:12 *a.* from commonwealth
Heb. 11:34 flight the armies of *a.*

ALIENATE, ED.

Eze. 23:17 her mind was *a.* from
18 my mind was *a.* from her as
22 from whom thy mind is *a.* 28
48:14 not *a.* first-fruits of land
Eph. 4:18 *a.* from life of G. thro'
Col. 1:21 that were sometime *a.*

ALIKE.

1 *Sam.* 30:24 they shall part *a.*
Job 21:26 lie down *a.* in dust

Ps. 33:15 fashion. their hearts *a.*
139:12 darkn. and light both *a.*
Ec. 9:2 all things come *a.* to all
11:6 whe. both shall be *a.* good
Rom. 14:5 esteemeth ev day *a.*

ALIVE.

Gen. 7:23 Noah remained *a.* and
12:12 kill me, and save thee *a.*
50:20 to save much people *a.*
Ex. 1:17 men-children *a.* 18
22 daughter ye shall save *a.*
22:4 if the theft be found *a.*
Lev. 10:16 was angry with
Aaron's sons left *a.*
Num. 16:33 went down *a.* into pit
22:33 slain thee, and sav. her *a.*
31:15 ye saved all the women *a.*
Deut. 4:4 *a.* every one this day
5:3 all of us *a.* here this day
6:24 might pres. us *a.* this day.
20:16 save *a.* noth. that breath.
32:39 and I make *a.* 1 *Sam.* 2:6
Jos. 2:13 ye save *a.* my father
14:10 the Lord hath kept me *a.*
Jud. 8:19 saved them *a.* I would
1 *Sam.* 15:8 he took Agag *a.*
27:9 left man nor woman *a.*
1 *K.* 20:18 peace or war take *a.*
21:15 Naboth is not *a.* but dead
2 *K.* 5:7 G. to kill and make *a.?*
7:4 if they save us *a.* we live
12 we shall catch them *a.*
10:14 and they took them *a.*
2 *Chr.* 25:12 other 10,000 left *a.*
Ps. 30:3 L. thou hast kept me *a.*
Prov. 1:12 swal. *a.* as the grave
Jer. 49:11 I will preserve *a.*
Eze. 13:18 the souls *a.* that come
19 souls *a.* that should not live
18:27 he shall save his soul *a.*
Dan. 5:19 whom would, kept *a.*
Mark 16:11 heard that he was *a.*
Luke 15:24 was dead and is *a.* 32
24:23 angels who said he was *a.*
Acts 1:3 *a.* after his passion
9:41 widows, presented her *a.*
20:12 brought the young man *a.*
25:19 whom P. affirmed to be *a.*
Rom. 6:11 *a.* to God through C.
13 as those *a.* from the dead
7:9 for I was *a.* without the law
1 *Cor.* 15:22 Christ all be made *a.*
1 *Thes.* 4:15 are *a.* and remain, 17
Rev. 1:18 I am *a.* forevermore
2:8 which was dead, and is *a.*
19:20 cast *a.* into lake of fire

Keep ALIVE. *See* KEEP.

Yet ALIVE.

Gen. 43:7 is your father *yet a. ?*

Gen. 45:27 he *yet a.?* 28 is *yet a.*
45:26 Joseph is *yet a.* 28
46:30 bec. thou art *yet a.*
Ex. 4:18 see they be *yet a.*
Deut. 31:27 I am *yet a.* with you
2 *Sam.* 12:18 child *yet a.* 21, 22
18:14 *yet a.* in midst of the oak
1 *K.* 20:32 he *yet a.?* he is my bro.
Ec. 4:2 than the living *yet a.*
Ezek. 7:13 sold, although *yet a.*
Mat. 27:63 said while *yet a.*

ALL.

Gen. 24:36 given *a.* that he hath
1 *Sam.* 9:19 tell thee *a.* in thy h.
30:8 and without fail recover *a.*
1 *K.* 20:4 I am thine, and *a.* I
Neh. 9:6 L. preservest them *a.*
Job 34:19 they *a.* are works of his
Ps. 14:3 are *a.* gone aside, a.
34:19 deliv. him out of them *a.*
44:17 *a.* this is come upon us
Prov. 22:2 L. is maker of them *a.*
Ezek. 20:40 *a.* of them shall serve
37:22 shall be king to them *a.*
Dan. 1:19 among *a.* none like D.
Hos. 5:2 a rebuker of them *a.*
Mal. 2:10 have we not *a.* one F.

Mat. 13:56 sisters, are they not *a.*
22:26 for they *a.* had her
Mark 12:44 *a.* she had, *Lu.* 21:4
Luke 4:7 if thou worship me, *a.*
15:31 son, *a.* that I have is thine
17:10 when ye have done *a.* say
John 4:39 told me *a.* ever I did
13:10 ye are clean, but not *a.*
17:21 that they *a.* may be one
Acts 4:33 great grace was on *a.*
16:28 thyself no harm, we are *a.*
1 *Cor.* 3:22 *a.* are yours, ye are
Phil 4:18 I have *a.* and abound
2 *Tim.* 3:11 out of them *a.* the L.
1 *Pet.* 3:8 be ye *a.* of one mind
1 *John* 2:19 were not *a.* of us

Above ALL. *See* ABOVE.

According to ALL.
Gen. 6:22 N. did *accor.* to *a.* 7:5
Ex. 31:11 *ac. to a.* L. commanded
36:1; 39:32. 42; 40:16; *Num.*
2:34; 8:20; 9:5; 29:40; *Deut.*
1:3, 41
Jos. 11:23 took the land *ac. to a.*
1 *K.* 8:56 given rest *ac. to a.* thy
11:37 shalt reign *ac. to a.* thy
22:53 *ac. to a.* his father had d.
2 *K.* 23:32, 37; 24:9, 19;
2 *Chr.* 26:4; 27:2
2 *K.* 10:30 *ac. to a.* in my heart
18:3 *ac. to a.* David, 2 *Chr.* 29:2
1 *Chr.* 17:15 *ac. to a.* these words
Neh. 5:19 for good, *ac. to a.* I h.
Jer. 42:20 *ac. to a.* L. shall say
50:29 *ac. to a.* Babyl. hath done
Eze. 24:24 *ac. to a.* he hath done

Before ALL.
Gal. 2:14 Peter *bef.* them *a.*

For ALL.
Phil. 2:21 *for a.* seek their own
Heb. 8:11 *for a.* shall know me
10:10 offering of Ch. once *for a.*

In ALL.
Gen. 21:12 *in a.* Sarah hath said
22 God with thee *in a.* thou
Deut. 29:9 prosp. *in a.* that ye do
1 *K.* 2:3 mayest prosper *in a.*
1 *Cor.* 12:6 God worketh all *in a.*
15:28 that God may be all *in a.*
Eph. 1:23 him that fill. all *in a.*
Col. 3:11 Christ is all *in a.*

ALL Night *See* NIGHT.

Over ALL.
2 *Sam.* 3:21 mayest reign *over a.*
1 *Chr.* 26:12 thou reignest *over a.*
Ps. 103:19 kingdom ruleth *over a.*
Mat. 24:47 ruler *over a. Lu.* 12:44
John 17:2 giv. him power *over a.*
Rom. 9:5 *over a.* God blessed for
10:12 Lord *over a.* is rich to all

To or **Unto ALL.**
Ps. 145:9 the Lord is good *to a.*
Ec. 2:14 one event *to a.* 9:3, 11
9:2 all things come alike *to a.*
Is. 36:6 Pharaoh *to a.* that trust
Mark 13:37 I say *unto a.* watch
Luke 12:41 speakest to us, *to a.?*
Acts 2:39 promise is *to a.* afar off
4:16 manifest *to a.* that dwell
Rom. 10:12 rich *unto a.* that call
13:7 render *to a.* their dues
1 *Cor.* 9:19 a servant *unto a.*
1 *Tim.* 4:15 profit. may app. *to a.*

Upon ALL.
Rom. 3:22 *upon a.* them that be.

ALL these.
Gen. 15:10 took to him *a. these*
Gen. 42:36 *a. these* are against me
Ex. 10:1 G. spake *a. these* words
Job 12:9 know. not that in *a. t.*
Hab. 2:6 shall not *a. t.* take up
Mat. 6:33 *a. t.* shall be, *Lu.* 12:31

ALL this.
Gen. 41:39 God showed thee *a. t.*
Deut. 32:27 hath not done *a. this*

Jud. 6:13 *a. this* befallen us!
1 *Sam.* 22:15 k. nothing of *a. t.*
2 *Sam.* 14: 19 of Joab in *a. this?*
Job 1:22 *a. t.* J. sinned not, 2:10
13:1 mine eye hath seen *a. this*
Ps. 44:17 *a. this* is come upon us
78:32 for *a. this* they sinned still
Ec. 8:9 *a. this* have I seen and
9:1 *a. this* I considered in heart
Is. 5:25 for *a. this* his anger is not
turned 9:12, 17, 21; 10:4
48:6 thou hast heard, see *a. this*
Dan. 5:22 thou knewest *a. this*
7:16 asked h. the truth of *a. t.*
Hos. 7:10 nor seek him for *a. t.*
Mic. 1:5 transgress. of Jac. is *a. t.*
Mat. 1:22 *a. t.* was done that prophets be fulfilled 21:4; 26:56
Luke 16:26 *a. t.* there is a gulf
24:21 *a. t.* to-day is the third d.

ALL that he had.
Gen. 12:20 P. and *a. t. h. h.*
13:1 A. out of E. and *a. t. h. h.*
25:5 Abr. gave *a. t. h. h.* to
31:21 Jacob fled with *a. t. h. h.*
39:4 *a. t. h. h.* into Joseph's
5 bl. of the L. was on *a. t. h. h.*
Mat. 18:25 he sold *a. t. he had*
Mark 5:26 she spent *a. t. she had*
12:44 cast in *a. t. s. h. Lu.* 21:4

ALL the while.
Job 27:3 *a. the w.* my breath

*See further other usual Substan-
tives:*

CONGREGATION DAY, EARTH, IS-
RAEL, MEN, PEOPLE, THINGS, *etc.*

ALLEGING.
Acts 17:3 *a.* C. must have suf.

ALLEGORY.
Gal. 4:24 which things are an *a.*

ALLELUIAH.
Rev. 19:1 great voice say *a.* 3, 4, 6

ALLOW.
Luke 11:48 that ye *a.* the deeds
Acts 24:15 themselves also *a.* that
Rom. 7:15 which I do, I *a.* not

ALLOWED (it.)
Rom. 14:22 that thing wh. he *a.*
1 *Thes.* 2:4 as were *a.* of God

ALLOWANCE.
2 *K.* 25:30 his *a.* was continual *a.*

ALLURE.
Hos. 2:14 *a.* her into the wild.
2 *Pet.* 2:18 they *a.* through lusts

ALMIGHTY.
Gen. 17:1 I am the *a.* God, walk
28:3 God *a.* bless thee and make
25:11 I am God *a.* be fruitful
43:14 God *a.* give you mercy
49:25 by *a.* who shall bless thee
Ex. 6:3 appeared by name God *a.*
Num. 24:4 saw the vision of *a.* 16
Ruth 1:20 *a.* hath dealt bitterly
21 the *a.* hath afflicted me
Job 5:17 desp. not chasten. of *a.*
6:4 arrows of the *a.* are with me
14 forsaketh the fear of the *a.*
8:3 doth the *a.* pervert justice?
5 thy supplication to the *a.*
11:7 find out *a.* to perfection?
12:3 surely I would speak to *a.*
15:25 strengtheneth ag. the *a.*
21:15 *a.* we should serve him
20 shall drink the wrath of *a.*
22:3 pleasure to *a.* thou art
17 what the *a.* do for them?
23 if thou return to the *a.* thou
25 the *a.* shall be thy defence
26 have thy delight in the *a.*
22:16 and the *a.* troubleth me
24:1 are not hid from the *a.*
27:2 *a.* who hath vexed my soul
10 delight himself in the *a.*
11 is with *a.* will I not conceal

29:5 w. the *a.* was yet with me
31:2 inheritance of *a.*
35 that the *a.* would answer me
32:8 inspiration of the *a.* giveth
33:4 breath of *a.* hath given me
34:10 far from *a.* to com. iniq.
12 neither will the *a.* pervert
35:13 the *a.* will not regard
37:23 the *a.* we cannot find him
40:2 contendeth with *a.* instruct
Ps. 68:14 when *a.* scattereth k.
Ps. 91:1 the shadow of the *a.*
Is. 13:6 destruction from the *a.*
Ezek. 1:24 voice of the *a.* 10:5
Joel 1:15 destruction from the *a.*
2 *Cor.* 6:18 my sons, saith L. *a.*
Rev. 1:8 was and is to come, *a.*
4:8 L. God *a.* which was, 11:17
15:3 Lord *a.* just and true, 16:7
21:22 G. *a.* and Lamb temple of

ALMOND, S.
Gen. 43:11 myrrh, nuts, and *a.*
Ex. 25:33 like to *a.* 34; 37:19, 20
Num. 17:8 rod of Aaron yield. *a.*
Ec. 12:5 *a.* tree shall flourish
Jer. 1:11 I see a rod of an *a.* tree

ALMOST.
Ps. 73:2 my feet were *a.* gone
94:17 my soul *a.* dwelt in silence
119:87 *a.* consumed me upon e.
Prov. 5:14 I was *a.* in all evil
Acts 13:44 came *a.* the whole city
19:26 but *a.* through all Asia
26:28 *a.* thou almost persuaded
29 were both *a.* and altogether
Heb. 9:22 *a.* all things by the law

ALMS.
Mat. 6:1 do not your *a.* before
2 doest thine *a.* do not sound
4 that thine *a.* may be in secret
Luke 11:41 give *a.* of such things
12:33 and give *a.* provide bags.
Acts 3:3 seeing P. and J. ask. *a.*
10:2 Cornelius gave much *a.*
4 thine *a.* for a memorial, 31
24:17 to bring *a.* to my nation

ALMSDEEDS.
Acts 9:36 Dorcas full of *a.*

ALMUG-TREES.
1 *K.* 10:11 fr. Ophir plenty of *a-t.*
12 made of *a-t.* pillars

ALOES.
Ps. 45:8 garments smell of *a.*
Prov. 7:17 perf. my bed with *a.*
Cant.. 4:14 myrrh, *a.* with spices
John 19:39 brought *a.* mix. of *a.*

ALONE.
Gen. 2:18 good man should be *a.*
Ex. 18:18 not able thyself *a.*
24:2 Moses *a.* shall come near
Num. 11:14 not able to bear all
this people *a. Deut.* 1:9, 12
23:9 the people shall dwell *a.*
Deut. 32:12 as Lord *a.* did lead h.
33:28 Isr. shall dwell in safety *a.*
2 *Sam.* 18:24 a man run. *a.* 26
1 *K.* 11:29 they two *a.* in field
2 *K.* 19:15 art God *a. Is.* 37:16;
Ps. 86:10
Job 1:15 escaped *a.* to t. 16, 17, 19
9:8 *a.* spreadeth out the heavens
15:19 to whom *a.* earth was giv.
31:17 have I eaten my morsel *a.*
Ps. 63:18 whose name *a.* is Jeh.
136:4 who *a.* doeth great wond.
148:13 his name *a.* is excellent
Ec. 4:8 one *a.* and not a second
10 that is *a.* when he falleth
Is. 2:11 L. *a.* shall be exalted, 17
14:31 none *a.* in appointed times
51:2 I called him *a.* and blessed
63:3 trodden the wine-press *a.*
Lam. 3:28 sitteth *a.* and keepeth
Mat. 4:4 live by bread *a. Lu.* 4:4
14:23 he was *a. Luke* 9:18
18:15 between thee and him *a.*

Mark 4:34 were *a*. he expounded
6:47 sea, and he *a*. on the land
Luke 5:21 forgive sins but G. *a*
6:4 but for the priests *a*.
9:18 as Jesus was *a*. praying
36 voice past, Jes. was found *a*.
John 6:15 into a mountain *a*.
22 discip. were gone away *a*.
8:16 for I am not *a*. but, 16:32
17:20 neither pray I for these *a*
Acts 19:26 that not *a*. at Ephesus
Rom. 4:23 written for his sake *a*.
Gal. 6:4 rejoicing in himself *a*
Heb. 9:7 went high-priest *a*. once
Jam. 2:17 faith is dead, being *a*.

Left ALONE.

Is. 49:21 I was *left a*. these where
John 8:9 Jesus was *left a*. and w.
29 Father hath not *left* me *a*.
Rom. 11:3 I am *left a*. and they

Let ALONE.

Job 10:20 *let* me *a*. that I take
Hos. 4:17 join. to idols, *l*. him *a*.
Mat. 15:14 *let* them *a*. blind lead
Mark 1:24 *let* us *a*. what have we
to do with thee, *Luke* 4:34
14:6 Jesus said, *let* her *a*.
Luke 13:8 *let* it *a*. this year also
John 11:48 if we *let* him *a*. all m.
12:7 *let* her *a*. against the day
Acts 5:38 refr. from these m. *l*. *a*.

ALOOF.

Ps. 38:11 my friends stand *a*.

ALOUD. *See* CRY, CRIED, SING.

ALPHA.

Rev. 1:8 I am *a*. 11 ; 21:6 ; 22:13

ALPHEUS.

Mat. 10:3 James, the son of A.
Mark 3:18 ; *Luke* 6:15 ; *Acts*
1:13
Mark 2:14 saw Levi the son of A.

ALREADY.

Ec. 1:10 it hath been *a*. of old
Mat. 17:12 Elias is come *a*.
John 3:18 condemned *a*.
Phil. 3:16 we have *a*. attained
Rev. 2:25 that ye have *a*. hold f.

ALSO.

Gen. 6:3 for that he *a*. is flesh
1 *Sam.* 14:44 S. answ. God do so,
and m. *a*. 2 *Sam.* 3:35 ; 19:13
Ps. 68:18 gifts for rebellious *a*.
Zec. 8:21 to seek Lord I will go *a*.
Mat. 6:21 w. heart be *a*. *Lu.* 12:34
26:73 thou art *a*. one of them
John 5:19 these *a*. doth the Son
12:26 where I am, there shall *a*.
14:3 where I am, ye may be *a*.
1 *Cor.* 15:8 he was seen of me *a*.
2 *Tim.* 1:5 persuaded in thee *a*.

ALTAR.

Gen. 8:20 Noah builded an *a*.
12:7 Abraham built an *a*. 22:9
35:1 Beth-el, make there an *a*.
Ex. 17:15 Moses built an *a*.
20:24 an *a*. of earth make to me
29:37 sanctify it, *a*. most holy
44 I will sanctify the *a*.
30:27 *a*. of incense
40:10 *a*. of burnt-offering
Lev. 6:9 fire of *a*. shall be burn.
Num. 7:84 dedication of the *a*.
18:3 shall not come nigh the *a*.
Jos. 22:34 called the *a*. Ed.
Jud. 6:25 throw down *a*. of B.
2 *Sam.* 24:18 rear an *a*. to the L.
1 *K.* 13:2 cried against the *a* O *a*.
18:30 Elijah repaired the *a*.
35 the water ran about the *a*.
2 *K.* 18:22 shall worship before
this *a*. *Is.* 36:7
Ps. 26:6 will I compass thine *a*.
43:4 then will I go to *a*. of God
Is. 19:19 an *a*. in midst of Egypt
27:9 stones of *a*. as chalk-sto.

56:7 sacri. accepted on mine *a*.
Lam. 2:7 Lord h. cast off his *a*.
Ezek. 8:16 between porch and *a*.
Joel 1:13 howl, ye minist. of *a*.
2:17 priests weep b. porch and *a*.
Amos 2:8 to pledge by every *a*.
Mal. 1:7 polluted bread on, *a*.
10 fire on mine *a*. for naught
2:13 covering *a*. with tears
Mat. 5:23 thou bring gift to the *a*.
23:18 swear by the *a*. it is n.
35 ye slew between the temple
and *a*. *Luke* 11:51
Acts 17:23 *a*. with this inscript.
1 *Cor.* 9:13 partak. with *a*. 10:18
Heb. 7:13 attendance at the *a*.
13:10 we have an *a*. whereof
Rev. 6:9 under the *a*. souls of
8:3 prayers on the golden *a*.
9:13 from horns of golden *a*.
See BUILT.

ALTARS.

1 *K.* 19:10 thrown down *a*. 14
Ps. 84:3 even thine *a*. O Lord.
Is. 17:8 shall not look to the *a*.
*Jer.*17:1 is graven on horns of *a*.
2 their children remem. *a*.
Ezek. 6:4 your *a*. shall be desol.
Hos. 8:11 *a*. to sin, *a*. shall be
12:11 *a*. as heaps in the furrows
Amos 3:14 visit the *a*. of Beth-el
Rom. 11:3 digged down thine *a*.

ALTER.

Ezr. 6:11 whoso. shall *a*. this
Ps. 89:34 not *a*. the thing gone

ALTERED.

Luke 9:29 countenance was *a*.

ALTOGETHER.

Ps. 14:3 *a*. filthy, 53:3
19:9 judgments are righteous *a*.
50:21 *a*. such a one as thyself
139:4 lo, thou knowest it *a*.
Cant. 5:16 yea, he is *a*. lovely
John 9:34 wast *a*. born in sins
Acts 26:29 alm. and *a*. such as I

ALWAY, S.

Job. 7:16 I would not live *a*.
27:10 will he *a*. call upon God ?
Ps. 16:8 have set L. *a*. before me
Ps. 103:9 he will not *a*. chide
Mat. 28:20 I am with you *a*.
Mark 14:7 ye have not *a*. *Jn.* 12:8
John 8:29 I do *a*. those things
11:42 thou hearest me *a*.
Phil. 1:4 *a*. in every prayer
20 as *a*. so now Christ shall
4:4 rejoice in the Lord *a*.
1 *Thes.* 2:16 fill up their sins *a*.

AM I.

Mat. 18:20 there *am I* in the m.

I AM, I AM that I AM.

Ex. 3:14 *I am that I am* hath
Job 9:32 he is not a man as *I am*
Is. 44:6 *I am* the first, *I am* the
last, 48:12 ; *Rev.* 1:11
47:8 *I am*, none else, Zep. 2:15
Luke 22:70 ye say that *I am*
John 8:58 before Abr. was, *I am*
12:26 where *I am* there shall my
17:24 with me where *I am*
Acts 26:29 altog. such as *I am*
1 *Cor.* 15:10 of G. *I am* what *I am*
Gal. 4:12 be as *I am*, for *I am* as

Here AM I, or Here I AM.

See HERE.

AMALEK.

Gen. 36:12 T. bare to Eliphaz A.
Ex. 17:8 then came A. and f.
14 the remembrance of A. 16
Num. 24:20 looked on A. he took
up his p. and said A. was
Deut. 25:17 A. did, 1 *Sam.* 15:2
. 19 out the remembrance of A.
Jud. 5:14 was a root against A.
1 *Sam.* 15:3 smite A.; 5 city of A.

28:18 exec. his wrath on A.
Ps. 83:7 Gebal, Ammon, A. are

AMANA. *Cant.* 4:8.

AMASA.

2 *Sam.* 17:25 A. capt. of the host
1 *K.* 2:5 what J. did to A. 32
1 *Chr.* 2:17 Abigail bare A.
2 *Chr.* 28:12 A. s. of H. stood up

AMAZED.

Job 32:15 *a*. answered no more
Is. 13:8 be *a*. one at another
Ezek. 32:10 people *a*. at thee
Mat. 19:25 the disciples were *a*.
Mark 2:12 were all *a*, *Luke* 5:26
14:33 he began to be sore *a*.
Luke 4:36 all *a*. and spake among
9:43 were all *a*. at mighty pow.
Acts 9:21 all that heard S. were *a*.

AMAZEMENT.

Acts 3:10 filled with *a*. at what
1 *Pet.* 3:6 not afraid with any *a*.

AMAZIAH.

2 *K.* 12:21 A. reign., 2 *Ch.* 24:27
13:12 fought against A. 14:15
14:11 but A. would not hear
15:3 A. had done, 2 *Chr.* 26:4
1 *Chr.* 6:45 A. son of Hilkiah
2 *Chr.* 25:27 A. did turn the L.
Amos 7:10 A. priest of Beth-el

AMBASSADOR.

Prov. 13:17 a faithful *a*. is health
Jer. 49:14 *a*. sent to heath. *Ob.* 1
Eph. 6:20 I am an *a*. in bonds

AMBASSADORS.

Jos. 9:4 as if they had been *a*.
2 *Chr.* 35:21 he sent *a*. saying
Is. 18:2 sendeth *a*. by the sea
30:4 his *a*. came to Hanes
33:7 *a*. of peace shall weep
Ezek. 17:15 rebelled in sending *a*.
2 *Cor.* 5:20 we are *a*. for Christ.

AMBASSAGE.

Luke 14:32 sendeth an *a*.

AMBER. *See* COLOR.

AMBUSH, ES.

Jos. 8:2 an *a*. for the city.
Jer. 51:12 prepare the *a*.

AMBUSHMENT, S.

2 *Chr.* 13:13 Jerob. caused an *a*.
20:22 Lord set *a*. against Am.

AMEN.

Num. 5:22 woman shall say *a*. *a*.
Deut. 27:15 people shall say *a*.
1 *K.* 1:36 Benaiah answered *a*.
1 *Chr.* 16:36 people said *a*. and
Ps. 41:13 everlasting, *a*. and *a*.
72:19 with his glory, *a*. and *a*.
89:52 blessed evermore, *a*. and *a*.
106:48 let all the people say *a*.
Jer. 28:6 even Jeremiah said *a*.
Mat. 6:13 the glory for ever, *a*.
1 *Cor.* 14:16 unlearned say *a*.
2 *Cor.* 1:20 in him yea and *a*.
Rev. 1:18 alive for evermore *a*.
3:14 these things saith the *a*.
5:14 the four beasts said *a*. 19:4
22:20 *a*. even so, come, L. Jesus

AMEND, S.

Lev. 5:16 he shall make *a*.
Jer. 7:3 *a*. ways, 5 ; 26:13 ; 35:15
John 4:52 when he began to *a*.

AMERCE.

Deut. 22:19 *a*. him in 100 shekels

AMETHYST. *See* AGATE and
JACINTH.

AMIABLE.

Ps. 84:1 how *a*. are thy taber.

AMISS.

2 *Chr.* 6:37 done *a*.
Dan. 3:29 speak any thing *a*.
Luke 23:41 hath done nothing *a*.
Jam. 4:3 because ye ask *a*.

AMMAH. 2 Sam. 2:24
AMMI. Hos. 2:1

AMMINADAB.
Ex. 6:23 Aaron took daugh. of A.
Ruth 4:20 A. begat N. Mat. 1:4

AMMI-NADIB. Cant. 6:12

AMMON.
Gen. 19:38 f. of children of A.

AMMONITE, 8.
Deut. 23:8 A. not enter congreg.
1 Sam. 11:11 slew A. till heat of
1 K. 11:1 S. loved women of A.
2 Chr. 26:8 A. gifts to Uzziah
Ezr. 9:1 the abomination of A.

AMNON.
2 Sam. 3:2 D's first-born was A.
13:2, 26, 28 ; 1 Chr. 3:1 ; 4:20

AMON.
1 K. 22:26 back to A.
2 K. 21:18 A. reigned ; 23 slain
2 Chr. 33:22 A. sacrificed to img.
Neh. 7:59 out of capt. child. of A.
Mat. 1:10 Manasses begat A.

AMORITE, S.
Gen. 15:16 iniq. of A. not full.
48:22 I took fr. A. with my sw.
Deut.20:17 utterly destroy the A.
Jos. 10:12 L. delivered up A.
Jud. 11:23 L. dispossessed the A.
1 Sam. 7:14 bet. Israel and A.
2 Sam.21:2 Gibeonites were of A.
Ezek. 16:3 fath. an A. moth., 45

AMOS, or AMOZ.
2 K. 19:2 Is. the son of A. 20;
20:1 ; 2 Chr. 26:22 ; 32:20, 32;
Is. 1:1 ; 2:1 ; 13:1 ; 20:2 ; 37:2,
21 ; 38:1
Amos 7:14 A. said I was no prop.
Luke 3:25 Matta. was son of A.

AMPHIPOLIS. Acts 17:1
AMPLIAS. Rom. 16:8

AMRAM.
Ex. 6:18 sons of Kohath, A.
1 Chr. 1:41 sons of Dishon, A.
6:3 children of A. Aaron
Ezr. 10:34 sons of B., Maadi, A.
ANAH. Gen. 36:24

ANAK.
Num. 13:28 children of A. 33
Deut. 9:2 bef. the children of A.?
Jos. 15:14 sons of A. Jud. 1:20

ANAKIM.
Deut. 2:10 people tall as A. 9:2
Jos. 11:22 none of the A. were
14:15 Arba was great among A.
ANAMMELECH. 2 K. 17:31 .

ANANIAS.
Acts 5:5 A. hearing fell down
9:12 vision A. coming, 22:12
23:2 A. commanded to smite
24:1 A. descended

ANATHEMA.
1 Cor. 16:22 be a. maran-atha

ANATHOTH.
Jos. 21:18 A. with her suburbs
1 K. 2:26 to A. to thine owe
1 Chr. 7:8 sons of Becher, A. and
Neh. 10:19 A. sealed the cov.
Is. 10:30 thy voice, O poor A.
Jer. 11:23 evil on the men of A.
29:27 reproved Jeremiah of A.
32:7 my field that is in A. 8.

ANCESTORS.
Lev. 26:45 covenant of their a.

ANCHOR, S.
Acts 27:30 would have cast a.
Heb. 6:19 hope we have as an a.

ANCIENT.
Deut. 33:15 things of a. moun.
Jud. 5:21 that a. river, Kishon
2 K. 19:25 a. times Is. 37:26
1 Chr. 4:22 these are a. things

Ezr. 3:12 a. men that had seen
Job. 12:12 with the a. is wisdom
Prov. 22:28 rem. not a. landmark
Is. 3:2 a. the Lord doth take
9:15 the a. and honorable he is
19:11 I am the son of a. kings
23:7 antiquity is of a. days
44:7 I appointed the a. people
47:6 the a. laid thy yoke
51:9 awake as in the a days
Jer. 18:15 stumble from a. paths
Ezek. 9:6 began at the a. man
Dan. 7:9 the a. of days did sit
13 like Son of man came to a.
22 till the a. of days came

ANCIENTS.
1 Sam. 24:13 proverb of the a.
Ps. 119:100 more than the a.
Is. 3:14 into judgment with a.
24:23 L. shall reign bef. his a.
Jer. 19:1 of a. of people and a.
Ezek. 7:26 shall per. from the a.
8:12 hast seen what the a. do?
27:9 a. of Gebal thy calkers

ANCLE-BONES.
Acts 3:7 a.-b. received strength.

ANCLES.
Ezek. 47:3 waters were to the a.

ANDREW.
Mark 13:3 A. asked privately
John 1:40 which heard was A.
ANDRONICUS. Rom. 16:7
ANER. Gen. 14:24 ; 1 Chr. 6:70

ANGEL.
Gen. 22:11 a. said, Abraham
24:7 send his a. before thee. 40
48:16 the a. who redeemed me
Ex. 23:20 send a. before thee,
23 ; 32:34 ; 33:2
Num. 20:16 sent an a.
Jud. 13:19 a. did wondrously
2 Sam. 24:16 the a. stretched out
his hand, the a. 1 Chr. 21:15
17 he saw the a. that smote
1 K. 13:18 a. spake by the word
19:5 an a. touched Elijah
1 Chr. 21:15 G. sent an a. to Jeru.
20 Ornan turned and saw the a.
27 Lord com. a. and he put up
2 Chr. 32:21 an a. which cut off
Ec. 5:6 bef. a. it was an error
Is. 63:9 the a. of his presence
Dan. 3:28 God who hath sent a.
6:22 sent his a. and shut up
Hos. 12:4 had power over the a.
Zec. 1:9 a. that talked, 4:5
3:4 stood before a.
Mat. 28:5 a. answer. the women
Luke 1:13 a. said, fear not, Zach.
19 a. answered, I am Gabriel
26 in sixth month the a. Gab'l
30 the a. said, Fear not, Mary
35 a. answ., Holy Ghost shall
2:10 a. said to the shepherds
13 suddenly with a. a multit.
21 so named of the a.
22:43 an a. strengthening him
John 5:4 a. went down at c. s.
12:29 an a. spake to him
Acts 6:15 as the face of an a.
7:35 a. that appear. in the bush
38 in wilderness with the a.
10:7 a. which spake to Cornel.
22 warned by a holy a. to send
11:13 he had seen a. in house
12:8 the a. said to Peter, bind
9 true which was done by a.
10 the a. departed from him
11 sent his a. and delivered me
15 then said they, it is his a.
23:8 say, neither a. nor spirit
9 if an a. hath spoken to him
2 Cor. 11:14 transf. into a. of l.
Gal. 1:8 though we or an a.
Rev. 1:1 sig. it by a. to John
2:1 a. of ch., 8, 12, 18 ; 3:1, 7, 14

5:2 I saw strong a. proclaiming
7:2 a. ascending from the east
8:3 a. came and stood at the al.
4 ascended out of the a. hand
5. a. took the censer
7 first a. sounded ; 8 second a.
8:10 third a. ; 12 fourth a.
13 I heard an a. flying through
9:1 fifth a. s. 13 sixth a.
11 the a. of the bottomless pit
14 sixth a. loose the four angs.
10:1 a. come down, 18:1 ; 20:1
5 a. which I saw stand on sea
7 in days of voice of seventh a.
8 take the book in hand of a.
11:15 seventh a. sounded
14:6 a. fly in the midst of heav.
8 another a. saying, Babylon is
19 the a. thrust in his sickle
16:1 a. poured out vial, 3, 4, etc.
5 a. of the waters
17:7 a. said, wherefore marvel?
18:21 mighty a. took up a stone
Rev. 19:17 an a. standing in the
21:17 of a man, that is of the a.
22:16 I Jesus have sent mine a.

ANGEL of God.
Ex. 14:19 a. of God removed
Jud. 13:6 counten. of a. of God
1 Sam. 29:9 good as an a. of God
2 Sam. 14:17 an a. of God, 19:27
20 accord. to wisd. of a. of G.
Acts 27:23 by me the a. of G.
Gal. 4:14 rec. me as an a. of God

ANGEL of the Lord.
Gen. 16:7 a. of the L. found Hag.
22:11 a. of the L. called 15
Num. 22:23 a. of the L. 25, 27
31 Balaam saw a. of Lord
Jud. 5:23 Meroz, said a. of L.
6:11 a. of the Lord sat under
12 a. of the L. appeared to G.
21 a. of L. put forth end of st.
13:3 a. of L. appeared to woman
16 he was an a. of L. 21
20 a. of the L. ascended
2 Sam. 24:16 a. of the L. was by
the thresh-pl. 1 Chr. 21:15
2 K. 19:35 a. of the L. smote in
camp, Is. 37:36
1 Chr. 21:12 a. of the L. destroy.
18 a. of the L. commanded G.
20 because of s. of a. of the L.
Ps. 34:7 a. of the L. encampeth
35:5 let a. of the L. chase them
6 let a. of the L. perse. them
Zec. 1:12 a. of the L. answered
3:5 a. of the L. stood by Joshua
6 a. of the L. protested
12:8 as the a. of the L. before
Mat.1:20 a. of L.ap.in dm. 2:13,9
24 Jos. did as a. of L. had bid.
28:2 a. of L. descended
Luke 1:11 Zacharias an a of L.
2:9 a. of L. came upon them
Acts 5:19 a. of L. opened prison
8:26 a. of the L. spake to Philip
12:23 a. of the L. smote Herod.

ANGELS.
Gen. 19:1 came two a. to Sodom
Ps. 8:5 low. than a. Heb. 2:7, 9
68:17 are thousands of a.
78:25 man did eat a.'s food
49 sending evil a. among them
Mat. 4:11 a. ministered.Mk. 1:13
13:39 the reapers are the a.
49 the a. shall sever the wick.
18:10 their a. behold face of G.
24:36 a. of heaven, Mark 13:32
25:31 all the holy a. with him
26:53 twelve legions of a.
Mark 8:38 Son of man cometh
with the holy a. Luke 9:26
12:25 are as the a. in heaven
Luke 2:15 as the a. were gone
16:22 was carried by the a.

20:36 equal unto the *a.*
24:23 also seen a vision of *a.*
John 20:12 seeth two *a.* in white
Acts 7:53 by disposition of *a.*
Rom. 8:38 nor *a.* able to separate
1 *Cor.* 4:9 spect. to world. to *a.*
  6:3 that we shall judge *a. ?*
  11:10 power because of the *a.*
  13:1 tongues of men and *a.*
Gal. 3:19 ordained by *a.*
Col. 2:18 in worship. of *a.*
2 *Thes.* 1:7 rev. with mighty *a.*
1 *Tim.* 3:16 of *a.* preached to Ge.
  5:21 before G. and the elect *a.*
Heb. 1:4 much better than the *a.*
  5 to which of the *a.* said he, 13
  7 who maketh his *a.* spirits
  2:2 word spoken by *a.* steadfast
  5 to the *a.* not put in subject.
  16 not nature of *a.* but seed
  12:22 innum. company of *a.*
  13:2 entertained *a.* unawares
1 *Pet.* 1:12 *a.* desire to look into
  3:22 *a.* and powers being subj.
2 *Pet.* 2:4 if God spared not the *a.*
  11 whereas a greater in power
Jude 6 *a.* kept not first estate
Rev. 1:20 stars *a.* of churches
  5:11 voice of many *a.* about th.
  7:1 four *a.* on the four corners
  2 with loud voice to the four *a.*
  11 the *a.* stood round the th.
  8:13 trumpet of *a.* yet to sound
  9:14 loose the four *a.* bound
  15 the *a.* were loosed
  14:10 torment. in pres. of h. *a.*
  21:12 and the gates twelve *a.*

ANGELS of God.
Gen. 28:12 *a.* of G. asc. *John* 1:51
32:1 Jacob went his way, and *a.*
  of God met him
Mat. 22:30 but as *a. of God* in
  heaven, *Mark* 12:25
Luke 12:8 him shall the Son confess before *a. of God*
  9 be denied before the *a. of G.*
  15:10 in presence of *a. of God*
Heb. 1:6 the *a. of God* worship

His ANGELS.
Job 4:18 *his a.* charged with
Ps. 91:11 give *his a.* charge, *Mat.* 4:6; *Luke* 4:10
103:20 ye *his a.* that excel
104:4 *his a.* spirits, *Heb.* 1:7
148:2 praise ye him all *his a.*
Mat. 13:41 shall send forth *his a.*
  16:27 glory of his F. with *his a.*
  24:31 *his a.* with s., *Mark* 13:27
  25:41 fire for devil and *his a.*
Rev. 3:5 will confess before *his a.*
  12:7 M. and *his a.* the dragon
  9 drag. was cast out, and *his a.*

ANGER, Verb.
Rom. 10:19 fool. nation I will *a.*

ANGER.
Gen. 27:45 thy brother's *a.* turn
44:18 let not thine *a.* burn
49:7 cursed be their *a.*
Ex. 32:19 Moses' *a.* waxed hot
Deut. 9:19 I was afraid of the *a.*
  13:17 the fierceness of his *a.*
  29:24 the heat of this great *a. ?*
Jud. 8:3 their *a.* was abated
Job 9:13 G. will not withdraw *a.*
Ps. 21:9 oven in time of thine *a.*
30:5 his *a.* endureth but a mom.
37:8 cease from *a.* and forsake
38:3 no soundness because of *a.*
69:24 wrathful *a.* take hold
74:1 why doth thy *a.* smoke
78:21 *a.* came up against Israel
  38 many a time turn. he his *a.*
  49 cast the fierceness of his *a.*
  50 he made a way to his *a.*
85:3 turned from fierceness of *a.*

  4 cause *a.* towards us to cease
  5 out *a.* to all generations
90:7 consumed by thine *a.*
  11 knoweth power of thine *a.*
103:9 his *a.* for ever, *Jer.* 3:5
Prov. 15:1 griev. words stir up *a.*
  19:11 discretion deferreth his *a.*
  21:14 a gift in secret pacifieth *a.*
22:8 the rod of his *a.* shall fail
27:4 and *a.* is outrageous
Ec. 7:9 *a.* resteth in bosom
Is. 5:25 his *a.* not turned away,
  9:12, 17, 21 : 10:4
  7:4 fear not for the *a.* of Resin
10:5 the rod of mine *a.* and staff
  25 my *a.* in their destruction
12:1 angry, thine *a.* is turned
13:9 cometh with fierce *a.*
  13 day of fierce *a. Lam.* 1:12
30:27 name of L. burn. with *a.*
  30 the indignation of his *a.*
42:25 on him fury of his *a.*
48:9 will I defer mine *a.*
66:15 come to render his *a.*
Jer. 2:35 his *a.* shall turn
  3:12 cause mine *a.* to fall on you,
  I will not keep mine *a.*
  4:26 cities brok. down by his *a.*
  7:20 *a.* be poured on this place
18:23 deal with them in thine *a.*
25:38 desolate because of his *a.*
32:31 city. provocat. of mine *a.*
36:7 great is the *a.* L. hath pron.
42:18 as mine *a.* on Jerusalem
44:6 mine *a.* was poured forth
49:37 evil on them, my fierce *a.*
Lam. 2:1 his footstool in day of *a.*
  6 in the indignation of his *a.*
  21 hast slain them in thine *a.*
  22 the Lord's *a.* none escaped
3:43 thou hast covered with *a.*
  4:11 poured out his fierce *a.*
Ezek. 5:13 thus *a.* be accompl.
  7:3 send mine *a.* upon thee
  8 accomp. *a.* on thee, 20:8, 21
  35:11 will do accord. to thine *a.*
Dan. 9:16 let thine *a.* be turned
Hos. 11:9 not execute mine *a.*
  14:4 for mine *a.* is turned away
Amos 1:11 his *a.* did tear
Jon. 3:9 God turn from fierce *a.*
Mic. 7:18 *a.* for ever
Nah. 1:6 who can abide his *a. ?*
Hab. 3:8 thine *a.* ag. the rivers
Zep. 3:8 to pour all my fierce *a.*
Mark 3:5 looked on them with *a.*
Eph. 4:31 *a.* be put, *Col.* 3:8

ANGER of the Lord.
Num. 25:4 fierce *a.* of the L.
32:14 to augment *a. of the L.*
Deut. 29:20 *a. of the L.* shall s.
Jud. 2:14 *a. of the L.* against Israel, 20 ; 3:8 ; 10:7

2 *K.* 24:20 thro' the *a. of the L.*
  it came to pass, *Jer.* 52:3
Jer. 4:8 *a. of the Lord* is not t.
  12:13 fierce *a. of the L.* 25:37
23:20 *a. of the L.* shall not, 30:24
51:45 from *a. of the L.*
Lam. 4:16 *a. of the L.* hath
Zep. 2:2 before *a. of the L.* come
  3 hid in day of *a. of the L.*

In ANGER.
Gen. 49:6 in *a.* they slew a man
Deut. 29:28 L. overthrew in *a.*
  28 the L. rooted them out in *a.*
Job 9:5 overturn. them in his *a.*
18:4 he teareth hims. in his *a.*
21:17 distributeth sorrows in *a.*
35:15 he hath visited in *a.*
Ps. 6:1 not in *a. Jer.* 10:24
  7:6 in thine *a.* lift up thyself
27:9 put not thy serv. away in *a.*
56:7 in *a.* cast down the people
77:9 in *a.* shut up his mercies ?
Is. 13:3 called mighty ones in *a.*

14:6 he that ruled nations in *a.*
63:3 I will tread them in *a.* 6
Jer. 21:5 against you, even in *a.*
32:37 driven them in mine *a.*
33:5 I have slain in mine *a.*
Lam. 2:1 Lord covered Zion with a cloud in his *a.*
  3 cut off in *a.* horn of Israel
3:66 destroy them in *a.*
Ezek. 5:15 execute judgm. in *a.*
  13:13 shower in mine *a.*
22:20 I gather you in *a.*
43:8 consumed them in mine *a.*
Dan. 11:20 destro'd, neither in *a.*
Hos. 13:11 gave a king in mine *a.*
Mic. 5:15 execute veng. in *a.*
Hab. 3:12 thresh heathen in *a.*

ANGER kindled.
Ex. 4:14 *a.* of L. *k.* against M.
Num. 11:1 *a.* of the Lord was *k.*
  10 ; 12:9 ; 22:22
  25:3 *a.* of the L. was *k.* against
  Israel. 32:13 ; *Jos.* 7:1 ; 2 *Sam.* 24:1 ; 2 *Kings* 13:3
Deut. 6:15 lest *a.* be *k.* against
  7:4 so will *a.* be *k.* against you
  29:27 *a.* of the L. *k.* against this
  31:17 *a.* be *k.* in that day, *Jos.* 23:16
32:29 *k.* in mine *a. Jer.* 15:14
2 *Sam.* 6:7 *a.* of the Lord was *k.* against Uzziah, 1 *Chr.* 13:10
12:5 David's *a.* *k.* against
Is. 5:25 *a.* of L. *k.* against
Jer. 17:4 have *k.* a fire in mine *a.*
Zec. 10:3 *a.* *k.* ag. the shepherds

Provoke or Provoked to ANGER.
Deut. 32:16 abominations *p. t. a.*
  21 they have *provoked* me *to a.*
Jud. 2:12 and *pr.* L. *to a.*
1 *K.* 16:2 *pr.* me *to a.* with sins,
  2 *K.* 17:11 ; *Jer.* 11:17 ; 32:29, 32 ; *Ezek.* 16:26
2 *K.* 21:15 *pr. to a.* since day
  22:17 forsaken me that they might *pro.* me *to a.* 2 *Chr.* 34:25 ; *Jer.* 25:7
Ps. 78:58 *pro.* him *to a.* with high places, 106:29
Prov. 20:2 whoso *pro. to a.*
Is. 1:4 *pro.* Holy One of Is. *to a.*
65:3 a people that *pro.* me *to a.*
Hos. 12:14 Ephr. *pro.* him *to a.*
Col. 3:21 *pro.* not your chil. *to a.*

Slow to ANGER.
Neh. 9:17 pardon, *slow* to *a.*
Ps. 103:8 *slow* to *a.* 145:8
Prov. 15:18 he s. *to a.* appeaseth
  16:32 s. *to a.* better than mighty
Joel 2:13 *slow* to *a.* of great kindness, *Jon.* 4:2
Nah. 1:3 Lord is sl. *to a.*

ANGERED.
Ps. 106:32 *a.* him at waters

ANGLE.
Is. 19:8 all they that cast *a.*
Hab. 1:15 they take up with *a.*

ANGRY.
Gen. 18:30 let not L. be *a.* 32
  45:5 be not *a.* that ye sold me
Lev. 10:16 Moses *a.* with Eleazar
Deut. 1:37 L. *a.* with me 4:21
  9:20 L. was very *a.* with Aaron
Jud. 18:25 lest *a.* fellows run on
1 *K.* 8:46 thou be *a.* 2 *Chr.* 6:36
  11:9 L. was *a.* with Solomon
2 *K.* 17:18 was *a.* with Israel
Ezr. 9:14 wouldst be *a.* with us
Ps. 2:12 kiss the S., lest he be *a.*
  7:11 God is *a.* with the wicked
  76:7 when thou art *a.*
Ps. 79:5 how long *a. ?* 80:4 ; 85:5
Prov. 14:17 soon *a.* dealeth fool
  21:19 than with an *a.* woman

22:24 friendship with an *a.* man
25:23 so doth an *a.* countenance
29:22 *a.* man stirreth up strife
Ec. 5:6 God be *a.* at thy voice?
7:9 be not hasty in spirit to be *a.*
Cant. 1:6 children were *a.*
Is. 12:1 thou wast *a.* with me
Ezek. 16:42 will be no more *a.*
Jon. 4:1 Jonah was very *a.*

4:4 doest thou well to be *a.?*
9 I do well to be *a.* unto death
Mat. 5:22 is *a.* with brother
Luke 14:21 master of h. being *a.*
15:28 *a.* and would not
John 7:23 are ye *a.* at me bec.
Eph. 4:26 be *a.* and sin not
Tit. 1:7 a bishop not soon *a.*
Rev. 11:18 the nations were *a.*

ANGUISH.
Ex. 6:9 not to M. for *a.*
Deut. 2:25 tremble, and be in *a.*
2 *Sam.* 1:9 slay me,for *a.* is come
Job 7:11 I will speak in *a.* of spir.
15:24 *a.* shall make him afraid
Ps. 119:143 and *a.* have taken
Prov. 1:27 when distress and *a.*
Is. 8:22 and behold dimness of *a.*
30:6 into land of trouble and *a.*
Jer. 4:31 the *a.* as of her that
John 16:21 no more her *a.* for joy
Rom. 2:9 tribulation and *a.* upon
2 *Cor.* 2:4 out of *a.* of heart

ANISE.
Mat. 23:23 pay tithe of mint, *a.*

ANNA. *Lu.* 2:36
ANNAS. *Lu.* 3:2; *John* 18:13, 24

ANOINT.
Ex. 28:41 ßhalt *a.* 30:30; 40:15
29:7 take oil and *a.* him, 40:13
36 shalt *a.* the altar, 40:10
30:26 *a.* the tabernacle, 40:9
Lev. 16:32 whom he shall *a.*
Deut. 28:40 shalt not *a.* thyself
Jud. 9:8 trees went to *a.* a king
15 if in truth ye *a.* me king
1 *Sam.* 9:16 *a.* him captain
15:1 sent me to *a.* thee king
16:3 *a.* him whom I name
12 L. said, Arise. *a.* him
2 *Sam.* 14:2 *a.* not thys. with oil
1 *K.* 1:34 Zadok *a.* him king
19:15 *a.* Hazael king
16 *a.* Elisha
Is. 21:5 princes, *a.* the shield
Dan. 9:24 and *a.* the most Holy
10:3 neither did I *a.* myself
Amos 6:6 *a.* themselves
Mic. 6:15 the olives, but not *a.*
Mat. 6:17 when thou fastest *a.*
Mark 14:8 is come to *a.* my body
16:1 spices that they might *a.*
Luke 7:46 head thou didst not *a.*
Rev. 3:18 *a.* thine eyes

ANOINTED.
Lev. 8:10 *a.* the tabernacle
11 *a.* the altar, *Num.* 7:1
12 A.'s head, and *a.* him
1 *Sam.* 10:1 the L. *a.* thee capt.
15:17 *a.* Saul
16:13 *a.* David, 2 *Sam.* 2:4, 7;
5:3, 17; 12:7; 2 *K.* 9:3, 6, 12;
1 *Chr.* 11:3; 14:8
2 *Sam.* 2:7 Judah have *a.* me k.
8:39 I am weak, though *a.* king
12:20 David arose, and *a.* hims.
23:1 David the *a.* of God said
Is. 61:1 *a.* me to preach, *Lu.* 4:18
Ezek. 28:14 *a.* cherub that covers
Luke 7:38 kissed his feet and *a.*
46 this woman hath *a.* my feet
John 9:6 he *a.* the eyes with clay
11:2 Mary which *a.* the Lord
12:3 Mary *a.* feet of Jesus
Acts 4:27 child J. thou hast *a.*
10:38 God *a.* Jesus of Nazar.
2 *Cor.* 1:21 hath *a.* us is God

ANOINTED Ones.
Zec. 4:14 *a.* ones which stand

His ANOINTED.
1 *Sam.* 2:10 exalt horn of *his a.*
12:3 against the L. and *his a.*
5 the L. and *his a.* is witness
2 *Sam.* 22:51 showeth mercy to
his a. Ps. 18:50
Ps. 2:2 and against *hts a.*
20:6 the Lord saveth *his a.*
28:8 saving strength of *his a.*
Is. 45:1 saith L. to *his a.* to C.

Lord's ANOINTED.
1 *Sam.* 16:6 *Lord's a.* is before
24:6 my master, the *Lord's a.*
10 my hand against *Lord's a.*

1 *Sam.* 26:9 L. *a.* and the guiltl.
16 have not kept the *Lord's a.*
2 *Sam.* 1:14 to destroy *L. a.*
19:21 he cursed *L. a.*
Lam. 4:20 *a.* of *L.* taken

Mine ANOINTED.
1 *Sam.* 2:35 walk before *mine a.*
1 *Chr.* 16:22 touch not *mine a.*
Ps. 132:17 a lamp for *mine a.*

ANOINTED with Oil.
2 *Sam.* 1:21 though not *a. with o.*
Ps. 45:7 *a. w. o.* of glad. *Heb.* 1:9
89:20 *with* holy *oil* have I *a.*
92:10 I shall be *a. with* fresh *o.*
Mark 6:13 *a. with oil* many sick

Thine ANOINTED.
2 *Chr.* 6:42 turn not away the
face of *thine a. Ps.* 132:10
Ps. 84:9 look on face of *thine a.*
89:38 been wroth with *thine a.*
51 footsteps of *thine a.*
Hab. 3:13 salvation with *thine a.*

ANOINTEST.
Ps. 23:5 *a.* my head with oil

ANOINTING.
Ex. 40:15 *a.* everlast. priesthood
Is. 10:27 destroyed bec. of *a.*
1 *John* 2:27 *a.* teacheth all things

ANOINTING Oil.
Ex. 37:29 made the holy *a. oil*
Lev. 8:12 *a. oil* on Aaron's head
10:7 *a. oil* of the L. is upon you
Num. 4:16 Elea. pertaineth *a. oil*
Jam. 5:14 *a.* with *o.* in name of L.

ANON.
Mat. 13:20 *a.* with joy receiv. it
Mark 1:30 mother lay sick and *a.*

ANOTHER.
1 *Sam.* 10:6 shalt be turned to *a.*
Job 19:27 shall behold and not *a.*
Ps. 109:8 let *a.* take, *Acts* 1:20
Prov. 25:9 dis. not a secret to *a.*
27:2 let *a.* praise thee, and not
Is. 42:8 my glory not to *a.* 48:11
65:15 his servants by *a.* name
Hos. 3:3 shalt not be for *a.* man
4:4 let no man reprove *a.*
Mat. 11:3 or do we look for *a.?*
Mark 14:19 *a.* said, Is it I?
Luke 16:7 to *a.* How much owest
2 *Cor.* 11:4 *a.* Jesus, *a.* spirit, or *a.*
Gal. 1:7 which is not *a.* but
6:4 rejoic. in himself, not in *a.*
Heb. 3:13 exhort one *a.* 10:25

One ANOTHER. *See* LOVE.

One against ANOTHER.
1 *Sam.* 2:25 if *one* man sin *a. a.*
Jer. 13:14 dash them *one a. a.*
1 *Cor.* 4:6 puffed up *one a. a.*
Jam. 5:9 grudge not *one a. a.*

One for ANOTHER.
1 *Cor.* 11:33 tarry *one for a.*
Jam. 5:16 pray *one for a.* that ye

ANSWER.
Gen. 41:16 Phar. an *a.* of peace

Deut. 20:11 if city make *a.*
2 *Sam.* 24:13 see what *a.* I ret'rn
Job 19:16 and he gave me no *a.*
32:3 found no *a.* and condem'd
35:12 cry, but none giveth *a.*
Prov. 15:1 soft *a.* turneth away
23 hath joy by the *a.* of his
16:1 *a.* of the tongue is from L.
24:26 lips that giveth right *a.*
Cant. 5:6 he gave no *a.*
Mic. 3:7 for there is no *a.* of God
Luke 20:26 marvelled at his *a.*
John 1:22 that we may give *a.*
19:9 Jesus gave him no *a.*
Rom. 11:4 what saith *a.* of God?
1 *Cor.* 9:3 mine *a.* is this
2 *Tim.* 4:16 at my first *a.*
1 *Pet.* 3:15 be ready to give an *a.*
21 the *a.* of a good conscience

ANSWERS.
Job 21:34 in your *a.* remaineth
34:36 his *a.* for wicked men
Luke 2:47 were aston. at his *a.*

ANSWER, Verb.
Gen. 30:33 righteousn. *a.* for me
Deut. 27:15 people shall *a.* amen
1 *K.* 18:29 voice, nor any to *a.*
Job 13:22 call thou, and I will *a.*
23:5 the words he would *a.* me
31:14 he visiteth what *a.* him?
33:12 will *a.* G. is greater, 35:4
40:2 reproveth God, let him *a.*
Ps. 27:7 have mercy and *a.* ßne
65:5 in right, wilt thou *a.* us?
86:7 will call, thou wilt *a.* me
102:2 when I call *a.* me speedily
108:6 thy right hand, and *a.* me
Ps. 143:1 in thy faithful. *a.* me
Prov. 15:28 heart studieth to *a.*
22:21 mightest *a.* words of truth
26:5 *a.* a fool accord. to his folly
Is. 14:32 what *a.* the messengers
50:2 was there none to *a.?* 66:4
58:9 shalt thou call, L. will *a.*
Dan. 3:16 not careful to *a.* thee
Hab. 2:1 what *a.* when reproved
Mat. 22:46 no man was able to *a.*
Mark 11:30 heaven or of men? *a.*
14:40 wist they what to *a.*
Luke 11:7 from within shall *a.*
12:11 ye shall *a.* or say
13:25 he shall *a.* I know you not
21:14 not to meditate what ye *a.*
2 *Cor.* 5:12 somewhat to *a.* them
Col. 4:6 how to *a.* every man

I will ANSWER.
Job 13:22 call, *I will a.* 14:15; *Ps.*
91:15; *Jer.* 33:3
Is. 65:24 they call *I will a.*

Not ANSWER.
2 *K.* 18:36 king's commandment
was *a.* him *not, Is.* 36:21
Job 9:3 *a.* him one of a thousand
Prov. 1:28 they shall call I *not a.*
26:4 *a. not* a fool accord. to his
29:19 understand, he will *not a.*
Is. 65:12 I called, ye did *not a.*
Jer. 7:27 they will *not a.* thee
Luke 14:6 they could *not a.* him
22:68 will *not a.* nor let me go

ANSWERED.
Jud. 8:8 *a.* as men of Succoth *a.*
1 *Sam.* 3:4 he *a.* Here am I, 16
1 *K.* 12:13 the king *a.* roughly,
2 *Chr.* 10:13
18:26 voice, nor any that *a.*
2 *Chr.* 25:9 *a.* the Lord is able
Job 11:2 multit. of words be *a.?*
Ezek. 37:3 I *a.* O L. thou knowest
Dan. 2:14 D. *a.* with counsel
Mat. 26:1 he *a.* nothing 14;
Mark 14:61; 15:3, 5; *Luke* 23:9
Mark 12:28 perceiv. he *a.* well
34 Jesus saw he *a.* discreetly
Acts 22:8 I *a.* Who art thou, L.?
25:8 he *a.* for himself, 26:1

ANSWERED, *meant of God.*
Gen. 35:3 *a.* me in my distress
Ex. 19:19 M. spake, and G. *a.*
2 *Sam.* 21:1 L. *a.* It is for Saul
1 *Chr.* 21:26 *a.* from heaven
28 David saw Lord had *a.* him
Ps. 81:7 I *a.* thee in the secret
99:6 on the L., and he *a.* them
118:5 the L. *a.* me and set me
Jer. 23:35 hath the Lord *a.* 37

ANSWERED not.
1 *Sam.* 4:20 *a. not* nor did regard
2 *Sam.* 22:42 looked, but *a.* them
not, Ps. 18:41
1 *K.* 18:21 people *a.* him *not*
2 *K.* 18:36; *Is.* 36:21
Jer. 7:13 called, ye *a. not,* 35:17
Mat. 15:23 he *a.* her *not* a word

ANSWEREDST.
Ps. 99:8 thou *a.* them, O Lord
138:3 when I cried thou *a.* me

ANSWEREST.
1 *Sam.* 26:14 *a.* thou not, Abner ?
Job 16:3 embold. that thou *a. ?*
Mat. 26:62 *a.* thou nothing? *Mark*
14:60 ; 15:4
John 18:22 *a.* thou the h.-p. so ?

ANSWERETH.
1 *Sam.* 28:15 God *a.* me no more
1 *K.* 18:24 God that *a.* by fire
Job 12:4 on God and he *a.* him
Prov. 18:13 that *a.* a matter
23 but the rich *a.* roughly
27:19 as face *a.* to face, so
Ec. 5:20 God *a.* him in the joy
10:19 but money *a.* all things
Gal. 4:25 and *a.* to Jerusalem

ANSWERING.
Luke 23:40 the other *a.* rebuked
Tit. 2:9 obedient, not *a.* again

ANT, S.
Prov. 6:6 the *a.* thou sluggard
30:25 *a.* are a people not strong

ANTICHRIST, S.
1 *John* 2:18 there are many *a.*
22 *a.* denieth Father and Son
4:3 spir. of *a.* whereof ye heard
2 *John* 7 is a deceiver and an *a.*

ANTIOCH.
Acts 11:19 as far as A. 22
26 called Christians first in A.
Gal. 2:11 Peter to A. I withstood

ANTIPAS. *See* MARTYR.
ANTIPATRIS. *Acts* 23:31

ANTIQUITY.
Is. 23:7 joyous city, whose *a.*

ANVIL.
Is. 41:7 him that smote *a.*

ANY.
Deut. 32:39 nor *a.* that can del.
1 *K.* 18:26 nor *a.* that answered
Job 33:27 if *a.* say, I have sinned
Ps. 4:6 who will show us *a.* good?
Is. 44:8 is no God, I know not *a.*
Amos 6:10 is there yet *a.*
Mark 8:26 nor tell it to *a.* in t.
11:25 have aught against *a.*
Acts 9:2 if he found *a.*

See FURTHER, GOD, MAN, MORE,
THING, TIME, WISE.

ANY *while. See* DEAD.
APACE. *See* FLEE, FLED.

APART.
Ex. 13:12 *a.* all that open
Lev. 15:19 she shall be put *a.*
18:19 as long as she is *a.*
Ps. 4:3 Lord hath set *a.* godly
Zec. 12:12 every family *a.* 14
Mat. 14:13 into a desert place *a.*
23 mountain *a.* 17:1; *Mark* 9:2
17:19 came the disciples to J. *a.*
Mark 6:31 come ye yourselves *a.*
Jam. 1:21 lay *a.* filthiness

APELLES. *Rom.* 16:10
APES. *See* PEACOCKS.

APHEK.
1 *Sam.* 4:1 pitched in A. 29:1
1 *K.* 20:30 the rest fled to A.
2 *K.* 13:17 the Syrians in A.

APIECE.
Num. 3:47 five shekels *a.*
17:6 gave him a rod *a.*
Luke 9:3 nor have two coats *a.*
John 2:6 two or three firkins *a.*

APOLLONIA. *Acts* 17:1

APOLLOS.
Acts 18:24 A. came to Ephesus
1 *Cor.* 1:12 and I of A. 3:4 ; 3:5
3:6 I planted, A. watered
4:6 in a figure transferred to A.
Tit. 3:13 bring Zenas and A.

APOLLYON. *Rev.* 9:11.

APOSTLE.
Rom. 1:1 Paul, called to be an *a.*
1 *Cor.* 1:1
11:13 am the *a.* of the Gentiles
1 *Cor.* 9:1 am I not an *a. ? 2*
15:9 not meet to be called an *a.*
2 *Cor.* 1:1 Paul an *a. Eph.* 1:1;
Col. 1:1 ; 1 *Tim.* 1:1 ; 2 *Tim.*
1:1 ; *Gal.* 1:1
12:12 the signs of an *a.*
1 *Tim.* 2:7 whereto I am ordained
an *a.* 2 *Tim.* 1:11
Tit. 1:1 a servant of G. and *a.*
Heb. 3:1 *a.* and high-priest of our

APOSTLES.
Mat. 10:2 names of the twelve *a.*
Mark 6:30 the *a.* gathered
Luke 6:13 whom he named *a.*
9:10 the *a.* when they returned
11:49 will send prophets and *a.*
17:5 the *a.* said, Increase
22:14 down, and the twelve *a.*
24:10 told these things to *a.*
Acts 1:26 with the eleven *a.*
2:43 signs by the *a.* 5:12
4:35 them at *a.* feet, 37 ; 5:2
5:18 laid their hands on the *a.*
8:1 all scattered except the *a.*
Rom. 16:7 of note among the *a.*
1 *Cor.* 4:9 set forth us the *a.* last
12:28 set first *a.* 29 are all *a.*
15:9 for I am the least of the *a.*
2 *Cor.* 11:5 chiefest *a.* 12:11
13 such are false *a.*
Gal. 1:17 to them *a.* before me
19 other of the *a.* saw I none
Eph. 3:5 revealed to his holy *a.*
4:11 he gave some *a.*
1 *Thes.* 2:6 burdensome as the *a.*
2 *Pet.* 3:2 command. of us the *a.*
Jude 17 words spoken bef. of *a.*
Rev. 2:2 which they say are *a.*
18:20 rejoice over her, ye holy *a.*

APOSTLESHIP.
Acts 1:25 take part of this *a.*
Rom. 1:5 received grace and *a.*
1 *Cor.* 9:2 the seal of mine *a.*
Gal. 2:8 effectually in P. to the *a.*

APOTHECARY.
Ex. 30:25 after art of *a.*
35 conf. after art of *a.* 37:29
Ec. 10:1 flies cause oint of *a.*

APPAREL.
2 *Sam.* 12:20 D. changed his *a.*
1 *K.* 10:5 attend. of his minis
ters and their *a.* 2 *Chr.* 9:4
Is. 3:22 changeable suits of *a.*
4:1 we will wear our own *a.*
63:1 who this glorious in his *a.*
Zep. 1:8 clothed in strange *a.*
Acts 1:10 men stood in white *a.*
20:33 no man's silver or *a.*
1 *Tim.* 2:9 women in modest *a.*
Jam. 2:2 man come in goodly *a.*
1 *Pet.* 3:3 or putting on *a.*
See ROYAL.

APPARELLED.
2 *Sam.* 13:18 daughters were *a.*
Luke 7:25 are gorgeously *a.*

APPARENTLY.
Num. 12:8 will I speak *a.*

APPEAL, ED.
Acts 25:11 I *a.* unto Cesar, 21
26:32 at liberty, if he had not *a.*
28:19 constrained to *a.* to Cesar

APPEAR.
Gen. 1:9 let the dry land *a.*
Ex. 23:15 none *a.* before me emp-
ty, 34:20 ; *Deut.* 16:16
34:24 when thou shalt go to *a.*
Deut. 31:11 Israel *a.* before L.
Ps. 42:2 shall I come and *a.*
90:16 work *a.* to thy servants
Cant. 2:12 flowers *a.* on earth
4:1 flock of goats that *a.* 6:5
Is. 1:12 ye come to *a.* before me
Jer. 13:26 that thy shame may *a.*
Ezek. 21:24 doings, your sins *a.*
Mat. 6:16 may *a.* to men to fast
23:28 ye outwardly *a.* righteous
24:30 *a.* the sign of the Son
Luke 11:44 as graves which *a.*
19:11 kingdom of God should *a.*
Acts 26:16 in which I will *a.*
Rom. 7:13 that it might *a.* sin
2 *Cor.* 5:10 *a.* before judg.-seat
Col. 3:4 Christ our life shall *a.*
1 *Tim.* 4:15 profiting may *a.*
Heb. 9:24 to *a.* in the presence
28 *a.* the second time
11:3 of things which do *a.*
1 *Pet.* 4:18 where shall ungod. *a.?*
5:4 when chief Sheph. shall *a.*
1 *John* 2:28 when he shall *a.*
3:2 not yet *a.* what we shall be,
when he shall *a.* we shall
Rev. 3:18 nakedness do not *a.*

APPEAR, *referred to God.*
Lev. 9:4 to-day L. will *a.* 6
16:2 I will *a.* in the cloud
1 *Sam.* 2:27 *a.* to the house
2 *Chr.* 1:7 did God *a.* to Solomon
Ps. 102:16 shall *a.* in his glory
Is. 66:5 he shall *a.* to your joy
Acts 26:16 in which I will *a.*

APPEARANCE.
Num. 9:15 as the *a.* of fire, 16
1 *Sam.* 16:7 looketh on outw. *a.*
Dan. 8:15 the *a.* of a man, 10:18
10:6 his face as *a.* of lightning
John 7:24 accord. to the *a.*
2 *Cor.* 5:12 which glory in *a.*
10:7 things after the outward *a.*
1 *Thes.* 5:22 abstain from all *a.*

APPEARED.
Ex. 4:1 L. hath not *a.* to thee
6:3 I *a.* by name of G. Almighty
1 *K.* 11:9 had *a.* to Solomon
Jer. 31:3 the L. hath *a.* of old
Mat. 2:7 what time the star *a.*
13:26 then *a.* the tares also
17:3 *a.* Moses and E. *Mark* 9:4
27:53 holy city, and *a.* to many
Mark 16:9 Jesus *a.* first to Mary
12 he *a.* in another form
14 after he *a.* to the eleven
Luke 1:11 there *a.* to him
9:31 who *a.* in glory, and spake
22:43 *a.* an angel, strengthening
24:34 L. is risen, *a.* to Simon
Acts 7:2 God *a.* to father Abra.
9:17 Jesus, that *a.* to thee in
26:16 I have *a.* for this purpose
27:20 neither sun nor stars *a.*
Tit. 2:11 grace of God hath *a.*
3:4 after the love of God *a.*
Heb. 9:26 he *a.* to put away sin
Rev. 12:1 there *a.* a great w. 3

APPEARETH
Ps. 84:7 in Zion *a.* before God
Prov. 27:25 the hay *a.*

Jer. 6:1 evil *a.* out of the north
Mal. 3:2 shall stand when he *a.*
Jam. 4:14 life as a vapor that *a.*

APPEARING.

1 *Tim.* 6:14 keep com. till *a.* L.
2 *Tim.* 1:10 manifest by the *a.*
  4:1 quick and dead at his *a.*
  8 to them also that love his *a.*
Tit. 2:13 looking for glorious *a.*
1 *Pet.* 1:7 to praise at the *a.* of J.

APPEASE.

Gen. 32:20 I will *a.* him

APPEASED, ETH.

Est. 2:1 Ahasuerus *a.*
Prov. 15:18 s. to anger, *a.* strife
Acts 19:35 town-clerk had *a.*

APPERTAIN.

Num. 16:30 swallow them, with
  all that *a.*
Jer. 10:7 for to thee doth it *a.*
See PERTAIN.

APPERTAINED.

Num. 16:32 that *a.* to Korah, 33

APPERTAINETH, ING.

Lev. 6:5 give it to whom it *a.*
Rom. 4:1 Abr. our father, as *a.*

APPETITE.

Job 38:39 fill the *a.* of lions
Prov. 23:2 a man given to *a.*
Ec. 6:7 yet *a.* not filled
Is. 29:8 and his soul hath *a.*

APPII-FORUM. *Acts* 28:15

APPLE of the eye.

Deut. 32:10 kept him as *a. of h. e.*
Ps. 17:8 keep me as *a. of eye*
Prov. 7:2 law as *a. of thine eye*
Lam. 2:18 let not *a. of thine eye*
Zec. 2:8 toucheth *a. of his eye.*

APPLE-TREE.

Cant. 2:3 as *a.-tree* among trees
  8:5 raised thee up under *a.-tree*
Joel 1:12 and *a.-tree* are withered

APPLES.

Prov. 25:11 like *a.* of gold in pic.
Cant. 2:5 comfort me with *a.*
  7:8 smell of thy nose like *a.*

APPLIED.

Ec. 7:25 I *a.* my heart to know
  8:9 I *a.* my heart to every work
  16 I *a.* heart to know wisdom

APPLY.

Ps. 90:12 *a.* our hearts to wisd.
Prov. 2:2 *a.* heart to understand
  22:17 *a.* thy heart to my know.
  23:12 *a.* thy heart to instruction

APPOINT.

Lev. 26:16 will *a.* over you terror
2 *Sam.* 6:21 to *a.* me ruler
  7:10 *a.* a place for my people
Job 14:13 *a.* me a set time
Is. 26:1 will God *a.* for walls
  61:3 to *a.* them that mourn in Z.
Jer. 15:3 *a.* over them four kinds
  49:19 who is *a* chosen man, I
    may *a.* Who will *a.* me the
    time? 50:44
Ezek. 21:19 *a.* thee two ways
  20 *a.* a way that the sword
Hos. 1:11 they shall *a.* one head
Mat. 24:51 *a.* his portion
Luke 12:46 *a.* his portion
  22:29 I *a.* you a kingdom
Acts 6:3 seven men whom we *a.*

APPOINTED.

Num. 9:2 passover in *a.* sea. 3
  7 offering of L. in his *a.* season
1 *Sam.* 13:11 not within days *a.*
1 *K.* 1:35 *a.* him to be ruler.
  20:42 a man *a.* to destruction
Neh. 6:7 thou hast *a.* prophets
  9:17 *a.* a captain to return, that
Job 7:3 wearisome nights are *a.*
  14:5 thou hast *a.* his bounds

  20:29 the heritage *a.* to him
  30:23 the house *a.* for all living
Ps. 44:11 like sheep *a.* for meat
  78:5 *a.* a law in Israel
  79:11 preserve those *a.* to die
  102:20 to loose those *a.* to death
Prov. 7:20 come home at day *a.*
  8:29 he *a.* the foundations
  31:8 as are *a.* to destruction
Is. 1:14 your *a.* feasts my soul
  44:7 I *a.* the ancient people
Jer. 5:24 reserveth the *a.* weeks
  47:7 sea-shore, there hath he *a.*
Ezek. 4:6 *a.* each day for a year
Mic. 6:9 and who hath *a.*
Luke 3:13 exact what is *a.* you
  10:1 Lord *a.* other seventy
  22:29 as Father *a.* me
Acts 1:23 they *a.* two, Joseph and
  17:31 he hath *a.* a day in which
1 *Cor.* 4:9 apostles last, *a.* to d.
1 *Thes.* 3:3 that we are *a.* thereto
  5:9 God hath not *a.* us to wrath
2 *Tim.* 1:11 *a.* a preacher
Heb. 3:2 faithful to him that *a.*
  9:27 *a.* to men once to die
1 *Pet.* 2:8 whereunto they were *a.*

APPOINTED, time and times.

1 *Sam.* 13:8 to set time Sam. *a.*
Job 7:1 an *a. time* to man
  14:14 all the days of my *a. time.*
Ps. 81:3 trumpet in *time a.*
Is. 14:31 be alone in his *a. time*
Jer. 8:7 knoweth her *a. times*
Dan. 8:19 at *time a.* the end
  10:1 but the *time a.* was long
  11:27 end be at the *time a.*
  29 at the *time a.* shall return
  35 it is yet for a *time a.*
Hab. 2:3 is yet for an *a. time*
Acts 17:26 determ. *times* bef. *a.*
Gal. 4:2 until *time a.*

APPOINTETH.

Ps. 104:19 *a.* moons for seasons
Dan. 5:21 *a.* whomsoever he will

APPOINTMENT.

Job 2:11 made *a.* together to c.

APPREHEND.

2 *Cor.* 11:32 garrison desir. to *a.*
Phil. 3:12 may *a.* that for which

APPREHENDED.

Acts 12:4 when he *a.* Peter
Phil. 3:12 I am *a.* of Christ J.
  13 count not myself to have *a.*

APPROACH.

Deut. 31:14 thy days *a.* that thou
Job 40:19 his sword to *a.* to him
Ps. 65:4 whom thou causest to *a.*
Jer. 30:21 engaged heart to *a.*
1 *Tim.* 6:16 in light no man c. *a.*

APPROACHETH, ING.

Is. 58:2 take delight in *a.* God
Luke 12:33 where no thief *a.*
Heb. 10:25 as ye see the day *a.*

APPROVE.

Ps. 49:13 posterity *a.* their say.
1 *Cor.* 16:3 shall *a.* by your let.
Phil. 1:10 that ye may *a.* things

APPROVED.

Acts 2:22 Jesus, a man *a.* of God
Rom. 14:18 accept to G. *a.* of m.
  16:10 Apelles *a.* in Christ
1 *Cor.* 11:19 they *a.* be made m.
2 *Cor.* 7:11 all things you have *a.*
  10:18 commendeth himself is *a.*
  13:7 that we should appear *a.*
2 *Tim.* 2:15 thyself *a.* unto God

APPROVEST, ETH.

Lam. 3:36 subvert a man, *a.* not
Rom. 2:18 *a.* things more excel.

APPROVING.

2 *Cor.* 6:4 in all things *a.* oursel.

APRON, S.

Gen. 3:7 fig-leaves, made *a.*
Acts 19:12 brought to the sick *a.*

APT.

1 *Tim.* 3:2 *a.* teach, 2 *Tim.* 2:24

AQUILA. *Acts* 18:2, 26 ; *Rom.*
  16:3 ; 1 *Cor.* 16:19 ; 2 *Tim.* 4:19
AR. *Num.* 21:28 ; *Deut.* 2:9 ; *Is.*
  15:1

ARABIA.

1 *K.* 10:15 had kings of A.
Is. 21:13 the burden upon A.
Jer. 25:24 the cup to kings of A.
Gal. 1:17 I went into A. 4:25

ARABIAN, S.

2 *Chr.* 17:11 the A. brought Jeh.
  26:7 helped Uzziah ag. the A.
Is. 13:20 nor shall A. pitch tent
Jer. 3:2 as A. in the wilderness
Acts 2:11 Cretes and A. we hear

ARAM.

Gen. 10:22 sons of Sh. Lud, A.
Num. 23:7 B. brought me fr. A.
Mat. 1:3 Esrom begat A. 4
Luke 3:32 Aminadab son of A.
See PADAN.

ARARAT. *Gen.* 8:4 ; *Jer.* 51:27
ARAUNAH. 2 *Sam.* 24:16, 23
ARBA. *Jos.* 14:15 ; 21:11

ARCHANGEL.

1 *Thes.* 4:16 with voice of A.
Jude 9 Michael the *a.* contend.

ARCHELAUS. *Mat.* 2:22

ARCHER.

Gen. 21:20 Ishmael became an *a.*
  49:23 the *a.* sorely grieved him
1 *Sam.* 31:3 *a.* hit him, 1 *Chr.* 10:3
Job 16:13 his *a.* comp. me round
Is. 22:3 rulers are bound by *a.*
Jer. 51:3 bendeth let *a.* bend bow

ARCHES.

Ezek. 40:16 windows to the *a.*

ARCHIPPUS. *Col.* 4:17 ; *Phile.* 2
ARCTURUS. *Job* 9:9 ; 38:32

ARE.

Num. 15:15 as ye *a.* so stranger
Job 38:35 say to thee, here we *a.*
Lam. 5:7 sinned, and *a.* not
Mat. 2:18 not comf. bec. they *a.*
Luke 13:25 whence you *a.* 27
  18:11 I am not as other men *a.*
John 17:11 may be one as we *a.*
1 *Cor.* 1:28 things which *a.* not
Rev. 1:19 the things which *a.*

AREOPAGITE. *Acts* 17:34
AREOPAGUS. *Acts* 17:19
ARETAS. 2 *Cor.* 11:32
ARGOB. *Deut.* 3:4, 13, 14 ; 1 *K.*
  4:13

ARGUING.

Job 6:25 what doth your *a.* rep.

ARGUMENTS.

Job 23:4 fill my mouth with *a.*

ARIEL.

Ezr. 8:16 I sent for E. and A.
Is. 29:1 woe to A. the city, 2, 7

ARIGHT.

Ps. 50:23 ord. his convers *a.*
  78:8 that set not their heart *a.*
Prov. 15:2 wise useth know. *a.*
  23:31 when it moveth itself *a.*
Jer. 8:6 I heark. they spake not *a.*

ARIMATHEA.

Mat. 27:57 Joseph of A. who
  was, *Mark* 15:43 ; *Luke* 23:51 ;
  John 19:38

ARIOCH.

Gen. 14:1 in the days of A. king
Dan. 2:25 A. brought Daniel

ARISE.

Jos. 1:2 a. go over this Jordan
Jud. 5:12 a. Barak, lead
2 *Sam.* 2:14 young men a.
1 *K.* 3:12 a. like thee
1 *Chr.* 22:16 a. be doing
Job 7:4 I a. and night be gone?
25:3 doth not his light a. ?
Ps. 10:33 a. O Lord, save me
7:6 a. O Lord, in thine anger
12:5 will I a. saith the Lord
44:26 a. for help, and redeem
68:1 let God a. let his enemies
88:10 shall dead a. praise thee ?
89:9 waves of sea a. thou stil.
102:13 a. and have mercy on Z.
Prov. 6:9 a. out of thy sleep ?
Cant. 2:13 a. my love, fair one
Is. 21:5 a. ye princes
26:19 my dead body shall a.
49:7 kings shall a. princes wor.
60:1 a. shine, thy light is come
60:2 Lord shall a. upon thee
Jer. 2:27 in trouble will say, a.
8:4 shall they fall, and not a. ?
31:6 a. ye, let us go up to Zion
Lam. 2:19 a. cry out in the night
Dan. 2:39 shall a. another kingd.
Amos 7:2 whom shall Jacob a. 5
Mic. 2:10 a. this is not your rest
4:13 a. and thresh, O daughter
7:8 enemy, I fall I shall a.
Hab. 2:19 to the dumb stone a.
Mal. 4:2 Sun of righteousness a.
Mat. 9:5 easier to say a. *Mark* 2:9
24:24 shall a. false Christs
Mark 7:41 damsel, a. *Luke* 8:54
Luke 7:14 L. said, young man a.
15:18 I will a. and go to my f.
24:38 thoughts a. in your hearts
John 14:31 a. let us go hence
Acts 9:40 said, Tabitha, a.
20:30 own selves shall men a.
22:16 a. and be baptized
Eph. 5:14 a. from the dead
2 *Pet.* 1:19 till the day-star a.

See RISE.

ARISETH.

1 *K.* 18:44 a. little cloud
Ps. 112:4 to the upright a. light
Is. 2:19 a. to shake terribly, 21
Mat. 13:21 persec. a. *Mark* 4:17
John 7:52 out of Galilee a.
Heb. 7:15 similitude of Melch. a.

See SUN

ARISTARCHUS.

Acts 19:29 caught Gaius and A.
20:4 A. accompanied Paul
27:2 one A. a Macedonian
Col. 4:10 A. f.-prisoner, *Phile.* 24

ARISTOBULUS. *Rom.* 16:10

ARK.

Gen. 6:14 an a. of gopher-wood
7:18 a. went on face of waters
Ex. 2:3 took an a. of bulrush.
25:16 put into the a. the testi-
    mony, 21 ; 40:3, 20
37:1 made the a. of shittim-w.
Num. 3:31 charge shall be the a
Jos. 4:11 a. of Lord. 6:12 ; 1 *Sam.*
    4:6 ; 6:1 ; 2 *Sam.* 6:9
1 *Sam.* 6:19 looked into a.
2 *Sam.* 11:11 a. and Israel abide
1 *K.* 2:26 bec. thou barest the a.
8:9 nothing in a. save the two
1 *Chr.* 6:31 the a. had rest
13:3 let us bring again the a.
    9 put forth hand to hold the a.
15:1 D. prepared a place for a.
2 *Chr.* 6:41 a. of thy strength,
    Ps. 132:8
8:11 whereunto a. hath come
Mat. 24:38 Noah ent. a. *Lu.* 17:27
Heb. 11:7 Noah prepared an a.
1 *Pet.* 3:20 G. waited while the a.
Rev. 11:19 in his temple the a.

Before the ARK.

Ex. 40:5 set altar of gold a.
Jos. 4:7 w. of Jordan cut off a.
7:6 J. fell on his face *be. the* a.
1 *Sam.* 5:3 D. was fallen *be. the* a.
1 *Chr.* 16: 37 left *before the* a. A.
2 *Chr.* 5:6 S. and congr. *be. the* a.

ARK of the Covenant.

Num. 10:33 a. of L. went bef.
Deut. 31:26 inside of a. c.
Jos. 4:7 waters cut off before a. c.
Jud. 20:27 a. c. of God was there
1 *Sam.* 4:3 let us fetch the a. c.
2 *Sam.* 15:24 Levites bearing a. c.
1 *Chr.* 17:1 a. c. under curtains
Jer. 3:16 shall say no more, a. c.
Heb. 9:4 tabern. which had a. c.

ARK of God.

1 *Sam.* 3:3 where a. of G. was
4:11 a. of G. was taken, 17, 22
6:3 if ye send away the a.
2 *Sam.* 6:7 there he died before a.
7:2 a. dwelleth within
15:25 a. of God into the city
1 *Chr.* 13:12 bring the a, home
15:2 none carry a. of G. but L.

ARM.

Ex. 15:16 greatness of thine a.
Deut. 33:20 teareth the a. with
1 *Sam.* 2:31 I will cut off thy a.
    and the a. of thy father's h.
2 *Chr.* 32:8 with him is a. of flesh
Job 26:2 savest a. that hath
31:22 a. fall from my shoulder
35:9 cry out by reason of the a.
38:15 high a. shall be broken
40:9 hast thou an a. like God?
Ps. 10:15 the a. of the wicked
44:3 nor their own a. save them
77:15 with thy a. red. thy peo.
89:13 thou hast a mighty a.
21 mine a. shall strengthen
98:1 his holy a. hath gotten him
Cant. 8:6 as a seal on thine a.
Is. 9:20 the flesh of his a.
33:2 be their a. every morning
40:10 his a. shall rule for him
    11 gather the lambs with a.
51:5 shall wait upon me, on
    mine a. shall they trust
9 put on strength, O a. of Lord
52:10 hath made bare his holy a.
53:1 to whom is the a. of the L.
    revealed ? *John* 12:38
59:16 his a. brought salv. 63:5
62:8 hath sworn by the a.
63:12 with his glorious a.
Jer. 17:5 that maketh flesh his a.
21:5 I will fight with strong a.
Ezek. 4:7 thine a. shall be unc.
30:21 broken a. of Pharaoh
31:17 into hell that were his a.
Dan. 11:6 retain power of the a.
Zec. 11:17 on his a. his a.
Luke 1:51 showed str. with his a.
Acts 13:17 with a high a. brought

ARM, Verb.

1 *Pet.* 4:1 a. yours. with same m.

Stretched-out ARM.

Ex. 6:6 with a *s.-out* a.
Deut. 4:34 assayed to take nation
    by a *stretched-out* a.
5.15 out thence with a a. 7:19 ;
    26:8 ; *Jer.* 32:21
2 Chr. 6:32 thy *stretched-out* a.
Ps. 136:12 a a. for his mercy
Jer. 27:5 made earth by a. 32:17
Ezek. 20:33 with a a. will I rule
    34 I will gather you with a a.

ARMS.

Gen. 49:24 a. of his hands
Deut. 33:27 the everlasting a.
2 *Sam.* 22:35 bow of steel is brok.
    by mine a. *Ps.* 18:34
Job 22:9 the a. of the fatherless

Ps. 37:17 a. of wicked broken
Prov. 31:17 strengtheneth her a.
Is. 44:12 with strength of a.
49:22 bring thy sons in their a.
51:5 my a. shall judge the peo.
Ezek. 13:20 tear from your a.
30:22 break Pharaoh's a. 24
24 strength. a. of king of B. 25
Dan. 2:32 and his a. of silver
10:6 his a. like polished brass
11:15 a. of south shall not
22 with the a. of a flood shall
31 a. shall stand on his part
Hos. 7:15 strengthened their a.
11:3 taking them by their a.
Mark 9:36 taken him in his a.
10:16 took them up in his a.
Luke 2:28 S. took C. in his a.

ARMAGEDDON. *Rev.* 16:16

ARMED.

Job 39:21 goeth on to meet a. m.
Ps. 78:9 children of E. being a.
Prov. 6:11 as an a. man, 24:34
Luke 11:21 a strong man a.

ARMENIA. 2 *K.* 19:37; *Is.*37:38

ARMHOLES.

Jer. 38:12 rotten rags under thy a.
Ezek. 13:18 sew pillows to a.

ARMIES.

Ex. 12:17 your a. out of E.
Num. 33:1 their a. under Mos.
1 *Sam.* 17:10 defy the a. of Israel
16 should defy the a. of God
45 name of God of a. of Israel
Job 25:3 any number of his a. ?
Ps. 44:9 forth with our a.
68:12 kings of a. did flee apace
Cant. 6:13 company of two a.
Is. 34:2 fury upon all their a.
Mat. 22:7 he sent forth his a.
Luke 21:20 Jerus. compa. with a.
Heb. 11:34 to flight a.
Rev. 19:14 a. in heaven followed
19 kings and their a. gathered

ARMOR.

1 *Sam.* 17:54 Goliah's a. in his
1 *K.* 22:38 washed his a.
2 *K.* 3:21 all able to put on a.
10:2 a fenced city also and a.
20:13 Hez. showed his precious
    things, h. of his a. *Is.* 39:2
Is. 22:8 look in that day to a.
Luke 11:22 his a. wherein he
Rom. 13:12 put on a. of light
2 *Cor.* 6:7 approv. by a. of right
Eph. 6:11 put on the a. of God
13 take the whole a. of God

ARMOR-BEARER.

Jud. 9:54 Abim. called his a.-b.
1 *Sam.* 14:7 a.-b. said, do all that
16:21 David became his a.-b.
31:6 Saul died, and his a.-b.

ARMORY.

Cant. 4:4 builded for an a.
Jer. 50:25 L. hath opened his a.

ARMY.

Deut. 11:4 he did to the a. of E.
Jud. 9:29 increase thine a.
1 *K.* 20:25 a. like the a. lost
2 *Chr.* 20:21 praise before a.
Job 29:25 dw. as a king in the a.
Cant. 6:4 as a. with banners, 10
Jer. 37:11 fear of Pharaoh's a.
Ezek. 29:18 a. to serve a great
37:10 an exceeding great a.
Dan. 4:35 according to his will
    in the a. of heaven
Joel 2:11 his voice before his a.
Zec. 9:8 encamp bec. of the a.
Acts 23:27 came I with an a.
Rev. 9:16 of a. of horsemen
19:19 sat on horse and his a.

ARNON.

Num. 21:14 brooks of A. 22:36
Deut. 2:24 over the river of A.
Jud. 11:26 by the coasts of A.
Is. 16:2 shall be at fords of A.
Jer. 48:20 tell ye it in A.

AROER.

Num. 32:34 child. of G. built A.
1 *Sam.* 30:28; 2 *Sam.* 24:5; 1 *Chr.* 5:8
Is. 17:2 cities of A. are forsaken
Jer. 48:19 inhabitant of A. stand

AROSE.

Gen. 37:7 and lo, my sheaf a.
Ex. 1:8 a. a new king over Eg.
  who knew not J. *Acts* 7:18
Jud. 2:10 a. a generation that
  knew not the Lord
5:7 till I Deborah a. a mother
20:8 the people a. as one man
1 *Sam.* 9:26 a. early, *Is.* 37:36
17:35 he a. against me
2 *K.* 23:25 aft. him a. there any
2 *Chr.* 36:16 wrath of the Lord a.
Job 29:8 aged a. and stood up
Ps. 76:9 God a. to judgment
Ec. 1:5 sun hasteth where he a.
Dan. 6:19 the king a. early
Mat. 2:14 he a. and took child,21
8:15 a. and ministered, *Lu.* 4:39
26 he a. and rebuked winds,
  Mark 4:39; *Luke* 8:24
9:9 a. and follow. 19; *Mark* 2:14
25 the hand, and the maid a.
27:52 saints which slept a.
Mark 9:27 J. lifted him up, he a.
Luke 6:48 when the flood a.
15:20 he a. and came to his f.
Acts 11:19 persec. which a. about
19:23 there a. no small stir
23:7 so said a. a dissension, 10
See ROSE.

AROSE and went.

1 *Sam.* 3:6 Samuel a. to Eli
1 *K.* 19:21 Elisha a. after Elijah
Jon. 3:3 so Jonah a. to Nineveh
Acts 9:39 Peter a. *and went*

ARPAD, ARPHAD.

2 *K.* 18:34 gods of A. *Is.* 36:19
19:13 king of A. ? *Is.* 37:13
Is. 10:9 is not Hamath as A. ?
Jer. 49:23 is confounded, and A.

ARPHAXAD.

Gen. 10:22 s. of Shem, A. 11:10
Luke 3:36 was the son of A.

ARRAY.

Job 6:4 terrors of God set in a.
Jer. 50:14 yourselves in a. ag. B.
See BATTLE.

ARRAY, Verb.

Est. 6:9 they may a. the man
Job 40:10 a. thyself with glory
Jer. 43:12 a. himself with land
1 *Tim.* 2:9 not with costly a.

ARRAYED.

Gen. 41:42 Pharaoh a. Joseph
2 *Chr.* 28:15 captives with sp. a.
Mat. 6:29 was not a. like one of
  these, *Luke* 12:27
Luke 23:11 Herod a. Christ
Acts 12:21 Herod a. in royal app.
Rev. 7:13 these a. in white
17:4 woman was a. in purple
19:8 to her was granted to be a.

ARROGANCY.

1 *Sam.* 2:3 let not a. come out
Prov. 8:13 pride and a. do I hate
Is. 13:11 cause a. of the proud
Jer. 48:29 M. his loftiness, his a.

ARROW.

1 *Sam.* 20:36 Jonathan shot a.
2 *K.* 9:24 a. went out at his h.
13:17 a. of Lord's deliverance

19:32 nor shoot an a. there, *Is.* 37:33
Job 41:28 a. cannot make him
Ps. 11:2 their a. on the string
64:7 an a. sudd. be wounded
91:5 nor afraid for a. that flieth
Prov. 25:18 witness is a sharp a.
Jer. 9:8 tongue as an a. shot out
Lam. 3:12 as a mark for the a.
Zec. 9:14 his a. go forth

ARROWS.

Num. 24:8 through with a.
Deut. 32:23 mine a. upon them
42 mine a. drunk with blood
1 *Sam.* 20:20 will shoot three a.
2 *Sam.* 22:15 sent out a. and scattered them, *Ps.* 18:14
2 *K.* 13:15 take bow and a.
18 take the a. and smite
Job 6:4 a. of Almighty are
Ps. 7:13 ordaineth a. against
21:12 thine a. against them
38:2 thine a. stick fast in me
45:5 a. sharp in heart of enem.
57:4 teeth are spears and a.
58:7 his bow to shoot his a.
64:3 their a. even bitter
76:3 brake he the a. of bow
77:17 thine a. also went abroad
120:4 sharp a. of the mighty
127:4 as a. in hand of a mighty
144:6 shoot thine a. and destroy
Prov. 26:18 man who cast a.
Is. 5:28 whose a. are sharp
7:24 with a. and bows shall m.
Jer. 50:9 a. as of expert man
14 at Babylon spare no a.
51:11 make bright the a.
Lam. 3:13 caused a. of his quiv.
Ezek. 5:16 send evil a. of fami.
21:21 he made his a. bright
39:3 cause thine a. to fall
9 Israel shall burn bows and a.
Hab. 3:11 light of thine a.

ART, Verb.

Gen. 32:17 whose a. thou ?
Jud. 8:18 as thou a.
1 *K.* 22:4 as thou a. 2 *K.* 3:7
Jer. 14:22 a. not thou he, O L.
Luke 7:19 a. he that should
Rev. 11:17 a. and w. and a. 16:5

ART, S, Substantive.

Ex. 30:25 ointment after the a.
2 *Chr.* 16:14 spices prep. by a.
Acts 17:29 stones graven by a.
19:19 which used curious a.

ARTAXERXES.

Ezr. 4:7; 6:14; 7:1, 11, 21
Neh. 2:1 in 20th year of A. wine
5:14 from 20th to 33d year of A.

ARTEMAS. *Tit.* 3:12

ARTIFICER, S.

Gen. 4:22 T.-Cain an instr. of a.
1 *Chr.* 29:5 works made by a.
2 *Chr.* 34:11 to a. gave they m.
Is. 3:3 away the cunning a.

ARTILLERY.

1 *Sam.* 20:40 Jonath. gave his a.

ASA.

1 *K.* 15:11 A. did right,2*Chr.*14:2, 12, 13; 2 *Chr.* 15:2, 17; 16:2
1 *Chr.* 9:16 Berechiah, son of A.
2 *Chr.* 14:11 A. cried to the Lord

ASAHEL.

2 *Sam.* 2:18, 21, 32; 1 *Chr.* 2:16
3:27 Abner died for blood of A.
23:24 A. was one, 1 *Chr.* 11:26

ASAIAH.

1 *Chr.* 4:36 Jeshohaiah and A.
6:30 sons of Merari, A. 9:5
2 *Chr.* 34:20 king Josiah sent A.

ASAPH.

2 *K.* 18:18 Joab the son of A. the
  recorder, 37; *Is.* 36:3, 22

1 *Chr.* 6:39 A. son of, 9:15; 15:17
16:7 delivered this psalm to A.
25:1 of the sons of A. 2; 26:1;
  2 *Chr.* 5:12; 20:14; 29:13;
  35:15; *Ezr.* 2:41; 3:10; *Neh.* 7:44; 11:17, 22; 12:35

ASCEND.

Jos. 6:5 people shall a. up
Ps. 24:3 a. into hill, *Rom.* 10:6
135:7 vap. to a. *Jer.* 10:13; 51:16
139:8 if I a. up into heaven
Is. 14:13 I will a. to heaven, 14
Ezek. 38:9 a. and come
John 6:62 Son of man a. up
20:17 I a. to my Father
Rev. 17:8 shall a. out of pit

ASCENDED.

Jud. 13:20 angel a. in the
Ps. 68:18 thou hast a. on high
Prov. 30:4 hath a. into heaven
John 3:13 no man hath a.
20:17 not yet a. to my Father
Acts 2:34 D. is not a. into the h
Eph. 4:8 when he a. up
9 that he a. 10 same that a.
Rev. 8:4 smoke of the incense a.
11:12 a. up to heaven

ASCENDETH.

Rev. 11:7 the beast that a. out
14:11 smoke of their torment a.

ASCENDING.

Gen. 28:12 the angels of God a.
1 *Sam.* 28:13 I saw gods a. out
Luke 19:28 before a. up to Jeru.
John 1:51 angels of God a. and
Rev. 7:2 angel a. from the east

ASCENT.

2 *Sam.* 15:30 Dav. went up by the a.
  of Olivet
1 *K.* 10:5 and his a. by which he
  went up, 2 *Chr.* 9:4

ASCRIBE.

Deut. 32:3 a. ye greatness
Job 36:3 I will a. to my Maker
Ps. 68:34 a. ye strength to God

ASCRIBED.

1 *Sam.* 18:8 a. to David 10,000

ASENATH. *Gen.* 41:45,50; 46:20

ASH.

Is. 44:14 he planteth an a.

ASHAMED.

Gen. 2:25 m. and w. were not a.
2 *Sam.* 10:5 men were greatly a
  1 *Chr.* 19:5
19:3 as people being a.
2 *K.* 2:17 till he was a.
8:11 countenance until a.
2 *Chr.* 30:15 the priests were a
Ezr. 9:6 I am a. to lift up
Job 6:20 came, and were a.
11:3 shall no man make a. ?
19:3 not a. to make
Ps. 34:5 and their faces not a.
74:21 not oppressed turn a.
Prov. 12:4 she that maketh a.
Is. 20:5 be a. of Ethiopia
24:23 the sun shall be a. when
30:5 a. of a people that could
33:9 L. is a. and hewn down
Jer. 2:26 as thief is a.
6:15 they a. ? at all a. 8:12
8:9 the wise men are a.
14:4 ploughmen were a.
48:13 a. of C. as Is. was a.
Ezek. 16:27 daughters of P. are a.
32:30 terror a. of their might
Luke 13:17 adversaries were a.
16:3 to beg I am a.
Rom. 1:16 not a. of the gospel
5:5 hope maketh not a.
6:21 whereof ye are now a. ?
2 *Cor.* 7:14 I am not a.
2 *Tim.* 1:12 neverth. I am not a.

ASHAMED

16 O. was not *a*. of my chain
Heb. 2:11 not *a*. to call them
11:16 not *a*. to be called
ASHAMED *and confounded. See* CONFOUNDED.

Be ASHAMED.

Ps. 6:10 let my enemies *be a*.
25:3 that wait on thee *be a*.
   let them *be a*. who transgress
31:1 let me never *be a*.
17 not *be a*. wicked *be a*. 35:26
69:6 wait *be a*. for my sake
86:17 wh. hate me, may *be a*.
109:28 let them *be a*.
119:78 let proud *be a*.
Is. 1:29 shall *be a*. of the oaks
23:4 *be* thou *a*. O Zidon
26:11 and *be a*. for their envy
42:17 *be* greatly *a*. that trust in
44:9 know, that they may *be a*.
   11 all his fellows shall *be a*.
45:24 against him shall *be a*.
65:13 rejoice, ye shall *be a*.
66:5 and they shall *be a*.
Jer. 2:36 shalt *be a*. of Egypt
3:3 refusedst *to be a*.
12:13 shall *be a*. of your rev.
17:13 forsake thee shall *be a*.
20:11 my persecuters shall *be a*.
48:13 Moab shall *be a*. of C.
50:12 your mother shall *be a*.
Ezek. 16:61 and *be a*.
43:10 they may *be a*. of their
Hos. 4:19 *be a*. bec. of their sac.
10:6 Is. *be a*. of his own counsel
Joel 1:11 *be* ye *a*. O ye husbandm.
2:26 shall never *be a*. 27
Zec. 9:5 expectation shall *be a*.
13:4 every one *be a*. of his vis.
Mark 8:38 *be a*. of me, *Luke* 9:26
2 *Cor.* 9:4 we (that we say not
   you) should *be a*.
Phil. 1:20 in nothing I shall *b. a*.
2 *Thes.* 3:14 that may *be a*.
Tit. 2:8 contrary part may *be a*.
1 *Pet.* 3:16 may *be a*. that falsely

Not be, or Be not ASHAMED.

Num. 12:14 she *b. a*. seven days?
Ps. 25:2 in thee, let me n. *b. a*.
31:17 let me *n. b. a*. 119:116
37:19 shall *n. b. a*. in the evil
119:6 a. when I have respect
   46 testimonies, and *n. be a*.
80 be sound, that I *b* e *n. a*.
127:5 shall *n. be a*. but speak
Is. 29:22 Jacob shall *not be a*.
45:17 *a*. world without end
49:23 shall *not be a*. that wait
50:7 like a flint, I shall *n. be a*.
54:4 for thou shalt *not be a*.
Zep. 3:11 that day shalt thou *a*.
Rom. 9:33 believ. shall *a*. 10:11
2 *Cor.* 10:8 I should *not be a*.
2 *Tim.* 1:8 *a*. of testimony of L.
2:15 that needeth *not be a*.
1 *Pet.* 4:16 as a Chr. let him *a*.
1 *John* 2:28 *a*. before him

ASHDOD

1 *Sam.* 5:1 the ark to A. 6
2 *Chr.* 26:6 wall of A. cit. ab. A.
Neh. 13:23 mar. wives of A. 24
Amos 1:8; 3:9; *Zep.*2:4; *Zec.* 9:6

ASHER

Gen. 30:13 L. called his name A.
49:20 out of A. his bread fat
Deut. 33:24 of A. he said A.
Jud. 5:17 A. on the sea-shore

Tribe of ASHER.

Num. 1:41 the *tribe of* A. 41,500
2:27 the *tribe of* A. shall
10:26 the host the *tribe of* A.
13:13 *tribe of* A. to spy, 34:27
Jos. 19:24 lot for *tribe of* A. 31
21:6 out of the *tribe of* A. 30
1 *Chr.* 6:62,74; *Luke* 2:36; *Rev.*7:6

ASHES.

Gen. 18:27 am but dust and *a*.
Lev. 6:11 the *a*. without camp
Num. 19:9 gather the *a*.
1 *K.* 13:3 and *a*. poured out
20:38 disguised himself with *a*.
Est. 4:3 lay in sackcloth and *a*.
Job 2:8 sat down among the *a*.
13:12 your rememb. like *a*.
30:19 become like dust and *a*.
42:6 and repent in dust and *a*.
Ps. 102:9 eaten *a*. like bread
147:16 the hoar-frost like *a*.
Is. 44:20 he feedeth on *a*.
58:5 to spread *a*. under him
61:3 to give them beauty for *a*.
Jer. 6:26 daughter, wallow in *a*.
Lam. 3:16 covered me with *a*.
Ezek. 28:18 bring thee to *a*. on
Jon. 3:6 king sat in *a*.
Mal. 4:3 wicked be *a*. under
Mat. 11:21 repented long ago in
   sackcloth and *a*. *Luke* 10:13
Heb. 9:13 if the *a*. of a heifer
2 *Pet.* 2:6 cities of Sodom into *a*.

ASHTAROTH.

Deut. 1:4 at A. *Jos.* 9:10; 12:4
Jud. 2:13 Is. served A. 10:6
1 *Sam.* 7:3 strange gods and A. 4
12:10 because we have served A.
31:10 S.'s armor in house of A.
1 *K.* 11.33 have worshipped A.
1 *Chr.* 6:71 Gershom was giv. A.

ASHUR, *or* ASSUR.

Gen. 10:11 A. went forth, 22
Num. 24:22 shall carry, 24
1 *Chr.* 2:24 H. wife bare him A.
4:5 A. had two wives, H. and
Ezr. 4:2 Esar-haddon. king of A.
Ps. 83:8 A. also is joined with
Ezek. 27:23 A. and Chil. 32:22
Hos. 14:3 A. shall not save us

ASIA.

Acts 6:9 of A. disputing Stephen
19:10 all they in A. heard
27 whom all A. worshippeth
1 *Pet.* 1:1 to strangers scat. in A.

ASIDE.

2 *K.* 4:4 set *a*. that which
Mark 7:33 *a*. from the multitude
John 13:4 laid *a*. his garments
Heb. 12:1 lay *a*. every weight
See GO, GONE, TURN, WENT, LAY.

ASK.

Gen. 32:29 w. *a*. after my name
34:12 *a*. me never so much dowry and gift, and I will give
Deut. 4:32 *a*. of the days that are
32:7 *a*. thy father
Jud. 18:5 *a*. counsel of God
1 *Sam.* 12:19 this evil to *a*. us
28:16 why dost thou *a*. of me
1 *K.* 3:5 God said, *a*. what I shall
   give thee, 2 *Chr.* 1:7
2 *K.* 2:9 *a*. what I shall do
2 *Chr.* 20:4 J. gathered to *a*. help
Job 12:7 *a*. the beasts
Ps. 2:8 *a*. of me, and I will give
Is. 7:11 *a*. thee a sign of L. *a*.
   12 I will not *a*. neither tempt
45:11 L. *a*. of things to come
58:2 they *a*. ordinances
Jer. 6:16 *a*. for the old paths
15:5 aside to *a*. how thou doest
18:13 *a*. among the heathen
38:14 I will *a*. thee a thing
48:19 *a*. him that fleeth
50:5 shall *a*. the way to Zion
Lam. 4:4 children *a*. bread
Dan. 6:7 shall *a*. a petition
Hos. 4:12 people *a*. counsel
Hag. 2:11 *a*. priests concerning
Zec. 10:1 *a*. rain in time
Mat. 6:8 need of, before ye *a*.
7:7 *a*. and it shall be. *Luke* 11:9

9 his son *a*. bread, *Luke* 11:11
   11 good things to them that *a*.
14:7 whatsoever she would *a*.
18:19 touch. any thing they *a*.
20:22 what ye *a*. *Mark* 10:38
21:22 whatsoever ye *a*.
22:46 *a*. him more questions,
   Mark 12:34 ; *Luke* 20:40
Mark 6:22 *a*. what thou wilt. 23
9:32 afraid to *a*. him, *Luke* 9:45
Luke 6:30 goods, *a*. them not
11:13 Holy S. to them that *a*.
12:48 of him they will *a*.
John 1:19 sent priests to *a*. him
9:21 he is of age, *a*. him, 23
11:22 whatsoever thou *a*. of G.
14:13 ye *a*. in my name, 15:16
   14 if yo *a*. in my name I will
15:7 abide in me, *a*. what ye
16:19 they were desirous to *a*.
John 16:23 ye shall *a*. me nothing
   24 *a*. and receive that your joy
   30 that any should *a*.
18:21 *a*. them which heard me
Acts 10:29 I *a*. for what intent
1 *Cor.* 14:35 *a*. their husbands
Eph. 3:20 above all we can *a*.
Jam. 1:5 lack wisdom, let him *a*.
   6 but let him *a*. in faith
4:2 ye have not, bec. ye *a*. not
   3 ye *a*. and rec. not, bec. ye *a*.
1 *John* 3:22 we *a*. we receive
5:14 we *a*. according to his will
   15 heareth us, whatever we *a*.
   16 not unto death, he shall *a*.
See COUNSEL.

ASKED.

Jud. 5:25 he *a*. water
13:6 I *a*. not whence he was
1 *Sam.* 1:17 petition thou *a*.
1 *K.* 3:11 thou *a*. this thing
2 *K.* 2:10 hast *a*. hard thing
Ezr. 5:10 we *a*. their names
Job 21:29 *a*. them that go by
Ps. 21:4 he *a*. life of thee
105:40 people *a*. he brought
Is. 30:2 not *a*. at my mouth
41:28 when I *a*. of them, could
65:1 sought of them that *a*. not
Dan. 2:10 no king that *a*.
7:16 *a*. him the truth
Mat. 16:13 he *a*. his disciples,
   Mark 8:27 ; *Luke* 9:18
22:23 Sadducees *a*. him, 35 ;
   Mark 9:11 ; 10:2 ; 12:18
Luke 18:40 when near he *a*.
John 4:10 wouldest have *a*.
16:24 have ye *a*. nothing
Rom. 10:20 to them that *a*. not

ASKELON, *or* ASHKELON.

Jud. 1:18 Judah took G. and A.
14:19 Samson went down to A.
1 *Sam.* 6:17 for A. one, for Gath
2 *Sam.* 1:20 in the streets of A.
Jer. 25:20 I made A. and Azzah
47:5 A. is cut off with rem. 7
Amos 1:8 holds sceptre from A.
Zep. 2:4 A. a desolation, 7
Zec. 9:5 A. shall see; A. shall

ASKEST.

Jud. 13:18 why *a*. after my name?
John 4:9 *a*. drink of me
18:21 why *a*. thou me?

ASKETH.

Ex. 13:14 thy son *a*. *Deut.* 6:20
Mic. 7:3 prince *a*. for a reward
Mat. 5:42 him that *a*. *Luke* 6:30
7:8 that *a*. receiv. *Luke* 11:10
John 16:5 none *a*. whither goest
1 *Pet.* 3:15 *a*. you a reason of

ASKING.

Ps. 78:18 tempting God by *a*.
Luke 2:46 *a*. them questions
John 8:7 they continued *a*.
1 *Cor.* 10:25 *a*. no question, 27

ASLEEP.
Jud. 4:21 Sisera was fast *a.*
Cant. 7:9 lips of those *a.* to speak
Jon. 1:5 Jonah was fast *a.*
Mat. 8:24 he was *a. Mark* 4:38
26:40 disciples *a. Mark* 14:40
Acts 7:60 Stephen fell *a.*
1 *Cor.* 15:6 but some are fallen *a.*
18 which are fallen *a.* in C.
1 *Thes.* 4:13 concerning them *a.*
15 prevent them that are *a.*
2 *Pet.* 3:4 since fathers fell *a.* all
ASNAPPAR. *Ezr.* 4:10.

ASP, S.
Deut. 32:33 wine is venom of *a.*
Job 20:14 meat is the gall of *a.*
16 he shall suck poison of *a.*
Is. 11:8 on the hole of the *a.*
Rom. 3:13 poison of *a.*

ASSAULT, ED.
Acts 14:5 and *a.* made of the G.
17:5 they *a.* the house of Jason

ASSAY, ED, ING.
Deut. 4:34 hath God *a.* to take
1 *Sam.* 17:39 David *a.* to go
Job 4:2 if we *a.* to commune
Acts 9:26 Saul *a.* to join himself
16:7 they *a.* to go to Bithynia
Heb. 11:29 the Egyptians *a.*

ASS.
Gen. 22:3 Abrah. saddled his *a.*
5 abide you here with the *a.*
49:14 Issachar is a strong *a.*
Ex. 13:13 firstling of an *a.*
23:4 if thou meet enemy's *a.*
12 thine ox and thine *a.*
Num. 16:15 not taken one *a.*
22:23 *a.* saw the angel, 25, 27
28 opened the mouth of *a.* 30
Deut. 22:10 with ox and *a.*
Jos. 15:18 lighted off her *a. Jud.*
1:14 ; 1 *Sam.* 25:23
Jud. 15:16 jawbone of an *a.*
1 *K.* 13:28 had not torn the *a.*
2 *K.* 6:25 *a.* head sold for 80 p.
Job 24:3 the *a.* of the fatherless
Prov. 26:3 a bridle for the *a.*
Is. 1:3 the *a.* his master's crib
32:20 send feet of the ox and *a.*
Jer. 22:19 the burial of an *a.*
Zec. 9:9 cometh lowly riding on
a. the foal of *a. Mat.* 21:5
14:15 so be the plague of the *a.*
Mat. 21:2 shall find an *a.* tied
Luke 13:15 each loose his *a.*
14:5 have an *a.* fallen into pit
John 12:14 had found a young *a.*
2 *Pet.* 2:16 dumb *a.* speaking
See SADDLE.

ASS'S COLT.
Gen. 49:11 binding his *a. c.*
Job 11:12 born like a wild *a. c.*
John 12:15 sitting on an *a. c.*

Wild ASS.
Job 6:5 *a.* bray when he hath g.
39:5 sent out *w. a.* free
Jer. 2:24 *w. a.* used to the w'ness
Hos. 8:9 *w. a.* alone by himself

ASSES.
Jud. 5:10 ride on w. *a.*
1 *Sam.* 8:16 will take your *a.*
9:3 *a.* of Kish were lost, 10:2
2 *Sam.* 16:2 *a.* for k. household
1 *Chr.* 27:30 over *a.* was Jehd.
2 *Chr.* 28:15 carried feeble on *a.*
Job 42:12 J.had a thousand she *a.*
Is. 21:7 he saw a chariot of *a.*
Ezek. 23:20 flesh as flesh of *a.*

Wild ASSES.
Job 24:5 as *wild a.* go they forth
Ps. 104:11 *w. a.* quench
Is. 32:14 shall be a joy of *w. a.*
Jer. 14:6 *wild a.* snuffed wind
Dan. 5:21 dwell. was with *w. a.*

Young ASSES.
Is. 30:6 riches on *young a.*
24 *y. a.* that ear the ground

ASSEMBLE.
Is. 11:12 he shall *a.* outcasts
45:20 *a.* and come, and draw n
48:14 all ye *a.* yourselves
Jer. 4:5 *a.* and let us go
8:14 why sit still ? *a.* let us
Ezek. 11:17 I will *a.* you out of
39:17 *a.* gather to my sacrifice
Hos. 7:14 *a.* for corn and wine
Joel 2:16 *a.* elders, gather
3:11 *a.* and come, all ye heathen
Amos 3:9 *a.* on mt. Samaria
Mic. 2:12 I will surely *a.* O J.
4:6 I will *a.* her that halteth
Zep. 3:8 I will *a.* the kingdoms

ASSEMBLED.
1 *Sam.* 2:22 lay with w. that *a.*
Ezr. 9:4 *a.* every one that trem.
Neh. 9:1 ch. of Is. *a.* with fast.
Ps. 48:4 lo the kings were *a.*
Is. 43:9 let the people be *a.* who
Jer. 5:7 *a.* by troops in harlot's h.
Mat. 28:12 when *a.* gave large
John 20:19 disciples *a.* for fear of
Acts 1.4 being *a.* not to depart
4:31 where they were *a.*
11:26 w. year *a.* with church
15:25 it seemed good to us *a.*

ASSEMBLING.
Heb. 10:25 forsake not the *a.*

ASSEMBLY.
Gen. 49:6 their *a.* mine honor
Ex. 16:3 kill *a.* with hunger
Lev. 4:13 from the eyes of the *a.*
Deut. 9:10 L. spake out of fire in
day of *a.* 10:4 ; 18:16
1 *Sam.* 17:47 *a.* shall know Lord
2 *Chr.* 30:23 *a.* took counsel
Ps. 22:16 the *a.* of the wicked
89:7 feared in *a.* of the saints
107:32 praise him in *a.*
111:1 I will praise him in *a.*
Prov. 5:14 was in all evil in *a.*
Jer. 6:11 on *a.* of young men
9:2 an *a.* of treacherous men
15:17 sat not in *a.* of mockers
Lam. 2:6 dest. places of the *a.*
Ezek. 13:9 shall not be in the *a.*
Acts 19:32 the *a.* was confused
39 deter. in a lawful *a.* 41
Heb. 12:23 to the general *a.*
Jam. 2:2 come to your *a.* a man

Solemn ASSEMBLY.
Lev. 23:36 eighth day is a *s. a.*
Num. 29:35 ; *Neh.* 8:18
Deut. 16:8 seventh day *s. a.* to L.
2 *K.* 10:20 a *s. a.* for Baal
2 *Chr.* 7:9 eighth d. made a *s. a.*
Joel 1:14 called a *s. a.* 2:15
Zep. 3:18 sorrowful for the *s. a.*

ASSEMBLIES.
Ps. 86:14 *a.* of violent men
Ec. 12:11 fas. by masters of *a.*
Is. 1:13 calling of *a.*
4:5 create on her *a.* a cloud
Ezek. 44:24 in all mine *a.*
Amos 5:21 not smell in your *a.*

ASSENTED.
Acts 24:9 Jews also *a.*

ASSOCIATE.
Is. 8:9 *a.* and be broken in p.

ASSUAGE, ED.
Gen. 8:1 and the w.ters *a.*
Job 16:5 mov. of lips should *a.*
6 my grief is not *a.*

ASSURANCE.
Deut. 28:66 shalt have none *a.*
Is. 32:17 effect of righteous. *a.*
Acts 17:31 he hath given *a.*
Col. 2:2 full *a* of understanding
1 *Thes.* 1:5 came in much *a.*

ASSURE.
1 *John* 3:19 shall *a.* our hearts

ASSURED.
Jer. 14:13 give you *a.* peace
2 *Tim.* 3:14 thou hast been *a.*

ASSUREDLY.
Acts 2:36 house of Israel know *a.*
16:10 *a.* gathering, L. called us

ASSYRIA.
Gen. 2:14 toward the east of A.
25:18 dwelt as thou goest to A.
2 *K.* 15:29 cap. to A. 17:6 ; 18:11
Is. 7:18 that is a land of A.
11:11 recover people from A. 16
19:23 out of Egypt to A. 24, 25
27:13 were ready to perish in A.
Jer. 2:18 in the way of A. ? 36
Ezek. 23:7 with men of A.
Hos. 7:11 to A. 8:9 up to A.
9:3 eat unclean things in A.
10:6 carried to A. for a present
11:11 dove out of the land of A.
Mic. 5:6 waste the land of A.
7:12 come to thee from A.
Zep. 2:13 destroy A. and Nin.
Zec. 10:10 g. them out of A. 11
See KING, KINGS.

ASTONISHED.
Lev. 26:32 enemies shall be *a.*
1 *K.* 9:8 shall be *a. Jer.* 18:16 ;
19:8 ; 49:17 ; 50:13
Ezr. 9:3 and sat down *a.*
Job 17:8 upright shall be *a.*
18:20 come after shall be *a.*
26:11 pillars of heaven are *a.*
Is. 52:14 many were *a.* at thee
Jer. 2:12 be *a.* O ye heavens
4:9 the priests shall be *a.*
14:9 why be as a man *a.*
Ezek. 3:15 I remained *a.* seven d.
4:17 *a.* one with another
26:16 shall tremble and be *a.*
28:19 know thee shall be *a.*
Dan. 3:24 Nebuchadnez. was *a.*
4:19 Daniel *a.* for one hour
5:9 his lords *a.*
8:27 Daniel was *a.* at the vision
Mat. 7:28 *a.* at his, 22:33 ; *Mark*
1:22 ; 6:2 ; 11:18 ; *Luke* 4:32
Mark 5:42 *a.* with great astonish.
7:37 beyond measure *a.* 10:26
10:24 disciples were *a.*
Luke 2:47 *a.* at his answers
5:9 was *a.* at draught of fishes
8:56 her parents were *a.* but he
24:22 certain women made us *a.*
Acts 9:6 Saul trembling and *a.*
10:45 which believed were *a.*
12:16 saw Peter. they were *a.*
13:12 deputy believed, being *a.*

ASTONISHMENT.
Deut. 28:28 shall smite with *a.*
37 become an *a.* and a proverb
2 *Chr.* 7:21 shall be an *a.*
29:8 hath delivered them to *a.*
Ps. 60:3 to drink the wine of *a.*
Jer. 8:21 I am black, *a.* hath
25:9 I will make them an *a.* 18
29:18 deliver them to be an *a.*
42:18 execra. and an *a.* 44:12
44:22 theref. is your land an *a.*
51:37 Babyl. shall become an *a.*
Ezek. 4:16 drink w. with *a.* 12:19
5:15 an *a.* to the nations
23:33 be filled with cup of *a.*
Zec. 12:4 smite horse with *a.*
ASTRAY. *See* WENT, GONE.

ASTROLOGERS.
Is. 47:13 let now *a.* star-gazers
Dan. 1:20 ten times better th. *a.*
2:27 cannot the *a.* show
4:7 came in magicians and *a.*

5:7 king cried to bring in the *a.*
ASUNDER. *See* CLEAVE, CUT,
  DIVIDE, PUT.
ASYNCRITUS. *Rom.* 16:14
ATAD. *Gen.* 50:10, 11

ATE.
Ps. 106:28 *a.* sacrifi. of the dead
Dan. 10:3 I *a.* no pleasant bread
Rev. 10:10 book, and *a.* it up

ATHALIAH.
2 *K.* 8:26 Ahaz. mother was A.
  11:1 A. destroyed, 2 *Chr.* 22:10
  2 hid Joash from A. 20
1 *Chr.* 8:26 Ben. Shehari. and A.
2 *Chr.* 24:7 the sons of A. 22:11
Ezr. 8:7 Jeshaiah son of A.
ATHENIANS. *Acts* 17:21

ATHENS.
Acts 17:15 bro't Paul to A. 16, 22
  18:1 Paul departed from A.
1 *Thes.* 3:1 good to be left at A.

ATHIRST.
Mat. 25:44 when saw we thee *a.*
Rev. 21:6 give to him that is *a.*
  22:17 let him that is *a.* come

ATONEMENT.
Ex. 30:16 shalt take *a.* money
Lev. 4:20 *a.* for them, 26, 31, 35 ;
  5:6 ; 6:7 ; 8:34 ; 12:8 ; 14:18 ;
  Num. 15:25
9:7 make *a.* for thyself, 16:24
16:10 the scape-goat to make *a.*
  17 there, when maketh *a.*
  34 to make *a.* once a year
23:28 no work, it is a day of *a.*
25:9 day of *a.* make trumpet
Num. 16:46 make *a.* for wrath
  31:50 ear-rings to make an *a.*
2 *Sam.* 21:3 wherewith make *a.*
Rom. 5:11 we have rec. *a.*

ATTAIN.
Ps. 139:6 I cannot *a.* unto it
Prov. 1:5 man of u. *a.* wisdom
Hos. 8:5 they *a.* to innocency ?
Phil. 3:11 might *a.* to resurrec.

ATTAINED.
Gen. 47:9 not *a.* to days of fath.
Rom. 9:30 G. have *a.* to right.
  31 Is. hath not *a.* to law
Phil. 3:12 I had already *a.*
  16 already *a.* let us walk
1 *Tim.* 4:6 whereto thou *a.*
ATTALIA. *Acts* 14:25

ATTEND.
Ps. 17:1 *a.* to my c. 61:1 ; 142:6
  55:2 *a.* to me, I mourn
  86:6 *a.* to the voice
Prov. 4:1 *a.* to know understand.
  20 son, *a.* to my words, 7:24
5:1 my son, *a.* to my wisdom
1 *Cor.* 7:35 *a.* on Lord

ATTENDANCE.
1 *Tim.* 4:13 give *a.* to reading
Heb. 7:13 gave *a.* at altar

ATTENDED.
Job 32:12 I *a.* none convinced J.
Ps. 66:19 hath *a.* to my prayer
Acts 16:14 she *a.* to things spok.

ATTENDING.
Rom. 13:6 ministers *a.* contin.

ATTENT.
2 *Chr.* 6:40 let thine ears be *a.*
7:15 shall be *a.* to the prayer

ATTENTIVE.
Neh. 1:6 let thine ear now be *a.*
  11 : *Ps.* 130:2
8:3 people were *a. Luke* 19:48

ATTENTIVELY.
Job 37:2 hear *a.* noise of his v.

ATTIRE.
Prov. 7:10 with *a.* of harlot
Jer. 2:32 a bride forget her *a.* ?
Ezek. 23:15 exceeding in dyed *a.*

AUDIENCE.
Ex. 24:7 and read in *a.*
1 *Chr.* 28:8 in *a.* of our God
Neh. 13:1 they read in the *a.*
Luke 7:1 his sayings in the *a.*
  20:45 in *a.* of the people
Acts 13:16 *ye* that fear G. give *a.*
  15:12 multitude gave *a.* 22:22
AUGHT. *See* OUGHT.

AUGMENT.
Num. 32:14 to *a.* fierce anger

AUGUSTUS.
Luke 2:1 decree from Cesar A.
Acts 25:21 P. appealed to A. 25
  27:1 Julius, a centurion of A.

AUNT.
Lev. 18:14 his wife, she is thy *a.*

AUSTERE.
Luke 19:21 thou art an *a.* man

AUTHOR.
1 *Cor.* 14:33 not *a.* of confusion
Heb. 5:9 became *a.* of salvation
  12:2 Jesus, the *a.* and finisher

AUTHORITY, IES.
Prov. 29:2 righteous are in *a.*
Mat. 7:29 having *a. Mark* 1:22
  8:9 a man under *a. Luke* 7:8
  20:25 exercise *a. Mark* 10:42
  21:23 by what *a. Mark* 11:28
Mark 1:27 for with *a.* com. unclean spirits, *Luke* 4:36.
  13:34 gave *a.* to his servants
Luke 9:1 power and *a.* over
  19:17 have thou *a.* over
  20:20 deliver him to *a.*
  22:25 exercise *a.* called benef.
John 5:27 *a.* to execute judgm.
Acts 8:27 eunuch of great *a.*
  9:14 hath *a.* to bind, 26:10, 12
1 *Cor.* 15:24 put down all *a.*
2 *Cor.* 10:8 boast more of *a.*
1 *Tim.* 2:2 suppli. for all in *a.*
  12 women to usurp *a.* over
Tit. 2:15 rebuke with all *a.*
1 *Pet.* 3:22 and *a.* made subject to
Rev. 13:2 gave him great *a.*

AVAILETH.
Gal. 5:6 Christ cir. *a.* not, 6:15
Jam. 5:16 prayer of right *a.*

AVEN.
Ezek. 30:17 men of A. fall
Hos. 10:8 high of A. *Amos* 1:5

AVENGE.
Lev. 19:18 thou shalt not *a.*
  26:25 *a.* the quarrel of my cov.
Num. 31:2 *a.* Is. of Midianites, 3
Deut. 32:43 *a.* blood of servants
1 *Sam.* 24:12 Lord *a.* me of thee
Isa. 1:24 *a.* me of mine enemies
Jer. 46:10 that he may *a.*
Hos. 1:4 will *a.* blood of Jezreel
Luke 18:3 *a.* me of mine adver.
  7 shall not God *a.* his own el.
  8 he will *a.* them speedily
Rom. 12:19 *a.* not yourselves
Rev. 6:10 dost thou *a.* our

AVENGED.
Gen. 4:24 Cain be *a.* seven-fold
Jos. 10:13 stayed till peo. had *a.*
Jud. 15:7 yet I will be *a.*
  16:28 *a.* of Philis. of my
1 *Sam.* 14:24 that I may be *a.*
  18:25 foreskins to be *a.*
  25:31 my Lord hath *a.* himself
2 *Sam.* 4:8 hath *a.* my lord
  18:19 the Lord hath *a.* him
Jer. 5:9 my soul be *a.* 29 ; 9:9
Acts 7:24 *a.* him oppressed
Rev. 18:20 God hath *a.* you
  19:2 *a.* blood of his servants

AVENGER.
Num. 35:12 from *a. Jos.* 20:3
Deut. 19:6 lest *a.* pursue
  12 the elders deliver him to *a.*
Jos. 20:5 if the *a.* pursue
Ps. 8:2 mightest still the *a.*
  44:16 by re. of the enemy and *a.*
1 *Thes.* 4:6 Lord is *a.* of all such

AVENGETH.
2 *Sam.* 22:48 G. *a.* me, *Ps.* 18:47

AVENGING.
Jud. 5:2 praise L. for *a.* of Isra.

AVERSE.
Mic. 2:8 as men *a.* from war

AVOID.
Prov. 4:15 *a.* it, pass not by it
Rom. 16:17 divisions, and *a.*
2 *Tim.* 2:23 unl. questions *a.*
Tit. 3:9 *a.* foolish questions

AVOIDING.
2 *Cor.* 8:20 *a.* this, that no man
1 *Tim.* 6:20 *a.* profane babblings

AVOUCHED.
Deut. 26:17 *a.* the Lord to be
  18 *a.* thee to be his people

AWAKE.
Jud. 5:12 *a.* Deb., *a. a.* utter
Job. 8:6 he would *a.* for thee
  14:12 be no more not *a.*
Ps. 7:6 *a.* for me, 35:23
  17:15 I *a.* with thy likeness
  44:23 *a.* why sleepest thou
  57:8 *a.* my glory, I w. *a.* 108:2
  59:4 they prepare, *a.* to help

Ps. 59:5 O L. *a.* to visit all the
Prov. 23:35 when shall I *a.*
Cant. 2:7 *a.* my love, 3:5 ; 8:4
  4:16 *a.* O north wind
Is. 26:19 *a.* ye that dwell
  51:9 *a. a.* put on strength, O
  arm of the Lord *a.* 52:1
  17 *a. a.* stand up, O Jerusalem
Jer. 51:57 perp. sleep, and not *a.*
Dan. 12:2 in the dust shall *a.*
Joel 1:5 *a.* ye drunkards, weep
Hab. 2:7 *a.* that shall vex thee
  19 that saith to the wood, *a.*
Zec. 13:7 *a.* O sword ag. my
Mark 4:38 and they *a.* him
Luke 9:32 when *a.* saw his glory
John 11:11 that I may *a.* him
Rom. 13:1 it is high time to *a.*
1 *Cor.* 15:34 *a.* to righteousness
Eph. 5:14 *a.* thou that sleepest

AWAKED.
1 *Sam.* 26:12 knew it, neither *a.*
1 *K.* 18:27 and must be *a.*
2 *K.* 4:31 the child is not *a.*
Ps. 3:5 I *a.* for L. sustained me
  78:65 L. *a.* as one out of sleep
Jer. 31:26 I *a.* and behold

AWAKEST.
Ps. 73:20 when thou *a.* shalt
Prov. 6:22 when thou *a.* it shall

AWAKETH, ING.

Ps. 73:20 dream when one *a.*
Is. 29:8 he *a.* and his soul
Acts 16:27 keeper of the prison *a.*

AWARE.

Cant. 6:12 I was *a.* my soul
Jer. 50:24 O, and was not *a.*
Luke 11:44 over them not *a.*

AWAY.

Is. 1:13 I cannot *a.* with
Luke 23:18 *a.* with this man
John 19:15 *a.* with h. *Acts* 21:36
Acts 22:22 *a.* with such a fellow

AWE.

Ps. 4:4 stand in *a.* and sin not
33:8 inhab. of world stand in *a.*
119:161 my heart standeth in *a.*

AWL.

Ex. 21:6 bore his ear with an *a.*
Deut. 15:17 thou shalt take an *a.*

AWOKE.

Mat. 8:25 discip. *a.* h. *Luke* 8:24

AXE.

Deut. 20:19 destroy trees by *a.*
Jud. 9:48 Abimelech took an *a.*
1 *Sam.* 13:20 went to sharp. *a.*

1 *K.* 6:7 hammer nor *a.* was h.
2 *K.* 6:5 *a.*-head fell into w.
Is. 10:15 shall the *a.* boast
Jer. 10:3 cuts a tree with the *a.*
51:20 thou art my battle-*a.*
Mat. 3:10 *a.* is laid, *Luke* 3:9

AXES.

1 *Sam.* 13:21 had a file for the *a.*
2 *Sam.* 12:31 he put them under
a. of iron, 1 *Chr.* 20:3
Ps. 74:5 fam. as he lifted up *a.*
6 break carved work with *a.*
Jer. 46:22 against her with *a.*
Ezek. 26:9 with *a.* break down

B

BAALAH. *Jam.* 15:9
BAAL-GAD. *Jos.* 11:17
BAAL-HERMON. *Jud.* 3:3

BAAL.

Num. 22:41 to high places of B.
Jud. 2:13 Is. served B. and Ash.
6:25 down the altar of B. 31
1 *K.* 16:31 B. and worshipped
18:21 if B. be God, follow him
19:18 7,000 in Israel which have
not bowed to B. *Rom.* 11:4
2 *K.* 10:19 sac. to do to B. 20
11:18 brake down house of B.
17:16 host of heaven served B.
21:3 Manas. reared altars for B.
23:4 bring all the vessels for B.
Jer. 2:8 proph. prophesied by B.
7:9 inc. to B. ? 11:13, 17; 32:29
2:16 to swear by B.
19:5 built high places of B.
23:13 prophesied in B. 27
Hos. 2:8 silver and gold for B.
13:1 Ephraim offended in B.
Zep. 1:4 cut off remnant of B.
BAAL-BERITH. *Jud.* 8:33
BAAL-HAMON. *Cant.* 8:11
BAALI. *Hos.* 2:16

BAALIM.

Jud. 2:11 Is. s. B. 3:7; 10:6, 10
8:33 Isr. went whoring after B.
1 *Sam.* 7:4 Israel put away B.
1 *K.* 18:18 hast followed B.
2 *Chr.* 17:3 J. sought not to B.
24:7 dedic. things on B. 28:2
33:3 M. reared altars for B.
34:4 brake the altars of B.
Jer. 2:23 have not gone after B.
9:14 have walked after B.
Hos. 2:13 on her days of B. 17
BAALIS. *Jer.* 40:14
BAAL-MEON. *Ezek.* 25:9

BAAL-PEOR.

Num. 25:3 Is. joined himself to
B. 5; *Ps.* 106:28; *Hos.* 9:10
Deut. 4:3 Lord did because of B.
BAAL-PERAZIM. 2 *Sam.* 5:20;
1 *Chr.* 14:11
BAAL-SHALISHA. 2 *K.* 4:42
BAAL-TAMAR. *Jud.* 20:33
BAAL-ZEBUB. 2 *K.* 1:2, 16
BAAL-ZEPHON. *Ex.* 14:2;
Num. 33:7

BAANAH.

2 *Sam.* 4:6 Rechab and B. esc.
23:29 Heleb the son of B.
1 *K.* 4:16 B. the son of H.
Ezr. 2:2 B. c. to. *Neh.* 7:7; 10:27

BAASHA.

1 *K.* 15:16, 19, 27; 16:1, 6, 11, 12;
21:22; 2 *K.* 9:9; 2 *Chr.* 16:3;
Jer. 41:9

BABBLER.

Ec. 10:11 and a *b.* is no better
Acts 17:18 what will this *b.* say ?

BABBLING, S.

Prov. 23:29 who hath *b.* ?
1 *Tim.* 6:20 avoiding vain *b.*
2 *Tim.* 2:16 profane and vain *b.*

BABE, S.

Ex. 2:6 behold the *b.* wept
Luke 1:41 *b.* leaped in her womb
44 *b.* leaped in my womb
2:12 find *b.* wrapped in swad.
16 the *b.* lying in a manger
Heb. 5:13 for he is a *b.*
Ps. 8:2 mouth of *b. Mat.* 21:16
17:14 leave substance to their *b.*
Is. 3:4 princes and *b.* shall rule
Mat. 11:25 rev. t. to *b. Luke* 10:21
Rom. 2:20 a teacher of *b.*
1 *Cor.* 3:1 as unto *b.* in Christ
1 *Pet.* 2:2 as new-born *b.* desire
BABEL. *Gen.* 10:10 ; 11:9

BABYLON.

Mat. 1:17 the carrying into B.
Acts 7:43 carry away beyond B.
1 *Pet.* 5:13 church at B. saluteth
Rev. 14:8 B. is fallen, is fallen
16:19 B. came in remembrance
17:5 B. the mother of harlots
18:10 alas, that city B. 21
See DAUGHTER.
BABYLONIANS. *Ezek.* 23:15, 17
BABYLONISH. *Jos.* 7:21
BACA. *Ps.* 84:6

BACK.

1 *K.* 14:9 behind t. *b. Ezek.* 23:35
Ps. 21:12 turn their *b.*
129:3 ploughed on my *b.*
Prov. 10:13 rod for *b.* 19:29 ; 26:3
Is. 38,17 my sins behind thy *b.*
50:6 my *b.* to the smiters
Jer. 2:27 have turned *b.* unto me
18:17 will show *b.* not the face
32:33 turned to me *b.* and not
48:39 turned the *b.* with shame
Rom. 11:10 bow down their *b.*

BACK, Adjective.

Ex. 33:23 shalt see my *b.* parts

BACKS.

Neh. 9:26 thy law behind their *b.*
Ezek. 8:16 their *b.* toward the
10:12 body, and *b.* full of
See TURNED.

BACKBITERS,

Rom. 1:30 *b.* haters of God

BACKBITETH.

Ps. 15:3 that *b.* not with his

BACKBITING, S.

Prov. 25:23 a *b.* tongue
2 *Cor.* 12:20 there be debates, *b.*

BACKSLIDER.

Prov. 14:14 *b.* in heart be filled

BACKSLIDING, S.

Jer. 2:19 thy *b.* shall reprove
3:6 what *b.* Israel hath done
8 whereby *b.* Israel com. ad.

3:11 *b.* Is. hath justified herself
12 return thou *b.* Israel,
14 O *b.* children, saith L. 22
5:6 because their *b.* increased
8:5 back by a perpetual *b.*
Jer. 14:7 for our *b.* are many
31:22 O *b.* daughter, 49:4
Hos. 4:16 Is. slideth back as a *b.*
11:7 are bent to *b.* from me
14:4 I will heal their *b.* I will

BACKWARD.

Gen. 9:23 *b.* their faces were *b.*
49:17 his rider shall fall *b.*
2 *K.* 20:10 return *b. Is.* 38:8
Job 23:8 *b.* I cannot perceive *b.*
Ps. 40:14 driven *b.* that wish me
70:2 turned *b.* that desire
Is. 1:4 they are gone away *b.*
28:13 they might go and fall *b.*
44:25 that turneth wise men *b.*
59:14 judgm. is turned away *b.*
Jer. 7:24 went *b.* not forward
15:6 thou art gone *b.* therefore
Lam. 1:8 sigheth and turn. *b.*
John 18:6 went *b.* and fell to

BAD.

Gen. 24:50 speak *b.* or good
31:24 to Jacob good or *b.* 29
Lev. 27:10 a good for a *b.* or a *b.*
Num. 13:9 land if good or *b.*
24:13 to do either good or *b.*
2 *Sam.* 13:22 spake good nor *b.*
14:17 to discern good or *b.*
1 *K.* 3:9 discern good and *b.*
Mat. 13:48 but cast the *b.* away
22:10 good and *b.* and the wed.
2 *Cor.* 5:10 whether good or *b.*

BADNESS.

Gen. 41:19 never saw in E. for *b.*

BADE, EST.

Gen. 27:19 have done as thou *b.*
Luke 14:9 he that *b.* thee, 10
16 a supper, and *b.* many
Acts 11:12 Spirit *b.* me go
18:21 but *b.* them farewell

BADGERS.

Ex. 26:14 cov. above of *b.* skins
35:7 skins dyed red, *b.* skins
Ezek. 16:10 I shod thee w. *b.* sk.

BAG.

Deut. 25:13 in thy *b.* div. weig.
1 *Sam.* 17:40 sm. stones in a *b.*
Job 14:17 trans. is sealed in a *b.*
Prov. 7:20 taken a *b.* of money
16:11 weights of *b.* are his w.
Is. 46:6 lavish gold out of the *b.*
Mic. 6:11 of deceitful weights
Hag. 1:6 wages to put in a *b.* w.
John 12:6 a thief, and had the *b.*
13:29 because Judas had the *b.*

BAGS.

2 *K.* 5:23 two talents in two *b.*
12:10 they put up in *b.*
Luke 12:33 prov. *b.* that wax not

BAHURIM.

2 *Sam.* 3:16 behind her to B.
16:5 when David came to B.
17:18 came to a house in B.
19:16 a Benj. of B. 1 *K.* 2:8

BAJITH.

Is. 15:2 he is gone up to B.

BAKE.

Ex. 16:23 b. that you will b.
Lev. 24:5 and b. twelve cakes
26:26 ten women shall b.
1 *Sam.* 28:24 woman at E. did b.
Ezek. 4:12 shall b. it with

BAKE-MEATS.

Gen. 40:17 b.-meats for Pharaoh

BAKEN.

1 *K.* 19:6 was b. on the coals

BAKER.

Gen. 40:1 b. had offended the k.
22 hanged b. as Jo. interpreted
41:10 in ward me and chief b.
Hos. 7:4 oven heated by the b.
6 their b. sleepeth all the n.

BAKERS.

Gen. 40:2 wroth ag. chief of b.
1 *Sam.* 8:13 daughters to be b.
Jer. 37:21 bread out of b. street

BAKETH.

Is. 44:15 he b. bread, yea, he

BALAAM.

Num. 22:5, 9, 14, 25, 31, 35 ; 23:4,
30 ; 24:2, 3, 25 ; 31:8, 16
Deut. 23:4 hired B. 5 ; *Neh.* 13:2
Jos. 24:9 B. sent and called B.
Mic. 6:5 rem. what B. answ.
2 *Pet.* 2:15 fol. the way of B.
Jude 11 greedily after error of B.
Rev. 2:14 hold the doctrine of B.

BALAK.

Num. 22:4, 16 ; 23:2, 7, 18 ; 2 4:13
Jos. 24:9 B. arose and warred
Jud. 11:25 better than B. ?
Mic. 6:5 remember what B. k.
Rev. 2:14 who taught B. to cast

BALD.

Lev. 13:40 he is b. yet clean, 41
2 *K.* 2:23 go up thou b. head
Jer. 16:6 make themselves b.
48:37 every head shall be b.
Ezek. 27:31 make themselves b.
29:18 every head was made b.
Mic. 1:16 make thee b. and poll

BALD-LOCUST.

Lev. 11:22 ye may eat the b.-l

BALDNESS.

Lev. 21:5 make b. on their head
Deut. 14:1 b. between your eyes
Is. 3:24 inst. of well-set hair, b.
15:2 on heads b. and beard cut
22:12 the Lord did call to b.
Jer. 47:5 b. is come upon Gaza.
Ezek. 7:18 b. on their h. *Am.* 8:10
Mic. 1:16 enlarge thy b.

BALANCE.

Job 31:6 be weighed in even b.
Ps. 62:9 laid in the b. are van.
Prov. 11:1 a false b. 20:23
16:11 just w. and b. are Lord's
Is. 40:12 weighed hills in a b.
15 as small dust of the b.
46:6 and weigh silver in the b.

BALANCES.

Lev. 19:36 just b. *Ezek.* 45:10
Job 6:2 calamity laid in the b.
Ezek. 5:1 take b. to weigh
Dan. 5:27 in the b. and found
Hos. 12:7 of deceit
Amos 8:5 falsifying the b.
Mic. 6:11 pure with wicked b. ?
Rev. 6:5 he that sat on h. had b.

BALANCINGS.

Job 37:16 kn. the b. of t. clouds

BALL.

Is. 22:18 will toss thee like a b.

BALM.

Gen. 37:25 Ishmaelites bearing b.
43:11 take a little b. and honey
Jer. 8:22 is there no b. in Gilead ?
46:11 to Gilead and take b. O
51:8 howl take b. for her pain
Ezek. 27:17 J. traded in honey b.

BAMAH. *Ezek.* 20:29

BAND, S.

Lev. 26:13 the b. of your yoke
Jud. 15:14 b. loosed off h. hands
2 *K.* 23:33 Phar. put Jeh. in b.
Job 38:9 darkness a swaddling b.
31 or loose the b. of Orion ?
39:5 the b. of the wild ass ?
10 the unicorn with his b. ?
Ps. 2:3 break their b. asunder
73:4 there are no b.
107:14 brake their b. in sunder
Ec. 7:26 snares, hands as b.
Is. 28:22 lest b. be made strong
52:2 loose from b. of thy neck
58:6 loose the b. of wickedness
Jer. 2:20 I have burst thy b.
Ezek. 3:25 shall put b. on thee
4:8 I will lay b. upon thee
34:27 broken the b. of their y.
Dan. 4:15 with a b. of iron, 23
Hos. 11:4 drew them with b.
Zec. 11:7 staves, beauty and b.
14 mine other staff, even b.
Luke 8:29 he brake b.
Acts 16:26 every one's b. were lo.
22:30 loosed Paul from his b.
Col. 2:19 all the body by b.

See BONDS.

BAND, S—*companies.*

Gen. 32:10 I am become two b.
1 *Sam.* 10:26 went with him a b.
2 *K.* 13:21 a man, spied a b.
24:2 L. sent b. of Chaldeans, b.
1 *Chr.* 12:18 made them cap. of b.
21 David ag. the b. of rovers
Job 1:17 Chald. made three b.
Ps. 119:61 b. of wicked robbed
Prov. 30:27 the locusts go by b.
Ezek. 12:14 will scatter all his b.
38:22 rain on him and his b.
Mat. 27:27 whole b. *Mark* 15:16
John 18:3 Judas having re. b.
12 the b. took Jesus
Acts 10:1 b. called the Italian b.
21:31 tid. came to cap. of the b.
27:1 to Jul. cent. of Augustus' b.

BANDED.

Acts 23:12 certain of the Jews b.

BANK.

Gen. 41:17 I stood on the b.
Deut. 4:48 Aroer by the b. of Arnon, *Jos.* 12:2 ; 13:9, 16
2 *Sam.* 20:15 a b. ag. the city
2 *K.* 2:13 E. stood by the b.
19:32 not cast a b. *Is.* 37:33
Ezek. 47:7 at b. of river
Dan. 12:5 one on this side, other
on that side of the b.
Luke 19:23 money into the b. ?

BANKS.

Jos. 3:15 Jord. overfl. his b. 4:18

BANNER.

Ps. 60:4 a b. to them that fear
Cant. 2:4 his b. over me was
Is. 13:2 lift ye up a b.

BANNERS.

Ps. 20:5 n. of G. set up our b.
Cant. 6:4 terr. as an army w. b.

BANISHED.

2 *Sam.* 14:13 fetch home his b.
14 that his b. be not expelled

BANISHMENT.

Ezr. 7:26 whether to death or b.
Lam. 2:14 have seen causes of b.

BANQUET.

Est. 5:4 Haman come to b. 5, 8
6 to Esther at b. of wine, 7:2
Job 41:6 make a b. of him
Amos 6:7 b. of them that

BANQUET-HOUSE.

Dan. 5:10 came into the b.-h.

BANQUETING, S.

Cant. 2:4 brought me to the b.
1 *Pet.* 4:3 we walked in lusts, b.

BAPTISM, S.

Mat. 3:7 Pharisees come to his b.
20:22 bap. with b. *Mark* 10:38
21:25 the b. of J.. whence was
it ? *Mark* 11:30 ; *Luke* 20:4
Mark 1:4 J. did baptize, and pre.
the b. of repent., *Luke* 3:3
Luke 7:29 publicans with b. of J.
12:50 a b. to be baptiz. with
Acts 1:22 beginning from b. of J.
10:37 after b. which J. preached
13:24 J. prea. b. of repentance
18:25 Apollos knowing only b.
19:3 they said unto John's b.
4 John bap. with b. of repent.
Rom. 6:4 buried with him by b.
Eph. 4:5 one L., one faith, one b.
Col. 2:12 buried with him in b.
Heb. 6:2 doctrine of b. and lay'g.
1 *Pet.* 3:21 whereunto, even b.

BAPTIST.

Mat. 3:1 came John b. preaching
11:11 hath not risen a greater
than J. the b. *Luke* 7:28
12 the days of John the b.
14:2 this is J. the b. he is risen
8 give me John the b. head
16:14 art J. the b. *Mark* 8:28
17:13 he spake of John the b.
Mark 6:14 John the b. was risen
25 give me head of John the b.
Luke 7:20 John the b. hath sent
33 J. the b. eating nor drink.
9:19 answering said, J. the b.

BAPTIZE.

Mat. 3:11 I b. with w.. he shall b.
with Holy Ghost, *Mark* 1:8 ;
Luke 3:16 ; *John* 1:26
Mark 1:4 J. did b. in wilderness
John 1:33 he that sent me to b.
1 *Cor.* 1:17 Ch. sent me not to b.

BAPTIZED.

Mat. 3:6 were b. in J. *Mark* 1:5
13 then cometh Jesus to be b.
14 I have need to be b. of thee
16 J. when he was b. went up
Mark 1:9 Jesus was b. of John
10:39 baptism I am b. withal
16:16 believeth and is b. shall
Luke 3:7 mult. came to be b.
12 came publicans to be b. 7:29
21 Jesus being b. and praying
7:30 lawyers, being not b.
John 3:22 he tarried, and b.
23 and they were b.
4:1 J. made and b. more disci.
2 though Jesus himself b. not
10:40 place where J. at first b.
Acts 1:5 J. b. with water, but ye
shall be b. with H. G. 11:16
2:38 be b. every one of you
41 received his word were b.
8:12 were b. both men and w.
13 Simon, and when he was b.
16 were b. in the name of J.
36 w. doth hinder me to be b. ?
38 P. and eunuch, and he b.
9:18 Saul arose and was b.
10:47 these should not be b.
48 P. commanded them to be b.
16:15 Lydia when she was b.
33 jailer was b. and all his
18:8 C. believed, and were b.

Acts 19:3 to what were ye *b.*
5 w. they heard this, were *b.*
22:16 arise, and be *b.* and wash
Rom. 6:3 *b.* into Jesus, *b.* into
1 *Cor.* 1:13 b. in the name of P.?
14 thank God that I *b.* none
16 I *b.* household of S. not *b.*
10:2 and were all *b.* to Moses
12:13 one Spirit *b.* into one body
15:29 are they *b.* for the dead
Gal. 3:27 as many as *b.* into Ch.

BAPTIZEST.
John 1:25 why *b.* thou

BAPTIZETH.
John 1:33 who *b.* with the H. G.
3:26 the same *b.* all men come

BAPTIZING.
Mat. 28:19 t. all nations, *b.* them
John 1:28 Jordan where J. was *b.*
31 am I come *b.* with water
3:23 John was also *b.* in Enon

BAR.
Neh. 7:3 shut the doors, *b.* them

BAR, Substantive.
Jud. 16:3 took doors, posts, *b.*
Amos 1:5 break *b.* of Damas

BARS.
Deut. 3:5 cit. fenced w. gates and
b. 2 K. 4:13 ; 2 *Chr.* 8:5 ; 14:7
1 *Sam.* 23:7 a town that hath *b.*
Job 17:16 to the *b.* of the pit
38:10 and set *b.* for the sea
40:18 Beh. his bones *b.* of iron
Ps. 107:16 *b.* of iron, *Is.* 45:2
147:13 strength, *b.* of thy gates
Prov. 18:19 cont. are like the *b.*
Jer. 49:31 neither gates nor *b.*
51:30 Babylon, her *b.* are brok.
Lam. 2:9 he hath broken her *b.*
Ezek. 38:11 having gates nor *b.*
Jon. 2:6 the earth with her *b.*
Nah. 3:13 fire shall dev. thy *b.*

BARACHEL. *Job* 32:2
BARABBAS. *Mat.* 27 ; *Mark* 15 ;
  Luke 23 ; *John* 18
BARACHIAS. *Mat.* 23:35
BARAK. *Jud.* 4:6, 9 ; 5:1, 12 ;
  Heb. 11:32

BARBARIAN.
1 *Cor.* 14:11 a *b.* and he a *b.*
Col. 3:11 nei. Greek nor Jew, *b.*

BARBARIANS.
Acts 28:4 *b.* saw venomous beast
Rom. 1:14 both to Greeks and *b.*

BARBAROUS.
Acts 28:2 *b.* people showed kind

BARBED.
Job 41:7 his skin with *b.* irons

BARBER.
Ezek. 5:1 take thee a *b.* razor

BARE—*carried.*
Ex. 19:4 I *b.* you on eagle's w.
Deut. 1:31 thy God *b.* thee as
Is. 53:12 he *b.* the sin of many
63:9 he *b.* them all the days
Mat. 8:17 *b.* our sicknesses
Luke 7:14 they that *b.* him stood
John 12:6 bag, *b.* what put th.
1 *Pet.* 2:24 his own self *b.* our s.

BARE.
Gen. 31:8 the cattle *b.* speckled
44:27 my wife *b.* me two sons
Ex. 6:20 Jochebed *b.* Moses
Jud. 13:2 Manoah's wife *b.* not
1 *Chr.* 4:9 Jabez, I *b.* him
Prov. 17:25 bitt. to her that *b.*
23:25 that *b.* thee shall rejoice
Cant. 6:9 ch. one of her that *b.*
8:5 that *b.* thee
Is. 51:2 look unto S. that *b.* you

Jer. 16:3 mother that *b.* them
20:14 the day my mother *b.* me
22:26 cast our mother that *b.*
50:12 *b.* you shall be ashamed
Luke 11:27 blessed is w. that *b.*
23:29 the wombs that never *b.*

BARE fruit.
Luke 8:8 and *b. f.* a hundred-fold
Rev. 22:2 tree of life *b. f.* twelve

BARE rule.
Neh. 5:15 their servants *b. r.* over

BARE witness, *and* **record.**
Mark 14:56 *b. f. w.* ag. him, 57
Luke 4:22 all *b.* him *w.* and won.
John 1:15 *b. w.* of him, 32, 34
5:33 John *b. witness* to the truth
12:17 the people with h. *b. rec.*
19:35 he that saw it *b. record*
Acts 15:8 kn. the hearts, *b. w.*
Rev. 1:2 *b. r.* of the word of God

BAREST.
Is. 63:19 thou never *b.* rule over
John 3:26 to whom thou *b.* witn.

BARE, Adjective.
Lev. 13:45 cli. rent, head *b.* 55
Is. 32:11 strip ye, make ye *b.*
47:2 make *b.* the leg, uncover
52:10 made *b.* his holy arm
Jer. 13:22 thy heels made *b.*
49:10 I have made Esau *b.*
Ezek. 16:7 wast naked and *b.* 22
  39 naked and *b.* 23:29
Joel 1:7 my fig-tree clean *b.*
1 *Cor.* 15:37 shall be, but *b.* grain

BAREFOOT.
2 *Sam.* 15:30 went *b.* and the p.
Is. 20:2 Is. did so, walking *b.* 3
  4 the Egyptians, naked and *b.*

BAR-JESUS. *Acts* 13:6
BAR-JONA. *Mat.* 16:17

BARK.
Is. 56:10 dumb dogs cannot *b.*

BARLEY.
Ex. 9:31 *b.* was smitten, for *b.*
Deut. 8:8 a land of wheat and *b.*
Jud. 7:13 a cake of *b.* tumbled
Ruth 1:22 begin. of *b.* harvest
3:2 B. winnoweth *b.* to-night
2 *Sam.* 14:30 Joab's field, *b.* there
  17:28 Barzillai brought beds, *b.*
2 *K.* 4:42 brought 20 loaves of *b.*
  7:1 two meas. of *b.* for sh. 16, 18
2 *Chr.* 2:10 20,000 measures of *b.*
  15 wheat, and *b.* let him send
  27:5 Am. gave 10,000 mea. of *b.*
Job 31:40 let co. grow inst. of *b.*
Is. 28:25 wheat, and appointed *b.*
Jer. 41:8 we have treasures of *b.*
Ezek. 4:9 take to thee wh. and *b.*
  12 shalt eat it as *b.* cakes
  13:19 handfuls of *b.*
Hos. 3:2 for a homer of *b.*
Joel 1:11 howl for wheat and *b.*
John 6:9 hath five *b.* loaves
  13 frag. of the five *b.* loaves
Rev 6:6 meas. of *b.* for a penny

BARN.
2 *K.* 6:27 out of the *b.* floor?
Job 39:12 g. thy seed into the *b.*
Hag. 2:19 is seed yet in *b.* vine
Mat. 13:30 g. wheat into my *b.*
Luke 12:24 no storehouse nor *b.*

BARNS.
Prov. 3:10 shall thy *b.* be filled
Joel 1:17 the *b.* are broken down
Mat. 6:26 nor gather into
Luke 12:18 will pull down my *b.*

BARNABAS.
Acts 4:36 ; 11:22, 30 ; 12:25 ;
  13:1, 2, 50 ; 14:12 ; 15:2, 12, 37
1 *Cor.* 9:6 or I only and B. have
Gal. 2:1 I went up with B. 9, 13

Col. 4:10 Marc. sister's son to B.

BARREL, 8.
1 *K.* 17:14 the *b.* of meal shall
  18:33 fill four *b.* with water

BARREM.
Gen. 11:30 but Sarai was *b.*
25:21 Reb. *b.* 29:31 Rachel *b.*
Ex. 23:26 cast young nor be *b.*
Deut. 7:14 male or female *b.*
Jud. 13:2 Man.'s wife was *b.* 3
1 *Sam.* 2:5 the *b.* hath borne sev.
2 *K.* 2:19 and the ground *b.*
  21 shall not be death, or *b.*
Job 24:21 evil entreateth the *b.*
  39:6 the *b.* land his dwellings
Ps. 113:9 the *b.* woman to keep
Prov. 30:16 *b.* womb not satis.
Cant. 4:2 and none is *b.* 6:6
Is. 54:1 sing, O *b.* that didst not
Joel 2:20 drive him into a land *b.*
Luke 1:7 Sec. Elizabeth was *b.*
  36 with her, who was called *b.*
  23:29 blessed are the *b.* and
Gal. 4:27 written, Rejoice thou *b.*
2 *Pet.* 1:8 neither *b.* nor unfruitful

BARRENNESS.
Ps. 107:34 fruitful land into *b.*

BARSABAS. *Acts* 1:23 ; 15:22
BARTHOLOMEW. *Mat.* 10:3 ;
  Mar. 3:18 ; *Lu.* 6:14 ; *Acts* 1:13
BARTIMEUS. *Mark* 10:46

BARUCH.
Neh. 3:20 B. son of Zab. repair.
Jer. 32:12 ; 36:4, 26 ; 43:3 ; 45:1
BARZILLAI. 2 *Sam.* 17:27 ; 19:32.
  39 ; 21:8 ; 1 *K.* 2:7 ; *Ezr.* 2:61

BASE.
Zec. 5:11 upon her own *b.*

BASE, Adjective.
2 *Sam.* 6:22 *b.* in mine own sight
Job 30:8 were children of *b.* men
Is. 3:5 *b.* against the honorable
Ezek. 17:14 kingdom might be *b.*
  29:14 shall be a *b.* kingdom
Mal. 2:9 I have made you *b.*
1 *Cor.* 1:28 *b.* things G. hath ch.
2 *Cor.* 10:1 who in presence am *b.*

BASER.
Acts 17:5 fellows of the *b.* sort

BASEST.
Ezek. 29:15 Patros *b.* of kingd.
Dan. 4:17 set. over it *b.* of men

BASHAN.
Num. 21:33 ; 32:33 ; *Deut.* 1:4 ; 3:1,
  3, 4, 10, 11 ; 4:47 ; *Jos.* 13:12
Ps. 22:12 strong bulls of B.
  68:15 B. a h. hill, B. why leap, 22
Is. 33:9 B. and Carmel shake
Jer. 22:20 lift up thy voice in B.
  50:19 feed on Carmel and B.
Ezek. 39:18 fatlings of B.
Amos 4:1 ye kine of B.
Mic. 7:14 let them feed in B.
Nah. 1:4 B. languished, Carmel

BASHEMATH.
Gen. 26:34 to wife B. 36:3

BASIN.
1 *Chr.* 28:17 gold for every *b.*
John 13:5 he poureth w. into a *b.*

BASINS.
2 *Sam.* 17:28 Barzillai brought *b.*
Jer. 52:19 *b.* captain took away

BASKET.
Gen. 40:17 in the *b.* all manner
  of bake-meats
Ex. 29:23 *b.* of unleavened bread,
  Lev. 8:2, 26 ; *Num.* 6:15, 17
Lev. 8:31 *b.* of consecrations
Deut. 28:5 blessed shall be thy *b.*
  17 cursed shall be thy *b.*
Jud. 6:19 Gid. put flesh in a *b.*

Jer. 24:2 one *b.* had good figs
Amos 8:1 a *b.* of summer fruit, 2
Acts 9:25 w. in a *b.* 2 *Cor.* 11:33

BASKETS.

Gen. 40:16 I had three white *b.*
18 the three *b.* are three days
2 *K.* 10:7 their heads in *b.*
Jer. 6:9 as g.-gatherer into the *b.*
24:1 *b.* of figs before the temple
Mat. 14:20 twelve *b.* *Mark* 6:43;
Luke 9:17; *John* 6:13
15:37 brok. meat 7 *b.* *Mark* 8:8
16:9 not rememb. how many *b.?*
10; *Mark* 8:9, 20

BASTARD, S.

Deut. 23:2 a *b.* shall not enter
Zec. 9:6 and a *b.* in Ashdod
Heb. 12:8 w. chast. them are *b.*

BAT, S.

Lev. 11:19 *b.* unclean, *Deut.* 14:18
Is. 2:20 idols to moles and *b.*

BATH.

Is. 5:10 ten a. shall yield one *b.*
Ezek. 45:10 a just ephah, a j. *b.*
11 ephah and *b.* of one meas.
14 offer the tenth part of a *b.*

BATHED.

Is. 34:5 my sword shall be *b.*

BATHS.

1 *K.* 7:26 molt. sea cont. 2,000 *b.*
38 one laver contained 40 *b.*
2 *Chr.* 2:10 give 2,000 *b.* of wine
4:5 the sea held 3,000 *b.*
Ezr. 7:22 *b.* of wine, 100 *b.* oil
Ezek. 45:14 ten *b.* are a homer

BATH-SHEBA. 2 *Sam.* 11:3;
12:24; 1 *K.* 1:15, 31; 2:13

BATTLE.

Deut. 20:3 O Israel you ap. to *b.*
5 lest he die in the *b.* 6, 7
Jud. 20:28 shall I yet go to *b.?*
1 *Sam.* 17:28 art come to see *b.*
47 *b.* is the L.'s, 2 *Chr.* 20:15
26:10 descend into *b.* and perish
28:1 thou shalt go with me to *b.*
2 *Sam.* 11:1 when kings go forth
to *b.* 1 *Chr.* 20:1
15 set Uriah in forefront of *b.*
19:10 Absalom is dead in *b.*
1 *K.* 8:44 thy people go to *b.*
20:39 thy serv. into midst of *b.*
22:4 go with me to *b.?* 2 *K.* 3:7
1 *Chr.* 5:20 cried to God in the *b.*
12:8 Gadites men fit for the *b.*
Job 15:24 a king ready to the *b.*
39:25 he smelleth the *b.* afar off
41:8 remem. the *b.* do no more
Ps. 18:39 girded with str. to *b.*
24:8 the Lord mighty in *b.*
55:18 deliv. my soul from the *b.*
76:3 br. the shield, and the *b.*
Ps. 89:43 not made to st. in the *b.*
Ec. 9:11 nor *b.* to the strong
Is. 9:5 every *b.* of the warrior
13:4 L. must. the host of the *b.*
22:2 slain are not dead in *b.*
27:4 set briars ag. me in *b.*
28:6 turn the *b.* to the gate
42:25 the strength of the *b.*
Jer. 8:6 horse rusheth into the *b.*
18:21 young men be slain in *b.*
50:22 a sound of *b.* is in land
Ezek. 7:14 none goeth to the *b.*
13:5 in the *b.* in the day of L.
Hos. 1:7 not save them by *b.*
2:18 break *b.* out of the earth
10:9 *b.* in Gibeah not overtake
Joel 2:5 strong people in *b.* array
Zec. 10:3 goodly horse in the *b.*
5 tread their enemies in the *b.*
14:2 all nations against J. to *b.*
1 *Cor.* 14:8 shall prep. to the *b.*
Rev. 9:7 like horses prepare to *b.*
9 chariots running to *b.*
16:14 *b.* of that great day, 20:8

Day of BATTLE.

Job 38:23 reserved ag. *d. of b.*
Ps. 78:9 Eph. turned in *d. of b.*
140:7 covered my head in *d. of b.*
Prov. 21:31 horse is prep. ag. *b.*

BATTLE-AXE. *See* AXE.

BATTLE-BOW.

Zec. 9:10 the *b.-bow* shall be cut
10:4 out of him came the *b.-b.*

BATTLES.

1 *Sam.* 18:17 fight the Lord's *b.*
25:28 my lord fighteth *b.* of L.
1 *Chr.* 26:27 spoils won in *b.* ded.
2 *Chr.* 32:8 is God, to fight our *b.*
Is. 30:32 and in *b.* of shaking

BATTERING.

Ezek. 4:2 and set *b.* rams round
21:22 to ap. *b.* rams ag. gates

BATTLEMENT, S.

Deut. 22:8 a *b.* for thy roof
Jer. 5:10 take away her *b.*

BAY.

Zec. 6:3 in fourth chariot *b.* h.
7 the *b.* went forth and sought

BAY-TREE.

Ps. 37:35 w. like a green *b.-t.*

BDELLIUM.

Gen. 2:12 in Havilah there is *b.*
Num. 11:7 color of manna as *b.*

BE.

Jud. 6:13 the Lord *be* with us
2 *Chr.* 36:23 L.*be* w. him, *Ezr.* 1:3
John 3:9 can these things *be ?*
Rom. 4:17 things which *be* not
8:31 if G. *be* for us, who can *be*
Gal. 4:12 *be* as I am, for I am

Shall BE, *or* shalt BE

Ec. 1:9 is that which *shall be*
Mat. 24:21 ever *sh. be, Mark* 13:19
Mark 9:19 how long *shall I be*
with you, *Luke* 9:41
John 14:17 with you, and *sh. be*
1 *John* 3:2 appear what we *sh. be*
Rev. 16:5 wast, and *shalt be*

Shall not, *or* shalt not BE.

Ps. 37:10 *shall not be, Jer.* 48:30 ;
Dan. 11:29; *Amos* 7:3, 6
Hos. 3:3 *shalt not be* for another
Mat. 16:22 *shall not be* to thee
20:26 *shall not be* so among you,
Mark 10:43; *Luke* 22:26

To BE.

Ec. 3:15 that *to be* hath already
BEEN. *See after* BEE.

BEACON.

Is. 30:17 left as a *b.* on the top

BEAM.

Jud. 16:14 went away with the *b.*
1 *Sam.* 17:7 spear was like a
weaver's *b.* 1 *Chr.* 11:23; 20:5
2 *K.* 6:2 J., and take thence a *b.*
5 was felling a *b.* axe-head
Hab. 2:11 the *b.* shall answer
Mat. 7:3 not *b.* *Luke* 6:41, 42
4 a *b.* is in thine own eye
5 cast out the *b.* *Luke* 6:42

BEAMS.

Ps. 104:3 layeth the *b.* in waters
Cant. 1:17 the *b.* of our house

BEANS.

2 *Sam.* 17:28 Barzillai brought *b.*
Ezek. 4:9 t. unto thee wheat *b.*

BEAR—carry, *or* endure.

Gen. 4:13 is greater than I can *b.*
13:6 not able to *b.* them, 36:7
43:9 let me *b.* the blame, 44:32
49:15 bowed his shoulder to *b.*
Ex. 18:22 shall *b.* the burden
25:27 to *b.* the table, 27:7 ; 30:4 ;
37:5 ; *Deut.* 10:8 ; *Jos.* 3:8, 13 ;
4:16 ; 2 *Sam.* 15:24
28:12 A. shall *b.* their names

Num. 11:14 *b.* all this, *Deut.* 1:9
14:27 how long *b.* with this
33 children shall *b.*your whoredoms, *Ezek.* 23:35
Deut. 1:31 a man doth *b.* his son
2 *K.* 14:34 put. on me, I will *b.*
Ps. 75:3 I *b.* pillars of the earth
89:50 how I do *b.* the reproach
91:12 *b.* thee up,*Mat.*4:6;*Lu.*4:11
Prov. 9:12 thou shalt *b.* it
18:14 w. spirit who can *b. ?*
30:21 for four which it cannot *b.*
Is. 1:14 feasts, I am weary to *b.*
46:4 I have made and will *b.* you
7 *b.* him upon the shoulder
52:11 clean that *b.* vessels of L.
Jer. 10:19 and I must *b.* it
17:21 *b.* no burden on Sab. 27
31:19 *b.* the reproach of my y.
44:22 Lord could no longer *b.*
Lam. 3:27 good he *b.* yoke
Ezek. 12:6 in their sight shalt *b.*
16:52 *b.* own shame, 54
34:29 *b.* shame of heath. 36:15
Mic. 6:16 *b.* rep. of my people
7:9 I will *b.* indignation of L.
Zec. 5:10 whither is the *b.* ephah ?
6:13 he shall *b.* glory, and rule
Mat. 3:11 shoes not worthy to *b.*
27:32 Simon to *b.* his cross, *Mar.*
15:21 ; *Luke* 23:26
Luke 14:27 doth not *b.* his cross
18:7 av. his elect, though he *b.*
John 16:12 ye cannot *b.* them
Acts 9:15 vessel to *b.* my name
15:10 nor we were able to *b.*
18:14 reason would I should *b.*
Rom. 15:1 *b.* infirm. of the weak
1 *Cor.* 3:2 hitherto not able to *b.*
10:13 that ye may be able to *b.*
15:49 *b.* the image
2 *Cor.* 11:1 would to G. ye could *b.*
4 ye might well *b.* with him
Gal. 6:2 *b.* one another's burd.
5 shall *b.* his own burden
17 *b.* in my body the marks
Jam. 3:12 fig-tree *b.* ol.-berries ?
Rev. 2:2 canst not *b.* them

BEAR—*bring forth.*

Gen. 17:17 S. 90 years old *b. ?*
18:13 shall I *b.* a child
Jud. 13:3 conceive and *b.* a son
1 *K.* 3:21 not my son I did *b.*
Cant. 4:2 ev. one *b.* twins, 6:6
Is. 7:14 a virgin shall con. and *b.*
54:1 sing, thou that didst not *b.*
Jer. 29:6 that they may *b.* sons
Luke 1:13 Elisab. shall *b.* a son
1 *Tim.* 5:14 marry, *b.* children

BEAR *fruit. See* FRUIT.

BEAR iniquity.

Ex. 28:38 A. may *b. in.* of holy
43 A. and his sons *b.* not *in.*
Lev. 5:1 he shall *b.* his *iniq.* 17;
7:18 ; 17:16 ; 19:8 ; 20:17
10:17 given to *b. in.* of the cong.
16:22 shall *b.* all their *in.*
20:19 shall *b.* their *in.* *Num.*
18:1, 23 ; *Ezek.* 44:10, 12
Num. 14:34 ye shall *b.* your *in.*
Is. 53:11 my righteous servant
shall *b.* their *in.*
Ezek. 4:4 shalt *b.* their *in.* 5, 6
18:20 son shall not *b. in.* of the

BEAR judgment.

Ex. 28:30 A. shall *b. j.*
Gal. 5:10 troub. you shall *b.* his *j.*

BEAR *record. See* RECORD.

BEAR rule.

Est. 1:22 every man should *b. r.*
in his own house
Prov. 12:24 of diligent *b. r.*
Jer. 5:31 priests *b. r.* by their m.

BEAR sin.

Lev. 24:15 shall *b*. his *sin*.
Ezek. 13:49 *b*. the *s*. of your idols
Heb. 9:28 once offered to *b*. *sin*

BEAR witness.

Ex. 20:16 not, *b*. false *w*. ag. thy.
*Deut.*5:20; *Mat.*19:18; *Rom.*13:9
1 *K.* 21:10 sons of B. to *b*. *wit*.
Mark 10:19 not *b*. f. *w. Luke* 18:20
Luke 11:48 ye *b*. *wit*. that
John 1:7 came for a wit. to *b. w*.
   8 to *b*. *witness* of that light
   3:28 ye *b*. me *w*. that I said
   5:31 if I *b*. *wit*. of myself
   36 *b*. *witness* of me, 10:25
   8:18 I am one that *b*. *witness*
   15:27 ye shall also *b*. *witness*
John 18:23 *b*. *witness* of the evil
   37 that I should *b*. *witness*
Acts 22:5 h.-priest doth *b*. me *w*.
   23:11 so must thou *b. w*. at R.
1 *John* 1:2 have seen it, and *b. w*.
   5:8 three that *b*. *witness*

BEAREST.

Ps. 106:4 favor thou *b*. to thy
John 8:13 *b*. record of thyself
Rom. 11:18 *b*. not the root,
Gal. 4:27 rej. barren that *b*. not

BEARETH.

Num. 11:12 a nursing father *b*.
Deut. 29:18 a root that *b*. gall
   23 it is not sown, nor *b*. nor
   32:11 as an eagle *b*. her young
Job 24:21 entreateth barren th. *b*.
Cant. 6:6 every one *b*. twins
Joel 2:22 for the tree *b*. her fruit
Mat. 13:23 which also *b*. fruit
John 15:2 ev. branch that *b*. not
Rom. 13:4 *b*. not the sword
1 *Cor.* 13:7 charity *b*. all things
Heb. 6:8 which *b*. thorns

BEARETH rule.

Prov. 29:2 wicked *b*. r. people m.

BEARETH witness.

Job 16:8 my leanness *b*. *witness*
Prov. 25:18 that *b*. false *witness*
John 5:32 another that *b*. *wit*.
   8:18 the Father *b*. *witness*
Rom. 8:16 S. *b. w*. with our sp.
1 *John* 5:6 it is the S. that *b. w*.

BEARING.

Gen. 1:29 every herb *b*. seed
   16:2 hath restrained me from *b*.
Jos. 3:3 *b*. the ark, 14; 2*Sam.*15:24
Ps. 126:6 forth *b*. precious seed
Mark 14:13 *b*. a pitcher of water,
     Luke 22:10
John 19:17 he *b*. his cross, went
Rom. 2:15 their conscience *b. w*.
   9:1 my con. also *b*. me witness
2 *Cor.* 4:10 *b*. in the body
Heb. 2:4 G. also *b*. them witness
   13:13 *b*. his reproach
1 *Tim.* 2:15 be saved in child-*b*.

BEAR, S.

1 *Sam.* 17:34 came a lion and a *b*.
   36 thy servant slew lion and *b*.
2 *Sam.* 17:8 chafed as a *b*. robbed
2 *K.* 2:24 came f. two she-*b*.
Prov. 17:12 a *b*. robbed of whelps
   28:15 and a ranging *b*.
Is. 11:7 cow and *b*. shall feed
   59:11 we roar all like *b*.
Lam. 3:10 he was to me as a *b*.
Dan. 7:5 a second like to a *b*.
Hos. 13:8 as a *b*. bereaved
Amos 5:19 a man did flee fr. a *b*.
Rev. 13:2 his feet were as of a *b*.

BEARD, S.

Lev. 13:29 plague on head or *b*.
   14:9 his hair off his head and *b*.
   19:27 mar corners of. 21:5
1 *Sam.* 17:35 caught him by *b*.
   21:13 let his spittle fall on *b*.

2 *Sam.* 10:5 tarry till *b*. be gr.
1 *Chr.* 19:5
   19:24 M. trimmed not his *b*.
   20:9 A. by the *b*. to kiss him
Ezr. 9:3 hair off my *b*.
Ps. 133:2 on the *b*. even A.'s *b*.
Is. 7:20 shall also consume *b*.
   15:2 and every *b*. cut off
Jer. 41:5 men *b*. shaven
   48:37 every head bald, *b*. clip.
Ezek. 5:1 to pass on thy *b*.

BEAST.

Gen. 1:24 earth bring forth *b*.
   3:1 more subtile than any *b*.
   37:20 evil *b*. hath devoured, 33
Ex. 13:12 firstling of a *b*.
   22:5 put his *b*. in another
   10 deliver any *b*. to keep
   19 lieth with a *b*. *Lev.* 18:23;
     20:15, 16; *Deut.* 27:21
   23:29 the *b*. multiply
Lev. 11:47 *b*. that may be eaten
Deut. 4:17 the likeness of any *b*.
Neh. 2:12 save the *b*. I rode on
Ps. 73:22 as a *b*. before thee
   147:9 giveth to the *b*. his food
Prov. 12:10 regards life of his *b*.
Ec. 3:19 pre-eminence above *b*.
Is. 43:20 the *b*. shall honor me
   63:14 as a *b*. that goeth
Dan. 4:16 let a *b*. heart be given
   7:11 till the *b*. was slain
   19 the truth of the fourth *b*.
Luke 10:34 on his own *b*.
Acts 28:5 Paul shook off the *b*.
Heb. 12:20 if so much as a *b*.
Rev. 4:7 first *b*. like a lion, sec. *b*.
   6:3 second *b*. say, Come

Rev. 11:7 *b*. that ascendeth out of
   13:1 a *b*. rise up out of the sea
   11 *b*. coming out of the earth
   15:2 got the victory over the *b*.
   16:13 unclean spirits out of *b*.
   17:8 *b*. that was, and is not, 11
   19:19 saw the *b*. and the kings
   20:10 the *b*. and false prophet

Every BEAST.

Gen. 1:30 to *ev*. *b*. I have given
   2:19 God formed *ev. b*.
   20 Adam gave names to *ev. b*.
   3:14 art cursed above *every b*.
   7:2 *every* clean *b*. by sevens, 8
   14 and *every b*. after his kind
   8:19 *every b*. went out
   20 of *every* clean *b*. he offered
   9:2 shall be on *every b*.
   5 blood at hand of *every b*.
   10 *every b*. I estab. covenant
   34:23 shall not *ev*. b. of theirs
Lev. 11:26 *ev*. *b*. which divideth
   the hoof, *Deut.* 14:6
Ps. 50:10 *every b*. of the forest
   104:11 give drink to *every b*.
Ezek. 34:8 flock meat to *every b*.
   39:17 speak to *every b*.

BEAST, joined with Man.

Gen. 6:7 destroy both *m*. and *b*.
Ex. 11:7 move tongue a. *m*. or *b*.
   12:12 smite first-born of *m*. and
     b. 13:15; *Ps.* 135:8
   13:2 first-born of *m*. and *b*. is
   mine, *Num.* 8:17
   19:13 *m*. or *b*. it shall not live
Ps. 36:6 preservest *m*. and *b*.
Jer. 7:20 fury on *m*. and *b*. 21:6
   36:29; *Ezek.* 14:13, 17, 19, 21;
   25:13; 29:8; *Zep.* 1:3
   27:5 I have made *man* and *b*.
   31:27 sow J. with seed of m.a.*b*.
   32:43 without *m*. or *b*. 33:10, 12;
   36:29; 51:62
   50:3 shall depart *m*. and *b*.
Ezek. 36:11 mul. on you *m*. and *b*.
Jon. 3:7 let not *m*. or *b*. taste

Unclean BEAST.

Lev. 5:2 touch any *u. b*. 7:21
   27:11 if it be *u. b*. of which, 27

Wild BEAST.

2 *K.* 14:9 *w. b*. in L. 2 *Chr.* 25:18
Job 39:15 forgetteth *w. b*.
Ps. 80:13 *w. b*. doth devour it
Hos. 13:8 the *w. b*. shall tear

BEASTS.

Gen. 31:39 torn of *b*. *Ex.* 22:31;
   Lev. 7:24; 17:15; 22:8
   36:6 Esau took all his *b*.
   45:17 lade your *b*. and go
Ex. 11:5 the first-b. of *b*.
Lev. 11:2 eat, *Deut.* 14:4
   3 chew cud among b. *Deut.*14:6
   26:6 will rid evil *b*. out of land
Deut. 32:24 will send teeth of *b*.
1 *K.* 4:33 Solomon spake of *b*.
Ezr. 1:4 help him with gold, *b*.
Job 12:7 ask the *b*. they teach
   18:3 are we counted as *b*.
   37:8 then the *b*. go into dens
Ps. 49:12 the *b*. that perish, 20
   104:20 wherein *b*. of forest creep
   25 sea, both small and great *b*.
   148:10 *b*. and all cattle, praise
Prov. 9:2 hath killed her *b*.
   30:30 lion strongest among *b*.
Ec. 3:18 themselves are *b*.
   19 befalleth men, before *b*.
Is. 30:6 of *b*. of the south
   40:16 nor *b*. thereof a burnt-off.
   46:1 idols on the *b*. and cattle
   66:20 upon swift *b*. to my holy
Jer. 9:10 *b*. fled, 12:4 consumed
Ezek. 5:17 send evil *b*. 14:15
   32:4 fill *b*. of whole earth
   '13 destroy all the *b*. 34:25, 28
Dan. 4:14 *b*. get away
   15 his portion be with the *b*.
   7:17 four great *b*. are kings
   8:4 no *b*. might stand before h.
Joel 1:18 how do the *b*. groan
Hab. 2:17 spoil of *b*.
Zep. 2:15 become a place for *b*.
Zec. 14:15 plague of all the *b*.
Acts 7:42 offered to me slain *b*.?
   23:24 *b*. that ye may set Paul
*Rom.*1:23 image made like to *b*.
1 *Cor.*15:32 I have fought with *b*.
Jam. 3:7 *b*. is tamed, but tongue
2 *Pet.* 2:12 as natural brute *b*.
Jude 10 naturally as brute *b*.
Rev. 4:6 four *b*. full of eyes
   8 four *b*. had each six wings
   9 when those *b*. give glory
   5:6 in midst of four *b*. stood a L.
   14 the four *b*. said, Amen
   6:1 *b*. saying, Come, 15:7
Rev. 7:11 stood about four *b*.
   14:3 song before the four *b*.
   19:4 and four *b*. fell down

BEASTS of the Earth.

Deut. 28:26 carc. meat to all *b*.
1 *Sam.* 17:46 carcasses of P. to *b*.
Job 5:22 nor be afraid of the *b*.
   35:11 teacheth us more than *b*.
Ps. 79:2 flesh of thy saints to *b*.
Is. 18:6 they shall be left to *b*.
Jer. 7:33 carc. of peop.meat for *b*.
   of the earth, 16:4; 19:7; 34:20
   15:3 I will appoint over them *b*.
Acts 10:12 of four-footed *b*. 11:6
Rev. 6:8 kill with hunger and *b*.

BEASTS of the Field.

Ex. 23:11 leave, *b*. may eat
Deut. 7:22 lest *b*. increase
1 *Sam.* 17:44 give thy flesh to *b*.
2 *Sam.* 21:10 nor *b*. *of the field*
Job 5:23 *b*. shall be at peace
   40:20 mountains where *b*. play
Ps. 8:7 put *b*. under his feet
Is. 56:9 ye *b*. come to devour
Jer. 12:9 assem. all *b*. *of the field*
   27:6 *b*. given, 28:14; *Dan.* 2:38

Ezek. 29:5 I have given thee for
    meat to the *b.* 34:5 ; 39:4
31:6 under branches *b.* bring
    13 *b.* shall be on his branches
38:20 *b.* shall shake
Dan. 4:12 the *b.* had shadow
    25 thy dwelling with *b.* 32
Hos. 2:18 cov. for them with *b.*
    4:3 shall land mourn with *b.*
Joel 1:20 cry also to thee
    2:22 ye *b.* pastures

Wild BEASTS.
Lev. 26:22 I will send *w. b.*
1 *Sam.* 17:46 carc. of Phil. to *w. b.*
Ps. 50:11 the *w. b.* are mine
Is. 13:21 *w. b.* shall lie there
    22 *wild b.* of the islands
34:14 *w.b.*of des. shall meet with
    w. b. of the island, *Jer.*50:39
Mark 1:13 C. was with the *w. b.*
Acts 10:12 wh. were all *w. b.* 11:6

BEAT.
Jud. 9:45 A. *b.* down the city
    19:22 sons of B. *b.* at the door
2 *Sam.* 22:43 I *b.* them, *Ps.* 18:42
Ps. 89:23 will *b.* down his foes
Prov. 23:14 *b.* him with the rod
Is. 2:4 *b.* their swords, *Mic.* 4:3
    3:15 that ye *b.* my people
    27:12 *b.* off from the channel
    41:15 mountains, *b.* them small
Joel 3:10 *b.* your ploughshares
Mic. 4:13 shalt *b.* in pieces
Mat. 7:25 *b.* on house, 27; *Luke*
    6:48, 49
    21:35 his servants and *b.* one,
    Mark 12:3 ; *Luke* 20:10, 11
Mark 4:37 waves *b.* into the ship
Luke 12:45 begin to *b.*
Acts 16:22 commanded to *b.* them
    18:17 took Sosthenes and *b.* him
    22:19 *b.* in every synagogue

BEATEN.
2 *Chr.* 34:7 *b.* images to powder
Prov. 23:35 they have *b.* me
Is. 28:27 fitches are *b.* with staff
Jer. 46:5 mighty ones are *b.*down
Mic. 1:7 images shall be *b.*
Mark 13:9 synag. ye shall be *b.*
Luke 12:47 did not shall be *b.*
Acts 5:40 apostles and *b.* them
    16:37 have *b.* us openly
2 *Cor.* 11:25 thrice was I *b.*

BEATEN Oil.
Ex. 27:20 *oil b. Lev.* 24:2
29:40 hin of *b. oil, Num.* 28:5

BEATEST.
Deut. 24:20 when thou *b.* thy ol.
Prov. 23:13 if thou *b.* him

BEATETH.
1 *Cor.* 9:26 as one that *b.* the air

BEATING.
1 *Sam.* 14:16 *b.* down one anoth
Mark 12:5 *b.* some and killing

BEAUTY.
Ex. 28:2 for glory and *b.*
2 *Sam.* 1:19 the *b.* of Israel
    14:25 praised as Absalom for *b.*
1 *Chr.* 16:29 *b.* of hol. *Ps.*29:2; 96:9
2 *Chr.* 20:21 praise *b.* of holiness
Est. 1:11 the people her *b.*
Job 40:10 array thyself with *b.*
Ps. 27:4 behold the *b.* of the L.
    39:11 made his *b.* to consume
    45:11 king greatly desire thy *b.*
    49:14 their *b.* shall consume
    50:2 the perfection of *b.*
    90:17 the *b.* of Lord be on us
Ps. 96:6 and *b.* in sanctuary
Prov. 6:25 lust not after her *b.*
    20:29 the *b.* of old is gray head
    31:30 favor is deceitful, *b.* is v.
Is. 3:24 burning instead of *b.*
    13:19 Babylon the *b.* of the C
    28:1 *b.* is a fading flower. 4

    5 a diadem of *b.* to residue
33:17 see the King in his *b.*
44:13 according to the *b.*
53:2 no *b.* that we should desire
    61:3 that mourn *b.* for ashes
Lam. 1:6 Zion all her *b.* is dep.
    2:1 from heaven the *b.* of Israel
    15 men call perfection of *b.* ?
Ezek. 7:20 *b.* of his ornament
    16:14 renown am. heath. for *b.*
    15 didst trust in thine own *b.*
    25 made thy *b.* to be abhorred
    27:3 I am of perfect *b.* 28:12
    4 builders perfected thy *b.* 11
    28:7 swords ag. the *b.* of thy
    17 lifted up beauty of *b.*
    31:8 no tree like Assyrian in *b.*
    32:19 whom dost pass in *b.*
Hos. 14:6 Israel's *b.* shall be
Zec. 9:17 how great is his *b.*
    11:7 staves, one I called *b.* 10

BEAUTIES.
Ps. 110:3 in the *b.* of holiness

BEAUTIFY.
Ezr. 7:27 king's heart, to *b.*
Ps. 149:4 *b.* the meek with salv.
Is. 60:13 *b.* place of my sanctu.

BEAUTIFUL.
Gen. 29:17 Rachel was *b.*
Deut. 21:11 am. cap. a *b.* woman
1 *Sam.* 16:12 was of a *b.* country
    25:3 Abigail was of a *b.* count.
2 *Sam.* 11:2 Bath. was very *b.*
Est. 2:7 Esther was fair and *b.*
Ps. 48:2 *b.* for situation is Zion
Ec. 3:11 every thing *b.*
Cant. 6:4 thou art *b.* O my love
    7:1 how *b.* thy feet with shoes
Is. 4:2 the branch of L. be *b.*
    52:1 O Zion, put on thy *b.* gar.
    7 how *b.* the feet, *Rom.* 10:15
    64:11 and *b.* house is burnt up
Jer. 13:20 where is thy *b.* flock ?
    48:17 broken, and the *b.* rod
Ezek. 16:12 *b.* crown on thy head
    13 thou wast exceeding *b.*
    23:42 Sabeans put *b.* crowns
Mat. 23:27 sepulch. which ap. *b.*
Acts 3:2 at the gate called *b.* 10

BECAME.
1 *Cor.* 9:20 to the Jews I *b.* a Jew
Heb. 7:26 such a High-priest *b.* us

BECAMEST.
1 *Chr.* 17:22 thou L. *b.* their God
Ezek. 16:8 and thou *b.* mine

BECKONED.
Luke 1:22 Zacharias *b.* speechl.
    5:7 they *b.* to their partners
John 13:24 Peter *b.* he should ask
Acts 19:33 Alex. *b.* and would
    21:40 P. stood on stairs, and *b.*

BECKONING.
Acts 12:17 Peter *b.* unto them
    13:16 Paul *b.* with his hand

BECOME.
Gen. 3:22 man is *b.* as one of us
Ex. 15:2 is *b.* my salvation, *Ps.*
    118:14 ; *Is.* 12:2
    32:1 as for M. we wot not what
    is *b.* of him, 23 ; *Acts* 7:40
Deut. 27:9 art *b.* the people
Mat. 21:42 is *b.* the head, *Mark*
    12:10 ; *Luke* 20:17 ; *Acts* 4:11
John 1:12 to *b.* the sons of God
2 *Cor.* 5:17 all things are *b.* new
Rev. 11:15 *b.* the kingd. of our L.

BECOMETH.
Ps. 93:5 holiness *b.* thy house
Prov. 10:4 *b.* poor that dealeth
    17:7 excell. speech *b.* not a fool
    18 void of understand. *b.* surety
Ec. 4:14 born in his kingd. *b.*
Mat. 3:15 it *b.* us to fulfil
    13:22 choketh the word, and he
    b. unfruitful, *Mark* 4:19

Rom. 16:2 receive P. as *b.* saints
Phil. 1:27 as *b.* gospel
1 *Tim.* 2:10 as *b.* women
Tit. 2:3 women as *b.* holiness

BED.
Gen. 47:31 bow. on *b.* 1 *K.* 1:47
    49:4 thy father's *b.* 1 *Chr.* 5:1
Ex. 21:18 but keepeth *b.*
1 *Sam.* 19:13 and laid it in *b.*
2 *Sam.* 4:5 who lay on *b.*
    11:2 David arose from his *b.*
2 *K.* 1:4 from that *b.* 6, 16
2 *K.* 4:10 set there for him a *b.*
Job 7:13 my *b.* shall comfort me
    17:13 my *b.* in the darkness
    33:15 slumberings upon the *b.*
Ps. 4:4 com. with heart on *b.*
    36:4 devis. mischief on his *b.*
    41:3 his *b.* in his sickness
    63:6 I rem. thee upon my *b.*
    132:3 into my *b.* till I find
    139:8 if I make my *b.* in hell
Prov. 7:16 decked my *b.* 17
    22:27 why take *b.* from under
    26:14 the slothful on his *b.*
Cant. 1:16 our *b.* is green
    3:1 on my *b.* I sought him
    7 his *b.* which is Solomon's
Is. 28:20 *b.* is shorter
    57:7 on mountain set thy *b.*
Amos 3:12 in the corner of a *b.*
Mat. 9:6 thy *b.* *Mark* 2:9, 11 ;
    John 5:11, 12
Mark 4:21 under a *b.* *Luke* 8:16
Luke 11:7 child. with me in *b.*
    17:34 two men in one *b.*
Rev. 2:22 will cast her into a *b.*

BED of love.
Ezek. 23:17 came to her in *b.*

BED of spices.
Cant. 5:13 his cheeks are as a *b.*
    6:2 my beloved is gone to thee *b.*

BED undefiled.
Heb. 13:4 honorable and the *b.*

BEDAD. *Gen.* 36:35
BEDAN. 1 *Sam.* 12:11; 1 *Chr.*7:17

BEDCHAMBER.
Ex. 8:3 frogs come into thy *b.*
2 *Sam.* 4:7 Ish. lay in his *b.*
2 *K.* 6:12 thou speakest in *b.*
    11:2 hid him in *b.* 2 *Chr.* 22:11
Ec. 10:20 the rich in *b.*

BEDS.
Ps. 149:5 sing aloud on *b.*
Is. 57:2 rest in their *b.* each
Hos. 7:14 they howled on *b.*
Amos 6:4 lie on *b.* of ivory
Mic. 2:1 that work evil on *b.*

BEDSTEAD.
Deut. 3:11 *b.* was a *b.* of iron

BEE, S.
Deut. 1:44 as *b.* in Seir
Jud. 14:8 swarm of *b.* in the lion
Ps. 118:12 me about like *b.*
Is. 7:18 hiss for the *b.* in As.

BEELZEBUB. *Mat.* 10:25; 12:24;
    Mark 3:22 ; *Luke* 11:15

Hath BEEN.
Ec. 3:15 which *h. been* is now

Have BEEN.
Job 10:19 *h. b.* as if I had not *b.*
Is. 66:2 all those things *h. b.*

Not BEEN.
Ob. 16 though they had *n. b.*

BEER. *Num.* 21:16
BEER-LAHAI-ROI. *Gen.* 16:14
BEERSHEBA. *Gen.* 21:14, 33:
    22:19 ; 26:33; 28:10 ; 1 *K.* 19:3

BEETLE.
Lev. 11:22 ye may eat, the *b.*

BEEVES.
Lev. 22:19 the *b.* of sheep
Num. 31:28 a tribute of the *b.*

BEFALL.

Gen. 42:4 lest mischief *b.* him
38 if mischief *b.* him, 44:29
49:1 what shall *b.* you, *Deut.*
31:29; *Dan.* 10:14
Deut. 31:17 evils shall *b.* them
Ps. 91:10 there shall no evil *b.*
Acts 20:22 things that shall *b.*

BEFALLEN.

Lev. 10:19 such things have *b.*
Num. 20:14 travail that hath *b.*
Deut. 31:21 when troubles are *b.*
Jud. 6:13 why is all this *b.*
1 *Sam.* 20:26 something had *b.*
Mat. 8:33 what was *b.*

BEFALLETH.

Ec. 3:19 *b.* men, *b.* beasts

BEFELL.

2 *Sam.* 19:7 than all that *b.* thee
Acts 20:19 *b.* me by lying in wait

BEFORE.

Jos. 10:14 like that *b.* it, or
Ps. 39:13 spare me *b.* I go
139:5 beset me behind and *b.*
Is. 43:13 *b.* the day was, I am
Mat. 24:25 I have told you *b.*
John 13:19 I tell you *b.* 14:29
Phil. 3:13 to things that are *b.*
1 *Thes.* 3:4 with you we told *b.*
Heb. 7:18 command going *b.*
Heb. 10:15 aft. that he had said *b.*
2 *Pet.* 3:17 know these things *b.*

Come BEFORE.

Ps. 100:2 *c. b.* presence
Mic. 6:6 shall I *c. b.* L?

BEFORE the people.

Ex. 13:22 pillar of fire from *b.*
17:5 L. said to Moses, go on *b.*
34:10 *b.* all *thy p.* I will do
1 *Sam.* 18:13 went out and in *b.*
Mark 8:6 discip. did set them *b.*
Luke 20:26 hold of his words *b.*
Rev. 10:11 prophesy *b. people*

BEFORE whom.

1 *K.* 17:1 as the Lord God of Isr.
liveth, *b. whom* I stand,18:15;
2 *K.* 3:14; 5:16
Acts 26:26 king *b. w.* I speak
See further, ALL, ARK, GOD, LORD,
MOUNT, STAND, STOOD, WENT.

BEFOREHAND.

Mark 13:11 take no thought *b.*
2 *Cor.* 9:5 make up *b.* your boun.
1 *Tim.* 5:24 men's s. are open *b.*
25 good works of some mani. *b.*
1 *Pet.* 1:11 testified *b.* sufferings

BEFORETIME.

Jos. 20:5 he hated him not *b.*
2 *Sam.* 7:10 nor afflict them as *b.*
Is. 41:26 *b.* that we may say
Acts 8:9 Simon which *b.* used

BEGAN.

Gen. 4:26 *b.* men call on name
2 *K.* 10:32 *b.* to cut Israel short
2 *Chr.* 34:3 *b.* to seek after God
Mat. 4:17 Jesus *b.* to preach
Luke 1:70 been since world *b.*
14:30 this man *b.* to build
John 4:52 when he *b.* to amend
9:32 since the world *b. Acts* 3:21;
Rom. 16:25
2 *Tim.* 1:9 in Christ before the
world *b. Tit.* 1:2
Heb. 2:3 at first to *b.* spoken

BEGAT.

Prov. 23:22 to thy father that *b.*
Jer. 16:3 their father that *b.* them
Dan. 11:6 and he that *b.* her
Zec. 13:3 and m. that *b.* him
Jam. 1:18 his own will *b.* he us
1 *John* 5:1 loveth him that *b.*

BEGET.

Gen. 17:20 princes shall he *b.*

Deut. 4:25 thou shalt *b.* children
28:41 *b.* sons
2 *K.* 20:18 sons thou shalt *b.* shall
they make eunuchs, *Is.* 39:7
Ec. 6:3 if a man *b.* 100 children
Jer. 29:6 take wives, and *b.* sons
Ezek. 18:10 if he *b.* a son
14 if he *b.* a son that seeth

BEGETTEST.

Gen. 48:6 issue which thou *b.*
Is. 45:10 to his father, what *b.*

BEGETTETH.

Prov. 17:21 *b.* a fool, doeth it
23:24 he that *b.* a wise child
Ec. 5:14 he *b.* a son

BEG.

Ps. 109:10 let his children *b.*
Prov. 20:4 sluggard *b.* in harvest
Luke 16:3 to *b.* I am ashamed

BEGGAR, LY.

1 *Sam.* 2:8 lifted *b.* from dungh.
Luke 16:20 a *b.* named Lazarus
22 the *b.* died and was carried
Gal. 4:9 to the *b.* elements

BEGGED.

Mat. 27:58 *b.* body of J. *Lu.* 23:52
John 9:8 he that sat and *b.*

BEGGING.

Ps. 37:25 seen his seed *b.* bread
Mark 10:46 Bart. sat *b. Lu.* 18:35

BEGIN.

Gen. 11:6 this they *b.* to do, and
Jos. 3:7 will I *b.* to magnify
1 *Sam.* 3:12 I *b.* I will make
22:15 did I then *b.* to inquire
Neh. 11:17 Mattan. to *b.* thanks.
Jer. 25:29 I *b.* to bring evil
Luke 3:8 *b.* not to say within
13:26 *b.* to say we have eaten
14:29 behold it, *b.* to mock him
21:28 things *b.* to come to pass
2 *Cor.* 3:1 do we *b.* to commend
1 *Pet.* 4:17 judgment must *b.* at
house of G., and if it first *b.*

BEGINNING, Part.

Mat. 14:30 *b.* to sink, L. save me
20:8 *b.* from last to first
Luke 24:47 all nations, *b.* at J.
John 8:9 *b.* at eldest
Acts 1:22 *b.* from baptism of J.

BEGINNING, Substantive.

Gen. 49:3 Reuben, *b.* of my st.
Ex. 12:2 the *b.* of months
Deut. 21:17 is *b.* of his strength
Job 8:7 thy *b.* was small
42:12 end of Job more than *b.*
Ps. 111:10 *b.* of wis. *Prov.* 9:10
Prov. 1:7 fear of L. *b.* of knowl.
17:14 *b.* of strife. as when one
Ec. 7:8 end of a thing than *b.*
10:13 *b.* of words is foolishness
Is. 64:4 since *b.* of world, men
Mic. 1:13 is *b.* of sin to daughter
Mat. 24:8 *b.* of sor. *Mark* 13:8
21 as was not since *b.*
Mark 1:1 the *b.* of the gospel
John 2:11 this *b.* of miracles
Col. 1:18 who is the *b.* the first-b.
Heb. 3:14 *b.* of our confidence
7:3 having neither *b.* of days
2 *Pet.* 2:20 is worse than the *b.*
Rev. 1:8 I am *b.* 21:6; 22:13
3:14 saith the *b.* of the creation

At the BEGINNING.

Ruth 3:10 kindness than at *b.*
1 *Chr.* 17:9 wicked. waste as *b.*
Prov. 20:21 in. gotten hastily *b.*
Is. 1:26 counsellors as *at the b.*
Dan. 9:23 *a. b.* of thy supplica.
Mat. 19:4 *at the b.* made them
John 16:4 I said not to you *b.*
Acts 11:15 H. G. as on us *a. t. b.*

From the BEGINNING.

Deut. 11:12 eyes of L. on it *b.*
Ps. 119:160 true *from the begin.*
Prov. 8:23 I was set up *f. b.*
Ec. 3:11 no man can find out the
work God maketh *f. t. b.*
Is. 18:2 peop. terrible *f. t. b.?*
40:21 been told *f. t. b.?*
41:26 hath declared *f. t. b.?*
46:10 declaring the end *f. t. b.*
48:16 not spoken in secret *f. t. b.*
Jer. 17:12 high throne *f. t. b.*
Mat. 19:8 *fr. the b.* it was not so
Luke 1:2 *f. b.* were eye-wit.
John 6:64 knew *f. b.* who believ.
8:25 same I said to you *f. b.*
44 a murderer *from the begin.*
15:27 have been with me *f. b.*
Eph. 3:9 *f. t. b.* of the world
2 *Thes.* 2:13 God hath *f. t. begin.*
chosen you to salvation
2 *Pet.* 3:4 continue as *fr. t. begin.*
1 *John* 2:7 ye have heard *b.* 3:11
13 known him that is *f. t. b.*
3:8 the devil sinneth *from f. t. b.*
2 *John* 5 that which we had *f. t. b*

In the BEGINNING.

Gen. 1:1 *i. t. b.* God created h.
Prov. 8:22 the Lord possessed me
in the begin, of his way
John 1:1 *in the b.* was the Word
2 the same was *in the b.*
Phil. 4:15 know *b.* of the gospel
Heb. 1:10 L. *b.* hast laid founda.

BEGINNINGS.

Num. 10:10 *b.* of your m. 28:11
Ezek. 36:11 bet. than at your *b.*

BEGINNEST.

Deut. 16:9 thou *b.* to put sickle

BEGOTTEN.

Num. 11:12 have I *b.* them?
Deut. 23:8 children *b.* of them
Jud. 8:30 Gideon had 70 sons *b.*
Job 38:28 hath *b.* drops of dew
Ps. 2:7 this day have I *b.* thee,
Acts 13:33; *Heb.* 1:5; 5:15
Is. 49:21 hath *b.* me these?
Hos. 5:7 have *b.* strange children
John 1:14 the only *b.* of the F.
18 only *b.* Son, he hath declar.
3:16 he gave his only *b.* Son
18 not believed in only *b.* Son
1 *Cor.* 4:15 *b.* you through gospel
Phile. 10 Onesi. whom I have *b.*
1 *Pet.* 1:3 *b.* us again
1 *John* 4:9 sent his only *b.* Son
5:1 loveth him *b.* of him
18 he that is *b.* of God

First-BEGOTTEN.

Heb. 1:6 he bringeth in *first-b.*
Rev. 1:5 who is *f.-b.* of the dead

BEGUILE.

Col. 2:4 lest any *b.* you
18 let no man *b.* you

BEGUILED, ING.

Gen. 3:13 serpent *b.* me
29:25 wherefore hast thou *b.*
Num. 25:18 they have *b.* you, in
the matter of Peor
Jos. 9:22 wherefore have ye *b.*
2 *Cor.* 11:3 as the serpent *b.* Eve
2 *Pet.* 2:14 cannot cease from sin,
b. unstable souls

BEGUN.

Deut. 3:24 *b.* to show thy great.
Mat. 18:24 he had *b.* to reckon
2 *Cor.* 8:6 had *b.* so would finish
10 for you who have *b.* before
Gal. 3:3 having *b.* in the Spirit
Phil. 1:6 hath *b.* a good work
1 *Tim.* 5:11 *b.* to wax wanton

BEHALF.

Ex. 27:21 a statute on *b.* of Is.
2 *Sam.* 3:12 Abner sent on his *b.*
2 *Chr.* 16:9 sh. hims. strong in *b.*
Job 36:2 yet to speak on God's *b.*
Dan. 11:18 prince for his own *b.*
Rom. 16:19 I am glad on your *b.*
1 *Cor.* 1:4 I thank God on your *b.*
2 *Cor.* 1:11 th. be given on our *b.*
   5:12 to glory on our *b.*
Phil. 1:29 given in *b.* of Christ
1 *Pet.* 4:16 glorify God on this *b.*

BEHAVE.

Deut. 32:27 lest adversaries *b.*
1 *Chr.* 19:13 let us *b.* valiantly
Ps. 101:2 I will *b.* wisely
Is. 3:5 child shall *b.* proudly
1 *Cor.* 13:5 not *b.* unseemly
1 *Tim.* 3:15 how thou oughtest
   to *b.* in the house of God

BEHAVED.

1 *Sam.* 18:5 D. *b.* wisely, 14, 15, 30
Ps. 35:14 I *b.* as he had been f.
  131:2 have *b.* as child weaned
Mic. 3:4 as they have *b.* ill
1 *Thes.* 2:10 unblamably we *b.*
2 *Thes.* 3:7 *b.* not disorderly

BEHAVETH.

1 *Cor.* 7:36 think he *b.* uncomely

BEHAVIOR.

1 *Sam.* 21:13 D. changed his *b.*
1 *Tim.* 3:2 a bishop of good *b.*
Tit. 2:3 women in *b.* as becom.

BEHEADED.

2 *Sam.* 4:7 Ish. and *b.* him
Mat. 14:10 *b.* John, *Mark.* 6:16,
  27; *Luke* 9:9
Rev. 20:4 I saw the souls of *b.*

BEHELD.

Num. 21:9 *b.* serpent of brass
  23:21 hath not *b.* iniquity in J.
1 *Chr.* 21:15 destroying, the L. *b.*
Job 31:26 if I *b.* the sun when
Ps. 119:158 I *b.* transgressors
  142:4 I *b.* but there was no man
Prov. 7:7 *b.* among the simple
Ec. 8:17 I *b.* all the work of God
Is. 41:28 I *b.* and there was no
  man, *Jer.* 4:25
Jer. 4:23 I *b.* the earth
Mark 15:47 *b.* where he was laid,
  Luke 23:55
Luke 10:18 I *b.* Satan as light.
  19:41 he *b.* the city and wept
John 1:14 we *b.* his glory
Acts 1:9 they *b.* J. was taken up
  17:23 and *b.* your devotions
Rev. 5:6 I *b.* and lo, a lamb
  11:12 their enemies *b.* them

BEHEMOTH.

Job 40:15 behold now *b.*

BEHIND.

Is. 38:17 all my sins *b.* thy back
1 *Cor.* 1:7 ye come *b.* in no gift
2 *Cor.* 11:5 whit *b.* chiefest, 12:11
Phil. 3:13 forgetting things *b.*
Col. 1:24 fill up what is *b.*

See BEFORE.

BEHOLD.

Gen. 28:15 *b.* I am with thee
Job 1:12 *b.* all he hath
  28:28 *b.* the fear of the Lord
  40:4 *b.* I am vile what shall I
Ps. 139:8 bed in hell, *b.* thou
Is. 8.18 *b.* I and chil. *Heb.* 2:13
  12:2 *b.* God is my salvation
  41:27 say to Zion, *b.* them
  65:1 I said, *b.* me, to a nation
Lam. 1:12 *b.* and see if any sor.
Zec. 9:9 *b.* thy King cometh,
  Mat. 21:5; *John* 12:15
Mark 16:6 *b.* place where they
Luke 24:39 *b.* my hands and feet
  49 *b.* I send prom. of my Fath.

John 1:29 *b.* the Lamb of God
  19:5 Pilate saith, *b.* the man
Acts 9:11 Saul, for *b.* he prayeth
1 *John* 3:1 *b.* what manner of love
Rev. 3:20 *b.* I stand at the door
  16:15 *b.* I come as a thief
  22:7 *b.* I come quickly, 12

BEHOLD it is.

Is. 52:6 I speak, *b. it is* I
Ezek. 7:10 *b.* the day, *b. it is* come
  39:8 *b. it is* come, and it is

Now BEHOLD, *or* BEHOLD now.

Job 16:19 n. *b.* my witness is in
Jer. 40:4 *now b.* I loose thee
Mat. 26:65 *b.* n. ye heard
Acts 13:11 n. *b.* hand of Lord
  20:22 *now b.* I go bound
2 *Cor.* 6:2 *b.* n. is the accepted t.

BEHOLD it was, BEHOLD there was.

See WAS.

BEHOLD, Verb.

Num. 12:8 simil. of L. shall he *b.*
  23:9 from the hills I *b.* him
  24:17 shall *b.* him, but not nigh
Deut. 3:27 *b.* it with thine eyes
Job 19:27 shall *b.* and not anoth.
  20:9 his place any more *b.* him
  23:9 work, but I cannot *b.* him
  34:29 his face, who can *b.?*
  36:24 magnify his work men *b.*
Ps. 11:4 his eyes *b.* his eyelids
  7 doth *b.* the upright
  17:2 let thine eyes *b.* things
  15 I will *b.* thy face in right.
  27:4 to *b.* the beauty of the L.
  37:37 perfect, *b.* the upright
  46:8 *b.* the works of the Lord
  59:4 awake to help me, and *b.*
  66:7 his eyes *b.* the nations
  80:14 look from heaven, *b.*
  91:8 eyes shalt thou *b.* and see
  102:19 from heaven did L. *b.*
  113:6 he humbleth hims. to *b.*
  119:18 mine eyes, that I may *b.*
Prov. 23:33 *b.* strange women
Ec. 11:7 pleasant it is to *b.*
Is. 26:10 will not *b.* the majesty
  38:11 I shall *b.* man no more
  41:23 do good or evil that we *b.*
  63:15 *b.* from habita. of thy holi.
Jer. 20:4 thine eyes shall *b.*
  29:32 nor *b.* the good I will do
  32:4 his eyes shall *b.* 34:3
  42:2 as thine eyes do *b.* us
Lam. 1:18 and *b.* my sorrow
  3:50 till Lord *b.* from heaven
  5:1 consider and *b.* our reproach
Ezek. 8:9 *b.* wicked abomina.
  28:17 that they may *b.*
  18 in sight of all that *b.*
  40:4 Son of man, *b.* 44:5
Dan. 9:18 and *b.* our desolations
Mic. 7:9 I shall *b.* his righteous.
  mine eyes shall *b.* her
Hab. 1:3 why cause me to *b.*
  13 purer eyes than to *b.* evil
Mat. 18:10 their angels *b.* face
Luke 14:29 all that *b.* it mock
  21:6 as for these *b.* the days
John 17:24 they may *b.* my glory
Acts 7:31 he drew near to *b.* it
  32 Moses durst not *b.*
2 *Cor.* 3:7 Is. could not *b.* face
1 *Pet.* 2:12 works they shall *b.*
  3:2 *b.* your chaste conversation
Rev. 17:8 when they *b.* the beast

BEHOLDEST.

Ps. 10:14 thou *b.* all mischief
Mat. 7:3 w. *b.* mote? *Luke* 6:41
Luke 6:42 *b.* not the beam

BEHOLDETH.

Job 24:18 he *b.* not the way

Ps. 33:13 Lord *b.* all the sons
Jam. 1:24 *b.* himself and goeth

BEHOLDING.

Ps. 119:37 mine eyes from *b.*
Prov. 15:3 *b.* the evil and good
Ec. 5:11 saving the *b.* of them
Mat. 27:55 women *b.* *Luke* 23:49
Mark 10:21 Jesus *b.* him, loved
Luke 23:35 people stood *b.*
  48 *b.* things done, smote breasts
Acts 4:14 and *b.* man healed
  23:1 and Paul *b.* the council
2 *Cor.* 3:18 *b.* as in a glass the g.
Col. 2:5 joying, and *b.* your order
Jam. 1:23 *b.* his natural face

BEHOVED.

Luke 24:46 thus it *b.* Christ
Heb. 2:17 *b.* him to be made

BEING.

Ps. 104:33 I have *b.* 146:2
Acts 17:28 move, and have our *b.*

BEKAH. *Ex.* 38:26
BEL. *Is.* 46:1; *Jer.* 50:2; 51:44

BELCH.

Ps. 59:7 beloold they *b.* out

BELIAL.

Deut. 13:13 children of B.
Jud. 19:22 certain sons of B.
  20:13 the children of B.
1 *Sam.* 1:16 a daughter of B.
  2:12 sons of Eli were sons of B
  10:27 children of B. said, how
  25:17 is such a son of B. 25
  30:22 then answ. the men of B.
2 *Sam.* 16:7 come out, man of B.
  20:1 a man of B.
  23:6 sons of B. shall be as th.
1 *K.* 21:10 two sons of B. 13
2 *Chr.* 13:7 Jerob. children of B.
2 *Cor.* 6:15 hath Christ with B.?

BELIED.

Jer. 5:12 they have *b.* the L.

BELIEF.

2 *Thes.* 2:13 of Spirit and *b.*

BELIEVE.

Ex. 4:5 may *b.* L. hath appeared
  19:9 may *b.* thee for ever
Num. 14:11 ere they *b.* me?
2 *Chr.* 20:20 *b.* in the L. his p.
Is. 43:10 may know and *b.* me.
Mat. 9:28 I am able to do this?
  18:6 ones which *b. Mark* 9:42
  21:32 that ye might *b.* him
  27:42 and we will *b.* him
Mark 1:15 repent and *b.* gospel.
  5:36 be not af. only *b. Lu.* 8:50
  9:23 if thou canst *b.* all things
  24 L. I *b.* help unb., *John* 9:38
  11:23 *b.* things he saith
  24 *b.* ye receive them, and ye
  15:32 descend, that we may *b.*
  16:17 signs fol. them which *b.*
Luke 8:12 the word lest they *b.*
  13 which for a while *b.*
  24:25 and slow of heart to *b.*
John 1:7 all thro' him might *b.*
  12 them that *b.* on his name
  3:12 shall ye *b.* if I tell you
  4:21 woman *b.* me
  42 we *b.* not bec. of thy saying
  5:44 can ye *b.* which receive
  47 how shall ye *b.* my words?
  6:29 that ye *b.* on him he sent
  7:5 did his brethren *b.* in him
  39 Spirit, which they that *b.*
  9:35 dost thou *b.* on S. of God?
  36 who is he that I might *b.*
  10:38 *b.* the w. that ye may *b.*
  11:15 to the intent ye may *b.*
  27 I *b.* thou art the Christ
  40 said I not, if wouldest *b.*
  42 may *b.* thou hast sent me
  48 let him alone all will *b.*

12:36 ye have light, *b.* in the l.
13:19 ye may *b.* I am he
14:1 ye *b.* in God, *b.* also in me
11 or *b.* for the work's sake
29 come to pass, ye might *b.*
16:30 we *b.* thou camest from G.
31 J. answered, Do ye now *b. ?*
17:20 for them which shall *b.*
21 world may *b.* thou sent me
19:35 that ye might *b.*
20:31 written that ye might *b.*
Acts 8:37 I *b.* J. C. is the S. of G.
13:39 by him all that *b.*
41 you shall in no wise *b.*
15:7 Gentiles by me should *b.*
11 *b.* thro' grace we sh. be sav.
16:31 *b.* on Jes. shalt be saved
19:4 *b.* on him that should come
21:20 seest how many Jews *b.*
25 touching Gentiles which *b.*
27:25 I *b.* God that it shall be
Rom. 3:22 on all that *b.*
4:11 of all that *b.*
24 if we *b.* on him
6:8 we *b.* we shall also live
10:9 shalt *b.* that G. raised him
14 how shall they *b.* in him
1 Cor. 1:21 to save that *b.*
14:22 tongues a sign, not to th.
that *b.* but prophesying
2 Cor. 4:13 we *b.* therefore speak
Gal. 3:22 promise to them that *b.*
Eph. 1:19 to us who *b.*
Phil. 1:29 given not only to *b.*
1 Thes. 1:7 ensamples to all th. *b.*
2:10 behaved am. you that *b.*
13 worketh in you that *b.*
4:14 if we *b.* Jesus died
2 Thes. 1:10 admi. in all that *b.*
2:11 that they should *b.* a lie
1 Tim. 1:16 pat. to them that *b.*
4:3 thanksg. of them that *b.*
10 Saviour, spec. of th. that *b.*
Heb. 10:39 *b.* to saving of soul
11:6 to God must *b.* that he is
Jam. 2:19 devils also *b.*
Pet. 1:21 by him do *b.* in God
2:7 to you wh. *b.* he is precious
John 3:23 com. that we *b.*
5:13 to you that *b.* ye may *b.*

BELIEVE not, *or* **not BE-
LIEVE.**
Ex. 4:1 they will *not b.* me
Deut. 1:32 ye did *not b.* the Lord
2 K. 17:14 fathers did *not b.* in L.
Job 9:16 I *not b.* he had heark.
Prov. 26:25 fair, *b.* him *not*
Is. 7:9 will *not b.* not be esta.
Jer. 12:6 *b. not*' they speak
Hab. 1:5 ye will not *b.*
Mat. 21:25 *not b.* him Mark 11:31
24:23 h. is C. *b.* n. 26; Mark 13:21
Luke 22:67 you will *not b.*
John 3:12 earthly th. and ye *b. n.*
4:48 ex. ye see signs will *not b.*
5:38 he hath sent, him ye *b. n.*
47 how shall ye *b.* my words *?*
6:36 ye have seen me and *b. not*
64 some of you which *b. not*
8:24 if ye *b. n.* I am he, die
45 tell the truth, ye *b.* me *not*
46 say the truth, why *n. b.* me
10:26 ye *b.* n. bec. not of my s.
37 do not works of F. *b.* me n.
38 ye *b. not* me, be. the works
12:30 could *not b.* because Isa.
47 hear words, and *b. not*
16:9 bec. they *b. not* on me
20:25 into his side, I will *n. b.*
Rom. 3:3 if some did *not b.*
15:31 from them that do *not b.*
1 Cor. 10:27 that *b. not* bid to a f.
14:22 sign to them that *b. not*
2 Cor. 4:4 blinded th. *b. not*
2 Tim. 2:13 if we *b. not*, he abid.
1 John 4:1 *b. not* every spirit

BELIEVED.
Gen. 15:6 he *b.* counted it, Rom.
4:3; Gal. 3:6; Jam. 2:23
Ex. 4:31 A. spake, people *b.*
14:31 they *b.* the L. and Moses
Ps. 27:13 fainted, unless I *b.*
106:12 then *b.* they his words
116:10 I *b.* therefore have I
spoken, 2 Cor. 4:13
119:66 I have *b.* thy command.
Is. 53:1 who hath *b.* our report *?*
John 12:38; Rom. 10:16
Dan. 6:23 bec. he *b.* in G.
Jon. 3:5 peo. of Nineveh *b.* G.
Mat. 8:13 *b.* so be it done to thee
21:32 publicans and harlots *b.*
Mark 16:13 neither *b.* they
Luke 1:1 things most surely *b.*
45 blessed is she that *b.* for
John 2:11 his disciples *b.* on him
22 they *b.* the scripture
4:50 the man *b.* word J. spoke
53 the father himself *b.*
5:46 had ye *b.* Moses
7:48 have Pharisees *b.* on him *?*
8:31 said Jesus to Jews that *b.*
11:45 seen things Jesus did, *b.*
12:11 many of the Jews *b.* on J.
16:27 loveth you, bec. you *b.*
17:8 have *b.* thou didst send me
20:8 other disciple, saw and *b.*
29 have not seen, and yet *b.*
Acts 2:44 all that *b.* were togeth.
4:4 many wh. h. the word *b.*
32 that *b.* were of one heart
8:12 *b.* Phil. preaching things
13 then Simon himself *b.*
10:45 who *b.* were astonished
11:17 like gift as to us who *b.*
21 a great number *b.* turned
13:12 then deputy *b.*
48 ordained to eternal life *b.*
14:1 both Jews and Greeks *b.*
23 to Lord on whom they *b.*
17:4 *b.* and consorted with Paul
34 certain clave to him and *b.*
18:8 Crispus chr. ruler of syn. *b.*
27 had *b.* through grace
19:2 rec. ye H. G. since ye *b. ?*
22:19 I beat them that *b.*
27:11 centur. *b.* master of ship
28:24 some *b.* and some *b. not*
Rom. 4:18 against hope *b.* in h.
13:11 nearer than when we *b.*
1 Cor. 3:5 minis. by whom ye *b.*
15:2 unless ye have *b.* in vain
11 so we preach, and so ye *b.*
Gal. 2:16 we have *b.* in Jesus C.
Eph. 1:13 after ye *b.* ye were
2 Thes. 1:10 our testim. was *b.*
1 Tim. 3:16 *b.* on in the world
2 Tim. 1:12 whom I have *b.*
Tit. 3:8 which have *b.* in God
Heb. 4:3 we which *b.* do enter
1 John 4:16 *b.* the love of God

Many BELIEVED.
John 2:23 at the pass. *many b.*
4:39 *many* of the Samaritans *b.*
11:45 *m.* Jews wh. came to M. *b.*
12:42 chief rulers also *many b.*
Acts 18:8 *m.* Corinth. hearing ***b.***

Acts 19:18 *m.* b. confess. their d.

BELIEVED not, *or* **not
BELIEVED.**
Gen. 45:26 h. fainted, he *b. not*
Num. 20:12 ye *b.* me *not*
Deut. 9:23 and *b.* him *not*
Job 39:12 they *b.* it *not*
Ps. 78:22 they *b.* not in God
32 *b. not* for his wond. works
106:24 despised land, *b. n.* his w.
Jer. 40:14 but G. *b.* them *not*
Lam. 4:12 world would *n.* have *b.*
Mat. 21:32 J. came, ye *b.* him *not*
Mark 16:11 he was alive, *b. not*
14 upbr. because they *b. not*

Luke 20:5 say, Why *b.* ye *not ?*
24:41 while they *b. not* for joy
John 3:18 because he hath *not b.*
6:64 Jesus knew who *b. not*
10:25 I told you, and ye *b. not*
12:37 miracles, yet they *b. not*
Acts 9:26 *b. not* he was a disc.
17:5 Jews wh. *b. not*
19:9 were hardened, *b. not*
Rom. 10:14 they have *not b.*
11:30 times past have *not b.* G.
31 these also now *not b.*
2 Thes. 2:12 damned who *b. not*
Heb. 3:18 his rest that *b. not*
11:31 R. per. not with them *b. n.*
Jude 5 destroyed them that *b. n.*

BELIEVERS.
Acts 5:14 *b.* were the more added
1 Tim. 4:12 an example of the *b.*

BELIEVEST.
Luke 1:20 dumb, bec. thou *b.* not
John 1:50 under the fig tree, *b.*
11:26 never die, *b.* thou this *?*
14:10 *b.* thou not I am in the F.
Acts 8:37 *b.* with all thy heart
26:27 *b.* thou the prophets *?*
Jam. 2:19 thou *b.* there is one God

BELIEVETH.
Job 15:22 *b.* he shall return
Prov. 14:15 simple *b.* every word
Is. 28:16 that *b.* not make haste
Mark 9:23 possible to him that *b.*
16:16 he that *b.* shall be saved,
he th. *b.* not shall be damn.
John 3:15 *b.* in him, 16
18 *b.* not is condemned already
36 *b.* hath everlasting life, 6:47
5:24 *b.* on him that sent me
6:35 *b.* on me shall never thirst
40 Son, and *b.* on him, hath l.
7:38 *b.* on me, out of his belly
11:25 *b.* though dead, yet shall
26 *b.* liv. me shall never die
12:44 *b.* not on me, but on him
46 whoso *b.* not abide in dark.
14:12 *b.* on me the works
Acts 10:43 *b.* receive remission
Rom. 1:16 of G. to ev. that *b.*
3:26 justifier of him that *b.* in J.
4:5 that worketh not, but *b.* on
9:33 whoso *b.* not be asha. 10:11
10:4 end of law to ev. one th. *b.*
10 the heart man *b.* to right.
14:2 one *b.* he may eat
1 Cor. 7:12 a wife that *b.* not
13:7 love *b.* all things
14:24 come in one that *b.* not
2 Cor. 6:15 hath he that *b.*
1 Tim. 5:16 if any that *b.*
1 Pet. 2:6 *b.* shall not be conf.
1 John 5:1 whoso *b.* J. is the C.
5 overcometh, but he that *b.*
10 *b.* on the Son; he that *b.* n.
G. bec. he *b.* not the record

BELIEVING.
Mat. 21:22 ask *b.* ye shall receive
John 20:27 not faithless, but *b.*
31 that *b.* ye might have life
Acts 16:34 *b.* in God
24:14 *b.* all things written
Rom. 15:13 joy and peace in *b.*
1 Tim. 6:2 that have *b.* masters
1 Pet. 1:8 yet *b.* ye rejoice

BELL, S.
Ex. 28:34 golden *b.* 39:26
Zec. 14:20 upon the *b.* of horses
BELLOW. *See* BULLS.

BELLOWS.
Jer. 6:29 the *b.* are burnt

BELLY.
Gen. 3:14 on thy *b.* shalt thou go
Lev. 11:42 goeth on the *b.*
Num. 5:21 and thy *b.* to swell
25:8 man and wom. through *b.*
Jud. 3:21 dag. thrust it in his *b.*

1 *K.* 7:20 pomeg. over against *b.*
Job 3:11 when I came out of *b.*
  15:2 fill his *b.* with east wind
  35 their *b.* prepareth deceit
  20:15 G. shall cast out of his *b.*
Job 20:20 not feel quietness in *b.*
  23 when about to fill his *b.*
  32:19 my *b.* is as wine which
Ps. 17:14 whose *b.* fillest
  22:10 from my mother's *b.*
  44:25 our *b.* cleaveth to earth
Prov. 13:25 *b.* of wicked
  18:8 innermost parts of *b.* 26:22
  20 a man's *b.* shall be satisfied
  20:27 inward parts of *b.*
  30 stripes inward parts of *b.*
Cant. 5:14 his *b.* is as br. ivory
  7:2 thy *b.* is like wheat
Is. 46:3 borne by me from the *b.*
Jer. 1:5 formed thee in *b.* 1 k.
  51:34 his *b.* with my delicates
Ezek. 3:3 cause thy *b.* to eat
Dan. 2:32 image's *b.* of brass
Jon. 1:17 in *b.* of fish, *Mat.* 12:40
  2:2 out of the *b.* of hell cried I
Hab. 3:16 my *b.* trembled
Mat. 15:17 into the *b.* and is cast
  out, *Mark* 7:19
Luke 15:16 his *b.* with the husks
John 7:38 out of his *b.* flow riv.
Rom. 16:18 serve their own *b.*
1 *Cor.* 6:13 meats for the *b.*
Phil. 3:19 whose God is their *b.*
Rev. 10:9 shall make thy *b.* bit.
  10 eaten it, my *b.* was bitter.

BELLIES.
Tit. 1:12 the Cretians are slow *b.*

BELONG.
Lev. 27:24 to whom it did *b.*
Deut. 29:29 secret things *b.* to G.
Ps. 47:9 shields of earth *b.* to G.
  68:20 to our God *b.* the issues
Prov. 24:2 these *b.* to the wise
Dan. 9:9 to the Lord *b.* mercies
Mark 9:41 bec. ye *b.* to Christ
Luke 19:42 which *b.* to thy p.
1 *Cor.* 7:32 things *b.* to Lord

BELONGED, EST.
1 *Sam.* 30:13 to whom *b.* thou ?
Luke 23:7 *b.* to Herod's jurisd.

BELONGETH.
Deut. 32:35 to me *b.* vengeance,
  Ps. 94:1; *Heb.* 10:30
Ps. 3:8 salvation *b.* unto the L.
  62:11 power *b.* unto God
  12 unto thee, O Lord, *b.* mercy
Dan. 9:7 righteousness *b.* to thee
  8 to us *b.* confusion of face
Heb. 5:14 strong meat *b.*

BELONGING.
Prov. 26:17 strife *b.* not to him

BELOVED.
Deut. 21:15 two wives, the one *b.*
  33:12 *b.* of Lord dwell in safety
Neh. 13:26 Solomon, *b.* of his G.
Ps. 60:5 thy *b.* may be d.108:6
  127:2 so he giveth his *b.* sleep
Prov. 4:3 only b. in sight of m.
Cant. 5:1 drink abundantly, O *b.*
  9 thy *b.* more than another *b.* ?
  61: whither is thy *b.* gone ?
  8:5 cometh leaning on her *b.* ?
Dan. 9:23 greatly *b.* 10:11, 19
Hos. 31 a woman *b.* of her. fr.
  9:16 I will slay the *b.* fruit
Acts 15:25 with *b.* B. and Paul
Rom. 1:7 all in Rome *b.* of God
  9:25 call her *b.* wh. was not *b.*
  11:28 are *b.* for Father's sake
  16:12 *b.* Persis who labored
Eph. 1:6 accepted in the *b.*
  6:21 T. a *b.* brother, *Col.* 4:7
Col. 3:12 elect of G. holy and *b.*
  4:9 Onesimus, a *b.* brother
  14 Luke the *b.* physician
1 *Thes.* 1:4 kn. *b.* your election

1 *Tim.* 6:2 serv. bec. they are *b.*
Phile. 16 a servant a brother *b.*
Heb. 6:9 *b.* we are persuaded
2 *Pet.* 3:8 *b.* be not ignorant
  15 even as our *b.* brother Paul
1 *John* 3:2 *b.* now we are the sons
  21 *b.* if our heart condemn
  4:1 *b.* believe not every spirit
  7 *b.* let us love one another
  11 *b.* if God so loved us, we
3 *John* 11 *b.* follow not evil,
Jude 20 but ye *b.* building up
Rev. 20:9 they compassed *b.* city

Dearly BELOVED. See DEARLY.

My BELOVED.
Cant. 1:14 my *b.* is to me a clus.
  16 art fair, my *b.* yea, pleasant
  2:3 the apple-tree, so is my *b.*
  9 my *b.* is like a roe or a hart
  16 my *b.* is mine, 6:3
  17 my *b.* and be like a roe
  4:16 let my *b.* come into his g.
  5:2 voice of my *b.* 5:8
  5 to open to my *b.* 6 I opened
Cant. 5:10 my *b.* is, 16 is my *b.*
  6:2 my *b.* is gone
  3 I am my *b.* my *b.* mine, 7:10
  7:13 laid up for thee, O my *b.*
Is. 5:1 song of my *b.* touching
Jer. 11:15 my *b.* to do in my h.
Mat. 3:17 this is my *b.* Son, 17:5 ;
  Mark 1:11 ; 9:7 ; *Luke* 3:22 ;
  9:35 ; 2 *Pet.* 1:17
  12:18 my *b.* in whom my soul
Luke 20:13 will send my *b.* Son
Rom. 16:8 greet Amplias my *b.*
1 *Cor.* 4:14 as my *b.* sons I warn
  17 Tim. my *b.* son, 2 *Tim.* 1:2
Jam. 1:16 do not err, my *b.* breth.

BELSHAZZAR. *Dan.* 5:1, 2, 9,
  22, 29, 30 ; 7:1 ; 8:1
BELTESHAZZAR. *Dan.* 1:7 ;
  2:26 ; 4:8, 18, 19 : 5:12 ; 10:1

BEMOAN, ED, ING.
Job 42:11 *b.* Job, and comfort.
Jer. 15:5 who shall *b.* thee, O J.
  16:5 neither lament. nor *b.*
  22:10 w. ye not for dead, nor *b.*
  31:18 heard Eph. *b.* himself
  48:17 all ye about him *b.* him
Nah. 3:7 N. who will *b.* her ?
BENAIAH. 2 *Sam.* 23:22 ; 1
  Chr. 11:24 ; *Ezek.* 11:1
BEN-AMMI. *Gen.* 19:38

BENCHES.
Ezek. 27:6 made thy *b.* of ivory

BEND.
Ps. 11:2 wicked *b.* their bow
  64:3 *b.* their bows to shoot
Jer. 9:3 they *b.* their tongue
  46:9 Lydians, that *b.* the bow
  50:14 *b.* bow shoot at her, 29
  51:3 bendeth, let the archer *b.*
Ezek. 17:7 vine did *b.* her roots

BENDETH, ING.
Ps. 58:7 when he *b.* his bow
Is. 60:14 that afflicted thee shall
  come *b.* to thee
Jer. 51:3 against him that *b.*

BENEATH.
Ex. 20:4 the earth *b. Deut.* 5:8
Deut. 4:39 earth *b.* there is none
  28:13 above only, and not be *b.*
Is. 51:6 look on the earth *b.*
John 8:23 ye are from *b.* I above

BENEFACTORS.
Luke 22:25 exer. auth. are call. *b.*

BENEFIT, Verb.
Jer. 18:10 wherewith I *b.* them

BENEFIT, S.
2 *Chr.* 32:25 Hezekiah rendered
  not according to *b.*

Ps. 68:19 loadeth us with *b.*
  103:2 forget not all his *b.*
  116:12 render for all his *b.* ?
2 *Cor.* 1:15 have a second *b.*
1 *Tim.* 6:2 partakers of the *b.*
Phile. 14 *b.* not be of necessity

BENEVOLENCE.
1 *Cor.* 7:3 render to the w. due *b.*

BEN-HADAD. 1 *K.* 15:18 ; 20:2 ;
  2 *K.* 6:24 ; 8:7 ; 13:3 ; *Jer.*
  49:27

BENJAMIN.
Gen. 35:18 his f. called him B.
  42:36 J. and will ye take B.
  46:21 the sons of B. *Num.* 26:38 ;
  1 *Chr.* 7:6 ; 8:1, 40 ; 9:7 ; *Neh.*
  11:7
  49:27 B. shall ravin as a wolf
Deut. 33:12 of B. Moses said, The
  beloved of the Lord
Jud. 20:20 went to battle ag't B.
Ps. 68:27 B. with their ruler
  80:2 before B. and Manasseh

See CHILDREN.

BENJAMIN with Judah.
Jud. 10:9 to fight J. and B.
1 *K.* 12:23 speak to the house of
  J. and B. 2 *Chr.* 11:3
1 *Chr.* 12:16 came of B. and J.
  2 *Chr.* 15:2 Asa all J. and B.
  31:1 the altars out of J. and B.
Ezr. 1:5 fathers of J. and B.

Land of BENJAMIN.
Jud. 21:21 go into *l. of* B.
1 *Sam.* 9:16 out of the *l. of* B.
2 *Chr.* 15:8 idols out of *l. of* B.
Jer. 17:26 come from *l. of* B.

Tribe of BENJAMIN.
Num. 1:37 of the *t. of* B.
Jos. 18:11 lot of *t. of* B. 21
Jud. 20:12 men thro' all *t. of* B.
1 *Sam.* 10:20 came near, *t. of* B.
Rom. 11:1 of *t. of* B. *Phil.* 3:5
Rev. 7:8 *t. of* B. sealed, 12,000

BENJAMITES.
Jud. 19:16 men of pl. were B.
  20:35 destroyed of the B.
1 *Sam.* 22:7 Hear now, ye B.
BENONI. *Gen.* 35:18

BENT.
Ps. 7:12 *b.* his *b. Lam.* 2:4 ; 3:12
  37:14 *b.* their bow to cast down
Is. 5:28 and all their bows *b.*
  21:15 for they fled from *b.* bow
Hos. 11:7 my people are *b.*
Zec. 9:13 when I have *b.* Judah

BEOR. *Gen.* 36:32 ; *Num.* 22:5 ;
  24:3 ; 31:8 ; *Deut.* 23:4 ; *Jos.*
  13:22 ; 24:9 ; 1 *Chr.* 1:43 ; *Mic.*
  6:5
BERACHAH. 1 *Chr.* 12:3 ; 2
  Chr. 20:26
BEREA. *Acts* 17:10, 13 ; 20:4

BEREAVE.
Ec. 4:8 and *b.* my soul of good
Jer. 15:7 I will *b.* them, 18:21
Ezek. 5:17 send evil beasts, and
  they shall *b.* thee
  36:12 no more *b.* them, 14
Hos. 9:12 yet will I *b.* them

BEREAVED.
Gen. 42:36 ye have *b.* of my ch.
  43:14 *b.* of my children, I am *b.*
Ezek. 36:13 thou land hast *b.*
Hos. 13:8 meet them as a bear *b.*

BEREAVETH.
Lam. 1:20 abroad the sword *b.*
BERITH. *Jud.* 9:46
BERNICE. *Acts* 25:13, 23 ; 26:30

BERRIES.
Is. 17:6 two or three *b.*
Jam. 3:12 fig-tree bear olive *b.*

BERYL.

Dan. 10:6 his body like the *b.*
Rev. 21:20 foundation was *b.*

BESEECH.

Ex. 33:18 I *b.* show me
Num. 12:13 her now, I *b.* thee
Ps. 80:14 return, we *b.* O God
116:4 O L. I *b.* thee, deliver
118:25 save, I *b.*
119:108 accept, I *b.* thee
Jer. 38:20 obey, I *b.* thee
Amos 7:2 forgive I *b.* thee
Jon. 1:14 we *b.* thee O Lord
4:3 take, I *b.* thee, my life
Mal. 1:9 *b.* God, he be gracious
Luke 8:28 J. I *b.* thee tor. me not
9:38 I *b.* thee look on my s.
Acts 26:3 I *b.* thee to hear me
Rom. 12:1 I *b.* you by mercies
1 *Cor.* 4:16 I *b.* ye be followers
2 *Cor.* 2:8 I *b.* you confirm
5:20 as tho' God did *b.* you
6:1 we *b.* you rec. not the grace
10:1 I Paul *b.* you by the meek
Gal. 4:12 I *b.* you, be as I am
Eph. 4:1 pris. of L. *b.* you walk
Phile. 9 yet for love's sake I *b.*
10 I *b.* thee for my son Onesi.
Heb. 13:19 I *b.* you the rather
1 *Pet.* 2:11 I *b.* you as strangers
2 *John* 5 now I *b.* thee, lady

See BRETHREN.

BESEECHING.

Mat. 8:5 centurion *b.* *Luke* 7:3
Mark 1:40 leper to him, *b.* him

BESET.

Jud. 19:22 sons of Bel. *b.* 20:5
Ps. 22:12 bulls of B. have *b.* me
139:5 *b.* me behind and before
Hos. 7:2 doings have *b.* them
Heb. 12:1 which doth so easily *b.*

BESIDE, B.

Gen. 19:12 hast thou here any *b.*
Luke 16:26 *b.* all this
24:21 *b.* all this
Phile. 19 thine own self *b.*

BESIDE, with self.

Mark 3:21 said he is *b.* himself
Acts 26:24 P. thou art *b.* thyself
2 *Cor.* 5:13 whether we be *b.*

BESIEGE.

Deut. 28:52 *b.* thee in thy gates
1 *K.* 8:37 enemies *b.* 2 *Chr.* 6:28
Is. 21:2 O Elam, *b.* O Media

BESIEGED.

2 *K.* 19:24 rivers of *b.* pl. *Is.* 37:25
Ec. 9:14 a great king and *b.* it
Is. 1:8 Zion is left as a *b.* city
Ezek. 6:12 *b.* shall die by famine

BESOM.

Is. 14:23 the *b.* of destruction

BESOR. 1 *Sam.* 30:9

BESOUGHT.

Gen. 42:21 *b.* us, we would not
Ex. 32:11 Moses *b.* L. *Deut.* 3:23
2 *Sam.* 12:16 D. G. for the child
1 *K.* 13:6 man of God *b.* the L.
2 *K.* 13:4 Jehoahaz *b.* the Lord
2 *Chr.* 33:12 Manasseh in affl. *b.*
Ezr. 8:23 *b.* our God for this
Jer. 26:19 Hezekiah *b.* the Lord
Mat. 8:31 the devils *b.* him.*Mark*
5:10, 12; *Luke* 8:31, 32
34 *b.* him to depart, *Luke* 8:37
Mark 5:23 Jairus *b.* *Luke* 8:41
John 4:40 S. *b.* he would tarry
47 nobleman of Caper. *b.* him
19:38 *b.* he might take the body
Acts 13:42 *b.* that these words
16:15 Lydia *b.* us saying
39 magistrates *b.* them
21:12 we *b.* him not to go to J.
2 *Cor.* 12:8 for this I *b.* the Lord

BEST.

Ps. 39:5 man at his *b.* state
Luke 15:22 bring forth the *b.*
1 *Cor.* 12:31 covet the *b.* gifts

BESTEAD.

Is. 8:21 pass thro' it hardly *b.*

BESTIR.

2 *Sam.* 5:24 hearest the sound *b.*

BESTOW.

Ex. 32:29 may *b.* on you
Deut. 14:26 *b.* money for what
2 *Chr.* 24:7 they did *b.* on Baalim
Ezr. 7:20 *b.* it out of k.'s treas.
Luke 12:17 to *b.* my fruits
1 *Cor.* 12:23 on these we *b.* more
13:3 though I *b.* all my goods

BESTOWED.

Is. 63:7 acc. to all Lord *b.* on us
John 4:38 to reap whereon ye *b.*
Rom. 16:6 Mary, who *b.* much
1 *Cor.* 15:10 grace *b.* not in vain
2 *Cor.* 1:11 gift *b.* on us by many
8:1 grace *b.* on the churches
Gal. 4:11 lest I *b.* labor in vain
1 *John* 3:1 manner of love F. *b.*

BETHABARA. *John* 1:28

BETHANY.

Mat. 21:17 went into B. 26:6
Mark 11:12; 14:3; *Luke* 19:29
Luke 24:50 led out as far as B.
John 11:1 Lazarus of B. 12:1

BETH-AVEN.

Jos. 7:2 Ai, which is beside B.
1 *Sam.* 14:23 passed over to B.
Hos. 4:15 nor go ye up to B.
5:8 cry aloud at B. after thee
10:5 because of the calves of B.

BETH-CAR. 1 *Sam.* 7:11
BETH-DAGON. *Jos.* 19:27
BETH-DIBLATHAIM. *Jer.* 48:22

BETH-EL.

Gen. 28:19 c. the place B. 35:15
31:13 I am God of B.
35:1 up to B. 3; 6 came to B.
Amos 3:14 will visit altars of B.
4:4 come to B. and transgress
5:5 B. shall come to naught, 6
7:13 proph. not any more at B.
BETH-ELITE. 1 *K.* 16:34
BETHER. *Cant.* 2:17
BETHESDA. *John* 5:2
BETH-EZEL. *Mic.* 1:11
BETH-GAMUL. *Jer.* 48:23
BETH-HACCEREM. *Jer.* 6:1

BETH-HORON.

Jos. 10:11 going down to B.
21:22 gave Lev. B. 1 *Chr.* 6:68
1 *Sam.* 13:18 comp. turned to B.
1 *K.* 9:17 S. built B. 2 *Chr.* 8:5
1 *Chr.* 7:24 Sherah built B.

BETH-JESHIMOTH.

1 *K.* 8:47 b. them. 2 *Chr.* 6:37

BETH-LEHEM.

2 *Sam.* 23:15 well of B. 1 *Ch.*11:17
Mat. 2:1 Jesus born in B. 6, 16

BETH-LEHEM EPHRA-TAH.

Mic. 5:2 B. E. though thou be
BETH-LEHEM JUDAH. *Jud.*
17:7; 19:1, 18; *Ruth* 1:1

BETH-LEHEMITE.

1 *Sam.* 16:1 J. the B. 18; 17:58
2 *Sam.* 21:19 B. slew G. brother

BETH-PEOR.

Deut. 3:29 valley over ag't B.
4:46 statutes over against B.
34:6 buried Moses over ag't B.
BETHPHAGE. *Mat.* 21:1; *Mark*
11:1; *Luke* 19:29

BETHSAIDA.

Mat. 11:21 thee. B. 1 *Luke* 10:13
Mark 6:45 disciples go to B. 8:22

Luke 9:10 a desert belong. to B.
John 1:44 Phil. was of B. 12:21
BETH-SHAN. 1 *Sam.* 31:10
BETH-SHEMESH. *Jud.* 1:33;
1 *Sam.* 6:9, 12, 19; 2 *K.* 14:11
BETHUEL. *Gen.* 22:22, 23;
24:24; 28:2

BETIMES.

Gen. 26:31 rose up *b.* and sware
2 *Chr.* 36:15 his messen. rising *b.*
Job 8:5 wouldest seek unto G. *b.*
24:5 as wild asses rising *b.*
Prov. 13:24 chasteneth him *b.*

BETRAY.

1 *Chr.* 12:17 come to *b.* me
Mat. 24:10 shall *b.* one another
26:16 sought opportunity to *b.*
Mark 14:11; *Luke* 22:6
21 one of you shall *b.* me,*Mark*
14:18; *John* 13:21
46 he is at hand that doth *b.*
Mark 13:12 brother shall *b.* bro.
John 6:64 should *b.* him, 13:11
13:2 into heart of Judas to *b.*

BETRAYED.

Mat. 10:4 J. who *b.* him, *Mark*
3:19
17:22 S. of m. shall be *b.* 20:18;
26:2, 45; *Mark* 14:41
26:24 Son of man is *b.* *Mark*
14:21; *Luke* 22:22
48 he that *b.* *Mark* 14:44
27:4 I *b.* innocent blood
Luke 21:16 be *b.* both by parents
John 18:2 *b.* him knew the place
1 *Cor.* 11:23 same night he was *b.*

BETRAYERS.

Acts 7:52 of whom ye the *b.*

BETRAYEST, ETH.

Mark 14:42 he that *b.* me
Luke 22:21 hand that *b.* me
48 S. Son of man with a kiss?
John 21:20 is he that *b.* thee?

BETROTH.

Deut. 28:30 shalt *b.* a wife
Hos. 2:19 *b.* thee to me
20 *b.* to me in faithfulness

BETROTHED.

Ex. 22:16 entice a maid not *b.*
Deut. 22:28
Lev. 19:20 lieth with a woman *b.*
Deut. 20:7 who hath *b.* a wife
22:23 find a virgin *b.* and lie
27 *b.* damsel cried, none to save

BETTER.

Gen. 29:19 *b.* I give her to thee
Ex. 14:12 *b.* serv. the Egyptians
Num. 14:3 *b.* to return to E. ?
Jud. 8:2 gleanings *b.* than vint.
11:25 art thou *b.* than Balak
1 *Sam.* 1:8 am not I *b.*than ten s.
27:1 nothing *b.* than go
1 *K.* 1:47 made name of k. Sol. *b.*
2:32 two men *b.* than he
19:4 am not *b.* than my fathers
21:2 give thee a *b.* vineyard
2 *K.* 5:12 rivers of Damascus *b.*
2 *Chr.*21:13 slain brethren *b.*than
Ps. 69:31 please *b.* than ox
Ec. 2:24 nothing *b.* than to eat
3:22 nothing *b.* than rejoice
4:3 *b.* is he than both they
9 two are *b.*
6:11 what is man *b.*?
7:10 former days were *b.*
10:11 and a babbler is no *b.*
Is. 56:5 a name *b.* than of sons
Lam. 4:9 that be slain are *b.*
Ezek. 36:11 settle you and do *b.*
Dan. 1:20 ten times *b.*
Hos. 2:7 then was it *b.* with me
Amos 6:2 be they *b.* than these
Nah. 3:8 art thou populous *b.* ?
Mat. 6:26 f. of the air, are ye not
b. than they? *Luke* 12:24

12:12 a man *b.* than a sheep?
18:6 *b.* that a millstone, *Mark*
9:42; *Luke* 17:2
Rom. 3:9 are we *b.* than they?
1 *Cor.* 7:38 marriage, doth *b.*
8:8 neither if we eat are we *b.*
9:15 *b.* for me to die
11:17 come together not for *b.*
Phil. 2:3 esteem other *b.* than
Heb. 1:4 much *b.* than the angels
6:9 persuaded *b.* things of you
7:7 the less is blessed of the *b.*
19 bringing in of a *b.* hope did
22 a surety of a *b.* testament
8:6 Mediator of a *b.* covenant,
established on *b.* promises
9:23 things with *b.* sacrifices
10:34 a *b.* and enduring sub.
11:16 desire a *b.* country
Heb. 11:35 obtain a *b.* resurrec.
40 some *b.* thing for us
12:24 *b.* things than that of A.
2 *Pet.* 2:21 *b.* not to have known

BETTER is.
Prov. 15:16 *b. is* little with f.of L.
17 *b. is* dinner of herbs
16:8 *b. is* a little with right.
16 *b. is* it to get wisdom
17:1 *b. is* a dry morsel
19:1 *b. is* poor 28:6
27:10 *b. is* a neighbor near
Ec. 4:6 *b. is* handful with quiet
13 *b. is* a poor wise child than
6:9 *b. is* the sight of the eyes
7:8 *b. is* the end than the beg.
Cant. 4:10 *b. is* thy love

Is BETTER, or is it BET-TER.
Jud. 9:2 whether is *b.* all reign
18:19 *is it b.* to be a priest
Ruth 4:15 thy daughter is *b.*
1 *Sam.* 15:22 to obey *is b.*
28 neighbor that *is b.*
2 *Sam.* 17:14 counsel of H. *is b.*
Est. 1:19 another that *is b.*
Ps. 37:16 righteous hath *is b.*
63:3 thy loving-kind. *is b.*
84:10 a day in thy courts *is b.*
119:72 *is b.* to me than gold
Prov. 3:14 wisdom *is b.*
8:11 wisdom *is b.* than rubies
19 my fruit *is b.* than gold
12:9 *is b.* than he that honoreth
16:32 that is slow to anger *is b.*
19:22 poor man *is b.* than a liar
27:5 rebuke *is b.* than secret l.
Ec. 6:3 an untimely birth *is b.*
7:1 a good name *is b.* than oint.
3 sorrow *is b.* than laughter,
by sad. of coun. h. *is made b.*
8 the patient in spirit *is b.*
9:4 a liv. dog *is b.* than a d. lion
16 wisdom *is b.* than strength
18 wisd. *is b.* than w. of war
Cant. 1:2 love *is b.* than wine
Luke 5:39 he saith, the old *is b.*
Phil. 1:23 with C. wh. *is far b.*

It is BETTER, or BETTER it is.
Ps. 118:8 *it is b.* to trust in L. 9
Prov. 16:19 *b.* to be of humble
21:9 *b.* to dwell in a, 25:24
19 *it is b.* to dwell in the wild.
25:7 *b. it is* it be said, Come up
Ec. 5:5 *b. it is* thou sh. not vow
7:2 *it is b.* to go to house of m.
5 *b.* to hear reb. of wise men
Jon. 4:3 *it is b.* for me, 8
Mat. 18:8 *it is b.* to enter into life
halt, 9; *Mark* 9:43, 45, 47
1 *Cor.* 7:9 *b.* to marry than to b.
1 *Pet.* 3:17 *b.* ye suffer for well-d.

BETTERED.
Mark 5:26 she was nothing *b.*

BETWIXT.
Phil. 1:23 I am in a strait *b.* two

BEULAH. *Is.* 62:4

BEWAIL.
Lev. 10:6 *b.* the burning L. kind.
Deut. 21:13 and *b.* her father
Jud. 11:37 *b.* my virginity, 38
Is. 16:9 will *b.* with the weep.
2 *Cor.* 12:21 *b.* many who have s.
Rev. 18:19 shall *b.* her

BEWAILED, ETH.
Jer. 4:31 daughter of Zion that *b.*
Luke 8:52 and all wept and *b.*
23:27 of women which also *b.*

BEWARE.
Gen. 24:6 *b.* bring not my son
Ex. 23:21 *b.* of him, obey his v.
Deut. 6:12 *b.* thou forget L. 8:11
15:9 *b.* there be not a thought
Jud. 13:4 *b.* drink no wine. 13
2 *Sam.* 18:12 *b.* none t. y. man
2 *K.* 6:9 *b.* thou pass not
Job 36:18 *b.* lest he take thee a.
Prov. 19:25 the simple will *b.*
Is. 36:18 *b.* lest H. persuade
Mat. 7:15 *b.* of false prophets
10:17 *b.* of men
16:6 *b.* of the leaven, 11; *Mark*
8:15; *Luke* 12:1
Mark 12:38 *b.* of s. *Luke* 20:46
Luke 12:15 *b.* of covetousness
Acts 13:40 *b.* lest that come
Phil. 3:2 *b.* of dogs, *b.* of evil w.
Col. 2:8 *b.* lest any man spoil
2 *Pet.* 3:17 *b.* lest being led

BEWITCHED.
Acts 8:9 Simon *b.* the people, 11
Gal. 3:1 who hath *b.* you?

BEWRAY.
Is. 16:3 *b.* not him that wand.

BEWRAYETH.
Prov. 27:16 oint. of right h. *b.*
29:24 cursing, and *b.* it not
Mat. 26:73 thy speech *b.* thee

BEYOND.
Num. 22:18 B. said, I cannot go
b. the word of the L. 24:13
Deut. 30:13 nor is it *b.* the sea
2 *Sam.* 10:16 *b.* the river, 1 *K.*
14:15; 1 *Chr.* 19:16; *Ezr.* 4:17,
20; 6:6, 8; 7:21, 25; *Neh.* 2:7,
9; *Is.* 7:20; 18:1; *Zep.* 3:10
Mark 6:51 amazed *b.* meas. 7:37
2 *Cor.* 8:3 *b.* their power willing
10:14 stretch not *b.* our meas.
Gal. 1:13 *b.* measure I persecut.
1 *Thes.* 4:6 that no man go *b.*

BEYOND *Jordan.* *See* JORDAN.

BEZALEEL. *Ex.* 31:2; 36:1;
38:22

BEZEK.
Jud. 1:4 slew in B. 10,000 men, 5
1 *Sam.* 11:8 Is. in B. 300,000

BIBBER. *See* WINE.

BICHRI. 2 *Sam.* 20:1, 2, 6, 22

BID.
1 *Sam.* 9:27 *b.* the servant pass
2 *Sam.* 2:26 *b.* the people return
2 *K.* 5:13 *b.* thee do great thing
10:5 all that thou shalt *b.* us
Zep. 1:7 L. hath *b.* his guests
Mat. 14:28 *b.* me come on the w.
22:9 find *b.* to the marriage
23:3 what they *b.* you observe
Luke 9:61 first *b.* farewell
10:40 *b.* her that help me
14:12 they also *b.* thee again
1 *Cor.* 10:27 any that bel. not *b.*
2 *John* 10 nor *b.* him God speed

BIDDEN.
1 *Sam.* 9:13 they eat that be *b.*
2 *Sam.* 16:11 for the L. hath *b.*
Mat. 1:24 as angel had *b.* him
22:3 to call them that were *b.*
4 tell them *b.* I have prepared
8 they *b.* were not worthy

Luke 7:39 Pharisee who had *b.*
14:7 to those who were *b.*
8 art *b.* lest a more hon. be *b.*
10 art *b.* sit in lowest room
24 none of those men *b.*

BIDDETH, ING.
1 *Sam.* 22:14 goeth at thy *b.*
2 *John* 11 that *b.* him God speed

BIDE.
Rom. 11:23 *b.* not still in unb.

BIDKAR. 2 *K.* 9:25

BIER.
2 *Sam.* 3:31 David followed the *b.*
Luke 7:14 and touched the *b.*

BIGTHAN. *Est.* 2:21; 6:2
BILDAD. *Job* 2:11; 8:1; 18:1;
25:1; 42:9
BILHAH. *Gen.* 29:29; 35:22, 25

BILL.
Luke 16:6 thy *b.* and write, 7
See DIVORCE.

BILLOWS.
Ps. 42:7 *b.* are gone over, *Jon.*
2:3

BIND.
Num. 30:2 an oath to *b.* his soul
Deut. 6:8 *b.* them for a sign
Jud. 15:10 to *b.* Samson
16:5 *b.* Samson to afflict him
Job 31:36 I will *b.* it as a crown
38:31 *b.* influence of Pleiades
39:10 canst thou *b.* the unicorn
40:13 *b.* their faces in secret
41:5 wilt thou *b.* Leviathan
Ps. 105:22 to *b.* his princes
118:27 *b.* the sacrifice
149:8 to *b.* their kings
Prov. 3:3 *b.* them about thy neck
6:21 *b.* them upon thy heart
7:3 *b.* them on thy fingers
Is. 8:16 *b.* up the testimony
49:18 *b.* them on thee as a bride
61:1 to *b.* up the broken-hearted
Ezek. 34:16 I will *b.* up broken
Hos. 6:1 smitten and will *b.* us
Mic. 1:13 *b.* the chariot
Mat. 12:29 first *b.* the strong
man, *Mark* 3:27
13:30 *b.* tares to burn them
16:19 shall *b.* on earth, 18:18
22:13 *b.* him hand and foot
23:4 *b.* heavy burdens grievous
Mark 5:3 no man could *b.* him
Acts 9:14 authority to *b.* all that
12:8 angel said *b.* on sandals
21:11 so shall the Jews *b.*

BINDETH.
Job 5:18 maketh sore and *b.* up
26:8 he *b.* up the waters
28:11 he *b.* floods from overfl.
30:18 *b.* me about as the collar
36:13 hyp. cry not when he *b.*
Ps. 129:7 he that *b.* sheaves
147:3 he healeth and *b.* up
Prov. 26:8 *b.* a stone in a sling
Is. 30:26 Lord *b.* up breach

BINDING.
Gen. 49:11 *b.* his foal to the vine
Acts 22:6 *b.* and delivering men

BIRD.
Gen. 7:14 every *b.* went into
Lev. 14:52 cleanse with living *b.*
Job 41:5 play as with a *b.*
Ps. 11:1 as a *b.* to mountain
124:7 our soul is escaped as a *b.*
Prov. 1:17 in sight of any *b.*
6:5 as a *b.* from the fowler
7:23 as a *b.* hasteth to the snare
26:2 as the *b.* by wandering
27:8 as a *b.* that wandereth
Ec. 10:20 *b.* shall tell the matter
12:4 rise at the voice of the *b.*

Is. 16:2 as a wandering *b.*
  46:11 ravenous *b.* from the east
Jer. 12:9 heritage as a speck. *b.*
Lam. 3:52 chased me like a *b.*
Hos. 9:11 fly away like a *b.*
  11:11 they shall tremble as a *b.*
Amos 3:5 a *b.* fall where no gin
Rev. 18:2 every unclean *b.*

BIRDS.
Gen. 15:10 the *b.* divided he not
  40:19 the *b.* shall eat thy flesh
Lev. 14:4 to take two *b.* alive
Deut. 14:11 clean *b.* shall eat
2 Sam. 21:10 to *b.* to rest by day
Ps. 104:17 the *b.* make nests
Ec. 9:12 as *b.* caught
Cant. 2.12 time of singing of *b.*
Is. 31:5 as *b.* flying
Jer. 4:25 *b.* of heaven were fled
  5:27 as a cage full of *b.* so are
  12:4 are consumed and the *b.*
  9 the *b.* round about
Ezek. 30:4 will gi. thee to rav. *b.*
Dan. 4:33 nails like *b.* claws
Mat. 8:20 *b.* have n. *Luke* 9:58
  13:32 *b.* lodge in the branches
Rom. 1:23 an image like to *b.*
1 Cor. 15:39 another of *b.*
Jam. 3:7 every kind of *b.* is tam.
BIRSHA. *Gen.* 14:2

BIRTH.
2 K. 19:3 children are come to
  the *b.* *Is.* 37:3
Job 3:16 as a hidden untimely *b.*
Ps. 58:8 like the untimely *b.*
Ec. 6:3 untimely *b.* is better
  7:1 better than day of one's *b.*
Is. 66:9 shall I bring to the *b.*
Ezek. 16:3 thy *b.* is of Canaan
Hos. 9:11 shall fly from the *b.*
Mat. 1:18 the *b.* of Jesus Christ
Luke 1:14 shall rejoice at his *b.*
Gal. 4:19 I travail in *b.*
Rev. 12:2 she cried, trav. in *b.*

BIRTHDAY.
Gen. 40:20 which was Ph.'s *b.*
Mat. 14:6 Herod's *b.* *Mark* 6:21

BIRTHRIGHT.
Gen. 25:31 this day thy *b.*
  33 sold his *b.* to Jacob
  34 thus Esau despised his *b.*
  27:36 took away my *b.*
  43:33 first-born ac. to his *b.*
1 Chr. 5:1 R.'s *b.* to sons of Jos.
Heb. 12:16 for morsel sold his *b.*

BISHOP, S.
Phil. 1:1 saints at Philippi, *b.*
1 Tim. 3:1 desire the office of a *b.*
  2 *b.* must be blamel. *Tit.* 1:7.
1 Pet. 2:25 to the *b.* of your souls

BISHOPRICK.
Acts 1:20 his *b.* let another take

BIT, S.
Ps. 32:9 must be held in with *b.*
Jam. 3:3 we put *b.* in horses' m.

BIT, Verb.
Num. 21:6 they *b.* people.
Amos 5:19 and a serpent *b.* him

BITE.
Ec. 10:8 a serpent shall *b.*
  11 *b.* without enchantment
Jer. 8:17 serpents, they shall *b.*
Amos 9:3 serp, and he shall *b.*
Mic. 3:5 the prophets that *b.*
Hab. 2:7 rise up that shall *b.*
Gal. 5:15 if ye *b.* and devour

BITETH.
Gen. 49:17 Dan an adder, that *b.*
Prov. 23:32 it *b.* like a serpent

BITHYNIA.
Acts 16:7 assayed to go into B.
1 Pet. 1:1 through Asia and B.

BITTEN.
Num. 21:8 is *b.* when he looks

BITTER.
Gen. 27:34 E. cried with *b.* cry
Ex. 1:14 made their lives *b.*
  12:8 with *b.* herbs, *Num.* 9:11
  15:23 waters, for they were *b.*
Deut. 32:24 dev. with *b.* destru.
  32 their clusters are *b.*
2 K. 14:26 affl. of Isr. it was *b.*
Job 3:20 why is life given to *b.* ?
  13:26 writest *b.* things
  23:2 to-day is my complaint *b.*
Ps. 64:3 arrows, even *b.* words
Prov. 5:4 *b.* as wormwood
  27:7 to hungry soul *b.* thing
Ec. 7:26 more *b.* than death
Is. 5:20 that put *b.* for sweet
  24:9 strong drink shall be *b.*
Jer. 2:19 an evil thing and *b.*
  4:18 thy wickedness, it is *b.*
  6:26 make most *b.* lamentation
  31:15 in Ramah, *b.* weeping
Amos 8:10 the end, as a *b.* day
Hab. 1:6 *b.* and hasty nation
Col. 3:19 be not *b.* against them
Jam. 3:14 if ye have *b.* envying
Rev. 8:11 men died of waters *b.*
  10:9 it shall make thy belly *b.*

BITTER with Water.
Num. 5:18 *b.* w. that causeth
Jam. 3:11 send sweet *w.* and *b.?*

BITTERLY.
Jud. 5:23 curse ye *b.* the inhab.
Ruth 1:20 Almighty hath dealt *b.*
Is. 22:4 I will weep *b.*
  33:7 amb. of peace shall weep *b.*
Ezek. 27:30 the pilots shall cry *b.*
Hos. 12:14 Eph. provoked him *b.*
Zep. 1:14 the mighty shall cry *b.*
Mat. 26:75 P. wept *b.* *Luke* 22:62

BITTERN.
Is. 14:23 posses. for the *b.* 34:11
Zep. 2:14 the *b.* shall lodge

BITTERNESS.
1 Sam. 1:10 Hannah was in *b.*
  15:32 the *b.* of death is past
2 Sam. 2:26 sword will be *b.*
Job 7:11 I will complain in the *b.*
  9:18 but filleth me with *b.*
  10:1 I will speak in *b.* of soul
  21:25 another dieth in *b.* of soul
Prov. 14:10 heart knoweth his *b.*
  17:25 a foolish son is *b.* to her.
Is. 38:15 softly in *b.* of my soul.
  17 for peace I had great *b.*
Lam. 1:4 afflic., and she is in *b.*
  3:15 he hath filled me with *b.*
Ezek. 3:14 and I went in *b.*
  21:6 *b.* sigh before their eyes
  27:31 weep for thee with *b.*
Zec. 12:10 in *b.* for him as one
  that is in *b.* for his first-born
Acts 8:23 art in the gall of *b.*
Rom. 3:14 full of cursing and *b.*
Eph. 4:31 let all *b.* be put away
Heb. 12:15 lest any root of *b.*

BLACK.
Lev. 13:31 there is no *b.* hair in it
1 K. 18:45 the heaven was *b.*
Job 30:30 my skin is *b.* upon me
Prov. 7:9 in the *b.* and dark n.
Cant. 1:5 I am *b.* but comely
  6 look not on me, I am *b.*
  5:11 his locks are *b* as a raven
Jer. 4:28 shall heavens be *b.*
  8:21 I am hurt, I am *b.*
  14:2 the gates thereof are *b.*
Lam. 5:10 our skin was *b.*
Zec. 6:2 in second chariot *b.* h.
  6 *b.* horses go forth into north
Mat. 5:36 one hair white or *b.*
Rev. 6:5 and lo, a *b.* horse
  12 the sun became *b.*

BLACKER.
Lam. 4:8 visage is *b.* than coal

BLACKISH.
Job 6:16 *b.* by reason of the ice

BLACKNESS.
Job 3:5 let *b.* of the day
Is. 50:3 clothe heavens with *b.*
Joel 2:6 shall gath. *b.* *Nah.* 2:10
Heb. 12:18 ye are not come to *b.*
Jude 13 to whom is reserved *b.*

BLADE.
Jud. 3:22 went in after the *b.*
Job 31:22 from my shoulder-*b.*
Mat. 13:26 *b.* was spr. *Mark* 4:28

BLAINS.
Ex. 9:9 a boil with *b.* 10

BLAME.
Gen. 43:9 bear the *b.* 44:32
2 Cor. 8:20 no man should *b.* us
Eph. 1:4 holy and without *b.*

BLAMED.
2 Cor. 6:3 the ministry be not *b.*
Gal. 2:11 bec. he was to be *b.*

BLAMELESS.
Jos. 2:17 *b.* of thine oath
Mat. 12:5 prof. Sab. and are *b.*
Luke 1:6 in ordin. of the L. *b.*
1 Cor. 1:8 *b.* in the day of our L.
Phil. 2:15 be *b.* and harmless
  3:6 in the law *b.*
1 Thes. 5:23 body be preserved *b.*
1 Tim. 3:2 bishop be *b.* *Tit.* 1:7
  10 use office of deacon being *b.*
  5:7 give in charge, they be *b.*
Tit. 1:6 if any be *b.* the husband
2 Pet. 3:14 ye may be found *b.*

BLASPHEME.
2 Sam. 12:14 enemies to *b.*
1 K. 21:10 didst *b.* God, 13
Ps. 74:10 shall the enemy *b.*
Mark 3:28 they shall *b*
  29 that shall be ag. Holy G.
Acts 26:11 I compelled them to *b.*
1 Tim. 1:20 may learn not to *b.*
Jam. 2:7 *b.* that worthy name
Rev. 13:6 to *b.* his name

BLASPHEMED.
Lev. 24:11 Israelitish wom. son *b.*
2 K. 19:6 servants of king of As-
  syria *b.* me, 22 ; *Is.* 37:6, 23
Ps. 74:18 have *b.* thy name
Is. 52:5 my name every day is *b.*
  65:7 and *b.* me on the hills
Ezek. 20:27 your fathers have *b.*
Acts 18:6 op. themselves and *b.*
Rom. 2:24 name of God is *b.*
1 Tim. 6:1 his doctrine be not *b.*
Tit. 2:5 that the word be not *b.*
Rev. 16:9 were scorched and *b.*
  11 *b.* because of their pains
  21 *b.* God because of the hail

BLASPHEMEST, ETH.
Lev. 24:16 whoso *b.* the Lord
Ps. 44:16 voice of him that *b.*
Mat. 9:3 scribes said, This m. *b.*
John 10:36 F. sanctified thou *b.*

BLASPHEMING.
Acts 13:45 J. contradicting and *b.*

BLASPHEMER, S.
Acts 19:37 are nei. *b.* of your god.
1 Tim. 1:13 who was before a *b.*
2 Tim. 3:2 men shall be *b.*

BLASPHEMY.
2 K. 19:3 a day of *b.* *Is.* 37:3
Mat. 12:31 all manner of *b.* shall
  be forgiven, but *b.* against
  26:65 heard his *b.* *Mark* 14:64
Mark 7:22 out of heart proceed *b.*
John 10:33 st. thee not but for *b.*
Col. 3:8 now ye also put off *b.*
Rev. 2:9 the *b.* of them that
  13:1 and upon his heads *b.*
  6 opened his mouth in *b.*

BLASPHEMIES.
Ezek. 35:12 have heard all thy *b.*
Mat. 15:19 out of the heart *b.*
Mark 2:7 man thus speak *b.* ?
3:28 *b.* they shall blaspheme
Luke 5:21 who is this speak. *b.* ?
Rev. 13:5 speaking *b.*

BLASPHEMOUS.
Acts 6:11 heard him speak *b.* w.
13 ceaseth not to speak *b.* w.

BLASPHEMOUSLY.
Luke 22:65 other things *b.* spake

BLAST.
Ex. 15:8 *b.* of thy nostrils
Jos. 6:5 a long *b.* with horns
2 *Sam.* 22:16 the *b.* of the breath
of his nostrils, *Ps.* 18:15
2 *K.* 19:7 *b.* on Sen. *Is.* 37:7
Job 4:9 by *b.* of God they perish
Is. 25:4 the *b.* of the terrible

BLASTED.
Gen. 41:6 thin ears *b.* 23;27
2 *K.* 19:26 as corn *Is.* 37:27

BLASTING.
Deut. 28:22 smite thee with *b.*
1 *K.* 8:37 there be a *b.* 2 *Chr.* 6:28
Amos 4:9 smitten you with *b.*
Hag. 2:17 I smote you with *b.*

BLASTUS. *Acts* 12:20

BLAZE.
Mark 1:45 *b.* abroad the matter

BLEATING, S.
Jud. 5:16 to hear *b.* of flocks
1 *Sam.* 15:14 this *b.* of sheep

BLEMISH.
Ex. 12:5 without *b.* *Lev.* 9:3;
14:10; 23:12; *Num.* 6:14
29:1 two rams with *b.* *Lev.* 5:15,
18; 6:6; 9:12; *Ezek.* 46:4
Lev. 1:3 male without *b.* 10;
22:19
21:17 hath *b.* not appr. 21:23
22:20 hath a *b.* *Deut.* 15:21
21 freewill-offering no *b.*
24:19 cause a *b.* in his neighbor
Num. 19:2 a red heifer with. *b.*
29:2 seven lambs without *b.*
2 *Sam.* 14:25 no *b.* in Absalom
Dan. 1:4 in whom was no *b.*
Eph. 5:27 holy and without *b.*
1 *Pet.* 1:19 of a lamb without *b.*

BLEMISHES.
Lev. 22:25 *b.* in them not accept.
2 *Pet.* 2:13 spots they are and *b.*

BLESS.
1 *Cor.* 10:16 cup of bless. we *b.*

BLESS, *God being agent.*
Gen. 12:2 I will *b.* thee, 16:3, 24
3 I will *b.* them that *b.* thee
17:16 will *b.* her, and give thee
22:17 I will *b.* *Heb.* 6:14
28:3 *b.* thee, and multiply thee
32:26 except thou *b.* me
48:16 *b.* the lads
49:25 by Alm. who shall *b.* thee
Ex. 20:24 and I will *b.* thee
23:25 he shall *b.* thy bread
Num. 6:24 Lord *b.* and keep thee
27 on Israel, and I will *b.* them
24:1 pleased the L. to *b.* Israel
Deut. 7:13 *b.* the fruit of thy w.
15:4 no poor, for L. shall *b.* t.
18 God shall *b.* thee, 30:16
16:15 bec. Lord shall *b.* thee
26:15 look down and *b.* Israel
28:8 *b.* thee in the land
12 *b.* all the work of thy hand
33:11 *b.* Lord, his substance
2 *Sam.* 7:29 to *b.* the house of
thy servant, 1 *Chr.* 17:27
1 *Chr.* 4:10 wouldst *b.* me indeed
Ps. 5:12 wilt *b.* the righteous
28:9 *b.* thine inheritance
29:11 *b.* his people with peace

67:6 our own God shall *b.* us, 7
115:12 L. will *b.* us, he will *b.*
the house of Israel, of Aaron
13 he will *b.* them that fear L.
128:5 shall *b.* thee out of Zion
132:15 abundantly *b.* her prov.
134:3 the Lord *b.* thee out of Z.
Is. 19:25 L. of hosts shall *b.*
Hag. 2:19 from this day will I *b.*
Acts 3:26 sent him to *b.* you

BLESS, *God being the object.*
Deut. 8:10 art full, shall *b.* Lord
Jud. 5:9 *b.* the L. *Ps.* 103:21; 134:1
1 *Chr.* 29:20 Dav. said, now *b.* L.
Neh. 9:5 stand up and *b.* L. for
Ps. 16:7 *b.* L. who hath given
26:12 in the cong. will I *b.* Lord
34:1 *b.* the Lord at all times
63:4 will I *b.* thee while I live
66:8 O *b.* our God
68:26 *b.* ye God in congregations
96:2 sing to the L. *b.* his name
100:4 *b.* his name, 103:1
103:1 *b.* L. O my soul, 2,22;
104:1, 35
20 *b.* ye his ang. 21 *b.* h. hosts
22 *b.* the Lord all his works
115:18 will *b.* L. from this time
134:2 lift up yourh. *b.* the L.
135:19 *b.* the L. O house of Is.
20 O Levi, *b.* the Lord
145:1 will *b.* thy name forever
2 every day will I *b.* thee
10 thy saints shall *b.* thee
21 let all flesh *b.* his holy n.
Jam. 3:9 therewith *b.* we God

BLESS, *Man agent and object.*
Gen. 27:4 *b.* thee before I die, 25
34 *b.* me, O my father, 38
48:9 bring them to me, I will *b.*
20 in thee shall Israel *b.* saying
Ex. 12:32 begone, and *b.* me also
Num. 6:23 on this wise *b.* Israel
23:20 I have received com. to *b.*
25 curse them nor *b.* them
Deut. 10:8 separ. Levi to *b.* 21:5
27:12 stand on Gerizim, to *b.*
29:19 heareth curse, he *b.* him
1 *Sam.* 9:13 doth not *b.* the sacrifice
2 *Sam.* 6:20 David returned to *b.*
his household, 1 *Chr.* 16:43
8:10 Joram his son to *b.* David
21:3 that ye *b.* inh. of the **Lord**
1 *K.* 1:47 came to *b.* our lord k. D.
1 *Chr.* 23:13 to *b.* in his name
Ps. 62:4 *b.* with their mouth
109:28 let them curse, but *b.*
129:8 *b.* you in the name of L.
Prov. 30:11 doth not *b.* their m.
Is. 65:16 *b.* himself in God
Jer. 4:2 nations shall *b.*
Mat. 5:44 *b.* that curse, *Luke* 6:28
Rom. 12:14 *b.* and curse not
1 *Cor.* 4:12 being reviled we *b.*
14:16 shall *b.* with the spirit

BLESSED, *Man agent and object.*
Gen. 14:19 Melchized. *b.* Abra.
24:60 they *b.* Rebekah
27:23 so Isaac *b.* Jacob, 27
29 *b.* be he that blesseth thee
33 have *b.* him, he shall be *b.*
41 his father *b.* him
28:1 Isaac called Jacob, *b.* him
30:13 daughters will call me *b.*
31:55 kissed his sons, and *b.*
47:7 *b.* Phar. 10; 48:15 Joseph
48:20 Jacob *b.* M. *Heb.* 11:21
49:28 Jacob *b.* his sons
Ex. 39:43 M. *b.* them, *Deut.* 33:1
Lev. 9:22 Aaron *b.* them
23 M. and A. *b.* the people
Num. 23:6 w. thou blesseth is *b.*
23:11 hast *b.* altogether, 24:10
Deut. 33:20 *b.* that enlargeth G.
24 Asher be *b.* with children

Jos. 22:6 *b.* sent them away, 7
24:10 Balaam *b.* you still
Jud. 5:24 *b.* above women J. be
1 *Sam.* 2:20 Eli *b.* Elkanah
25:33 *b.* be thy advice
26:25 Saul said *b.* be thou
2 *Sam.* 13:25 but *b.* him
1 *K.* 2:45 Solomon shall be *b.*
8:14 Solomon *b.* congreg. 55
66 congreg. *b.* Sol. 2 *Chr.* 6:3
Job 29:11 ear heard me, *b.* me
31:20 his loins have not *b.* me
Ps. 49:18 lived he *b.* his soul
72:17 men be *b.* in him
113:26 *b.* be he that cometh in
name of the L. we ha. *b.* you
Prov. 31:28 children call her *b.*
Ec. 10:17 *b.* art thou, O land
Cant. 6:9 the daughters *b.* her
Is. 66:3 as if he *b.* an idol
Jer. 20:14 let not the day be *b.*
Mal. 3:12 all nations call you *b.*
Mark 11:10 *b.* be king. of our f.
Luke 1:48 gen. shall call me *b.*
2:34 Simeon *b.* them, and **said**
Acts 20:35 it is more *b.* to give
Tit. 2:13 looking for that *b.* hope
Heb. 7:1 met Abraham *b.* him, **6**
7 the less is *b.* of the better

BLESSED, *God the agent.*
Gen. 1:22 *b.* Be fruitful, 28; 5:2
2:3 *b.* seventh day, *Ex.* 20:11
12:3 in thee shall all families be
b. 18:18; 22:18; 26:4; 28:14;
Acts 3:25; *Gal.* 3:8
17:20 *b.* Ish. 24:1 *b.* Abraham
24:31 thou *b.* of the Lord
25:11 God *b.* Isaac, 26:12
26:29 thou art now the *b.* of L.
27:27 which the Lord hath *b.*
30:27 hath *b.* me for thy sake
30 L. *b.* thee since my coming
32:29 *b.* J. there, 35:9; 48:3
39:5 Lord *b.* Egyptian's house
Num. 22:12 for the people are *b.*
23:20 *b.* I cannot reverse it
Deut. 2:7 thy God hath *b.* thee,
12:7; 15:14; 16:10
7:14 shalt be *b.* above all people
28:3 *b.* shalt thou be in city, *b.*
4 *b.* be fruit of body, 5 basket
33:13 of Joseph he said, *b.* of L.
Jos. 17:14 the Lord hath *b.* me
Jud. 13:24 Lord *b.* Samson
Ruth 3:10 *b.* be thou my daught.
1 *Sam.* 23:21 *b.* be ye, 2 *Sam.* 2:5
2 *Sam.* 6:11 *b.* Obed-edom, 12; 1
Chr. 13:14; 26:5
7:29 house of thy servant be *b.*
1 *Chr.* 17:27 blessest, it shall be *b.*
2 *Chr.* 31:10 hath *b.* his people
Job 1:10 *b.* the work of his hands
42:12 Lord *b.* latter end of Job
Ps. 21:6 hast made him most *b.*
33:12 *b.* is the nation whose God
37:22 as be *b.* of him shall inh.
26 lendeth. and his seed is *b.*
41:2 and he shall be *b.*
45:2 therefore God hath *b.* thee
89:15 *b.* is the people that know
112:2 gen. of upright shall be *b.*
115:15 you are *b.* of the Lord
119:1 *b.* are the undefiled

Ps. 128:1 *b.* is every one that fear.
4 man be *b.* that fear. the L.
147:13 he hath *b.* thy children
Prov. 5:18 let thy fountain be *b.*
10:7 memory of the just is *b.*
20:7 just man's children are *b.*
21 end thereof shall not be *b.*
22:9 bountiful eye shall be *b.*
Is. 19:25 *b.* be Egypt my people
51:2 I called him alone and *b.*
61:9 seed Lord hath *b.* 65:23
Mat. 5:3 *b.* poor in spirit, 5 meek
7 merciful, 8 pure in heart

9 peacemakers, 10 persecuted
13:16 *b.* are y. eyes, *Luke* 10:23
14:19 *b.* and br. 26:26; *Mark*
  6:41; 14:22; *Luke* 9:16; 24:30
16:17 *b.* art thou, S. Bar-jona
24:46 *b.* is that serv. *Luke* 12:43
25:34 come, ye *b.* of my Father
Mark 10:16 in his arms and *b.*
14:61 thou Christ, son of the *b.*
Luke 1:28 *b.* among women, 42
  45 *b.* is that believed
6:20 *b.* be ye poor
11:27 *b.* is womb that bare thee
12:37 *b.* are serv. watching, 38
14:14 thou shalt be. not rec.
19:38 *b.* be the king that com.
23:29 *b.* are the barren
24:50 he *b.* them, 51 while he *b.*
Gal. 3:9 *b.* with faithful Abrah.
Eph. 1:3 *b.* us with spiritual bl.
Jam. 1:25 shall be *b.* in his deed
Rev. 14:13 *b.* are the dead

BLESSED, *God the object.*
Gen. 14:20 *b.* be most high God
Jos. 22:33 children of Is. *b.* God
2 *Sam.* 22:47 *b.* be my r. *Ps.* 18:46
1 *Chr.* 29:10 D. *b.* the L. *b.* be L.
  20 all the cong. *b.* the Lord God
2 *Chr.* 20:26 for there they *b.* L.
Neh. 9:5 *b.* be thy glo. n. *Ps.* 72:19
Job 1:21 *b.* be name, *Ps.* 113:2
Ps. 66:20 *b.* be G. 68:35; 2 *Cor.* 1:3
119:12 *b.* art thou, O Lord
Ezek. 3:12 saying, *b.* the glory
Dan. 2:19 *b.* the G. of heaven, 20
  4:34 Nebuch. *b.* the Most High
Luke 2:28 in his arms and *b.* God
John 12:13 *b.* is the King of Is.
Rom. 1:25 who is *b.* for ever
  9:5 over all, God *b.* for ever
2 *Cor.* 11:31 is *b.* for evermore
Eph. 1:3 *b.* be the F. 1 *Pet.* 1:3
1 *Tim.* 1:11 gospel of the *b.* God
  6:15 *b.* and only Potentate

BLESSED are they.
Ps. 2:12 *b. a. t.* that trust
84:4 *b. a. t.* that dwell in thy h.
106:3 *b. a. they* that keep judg.
119:2 *b. a. t.* that keep his testi.
Prov. 8:32 *b. a. t.* that keep my w.
Is. 30:18 *b. are t.* that wait for h.
Mat. 5:4 *b. are they* that mourn
  6 *b.* who hunger, 10 persecuted
Luke 11:28 rather *b.* hear the w.
John 20:29 *b.* have not seen
Rom. 4:7 *b. are they* whose iniq.
Rev. 19:19 *b.* called to mar. sup.
22:14 *b. a. t.* do his command.

BLESSED are ye.
Is. 32:20 *b. a. ye* sow beside w.
Mat. 5:11 *b.* when m. shall revile
Luke 6:21 *b. are ye* that hunger,
  be filled; *b. a. ye* that weep
  22 *b. a. ye* when men shall hate

BLESSED is he.
Num. 24:9 *b. is he* that blesseth
Ps. 32:1 *b. is he* who transg.
  41:1 *b. is he* that considerch p.
Dan. 12:12 *b. is he* that waiteth
Mat. 11:6 *b. is he* whoso. shall not
  be offended, *Luke* 7:23
21:9 *b. is he* that cometh in the
  name of the Lord, 23:39;
  Mark 11:9; *Luke* 13:35
Luke 14:15 *b.* shall eat bread
Rev. 1:3 *b. is he* that readeth
16:15 *b. is he* that watcheth
20:6 *b.* that hath part in first res.
22:7 *b.* keepeth sayings

BLESSED is the man.
Ps. 1:1 *b. is the m.* that walk. not
32:2 *b. is the m.* to whom the L.
  impu. not iniquity, *Rom.* 4:8
34:8 *b. is the m.* trusteth in him,
  84:12; *Jer.* 17:7
40:4 *b. m.* that maketh Lord

65:4 *b. is t. m.* whom thou ch.
84:5 *b. m.* whose str. is in thee
94:12 *b. is m.* whom thou chast.
112:1 *b. is th. m.* that feareth L.
Prov. 8:34 *b. m.* that heareth me
Is. 56:2 *b. is th m.* that doeth this
Jam. 1:12 *b.* that end. temptation

BLESSEDNESS.
Rom. 4:6 as D. describeth the *b.*
  9 cometh this *b.* on cir. only
Gal. 4:15 the *b.* ye spake of

BLESSEST.
Num. 22:6 whom thou *b.* is bl.
1 *Chr.* 17:27 thou *b.* O Lord
Ps. 65:10 thou *b.* the springing

BLESSETH.
Gen. 27:29 that *b.* thee, *Num.* 24:9
Deut. 15:6 *b.* thee as he promised
Ps. 10:3 *b.* covetous
107:38 he *b.* they are multiplied
Prov. 3:33 *b.* habita. of the just
27:14 *b.* his friend with a loud
Is. 65:16 *b.* himself in the earth

BLESSING, Substantive.
Gen. 12:2 thou shalt be a *b.*
22:17 in *b.* I will bl. *Heb.* 6:14
27:12 a curse on me, not a *b.*
  35 thy brother taken thy *b.*
  38 but one *b.* my father?
28:4 give thee *b.* of Abraham
33:11 my *b.* that is brought
39:5 *b.* was on all he had
49:28 ev. one ac. to his *b.* he bl.
Ex. 32:29 bestow on you a *b.*
Lev. 25:21 I com. my *b.* on you
Deut. 11:26 before you a *b.* 30:19
  27 a *b.* if ye obey the com.
  29 shalt put the *b.* on Gerizim
12:15 ac. to *b.* of the L. 16:17
23:5 turned the curse into a *b.*
28:8 com. a *b.* on storehouse
33:1 *b.* wherewith Moses bl. 7
  16 let the *b.* come upon Joseph
  23 Naphtali full with the *b.*
Jos. 15:19 g. me a *b. Jud.* 1:15
1 *Sam.* 25:27 this *b.* thy handm.
2 *Sam.* 7:29 thy *b.* let the house
2 *K.* 5:15 take a *b.* of thy serv.
Neh. 9:5 exalted above all *b.*
13:2 God turned curse into a *b.*
Job 29:13 *b.* of him ready to per.
Ps. 3:8 thy *b.* is on thy people
24:5 shall receive *b.* from Lord
109:17 he delighteth not in *b.*
129:8 *b.* of the L. be upon you
133:3 L. comm. the *b.* even life
Prov. 10:22 *b.* of L. maketh rich
11:11 by the *b.* of the upright
  26 a *b.* on him that selleth it
24:25 a good *b.* on them
Is. 19:24 a *b.* in midst of the l.
44:3 my *b.* on thy offspring
65:8 destroy it not, a *b.* is in it
Ezek. 34:26 about my hill a *b.*
  there shall be showers of *b.*
44:30 *b.* to rest in thy house
Joel 2:14 leave a *b.* behind him
Zec. 8:13 and ye shall be a *b.*
Mal. 3:10 and pour you out a *b.*
Luke 24:53 in the temple *b.* God
Rom. 15:29 fulness of the *b.*
1 *Cor.* 10:16 the cup of *b.* we bless
Gal. 3:14 *b.* of Ab. might come
Heb. 6:7 earth receiveth *b.*
  12:17 have inherited the *b.*
Jam. 3:10 same mouth *b.* cursing
1 *Pet.* 3:9 but contrariwise *b.* that
  ye should inherit a *b.*
Rev. 5:12 worthy to receive *b.*
  13 *b.* to him that sitteth on th.
7:12 *b.* and glory to our God

BLESSINGS.
Gen. 49:25 *b.* of the heav. above,
  b. of the deep, *b.* of t. breasts
26 *b.* of thy fath. above *b.* of my
Deut. 28:2 all these *b.* shall come

Jos. 8:34 he read the *b.* and curs.
Ps. 21:3 prev. him with the *b.*
Prov. 10:6 *b.* are upon the just
28:20 shall abound with *b.*
Mal. 2:2 and will curse your *b.*
Eph. 1:3 with all spiritual *b.*

BLEW.
Jos. 6:8 priests passed and *b.*
Jud. 3:27 Ehud *b.* a trumpet
  6:34 Gideon, *b.* a trumpet
  7:19 *b.* the trumpets, 20, 22
1 *Sam.* 13:3 Saul *b.* let Hebrews
2 *Sam.* 2:28 Joab *b.* 18:16; 20:22
20:1 Sheba a Benjamite *b.*
1 *K.* 1:39 *b.* people said, God save
  king Sol. 2 *K.* 9:13; 11:14
Mat. 7:25 *b.* on that house, 27
John 6:18 a great wind that *b.*
Acts 27:13 south-wind *b.* 28:13

BLIND, Adjective.
Ex. 4:11 who maketh the *b.?*
Lev. 19:14 stumb.-block before *b.*
21:18 a *b.* man shall not app.
22:22 offer the *b. Deut.* 15:21
Deut. 27:18 maketh *b.* to wander
28:29 as *b.* gropeth in darkness
2 *Sam.* 5:6 ex. thou take away *b.*
2 *Sam.* 5:8 *b.* hated of D. b. not
Job 29:15 I was eyes to the *b.*
Ps. 146:8 openeth the eyes of *b.*
Is. 29:18 eyes of *b.* shall see, 35:5
  42:7 light to open the *b.* eyes
  16 *b.* by a way they knew not
  18 look, ye *b.* that ye may see
  19 who is *b.?* who is *b.* as he
  that is perfect, and *b.*
43:8 *b.* people that have eyes
56:10 his watchmen are *b.*
59:10 we grope for wall like *b.*
Jer. 31:8 the *b.* and lame
Lam. 4:14 wandered as *b.* men
Zep. 1:17 walk like *b.* men
Mal. 1:8 *b.* for sacrifice
Mat. 9:27 two *b* men, 20:30
  11:5 *b.* rec. sight, 12:22; *Luke* 7:22
15:14 *b.* leaders of *b.* if the *b.* lead
  the *b. Luke* 6:39
23:16 woe to you, ye *b.* guides
  17 ye *b.* whether is greater, 19
  26 thou *b.* Pharisee
Mark 8:23 took *b.* man by the h.
10:46 *b.* Bartimeus sat begging
Luke 4:18 recovery of sight to *b.*
  7:21 to many *b.* he gave sight
  14:13 makest a feast call the *b.*
John. 5:3 a great multitude of *b.*
  9:1 he saw a man that was *b.*
  39 which see might be made *b*
  40 are we *b.* 41 if ye were *b.*
10:21 can a *b.* open eyes of *b.?*
Acts 13:11 thou shalt be *b.*
Rom. 2:19 art a guide to the *b.*
2 *Pet.* 1:9 lack. these things is *b.*
Rev. 3:17 knowest not thou art *b.*

BLIND, Verb.
Deut. 16:19 gift doth *b.* the eyes
1 *Sam.* 12:3 a bribe to *b.*

BLINDED, ETH.
Ex. 23:8 for a gift *b.* the wise
John 12:40 he hath *b.* their eyes
Rom. 11:7 the rest were *b.*
2 *Cor.* 3:14 their minds were *b.*
  4:4 god of this world hath *b.*
1 *John* 2:11 dark. hath *b.* his eyes

BLINDFOLDED.
Luke 22:64 when they had *b.* him

BLINDNESS.
Gen. 19:11 at the door with *b.*
Deut. 28:28 smite thee with *b.*
2 *K.* 6:18 E. prayed, Smite this
  people, I pray thee, with *b.*
Zec. 12:4 every horse with *b.*
Rom. 11:25 *b.* in part has hap.
Eph. 4:18 because ot *b.* of their h.

BLOCK. *See* STUMBLING.

BLOOD.

Where marked with † it is in the original BLOODS.

Gen. 4:10† thy brother's *b.*
9:4 life which is the *b.* not eat
5 *b.* of your lives will I require
37:31 and dipped the coat in *b.*
Ex. 4:9 water shall become *b.*
7:17 waters be turned into *b.*
12:13 *b.* a token, when I see *b.*
23:18 the *b.* with leaven, 34:25
Lev. 15:19 in her flesh be *b.*
17:4 *b.* imputed unto that man
11 it is *b.* maketh atonement
19:16 stand ag. *b.* of neighbor
Num. 23:24 and drink *b.* of slain
35:33 by *b.* of him that shed it
Deut. 17:8 *b.* and *b.* 2 *Chr.* 19:10
21:8 *b.* shall be forgiven them
32:43 avenge *b.* of his servants
Jud. 9:24 their *b.* on Abimelech
1 *Sam.* 26:20 my *b.* fall to the e.
2 *Sam.* 1:16 thy *b.* be on thy h.
22 from the *b.* of the slain
16:7† come out. thou man of *b.*
8 returned upon thee all the *b.*
20:12 Amasa wallowed in *b.*
23:17 *b.* of the m. 1 *Chr.* 11:19
1 *K.* 2:5 *b.* of war on his girdle
18:28 till the *b.* gushed out
2 *K.* 3:22 saw the water red as *b.*
23 said, This is *b.* the kings
9:26† I have seen *b.* of Naboth
Job 16:18 earth, cover not my *b.*
39:30 eagles' young suck up *b.*
Ps. 30:9 what profit in my *b.* ?
50:13 will I drink *b.* of goats ?
58:10 wash his feet in *b.* of w.
68:23 dipped in *b.* of thine ene.
72:14 precious their *b.*
Prov. 28:17 violence to *b.* of any
Is. 1:15† hands are full of *b.*
4:4 L. purge *b.* of Jerusalem
9:5 and garments rolled in *b.*
15:9 waters of Dimon full of *b.*
26:21† earth shall disclose her *b.*
33:15† his ear from hearing *b.*
34:3 mount. melted with their *b.*
Jer. 2:34 *b.* of the poor innocents
18:21 pour out their *b.* by force
48:10 keepeth his sword from *b.*
51:35 my *b.* be on the inh. of C.
Lam. 4:14 pol. thems. with *b.*
Ezek. 5:17 pestilence and *b.* pass
9:9 the land is full of *b.*
14:19 my fury upon it in *b.*
16:6 when thou wast in thy *b.*
9† I washed away thy *b.*
38 I will give thee *b.* in fury
18:10 son that is a shedder of *b.*
13† he shall die, his *b.* shall be
19:10 a vine in thy *b.*
21:32 thy *b.* in midst, 22:13
22:3 sheddeth *b.* in midst of it
23:37 *b.* is in their hands, 45
24:8 her *b.* on the top of a rock
28:23 send *b.* into her streets
32:6 water with thy *b.* the land
35:6 to *b.* thou hast not hated *b.*
even *b.* shall pursue thee
44:7 the fat and the *b.* 15
Hos. 1:4 avenge the *b.* of Jezreel
4:2† and *b.* toucheth *b.*
Joel 2:30 *b.* fire, pillars of smoke
31 moon turn. into *b.* *Acts* 2:20
3:21 I will cleanse their *b.*
Zep. 1:17 their *b.* poured out
Mat. 9:20 w. with an issue of *b.*
12 yrs. *Mark* 5:25; *Luke* 8:43
16:17 *b.* hath not revealed it
23:30 in the *b.* of prophets
35 *b.* of right. Abel, *Luke* 11:51
26:28 *b.* of new test. *Mark* 14:24
27:6 because it is price of *b.*
8 called the field of *b.* *Acts* 1:19
24 inn. of *b.* this just pers.
Luke 13:1 whose *b.* P. mingled
22:20 test. in my *b.* 1 *Cor.* 11:25

44 sweat as great drops of *b.*
John 1:13 born not of *b.*
6:54 and drinketh my *b.* 56
55 and my *b.* is drink indeed
19:34 forth. came there out *b.*
Acts 5:28 to bring this man's *b.*
15:20 abstain from *b.* 29; 21:25
17:26 made of one *b.* all nations
18:6 *b.* be on your own heads
20:26 pure from *b.* of all men
Cor. 11:27 the body and *b.*
15:50 flesh and *b.* cannot inherit
Eph. 6:12 against flesh and *b.*
Col. 1:20 through *b.* of his cross
Heb. 2:14 partak. of flesh and *b.*
9:7 without *b.* which he offered
12 *b.* of goats, but by his own *b.*
13 if the *b.* of bulls sanctifieth
20 the *b.* of the testament
22 without shedding of *b.*
10:19 holiest by the *b.* of Jesus
11:28 and sprinkling of *b.*
12:4 not yet resisted unto *b.*
24 *b.* of sprinkling that speak.
13:11 whose *b.* is brought into
1 *Pet.* 1:2 sprinkling of the *b.*
1 *John* 1:7 *b.* of J. C. cleanseth
5:6 came by water and *b.*
8 the Spirit, water, and *b.*
Rev. 5:9 redeemed us by thy *b.*
6:10 avenge our *b.*
12 and the moon became as *b.*
7:14 in the *b.* of the Lamb
8:8 part of sea became *b.* 16:3
11:6 to turn the waters into *b.*
12:11 overcame by *b.* of the L.
14:20 *b.* came out of wine-press
16:6 hast given them *b.* to drink
18:24 the *b.* of the prophets
19:2 avenged the *b.* in his serv.
13 with a vesture dipped in *b.*
See AVENGER, REVENGER.

BLOOD be upon.
Lev. 20: 9 curs. father, his *b.* him
11 incest, 13 sodomy, 16 bestiality, 27 wizard, their *b.* be u. them
Ezek. 18:13 abom. his *b.* be upon
33:5 his *b.* shall be upon him

BLOOD, with bullock.
Is. 1:11 I del. not in *b.* of bull.

BLOOD of Christ.
1 *Cor.* 10:6 com. of *b.* of C.
Eph. 2:13 made nigh by *b.* of C.
Heb. 9:14 shall *b.* purge?
1 *Pet.* 1:19 with precious *b.* of C.
1 *John* 1:7 the *b.* of J. C. cleanseth

BLOOD of the Covenant.
Ex. 24:8 M. said Behold the *b.*
Zec. 9:11 for thee also by *b.* of c.
Heb. 10:29 *b.* of cov. unholy thing
13:20 *b.* of the everlasting cov.

BLOOD, with eat.
Lev. 3:17 eat neither fat nor *b.*
7:26 eat no manner of *b.* 27;
17:14; *Deut.* 12:16, 23; 15:23
27 eateth *b.* soul cut off, 17:10
1 *Sam.* 14:32 eat them with the *b.*
Ezek. 33:25 ye eat with *b.*

For BLOOD.
2 *Chr.* 24:25 for the *b.* of sons
Ps. 9:12 maketh inquis. for *b.*
Prov. 1:11 lay wait for *b.* 18
12:6 are to lie in wait for *b.*
Mic. 7:2 lie in wait for *b.*

His BLOOD.
Gen. 37:26 and conceal his *b.*
42:22 behold his *b.* is required
Jos. 2:19 his *b.* be upon his head
2 *Sam.* 4:11 shall I not req. his *b.*
1 *K.* 2:32 shall return his *b.*
Ezek. 3:18 his *b.* will I require at
thy hand, 20; 33:4, 6, 8
Hos. 12:14 leave his *b.* on him
Mat. 27:25 his *b.* be on us

Acts 20:28 ch. purchased with *h.b.*
Rom. 3:25 thro' faith in his *b.*
5:9 justified by his *b.*
Eph. 1:7 red. thro' his *b.* *Col.* 1:14
Heb. 9:12 by his own *b.* he ent.
13:12 sanct. the people with *h. b.*
Rev. 1:5 and washed us in his *b.*

Innocent BLOOD.
Deut. 19:10 that in. *b.* be not shed
13 put away guilt of in. *b.* 21:9
21:8 in. *b.* to thy people's ch.
1 *Sam.* 19:5 sin against in. *b.*
1 *K.* 2:31 take away in. *b.*
2 *K.* 21:16 Man. shed in. *b.* 24:4
Ps. 94:21 they condemn in. *b.*
106:38 in. *b.* even *b.* of sons
Prov. 6:17 hateth hands sh. in. *b.*
Is. 59:7 haste to shed in. *b.*
Jer. 7:6 shed not innocent *b.*
22:17 are to shed innocent *b.*
26:15 shall surely bring inno. *b.*
Joel 3:19 bec. they shed inno. *b.*
Jon. 1:14 L. lay not on us inno. *b.*
Mat. 27:4 I betrayed innocent *b.*

Shed BLOOD.
Gen. 9:6 m's *b.* by m. h. *b.* be s.
37:22 Reuben said, shed no *b.*
Lev. 17:4 shed *b.* shall be cut off
Num. 35:33 cl. of *b. s.* but by *b.*
Deut. 21:7 hands not shed this *b.*
1 *K.* 2:5 shed *b.* of war in peace
1 *Chr.* 22:8 shed *b.* much *b.* 28:3
Ps. 79:3 their *b.* shed like water
10 reveng. *b.* of thy servants *sh.*
Prov. 1:16 h. to shed *b.* *Rom.* 3:15
Lam. 4:13 shed the *b.* of the just
Ezek. 16:38 women that s. *b.* 23:45
22:4 guilty in *b.* th. hast shed, 6
33:25 ye s. *b.* and shall ye pos.
36:18 for the *b.* shed
Mat. 23:35 the righteous *b. s.*
Mark 14:24 this is my *b.* which
is shed, *Luke* 22:20
Luke 11:50 *b.* of all the proph. *s.*
Acts 22:20 when *b.* of S. was *s.*
Rev. 16:6 *s.* the *b.* of the saints

Sprinkle BLOOD.
Ex. 29:20 sprinkle *b.* on altar,
Lev. 1:5, 11; 3:2, 8, 13; 7:2;
17:6; *Num.* 18:17.

BLOOD sprinkled.
Ex. 24:8 M. *sp. b.* on the people
Is. 63:3 their *b.* shall be sprinkled
on my garment
Heb. 9:21 he *sp.* with *b.*

With BLOOD.
Ex. 30:10 A. make atone. *with b.*
Lev. 19:26 not eat any th. *with b.*
1 *K.* 2:9 bring thou down *with b.*
Ps. 106:38 land was pol. *with b.*
Is. 34:6 sword of L. filled *with b.*
7 land shall be soaked *with b.*
49:26 drunken *with* their own *b.*
59:3 hands are defiled *with b.*
Jer. 19:4 this place *w. b.* of innoc.
46:10 drunk *with* their *b.*
Lam. 4:14 pol. thems. *with b.*
Ezek. 38:22 plead ag. him *with b.*
Hos. 6:8 Gilead polluted *with b.*
Mic. 3:10 build up Zion *with b.*
Hab. 2:12 build. a town *with b.*
Gal. 1:16 I conferred not *with b.*
Heb. 9:22 the law purged *with b.*
Rev. 8:7 fire, mingled *with b.*
17:6 the woman drunken *w. b.*

BLOOD-GUILTINESS.
Ps. 51:14 deliver me from *b.-g.*

BLOOD-THIRSTY.
Prov. 29:10 *b.-th.* hate upright

BLOODY.
Ex. 4:25 a *b.* hush. art thou, 26
2 *Sam.* 16:7 Sh. said, Thou *b.* man
21:1 famine is for S. his *b.* house
Ps. 5:6 L. will abhor the *b.* man
26:9 gather not my life with *b.m.*

Ps. 55:23 *b.* m. not live half th. d.
59:2 and save me from *b.* men
139:19 depart from me, ye *b.* m.
Ezek. 7:23 full of *b.* crimes
22:2 wilt thou judge the *b.* city?
24:6 the *b.* city, 9; *Nah.* 3:1
Acts 28:8 lay sick of a *b.* flux

BLOOMED.
Num. 17:8 A. rod *b.* blossoms.

BLOSSOM, S.
Gen. 40:10 her *b.* shot forth
Is. 5:25 *b.* shall go up as dust

BLOSSOM, ED.
Num. 17:5 the man's rod shall *b.*
Is. 27:6 Israel shall *b.* and bud
35:1 desert shall *b.* as the rose
2 it shall *b.* abundantly
Ezek. 7:10 the rod hath *b.*
Hab. 3:17 fig-tree shall not *b.*

BLOT.
Job 31:7 if any *b.* hath cleaved
Prov. 9:7 wicked, getteth a *b.*

BLOT out.
Ex. 32:32 *b.* me *out* of thy b.
33 him will I *b. out*
Deut. 9:14 alone that I *b. out*
25:19 *b. out* reme. of Amalek
29:20 *b. out* his name
2 *K.* 14:27 would *b. out* name
Ps. 51:1 *b. out* transgress.
9 *b. out* all my iniquity
Jer. 18:23 nor *b. out* their sin
Rev. 3:5 not *b.* his name *out*

BLOTTED.
Neh. 4:5 let not their sin be *b.*
Ps. 69:28 *b.* out of book of the l.
109:13 let their name be *b.* out
14 sin of his mother be *b.* out
Is. 44:22 *b.* out as a thick cloud
Acts 3:19 that your sins be *b.* out

BLOTTETH, ING.
Is. 43:25 *b.* out thy transgress.
Col. 2:14 *b.* out the handwriting

BLOW, Substantive.
Ps. 39:10 consumed by the *b.*
Jer. 14:17 with a grievous *b.*

BLOW, Verb.
Ex. 15:10 *b.* with thy wind
Jud. 7:18 when I *b.* then *b.* ye
Ps. 78:26 caused east-wind to *b.*
147:18 causeth his wind to *b.*
Cant. 4:16 come, thou south, *b.*
Is. 40:24 *b.* upon them
Ezek. 21:31 will *b.* ag. thee, 22:21
Hos. 5:8 *b.* cornet in Gibeah
Hag. 1:9 I did *b.* upon it
Luke 12:55 see the south-wind *b.*
Rev. 7:1 that wind should not *b.*

See TRUMPET.

BLOWETH.
Is. 40:7 S. of the Lord *b.* on it
54:16 created the smith that *b.*
John 3:8 wind *b.* where it listeth

BLOWN.
Job 20:26 fire not *b.* consume

BLUE.
Ex. 25:4 *b.* 26:1, 31, 36; 27:16
2 *Chr.* 2:7 cunning to w. in *b.* 14
Est. 1:6 *b.* hangings, *b.* marble
8:15 Mordecai in apparel of *b.*
Ezek. 23:6 Assyr. clothed with *b.*

See PURPLE, LINEN, LACE, LOOPS.

BLUENESS.
Prov. 20:30 *b.* of a wound

BLUNT.
Ec. 10:10 if iron be *b.* and he

BLUSH.
Ezr. 9:6 I *b.* to lift up my face
Jer. 6:15 nor could they *b.* 8:12

BOANERGES. *Mark* 3:17

BOAR.
Ps. 80:13 *b.* out of the wood

BOARDS.
Cant. 8:9 inclose her with *b.*
Acts 27:44 on *b.* came to land

BOAST, Substantive.
Ps. 34:2 shall make her *b.*
Rom. 2:17 makest thy *b.* of God
23 makest thy *b.* of the law

BOAST, Verb.
1 *K.* 20:11 *b.* as he
2 *Chr.* 25:19 lifteth thee up to *b.*
Ps. 44:8 in God we *b.* all the day
49:6 *b.* themselves
94:4 workers of iniquity *b.*
97:7 confounded that *b.* of idols
Prov. 27:1 *b.* not of to-morrow
Is. 10:15 shall the axe *b.* itself
61:6 in their glory shall you *b.*
Rom. 11:18 *b.* not ag. branches
2 *Cor.* 9:2 I *b.* to them of Maced.
10:13 *b.* without our measure
16 to *b.* in another man's line
11:16 receive me that I may *b.*
Eph. 2:9 of works, lest any *b.*

BOASTED.
Ezek. 35:13 with mouth ye h. *b.*
2 *Cor.* 7:14 if I have *b.* any thing

BOASTERS.
Rom. 1:30 *b.* inventors of evil th.
2 *Tim.* 3:2 covetous, *b.* proud

BOASTEST, ETH.
Ps. 10:3 wicked *b.* of his heart's
52:1 why *b.* thyself in mischief
Prov. 20:14 then he *b.*
25:14 whoso *b.* of a false gift
Jam. 3:5 tongue *b.* great things

BOASTING, Participle.
Acts 5:36 Theudas *b.* himself
2 *Cor.* 10:15 not *b.* without meas.

BOASTING, Substantive.
Rom. 3:27 where is *b.* then?
2 *Cor.* 7:14 our *b.* before Titus
8:24 show you the proof of our *b.*
9:3 lest our *b.* of you be in vain
4 in this same confident *b.*
11:10 no man stop me of this *b.*
17 in this confidence of *b.*
Jam. 4:16 ye rejoice in your *b.*

BOAT, S.
John 6:22 no other *b.* there, Jesus
went not into the *b.*
23 came other *b.* from Tiberias
Acts 27:16 work to come by the *b.*
30 they had let down the *b.*
32 cut off the ropes of the *b.*

BOAZ. 1 *K.* 7:21; 2 *Chr.* 3:17;
Ruth 2:1, 19; 3:2; 4:1; *Lu.* 3:32

BOCHIM.
Jud. 2:1 angel came up to B. 5

BODY.
Ex. 24:10 as the *b.* of heaven
1 *Sam.* 31:12 *b.* of S. 1 *Chr.* 10:12
Job 19:17 child.'s sake of my *b.*
26 worms destroy *b.*
20:25 and cometh out of the *b.*
Prov. 5:11 flesh and *b.* are cons.
Is. 10:18 consume soul and *b.*
51:23 hast laid thy *b.* as ground
Ezek. 10:12 whole *b.* full of eyes
Dan. 7:15 in midst of my *b.*
Mat. 5:29 *b.* be cast into hell, 30
6:22 light of *b.* *Luke* 11:34;
full of light, *Luke* 11:34, 36
23 *b.* shall be full of darkness
25 thought for *b.* *Luke* 12:22
10:28 kill the *b.* *Luke* 12:4
14:12 John's discip. took the *b.*
26:12 this ointment on my *b.*
26 this is my *b.* *Mark* 14:22;
Luke 22:19; 1 *Cor.* 11:24
27:58 Joseph begged the *b.* of J.
Mark 15:43; *Luke* 23:52

Mark 5:29 she felt in her *b.*
14:8 aforehand to anoint my *b.*
51 linen cloth cast about his *b.*
15:45 P. gave the *b.* *Mat.* 27:58
Luke 12:23 *b.* more than raiment
17:37 *b.* is, thither the eagles
24:3 found not the *b.* of Lord
John 20:12 *b.* of Jesus had lain
Rom. 6:6 *b.* of sin be destroyed
7:4 dead to the law by *b.* of C.
24 from the *b.* of this death
8:10 *b.* is dead because of sin
13 Spirit mortify deeds of *b.*
23 the redemption of our *b.*
1 *Cor.* 6:13 *b.* is not for fornication, but for L. and L. for *b.*
18 every sin is without the *b.*
6:19 your *b.* is the temple
7:4 no power over her own *b.*
9:27 I keep under my *b.* and
10:16 communion of the *b.* of C.
11:27 guilty of the *b.* and blood
29 not discerning the Lord's *b.*
12:14 the *b.* is not one member
15 therefore not of the *b.*? 16
17 if whole *b.* were an eye
19 wh. were the *b.*? 20 one *b.*
27 now ye are the *b.* of Christ
13:3 I give my *b.* to be burned
15:35 w. what *b.* do dead come?
37 sowest not that *b.* that shall
38 God giveth a *b.* as it hath
44 sown a nat. *b.* raised spir. *b.*
2 *Cor.* 5:8 to be absent from *b.*
Eph. 3:6 heirs of the same *b.*
4:12 the edifying of *b.* of Christ
16 from whom the whole *b.*
5:23 he is the Saviour of the *b.*
Phil. 3:21 shall change vile *b.*
Col. 1:18 head of the *b.* the ch.
2:11 in putting off the *b.* of sins

Col. 2:17 shadow, the *b.* is of Ch.
19 from which the *b.* by joints
23 a show of wisdom in neg. *b.*
1 *Thes.* 5:23 your soul and *b.*
Heb. 10:5 a *b.* hast thou prepared
10 offering of the *b.* of Jesus
Jam. 2:16 things needful to *b.*
26 the *b.* without the spirit
3:2 to bridle the whole *b.*
3 we turn about their whole *b.*
6 tongue defileth the whole *b.*
Jude 9 disputed about. *b.* of M.

Dead BODY.
Num. 19:11 *d. b.* unclean, 16
2 *K.* 8:5 he had restored *d. b.* ?
Is. 26:19 my *d. b.* sh. they arise
Jer. 26:23 cast his *b.* into gra.
36:30 *dead b.* shall be cast out

Fruit of the BODY.
Deut. 28:4 blessed be *f. of thy b.*
18 cursed shall be *fr. of thy b.*
53 shalt eat the *fr. of thy b.*
Ps. 132:11 *f. b.* will I set on thy
Mic. 6:7 *f. of my b.* for sin of soul

His BODY.
1 *Sam.* 31:10 fast. *his b.* to wall
Dan. 4:33 *his b.* wet w. dew, 5:21
7:11 beast was slain, and *his b.*
10:6 *his b.* was like the beryl
Luke 23:55 b. how *his b.* was laid
24:23 they found not *his b.*
John 2:21 temple of *his b.*
Acts 19:12 from *his b.* were br.
Rom. 4:19 con. not *h. b.* now d.
1 *Cor.* 6:18 sinneth against *his b.*
7:4 power of *his* own *b.*
2 *Cor.* 5:10 things done in *his b.*
Eph. 1:23 which is *his b.* fulness
Phil. 3:21 like *his* glorious *b.*
Col. 1:24 for *his b.* sake
1 *Pet.* 2:24 bare our sins in *his b.*

In BODY.
Lam. 4:7 *in b.* than rubies
Rom. 6:12 *in* your mortal *b.*
1 *Cor.* 5:3 I verily as absent *in b.*

BODY

6:20 glorify God *in* your *b.*
7:34 that she may be holy *in b.*
12:18 members every one *in b.*
25 no schism *in* the *b.*
2 *Cor.* 4:10 *in b.* the dy. of the L.
  that life be manif. *in* our *b.*
5:6 whilst we are at home *in b.*
12:2 whether *in b.* or out of *b.*
Gal. 6:17 I bear *in b.* the marks
Phil. 1:20 be magnified *in* my *b.*
Col. 1:22 *in b.* of his flesh
Heb. 13:3 being yours. *in* the *b.*

One BODY.

Rom. 12:4 members *in one b.*
5 are *one b.* in C. 1 *Cor.* 10:17
1 *Cor.* 6:16 joined to a h. is *one b.*
12:12 as the *b. is one*, and hath
13 we are baptized into *one b.*
20 many members, yet *one b.*
Eph. 2:16 rec. both to G. in *one b.*
4:4 there is *one b.* and one S.
Col. 3:15 also called in *one b.*

BODIES.

Job 13:12 your *b.* like *b.* of clay
Ezek. 1:11 wings covered *b.* 23
Dan. 3:27 on *b.* fire had no power
Mat. 27:52 *b.* of saints arose
John 19:31 *b.* should not remain
Rom. 1:24 dishonor their own *b.*
8:11 quicken your mortal *b.*
12:1 your *b.* a living sacrifice
1 *Cor.* 6:15 your *b.* members
15:40 celestial *b.* and *b.*
Eph. 5:28 love wives as own *b.*
Heb. 10:22 *b.* washed with pure
13:11 *b.* of beasts, whose blood

Dead BODIES.

2 *Chr.* 20:24 were *d. b.* fallen
Ps. 79:2 *d. b.* of thy servants
110:6 fill places with *d. b.*
Jer. 31:40 valley of *dead b.*
33:5 to fill them with *d. b.*
34:20 *d. b.* shall be for meat
41:9 Ishm. cast *dead b.* of men
Amos 8:3 *d. b.* in every place
Rev. 11:8 *dead b.* in the street
9 their *dead b.* three days and
  a half, nor suffer *d. b.*

BODILY.

Luke 3:22 desc. in a *b.* shape
2 *Cor.* 10:10 *b.* presence is weak
Col. 2:9 fulness of the Godh. *b.*
1 *Tim.* 4:8 *b.* exer. profiteth little

BOIL, S, Substantive.

Ex. 9:10 it became a *b.*
2 *K.* 20:7 figs on *b.* *Is.* 38:21
Job 2:7 Satan smote Job with *b.*

BOIL.

Job 41:31 the deep to *b.* like a pot
Is. 64:2 fire causeth waters to *b.*
Ezek. 24:5 make it *b.* well, 46.20

BOILED.

1 *K.* 19:21 yoke of oxen and *b.*
2 *K.* 6:29 so we *b.* my son
Job 30:27 my bowels *b.*

BOISTEROUS.

Mat. 14:30 he saw the wind *b.*

BOLD.

Prov. 28:1 right. are *b.* as a lion
Acts 13:46 P. and Bar. waxed *b.*
Rom. 10:20 Esaias is very *b.*
2 *Cor.* 10:1 being absent, am *b.*
2 wherewith I think to be *b.*
11:21 any is *b.* I am *b.* also
Phil. 1:14 are much more *b.*
1 *Thes.* 2:2 we were *b.* in our G.
Phile. 8 I might be much *b.* in C.

BOLDLY.

Mark 15:43 Joseph went in *b.*
John 7:26 he speaketh *b.*
Acts 9:27 preached *b.* at Dam.
29 he spake *b.* in name of L. J.
14:3 abode they, speaking *b.*
18:26 Apollos began to speak *b.*

19:8 spake *b.* for three months
Rom. 15:15 written more *b.*
Eph. 6:19 open my mouth *b.*
20 I may speak *b.* as I ought
Heb. 4:16 *b.* to the thr. of grace
13:6 *b.* say, Lord is my helper

BOLDNESS.

Ec. 8:1 *b.* of his face be changed
Acts 4:13 *b.* of Peter and John
29 with all *b.* they may speak
31 spake word of God with *b.*
2 *Cor.* 7:4 great is my *b.* of speech
Eph. 3:12 we have *b.* and access
Phil. 1:20 with all *b.* as always
1 *Tim.* 3:13 they purchase gr. *b.*
Heb. 10:19 *b.* to enter into holiest
1 *John* 4:17 may have *b.* in judg.

BOLSTER.

1 *Sam.* 19:13 goats' hair for *b.* 16
26:7 spear at *b.* 11, 12 ; 16 water

BOND, Adjective.

1 *Cor.* 12:13 one body, *b.* or free
See FREE.

BOND.

Ezek. 20:37 bring you into *b.*
Luke 13:16 from his *b.* on sab.
Acts 8:23 art in the *b.* of iniquity
Eph. 4:3 Spirit, in *b.* of peace
Col. 3:14 charity, *b.* of perfect.

BONDS.

Job 12:18 looseth the *b.* of kings
Ps. 116:16 hast loosed my *b.*
Jer. 5:5 the yoke, and burst the *b.*
27:2 make thee *b.* and yokes
30:8 his yoke, and burst thy *b.*
Nah. 1:13 I will burst thy *b.*
Acts 20:23 that *b.* and aff. abide
23:29 wor. of death or *b.* 26:31
25:14 a certain man left in *b.*
26:29 as I am, except these *b.*
Eph. 6:20 am an ambassa. in *b.*
Phil. 1:7 in *b.* ye are all partak.
13 so my *b.* in C. are manifest
14 waxing confident by my *b.*
16 to add affliction to my *b.*
Col. 4:3 in *b.* ; 18 rem. my *b.*
2 *Tim.* 2:9 suffer trouble even to *b.*
Phile. 10 begotten in my *b.*
13 in the *b.* of the gospel
Heb. 10:34 compassion of me in *b.*
11:36 others had trial of *b.* and
13:3 rem. them in *b.* as bound

BONDAGE.

Ex. 1:14 bitter with hard *b.*
2:23 Israel sighed by reason of *b.*
13:14 Lord brought us out of the
  house of *b.* 20:2 ; *Deut.* 5:6 ;
  6:12 ; 8:14 ; 13:5, 10 ; *Jos.*
  24:17 ; *Jud.* 6:8
Deut. 26:6 E. laid on us hard *b.*
Neh. 9:17 captain to return to *b.*
Is. 14:3 rest from thy hard *b.*
Rom. 8:15 received spirit of *b.*
21 from *b.* of corruption
Gal. 4:24 which gendereth to *b.*
5:1 not entangled with y. of *b.*
Heb. 2:15 lifetime subject to *b.*

In, into, or under BONDAGE.

Ezr. 9:8 reviving *in* our *b.*
9 God hath not fors. us *in b.*
John 8:23 never *in b.* to any
Acts 7:6 bring them *into b.*
7 to whom they shall be *in b.*
1 *Cor.* 7:15 is not *under b.*
2 *Cor.* 11:20 man bring you *into b.*
Gal. 2:4 might bring us *into b.*
4:3 *in b.* under the elements
9 ye desire to be *in b.*

Gal. 4:25 answ. to J. which is *in b.*
2 *Pet.* 2:19 is he brought *into b.*

BONDMAID.

Gal. 4:22 one by a *b.* the other

BONDMAN.

Deut. 15:15 wast a *b.* in Egypt,
  L. red. thee, 16:12 ; 24:18, 22
Rev. 6:15 every *b.* hid themselves

BONDMEN.

Lev. 25:44 *b.* shall ye be of the h.
Deut. 28:68 ye sh. be sold for *b.*
2 *K.* 4:1 my two sons to be *b.*
2 *Chr.* 28:10 children of J. for *b.*
Ezr. 9:9 we were *b.* yet God
Est. 7:4 had been sold for *b.*
Jer. 34:13 out of the house of *b.*

BONDSERVICE.

1 *K.* 9:21 a tribute of *b.*

BONDWOMAN.

Gen. 21:10 cast out this *b.* and
  her son, *Gal.* 4:30
13 son of *b.* will I make a nat.
Gal. 4:23 son of *b.* born
31 are not children of the *b.*

BONDWOMEN. *See* BONDMEN.

BONE.

Gen. 2:23 this is *b.* of my bones
29:14 art my *b.* and my flesh
Ex. 12:46 neither shall ye break
  a *b.* *Num.* 9:12
2 *Sam.* 5:1 are thy *b.* 1 *Chr.* 11:1
Job 2:5 touch his *b.* and flesh
19:20 my *b.* cleav. to my skin
31:22 my arm be bro. from the *b.*
Prov. 25:15 tongue breake. the *b.*
Ezek. 37:7 together, *b.* to his *b.*
John 19:36 a *b.* of him sh. n. be b.

BONES.

Ex. 13:19 M. took *b.* of Joseph
Jos. 24:32 *b.* of Joseph buried
2 *Sam.* 21:12 took *b.* of Saul
1 *K.* 13:2 men's *b.* shall be burnt
2 *K.* 13:21 touched *b.* of Elisha
23:20 burnt men's *b.*
2 *Chr.* 34:5 burnt *b.* of the priests
Job 10:11 hast fenced me with *b.*
Ps. 51:8 *b.* thou hast broken
53:5 G. scattereth the *b.* of him
141:7 *b.* are scat. at grave's m.
Prov. 3:8 marrow to thy *b.*
14:30 the rottenness of the *b.*
15:30 good report maketh *b.* fat
16:24 pleas. words health to *b.*
17:22 broken spirit drieth the *b.*
Ec. 11:5 how the *b.* do grow
Is. 58:11 shall make fat thy *b.*
66:14 your *b.* shall flourish
Jer. 8:1 *b.* of the kings, priests,
  prophets, inhabitants
Ezek. 6:5 scat. your *b.* about
24:4 choice *b.* ; 5 burn *b.* 10
37:1 valley full of *b.* ; 3 *b.* live ?
4 prophesy and say, O ye dry *b.*
11 *b.* are house of Isr. our *b.*
Amos 6:10 to bring out the *b.*
Zep. 3:3 they gnaw not the *b.*
Mat. 23:27 full of dead men's *b.*
Luke 24:39 a spirit hath not *b.*

His BONES.

1 *K.* 13:31 lay my *b.* beside *his b.*
2 *K.* 23:18 no man move his *b.*
Job 20:11 *his b.* are full
21:24 *his b.* moistened
33:19 *his b.* with strong pain
21 and *his b.* stick out
40:18 *his b.* as br. *his b.* as iron
Ps. 34:20 he keepeth all *his b.*
109:18 come like oil into *his b.*
Prov. 12:4 rottenness in *his b.*
Eph. 5:30 members of *his b.*
Heb. 11:22 com. concern. *his b*

My BONES.

Gen. 50:25 up my *b.* *Ex.* 13:19
2 *Sam.* 19:12 are *my b.* and flesh
1 *K.* 13:31 my *b.* beside his *b.*
Job 4:14 made all *my b.* to shake
30:17 *my b.* are pierced in me
30 and *my b.* burnt with heat

Ps. 6:2 heal me, *my b.* are vexed
22:14 all my *b.* are out of joint
17 I may tell all *my b.*
31:10 *my b.* are consumed
32:3 *my b.* waxed old
35:10 *my b.* shall say, Lord
38:3 neither any rest in *my b.*
42:10 as with a sword in *my b.*
102:3 *my b.* are burnt as a hearth
5 *my b.* cleave to my skin
Is. 38:13 will he break all *my b.*
Jer. 20:9 a burning fire in *my b.*
23:9 all *my b.* shake
Lam. 1:13 sent fire into *my b.*
3:4 he hath broken *my b.*
Hab. 3:16 entered into *my b.*

Their BONES.

Num. 24:8 Is. shall break *their b.*
1 *Sam.* 31:13 *their b.* buried them
Lam. 4:8 skin cleaveth to *their b.*
Ezek. 32:27 iniquity on *their b.*
Dan. 6:24 lions brake all *their b.*
Mic. 3:2 flesh from *their b.*

BONNETS.

Is. 3:20 L. will take away the b.
Ezek. 44:18 shall have linen b.

BOOK.

Ex. 17·14 memorial in a *b.*
32:32 blot me out of thy *b.*
33 will I blot out of my *b.*
Num. 21:14 *b.* of the wars
Deut. 17:18 of this law in a *b.*
Jos. 10:13 *b.* of J. 2 *Sam.* 1:18
1 *Sam.* 10:25 S. wrote it in a *b.*
1 *K.* 11:41 *b.* of acts of Solomon
2 *K.* 22:8 Hilk. gave *b.* to Shap.
23:24 perform words in *b.*
Ezr. 4:15 s. may be made in *b.*
Neh. 8:5 Ezra opened the *b.*
Job 19:23 they were prin. in a *b.*
31:35 adver. had written a *b.*
Ps. 40:7 vol. of the *b. Heb.* 10:7
56:8 are they not in thy *b. ?*
69:28 blotted out of *b.*
139:16 in thy *b.* all my members
Is. 29:11 as words of a *b.* sealed
12 *b.* is deliv. to him not learn.
18 shall hear words of the *b.*
30:8 now go and note it in a *b.*
34:16 seek ye out of the *b.* of L.
Jer. 30:2 write the words in a *b.*
36:2 roll of a *b.* ; 10 read in *b.*
45·1 words in a *b.* from Jerem.
Ezek. 2:9 roll of a *b.* was therein
Dan. 12:1 ev. one writ. in the *b.*
4 O Daniel, seal the *b.*
Nah. 1:1 *b.* of vision of Nahum
Mal. 3:16 a *b.* of remembrance
Mat. 1:1 *b.* of the gen. of Jesus
Luke 3:4 written in the *b.* of E.
4:17 deliv. to J. the *b.* of Esaias,
when he opened the *b.*
20 he closed the *b.* and gave it
20:42 in *b.* of Psalms, *Acts* 1:20
Acts 7:42 in *b.* of the prophets
Heb. 9:19 sprinkled the *b.* and
Rev. 1:11 write in a *b.*
5:1 a *b.* written within, on the
2 is worthy to open the *b.* 3
10:2 in his hand a little *b.* open
9 little *b.* ; 10 I took the *b.*
20:12 *b.* was opened, of life
22:19 if any take from w. of *b.*

See COVENANT.

BOOK of the Law.

Deut. 31:26 *b. of l.* put it in ark
Jos. 1:8 *b. of law* shall not depart
2 *K.* 22:8 I have found *b. of law*
Neh. 8:8 read in the *b. of law*
Gal. 3:10 in *b. of l.* to do them

BOOK of Life.

Phil. 4:3 writ. in the *b. of life*
Rev. 3:5 name out of *b. of l.*
13:8 not writ. in *b. of life,* 17:8
20:12 an. *b.* opened, *b. of life*
15 not written in *b. of life*

21:27 written in L.'s *b. of life*
22:19 part out of the *b. of life*

BOOK of Moses.

2 *Chr.* 25:4 as in *b. of M.* 35:12
Ezr. 6:18
Neh. 13:1 read in the *b. of M.*
Mark 12:26 ye not read in *b.*

This BOOK.

Deut. 28:58 it *t. b.* 2 *Chr.* 34:21
2 *K.* 22:13 to the words of *t. b.*
23:3 perf. the words in *this b.*
Jer. 25:13 ah that is in *this b.*
51·63 an end of reading *this b.*
John 20:30 not written in *this b.*
Rev. 22:9 keep the say. of *this b.*
10 the sayings of *this b.*
18 plagues in *this b.*
19 things in *this b.*

BOOKS.

Ec. 12;12 of making *b.*
Dan. 7:10 *b.* were op. *Rev.* 20:12
John 21:25 could not cont. the *b.*
Acts 19:19 their *b.* and burned
2 *Tim.* 4:13 bring the *b.* espec.
Rev. 20:12 out of things in *b.*

BOOTH.

Job 27:18 as a *b.* the keeper
Jon. 4:5 Jonah made him a *b.*

BOOTHS.

Gen. 33:17 and Jacob made *b.*
Lev. 23:42 dwell in *b.* seven days
43 I made Is. dwell in *b.*
Neh. 8:14 Isr. should dwell in *b.*

BOOTY, IES.

Jer. 49:32 camels shall be a *b.*
Hab. 2:7 be for *b.* unto them
Zep. 1:13 goods shall bec. a *b.*

BORDER.

Ex. 19:12 touch *b.* of mount
Deut. 12:20 w. L. enlarge thy *b.*
1 *K.* 4:21 Solomon reigned unto
b. of Egypt, 2 *Chr.* 9:26
Ps. 78:54 *b.* of his sanctuary
Prov. 15:25 establish *b.* of widow
Is. 37:24 the height of his *b.*
Jer. 31:17 chil. again to their *b.*
Joel 3:6 remove them from *b.*
Amos 1:13 enlarge their *b.*
6:2 their *b.* great. than your *b.*
Ob. 7 even to the *b.*
Zep. 2:8 magnified ag. their *b.*
Mal. 1:4 the *b.* of wickedness
5 L. will be mag. fr. *b.* of Isr.
Mark 6:56 if it were but *b.*
Luke 8:44 touched *b.* of garment

See EAST, SOUTH.

BORDER, Verb.

Zec. 9:2 H. shall *b.* thereby

BORDERS.

Ex. 16:35 come to *b.* Canaan
34:24 I will enlarge thy *b.*
2 *K.* 19:23 enter lodg. of his *b.*
Ps. 74:17 set the *b.* of the earth
147:14 maketh peace in thy *b.*
Cant. 1:11 will make *b.* of gold
Is. 54:12 *b.* of pleasant stones
Jer. 15:13 thy sins in all thy *b.*
Ezek. 45:1 be holy in all the *b.*
Mic. 5:6 treadeth within our *b.*
Mat. 4:13 in the *b.* of Zebulun
23:5 enlarge *b.* of their garments

BORE.

Ex. 21:6 master shall *b.* his ear
Job 41:2 *b.* his jaw with thorn?

BORN, *for brought forth.*

Gen. 17:17 *b.* him 100 yrs. old, 21:5
Ex. 1:22 every son *b.* into river
Lev. 19:34 as one *b.* among
Num. 15:29 one law for him *b.*
Jos. 8:33 the stranger as he *b.*
Jud. 13:8 child that shall be *b.*
2 *Sam.* 12:14 the child *b.* shall die

---

1 *K.* 13:2 a child shall be *b.* to
the house of David
1 *Chr.* 22:9 son shall be *b.* to thee
Job 3:3 day perish wh. I was *b.*
5:7 yet man is *b.* to trouble
11:12 *b.* like a wild ass's colt
15:7 first man that was *b. ?*
38:21 bec. thou wast then *b. ?*
Ps. 22:31 people that shall be *b.*
58:3 as soon as they be *b.*
78:6 children that should be *b.*
87:4 *b.* there, 6 ; 5 that man *b.*
Prov. 17:17 a brother is *b.*
Ec. 3:2 a time to be *b.*
4:14 *b.* in his kingdom
Is. 9:6 unto us a child is *b.*
66:8 shall a nat. be *b.* at once?
Jer. 16:3 con. sons and daugh. *b.*
20:14 cursed be day I was *b.*
22:26 where not *b.* shall ye die
Ezek. 16:4 the day thou wast *b.*
5 loath. of thy person in day *b.*
Mat. 2:2 is *b.* king of the Jews
4 where Christ should be *b.*
19:12 some eunuchs were so *b.*
26:24 good if not *b. Mark* 14:21
Luke 1:35 thing that shall be *b.*
2:11 to you is *b.* this day
John 3:4 be *b.* when he is old ?
5 except a man be *b.* of water
6 *b.* of flesh is flesh, that *b.*
8 so is every one *b.* of the Sp.
8:41 we be not *b.* of fornication
9:2 did sin, that he was *b.* blind
34 wast altogether *b.* in sins
16:21 for joy that a man is *b.*
18:37 to this end was I *b.*
Acts 2:8 wherein we were *b.*
7:20 which time Moses was *b.*
22:3 *b.* in T. ; 28 I was free *b.*
Rom. 9:11 chil. being not yet *b.*
1 *Cor.* 15:8 *b.* out of due time
Gal. 4:23 *b.* after the flesh, 29
Heb. 11:23 by faith M. when *b.*
1 *Pet.* 2:2 as new *b.* babes desire
1 *John* 2:29 righte. is *b.* of him
Rev. 12:4 dev. child as soon as *b.*

BORN again.

John 3:3 except a man be *b. a.* 5
7 ye must be *b. again*
1 *Pet.* 1:23 *b. a.* not of corruptible

See FIRST-BORN, WITNESS.

BORN of God.

John 1:13 *b.* n. of blood, but *of G.*
1 *John* 3:9 *b. of God* not com. sin

1 *John* 4:7 one that lov. *b. of G.*
5:1 Jesus is Christ is *b. of God*
4 whatsoever is *b. of God*
18 whosoever is *b. of God*

BORN in the house.

Gen. 15:3 *b. in my h.* is my heir
Ec. 2:7 had serv. *b. in my h.*

BORN in the land.

Ex. 12:48 stran. as one *b. in l.*
Num. 9:14 one ordin. for *b. in l.*

BORN of a woman, *or* **women.**

Job 14:1 man *b. of a w.*
15:14 *b. of a w.* that he
25:4 that is *b. of a w. ?*
Mat. 11:11 are *b. of w. Luke* 7:28

BORNE, *brought forth.*

Gen. 21:7 *b.* him son in old age
29:34 I have *b.* three sons
30:20 because I have *b.* six sons
1 *Sam.* 2:5 barren hath *b.* seven
4:20 thou hast *b.* a son
Jer. 15:9 *b.* seven languisheth
10 that thou hast *b.* me
Ezek. 16:20 thy sons *b.* to me

BORNE, *carried.*

Is. 46:3 *b.* by me from the belly
66:12 be *b.* upon her sides
Jer. 10:5 they must be *b.* because
Amos 5:26 have *b.* tab. of Moloch
Mark 2:3 one sick of palsy was *b.*

John 20:15 *b.* him hence tell me
Acts 21:35 was *b.* of the soldiers
1 *Cor.* 15:49 *b.* image of the e.

BORNE, *endured.*
Job 34:31 I have *b.* chastisement
Ps. 55:12 then I could have *b.*
69:7 thy sake I have *b.* reproach
Is. 53:4 surely he hath *b.* griefs
Lam. 3:28 hath *b.* it upon him
5:7 we have *b.* their iniquities
Ezek. 16:58 hast *b.* thy lewd.
32:24 *b.* shame, 36:6 ; 39:26
Mat. 20:12 *b.* burden and heat
23:4 griev. to be *b.* *Luke* 11:46
Rev. 2:3 hast *b.* and hast patience

BORROW.
Ex. 3:22 ev. wom. shall *b.* 11:2
22:14 if a man *b.* aught
Deut. 15:6 shalt not *b.* 28:12
2 *K.* 4:3 E. said, Go *b.* vessels
Mat. 5:42 him that would *b.*

BORROWED.
Ex. 12:35 *b.* of Egyptians
2 *K.* 6:5 master, for it was *b.*

BORROWER.
Prov. 22:7 *b.* is servant to lender
Is. 24:2 with lender, so with *b.*

BORROWETH.
Ps. 37:21 *b.* and payeth not

BOSOM.
Gen. 16:5 my maid into thy *b.*
Ex. 4:6 put hand into thy *b.* 7
Num. 11:12 carry th. in thy *b.*
Ruth 4:16 Naomi laid it in her *b.*
2 *Sam.* 12:3 and lay in his *b.*
8 master's wives into thy *b.*
1 *K.* 1:2 let her lie in thy *b.*
3:20 laid it in her *b.* and laid her dead child in my *b.*
17:19 E. took him out of her *b.*
Job 31:33 hiding iniq. in my *b.*
Ps. 35:13 returned to my *b.*
74:11 thy right hand out of *b.*
79:12 sevenfold into their *b.*
89:50 I do bear in my *b.*
129:7 bindeth sheaves, his *b.*
Prov. 5:20 emb. *b.* of stranger?
6:27 man take fire in his *b.* ?
17:23 a gift out of the *b.*
19:24 his hand in *b.* 26:15
21:14 a reward in the *b.*
Ec. 7:9 resteth in *b.* of fools
Is. 40:11 the lambs in his *b.*
65:6 recompense into their *b.*
7 former work into their *b.*
Jer. 32:18 iniq. of fathers into *b.*
Lam. 2:12 soul into mother's *b.*
Mic. 7:5 lieth in thy *b.*
Luke 6:38 good m. into your *b.*
16:22 by angel's into Ab.'s *b.*
23 Abrah. and Laz. in his *b.*
John 1:18 the *b.* of the Father
13:23 leaning on Jesus' *b.*

BOSSES.
Job 15:26 thick *b.* of his bucklers

BOTCH.
Deut. 28:27 smite with the *b.* 35

BOTTLE.
Gen. 21:14 *b.* of water gave it H.
15 w. spent in *b.* ; 19 filled *b.*
Jud. 4:19 opened a *b.* of milk
1 *Sam.* 1:24 H. took *b.* of wine
10:3 another carrying *b.* of w.

1 *Sam.* 16:20 Jesse took a *b.* of w.
Ps. 56:8 my tears into thy *b.*
119:83 like a *b.* in the smoke
Jer. 13:12 every *b.* filled with w.
19:1 a potter's *b.* ; 10 break *b.*
Hab. 2:15 puttest thy *b.* to him

BOTTLES.
Jos. 9:4 Gibeonites took wine *b.*
13 these *b.* of wine were new
Job 32:19 to burst like new *b.*
38:37 can stay *b.* of heaven?

Hos. 7:5 sick with *b.* of wine
Mat. 9:17 new wine into old *b.*
else *b.* break, *Mark* 2:22 ;
Luke 5:37, 38

BOTTOM.
Ex. 15:5 they sank into the *b.*
Job 36:30 covereth *b.* of the sea
Cant. 3:10 made the *b.* of gold
Dan. 6:24 they came at *b.*
Amos 9:3 from my sight in *b.*
Jon. 2:6 to *b.* of the mount.
Zec. 1:8 myrtle-trees in *b.*
Mat. 27:51 veil rent from top to *b.*
Mark 15:38

BOTTOMLESS.
Rev. 9:1 to him key of the *b.* pit
2 he opened *b.* pit, arose smoke
11 had a king, angel of *b.* pit
11:7 that ascend. out of *b.* pit
17:8 ascend out of the *b.* pit
20:1 an angel hav. key of *b.* pit
3 cast him into the *b.* pit

BOUGH.
Gen. 49:22 Joseph is fruitful *b.*
Jud. 9:48 Abim. cut down a *b.*
49 cut down every man his *b.*
Is. 10:33 Lord shall lop *b.*
17:6 in top of uppermost *b.*
9 cities be as a forsaken *b.*

BOUGHS.
Lev. 23:40 *b.* of goodly trees, *b.* of
Deut. 24:20 go over the *b.*
2 *Sam.* 18:9 mule went under *b.*
Job 14:9 brought forth *b.*
Ps. 80:10 *b.* like goodly cedars
11 sent out her *b.* to the sea
Cant. 7:8 take hold of the *b.*
Is. 27:11 when the *b.* are with.
Ezek. 17:23 it shall bring forth *b.*
31:3 his top among thick *b.* 14
6 nests in his *b.* *Dan.* 4:12

BOUGHT.
Gen. 33:19 J. *b.* field, *Jos.* 24:32
39:1 Potiphar *b.* Joseph
47:20 Joseph *b.* all land of E. 23
49:30 Abr. *b.* 50:13 ; *Acts* 7:16
Lev. 27:24 of whom it was *b.*
Deut. 32:6 father that *b.* thee?
2 *Sam.* 12:3 ewe-lamb he had *b.*
24:24 David *b.* threshing-floor
1 *K.* 16:24 O. *b.* hill Samaria
Neh. 5:16 nor *b.* we any land
Jer. 32:9 I *b.* field of Hanameel
Hos. 3:2 so I *b.* her for fifteen p.
Mat. 13:46 sold all. *b.* that field
21:12 sold and *b.* in the temple, *Mark* 11:15 ; *Luke* 19:45
27:7 *b.* with them potter's field
Mark 15:46 Joseph *b.* fine linen
16:1 *b.* sweet spices to anoint
Luke 14:18 have *b.* a piece of gro.
19 I have *b.* five yoke of oxen
17:28 drank, they *b.* and sold
1 *Cor.* 6:20 ye are *b.* 7:23
2 *Pet.* 2:1 deny L. that *b.* them

BOUND, *actively.*
Gen. 22:9 *b.* Isaac his son
42:24 took Simeon, and *b.* him
Num. 30:4 had *b.* her soul, 11
Jud. 15:13 *b.* Samson with new
16:8 withs ; 12 ropes ; 21 fetters
2 *K.* 5:23 he *b.* two talents
17:4 he shut up Hoshea and *b.*
25:7 Zedekiah with fetters
2 *Chr.* 33:11 b. Manasseh
36:6 *b.* Jehoiakim
Prov. 30:4 *b.* waters in a garm.
Hos. 7:15 I have *b.* their arms
Mat. 14:3 H. *b.* John, *Mark* 6:17
27:2 *b.* J. *Mark* 15:1 ; *John* 18:12
Luke 13:16 daughter S. hath *b.*
Acts 21:11 Agabus *b.* his hands
22:25 as they *b.* Paul, 29
23:12 *b.* them under, 14:21
Rev. 20:2 *b.* S. a thousand years

BOUND, *passively.*
Gen. 39:20 king's pris. are *b.*
42:19 one of your brethren be *b.*
Jud. 16:6 mightest be *b.* 10, 13
1 *Sam.* 25:29 soul of my lord be *b.*
2 *Sam.* 3:34 thy hands were not *b.*
Job 36:8 if they be *b.* in fetters
Ps. 107:10 being *b.* in affliction
Prov. 22:15 foolish. is *b.* in heart
Is. 22:3 *b.* by archers, all are *b.*
61:1 opening of pris. to them *b.*
Lam. 1:14 yoke of my tran. is *b.*
Dan. 3:21 in their coats
24 three men *b.* into furnace?
Mat. 16:19 in heaven, 18:18
Mark 15:7 Barabbas which lay *b.*
John 11:44 *b.* h. and foot, face *b.*
18:24 Annas had sent him *b.*
Acts 9:2 bring them *b.* 21 ; 22:5
12:6 Peter *b.* ; 24:27 left Paul *b.*
20:22 I go *b.* in the Spirit to J.
21:13 I am ready not to be *b.*
Rom. 7:2 is *b.* by the law to her husband, 1 *Cor.* 7:39
1 *Cor.* 7:27 *b.* unto a wife
2 *Thes.* 1:3 *b.* to thank God, 2:13
2 *Tim.* 2:9 word of God is not *b.*
Heb. 13:3 in bonds, as *b.* with
Rev. 9:14 loose the angels *b.*

BOUND with chains.
Ps. 68:6 G. bring. out th. *b. w. c.*
Jer. 39:7 b. Zed. *with c.* 52:11
40:1 Jeremiah *b. with c.*
Nah. 3:10 her great men *b. w. c.*
Mark 5:4 had been often *b. w. c.*
Luke 8:29 was kept *b. with c.*
Acts 21:33 com. P. to be *b. w. 2 c*
28:20 for hope of Israel I am *b.*

BOUND up.
Gen. 44:30 life is *b. up* in lad's
Is. 1:6 have not been *b. up*
Jer. 30:13 none to plead, that thou mayest be *b. up*
Ezek. 30:21 be *b. up* to be healed
34:4 have ye *b. up* that broken
Hos. 4:19 wind hath *b.* her *up*
13:12 iniq. of Ephraim is *b. up*
Luke 10:34 he *b. up* his wounds

BOUND, Substantive.
Gen. 49:26 *b.* of the everlasting
Job 38:20 take it to the *b.* there.
Ps. 104:9 the waters set a *b.*
Jer. 5:22 sand for *b.* of the sea
Hos. 5:10 them that remove *b.*

BOUNDS.
Ex. 19:23 about the mount
23:31 thy *b.* from the Red sea
Deut. 32:8 set of the people
Job 14:5 *b.* that he cannot pass
26:10 comp. the waters with *b.*
Is. 10:13 rem. *b.* of the people
Acts 17:26 hast determined the *b.*

BOUNTY.
2 *Cor.* 9:5 make up before h.y. *b.*

BOUNTIFUL.
Prov. 22:9 hath a *b.* eye
Is. 32:5 churl be said to be *b.*

BOUNTIFULNESS.
2 *Cor.* 9:11 enriched to all *b.*

BOUNTIFULLY.
Ps. 13:6 hath dealt *b.* with me
116:7 Lord hath dealt *b.*
119:17 deal *b.* with thy servant
142:7 shalt deal *b.* with me
2 *Cor.* 9:6 soweth *b.* shall reap *b.*

BOW, Substantive.
Gen. 9:13 set my *b.* in the cloud
27:3 take thy quiver and *b.*
48:22 I took of Amorite with *b.*
49:24 his *b.* abode in strength
Jos. 24:12 but not with thy *b.*
2 *Sam.* 1:22 *b.* of Jon. turned not

1 *K.* 22:34 a certain man drew a
  b. at a venture, 2 *Chr.* 18:33
2 *K.* 13:15 take *b.* and ar. took *b.*
Job 29:20 my *b.* was renewed
Ps. 44:6 will not trust in my *b.*
  46:9 he breaketh the *b.* cutteth
  76:3 there brake he arrows of *b.*
  78:57 aside like a deceitful *b.*
Is. 41:2 as stubble to his *b.*
Jer. 6:23 shall lay hold on *b.*
  49:35 I will break the *b.* of E.
Lam. 2:4 bent his *b.*
Ezek. 1:28 as the *b.* in the cloud
Hos. 1:5 I will break *b.* of Israel
  7 will not save them by *b.*
  2:18 I will break the *b.*
  7:16 they are like a deceitful *b.*
Amos 2:15 he that handleth *b.*
Hab. 3:9 *b.* made quite naked
Zec. 9:13 filled the *b.* with Eph.
Rev. 6:2 sat on wh. horse had *b.*

See BEND, BENT, BATTLE-BOW.

BOWS.

1 *Sam.* 2:4 the *b.* of mighty
Neh. 4:16 half of them held *b.*
Ps. 37:15 *b.* shall be broken
Is. 7:24 with *b.* shall men come
  13:18 their *b.* shall dash young
Jer. 51:56 every one of their *b.*
Ezek. 39:9 they shall burn the *b.*

BOW-SHOT.

Gen. 21:16 as it were a *b.-s.*

BOW, Verb.

Jos. 23:7 nor *b.* yourselves to
  their gods, 2 *K.* 17:35
2 *K.* 5:18 I *b.* in house of Rim.
Job 39:3 *b.* themselves
Ps. 22:29 to the dust shall *b.*
  72:9 in wilder. sh. *b.* before him
  144:5 *b.* thy heavens, O Lord
Prov. 5:1 *b.* thine ear
  14:19 evil *b.* before the good
Ec. 12:3 strong men shall *b.*
Mic. 6:6 *b.* myself bef. high G. ?
Hab. 3:6 perpetual hills did *b.*
Eph. 3:14 *b.* my knees to the F.

BOW down.

Gen. 27:29 nations *b. down*
  37:10 mother, brethren *b. down*
  49:8 father's children shall *b. d.*
Ex. 11:8 serv. shall *b. d.* to me
  20:5 not *b. d. Deut.* 5:9
  23:24 shalt not *b. d.* to their g.
Lev. 26:1 any image to *b. d.* to it
Jud. 2:19 other gods to *b. d.*
2 *K.* 5:18 *b. d.* in house of Rim.
  19:16 L. *b. d.* thine ear, *Ps.* 86:1
Job 31:10 others *b. d.* upon her
Ps. 31:2 *b. d.* th. ear, *Prov.* 22:17
  95:6 worship and *b. down*
Is. 10:4 without me *b. down*
  46:2 they stoop, they *b. down*
  49:23 kings and queens sh. *b. d.*
  51:23 *b. d.* that we may go over
  58:5 to *b. d.* head as a bulrush ?
  60:14 despised thee shall *b. d.*
  65:12 all *b. d.* to slaughter
Rom. 11:10 *b. d.* their back

BOW knee.

Gen. 41:43 before him *b.* the *k.*
Is. 45:23 *k.* shall *b. Rom.* 14:11
Eph. 3:14 I *b.* my knee to F.
Phil. 2:10 every *knee* shall *b.*

BOWED.

Gen. 43:26 Jos. brethren *b.*
  49:15 Issachar *b.* shoulder
Jos. 23:16 served other gods, and
  b. to them, *Jud.* 2:12, 17
Jud. 5:27 at her feet he *b.*
2 *Sam.* 19:14 David *b.*
  22:10 he *b.* heavens, *Ps.* 18:9
1 *K.* 19:18 not *b.* to B. *Rom.* 11:4
2 *K.* 2:15 prophets *b.* before E.
2 *Chr.* 7:3 *b.* upon the pavement
  29:29 king and all present *b.*

Est. 3:5 Mordecai *b.* not
Mat. 27:29 *b.* the knee
Luke 13:11 spirit of infir. and *b.*

BOWED down.

Gen. 42:6 J. brethren *b. d.* 43:28
Jud. 7:6 rest of the people *b. d.*
Ps. 35:14 I *b. d.* heavily as one
  38:6 I am *b. d.* greatly,
  44:25 soul is *b. d.* to the dust
  57:6 my soul is *b. d.*
  145:14 rais. up all *b. d.* 146:8
Is. 2:11 haught. of men be *b. d.*
  17 lofti. of man shall be *b. d.*
  21:3 was *b. d.* at hearing of it
Luke 24:5 and *b. d.* their faces

BOWED head.

Gen. 43:28 they *b.* their *heads*
Ex. 4:31 they *b.* their *heads* and
  worship. 12:27 ; *Neh.* 8:6
  34:8 Mos. made haste and *b. h.*
Num. 22:31 Balaam *b.* his *head*
1 *Chr.* 29:20 *b.* down their *head*
2 *Chr.* 20:18 Jehosh. *b.* his *head*
  29:30 praises and *b.* their *head*
John 19:30 Jesus *b.* his *head*

BOWED himself.

Gen. 18:2 A. *b. himself*, 23:7, 12
  19:1 Lot *b. him-ilf*
  33:3 Jacob *b. himself* 47:31
  48:12 Joseph *b. himself*
Jud. 16:30 S. *b. h.* with might
2 *Sam.* 24:20 A. *b. h.* 1 *Chr.* 21:21
1 *K.* 1:23 N. *b. h.* ; 47 king *b. h.*
  43 Adonijah *b. h.* to king Sol.
  2:19 Solomon *b. h.* to his mother

BOWETH.

Jud. 7:5 that *b.* on knees
Is. 2:9 m. man *b.* ; 46:1 Bel. *b.*

BOWING.

Gen. 24:52 Eliezer *b.* h. to earth
Ps. 17:11 set their eyes, *b.* down
  62:3 as a *b.* wall shall ye be
Mark 15:19 spit on him, *b.* knees

BOWELS.

Gen. 15:4 out of own *b.* thy heir
  25:23 manner of people from *b.*
  43:30 *b.* did yearn on brother
2 *Sam.* 7:12 which pro. out of *b.*
  16:11 which came forth of my *b.*
2 *Sam.* 20:10 Jo. sh. Amasa's *b.*
1 *K.* 3:26 *b.* yearned on her son
2 *Chr.* 21:15 sick. by disease of *b.*
  21:18 smote him in *b.* 19
  32:21 of his own *b.* slew him
Job 20:14 meat in his *b.* is turn.
  30:27 *b.* boiled, and rested not
Ps. 22:14 it is melted in my *b.*
  71:6 out of my mother's *b.*
  109:18 come into his *b.*
Cant. 5:4 *b.* were moved for him
Is. 16:11 *b.* sound like a harp
  48:19 the offspring of thy *b.*
  49:1 from *b.* of my mother
  63:15 sounding of thy *b.*
Jer. 4:19 my *b.* I am pained
  31:20 my *b.* are troubled
Lam. 1:20 *b.* are troubled, 2:11
Ezek. 3:3 fill thy *b.* with this roll
  7:19 their souls, nor fill their *b.*
Acts 1:18 J. burst, and all his *b.*
2 *Cor.* 6:12 strait. in your own *b.*
Phil. 1:8 in *b.* of Christ
  2:1 if there be any *b.*
Col. 3:12 put on *b.* of mercies
Phile. 7 *b.* of saints are refreshed
  12 rec. him that is my own *b.*
  20 refresh my *b.* in the Lord
1 *John* 3:17 shut. up *b.* of comp.

BOWL.

Jud. 6:38 a *b.* full of water
Ec. 12:6 or golden *b.* be broken
Zec. 4:2 candlestick with a *b.*

BOWLS.

Amos 6:6 that drink wine in *b.*

Zec. 9:15 shall be filled like *b.*
  14:20 the pots shall be like *b.*

BOWMEN.

Jer. 4:29 for the noise of the *b.*

BOX.

2 *K.* 9:1 take this *b.* of oil, 3
Mat. 26:7 alaba. *b. Mark* 14:3
Mark 14:3 brake the *b. Luke* 7:37

BOX-TREE.

Is. 41:19 set in the desert *b.-tree*
  60:13 glory of Lebanon *b.-trees*

BOY, S.

Gen. 25:27 the *b.* grew
Joel 3:3 given a *b.* for a harlot
Zec. 8:5 shall be full of *b.*

BOZRAH.

Is. 34:6 hath a sacrifice in B.
  63:1 dyed garments from B.
Jer. 48:24 judg. is come upon B.
  48:13 B. shall bec. desolation, 22
Amos 1:12 dev. the palaces of B.
Mic. 2:12 put as the sheep of B.

BRACELET, S.

Gen. 24:30 *b.* on sister's hands
  38:18 signet, *b.* and staff, 25
Ex. 35:22 brought *b. Num.* 31:50
2 *Sam.* 1:10 the *b.* on his arm
Is. 3:19 I will take away the *b.*
Ezek. 16:11 I put *b.* on thy hands

BRAKE.

Ex. 32:19 tables out of his hands
  and *b.* them, *Deut.* 9:17
Jud. 7:19 they *b.* pitchers, 20
  16:9 *b.* withs. 12 *b.* new ropes
1 *Sam.* 4:18 Eli fell, his neck *b.*
1 *K.* 19:11 a strong wind *b.* in
  pieces the rocks
2 *K.* 11:18 Baal's images *b.* they
  18:4 *b.* images, *b.* brazen serp.
  23:14 Josi. *b.* images, 2 *Chr.* 34:4
2 *Chr.* 21:17 Arabians *b.* into J.
Job 38:8 shut sea wh. it *b.* forth ?
  10 *b.* up for it my decreed place
Ps. 76:3 there *b.* he the arrows
  105:16 *b.* the whole staff of bread
  33 *b.* trees of their coast
  106:29 plague *b.* in upon them
  107:14 *b.* their bands in sunder
Jer. 28:10 yoke from Jer. *b.* it
  31:32 my covenant they *b.*
Ezek. 17:16 and covenant he *b.*
Dan. 2:1 sleep *b.* from him 34
  6:24 the lions *b.* all their bones
  7:7 fourth beast *b.* in pieces
  8:7 ram, and *b.* his two horns
Mat. 14:19 he blessed and *b.* and
  gave the loaves, 15:36 ; 26:26 ;
    Mark 6:41 ; 8:6 ; 14:22 ; *Luke*
    9:16 ; 22:19; 24:30; 1 *Cor.* 11:24
Mark 8:19 1 *b.* the five loaves
  14:3 she *b.* the box, and poured
Luke 5:6 net *b.* ; 8:29 *b.* the bands
John 19:32 soldiers *b.* legs
  33 they *b.* not his legs

BRAKE down.

2 *K.* 10:27 *b. down* image of Baal,
  2 *Chr.* 23:17
  11:18 *b. down* the house of Baal
2 *K.* 14:13 *b. down* w. of J. 2 *Chr.*
  25:23 ; 36:19 ; *Jer.* 39:8 ; 52:14
  23:7 *b. d.* houses of Sodomites
2 *Chr.* 26:6 Uzziah *b. d.* wall of G.
  34:4 *b. down* altars of Baalim

BRAKEST.

Ex. 34:1 first table *b. Deut.* 10:2
Ps. 74:13 *b.* heads of dragons, 14
Ezek. 29:7 leaned on thee, thou *b.*

BRAMBLE, S.

Jud. 9:14 said trees to the *b.*
  15 let fire come out of the *b.*
Is. 34:13 *b.* shall come up
Luke 6:44 of a *b.*-bush grapes

BRANCH.

Num. 13:23 cut a *b.*
Job 8:16 his *b.* shooteth forth
14:7 tender *b.* thereof not cease
15:32 his *b.* shall not be green
18:16 shall his *b.* be cut off
29:19 lay all night on my *b.*
Ps. 80:15 *b.* thou madest strong
Prov. 11:28 shall flour. as a *b.*
Is. 4:2 shall *b.* of the L. be beau.
9:14 Lord will cut off *b.*
11:1 a *b.* shall grow out
14:19 cast out like abomina. *b.*
17:9 cities as an uppermost *b.*
19:15 work, *b.* or rush may do
25:5 the *b.* of terrible ones low
60:21 the *b.* of my planting
Jer. 23:5 to David a righteous *b.*
33:15 cause *b.* of righteousness
Ezek. 8:17 put it. to her nose
15:2 more than any *b.* ?
17:3 took the highest *b.* 22
Dan. 11:7 a *b.* of her roots
Zec. 3:8 forth my servant the *b.*
6:12 man whose name is the *b.*
Mal. 4:1 it shall leave root nor *b.*
Mat. 24:32 *b.* yet t. *Mark* 13:28
John 15:2 every *b.* that beareth
4 as *b.* cannot bear fruit
6 he is cast forth as a *b.*

BRANCHES.

Gen. 40:12 the three *b.* are three
49:22 bough, whose *b.* run over
Lev. 23:40 *b.* of tree, *Neh.* 8:15
Job 15:30 shall dry up his *b.*
Ps. 80:11 sent out her *b.* to river
104:12 sing among the *b.*
Is. 16:8 Moab's *b.* are stretched
17:6 four or five in outmost *b.*
18:5 he shall cut down the *b.*
27:10 there lie and consume *b.*
Jer. 11:16 and *b.* of it are broken
Ezek. 17:6 spread. vine whose *b.*
19:10 fruitful and full of *b.*
14 fire out of a rod of her *b.*
31:8 not like the Assyrian's *b.*
36:8 O mount. ye shall shoot *b.*
Dan. 4:14 cut off his *b.*
Hos. 11:6 consume Ephraim's *b.*
14:6 his *b.* shall spread, and
Joel 1:7 *b.* thereof are m. white
Nah. 2:2 marred their vine *b.*
Zec. 4:12 these two olive *b.* ?
Mat. 13:32 lodge in *b.* *Luke* 13:19
21:8 cut *b.* *Mark* 11:8; *John* 12:13
Mark 4:32 shooteth *b.*
John 15:5 the vine, ye the *b.*
Rom. 11:16 if root be holy so *b.*
17 if some *b.* be broken off, 19
18 boast not against the *b.*
21 spared not the natural *b.*

BRAND, S.

Jud. 15:5 had set the *b.* on fire
Zec. 3:2 *b.* plucked out of fire?

BRANDISH.

Ezek. 32:10 when I *b.* my sword.

BRASS.

Ex. 38:29 *b.* of offer. 70 talents
Num. 21:9 serpent of *b.* when he
beheld serpent of *b.* he lived
Deut. 8:9 thou mayest dig *b.*
28:23 the heaven shall be *b.*
1 *Sam.* 17:6 greaves of *b.* on legs
2 *Sam.* 8:8 David took much *b.*
1 *Chr.* 18:8
1 *K.* 7:14 Hiram worker in *b.*
2 *K.* 25:7 Zed. with fetters of *b.*
13 *b.* to Babylon, *Jer.* 52:17
1 *Chr.* 15:19 with cymbals of *b.*
22:3 David prepared *b.* 29:7
29:2 prepared *b.* for things of *b.*
Job 6:12 or is my flesh *b.* ?
40:18 as strong pieces of *b.*
41:27 esteemeth *b.* as rotten
Ps. 107:16 broken the gates of *b.*
Is. 45:2 in pieces the gates of *b.*

60:17 for wood *b.* for *b.* gold
Ezek. 24:11 the *b.* may be hot
Dan. 2:32 his thighs were of *b.*
39 third kingdom of *b.*
7:19 the fourth beast nails of *b.*
Dan. 10:6 like in color to pol. *b.*
Mic. 4:13 will make thy hoofs *b.*
Zec. 6:1 were mountains of *b.*
Mat. 10:9 neither gold nor *b.*
1 *Cor.* 13:1 I am as sounding *b.*
Rev. 1:15 feet like fine *b.* 2:18
9:20 not worship idols of *b.*

Iron and BRASS.

Gen. 4:22 T.-cain instruc. in *b.*
Lev. 26:19 heaven iron, earth *b.*
Num. 31:22 *b. i.* may abide fire
Deut. 33:25 shall be *iron and b.*
Jos. 22:8 ret. with *b. and iron*
1 *Chr.* 22:14 *b. i.* with weight, 16
2 *Chr.* 2:7 a cun. man in *b. ir.* 14
24:12 such as wrought in *ir. b.*
Job 28:2 *iron* taken out *b.*
Is. 48:4 neck *ir.* sin. *and* brow *b.*
60:17 for *b.* gold, for *iron* silver
Jer. 6:28 they are *b. i. Ezek.* 22:18
Ezek. 22:20 gather *iron and b.*
Dan. 2:35 was *iron b.* broken, 45
4:15 with hand of *iron and b.* 23
5:4 praised gods of silver, *b. i.*

Vessels of BRASS.

Jos. 6:19 all v. *of b.* are consec.
2 *K.* 25:16 the *b.* of all these
ves. was with. w. *Jer.* 52:20
Ezek. 27:13 in v. *of b. Rev.* 18:12

BRAVERY.

Is. 3:18 will take away their *b.*

BRAWLER, S.

1 *Tim.* 3:3 bishop must be no *b.*
Tit. 3:2 to be no *b.*

BRAWLING.

Prov. 25:24 a *b.* woman, 21:19

BRAY, ED, ETH.

Job 6:5 doth the wild ass *b.*
30:7 among the bushes they *b.*
Prov. 27:22 *b.* a fool in a mortar

BRAZEN.

2 *K.* 18:4 brake the *b.* serpent
25:13 *b.* sea Chal. *Jer.* 52:17
2 *Chr.* 6:13 Sol. made a *b.* scaf.
Jer. 1:18 made thee this day *b.*
15:20 make thee a fenced *b.* wall
52:20 *b.* bulls; *Mark* 7:4 *b.* ves.
See ALTAR.

BREACH.

Gen. 38:29 midwife said, this *b.*
Lev. 24:20 *b.* for *b.* eye for eye.
Num. 14:34 my *b.* of promise
Jud. 21:15 a *b.* in the tribes
2 *Sam.* 5:20 forth as *b.* of waters
6:8 *b.* on Uzzah, 1 *Chr.* 13:11
2 *K.* 12:5 wheresoever any *b.*
1 *Chr.* 15:13 L. made a *b.* on us
Neh. 6:1 and there was no *b.*
Job 16:14 with *b.* upon *b.*
Ps. 106:23 not Moses stood in *b.*
Prov. 15:4 perverseness is a *b.*
Is. 7:6 a *b.* for us,
30:13 this iniq. shall be as a *b.*
26 in the day L. bindeth up *b.*
58:12 called the repairer of the *b.*
Jer. 14:17 is broken with a *b.*
Lam. 2:13 thy *b.* is great
Ezek. 26:10 city wherein a *b.*

BREACHES.

Jud. 5:17 Asher abode in his *b.*
1 *K.* 11:27 rep. *b.* of city of Dav.
2 *K.* 12:5 let them repair the *b.*
6 priests had not repaired the *b.*
Ps. 60:2 heal the *b.* for it shaketh
Is. 22:9 have seen *b.* of the city
Amos 4:3 shall go out at the *b.*
6:11 smite great house with *b.*
9:11 close up the *b.* thereof

BREAD.

Gen. 14:18 king of S. brought *b.*
18:5 will fetch a morsel of *b.*
21:14 Abraham took *b.* gave **H.**
25:34 then Jacob gave Esau *b.*
27:17 savory meat and *b.* to **J.**
41:54 in Egypt there was *b.*
55 cried to Pharaoh for *b.*
43:31 set on *b.* ; 45:23 *b.* for **f.**
47:15 give us *b.* ; 17 *b.* for h.
19 buy us and our land for *b.*
49:20 out of Asher his *b.* be fat
Ex. 16:4 I will rain *b.* from heav.
8 in morning *b.* to the full, 12
29 sixth day the *b.* of two days
32 may see the *b.* I fed you
23:25 he shall bless thy *b.*
40:23 he set the *b.* in order
Lev. 8:32 what remaineth of *b.*
21:6 *b.* of their G. 8, 17, 21, 22
26:26 ten women shall bake *b.*
Num. 4:7 continual *b.* be thereon
14:9 people of the land are *b.*
21:5 soul loatheth this light *b.*
Deut. 8:3 man doth not live by *b.*
only, *Mat.* 4:4; *Luke* 4:4

Deut. 23:4 met you not with *b.*
29:6 ye have not eaten *b.* nor
Jos. 9:5 *b.* was dry and mouldy
12 this cur *b.* we took hot
Jud. 7:13 a cake of *b.* tumbled
8:6 give *b.* to thy army, 15
19:5 comfort thy heart with *b.*
19 there is *b.* and wine also
Ruth 1:6 in giving them *b.*
1 *Sam.* 2:5 hired out them. for *b.*
36 crouch for a morsel of *b.*
9:7 the *b.* is spent in our vessels
21:4 hallowed *b.* ; 5 *b.* is com.
6 priest gave him hallowed *b.*
22:13 hast given him *b.* and
28:22 let me set a morsel of *b.*
2 *Sam.* 3:29 J. one that lacketh *b.*
35 taste *b.* till sun be down
6:19 to every one a cake of *b.*
1 *K.* 13:22 back and hast eaten *b.*
17:6 ravens brought *b.* and flesh
11 bring me a morsel of *b.*

2 *K.* 4:42 brought man of God *b.*
18:32 a land of *b. Is.* 36:17
Neh. 5:14 *b.* of governor
9:15 gavest them *b.* from h.
13:2 they met not Israel with *b.*
Job 15:23 wand. abroad for *b.*
22:7 withholden *b.* from hungry
27:14 not be satisfied with *b.*
28:5 out of it cometh *b.*
33:20 his life abhorreth *b.*

Ps. 37:25 his seed begging *b.*
78:20 can he give *b.* ?
80:5 with *b.* of tears
102:9 eaten ashes like *b.*
104:15 *b.* which stren. man's h.
105:40 satisfied them with *b.*
109:10 seek their *b.*
132:15 satisfy her poor with *b.*
Prov. 9:17 *b.* eaten in secret
12:9 hon. hims. and lacketh *b.*
11 land satisfied with *b.* 28:19
20:13 shalt be satisfied with *b.*
17 *b.* of deceit is sweet
22:9 he giveth of his *b.*
31:27 eateth not *b.* of idleness
Ec. 9:11 nor *b.* to wise
11:1 cast thy *b.* upon the waters
Is. 3:1 away the whole stay of *b.*
7 in my house is neither *b.* nor
21:14 with their *b.* him that
30:20 Lord give *b.* of adversity
33:16 his *b.* shall be given him
44:15 baketh *b.* on the coals, 19
51:14 nor that his *b.* should fail
55:2 that which is not *b.*
10 that it may give *b.* to eater
58:7 deal thy *b.* to hungry?
Jer. 42:14 nor have hunger of *b.*

Lam. 1:11 they seek *b.*
4:4 young children ask *b.*
5:6 Egyptians to be sat. with *b.*
9 we gat our *b.* with peril
Ezek. 4:15 prep. thy *b.* therewith
17 they may want *b.* and water
16:49 pride, fulness of *b.* and
18:7 his *b.* to the hungry, 16
44:7 strang. when ye offer my *b.*
Hos. 2:5 lovers that give me *b.*
9:4 sacrifices as *b.* of mourners
Amos 4:6 given you want of *b.*
8:11 not famine of *b.*
Hag. 2:12 his skirt do touch *b.*
Mal. 1:7 ye offer polluted *b.*
Mat. 4:3 st. be made *b. Luke* 4:3
6:11 our daily *b. Luke* 11:11
7:9 if his son ask *b.* will he give
15:26 children's *b. Mark* 7:27
33 so much *b.? Mark* 8:4
16:5 forgot. to take *b. Mark* 8:14
11 spake it not concerning *b.*
12 not beware of leaven of *b.*
26:26 Jesus took *b. Mark* 14:22
Luke 7:33 Bapt. neither eating *b.*
9:3 for your journey, neither *b.*
15:17 servants have *b.* enough
22:19 took *b.* gave thanks, 24:30
24:35 in breaking *b.*
John 6:7 two hun. pennyw. of *b.*
  32 M. gave you not that *b.*
  from h. my F. giveth true *b.*
  33 the *b.* of God is he
  34 Lord, give us this *b.*
  35 I am the *b.* of life, 48
  41 *b.* which came down, 50
  58 eateth of this *b.* shall live
13:18 eateth *b.* hath lifted
21:9 fish laid thereon and *b.*
  13 J. then taketh *b.* and giveth
Acts 2:42 con. in breaking of *b.*
  46 break. *b.* from house to ho.
20:7 disciples came to break *b.*
  11 when he had bro'ken *b.*
27:35 he took *b.* and gave tha.
1 *Cor.* 10:16 *b.* we break is it not
  17 being many are one *b.*
11:23 in wh. he was bet. took *b.*
2 *Cor.* 9:10 min. *b.* to your food
See AFFLICTION.

BREAD-CORN.
Is. 28:28 *b.-c.* is bruised because

BREAD, with eat.
Gen. 3:19 in sweat of face *e. b.*
28:20 if L. give me *b.* to *eat*
31:54 Jacob called breth. to *e. b.*
37:25 J.'s brethren sat to *e. b.*
39:6 save *b.* he *eat*
43:32 Egyptians not *e. b.* w. H.
Ex. 2:20 that he may *e. b.*
16:3 when we *eat b.* to the ful.
  15 *b.* L. ha. giv. you to *e.*
18:12 to *e.* with M.s' f-in law
34:28 *e. b.* 40 da. *Deut.* 9:9, 18
Lev. 21:22 shall *e.* the *b.* of God
26:5 ye shall *eat b.* to the full
Deut. 8:9 *eat b.* without scarce.
Ruth 2:14 meal-time come *eat b.*
2 *Sam.* 9:7 *eat b.* at my table, 10
12:21 didst rise and *eat b.*
1 *K.* 13:8 nor will I *eat b.*
  15 come home with me *eat b.*
2 *K.* 4:8 const. Elisha to *e. b.*
6:22 *eet b.* and w. they may *e.*
25:29 did *e. b.* bef. h. *Jer.* 52:33
Job 42:11 and did *eat b.* with Job
Ps. 14:4 people as they *e. b.* 53:4
41:9 *eat* of my *b.* hath lift. heel
102:4 I forgot to *eat* my *b.*
127:2 to *eat* the *b.* of sorrows
Prov. 4:17 *e. b.* of wickedness
9:5 come *eat* of my *b.* and drink
23:6 *e.* not *b.* of him hath evil
25:21 if thy en. hunger give *b.*
Ec. 9:7 go *eat* thy *b.* with joy
Is. 4:1 we will *eat* our *b.*

Jer. 5:17 they shall eat up thy *b.*
41:1 I did *eat b.* together in Mi.
Ezek. 4:13 shall *eat* defiled *b.*
  16 they shall *eat b.* by weight
12:18 *e. b.* with quaking; 19 care
24:17 and *eat* not *b.* of men, 22
44:3 prince sit in it to *eat b.*
Amos 7:12 flee into J. there *e. b.*
Ob. 7 *eat* thy *b.* have laid a w.
Mat. 15:2 w. not when they *e. b.*
Mark 3:20 not so much as *e. b.*
6:36 buy *b.* have nothing to *e.*
7:2 discip. *eat b.* with defiled, 5
Luke 14:1 to Phar.'s house to *e. b.*
  15 he shall *e.* in kingdom
John 6:5 whence shall we buy *b.*
  23 place where they did *eat b.*
  31 gave them *b.* from hea. to *e.*
  51 if any *e.* of this *b.* he shall l.
1 *Cor.* 11:26 often as ye *e.* this *b.*
  27 whosoever shall *eat* this *b.*
2 *Thes.* 3:8 we eat *b.* for naught?
  12 with quietness they *eat b.*

Leavened BREAD.
Ex. 13:3 shall no *l. b.* eaten
  7 no leav. *b. Deut.* 16:3, 4
Lev. 7:13 he shall offer *leavened b.*

Loaf, or Loaves of BREAD.
Jud. 8:5 give *l. of b.* to people
1 *Sam.* 10:3 ano. car three *l. of b.*
  4 will give thee two *l. of b.*
21:3 five *l. of b.* in my hand
Chr. 16:3 to every one *l. of b.*

No BREAD.
Gen. 47:13 *no b.* in all the land
Num. 21:5 *no b.* and our soul
1 *Sam.* 21:4 there is *no com. b.*
  6 *no b.* there but showbread
28:20 S. had eaten *no b.* all day
30:12 Egyp. had eat *no b.* 3 days
1 *K.* 13:9 eat *no b.* 17:22
2 *K.* 25:3 *no b.* for peo. *Jer.* 52:6
Jer. 38:9 there is *no more b.*
Dan. 10:3 I ate *no pleasant b.*
Mat. 16:7 because we have taken
  no b. 8; *Mark* 8:16, 17
Mark 6:8 take no scrip, no *b.*

Piece, or Pieces of BREAD.
1 *Sam.* 2:36 I may eat a *p. of b.*
Prov. 6:26 to a *piece of b.*
28:21 for a *p. of b.* that man
Jer. 37:21 Jerem. daily a *p. of b.*
Ezek. 13:19 ye pollute me for *p. b.*

SHOWBREAD. *See* SHOW.

Staff of BREAD.
Lev. 26:26 I have broken *st. b.*
Ps. 105:16 he bra'ke whole *st. of b.*
Ezek. 4:16 break *st. b.* 5:16; 14:13

Unleavened BREAD.
Ex. 12:18 eat w. *u. b. Num.* 9:11
  15 sev. days eat *unl. b.* 13:6, 7;
  23:15; 34:18; *Lev.* 23:6; *Num.*
  28:17; *Deut.* 16:3
Deut. 16:8 six days sh. eat *un. b.*
1 *Sam.* 28:24 witch of E. b. *u. b.*
Ezek. 45:21 passover of *un. b.*
Mark 14:12 first day of *un. b.*
Luke 22:7 day of *u. b. Acts* 12:3
Acts 20:6 after days of *u. b.*
1 *Cor.* 5:8 with *u. b.* of sincerity
See BASKET, FEAST.

BREADTH.
Gen. 13:7 through land in *b.* of it
Deut. 2:5 so much as a foot *b.*
Jud. 20:16 could sling at a h. *b.*
Job 37:10 *b.* of waters is strait.
38:18 perceived *b.* of the earth?
Is. 8:8 his wings shall fill the *b.*
Hab. 1:6 march through *b.* of la.
Zec. 2:2 measure J. to see the *b.*
  5:2 I see a flying roll, the *b.*
Eph. 3:18 the *b.* and length
Rev. 20:9 up on *b.* of the earth
21:16 length of city is as the *b.*

2 *Sam.* 2:32 J. came at *b.* of day
Acts 20:11 talked till *b.* of day

BREAK.
Gen. 27:40 *b.* his yoke off thy n.
Ex. 12:46 *b.* a bone, *Num.* 9:12
34:13 ye shall *b.* their images
Lev. 26:19 I will *b.* pride
Num. 24:8 Is. shall *b.* their bones
30:2 if a man vow, not *b.* word
Deut. 12:3 shall *b.* their pillars
1 *Sam.* 25:10 *b.* eve. man from m.
Ezr. 9:14 should we again *b.*
Job 13:25 wilt *b.* a leaf driven
39:15 t. wild beast may *b.* them
Ps. 2:3 let us *b.* their bands
  9 *b.* them with rod of iron
  10:15 *b.* the arm of the wicked
  58:6 *b.* their teeth, O God
  89:31 if they *b.* my statutes
141:5 which shall not *b.* my head
Cant. 2:17 until day *b.* 4:6
Is. 14:25 I will *b.* the Assyrian
28:24 *b.* the clods; 28 nor *b.* it
30:14 *b.* it as of the potters' ves.
38:13 as a lion so will he *b.* all
42:3 reed not *b. Mat.* 12:20
58:6 that ye *b.* every yoke?
Jer. 15:12 iron *b.* the north. iron
19:10 *b.* bottle, so will I *b.* 11
28:4 *b.* yoke 11 : 30:8
49:35 I will *b.* the bow of Elam
Ezek. 4:16 I will *b.* the staff of
  bread, 5:16 ; 14:13
16:38 as a woman that *b.* wed.
23:34 shalt *b.* the sherds
29:7 hold of thee thou didst *b.*
30:18 when I *b.* yokes of Egypt
  22 will *b.* Pharaoh's arms, 24
Hos. 1:5 will *b.* the bow of Israel
  2:18 I will *b.* the bow
10:11 Jacob shall *b.* his clods
Joel 2:7 and not *b.* their ranks
Amos 1:5 *b.* the bar of Damascus
Mic. 3:3 who *b.* their bones
Nah. 1:13 will I *b.* his yoke off
Zec. 11:14 *b.* the brotherhood
Mat. 5:19 *b.* one of least com.
  9:17 the bottles *b.* and the wine
Acts 20:7 came tog. to *b.* bread
21:13 mean ye to *b.* my heart?
1 *Cor.* 10:16 bread we *b.* is it not

BREAK covenant.
Lev. 26:44 I will not *b.* my cov.
Deut. 31:16 will *b.* my c.* 20
Jud. 2:1 I will never *b.* my c.
Ps. 89:34 my cov. will I not *b.*
Jer. 14:21 *b.* not thy cov. with us
33:20 if ye can *b.* my c.
Ezek. 17:15 *b.* cov. and be deliv.
Zec. 11:10 I might *b.* my cov.

BREAK down.
Ex. 23:24 quite *b. d. Deut.* 7:5,
Jud. 8:9 I will *b. down* tower
Neh. 4:3 shall *b. d.* stone wall
Ps. 74:6 *b. down* carved work
Ec. 3:3 a time to *b. d.*
Is. 5:5 I will *b. d.* wall of vine.
Jer. 31:28 over them to *b. d.*
  45:4 I have built will I *b. down*
Ezek. 13:14 so will I *b. down* w.
26:4 shall *b. down* towers of T.
Hos. 10:2 he shall *b. d.* their al.

BREAK forth.
Ex. 19:22 L. *b. f.* on them, 24
Is. 14:7 they *b. forth* into singing, 44:23 ; 49:13 ; 54:1
52:9 *b. f.* into joy ye w. places
54:3 shalt *b. f.* on the right hand
55:12 hills shall *b. f.* into sing.
58:8 light *b. f.* as the morning
Jer. 1:14 an evil shall *b. forth*
Gal. 4:27 *b. forth* that trav. not

BREAK off.
Gen. 27:40 *b.* his y. *off* the neck
Dan. 4:27 O king, *b. off* thy sins

BREAK out.
Ps. 58:6 b. *out* the great teeth
Is. 35:6 shall waters b. *out*
Hos. 4:2 they b. *out* and blood, 4
Amos 5:6 lest he b. *out* like fire

BREAK in pieces.
Job. 19:2 b. me *in pieces*
34:24 b. *in pieces* mighty men
Ps. 72:4 he shall b. *in p.* the op.
94:5 they b. *in p.* thy people
Is. 45:2 I will b. *in p.* gates of b.
Jer. 51:20 will I b. *in p.* nations
21 with thee b. *in p.* horse a. r.
22 b. *in p.* man, woman
Dan. 2:40 shall it b. *in pieces* and
bruise kingdoms, 44
7:23 shall b. *in p.* whole earth

BREAK through.
Ex. 19:21 b. *th.* to gaze, 24
2 *K.* 3:26 b. *th.* to king of Edom
Mat. 6:19 th. b. *th.* ; 20 b. not *th.*

BREAK up.
Jer. 4:3 b. *u.* yo. f.-gr. *Hos.* 10:12

BREAKER, S.
Mic. 2:13 b. is come up before
Rom. 1:31 covenant-*breakers*
2:25 if thou be a b. of the law

BREAKEST, ETH.
Gen. 32:26 let me go, for day b.
Job 9:17 he b. me with tempest
12:14 he b. it cannot be built
16:14 he b. me with breach
28:4 flood b. out from inhabit.
Ps. 29:5 b. the ced. ; 46:9 b. bow
48:7 thou b. ships of Tarshish
119:20 my soul b. for longing
Prov. 25:15 a soft tongue b. the
Ec. 10:8 b. a hedge, a serpent
Is. 59:5 crushed b. into a viper
Jer. 19:11 as one b. potter's ves.
23:29 a hammer that b. rock ?
Lam. 4:4 ask bread, no man b.
Dan. 2:40 for as much as iron b.

BREAKING.
Gen. 32:24 wrestled till b. of day
1 *Chr.* 14:11 like b. forth of wa.
Job 30:14 as a wide b. in of wat.
41:25 by reason of b. they purify
Ps. 144:14 that there be no b. in
Is. 22:5 b. down walls, of crying
30:13 whose b. cometh suddenly
14 as b. of the potter's vessel
Ezek. 16:59 oath in b. cov. 17:18
21:6 with the b. of thy loins
Hos. 13:13 place of b. forth
Luke 24:35 known in b. of bread
Acts 2:42 continued in b. of bre.
46 b. bread from house to ho.
Rom. 2:23 through b. law.

BREAST.
Job 24:9 pluck fatherless from b.
Is. 60:16 shall suck b. of kings
Lam. 4:3 monsters draw out b.
Dan. 2:32 head of gold, his b.
Luke 18:13 publican smote his b.
John 13:25 lying on J.'s b. 21:20

BREASTS.
Gen. 49:25 with blessings of b.
Job 3:12 b. that I should suck
21:24 his b. full of milk
Ps. 22:9 when on mother's b.
Prov. 5:19 let her b. satisfy thee
Cant. 1:13 all night bet. my b.
4:5 thy two b. like roes, 7:3
7:7 b. like clusters of grapes
8 thy b. as clusters of the vine
8:1 sucked the b. of my mother
8 little sister, she hath no b.
10 and my b. like towers
Is. 28:9 weaned from m. from b.
66:11 with b. of her consolations
Ezek. 16:7 thy b. are fashioned
23:3 there were their b. pressed
8 bruised the b. of her virgin.

---

34 shalt pluck off thine own b.
Hos. 2:2 adulteress from b. her b.
9:14 give them dry b.
Joel 2:16 gather those suck the b.
Nah. 2:7 doves taber. on their b.
Luke 23:48 people smote their b.
Rev. 15:6 having their b. girded

BREASTPLATE.
Ex. 25:7 sto. to be set in b. 35:9
28:4 shall make a b. 15 ; 39:8
29 the names of Israel in b.
30 put in b. the Urim, *Lev.* 8:8
Is. 59:17 he put on right. as a b.
Eph. 6:14 the b. of righteousness
1 *Thes.* 5:8 the b. of faith and lo.
Rev. 9:9 b. as it were b. of iron.
17 having b. of fire, of jacinth

BREATH.
Gen. 2:7 into his nostrils b. of l.
6:17 to destroy all flesh whose b.
7:15 wherein is b.
22 all in whose nostrils was b.
2 *Sam.* 22:16 found. discov. at b.
of his nostrils, *Ps.* 18:15
1 *K.* 17:17 no b. left in him
Job 4:9 by b. of his nostrils
9:18 not suffer me to take my b.
12:10 in whose hand is b. of all
15:30 b. of his mouth go away
17:1 my b. is corrupt, my days
19:17 b. is strange to my wife
27:3 while my b. is in me
33:4 the b. of Alm. hath given
34:14 gather his spirit and b.
37:10 by b. of God frost is given
41:21 his b. kindleth coals
Ps. 33:6 made by the b. of his
104:29 takest away b. they die
135:17 any b. in their mouths
146:4 his b. goeth forth
150:6 that hath b. praise the L.
Ec. 3:19 they have all one b
Is. 2:22 b. in his nostrils
11:4 with b. of lips slay wicked
30:8 his b. as overflowing str.
33 b. of L. like stream of brim.
33:11 your b. as fire shall devour
42:5 giveth b. to people upon it
Jer. 10:14 no b. in them, 51:17
Lam. 4:20 the b. of our nostrils
Ezek. 37:5 b. to enter you
6 with skin, and put b. in you
8 no b. in them ; 9 come, O b.
10 the b. came they lived
Dan. 5:23 in whose hand thy b.
10:17 neither is b. left in me
Hab. 2:19 b. in midst of image
Acts 17:25 giv. to all life and br.

BREATHE.
Jos. 11:11 not any left to b. 14
Ps. 27:12 such as b. out cruelty
Ezek. 37:9 O breath, b. on these

BREATHED.
Gen. 2:7 b. into nostrils b. of life
Jos. 10:40 destroyed all that b.
John 20:22 b. on them.

BREATHETH, ING.
Deut. 20:16 save alive n. that b.
Lam. 3:56 hide not ear at my b.
Acts 9:1 Saul yet b. threatenings

BRED.
Ex. 16:20 and it b. worms

BREECHES.
Ex. 28:42 make linen b. 39:28
Ezek. 44:18 shall have linen b.

BREED.
Deut. 32:14 rams of b. of Bashan

BREED, ING.
Gen. 8:17 may b. abundantly
Zep. 2:9 as Sodom b. of nettles

BRETHREN.
Gen. 13:8 no strife, for we be b.
19:7 Lot said, b. do not so wick.

24:27 Lord led me to master's b.
34:25 D. s b. took each his sword
42:6 b. bowed ; 13 twelve b. 32
45:16 b. are c. ; 49:5 b. of cruel.
Num. 27:7 posses. am. father's b.
10 no b. give it to his fath.'s b.
Deut. 25:5 if b. dwell together
Jos. 6:23 brought out Rahab b.
17:4 inheritance among the b.
Jud. 9:1 A. went to mother's b.
2 *K.* 10:13 we are b. of Ahaziah
2 *Chr.* 21:2 had b. sons of Jehos.
Ps. 133:1 b. to dwell in unity
Prov. 6:19 soweth discord am. b.
17:2 shall have part among b.
19:7 b. of the poor to hate
Mat. 4:18 Jesus saw two b. 21
19:29 hath forsaken houses, b.
24:24 indignation ag'st two b.
22:25 seven b. *Mark* 12:20
23:8 one is Master, ye are b.
Mark 10:29 no man hath left b.
for my sake, *Luke* 18:29
30 shall receive houses, b.
Luke 14:26 hate not children b.
16:28 for I have five b.
21:16 ye shall be betrayed by b.
John 21:23 went among the b.

Acts 3:17 b. I wot through ignor.
6:3 b. look out seven men
7:26 sirs, ye are b. ; 9:30 b. knew
10:23 b. from Joppa accom. him
11:12 six b. accompanied me
29 to send relief to the b.
12:17 show these things to b.
14:2 evil affected against the b.
15:1 men from Judea taught b.
3 caused great joy to all the b.
22 and Silas chief among the b.
23 and b. send greeting to the
b. of the Gentiles in Antioch
32 exhorted the b. 1 *Thes.* 5:14
33 let go in peace from b.

Acts 15:40 re. by b. to grace of G.
16:2 Tim. well reported of by b.
40 had seen b. they comfort.
17:6 drew Jason and certain b.
10 b. im. sent away Paul, 14
18:18 Paul took leave of the b.
27 b. wrote to receive Apollos
20:32 b. I commend you to God
21:7 Ptolemais, saluted the b.
16 to Jerus. b received us
22:5 I received letters to the b.
23:5 I wist not, b. he was h.-pri.
28:14 where we found b.
15 b. heard of us
21 any of the b. spake harm

Rom. 1:13 not have you ignor. b.
11:25 ; 1 *Cor.* 10:1 ; 12:1 ; 1 *Thes.*
4:13
7:1 know ye not, b. law hath
8:12 b. we are debtors
29 first-born among many b.
10:1 b. my prayer to God for b.
12:1 b. by the mercies of God,
15:30 ; 16:17 ; 1 *Cor.* 1:10 ;
16:15 ; *Gal.* 4:12 ; *Heb.* 13:22

1 *Cor.* 1:26 see your calling, b.
2:1 I, b. when I came to you
3:1 I, b. could not speak to you
4:6 these things, b.
7:29 b. the time is short, 15:50
8:12 ye sin so against the b.
9:5 b. of the Lord and Cephas
11:2 b. that ye remember me
14:26 b. when ye come together
15:6 he was seen of above 500 b.
58 b. be steadfast, *Jam.* 2:5
16:11 I look for him with b.
20 the b. greet you, *Phil.* 4:21
2 *Cor.* 9:3 I sent b. lest our boast.
5 necessary to exhort the b.
11:9 b. from Macedonia supplied
26 been in perils among false b.
13:11 finally, b. farewell

Gal. 1:2 *b.* with me to churches
2:4 because of false *b.* brought
Eph. 6:23 peace be to the *b.* and
Phil. 1:14 *b.* waxing confident
Col. 1:2 to faithful *b.* in Christ
1 *Thes.* 4:1 we beseech you *b.* 10;
5:12; 2 *Thes.* 2:1
10 to all *b.* in Macedonia
5:15 *b.* pray for us, 2 *Thes.* 3:1
26 greet *b.* with a holy kiss
27 this epistle be read to *b.*
1 *Tim.* 4:6 put the *b.* in remem.
5:1 entreat younger men as *b.*
6:2 because they are *b.*
Heb. 2:11 not ash. to call them *b.*
3:1 holy *b.* consider the apostle
1 *Pet.* 1:22 unfeigned love of *b.*
3:8 love as *b.* be pitiful
1 *John* 3:14 because we love *b.*
16 to lay down our lives for *b.*
3 *John* 3 rej. when *b.* tes. of tru.
5 whatso. thou doest to the *b.*
10 neit. doth he receive the *b.*

His BRETHREN.

Gen. 9:25 servant of serv. to *h. b.*
16:12 he shall dwell in presence
of *his b.* 25:18
27:37 *his b.* to him for servants
37:5 a dream and told it to *his b.*
11 *his b.* envied him, his father
38:11 lest he die also as *his b.*
47:12 Joseph nourished *his b.*
49:26 sep. from *b. Deut.* 33:16
Ex. 2:11 smiting one of *his b.*
Num. 25:6 to *h. b.* a Midian. w.
27:9 give his inheritance to *h. b.*
Deut. 10:9 L. no part with *his b.*
17:20 not lifted above *his b.*
20:8 lest *his b.* heart faint as
24:7 stealing any of *his b.*
33:9 nor did he acknow. *his b.*
24 let A. be acceptable to *his b.*
Jud. 9:5 Abimelech slew *his b.*
11:3 Jephthah fled from *his b.*
Ruth 4:10 not cut off from *b.*
1 *Sam.* 16:13 anointed in m. of
22:1 *his b.* and father heard it
2 *K.* 9:2 rise up from among *h. b.*
1 *Chr.* 4:9 J. more hon. than *h. b.*
5:2 Judah prevailed above *his b.*
7:22 Ephraim mourned *his b.*
25:9 *his b.* and sons twelve
2 *Chr.* 21:4 Jehor. slew all *his b.*
Est. 10:3 Mord. accepted of *his b.*
Hos. 13:15 fruitful among *his b.*
Mic. 5:3 rem. of *h. b.* return to I.
Mat. 12:46 *his b.* stood without,
Mark 3:31; *Luke* 8:19
John 7:5 *his b.* believe in him
Acts 7:13 was made known to *h.b.*
23 into M.'s heart to visit *h. b.*
25 supposed *his b.* understood
1 *Cor.* 6:5 judge between *his b.*
Heb. 2:17 beh. to. be like to *his b.*

Men and BRETHREN.

Acts 1:16 *m. b.* this scripture
2:29 *m. b.* let me fr. speak
37 *m. and b.* what shall we do ?
7:2 *m. b.* and fathers, hearken
13:15 *m. and b.* if ye have any
26 *m. b.* children of stock of A.
38 *m. and b.* through this man
15:7 *m. and b.* God made choice
13 James answered, *m. and b.*
22:1 *m. and b.* and fathers
23:1 *m. b.* I have lived in all g.
6 *men and b.* I am a Pharisee
28:17 *m. and b.* though I have
committed nothing

My BRETHREN.

Gen. 29:4 *my b.* whence be ye ?
37:16 I seek *my b.* tell me
46:31 *my b.* are come, 47:1
Ex. 4:18 let me return to *my b.*
Jos. 2:13 will save alive *my b.*
Jud. 8:19 they were *my b.*
19:23 *my b.* do not so wickedly

1 *Sam.* 20:29 let me see *my b.*
30:23 ye shall not do so, *my b.*
2 *Sam.* 19:12 ye are *my b.*
1 *Chr.* 28:2 Hear me, *my b.*
Neh. 4:23 *my b.* put off clothes
Job 6:15 *my b.* have dealt deceit.
19:13 put *my b.* far from me
Ps. 22:22 to *my b. Heb.* 2:12
69:8 I am a stranger to *my b.*
122:8 for *my b.* sake, I will say
Mat. 12:48 are *my b. Mark* 3:33
49 m. and *my b. Mark* 3:34
25:40 to least of these *my b.*
28:10 tell *my b.* go into Galilee
Luke 8:21 *my b.* are which hear
John 20:17 *my b.* and say
Rom. 9:3 ac. from C. for *my b.*
Jam. 5:10 take *my b.* the prop.

Our BRETHREN.

Num. 20:3 when *our b.* died
1 *Chr.* 13:2 let us send to *our b.*
Neh. 5:5 as flesh of *our b.*
8 have redeemed *our b.* the J.
Acts 15:36 *our b.* in every city
2 *Cor.* 8:23 *our b.* be inquired of
Rev. 10:12 accuser of *our b.*

Their BRETHREN.

Deut. 18:18 a prophet from *th. b.*
Jud. 21:22 *th. b.* come to comp.
2 *Sam.* 2:26 from following *th. b.*
1 *Chr.* 12:32 *th. b.* at their com.
2 *Chr.* 28:15 brought them to *th. b.*
Neh. 13:13 to distribute to *th. b.*
Job 42:15 inheritance am. *th. b.*
Jer. 41:8 sl. them not am. *th. b.*
Heb. 7:5 people that is of *their b.*
Rev. 6:11 *th. b.* should be killed

Thy BRETHREN.

Gen. 27:29 be lord over *thy b.*
37:10 I and *thy b.* come to bow
13 do not *thy b.* feed the flock ?
14 whet. it be well with *thy b.*
48:22 one portion above *thy b.*
49:8 whom *thy b.* shall praise
Deut. 15:7 a poor man of *thy b.*
17:15 from among *t. b.* set king
18:15 raise up a proph. of *thy b.*
24:14 not oppress poor of *thy b.*
Jos. 2:18 bring *thy b.* home
1 *Sam.* 17:17 to camp to *thy b.*
2 *Sam.* 15:20 take back *thy b.*
2 *Chr.* 21:13 hast slain *thy b.* better than thyself
Jer. 12:6 *thy b.* have dealt treac.
Ezek. 11:15 *thy b.* even *thy b.*
Mat. 12:47 mother and *thy b.* st.
with. *Mark* 3:32; *Luke* 8:20
Luke 14:12 call not *thy b.*
22:32 strengthen *thy b.*
Rev. 19:10 I am of *thy b.* 22:9

Your BRETHREN.

Gen. 42:33 leave one of *your b.*
Lev. 10:4 carry *y. b.* from sanct.
6 let *your b.* bewail the burn.
25:46 *your b.* ye shall not rule
Num. 32:6 *your b.* go to war
Deut. 1:16 causes between *y. b.*
3:20 rest to *your b. Jos.* 1:15
Jos. 22:4 given rest to *your b.*
8 divide the spoil with *your b.*
1 *K.* 12:24 not fi. *y. b.* 2 *Chr.* 11:4
2 *Chr.* 19:10 *your b.* and so wrath
come upon you and *your b.*
28:11 deliver captives of *your b.*
30:7 be not like *y. b.* which tres.
9 if ye turn, *y. b.* shall find
Neh. 4:14 fight for *your b.* sons
5:8 will you even sell *your b.*
Is. 66:5 *your b.* that hated you
20 *your b.* for an offering to L.
Jer. 7:15 have cast out all *y. b.*
Hos. 2:1 say to *your b.* Ammi
Mat. 5:47 if ye salute *your b.*

Acts 3:22 proph. of *your b.* 7:37
1 *Cor.* 6:8 defraud that *your b.*
1 *Pet.* 5:9 same afflic. in *your b.*

BRIBE, S.

1 *Sam.* 8:3 Samuel's sons took *b.*
12:3 hand have I received any *b.*
Ps. 26:10 right hand full of *b.*
Is. 33:15 hands from holding *b.*
Amos 5:12 they take a *b.* and

BRIBERY.

Job 15:34 consume taber. of *b.*

BRICK, S.

Gen. 11:3 make *b.* had *b.* for st
Ex. 1:14 their lives bitter in *b.*
5:7 give straw to make *b.* 16
8 tale of *b.* lay on them
18 yet deliver the tale of *b.* 19
Is. 9:10 the *b.* are fallen down
65:3 incense on altars of *b.*

BRICKKILN.

2 *Sam.* 12:31 make pass thro' *b.*
Jer. 43:9 hide stones in clay in *b.*
Nah. 3:14 make strong the *b.*

BRIDE.

Is. 49:18 bind them, as a *b.* doth
61:10 as a *b.* adorn. with jewels
62:5 bridegroom rejoic. over *b.*
Jer. 2:32 can a *b.* forget ?
7:34 voice of the *b.* 16:9 ; 25:10
33:11 shall be heard voice of *b.*
Joel 2:16 b. go out of her closet
John 3:29 he that hath the *b.* is
Rev. 18:23 voice of *b.* heard
21:2 b. adorned for her husband
9 show the *b.* the Lamb's wife
22:17 Sp. and the *b.* say, Come

BRIDECHAMBER.

Mat. 9:15 can children *b.* mourn
Mark 2:19 child. of *b. f. Luke* 5:34

BRIDEGROOM.

Ps. 19:5 as a *b.* coming out
Is. 61:10 as a *b.* decketh himself
62:5 as *b.* rejoiceth over bride
Mat. 9:15 while the *b.* is with
them, *Mark* 2:19 ; *Luke* 5:34
25:1 ten virgins to meet the *b.*
5 *b.* tarried ; 6 *b.* cometh, 10
John 2:9 governor called the *b.*
3:29 friend of the *b.* rejoiceth
greatly because of the *b.* voi.

See **BRIDE.**

BRIDLE.

2 *K.* 19:28 *b.* in thy lips, *Is.* 37:29
Job 30:11 have let loose the *b.*
41:13 to him with his double *b.*
Ps. 32:9 must be held with the *b.*
39:1 keep my mouth with a *b.*
Prov. 26:3 a *b.* for the ass
Is. 30:28 a *b.* in jaws of people
Jam. 1:26 and *b.* not his tongue
3:2 able also to *b.* whole body
Rev. 14:20 blood to the horse *b.*

BRIEFLY.

Rom. 13:9 it is *b.* comprehended
1 *Pet.* 5:12 by Sylv. I have writ. *b.*

BRIER.

Is. 55:13 instead of the *b.*
Ezek. 28:24 no more a pricking *b.*
Mic. 7:4 best of them is as a *b.*

BRIERS.

Jud. 8:7 tear your flesh with *b.*
16 he took the elders and *b.*
Is. 5:6 there shall come up *b.*
7:23 shall even be for *b.* and
24 shall become *b.* and thorns
25 come thither the fear of *b.*
9:18 wicked. shall devour the *b.*
10:17 devour his *b.* in one day
27:4 set *b.* against me in battle ?
32:13 on land shall come up *b.*
Ezek. 2:6 though *b.* be with thee
Heb. 6:8 which beareth *b.* is rej.

BRIGANDINE.

Jer. 46:4 and put on the *b.*
51:3 lifteth up himself in his *b.*

BRIGHT.

Job 37:11 scattereth his *b.* cloud
21 see not *b.* light in the clouds

Cant. 5:14 his belly is as *b.* ivory
Jer. 51:11 make *b.* the arrows
Ezek. 1:13 fire was *b.* and out
21:15 the sword is made *b.*
21 made his arrows *b.*
27:19 *b.* iron in thy market
32:8 *b.* lights I will make dark
Nah. 3:3 lifteth up the *b.* sword
Zec. 10:1 make *b.* clouds
Mat. 17:5 a *b.* cloud overshad.
Luke 11:36 *b.* shining of a candle
Acts 10:30 stood in *b.* clothing
Rev. 22:16 *b.* and morning star

BRIGHTNESS.
2 *Sam.* 22:13 thro' *b.* before him
were coals kindled, *Ps.* 18:12

Job 31:26 moon walking in *b.*
Is. 59:9 we wait for *b.* but walk
60:3 kings to the *b.* of thy rising
19 for *b.* the moon give light
62:1 righteousness go forth as *b.*
Ezek. 1:4 and *b.* was about it, 27
28 so appearance of the *b.* 8:2
10:4 court full of the *b.* of glory
28:7 strangers shall defile thy *b.*
17 hast corrupted by thy *b.*
Dan. 2:31 image, *b.* was excell.
4:36 my *b.* returned unto me
12:3 shine as *b.* of firmament
Amos 5.20 day of L. no *b.* in it
Hab. 3:4 his *b.* was as the light
Acts 26:13 above *b.* of the sun
2 *Thes.* 2:8 the *b.* of his coming
Heb. 1:3 being the *b.* of his glory

BRIM.
Jos. 3:15 dipped in *b.* of water
John 2:7 filled them to the *b.*

BRIMSTONE.
Gen. 19:24 on G. *b. Luke* 17:29
Deut. 29:23 the whole land is *b.*
Job 18:15 *b.* scattered on his hab.
Ps. 11:6 on the wicked snares,
fire and *b. Ezek.* 38:22
Is. 30:33 like a stream of *b.*
34:9 dust thereof into *b.*
Rev. 9:17 out of their mouths *b.*
18 third part killed by the *b.*
14:10 shall be tormented with *b.*
19:20 burning with *b.* 20:10
21:8 part in the lake which
burneth with fire and *b.*

BRING.
Gen. 6:17 *b.* a flood on the earth
19 two of every sort *b.* into ark
9:14 I *b.* a cloud over earth
18:16 Abra. did *b.* on their way
19 *b.* on A. what he hath spo.
27:12 I shall *b.* a curse on me
42:20 *b.* youngest brother, 34
37 if I *b.* him not, 43:9 ; 44:32
43:16 *b.* these men home
45:19 take wag. and *b.* your fa.
48:9 *b.* them, and I will bless
Ex. 13:5 L. shall *b.* thee, 11
18:19 mayest *b.* the causes to G.
21:6 master *b.* him to judges
23:19 first of first-fruits *b.* 34:26
23:20 send an angel to *b.* thee
35:5 a willing heart, let him *b.*
36:5 people *b.* more than enough
Num. 14:8 if L. del. in us, will *b.*
14:16 able to *b. Deut.* 9:28
24 Caleb will I *b.* into the land
20:12 ye shall not *b.* this cong.
Deut. 1:17 cause too hard, *b.*
7:1 Lord shall *b.* thee into land
21:12 shalt *b.* her to thy house
30:12 *b.* it to us that we may, 13
33:7 *b.* Judah to his people
1 *Sam.* 1:22 weaned, I will *b.* him
9:7 said Saul, what *b.* the man?
23 *b.* the portion I gave thee
20:8 why *b.* thee to thy father
2 *Sam.* 3:12 to *b.* all Israel to thee
13 except thou *b.* Michal when

14:10 saith aught, *b.* him to me
19:11 last to *b.* the king back
1 *K.* 8:32 *b.* his way on his head
13:18 *b.* him back to thy house
17:11 *b.* me a morsel of bread
20:33 he said, Go ye, *b.* him
2 *K.* 2:20 *b.* me a new cruse
6:19 *b.* you to whom ye seek
2 *Chr.* 16:29 *b.* an offering
Neh. 13:18 our God *b.* this evil
Job 6:22 did I say, *b.* unto me
10:9 wilt thou *b.* me into dust
14:4 who can *b.* a clean thing
18:14 *b.* him to king of terrors
30:23 thou wilt *b.* me to death
33:30 *b.* back his soul from pit
Ps. 43:3 *b.* me to thy holy hill
60:9 *b.* me into a str. city, 108:10
72:3 shall *b.* peace to people
94:23 *b.* on them their own
Prov. 29:8 scornful *b.* a city
Ec. 3:22 shall *b.* him to see
11:9 God will *b.* thee into judg.
12:14 *b.* every work into judg.
Cant. 8:2 *b.* thee into my m.
Is. 7:17 Lord shall *b.* on thee
14:2 *b.* them to their place
15:9 for I will *b.* more upon D.
25:12 shall *b.* to the ground
45:21 tell ye and *b.* them near
46:13 I *b.* near my righteousn.
56:7 will I *b.* to my holy moun.
58:7 *b.* the poor to thy house
60:17 for brass *b.* gold, for iron *b.*
66:4 *b.* their fears upon them
Jer. 3:14 I will *b.* you to Zion
10:24 last thou *b.* me to nothing
Jer. 11:8 I will *b.* words of this
17:18 *b.* on them day of evil
31:8 *b.* them from the north
32:42 *b.* on them all the good
33:6 I will *b.* it health and cure
11 shall *b.* sacrifice of praise
49:5 I will *b.* a fear upon them
Ezek. 6:3 *b.* a sword upon you
11:9 *b.* you out of the midst
20:15 I would not *b.* them
21:29 will *b.* on necks of them
23:22 *b.* them against thee on
34:13 *b.* to own, 36:24 ; 37:21
38:17 *b.* thee against them
Hos. 2:14 and *b.* her to wildern.
Amos 4:1 *b.* and let us drink, 4
Mic. 1:15 will I *b.* an heir to thee
Zec. 8:8 I will *b.* them, and they
Mat. 2:13 be there till I *b.* word
5:23 *b.* thy gift to the altar
17:17 *b.* him to me, *Mark* 9:19
21:2 *b.* them to me, *Mark* 11:2 ;
Luke 19:30
Mark 7:32 *b.* to him one deaf
Luke 2:10 I *b.* good tidings
8:14 *b.* no fruit to perfection
12:11 *b.* you into the synagog.
John 10:16 other sheep I must *b.*
14:26 *b.* all things to rememb.
18:29 what accusation *b.* you?
Acts 5:28 to *b.* this man's blood
7:6 should *b.* them into bondage
9:2 he might *b.* them bound, 21
22:5 I went to *b.* them bound
23:10 to *b.* Paul into the castle
17 *b.* this young man to capt.
1 *Cor.*:1:19 I will *b.* to nothing
28 to *b.* to naught
4:17 *b.* you into remembrance
9:27 body, I *b.* into subjection
16:6 may *b.* me on my journey
2 *Cor.* 11:20 if a man *b.* you
Gal. 3:24 schoolm. to *b.* us to C.
1 *Thes.* 4:14 sleep, will God *b.*
1 *Pet.* 3:18 he might *b.* us to G.
2 *John* 10 if any *b.* not this doc.
3 *John* 6 if thou *b.* on journey
Rev. 21:24 do *b.* their glory to it
26 *b.* the glory of nations into

See HOME, HITHER.

BRING again.
Gen. 24:6 *b.* not my son *again,* 8
28:15 *b.* thee *a.* into land, 48:21
42:37 I will *b.* him *again*
Ex. 23:4 *b.* it back to him *again*
Num. 22:8 I will *b.* word *again*
Deut. 1:22 *b.* us word *again* what
28:68 L. shall *b.* thee into E. *a.*
Jud. 11:9 if ye *b.* me home *a.*
19:3 her husb. went to *b.* her *a.*
2 *Sam.* 12:23 can I *b.* him *again*
14:21 *b.* the young man Ab. *a.*
15:8 if Lord *b.* me *a.* to Jerus.
25 *b.* me *again* and show me
1 *K.* 8:34 forg. and *b. a.* 2 *Chr.*6:25
1 *Chr.* 13:3 let us *b. a.* the ark
21:12 what word I shall *b. a.*
2 *Chr.* 24:19 proph. to *b.* them *a.*
Neh. 9:29 mightest *b. again*
Ps. 68:22 *b. again* from B. I will
b. my people from depths of
Prov. 19:24 as *b.* it to mouth *a.*
26:15 grieveth to *b.* it *again*
Is. 38:8 *b. again* shadow
46:8 *b.* it *again* to mind
49:5 saith Lord to *b.* Jac. *again*
52:8 Lord shall *b. again* Zion
Jer. 12:15 will *b.* them *a.* 50:19
15:19 will I *b.* thee *again*
16:15 *b. a.* to their l. 24:6 ; 32:37
23:3 *b. again* into their folds
28:4 I will *b. again* Jeconiah, 6
30:3 *b. again* the captivity, 18 ;
31:23 ; *Ezek.* 39.25 ; *Amos* 9:14
48:47 *b. a.* captivity of Moab
49:6 *of* Ammon ; 39 *of* Elam
Ezek. 16:53 when I *b. a.* their
29:14 I will *b. again* captivity
34:16 will *b. again* that driven
Zep. 3:20 at that time *b.* you *a.*
Zec. 10:6 *b.* them *again* to place
10 I will *b.* them *a.* out of E.
Mat. 2:8 *b.* word *a.* that I may

See CAPTIVITY.

BRING down.
Gen. 42:38 *b. d.* gray h. 44:29, 31
43:7 say, *b.* brother *down,* 44:21
45:13 and *b. down* my father
Deut. 9:3 *b.* them *down* before
2 *Sam.* 22:28 on haughty to *b. d.*
1 *K.* 1:33 Solomon, *b. d.* to G.
2:9 his hoar head *b.*thou *d.*
Ps. 18:27 *b. down* high looks
55:23 shalt *b. d.* to pit of dest.
Is. 25:5 shalt *b. d.* the noise
11 he shall *b. d.* their pride
Is. 25:12 high fort shall he *b. d.*
63:6 *b. d.* their strength to earth
Jer. 49:16 *b.* thee *d.* from th. *Ob.* 4
51:40 will *b.* them *d.* like lambs
Ezek. 26:20 shall *b.* thee *down*
28:8 shall *b.* thee *d.* to the pit
Hos. 7:12 *b.* them *d.* as fowls
Joel 3:2 *b. d.* to valley of Jehosh.
Amos 3:11 he shall *b. d.* thy str.
9:2 climb to heaven, *b.* them *d.*
Ob. 3 Who shall *b.* me *down*
Acts 23:15 that he *b.* him *down*
20 thou wouldest *b. down* Paul
Rom. 10:6 to *b.* Christ *down*

See EVIL.

BRING forth.
Gen. 1:11 earth *b. f.* 24 ; 20 waters
3:16 in sor. shall *b. f.* children
18 th. and thist. sh. it *b. f.*
8:17 *b. f.* every living thing
9:7 *b. f.* abundantly in the earth
38:24 *b.* her *f.* let her be burnt
Ex. 3:10 may. *b. f.* my people Is.
11 who am I that sh. *b. f.?* Is.
7:4 I may *b. forth* my armies
Lev. 26:10 *b. f.* old, bec. of new
Num. 20:8 *b. f.* w. out of the ro.
Jos. 2:3 *b. f.* men that are come
Jud. 6:18 I *b. forth* my present
19:22 *b. f.* man came to thy h.

2 *K.* 19:3 no str. to *b. f. Is.* 37:3
Job 14:9 *b. f.* boughs like a plant
  15:35 conc. mischief, *b. f.* vanity
  38:32 canst thou *b. f.* Mazzaroth
  39:1 the wild goats *b. f.* 2, 3
  40:20 mountains *b.* him *f.* food
Ps. 37:6 he shall *b. f.* thy right.
  92:14 shall *b. f.* fruit in old age
  104:14 *b. f.* food out of earth
  144:13 our sheep may *b. f.*
Prov. 27:1 what a day may *b. f.*
Is. 5:2 should *b. f.* grapes, 4
  3:4 I, nor *b. f.* children
  33:11 conceive chaff, and *b. f.*
  41:21 *b. forth* your strong reas.
  42:1 he shall *b. f.* judg. to Gen.
  3 he shall *b. f.* judgment
  43:8 *b. f.* the blind
  9 let them *b. f.* their witnesses
  45:8 and let them *b. f.* salvation
  55:10 water. maketh it *b. forth*
  59:4 conceive mischief and *b. f.*
  65:9 I will *b. f.* seed out of J.
  23 nor *b. forth* for trouble
  66:8 earth to *b. f.* in one day?
  9 and not cause to *b. f.?*
Jer. 12:2 grow, yea *b. f.* fruit
  5:44 I will *b. f.* what he swal.
Ezek. 12:4 shalt *b. f.* thy stuff.
  17:23 it shall *b. forth* boughs
  20:6 to *b.* them *f.* of land of E.
  38 *b.* them *f.* out of country
  47:12 it shall *b. f.* new fruit
Hos. 9:13 Eph. sh. *b. f.* his chil.
  16 though they *b. f.* yet will I
Mic. 4:10 labor to *b. f.* O Zion
  7:9 he will *b.* me *f.* to the light
Zep. 2:2 before decree *b. f.*
Zec. 3:8 *b. f.* my servant
  4:7 *b. f.* headstone with shout.
  5:4 *b. f.* a curse, it shall enter
Mat. 1:23 virg. sh. *b. f.* a son, 21
  3:8 *b. f.* fruits meet, *Luke* 3:8
  7:18 cannot *b. f.* evil, *Luke* 6:43
Mark 4:20 *b. f.* fruit
Luke 1:31 *b. f.* a son shalt call J.
  8:15 having heard word, *b. f.*
  15:22 *b. f.* best robe
John 15:2 it may *b. f.* more fruit
  16 I ord. you, should *b. f.* fruit
  19:4 I *b.* him *f.* that ye may
Acts 12:4 after Easter to *b.* him *f.*
Rom. 7:4 that we shall *b. f.* fruit
  5 motions of sin to *b. f.*

BRING in.
Ex. 6:8 *b.* you *into* land
  15:17 shalt *b. in* and plant them
  23:23 my Angel shall *b.* thee *in*
Num. 14:31 lit. ones, will I *b. in*
Jer. 17:24 *b. in* no burden on sab.
Dan. 2:24 *b.* me *in* before the k.
  9:24 to *b. in* everlasting right.
Hag. 1:6 s. much and *b. in* little
Luke 5:18 means to *b.* him *in*
  14:21 *b. in* hither the poor
2 *Pet.* 2:1 *b. in* damnable here.

BRING out.
Gen. 40:14 *b.* me *out* of this ho.
  50:24 G. will *b.* you *out* of this l.
Ex. 6:6 *b.* you *out* from under
  13 *b.* chil. of Is. *out* of E. 26:27 ;
  7:5 ; 12:51 ; *Jer.* 31:32
Deut. 22:21 *b.* o. d. ; 24 *b.* both *o.*
Jos. 6:22 *b. o.* thence Rahab
Jud. 6:30 *b. o.* thy son
Ps. 25:17 O *b.* me *o.* of my dis.
Ps. 142:7 *b.* my soul *out* of prison
  143:11 *b.* my soul *cut* of trou.
Is. 42:7 to *b. o.* the prisoners
Ezek. 11:7 *b.* you *out* of midst
  20:34 *b.* you *o.* from peo. 34:13
  41 ac. you, when I *b.* you *out*
  24:6 *b.* it *out* piece by piece
Acts 17:5 sought to *b.* them *out*

BRING to pass.
Gen. 41:32 God will *b.* it *to p.*
  50:20 to *b. t. p.* as at this day

Ps. 37:5 he shall *b.* it *t. p.*
Is. 28:21 *b. to p.* his act
  46:11 I will also *b.* it *to p.*

BRING up.
Gen. 46:4 I will *b.* thee *up* again
Ex. 3:17 I will *b.* you *up* out of
  33:12 sayest, *b. up* this people
Num. 20:25 *b. up* Aaron to m. H.
Jud. 6:13 did not L. *b. us up*
1 *Sam.* 19:15 *b.* him *up* in the b.
  28:11 he said, *b.* me *up* Samuel
2 *Sam.* 6:2 to *b. up* ark of G. 1 *K.*
  8:1, 4 ; 1 *Chr.* 13:6 ; 15:3, 12,
  14, 25 ; 2 *Chr.* 5:2, 5
1 *Chr.* 17:5 since I *b. up* Israel
Is. 23:4 nor *b. up* virgins
Jer. 27:22 then will I *b.* them *up*
Ezek. 16:40 *b. up* a company ag.
  23:46 I will *b. up* a company
  37:6 I will *b. up* flesh on you
Hos. 9:12 they *b. up* children
Rom. 10:7 to *b. up* C. from the d.
Eph. 6:4 *b.* them *up* in nurture

BRINGERS.
2 *K.* 10:5 *b. up* of chil. sent to J.

BRINGEST.
Job 14:3 *b.* me into judgment
Is. 40:9 O Jer. that *b.* good tid.
Acts 17:20 *b.* strange things

BRINGETH.
Ex. 6:7 *b.* you from under burd.
Lev. 11:45 L. that *b.* you out
Deut. 8:7 L. *b.* thee into a good
1 *Sam.* 2:6 he *b.* down to the gr.
  7 Lord *b.* low, and lifteth up
2 *Sam.* 22:48 *b.* me people under
  49 *b.* me forth from mine ene.
Job 12:6 into whose hand G. *b.*
  22 *b.* to light shadow of death
  19:29 wrath *b.* punis. of the sw.
  28:11 thing hid *b.* he to light
Ps. 1:3 *b.* forth his fruit
  14:7 when L. *b.* back cap. 53:6
  33:10 *b.* coun. of hea. to naught
  37:7 *b.* wicked devices to pass
  68:6 *b.* out them that are bound
  107:28 *b.* them out of their dist.
  30 *b.* them to desired haven
  135:7 *b.* wind, *Jer.* 10:3 ; 51:16
Prov. 10:31 mouth of just *b.* wis.
  16:30 moving his lips, he *b.* evil
  18:16 *b.* him before great men
  19:26 son that *b.* reproach
  20:26 king *b.* wheel over them
  29:15 *b.* mother to shame
  21 delicately *b.* up his servant
  25 the fear of man *b.* a snare
  31:14 she *b.* her food from afar
Is. 8:7 L. *b.* on them the waters
  26:5 *b.* down them dwell on h.
  40:23 *b.* the princes to nothing
  26 *b.* out their host by number
  43:17 *b.* forth chariot and horse
  54:16 the smith that *b.* forth
  61:11 the earth *b.* forth her bud
Jer. 4:31 *b.* forth her first child
Ezek. 29:16 *b.* iniquity to rem.
Hos. 10:1 Is. *b.* forth fruit to him.
Hag. 1:11 which ground *b.* forth
Mat. 3:10 every tree that *b.* not
  forth g. fruit, 7:19 ; *Luke* 3:9
  7:17 good tree *b.* forth g. fruit
  12:35 a good man *b.* forth good,
  evil *b.* evil things, *Luke* 6:45
  13:23 *b.* forth some a h.-fold
  52 *b.* out of treas. things new
  17:1 Jesus *b.* them to high m.
Mark 4:28 the earth *b.* forth fr.
Luke 6:43 good tree *b.* not cor.
John 12:24 if it die it *b.* 15:5
Col. 1:6 gospel *b.* forth fruit
Tit. 2:11 grace of G. that *b.* sal.
Heb. 1:6 *b.* first-begot. into world
  6:7 the earth *b.* forth herbs
Jam. 1:15 *b.* forth sin, and sin *b.*
See TIDINGS.

Ex. 12:42 observed for *b.* them
  36:6 were restrained from *b.*
Num. 14:36 by *b.* up a slander
2 *Sam.* 19:10 of *b.* the king, 43
2 *K.* 21:12 I am *b.* such evil
Ps. 126:6 rejoic. *b.* his sheaves
Ezek. 20:9 known in *b.* them
Dan. 9:13 *b.* upon us great evil
Mat. 21:43 a nation *b.* forth fruit
Rom. 7:23 *b.* me into captivity
2 *Cor.* 10:5 *b.* into capti. ev. tho.
Heb. 2:10 in *b.* many sons.
  7:19 *b.* in of a better hope did
2 *Pet.* 2:5 *b.* in the flood on world

BRINK.
Ex. 2:3 laid the ark by river's *b.*
Jos. 3:8 when come to *b.* of J.
Ezek. 47:6 caused me return to *b.*

BROAD.
Neh. 3:8 they fortified Jerusalem
  to the *b.* wall, 12:38
Job 36:16 out of strait into *b.* pl.
Ps. 119:96 thy com. is exceed. *b.*
Cant. 3:2 in *b.* ways I will seek
Is. 33:21 be a place of *b.* rivers
Jer. 5:1 seek in *b.* places thereof
  51:58 *b.* walls of Babylon
Nah. 2:4 chariots justle in *b.* w.
Mat. 7:13 *b.* way to destruction
  23:5 make *b.* their phylacteries

BROADER.
Job 11:9 meas. is *b.* than the sea

BROIDERED.
Ezek. 16:13 raim. was of *b.* work
  18 *b.* garments and coveredst
  27:7 with *b.* work to be thy sail
  16 in thy fairs with *b.* work
  24 thy merchants in *b.* work
1 *Tim.* 2:9 nor with *b.* hair

BROILED.
Luke 24:42 a piece of a *b.* fish

BROKEN.
Gen. 17:14 *b.* my cov. *Ps.* 55:20 ;
  Is. 24:5 ; 33:8 ; *Jer.* 11:10
Lev. 21:19 m. *b.* footed, *b.* hand.
  20 hath his stones *b.* not offer
  22:22 *b.* ye shall not offer, 24
  26:13 *b.* the hands of your yoke
  26 when I have *b.* staff of bread
Jud. 5:22 the horse-hoofs *b.* by
1 *Sam.* 2:4 bows of mighty are *b.*
2 *Sam.* 22:35 *b.* of st. *b. Ps.* 18:34
1 *Chr.* 14:11 *b.* in upon mine ene.
2 *Chr.* 20:37 *b.* thy works, sh. *b.*
  32:5 he built up all the wall *b.*
Job 4:10 teeth of y. lions are *b.*
  7:5 skin is *b.* and loathsome
  16:12 he hath *b.* me asunder
  22:9 arms of fatherless been *b.*
  24:20 wickedness shall be *b.*
  31:22 arm be *b.* from the bone
  38:15 the high arm shall be *b.*
Ps. 3:7 *b.* teeth of the ungodly
  31:12 I am like a *b.* vessel
  34:18 them of a *b.* heart, 51:17
  20 not one of them is *b.*
  37:15 their bows be *b.* ; 17 arms
  38:8 I am feeble and sore *b.*
  44:19 *b.* us in place of dragons
  51:8 bones thou hast *b.* may rej.
  17 sacrifices of G. are a *b.* spi.
  60:2 earth to tremble hast *b.*
  69:20 repr. hath *b.* my heart
  107:16 *b.* the gates of brass
  109:16 slay the *b.* in heart
  124:7 snare is *b.* we are escaped
  147:3 he healeth the *b.* in heart
Prov. 6:15 suddenly sh. he be *b.*
  15:13 by sor. of heart spirit is *b.*
  17:22 *b.* spirit drieth the bones
  25:19 is like a *b.* tooth
Ec. 4:12 threefold cord is not *b.*
  12:6 or the golden bowl be *b.*
Is. 5:27 latchet of their shoes *b.*
  7:8 shall Eph. be *b.*

8:15 among them shall be *b.*
9:4 *b.* the yoke of his burden
14:5 *b.* the staff of the wicked
  29 rod of him smote thee is *b.*
19:10 shall be *b.* in purposes
21:9 all the images he hath *b.*
28:13 fall backward and be *b.*
33:8 *b.* the covenant
  10 any of the cords be *b.*
36:6 trustest in staff of *b.* reed
Jer. 2:13 *b.* cisterns that hold no
  16 *b.* the crown of thy head
  20 of old I have *b.* thy yoke
5:5 these have *b.* the yoke and
10:20 all my cords are *b.*
11:16 the branches of it are *b.*
14:17 virgin of my people is *b.*
22:28 is this man C. a *b.* idol?
23:9 my heart is *b.*
28:2 *b.* yoke of king of Babylon
33:21 then may also my covenant be *b.* with David
48:17 how is the strong staff *b.*
  38 I have *b.* Moab like a vessel
50:17 Nebuch. *b.* Israel's bones
  23 hammer of whole earth *b.*
51:58 broad walls of B. sh. be *b.*
Lam. 2:9 he hath *b.* her bars
3:4 hath *b.* my bones ; 16 teeth
Ezek. 6:9 *b.* with their wh. heart
17:19 covenant that he hath *b.*
19:12 her strong rods were *b.*
26:2 Aha, she is *b.*
27:26 east wind *b.* thee
  34 shalt be *b.* by the seas
30:21 *b.* the arm of Pharaoh
  22 break the strong and that *b.*
31:12 his boughs are *b.* by rivers
32:28 be *b.* in midst of uncir.
34:4 nor have ye bound up *b.*
  16 and I will bind up that *b.*
  27 *b.* the bands of their yoke
44:7 they have *b.* my covenant
Dan. 2:42 kingdom partly *b.*
8:8 the great horn was *b.* 22
  25 he shall be *b.* without hand
11:4 his kingdom shall be *b.*
  22 with arms of a flood be *b.*
Hos. 5:11 Eph. is *b.* in judgment
Zec. 11:11 it was *b.* in that day
  16 shep. shall not heal that *b.*
Mat. 15:37 *b.* meat. *Mark* 8:8
21:44 fall on this stone, shall be
  b. Luke 20:18
Luke 12:39 suff. house to be *b.*
John 5:18 not only *b.* the Sab.
7:23 law of M. should not be *b.*
10:35 the scripture cannot be *b.*
19:31 their legs might be *b.*
  36 bone of him shall not be *b.*
21:11 yet was not the net *b.*
Acts 20:11 *b.* bread and talked
27:35 had *b.* it, he began to eat
1 *Cor.* 11:24 my body *b.* for you
Rev. 2:27 as ves. shall they be *b.*

BROKEN down.

2 *K.* 11:6 that it be not *b. d.*
Neh. 2:13 I viewed the walls *b. d.*
Ps. 80:12 why *b. d.* her hedges ?
89:40 hast *b. d.* all his hedges
Prov. 24:31 wall was *b. down*
25:28 is like a city *b. down*
Is. 16:8 *b. d.* principal plants
22:10 houses *b. d.* to fortify wall
24:10 city of confusion is *b. d.*
  19 is utterly *b. down.*
Jer. 4:26 cities *b. d.* ; 48:20 M. 39
Ezek. 30:4 foundation sh. be *b. d.*
Joel 1:17 the barns are *b. d.*
Eph. 2:14 *b. d.* middle wall

BROKEN forth.

Gen. 38:29 how hast thou *b. forth*
2 *Sam.* 5:20 L. *b. f.* on mine ene.

BROKEN in.

1 *Chr.* 14:11 *b. in* on mine ene.

BROKEN off.

Job 17:11 my purposes are *b. off*
Is. 27:11 boughs withered *b. off*
Rom. 11:17 and if some be *b. off*
  20 bec. of unbelief, *b. off*, 19

BROKEN in, or to pieces.

1 *Sam.* 2:10 adv. shall be *b. to p.*
2 *Chr.* 25:12 from rock, were *b.*
Ps. 89:10 thou has *b.* R. *in p.*
Is. 8:9 ye shall *b. in p.*
30:14 as a potter's ves. *b. in p.*
Hos. 8:6 calf of Sam. shall *b. p.*

BROKEN up.

Gen. 7:11 fount. of deep *b. up*
2 *K.* 25:4 J. *b. up, Jer.* 39:2 ; 52:7
2 *Chr.* 24:7 *b. up* house of God
Prov. 3:20 depths *b. up*
Mat. 24:43 house to be *b. up*
Mark 2:4 they had *b.* roof *up*
Acts 13:43 when cong. was *b. up*

BROKEN-HEARTED.

Is. 61:1 to bind up the *b.-h.*
Luke 4:18 to heal the *b.-h.*

BROOD.

Luke 13:34 hen doth gather *b.*

BROOK.

Gen. 32:23 sent them over the *b.*
Lev. 23:40 take willows of the *b.*
Num. 13:23 to *b.* Eschol. cut br.
Deut. 2:13 over the *b.* Zered, 14
9:21 cast the dust into the *b.*
1 *Sam.* 17:40 stones out of the *b.*
2 *Sam.* 15:23 passed *b.* Kidron
  17:20 they be gone over the *b.*
1 *K.* 2:37 day thou passest ov. *b.*
17:3 hide by the *b.* Cherith, 5
  6 he drank of the *b.*
18:40 Elijah brought to *b.* Kish.
2 *Chr.* 20:16 find them at e. of *b.*
29:16 carried it to the *b.* Kidron
32:4 gathered and stopped the *b.*
Neh. 2:15 by *b.* and viewed the
Job 6:15 dealt deceitfully as a *b.*
40:22 willows of *b.* compass him
Ps. 83:9 as to Jabin at the *b.* K.
110:7 drink of the *b.* in way
Prov. 18:4 wisdom as a *b.*
Is. 15:7 carry to *b.* of willows
Jer. 31:40 fields to *b.* Kid. holy
John 18:1 went over *b.* Cedron

BROOKS.

Num. 21:14 in the *b.* of Arnon
Deut. 8:7 a land of *b.* of water
2 *Sam.* 23:30 *b.* of G. 1 *Chr.* 11:32
1 *K.* 18:5 A. said, Go unto all *b.*
Job 6:15 as stream of *b.* pass
20:17 shall not see the *b.*
22:24 gold as stones of *b.*
Ps. 42:1 hart pant. after wat.-*b.*
Is. 19:6 *b.* of defence be emptied
  7 paper-reeds by the *b.* shall
  8 cast angle into *b.* shall lam.

BROTH.

Jud. 6:19 G. put the *b.* in a pot
Is. 65:4 *b.* of abominable things

BROTHER.

Gen. 9:5 of every man's *b.*
29:12 he was her father's *b.*
43:6 ye had a *b.* the man asked,
  have ye another *b.* 44:19
Deut. 25:5 husb. *b.* shall go in
Jud. 21:6 I. repen. for B. their *b.*
Job 1:13 in the eldest *b.* ho. 18
30:29 I am a *b.* to dragons
Prov. 17:17 a *b.* is born for adv.
18:9 slothful is *b.* to him
  19 a *b.* offended is harder
  24 sticketh closer than a *b.*
27:10 better a neigh. than *b.* far
Ec. 4:8 hath neither child nor *b.*
Jer. 9:4 tr. not in any *b.* for ev. *b.*
Ezek. 44:25 for *b.* they may defile
Mal. 1:2 was not E. Jacob's *b.* ?
Mat. 10:21 *b.* de. up *b. Mark* 13:12

Mark 12:19 if m.'s *b.* die, *Luke* 20:28
John 11:19 J. came to co. con. *b.*
Acts 9:17 b. Saul receiv. 22:13
12:2 killed James the *b.* of John
21:20 *b.* how many thous. bel.
1 *Cor.* 5:11 called a *b.* be a forn.
6:6 *b.* go -th to law with *b.*
7:12 *b.* hath a wife
  15 a *b.* is not under bondage
8:11 thy know. weak *b.* perish
2 *Cor.* 8:18 sent with him the *b.*
2 *Thes.* 3:6 withdraw from ev. *b.*
  15 but admonish him as a *b.*
Phile. 7 saints refresh. by thee, *b.*
  16 above a servant a *b.* beloved

His BROTHER.

Gen. 25:26 after that came *his b.*
42:38 *his b.* is dead, 44:20
Ex. 32:27 slay ev. man *his b.*
Deut. 19:19 to have done to *b.*
  28:54 eye be evil toward *his b.*
Neh. 5:7 usury ev. one of *his b.*
Ps. 49:7 by any means red. *his b.*
Is 3:6 shall take hold of *his b.*
9:19 no man shall spare *his b.*
19:2 fight every -one ag. *his b.*
41:6 to *his b.* be of good cour.
Jer. 31:34 teach no more every
  man *his b. Heb.* 8:11
34:9 serve himself of a J. *his b.*
  17 liberty every one to *his b.*
Ezek. 18:18 spoiled *his b.* by vio.
33:30 every one to *his b.*
Hos. 12:3 *b.* by the heel in the w.
Amos 1:11 he did pursue *h. b.*
Mic. 7:2 hunt every man *his b.*
Hag. 2:22 by sword of *his b.*
Zec. 7:9 mercy ev. man to *h. b.*
  10 imagine evil against *his b.*
Mal. 2:10 treacherously ag'st *b.*
Mat. 5:22 sayeth Raca to *his b.*
18:35 if ye forgive not every one
  his b. their trespasses
22:24 seed to *b. Mark* 12:19 ;
  Luke 20:28
  25 left his wife to *his b.*
John 1:41 he findeth *his b.* Simon
Rom. 14:13 to fall in *his b.* way
1 *Thes.* 4:6 no man def. *his b.*
Jam. 4:11 evil of and jud. *his b.*
1 *John* 2:9 and hateth *his b.* 11
  10 loveth *his b.* abideth in lig.
3:10 that loveth not *his b.* 14
  12 not as Cain. who sle. *his b.*
  15 hateth *his b.* is a murd. 4:20
4:21 love God, love *his b.* also
5:16 if any see *his b.* sin a sin

My BROTHER.

Gen. 4:9 C. said, Am I *my b.* kee.
20:5 he is *my b.* 13 ; 1 *K.* 20:32
27:41 will I slay *my b.* Jacob
29:15 because thou art *my b.*
2 *Sam.* 1:26 *my b.* Jonathan
1 *K.* 13:30 saying, Alas, *my b.*
Ps. 35:14 tho. he had been *my b.*
Cant. 8:1 wert as *my b.*
Jer. 22:18 saying, Ah, *my b.*
Mat. 12:50 is *my b. Mark* 3:35
18:21 how oft shall *my b.* sin
Luke 12:13 speak to *my b.*
John 11:21 *my b.* had not died
1 *Cor.* 8:13 if meat make *my b.*
2 *Cor.* 2:13 found not Tit. *my b.*

Our BROTHER.

Gen. 37:26 wh. profit if sl. *our b.*
  27 for he is *our. b. Jud.* 9:3
42:21 guilty concerning *our b.*
2 *Cor.* 8:22 sent with them *our b.*
Phile. 1 Tim. *our b.* to Philem.

Thy BROTHER.

Gen. 4:9 Where is Abel *thy b.*
  10 voice of *thy b.* blood crieth
27:40 and shalt serve *thy b.*
38:8 *b.* wife r. up seed to *thy b.*
Ex. 4:14 is not Aaron *thy b.* ?

Lev. 19:17 shalt not hate *thy b.*
25:36 that *thy b.* may live
Deut. 13:6 if *thy b.* entice secretly
15:11 open thy h. wide to *thy b.*
12 *thy b.* a Heb. be sold to thee
22:3 all lost things of *thy b.*
23:7 not abhor Edom. he is *t. b.*
2 *Sam.* 2:22 my face to J. *thy b.*
13:20 h. thy peace, he is *thy b.*
1 *K.* 20:33 said, *thy b.* Benhadad
Job 22:6 pledge from *thy b.*
Ps. 50:20 speakest against *thy b.*
Prov. 27:10 into *thy b.* house
Ob. 10 violence against *t. b.* J.
Mat. 5:23 that *t. b.* hath aught
24 first be reconciled to *thy b.*
7:3 in *t. b.* eye, 5; *Luke* 6:41, 42
18:15 gained *t. b.* *Luke* 17:3
John 11:23 *thy b.* shall rise
Rom. 14:10 set at naught *thy b.*

Your BROTHER.
Gen. 42:34 will I deliver you *y. b.*
45:4 I am Joseph, *your b.*
Jud. 9:18 Ab'm. bec. he is *y. b.*
Rev. 1:9 I John who also am *y. b.*

BROTHERHOOD.
Zec. 11:14 break *b.* between J.
1 *Pet.* 2:17 love the *b.* fear God

BROTHERLY.
Amos 1:9 remember not *b.* cove.
Rom. 12:10 affect. with *b.* love
1 *Thes.* 4:9 as touching *b.* love
Heb. 13:1 let *b.* love continue
2 *Pet.* 1:7 to godliness *b.* kindness

BROUGHT.
Gen. 20:9 *b.* on me a great sin
27:20 Lord thy God *b.* it to me
Ex. 18:26 hard causes they *b.*
19:4 how I *b.* you to myself
32:1 that *b.* us up out, 23
21 thou hast *b.* so great a sin
Num. 14:3 *b.* us to this land
16:10 hath *b.* thee near to him
27:5 M. *b.* their cause before L
Deut. 5:15 *b.* thee out thence
26:13 *b.* away the hal. things
Jos. 7:24 *b.* them to valley of A.
24:7 Lord *b.* the sea upon them
Jud. 2:1 *b.* you unto the land
18:3 who *b.* thee hither?
1 *Sam.* 1:24 *b.* Sam. to house of L.
10:27 and *b.* him no presents
15:35 D. received what she *b.*
2 *Sam.* 7:18 that thou hast *b.* me
hitherto, 1 *Chr.* 17:16
1 *K.* 9:9 *b.* this evil, 2 *Chr.* 7:22
17:20 *b.* evil upon the widow?
2 *K.* 5:20 in not receiv. what he *b.*
17:4 Hoshea *b.* no present
20:11 *b.* the shadow backward
1 *Chr.* 11:19 with jeop. of lives *b.*
14:17 L. *b.* fear of him on all
2 *Chr.* 13:18 chil. of Isr. were *b.*
22:9 *b.* Ahaziah to Jehu
32:23 many *b.* gifts to L. to Jer.
Ezra 8:18 *b.* us a man of underst.
Neh. 4:15 *b.* their counsel
9:33 in all that is *b.* upon us
13:12 Judah *b.* tithe of corn
Job 4:12 was secretly *b.* to me
21:32 yet shall he be *b.* to grave
Ps. 35:4 be *b.* to confusion, 26
45:15 with gladness shall he *b.*
71:24 *b.* to shame seek my hurt
Prov. 6:26 a man is *b.* to piece
Cant. 3:4 *b.* to banquet-house
Is. 15:1 Ar *b.* Kir *b.* to silence
23:13 *b.* the land of C. to ruin
29:20 terrible one is *b.* to naught
43:23 *b.* me the small cattle, 24
48:15 called him. I have *b.* him
53:7 he is *b.* as a lamb
59:16 his arm *b.* salvation, 63:5
60:11 that their kings may be *b.*
62:9 they that *b.* it shall drink it
Jer. 15:8 I have *b.* on them

32:42 as I have *b.* all this evil on
40:3 now the Lord hath *b.* it
Ezek. 14:22 comf. concer. evil I *b.*
29:5 shalt not be *b.* together
40:4 art thou *b.* hither
Dan. 7:13 *b.* him near Ancient
9.14 watched evil and *b.* it on
11:6 and they that *b.* her
Hag. 1:9 ye *b.* it home
Mat. 10:18 shall be *b.* before kings,
Mark 13:9; *Luke* 21:12
12:25 is *b.* to desol. *Luke* 11:17
17:16 *b.* him to disciples
18:24 was *b.* owed 10,000 talents
19:13 *b.* little chil. *Mark* 10:13
Mark 10:13 rebuke.l those *b.* them
Luke 2:22 *b.* him to Jerusalem
10:34 *b.* him to an inn
John 7:45 have ye not *b.* him?
Acts 5:21 prison to have them *b.*
9:27 *b.* him to apostles
15:3 *b.* on their way
16:20 *b.* them to the magistrates
19:37 *b.* these men, no robbers
20:12 *b.* the young man alive
21:5 they all *b.* us on our way
25:6 commanded Paul to be *b.*
27:24 must be *b.* before Cesar
Rom. 15:24 to be *b.* thither
1 *Cor.* 6:12 not be *b.* under power
2 *Cor.* 1:16 be *b.* on my way to J.
2 *Tim.* 1:10 *b.* life and immortal.
1 *Pet.* 1:13 grace that is *b.* to you
2 *Pet.* 2:19 of same is he *b.*

BROUGHT again.
Gen. 14:16 Abram *b.* again Lot
Ex. 15:19 L. *b. a.* waters of sea
Deut. 1:25 *b.* us word *again*
Ruth 1:21 L. *b.* me home *again*
1 *Sam.* 6:21 Philistines *b. again*
2 *Chr.* 33:13 L. *b.* Manas. *a.* to J.
Ezek. 34:4 *b. a.* what was driven
39:27 *b.* them *ag.* from the dead
Heb. 13:20 *b. ag.* from the dead

BROUGHT back.
1 *K.* 13:23 prophet he had *b. back*
2 *Chr.* 19:4 Jehos. *b.* them *b.* to L.
Ps. 85:1 *b. back* the captivity
Ezek. 38:8 land *b. b.* from the sw.

BROUGHT down.
Gen. 39:1 was *b. d.* into Egypt
1 *Sam.* 30:16 *b.* him *d.* they were
Ps. 20:8 they are *b. d.* and fallen
107:12 he *b. d.* their heart
Is. 5:15 mean man shall be *b. d.*
14:11 thy pomp is *b. down*
15 shall be *b. down* to hell
29:4 shall be *b. d.* speak out
43:14 *b. down* all the nobles
Lam. 2:2 *b.* them *d.* to the gro.
Ezek. 17:24 have *b. d.* high tree
31:18 be *b. d.* with trees of Eden
Zec. 10:11 pride of Assy. be *b. d.*
Mat. 11:23 Capern. *b. d.* to hell
Acts 9:30 brethren *b.* him *d.* to C.

BROUGHT forth.
Gen. 1:12 the earth *b. forth* grass
21 waters *b. forth* abundantly
14:18 king of Salem *b. f.* bread
15:5 Lord *b. forth* Abram
19:16 angels *b.* Lot *forth*
41:47 the earth *b. forth* by hand.
Ex. 3:12 thou hast *b. f.* peop.
16:3 ye have *b.* us *f.* into wild.
29:46 I am L. *b.* them *f.* *Lev.*
25:38; 26:13, 45
Num. 24:8 God *b.* him *f.*
Deut. 6:12 Lord *b.* thee *f.* 8:14
9:12 people *b. f.* have corrupted
26:8 L. *b.* us *f.* with a mighty h.
33:14 fruits *b. forth* by sun
Jud. 6:8 *b.* you *f.* out of house
2 *Sam.* 22:20 *b.* me *forth* into a
large place, *Ps.* 18:19
1 *K.* 9:9 forsook Lord who *b. f.*
their fathers, 2 *Chr.* 7:22

Job 10:18 hast thou *b.* me *f.*
21:30 be *b. f.* to day of wrath
Ps. 7:14 *b. forth* falsehood
90:2 before mountains were *b. f.*
105:30 their land *b. f.* frogs
43 *b. forth* his people with joy
Prov. 8:24 no depths, I was *b. f.*
25 before the hills was I *b. f.*
Cant. 8:5 thy mother *b.* thee *f.*
Is. 5:2 it *b. forth* wild grapes
26:18 *b. f.* wind; 45:10 *w. b. f.*
51:18 among sons she hath *b. f.*
66:7 before she trav. she *b. f.*
8 as soon as Z. trav. she *b. f.*
Jer. 2:27 thou hast *b.* me *f.*
11:4 I *b.* them *forth*, 34:13
20:3 Pashur *b. f.* J. out of stocks
32:21 *b. forth* Israel with signs
50:25 Lord *b. f.* weap. of indig.
51:10 L. hath *b. f.* our right.
Ezek. 12:7 I *b. f.* my stuff by day
14:22 a remnant *b. f.* sons
Mic. 5:3 which trav. hath *b. f.*
Hag. 2:19 olive-tree hath not *b. f.*
Mat. 1:25 she had *b. f.* first-born
Mat. 13:8 good gr. *b. f.* *Mark* 4:8
Luke 1:57 Elizabeth *b. f.* a son
2:7 she *b. f.* her first-born son
12:16 ground of a rich man *b. f.*
John 19:13 Pilate *b. forth* Jesus
Acts 5:19 doors and *b.* them *f.*
12:6 Herod would have *b.* him *f.*
25:17 com. the man to be *b. f.*
Jam. 5:18 earth *b. forth* fruit
Rev. 12:5 she *b. f.* a man-child
13 persecuted woman wh. *b. f.*

BROUGHT in.
Gen. 39:14 *b.* in a Hebrew
47:7 Jos. *b.* in Jacob his father
Deut. 9:4 my right L. *b.* me *in*
11:29 L. hath *b. in* unto land
Neh. 13:19 no burden *b. in*
Ps. 78:26 *b. in* the south wind
Acts 7:45 *b. in* with Jesus
Gal. 2:4 brethren unawares *b. in*

BROUGHT into.
Num. 16:14 not *b.* us *into* a land
1 *Sam.* 20:8 *b.* thy serv *into* a cov.
Ps. 22:15 *b.* me *into* dust
Cant. 1:4 king *b.* me *i.* his cham.
Jer. 2:7 *b.* you *i.* a plen. country
Lam. 3:2 *b.* me *into* darkness
Ezek. 44:7 *b. in.* my sanctuary
Acts 9:8 *b.* him *into* Damascus
21:28 *b.* Greeks *into* the temple
1 *Tim.* 6:7 *b.* nothing *into* world
Heb. 13:11 whose blood is *b. into*

BROUGHT low.
Jud. 11:35 dau. *b.* me very *low*
2 *Chr.* 28:19 Lord *b.* Judah *low*
Job 14:21 they are *b. low*
24:24 are gone and *b. low*
Ps. 79:8 for we are *b.* very *low*
106:43 *b. low* for their iniquity
107:39 *b. low* thro' oppression
116:6 I was *b. low*, he helped
142:6 for I am *b.* very *low*
Ec. 12:4 daug. of music be *b. low*
Is. 2:12 shall be *b. low*
25:5 of terrible ones *b. low*
Luke 3:5 every mountain and hill
b. low, *Is.* 40:4

BROUGHT out.
Gen. 15:7 *b.* thee *o.* of Ur of Cha.
43:23 he *b.* S. *out* unto them
Ex. 13:3 L. *b.* you *out*, 9, 14, 16
20:2 L. *b.* thee *out*, *Lev.* 19:36;
*Num.*15:41; *Deut.*5:6; *Ps.*81:10
Lev. 23:43 I *b.* them *o.* 1 *K.* 8:21
Deut. 5:15 that L. *b.* thee *out*
9:28 *b.* out to slay them
Jos. 6:23 *b. out* Rahab and all
24:5 and afterward I *b.* you out
2 *Sam.* 13:18 *b.* her *o.* and bolted
2 *Chr.* 23:11 *b. out* the king's son

BROUGHT

Ps. 78:16 he *b.* str. *out* of rock
80:8 hast *b.* a vine *out* of Egypt
107:14 *b.* them *out* of darkness
136:11 *b. out* Isr. from among
Jer. 7:22 in the day I *b.* them *out*
Dan. 5:13 king *b. o.* of Jewry?
Hos. 12:13 prophet L. *b.* Isr. *out*
Acts 7:40 M. wh. *b.* us *out* of Eg.
12:17 L. *b.* him *out* of prison
13:17 a high arm *b.* them *out*
16:30 *b. o.* and said. wh. m. I do?
39 bes. them and *b.* them *out*

BROUGHT to pass.

2 *K.* 19:25 I *b.* it *to p. Is.* 37:26
Ezek. 21:7 and shall be *b. to p.*
1 *Cor.* 15:54 then be *b. to p.*

BROUGHT up.

Ex. 17:3 wh. *b.* us *up, Num.* 21:5
32:1 as for M. that *b.* us *up*
4 thy gods *b.* th. *up,* 8; 1 *K.* 12:28
Num. 16:13 hast *b.* us *up*
20:4 why have ye *b.* us *up*
Deut. 20:1 with thee *b.* thee *up*
Jos. 24:17 he it is that *b.* us *up*
Jud. 6:8 *b.* you *u.* 1 *Sam.* 10:18
15:13 *b.* Samson *u.* ; 16:31
1 *Sam.* 8:8 since the day I *b. up ;*
2 *Sam.* 7:6 ; 1 *Chr.* 17:5
12:6 L. that *b.* your fathers *up*
2 *Sam.* 6:12 *b. up* the ark, 15 ; 1
K. 8:4 ; 1 *Chr.* 13:28 ; 2 *Chr.* 1:4
21:13 *b. up* the bones of Saul
2 *K.* 17:7 sin. ag. L. *b.* them *up*
36 Lord who *b.* you *up*
25:6 *b. up* Z. to king, *Jer.* 39:5
2 *Chr.* 8:11 Sol. *b. up* dau. of P.
10:8 men *b. up* with him, 10
Neh. 9:18 is thy God *b.* thee *up*
Est. 2:7 he *b. up* Esther
20 like as when *b. up* with him
Job 31:18 he was *b. up* with me
Ps. 30:3 *b. up* my soul
40:2 *b.* me *up* out of horrible pit
Prov. 8:30 one *b. up* with him
Is. 1:2 nourished and *b. up* chil.
49:21 who hath *b. up* these

Is. 51:18 her of sons she *b. up*
63 11 he *b.* them *up, Jer.* 2:6
Jer. 11:7 in day I *b.* them *up*
16:14 L. that *b. u.* Israel, 23:8
15 *b. up* Israel from the n. 23:8
Lam. 2:22 those I *b. up* my en.
4:5 *b. up* in scarlet, embrace
Ezek. 19:3 *b. up* one of her whelps
37:13 *b.* you *up* out of your gr.
Amos 2:10 I *b.* you *u.* 3:1 ; 9:7 ;
Mic 6:4
Jon. 2:6 *b. up* my life from cor.
Luke 4:16 N. where he been *b. u.*
Acts 13:1 I been *b. up* with Herod
22:3 *b. up* at the feet of Gamal.
1 *Tim.* 5:10 widow, if she *b. up*

BROUGHTEST.

Ex. 32:7 people *b.* out have cor.
Num. 14:13 *b.* up this people
Deut. 9:28 lest land whence *b.* us
29 inherit. *b.* out, 1 *K.* 8:51
2 *Sam.* 5:2 he *b.* in Isr. 1 *Chr.* 11:2
1 *K.* 8:53 when *b.* our fathers out
Neh. 9:7 *b.* him forth out of Ur.
15 *b.* forth water out of rock
23 *b.* them into the land
Ps. 66:11 thou *b.* us into the net
12 *b.* us out into a wealthy pl.

BROW.

Is. 48:4 thy neck iron, *b.* brass
Luke 4:29 led him to *b.* of the hill

BROWN.

Gen. 30:32 all *b.* cattle, 35, 40
33 every o. not *b.* accounted st.

BRUISE, Substantive.

Jer. 30:12 L. thy *b.* is incurable
Nah. 3:19 no healing of thy *b*

BRUISES.

Is. 1:6 but wounds and *b.*

BRUISE, Verb.

Gen. 3:15 *b.* thy head, *b.* his heel
Is. 28:28 nor *b.* it with horsemen
53:10 pleased the Lord to *b.* him
Dan. 2:40 as iron shall it *b.*
Rom. 16:20 G. of peace shall *b.* S.

BRUISED.

Lev. 22:24 not offer what is *b.*
2 *K.* 18:21 trustest this *b.* reed
Is. 42:3 a *b.* reed shall he not
break, *Mat.* 12:20
53:5 he was *b.* for our iniquities
Ezek. 23:3 in Egypt *b.* the teats
8 *b.* the breasts of her virginity
Luke 4:18 set at liberty them *b.*

BRUISING.

Ezek. 23:21 in *b.* thy teats by E.
Luke 9:39 the spirit *b.* him

BRUIT.

Jer. 10:22 noise of the *b.* is come
Nah. 3:19 all that hear *b.* of thee

BRUTE. *See* BEASTS.

BRUTISH.

Ps. 49:10 fool and *b.* person
92:6 a *b.* man knoweth not
94:8 unwiser. ye *b.* am. the peo.
Prov. 12:1 hateth reproof is *b.*
30:2 I am more *b.* than any
Is. 19:11 the counsel of the counsellors of Phar. is become *b.*
Jer. 10:8 they are altogether *b.*
14 man is *b.* 51:17 ; 21 pastors
Ezek. 21:31 into the hand of *b.*

BUCKET, S.

Num. 24:7 water out of his *b.*
Is. 40:15 nat. are as drop of a *b.*

BUCKLER.

2 *Sam.* 22:31 a *b.* to all that trust
in him, *Ps.* 18:30
1 *Chr.* 5:18 men able to bear a *b.*
12:8 Gadites that could h. *b.*
Ps. 18:2 Lord is my God, my *b.*
35:2 take hold of shield and *b.*
91:4 his truth shall be thy *b.*
Prov. 2:7 *b.* to them walk upr.
Jer. 46:3 order ye *b.* and shield
Ezek. 23:24 set against thee *b.*
26:8 he shall lift up *b.* against

BUCKLERS.

2 *Chr.* 23:9 Jehoiada delivered *b.*
Job 15:26 run. on bosses of his *b.*
Cant. 4:4 there hanged 1,000 *b.*
Ezek. 38:4 great company with *b.*
39:9 they shall set on fire *b.*

BUD, Substantive.

Job 38:27 *b.* of tender herb
Is. 18:5 when the *b.* is perfect
61:11 as earth bringeth forth *b.*
Ezek. 16:7 multiply as *b.* of field
Hos. 8:7 *b.* shall yield no meal

BUDS.

Num. 17:8 Aaron's rod *b.* forth *b.*

BUD, Verb.

Job 14:9 thr. scent of water, *b.*
Ps. 132:17 horn of David to *b.*
Cant. 7:12 see if pomegranates *b.*
Is. 27:6 Is. shall blossom and *b.*
55:10 maketh the earth to *b.*
Ezek. 29:21 cause horn of Is. to *b.*

BUDDED.

Gen. 40:10 was as though it *b.*
Num. 17:8 A. rod for house of L. *b.*
Cant. 6:11 to see whether pom. *b.*
Ezek. 7:10 pride hath *b.*
Heb. 9:4 ark wherein rod that *b.*

BUFFET.

2 *Cor.* 12:7 mes. of Satan to *b.* me

BUFFETED.

Mat. 26:67 *b.* him, *Mark* 14:65
1 *Cor.* 4:11 to present hour *b.*
1 *Pet.* 2:20 when *b.* for your f.

BUILD, *referred to God.*

1 *Sam.* 2:35 *b.* him a sure h. 2
Sam. 7:27 ; 1 *K.* 11:38
1 *Chr.* 17:10 will *b.* thee a house
25 told wilt *b.* him a house
Ps. 28:5 and not *b.* them up
51:18 *b.* thou the walls of Jer.
69:35 will *b.* the cities of Judah
89:4 *b.* up thy throne to all gen.
102:16 when L. shall *b.* up Zion
127:1 except the L. *b.* the house
147:2 Lord doth *b.* up Jerusalem
Jer. 18:9 con. a nation to *b.* it
24:6 I will *b.* not pull d. 31:28
31:4 I will *b.* thee, O virgin
33:7 I will *b.* Judah and Israel
42:10 if ye abide, I will *b.* you
Ezek. 36:36 that I *b.* ruined pl.
Amos 9:11 *b.* it as in days of old
Mat. 16:18 on this rock *b.* my ch.
26:61 *b.* it in three d. *Mark* 14:58
Acts 15:16 *b.* again tabernacle

BUILD, *Man the Agent.*

Gen. 11:4 go to, let us *b.* a city
Num. 32:24 *b.* ye cities
Deut. 20:20 shalt *b.* bulwarks
1 *K.* 9:24 then did *b.* Millo
11:7 Solom. did *b.* a high place
16:34 did Hiel *b.* Jericho
1 *Chr.* 22:19 *b.* ye the sanctuary
29:19 give Sol. a heart to *b.*
2 *Chr.* 14:7 let us *b.* these cities
Ezr. 4:2 let us *b.* with you
Neh. 2:17 let us *b.* the wall
4:3 which they *b.* if a fox go up
10 so we are not able to *b.*
Ec. 3:3 a time to *b.* up
Cant. 8:9 we will *b.* on her
Is. 9:10 fallen, but we will *b.*
45:13 he shall *b.* my city
58:12 *b.* old waste places, 61:4
60:10 sons of strangers, *b.* walls
65:22 not *b.* and another inhabit
Jer. 1:10 set over nations to *b.*
Ezek. 4:2 *b.* a fort against, 21:22
Dan. 9:25 to *b.* Jerusalem
Amos 9:11 I will *b.* as in days
14 Isr. shall *b.* the waste cities
Mic. 3:10 *b.* Zion with blood
Zec. 6:12 shall *b.* the temple, 13
15 they far off sh. *b.* in temple
9:3 Tyrus did *b.* a stronghold
Mal. 1:4 *b.* but I will throw d.
Mat. 23:29 ye *b.* tombs of proph.
Luke 11:47, 48
Luke 12:18 barns and *b.* greater
14:28 intending to *b.* a tower
30 to *b.* and not able to finish
Acts 20:32 word of his grace able
to *b.* you up
Rom. 15:20 lest I *b.* on ano. man's
1 *Cor.* 3:12 *b.* on this foundation
Gal. 2:18 if I *b.* again things

BUILD altar, s.

Ex. 20:25 *b. altar* of hewn stone
Num. 23:1 *b.* me here sev. *a.* 29
Deut. 27:5 there *b.* an *altar* to L.
6 shalt *b.* the *a.* of whole st.
Jos. 22:29 God forbid we sh. *b. a.*

See BEGAN.

BUILD, *joined with House, s.*

Deut. 25:9 will not *b.* brother's *h.*
28:30 *b.* a *h.* Zep 1:13
Ruth 4:11 which two did *b. h.*
2 *Sam.* 7:5 *b.* me *h.* to dwell in
7 why *b.* ye not me a *h.*
13 thy seed shall *b.* a *h.* 1 *K.* 5:5 ;
8:19 ; 1 *Chr.* 17:12 ; 22:10
1 *K.* 2:36 *b.* thee a *h.* in Jerus.
5:3 D. not *b.* a *h.* for the wars
5 I purp. to *b.* a *h.* to L. 2 *Chr.* 2:1
8:16 no city to *b. h.* 2 *Chr.* 6:5
17 it was in heart of D. to *b.* a
h. 1 *Chr.* 28:2 ; 2 *Chr.* 6:7
1 *Chr.* 17:12 shall *b.* a *h.* 2 *Chr.* 6:9
22:8 not *b.* a *h.* thou shed blood

1 *Chr.* 22:11 son, *b.* the *h.* of the L.
28:6 Sol. shall *b.* my *h.*
2 *Chr.* 2:4 behold, I *b.* a *h.*
5 *h.* I *b.* is great, for great is G.
6 who able to *b.* him a *h.*
36:23 ch. me to *b.* a *h. Ezr.* 1:2
Ezr. 1:3 go to Jerusalem *b. h.*
5:3 comman. you to *b.* this *h.* 9
6:7 let governor of Jews *b. h.*
Ps. 127:1 labor in vain that *b. h.*
Prov. 24:27 afterwards *b.* thy *h.*
Is. 65:21 shall *b. h.* and inhabit
66:1 where is *h.* ye *b.* unto me?
Jer. 22:14 I will *b.* me a wide *h.*
29:5 *b. h.* and dwell in them, 28
35:7 nei. shall ye *b. h.* nor sow
Ezek. 11:3 is not near, let us *b. h.*
28:26 and shall *b. h.*
Hag. 1:8 bring wood, *b.* the *h.*
Zec. 5:11 to *b.* it a *h.* in Shinar
Acts 7:49 what *h.* will ye *b.* me

BUILDED.

Gen. 4:17 C. *b.* city called Enoch
8:20 Noah *b.* an altar to the L.
10:11 Ashur *b.* Nineveh and
11:5 L. come to see tower men *b.*
Jos. 22:16 you *b.* an altar
1 *K.* 8:27 house I have *b.* 43
15:22 stones wh. Baasha had *b.*
2 *K.* 23:13 Solo. *b.* for Ashtoreth
1 *Chr.* 22:5 *b.* must be magnifical
Ezr. 4:13 if city be *b.* 16
5:8 to the house of great God *b.*
11 we build house *b.* years ago
15 let the house of G. be *b.* 6:3
6:14 elders of Jews *b.* and pros.
Job 20:19 a house he *b.* not
Ps. 122:3 J. is *b.* a city compact
Prov. 9:1 wisdom hath *b.* her *h.*
24:3 thr. wisdom is a house *b.*
Ec. 2:4 I *b.* me houses, I planted
Cant. 4:4 David *b.* for an armory
Jer. 30:18 city be *b.* on her heap
Lam. 3:5 he hath *b.* against me
Ezek. 36:10 wastes shall be *b.* 33
Luke 17:28 they planted, they *b.*
Eph. 2:22 in whom ye are *b.* tog.
Heb. 3:3 *b.* house hath more hon.
4 every house is *b.* by some m.

BUILDEDST.

Deut. 6:10 cities thou *b.* not

BUILDER, S.

1 *K.* 5:18 Solomon's and H.'s *b.*
2 *K.* 22:6 give it to *b.* 2 *Chr.* 34:11
Ezr. 3:10 when *b.* laid found.
Neh. 4:5 to anger before the *b.*
Ps. 118:22 stone *b.* refu. *Mat.* 21:42; *Mark* 12:10; *Luke* 20:17;
Acts 4:11
Ezek. 27:4 thy *b.* have perfected
Heb. 11:10 city whose *b.* is God
1 *Pet.* 2:7 the stone *b.* disallowed

Master-BUILDER.

1 *Cor.* 3:10 as a wise *m.-b.* I have

BUILDEST.

Deut. 22:8 *b.* a new house
Neh. 6:6 for wh. cause *b.* the wall
*Ezek.*16:31 *b.* thine eminent place
Mat. 27:40 that destroyest the temple and *b.* it, *Mark* 15:29

BUILDETH.

Jos. 6:26 cursed be man *b.* this c.
Job 27:18 *b.* his house as a moth
Prov. 14:1 wise woman *b.* her *h.*
Jer. 22:13 woe to him *b.* by un.
Hos. 8:14 for. maker, *b.* temples
Amos 9:6 *b.* his stories in heaven
Hab. 2:12 *b.* a town with blood
1 *Cor.* 3:10 another *b.* thereon

BUILDING, Participle.

1 *K.* 3:1 end of *b.* his own house
6:7 no tool of iron heard wh. *b.*
38 seven years in *b.* it
Ezr. 4:12 *b.* the rebellious city
Ezek. 17:17 *b.* forts to cut off

John 2:20 temple was 46 y. in *b.*
Jude 20 *b.* up on most holy faith

BUILDING, Substantive.

1 *K.* 9:1 when Sol. finished the *b.*
1 *Chr.* 28:2 made ready for the *b.*
2 *Chr.* 3:3 instructed for the *b.*
Ec. 10:18 slothful. *b.* decayeth
Ezek. 40:5 measured *b.* 41:15
46:23 a row of *b.* round about
1 *Cor.* 3:9 ye are God's *b.*
2 *Cor.* 5:1 we have a *b.* of God
Eph. 2:21 in whom *b.* fitly fra.
Heb. 9:11 tabernacle not of th. *b.*
Rev. 21:18 *b.* of wall was jasper

BUILDINGS.

Mat. 24:1 show him *b.* of temple
Mark 13:1 see what *b.* are here, 2

BUILT.

Deut. 13:16 it shall not be *b.*
1 *K.* 22:39 cities that Ahab *b.*
2 *Chr.*14:7 they *b.* and prospered
20:8 *b.* thee a sanctuary therein
26:9 Uzziah *b.* towers in Jer. 10
27:4 Joth. *b.* castles and towers
Job 3:14 who *b.* desolate places
12:14 and it cannot be *b.* again
22:23 if return shalt be *b.* up
Ps. 78:69 *b.* his sanc. like high p.
89:2 mercy shall be *b.* up
Is. 5:2 *b.* a tower in the midst
44:28 to Jeru. thou shalt be *b.*
Jer. 12:16 then shall they be *b.*
31:4 thou shalt be *b.* O virgin
32:31 prov. from day they *b.* it
45:4 which I *b.* will break it
Ezek. 16:24 hast *b.* eminent place
26:14 thou shalt be *b.* no more
Dan. 4:30 gr. Babylon I have *b.*?
9:25 street shall be *b.* again
Zec. 8:9 that temple be *b.*
Mat. 21:33 *b.* a tower, *Mark* 12:1
Luke 7:5 hath *b.* us a synagogue
1 *Cor.* 3:14 abide wh. he hath *b.*
Eph. 2:20 *b.* on found. of apost.
Col. 2:7 rooted and *b.* up in him
Heb. 3.4 that *b.* all things is God

BUILT altar.

Ex. 17:15 *b. a.* 24:4; 32:5 Aaron
Jos. 8.30 I *b. a.* ; 22:10 half tr.
Jud. 6:24 G. *b. a.*; 21:4 peo. *b. a.*
1 *Sam.* 7:17 S. *b. a.* ; 14:35 Saul *b.*
2 *Sam.* 24:25 D. *b. a.* to the Lord
1 *K.* 9:25 Solo. offered on *a.* he *b.*
18:32 with stones Elijah *b. a.*
2 *K.* 16:11 Urijah the priest *b. a.*

BUILT altars.

Num. 23:14 Balak *b.* seven *a.*
2 *K.* 21:4 he *b. a.* in house of L.
5 *b. a.* for host of h. 2 *Chr.* 33:5
2 *Chr.* 33:15 away *a.* he had *b.* in

BUILT city.

Num. 21:27 let *city* of Sihon be *b.*
Jos. 19:50 Joshua *b. c.* and dwelt
1 *Chr.* 11:8 David *b. c.* from Millo
Is. 25:2 to be no *c.* never be *b.*
Jer. 31:38 *city* shall be *b.* to Lord
Luke 4:29 hill whereon *c.* was *b.*

BUILT cities.

Ex. 1:11 *b.* for Phar. treasure-*cit.*
Jos. 24:13 *cities* which ye *b.* not
2 *Chr.* 14:6 Asa *b.* fenced *c.* in J.
17:12 Jehosh. *b. cities* of store
27:4 Jotham *b. c.* in mountains
Is. 44:26 *c.* of J. ye shall be *b.*

BUILT house, *or* houses.

Deut. 8:12 when hast *b.* goodly *h.*
20:5 what man hath *b.* new *h.*
1 *K.* 3:2 no *h.* was *b.* to name of Lord
6:9 Sol. *b. h.* 14 ; 8:13 *b.* th. a *h.*
8:20 have *b. h.* for name of L.
44 toward the *h.* I have *b.* 48;
2 *Chr.* 6:34, 38
1 *Chr.* 17:6 why not *b.* me a *h.*?
2 *Chr.* 6:18 less this *h.* I have *b.*?

Amos 5:11 ye *b. h.* of hewn stone
Hag. 1:2 Lord's *h.* should be *b.*
Zec. 1:16 my *h.* shall be *b.* in it
Mat. 7:24 *b. h.* on a r. *Luke* 6:48
26 *b.* his *h.* on sand, *Luke* 6:49
Acts 7:47 Solomon *b.* him a *h.*
1 *Pet.* 2:5 *b.* up a spiritual *house*

BUILT high places.

1 *K.* 14:23 Jud. *b. h. p.* and ima.
2 *K.* 17:9 chil. of Israel *b. h. p.*
Jer. 7:31 *b. h. p.* of Tophet ; 19:5 of Baal, 32:35

BUILT wall, *or* walls.

2 *Chr.* 27:3 on *w.* of O. *b.* much
32:5 Hezekiah *b.* up *w.* broken
33:14 Manas. *b. w.* without city
Neh. 4:6 so *b.* we the *w.* 7:1
Ezek. 13:10 one *b.* up the *w.*
Dan. 9:25 street *b.* ag. and the *w.*
Mic. 7:11 thy *walls* are to be *b.*

BUL. 1 *K.* 6:38

BUL.

Job 21:10 their *b.* gendereth
Is. 51:20 as a wild *b.* in a net

BULLS.

Ps. 22:12 many *b.* have compassed me, strong *b.*
50:13 will I eat the flesh of *b.*
68:30 rebuke the multitude of *b.*
Is. 34:7 with *b.* shall come down
Jer. 50:11 because ye bellow as *b.*
52:20 brazen *b.* under the bases
Heb. 9:13 if blood of *b.* and goats
10:4 blood of *b.* take away sins

BULLOCK.

Ex. 29:11 kill the *b. Lev.* 1:5; 9:18
Deut. 33:17 like firstling of *b.*
Jud. 6:25 take the young *b.* 26
1 *K.* 18:23 choose one *b.* 25
1 *K.* 18:33 E. cut the *b.* in pieces
Ps. 50:9 no *b.* out of thy house
69:31 than a *b.* that hath hor.
Is. 65:25 lion eat straw like *b.*
Jer. 31:18 a *b.* unaccus. to yoke

BULLOCK *with* Sin-offering.

Ex. 29:36 eve. day a *b.* for *sin-o.*
Ezek. 45:22 prepare a *b.* for *sin-o.*

See BLOOD.

Young BULLOCK.

Lev. 16:3 holy place with a *y. b.*
Num. 7:15 one *y. b.* 21, etc. to 81
2 *Chr.* 13:9 consecrate with *y. b.*
Ezek. 45:18 *y. b.* and clea. sanct.
46:6 day of new moon a *y. b.*

BULLOCKS.

1 *Chr.* 29:21 offered a thousand *b.*
Ezr. 6:17 the dedication 100 *b.*
Ps. 51:19 offer *b.* on thy altar
66:15 I will offer unto thee *b.*
Is. 1:11 'I delight not in bl. of *b.*
34:7 the *b.* shall come down
Jer. 46:21 hired men like fatted *b.*
50:27 slay all her *b.* let them go
Ezek. 39:18 drink the blood of *b.*
Hos. 12:11 they sacrifice *b.* in G.

See SEVEN.

BULRUSH, ES.

Ex. 2:3 an ark of *b.*
Is. 18:2 ambas. in vessels of *b.*
58:5 to bow his head like a *b.*?

BULWARKS.

Deut. 20:20 *b.* against the city
2 *Chr.* 26:15 engines on the *b.*
Ps. 48:13 mark well her *b.*
Ec. 9:14 a great king built *b.*
Is. 26:1 salvation appoint for *b.*

BUNCH, ES.

Ex. 12:22 take a *b.* of hyssop
1 *Chr.* 12:40 Zebulun brought *b.*
Is. 30:6 treas. upon *b.* of camels

BUNDLE, S.

Gen. 42:35 every man's b.
1 *Sam.* 25:29 bound in b. of life
Cant. 1:13 a b. of myrrh is my b.
Mat. 13:30 bind the tares in b.
Acts 28:3 P. gathered a b. of s.

BURDEN, Substantive.

Ex. 18:22 b. with th. *Num.* 11:17
23:5 ass lying under b.
Num. 4:19 appoint each to his b.
11:11 b. of all this people on me
Deut. 1:12 can I bear alone b. ?
2 *Sam.* 15:33 shalt be a b. to me
19:35 thy servant be a b. ?
2 *K.* 8:9 forty camels b. to Elisha
2 *Chr.* 35:3 not be a b.
Neh. 13:19 no b. on the Sabbath
Job 7:20 I am a b. to myself
Ps. 38:4 as a b. they are too h.
55:22 cast thy b. on the Lord
81:6 rem. his shoulder from b.
Ex. 12:5 grasshop. shall be a b.
Is. 9:4 broken the yoke of his b.
10:27 b. taken off thy shoulder
13:1 b. of Babylon
14:25 his b. depart off
28 year Ahaz died, was this b.
15:1 b. of Moab; 17:1 Damascus
19:1 b. of Egypt; 23:1 b. of T.
21:1 b. of the desert of the sea
11 b. of Du. 13 b. on Arabia
22:1 b. of the valley of vision
25 b. upon it shall be cut off
30:6 b. of beasts of the south
27 the b. thereof is heavy
46:1 a b. to weary beast
2 they could not deliver the b.
Jer. 17:21 no b. on Sabbath, 22, 27
23:33 what is the b. of the L. ?
36 b. of the Lord
38 but since ye say, b. of the L.
Ezek. 12:10 b. concerning prince
Hos. 8:10 for b. of the king
Nah. 1:1 the b. of Nineveh
Zep. 3:18 rep. of it was a b.
Mat. 11:30 and my b. is light
20:12 the b. and heat of the day
Acts 15:28 to lay no greater b.
21:3 ship was to unlade her b.
Gal. 6:5 man bear his own b.
Rev. 2:24 upon you none other b.

BURDEN, ED.

Zec. 12:3 I themes. be cut in p.
2 *Cor.* 5:4 we groan being b.
8:13 others be eased, and you b.
12:16 be it so, I did not b. you

BURDENS.

Gen. 49:14 couching bet. two b.
Ex. 2:11 M. looked on their b.
5:4 king said, get you to your b.
6:6 under b. of Egyptians, 7
Num. 4:27 appoint all their b.

Neh. 4:17 bare b. held a weapon
Is. 58:6 to undo the heavy b.
Lam. 2:14 seen for thee false b.
Mat. 23:4 heavy b. *Luke* 11:46
Gal. 6:2 bear ye one another's b.

BURDENSOME.

Zec. 12:3 Jerusalem a b. stone
2 *Cor.* 11:9 kept from being b.
12:13 that I was not b. to you
14 I will not be b. to you
1 *Thes.* 2:6 might been b.

BURIAL.

Ec. 6:3 also that he have no b.
Is. 14:20 not j. with them in b.
Jer. 22:19 with the b. of an ass
Mat. 26:12 she did it for my b.
Acts 8:2 carried Stephen to his b.

BURIED.

Gen. 25:10 there was Abraham b.
49:31 there they b. Abra., Sarah,
Isaac, Rebekah, there I b. L.
Num. 11:34 b. the people
20:1 Miriam died, was b. there

33:4 Egyptians b. all first-born
Deut. 10:6 Aaron, there he was b.
Jos. 24:32 bones of J. b. in She.
Ruth 1:17 and there will I be b.
2 *Sam.* 4:12 b. head of Ish-bosh.
21:14 bones of Saul b. in Zelah
1 *K.* 13:31 wherein man of G. b.
Ec. 8:10 so I saw the wicked b.
Jer. 8:2 nor b. 16:6; 20:6; 25:33
16:4 shall not be lamented nor b.
22:19 be b. with burial of an ass
Ezek. 39:15 till buriers have b.
Mat. 14:12 took body and b. it
Luke 16:22 died and was b.
Acts 2:29 D. is both dead and b.
5:9 feet of them which b.
Rom. 6:4 b. with him by baptism
1 *Cor.* 15:4 that he was b. and r.
Col. 2:12 b. with him in baptism

BURIED him.

Deut. 34:6 he b. him in val. in M.
2 *Sam.* 2:5 blessed be ye b. Saul
1 *K.* 14:18 b. All Isr. mourned
Acts 5:6 the young men b. him

BURIED in.

Gen. 15:15 b. in a good old age
1 *K.* 2:10 D. was b. in city of D.
Job 27:15 shall be b. in death.

BURIERS.

Ezek. 39:15 till b. have buried

BURN.

Gen. 44:18 let not thine anger b.
Ex. 27:20 lamp to b. *Lev.* 24:2
2 *Chr.* 2:6 save only to b. sacrif.
13:11 b. to Lord every morning
Is. 1:31 shall both b. together
10:17 b. and devour his thorns
27:4 I would b. them together
40:16 Lebanon is not suf. to b.
44:15 shall it be for man to b.
Jer. 7:20 my fury shall b.
34:5 so shall they b. odors
36:25 king would not b. roll
Ezek. 24:5 b. also bones under it
11 that the brass of it may b.
39:9 and b. the weapons
Nah. 2:13 I will b. her chariots
Mal. 4:1 that shall b. as oven
Mat. 13:30 in bundles to b. them
Luke 3:17 the chaff he will b.
24:32 did not our hearts b. in us
1 *Cor.* 7:9 bet. to marry than to b.
2 *Cor.* 11:29 offend. and I b. not?

BURN joined with fire.

Deut. 5:23 mount. did b. with f.
32:22 a f. shall b. to the lowest
hell, *Jer.* 17:4
Jos. 11:6 b. chariots with fire
Jud. 9:52 to b. it with fire
12:1 b. h. with f.; 14:15 b. thee f.
Ps. 79:6 thy jealousy b. like f.
89:46 thy wrath b. like fire?
Is. 47:14 as stubble f. shall b.
Jer. 4:4 like f. and b. 21:12
7:31 b. sons and dau. in f. 19:5
21:10 N. b. this city with fire,
32:29 ; 34:2, 22 ; 37:8. 10 ; 38:18
Ezek. 5:2 b. with fire a third part
16:41 b. thy h. with fire. 23:47
Mat. 3:12 b. up the chaff with
unquench. fire, *Luke* 3:17
Rev. 17:16 and b. her with fire

BURN incense.

Ex. 30:7 A. shall b. sweet i. 8.
1 *K.* 13:1 Jeroboam stood to b. i.
2 *K.* 18:4 chil. of Is. did b. i. to
1 *Chr.* 23:13 for ever to b. i.
2 *Chr.* 2:4 to b. sweet incense
13:11 b. every morn. sweet inc.
26:16 U. went to b. incense, 19
29:11 L. hath chosen you to b. i.
32:12 one altar and b. inc. on it
Jer. 7:9 b. i. to Baal? 11:13
44:17 b. i. to queen of heaven
Hos. 4:13 b. incense on hills
Hab. 1:16 b. i. to their dragon

Luke 1:9 Zach. his lot to b. inc.

BURNED.

Ex. 3:2 bush b. was not cons.
Deut. 9:15 the mount b. with fire
Jos. 7:25 b. them with fire
2 *Chr.* 34:25 forsaken me b. inc.
Est. 1:12 king's anger b. in him
Ps. 39:3 while musing the fire b.
Is. 24:6 inhab. of the earth are b.
42:25 it b. him, laid it not to h.
Lam. 2:3 b. ag. J. like flaming
John 15:6 withered branches b.
Acts 19:19 books, and b. them
Rom. 1:27 b. in their lust
1 *Cor.* 13:3 th. I give body to b.
Heb. 6:8 whose end is to be b.
12:18 not come to mount that b.
Rev. 1:15 his feet as if they b.

BURNETH.

Ps. 46:9 b. chariot in the fire
83:14 as the fire b. the wood
97:3 a fire b. up his enemies
Is. 9:18 wickedness b. as the fire
44:16 he b. part thereof in fire
62:1 salvation as a lamp that b.
64:2 as when melting fire b.
65:5 these are a fire b. all day
66:3 b. incense as if he blessed
Jer. 48:35 him that b. incense
Joel 2:3 behind them a flame b.
Rev. 21:8 lake which b. with fire

BURNING.

Gen. 15:17 a b. lamp passed bet.
Lev. 26:16 will appoint b. ague
Deut. 28:22 with extreme b.
32:24 be devoured with b. heat
Job 41:19 out of mo. go b. lamps
Ps. 140:10 b. coals fall upon them
Prov. 16:27 in his lips as b. fire
26:21 as coals to b. coals
23 b. lips and a wicked heart
Is. 30:27 name of L. com. far, b.
34:9 land shall become b. pitch
Jer. 20:9 his word was as a b. fire
Ezek. 1:13 appearance like b. c.
Dan. 3:6 cast into b. furnace, 11
7:9 and his wheels were as b. f.
Hab. 3:5 b. coals forth at his feet
Luke 12:35 loins girded, lights b.
John 5:35 John b. and shin. light
Rev. 4:5 lamps b. before throne
8:8 great mountain b. with fire
10 there fell a great star b.
19:20 cast alive into a lake b.

BURNING, Substantive.

Ex. 21:25 b. for b. wound for w.
Lev. 10:6 bewail b. which Lord
Deut. 29:23 brimstone, salt, b.
2 *Chr.* 16:14 great b. for him
21:19 people made no b. like b.
Is. 3:24 be b. instead of beauty
4:4 purged Jeru. by spirit of b.
9:5 this shall be with b. and f.
10:16 under his glory kindle b.
33:12 people as the b. of lime
Amos 4:11 a firebrand out of b.
Rev. 18:9 see smoke of her b.

BURNINGS.

Is. 33:14 dwell with everla. b. ?
Jer. 34:5 with b. of thy fathers

BURNISHED.

Ezek. 1:7 like color of b. brass

BURNT.

Gen. 34:29 let her be b.
Ex. 3:3 why the bush is not b.
Deut. 32:24 be b. with hunger
1 *K.* 13:2 men's bones be b.
15:13 b. her idol, 2 *Chr.* 15:16
2 *K.* 23:16 out of sepulc. b. them
25:9 b. house of the L. 2 *Chr.*
36:19 ; *Jer.* 52:13
Job 30:30 my bones are b.
Ps. 102:3 my bones b. as hearth
Prov. 6:27 his clothes not be b. ?
28 and his feet not be b. ?

Jer. 2:15 cities *b.; 6:29 bellows *b.*
36:28 in the roll Jehoiakim *b.*
51:25 make thee a *b.* mountain
Ezek. 20:47 all faces be *b.* therein
24:10 and let the bones be *b.*
Joel 1:19 the flame *b.* all the trees
Amos 2:1 bec. he *b.* bones of k.
Nah. 1:5 earth is *b.* at his pres.
1 *Cor.* 3:15 man's work be *b.*
Heb. 13:11 *b.* without the camp

BURNT *joined with* **fire.**
Lev. 6:30 sin-offer. *b.* in the *fire*
20:14 if a man take a wife and
her mother, shall be *b. w. f.*
21:9 if daughter of any priest
pro. herself, be *b.* with *fire*

Num. 11:1 *fl.* of L. *b.* 3
Deut. 4:11 mountain *b.* with *fire*
12:31 sons and d. they *b.* in *fire*
Jos. 7:15 he taken with accursed
thing be *b.* with *fire*
Jud. 15:6 *b.* her and fath. with *fl.*
14 cords bec. as flax *b.* with *fl.*
2 *Sam.* 23:7 shall be *b.* with *fire*
1 *K.* 16:18 *b.* king's house with *f.*
2 *K.* 1:14 *fire b.* up two captains
17:31 Seph. *b.* children in *fire*
23:11 *b.* chariots of sun with *fl.*
25:9 great man's house *b. w. fl.*
1 *Chr.* 14:12 gods were *b.* with *fl.*
2 *Chr.* 28:3 Á. *b.* his child. in *fl.*
Neh. 1:3 gates *b.* with *fl.* 2:17
Ps. 80:16 it is *b.* with *fire*
Is. 1:7 cities are *b.* with *fire*
43:2 walkest thr. *fire* not be *b.*
64:11 house is *b.* with *fire*
Jer. 38:17 city not be *b.* with *fl.*
49:2 her dau. shall be *b.* with *fl.*
51:32 reeds may have *b.* with *fl.*
58 high gates be *b.* with *fire*
Rev. 18:8 utterly *b.* with *fire*

BURNT Incense.
Ex. 40:27 he *b.* sweet *incense*
1 *K.* 9:25 Solomon *b. i.* upon alt.
12:33 Jerob. offered, and *b. i.*
22:43 people yet *b. i.* 2 *K.* 12:3 ;
14:4 ; 15:4, 35
2 *Chr.* 29:7 and have not *b. i.*
Is. 65:7 *b. i.* on the mountains
Jer. 18:15 my people *b. i.*
44:15 that their wives had *b. i.*
Hos. 2:13 she *b. i.* to them
11:2 and *b. i.* to graven images

BURNT-OFFERING.
Gen. 22:7 where is l. for a *b.-o. ?*
8 G. will provide lamb for *b.-o.*
Lev. 6:9 law of the *b.-o.* 7:37
9:2 ram for *b.-o.* 16:3, 5 ; 23:18
Num. 7:15 one lamb for *b.-o.* 21
to 81 ; *Ezek.* 45:15
28:10 the *b.-o.* of every sabbath
Jos. 22:26 altar not for a *b.-o.*
Jud. 13:23 not have rec. *b.-o.*
1 *Sam.* 7:10 as S. was off. *b.-o.*
13:12 forced myself and off. *b.-o.*
2 *K.* 3:27 offered him for a *b.-o.*
2 *Chr.* 7:1 fire consumed the *b.-o.*
29:24 the *b.-o.* sh. be made
Ps. 40:6 *b.-o.* hast thou not req.
51:16 delightest not in *b.-o.*
19 pl. with *b.-o.* whole *b.-o.*
Is. 40:16 nor beasts th. for *b.-o.*
61:8 L. hate robbery for *b.-o.*
Ezek. 46:13 daily prepare a *b.-o.*

**Continual BURNT-OFFER-
ING.**
Ex. 29:42 a con. *b.-o. Num.* 28:3,
6, 10, 15, 24, 31 ; 29:11, 16, 19,
22 ; *Ezr.* 3:5 ; *Neh.* 10:33 ;
Ezek. 46:15

Offer BURNT-OFFERING.
Gen. 22:2 take I. for *b.-o.*
Jud. 11:31 o. it up for *b.-o.*
13:16 *b.-o offer* it to the Lord

---

1 *Sam.* 6:14 *offer* kine for *b.-o.*
7:9 *off.* sucking lamb for *b.-o.*
2 *Chr.* 29:27 Hez. com. to o. *b.-o.*
Job 42:8 o. for yourselves a *b.-o.*

BURNT-OFFERINGS.
Gen. 8:20 N. offered *b.-o.* on altar
Num. 10:10 trumpets over *b.-o.*
1 *Sam.* 15:22 delight in *b.-o.*
1 *K.* 3:15 Solomon offered *b.-o.*
2 *Chr.* 2:4 b. a house for *b.-o.*
29:34 not slay all the *b.-o.*
35:14 busied in offering *b.-o.*
Ezr. 6:9 have need for *b.-o.*
Job 1:5 off. *b.-o.* accor. to num.
Ps. 50:8 not re. thee for *b.-o.*
66:13 into thy house with *b.-o.*
Is. 1:11 full of *b.-o.* of rams
43:23 small cattle of thy *b.-o.*
56:7 *b.-o.* shall be accepted
Jer. 6:20 *b.-o.* are not acceptable
7:21 put your *b.-o.* to your sacri.
17:26 from south bringing *b.-o.*
19:5 burn sons for *b.-o.* to Baal
Hos. 6:6 know. of G. m. than *b.-o.*
Mic. 6:6 before him with *b.-o. ?*
Mark 12:33 to love neighbor is
more than *b.-o.*
Heb. 10:6 in *b. o.* for sin

Offer BURNT-OFFERINGS.
2 *Sam.* 24:24 o. *b.-o.* of that cost
me nothing, 1 *Chr.* 21:24
1 *K.* 3:4 1000 *b.-o.* did Solomon *of.*
Jer. 33:18 want man to o. *b.-o.*
Amos 5:22 ye *offer* me *b.-o.*

BURNT-SACRIFICE.
Num. 23:6 he stood by his *b.-s.*
Deut. 33:10 shall put whole *b.-s.*
2 *Sam.* 24:22 oxen for *b.-s.*
1 *K.* 18:38 fire fell and c. *b.-s.*
Ps. 20:3 accept thy *b.-s.*

BURNT-SACRIFICES.
1 *Chr.* 23:31 to offer all *b.-s.*
2 *Chr.* 13:11 morn. and eve. *b.-s.*
Ps. 66:15 I will offer *b.-s.*

BURNT up.
Jud. 15:5 foxes *b. up* the shocks
2 *K.* 1:14 fire *b. up* two captains
Job 1:16 fire of God *b. up* sheep
Ps. 74:8 have *b. up* synagogue
106:18 flame *b. up* the wicked
Is. 64:11 beautiful house *b. up*
Jer. 9:10 *b. up* none can pass, 12
Mat. 22:7 king *b. up* their city
2 *Pet.* 3:10 earth and w. be *b. up*
Rev. 8:7 third part of trees and
all green grass was *b. up*

BURST.
Job 32:19 I am ready to *b.* like
Prov. 3:10 *b.* with new wine
Jer. 2:20 I have *b.* thy bands,
5:5 ; 30:8 ; *Nah.* 1:13
Mark 2:22 wine *b.* bot. *Lu.* 5:37
Acts 1:18 he *b.* asunder in midst

BURSTING.
Is. 30:14 in the *b.* of it a sherd

BURY.
Gen. 23:4 *b.* my d.; 6 *b.* dead, 11:15
47:29 *b.* me not in Egypt, 49:29
50:5 let me go and *b.* my father
1 *K.* 2:31 fall on Joab and *b.* him
13:29 old proph. came to *b.* him
31 *b.* me in the sepulchre
14:13 Israel shall *b.* him
2 *K.* 9:10 shall be none to *b.* her
34 this cursed woman *b.* her
35 went to *b.* her
Ps. 79:3 was none to *b.* them
Jer. 7:32 shall *b.* in Tophet, 19:11
14:16 shall have none to *b. G.*
Ezek. 39:11 there shall they *b.* G.
13 all the people shall *b.* them
Hos. 9:6 Memphis shall *b.* them
Mat. 8:21 go *b.* father, *Lu.* 9:59
22 dead *b.* their dead, *Lu.* 9:60
27:7 potter's field, to *b.* strang.

John 19:40 manner of J. is to *b.*

BURYING.
Gen. 23:4 *b.* pl. 9 ; 49:30 ; 50:13
2 *K.* 13:21 as they were *b.*
Ezek. 39:12 sev. mon. *b.* of them
Mark 14:8 anoint my body to *b.*
John 12:7 against my *b.* she kept

BUSH, ES.
Ex. 3:2 in the *b. Acts* 7:30
4 God called to him out of *b.*
Deut. 33:16 good-w. of him in *b.*
Job 30:4 cut mallows by the *b.*
7 among the *b.* they brayed
Is. 7:19 and rest upon all *b.*
Mark 12:26 how in *b.* God spake
Luke 6:44 nor of bramble-*b.*
20:37 dead r. Moses showed at *b.*
Acts 7:35 angel which app. in *b.*

BUSHEL.
Mat. 5:15 a candle and put it under a *b. Mark* 4:21 ; *Lu.* 11:33

BUSHY.
Cant. 5:11 his locks are *b.*

BUSINESS.
Gen. 39:11 J. went to do his *b.*
Deut. 24:5 nor be charged with *b.*
Jos. 2:14 utter not this our *b.*
Jud. 18:7 had no *b.* with any, 28
1 *Sam.* 20:19 hide wh. *b.* in hand
21:2 let no man know of the *b.*
8 the king's *b.* required haste
2 *Chr.* 13:10 wait on their *b.*
32:31 in *b.* of the ambassadors
Neh. 13:30 every man in his *b.*
Est. 3:9 that have charge of *b.*
Ps. 107:23 do *b.* in great waters
Prov. 22:29 a man dilig. in his *b.*
Ec. 5:3 through mult. of *b.*
Dan. 8:27 did the king's *b.*
Luke 2:49 about my Father's *b.*
Acts 6:3 may appoint over this *b.*
Rom. 12:11 not slothful in *b.*
16:2 assist in *b.* she hath need
1 *Thes.* 4:11 to do your own *b.*

BUSY, IED.
1 *K.* 20:40 as thy serv. was busy
2 *Chr.* 35:14 sons of Aaron *b.*

BUSYBODY, IES.
2 *Thes.* 3:11 are *b.* 1 *Tim.* 5:13
1 *Pet.* 4:15 let none suffer as a *b.*

BUTLER, S.
Gen. 40:9 *b.* told dream to Jos.
21 restored the chief *b.* to his
41:9 *b.* said, I remem. my faults

BUTTER.
Gen. 18:8 Abra. took *b.* and milk
Deut. 32:14 *b.* of kine
Jud. 5:25 bro. *b.* in lordly dish
2 *Sam.* 17:29 Barzillai brought *b.*
Job 20:17 brooks of honey and *b.*
29:6 I washed my steps with *b.*
Ps. 55:21 smoother than *b.*
Prov. 30:33 churn. of milk bri. *b.*
Is. 7:15 *b.* shall he eat, 22

BUTTOCKS.
2 *Sam.* 10:4 garm. to *b.* 1 *Chr.* 19:4
Is. 20:4 *b.* uncov. to shame of E.

BUY.
Gen. 42:7 fr. Can. to *b.* food, 43:20
47:19 *b.* us and our land
Ex. 21:2 if *b.* Hebrew servant
Lev. 25:44 shall *b.* bondmen, 45
Deut. 2:6 ye shall *b.* meat
28:68 and no man shall *b.* you
Ruth 4:5 must *b.* it also of Ruth
2 *Sam.* 24:21 D. said, to *b.* the
thresh.-floor, 24 ; 1 *Chr.* 21:24
Neh. 10:31 not *b.* it on sabbath
Is. 55:1 *b.* eat, *b.* wine and milk
Jer. 32:7 *b.* my field in Anathoth
44 men shall *b.* fields for money

Mat. 14:15 *b.* victuals, *Mark* 6:36
25:9 go to them that sell, and *b.*
10 went to *b.* bridegroom came
Mark 6:37 sh. we *b.* 200 p. worth
Luke 9:13 *b.* meat for this peo.
22:36 let him sell garm. and *b.*
John 4:8 were gone to *b.* meat
6:5 whence shall we *b.* bread
13:29 *b.* things we have need of
1 *Cor.* 7:30 *b.* as though they pos.
Jam. 4:13 *b.* and sell and get gain
Rev. 3:18 to *b.* of me gold tried
13:17 no man might *b.* or sell

BUY corn.

Gen. 41:57 all came to Jos. to *b. c.*
42:3 Joseph's brethren to *b. c.* 5
Neh. 5:3 mort. our lands to *b. c.*

BUY poor.

Amos 8:6 may *b.* the *poor* for sil.

BUY truth.

Prov. 23:23 *b. truth*, sell it not

BUYER.

Prov. 20:14 it is naught, saith *b.*
Is. 24:2 as with the *b.* so the s.
Ezek. 7:12 let not *b.* rejoice, nor

BUYEST.

Lev. 25:14 and if thou *b.* aught
Ruth 4:5 day *b.* field of Naomi

BUYETH.

Prov. 31:16 consider. field, *b.* it
Mat. 13:44 he selleth all, *b.* field
Rev. 18:11 no man *b.* her mer.

BUZ.

Gen. 22:21 M. bare to Nahor B.
1 *Chr.* 5:14 Jahdo, the son of B
Jer. 25:23 B. to drink the cup

BUZI.   *Ezek.* 1:3.
BUZITE.   *Job* 32:2, 6

BY and BY.

Mat. 13:21 *b. and b.* he is off.
Mark 6:25 give me *b. and b.* head
Luke 17:7 *b. and b.* sit down
21:9 the end is not *b. and b.*

BY-WAYS.

Jud. 5:6 walked through *b.-w.*

BYWORD.

Deut. 28:37 a *b.* among nations
1 *K.* 9:7 be *b.* among all people
2 *Chr.* 7:20 make this house a *b.*
Job 17:6 made me a *b.* of the
30:9 yea I am their *b.*
Ps. 44:14 a *b.* among heathen

C

CABINS.

Jer. 37:16 when J. entered into *c.*
CABUL.   1 *K.* 9:13.

CAGE.

Jer. 5:27 as a *c.* is full of birds
Rev. 18:2 *c.* of every uncl. bird
CAIAPHAS.   *Mat.* 26:3, 7; *John*
11:49; 18:14, 28.

CAIN.

Gen. 4:2, 5, 15, 25; *Jos.* 15:57.
Heb. 11:4 excel. sacrifice than C.
1 *John* 3:12 not as C. who was of
Jude 11 gone in the way of C.

CAINAN.

Luke 3:36 the son of C. 37

CALEB, S.

Lev. 24:5 bake twelve *c.* thereof
Jud. 7:13 a *c.* tumbled into host
2 *Sam.* 6:19 D. dealt to each a *c.*
2 *Sam.* 13:6 Tam. m. couple of *c.*
1 *K.* 17:12 I have not a *c.*
19:6 there was a *c.* baken
Ezek. 4:12 shalt eat it as barley *c.*
Hos. 7:8 Ephr. is a *c.* not turned
See FIGS, UNLEAVENED.
CALAH.   *Gen.* 10:12.

CALAMITY, IES.

Deut. 32:35 their *c.* is at hand
2 *Sam.* 22:19 day of *c. Ps.* 18:18
Job 6:2 my *c.* laid in balances
30:13 they set forward my *c.*
Ps. 57:1 until these *c.* be overp.
141:5 my prayer be in their *c.*
Prov. 1:26 I will laugh at your *c.*
6:15 his *c.* shall come suddenly
17:5 he glad at *c.* not be unpun.
19:13 foolish son is *c.* of father
24:22 *c.* shall rise suddenly
27:10 nor go to brother's h. in *c.*
Jer. 18:17 the back in day of *c.*
46:21 day of their *c.* was come
48:16 *c.* of Moab is near to come
49:8 bring *c.* of Esau upon him
32 bring their *c.* from all sides
Ezek. 35:5 shed blood of Israel
by sword in day of their *c.*
Ob. 13 sub. in day of their *c.*

CALAMUS.

Ex. 30:23 sweet *c.* 250 shekels
Cant. 4:14 spikenard, saffron, *c.*
Ezek. 27:19 *c.* in market of Tyrus

CALDRON.

1 *Sam.* 2:14 he struck it into *c.*
Job 41:20 smoke, as out of a *c.*
Ezek. 11:3 this city is the *c.* 7
Mic. 3:3 chop them as flesh in *c.*

CALDRONS.

2 *Chr.* 35:13 offering sod in *c.*
Jer. 52:18 *c.* took they away, 19

CALEB.

Num. 13:6, 30; 14:24, 38; 34:19
Jos. 14:13 Josh. gave C. Hebron
15:14 C. drove sons of Anak, 16
1 *Sam.* 25:3 N. was of house of C.
30:14 south of C. burnt Ziklag
CALEB-EPHRATAH.   1 *Chr.*
2:24

CALF.

Gen. 18:7 Abraham fetched a *c.*
Ex. 32:20 Moses burnt *c.*
Deut. 9:16 made you a molten *c.*
Neh. 9:18; *Ps.* 106:19
Job 21:10 their cow casteth not *c.*
Ps. 29:6 maketh to skip like a *c.*
Is. 11:6 *c.* and young lion
27:10 there sh. *c.* feed and lie
Jer. 34:18 when cut *c.* in twain
Ezek. 1:7 their feet like *c.* foot
Hos. 8:5 thy *c.* O S. cast thee off
6 *c.* of Samaria shall be broken
Luke 15:23 bring hither fatted *c.*
27 killed fatted *c.* 30
Acts 7:41 make a *c.* in those days
Rev. 4:7 second beast like a *c.*

CALKERS.

Ezek. 27:9 ancients of Geb. thy *c.*
27 thy *c.* shall fall into seas

CALL.

Gen. 2:19 what A. would *c.* them
Num. 22:20 if the men *c.* thee
Deut. 4:7 God is in all we *c.* for
26 I *c.* heaven and earth to
wit.' ag. you, 30:19; 31:28
Jud. 21:13 to *c.* peaceably
1 *Sam.* 3:6 thou didst *c.* me, 8
1 *K.* 8:52 hearken in all they *c.*
18:24 *c.* ye on your gods
Job 5:1 *c.* now if any
13:22 *c.* I will answer, 14:15
Ps. 4:1 hear when I *c.* O God
3 the Lord will hear when I *c.*
14:4 who eat my peo. and *c.* not
20:9 let king hear us when we *c.*
49:11 *c.* lands after their names
77:6 I *c.* to rem. my song in n.
86:5 plen. in m. to all *c.* on thee
99:6 among them *c.* on name
102:2 when I *c.* answer me sp.
145:18 L. is nigh all that *c.*
Prov. 8:4 to you, O men, I *c.*
9:15 *c.* passengers who go right
31:28 her children *c.* her blessed
Is. 5:20 them that *c.* evil good
45:3 *c.* thee by thy name
48:2 *c.* themselves of holy city
13 when I *c.* they stand up

55:6 *c.* on him while he is near
58:5 wilt thou *c.* this a fast
13 *c.* the sabbath a delight
65:15 *c.* his serv. by ano. name
24 before they *c.* I will answer
Jer. 33:3 *c.* to me, I will ans. thee
Lam. 2:15 men *c.* perfection
Hos. 1:4 L. said, *c.* his n. Jezreel
6 *c.* his name Lo-ruhamah
9 *c.* his name Lo-ammi
7:11 *c.* to Egypt, go to Assy.
Joel 1:14 *c.* a sol. assembly, 2:15
Jon. 1:6 sleeper *c.* on thy God
Zec. 3:10 *c.* ev. man his neighbor
Mal. 3:15 we *c.* the proud happy
Mat. 9:13 not come to *c.* righteous, *Mark* 2:17; *Luke* 5:32
22:3 servants to *c.* them bidden
43 D. in spirit *c.* him Lord
23:9 *c.* no man father on earth
Luke 6:46 why *c.* me Lord
14:13 makest feast *c.* the poor
John 13:13 ye *c.* me Master
Acts 9:14 all *c.* on thy name
19:3 to *c.* over them had evil spi.
24:14 after way they *c.* heresy
Rom. 10:12 to all that *c.* on him
2 *Cor.* 1:23 I *c.* God for a record
2 *Tim.* 2:22 peace wi. th. *c.* on L.
Heb. 2:11 not asha. to *c.* them
10:32 *c.* to remem. former days
Jam. 5:14 let him *c.* the elders
1 *Pet.* 1:17 if ye *c.* on the Father

**CALL on the name of the
Lord.**

Gen. 4:26 began men to *c. on L.*
1 *K.* 18:24 I will *c. L. Ps.* 116:17
2 *K.* 5:11 will come and *c. on L.*
1 *Chr.* 16:8 *c.* upon his name, *Ps.*
105:1; *Is.* 12:4
Joel 2:32 whosoever shall *c. on
L. Acts* 2:21; *Rom.* 10:13
Zep. 3:9 they may all *c. on L.*
1 *Cor.* 1:2 in every place *c. L.*

Not CALL.

Ruth 1:20 *c.* me *not* N. *c.* me M.
Ps. 14:4 *c.* not upon the Lord
Is. 31:2 will *not c.* back his w.
Jer. 10:25 fury upon the families
that *c. not* on thy name
Luke 14:12 *c. not* thy friends nor
John 15:15 I *c.* you *not* servants
Acts 10:15 *c. not* common, 11:9
28 *not* to *c.* any man common

Shall, or shalt CALL.

Deut. 30:1 *shalt c.* them to mind
33:19 *shalt c.* people to moun.
Job 14:15 *shalt c.* I will answer
Ps. 50:4 *shall c.* to the heavens
72:17 nations *s. c.* him blessed

Is. 7:14 *s. c.* Imman. *Mat.* 1:23
41:25 rising of sun *shall* he *c.*
44:5 *s. c.* himself by name of J.
7 and who, as I, *shall c.* and
55:5 *shall c.* a nation
58:9 *shalt c.* and L. shall answer
60:14 *shall c.* thee city of Lord
18 *shalt c.* thy walls salvation
61:6 men *s. c.* you min. of our G.
62:12 *shalt c.* them holy people
Jer. 3:17 *s. c.* Jer. throne of Lord
19 thou *shalt c.* me, my father
7:27 *shalt c.* to them, not answ.
Hos. 2:16 *shalt c.* me no more B.
Joel 2:32 the remnant L. *shall c.*
Zec. 13:9 they *shall c.* I will hear
Mal. 1:4 *s. c.* them bord. of wick.
3:12 nations *shall c.* you blessed
Mat. 1:21 *shalt c.* his name Jesus
10:25 much more *s. c.* them
Luke 1:13 *shalt c.* his name John
48 generations *s. c.* me blessed
Acts 2:39 as many as the L. *s. c.*
Rom. 10:14 how *s.* they *c.* on him

Will CALL.

1 *Sam.* 12:17 I *will c.* to Lord.
2 *Sam.* 22:4 I *will c.* Lord, *Ps.* 18:3
Job 27:10 *will* hypocrite *c.* on G.
Ps. 55:16 I *will c.* on God, 86:7
80:18 quicken us, we *will c.*
116:2 *w.* I *c.* on him
Is. 22:20 that I *w. c.* my ser. E.
Jer. 1:15 I *will c.* fam. of north
Rom. 9:25 I *w. c.* them my peo.

CALL upon me.

Ps. 50:15 *c. u. m.* in d. of trouble
91:15 he shall *c. upon me*
Prov. 1:28 *c. u. m.* but I will
Jer. 29:12 then shall ye *c. u. m.*

CALLED.

Gen. 11:9 name of it *c.* Babel
21:17 *c.* to Hagar out of heaven
22:11 *c.* to Abrah. out of heaven
35:10 not be *c.* any more Jacob
18 his father *c.* him Benjamin
Ex. 8:8 Pharaoh *c.* for Moses, 25 ;
9:27 ; 10:16, 24 ; 12:31
Deut. 5:1 Moses *c.* all Israel, 29:2
15:2 it is *c.* the Lord's release
28:10 thou art *c.* by name of L.
Jud. 14:15 S. wife, have ye *c.* us
15:17 cast away jawb. *c.* place
Jud. 15:18 w. athirst, and *c.* on L.
16:28 Samson *c.* to the Lord
1 *Sam.* 9:9 now *c.* a proph. was *c.*
2 *Sam.* 6:2 name is *c.* by name
12:28 city be *c.* after my name
1 *K.* 1:9 Adonijah *c.* breth. 19, 25
18:3 Ahab *c.* Obadiah the gov.
26 they *c.* on the name of Baal
1 *Chr.* 4:10 Jabez *c.* on God
13:6 whose name is *c.* on it
21:26 David *c.* on Lord
Est. 2:14 except that she were *c.*
4:11 I have not been *c.* to come
Ps. 53:4 they have not *c.* on God
79:6 kingd. not *c.* on thy name
Is. 43:22 hast not *c.* on me, O J.
48:1 ver. *c.* by the name of Israel
12 O Jacob, my *c.*
61:3 be *c.* trees of righteousness
Lam. 1:21 bring day thou hast *c.*
2:22 thou hast *c.* my terrors
Ezek. 20:29 name is *c.* Bamah
Dan. 5:12 now let Daniel be *c.*
Mat. 1:16 Jesus who is *c.* Christ
13:55 is not his mother *c.* Mary ?
18:2 *c.* a little child unto him
20:16 many be *c.* few cho. 22:14
32 Jesus stood still and *c.* them
23:8 be not ye *c.* Rabbi, 10
27:17 shall I release J. *c.* C. 22
Mark 10:49 J. com. him to be *c.*
14:72 P. *c.* to mind word J. said
Luke 1:61 none of thy kind. is *c.*
62 how he would have him *c.*

15:19 worthy to be *c.* thy son, 21
19:15 he com. servants to be *c.*
23:33 place that is *c.* Calvary
John 1:48 before Philip *c.* thee I
4:25 cometh which is *c.* Christ
9:11 a man *c.* Jesus made clay
Acts 9:11 go into str. *c.* Straight
11:26 disciples first *c.* Christians
13:7 *c.* for Barnabas and Saul
15:17 on whom my name is *c.*
19:40 *c.* in quest. for this day's
23:6 I am *c.* in question, 24:21
18 Paul the prisoner *c.* me
Rom. 1:1 P. *c.* to be apos. 1 *Cor.* 1:1
6 are ye also the *c.* of Jesus
7 *c.* to be saints, 1 *Cor.* 1:2
2:17 thou art *c.* a Jew
8:28 the *c.* acc. to his purpose
1 *Cor.* 1:9 were *c.* to fellowship
· 24 *c.* both Jews and Greeks
26 not many noble are *c.*
5:11 *c.* a brother be a fornicator
7:18 *c.* being circum.? is any *c.*
21 art thou *c.* being a servant?
24 wherein he is *c.*
Gal. 1:6 removed from him *c.* you
5:13 ye have been *c.* to liberty
Eph. 2:11 *c.* uncircum. by that *c.*
4:1 vocation wherew. ye are *c.*
4 even as ye are *c.* in one hope
Col. 3:15 to the which ye are *c.*
2 *Thes.* 2:4 exalteth above all *c.*
1 *Tim.* 6:12 et. life, wher. art *c.*
20 science falsely so *c.*
Heb. 3:13 while it is *c.* to-day
9:15 they *c.* might rec. promise
11:16 not ash. to be *c.* their G.
24 to be *c.* son of Phar. daught.
Jam. 2:7 name by wh. ye are *c.*
1 *Pet.* 2:9 *c.* you out of darkness
even hereunto were ye *c.*
3:9 that ye are thereunto *c.*
2 *Pet.* 1:3 that hath *c.* us to glory
1 *John* 3:1 sh. be *c.* the sons of G.
Jude 1 preserved in J. Ch. and *c.*
Rev. 8:11 star is *c.* Wormwood
11:8 city spiritually *c.* Sodom
17:18 they with him are *c.*
19:9 blessed are *c.* to mar. sup.

CALLED, *joined with* God *or* Lord.

Gen. 1:5 God *c.* the light Day
5:2 and *c.* their name Adam
Ex. 3:4 God *c.* to him
19:3 L. *c.* to him out of mount.
20 L. *c.* Moses to top of mount
Num. 12:5 L. *c.* Aaron and Mir.
1 *Sam.* 3:4 L. *c.* Samuel, 6, 8, 10
Ps. 50:1 *c.* earth from the rising
Is. 41:2 Lord *c.* him to his foot
42:6 I have *c.* thee in righteous.
49:1 L. hath *c.* me
54:6 *c.* thee as a woman fors.
Jer. 11:16 *c.* name green olive-t.
20:3 not *c.* thy name Pashur
Amos 7:4 God *c.* to contend
Acts 16:10 gath. that Lord *c.* us
1 *Cor.* 7:15 G. hath *c.* us to peace
17 L. hath *c.* every one, so let
Gal. 1:15 who *c.* me by grace
1 *Thes.* 2:12 *c.* you to his kingd.
4:7 hath not *c.* us to unclean.
2 *Thes.* 2:14 God *c.* you
1 *Tim.* 1:9 *c.* us with a holy call.
Heb. 5:4 *c.* of God as was Aaron
10 *c.* of God a high-priest after
1 *Pet.* 5:10 G. who hath *c.* us

He CALLED.

Gen. 26:18 *c.* names as hi· *f. c.*
35:10 he *c.* his name Isr·
Ex. 24:16 *c.* to M. out of ·oud
2 *K.* 4:36 *c.* to Gehazi, s· ·e *c.*
Ps. 105:16 he *c.* for a fam··e on
Lam. 1:15 *c.* an assembly
Mat. 10:1 *c.* twelve; 15:10 mult.
Mark 1:20 he *c.* them
Luke 13:12 Jesus saw her, he *c.*

John 10:35 if he *c.* then gods
Acts 9:41 had *c.* saints and wid.
10:23 *c.* he them in, and lodged
23:23 he *c.* unto him two centur.
Rom. 8:30 he also *c.* whom he *c.*
9:24 even us whom *he* hath *c.*
1 *Pet.* 1:15 hath *c.* you is holy

See CALLED *the name.*

I CALLED, *or* I have CALLED.

Num. 24:10 I *c.* thee to curse
1 *Sam.* 3:5 Eli said, I *c.* not, 6
28:15 therefore I *have c.* thee
2 *Sam.* 22:7 in my distress I *c.*
Ps. 18:6 ; 118:5
Job 9:16 if I *had c.* and he answ.
19:16 I *c.* my servant, no answ.
Ps. 17:6 I *have c.* on thee, for
31:17 not be ashamed, I *have c.*
88:9 I *have c.* daily upon thee
116:4 then *c.* I on name of Lord
Prov. 1:24 I *have c.* and ye ref.
Cant. 5:6 I *c.* him
Is. 13:3 I *have c.* my mighty
41:9 I *have c.* thee from chief
43:1 I *c.* thee by thy name, 45:4
48:15 yea, I *have c.* him
50:2 I *c.* was there none to ans.
51:2 for I *c.* him alone
65:12 I *c.* ye did not a. *Jer.* 7:13
66:4 when I *c.* none did answer
Jer. 35:17 I *have c.* to them, but
Lam. 1:19 I *c.* for my lovers, but
3:55 I *c.* out of the low dungeon
57 drewest near in day I *c.* on
Hos. 11:1 then I *c.* my son out of
Egypt, *Mat.* 2:15
Zec. 11:7 one I *c.* b. other I *c.*
John 15:15 I *have c.* you friends
Acts 13:2 work wh. I *have c.* them
28:20 have I *c.* for you, to see

CALLED by my name.

2 *Chr.* 7:14 if my people which
are *c.* by my name humble
Is. 43:7 even every one *c.* n.
65:1 to nation not *c.* my n.
Jer. 7:10 this house *c. b. m. name,*
11, 14, 30 ; 32:34 ; 34:15
25:29 evil on city *c. by n.*
Amos 9:12 remnant of heath. *c. n.*

CALLED by thy name,

1 *K.* 8:43 house *c. b. t. n.* 2 *Chr.* 6:33
Is. 4:1 let us be *c. by t. n.* to take
43:1 I have *c.* thee *by t. n.* 45:4
63:19 were not *c. by thy name*
Jer. 14:9 we are *c. by thy n.*
15:16 am *c. t. n.* O L. G. of hosts
Dan. 9:18 the city *c. by thy n.*
19 for thy people are *c. n.*

CALLED his name.

Gen. 35:10 *c.* n. Is.; 18 Benoni
1 *Chr.* 4:9 Jabez; 7:16 Peresh; 23 Ber.
Mat. 1:25 he *c. his name* Jesus
Rev. 19:13 n. is *c.* the word of G.

Sent and CALLED.

Acts 20:17 *s.* to Ephesus *c.* elders

Shall be CALLED.

Gen. 2:23 *s. c.* Woman, because
17:5 name *shall be c.* Abraham
21:12 in Isaac *shall* thy seed *be*
c. Rom. 9:7 ; *Heb.* 11:18
32:28 *shall be c.* no more Jacob
48:6 issue *s. c.* after their breth.
Prov. 16:21 wise in heart *s. c.*
24:8 deviseth evil *s. c.* mischief.
Is. 4:3 remain. in Jer. *s. c.* holy
9:6 his name *s. be c.* Wonderful
32:5 no more *shall be c.* liberal
35:8 *s. be c.* the way of holiness
54:5 G. of whole earth *s.* he *be c.*
56:7 *s. c.* h. of prayer, *Mat.* 21:13
Jer. 23:6 *s. c.* L. our right. 33:16
Zec. 8:3 J. *s. be c.* city of truth
Mat. 2:23 *shall be c.* a Nazarene
5:9 peacemakers *s. c.* child. of G.
19 *s. be c.* least in kingdom

Luke 1:32 *s. c.* Son of the Highest
35 holy thing *s. be c.* the Son
60 but he *shall be c.* John
2:23 every male *shall be c.* holy
Rom. 9:26 *s. be c.* children of G.

Shalt be CALLED.

Is. 1:26 *s. c.* city of righteousness
47:1 *shalt be c.* no more tender
5 *s.* no more *be c.* a lady of k.
58:12 *s. be c.* repairer of the br.
62:2 *s. be c.* by a new name
4 *s. c.* Hephzi-bah, thy land B.
12 *s. be c.* Sought out, A city n.
Luke 1:76 *s. c.* proph. of Highest
John 1:42 thou *shalt be c.* Cephas

They CALLED.

*Num.*25:2 *t. c.* people to sacrifices
Est. 9:26 *they c.* these days Pur.
Ps. 99:6 *t. c.* upon the Lord, and
Jer. 12:6 *t. c.* a multitude
30:17 bec. *t. c.* thee an outcast
Hos. 11:2 as *they c.* them, so they
7 *t. c.* them to Most High
Mat. 10:25 *t. c.* master Beelzebub
Luke 1:59 *t. c.* him Zacharias
John 9:18 *t. c.* parents of him
24 *c. they* man that was blind
Acts 4:18 *t. c.* com. not to speak
5:40 when *t. had c.* the apostles
14:12 *they c.* Barnabas Jupiter

Was CALLED.

Is. 48:8 *was c.* a transgressor
Luke 2:21 his name *was c.* Jesus
John 2:2 J. *w. c.* and his discip.
*Acts*24:2 he *w. c.* forth, Tertullus
1 *Cor.* 7:20 calling wh. he *w. c.*
Heb. 11:8 A. wh. he *w. c.* obeyed
Jam. 2:23 *w. c.* the friend of God
Rev. 19:11 sat on him *w. c.* faith.

CALLEDST, EST.

Jud. 8:1 *c.* us not when wentest
1 *Sam.* 3:5 here am I, thou *c.* me
Ps. 81:7 thou *c.* in trouble
Mat. 19:17 w. *c.* thou me good?
Mark 10:18 ; *Luke* 18:19

CALLETH.

1 *K.* 8:43 do accor. to all stranger
c. to thee for, 2 *Chr.* 6:33
Job 12:4 *c.* on God, and he ans.
Ps. 42:7 deep *c.* unto deep
147:4 *c.* them, *Is.* 40:26
Prov. 18:6 mouth *c.* for strokes
Is. 21:11 he *c.* to me out of Seir
59:4 none *c.* for justice, nor any
64:7 none that *c.* on thy name
Hos. 7:7 none that *c.* to me
Amos 5:8 *c.* for waters of sea, 9:6
Mat. 27:47 *c.* for E. *Mark* 15:35
Mark 3:13 *c.* to him whom he w.
6:7 *c.* to him the twelve
8:1 Jesus *c.* his disciples
10:49 arise, he *c.* thee
12:37 David *c.* him L. *Luke* 20:44
Lu. 15:6 he *c.* together his friends
9 *c.* her friends and neighbors
20:37 when he *c.* L. the G. of A.
John 10:3 *c.* his sheep by name
11:28 the Master *c.* for thee
Rom. 4:17 *c.* things which be not
9:11 election m. stand of him *c.*
1 *Cor.* 12:3 by Spirit *c.* Jesus
Gal. 5:8 not of him that *c.*
1 *Thes.* 5:24 faithful is he *c.* you
Rev. 2:20 *c.* herself a prophetess

CALLING, Substantive.

Is. 1:13 *c.* of assemblies I cannot
Ezek. 23:19 *c.* to rem. her youth
Rom. 11:29 *c.* of God without
1 *Cor.* 1:26 ye see your *c.* breth.
7:20 ev. man abide in same *c.*
Eph. 1:18 the hope of his *c.*
4:4 called in one hope of your *c.*
Phil. 3:14 the high *c.* of God
2 *Thes.* 1:11 worthy of this *c.*
2 *Tim.* 1:9 called us w. a holy *c.*

Heb. 3:1 partakers of heavenly *c.*
2 *Pet.* 1:10 your *c.* and election

CALLING, Participle.

Is. 41:4 *c.* gen. from beginning
46:11 *c.* ravenous bird from east
Mat. 11:16 *c.* to fell. *Luke* 7:32
Mark 11:21 P. *c.* to remembrance
Acts 7:59 stoned Stephen *c.* on G.
22:16 thy sins, *c.* on Lord
1 *Pet.* 3:6 S. obeyed A. *c.* him lord

CALM.

Ps. 107:29 maketh storm a *c.*
Jon. 1:11 sea may be *c.* unto us
12 cast me forth, so sea be *c.*
*Mat.*8:26 gr.*c. Mark* 4:39 ; *Lu.*8:24

CALNEH.

Gen. 10:10 Babel and C. in land
Amos 6:2 pass ye unto C. from

CALNO. *Is.* 10:9

CALVARY. *Luke* 23:33

CALVE, ED, ETH.

Job 21:10 their cow *c.* casteth n.
39:1 mark when hinds do *c.*

Ps. 29:9 make hinds to *c.*
Jer. 14:5 the hind *c.* in the field

CALVES.

1 *Sam.* 6:7 bring *c.* home
1 *K.* 12:28 king made 2 *c.* of gold
32 sacrificing to *c.* he had m.
2 *K.* 10:29 dep. not from gold. *c.*
2 *Chr.* 11:15 ord. priests for the *c.*
13:8 there be with you golden *c.*
Ps. 68:30 rebuke bulls with the *c.*
Hos. 10:5 because of *c.* of Beth.
13:2 that sacrifice kiss the *c.*
14:2 render the *c.* of our lips
Amos 6:4 eat *c.* out of the stall
Mic. 6:6 with *c.* of a year old?
Mal. 4:2 ye shall grow up as *c.*
Heb. 9:12 nor by the blood of *c.*
19 blood of *c.* and sprinkled

CAME.

Gen. 27:35 brother *c.* w. subtilty
32:6 we *c.* to thy brother Esau
Num. 22:9 God *c.* to Balaam, 20
24:2 spirit of God *c.* upon him,
Jud. 3:10 ; 1 *Sam.* 10:10
Deut. 33:2 Lord *c.* from Sinai
Jud. 13:10 man that *c.* other day
1 *Sam.* 2:27 *c.* a man of G. to Eli
4:1 word of Samuel *c.* to all Isr.
2 *Sam.* 20:12 every one that *c.*
1 *K.* 1:42 while he spake Jon. *c.*
4:34 *c.* of all people to hear Sol.
13:10 returned not by way he *c.*
2 *K.* 6:32 ere the messe. *c.* he s.
10:21 all worshippers of Baal *c.*
17:28 one of priests *c.* to Bethel
19:33 by the way he *c.* return
24:3 at com. of Lord *c.* this on J.
1 *Chr.* 5:2 of Judah *c.* chief ruler
2 *Chr.* 11:14 Levites *c.* to Judah
14:14 fear of L. *c.* upon them
25:20 A. not hear, for it *c.* of G.
Est. 1:17 but Vashti *c.* not
Job 3:26 yet trouble *c.*
29:13 him ready to perish *c.*
30:26 I looked for good, evil *c.*
Ps. 18:6 my cry *c.* before him
27:2 when my foes *c.* upon me
78:31 wrath of G. *c.* upon them
88:17 they *c.* about me daily
105:19 until the time his w. *c.*
Ec. 5:15 to go as he *c.* 16
Is. 41:5 ends of earth were af. *c.*
Jer. 7:31 nor *c.* it into my mind,
19:5 ; 32:35
8:15 for peace, but no good *c.*
44:21 *c.* it not into his mind?
Ezek. 33:22 afore he that esc. *c.*
43:2 glory of G. *c.* from east
Dan. 4:28 all this *c.* on Nebuch.
Amos 6:1 to whom house of Is. *c.*
Hab. 3:3 G. *c.* from Teman, and

Mat. 3:1 in those days *c.* J. B.
9:1 and *c.* into his own city
20:28 *c.* not to be ministered to
21:30 he *c.* to second, said lik.
32 John *c.* in way of right.
25:36 in prison, ye *c.* to me
28:13 disciples *c.* by night
Mark 9:21 since this *c.* to him ?
Luke 9:35 *c. a* voice out of cloud
15:17 when *c.* to himself, he said
20 he arose and *c.* to his father
John 1:11 he *c.* to his own
17 grace and truth *c.* by J. Chr.
3:2 same *c.* to Jesus, 7:50 ; 19:39
4:27 upon this *c.* his disciples
12:30 voice *c.* not because of me
20:19 at even *c.* J. in the midst
Acts 9:21 *c.* hither for that intent
19:18 many that believed *c.* and
Rom. 5:18 free gift *c.* on all men
7:9 when com. *c.* sin revived
9:5 whom con. the flesh C. *c.*
1 *Cor.* 15:21 since by man *c.* death
Gal. 2:12 certain *c.* from James
1 *Thes.* 1:5 gospel *c.* not in word
1 *Tim.* 1:15 that J. C. *c.* to save
2 *Pet.* 1:17 *c.* such a voice to him
18 this voice *c.* from heaven
21 proph. *c.* not by will of man
1 *John* 5:6 that *c.* by water and

See Spirit of the LORD.

CAME again.

Jud. 13:9 angel *c. a.* to the wom.
15:19 spirit *c. a.* 1 *Sam.* 30:12
1 *K.* 17:22 soul of the child *c. a.*
19:7 angel *c. a.* the second time
Luke 8:55 her spirit *c. again*
John 8:2 he *c. a.* into temple

CAME down.

Gen. 11:5 L. *c. down* to see tower
Ex. 19:20 L. *c. d.* on mount Sinai
34:29 Moses *c. d.* from mount S.
2 *Sam.* 22:10 bowed the heavens
and *c. down, Ps.* 18:9
Lam. 1:9 she *c. down* wonderf.
Dan. 4:13 holy one *c. d.* from h.
Mic. 1:12 evil *c. down* from the L.
Mat. 17:9 as *c. d.* fr. m. *Mark* 9:9
John 3:13 he that *c. d.* fr. heav.
6:38 I *c. down* from heaven
41 bread which *c. d.* 51, 58
Acts 15:1 which *c. down* from J.

CAME forth.

Num. 11:20 *c.* we *f.* out of Eg. ?
Jud. 14:14 out of eater *c. f.* meat,
out of strong *c. f.* sweetness
2 *Sam.* 16:11 son which *c. f.* of
my bowels seeketh my life
2 *Chr.* 32:21 *c. f.* of his bowels
Prov. 7:15 *c.* I *forth* to meet thee
Ec. 5:15 as he *c. f.* naked
Jer. 20:18 *c.* I *f.* out of womb?
Zec. 10:4 of him *c. f.* the corner
Mark 1:38 for therefore *c.* I *f.*,
John 16:28 I *c. f.* from the Father
19:5 J. *c. f.* wearing the crown

I CAME.

Gen. 30:30 thou hadst before *I c.*
1 *K.* 10:7 I believed not till *I c.*
half was not told, 2 *Chr.* 9:6
Is. 50:2 *I c.* was there no man?
Ezek. 3:15 *I c.* to them of capt.
Mat. 10:34 *I c.* not to send peace
Mark 2:17 *I c.* not to call, *Lu.* 5:32
John 8:14 I know whence *I c.*
42 *I c.* from G. nor *c.* I of mys.
12:27 for this cause *c.* I
47 *I c.* not to judge the world
18:37 for this cause *c.* I into w.
Acts 10:29 *c.* I, as soon as sent I.
20:18 from first day *I c.* into A.
22:11 *I c.* into Damascus
1 *Cor.* 2:1 *I c.* not with excellency
2 *Cor.* 1:23 to spare you *I c.* not
2:3 when *I c.* I sh. have sorrow

CAME in.

Gen. 6:4 sons of God *c. in*
19:5 where men *c. in* to thee
38:18 Judah *c. in* unto her
1 *Sam.* 18:13 David went out and
   c. in before the people, 16
2 *Sam.* 11:4 she *c. in* to him
2 *Chr.*15:5 no p. to him that went
   out nor him *c. in, Zec.* 8:10
Est. 2:14 *c. in* to king no more
Jer. 37:4 Jer. *c. in* and went out
Mat. 22:10 k. *c. in* to see guests
Luke 1:28 angel *c. in* to Mary
   7:45 since I *c. in* kissed my feet
Gal. 2:4 who *c. in* privily

CAME near.

Ex. 14:20 *c.* not n. other all night
Deut. 1:22 ye *c. n.* to me, 5:23
Jos. 17:4 they *c. n.* bef. El. 21:1
1 *K.* 18:36 Elijah *c. n.* and said
Jer. 42:1 least to the greatest *c. n.*
Acts 9:3 as he *c. n.* Damascus

CAME nigh.

Mat. 15:29 Jesus *c. n.* to sea of G.
Mark 11:1 when they *c. n.* to J.
Luke 7:12 when he *c. n.* to gate

CAME out.

Gen. 38:28 m. said this *c. o.* first
Ex. 13:3 remember day ye *c. o.* 4
Num. 16:27 Dathan and Ab. *c. o.*
2 *Sam.*6:20 Michal *c. o.* to meet D.
18:4 people *c. out* by hundreds
Job 1:21 naked *c. I out* of womb
   3:11 when I *c. out* of the belly
Jer. 17:16 which *c. o.* of my lips
Mat. 8:34 whole city *c. o.*
   12:44 return to m. house whence
   I *c. out, Luke* 11:24
   27:32 they *c. out* found Simon
   53 *c. o.* of graves after his res.
Mark 1:26 unc. spirit *c. out,* 9:26
9:7 a voice *c. out* of the cloud
Luke 1:22 he *c. o.* could not speak
   4:35 *c. out* of him, hurt his not
John 16:27 because ye believed I
   c. out from God
   17:8 that I *c. out* from thee
   19:34 forthwith *c. o.* blood
Acts 8:7 uncl. spir. *c. o.* of many
   16:18 spirit *c. o.* the same hour
1 *Cor.* 14:36 *c.* word of G. *o.* from
Heb. 3:16 not all that *c. o.* of Eg.
Rev. 7:14 these *c. o.* of great trib.

CAME over.

Jos. 4:22 Is. *c. o.* J. on dry land
Mark 5:1 *c. over* to other side

CAME to pass.

Ex. 12:41 it *c. to p.* at end of 430
   years, self-s. day it *c. to p.*51
Deut. 2:16 *c. to p.* 1 *Sam.* 13:22 ;
   2 *K.* 15:12; *Est.*2:8; *Acts*27:44
Jos. 21:45 L. had spoken all *c. p.*
1 *Sam.* 1:20 it *c. p.* wh. time was
   10:9 all those signs *c. to pass*
2 *Sam.* 2:1 it *c. to p.* after, 8:1 ;
   10:1 ; 2 *K.* 6:24 ; 2 *Chr.* 20:1
2 *K.*8:15 it *c. to p.* on the morrow,
   1 *Chr.* 10:8 ; *Jer.* 20:3 ; *Acts* 4:5
Is. 48:3 and they *c. to pass*
   5 before it *c. to p.* I showed it
1 *Thes.* 3:4 as it *c. to pass.*

Then CAME.

2 *Sam.* 5:1 *then c.* all the tribes
2 *Chr.* 12:5 *t. c.* Shemaiah to R.
Job 30:26 for good *then* evil *c.*
Jer. 19:14 *t. c.* Jer. from Tophet
   38:27 *t. c.* all the princes to Jer.
Mat. 9:14 *t. c.* disciples of John
   15:1 *t. c.* to Jesus scribes and
   12 *then c.* his disciples, 17:19
   18:21 *then c.* Peter to him
John 7:45 *t. c.* officers to ch. prl.
   12:28 *t. c.* a voice from heaven
   20:26 *t. c.* Jesus, doors being

They CAME, *or* CAME they.

Gen. 11:31 *they c.* to Haran
   12:5 into land of Canaan *they c.*
   22:9 *t. c.* to place G. told him of
Ex. 16:35 till *t. c.* to a land
1 *K.* 2:7 so *t. c.* to me when I
2 *K.* 20:14 men wh. *t. c. Is.* 39:3
2 *Chr.* 20:4 *t. c.* to seek the Lord
Neh. 13:21 *c. t.* no more on sab.
Job 6:20 *t. c.* thither
   30:14 *t. c.* as a wide breaking
Ps. 88:17 *t. c.* round me like w.
Jer. 43:7 thus *c. t.* to Tahpanhes
Ezek. 23:40 and lo, *they c.*
Mat. 1:18 before *they c.* together
   14:34 *t. c.* into l. of Gennesaret
   26:73 after a while *c. they*
Mark. 1:45 *t. c.* from every quar.
   3:13 whom he would and *t. c.*
Luke 2:16 *t. c.* with haste found
John 12:9 *t. c.* not for Jes. sake
Acts 12:20 *t. c.* with one accord
   17:13 *they c.* thither also
   23:14 *they c.* to the chief priests
Rev. 7:13 whence *c. they?*

Word of the Lord CAME.

Gen. 15:1 the *w. L. c.* to Abr. 4
1 *Sam.* 15:10 *w. L. c.* to Samuel
2 *Sam.* 24:11 Gad ; 1 *K.* 6:11 Solo.
   16:1 Jehu, 7 ; 17:2 Elijah, 8 ;
   18:1 ; 19:9 ; 21:17, 28
   18:31 to whom *word of the L. c.*
   saying, Israel be thy name
1 *K.* 12:22 Shema, 2 *Chr.*11:2 ; 12:7
2 *K.* 20:4 Isaiah, *Is.* 38:4
1 *Chr.* 17:3 Nathan ; 22:8 David
Jer. 1:2 *w. L. c.* to Jere. 4 ; 2:1 ;
   14:1 ; 29:30 ; 33:1, 19 ; *Dan.* 9:2
Ezek. 1:3 expressly to Ezek. 3:16
Hos. 1:1 Hosea ; *Joel* 1:1 Joel
Jon. 1:1 Jon. 3:1 ; *Mic.* 1:1 Mic.
Zep. 1:1 Zeph. ; *Hag.* 1:1 Hag.
Zec. 7:4 *c. w.* L. of hosts, 8:1

CAMEL.

Gen. 24:64 Reb. lighted off the *c.*
Lev. 11:4 not *c.* the *c. Deut.* 14:7
1 *Sam.* 15:3 slay infant, ox, and *c.*
Zec. 14:15 so be plague of *c.*
Mat. 19:24 is easier for a *c. Mark*
   10:25 ; *Luke* 18:25
   23:24 strain at a gnat, swallow *c*

CAMELS.

Gen. 12:16 Abram had *c.*
   24:19 draw water for thy *c.* 44
   30:43 J. had much cattle, *c.*
   31:34 put them in *c.* furniture
   37:25 Ishmaelites came with *c.*
Ex. 9:3 hand of the L. on the *c.*
Jud. 6:5 *c.* without number, 7:12
   8:21 took ornam. on *c.* necks, 26
1 *Sam.* 27:9 David took away *c.*
   30:17 save 400 which rode on *c.*
1 *K.* 10:2 to Jer. with *c.* 2 *Chr.*9:1
2 *K.* 8:9 a present forty *c.* burden
1 *Chr.* 5:21 Reu. took of *c.* 50,000
   12:40 brought bread on *c.*
   27:30 over the *c.* was Obil
Ezr. 2:67 their *c.* 435, *Neh.* 7:69
Est. 8:10 letters by post on *c.* 14.
Job 1:3 his substance was 3,000 *c.*
   17 Chaldeans fell upon the *c.*
Is. 21:7 he saw a chariot of *c.*
   30:6 treasures on bunches of *c.*
   60:6 mult. of *c.* shall cover thee
Jer. 49:29 shall take their *c.*
   32 their *c.* shall be a booty
Ezek. 25:5 Rabbah a stable for *c.*
Mat. 3:4 raim. of *c.* hair, *Mark* 1:6

CAMEST.

Gen. 16:8 Hagar, whence *c.* thou
   27:33 eaten of all before thou *c.*
Num. 22:37 wherefore *c.* thou not
Deut. 16:3 rem. day *c.* out of Eg
1 *Sam.* 13:11 *c.* not within days
   17:28 why *c.* thou down hither

2 *Sam.* 15:20 whereas *c.* but yes.
1 *K.* 13:9 nor return by way *c.* 17
   14 man of God that *c.* from J.?
2 *K.* 19:28 I will turn thee back
   by way thou *c. Is.* 37:29
Neh. 9:13 *c.* down also on M. Si.
Is. 64:3 *c.* down, mount. flowed
Jer. 1:5 before thou *c.* forth out of
   the womb I sancti. thee
Ezek. 32:2 *c.* forth with thy rivers
Mat. 22:12 friend, how *c.* in hit.
John 6:25 Rabbi, when *c.* hither
   16:30 we believe thou *c.* from G.
Acts 9:17 in the way as thou *c.*

CAMON. *Jud.* 10:5

CAMP.

Ex. 14:19 ang. of L. went bef. *c.*
   32:17 a noise of war in *c.*
   27 *c.* slay every man brother
   36:6 proclaimed through the *c.*
Lev. 24:10 strove together in *c.*
Num. 4:5 when *c.* setteth forw.
   11:1 con. in utmost parts of *c.*
   26 Eld. and Med. prophes. in *c.*
Deut. 23:14 in midst of thy *c.*
Jos. 6:18 made *c.* of Isr. a curse
Jud. 13:25 spirit of God began to
   move Samson in the *c.*
   21:8 none to the *c.* from Jabesh
1 *Sam.* 4:6 noise of shout in the *c.*
   17:17 run to *c.* to thy brethren
2 *K.* 6:8 in such a place be my *c.*
   7:7 left *c.* as it was, fled for life
   8 when these lepers came to *c.*
   19:35 angel of L. smote in *c.* of
   Assyr. 185,000, *Is.* 37:36
Ps. 78:28 let it fall in midst of *c.*
   106:16 envied M. also in the *c.*
Ezek. 4:2 set the *c.* also against it
Joel 2:11 for his *c.* is very great
Rev. 20:9 compassed *c.* of saints

CAMP, Verb.

Is. 29:3 I will *c.* against thee
Jer. 50:29 bend the bow *c.* ag. it
Nah. 3:17 *c.* in hedges in cold day

CAMPED.

Ex. 19:2 Israel *c.* before mount

Into the CAMP.

1 *Sam.* 4:7 God is come *into c.*

Out of the CAMP.

Ex. 19:17 M. brought people *o. c.*
Lev. 10:4 your brethren *out c.*
   24:23 had cursed *out c.*
Num. 14:44 M. departed not *o. c.*
Deut. 23:10 unclean shall go *o. c.*
1 *Sam.* 13:17 spoilers *o. c.* of Phil.
2 *Sam.* 1:2 came *o. c.* from Saul

Round about the CAMP.

Num. 11:31 quails *r. a. c.* 32

Without the CAMP.

Ex. 29:14 bullock burn *w. c. Lev.*
   8:17 ; 9:11 ; 16:27
   33:7 sought the L. went *w. t. c.*
Deut. 23:12 have a place *w. c.*
Jos. 6:23 R. left kindred *w. c.*
Heb. 13:11 beasts burnt *w. the c.*
   13 go forth to him *w. the c.*

CAMPS.

Num. 10:2 trum. for journey of *c.*
Amos 4:10 stink of your *c.* come

CAMPHIRE.

Cant. 1:14 my beloved is as *c.*
   4:13 thy plants an orchard of *c.*

CAN.

Mat. 27:65 as sure as you *c.*
John 15:4 no more *c.* ye except
Rom. 8:7 subject to law, nor *c.* be

How CAN.

John 3:9 said, *h. c.* these th. be?
Acts 8:31 *h. c.* I exc. some guide?

CANA.

John 2:1 marriage in C. 11
4:46 Jesus came again into C.
21:2 Thomas and Nath. of C.

CANAAN.

Gen. 9:18, 22; 10:15; 28:1
Ex. 15:15 the inhabitants of C.
Jud. 3:1; 4:2, 23; 5:19
Ps. 106:38 to the idols of C.
135:11 smote all kingdoms of C.
Is. 19:18 speak language of C.
Zep. 2:5 C. I will destroy thee
Mat. 15:22 a woman of C. cried

Land of CANAAN.

Gen. 12:5 to go into *land of* C.

CANAANITE.

Gen. 12:6; 15:21; 24:3; 34:30
Ex. 23:28 drive out C. 33:2; 34:11
Num. 21:3 deliv. up C. *Neh.* 9:24
Mat. 10:4 Simon the C. *Mark* 3:18

CANAANITESS. 1 *Chr.* 2:3
CANDACE. *Acts* 8:27

CANDLE.

Job 18:6 his c. be put out
21:17 c. of wicked put out?
29:3 his c. shined on my head
Ps. 18:28 thou wilt light my c.
Prov. 20:27 spirit of man is c.
24:20 c. of wicked be put out
31:18 c. goeth not out by night
Jer. 25:10 from them light of c.
Mat. 5:15 put c. under a bushel,
Mark 4:21; *Luke* 8:16; 11:33
Luke 11:36 bright shining of a c.
15:8 a c. and sweep the house
Rev. 18:23 c. shine no more
22:5 need no c. nor light of sun

CANDLES.

Zep. 1:12 will search Jer. with c.

CANDLESTICK.

Ex. 25:31 make c. 37:17 ; *Num.* 8:4
40:24 put c. in tent of congreg.
Lev. 24:4 lamps on c. continually
Num. 3:31 their charge shall be c.
2 *K.* 4:10 let us set for him a c.
1 *Chr.* 28:15 gold for every c.
2 *Chr.* 13:11 set they in order c.
Dan. 5:5 wrote over ag. the c.
Zec. 4:2 behold a c. all of gold
11 olive-trees on right side of c.
Mat. 5:15 on a c. and it giveth
light to all, *Luke* 8:16 ; 11:33
Mark 4:21 not be set on c. ?
Heb. 9:2 first wherein was the c.
Rev. 2:5 else I will remove thy c.

CANDLESTICKS.

1 *K.* 7:49 c. of p. gold, 2 *Chr.* 4:7
Jer. 52:19 he took away the c.
Rev. 11:4 two c. standing bef. G.
See SEVEN.

CANE.

Is. 43:24 brought me no sweet c.
Jer. 6:20 c. from far country

CANKER, ED.

2 *Tim.* 2:17 will eat as c.
Jam. 5:3 your gold and silver is c.

CANKER-WORM.

Joel 1:4 c. eat. and c.-w. left, 2:25
Nah. 3:15 like c.-w. make thyself
many as the c.-w.
16 c.-w. spoileth and flieth

CANNOT.

Is. 1:13 calling of assemblies I c.
Jer. 18:6 c. I do with you
Luke 16:26 from hence to you c.

CANST.

Mat. 8:2 *thou* c. make me clean
Mark 9:22 if thou c. do any thing

CAPERNAUM. *Mat.* 4:13 ; 8:5;
11:23; 17:24; *Luke* 4:23; 10:15;
John 2:12; 4:46; 6:17, 24, 59
CAPHTOR. *Jer.* 47:4 ; *Amos* 9:7

CAPPADOCIA.

Acts 2:9 dwellers in C. we hear
1 *Pet.* 1:1 strangers throughout C.

CAPTAIN.

Gen. 37:36 sold him to Potiph. c.
40:4 c. charged Jos. with them
Num. 14:4 make a c. *Neh.* 9:17
Jos. 5:14 as c. of host of the L.
15 c. of the L. host said to Jos.
Jud. 4:2 c. of Jabin's host was
Sisera, 7 ; 1 *Sam.* 12:9
11:6 said to Jephthah, be our c.
11 made him c. over them
1 *Sam.* 9:16 anoint him c. 10:1
13:14 Lord com. him to be c.
17:18 carry th. ten cheeses to c.
22:2 David became c. over them
2 *Sam.* 5:2 shalt be c. over Israel
8 he shall be c. 1 *Chr.* 11:6
19:13 if thou be not c. of the
23:19 Abishai was therefore c.
1 *K.* 16:16 Isr. made Omri c. king
2 *K.* 1:9 king sent a c. with fifty
4:13 wouldest be spo. for to c. ?
5:1 Naaman c. of host of Syria
9:5 an errand to thee, O c.
15:25 Pekah a c. of his conspired
18:24 face of one c. *Is.* 36:9
20:5 Hezekiah c. of my people
25:8 Nebuzar-adan. c. *Jer.* 52:12
1 *Chr.* 11:21 honorable, he was c.
27:5 c. for 3d month Benaiah
2 *Chr.* 13:12 God himself is our c.
Is. 3:3 doth take away c. of fifty
Jer. 37:13 a c. Irijah took Jer.
40:5 c. gave Jer. victuals
51:27 appoint a c. against her
John 18:12 band and c. took Jes.
Acts 5:26 c. with officers brought
Heb. 2:10 c. of their salvation

CAPTAINS.

Ex. 15:4 chosen c. are drowned
Deut. 1:15 I made wise men c.
20:9 make c. to lead the p.
1 *Sam.* 8:12 he will appoint him c.
22:7 son of Jesse make you c. ?
2 *Sam.* 18:5 c. charge con. Absal.
23:8 that sat chief among the c.
1 *K.* 2:5 what Joab did to the c.
20:24 kings away, and put c.
22:33 when c. perceived he was
not the king, 2 *Chr.* 18:32
1 *Chr.* 11:15 three of 30 c. went
2 *Chr.* 33:11 brought on them c.
Job 39:25 the thunder of the c.
Jer. 13:21 taught them to be c.
51:23 I will break in pieces c.
57 I will make drunk her c.
Ezek. 21:22 c. to open the mouth
23:6 c. all desirable men, 12, 23
Nah. 3:17 thy c. as great grassh.
Mark 6:21 H. made a supper to c.
Luke 22:4 J. communed with c.
Rev. 19:18 may eat the flesh of c.

CAPTIVE.

Gen. 14:14 brother was taken c.
34:29 their wives took they c.
Ex. 12:29 unto first-born of c.
2 *K.* 5:2 bro. away c. a little m.
6:22 those thou hast taken c.
Is. 49:21 I am desolate, a c.
24 shall lawful c. be delivered
51:14 c. exile hasteneth
52:2 loose thys. O c. dau. of Z.
Amos 6:7 c. with first that go c.
2 *Tim.* 2:26 taken c. by him

Carry *or* **carried CAPTIVE,**
or **CAPTIVES.**

Gen. 31:26 *car.* my daughters c.
Num. 24:22 until A. *car.* thee c.
1 *K.* 8:46 *car.* them c. 2 *Chr.* 6:36
47 they bethink thems. in land
whither *carried* c. 2 *Chr.* 6:37
2 *K.* 15:29 T.-pileser *car.* them c.
16:9 c. peo. of Damas. c. to Kir
1 *Chr.* 5:6 king of Assyria c. c.

2 *Chr.* 25:12 10,000 did Judah c. c.
28:5 *car.* a great multitude c.
8 Is. *car.* c. of brethren 200,000
Ps. 106:46 pitied of th. c. them c.
137:3 c. us c. required a song
Jer. 13:17 Lord's flock is *car.* c.
19 J. shall be wholly c. away c.
20:4 shall c. them c. to Babylon
24:5 acknowledge them *car.* c.
29:4 saith the Lord to all *car.* c.
14 bring you into place whence
I caused you to be *car.* c.
41:10 Ishm. c. c. all the residue
43:12 *carry* the Egyptians c.
52:29 c. c. from Jer. 832 persons
30 c. c. of the Jews 745 persons
Ezek. 6:9 nations whither be c. c.
Dan. 11:8 also c. c. into Egypt
Amos 1:6 bec. they c. c. captivity
Ob. 11 in day strangers *car.* c.

Carrying CAPTIVE.

Jer. 1:3 to *car.* of Jerusalem c.

Lead, *or* **led CAPTIVE.**

Jud. 5:12 *lead* thy captivity c.
1 *K.* 8:48 return unto thee in land
of enemies which *l.* them c.
2 *Chr.* 30:9 shall find compassion
before them that *lead* c.
Ps. 68:18 *led* captivity c. *Eph.* 4:8
Jer. 22:12 die whither *led* him c.
Amos 7:11 Israel shall be *led* c.
Nah. 2:7 Huzzab shall be *led* c.
Luke 21:24 shall be *led* away c.
2 *Tim.* 3:6 *lead* c. silly women

CAPTIVES.

Num. 31:9 women of Midian c.
12 brought c. ; 19 purify your c.
Deut. 21:11 am. c. a beauti. wo.
32:42 drunk with blood of c.
1 *Sam.* 30:5 David's two wives c.
2 *K.* 24:14 from Jerus. 10,000 c.
2 *Chr.* 28:11 deliver the c. again
13 ye shall not bring in c.
Is. 14:2 take them c. whose c.
20:4 the Ethiopians c.
45:13 let go my c. not for price
49:25 c. of mighty be taken
61:1 liberty to the c. *Luke* 4:18
Jer. 48:46 thy sons and d. are c.
50:33 took them c. held them
Ezek. 1:1 as I was among c.
16:53 captivity of thy c.
Dan. 2:25 found a man of c. of J.

CAPTIVITY.

Num. 21:29 his daughters into c.
Deut. 21:13 raiment of c. from of
30:3 Lord will turn thy c.
2 *K.* 24:15 carried he into c. to B.
25:27 37th year of c. *Jer.* 52:31
1 *Chr.* 5:22 dwelt in steads until c.
6:15 Jehozadak went into c.
2 *Chr.* 6:37 pray in land of c.
38 if they return to thee in c.
29:9 our sons and wives are in c.
Ezr. 9:7 have been delivered to c.
Neh. 1:2 Jews wh. were left of c.
4:4 for a prey in land of their c.
Est. 2:6 Mordecai carried with c.
Job 42:10 L. turned the c. of Job
Ps. 14:17 Lord bring back c. 85:1
78:61 deliv. his strength into c.
126:1 when L. turned ag. c. of Z.
4 turn again our c. O L. as str.
Is. 5:13 my peo. are gone into c.
22:17 carry thee with mighty c.
46:2 themselves are gone into c.
Jer. 15:2 for the c. to the c. 43:11
29:14 I will turn away your c.
30:3 ; 32:44 ; 33:7, 11, 26
20 hear all of c. ; 28 c. is long
22 taken up a curse by all c.
31 send to all them of c.
30:10 seed from land of c. 46:27
48:11 hath Moab gone into c.
Lam. 1:3 Judah is gone into c.
5 her children are gone into c.

2:14 discov. to turn away thy *c.*
4:22 no more carry thee into *c.*
Ezek 1:2 fifth y. of Jehoiac. *c.*
3:11 get to them of *c.* and speak
11:25 I spake to them of *c.* all
12:7 my stuff, as stuff for *c.*
16:53 bring again their *c.* the *c*
of Sodom and Samaria
25:3 went into *c.* thou saidst
33:21 in 12th year of *c.* one esc.
39:23 house of Isr. went into *c.*
40:1 in the 25th year of our *c.*
Dan. 6:13 D. of the *c.* of Judah
11:33 shall fall by *c.* many days
Hos. 6:11 returned *c.* of my peo.
Ob. 20 *c.* of this host, *c.* of Jer.
Mic. 1:16 gone into *c.* from thee
Nah. 3:10 No went into *c.* her ch.
Hab. 1:9 gather *c.* as the sand
Zep. 2:7 shall turn away *c.* 3:20
Zec. 6:10 take of them of the *c.*
Rom. 7:23 *c.* to the law of sin
2 *Cor.* 10:5 into *c.* every thought

See CAPTIVE.

Bring CAPTIVITY.

Ps. 53:6 when God *b.* back *c.*
Jer. 30:18 *b.* ag. *c.* of Jacob's t
31:23 I shall *b.* again their *c.*
48:47 *bring* again *c.* of Moab
49:6 I will *b.* again *c.* of Ammon
39 will *bring* again *c.* of Elam
Ezek. 29:14 *b.* again *c.* of Egypt
39:25 now will I *b.* again *c.* of J.
Joel 3:1 I *b.* again *c.* of Judah
Amos 9:14 *b.* again *c.* of my peo.

Children of CAPTIVITY.

Ezr. 4:1 *c. c.* builded temple
10:7 proclamation to the *c. c.*
16 *c.* of *c.* did so, all were sep.
Dan. 5:13 which art *c. c.* of Ju.

Go into CAPTIVITY.

Deut. 28:41 sons and daugh. *g. c.*
Jer. 20:6 and house shall *go c.*
22:22 thy lovers shall *go into c.*
30:16 adver. every one shall *go c.*
46:19 O daugh. furnish to *go c.*
48:7 Chem. shall *c.;* 49:3 king
Ezek. 12:4 go as they that *go c.*
30:17 these cities shall *go into c.*
18 Egypt, her dau. shall *go c.*
Amos 1:5 people of S. shall *go c.*
15 their king shall *go into c.*
5:5 Gilgal shall surely *go into c.*
27 I cause you to *go into c.*
7:17 Is. shall surely *go into c.*
9:4 they *go c.* before enemies
Zec. 14:2 city shall *go into c.*
Rev. 13:10 lead. into *c.* shall *go c*

Out of CAPTIVITY.

Ezr. 2:1 went up *o. c. Neh.* 7:6
6:21 come *out c.* kept the feast
8:35 come *out of c.* offered

CARBUNCLE, S.

Ex. 28:17 first row a *c.* 39:10
Is. 54:12 make thy gates of *c.*
Ezek. 28:13 and *c.* thy covering

CARCASS.

Lev. 5:2 touch *c.* unclean thing
11:8 *c.* not touch, *Deut.* 14:8
Deut. 28:26 *c.* be meat to fowls
Jos. 8:29 should take his *c.* down
Jud. 14:8 to see *c.* of lion honey
1 *K.* 13:22 thy *c.* not come
24 a lion stood by the *c.*
2 *K.* 9:37 *c.* of Jez. be as dung
Is. 14:19 cast out as *c.* trodden
Mat. 24:28 *c.* is there will eagles

CARCASSES.

Gen. 15:11 fowls came on *c.*
Lev. 11:11 *c.* in abomination, 26
26:30 cast your *c.* on *c.* of idols
Num. 14:29 *c.* shall fall in wilder.
1 *Sam.* 17:46 I will give *c.* of Ph.
Is. 5:25 their *c.* torn in streets
34:3 stink come up out of *c.*

66:24 *c.* of them transgressed
Jer. 7:33 *c.* of this people be
meat for fowls, 16:4 ; 19:7
16:18 filled mine inh. with the *c.*
Ezek. 6:5 lay *c.* of Isr. before id.
43:9 *c.* of their kings far from
Nah. 3:3 a great number of *c.*
Heb. 3:17 *c.* fell in wilderness

CARCHEMISH.

2 *Chr.* 35:20 to fight against C.
Is. 10:9 is not Calno as C. ?
Jer. 46:2 river Euphrates in C.

CARE.

1 *Sam.* 10:2 father left *c.* of asses
2 *K.* 4:13 careful with all this *c.*
Jer. 49:31 the nation without *c.*
Ezek. 4:16 shall eat bread with *c.*
Luke 10:34 he took *c.* of him
35 said, Take *c.* of him
1 *Cor.* 9:9 God take *c.* for oxen ?
12:25 same *c.* one for another
2 *Cor.* 7:12 *c.* for you might ap.
8:16 same earnest *c.* in Titus
11:28 *c.* of all the churches
1 *Tim.* 3:5 how take *c.* of church
1 *Pet.* 5:7 casting your *c.* on him

CARE, ED.

2 *Sam.* 18:3 if we flee, not *c.* for
Ps. 142:4 no man *c.* for my soul
Luke 10:40 *c.* that my sister left
John 12:6 he *c.* for the poor
Acts 18:17 G. *c.* for none of those
1 *Cor.* 7:21 a servant? *c.* not
Phil. 2:20 natur. *c.* for your state

CAREFUL.

2 *K.* 4:13 thou hast been *c.* for us
Jer. 17:8 *c.* in year of drought
Dan. 3:16 we are not *c.* to answer
Luke 10:41 *c.* about many things
Phil. 4:6 be *c.* for nothing, but
10 *c.* but lacked opportunity
Tit. 3:8 *c.* to maintain good w.

CAREFULLY.

Deut. 15:5 thou *c.* hearken to L.
Mic. 1:12 inha. of M. waited *c.*
Phil. 2:28 I sent him the more *c.*
Heb. 12:17 sought it *c.* with tears

CAREFULNESS.

Ezek. 12:18 drink water with *c.*
19 shall eat their bread with *c.*
1 *Cor.* 7:32 have you without *c.*
2 *Cor.* 7:11 what *c.* it wrought

CARELESS.

Jud. 18:7 saw how they dwelt *c.*
Is. 32:9 hear, ye *c.* daughters
10 ye *c.* women ; 11 ye *c.* ones
Ezek. 30:9 *c.* Ethiopians afraid

CARELESSLY.

Is. 47:8 thou that dwellest *c.*
Ezek. 39:6 fire am. them dwell *c.*
Zep. 2:15 rejoicing city dwelt *c.*

CARES.

Mark 4:19 *c.* of this world choke
Luke 8:14 chok. with *c.* and rich.
21:34 overcharged with *c.* of life

CAREST, ETH, ING.

Deut. 11:12 a land which L. *c.*
Mat. 22:16 *c.* thou for any man
Mark 4:38 *c.* thou not we perish
12:14 art true, and *c.* for no man
John 10:13 hireling *c.* not for sh.
1 *Cor.* 7:32 is unmarried *c.* 34
33 is married, *c.* for world, 34
1 *Pet.* 5:7 for he *c.* for you

CARMEL.

1 *Sam.* 25:2 posses. in C. 7, 40
1 *K.* 18:19 gather all Is. to mt. C.
Cant. 7:5 head u. thee is like C.
Is. 35:2 excellency of C.
Jer. 46:18 as C. by the sea
Amos 1:2 C. shall wither, 9:3
Mic. 7:14 in the midst of C.

CARMELITE.

1 *Sam.* 30:5 N. *c.* 2 *Sam.* 2:2 ; 3:3
2 *Sam.* 23:35 Hezrai C. one of D.

CARMI. *Gen.* 46:9; *Jos.* 7:1 ; 1
Chr. 2:7 ; 4:1

CARNAL.

Rom. 7:14 I am *c.* sold under sin
8:7 *c.* mind is enmity against G.
15:27 to minister in *c.* things
1 *Cor.* 3:1 unto *c.* even to babes
3 are yet *c.* ; 4 are ye not *c.?*
9:11 if we reap your *c.* things
2 *Cor.* 10:4 w. of warfare not *c.*
Heb. 7:16 law of a *c.* command.
9:10 stood in *c.* ordinances

CARNALLY.

Lev. 18:20 not lie *c.* with n. wife
19:20 lieth *c.* with a bondmaid
Num. 5:13 man lie with her *c.*
Rom. 8:6 *c.* minded is death

CARPENTER, S.

2 *Sam.* 5:11 *c.* to D. 1 *Chr.* 14:1
2 *Chr.* 24:12 hired *c. Ezr.* 3:7
Is. 41:7 *c.* encouraged goldsmith
44:13 *c.* stretcheth out his rule
Jer. 24:1 *c.* he carried away, 29:2
Zec. 1:20 Lord showed me four *c.*
Mat. 13:55 is not this the *c.* son?
Mark 6:3 is not this the *c.*

CARPUS. 2 *Tim.* 4:13

CARRIAGE, S.

1 *Sam.* 17:22 David left his *c.*
Is. 10:28 Michmash laid up *c.*
46:1 your *c.* were heavy laden
Acts 21:15 we took up our *c.*

CARRY.

Gen. 50:25 *c.* up my b. *Ex.* 13:19
Ex. 33:15 pres. go not, *c.* us
Lev. 10:4 *c.* your breth. out of c.
Num. 11:12 *c.* them in bosom
Deut. 14:24 too long to *c.* it
Jos. 4:3 *c.* the twelve stones
1 *Sam.* 30:40 *c.* them to the city
2 *Sam.* 19:18 *c.* king's household
1 *K.* 18:12 spirit of L. sh. *c.* thee
2 *K.* 4:19 *c.* him to his mother
9:2 *c.* Jehu to an inner chamber
17:27 *c.* thith. one of the priests
1 *Chr.* 15:2 none ought to *c.* ark
23:26 L. no more *c.* tabernacle
2 *Chr.* 36:6 *c.* him to B. *Jer.* 39:7
Ec. 10:20 a bird shall *c.* the v.
Is. 23:7 own feet *c.* her afar off
30:6 *c.* riches on young asses
40:11 *c.* lambs in his bosom
46:4 to hoary hairs will I *c.* you
7 *c.* him, set him in his place
Jer. 20:5 and *c.* them to Babylon
39:14 should *c.* Jeremiah home
Ezek. 22:9 thee are men *c.* tales
Mark 6:55 began to *c.* in beds
11:16 to *c.* a vessel th. temple
Luke 10:4 *c.* nei. purse nor scrip
John 5:10 not lawful to *c.*
21:18 *c.* thee whit. wouldst not

CARRY away.

2 *K.* 18:11 king of A. did *c. a.* Is.
25:11 fugitives did N. *c. away*
2 *Chr.* 20:25 more than could *c. a.*
Job 15:12 thy heart *c.* thee *a. ?*
Ps. 49:17 dieth he sh. *c.* noth. *a.*
Ec. 5:15 noth. wh. he may *c. a.*
Is. 5:29 shall *c.* prey *away* safe
15:7 shall they *c. away*
22:17 Lord will *c.* thee *away*
41:16 wind *c.* them *a.* 57:13
Lam. 4:22 *c.* thee *a.* O Zion
Ezek. 38:13 art come to *c. a.*
Acts 7:43 *c.* you *a.* bey. Babylon

See CAPTIVE.

CARRY back.

2 *Sam.* 15:25 *c. back* ark
1 *K.* 22:26 *c.* Mic. b. 2 *Chr.* 18:25

CARRY forth.
Ex. 12:46 not *c. forth* aught
14:11 *c.* us *forth* out of Egypt
Lev. 4:12 whole bullock *c. f.* 21
2 *Chr.* 29:5 *c. f.* the filthiness
Jer. 17:22 nor *c. f.* a burden
Ezek. 12:6 *c.* it *f.* in the twilight

CARRY out.
Gen. 47:30 *c.* me *out* of Egypt
Deut. 28:38 *c.* much seed *out*
1 *K.* 22:34 *c.* me *o.* 2 *Chr.* 18:33
Ezek. 12:5 dig wall, *c. o.* thereby
Acts 5:9 at door, shall *c.* thee *o.*
1 *Tim.* 6:7 we *c.* nothing *out*

CARRIED.
Gen. 46:5 sons of Is. *c.* Jac. 50:13
Lev. 10:5 *c.* them in their coats
Jud. 16:3 Samson *c.* them up
1 *Sam.* 5:8 let ark be *c.* to Gath
2 *Sam.* 6:10 *c.* ark, 1 *Chr.* 13:13
15:29 Abiathar *c.* ark to Jerusa.
1 *K.* 17:19 he *c.* him into a loft
2 *K.* 20:17 have laid up in store
shall be *c.* to Baby. *Is.* 39:6
24:13 he *c.* out all the treasures
25:7 *c.* Zedekiah to Babylon
2 *Chr.* 28:15 *c.* all the feeble
33:11 *c.* Manasseh to Babylon
36:4 Necho. *c.* Jehoahaz to Eg.
Job 5:13 the froward is *c.* headlo.
10:19 I should been *c.* from w.
Ps. 46:2 mount. be *c.* into sea
Is. 46:3 remnant *c.* from the w.
49:22 daugh. be *c.* on shoulders
53:4 he hath *c.* our sorrows
63:9 *c.* them all the days of old
Jer. 27:22 be *c.* to Babylon, 28:3;
52:11, 17
Ezek. 17:4 he *c.* twigs into a land

Ezek. 37:1 *c.* me out in Sp. of L.
Dan. 1:2 *c.* into land of Shinar
Hos. 10:6 also *c.* unto Assyria
12:1 and oil is *c.* into Egypt
Joel 3:5 *c.* into your temples
Luke 7:12 dead man *c.* out
16:22 was *c.* by the angels
24:51 was *c.* up into heaven
Acts 3:2 one lame from womb *c.*
5:6 young men *c.* Ananias out
7:16 fathers were *c.* to Sychem
8:2 *c.* Stephen to his burial
21:34 com. to be *c.* into castle
Eph. 4:14 *c.* with every wind
Heb. 13:9 *c.* with divers doctrines
2 *Pet.* 2:17 *c.* with a tempest
Jude 12 clouds without water *c.*
See CAPTIVE.

CARRIED away.
Gen. 31:18 J. *c. a.* all his cattle
26 *c. a.* my daughters
1 *Sam.* 30:2 *c.* them *a.* 18.
2 *K.* 17:6 *c.* Is. into Assyria, 23
11 heathen whom the L. *c. a.*
28 one of priests they had *c. a.*
24:14 *c. a.* all Jerusalem
15 *c. a.* Jehoiachin to Babylon
25:21 so Judah was *c. a.* out of
1 *Chr.* 5:26 *c. a.* the Reubenites
6:15 when L. *c. a.* J. and Jerus.
9:1 *c. a.* for their transgression
2 *Chr.* 14:13 Asa *c. away*, 21:17
Ezr. 2:1 been *c. a.* *Neh.* 7:6
9:4 transg. of those *c. a.* 10:6
Jer. 29:4 caused to be *c. a.*
Dan. 2:35 wind *c.* them *away*
Nah. 3:10 No was *c. a.* into cap.
Mat. 1:11 about time *c.* a. to B.
Mark 15:1 *c.* Jesus *a.* to Pilate
1 *Cor.* 12:2 G. *c. a.* dumb idols
Gal. 2:13 Barnabas *c. a.*
Rev. 12:15 be *c. a.* of flood
17:3 *c.* me *a.* in spirit, 21:10

CARRIEST, ETH, ING.
Job 21:18 as chaff storm *c.* away
27:21 east wind *c.* rich away ·

Ps. 78:9 Ephraim *c.* bows turned
90:5 *c.* them away with flood
Mat. 1:17 till the *c.* into Babylon
Rev. 17:7 mystery of beast th. *c.*

CART.
1 *Sam.* 6:7 makes a new *c.* and
2 *Sam.* 6:3 set ark on a new *c.*
1 *Chr.* 13:7 Uzziah drave the *c.*
Is. 28:28 corn with wheel of *c.*
Amos 2:13 as a *c.* is pressed

CART-ROPE.
Is. 5:18 draw sin as with a *c.-r.*

CART-WHEEL.
Is. 28:27 nor is *c.-w.* turned

CARVED, ING, INGS.
Ex. 31:5 Bezaleel in *c.* 35:33
Jud. 18:18 fetched the *c.* image
1 *K.* 6:18 cedar within was *c.*
2 *Chr.* 33:7 *c.* image in house G.
34:4 Josiah cut down *c.* images
Ps. 74:6 they break *c.* work
Prov. 7:16 my bed with *c.* work

CASE, S.
Ex. 5:19 did see were in evil *c.*
Ps. 144:15 happy p. in such a *c.*
Mat. 5:20 in no *c.* enter kingdom
19:10 *c.* of man be so with wife
John 5:6 long time in that *c.*
1 *Cor.* 7:15 bondage in such *c.*

CASEMENT
Prov. 7:6 looked through my *c.*

CASIPHIA *Ezr.* 8:17

CASSIA.
Ex. 30:24 of *c.* 500 shekels
Ps. 45:8 garments smell of *c.*
Ezek. 27:19 *c.* in thy market

CAST, *passive.*
Job 18:8 he is *c.* into a net
Ps. 22:10 I was *c.* on thee
76:6 are *c.* into a dead sleep
140:10 let them be *c.* into fire
Prov. 16:33 the lot is *c.* into lap
Is. 25:7 covering *c.* over all
Jer. 22:28 *c.* into a land know not
38:11 old *c.* clouts and rags
Dan. 3:6 *c.* into fiery furnace
6:7 be *c.* into den of lions, 24
Jon. 2:4 am *c.* out of thy sight
Mat. 4:12 John was *c.* into prison
5:25 and thou be *c.* into prison
29 body be *c.* into hell, 30
6:30 *c.* into the oven, *Lu.* 12:28
21:21 mountain, Be *c.* into sea
Mark 9:42 *c.* into sea, *Luke* 17:2
45 to be *c.* into hell, 47
Luke 3:9 *c.* it into, *Mat.* 3:10 ; 7:19
23:19 *c.* into prison, 25

John 3:24 not yet *c.* into prison
Acts 27:26 *c.* on a certain island
Rev. 8:7 hail and fire *c.* on earth
8 mountain burning *c.* into sea
12:13 dragon was *c.* unto earth
19:20 both *c.* alive into the lake
20:10 the devil was *c.* into lake
14 death and hell *c.* into lake
15 not found in book of life, *c.*

CAST, *active.*
Gen. 31:38 she-goats have not *c.*
37:20 *c.* him into some pit
39:7 *c.* eyes on Joseph
Ex. 1:22 every son *c.* into river
4:3 he *c.* rod on the ground
15:4 Ph. chariots he *c.* into sea
25 had *c.* tree into the waters
22:31 flesh torn, *c.* it to the dogs
23:26 nothing *c.* their young
25:12 *c.* 4 rings, 37:3, 13 ; 38:5
32:19 Moses *c.* tables out
Num. 35:23 *c.* it on him
Deut. 29:28 L. *c.* into an. land
Jos. 8:29 *c.* king of Ai at gate
10:27 *c.* them into cave
Jud. 9:53 a woman *c.* a piece of
millstone, 2 *Sam.* 11:21

1 *Sam.* 18:11 S. *c.* javelin, 20:33
2 *Sam.* 16:6 S. *c.* stones at Dav.
18:17 *c.* Absalom into a pit
1 *K.* 7:46 *c.* them, 2 *Chr.* 4:17
14:9 *c.* me behind thy back
19:19 E. *c.* his mantle on him
2 *K.* 2:16 *c.* him on some mount,
21 spring, and *c.* salt in there
3:25 *c.* each his stone
4:41 meal he *c.* into the pot
6:6 he *c.* in stick, iron swam
9:25 *c.* into portion of N. 26
13:21 *c.* into sepulchre of Elisha
23 *c.* from his presence as yet
19:18 *c.* gods into fire, *Is.* 37:19
32 *c.* a bank ag. it, *Is.* 37:33
Neh. 9:26 *c.* law behind
Est. 3:7 *c.* Pur, 9:24
Job 20:23 shall *c.* fury of wrath
27:22 God shall *c.* upon him
30:19 hath *c.* me into mire
40:11 *c.* abroad rage of wrath
Ps. 55:3 they *c.* iniquity on me
22 *c.* thy burden on the Lord
74:7 *c.* fire into thy sanctuary
78:49 *c.* on them his wrath
Prov. 1:14 *c.* in thy lot among us
Ec. 11:1 *c.* thy bread on waters
Is. 2:20 shall *c.* his idols to bats
38:17 has *c.* all my sins behind
Jer. 26:23 *c.* Urijah's body into
36:23 *c.* it into fire on hearth
38:6 *c.* Jerem. into dungeon, 9
41:7 Ishmael *c.* them into pit
Lam. 3:53 *c.* a stone upon me
Ezek. 11:16 I have *c.* them far off
23:35 *c.* me behind thy back
28:17 I will *c.* thee to ground
Dan. 3:20 *c.* them into furnace
24 did not we *c.* three into fire
6:24 *c.* them into den of lions
Jon. 2:3 *c.* me into the deep
Mic. 4:7 I will make her *c.* off
7:19 *c.* all their sins into sea
Nah. 3:6 I will *c.* filth on thee
Zec. 5:8 *c.* it into the ephah, *c.*
11:13 *c.* it unto potter, *c.* them
Mal. 3:11 nor vine *c.* fruit before
Mat. 3:10 is *c.* into fire, 7:19
5:29 *c.* it from thee, 30 ; 18:8, 9
7:6 nor *c.* pearls before swine
15:26 *c.* it to dogs, *Mark* 7:27
17:27 *c.* a hook and take up fish
18:30 *c.* into prison till he pay
22:13 *c.* into outer dark. 25:30
27:44 *c.* same in his teeth
Mark 9:22 *c.* him into fire
11:7 *c.* gar. on him, *Luke* 19:35
12:4 at him they *c.* stones
41 *c.* money into t. *Luke* 21:4
43 widow hath *c.* more in, 44
Luke 12:5 to *c.* into hell
19:43 enemies shall *c.* a trench
John 8:7 first *c.* a stone at her
21:7 Peter *c.* himself into sea
Acts 12:8 *c.* garment about thee
16:23 *c.* Paul and S. into prison
27:43 who could swim, *c.* th.
1 *Cor.* 7:35 may *c.* a snare on you
Rev. 2:10 devil *c.* some into prison
14 Balak to *c.* stumbling-block
22 I will *c.* her into a bed
4:10 elders *c.* their crowns
18:21 and *c.* it into sea

CAST away.
Lev. 26:44 I will not *c.* them *a.*
2 *Sam.* 1:21 sh. of mighty is *c. a.*
2 *K.* 7:15 vessels Syrians *c. a.*
2 *Chr.* 29:19 vessels Ahaz *c. a.*
Job 8:4 *c.* them *a.* for transgress
Job 8:20 G. will not *c. a.* perfect
Ps. 2:3 *c. a.* their cords
51:11 *c.* me not *a.* from presence
Ec. 3:5 a time to *c. a.* stones, 6
Is. 5:24 because they have *c. a.*
30:22 *c. a.* as menstruous cloth
31:7 *c. a.* his idols of silver

41:9 chosen and not *c.* thee *a.*
Jer. 7:29 cut thy hair and *c.* it *a.*
33:26 *c. a.* seed of Jacob
Ezek. 18:31 *c. a.* all transgress.
20:8 did not *c. a.* abominations
Hos. 9:17 God will *c.* them *a.*
Mat. 13:48 but *c.* the bad *away*
Luke 9:25 if a man be *c. away*
Rom. 11:1 God *c. a.* his people ?
2 not *c. away* people
Heb. 10:35 *c.* not *a.* your confid.

CASTAWAY.

1 *Cor.* 9:27 lest I myself be a *c.*

CAST down.

Ex. 7.10 Aaron *c. down* his rod
Jos. 10:11 L. *c. d.* great stones
Jud. 6:28 Baal was *c. down*
1 *K.* 18:42 Elijah *c.* himself *d.*
2 *Chr.* 25:8 G. hath power to *c. d.*
12 *c.* them *d.* from top of rock
Neh. 6:16 *c. d.* in their own eyes
Job 18:7 counsel sh. *c.* him *d.*
22:29 when men are *c. down*
29:24 my count. they *c.* not *d.*
41:9 be *c. d.* at sight of him ?
Ps. 17:13 disap. him, *c.* him *d.*
36:12 they are *c. down*
37:14 bent bow to *c. d.* needy
24 shall not be utterly *c. d.*
42:5 *c. d.* O my soul ? 11 ; 43:5
6 my soul is *c. d.* within me
56:7 in thine anger *c. d.* people
62:4 consult to *c.* him *down*
89:44 *c.* his throne *d.* to ground
102:10 lifted me up, and *c. d.*
Prov. 7:26 *c. d.* many wounded
Is. 28:2 shall *c. d.* with his hand
Jer. 6:15 shall be *c. down,* 8:12
Lam. 2:1 *c. d.* the beauty of Isr.
Ezek. 6:4 *c. d.* your slain
19:12 thy mother was *c. d.*
31:16 when I *c.* Assyrian *d.*
32:18 wail for E. and *c.* her *d.*
Dan. 7:9 the thrones were *c. d.*
8:7 he-goat *c. d.* ram to the gr.
10 it *c. d.* some of host
12 *c. down* truth to ground
11:12 he shall *c. d.* ten thous.
Mat. 4:6 *c.* thyself *d. Luke* 4:9
15:30 *c.* them *d.* at Jesus' feet
27:5 he *c. d.* pieces of silver
Luke 4:29 *c.* Jesus *d.* headlong
2 *Cor.* 4.9 *c. d.* but not destroyed
7:6 that comforteth those *c. d.*
2 *Pet.* 2:4 *c.* angels *down* to hell
Rev. 12:10 the accuser is *c. d.*

CAST forth.

Neh. 13:8 I *c.* forth household
Ps. 144:6 *c. f.* lightning
Jer. 22:19 Jehoi. *c. f.* beyond g.
Ezek. 32:4 *c.* thee *f.* on op. field
Hos. 14:5 *c. f.* his roots at Leb.
Jon. 1:15 *c. f.* Jonah into sea
Mark 7:26 *c. f.* devil
John 15:6 he is *c. f.* as a branch

CAST lots.

Lev. 16:8 *c. lots* on the two g.
Jos. 18:10 Joshua *c. lots* in Sh.
1 *Sam.* 14:42 *c. l.* bet. me and Jon.
1 *Chr.* 26:13 *c. l.* as well small
Ps. 22:18 *c. l.* upon my vesture,
    Mat. 27:35 ; *John* 19:24
Is. 34:17 he hath *c. lots*
Joel 3:3 *c. lots* for my people
Ob. 11 foreigners *c. l.* on Jer.
Jon. 1:7 *c. lots* that we may k.
Nah. 3:10 *c. l.* for her hon. men

CAST off.

2 *K.* 23:27 I will *c. off* Jerusa.
1 *Chr.* 28:9 *c.* thee *off* forever
2 *Chr.* 11:14 J. had *c.* them *off*
Job 15:33 *c. off* his flower
Ps. 43:2 why dost *c.* me *off* ?
44:9 but thou hast *c. off,* 60:1,
    10 ; 89:38 ; 108:11
23 Lord *c.* us not *off* for ever

71:9 *c.* me not *off* in old age
74:1 why hast *c.* us *off* for ever ?
77:7 will Lord *c. off* for ever ?
94:14 not *c. o.* his p. *Lam.* 3:31
Jer. 28:16 I will *c.* Hananiah *off*
31:37 *c. off* seed of Isr. 33:24
Lam. 2:7 L. hath *c. off* his altar
Hos. 8:3 Is. hath *c. off* thing good
5 thy calf, O Sam. *c.* thee *off*
Amos 1:11 bec. he *c. off* all pity
Zec. 10:6 tho' I not *c.* them *off*
Acts 22:23 and *c. off* their clothes
Rom. 13:12 let us *c. off* works
1 *Tim.* 5:12 *c. off* their first faith

CAST out.

Gen. 21:10 *c. o.* this bondwoman
Ex. 34:24 *c. out* the nations
Lev. 18:24 nations I *c. o.* 20:23 ;
    Deut. 7:1
Deut. 9:17 *c.* tables *out*
1 *K.* 9:7 this house will I *c. out*
    of my sight, 2 *Chr.* 7:20
21:26 Amorites *c. out,* 2 *K.* 16:3
2 *K.* 10:25 captains *c.* them *out*
    17:20 *c.* them *out,* 24:20
2 *Chr.* 13:9 have ye not *c. out*
20:11 to *c.* us *out* of thy posses.
Neh. 1:9 there were of you *c. out*
Job 20:15 *c.* them *out* of his belly
39:3 they *c. out* their sorrows
Ps. 5:10 *c.* them *out* in trans.
18:42 did *c.* them *out* as dirt in
44:2 afflict people, and *c.* th. *o.*
60:8 will I *c. out* my shoe, 108:9
78:55 he *c. out* the heathen, 80:8
Prov. 22:10 *c. out* the scorner
Is. 14:19 art *c. out* of thy grave
16:52 as a wandering bird *c. out*
26:19 earth shall *c. out* the dead
34:3 their slain shall be *c. out*
58:7 that thou bring poor *c. out*
66:5 *c.* you *out* for my name's s.
Jer. 7:15 *c.* you *out* of my sight
9:19 our dwellings have *c.* us *o.*
15:1 *c. out* of my s. 23:39 ; 52:3
16:13 will I *c.* you *out*
22:26 I will *c.* thee *out*
36:30 dead body shall be *c. out*
51:34 Nebuch. hath *c.* me *out*
Ezek. 16:5 wast *c. o.* in open field
28:16 *c.* thee *out* of mountain
Amos 8:8 *c. out* and drowned
Mic. 2:9 women have ye *c. out*
Zep. 3:15 hath *c. o.* thine enemy
Zec. 1:21 to *c. out* horns of Gen.
9:4 Lord will *c.* her *out*
Mat 5:13 unsav. *c. o. Luke* 14:35
7:5 first *c. out* beam, *Luke* 6:42
22 in thy name *c. out* devils ?
8:12 child. of kingdom be *c. out*
16 *c. out* spirits with his word
31 if thou *c.* us *out* suffer us
9:33 devil was *c. o.* dumb spake
10:1 power against spir. to *c. o.*
8 raise dead, *c. out* devils
12:24 *c. o.* but by B. *Luke* 11:18
26 if Satan *c. out* Satan
28 by spirit of God *c. o.* devils
15:17 and is *c. out* into draught
17:19 we *c.* him *o.* ? *Mark* 9:28
21:12 Jesus *c.* all that sold,
    Mark 11:15 ; *Luke* 19:45
39 *c. o.* v. *Mark* 12:8 ; *Luke* 20:15
Mark 1:34 *c. o.* m. dev. 39 ; 6:13
3:15 have power to *c. out* devils
23 how can Satan *c. o.* Satan ?
16:9 out of whom *c.* 7 devils
17 shall *c. out* devils
Luke 6:22 *c. out* your name
11:20 with finger of G. *c. o.* dev.
13:32 I *c. out* devils and do cures
20:12 wounded him *c.* him *out*
John 6:37 I will in no wise *c. out*
9:34 teach us ? they *c.* him *out*
12:31 pr. of this world be *c. out*
Acts 7:19 *c. out* their young
21 when Moses was *c. out*

58 *c.* Stephen *out* and stoned
27:19 we *c. out* tackling of ship
Gal. 4:30 *c. out* the bondwoman
Rev. 12:9 great dragon was *c. out*
15 serpent *c. out* water, 16

Lord CAST out.

1 *K.* 14:24 L. *c. o.* bef. ch. of Isr.
    2 *K.* 16:3 ; 2 *Chr.* 28:3 ; 33:2
2 *K.* 17:8 L. *c. o.* before Is. 21:2
Zec. 9:4 behold L. will *c.* her *out*

CAST up.

2 *Sam.* 20:15 *c. up* bank ag. city
Is. 57:14 *c.* ye *up,* pre. way, 62:10
20 whose waters *c. up* mire
Jer. 18:15 in way not *c. up*
50:26 *c.* her *up* as heaps
Lam. 2:10 *c. up* dust. *Ezek.* 27:30
Dan. 11:15 shall *c. up* a mount

CASTEST, ETH.

Job 15:4 yea thou *c.* off fear
21:10 cow *c.* not her calf
Ps. 50:17 *c.* my words behind
73:18 *c.* them into destruction
88:14 why *c.* thou off my soul
147:6 Lord *c.* the wicked down
17 he *c.* forth his ice
Prov. 10:3 *c.* away subst. of w.
19:15 slothful. *c.* into deep sleep
21:22 *c.* down strength
26:18 a madman *c.* firebrands
Jer. 6:7 so she *c.* out wickedness
Mat. 9:34 he *c.* out devils, *Mark*
    3:22 ; *Luke* 11:15
1 *John* 4:18 per. love *c.* out fear
3 *John* 10 *c.* them out of church
Rev. 6:13 fig-tree *c.* untimely figs

CASTING.

Ez. 10:1 *c.* himself down
Job 6:21 ye see my *c.* down
Ps. 74:7 by *c.* down dwelling-p.
89:39 profaned crown by *c.* it
Mic. 6:14 thy *c.* down be in mid.
Mat. 27:35 *c.* lots, *Mark* 15:24
Mark 9:38 *c.* out dev. *Luke* 9:49
Luke 21:2 wid. *c.* in two mites
Rom. 11:15 if *c.* away be recon.
2 *Cor.* 10:5 *c.* down imaginations
1 *Pet.* 5:7 *c.* all your care on him

CASTLE.

1 *Chr.* 11:5 David took *c.* of Zion
7 David dwelt in *c.* city of D.
Prov. 18:19 like bars of a *c.*
Acts 21:34 Paul to be carried into
    the *c.* 37 ; 22:24 ; 23:10
23:16 entered into *c.* told Paul

CASTLES.

Gen. 25:16 names by their *c.*
Num. 31:10 burnt their goodly *c.*
2 *Chr.* 17:12 Jehoshaphat built *c.*
27:4 in the forest build *c.*

CASTOR. *See* SIGN.

CATCH.

1 *K.* 20:33 men did hastily *c.*
2 *K.* 7:12 we shall *c.* them alive
Ps. 10:9 in wait to *c.* the poor
35:8 let his net *c.* himself
109:11 extor. *c.* all he hath
Jer. 5:26 set a trap they *c.* men
Ezek. 19:3 it learned to *c.* prey, 6
Hab. 1:15 *c.* them in their net
Mark 12:13 to *c.* him in his wo.
Luke 5:10 from hencef. *c.* men
11:54 to *c.* something

CATCHETH,

Mat. 13:19 *c.* what was sown
John 10:12 wolf *c.* the sheep

CATERPILLAR, S.

1 *K.* 8:37 if any *c.* 2 *Chr.* 6:28
Ps. 78:46 their increase to *c.*
105:34 he spake, and *c.* came
Is. 33:4 like gathering of *c.*
Jer. 51:14 with men as *c.*
27 horses come up as rough *c.*

Joel 1:4 c.-w. left hath c. eaten
2:25 restore years c. hath eaten

CATTLE.

Gen. 1:25 God made the c.
3:14 art cursed above all c.
8:1 God remembered c. in ark
9:10 establish covenant with c.
13:2 Abram was rich in c.
31:9 taken away c. of your fath.
43 these c. are my c. and all
34:5 his sons were with his c.
46:32 their trade to feed c.
47:6 make them rulers over c.
17 Joseph gave bread for c.
Ex. 9:4 sever. bet. c. of Is. and c.
20 and c. flee into the houses
12:29 smote first-born of c.
Num. 3:41 take c. of Levi
20:19 c. drink, I will pay for it
32:4 land for c. and thy servants
Job 36:33 c. concerning vapor
Ps. 50:10 c. on a thousand hills
104:14 grass to grow for the c.
148:10 all c. praise the Lord
Ec. 2:7 great and small c.
Is. 7:25 for treading of lesser c.
43:23 not brought me small c.
46:1 their idols were upon c.
Jer. 9:10 nor hear voice of the c.
Ezek. 34:17 judge bet. c. 20:22
Hag. 1:11 for a drought upon c.
Zec. 2:4 for multitude of c.
13:5 man taught me to keep c.
Luke 17:7 servants feeding c.
John 4:12 dr. thereof, and his c.

Much CATTLE.

Gen. 30:43 Jacob had much c.
Ex. 12:38 out of Egy. with m. c.
Deut. 3:19 ye have much c.
Jos. 22:8 with very much c.
2 *Chr.* 26:10 Uzziah had much c.
Jon. 4:11 Nin. wherein is m. c.

Our CATTLE.

Ex. 10:26 our c. shall also go
17:3 kill our c. with thirst
Num. 32:16 sheepfolds for o. c.
Jos. 21:2 with suburbs for our c.
Neh. 10:36 bring first-born of o. c.

Their CATTLE.

Gen. 34:23 shall not their c.
Num. 35:3 sub. for t. c. *Jos.* 14:4
Jud. 6:5 Midian. came with t. c.
1 *Sam.* 23:5 brought away t. c.
Ps. 78:48 he gave up their c.
107:38 suff. not their c. to dec.
Jer. 49:32 a booty, t. c. a spoil

Thy CATTLE.

Gen. 30:29 thy c. was with me
31:41 served thee 6 years for t. c.
Ex. 9:19 and gather t. c.
20:10 t. c. do any w. *Deut.* 5:14.
34:19 firstling among thy c.
Lev. 25:7 sab. be meat for thy c.
Deut. 11:15 send grass for thy c.
28:4 fruit of t. c. 11; 30:9
51 he shall eat fruit of thy c.
Is. 30:23 t. c. feed in large past.

Your CATTLE.

Gen. 47:16 bread for your c.
Deut. 3:19 y. c. in c. *Jos.* 1:14
7:14 be barren among your c.

CAUGHT.

Gen. 22:13 behind him a ram c.
Ex. 4:4 and c. the serpent
Num. 31:32 prey men had c.
Jud. 8:14 c. young man of Suc.
21:23 danced, whom they c.
1 *Sam.* 17:35 I c. him by his bea.
2 *Sam.* 2:16 c. every one his fellow
18:9 Absalom's head c. hold of
1 *K.* 1:50 Adon. c. hold on altar
2:28 J. c. hold on horns of altar
11:30 Ahijah c. new garment
2 *K.* 4:27 she c. Elisha by feet
2 *Chr.* 22:9 they c. Ahaziah

Prov. 7:13 so she c. him
Jer. 50:24 O Babylon, thou art c.
Mat. 14:31 Jesus c. Peter
21:39 the husbandmen c. him
Mark 12:3 they c. the servant
Luke 8:29 oftentimes it c. him
John 21:3 that night c. nothing
Acts 6:12 Stephen and c. him
8:39 the spirit c. away Philip
16:19 they c. Paul and Silas
26:21 the J. c. me in the temple
27:15 when ship was c. we let
2 *Cor.* 12:2 I knew a man c. up
4 he was c. up into paradise
16 crafty I c. you with guile
1 *Thes.* 4:17 we shall be c. up
Rev. 12:5 child was c. up to God

CAUL, S.

Ex. 29:13 c. above the liver, 22;
  Lev. 3:4, 10, 15; 4:9; 7:4; 8:16,
  25; 9:10, 19
Is. 3:18 will take away their c.
Hos. 13:8 rend c. of their heart.

CAUSE, Substantive.

Ex. 22:9 c. of both before judges
23:2 nor speak in a c. to decline
3 counten. a poor man in his c.
6 wrest judg. of poor in his c.
Num. 16:11 for which c. thou
and all thy company are ga.
27:5 Moses brought c. before L.
Deut. 1:17 the c. too hard for you
1 *Sam.* 17:29 is there not a c. ?
25:39 L. pleaded c. of my rep.
2 *Sam.* 13:16 there is no c.
15:4 hath any c. might come
1 *K.* 8:45 maintain their c. 49,59;
  2 *Chr.* 6:35, 39
11:27 c. that he lift up his hand
12:15 c. was Fr. L. 2 *Chr.* 10:15
1 *Chr.* 21:3 a c. of tresp. to Is. ?
2 *Chr.* 19:10 what c. shall come
Job 5:8 would I commit my c.
13:18 I have ordered my c.
23:4 order my c. before him
29:16 c. I knew not I searched
31:13 if I did despise c. of serv.
Ps. 9:4 hast maintained my c.
35:23 awake to my c. my God
140:12 Lord will maintain the c.
Prov. 18:17 he first in his own c.
25:9 debate thy c. with neighbor
25:7 considereth c. of poor
31:8 for the dumb in the c.
Ec. 7:10 say not. what is the c.
Is. 1:23 nor c. of widow come
41:21 produce your c. saith Lord
51:22 God that pleadeth the c.
Jer. 5:28 judge not c. of fatherl.
11:20 to thee revealed my c.
20:12 unto thee I opened my c.
22:16 he judged the c. of poor
Lam. 3:36 subv. a man in his c.
59 seen my wrong, jud. my c.
Jon. 1:7 for whose c. 8
Mat. 5:32 saving for c. of forni.
19:3 put aw. his wife for ev c.
Luke 23:22 no c. of death in him
Acts 10:21 c. where. ye are come
13:28 found no c. of death
28:18 was no c. of death in me
2 *Cor.* 4:16 which c. we faint not
5:13 we be sober, it is for yo. c.
2 *Cor.* 7:12 his c. that h. done w.
Phil. 2:18 same c. do ye joy
2 *Tim.* 1:12 for which c. I suffer
Heb. 2:11 c. he is not ashamed to

Plead CAUSE.

1 *Sam.* 24:15 Lord plead my c. *Ps.*
  35:1; 43:1; 119:154
Ps. 74:22 plead thine own c.
Prov. 22:23 will plead their c.
23:11 plead their c. with thee
31:9 p. the c. of poor and needy
Jer. 30:13 none to plead thy c.
50:34 Lord thor. plead their c.

51:36 behold I will plead thy c.
Mic. 7:9 until he plead my c.

For this CAUSE.

Ex. 9:16 f. t. c. raised up Ph.
John 12:27 f. t. c. came I
18:37 f. t. c. came I into the w.
Rom. 15:9 f. c. I will confess
1 *Cor.* 11:30 f. this c. many
Eph. 3:14 f. this c. I bow
1 *Thes.* 2:13 f. this c. thank we
1 *Tim.* 1:16 f. t. c. I obtained
Heb. 9:15 f. this c. he is med.
1 *Pet.* 4:6 f. t. c. was gospel pr.

Without CAUSE.

1 *Sam.* 19:5 slay D. without a c.
Job 2:3 to destroy him without c.
9:17 multipli. my wounds w. c.
Ps. 7:4 that w. c. is my enemy
25:3 that transgress w. c.
35:7 w. c. dig. a pit without c.
19 w. c. 69:4 ; *John* 15:25
109:3 fought ag. me with. a c.
119:78 perv. with me with. c.
161 persecuted me with. c.
Prov. 1:11 lurk for innocent w.'c.
3:30 st. not with a man with. c.
23:29 hath wounds without c.
24:28 be not witness without c.
Is. 52:4 oppressed them w. c.
Lam. 3:52 chased me sore w. c.
Ezek. 14:23 have not done w. c.
Mat. 5:22 angry with bro. w. c.

CAUSE.

Gen. 45:1 c. every man to go out
Num. 16:5 will c. him to come
Deut. 1:38 c. to inh. 3:28; 31:7
12:11 c. his name to dwell there
2 *Sam.* 13:13 c. my shame to go
Est. 3:13 c. to perish, 8:11
Job 6:24 c. me to understand
34:11 c. every man to find
Ps. 10:17 wilt c. thine ear
67:1 c. his face to sh. 80:3. 7, 19
76:8 c. judgment to be heard
143:8 c. me to hear
Prov. 4:16 unless c. some to fall
Ec. 5:6 to c. thy flesh to sin
Cant. 8:13 voice, c. me to hear it
Ps. 3:12 lead c. thee to err, 9:16
27:6 c. them of Jacob take root
30:30 c. his glor. voice be heard
42:2 nor c. his voice to be heard
58:14 c. thee to ride on high
61:11 c. righteousness to spring
66:9 and not c. to bring forth
Jer. 3:12 not c. mine anger
7:3 c. to dwell in this place, 7
23:27 c. people forget my name
31:2 I went to c. him to rest
9 c. to walk by rivers of waters
Lam. 3:32 but though he c. grief
Ezek. 20:37 c. to pass under rod
34:15 I will c. them to lie down
36:12 c. men to walk upon you
Dan. 9:17 G. c. thy face to shine
Joel 3:11 thither c. mighty ones
Hab. 1:3 why c. me behold
Mat. 10:21 c. par. to be put to d.
  Mark 13:12; *Luke* 21:16
Rom. 16:17 mark them c. divi.
Col. 4:16 c. it be read in church
AUSE to cease. See CEASE.

CAUSED.

Gen. 2:21 Lord c. a deep sleep
20:13 God c. me wander
Deut. 34:4 the land c. thee
2 *Sam* 7:11 c. thee to rest
2 *Chr.* 34:32 c. all to stand to it
Ezr. 6:12 c. his name to dwell
Job 31:16 c. eyes of widow
Ps. 66:12 c. men to ride over
119:49 on which c. me to hope
Is. 19:14 have c. Egypt to err
68:14 Sp. of Lord c. him to rest
Jer. 12:14 c. my people to inher.
13:11 c. to cleave house of Isr.

29:31 c. you to trust in a lie
32:23 thou hast c. all this evil
48:4 little ones have c. a cry
Zec. 3:4 c. thy iniquity to pass
Mal. 2:8 c. many to stumble
John 11:37 c. this man not died
Acts 15:3 c. great joy to brethren
2 Cor. 2:5 if any have c. grief

CAUSELESS.
1 Sam. 25:31 hast shed blood c.
Prov. 26:2 curse c. shall not co.

CAUSES.
Ex. 18:19 bring c. to God
26 hard c. brought to Moses
Deut. 1:16 c. between brethren
Jer. 3:8 c. whereby backsliding
Lam. 3:58 pleaded c. of my soul
Acts 26:21 c. the Jews caught me

CAUSEST.
Job 30:22 c. me to ride on wind
Ps. 65:4 blessed c. approach thee

CAUSETH.
Job 20:3 spirit of under. c. me
37:13 c. it come for correction
Ps. 135:7 he c. vapors to ascend,
Jer. 10:13 ; 51:16
Prov. 10:5 son c. sh. 17:2 ; 19:26
17:2 rule over a son c. shame
19:27 instruction that c. to err
28:10 c. righteous to go ast.
Mat. 5:32 c. her to commit adul.
2 Cor. 2:14 which c. us triumph
9:11 c. through us thanksgiving

CAUSEWAY.
1 Chr. 26:16 lot came by the c.

CAUSING.
Cant. 7:9 c. lips of those asleep
Jer. 29:10 in c. you to return

CAVE, S.
Gen. 19:30 Lot dwelt in a c. he
23:19 buried Sarah in the c.
49:29 bury me in the c.
Jos. 10:16 kings hid in a c. 17
Jud. 6:2 Israel made c.
1 Sam. 13:6 Israel did hide in c.
22:1 David escaped to the c.
24:10 delivered thee in the c.
1 K. 18:4 prophets hid in c. 13
19:9 Elijah came to a c. and
Is. 2:19 go into c. for fear of L.
Ezek. 33:27 die that be in the c.
John 11:38 it was a c. a stone
Heb. 11:38 they wandered in c

CEASE.
Gen. 8:22 day and night not c.
Num. 8:25 age of fifty years. c.
11:25 prophesied, did not c.
17:5 to c. the murmurings
Deut. 15:11 poor shall never c.
32:26 rememb. of them to c.
Jos. 22:25 child. c. from fearing
20:28 ag. go up, or shall I c. ?
1 Sam. 7:8 c. not to cry to G.
2 Chr. 16:5 B. let his work c.
Ezr. 4:23 to c. by force
Neh. 6:3 why should the work c.
Job 3:17 c. from troubling
10:20 my days few ? c. then
14:7 tender branch will not c.
Ps. 37:8 c. from anger
46:9 he maketh wars to c.
89:44 hast made his glory to c.
Prov. 19:27 c. to hear instruction
20:3 an honor to c. from strife
22:10 and reproach shall c.
23:4 c. from thy wisdom.
Ec. 12:3 grinders c. bec. few
Is. 1:16 c. to do evil
2:22 c. ye from man whose br
10:25 and indignation shall c.
16:10 vintage shouting to c.
17:3 fortress c. from Ephraim
21:2 all the sighing made to c.
33:1 shalt c. to spoil, be spoiled

Jer. 14:17 let tears not c.
17:8 nor c. from yielding fruit
31:36 seed of Israel shall c.
Lam. 2:18 apple of thine eye c.
Ezek. 6:6 that your idols may c.
7:24 pomp of the strong to c.
12:23 will make this proverb c.
23:27 make thy lewdness to c.
30:10 multitude of Egypt to c.
18 pomp of her str. c. 33:28
Amos 7:5 Lord c. I beseech thee
Acts 13:10 not c. to pervert right
1 Cor. 13:8 tongues they shall c.
Eph. 1:16 I c. not to give thanks
Col. 1:9 not c. to pray for you
2 Pet. 2:14 cannot c. from sin

Cause to CEASE.
Ezr. 5:5 could not c. them c.
Neh. 4:11 cause the work to c.
Ps. 85:4 cause thine anger to c.
Prov. 18:18 c. contentions to c.
Is. 13:11 c. arrog. of proud to c.
30:11 cause H. O. of Israel to c.
Jer. 7:34 c. mirth to c. Hos. 2:11
36:29 cause to c. man and beast
48:35 c. to c. him that offereth
Ezek. 23:48 cause lewdness to c.
Ezek. 26:13 cause n. of songs to c.
30:13 cause their images to c.
34:10 c. to c. from feeding, 25
Dan. 9:27 shall c. oblation to c.
11:18 cause reproach offered to c.
Hos. 1:4 c. to c. kingdom of Isr.

CEASED.
Gen. 18:11 it c. to be with Sarah
Jud. 2:19 c. not from their d.
5:7 inhabitants of villages c.
1 Sam 2:5 that were hungry c.
25:9 in name of David and c.
Ezr. 4:24 then c. work of house
Job 32:1 three men c. to answer
Ps. 35:15 did tear me and c. not
77:2 my sore ran and c. not
Is. 14:4 opp. c. golden city c.
Lam. 5:14 elders have c.
15 the joy of our heart is c.
Jon. 1:15 sea c. from raging
Mat. 14:32 w. c. Mark 4:39 ; 6:51
Luke 7:45 not c. to kiss my feet
11:1 was praying, when he c.
Acts 5:42 c. not to preach Jesus
20:1 after uproar was c. Paul
31 three years I c. not to warn
21:14 not be persuaded, we c.
Gal. 5:11 offence of cross c.
Heb. 4:10 c. from his own works
10:2 not have c. to be offered
1 Pet. 4:1 hath c. from sin

CEASETH.
Ps. 12:1 for the godly man c.
49:8 redemption precious, it c.
Prov. 26:20 talebearer, strife c.
Is. 16:4 the spoiler c.
24:8 tabrets c. joy of the harp c.
33:8 the wayfaring man c.
Lam. 3:49 eye trickleth, c. not
Acts 6:13 c. not to speak blasph.

CEASING.
1 Sam. 12:23 sin in c. to pray
Acts 12:5 prayer made without c.
Rom. 1:9 c. make m. 1 Thes. 1:3
1 Thes. 2:13 we think G. w. c.
5:17 pray without c.
2 Tim. 1:3 without c. I have re.

CEDAR.
2 Sam. 7:2 I dwell in house of c.
7 wl y build ye not house of c.
1 K. 4:3 he spake from the c.
5:8 I will do thy desire conc. c.
2 K. 14:9 sent to c. 2 Chr. 25:18
Job 40:17 moveth tail like a c.
Ps. 92:12 righteous grow like c.
Cant. 1:17 beams of our house c.
8:9 inclose her with boards of c.
Is. 41:19 in wilderness the c.
Jer. 22:14 it is ceiled with c.

15 because closest thyself in c.
Ezek. 17:3 took highest br. of c.
23 it shall be a goodly c.
27:24 chests made of c. among
31:3 Assyrian was a c.
Zep. 2:14 shall uncover c. work
Zec. 11:2 howl, for c. is fallen

CEDAR-TREES.
Num. 24:6 Is. tabernac. as c.-t.
2 Sam. 5:11 H. sent c.-t to Dav.
1 K. 5:6 they hew me c.-t.
10 H. gave Solomon c.-t. 9:11
2 K. 19:23 cut down tall c.-t.
1 Chr. 22:4 David prepared c.-t.
2 Chr. 1:15 c. as sycamo. 9:27
2:8 send me c.-t. out of Lebanon
Ezr. 3:7 gave mon. to bring c.-t.

CEDAR-WOOD.
Lev. 14:4 take c.-w. 6, 49, 51, 52
Num. 19:6 priest shall take c.-w.
1 Chr. 22:4 much c.-w. to David

CEDARS.
1 K. 10:27 c. as sycamore-trees
1 Chr. 17:1 dwell in a house of c.
2 Chr. 2:3 didst send c. to build
Ps. 29:5 voice of L. breaketh c.
80:10 the boughs like goodly c.
148:9 praise him all c.
Cant. 5:15 his countenance as c.
Is. 9:10 change them into c.
37:24 I will cut down the tall c.
44:14 heweth him down c.
Jer. 22:7 cut down thy choice c.
23 makest thy nest in the c.
Ezek. 31:8 c. in garden
Amos 2:9 Amor. height of the c.
Zec. 11:1 fire may devour thy c.

CEDARS of Lebanon.
Jud. 9:15 bramble dev. c. of Leb.
Ps. 104:16 c. of Leb. he planted
Is. 2:13 Lord on all c. of Leb.
14:8 c. of Leb. rejoice at thee
Ezek. 27:5 c. from Leb. to make
CEDRON. John 18:1

CEILED.
2 Chr. 3:5 he c. the greater house
Jer. 22:14 it is c. with cedar
Hag. 1:4 to dwell in c. houses ?

CEILING.
1 K. 6:15 he built walls of the c.

CELEBRATE.
Lev. 23:32 even c. sabbath, 41
Is. 38:18 death cannot c. thee

CELESTIAL.
1 Cor. 15:40 c. bodies, glory of c.

CELLARS.
1 Chr. 27:28 over the c. of oil

CENCHREA.
Acts 18:18 shorn his head in C.
Rom. 16:1 serv. of church at C.

CENSER, S.
Lev. 10:1 sons of Aaron took c.
16:12 a c. full of burning coals
Num. 16:6 take ye c. 17
39 Eleazar took the brazen c.
1 K. 7:50 c. of gold, 2 Chr. 4:22
2 Chr. 26:19 Uzziah had a c.
Ezek. 8:11 with every man his c.
Heb. 9:4 holiest had the golden c.
Rev. 8:3 angel having a golden c.
5 angel took the c. and filled it

CENTURION, S.
Mat. 8:5 came unto him a c.
8 c. said, L. I am not worthy
27:54 when c. saw earthquake
Luke 7:2 c. servant was sick
23:47 c. saw what was done
Acts 10:1 Cornelius was a c.
22 Cornelius the c. a just man
21:32 immediately took c.
22:26 when the c. heard that
23:17 Paul called one of the c.
23 he called to him two c.

24:23 command. a *c.* to keep P.
27:1 J. a *c.* against band
11 *c.* believ. m. more than P.
43 *c.* willing to save Paul
28:16 *c.* delivered the prisoners

CEPHAS.
John 1:42 shalt be called C.
1 *Cor.* 1:12 I am of C. 3:22
9:5 breth. of the L. and C. 15:5
Gal. 2:9 James, C. and John

CEREMONIES.
Num. 9:3 passover accord. to *c.*

CERTAIN, *some.*
Deut. 13:13 *c.* men children of B.
25:2 beaten by *c.* number
Jer. 41:5 came *c.* from Shechem
52:15 carried away *c.* poor
Dan. 8:27 D. was sick *c.* days
Mat. 20:20 desiring *c.* thing
Mark 14:57 *c.* bare false witness
Luke 5:12 he was in a *c.* city
11:27 a *c.* woman lift up voice
18:9 parable to *c.* who trusted
24:22 *c.* women made us aston.
24 *c.* with us went to sepulchre
John 5:4 went at a *c.* season
Acts 9:19 Saul *c.* days with disc.
10:48 Peter to tarry *c.* days
12:1 to vex. *c.* of the church
15:24 *c.* which went from us
17:28 as *c.* of your own poets
Rom. 15:26 to make a *c.* contrib.
Gal. 2:12 before *c.* came from J.
Heb. 2:6 one in a *c.* place testified
4:4 in *c.* place of seventh day
7 he limiteth a *c.* day, saying
10:27 *c.* looking for of judgm.
Jude 4 *c.* men crept in unawares

A CERTAIN man. *See* MAN.

CERTAIN, *sure.*
Deut. 13:14 the thing *c.* 17:4
1 *K.* 2:37 kn. for *c.* 42; *Jer.* 26:15
Dan. 2:45 the dream is *c.*
Acts 25:26 no *c.* thing to write
1 *Cor.* 4:11 no *c.* dwelling-place
1 *Tim.* 6:7 it is *c.* we can carry

CERTAINLY.
Gen. 18:10 will *c.* return to thee
26:28 saw *c.* L. was with thee
43:7 *c.* know he would say
Ex. 3:12 *c.* I will be with thee
Jos. 9:24 it was *c.* told thy serv.
1 *Sam.* 20:9 if I knew *c.* evil
25:28 *c.* make my lord a sure
1 *K.* 1:30 so will I *c.* do this day
2 *K.* 8:10 thou mayest *c.* recover
2 *Chr.* 18:27 if *c.* return in peace
Jer. 8:8 lo *c.* in vain made he it
42:19 *c.* I have admonished
44:17 *c.* do what goeth out
Lam. 2:16 *c.* this is day looked
Dan. 11:10 *c.* come and over. 13
Luke 23:47 *c.* this was a r. man

CERTAINTY.
Jos. 23:13 *c.* Lord will no more
1 *Sam.* 23:23 with the *c.*
Prov. 22:21 *c.* of words of truth
Dan. 2:8 *c.* ye would gain time
Luke 1:4 know *c.* of those things
Acts 22:30 would have known *c.*

CERTIFY, IED.
Ezr. 4:14 we have *c.* the king
16 *c.* king that if city be built
Gal. 1:11 I *c.* you the gospel

CESAR.
Mat. 22:17 tribute to C. *Mark*
12:14 ; *Luke* 20:21, 22
Luke 2:1 a decree from C.
John 19:12 not C.'s friend; ag. C.
Acts 17:7 dec. of C. 25:8, 11, 21
Phil. 4:22 they that are of C.

CESAREA.
Mat. 16:13 into coasts of C.
Mark 8:27 into the towns of C.
Acts 8:40 ; 9:30 ; 10:24 ; 23:23 ; 25:4

CHAFED.
2 *Sam.* 17:8 they be *c.* as a bear

CHAFF.
Job 21:18 as *c.* storm carrieth
Ps. 1:4 like the *c.* which wind
35:5 be as *c.* before the wind
Is. 5:24 as flame consumeth *c.*
17:13 nations be chased as *c.*
29:5 terrible ones shall be as *c.*
33:11 conc. *c.* and bring forth
41:15 shalt make the hills as *c.*
Jer. 23:28 what is *c.* to the wheat
Dan. 2:35 *c.* of threshing floor
Hos. 13:3 as *c.* driven with wh.
Zep. 2:2 day pass as the *c.*
Mat. 3:12 b. up the *c. Luke* 3:17

CHAIN.
Gen. 41:42 put a gold *c.* about his
neck, *Dan.* 5:7, 16, 29.
Ps. 73:6 pride compasseth as a *c.*
Cant. 4:9 ravished me with one *c.*
Lam. 3:7 he made my *c.* heavy
Ezek. 7:23 *c.* land is full of crim.
16:11 I put a *c.* on thy neck
Acts 28:20 for hope bound with *c.*
2 *Tim.* 1:16 O. not ashamed of *c.*
Rev. 20:1 angel *c.* in his hand

CHAINS.
Jud. 8:26 *c.* about camels' necks
1 *K.* 6:21 *c.* of gold before oracle
Ps. 149:8 to bind kings with *c.*
Prov. 1:9 instruction shall be *c.*
Cant. 1:10 neck comely with *c.*
Is. 3:19 L. will take away thy *c.*
40:10 goldsmith casteth silver *c.*
45:14 come after thee in *c.*
Jer. 40:4 I. thee this day from *c.*
Ezek. 19:4 brought him with *c.*
9 they put him in ward in *c.*
Mark 5:3 no not with *c.*
Acts 12:7 Peter's *c.* fell off
2 *Pet.* 2:4 deliv. into *c.* of dark.
Jude 6 reserved in everlasting *c.*
See BOUND.

CHALCEDONY.
Rev. 21:19 foundation was a *c.*

CHALCOL.
1 *K.* 4:31 Sol. was wiser than C.
1 *Chr.* 2:6 sons of Z. Heman, C.

CHALDEA.
Jer. 50:10 C. shall be a spoil
51:24 to inhabitants of C. 35
Ezek. 16:29 thy fornication to C.
23:16 messeng. to them into C.

CHALDEAN.
Ezr. 5:12 them into hand of C.
Dan. 2:10 such things at any C.

CHALDEANS.
Job 1:17 C. made out three bands
Is. 23:13 C. the Assyrian foun.
Dan. 1:4 ; 2:2 ; 3:8 ; 4:7 ; 5:7, 11
Hab. 1:6 lo, I raise up the C.
Acts 7:4 out of the land of the C.

CHALDEES.
2 *K.* 24:2 C. the C. 25:4, 10, 26
2 *Chr.* 36:17 the king of the C.
Is. 13:19 Bab. the beauty of C.

CHALK-STONES.
Is. 27:9 stones of altar as *c.-s.*

CHALLENGETH.
Ex. 22:9 another *c.* to be his

CHAMBER.
Gen. 43:30 J. entered into his *c.*
Jud. 15:1 my wife into the *c.*
16:9 in wait abiding in *c.* 12
2 *K.* 4:11 Elisha turned into *c.*
Neh. 13:5 prepared for Tobiah *c.*
Ps. 19:5 as bridegroom out of *c.*
Cant. 3:4 *c.* of her conceived me
Jer. 36:10 book in *c.* of Gemariah
20 laid roll in *c.* of Elishama
Ezek. 40:45 *c.* prospect to south
Dan. 6:10 windows open in his *c.*

Joel 2:16 bridegr. go forth of *c.*

Inner CHAMBER.
1 *K.* 20:30 Benh. came into in. *c.*
22:25 *inner c.* 2 *Chr.* 18:24
2 *K.* 9:2 carry Jehu into *inner c.*

Little CHAMBER.
2 *K.* 4:10 a *little c.* on the wall
Ezek. 40:7 *little c.* one reed, 13

Side CHAMBER.
Ezek. 41:5 every *side c.* four cub.

Upper CHAMBER.
2 *K.* 1:2 thro' a lattice in u. *c.*
23:12 altars on top of *upper c.*
Acts 9:37 Dorcas in an *upper c.*
39 P. when come into *upper c.*
20:8 many lights in *upper c.*

CHAMBERS.
1 *K.* 6:5 against the wall built *c.*
1 *Chr.* 9:26 porters over *c.* 23:28
2 *Chr.* 31:11 com. to prepare *c.*
Job 9:9 maketh *c.* of the south
Ps. 104:3 beams of *c.* in waters
13 watereth hills from *c.*
105:30 in the *c.* of their kings
Prov. 7:27 down to *c.* of death
24:4 by knowledge *c.* be filled
Cant. 1:4 brought me into his *c.*
Is. 26:20 *c.* and shut thy doors
Jer. 22:13 buildeth *c.* by wrong
14 a wide house and large *c.*
35:2 Rechabites into one of *c.*
Ezek. 8:12 in *c.* of his imagery
21:14 sword entereth privy *c.*
42:13 holy *c.* where priests eat
Mat. 24:26 he is in secret *c.*

CHAMBERING.
Rom. 13:13 *c.* and wantonness

CHAMBERLAIN, S.
2 *K.* 23:11 Nathan-melech the *c.*
Est. 1:10 seven *c.* that served
2:21 king's *c.* were wroth
Acts 12:20 Blastus the king's *c.*
Rom. 16:23 Erastus *c.* saluteth

CHAMELEON.
Lev. 11:30 be unclean, the *c.*

CHAMOIS.
Deut. 14:5 ye shall eat, the *c.*

CHAMPAIGN.
Deut. 11:30 in *c.* over against G.

CHAMPION.
1 *Sam.* 17:4 there went out a *c.*
51 saw their *c.* was dead

CHANCE.
1 *Sam.* 6:9 *c.* that happened to us
Ec. 9:11 time and *c.* happeneth
Luke 10:31 by *c.* a priest came
1 *Cor.* 15:37 it may *c.* of wheat

CHANCELLOR.
Ezr. 4:8 Rehum the *c.* 9, 17

CHANGE.
Gen. 45:22 each *c.* to Ben. five *c.*
Jud. 14:12 *c.* of garments, 13
2 *K.* 5:5 took ten *c.* of raiment
22 two *c.* of garments
23 bound two *c.* of garments
Job 10:17 *c.* and war are ag. me
14:14 I wait till my *c.* come
Ps. 55:19 no *c.* they fear not
Prov. 24;21 them given to *c.*
Heb. 7:12 of necessity a *c.* of law

CHANGE, Verb.
Gen. 35:2 and *c.* your garments
Lev. 27:10 he shall not *c.* it
33 nor *c.* it, if he *c.*
Job 17:12 *c.* the night into the day
Ps. 102:26 as vesture *c.* them
Is. 9:10 will *c.* them into cedars
Jer. 2:36 so much to *c.* thy way?
13:23 can Ethiopian *c.* his skin
Dan. 7:25 think to *c.* times
Hos. 4:7 *c.* their glory to shame
Hab. 1:11 his mind *c.* and pass

Mal. 3:6 I am the Lord I *c.* not
Acts 6:14 shall *c.* the customs
Rom. 1:26 women did *c.* the use
Gal. 4:20 I desire to *c.* my voice
Phil. 3:21 C. shall *c.* our vile b.

CHANGED, ETH.
Gen. 31:7 your father *c.* wages
41:14 Joseph *c.* his raiment
Lev. 13:16 flesh turn and be *c.*
55 plague have not *c.* his color
1 *Sam.* 21:13 *c.* behavior before
2 *Sam.* 12:20 Dav. *c.* his apparel
2 *K.* 24:17 *c.* name to Zedekiah
25:29 *c.* prison gar. *Jer.* 52:33
Job 30:18 is my garment *c.*
Ps. 15:4 sweareth to hurt. *c.* not
102:26 as a vesture *c. Heb.* 1:12
106:20 *c.* their glory to an ox
Ec. 8:1 bold. of face shall be *c.*
Is. 24:5 *c.* the ordinance

Jer. 2:11 *c.* their gods, my people
48:11 and his scent is not *c.*
Lam. 4:1 how is the fine gold *c.*
Ezek. 5:6 hath *c.* my judgments
Dan. 2:9 to speak till time be *c.*
21 he *c.* times and seasons
3:19 form of his visage was *c.*
27 coats *c.* nor smell of fire
4:16 heart be *c.* from man's
6:8 writing that it be not *c.*
15 no decree may be *c.*
Mic. 2:4 *c.* portion of my people
Acts 28:6 barbarians *c.* their m.
Rom. 1:23 *c.* glory of uncor. God
25 *c.* truth of God into a lie
1 *Cor.* 15:51 we shall all be *c.* 52
2 *Cor.* 3:18 *c.* into same image
Heb. 7:12 for priesthood being *c.*

**CHANGEST, ED, counte-
nance.**
Job 14:20 *c.* his *c.* and sendest
Dan. 5:6 king's *c.* was *c.* 9
7:28 my *countenance c.* in me

CHANGERS.
Mat. 21:12 tables of money *c.*
Mark 11:15; *John* 2:14, 15

CHANGING.
Ruth 4:7 manner concerning *c.*

CHANNEL, S.
2 *Sam.* 22:16 *c.* of the s. *Ps.* 18:15
Is. 8:7 shall come up over his *c.*
27:12 beat off from *c.* of the riv.

CHANT.
Amos 6:5 *c.* to sound of the viol

CHAPEL.
Amos 7:13 it is the king's *c.*

CHAPITER, S.
Ex. 36:38 *c.* with gold, 38:28
38:17 overlaying of *c.* 19
2 *K.* 7:16 *c.* of brass, 2 *K.* 25:17;
2 *Chr.* 4:12, 13; *Jer.* 52:22

CHAPMEN.
2 *Chr.* 9:14 what *c.* brought

CHAPPED.
Jer. 14:4 because the ground is *c.*

CHARGE, Substantive.
Gen. 26:5 Abraham kept my *c.*
28:6 Isaac gave Jacob a *c.*
Ex. 6:13 Moses and Aaron a *c.*
Num. 9:19 kept the *c.* of L. 23
27:23 Joshua a *c. Deut.* 31:23
Jos. 22:3 Reubenites kept *c.*
2 *Sam.* 18:5 *c.* concerning Abs.
1 *K.* 11:28 Jeroboam ruler over *c.*
2 *K.* 7:17 lord *c.* of the gate
1 *Chr.* 9:27 bec. *c.* was on them
Neh. 7:2 Hanani *c.* over Jerus.
Job 34:13 *c.* over the earth?
Ps. 35:11 *c.* things I knew not
*Jer.*39:11 *c.* concerning Jeremiah
47:7 seeing L. hath given it *c.*
Ezek. 9:1 have *c.* over the city
44:8 not kept *c.* of holy things
15 kept *c.* of my sanctuary

48:11 my *c.* went not astray
Acts 7:60 lay not sin to their *c.*
8:27 had *c.* of treasure
16:24 rec. *c.* thrust into prison
23:29 to his *c.* worthy of death
Rom. 8:33 to *c.* of God's elect?
1 *Cor.* 9:18 gospel without *c.*
1 *Tim.* 1:18 *c.* I commit to thee
2 *Tim.* 4:16 not be laid to their *c.*
See KEEP.

Give CHARGE.
Num. 27:19 *give* Joshua a *c.*
Deut. 31:14 call J. *give* him a *c.*
2 *Sam.* 14:8 I will *g. c.* con. thee
1 *Chr.* 22:12 L. *g.* thee wis. and *c.*
Ps. 91:11 *g.* ang. *c. Mat.* 4:6;
Luke 4:10
1 *Tim.* 5:7 these things *give* in *c.*
6:13 *give* thee *c.* in sight of God

CHARGE, Verb.
Ex. 19:21 go down *c.* the people
Deut. 3:28 *c.* Joshua encourage
Neh. 10:32 to *c.* ourselves yearly
Cant. 2:7 I *c.* dau. 3:5; 5:8; 8:4
5:9 that thou dost so *c.* us
Mark 9:25 I *c.* thee, come out
1 *Tim.* 1:3 *c.* that they teach no
5:21 *c.* thee bef. God, 2 *Tim.* 4:1
6:17 *c.* them that are rich

CHARGEABLE.
2 *Sam.* 13:25 not all go, lest be *c.*
Neh. 5:15 governors were *c.*
2 *Cor.* 11:9 I was *c.* to no man
1 *Thes.* 2:9 we would not be *c.*
2 *Thes.* 3:8 might not be *c.* to any

CHARGED.
Gen. 26:11 Abimelech *c.* his peo.
28:1 Isaac called J. and *c.* him
40:4 captain *c.* Jos. with them
49:29 Jacob *c.* his sons, and said
Ex. 1:22 Pharaoh *c.* his people
Deut. 1:16 I *c.* your judges
24:5 nor be *c.* with business
27:11 Moses *c.* people *same day*
1 *Sam.* 14:27 heard not when S. *c.*
2 *Sam.* 18:12 hearing, king *c.*
1 *K.* 2:1 David *c.* Solomon
13:9 so *c.* me by word of Lord
2 *Chr.* 36:23 *c.* me to b. *Ezr.* 1:2
Job 1:22 nor *c.* God foolishly
4:17 angels he *c.* with folly
Jer. 32:13 I *c.* Baruch saying
35:8 obeyed Jonadab in all *he c.*
Mat. 9:30 *c.* that no man known
Mark 5:43 ; *Luke* 9:21
11:16 J. *c.* not to make known
Mark 7:36 *c.* not to tell, 8:30; 9:9;
Luke 5:14 ; 8:56
10:48 *c.* him should hold peace
1 *Thes.* 2:11 *c.* every one of you
1 *Tim.* 5:16 let not church be *c.*

CHARGEDST.
Ex. 19:23 *c.* us, saying

CHARGER, S.
Num. 7:13 offering silver *c.* 19-79
85 each *c.* of silver 130 shekels
Ezr. 1:9 one thousand *c.*
Mat. 14:8 head in a *c. Mark* 6:25

CHARGES.
2 *Chr.* 8:14 Levites to their *c.*
31:17 twenty years in their *c.*
35:2 set priests in their *c.*
Acts 21:24 be at *c.* with them
1 *Cor.* 9:7 warfare at his own *c.* ?

CHARGING.
Acts 16:23 *c.* jailer to keep safely
2 *Tim.* 2:14 *c.* strive not about w.

CHARIOT.
Gen. 41:43 ride in second *c.*
Ex. 14:25 Lord took off *c.* wheels
1 *K.* 18:44 prep. ran *c.* get down
20:25 number *c.* for *c.*
22:35 the blood thy into *c.*
2 *K.* 2:11 appeared a *c.* of fire
12 cried, *c.* of Israel, 13:14

5:21 from *c.* to meet Gehazi
9:16 J. rode in *c.* ; 27 smite in *c.*
28 carried him in a *c.* 23:30
2 *Chr.* 35:24 took him out of *c.*
Ps. 46:9 he burneth the *c.* in fire
76:6 *c.* and horse cast into sleep
Cant. 3:9 *c.* of wood of Lebanon
Is. 21:7 saw a *c. c.* of asses
Jer. 51:21 will I break in pieces *c.*
Mic. 1:13 bind *c.* to swift beast
Zec. 6:2 first *c.* red horses
9:10 cut off *c.* from Ephraim
Acts 8:29 join thyself to this *c.*
38 commanded *c.* to stand still

His CHARIOT.
Gen. 46:29 J. made ready *his c.*
Ex. 14:6 Ph. made ready *his c.*
Jud. 4:15 Sisera lighted off *his c.*
5:28 *his c.* so long in coming
1 *K.* 12:18 to *his c.* 2 *Chr.* 10:18
22:34 to driver of *his c.*
2 *K.* 5:9 Naaman came with *h. c.*
9:21 went out each in *his c.*
24 Jehoram sunk down in *h. c.*
10:16 made him ride in *his c.*
Ps. 104:3 maketh clouds *his c.*
Jer. 4:13 *his c.* like whirlwind
Acts 8:28 in *his c.* read Esaias

CHARIOT-CITIES.
2 *Chr.* 1:14 placed in *c.-c.*
8:6 Solomon built all *c.-c.*
9:25 bestowed the *c.-c.*

CHARIOT-HORSES.
2 *Sam.* 8:4 hou. *c.-h.* 1 *Chr.* 18:4
2 *K.* 7:14 they took two *c.-h.*

CHARIOT-MAN.
2 *Chr.* 18:33 to *c.-m.* turn thy h.

CHARIOTS.
Gen. 50:9 went with Joseph *c.*
Ex. 14:7 Pharaoh took 600 *c.*
28 waters covered all the *c.*
15:4 Ph.'s *c.* cast into sea, 19
Jos. 17:16 *c.* of iron 18; *Jud.* 1:19
4:3
Jud. 5:28 wheels of his *c.*
1 *Sam.* 8:11 king appoint for his *c.*
13:5 to fight Israel 30,000 *c.*
2 *Sam.* 1:6 the *c.* followed Saul
1 *K.* 10:26 Solomon had 1,400 *c.*
22:32 captains of *c.* saw Jeh.
2 *K.* 13:7 left but ten *c.*
18:24 trust on E. for *c. Is.* 36:9
Ps. 68:17 *c.* of God are 20,000
Cant. 6:12 my soul like *c.* of Am
Is. 2:7 nor any end of their *c.*
22:18 *c.* of thy glory be shame
31:1 woe to them that trust in *c.*
37:24 by mul. of *c.* am I come
66:15 with *c.* like whirlwind.
Jer. 4:13 ; *Dan.* 11:40
Jer. 47:3 at rushing of his *c.*
Ezek. 23:24 against thee with *c.*
26:10 walls shake at noise of *c.*
Joel 2:5 like noise of *c.* shall leap
Mic. 5:10 I will destroy thy *c.*
Nah. 2:3 *c.* shall be with torches
4 *c.* shall rage in the streets
13 I will burn her *c.* in smoke
Hag. 2:22 I will overthrow the *c.*
Rev. 9:9 sound of wings as of *c.*

CHARIOTS with horses.
Deut. 11:4 he did to *h.* and *c.*
20:1 seest *horses* and *c.* fear not
Jos. 11:6 hough their *h.* burn *c.*
9 Josh. burnt their *c.* with fire
2 *Sam.* 15:1 Absal. pre. *h.* and *c.*
1 *K.* 20:1 Samaria with *c.* and *h.*
2 *K.* 6:17 mount. full of *c.* and *h.*
7:6 to hear a noise of *h.* and *c.*
10:2 with you *c.* and *horses*
Ps. 20:7 trust in *c.* some in *h.*
Cant. 1:9 comp. to *h.* in Phar. *c.*
Is. 66:20 bring brethren in *c.*
Jer. 17:25 princes in *c.* 22:4
46:9 come up, ye *h.* rage ye *c.*
50:37 on their *horses* and *c.*

Ezek. 26:7 Tyrus Neb. with *c.*
39:20 at table with *h.* and *c.*
Nah. 3:2 *h.* and jumping *c.*
Hab. 3:8 thy *c.* of salvation
Rev. 18:13 buys their *h.* and *c.*

CHARITABLY.
Rom. 14:15 now walkest not *c.*

CHARITY.
1 *Cor.* 8:1 but *c.* edifieth
13:1 and have not *c,* 2, 3
4 *c.* suffereth long, *c.* env. not
13 faith, hope, *c.* greatest is *c.*
14:1 follow *c.* desire spir. gifts
16:14 let all be done with *c.*
Col. 3:14 above all put on *c.*
1 *Thes.* 3:6 good tidings of your *c.*
2 *Thes.* 1:3 *c.* to each other
1 *Tim.* 1:5 end of command. is *c.*
2:15 if continue in faith and *c.*
4:12 example in *c.* in spirit
2 *Tim.* 2:22 follow righteous. *c.*
3:10 known my life, faith, *c.*
Tit. 2:2 aged men be sound in *c.*
1 *Pet.* 4:8 fervent *c. c.* cover sins
5:14 greet with a kiss of *c.*
2 *Pet.* 1:7 brotherly kindness *c.*
3 *John* 6 borne witness of thy *c.*
Jude 12 spots in your feasts of *c.*
Rev. 2:19 I know thy works, *c.*

CHARMED.
Jer. 8:17 wh. will not be *c.*

CHARMER, S.
Deut. 18:11 not be found a *c.*
Ps. 58:5 not hearken to *c.*

CHARRAN. *Acts* 7:2, 4

CHASE.
Lev. 26:8 shall *c.* a hundred, 36.
Deut. 32:30 *c.* 1,000, *Jos.* 23:10
Ps. 35:5 angel of L. *c.* them

CHASED, ETH, ING.
Deut. 1:44 Amorites *c.* you
Jud. 9:40 Abimelech *c.* him
Neh. 13:28 I *c.* him from me
Job 18:18 be *c.* out of the world
20:8 be *c.* as a vision of night
Prov. 19:26 *c.* away his mother
Is. 13:14 shall be as the *c.* roe
17:13 they shall be *c.* as chaff
Lam. 3:52 *c.* me sore like a bird

CHASTE.
2 *Cor.* 11:2 pres. you as *c.* virgin
Tit. 2:5 young women be *c.*
1 *Pet.* 3:2 your *c.* conversation

CHASTEN.
2 *Sam.* 7:14 *c.* with rod of men
Ps. 6:1 *c.* me in hot displ. 38:1
Prov. 19:18 *c.* son while hope
Dan. 10:12 *c.* thyself before God
Rev. 3:19 I rebuke and *c.*

CHASTENED.
Deut. 21:18 they have *c.* him
Job 33:19 is *c.* also with pain
Ps. 69:10 *a.* my soul
73:14 and *c.* every morning
118:18 Lord hath *c.* me sore
1 *Cor.* 11:32 *c.* that we be not
2 *Cor.* 6:9 as *c.* and not killed
Heb. 12:10 for a few days *c.* us

CHASTENEST, ETH, ING.
Deut. 8:5 *c.* his son, so L. *c.* thee
Job 5:17 *c.* of Almighty, *Prov.*
3:11; *Heb.* 12:5.
Ps. 94:12 bless. is whom thou *c.*
Prov. 13:24 lov. him, *c.* betimes
Is. 26:16 *c.* was on them
Heb. 12:6 whom Lord loveth he *c.*
Heb. 12:7 if ye end. *c.* what son
11 no *c.* seemeth to be joyous

CHASTISE, ED, ETH.
Lev. 26:28 I will *c.* seven times
Deut. 22:18 elders shall *c.* him

---

1 *K.* 12:11 I will *c.* you with scor-
pions, 14; 2 *Chr.* 10:11, 14
Ps. 94:10 he that *c.* heathen
Jer. 31:18 *c.* me, and I was *c.*
Hos. 7:12 I will *c.* them as cong.
10:10 I should *c.* them
Luke 23:16 *c.* him and release, 22

CHASTISEMENT.
Deut. 11:2 have not seen the *c.*
Job 34:31 I have borne *c.*
Is. 53:5 *c.* of our peace
Jer. 30:14 with *c.* of a cruel one
Heb. 12:8 with, *c.* then bastards

CHATTER.
Is. 38:14 so did I *c.*

CHEBAR. *Ezek.* 1:1, 3; 3:15, 23;
10:15, 20

CHECK.
Job 20:3 heard *c.* of my reproach

CHECKER-WORK.
1 *K.* 7:17 Hir. made nets of *c.*

CHEDORLAOMER. *Gen.* 14:4

CHEEK.
1 *K.* 22:24 Zed. smote Mic. on *c.*
Job 16:10 smitten me on the *c.*
Lam. 3:30 *c.* to him that smiteth
Mic. 5:1 smite the judge on the *c.*
Mat. 5:39 right *c.* turn other
Luke 6:29 to him smiteth one *c.*

CHEEKBONE.
Ps. 3:7 smitten enemies on *c.*

CHEEKS.
Cant. 1:10 thy *c.* comely
5:13 his *c.* are as a bed of spices
Is. 50:6 my *c.* to them
Lam. 1:2 her tears are on her *c.*

CHEEKTEETH.
Joel 1:6 he hath *c.* of a great lion

CHEER.
Deut. 24:5 shall *c.* up his wife
Ec. 11:9 thy heart *c.* thee

Good CHEER.
Mat. 9:2 son, be of *g. c.*
14:27 be of *g. c. Mark* 6:50
John 16:33 be of *g. c.* I have
Acts 23:11 be of *good c.* Paul
27:22 to be of *good c.* 25, 36

CHEERETH.
Jud. 9:13 which *c.* God and man

CHEERFUL.
Prov. 15:13 a *c.* countenance
Zec. 8:19 be to Judah *c.* feasts
9:17 corn make young men *c.*
2 *Cor.* 9:7 God loveth a *c.* giver

CHEERFULLY.
Acts 24:10 *c.* answer for myself

CHEERFULNESS.
Rom. 12:8 showeth mercy with *c.*

CHEESE, S.
1 *Sam.* 17:18 carry ten *c.* to capt.
2 *Sam.* 17:29 of kine for David
Job 10:10 curdled me like *c.*

CHEMARIM. *Zep.* 1:4

CHEMOSH.
Num. 21:29 O people of C.
Jud. 11:24 what C. giveth?
1 *K.* 11:7, 33; *Jer.* 48:7, 13, 46

CHENAANAH. 1 *K.* 22:24;
2 *Chr.* 18:23.

CHENANIAH.
1 *Chr.* 15:22 C. chief of Lev. 27

CHERETHIM. *Ezek.* 25:16

CHERETHITES.
1 *Sam.* 30:14 invasion on the C.
2 *Sam.* 8:18 the C. 20:23; 1 *Chr.*
18:17.
Zep. 2:5 woe unto nation of C.

CHERISH, ED, ETH.
1 *K.* 1:2 let her *c.* him. and lie
4 damsel *c.* the king

Eph. 5:29 *c.* flesh, as L. church
1 *Thes.* 2:7 as a nurse *c.* children

CHERITH. *K.* 17:3.

CHERUB.
Ex. 25:19 *c.* on one end *c.* 37:8
2 *Sam.* 22:11 on a *c. Ps.* 18:10
1 *K.* 6:25 other *c.* was ten cubits
Ezek. 9:3 gone up from *c.* 10:4
10:14 first face was face of a *c.*
28:16 destroy thee, O covering *c.*
41:18 every *c.* had two faces

CHERUBIM.
Gen. 3:24 placed the *c.* east

Ex. 37:7 made two *c.* of gold
1 *K.* 6:25 both the *c.* of one meas.
8:7 *c.* covered ark, 2 *Chr.* 5:8;
Heb. 9:5
2 *Chr.* 3:10 most holy house two *c.*
Ezek. 10:16 *c.* went wheels went
19 the *c.* lifted wings, 11:22

Between the CHERUBIM.
Ex. 25:22 from *b.* two *c.*
Num. 7:89 *betw.* the two *c.*
1 *Sam.* 4:4 wh. dw. *bet. c.* 2 *Sam.*
6:2; 2 *K.* 19:15; *Is.* 37:16
Ps. 80:1 dwellest *bet. c.* shine
99:1 he sitteth *bet. t. c.*
Ezek. 10:2 fire from *bet. t. c.* 6
7 hand from *betw. the c.*

CHESED. *Gen.* 22:22

CHESNUT-TREE, S.
Gen. 30:37 Jac. took rods of *c.-t.*
Ezek. 31:8 *c.-t.* not like his bran.

CHEST, S.
2 *K.* 12:9 a *c.* and bored a hole
2 *Chr.* 24:8 at king's com. made *c.*
Ezek. 27:24 thy merchants in *c.*

CHEW, ED, ETH.
Lev. 11:4 *c.* the cud, *Deut.* 14:7
7 *c.* not the cud, *Deut.* 14:8
Num. 11:33 ere flesh *c.* wrath

CHICKENS.
Mat. 23:37 hen gathereth her *c.*

CHIDE.
Ex. 17:2 people did *c.* why *c.*
Jud. 8:1 Eph. did *c.* with Gid.
Ps. 103:9 he will not always *c.*

CHIDING.
Ex. 17:7 Meribah, because of *c.*

CHIEF.
Gen. 40:21 restored the *c.* butler
22 but he hanged the *c.* baker
Num. 3:32 Eleazar *c.* over the *c.*
2 *Sam.* 23:18 Abishai was *c.*
1 *Chr.* 5:2 of Judah came *c.* ruler
11:6 smit. Jebusites be *c.* ruler
18:17 the sons of David were *c.*
26:10 though not first-born *c.*
Ezr. 9:2 rulers *c.* in this trespass
Job 12:24 taketh away heart of *c.*
29:25 chose out their way, sat *c.*
40:19 behemoth is *c.* of ways
Ps. 78:51 *c.* of strength, 105:36
137:8 Jerusalem above my *c.* joy
Prov. 1:21 crieth in *c.* places
16:28 whisperer sep. *c.* friends
Is. 14:9 helt stirreth up *c.* ones
Jer. 13:21 taught them as *c.* over
31:7 shout among *c.* of nations
Lam. 1:5 her adversaries are *c.*
Dan. 11:41 *c.* of children of Am.
Amos 6:1 *c.* of the nations
Mat. 20:27 whosoever will be *c.*
23:6 love *c.* seats, *Mark* 12:39
Mark 6:21 supper to his *c.* estates
Lu. 11:15 cast. out devils thro' *c.*
14:1 house of one of *c.* Pharisees
7 they chose *c.* rooms, 20:46
22:26 he *c.* as he that serveth
John 12:42 *c.* rulers many believ.
Acts 14:12 he was the *c.* speaker
17:4 of *c.* women not a few
Eph. 2:20 *c.* corner-st. 1 *Pet.* 2:6

CHIEF captain.

2 Sam. 5:8 he shall be c. and cap.
Acts 21:31 came to c. captain
33 saw c. captain they left
23:17 bring young man to c. c.
24:7 c. captain L. came upon us
22 c. c. shall come, I will know

CHIEF captains.

2 Sam. 23:8 sat c. among the c.
2 Chr. 8:9 Is. c. of Solomon's cap.
Acts 25:23 Ag. entered with c. c.
Rev. 6:15 c. c. hid themselves

CHIEF fathers.

Num. 31:26 c. f. of the congreg.
1 Chr. 9:34 c. fathers of Levites
24:31 c. fathers of priests
26:32 c. f. D. made rulers
2 Chr. 26:12 number of c. fathers
Ezr. 1:5 rose up c. fath. of Jud.
Neh. 7:70 c. of f. gave to work, 71

CHIEF house.

Jos. 22:14 c. h. a prince was sent

CHIEF man, or men.

Lev. 21:4 not defile him. a c. m.
1 Chr. 7:3 sons of Uzzi c. men.
24:4 more c. men of Eleazar
Ezr. 7:28 I gath. c. m. to go up
Is. 41:9 I called thee from c. m.
Acts 13:50 Jews stirred up c. m.
15:22 Judas and Silas c. men
Acts 28:7 poss. of c. man of isl.

CHIEF priest.

2 K. 25:18 took Ser. the c. priest
1 Chr. 27:5 Benaiah a c. priest
29:22 anointed Z. to be c. priest
2 Chr. 19:11 Amariah c. priest
26:20 Azariah c. p. looked on

CHIEF priests.

Ezr. 10:5 c. p. and all Israel
Mat. 16:21 suffer of the c. priests
26:47 multitude from c. priests
27:12 accu. of c. p. Mark 15:3
41 c. p. mocking, Mark 15:31
Mark 14:1 c. p. sought. 55 ; Mat.
26:59 ; Luke 9:22 ; 22:2.
Luke 23:23 voices of c. p. prev.
John 7:32 c. p. sent officers, 18:3
Acts 9:14 auth. from c. p. 26:10
22:30 commanded c. p. to appear

CHIEF prince, or princes.

1 Chr. 7:40 children of A. c. of p.
Ezek. 38:2 Gog c. prince, 3 ; 39:1
Dan. 10:13 Michael one of c. p.

CHIEF singer, or singers.

Neh. 12:46 in days of D. c. of s.
Hab. 3:19 to c. singer on instru.

CHIEFEST.

1 Sam. 2:29 yoursel. fat with c.
9:22 Sam. made sit in c. place
2 Chr. 32:33 in c. of sepulchres
Cant. 5:10 the c. among 10,000
Mark 10:44 c. shall be servant
2 Cor. 11:5 c. apostles, 12:11

CHIEFLY.

Rom. 3:2 c. because to them
Phil. 4:22 c. they of Cesar's h.
2 Pet. 2:10 c. them walk after fl.

CHILD.

Gen. 21:16 not see death of c.
37:30 c. is not, and I whither
42:22 do not sin against the c.
Ex. 2:8 maid called c. mother
22:22 not afflict any fatherless c.
Jud. 11:34 his daughter, only c.
13:8 teach us what we do to c.
1 Sam. 1:25 brought the c. to Eli
3:8 Eli perc. L. had called c.
2 Sam. 12:14 the c. born shall die
15 L. stru. c. Uriah's wife bare
16 David besought God for c.
1 K. 3:25 divide living c. in two

14:3 what shall become of c.
17:22 soul of the c. came
2 K. 4:31 told c. is not awaked
35 c. sneezed, c. opened eyes
Prov. 22:13 correction from c.
Ec. 4:8 hath neither c. nor bro.
15 second c. that shall stand
Is. 3:5 c. shall behave proudly
7:16 before c. know to refuse
8:4 before c. know to cry
11:8 c. put hand on cockatrice
65:20 c. shall die 100 years old
Jer. 4:31 bring. forth her first c.
31:20 Eph. is he a pleasant c. ?
44:7 cut off man, woman, and c.
Mat. 10:21 deliver c. to death
17:18 c. was cured from that h.
23:15 more the c. of hell
Luke 1:59 came to circumcise c.
1:66 what manner of c.
76 c. called prophet of Highest
80 c. grew, waxed strong, 2:40
2:27 parents brought in c. Jesus
9:38 look on my son, only c.
John 4:49 come down ere c. die
16:21 as soon as delivered of c.
Acts 4:27 against thy holy c. J.
30 done by name of thy c. J.
13:10 Saul said, Thou c. of devil
Rev. 12:4 to devour her c. as soon
5 her c. was caught up to God

A CHILD.

Gen. 18:13 bear a c. who am old ?
44:20 and a c. of his own age
Ex. 2:2 a goodly c. Heb. 11:23
1 Sam. 2:18 c. girded with linen
1 K. 13:2 a c. born to house of D
Job 33:25 flesh fresher than a c.
Ps. 131:2 as a c. as a weaned c.
Prov. 20:11 a c. is known
22:6 train up a c. in way he
15 foolish. is in heart of a c.
21 bringing up serv. from a c.
Ec. 4:13 better is a wise c. than
10:16 when thy king is a c.
Is. 9:6 for unto us a c. is born
10:19 a c. may write
Jer. 1:6 for I am a c. 7
20:15 a man c. is born to thee
Hos. 11:1 Is. a c. I loved him
Mark 9:21 he said of a c.
36 took a c. set it, Luke 9:47
1 Cor. 13:11 a c. I spake as a. c.
Gal. 4:1 as long as he is a c.

2 Tim. 3:15 from a c. known sc.
Heb. 11:11 S. deliv. of a c. past a.
Rev. 12:5 a man c. to rule nations

Little CHILD.

1 K. 3:7 I am but a l. c.
11:17 H. fled being yet a little c.
2 K. 5:14 the flesh of a little c.
Is. 11:6 a little c. shall lead them
Mat. 18:2 J. called a little c. to him
5 receive one such l. c. in my
Mark 10:15 whoso not rec. kingdom of G. as lit. c. Luke 18:17

No CHILD.

Gen. 11:30 Sarai had no c.
Lev. 22:13 priest's dau. have n. c.
Deut. 25:5 brother die, have n. c.
2 Sam. 6:23 Michal had no c.
2 K. 4:14 verily she hath no c.
Luke 1:7 they had no. c. bec. E.
Acts 7:5 when he had no c.

Sucking CHILD.

Num. 11:12 beareth sucking c.
Is. 11:8 suck. c. play on hole
49:15 woman forget suck. c.
Lam. 4:4 tongue of suck. c.

This CHILD.

Luke 2:17 told concerning this c.
34 c. is set for fall and rising
9:48 receive t. c. in my name

With CHILD.

Gen. 16:11 Hagar thou art w. c.
19:36 daughters of Lot with c.
38:24 T. thy daughter is w. c.
25 whose these are, am I w. c.
Ex. 21:22 hurt a woman w. c.
1 Sam. 4:19 Phin. wife was w. c.
2 Sam. 11:5 B. said, I am w. c.
2 K. 8:12 wilt rip up their woman with c. 15:16
Ec. 11:5 in womb of her w. c.
Is. 26:17 with c. that, draweth
18 we have been with c.
54:1 that didst not trav. with c.
Jer. 30:6 whe. a man trav. w. c.
31:8 the woman with c.
Hos. 13:16 with c. shall be rip.
Amos 1:13 rip. up woman, w. c.
Mat. 1:18 with c. of the H. Ghost
23 a virgin shall be with c.
24:19 woe to them that are w. c.
Mark 13:17 ; Luke 21:23
Luke 2:5 Mary, great with c.
1 Thes. 5:3 travail on wom. w. c.
Rev. 12:2 and she being with c.

Young CHILD.

1 Sam. 1:24 the c. was young
Mat. 2:8 search dilig. for y. c.
13 take young c. and his moth.

CHILD-BEARING.

1 Tim. 2:15 shall be saved in c.-b.

CHILDHOOD.

1 Sam. 12:2 before you from c.
Ec. 11:10 c. and youth are vanity

CHILDISH.

1 Cor. 13:11 I put away c. things

CHILDLESS.

Gen. 15:2 seeing I go c.
Lev. 20:20 they shall die c.
1 Sam. 15:33 as thy sword made
women c. so thy mother be c.
Jer. 22:30 write ye this man c.
Luke 20:30 sec. took her, died c.

CHILDREN.

Gen. 3:16 in sorrow bring forth c.
16:2 I may obtain c. by her
25:22 the c. struggled within her
30:1 give me c. or I die
33:5 c. God hath given
49:8 thy father's c. shall bow
Ex. 20:5 iniq. of fath. on c. 34:7 ;
Num. 14:18 ; Deut. 5:9
21:4 c. shall be her masters
Num. 13:28 saw c. of Anak there
26:11 c. of Korah died not
Deut. 9:2 before c. of Anak?
13:13 c. of Belial are gone out
14:1 ye are the c. of the Lord
23:8 c. begotten of them
24:16 fath. not put to death for
c. nor c. for fath. 2 Chr. 25:4
32:20 c. in whom there is no f.
33:24 Asher be blessed with c.
Jud. 8:18 resembled c. of king
20:13 deliver us the c. of Belial
1 Sam. 2:5 she that hath many c.
is waxed feeble
2 Sam. 7:10 c. of wickedness affl.
any more, 1 Chr. 17:9
1 K. 21:13 came in two c. of Bel.
2 K. 2:24 she-bears tare 42 c.
10:13 c. of king c. of queen
14:6 c. of murderers, 2 Chr. 25:4
17:34 as Lord com. c. of Jacob
19:3 c. are come to b. Is. 37:3

1 Chr. 2:30 Seled died without c.
32 and Jether died without c.
4:27 Shimei's bre. not many c.
16:13 ye c. of Jacob, Ps. 105:6
2 Chr. 13:7 to Jeroboam c. of B.
25:7 L. is not with all c. of E.
Ezra 10:44 by whom had c.
Neh. 9:23 c. multipledst as stars
Job 19:17 I entreated for c. sake
30:8 c. of fools, yea c. of base

41:34 king over all *c.* of pride
Ps. 17:14 they are full of *c.*
34:11 come ye *c.* hearken to me
69:8 an alien to my mother's *c.*
72:4 he shall save *c.* of needy
78:6 *c.* wh. sh. be born might
82:6 all of you *c.* of Most High
83:8 holpen *c.* of Lot, Selah
102:28 *c.* of thy serv. continue
113:9 barren to be mother of *c.*
127:3 *c.* are a heritage of Lord
4 as arrows in hand, so are *c.*
137:7 remember, *c.* of Edom
148:12 old men and *c.* praise L.
149:2 let *c.* of Zion be joyful
Prov. 4:1 hear, ye *c.* the instruction, 5:7; 7:24; 8:32
17:6 glory of *c.* are their fathers
31:28 her *c.* call her blessed
Ec. 6:3 if a man beget 100 *c.*
Cant. 1:6 my mother's *c.* angry
Is. 1:2 brought up *c.* they reb.
4 *c.* that are corrupters
2:6 in the *c.* of strangers
3:4 give *c.* to be their princes
12 *c.* are their oppressors
8:18 *c.* Lord hath giv. *Heb.* 2:13
13:18 eyes shall not spare *c.*
21:17 mighty of *c.* of K. dimin.
23:4 nor bring forth *c.*
30:1 woe to rebellious *c.*
9 lying *c. c.* will not hear law
38:19 father to *c.* make known
47:8 neither know loss of *c.*
9 loss of *c.* widowhood
49:20 *c.* shalt have, shall say
54:1 are *c.* of desolate than *c.* of
married wife, *Gal.* 4:27
57:4 are ye not *c.* of transg.
5 slaying the *c.* in the valleys
63:8 *c.* that will not lie
66:8 Zion brought forth *c.*
Jer. 3:14 O blacksliding *c.* 22
19 how put these among the *c.*
4:22 my people are sottish *c.*
6:11 pour it out on *c.* abroad
7:18 *c.* gather wood, fathers
9:21 death entered to cut off *c.*
15:7 I will bereave them of *c.*
31:15 R. weep. for *c.* *Mat.* 2:18
Lam. 2:20 shall the women eat *c.*
5:13 *c.* fell under the wood
Ezek. 2:4 are imprudent *c.*
20:21 the *c.* rebelled against me
33:30 *c.* talking against thee
47:22 to strangers that beget *c.*
Dan. 1:4 *c.* in whom no blemish
17 four *c.* God gave knowledge
12:1 Michael shall stand for *c.*
Hos. 1:2 take *c.* of whoredoms
2:4 not have mercy on her *c.*
11:10 *c.* shall tremble
13:13 breaking forth of *c.*
Joel 2:16 gather *c.* and those
23 be glad, then, ye *c.* of Zion
Amos 9:7 *c.* of the Ethiopians?
Mic. 1:16 poll thee for delicate *c.*
Zep. 1:8 I will punish king's *c.*
Mal. 4:6 heart of fathers to *c.* of *c.*
to fathers, *Luke* 1:17
Mat. 2:16 Herod slew all the *c.*
3:9 to raise up *c.* *Luke* 3:8
5:45 be the *c.* of your Father
8:12 but the *c.* shall be cast out
9:15 *c.* of bridechamber mourn,
Mark 2:19; *Luke* 5:34
10:21 *c.* ag. parents, *Mark* 13:12
11:19 justi. of her *c.* *Luke* 7:35
13:38 good seed are *c.* of kingd.
15:26 *c.* bread, *Mark* 7:27
17:26 then are the *c.* free
19:29 forsaken *c.* *Mark* 10:29
20:20 mother of Zebedee's *c.*
21:15 saw *c.* crying in temple
Mark 7:27 let the *c.* first be filled
28 dogs eat of the *c.* crumbs
9:37 receive one of such *c.* 41
Luke 6:35 shall be *c.* of Highest

16:8 *c.* of this world are wiser
20:29 the first died without *c.*
34 the *c.* of this world marry
John 8:39 were Abraham's *c.*
Acts 3:25 ye are *c.* of prophets
Rom. 8:17 if *c.* then heirs, heirs
9:7 seed of Abra. are they all *c.*
11 the *c.* being not yet born
1 *Cor.* 14:20 not *c.* in understand.
2 *Cor.* 12:14 *c.* not lay up
Gal. 3:7 of faith, are *c.* of Abra.
4:3 when *c.* were in bondage
25 Jeru. in bondage with her *c.*
31 we are not *c.* of bondwoman
Eph. 1:5 to the adoption of *c.*
2:2 in *c.* of disobedience
3 were by nature *c.* of wrath
4:14 we be no more *c.* tossed
5:1 followers of God as dear *c.*
6 wrath on *c.* of dis. *Col.* 3:6
6:1 *c.* obey your par. *Col.* 3:20
1 *Tim.* 5:4 if any widow have *c.*
10 if she brought up *c.*
Heb. 2:14 as *c.* are partakers
12:5 speaketh to you as *c.*
1 *Pet.* 1:14 as obedient *c.*
2 *Pet.* 2:14 cursed *c.*
2 *John* 1 to elect lady and her *c.*
13 *c.* of elect sister greet thee
Rev. 2:23 I will kill her *c.*

See AMMON, CAPTIVITY.

CHILDREN of Benjamin.
Jud. 20:13 *c.* of *B.* would not
20 2 *Sam.* 2:25 *c.* of *B.* gathered
1 *Chr.* 12:16 *c.* of *B.* to hold to D.
Jer. 6:1 O ye *c.* of *B.* gather

Children's CHILDREN.
Gen. 45:10 thou and thy *c. c.*
Ex. 34:7 iniq. of fathers on *c. c.*
Deut. 4:25 beget *c.* and *c. c.*
2 *K.* 17:41 served images *child. c.*
Ps. 103:17 righteousness to *c. c.*
128:6 shalt see thy *c. c.*
Prov. 13:22 inherit. to his *c. c.*
17:6 *child. c.* crown of old men
Jer. 2:9 with your *c. c.* will I pl.
Ezek. 37:25 and *c. c.* for ever

Fatherless CHILDREN.
Ps. 109:12 to favor his *f. c.*
Jer. 49:11 leave thy *f. c.*

CHILDREN of God.
Mat. 5:9 peacemakers *c.* of God
Luke 20:36 *c.* of God being *c.*
John 11:52 in one the *c.* of God
Rom. 8:16 we are the *c.* of God
21 glor. liberty of the *c.* of G.
9:8 *c.* of the flesh, not *c.* of G.
26 called *c.* of the living God
Gal. 3:26 *c.* of God by faith in C.
John 3:10 *c.* G. manifest, *c.* of *c.*
5:2 know we love *c.* of God

His CHILDREN.
Gen. 18:19 Abra. will com. *h. c.*
Deut. 17:20 pro. days and *his c.*
32:5 is not spot of *his c.*
33:9 nor knew *his own c.*
2 *Sam.* 12:3 ewe-l. grew with *h. c.*
2 *Chr.* 28:3 give a light, and to *h. c.*
21:3 burnt *h. c.* after h.
33:6 *his c.* to pass through fire
Job 5:4 *his c.* are far from safety
17:5 eyes of *his c.* shall fail
20:10 *h. c.* shall seek to please
21:19 iniquity for *his c.*
27:14 if *his c.* be multiplied
Ps. 89:30 if *his c.* forsake
103:13 as a father pitieth *his c.*
109:9 let *his c.* be fatherless
10 let *his c.* be vagabonds
Prov. 14:26 *his c.* shall have ref.
20:7 *his c.* are blessed after him
Is. 14:21 slaughter for *his c.*
29:23 seeth *his c.* in midst
Hos. 9:13 shall bring forth *his c.*

John 4:12 *his c.* drank thereof
1 *Thes.* 2:11 ch. you as fath. *h. c.*
1 *Tim.* 3:4 *his c.* in subjection

CHILDREN of Israel.
Ex. 1:7 *c.* of *I.* were fruitful
12 grieved bec. of the *c.* of *I.*
2:25 God looked on *c.* of *Israel*
4:31 heard L. had visited *c.* of *I.*
6:13 *c.* of *I.* o. of Eg. 26, 27; 12:51
29:43 I will meet with *c.* of *I.*
Lev. 25:55 *c.* of *I.* are servants
Num. 14:10 gl. of L. ap. bef. *c. I.*
Jos. 7:12 *c. I.* not stand bef. enc.
2 *Sam.* 21:2 Gib. not of *c.* of *I.*
2 *K.* 17:24 instead of the *c.* of *I.*
Ps. 103:7 his acts to the *c.* of *I.*
148:14 *c.* of *I.* a people near
Is. 27:12 gath. one by one, *c. I.*
Ezek. 44:15 *c. I.* w. astray, 48:11
Amos 2:11 thus, O *c.* of *I.*?
4:5 liketh you, O ye *c.* of *I.*
Luke 1:16 *c.* of *Is.* shall turn
Acts 7:23 visit breth. the *c.* of *I.*
37 Moses which said to *c.* of *I.*
9:15 bear my name bef. *c.* of *I.*
10:36 word of G. sent to *c. I.*
Rom. 9:27 *c.* of *I.* be as the sand.
Heb. 11:22 mention of *d.* of *c. I.*
Rev. 7:4 sealed 144,000 of *c.* of *I.*
21:12 twelve tribes of *c.* of *I.*

CHILDREN of Judah.
Num. 1:26 *c.* of *J.* by their gen.
Jos. 14:6 *c.* of *J.* came to Joshua
2 *Sam.* 1:18 teach *c.* of *J.*
2 *Chr.* 13:18 *c.* of *J.* prevailed
28:10 keep under the *c.* of *Jud.*
Jer. 50:4 they and *c.* of *Judah*
33 Is. and *c.* of *J.* were oppres.
Joel 3:19 for violence ag. *c.* of *J.*

CHILDREN of light.
Luke 16:8 wiser than *c.* of *light*
John 12:36 ye may be the *c.* of *l.*
Eph. 5:8 walk as *c.* of *light*
1 *Thes.* 5:5 ye are all the *c.* of *l.*

Little CHILDREN.
Num. 16:27 *l. c.* stood in the door
2 *K.* 2:23 came *l. c.* and mocked
Est. 3:13 to destroy *l. c.*
Ezek. 9:6 slay maids, *little c.*
Mat. 18:3 except bec. as *little c.*
19:13 brought to him *little c.*
14 suffer *l. c.* to come unto me,
Mark 10:14; *Luke* 18:16
John 13:33 *l. c.* yet a little while
Gal. 4:19 *l. c.* of whom I travail
1 *John* 2:1 my *little c.* 12, 13
4:4 ye are of God *little c.*
5:21 *little c.* keep from idols

CHILDREN of men.
1 *Sam.* 26:19 if *c. m.* cursed be
2 *Sam.* 7:14 the stripes of *c. m.*
1 *K.* 8:39 knowest hearts of *c.* of
men, 2 *Chr.* 6:30
Ps. 11:4 his eyelids try *c. m.*
12:1 faith. fail from among *c. m.*
14:2 heaven upon *c. m.* 53:2
36:7 *c. m.* put trust under sha.
45:2 fairer than the *c.* of *men*
90:3 return ye *c.* of *men*
107:8 works to *c. m.* 15, 21, 31
115:16 given to *c.* of *men*
Prov. 15:11 hearts of *c.* of *men*
Lam. 3:33 doth not grieve *c. m.*
Dan. 2:38 wherever the *c.* of *men*

Men-CHILDREN.
Ex. 1:17 midw. saved *men-c.* 18
34:23 *men-c.* shall app. bef. L.

Men, Women, and CHIL-DREN.
Deut. 3:6 in B. we dest. *m. w. c.*
31:12 gather *m. w.* and *c.*
Ezra 10:1 great cong. of *m. w. c.*
Jer. 40:7 to Gedaliah *m. w. c.*
Mat. 14:21 eaten, were 5,000 *m.*
beside *women* and *c.* 15:38

My CHILDREN.

Gen. 30:26 give me *my c.*
31:43 these *c.* are *my c.* and
42:36 me ye have ber. of *my c.*
43:14 if bereaved of *my c.* I am
Ex. 21:5 I love my master *my c.*
1 *K.* 20:7 he sent to me for *my c.*
Job 29:5 *my c.* were about me
Is. 49:21 I have lost *my c.*
Jer. 10:20 *my c.* gone forth of me
Lam. 1:16 my *c.* are desolate
*Ezek.*16:21 thou hast slain *my c.?*
Luke 11:7 *my c.* are with me
2 *Cor.* 6:13 speak as to *my c.*
3 *John* 4 that *my c.* walk in truth

No CHILDREN.

Gen. 16:1 Sarai bare him *no c.*
30:1 Rachel saw she bare *no c.*
1 *Sam.* 1:2 but Hannah had *no c.*
Mat. 22:24 having *no c.* Mark
12:19; *Luke* 20:31 seven left

Our CHILDREN.

Gen. 31:16 riches ours and *our c.*
Num. 14:3 that *our c.* be a prey
Deut. 29:29 bel. to us and *our c.*
Jos. 22:24 *c.* might sp. to *our c.*
22:25 your *c.* make *o. c.* cease
Neh. 5:5 *our c.* as their children
Mat. 27:25 his blood be on *our c.*

CHILDREN of promise.

Rom. 9:8 *c. prom.* counted
Gal. 4:28 as Isaac, are *c. of prom.*

Strange CHILDREN.

Ps. 144:7 rid me from *str. c.* 11
Hos. 5:7 have begotten *strange c.*

Their CHILDREN.

Gen. 31:43 can I do to their *c.?*
Deut. 4:10 may teach *their c.*
5:29 might be well with *their c.*
31:13 *their c.* may learn
2 *K.* 8:12 thou wilt dash *their c.*
17:31 burnt *their c.* to the gods
41 *t. c.* served images
2 *Chr.* 20:13 before L. with *th. c.*
25:4 he slew not *their c.*
Neh. 9:23 *their c.* multi. as stars
13:24 *their c.* spake
Job 21:11 *their c.* dance
24:5 yieldeth food for *their c.*

Ps. 78:4 not hide them from *t. c.*
6 and declare them to *their c.*
90:16 let thy glory appear to *t. c.*
132:12 *t. c.* sh. sit on thy throne
Is. 13:16 *t. c.* be dashed to pieces
Jer. 17:2 *t. c.* remember altars
18:21 deliver *their c.* to famine
30:20 *t. c.* shall be as aforetime
32:18 into bosom of *their c.*
39 good of them and *their c.*
47:3 not look back to *their c.*
Lam. 4:10 have sodden *their c.*
Ezek. 20:18 I said to *their c.*
23:39 when had slain *their c.*
37:25 they and *their c.* sh. dwell
Hos. 9:12 *t. c.* yet I will bereave
Joel 1:3 your *c.* tell *t. c.* and *t. c.*
Mic. 2:9 from *their c.* taken
Zec. 10:7 *t. c.* shall see it
9 live with *their c.* and turn
Acts 13:33 same to us *their c.*
1 *Tim.* 8:12 ruling *their c.* well
Tit. 2:4 women to love *their c.*

Thy CHILDREN.

Deut. 4:40 w. with *thy c.* 12:25, 28
6:7 shalt teach them to *thy c.*
30:2 thou and *thy c.* obey with
Jos. 14:9 *be* thine and *thy c.*
1 *Sam.* 16:11 are here all *thy c.*
1 *K.* 2:4 if *thy c.* take heed
8:25 *thy c.* take h. 2 *Chr.* 6:16
20:3 thy wives and *thy c.*
2 *K.* 10:30 *c.* of fourth gen.
2 *Chr.* 21:14 L. shall smite *thy c.*
Job 8:4 if *thy c.* have sinned
Ps. 45:16 inst. of fathers be *thy c.*

73:15 offend ag. gen. of *thy c.*
128:3 *thy c.* like olive-plants
132:12 if *thy c.* keep covenant
147:13 blessed *thy c.* within thee
Is. 49:17 *thy c.* shall make haste
54:13 all *thy c.* be taught of L.
and great be peace of *thy c.*
Jer. 5:7 *thy c.* have forsaken me
31:17 that *thy c.* come again
38:23 bring out *thy c.* to Chald.
Ezek. 16:36 by the blood of *thy c.*
Hos. 4:6 I will also forget *thy c.*
Mat. 23:37 how oft. would I have
gath. *thy c. Luke* 13:34
Luke 19:44 lay *thy c.* within thee
2 *John* 4 *thy c.* walking in truth

Your CHILDREN.

Ex. 12:26 *your c.* shall say
22:24 *your c.* shall be fatherless
Lev. 26:22 beasts rob you of *y. c.*
Deut. 1:39 *your c.* shall go in
11:2 I speak not with *your c.*
19 ye shall teach *your c.*
21 days of *your c.* be multiplied
32:46 com. *your c.* to observe
Jos. 4:22 then let *your c.* know
1 *K.* 9:6 if *y. c.* turn from fol. me
1 *Chr.* 28:8 inh. to *y. c. Ezr.* 9:12
2 *Chr.* 30:9 *your c.* shall find
Ps. 115:14 you and *your c.*
Jer. 2:30 have I smitten *y. c.*
Mat. 7:11 gifts to *y. c. Luke* 11:13
12:27 by whom do *y. c.* cast out
Luke 23:28 weep for *y.* and *y. c.*
Acts 2:39 is to you and *y. c.*
1 *Cor.* 7:14 were *your c.* unclean
Eph. 6:4 pro. not *y. c. Col.* 3:21

Young CHILDREN.

Job 19:18 *young c.* despised me
Lam. 4:4 *y. c.* ask bread
Nah. 3:10 *young c.* were dashed
Mark 10:13 brought *y. c.* to him
Acts 7:19 they cast out *y. c.*

CHILEAB. 2 *Sam.* 3:3
CHILION. *Ruth* 1:2, 5
CHILMAD. *Ezek.* 27:23

CHIMHAM.

2 *Sam.* 19:37 C. let him go, 38, 40
Jer. 41:17 habitation of C.

CHIMNEY.

Hos. 13:3 be as smoke out of *c.*
CHIOS. *Acts* 20:15
CHISLEU. *Neh.* 1:1; *Zec.* 7:1

CHITTIM.

Num. 24:24 from coasts of C.
Is. 23:1 from the land of C. 12
Jer. 2:10 pass over the isles of C.
Ezek. 27:6 ivory out of isles of C.
Dan. 11:30 ships of C. shall come
CHIUN. *Amos* 5:26
CHLOE. 1 *Cor.* 1:11

CHODE.

Gen. 31:36 Jacob *c.* with Laban
Num. 20:3 people *c.* with Moses

CHOICE.

1 *Sam.* 9:2 Saul a *c.* young man
2 *Sam.* 10:9 *c.* of Is. 1 *Chr.* 19:10
2 *Chr.* 25:5 300,000 *c.* men
Cant. 6:9 *c.* one of her that bare
Acts 15:7 God made *c.* among us

CHOICEST.

Is..5:2 planted with the *c.* vine
22:7 *c.* valleys full of chariots

CHOKE.

Mat. 13:22 deceitfulness of riches
c. the word, *Mark* 4:19

CHOKED.

*Mat.*13:7 thorns *c.Mar.*4:7;*Lu.*8:7
Mark 5:13 *c.* in sea, *Luke* 8:33
Luke 8:14 and are *c.* with cares

CHOLER.

Dan. 8:7 he-goat moved with *c.*
11:11 k. of south moved with *c.*

CHOOSE, as an act of God.

*Num.*16:7 man L. doth *c.* be holy
Deut. 7:7 did not *c.* you because
12:5 place Lord shall *c.* 11, 14,
18, 26; 14:23, 24, 25; 15:20;
16:2, 6, 7, 15, 16; 17:8, 10;
18:6; 26:2; 31:11; *Jos.* 9:27
17:15 king, whom Lord shall *c.*
1 *Sam.* 2:28 did I *c.* him of all
2 *Sam.* 16:18 and this people *c.*
21:6 hang in G. whom L. did *c.*
1 *K.* 14:21 the city the L. did *c.*
Neh. 9:7 God who didst *c.* Abram
Ps. 25:12 teach in way he shall *c.*
47:4 he shall *c.* our inheritance
Is. 14:1 Lord will yet *c.* Israel
49:7 Holy One of Israel shall *c.*
66:4 I will *c.* their delusions
Zec. 1:17 Lord shall *c. Jer.* 2:12

CHOOSE.

Deut. 23:16 in place he shall *c.*
30:19 therefore *c.* life that both
Jos. 24:15 *c.* this day whom serve
1 *Sam.* 17:8 *c.* you a man for you
2 *Sam.* 17:1 let me *c.* 12,000 men
24:12 three, *c.* one, 1 *Chr.* 21:10
Job 9:14 *c.* my words to reason
34:4 let us *c.* to us judgment
33 or whether thou *c.*
Prov. 1:29 did not *c.* fear of L.
3:31 and *c.* none of his ways
Is. 7:15 know to *c.* good, 16
56:4 eunuchs *c.* things
65:12 did *c.* wherein I del. not
Ezek. 21:19 *c.* a place *c.* it
Phil. 1:22 what I shall *c.* I wot n.

CHOOSEST, ETH, ING.

Job 7:15 my soul *c.* strangling
15:5 thou *c.* tongue of crafty
Ps. 65:4 blessed is man thou *c.*
Is. 40:20 *c.* a tree will not rot
41:24 abomination is he *c.* you
Heb. 11:25 *c.* to suffer affliction

CHOP.

Mic. 3:3 *c.* bones of my people
CHORAZIN.*Mat.*11:21; *Lu.*10:13

CHOSE.

Ex. 18:25 Moses *c.* able men
Deut. 4:37 he *c.* their seed, 10:15
Jos. 8:3 J. *c.* 30,000 mighty
Jud. 5:8 they *c.* new gods
2*Sam.*6:21 *c.* me before thy fath.
1 *K.* 8:16 I *c.* no city to build a
house, 2 *Chr.* 6:5
1 *Chr.* 28:4 Lord *c.* me before all
Job 29:25 I *c.* out their way
Ps. 78:67 *c.* not tribe of Ephr.
68 but *c.* the tribe of Judah
70 he *c.* David also his servant
Is. 66:4 *c.* that I delighted not
Ezek. 20:5 in the day I *c.* Israel
Luke 6:13 he *c.* twelve apostles
14:7 how they *c.* chief rooms
Acts 6:5 *c.* Stephen, full of faith
13:17 G. of Israel *c.* our fathers
15:40 Paul *c.* Silas and departed

CHOSEN.

Num. 16:5 him *c.* cause to come
Jos. 24:22 have *c.* you the Lord
Jud. 10:14 cry to gods ye have *c.*
1 *Sam.* 8:18 king ye have *c.* 12:13
20:30 hast *c.* the son of Jesse
1 *K.* 3:8 hast *c.* a great people
8:44 city *c.* of 48; 2 *Chr.* 6:34, 38
1 *Chr.* 16:13 children of J. *c.* ones
Job 36:21 *c.* rather than affliction
Ps. 33:12 *c.* for his inheritance
89:3 a covenant with my *c.*
19 exalted one *c.* out of people
105:6 ye child. of Jacob, his *c.*
43 forth his *c.* with gladness
106:5 I may see good of thy *c.*
23 had not Moses his *c.* stood

Prov. 16:16 underst. rather *c.*
22:1 a good name rather *c.*
Is. 43:20 to give drink to my *c.*
65:15 name a curse to my *c.*
66:3 have *c.* their own ways
Jer. 8:3 death shall be *c.* rather
49:19 who is a *c.* man, 50:44
Mat. 20:16 but few *c.* 22:14
Mark 13:20 elect whom hath *c.*
Luke 10:42 M. hath *c.* good part
Acts 1:24 whether thou hast *c.*
9:15 for he is a *c.* vessel to me
Rom. 16:13 Rufus *c.* in Lord
2 *Cor.* 8:19 *c.* of churches to trav.
2 *Tim.* 2:4 *c.* him to be a soldier
1 *Pet.* 2:9 ye are a *c.* generation
Rev. 17:14 they are called, and *c.*

CHOSEN of God.
Luke 23:35 if C. the *c. of* God
Acts 10:41 witnesses *c.* bef. *of* G.
1 *Pet.* 2:4 living stone *c. of* God

God hath CHOSEN.
Deut. 12:21 *G. h. c.* to put, 16:11
21:5 *G. h. c.* to minister
1 *Chr.* 29:1 Sol. whom al. *G. h. c.*
Acts 22:14 *G.* of fathers *h. c.*
1 *Cor.*1:27 *G.h.c.* foolish th. *G.h.c.*
28 things despised *G. h. c.*
2 *Thes.* 2:13 *G.* from begin. *h. c.*
Jam. 2:5 *h.* not *G. c.* poor of w.

I have CHOSEN.
1 *K.* 11:13 Jer. sake which *I h. c.*
2 *K.* 21:7; 23:27; 2 *Chr.* 6:6
32 *I h. c.* out of all tribes
Neh. 1:9 *I h. c.* to set my name
Ps. 119:30 *I h. c.* way, 173
Is. 41:8 Jacob whom *I have c.*
9 *I have c.* and not cast away
43:10 my serv. *I h. c. Mat.* 12:18
44:1 Israel whom *I h. c.* 2 Jesn.
48:10 *I have c.* thee in furnace
58:5 the fast that *I have c. ?* 6
Hag. 2:23 *I have c.* thee
John 13:18 whom *I have c.*
15:16 ye have not *c.* me, *I h. c.*
19 *I have c.* you out of world

Lord hath CHOSEN.
*Deut.*7:6 *L.h.c.* thee a sp. peo. 14:2
18:5 *L. h. c.* him out of all
1 *Sam.* 10:24 see ye him *L. h. c.*
16:10 Samuel said, *L. h.* not *c.*
1 *Chr.* 28:4 *Lord hath c.* Judah
5 *L. h. c.* Sol. to sit on throne,10
2 *Chr.* 29:11 *L. h. c.* you to serve
Ps. 105:26 A. whom he had *c.*
132:13 *L. c.* Zion ; 135:4 *L. c.* J.
Jer. 33:24 two families *L. h. c.*
Zec. 3:2 L. that *h. c.* Jeru. reb.
Eph. 1:4 acc. as he *hath c.* us

CHOSEN men.
Jud. 20:16 700 *c. m.* left-handed
2 *Chr.* 13:3 Ab. with 400,000 *c.m.*
Jeroboam with 800,000 *c.m.*
Ps. 78:31 smote *c. m.* of Israel
Acts 15:22 to send *c. men,* 25

CHRIST.
Mat. 2:4 where C. sh. be born
16:16 thou art C. the Son
23:8 one is Master, even C. 16
24:5 saying I am C. *Mark* 13:6 ;
Luke 21:8
26:68 prophesy to us, thou C.
Mark 9:41 bec. ye belong to C.
15:32 let C. descend from cross
Luke 2:26 before he had seen C.
4:41 devils knew he was C.
23:35 save himself, if he be C.
39 if.C. save thyself and us
24:26 ought not C. to have suff.
46 it behooved C. to suffer
John 4:25 Mes. cometh called C.
7:27 C. cometh, 31
41 C. come out of Galilee ?
42 C. cometh of seed of David
9:22 did confess he was C.
12:34 heard C. abideth for ever

Acts 2:30 would raise up C. to sit
36 Jesus both Lord and C.
3:18 showed C. should suffer
8:5 Philip preached C. to them
9:20 straightway preached C.
17:3 C. must needs have suff.
26:23 C. should suffer
Rom. 5:6 in due time C. died
8 yet sinners, C. died for us
6:4 C. was raised from dead
9 C. being raised dieth no m.
7:4 by the body of C.
8:9 have not the spirit of C.
10 if C. be in you, body is d.
11 raised up C. from dead
9:3 accursed from C.
5 of whom C. came
10:4 C. is end of law for right.
6 to bring C. down from above
7 that is, to bring C. up again
14:9 to this end C. both died
15 not him for whom C. died
18 in these things serveth C.
15:3 C. pleased not himself
7 as C. also received us
Rom. 15:18 wh. C. not wrought
20 not where C. was named
16:5 Epenetus first-fruits to C.
1 *Cor.* 1:23 we preach C. crucif.
24 C. the power of God, and
3:23 ye are C. and C. is God's
5:7 C. our passover sacrificed
8:11 perish, for whom C. died
9:21 under law to C. that I m.
10:4 and that Rock was C.
9 nor let us tempt C.
15:3 how C. died for our sins
12 if C. be preached
16 rise not, is not C. raised
17 if C. not raised, faith is v.
23 in his order, C. first-fruits
2 *Cor.* 3:4 thro' C. to God-ward
5:16 known C. after flesh
6:15 what concord C. with B.
11:2 as a chaste virgin to C.
Gal. 2:20 C. liveth in me
21 then C. is dead in vain
3:13 C. redeemed us from curse
24 schoolmaster to br. us to C.
29 if ye be C. then Abr.'s seed
4:7 heir of God through C.
19 till C. be formed in you
5:1 wherewith C. m. us free
2 if circum. C. profit nothing
4 C. is of none effect unto you
24 that are C. have crucified
Eph. 2:12 without C.
3:17 that C. may dwell by faith
4:15 which is the head, even C.
20 ye have not so learned C.
5:2 as C. also loved us
14 C. shall give thee light
23 as C. is head of the church
24 as church is subject to C.
25 love wives as C. loved ch.
32 concerning C. and church
6:5 singlen. of heart as to C.
Phil. 1:15 some preach C.
16 preach C. of contention
18 C. is preached, and I rejoice
20 C. be magnified in my body
3:8 dung that I may win C.
4:13 I can do all through C.
Col. 2:8 world, and not after C.
3:1 C. sitteth on right hand
4 C. who is our life shall ap.
11 but C. is all and in all
13 as C. forgave you, so do ye
24 for ye serve the Lord C.
Heb. 3:6 C. as a son
5:5 so C. glorified not himself
9:11 C. a high-priest of good
24 C. is not entered into holy
28 C. was once offered to our
1 *Pet.* 2:21 C. also suffered for us
3:18 C. once suffered for sins
4:1 as C. suffered in the flesh

Rev. 11:15 kingdom of L. and C.
12:10 is come power of his C.

Against CHRIST.
Acts 4:26 kings gath. *a.* his C.
1 *Cor.* 8:12 brethren, ye sin *a.* C.
1 *Tim.* 5:11 wax wanton *a.* C.

By CHRIST.
2 *Cor.* 1:5 aboundeth *by* C.
Gal. 2:17 to be justified *by* C.
Eph. 3:21 glory in church *by* C.

For CHRIST.
1 *Cor.* 1:17 C. sent me not to b.
4:10 we are fools *for* C. sake
2 *Cor.* 5:20 ambassadors *for* C.
12:10 in distresses *for* C.
Eph. 4:32 as God *for* C. sake
Phil. 3:7 I counted loss *for* C.
2 *Thes.* 3:5 patient waiting *for* C.

Jesus, *with* CHRIST.
Mat. 1:16 J. called C. 27:17, 22
John 1:17 and truth by J. C.
17:3 may know thee, and J. C.
Acts 2:38 in name of J. C.
3:6 in name of J. C. rise up
20 J. C. who was preached
4:10 of J. C. doth this man
5:42 ceased not to preach J. C.
8:12 Philip preach. things concern. the name of J. C.
37 I believe J. C. is Son of God
9:34 J. C. maketh thee whole
10:36 preaching peace by J. C.
16:18 in name of J. C. come out
17:3 *Jesus* I preach to you is C.
18:5 testified that *Jesus* was C.
28 by scripture. *Jesus* was C.
19:4 should believe on C. *Jesus*
Rom. 1 serv. of J. C. *Phil.* 1:1
3 concerning his son J. C.
6 are ye the called of *Jesus* C.
8 I thank God through J. C.
2:16 secrets of men by J. C.
3:22 by faith of J. C.
24 redemption in *Jesus* C.
Rom. 5:15 gr. by one man J. C.
17 reign in life by one J. C.
6:3 baptized into *Jesus* C.
8:1 to them in C. *Jesus*
2 C. J. made me free
16:3 my helpers in C. *Jesus*
1 *Cor.* 1:1 J. C. 2 *Cor.* 1:1; *Eph.* 1:1
2 call on name of J. C.
4 grace given you by J. C.
30 of him are ye in C. *Jesus*
2:2 save J. C. crucified
4:15 in C. J. have I begotten
2 *Cor.* 4:6 in face of J. C.
13:5 that *Jesus* C. is in you
*Gal.*2:16 justified by faith of J. C.
3:14 blessings on G.through J.C.
28 ye are all one in C. *Jesus*
4:14 me as an angel, as C. J.
Eph. 2:6 heav. places in C. J.
20 J. C. chief corner-stone
Phil. 1:8 I in bowels of *Jesus* C.
2:5 mind in you, was in C. J.
11 J. C. is Lord to glory of G.
21 seek not th. wh. are J. C.
3:8 for excellency of C. J.
12 I am apprehended of C. J.
4:19 riches in glory by C. J.
Col. 2:6 rec. C. J. so walk ye
1 *Tim.* 1:15 C. J. ca. to save sin.
2:5 one mediator, the man C.J.
6:13 C. *Jesus* who witnessed
2 *Tim.* 1:9 grace given us in C. J.
13 faith and love in C. *Jesus*
Phile. 1 P. a priso. of J. C. 9, 23
Heb. 13:8 *Jesus* C. the same yes.
1 *John* 1:7 blood of *Jesus* C.
2:1 an advocate *Jesus* C.
5:6 by water and blood J. C.
20 even in *Jesus* C.

Lord Jesus CHRIST.

Acts 11:17 believed on L. J. C.
15:11 through grace of L. J. C.
16:31 believe on L. J. C.
20:21 faith toward L. J. C.
Rom. 5:1 p. with G. thro' L J. C.
11 joy in God through L. J. C.
6:23 eternal life through L. J. C.
8:39 love of G. in C. J. our L
13:14 put ye on the L. J. C.
16:20 grace of L. J. C. be w. you,
24; 2 *Cor.* 13:14; *Gal.* 6:18;
2 *Thes.* 3:18; *Rev.* 22:21
1 *Cor.* 1:7 coming of our L. J. C.
8:6 one L. J. C. by whom are
15:57 victory thro' our L. J. C.
16:22 if any love not L. J. C.
2 *Cor.* 1:2 from G. and L. J. C.
Gal. 1:3; *Eph.* 1:2; *Col.* 1:2
8:9 ye know grace of L J. C.
Gal. 6:14 in cross of L. J. C.
Eph. 1:3 Father of L. J. C.
17 God of L J. C.
1 *Thes.* 1:3 hope in L. J. C.
2:19 in presence of L. J. C.
3:13 at coming of L. J. C.
5:23 pres. to coming of L. J. C.
2 *Thes.* 2:1 by coming of L. J. C.
16 our L. J. C. who hath
1 *Tim.* 5:21 I charge thee before
L. J. C. 2 *Tim.* 4:1
2 *Tim.* 4:22 L. J. C. be with thy
2 *Pet.* 1:11 kingdom of L. J. C.
3:18 in knowledge of L. J. C.

In CHRIST.

Acts 24:24 concerning faith *in* C.
Rom. 9:1 I say the truth *in* C.
12:5 many, are one body *in* C.
16:7 were *in* C. before me
9 Urbane our helper *in* C.
10 Apelles approved *in* C.
1 *Cor.* 3:1 as unto babes *in* C.
4:10 but ye are wise *in* C.
15:18 asleep *in* C.
19 in this life hope *in* C.
22 *in* C. all be made alive
2 *Cor.* 1:21 establish us *in* C.
2:14 to triumph *in* C.
17 in sight of God speak *in* C.
3:14 veil is done away *in* C.
5:17 *in* C. he is a new creature
19 *in* C. reconciling the world
20 *in* C. stead, be reconciled
12:2 a man *in* C. 14 years
19 we speak before God *in* C.
Gal. 1:22 to churches of J. *in* C.
3:17 confirmed of God *in* C.
27 as many as baptized *in* C.
Eph. 1:3 spiritual bless. *in* C.
10 in one all things *in* C.
12 who first trusted *in* C.
20 *in* C. when he raised
3:6 his promise *in* C.
Phil. 1:13 my bonds *in* C.
2:1 if any consolation *in* C.
Col. 2:5 your faith *in* C.
1 *Thes.* 4:16 dead *in* C. rise first
1 *Tim.* 2:7 I speak the truth *in* C.
1 *Pet.* 3:16 good conversation *in* C.

Is CHRIST.

Mat. 24:23 h. *is* C. *Mark* 13:21
Mark 12:35 C. *is* son. *Luke* 20:41.
Luke 2:11 a Saviour, wh. *is* C.
23:2 saying, that he *is* C.
John 7:41 said this *is* the C.
Acts 9:22 Saul proving this *is* C.
17:3 Jesus I preach to you *is* C.
Rom. 8:34 it *is* C. that died
1 *Cor.* 1:12 *is* C. divided?
7:22 being free *is* C. servant
11:3 head of every man *is* C.
12:12 are one body, so *is* C.
15:13 if dead rise not, *is* C. 16
20 now *is* C. risen from dead
2 *Cor.* 10:7 if any trust he *is* C.
Gal. 2:17 *is* C. minister of sin?
3:16 to thy seed, which *is* C.

Phil. 1:21 to live *is* C.
Col. 1:27 *is* C. in you hope

Of CHRIST.

Mat. 11:2 John heard works *of* C.
22:42 what think ye *of* C.?
Rom. 8:9 any have not S. *of* C.?
35 sep. us from love *of* C.?
14:10 judgment-seat *of* C.
1 *Cor.* 1:17 cross *of* C. be made
2:16 we have the mind *of* C.
6:15 your bodies members *of* C.
10:16 communion of blood *of* C.
11:1 be foll. of me as I *of* C.
3 the head *of* C. is God
12:27 ye are the body *of* C.
2 *Cor.* 1:5 as sufferings *of* C.
2:10 forgave I it in person *of* C.
15 we are a sweet savor *of* C.
3:3 epistle *of* C. ministered
4:4 light of gospel *of* C. shine
5:14 love *of* C. constraineth us
8:23 they are glory *of* C.
10:1 by the meekness *of* C.
5 bringing to obedience *of* C.
11:10 the truth *of* C. is in me
12:9 power *of* C. *Rev.* 12:10
13:3 proof *of* C. speaking
Gal. 1:10 be servant *of* C.
2:16 be justified by faith *of* C.
6:12 persecution for cross *of* C.
Eph. 2:13 by the blood *of* C.
3:4 in mystery *of* C.
8 the unsearchable riches *of* C.
19 love *of* C. which passeth
4:7 measure of gift *of* C.
5:5 inheritance in king. *of* C.
6:6 as servants *of* C.
Phil. 1:10 till the day *of* C.
29 it is given in behalf *of* C.
2:16 rejoice in the day *of* C.
30 work *of* C. nigh to death
3:18 enemies of the cross *of* C.
Col. 1:24 afflictions *of* C.
2:2 mystery of God, and *of* C.
17 but the body is *of* C.
3:16 let the word *of* C. dwell
4:3 to speak the mystery *of* C.
2 *Tim.* 2:19 the name *of* C.
Heb. 3:14 made partakers *of* C.
9:14 more, blood *of* C. purge
11:26 reproach *of* C. greater
1 *Pet.* 1:11 Spirit *of* C. did signify
19 with precious blood *of* C.
4:13 partakers *of* C. sufferings
14 reproached for name *of* C.
Rev. 20:6 priests of G. and *of* C.

That CHRIST.

John 1:25 if thou be not *that* C
6:69 sure that thou art *that* C

The CHRIST.

Mat. 16:20 he was the C.
26:63 whether thou be *the* C.
Mark 8:29 saith, thou art *the* C.
14:61 *the* C. son of the B.?
Luke 3:15 whether he were *t.* C.
9:20 Peter said thou art *the* C.
22:67 saying art thou *the* C.
John 1:20 I am not *the* C.
41 found the Messias, *the* C.
3:28 I said I am not *the* C.
4:29 is not this *the* C.?
42 this is indeed *the* C. 7:26
7:41 others said, this is *the* C.
10:24 be *the* C. tell us plainly
11:27 I believe thou art *the* C
20:31 believe Jesus is *the* C.
1 *John* 2:22 Jesus is *the* C.
5:1 believeth Jesus is *the* C.

With CHRIST.

Rom. 6:8 if we be dead *with* C.
8:17 then joint-heirs *with* C.
Gal. 2:20 I am crucified *with* C.
Eph. 2:5 quickened us tog. *w.* C.
Phil. 1:23 a desire to be *with* C.
Col. 2:20 if dead *with* C.
3:1 if risen *w.* C. seek things

Col. 3:3 your life is hid *with* C.
Rev. 20:4 reigned *with* C.

CHRISTIAN, S.

Acts 11:26 called *c.* at Antioch
26:28 almost pers. me to be a *c.*
1 *Pet.* 4:16 if any suffer as a *c.*

CHRISTS.

Mat. 24:24 false *c.* *Mark* 13:22

CHRONICLES.

1 *Chr.* 27:24 number put in *c.*
Est. 6:1 to bring the book of *c.*
See BOOK.

CHRYSOLITE.

Rev. 21:20 seventh found. a *c.*

CHRYSOPRASUS.

Rev. 21:20 tenth foundation a *c.*

CHURCH.

Mat. 16:18 on this rock b. my *c.*
18:17 tell it to the *c.*
Acts 2:47 added to *c.* daily such
5:11 great fear came on *c.*
8:1 persecution against *c.*
11:26 assembled with the *c.*
14:23 ordained elders in every *c.*
27 had gathered *c.* together
15:3 brought on way by the *c.*
22 it pleased elders with the *c.*
18:22 when he had saluted *c.*
Rom. 16:5 greet *c.* in their house
1 *Cor.* 4:17 as I teach in every *c.*
14:4 prophesieth edifieth *c.*
5 that *c.* may receive edifying
23 if *c.* be come into one place
16:19 *c.* in their house
Eph. 1:22 head over all to the *c.*
3:10 known by *c.* wisdom of G.
5:24 as *c.* is subject to Christ
25 as Christ loved the *c.*
27 might present a glorious *c.*
29 cherisheth it, as Lord the *c.*
32 speak concern. Christ and *c.*
Phil. 3:6 persecuting the *c.*
4:15 no *c.* communicated
Col. 1:18 head of the body the *c.*
24 for his body's sake, the *c.*
4:15 salute *c.* in Nymphas' ho.
1 *Tim.* 5:16 let not *c.* be charged
Phile. 2 Paul to *c.* in thy house
Heb. 12:23 to *c.* of first-born
1 *Pet.* 5:13 *c.* at Babylon saluteth
3 *John* 6 thy charity before *c.*
9 I wrote to the *c.* but Diotre

In the CHURCH.

Acts 7:38 that was *in* the *c.*
13:1 proph. *in* the *c.* at Antioch
1 *Cor.* 6:4 least esteemed *in* the *c.*
11:18 come together *in* the *c.*
12:28 hath set some *in* the *c.*
14:19 yet *in* the *c.* I had rather
28 keep silence *in* the *c.*
35 sh. for wo. to speak *in* the *c.*
Eph. 3:21 be glory *in* the *c.*
Col. 4:16 to be read *in* the *c.*

Of the CHURCH.

Acts 8:3 S. made havoc *of* the *c.*
11:22 came to ears *of* the *c.*
12:1 H. vexed certain *of* the *c.*
5 prayer was made *of* the *c.*
15:4 were received *of* the *c.*
20:16 Paul called elders *of* the *c.*
Rom. 16:1 P. a servant *of* the *c.*
23 Gaius my host and *of* the *c.*
1 *Cor.* 14:12 excel to edify. *of* c.
5:23 as C. is head *of* the *c.*
Heb. 2:12 in midst *of* the *c.*
3 *John* 10 D. casteth out *of* c.
Rev. 2:1 angel *of* c. *of* Ephesus
8 Smyrna; 12 Perga.; 18 Thya.
3:1 Sardis; 7 Philad.; 14 Laodi.

CHURCH of God.

Acts 20:28 feed the *c.* of God
1 *Cor.* 1:2 to *c. of* God at Corinth
10:32 none offence to *c. of* God

11:22 despise ye the *c. of God*
15:9 I pers. *c. of God, Gal.* 1:13
1 *Tim.* 5:3 take care of *c. of God*

CHURCHES.

Acts 9:31 then had the *c.* rest
15:41 Paul confirming the *c.*
16:5 *c.* established in the faith
19:37 these neither robbers of *c.*
Rom. 16:4 all *c.* gave thanks
16 the *c.* of Christ salute you
1 *Cor.* 7:17 so ordain I in all *c.*
11:16 such custom, nei. the *c.*
14:33 author of peace as in all *c.*
34 women keep silence in *c.*
16:1 order to *c.* of Galatia
19 the *c.* of Asia salute you
2 *Cor.* 8:1 grace bestow. on the *c.*
19 chosen of the *c.* to travel
23 they are messengers of *c.*
11:8 I robbed other *c.*

2 *Cor.* 11:28 the care of all the *c.*
12:13 inferior to other *c. ?*
Gal. 1:22 unknown by face to *c.*
1 *Thes.* 2:14 fol. of the *c.* of God.
2 *Thes.* 1:4 glory in you in *c.*
Rev. 1:4 John to the seven *c.*
11 send it to the seven *c.*
20 seven stars are angels of *c.*
candlesticks are the seven *c.*
2:7 what the Spirit saith unto the *c.* 11, 17, 29: 3:6, 13, 22
23 *c.* know I am he searcheth
22:16 testify these things in *c.*

CHURL.

Is. 32:5 *c.* said to be bountiful
7 instruments of *c.* are evil

CHURLISH.

1 *Sam.* 25:3 Nab. was *c.* and evil

CHURNING.

Prov. 30:33 surely *c.* of m. bring-eth butter

CHUSHAN-RISHATHAIM.

Jud. 3:8 sold Is. into hand of C.

CHUZA. *Luke* 8:3

CILICIA.

Acts 6:9; 15:23, 41; 21:39; 22:3;
23:34; 27:5
Gal. 1:21 into regions of C.

CINNAMON.

Ex. 30:23 sweet *c.*
Prov. 7:17 perf. bed with *c.*
Cant. 4:14 are an orchard of *c.*
Rev. 18:13 buyeth her *c.*

CIRCLE.

Is. 40:22 sitteth on *c.* of earth

CIRCUIT, S.

1 *Sam.* 7:16 year to year in *c.*
Job 22:14 in *c.* of heaven
Ps. 19:6 his *c.* unto the ends
Ec. 1:6 according to his *c.*

CIRCUMCISE.

Gen. 17:11 ye shall *c.* foreskin
Deut. 10:16 *c.* foreskin
30:6 Lord will *c.* thy heart
Jos. 5:2 *c.* again children of Isr.
Jer. 4:4 *c.* yourselves to the L.
Luke 1:59 came to *c.* the child
John 7:22 on Sabbath *c.* a man
Acts 15:5 needful to *c.* them
21:21 they ought not to *c.*

CIRCUMCISED.

Gen. 17:10 every man-child be *c.*
14 not *c.* shall be cut off
26 Abraham was *c.* and Ishm.
34:15 every male *c.*
24 every male was *c. Ex.* 12:48
Jos. 5:3 J. *c.* children of Israel
Jer. 9:25 punish all *c.* with uncir.
Acts 15:1 except *c.* not saved, 24
16:3 Paul *c.* Timothy
Rom. 4:11 though not *c.*
1 *Cor.* 7:18 being *c. ?* in uncir-cision ? let him not be *c.*

Gal. 2:3 Titus compelled to be *c.*
5:2 if *c.* C. shall profit nothing
6:12 they constrain you to be *c.*
13 they *c.* keep not the law
Phil. 3:5 *c.* eighth day
Col. 2:11 in whom also ye are *c.*

CIRCUMCISING.

Luke 2:21 days accomp. for *c.*

CIRCUMCISION.

John 7:22 M. gave unto you *c.*
23 if on the sabbath receive *c.*
Rom. 2:25 *c.* profiteth, if thou keep the law ; thy *c.* is made
28 nor is that *c.* which is outw.
29 *c.* is that of the heart
3:30 shall justify *c.* by faith
4:9 this blessedness on *c.* only ?
10 when he was in *c. ?* not in *c.*
1 *Cor.* 7:19 *c.* is keeping of com.
Gal. 2:9 they should go unto *c.*
5:6 neither *c.* availeth, 6:15
11 and I, if I yet preach *c.*
Eph. 2:11 by that called *c.*
Phil. 3:3 *c.* which worship God
Col. 2:11 *c.* without hands, by *c.*
3:11 there is nei. *c.* nor uncir.

Of CIRCUMCISION.

Ex. 4:26 bloody hus. bec. *of c.*
Acts 7:8 Abrah. covenant *of c.*
10:45 they *of c.* were astonished
11:2 *of c.* contended with Peter
Rom. 3:1 what profit *of c. ?*
4:11 he received the sign *of c.*
12 *of c.* to them not *of c.*
15:8 J. C. was a minister *of c.*
Gal. 2:7 gospel *of c.* com. to Pe.
8 in Peter to apostleship *of c.*
Col. 4:11 who are of the *c.* salute
Tit. 1:10 unruly, especially *of c.*

CIRCUMSPECT, LY.

Ex. 23:13 in all things be *c.*
Eph. 5:15 see that ye walk *c.*

CISTERN, S.

2 *K.* 18:31 drink ev. one of his *c.*
Prov. 5:15 drink of thine own *c.*
Ec. 12:6 wheel broken at the *c.*
Is. 36:16 every one of own *c.*
Jer. 2:13 hewed out *c.* of brok. *c.*

CITY.

Gen. 4:17 Cain builded a *c.*
11:4 build *c.* and a tower
5 Lord came down to see *c.*
8 they left off to build the *c.*
18:26 find fifty righteous in *c.*
34:25 came upon the *c.* boldly
Num. 21:28 flame is gone from *c.*
Deut. 2:36 not one *c.* too strong
3:4 not a *c.* we took not from
13:15 smite inhabit. of that *c.*
Jos. 3:16 very far from *c.* Adam
6:3 compass the *c.* six days, 7
24 burnt *c. Deut.* 13:16 *Jos.* 8:8,
19 ; *Jud.* 1:8 ; 18:27
8:2 lay ambush for *c.* behind
20 smoke of *c.* ascended to h.
15:13 *c.* of Arba, which *c.* is H.
19:50 gave Joshua *c.* he asked
Jud. 6:27 he feared men of *c.*
9:45 *c.* and sowed it with salt
20:40 flame of the *c.* ascended
Ruth 1:19 all the *c.* was moved
3:11 for *c.* of my people know
1 *Sam.* 1:3 out of *c.* yearly to w.
4:13 told it, all the *c.* cried out
8:22 every man to his *c.* 1 *K.*
22:36 ; *Ezr.* 2:1 ; *Neh.* 7:6
26:3 Israel b. him in his own *c.*
2 *Sam.* 12:1 two men in one *c.*
15:2 of what *c.* art thou ?
19:37 I may die in my own *c.*
20:19 seekest to destroy a *c.*
1 *K.* 1:45 so that *c.* rang again
11:32 *c.* I have chosen, 36
2 *K.* 6:19 neither is this the *c.*
11:20 and the *c.* was in quiet

24:10 *c.* Jer. was besieged, 25:2
2 *Chr.* 15:6 *c.* was destroyed of *c.*
19:5 and he set judges *c.* by *c.*
30:10 posts passed from *c.* to *c.*
32:18 that they might take *c.*
Ezr. 4:12 building rebellious *c,*
Neh. 2:3 *c.* why not sad, *c.* waste, 5
11:9 Judah was second over *c.*
Est. 8:15 the *c.* Shushan rejoiced
Ps. 48:2 *c.* of gr. king, *Mat.* 5:35
59:6 go round about the *c.* 14
72:16 thay of *c.* shall flourish
107:4 found no *c.* to dwell in
122:3 Jerusalem as a *c.* compact
127:1 except the Lord keep *c.*
Prov. 8:3 crieth at entry of *c.*
10:15 his strong *c.* 18:11
11:10 the *c.* rejoiceth
11 by blessing of upright *c.*
16:32 than he that taketh a *c.*
25:28 like a *c.* broken down
29:8 scornful bring *c.* into snare
Ec. 9:14 there was a little *c.*
15 poor wise man delivered *c.*
Is. 1:26 *c.* of right. faithful *c.* 21
14:31 howl, O gate, cry O *c.*
17:1 Damascus from being a *c.*
19:2 shall fight, *c.* against *c.*
24:10 *c.* of confusion is broken
25:2 of a *c.* a heap, to be no *c.*
33:20 Zion *c.* of our solemnities
60:14 shall call thee *c.* of Lord
62:12 a *c.* not forsaken
Jer. 3:14 take you one of a *c.*
4:29 *c.* shall flee for the noise
19:12 make this *c.* as Tophet
25:29 *c.* called by my name
32:24 come to *c.* and *c.* is given
39:2 the *c.* was broken up, 52:7
46:8 I will destroy the *c.*
49:25 how *c.* of praise not left
Lam. 1:1 how doth *c.* sit solitary
2:15 *c.* men call perf. of beauty
Ezek. 4:1 portray *c.* Jerusalem
7:23 the *c.* is full of violence
9:1 that have charge over *c.*
4 go thro' midst of *c.* Jerusa.
9 *c.* is full of perverseness
10:2 coals of fire over the *c.*
27:32 what *c.* is like Tyrus
33:21 saying, the *c.* is smitten
48:35 name of *c.* be, L. is there
Dan. 9:18 *c.* called by thy na. 19
Hos. 6:8 G. *c.* of th. work iniq.
Amos 4:7 to rain on one *c.*
5:3 *c.* that went up by thous.
Mic. 6:9 Lord's voice crieth to *c.*
Hab. 2:12 stablish a *c.* by iniq.
Zep. 3:1 woe to the oppressing *c.*
Zec. 8:3 Jerusalem a *c.* of truth
5 streets of *c.* be full of boys

Zec. 14:2 the *c.* shall be taken
Mat. 5:14 a *c.* set on hill cannot
35 Jerusalem is *c.* of great King
8:34 *c.* came out to meet Jesus
10:11 whatsoever *c.* ye enter
15 that *c. Mark* 6:11 ; *Luke* 10:12
21:10 all the *c.* was moved
22:7 king burnt up their *c.*
23:34 persecute from *c.* to *c.*
Mark 1:33 *c.* was gathered
5:14 told it in the *c. Luke* 8:34
Luke 2:3 taxed, ev. one to own *c.*
7:12 much people of *c.* with her
19:41 he beheld the *c.* and wept
23:51 he was of Arimathea a *c.*
John 4:39 many of th. *c.* believed
Acts 8:8 was great joy in that *c.*
13:44 almost whole *c.* to h.
16:12 in that *c.* certain days
17:5 set all the *c.* in an uproar
19:29 *c.* was filled with confus.
21:30 all the *c.* was moved
Heb. 11:10 *c.* that hath found.
16 hath prepared for them a *c.*
12:22 the *c.* of the living God
13:14 we have no continuing *c.*

Jam. 4:13 will go into such a *c.*
Rev. 20:9 comp. the beloved *c.*
21:14 wall of *c.* had foundations
18 the *c.* was pure gold
23 *c.* had no need of the sun

Bloody CITY.
Ezek. 22:2 judge the *bloody c. ?*
24:6 *bloody c.* 9; *Nah.* 3:1

Defenced CITY.
Is. 25:2 of a *defenced c.* a ruin
27:10 the *d. c.* shall be desolate
Jer. 1:18 thee this day a *d. c.*

CITY of David.
2 *Sam.* 5:9 *c. of D.* 1 *Chr.* 11:7
6:10 remove ark into *c. of D.*
12 brought ark into *c. of D.* 16
1 *K.* 2:10 D. was buried in *c. D.*
3:1 Sol. brought her to *c. of D.*
8:1 out of *c. of D.* 2 *Chr.* 5:2.
11:43 bur. in *c. D.* 2 *Chr.* 9:31
14:31 R. bur. *c. D.* 2 *Chr.* 12:16
15:8 bur. A. *c. of D.* 2 *Chr.* 14:1
22:50 J. bur. *c. D.* 2 *Chr.* 21:1
2 *K.* 8:24 J. bur. *c. D.* 2 *Chr.* 21:20
9:28 A. was buried in *c. of D.*
12:21 J. bur. *c. D.* 2 *Chr.* 24:25
14:20 Amaziah ; 15:7 Azariah
15:38 Jot. 2 *Chr.* 27:9 ; 28:27 Ahaz
2 *Chr.* 24:16 bur. Jeh. in *c. of D.*
Is. 22:9 breaches of *c. of D.*
29:1 woe to A. *c.* where *David*
Luke 2:4 Joseph went to *c. of D.*
11 born in *c. of D.* a Saviour

Elders, with CITY.
Deut. 19:12 *elders* of his *c.*
21:6 *elders* of that *c.* next
20 say to *e.* of *c.* our son is
22:17 cloth before *elders* of *c.*
25:8 *elders* of his *c.* shall call
Jos. 20:4 dec. his cause to *e.* of *c.*
Jud. 8:16 Gideon took *elders* of *c.*
Ruth 4:2 took ten men of *e. of c.*
Ezr. 10:14 *elders* of every *c*

Every CITY.
2 *K.* 3:19 smite *every* fenced *c.*
2 *Chr.* 31:19 of sons of A. in *e. c.*
Jer. 4:29 *every c.* shall be forsak.
48:8 spoiler shall come on *e. c.*
Mat. 12:25 *e. c.* divided ag. itself
Luke 10:1 two into *every c.*
Acts 15:21 in *e. c.* them that p.
36 visit brethren in *every c.*
20:33 H. G. witnesseth in *e. c.*
Tit. 1:5 ordain elders in *every c.*

Fenced CITY.
2 *K.* 10:2 with you a *fenced c.*
17:9 tower of watchmen to *f. c.*
2 *Chr.* 11:23 he dispersed of chil.
unto every *fenced c.*

CITY of God.
Ps. 46:4 make glad *c. of God*
48:1 to be praised in *c. of God*
8 *c. of God* will establish it
87:3 glorious things spoken of
thee, O *c. of God*
Heb. 12:22 *c. of* living God
Rev. 3:12 name of *c. of* my *God*

Great CITY.
Gen. 10:12 builded R. a *great c.*
Jos. 10:2 Gibeon was *great c.*
Neh. 7:4 *c.* was large and *great*
Jer. 22:8 done thus to *great c.*
Jon. 1:2 Nineveh that *g. c.* 3:2
3:3 N. was an exceeding *g. c.*
Rev. 11:8 in street of *great c.*
14:8 Bab. *g. c.* 18:10, 16, 19, 21
16:19 *great c.* was divided
17:18 woman is that *great c.*
21:10 he showed me that *g. c.*

Holy CITY.
Neh. 11:1 Jerusalem the *holy c.*
Is. 48:2 call themselves of *holy c.*
52:1 put on beau. garm. O *h. c.*
Dan. 9:24 seventy w. on thy *h. c.*

Mat. 4:5 devil taketh him to *h. c.*
27:53 went to *h. c.* and appeared
Rev. 11:2 *holy c.* shall they tread
21:2 1 John saw the *h. c.* coming
22:19 take his part out of *h. c.*

In, *or* into the CITY.
Gen. 19:12 hast in the *c.* bring
Deut. 20:14 all in the *c.* take
28:3 blessed shalt be in the *c.*
16 cursed shalt be in the *c.*
Jos. 6:21 destroyed all in the *c.*
8:19 into *c.* and set it on fire
Jud. 1:24 entrance into *c.*
2 *Sam.* 15:25 car. back ark into *c.*
27 return into the *c.*
1 *K.* 14:11 dieth of Jerob. in *c.*
12 when thy feet enter into *c.*
16:4 that dieth of Baasha in *c.*
2 *K.* 7:4 we will enter into *c.*
12 catch them, get into *c.*
Ps. 31:21 showed me his marvellous kindness in a strong *c.*
55:9 seen violence in the *c.*
Prov. 1:21 in *c.* wisdom uttereth
Ec. 7:19 mighty men in the *c.*
8:10 wicked were forgotten in *c.*
Is. 24:12 in the *c.* is left deso.
Jer. 14:18 if I enter into the *c.*
38:9 no more bread in the *c.*
52:6 famine was sore in the *c.*
Lam. 1:19 gave up ghost in *c.*
Hos. 11:9 not enter into the *c.*
Joel 2:9 run to and fro in the *c.*
Amos 3:6 be blown in the *c.* shall
there be evil in a *c.*
7:17 thy wife be harlot in *c.*
Jon. 3:4 J. began to enter into *c.*
Mat. 9:1 came into his own *c.*
10:5 *c.* of the Samaritans
11 into whatsoever *c.* ye enter
26:18 go into *c.* to such a man
28:11 some of watch came into *c.*
Mark 14:13 into the *c.* *Acts* 9:6
Luke 2:3 every one into his *c.*
7:37 a woman in the *c.* a sinner
18:2 there was in a *c.* a judge
22:10 ye are entered into *c.*
24:49 tarry ye in *c.* of Jerusalem
John 4:8 disciples gone into *c.*
Acts 11:5 in the *c.* of Joppa
14:20 he came into the *c.*
21:29 with him in the *c.*
24:12 synagogues nor in the *c.*
2 *Cor.* 11:26 in perils in the *c.*
Rev. 22:14 through gates into *c.*

CITY of the Lord.
Ps. 101:8 cut off all wicked doers
from *c. of the Lord.*
Is. 60:14 call thee *c. of Lord*

Out of the CITY.
Gen. 44:4 gone *out-of* the *c.*
Ex. 9:29 soon as I am *out of c.*
33 Moses went *out of* the *c.*
Jos. 8:22 issued *out of* the *c.*
Jud. 1:24 saw man come *o. of c.*
2 *Sam.* 18:3 succor us *out of c.*
20:16 wise woman *out of* the *c.*
2 *K.* 7:12 they come *out of c.*
9:15 none escape *out of* the *c.*
Job 24:12 groan from *out of t. c.*
Jer. 39:4 Zed. went *o. of c.* 52:7
Ezek. 48:30 are goings *o.* of the *c.*
Mic. 4:10 go forth *out of* the *c.*
Mat. 21:17 went *out of* the *c.*
Mark 11:19 he went *out of c.*
Luke 4:29 thrust him *out of t. c.*
9:5 go *out of c.* shake off dust
John 4:30 they went *out of c.*
Acts 7:58 cast Steph. *out of* the *c.*
14:19 drew him *out of c.*
16:13 we went *out of* the *c.*
21:5 brought us till *out of* the *c.*

CITY of Refuge.
Num. 35:25 rest. him to *c. of ref.*
Jos. 21:13 *c. of r.* 1 *Chr.* 6:57
21 Shech. ; 27 Golan ; 32 Ked.

This CITY.
Gen. 19:14 L. will destroy *this c.*
20 *this c.* is near to flee unto
21 I will not overthrow *this c.*
Jos. 6:26 buildeth *this c.*
Jud. 19:11 turn into *this c.*
1 *Sam.* 9:6 in *this c.* a man of G.
2 *K.* 2:19 *this c.* is pleasant
18:30 *t. c.* not be deliv. *Is.* 36:15
19:32 into *this c.* 33 ; *Is.* 37:34
34 def. *t. c.* 20:6 ; *Is.* 37:35 ; 38:6
23:27 cast off *this c.* Jerusalem
2 *Chr.* 6:34 pray toward *this c.*
Ezr. 4:13 if *this c.* be builded, 16
Neh. 13:18 bring evil on *this c. ?*
Jer. 6:6 *this* is the *c,* to be visited
17:25 *this c.* shall remain
19:8 will make *this c.* desolate
15 bring on *this c.* all the evil
20:5 deliver strength of *this c.*
21:9 abideth in *this c.* shall die
10 set my face against *this c.*
22:8 why L. done thus unto *t. c.*
26:6 I will make *this c.* a curse
15 innocent blood on *this c.*
27:17 *this c.* be laid waste
32:3 give *t. c.* to Chald. 28 ; 34:2
31 *this c.* been as a provocation
33:5 hid my face from *this c.*
34:22 cause them return to *t. c.*
38:17 *this c.* shall not be burnt
39:16 words on *this c.* for evil
Ezek. 11:3 *this c.* is the caldron, 7
Mat. 10:23 persecute in *this c.*
Acts 18:10 much people in *this c.*
22:3 brought up in *this c.* at feet

Without CITY.
Gen. 19:16 men set Lot *with. c.*
Num. 35:5 measure from *w. c.*
Rev. 14:20 w.-press trodden *w. c.*

CITIES.
Gen. 19:29 when God destroy. *c.*
35:5 terror of God on *c.* round
47:21 he rem. people to *c.*
Num. 13:19 what *c.* they dwell in
35:8 give of his *c.* to Levites
Deut. 2:37 nor to *c.* in mountains
3:19 abide in *c.* I have given you
6:10 to give thee goodly *c.*
19:5 flee to one of these *c.*
Jos. 10:19 suf. th. not to enter *c.*
11:13 as for *c.* still in strength
18:9 described it by *c.* in a book
Jud. 20:48 set on fire *c.*
21:23 they repaired the *c.*
1 *Sam.* 31:7 Israelites forsook *c.*
2 *Sam.* 10:12 *c.* our God, 1 *Chr.*
19:13
1 *K.* 9:12 Hiram came to see *c.*
20:34 *c.* father took I restore
Job 15:28 dwell. in desolate *c.*
Ps. 9:6 O enemy, destroyed *c.*
Is. 6:11 Until *c.* be wasted
14:21 nor fill world with *c.*
19:18 day shall five *c.* in E.
33:8 he hath despised the *c.*
64:10 thy holy *c.* a wilderness
Jer. 2:15 his *c.* are burnt
28 number of thy *c.* 11:13
13:19 *c.* of south be shut up
20:16 be as the *c.* L. overthrew
31:21 O virgin, to these thy *c.*
49:13 *c.* be perpetual wastes
50:32 I will kindle fire in his *c.*
Ezek. 26:19 like *c.* not inhabited
30:17 these *c.* into captivity
35:9 thy *c.* shall not return
Hos. 8:14 send fire upon his *c.*
11:6 sword shall abide on his *c.*
Amos 4:8 three *c.* to one for wat.
Mic. 5:14 so will I destroy thy *c.*
Zep. 3:6 their *c.* are destroyed
Zec. 1:17 my *c.* shall yet spread
Nat. 10:23 not have gone over *c.*
11:1 to preach in their *c.*
Acts 26:11 persec. to strange *c.*

2 *Pet.* 2:6 *c.* of S. and G. to **ashes**
Jude 7 *c.* about them in like m.
Rev. 16:19 *c.* of the nations fell

All CITIES.
Num. 21:25 Is. took *all* these *c.*
Deut. 2:34; 3:4; *Jos.* 10:39
31:10 burnt their *c. Jud.* 20:48
Deut. 20:15 thus do to *all c.* afar
Jos. 11:12 *all c.* of kings destr.
21:19 *all c.* of Aaron were 13 *c.*
41 *all c.* of Levites were 48 *c.*
1 *Sam.* 18:6 came out of *all c.*
2 *Sam.* 24:7 came to *all c.* of Hiv.
Neh. 10:37 tithes in *all* the *c.*
Jer. 4:26 *all* the *c.* broken down
33:12 in *all c.* habita. of sheph.
Hos. 13:10 save thee in *all* thy *c.*
Acts 8:40 he preached in *all* the *c.*

Defenced CITIES.
Is. 36:1 Sennacherib ag. *def. c.*
37:26 to lay waste *defenced c.*
Jer. 4:5 go to *defenced c.* 8:14
34:7 *defenced c.* remained of J.

Fenced CITIES.
Num. 32:17 ones in *fenced c.*
Deut. 3:5 *c. fenced* with high w.
9:1 *c. f.* to heaven, *Jos.* 14:12
Jos. 10:20 entered into *fen. c.*
2 *Sam.* 20:6 get him *fenced c.*
2 *Chr.* 12:4 Shishak took *fen. c.*
14:6 Asa built *fenced c.* in Jud.
21:3 Jehosh. gave sons *fen. c.*
Jer. 5:17 impoverish thy *fen. c.*
Dan. 11:15 k. of north take *f. c.*
Hos. 8:14 J. multiplied *fenced c.*
Zep. 1:16 day of alarm ag. *f. c.*

CITIES of Judah.
2 *Sam.* 2:1 I go up to *c.* of J. **?**
2 *K.* 23:5 burnt inc. in *c.* of J.
1 *Chr.* 6:57 sons of Aaron *c. of J.*
2 *Chr.* 17:7 to teach in *c. of J.* 13
19:5 set judges in the *c.* of J.
23:2 gather Lev. out of *c. of J.*
Neh. 11:3 in *c.* of *Judah* each
Ps. 69:35 will build *c. of Judah*
Is. 40:9 *c. of Jud.* behold your G.
44:26 *c. of J.* ye shall be built
Jer. 1:15 fam. of north ag. *c. of J.*
4:16 voice against *c. of J.*
7:17 what they do in *c. of J.*
9:11 *c. of J.* des. 10:22; 34:22
11:12 *c. of Judah* cry to gods
32:44 witness in the *c. of J. Judah*
33:10 man and beast in *c. of J.*
13 in the *c. of Ju.* shall flocks
44:6 fury kindled in *c. of Jud.*
21 incense ye burn in *c. of J.*
Zec. 1:12 not mercy on *c. of J.*

CITIES of Refuge.
Num. 35:6 six *c.* for *ref.* 13,14
11 ap. *c. of refuge, Jos.* 20:2
1 *Chr.* 6:67 to sons of K. of *c. r.*

Six CITIES.
Jos. 15:59 mount. of Jud. *six c.*

CITIES, with Suburbs.
Lev. 25:34 *sub.* of *c.* not be sold
Num. 35:2 give to L. *sub.* for *c.*
Jos. 21:3 to Levites *c.* with *s.*

CITIES, with Villages.
1 *Sam.* 6:18 *c.* and of country *v.*
Mat. 9:35 J. went about all *c.* and
villages teaching, *Luke* 13:22
Mark 6:56 into *villages* or *c.*

CITIES, with waste.
Lev. 26:31 your *c.* waste, 33
Is. 61:4 shall repair *waste c.*
Jer. 4:7 *c.* shall be laid *waste*
Ezek. 6:6 in dwell. *c.* shall be *w.*
19:7 w. their *c.* ; 35:4 thy *c. w.*
36:35 *w. c.* are become fenced
38 *w. c.* be filled with flocks
Amos 9:14 build the *waste c.*

Your CITIES.
Is. 1:7 *your c.* are burnt

Jer. 40:10 dwell in *your c.*

CITIZEN, S
Luke 15:15 prodigal joined to *c.*
19:14 his *c.* hated him, and
Acts 21:39 a *c.* of no mean city
Eph. 2:19 fellow-*c.* with saints

CLAD.
1 *K.* 11:29 Jerob. had *c.* himself
Is. 59:17 *c.* with zeal as a cloak

CLAMOR, OUS.
Prov. 9:13 a foolish woman is *c.*
Eph. 4:31 let all *c.* be put away

CLAP hands.
Job 27:23 shall *c.* their *hands*
Ps. 47:1 *c.* your *h.* all ye people
98:8 let the floods *c.* their *hands*
Is. 55:12 trees of field *c.* their *h.*
Lam. 2:15 *c.* their *h.* at thee
Nah. 3:19 bruit of thee *c.* their *hands*

CLAPPED, ETH.
2 *K.* 11:12 *c.* their hands
Ezek. 25:6 hast *c.* thy hands
Job 34:37 *c.* his hands among us

CLAVE, cleft.
Gen. 22:3 A. *c.* wood for bur.-off.
Num. 16:31 ground *c.* asunder
Jud. 15:19 God *c.* hollow in jaw
1 *Sam.* 6:14 *c.* wood of cart
Ps. 78:15 *c.* rocks, *Is.* 48:21

CLAVE, adhered.
Gen. 34:3 his soul *c.* to Dinah
Ruth 1:14 R. *c.* to mother-in-law
2 *Sam.* 20:2 Jud. *c.* to their king
23:10 till his hand *c.* to sword
1 *K.* 11:2 Sol. *c.* to these in love
2 *K.* 18:6 Hezekiah *c.* to the Lord
Neh. 10:29 *c.* to their brethren
Acts 17:34 certain men *c.* to Paul
CLAUDA. *Acts* 27:16
CLAUDIA. 2 *Tim.* 4:21

CLAWS.
Deut. 14:6 the cleft into two *c.*
Dan. 4:33 his nails like birds' *c.*
Zec. 11:16 he shall tear their *c.*

CLAY.
Job 4:19 dwell in houses of *c.*
10:9 hast made me as the *c.*
13:12 are like to bodies of *c.*
27:16 prepare raiment as *c.*
33:6 I am formed out of *c.*
38:14 it is turned as *c.* to seal
Ps. 40:2 up out of the miry *c.*
Is. 64:6 esteem. as potter's *c.*
Is. 41:25 as potter treadeth *c.*
45:9 *c.* say to him fashioneth it
64:8 we the *c.* thou our potter
Jer. 18:4 vessel made of *c.* marred
6 as *c.* is in the potter's hand
43:9 stones, hide them in *c.*
Dan. 2:33 his feet, part *c.* 34, 42
Nah. 3:14 go into *c.* and tread
Hab. 2:6 ladeth with thick *c.*
John 9:6 he made *c.* of spittle
15 he put *c.* on mine eyes
Rom. 9:21 potter power over *c.* **?**

CLAY-GROUND.
1 *K.* 7:46 into *c.-g.* 2 *Chr.* 4:17

CLEAN.
Lev. 23:22 not make *c.* riddance
Jos. 3:17 *c.* over Jordan, 4:1, 11
Ps. 77:8 is his mercy *c.* gone
Is. 24:19 earth is *c.* dissolved
Joel 1:7 he hath made it *c.* bare
2 *Pet.* 2:18 those *c.* escaped

CLEAN, Adjective.
Gen. 8:20 took of every *c.* beast
35:2 be *c.* and change garments
Lev. 7:19 all *c.* shall eat thereof
10:10 difference betw. *c.* 11:47 ;
20:25 ; *Ezek.* 22:26 ; 44:23
16:30 be *c.* from all your sins
22:4 not eat holy things till *c.*
Num. 19:18 a *c.* person take hys.

Deut. 12:15 *c.* may eat, 15:22
1 *Sam.* 20:26 surely he is not *c.*
2 *K.* 5:10 flesh come ag. be *c.* 14
12 wash in them and be *c.*
13 he saith, Wash and be *c.*
Job 11:4 I am *c.* in thine eyes
14:4 *c.* thing out of an unclean **?**
15:14 what is man he sh. be *c.* **?**
15 heavens not *c.* in his sight
25:4 he be *c.* born of a woman
33:9 I am *c.* without transgr.
Prov. 16:2 *c.* in his own eyes
Ec. 9:2 alike to *c.* and unclean
Is. 1:16 wash ye, make you *c.*
28:8 so there is no place *c.*
52:11 be ye *c.* that bear vessels
Jer. 13:27 wilt not be made *c.* **?**
Ezek. 36:25 sprinkle *c.* water on
Mat. 8:2 thou canst make me *c.*
Mark 1:40 ; *Luke* 5:12
3 thou *c. Mark* 1:41 ; *Lu.* 5:13
23:25 *c.* the outside, *Luke* 11:39
Luke 11:41 all things are *c.*
John 13:11 Ye are not all *c.*
15:3 ye are *c.* through the word
Acts 18:6 own heads, I am *c.*
Rev. 19:8 linen, *c.* and white, 14

CLEAN hands.
Job 9:30 make *hands* never so *c.*
17:9 *c. hands* shall be stronger
Ps. 24:4 he that hath *c. hands*

CLEAN heart.
Ps. 51:10 create in me a *c. heart*
73:1 God is good to such of *c. h.*
Prov. 20:9 made my *heart c.* **?**

Is CLEAN.
Lev. 13:13 he is *c.* 17, 37, 39
Ps. 19:9 fear of the Lord *is c.*
Prov. 14:4 no oxen are, crib *is c.*
John 13:10 but *is c.* every whit

Pronounce CLEAN.
Lev. 13:6 *pronounce* him *c.* 14:7

Shall be CLEAN.
Lev. 11:36 wh. is water *s. be c.*
12:8 she *s. be c.* 15:28 ; 13:58 it *s.*
be c.
14:20 he *s. be c.* 53 ; 15:13 ; 17:15 ;
22:7 ; *Num.* 19:12, 19
Num. 31:24 *shall be c. Ezek.* 36:25
Ps. 51:7 hyssop and I *shall be c.*

CLEANNESS.
2 *Sam.* 22:21 *c.* of my hands recompensed me, *Ps.* 18:20
25 *c.* in his eyesight, *Ps.* 18:24
Amos 4:6 give you *c.* of teeth

CLEANSE.
Ex. 29:36 *c.* the alt. *Lev.* 16:19
Num. 8:6 take Lev. and *c.* them
2 *Chr.* 29:15 *c.* house of Lord, 16
Neh. 13:22 Levites should *c.* th.
Ps. 19:12 *c.* from secret faults
51:2 and *c.* me from my sin
119:9 a young man *c.* his way **?**
Jer. 4:11 a dry wind not to *c.*
33:8 *c.* them, *Ezek.* 37:23
Ezek. 36:25 from idols will I *c.*
39:12 that they may *c.* land, 16
45:18 and *c.* the sanctuary
Joel 3:21 *c.* their blood
Mat. 10:8 heal the sick, *c.* lepers
23:26 *c.* first within the cup
2 *Cor.* 7:1 *c.* ourselves
Eph. 5:26 *c.* it with washing
Jam. 4:8 *c.* your hands, ye sinn.
1 *John* 1:9 *c.* us from unright.

CLEANSED.
Lev. 14:14 to be *c.* 17, 18, 25, 28
Num. 35:33 land cannot be *c.*
Jos. 22:17 we are not *c.*
2 *Chr.* 29:18 *c.* all the house of L.
30:19 his heart though not *c.*
34:5 Josiah *c.* Judah and Jerus.
Neh. 13:9 they *c.* the chambers
Job 35:3 what profit if I be *c.*

Ps. 73:13 *c.* my heart in vain
Ezek. 22:24 art the land not *c.*
44:26 he is *c.* reck. seven days
Dan. 8:14 then sanctuary be *c.*
Mat. 8:3 his leprosy was *c.*
11:5 lepers are *c. Luke* 7:22
Mark 1:42 leprosy dep. he was *c.*
Luke 4:27 none *c.* save Naaman
17:17 were not ten *c.* but where
Acts 10:15 what God hath *c.* 11:9

CLEANSETH, ING.
Job 37:21 but the wind *c.* them
Prov. 20:30 blueness of a wo. *c.*
1 *John* 1:7 bl. of Jesus Christ *c.*
Mark 1:44 offer for *c. Luke* 5:14

CLEAR.
Gen. 44:16 how shall we *c.* ours.
Exod. 34:7 by no means *c.* guilty
2 *Sam.* 23:4 *c.* shining after rain
Ps. 51:4 *c.* when thou judgest
Cant. 6:10 *c.* as the sun
Is. 18:4 like a *c.* heat on herbs
Amos 8:9 darken earth in *c.* day
Zec. 14:6 light shall not be *c.*
2 *Cor.* 7:11 ap. yourselves to be *c.*
Rev. 21:11 *c.* as crystal, 22:1
18 pure gold like to *c.* glass

CLEARER.
Job 11:17 shall be *c.* than noon

CLEARING.
Num. 14:18 no means *c.* guilty
2 *Cor.* 7:11 what *c.* of yourselves

CLEARLY.
Job 33:3 utter knowledge *c.*
Mat. 7:5 *c.* to pull, *Luke* 6:42
Mark 8:25 and saw every man *c.*
Rom. 1:20 from creation *c.* seen

CLEARNESS.
Exod. 24:10 body of heaven in *c.*

CLEAVE.
Lev. 1:17 *c.* it with the wings
Ps. 74:15 didst *c.* the fountain
Hab. 3:9 *c.* the earth with rivers
Zec. 14:4 mount shall *c.* in midst
Gen. 2:24 shall *c.* to his wife,
Mat. 19:5 ; *Mark* 10:7
Deut. 4:4 ye that did *c.* to the L.
10:20 to him shalt thou *c.* 11:22 ;
13:4 ; 30:20 ; *Jos.* 22:5
Jos. 23:8 *c.* to Lord your God
Job 38:38 the clods *c.* together
Ps. 101:3 hate work, not *c.*
102:5 my bones *c.* to my skin
137:6 let my tongue *c.* to roof
Is. 14:1 *c.* to house of Jacob
Jer. 13:11 caused to *c.* to me Is.
Ezek. 3:26 make thy tongue *c.*
Dan. 2:43 not *c.* one to another
11:34 *c.* to them with flatteries
Acts 11:23 heart *c.* to Lord
Rom. 12:9 *c.* to that wh. is good

CLEAVED.
2 *K.* 3:3 J. *c.* to Jeroboam's sins
Job 29:10 their tongue *c.* to roof
31:7 blot hath *c.* to my hands

CLEAVETH.
Job 19:20 my bone *c.* to my skin
Ps. 22:15 tongue *c.* to my jaws
41:8 an evil disease *c.* to him
44:25 our belly *c.* to the earth
119:25 my soul *c.* to the dust
Jer. 13:11 as girdle *c.* to loins
Lam. 4:4 tongue of suck. child *c.*
8 their skin *c.* to their bones
Luke 10:11 dust of city which *c.*

CLEAVETH, *divideth.*
Deut. 14:6 beast that *c.* the cleft
Job 16:13 he *c.* my reins asunder
Ps. 141:7 as when one *c.* wood
Ec. 10:9 *c.* wood be endangered

CLEFT.
Mic. 1:4 valleys sh. be *c.* as wax

CLEFTS.
Cant. 2:14 that art in *c.*

Is. 2:21 to go into *c.* for fear
Jer. 49:16 dw. in the *c. Ob.* 3
Am. 6:11 smite house with *c.*

CLEMENCY.
Acts 24:4 hear us of thy *c.*
CLEMENT. *Phil.* 4:3
CLEOPAS. *Lu.* 24:18 ; *Jo.* 19:25

CLERK.
Acts 19:35 town *c.* had appeased

CLIFT, S.
Ex. 33:22 will put thee in a *c.*
2 *Chr.* 20:16 come by *c.* of Ziz
Job 30:6 to dwell in *c.* of valleys
Is. 57:5 slay. children under *c.*

CLIMB, ED, ETH.
1 *Sam.* 14:13 Jonathan *c.* up
Jer. 4:29 they shall *c.* up rocks
Joel 2:7 *c.* wall like men of war
9 they shall *c.* up on houses
Amos 9:2 though *c.* up to heaven
Luke 19:4 Zaccheus *c.* up a tree
John 10:1 *c.* up some other way

CLIPPED.
Jer. 48:37 every beard shall be *c.*

CLOAK.
Is. 59:17 clad with zeal as a *c.*
Mat. 5:40 let him have *c.* also
Luke 6:29 taketh *c.* forbid not
John 15:22 no *c.* for their sin
1 *Thes.* 2:5 nor used *c.* of covet.
2 *Tim.* 4:13 *c.* I left at Troas
1 *Pet.* 2:16 lib. for *c.* of maliciousn.

CLODS.
Job 7:5 clothed with *c.* of dust
21:33 *c.* of valley be sweet
38:38 *c.* cleave fast together
Is. 28:24 ploughm. break the *c.*
Hos. 10:11 J. shall break his *c.*
Joel 1:17 seed is rotten under *c.*

CLOSE.
Num. 5:13 kept *c.* from husband
2 *Sam.* 22:46 afraid out of their *c.*
places, *Ps.* 18:45
1 *Chr.* 12:1 David kept himself *c.*
Job 28:21 kept *c.* from fowls
Jer. 42:16 follow *c.* after you
Amos 9:11 *c.* up the breaches
Luke 9:36 they kept it *c.*

CLOSED.
Num. 16:33 earth *c.* upon them
Is. 1:6 they have not been *c.*
29:10 Lord hath *c.* your eyes
Dan. 12:9 the words are *c.* up
Jon. 2:5 the depth *c.* me around
Mat. 13:15 eyes *c. Acts* 28:27
Luke 4:20 and he *c.* the book

CLOSER.
Prov. 18:24 a friend sticketh *c.*

CLOSEST.
Jer. 22:15 thou *c.* thyself in ced.

CLOSET.
Joel 2:16 bride go out of her *c.*
Mat. 6:6 prayest, enter thy *c.*
Luke 12:3 spok. in the ear in *c.*

CLOTH.
Num. 4:8 spread a *c.* of scarlet
Deut. 22:17 spread *c.* bef. elders
1 *Sam.* 19:13 M. cov. im. with *c.*
21:9 sword is wrapt in a *c.*
2 *Sam.* 20:12 cast a *c.* on Amasa
2 *K.* 8:15 Hazael took a thick *c.*
Is. 30:22 as a menstruous *c.*
Mat. 9:16 new *c. Mark* 2:21
27:59 wrapped it in a linen *c.*
Mark 14:51 linen *c.* about body

CLOTHE.
Ex. 40:14 his sons and *c.* them
Est. 4:4 raiment to *c.* Mordecai
Ps. 132:16 *c.* priests with salva.
18 his enemies *c.* with shame
Prov. 23:21 drowsiness *c.* with
Is. 22:21 *c.* him with thy robe

49:18 shalt *c.* thee with them
50:3 *c.* heavens with blackness
Ezek. 20:16 *c.* with trembling
34:3 *c.* you with the wool
Hag. 1:6 ye *c.* but none warm
Zec. 3:4 I will *c.* thee
Mat. 63:0 if God so *c.* the grass,
much more *c.* you, *Lu.* 12:28

CLOTHED.
Gen. 3:21 coats of skins, *c.* them
Lev. 8:7 Moses *c.* A. with robe
2 *Sam.* 1:24 *c.* with scarlet
1 *Chr.* 21:16 Israel *c.* with sack.
2 *Chr.* 6:41 priests be *c.* with salv.
18:9 king of Israel and Judah *c.*
28:15 *c.* all that were naked
Est. 4:2 king's gate *c.* with
Job 7:5 my flesh *c.* with worms
10:11 *c.* me with skin and flesh
29:14 righteousness *c.* me
39:19 *c.* his neck with thunder ?
Ps. 35:26 be *c.* with sh. 109:29
65:13 pastures *c.* with flocks
93:1 Lord is *c.* with majesty
104:1 thou art *c.* with honor
109:18 *c.* himself with cursing
132:9 priests be *c.* with right.
Prov. 31:21 *c.* with scarlet
Is. 61:10 *c.* me with garm. of sal.
Ezek. 16:10 *c.* thee vi. broidered
Dan. 5:29 *c.* Daniel with scarlet
Zep. 1:8 *c.* with strange apparel
Zec. 3:3 *c.* with filthy garments
Mat. 11:8 *c.* in soft, *Luke* 7:25
25:36 and ye *c.* me not, 43
Mark 1:6 *c.* with camel's hair
5:15 they see him *c. Luke* 8:35
15:17 they *c.* Jesus with purple
Luke 16:19 rich man *c.* in purple
2 *Cor.* 5:2 desiring to be *c.* upon
3 if so being *c.* not be naked
1 *Pet.* 5:5 be *c.* with humility
Rev. 3:18 that thou mayest be *c.*
10:1 saw angel *c.* with a cloud
11:3 prophesy *c.* in sackcloth
12:1 a woman *c.* with the sun
19:13 was *c.* with vesture

CLOTHED, *with* linen.
Ezek. 9:2 one man was *c.* with *l.*
44:17 shall be *c.* with *l.* garm.
Dan. 10:5 certain man *c.* with *l.*
12:6 one said to man *c.* in *linen*
Rev. 15:6 *c.* in wh. *l.* 18:16 ; 19:14

Shall be CLOTHED.
Job 8:22 *shall be c.* with shame
Ezek. 7:21 *s. be c.* with desola.
Dan. 5:7 read this writ. *s. be c.*
Mat. 6:31 wherewithal *s.* we *b. c.*
Rev. 3:5 overcometh *s.* be *c.* 4:4

CLOTHES.
Gen. 49:11 his *c.* in blood of gr.
Ex. 35:19 *c.* of service, 39:1, 41
Lev. 10:6 nor rend your *c.* 21:10
Deut. 29:5 *c.* not old, *Neh.* 9:21
1 *Sam.* 19:24 S. stripped off his *c.*
1 *K.* 1:1 covered David with *c.*
2 *K.* 2:12 took own *c.* and rent
2 *Chr.* 34:27 didst rend thy *c.*
Neh. 4:23 none of us put off *c.*
Job 9:31 my *c.* shall abhor me
Prov. 6:27 his *c.* not be burnt
Ezek. 16:39 strip thee of *c.* 23:26
Mat. 24:18 not return to take *c.*
Mark 5:28 If I touch but his *c.* I
15:20 put his own *c.* on him
Luke 2:7 in swaddling *c.* 12
8:27 ware no *c.* neither abode
19:36 spread their *c.* in way
24:12 beheld linen *c. John* 20:5
John 11:44 bound with grave-*c.*
19:40 and wound it in linen *c.*
20:7 napkin not with linen *c.*
Acts 7:58 laid their *c.* at S.'s feet
22:23 as they cried, cast off *c.*

Rent CLOTHES.
Gen. 37:29 Reuben ; 34 Jacob
44:13 Joseph's brethren *rent c.*
Num. 14:6 Joshua and C. *rent c.*
Jos. 7:6 Josh. ; *Jud.* 11:35 Jeph.
2 *Sam.* 3:31 r. *c.* gird with sack.
1 *K.* 21:27 Ahab ; 2 *K.* 5:8 king
2 *K.* 11:14 Atha. 2 *Chr.* 23:13
19:1 Hezekiah *rent c. Is.* 37:1
Est. 4:1 Mordecai *rent* his *c.*
Mat. 26:65 h.-pr. *r. c. Mark* 14:63
Acts 14:14 Bar. and Paul *rent c.*
16:22 magistrates *r.* off their *c.*

CLOTHES rent.
Lev. 13:45 leper's *c.* shall be *rent*
1 *Sam.*4:12 came to Shiloh *c. r.*
2 *Sam.* 1:2 man from Saul *c. r.*
13:31 servants stood with *c. r.*
2 *K.* 18:37 to Hez. *c. r. Is.* 36:22
Jer. 41:5 to Mizpah with *c. rent*

Wash CLOTHES.
Ex. 19:10 *wash* the. *c. Num.* 8:7
Lev. 11:25 *w.* his *c.* 40 ; 13:6 ; 14:8,
9, 47 ; 15:5, 8, 11, 22 ; 16:26,
28 ; *Num.* 19:10, 21 ; 31:24

Washed CLOTHES.
Ex. 19:14 people *wash.* their *c.*
Num. 8:21 Levi. *washed* their *c.*
2 *Sam.* 19:24 Mephib. *w.* not *c.*

CLOTHEST.
Jer. 4:30 though *c.* with crimson

CLOTHING.
Job 22:6 hast stripped naked. of *c.*
24:7 naked to lodge without *c.*
31:19 any perish for want of *c.*
Ps. 35:13 my *c.* was sackcloth
45:13 king's daughter, her *c.*
Prov. 27:26 lambs for thy *c.*
31:22 virtuous wom.'s *c.* is silk
25 strength and honor her *c.*
Is. 3:6 thou hast *c.* be thou ruler
7 for in my house is neither *c.*
23:18 merchandise be for dur. *c.*
59:17 garments of veng. for *c.*
Jer. 10:9 and purple is their *c.*
Mat. 7:15 sheep's *c. ;* 11:8 soft *c.*
Mark 12:38 scribes love long *c.*
Acts 10:30 man stood in bright *c.*
Jam. 2:3 to him weareth gay *c.*

CLOUD.
Gen. 9:13 set my bow in the *c.*

Ex. 14:20 it was a *c.* to them
16:10 glory of L. appeared in *c.*
19:9 lo, I come in a thick *c.*
24:15 a *c.* covered the mount
16 God called to Mos. out of *c.*
34:5 L. desc. in *c. Num.* 11:25
40:34 a *c.* covered tent of cong.
38 *c.* on tabernacle by day
Lev. 16:2 I will appear in the *c.*
Num. 9:19 *c.* tarried long
10:34 *c.* was upon them by day
1 *K.* 8:10 *c.* filled house of Lord,
2 *Chr.* 5:13 ; *Ezek.* 10:4
18:44 a little *c.* like a man's h.
Job 3:5 that day let *c.* dwell
22:13 judge through dark *c. ?*
30:15 my welf. passeth as a *c.*
38:9 I made *c.* the garment
Ps. 78:14 daytime led with *c.*
105:39 he spread a *c.* for a cov.
Prov. 16:15 is as *c.* of rain
Is. 4:5 create on assemblies a *c.*
18:4 like a *c.* of dew in harvest
19:1 Lord rideth upon a swift *c.*
44:22 as a thick *c.* thy transgressions, as a *c.* thy sins
60:8 who are these flee as a *c.*
Lam. 2:1 dau. of Zion with a *c.*
3:44 covered thyself with a *c.*
Ezek. 1:4 *c.* and fire infolding it
28 as appearance of bow in *c.*
8:11 thick *c.* of incense went up
10:4 house was filled with the *c.*
30:18 as for her, a *c.* cover her
32:7 I will cover sun with a *c.*

38:9 like *c.* to cover land, 16
Mat. 17:5 *c.* ov. *Mark* 9:7 ; *Luke*
9:34 v. out of *c. Luke* 9:35
Luke 12:54 when ye see a *c.*
21:27 Son of man coming in *c.*
Acts 1:9 a *c.* received him
1 *Cor.* 10:1 our fathers under *c.*
2 baptized to Moses in the *c.*
Heb. 12:1 so great a *c.* of witn.
Rev. 10:1 angel clothed with a *c.*
11:12 they ascended in a *c.*
14:14 white *c.* on *c.* 15, 16

CLOUD abode.
Ex. 40:35 a *c. abode* therein
Num. 9:17 *c. abode* there

Morning CLOUD.
Hos. 6:4 goodness as *morning c.*
13:3 be as *m. c.* and early dew

Pillar of CLOUD.
Ex. 13:21 in a *pillar of c.*
14:24 on Egyp. through *pil. of c.*
Num. 12:5 down in *pillar of c.*
Deut. 31:15 L. app. in *p. of c.*
Neh. 9:19 the *pil. of c.* dep. not

CLOUD taken up.
Ex. 40:36 *c. t. up, Num.* 9, 17
37 *c.* not *t. up* journeyed not

CLOUDS.
Deut. 4:11 *c.* and thick darkness
Jud. 5:4 *c.* dropped with water
2 *Sam.* 22:12 about him thick *c.*
23:4 as a morning without *c.*
1 *K.* 18:45 heaven black with *c.*
Job 20:6 his head reached to *c.*
22:14 thick *c.* covering to him
26:8 bindeth up water in *c.*
36:29 spreading of *c. ?*
37:16 balancings of the *c. ?*
38:37 number *c.* in wisdom ?
Ps. 36:5 thy faithfulness to *c.*
57:10 thy truth to the *c.* 108:4
68:34 his strength is in the *c.*
77:17 the *c.* poured out water
78:23 tho' he com. *c.* from ab.
97:2 *c.* and darkness about him
104:3 maketh *c.* his chariot
147:8 covereth heaven with *c.*
Prov. 3:20 *c.* drop down
8:28 he established the *c.*
25:14 *c.* without rain
Ec. 11:4 reg. *c.* shall not reap
12:2 nor *c.* return after rain
Is. 5:6 *c.* that they rain not
14:14 I will ascend above the *c.*
Jer. 4:13 he shall come up as *c.*
Dan. 7:13 S. of man came with *c.*
Joel 2:2 a day of *c. Zep.* 1:15
Nah. 1:3 the *c.* dust of his feet
Zec. 10:1 shall make bright *c.*
Mat. 24:30 Son of man com. in *c.*
26:64 ; *Mark* 13:26 ; 14:62
1 *Thes.* 4:17 caught up in *c.*
2 *Pet.* 2:17 they are *c.* carried
Jude 12 *c.* they are without wat.
Rev. 1:7 he cometh with *c.*

CLOUDY.
Ex. 33:9 the *c.* pillar descended
Neh. 9:12 leddest by a *c.* pillar
Ps. 99:7 he spake in *c.* pillar
Ezek. 30:3 day of L. near, a *c.* day
34:12 been scattered in *c.* day

CLOUTED.
Jos. 9:5 took old shoes and *c.*

CLOUTS.
Jer. 38:11 Ebed. took old cast *c.*

CLOVEN.
Lev. 11:3 *c.* footed that eat
7 swine *c.* footed, unclean
Acts 2:3 appeared *c.* tongues

CLUSTER.
Num. 13:23 branch with one *c.*
Cant. 1:14 as a *c.* of camphire
Is. 65:8 new wine is found in *c.*
Mic. 7:1 there is no *c.* to eat

CLUSTERS.
Gen. 40:10 *c.* bro. forth ripe gr.
Deut. 32:32 their *c.* are bitter
Cant. 7:7 thy breasts two *c.* 8
Rev. 14:18 gather *c.* of vine

COAL.
2 *Sam.* 14:7 quench my *c.* left
Is. 6:6 ser. hav. live *c.* in hand
47:14 shall not be *c.* to warm at
Lam. 4:8 visage blacker than a *c.*

COALS.
Lev. 16:12 take a cen. full of *c.*
1 *K.* 19:6 a cake baken on *c.*
Job 41:21 his breath kindleth *c.*
Ps. 18:8 *c.* were kindled by it
12 hailstones and *c.* of fire
120:4 arrows with *c.* of juniper
140:10 burning *c.* fall on them
Prov. 6:28 can one go on hot *c.*
25:22 *c.* of fire, *Rom.* 12:20
26:21 as *c.* to burning *c.*
Cant. 8:6 *c.* thereof are *c.* of fire
Is. 44:12 smith worketh in *c.*
19 baked bread on *c.* thereof
54:16 smith that bloweth the *c.*
Ezek. 1:13 appearance burning *c.*
10:2 fill thy hand with *c.* of fire
24:11 set it empty on the *c.*
Hab. 3:5 burning *c.* forth
John 18:18 serv. made fire of *c.*
21:9 saw fire of *c.* and fish laid

COAST.
Num. 24:24 ships from *c.* of Chit.
Deut. 11:24 uttermost sea your *c.*
19:8 if the Lord enlarge thy *c.*
Jos. 1:4 down *c.* of sun be your *c.*
Jud. 11:20 Is. to pass through *c.*
1 *Sam.* 6:9 if it go by his own *c.*
7:13 no more into *c.* of Israel
27 1 seek me in any *c.* of Isr.
3v 14 invasion on *c.* of Judah
2 *K.* 14:25 Jeroboam restored *c.*
1 *Chr.* 4:10 enlarge my *c.*
Zep. 2:7 *c.* for remnant of Judah

Sea-COAST.
Ezek. 25:16 dest. remnant of *s.-c.*
Zep. 2:6 *sea-c.* dwell. for sheph.
Mat. 4:13 J. dwelt in C. on *s.-c.*
Luke 6:17 from *sea-c.* came

COASTS.
Deut. 2:4 through *c.* of your bre.
18:3 divide *c.* of thy land
1 *Sam.* 7:14 *c.* did Israel deliver
11:3 send mess. into all *c.* 7
2 *Sam.* 21:5 be destroyed from *c.*
1 *Chr.* 21:12 a destroy. throu. *c.*
2 *Chr.* 11:13 to Rehob. out of *c.*
Ps. 105:31 lice in all their *c.*
33 he brake trees of their *c.*
Jer. 25:32 a whirlwind from *c.*
Ezek. 33:2 take a man of their *c.*
Joel 3:4 all the *c.* of Palestine?
Mat. 2:16 H. slew child. in all *c.*
8:34 out of their *c. Mark* 5:17
15:21 departed into *c.* of Tyre
Mark 7:31 dep. from *c.* of Tyre
Acts 13:50 expelled them out of *c.*

COAT.
Gen. 37:3 *c.* of many colors, 32
Ex. 28:4 Aaron, a broidered *c.*
Lev. 8:7 he put on him the *c.*
16:4 put on the holy linen *c.*
1 *Sam.* 2:19 made him a little *c.*
17:5 Goliah *c.* of mail, 38
2 *Sam.* 15:32 Hushai came *c.* rent
Job 30:18 bindeth as *c.* of my *c.*
Cant. 5:3 I have put off my *c.*
Mat. 5:40 take away thy *c.*
Luke 6:29 forbid not to take *c.*
John 19:23 *c.* was without seam
21:7 Peter girt his fisher's *c.*

COATS.
Gen. 3:21 God made *c.* of skins
Lev. 8:13 put *c.* upon A.'s sons
10:5 their *c.* out of camp

Dan. 3:21 were bound in their *c.*
27 nor were their *c.* changed
Mat. 10:10 neither provide two *c.*
Mark 6:9 and put not on two *c.*
Luke 3:11 hath two *c.* impart
Acts 9:39 *c.* which Dorcas made

COCK.

Mat. 26:34 *c.* crow, 75; *Mark*
14:30, 72; *Luke* 22:34, 61
74 *c.* crew, *Lu.* 22:60; *John* 18:27
Mark 13:35 cometh at *c.* crowing
14:68 and the *c.* crew, 72
John 13:38 *c.* not crow till thou
hast denied me thrice

COCKATRICE, S.

Is. 11:8 put his hand on *c.* den
14:29 of serpent's root come *c.*
59:5 they hatch *c.* eggs
Jer. 8:17 will send *c.* among you

COCKLE.

Job 31:40 *c.* grow inst. of barley

COFFER.

1 *Sam.* 6:8 put jewels in a *c.*
11 laid the *c.* on the cart

COFFIN.

Gen. 50:26 Joseph was put in a *c.*

COGITATIONS.

Dan. 7:28 *c.* much troubled me

COLD.

Gen. 8:22 *c.* and heat not cease
Job 24:7 naked no covering in *c.*
37:9 *c.* cometh out of north
Ps. 147:17 stand before his *c. ?*
Prov. 20:4 not plough by re. of *c.*
25:13 as *c.* of snow in harvest
20 taketh away garment in *c.*
25 *c.* waters to a thirsty soul
Jer. 18:14 *c.* water be forsaken ?
Nah. 3:17 in hedges in *c.* day
Mat. 10:42 a cup of *c.* water
24:12 love of many wax *c.*
John 18:18 a fire, for it was *c.*
Acts 28:2 received us, bec. of *c.*
2 *Cor.* 11:27 in *c.* and nakedness
Rev. 3:15 neither *c.* nor hot, 16

COLLAR, S.

Jud. 8:26 jewels beside *c.*
Job 30:18 disease bindeth as *c.*

COLLECTION.

2 *Chr.* 24:6 to bring in the *c.* 9
1 *Cor.* 16:1 conc. *c.* for saints

COLLEGE.

2 *K.* 22:14 in *c.* 2 *Chr.* 34:22

COLLOPS.

Job 15:27 *c.* of fat on his flanks

COLONY.

Acts 16:12 and a *c.*

COLOR, S.

Gen. 37:3 a coat of many *c.*
Num. 11:7 the *c.* as bdellium
Jud. 5:30 a prey of divers *c.*
2 *Sam.* 13:18 garm. of divers *c.*
1 *Chr.* 29:2 stones of divers *c.*
Is. 54:11 lay stones with fair *c.*
Prov. 23:31 giveth his *c.* in cup
Ezek. 1:4 midst as *c.* of amber
7 like *c.* of brass, *Dan.* 10:6
16 like *c.* of beryl, *Dan.* 10:9
22 firmament as *c.* of crystal
16:16 places with divers *c.*
17:3 eagle with divers *c.* to L.

COLOSSE. *Col.* 1:2

COLT, S.

Gen. 32:15 thirty camels with *c.*
49:11 binding ass's *c.* to vine
Jud. 10:4 thirty s. rode on 30 *c.*
12:14 Abdon's sons ro. on 70 *c.*
Job 11:12 man be born like *c.*
Zec. 9:9 riding upon a *c. Mat.*
21:5; *John* 12:15
Mat. 21:2 find an ass tied, a *c.*
Mark 11:2; *Luke* 19:30

7 brought ass and *c. Mark* 11:7
Mark 11:5 loos. *c. ? Luke* 19:33
Luke 19:35 cast their garm. on *c.*

COME.

Gen. 26:27 wherefore *c.* ye to me
42:7 whence *c.* ye ? *Jos.* 9:8
49:10 sceptre until Shiloh *c.*
Num. 10:29 *c.* thou with us
24:19 out of Jacob shall *c.* he
that shall have dominion
Deut. 18:6 if a L. *c.* with desire
1 *Sam.* 2:34 *c.* on thy two sons
10:8 thou shalt tarry till I *c.*
17:45 I *c.* to thee in name of **L.**
20:21 then *c.* there is peace
2 *Sam.* 19:33 *c.* thou over
2 *K.* 5:8 let him *c.* now to me
18:32 till I *c. Is.* 36:17
1 *Chr.* 29:14 all things *c.* of thee
Job 13:13 let *c.* on me what will
14:14 wait till my change *c.*
21 his sons *c.* to honor
37:13 to *c.* for correction
38:11 hitherto shalt thou *c.*
Ps. 40:7 lo, I *c. Heb.* 10:7, 9

Ps. 42:2 when shall I *c.* and app.
50:3 our God shall *c.* and not
65:2 unto thee shall all flesh *c.*
80:2 and *c.* and save us
86:9 all nations shall *c.*
101:2 when wilt thou *c.* to me
109:17 loved cursing, so let it *c.*
119:41 let thy mercies *c.* 77
Ec. 9:2 all things *c.* alike
Cant. 2:10 love, *c.* away, 13
Is. 13:5 *c.* from a far country
6 day of L. *c.* as destruction
21:12 inquire ye, return, *c.*
26:20 *c.* my people, enter
35:4 your G. will *c.* with veng.
40:10 will *c.* with strong hand
41:25 raised up one, he shall *c.*
44:7 things coming, and shall *c.*
45:20 assem. and *c.* draw near
24 even to him shall men *c.*
51:11 redeemed shall *c.* to Z.
55:1 *c.* ye to the waters, *c.* ye
3 *c.* unto me, hear
59:20 Redeemer shall *c.* to Z.
60:3 Gentiles *c.* to thy light, 5
66:15 Lord will *c.* with fire
Jer. 2:31 will *c.* no more to thee
3:22 we *c.* to thee
13:22 wherefore *c.* these things
17:15 word of Lord ? let it *c.*
40:4 seem good to *c.* if ill to *c.*
46:18 as Carmel so shall he *c.*
49:4 who shall *c.* unto me ?
Lam. 1:4 none *c.* to solemn fea.
Ezek. 21:27 till he *c.* whose right
33:31 *c.* to thee as the people
33 it will *c.* then shall know
36:8 they are at hand to *c.*
Hos. 6:1 *c.* let us return to Lord
3 he shall *c.* to us as the rain
10:12 time to seek L. till he *c.*
Joel 1:15 as destruction sh. it *c.*
2:31 be. terrible day of Lord *c.*
Hab. 2:3 it will *c.* and not tarry
Zec. 1:21 what *c.* these to do ?
14:5 God shall *c.* and all saints
Mal. 3:1 the Lord ye seek shall *c.*

Mat. 2:6 out of thee *c.* Governor
6:10 thy kingdom *c. Luke* 11:2
8:9 *c.* and he cometh, *Luke* 7:8
11 many shall *c.* from the east
11:3 he that sh. *c. ? Luke* 7:19, 20
28 *c.* all ye that labor
16:24 if any man will *c.* after me
17:10 Elias must first *c. ?* 11
24:14 then shall the end *c.*
42 know not hour Lord doth *c.*
25:34 *c.* ye blessed of my Father
Mark 8:34 if any will *c.* after me,
Luke 9:23 ; 14:27
10:14 child. to *c. Luke* 18:16

Luke 10:1 place whither he w. *c.*
17:20 when kingdom should *c.*
19:13 occupy till I *c.*
22:18 till king. of God shall *c.*
John 1:39 he saith, *c.* and see
3:26 baptizeth, and all men *c.*
5:14 lest worse thing *c.* to thee
40 ye will not *c.* to me that ye
6:37 F. giveth shall *c.* to me
44 no man can *c.* except F. 65
7:34 I am, thither ye cannot *c.*
37 if any man thirst, let him *c.*
8:14 ye cannot tell whence I *c.*
13:19 before it *c.* that when *c.*
14:18 I will *c.* unto you
23 and we will *c.* unto him
17:11 I *c.* to thee, 13
21:22 I will he tarry till I *c.* 23
Acts 1:11 this Jesus shall so *c.* as
2:20 before great day of Lord *c.*
8:24 pray none of these things *c.*
9:38 he would not delay to *c.*
13:40 lest that *c.* upon you
16:9 *c.* over into Macedonia
19:4 believe on him should *c.*
26:22 Moses did say should *c.*
Rom. 3:8 do evil th. good may *c.*
1 *Cor.* 4:5 judg nothing till I *c.*
11:26 show L.'s death till he *c*
34 will I set in order when L *c.*
2 *Cor.* 1:15 I was minded to *c.*
12:20 for I fear, lest when I *c.*
2 *Thes.* 1:10 shall *c.* to be glori.
2:3 except *c.* a falling away
1 *Tim.* 4:8 life now is, and to *c.*
2 *Tim.* 4:3 time will *c.* they will
Heb. 4:16 *c.* boldly to throne.
7:25 able to save them *c.* to God
10:37 he that shall *c.* will *c.*
Rev. 2:5 else I will *c.* quickly
25 ye have, hold fast till I *c.*
3:11 I *c.* quickly, 22:7, 20
6:1 saying, *c.* and see, 3, 5, 7
22:17 and let him athirst *c.*

COME again.

Gen. 28:21 so that I *c. ag.*
Ex. 14:26 waters *c. a.* on E.
Jud. 8:9 I *c. a.* in peace
13:8 let man of God *c. again*
1 *K.* 2:41 Shimei was *c. again*
12:5 thr. d. and *c. a.* 2 *Chr.* 10:5
17:21 let this child's soul *c. a.*
Ps. 126:6 he shall *c. again*
Prov. 3:28 say not, Go and *c. a*
Luke 10:35 I *c. ag.* will repay
John 14:3 I will *c. aga.* and rec.
28 I go away, and *c. a.*
2 *Cor.* 2:1 not *c. a.* in heaviness
12:21 I *c. a.* God will humble
13:2 if I *c. a.* I will not spare

COME down.

Gen. 45:9 saith Jos. *c. d.* to me
Ex. 3:8 I am *c. d.* to deliver
19:11 Lord will *c. d.* on Sinai
Num. 11:17 I will *c. d.* and talk
Deut. 28:24 it shall *c. d.*
Jud. 7:24 *c. d.* against Midian
1 *Sam.* 23:11 S. *c. d. ?* will *c. d.*
20 *c. d.* according to desire
2 *K.* 1:4 not *c. d.* from, 6, 16
9 then man of God *c. down*
Neh. 6:3 I cannot *c. d.*
Ps. 7:16 *c. d.* on his own pate
72:6 shall *c. down* like rain
144:5 bow thy heavens and *c. d.*
Is. 47:1 *c. down* O virgin
64:1 that thou wouldst *c. d.*
Jer. 13:18 principali. shall *c. d.*
21:13 who shall *c. d.* ag. us ?
48:18 *c. down* from thy glory
Ezek. 26:16 prin. of sea shall *c. d.*
30:6 pride of power shall *c. d.*
Joel 3:11 thy mighty ones to *c. d.*
Mat. 24:17 on house-top not *c. d.*
27:40 *c. d.* fr. cr. 42; *Mark* 15:30
Luke 19:5 J. said, Zaccheus *c. d.*

John 4:49 *c. down* ere child die

COME forth.

Gen. 15:4 *c. f.* of thy bowels
1 *Sam.* 14:11 Hebrews *c. f.*
1 *K.* 2:30 saith the king, *c. forth*
2 *K.* 10:25 slay, let none *c. forth*
Job 23:10 I shall *c. f.* as gold
Ps. 17:2 let my sentence *c. f.*
88:8 I cannot *c. forth*
Ec. 7:18 feareth God shall *c. f.*
Is. 11:1 *c. f.* rod out stem of J.
48:1 art *c. forth* of waters of J.
Jer. 46:9 let mighty men *c. forth*
Ezek. 21:19 twain *c. forth*
Dan. 3:26 ye serv. of God, *c. f.*
Joel 3:18 a fountain shall *c. forth*
Mic. 5:2 out of thee *c. forth* ruler
Mat. 15:18 *c. f.* from heart
Mark 9:29 *c. f.* by prayer
Luke 12:37 will *c. f.* and serve
John 5:20 *c. f.* they done good
11:43 he cried, Lazarus, *c. forth*
Acts 7:7 shall *c. f.* and serve me

COME hither.

Gen. 15:16 the fourth gen. *c. h.*
Jud. 16:2 Samson *c. hither*
1 *Sam.* 10:22 man should *c. h.*
16:11 not sit down till he *c. h.*
2 *Sam.* 20:16 say to Joab, *c.h.*
Prov. 25:7 bet. be said, *c. up h.*
Dan. 3:26 servants of G. *c. h.*
John 4:16 call husband and *c. h.*
Acts 17:6 turned world, are *c. h.*
Rev. 4:1 *c. up hither* 11:12; 17:1;
21:9

COME in *or* **into.**

Gen. 19.31 not a man to *c. in*
24:31 *c. in* thou blessed of Lord
Num. 27:21 his word shall *c. in*
Deut. 31:2 I can no more *c. in*
Jos. 14:11 my strength to *c. in*
1 *K.* 1:14 I will *c. in* after thee
3:7 I know not how to *c. in* or
14:6 *c. in* thou wife of Jeroboam
15:17 any to go out or *c. in*
2 *K.* 4:4 when *c. in*, shut door
11:9 each his men to *c. in* and
2 *Chr.* 1:10 and *c. in* before peo.
16:1 none go out or *c. in* to A.
23:6 *c. into* house, save priests
Neh. 2:7 till I *c. into* Judah
Est. 6:5 said, let Haman *c. in*
Ps. 24:7 king of glory *c. in*, 9
69:1 for the waters are *c. in*
96:8 and *c. into* his courts
Is. 19:1 Lord shall *c. into* Egypt
19:23 Assyrian sh. *c. into* E.
24:10 no man *c. in*
Jer. 17:19 kings of Judah *c. in*
51:50 Jerus. *c. into* your mind
Mic. 5:5 Assyrian shall *c. into*
Mat. 16:27 Son of man sh. *c. in*
24:5 many sh. *c. in* my name,
Mark 13:6; *Luke* 21:8
25:31 Son of man shall *c. in*
Luke 11:33 wh. *c. in* may see

Luke 12:46 *c. in* a d. he look. n.
14:23 compel them to *c. in*
John 5:43 I am *c. in* my Father's
name, if another shall *c.*
6:14 prophet, that sh. *c.* 11:27
Acts 16:15 *c. into* my house
Rom. 11:25 fulness of G. be *c. in*
1 *Cor.* 14:23 *c. in* those unlearned
24 if *c. in* one believeth not
Jam. 2:2 there *c. in* a poor man
Rev. 3:20 *c. in* to him, and sup

COME near.

Gen. 20:4 Abime. had not *c. n.*
Ex. 16:9, say *c. n.* bef. the L.
Num. 16:5 cause him to *c. near*
1 *Sam.* 10:20 tribes to *c. near*
Ps. 32:9 lest they *c. n.* thee
119:169 let my cry *c. near* thee
Is. 41:1 *c. near* to judgment
48:16 *c.* ye near hear ye this

50:8 mine adversary ? *c. near*
Ezek. 40:46 *c. near* to L. to min
44:15 *c. near* to me to minister
Mal. 3:5 *c. near* to you to judg.
Luke 19:41 *c. near* he beheld city
Acts 23:15 or ever he *c. near*

COME nigh.

Ex. 34:30 were afraid to *c. n.*
Lev. 10:3 he sanc. in all *c. nigh*
Luke 10:9 kingdom of G. *c. n.* 11

COME not.

Ex. 24:2 they shall *not c.* nigh
Num. 16:12 we will n. *c.* up, 14
Jos. 3:4 *c. not* near unto ark
23:7 ye *c. not* among nations
2 *Sam.* 14:29 Joab would *not c.*
2 *K.* 19:32 king of Assyria *not c.*
into city, 33; *Is.* 37:33, 34
2 *Chr.* 35:21 I *c. not* against thee
Ezr. 10:8 *not c.* within
Job 3:16 hypocrite *n. c.* before
Ps. 32:6 they shall *not c.*
63:27 let them *not c.* into
91:7 it shall *not c.* nigh thee
Prov. 5:8 *c. not* nigh door of h.
Is. 1. shall bring days *not c.*
32:10 gathering shall *not c.*
54:14 terror shall *not c.* near
65:5 which say, *c. not* near me
Ezek. 16:16 things shall *not c.*
Hos. 4:15 *c. not* ye unto Gilgal
9:4 soul shall *n. c.* into house
Zec. 14:18 if fam. of E. *c. not*
Mat. 22:3 and they would *not c.*
Mark 2:4 not for pr. *Luke* 8:19
Luke 14:20 married, I cannot *c.*
John 5:24 *not c.* into condemn.
40 *not c.* that ye might
7:34 thither ye *cannot c.* 36
15:22 if I had *not c.* not had sin
16:7 the Comforter will *not c.*
1 *Cor.* 4:18 as tho. I would *not c.*

COME out.

Gen. 15:14 *c. o.* with substance
17.6 kings *c. out* of thee, 35:11
Num. 11:20 it *c. out* at nostrils
12:4 *c. out* ye three to tabern.
22.5 people *c. out* of Egypt, 11
Deut. 28:7 *c. out* one way
Jud. 9:29 in. army and *c. out*
1 *Sam.* 11:3 to mor. will *c. out*, 10
24:14 after whom is king *c. out* ?
2 *Sam.* 16:7 *c. out*, bloody man
1 *K.* 6:1 480th year after Isr. *c. o.*
20:17 men *c. out* of Samaria
2 *K.* 5:11 he will *c. out* to me
18:31 agree. and *c. out*, *Is.* 36:16
Ps. 14:7 O that salva. *c. out* of Z.
68:31 princes shall *c. out* of E.
Nah. 1:11 one *c. out* imagineth
Mat. 5:26 not *c. out* till thou hast
26:55 are ye *c. out* as ag. a thief ?
Mark 14:48 ; *Luke* 22:52
Mark 1:25 *c. o.* of him, *Luke* 4:35
5:8 *c. out* unclean, *Luke* 8:29
John 1:46 any good *c. out* of N.
7:41 Christ *c. out* of Galilee ?
Acts 16:18 to *c. out* of her
Rom. 11:26 *c. out* of Zion Deliv.
2 *Cor.* 6:17 *c. out* from among
Heb. 7:5 *c. out* of loins of Abra.
Rev. 16:13 spirits *c. out* of drag.
18:4 *c. out* of her, my people

COME to pass.

Num. 11:23 my word *c. to p.*
Deut. 13:2 wonder *c. to pass*
Jos. 23:14 all *c. to pass*
Jud. 13:12 M. said, words *c. to p.*
21:3 why is this *c. to pass*
1 *K.* 13:32 saying shall *c. to pass*
Is. 7:7 not stand, nor *c. to p.*
14:24 so shall it *c. to p.*
42:9 former things are *c. to p.*
Jer. 32:24 has spoken is *c. to p.*
Ezek. 12:25 I speak shall *c. to p.*
24:14 spoken, it shall *c. to p.*

Dan. 2:29 what shall *c. to p.*
Zec. 6:15 this shall *c. to p.*
7:13 *c. to pass* that as he **cried**
Mat. 24:6 these must *c. to pass*
Mark 11:23 th. he saith sh. *c. to* **p**
13:29 see these things *c. to p.*
Luke 2:15 see this thing *c. to p.*
21:7 when these *c. to pass ?* 28
24:12 wond. at what was *c. to p.*
18 not known things *c. to pass*
John 13:19 *c. to p.* may b. 14:29
Rev. 1:1 must shortly *c. to pass*

COME short.

Rom. 3:23 all *c. sh.* of glory of G.
Heb. 4:1 seem to *c. short* of it

COME together

Job 9:32 should *c. t.* in judgment
19:12 troops *c. t.* against me
Jer. 3:18 *c. t.* out of land of north
50:4 Israel and Judah shall *c. t.*
Acts 1:6 wh. they were *c. t.* 28:17
10:27 he found many *c. together*
19:32 knew not wherefore. *c. t.*
21:22 multitude must needs *c. t.*
1 *Cor.* 7:5 *c. together* again,
11:17 you *c. t.* not for the better
18 when ye *c. t.* 20, 33 ; 14:26
34 ye *c. not t.* to condemna.
14:23 if whole church be *c. t.*

COME up.

Ex. 19:24 *c. up* thou and Aaron
24:12 *c. up* to me into mount
33:5 I will *c. up* in a moment
34:3 no man shall *c. up* with
Num. 20:5 why *c. up* out of E.
Jos. 10:6 *c. up* to us quickly
Jud. 1:3 Jud. said *c. up* with me
15:10 why are ye *c. up* ag. us ?
16:18 Del. sent, *c. up* this once
1 *Sam.* 14:10 if they say *c. up*
17:25 seen man that is *c. up ?*
1 *K.* 1:35 then *c. up* after him
20:22 will *c. up* against thee
2 *K.* 18:25 am I *c. u. Is.* 36:10
Job 7:9 to grave *c. up* no more
Prov. 25:7 better said, *c. up*
Is. 8:7 *c. up* over his channels
14:8 no feller is *c. up* against us
60:7 *c. up* with acceptance
Jer. 49:19 he shall *c. up*, 50:44
22 shall *c. up* and fly as eagle
Ezek. 38:16 *c. up* aga. my people
Hos. 1:11 shall *c. up* out of land
13:15 wind of the L. shall *c. up*
Ob. 21 saviors shall *c. up* on Z.
Zec. 14:17 whose will not *c. up*
18 if family of Egypt *c. not up*
Acts 8:31 Philip to *c. up* and sit
10:4 Cornel. the alms are *c. up*
Rev. 4:1 *c. up hither*, 11:12

COME, passive.

Gen. 6:13 the end of all flesh is *c.*
18:5 are ye *c.* to your servant
21 accord. to cry wh. *c.* to me
Ex. 3:9 cry of Israel is *c.* to me
Num. 22:11 there is a people *c.*
Jos. 5:14 as captain am I *c.*
Jud 16:2 Samson is *c. hither*
1 *Sam.* 4: i G. is *c.* into the **camp**
9:16 bec. their cry is *c.* to me
2 *K.* 8:7 man of God is *c. hither*
Ezr. 9:13 after all that is *c.*
Job 3:25 thing I feared is *c.* 4:5
Ps. 44:17 all this is *c.* on us, yet
53:6 O that salvation were *c.*
55:5 fear. and trembling are *c*
69:2 I am *c.* into deep waters
102:13 yea, the set time is *c.*
Is. 10:28 he is *c.* to Aiath
56:1 my salvation near to *c*
60:1 shine, for thy light is *c.*
63:4 year of my redeemed is *c.*
Jer. 40:3 theref. this is *c.* on you
50:27 their day is *c.*
31 thy day is *c.* I will visit thee
51:13 on waters, thy end is *c.*

Lam. 4:18 our end is *c.*
5:1 rememb. what is *c.* upon us
Ezek. 7:2 an end is *c.* on land, 6
   7 the morning is *c.* upon thee
   10 day, behold it is *c.* 39:8
21:25 whose day is *c.* 29
Dan. 9:13 all this evil is *c.* on us
Amos 8:2 the end is *c.* on Israel
Mic. 1:9 *c.* to gate of my people
Mat. 12:28 kingdom of God is *c.*
18:11 Son of man is *c.* to save
Mark 14:41 hour is *c.*
Luke 19:10 *c.* to seek and to save
John 4:25 is *c.* he will tell us all
11:28 Master is *c.* and calleth
12:23 J. answ. the hour is *c.* 17:1
1 *Cor.* 13:10 when that perf. is *c.*
Col. 1:6 which gospel is *c.* to you
1 *John* 4:3 that confesseth n. C.
   is *c.* in the flesh, 2 *John* 7

1 *John* 5:20 we k. Son of G. is *c.*

I am COME, *or* am I COME
Ex. 18:6 I Jethro am *c.* to thee
Num. 22:38 Bal. said, lo, *I am c.*
2 *Sam.* 14:32 am *I c.* fr. Gesh. ?
Ps. 69:2 *I am c.* into deep wat.
Ec. 1:16 lo, *I am c.*
Dan. 9:23 *I am c.* to show, 10:14
10:12 *I am c.* for thy words
Mat. 5:17 *I am c.* to destroy law
9:13 *I am* not *c.* to call right.
10:34 not *I am c.* to send peace
   35 *I am c.* to set at variance
Luke 12:51 *I am c.* to give peace ?
John 1:31 therefore *am I c.*
5:43 *I am c.* in my F.'s name
7:28 *I am* not *c.* of myself
9:39 for judgment *I am c.*
10:10 *I am c.* th. might ha. life
12:46 *I am c.* a light into world
16:28 *I am c.* again I leave wor.

COME, joined with Time.
Gen. 30:33 answer in *t.* to come
Ex. 13:14 asketh in *time* to c.
   Deut. 6:20 ; *Jos.* 4:6, 21
Ps. 102:13 the set *time* is c.
Prov. 31:25 rejoice in *t.* to c.
Cant. 2:12 *t.* of sing. of birds *c.*
Is. 13:22 her *time* is near to c.
30:8 be for *time* to c.
42:23 will hear for *time* to c. ?
Ezek. 7:7 *t.* is *c.* 12 ; *Hag.* 1:2
   not *c.*
Luke 9:51 *t.* he sh. be received
Gal. 4:4 when fulness of *t.* w. *c.*
1 *Tim.* 6:19 founda. aga. *t.* to c.
1 *Pet.* 4:17 *t.* is *c.* judgm. must b.

Yet COME.
Deut. 12:9 not *yet c.* to the rest
John 2:4 my hour is not *yet c.*
7:6 my time is not *yet c.*
   30 hour was not *yet c.* 8:20
11:30 J. was not *y. c.* into town
Rev. 17:10 the other is not *yet c.*

COMELINESS.
Is. 53:2 hath no form nor *c.*
Ezek. 16:14 perfect through my *c.*
27:10 they of Lud set fo. thy *c.*
Dan. 10:8 my *c.* into corruption
1 *Cor.* 12:23 more abundant *c.*

COMELY.
1 *Sam.* 16:18 David a *c.* person
Job 41:12 con. his *c.* proportion
Ps. 33:1 praise is *c.* for, 147:1
Prov. 30:29 four are *c.* in going
Ec. 5:18 it is *c.* for one to eat
Cant. 1:5 I am black, but *c.*
   10 cheeks are *c.* with jewels
2:14 thy countenance is *c.*
4:3 thy speech is *c.*
6:4 art *c.* O my love, as Jerus.
Is. 4:2 the fruit shall be *c.*
Jer. 6:2 daugh. of Zion to a *c.* w.
1 *Cor.* 7:35 I speak for that *c.*
12:24 *c.* parts have no need

COMERS.
Heb. 10:1 *c.* thereunto perfect

COMEST.
Deut. 28:6 blessed when thou *c.*
   19 cursed when thou *c.* in
Jud. 17:9 Mic. said, whence *c.*
   19:17 old man said, whence *c.*
1 *Sam.* 16:4 *c.* peacea. ? 1 *K.* 2:13
   17:45 thou *c.* to me w. a sword
2 *K.* 5:25 whence *c.* th. Gehazi ?
Job 1:7 whence *c.* thou ? 2:2
Jon. 1:8 whence *c.* thou ?
Mat. 3:14 and *c.* thou to me ?
Luke 23:42 wh. *c.* into thy king.

COMETH.
Deut. 23:13 that *c.* from thee
1 *Sam.* 4:3 when ark *c.*
9:6 all he saith *c.* surely to pass
20:29 he *c.* not to king's table
Job 28:20 wh. then *c.* wisdom ?
Ps. 30:5 but joy *c.* in morning
75:6 promotion *c.* not from east
96:13 for he *c.* to judge
118:26 blessed is he *c.* in name
121:2 my help *c.* from the Lord
Ec. 6:4 he *c.* in with vanity
Cant. 2:8 he *c.* leaping on mou.
Is. 13:9 day of L. *c.* with wrath
30:27 name of L. *c.* from far
62:11 Zion thy salvation *c.*
63:1 who is this *c.* from Edom
Jer. 17:6 not see when good *c.*
43:11 *c.* he shall smite Egypt
Lam. 3:37 and it *c.* to pass
Ezek. 20:32 *c.* in your mind
21:7 because it *c.* behold it *c.*
24:24 when this *c.* kn. I am L.
33:31 they come as people *c.*
33 when this *c.* to pass, then
Dan. 12:12 *c.* to 1,335 days

Joel 2:1 day of L. *c.* Zec. 14:1 ;
   Thes. 5:2
Mal. 4:1 day *c.* that shall burn
Mat. 3:11 he that *c.* after is mig.
   Mark 1:7 ; *Luke* 3:16
5:37 more than these *c.* of evil
8:9 come, and he *c.* *Luke* 7:8
21:5 thy king *c.* *John* 12:15
   9 ble. is he *c.* in name of Lord,
   Mark 11:9 ; *Luke* 13:35 ; 19:38
25:19 after long time Lord *c.*
Mark 8:38 when he *c.* in glory
9:12 Elias *c.* first and restoreth
14:43 while he spake *c.* Judas
Luke 6:47 whoso *c.* to me, and
12:37 he *c.* shall find watching
   40 *c.* at an hour ye think not
43 when he *c.* shall find
55 will be heat, and it *c.*
17:20 *c.* not with observation
18:8 *c.* shall he find faith
John 3:8 canst not tell wh. it *c.*
   20 nor *c.* to the light
4:21 woman, hour *c.* 23 ; 16:32
6:35 *c.* to me never hunger, 37
45 learned of Father, *c.* to me
7:27 C. *c.* no man knoweth, 31
   42 Christ *c.* of seed of David
9:4 night *c.* no man can work
14:6 no man *c.* to Father but
16:32 hour *c.* ye shall be scat.
Acts 10:32 when he *c.* shall speak
1 *Cor.* 15:24 then *c.* the end
2 *Cor.* 11:28 beside wh. *c.* on me
1 *Thes.* 5:2 day of L. *c.* as a thief
Heb. 11:6 *c.* to G. must believe
Jude 14 L. *c.* with 10,000 saints
Rev. 1:7 he *c.* with clouds
17:10 *c.* continue a short space

COMETH down.
Is. 55:10 rain *c. d.* from heaven
John 6:33 he *c.* *down,* 50
Jam. 1:17 every good gift *c. d.*
Rev. 3:12 new Jeru. which *c. d.*

COMETH forth.
Ex. 4:14 *c. forth* to meet thee

Jud. 11:31 *c. forth* of doors
1 *Sam.* 11:7 *c.* not *f.* after S.
Job 5:6 affliction *c.* not *forth*
   14:2 he *c. forth* like a flower
Is. 28:29 this also *c. forth*
Ezek. 33:30 what word *c. forth*
Mic. 1:3 L. *c. f.* out of his place

COMETH nigh.
Num. 1:51 stranger that *c. n.* be
   put to death, 3:10, 38 ; 18:7

COMETH out.
Deut. 28:57 young one *c. out*
Is. 26:21 Lord *c. out* of his place
42:5 earth, and what *c. out*
Mat. 15:11 *c. out* of mouth, this
   defileth a man, *Mark* 7:20

COMETH up.
1 *Sam.* 28:14 an old man *c. up*
Cant. 8:5 *c.* up. from wilderness ?
Jer. 46:7 that *c. up* as a flood ?
50:3 out of north *c. up* a nation

COMFORT.
Job 6:10 then should I yet have *c.*
10:20 alone that I may take *c.*
Ps. 119:50 my *c.* in affliction
   76 let kindness be for my *c.*
Is. 57:6 sh. I receive *c.* in these?
Ezek. 16:54 thou art a *c.* to them
Mat. 9:22 be of good *c.* *Luke* 8:48
Mark 10:49 be of g. *c.* he calleth
Acts 9:31 walking in *c.* of H. G.
Rom. 15:4 *c.* of the scriptures
1 *Cor.* 14:3 speaketh to ex. and *c.*
2 *Cor.* 1:3 blessed be God of all *c.*
   4 *c.* wherewith we are comfort.
7:4 I am filled with *c.*
   13 were comforted in your *c.*
13:11 brethren, be of good *c.*
Phil. 2:1 if any *c.* of love
   19 of good *c.* when I know
Col. 4:11 been *c.* to me

COMFORT, Verb.
Gen. 5:29 *c.* us concerning work
18:5 *c.* ye your hearts
27:42 Esau doth *c.* himself
37:35 sons rose to *c.* him
Jud. 19:5 *c.* heart with bread, 8
2 *Sam.* 10:2 David sent to *c.* him
1 *Chr.* 7:22 came to *c.* him
Job 2:11 friends came to *c.* him
7:13 say, My bed shall *c.* me
9:27 if I say, I will *c.* myself
21:34 how then *c.* ye me in vain
Ps. 23:4 thy staff, they *c.* me
71:21 shalt *c.* me on every side
119:82 when wilt thou *c.* me ?
Cant. 2:5 *c.* me with apples
Is. 22:4 labor not to *c.* me
40:1 *c.* ye, *c.* ye my people

Is. 51:3 L. shall *c.* Zion, *c.* was.
   19 by whom shall I *c.* thee ?
61:2 to *c.* all that mourn
66:13 so will I *c.* you in Jeru.
Jer. 8:18 when I would *c.* myself
16:7 nor men tear to *c.* them
31:13 I will *c.* and make rejoice
Lam. 1:2 hath none to *c.* her, 17
   21 there is none to *c.* me
2:13 equal, that I may *c.* thee ?
Ezek. 14:23 *c.* when ye see ways
Zec. 1:17 Lord shall yet *c.* Zion
10:2 they *c.* in vain
John 11:19 to *c.* them concerning
2 *Cor.* 1:4 may be able to *c.* them
2:7 ye ought rather to comfort
Eph. 6:22 might *c.* your hearts
Col. 4:8 and *c.* your hearts
1 *Thes.* 3:2 to *c.* you conc. faith
4:18 *c.* one another
5:11 wherefore *c.* yourselves
   14 *c.* the feeble-minded
2 *Thes.* 2:17 L. J. *c.* your hearts

COMFORTABLE.
2 *Sam.* 14:17 w. of L. now be *c.*
Zec. 1:13 L. answ. with *c.* words

COMFORTABLY.

2 *Sam.* 19:7 speak *c.* to thy serv.
2 *Chr.* 30:22 spake *c.* to Levites
32:6 set captains, and spake *c.*
Is. 40:2 speak ye *c.* to Jerusalem
Hos. 2:14 I will speak *c.* to her

COMFORTED.

Gen. 24:67 Isaac was *c.*
37:35 Jacob refused to be *c.*
38:12 Judah was *c.*
50:21 Joseph *c.* his brethren
Ruth 2:13 for hast *c.* me
2 *Sam.* 12:24 David *c.* Bath-sheba
13:39 he was *c.* concerning A.
Job 42:11 brethren *c.* him.
Ps. 77:2 my soul refused to be *c.*
86:17 bec. thou L. hast *c.* me
119:52 and have *c.* myself
Is. 49:13 God *c.* his people, 52:9
54:11 Oh thou afflicted, not *c.*
66:13 shall be *c.* in Jerusalem
Jer. 31:15 Rachel refused to be *c.*
Ezek. 5:13 fury to rest, I w. be *c.*
14:22 be *c.* concerning
31:16 all that drink water be *c.*
32:31 Pharaoh shall be *c.*
Mat. 2:18 not be *c.* bec. were not
5:4 mourn, for they shall be *c.*
Luke 16:25 he is *c.* thou torm.
John 11:31 the Jews which *c.* her
Acts 16:40 seen brethren, *c.* them
20:12 brought man alive, were *c.*
Rom. 1:12 I may be *c.* with you
1 *Cor.* 14:31 and all be *c.*
2 *Cor.* 1:4 we are *c.* of God
7:6 God *c.* us by coming of Titus
7 consola. wh. he was *c.* in you
13 we are *c.* in your comfort
Col. 2:2 hearts be *c.* being knit
1 *Thes.* 2:11 know how he *c.* you
3:7 we were *c.* in our affliction

COMFORTEDST.

Is. 12:1 and thou *c.* me.

COMFORTER, S.

2 *Sam.* 10:3 sent *c.* 1 *Chr.* 19:3
Job 16:2 miserable *c.* are ye all
Ps. 69:20 I looked for *c.* but
Ec. 4:1 oppressed, had no *c.*
Lam. 1:9 she had no *c.*
16 *c.* that should relieve is far
Nah. 3:7 whence shall I seek *c.*
John 14:16 give you another *C.*
26 *C.* which is the Holy Ghost
15:26 when the *C.* is come
16:7 *C.* will not come

COMFORTETH.

Job 29:25 as one that *c.* mourners
Is. 51:12 I am he that *c.* you
66:13 as one his mother *c.* so
2 *Cor.* 1:4 who *c.* us in tribula.
7:6 God that *c.* those cast down

COMFORTLESS.

John 14:18 I will not leave you *c.*

COMFORTS.

Ps. 94:19 thy *c.* delight my soul
Is. 57:18 and restore *c.* to him.

COMING.

Gen. 30:30 since my *c.*
Num. 22:16 let noth. hinder *c.*
Jud. 5:28 chariot so long in *c.* ?
1 *Sam.* 16:4 trembled at his *c.*
29:6 thy *c.* in with me is good
2 *Sam.* 3:25 to know thy *c.* in
2 *K.* 19:27 know thy *c.* *Is.* 37:28
Ps. 37:13 seeth his day is *c*
121:8 L. shall preserve thy *c.* in
Is. 44:7 things *c.* let them show
Jer. 8:7 observe time of their *c.*
Mic. 7:15 accord. to days of thy *c.*

Mal. 3:2 abide day of his *c.* ?
4:5 before *c.* of the great day
Mat. 16:28 till see Son of man *c.*
24:3 shall be sign of thy *c.* ?
27 *c.* of Son of man be, 37, 39

30 Son of man *c.* 26:64; *Mark*
13:26; 14:62; *Luke* 21:27
48 Lord delayeth *c.* *Luke* 12:45
25:27 at *c.* received my own,
Luke 19:23
Mark 6:31 many *c.* and going
Luke 18:5 continual *c.* she w. me
John 5:7 I am *c.* another step.
25 hour is *c.* 28; 10:12 wolf *c.*
Acts 7:52 before *c.* of Just One
9:28 Saul was with them *c.* in.
13:24 preached before his *c.*
1 *Cor.* 1:7 waiting for *c.* of L. J.
15:23 that are Christ's at his *c.*
16:17 glad of *c.* of Stephanas
2 *Cor.* 7:6 G. comf. us by *c.* of T.
7 not by his *c.* only
Phil. 1:26 abundant, by my *c.*
1 *Thes.* 2:19 rejoicing at his *c.* ?
3:13 unblameable at *c.* of Lord
4:15 which remain to *c.* of L.
5:23 blameless to *c.* of our Lord
2 *Thes.* 2:1 we beseech by *c.* of L.
8 destroy with brightness of *c.*
9. *c.* is after working of Satan
Jam. 5:7 be patient to *c.* of Lord
8 *c.* of Lord draweth nigh
1 *Pet.* 2:4 *c.* as unto a live stone
2 *Pet.* 1:16 power and *c.* of L. J.
3:4 the promise of his *c.* ?
12 hasting to *c.* of day of God
1 *John* 2:28 not be ash. at his *c.*
Rev. 13:11 another beast *c.* up
21:2 new Jer. *c.* down from G.

COMINGS.

Ezek. 43:11 show them the *c.* in

COMMAND, Substantive.

Job 39:27 eagle mount at thy *c.*

COMMAND, Verb.

Gen. 18:19 Ab. will *c.* children
Ex. 18:23 and God *c.* thee so
Num. 9:8 I will hear what L. *c.*
36:6 the thing Lord doth *c.*
Deut. 28:8 Lord *c.* blessing
32:46 *c.* children to observe
Jos. 11:15 so did Moses *c.* Joshua
Ps. 42:8 L. *c.* his loving-kindness
44:4 *c.* deliverance for Jacob
Is. 45:11 work of my hands, *c.*
Jer. 27:4 *c.* to say to masters
Lam. 1:10 *c.* should not enter
Mat. 19:7 why did Moses *c.*
27:64 *c.* sepulchre be made sure
Mark 10:3 what did Moses *c.* you
Luke 8:31 not *c.* to go into deep
9:54 wilt thou we *c.* fire
Acts 5:28 we straitly *c.* you
15:5 to *c.* to keep law of Moses
2 *Thes.* 3:4 will do things we *c.*
6 we *c.* you in name of Lord
12 such we *c.* and exhort
1 *Tim.* 4:11 these things *c.*

I COMMAND.

Ex. 7:2 all I *c.* *Jer.* 1:7, 17
34:11 obs. what I *c.* *Deut.* 12:28
Lev. 25:21 I will *c.* my blessing
Deut. 4:2 not add to word I *c.* you
7:11 wh. I *c.* 8:11; 10:13; 11:8,
27; 13:18; 30:8
24:18 I *c.* thee to do this, 22
30:16 I *c.* thee this day love L.
Jer. 11:4 do all which I *c.* you
Amos 9:9 I will *c.* and sift house
John 15:14 if ye do what I *c.* you
17 I *c.* you, that ye love
Acts 16:18 I *c.* thee in na. of J.

COMMANDED.

Gen. 50:12 J.'s sons did as he *c.*
Ex. 1:17 did not as k. *c.*
Deut. 1:18 I *c.* you, 3:18
Jos. 4:8 child. of I. did as J. *c.*
22:2 obeyed my voice in all I *c.*
Jud. 13:14 all I *c.* let her observe
1 *Sam.* 20:29 *c.* me to be there
21:2 the king *c.* me a business

2 *Sam.* 21:14 perform all king *c.*
2 *K.* 11:9 accor. to all Jehoiada *c.*
16:16 according to all Ahaz *c.*
2 *Chr.* 8:14 so had David *c.*
14:4 Asa *c.* Judah to seek Lord
32:12 Hezekiah; 33:16 Manas.
Est. 4:17 Mord. did as Esther *c.*
8:9 writ. accor. to all Mord. *c.*
Job 38:12 hast thou *c.* morning
Jer. 35:6 Jon. *c.* us, 10,14, 16, 18
Ezek. 12:7 I did as I was *c.* 37:7
Dan. 3:4 to you it is *c.* O people
Mat. 14:19 *c.* multitude to sit,
15:35; *Mark* 6:39
18:25 his lord *c.* him to be sold
21:6 disciples did as Jesus *c.*
Mat. 28:20 teac. to observe all I *c.*
Luke 9:21 *c.* them to tell no man
Acts 25:6 Festus *c.* Paul to be b.
1 *Cor.* 14:34 *c.* to be under obed.
1 *Thes.* 4:11 work as we *c.*
Heb. 12:20 not endure that *c.*

God COMMANDED.

Gen. 6:22 according to al. *G. c.*
7:9 as *God* had *c.* 16; 21:4;
Deut. 30:17; *Jos.* 10:40
Deut. 5:32 observe to do as *God c.*
6:1 *God c.* to teach 20; 13:5
26:16 day *God c.* thee to keep
1 *Chr.* 14:16 David did as *God c.*
Ezr. 7:23 whatsoever is *c.* by *G.*
Ps. 68:28 *God* hath *c.* thy str.
Acts 10:33 all *c.* thee of God
2 *Cor.* 4:6 *God* who *c.* light shine

Lord COMMANDED.

2 *Sam.* 24:19 D. went up as *L. c.*
Ps. 106:34 whom *L. c.* them
133:3 for there *L. c.* blessing
Lam. 1:17 L. hath *c.* concern. J.
Acts 13:47 turn to Gent. so *L. c.*

Lord or God COMMANDED, implicitly

Ex. 23:15 as I *c.* in time ap.
Deut. 17:3 I have not *c.* 18:20;
Jer. 19:5; 23:32; 29:23
Jos. 1:9 have not I *c.* thee ? be
1 *K.* 11:10 *c.* Sol. concerning this
1 *Chr.* 16:15 word he *c.* to 1000
generations, *Ps.* 105:8
Ps. 7:6 awake to judgm. hast *c.*
33:9 he *c.* and it stood fast
111:9 he hath *c.* his covenant
119:4 *c.* us to keep thy precepts
138 testimonies hast *c.* are r.
148:5 he *c.* they were created
Is. 13:3 *c.* my sanctified ones
34:16 for my mouth it hath *c.*
45:12 heavens and host have I *c.*
Jer. 7:31 I *c.* not, 19:5; 32:35
Lam. 2:17 he *c.* in days of old
Ezek. 9:11 I have done as thou *c.*
24:18 I did in morn. as *c.* 37:10
Zec. 1:6 words I *c.* did they not
Mal. 4:4 rem. law I *c.* in Horeb
Luke 14:22 Lord, it is done as *c.*
Acts 10:42 he *c.* us to preach

Moses COMMANDED.

Deut. 31:29 turn from way I *c.*
33:4 *Moses c.* us a law, even
Jos. 1:7 observe to do all *Moses c.*
22:2 ye have kept all *Moses c.*
Mat. 8:4 offer the gift *Moses c.*
Mark 1:44 of. for thy cleansing
things *Moses c. Luke* 5:14
John 8:5 *Moses c.* such be stoned

COMMANDEDST.

Neh. 9:14 thou *c.* them precepts
Jer. 32:23 done nothing thou *c.*

COMMANDER.

Is. 55:4 and *c.* to the people

COMMANDEST.

Jos. 1:16 all thou *c.* us we will do
18 not hearken in all thou *c.*
Jer. 32:23 done nothing of all *c.*
Acts 23:3 *c.* me to be smitten

COMMANDETH.

Num. 32:25 will do as my lord *c.*
Job 9:7 *c.* sun, and it riseth not
37:12 may do whatever he *c.*
Lam. 3:37 when L. *c.* not ?
Mark 1:27 *c.* spirits, *Luke* 4:36
Acts 17:30 *c.* all men to repent

COMMANDING.

Gen. 49:33 Jacob an end of *c.*
Mat. 11:1 Jesus made end of *c.*

COMMANDMENT.

Ex. 34:32 *c.* all L. had spoken
Num. 15:31 broken *c.* be cut off
23:20 have received *c.* to bless
27:14 rebelled against my *c.*
Deut. 30:11 this *c.* I command
1 *K.* 2:43 why hast not kept *c.*
1 *Chr.* 12:32 were at their *c.*
28:21 people will be at thy *c.*
2 *Chr.* 19:10 between law and *c.*
30:12 one heart to do *c.* of king
31:5 as soon as *c.* came abroad
Ezr. 8:17 I sent with *c.* to Iddo
10:3 of those tremble at *c.*
Neh. 11:23 king's *c.* conc. them
Est. 1:12 refused to come at *c.*
3:3 why transgressest king's *c.* ?
9:1 when king's *c.* drew nigh
Job 23:12 nor gone back from *c.*
Ps. 119:96 *c.* exceeding broad
147:15 forth his *c.* upon earth
Prov. 6:23 the *c.* is a lamp
8:29 waters not pass his *c.*
13:13 feareth *c.* be rewarded
19:16 keepeth *c.* keepeth soul
Ec. 8:5 keepeth *c.* feel no evil

Jer. 35:14 obey their father's *c.*
Dan. 3:22 king's *c.* was urgent
9:23 the *c.* came forth, and I am
Hos. 5:11 he walked after *c.*
Mal. 2:1 O priests, *c.* is for you
4 I have sent this *c.* to you
Mat. 15:3 transgress *c.* of God ?
6 the *c.* of God of no effect
22:36 which is the great *c.*
38 this is great *c. Mark* 12:30
Mark 7:8 laying aside *c.* of God
9 full well ye reject *c.* of God
12:31 no *c.* greater than these
Luke 15:29 nor transgressed I *c.*
23:56 rested sab. accord. to *c.*
John 10:18 this *c.* I received of
12:49 what I should say
50 his *c.* is life everlasting
14:31 Father gave me *c.* so I do
15:12 *c.* that ye 1. 1 *John* 3:23
Acts 15:24 we gave no such *c.*
23:30 gave *c.* to his accusers
Rom. 7:8 occasion by the *c.* 11
9 *c.* came, sin revived
10 *c.* which was ordained to l.
12 *c.* is holy, just, and good
13:9 if any other *c.* it is
16:26 accord. to *c.* of everl. God
1 *Cor.* 7:6 I speak this, not of *c.*
2 *Cor.* 8:8 not by *c.* but by occa.
Eph. 6:2 first *c.* with promise
1 *Tim.* 1:1 by *c.* of G. *Tit.* 1:3
5 end of the *c.* is charity out of
Heb. 7:16 after law of a carnal *c.*
18 disannulling of the *c.*
11:23 not afraid of king's *c.*
2 *Pet.* 2:21 turn from holy *c.*
3:2 mindful of *c.* of us apos.
1 *John* 2:7 but an old *c.*
3:23 this is his *c.*
4:21 this *c.* have we from him,
2 *John* 4 received a *c.* from Fath.
6 this is the *c.*

Give or given COMMANDMENT.

Ex. 25:22 I will *give* in *c.*
Deut. 1:3 Lord had *g.* him in *c.*
Ezr. 4:21 *g. c.* till ano. *c.* be *g.*
Ps. 71:3 hast *given c.* to save
Is. 23:11 hath *g. c.* against city

Nah. 1:14 L. hath *g. c.* con. thee
John 11:57 *g. c.* if any knew

Keep COMMANDMENT.

See KEEP.

COMMANDMENT of the Lord

Num. 24:13 can. go bey. *c. of L.*
Jos. 22:3 charge of *c. of the L.*
1 *Sam.* 12:14 against *c. of the L.*
15 but rebel ag. *c. of the L.*
13:13 hast not kept *c. of the L.*
15:13 S. said, I perf. *c. of the L.*
24 I have trans. *c. of the L.*
2 *Sam.* 12:9 despised *c. of the L.*
2 *K.* 24:3 at *c. of L.* came on J.
2 *Chr.* 29:25 was *c. of the Lord*
Ps. 19:8 the *c. of the Lord* is pure
1 *Cor.* 7:25 I have no *c. of the L.*

New Commandment.

John 13:34 a *new c.* I give
1 *John* 2:7 no *new c.* ; 8 a *new c.*
2 *John* 5 not as tho' I wrote *n. c.*

Rebelled against the COMMANDMENT.

Num. 27:14 *rebelled against* my *c.*
Deut. 1:26 ye *r. a. c.* of L. 43
9:23 then ye *r. a. the c.* of Lord
Lam. 1:18 I have *reb. ag.* his *c.*

COMMANDMENTS.

Gen. 26:5 Abraham kept my *c.*
Ex. 15:26 if give ear to his *c.*
34:28 ten *c. Deut.* 4:13 ; 10:4
Lev. 4:13 against any *c.* 27
5:17 commit sin forbidden by *c.*
27:34 these are *c.* L. command.
Num. 15:39 rem. all *c.* of Lord
Deut. 8:11 in not keeping his *c.*
11:13 if you shall hearken to my
c. 28:13 ; *Jud.* 3:4
27 if ye will obey the *c.* of L.
28 if ye will not obey the *c.*
1 *Sam.* 15:11 Saul not perf. my *c.*
1 *K.* 11:34 b. he hath kept my *c.*
14:8 David who kept my *c.*
18:18 ye have forsaken *c.*
2 *K.* 17:16 they left all the *c.*
19 Judah kept not *c.* of the L.
18:6 kept his *c.* which he com.
2 *Chr.* 7:19 if ye forsake my *c.*
24:20 why transgress ye the *c.*
Ezr. 9:10 have forsaken thy *c.*
14 sh. we again break thy *c.*
Ps. 89:31 if they keep not my *c.*
111:7 all his *c.* are sure
112:1 blessed he delighteth in *c.*
119:10 not wander from *c.*

Ps. 119:19 hide not thy *c.* from me
35 to go in path of thy *c.*
47 I will delight in thy *c.*
66 for I have believed thy *c.*
73 that I may learn thy *c.*
86 *c.* are faithful ; 151 truth
98 through *c.* made me wiser
127 I love thy *c.* ; 131 I longed
143 thy *c.* my delights ; 172 right.
166 done thy *c. ;* 176 not forget
Prov. 2:1 wilt hide my *c.*
7:1 lay up my *c.* with thee
10:8 wise in heart will rec. *c.*
Is. 48:18 hadst hearkened to *c.*
Mat. 5:19 whoso. break least *c.*
15:9 teach. *c.* of men, *Mark* 7:7
22:40 on these two *c.* hang law
Mark 10:19 thou knowest *c.*
Luke 18:20
12:29 first of *c.* is, Hear, O Is.
Luke 1:6 walking in *c.* blameless
John 14:21 he that hath my *c.*
15:10 if keep my *c.* as I kept
1 *Cor.* 7:19 nothing, but keep. *c.*
14:37 things I write you are *c.*
Col. 2:22 *c.* and doctr. of men
1 *Thes.* 4:2 ye know *c.* we gave
1 *John* 2:4 keepeth not *c.* is a liar
3:24 that keepeth *c.* dwelleth
2 *John* 6 this is love, walk after *c.*

Do COMMANDMENTS

Num. 15:40 *do* all my *c.*
Deut. 6:25 to *do* all *c.* 15:5
1 *Chr.* 28:7 to *do* my *c.*
Ps. 103:18 that rem. his *c.* to *do*
111:10 understanding that *do c.*
Rev. 22:14 blessed are they *do c.*

Not do COMMANDMENTS.

Lev. 26:14 if ye will *not do c.*

See KEEP.

COMMEND.

Luke 23:46 into thy hands I *c.*
Acts 20:32 breth. I *c.* you to God
Rom. 3:5 unrigh. *c.* right. of G.
16:1 I *c.* unto you Phebe
2 *Cor.* 3:1 we begin again to *c.*
5:12 for we *c.* not ourselves
10:12 compare with some that *c.*

COMMENDATION.

2 *Cor.* 3:1 need we epistles of *c.*

COMMENDED.

Gen. 12:15 princes *c.* Sarai
Prov. 12:8 man *c.* accor. to wisd.
Ec. 8:15 then I *c.* mirth
Luke 16:8 Lord *c.* unjust steward
Acts 14:23 *c.* them to Lord
2 *Cor.* 12:11 have been a *c.* of you

COMMENDETH.

Rom. 5:8 God *c.* his love tow. us
1 *Cor.* 8:8 meat *c.* us not to God
2 *Cor.* 10:18 *c.* himself is approv.

COMMENDING.

2 *Cor.* 4:2 *c.* ourselves

COMMISSION, S.

Ezra 8:36 delivered the king's *c.*
Acts 26:12 as I went with *c.*

COMMIT.

Ex. 20:14 not *c.* adult. *Deut.* 5:18 ;
Mat. 5:27 ; 19:18 ; *Rom.* 13:9
Lev. 5:17 *c.* things forbidden
18:29 *c.* any of these abomina.
Num. 5:6 *c.* any sin that men *c.*
Deut. 19:20 *c.* no more such evil
2 *Chr.* 21:11 J. to *c.* fornication
Job 5:8 would I *c.* my cause
Ps. 31:5 thy hand I *c.* my spirit
37:5 *c.* thy way to the Lord
Prov. 16:3 *c.* thy works unto Lord
12 to kings to *c.* wickedness
Is. 22:21 I will *c.* thy government
Jer. 44:7 why *c.* ye this evil?
Ezek. 8:17 *c.* abomina. they *c.* h.
16:43 shalt not *c.* this lewdness
22:9 in midst of thee *c.* lewdness
Hos. 6:9 priests *c.* lewdness
7:1 for they *c.* falsehood
Luke 12:48 *c.* worthy of stripes
16:11 *c.* the true riches ?
John 2:24 Jes. did not *c.* himself
Rom. 1:32 *c.* such worthy of d.
2:2 is ag. them *c.* such things
22 dost thou *c.* sacrilege ?
1 *Cor.* 10:8 nei. let us *c.* fornica.
1 *Tim.* 1:18 charge I *c.* to thee
2 *Tim.* 2:2 *c.* to faithful men
Jam. 2:9 respect to persons ye *c.*
1 *Pet.* 4:19 *c.* keeping of souls
1 *John* 3:9 born of God, not *c.* sin
Rev. 2:14 taught Is. to *c.* fornica.
20 my servants to *c.* fornica.

See ADULTERY.

COMMIT iniquity.

2 *Sam.* 7:14 *c. i.* I will chasten
Job 34:10 Almighty he sh. *c. i.*
Jer. 9:5 weary th. to *c. iniquity*
Ezek. 3:20 right. and *c. i.* 33:13

COMMIT trespass.

Lev. 5:15 if a soul *c. t.* thro' ig.
Num. 5:12 if a man's wife *c. tres.*
31:16 caused Israel to *c. trespass*
Jos. 22:20 Achan *c.* a *trespass*

COMMIT whoredom, or whoredoms.

Lev. 20:5 that c. w. with Molech
Num. 25:1 to c. w. with dau. of M.
Ezek. 16:17 c. w. with images
34 followeth to c. whoredom
20:30 c. ye w. after their abo. ?
23:43 will they c. w. with her
Hos. 4:10 c. w. and not increase
13 your daugh. shall c. w. 14

COMMITTED

Gen. 39:8 c. all he hath to my h.
22 c. to Joseph the prisoners
Lev. 20:23 c. these and I abhorr.
Jud. 20:6 c. lewdness in Israel
1 K. 8:47 we have c. wickedness
14:22 with sins they c.
Jer. 2:13 my people c. two evils
5:30 a horrible thing is c.
16:10 what is our sin we c.
44:3 c. to provoke me, 9
Ezek. 16:26 hast also c. fornica.
51 nor Sam. c. half of thy sins
18:21 from sins he c. 22, 28
23:3 c. whored. in Eg. in youth
7 c. her whoredoms with them
33:16 none of sins he c.
Hos. 1:2 land hath c. great who.
4:18 they have c. whoredom
Mark 15:7 who had c. murder
Luke 12:48 have c. much, of him
John 5:22 c. all judgment to Son
Acts 8:3 c. them to prison
25:11 if I have c. any th. worthy
25 found he c. nothing worthy
27:40 c. themselves to the sea
28:17 c. nothing against people
Rom. 3:2 were c. oracles of God
2 Cor. 5:19 c. to us word of rec.
12:21 lasciviousness they c.
Gal. 2:7 gospel of the uncircum.
was c. to me, 1 Tim. 1:11
1 Tim. 6:20 what is c. to thee
2 Tim. 1:12 to keep what I c.
Jam. 5:15 if he c. sins be forgiv.
1 Pet. 2:23 c. himself to him jud.
Jude 15 ungodly deeds they c.
Rev. 18:17 c. forni. 18:3, 9

See ABOMINATIONS.

COMMITTED iniquity.

Ps. 106:6 we have c. iniquity
Ezek. 33:13 iniqui. he shall die
Dan. 9:5 c. i. and done wickedly

COMMITTED trespass.

Jos. 7:1 Is. c. t. in accurs. thing
22:16 what t. is this ye have c.
31 because not c. this t. aga. L.
Ezek. 15:8 have c. t. I will make
20:27 in that they c. a t. ag. me

COMMITTEST, ETH, ING.

Ps. 10:14 c. himself to thee
Ezek. 8:6 abomination Is. c.
33:15 without c. iniquity, 18
Hos. 4:2 by lying, c. adultery
5:3 O Ephraim, c. whoredom
John 8:34 c. sin, is servant of sin
1 Cor. 6:18 c. fornication sinneth
1 John 3:4 c. sin transgresseth l.
8 he that c. sin is of the devil

COMMODIOUS.

Acts 27:12 the haven was not c.

COMMON.

1 Sam. 21:4 there is no c. bread
Ec. 6:1 there is an evil, it is c.
Jer. 31:5 eat them as c. things
Ezek. 23:42 with men of c. sort
Acts 2:44 had all things c. 4:32
10:14 eaten any thing c. 11:8
15 cleansed, call not c. 11:9
28 should not call any man c.
1 Cor. 10:13 no temptation but c.
Tit. 1:4 my son after c. faith
Jude 3 to write of c. salvation

COMMON people.

Jer. 26:23 the graves of c. people

Mark 12:37 c. peo. heard him

COMMONLY. See REPORTED.

COMMONWEALTH.

Eph. 2:12 aliens from the c. of Is.

COMMOTION, S.

Jer. 10:22 a great c. out of north
Luke 21:9 when ye hear of c. be

COMMUNE.

Ex. 25:22 there c. with thee
1 Sam. 18:22 c. with D. secretly
1 Sam. 19:3 I will c. with my fa.
Job 4:2 if assay to c. with thee
Ps. 4:4 c. with your own heart
64:5 c. of laying snares privily
77:6 night I c. with my heart

COMMUNED.

Gen. 23:8 Abra. ; 34:6 Hamor, 8
42:24 Joseph ; Jud. 9:1 Abim.
1 Sam. 9:25 Samuel ; 25:39 David
1 K. 10:2 the queen of Sheba c.
with Solomon, 2 Chr. 9:1
2 K. 22:14 c. with Huldah
Ec. 1:16 I c. with my own heart
Dan. 1:19 king c. with them
Luke 6:11 c. what do to Jesus
24:15 while c. Jesus drew nigh
Acts 24:26 Felix c. the oftener

COMMUNICATE.

Gal. 6:6 c. to him that teacheth
Phil. 4:14 c. with my affliction
1 Tim. 6:18 be willing to c.
Heb. 13:16 and to c. forget not

COMMUNICATED.

Gal. 2:2 c. to them that gospel
Phil. 4:15 no church c. with me.

COMMUNICATION, S.

2 Sam. 3:17 A. had c. with elders
2 K. 9:11 ye know his c.
Mat. 5:37 let your c. be yea, yea
Luke 24:17 what manner of c.
1 Cor. 15:33 evil c. corrupt good
Eph. 4:29 no corrupt c. Col. 3:8
Phile. 6. c. of thy faith effectual

COMMUNING.

Gen. 18:33 left c. with Abraham
Ex. 31:18 an end of c. on Sinai

COMMUNION.

1 Cor. 10:16 c. of blood, c. of body
2 Cor. 6:14 wh. c. light with dark.
13:14 c. H. G. be with you all

COMPACT.

Ps. 122:3 Jerusalem is a city c.

COMPACTED.

Eph. 4:16 the whole body c.

COMPANY, Substantive.

Gen. 32:8 E. come to the one c.
35:11 c. of nations be of thee
Num. 16:16 thou and all thy c.
40 be not as Korah and his c.
22:4 this c. lick up all round
26:9 strove in c. of Korah, 27:3
Jud. 9:37 another c. by plain
18:23 comest with such a c. ?
1 Sam. 30:15 bring me to this c. ?
2 K. 5:15 his c. came to Elisha
9:17 he spied the c. of Jehu
2 Chr. 24:24 Syrians with small c.
Job 16:7 made desolate all my c.
34:8 in c. with workers of iniq.
Ps. 55:14 to house of God in c.
68:30 rebuke the c. of spearmen
106:17 covered c. of Abiram
18 fire was kindled in their c.
Prov. 29:3 keepeth c. with harl.
Cant. 1:9 to a c. of horses in Ph.
6:13 as it were c. of two armies
Ezek. 16:40 bring a c. against thee
23:46 I will bring a c. on them
32:22 Ashur is there and her c.
38:7 prepare, thou and thy c.
Hos. 6:9 so c. of priests murder
Luke 2:44 suppos. him in the c.
6:17 and c. of his disciples
22 separate you from their c.

9:14 sit by fifties in a c.
38 a man of the c. cried out
24:22 a woman of our c. made
Acts 4:23 went to their own c.
10:28 unl. for a Jew to keep c.
15:22 to send chosen men of c.
17:5 gathered a c. and set city
21:8 we of Paul's c. departed
Rom. 15:24 filled with your c.
1 Cor. 5:11 not to keep c. with
2 Thes. 3:14 have no c. with him
Heb. 12:22 an innum. c. of angels
Rev. 18:17 c. in ships afar off

Great COMPANY.

Gen. 50:9 with Joseph a great c.
2 Chr. 9:1 queen of S. with g. c.
20:12 no might ag. this great c.
Ps. 68:11 g. was c. of those pub.
Jer. 31:8 a great c. return thither
Ezek. 17:17 Pharaoh with great c.
John 6:5 saw a great c. come
Acts 6:7 g. c. of priests obedient

COMPANY, Verb.

1 Cor. 5:9 not to c. with fornica.

COMPANIED.

Acts 1:21 which have c. with us

COMPANIES.

Jud. 7:16 300 into three c.
1 Sam. 11:11 Saul put in three c.
13:17 spoilers in three c.
2 K. 5:2 Syrians gone by c.
Neh. 12:31 c. gave thanks, 40
Job 6:19 the c. of Sheba waited
Is. 21:13 O ye travelling c.
57:13 let thy c. deliver thee
Mark 6:39 to make all sit by c.

COMPANION.

Ex. 32:27 slay every man his c.
Jud. 14:20 S.'s wife to c. 15:6
1 Chr. 27:33 Hushai king's c.
Job 30:29 I am a c. to owls
Ps. 119:63 c. to all that fear thee
Prov. 13:20 c. of fools be destroy.
28:7 c. of riotous shameth fath.
24 same c. of a destroyer
Mal. 2:14 she is thy c. wife of
Phil. 2:25 Epaph. my c. in labor
Rev. 1:9 I John your c. in tribu.

COMPANIONS.

Jud. 11:38 went with c.
14:11 thirty c. to be with him
Job 34:4 will answer thee and c.
41:6 c. make a banquet of him ?
Ps. 45:14 her c. shall be brought
122:8 for my c. sake I will say
Cant. 1:7 aside by flocks of thy c.
8:13 c. hearken to thy voice
Is. 1:23 princes c. of thieves
Ezek. 37:16 Judah and Isr. his c.
Dan. 2:17 thing known to his c.
Acts 19:29 caught Paul's c.
Heb. 10:33 c. of them so used

COMPARABLE.

Lam. 4:2 sons of Zion c. to gold

COMPARE, ED, ING.

Ps. 89:6 who in heaven c. to L. ?
Prov. 3:15 not be c. 8:11
Cant. 1:9 I have c. thee
Is. 40:18 wh. likeness c. to him ?
46:5 to whom will ye c. me
Rom. 8:18 to be c. with the glory
1 Cor. 2:13 c. spiritual things
2 Cor. 10:12 c. ours. with some
that com. c. thems. amongst

COMPARISON.

Jud. 8:2 I done in c. of you ? 3
Hag. 2:3 in your eyes in c. of it
Mark 4:30 with what c. shall we

COMPASS.

2 Sam. 5:23 but fetch a c. behind
2 K. 3:9 fetched a c. of 7 days
Prov. 8:27 c. on face of the deep
Is. 44:13 marketh it with c.
Acts 28:13 fetched a c. to Rheg.

COMPASS, Verb.

Num. 21:4 c. the land of Edom
Jos. 6:3 ye shall c. the city
2 *K.* 11:8 c. the king: 2 *Chr.* 23:7
Job 16:13 his archers c. me about
40:22 willows of brook c. him
Ps. 5:12 with favor c. as a shield
7:7 congregation c. thee about
17:9 deadly enemies who c. me
26:6 so will I c. thine altar
32:7 c. me with songs of deliv.
10 trust. in Lord mercy c. him
49:5 iniquity of my heels c. me
140:9 as for head of those c. me
142:7 the righteous shall c. me
Is. 50:11 c. yoursel. with sparks
Jer. 31:22 a wom. shall c. a man
Hab. 1:4 wicked c. righteous
Mat. 23:15 for ye c. sea and land
Luke 19:43 thine enemies shall c.

COMPASSED.

Deut. 2:1 we c. Seir many days
Jos. 6:11 so the ark c. the city
Jud. 11:18 c. the land of Edom
16:2 they c. Samson in
1 *Sam.* 23:26 Saul c. David and
2 *Sam.* 22:5 when waves of death
   c. me, *Ps.* 18:4; 116:3
2 *K.* 6:15 behold a host c. city
2 *Chr.* 21:9 Edomites which c.
Job 19:6 God c. me with his net
26:10 c. waters with bounds
Ps. 17:11 now c. us in our steps
22:12 bulls c. me; 16 dogs
Lam. 3:5 c. me with gall and
Luke 21:20 when ye see Jer. c.
Heb. 5:2 himself c. with infirmity

COMPASSED about.

2 *Sam.* 18:15 c. Absalom *about*
22:6 c. me *ab. Ps.* 18:5
2 *K.* 6:14 Syrians c. city *about*
2 *Chr.* 18:31 c. about Jehoshaph.
Ps. 40:12 innum. evils c. me *ab.*
88:17 c. me *ab.* 109:3; 118:11, 12
118:10 all nations c. me *about*
Jon. 2:3 floods c. me *about*
Heb. 11:30 after c. a. seven days
12:1 c. a. with such cloud of w.
Rev. 20:9 c. camp of saints *about*

COMPASSEST, ETH.

Gen. 2:11 c. Havilah ; 13 Ethio.

Ps. 73:6 pride c. them as a chain
139:3 thou c. my path, and
Hos. 11:12 Ephraim c. with lies

COMPASSION.

1 *K.* 8:50 give them c. before
2 *Chr.* 30:9 children shall find c.
Mat. 9:36 Jesus moved with c.
   14:14 ; *Mark* 1:41 ; 6:34
18:27 lord was moved with c.
1 *Pet.* 3:8 hav. c. one of another
1 *John* 3:17 shut. his bowels of c.

Full of COMPASSION.

Ps. 78:38 he being *full of* c.
86:15 G. *f. of* c. 111:4; 112:4;
   145:8

Have *or* had COMPASSION.

Ex. 2:6 babe wept, she *had* c.
Deut. 13:17 L. may *h. c.* on thee
30:3 Lord will *have* c. on thee
1 *Sam.* 23:21 for ye *have* c. on me
1 *K.* 8:50 they may *h.* c. on them
2 *K.* 13:23 Lord *had* c. on them
2 *Chr.* 36:15 *had* c. on his people
17 Chaldees *had* no c. on man
Is. 49:15 she not *have* c. on son
Jer. 12:15 I will *have* c. on them
Lam. 3:32 he *have* c. *Mic.* 7:19
Mat. 15:32 c. on mult. *Mark* 8:2
18:33 c. on thy fellow-servant
20:34 so Jesus *had* c. on them
Mark 5:19 how L. *had* c. on thee
9:22 *have* c. on us and help us
Luke 7:13 L. saw her, he *had* c.
10:33 Samaritan *had* c. on him

15:20 father *had* c. and ran and
Rom. 9:15 will *have* c. on whom
Heb. 5:2 can *have* c. on ignorant
10:34 *had* c. of me in my bonds
Jude 22 of some *have* c. making

COMPASSIONS.

Lam. 3:22 because his c. fail not
Zec. 7:9 show c. ev. man to bro.

COMPEL.

Mat. 5:41 c. thee to go a mile go
Mark 15:21 c. one Simon to bear
Luke 14:23 c. them to come in

COMPELLED, EST.

2 *Chr.* 21:11 c. Judah thereto
Mat. 27:32 him c. to bear cross
Acts 26:11 c. them to blaspheme
2 *Cor.* 12:11 glorying, ye c. me
Gal. 2:3 c. to be circumcised
   14 c. Gentiles to live as Jews?

COMPLAIN, ED, ING.

Num. 11:1 c. it displeased Lord
Jud. 21:22 bre. come to us to c.
Job 7:11 I will c. in bitterness
   31:38 the furrows thereof c.
Ps. 77:3 I c. and my spirit was
144:14 be no c. in our streets
Lam. 3:39 doth a living man c. ?

COMPLAINERS.

Jude 16 these are murmurers, c.

COMPLAINT, S.

1 *Sam.* 1:16 abundance of my c.
Job 7:13 couch shall ease my c.
   9:27 if I say, I will forget my c.
10:1 I will leave c. on myself
21:4 is my c. to man ?
23:2 even to-day is my c. bitter
Ps. 55:2 I mourn in my c.
142:2 I poured out my c.
Acts 25:7 c. against Paul

COMPLETE.

Lev. 23:15 seven sabbaths be c.
Col. 2:10 and ye are c. in him
4:12 that ye may stand c. in all

COMPOSITION.

Ex. 30:32 any like it after c. 37

COMPOUND, ETH.

Ex. 30:25 an ointment c.
   33 whosoever c. any like it

COMPREHEND.

Job 37:5 doeth he, we cannot c.
Eph. 3:18 able to c.

COMPREHENDED.

Is. 40:12 c. dust of the earth
John 1:5 the darkness c. it not
Rom. 13:9 it is briefly c. in this

CONCEAL, ED, ETH.

Gen. 37:26 bro. and c. his blood
Deut. 13:8 spare, neither c. him
Job 6:10 I have not c. the words
   27:11 Almighty will I not c.
41:12 I will not c. his parts
Ps. 40:10 not c. thy loving-kind.
Prov. 11:13 of a faithful spirit c.
12:23 prudent c. knowledge
25:2 glory of God to c. a thing
Jer. 50:2 publish and c. not

CONCEIT, S.

Prov. 18:11 as high wall in own c.

Prov. 26:5 he be wise in own c.
   12 a man wise in his own c. ?
16 sluggard wiser in own c.
28:11 rich is wise in own c.
Rom. 11:25 in your own c.
12:16 be not wise in own c.

CONCEIVE.

Gen. 30:38 c. when came to drink
Jud. 13:3 shalt c. and bear a son,
   5:7; *Luke* 1:31
Job 15:35 c. mischief, *Is.* 59:4
Ps. 51:5 in sin did mother c. me
Is. 7:14 a virgin shall c. and
33:11 c. chaff; 59:13 c. falsehood
Heb. 11:11 Sarah rec. str. to c.

CONCEIVED.

Gen. 4:1 Eve c.; 17 Cain's wife c.
16:4 Hagar c. ; 21:2 Sarah c.
25:21 Reb. c. ; 29:32 Leah, 33
30:5 Bilhah c.; 23 Rachel c.
   39 flocks c.; 38:3 Shuah c.
38:18 Tamar c. ; *Ex.* 2:2 Joch. c.
Lev. 12:2 have c. seed. and borne
Num. 11:12 have I c. all this ?
1 *Sam.* 1:20 Hannah c. 2:21
2 *Sam.* 11:5 Bath-sheba c.
2 *K.* 4:17 Shun.; *Is.* 8:3 proph.
Job 3:3 there is a man-child c.
Ps. 7:14 c. mischief, brought
Cant. 3:4 chamber of her c. me
Jer. 49:30 c. a purpose ag. you
Hos. 1:3 Gomer c.
   2:5 c. hath done shamefully
Mat. 1:20 c. in her is of Holy G.
Luke 1:36 Elizabeth hath c. a son
   2:21 so named before he was c.
Acts 5:4 c. this in thy heart ?
Rom. 9:10 Rebecca had c.
Jam. 1:15 when lust hath c.

CONCEPTION.

Gen. 3:16 multiply thy c.
Ruth 4:13 the Lord gave her c.
Hos. 9:11 glory flee from the c.

CONCERN, ETH.

Ps. 138:8 L. perfect that c. me
Acts 28:31 things which c. Christ
2 *Cor.* 11:30 c. mine infirmities

CONCERNING.

Gen. 19:21 accepted thee c. this
Num. 10:29 spoken good c. Isr.
1 *K.* 11:10 command him c. this
Ec. 7:10 inquire wisely c. this
Is. 30:7 therefore I cried c. this
Ezek. 21:28 saith L. c. Ammon.
   47:14 c. which lifted my hand
Luke 24:27 exp. things c. hims.
   44 written in Psalms c. me
Acts 13:34 as c. he raised him
Rom. 9:5 as c. flesh Christ came
   11:28 as c. gospel enemies for
2 *Cor.* 11:21 I sp. as c. reproach
Eph. 5:32 but I speak c. Christ
Phil. 4:15 as c. giving and receiv.
1 *Thes.* 5:18 will of God in C. c.

CONCISION.

Phil. 3:2 beware of the c.

CONCLUDE.

Rom. 3:28 c. a man is justified

CONCLUDED.

Acts 21:25 touching Gent. we c.
Rom. 11:32 c. them all in unbel.
Gal. 3:22 hath c. all under sin

CONCLUSION.

Ec. 12:13 hear c. of matter

CONCORD.

2 *Cor.* 6:15 what c. Ch. with B.

CONCOURSE.

Prov. 1:21 crieth in place of c.
Acts 19:40 give acc. of this c.

CONCUBINE.

Jud. 19:2 c. played the whore
   29 c. and divided her, 20:6
20:4 I and my c. to lodge
2 *Sam.* 3:7 unto my father's c. ?
21:11 that Rizpah c. of Saul

CONCUBINES.

Gen. 25:6 to sons of c. gave gifts
2 *Sam.* 5:13 David took more c.
   16:22 Abs. went in to father's c.
19:5 and the lives of thy c.
20:3 king put his c. in ward
1 *K.* 11:3 Solomon had 300 c.
2 *Chr.* 11:21 took threescore c.
Est. 2:14 Shaashgaz kept c.
Cant. 6:8 there are eighty c.
   9 and c. they praised her
Dan. 5:3 c. drank in them, 23

CONCUPISCENCE.
Rom. 7:8 sin wr. all **manner** of *c*.
Col. 3:5 mortify evil *c*.
1 *Thes.* 4:5 not in the lust of *c*.

CONDEMN.
Ex. 22:9 whom judges shall *c*
Deut. 25:1 judges shall *c*. wicked
Job 9:20 my mouth shall *c*. me
10:2 I will say, Do not *c*. me
34:18 wilt th. *c*. him most just?
40:8 wilt thou *c*. me, that
Ps. 37 33 nor *c*. him
94:21 they *c*. innocent blood
109:31 those that *c*. his soul
Prov. 12:2 wick. devices will he *c*.
Is. 50:9 who is he shall *c*. me?
54:17 that rise against thee *c*.
Mat. 12:41 shall *c*. it, *Luke* 11:32
42 queen of south shall *c*. it
20:18 *c*. him to d. *Mark* 10:33
Luke 6:37 *c*. not, sh. not be con.
John 3:17 his Son to *c*. the world
8:11 neither do I *c*. thee, go
2 *Cor.* 7:3 I speak not this to *c*.
1 *John* 3:20 if our heart *c*. us
21 if our heart *c*. us not, we

CONDEMNATION.
Luke 23:40 thou art in same *c*.
John 3:19 *c*. that light is come
5:24 believeth, not come into *c*.
Rom. 5:16 judgment by one to *c*.
18 judgment came to *c*.
8:1 there is no *c*. to them in C.
1 *Cor.* 11:34 come not togeth. to *c*.
2 *Cor.* 3:9 minist. of *c*. be glory
1 *Tim.* 3:6 lest he fall into *c*. of
Jam. 3:1 receive the greater *c*.
5:12 be nay, lest ye fall into *c*.
Jude 4 of old ordained to this *c*.

CONDEMNED.
Job 32:3 yet had *c*. Job
Ps. 109:7 judged, let him be *c*.
Amos 2:8 they drink wine of *c*.
Mat. 12:7 not have *c*. guiltless
37 by thy words shalt be *c*.
27:3 J. when he saw he was *c*.
Mark 14:64 *c*. him to be guilty
Luke 24:20 delivered him to be *c*.
John 3:18 believ. on him, is not
c. believ. not, is *c*. already
8:10 hath no man *c*. thee?
Rom. 8:3 for sin *c*. sin in flesh
1 *Cor.* 11:32 not be *c*. with world
Tit. 2:8 speech that cannot be *c*.
3:11 sinneth, being *c*. of hims.
Heb. 11:7 by which he *c*. world
Jam. 5:6 *c*. and killed the just
9 grudge not, lest ye be *c*.
2 *Pet.* 2:6 *c*. with overthrow

CONDEMNEST, ETH, ING.
1 *K.* 8:32 *c*. wicked
Job 15:6 own mouth *c*. thee
Prov. 17:15 he that *c*. the just
Acts 13:27 fulfilled them in *c*. him
Rom. 2:1 judgest thou *c*. thyself
8:34 who is he that *c*.?
14:22 *c*. not himself in thing

CONDESCEND.
Rom. 12:16 *c*. to men of low est.

CONDITION, S.
1 *Sam.* 11:2 on this *c*. make cov.
Luke 14:32 desireth *c*. of peace

CONDUCT, ED.
2 *Sam.* 19:15 *c*. king over Jor. 31
40 people of Judah *c*. king
Acts 17:5 that *c*. Paul brought
1 *Cor.* 16:11 but *c*. him in peace

CONDUIT.
2 *K.* 18:7 stood by *c*. Is. 36:2
20:20 how he made a pool and *c*.
Is. 7:3 to meet Ahaz at end of *c*.

CONFECTION.
Ex. 30:35 make a *c*. after art

CONFECTIONARIES.
1 *Sam.* 8:13 your dau. to be *c*.

CONFEDERACY.
Is. 8:12 *c*. to whom people say *c*.
Ob. 7 men of thy *c*. brought

CONFEDERATE.
Gen. 14:13 these *c*. with Abram
Ps. 83:5 they are *c*. against thee
Is. 7:2 Syria is *c*. with Ephraim

CONFERENCE.
Gal. 2:6 they in *c*. added nothing

CONFERRED.
1 *K.* 1:7 Adonijah *c*. with Joab
Acts 4:15 *c*. among themselves
25:12 Festus, when he had *c*.
Gal. 1:16 I *c*. not with flesh and

CONFESS.
Lev. 5:5 *c*. that he hath sinned
16:21 *c*. over him all the iniq.
26:40 if they *c*. their iniquity
Num. 5:7 they shall *c*. their sin
1 *K.* 8:33 *c*. thy name, 35; 2 *Chr.* 6:24, 26
Neh. 1:6 *c*. sins of children of Is.
Job 40:14 *c*. thy hand can save
Ps. 32:5 I said, I will *c*. my tr.
Mat. 10:32 *c*. me before, *Lu.* 12:8
John 9:22 if *c*. that he was Christ
12:42 did not *c*. him, lest they
Acts 23:8 but Pharisees *c*. both
24:14 I *c*. after the way
Rom. 10:9 *c*. with thy mouth
14:11 every tongue shall *c*.
15:9 *c*. to thee among Gentiles
Phil. 2:11 every tongue should *c*.
Jam. 5:16 *c*. your faults
1 *John* 1:9 if we *c*. our sins
4:15 *c*. Jesus is the Son of God
2 *John* 7 *c*. not Jesus Christ
Rev. 3:5 *c*. his name bef. my Fa.

CONFESSED, ETH, ING.
Ezr. 10:1 Ezra had *c*. weeping
Neh. 9:2 stood and *c*. their sins
Prov. 28:13 whoso *c*. and forsak.
Dan. 9:20 *c*. my sin and the sin
Mat. 3:6 baptized *c*. their sins
John 1:20 *c*. I am not the Christ
Acts 19:18 many *c*. and showed
Heb. 11:13 *c*. they were strangers
1 *John* 4:2 spirit that *c*. Christ
3 *c*. not Jesus Christ is come

CONFESSION.
Jos. 7:19 and make *c*. to God
2 *Chr.* 30:22 offer, and making *c*.
Ezr. 10:11 make *c*. to the Lord
Dan. 9:4 I prayed and made *c*.
Rom. 10:10 with mouth *c*. is m.
1 *Tim.* 6:13 witnessed a good *c*.

CONFIDENCE.
Jud. 9:26 Shech. put *c*. in Gaal
2 *K.* 18:19 what *c*. is this? *Is.* 36:4
Job 4:6 is not this thy fear, thy *c*.
31:24 fine gold thou art my *c*.
Ps. 65:5 art *c*. of all the earth
118:8 than put *c*. in man
9 than to put *c*. in princes
Prov. 3:26 Lord shall be thy *c*.
14:26 fear of Lord is strong *c*.
21:22 strength of *c*.
25:19 *c*. in unfaithful
Is. 30:15 in *c*. be your strength
Jer. 48:13 ashamed of B. their *c*.
Ezek. 28:26 shall dwell with *c*.
29:16 E. be no more *c*. of Israel
Mic. 7:5 put ye not *c*. in a guide
Acts 28:31 preaching with all *c*.
2 *Cor.* 1:15 in this *c*. minded
2:3 *c*. that my joy is the joy
7:16 that I have *c*. in you
8:22 great *c*. I have in you
10:2 the *c*. I think to be bold
11:17 as foolishly in this *c*.
Gal. 5:10 I have *c*. in you
Eph. 3:12 access with *c*. by faith
Phil. 1:25 having this *c*.

3:3 we have no *c*. in the flesh
4 I might have *c*. in flesh
2 *Thes.* 3:4 *c*. in L. touching you
Phile. 21 in thy obedience
Heb. 3:6 if we hold fast *c*.
14 beginning of our *c*. steadf.
10:35 cast not away your *c*.
1 *John* 2:28 we may have *c*.
3:21 then have we *c*. toward G.
5:14 the *c*. we have in him

CONFIDENCES.
Jer. 2:37 Lord rejected thy *c*.

CONFIDENT.
Ps. 27:3 in this I be *c*.
Prov. 14:16 fool rageth and is *c*.
Rom. 2:19 art *c*. thou art a guide
2 *Cor.* 5:6 we are always *c*.
8 *c*. and willing to be absent
9:4 ashamed in same *c*. boasting
Phil. 1:6 *c*. of this very thing
14 waxing *c*. by my bonds

CONFIDENTLY.
Luke 22:59 *c*. affirmed, This fel.

CONFIRM.
Ruth 4:7 manner to *c*. all things
1 *K.* 1:14 I will *c*. thy words
2 *K.* 15:19 to *c*. the kingdom in
Est. 9:31 to *c*. these days of P.
Ps. 68:9 *c*. thine inheritance
Is. 35:3 and *c*. the feeble knees
Ezek. 13:6 they would *c*. the w.
Dan. 9:27 *c*. cov. for one week
11:1 I stood to *c*. him
Rom. 15:8 to *c*. promises made
1 *Cor.* 1:8 also *c*. you to the end
2 *Cor.* 2:8 ye would *c*. your love

CONFIRMATION.
Phil. 1:7 in the *c*. of the gospel
Heb. 6:16 an oath for *c*. is an end

CONFIRMED.
2 *Sam.* 7:24 *c*. to thyself Israel
2 *K.* 14:5 as soon as king was *c*.
1 *Chr.* 14:2 Lord had *c*. him k.
16:17 *c*. same to J. *Ps.* 105:10
Est. 9:32 Esther *c*. mat. of Pur.
Dan. 9:12 *c*. words he spake

Acts 15:32 exhorted and *c*. them
1 *Cor.* 1:6 testim. of C. *c*. in you
Gal. 3:15 if *c*. no man disannul.
17 the covenant that was *c*.
Heb. 2:3 was *c*. to us by them
6:17 he *c*. it by an oath

CONFIRMETH, ING.
Num. 30:14 bonds on her, he *c*.
Deut. 27:26 cursed be he *c*. not
Is. 44:26 *c*. word of his servant
Mark 16:20 *c*. the word
Acts 14:22 *c*. souls of disciples
15:41 Syria *c*. the churches

CONFISCATION.
Ezr. 7:26 judgm. be exec. to *c*.

CONFLICT.
Phil. 1:30 same *c*. ye saw in me
Col. 2:1 knew what *c*. I have

CONFORMABLE.
Phil. 3:10 made *c*. to his death

CONFORMED.
Rom. 8:29 *c*. to image of his Son
12:2 be not *c*. to this world

CONFOUND.
Gen. 11:7 *c*. their language, 9
Jer. 1:17 lest I *c*. thee before
1 *Cor.* 1:57 to *c*. the wise, to *c*.

CONFOUNDED.
2 *K.* 19:26 inhab. were *c*. Is. 37:27
Job 6:20 *c*. bec. they had hoped
Ps. 35:4 be *c*. that seek my soul
69:6 let not those seek L. be *c*.
71:13 be *c*. that are adversaries
24 are *c*. that seek my hurt
83:17 let them be *c*. for ever
97:7 *c*. be all that serve images
129:5 let all be *c*. that hate Zion

Is. 1:29 *c.* for the gardens
19:9 that weave net-work be *c.*
37:27 inhabitants were *c.*
Jer. 9:19 *c.* bec. we have forsaken
10:14 founder *c.* by image, 51:17
17:18 be *c.* that persecute me
46:24 dau. of E. *c.;* 48:20 Moab
49:23 Hamath is *c.;* 50:2 Bel.
50:12 your mother be sore *c.*
51:47 Babylon whole land be *c.*
   51 *c.* bec. we heard reproach
Ezek. 16:52 be thou *c.* 54, 63
Mic. 7:16 nations *c.* at their m.
Zec. 10:5 riders and horses be *c.*
Acts 2:6 multitude were *c.*
   9:22 Saul *c.* Jews at Damascus

Ashamed and CONFOUNDED.

Ps. 40:14 *ash. c.* seek soul, 70:2
Is. 24:23 moon be *c.* sun be *ash.*
41:11 inc. ag. thee be *a. and c.*
45:16 idol mak. be *ash. and c.*
54:4 not be *asham.* neither *c.*
Jer. 14:3 nob. and lit. ones *a. c.*
15:9 borne seven been *a. and c.*
22:22 shalt be *ashamed and c.*
31:19 *ash.* yea *c.* bec. I did bear
Ezek. 36:32 be *a. a. c.* for your w.
Mic. 3:7 scers be *a.* diviners *c.*

Not CONFOUNDED.

Ps. 22:5 were *not c.*
Is. 45:17 nor *c.* world with. end
50:7 God will help, I *not* be *c.*
1 *Pet.* 2:6 believeth shall *not* be *c.*

CONFUSED.

Is. 9:5 battle is with *c.* noise
Acts 19:32 the assembly was *c.*

CONFUSION.

Lev. 18:23 a beast to lie, it is *c.*
20:12 they have wrought *c.*
1 *Sam.* 20:30 chosen D. to thy *c.*
Ezr. 9:7 delivered to *c.* of face
Job 10:15 I am full of *c.*
Ps. 35:4 to *c.* that devise
   44:15 my *c.* is cont. before me
   70:2 to *c.* that desire my hurt
   71:1 let me never be put to *c.*
   109:29 cover with their own *c.*
Is. 24:10 the city of *c.* is broken
30:3 trust in shadow of Egypt *c.*
34:11 stretch on it line of *c.*
41:29 their molten images are *c.*
45:16 makers of idols go to *c.*
61:7 for *c.* they shall rejoice in
Jer. 3:25 and our *c.* covereth us
   7:19 provoke to the *c.*
Dan. 9:7 belongeth *c.* of faces, 8
Acts 19:29 city was filled with *c.*
1 *Cor.* 14:33 God not author of *c.*
Jam. 3:16 where strife is, is *c.*

CONGEALED.

Ex. 15:8 depths were *c.* in sea

CONGRATULATE.

1 *Chr.* 18:10 his welfare, and *c.*

CONGREGATION.

Lev. 10:17 to bear iniquity of *c.*
16:33 atonement for all the *c.*
Num. 1:16 the renowned of *c.*
14:27 bear with this evil *c. ?*
15:15 one ordinance be for *c.*
16:21 sep. yours. from this *c.*
   45 get you up from am. this *c.*
   47 Aaron ran into midst of *c.*
27:16 Lord set a man over *c.*
35:12 bef. *c.* for judg. *Jos.* 20:6
Jud. 20:1 *c.* gath. as one man
21:5 came not up with *c.* to L.
1 *K.* 12:20 called Jeroboam to *c.*
Ezr. 10:8 himself sep. from *c.*
Neh. 13:1 Moab. not come into *c.*
Job 15:34 *c.* of hypoc. desolate
30:28 and I cried in the *c.*
Ps. 1:5 nor sinners in *c.* of right.

22:22 midst of *c.* will I praise
26:5 hated the *c.* of evil-doers
58:1 speak righteousness, O *c. ?*
74:2 rem. *c.* thou hast purch.
   19 forget not the *c.* of thy poor
75:2 when I receive the *c.*
82:1 G. standeth in *c.* of mighty
89:5 thy faithfulness in *c.*
107:32 exalt him also in *c.*
111:1 praise the Lord in *c.*
Prov. 5:14 in midst of *c.*
   21:16 remain in *c.* of the dead
Is. 14:13 will sit on mount of *c.*
Jer. 6:18 O *c.* what is among
30:20 *c.* be established before
Lam. 1:10 not enter into *c.*
Hos. 7:12 chas. them as their *c.*
Joel 2:16 sanctify the *c.*
Acts 13:43 when *c.* was broken

All the CONGREGATION.

Lev. 8:3 gather *all the c.*
16:17 atonement for *all the c.*
Num. 16:3 *all the c.* are holy
   22 be wroth with *all the c. ?*
20:27 sight of *all the c.* 25:6
Jos. 22:20 wrath fell on *all the c.*
1 *K.* 8:14 king blessed *all the c.* 55
1 *Chr.* 29:20 *all the c.* blessed L.
2 *Chr.* 23:3 *a. t. c.* made covenant
29:8 *all the c.* worshipped
Neh. 5:13 *all the c.* said, Amen
8:17 *all the c.* come again

Elders of the CONGREGATION.

Lev. 4:15 *e. of c.* shall lay hands

Great CONGREGATION.

1 *K.* 8:65 Sol. held feast, and all
    Is. a *gr. c.* 2 *Chr.* 7:8; 30:13
Ezr. 10:1 assem. to him a *gr. c.*
Ps. 22:25 pr. be of thee in *g. c.*
35:18 give thee thanks in *g. c.*
40:9 preached right. in *g. c.*
   10 not conc. truth from *great c.*

CONGREGATION of Israel.

Lev. 4:13 if *c. of Is.* sin
2 *Chr.* 24:6 accord. to com. of *c. I.*

CONGREGATION of the Lord.

Num. 16:3 you above *c. L.*
27:17 *c. of L. Lord.* not as sheep
Deut. 23:1 not en. *c. of L.* 2, 3
1 *Chr.* 28:8 in sight of *c. L.*

Tabernacle of the CONGREGATION.

Ex. 29:44 sanctify *t. of t. c.*
33:7 called it the *tab. of the c.*
Lev. 16:33 atone. for *t. of the c.*
Num. 4:3 *ta. of the c.* 23, 25
8:9 Levites before *t. of the c.*
12:4 come out to *t. of t. c.*
14:10 glory of L. ap. in *t. of c.*
18:4 charge of *taber. of the c.*
Deut. 31:14 pres. yours. in *t. of c.*
Jos. 18:1 set up *t. of t. c.* at Shil.
1 *K.* 8:4 bro. up the *t.* 2 *Chr.* 5:5
2 *Chr.* 1:3 there was *t. of the c.*

See DOOR.

Tent of the CONGREGATION.

Ex. 39:32 *tent of the c.* finished
40:34 a cloud cov. *tent of the c.*
   35 M. not able to enter *t. of c.*

Whole CONGREGATION.

Ex. 16:2 *w. c.* of Isa. murmured
Num. 3:7 keep charge of *whole c.*
Jos. 22:18 wroth with *w. c.*
Num. 21:13 *wh. c.* sent to Benj.
2 *Chr.* 6:3 king blessed *whole c.*
Ezr. 2:64 *whole c.* 42,360, *Neh.* 7:66
Prov. 26:26 be showed bef. *w. c.*

CONGREGATIONS.

Ps. 26:12 in *c.* will I bless L.
68:26 bless ye God in the *c.*
74:4 enemies roar in thy *c.*

CONIAH. *Jer.* 22:24, 28; 37:1

CONQUER.

Rev. 6:2 conquering and to *c.*

CONQUERORS.

Rom. 8:37 we are more than *c.*

CONSCIENCE.

John 8:9 convicted by own *c.*
Acts 23:1 I have lived in good *c.*
24:16 a *c.* void of offence
Rom. 2:15 *c.* bearing witness
9:1 my *c.* bearing witness
13:5 be subject for *c.* sake
1 *Cor.* 8:7 with *c.* of idol eat it
   10 weak *c.* be emboldened
   12 wound weak *c.* ye sin
10:25 no question for *c.* sake, 27
   28 eat not, for his and *c.* sake
   29 *c.* I say, not thine own, but
2 *Cor.* 1:12 testimony of our *c.*
4:2 com- to every man's *c.*
1 *Tim.* 1:5 and of a good *c.*
   19 holding faith and a good *c.*
3:9 mystery of faith in pure *c.*
4:2 *c.* seared with a hot iron
2 *Tim.* 1:3 whom I serve with *c.*
Tit. 1:15 but their *c.* is defiled
Heb. 9:9 as pertaining to *c.*
   14 purge *c.* from dead works
10:2 worshippers no more *c.*
   22 sprinkled from an evil *c.*
13:18 trust we have good *c.*
1 *Pet.* 2:19 for *c.* endure grief
3:16 having a good *c.*
   21 but the answer of a good *c.*

CONSCIENCES.

2 *Cor.* 5.11 manifest in your *c.*

CONSECRATE.

Ex. 29:9 *c.* A. and sons, 30:30
32:29 *c.* yourselves this day to L.
1 *Chr.* 29:5 *c.* his service to Lord
Ezek. 43:26 shall *c.* themselves
Mic. 4:13 I will *c.* their gain

CONSECRATED.

Jud. 17:5 M. *c.* one of sons, 12
1 *K.* 13:33 whosoever would, he *c.*
2 *Chr.* 29:31 *c.* yourselves to Lord
   33 *c.* things six hundred oxen
31:6 tithe of holy things *c.*
Heb. 7:28 Son, who is *c.* evermore
10:20 by a living way *c.* for us

CONSECRATION, S.

Ex. 29:22 for it is a ram of *c.*
Lev. 7:37 this is law of the *c.*
8:28 *c.* for sweet savor to Lord
   31 with bread in basket of *c.*
   33 days of your *c.* be at end
Num. 6:9 defiled head of his *c.*

CONSENT, ED, ING.

Gen. 34:23 only let us *c.* to them
Deut. 13:8 shalt not *c.* to him
1 *K.* 20:8 hearken not, nor *c.*
Ps. 50:18 sawest thief, thou *c.*
Prov. 1:10 entice thee, *c.* thi. not
Dan. 1:14 so he *c.* in this matter
Luke 23:51 same had not *c.*
Acts 8:1 *c.* his death, 22:20
   18:20 to tarry longer, he *c.* not
Rom. 7:16 I *c.* to law
1 *Tim.* 6:3 *c.* not to whole. words

CONSENT, Substantive.

1 *Sam.* 11:7 came out with one *c.*
Ps. 83:5 consulted with one *c.*
Hos. 6:9 of priests murder by *c.*
Zep. 3:9 serve him with one *c.*
Luke 14:18 one *c.* began to make excuse
1 *Cor.* 7:5 ex. with *c.* for a time

CONSIDER.

Deut. 4:39 *c.* it in thy heart
32:29 wise to *c.* latter end
Jud. 18:14 *c.* what ye have to do
1 *Sam.* 12:24 *c.* how great things
25:17 *c.* what thou wilt do
Job 11:11 will he not then *c.* it?
   23:15 I *c.* I am afraid of him

34:27 would not *c.* his ways
37:14 *c.* wondrous works of God
Ps. **5:1** *c.* my meditation
8:3 when I *c.* thy heavens
13:3 *c.* and hear, 45:10
25:19 *c.* my enemies
37:10 diligently *c.* his place
48:13 *c.* her palaces, that ye
50:22 *c.* this, ye that forget God
64:9 wisely *c.* of his doing
119:95 I will *c.* thy testimonies
153 *c.* mine affliction, deliver
159 *c.* how I love thy precepts
Prov. **6:6** go to ant. *c.* her ways
23:1 *c.* what is before thee
24:12 that pondereth heart *c.* it ?
Ec. **5:1** *c.* not that they do evil
7:13 *c.* work of God, who can
14 but in day of adversity *c.*
Is. **1:3** my people doth not *c.*
5:12 *c.* operation of his hands
Is. **14:16** shall narrowly *c.* thee
18:4 *c.* in my dwelling-place
41:20 that they may see, and *c.*
43:18 nor *c.* the things of old
52:15 not heard shall they *c.*
Jer. **2:10** *c.* if there be such thing
23:20 in the latter days ye sh. *c.*
it perfectly, 30:24
Lam. **2:20** *c.* to whom done this
5:1 O Lord, *c.* our reproach
Ezek. **12:3** it may be they will *c.*
Dan. **9:23** and *c.* the vision
Hos. **7:2** *c.* not that I remember
Hag. **1:5** *c.* your ways, 7
2:15 I pray *c.* from this day, 18
Mat. **6:28** *c.* the lilies, *Lu.* 12:27
Luke **12:24** *c.* the ravens
John **11:50** nor *c.* it is expedient
Acts **15:6** elders came to *c.* of this
2 *Tim.* **2:7** *c.* and L. give thee
Heb. **3:1** brethren *c.* the Apostle
7:4 *c.* how great this man was
10:24 let us *c.* one another
12:3 *c.* him endured such con.

CONSIDERED, EST.

1 *K.* **5:8** I have *c.* things
Job **1:8** hast thou *c.* Job ? 2:3
Ps. **31:7** hast *c.* my trouble
Prov. **24:32** then I *c.* it well
Ec. **4:1** I *c.* all the oppressions
4 again I *c.* all travail, and
9:1 all this I *c.* to declare this
Jer. **23:24** *c.* not people have spo.
Acts **12:12** when Peter had *c.*
Rom. **4:19** *c.* not his body dead

CONSIDERETH, ING.

Ps. **33:15** he *c.* all their works
41:1 blessed is he *c.* the poor
Prov. **21:12** *c.* house of wicked
28:22 *c.* not poverty shall come
29:7 righteous *c.* cause of poor
31:16 she *c.* a field, buyeth it
Is. **44:19** none *c.* to say, I burnt
57:1 none *c.* right. is tak. away
Ezek. **18:14** *c.* and doeth not, 28
Gal. **6:1** *c.* lest also be tempted
Heb. **13:7** *c.* end of their conver.

CONSIST, ETH.

Luke **12:15** life *c.* not in abund.
Col. **1:17** by him all things *c.*

CONSOLATION.

Jer. **16:7** nor give them cup of *c.*
Luke **2:25** Simeon waiting for *c.*
6:24 woe to you rich, rec. yo. *c.*
Acts **4:36** interpreted, son of *c.*
15:31 they rejoiced the he *c.*
Rom. **15:5** God of *c.* grant you
2 *Cor.* **1:5** our *c.* aboundeth by C.
6 afflicted for your *c.* comforted
7 so ye be partakers of the *c.*
7:7 *c.* wherewith we was comf.
Phil. **2:1** if any *c.* in Christ
2 *Thes.* **2:16** given us everlast. *c.*
Phile. **7** joy and *c.* in thy love

Heb. **6:18** might have strong *c.*

CONSOLATIONS.

Job **15:11** are *c.* of God small
21:2 and let this be your *c.*
Is. **66:11** with breasts of her *c.*

CONSORTED.

Acts **17:4** *c.* with Paul and Silas

CONSPIRACY.

2 *Sam.* **15:12** Absalom's *c.* strong
2 *K.* **12:20** a *c.* and slew Joash
14:19 *c.* ag. A. 2 *Chr.* 25:27
15:15 acts of Shallum and *c.*
17:4 found *c.* in Hoshea
Jer. **11:9** *c.* among men of Judah
Ezek. **22:25** a *c.* of her prophets
Acts **23:13** forty which made *c.*

CONSPIRATORS.

2 *Sam.* **15:31** Ahith. is among *c.*

CONSPIRED.

Gen. **37:18** *c.* ag. Jos. to slay him
1 *Sam.* **22:13** *c.* thou and son of J.
1 *K.* **15:27** Baasha *c.* aga. Nadab
16:9 Zimri *c.* against Elah, 16
2 *K.* **9:14** Jehu *c.* against Joram
10:9 *c.* against my master
15:10 Shallum *c.* ag. Zechariah
25 Pekah *c.* against Pekahiah
21:23 serv. of Amon *c.* ag. him
24 *c.* against him. 2 *Chr.* 33:25
2 *Chr.* **24:21** *c.* against Jehoiada
25 serv. of Joash *c.* ag. him, 26
Neh. **4.8** *c.* all to come and fight
Amos **7:10** Amos hath *c.* ag. thee

CONSTANT, LY.

1 *Chr.* **28:7** if he be *c.* to do com.
Prov. **21:28** heareth. speaketh *c.*
Acts **12:15** she *c.* affirmed it was
Tit. **3:8** I will thou affirm *c.*

CONSTELLATIONS.

Is. **13:10** *c.* thereof

CONSTRAIN, ED, ETH.

2 *K.* **4:8** women *c.* him to eat
Job **32:18** the spirit in me *c.* me
Mat. **14:22** J. *c.* disc. *Mark* 6:45
Luke **24:29** *c.* him, saying, Abide
Acts **16:15** Lydia *c.* us to come
28:19 I was *c.* to appeal to
2 *Cor.* **5:14** love of Christ *c.* us
Gal. **6:12** *c.* you to be circum.

CONSTRAINT.

1 *Pet.* **5:2** oversight, not by *c.*

CONSULTATION.

Mark **15:1** chief priests held a *c.*

CONSULT, ED, ETH.

1 *K.* **12:6** Rehoboam *c.* 8
1 *Chr.* **13:1** D. *c.* with captains
2 *Chr.* **20:21** Jeh. *c.* with people
Neh. **5:7** then I *c.* with myself
Ps. **62:4** *c.* to cast him down
83:3 *c.* against hidden ones
5 have *c.* with one consent
Ezek. **21:21** king of B. *c.* images
Dan. **6:7** presidents and capt. *c.*
Mic. **6:5** rem. what Balak *c.*
Hab. **2:10** *c.* shame to thy house
Mat. **26:4** *c.* might take Jesus
Lu. **14:31** *c.* w. able with 10,000
John **12:10** *c.* to put L. to death

CONSULTER.

Deut. **18:11** a *c.* with spirits

CONSUME.

Ex. **33:3** lest I *c.* thee in way, 5
Deut. **5:25** this fire will *c.* us
7:16 shalt *c.* all the people
28:38 locust shall *c.* it, 42
32:22 fire kindled in anger *c.*
Jos. **24:20** *c.* after done you good
1 *Sam.* **2:33** to *c.* thine eyes
2 *K.* **1:10** let fire *c.* thy fifty, 12
Job **15:34** fire *c.* tabern. of brib.
20:26 a fire not blown *c.* him
24:19 and heat *c.* snow waters
Ps. **37:20** *c.* into smoke shall *c.*

39:11 his beauty to *c.* away
49:14 their beauty *c.* in grave
78:33 their days did he *c.*
Is. **7:20** it shall *c.* the beard
10:18 *c.* glory of his forest
27:10 shall calf *c.* branches
Jer. **49:27** fire *c.* pal. of Ben-ha
Ezek. **4:17** *c.* away for iniquity
13:13 great hailstones to *c.* it
21:28 sword is furbished to *c.*
22:15 I will *c.* thy filthiness
24:10 kindle fire, *c.* the flesh
35:12 they are giv. us to *c.*
Dan. **2:44** it shall *c.* these kingd.
Hos. **11:6** sword *c.* his branches
Zep. **1:2** I will *c.* all off land
3 I will *c.* man and beast
Zec. **5:4** in house and *c.* it
14:12 tongue shall *c.* away
2 *Thes.* **2:8** whom L. shall *c.*
Jam. **4:3** may *c.* it on your lusts

CONSUME them.

Ex. **32:10** that I may *c.* t. 12
Num. **16:21** *c.* t. in a moment, 45
Deut. **7:22** mayest not *c.* t.
Neh. **9:31** not utterly *c. them*
Est. **9:24** H. cast lot to *c. them*
Ps. **59:13** *c.* t. in wrath, *c. them*
Jer. **8:13** I will utterly *c.* t.
14:12 I will *c.* them by sword
Ezek. **20:13** fury on them to *c.* t.
Luke **9:54** fire to *c. them*

CONSUMED.

Gen. **19:15** be *c.* in the iniquity
17 escape to mount. lest be *c.*
31:40 in day drought *c.* me
Ex. **3:2** behold, bush was not *c.*
15:7 wrath *c.* them as stubble
22:6 if corn be *c.* therewith
Num. **11:1** *c.* them were in utter.
12:12 of whom flesh is half *c.*
16:26 lest ye be *c.* in their sins
35 fire *c.* the 250 men
21:28 fire hath *c.* Ar of Moab
25:11 that I *c.* not child. of Isr.
32:13 gener. done evil was *c.*
Deut. **2:16** men of war were *c.*
Jud. **6:21** fire out of rock *c.* flesh
2 *Sam.* **21:5** the man that *c.* us
1 *K.* **18:38** fell and *c.* 2 *Chr.* 7:1
2 *K.* **1:10** fire *c.* his fifty, 12
2 *Chr.* **8:8** children of Isr. *c.* not
Neh. **2:3** gates thereof are *c.* 13
Job **1:16** fire of God *c.* sheep
4:9 by breath of his nostrils *c.*
6:17 snow and ice are *c.*
7:9 as cloud is *c.* and vanisheth
19:27 reins *c.* ; 33:21 flesh is *c.*
Ps. **6:7** mine eye *c.* 31:9
10 my bones *c.* 102:3
39:10 *c.* by blow of thy hand
71:13 let them be *c.* that are
Ps. **73:19** utterly *c.* with terrors
78:63 fire *c.* their young men
90:7 we are *c.* by thine anger
104:35 let sinners by *c.* out of
119:87 almost *c.* me upon earth
139 my zeal hath *c.* me, becau.
Prov. **5:11** flesh and body are *c.*
Is. **16:4** oppressors *c.* out of land
29:20 the scorner is *c.* and all
64:7 *c.* us because of iniquities
Jer. **5:3** *c.* refused correction
6:29 lead is *c.* ; 12:4 beasts
20:18 should be *c.* with shame
36:23 till all the roll was *c.*
44:18 we have been *c.* by sword
Lam. **2:22** those I swad. enemy *c.*
3:22 of Lord's mercies not *c.*
Ezek. **19:12** rods fire *c.* 22:31
24:11 scum of it may be *c.*
43:8 wherefore I have *c.* them
Mal. **3:6** sons of Jacob are not *c.*
Gal. **5:15** ye be not *c.*

Shall be CONSUMED.

Num. **14:35** wilder. *sh.* they *be c.*

17:13 *shall* we *be c.* with dying ?
1 *Sam.* 12:25 ye *s, be c.*
Is. 1:28 that forsake L. *sh. be c.*
66:17 eat swine's flesh, *s. be c.*
Jer. 16:4 *s. be c.* by sw. 44:12, 27
Ezek. 5:12 with famine *shall be c.*
13:14 and ye *shall be c.*
34:29 *sh. be* no more *c.*
47:12 nor *shall* fruit thereof *be c.*
Dan. 11:16 land which *shall be c.*

CONSUMED, *with* till *or* until.

Deut. 2:15 *until c. Jos.* 5:6
28:21 *until* he have *c.* thee
Jos. 10:20 slaying them *till c.*
1 *Sam.* 15:18 *until* they be *c.*
2 *Sam.* 22:38 I turned not *until* I
had *c.* them, *Ps.* 18:37
1 *K.* 22:11 push Syr. *u. c.* them,
2 *K.* 13:17, 19 ; 2 *Chr.* 18:10
Ezr. 9:14 angry *till* hadst *c.* us
Jer. 9:16 send a sword *till* I have
c. them, 24:10 ; 27:8 ; 49:37

CONSUMETH, ING.

Deut. 4:24 a *c.* fire, *Heb.* 12:29
9:3 L. goeth bef. thee as *c.* fire
Job 13:28 he *c.* as a garment that
22:20 remnant of them fire *c.*
31:12 fire that *c.* to destruction
Is. 5:24 as the flame *c.* chaff

CONSUMMATION.

Dan. 9:27 desolate until *c.*

CONSUMPTION.

Lev. 26:16 appoint over you *c.*
Deut. 28:22 smite thee with *c.*
Is. 10:22 *c.* dec. shall overflow
23 the Lord shall make a *c.*
28:22 I have heard from L. a *c.*

CONTAIN.

1 *K.* 8:27 heaven of heav. cannot
c. thee, 2 *Chr.* 2:6 ; 6:18
John 21:25 world not *c.* the books
1 *Cor.* 7:9 if cannot *c.* marry

CONTAINED, ETH, ING.

Ezek. 23:32 thy sister's cup *c.*
Rom. 2:14 by nat. thi. *c.* in law
Eph. 2:15 abol. law *c.* in ordin.
1 *Pet.* 2:6 it is *c.* in scripture

CONTEMN, ED, ETH.

Ps. 10:13 wicked *c.* God ?
15:4 eyes a vile person is *c.*
107:11 *c.* counsel of Most High
Cant. 8:7 substance would be *c.*
Is. 16:14 glory of Moab be *c.*
Ezek. 21:10 it *c.* rod of my son

CONTEMPT.

Est. 1:18 thus arise too much *c.*
Job 12:21 *c.* on princes, *Ps.* 107:40
31:34 *c.* of families terrify me
Ps. 119:22 remove from me *c.*
123:3 we are ex. filled with *c.*
4 soul filled with *c.* of proud
Prov. 18:3 wicked com. then *c.*
Is. 23:9 into *c.* the honorable
Dan. 12:2 awake to everlast. *c.*

CONTEMPTIBLE.

Mal. 1:7 say, table of Lord is *c.*
12 meat *c.* ; 2:9 I made you *c.*
2 *Cor.* 10:10 his speech *c.*

CONTEMPTUOUSLY.

Ps. 31:18 speak *c.* against right.

CONTEND.

Deut. 2:9 neither *c.* in battle, 24
Job 9:3 if *c.* he cannot answer
13:8 will ye *c.* for God ?
Prov. 28:4 such as keep law *c.*
Ec. 6:10 may he *c.* with him
Is. 49:25 I will *c.* with him
50:8 who will *c.* with me ?
Is. 57:16 I will not *c.* for ever, nor
Jer. 12:5 how *c.* with horses ?
18:19 to voice of them that *c.*
Amos 7:4 Lord called to *c.* by fire

Mic. 6:1 *c.* thou bef. the mount.
Jude 3 earnestly *c.* for the faith

CONTENDED.

Neh. 13:11 *c.* I with rulers, 17
Job 31:13 servants when they *c.*
Is. 41:12 not find them that *c.*
Acts 11:2 they of circum. *c.* with

CONTENDEST.

Job 10:2 show me wherefore *c.*

CONTENDETH.

Job 40:2 that *c.* with Almighty
Prov. 29:9 if wise *c.* with foolish

CONTENDING.

Jude 9 when *c.* with the devil

CONTENT.

Gen. 37:27 sell him, brethren *c.*
Lev. 10:20 heard that, he was *c.*
Jos. 7:7 would we had been *c.*
2 *K.* 6:3 one said, Be *c.* and go
Job 6:28 now therefore be *c.*
Prov. 6:35 nor will he rest *c.*
Mark 15:15 Pilate willing to *c.*
Luke 3:14 be *c.* with your wages
Phil. 4:11 in every state to be *c.*
1 *Tim.* 6:8 raiment, let us be *c.*
Heb. 13:5 be *o.* with such things
3 *John* 10 not *c.* with prating

Prov. 13:10 by pride cometh *c.*
17:14 leave off *c.* before it be
18:6 a fool's lips enter into *c.*
22:10 cast out scorner, *c.* sh. go
Jer. 15:10 borne me a man of *c.*
Hab. 1:3 that raise up *c.*
Acts 15:39 the *c.* was so sharp
Phil. 1:16 preach Christ of *c.*
1 *Thes.* 2:2 speak gospel with *c.*

CONTENTIONS.

Prov. 18:18 causeth *c.* to cease
19 *c.* like bars of a castle
19:13 *c.* of a wife, 27:15
23:29 who hath *c.* ?
1 *Cor.* 1:11 there are *c.* am. you
Tit. 3:9 avoid *c.* and strivings

CONTENTIOUS.

Prov. 21:19 with *c.* woman
26:21 a *c.* man to kindle strife
27:15 dropping and *c.* woman
Rom. 2:8 to them that are *c.*
1 *Cor.* 11:16 if any seem to be *c.*

CONTENTMENT.

1 *Tim.* 6:6 godli. with *c.* is gain

CONTINUAL.

Ex. 29:42 be a *c.* burnt-offering
2 *Chr.* 2:4 for *c.* show-bread
Prov. 15:15 merry heart a *c.* feast
Is. 14:6 smote with a *c.* stroke
Jer. 48:5 *c.* weeping shall go up
Ezek. 39:14 men of *c.* employm.
Luke 18:5 lest by her *c.* coming
Rom. 9:2 *c.* sorrow in my heart

See BURNT-OFFERING.

CONTINUALLY.

Gen. 6:5 imagination was evil *c.*
Ex. 28:30 on heart before L. *c.*
1 *Chr.* 16:11 seek his face *c.*
Job 1:5 thus did Job *c.*
Ps. 34:1 his praise be *c.* 71:6
35:27 *c.* L. be mag. 40:16 ; 70:4
38:17 sorro *v c.* before me
40:11 truth *c.* preserve me
42:3 *c.* say, Where is thy God ?
44:15 confusion *c.* before me
50:8 burnt-offer. *c.* before me
52:1 goodness of G. endureth *c.*
71:3 whereunto I may *c.* resort
6 my praise be *c.* of th
14 but I will hope *c.* and yet
73:23 I am *c.* with thee, 'hou
74:23 the tumult increaseth *c.*
109:15 let them be before L. *c.*
119:44 shall I keep thy law *c.*
109 my soul is *c.* in my hand

117 respect to thy statutes *c.*
140:2 *c.* are gathered for war
Prov. 6:14 deviseth mischief *c.*
21 bind them *c.* on thy heart
Is. 21:8 *c.* upon the watch-tower
49:16 thy walls are *c.* before me
51:13 hast feared *c.* because
52:5 my name *c.* is blasph.
58:11 L. shall guide thee *c.*
60:11 gates shall be open *c.*
65:3 provoketh me to anger *c.*
Jer. 6:7 before me *c.* is grief
Dan. 6:16 G. whom servest *c.* 20
Hos. 12:6 wait on thy God *c.*
Ob. 16 heathen drink *c.*
Nah. 3:19 thy wick. passed *c.* ?

Luke 24:53 *c.* in temple
Acts 6:4 ourselves *c.* to prayer
Rom. 13:6 *c.* on this very thing
Heb. 7:3 abideth a priest *c.*
10:1 sacrifices year by year *c.*
13:15 the sacrifice of praise *c.*

CONTINUANCE.

Deut. 28:59 plag. and of long *c.*
Ps. 139:16 in *c.* were fashioned
Is. 64:5 in those is *c.*
Rom. 2:7 patient *c.* in well-doing

CONTINUE.

Ex. 21:21 if he *c.* a day or two
1 *Sam.* 12:14 *c.* following the L.
13:14 thy kingdom not *c.*
2 *Sam.* 7:29 it may *c.* for ever
1 *K.* 2:4 L. may *c.* word he spake
Job 15:29 neither substance *c.*
17:2 eye *c.* in their provocation ?
Ps. 36:10 O *c.* thy loving-kind.
49:11 that their houses shall *c.*
102:28 children of thy serv. *c.*
119:91 *c.* according to thy ordin.
Is. 5:11 *c.* till night, till wine
Jer. 32:14 may *c.* many days
Dan. 11:8 *c.* more years than k.
Mat. 15:32 *c.* now three days
John 8:31 if ye *c.* in my word
15:9 *c.* ye in my love
Acts 13:43 to *c.* in grace of God
14:22 exhorting to *c.* in faith
26:22 I *c.* unto this day
Rom. 6:1 shall we *c.* in sin
11:22 if thou *c.* in his goodness
Gal. 2:5 truth of gospel might *c.*
Phil. 1:25 I shall *c.* with you all
Col. 1:23 if ye *c.* in the faith
4:2 *c.* in prayer, and watch
1 *Tim.* 2:15 if they *c.* in faith
4:16 doctrine, *c.* in them
2 *Tim.* 3:14 *c.* in things hast
Heb. 7:23 not suffer to *c.*
13:1 let brotherly love *c.*
Jam. 4:13 *c.* there a year
2 *Pet.* 3:4 things *c.* as they were
1 *John* 2:24 ye shall *c.* in the Son
Rev. 13:5 power to *c.*
17:10 he must *c.* a short space

CONTINUED.

Ps. 72:17 his name be *c.* as sun
Dan. 1:21 Daniel *c.* to year of C.
Luke 6:12 *c.* all night in prayer
22:28 ye *c.* with me in tempt.
Acts 1:14 these *c.* in prayer
2:42 *c.* stead. in apostles' doc.
8:13 Simon *c.* with Philip
20:7 P. *c.* speech until midnight
Heb. 8:9 *c.* not in my covenant
1 *John* 2:19 no doubt *c.* with us

CONTINUETH, ING.

Job 14:2 as shadow, and *c.* not
Jer. 30:23 a *c.* whirlwind, it
Acts 2:46 *c.* daily with one ac.
Rom. 12:12 *c.* instant in prayer
Gal. 3:10 cursed *c.* not in all th.
1 *Tim.* 5:5 *c.* in supplications
Heb. 7:24 because he *c.* ever
13:14 we have no *c.* city, but
Jam. 1:25 perfect law, *c.* in it

CONTRADICTING.
Acts 13:45 with envy *c.* blasph.

CONTRADICTION.
Heb. 7:7 without *c.* less is blessed
12:3 endured such *c.* of sinners

CONTRARIWISE.
2 *Cor.* 2:7 *c.* rather to forgive him
Gal. 2:7 *c.* when saw gospel was
1 *Pet.* 3:9 railing, but *c.* blessing

CONTRARY.
Lev. 26:24 will I walk *c.* 28, 41
Est. 9:1 though turned to *c.*
Ezek. 16:34 *c.* is in thee, art *c.*
Mat. 14:24 for the wind was *c.*
Acts 77:7 these do *c.* to decrees
18:13 to worship God *c.* to law
23:3 to be smitten *c.* to the law
26:9 *c.* to the name of Jesus
Rom. 11:24 graffed *c.* to nature
16:17 *c.* to doctrine ye learned
Gal. 5:17 *c.* one to the other
Col. 2:14 handwriting *c.* to us
1 *Thes.* 2:15 and are *c.* to all men
1 *Tim.* 1:10 *c.* to sound doctrine
Tit. 2:8 he of a *c.* part be asham.

CONTRIBUTION.
Rom. 15:26 *c.* for the poor saints

CONTRITE.
Ps. 34:18 such as of *c.* spirit
51:17 *c.* heart, wilt not despise
Is. 57:15 of a *c.* spirit, to revive heart of the *c.* ones
66:2 of *c.* spirit and trembleth

CONTROVERSY.
Deut. 17:8 being matters of *c.*
Deut. 19:17 between whom *c.* is
21:5 by their word *c.* be tried
25:1 if there be a *c.* betw. men
2 *Sam.* 15:2 that had a *c.* came
2 *Chr.* 19:8 set the Levites for *c.*
Is. 34:8 year of recom. for *c.*
Jer. 25:31 hath *c.* with nations
Ezek. 44:24 in *c.* they shall stand
Hos. 4:1 L. hath a *c.* with inhab.
12:2 Lord hath a *c.* with Judah
Mic. 6:2 L. hath *c.* with people
1 *Tim.* 3:16 with. *c.* great is mys.

CONVENIENT, LY.
Prov. 30:8 with food *c.* for me
Jer. 40:4 it seemeth *c.* to go, 5
Mark 6:21 a *c.* day was come
14:11 might *c.* betray him
Acts 24:25 a *c.* season, I will call
Rom. 1:28 to do things not *c.*
1 *Cor.* 16:12 when have *c.* time
Eph. 5:4 talking, nor jesting, *c.*
Phile. 8 to enjoin thee that *c.*

CONVERSANT.
Jos. 8:35 strangers *c.* am. them
1 *Sam.* 25:15 long as we were *c.*

CONVERSATION.
Ps. 37:14 as be of upright *c.*
59:23 ordereth his *c.* aright
2 *Cor.* 1:12 in godly sinc. had *c.*
Gal. 1:13 ye have heard of my *c.*
Eph. 2:3 had our *c.* in times past
4:22 concerning the former *c.*
Phil. 1:27 *c.* as becometh gospel
3:20 for our *c.* is in heaven
1 *Tim.* 4:12 be an example in *c.*
Heb. 13:5 *c.* be without covet.
7 considering end of their *c.*
Jam. 3:13 show out of a good *c.*
1 *Pet.* 1:15 in all manner of *c.*
18 not redeemed from vain *c.*
2:12 *c.* honest among Gentiles
3:1 may be won by *c.* of wives
2 while they behold chaste *c.*
16 falsely accuse your good *c.*
2 *Pet.* 2:7 vexed with the filthy *c.*
3:11 to be in all holy *c.*

CONVERSION.
Acts 15:3 declaring *c.* of Gentiles

CONVERT, ED.
Ps. 51:13 sinners be *c.* unto thee
Is. 6:10 lest *c.* and be healed
60:5 abundance of sea be *c.*
Mat. 13:15 be *c.* *Mark* 4:12
18:3 *c.* and become as children
Luke 22:32 when *c.* strengthen
John 12:40 be *c.* *Acts* 28:27
Acts 3:19 repent ye and be *c.*
Jam. 5:19 do err, and one *c.* him

CONVERTETH, ING.
Ps. 19:7 law is perfect, *c.* soul
Jam. 5:20 he which *c.* a sinner

CONVERTS.
Is. 1:27 her *c.* be redeemed with

CONVEY, ED.
1 *K.* 5:9 I will *c.* them by sea
Neh. 2:7 *c.* me over till I come
John 5:13 Jesus *c.* himself away

CONVICTED.
John 8:9 *c.* by their consistence

CONVINCE, ED, ETH.
Job 32:12 none of you *c.* Job
John 8:46 which of you *c.* me
Acts 18:28 mightily *c.* the Jews
1 *Cor.* 14:24 he is *c.* of all, he is
Tit. 1:9 be able to *c.* gainsayers
Jam. 2:9 *c.* of law as transgres.
Jude 15 to *c.* all that are ungodly

CONVOCATION.
Ex. 12:16 a holy *c.* *Lev.* 23:7, 24, 35; *Num.* 28:18; 29:1
Num. 28:26 first-fruit a holy *c.*

CONY, IES.
Lev. 11:5 *c.* chew. cud, *Deut.* 14:7
Ps. 104:18 a refuge for the *c.*
Prov. 30:26 the *c.* a feeble folk

COOK, S.
1 *Sam.* 8:13 daughters to be *c.*
9:23 Sam. said to the *c.* Bring

COOL.
Gen. 3:8 walking in *c.* of day
Luke 16:24 and *c.* my tongue

COPIED.
Prov. 25:1 men of Hezekiah *c.*

COPING.
1 *K.* 7:9 from foundation to *c.*

COPPER.
Ezr. 8:27 two vessels of fine *c.*

COPPERSMITH.
2 *Tim.* 4:14 Alexander the *c.* did

COPULATION.
Lev. 15:16 seed of *c.* 17, 18

COPY.
Deut. 17:18 write a *c.* of law
Jos. 8:32 *c.* of law of Moses
Ezr. 4:11 *c.* of letter sent, 5:6
Est. 3:14 *c.* of writing, 8:13

COR.
Ezek. 45:14 a bath out of the *c.*

CORAL.
Job 28:18 no mention made of *c.*
Ezek. 27:16 Syria merchant in *c.*

CORBAN.
Mark 7:11 it is *c.* that is, a gift

CORD.
Jos. 2:15 let spies down by a *c.*
Job 30:11 he hath loosed my *c.*
41:1 dr. out tongue with a *c.*?
Ec. 4:12 threefold *c.* not quickly
12:6 or ever silver *c.* be loosed
Is. 54:2 lengthen thy *c.*
Mic. 2:5 a *c.* by lot in the congr.

CORDS.
Jud. 15:13 Samson with new *c.*
Job 36:8 in *c.* of affliction
Ps. 2:3 let us cast away their *c.*
118:27 bind the sacrifice with *c.*
129:4 hath cut *s.* of the wicked
140:5 proud have hid *c.* for me
Prov. 5:22 with *c.* of his sins

CONVERT, ED. — *(continued)*
Is. 5:18 draw iniquity with *c.*
33:20 any of the *c.* be broken
Jer. 10:20 spoiled, and all my *c.*
38:13 drew up Jeremiah with *c.*
Ezek. 27:24 apparel bound with *c.*
Hos. 11:4 drew with *c.* of a man
John 2:15 a scourge of small *c.*

CORIANDER.
Ex. 16:31 *c.* seed, *Num.* 11:7

CORINTH.
Acts 18:1 after, Paul came to C.
19:1 while Apollos was at C.
1 *Cor.* 1:2; 2 *Cor.* 1:1, 23
2 *Tim.* 4:20 Erastus abode at C.

CORINTHIANS.
Acts 18:8 of the C. 2 *Cor.* 6:11

CORMORANT.
Lev. 11:17 owl and *c. Deut.*14:17
Is. 34:11 *c.* possess it, *Zep.* 2:14

CORN.
Gen. 41:57 all came to buy *c.*
42:2 *c.* in Egypt, *Acts* 7:12
Ex. 22:6 stacks of *c.* be consum
Lev. 2:16 burn part of beaten *c.*
23:14 eat bread nor parched *c.*
Num. 18:27 *c.* of threshing-floor
Deut. 16:9 put sickle to *c.*
25:4 not muzzle ox treadeth *c.* 1 *Cor.* 9:9; 1 *Tim.* 5:18
Jos. 5:11 did eat of old *c.* 12
Ruth 3:7 lie down at heap of *c.*
1 *Sam.* 17:17 for breth. parched *c.*
25:18 Abigail took of parched *c.*
2 *Sam.* 17:28 brought parched *c.*
2 *K.* 19:26 blasted *c. Is.* 37:27
Neh. 5:2 we take up *c.* for them
Job 5:26 as a shock of *c.* cometh
24:6 reap every one *c.* in field
39:4 young grow up with *c.*
Ps. 65:9 thou preparest them *c.*
13 the valleys covered with *c.*
72:16 handful of *c.* in the earth
78:24 given of the *c.* of heaven
Prov. 11:26 with. *c.* people curse
Is. 17:5 harvestman gather. *c.*
21:10 and *c.* of my floor
62:8 no more give *c.* to enemies
Ezek. 36:29 I will call for *c.* and
Hos. 2:9 I will take away my *c.*
10:11 Ephraim loveth to tread *c.*
14:7 shall revive as the *c.* and
Joel 1:10 for the *c.* is wasted
17 the *c.* is withered
Amos 8:5 that we may sell *c.*
9:9 like as *c.* sifted in sieve
Mark 4:28 after that the full *c.*
John 12:24 except *c.* of wheat

Ears of CORN.
Gen. 41:5 seven *ears of c.* came
Lev. 2:14 offer green *ears of c.*
Ruth 2:2 glean *ears of c.*
2 *K.* 4:42 brought full *ears of c.*
Job 24:24 cut off as *ears of c.*
Mat. 12:1 pluck *ears of c. Mark* 2:23 ; *Luke* 6:1

CORN-FLOOR.
Hos. 9:1 reward on every *c.-fl.*

Standing CORN.
Ex. 22:6 so that *s. c.* be consum.
Deut. 23:25 *stand. c.* of neighbor
Jud. 15:5 foxes go into *s. c.*

CORN and wine.
Gen. 27:28 G. gave plenty of *c. w.*
37 with *c.* and w. I sust. him
Deut. 7:13 bless thy *c.* and wine
Deut. 11:14 gather in thy *c. w.*
12:17 tithe of thy *c. w.* 14:23
18:4 first fruit of *c.* and wine
28:51 leave thee *c.* and wine
33:28 J. shall be on land of *c. w.*
2 *K.* 18:32 land of *c. w. Is.* 36:17
2 *Chr.* 31:5 first-fruits of *c. w.*
32:28 storehouses for *c.* and *w.*
Neh. 5:11 part of *c.* and wine
10:39 offer. of *c.* and *w.* 13:5, 12

Ps. 4:7 in time *c. w.* increased
Lam. 2:12 Where is *c. and w.?*
Hos. 2:8 I gave her *c. and wine*
  22 the earth shall hear *c. w.*
  7:14 assemble for *c. and wine*
Joel 2:19 I will send you *c. a. w.*
Hag. 1:11 drought on *c. and w.*
Zec. 9:17 *c.* make men cheer. *w.*

CORNELIUS. *Acts* 10:1, 7, 25, 31

CORNER.

Lev. 21:5 nor shave off *c* of beard
2 *Chr.* 28:24 altars in every *c.*
Ps. 118:22 is head stone of *c.*
Prov. 7:8 passing near her *c.*
  12 she lieth in wait at every *c.*
  21:9 better to dwell in *c.* 25:24
Is. 30:20 thy teachers into a *c.*
Jer. 31:38 city built to gate of *c.*
  48:45 devour *c.* of Moab
  51:26 nor take a stone for a *c.*
Ezek. 46:21 in every *c.* of court
Amos 3:12 in S. in *c.* of a bed
Zec. 10:4 out of him came *c.*
Mat. 21:42 same is bec. head of *c.*
  Ps. 118:22; *Mark* 12:10; *Luke*
  20:17; *Acts* 4:11; 1 *Pet.* 2:7
Acts 26:26 was not done in a *c.*

CORNER-GATE.

Zec. 14:10 be inhabited to *c.-g.*

CORNER-STONE, S.

Job 38:6 who laid *c.-s.* thereof?
Ps. 144:12 daughters as *c.-stone*
Is. 28:16 in Zion a *c.-s.* 1 *Pet.* 2:6
Eph. 2:20 Christ being chief *c.-s.*

CORNERS.

Lev. 19:9 not reap the *c.* 23:22
  27 not round *c.* of your heads
Num. 24:17 smite *c.* of Moab
Deut. 32:26 I will scatter into *c.*
Neh. 9:22 divide them into *c.*
Job 1:19 smote four *c.* of house
Is. 11:12 gather disp. from four *c.*
Jer. 9:26 I will punish all in ut-
  termost *c.* 25:23; 49:32
Ezek. 7:2 end is come upon four *c.*
  45:19 put blood upon four *c.*
Mat. 6:5 they love to pray in *c.*
Acts 10:11 knit at four *c.* 11:5
Rev. 7:1 four angels on four *c.*

CORNET.

1 *Chr.* 15:28 ark with sound of *c.*
Ps. 98:6 of *c.* make a joyful noise
Dan. 3:5 time ye hear *c.* 15
Hos. 5:8 blow ye the *c.* in Gibeah

CORNETS.

2 *Sam.* 6:5 David played on *c.*
2 *Chr.* 15:14 shouting with *c.*

CORPSE. S.

2 *K.* 19:35 all dead *c. Is.* 37:36
Nah. 3:3 no end of their *c.* they
Mark 6:29 took up John's *c.* and

CORRECT.

Ps. 39:11 *c.* man for iniquity
  94:10 shall not he *c.?*
Prov. 29:17 *c.* thy son
Jer. 2:19 own wickedness *c.* thee
  10:24 O Lord, *c.* me, but with
  30:11 *c.* thee in measure 46:28

CORRECTED, ETH.

Job 5:17 happy is man God *c.*
Prov. 3:12 whom L. loveth he *c.*
  29:19 servant not be *c.* by words
Heb. 12:9 fathers which *c.* us

CORRECTION.

Job 37:13 rain whether for *c.*
Prov. 3:11 nei. be weary of his *c.*
  7:22 goeth as a fool to the *c.*
  15:10 *c.* grievous to him
  22:15 rod of *c.* drive it from him
  23:13 withhold not *c.* from child
Jer. 2:30 children received no *c.*
  5:3 have refused to receive *c.*
  7:28 nation receiveth not *c.*
Hab. 1:12 establish them for *c.*

Zep. 3:2 she received not *c.*
2 *Tim.* 3:16 scrip. profitable for *c.*

CORRUPT, Adjective.

Gen. 6:11 the earth also was *c.* 12
Job 17:1 my breath is *c.*
Ps. 14:1 they are *c.* 53:1; 73:8
  38:5 my wounds are *c.* because
Prov. 25:26 as a *c.* spring
Ezek. 20:44 not accor. to *c.* doings
  23:11 *c.* in her inordinate love
Dan. 2:9 ye have prep. *c.* words
Mal. 1:14 sacrificeth a *c.* thing
Mat. 7:17 a *c.* tree evil fruit
  18 *c.* tree good fruit, *Luke* 6:43
  12:33 or else make tree *c.* and
Eph. 4:22 put off the old man *c.*
  29 let no *c.* communication
1 *Tim.* 6:5 disputings of men of *c.*
2 *Tim.* 3:8 men of *c.* minds

CORRUPT, Verb.

Deut. 4:16 lest ye *c.* yours. 25
  31:29 after my death ye will *c.*
Dan. 11:32 sh. he *c.* by flatteries
Mal. 2:3 I will *c.* your seed
Mat. 6:19 moth and rust doth *c.*
  20 moth nor rust doth *c.*
1 *Cor.* 15:33 evil communica. *c.*
2 *Cor.* 2:17 that *c.* the word
Jude 10 in those things they *c.*
Rev. 19:2 *c.* earth with her forn.

CORRUPTED, ETH.

Gen. 6:12 all flesh had *c.* his way
Ex. 32:7 people have *c.* them-
  selves, *Deut.* 9:12; 32:5
Jud. 2:19 *c.* more than fathers
Ezek. 16:47 *c.* more than they
  28:17 hast *c.* thy wisdom
Hos. 9:9 deeply *c.* themselves
Zep. 3:7 and *c.* their doings
Mal. 2:8 *c.* covenant of Levi
Luke 12:33 nor moth *c.*
2 *Cor.* 7:2 wronged *c.* no man
  11:3 your minds be *c.*
Jam. 5:2 your riches are *c.*

CORRUPTERS.

Is. 1:4 children that are *c.*
Jer. 6:28 they are all *c.*

CORRUPTIBLE.

Rom. 1:23 image like to *c.* man
1 *Cor.* 9:25 to obtain a *c.* crown
  15:53 *c.* must put on incorrup.
1 *Pet.* 1:18 not redeemed with *c.*
  23 born again, not of *c.* seed
  3:4 be in that which is not *c.*

CORRUPTING.

Dan. 11:17 dau. of women *c.* her

CORRUPTION.

Lev. 22:25 their *c.* is in them
2 *K.* 23:13 right of mount of *c.*
Job 17:14 I said to *c.* my father.
Ps. 16:10 nei. suffer thy H. One
  to see *c. Acts* 2:27; 13:35
  49:9 live and not see *c.*
Is. 38:17 deliv. it from pit of *c.*
Dan. 10:8 comeliness into *c.*
Jon. 2:6 br. up my life from *c.*
Acts 2:31 nei. his flesh did see *c.*
  13:34 no more to return to *c.*
  36 David saw *c.*
  37 whom God raised saw no *c.*
Rom. 8:21 from bondage of *c.*
1 *Cor.* 15:42 is sown in *c.* raised
  50 *c.* inherit incorruption
Gal. 6:8 of the flesh reap *c.*
2 *Pet.* 1:4 escaped the *c.* that is
  2:12 perish in their own *c.*
  19 they are servants of *c.*

CORRUPTLY.

2 *Chr.* 27:2 people did yet *c.*
Neh. 1:7 we have dealt *c.* ag. thee

COST.

2 *Sam.* 19:42 eaten of king's *c.?*
  24:24 offer of that *c.* nothing
1 *Chr.* 21:24 b.-offering without *c.*

Luke 14:28 and counteth the *c.*

COSTLINESS.

Rev. 18:19 made rich by her *c.*

COSTLY.

1 *K.* 7:9 all these were of *c.* stones
John 12:3 took spikenard, *c.*
1 *Tim.* 2:9 not with *c.* array

COTES.

2 *Chr.* 32:28 Hezekiah made *c.*

COTTAGE, S.

Is. 1:8 dau. of Zion is left as a *c.*
  24:20 earth be removed like a *c.*
Zep. 2:6 coasts be *c.* for sheph.

COUCH, ES.

Gen. 49:4 Reuben went to my *c.*
Job 7:13 I say my *c.* shall ease
Ps. 6:6 I water *c.* with tears
Amos 3:12 in Damascus in a *c.*
  6:4 that stretch upon their *c.*
Luke 5:19 tiling with his *c.*
  24 arise take up thy *c.* and go
Acts 5:15 laid sick folks on *c.*

COUCH, ED.

Job 38:40 when they *c.* in dens
Gen. 49:9 Judah *c.* as a lion
Num. 24:9 he *c.* he lay as a lion

COUCHETH, ING.

Gen. 49:14 a strong ass *c.* down
Deut. 33:13 deep that *c.* beneath
Ezek. 25:5 a *c.* place for flocks

COULD.

Ps. 37:36 but he *c.* not be found
Jer. 15:1 *c.* not be toward this p.
Mark 9:18 they *c.* not, *Lu.* 9:40
  14:8 she hath done what she *c.*

COULTER.

1 *Sam.* 13:20 sharpen each his *c.*

COUNCIL.

Ps. 68:27 princes of J. and *c.*
Mat. 5:22 Raca, in danger of *c.*
  12:14 Pharisees held a *c.*
  26:59 *c.* so. false wit. *Mark* 14:55
Mark 15:1 *c.* bound Jesus
Luke 22:66 led Jesus into their *c.*
John 11:47 gather *c. Acts* 5:21
Acts 4:15 com. to go out of *c.*
  5:27 and set them before *c.*
  34 stood up in *c.* a Pharisee
  41 departed from *c.* rejoicing
  6:12 brought Stephen to *c.*
  22:30 he com. their *c.* to appear
  23:15 ye with *c.* sig. to captain
  24:20 evil in me, while before *c.*

COUNCILS.

Mat. 10:17 del. to *c. Mark* 13:9

COUNSEL.

Ex. 18:19 I will give thee *c.*
Num. 27:21 Eleazar ask *c.*
  31:16 *c.* of Balaam to trespass
Deut. 32:28 a nation void of *c.*
Jos. 9:14 asked not *c.* at the L.
Jud. 20:7 give here your *c.*
2 *Sam.* 15:31 *c.* of A. foolishness
  16:23 all *c.* of Ahith. with D.
  17:14 defeated good *c.* of Ah.
  20:18 surely ask *c.* at Abel
1 *K.* 1:12 let me give thee *c.*
  12:8 forsook *c.* 2 *Chr.* 10:8
2 *K.* 6:8 took *c.* with his servants
  18:20 I have *c.* for war, *Is.* 36:5
1 *Chr.* 10:13 died for asking *c.*
2 *Chr.* 22:5 Ahaziah after their *c.*
  25:16 art thou made of king's *c.*
Ezr. 10:8 accord. to *c.* of princes
Neh. 4:15 brought *c.* to naught
Job 5:13 *c.* of froward headlong
  10:3 shine on *c.* of the wicked
  12:13 hath *c.* and understand.
  21:16 *c.* of wicked is far, 22:18
  38:2 darkeneth *c.* by words?
  42:3 hideth *c.* without knowl.?

Ps. 1:1 not in *c.* of ungodly
14:6 shamed the *c.* of poor
16:7 who hath given me *c.*
20:4 the Lord fulfil all thy *c.*
31:13 they took *c.* against me
33:10 *c.* of heathen to naught
55:14 we took sweet *c.* together
64:2 from secret *c.* of wicked
73:24 guide me with thy *c.*
83:3 crafty *c.* against thy people
106:13 waited not for his *c.* but
43 provoked him with their *c.*
107:11 contemned *c.* of M. High
Prov. 8:14 *c.* is mine, and wisd.
11:14 where no *c.* is, people fall
12:15 hearkeneth to *c.* is wise
15:22 without *c.* purposes disap.
19:20 hear *c.* receive instruction
20:5 *c.* in man like deep water
18 purpose established by *c.*
21:30 no wisdom nor *c.* ag. L.
24:6 by wise *c.* shalt make war
27:9 friend by hearty *c.*
Is. 5:19 *c.* of Holy One
7:5 taken evil *c.* against thee
11:2 spirit of *c.* rest upon him
19:3 I will destroy *c.* of Egypt
11 *c.* of counsellors brutish
23:8 hath taken this *c.* ag. T. ?
28:29 which is wonderful in *c.*
29:15 to hide *c.* from Lord
40:14 with whom took he *c.*
44:26 performeth *c.* of his mes.
Jer. 18:18 nor *c.* perish from w.
23 knowest all their *c.* ag. me
19:7 make void the *c.* of Judah
32:19 mighty God, great in *c.*
38:15 if I give *c.* wilt not thou
49:7 is *c.* perished from prudent
30 king of Babylon taken *c.*
Ezek. 7:26 *c.* perish from ancients
11:2 give wicked *c.* in this city
Dan. 2:14 D. answered with *c.*
Hos. 4:12 my people ask *c.*
Mic. 4:12 understand his *c.*
Zec. 6:13 *c.* of peace between
Mark 3:6 *c.* ag. Jes. *John* 11:53
Luke 23:51 not consented to *c.* of
John 18:14 now Caiaphas gave *c.*
Acts 4:28 thy *c.* determined bef.
5:33 they took *c.* to slay them
38 if this *c.* be of men
9:23 Jews took *c.* to kill him

Acts 27:42 soldiers *c.* to kill pris.
Eph. 1:11 after *c.* of his own will
Heb. 6:17 immutability of his *c.*

COUNSEL of God, or Lord.
Jud. 18:5 said, Ask *c.* of God
20:18 chil. of Is. asked *c.* of G
1 *Sam.* 14:37 Saul asked *c.* of G
Ps. 33:11 *c.* of L. *Prov.* 19:21
Is. 19:17 bec. of the *c.* of Lord
Jer. 23:18 stood in *c.* of Lord
49:20 hear *c.* of Lord, 50:45
Luke 7:30 rejected *c.* of God
Acts 2:23 determinate *c.* of God
20:27 to declare all *c.* of God

My COUNSEL.
2 *Chr.* 25:16 not heark. to *my c.*
Job 29:21 kept silence at *my c.*
Prov. 1:25 set at naught *my c.*
30 they would none of *my c.*
Is. 46:10 *my c.* shall stand
11 executeth *my c.*
Jer. 23:22 had stood in *my c.*
Dan. 4:27 O king, let *my c.* be

Own COUNSEL.
Job 18:7 his *own c.* cast down
Hos. 10:6 ashamed of his *own c.*

Take COUNSEL.
Neh. 6:7 come now, let us *take c.*
Ps. 2:2 rulers *t. c.* against Lord
13:2 how long *t. c.* in my soul
71:10 wait for my soul, *take c.*
Is. 8:10 *t. c.* it come to naught
16:3 *take c.* execute judgment

30:1 that *take c.* but not of **me**
45:21 yea, let them *take c.*

COUNSEL, LED.
2 *Sam.* 16:23 which Ahith. *c.*
17:15 Ahithophel *c.* thus I *c.* 21
Job 26:3 how *c.* him hath no wis.
Ec. 8:21 *c.* thee to keep
Rev. 3:18 I *c.* to buy of me gold

COUNSELLOR.
2 *Sam.* 15:12 D.'s *c.* 1 *Chr.* 27:33
1 *Chr.* 26:14 Zechariah a wise *c.*
27:32 Jonathan was a *c.*
2 *Chr.* 22:3 Athaliah was his *c.*
Is. 3:3 Lord taketh away *c.*
9:6 be called Wonderful, *C.*
40:13 or who being his *c.* hath
41:28 for I beheld, was no *c.*
Mic. 4:9 is thy *c.* perished ?
Nah. 1:11 out of thee-a wicked *c.*
Mark 15:43 J. a *c.* *Luke* 23:50
Rom. 11:34 hath been his *c.*

COUNSELLORS.
2 *Chr.* 22:4 *c.* after father's death
Ezr. 4:5 hired *c.* against them
7:14 sent of king and his sev. *c.*
28 ext. mercy to me before *c.*
Job 3:14 at rest with *c.* of earth
12:17 leadeth *c.* away spoiled
Ps. 119:24 thy testimonies my *c.*
Prov. 11:14 multitude of *c.* 24:6
12:20 to *c.* of peace is joy
15:22 in multitude of *c.* estab.
Is. 1:26 restore thy *c.* as at begin.
19:11 wise *c.* of Pharaoh brutish
Dan. 3:27 the king's *c.* saw these
4:36 my *c.* sought unto me
6:7 all the *c.* have consulted

COUNSELS.
Job 37:12 turned about by his *c.*
Ps. 5:10 fall by their own *c.*
81:12 walked in their own *c.*
Prov. 1:5 shall attain to wise *c.*
12:5 *c.* of wicked are deceit
22:20 excellent things in *c. ?*
Is. 25:1 *c.* of old are faithful
47:13 wearied in mul. of thy *c.*
Jer. 7:24 in *c.* of their evil heart
Hos. 11:6 because of their own *c.*
Mic. 6:16 in *c.* of house of Ahab
1 *Cor.* 4:5 manifest *c.* of heart

COUNT.
Lev. 23:15 *c.* from morrow after
25:27 let *c.* years of sale, 52
Num. 23:10 can *c.* dust of Jacob
1 *Sam.* 1:16 *c.* not. me dau. of B.
Job 19:15 maids *c.* me a stranger
31:4 doth not he *c.* all my steps
Ps. 87:6 *L. c.* when he writeth
139:18 if I *c.* them, more than sand
22 I *c.* them mine enemies
Mic. 6:11 shall I *c.* them pure
Acts 20:24 neither *c.* I my life
Phil. 3:8 I *c.* all loss, *c.* but dung
13 I *c.* not to have apprehend.
2 *Thes.* 1:11 *c.* you worthy
3:15 *c.* him not as an enemy
1 *Tim.* 6:1 *c.* masters worthy of
Phile. 17 if thou *c.* me a partner
Jam. 1:2 *c.* it joy when ye fall
5:11 we *c.* happy which endure
2 *Pet.* 2:13 *c.* it pleasure to riot
2 *Pet.* 3:9 as some men *c.* slackn.
Rev. 13:18 *c.* number of beast

COUNTED.
Gen. 15:6 *c.* it to him *Ps.* 106:31 ;
Rom. 4:3 ; *Gal.* 3:6
30:33 be *c.* stolen with me
31:15 are we not *c.* strangers
1 *K.* 3:8 cannot be *c.* for multi.
1 *Chr.* 21:6 Benjamin *c.* he not
Neh. 13:13 were *c.* faithful
Job 18:3 where. are we *c.* as beas.
41:29 darts are *c.* as stubble
Ps. 44:22 we are *c.* as sheep for
88:4 *c.* with them go to the pit

Prov. 17:28 hold. peace is *c.* wise
27:14 be *c.* a curse to him
Is. 5:28 hoofs be *c.* like flint
32:15 field be *c.* for a forest
33:18 where is he *c.* towers
40:15 nations *c.* as small dust
17 nations *c.* less than nothing
Hos. 8:12 were *c.* as strange
Mat. 14:5 *c.* him, *Mark* 11:32
Luke 21:36 *c.* worthy to escape
Acts 5:41 rejoic. were *c.* worthy
19:19 burn books, and *c.* price
Rom. 2:26 uncir. be *c.* for circ.
4:5 his faith is *c.* for right.
9:8 child. of promise *c.* for seed
Phil. 3:7 those I *c.* lost for Christ
2 *Thes.* 1:5 *c.* worthy of kingdom
1 *Tim.* 1:12 he *c.* me faithful
5:17 elders *c.* worthy
Heb. 3:3 *c.* worthy of more glory
7:6 he whose descent is not *c.*
10:29 *c.* blood of cov. unholy
See ACCOUNTED

COUNTETH, ING.
Job 19:11 *c.* me of enem. 33:10
Ec. 7:27 *c.* one by one, to find
Luke 14:28 and *c.* the cost

COUNTENANCE, Verb.
Ex. 23:3 neither *c.* a poor man

COUNTENANCE.
Gen. 4:5 Cain was wroth, *c.* fell
31:2 Jacob beheld *c.* of Laban
5 father's *c.* not toward me
Num. 6:26 lift up his *c.* on thee
Deut. 28:50 a nation of fierce *c.*
Jud. 13:6 his *c.* like *c.* of angel
1 *Sam.* 1:18 her *c.* no more sad
16:7 look not on his *c.* or height
12 David was of beau. *c.* 17:42
25:3 Abigail ; 2 *Sam.* 14:27 Tam.
2 *K.* 8:11 he settled his *c.* on H.
Neh. 2:2 why is thy *c.* sad
3 why not *c.* sad, when city
Job 14:20 thou changest his *c.*
29:24 light of *c.* cast not down
Ps. 4:6 lift light of thy *c.* on us
10:4 pride of *c.* not seek God
11:7 *c.* doth behold upright
21:6 made him glad with thy *c.*
42:5 praise him for help of his *c.*
11 who is health of my *c.* 43:5
44:3 light of thy *c.* did save
80:16 perish at rebuke of thy *c.*
89:15 walk in light of thy *c.*
90:8 secret sins in light of thy *c.*
Prov. 15:13 maketh a cheerful *c.*
16:15 in light of king's *c.* is life
25:23 so angry *c.* a backbiting
27:17 so man sharpeneth *c.* of
Ec. 7:3 by sadness of *c.*
Cant. 2:14 see *c.* thy *c.* is comely
5:15 his *c.* is as Lebanon
Is. 3:9 *c.* doth witness ag. them
Ezek. 27:35 be troubled in their *c.*
Dan. 5:6 king's *c.* was changed
8:23 king of fierce *c.* stand up
Mat. 6:16 as hypocrites, of sad *c.*
28:3 *c.* like lightning, *Luke* 9:29
Acts 2:28 full of joy with thy *c.*
2 *Cor.* 3:7 not behold Mos. for *c.*
Rev. 1:16 *c.* was as sun shineth
See CHANGED.

COUNTENANCES.
Dan. 1:13 let our *c.* be looked on
15 their *c.* appeared fairer and

COUNTERVAIL.
Est. 7:4 not *c.* the k.'s damage

COUNTRY.
Gen. 24:4 thou shalt go to my *c.*
29:26 be so done in our *c.*
30:25 that I may go to my *c.*
42:33 lord of *c.* said unto us
Num. 15:13 born in *c.* shall do
32:4 *c.* Lord smote before Israel
Deut. 26:3 come into *c.* L. sware

Jos. 2:2 to search out the *c.* 3
7:2 go up and view the *c.*
Jud. 11:21 Isr. possessed that *c.*
16:24 the destroyer of our *c.*
Ruth 1:2 came into *c.* of Moab
2 *Sam.* 15:23 all the *c.* wept
1 *K.* 20:27 Syrians filled the *c.*
2 *K.* 3:20 *c.* filled with water
Is. 1:7 *c.* is desolate, cities burnt
22:18 like a ball in a large *c.*
Jer. 22:10 not see his native *c.*
31:8 bring them from north *c.*
48:21 judgment upon plain *c.*
50:9 an assembly from north *c.*
Ezek. 20:38 bring them forth of *c.*
25:9 glory of *c.* Beth-jeshimoth
47:22 be to you as born in the *c.*
Jon. 4:2 when yet in my *c.*
Mat. 9:31 his fame in all that *c.*
Mark 5:10 not send th. out of *c.*
14 told it in the *c. Luke* 8:34
Luke 15:15 joined to cit. of th. *c.*
Acts 12:20 their *c.* was nourished
27:27 they drew near to some *c.*
Heb. 11:9 as in a strange *c.*
14 plainly that they seek a *c.*
15 been mindful of that *c.*
16 desire better *c.* a heavenly

Far COUNTRY.

Jos. 9:6 we be come from *f. c.* 9
1 *K.* 8:41 out of a *far c.* for thy
sake, 2 *Chr.* 6:32
2 *K.* 20:14 *fr. f. c.* fr. Bab. *Is.* 39:3
Prov. 25:25 good news from *f. c.*
Is. 13:5 from *f. c.* to destroy
46:11 exec. counsel from *far c.*
Jer. 4:16 watchers come fr. *far c.*
8:19 because of them in a *far c.*
Mat. 21:33 householder went into
far c. Mark 12:1
25:14 a man trav. into a *far c.*
Luke 15:13 journey into a *far c.*

Own COUNTRY.

Lev. 16:29 one of *own c.* 24:22
1 *K.* 10:13 went to her *o. c.*
11:21 I may go to my *own c.*
22:36 every man to *own c.*
Jer. 51:9 every one into his *o. c.*
Mat. 2:12 dep. into their *own c.*
13:57 without honor save in his
o. c. Mark 6:4 ; *Luke* 4:24
Mark 6:1 came into his *own c.*
John 4:44 proph. no honor in *o. c.*

Thy COUNTRY.

Gen. 12:1 out of *thy c. Acts* 7:3
32:9 return to *t. c.* and kindred
Num. 20:17 let us pass thro' *t. c.*
Jon. 1:8 what is *thy c.* ?
Luke 4:23 do here in *thy c.*

COUNTRY Villages.

1 *Sam.* 6:18 both of *c. villages*

COUNTRYMEN.

2 *Cor.* 11:26 in perils by *own c.*
1 *Thes.* 2:14 like things of your *c.*

COUNTRIES.

Gen. 26:3 to thy seed these *c.* 4
41:57 all *c.* came to buy corn
1 *Chr.* 22:5 glory through *c.*
2 *Chr.* 20:29 fear of G. on all *c.*
Ezr. 3:3 because of people of *c.*
4:20 which ruled over all *c.*
Ps. 110:6 wound over many *c.*
Is. 8:9 give ear ye of far *c.*
Jer. 23:3 I will gather my flock
out of all *c.* 8 ; 32:37
28:8 prophesied against many *c.*
Ezek. 5:5 Jerusalem in midst of *c.*
6 changed statutes more th. *c.*
6:8 when scattered through *c.*
11:16 I scattered them among
c. little sanctuary in *c.*
17 out of *c.* 20:34, 41
22:4 a mocking to all *c.*
25:7 to perish out of *c.*
29:12 disperse through *c.* 36:19

35:10 these two *c.* shall be mine
Dan. 11:40 he shall enter into *c.*
42 forth his hand upon the *c.*
Zec. 10:9 remember me in far *c.*
Luke 21:21 that are in *c.* enter

COUPLED.

1 *Pet.* 3:2 conversation *c.* with f.

COURAGE.

Jos. 2:11 nor any more *c.* in any
2 *Chr.* 15:8 took *c.* put away idols
Dan. 11:25 stir up *c.* ag. king
Acts 28:15 thanked God took *c.*

Good COURAGE.

Num. 13:20 *good c.* bring fruit
Deut. 31:6 strong and of *good c.* 7,
23 ; *Jos.* 1:6, 9, 18 ; 10:25 ; 1
Chr. 22:13 ; 28:20
2 *Sam.* 10:12 be of *g. c.* 1 *Chr.*
19:13 ; *Ezr.* 10:4 ; *Is.* 41:6
Ps. 27:14 be of *g. c.* he shall stre.
thy heart, 31:24

COURAGEOUS, LY.

Jos. 1:7 be *c.* 23:6 ; 2 *Chr.* 32:7
2 *Sam.* 13:28 be *c.* valiant
2 *Chr.* 19:11 deal *c.*
Amos 2:16 he *c.* shall flee naked

COURSE.

1 *Chr.* 27:1 of every *c.* 24,000
2 *Chr.* 5:11 did not wait by *c.*
Ezr. 3:11 sang together by *c.*
Ps. 82:5 foundations out of *c.*
Jer. 8:6 every one turned to his *c.*
23:10 their *c.* is evil, their force
Luke 1:5 Zacharias *c.* of Abia
8 in the order of his *c.*
Acts 13:25 John fulfilled his *c.*
16:11 with straight *c.* 21:1
20:24 finish my *c.* with joy
21:7 finished *c.* from Tyre
1 *Cor.* 14:27 by three, by *c.*
2 *Thes.* 3:1 may have free *c.*
2 *Tim.* 4:7 I have finished my *c.*
Jam. 3:6 on fire the *c.* of nature

See WATERCOURSE.

COURSES.

Jud. 5:20 the stars in their *c.*
1 *Chr.* 23:6 the Levites into *c.*
2 *Chr.* 23:8 Jeh. dismissed not *c.*
31:2 Hezekiah appointed *c.*
35:10 Levites stood in their *c.*

COURT.

Ex. 27:9 shalt make the *c.*
40:8 thou shalt set up the *c.*
2 *K.* 20:4 afore Isaiah was into *c.*
2 *Chr.* 20:5 Jehosh. bef. new *c.*
24:21 stoned Zechariah in *c.*
29:16 brought unclean. into *c.*
Est. 6:5 beh. H. standeth in *c.*
Is. 34:13 shall be a *c.* for owls
Jer. 19:14 Jeremiah stood in *c.*
26:2 stand in *c.* of Lord's house
32:2 Jeremiah was shut up in *c.*
of prison, 33:1 ; 39:15
Ezek. 8:7 brou. me to door of *c.* 16
10:3 the cloud filled inner *c.*
40:17 to outward *c.* 42:1 ; 46:21
28 he brought me to inner *c.*
43:5 brought me to inner *c.*
46:21 in every cor. of *c.* was a *c.*
Amos 7:13 and it is the king's *c.*
Rev. 11:2 *c.* without the temple

COURTS.

2 *K.* 21:5 built altars for hosts of
heav. in two *c.* 2 *Chr.* 33:5
1 *Chr.* 23:28 office to wait in *c.*
28:6 Solomon shall build my *c.*
2 *Chr.* 23:5 all the people be in *c.*
Ps. 65:4 he may dwell in thy *c.*
84:2 soul fainteth for *c.* of Lord
92:13 flourish in *c.* of our God
96:8 bring offering come into *c.*
100:4 enter his *c.* with praise
116:19 pay vows in the *c.*
135:2 ye that stand in the *c.* of

Is. 1:12 to tread my *c.* ?
62:9 drink it in *c.* of holiness
Ezek. 9:7 fill *c.* with the slain
Zec. 3:7 shalt also keep my *c.*
Luke 7:25 delicately in king's *c.*

COURTEOUS, LY.

Acts 27:3 Julius *c.* entreated P.
28:7 and Publius lodged us *c.*
1 *Pet.* 3:8 love as brethren, be *c.*

COUSIN, S.

Luke 1:36 thy *c.* Elisabeth
1:58 her *c.* heard how

COVENANT.

Gen. 9:12 tok. of *c.* 13, 17 ; 17:11
17:4 my *c.* is with thee
13 my *c.* be in your flesh
14 hath broken my *c.*
Ex. 31:16 sab. a perpetual *c.*
34:28 wrote upon tables the *c.*
Lev. 26:15 that ye break my *c.*
Num. 25:12 my *c.* of peace
13 *c.* of everlasting priesthood
Deut. 4:13 dec. unto you his *c.*
23 lest ye forget *c.* of Lord
31 Lord not forget *c.*
9:11 Lord gave me tables of *c.*
29:1 these are the words of *c.*
12 thou shouldest enter into *c.*
21 ac. to all curses of *c.*
25 because ye have forsaken *c.*
31:20 they will break my *c.*
Jud. 2:1 I will never break *c.*
1 *Sam.* 20:8 thy serv. in *c.* of L.
1 *K.* 19:10 Israel forsaken *c.* 14
20:34 send thee aw. with this *c.*
2 *K.* 11:23 bec. of *c.* with Abrah.
23:3 to perform *c.* all the people
stood to *c.* 2 *Chr.* 34:31
1 *Chr.* 16:15 be mindful of his *c.*
2 *Chr.* 15:12 into *c.* to seek Lord
Neh. 13:29 defiled *c.* of priesthoo.
Ps. 25:14 will show them his *c.*
50:16 take my *c.* in thy mouth
55:20 he hath broken his *c.*
74:20 respect to *c.* for dark pla.
Ps. 78:37 neit. were stead. in his *c.*
89:28 my *c.* st. fast with him
34 my *c.* will I not break, nor
39 made void *c.* of thy servant
111:5 ever be mindful of his *c.*
9 commanded his *c.* for ever
Prov. 2:17 forgetteth *c.* of her G.
Is. 28:18 *c.* with death be disan.
33:8 broken *c.* he hath despised
42:6 for *c.* of people, 49:8
54:10 nor *c.* of my peace be rem.
56:4 eunuchs hold of my *c.* 6
59:21 as for me this is my *c.*
Jer. 11:2 hear ye words of *c.* 6
3 cursed obeyeth not w. of *c.*
14:21 break not thy *c.* with us
22:9 bec. they have forsaken *c.*
31:32 which my *c.* they break
33:20 if you can break *c.* of day
21 may *c.* be broken with Da.
25 if my *c.* be not with day
34:18 not performed words of *c.*
50:5 join to L. in perpetual *c.*
Ezek. 16:8 into a *c.* with thee
59 in breaking *c.* 17:18
61 give th. for daugh. not by *c.*
17:15 or break *c.* and be deliv. ?
16 whose *c.* he brake
19 my *c.* he hath broken, it
20:37 bring you into bond of *c.*
44:7 they have broken my *c.*
Dan. 9:27 confirm *c.* for one week
11:22 also the prince of *c.*
28 his heart be against holy *c.*
30 indignation against holy *c.*
32 do wickedly against *c.*
Hos. 10:4 falsely in making a *c.*
Zec. 11:10 I might break my *c.*
Mal. 2:4 my *c.* be with Levi, 5
8 ye have corrupted *c.* of Levi

10 by profaning c. of fathers
14 she is the wife of thy c.
3:1 messenger of c. ye delight in
Acts 3:25 children of c. G. made
7:8 gave him c. of circumcision
Rom. 1:31 c. breakers
11:27 this is my c. when I take
Gal. 3:15 tho' it be but a m.'s c.
17 the c. confirmed bef. of God
Heb. 8:6 mediator of a better c.
7 if first c. had been faultless
9 they continued not in my c.
9:1 first c. had also ordinances
4 and the tables of the c.
See ARK, BLOOD, BREAK.

Book of the COVENANT.
Ex. 24:7 Moses took book of c.
2 *K.* 23:2 Josiah read all the w. of book of c. 2 *Chr.* 34:30

Establish COVENANT.
Gen. 6:18 establish my c. 9:9
17:7 est. c. bet. me and Abra.
19 esta. c. with I. and seed, 21
Ezek. 16:60 e. to thee an everl. c.

Everlasting COVENANT.
Gen. 9:16 I may remember e. c.
17:13 your flesh for everlast. c.
19 c. with Isaac for an ever. c.
2 *Sam.* 23:5 an ever. c. ordered
1 *Chr.* 16:17 confirmed to Israel for an everlast. c. *Ps.* 105:10
Is. 24:5 have broken everlast. c.
55:3 e. c. w. you, 61:8 ; *Jer.* 32:40
Ezek. 37:26 everlast. c. with them
Heb. 13:20 thro' blood of ever. c.

Keep, keepeth, *or* kept COVENANT.
Gen. 17:9 thou shalt keep my c.
Ex. 19:5 if ye will keep my c.
Deut. 7:9 God wh. k. c. 12 : 1 *K.* 8:23 ; 2 *Ch.* 6:14; *Neh.* 1:5; 9:32
29:9 keep words of this c. and do
33:9 they have kept thy c.
1 *K.* 11:11 hast not k. c. *Ps.* 78:10
Ps. 25:10 to such as k. c. 103:18
132:12 if thy child. keep my c.
Ezek. 17:14 by k. c. it might
Dan. 9:4 keep c. and mercy

Made COVENANT.
Gen. 15:18 same day L. m. c.
21:27 Abra. and Abim. m. c. 32
Deut. 5:2 L. m. a c. with us in H.
3 m. not c. with fa. *Heb.* 8:9
29:1 besides c. he made in Ho
31:16 will break my c. I made
Jos. 24:25 Joshua m. a c.
1 *Sam.* 18:3 J. and D. m. c. 23:18
20:16 J. m. c. with house of D.
1 *K.* 8:21 ark w. is c. of L. he m.
20:34 Ahab made c. with Benj.
2 *K.* 11:4 Jehoiada m.
17 made c. bet. Lord and king
17:15 c. made with fathers
38 c. made with you not forget
23:3 Josiah m. c. 2 *Chr.* 34:31
1 *Chr.* 11:3 David m. c. with eld.
1 *Chr.* 16:16 mind. of c. he made with A. *Neh.* 9:8 ; *Ps.* 105:9
2 *Chr.* 21:7 c. he had m. with D.
23:3 m. a c. with king Joash
Job 31:1 m. a c. with mine eyes
Ps. 50:5 m. a c. with me
89:3 made a c. with my chosen
Is. 28:15 m. a c. with death
57:8 enlarg. thy bed and m. a c.
Jer. 11:10 broke c. I m.
31:32 not a c. to c. I m. with fa.
34:8 Zed. m. c. with people, 15
13 I made a c. with your fath.
15 ye had made c. before me
Ezek. 17:13 made a c. with him

Make COVENANT.
Gen. 17:2 m. c. bet. me and thee
26:28 m. c. with thee, 31:44
Ex. 23:32 m. no c. *Deut.* 7:2

34:10 I m. c. before thy people
12 m. c. with inhabitants, 15
Deut. 29:14 nor with you m. c.
1 *Sam.* 11:2 on this cond. I m. c.
2 *Chr.* 29:10 in my he. to m. a c.
Neh. 9:38 we make a sure c.
Job 41:4 will he m. a c.
Jer. 31:33 this is the c. I will m. *Heb.* 8:10; 10:16
Ezek. 34:25 m. c. of peace, 37:26
Hos. 2:18 m. c. for them.
12:1 do m. c. with Assyrians

New COVENANT.
Jer. 31:31 n. c. with Is. *Heb.* 8:8
Heb. 8:13 a new c. the first old
12:24 mediator of the new c.

Remember COVENANT.
Gen. 9:15 I will r. my c. *Lev.* 26:42 ; *Ezek.* 16:60
Lev. 26:45 for their sakes r. c.
Ps. 105:8 he hath r. his c. 106:45
Amos 1:9 rem. not the broth. c.
Luke 1:72 and to rem. his holy c.

COVENANT of Salt.
Lev. 2:13 salt of c. to be lacking
Num. 18:19 it is a c. of s.
2 *Chr.* 13:5 to David by c. of salt

Transgressed, ing COVENANT.
Deut. 17:2 wickedness in t. his c.
Jos. 7:11 transgressed my c.
15 because he t. c. of the Lord, *Jud.* 2:20 ; 2 *K.* 18:12
23:16 ye have trans. c. of Lord
Jer. 34:18 men that trans. my c.
Hos. 6:7 like men trans. the c.
8:1 they have trans. my c.

COVENANTED.
2 *Chr.* 7:18 as I have c. with D.
Hag. 2:5 word I c. with you
Mat. 26:15 c. for thirty pieces.
Luke 22:5 c. to give him money

COVENANTS.
Rom. 9:4 to whom pertaineth c.
Gal. 4:24 two c. one from Sinai
Eph. 2:12 strangers from c.

COVER.
Ex. 33:22 c. thee while I pass
Num. 22:5 they c. face of earth
Deut. 23:13 c. wh. com. from thee
33:12 shall c. him all the day
1 *Sam.* 24:3 S. went to c. his feet
Neh. 4:5 c. not their iniquity
Job 16:18 earth. c. not thy blood
21:26 worms shall c. them
22:11 waters c. thee, 38:34
40:22 the shady trees c. him
Ps. 91:4 c. thee with his feath.
104:9 they turn not to c. earth
109:29 c. with own confusion
139:11 darkness shall c. me
140:9 mischief of lips c. them
Is. 11:9 waters c. sea, *Hab.* 2:14
14:11 worms c. thee
22:17 L. will surely c. thee
26:21 earth no more c. her s.a.n
30:1 c. with a covering, but
58:7 naked, that thou c. him
59:6 nor c. themsel. with works
60:2 darkness shall c. the earth
6 multi. of camels shall c. thee
Jer. 46:8 I will c. the earth
Ezek. 7:18 horror shall c. them
12:6 thou shalt c. thy face
12 he shall c. his face, that
24:7 pour. it not on the gr. to c.
17 c. not thy lips,
22 ye shall not c. your lips
26:10 horses, their dust c. thee
19 when waters shall c. thee
30:18 as for her a cloud c. her
32:7 I will c. the heaven, sun
37:6 c. you with skin and
38:9 be like cloud to c. land, 16
Hos. 2:9 flax given to c. her

10:8 mount. c. us, *Luke* 23:30
Ob. 10 shame shall c. thee
Mic. 3:7 shall all c. their lips
7:10 shame c. her said to me
Hab. 2:17 violence of L. c. thee
Mark 14:65 and c. his face
1 *Cor.* 11:7 man not to c. head
1 *Pet.* 4:8 charity c. mult. of sins

COVERED.
Gen 7:19 mountains were c. 20
9:23 c. naked. of their father
24:65 Rebekah c. herself
38:14 Tam. c. her with a veil
Ex. 14:28 waters c. chariots
15:5 the depths c. them
10 the sea c. them, *Jos.* 24:7
24:15 a cloud c. the mount. 16
37:9 c. with wings mercy-seat
40:21 veil c. ark of testimony
Num. 4:20 when holy things c.
Deut. 32:15 art c. with fatness
Jud. 4:18 Jael c. Sisera,
1 *Sam.* 19:13 Mich. c. the image
28:14 old man cometh up c.
1 *K.* 1:1 c. David with clothes
8:7 cher. c. the ark, 2 *Chr.* 5:8
2 *K.* 19:1 Hezekiah c. himself with sackcloth, *Is.* 37:1
Job 23:17 c. dark. from my face
31:33 if I c. my transgressions
Ps. 44:15 shame of face c. me
19 c. us with shadow of death
65:13 valleys c. over with corn
68:13 w. of dove c. with silver
71:13 c. with reproach that seek
89:45 hast c. him with shame
106:17 c. company of Abiram
139:13 c. me in mother's womb
Prov. 26:23 a potsherd c. with
26 whose hatred is c. by deceit
Ec. 6:4 his name c. with dark.
Is. 6:2 with twain he c. his face
29:10 the seers hath he c.
51:16 I have c. thee in shadow
61:10 c. me with robe
Jer. 51:42 she is c. with waves
Lam. 2:1 c. dau. of Z. with clo.
3:16 he hath c. me with ashes
43 hast c. with anger
44 c. thyself with a cloud
Ezek. 1:11 two wings c. bod. 23
16:8 and c. thy nakedness
10 I c. thee with silk
18:7 and hath c. the naked, 16
24:8 her blood should not be c.
27:7 blue and purple c. thee
31:15 I c. the deep for him
37:8 and skin c. them above
Jon. 3:8 and beast he c. with sa.
Hab. 3:3 his glory c. heavens
Mat. 8:24 was c. with waves
10:26 nothing c. that shall not be revealed, *Luke* 12:2
1 *Cor.* 11:6 the woman be not c.

COVERED face.
Gen. 38:15 Tamar had c. her fac.
2 *Sam.* 19:4 but David c. his face
Est. 7:8 they c. Haman's face
Ps. 69:7 shame hath c. my face
Prov. 24:31 nettles c. face there.
Is. 6:2 with twain he c. his face
Jer. 51:51 shame hath c. our face.

Head COVERED.
2 *Sam.* 15:30 David had his h. c.
Est. 6:12 Haman, his head c.
Ps. 140:7 c. my head in battle
Jer. 14:3 and their heads, 4
1 *Cor.* 11:4 ev. man praying, h. c.

COVERED sin
Ps. 32:1 sin is c. *Rom.* 4:7
85:2 thou hast c. all their sin

COVEREDST.
Ps. 104:6 c. it with deep
Ezek. 16:18 br. garm. and c. them

COVEREST.
Deut. 22:12 vesture wherewith *c.*
Ps. 104:2 *c.* thyself with light

COVERETH.
Num. 22:11 *c.* face of the earth
Jud. 3:24 surely he *c.* his feet
Job 9:24 he *c.* faces of judges
15:27 *c.* his face with fatness
36:30 he *c.* bottom of the sea
32 with clouds he *c.* the light
Ps. 73:6 violence *c.* as garment
109:19 garment which *c.* him
147:8 *c.* heaven with clouds
Prov. 10:6 vio. *c.* the mouth, 11
12 love *c.* all sins
12:16 prudent man *c.* shame
17:9 *c.* transgression seek. love
28:13 *c.* his sins, shall not pros.
Jer. 3:25 our confusion *c.* us
Ezek. 28:14 art cherub that *c.*
Mal. 2:16 for one *c.* violence
Luke 8:16 candle *c.* it with ves.

COVERING, Participle.
Ex. 25:20 *c.* mercy-seat with
Num. 4:5 shall take down *c.* veil
Ezek. 28:16 O *c.* cherub
Mal. 2:13 *c.* the altar with tears

COVERING, Substantive.
Gen. 20:16 thee a *c.* of the eyes
Ex. 22:27 it is his *c.* for his skin
Lev. 13:45 put *c.* on upper lip
2 *Sam.* 17:19 *c.* over well's mou.
Job 22:14 thick clouds *c.* to him
24:7 naked have no *c.* in cold
26:6 destruction hath no *c.*
31:19 any poor without *c.*
Ps. 105:39 he spread cloud for *c.*
Cant. 3:10 he made *c.* of purple
Is. 22:8 discovered *c.* of Judah
25:7 *c.* cast over all people
28:20 *c.* narrower, than can wr.
30:1 with *c.* not of my Spirit
22 ye shall defile *c.* of images
50:3 I make sackcloth their *c.*
Ezek. 28:13 precious stone thy *c.*
1 *Cor.* 11:15 hair is given for *c.*
See BADGER.

COVERINGS.
Prov. 7:16 deck. my bed with *c.*
31:22 maketh herself *c.* of tap.

COVERS.
Ex. 25:29 make *c.* 37:16
Num. 4:7 put *c.* to cover withal

COVERT.
2 *K.* 16:18 *c.* for the sabbath,
Ahaz took down
Job 38:40 when lions abide in *c.*
40:21 behemoth lieth in *c.* of
Ps. 61:4 trust in *c.* of thy wings
Is. 4:6 a tabernacle for a *c.*
16:4 be thou a *c.* from spoiler
32:2 a man be *c.* from tempest
Jer. 25:38 forsaken his *c.*

COVET.
Ex. 20:17 thou shalt not *c. Deut.*
5:21 ; *Rom.* 7:7; 13:9
Mic. 2:2 they *c.* fields and take
1 *Cor.* 12:31 but *c.* the best gifts
14:39 *c.* to prophesy

COVETED.
Jos. 7:21 then I *c.* them, and
Acts 20:33 I *c.* no man's silver
1 *Tim.* 6:10 while some *c.* after

COVETETH.
Prov. 21:26 *c.* all the day long
Hab. 2:9 woe to him *c.* evil cov.

COVETOUS.
Ps. 10:3 wicked blesseth *c.*
Luke 16:14 Pharis. who were *c.*
1 *Cor.* 5:10 yet not altog. with *c.*
11 *c.* with such not to eat
6:10 nor *c.* inherit, *Eph.* 5:5
1 *Tim.* 3:3 bishop must not be *c.*
2 *Tim.* 3:2 in last times m. be *c.*

2 *Pet* 2:14 exer. with *c.* practices

COVETOUSNESS.
Ex. 18:21 men hating *c.*
Ps. 119:36 incline not heart to *c.*
Prov. 28:16 hateth *c.* sh. prolong
Is. 57:17 for iniquity of his *c.*
Jer. 6:13 given to *c.* 8:10
22:17 eyes are not but for thy *c.*
51:13 and measure of thy *c.*
Ezek. 33:31 heart goeth after *c.*
Hab. 2:9 that coveteth an evil *c.*
Mark 7:22 out heart proceed. *c.*
Luke 12:15 he said, beware of *c.*
Rom. 1:29 filled with all *c.*
2 *Cor.*9:5 as a matter not of *c.*
Eph. 5:3 *c.* let it not be named
Col. 3:5 mortify *c.* wh. is idola.
1 *Thes.* 2:5 nor used cloak of *c.*
Heb. 13:5 conver. be without *c.*
2 *Pet.* 2:3 through *c.* make mer.

COW.
Lev. 22:28 *c.* or ewe, sh. not kill
Num. 18:17 firstling of *c.*
Job 21:10 their *c.* casteth not
Is. 7:21 nourish a young *c.*
11:7 *c.* and the bear shall feed
Ezek. 4:15 given thee *c.* dung for
Amos 4:3 every *c.* at that before

COZBI. *Num.* 25:15, 18

CRACKLING.
Ec. 7:6 *c.* of thorns under pot

CRACKNELS.
1 *K.* 14:3 take with thee *c.*

CRAFT.
Dan. 8:25 cause *c.* to prosper
Mark 14:1 take him by *c.*
Acts 18:3 he was of same *c.*
19:27 not only our *c.* is in dan.
Rev. 18:22 whatsoever *c.* he be

CRAFTINESS.
Job 5:13 in their *c.* 1 *Cor.* 3:19
Luke 20:23 he perceived their *c.*
2 *Cor.* 4:2 not walking in *c.* nor
Eph. 4:14 carried by cunning *c.*

CRAFTY.
Job 5:12 he disap. devices of *c.*
15:5 thou choosest tongue of *c.*
Ps. 83:3 *c.* counsel against
2 *Cor.* 12:16 being *c.* I caught

CRAFTSMAN.
Deut. 27:15 the work of the *c*
Rev. 18:22 no *c.* be found.

CRAFTSMEN.
2 *K.* 24:14 carried away *c.* 16
1 *Chr.* 4:14 for they were *c.*
Neh. 11:35 the valley of *c.*
Hos. 13:2 the work of *c.*
Acts 19:24 no small gain to *c.*
38 *c.* have matter against any

CRAG.
Job 39:28 eagle abideth on *c.*

CRANE.
Is. 38:14 like *c.* so did I chatter
Jer. 8:7 *c.* obs. time of coming

CRASHING.
Zep. 1:10 great *c.* from hills

CRAVED, ETH.
Prov. 16:26 for his moutn *c.* it
Mark 15:43 Joseph *c.* body of J.

CREATE.
Ps. 51:10 *c.* in me a clean heart
Is. 4:5 *c.* on every d.-p. a cloud
45:7 *c.* darkness, I *c.* evil
57:19 I *c.* the fruits of the lips
65:17 I *c.* new heavens
18 rejoice in that which I *c.*

CREATED.
Gen. 1:1 in the begin. God *c.* he
21 God *c.* great whales
27 God *c.* man in his own image, male and female, 5:2
2:3 in it rested from all he *c.*

6:7 will destroy man I have *c.*
Deut. 4:32 day God *c.* man
Ps. 89:12 north and south h. *c.*
102:18 people to be *c.*
104:30 forth spirit they are *c.*
148:5 com. and they were *c.*
Is. 40:26 hath *c.* these things
41:20 Holy One of Is. hath *c.* it
42:5 he that *c.* the heavens
43:1 Lord that *c.* thee, O Jacob
7 I have *c.* him for my glory
45:8 I the Lord have *c.* it
12 I have *c.* man upon it
18 he *c.* it not in vain
48:7 *c.* now, not from begin.
54:16 have *c.* smith, *c.* waster
Jer. 31:22 L. hath *c.* a new thing
Ezek. 21:30 judge where wast *c.*
28:13 in day thou wast *c.*
15 from day thou wast *c.*
Mal. 2:10 hath not one God *c.*
Mark 13:19 creation G. *c.*
1 *Cor.* 11:9 man *c.* for the wom.
Eph. 1:10 workmanship *c.* in C.
3:9 who *c.* all things by Jes. C.
4:24 God is *c.* in righteousness
Col. 1:16 were all things *c.*
3:10 after image of him *c.* him
1 *Tim.* 4:3 G. *c.* to be received
Rev. 4:11 hast *c.* all things, for
thy pleasure are and were *c.*
10:6 who *c.* heaven and the

CREATETH.
Amos 4:13 *c.* w. L. is his name

CREATION.
Mark 10:6 from *c.* male and fe.
13:19 as was not from the *c.*
Rom. 1:20 from *c.* are clearly
8:22 that whole *c.* groaneth
2 *Pet.* 3:4 continue as from the *c.*
Rev. 3:14 beginning of *c.* of God

CREATOR.
Ec. 12:1 remember *c.* in youth
Is. 40:28 *c.* of ends of the earth
43:15 I am the Lord, *c.* of Israel
Rom. 1:25 creature more than *c.*
1 *Pet.* 4:19 as to a faithful *c.*

CREATURE.
Gen. 1:20 bring forth moving *c.*
Lev. 11:46 this is law of every *c.*
Mark 16:15 gospel to every *c.*
Col. 1:23
Rom. 8:19 expectation of *c.*
20 *c.* made subject to vanity
21 *c.* be delivered from bond.
39 any *c.* able to separate us
2 *Cor.* 5:17 he is a new *c.*
Gal. 6:15 nor uncir. but new *c.*
Col. 1:15 first-born of every *c.*
1 *Tim.* 4:4 every *c.* of G. is good
Heb. 4:13 any *c.* not manifest
Rev. 5:13 every *c.* in heaven

Living CREATURE.
Gen. 1:21 God created every *l. c.*
24 let earth bring forth *liv. c.*
2:19 Adam called every *liv. c.*
9:10 cov. with every *living c.*
12 between me and ev. *l. c.* 15
Lev. 11:46 law of every *living c.*
Ezek. 1:20 spirit of *l. c.* 21 ; 10:17
10:15 *l. c.* I saw by Chebar, 20

CREATURES.
Is. 13:21 houses full of doleful *c.*
Jam. 1:18 first-fruits of his *c.*
Rev. 8:9 third of *c.* in sea died

Living CREATURES.
Ezek. 1:5 likeness of four *liv. c.*
14 *l. c.* ran, returned as light.
19 *l. c.* went the wheels went
3:13 noise of wings of *living c.*

CREDITOR, S.
Deut. 15:2 *c.* that lendeth should
2 *K.* 4:1 *c.* to take my two sons
Is. 50:1 to which of my *c.*

Luke 7:41 *c.* had two debtors

CREEK.
Acts 27:39 discovered a certain *c*

CREEP.
Lev. 11:31 unclean all that *c.*
Ps. 104:20 beasts of forest *c.*
2 *Tim.* 3:6 of this sort *c.* into

CREEPETH.
Gen. 1:25 every thing that *c.* 26
30 given to every thing *c.* herb
7:8 *c.* went in two and two, 14
21 of thing that *c.*
8:17 bring forth every thing *c.*
19 whatsoever *c.* went forth
Lev. 11:41 that *c.* shall be an
abomination, 43, 44 ; 20:25
Deut. 4:18 of any thing that *c.*

CREEPING thing, s.
Gen. 1:26 dominion over ev. *c. t.*
Lev. 5:2 unclean *c. thing*
11:21 ye eat, of every *c. thing*
22:5 or whoso. toucheth any *c. t.*
Deut. 14:19 *c. thing* that flieth
1 *K.* 4:33 he spake of *c. t.* fishes
Ps. 104:25 *c. things* innumerable
148:10 all *c. things* praise the L.
Ezek. 8:10 form of *c. t.* portrayed
38:20 all *c. t.* shake at my pres.
Hos. 2:18 covenant with *c. things*
Hab. 1:14 men as *c. things*
Acts 10:12 P. saw *c. things,* 11:6
Rom. 1:23 like to *c. things*

CREPT.
Jude 4 certain *c.* in unawares

CRESCENS. 2 *Tim.* 4:10
CRETE. *Acts* 27:7, 12, 21 ; *Tit.*1:5
CRETES. *Acts* 2:11
CRETIANS. *Tit.* 1:12

CREW.
Mat. 26:74 the cock *c.* *Mar.* 14:68 ;
Luke 22:60 ; *John* 18:27

CRIB.
Job 39:9 unicorn abide by thy *c. ?*
Prov. 14:4 no oxen are *c.* is clean
Is. 1:3 ass know. his master's *c.*

CRIED. *See after* CRY.

CRIME, S.
Job 31:11 his is a heinous *c.*
Ezek. 7:23 land is full of bloody *c.*
Acts 25:16 conc. *c.* laid ag. him
27 not to signify the *c.* laid

CRIMSON.
2 *Chr.* 2:7 cun. to work in *c.* 14
3:14 he made the veil of *c.*
Is. 1:18 your sins be like *c.*
Jer. 4:30 thou clothest with *c.*

CRIPPLE.
Acts 14:8 being a *c.* from womb

CRISPING-PINS.
Is. 3:22 L. will take away *c.-p.*

CRISPUS. *Acts* 18:8 ; 1 *Cor.* 1:14

CROOK-BACKED.
Lev. 21.20 *c.-b.* not approach

CROOKED.
Deut. 32:5 are a *c.* generation
Job 26:13 formed the *c.* serpent
Ps. 125:5 aside to their *c.* ways
Prov. 2:15 whose ways are *c.*
Ec. 1:15 *c.* not be m. stra. 7:13
Is. 27:1 pun. lev. that *c.* serpent
40:4 *c.* be made, 42:16 ; *Luke* 3:5
45:2 make the *c.* places straight.
59:8 have made them *c.* paths
Lam. 3:9 hath made my paths *c.*
Phil. 2:15 midst of a *c.* nation

CROP.
Lev. 1:16 he shall pluck away *c.*

CROPPED.
Ezek. 17:4 *c.* off top of y. twigs, 22

CROSS.
Mat. 10:38 taketh not his *c.* is not
worthy of me, *Luke* 14:27
16:24 *c.* and follow me, *Mark*
8:34 ; 10:21 ; *Luke* 9:23
27:32 compelled to bear *c. Mark*
15:21 ; *Luke* 23:26
40 if S. of God come down from
the *c.* 42 ; *Mark* 15:30, 32
John 19:17 bearing *c.* went forth
19 wrote title, and put it on *c.*
25 stood by the *c.* his mother
31 not remain on *c.* on sabbath
1 *Cor.* 1:17 lest *c.* be of none ef.
18 preaching of *c.* foolishness
Gal. 5:11 offence of the *c.* ceased
6:12 suf. persecution for *c.* of C.
14 should glory, save in the *c.*
Eph. 2:16 reconcile both by *c.*
Phil. 2:8 obedient to death of *c.*
3:18 are enemies of *c.* of Christ
Col. 1:20 through blood of *c.*
2:14 nailing it to his *c.*
Heb. 12:2 endured the *c.*

CROSS-WAY.
Ob. 14 nor have stood in *c.-w.*

CROUCH, ETH.
1 *Sam.* 2:36 *c.* for piece of silver
Ps. 10:10 he *c.* and humbleth

CROW, CROWING. *See* COCK.

CROWN.
Ex. 25:25 a golden *c.* to border
29:6 holy *c.* upon the mitre
Lev. 8:9 on his forefront holy *c.*
21:12 *c.* of anointing oil
2 *K.* 11:12 *c.* on J. 2 *Chr.* 23:11
Est. 1:11 Vashti with *c.* royal
Job 31:36 bind it as a *c.* to me
Ps. 89:39 hast profaned his *c.*
132:18 upon himself *c.* flourish
Prov. 4:9 *c.* of glory deliver
12:4 a virtuous woman is a *c.*
14:24 *c.* of wise is their riches
16:31 hoary head is *c.* of glory
17:6 children's child, *c.* of old
27:24 *c.* endure to every genera.
Cant. 3:11 behold S. with the *c.*
Is. 28:1 woe to the *c.* of pride
5 shall be for a *c.* of glory
62:3 shalt also be a *c.* of glory
Jer. 13:18 *c.* of glory come down
Ezek. 21:26 take off the *c.*
Zec. 9:16 as the stones of a *c.*
John 19:5 J. wearing *c.* of thorns
1 *Cor.* 9:25 a corruptible *c.*
Phil. 4:1 beloved, my joy and *c.*
1 *Thes.* 2:19 our *c.* of rejoicing
2 *Tim.* 4:8 *c.* of righteousness
Jam. 1:12 shall rec. *c.* of life
1 *Pet.* 5:4 shall receive *c.* of glory
Rev. 2:10 give thee a *c.* of life
3:11 that no man take thy *c.*
6:2 a *c.* was given to him

CROWN of gold.
Ex. 25:11 *c.* of *g.* round about,
24 ; 30:3 ; 37:2 ; 11, 12, 26
Est. 8:15 Mordecai with *c.* of *g.*
Ps. 21:3 *c.* of *g.* on his head

CROWN, with Head.
Gen. 49:26 on *c.* of Joseph's *h.*
Deut. 33:20 teareth arm with *c.*
2 *Sam.* 1:10 the *c.* on his *head*
12:30 *c.* from *h.* 1 *Chr.* 20:2
14:25 sole to *c.* of *h. Job* 2:7
Est. 2:17 king set *c.* on her *h.*
6:8 *c.* royal set upon his *head*
Job 19:9 taken *c.* from my *head*
Is. 3:17 smite with a scab *c.* of *h.*
Jer. 2:16 broken *c.* of thy *head*
48:45 *c.* of h. of tumultuous ones
Lam. 5:16 *c.* fallen from our *head*
Ezek. 16:12 beautiful *c.* on thy *h.*
Mat. 27:29 put a *c.* of thorns,
Mark 15:17 ; *John* 19:2
Rev. 12:1 a *c.* of twelve stars
14:14 on his *head* a golden *c.*

CROWNED.
Ps. 8:5 hast *c.* him with glory
Prov. 14:18 *c.* with knowledge
Cant. 3:11 his mother *c.* him
Nah. 3:17 thy *c.* are as locusts
2 *Tim.* 2:5 not *c.* except he strive
Heb. 2:9 Jesus *c.* with glory

CROWNEDST.
Heb. 2:7 *c.* him with glory and

CROWNEST, ETH.
Ps. 65:11 *c.* year with thy goodn.
103:4 *c.* thee with loving-kind.

CROWNING.
Is. 23:8 against Tyre the *c.* city

CROWNS.
Ezek. 23:42 beau. *c.* on their h.
Zec. 6:11 make *c.* ; 14 *c.* to Helem.
Rev. 4:4 elders had *c.* of gold
10 cast their *c.* before throne
9:7 on locusts' heads were *c.*
12:3 dragon having seven *c.*
13:1 upon his horns ten *c.*
19:12 on his head many *c.*

CRUCIFY.
Mat. 20:19 to Gentiles, to *c.* him
23:34 some of them ye shall *c.*
27:31 to *c.* him, *Mark* 15:20
Mark 15:13 cried again *c.* him, 14
Luke 23:21 *c.* him, *c. John* 19:6, 15
Heb. 6:6 *c.* Son of God afresh

CRUCIFIED.
Mat. 26:2 bet. to be *c. Luke* 24:7
27:22 said, Let him be *c.* 23
26 del. him to be *c. John* 19:16
35 *c.* him, *John* 19:23
38 thieves *c.* 44 ; *Mark* 15:32;
Luke 23:33 ; *John* 19:18
28:5 Jesus w. was *c. Mark* 16:6
John 19:20 where Jesus was *c.* 41
Acts 2:23 by wicked hands *c.*
36 made J. whom ye *c.* L. 4:10
Rom. 6:6 old man is *c.* with him
1 *Cor.* 1:13 was Paul *c.* for you ?
23 preach Christ *c.* unto Jews
2:2 Jesus Christ and him *c.*
3 not have *c.* Lord of glory
2 *Cor.* 13:4 tho' *c.* through weak.
Gal. 2:20 I am *c.* with Christ
3:1 Chr. set forth, *c.* among you
5:24 are Christ's have *c.* flesh
6:14 by whom the world is *c.*
Rev. 11:8 where Lord was *c.*

CRUEL.
Gen. 49:7 wrath, for it was *c.*
Ex. 6:9 for *c.* bondage
Deut. 32:33 *c.* venom of asps
Job 30:21 art become *c.* to me
Ps. 25:19 hate me with *c.* hatred
71:4 deliver out of hand of *c.*
Prov. 5:9 thou give years to *c.*
11:17 he *c.* troubleth own flesh
12:10 mercies of wicked are *c.*
17:11 *c.* messenger be sent
27:4 wrath is *c.*
Cant. 8:6 jealousy is *c.*
Is. 13:9 day of Lord cometh *c.*
19:4 Egyptians give to *c.* lord
Jer. 6:23 they are *c.* 50:42
30:14 chastisement of *c.* one
Lam. 4:3 daughter of my peo. *c.*
Heb. 11:36 trial of *c.* mockings

CRUELLY.
Ezek. 18:18 bec. he *c.* oppressed

CRUELTY.
Gen. 49:5 instruments of *c.*
Jud. 9:24 *c.* to sons of Jerubbaal
Ps. 27:12 such as breathe out *c.*
74:20 are full of habitations of *c.*
Ezek. 34:4 with *c.* ye ruled them

CRUMBS.
Mat. 15:27 eat of *c. Mark* 7:28
Luke 16:21 to be fed with the *c.*

CRUSE.
1 *Sam.* 26:11 take the *c.* of water
12 so David took the *c.* 16

CRUSE

1 *K.* 14:3 take a *c.* of honey
17:12 I have a little oil in *c.*
14 nor *c.* of oil fail till, 16
19:6 Elijah had *c.* of water
2 *K.* 2:20 bring me a new *c.*

CRUSH.

Job 39:15 forgetteth foot may *c.*
Lam. 1:15 to *c.* my young
3:34 to *c.* all the prisoners
Amos 4:1 which *c.* the needy

CRUSHED.

Lev. 22:24 not offer what is *c.*
Num. 22:25 ass *c.* Balaam's foot
Deut. 28:33 and *c.* alway
Job 4:19 are *c.* before the moth
5:4 his children *c.* in the gate
Is. 59:5 *c.* breaketh into a viper
Jer. 51:34 Nebuch. hath *c.* me

CRY, Substantive.

Gen. 18:21 accord. to *c.* come up
Ex. 2:23 their *c.* came up, 3:9
3:7 I have heard their *c.* ?
Num. 16:34 Is. fled at *c.* of them
1 *Sam.* 5:12 *c.* of city went up
9:16 because their *c.* is come up
2 *Sam.* 22:7 my *c.* did enter
1 *K.* 8:28 hearken to *c.* and
prayer, 2 *Chr.* 6:19
Neh. 5:6 angry when I heard *c.*
9:9 heardest *c.* by Red sea
Est. 4:1 cried with bitter *c.*
9:31 of fastings and their *c.*
Job 16:18 let my *c.* have no place
34:28 *c.* of poor to come to him,
he heareth *c.* of afflicted
Ps. 5:2 hearken to my *c.* my K.

Ps. 9:12 forget. not *c.* of humble
17:1 O Lord attend unto my *c.*
18:6 my *c.* came before him
34:15 his ears open to their *c.*
39:12 O Lord, give ear to my *c.*
40:1 inclined and heard my *c.*
88:2 incline thine ear to my *c.*
102:1 let my *c.* come unto thee
106:44 when he heard their *c.*
119:169 let my *c.* come near
142:6 attend to my *c.* I am
Prov. 21:13 at *c.* of poor
Ec. 9:17 more than *c.* of him
Is. 5:7 for right. behold a *c.*
15:5 raise up *c.* of destruction
8 *c.* gone about borders of Mo.
30:19 will be gracious at thy *c.*
43:14 whose *c.* is in the ships
Jer. 7:16 neither lift up *c.* 11:14
8:19 voice of *c.* of my people
14:2 *c.* of Jerusalem is gone up
18:22 *c.* be heard from houses
25:36 *c.* of shepherds be heard
46:12 thy *c.* hath filled land
48:4 little ones caused a *c.*
5 enem. heard *c.* of destruction
49:21 moved at *c.* of Edom
50:46 *c.* heard at taking of Bab.
51:54 sound of *c.* from Babylon
Lam. 3:56 hide not ear at my *c.*
Ezek. 27:28 shake at *c.* of pilots
Zep. 1:10 be a *c.* from fish-gate
Mat. 25:6 midnight was *c.* made

Great CRY.

Gen. 18:20 *c.* of S. is great, 19:13
27:34 Esau cried with a great *c.*
Ex. 11:6 be a great *c.* thro' Egy.
12:30 there was great *c.* in Eg.
Neh. 5:1 a g. *c.* of the people
Acts 23:9 so said, arose a great *c.*

Hear CRY.

Ex. 22:23 I will *hear* their *c.*
Job 27:9 *hear c.* when trouble
Ps. 61:1 *hear* my *c.* O God
145:19 he also will *hear* their *c.*
Jer. 14:12 I will not *h.* their *c.*
20:16 *hear c.* in the morning

CRIES.

Jam. 5:4 of them that reaped

CRY, Verb.

Ex. 5:8 idle therefore they *c.*
22:23 if thou afflict and they *c.*
32:18 voice of them that *c.*
Lev. 13:45 and *c.* Unclean
Jud. 10:14 go *c.* to the gods
2 *Sam.* 19:28 right have I to *c.*
2 *K.* 8:3 to *c.* for her house
2 *Chr.* 20:9 *c.* in afflict. wilt hear
Job 30:20 I *c.* thou dost not hear
24 they *c.* in his destruction
35:9 oppressed to *c.* they *c.* out
12 they *c.* none giveth answer
36:13 *c.* not when he bindeth
38:41 his young ones *c.* to God
Ps. 22:2 I *c.* in the daytime
27:7 O Lord, when I *c.* 28:2
28:1 to thee will I *c.* 2
34:17 righteous *c.* Lord heareth
56:9 when I *c.* mine enem. turn
57:2 I will *c.* to God most high
61:2 from end of earth will I *c.*
86:3 be merciful, for I *c.* daily
89:26 shall *c.* thou art my father
141:1 Lord I *c.* make haste
147:9 to young ravens which *c.*
Prov. 8:1 doth not wisdom *c.* and
21:13 shall *c.* but not be heard
Is. 8:4 before child *c.* My father
13:22 beasts of islands shall *c.*
14:31 *c.* O city, thou Palestina
15:4 and Heshbon shall *c.* and
33:7 their valiant ones shall *c.*
34:14 satyr shall *c.* to fellow
40:2 *c.* to Jerus. warfare accom.
6 voice said, *c.* what shall I *c.* ?
42:2 he shall not *c.* nor lift voice
13 he shall *c.* yea, prevail
14 I *c.* like travailing woman
46:7 one shall *c.* to him, yet can
58:9 *c.* he shall say, Here I am
65:14 shall *c.* for sorrow of heart
Jer. 2:2 go and *c.* in ears of Jer.
3:4 wilt not from this time *c.*
4:5 blow trumpet, *c.* gather
11:11 though they *c.* to me
12 *c.* to gods
14 not hear when *c.* *Ezek.* 8:18
22:20 go up to Lebanon, and *c.*
25:34 and *c.* 48:20; *Ezek.* 21:12
31:6 watchmen on Ephraim *c.*
Lam. 3:8 when I *c.* he shutteth
Ezek. 9:4 *c.* for abominations
24:17 forbear to *c.* make no
26:15 shake, when wounded *c.*
27:30 *c.* bitterly for Tyrus
Hos. 8:2 Israel *c.* we know thee
Joel 1:19 Lord, to thee will I *c.*
20 the beasts *c.* unto thee
Jon. 3:8 man and beast *c.* to G.
Mic. 3:5 bite with teeth, *c.* peace
Nah. 2:8 *c.* but none look back
Zep. 1:14 mighty sh. *c.* bitterly
Zec. 1:14 angel said, *c.* thou
Mat. 12:19 not strive nor *c.*
Luke 18:7 avenge elect, which *c.*
Rom. 8:15 whereby we *c.* Abba
Gal. 4:27 *c.* that travailest not

CRY against.

Deut. 15:9 *c.* to L. *a.* thee, 24:15
2 *Chr.* 13:12 to *c.* alarm *ag.* you
Job 31:38 if my land *c. ag.* me
Jon. 1:2 go to Nineveh, *c. ag.* it

CRY aloud.

1 *K.* 18:27 Elijah said, *c. aloud*
Job 19:7 I *c. aloud* but no judgm.
Ps. 55:17 at noon will I *c. aloud*
Is. 24:14 *c. aloud* from the sea
54:1 break forth into sing. *c. a.*
58:1 *c. aloud* spare not
Hos. 5:8 *c.* at Beth-a. after
Mic. 4:9 why *c. a.* ? is there no

CRY to the Lord.

1 *Sam.* 7:8 cease not to *c.* for us
Ps. 107:19 *c.* to the Lord, 28
Is. 19:20 *c.* to L. bec. of oppres.

Joel 1:14 sanctify fast, *c.* to the L.
Mic. 3:4 *c.* to the L.* he will not

CRY out.

1 *Sam.* 8:18 ye shall *c. out*
Job 19:7 I *c. out* of wrong,
35:9 *c. o.* by r. of arm of mighty
Is. 12:6 *c. out* and shout
18:4 soldiers of M. shall *c. out*
5 my heart shall *c. out* for M.
29:9 wonder, *c. out*, and cry
Jer. 48:31 I will *c. out* for Moab
Lam. 2:19 *c. out* in the night
Amos 3:4 y. lion *c. out* of den ?
Hab. 1:2 I *c. out* to thee
2:11 stone shall *c. out* of wall
Mark 10:47 *c. out*, Have mercy
Luke 19:40 stones would *c. out*

CRIED.

Gen. 27:34 E. *c.* with bitter cry
39:15 he heard that I *c.*
41:55 *c.* to Pharaoh for bread
Num. 11:2 *c.* to Moses
Deut. 22:24 dam. bec. she *c.* not
27 damsel *c.* and none to save
Jud. 5:28 mother *c.* through lat.
7:21 all the host ran, and *c.*
10:12 ye *c.* and I delivered you
i Sam. 17:8 G. *c.* to armies of Isr.
20:37 Jonathan *c.* after lad, 38
ﬔ *Sam.* 20:16 then *c.* a wise w.
22:7 I *c.* to my G. he did hear
ﬔ *K.* 13:2 *c.* against altar, 4, 32
18:28 *c.* aloud and cut them.
2 *K.* 2:12 Elisha *c.* My father
6:5 he *c.* Alas, it was borrowed
8:5 woman *c.* to king for house
11:14 Athaliah *c.* Treason
1 *Chr.* 5:20 *c.* to God in the battle
2 *Chr.* 32:20 Isaiah *c.* to heaven
Neh. 9:27 they *c.* thou heard. 28
Job 29:12 I delivered poor that *c.*
30:5 they *c.* as after a thief
Ps. 18:6 in my distress I *c.* to G.
41 *c.* but none to save them
22:5 they *c.* and were delivered
24 *c.* unto him, he heard
30:2 O Lord I *c.* to thee
8 I *c.* to thee O Lord and made
31:22 heardest sup. when I *c.*
34:6 this poor man *c.* and the L.
66:17 I *c.* with my mouth, 77:1
88:1 I *c.* day and night
13 I *c.* O Lord, in the morning
119:145 I *c.* with whole heart
130:1 out of the depths have I *c.*
138:3 I *c.* thou answeredst
Is. 6:4 moved at voice of him *c.*
30:7 have I *c.* concerning this
Jer. 4:20 destru. on destru. is *c.*
Ezek. 9:8 I fell on my face, and *c.*
10:13 it was *c.* to them
Dan. 6:20 he *c.* O Daniel
Hos. 7:14 not *c.* to me with heart
Jon. 1:5 mariners *c.* ev. man to
2:2 I *c.* by reason of affliction to
L. out of belly of hell *c.* I
Zec. 7:13 as he *c.* and they would
not hear, so they *c.*
Mat. 14:30 Peter *c.* Lord save me
20:31 *c.* the more, Have mercy,
Mark 10:48; *Luke* 18:39
Mark 9:26 spirit *c.* and rent him
John 7:37 Jesus *c.* If any thirst
Acts 19:32 some *c.* one th. 21:34
22:24 wheref. they *c.* so ag. him
Rev. 10:3 he *c.* seven thunders
12:2 and she *c.* travailing
Rev. 14:18 *c.* to him that had sic.
18:2 he *c.* mightily, 18
19 they *c.* weeping and wailing

CRIED to the Lord.

Ex. 8:12 Moses *c.* to the L. 15:25;
17:4; *Num.* 12:13
14:10 Israel *c.* to the Lord, *Jud.*
3:9, 15; 4:3; 6:7; 10:1
Num. 20:16 we *c.* to the Lord he
heard, *Deut.* 26:7

Jos. 24:7 c. to the L. he put dark.
1 *Sam.* 7:9 S. c. to the L. 15:11
2 *Chr.* 13:14 they c. to the L. Ps.
107:6, 13; *Jon.* 1:14
14:11 Asa c. to the Lord
Ps. 3:4 I c. to the L. 120:1; 142:1
Lam. 2:18 c. to L. O dau. of Z.

CRIED with a loud voice.
1 *Sam.* 28:12 En-dor c. w. l. v.
2 *Sam.* 19:4 D. c. w. l. v. O Absa.
Neh. 9:4 Levites; *Ezek.* 11:13 Ez.
Mat. 27:46 ninth hour J. c. w. l. v.
50; *Mark* 15:34, 37; *Luke*
23:46; *John* 11:43
Mark 1:26 evil spirit c. w. a l. v.
Acts 7:60 S. c. w. a loud voice
16:28 Paul c. with a loud voice
Rev. 6:10 c. w. a l. v. How long
7:2 angel c. w. l. v. 10:3 : 19:17
10 stood bef. Lamb c. w. l. v.

CRIED out.
1 *Sam.* 4:13 city c. out ; 5:10 Ek.
1 *K.* 22:32 Jehosh. 2 *Chr.* 18:31
Jer. 20:8 I c. out I cried violence
Mat. 8:29 spirits c. out, Luke 4:33
14:26 c. o. for fear, *Mark* 6:49
20:30 blind men c. out
Mark 1:23 unclean spirit c. out
9:24 father c. out, *Luke* 9:38
15:13 c. o. again, *Mat.* 27:23 ;
Luke 23:18; *John* 19:6
Acts 19:28 c. out Great is D. 34
22:23 c. out and threw dust
23:6 Paul c. out I am a Pharisee

Gen. 4:10 brother's blood c.
Ex. 14:15 where. c. thou to me?
22:27 when he c. I will hear
1 *Sam.* 26:14 that c. to the king?
Job 24:12 soul of wounded c.
Ps. 72:12 del. needy when he c.
84:2 c. out for living God
Prov. 1:20 wisdom c. 8:3 ; 9:3
2:3 if thou c. after knowledge
Is. 26:17 as a woman c. out
40:3 that c. in the wilderness
57:13 c. let companies deliver
Jer. 12:8 my heritage c. ag. me
30:15 why c. thou
Mic. 6:9 Lord's voice c. to city
Mat. 15:23 for she c. after us
Luke 9:39 he c out
Rom. 9:27 Esa. as also c.
Jam. 5:4 hire of laborers c

CRYING.
1 *Sam.* 4:14 Eli heard noise of c.
2 *Sam.* 13:19 Tamar went on c.
Job 39:7 nor reg. he c. of driver
Prov. 19:18 soul spare for his c.
30:15 horseleech dau. c. Give
Is. 22:5 day of c. to mountains
24:11 a c. for wine in streets
65:19 of c. no more heard in her
Jer. 48:3 of c. be from Horonaim
Zec. 4:7 the headstone with c.
Mal. 2:13 covering altar with c.
Mat. 3:3 c. in wilderness, *Mark*
1:3 ; *Luke* 3:4 ; *John* 1:23
21:15 children c. in the temple
Acts 8:7 c. spirits came out
14:14 ran among people c. out
21:28 c. out, Men of Israel, help
36 multitude c. away with him
Gal. 4:6 c. Abba, Father
Heb. 5:7 prayers with strong c.
Rev. 21:4 no more death, nor c.

CRYSTAL.
Job 28:17 and c. cannot equal it
Ezek. 1:22 as color of terrible c.
Rev. 4:6 a sea of glass, like c.
21:11 light of city clear as c.
22:1 a pure river, clear as c.

CUBIT.
Deut. 3:11 after the c. of a man
Ezek. 43:13 the c. is a c.
Mat. 6:27 one c. to stat. Lu. 12:25

CUBITS.
Gen. 6:15 length of the ark 300 c.
1 *Sam.* 17:4 Gol.'s height, six c.
1 *K.* 6:2 length of the house 60 c.
2 *K.* 14:13 brake wall of Jerusa-
lem, 400 c. 2 *Chr.* 25:23
Est. 5:14 gallows 50 c. high, 7:9
Ezek. 40:23 gate to gate 100 c.
43:17 the settle fourteen c.
Dan. 3:1 height of image 60 c.
John 21:8 were from land, 200 c.
Rev. 21:17 wall of city 144 c.

CUCKOO.
Lev. 11:16 c. ab. *Deut.* 14:15

CUCUMBERS.
Num. 11:5 we remember the c.
Is. 1:8 as lodge in garden of c.
CUD. See CHEW and CHEWETH.

CUMBERED, ETH.
Luke 10:40 c. about much serv.
13:7 why c. it the ground ?

CUMBRANCE.
Deut. 1:12 I alone bear your c. ?

CUMMIN.
Is. 28:25 doth he not scatter c.
27 on c. but c. is beaten
Mat. 23:23 ye pay tithe of c.

CUNNING.
Gen. 25:27 Esau was a c. hunter
Ex. 31:4 to devise c. works
1 *Sam.* 16:18 son of J. c. in play.
1 *Chr.* 25:7 c. in songs, were 288
2 *Chr.* 2:13 I sent a c. man of H.
Ps. 137:5 right hand forget her c.
Cant. 7:1 work of a c. workman
Is. 3:3 take away c. artificer
40:20 he seeketh a c. workman
Jer. 9:17 send for c. women
10:9 all the work of c. men
Dan. 1:4 children c. in knowl.
Eph. 4:14 car. by c. craftiness

CUNNINGLY.
2 *Pet.* 1:16 c. devised fables

CUP.
Gen. 40:11 Phar.'s c. in my hand
44:2 silver c. in sack's mouth
2 *Sam.* 12:3 drank of his own c.
Ps. 11:6 be portion of their c.
16:5 L. is the portion of my c.
23:5 my c. runneth over
73:10 waters of a full c. wrung
75:8 in hand of Lord is a c.
116:13 I will take c. of salvation
Prov. 23:31 giveth its color in c.
Is. 51:17 hast drunk the c. the
dregs of the c. of trembling
22 taken out of thy hand c. of
Jer. 16:7 give c. of consolation
25:15 take wine c. of this fury
17 took I c. at Lord's hand
28 they refuse c. at thy hand
49:12 judgment not to drink c.
51:7 Babylon been a golden c.
Lam. 4:21 c. also pass through
Ezek. 23:31 her c. into thy hand
32 drink of thy sister's c. deep
Hab. 2:16 c. of L. right hand
Zec. 12:2 Jerus. c. of trembling
Mat. 10:42 c. of c. wat. *Mark* 9:41
20:22 to drink c. *Mark* 10:38
23 indeed of my c. *Mark* 10:39
23:25 make clean outside of c.
26 cleanse first that within c.
26:27 he took the c. gave thanks,
Mark 14:23 ; *Luke* 22:17, 20 ;
1 *Cor.* 11:25.
39 let this c. pass from me,
Mark 14:36 ; *Luke* 22:42
42 if c. may not pass from me
Luke 22:20 this c. is new testament in my bl. 1 *Cor.* 11:25
John 18:11 c. Father hath given
1 *Cor.* 10:16 c. of blessing
21 cannot drink c. of L. and c.

11:26 as often as ye drink of c.
27 drink c. of Lord unworthily
Rev. 14:10 without mixt. into c
16:19 to her c. of his wrath
17:4 woman having golden c.
18:6 in c. fill to her double

CUP-BEARER.
Neh. 1:11 I was the king's c.-b.

CUP-BEARERS.
1 *K.* 10:5 saw c.-b. 2 *Chr.* 9:4

CUPS.
1 *Chr.* 28:17 pure gold for the c.
Is. 22:24 hang the vessels of c.
Jer. 52:19 Chaldeans took aw. c.
Mark 7:4 as washing of c. 8

CURDLED.
Job 10:10 c. me like cheese ?

CURE, Substantive.
Jer. 33:6 I will bring it c.

CURE, ED.
Jer. 33:6 I will c. them, and
46:11 O Egypt, shalt not be c.
Hos. 5:13 could he not c. you
Mat. 17:16 disciples, not c. him
18 child c. that very hour
Luke 7:21 same hour he c. many
9:1 gave power to c. diseases
John 5:10 Jews said to him c.

CURES.
Luke 13:32 I do c. to-day

CURIOUS, LY.
Ex. 28:8 c. girdle, 27, 28 ; 29:5 ;
39:5 ; *Lev.* 8:7
35:32 and to devise c. works
Ps. 139:15 c. wrought in lowest
Acts 19:19 that used c. arts

CURRENT.
Gen. 23:16 c. money with mer.

CURSE, Substantive.
Gen. 27:12 bring c. on me
13 mother said, Upon me be c.
Num. 5:18 bitter water that causeth the c. 19, 22, 24, 27
27 woman be c. am. her peo.
Deut. 11:26 a bless. and c. 30:1
28 a c. if ye will not obey
29 and put the c. upon Ebal
23:5 c. into blessing, *Neh.* 13:2
29:19 heareth words of this c.
Jos. 6:18 camp of Israel a c.
Jud. 9:57 came c. of Jotham
1 *K.* 2:8 with a grievous c.
2 *K.* 22:19 should become a c.
Neh. 10:29 they entered into a c.
Job 31:30 wishing c. to his soul
Prov. 3:33 c. of L. in ho. of wic.
26:2 so c. canseless not come
27:14 be counted a c. to him
28:27 hid. eyes have many a c.
Is. 24:6 therefore c. dev. earth
34:5 down on people of my c.
43:28 given Jacob to the c.
65:15 leave your name for a c.
Jer. 24:9 deliv. them to be a c.
25:18 ; 29:18 ; 42:18 ; 44:8
26:6 this city a c. to all nations
44:22 therefore is your land a c.
49:13 Bozrah shall become a c.
Lam. 3:65 give thy c. unto them
Dan. 9:11 the c. is poured upon
Zec. 5:3 this is c. that goeth
8:13 ye were c. among heathen
Mal. 2:2 I will send c.
3:9 ye are cursed with a c. ye
4:6 lest I smite earth with a c.
Acts 23:12 bound under a c. 14
Gal. 3:10 of law are under c.
13 redeemed us from c. of law
Rev. 22:3 shall be no more c.

CURSE, Verb.
Gen. 8:21 I will not c. ground
12:3 will c. him curseth thee
Ex. 22:28 not c. ruler of thy peo.
Lev. 19:14 shalt not c. the deaf

Num. 22:6 *c.* me this people, 17
11 now *c.* me them, 23:7, 13
12 God said, Thou shalt not *c.*
23:8 how I *c.* whom God hath
11 I took thee to *c.* enem. 24:10
25 neither *c.* at all, nor bless
Deut. 23:4 Bal. to *c.* thee. *Neh.* 13:2
27:13 shall stand on Ebal to *c.*
Jos. 24:9 B. called Bal. to *c.* you
Jud. 5:23 *c.* Meroz, said angel, *c.*
2 *Sam.* 16:9 dead dog *c.* king?
10 let him *c.* L. hath said, *c.* D.
Job 1:11 *c.* thee to thy face, 2:5
2:9 said his wife, *c.* God and die
3:8 let them *c.* it that *c.* day
Ps. 62:4 but they *c.* inwardly
109:28 let them *c.* but bless thou
Prov. 11:26 people shall *c.* him
24:24 him shall the people *c.*
30:10 accuse not serv. lest he *c.*
Ec. 7:21 hear servant *c.* thee
10:20 *c.* not king, *c.* not the rich
Is. 8:21 *c.* their king, and God
Jer. 15:10 every one doth *c.* me
Mal. 2:2 I will *c.* your blessings
Mat. 5:44 bl. th. that *c.* Lu. 6:28
26:74 began to *c.* Mark 14:71
Rom. 12:14 bless, and *c.* not
Jam. 3:9 therewith *c.* we men

CURSED.

Gen. 3:14 serpent *c.* ; 17 ground
4:11 Cain *c.* ; 9:25 *c.* be Canaan
5:29 bec. of ground Lord hath *c.*
27:29 *c.* that curseth, *Num.* 24:9
49:7 *c.* be their anger, for
Lev. 20:9 hath *c.* his father or
24:11 Israelitish woman's son *c.*
14 bring forth him hath *c.* 23
Num. 22:6 wh. thou cursest is *c.*
Deut. 27:15 *c.* be he, 16–26
28:16 *c.* be in city, *c.* in field
17 *c.* shalt be thy basket and
18 *c.* be fruit of thy body
19 *c.* when comest in and goest
Jos. 6:26 *c.* be man bu. Jericho
9:23 ye Gibeonites are *c.*
Jud. 9:27 and *c.* Abimelech
21:18 *c.* giveth a wife to Benj.
1 *Sam.* 14:24 *c.* that eateth
17:43 Goliath *c.* David

1 *Sam.* 26:19 if men, *c.* be they
2 *Sam.* 16:5 Shimei *c.* still, 7, 13
19:21 he *c.* Lord's anointed
1 *K.* 2:8 *c.* me with grievous *c.*
2 *K.* 2:24 *c.* them in name of Lord
9:34 go see now this *c.* woman
Neh. 13:25 I *c.* them
Job 1:5 it may be my sons *c.* G.
3:1 then Job *c.* his day
5:3 suddenly I *c.* his habitation
24:18 portion is *c.* in the earth
Ps. 37:22 *c.* of him shall be cut
119:21 rebuked proud that are *c.*
Ec. 7:22 likewise hast *c.* others
Jer. 11:3 *c.* obeyeth not covenant
17:5 *c.* man that trust. in man
20:14 *c.* be the day I was born
15 *c.* man brought tid. to father
48:10 *c.* doeth Lord's work dec.
c. keepeth back sword
Mal. 1:14 but *c.* be the deceiver
2:2 *c.* your blessings already
3:9 ye are *c.* with a curse for
Mat. 25:41 depart from me ye *c.*
John 7:49 know not law are *c.*
Gal. 3:10 *c.* that continueth not
13 *c.* every one hang. on a tree
2 *Pet.* 2:14 *c.* children, who have

CURSED thing.

Deut. 7:26 lest thou be a *c. thing,*
for it is a *c. thing.*
13:17 cleave naught of *c. thing*

CURSEDST.

Jud. 17:2 silver about which *c.*
Mark 11:21 fig-tree thou *c.* is

CURSES.

Num. 5:23 priest write these *c.*
Deut. 28:15 th. *c.* shall come, 45
29:20 all the *c.* written in this
book, 27: ; 2 *Chr.* 34:24
21 accord. to all the *c.* of cov.
30:7 put these *c.* on enemies

CURSETH.

Ex. 21:17 he that *c.* his father,
Lev. 20:9 ; *Prov.* 20:20
Lev. 24:15 whoso *c.* his God
Prov. 30:11 genera. *c.* their father
Mat. 15:4 *c.* his father or mother,
let him die, *Mark* 7:10

CURSING.

Num. 5:21 charge with oath of *c.*
Deut. 28:20 shall send on thee *c.*
30:19 before you blessing and *c.*
2 *Sam.* 16:12 good for his *c.*
Ps. 10:7 full of *c. Rom.* 3:14
59:12 *c.* and lying they speak
109:17 loved *c.* so let it come
18 he clothed himself with *c.*
Prov. 29:24 hear *c.* bewrayeth not
Heb. 6:8 thorns, is nigh to *c.*
Jam. 3:10 out of same mouth *c.*

CURSINGS.

Jos. 8:34 read blessings and *c.*

CURTAIN.

Ps. 104:2 stretchest out the heavens like a *c. Is.* 40:22

CURTAINS.

Ex. 26:1 with ten *c.* 2 ; 36:9
Num. 4:25 Gershonites bear *c.*
2 *Sam.* 7:2 within *c.* 1 *Chr.* 17:1
Cant. 1:5 comely as *c.* of Solom.
Is. 54:2 stretch forth the *c.*
Jer. 4:20 my *c.* spoiled in a mom.
10:20 none to set up my *c.*
49:29 shall take their *c.*
Hab. 3:7 *c.* of Midian did tremble

CUSH.

Gen. 10:6 Ham, C. 7; 1 *Ch.* 1:8, 9
Is. 11:11 remnant left from C.
CUSHAN. *Hab.* 3:7

CUSHI.

2 *Sam.* 18:21 C. tell the king, 23
Jer. 36:14 princes sent son of C.
Zep. 1:1 Zephaniah, son of C.

CUSTODY.

Num. 3:36 *c.* of sons of Merari
Est. 2:3 virgins to *c.* of Hege, 8
14 to *c.* of Shaashgaz

CUSTOM.

Gen. 31:35 *c.* of women is on me
Jud. 11:39 was a *c.* in Israel
1 *Sam.* 2:13 the priest's *c.* was
Ezr. 3:4 accord. to *c. Jer.* 32:11
4:13 then will they not pay *c.*
20 and *c.* was paid to them
7:24 not impose *c.* on priests
Mat. 9:9 saw Matthew at receipt
of *c. Mark* 2:14 : *Luke* 5:27
17:25 whom do kings take *c.*?
Luke 1:9 ac. to *c.* of priest's office
2:27 do for him after *c.* of law
42 Jerusalem after *c.* of feast
Luke 4:16 as J. *c.* was, he went
John 18:39 *c.* I should release one
Rom. 13:7 *c.* to whom *c.* is due
1 *Cor.* 11:16 we have no such *c.*

CUSTOMS.

Lev. 18:30 these abominable *c.*
Jer. 10:3 *c.* of this people
Acts 6:14 shall change *c.* of M.
16:21 *c.* not lawful to receive
21:21 ought not to walk after *c.*
26:3 thee to be expert in all *c.*
28:17 I com. nothing against *c.*

CUT, Participle.

Lev. 22:24 not offer what is *c.*
Ezek. 16:4 thy navel was not *c.*

Acts 5:33 *c.* to the heart, 7:54

CUT, Verb.

Deut. 14:1 shall not *c.* yourselves
Jud. 20:6 concubine, and *c.* her
1 *K.* 18:28 *c.* thems. after manner
2 *K.* 24:13 he *c.* all the vessels of
gold, 2 *Chr.* 28:24
1 *Chr.* 20:3 he *c.* peop. with saws
Ps. 58:7 let them be as *c.*
107:16 *c.* bars of iron *Is.* 45:2
Is. 51:9 art thou not it *c.* Rahab
Jer. 16:6 nor *c.* themselves
36:23 he *c.* roll with penknife
41:5 having *c.* themselves
47:5 how long wilt *c.* thyself
Dan. 2:5 ye will not shall be *c.*
3:29 speak ag. God shall be *c.*
Amos 9:1 *c.* them in the head
Zec. 12:3 bur. them with it be *c.*

CUT asunder.

Ps. 129:4 *c. a.* cords of wicked
Jer. 50:23 hammer of earth *c. a.*
Zec. 11:10 Beauty and *c.* it *a.*
14 I *c. asun.* mine other staff
Mat. 24:51 *c.* him *a. Luke* 12:46

CUT down.

Ex. 34:13 *c. down* their groves,
Deut. 7:5 ; 2 *K.* 18:4 ; 23:14
Num. 13:23 *c. down* a branch, 24
Deut. 20:19 tr. for meat not *c. d.*
Job 8:12 in greenness not *c. d.*
14:2 like a flower, and is *c. d.*
7 hope of a tree if it be *c. d,*
22:16 wicked *c. d.* out of time
20 our substance is not *c. d.*
Ps. 37:2 shall soon be *c. down*
80:16 branch is burnt, it is *c. d.*
90:6 in the even. it is *c. down*
Is. 9:10 sycamores are *c. down*
14:12 how art thou *c. d.* to gr.
22:25 the nail shall be *c. down*
Jer. 22:7 *c. d.* thy choice cedars
25:37 habitations *c. down*
48:2 shalt be *c. d.* O Madmen
Nah. 1:12 thus shall be *c. down*
Zep. 1:11 merch. people *c. down*
Mat. 21:8 *c. d.* bra. *Mark* 11:8
Luke 13:7 *c.* it *down*
9 thou shalt *c.* it *down*

CUT off.

Gen. 9:11 nor all flesh be *c. off*
Ex. 12:15 that soul be *c. off,* 19 ;
31:14 ; *Num.* 15:30 ; 19:13
23:23 and I will *c.* them *off*
30:33 be *c. off* from his people,
38 ; *Lev.* 7:20, 27 ; 17:4, 9 ;
19:8 ; 23:29 ; *Num.* 9:13
Lev. 17:10 will *c.* him *off,* 18:29 ;
20:3, 6, 18 ; *Num.* 19:20
14 eateth blood shall be *c. off*
20:17 *c. off* in sight of people
Num. 4:18 *c.* not *off* tribe of K.
15:31 that soul utterly be *c. off*
Deut. 12:29 G. shall *c. off* nations
19:1 God hath *c. off* nations
23:1 hath privy member *c. off*
25:12 *c. off* her hand pity not
Jos. 3:13 the waters of Jordan
shall be *c. off,* 16 ; 4:7
7:9 and shall *c. off* our name
11:21 Joshua *c. off* Anakim
Jud. 21:6 one tribe *c. off*
Ruth 4:10 dead be not *c. off*
1 *Sam.* 2:31 I will *c. off* thy arm
33 man whom I shall not *c. off*
17:51 David *c. off* Goliath's head
20:15 not *c. off* thy kind. ; 24:21
when L. *c. off* enemies of D.
24:4 David *c. off* the skirt of, 5
28:9 how Saul *c. off* wizards
31:9 and they *c. off* Saul's head
2 *Sam.* 4:12 and *c. off* their hands
10:4 H. *c. off* their garments in
the middle, 1 *Chr.* 19:4
20:22 *c. off* the head of Sheba

1 *K*. 9:7 will I *c. off* Is. out of
11:16 *c. off* every male in Edom
13:34 to *c. off* Jer. house, 14:14
14:10 *c. off* Jeroboam him
18:4 Jezebel *c. off* prophets

1 *K*. 21:21 *c. off* from Ahab him
    that pisseth, 2 *K*. 9:8
1 *Chr*. 17:8 *c. off* all thine enem.
2 *Chr*. 22:7 *c. off* of Ahab
32:21 angel *c. off* mighty men
Job 4:7 where were right. *c. off ?*
6:9 loose his hand, and *c. me off*
8:14 whose hope shall be *c. off*
11:10 if he *c. off* who can hinder
18:16 above, his branch be *c. off*
23:17 I was not *c. off* before
24:24 *c. off* as tops of ears of c.
36:20 people *c. off* in their place
Ps. 12:3 *c. off* flattering lips
31:22 *c. off* from bef. thine eyes
34:16 to *c. off* remem. of them
37:9 evil-doers shall be *c. off*
22 they cursed of him be *c. off*
28 seed of wicked sh. be *c. off*
34 wicked are *c. off* shalt see it
38 end of wicked shall be *c. off*
54:5 *c. them off* in thy truth
75:10 horns of wick. will I *c. off*
76:12 *c. off* spirit of princes
83:4 said, let us *c. them off*
88:5 are *c. off* from thy hand
16 terrors have *c. me off*
94:23 *c. them off* in their wick.
101:5 slandereth will I *c. off*
   8 *c. off* wicked doers from city
109:13 let his posterity be *c. off*
   15 Lord may *c. off* memory
143:12 *c. off* enemies
Prov. 2:22 wicked shall be *c. off*
23:18 expect. not be *c. off*, 24:14
Is. 9:14 will *c. off* head and tail
10:7 to *c. off* nations not a few
11:13 adversary of Jud. be *c. off*
14:22 *c. off* from Babylon
15:2 every beard *c. off*
29:20 watch for iniquity *c. off*
38:12 *c. me off* with pining
48:9 that I *c. thee not off*
   19 should not been *c. off*
53:8 he was *c. off* out of land
55:13 that shall not be *c. off*
66:3 as if he *c. off* a dog's neck
Jer. 7:28 truth is *c. off* fr. mouth
29 *c. off* thy hair, O Jerusalem
9:21 to *c. off* children fr. without
11:19 let us *c. him off* from land
44:7 *c. off* man and woman
11 to *c. off* all Judah
47:4 to *c. off* from Tyrus
   5 Ashkelon is *c. off*
48:2 *c. it off* from being a nation
25 the horn of Moab is *c. off*

49:26 men of war shall be *c. off*
50:16 *c. off* sower from Babylon
51:6 be not *c. off* in her iniquity
62 this place, to *c. it off*
Lam. 2:3 *c. off* in anger
3:53 *c. off* my life
Ezek. 14:8 *c. him off* from people
13 *c. off* man and beast, 17, 19,
    21; 25:13; 29:8
17:9 not *c. off* fruit thereof
17 forts to *c. off* many persons
21:3 *c. off* right. and wicked, 4
25:7 I will *c. thee off* from péo.
16 I will *c. off* Cherethim
30:15 *c. off* multitude of No
31:12 ter. of nations *c. him off*
35:7 I will *c. off* from Seir him
37:11 we are *c. off* for our parts
Dan. 4:14 *c. off* his branches
9:26 Messiah shall be *c. off*
Hos. 8:4 that they may be *c. off*
10:7 king is *c. off* as foam, 15
Joel 1:5 the new wine is *c. off*, 9
16 meat *c. off* before our eyes ?
Amos 1:5 *c. off* inhabitant, 8
2:3 I will *c. off* judge from midst
3:14 horns of altar shall be *c. off*
Ob. 5 how art thou *c. off ?*
   9 every one of E. may be *c. off*
10 shalt be *c. off* for ever
14 to *c. off* those did escape
Mic. 5:9 thine enemies be *c. off*
10 horses ; 12 witchcrafts
13 will I *c. off*, *Nah*. 1:14
Nah. 1:15 wicked is utterly *c. off*
2:13 *c. off* thy prey from earth
3:15 the sword shall *c. thee off*
Hab. 3:17 tho' the flock be *c. off*
Zep. 1:3 *c. off* man from land
   4 *c. off* a remnant of Baal
11 that bear silver *c. off*
3:6 I have *c. off* the nations
7 so dwellings sh. not be *c. off*
Zec. 5:3 sweareth, shall be *c. off*
9:6 *c. off* pride of Philistines
10 *c. off* chariot from Ephraim
11:8 three shepherds also I *c. off*
   9 to be *c. off*, let it be *c. off*
13:2 I will *c. off* names of idols
8 two parts shall be *c. off*
14:2 residue shall not be *c. off*
Mal. 2:12 Lord will *c. off* man
Mat. 5:30 if right hand offend *c.*
   it *off*, 18:8 ; *Mark* 9:43, 45
Mark 14:47 *c. off* his ear, *Luke*
   22:50 ; *John* 18:10, 26
Rom. 11:22 shalt also be *c. off*
2 *Cor*. 11:12 I may *c. off* occasion
Gal. 5:12 I would they were *c. off*

CUT out.

Prov. 10:31 fro. tongue be *c. out*

Dan. 2:34 a stone was *c. out*, 45
Rom. 11:24 *c. out* of olive tree

CUT short.

2 *K*. 10:32 began to *c. Israel sh.*
Rom. 9:28 *c. it short* in right.

CUT up.

Job 30:4 who *c. up* mallows
Is. 33:12 as thorns *c. up* shall

CUTTEST, ETH.

Deut. 24:19 when thou *c. harvest*
Job 28:10 he *c. out* rivers
Ps. 46:9 he *c. the spear in sunder*
141:7 as when one *c. wood*
Prov. 26:6 mess. by fool, *c. off*
Jer. 10:3 for one *c. a tree out of*
22:14 and *c. him out windows*

CUTTING.

Ex. 31:5 in *c. of stones*, **35:33**
Is. 38:10 I said in *c. off of days*
Hab. 2:10 by *c. off many people*
Mark 5:5 *c. himself with stones*

CUTTINGS.

Lev. 19:28 not make any *c.* 21:5
Jer. 48:37 upon all hands be *c.*

CYMBAL.

1 *Cor*. 13:1 I am as tinkling *c.*

CYMBALS.

2 *Sam*. 6:5 play. on *c.* 1 *Chr*. 13:8
1 *Chr*. 15:16 harps and *c.* 16:42
16:5 Asaph made sound with *c.*
25:6 these were to sound with *c.*
2 *Chr*. 5:13 lift up voice with *c.*
29:25 Levites in house with *c.*
Ezr. 3:10 sons of Asaph with *c.*
Ps. 150:5 upon high sounding *c.*

CYPRESS.

Is. 44:14 he taketh the *c.*

CYPRUS.

Acts 4:36 country of C. 11:**20**
13:4 from Seleucia sailed to C.
15:39 Mark, and sailed to C.
27:4 we sailed under C.

CYRENE.

Mat. 27:32 found a man of C.
Acts 2:10 parts of Libya about C.
11:20 men of Cyprus and C.
13:1 Lucius of C. was in **church**

CYRENIAN.   *Mark* 15:21
CYRENIANS.   *Acts* 6:9
CYRENIUS.   *Luke* 2:2

CYRUS.

2 *Chr*. 36:22 the first year of C.
Ezr. 1:7 ; 3:7 ; 4:3 ; 5:13
Is. 44:28 that saith of C. **45:1**
Dan. 1:21 to the first year of C.
6:28 Dan. prosp. in reign of C
10:1 in the third year of C.

D

DABBASHETH.   *Jos*. 19:11
DABERATH. *Jos*. 19:12 ; 1 *Ch*.
   6:72

DAGGER.

Jud. 3:16 Ehud made him a *d.*
21 took *d.* from right thigh, 22
DAGON. *Jud*. 16:23 ; 1 *Sam*.
   5:2, 3, 7 ; 1 *Chr*. 10:10
DAILY. See after **DAYS.**

DAINTY, IES.

Gen. 49:20 Asher yield royal *d.*
Job 33:20 abhorreth *d.* meat
Ps. 141:4 let me not eat of *d.*
Prov. 23:3 be not desirous of *d.*
   6 neither desire his *d.* meats
Rev. 18:14 are departed

DALE.

Gen. 14:17 valley of S. king's *d.*

2 *Sam*. 18:18 a pillar in king's *d.*
DALMATIA.   2 *Tim*. 4:10
DALMANUTHA. *Mark* 8:10

DAM.

Ex. 22:30 seven days with *d.*
       Lev. 22:27
Deut. 22:6 not take *d.* with you.

DAMAGE.

Ezr. 4:22 why should *d.* grow
Est. 7:4 not count. king's *d.*
Prov. 26:6 and drinketh *d.*
Dan. 6:2 should have no *d.*
Acts 27:10 voy. will be with *d.*
2 *Cor*. 7:9 *d.* by us in nothing

DAMARIS.   *Acts* 17:34

DAMASCUS.

Gen. 15:2 Eliezer of D.
2 *Sam*. 8:6 put garrisons in D.

2 *K*. 5:12 Pharpar rivers of D.
8:7 E. came to D. 14:28 ; 16:9
Is. 7:8 ; 8.4 ; 10:9 ; 17:1, 3
Ezek. 27:18 ; *Amos* 1:3 ; 3:12 ; 5:27
Acts 9:2 desired letters to D. 10,
   19, 22, 27 ; 22:6, 10 ; 26:12
2 *Cor*. 11:32 in D. the gov. desir.
Gal. 1:17 I returned again to D.

DAMNABLE.

2 *Pet*. 2:1 who bring in *d.* heres.

DAMNATION.

Mat. 23:14 shall receive greater
   d. Mark 12:40 ; *Luke* 20:47
33 can ye escape *d.* of hell
Mark 3:29 in danger of eternal *d.*
John 5:29 to the resurrection of *d.*
Rom. 3:8 whose *d.* is just
13:2 receive to themselves *d.*
1 *Cor*. 11:29 eateth and drink. *d.*

1 *Tim.* 5:12 having *d.* because
2 *Pet.* 2:3 their *d.* slumbereth not

DAMNED.

Mark 16:16 believeth not be *d.*
Rom. 14:23 doubteth is *d.*
2 *Thes.* 2:12 *d.* who believed not

DAMSEL.

Gen. 24:55 said, Let the *d.* abide
34:3 he loved *d.* spake kindly, 12
Deut. 22:15 tokens of *d.* virginity
21 bring out *d.* and stone her
Jud. 5:30 to ev. man a *d.* or two?
19:4 the *d.* father retained him
Ruth 2:6 it is the Moabitish *d.*
1 *K.* 1:4 and the *d.* cherished h.
Mat. 14:11 given to *d. Mark* 6:28
26:69 *d.* came to P. *John* 18:17
Mark 5:39 *d.* is not dead, but
40 he entereth in where *d.* was
Acts 12:13 a *d.* came to hearken
16:16 *d.* possessed met us

DAMSELS.

Gen. 24:61 Rebekah arose and *d.*
1 *Sam.* 25:42 Abigail rode with *d.*
Ps. 68:25 among them *d.* playing

DAN, *a person*

Gen. 30:6; 35:25; 49:16, 17
Deut. 33:22 of D. he said, D. is a
Jud. 5:17 why did D. remain?

DAN, *a place.*

Gen. 14:14 pursued them unto D.
Deut. 34:1 Moses all Gil. unto D.

Tribe of DAN.

Num. 1:38 num. of D. 13:12; 34:22
Jos. 19:40 came out for D. 21:5
Jud. 18:30 priests to D. till cap.

DANCE, Substantive.

Ps. 149:3 praise him in *d.* 150:4
Jer. 31:13 virgin rejoice in the *d.*
Lam. 5:15 our *d.* is turned into.

DANCE, Verb.

Jud. 21:21 if dau. of S. come to *d.*
Job 21:11 their children *d.*
Ec. 3:4 and a time to *d.*
Is. 13:21 satyrs shall *d.* there

DANCED.

Jud. 21:23 number that *d.*
2 *Sam.* 6:14 David *d.* bef. Lord
Mat. 11:17 have not *d. Luke* 7:32
14:6 dau. of Herod. *d. Mark* 6:22

DANCES.

Jud. 11:34 daugh. came with *d.*
1 *Sam.* 21:11 sing of h. in *d.* 29:5
Jer. 31:4 shalt go forth in the *d.*

DANCING.

Ex. 32:19 he saw calf and *d.*
1 *Sam.* 18:6 women came out of
30:16 spread on all the earth *d.*
2 *Sam.* 6:16 Dav. *d.* 1 *Chr.* 15:29
Ps. 30:11 my mourning into *d.*
Luke 15:25 as he came heard *d.*

DANDLED.

Is. 66:12 be *d.* upon her knees

DANGER.

Mat. 5:21 in *d.* of judgment, 22
22 in *d.* of council, of hell-fire
Mark 3:29 in *d.* of eternal dam.
Acts 19:27 not only craft is in *d.*
40 *d.* to be called in question

DANGEROUS.

Acts 27:9 sailing was now *d.*

DANIEL.

Ezek. 14:14 though Noah, D. and
Mat. 24:15 spo. by D. *Mark* 13:14

DARE.

Job 41:10 none *d.* stir him up
Rom. 5:7 would even *d.* to die
15:18 *d.* to speak of anything
1 *Cor.* 6:1 any of you go to l.
2 *Cor.* 10:12 *d.* not make ourselv.

DARIUS.

Ezr. 4:5; 5:5; 6:1, 15; *Neh.* 12:22

Dan. 5:31; 6:9, 25; 9:1
Zec. 7:1 in fourth year of D.

DARK.

Gen. 15:17 when it was *d.*
Lev. 13:6 plague be *d.* 21, 56
Num. 12:8 speak not in *d.* sp.
Jos. 2:5 when *d.* men went out
2 *Sam.* 22:12 *d.* waters, *Ps.* 18:11
Neh. 13:19 gates began to be *d.*
Job 3:9 let stars of twilight be *d.*
12:25 they grope in the *d.*
18:6 light be *d.* in his tabernac.
22:13 judge through *d.* cloud?
24:16 in *d.* they dig thro' houses
Ps. 35:6 let their way be *d.*
49:4 open *d.* saying on harp
74:20 *d.* places full of cruelty
78:2 utter *d.* sayings of old
88:12 wonders be known in *d.* ?
105:28 sent darkness, made it *d.*
Prov. 1:6 and their *d.* sayings
7:9 in the black and *d.* night
Is. 29:15 their works are in the *d.*
45:19 not spoken in a *d.* place
Jer. 13:16 feet stumble on *d.* m.
Lam. 3:6 set me in *d.* places
Ezek. 8:12 house of Israel in *d.*
32:7 make stars thereof *d.*
8 bright lights of heaven *d.*
34:12 in cloudy and *d.* day
Dan. 8:23 understand. *d.* senten.
Joel 2:10 sun and moon be *d.*
Amos 5:8 maketh the day *d.* 20
Mic. 3:6 *d.* to you, day shall be *d.*
Zec. 14:6 light not clear nor *d.*
Luke 11:36 having no part *d.*
John 6:17 and it was now *d.*
20:1 Mary came when yet *d.*
2 *Pet.* 1:19 shineth in a *d.* place

DARKEN.

Amos 8:9 *d.* earth in clear day

DARKENED.

Ex. 10:15 so that land was *d.*
Ps. 69:23 eyes be *d. Rom.* 11:10
Ec. 12:2 moon or stars be not *d.*
3 look out of windows be *d.*
Is. 5:30 light is *d.* in heavens
9:19 land; 13:10 sun, *Joel* 3:15
24:11 all joy is *d.* mirth gone
Ezek. 30:18 at Tehaph, day be *d.*
Zec. 11:17 right eye be utterly *d.*
Mat. 24:29 sun be *d. Mark* 13:24
Luke 23:45 and the sun was *d.*
Rom. 1:21 foolish heart was *d.*
Eph. 4:18 the understanding *d.*
Rev. 8:12 so as third part was *d.*
9:2 sun and the air were *d.*

DARKENETH.

Job 38:2 who is this *d.* counsel

DARKLY.

1 *Cor.* 13:12 we see thro' a glass *d.*

DARKNESS.

Gen. 1:2 *d.* was upon the deep
5 the *d.* he called Night
18 to divide the light from *d.*
15:12 horror of *d.* fell on Abram
Ex. 10:22 *d.* in all Egypt
14:20 *d.* to them, but light
20:21 Moses drew near to *d.*
Deut. 4:11 mount. burnt with *d.*
5:22 words Lord spake out of *d.*
Jos. 24:7 *d.* bet. you and Egypt,
2 *Sam.* 22:10 *d.* under, *Ps.* 18:9
12 *d.* his pavilions
29 enlighten my *d. Ps.* 18:28
Job 3:5 let *d.* stain it
6 for that night, let *d.* seize it
5:14 meet with *d.* in daytime
10:22 a land of *d.* as *d.* itself
19:8 hath set *d.* in my paths
20:26 all *d.* be hid
22:11 or *d.* that canst not see
23:17 not cut off before *d.* neith.
hath he covered the *d.*
28:3 an end to *d.* stones of *d.*

34:22 no *d.* where may hide
37:19 not order speech for *d.*
38:9 thick *d.* a swaddling-band
19 as for *d.* where is the place
Ps. 18:11 *d.* his secret place
88:18 mine acquaint. into *d.*
97:2 clouds and *d.* about him
104:20 makest *d.* and it is night
105:28 sent *d.* made it dark
139:11 surely *d.* shall cover me
12 *d.* hideth not from thee
Prov. 2:13 to walk in *d.* ways of *d.*
4:19 way of the wicked is as *d.*
Ec. 6:4 name be covered with *d.*
Is. 5:30 look to land, behold *d.*
8:22 shall look, and behold *d.*
45:3 give thee treasures of *d.*
47:5 get thee into *d.* O Daughter
60:2 *d.* shall cover the earth, and
gross *d.* the people
Jer. 13:16 before he cause *d.* and
make light gross *d.*
Ezek. 32:8 set *d.* upon thy land
Joel 2:2 a day of clouds and *d.*
31 sun be turned to *d. Acts* 2:20
Amos 4:13 maketh morning *d.*
Nah. 1:8 *d.* pursue his enemies
Mat. 6:23 full of *d. Luke* 11:34
8:12 outer *d.* 22:13; 25:30
27:45 sixth hour *d. Mark* 15:33
Luke 22:53 and power of *d.*
23:44 was *d.* over all the earth
Acts 13:11 on him mist and *d.*
Eph. 5:11 with works of *d.*
6:12 rulers of *d.* of this world
Col. 1:13 from power of *d.*
1 *Thes.* 5:5 not of night nor of *d.*
Heb. 12:18 are not come to *d.*
2 *Pet.* 2:4 deliv. into chains of *d.*
17 mist of *d.* is reserved
1 *John* 2:11 *d.* hath blinded
Jude 6 everlast. chains under *d.*
13 is reserved blackness of *d.*
Rev. 16:10 kingd. was full of *d.*

DARKNESS, *with day.*

Job 3:4 let that *day* be *d.*
15:23 that *day* of *d.* is at hand
Ec. 11:8 remember *days* of *d.*
Is. 58:10 thy *d.* be as noon-*day*
Joel 2:2 a *day* of *d. Zep.* 1:15
Amos 5:20 *day* of Lord be *d.* ?

In DARKNESS.

Deut. 28:29 grope as blind *in d.*
1 *Sam.* 2:9 wicked be silent *in d.*
1 *K.* 8:12 L. said he would dwell
in thick *d.* 2 *Chr.* 6:1
Job 17:13 made my bed *in d.*
Ps. 82:5 they walk on *in d.*
88:6 laid me *in d.* in deeps
91:6 pestilence that walketh *i. d.*
107:10 such as sit *in d.*
143:3 made me dwell *in d.*
Prov. 20:20 out *in* obscure *d.*
Ec. 2:14 fool walketh *in d.*
5:17 eateth; 6:4 departeth *in d.*
Is. 42:7 sit *in d.* out of prison
49:9 to them *in d.* show yoursel.
59:9 light, but we walk *in d.*
Jer. 23:12 as slippery ways *in d.*
Dan. 2:22 knoweth what is *in d.*
John 8:12 not walk *in d.*
12:35 walketh *in d.* know. not
46 shall not abide *in d.*
1 *Thes.* 5:4 but ye are not *in d.*
1 *John* 1:6 and walk *in d.* we lie
2:9 hateth brother, is *in d.* 11

Land of DARKNESS.

Job 10:21 bef. I go to *land of d.*
22 *land of d.* as *d.* itself.
Jer. 2:31 been to Israel *l. of d.*

DARKNESS, *with light.*

Gen. 1:4 G. divided *light* from *d.*
18 to divide *light* from *d.*
Job 10:22 where *light* is as *d.*
17:12 *light* is short because of *d.*
18:18 driven from *light* into *d.*

29:3 by his *light* I walk. thro' d.
30:26 I waited for *light* came d.
Ps. 112:4 ariseth *light* in d.
139:12 d. and *l.* are both alike
Ec. 2:13 as *light* excelleth d.
Is. 5:20 that put d. for *l. l.* for d.
42 peo. that walk. in d. have
  seen a great *l. Mat.* 4:16
42:16 make d. *light* before them
45:7 I form *light* and create d.
50:10 walketh in d. hath no *l.*
Jer. 13:16 look for *l.* he make it d.
Lam. 3:2 bro't me into d. not *l.*
Amos 5:18 is d. and not *light*
Mic. 7:8 I sit in d. L. be a *light*
Mat. 6:23 *l.* be d. how gr. that d.
10:27 what I tell in d. speak in *l.*
  Luke 12:3
Luke 1:79 *l.* that sit d. *Rom.* 2:19
11:35 that *light* in thee be not d.
John 1:5 *l.* shineth in d. d. com.
3:19 loved d. rather than *light*
12:35 while ye have *l.* lest d.
Acts 26:18 from d. to *light*
Rom. 13:12 works of d. put on *l.*
1 *Cor.* 4:5 to *l.* hid. things of d.
2 *Cor* 4:6 *l.* to shine out of d.
6:14 communion *light* with d.
1 *Pet.* 2:9 out of d. into marv. *l.*
1 *John* 1:5 in Him is no d. at all
2:8 d. is passed true *l.* shineth

Out of DARKNESS.
Deut. 5:23 voice *out of* the d.
Job 12:22 deep things *out of* d.
Job 15:22 he shall return *out of* d.
30 shall not depart *out of* d.
Ps. 107:14 brought them *out of* d.
Is. 29:18 blind see *out of* d.

DARLING.
Ps. 22:20 d. from power of dog
35:17 rescue my d. from lions

DART, S.
2 *Sam.* 18:14 Joab took three d.
2 *Chr.* 32:5 Hezekiah made d.
Job 41:26 nor the d. cannot hold
29 d. are counted as stubble
Prov. 7:23 till d. strike thro' liver
Eph. 6:16 to quench fiery d. of
Heb. 12:20 thrust thro' with a d.

DASH.
2 *K.* 8:12 wilt d. their children
Ps. 2:9 d. in pieces like a pot.
91:12 lest thou d. foot against a
  stone, *Mat.* 4:6; *Luke* 4:11
Is. 13:18 shall d. young men
Jer. 13:14 will d. one ag. another

DASHED.
Ex. 15:6 thy right hand, O L. d.
Is. 15:16 child. be d. to pieces,
  Hos. 13:16; *Nah.* 3:10
Hos. 10:14 mo. was d. on child.

DASHETH.
Ps. 137:9 d. little ones ag. stones

DATHAN. *See* ABIRAM.

DAUB, ED, ING.
Ex. 2:3 she d. ark with slime
Ezek. 13:10 d. it with untempered
22:28 her prophets d. them

DAUGHTER.
Gen. 20:12 d. of my father, not d.
24:23 whose d. art thou, 47
48 master's brother's d. to son
34:7 in lying with Jacob's d.
8 my son longeth for your d.
Ex. 1:16 if a d. she shall live
21:31 have gored a son or a d.
Lev. 12:6 days fulfilled for a d.
18:17 nor take her daughter's d.
21:9 if d. of priest profane
Num. 27:9 if no d. give his inh.
36:8 d. that possess. an inher.
Deut. 27:22 lieth with d. of father
28:56 eye be evil toward her d.

Jud. 11:40 lament Jephthah's d.
1 *Sam.* 1:16 handmaid a d. of B.
18:19 Saul's d. should been giv.
2 *Sam.* 12:3 lamb unto him as a d.
1 *K.* 3:1 Solo. took Pharaoh's d.
11:1 many with d. of Pharaoh
2 *K.* 8:18 d. Jehoram's wife
9:34 bury her, she is a king's d.
1 *Chr.* 2:49 d. of Caleb Achsa
Est. 2:7 uncle's d. for his own
Ps. 45:10 O d. and consider, and
  13 king's d. glorious within.
Cant. 7:1 shoes, O prince's d.
Jer. 31:22 backsliding d. 49:4
46:19 O d. in Egypt, furnish
48:18 d. dost inhabit Dibon
Ezek. 14:16 deliv. son nor d. 18, 20
16:44 as mother, so is her d.
45 art mother's d. that loatheth
Dan. 11:6 king's d. of south come
17 shall give him d. of women
Hos. 1:6 conce. ag. and bare a d.
Mic. 5:1 O d. of troops
7:6 d. riseth up ag. mother, *Mat.*
  10:35; *Luke* 12:53
Zep. 3:10 d. of my dispersed
Mal. 2:11 mar. d. of strange god
Mat. 9:22 d. be of good comfort,
  Mark 5:34; *Luke* 8:48
10:37 loveth d. more than me
14:6 d. of Herodias danced
15:28 her d. was made whole
Mark 7:26 cast devil out of her d.
Luke 8:42 he had one only d.
13:16 this woman being a d.
Acts 7:21 Pharaoh's d. nourished
Heb. 11:24 son of Pharaoh's d.

DAUGHTER of Babylon.
Ps. 137:8 O d. of B. to be destr
Is. 47:1 O d. of B.sit on ground
Jer. 50:42 battle ag. thee d. of B.
51:33 d. of B. like a thr.-floor
Zec. 2:7 dwellest with d. of B.

**DAUGHTER of the
Chaldeans.**
Is. 47:1 throne, O d. of Chal.
5 into darkness, d. of Chal.

DAUGHTER of Edom.
Lam. 4:21 be glad, d. of E.
22 thine iniquity, O d. of E.

DAUGHTER of Egypt.
Jer. 46:11 go into G. d. of Eg.
24 d. of Egypt be confounded

DAUGHTER of Gallim.
Is. 10:30 thy voice d. of Gallim

His DAUGHTER.
Ex. 21:7 sell his d. to be servant
Num. 27:8 to pass to his d.
30:16 statutes bet. fa. and his d.
Deut. 7:3 nor his d. take
18:10 his d. pass, 2 *K.* 23:10
Jud. 21:1 not give his d. to B.
1 *Sam.* 17:25 king give him his d.

DAUGHTER of Jerusalem.
2 *K.* 19:21 d. of J. hath shaken
  her head at thee, *Is.* 37:22
Lam. 2:13 liken to thee, d. of J.
15 wag their head at d. of J.
Mic. 4:8 shall come to d. of J.
Zep. 3:14 rej. with heart, d. of J.
Zec. 9:9 d. of J. thy king cometh

DAUGHTER of Judah.
Lam. 1:15 hath trodden d. of J.
2:2 strong-holds of d. of J.
5 inc. in d. of J. mourning

DAUGHTER-IN-LAW.
Gen. 38:16 she was d.-in-law
  24 Tamar thy d.-in-law played
Lev. 18:15 naked. of thy d.-in-law
20:12 man lie with his d.-in-l.
Ruth 4:15 d.-in-l. which lov. thee
1 *Sam.* 4:19 d.-in-law with child
Ezek. 22:11 defileth his d.-in-l.

Mic. 7:6 d. aga. mother-in-law,
  Mat. 10:35; *Luke* 12:53

My DAUGHTER.
Deut. 22:17 tokens of my d. virg.
Jos. 15:16 him will I give my d.
Jud. 11:35 my d. hast brou. me
  19:24 here is my d. a maiden
Ruth 2:2 she said, Go my d.
  3:10 blessed be thou my d.
Mat. 9:18 my d. is even now d.
  15:22 my d. is vexed
Mark 5:23 my d. at point of d.

DAUGHTER of my people.
Is. 22:4 spoiling of d. of p.
Jer. 4:11 wind toward d. of p.
6:14 healed d. of p. 8:11
  26 O d. of my p. gird with sack.
8:19 the cry of d. of my p.
  21 for hurt of d. of my p.
  22 health of d. of p. recovered
9:1 weep for slain of d. of p.
  7 shall I do for d. of my p.
14:17 virgin d. of p. is broken
Lam. 2:11 destr. of d. of p. 3:48
4:3 the d. of my p. is bec. cruel
  6 iniquity of d. of my p.
  10 in destruction of d. of p.

DAUGHTER of Tarshish.
Is. 23:10 as river, d. of T.

Thy DAUGHTER.
Gen. 29:18 serve 7 y. for thy d.
Ex. 20:10 nor thy d. *Deut.* 5:14
Lev. 18:10 nakedness of thy d.
  19:29 do not prostitute thy d.
Deut. 7:3 thy d. not give
  13:6 if thy d. entice thee
  22:17 found not thy d. a maid
2 *K.* 14:9 give thy d. to my son
Mark 5:35 t. d. is dead, *Luke* 8:49
7:29 devil is gone out of thy d.

DAUGHTER of Tyre.
Ps. 45:12 d. of T. be there

DAUGHTER of Zidon.
Is. 23:12 O oppressed d. of Z.

DAUGHTER of Zion.
2 *K.* 19:21 d. of Z. desp. *Is.* 37:22
Ps. 9:14 in gates of d. of Zion
Is. 1:8 d. of Z. left as a cottage
  4:4 washed away filth of d. of Z.
  10:32 mount of d. of Z. 16:1
  52:2 thyself captive d. of Zion
  62:11 d. of Zion thy sal. cometh
Jer. 4:31 voice of d. of Zion
  6:2 d. of Z. to a comely woman
  23 men of war ag. thee, d. of Z.
Lam. 1:6 d. of Zion beauty dep.
2:1 L. cover d. of Z. with cloud
  4 tabernacle of d. of Zion
  8 destroy wall of d. of Z.
  10 elders of d. of Zion
  13 equal to thee, d. of Zion
  18 O wall of d. of Zion
4:22 accomplished d. of Zion
Mic. 1:13 sin to d. of Zion
4:8 strong-hold of d. of Zion
  10 to bring forth, d. of Zion
  13 arise and thresh, O d. of Z.
Zep. 3:14 sing, O d. of Zion
Zec. 2:10 rejoice, d. of Zion, 9:9
Mat. 21:5 d. of Zion king cometh
John 12:15 fear not d. of Zion

DAUGHTERS.
Gen. 6:2 sons of God saw d.
Gen. 19:36 both d. of Lot with c.
24:3 d. of Can. 37; 28:1, 6
  13 d. came out to draw water
27:46 weary of life bec. of d.
30:13 d. will call me blessed
31:26 hast carried away my d.
  43 d. my d.; 50 if afflict my d.
34:1 Dinah went out to see d.
  9 give your d. take our d.

Ex. 2:16 priest of Midan had 7 *d.*
21:9 deal after the manner of *d.*
34:16 *d.* go a whoring after gods
Lev. 26:29 flesh of *d.* shall ye eat
Num. 26:33 *d.* of Zeloph. *Jos.* 17:3
27:7 *d.* of Zeloph, speak right
36:10 so did *d.* of Zelophehad
Deut. 23:17 no whore of *d.* of Is.
Jud. 3:6 took *d.* to be wives
21:7 not give them of our *d.* 18
Ruth 1:11 turn again my *d.* 12
1 *Sam.* 8:13 *d.* confectionaries
Neh. 5:5 our *d.* into bondage
7:63 one of *d.* of B. *Ezr.* 2:61
10:30 not give *d.* to peo. of land
Job 42:15 none so fair as *d.* of J.
Ps. 45:9 king's *d.* am. hon. wom.
144:12 *d.* be as corner-stones
Prov. 31:29 *d.* done virtuously
Cant. 2:2 so is my love among *d.*
6:9 the *d.* saw and blessed her
Is. 32:9 ye careless *d.* give ear
60:4 *d.* be nursed at thy side
Jer. 9:20 teach your *d.* wailing
29:6 give your *d.* to husbands
49:2 her *d.* be burnt with fire
3 cry, ye *d.* of Rabbah, gird ye
Lam. 3:51 bec. of *d.* of my city
Ezek. 13:17 set face ag. *d.* of peo.
16:46 Samaria and her *d.* Sod.
49 idlen. was in her, and in *d.*
55 sister Sodom and *d.* return
61 give them unto thee for *d.*
23:2 two wom. *d.* of one mother
26:6 her *d.* be slain in field, 8
30:18 her *d.* go into captivity
32:16 *d.* of nations lament her
Hos. 4:13 *d.* shall commit whor.
14 I will not punish your *d.*
Luke 1:5 his wife of *d.* of Aaron
Acts 21:9 had four *d.* virgins
1 *Pet.* 3:6 whose *d.* ye are as long

DAUGHTERS of Israel.
Deut. 23:17 no whore of *d.* of I.
Jud. 11:40 *d.* of I. yearly to lam.
2 *Sam.* 1:24 *d.* of I. weep over S.

DAUGHTERS of Jerusalem.
Cant. 1:5 comely, O *d.* of J.
2:7 you *d.* of J. 3:5; 5:8; 8:4
3:10 paved with love for *d.* of J.
5:16 my beloved, O *d.* of J.
Luke 23:28 *d.* of J. weep not

DAUGHTERS of Judah.
Ps. 48:11 let *d.* of Judah be glad
97:8 the *d.* of Judah rejoiced

DAUGHTERS-IN-LAW.
Ruth 1:8 Naomi said *d.-in-law*

DAUGHTERS of Moab.
Num. 25:1 whore. with *d.* of M.
Is. 16:2 *d.* be at fords of Arnon

DAUGHTERS of music.
Ec. 12:4 *d.* of m. be bro. low

DAUGHTERS of the Philistines.
2 *Sam.* 1:20 lest the *d.* of P. rej.
Ezek. 16:27 deliver thee to *d.* of P.
57 the *d.* of P. which despise

DAUGHTERS of Shiloh.
Jud. 21:21 if *d.* of Shiloh come

DAUGHTERS, *joined with*
sons.
Gen. 5:4 begat *s. d.* 7, 10; 11:11
19:12 thy *sons* and *d.* bring out
31:28 not suff. to kiss *s.* and *d.*
55 kissed his *sons* and *d.*
37:35 *sons* and *d.* rose to comfort
Ex. 10:9 with *s.* and *d.* will we
21:4 have borne him *sons* or *d.*
34:16 take of their *d.* to thy *s.*
Num. 21:29 *sons* and *d.* into captiv.
26:33 no *sons* but *d. Jos.* 17:3
Deut. 12:12 and *s.* and *d.* rejoice
31 *sons* and *d.* they have burnt,
2 *K.* 17:17; *Jer.* 7:31; 32:35

28:32 *s. d.* given to another peo.
41 begat *sons d.* but not enjoy
53 eat flesh of *sons* and *d.*
32:19 provoking of his *s.* and *d.*
Jos. 7:24 brought Ach. *s.* and *d.*
17:6 *d.* of Manasseh inh. am. *s.*
Jud. 3:6 gave their *d.* to their *s.*
12:9 Ibzan 30 *d.* for his *sons*
1 *Sam.* 30:19 noth. lack. *s.* nor *d.*
1 *Chr.* 23:22 Ele. had no *s.* but *d.*
25:5 God gave Heman 14 *s.* 3 *d.*
2 *Chr.* 11:21 Rehob. had 28 *s.* 60 *d.*
13:21 Abijah begat 22 *sons* 16 *d.*
Ezr. 9:12 *d.* to their *s. Neh.* 13:25
Neh. 4:14 fight for your *s.* and *d.*
5:2 our *sons* and *d.* are many
10:28 *s.* and *d.* clave to brethren
Job 1:2 born to Job 7 *s.* 3 *d.* 42:13
Ps. 106:37 sacrificed *sons* and *d.*
38 shed blood of their *s.* and *d.*
Is. 43:6 bring my *s.* from far. *d.*
49:22 bring thy *sons* in arms, *d.*
56:5 better than *sons* and *d.*
Jer. 3:24 shame dev. *sons* and *d.*
16:2 nor shalt have *sons* nor *d.*
19:9 cause eat flesh of *s.* and *d.*
29:6 wives, beget *sons* and *d.*
48:46 *s.* and *d.* taken captive
Ezek. 14:16 deliver *sons* nor *d.*
16:20 *s.* and *d.* and sacrificed
23:4 mine, bare *sons* and *d.*
46 shall slay their *sons* and *d.*
24:21 *s. d.* fall by sw. *Amos* 7:17
25 when I take their *s.* and *d.*
Joel 2:28 *s.* and *d.* prop. *Acts* 2:17
3:8 sell *sons* and *d.* to Judah
2 *Cor.* 6:18 be my *s.* and *d.* saith L.

Two DAUGHTERS.
Gen. 19:8 I have *two d.* let me
15 take thy wife and *two d.*
29:16 Laban had *two d.* Leah
31:41 I served for thy *two d.*
Ruth 1:7 N. went out with *t. d.*
1 *Sam.* 2:21 Hannah bare *two d.*
14:49 Saul's *two d.* were Merab
Prov. 30:15 horseleech hath *t. d.*

DAUGHTERS of the uncircumcised.
2 *Sam.* 1:20 lest *d.* of *u.* triumph

DAUGHTERS of Zion.
Cant. 3:11 go forth, O ye *d.* of Z.
Is. 3:16 *d.* of Zion are haughty
4:4 filth of *d.* of Zion

DAVID.
Ruth 4:22 Jesse begat *D. Mat.*
1:6; *Luke* 3:31
1 *Sam.* 16:13 came upon *D.*
2 *Sam.* 5:1 all tribes of Is. to *D.*
1 *K.* 2:10 *D.* slept, 1 *Chr.* 29:28
Ps. 72:20 prayers of *D.* son of J.
Mat. 9:27 son of *D.* 15:22; 20:30;
Mark 10:47; *Luke* 18:38
12:3 *D.* did when h'ngered,
Mark 2:25; *Luke* 20:41
21:9 S. of *D.* 15; 22:42; *Mark* 12:35
Rom. 1:3 C. seed of *D.* 2 *Tim.* 2:8
Heb. 4:7 saying in *D.* to-day
Rev. 3:7 key of *D.*;*5:5 root, 22:16

Hand of DAVID.
1 *Sam.* 20:16 Lord req. at *h.* of *D.*
2 *Sam.* 3:8 not into *hand* of *D.* 18
21:22 fell by *h.* of *D.* 1 *Chr.* 20:8

House of DAVID.
1 *K.* 12:19 fol. *D.* but J. 2 *Chr.* 10:19
Ps. 122:5 thrones of the *h.* of *D.*
Is. 7:2 it was told *house* of *D.* 13
22:22 key of *h.* of *D.* I wil lay
Zec. 12:7 gl. of *h.* of *D.* 8, 10, 12
13:1 fountain opened to *h.* of *D.*
Luke 1:27 Joseph, of *h.* of *D.* 69
2:4 the *house* and lineage of *D.*

DAVID, *joined with* **king.**
1 *Sam.* 21:11 this *D. k.* of land?
2 *Sam.* 2:4 anointed *D. k.* over J.
Jer. 30:9 Lord and *D.* the *king*

Hos. 3:5 seek L. and *D.* their *k.*
Mat. 1:6 *D.* the *k.* and *D.* the *k.*
Acts 13:22 raised *D.* to be the *k.*

Servant DAVID.
2 *Sam.* 7:5 my *servant D.* 8, 26
1 *K.* 8:25 thy *s. D.* 2 *Chr.* 6:16
11:13 for *D. s.* sake, *Ps.* 132:10;
Is. 37:35
Ps. 78:70 *D.* his *servant,* 89:20
Jer. 33:21 brok. with *D.* my *s.* 22
Ezek. 34:23 even my *servant D.*
37:24 *D.* my *ser.* shall be king
Luke 1:69 salva. in house of *s. D.*
Acts 4:25 mouth of thy *serv. D.*

DAWN, ING.
Jos. 6:15 rose about *d.* of day
Jud. 19:26 came woman in *d.*
Job 3:9 nor let it see *d.* of day
7:4 I am full of tossings to *d.*
Ps. 119:147 I prevented the *d.*
Mat. 28:1 as it began to *d.*
2 *Pet.* 1:19 till the day *d.* and the

DAY.
Gen. 1:5 God called the light *d.*
32:26 let me go, *d.* breaketh
Lev. 23:37 every thing on his *d.*
Num. 14:34 each *d.* for a year
Deut. 4:10 *d.* thou stoodest be. L.
9:24 rebellious from *d.* I knew
24:15 at his *d.* give him his hire
Jos. 10:13 sun not down ab. a *d.*
14 was no *d.* like that
Jud. 16:2 when it is *d.* kill Sam.
1 *Sam.* 9:15 told S. a *d.* before
24:4 *d.* of which Lord said
26:10 or his *d.* shall come to die
2 *Sam.* 3:35 while yet *d. Jer.* 15:9
1 *K.* 2:37 on *d.* thou goest out
2 *K.* 4:8 fell on a *d.* Elisha, 11, 18
Neh. 4:2 make an end in a *d.?*
Job 1:4 feasted, every one his *d.*
6 was a *d.* when sons, 13; 2:1
3:3 *d.* per. wherein I was born
14:6 till he accomplish his *d.*
18:20 be astonished at his *d.*
19:25 stand at latter *d.* on earth
21:30 reserved to *d.* of destruction
Ps. 19:2 *d.* unto *d.* uttereth
37:13 he seeth his *d.* is coming
78:42 nor rem. *d.* he delivered
84:10 a *d.* in thy courts better
119:164 7 times a *d.* I praise
Prov. 4:18 and more to perfect *d.*
7:20 home at the *d.* appointed
27:1 what a *d.* may bring forth
Cant. 2:17 till the *d.* break, 4:6
Is. 7:17 from *d.* Ephraim dep.
43:13 before *d.* was, I am he
58:5 a *d.* to afflict soul? call this
an acceptable *d.* to Lord?
61:2 *d.* of vengeance of G. 63:4
Jer. 12:3 prep. for *d.* of slaughter
17:22 there be till *d.* I visit
32:31 from the *d.* they built it
36:2 from the *d.* I spake to thee
38:28 *d.* Jerusalem was taken
47:4 of *d.* that cometh to spoil
50:27 woe, for their *d.* is come
Ezek. 4:6 each *d.* for a year
7:10 behold the *d.* it is come
21:25 prince, whose *d.* is come
28:15 from *d.* thou wast created
30:2 woe worth the *d.;* 3 near
18 at Tehaphne. *d.* be darken.
Dan. 6:10 petition 3 times a *d.*
Hos. 9:5 what do in solemn *d.?*
Joel 2:2 a *d.* of darkness and
Amos 5:8 maketh *d.* dark
8:10 end thereof as a bitter *d.*
Mic. 3:6 *d.* be dark over them
7:4 the *d.* of thy watchmen
Zep. 2:2 before *d.* pass as chaff
3:8 till *d.* I rise up to the prey
Zec. 4:10 desp. *d.* of small things
Mal. 3:2 abide *d.* of his coming?
4:1 *d.* cometh that shall burn

Mat. 24:38 *d.* Noe ent. *Luke* 17:27
50 L. shall come in a *d.* when
he looketh not, *Luke* 12:46
25:13 know the *d.* nor the hour
Mark 1:35 great while before *d.*
Luke 1:20 *d.* these be performed
80 *d.* of his showing to Israel
17:4 trespass seven times in a *d.*
24 so Son of man be in his *d.*
John 6:39 raise it ag. at last *d.*
40 raise him at last *d.* 44, 54
8:56 Abra. rejoiced to see my *d.*
9:4 work while it is *d.*
Acts 1:2 until *d.* he was tak. up
12:21 on a set *d.* Herod sat
16:35 it was *d.* 28:12 ; 27:39
17:31 he hath appointed a *d.*
27:29 they wished for *d.*
Rom. 2:5 wrath ag. *d.* of wrath
13:12 *d.* is at hand, let us
14:6 regardeth *d.* to the Lord
1 *Cor.* 3:13 the *d.* shall declare it
2 *Cor.* 6:2 now is the *d.* of salv.
Eph. 4:30 sealed to *d.* of redem.
Phil. 1:6 perf. it un. the *d.* of C.
1 *Thes.* 5:5 children of the *d.*
8 who are of the *d.* be sober
Heb. 4:7 he limiteth a certain *d.*
8 have not spoken of anoth. *d.*
10:25 see the *d.* approaching
2 *Pet.* 1:19 till the *d.* dawn, and
3:12 to coming of *d.* of God
Rev. 9:15 were prepared for a *d.*

See ATONEMENT, BATTLE, CALAM-
ITY, DARKNESS, EVIL, HOLY,
LAST.

All the DAY.

Ps. 25:5 do I wait *all the d.*
71:15 thy salvation *all the d.*
89:16 rejoice *all the d.*
102:8 reproach me *all the d.*
119:97 meditation *all the d.*
Is. 28:24 ploughman plo. *a. d.*
65:2 spread out hands *all the d.*
5 a fire burneth *all the d.*
Lam. 1:13 desolate *all the d.*
3:3 his hand ag. me *all t. d.*
14 derision to people *all the d.*
62 their devices ag. me *a. t. d.*
Mat. 20:6 stand *all the d.* idle

All the DAY long.

Deut. 28:32 longinge *a. t. d. l.*
33:12 cover him *all the d. l.*
Ps. 32:3 my roaring *all the d. l.*
35:28 thy praise *all the d. l.*
38:6 mourning *all the d. long*
12 imagine deceits *all the d. l.*
44:8 we boast *all the d. long*
22 are killed *all t. d. l.*
71:24 thy righteousness *a. t. d. l.*
73:14 *a. t. d. l.* have I been pla.
Prov. 21:26 coveteth *all the d.*
23:17 in fear of Lord *all the d.*
Rom. 10:21 *a. t. d. l.* stret. my h.

By DAY.

Gen. 39:10 spake to Jos. *d. by d.*
Ex. 13:21 L. went be. them *by d.*
40:38 cloud was upon the taber-
nacle *by d. Num.* 9:16
Num. 10:34 cloud on them *by d.*
14:14 ; *Deut.* 1:33 ; *Neh.* 9:19
Jud. 6:27 could not do it *by d.*
2 *Chr.* 30:21 praised L. *d. by d.*
Ezr. 6:9 let it be given *d. by d.*
Neh. 8:18 *d. by d.* he read in law
Ps. 91:5 nor arrow flieth *by d.*
121:6 sun not smite thee *by d.*
136:8 sun to rule *by d.* for
Is. 60:19 no more thy light *by d.*
Jer. 31:35 sun for a light *by d.*
Ezek. 12:3 remove *by d.* in sight
Luke 11:3 give us *d. by d.* bread
2 *Cor.* 4:16 is renewed *d. by d.*
Rev. 21:25 g. not to be shut *by d.*

Day of DEATH.

Gen. 27:2 I know not *d. of* my *d.*

Jud. 13:7 Nazarite to *d. of d.*
1 *Sam.* 15:35 Saul till *d. of d.*
2 *Sam.* 20:3 shut up to *d. of d.*
2 *K.* 15:5 Uzziah lep. to *d. of d.*
Ec. 7:1 *d. of d.* better than birth
8:8 nor ha. he power in *d. of d.*
Jer. 52:11 in prison, till *d. of d.*
34 a portion till *d. of d.*

Every DAY.

Ps. 7:11 angry with wicked *e. d.*
56:5 *e. d.* they wrest my words
145:2 *every d.* will I bless thee
Is. 51:13 hast feared *every d.*
52:5 my name *e. d.* blasphemed
Luke 16:19 sumptuously *every d.*
Rom. 14:5 esteem. *every d.* alike

Feast DAY.

Ps. 81:3 blow trumpet on *feast-d.*
Mat. 26:5 Not on *f.-d. Mark* 14:2
John 2:23 in *feast-d.* many bel.

First DAY.

Gen. 1:5 evening and morn. *f. d.*
Neh. 8:18 from *f.* unto last *d.*
Dan. 10:12 from *f. d.* thou didst
Mat. 26:17 *f. d.* of unl. b. *Mark*
14:12
Acts 20:18 *f. d.* I came into A.
Phil. 1:5 fellowship from *f. d.*

See WEEK.

Third DAY.

Hos. 6:2 *third d.* he will raise us
Mat. 16:21 be raised again the
third d. 17:23 ; *Luke* 9:22
20:19 and the *third d.* he shall
rise again, *Mark* 9:31 ; 10:34 ;
Luke 18:33 ; 24:7, 46
Luke 13:32 *t. d.* I shall be perf.
24:21 to-day is the *third d.*
1 *Cor.* 15:4 he rose again *third d.*

Seventh DAY.

Gen. 2:3 G. bless. *s. d. Ex.* 20:11
Ex. 12:15 fr. first *d.* to *s. d.* 13:6
16:26 *s. d.* is the sabbath, 20:10 ;
Lev. 23:3 ; *Deut.* 5:14
27 there went out some on *s. d.*
31:17 on *seventh d.* God rested
Heb. 4:4 spake of *s. d.*

Eighth DAY.

Lev. 12:3 on *eighth d.* be circum.
Luke 1:59 *e. d.* came to circumcise ch. *Acts* 7:8 ; *Phil.* 3:5

Good DAY.

1 *Sam.* 25:8 we co. in a *good d.*
Est. 8:17 J. had a *good d.* 9:19
9:22 mourning into a *good d.*

Great DAY.

Jer. 30:7 alas, that *d.* is *great*
Hos. 1:11 *great* shall be *d.* of J.
Joel 2:11 *d.* of L. is *great* and te.
31 bef. the *great* and terrible *d.*
of the Lord come, *Acts* 2:20
Zep. 1:14 *g. d.* of the L. is near
Mal. 4:5 before coming of *g. d.*
John 7:37 *great d.* of feast
Rev. 6:17 *g. d.* of his wrath
16:14 to gather to battle of *g. d.*

In the DAY.

Gen. 2:4 *i. t. d.* L. made the ear.
Gen. 2:17 *in the d.* thou eatest
3:5 *in the d.* ye eat
31:40 *in d.* drought consumed
35:3 *in the d.* of my distress
Ex. 32:34 *in the d.* when I. visit
Job 20:28 away *in d.* of wrath
Ps. 95:8 *in d.* of temp. *Heb.* 3:8
102:2 hide not face *in d.* of tro.
in the d. when I call
110:3 *in the d.* of thy power
5 kings *in the d.* of his wrath
137:7 Edom, *in the d.* of Jerus.
138:3 *in d.* I cried, thou answ.
Prov. 6:34 not spare *in d.* of ven.
11:4 riches profit not *in d.* of w.
24:10 *in the d.* of adversity

Ec. 7:14 *in the d.* of prosperi. be
joyful, *in d.* of adversity
8:8 nor hath power *in d.* of d.
12:3 *in the d.* keepers sh. trem.
Cant. 3:11 *in d.* of his espousals
8:8 *in the d.* she shall be spok.
Is. 9:4 as *in the d.* of Midian
10:3 what do *in the d.* of visit.
11:16 *d.* come out Eg. *Hos.* 2:15
13:13 remove, *in d.* of his anger
17:11 *in the d.* shalt make thy
plant grow, *in the d.* of grief
30:25 *in the d.* of great slaught.
26 *in the d.* Lord bindeth up
58:3 *in d.* of your fast
Jer. 16:19 *in t. d.* of affliction
17:17 my hope *in the d.* of evil
18:17 *in the d.* of calamity
36:30 body be cast out *in t. d.*
Lam. 1:12 *in d.* of anger
2:1 footstool *in d.* of anger
3:57 drewest near *in the d.*
Ezek. 7:19 gold not deliver *i. t. d.*
16:4 *in the d.* thou wast born, 5
56 Sod. not men. *in d.* of pride
27:27 fall *in the d.* of thy ruin
30:9 as *in d.* of Egypt
32:10 *in the d.* of thy fall
33:12 *in t. d.* he turneth from
wick. not able to live *in d.*
Hos. 2:3 *in the d.* she was born
4:5 therefore shalt fall *in the d.*
Amos 1:14 *in the d.* of whirlwind
8:9 the earth *in the d.* clear *d.*
Ob. 11 *in d.* stoodest
12 nor rejoiced *in d.* of destr.
Mal. 4:3 *in t. d.* that I shall do
Luke 17:30 *in the d.* Son is rev.
John 11:9 if any walk *in the d.*
Rom. 2:16 *in d.* G. shall judge
13:13 walk honestly as *in the d.*
1 *Cor.* 1:8 blameless *in t. d.* of L.
2 *Cor.* 6:2 *in d.* of salvat. I suc.
Phil. 2:16 rejoice *in d.* of Chr.
Heb. 8:9 *in d.* I took them
1 *Pet.* 2:12 glorify G. *in d.* of vis.

DAY of Judgment.

Mat. 10:15 more tolerable for S.
in d. of j. 11:24 ; *Mark* 6:11
11:22 Tyre and Sidon at *d. of j.*
12:36 account in the *d. of ju.*
2 *Pet.* 2:9 res. unjust to *d. of ju.*
3:7 res. unto fire aga. *d. of ju.*
1 *John* 4:17 boldness in *d. of ju.*

DAY of the Lord.

Is. 2:12 *d. of* L. be on every one
13:6 is at ha. *Joel* 1:15 ; *Zep.* 1:7
9 cometh, *Joel* 2:1 ; *Zec.* 14:1
34:8 *d. of* Lord's vengeance
Jer. 46:10 *d. of* L. G. of hosts
Lam. 2:22 *d. of* L. anger
Ezek. 13:5 battle *d. of* the Lord
30:3 *d.* is near, *Joel* 3:14 ; *Ob.* 15
Amos 5:18 desired *d. of* L.
Zep. 1:8 *d. of* Lord's sacrifice
18 deliver them in *d. of* L.
2:2 before *d. of* the L. anger
3 in *d. of* the Lord's anger
Mal. 4:5 coming of *d. of* Lord
1 *Cor.* 5:5 saved in *d. of* Lord
2 *Cor.* 1:14 ye are ou. in *d. of* L.
1 *Thes.* 5:2 as a thief, 2 *Pet.* 3:10
Rev. 1:10 the Spirit on Lord's *d.*

See Great DAY.

DAY, joined with Night.

Gen. 1:14 to divide *d.* from *n.*
18 rule over the *d.* and *night*
8:22 *d.* and night shall not cea.
31:39 whether stolen by *d.* or *n.*
Ex. 13:21 to go by *d.* and *n.*
Num. 11:32 that *d.* and all *n.*
Deut. 28:66 shalt fear *d.* and *n.*
Jos. 1:8 shalt meditate therein *d.*
and *night, Ps.* 1:2
1 *Sam.* 19:24 naked all *d.* and *n.*

1 *K.* 8:29 eyes be opened towards
house *n.* and *d.* 2 *Chr.* 6:20
Neh. 1:6 I pray *d.* and *night*
Job 17:12 change *night* into *d.*
26:10 *d.* and *n.* come to an end
Ps. 39:4 *d.* an. thy hand
42:3 tears my meat *d.* and *night*
55:10 *d.* and *night* they go abo.
74:16 *d.* is thine, *n.* also is thi.
88:1 I have cried *d.* and *n.*
139:12 *night* shineth as the *d.*
Ec. 8:16 *d.* nor *night* seeth
Is. 4:5 sm. by *d.* fla. fire by *n.*
27:3 L. will keep it *d.* and *n.*
34:10 not be quenched *d.* nor *n.*
38:12 sickness from *d.* to *n.*
13 *d.* to *n.* wilt make an end
60:11 gates not be sh. *d.* nor *n.*
62:6 hold their peace *d.* nor *n.*
Jer. 9:1 weep *d.* and *night*
14:17 tears *d.* and *n. Lam.* 2:18
16:13 serve other gods *d.* and *n.*
33:20 should not be *d.* nor *n.*
Zec. 14:7 *d.* kn. to L. not *d. n. n.*
Mark 4:27 and rise, *n.* and *d.*
5:5 *d.* and *n.* he was in mount.
Luke 2:37 prayers *night* and *d.*
18:7 which cry *d.* and *night*
Acts 9:24 watched gates *n.* and *d.*
20:31 cease not to warn *n.* a. *d.*
26:7 instantly serv. *G.* and *n.*
1 *Thes.* 2:9 laboring *d.* and *n.*
3:10 *n.* and *d.* pray. 1 *Tim.* 5:5
2 *Thes.* 3:8 labor *night* and *d.*
2 *Tim.* 1:3 in prayers *n.* and *d.*
Rev. 4:8 rest not *d.* and *night*
7:15 serve him *d.* and *n.*
8:12 *d.* shone not for a third p.
12:10 accused bef. *G. d.* and *n.*
14:11 have no rest *d.* nor *night*
20:10 torment. *d.* and *n.* for ev.

One DAY.

Gen. 27:45 dep. of both in *o. d. ?*
1 *Sam.* 2:34 in *one d.* shall die
27:1 *one d.* perish by hand of S.
Is. 9:14 bra. and rush in *one d.*
10:17 dev. thorns and br. in *o. d.*
47:9 two things sh. co. in *o. d.*
66:8 earth bring forth in *one d. ?*
Zec. 3:9 remove iniquity in *o. d. ?*
14:7 *o. d.* which shall be known
Acts 21:7 abode with breth. *o. d.*
Rom. 14:5 esteemeth *o. d.*
1 *Cor.* 10:8 fell in *one d.* 23,000
2 *Pet.* 3:8 *o. d.* with L. as 1,000 y.
Rev. 18:8 plagues come in *one d.*

Sabbath DAY.

Ex. 16:26 seventh *d.* is *sa.* 20:10
20:8 *s.-d* to keep it h. *Deut.* 5:12
11 Lord blessed the *s.-d.*
31:15 doeth any work on *s.-d.*
35:3 shall kindle no fire on *s.-d.*
Num. 15:32 gath. sticks on *s.-d.*
Deut. 5:15 God com. to keep *s.-d.*
Neh. 13:15 burdens to J. on *s.-d.*
17 and profane the *s.-d.*
22 keep gates, to sanctify *s.-d.*
Jer. 17:21 bear no burd. on *s.-d.*
Ezek. 46:4 prince sh. offer in *s.-d.*
Mat. 12:1 Jesus went on *s.-d* th.
corn-fields, *Mark* 2:23
8 for Son of man is Lo. of *s.-d.*
11 into a pit on *s.-d. Luke* 14:5
24:20 pray flight be not on *s.-d.*
Mark 2:24 *s.-d.* that not lawful
3:2 heal on *s.-d. Luke* 6:7
6:2 went into the synagogue on
s.-d. Luke 4:17; *Acts* 13:4
Luke 13:16 this bond on *s.-d.*
14:1 went to eat bread on *s.-d.*
23:56 and rested the *s.-d.*
John 5:10 *s.-d* not lawful
16 because done these on *s.-d.*
7:22 on *s.-d.* circumcise a man
9:14 it was *s.-d.* J. made clay
19:31 not rem. on cross on *s.-d.*

Acts 13:27 read every *s.-d.* 15:21
44 next *s.-d.* came the wh. city

Same DAY.

Ezek. 24:2 the name of this *s. d.*
Zep. 1:9 *s. d.* will I punish those
Luke 23:12 *s. d.* P. and H. frien.
John 5:9 on *s. d.* was thesabbath
20:19 *same d.* J. stood in midst
Acts 1:22 *sa. d.* he was taken up
2:41 *s. d.* were added 3,000 souls

Since the DAY.

Deut. 4:32 *s. the d.* God created
1 *Sam.* 8:8 *s. t. d.* I bro. them o.
of E. 1 *K.* 8.16; 1 *Chr.* 17:5
Jer. 7:25 *s. the d.* fathers came
Col. 1:6 *since the d.* ye hea. of it
9 *s. thé d.* we heard it

That DAY.

Ex. 10:28 *t. d.* seest my face
14:30 Lord saved Israel *th. d.*
Deut. 31:23 bury him *t. d.*
31:18 hide my face in *that d.*
1 *Sam.* 8:18 shall cry out in *t. d.*
and Lord will not hear you
14:23 Lord saved **Israel** *that d.*
1 *Sam.* 14:37 S. ask. he a. not *t. d.*
16:13 Spirit of L. on D. fro. *t. d.*
18:9 Saul eyed David from *t. d.*
2 *Sam.* 6:9 D. afraid of L. *that d.*
11:12 Uriah abode in Jeru. *t. d.*
Job 3:4 let *that d.* be darkness
Ps. 146:4 in *t. d.* his thoughts
Is. 2:11 L. alone exalted in *t. d.*
19:21 E. shall know L. in *t. d.*
24:21 in *t. d.* L. shall punish
26:1 in *t. d.* this be sung in Ju.
29:18 in *t. d.* shall deaf hear
52:6 shall know in *that d.*
Jer. 39:16 accomplished in *t. d.*
17 I will deliver thee in *t. d.*
Ezek. 29:21 in *t. d.* Is. be exalted
38:19 in *t. d.* be a great shaking
39:22 know I am L. from *t. d.*
Hos. 2:18 in *t. d.* make a cov.
Joel 3:18 in *t. d.* mount. drop wine
Amos 2:16 flee away nak. in *t. d.*
8:3 songs be howlings in *t. d.*
Zep. 1:15 *that d.* is a day of wra.
Zec. 2:11 joined to L. in *t. d.*
9:16 G. shall save them in *t. d.*
11:11 covenant, broken in *t. d.*
12:8 feeble at *t. d.* sh. be as D.
11 in *that d.* be a great mour.
13:1 in *t. d.* be a foun. opened
14:4 his feet *t. d.* on the mount.
9 *t. d.* be one L. his name one
Mal. 3:17 *t. d.* I make up jewels
Mat. 7:22 will say in *that d.* Lo.
24:36 *t. d.* kn. no m. *Mark* 13:32
26:29 *t. d.* I drink, *Mark* 14:25
Luke 6:23 rejoice in *th. d.*
10:12 more tol. in *t. d.* for Sod.
21:34 so *that d.* come unawares
23:54 *t. d.* was the preparation
John 1:39 abode with him *that d.*
11:53 from *t. d.* they took coun.
14:20 *t. d.* know I am in the F.
16:23 in *th. d.* shall ask me no.
26 *t. d.* shall ask in my name
1 *Thes.* 5:4 *t. d.* overtake as thi.
2 *Thes.* 1:10 believed in *t. d.*
2:3 *that d.* shall not come
2 *Tim.* 1:12 com. to h. ag. *t. d.*
18 find mercy of L. in *that d*
4:8 L. shall give me at *t. d.*

This DAY.

Gen. 48:15 who fed me *t. a.*
Ex. 12:14 *t. d.* for a memorial
17 observe *t. d.* in your gener.
13:3 remem. *t. d.* ye came out, 4
Deut. 4:4 alive every one *t. d.* 5:3
5:24 *t. d.* God talk with man
6:24 at *t. d.* 8:18; *Exr.* 9:7
11:8 I com. you *t. d.* 13:27, 28;
13:18; 15:5; 19:9; 27:1, 4
26:17 avou. *t. d.* L. to be thy G.

27:9 *t. d.* art bec. people of Lord
29:4 not ears to hear, to *this d.*
10 ye stand *this d.* before L.
30:15 *this d.* life and death, 19
16 I command thee *t. d.*
31:27 I am yet alive *this d.*
Jos. 14:11 I am as strong *t. d.*
22:17 are not cleansed till *t. d.*
22 save us not *this d.*
23:8 as done unto *t. d.*
24:15 choose *this d.* whom serv.
Jud. 10:15 deliver us only *this d.*
19:30 since Isr. came out of E.
to *th. d.* 1 *Sam.* 8:8; 2 *Sam.*
7:6; 2 *K.* 21:15; 1 *Chr.* 17:5;
Jer. 7:25
1 *Sam.* 10:19 *t. d.* rejected y. G.
14:45 J. wrought with God *t. d.*
17:10 I defy armies of Is. *this d.*
18:21 *this d.* be my son-in-law
22:8 lie in wait as at *t. d. ?* 13
25:33 *t. d.* from com. to shed bl.
26:21 my soul precious *this d.*
2 *Sam.* 3:39 I *this d.* weak
1 *K.* 8:61 to keep com. as at *t. d.*
2 *K.* 7:9 *t. d.* day of good tidings
17:34 to *t. d.* do after former
2 *Chr.* 5:9 there it is unto *t. d.*
35:21 I come not ag. thee *t. d.*
Neh. 9:36 we are servants *this d.*
Ps. 2:7 my S. *t. d* have I begot.
thee, *Acts* 13:33; *Heb.* 1:5
118:24 *t.* is the *d.* L. hath made
119:91 continue *t. d.* accord. to
Prov. 7:14 *this d.* I paid my vo.
22:19 known to thee *this d.*
Is. 38:19 praise thee *this d.*
56:12 to-mor. shall be as *this d.*
Jer. 25:18 hiss. as at *t. d.* 44:22
36:2 from Josiah even to *this d.*
44:10 are not humbled to *this d.*
Lam. 2:16 *this* is *d.* we looked f.
Ezek. 39:8 *t.* the *d.* I have spok.
Dan. 9:7 conf. of faces as at *t. d.*
Hag. 2:15 consider from *t. d.* 18
19 from *this d.* will I bless you
Mat. 6:11 give us *this d.* daily b.
11:23 Sodom remain. to *this d.*
28:15 among Jews to *this d.*
Luke 2:11 is born *t. d.* a Saviour
4:21 *this d.* scripture fulfilled
19:9 *t. d.* salvation to this house
42 at least in *this* thy *d.*
Acts 22:3 as ye are all *t. d.*
23:1 good conscience till *t. d.*
24:21 called in question *this d.*
26:22 continue to *t. d.* witness.
29 all that hear me *t. d.*
Rom. 11:8 sh. not hear to *t. d.*

To-DAY.

Gen. 21:26 heard I of it but *to-d.*
Ex. 2:18 come so soon *to-d. ?*
14:13 salvation show you *to-d.*
Lev. 9:4 *to-d.* Lord will appear
1 *Sam.* 11:13 *to-d.* Lord wrought
24:10 how Lord delivered thee
to-d. into my hand, 26:23
2 *Sam.* 18:4 lean from d. *to-d. ?*
16:3 *to-d.* house of Is. resto. me
1 *K.* 18:15 will show myself *to-d.*
22:5 inq. at L. *to-d.* 2 *Chr.* 18:4
2 *K.* 4:23 why go to him *to-d. ?*
1 *Chr.* 16:23 show from day *to-d.*
his salvation, *Ps.* 96:2
Job 23:2 *to-d.* my complaint
Ps. 95:7 *to-d.* if ye will hear his
voice, *Heb.* 3:7, 15; 4:7
Zec. 9:12 *to-d.* do I declare
Mat. 6:30 *to-d.* is. and to-mor.
is cast into oven, *Luke* 12:28
21:28 work *to-d.* in vineyard
Luke 5:26 strange things *to-d.*
13:32 I do cures *to-d.* and to-mo.
33 must walk *to-d.* and d. fol.
19:5 *to-d.* I abide at thy house
23:43 *to-d.* be with me in para.
24:21 *to-d.* is the third day

Heb. 3:13 while it is called *to-d.*
5:5 *to-d.* have I begotten thee
13:8 the same yesterday, *to-d.*
Jam. 4:13 that say *to-d.* or
2 *Pet.* 2:8 vexed his soul *b. to-d.*

DAY of trouble.
2 *K.* 19:3 this is *d. of t.* Is. 37:3
Ps. 20:1 L. hear thee in *d. of t.*
50:15 call upon me in *d. of t.*
59:16 my refuge in *d. of trou.*
77:2 in *d. of t.* I sought the L.
86:7 in *d. of t.* I will call
Is. 22:5 it is a *d. of trouble*
Jer. 51:2 *d. of t.* shall be ag. her
Ezek. 7:7 time is come, *d. of tr.*
Nah. 1:7 strong-hold in *d. of t.*
Hab. 3:16 I might rest *in d. of t.*
Zep. 1:15 that day is a *d. of t.*

DAYTIME.
Job 5:14 meet with dark. in *d.*
24:16 houses they marked in *d.*
Ps. 22:2 I cry in *d.* hearest not
42:8 his loving kindness in *d.*
78:14 in *d.* led with a cloud
Is. 4:6 a taber. for shadow in *d.*
21:8 on watch-tower in the *d.*
Luke 21:37 in *d.* he was teaching
2 *Pet.* 2:13 pleasure to riot in *d.*

DAYS.
Gen. 8:3 after 150 *d.* waters ab.
27:41 *d.* of mourning for my f.
47:9 *d.* of my pilgrimage
50:4 *d.* of his mourning past
Deut. 4:32 ask now of the *d.* past
10:10 I stayed in mount forty *d.*
1 *Sam* 13:11 came not within *d.*
18:26 the *d.* were not expired
29:3 been with me these *d.*
1 *Chr.* 23:1 David was full of *d.*
29:15 *d.* as a shadow, *Job* 8:9
28 he died full of *d.* riches, and
2 *Chr.* 24:15 Jehoiada full of *d.*
Ezr. 9:7 since *d.* of fathers
Neh. 1:4 I mourned certain *d.*
Est. 9:26 they called these *d.*
Job 3:6 not joined to *d.* of year
7:1 his *d.* like *d.* of a hireling ?
12:12 length of *d.* understand.
21:13 spend their *d.* in wealth
30:16 *d.* of afflict. taken hold
27 *d.* of affliction prevent. me
32:7 I said, *d.* should speak
33:25 return to *d.* of his youth
36:11 spend their *d.* in prosper.
42:17 so Job died, full of *d.*
Ps. 21:4 gavest him length of *d.*
37:18 L. knoweth *d.* of upright
44:1 work thou didst in their *d.*
55:23 not live half their *d.*
75:5 considered the *d.* of old
78:33 their *d.* did he consume
89:29 his throne as *d.* of heaven
45 *d.* of his youth shortened
90:9 all our *d.* are passed away
10 *d.* of our years threescore
Ps. 90:12 so tea. us to nu. our *d.*
14 we may be glad all our *d.*
94:13 rest from *d.* of adversity
119:84 many are *d.* of thy ser.
143:5 I remember the *d.* of old
Prov. 3:2 leng. of *d.* add to thee
16 length of *d.* is in right hand
Ec. 5:20 not much remember *d.*
7:10 that former *d.* were better
8:15 abide with him *d.* of his li.
11:8 remember *d.* of darkness
12:1 while the evil *d.* come not
Is. 23:7 antiquity of ancient *d.*
15 according to *d.* of one king
60:20 *d.* of mourn. shall be end.
65:20 be no more infant of *d.*
22 as *d.* of a tree *d.* of my peo.
Jer. 2:32 *d.* without number
6:11 aged with him full of *d.*
31:33 after those *d.* put my law
36:2 *d.* of Josiah to this day

Lam. 4:18 our *d.* are fulfilled,
Ezek. 12:23 *d.* at hand, effect of
16:22 rem. *d.* of thy youth, 43
Dan. 8:14 unto 2,300 *d.* sanctuary
12:11 set up shall be 1,290 *d.*
12 blessed waiteth to 1,335 *d.*
Hos. 2:13 visit on her *d.* of Baal.
9:7 *d.* of visitation, recompense
10:9 sinned from *d.* of Gibeah
Mic. 7:15 acc. to *d.* of thy com.
Zec. 8:9 ye that hear in these *d.*
11 I will not be as in former *d.*
15 thought in these *d.*
Mal. 3:7 *d.* of fat, ye are gone
Mat. 11:12 *d.* of John Baptist
24:22 those *d.* be shortened, no
flesh be saved, *Mark* 13:20
37 as *d.* of Noe, so com. of S.
Luke 21:22 these be *d.* of veng.
Acts 3:24 foretold of these *d.*
5:36 bef. these *d.* rose up Theu.
12:3 *d.* of unleav. bread, 20:6
Gal. 4:10 ye observe *d.* months
Eph. 5:16 because the *d.* are evil
Heb. 7:3 beg. of *d.* nor end of life
10:32 call to remem. former *d.*
1 *Pet.* 3:10 see good *d.* let refrain
Rev. 11:3 shall prophesy 1,260 *d.*
12:6 feed her there 1,260 *d.*

See DAVID, LAST, OLD, JOURNEY.

All the DAYS.
Gen. 5:5 *all t.* A. lived 930 ye.
8 *d.* of Seth ; 11 of Enos
14 of Cainan ; 23 Enoch
27 Methusclah ; 9:29 Noah
Deut. 4:9 they depart *all the d.*
10 to fear me *all t. d.* 1 *K.* 8:40
12:1 to possess it *all the d.*
Jos. 24:31 served L. *all t. d.* of J.
1 *Sam.* 1:11 give him to L. *a. t. d.*
1 *K.* 4:25 safely *all t. d.* of Sol.
Job 14:14 *all d.* of my ap. time
Ps. 23:6 mercy fol. me *all t. d.*
27:4 house of L. *all d.* of my life
Prov. 15:15 *all t. d.* of afflicted
31:12 good *all the d.* of her life
Luke 1:75 holi. *all t. d.* of our life
See His LIFE, *Thy* LIFE.

DAYS come.
Is. 7:17 *d.* that have not *come*
Jer. 23:5 behold *d.* c. 7 ; 31:31
Amos 4:2 *d. c.* he will take you
Mat. 9:15 *d. c.* brideg. shall be
taken, *Mark* 2:20 ; *Luke* 5:35
Luke 17:22 *d. c.* ye sh. des. to see
21:6 *d. c.* there shall not be left
Heb. 8:8 *d. c.* I will make new c.

Few DAYS.
Gen. 29:20 seemed but a *few d.*
47:9 *f.* and evil *d.* of my pilgr.
Job 14:1 man b. of wo. is of *f. d.*
Ps. 109:8 let his *d.* be *few*
Dan. 11:20 *f. d.* he be destroyed
Heb. 12:10 for a *f. d.* chasten. us

His DAYS.
Gen. 6:3 his *d.* shall be 120 years
10:25 in *h. d.* was earth divided
Deut. 22:19 put her away all *h. d.*
1 *K.* 15:14 A. was perf. all *h. d.*
21:29 not bring the evil in *h. d.*
2 *K.* 8:20 in *his d.* Edom revolted
12:2 Jehoash did right all *h. d.*
1 *Chr.* 22:9 and quietness in *h. d.*
Job 14:5 seeing *h. d.* determined
15:20 travail with pain all *h. d.*
24:1 know him, not see *his d. ?*
Ps. 72:7 in *his d.* right. flourish
103:15 man, *his d.* are as grass
144:4 *his d.* are as a shadow
Ec. 2:23 all *his d.* are sorrows
5:17 all *h. d.* eateth in darkness
Is. 65:20 hath not filled *his d.*
Jer. 17:11 in the midst of *his d.*
22:30 a man not prosper in *h. d.*
23:6 in *his d.* J. shall be saved

In the DAYS.
1 *K.* 10:21 silver noth. accounted
of *d.* of Sol. 2 *Chr.* 9:20
1 *Chr.* 13:3 inq. not *in d.* of Saul
2 *Chr.* 26:5 sought G. *in d.* of Z.
32:26 came not *in d.* of Hezek.
Job 29:2 *in d.* God preserved me
4 as I was *in the d.* of my you.
Ps. 37:19 *in d.* of famine eatis.
49:5 wherefore fear *in d.* of evil
Ec. 2:16 *in d.* to come be forgot.
11:9 heart cheer thee *in the d.*
12:1 remember thy Creator *in d.*
Lam. 1:7 Jer. remembered *in d.*
Ezek. 16:60 remem. my cov. *in d.*
22:14 hands be strong *in the d.*
Dan. 2:44 *in the d.* of these kings
5:11 *in the d.* of thy father
Hos. 2:15 as *in d.* of her youth
9:9 corrupted as *in d.* of Gibeah
12:9 *in the d.* of solemn feasts
Joel 1:2 *in d.* of your fathers
Mat. 2:1 J. was born *in d.* of H.
23:30 been *in d.* of our fathers
24:38 for as *in the d.* bef. flood
Mark 2:26 *in the d.* of Abiathar
Luke 1:25 L. dealt with me *in d.*
4:25 widows *in d.* of Elias
17:26 *in the d.* of Noe ; 28 Lot
Acts 5:37 Judas *in d.* of taxing
11:28 *in t. d.* of Claudius Cesar
Heb. 5:7 who *in t. d.* of his flesh
1 *Pet.* 3:20 waited *in the d.* of N.
Rev. 10:7 *in d.* of seventh angel

In those DAYS.
1 *Sam.* 3:1 precious *in those d.*
Jer. 33:16 *in those d.* J. be saved
50:4 *in th. d.* Isr. shall seek God
20 *in th. d.* iniquity be sought
Joel 2:29 *in th. d.* will I pour out
my Spirit, *Acts* 2:18
Luke 1:39 Mary arose *in those d.*
20:1 one of *th. d.* as he taught

Latter DAYS.
Num. 24:14 peo. do to pe. in *l. d.*
Deut. 4:30 *l. d.* if thou turn to L.
31:29 evil befall you in *latter d.*
Jer. 23:20 in *lat. d.* con. it, 30:24
48:47 captivity of Moab in *l. d.*
49:39 captivity of Elam in *l. d.*
Ezek. 38:16 ag. my people in *l. d.*
Dan. 2:28 what shall be in *l. d.*
10:14 befall thy people in *l. d.*
Hos. 3:5 shall fear Lord in *l. d.*

Many DAYS.
Gen. 37:34 J. mourned *many d.*
1 *K.* 17:15 she and he *d.* eat *m. d.*
Ps. 31:12 he that loveth *m. d. ?*
119:84 *m.* are *d.* of thy serv. ?
Ec. 6:3 *d.* of his years be *many*
11:1 shalt find it after *many d.*
Is. 24:22 after *many d.* shall they
be visited, *Ezek.* 38:8
32:10 *m. d.* shall ye be troubled
Jer. 32:14 continue *many d.* 35:7
37:16 Jer. had remained *m. d.*
Ezek. 12:27 vision that he seeth
is for *m. d. Dan.* 8:26 ; 10:14
Dan. 11:33 fall by captivity *m. d.*
Hos. 3:3 abide for me *many d.*
4 Is. abide *m. d.* witho. a king
Luke 15:13 *m. d.* after younger
John 2:12 continued not *many d.*
Acts 1:5 baptized not *many d.*
13:31 he was seen *many d.*
16:18 this did she *many d.*
27:20 nor stars in *m. d.* appear.

My DAYS.
2 *K.* 20:19 if truth be in *my d. ?*
Job 7:6 *my d.* swifter th. shuttle
16 let alone, *my d.* are vanity
9:25 *my d.* swifter than a post
10:20 are not *my d.* few ?
17:1 *my d.* are extinct
11 *my d.* are past. my purposes
29:18 multiply *my d.* as sand

DAYS

Ps. 39:4 the measure of *my d.*
5 *my d.* as a handbreadth
102:3 *m. d.* consum. like smoke
11 *my d.* are like a shadow
23 he shortened *my d.*
24 not away in midst of *my d.*
Is. 38:10 in cutting off *my d.*
39:8 be peace and truth in *m. d.*
Jer. 20:18 *my d.* consu. with sh.

Prolong, ed, eth DAYS.

Deut. 4:26 not p. your *d.* 30:18
40 mayest *prolong* thy *d.* 22:7
5:16 thy *d.* may be *prolong.* 6:2
33 that ye may *prolong.* 11:9
17:20 he may *prolong* his *d.*
32:47 ye shall *prolong* your *d.*
Prov. 10:27 fear of the L. *prol. d.*
28:16 hateth covetous. p. his *d.*
Ec. 8:12 tho' sinner's *d.* be *pro.*
13 nei. shall wicked *pro.* his *d.*
Is. 13:22 her *d.* shall not be *p.*
53:10 his seed, he shall *pro. d.*
Ezek. 12:22 *d.* are *p.* vision fail.

Sabbath DAYS.

Mat. 12:15 on *sab. d.* priests dep.
10 lawful to heal on *sab. d.?*
12 lawful to do well on *s. d.?*
Mark 3:4 good on *s. d.? Lu.* 6:9
Luke 4:31 taught them on *sab. d.*
6:2 not lawful to do on *sab. d.*
Acts 17:2 three *sabbath d.* reason.
Col. 2:16 judge in respect of *s. d.*

Thy DAYS.

Ex. 20:12 hon. thy father that *t. d.* may be long, *Deut.* 25:15
23:26 the number of *t. d.*
Deut. 23:6 seek peace all *thy d.*
30:20 thy life, length of *thy d.*
31:14 *thy d.* ap. thou must die
33:25 as *thy d.* so thy strength
1 *Sam.* 25:28 not found all *thy d.*
2 *Sam.* 7:12 when *thy d.* be ful.
1 *K.* 3:13 any like thee all *thy d.*
14 then will I lengthen *thy d.*
11:12 in *thy d.* I will not do it
2 *K.* 20:6 add to *thy d. Is.* 38:5
1 *Chr.* 17:11 when *thy d.* be exp.
Job 10:5 *thy d.* as the *d.* of man
38:12 morning since *thy d.*
21 number of *thy d.* is great
Prov. 9:11 *thy d.* be multiplied
Ezek. 22:4 caused *t. d.* draw near

Two DAYS.

Num. 9:22 whe. *two d.* or mon.
11:19 not eat one, nor *two d.*
Hos. 6:2 after *two d.* will revive
Mat. 26:2 *t. d.* is feast, *Mark* 14:1
John 4:40 he abode there *two d.*
11:6 he abode *two d.* still

Three DAYS.

Gen. 40:12 branches are *three d.*
18 three baskets *three d.*
42:17 put all into ward *three d.*
Ex. 3:18 *three d.* journey into
wilderness, 5:3; 8:27; 15:22
10:23 nor rose any for *three d.*
Jos. 1:11 within *t. d.* ye sh. pass
2:16 hide here *three d.* 22
Jud. 19:4 abode with him *th. d.*
1 *Sam.* 21:5 kept fr. us these *t. d.*
30:12 eaten no bread *three d.*
13 *three d.* agone I fell sick
2 *Sam.* 20:4 assemble J. in *t. d.*
24:13 *th. d.* pestil. 1 *Chr.* 21:12
1 *K.* 12:5 dep. for *t. d.* 2 *Chr.* 10:5
2 *K.* 2:17 sought him *three d.*
Ezr. 10:8 not come in *three d.* 9
Jon. 1:17 in fish *th. d. Mat.* 12:40
Mat. 15:32 they continue with
me *three d. Mark* 8:2
26:61 destroy the temple, and to
build it in *t. d.* 27:40; *Mark*
14:58; 15:29; *John* 2:19
27:63 after *t. d.* I will, *Mark* 8:31
Luke 2:46 after *t. d.* found in t.

Acts 9:9 S. *th. d.* without sight
28:7 Publius lodged us *t. d.*
Rev. 11:9 *three d.* and a half
11 after *t. d.* spirit of life ent.

Four DAYS.

John 11:39 he ha. been dead *f. d.*
Acts 10:30 *f. d.* ago I was fasting

Five DAYS.

Num. 11:19 nor *five d.* nor ten *d.*

Six DAYS.

Ex. 20:9 *six d.* shalt thou labor,
23:12; 34:21; *Deut.* 5:13
11 in *s. d.* made heaven, 31:17
31:15 *six d.* may work be done,
35:2; *Lev.* 23:3
Jos. 6:3 thus shalt do *six d.*
Ezek. 46:1 shut *six* working *d.*
Luke 13:14 *six d.* ought to work
John 12:1 J. *six d.* bef. passover

Seven DAYS.

Is. 30:26 light of sun as of *s. d.*
Ezek. 3:15 I remained aston. *s. d.*
Heb. 11:30 compassed *seven d.*

Eight DAYS.

Gen. 17:12 *e. d.* old, be cir. 21:4
Luke 2:21 when *e. d.* were ac.
John 20:26 after *eight d.* J. came

Ten DAYS.

Dan. 1:12 prove thy servant *t. d.*
Rev. 2:10 have tribulation *ten d.*

Forty DAYS.

Ex. 24:18 Moses in mount *forty
d.* 34:28; *Deut.* 9:9; 10:10
Num. 13:25 after *forty d.* 14:34
Deut. 9:25 I fell before L. *f. d.*
Ezek. 4:6 bear iniquity of J. *f. d.*
Jon. 3:4 yet *f. d.* Ninev. be over.
Mat. 4:2 he had fasted *forty d.*

Mark 1:13 *f. d.* tempted, *Lu.* 4:2
Acts 1:3 seen of them *forty d.*

Your DAYS.

Deut. 11:21 *y. a* may be multi.
Jer. 16:9 cease in *your d.* mirth
35:7 *y. d.* ye sh. dwell in tents
Ezek. 12:25 in *your d.* will I say
Joel 1:2 hath this been in *your d.*
Hab. 1:5 in *your d. Acts* 13:41

DAILY.

Jud. 16:16 she pressed him *d.*
Est. 3:4 spake *d.* he heark. not
Ps. 13:2 sorrow in my heart *d.*
42:10 *d.* to me, Wh. is thy God?
56:1 fighting *d.* oppresseth me
2 would *d.* swallow me up
61:8 I may *d.* perform my vows
68:19 Lord, who *d.* loadeth us
72:15 and *d.* shall he be praised
74:22 foolish reproach. thee *d.*
86:3 I cry *d.* ; 88:9 I called *d.*
88:17 about me *d.* like water
Prov. 8:30 I was *d.* his delight
34 watching *d.* at my gates
Is. 58:2 yet they seek me *d.*
Jer. 7:25 *d.* rising up early
20:7 I am in derision *d.* 8
Ezek. 30:16 N. have distresses *d.*
Dan. 8:11 by him the *d.* sacrifice
was tak. away, 11:31 ; 12:11
Hos. 12:1 Eph. *d.* increaseth
Mat. 6:11 *d.* bread, *Luke* 11:3
26:55 I sat *d.* with you, *Mark*
14:49 ; *Luke* 19:47 ; 22:53
Luke 9:23 take up his cross *d.*
Acts 2:46 continuing *d.* with one
47 Lord added to church *d.*
6:1 neglected in *d.* ministration
16:5 the churches increased *d.*
17:11 searched the scriptures *d.*
1 *Cor.* 15:31 I die *d.*
Heb. 3:13 but exhort *d.*
7:27 needeth not *d.* to offer
Jam. 2:15 sister desti. of *d.* food

DAYSMAN.

Job 9:33 nor any *d.* betwixt us

DAYSPRING.

Job 38:12 *d.* to know his place
Luke 1:78 *d.* from on high visited

DAYSTAR.

2 *Pet.* 1:19 *d.* arise in your hearts

DEACON, S.

Phil. 1:1 the saints with the *d.*
1 *Tim.* 3:8 *d.* must be grave
10 then use office of a *d.* 13
12 *d.* the husband of one wife

DEAD.

Gen. 20:3 thou art but a *d.* man
23:3 A. stood up from before *d.*
Ex. 4:19 *d.* which sought thy li.
9:7 not one of Israel. cattle *d.*
12:30 where was not one *d.*
33 Eg. said, We be all *d.* men
14:30 Egyptians *d.* on the shore
21:34 *d.* beast shall be his, 36
35 *d.* ox they shall divide
Lev. 22:4 unclean by the *d.*
Num. 5:2 whoso. is defiled by *d.*
12:12 let her not be as one *d.*
16:48 he stood bet. *d.* and living
Jud. 3:25 their lord was *d.*
4:22 behold, Sisera lay *d.*
16:30 *d.* he slew at death more
Ruth 4:5 raise up name of the *d.*
1 *Sam.* 4:17 Hophni and P. are *d.*
24:14 pursue after a *d.* dog
2 *Sam.* 9:8 look on such *d.* dog
13:33 think all king's sons *d.*
16:9 this *d.* dog curse my lord?
19:28 father's house but *d.* men
1 *K.* 3:22 the *d.* is thy son, 23
13:31 when I am *d.* bury me
21:15 arise, for Naboth is *d.*
Job 26:5 *d.* formed from under
Ps. 31:12 forgotten as a *d.* man
76:6 chariot and horses in *d.* sl.
88:5 among the *d.* like slain
10 show wonders to the *d.?*
106:28 ate sacrifices of the *d.*
115:17 *d.* praise not the Lord
143:3 as those been long *d.*
Prov. 2:18 her paths unto the *d.*
9:18 knoweth not *d.* are there
21:16 remain in cong. of the *d.*
Ec. 4:2 I praised *d.* already *d.*
9:3 after that they go to *d.*
4 liv. dog better than *d.* lion
5 the *d.* know not any thing
Is. 8:10 for living to the *d.?*
14:9 it stirreth up *d.* for thee
22:2 not slain nor *d.* in battle
26:14 are *d.* they shall not live
19 thy *d.* men shall live, with
59:10 desolate places as *d.* men
Lam. 3:6 they that be *d.* of old

Ezek. 44:25 come at no *d.* person
Mat. 2:20 are *d.* sou. child's life
8:22 let the *d.* bury their *d.*
9:24 maid is not *d.* but sleepeth,
Mark 5:39 ; *Luke* 8:52
10:8 heal the sick, raise the *d.*
11:5 *d.* are raised, *Luke* 7:22
22:31 touch. res. of *d. Mar.* 12:26
32 God is not the God of the *d.*
Mark 12:27; *Luke* 20:38
23:27 full of *d.* men's bones
28:4 keepers became as *d.* men
Mark 9:26 was as one *d.* he is *d.*
15:44 Pilate marv. if he were *d.*
Luke 7:12 a *d.* man carried out
10:30 leaving him half *d.*
24:5 why seek living am. *d.?*
John 5:21 Father raiseth up *d.*
25 *d.* shall hear voi. of S. of G.
6:49 eat manna, and are *d.* 58
11:25 though *d.* yet shall live
Acts 2:29 patriarch David is *d.*
10:42 ordained to be judge of
quick and *d.* 2 *Tim.* 4:1

14:19 supposing he had been *d.*
20:9 Eutychus was taken up *d.*
26:8 God should raise the *d.*
28:6 have swollen, or fallen *d.*
Rom. 4:17 quickeneth the *d.*
   19 considered not his body *d.*
5:15 offence of one, many be *d.*
6:2 we that are *d.* to sin, live
   8 if we be *d.* with Christ, we
  11 reckon ye to be *d.* to sin
7:2 if husb. be *d.* 3 ; 1 *Cor.* 7:39
   4 ye also *d.* to law, *Gal.* 2:19
14:9 Lord of the *d.* and living
1 *Cor.* 15:15 if so be *d.* rise not
  35 will say, How are *d.* raised
  52 *d.* be raised incorruptible
2 *Cor.* 1:9 God who raiseth *d.*
   5:14 for all, then were all *d.*
Eph. 2:1 *d.* in tres. 5 ; *Col.* 2:13
Col. 2:20 if *d.* with C. 2 *Tim.* 2:11
3:3 ye are *d.* and your life hid
1 *Thes.* 4:16 *d.* in Chr. shall rise
Heb. 6:1 repent. from *d.* works
9:14 purge consc. from *d.* works
  17 is of force after men are *d.*
11:4 he being *d.* yet speaketh
  12 and him as good as *d.*
  35 women received *d.* raised
1 *Pet.* 2:24 we being *d.* to sin
4:5 ready to judge quick and *d.*
  6 gospel preached to them *d.*
Jude 12 twice *d.* plucked by
Rev. 1:5 J. first-begotten of *d.*
  17 I fell at his feet as *d.*
3:1 thou livest, and art *d.*
14:13 blessed are *d.* die in Lord
16:3 sea, as blood of a *d.* man
20:5 rest of *d.* lived not again
  12 I saw the *d.* stand bef. God ;
    the *d.* were judged
  13 sea gave up *d.*

See BODY, BURY, CARCASS,
   CORPSE, RESURRECTION.

For the DEAD.

Lev. 19:28 not make cut. *f. t. d.*
Deut. 14:1 any baldness *f. d.*
  26:14 not give aught *for the d.*
2 *Sam.* 14:2 had mourned *for d.*
Jer. 16:7 to comfort for *t. d.*
22:10 weep ye not *for the d.*
Ezek. 24:17 no mourning *f. t. d.*
1 *Cor.* 15:29 are baptized *for the*
   d. why baptized for *d. ?*

From the DEAD.

Mat. 14:2 J. is risen *from the d.*
Mark 9:10 rising *from the d.*
Luke 16:31 though one rose *f. d.*
24:46 *fr. t. d.* day, *John* 20:9
Acts 10:41 after he rose *f. t. d.*
  26:23 that should rise *from t. d.*
Rom. 6:13 those alive *from the d.*
  10:7 to bring up Christ *f. t. d.*
  11:15 rec. of them be life *f. t. d.*
1 *Cor.* 15:12 he rose *from the d.*
Eph. 5:14 arise *f. d.* C. give light
Col. 1:18 first-born *from d.*
Heb. 11:19 to raise him *from t. d.*
13:20 brought again *f. t. d.*

See RAISED, RISEN.

Is DEAD.

Gen. 42:38 his brother *is d.* 44:20
Jos. 1:2 Moses my servant *is d.*
Jud. 20:5 forced that she *is d.*
2 *Sam.* 2:7 S. 4:10 ; 11:21 Uriah
  12:18 child ; 13:32 Amnon only
14:5 my husband *is d.* 2 *K.* 4:1
18:20 because king's son *is d.*
19:10 Absa. ; 1 *K.* 21:14 Naboth
Ezek. 44:31 that is *d.* of itself
Mat. 9:18 my daugh. *is d. Mark*
  5:35; *Luke* 8:49 .
Mark 9:26 many said, He *is d.*
John 8:52 Abraham *is d.* 53
11:14 said Jesus, Lazarus *is d.*
Rom. 6:7 he *is d.* is freed fr. sin
  8:10 if C. be in you, body *is d.*

Gal. 2:21 if right. by law C. *is d.*
1 *Tim.* 5:6 is *d.* while she liveth.
Jam. 2:17 without works *is d.* 20
  26 as body without spirit *is d.*

Was DEAD.

Jud. 2:19 when the judge *was d.*
  9:55 Israel saw Abimelech *w. d.*
1 *Sam.* 17:51 saw champion *w. d.*
31:5 Saul *was d.* 1 *Chr.* 10:5
2 *Sam.* 4:1 heard Abner *was d.*
  11:26 Bath. heard her h. *was d.*
  12:19 D. perceived child *was d.*
  13:39 Amnon, seeing he *was d.*
1 *K.* 3:21 give child suck, it *w. d.*
2 *K.* 4:32 behold the child *was d.*
11:1 Athaliah saw her son *w. d.*
Mat. 2:19 when Herod *was d.*
Luke 7:15 he that *was d.* sat up
8:53 knowing that she *was d.*
15:24 this my son *was d.*
  32 thy bro. *was d.* and is alive
John 11:44 he that *was d.* came
19:33 Jesus *was d.* brake not
Acts 25:19 Jesus which *was d.*
Rom. 7:8 without law sin *was d.*
Rev. 1:18 liveth and *was d.*

DEADLY.

1 *Sam.* 5:11 *d.* destruction
Ps. 17:9 from my *d.* enemies
Ezek. 30:24 of a *d.* wounded man
Mark 16:18 drink *d.* thing
Jam. 3:8 tongue full of *d.* poison
Rev. 13:3 *d.* wound healed, 12

DEADNESS.

Rom. 4:19 nor *d.* of Sar.'s womb

DEAF.

Ex. 4:11 who maketh the *d.*
Lev. 19:14 shalt not curse the *d.*
Ps. 38:13 as a *d.* man, heard not
58:4 they are like the *d.* adder
Is. 29:18 *d.* hear words
35:5 ears of the *d.* be unstopped
42:18 hear, ye *d.* look, ye blind
  19 who is *d.* as my messenger
43:8 bring *d.* that have ears
Mic. 7:16 their ears shall be *d.*
Mat. 11:5 the *d.* hear, *Luke* 7:22
Mark 7:32 brought to him one *d.*
  37 he maketh the *d.* to hear
9:25 thou *d.* spirit come out

DEAL.

Gen. 19:9 *d.* worse with thee
24:49 if ye *d.* truly with master
32:9 I will *d.* well with thee
34:31 *d.* with sister as harlot ?
Ex 1:10 *d.* wisely with them
21:9 *d.* with her after manner
23:11 like manner *d.* with vine
Lev. 19:11 not steal nor *d.* falsely
Num. 11:15 if *d.* thus, kill me
Deut. 7:5 shall ye *d.* with them
2 *Chr.* 2:3 as thou didst *d.* with
   David, so *d.* with me
Job 42:8 lest I *d.* after your folly
Ps. 75:4 to fools, *d.* not foolishly
119:17 *d.* bountifully with, 142:7
  124 *d.* with me acco. to thy m.
Prov. 12:22 they that *d.* truly
Is. 26:10 land of uprightness *d.*
52:13 my servant *d.* prudently
58:7 to *d.* thy bread to hungry
Jer. 18:23 *d.* thus in thine anger
21:2 Lord will *d.* with us
Ezek. 8:18 will I also *d.* in fury
16:59 *d.* with thee as hast done
22:14 in days I *d.* with thee ?
23:25 *d.* furiously with thee
31:11 shall surely *d.* with him
Dan. 1:13 *d.* with thy servants
11:7 and shall *d.* against them

See TREACHEROUSLY.

DEAL, Substantive.

Ex. 29:40 *d.* of flour, *Lev.* 14:21 ;
  Num. 15:4 ; 28:13 ; 29:4
Mark 10:48 cried more a great *d.*

DEALER, S.

Is. 21:2 treacherous *d.* dealeth
24:16 *d.* dealt treacherously

DEALEST, ETH, ING, S.

Jud. 18:4 thus *d.* Micah with me
1 *Sam.* 2:23 I hear of your evil *d.*
  23:22 that he *d.* subtilely
Ps. 7:16 violent *d.* on his pate
Prov. 10:4 poor that *d.* w. slack
13:16 prudent *d.* with knowl.
14:17 he soon angry *d.* foolishly
21:24 who *d.* in proud wrath
Is. 21:2 treacherous dealer *d.*
33:1 woe to thee *d.* treacher.
Jer. 6:13 from prophet to priest,
   every one *d.* falsely, 8:10
John 4:9 no *d.* with Samaritans
Heb. 12:7 God *d.* as with sons

DEALT.

Gen. 16:6 Sar. *d.* hardly with her
33:11 God hath *d.* graciously
43:6 *d.* ye so ill with me
Ex. 1:20 God *d.* well with midw.
14:11 wherefore *d.* so ill with us
18:11 in thing they *d.* proudly
Jud. 9:16 if *d.* well with Jerub.
Ruth 1:8 ye have *d.* with dead
  20 Almig. *d.* bitterly with me
1 *Sam.* 24:18 *d.* well with me
25:31 L. have *d.* well with thee
2 *Sam.* 6:19 he *d.* am. the people
2 *K.* 12:15 they *d.* faithfu. 22:7
21:6 *d.* with fam. sp. 2 *Chr.* 33:6
2 *Chr.* 6:37 we have *d.* wickedly
11:23 Rehoboam *d.* wisely
Neh. 1:7 *d.* corrupt. against thee
9:10 knewest *d.* proudly, 16, 29
Job 6:15 brethren *d.* deceitfully
Ps. 13:6 *d.* bountifully with me
44:17 nor *d.* falsely in thy cov.
78:57 *d.* unfaithfully like fathers
103:10 *d.* with us after our sins
116:7 L. *d.* bountifully with thee
119:65 *d.* well with thy servant
  78 *d.* perversely without cause
147:20 not *d.* so with any nation
Is. 24:16 *d.* very treach. *Jer.* 3:20 ;
  5:11 ; 12:6 ; *Lam.* 1:2
Ezek. 22:7 in thee *d.* by oppres.
25:12 Edom hath *d.* ag. Judah
  15 Philis. have *d.* by revenge
Hos. 5:7 they have *d.* treach.
6:7 *d.* treacherously against me
Joel 2:26 God that *d.* wondrously
Zec. 1:6 thought, so *d.* with us
Mal. 2:11 Judah *d.* treacherously
  14 whom hast *d.* treacherously
Luke 1:25 hath L. *d.* with me
2:48 son, why thus *d.* with us
Acts 7:19 *d.* subtil. with kindred
25:24 mult. of Jews have *d.*
Rom. 12:3 G. hath *d.* to ev. man

Jer. 31:20 is Ephraim my *d.* son
Luke 7:2 servant who was *d.*
Acts 20:24 neither count I life *d.*
Eph. 5:1 foll. of God, as *d.* child.
Col. 1:7 Epaphras our *d.* fel.-ser.
  13 into kingdom of his *d.* Son
1 *Thes.* 2:8 bec. ye were *d.* to us

DEARLY beloved.

Jer. 12:7 given *d. belov.* to enem.
Rom. 12:19 *d. beloved* avenge not
1 *Cor.* 10:14 my *d. b. Phil.* 4:1;
  2 *Tim.* 1:2
2 *Cor.* 7:1 *d. belov.* 12:19; *Phil.*
  4:1 ; 1 *Pet.* 2:11
Phile. 1 unto Philemon our *d. b.*

DEARTH.

Gen. 41:54 *d.* was in all lands
2 *K.* 4:38 was a *d.* in the land
2 *Chr.* 6:28 if there be *d.* mildew
Neh. 5:3 buy corn because of *d.*
Jer. 14:1 word came to J. conc. *d.*
Acts 7:11 came a *d.* over all land
11:28 there should be a great *d.*

DEATH.

Gen. 21:16 let not see *d.* of child
24:67 after his mother's *d.*
27:7 bless thee before my *d.*
10 bless thee before his *d.*
Ex. 10:17 take me from this *d.*
Num. 16:29 common *d.* of all
23:10 let me die *d.* of righteous
35:31 of a murderer guilty of *d.*
Deut. 30:15 I have set before **you**
life and *d.* 19; *Jer.* 21:8
31:27 more rebel after my *d.*
29 after my *d.* ye will corrupt
33:1 Moses blessed Isr. before *d.*
Jud. 5:18 their lives to the *d.*
16:16 his soul vexed unto *d.*
30 dead he slew at his *d.* more
Ruth 1:17 if aught but *d.* part
1 *Sam.* 4:20 about time of her *d.*
15:32 bitterness of *d.* is past
20:3 a step between me and *d.*
22:22 *d.* of father's house
2 *Sam.* 1:23 in *d.* were not divid.
15:21 in *d.* or life, there
22:5 when waves of *d.* compassed me, *Ps.* 18:4; 116:3
6 snares of *d.* *Ps.* 18:5
2 *K.* 2:21 sh. not be any more *d.*
4:40 is in the pot
1 *Chr.* 22:5 D. prepared before *d.*
2 *Chr.* 22:4 after *d.* of father
32:33 did him honor at his *d.*
Ezr. 7:26 *d.* or banishment
Job 3:21 long for *d.* it com. not
7:15 my soul chooseth *d.*
18:13 first-born of *d.* devour
Job 27:15 remain be buried in *d.*
28:22 destruction and *d.* say
30:23 thou wilt bring me to *d.*
Ps. 6:5 in *d.* no remem. of thee
7:13 prepared instruments of *d.*
13:3 lest I sleep the sleep of *d.*
22:15 brought me into dust of *d.*
48:14 God be our guide unto *d.*
49:14 *d.* shall feed on them
55:4 terrors of *d.* fallen on me
15 let *d.* seize on them
73:4 no bands in their *d.*
89:48 and shall not see *d.* ?
102:20 to loose those ap. to *d.*
116:15 precious is *d.* of saints
118:18 not given me over to *d.*
Prov. 2:18 house inclineth to *d.*
5:5 her feet go down to *d.*
7:27 down to chambers of *d.*
8:36 they that hate me, love *d.*
11:19 pursueth it to his own *d.*
12:28 in pathways there is no *d.*
13:14 from snares of *d.* 14:27
14:12 end, ways of *d.* 16:25
32 right. hath hope in his *d.*
16:14 wrath of king as m. of *d.*
18:21 life in power of tongue
21:6 van. tossed of them seek *d.*
24:11 deliver them drawn to *d.*
26:18 madman who casteth *d.*
Ec. 7:26 bitter than *d.*
Cant. 8:6 for love is strong as *d.*
Is. 25:8 swallow up *d.* in victory
38:18 *d.* cannot celebrate thee
53:9 with the rich in his *d.*
12 poured out his soul unto *d.*
Jer. 8:3 *d.* chosen rather than life
9:21 *d.* come up to windows
15:2 as are for *d.* to *d.* 43:11
Lam. 1:20 at home there is as *d.*
Ezek. 18:32 I have no pleasure in
d. of the wicked, 33:11
31:14 are all delivered unto *d.*
Hos. 13:14 O *d.* I be thy plagues
Jon. 4:9 to be angry unto *d.*
Hab. 2:5 is as *d.* not satisfied
Mat. 2:15 there till *d.* of Herod
10:21 del. bro. to *d.* *Mark* 13:12
15:4 curseth fath. or moth. let
him die the *d.* *Mark* 7:10
16:28 some here shall not taste
of *d.* *Mark* 9:1; *Luke* 9:27

20:18 con. him to *d.* *Mark* 10:33
26:38 sorrowf. to *d.* *Mark* 14:34
66 guilty of *d.* *Mark* 14:64
Mark 5:23 daugh. at point of *d.*
Luke 2:26 not see *d.* bef. seen C.
22:33 to prison and *d.*
23:22 I found no cause of *d.*
John 4:47 he was at point of *d.*
8:51 he shall never see *d.* 52
11:4 this sickness not unto *d.*
13 Jesus spake of his *d.*
12:33 signifying what *d.* 18:32
21:19 by what *d.* glorify God
Acts 2:24 loosed the pains of *d.*
8:1 consenting to his *d.* 22:20
13:28 no cause of *d.* in him
22:4 I pers. this way to the *d.*
Rom. 5:10 reconciled to God by
the *d.* of his Son, *Col.* 1:22
12 and *d.* by sin, so *d.* passed
14 *d.* reigned from Adam to M.
21 as sin hath reigned unto *d.*
6:3 were baptized into his *d.*
4 buried by baptism into *d.*
5 planted in likeness of his *d.*
9 *d.* no more domin. over him
16 whether of sin unto *d.*
21 end of those things is *d.*
23 for the wages of sin is *d.* but
7:5 to bring forth fruit unto *d.*
10 com. to life I found unto *d.*
13 that good made *d.* unto me ?
24 from body of this *d.* ?
8:2 free from law of sin and *d.*
6 to be carnally minded is *d.*
38 *d.* nor life separ. from love
1 *Cor.* 3:22 life or *d.* all are yours
4:9 were appointed to *d.*
11:26 ye do show the Lord's *d.*
15:21 for since by man came *d.*
26 last enemy be destroy. is *d.*
54 *d.* is swallowed up in vict.
55 O *d.* where is thy sting ?
56 the sting of *d.* is sin
2 *Cor.* 1:9 sentence of *d.*
10 del. us from so great a *d.*
2:16 the savor of *d.* unto *d.*
3:7 if ministration of *d.* glorious
4:11 del. to *d.* for Jesus' sake
12 so then *d.* worketh in us
7:10 sorrow of world worketh *d.*
Phil. 1:20 whether by life or *d.*
2:8 obedient to *d.* the *d.* of cross
27 Epaph. sick nigh unto *d.*
30 work of C. he was nigh *d.*
3:10 made conformable to his *d.*
2 *Tim.* 1:10 hath abolished *d.*
Heb. 2:9 suffering of *d.* crowned,
that he taste *d.* for ev. man
14 through *d.* destroy him that
had power of *d.*
15 who through fear of *d.*
7:23 to continue, by reason of *d.*
9:15 by means of *d.* for redem.
16 of necessity of testator
11:5 that he should not see *d.*
Jam. 1:15 sin, bringeth forth *d.*
1 *John* 3:14 not abideth in *d.*
5:16 sin unto *d.* ; 17 not unto *d.*
Rev. 1:18 keys of hell and of *d.*
2:10 be faithful unto *d.*
11 not be hurt of second *d.*
6:8 his name sat on him was *d.*
9:6 shall seek *d.* *d.* shall flee
12:11 loved not lives to the *d.*
13:3 as it were wounded to *d.*
18:8 her plagues in one day, *d.*
20:6 second *d.* hath no power
13 *d.* and hell deliver. up dead
14 *d.* cast into lake, second *d.*
21:4 there shall be no more *d.*

See DAY.

From DEATH.

Jos. 2:13 deliver our lives *f. d.*
Job 5:20 redeem thee *f. d.*
Ps. 33:19 to del. their soul *f. d.*
56:13 del. my soul *f. d.* 116:8

68:20 to L. belong issues *f. d.*
78:50 spared not their soul *f. d.*
Prov. 10:2 delivereth *f. d.* 11:4
Hos. 13:14 redeem them *f. d.*
John 5:24 *fr. d.* 1 *John* 3:14
Heb. 5:7 able to save *from d.*
Jam. 5:20 shall save a soul *f. d.*

Gates of DEATH.

Job 38:17 *g. of d.* been opened
Ps. 9:13 liftest me from *g. of d.*
107:18 draw near to *gates of d.*

Put to DEATH.

Gen. 26:11 this man *p. to d.*
Ex. 35:2 who. doth work, *p. to d.*
Lev. 19:20 not be *p. to d.*
24:21 be *p. to d.* *Num.* 35:30
Num. 1:51 stranger that cometh
nigh *p. to d.* 3:10, 38 ; 18:7
Deut. 13:5 dreamer be *put to d.*
17:6 one witness not be *p. to d.*
24:16 the fathers not be *put to d.*
for children, 2 *K.* 14:6
Jos. 1:18 ag. thy com. *p. to d.*
Jud. 6:31 plead. for B. be *p. to d.*
20:13 may *p. to d.* 1 *Sam.* 11:12
1 *Sam.* 11:13 be *put to d.*
2 *Sam.* 8:2 two lines to *p. to d.*
19:21 shall no Shi. be *put to d.*
1 *K.* 2:8 I will not *put* thee to *d.*
24 Adonijah shall be *put to d.*
26 at this time *put* thee to *d.*
2 *Chr.* 15:13 seek L. be *put to d.*
23:7 cometh into house, *p. to d.*
Est. 4:11 law to *put* him to *d.*
Jer. 18:21 their men be *put to d.*
26:15 know, if ye *put* me to *d.*
19 did J. *put* him at all to *d.* ?
38:4 this man be *put to d.*
16 not *put* thee to *d.*
52:27 *put* them *to d.* in Riblah
Mat. 10:21 cause them to be *p. to*
d. *Mark* 13:12 ; *Luke* 21:16
14:5 have *put* him *to d.*
26:59 sou. false wit. ag. J. to *p.*
him *to d.* 27:1 ; *Mark* 14:55
Mark 14:1 and *put* him *to d.*
Luke 18:33 shall *put* him *to d.*
23:32 malefac. to be *put to d.*
John 11:53 to *put* him *to d.*
12:10 might *put* Lazarus *to d.*
18:31 not lawful to *p.* any *to d.*
Acts 12:19 keepers to be *put to d.*
26:10 *put to d.* I gave my voice
1 *Pet.* 3:18 *put to d.* in the flesh

See SURELY.

Shadow of DEATH.

Job 3:5 the *shadow of d.* stain it
10:21 land of dark. and *s. of d.*
12:22 bringeth to light *s. of d.*
16:16 on eyelids is *shadow of d.*
24:17 is as the *shad. of d.*
28:3 searcheth out *shad. of d.*
34:22 no *s. of d.* sinners
38:17 doors of the *shad. of d.* ?
Ps. 23:4 valley of *shad. of d.*
44:19 covered us with *s. of d.*
107:10 darkness and in *s. of d.*
14 darkness and *shad. of d.*
Is. 9:2 in land of *shad. of d.*
Jer. 2:6 land of the *shad. of d.*
13:16 he turn it to *shad. of d.*
Amos 5:8 *s. of d.* into the morn.
Mat. 4:16 that sat in *s. of d.*
Luke 1:79 light to them in *s. of d.*

With DEATH.

Is. 28:15 have made cov. *w. d.*
18 cov. *w. d.* be disannulled
Rev. 2:23 kill her children *w. d.*
6:8 power given to kill *with d.*

Worthy of DEATH.

Deut. 17:6 is *w. of d.*
19:6 he was not *w. of d.*
21:22 have com. sin *w. of d.*
1 *K.* 2:26 Abiathar, art *w. of d.*
Luke 23:15 nothing *w. of d.*

Acts 23:29 to his charge *w. of d.*
25:11 any thing *wor. of d.*
25 committed nothing *w. of d.*
26:31 doth nothing *w. of d.*
Rom. 1:32 com. such *wor. of d.*

DEATHS.

Jer. 16:4 shall die of grievous *d.*
Ezek. 28:8 die *d.* of them slain
10 die *d.* of uncircumcised
2 *Cor.* 11:23 in *d.* oft

DEBASE.

Is. 57:9 *d.* thyself unto hell

DEBATE, Verb.

Prov. 25:9 *d.* cause with neigh.
Is. 27:8 in measure wilt *d.*

DEBATE, S.

Is. 58:4 fast for strife and *d.*
Rom. 1:29 full of envy, *d.*
2 *Cor.* 12:20 lest there be *d.*

DEBORAH.

Gen. 35:8 D. died, was buried
Jud. 4:4 and D. judged Israel
5:7 D. a mother in Isr. 12, 15

DEBT, S.

1 *Sam.* 22:2 ev. one in *d.* w. to D.
2 *K.* 4:7 sell oil, pay thy *d.*
Neh. 10:31 exaction of every *d.*
Prov. 22:26 are sureties for *d.*
Mat. 6:12 forgive us our *d.* as
18:27 forgave him the *d.*
30 into prison till he pay *d.*
32 I forgave all that *d.*
Rom. 4:4 reward reckoned of *d.*

DEBTOR.

Ezek. 18:7 restored to *d.* pledge
Mat. 23:16 swear by gold, is a *d.*
Rom. 1:14 I am *d.* to the Greeks
Gal. 5:3 a *d.* to do the whole law

DEBTORS.

Mat. 6:12 as we forgive our *d.*
Luke 7:41 a creditor had two *d.*
16:5 he called his lord's *d.*
Rom. 8:12 therefore, we are *d.*
15:27 and their *d.* they are

DECAPOLIS.

Mat. 4:25 followed him from D.
Mark 5:20 to publish in D. 7:31

DECAY, ED, ETH.

Lev. 25:35 if brother fallen in *d.*
Neh. 4:10 strength of bearers *d.*
Job 14:11 and as the flood *d.*
Ec. 10:18 by sloth. building *d.*
Is. 44:26 I will raise up *d.* places
Heb. 8:13 *d.* is ready to vanish

DECEASE.

Luke 9:31 and spake of his *d.*
2 *Pet.* 1:15 after my *d.* in rem.

DECEASED.

Is. 26:14 *d.* they shall not rise
Mat. 22:25 when he married, *d.*

DECEIT, S.

Job 15:35 belly prepareth *d.*
27:4 nor my tongue utter *d.*
31:5 or if my foot hasted to *d.*
Ps. 10:7 his mouth is full of *d.*
36:3 words of his mouth are *d.*
38:12 imagine *d.* all the day
50:19 thy tongue frameth *d.*
55:11 *d.* and guile depart not
72:14 redeem their soul from *d.*
101:7 worketh *d.* not dwell
119:118 their *d.* is falsehood
Prov. 12:5 coun. of wicked are *d.*
17 false witness showeth *d.*
20 *d.* is in them that imag. ev.
14:8 the folly of fools is *d.*
20:17 bread of *d.* is sweet
26:24 hateth layeth up *d.*
26 hatred is covered by *d.*
Is. 30:10 speak smooth, proph. *d.*
53:9 nor any *d.* in his mouth
Jer. 5:27 their houses full of *d.*
8:5 they hold fast *d.* they refuse

9:6 through *d.* refuse to know
8 their tongue, it speaketh *d.*
14:14 prophesy *d.* of their heart
23:26 are prophets of the *d.* of
Hos. 11:12 compasseth me w. *d.*
12:7 balances of *d.* in his hand
Amos 8:5 falsify. balances by *d.*
Zep. 1:9 masters' houses with *d.*
Mark 7:22 out of he. proceed *d.*
Rom. 1:29 full of debate, *d.*
3:13 with tongues have used *d.*
Col. 2:8 spoil you thro. vain *d.*
1 *Thes.* 2:3 exhortation not of *d.*

DECEITFUL.

Ps. 5:6 Lord will abhor *d.* man
35:20 devise *d.* matters ag. th.
43:1 deliver me from *d.* man
52:4 O thou *d.* tongue
55:23 *d.* not live half their days
78:57 turned aside like *d.* bow
109:2 mouth of *d.* opened ag. me
120:2 del. my soul fr. *d.* tongue
Prov. 11:18 worketh a *d.* work
14:25 *d.* witness speaketh lies
23:3 his dainties are *d.* meat
27:6 kisses of enemy are *d.*
29:13 poor and *d.* meet together
31:30 favor is *d.* beauty vain
Jer. 17:9 heart is *d.* above all
Hos. 7:16 they are like a *d.* bow
Mic. 6:11 with bag of *d.* weights
12 tongue is *d.* in their mouth
Zep. 3:13 nor *d.* tongue be found
2 *Cor.* 11:13 such are *d.* workers
Eph. 4:22 according to *d.* lusts

DECEITFULLY.

Gen. 34:13 answered Hamor *d.*
Ex. 8:29 let not Pharaoh deal *d.*
Lev. 6:4 or the thing *d.* gotten
Job 6:15 brethren dealt *d.*
13:7 will you talk *d.* for God
Ps. 24:4 nor sworn *d.*
52:2 like a razor, working *d.*
Jer. 48:10 doeth work of Lord *d.*
Dan. 11:23 after league work *d.*
2 *Cor.* 4:2 handling word of G. *d.*

DECEITFULNESS.

Mat. 13:22 the *d.* of rich. choke
the word, *Mark* 4:19
Heb. 3:13 hardened thro' *d.* of sin

DECEIVABLENESS.

2 *Thes.* 2:10 all *d.* of unrighte.

DECEIVE.

2 *Sam.* 3:25 Abner came to *d.* th.
2 *K.* 4:28 say, do not *d.* me
18:29 let not Hezekiah *d.* you,
2 *Chr.* 32:15 ; *Is.* 36:14
19:10 let not God *d.* *Is.* 37:10
Prov. 24:28 *d.* not with thy lips
Jer. 9:5 *d.* every one his neigh.
29:8 diviners in midst *d.* you
37:9 saith L. *d.* not yourselves
Zec. 13:4 rough garment to *d.*
Mat. 24:4 no m. *d. Mark* 13:5
5 *d.* many, 11 ; *Mark* 13:6
24 they shall *d.* the very elect
Rom. 16:18 f. speeches *d.* simple
1 *Cor.* 3:18 let no man *d.* himself
Eph. 4:14 they lie in wait to *d.*
5:6 let no man *d.* you, 2 *Thes.*
2:3 ; 1 *John* 3:7
1 *John* 1:8 have no sin, we *d.*
Rev. 20:3 *d.* the nations no more
8 go to *d.* nations

DECEIVED.

Gen. 31:7 your father hath *d.* me
Lev. 6:2 or if *d.* his neighbor
Deut. 11:16 your heart be not *d.*
1 *Sam.* 19:17 why *d.* me? 28:12
2 *Sam.* 19:26 my servant *d.* me
Job 12:16 *d.* and deceiver are his
15:31 let not *d.* trust in vanity
31:9 if been *d.* by a woman
Is. 19:13 princes of Noph are *d.*
44:20 a *d.* heart turned him

Jer. 4:10 greatly *d.* this people
20:7 O Lord thou hast *d.* me
49:16 thy terribleness *d.* thee
Lam. 1:19 my lovers, they *d.* me
Ezek. 14:9 if proph. be *d.* I. *d.* h.
Ob. 3 pride of heart *d.* thee
7 men at peace with thee *d.*
Luke 21:8 take heed ye be not *d.*
John 7:47 answ. Are ye also *d.*
Rom. 7:11 for sin *d.* me
1 *Cor.* 6:9 not *d.* 15:33 ; *Gal.* 6:7
1 *Tim.* 2:14 Adam was not *d.* but
2 *Tim.* 3:13 deceiv. and being *d.*
Tit. 3:3 were foolish. *d.*
Rev. 18:23 all nations were *d.*
19:20 *d.* them received the mark
20:10 devil that *d.* was cast

DECEIVER.

Gen. 27:12 to my father as a *d.*
Job 12:16 deceived and *d.* are his
Mal. 1:14 cursed *d.* hath a male
Mat. 27:63 we rem. that *d.* said
2 *John* 7 this is a *d.* and antich.

DECEIVERS.

2 *Cor.* 6:8 as *d.* and yet true
Tit. 1:10 many *d.* especially
2 *John* 7 for many *d.* are entered

DECEIVETH.

Prov. 26:19 so is man *d.* neighbor
John 7:12 said, he *d.* the people
Gal. 6:3 nothing, he *d.* himself
Jam. 1:26 but *d.* his own heart
Rev. 12:9 serpent which *d.*
13:14 and *d.* them that dwell

DECEIVING, S.

1 *Tim.* 3:13 and being deceiv.
Jam. 1:22 not hearers only, *d.*
2 *Pet.* 2:13 sporting with their *d.*

DECENTLY.

1 *Cor.* 14:40 done *d.* and in order

DECIDED.

1 *K.* 20:40 thyself hast *d.* it

DECISION.

Joel 3:14 multi. in valley of *d.*

DECK, ED.

Job 40:10 *d.* thyself with majesty
Prov. 7:16 I have *d.* my bed
Jer. 10:4 they *d.* it with silver
Ezek. 16:11 I *d.* thee with orna.
13 thus wast thou *d.* with gold
Hos. 2:13 she *d.* with ear-rings
Rev. 17:4 wom. was *d.* with gold
18:16 alas, city that was *d.*

DECKEDST.

Ezek. 16:16 *d.* thy high places
23:40 and *d.* with ornaments

DECKEST, ETH.

Is. 61:10 as a bridegroom *d.*
Jer. 4:30 though thou *d.* with g.

DECLARATION.

Job 13:17 hear my *d.* with ears
Luke 1:1 set forth in order a *d.*
2 *Cor.* 8:19 to *d.* of ready mind

DECLARE.

Jos. 20:4 *d.* cause in ears
Jud. 14:12 ye *d.* it in 7 days
1 *K.* 22:13 proph. *d.* good to k.
1 *Chr.* 16:24 *d.* his glory among
the heathen, *Ps.* 96:3
Job 12:8 fishes shall *d.* unto thee
21:31 *d.* his way to his face
28:27 did he see it and *d.* it
31:37 *d.* to him numb. of steps
38:4 *d.* if hast understanding
40:7 *d.* thou to me, 42:4
Ps. 9:11 *d.* among people
19:1 the heavens *d.* glory of G.
22:31 *d.* his right. 50:6 ; 97:6
30:9 shall dust *d.* thy truth?
40:5 I wo. *d.* and speak of them
50:16 to do to *d.* my statutes?
64:9 all shall *d.* work of God

73:28 I may *d.* all thy works
75:1 thy wondrous works *d.*
78:6 *d.* them to their children
102:21 to *d.* name of Lord in Z.
107:22 *d.* works with rejoicing
118:17 live and *d.* works of L.
145:4 shall *d.* thy mighty acts
Ec. 9:1 considered to *d.* all this
Is. 3:9 *d.* thy sins as Sodom
12:4 *d.* his doings am. people
21:6 let him *d.* what he seeth
41:22 *d.* to us things to come
42:9 new things do I *d.* before
12 *d.* his praise in the islands
43:9 who among them can *d.*
26 *d.* thou mayest be justified
44:7 and who, as I, shall *d.* it
45:19 I the Lord *d.* things right
48:6 and will not ye *d.* it?
53:8 *d.* his generat.? *Acts* 8:33
66:19 *d.* my glory among Gent.
Jer. 5:20 *d.* this in house of Jac.
9:12 spoken that he may *d.*
31:10 *d.* it in the isles a'ar off
38:15 if I *d.* it to thee wilt thou
42:20 what God say *d.* to us
50:28 *d.* in Z. vengeance of L.
51:10 *d.* in Zion work of Lord
Ezek. 12:16 *d.* their abom. 23:36
40:4 *d.* all thou seest to Israel
Mic. 3:8 *d.* to Jacob his transg.
Zec. 9:12 I *d.* that I will render
Mat. 13:36 *d.* parable of tares
15:15 said Peter, *d.* this parable
Acts 13:32 we *d.* glad tidings
41 though a man *d.* it to you
17:23 worship, him *d.* I to you
20:27 *d.* to you counsel of God
Rom. 3:25 to *d.* his righteous. 26
1 *Cor.* 3:13 the day shall *d.* it
11:17 that I *d.* I praise you not
15:1 I *d.* unto you the gospel
Col. 4:7 my state shall Tych. *d.*
Heb. 11:14 *d.* plainly they seek
1 *John* 1:3 have seen *d.* we to y.
5 message we *d.* unto you.

I will DECLARE.

Job 15:17 I have seen *I will d.*
Ps. 2:7 *I will d.* the decree
22:22 *I w. d.* name, *Heb.* 2:12
Ps. 38:18 *I will d.* mine iniquity
66:16 *I will d.* what done
75:9 but *I will d.* forever, I will
145:6 *I will d.* thy greatness
Is. 57:12 *I will d.* thy right.
Jer. 42:4 *I will d.* it
John 17:26 and *will d.* it

DECLARE ye.

Is. 48:20 voice of singing *d.* ye
Jer. 4:5 *d. ye* in Judah, publish
46:14 *d. ye* in Egypt, publish
50:2 *d. ye* among the nations
Mic. 1:10 *d. ye* it not at Gath

DECLARED.

Ex. 9:16 my name may be *d.*
Deut. 4:13 *d.* to you his covenant
Job 26:3 plentifully *d.* the thing
Ps. 40:10 *d.* thy faithfulness
71:17 I *d.* thy wondrous works
77:14 *d.* thy strength am. peop.
88:11 thy loving-kindness be *d.*
119:13 have I *d.* all judgments
26 I have *d.* my ways, and th.
Is. 21:2 grievous vision is *d.*
10 what I heard of G. have I *d.*
41:26 *d.* from beginning, 45:21
43:12 I have *d.* 44:8; 48:5
48:3 I have *d.* former things
14 which *d.* these things?
Jer. 36:13 Michaiah *d.* words
42:21 I this day *d.* it to you
Luke 8:47 she *d.* to him before all
John 1:18 seen God; Son *d.* him
17:26 *d.* to them thy name
Acts 9:27 he *d.* how he had seen
10:8 he had *d.* these things

12:17 *d.* how Lord brought him
15:4 *d.* all God hath done
14 Simeon *d.* how God at first
25:14 Festus *d.* Paul's cause to
Rom. 1:4 *d.* to be the Son
9:17 my name might be *d.*
1 *Cor.* 1:11 been *d.* to me of you
2 *Cor.* 3:3 ye are *d.* to be the ep.
Col. 1:8 who *d.* to us your love
Rev. 10:7 mys. finished, as he *d.*

DECLARETH, ING.

Is. 41:26 there is none that *d.*
46:10 *d.* the end from beginning
Jer. 4:15 a voice *d.* from Dan
Hos. 4:12 their staff *d.* unto them
Amos 4:13 *d.* to man his thought
Acts 15:3 *d.* conversion of Gent.
12 *d.* what miracles God wro.
1 *Cor.* 2:1 *d.* to you testimony

DECLINE.

Ex. 23:2 to *d.* after many
Deut. 17:11 nor *d.* from sentence
Ps. 119:157 *d.* from thy testi.
Prov. 4:5 not *d.* from words of my
7:25 let not heart *d.* to her ways

DECLINED, ETH.

2 *Chr.* 34:2 *d.* neither to right
Job 23:11 his way I kept, not *d.*
Ps. 44:18 nor have our steps *d.*
102:11 days as shadow that *d.*
109:23 like shadow when it *d.*
119:51 yet not *d.* from thy law

DECREASE, ED.

Gen. 8:5 waters *d.* continually
Ps. 107:38 not their cattle to *d.*
John 3:30 he must increase, I *d.*

DECREE, S.

Ezr. 5:13 Cyrus made a *d.* 17
6:1 Darius, 12; 7:21 Artaxerxes
Est. 3:15 *d.* in Shushan, 9:14
9:32 the *d.* of Esther confirmed
Job 28:26 made a *d.* for the rain
Ps. 2:7 declare *d.* Lord hath said
148:6 hath made a *d.* not pass
Prov. 8:29 gave to the sea his *d.*
Is. 10:1 decree unrighteous *d.*
Jer. 5:22 bound of sea by per. *d.*
Dan. 2:9 but one *d.* for you
4:17 this is by *d.* of watchers
24 this is *d.* of the Most High
6:8 now, O king, establish *d.*
13 Daniel regardeth not the *d.*
26 I make *d.* that in every do.
Jon. 3:7 *d.* of king and nobles
Mic. 7:11 in that day *d.* far rem.
Zep. 2:2 before the *d.* bring forth
Luke 2:1 a *d.* from C. Augustus
Acts 16:4 delivered *d.* to keep
17:7 do contrary to *d.* of Cesar

DECREE, ED.

Est. 2:1 rememb. what was *d.*
Job 22:28 shalt *d.* and it shall be
38:10 break up for it *d.* place
Prov. 8:15 princes *d.* justice
Is. 10:22 consumption *d.*
1 *Cor.* 7:37 hath so *d.* he will k.

DEDAN.

Gen. 10:7 sons of Raamah, D.
1 *Chr.* 1:9 Sheba, D. 32
Jer. 25:23 I made D. drink, 49:8
Ezek. 25:13 D. fall by sw. 27:20

DEDANIM. *Is.* 21:13

DEDICATE.

1 *Chr.* 26:27 spoils did they *d.*
2 *Chr.* 2:4 I build to *d.* it to God

DEDICATED.

Deut. 20:5 a new house, not *d.* it
1 *K.* 7:51 which D. his father had
8 *d.* 1 *Chr.* 18:11; 2 *Chr.* 5:1
8:63 *d.* the house, 2 *Chr.* 7:5
15:15 Asa bro. in the things his
father had *d.* 2 *Chr.* 15:18
2 *Chr.* 24:7 *d.* things did bestow
31:12 brought *d.* things faith.

Ezek. 44:29 ev. *d.* thing be theirs
Heb. 9:18 nor *d.* without blood

DEDICATION.

Ezr. 6:17 at *d.* of this house
John 10:22 at Jerus. feast. of *d.*

DEED.

Gen. 44:15 what *d.* is this
Ex. 9:16 very *d.* for this cause
Jud. 19:30 no such *d.* done
1 *Sam.* 26:4 was come in very *d.*
2 *Sam.* 12:14 by this *d.* given
Est. 1:17 *d.* of queen come
Luke 23:51 not consented to *d.*
24:19 J. who was mighty in *d.*
Acts 4:9 examined of good *d.*
Rom. 15:18 Gentiles obe. by *d.*
1 *Cor.* 5:2 hath done this *d.*
3 hath so done this *d.*
Col. 3:17 ye do in word or *d.*
Jam. 1:25 be blessed in his *d.*
1 *John* 3:18 in word, but in *d.*

DEEDS.

Gen. 20:9 done *d.* ought not to
1 *Chr.* 16:8 make known his *d.*
among the people, *Ps.* 105:1
Ezr. 9:13 all is come for evil *d.*
Neh. 6:19 reported his good *d.*
13:14 wipe not out my good *d.*
Ps. 28:4 give them ac. to their *d.*
Is. 59:18 ac. to *d.* he will repay
Jer. 5:28 overpass *d.* of wicked
25:14 recompense accord. to *d.*
Luke 11:48 ye allow *d.* of fathers
23:41 receive reward of our *d.*
John 3:19 their *d.* were evil
20 his *d.* should be reproved
21 *d.* may be made manifest
8:41 ye do *d.* of your father
Acts 7:22 Moses was mighty in *d.*
9:36 Dorcas was full of alms-*d.*
19:18 many showed their *d.*
24:2 worthy *d.* are done
Rom. 2:6 to every man acc. to *d.*
3:20 by *d.* of law no flesh justi.
28 justified by faith without *d.*
8:13 mortify *d.* of body
2 *Cor.* 12:12 signs and mighty *d.*
Col. 3:9 off old man with his *d.*
2 *Pet.* 2:8 vexed with unlawful *d.*
3 *John* 11 partaker of his evil *d.*
3 *John* 10 I will remember his *d.*
Jude 15 conv. of their ungod. *d.*
Rev. 2:6 hatest *d.* of Nicolaitans
22 except repent of *d.*
16:11 repented not of their *d.*

DEEMED.

Acts 27:27 the shipmen *d.* drew

DEEP, Substantive.

Gen. 1:2 darkness on face of *d.*
7:11 fountains of the *d.* were brok.
8:2 fountains of *d.* were stop.
49:25 with blessings of the *d.*
Deut. 33:13 *d.* that coucheth ben.
Job 38:30 face of *d.* is frozen
41:31 the *d.* to boil like a pot
32 think the *d.* to be hoary
Ps. 36:6 judgments a great *d.*
42:7 *d.* calleth to *d.* at noise of
69:15 nor let *d.* swallow me up
104:6 coveredst it with the *d.* as
107:24 see his wonders in the *d.*
Prov. 8:28 strength. fount. of *d.*
Is. 44:27 saith to the *d.* Be dry
51:10 which dried waters of *d.*
63:13 led them through the *d.*
Ezek. 26:19 bring up *d.* on thee
31:4 *d.* set him on high
15 I covered the *d.* for him
Amos 7:4 devoured the great *d.*
Jon. 2:3 hadst cast me into *d.*
Hab. 3:10 *d.* uttered his voice
Luke 5:4 launch out into the *d.*
8:31 command to go into *d.*
Rom. 10:7 who descend into *d.*
2 *Cor.* 11:25 night and day in *d.*

DEEP, Adjective.

Job 12:22 discovereth *d.* things
Ps. 64:6 and the heart is *d.*
Ps. 69:2 I sink in *d.* mire, *d.* wat.
 14 be delivered out of *d.* wat.
 80:9 didst cause it take *d.* root
 92:5 thy thoughts are very *d.*
 95:4 in his hands are *d.* places
 135:6 in seas, and all *d.* places
 140:10 be cast into *d.* pits
Prov. 18:4 words are as *d.* waters
 20:5 counsel like *d.* water
 22:14 of strange woun. is a *d.* pit
 23:27 for a whore is a *d.* ditch
Ec. 7:24 exceeding *d.* who can
Is. 29:15 seek *d.* to hide counsel
 30:33 he hath made Tophet *d.*
Jer. 49:8 dwell *d.* O inhab. of D.
Ezek. 23:32 drink sister's cup *d.*
 32:14 make their waters *d.*
 34:18 drunk of *d.* waters
Dan. 2:22 revealeth *d.* things
Luke 6:48 and digged *d.*
John 4:11 and the well is *d.*
1 *Cor.* 2:10 search. *d.* things
2 *Cor.* 8:2 *d.* poverty abounded

DEEP sleep.

Gen. 2:21 a *d. sleep* to fall on A.
 15:12 a *d. sleep* fell on Abram
1 *Sam.* 26:12 *d. s.* was on them
Job 4:13 *d. sleep* falleth 33:15
Prov. 19:15 sloth. casteth in *d. s.*
Is. 29:10 spirit of *d. sleep*
Dan. 8:18 I was in a *d. s.* 10:9
Acts 20:9 Eutychus into *d. sleep*

DEEPER.

Job 11:8 it is *d.* than hell, what
Is. 33:19 a people of *d.* speech

DEEPLY.

Is. 31:6 Israel have *d.* revolted
Hos. 9:9 they have *d.* corrupted
Mark 8:12 Jesus sighed *d.*

DEEPNESS.

Mat. 13:5 had no *d.* of earth

DEEPS.

Neh. 9:11 persecutors into *d.*
Ps. 88:6 hast laid me in the *d.*
 148:7 praise the Lord, all *d.*
Zec. 10:11 *d.* of river shall dry

DEER.

Deut. 14:5 ye shall eat fallow *d.*
1 *K.* 4:23 Solomon had *d.*

DEFAMED, ING.

1 *Cor.* 4:13 being *d.* we entreat
Jer. 20:10 I heard *d.* of many

DEFEAT.

2 *Sam.* 15:34 *d.* coun. of A. 17:14

DEFENCE.

Num. 14:9 their *d.* is departed
Job 22:25 Almighty be thy *d.*
Ps. 7:10 my *d.* is of God, who
 31:2 be thou for house of *d.*
 59:9 God is my *d.* 17; 62:2, 6
 16 hast been my *d.* in trouble
 89:18 L. is our *d.*; 94:22 my *d.*
Ec. 7:12 wisdom is a *d.* money
Is. 4:5 on glory shall be a *d.*
 19:6 brooks of *d.* be emptied
 33:16 his *d.* munitions of rocks
Nah. 2:5 *d.* shall be prepared
Acts 19:33 made his *d.*
 22:1 hear ye my *d.* I make now
Phil. 1:7 and in *d.* of the gospel
 17 I am set for *d.* of gospel

DEFENCED. *See* CITY, CITIES.

DEFEND.

Jud. 10:1 Tola son of Puah arose
 to *d.* Israel
2 *K.* 19:34 I will *d.* this city, 20:6;
 Is. 37:35; 38:6
Ps. 20:1 name of G. of Jacob *d.*
 59:1 *d.* me from them rise up
 82:3 *d.* the poor and fatherless
Is. 31:5 so will Lord *d.* Jerusal.

Zec. 9:15 Lord sl all *d.* them
 12:8 in that day L. *d.* inhabit.

DEFENDED, EST, ING.

2 *Sam.* 23:12 Shammah *d.* ground
Ps. 5:11 because thou *d.* them
Is. 31:5 *d.* Jerus. will deliver it
Acts 7:24 he *d.* him, and aveng.

DEFER, RED, ETH.

Prov. 13:12 hope *d.* maketh sick
 19:11 discretion *d.* anger
Ec. 5:4 vowest *d.* not to pay it
Is. 48:9 will I defer mine anger
Dan. 9:19 *d.* not, for own sake
Acts 24:22 Felix *d.* them

DEFY, IED.

Num. 23:7 curse me Jacob, *d.* Is.
 8 how I *d.* whom L. not *defied ?*
1 *Sam.* 17:10 I *d.* armies of Israel
 25 to *d.* Israel is he come up
 26 that he should *d.* the armies
 36 *d.* armies of living God
 45 God of Israel whom hast *d.*
2 *Sam.* 21:21 when he *d.* Is. Jonathan slew him, 1 *Chr.* 20:7
 23:9 when they *d.* Philistines

DEFILE.

Lev. 11:44 nor *d.* yours. 18:24
 18:28 spue not out when ye *d.*
Num. 35:34 *d.* not land ye sh. in.
Cant. 5:3 how shall I *d.* them ?
Is. 30:22 *d.* covering of images
Ezek. 7:22 robbers shall *d.* it
 9:7 *d.* the house
 20:7 *d.* not with the idols, 18
 28:7 shall *d.* thy brightness
 33:26 *d.* every man neigh. wife
 37:23 *d.* themselves any more
 43:7 my name Israel no more *d.*
Dan. 1:8 not *d.* with king's meat
Mat. 15:18 *d.* the man, *Mark* 7:15
1 *Cor.* 3:17 if any *d.* temple
1 *Tim.* 1:10 law is for them *d.*
Jude 8 filthy dreamers *d.* flesh

DEFILED.

Gen. 34:2 Shechem *d.* Dinah
Lev. 18:24 in all these, nations *d.*
1 *Chr.* 5:1 as he *d.* his father's b.
Job 16:15 *d.* my horn in the dust
Ps. 74:7 *d.* the dwelling-pl. 79:1
 106:39 *d.* with their own works
Is. 24:5 earth is *d.* under inhab.
 59:3 your hands *d.* with blood
Jer. 2:7 entered ye *d.* my land
 16:18 because they *d.* my land
Ezek. 4:13 shall Isr. eat *d.* bread
 5:11 because *d.* my sanctuary
 7:24 their holy places shall be *d.*
 18:6 nor *d.* neighbor's wife, 15
 20:43 doings wherein been *d.*
 22:4 *d.* thyself in idols, 23:7
 11 another *d.* daughter-in-law
 23:38 *d.* my sanctuary same day
 28:18 hast *d.* thy sanctuaries
 43:8 *d.* my holy name
Hos. 5:3 and Israel is *d.* 6:10
Mic. 4:11 say, let her be *d.*
Mark 7:2 disc. eat with *d.* hands
John 18:28 went not in, lest be *d.*
1 *Cor.* 8:7 conscience weak, is *d.*
Tit. 1:15 them that are *d.* their
 mind and conscience is *d.*
Heb. 12:15 thereby many be *d.*
Rev. 3:4 not *d.* their garments
 14:4 were not *d.* with women

DEFILEDST, ETH.

Gen. 49:4 father's bed, *d.* it
Ex. 31:14 *d.* sab. put to death
Mat. 15:11 goeth into mouth *d.*
 20 with unwashen hand *d.* not
Mark 7:20 that cometh out *d.*
Jam. 3:6 tongue, it *d.* whole bo.
Rev. 21:27 enter anything *d.*

DEFRAUD, ED.

Lev. 19:13 shalt not *d.* neighbor
1 *Sam.* 12:3 whom have I *d. ?*

Mark 10:19 *d.* not
1 *Cor.* 6:7 rather suffer to be *d.*
 8 you *d.* your brethren
 7:5 *d.* not, except with consent
2 *Cor.* 7:2 we have *d.* no man
1 *Thes.* 4:6 no man *d.* his brother

DEGENERATE.

Jer. 2:21 turned into *d.* plant

DEGREE, S.

2 *K.* 20:9 back. ten *d.* 38:8
1 *Chr.* 17:17 a man of high *d.*
Ps. 62:9 low *d.* vanity, high *d.*
Luke 1:52 exalted them of low *d.*
1 *Tim.* 3:13 purchase a good *d.*
Jam. 1:9 brother of low *d.* rej.

DELAY, ED, ETH.

Ex. 22:29 not *d.* to offer fl.-fruits
 32:1 Moses *d.* to come down
Ps. 119:60 *d.* not to keep com.
Mat. 24:48 Lord *d.* *Luke* 12:45
Acts 9:38 not *d.* to come to them
 25:17 without *d.* morrow I sat

DELECTABLE.

Is. 44:9 their *d.* things not profit

DELICACIES.

Rev. 18:3 merc. rich thro' her *d.*

DELICATE.

Deut. 28:54 the *d.* man or w. 56
Is. 47:1 no more be called *d.*
Jer. 6:2 likened Zion to *d.* wom.
Mic. 1:16 bald for thy *d.* child.

DELICATES.

Jer. 51:34 filled belly with my *d.*

DELICATELY.

1 *Sam.* 15:32 Agag came *d.*
Prov. 29:21 that *d.* bringeth up
Lam. 4:5 did feed *d.* are desolate
Luke 7:25 live *d.* are in kings'

DELICATENESS.

Deut. 28:56 foot on ground for *d.*

DELICIOUSLY.

Rev. 18:7 she lived *d.* 9

DELIGHT, Substantive.

Deut. 10:15 L. had *d.* in thy fath.
1 *Sam.* 15:22 great *d.* in offering
 18:22 the king hath *d.*
2 *Sam.* 15:26 I have no *d.* in thee
Job 22:26 have *d.* in Almighty
Ps. 1:2 his *d.* is in law of the L.
 16:3 in whom is all my *d.*
 119:24 testimonies are my *d.*
 77 for thy law is my *d.* 174
Prov. 8:30 I was daily his *d.*
 11:1 just weight is Lord's *d.*
 20 such as upright, are his *d.*
 12:22 deal truly are his *d.*
 15:8 prayer of upright is his *d.*
 16:13 righteous lips *d.* of kings
 18:2 a fool no *d.* in unders.
 19:10 *d.* not seemly for a fool
 24:25 to them that reb. sh. be *d.*
 29:17 he give *d.* to thy soul
Cant. 2:3 under sha. wi. great *d.*
Is. 58:2 take *d.* in app. to God
 13 if thou call sabbath a *d.*
Jer. 6:10 no *d.* in word of Lord

DELIGHT, Verb.

Num. 14:8 if Lord *d.* in us
2 *Sam.* 24:3 why should king *d.*
Job 27:10 he *d.* in Almighty ?
 34:9 should *d.* himself with G.
Ps. 37:4 *d.* thyself also in Lord
 11 *d.* in abundance of peace
 40:8 I *d.* to do thy will, O God
 62:4 *d.* in lies; 68:30 *d.* in war
 94:19 thy comforts *d.* my soul
 119:16 *d.* in thy statutes, 35
 47 *d.* in thy com.; 70 *d.* in law
Prov. 1:22 long will scorners *d.*
 2:14 *d.* in frowardness
Is. 1:11 I *d.* not in blood of bul.
 13:17 as for gold, not *d.* in it
 55:2 let your soul *d.* in fatness

58:2 they *d.* to know my ways
14 shalt *d.* thyself in the Lord
Jer. 9:24 in these things I *d.*
Mal. 3:1 messenger of cov. ye *d.*
Rom. 7:22 I *d.* an law after in. m.

DELIGHTED.

1 *Sam.* 19:2 Jonath. *d.* in David
2 *Sam.* 22:20 *d.* in me, *Ps.* 18:19
1 *K.* 10:9 L. *d.* in thee, 2 *Chr.* 9:8
Neh. 9:25 *d.* in thy great goodn.
Est. 2:14 except king *d.* in her
Ps. 22:8 seeing he *d.* in him
109:17 as he *d.* not in blessing
Is. 65:12 did choose that wherein
I *d.* not, 66:4
66:11 be *d.* with her glory

DELIGHTEST, ETH.

Est. 6:6 *d.* to honor, 7, 9, 11
Ps. 37:23 and he *d.* in his way
51:16 *d.* not in burnt-offering
112:1 *d.* greatly in his command
147:10 *d.* not in stor. of horse
Prov. 3:12 son in whom he *d.*
Is. 42:1 in whom my soul *d.*
62:4 for the Lord *d.* in thee
66:3 soul *d.* in abominations
Mic. 7:18 because he *d.* in mercy
Mal. 2:17 G. *d.* in them do evil

DELIGHTS.

2 *Sam.* 1:24 clothed you with *d.*
Ps. 119:92 law been my *d.*
143 yet thy comman. are my *d.*
Prov. 8:31 my *d.* with sons of m.
Ec. 2:8 I gat me the *d.* of men
Cant. 7:6 how pleasant for *d.*

DELIGHTSOME.

Mal. 3:12 ye shall be a *d.* land

DELILAH. *Jud.* 16:4, 12

DELIVER.

Ex. 23:31 I will *d.* the inhabit.
Num. 21·2 indeed *d.* this people
Deut. 7:24 *d.* kings into thy h.
32:39 neither any that can *d.* out
of my hand, *Is.* 43:13
Jos. 2:13 *d.* our lives from death
Jud. 7:7 by the 300 will I *d.* M.
1 *Sam.* 12:21 cannot profit nor *d.*
24:4 *d.* enemy into thy hand
28:19 L. will *d.* Is. to Phil.
1 *K.* 20:13 I will *d.* this multi.
22:6 *d.* into king's hand, 12, 15;
2 *Chr.* 18:5, 11
2 *K.* 3:18 he will *d.* Moabites
18:35 should *d.* Jer. *Is.* 36:20
2 *Chr.* 25:15 could not *d.* own p.
32:13 able to *d.* their lands?
14 that your God should *d.* you
Job 10:7 none can *d.* out
22:30 shall *d.* island of innocent
33:28 *d.* soul from going into pit
Ps. 6:4 *d.* my soul, 17:13; 22:20;
116:4; 120:2
Ps. 7:2 none to *d.* 50:22
33:17 *d.* any by his great str.
19 to *d.* their soul from death
56:13 *d.* my feet from falling?
72:12 *d.* needy when he
74:19 *d.* not soul of turtle-dove
82:4 *d.* needy out of the hand
89:48 *d.* his soul from grave
Prov. 4:9 a crown shall she *d.* to
6:3 do this now *d.* thyself
23:14 shalt *d.* his soul from hell
Ec. 8:8 wick. *d.* those given
Is. 5:29 none shall *d.* prey
29:11 men *d.* to one learned
31:5 defending also he will *d.* it
44:20 that he cannot *d.* his soul
46:2 they could not *d.* burden
47:14 not *d.* thems. from flame
50:2 have I no power to *d.?*
Jer. 15:9 residue will I *d.*
18:21 *d.* their children to famine
20:5 *d.* strength of this city
21:7 *d.* Zedekiah from sword
22:3 *d.* spoiled out of hand of

43:11 *d.* such as are for death
51:6 *d.* every man his soul, 45
Ezek. 13:21 I will *d.* my peo. 23
14:14 *d.* but their own souls
16 shall *d.* sons nor dau. 18:20
33:5 taketh warning *d.* his soul
34:10 *d.* flock from their mouth
Dan. 3:29 no god *d.* after this
8:4 nor any could *d.* from ram
Hos. 2:10 none *d.* her out of hand
Amos 2:14 nor mighty *d.* himself
6:8 *d.* city with a therein
Mic. 5:8 teareth, and none can *d.*
6:14 shalt take hold, but not *d.*
Zec. 2:7 *d.* thyself, O Zion
11:6 *d.* every one into n. hand
Mat. 10:21 bro. *d.* bro. to death
Acts 25:16 to *d.* any man to die
1 *Cor.* 5:5 *d.* such a one to Satan
2 *Cor.* 1:10 death, and doth *d.*
2 *Pet.* 2:9 Lord know. how to *d.*

DELIVER him.

Gen. 37:22 *d. him* to his father
1 *Sam.* 23:20 part be to *d. him*
2 *Sam.* 14:7 *d. him* smote his bro.
20:21 *d. him,* and I will depart
Job 33:24 *d. h.* from going to pit
Ps. 22:8 *d. him,* let him *d. him*
41:1 L. *d. him* in time of troub.
2 not *d. h.* to will of enemies
71:11 for there is none to *d. h.*
91:14 his love on me, I *d. him*
15 be with him, I will *d. him*
Prov. 19:19 if *d. him* must do it
Jer. 21:12 *d. him* spoiled
Ezek. 33:12 shall not *d. him*
Mat. 20:19 *d. him* to G. *Mark*
10:33; *Luke* 20:20; *Acts* 21:11
26:15 and I will *d. him*
27:43 let him *d. him* now

DELIVER me.

Gen. 32:11 *d. me* from Esau
1 *Sam.* 17:37 *d. me* from Goliath
23:11 men of Keilah *d. me* up?
24:15 Lord be judge and *d. me*
26:24 *d. me* out of all tribulat.
Job 6:23 *d. me* from enemies, *Ps.*
31:15; 59:1
Ps. 7:1 save me from them, *d. m.*
25:20 keep my soul, and *d. me*
27:12 *d. me* not to will of enem.
31:2 *d. me* speedily
39:8 *d. me* from all my transg.
40:13 be pleased to *d. me*
43:1 O *d. me* from the deceitful
51:14 *d. me* from blood-guilti.
59:2 *d. me* from workers of iniq.
69:14 *d. me* out of the mire
18 draw nigh to my soul, *d. me*
70:1 make haste to *d. me*
71:2 *d. me* in thy righteous. 31:1
4 *d. me* out of hand of wicked
109:21 mercy is good, *d.* thou *me*
119:134 *d. me* from op. of man
153 consider affliction, *d. me*
154 plead my cause, and *d. me*
170 *d. me* according to thy w.
140:1 *d. me* from the evil man
142:6 *d. me* from my persecutors
143:9 *d. me* from mine enemies
144:7 *d. me* out of great waters
11 *d. me* from strange children
Is. 44:17 *d. me,* thou art my God
Jer. 38:19 afraid lest Jews *d. me*
Acts 25:11 no man may *d. me*
Rom. 7:24 *d. me* from body of d.?
2 *Tim.* 4:18 *d. me* from evil work

DELIVER thee.

Deut. 23:14 in camp to *d. thee*
1 *Sam.* 17:46 *d. thee* into
2 *K.* 20:6 *d. t.* and city, *Is.* 38:6
Job 5:19 *d. t.* in six troubles
Job 36:18 ransom cannot *d. thee*
Ps. 50:15 *d. t.* thou shalt glorify
91:3 *d. thee* from snare of fowler
Prov. 2:12 *d. t.* from way of evil

16 *d. t.* from strange woman
Is. 57:13 thy companies *d. thee*
Jer. 1:8 with thee to *d. t.* 15:20
38:20 J. said they shall not *d. t.*
39:17 I will *d. thee* in that day
Ezek. 21:31 *d. thee* to brutish
23:28 *d. t.* to them thou hatest
25:4 I will *d. t.* to men of east
7 I will *d. thee* for spoil
Dan. 6:16 thy G. will *d. thee*
Hos. 11:8 how shall I *d. thee,* Is.
Mat. 5:25 judge *d. t.* *Luke* 12:58

DELIVER them.

Ex. 3:8 down to *d. t.* *Acts* 7:34
Deut. 7:2 Lord shall *d. them,* 23
Jos. 11:6 *d.* them up all slain
Jud. 20:28 to-morrow I will *d. t.*
1 *Sam.* 14:37 wilt thou *d. them,*
2 *Sam.* 5:19; 1 *Chr.* 14:10
1 *K.* 8:46 *d. t.* to ene. 2 *K.* 21:14
2 *Chr.* 25:20 came to G. to *d. t.*
Neh. 9:28 didst *d. them*
Job 5:4 neither any to *d. them*
Ps. 22:4 didst *d. them*
37:40 the L. shall *d. them*
106:43 many times did he *d. t.*
Prov. 11:6 right. of upr. sha. *d. t.*
12:6 the mouth of upright *d. t.*
24:11 forbear to *d. them*
Is. 19:20 a Saviour and *d. them*
Ezek. 7:19 not *d. them, Zep.* 1:18
34:12 my sheep and *d. them*
Acts 7:25 God by his hand *d. t.*
Heb. 2:15 *d. t.* who through fear

DELIVER us.

Jud. 10:15 *d. us* only, this day
20:13 *d. us* children of Belial
1 *Sam.* 4:8 who shall *d. us*
12:10 now *d. us* from enemies
2 *K.* 18:30 will *d. us, Is.* 36:15
1 *Chr.* 16:35 *d. us* from heathen
2 *Chr.* 32:11 Lord shall *d. us*
Ps. 79:9 *d. us,* purge away sins
Jer. 43:3 to *d. us* to Chaldeans
Lam. 5:8 none that doth *d. us*
Dan. 3:17 able and will *d. us*
Mat. 6:13 *d. us* fr. evil, *Luke* 11:4
2 *Cor.* 1:10 he will yet *d. us*
Gal. 1:4 *d. us* from evil world

DELIVER you.

Jud. 10:13 I will *d. you* no more
14 *d. you* in tribulation
2 *Chr.* 32:14 *d. you* out of hand
Is. 36:14 H. not be able to *d. you*
46:4 I will carry and *d. you*
Ezek. 11:9 *d. you* to strangers
Dan. 3:15 that God sh. *d. you*
Mat. 10:17 *d. you* up, *Mark* 13:9

DELIVERANCE, S.

Gen. 45:7 to save by a great *d.*
Jud. 15:18 given this great *d.*
2 *K.* 5:1 had given *d.* to Syria
13:17 arrow of Lord's *d.* of *d.*
1 *Chr.* 11:14 saved by a great *d.*
2 *Chr.* 12:7 I will grant some *d.*
Ezr. 9:13 given such *d.* as this
Est. 4:14 then *d.* arise to Jews
Ps. 18:50 great *d.* giveth to king
32:7 compass with songs of *d.*
44:4 command *d.* for Jacob
Is. 26:18 not wrought any *d.*
Joel 2:32 in Z. and in Jeru. be *d.*
Ob. 17 upon Zion shall be *d.*
Luke 4:18 to preach *d.* to capt.
Heb. 11:35 not accepting *d.*

DELIVERED.

Gen. 9:2 into your h. are they *d.*
14:20 blessed be God who *d.*
25:24 her days to be *d.* fulfilled
Ex. 1:19 *d.* ere midwives come
5:23 nor hast *d.* thy people
12:27 and *d.* our houses
Deut. 2:36 Lord *d.* all unto us
1 *Sam.* 4:19 P. wife near to be *d,*
17:35 *d.* it of his mouth
30:23 *d.* company came ag. us
1 *K.* 3:17 *d.* of a child with her

2 K. 19:11 and shalt thou be d.
Job 22:30 d. by puren. of hands
23:7 be d. for ever from judge
29:12 I d. the poor that cried
Ps. 22:5 they cried and were d.
33:16 not d. by much strength
55:18 d. my soul in peace
56:13 d. soul, 86:13; 116:8
60:5 beloved may be d. 108.6
69:14 d. from them that hate me
78:61 d. his strength into capt.
Prov. 11:8 is d. out of trouble
9 through knowledge just be d.
21 seed of righteous shall be d.
28:26 walk. wisely, shall be d.
Ec. 9:15 by wisdom he d. city
Is. 36:19 d. Samaria out
38:17 d. it from pit of corrupt.
49:24 or lawful captive be d. ?
66:7 was d. of a man-child
Jer. 20:13 d. soul of the poor
Ezek. 3:19 d. thy soul, 33:9
14:16 they only shall be d.
17:15 break cov. and be d. ?
31:14 all d. unto death
32:20 she is d. to the sword
Dan. 3:28 d. serv. that trusted
6:27 who d. Daniel from lions
12:1 thy people be d.
Joel 2:32 call on L. shall be d.
Amos 9:1 shall not be d.
Mic. 4:10 go to Bab. there be d.
Hab. 2:9 d. from power of evil
Mal. 3:15 tempt God are even d.
Mat. 11:27 all things are d. to me
of my Father, Luke 10:22
27:58 Pilate com. body to be d.
Mark 10:33 be d. to chief priests
15:15 and d. Jesus, Luke 23:25
Luke 1:57 she should be d. 2:6
4:6 that is d. to me
17 d. to book of Esaias
9:44 Son be d. into hands of m.
12:58 give dilig. mayest be d.
18:32 he shall be d. to Gentiles
John 16:21 as soon as she is d.
18:36 should not be d. to Jews
Acts 2:23 d. by counsel of God
15:30 Judas and Silas d.
27:1 they d. Paul to one Julius
28:17 d. prisoner from Jerusal.
Rom. 4:25 was d. for our offenc.
7:6 now we are d. from the law
8:21 creature itself shall be d.
15:31 d. from them not believe
2 Cor. 4:11 are always d. to dea.
2 Thes. 3:2 d. from unreas. men
1 Tim. 1:20 whom I ha. d. to S.
2 Tim. 4:17 I was d. out of the
mouth of the lion
Heb. 11:11 by faith Sarah was d.
2 Pet. 2:7 and d. just Lot, vexed
21 turned from the com. d.
Jude 3 faith once d. to the sain.
Rev. 12:2 and pained to be d.

See HAND, HANDS.

DELIVERED him.
Gen. 37:21 Reuben d. him
Deut. 2:33 God d. him before us
1 K. 13:26 Lord d. h. to the lion
17:23 Elijah d. h. to his mother
Ps. 7:4 d. h. that is mine enemy
Mat. 18:34 d. him to tormentors
27:2 d. him to P. Pilate, Mark
15:1
18 for envy d. him, Mark 15:10
26 d. h. to be cruc. John 19:16
Luke 7:15 Jesus d. h. to his mot.
24:20 how our rulers d. him
John 18:30 wo. not d. h. to thee
Acts 7:10 d. h. out of afflictions
12:4 d. h. to four quarternions

DELIVERED me.
Ex. 18:4 d. me fr. swo. of Pha.
Job 12:3 I saw ye d. me not

2 Sam. 22:18 he d. me from my
strong enemy, Ps. 18:17
20 he d. me because he delighted in me, Ps. 18:19
49 d. me from vio. Ps. 18:48
Job 16:11 d. me to the ungodly
Ps. 18:43 d. me from striv. of pe.
34:4 L. d. me from all my fears
54:7 d. me out of all my trouble
John 19:11 d. me hath great. sin
2 Tim. 3:11 of them all L. d. me

DELIVERED thee.
1 Sam. 24:10 d. t. to-d. into m. h.
2 Sam. 12:7 I d. thee out of the h.
Ps. 81:7 calledst and I d. thee
Ezek. 16:27 I d. t. to them th. h.
John 18:35 ch. priests d. t. to me

DELIVERED them.
Ex. 18:8 Mos. told how L. d. t.
Jud. 3:9 r. up. deliv. who d. th.
2 K. 19:12 gods d. th. Is. 37:12
2 Chr. 29:8 d. them to trouble
Ps. 78:42 he d. th. from enemy
107:6 he d. th. out of distresses
20 he d. th. from destructions
Is. 34:2 hath d. th. to slaughter
Mat. 25:14 d. to them his goods
Luke 1:2 as they d. them un. us
Acts 16:4 d. t. decrees for to ke.
1 Cor. 11:2 keep ordin. as I d. t.
2 Pet. 2:4 d. t. into chains of d.

DELIVERED up.
Num. 21:3 Lord d. up the Can.
2 Sam. 18:28 d. up men that lift
Ob. 14 nor d. up those that rem.

Acts 3:13 glorified Son ye d. up
Rom. 8:32 but d. him up for us
1 Cor. 15:24 have d. up kingdom
Rev. 20:13 and hell d. up dead

DELIVERED us.
Ex. 2:19 Egyp. d. us fr. shep.
Acts 6:14 ch. customs Mos. d. us
2 Cor. 1:10 d. us from so gr. dea.
Col. 1:13 d. us. fr. pow. of dark.
1 Thes. 1:10 who d. us fr. wrath

DELIVERED you.
Rom. 6:17 obeyed doctrine d. y.
1 Cor. 11:23 that I d. y. 15:3

DELIVEREDST, EST.
Ps. 35:10 d. poor fr. him spoil.
Mic. 6:14 what d. I give to swo.

DELIVERER.
Jud. 3:9 L. raised up d. to Is. 15
18:28 there was no d.
2 Sam. 22:2 L. is my d. Ps. 18:2
Ps. 40:17 thou art my d. 70:5
144:2 my fortress and my d.
Acts 7:35 did God send to be a d.
Rom. 11:26 come out of Sion d.

DELIVERETH.
Job 36:15 d. poor in his affliction
Ps. 18:48 d. me from enemies
34:7 that fear him, and d. them
17 d. them out of troubles, 19
97:10 d. out of hand of wicked
144:10 who d. David from swo.
Prov. 10:2 right. d. fr. d. 11:4
14:25 a true witness d. souls
Is. 42:22 are for a prey, none d.
Dan. 6:27 God d. and rescueth

DELIVERING.
Luke 21:12 d. you up to synag.
Acts 22:4 d. men and women
26:17 d. thee from the Gentiles

DELIVERY.
Is. 26:17 near the time of her d.

DELUSION, S.
Is. 66:4 I will choose their d.
2 Thes. 2:11 send them strong d.

DEMAND.
Dan. 4:17 d. by word of h. ones.

DEMAND, ED.
Job 38:3 d. of thee, 40:7; 42:4

Mat. 2:4 d. wh. C. sh. be born
Luke 3:14 Soldi. d. what shall
17:20 when he was d. of Phar.
Acts 21:33 cap. d. who he was

DEMAS.
Col. 4:14 ; Phile. 24
2 Tim. 4:10 D. hath forsaken me

DEMETRIUS.
Acts 19:24 D. a silver. 3 John 12

DEMONSTRATION.
1 Cor. 2:4 but in d. of the Spirit

DEN, S.
Jud. 6:2 Israel made them a.
Job 37:8 th. the beasts go into d.
38:40 when they couch in d.
Ps. 10:9 lieth as a lion in his d.
104:22 lay them. down in d.
Cant. 4:8 look from the lions' d.
Is. 11:8 hand on cockatrice d.
32:14 towers be for d. forever
Jer. 7:11 house a d. of robbers
9:11 Jerusalem a d. of dragons
10:22 cit. of Judah a d. of drag.
Dan. 6:16 cast him into d. of li.
24 cast them into d. of lions
Amos 3:4 y. lion cry out of d. ?
Nah. 2:12 filled d. with ravin
Mat. 21:13 a d. of th. Mark 11:17
Heb. 11:38 they wandered in d.
Rev. 6:15 bond and free hid in d.

DENY.
Jos. 24:27 lest ye d. your God
1 K. 2:16 d. me not, Prov. 30:7
Job 8:18 then it shall d. him
Prov. 30:9 lest I be full and d.
Mat. 10:33 d. me, him will I d.
16:24 let him d. himself, Mark
8:34 ; Luke 9:23
26:34 d. me thrice, 75 ; Mark
14:30, 72
Luke 20:27 d. th. is any resur.
2 Tim. 2:12 d. him. he will d. us
13 he cannot d. himself
Tit. 1:16 in works they d. him

DENIED.
1 K. 20:7 sent and I d. him not
Job 31:28 I sh. have d. God above
Mat. 26:70 Peter d. before all, 72 ;
Mark 14:70; Luke 22:57 ;
John 18:25, 27
Luke 8:45 all d. th. touched him
12:9 be d. bef. angels of God
John 1:20 John d. not
Acts 3:13 wh. d. in pres. of Pi.
14 but ye d. the Holy One
1 Tim. 5:8 he hath d. the faith
Rev. 2:13 hast not d. my faith
3:8 and hast not d. my name

DENIEDST, ING.
Luke 12:9 that d. me before men
2 Tim. 3:5 d. the power thereof
Tit. 2:12 that d. ungodliness
2 Pet 2:1 d. L. that bought them
1 John 2:22 a liar d. esus is C.
23 who d. Son, hath not Fath.
Jude 4 and d. the only Lord God

DENOUNCE.
Deut. 30:18 I d. this day

DEPART.
Ex. 33:1 d. thou and the peo.
1 Sam. 22:5 abide not in hold, d.
29:10 as soon as ye be up, d.
2 Sam. 15:1· speed to d. lest he
1 K. 12:5 d. for three days
Job 20:28 incr. of his house d.
Is. 11:13 envy of Ephr. shall d.
52:11 d. ye, d. ye, Lam. 4:15
54:10 the mountains shall d.
Jer. 50:3 d. both man and beast
Mic. 2:10 d. this is not your rest
Zec. 10:11 sceptre of Eg. shall d.
Mat. 8:34 d. out of c. Mark 5:17
10:14 when ye d. out of that ho.
Mark 6:11 ; Luke 9:4

Luke 2:29 thy serv. *d.* in peace
13:31 *d.* Herod will kill thee
21:21 let them in midst *d.* out
John 7:3 said *d.* go into Judea
16:7 but if I *d.* I will send him
Acts 16:36 *d.* and go in peace
  39 desired them to *d.* out of ci.
20:7 Paul preached ready to *d.*
22:21 *d.* I will send thee to Gen.
25:4 would *d.* shortly thither
27:12 more part advised to *d.*
1 *Cor.* 7:15 if unb. *d.* let him *d.*
Phil. 1:23 *d.* and to be with Chr.
Jam. 2:16 *d.* in peace, be clothed

DEPART from.

Num. 16:26 *d. f.* tents of these
Deut. 4:9 they *d. fr.* thy heart
Jud. 7:3 fearful *d. from* Gilead
2 *Sam.* 12:10 sw. never *d. f.* ho.
20:21 del. Sheba, and I will *d. f.*
2 *Chr.* 18:31 G. moved to *d. f.* h.
Job 21:14 say to G. *d. f.* us, 22:17
28:28 to *d. f.* evil is unders.
Ps. 6:8 *d. from* me, wo. of iniq.
  Mat. 7:23 ; *Luke* 13:27
34:14 *d. f.* evil, do good, 37:27
101:4 a froward heart *d. f.* me
119:115 *d. f.* me, ye evil-doers
139:19 *d. f.* me ye bloody men
Prov. 3:7 fear Lord, *d. from* evil
13:14 *d. fr.* sna. of death, 14:27
  19 abom. to fools to *d. f.* evil
15:24 he may *d. from* hell ben.
16:6 by fear of L. men. *d. f.* ev.
17:13 evil, is to *d. from* evil
Is. 14:25 burden *d. f.* shoulders
Jer. 6:8 lest my soul *d. f.* thee
17:13 *d. fr.* me be wri. in earth
31:36 if ordin. *d. f.* before me
Ezek. 16:42 my jeal. *d. fr.* thee
Hos. 9:12 woe to th. wh. I *d. f.*
Mat. 25:41 *d. f.* me, ye cursed
Mark 6:10 abide, till ye *d. f.*
Luke 5:8 *d. f.* me, I am sinful
8:37 Gadar. besou. him to *d. fr.*
Acts 14:4 should not *d. f.* Jerus.
18:2 com. Jews to *d. f.* Rome
2 *Cor.* 12:8 that it might *d. f.* me
1 *Tim.* 4:1 some shall *d. f.* faith
2 *Tim.* 2:19 nameth C. *d. f.* iniq.

Not DEPART.

Gen. 49:10 sceptre *not d.* from J.
Jos. 1:8 book of law shall *not d.*
Jud. 6:18 *d. n.* hence till I come
2 *Sam.* 7:15 mercy *n. d.* from hi.
22:23 sta. I did *n. d.* from them
Job 7:19 long *not d.* from me
15:30 he shall not *d.* out
Ps. 55:11 guile *d. not* from str.
Prov. 3:21 *not d.* from eyes, 4:21
5:7 *d. not* from words of my m.
17:13 evil *not d.* from his house
22:6 when old, he will *not d.*
27:22 will *not* his foolishness *d.*
Is. 54:10 kindness shall *not d.*
59:21 my Spirit and wo. *not d.*
Jer. 32:40 shall *not d.* from me
37:9 the Chalde. shall *not d.*
Mat. 14:16 they need *not d.* give
Luke 4:42 that he should *not d.*
12:59 *not d.* till thou hast paid

DEPARTED.

Gen. 12:4 so Abraham *d.*
Num. 12:9 kindled, and he *d.*
Ps. 105:38 E. glad when they *d.*
Is. 38:12 mine age is *d.*
Lam. 1:6 all her beauty is *d.*
Mat. 2:9 the wise men *d.* 12
  14 Joseph and Mary *d.* in E.
4:12 Jesus *d.* 9:27 ; 11:1 ; 12:9 ;
  13:53 ; 14:13 ; 15:21, 29 ; 16:4 ;
  19:15 ; *Mark* 1:35 ; 6:46 ; 8:1. ;
  Luke 4:42 ; *John* 4:3, 43 ;
  6:15 ; 12:36
Luke 5:25 he *d.* to his own house

7:24 messengers of John were *d.*
10:30 thieves wounded him, *d.*
Acts 15:39 Paul and Barna. *d.*
Phile. 15 perhaps he therefore *d.*
Rev. 6:14 heaven *d.* as a scroll

DEPARTED from.

Gen. 31:40 sleep *d. f.* mine eyes
Num. 14:9 defence is *d. f.* them
33:3 they *d. f.* Rameses, 3-49
Deut. 1:19 when we *d. f.* Horeb
Jud. 16:20 wist not L. was *d. f.*
1 *Sam.* 4:21 glory is *d. f.* Isr. 22
16:14 Spirit *d. f.* Saul, 18:12
  23 the evil spirit *d. from* him
28:15 God is *d. from* me
Ps. 18:21 not wicked *d. f.* my G.
Is. 7:17 Ephraim *d. fr.* Judah
Dan. 4:31 kingdom is *d. f.* thee
Hos. 10:5 glory of Sam. *d. fr.* it
Mat. 28:8 *d.* quickly *f.* sepulc.
Luke 4:13 *d. f.* him for a season
Rev. 18:14 fruits thy soul lusted
  after are *d. from* thee

DEPARTED not from.

2 *Sam.* 22:22 not *d. f.* my G. *Ps.*
  18:21
2 *K.* 3:3 he *d. not* therefrom, 13:2
10:29 *d. n. f.* sins of Jer. 31:13,
  6:11 ; 14:24 ; 15:9, 18 ; 17:22
18:6 H. *d. n. f.* following Lord
2 *Chr.* 34:33 they *d. n. f.* fol. L.
Ps. 119:102 *n. d. f.* thy judgm.
Luke 2:37 Anna *d. not f.* temple

DEPARTED out.

Jud. 6:21 an. *d. o.* of his sight
Mal. 2:8 ye are *d. o.* of the way
Mat. 17:18 rebuked *d.* and he
  d. out

DEPARTETH.

Job 27:21 w. car. away and he *d.*
Prov. 14:16 wise man *d.* fr. evil
Ec. 6:4 *d.* in darkness
Is. 59:15 that *d.* fr. evil, a prey
Jer. 3:20 as a wife treach. *d.*
  17:5 whose heart *d.* from Lord
Nah. 3:1 the prey *d.* not
Luke 9:39 bruis. him hardly *d.*

DEPARTING.

Is. 59:13 in *d.* away from God
Dan. 9:5 *d.* from thy precepts
Hos. 1:2 whoredom, *d.* from Lo.
Mark 6:33 people saw them *d.*
Acts 20:29 aft. my *d.* sh. wolves
Heb. 3:12 in *d.* from living God
11:22 mention of the *d.* of Isra.

DEPARTURE.

Ezek. 26:18 be troubled at thy *d.*
2 *Tim.* 4:6 time of my *d.* is at h.

DEPOSED.

Dan. 5:20 he was *d.* from throne

DEPRIVED.

Gen. 27:45 *d.* of both in one day
Job 39:17 God *d.* her of wisdom
Is. 38:10 *d.* of residue of years

DEPTH.

Job 28:14 *d.* saith, It is not in me
38:16 or walked in search of *d. ?*
Ps. 33:7 the *d.* in storehouses
Prov. 8:27 compass on face of *d.*
  25:3 and the earth for *d.*
Is. 7:11 ask it either in the *d.*
Jon. 2:5 *d.* closed me round ab.
Mat. 18:6 drowned in *d.* of sea
Mark 4:5 no *d.* of earth wither.
Rom. 8:39 nor *d.* sep. us fr. love
11:33 O the *d.* of the riches bot.
Eph. 3:18 *d.* of the love of Christ

DEPTHS.

Ex. 15:5 *d.* have covered them
  8 *d.* congealed in heart of sea
Deut. 8:7 *d.* spring out of valleys
Ps. 68:22 br. peo. from *d.* of sea
71:20 br. me up fr. *d.* of earth
77:16 the *d.* were troubled

78:15 drink, as out of great *d.*
106:9 led them through the *d.*
107:26 they go down again to *d.*
130:1 out of the *d.* have I cried
Prov. 3:20 by his knowl. *d.* bro.
8:24 when no *d.* I was br. forth
9:18 her guests are in *d.* of hell
Ezek. 27:34 shalt be broken in *d.*
Mic. 7:19 cast sins into *d.* of sea
Rev. 2:24 not known *d.* of Satan

DEPUTED.

2 *Sam.* 15:3 no man *d.* of the ki.

DEPUTY.

1 *K.* 22:47 a *d.* was king
Acts 13:8 to turn *d.* fr. the faith
18:12 Gallio was *d.* of Achaia

DEPUTIES.

Acts 19:38 are *d.* let th. implead
DERBE. *Acts* 14:6

DERIDE, ED.

Hab. 1:10 sh. *d.* ev. strong-hold
Luke 16:14 the Pharisees *d.* him
23:35 rulers also with peo. *d.*

DERISION.

Job 30:1 younger, have me in *d.*
Ps. 2:4 L. shall have them in *d.*
44:13 a *d.* to them ab. us, 79:4
59:8 shalt have heathen in *d.*
119:51 proud have had me in *d.*
Jer. 20:7 in *d.* daily ; 8 a *d.* daily
48:26 Moab shall be in *d.* 39
  27 was not Israel a *d.* to thee
Lam. 3:14 a *d.* to all my people
Ezek. 23:32 shalt be had in *d.*
36:4 to cities which bec. a *d.*
Hos. 7:16 be their *d.* in Egypt

DESCEND.

Ps. 49:17 glory nor *d.* after him
Ezek. 26:20 that *d.* into plt, 31:16
Mark 15:32 let C. *d.* from cross
Acts 11:5 I saw a vision, ves. *d.*
Rom. 10:7 who *d.* into the deep ?
1 *Thes.* 4:16 L. sh. *d.* fr. heaven

DESCENDED.

Ex. 19:18 L. *d.* on Sinai in fire
  34:5 L. *d.* in the cloud
Ps. 133:3 as dew that *d.* on Zion
Prov. 30:4 as. to heaven or *d. ?*
Mat. 7:25 rain *d.* floods came, 27
28:2 angel of L. *d.* from heaven
Luke 3:22 H. G. *d.* in bod. shape
Acts 24:1 Ananias high-priest *d.*
Eph. 4:10 he that *d.* is the same

DESCENDETH, ING.

Gen. 28:12 the angels of God as-
  cending and *d.* *John* 1:51
Mat. 3:16 saw Sp. *d.* *Mark* 1:10
John 1:32 Spirit *d.* like a dove
  33 on whom shalt see spirit *d.*
Acts 10:11 a vessel *d.* as a sheet
Jam. 3:15 this wisdom *d.* not
Rev. 21:10 city *d.* out of heaven

DESCENT.

Luke 19:37 *d.* of mount of Olives
Heb. 7:3 Melchizedek without *d.*
  6 *d.* is not counted from them

DESCRIBE, ED, ETH.

Jos. 18:4 go th. land and *d.* it
Jud. 8:14 *d.* to him the princes
Rom. 4:6 as D. *d.* the blessedn.
10:5 Mos. *d.* righteousn. of law

DESERT, Wilderness.

Ex. 5:3 three days jour. into *d.*
Num. 27:14 rebelled in *d.* of Zin
Job 24:5 as wild asses in *d.* go
Ps. 78:40 grieve him in *d.*
102:6 I am like an owl of *d.*
106:14 tempted God in the *d.*
Is. 13:21 wild beasts of *d.* shall
  lie there, 34:14 ; *Jer.* 50:39
21:1 so it cometh from the *d.*

35:1 the *d.* shall rejoice
6 streams in the *d.*
40:3 straight in *d.* a highway
41:19 I will set in *d.* the fir-tree
43:19 make rivers in the *d.* 20
51:3 her *d.* like garden of Lord
Jer. 17:6 sh. be like heath in *d.*
25:24 peo. dwell in *d.* sh. drink
50:12 Chaldea shall be a *d.*
Ezek. 47:8 these waters go in. *d.*
Mat. 24:26 behold, he is in the *d.*
John 6:31 did e. manna in the *d.*

DESERT land.
Deut. 32:10 found him in a *d. l.*

DESERT place.
Mark 6:31 come ye into a *d. p.*
32 departed into a *d. place,*
Mat. 14:13 ; *Luke* 4:42
Luke 9:10 aside priv. into a *d. p.*

DESERTS.
Is. 48:21 he led them through *d.*
Jer. 2:6 led us thro. a land of *d.*
Ezek. 13:4 proph. like foxes in *d.*
Luke 1:80 J. was in the *d.* till
Heb. 11:38 they wandered in *d.*

DESERT, S.
Ps. 28:4 render to them their *d.*
Ezek. 7:27 ac. to *d.* will I judge

DESERVE, ETH, ING.
Jud. 9:16 ac. to *d.* of his hands
Ezr. 9:13 less than our iniq. *d.*
Job 11:6 less than thy iniq. *d.*

DESIRABLE.
Ezek. 23:6 *d.* young men, 12, 23

DESIRE, Substantive.
Gen. 3:16 *d.* shall be to thy hus.
4:7 to thee shall be his *d.*
Deut. 18:6 all *d.* of his mind
1 *Sam.* 9:20 on whom *d.* of Isra.
2 *Sam.* 23:5 salva. and all my *d.*
1 *K.* 10:13 queen of S. all her *d.*
2 *Chr.* 15:15 with their whole *d.*
Job 14:15 *d.* to work of thy han.
31:16 if withheld poor from *d.*
35 *d.* is Almigh. would answer
34:36 *d.* is Job be tried to end
Ps. 10:3 boast. of his heart's *d.*
17 hast heard *d.* of humble
21:2 given him his heart's *d.*
38:9 all my *d.* is before thee
54:7 seen *d.* on enemies, 92:11
59:10 let me see *d.* on enemies
78:29 gave them their own *d.*
92:11 sh. hear my *d.* of wicked
112:8 till he see *d.* on enemies
10 *d.* of wicked shall perish
118:7 shall I see my *d.* on them
145:16 satisfiest *d.* of ev. living
19 fulfil *d.* of them fear him
Prov. 10:24 *d.* of righte. be gr.
11:23 *d.* of righte. is only good
13:12 *d.* cometh, a tree of life
19 *d.* accomplished is sweet
19:22 *d.* of a man is his kindn.
21:25 *d.* of slothful killeth him
Ec. 6:9 than wandering of *d.*
12:5 what *d.* shall fail, because
Cant. 7:10 his *d.* is towards me
Is. 26:8 *d.* of soul to thy name
Jer. 44:14 ye have a *d.* to return
Ezek. 24:16 take *d.* of thine eyes
21 profane *d.* of your eyes, 25
Dan. 11:37 nor reg. *d.* of women
Hos. 10:10 my *d.* I should chas.
Mic. 7:3 uttereth mischievous *d.*
Hab. 2:5 enlargeth his *d.* as hell
Hag. 2:7 *d.* of all nations shall
Luke 22:15 with *d.* I des. to eat
Rom. 10:1 my heart's *d.* for Isr.
15:23 having great *d.* to come
2 *Cor.* 7:7 told us your earnest *d.*
11 what vehement *d.* yea, what
Phil. 1:23 having a *d.* to depart
1 *Thes.* 2:17 see yo. face with *d.*

DESIRE, Verb.
Ex. 10:11 for that ye did *d.*
34:24 nor shall any *d.* thy land
Deut. 5:21 nor *d.* neighbor's wife
7:25 not *d.* the silver or gold
1 *K.* 2:20 I *d.* one small petition
2 *K.* 4:28 *d.* a son of my lord ?
Neh. 1:11 *d.* to fear thy name
Job 13:3 I *d.* to reason with God
21:14 *d.* not knowl. of thy ways
33:32 for I *d.* to justify thee
36:20 *d.* not the night, when
Ps. 40:6 offer. thou didst not *d.*
45:11 greatly *d.* thy beauty
70:2 to confusion *d.* my hurt
73:25 none I *d.* beside thee
Prov. 3:15 canst *d.* not to be co.
23:6 neither *d.* his dainty meats
24:1 nor *d.* to be with them
Is. 53:2 no beauty we sh. *d.* him
Jer. 22:27 iand they *d.* to return
Dan. 2:18 *d.* mercies of G. of h.
Amos 5:18 woe to you *d.* day of
Mark 9:35 any *d.* to be first
10:35 for us whatev. we sh. *d.*
11:24 what ye *d.* when ye pray
15:8 *d.* to do as he had done
Acts 28:22 *d.* to hear what think.
1 *Cor.* 14:1 *d.* spiritual gifts
2 *Cor.* 11:12 from them *d.* occas.
Gal. 4:9 *d.* ag. to be in bondage
20 I *d.* to be present with you
21 ye that *d.* to be under law
6:12 as *d.* to make a fair show
Eph. 3:13 I *d.* that ye faint not
Phil. 4:17 not because *d.* a gift
1 *Tim.* 3:1 *d.* office of a bishop
Heb. 6:11 *d.* ev. one of you do
11:16 they *d.* a better country
Jam. 4:2 ye *d.* to have, not obt.
1 *Pet.* 1:12 angels *d.* to look into
2:2 as babes, *d.* the sincere milk
Rev. 9:6 men shall *d.* to die, and

DESIRED.
Gen. 3:6 tree to be *d.* to m. wise
1 *Sam.* 12:13 behold king ye *d.*
1 *K.* 9:19 Solom. *d.* 2 *Chr.* 8:6
Est. 2:13 what. she *d.* was giv.
Job 20:20 not save of that he *d.*
Ps. 19:10 more to be *d.* th. gold
27:4 one thing I *d.* of the Lord
107:30 bringeth to th. *d.* haven

Ps. 132:13 *d.* it for his habitation
14 here dwell for I have *d.* it
Prov. 8:11 *d.* not to be compared
21:20 there is a treasure to be *d.*
Ec. 2:10 what my eyes *d.* I kept
Is. 26:9 with my soul I *d.* thee
Jer. 17:16 neither *d.* woful day
Hos. 6:6 I *d.* mercy, not sacrifice
Zep. 2:1 O nation not *d.*
Mat. 13:17 righte. have *d.* to see
Mark 15:6 one pris. whom th. *d.*
Luke 9:9 and he *d.* to see him
10:24 kings have *d.* to see those
22:31 Satan hath *d.* to sift you
Acts 12:20 they *d.* peace
13:7 Sergius Paulus *d.* to hear
21 afterward they *d.* a king
28 *d.* Pilate he should be slain
16:39 *d.* to depart out of city
25:3 *d.* favor against Paul
1 *Cor.* 16:12 *d.* him to come
1 *John* 5:15 have petitions we *d.*

DESIREDST, EST.
Deut. 18:16 acc. to all thou *d.*
Ps. 51:6 *d.* truth in inw. parts
16 thou *d.* not sacrifice, else
Mat. 18:32 forgave bec. thou *d.*

DESIRES.
Ps. 37:4 give thee *d.* of thy h.
140:8 grant not *d.* of wicked
Eph. 2:3 fulfilling *d.* of the flesh

DESIRETH.
1 *Sam.* 20:4 wh. thy soul *d.* will

2 *Sam.* 3:21 reign over all h. *d.*
Job 7:2 as a serv. *d.* the shadow
23:13 his soul *d.* that he doeth
Ps. 34:12 wh. man is he that *d.*
68:16 hill God *d.* to dwell in
Prov. 12:12 wicked *d.* net of evil
13:4 sluggard *d.* and hath not
21:10 soul of wicked *d.* evil
Ec. 6:2 nothing of all that he *d.*
Luke 5:39 drunk old w. *d.* new
14:32 he *d.* conditions of peace
1 *Tim.* 3:1 bishop, *d.* a good w.

DESIRING.
Mat. 12:46 *d.* to speak with him
20:20 *d.* a certain thing of him
Luke 8:20 breth. *d.* to see thee
2 *Cor.* 5:2 *d.* to be clothed upon
1 *Thes.* 3:6 *d.* greatly to see us
2 *Tim.* 1:4 greatly *d.* to see thee

DESIROUS.
Prov. 23:3 not *d.* of his dainties
Luke 23:8 H. was *d.* to see him
2 *Cor.* 11:32 *d.* to apprehend me
Gal. 5:26 not be *d.* of vain-glory
1 *Thes.* 2:8 affectiona. *d.* of you

DESOLATE.
2 *Sam.* 13:20 Tamar remained *d.*
Job 15:28 dwelleth in *d.* cities
16:7 made *d.* all my company
30:3 wildern. in former times *d.*
38:27 to satisfy the *d.* ground
Ps. 25:16 mercy, for I am *d.*
40:15 be *d.* for a reward
69:25 let their habitation be *d.*
143:4 my heart within me is *d.*
Is. 1:7 your country is *d.*
3:26 she *d.* shall sit on ground
7:19 shall rest all in *d.* valleys
13:22 beasts sh. cry in *d.* houses
24:6 that dwell therein are *d.*
49:8 to inherit *d.* heritages
21 lost my children, and am *d.*
54:1 chil. of *d. Gal.* 4:27
3 *d.* cities to be inhabited
Jer. 2:12 be ye very *d.* saith L.
6:8 lest I make thee *d.* a land
9:11 I will make the cities of J.
d. 10:20 ; 33:10 ; 44:6
10:25 made his habitation *d.*
12:11 and being *d.* it mourneth
19:8 this city *d.* and a hissing
32:43 is *d.* without man, 33:12
49:20 their habitations *d.* 50:45
Lam. 1:13 *d.* all day, 3:11
16 my children are *d.*
4:5 did feed delicately are *d.*
5:18 mount. of Zion which is *d.*
Ezek. 6:6 altars may be made *d.*
19:7 he knew their *d.* palaces
20:26 make them *d.* to the end
35:3 Seir, I will make thee *d.*
15 didst rejoice, bec. it was *d.*
36:3 made you *d.* and swal.
35 *d.* cities are fenced and inh.
36 I the L. plant that was *d.*
Dan. 9:17 to shine on sanct. *d.*
11:31 abomi. th. maketh *d.* 12:11
Hos. 13:16 Sam. shall become *d.*
Joel 1:17 the garners are laid *d.*
18 flocks of sheep are made *d.*
Mic. 1:7 id. thereof will I lay *d.*
6:13 making thee *d.* bec. of sins

Zep. 3:6 their towers are *d.*
Mat. 23:38 is left *d. Luke* 13:35
Acts 1:20 let his habitation be *d.*
1 *Tim.* 5:5 a wid. indeed, and *d.*
Rev. 17:16 and make her *d.*
18:19 in one hour is she made *d.*

Land DESOLATE.
Lev. 26:34 enjoy sab. as long as
it lieth *d.* 35:43 ; 2 *Chr.* 36:21
Is. 6:11 until the *land* be unt. *d.*
13:9 of L. cometh to lay *land d.*
62:4 nor thy *l.* more be term. *d.*
Jer. 4:7 gone to make thy *l. d.*
27 Lord said, whole *l.* sh. be *d.*

7:34 cease mirth for *l*. sh. be *d*.
12:11 whole *land* is made *d*.
18:16 their *l*. *d*. and a hissing
25:38 *l*. is *d*. bec. of his anger
32:43 *l*. whereof ye say, It is *d*.
50:3 nation sh. make her *l*. *d*.
Ezek. 6:14 the *l*. *d*. yea more *d*.
12:19 *l*. may be *d*. fr. all therein
15:8 and I will make the *l*. *d*.
19:7 *land* was *d*. and fulness
29:9 *l*. of E. be *d*. 30:7 ; 32:15
33:29 wh. I have laid *l*. most *d*.
36:34 *d*. *l*. sh. be tilled, it lay *d*.
35 *l*. that was *d*. is like Eden
Joel 2:20 drive him to *a land d*.
Zec. 7:14 laid the pleas. *land d*.

DESOLATE places.

Job 3:14 built *d*. *p*. for thems.
Ps. 109:10 seek bread out of *d*. *p*.
Is. 49:19 thy *d*. *places* be too nar.
59:10 in *d*. *p*. as dead men
Ezek. 6:6 high *p*. shall be *d*.
26:20 set thee in *d*. *p*. of old
38:12 turn thy hand on *d*. *p*.
Amos 7:9 h. *p*. of Isaac sh. be *d*.
Mal. 1:4 ret. and build the *d*. *p*.

**Shall be, or shall be DESO-
LATE.**

Lev. 26:33 your land *shall be d*.
Job 15:34 cong. of hyp. *sh. be d*.
Ps. 34:21 hate righte. *sh. be d*.
22 none th. trust in him *s. be d*.
Is. 5:9 many houses *shall be d*.
15:6 waters of Nimrim *sh. be d*.
Jer. 36:9 this city *s. be d*. with.
33:10 which ye say *shall be d*.
49:2 Rabbah *shall be* a *d*. heap
50:13 Babylon *sh. be* wholly *d*.
51:26 thou *shalt be d*. for ever
Ezek. 6:4 your altars *shall be d*.
29:12 cities of Eg. *shall be d*.
33:28 mountains of Isr. *s. be d*.
35:4 O mount Seir, thou *sh. be d*.
Hos. 5:9 Eph. *shall be d*. in the

DESOLATE wilderness.

Jer. 12:10 pleas. portion a *d. w*.
Joel 2:3 and behind it is a *d. w*.
3:19 and Edom shall be a *d. w*.

DESOLATION.

Lev. 26:32 will br. land into *d*.
2 *K*. 22:19 should become a *d*.
2 *Chr*. 30:7 up to *d*. as ye see
Job 30:14 in *d*. they rolled
Ps. 73:19 how brought into *d*.
Prov. 1:27 fear cometh as *d*.
3:25 be not af. of *d*. of wicked
Is. 17:9 in that day shall be *d*.
24:12 in the city is left *d*.
47:11 *d*. come on thee sud.
51:19 two things are come, *d*.
64:10 Jerusalem a *d*.
Jer. 22:5 this house sh. bec. a *d*.
25:18 Jerus. and Judah a *d*.
44:2 this day they are a *d*.
22 therefore is your land a *d*.
49:13 Bozra a *d*.; 17 Edom a *d*.
50:23 how is Bab. become a *d*.
51:43 her cities are a *d*.
Lam. 3:47 fear is come on us, *d*.
Ezek. 7:27 prince clothed with *d*.
23:33 be filled with cup of *d*.
Dan. 8:13 the transgression of *d*.
Hos. 12:1 Eph. daily inc. *d*.
Joel 3:19 Egypt shall be a *d*.
Mic. 6:16 should make thee *d*.
Zep. 1:15 day of wasten. and *d*.
2:4 Ashkelon be a *d*.; 9 Moab
13 he will make Nineveh a *d*.
14 *d*. shall be in the thresholds
Mat. 12:25 ev. kingd. divided ag.
itself is br. to *d*. *Luke* 11:17
24:15 abom. of *d*. *Mark* 13:14
Luke 21:20 *d*. thereof is nigh

DESOLATIONS.

Ezr. 9:9 to repair *d*. thereof
Ps. 46:8 what *d*. made in earth
74:3 lift up thy feet to perp. *d*.

Is. 61:4 shall raise up former
d. the *d*. of many generat.
Jer. 25:9 these nations perp. *d*.
12 Chaldeans' land perp. *d*..
Ezek. 35:9 m. Seir perpetual *d*.

Dan. 9:2 70 years in *d*. of Jeru.
18 and behold our *d*.
26 to end of war *d*. determined

DESPAIR.

1 *Sam*. 27:1 Saul shi. *d*. of me
Ec. 2:20 to cause my heart to *d*.
2 *Cor*. 4:8 perplexed, not in *d*.

DESPAIRED.

2 *Cor*. 1:8 that we *d*. even of life

DESPERATE, LY.

Job 6:26 speeches of one that is *d*.
Is. 17:11 in the day of *d*. sorrow
Jer. 17:9 the heart is *d*. wicked

DESPISE.

Lev. 26:15 if ye *d*. my statutes
1 *Sam*. 2:30 *d*. me, be lightly est.
2 *Sam*. 19:43 why did ye *d*. us
Est. 1:17 shall *d*. their husb.
Job 5:17 *d*. not chast. Almighty,
Prov. 3:11 ; *Heb*. 12:5
9:21 I would *d*. my life
10:3 who. *d*. work of thy hands
31:13 if *d*. cause of man-servant
Ps. 51:17 contrite h. wilt not *d*.
73:20 thou shalt *d*. their image
102:17 will not *d*. their prayer
Prov. 1:7 but fools *d*. wisdom
6:30 men do not *d*. a thief, if
23:9 a fool will *d*. the wisd. of
22 *d*. not thy mother when old
Is 30:12 because ye *d*. this word
Jer. 4:30 thy lovers will *d*. thee
23:17 say to them that *d*. me
Lam. 1:8 all that honored, *d*. her
Ezek. 28:26 judgm. on all *d*. th.
Amos 5:21 I *d*. your feast-days
Mal. 1:6 O priests, *d*. my name
Mat. 6:24 *d*. the other, *Luke* 16:13
18:10 *d*. not one of these little
Rom. 14:3 *d*. him th. eateth not
1 *Cor*. 11:22 or *d*. ye church of G.
16:11 let no man there. *d*. him
1 *Thes*. 5:20 *d*. not prophesyings
1 *Tim*. 4:12 let none *d*. thy youth
6:2 not *d*. them bec. brethren
Tit. 2:15 let no man *d*. thee
2 *Pet*. 2:10 that *d*. government
Jude 8 *d*. dominion

DESPISED.

Gen. 16:4 mistress *d*. in her eyes
25:34 Esau *d*. his birthright
Lev. 26:43 they *d*. my judgm.
Num. 11:20 ye have *d*. the Lord
14:31 know land ye have *d*.
15:31 bec. he *d*. word of Lord
1 *Sam*. 10:27 they *d*. him
2 *Sam*. 6:16 *d*. him in her heart
2 *K*. 19:21 daughter of Zion hath
d. thee, *Is*. 37:22
2 *Chr*. 36:16 mocked, *d*. his words
Neh. 4:4 hear, O G. for we are *d*.
Job 12:5 is as a lamp *d*. of him
19:18 yea, young children *d*. me
Ps. 22:6 I am *d*. of peo. *Is*. 53:3
24 not *d*. affliction of afflicted
53:5 because God hath *d*. them
106:24 they *d*. pleasant land
119:141 I am small and *d*. yet
Prov. 1:30 they *d*. all my reproof
5:12 my heart *d*. reproof
12:8 he of perverse heart be *d*.
9 he that is *d*. and hath a serv.
Ec. 9:16 poor man's wisd. is *d*.
Cant. 8:1 yet, I should not be *d*.
Is. 5:24 *d*. word of H. O. of Israel
33:8 he hath *d*. the cities
53:3 he is *d*. and rej. of men, *d*.
60:14 that *d*. thee shall bow
Jer. 22:28 Con. a *d*. broken idol ?
33:24 they have *d*. my people
49:15 make thee *d*. among men

Lam. 2:6 hath *d*. in indignation
Ezek. 16:59 which hast *d*. the
oath, 17:16, 18, 19
20:13 *d*. my judgments, 16
22:8 hast *d*. my holy things
Amos 2:4 bec. they *d*. law of L.
Ob. 2 thou art greatly *d*.
Zec. 4:10 *d*. day of small things
Mal. 1:6 wherein *d*. we thy n. ?
Luke 18:9 righte. and *d*. others
Acts 19:27 temple of Diana be *d*.
1 *Cor*. 1:28 things *d*. God chosen
4:10 ye honorable, we are *d*.
Gal. 4:14 my tempta. ye *d*. not
Heb. 10:28 that *d*. Moses' law
Jam. 2:6 but ye have *d*. the poor

DESPISERS.

Acts 13:41 behold, ye *d*. wonder
2 *Tim*. 3:3 fierce, *d*. of those good

DESPISEST, ETH, ING.

Job 36:5 behold, God *d*. not any
Ps. 69:33 L. *d*. not his prisoners
Prov. 11:12 void of wisdom *d*.
13:13 *d*. word shall be destroyed
Prov. 14:2 perv. in ways, *d*. him
21 *d*. his neighbor sinneth
15:5 fool *d*. father's instruction
20 foolish man *d*. his mother
32 refuseth instruction *d*. soul
19:16 that *d*. his ways shall die
30:17 eye that *d*. to obey mother
Is. 33:15 *d*. gain of oppressions
49:7 to him whom man *d*.
Luke 10:16 *d*. you *d*. me ; *d*. me *d*.
Rom. 2:4 *d*. riches of his goodn.
1 *Thes*. 4:8 that *d*. *d*. not man
Heb. 12:2 cross *d*. the shame

DESPITE.

Ezek. 25:6 thy *d*. against Judah
Het 10:29 done *d*. to Sp. of gr.

DESPITEFUL, LY.

Ezek. 25:15 veng. with a *d*. heart
36:5 with *d*. minds
Mat. 5:44 *d*. use you, *Luke* 6:28
Acts 14:5 assault to use them *d*.
Rom. 1:30 haters of God *d*.

DESTITUTE.

Gen. 24:27 not left *d*. my master
Ps. 102:17 regard prayer of *d*.
141:8 leave not my soul *d*.
Prov. 15:21 to him *d*. of wisdom
Ezek. 32:15 *d*. of which it was
1 *Tim*. 6:5 men *d*. of the truth
Heb. 11:37 being *d*. afflicted,
Jam. 2:15 if a bro. or sister be *d*.

DESTROY.

Gen. 18:23 *d*. right. wi. wicked ?
28 *d*. all city for lack of five ?
19:13 we will *d*. this place
Deut. 6:15 lest anger of Lord *d*.
7:24 *d*. name from un. heaven
9:14 let me alone, I may *d*.
31:3 he will *d*. these nations
32:25 *d*. young man and virgin
33:27 shall say, *d*. them
2 *Sam*. 14:7 we will *d*. heir also
16 would *d*. me and my son
20:20 far be it fr. me I should *d*.
22:41 *d*. th. hate me, *Ps*. 18:40
2 *K*. 10:19 *d*. worship. of Baal
18:25 go ag. this land and *d*.
Ezr. 6:12 *d*. kings put to hand
Job 8:18 if *d*. him fr. his place
10:8 yet thou dost *d*. me
19:26 worms *d*. this body
Ps. 5:6 *d*. them speak leasing
10 *d*. thou them, O God
21:10 their fruit shalt thou *d*.
28:5 he shall *d*. not build up
52:5 likewise *d*. thee for ever
55:9 *d*. and divide their tongues
69:4 would *d*. me are mighty
74:8 Let us *d*. them together
143:12 *d*. all afflict my soul
144:6 shoot arrows, *d*. them
145:20 all wicked will he *d*.

Prov. 1:32 prosp. of fools *d.* th.
11:3 perverseness of transgr. *d.*
15:25 L. will *d.* house of proud
21:7 robberies shall *d.* them
Ec. 5:6 *d.* work of thy hands ?
7:16 why shouldest *d.* thyself ?
Is. 3:12 *d.* way of thy paths
11:9 ner *d.* in holy mount. 65:25
13:9 shall *d.* sinners thereof
25:7 *d.* in this mount. the face
Jer. 5:10 go upon walls, and *d.*
6:5 by night *d.* her palaces.
12:17 I will *d.* that nation
13:14 I will not spare, but *d.*
15:6 stretch my hand, and *d.*
17:18 *d.* with double destruct.
23:1 pastors that *d.* the sheep
49:9 I'f thieves. they will *d.*
Lam. 3:66 persecute and *d.* them
Ezek. 9:8 *d.* all residue of Israel ?
Dan. 8:25 by peace shall he *d.*
9:26 shall *d.* city and sanctuary
11:26 feed on his meat, *d.* him
Ob. 8 *d.* wise men out of Eden ?
Mic. 2:10 polluted, it shall *d.* you
Mat. 12:14 how they might *d.*
him, *Mark* 3:6 ; 11:18
21:41 *d.* those wicked men
27:20 ask Barab. and *d.* Jesus
Mark 12:9 *d.* husband. *Lu.* 20:16
John 2:19 J. said, *d.* this temple
Acts 6:14 this Jesus *d.* this place
1 *Cor.* 6:13 *d.* both it and them
2 *Thes.* 2:8 shall *d.* with brightn.
Heb. 2:14 *d.* him had power
1 *John* 3:8 might *d.* works of *d.*
Rev. 11:18 *d.* th. wh. *d.* the earth

I will, *or* **will I DESTROY.**
Gen. 6:7 *I will d.* man whom I
Ex. 23:27 *I will d.* the people
Ps. 101:8 *I will* early *d.* wicked
118:10 in n. of L. *d.* them, 11, 12
Is. 19:3 *I will d.* counsel thereof
42:14 *I will d.* and dev. at once

Jer. 15:7 *I will d.* my people
Ezek. 25:7 *I will d.* thee, 28:16 ;
Zep. 2:5
30:13 saith Lord *I will d.* idols
Amos 9:8 *I will d.* sinf. kingdom
Mark 14:58 *I will d.* this temple
1 *Cor.* 1:19 *I will d.* wisd. of wise

Not DESTROY.
Gen. 18:31 not *d.* it for 20's sake
Deut. 4:31 not fors. thee, nor *d.*
9:26 *d. not* thy people
10:10 Lord would *not d.* thee
1 *Sam.* 24:21 not *d.* my name
2 *K.* 8:19 n. *d.* Jud. for Dav. sake
13:23 would *not d.* them, nor
2 *Chr.* 12:12 *not d.* him. altog.
21:7 *not d.* the house of David
35:21 forbear Fr. G. he *d. not*
Ps. 106:34 did *not d.* nations
Is. 65:8 *d.* it *not,* bless. is in it
Dan. 2:24 *d.* n. wise men of Ba.
Rom. 14:20 *d.* n. work of God

To DESTROY.
Gen. 19:13 hath sent us *to d.* it
Deut. 9:19 was wroth *to d.* you
28:63 L. will rejoice *to d.* you
1 *Sam.* 26:15 came one *to d.* ki.
2 *Sam.* 1:14 not af. *to d.* anoint.
20:19 *to d.* city and c. mother
24:16 hand on Jerusa. *to d.* i
1 *Chr.* 21:15 angel *to* Jeru. *to d.*
2 *Chr.* 25:16 determin. *to d.* thee
Est. 3:6 *to d.* all the Jews, 13 ;
4:7, 8 ; 9:34
Job 2:3 *to d.* him without cause
6:9 it would p. God *to d.* me
Ps. 40:14 seek soul *to d.* it, 63:9
119:95 wicked waited *to d.* me
Is. 10:7 it is in his heart *to d.*
13:5 they come from far *to d.*
23:11 Lord given a com. *to d.*
32:7 wicked devices *to d.* poor

51:13 as if oppressor ready *to d.*
54:16 created the waster *to d.*
Jer. 1:10 set *to d.* 18:7 ; 31:28
51:11 device ag. Baby. *to d.* it
Ezek. 22:27 *to d.* souls, to get
25:15 despiteful heart *to d.* it
Dan. 2:12 *to d.* wise of Bab. 24
7:26 *to d.* his domin. unto end
11:44 go forth with fury *to d.*
Hos. 11:9 not return *to d.* Eph
Zec. 12:9 seek *to d.* all nations
Mat. 2:13 Herod seek child *to d.*
5:17 not come *to d.* but to fulfil
10:28 fear him, able *to d.* both
26:61 I am able *to d.* temple
Mark 1:24 art thou come *to d.*
Luke 6:9 to save life or *d.* it ?
9:56 not come *to d.* men's lives
19:47 chief sought *to d.* him
John 10:10 thief cometh *to d.*
Jam. 4:12 one lawgiver able *to d.*

DESTROYED.
Gen. 19:29 *d.* cities of plain
Ex. 10:7 knowest not E. is *d.* ?
Deut. 2:21 *d.* them bef. them, 4:3 ;
11:4 ; 2 *K.* 21:9 ; 2 *Chr.* 33:9
9:8 Lord angry to have *d.* you
28:20 until thou be *d.* 24, 45
Jud. 20:21 Ben. *d.* that day, 25
2 *Sam.* 21:5 devised we sh. be *d.*
21:16 angel that *d.* 1 *Chr.* 21:15
2 *K.* 10:28 thus Jehu *d.* Baal
2 *Chr.* 14:13 were *d.* before Lord
15:6 nation was *d.* of nation
Ezr. 4:15 which cause city *d.*
Job 19:10 *d.* me on every side
Ps. 9:5 thou hast *d.* the wicked
73:27 *d.* all that go a whoring
137:8 O daugh. Bab. to be *d.*
Prov. 13:23 *d.* for want of judg.
Is. 14:20 because *d.* thy land
26:14 theref. hast thou *d.* them
Jer. 12:10 many pastors have *d.*
48:4 Moab ; 51:8 Babylon is *d.*
51:55 hath *d.* out of Babylon the
Lam. 2:5 *d.* his strong-holds
Ezek. 27:32 like *d.* in the sea
Hos. 13:9 O Israel, *d.* thyself
Amos 2:9 yet *d.* I the Am. I *d.*
Mat. 22:7 he *d.* those murderers
Luke 17:27 flood came, and *d.*
Acts 9:21 *d.* them that called
13:19 *d.* seven nations in Can.
19:27 her magnificence be *d.*
Rom. 6:6 body of sin might be *d.*
1 *Cor.* 10:9 *d.* of serpents
Gal. 1:23 preacheth faith he *d.*
2:18 if I build again things I *d.*
Heb. 11:28 lest he *d.* first-born
2 *Pet.* 2:12 beasts made to be *d.*
Jude 5 *d.* them that believed not

Are DESTROYED.
Job 4:20 *are d.* from morn. to n
34:25 so that they *are d.*

Is. 9:16 they led of them *are d.*
Jer. 22:20 thy lovers *are d.*
Hos. 4:6 a. for lack of knowl.
Zep. 3:6 their cities *are d.*

Not DESTROYED.
2 *Chr.* 26:10 *d.* th. n. *Ps.* 78:38
Dan. 7:14 his kingdom *not* bed.
2 *Cor.* 4:9 cast down, but *not d.*

Shall be DESTROYED.
Gen. 34:30 I *shall be d.* I and
Est. 4:14 father's house *s. be d.*
Ps. 37:38 transgressors *sh. be d.*
92:7 they *s. be d.* forever
Prov. 13:13 des. word *s. be d.*
20 companion of fools *s. be d.*
29:1 hardeneth his neck *s. be d.*
Is. 10:27 yoke *shall be d.* bec.
Jer. 48:8 the plain *shall be d.*
Ezek. 30:8 her helpers *s. be d.*
Dan. 2:44 *sh.* never *be d.* 6:26
11:20 within few days *s. be d.*

Hos. 10:8 the sin of Is. *sh. be d.*
Acts 3:23 will not hear *s. be d.*
1 *Cor.* 15:26 last ene. that *s. be d.*

Utterly DESTROYED.
Deut. 4:26 shall be *u. d.*
Is. 34:2 L. hath *ut. d.* all nations

DESTROYER.
Ex. 12:23 *d.* come into houses
Jud. 16:24 the *d.* of our country
Job 15:21 in prosperity *d.* come
Ps. 17:4 kept from paths of *d.*
Prov. 28:24 is companion of a *d.*
Jer. 4:7 *d.* of Gentiles is
1 *Cor.* 10:10 were destroyed of *d.*

DESTROYERS.
Job 33:22 life draweth near to *d.*
Is. 49:19 thy *d.* go forth of thee
Jer. 22:7 prepare *d.* against thee
50:11 O *d.* of my heritage

DESTROYEST, ETH.
Deut. 8:20 as nat. which L. *d.*
Job 9:22 he is *d.* perfect and wick.
12:23 incr. nat. and *d.* them
14:19 thou *d.* hope of man
Prov. 6:32 doeth it, *d.* own soul
11:9 with mouth *d.* neighbor
31:3 thy ways to that *d.* kings
Ec. 7:7 and a gift *d.* the heart
9:18 one sinner *d.* much good
Jer. 51:25 O mountain, *d.* earth
Mat. 27:40 *d.* temple, *Mark* 15:29

DESTROYING.
1 *Chr.* 21:15 as he was *d.* L. rep.
Is. 28:2 strong one, as *d.* storm
Jer. 2:30 sword like a *d.* lion
51:1 a *d.* wind ; 25 O *d.* mount.
Lam. 2:8. not withd. hand fr. *d.*
Ezek. 9:1 *d.* weapon in his hand
20:17 eye spared from *d.* them

See **UTTERLY.**

DESTRUCTION.
Deut. 7:23 with a mighty *d.*
32:24 devoured with bitter *d.*
1 *Sam.* 5:9 ag. city with great *d.*
11 was a deadly *d.* thro. city
1 *K.* 20:42 appointed to utter *d.*
2 *Chr.* 22:4 counsellors to his *d*
7 *d.* of Ahaziah was of God
26:16 heart lifted up to his *d.*
Est. 8:6 to see *d.* of my kindred
Job 5:21 neither be afraid of *d.*
22 *d.* and famine shalt laugh
18:12 *d.* sh. be ready at his side
21:17 how oft cometh *d.*
20 his eyes shall see his *d.*
30 wicked reserved to day of *d.*
26:6 *d.* hath no covering
28:22 *d.* and death say, We
30:12 ag. me ways of their *d.*
24 though they cry in his *d.*
31:3 is not *d.* to the wicked ?
12 a fire that consumeth to *d.*
23 *d.* from God terror to me
29 if I rejoiced at the *d.* of him
Ps. 35:8 let *d.* come unawares,
into that very *d.* let him fall
55:23 shalt bring to pit of *d.*
73:18 castedst th. down into *d.*
88:11 faithfuln. declared in *d.*
90:3 thou turnest man to *d.*
91:6 *d.* that wasteth at noon-d.
103:4 redeemeth thy life fr. *d.*
Prov. 1:27 your *d.* as a whirlw.
10:14 mouth of foolish near *d.*
15 *d.* ot the poor is poverty
29 *d.* to workers of iniq. 21:15
13:3 wide his lips shall have *d.*
14:28 want of people is *d.* of
15:11 hell and *d.* are bef. Lord
16:18 pride goeth before *d.*
17:19 exalteth gate seeketh *d.*
18:7 a fool's mouth is his *d.*
12 before *d.* heart is haughty

Prov. 24:2 for their heart stu. *d.*
27:20 hell and *d.* are never full
31:8 such as are appointed to *d.*
Is. 1:28 of transgr. together
10 25 answer cease in their *d.*
13:6 as *d.* from the Almighty
14:23 Bab. with bosom of *d.*
15:5 shall raise up a cry of *d.*
19:18 shall be called city of *d.*
24:12 gate is smitten with *d.*
49:19 land of thy *d.* too narrow
51:19 desol. and *d.* are come
59:7 wast. and *d.* are in th. paths
60.18 *d.* no more be heard in
Jer. 4:6 from north a gr. *d.* 6:1
20 *d.* upon *d.* is cried, for
17:18 dest. th. with double *d.*
46:20 *d.* cometh out of north
48:3 a voice, spoiling and *d.* 5
50:22 sound of gr. *d.* in land
Lam. 2:11 *d.* of dau. of my p. 3:48
3:47 and *d.* is come upon us
4:10 in *d.* of daugh of my peo.
Ezek. 7:25 *d.* cometh, seek peace
Hos. 7:13 *d.* to them, transgr.
9:6 are gone, because of *d.*
13:14 O grave, I will be thy *d.*
Joel 1:15 as *d.* from Almighty
Ob. 12 neither rej. in their *d.*
Mic. 2:10 dest. you with sore *d.*
Zec. 14:11 be no more utter *d.*
Mat. 7:13 br. is way lead. to *d.*
Rom. 3:16 *d.* and mis. in ways
9:22 ves. of wrath fitted to *d.*
1 *Cor.* 5:5 Satan for *d.* of flesh
2 *Cor.* 10:8 not for your *d.* 13:10
Phil. 3:19 walk, whose end is *d.*
1 *Thes.* 5:3 then sud. *d.* cometh
2 *Thes.* 1:9 pun. with everlas. *d.*
1 *Tim.* 6:9 drown men in *d.*
2 *Pet.* 2:1 and bring swift *d.*
3:16 unstable wrest to own *d.*

DESTRUCTIONS.
Ps. 9:6 *d.* come to perp. end
35:17 rescue my soul from *d.*
107:20 delivereth from their *d.*

DETAIN, ED.
Jud. 13:16 *d.* me I will not eat
1 *Sam.* 21:7 D. was that day *d.*

DETERMINATE.
Acts 2:23 *d.* counsel of God

DETERMINATION.
Zep. 3:8 *d.* is to gather nations

DETERMINED.
1 *Sam.* 20:7 be sure evil is *d.*
25:17 evil is *d.* ag. our master
2 *Sam.* 13:32 by Absal. been *d.*
2 *Chr.* 25:16 *d.* to destroy thee
Est. 7:7 evil *d.* against him
Job 14:5 seeing his days are *d.*
Is. 19:17 counsel he hath *d.*
Dan. 9:24 seventy weeks are *d.*
11:36 that is *d.* shall be done
Luke 22:22 goeth, as it was *d.*
Acts 3:13 Pil. *d.* to let him go
4:28 what thy counsel *d.* bef.
11:29 ev. man *d.* to send relief
15:2 *d.* Paul and B. to go to Je.
37 Barn. *d.* to take John
17:26 *d.* times to be appointed
19:39 be *d.* in a lawful assembly
25:25 *d.* to send him to August.
1 *Cor.* 2:2 I *d.* not to know sa. J.
2 *Cor.* 2:1 I *d.* this with myself

DETEST.
Deut. 7:26 thou shalt utterly *d.* it

DETESTABLE things.
Ezek. 11:18 shall take away *d.* t.
21 heart walk. after their *d.* th.
37:23 no more defile with *d.* t.

DEVICE.
2 *Chr.* 2:14 to find out every *d.*
Est. 9:25 *d.* return on his head
Ps. 21:11 imag. mischievous *d.*
140:8 further not his wicked *d.*

Ec. 9:10 no work nor *d.*
Jer. 18:11 I devise a *d.* ag. you
51:11 his *d.* is ag. Bab. to dest.
Lam. 3:62 their *d.* ag. me all *d.*
Acts 17:29 graven by man's *d.*

DEVICES.
Job 5:12 disappoint. *d.* of crafty
21:27 *d.* ye wrongfully imagine
Ps. 10:2 let them be taken in *d.*
33:10 *d.* of people of none effect
37:7 bringeth wicked *d.* to pass
Prov. 1:31 be filled with own *d.*
12:2 of wicked *d.* will he cond.
19:21 many *d.* in a man's heart
Is. 32:7 wicked *d.* to dest. poor
Jer. 11:19 had devised *d.* ag. me
18:12 walk after our own *d.*
18 let us devise *d.* ag. Jeremi.
Dan. 11:24 shall forecast his *d.*
2 *Cor.* 2:11 not ignorant of his *d.*

DEVIL.
Mat. 4:1 to be tempted of the *d.*
9:32 man poss. with *d.* 12:22
11:18 he hath a *d. Luke* 7:33
13:39 that sowed them is the *d.*
15:22 is vexed with a *d.*
17:18 Jesus rebuked the *d.*
25:41 fire, prepared for the *d.*
Mark 5:15 poss. with *d.* 16, 18
7:29 *d.* is gone out of thy dau.
Luke 4:2 forty days tempt. of *d.*
13 when *d.* had ended tempt.
33 a spirit of an unclean *d.*
35 *d.* had thrown him
8:12 *d.* taketh away the word
29 driven of *d.* into wilderness
9:42 the *d.* threw him down
11:14 when the *d.* was gone out
John 6:70 and one of you is a *d.*
7:20 said, Thou hast a *d.* 8:48
8.44 ye are of your father the *d.*
49 I have not a *d.* ; 52 hast a *d.*
10:20 many said, He hath a *d.*
21 words of him that hath a *d.*
13:2 *d.* having put into Judas
Acts 10:38 heal. all oppr. with *d.*
13:10 thou child of the *d.*
Eph. 4:27 neither give pla. to *d.*
6.11 to stand aga. wiles of *d.*
1 *Tim.* 3 6 fall into cond. of *d.*
7 lest he fall into snare of *d.*
2 *Tim.* 2:26 rec. out of sna. of *d.*
Heb. 2:14 p. of death, that is *d.*
Jam. 4:7 resist *d.* and he will fl.
1 *Pet.* 5:8 your adversary the *d.*
1 *John* 3:8 commit. sin is of *d.*
might destroy works of *d.*
10 children of *d.* are manifest
Jude 9 Mich. contend. with *d.*
Rev. 2:10 *d.* cast some into pris.
12:9 old serpent called the *d.*
12 *d.* is come down
20:2 old serpent which is the *d.*
10 *d.* that deceived, was c. out

DEVILISH.
Jam. 3:15 this wisd. earthly, *d.*

DEVILS.
Lev. 17:7 no more of. sac. to *d.*
Deut. 32:17 they sacrified to *d.*
2 *Chr.* 11:15 ordained prie. f. *d.*
Ps. 106:37 sacrificed sons to *d.*
Mat. 4:24 poss. with *d.* 8:16, 28,
33 ; *Mark* 1:32 ; *Luke* 8:36
8:31 the *d.* besought, *Mark* 5:12
Mark 9:38 saw one casting out
d. in thy name, *Luke* 9:49
16:17 in my name cast out *d.*
Luke 4:41 *d.* came out of many
8:2 out of whom went seven *d.*
36 by what means he pos. of *d.*
9:1 authority over all *d.*
10:17 even *d.* are subject to us
13:32 tell that fox, I cast out *d.*

---

1 *Cor.* 10:20 Gent. sacrifice to *d.* I
wo. not ye have fel. with *d.*
21 the cup of *d.* of the Lord's
table, and of the table of *d.*
1 *Tim.* 4:1 heed to doctr. of *d.*
Jam. 2:19 *d.* believe and tremble
Rev. 9:20 should not worship *d.*
16:14 the spirits of *d.* working
18:2 become habitation of *d.*

See CAST.

DEVISE.
2 *Sam.* 14:14 *d.* means that ban.
Ps. 35:4 confusion, *d.* my hurt
20 *d.* deceitful matters ag. th.
41:7 ag. me do they *d.* my hurt
Prov. 3:29 *d.* not evil ag. neigh.
14:22 that *d.* evil? but mercy
and truth be to them *d.* good
16:30 shutteth eyes to *d.* frow.
Jer. 18:11 *d.* a device against you
18 let us *d.* devices ag. Jerem.
Ezek. 11:2 men that *d.* mischief
Mic. 2:1 woe to them *d.* iniquity
3 ag. this fam. do I *d.* an evil

DEVISED.
2 *Sam.* 21:5 that *d.* against us
1 *K.* 12:33 month which he *d.*
Est. 8:3 device he had *d.* ag. J.
Ps. 31:13 *d.* to take my life
Jer. 11:19 *d.* devices against me
51:12 *d.* and done, *Lam.* 2:17
2 *Pet.* 1:16 cunningly *d.* fables

DEVISETH.
Ps. 36:4 *d.* mischief on his bed
52:2 thy tongue *d.* mischiefs
Prov. 6:14 *d.* mischief contin.
18 *d.* wicked imaginations
16:9 a man's heart *d.* his way
24:8 *d.* evil be called mischievous
Is. 32:7 he *d.* wicked devices to
8 the liberal *d.* liberal things

DEVOTED.
Lev. 27:28 *d.* thing is most holy
Num. 18:14 every thing *d.*
Ps. 119:38 *d.* is *d.* to thy fear

DEVOTIONS.
Acts 17:23 as I beheld your *d.*

DEVOUR.
Gen. 49:27 in morning *d.* prey
Deut. 32:42 sword shall *d.* flesh
2 *Sam.* 2:26 sh. sw. *d.* for ever ?
Job 18:13 first-born of death *d.*
Ps. 80:13 wild beast doth *d.* it
Is. 1:7 land, strangers *d.* it
9:12 *d.* Israel with open mouth
18 wickedness sh. *d.* briers
31:8 sword, not of mean man *d.*
42:14 destroy and *d.* at once
56:9 ye beasts of the field, come
to *d. Jer.* 12:9 ; 15:3
Jer. 2:3 all *d.* Israel shall offend
12:12 sw. of L. shall *d.* 46:10, 14
30:16 all that *d.* thee be dev.
Ezek. 36:14 shalt *d.* men no mo.
Dan. 7:5 *d.* much flesh
23 *d.* the whole earth
Hos. 5:7 month *d.* with portions
13:8 will I *d.* them like a lion
Amos 1:4 fire *d.* palaces, 7, 10, 12
Ob. 18 kindle in them, and *d.*
Nah. 2:13 sw. *d.* the young lions
Hab. 3:14 rejoic. to *d.* the poor
Zec. 12:6 *d.* all people ·
Mat. 23:14 ye *d.* widows' houses,
Mark 12:40 ; *Luke* 20:47
2 *Cor.* 11:20 if a man *d.* you
Gal. 5:15 if bite and *d.* one ano.
Heb. 10:27 shall *d.* adversaries
1 *Pet.* 5:8 seeking wh. he may *d.*
Rev. 12:4 to *d.* her child as soon

Fire DEVOUR.
Jud. 9:15 let *fire d.* the cedars
20 let *fire d.* the men of Shec.

Ps. 21:9 the *fire* shall *d.* them
50:8 a *fire* shall *d.* before him
Is. 26:11 *f.* of enemies *d.* them
33:11 your breath as *fire d.* you
Ezek. 15:7 another *fire d.* them
23:37 through the *fire* to *d.*
Amos 5:6 break out like *f., d.* it
Nah. 3:13 *fire* shall *d.* thy bars
Zec. 11:1 *fire* may *d.* thy cedars

It shall DEVOUR.

Job 18:13 i. *s. d.* strength of skin
Is. 10:17 *it shall d.* his thorns
Jer. 5:14 fire, *it s. d.* them
17:27 and *it shall d.* the palaces
  of Jerusalem, *Amos* 2:5
Hos. 8:14 *it s. d. Amos* 1:14 ; 2:2

DEVOURED.

Gen. 37:20 some evil beast *d.* h.
Lev. 10:2 fire from Lord *d.* them
Num. 26:10 fire *d.* 250 men
Deut. 31:17 hide face shall be *d.*
  32:24 be *d.* with burning heat
2 *Sam.* 18:8 wood *d.* more than
  22:9 his mouth *d. Ps.* 18:8
Ps. 79:7 for they have *d.* Jacob
Is. 1:20 be *d.* with the sword
  24:6 therefore curse *d.* earth
Jer. 2:30 your sword *d.* prophets
  3:24 shame hath *d.* the labor
  8:16 and have *d.* the land
  10:25 eaten up Jacob, *d.* him
  30:16 devour thee shall be *d.*
  50:7 all that found *d.* them
  17 the king of Assyr. hath *d.*
  51:34 Nebuchadnezzar *d.* me
Lam. 4:11 hath *d.* found. thereof
Ezek. 15:5 when fire hath *d.* it
  16:20 sacrificed sons to be *d.*
  19:3 to catch prey, it *d.* men, 6
  14 fire hath *d.* her fruit
  22:25 a roaring lion, *d.* souls
  23:25 the residue be *d.* by fire
  33:27 I will give to be *d.* 39:4
Dan. 7:7 it *d.* and brake, 19
Hos. 7:7 have *d.* their judges
  9 strangers have *d.* his streng.
Joel 1:19 fire *d.* pastures, 20
Amos 4:9 palmer worm *d.* trees
  7:4 and it *d.* the great deep
Nah. 1:10 shall be *d.* as stubble
Zep. 1:18 be *d.* by jealousy
  3:8 earth shall be *d.* with fire
Zec. 9:4 shall be *d.* with fire
Mat. 13:4 fowls came *d.* them,
  Mark 4:4 ; *Luke* 8:5
Rev. 20:9 fire came and *d.* them

DEVOURER.

Mal. 3:11 I will rebuke the *d.*

DEVOUREST, ETH.

Ezek. 36:13 thou land *d.* up men
2 *Sam.* 11:25 sword *d.* one
Prov. 19:28 wicked *d.* iniquity

Prov. 20:25 a snare to man *d.*
Is. 5:24 fire *d.* stubble, *Joel* 2:5
Lam. 2:3 flaming fire, which *d.*
Ezek. 15:4 fire *d.* both ends of it
Joel 2:3 a fire *d.* before them
Hab. 1:13 wicked *d.* more right
Rev. 11:5 fire *d.* their enemies

DEVOURING.

Ex. 24:17 appearance *d.* fire
Ps. 52:4 lovest all *d.* words
Is. 29:6 visit. with *d.* fire, 30:30
  30:27 his tongue as a *d.* fire
  33:14 who dwell with *d.* fire?

DEVOUT.

Luke 2:25 Sim. was just and *d.*
Acts 2:5 at Jerusal. Jews *d.* men
  8:2 *d.* men car. Steph, to burial
  10:2 Cornelius ; 7 *d.* soldier
  13:50 Jews stirred up *d.* women
  17:4 of *d.* Greeks a great mult.
  17 P. disputed with *d.* persons
  22:12 Ananias a *d.* man

DEW.

Gen. 27:28 G. give thee of the *d.*
Ex. 16:13 morning the *d.* lay
Num. 11:9 when *d.* fell on camp
Deut. 32:2 my speech distil as *d.*
  33:13 blessed is J.'s land for *d.*
  28 his heavens shall drop *d.*
Jud. 6:37 if *d.* on fleece only
  39 on ground let there be *d.*
2 *Sam.* 1:21 be no *d.* upon you
  17:12 light on him as *d.* falleth
1 *K.* 17:1 there shall not be *d.*
Job 29:19 *d.* lay on my branch
  38:28 hath begot drops of *d.?*
Ps. 110:3 hast *d.* of thy youth
  133:3 as the *d.* of thy Hermon
Prov. 3:20 clouds drop down *d.*
  19:12 but his favor is as *d.*
Cant. 5:2 head is filled with *d.*
Is. 18:4 cloud of *d.* in harvest
  26:19 thy *d.* as *d.* of herbs
Dan. 4:33 body wet with *d.* 5:21
Hos. 6:4 early *d.* it goeth, 13:3
  14:5 I will be as the *d.* to Israel
Mic. 5:7 Jacob shall be as the *d.*
Hag. 1:10 heaven stayed from *d.*
Zec. 8:12 heavens give their *a.*

DIADEM.

Job 29:14 my judgment as a *d.*
Is. 28:5 and for a *d.* of beauty
  62:3 a royal *d.* in hand of God
Ezek. 21:26 remove the *d.*

DIAL.

2 *K.* 20:11 down in the *d. Is.* 38:8

DIAMOND.

Ex. 28:18 second row a *d.* 39:11
Jer. 17:1 sin is written with a *d.*

DIANA. *Acts* 19:24, 35
DIBON. *Num.* 21:30 ; *Jos.* 13:17 ;
  Neh. 11:25 ; *Is.* 15:2 ; *Jer.*
  48:18, 22
DIBON-GAD. *Num.* 33:45, 46

Neh. 2:16 knew not what I *d.*
Mat. 12:3 read what David *d.?*
  21:15 wond. things that he *d.*
Mark 3:8 great things he *d.*
John 4:29 told me all ever I *d.* 39
  9:26 said, What *d.* he to thee?
  15:24 works none other man *d.*
Acts 3:17 ye *d.* it as *d.* rulers
  26:10 which thing I *d.* in Jerus.
2 *Cor.* 8:5 *d.* not as we hoped
1 *Pet.* 2:22 who *d.* no sin, nor

DID, joined with as.

Ex. 7:6 *d. as* L. com. 10, 20:
  12:28, 50 ; 39:32 ; *Lev.* 8:4:
  16:34 ; 24:23 ; *Num.* 1:54:
  2:34 ; 20:27 ; 27:22 : 31:31
Jud. 15:11 as they *d.* to me
2 *Sam.* 3:36 *as* what king *d.*
  5:25 David *d. as* L. commanded
2 *K.* 17:41 as *d.* fathers, so do
1 *Chr.* 11:16 David *d. as* G. com.
Mat. 21:6 *d. as* Jesus com. 26:19
  28:15 so watch *d. as.,* taught
Luke 9:54 con. them *as* Elias *d.*
Acts 3:17 ignor. *as d.* your rulers
  7:51 *as* your fathers *d.* so do ye
Heb. 4:10 ceased, *as* God *d.*

DID, joined with evil.

Gen. 50:15 he req. us *evil* we *d.*
Jud. 2:11 *d. evil* in sight of L.
  3:7, 12 ; 4:1 ; 6:1 ; 10:6 ; 13:1 :
  1 *K.* 14:22 ; 15:26, 34 ; 16:7, 30 :
  2 *K.* 8:27 ; 13:2, 11 ; 14:24 :
  15:9, 18, 24, 28 ; 17:2 ; 2 *Chr.*
  22:4
1 *K.* 11:6 Solomon *d. evil*
2 *K.* 21:2 Manasseh, 2 *Chr.* 33:2
  23:32 Jehoahaz ; 37 Jehoiakim
  24:9 Jehoiachin ; 19 Zedekiah
2 *Chr.* 12:14 Rehob. ; 33:22 Amon
Neh. 9:28 had rest, they *d. evil*
Is. 65:12 *d. evil* bef. m. eyes, 66:4
2 *Tim.* 4:14 Alex. *d.* me much *e.*

DID not.

2 *K.* 16:2 Ahaz *d. not* right
Jer. 11:8 but they *d.* them *not*
Mat. 13:58 he *d. not* many works
  25:45 *d.* it *not* to one of these
John 8:40 this *d. not* Abraham
2 *Cor.* 7:12 I *d.* it *not* for his cau.

Thus DID.

Job 1:5 thus *d.* Job continually

DIDST.

2 *Sam.* 12:12 thou *d.* it secretly
Ps. 39:9 dumb, because thou *d.*
  44:1 work thou *d.* in their days
Is. 64:3 *d.* terrible things

DIDYMUS.

John 11:16 T. cal. D. 20:24 ; 21:2

DIE.

See on DEAD and DEATH.

Gen. 6:17 every thing shall *d.*
  44:22 his father would *d.*
  46:30 now let me *d.*
  47:29 that Israel must *d.*
Ex. 9:4 nothing *d.* of Israel's
  10:28 seest my face, shalt *d.*
  11:5 first-born in Egypt shall *d.*
Num. 14:35 in wilder. they sh. *d.*
  16:29 if these *d.* common death
  20:26 and Aaron shall *d.* there
  23:10 let me *d.* death of right.
Deut. 25:5 if one *d.* and have no
  children, *Mark* 12:19
  31:14 days approach th. must *d.*
  32:50 and *d.* in the mount
Jud. 16:30 let me *d.* with Phil.
1 *Sam.* 2:33 increase of house *d.*
  34 sons in one day shall *d.*
  14:45 said, Shall Jonathan *d.*
2 *Sam.* 18:3 nor if half of us *d.*
1 *K.* 14:12 feet enter child sha. *d.*
2 *K.* 20:1 shalt *d.* and not live
2 *Chr.* 25:4 every man shall *d.* for
  his own sin, *Jer.* 31:30
Job 2:9 said, Curse God and *d.*
  4:21 they *d.* without wisdom
  12:2 wisdom shall *d.* with you
  14:8 and the stock thereof *d.*
  14 if man *d.* shall he live ag.
  34:20 in a moment shall they *d.*
  36:12 shall *d.* without knowl.
  14 they *d.* in youth, their life
Ps. 49:10 seeth that wise men *d.*
  104:29 aw. their breath, they *d.*
Prov. 10:21 fools *d.* for want of
Ec. 7:17 *d.* before thy time
  9:5 living know they shall *d.*
Is. 22:18 large country, there *d.*
  51:6 that dwell therein shall *d.*
  12 afraid of a man that shall *d.*
  65:20 child shall *d.* 100 years old
Jer. 11:22 youn. man shall *d.* by
  sw. sons and dau. by famine
  16:4 shall *d.* of grievous deaths
  6 great and the small shall *d.*
  28:16 this year thou shalt *d.*
  34:5 but thou shalt *d.* in peace
Ezek. 18:4 soul sin. shall *d.* 20
  28:8 *d.* deaths of them slain
  33:8 that wicked man shall *d.*
  27 in caves *d.* of the pestilence
Amos 2:2 Moab shall *d.*
  6:9 they shall *d.*
  7:17 shalt *d.* in a polluted land
  9:10 sinners of my people *d.*
Zec. 11:9 that dieth, let it *d.*
  13:8 two parts be cut off and *d.*
Mat. 15:4 curs. father or mother
  let him *d. Mark* 7:10
  22:24 *d.* hav. no s. *Luke* 20:28
Luke 20:36 nei. can *d.* any more
John 4:49 come ere my child *d.*
  11:50 one *d.* for the peo. 18:14
  51 J. should *d.* for that nation
  12:24 except a corn of wheat *d.*
Rom. 5:7 for a r. man will one *d.*
1 *Cor.* 15:22 as in Adam all *d.*
  36 not quickened except it *d.*

Heb. 7:8 that *d.* receive tithes
Rev. 14:13 blessed that *d.* in L.

He DIE.

Gen. 38:11 lest *he d.* as bre. did
Num. 35:16 if he smite him that
    he d. 20, 21, 23 ; *Deut.* 13:10 ;
    19:5, 11 ; 21:21
Deut. 20:5 lest *he d.* in battle
Jud. 6:30 bring son, that *he d.*
2 *Sam.* 11:15 that Uriah may *d.*
1 *K.* 1:52 if wick. in h*i*m *he* sh. *d.*
2:1 David, that *he* should *d.*
19:4 E. requested he might *d.*
Ps. 41:5 when shall *he d.* and
Prov. 5:23 *he d.* without instruc.
15:10 *he* that hateth rep. shall *d.*

Prov. 19:16 he de. his ways sh. *d.*
Jer. 22:12 *he d.* whither led cap.
38:10 take up Jer. before *he d.*
Ezek. 3:19 *he* shall *d.* in his iniq.
    18:18 ; 33:9, 13, 18
12:13 not see it, though *he d.*
17:16 in Babylon *he* shall *d.*
John 12:33 death *he* sh. *d.* 18:32

I DIE.

Gen. 26:9 Lest *I die.* for her
27:4 may bless thee before *I d.*
30:1 give me children or *I d.*
45:28 see him before *I d.*
48:21 Israel said to Joseph, *I d.*
50:5 lo, *I d.* ; 24 Jos. said, *I d.*
Deut. 4:22 *I* must *d.* in this land
Jud. 15:18 shall *I d.* for thirst
Ruth 1:17 where diest will *I d.*
1 *Sam.* 14:43 and lo, *I* must *d.*
2 *Sam.* 19:37 *I d.* in n. own city
1 *K.* 2:30 nay, *I* will *d.* here
Job 27:5 justify you ; till *I d.*
29:18 *I* shall *d.* in my nest
Prov. 30:7 deny me not bef. *I d.*
Jer. 37:20 not return, lest *I d.*
Mat. 26:35 *I* sh. *d. Mark* 14:31
1 *Cor.* 15:31 *I d.* daily

Not DIE.

Gen. 42:20 be verified *not d.*
Deut. 18:16 see fire, that *I d. not*
33:6 let Reuben live and *not d.*
Jud. 6:23 shalt *not d.* 1 *Sam.* 20:2 ;
    2 *Sa.* 12:13 ; 19:23 ; *Jer.* 38:24
1 *Sam.* 12:19 pray that we *d. not*
20:14 kind. of Lord that I *d. not*
2 *K.* 18:32 ye may live and *not d.*
2 *Chr.* 25:4 fath. *n. d.* for child.
Ps. 118:17 I shall *n. d.* but live
Prov. 23:13 shalt *n. d. Ezek.* 18:17,
    21, 28 ; 33:15 ; *John* 21:23
Is. 51:14 he should *not d.*
66:24 their worm shall *not d.*
Jer. 11:21 *d. not* by our hand
34:4 shalt *not d.* by the sword
Ezek. 13:19 souls should *not d.*
Hab. 1:12 we shall *not d.* Lord
John 6:50 eat thereof and *not d.*
21:23 that disciple should *not d.*

Surely DIE.

Gen. 2:17 *s. d.* 20:7 ; 1 *Sam.* 14:44 ;
    22:16 ; 1 *K.* 2:37, 42 ; *Jer.* 26:8 ;
    Ezek. 3:18 ; 33:8, 14
3:4 ye shall not *surely d.*
Num. 26:65 they shall *surely d.*
Jud. 13:22 *s. d.* bec. we ha. seen
1 *Sam.* 14:39 he shall *s. d.* 20:31 ;
    2 *Sam.* 12:5 ; 2 *K.* 8:10 ; *Ezek.*
    18:13
2 *Sam.* 12:14 child born shall *s. d.*
2 *K.* 1:4 but shalt *surely d.* 6, 16

To DIE.

Gen. 25:32 I am at point *to d.*
Ex. 14:11 *to d.* in wil. *Num.* 21:5
Num. 35:30 test. to cau. him *to d.*
1 *Sam.* 26:10 or his day co. *to d.*
28:9 a snare to cause me *to d.*
2 *Chr.* 32:11 give yoursel. *to d.*
Ps. 79:11 that are appointed *to d.*
88:15 and ready *to d.* from youth

Ec. 3:2 born, and a time *to d.*
Jer. 26:11 worthy *to d.* ; 16 not
38:9 he is like *to d.* for hunger
26 to Jonathan's house *to d.*
Jon. 4:3 better for me *to d.*
8 Jonah wished in himself *to d.*
Luke 7:2 centu. serv. ready *to d.*
John 19:7 by law he ought *to d.*
Acts 21:13 I am ready also *to d.*
25:11 I refuse not *to d.*
16 of Romans to del. any *to d.*
Rom. 5:7 some would dare *to d.*
1 *Cor.* 9:15 better for me *to d.*
2 *Cor.* 7:3 in our hearts *to d.*
Phil. 1:21 to live is C *to d.* is
Heb. 9:27 app. to men once *to d.*
Rev. 3:2 that are ready *to d.*
9:6 desire *to d.* and death flee

We DIE.

Gen. 47:15 we *d.* in thy pres. 19
Ex. 14:12 than we sh. *d.* in wil.
20:19 speak lest *we d. Deut.* 5:25
Num. 17:12 *we d.* we all perish
20:4 that *we* and cattle *d.* there
1 *Sam.* 12:19 pray that *we d.* not
2 *Sam.* 14:14 for *we* must needs *d.*
1 *K.* 17:12 *we* may eat it and *d.*
2 *K.* 7:3 why sit here till *we d.?*
4 if kill us, *we* shall but *d.*
Is. 22:13 for to-morrow *we* sh. *d.*
    1 *Cor.* 15:32
John 11:16 *we* may *d.* with him
Rom. 14:8 *we d.* *we d.* unto the L.

Ye DIE.

Gen. 3:3 nor touch it lest *ye d.*
Ps. 82:7 *ye* shall *d.* like men
Is. 22:14 not be purged till *ye d.*
Jer. 22:26 there shall *ye d.* 42:16
27:13 why will *ye d. Ezek.* 18:31 ;
    33:11
42:22 *ye* shall *d.* by the sword
John 8:21 *ye* sh. *d.* in yo. sins, 24
Rom. 8:13 if live after flesh *ye d.*

DIED.

Gen. 7:21 all flesh *d.* 22
23:2 Sarah *d.* ; 25:8 Abraham
25:17 Ishmael ; 35:8 Deborah
35:18 Rachel, 48:7 ; 35:29 Isaac
50:16 Jacob ; 26 Jos. *Ex.* 1:6
Ex. 2:23 the king of Egypt *d.*
16:3 would to God we had *d.* in
    Eg. *Num.* 14:2 ; 20:3 ; 26:10
Lev. 10:2 Nad. and Ab. *d.* 16:1 ;
    Num. 3:4 ; 26:61 ; 1 *Chr.* 24:2
Num. 14:37 searchers of land *d.*
20:28 Aaron *d.* 33:38, 39'
16:49 now they that *d.* besides
20:1 Miriam ; 21:6 much peo.
25:9 *d.* in the plague were 24,000
26:11 children of Korah *d.* not
27:3 our father *d.* in the wilder-
    ness but *d.* in his own sin
Deut. 34:5 Moses *d.*
Jos. 5:4 all the men of war *d.*
24:29 Joshua *d. Jud.* 2:8
1 *Sam.* 25:1 Sam. : 37 Nab. heart
31:5 Saul and his armor-bearer
    d. 6 ; 1 *Chr.* 10:5, 13
2 *Sam.* 3:33 *d.* Abner as a fool
6:7 there Uzzah *d.* 1 *Chr.* 13:10
11:17 Uriah the Hittite *d.*
12:18 on seventh day child *d.*
18:33 I had *d.* for thee, O Ab.
19:6 and all we had *d.* this day
24:15 *d.* of peo. even from Dan
1 *K.* 3:19 this woman's child *d.*
14:17 came to threshold, child *d.*
2 *K.* 4:20 sat on her knees, *d.*
13:14 Elisha. 20 ; 24 Haz el
2 *Chr.* 24:22 he *d.* said. L. look
Job 3:11 why *d.* I not fr. womb?
42:17 so Job *d.* being old
Is. 6:1 Uzziah *d.* ; 14:28 Ahaz *d.*
Ezek. 24:18 at even my wife *d.*
Hos. 13:1 offended in Baal, he *d.*

Mat. 22:27 last of all woman *d.*
Mark 12:22 ; *Luke* 20:32
Luke 16:22 beggar *d.* rich man *d.*
John 11:21 my bro. had not *d.* 32
37 even this man sh. not ha. *d.*
Acts 9:37 Dorcas was sick and *d.*
Rom. 5:6 in due time Christ *d.* 8
7:9 sin revived and I *d.*
8:34 it is Christ that *d.*
14:9 to this end Christ both *d.*
15 for whom C. *d.* 1 *Cor.* 8:11
1 *Cor.* 15:3 how C. *d.* for our sins
2 *Cor.* 5:14 if one *d.* for all, then
15 live to him who *d.* for them
1 *Thes.* 4:14 if we believe Jesus *d.*
5:10 *d.* for us, that we sho. live
Heb. 10:28 desp. Moses' law *d.*
11:13 these all *d.* in faith, not
22 by faith Joseph when he *d.*
Rev. 8:9 the third part *d.*
11 many men *d.* of wa. bitter
16:3 every living soul *d.* in sea

And he, So he, That he DIED.

Gen. 5:5 *and* Adam *d.*
Jud. 4:21 nail into tem. *so he d.*
1 *Sam.* 4:18 E. neck bra. *a. he d.*
14:45 rescued Jon. *th. he d.* not
2 *Sam.* 11:21 sm. Abim. *th. he d.*
2 *K.* 1:17 Ahaziah *d.* according
8:15 cl. on his face. *so th. he d.*
2 *Chr.* 13:20 struck him, *a. he d.*
Luke 20:29 *a. he d.* without chil.
Acts 7:15 *he d.* in Egypt, he and
Rom. 6:10 in *th. he d. he d.* to
2 *Cor.* 5:15 *t. he d.* for all, th. they

DIEST.

Ruth 1:17 wh. thou *d.* I will die

DIET.

Jer. 52:34 for his *d.* continual *d.*

DIETH.

Lev. 22:8 wh. *d.* of itself, not eat
2 *Sam.* 3:33 died A. as a fool *d.*
1 *K.* 14:11 him *d.* in city dogs eat
16:4 *d.* in field fowls eat, 21:24
Job 14:10 man *d.* wasteth away
14:14 if a man *d.* shall he live?
21:23 one *d.* in his full strength
    25 *d.* in bitterness of soul
Ps. 49:17 when he *d.* carry noth.
Prov. 11:7 wicked *d.* his expect.
Ec. 2:16 how *d.* the wise man?
3:19 as one *d.* so *d.* the other
Is. 50:2 their fish *d.* for thirst
59:5 that eateth of their eggs *d.*
Ezek. 18:26 iniquity. *d.* in them
32 no pleas. in death of him *d.*
Zec. 11:9 that *d.* let it die
Mark 9:44 worm *d.* not, 46, 48
Rom. 6:9 Christ *d.* no more
14:7 no man *d.* to himself

DYING.

Num. 17:13 be consumed wi. *d. ?*
Mark 12:20 first *d.* left no seed
Luke 8:42 Jairus' dau. lay a *d.*
2 *Cor.* 4:10 in body the *d.* of Jesus
6:9 as *d.* and behold we live
Heb. 11:21 by faith Jac. when *a.*

DIFFER.

1 *Cor.* 4:7 who maketh thee to *d.*

DIFFERENCE, S.

Ex. 11:7 L. put *d.* b. Eg. and Is.
Lev. 10:10 *d.* bet. holy and unh.
Ezek. 22:26 they have put no *d.*
44:23 teach my people the *d.*
Acts 15:9 no *d.* bet. us and them
Rom. 3:22 their believe, for no *d.*
10:12 no *d.* bet. Jew and Greek
1 *Cor.* 12:5 *d.* of administrations
Jude 22 compassion, making a *d.*

DIFFERETH, ING.

Rom. 12:6 gifts *d.* acc. to grace
1 *Cor.* 15:41 one star *d.* from ano.
Gal. 4:1 the heir when a child *d.*

DIG.

Job 3:21 *d.* for it more than for
6:27 ye *d.* a pit for your friend
11:18 thou shalt *d.* about thee
24:16 in dark *d.* thro' houses
Ezek. 8:8 *d.* now in the wall
12:5 *d.* thro' wall in their sight
Amos 9:2 tho' they *d.* into hell
Luke 13:8 let it alone till I *d.*
16:3 I cannot *d.*

DIGGED.

Gen. 49:6 in self-will *d.* down
50:5 my grave I have *d.* for me
Num. 21:18 princes *d.* the well
Deut. 6:11 wells *d.* diggedst not
2 *K.* 19:24 I have *d.* and drunk
strange waters, *Is.* 37:25
Ps. 7:15 a pit and *d.* it, 57:6
35:7 they *d.* a pit for my soul
94:13 till pit be *d.* for wicked
119:85 proud *d.* pits for me
Is. 5:6 not be pruned nor *d.*
7:25 on hills *d.* with mattock
51:1 hole of pit whence ye are *d.*
Jer. 18:20 *d.* pit for my soul, 22
Mat. 21:33 *d.* a wine-press in it
25:18 *d.* and hid lord's money
Luke 6:48 *d.* and laid foundation
Rom. 11:3 *d.* down thine altars

DIGGETH.

Prov. 16:27 ungodly *d.* up evil
26:27 *d.* pit shall fall, *Ec.* 10:8

DIGNITY, IES.

Gen. 49:3 Reu. excellency of *d.*
Est. 6:3 what *d.* to Mordecai
Ec. 10:6 folly is set in great *d.*
Hab. 1:7 *d.* proceed of themsel.
2 *Pet.* 2:10 sp. evil of *d. Jude* 8

DILIGENCE.

Prov. 4:23 keep heart with all *d.*
Luke 12:58 art in way, give *d.*
Rom. 12:8 that ruleth, with *d.*
2 *Cor.* 8:7 as ye abound in all *d.*
3 *Tim.* 4:9 do thy *d.* to come, 21
Heb. 6:11 ev. one do sh. same *d.*
2 *Pet.* 1:5 giv. all *d.* add to faith
10 *d.* to make calling sure
Jude 3 I gave all *d.* to write

DILIGENT.

Deut. 19:18 make *d.* inquisition
Jos. 22:5 take *d.* heed to do com.
Ps. 64:6 accomplish a *d.* search
77:6 my spirit made *d.* search
Prov. 10:4 hand of *d.* mak. rich
12:24 hand of *d.* shall bear rule
27 substance of *d.* is precious
13:4 soul of *d.* sh. be made fat
21:5 thoughts of *d.* tend to pl.
22:29 seest a man *d.* in busi.
27:23 be *d.* to know state of fl.
2 *Cor.* 8:22 whom we have often
proved *d.* how much more *d.*
2 *Pet.* 3:14 *d.* ye be fou. in peace

DILIGENTLY.

Ex. 15:26 if wilt *d.* heark. *Deut.*
11:13 ; 28:1 ; *Jer.* 17:24
Deut. 4:9 and keep thy soul *d.*
6:7 teach them *d.* to thy child.
17 *d.* keep commandm. 11:22
13:14 ask *d.* and if it be truth
Ezr. 7:23 *d.* done for house of G.
Job 13:17 hear *d.* my sp. 21:2
Ps. 37:10 *d.* consider his place
119:4 to keep thy precepts *d.*
Prov. 7:15 *d.* to seek thy face
11:27 he that *d.* seeketh good
23:1 consider *d.* what is before
Is. 21:7 he hearkened *d.*
55:2 hearken *d.* to, me, and eat
Jer. 2:10 consider *d.* see if
12:16 *d.* learn ways of my peo.
Zec. 6:15 if *d.* obey voice of L.
Mat. 2:8 search *d.* for yo. child
16 *d.* inquired of the wise men
Luke 15:8 seek *d.* till she find it

Acts 18:25 taught *d.* things of L.
1 *Tim.* 5:10 she followed *d.* every
2 *Tim.* 1:17 in Ro. sought me *d.*
Heb. 11:6 rew. of them *d.* seek
12:15 looking *d.* lest any fail
1 *Pet.* 1:10 prophets searched *d.*

DIM.

Gen. 27:1 Is. was old, his eyes *d.*
48:10 the eyes of Israel were *d.*
Deut. 34:7 Moses' eye was not *d.*
1 *Sam.* 3:2 Eli's eyes wax *d.* 4:15
Job 17:7 mine eye is *d.* by sorrow
Is. 32:3 that see, shall not be *d.*
Lam. 4:1 how is gold become *d.*
5:17 these things our eyes *d.*

DIMINISH, ED, ING.

Ex. 5:8 you shall not *d.* aught
Lev. 25:16 acc. to years shalt *d.*
Deut. 4:2 nor *d.* aught, 12:32
Prov. 13:11 w. got. by vanity *d.*
Is. 21:17 men of Kedar sh. be *d.*
Jer. 26:2 I com.*d.* not a word
29:6 may be inc. and not *d.*
Ezek. 5:11 therefore also *d.* thee
16:27 I have *d.* thine ordi. food
29:15 I will *d.* them
Rom. 11:12 *d.* of them the riches

DIMNESS.

Is. 8:22 behold, *d.* of anguish
9:1 *d.* not be such as in her

DIMON. *Is.* 15:9
DINAH. *Gen.* 30:21 ; 34:5

DINE, D.

Gen. 43:16 *d.* with me at noon
Luke 11:37 Pha. bes. him to *d.*
John 21:12 J. saith, Come and *d.*
15 had *d.* Jesus saith to Simon

DINNER.

Prov. 15:17 better is a *d.* of herbs
Mat. 22:4 I have prepared my *d.*
Luke 11:38 not washed before *d.*
14:12 when thou makest a *d.*

DIONYSIUS. *Acts* 17:34
DIOTREPHES. 3 *John* 9

DIP.

Deut. 33:24 Asher *d.* foot in oil
Ruth 2:14 *d.* morsel in vinegar
Luke 16:24 that he may *d.* finger

DIPPED, ETH.

Gen. 37:31 *d.* coat in the blood
Lev. 9:9 and he *d.* finger in bl.
Jos. 3:15 priest's feet *d.* in brim
1 *Sam.* 14:27 *d.* rod in honey-co.
2 *K.* 5:14 Naaman *d.* in Jordan
Ps. 68:23 thy foot be *d.* in blood
Mat. 26:23 *d.* wi. me, *Mark* 14:20
John 13:26 have *d.* it, when he *d.*
Rev. 19:13 with vesture *d.* in bl.

DIRECT.

Gen. 46:28 *d.* his face to Goshen
Ps. 5:3 morning *d.* my prayer
Prov. 3:6 he shall *d.* thy paths
11:5 righte. of the perf. shall *d.*
Ec. 10:10 wisd. is profitable to *d.*
Is. 45:13 I will *d.* all his ways
61:8 *d.* their work in truth
Jer. 10:23 to *d.* his steps
1 *Thes.* 3:11 J. C. *d.* our way to
2 *Thes.* 3:5 L. *d.* hearts into love

DIRECTED, ETH.

Job 32:14 not *d.* his words aga.
37:3 *d.* it under whole heaven
Ps. 119:5 ways were *d.* to keep
Prov. 16:9 the Lord *d.* his steps
21:29 upright, he *d.* his way
Is. 40:13 who hath *d.* the Spirit

DIRT.

Jud. 3:22 and the *d.* came out
Ps. 18:42 I cast them out as *d.*
Is. 57:20 whose waters cast up *d.*

DISALLOW, ED.

Num. 30:5 father *d.* her not, 8, 11

---

1 *Pet.* 2:4 *d.* indeed of men, but
7 stone builders *d.* is made h.

DISANNUL.

Job 40:8 wilt thou *d.* my judg. ?
Is. 14:27 L. purposed, who *d.* it ?
Gal. 3:17 coven. law cannot *d.*

DISANNULLED, ETH, ING.

Is. 28:18 coven. with death be *d.*
Gal. 3:15 no man *d.* or addeth
Heb. 7:18 there is a *d.* of com.

DISAPPOINT, ED, ETH.

Job 5:12 *d.* devices of crafty
Ps. 17:13 arise, O Lord, *d.* him
Prov. 15:22 purposes are *d.*

DISCERN.

Gen. 31:32 *d.* thou what is thine
2 *Sam.* 14:17 so is my Lord to *d.*
19:35 can I *d.* bet. good and ev. ?
1 *K.* 3:9 I may *d.* betw. good
11 asked unders. to *d.* judg.
Ezr. 3:13 not *d.* noise of joy
Job 4:16 not *d.* form thereof
6:30 taste *d.* perverse things ?
Ezek. 44:23 cause *d.* bet. uncl.
Jon. 4:11 *d.* bet. right and left
Mal. 3:18 *d.* bet. right. and wick.
Mat. 16:3 can *d.* sky, *Luke* 12:56
Heb. 5:14 senses exer. to *d.* good

DISCERNED, ETH.

1 *K.* 20:41 king of Israel *d.* him
Prov. 7:7 I *d.* among the youths
Ec. 8:5 wise *d.* time and judg.
1 *Cor.* 2:14 because spiritually *d.*

DISCERNER.

Heb. 4:12 is a *d.* of the thoughts

DISCERNING.

1 *Cor.* 11:29 not *d.* the L. body
12:10 to another, *d.* of spirits

DISCHARGE, D.

1 *K.* 5:9 will cause he *d.* there
Ec. 8:8 there is no *d.* in that war

DISCIPLE.

Mat. 10:24 *d.* is not above his
master, *Luke* 6:40
42 give cup of cold water to *d.*
27:57 Joseph also was Jesus' *d.*
John 9:28 art his *d.* we are Mo.
18:16 went out that other *d.*
19:26 *d.* standing by, Je. loved
27 to that *d.* Behold thy mo.
38 being a *d.* but secretly
20:2 *d.* Jesus loved, 21:7, 20
4 the other *d.* did outrun Pet.
8 went in also that other *d.*
21:23 that that *d.* should not die
24 this is the *d.* which testifi.
Acts 9:10 a certain *d.* at Damas.
26 believed not that he was *d.*
36 Joppa a *d.* named Tabitha
21:16 old *d.* with whom lodge

My DISCIPLE.

Luke 14:26 not be *my d.*
27 bear cross cannot be *my d.*
33 fors. not all, not be *my d.*

DISCIPLES.

Mat. 9:14 then came *d.* of John
11:1 end of commanding his *d.*
14:26 when *d.* saw him on sea
17:6 *d.* heard it, fell on th. face
19:13 *d.* reb. them, *Mark* 10:13
20:17 twelve *d.* apart in way
22:16 Pharisees sent their *d.*
26:26 J. took bread, gave to *d.*
35 likewise also said all the *d.*
56 *d.* forsook him and fled
Mark 2:18 why *d.* of John and of
Pharisees fast, *Luke* 5:33
8:14 *d.* forgotten to take bread
Luke 19:37 *d.* began to rejoice
John 3:25 betw. John's *d.* and
4:1 Je. bap. more *d.* that John
9:28 but we are Moses' *d.*
13:5 began to wash the *d.* feet

18:17 art one of this man's *d.?*
20:18 told *d.* she had seen Lord
Acts 9:1 breath. slaughter ag. *d.*
26 Saul assayed to join the *d.*
11:26 *d.* called Christians first
19:1 Ephesus, finding certain *d.*
30 the *d.* suffered him not
20:7 *d.* came to break bread
30 to draw away *d.* after them

His DISCIPLES.
Mat. 8:25 *his d.* awoke him
9:19 Jes. followed, so did *his d.*
28:7 tell *his d.* he is risen
13 say ye, *h. d.* came by night
Luke 5:30 murmur against *h. d.*
6:20 lifted up his eyes on *his d.*
11:1 as John taught *his d.*
John 2:11 *his d.* believed on him
4:2 Jes. baptized not but his *d.*
27 came *his d.* and marvelled
6:22 *his d.* were gone away
9:27 will ye also be *his d.?*
18:1 with *his d.* over Cedron
20:26 again *his d.* were within

Of his DISCIPLES.
Mat. 11:2 sent two *of his d. Mark*
11:1; 14:13; *Luke* 19:29
Mark 7:2 *d.* cat with unw. hands
John 6:66 many *of his d.* went
18:19 high-p. asked J. *of his d.*
25 art not th. also one *of h. d.*
21:12 none *of his d.* durst ask

To his DISCIPLES.
Mat. 14:19 gave loaves *to his d.*
Mark 4:34 expounded all *to h. d.*
Luke 10:23 he turned *to his d.*
John 21.14 showed hims. *to h. d.*

My DISCIPLES.
Is. 8:16 seal law among *my d,*
Mat. 26:18 keep passover with
my d. Mark 14:14; *Luke* 22:11
John 8:31 *my d.* indeed, 13:35
15:8 so shall ye be *my d.*

Thy DISCIPLES.
Mat. 9:14 *t. d.* fast not, *Mark* 2:18
12:2 *thy d.* do what is not lawf.
15:2 *t. d.* transgress tradition?
17:16 *d.* they could not cure
Mark 7:5 walk not *t. d.* accor. to
9:18 *t. d.* to cast him, *Luke* 9:40
Luke 19:39 Master rebuke *thy d.*
John 7:3 *t. d.* see works thou

DISCIPLINE.
Job 36:10 openeth their ears to *d.*

DISCLOSE.
Is. 26:21 earth shall *d.* her blood

DISCOMFITED.
Jos. 10:10 L. *d.* them before Is.
Jud. 4:15 the Lord *d.* Sisera
8:12 Gideon *d.* all the host
1 *Sam.* 7:10 thundered on Ph. *d.*
2 *Sam.* 22:15 *d.* them. *Ps.* 18:14
Is. 31:8 young men shall be *d.*

DISCOMFITURE.
1 *Sam.* 14:20 was a very great *d.*

DISCONTENTED.
2 *Sam.* 22:2 *d.* gathered to David

DISCONTINUE.
Jer. 17:4 *d.* from thy heritage

DISCORD.
Prov. 6:14 he soweth *d.*
19 soweth *d.* among brethren

DISCOVER.
1 *Sam.* 14:8 *d.* ourselves to them
Job 41:13 *d.* face of his garment?
Prov. 18:2 his heart may *d.* itself
25:9 *d.* not a secret to another
Is. 3:17 L. will *d.* th. secret parts
Jer. 13:26 *d.* thy skirts, *Nah.* 3:5
Lam. 4:22 he will *d.* thy sins
Ezek. 16:37 I will *d.* thy nakedn.
Hos. 2:10 will I *d.* her lewdness

Mic. 1:6 I will *d.* the foundations

DISCOVERED.
1 *Sam.* 14:11 *d.* thems. to garri.
22:6 Saul heard David was *d.*
2 *Sam.* 22:16 foundations of the
world were *d. Ps.* 18:15
Is. 22:8 he *d.* covering of Judah
57:8 hast *d.* thyself to another
Jer. 13:22 thy skirts *d.*
Lam. 2:14 not *d.* thine iniquity
Ezek. 13:14 foundat. shall be *d.*
16:36 nakedness *d.* thro' whor.
57 before thy wickedn. was *d.*
21:24 that your transgr. are *d.*
22:10 *d.* their father's nakedn.
23:10 these *d.* her nakedness
Hos. 7:1 iniq. of Ephraim was *d.*

DISCOVERETH, ING.
Job 12:22 he *d.* deep things out
Ps. 29:9 voice of Lord *d.* forests
Hab. 3:13 *d.* foundation to neck

DISCOURAGE, D.
Num. 21:4 soul of people was *d.*
32:7 why *d.* heart of people? 9
Deut. 1:21 fear not, nor be *d.*
28 brethren have *d.* our heart
Is. 42:4 shall not fail nor be *d.*
Col. 3:21 children, lest they be *d.*

DISCREET.
Gen. 41:39 none so *d.* and wise
Tit. 2:5 teach yo. women to be *d.*

DISCREETLY.
Mark 12:34 Jesus saw he ans. *d.*

DISCRETION.
Ps. 112:5 guide affairs with *d.*
Prov. 1:4 to the young man *d.*
2:11 *d.* shall preserve thee
3:21 keep wisdom and *d.*
5:2 thou mayest regard *d.*
11:22 a fair woman without *d.*
19:11 *d.* deferreth his anger
Is. 28:26 God instruct him to *d.*
Jer. 10:12 stretched heav. by *d.*

DISDAINED.
1 *Sam.* 17:42 Goliah *d.* David
Job 30:1 fathers I would have *d.*

DISEASE.
2 *K.* 1:2 if I sh. recov. of this *d.*
8:8 shall I recover of this *d.?* 9
2 *Chr.* 16:12 in his *d.* he sought
21:15 have *d.* of thy bowels
18 L. smote him with incur. *d.*
Job 30:18 by *d.* garment changed
Ps. 38:7 filled with loathsome *d.*
41:8 an evil *d.* say they, cleav.
Ec. 6:2 this is vanity, an evil *d.*
Mat. 4:23 healing *d.* 9:35; 10:1
John 5:4 whole of whatsoever *d.*

DISEASES.
Ex. 15:26 none of these *d.*
Deut. 28:60 bring on thee *d.*
2 *Chr.* 21:19 he died of sore *d.*
24:25 they left him in great *d.*
Ps. 103:3 who healeth all thy *d.*
Mat. 4:24 were taken with divers
d. Mark 1:34; *Luke* 4:40
Luke 9:1 gave power to cure *d.*
Acts 19:12 *d.* departed from them
28:9 had *d.* in island, came

DISEASED.
1 *K.* 15:23 Asa was *d.* in his feet
Ezek. 34:4 *d.* not strengthened
21 because ye have pushed *d.*
Mat. 9:20 woman *d.* with issue
14:35 brought all *d. Mark* 1:32
John 6:2 miracles he did on *d.*

DISFIGURE.
Mat. 6:16 hypocrites *d.* faces

DISGRACE.
Jer. 14:21 do not *d.* the throne

DISGUISE, ED, ETH.
1 *Sam.* 28:8 and Saul *d.* himself

1 *K.* 14:2 Jerob. said, *d.* thyself
20:38 one of prophets *d.* himself
22:30 *d.* myself, 2 *Chr.* 18:29
2 *Chr.* 35:22 Josiah *d.* to fight
Job 24:15 adulterer *d.* his face

DISH, ES.
Jud. 5:25 butter in a lordly *d.*
2 *K.* 21:13 as a man wipeth a *d.*
Mat. 26:23 dip. in *d. Mark* 14:20

DISHONEST. See GAIN.

DISHONESTY.
2 *Cor.* 4:2 renounced things of *d.*

DISHONOR.
Ezr. 4:14 to see king's *d.*
Ps. 35:26 clothed with *d.* 71:13
69:19 thou hast known my *d.*
Prov. 6:33 and *d.* shall he get
Rom. 9:21 another vessel to *d.*
1 *Cor.* 15:43 sown in *d.* raised in
2 *Cor.* 6:8 by honor and *d.*
2 *Tim.* 2:20 are vess. some to *d.*

DISHONOR, EST, ETH.
Mic. 7:6 the son *d.* the father
John 8:49 Father, and ye *d.* me
Rom. 1:24 to *d.* their own bodies
2:23 breaking law, *d.* God
1 *Cor.* 11:4 man *d.* head; 5 wom.

DISINHERIT.
Num. 14:12 I will *d.* them

DISMAYED.
Deut. 31:8 nor be *d. Jos.* 1:9; 8:1;
10:25; 1 *Chr.* 22:13; 28:20;
2 *Chr.* 20:15, 17; 32:7
1 *Sam.* 17:11 they were *d.* 2 *K.*
19:26; *Is.* 37:27
Is. 21:3 I was *d.* at seeing of it
41:10 not *d. Jer.* 1:17; 10:2; 23:4·
30:10; 46:27; *Ezek.* 2:6; 3:9
23 that we may be *d.*
Jer. 8:9 the wise men are *d.* 10:2
17:18 let them be *d.* let not me
46:5 have I seen them *d.* and
48:1 M. is *d.;* 49:37 Elam be *d.*
50:36 mighty of Babylon be *d.*
Ob. 9 mighty men shall be *d.*

DISMAYING.
Jer. 48:39 Moab shall be a *d.*

DISMISSED.
Acts 15:30 *d.* they came to Anti
19:41 spoken, he *d.* assembly

DISOBEDIENCE.
Rom. 5:19 by one man's *d.*
2 *Cor.* 10:6 readiness to rev. *d.*
Eph. 2:2 worketh in child. of *d.*
5:6 on children of *d. Col.* 3:6
Heb. 2:2 *d.* received just recom.

DISOBEDIENT.
1 *K.* 13:26 man of G. who was *d.*
Neh. 9:26 they were *d.* rebelled
Luke 1:17 turn *d.* to wis. of just
Acts 26:19 not *d.* to heav. vision
Rom. 1:30 *d.* to par. 2 *Tim.* 3:2
10:21 forth my hands to *d.* peo.
1 *Tim.* 1:9 law was made for *d.*
Tit. 1:16 deny him, being *d.*
3:3 we also were sometimes *d.*
1 *Pet.* 2:7 to them *d.* the stone
8 stumble at word, being *d.*
3:20 which sometime were *d.*

DISOBEYED.
1 *K.* 13:21 as hast *d.* mouth of L.

DISORDERLY.
2 *Thes.* 3:6 withd. from broth. *d.*
2 *Thes.* 3:7 behaved not ours. *d.*
11 some walk among you *d.*

DISPATCH.
Ezek. 23:47 *d.* them with swords

DISPENSATION.
1 *Cor.* 9:17 a *d.* of gospel
Eph. 1:10 *d.* of fulness of times
3:2 heard of *d.* of grace of God
Col. 1:25 minister acc. to *d.* of G.

DISPERSE, ED.
2 Chr. 11:23 Rehob. *d.* of child.
Est. 3:8 certain people *d.* among
Ps. 112:9 he hath *d.* 2 *Cor.* 9:9
Prov. 5:16 let thy fountains be *d.*
15:7 lips of wise *d.* knowledge
. 11:12 gather *d.* of Judah
Izek. 12:15 *d.* them in the coun.
20:23 ; 29:12 ; 30:23, 26
22:15 *d.* thee in the countries
36:19 were *d.* through countries
Zep. 3:10 my *d.* shall bring
John 7:35 will he go to the *d.*
Acts 5:37 obeyed him, were *d.*

DISPERSIONS.
Jer. 25:34 days of *d.* accomp.

DISPLAYED.
Ps. 60:4 ban. that it may be *d.*

DISPLEASE.
Num. 22:34 if it *d.* thee
1 *Sam.* 29:7 *d.* not the lords
2 *Sam.* 11:25 Joab, let not this *d.*
Prov. 24:18 L. see it, it *d.* him

DISPLEASED.
Gen. 48:17 hand on Ephr. it *d.*
Num. 11:1 complained, it *d.* L.
10 Moses also was *d.*
1 *Sam.* 8:6 the thing *d.* Samuel
18:8 saying *d.* Saul, and he said
2 *Sam.* 11:27 th. D. had done, *d.*
1 *K.* 1:6 father had not *d.* him
20:43 went to his house *d.* 21:4
1 *Chr.* 21:7 God was *d.* with this
Ps. 60:1 thou hast been *d.*
Is. 59:15 it *d.* him
Dan. 6:14 king *d.* with himself
Jon. 4:1 it *d.* Jonah exceedingly
Hab. 3:8 Lord *d.* against rivers
Zec. 1:2 L. been *d.* with fathers
15 sore *d.* with heathen at ease,
for I was but a little *d.*
Mat. 21:15 scribes saw, were *d.*
Mark 10:14 Jesus saw it, was *d.*
41 *d.* with James and John
Acts 12:20 Herod highly *d.* with

DISPLEASURE.
Deut. 9:19 I was afraid of hot *d.*
Jud. 15:3 though I do them a *d.*
Ps. 2:5 vex them in his sore *d.*
6:1 chasten me in hot *d.* 38:1

DISPOSED, ING.
Job 34:13 who *d.* whole world ?
37:15 know when God *d.* them
Prov. 16:33 *d.* thereof is of L.
1 *Cor.* 10:27 feast, ye be *d.* to go

DISPOSITION.
Acts 7:53 law by *d.* of angels

DISPOSSESS, ED.
Num. 32:53 shall *d.* the inhabi.
Deut. 7:17 How can I *d.* them ?
Jud. 11:23 God hath *d.* the A.

DISPUTATION, S.
Acts 15:2 had no small *d.*
Rom. 14:1 but not to doubtful *d.*

DISPUTE, ED.
Job 23:7 righteous might *d.*
Mark 9:34 *d.* who sh. be greatest
Acts 9:29 S. *d.* ag. the Grecians
17:17 Paul *d.* in the synagogue
Jude 9 Mich. *d.* about body of M.

DISPUTER.
1 *Cor.* 1:20 where is *d.* of world ?

DISPUTING, S.
Acts 6:9 *d.* with Stephen
15:7 been much *d.* Peter rose
19:8 *d.* and persuading, 9
24:12 they neither found me *d.*
Phil. 2:14 all things without *d.*
1 *Tim.* 6:5 perverse *d.*

DISQUIET, ED, NESS.
1 *Sam.* 28:15 why hast thou *d.*
Ps. 38:8 roared by reason of *d.*
39:6 surely are *d.* in vain

42:5 O my soul, why art thou *d.*
within me ? 11 ; 43:5
Prov. 30:21 earth is *d.*
Jer. 50:34 *d.* inhabitants of Bab.

DISSEMBLED, ETH.
Jos. 7:11 stolen. and *d.* also
Prov. 26:24 he that hateth *d.*
Jer. 42:20 for ye *d.* when ye sent
Gal. 2:13 other Jews *d.* likewise

DISSEMBLERS.
Ps. 26:4 nor will I go in with *d.*

DISSENSION.
Acts 15:2 had no small *d.*
23:7 arose a *d.* between Phari.

DISSIMULATION.
Rom. 12:9 let love be without *d.*
Gal. 2:13 carried away with *d.*

DISSOLVE, ED, EST.
Job 30:22 thou *d.* my substance
Ps. 75:3 inhab. thereof are *d.*
Is. 14:31 thou Palestina art *d.*
24:19 the earth is clean *d.*
34:4 the host of heaven be *d.*
Dan. 5:16 thou canst *d.* doubts
Nah. 2:6 palace shall be *d.*
2 *Cor.* 5:1 house of this taber. *d.*
2 *Pet.* 3:11 all these things be *d.*
12 heavens on fire shall be *d.*

DISTAFF.
Prov. 31:19 her hands hold *d.*

DISTIL.
Deut. 32:2 my speech *d.* as dew
Job 36:28 the clouds *d.* on man

DISTINCTION.
1 *Cor.* 14:7 exc. *d.* in the sounds

DISTINCTLY.
Neh. 8:8 in book of the law *d.*

DISTRACTED, ION.
Ps. 88:15 I suff. thy ter. I am *d.*
1 *Cor.* 7:35 attend without *d.*

DISTRESS, Substantive.
Gen. 35:3 answered me in my *d.*
42:21 therefore is this *d.* come
Jud. 11:7 ye come when in *d.*
1 *Sam.* 22:2 in came to David
2 *Sam.* 22:7 in my *d.* I called on
L. *Ps.* 18:6 ; 118:5 ; 120:1
1 *K.* 1:29 redeemed soul out of *d.*
2 *Chr.* 28:22 in *d.* Ahaz trespass.
Neh. 2:17 ye see the *d.* we are in
9:37 and we are in great *d.*
Ps. 4:1 enlarged me when in *d.*
Prov. 1:27 mock when *d.* cometh
Lam. 1:20 O Lord, for I am in *d.*
Ob. 12 nor spoken proudly in *d.*
14 nor deliv. those in day of *d.*
Zep. 1:15 that day is a day of *d.*
17 I will bring *d.* upon men
Luke 21:23 great *d.* in land
25 on the earth *d.* of nations
Rom. 8:35 love of C. ? shall *d.*
1 *Cor.* 7:26 good for the present *d.*
1 *Thes.* 3:7 comforted in your *d.*

DISTRESS, ED.
Gen. 32:7 Jacob was greatly *d.*
Deut. 2:9 not the Moabites
19 *d.* not the Ammonites
28:53 wherewith *d.* thee, 55, 57
Jud. 2:15 Israel *d.* 10:9
1 *Sam.* 13:6 the people were *d.*
14:24 men of Is. *d.* ; 28:15 Saul
30:6 David *d.* for people spake
2 *Sam.* 1:26 *d.* for thee, Jonathan
2 *Chr.* 28:20 king of Assy. *d.* A.
Is. 29:2 yet I will *d.* Ariel
7 that *d.* her be as a dream
Jer. 10:18 will *d.* the inhabitants
2 *Cor.* 4:8 troubled yet not *d.*

DISTRESSES.
Ps. 25:17 O bring me out of *d.*
107:6 he deliv. them out of *d.*
13 he saved them out of *d.* 19

---

28 bringeth them out of *d.*
Ezek. 30:16 Noph have *d.* daily
2 *Cor.* 6:4 approv. ourselves in *d.*
12:10 I take pleasure in *d.* for

DISTRIBUTE.
Neh. 13:13 their office was to *d.*
Luke 18:22 sell all and *d.* to poor
1 *Tim.* 6:18 rich to be ready to *d.*

DISTRIBUTED, ETH, ING.
Job 21:17 God *d.* sorrows
John 6:11 Je. *d.* to the disciples
Rom. 12:13 *d.* to neces. of saints
1 *Cor.* 7:17 God hath *d.* to every
2 *Cor.* 10:13 ac. to rule G. hath *d.*

DISTRIBUTION.
Acts 4:35 *d.* made to every one
2 *Cor.* 9:13 for your liberal *d.*

DITCH, ES.
3 *K.* 3:16 make valley full of *d.*
Job 9:31 plunge me in the *d.*
Ps. 7:15 fallen into *d.* he made
Prov. 23:27 a whore is a deep *d.*
Is. 22:11 a *d.* between two walls
Mat. 15:14 fall into *d.* *Luke* 6:39

DIVERS, E.
Deut. 22:9 not sow with *d.* seed
11 not wear garment of *d.* sorts
25:13 shalt not have *d.* weights
Deut. 25:11 in house *d.* measures
Jud. 5:30 to S. a prey of *d.* colors
2 *Sam.* 13:18 gar. of *d.* colors, 19
1 *Chr.* 29:2 stones of *d.* colors
2 *Chr.* 30:11 *d.* of Asher humbled
Est. 3:8 their laws *d.* from all
Ps. 78:45 sent *d.* sort of flies
105:31 came *d.* sorts of flies
Prov. 20:10 *d.* weights, *d.* meas.
23 *d.* weights are abomination
Ec. 5:7 there are also *d.* vanities
Ezek. 17:3 a great eagle *d.* colors
Dan. 7:3 beasts *d.* one from ano.
23 *d.* from all kingdoms
Mat. 4:24 sick with *d.* diseases,
Mark 1:34 ; *Luke* 4:40
24:7 earthquakes in *d.* places,
Mark 13:8 ; *Luke* 21:11
Mark 8:3 for *d.* came from far
Acts 19:9 when *d.* were hardened
1 *Cor.* 12:10 *d.* kinds of tongues
2 *Tim.* 3:6 led away with *d.* lusts
Tit. 3:3 serving *d.* lusts and ple.
Heb. 1:1 in *d.* manners spake
2:4 witness with *d.* miracles
9:10 *d.* washings ; 13:9 *d.* doct.
Jam. 1:2 fall into *d.* temptations

DIVERSITIES.
1 *Cor.* 12:4 *d.* of gifts ; 6 opera.
28 set in church *d.* of tongues

DIVIDE.
Gen. 1:6 let firmament *d.* waters
14 be lights to *d.* the day, 18
49:27 at night he shall *d.* spoil
Ex. 14:16 over the sea and *d.* it
26:33 veil shall *d.* between holy
Num. 31:27 *d.* the prey into two
Jos. 1:6 *d.* for inheritance, 18:5
22:8 *d.* the spoil with brethren
2 *Sam.* 19:29 thou and Z. *d.* land
1 *K.* 3:25 *d.* living child, 26
Neh. 9:11 didst *d.* sea, *Ps.* 74:13
22 didst *d.* them into corners
Job 27:17 innocent shall *d.* silver
Ps. 55:9 and *d.* their tongues
Prov. 16:19 to *d.* spoil with proud
Is. 9:3 rejoice when *d.* the spoil
53:12 shall *d.* spoil with strong
Ezek. 5:1 take balances, and *d.*
45:1 *d.* land by lot, 47:21, 22
48:29 this is land ye shall *d.*
Dan. 11:39 he shall *d.* land
Luke 12:13 that he *d.* the inheri.
22:17 *d.* it among yourselves

I will DIVIDE.
Gen. 49:7 *I will d.* them in Jacob

Ex. 15:9 said, *I will d.* spoil
Ps. 60:6 *I will d.* Shech. 108:7
Is. 53:12 *will I d.* him a portion

DIVIDED.

Gen. 1:4 *d.* light; 7 *d.* waters
10:5 were isles of Gentiles *d.*
25 in his days was the earth *d.*
32 nations *d.* after the flood
14:15 Abram *d.* himself ag. them
15:10 *d.* Abram *d.* them in midst
32:7 Jacob *d.* people
Ex. 14:21 the waters were *d.*
Deut. 4:19 which God hath *d.*
32:8 Most High *d.* to nations
Jos. 14:5 they *d.* land, 18:10
Jud. 5:30 *d.* the prey to every
19:29 the Levite *d.* her
2 *Sam.* 1:23 in death were not *d.*
1 *K.* 16:21 were people of Isr. *d.*
K. 6 Ahab and Ob. *d.* the land
2 *K.* 2:8 waters were *d.* hither
Job 38:25 hath *d.* a watercourse
Ps. 68:12 she that tar. *d.* spoil
78:13 he *d.* the sea, and caused
55 *d.* them an inheritance by
line, *Acts* 13:19
136:13 to him which *d.* Red sea
Is. 33:23 prey of great spoil *d.*
34:17 his hand *d.* it by line
51:15 I am the Lord that *d.* sea
Lam. 4:16 anger of Lord *d.* them
Ezek. 37:22 nor be *d.* into two k.
Dan. 2:41 kingdom shall be *d.*
5:28 kingdom *d.* given to M.
11:4 kingdom *d.* toward four w.
Hos. 10:2 their heart is *d.*
Amos 7:17 thy land shall be *d.*
Mic. 2:4 he hath *d.* our fields
Zec. 14:1 spoil be *d.* in midst
Mat. 12:25 house *d.* not stand,
Mark 3:24 ; *Luke* 11:17
Luke 12:52 five in one house *d.*
53 father be divided aga. son
15:12 *d.* unto them his living
Acts 14:4 multi. was *d.* 23:7
1 *Cor.* 1:13 is Christ *d.* ? was P.
Rev. 16:19 city was *d.*

DIVIDER.

Luke 12:14 made me *d.* over you

DIVIDETH.

Job 26:12 *d.* sea with his power
Ps. 29:7 voice of L. *d.* flames
Jer. 31:35 *d.* sea when waves roar.
Mat. 25:32 *d.* his sheep fr. goats
Luke 11:22 and *d.* his spoils

DIVIDING.

Is. 63:12 *d.* water before them
Dan. 7:25 and a *d.* of time
1 *Cor.* 12:11 *d.* to every man
2 *Tim.* 2:15 rightly *d.* the word
Heb. 4:12 to *d.* asunder of joints

DIVINATION, S.

Num. 22:7 rewards of *d.*
23:23 nor any *d.* against Israel
Deut. 18:10 useth *d.* 2 *K.* 17:17
Jer. 14:14 they prophesy *d.*
Ezek. 12:24 nor flattering *d.* in Is.
13:7 not spoken a lying *d.*
23 see no more divine *d.*
21:21 the king of Babylon stood
to use *d.*
Acts 16:16 pos. with spirit of *d.*

DIVINE, Verb.

Gen. 44:15 a man as I can *d.* ?
1 *Sam.* 28:8 *d.* to me by fam. sp.
Ezek. 13:9 prophets that *d.* lies
21:29 while they *d.* a lie
Mic. 3:6 that ye shall not *d.*
11 prophets *d.* for money

DIVINE, Adjective.

Prov. 16:10 *d.* sentence in lips
Heb. 9:1 ordinances of *d.* service
2 *Pet.* 1:3 *d.* power hath given
4 be partakers of *d.* nature

DIVINER, S.

Deut. 18:14 hearkened to *d.*
1 *Sam.* 6:2 Philis. called for *d.*
Is. 44:25 that maketh *d.* mad
Jer. 27:9 hearken not to your *d.*
29:8 let not your *d.* deceive you
Mic. 3:7 and the *d.* confounded
Zec. 10:2 the *d.* have seen a lie

DIVINETH, ING.

Gen. 44:5 this it whereby he *d.* ?
Ezek. 22:28 and *d.* lies to them

DIVISION, S.

Ex. 8:23 put a *d.* between
Jud. 5:15 for *d.* of Reuben, 16
Luke 12:51 nay but rather *d.*
John 7:43 there was a *d.* among
the people, 9:16 ; 10:19
Rom. 16:17 mark them wh. ca. *d.*
1 *Cor.* 1:10 be no *d.* among you
3:3 whereas there is am. you *d.*
11:18 I hear there be *d.* am. you

DIVORCE, ED.

Jer. 3:8 given her a bill of *d.*
Mat. 5:32 shall marry her *d.*

DIVORCEMENT.

Deut. 24:1 write her bill of *d.* 3
Is. 50:1 your mother's *d.* ?
Mark 10:4 M. suffered bill of *d.*

See WRITING.

DO.

Gen. 18:25 Judge of all *d.* right?
31:16 what God hath said, *d.*
41:25 what he is to *d.* 28
Ex. 4:15 teach you what ye sh. *d.*
19:8 all L. hath spok. we will *d.*
Lev. 18:5 if man *d.* he shall live,
Neh. 9:29 ; *Ezek.* 20:11, 13, 21
Num. 22:20 word I say shalt *d.*
24:14 this peo. *d.* to thy people
Deut. 7:11 command. to *d.* them
19:19 *d.* to him as he thought to
27:26 words of law, to *d.* them
30:12 may hear it and *d.* it ? 13
Jos. 7:9 *d.* to thy great name ?
22:24 what have ye to *d.* with L.
23:6 *d.* all written in the law,
1 *Chr.* 16:40 ; 2 *Chr.* 34:21
Jud. 7:17 as I *d.* so shall ye *d.*
8:3 to *d.* in comparison of you ?
10:15 *d.* to us what seem. good
18:18 the priest, What *d.* ye ?
1 *Sam.* 16:3 show thee what *d.*
22:3 what God will *d.* for me
26:25 thou shalt *d.* great things
2 *Sam.* 3:18 now then *d.* it
15:26 *d.* to me as seemeth good
1 *K.* 2:6 *d.* acc. to thy wisdom
8:32 *d.* and judge thy servants.
59 forgive, and *d.* 2 *Chr.* 6:23
11:33 to *d.* right, 38 ; 14:8
2 *K.* 9:18 to *d.* with peace? 19
17:34 *d.* after former manners
20:9 L. will *d.* as he hath spok.
1 *Chr.* 17:2 *d.* all in thy heart
23 and *d.* as thou hast said
21:8 *d.* away iniq. of thy serv.
2 *Chr.* 19:6 take heed what ye *d.*
20:12 nor know we what to *d.*
25:8 if thou wilt go, *d.* it
Ezr. 4:2 we seek God as ye *d.*
7:10 to seek law and to *d.* it
Neh. 2:12 put in my heart to *d.*
9:24 *d.* with them as they
Job 7:20 *d.* to thee ? O Preserver
11:8 high as heav. what *d.* ?
13:20 *d.* not two things to me
Ps. 40:8 I delight to *d.* thy will
50:16 to *d.* to dec. my statutes ?
109:21 but *d.* thou for me
119:132 to *d.* to those
143:10 teach me to *d.* thy will
Prov. 3:27 power of hand to *d.*
Ec. 9:10 *d.* it with thy might
Is. 10:3 *d.* in day of visitation ?
45:7 Lord *d.* all these things

Jer. 5:31 *d.* in the end thereof ?
11:4 obey my voice and *d.* them
14:7 *d.* it for thy name's sake
39:12 *d.* to him as he shall say
42:3 show thing we may *d.*
50:15 hath done, *d.* to her, 29
Lam. 1:22 *d.* to them as they
Ezek. 8:6 seest thou what they *d.*
24:22 ye shall *d.* as I have done
36:37 be inquired of, to *d.* it for
Dan. 9:19 Lord, hearken and *d.*
11:3 *d.* accord. to his will, 16, 36
Hos. 10:3 should king *d.* to us?
Amos 3:7 Lord *d.* nothing
Jon. 4:9 I *d.* well to be angry
Mic. 6:8 but to *d.* justly
Zec. 1:21 what come these to *d.* ?
8:16 these are things ye shall *d.*
Mat. 5:19 shall *d.* and teach
47 what *d.* ye more than oth. ?
8:29 wh. have we to *d.* wi. thee ?
Mark 1:24 ; *Luke* 4:34
12:50 whosoever sh. *d.* the will
of my Father, *Mark* 3:35
20:15 *d.* what I will with own
32 wh. will ye I *d.* *Mark* 10:36
21:27 author. I *d.* these things,
Mark 11:33 ; *Luke* 20:8
23:5 works they *d.*
27:19 to *d.* with that just man
Mark 7:8 such like ye *d.* 13
Luke 4:23 *d.* also in thy country
6:2 why *d.* that not lawful
11 what they might *d.* to Jes.
31 as ye would that men sh. *d.*
8:21 hear word of God and *d.* it
16:4 I am resolved what to *d.*
17:10 done what was duty to *d.*
23:34 know not what they *d.*
John 2:5 whatsoever he saith *d.*
4:34 my meat is to *d.* will
5:30 I can of myself *d.* nothing
6:6 he knew what he would *d.*
28 what shall we *d.* ? *Acts* 2:37
7:17 if any man will *d.* his will
8:29 I *d.* those things please
9:33 of G. he could *d.* nothing
11:47 Pharisees said, What *d.* ?
13:7 what I *d.* knowest not
15 ye shall *d.* as I have done
17 happy are ye if ye *d.* them
14:12 works I *d.* shall he *d.* also
14 ask in my name, I will *d.* it
15:14 if ye *d.* what I command
21 will they *d.* unto you, 16:3
17:4 work thou gavest me to *d.*
21:21 what shall this man *d.* ?
Acts 1:1 of all Jesus began to *d.*
4:28 *d.* whatsoever thy counsel
9:6 what wilt thou have me *d.* ?
10:6 what thou oughtest to *d.*
14:15 why *d.* ye these things?
Rom. 1:32 not only *d.* the same
2:14 *d.* by nature things in law
7:15 for what I *d.* I allow not,
but what I hate, that *d.* I
1 *Cor.* 7:36 let him *d.* what he
10:31 ye *d.* all to glory of God
2 *Cor.* 8:10 not only to *d.* but
Gal. 3:10 writ. in law to *d.* them
5:21 *d.* such shall not inherit
Eph. 6:21 know and how I *d.*
Phil. 2:13 G. worketh both to *d.*
4:9 heard and seen in me, *d.*
Col. 3:17 whatsoe. ye *d.* in word
or deed, *d.* all in na. of L. J.
23 whats. ye *d.* *d.* it heartily
1 *Thes.* 4:10 ye *d.* it tow. breth.
5:11 edify, even as also ye *d.*
24 faithful who also will *d.* it
2 *Thes.* 3:4 ye both *d.* and will *d.*
Phile. 21 wilt *d.* more than I say
Heb. 4:13 whom we have to *d.*
10:7 lo, I come to *d.* thy will, 9
13:6 not fear what man shall *d.*
21 perfect to *d.* his will
2 *Pet.* 1:10 if ye *d.* these, never

1 *John* 3:22 and *d.* those things
Rev. 2:5 and *d.* the first works

Can, *or* canst DO.

Job 22:17 what *can* Almighty *d.*
Job 42:2 thou c. *d.* every thing
Ps. 11:3 *can* the righteous *d.?*
56:4 fear what flesh *can d.* 11
118:6 not fear what man *can d.*
Mark 9:22 if *canst d.* anything
Luke 12:4 no more they *can d.*
John 5:19 Son *can d.* nothing, 30
15:5 without me ye *can d.* noth.
Phil. 4:13 I *can d.* all through C.

See DO COMMANDMENTS.

DO, *with evil.*

Ex. 23:2 not fol. a mult. to *d. e.*
Lev. 5:4 soul swear to *d. evil*
Deut. 31:29 bec. ye will *d. evil*
2 *Sam.* 12:9 despised L. to *d. e.*
2 *K.* 8:12 *evil* thou wilt *d.*
17:17 sold themselves to *d. evil*
21:9 Man. seduced to *d.* more *e.*
Ps. 34:16 face ag. them *d. evil*
37:8 fret not thyself to *d. evil*
Prov. 2:14 who rejoice to *d. evil*
24:8 he that deviseth to *d. evil*
Ec. 5:1 consider not they *d. evil*
8:11 fully set in them to *d. evil*
12 a sinner *d. evil* 100 times
Is. 1:16 wash ye, cease to *d. evil*
41:23 *d.* good or *evil* that we
Jer. 4:22 people are wise to *d. e.*
10:5 for they cannot *d. evil*
13:23 accustomed to *d. evil*
18:10 if it *d. evil* in my sight
Ezek. 6:10 I would *d.* this *evil*
Mic. 7:3 *d. evil* with both hands
Zep. 1:12 nor will he *d. evil*
Mark 3:4 to *d. evil?* *Luke* 6:9
Rom. 3:8 *d. evil* that good come
13:4 if thou *d. evil* be afraid
2 *Cor.* 13:7 I pray that ye *d.* no *e.*
1 *Pet.* 3:12 against them that *d. e.*

DO, *joined with good.*

Gen. 27:46 *g.* shall my life *d.*
Num. 24:13 to *d. g.* or bad
Deut. 8:16 to *d.* thee *good*
28:63 Lord rejoice to *d.* you *g.*
30:5 and he will *d.* thee *good*
Jud. 17:13 Lord will *d.* me *good*
1 *Sam.* 1:23 *d.* what seemeth *g.*
14:36, 40 ; 2 *Sam.* 19:27, 37
3:18 the Lord *d.* what seemeth
him *good*, 2 *Sam.* 10:12
2 *K.* 10:5 *d.* that *g.* in thine eyes
1 *Chr.* 19:13 Lord *d.* what is *g.*
Neh. 5:9 it is not *g.* that ye *d.*
Ps. 34:14 *d. g.* 37:3, 27 ; 51:18 ;
125:4 ; *Mat.* 5:44 ; *Luke* 6:9, 35
36:3 he hath left off to *d. g.*
Prov. 31:12 she will *d.* him *g.*
Ec. 3:12 for a man to *d. good*
Is. 41:23 yea, *d. good*, or *d.* evil
Jer. 4:22 to *d. good* no knowl.
10:5 nei. is it in them to *d. g.*
13:23 then may ye *d. good*
26:14 *d.* with me as seemeth *g.*
29:32 nor behold the *g.* I will *d.*
32:40 turn away to *d.* them *g.*
41 rejoice over them to *d. g.*
33:9 hear all the *good* I *d.*
Mic. 2:7 words *d. g.* to upright
Zep. 1:12 he L. will not *d. good*
Mark 3:4 is it lawful to *d. g.* on
the sabbath days? *Luke* 6:9
14:7 poor, ye may *d. g.* to them
Luke 6:33 if ye *d. g.* to them that
d. good to you
Rom. 7:19 *g.* that I would, I *d.*
21 when I would *d. g.* evil is
13:3 *d. g.* thou shalt have
Gal. 6:10 *d. good* unto all men
1 *Tim.* 6:18 that they *d. g.* and communn.
Heb. 13:16 to *d. g.* and commun.
Jam. 4:17 knoweth to *d. good*
1 *Pet.* 3:11 eschew evil, and *d. g.*

What have I to DO.

2 *Sam.* 16:10 *w. d.* with? 19:22
1 *K.* 17:18 *w. h. I to d.* with thee?
2 *K.* 3:13 ; 2 *Chr.* 35:21 ; *Mark*
5:7 ; *Luke* 8:28 ; *John* 2:4
Hos. 14:8 *w. d.* any more
1 *Cor.* 5:12 what *d.* to judge

I shall, I will, will I, *or*
shall I DO.

Gen. 27:37 what *s. I d.* now
Num. 22:17 *I will d.* what sayest
33:56 *I s. d.* to you, as I th. to *d.*
1 *Sam.* 3:11 *I w. d.* a thing in Isr.
20:4 thy soul desireth, *I will d.*
28:15 known wh. *I s. d.*
2 *Sam.* 18:4 best *I will d.* 19:38
Job 31:14 *what d.* when G. riseth
34:32 *I will d.* no more
Prov. 24:29 *I will d.* so to him
Is. 5:5 *I w. d.* to my vineyard
43:19 *I will d.* a new thing
46:10 *I will d.* all my pleasure
11 have purposed, *I will al. d.*
48:11 for own sake *will I d.*
Jer. 29:32 good *I will d.* for my
Ezek. 5:9 *I will d.* in thee what I
7:27 *d.* to them after their way
22:14 spoken, and *will d.* it
24:14 ; 36:36
Hos. 6:4 what *shall I d.* to thee?
Amos 4:12 thus *will I d.* to thee
Mat. 19:16 good thing *shall I d.*
27:22 what *shall I d.* with J.?
Luke 16:3 what *shall I d.?* 20:13 ;
Acts 22:10
John 14:13 ask, that *will I d.*
14 ask in my name, *I will d.* it
2 *Cor.* 11:12 what I do, *I will d.*

See JUDGMENT.

Must DO.

Num. 23:26 that I *must d.*
Acts 16:30 wh. *m. I d.* to be sav.?

DO, *joined with no or not.*

Ex. 20:10 in it thou shalt *not d.*
any work, *Lev.* 23:31
23:24 *not d.* after their works
Lev. 16:29 *d.* no work, 23:3, 28 ;
Deut. 15:19 ; *Jer.* 17:24
18:3 after their doings, *not d.*
Num. 33:31 all the *d.*, *d.* it?
Deut. 12:8 n. *d.* after all we *d.*
1 *K.* 11:12 *not d.* it for D.'s sake
2 *K.* 7:9 said, We *d. not* well
17:15 should *not d.* like them
18:12 nor hear nor *d.* them
Ezr. 7:26 whoso will *not d.* law
Job 13:20 only *d. not* two things
34:12 God will *not d.* wickedly
41:8 remem. battle, *d. no* more
Ps. 119:3 also *d. no* iniquity
Jer. 18:6 *d.* with you
32:5 *nôt d.* any more
Mat. 5:46 *d. n.* publ. the same?
6:1 *d. not* your alms before men
12:2 *d.* that *not* lawful to *d.*
20:13 I *d.* thee *no* wrong
23:3 they say and *d. not*
Mark 6:5 *d.* no mighty work
Luke 6:46 *d. not* the things I say
John 6:38 *not* to *d.* mine own
10:37 if I *d. not* works of my F.
Rom. 7:15 that *d.* I *not*, 19
8:3 what the law could *not d.*
Gal. 5:17 ye cannot *d.* the things
Rev. 19:10 see thou *d.* it *not*, 22:9

Observe, *with* DO.

Deut. 5:32 *ob.* to *d.* 8:1 ; 11:32 ;
12:1 ; 24:8 ; 2 *K.* 17:37
6:3 *ob.* to *d.* it, 12:32 ; 28:13, 15,
58 ; 31:12 ; 32:46
25 if we *obs.* to *d.* these com.
15:5 to *ob.* to *d.* all these com.
Jos. 1:7 *ob.* to *d.* all the law
Ezek. 37:24 *observe* and *d.* them
Mat. 23:3 you, that *obser.* and *d.*

Will we, *or* we will DO.

Ex. 19:8 said, *we w. d.* 24:3, 7
Deut. 5:27 *w. w.* hear it, and *d.*
Jos. 1:16 command. us, *w. w. d.*
2 *K.* 10:5 *d.* all thou shalt bid
Jer. 42:20 and *w. w. d.* it
44:17 *we will* certainly *d.*

Shall we, *or* we shall DO.

Jud. 13:8 what *we shall d.*
2 *Sam.* 16:20 what *we shall d.*
17:6 *sh. we d.* after his saying?
2 *K.* 6:15 alas, how *shall we d.?*
Est. 1:15 what *sh. we d.* to V. ?
Ps. 60:12 through God *w. sh. d.*
valiantly, 108:13
Cant. 8:8 what *sh. we. d.*
Jon. 1:11 what *shall we d.?*
Luke 3:10 what *s. we d. ?* 12, 14
John 6:28 *d.* th. we might work?
Acts 2:37 what *shall we d.?*
4:16 what *sh. we d.* to these m. ?

DO, *joined with so.*

Num. 22:30 wont to *d. so* to th. ?
32:23 not *d. so*, ye have sinned
Deut. 12:30 *so* will I *d.*
1 *Sam.* 8:8 served oth. gods, *so d.*
1 *K.* 17:41 as fathers, *so d.* they
Prov. 24:29 I will *d. so* to him
Is. 10:11 *so d.* to Jerusalem
Jer. 28:6 L. *so.* L. perform
Mat. 7:12 sh. *d.* to you, *so d.* ye
18:35 *so* shall Father *d.* to you
John 14:31 Fa. gave com. *so I d.*
Acts 7:51 fathers did, *so d.* ye
Col. 3:13 forgave you, *so d.* ye
Jam. 2:12 *so d.* ye, as they that

DO, *joined with this.*

Gen. 42:18 this *d.* and live
2 *K.* 19:31 zeal of the Lord shall
d. this, *Is.* 37:32
Mat. 8:9 *d. this*, *Luke* 7:8
9:28 I am able to *d. this?*
Mark 11:3 Why *d. this?*
Luke 10:28 th. *d.* and thou sh. l.
22:19 *this d.* in remembrance of
me, 1 *Cor.* 11:24, 25
1 *Cor.* 9:17 for if I *d. this*
Heb. 6:3 *this* will we *d.*
13:19 rather to *d. this.*
Jam. 4:15 we will *d. this*

See THING.

DO well.

Is. 1:17 cease *d.* evil, lea. *d. well*
Jon. 4:9 I *d. well* to be angry
Zec. 8:15 to *d. well* to Jerusalem
Mat. 12:12 to *d. well* on sabbath
John 11:12 he shall *d. well*
1 *Pet.* 2:14 them that *d. w.*
20 if ye *d. well* and suffer for it
2 *Pet.* 1:19 ye *d. w.* that ye take
3 *John* 6 if bring shalt *d. well*

DOER.

Gen. 39:22 Joseph *was d.* of it
2 *Sam.* 3:39 reward *d.* of evil
Ps. 31:23 rewardeth the proud *d.*
Prov. 17:4 wicked *d.* giveth heed
Jam. 1:23 be not *d.* of word
25 not a forgetful hearer, but *d.*
4:11 thou art not a *d.* of the law

DOERS.

2 *K.* 22:5 give it to *d.* of work
Ps. 101:8 cut off all wicked *d.*
Rom. 2:13 *d.* of law be justified
Jam. 1:22 be ye *d.* of the word

See EVIL-DOER, S.

DOEST.

Gen. 4:7 if *d.* well ; if not well
21:22 with thee in all thou *d.*
Deut. 12:28 when thou *d.* good
1 *K.* 2:3 prosper in all thou *d.*
19:9 what *d.* here, Elijah ? 13
20:22 mark and see what *d.*
Job 9:12 say, What *d.* thou ?
35:6 what *d.* against him ?

Ps. 49:18 *d.* well to thyself
77: 14 the God that *d.* wonders
86:10 and *d.* wondrous things
119:68 art good, and *d.* good
Ec. 8:4 what *d.* thou *? Dan.* 4:35
Jer. 11:15 *d.* evil, then rejoicest
15:5 to ask how thou *d. ?*
Ezek. 12:9 house said, What *d. ?*
16:30 seeing, *d.* all these things
John 2:18 thou *d.* these things *?*
13:27 that thou *d.* do quickly
Acts 22:26 take heed what th. *d.*
Rom. 2:1 judg. *d.* same things, 3
Jam. 2:19 believest, thou *d.* well
3 *John* 5 *d.* faithfully what th. *d.*

DOETH.

Ex. 31:14 for whosoever *d.* any
work therein, 15 ; *Lev.* 23:30
Job 5:9 great things, 9:10 ;
37:5 ; *Ps.* 72:18 ; 136:4
23:13 soul desireth, that he *d.*
Ps. 1:3 what. he *d.* shall prosper
14:1 none *d.* 3 ; 53:1, 3 ; *Ro.* 3:12
15:5 *d.* these never be moved
118:15 hand *d.* valiantly, 16
Ec. 2:2 said of mirth, What *d.* it
3:14 whatsoever God *d.* it shall
be for ever, and God *d.* it
7:20 not a man that *d.* good
8:3 he *d.* whatso. pleaseth him
Is 56:2 blessed is man *d.* this
Dan. 4:35 *d.* accord. to his will
9:14 L. is righteous in all he *d.*
Mal. 2:12 L. cut off man *d.* this
Mat. 6:3 left know what right *d.*
7:24 sayings and *d.* them
26 and *d.* not, *Luke* 6:49
8:9 and he *d.* it, *Luke* 7:8
John 5:19 he *d.* these *d.* the Son
7:51 before it know what he *d.*
9:31 *d.* his will, him he heareth
15:15 knoweth not what lord *d.*
Rom. 10:5 that *d.* these things
shall live by them, *Gal.* 3:12
Eph. 6:8 good thing any man *d.*

DOCTOR, S.

Luke 2:46 J. in midst of the *d.*
5:17 *d.* of the law sitting by
Acts 5:34 Gamaliel a *d.* of law

DOCTRINE.

Is. 28:9 make to understand *d.*
29:24 murmured, shall learn *d.*
Jer. 10:8 stock is *d.* of vanities
Mat. 7:28 aston. at his *d.* 22:33 ;
Mark 1:22 ; 11:18 ; *Luke* 4:32
16:12 beware of *d.* of Pharisees
Mark 1:27 what new *d.* is this *?*
4:2 in his *d.* 12:38
John 7:17 shall know of the *d.*
18:19 asked Jesus of his *d.*
Acts 2:42 conti. in apostles' *d.*
5:28 filled Jerus. with your *d.*
13:12 being astonished at the *d.*
17:19 what this new *d.* is *?*
Rom. 6:17 that form of *d.*
16:17 contrary to the *d.*
1 *Cor.* 14:6 except I speak by *d.*
26 every one of you hath a *d.*
Eph. 4:14 with every wind of *d.*
1 *Tim.* 1:3 teach no other *d.*
4:13 give attendance to *d.*
16 heed to thyself to thy *d.*
5:17 who labor in word and *d.*
6:1 his *d.* be not blasphemed
3 the *d.* according to godliness
2 *Tim.* 3:16 is profitable for *d.*
4:2 exhort with long suf. and *d.*
Tit. 2:7 in *d.* showing incorrupt.
10 adorn *d.* of God our Saviour
Heb. 6:1 principles of the *d.*
2 of the *d.* of baptisms, and
2 *John* 9 abideth not in the *d.* of
Christ ; abideth in *d.*
Rev. 2:14 that hold *d.* of Balaam
15 that hold *d.* of Nicolaitans

Good DOCTRINE.

Prov. 4:2 I give you *good d.*

---

1 *Tim.* 4:6 in words of *good d.*

My DOCTRINE.

Deut. 32:2 *my d.* drop as rain
Job 11:4 *my d.* is pure
John 7:16 *my d.* is not mine
2 *Tim.* 3:10 fully known *my d.*

Sound DOCTRINE.

1 *Tim.* 1:10 contrary to *sound d.*
2 *Tim.* 4:3 not endure *sound d.*
Tit. 1:9 by *sound d.* to exhort
2:1 speak things become *s. d.*

This DOCTRINE.

2 *John* 10 and bring not *this d.*
Rev. 2:24 as have not *this d.*

DOCTRINES.

Mat. 15:9 for *d.* com. *Mark* 7:7
Col. 2:22 comm. and *d.* of men
1 *Tim.* 4:1 heed to *d.* of devils
Heb. 13:9 not carried with str. *d.*

DOEG. 1 *Sam.* 21:7 ; 22:18, 22

DOG.

Ex. 11:7 ag. Is. not a *d.* move
Deut. 23:18 a *d.* into house
Jud. 7:5 as a *d.* lappeth
1 *Sam.* 17:43 am I a *d. ? 2 K.* 8:13
24:14 wh. dost purs. *?* after a *d. ?*
2 *Sam.* 3:8 am I a *d.* head *?*
9:8 upon such a dead *d.* as I am
16:9 this dead *d.* curse my lord *?*
Ps. 22:20 from power of *d.*
59:6 make a noise like a *d.* 14
Prov. 26:11 as a *d.* returneth to
his vomit, 2 *Pet.* 2:22
17 taketh a *d.* by the ears
Ec. 9:4 a living *d.* is better than
Is. 66:3 as if he cut off a *d.* neck

DOGS.

Ex. 22:31 cast it to the *d.*
15:26 ; *Mark* 7:27
1 *K.* 14:11 *d.* eat, 16:4 ; 21:24
21:19 the place where *d.* licked
23 *d.* shall eat J. 2 *K.* 9:10, 36
22:38 *d.* licked up his blood
Job 30:1 I disd. to set with *d.*
Ps. 22:16 *d.* have compassed me
68:23 and the tongue of thy *d.*
Is. 56:10 dumb *d.* ; 11 greedy *d.*
Jer. 15:3 and the *d.* to tear
Mat. 7:6 which is holy unto *d.*
15:27 *d.* eat of cru. *Mark* 7:28
Luke 16:21 the *d.* licked his sores
Phil. 3:2 beware of *d.*
Rev. 22:15 for without are *d.*

DOING.

Ex. 15:11 *d.* wonders
1 *K.* 22:43 *d.* right, 2 *Chr.* 20:32
1 *Chr.* 22:16 arise and be *d.*
Job 32:22 in so *d.* my Maker
Ps. 64:9 wisely consider of his *d.*
66:5 he is terrible in his *d.*
118:23 the L.'s *d.* it is marvellous, *Mat.* 21:42 ; *Mark* 12:11
Is. 56:2 keepeth hand from *d.* ev.
Mat. 24:46 find so *d. Luke* 12:43
Acts 10:38 went about *d.* good
24:20 found any evil *d.* in me
Rom. 12:20 in so *d.* shalt heap
2 *Cor.* 8:11 perform the *d.* of it
Eph. 6:6 *d.* the will of God
1 *Tim.* 4:16 in *d.* this,

Well-DOING.

Rom. 2:7 continuance in *w.-d.*
Gal. 6:9 w. in *w.-d.* 2 *Thes.* 3:13
1 *Pet.* 2:15 with *w.-d.* ye silence
3:17 better suffer for *w.-d.*
4:19 com. souls to him in *w.-d.*

DOINGS.

Lev. 18:3 after *d.* of Egypt and
Canaan, shall ye not do
Deut. 28:20 wickedness of thy *d.*
Jud. 2:19 ceased not from own *d.*
2 *Chr.* 17:4 not after *d.* of Israel
Ps. 9:11 declare his *d. Is.* 12:4
77:12 I will also talk of thy *d.*

Prov. 20:11 known by his *d.*
Is. 1:16 put away evil of your *d.*
3:8 their *d.* are against the L.
10 shall eat the fruit of their *d.*
Jer. 4:4 because of evil of your
d. 21:12 ; 26:3 ; 44:22
18 thy *d.* have procured these
7:3 am. your *d.* 5 ; 26:13 ; 35:15
11:18 showedst me their *d.*
17:10 fruit of his *d.* 21:14
18:11 and make your *d.* good
23:2 visit on you evil of your *d.*
22 evil of *d.* 25:5 ; *Zec.* 1:4
32:19 give accord. to fruit of *d.*
Ezek. 14:22 ye shall see their *d.*
20:43 shall ye remember *d.*
44 nor according to corrupt *d.*
21:24 in all your *d.* sins do ap.
24:14 thy *d.* shall judge
36:17 defiled it by their own *d.*
19 according to *d.* I judged th.
31 shall remember *d.* not good
Hos. 4:9 reward them their *d.*
5:4 not frame *d.* to turn to God
7:2 their own *d.* have beset th.
9:15 for wicked. of *d.* I will dr.
12:2 acc. to *d.* will he recomp.
Mic. 2:7 are these his *d. ?*
3:4 have behaved ill in their *d.*
7:13 be desolate, for fruit of *d.*
Zep. 3:7 corrupted all their *d.*
11 not be ashamed for thy *d. ?*
Zec. 1:6 accord. to our *d.* so d.

DOLEFUL.

Is. 13:21 full of *d.* creatures
Mic. 2:4 with a *d.* lamentation

DOMINION.

Gen. 1:26 *d.* over the fish, 28
27:40 thou shalt have the *d.*
37:8 shalt thou have *d.* over us *?*
Num. 24:19 he that shall have *d.*
Jud. 5:13 have *d.* over nobles
1 *K.* 4:24 Solomon had *d.*
1 *Chr.* 18:3 to establish his *d.*
Neh. 9:37 have *d.* over our bod.
Job 25:2 *d.* and fear are with him
38:33 thou set the *d.* thereof
Ps. 8:6 to have *d.* over the works
19:13 sins, let them not have *d.*
49:14 the upright shall have *d.*
72:8 have *d.* from sea to sea
103:22 in all places of his *d.*
114:2 and Israel his *d.*
119:133 let not any, iniq. have *d.*
145:13 thy *d.* endureth
Is. 26:13 other lords have had *d.*
Dan. 4:3 his *d.* from generation
22 *d.* reacheth to end of earth
34 *d.* is an everlasting *d.* 7:14
6:26 his *d.* be even unto the end
7:6 *d.* was given to the beast
12 beasts had *d.* taken away
14 was given him *d.* and glory
26 they shall take away his *d.*
27 *d.* sh. be given to the saints
11:3 shall rule with great *d.* 5
Mic. 4:8 to thee, even the first *d.*
Zec. 9:10 his *d.* be from sea
Mat. 20:25 princes exercise *d.*
Rom. 6:9 death hath no more *d.*
14 sin not have *d.* over you
7:1 law hath *d.* over a man
2 *Cor.* 1:24 *d.* over your faith
Eph. 1:21 above might and *d.*
1 *Pet.* 4:11 to whom be praise and
d. for ever, 5:11 ; *Rev.* 1:6
Jude 8 despise *d.*
25 to the only wise God be *d.*

DOMINIONS.

Dan. 7:27 all *d.* shall serve him
Col. 1:16 whether thrones or *d.*

DONE.

Ex. 18:9 goodness L. had *d.* to I.
31:15 six days may work be *d.*
35:2 ; *Lev.* 23:3
Lev. 5:17 things forbid. to be *d.*

Num. 22:2 saw all Israel had *d.*
27:4 name of our father *d.* aw. ?
32:13 all had *d.* evil were cons.
Deut. 10:21 thy God that hath *d.*
29:24 wherefore hath the L. *d.*
thus, 1 *K.* 9:8; 2 *Chr.* 7:21
2 *Sam.* 13:12 to be *d.* in Israel
24:17 they *d. ?* 1 *Chr.* 21:17
Neh. 9:33 we have *d.* wickedly,
Ps. 106:6; *Dan.* 95, 15
Est. 6:6 shall be *d.* to the man
Job 21:31 repay what he hath *d. ?*
Ps. 33:9 he spake, and it was *d.*
71:19 hast *d.* gr. things, 106:21;
126:2, 3
120:3 *d.* to thee, false tongue ?
Ec. 1:9 is *d.* is what shall be *d.*
2:12 hath been already *d.*
Is. 41:4 who hath *d.* it ?
44:23 for the Lord hath *d.* it
Jer. 48:19 him fleeth, what is *d.*
Ezek 39:8 it is *d.* saith the Lord
Dan. 11:36 determined sh. be *d.*
Mat. 6:10 thy will be *d.* 26:42;
Luke 11:2; 22:42
8:13 so be it *d.* to thee
11:21 works *d.* in you, had been
d. in Tyre, *Luke* 10:13
18:19 it shall be *d.* for them
23:23 these ought ye to have *d.*
Luke 11:42
25:21 well *d.* good servant, 23
40 as ye have *d.* it to one of
these, **ye** have *d.* it to me
27:54 things that were *d.* 28:11
Mark 5:19 things the L. hath *d.*
for thee, 20; *Luke* 8:39
6:30 told him what they had *d.*
9:13 *d.* to him what. they listed
13:30 not pass till these be *d.*
15:8 to do, as he had ever *d.*
Luke 1:49 hath *d.* great things
3:19 evils Herod had *d.*
8:56 tell no man what was *d.*
9:10 told him all they had *d.*
14:22 it is *d.* as thou hast com.
17:10 we have *d.* that which was
our duty to do
John 5:29 they that have *d.* good
to life ; they that have *d.* ev.
15:7 what ye will, it shall be *d.*
Acts 4:16 determ. before to be *d.*
14:27 rch. all G. had *d.* 15:4
21:14 the will of the Lord be *d.*
Rom. 9:11 *d.* any good or evil
1 *Cor.* 9:15 nor be so *d.* unto me
13:10 in part shall be *d.* away
14:26 let all be *d.* to edifying
40 be *d.* decently
16:14 be *d.* with charity
2 *Cor.* 5:10 things *d.* in body
Eph. 6:13 having *d.* all to stand
Phil. 2:3 nothing be *d.* through
strife
Col. 4:9 known all things *d.*
Rev. 16:17 saying, It is *d.* 21:6
22:6 which must shortly be *d.*

Have I DONE.

Num. 22:28 what h. *I d.* to thee,
1 *K.* 19:20; *Mic.* 6:3
Jud. 8:2 what *have I* now *d. ?*
1 *Sam.* 17:29
1 *Sam.* 20:1 what *have I d. ?*
26:18 ; 29:8 ; *Jer.* 8:6

He hath, or hath he DONE.

Lev. 24:19 as *h. d.* so be done
Jud. 15:10 as *he hath d.* to us
1 *Sam.* 6:9 *h. h. d.* us this gr. ev.
12:24 great things *he hath d.*
20:32 what *hath he d. ?*
1 *Chr.* 16:12 rem. his works *he hath d. Ps.* 78:4 ; 98:1 ; 105:5
Ps. 66:16 declare wha. *he hath d.*
115:3 *he h. d.* what he pleased
Prov. 24:29 as *he hath d.* to me
Is. 12:5 *he hath d.* excel. things

Ezek. 24:24 that *he hath d.* shall
ye do
33:16 *he hath d.* that is lawful
Joel 2:20 *he hath d.* great things
Mark 7:37 *he hath d.* all things
2 *Cor.* 5:10 receive accor. *h. h. d.*

I have DONE.

Gen. 28:15 till *I have d.* that *I* h.
Jos. 24:7 seen what *I have d.*
Jud. 1:7 as *I h. d.* so G. req. me
15:11 as th. did to me, so *h. I d.*
2 *Sam.* 14:21 *I have d.* this thing
24:10 *I h. d.* foolishly, 1 *Chr.* 21:8
2 *K.* 19:25 how *I have d.* it ?
Job 34:32 if *I have d.* iniquity
Ps. 7:3 O L. if *I have d.* this
119:121 *I h. d.* judgment
Is. 10:13 by st. of hand *I h. d.* it
33:13 what *I have d.*
37:26 heard how *I have d.* it ?
Ezek. 12:11 as *I h. d.* so be done
14:23 *I have* not *d.* without ca.
all *I have d.* in it
John 13:12 what *I have d.* to you ?
15 do as *I have d.* to you

Hast thou DONE.

Gen. 4:10 what h. *t. d. ?* 31:26 ;
Num. 23:11 ; 1 *Sam.* 31:11 ;
2 *Sam.* 3:24 ; *John* 18:35
20:9 what h. *th. d. ?* *Jud.* 15:11
2 *Sam.* 7:21 to thy heart *h. t. d.*
16:10 wherefore *hast thou d.* so ?
1 *K.* 1:6 saying, Why *h. t. d.* so ?
1 *Chr.* 17:19 *h. t. d.* all this
Ps. 60:21 these things *h. thou d.*
Jon. 1:10 why *hast thou d.* this ?

Thou hast DONE.

Gen. 3:13 what is this *thou h. d. ?*
12:18 ; 26:10 ; 29:25 ; *Jud.*
15:11 ; 2 *Sam.* 12:21
14 because *thou hast d.* this,
22:16 ; 2 *Chr.* 25:16
20:9 *t. h. d.* deeds ou. n. to be *d.*
27:45 he forget what *t. h. d.*
31:28 *thou h. d.* foolish. 1 *Sam.*
13:13 ; 2 *Chr.* 16:9
Jos. 7:19 tell me what *thou hast
d.* 1 *Sam.* 14:43
Ps. 40:5 wonderful works *t. h. d.*
52:9 praise thee bec. *t. h. d.* it
109:27 know that *thou h. d.* it
Jer. 2:23 know what *thou hast d.*
Lam. 1:21 are glad *thou h. d.* it
22 as *thou hast d.* unto me
2:20 consider to whom *t. h. d.*
Ezek. 16:48 Sod. not *d.* as *t. h. d.*
59 deal with these as *thou h. d.*
Ob. 15 as *t. h. d.* be done to thee
Jon. 1:14 *t. h. d.* as it pleaseth

Not DONE.

Gen. 20:9 deeds ought *not* be *d.*
Num. 16:28 *not* of *d.* of mine own
Deut. 32:27 Lord hath *not d.* all
Is. 5:4 done that I have *not d. ?*
46:10 declaring things *not* yet *d.*
Jer. 3:16 neither shall that be *d.*
Ezek. 5:9 that I have *not d.*
Dan. 9:12 *not* been *d.* as on Jer.
11:24 do what his fat. *not d.*
Amos 3:6 in city, L. *not d.* it ?
Acts 26:26 was *not d.* in a corner

DONE, with this.

Gen. 21:26 wot n. who hath *d. t.*
42:28 what is *this* God hath *d.*
Jud. 2:2 not obeyed, why *d. t. ?*
6:29 Who hath *d. this ?* 15:6
1 *Sam.* 28:18 hath Lord *d. this*
Ps. 7:3 O Lord, if I have *d. this*
22:31 declare that he hath *d. th.*
51:4 and *d. this* evil in my sight
Is. 41:20 hand of Lord hath *d.
this*
Ezek. 23:38 moreover *this* they
have *d.* unto me
Mark 5:32 her that had *d. this*

Acts 4:7 by what p. ha. ye *d. t. ?*

DOOR.

Gen. 4:7 sin lieth at the *d.*
19:9 came near to break the *d.*
Ex. 12:23 will pass over the *d.*
Deut. 15:17 thrust it through ear
to *d.*
2 *Sam.* 13:17 bolt the *d.* after h.
2 *K.* 4:15 she stood in the *d.*
9:3 then open the *d.* and flee
Est. 2:21 which kept the *d.* 6:2
Job 31:9 laid wait at neighb. *d.*
34 I went not out of the *d. ?*
Ps. 141:3 keep the *d.* of my lips
Prov. 26:14 as *d.* turneth
Cant. 5:4 in hand by hole of *d.*
8:9 if she be a *d.* we will inclose
Ezek. 8:8 in wall, behold a *d.*
10:19 stood at *d.* of the east gate
11:1 at *d.* of the gate 25 men
41:2 breadth of *d.* ten cubits
46:3 peo. shall worship at the *d.*
Hos. 2:15 valley of A. *d.* of hope
Amos 9:1 smite the lint. of the *d.*
Mat. 27:60 rolled great stone to
d. of sepulchre. *Mark* 15:46
28:2 rolled stone from the *d.*
Mark 1:33 city was gather. at *d.*
2:2 no room, no not about the *d.*
16:3 who roll us stone from *d. ?*
John 10:1 entereth not by the *d.*
2 that entereth in by the *d.*
7 I am the *d.* 9.
18:16 but Peter stood at the *d.*
Acts 5:9 feet at *d.* to carry thee
12:13 as Peter knocked at the *d.*
14:27 opened *d.* of faith to Gen.
1 *Cor.* 16:9 great *d.* and effectual
2 *Cor.* 2:12 a *d.* was opened to me
Col. 4:3 open a *d.* of utterance
Jam. 5:9 judge standeth bef. *d.*
Rev. 3:8 before thee an open *d.*
20 stand at *d.* if any man open
4:1 a *d.* was open in heaven

DOOR, with house.

Gen. 19:11 that were at *d.* of *h.*
43:19 communed at *d.* of *house*
Ex. 12:22 no. of you go out at *d.*
Jud. 19:26 fell down at *d.* 27
2 *Sam.* 11:9 slept at *d.* of *house*
2 *K.* 5:9 Naam. stood at *d.* of *h.*
Neh. 3:21 Meremoth rep. from *d.*
Prov. 5:8 not nigh *d.* of her *h.*
9:14 she sitteth at *d.* of her *h.*
Ezek. 8:14 to *d.* of Lord's *h.* 47:1

DOOR, with keeper, s.

2 *K.* 25:18 captain of the guard
took the three *k.* of *d.* *Jer.*
52:24
1 *Chr.* 15:24 Obed. and Jeh. *d.-k.*
Est. 6:2 *k.* of *d.* sought to lay
Ps. 84:10 I had rather be a *d.-k.*
Jer. 35:4 Maaseiah keep. of the *d.*

DOOR, with posts.

Ex. 12:7 blood on upper *d.-p.*
21:6 master bring him to *d.-p.*
Deut. 11:20 write them on *d.-p.*
Is. 6:4 *p.* of *d.* moved at the vo.
Ezek. 41:3 he measured *p.* of *d.*
16 measured the *d.-p.*

DOOR, with shut.

Gen. 19:6 L. *s. d.* ; 10 ang. *s. d.*
2 *K.* 4:4 shalt *shut d.* upon thee
6:32 *shut d.* hold him fast at *d.*
Mat. 6:6 hast *shut* thy *d.* pray
25:10 *d.* was *s.* ; *Luke* 11:7 *d.* is
now *s.*
Luke 13:25 hath *s.* to the *d.*
Rev. 3:8 open *d.* no man can *s.*

DOOR, with tabernacle.

Ex. 29:4 bring to *d.* of *tab.* 40:12 ;
Lev. 4:4 ; 8:3, 4 ; 12:6 ; *Num.*
6:10

11 by *d.* of *t.* 32; 40:29; *Lev.*
1:5; *Num.* 27:2
42 burnt-offering at *d.* of *t.* 33:9,
10; 38:8; 40:28; *Lev.* 1:3; 3:2;
4:7, 18
40:6 *d.* of *taber. Num.* 25:6
Lev. 8:31 at *d.* of *t.* 35; 14:11;
16:7; 17:6; *Num.* 6:18; 10:3;
Jos. 19:51
33 shall not go out of *d.* of *t.*
10:7 not go out from *d.* of *t.*
14:23 *d.* of *t.* 15:14, 29; 19:21;
Num. 6:13; 16:19, 50; 20:6
17:4 bring. it not to *d.* of *tab.* 9
Num. 12:5 in *d.* of *tab.* 16:18
Deut. 31:15 pillar of cloud ov. *d.*

DOOR, *joined with* tent.
Gen. 18:1 Abra. sat in the *tent d.*
10 Sarah heard it in the *tent d.*
Ex. 33:8 ev. man at his *t. d.* 10
Num. 11:10 weep. ev. man in *d.*
16:27 Abiram stood in *t. d.*
Jud. 4:20 Stand in *d.* of *tent*

DOORS.
Jos. 2:19 whosoever go out of *d.*
Jud. 3:25 opened not *d.* of parlor
11:31 cometh forth of *d.*
16:3 Samson took *d.* of the city
1 *Sam.* 3:15 Samuel opened t. *d.*
21:13 D. scrabbled on *d.* of gate
Job 31:32 opened *d.* to traveller
38:10 set bars and *d.* to the sea
17 seen *d.* of shadow of death?
41:14 who open. *d.* of his face?
Ps. 24:7 up, ye everlasting *d.* 9
78:23 though opened *d.* of heav.
Prov. 8:3 wisdom crieth at the *d.*
34 waiting at posts of my *d.*
Is. 57:8 behind *d.* set up
Ezek. 33:30 talking in the *d.*
Mic. 7:5 *d.* of mouth from her
Zec. 11:1 open thy *d.* O Lebanon
Mat. 24:33 at the *d. Mark* 13:29
Acts 5:19 angel opened prison *d.*
23 keepers standing before *d.*
16:26 all the *d.* were opened
27 keeper seeing prison *d.* op.

Shut DOORS.
Jud. 3:23 Ehud *shut d.* of parlor
2 *Chr.* 28:24 *s.* up *d.* of L.'s ho.
29:7 have *shut d.* of the porch
Neh. 6:10 let us *shut d.* of temple
7:3 *shut* the *d.* and bar them
Job 3:10 *shut* not up *d.* of womb
38:8 shut up the sea with *d.?*
Ec. 12:4 be *s.* in the streets
Is. 26:20 enter. and shut thy *d.*
Mal. 1:10 *shut d.* for naught
John 20:19 *d. sk.* Jesus came, 26
Acts 21:30 the *d.* were *shut*
DOR. *Jud.* 1:27; 1 *K.* 4:11
DORCAS. *Acts* 9:36, 39

DOTE, ED, ING.
Jer. 50:36 and they shall *d.*
Ezek. 23:5 Aholah *d.* on Assyri.
1 *Tim.* 6:4 *d.* about questions
DOTHAN. *Gen.* 37:17; 2 *K.* 6:13

DOUBLE.
Gen. 43:12 and take *d.* money
Ex. 22:4 theft be found, rest. *d.*
7 if found, let him pay *d.*
Deut. 15:18 worth a *d.* hired ser.
21:17 giving him a *d.* portion
2 *K.* 2:9 *d.* portion of thy spirit
1 *Chr.* 12:33 were not of *d.* heart
Job 11:6 *d.* to that which is
Job 41:13 to him with *d.* bridle?
Ps. 12:2 with a *d.* heart do speak
Is. 40:2 rec. *d.* for all her sins
61:7 your shame have *d.* in their
land they shall possess *d.*
Jer. 16:18 recomp. their sin *d.*
17:18 with *d.* destruction

Zec. 9:12 I will render *d.* to thee
1 *Tim.* 3:8 deacons not *d.*-tong.
5:17 worthy of *d.* honor
Rev. 18:6 *d.* unto her in *d.* cup
she hath filled, fill to her *d.*

DOUBLE-MINDED.
Jam. 1:8 *d.-m.* man is unstable
4:8 purify your hearts, ye *d.-m.*

DOUBLED.
Gen. 41:32 dream was *d.* twice
Ex. 28:16 four-square, being *d.*
39:9 span was breadth, being *d.*
Ezek. 21:14 sword be *d.* third ti.

DOUBT, S.
Deut. 28:66 thy life hang in *d.*
Dan. 5:16 thou canst dissolve *d.*
Acts 28:4 no *d.* this man is a mur.
Gal. 4:20 for I stand in *d.* of you
1 *John* 2:19 wo. no *d.* have con.

DOUBT.
Mal. 14:31 wheref. didst thou *d.?*
21:21 if ye have faith and *d.* not
Mark 11:23 not *d.* in his heart
John 10:24 how long make us *d.?*

DOUBTED, ETH.
Mat. 28:17 but some *d.*
Acts 5:24 *d.* where. would grow
10:17 Peter *d.* in himself
25:20 I *d.* of such questions
Rom. 14:23 *d.* is damned

DOUBTFUL.
Luke 12:29 nei. be ye of *d.* mind
Rom. 14:1 not to *d.* disputations

DOUBTING.
John 13:22 *d.* of whom he spake
Acts 10:20 go, nothing *d.* 11:12
1 *Tim.* 2:8 men pray without *d.*

DOUBTLESS.
Ps. 126:6 *d.* come again rejoicing
Is. 63:16 *d.* thou art our father
1 *Cor.* 9:2 yet *d.* I am to you
Phil. 3:8 *d.* I count all but loss

DOUGH.
Ex. 12:39 unleavened cakes of *d.*
Num. 15:20 offer a cake of *d.* 21
Neh. 10:37 firsc-fruits of our *d.*
Jer. 7:18 women knead their *d.*
Ezek. 44:30 give priest first of *d.*
Hos. 7:4 after he hath kneaded *d.*

DOVE.
Gen. 8:8 N. sent forth a *d.* 10, 12
9 the *d.* found no rest
Ps. 55:6 that I had w. like a *d.*
68:13 ye shall be as w. of a *d.*
Cant. 1:15 thou hast *d.* eyes, 4:1
2:14 my *d.* let me see thy coun.
5:2 my sister, my *d.*
6:9 my *d.* my undefiled
Is. 38:14 I did mourn as a *d.*
Jer. 48:28 and be like the *d.*
Hos. 7:11 Eph. is like a silly *d.*
11:11 they shall tremble as a *d.*
Mat. 3:16 like a *d. Mark* 1:10;
Luke 3:22; *John* 1:32

DOVES.
2 *K.* 6:25 of a cab of *d.* dung
Cant. 5:12 eyes are as eyes of *d.*
Is. 59:11 we mourn sore like *d.*
60:8 flee as a *d.* to their windows.
Ezek. 7:16 like *d.* of the valleys
Nah. 2:7 lead as with voice of *d.*
Mat. 10:16 harmless as *d.*
21:12 that sold *d. Mark* 11:15
John 2:14 those that sold *d.*

Up and DOWN.
Job 1:7 walking *up and d.* 2:2
Ps. 59:15 wander *up and d.*
109:23 I am tossed *up and d.*
Ezek. 28:14 *up a. d.* in midst
Zec. 10:12 shall walk *up a. d.*
Acts 27:27 were driven *up and d.*

DOWNSITTING.
Ps. 139:2 thou knowest my *d.*

DOWNWARD.
2 *K.* 19:30 take root *d. Is.* 37:31
Ec. 3:21 spirit of beast goeth *d.*
Ezek. 1:27 appear. of loins *d.* 8:2

DOWRY.
Gen. 30:20 end. me with good *d.*
34:12 ask me never so much *d.*
Ex. 22:17 according to the *d.*
1 *Sam.* 18:25 king desireth not *d.*

DRAG.
Hab. 1:15 gather them in their *d.*
16 burn incense to their *d.*

DRAGGING.
John 21:8 *d.* the net with fishes

DRAGON.
Ps. 91:13 *d.* shalt thou trample
Is. 27:1 slay *d.* that is in sea
51:9 cut Rahab and wounded *d.*
Jer. 51:34 swallow. me up like *d.*
Ezek. 29:3 Pharaoh, the great *d.*
Rev. 12:3 behold, a great red *d.*
9 *d.* was cast out, 13
17 *d.* was wroth with the wom.
13:2 the *d.* gave him his power
4 they worshipped the *d.*
11 he spake as a *d.*
16:13 come out of mouth of *d.*
20:2 he laid hold on the *d.*

DRAGON-WELL.
Neh. 2:13 I went out before *d.-w.*

DRAGONS.
Deut. 32:33 wine is poison of *d.*
Job 30:29 I am a brother to *d.*
Ps. 44:19 brok. us in place of *d.*
74:13 breakest the heads of *t. d.*
148:7 praise the Lord, ye *d.*
Is. 13:22 *d.* in pleasant palaces
34:13 he habitation for *d.* 35:7
43:20 *d.* and owls shall hon. me
Jer. 9:11 Jerusalem a den of *d.*
10:22 cities of Judah a den of *d.*
14:6 snuffed up wind like *d.*
51:37 Babylon a dwelling for *d.*
Mic. 1:8 make wailing like *d.*
Mal. 1:3 heritage waste for the *d.*

DRAMS.
1 *Chr.* 29:7 gave of gold 10,000 *d.*
Ezr. 2:69 gave 61,000 *d.* of gold
8:27 20 basins of gold, of 1,000 *d,*
Neh. 7:70 gave to treas. 1,000 *d.*
71 gave 20,000 *d.* of gold, 72

DRANK.
Gen. 9:21 Noah *d.* of the wine
24:46 I *d.* made camels drink
27:25 brought wine and he *d.*
Num. 20:11 the congregation *d.*
Deut. 32:38 *d.* wine of drink-of.
1 *Sam.* 30:12 nor *d.* water
2 *Sam.* 12:3 *d.* of his own cup
1 *K.* 13:19 eat bread in h. *d.* wa.
17:6 and he *d.* of brook
Dan. 1:5 king ap. of wine he *d.*
5:1 *d.* before the thousand
3 his concubines *d.* in them
Mark 14:23 and they all *d.* of it
Luke 17:27 they eat, they *d.* 28
John 4:12 Jacob *d.* thereof
1 *Cor.* 10:4 *d.* of that spirit. rock

DRAUGHT.
Mat. 15:17 out in *d. Mark* 7:19
Luke 5:4 let down nets for a *d.*
9 astonished at *d.* of fishes

DRAUGHT-HOUSE.
2 *K.* 10:27 made Baal's house a *d.*

DRAVE.
Ex. 14:25 they *d.* them heavily
Jos. 16:10 *d.* not out Cananites
24:12 and *d.* them out from before you, *Jud.* 6:9
18 Lord *d.* out before us
Jud. 1:19 J. *d.* out inhabitants
2 *Sam.* 6:3 *d.* the cart, 1 *Chr.* 13:7
2 *K.* 17:21 Jeroboam *d.* Israel
from following the Lord

Acts 7:45 whom God *d.* out
18:16 *d.* them from judgm.-seat
See **DROVE.**

DRAW.

Gen. 24:44 will *d.* for thy camels
Ex. 15:9 I will *d.* my sword
Jud. 4:7 I will *d.* to thee Sisera
9:54 *d.* thy sword, and slay me,
    1 *Sam.* 31:4 ; 1 *Chr.* 10:4
20:32 *d.* from city to highways
2 *Sam.* 17:13 *d.* city into t. river
Job 21:33 every man *d.* after him
Ps. 28:3 *d.* me not with the w.
Cant. 1:4 *d.* me, we will run aft.
Is. 5:18 *d.* iniquity with cords
66:19 nations that *d.* the bow
Ezek. 21:3 will *d.* forth my sw.
28:7 strangers *d.* their swords
30:11 *d.* their swords ag. Egypt
32:20 *d.* her and all her multi.
John 4:11 hast nothing to *d.* w.
    15 nor come hither to *d.*
6:44 except the Father *d.* him
12:32 I will *d.* all men unto me
21:6 were not able to *d.* it
Acts 20:30 to *d.* away disciples
Jam. 2:6 *d.* you before judg.-seat

DRAW back.

Heb. 10:38 but if any *d.* back
    39 not of them who *d.* back

DRAW near.

1 *Sam.* 14:36 let us *d.* near to G.
1 *Sam.* 14:38 *d.* ye n. h. all t. ch.
Ps. 73:28 good to *d.* n. to God
107:18 *d.* near to gates of death
Is. 29:13 *d.* near with their lips
45:20 *d. n.* ye that are escaped
57:3 *d. near* ye sons of sorceress
Jer. 30:21 cause him to *d. near*
46:3 and *d. near* to battle
Ezek. 9:1 charge ov. city, to *d. n*
22:4 caused thy days to *d. neap*
Joel 3:9 let all men of war *d. n.*
Heb. 10:22 *d. n.* with true heart

DRAW nigh.

Ex. 3:5 said *d.* not *nigh* hither
Ps. 69:18 *d. nigh* to my soul
119:150 *d. nigh* that fol. misch.
Ec. 12:1 nor years *d. nigh*
Is. 5:19 coun. of Holy One *d. n.*
Heb. 7:19 by the which we *d. n.*
Jam. 4:8 *d. n.* to G. he will *d. n.*

DRAW out.

Ex. 12:21 *d. out* and take a lamb
Lev. 26:33 *d. out* a sword after
Jud 3:22 not *d.* dagger *out* of
Job 41:1 canst *d. out* leviathan ?
Ps. 35:3 *d. out* also the spear
85:5 wilt thou *d. o.* thine anger
Prov. 20:5 m. of und. will *d.* it *o.*
Is. 57:4 do ye *d. o.* tongue
58:10 *d. out* soul to the hungry
Jer. 49:20 *d.* them *out*, 50:45
Lam. 4:3 sea-monster *d. out*
Ezek. 5:2 I will *d. out* a sword
    after them, 12 ; 12:14
Hag. 2:16 to *d. out* fifty vessels
John 2:8 *d. out* now, and bear

DRAW up.

Job 40:23 he can *d. up* Jordan

DRAW, *joined with* **water.**

Gen. 24:13 dau. come to *d. wa.*
1 *Sam.* 9:11 maid going to *d. wa.*
Is. 12:3 with joy shall ye *d. wa.*
Nah. 3:14 *d. waters* for the siege
John 4:7 woman of S. to *d. wa.*

DRAWN.

Num. 22:23 his sword *d.* 31 ; *Jos.*
    5:13 ; 1 *Chr.* 21:16
Deut. 30:17 *d.* away, and w. gods
Jos. 8:6 till *d.* them from city
Job 20:5 it is *d.* and cometh out
Ps. 37:14 wicked *d.* out sword
55:21 than oil, yet *d.* swords
Prov. 24:11 that are *d.* to death

Is. 21:15 fled from *d.* swords
28:9 that are *d.* from breasts
Jer. 31:3 with loving-kindness *d.*
Lam. 2:3 *d.* back his right hand
Ezek. 21:5 Lord *d.* my sword, 28
Acts 11:10 *d.* up again to heaven
Jam. 1:14 *d.* away of his own

DRAWER, S.

Deut. 29:11 to *d.* of water
Jos. 9:21 be *d.* of water, 23, 27

DRAWETH.

Deut. 25:11 the one *d.* near
Jud. 19:9 day *d.* towards even.
Job 24:22 he *d.* the mighty
33:22 his soul *d.* near to grave
Ps. 10:9 *d.* him into his net
88:3 life *d.* nigh to the grave
Is. 26:17 *d.* near delivery
Ezek. 7:12 the day *d.* near
Mat. 15:8 *d.* nigh with their lips
Luke 21:8 the time *d.* near
    28 your redemption *d.* nigh
Jam. 5:8 coming of L. *d.* nigh

DRAWING.

Jud. 5:11 in places of *d.* water
John 6:19 Jesus *d.* nigh to ship

DREAD, Substantive.

Gen. 9:2 *d.* of you be on ev. beast
Ex. 15:16 *d.* shall fall upon them
Deut. 2:25 to put *d.* of thee upon
    the nations, 11:25
Job 13:11 his *d.* fall upon you ?
    21 let not thy *d.* make me afr.
Is. 8:13 and let him be your *d.*

DREAD, Verb.

Deut. 1:29 I said to you, *d.* not
1 *Chr.* 22:13 be strong, *d.* not

DREADFUL.

Gen. 28:17 how *d.* is this place
Job 15:21 a *d.* sound is in his ears
Ezek. 1:18 rings, they were *d.*
9:4 O Lord the great and *d.* God
Dan. 7:7 a fourth beast *d.* 19
Hab. 1:7 the Chaldeans are *d.*
Mal. 1:14 name *d.* among heath.
4:5 great and *d.* day of the Lord

DREAM, Substantive.

Gen. 20:3 to Abimelech in a *d.*
31:10 Jacob saw in a *d.* the ram
    24 God came to Laban in a *d.*
37:5 Joseph dreamed a *d.* 9, 10
Gen. 40:5 but. and ba. a *d.* both
41:7 it was a *d.* 1 *K.* 3:15
    25 *d.* of Pharaoh is one, 26
Num. 12:6 L. will speak in a *d.*
Jud. 7:13 told a *d.* to his fellow
1 *K.* 3:5 to Solomon in a *d.*
Job 20:8 he shall fly away as a *d.*
33:15 in a *d.* openeth ears
Ps. 73:20 as a *d.* when one awak.
Ec. 5:3 a *d.* com. through busin.
Is. 29:7 fight ag. Ariel be as a *d.*
Jer. 23:28 hath *d.* let him tell *d.*
Dan. 2:4 tell thy servants the *d.*
    36 this is the *d.*
d. 19 *d.* be to th. that hate thee
7:1 Daniel had a *d.* wrote *d.*
Mat. 1:20 angel of Lord app. to
    Joseph in a *d.* 2:13, 19
2:12 warned of God in a *d.* 22
27:19 I have suffered in a *d.*

DREAM, Verb.

Ps. 126:1 were like them that *d.*
Joel 2:28 old men *d.* *Acts* 2:17

DREAMED.

Gen. 28:12 Jac. *d.* ; 37:5 Jos. *d.*
40:5 officers *d.* ; 41:1 Phar. 15
Jer. 23:25 proph. said, I have *d.*
29:8 dreams you cause to be *d.*
Dan. 2:1 Nebuchadnezzar *d.*

DREAMER, S.

Gen. 37:19 said, This *d.* cometh
Deut. 13:3 not hearken to *d.*
    5 *d.* shall be put to death
Jer. 27:9 hearken not to your *d.*

Jude 8 filthy *d.* defile the flesh

DREAMS.

Gen. 37:8 hated him for his *d.*
    20 what will become of his *d.*
41:12 and he interpreted our *d.*
42:9 Joseph remembered the *d.*
1 *Sam.* 28:6 answer. not by *d.* 15
Job 7:14 thou scarest me with *d.*
Ec. 5:7 in multitude of *d.* are
Jer. 23:27 forget my name by *d.*
    32 that prophesy false *d.*
Dan. 1:17 understand. in *d.* 5:12
Zec. 10:2 diviners told false *d.*

DREAMETH.

Is. 29:8 hungry man *d.* a thirsty

DREGS.

Ps. 75:8 *d.* wicked shall drink
Is. 51:17 drunken *d.* of cup, 22

DRESS.

Gen. 2:15 into garden to *d.* it
18:7 young man hasted to *d.* it
Deut. 28:39 plant viney. *d.* them
2 *Sam.* 12:4 to *d.* for wayfaring
13:5 Tamar *d.* meat in my sight
1 *K.* 18:25 Elijah said, *d.* it first

DRESSED.

2 *Sam.* 12:4 poor man's lamb
19:24 Mephib. not *d.* his feet
Heb. 6:7 for them by wh. it is *d.*

DRESSER.

Luke 13:7 said to *d.* of vineyard

DREW.

Gen. 24:20 Rebekah *d.* water, 45
37:28 they *d.* up Joseph
38:29 as Zarah *d.* back his hand
Ex. 2:10 I *d.* him out of water
    16 Jethro's daughters *d.* water
Jos. 8:26 Jos. *d.* not hand back
Jud. 8:10 fell 120,000 *d.* sword
    20 the youth *d.* not his sword
20:2 400,000 that *d.* sword
Ruth 4:8 so he *d.* off his shoe
2 *Sam.* 22:17 he *d.* me out of
    many waters, *Ps.* 18:16
23:16 mighty men *d.* water out
    well Beth. 1 *Chr.* 11:18
24:9 in Israel 800,000 *d.* sword
1 *K.* 22:34 *d.* a bow, 2 *Chr.* 18:33
2 *K.* 9:24 Jehu *d.* bow
1 *Chr.* 19:16 *d.* forth the Syrians
21:5 Israel were 1,100,000 that *d.*
    sword, Judah 470,000
Jer. 38:13 *d.* up Jeremiah
Hos. 11:4 *d.* with cords of a man
Mat. 13:48 *d.* to shore, *Mark* 6:53
26:51 Peter *d.* his sword, *Mark*
    14:47 ; *John* 18:10
Luke 23:54 and the sabbath *d.* on
John 2:9 servants *d.* the water
21:11 *d.* the net full of fishes
Acts 5:37 *d.* away much people
14:19 *d.* Paul out of the city
16:19 *d.* P. and S. into mark.-pl.
    27 jailer *d.* his sword
17:6 *d.* Jason and certain breth.
19:33 they *d.* Alexander out
21:30 *d.* Paul out of temple
Rev. 12:4 *d.* third part of stars

DREW near, or nigh.

Gen. 47:29 time *d. n.* Is. m. die
1 *Sam.* 17:40 David *d. n.* to Goli.
2 *Sam.* 18:25 Ahimaaz *d. near*
Zep. 3:2 *d.* not *near* to her God
Mat. 21:1 when they *d. n.* to Jer.
    34 time of fruit *d. near*, he sent
Luke 15:25 elder son *d. n.* to ho.
22:47 Judas *d. n.* to J. to kiss
24:15 Jesus himself *d. near*
    28 they *d. nigh* to the village
Acts 7:17 time of promise *d. n.*
    31 as Mos. *d. near* to behold it
27:27 *d. near* some country

DREWEST.

Lam. 3:57 *d.* near in day I called
DRIED. See after **DRY.**

DRINK, Substantive.

Gen. 21:19 and gave the lad *d.*
24:14 thy camels *d.* also, 46
Lev. 11:34 *d.* drunk in such ves.
Num. 20:8 give congregation *d.*
Jud. 4:19 she gave Sisera *d.*
Est. 1:7 *d.* in vessels of gold
Ps. 78:15 *d.* as out of gr. depths
102:9 mingled my *d.* with weep.
104:11 gave *d.* to every beast
Is. 32:6 cause *d.* of thirsty
43:20 to give *d.* to my people
Hos. 2:5 lovers that give me *d.*
4:18 their *d.* is sour
Hab. 2:15 giveth his neighbor *d.*
Hag. 1:6 ye are not filled with *d.*
Mal. 25:35 and ye gave me *d.*
37 g. thee *d.* ; 42 gave me no *d.*
John 4:9 a Jew, askest *d.* of me
6:55 my blood is *d.* indeed
Rom. 12:20 enemy thirst, give *d.*
14:17 kingdom not meat and *d.*
1 *Cor.* 10:4 drink same spirit. *d.*
Col. 2:16 judge in meat or in *d.*

Strong DRINK.

Lev. 10:9 do not drink *strong d.*
Num. 6:3 Nazarite sep. fr. *s. d.*
Deut. 14:26 money for *str. d.*
29:6 nor drunk *s. d.* forty years
Jud. 13:4 wife not drink *s. d.*
1 *Sam.* 1:15 wine nor *str. d.*
Prov. 20:1 *strong d.* is raging
31:4 princes to drink *str. d.*
6 *s. d.* to him ready to perish
Is. 5:11 may follow *strong d.*
22 men of strength min. *s. d.*
24:9 *str. d.* bitter to them
28:7 erred through *st. d.* they
are out of the way thro' *s. d.*
29:9 stag. but not with *strong d.*
56:12 fill ourselves with *str. d.*
Mic. 2:11 prophesy of *strong d.*
Luke 1:15 shall not drink *s. d.*

DRINK-OFFERING.

Ex. 29:40 for a *d.-o. Num.* 15:5
Lev. 23:13 *d.-o.* shall be of wine
Is. 57:6 hast poured *d.-o.*
65:11 furnish *d.-o.*
Joel 1:9 *d.-o.* cut off
13 the *d.-o.* is withholden
2:14 return, and leave a *d.-o.*

DRINK-OFFERINGS.

Lev. 23:18 with *d.-o.* 37 ; *Num.*
6:15 ; 28:31 ; 29:11, 18, 19, 21,
24, 30, 33, 37, 39
Num. 28:14 *d.-o.* half a hin of w.
Deut. 32:38 drank wine of *d.-o.*
Ezr. 7:17 buy speedily *d.-o.*
Ps. 16:4 their *d.-o.* of blood
Jer. 7:18 *d.-o.* to oth. gods, 19:13 ;
32:29
44:17 *d.-o.* to qu. of heaven, 18
Ezek. 20:28 there poured out *d.-o.*
45:17 princes part to give *d.-o.*

DRINK, Verb.

Gen. 24:18 *d.* my lord, 46
30:38 when flocks came to *d.*
Ex. 15:24 what shall we *d.* ?
32:20 made children of Israel *d.*
Lev. 10:9 do not *d.* wine nor
Num. 6:3 nor *d.* liquor of grapes
Jud. 7:5 boweth down to *d.*
Ruth 2:9 go to the vessels, and *d.*
2 *Sam.* 23:16 would not *d.* thereof, 17 ; 1 *Chr.* 11:18, 19
1 *K.* 17:4 shalt *d.* of the brook
Est. 5:13 king and Haman to *d.*
Job 21:20 *d.* wrath of Almighty
Ps. 36:8 *d.* of river of thy pleas.
60:3 *d.* wine of astonishment
69:21 gave me vinegar to *d.*
75:8 wicked of earth shall *d.*
78:44 into blood that not *d.*
80:5 givest them tears to *d.*
110:7 *d.* of the brook
Prov. 4:17 they *d.* wine

31:5 lest they *d.* and forget law
7 *d.* and forget his poverty
Cant. 5:1 *d.* yea, *d.* abundantly
Is. 24:9 drink bit. to them *d.* it
Is. 51:22 no more *d.* it again
62:9 *d.* it in courts of holiness
65:13 my servant shall *d.*
Jer. 16:7 cup of consolation to *d.*
23:15 make *d.* water of gall
25:15 cause nations to *d.* it
16 they shall *d.* and be moved
27 *d.* ye, be drunken, and spue
28 Ye shall certainly *d.*
35:14 to this day they *d.* none
49:12 whose judgm. was not to
d. of cup, but thou shalt *d.*
Ezek. 4:11 time to time shalt *d.*
23:32 *d.* of thy sister's cup
34:19 *d.* that ye have fouled
Dan. 5:2 concubines might *d.*
Amos 4:1 masters, Let us *a.*
Ob. 16 the heathen *d.* continually, yea, they shall *d.*
Hab. 2:16 *d.* and let thy foreskin
Hag. 1:6 ye are not filled
Zec. 9:15 *d.* and make a noise
Mat. 10:42 whoso giveth to *d.* to
20:22 are ye able to *d.* of the cup
I shall *d.* of ? *Mark* 10:38
23 shall *d.* indeed, *Mark* 10:39
26:27 saying, *d.* ye all of it
29 not *d.* till that day I *d.* it,
Mark 14:25 ; *Luke* 22:18
42 may not pass, except I *d.* it
27:34 gave him vinegar to *d.*
48 put it on a reed, and gave
him to *d. Mark* 15:36
Mark 16:18 if *d.* any deadly th.
John 4:10 saith, Give me to *d.*
7:37 let him come to me and *d.*
18:11 shall I not *d.* ?
1 *Cor.* 10:4 did all *d.* the same
21 *d.* cup of L. and of devils
11:25 this do, as oft as ye *d.* it
12:13 all to *d.* into one Spirit

DRINK water, or waters.

Gen. 24:43 *w.* of thy pitcher to *d.*
Ex. 7:24 for w. to *d.*
15:23 could not *d. waters* of M.
17:1 no *water* for the peo. to *d.*
Num. 5:24 *d.* bitter *water,* 26, 27
20:5 neither any *w.* to *d.* 33:14
17 nor *d. water* of wells, 21:22
Deut. 2:6 wa. for money, *d.* 28
Jud. 4:19 *w.* to *d.* for I am thir.
7:6 rest bowed to *d. water*
1 *Sam.* 30:11 Egyptian *d. w.*
2 *Sam.* 23:15 give me to *d.* of w.
of Bethlehem, 1 *Chr.* 11:17
1 *K.* 13:8 nor will I *d. water,* 9
17:10 a little w. that I may *d.*
2 *K.* 3:17 val. fill. with w. may *d.*
18:31 *d.* ev. one wa. cis. *Is.* 36:16
Job 22:7 given *w.* to weary to *d.*
Prov. 5:15 *d. wa.* out of thy cist.
25:21 give *w.* to *d.*
Jer. 2:18 *d. water* of Sihor
8:14 *w.* of gall to *d.* 9:15
Ezek. 4:11 *d. water* by meas. 16
12:18 *d.* thy *water* with tremb.
19 *d.* their *wa.* with astonish.
31:14 their trees that *d. w.* 16
Dan. 1:12 pulse to eat, *wat.* to *d.*
Amos 8:4 wandered to *d. water*
Jon. 3:7 let not feed nor *d. w.*
Mark 9:41 cup of w. to *d.*
John 4:7 Give me w. to *d.*
1 *Tim.* 5:23 *d.* no longer *water*

DRINK, with wine.

Gen. 19:32 our father *d.* wine
Lev. 10:9 not *d.* wine when go
Num. 6:3 *d.* no vinegar of *w.*
20 Nazarite may *d. w.*
Deut. 28:39 plant vineyards, but
not *d.* of *wine, Amos* 5:11
Jud. 13:4 M. wife *d.* no *w.* 7, 14
2 *Sam.* 16:2 *w.* such as faint m. *d.*

Ps. 60:3 *d. wine* of astonishment
Prov. 4:17 *d. wine* of violence
9:5 *d.* of *wine* I have mingled
31:4 it is not for kings to *d. w.*
Ec. 9:7 *d.* thy *w.* with a merry
Cant. 8:2 *d.* of spiced *w.*
Is. 5:22 are mighty to *d. wine*
24:9 shall not *d. w.* with a song
62:8 sons of stranger not *d. w.*
Jer. 35:2 give Rechabites *w.* to *d.*
6 *d.* no *w.* ye shall *d.* no *w.*
Ezek. 44:21 nor any priest *d. w.*
Dan. 1:16 *wine* they should *d.*
Joel 3:3 sold a girl for *w.* to *d.*
Amos 2:8 *d. w.* of condemned
12 ye gave Nazarites *wine* to *d.*
6:6 that *d. wine* in bowls
9:14 plant vineyards and *d. w.*
Mic. 6:15 not *d. wine,* Zep. 1:13
Mark 15:23 gave to *d. w.* mingled
Luke 1:15 J. shall *d.* neither *w.*
Rom. 14:21 not good to *d. wine*
Rev. 14:8 all nations *d.* of *w.*
10 *d.* of *wine* of wrath of G.

DRINKERS.

Joel 1:5 howl, all ye *d.* of wine

DRINKS.

Heb. 9:10 only in meats and *d.*

DRINKETH.

Gen. 44:5 in which my lord *d.* ?
Deut. 11:11 land *d.* water of rain
Job 6:4 poison *d.* up my spirit
15:16 *d.* iniquity like water
34:7 like Job who *d.* scorning
40:23 behold, he *d.* up a river
Prov. 26:6 *d.* damage
Is. 29:8 he *d.* but he awaketh
44:12 the smith, he *d.* no water
Mark 2:16 *d.* with publicans ?
John 4:13 *d.* this wa. shall thirst
14 *d.* of water I shall give him
6:54 *d.* my blood hath eter. life
56 *d.* my blood, dwelleth in me
1 *Cor.* 11:29 *d.* unworth. *d.* dam.
Heb. 6:7 which *d.* in the rain

DRINKING.

Gen. 24:22 camels had done *d.*
Ruth 3:3 till Boaz have done *d.*
1 *Sam.* 30:16 were eating and *d.*
1 *K.* 4:20 Judah and Israel *d.*
10:21 Solomon's *d.* vessels
16:9 E. was *d.* ; 20:12 Benhad.
1 *Chr.* 12:39 with D. three days *d.*
Est. 1:8 *d.* was according to law
Job 1:13 sons and daughters *d.*
Is. 22:13 eating flesh, and *d. w.*
Mat. 11:18 John came neither
eating nor *d. Luke* 7:33
19 eating and *d. Luke* 7:34
24:38 and *d.* till the flood came
Luke 10:7 *d.* such as they give

DRIVE.

Ex. 6:1 with a strong hand *d.* out
23:28 hornets, which shall *d.*
29 I will not *d.* out in one year
30 by little and little I will *d.*
33:2 I will *d.* out the Canaanite
34:11 behold, I *d.* out Amorite
Num. 22:6 I may *d.* them out
11 able to overcome, and *d.*
33:55 if ye will not *d.* out the
Deut. 4:38 *d.* out nations from
bef. thee, 9:4, 5 ; *Jos.* 3:10
9:3 so shalt thou *d.* them out
11:23 then will the Lord *d.* out
18:12 Lord doth *d.* them out
Jos. 13:6 them will I *d.* out
14:12 then I shall be able to *d.*
15:63 Judah could not *d.* out
17:12 Manasseh could not *d.* out
13 not utterly *d.* out, *Jud.* 1:28
18 shalt *d.* out the Canaanites
23:5 *d.* them out of your sight
13 no more *d.* out, *Jud.* 2:3, 21

DRIVE

Jud. 1:19 Judah could not *d.* out
21 Benjamin not *d.* out Jebus.
27 Manasseh ; 29 Ephraim
31 Asher ; 33 Naphtali
11:24 whom Lord shall *d.* out
2 *K.* 4:24 *d.* slack not thy riding
2 *Chr.* 20:7 *d.* out inhabitants
Job 18:11 ter. *d.* him to his feet
24:3 *d.* away ass of fatherless
Ps. 44:2 didst *d.* out heathen
68:2 as smoke, so *d.* them away
Ps. 22:15 rod of correction *d.* it
Is. 22:19 *d.* thee from thy station
Jer. 24:9 be a curse whither I *d.*
27:10 I should *d.* you out, 15
46:15 Lord did *d.* them
Ezek. 4:13 whether I will *d.* them
Dan. 4:25 *d.* thee from men, 32
Hos. 9:15 *d.* th. out of my house
Joel 2:20 *d.* the northern army
Zep. 2:4 *d.* out Ashd. at noonday
Acts 27:15 ship, we let her *d.*

DRIVEN.

Gen. 4:14 hast *d.* me out this day
Ex. 10:11 *d.* from Pharaoh's pre.
22:10 the beast be *d.* away
Num. 32:21 *d.* out his enemies
Deut. 4:19 be *d.* to worship them
30:1 whither Lord hath *d.*
4 if any of thine be *d.* out
Jos. 23:9 L. *d.* out great nations
1 *Sam.* 26:19 *d.* me out this day
Job 6:13 wisdom *d.* from me ?
13:25 break leaf *d.* to and fro ?
18:18 *d.* from light to darkness
30:5 *d.* forth from among men
Ps. 40:14 let be *d.* backward
68:2 as smoke is *d.* away, so
114:3 Jordan was *d.* back, 5
Prov. 14:32 wicked is *d.* away
Is. 8:22 shall be *d.* to darkness
19:7 sown by brooks *d.* away
41:2 as *d.* stubble to his bow
Jer. 8:3 in places whither *d.*
23:3, 8 ; 29:14, 18 ; 32:37
16:15 from all lands whither *d.*
Jer. 23:2 *d.* them away not visit.
12 be *d.* on, and fall therein
40:12 places whither *d.* 43:5
46:28 end of nations, whither *d.*
49:5 shall be *d.* out every man
50:17 lions have *d.* him away
Ezek. 31:11 I have *d.* him out for
34:4 brought that *d.* away, 16
Dan. 4:33 *d.* from men, 5:21
9:7 through all countries *d.*
Hos. 13:3 as chaff *d.* with whirl.
Mic. 4:6 gather her *d.* Zep. 3:19
Luke 8:29 *d.* of devil into wilder.
Acts 27:17 and so were *d.*
27 *d.* up and down in Adria
Jam. 1:6 like wave *d.* with wind
3:4 though *d.* of fierce winds

DRIVER.

Job 39:7 nor regard. crying of *d.*

DRIVETH.

2 *K.* 9:20 for he *d.* furiously
Ps. 1:4 like chaff wind *d.*
Prov. 25:23 wind *d.* away rain
Mark 1:12 *d.* him to wilderness

DRIVING.

Jud. 2:23 *d.* them out hastily
2 *K.* 9:20 *d.* is like *d.* of Jehu
1 *Chr.* 17:21 by *d.* out nations

DROMEDARY, IES.

1 *K.* 4:28 brought barley for *d.*
Est. 8:10 sent letters on young *d.*
Is. 60:6 *d.* of Midian cover thee
Jer. 2:23 thou art a swift *d.*

DROP, S.

Job 36:27 maketh small the *d.*
38:28 who begotten *d.* of dew ?
Cant. 5:2 locks with *d.* of night
Is. 40:15 nat. are as *d.* of bucket
Luke 22:44 as great *d.* of blood

DROP.

Deut. 32:2 doctrine *d.* as rain
33:28 heav. *d.* dew, *Prov.* 3:20
Job 36:28 which the clouds do *d.*
Ps. 65:11 thy paths *d.* fatness
12 *d.* on pastures of wilderness
Prov. 5:3 lips of a str. woman *d.*
Cant. 4:11 lips *d.* as honey-comb
Is. 45:8 *d.* down, ye heavens
Ezek. 20:46 *d.* thy word
21:2 *d.* thy word to holy places
Joel 3:18 mountains shall *d.*
down new wine, *Amos* 9:13
Amos 7:16 *d.* not thy word ag. Is.

DROPPED, ETH.

Jud. 5:4 heavens *d.* clouds *d.*
1 *Sam.* 14:26 the honey *d.*
2 *Sam.* 21:10 water *d.* on them
Job 29:22 my speech *d.* on them
Ps. 68:8 heavens *d.* at pres. of G.
Ec. 10:18 thr. idleness house *d.*
Cant. 5:5 hands *d.* with myrrh

DROPPING.

Prov. 19:13 a continual *d.* 27:15
Cant. 5:13 his lips *d.* myrrh

DROPSY.

Luke 14:2 a man wh. had the *d.*

DROSS.

Ps. 119:119 the wicked like *d.*
Prov. 25:4 take *d.* from silver
26:23 covered with silver *d.*
Is. 1:22 thy silver is become *d.*
25 purely purge away thy *d.*
Ezek. 22:18 house of Israel *d.* 19

DROUGHT.

Gen. 31:40 in day *d.* consumed
Deut. 8:15 fiery serpents and *d.*
Job 24:19 *d.* consu. snow-waters
Ps. 32:4 my moisture into the *d.*
Is. 58:11 L. satisfy thy soul in *d.*
Jer. 2:6 through a land of *d.*
17:8 not be careful in year of *d.*
50:38 a *d.* is upon her waters
Hos. 13:5 know thee in land of *d.*
Hag. 1:11 and I called for a *d.*

DROVE.

Gen. 32:16 ev. *d.* by themselves
33:8 what meanest by all this *d.*

DROVE, Verb.

Gen. 3:24 so God *d.* out the man
15:11 Abram *d.* fowls away
Ex. 2:17 shepherds *d.* them
Num. 21:32 *d.* out the Amorites
Hab. 3:6 *d.* asunder the nations
John 2:15 *d.* them out of temple

DROWN.

Cant. 8:7 neither can floods *d.* it
1 *Tim.* 6:9 *d.* men in perdition

DROWNED.

Ex. 15:4 are *d.* in Red sea
Amos 8:8 *d.* as by flood of E. 9:5
Mat. 18:6 better *d.* in the sea
Heb. 11:29 Egyptians were *d.*

DROWSINESS.

Prov. 23:21 *d.* shall clo. with rags

DRUNK.

Deut. 29:6 nor have you *d.* wine
32:42 my arrows *d.* with blood
Jud. 15:19 *d.* his spirit came ag.
1 *Sam.* 1:15 I have *d.* nei. wine
2 *Sam.* 11:13 Dav. made Uriah *d.*
1 *K.* 13:22 hast eaten and *d.*
16:9 Elah drinking himself *d.*
20:16 Benha. drinking hims. *d.*
2 *K.* 6:23 eat. and *d.* he sent aw.
19:24 *d.* strange wat. *Is.* 37:25
Cant. 5:1 *d.* my wine
Is. 51:17 hast *d.* cup of his fury
63:6 make them *d.* in my fury
Jer. 46:10 he *d.* with their blood
51:57 I will make *d.* her princes
Ezek. 34:18 *d.* of the deep waters
Dan. 5:4 *d.* praised gods of gold-

23 thou and concubines have *d.*
Ob. 16 *d.* on my holy mountain
Luke 5:39 having *d.* old wine
13:26 eaten and *d.* in thy pres.
John 2:10 well *d.* then worse
Eph. 5:18 *d.* wherein is excess
Rev. 17:2 *d.* with wine of fornic.
18:3 all nations *d.* of wine

DRUNKARD.

Deut. 21:20 this our son is a *d.*
Prov. 23:21 *d.* sh. come to pov.
26:9 as a thorn into hand of *d.*
Is. 24:20 the earth reel like a *d.*
1 *Cor.* 5:11 with bro. a *d.* eat not

DRUNKARDS.

Ps. 69:12 I was song of the *d.*
Is. 28:1 woe to *d.* of Ephraim, 3
Joel 1:5 awake, ye *d.* and weep
Nah. 1:10 while drunken as *d.*
1 *Cor.* 6:10 nor *d.* inherit kingd.

DRUNKEN.

Gen. 9:21 Noah was *d.*
1 *Sam.* 1:14 How long be *d.* ?
25:36 Nabal was very *d.*
Job 12:25 stag. like *d. Ps.* 107:27
Is. 19:14 as a *d.* man staggereth
29:9 *d.* but not with wine, 51:21
49:26 be *d.* with their own blood
51:17 *d.* dregs of cup of tremb.
Jer. 23:9 I am like a *d.* man
25:27 be *d.* and spue. and fall
48:26 *d.* for he magnified hims.
49:12 they have assuredly *d.*
51:7 golden cup made earth *d.*
39 make *d.* that they may sleep
Lam. 3:15 *d.* with wormwood
4:21 thou shalt be *d. Nah.* 3:11
5:4 *d.* our water for money
Ezek. 39:19 dri. blood till ye be *d.*
Nah. 1:10 while *d.* as drunkards
Hab. 2:15 and makest him *d.* also
Mat. 24:49 begin to eat and drink
with the *d. Luke* 12:45
Luke 17:8 serve me till I have *d.*
Acts 2:15 not *d.* as ye suppose
1 *Cor.* 11:21 and another is *d.*
1 *Thes.* 5:7 be *d.* are *d.* in night
Rev. 17:6 woman *d.* with blood

DRUNKENNESS.

Deut. 29:19 to add *d.* to thirst
Ec. 10:17 eat for strength not *d.*
Jer. 13:13 fill inhabitants with *d.*
Ezek. 23:33 shalt be filled with *d.*
Luke 21:34 overcharged with *d.*
Rom. 13:13 not in rioting and *d.*
Gal. 5:21 works of flesh are *d.*

DRUSILLA. *Acts* 24:24

DRY.

Lev. 13:30 it is a *d.* scall
Jos. 9:5 bread was *d.* 12
Jud. 6:37 it be *d.* on all the earth
39 let it be *d.* only on fleece
Job 13:25 pursue the *d.* stubble ?
Ps. 105:41 they ran in *d.* places
Prov. 17:1 better is a *d.* morsel
Is. 25:5 as the heat in a *d.* place
32:2 be as rivers in a *d.* place
44:27 saith to the deep, Be *d.*
56:3 say, I am a *d.* tree
Jer. 4:11 a *d.* wind, not to fan
51:36 I will make her springs *d.*
Ezek. 17:24 made *d.* tree flourish
20:47 devour every *d.* tree
30:12 I will make the rivers *d.*
37:2 bones *d.* ; 4 O ye *d.* bones
Hos. 9:14 give them *d.* breasts
13:15 his spring shall become *d.*
Nah. 1:4 rebuk. sea, maketh it *d.*
10 be dev. as stubble fully *d.*
Zep. 2:13 make Nineveh *d.* like
Mat. 12:43 *d.* places, *Luke* 11:24
Luke 23:31 be done in the *d.* ?

DRY ground.

Gen. 8:13 face of *ground* was *d.*
Ex. 14:16 on *g.* in sea, 22

Jos. 3:17 the priests stood firm
   on *d. ground* in Jordan
2 K. 2:8 Elisha went over on *d. g.*
Ps. 107:33 water-spr. into *d. g.*
   53 turneth *g.* into water-sp.
Is. 44:3 will pour floods on *d. g.*
   53:2 as a root out of a *d. g.*
Ezek. 19:13 planted in a *d. g.*
See LAND.

DRY, Verb.

Job 12:15 waters, they *d.* up
   15:30 flame *d.* up his branches
Is. 42:15 will *d.* up herbs, pools
   44:27 *d.* up thy rivers; 50:2 sea
Jer. 51:36 I will *d.* up her sea
Zec. 10:11 deeps of river shall *d.*

DRIED.

Gen. 8:7 until waters were *d.* up
Lev. 2:14 green ears of corn *d.* by
Num. 6:3 moist grapes or *d.*
   11:6 our soul is *d.* away
Jos. 2:10 Lord *d.* up Red sea
   4:23 *d.* up waters of Jordan
   5:1 heard Lord had *d.* up Jord.
Jud. 16:7 with withs never *d.*
1 K. 13:4 Jeroboam's hand *d.*
   17:7 brook *d.* because no rain
2 K. 19:24 with sole of feet have
   I *d.* the rivers, *Is.* 37:25
Job 18:16 his roots be *d.* beneath
   28:4 they are *d.* up
Ps. 22:15 my strength is *d.*
   69:3 my throat is *d.* eyes fail
   106:9 Red sea, it was *d.* up
Is. 5:13 multi. *d.* up with thirst
   19:5 river be wasted and *d.* up
   6 brooks of defence be *d.* up
   51:10 it which hath *d.* the sea?
Jer. 23:10 places of wilder. *d.* up
   50:38 her waters shall be *d.* up
Ezek. 17:24 *d.* up the green tree
   19:12 east wind *d.* up her fruit
   37:11 they say, Our bones are *d.*
Hos. 9:16 their root is *d.* up
   13:15 his fountain be *d.* up
Joel 1:10 the new wine is *d.* up
   12 vine is *d.;* 20 rivers are *d.*
Zec. 11:17 arm be clean *d.* up
Mark 5:29 fount. of her blood *d.*
   11:20 saw the fig-tree *d.* up
Rev. 16:12 Euphrates was *d.* up

DRIEDST, ETH.

Job 14:11 and as the flood *d.* up
Ps. 74:15 *d.* up mighty rivers
Prov. 17:22 broken spirit *d.* bon.
Nah. 1:4 Lord *d.* up all the riv.

DRY-SHOD.

Is. 11:15 make men go over *d.-s.*

DUE.

Lev. 10:13 thy *d.* thy sons' *d.* 14
Deut. 18:3 shall be the priest's *d.*
1 Chr. 15:13 sought not after *d.*
   16:29 the glory *d.* to his name,
   Ps. 29:2; 96:8
Prov. 3:27 with. not to whom *d.*
Mat. 18:34 pay all that was *d.*
Luke 23:41 we receive *d.* reward
Rom. 13:7 to whom tribute is *d.*
1 Cor. 7:3 to the wife *d.* benevol.

DUE season.

Lev. 26:4 in *d. s. Deut.* 11:14
Num. 28:2 to offer to me in *d. s.*
Ps. 104:27 meat in *d. s.* 145:15
Prov. 15:23 a word spoken in *d. s.*
Ec. 10:17 princes eat in *d. s.*
Mat. 24:45 in *d. s. Luke* 12:42
Gal. 6:9 in *d. s.* we shall reap

DUE time.

Deut. 32:35 foot slide in *d. time*
Rom. 5:6 in *d. time* Christ died
1 Cor. 15:8 one born out of *d. t.*
1 Tim. 2:6 be testified in *d. t.*
Tit. 1:3 in *d. time* manifested
1 Pet. 5:6 he may exalt you in *d. t.*

DUES.

Rom. 13:7 render to all their *d.*

DUKE, S.

Gen. 36:15 *d.* of sons of Esau, 19
   21 *d.* of the Horites, 29
   40 *d.* Alvah, *d.* Jetheth
Ex. 15:15 *d.* of Edom amazed
Jos. 13:21 Hur and Reba, *d.*

DULCIMER.

Dan. 3:5 *d.* and music, 10, 15

DULL.

Mat. 13:15 ears are *d. Acts* 28:27
Heb. 5:11 ye are *d.* of hearing

DUMAH.

Gen. 25:14; *Jos.* 15:52; *Is.* 21:11

DUMB.

Ex. 4:11 or who maketh the *d.*
Ps. 38:13 I was as a *d.* man
   39:2 I was *d.* with silence, 9
Prov. 31:8 open thy mouth for *d.*
Is. 35:6 tongue of *d.* shall sing
   53:7 sheep before shearers is *d.*
   56:10 his watchmen all *d.* dogs
Ezek. 3:26 *d.* and not be reprover
   24:27 speak, and be no more *d.*
   33:22 and I was no more *d.*
Dan. 10:15 to the grou. I bec. *d.*
Hab. 2:18 to make him *d.* idols
   19 saith to *d.* stone, Arise
Mat. 9:32 bro. to him a *d.* man
   33 the *d.* spake, *Luke* 11:14
   12:22 and *d.* and he healed
   15:30 having with them those *d.*
   31 saw the *d.* speak, *Mark* 7:37
Mark 9:25 thou *d.* spirit, come
Luke 1:20 shalt be *d.* until the
Acts 8:32 lamb *d.* before shearer
1 Cor. 12:2 carried away to *d.*
2 Pet. 2:16 the *d.* ass speaking

DUNG, Substantive.

Ex. 29:14 and *d.* burn, *Lev.* 4:11:
   8:17; 16:27; *Num.* 19:5
1 K. 14:10 as taketh away *d.*
2 K. 6:25 cab of doves' *d.*
   9:37 carcass of Jezebel be as *d.*
   18:27 eat their own *d. Is.* 36:12
Job 20:7 perish like his own *d.*
Ps. 83:10 they became as *d.*
Jer. 8:2 be for *d.* on the earth
   9:22 carcasses fall as *d.*
   16:4 shall be as *d.;* 25:33 be *d.*
Ezek. 4:12 shalt bake it with *d.*
   15 given cow's *d.* for man's *d.*
Zep. 1:17 their flesh be as the *d.*
Mal. 2:3 spread *d.* on your faces,
   even *d.* of solemn feasts
Phil. 3:8 I count all things but *d.*

DUNG, Verb.

Luke 13:8 dig about, and *d.* it

DUNG-GATE.

Neh. 3:13 Ha. rep. to *d.-g.* 12:31

DUNGHILL, S.

1 Sam. 2:8 beg. from *d. Ps.* 113:7
Ezr. 6:11 let his house be a *d.*
Is. 25:10 as straw trodden for *d.*
Lam. 4:5 embrace *d.*
Dan. 2:5 houses be made a *d.*
   3:29 their houses be made a *d.*
Luke 14:35 salt not fit for the *d.*

DUNGEON.

Gen. 40:15 should put me into *d.*
   41:14 Joseph hastily out of *d.*
Ex. 12:29 to first-born in *d.*
Jer. 37:16 Jeremiah entered *d.*
   38:6 cast him into the *d.*
   10 take up Jere. out of the *d.*
   11 let them lift up Jerem.
Lam. 3:53 cut off my life in *d.*
   55 called on thy name out of *d.*

DURA. *Dan.* 3:1

DURABLE.

Prov. 8:18 *d.* riches are with me
Is. 23:18 be for *d.* clothing

DURETH.

Mat. 13:21 but *d.* for a while

DURST.

Est. 7:5 that *d.* presume to do so
Job 32:6 *d.* not show my opinion
Mat. 22:46 *d.* not ask more ques.
   Mark 12:34; *Luke* 20:40
John 21:12 none *d.* ask him
Acts 5:13 *d.* no man join to them
   7:32 then Moses *d.* not behold
Jude 9 *d.* not bring a railing ac.

DUST.

Gen. 3:14 *d.* shalt eat all the *d.*
   19 *d.* thou art, to *d.* shalt ret.
   13:16 if number the *d.* of earth
   18:27 who am but *d.* and ashes
Ex. 8:16 say to Aaron, smite *d.*
   9:9 it shall become small *d.*
Lev. 14:41 pour out *d.*
   17:13 blood, and cover it with *d.*
Num. 23:10 who can count *d.*
Deut. 9:21 I cast *d.* into brook,
   2 K. 23:12
   28:24 make rain of thy land *d.*
Jos. 7:6 elders put *d.* on heads
2 Sam. 16:13 Shimei cast *d.*
1 K. 18:38 fire of L. consumed *d.*
   20:10 if the *d.* of Samaria suffice
2 Chr. 34:4 made *d.* of images
Job 2:12 sprinkled *d.* upon heads
   7:5 flesh clothed with clods of *d.*
   10:9 bring me into *d.* again?
   28:6 earth, it hath *d.* of gold
   34:15 shall turn again to *d.*
   38:38 *d.* groweth into hardness
   42:6 and repent in *d.* and ashes
Ps. 22:15 brought me into the *d.*
   30:9 shall *d.* praise thee, shall
   72:9 enemies shall lick the *d.*
   78:27 rained flesh on them as *d.*
   Ps. 102:14 serva. favor *d.* thereof
   103:14 remembereth we are *d.*
Ec. 12:7 shall *d.* return to earth
Is. 34:7 their *d.* shall be made fat
   9 *d.* be turned into brimstone
   40:12 comprehended *d.* of earth
   49:23 lick up the *d.* of thy feet
   52:2 shake thyself from the *d.*
   65:25 *d.* be the serpent's meat
Lam. 2:10 cast *d.* on their heads,
   Ezek. 27:30
Ezek. 24:7 to cover it with *d.*
   26:4 I will scrape her *d.* from
   10 their *d.* shall cover thee
Amos 2:7 pant after *d.* of earth
Mic. 7:17 they shall lick the *d.*
Nah. 1:3 clouds are *d.* of his feet
Hab. 1:10 for they shall heap *d.*
Mat. 10:14 sha. off the *d.* of your
   feet, *Mark* 6:11; *Luke* 9:5
Luke 10:11 the *d.* we do wipe off
Acts 13:51 they shook off the *d.*
   22:23 as threw *d.* into the air
Rev. 18:19 cast *d.* on their heads

As the DUST.

Gen. 13:16 thy seed *as the d.* of
   the earth, 28:14; *2 Chr.* 1:9
Deut. 9:21 calf small *as the d.*
2 Sam. 22:43 I beat them as small
   as the d. Ps. 18:42
Job 22:24 lay up gold *as the d.*
   27:16 heap up silver *as d.*
Is. 5:24 their blossom go up *as d.*
   40:15 nations *as small d.* of bal.
   41:2 he gave *as d.* to his sword
Zep. 1:17 blood be pour. out *as d.*
Zec. 9:3 heaped up silver *as d.*

In the DUST.

Job 4:19 foundation is *in the d.*
   7:21 now shall I sleep *in the d.*
   16:15 defiled my horn *in the d.*
   17:16 rest together is *in the d.*
   20:11 lie down with him *in t. d.*
   21:26 lie down alike *in the d.*
   39:14 warmeth eggs *in the d.*
   40:13 hide them *in the d.* toget.

Ps. 7:5 lay my honor *in the d.*
Is. 2:10 hide thee *in the d.*
26:19 and sing, ye *in the d.*
47:1 and sit *in the d.* O virgin
Lam. 3:29 putteth mouth *in t. d.*
Dan. 12:2 sleep *in d.* shall awake
Mic. 1:10 roll thyself *in the d.*
Nah. 3:18 nobles shall dwell *in d.*

Like the DUST.
2 *K.* 13:7 *like the d.* by thresh.
Is. 29:5 thy strangers be *like d.*

Of the DUST.
Gen. 2:7 L. formed man *of the d.*
Num. 5:17 take *of d.* in the tab.
Deut. 32:24 serpents *of d.*
1 *Sam.* 2:8 out *of d. Ps.* 113:7
Job 5:6 cometh not *of the d.*
Prov. 8:26 highest part *of d.*
Ec. 3:20 all are *of the d.*
Is. 29:4 be low out *of d.*

To the DUST.
Ps. 22:29 that go down *to the d.*
44:25 soul is bowed down *to d.*
104:29 they die and return *to d.*
119:25 soul cleaveth *to the d.*
Ec. 3:20 all turn *to the d.*
Is. 25:12 bring fortress *to d.*
26:5 bringeth city even *to the d.*

DUTY.
Ex. 21:10 *d.* of mar. not dimin.
Deut. 25:5 *d.* of a husband's bro.
Ec. 12:13 whole *d.* of man
Luke 17:10 that which was *d.*
Rom. 15:27 their *d.* to minister

DWARF.
Lev. 21:20 a *d.* shall not come

DWELL.
Gen. 9:27 Japhet *d.* in tents of
Ex. 2:21 content to *d.* with man
29:45 I will *d.* amongst Israel
Lev. 18:46 unclean shall *d.* alone
Num. 23:9 the people sh. *d.* alone
35:34 L. *d.* am. child. of Israel
Deut. 12:11 cause his name *d.*
33:12 *d.* between his shoulders
Jud. 9:41 Gaal not *d.* in Shech.
17:10 M. said Levite *d.* with me
1 *Sam.* 27:5 that I may *d.* there
1 *K.* 6:13 I will *d.* among Israel
8:12 he would *d.* in thick dark.
17:9 get to Zareph. and *d.* there
2 *K.* 4:13 *d.* among mine own p.
Job 3:5 let a cloud *d.* upon it
11:14 not wickedness *d.* in tab.
18:15 shall *d.* in his tabernacle
30:6 *d.* in clefts of the valleys
Ps. 5:4 nei. sh. evil *d.* with thee
15:1 who sh. *d.* in thy holy hill
25:13 his soul shall *d.* at ease
Ps. 37:27 depart from evil, and *d.*
65:4 that he may *d.* in thy cou.
8 that *d.* in the uttermost pa.
68:16 hill God desireth to *d.* in
18 Lord might *d.* among them
72:9 that *d.* in wilderness
84:10 than *d.* in tents of wicked.
101:6 faithful, that they may *d.*
120:5 that I *d.* in tents of Kedar
132:14 my rest, here will I *d.*
139:9 I *d.* in uttermost parts
143:3 made me to *d.* in darkness
Prov. 1:33 whoso hearken. sh. *d.*
8:12 I wisdom *d.* with prudence
21:19 better to *d.* in wilderness
Is. 6:5 I *d.* in midst of a people
11:6 wolf shall *d.* with lamb
13:21 owls shall *d.* there
26:5 bringeth down them th. *d.*
19 awake ye that *d.* in the dust
30:19 the people shall *d.* in Z.
32:16 judgment shall *d.* in wil.
18 people *d.* in a habitation
33:14 *d.* with devouring fire?
16 he shall *d.* on high
24 the people that *d.* therein
34:11 the owl and raven sh. *d.*

40:22 spread. out as tent to *d.* in
49:20 place to me that I may *d.*
58:12 restorer of paths to *d.* in
65:9 my servants shall *d.* there
Jer. 49:8 *d.* deep, O inhabitants
Ezek. 2:6 dost *d.* among scorp.
43:7 *d.* in midst, 9; *Zec.* 2:10,11
Hos. 12:9 I make to *d.* in taber.
14:7 that *d.* under his shadow
Joel 3:20 Judah shall *d.* for ever
Mic. 4:10 shalt *d.* in the field
7:14 flock which *d.* solitarily
Nah. 3:18 O Assy. nobles sh. *d.*
Hag. 1:4 to *d.* in ceiled houses?
Zec. 9:6 a bastard sh. *d.* in Ash.
Mat. 12:45 *d.* there, *Luke* 11:26
Luke 21:35 that *d.* on the face of
    the earth, *Acts* 17:26
Acts 7:4 land wherein ye now *d.*
28:16 P. suff. to *d.* by himself
Rom. 8:9 Sp. of G. *d.* in you, 11
1 *Cor.* 7:12 she pleased to *d.* with
2 *Cor.* 6:16 G. hath said I will *d.*
Eph. 3:17 C. *d.* in hearts by faith
Col. 1:19 in him sh. all fulness *d.*
3:16 let word of C. *d.* in you
1 *Pet.* 3:7 husbands *d.* with them
1 *John* 4:13 we *d.* in him
Rev. 7:15 he on throne shall *d.*
12:12 ye heavens, and ye that *d.*
13:6 against them that *d.*
21:3 and he will *d.* with them

DWELL, with earth.
1 *K.* 8:27 will God *d.* on *earth?*
    2 *Chr.* 6:18
Dan. 4:1 languages that *d.* in all
    the *earth*, 6:25
Rev. 3:10 try them that *d.* in *e.*
6.10 blood on them that *d.* on *e.*
13:8 all that *d.* on *e.* shall wors.
14 deceiveth them that *d.* on *e.*
14:6 preach to them th. *d.* on *e.*
17:8 they that *d.* on *earth*

DWELL, with house.
Deut. 28:30 build *house* and not
    d. *Amos* 5:11
2 *Sam.* 7:2 I *d.* in a *house* of
    cedar, 1 *Chr.* 17:1
5 build *ho.* to *d.* 1 *Chr.* 17:1
1 *K.* 2:36 build *h.* in Jer. and *d.*
3:17 I and th. wom. *d.* in one *h.*
8:13 surely built *h.* to *d.* in
Job 4:19 that *d.* in *h.* of cl.
19:15 *d.* in *h.* count stranger
Ps. 23:6 *d.* in *h.* of the Lord
27:4 that I may *d.* in *h.* of Lord
84:4 they that *d.* in thy *house*
101:7 work deceit not *d.* my *h.*
Prov. 21:9 better *d.* in the corner
    of a *house*, 25:24
Jer. 29:5 build *h. d.* in them, 28

DWELL, with Jerusalem.
1 *Chr.* 23:25 that ye may *d.* in *J.*
Neh. 11:2 offered them. to *d.* at *J.*
Jer. 33:16 *J.* shall *d.* safely
Zec. 8:3 I will *d.* in midst of *J.*
Acts 2:14 all ye that *d.* at *Jerus.*
4:16 manifest to all that *d.* in *J.*

DWELL, with land.
Gen. 24:37 Canaan. in wh. I. *d.*
26:2 *d.* in *l.* which I shall tell
34:21 let them *d.* in the *land*
45:10 shalt *d.* in *l.* of Goshen
46:34 may *d.* in *l.* of Goshen
47:6 in *l.* of Goshen let them *d.*
Ec. 8:22 *l.* in wh. my people *d.*
Lev. 25:18 shall *d.* in *l.* in safety
26:5 and *d.* in your *l.* safely
Num. 35:34 defile not *l.* wh. I *d.*
Deut. 30:20 thou mayest *d.* in *l.*
Jos. 17:12 the Canaanites would
    d. in that *land*, *Jud.* 1:27
2 *K.* 25:24 fear not to *d.* in *land*,
    Jer. 25:5; 40:9
Ps. 37:3 so thou shalt *d.* in *l.*
68:6 rebellious *d.* in a dry *land*
85:9 that glory may *d.* in our *l.*

Is. 9:2 *d.* in *l.* of shadow of death
Jer. 50:3 *l.* desol. none shall *d.*
Ezek. 28:25 they *d.* in their *land*
38:12 the people that *d.* in *land*
Hos. 9:3 shall not *d.* in Lord's *l.*

DWELL, with place.
Ex. 15:17 in *p.* th. hast ma. to *d.*
1 *Sam.* 12:8 *d.* in this *place*
2 *K.* 6:1 the *p.* we *d.* is strait
2 a *place* where we may *d.*
1 *Chr.* 17:9 shall *d.* in their *pla.*
Is. 57:15 *d.* in high and holy *p.*

DWELL safely.
Prov. 1:33 to me shall *d.* safely
Jer. 23:6 Israel shall *d.* safely,
    Ezek. 28:26; 34:25, 28; 38:8
32:37 cause them to *d.* safely
Ezek. 38:11 them that *d.* safely

DWELL in safety.
Lev. 25:18 ye shall *d.* in the land
    in *safety*, 19; *Deut.* 12:10
Deut. 33:12 beloved of the Lord
    shall *d.* in *safety*
28 Israel shall *d.* in *safety*
Ps. 4:8 L. makest me to *d.* in *s.*

DWELL therein.
Num. 14:30 to make you *d. t.*
33:53 shall *d. t. Deut.* 11:31
Ps. 24:1 and they that *d. therein*
37:29 the righteous shall *d. th.*
69:36 love his name shall *d. t.*
Is. 33:24 people that *d. therein*
51:6 that *d. therein* shall die
Jer. 4:29 and not a man *d. th.*
12:4 wick. of them. that *d. t.*
48:9 cities without any to *d. t.*
50:39 the owls shall *d. therein*
Acts 1:20 let no man *d. therein*

DWELL together.
Ps. 133:1 brethren to *d. together*

DWELLERS.
Is. 18:3 ye *d.* on earth, see ye
Acts 1:19 was known to *d.* at Jef.
2:9 *d.* in Mesopotamia we do

DWELLEST.
2 *K.* 19:15 which *d.* betw. cheru-
    bim, *Ps.* 80:1; *Is.* 37:16
Ps. 123:1 thou that *d.* in heaven
Jer. 49:16 *d.* in the clefts, *Ob.* 3
51:13 thou that *d.* upon waters
Ezek. 12:2 thou *d.* in midst
John 1:38 Master, where *d.* th.?
Rev. 2:13 works where thou *d.*

DWELLETH.
Lev. 19:34 stranger that *d.*
25:39 brother that *d.* poor, 47
Deut. 33:20 God *d.* as a lion
Jos. 6:25 Rahab *d.* in Israel
22:19 the Lord's tabernacle *d.*
1 *Sam.* 4:4 who *d.* bet. cherubim,
    2 *Sam.* 6:2; 1 *Chr.* 13:6
2 *Sam.* 7:2 the ark *d.* within
Job 15:28 he *d.* in desolate cities
38:19 way where light *d.?*
Ps. 9:11 sing to the Lord who *d.*
26:8 place where thine honor *d.*
91:1 he that *d.* in secret places
113:5 L. our G. who *d.* on high
135:21 blessed L. who *d.* at Jer.
Is. 8:18 L. who *d.* in mount Z.
33:5 the Lord, for he *d.* on high
Jer. 44:2 desolation, no man *d.*
49:31 that *d.* without care
Lam. 1:3 J. *d.* among heathen
Ezek. 16:46 sister *d.* at right ha.
Dan. 2:22 and light *d.* with him
Hos. 4:3 every one that *d.* there.
    shall mourn, *Amos* 8:8
Joel 3:21 I cleanse, for L. *d.* in Z.
Mat. 23:21 sweareth by him *d.*
John 6:56 my blood *d.* in me
14:10 Father that *d.* in me
17 the Spirit, for he *d.* in you
Acts 7:48 *d.* not in temples made
    with hands, 17:24

Rom. 7:17 I, sin th. *d.* in me, 20
18 in my flesh *d.* no good th.
8:11 quicken by Spirit that *d.*
1 *Cor.* 3:16 Spirit of G. *d.* in you
Col. 2:9 *d.* the fulness of God
2 *Tim.* 1:14 H. G. *d.* in us
Jam. 4:5 spirit that *d.* in us
2 *Pet.* 3:13 earth where. *d.* right.
1 *John* 3:17 how *d.* love of G.?
24 that keepeth com. *d.* in him
4:12 if we love, God *d.* in us
15 J. is S. of G. God *d.* in him
1 *John* 4:16 he that *d.* in love, *d.*
2 *John* 2 which *d.* in us
Rev. 2:13 slain am. you, Satan *d.*

DWELLING, Substantive.
Gen. 27:39 thy *d.* shall be fatness
2 *Chr.* 6:2 built place for thy *d.*,
Ps. 49:14 cons. in grave from *d.*
91:10 no plague come nigh *d.*
Prov. 21:20 in the *d.* of the wise
24:15 against *d.* of the righteous
Dan. 2:11 gods *d.* not with flesh
4:25 thy *d.* with beasts, 32 ; 5:21
Zep. 3:7 *d.* should not be cut off
Nah. 2:11 wh. is *d.* of the lions ?
Mark 5:3 his *d.* among tombs

DWELLING.
Gen. 25:27 plain man, *d.* in tents
Lev. 25:29 if a man sell a *d.* hou.
Num. 24:21 strong is thy *d.* place
1 *K.* 8:30 in heaven thy *d.* place
39, 43, 49 ; 2 *Chr.* 6:21, 30, 39
2 *Chr.* 30:27 prayer up to holy *d.*
36:15 compassion on *d.* place
Job 8:22 *d.* place of the wicked
21:28 *d.* places of the wicked ?
Ps. 49:11 *d.* places to all genera.
52:5 shall pluck thee out of *d.*
74:7 cast. *d.* place of thy name
76:2 his *d.* place in Zion
79:7 laid waste his *d.* place
90:1 hast been our *d.* place
Is. 4:5 create on every *d.* place
18:4 will consider in my *d.* pla.
Jer. 49:19 daughter *d.* in Egypt
51:30 have burnt their *d.* places
37 Babylon shall become a *d.*
Ezek. 38:11 all them *d.* without
Joel 3:17 Lord your God *d.* in Z.

Hab. 1:6 possess *d.* places
Acts 2:5 were *d.* at Jerusalem
19:17 known to Greeks *d.* at **E.**
1 *Cor.* 4:11 no certain *d.* place
1 *Tim.* 6:16 *d.* in light
Heb. 11:9 *d.* in taberna. with I.
2 *Pet.* 2:8 Lot, righteous man *d.*

DWELLINGS.
Ex. 10:23 child, of Isr. li. in *d.*
Lev. 3:17 a perpet. statute thro'
all *d.* 23:14 : *Num.* 35:29
7:26 art no blood in any of *d.*
23:3 do no work in all your *d.* 31
Job 18:21 the *d.* of wicked
39:6 made barren land his *d.*
Ps. 55:15 wicked. is in their *d.*
87:2 gates of Z. than all *d.* of J.
Is. 32:18 people dwell in sure *d.*
Ezek. 25:4 men of east make *d.*
Zep. 2:6 coast shall be *d.*

DWELT.
Gen. 11:2 and they *d.* there, 31 ;
26:17 ; 2 *K.* 16:6 ; 1 *Chr.* 4:43 ;
2 *Chr.* 28:18
Num. 31:10 they *d.* 2 *K.* 17:29
1 *K.* 13:11 *d.* old proph. in B. 25
Job 29:25 and I *d.* as a king
Ps. 74:2 Z. wherein thou hast *d.*
Is. 29:1 the city where David *d.*
Jer. 2:6 a land where no man *d.*
39:14 J. *d.* among the people
Ezek. 3:15 that *d.* by river Cheb.
31:6 und. shadow *d.* nations, 17
Dan. 4:21 beasts of field *d.*
Zep. 2:15 rejoicing city that *d.*
Luke 1:65 fear ca. on all that *d.*
John 1:14 W. made flesh and *d.*
39 and saw where he *d.*
Acts 13:17 they *d.* as strangers
28:30 Paul *d.* in hired house
Rev. 11:10 torm. them that *d.*

DWELT at.
Gen. 22:19 and Abraham *d.* at **B.**
Jud. 9:41 Abimelech *d.* at **A.**
1 *K.* 15:18 Benhad. *d.* at Damas.
2 *Chr.* 16:2
2 *K.* 19:36 Sen. *d.* at N. *Is.* 37:37
1 *Chr.* 2:55 scribes which *d.* at **J.**
9:34 Levites *d.* at Jerusalem
Acts 9:22 S. conv. Jews that *d.* at
32 saints who *d.* at Lydda

DWELT in.
Num. 20:15 we have *d.* in Egypt
21:31 Is. *d.* in land of Amorites
Deut. 2:12 *d.* in their stead, 21,
22, 23 ; 1 *Chr.* 5:22
13:16 of him that *d.* in bush
Jud. 8:11 of them *d.* in tents
2 *Sam.* 7:6 not *d.* in any house
since I b. Is. out, 1 *Chr.* 17:5
9:12 all that *d.* in house of Ziba
14:28 Absalom *d.* 2 years in J.
1 *K.* 2:38 Shimei *d.* in Jerusalem
12:2 J. fled from Sol. *d.* in **E.**
2 *K.* 13:5 Israel *d.* in their tents
15:5 A. *d.* in house, 2 *Chr.* 26:21
22:14 H. the prophetess *d.* in
Jer. in college, 2 *Chr.* 34:22
Ezr. 2:70 Levites, Nethinim, *d.*
in cities, *Neh.* 3:26 ; 11:21
Neh. 7:73 Israel *d.* in their cities
Ps. 94:17 almost *d.* in silence
Is. 13:20 shall it be *d.* in from
generation, *Jer.* 50:39
Jer. 35:10 we have *d.* in tents
Ezek. 36:17 Israel *d.* in own land
39:26 *d.* safely in their land
Dan. 4:12 the fowls *d.* in boughs
Mat. 2:23 Joseph *d.* in city Naz.
4:13 Jesus *d.* in Capernaum
Luke 13:4 above all that *d.* in J.
Acts 7:2 Abraham *d.* in Charr. 4
19:10 they who *d.* in Asia heard
2 *Tim.* 1:5 *d.* in grandmother

DWELT therein.
Deut. 2:10 E. *d. t.* ; 20 giants *d. t.*
1 *K.* 11:34 went to Dam. and *d. t.*
12:25 Jerob. built S. and *d. th.*
Neh. 13:16 *d.* men of Tyre *th.*
Ps. 68:10 congregation hath *d. t.*

DWELT with.
Ruth 2:23 and Ruth *d. with* her
1 *Sam.* 22:4 moth. *d. w.* k. of M.
1 *Chr* 4:23 they *d. with* king
Ps. 120:6 my soul hath long *d. w.*
Jer. 40:6 J. *d. w.* him among peo.

DYED.
Is. 63:1 with *d.* garm. from Boz.
Ezek. 23:15 *d.* attire upon heads
DYING. *See after* DIE.

E

EACH.
Gen. 15:10 Abraham laid *e.* piece
34:25 Sim. and Levi took *e.* man
40:5 *e.* his dr. 45:22 *e.* changes
Ex. 18:7 asked *e.* other of welf.
Num. 1:44 *e.* one was for house
7:3 they brought for *e.* one an ox
16:17 Aaron *e.* of you his censer
Jos. 22:14 of *e.* chief house *e.* one
Jud. 21:22 reserved not to *e.* man
Ruth 1:9 may find rest *e.* of you
1 *K.* 4:7 *e.* man his month
22:10 kings *e.* sat on his throne
2 *K.* 15:20 of *e.* man fifty shekels
Ps. 85:10 right. and pe. kissed *e.*
Is. 2:20 they made *e.* one
6:2 seraphim, *e.* had six wings
35:7 where *e.* lay, shall be grass
57:2 *e.* one walking in his upr.
Ezek. 4:6 thee *e.* day for a year
Luke 13:15 doth not *e.* on sabbath
Acts 2:3 tongues sat upon *e.* of
Phil. 2:3 let esteem other better
2 *Thes.* 1:3 charity toward *e.* oth.
Rev. 4:8 beasts had *e.* six wings

EAGLE.
Lev. 11:13 *e.* have, *Deut.* 14:12
Deut. 28:49 swift as the *e.* flieth
32:11 as an *e.* stirreth her nest
Job 9:26 *e.* that hasteth to prey

39:27 doth the *e.* mount up ?
Prov. 23:5 riches fly away as an *e.*
30:19 way of an *e.* in the air
Jer. 48:40 shall fly as an *e.*
14:16 make thy nest high as *e.*
Ezek. 1:10 had face of an *e.* 10:14
17:3 a great *e.* with gr. wings, 7
Dan. 4:33 hairs gro. like *e.* feath.
7:4 a lion, and had *e.* wings
Hos. 8:1 as an *e.* aga. the house
Mic. 1:16 thy baldness as the *e.*
Hab. 1:8 Chaldeans shall fly as *e.*
Rev. 4:7 fourth beast like fly. *e.*
12:14 to woman wings of gr. *e.*

EAGLES.
Ex. 19:4 I bare you on *e.* wings
2 *Sam.* 1:23 were swifter than *e.*
Ps. 103:5 thy youth is ren. like *e.*
Prov. 30:17 young *e.* shall eat it
Is. 40:31 mount with wings as *e.*
Jer. 4:13 his horses swifter th. *e.*
Lam. 4:19 pers. swifter than *e.*
Mat. 24:28 *e.* be gath. *Luke* 17:37

EAR.
Ex. 21:6 bore *e.* *Deut.* 15:17
1 *Sam.* 9:15 L. hath told S. in *e.*
2 *K.* 19:16 bow down *e.* *Ps.* 31:2 ;
86:1
Neh. 1:6 let thine *e.* be attent. 11

Job 4:12 and mine *e.* received
12:11 *e.* try words ? 34:3
13:1 mine *e.* hath heard
29:11 when the *e.* heard me
21 to me men gave *e.* waited
36:10 he openeth also their *e.*
42:5 I heard by hearing of *e.*

Ps. 10:17 will cause thine *e.*
31:2 bow down thine *e.* to me
58:4 like adder that stoppeth *e.*
77:1 and he gave *e.* unto me
94:9 he that planted the *e.*
Ps. 116:2 he hath inclined his *e.*

Prov. 5:1 and bow thine *e.* to
5:13 incline mine *e.* to them
15:31 the *e.* that heareth
17:4 and a liar giveth *e.* to
18:15 the *e.* of the wise seeketh
20:12 hearing *e.* seeing eye
22:17 thine *e.* hear the words
25:12 reprover on obedient *e.*
28:9 turneth away *e.* from hear.

Ec. 1:8 nor is the *e.* filled with

Is. 48:8 time thine *e.* was not
50:4 he wakeneth my *e.* to hear
5 Lord hath opened mine *e.*
59:1 *e.* heavy that it cannot h.
64:4 nor perceived by the *e.*

Jer. 6:10 their *e.* is uncircumc.
  7:24 inclined their *e.* 26; 11:8;
    17:23; 25:4; 34:14; 44:5
  9:20 let your *e.* receive the word
  35:15 ye have not inclined *e.*
Lam. 3:56 hide not *e.*
Amos 3:12 fr. the lion piece of *e.*
Mat. 10:27 what ye hear in the *e.*
  26:51 smote off hiss *e. Mark* 14:47
Luke 12:3 ye have spoken in *e.*
  22:51 touched his *e.* and healed
John 18:26 servant whose *e.* Pet
  1 *Cor.* 2:9 not seen, nor *e.* heard
  12:16 if the *e.* shall say
Rev. 2:7 he that hath *e.* let hear,
  11, 17, 29 ; 3:6, 13, 22 ; 13:9

Incline EAR.
Ps. 17:6 in. thine *e.* to me, 71:2 ;
  88:2 ; *Is.* 37:17 ; *Dan.* 9:18
  45:10 O daughter, *incline* th. *e.*
  49:4 I will *incline* mine *e.* to
Prov. 2:2 that thou in. thine *e.*
  4:20 *in. thine. e.* to my saying
Is. 55:3 *in.* your *e.* and come

Give EAR.
Ex. 15:26 if thou wilt *give e.*
Deut. 1:45 not *g. e.* to your voice,
  2 *Chr.* 24:19 ; *Neh.* 9:30
  32:1 *give e.* O heavens
Jud. 5:3 *give e.* O ye princes
Job 34:2 *give e.* to me
Ps. 5:1 *g. e.* to my words, 54:2
  17:1 *g. e.* to my pra. 55:1 ; 86:6
  39:12 *give e.* to my cry, 141:1
  49:1 *give. e.* all ye inhabitants
  78:1 *g. e.* O p. ; 80:1 *g. e.* sheph.
  84:8 *give e.* O God of Jacob
  143:1 *g. e.* to my supplications
Is. 1:2 *give e.* O earth
  10 *g. e.* to the law of our God
  8:9 *give e.* all of far countries
  28:23 *give ye e.* and hear
  42:23 who among you will *g. e. ?*
  51:4 hearken and *g. e.* to me
Jer. 13:15 *give e.* be not proud
Hos. 5:1 and *give ye e.* O house
Joel 1:2 *g. e.* all ye inhabitants

Right EAR.
Ex. 29:20 tip of *right e. Lev.* 8:23,
  24 ; 14:14, 17, 25, 28
Luke 22:50 c. off *ri. e. John* 18:10

EAR, *of corn.*
Ex. 9:31 for barley was in the *e.*
Mark 4:28 the *e.* full corn in *e.*

EAR, Verb.
1 *Sam.* 8:12 set them to *e.* ground
Is. 30:24 oxen that *e.* the ground

EARED, ING.
Gen. 45:6 neither *e.* nor harvest
Ex. 34:21 in *e.* time and harvest
Deut. 21:4 valley neither *e.* sown

EARLY.
Gen. 19:2 ye shall rise *e.* and go
Jud. 7:3 let him depart *e.*
Ps. 46:5 God shall help right *e.*
  57:8 I will awake *e.* 108:2
  63:1 my God, *e.* will I seek thee
  78:34 they inquired *e.* after God
  90:14 satisfy us *e.* with mercy
  101:8 *e.* destroy the wicked
Prov. 1:28 they shall seek me *e.*
  8:17 seek me *e.* shall find me
Hos. 5:15 they will seek me *e.*
  6:4 as *e.* dew it goeth, 13:3
Luke 24:22 woman *e.* at sepulch.
John 18:28 led J. and it was *e.*
  20:1 com. Mary Magdalene *e.*
Jam. 5:7 till he receive *e.* rain

See AROSE, RISE, RISEN, RISING,
  ROSE, MORNING.

EAR-RING.
Gen. 24:22 took a golden *e.-r.*
  30 when Laban saw *e.-r.*
  47 I put *e.-r.* upon her face
Job 42:11 ev. one gave J. an *e.-r.*
Prov. 25:12 a *e.-r.* of gold

EAR-RINGS.
Gen. 35:4 gave J. all their *e.-r.*
Ex. 32:2 break off the gold. *e.-r.*
  35:22 brought *e.-r.* for offering
Num. 31:50 we have broug. *e.-r.*
Jud. 8:24 give ev. man the *e.-r.*
Is. 3:20 L. will take away *e.-r.*
Ezek. 16:12 I put *e.-r.* in th. ears
Hos. 2:13 decked hers. with *e.-r.*

EARS.
Gen. 44:18 speak in my lord's *e.*
  50:4 speak in the *e.* of Pharaoh
Ex. 10:2 mayest tell in *e.* of son
  17:14 rehearse in *e.* of Joshua
Jud. 9:2 in *e.* of men of Shech. 3
  1 *Sam.* 3:11 the *e.* shall tingle,
    2 *K.* 21:12 ; *Jer.* 19:3
2 *Sam.* 7:22 we heard with our *e.*
  1 *Chr.* 17:20
  22:7 my cry did enter into his *e.*
Job 15:21 dreadful sound in his *e.*
  28:22 heard fame with our *e.*
  33:16 he openeth the *e.* of men
Ps. 18:6 cry came into his *e.*
  34:15 his *e.* are open
  44:1 we heard with our *e.*
  115:6 have *e.* hear not, 135:17
Prov. 21:13 whoso stop. his *e.*
  23:9 speak not in the *e.* of a fool
  26:17 taketh a dog by the *e.*
Is. 11:3 the hearing of his *e.*
  32:3 the *e.* of them that hear
  33:15 stoppeth *e.* from hearing
  35:5 *e.* of deaf shall be unstop.
  43:8 and deaf that have *e.*
Jer. 2:2 and cry in the *e.* of Jer.
  5:21 O people, which have *e.*
  29:29 Zep. read in the *e.* of Jer.
Mat. 28:14 come to governor's *e.*
Mark 7:33 put fingers into his *e.*
  35 his *e.* were opened
  8:18 having *e.* hear ye not ?
Acts 7:51 uncirc. in heart and *e.*
  17:20 bring. strange things to *e.*
Rom. 11:8 hath given *e.*
2 *Tim.* 4:3 having itching *e.*
Jam. 5:4 *e.* of Lord of sabaoth
1 *Pet.* 3:12 and his *e.* are open to

EARS to hear.
Deut. 29:4 L. hath not *g. e.* to *h.*
Ezek. 12:2 they have *e.* to hear
Mat. 11:15 *e.* to *h.* 13:9, 43 ; *Mark*
  4:9, 23 ; 7:16 ; *Luke* 8:8 ; 14:35

Mine EARS.
Num. 14:28 have spoken in *m. e.*
Jud. 17:2 spakest of in *m. e.*
  1 *Sam.* 15:14 bleat. of sh. in *m. e.*
  2 *K.* 19:28 tumult come into *mine*
    e. Is. 37:29
Ps. 40:6 *m. e.* hast thou opened
  92:11 *mine e.* shall hear
Is. 5:9 in *mine e.* said the Lord
  22:14 revealed in *mine e.*
Ezek. 8:18 tho' they cry in *m. e.*
  9:1 he cried also in *mine e.*
Luke 1:44 salut. sounded in *m. e.*

EARS of the People.
Ex. 11:2 speak in *e.* of the peo.
Deut. 32:44 M. spake in *e.* of *pe.*
Jud. 7:3 proclaim in *e.* of *pe*
  1 *Sam.* 11:4 told tid. in *e.* of *p.*
2 *K.* 18:26 not in *e. Is.* 36:11
Neh. 8:3 *e.* of *p.* were attentive

Their EARS.
Gen. 35:4 ear-rings wear in *t. e.*
Ex. 32:3 ear-rings in *their e.*
2 *K.* 23:2 read in *their e.* 2 *Chr.*
  34:30 ; *Jer.* 36:15

Is. 6:10 *t. e.* heavy, lest hear with
  t. e. Mat. 13:15 ; *Acts* 28:27
Mic. 7:16 *their e.* shall be deaf
Zec. 7:11 stopped *t. e. Acts* 7:57
2 *Tim.* 4:4 turn *it. e.* from truth

Thine EARS.
Ps. 10:17 cause *thine e.* to hear
Prov. 23:12 apply *thine e.*
Is. 30:21 *thine e.* shall hear
  49:20 children say in *thine e.*
Ezek. 3:10 hear w. *th. e.* 40:4 ; 44:5
  16:12 I put ear-rings in *thine e.*
  23:25 shall take away *thine e.*
  24:26 to hear with *thine e.*

Your EARS.
Job 13:17 declaration with *y. e.*
Ps. 78:1 incline *your e.* to words
Jer. 26:11 as heard with *your e.*
  15 Lord sent to speak in *your e.*
Mat. 13:16 but blessed are *your e.*
Luke 4:21 scripture fulfil. in *y. e.*
  9:44 let sayings sink in *your e.*

EARS of Corn.
Gen. 41:5 seven *e.* of corn, 22
Lev. 2:14 meat-offering, green *e.*
  23:14 not eat green *e. of corn*
Deut. 23:25 mayest pluck the *e.*
  Ruth 2:2 go and glean *e. of*
2 *K.* 4:42 brought full *e. of corn*
Mat. 12:1 discip. began to pluck
  e. of c. Mark 2:23 ; *Luke* 6:1

See SEVEN.

EARNEST, Substantive.
2 *Cor.* 1:22 *e.* of the Spirit, 5:5
Eph. 1:14 *e.* of our inheritance

EARNEST, Adjective.
Rom. 8:19 *e.* expecta. of creature
2 *Cor.* 7:7 when he told *e.* desire
  8:16 put same *e.* care into Titus
Phil. 1:20 accord. to my *e.* expec.
Heb. 2:1 to give more *e.* heed

EARNESTLY.
Num. 22:37 did I not *e.* send
1 *Sam.* 20:6 D. *e.* asked leave, 28
Job 7:2 serv. *e.* desireth shadow
Jer. 11:7 I *e.* protested to fathers
  31:20 I do *e.* remember him still
Mic. 7:3 evil with both hands *e.*
Luke 22:44 he prayed *e.*
  56 a certain maid *e.* looked
Acts 3:12 why look ye so *e.*
  23:1 Paul *e.* beholding council
1 *Cor.* 12:31 covet *e.* the best gifts
2 *Cor.* 5:2 we groan *e.* desiring
Jam. 5:17 pray. *e.* that it not rain
Jude 3 should *e.* con. for faith

EARNETH.
Hag. 1:6 *e.* wages *e.* to put in bag

EARTH.
Gen. 1:2 the *e.* was without form
  10 God called the dry land *e.*
  11 let *e.* bring forth, 24
  12 *e.* brought forth grass
  28 replenish the *e.* 9:1
  6:11 *e.* was corrupt before God
  7:17 the ark was lifted above *e,*
  8:14 in second mo. was *e.* dried
  22 *e.* rem. seed-time not cease
  10:25 the *e.* divided, 1 *Chr.* 1:19
  18:18 all nations of *e.* blessed in
    him, 22:18 ; 26:4 ; 28:14
  27:28 God give thee fatness of *e.*
  41:47 *e.* brought forth by hand.
Ex. 9:29 *e.* is the Lord's, *Deut*
    10:14 ; *Ps.* 24:1 ; 1 *Cor.* 10:26
  15:12 the *e.* swallowed them
  20:24 altar of *e.* thou shalt make
Num. 16:30 *e.* open her mouth
  32 *e.* opened mouth and swal-
    lowed, 26:10 ; *Ps.* 106:17
  34 lest *e.* swallow us up

Deut. 28:23 *e.* under thee be iron
32:1 hear, O *e.* the words
13 ride on high places of *e.*
22 a fire shall consume the *e.*
1 *Sam.* 2:8 pil. of the *e.* are L.'s
4:5 so that the *e.* rang again
14:15 and the *e.* quaked
2 *Sam.* 1:2 with *e.* on head, 15:32
22:8 then the *e.* sh.ook, *Ps.* 18:7
1 *K.* 1:40 so that the *e.* rent
2 *K.* 5:17 two mules' burden of *e.*
1 *Chr.* 16:31 let *e.* rej. *Ps.* 96:11
33 cometh to judge the *e. Ps.*
96:13 ; 98:9
Neh. 9:6 thou made *e. Is.* 45:12
Job. 15:47 offspring as grass of *e.*
9:6 shaketh *e.* out of her place
24 *e.* given into hand of wicked
11:9 measure longer than *e.*
15:19 to whom *e.* was given
16:18 O *e.* cover not my blood
24:4 the poor of the *e.* hide
26:7 hangeth *e.* upon nothing
30:6 to dwell in caves of the *e.*
8 were viler than the *e.*
37:17 when he quieteth the *e.*
38:4 I laid foundations of the *a.*
18 the breadth of the *e.* ?
Ps. 2:8 uttermost parts of the *e.*
10 be instr. ye judges of the *e.*
12:6 silver tried in furnace of *e.*
25:13 his seed shall inherit the *e.*
33:5 *e.* is full of goodness of L.
37:9 wait on L. inherit *e.* 11, 22
46:2 though the *e.* be removed
6 uttered voice, the *e.* melted
47:9 the shields of the *e.*
48:2 joy of whole *e.* is mount Z
60:2 made the *e.* to tremble
63:9 the lower parts of the *e.*
65:9 thou visitest the *e.*
67:6 *e.* yield incr. *Ezek.* 34:27
68:8 *e.* shook, heavens dropped
32 sing, kingdoms of *e.*
71:20 from the depths of the *e.*
72:6 showers that water the *e.*
75:3 *e.* and inhabit. *Is.* 24:19
8 wicked of the *e.* shall wring
76:8 *e.* feared ; 77:18 *e.* tre. 97:4
82:8 O God, judge the *e.*
90:2 or ever thou hadst form. *a*
Ps. 97:1 let the *e.* rejoice
99:1 let the *e.* be moved
102:25 laid the founda. of the *e.*
104:5 ; *Prov.* 8:29 ; *Is.* 48:13
148:13 his glory is above the *e.*
Prov. 3:19 L. founded *e. Is.* 24:1
8:23 or ever *e.* was
26 not made the *e.* nor fields
25:3 *e.* for depth unsearchable
30:16 the *e.* not filled with wat.
21 for three things *e.* disquiet.
Ec. 1:4 the *e.* abideth for ever
5:9 the profit of the *e.* for all
Is. 4:2 fruit of *e.* excellent
11:4 smite the *e.* with rod
9 *e.* full of knowledge of Lord
24:1 the *e.* mourneth, 33:9
19 *e.* broken, *e.* is dissolved
20 *e.* shall reel ; 26:19 cast out
26:21 *e.* shall disclose blood
40:22 sit. on the circle of the *e.*
28 the Creator of ends of the *e.*
45:8 let *e.* open ; 12 I m. the *e.*
he saved, all ends of the *e.*
51:6 look on *e. e.* shall wax old
66:1 the *e.* is my footstool
Jer. 4:23 I beheld *e.* with. form
28 for this shall the *e.* mourn
6:19 hear, O *e.* I will bring evil
22:29 O *e. e.* hear the word of
the Lord, *Mic.* 1:2
46:8 saith, I will cover the *e.*
49:21 the *e.* is moved, 50:46
Ezek. 7:21 give to wick. of the *e.*
9:9 Lord hath forsaken the *e.*
43:2 *e.* shined with his glory
Hos. 2:22 the *e.* shall hear corn

Amos 8:9 I will darken the *e.*
Jon. 2:6 the *e.* with her bars
Mic. 7:17 like worms of the *e.*
Nah. 1:5 the *e.* is burnt up
Hab. 2:14 *e.* filled with knowl.
3:3 *e.* was full of his praise
9 didst clea. the *e.* with rivers
Zec. 1:10 to and fro thro. *e.* 6:7
4:10 eyes wh. run through the *e.*
Mal. 4:6 I smite *e.* with curse
Mat. 5:5 meek shall inherit the *e.*
35 sw. not by *e.* it is footstool
13:5 had not much *e. Mark* 4:5
Mark 4:28 *e.* bringeth forth fruit
John 3:31 of the *e.* is earthly
1 *Cor.* 15:47 first man of *e.*
2 *Tim.* 2:20 ves. of wood and *e.*
Heb. 12:26 whose voice shook *e.*
Jam. 5:7 precious fruit of the *e.*
2 *Pet.* 3:10 *e.* and works therein
Rev. 7:3 hurt not the *e.* nor sea
11:6 have power to smite the *e.*
12:16 the *e.* opened her mouth
13:12 caus. *e.* to worship beast
18:1 and the *e.* was lightened
19:2 whore which did corrupt *e.*
20:11 from whose face the *e.* fled
    See BEASTS, DUST, ENDS, FACE,
KINGS, HEAVEN, PEOPLE, WHOLE.

All the EARTH.
Gen. 1:26 dominion over *all the e.*
7:3 seed on the face of *all t. e.*
11:9 confound lang. of *all t. e.*
18:25 Judge of *all t. e.* do right?
19:31 after manner of *all the e.*
Ex. 19:5 for *all the e.* is mine
34:10 not been done in *all the e.*
Num. 14:21 *all t. e.* filled with gl.
Jos. 3:11 *all t. e.* 13 ; *Zec.* 6:5
23:14 way of *all the e.* 1 *K.* 2:2
1 *Chr.* 16:14 judgments in *all the
e. Ps.* 105:7
30 fear *a. t. e. Ps.* 33:8 ; 96:9
Ps. 8:1 excellent in *all the e.* 9
47:2 k. over *all e.* 7 ; *Zec.* 14:9
57:5 be above *all e.* 11 ; 108:5
66:4 *all the e.* shall worship
83:18 high over *all the e.* 97:9
Is. 10:14 I gathered *all t. e.*
12:5 this is known in *all the e.*
Jer. 26:6 city a curse to *all the e.*
51:7 made *all the e.* drunken
Dan. 2:39 kingd. rule over *a. t. e.*
Hab. 2:20 let *all the e.* keep sil.
Zec. 1:11 *all the e.* sitteth still
Luke 23:44 dark. over *all the e.*
Rom. 10:18 sou. went into *a. t. e.*
Rev. 5:6 sp of G. sent into *all e.*

From the EARTH.
Gen. 2:6 went up a mist *f. the e.*
7:23 destroyed *from the e.*
8:11 waters abated *from the e.*
Ex. 9:15 *from the e. Jos.* 7:9 ; *Ps.*
199:15 ; *Prov.* 2:22 ; *Nah.* 2:13
2 *Sam.* 12:20 D. arose *from the e.*
Job 18:17 rememb. perish *f. t. e.*
Ps. 148:7 praise Lord *from the e.*
Amos 3:5 snare *from the e.*
John 12:32 if lifted up *f. the e.*
Acts 8:33 his life is taken *f. the e.*
Acts 9:8 Saul arose *from the e.*
22:22 away with fellow *f. the e.*
Rev. 6:4 to take peace *f. the e.*
14:3 144,000 redeemed *f. the e.*

In the EARTH.
Gen. 1:22 let fowl mult. *in the e.*
4:12 a vagabond *in the e.* 14
6:5 wickedness great *in the e.*
10:8 Nim. mighty one *in the e.*
19:31 not a man *in t. e.*
45:7 pres. a posterity *in the e.*
Ex. 20:4 *in the e.* beneath
2 *Sam.* 7:9 name like great men
in the e. 1 *Chr.* 17:8
23 what nation *in t. e.* like Israel?
1 *Chr.* 17:21
14:20 know all things *in the e.*

1 *Chr.* 29:11 *all in the e.* is thine
2 *Chr.* 6:14 no G. like thee *in t. e.*
Job 1:7 to and fro in *the e.* 2:2
8 none like Job *in the e.* 2:3
14:8 root wax old *in the e.*
24:18 portion cursed *in the e.*
39:14 ostrich leav. eggs *in the e.*
Ps. 16:3 saints that are *in the e.*
46:8 desolations made *in the e.*
10 I will be exalted *in the e.*
58:11 God that judgeth *in the e.*
72:16 a handful of corn *in the e.*
119:19 I am a stranger *in the e.*
Is. 26:9 thy judgm. are *in the e.*
18 not wrought deliver. *in t. e.*
40:24 stock not take root *in t. e.*
42:4 he set judgment *in the e.*
62:7 Jerusalem a praise *in the e.*
65:16 blesseth himself *in the e.*
sweareth *in the e.*
Jer. 31:22 a new thing *in the e.*
Joel 2:30 show wonders *in the e.*
Mat. 25:18 digged *in the e.*
25 hid thy talent *in the e.*
Mark 4:31 mustard seed sown *in
t. e.* less than all seeds *in t. e.*
1 *John* 5:8 three that witn. *i. t. e.*

On, *or* upon the EARTH.
Gen. 6:12 God looked *upon the e.*
7:4 I will cause rain *upon the e.*
8:17 multiply *upon the e.* and
19:23 sun was risen *upon the e.*
28:12 ladder set *upon the e.*
Ex. 10:6 since they were *u. the e.*
Deut. 4:10 live *up. e.* 12:1, 19
36 *upon the e.* showed great fire
12:16 pour it *upon the e.* 24
2 *Sam.* 12:16 David lay *u. the e.*
1 *K.* 8:27 will God dwell *on the
e.* ? 2 *Chr.* 6:18
17:14 L. sends rain *upon the e.*
1 *Chr.* 29:15 days *on e. Job* 8:9
Job 7:1 time to man *on e.* ?
19:25 stand at latter day *u. t. e.*
20:4 man was placed *on the e.*
37:6 snow, be thou *on the e.*
41:33 *on e.* there is not his like
Ps. 7:5 enemy tread life *on the e.*
67:2 thy way known *upon the e.*
73:25 none *upon e.* I desire bes.
Prov. 30:24 four th. little *u. the e.*
Ec. 7:20 not a just man *u. the e.*
10:7 princes as serv. *upon the e.*
11:3 clouds empty th. *upon t. e.*
Cant. 2:12 flowers appear *on t. e.*
Is. 28:22 consumption *upon the e.*
Jer. 9:3 not valiant for truth *u. e.*
Lam. 2:11 liver poured *u. the e.*
Amos 3:5 fall in snare *u. the e.*
Mat. 6:19 lay not up treas. *on e.*
9:6 Son hath power *on e.* to forgive, *Mark* 2:10 ; *Luke* 5:24
10:34 come to send peace *on e.*
16:19 thou shalt bind *on e.* 18:18
23:9 call no man father *u. the e.*
Mark 9:3 no fuller *on e.* can wh.
Luke 2:14 glory to God, *on e.*
12:49 come to send fire *o. t. e.*
51 come to give peace *on e.* ?
18:8 shall he find faith *on e.* ?
John 17:4 glorified thee *on the e.*
Rom. 9:28 a short work *on the e.*
Col. 3:2 affec. not on things *on e.*
5 mortify your members *o. t. e.*
Heb. 8:4 *on e.* not be a priest
11:13 strangers *on the e.*
12:25 ref. him that spake *on e.*
Jam. 5:5 lived in pleas. *on the e.*
17 it rained not *on the e.*
Rev. 3:10 that dwell *upon the e.*
5:10 we shall reign *on e.*
8:7 hail and fire cast *upon the e.*
11:10 dw. *on e.* 13:8 ; 14:6 ; 17:8
16:2 poured vial *upon the e.*

Out of the EARTH.
1 *Sam.* 28:13 ascend. *out of the e.*
2 *Sam.* 23:4 grass *out of the e.*

EARTH (cont.)

Job 28:2 iron is taken *out of the e.*
5 *e. out of* it cometh bread
Ps. 85:11 truth sh. spr. *o. of t. e.*
104:35 sinners be cons. *o. of t. e.*
Dan. 7:17 four kings *out of the e.*
Hos. 2:18 battle *out of the e.*
Mic. 7:2 good perish *out of the e.*
Rev. 13:11 beast up *out of the e.*

To, or unto the EARTH.
Gen. 24:52 bow. himself *to the e.*
42:6 they bowed *to the e.* 43:26
Jos. 5:14 Josh. fell *to the e.* 7:6
1 *Sam.* 5:3 D. on his face *to the e.*
17:49 Goliath his face *to the e.*
25:41 bow. herself *to e.* 1 *K.* 1:31
26:8 smite him *to the e.*
20 let not my blood fall *to t. e.*
2 *Sam.* 14:11 not one hair shall
fall *to the e.* 1 *K.* 1:52
2 *K.* 10:10 fall *to t. e.* no word
Job 12:8 or speak *to the e.*
Ps. 17:11 bowing down *to the e.*
44:25 belly cleaveth *unto the e.*
50:4 he shall call *to the e.*
146:4 he returneth *to his e.*
Ec. 3:21 sp. of beast goeth *to e.*
12:7 dust ret. *to t. e.* spirit to G.
Jer. 15:10 conten. *to the whole e.*
Hos. 6:3 and former rain *to the e.*
Acts 9:4 and Saul fell *to the e.*
10:11 great sheet down *to the e.*
Rev. 6:13 stars of heav. fell *t. t. e.*
12:13 dragon cast *unto the e.*

EARTHEN.
Lev. 6:28 e. ves. wherein sodden
11:33 e. vessel wherein falleth
14:5 birds killed in e. vessel, 50
Num. 5:17 water in e. vessel
Jer. 19:1 a potter's e. bottle
32:14 evidences in an e. vessel
Lam. 4:2 esteemed as e. pitchers
2 *Cor.* 4:7 treasure in e. vessels

EARTHLY.
John 3:12 if I told you e. things
31 he that is of the earth is e.
2 *Cor.* 5:1 our e. house of tabern.
Phil. 3:19 who mind e. things
Jam. 3:15 this wisd. is e. sensual

EARTHQUAKE.
1 *K.* 19:11 an e. L. was not in e.
12 after the e. a fire
Is. 29:6 visited of Lord with e.
Amos 1:1 two years before the e.
Zec. 14:5 ye fled before the e.
Mat. 27:54 centurion saw the e.
28:2 a great e. *Acts* 16:26; *Rev.*
6:12; 11:13
Rev. 8:5 thunder. and e. 11:19
16:18 great e. so mighty an e.

EARTHQUAKES.
Mat. 24:7 famines and e. *Mark*
13:8; *Luke* 21:11

EARTHY.
1 *Cor.* 15:47 first man of earth, e.
49 have borne image of e.

EASE, Substantive.
Deut. 28:65 shalt thou find no e.
Jud. 20:43 trod down with e.
Job 12:5 of him that is at e.
16:12 at e. ; 21:23 being at e.
Ps. 25:13 soul shall dwell at e.
123:4 scorning of those at e.
Is. 32:9 rise up, ye women at e.
11 tremble, ye women at e.
Jer. 48:11 Moab hath been at e.
Ezek. 23:42 voice of multi. at e.
Amos 6:1 woe to them at e. in Z.
Luke 12:19 take thine e. eat

EASE, Verb.
Deut. 23:13 thou wilt e. thyself
2 *Chr.* 10:4 e. thou somewhat, 9
Is. 1:24 e. me of adversaries

EASED.
Job 16:6 forbear, what am I e. ?

---

2 *Cor.* 8:13 that other men be e.

EASIER.
Ex. 18:22 be e. for thyself
Mat. 9:5 whether is e. to say,
Mark 2:9; *Luke* 5:23
19:24 e. for camel to go thro' eye,
Mark 10:25; *Luke* 18:25
Luke 16:17 e. for heaven to pass

EASILY.
1 *Cor.* 13:5 is not e. provoked
Heb. 12:1 sin which doth e. beset

EAST.
Gen. 3:24 e. of garden of Eden
13:11 Lot journeyed e.
28:14 abroad to the west and e.
29:1 land of the people of the e.
Num. 23:7 brought me out of e.
Jud. 6:3 children of the e. 33 ;
7:12 ; 8:10 ; 1 *K.* 4:30
1 *K.* 7:25 three tow. e. 2 *Chr.* 4:4
1 *Chr.* 9:24 the porters toward e.
1 *Chr.* 12:15 to flight them to. e.
Job 1:3 of all the men of the e.
Ps. 75:6 promotion not from e.
103:12 far as the e. is from west
107:3 gathered them from e.
Is. 11:14 sp. them of e. *Jer.* 49:28
41:2 righteous man from the e.
43:5 seed from e. *Zec.* 8:7
46:11 bird from the e. the man
Ezek. 8:16 faces toward the e.
40:6 gate toward the e. 22 ; 43:1 ;
44:1 ; 46:1, 12
47:8 waters issue toward the e.
48:10 toward the e. ten thousa.
Dan. 8:9 horn great toward e.
11:44 tidings out of the e.
Zec. 14:4 mo. sh. cleave tow. e.
Mat. 2:1 wise men from the e.
2 seen his star in the e. 9
8:11 come from e. *Luke* 13:29
24:27 as lightning out of the e.
Rev. 7:2 angel ascending from e.
16:12 the way of kings of e.
21:13 on the e. three gates

EAST border.
Num. 34:10 point out your e. bor.
Jos. 4:19 encamped in the e. bor.
15:5 the e. border was salt sea

EASTER.
Acts 12:4 after e. to bring him

EAST gate.
Neh. 3:29 Shem. keeper of e. gate
Jer. 19:2 entry of the e. gate
Ezek. 10:19 stood at door of e. g.
11:1 Spirit brought to the e. g.

EAST side.
Num. 2:3 on e. side shall J. pitch
Jos. 7:2 Ai, on e. side of Bethel
Jud. 11:18 came by e. side of M.
Ezek. 48:2 fr. the e. s. even unto,
3, 4, 5, 6, 7, 8, 23, 24, 25, 26, 27
Jon. 4:5 Jonah sat on e. s. of city

EASTWARD.
Gen. 13:14 th. eyes e. *Deut.* 3:27
2 *K.* 13:17 open the window e.
1 *Chr.* 26:17 e. were six Levites
Ezek. 47:3 man with line went e.

EAST wind.
Gen. 41:6 blasted with e. w. 23, 27
Ex. 10:13 brought an e. w. 14:21
Job 15:2 fill his belly with e. w.
38:24 scattereth the e. wind
Ps. 48:7 breakest ship with e. w.
78:26 caused e. wind to blow
Is. 27:8 rough in day of e. w.
Ezek. 17:10 the e. wind touch. it
19:12 and the e. wind drieth up
27:26 the e. wind hath broken
Hos. 12:1 Ephra. follow. e. w.
13:15 an e. wind shall come
Jon. 4:8 God prepared e. wind
Hab. 1:9 faces sup. up as e. wind

EASY.
Prov. 14:6 knowledge is e. to h.
Mat. 11:30 my yoke is e.
1 *Cor.* 14:9 e. to be understood
Jam. 3:17 wisdom from ab. is e.

EAT.
Gen. 2:16 of ev. tree thou may. e.
3:5 day ye e. eyes sh. be opened
6 Eve did e. ; 12 I did e. 13
14 and dust shalt thou e.
16 in sorrow shalt thou e.
27:4 savory meat that I may e.
31:46 and they did e. there
40:17 the birds did e. them
43:32 Egyptians e. by themsel.
Ex. 10:5 the locusts shall e.
12 locusts may e. every herb
12:8 bitter herbs they shall e.
43 no str. sh. e. 48 ; *Lev.* 22:13
44 then shall he e. thereof
16:25 e. that to-day
35 e. manna, *John* 6:31, 49, 58
29:32 Aaron and sons shall e.
Lev. 6:16 ; 8:31
Lev. 6:18 all males shall e. 29 ;
7:6 ; *Num.* 18:10
7:19 clean shall e. *Num.* 18:11
24 but in no wise e. of it
10:12 e. it without leaven
11:21 ye may e. 22 ; *Deut.* 14:20
24:9 Aaron and his sons shall e.
25:20 what shall we e. sev. year
26:16 your enemies shall e.
Num. 11:5 fish we did e. freely
13 flesh that we may e.
23:24 till he e. of the prey
25:2 the peo. did e. of sacrifices
Deut. 12:15 e. in gates, 21 ; 15:22
15 unc. and clean e. 22 ; 26:12
18 must e. bef. L. 14:26 ; 15:20
20 I will e. flesh
14:21 give to stra. th. he may e.
23:24 thou mayest e. grapes
Deut. 28:29 for worms shall e. th.
53 e. fruit of body, *Lam.* 2:20
32:38 e. fat of sacrifices
Jos. 5:11 they e. of old corn
Jud. 19:8 they tarried, and did e.
1 *Sam.* 1:18 Hannah did e.
9:13 they e. that be bidden
14:34 and e. and sin not
20:34 Jonathan did e. no meat
2 *Sam.* 9:11 e. at table, 1 *K.* 2:7
1 *K.* 14:11 him that dieth of J.
dogs e. 16:4 ; 21:23 ; 2 *K.*
9:10, 36
17:12 that we may e. and die
19:5 arise e. *Acts* 10:13 ; 11:7
2 *K.* 4:43 they shall e. and
44 they did e. and left thereof
6:28 give son that we may e.
29 we boiled my son, and did e.
18:31 e. eve. m. of vine, *Is.* 36:16
2 *Chr.* 30:18 yet did e. passover
Neh. 5:2 that we may e.
9:25 so they did e. *Ps.* 78:29
Job 3:24 sighing cometh before
I e.
31:8 and let another e.
Ps. 22:26 meek shall e.
29 fat on earth shall e.
50:13 will I e. the flesh of bulls
78:25 man did e. angels' food
128:2 thou shalt e. the labor
Prov. 1:31 e. fruit, *Is.* 3:10
18:21 they that love shall e. fruit
24:13 my son, e. thou honey
30:17 young eagles shall e. it
Ec. 2:25 for who can e. ?
5:11 are increased that e. them
12 whether he e. little or much
10:16 princes e. in the morning
17 princes e. in due season
Cant. 4:16 come into gar. and e.
Is. 4:1 we will e. our own bread
7:15 butter and honey sh. he e.
22 butter and honey sh. one e.

9:20 *e.* on left hand, *e.* flesh
11:7 lion shall *e.* straw, 65:25
30:24 oxen and asses shall *e.*
37:30 plant vineyards, and *e.* the
   fruit, 65:21; *Jer.* 29:5, 28
51:8 worms shall *e.* them
55:1 come ye, buy and *e.*
   2 hearken to me, and *e.* good
65:4 peo. which *e.* swine's flesh
   13 my servants shall *e.*
   22 not plant and another *e.*
Jer. 15:16 found, and I did *e.*
19:9 shall *e.* the flesh of friend
Ezek. 2:8 open thy mouth and *e.*
3:1 *e.* that thou findest, *e.* roll
4:10 *e.* by wei.; 5:10 fath. *e.* so.
16:13 thou didst *e.* fine flour
34:3 ye *e.* the fat
Dan. 4:33 Nebuch. did *e.* grass
Hos. 4:10 shall *e.* and not have
   enough, *Mic.* 6:14; *Hag.* 1:6.
9:3 shall *e.* unclean things
   4 *e.* thereof shall be polluted
Amos 6:4 that *e.* the lambs
Mic. 3:3 who also *e.* the flesh
Zec. 11:9 let the rest *e.*
Mat. 12:4 David did *e.* shew-bre.
14:20 did all *e.* 15:37; *Mark* 6:42;
   8:8; *Luke* 9:17
15:27 dogs *e.* of cru. *Mark* 7:28
   38 they that did *e.* were 4,000
26:21 as they did *e.* he said.
   Mark 14:18, 22
   26 take *e.* this my body, *Mark*
   14:22; 1 *Cor.* 11:24
Mark 2:16 *e.* with publicans
6:44 that did *e.* were above 5,000
11:14 no man *e.* fruit of thee
14:12 mayest *e.* the passover. 14;
   Luke 22:8, 11; *John* 18:28
Luke 6:1 did *e.* rubbing them
10:8 *e.* such things as are set
15:23 let us *e.* and be merry
24:43 he took it, and did *e.*
John 4:31 saying, Master, *e.*
6:26 because ye did *e.* of loaves
53 exc. ye *e.* fle. of Son of m.
Acts 2:46 they did *e.* their meat
11:3 and didst *e.* with them
23:14 *e.* nothing till slain Paul
Rom. 14:2 believeth he may *e.* all
23 doubteth is damned if he *e.*
1 *Cor.* 8:8 *e.* are better, if we *e.* n.
13 I will *e.* no flesh while
10:18 who *e.* of the sacrifices
25 what. sold in shamb. that *e.*
27 *e.* asking no question
2 *Thes.* 3:10 work not, neither *e.*
2 *Tim.* 2:17 word will *e.* as cank.
Jam. 5:3 and shall *e.* your flesh
Rev. 17:16 shall *e.* her flesh
19:18 that *e.* flesh of kings

See BLOOD BREAD, FAT.

EAT, *with* drink.

Gen. 24:54 *e.* and *drink*, 26:30;
   Ex. 24:11; *Jud.* 9:27; 19:4
Ex. 32:6 to *e.* and *d.* 1 *Cor.* 10:7
34:28 *e.* br. nor *d. Deut.* 9:9, 18
2 *Sam.* 11:11 to *e.* and *d. f*
12:3 *e.* of his meat and *drink*
19:35 taste what I *e.* or *drink f*
1 *K.* 13:8 nor *e.* bread nor *drink*
   water, 9, 17, 22
18:41 E. said, *e.* and *drink*
2 *K.* 6:22 th. they may. *e.* and *d.*
18:27 *e.* du. and *d.* piss, *Is.* 36:12
Ezr. 10:6 E. *e.* no bread nor *dr.*
Neh. 8:10 *e.* the fat and *d.* the s.
Est. 4:16 nor *e.* nor *d.* three days
Job 1:4 called sisters to *e.* and *d.*
   and *drink*, 3:13; 5:18; 8:15
Cant. 5:1 *e.* O friends, yea, *dri.*
Is. 5:3 *e.* *drink*, ye princes
22:13 *e.* and *drink*, 1 *Cor.* 15:32
Ezek. 25:4 *e.* fruit and *dr.* milk
39:17 *e.* flesh and *drink* blood

Dan. 1:12 pulse to *e.* water to *d.*
Mat. 6:25 *e.* or *d.* 31; *Luke* 12:29
24:49 *e.* and *d.* w. d. *Luke* 12:45
Luke 5:30 *e.* and *d.* with publi. ?
   33 thy disciples *e.* and *drink*
12:19 take thine ease, *e.* *drink*
17:27 they did *e.* they *drank*. 28
Acts 9:9 did neither *e.* nor *drink*
23:12 *e.* nor *d.* till killed P. 21
Rom. 14:21 *e.* flesh nor *d.* wine
   1 *Cor.* 9:4 power to *e.* and to *d.*
10:31 whether ye *e.* or *drink*
11:22 houses to *e.* and *drink* in ?
   26 ye *e.* bread and *drink* cup
   27 *e.* and *drink* unworthily
28 so let him *e.* and *drink*

He did EAT.

Gen. 25:28 *he did e.* of his ven.
27:25 to Isaac, and *he did e.*
39:6 save the bread *he did e.*
Mark 1:6 John did *e.* locusts
Luke 4:2 days *he did e.* nothing
Gal. 2:12 *he did e.* with Gentiles

EAT not.

Gen. 2:17 shall *not e.* 3:1, 3
3:11 I commanded *not* to *e.* 17
9:4 blood *not e. Lev.* 19:26; *Deut.*
   12:16, 23–25; 15:23
32:32 child, of Is. *e. not* of sinew
43:32 Egyptians might *not e.*
Ex. 12:9 *e.* n. of raw nor sodden
   45 foreigner shall *not e.* thereof
Lev. 22:4 leper n. *e.* 6:10, 12
Deut. 14:21 *not e.* of thing that
   dieth, *Ezek.* 44:31
Jud. 13:4 *e. not* unc. thing, 7, 14
1 *Sam.* 9:13 the people will *not e.*
28:23 Saul refused, I will *not e.*
2 *K.* 7:2 but *not e.* thereof, 19
Ezr. 2:63 *not e. Neh.* 7:65
Ps. 141:4 let me *not e.*
Prov. 23:6 *e. not* bread of him
Mark 7:3 exc. they wash *e. not*, 4
Luke 22:16 I will *not e.* thereof
1 *Cor.* 5:11 with such no *not* to *e.*
10:28 *e. not* for his sake

Shall ye EAT.

Ex. 12:11 *s.* ye *e.* with loins gird.
   15 seven days *shall ye e.* 20
22:31 *shall ye e.* any flesh torn
Lev. 10:14 wave-breast *shall ye e.*
11:3 cheweth the cud, that *shall*
   ye e. Deut. 14:4, 6
19:25 in the fifth year *shall ye e.*

Ye shall EAT.

Ex. 12:11 *ye shall e.* it with haste
   18 *ye shall e.* unleavened bread
16:12 at even *ye shall e.* flesh
Lev. 7:23 *ye shall e.* no fat, 24
   26 *ye shall e.* no blood, 17:14
23:14 *ye shall e.* neither bread
25:12 *ye shall e.* the increase
   19 *ye shall e.* your fill
22 *ye sh. e.* of old store, 26:10
Deut. 14:11 clean birds *ye sh. e.*
2 *K.* 19:29 *e.* this year, *Is.* 37:30
Is. 1:19 if obedient *ye shall e.*
61:6 *ye sh. e.* riches of Gentiles
Joel 2:26 *ye shall e.* in plenty
Luke 22:22 what *ye s. e.*

To EAT.

Ex. 16:8 L. shall give flesh to *e.*
Deut. 12:20 longeth to *e.* flesh
2 *K.* 4:40 poured out for m. to *e.*
2 *Chr.* 31:10 had enough to *e.*
Neh. 9:36 land thou gavest to *e.*
Ps. 78:24 manna on them to *e.*
Prov. 23:1 sit. to *e.* with a ruler
25:27 not good to *e.* much honey
Ec. 5:19 given power to *e.*
Is. 33:18 shall be for them to *e.*
Jer. 19:9 cause th. to *e.* the flesh
Ezek. 3:2 caused me to *e.* th. roll
   3 cause thy belly to *e.*
Dan. 4:25 to *e.* grass, 32
Mic. 7:1 there is no cluster to *e.*

Hab. 1:8 eagle that hasteth *to e.*
Mat. 12:1 to pluck ears and *to e.*
   4 not lawful to *e. Mark* 2:26;
   Luke 6:4
14:16 give them to *e. Mark* 6:37;
   Luke 9:13
15:20 to *e.* with unwash. hands
   32 nothing to *e. Mark* 8:1, 2
26:17 prepare to *e.* passover?
Mark 5:43 given her to *e.*
6:31 no leisure to *e.*
Luke 22:15 to *e.* this passover
John 4:32 meat to *e.* ye know not
   33 brought him aught to *e. f*
6:52 man give us his flesh to *e. f*
1 *Cor.* 8:10 embolden to *e.* things
11:20 not to *e.* Lord's supper
Heb. 13:10 an altar no right to *e.*
Rev. 2:7 to *e.* of the tree of life
   14 to *e.* things sacrificed, 20
   17 to *e.* of hidden manna

EAT up.

Gen. 41:4 did *e. up* seven fat, 20
Num. 24:8 he shall *e. up* nations
Ps. 27:2 enemies came to *e. up*
   105:55 did *e. up* all the herbs
Is. 50:9 moth shall *e. up*, 51:8
Jer. 5:17 *e. up* thy harvest, *e. up*
   flocks, *e. up* vines
22:22 wind *e. up* all pastures
Hos. 4:8 they *e. up* the sin of
Nah. 3:15 shall *e. up* like canker
Rev. 10:9 take it, and *e.* it *up*

EATEN.

Gen. 3:11 hast thou *e.* of tree
14:24 which young men have *e.*
41:21 when they had *e.* them
Ex. 12:46 in one ho. sh. it be *e.*
13:3 no leavened br. be *e.* 7
21:28 his flesh shall not be *e.*
29:34 not be *e.* because it is ho.
Lev. 6:16 shall be *e.* in the holy
   place, 26; 7:6
   23 wholly burnt not be *e.* 7:19
   30 no sin-offering shall be *e.*
   7:15 shall be *e.* the same day, 16
10:17 why not *e.* sin offering?
11:13 not be *e.* 41; *Deut.* 14:19
19:6 shall be *e.* same day, 22:30
Num. 28:17 br. be *e. Ezek.* 45:21
Deut. 6:11 shalt have *e.* 8:10, 12
26:14 I have not *e.* in mourning
29:6 ye have not *e.* bread
31:20 when they shall have *e.*
Jos. 5:12 had *e.* of old corn.
Ruth 3:7 when Boaz had *e.* and
1 *Sam.* 28:20 *e.* no bread all day
   30:12 had *e.* his spirit came
1 *K.* 13:28 lion not *e.* the carcass
Neh. 5:14 have not *e.* the bread
Job 6:6 unsavory *e.* without salt
31:17 or have *e.* my morsel
   39 if I have *e.* the fruits
Ps. 69:9 zeal of thy house hath *e.*
   me up, *John* 2:17
102:9 I have *e.* ashes like bread
Prov. 9:17 bread *e.* in secret
23:8 morsel *e.* shalt thou vomit
Cant. 5:1 I have *e.* my honey-co.
Is. 3:14 ye have *e.* up vineyard
Jer. 10:25 they have *e.* up Jacob
24:2 could not be *e.* 3:8; 29:17
31:29 *e.* sour grapes, *Ezek.* 18:2
Hos. 10:13 ye have *e.* the fruit
Joel 1:4 locust left c.-w. *e.* 25
Mat. 14:21 and they that had *e.*
   Mark 8:9
Luke 13:26 we have *e.* and drunk
17:8 I have *e.* afterward thou *e.*
Acts 10:10 would have *e.*
   14 I have nev. *e.* anyth. com.
12:23 he was *e.* of worms
27:38 when they had *e.* enough
Rev. 10:10 had *e.* it, belly bitter

EATER, S.

Jud. 14:14 out of *e.* came forth
Prov. 23:30 riotous *e.* of flesh

Is. 55:10 give bread to the *e.*
Nah. 3:12 fall into mouth of *e.*

EATEST.
Gen. 2:17 day thou *e.* thou shalt
1 *Sam.* 1:8 why *e.* thou not ?

EATETH.
Ex. 12:15 who *e.* leav. bread, 19
Lev. 7:18 that *e.* 20, 25 ; 17:10
Num. 13:2 land *e.* up inhabit.
1 *Sam.* 14:24 cursed m. that *e.* 28
Job 5:5 harvest the hungry *e.* up
21:25 never *e.* with pleasure
40:15 behemoth *e.* grass as an ox
Ps. 106:20 an ox that *e.* grass
Prov. 13:25 righteous *e.* to satisfy
Prov. 30:20 she *e.* and wipeth m.
31:27 she *e.* not bread of idlen.
Ec. 4:5 fool *e.* his own flesh
Is. 29:8 he *e.* but awaketh
44:16 with part he *e.* flesh
59:5 that *e.* of their eggs
Mat. 9:11 why *e.* your master,
Mark 2:16 ; *Luke* 15:2
John 6:54 whoso *e.* my flesh
56 that *e.* my flesh dwelleth in
57 so he that *e.* me shall live
58 he that *e.* of this bread
Rom. 14:2 another weak *e.* herbs
3 let not him that *e.* despise
6 *e.* to L. that *e.* not, to L. *e.* n.
20 evil for who *e.* with offence
23 because *e.* not of faith
1 *Cor.* 9:7 planteth vineyard and
e. not ? and *e.* not of milk
11:29 that *e.* unworth. *e.* damn.
See DRINKING.

EATING.
Ex. 12:4 ev. man to his *e.* 16:18
Jud. 14:9 Samson went on *e.*
1 *Sam.* 14:34 sin not in *e.* with b.
2 *K.* 4:40 as they were *e.* pottage
Job 20:23 upon him while he is *e.*
Is. 66:17 *e.* swine's flesh
Amos 7:2 made an end of *e.* grass
Mat. 26:26 were *e.* Jes. took br.
1 *Cor.* 8:4 *e.* of things sacrificed
11:21 in *e.* ev. one tak. own sup
See DRINKING.

EBAL.
Deut. 11:29 mount E. 27:4, 13
Jos. 8:30 an altar in mount E.

EBED.   *Jud.* 9:30 ; *Ezr.* 8:6

EBED-MELECH.
Jer. 38:8 E. spake to king, 39:16

EBEN-EZER.
1 *Sam.* 4:1 and pitched beside E.
5:1 bro. the ark from E. 7:12

EBER.   *Gen.* 10:21, 25 ; *Num.*
24:24

ED.   *Jos.* 22:34

EDEN.
Gen. 2:15 man into garden of E.
Is. 51:3 her wilderness like E.
Ezek. 28:13 ; 31:9, 16, 18 ; 36:35
Joel 2:3 is as the garden of E.
Amos 1:5 cut off sceptre from E.

EDGE.
Ex. 13:20 *e.* of wild. *Num.* 33:6
26:10 loops in the *e.* of curtain
Ec. 10:10 do not whet the *e.*

See TEETH.

EDGE of the sword.
Gen. 34:26 slew H. with *e. of s.*
Ex. 17:13 Amalek with *e. of s.*
Num. 21:24 smote S. with *e. of s.*
Jos. 8:24 smote Ai. with *e. of s.*
Jud. 4:15 Sisera ; 21:10 Jabe.-gil.
Job 1:15 Job's ser. with *e. of s.* 17
Ps. 89:43 turned the *e. of the s.*
Jer. 21:7 smite them with *e. of s.*
Luke 21:24 Jews fall by *e. of sw.*
Heb. 11:34 thro' faith esca. *e. of s.*

EDGED.
Ps. 149:6 two-*e.* sword in hand

Prov. 5:4 sharp as a two-*e.* sword
Heb. 4:12 word of God sharper
than two-*e.* sword
Rev. 1:16 mouth sharp two-*e.* 6

EDGES.
Ex. 28:7 joined at two *e.* 39:4
Jud. 3:16 Eh.'s dag. had two *e.*
Rev. 2:12 sharp sw. with two *e.*

EDIFICATION.
Rom. 15:2 please neighbor to *e.*
1 *Cor.* 14:3 speaketh to men to *e.*
2 *Cor.* 10:8 L. hath given us for *e.*
13:10 Lord hath given me to *e.*

EDIFIED.
Acts 9:31 churches had rest, *e.*
1 *Cor.* 14:17 the other is not *e.*

EDIFIETH.
1 *Cor.* 8:1 knowledge puffeth
charity *e.*
14:4 he that speaks *e.* hims. he
that prophes. *e.* the church

EDIFY.
Rom. 14:19 one may *e.* another
1 *Cor.* 10:23 lawful but *e.* not
1 *Thes.* 5:11 *e.* one another.

EDIFYING.
1 *Cor.* 14:5 church may receive *e.*
12 that ye may excel to the *e.*
14:26 let all things be done to *e.*
2 *Cor.* 12:19 all thin. for your *e.*
Eph. 4:12 *e.* of body of Christ
16 the body to the *e.* of itself
29 good to the use of *e.*
1 *Tim.* 1:4 quest. rather than *e.*

EDOM.
Gen. 25:30 was called E. 36:1
Ex. 15:15 dukes of E. amazed
Num. 20:21 E. refused to give Is-
rael passage, 24:18
2 *Sam.* 8:14 gar. in E. 1 *Chr.* 18:13
2 *K.* 8:20 E. revolted, 14:10 ; 2
Chr. 25:20
Ps. 60:8 over E. cast shoe, 108:9
Is. 63:1 that cometh from E. ?
Jer. 49:7 concerning E. saith
Lord, *Ezek.* 25:12
Amos 2:1 king of E. 9:12
Ob. 8 dest. wise men out of E.

EDOMITE. *Deut.* 23:7 ; 2 *K.* 8:21
EDREI. *Deut.* 1:4

EFFECT, Substantive.
Num. 30:8 make vow of no *e.*
Ps. 33:10 devices of peo. of no. *e.*
Is. 32:17 the *e.* of righteousness
Ezek. 12:23 and *e.* of every vision
Mat. 15:6 com. of G. of none *e.*
Mark 7:13 word of God of none *e.*
Rom. 3:3 unbelief make the faith
of God without *e.*
4:14 prom. of none *e. Gal.* 3:17
9:6 word hath taken none *e.*
1 *Cor.* 1:17 cr. of C. be of none *e.*
Gal. 5:4 Chr. is become of no *e.*

EFFECT, Verb.
Jer. 48:30 lies shall not so *e.* it

EFFECTED.
2 *Chr.* 7:11 Sol. prosperously *e.*

EFFECTUAL.
1 *Cor.* 16:9 a great door and *e.*
2 *Cor.* 1:6 is *e.* in enduring suff.
Eph. 3:7 by the *e.* working of
4:16 according to *e.* working
Phile. 6 faith may become *e.*
Jam. 5:16 the *e.* prayer of right.

EFFECTUALLY.
Gal. 2:8 he that wrought *e.* in P.
1 *Thes.* 2:13 the word *e.* worketh

EFFEMINATE.
1 *Cor.* 6:9 nor *e.* shall inherit

EGG.
Job 6:6 any taste in white of *e.* ?
Luke 11:12 ask *e.* will offer scor. ?

EGGS.
Deut. 22:6 whet. young ones or *e.*
Job 39:14 ostr. leaveth *e.* in earth
Is. 10:14 one gathereth *e.*
59:5 hatch cockatrice's *e.*
Jer. 17:11 partridge sitteth on *e.*

EGLAH.   2 *Sam.* 3:5
EGLAIM.   *Is.* 15:8
EGLON.   *Jud.* 3:14, 17

EGYPT.
Gen. 15:18 from the river of E.
45:19 made me lord of all E.
Ex. 3:20 will smite E. 7:4 ; 10:7
2 *K.* 18:21 thou trustest on E. 24
Is. 19:16 E. like unto women, 24
Jer. 2:18 in way of E. ? 36
Ezek. 29:2 ag. E. 30:15 ; 32:12
Joel 3:19 E. a desolat. *Zec.* 10:11
Nah. 3:9 Ethiopia and E. were
Acts 7:10 governor over E.
Heb. 11:27 by faith he forsook E.
Rev. 11:8 is called Sodom and E.

In, *and* into EGYPT.
Gen. 46:4 go down with thee i. E.
Ex. 10:2 things I wrought in E.
12:30 cry in E. ; 14:11 graves in E.
Num. 11:18 well with us in E.
14:3 for us to return *into* E. 4
29:15 and we have dwelt in E.
Deut. 1:30 did for you in E. 4:34
Jos. 9:9 all that he did in E.
Is. 19:1 Lord shall come *into* E.
Jer. 26:21 fled and went *into* E.
41:17 to go *into* E. 42:15
42:19 Go ye not *into* E. 43:2
Mat. 2:13 flee *into* E. 14

Land of EGYPT.
Gen. 13:10 ; 41:19. 54 ; 45:18 ; 47:6
Ps. 78:12 marvel. th. in E. 81:5
Heb. 8:9 out of the *land of* E.
Jude 5 saved peo. out of *l. of* E.

Out of EGYPT.
Gen. 13:1 Abraham *out of* E.
47:30 carry me *out of* E.
Ex. 3:11 ; 12:39 ; 13:9, 16
Num. 11:20 came forth *out of* E.
22:11 is a people come *out of* E.
Jud. 2:1 made you go *out of* E.
Heb. 3:16 all that came *out of* E.

To EGYPT.
Is. 19:21 L. shall be known *to* E.
31:1 woe to them that go *to* E.
Hos. 7:11 they call *to* E.

EGYPTIAN, S.
Gen. 16:1, 3 ; 21:9 ; 39:1, 5 ; 41:55
Ex. 2:11 E. smiting Heb. 12, 19
3:22 shall spoil the E. 12:36
14:9 E. pursued after, 10, 13, 25
19:4 seen what I did to the E.
32:12 wherefore should the E.
Num. 14:13 M. said, Then the E.
20:15 and E. vexed us and our
1 *Sam.* 30:11 found an E. in field
Is. 19:2 I will set the E. 4, 21, 23
Acts 21:38 art not thou that E. ?
Heb. 11:29 E. assaying to do

EHUD.
Jud. 3:15 raised up E. 16, 23, 26
1 *Chr.* 7:10 sons of Bilham, E. 8:6

EIGHT.
Gen. 17:12 he that is *e.* days old,
21:4 ; *Luke* 2:21
22:23 these *e.* Milcah did bear
Num. 29:29 *e.* bullocks, two rams
Jud. 3:8 Israel served *e.* years
12:14 Abdon judged Is. *e.* y.
1 *K.* 7:10 of stones of *e.* cubits
2 *K.* 8:17 Jehor. reigned *e.* years
22:1 Josi. was *e.* years old, 2 *Chr.*
34:1
2 *Chr.* 29:17 sanct. L. in *e.* days
Ec. 11:2 to seven, also to *e.*
Ezek. 40:31 had *e.* steps, 34:37
41 *e.* tables slew sacrifices
Mic. 5:5 seven shepherds, *e.* men

Luke 9:28 about an *e*. days after
John 20:26 after *e*. days
Acts 9:33 E. kept his bed *e*. years
1 *Pet.* 3:20 *e*. souls were saved

EIGHTH.
Lev. 25:22 shall sow *e*. year
1 *K*. 6:38 which the *e*. month
1 *Chr.* 24:10 the *e*. lot came forth
Zec. 1:1 in *e*. month word came
2 *Pet.* 2:5 saved Noah the *e*. per.
Rev. 17:11 beast that was, is the *e*.
21:20 *e*. foundation was a beryl
See DAY, DAYS.

EIGHT hundred.
Gen. 5:4 Adam lived *e. h.* years

EIGHTEEN.
1 *K*. 7:15 two pillars of brass *e*.
cubits, 2 *K*. 25:17; *Jer.* 52:21
2 *Chr.* 11:21 Reho. took *e*. wives
Luke 13:4 *e*. on whom tower fell
16 Satan hath bound *e*. years

EIGHTEENTH.
1 *K*. 15:1 *e*. year of Jer. 2 *Chr.* 13:1
1 *Chr.* 24:15 *e*. lot came forth
25:25 the *e*. to Hanani
Jer. 32:1 was *e*. year of Nebuch.

EITHER.
John 19:18 crucifi. on *e*. side one
Rev. 22:2 *e*. side river tree of life

EKRON.
1 *Sam.* 5:10 as ark came to E.
2 *K*. 1:2 the god of E. 3:6, 16
Amos 1:9 my hand against E.
Zep. 2:4 E. shall be rooted up
Zec. 9:5 E. very sorrowful, 7

EKRONITES.
Jos. 13:3 the land of the E. not
1 *Sam.* 5:10 ark ca. to Ekron, E.

ELAH.
Gen. 36:41 duke E. 1 *K*. 4:18
1 *Sam.* 17:2 by the valley of E.
21:9 Goliath in valley of E.
1 *K*. 16:8 E. son of Baasha
2 *K*. 15:30 son of E. 17:1; 18:1, 9
1 *Chr.* 4:15 son of Caleb, E. 9:8

ELAM.
Gen. 10:22 children of Shem, E.
14:1 Chedorlaomer king of E.
Is. 11:11 recover people from E.
21:2 go up, O E. ; 22:6 E. bare
Jer. 25:25 kings of E. 49:34, 36, 39
Ezek. 32:24 there is E. and all
Dan. 8:2 in the province of E.

ELAMITES.
Ezr. 4:9 E. wrote letter, *Acts* 2:9
ELATH. 1 *K*. 14:22; 16:6
EL-BETHEL. *Gen.* 35:7
ELDAD. *Num.* 11:26, 27

ELDER.
Gen. 10:21 S. brother of Ja. the *e*.
25:23 *e*. serve young. *Rom.* 9:12
1 *K*. 2:22 he is the *e*. brother
Job 15:10 much *e*. than father
Ezek. 16:46 thy *e*. sister is Sama.
Luke 15:25 his *e*. son was in field
1 *Tim.* 5:2 entreat the *e*. women
1 *Pet.* 5:5 younger, submit to *e*.

ELDER, *for ruler.*
1 *Tim.* 5:1 rebuke not an *e*.
19 against *e*. receive not accu.
1 *Pet.* 5:1 who am also an *e*.
2 *John* 1 the *e*. to the elect lady
3 *John* 1 the *e*. unto Gaius

ELDERS.
Gen. 50:7 *e*. of his house went
Lev. 4:15 *e*. of congr. lay hands
Num. 11:25 L. gave spirit to 70 *e*.
Deut. 29:10 before the L. your *e*.
31:28 gather to me all *e*.
32:7 ask thy father and *e*.
1 *Sam.* 16:4 *e*. of the town
1 *K*. 21:11 *e*. did as Jezebel sent
2 *K*. 6:32 Elisha and *e*. sat

10:1 Jehu sent to *e*. of Jezreel
19:2 Hezekiah sent *e*. *Is.* 37:2
Ps. 107:32 in assembly of *e*.
Prov. 31:23 known among *e*.
Lam. 1:19 *e*. gave up the ghost
2:10 *e*. of Zion sit upon ground
4:16 favored not *e*. 5:12
Ezek. 8:1 and the *e*. of Judah sat
Joel 1:14 gather the *e*. 2:16
Mat. 15:2 tradition of the *e*. ?
16:21 suffer things of *e*. 27:12
26:59 *e*. sought false witness
27:20 *e*. persuaded the multit.
41 mocking with the *e*. said
28:12 assembled with the *e*.
Mark 7:3 tradition of the *e*.
8:31 rejected of the *e*. *Luke* 9:22
15:1 held a consultation with *e*.
Acts 4:5 *e*. were gath. together
23 all that the *e*. had said
6:12 stirred up the peo. and *e*.
11:30 sent it to the *e*. by Barna.
14:23 ordained *e*. in ev. church
15:4 of the church and of the *e*.
6 the apostles and *e*. came
23 apostles, *e*. and brethren
16:4 decrees ordained of the *e*.
20:17 the *e*. of the church
1 *Tim.* 5:17 *e*. rule well
Tit. 1:5 ordain *e*. in every city
Heb. 11:2 by faith the *e*. obtained
Jam. 5:14 call for *e*. of church
1 *Pet.* 5:1 *e*. which are am. you
Rev. 4:4 I saw twenty-four *e*.
10:24 *e*. fall, 5:8, 14 ; 11:16 ; 19:4
5:5 and one of *e*. saith
6 in midst of *e*. stood a Lamb
7:11 angels stood about the *e*.
13 one of the *e*. answered

ELDERS, *with city.*
Deut. 19:12 *e*. of *city* shall fetch
21:3 *e*. of *city* shall take heifer
6 *e*. of that *city* shall wash
21:19 bring son to *e*. of his *city*
Jud. 8:16 he took *e*. of the *city*
Ruth 4:2 B. took men of *e*. of *c*.
Ezr. 10:14 the *e*. of every *city*

ELDERS of *Israel.*
Ex. 3:16 gather the *e*. of *Israel*
12:21 M. called for *e*. of *Israel*
18:12 *e*. of *Israel* came to eat
24:1 seventy of *e*. 9 ; *Num.* 11:16
Deut. 27:1 *e*. of *Isr*. commanded
31:9 delivered law to *e*. of *Isr*.
Jos. 7:6 *e*. of *Isr*. put dust on
2 *Sam.* 5:3 *e*. of *Isr*. came to king at
Hebron, 1 *K*. 8:3 ; 2 *Chr.* 5:4
17:4 pleased all *e*. of *Israel*
15 Ahithophel counsel *e*. of *Is.*
Ezek. 20:1 *e*. of *I*. came to inqu.
Acts 4:8 rulers of peo. and *e*. of *I*:

ELDERS, *with people.*
Num. 11:24 M. gathered seventy
men of the *e*. of the *people*
1 *Sam.* 15:30 honor before *e*. of *p*.
Mat. 21:23 the *e*. of *people* came,
Luke 22:66
27:1 *e*. of the *peo*. took counsel

ELDEST.
Gen. 24:2 Ab. said to his *e*. serv.
27:1 Isaac called Es. his *e*. son
44:12 began at the *e*.
Num. 1:20 Reuben *e*. son, 26:5
1 *Sam.* 17:13 sons of Jesse, 14
28 Eliab his *e*. brother
2 *K*. 3:27 he took his *e*. son
Job 1:13 in *e*. brother's house, 18
John 8:9 one by one, begin. at *e*.
ELEALEH. *Num.* 32:37 ; *Is.*
15:4 ; 16:9 ; *Jer.* 48:34

ELEAZAR.
Ex. 6:25 ; 28:1 ; *Num.* 3:2 ; 26:60 ;
1 *Chr.* 6:3 ; 24:1 ; *Ezr.* 8:33
Lev. 10:16 M. was angry with E.
Num. 3:4 E. minister. in priests'

34:17 E. and Joshua shall divide
Jos. 17:4 ca. near bef. E. 24:33
1 *Sam.* 7:1 they sanctified E. to
Neh. 12:42 Shemaiah and E.
Mat. 1:15 Eliud begat E. and E.

ELECT.
Is. 42:1 mine *e*. in whom my
45:4 Israel mine *e*. I have called
65:9 mine *e*. shall inherit it
22 mine *e*. shall long enjoy
Mat. 24:22 for the *e*. those days
shall be short. *Mark* 13:20
24 dec. the very *e*. *Mark* 13:22
31 angels gather *e*. *Mark* 13:27
Luke 18:7 G. avenge his own *e*. ?
Rom. 8:33 to charge of God's *e*. ?
Col. 3:12 put on as *e*. of G. bow,
1 *Tim.* 5:21 before the *e*. angels
2 *Tim.* 2:10 endure for the *e*. sak
Tit. 1:1 to the faith of God's *e*.
1 *Pet.* 1:2 *e*. according to foreknn.
2:6 chief corner-stone, *e*. prec.
2 *John* 1 the elder to the *e*. lady
13 the children of thy *e*. sister

ELECTED.
1 *Pet.* 5:13 church at Bab. *e*. with

ELECTION.
Rom. 9:11 purpose accord. to *e*.
11:5 remn. according to the *e*.
7 the *e*. hath obtained it
28 the *e*. they are 'eloved
1 *Thes.* 1:4 knowing your *e*. of G
2 *Pet.* 1:10 your calling and *e*.

EL-ELOHE-*Israel*. *Gen.* 33:20

ELEMENTS.
Gal. 4:3 under *e*. of the world
9 the weak and beggarly *e*.
2 *Pet.* 3:10 *e*. melt with heat, 12

ELEVEN.
Gen. 32:22 Jacob took his *e*. sons
37:9 sun, moon, and *e*. stars
Ex. 26:7 *e*. curtains shalt make
36:14 *e*. curt. ; 15 *e*. of one size
Num. 29:20 *e*. bullocks, two rams
Deut. 1:2 *e*. days' journey fr. H.
Jos. 15:51 *e*. cities with villages
Jud. 16:5 *e*. hun. pieces of silver
17:2 *e*. hundred shekels of silv.
2 *K*. 23:36 Jehoiakim reigned *e*.
years in Jeru. 2 *Chr.* 36:5
24:18 Zedekiah reigned *e*. years,
2 *Chr.* 36:11 ; *Jer.* 52:1
Mat. 28:16 *e*. disciples went to G.
Mark 16:14 he appeared to the *e*.
Luke 24:9 told to the *e*. and rest
33 found the *e*. gath. together
Acts 1:26 numb. with *e*. apostles
2:14 P. with the *e*. said to them

ELEVENTH.
1 *K*. 6:38 *e*. year was ho. finished
1 *Chr.* 24:12 the *e*. lot came forth
25:18 the *e*. to Azareel
27:14 *e*. capt. for the *e*. month
Jer. 1:3 Jer. proph. *e*. year of Z.
39:2 in *e*. year city was bro. up
Ezek. 26:1 word of L. came to E.
in *e*. year, 30:20 ; 31:1
Mat. 20:6 about *e*. hour he went
9 were hired about the *e*. hour
Rev. 21:20 *e*. foundat. of the city
ELHANAN. 2 *Sam.* 21:19 ; 23:24 ;
1 *Chr.* 11:26 ; 20:5

ELI.
1 *Sam.* 1:25 brou. the child to E.
2:12, 27 ; 3:5, 6, 8, 12, 14 ; 4:14
1 *K*. 2:27 spake concerning E.
Mat. 27:46 cried, E. E. lama,
Mark 15:34

ELIAB.
Num. 1:9 ; 2:7 ; 7:24, 29 ; 10:16
16:1 sons of E. 12 ; 26:8, 9
Deut. 11:6 he did to sons of E.
1 *Sam.* 17:28 E. heard, 1 *Chr.* 2:13
1 *Chr.* 6:27 E. the son of Nahath
15:18 E. port. 20 ; 16:5 E. with

2 *Chr.* 11:18 took daughter of E.

ELIADA.
2 *Sam.* 5:16; 1 *Chr.* 3:8; 2 *Chr.* 17:17

ELIAKIM.
2 *K.* 18:18 out to Rab-shakeh E.
 23:34 made E. son, 2 *Chr.* 36:4
Is. 22:20; 36:3; 37:2
Mat. 1:13 Abiud begat E. and E.

ELIAM. 2 *Sam.* 11:3; 23:34

ELIASHIB.
Ezr. 10:6 the son of E. 24, 27, 36
Neh. 3:1; 12:10, 23; 13:4, 7, 28

ELIEZER.
Gen. 15:2 steward of house is E.
Ex. 18:4 name of Moses' son E.
1 *Chr.* 7:8; 15:24; 23:15, 17; 27:16
2 *Chr.* 20:37 E. prophesied aga.
Ezr. 10:18 E. had taken, 23, 31
Luke 3:29 Jose was the son of E.

ELIHOREPH. 1 *K.* 4:3

ELIHU.
1 *Chr.* 12:20; 26:7; 27:18; *Job* 32:2

ELIJAH, or ELIAS.
1 *K.* 17:1 E. the Tishbite, 15, 22
 23 E. took the child down
 18:2 E. went to A. 7, 16, 40, 46
 19:1 E. had done, 9:20; 21:20
2 *K.* 1:8 is E. the Tishbite, 13, 17
 2:1 E. into heaven, 8, 11, 14, 15
 3:11 poured wa. on hands of E.
2 *Chr.* 21:12 came a writing fr. E.
Mal. 4:5 behold I will send you E.
Mat. 11:14 which was to come
 16:14 say E. *Mark* 6:15; *Lu.* 9:8
 17:3 app. E. *Mark* 9:4; *Lu.* 9:30
 11 E. shall come, *Mark* 9:12
 12 E. come already, *Mark* 9:13
 27:47 calleth for E. *Mark* 15:35
 49 E. will come, *Mark* 15:36
Luke 1:17 before in power of E.
 9:54 fire to consume as E. did
John 1:21 art thou E. ? art th. 25
Rom. 11:2 scripture saith of E.
Jam. 5:17 E. was a man subject

ELIM.
Ex. 15:27; 16:1; *Num.* 33:9, 10

ELIMELECH.
Ruth 1:2 name E. 3; 2:1; 4:9

ELIPHALET.
2 *Sam.* 5:16; 1 *Chr.* 3:6, 8

ELIPHAZ.
Gen. 36:4, 10, 11, 12, 15; 1 *Chr.* 1:35
Job 2:11; 4:1; 15:1; 22:1; 42:9

ELISABETH. *Luke* 1:5,24,40,57

ELISHA, ELISEUS.
1 *K.* 19:16 E. to be proph. 17, 19
2 *K.* 2:5 proph. came to E. 12, 15
 3:11 Here is E. 4:1, 8, 17
 5:9 Naaman stood at door of E.
 6:20 E. said, open the eyes, 31
 8:4 that E. hath done 5, 14
 13:14 E. fallen sick, 16, 17, 21
Luke 4:27 lepers in days of E.

ELISHAH. *Ezek.* 27:7

ELISHAMA.
Num. 1:10; 2:18; 7:48, 53; 10:22
2 *Sam.* 5:16 E. David's son
1 *Chr.* 2:41; 3:6, 8; 7:26; 14:7
2 *Chr.* 17:8 he sent with them E.
Jer. 36:12 E. the scribe, 41:1

ELISHEBA. *Ex.* 6:23

ELISHUA.
2 *Sam.* 5:15 E. D. sons, 1 *Chr.*14:5

ELIUD. *Mat.* 1:14, 15

ELKANAH.
Ex. 6:24 Korah, Assir, and E.
1 *Sam.* 1:1 name was E. 21; 2:11
1 *Chr.* 6:23 son of E. 26, 34, 35
 12:6 the Korhite, 9:16
 15:23 E. was door-keeper for ark
2 *Chr.* 28:7 E. was next to king

ELMODAM. *Luke* 3:28

ELNATHAN.
2 *K.* 24:8 the daughter of E.
Ezr. 8:16 I sent for E. and Jarib
Jer. 26:22 sent E. into, 36:12, 25

ELON.
Gen. 26:34 daughter of E. 36:2
 46:14 the sons of Zebulun, E.
Jud. 12:11 E. judged Israel, 12

ELOQUENT.
Ex. 4:10 O my lord, I am not *e.*
Is. 3:3 doth take away *e.* orator
Acts 18:24 Apollos, an *e.* man

ELSE.
Deut. 4:35 God, there is none *e.*
 39; 1 *K.* 8:60; *Is.* 45:5, 6, 14,
 18, 21, 22; 46:9; *Joel* 2:27
Jud. 7:14 noth. *e.* save sw. of Gid.
1 *Chr.* 21:12 or *e.* three days
Ps. 51:16 not sacrifice *e.* give it
Is. 47:8 none *e.* beside me, 10
John 14:11 or *e.* believe me
Rom. 2:15 accusing or *e.* excus.
Rev. 2:5 repent, or *e.* I come, 16

ELUL. *Neh.* 6:15

ELYMAS. *Acts* 13:8

EMBALM, ED.
Gen. 50:2 Jos. commanded physician to *e.* his father; physicians *e.* Israel
 26 they *e.* Joseph in Egypt

EMBOLDENED, ETH.
Job 16:3 *e.* thee that answerest ?
1 *Cor.* 8:10 the conscience be *e.*

EMBRACE.
2 *K.* 4:16 thou shalt *e.* a son
Prov. 4:8 when thou dost *e.* her
 5:20 why wilt thou *e.* bosom ?
Ec. 3:5 to *e.* and to refrain
Cant. 2:6 hand doth *e.* me, 8:3
Lam. 4:5 in scarlet, *e.* dunghills

EMBRACED.
Gen. 29:13 Laban *e.* Jacob
 33:4 Esau ran and *e.* Jacob
 48:10 Jacob *e.* Joseph's sons
Acts 20:1 Paul *e.* disciples
Heb. 11:13 and *e.* the promises

EMBRACING.
Ec. 3:5 time to refrain from *e.*
Acts 20:10 Paul *e.* Eutychus

EMBROIDER.
Ex. 28:39 thou shalt *e.* the coat

EMBROIDERER.
Ex. 35:35 work of the *e.*
 38:23 Aholiab, an *e.* in blue

EMERALD, S.
Ex. 28:18 second row *e.* 39:11
Ezek. 27:16 Syria in fairs with *e.*
 28:13 precious stone, the *e.*
Rev. 4:3 rainbow like unto an *e.*
 21:19 fourth found. was an *e.*

EMERODS.
Deut. 28:27 smite thee with *e.*
1 *Sam.* 5:6 smote Ashdod with *e.*
 9 *e.* in their secret parts
 12 were smitten with *e.*
 6:4 answered, Five golden *e.* 17
 5 make images of your *e.* 11

EMIM.
Gen. 14:5 sm. the E. *Deut.* 2:10

EMINENT.
Ezek. 16:24 built an *e.* place, 31
 39 throw down thine *e.* place
 17:22 a high and *e.* mountain

EMMANUEL.
Is. 7:14 his name E. *Mat.* 1:23
 8:8 breadth of thy land, O E.

EMMAUS. *Luke* 24:13

EMMOR. *Acts* 7:16

EMPIRE.
Est. 1:20 publish. throughout *e.*

EMPLOY, ED.
Deut. 20:19 tree, to *e.* in siege
1 *Chr.* 9:33 sing. *e.* day and night

EMPLOYMENT.
Ezek. 39:14 sever out men of *e.*

EMPTY, Adjective.
Gen. 31:42 hadst sent me away *e.*
 37:24 pit was *e.* no water in it
 41:27 the seven *e.* ears blasted
Ex. 23:15 none shall appear before me *e.* 34:20; *Deut.* 16:16
Jud. 7:16 in hand *e.* pitchers
Ruth 1:21 brought me home *e.*
 3:17 go not *e.* to mother-in-law
1 *Sam.* 6:3 send not ark away *e.*
 20:18 thy seat will be *e.* 25:27
2 *Sam.* 1:22 sword return. not *e.*
2 *K.* 4:3 borrow thee *e.* vessels
Job 22:9 sent widows away *e.*
 26:7 the north over the *e.* place
Is. 24:1 Lord maketh earth *e.*
 29:8 hungry man awak. soul *e.*
 32:6 to *e.* the soul of the hung.
Hos. 10:1 Israel is an *e.* vine
Nah. 2:10 Nineveh is *e.* and void
Mat. 12:44 he findeth it *e.*
Mark 12:3 away *e.* *Luke* 20:10
Luke 1:53 rich he sent *e.* away

EMPTY, Verb.
Lev. 14:36 that they *e.* the house
Ec. 11:3 clouds *e.* themselves
Jer. 51:2 fanners shall *e.* her land
Hab. 1:17 shall they *e.* their net
Zec. 4:12 which *e.* the golden oil

EMPTIED.
Gen. 42:35 they *e.* their sacks
2 *Chr.* 24:11 officer *e.* the chest
Is. 24:3 land shall be utterly *e.*
Jer. 48:11 Moab not been *e.*
Nah. 2:2 emptiers have *e.* them

EMPTIERS.
Nah. 2:2 have emptied them

EMPTINESS.
Is. 34:11 out upon it stones of *e.*

EMULATION, S.
Rom. 11:14 prov. to *e.* my breth.
Gal. 5:20 works of the flesh are *e.*

ENABLED.
1 *Tim.* 1:12 Ch. Jesus hath *e.* me

ENCAMP.
Ex. 14:2 *e.* before Pi-hahiroth
Num. 2:17 as they *e.* so shall th.
 3:38 *e.* before the tabernacle
 10:31 how we are to *e.* in wild.
2 *Sam.* 12:28 *e.* against Rabbah
Job 19:12 his troops *e.* about tab.
Ps. 27:3 a host *e.* against me
Zec. 9:8 I will *e.* about my house

ENCAMPED.
Ex. 13:20 *e.* in Etham
 15:27 *e.* by the waters
 18:5 Moses *e.* at mount of G.
Num. 33:10 from E. *e.* by Red sea
 11 from Red sea, *e.* in Sin
Jos. 4:19 peo. *e.* in Gilgal, 5:10
Jud. 6:4 Midianites *e.* ag. Israel
 9:50 Abimelech *e.* ag. Thebez

ENCAMPETH.
Ps. 34:7 angel of Lord *e.* round
 53:5 bones of him that *e.* ag. th.

ENCHANTER, S.
Deut. 18:10 not be found an *e.*
Jer. 27:9 heark. not to dr. or *e.*

ENCHANTMENT, S.
Ex. 7:11 magicians did so with
 their *e.* 22; 8:7, 18
Lev. 19:26 nor shall ye use *e.*
Num. 22:23 there is no *e.* aga. J.
 24:1 B. went not to seek for *e.*

2 *K.* 17:17 used *e.* and did evil
21:6 Manas. used *e.* 2 *Chr.* 33:6
Ec. 10:11 serpent will bite w. *e.*
Is. 47:9 great abund. of thine *e.*
12 stand now with thine *e.*

ENCLOSE, ED.
Ex. 39:6 onyx-sto. *e.* in gold, 13
Ps. 17:10 they are *e.* in their fat.
22:16 assem. of wicked have *e.*
Cant. 4:12 a garden *e.* is my sis.
8:9 we will *e.* her with cedar
Lam. 3:9 he hath *e.* my ways
Luke 5:6 *e.* great multi. of fishes

ENCLOSINGS.
Ex. 28:20 stones in gold *e.* 39:13

ENCOUNTERED.
Acts 17:18 philosophers *e.* him.

ENCOURAGE.
Deut. 1:38 *e.* him, sh. cause, 3:28
2 *Sam.* 11:25 and *e.* thou him
Ps. 64:5 they *e.* themselves

ENCOURAGED.
1 *Sam.* 30:6 David *e.* himself
2 *Chr.* 31:4 Levites might be *e.*
35:2 Josiah *e.* th. to serv. of L.
Is. 41:7 carpenter *e.* goldsmith

END.
Gen. 6:13 *e.* of all flesh is come
47:21 one *e.* of Egypt to other *e.*
Ex. 25:19 on one *e.* other *e.*
Deut. 28:64 L. scatter from one *e.*
Jud. 16:21 angel put *e.* of his staff
19:9 day groweth to an *e.*
1 *Sam.* 14:27 Jonath. put *e.* of rod
2 *K.* 10:21 Baal full from *e.*
2 *Chr.* 21:19 after *e.* of two years
Job 6:11 what is my *e.* that I
16:3 shall vain words have *e.* *f*
26:10 until night come to an *e.*
28:3 he setteth an *e.* to darkness
Ps. 7:9 wickedness come to an *e.*
9:6 are come to a perpetual *e.*
19:6 going forth from *e.* of heav.
37:37 *e.* of that man is peace
38 *e.* of wicked shall be cut off
39:4 make me know mine *e.*
73:17 I understood their *e.*
102:27 thy years have no *e.*
119:96 seen an *e.* of perfection
Prov. 5:4 *e.* bitter ; 23:18 the. is *e.*
14:12 *e.* thereof are ways of d.
Ec. 4:8 no *e.* of all his labor
16 there is no *e.* of all the peo.
7:2 *e.* of men ; 8 better *e.*
10:13 *e.* of his talk is madness
12:12 of mak. books th. is no *e.*
Is. 2:7 any *e.* of their treasures,
any *e.* of their chariots
9:7 of his governm. sh. be no *e.*
13:5 come from the *e.* of heaven
16:4 the extortioner is at an *e.*
23:15 after *e.* of seventy y. 17
42:10 his praise from *e.* of earth
45:17 world without *e.*
46:10 the *e.* from the beginning
Jer. 12:12 one *e.* to other *e.* 25:33
17:11 at his *e.* he shall be a fool
29:11 to give you an expected *e.*
31:17 there is hope in thine *e.*
51:13 dwellest, thine *e.* is come
31 his city is taken at one *e.*
Lam. 4:18 our *e.* near, *e.* come
Ezek. 7:2 an *e.* the *e.* is come, 3, 6
21:25 iniquity have *e.* 29 ; 35:5
Dan. 7:28 is the *e.* of the matter
8:17 time of *e.* shall be the vis.
19 at the time *e.* shall be, 11:27
9:26 the *e.* thereof be with flood
11:6 and in the *e.* of years
35 even to the time of the *e.*
40 time of *e.* king of sou.
45 yet he shall come to his *e.*
12:4 seal the book even to the *e.*
8 O Lord, what shall be the *e.*

---

9 words are clos. up, till the *e.*
13 go thy way till the *e.* be
Amos 3:15 houses sha. have an *e.*
5:18 to what *e.* is it for you
8:2 *e.* is come upon people of Is.
Nah. 2:9 there is none *e.* of store
3:3 there is none *e.* of corpses
Mat. 13:39 harvest is *e.* of world
24:3 sign of *e.* of the world ?
14 then shall the *e.* come
31 gath. from one *e.* of heaven
26:58 Peter sat to see the *e.*
28:1 in the *e.* of the sabbath
Luke 1:33 his kingdom be no *e.*
18:1 a para. to them, to this *e.*
22:37 concern. me have an *e.*
John 18:37 to this *e.* was I born
Rom. 6:21 *e.* of those th. is death
22 the *e.* everlasting life
10:4 Christ is the *e.* of the law
14:9 to this *e.* Christ hath died
2 *Cor.* 11:15 *e.* according to works
Eph. 3:21 glory, world without *e.*
Phil. 3:19 whose *e.* is destruction
1 *Tim.* 1:5 *e.* of com. is charity
Heb. 6:8 whose *e.* is to be burned
16 an oath is an *e.* of all strife
7:3 neither begin. nor *e.* of life
9:26 in the *e.* hath appeared
13:7 the *e.* of their conversation
Jam. 5:11 ye have seen *e.* of Lord
1 *Pet.* 1:9 receiv. *e.* of your faith
4:17 *e.* of them that obey Lord
Rev. 21:6 Alpha and Omega, the
beginning and the *e.* 22:13

At the END.
Deut. 15:1 at *e.* of sev. ye. rel.
Ps. 107:27 are at their wit's *e.*
Dan. 12:13 stand in lot at the *e.*
Hab. 2:3 at the *e.* it shall speak
Mat. 13:40 so be in *e.* of world

But the END.
Prov. 14:12 *but the e.* thereof are
the ways of death, 16:25
20:21 *the e.* thereof not be bles.
Mat. 24:6 *but the e.* is not yet,
Mark 13:7 ; *Luke* 21:9
1 *Pet.* 4:7 *but e.* of all things

Last END.
Num. 23:10 let my *l. e.* be like h.
Jer. 12:4 shall not see our *last e.*
Lam. 1:9 remembereth not *l. e.*
Dan. 8:19 known what be in *l. e.*

Latter END.
Num. 24:20 *l. e.* be that he per.
Deut. 8:16 to do thee good at *l. e.*
32:29 consider their *l. e.*
Ruth 3:10 kindness in *latter e.*
2 *Sam.* 2:26 bitterness in *lat. e.*
Job 8:7 thy *latter e.* greatly incr.
42:12 L. blessed *latter e.* of Job
Prov. 19:20 mayest be wise in *l. e.*
Is. 41:22 consid. them, know *l. e.*
47:7 nor didst remember *lat. e.*
2 *Pet.* 2:20 *l. e.* worse than begin.

Made an END.
Gen. 27:30 Isaac *m. e.* of blessing
Deut. 32:45 *m. e.* of speaking,
Jud. 15:17 ; 1 *Sam.* 18:1 ;
24:16 ; 2 *Sam.* 13:36 ; 1 *K.* 1:41 ;
3:1 ; *Jer.* 26:8 ; 43:1 ; 51:63
Mat. 11:1 *m. e.* of com. discip.

Make an END.
1 *Sam.* 3:12 I will also *m. an e.*
Neh. 4:2 will they *m. an e.* *f*
Job 18:2 ere you *m. an e.* *f*
Is. 38:12 *make e.* of me, 13
Ezek. 20:17 nor did I *make e.*
Dan. 9:24 70 weeks to *m. e.*
Nah. 1:8 make utter *e.* 9

Make a full END.
Jer. 4:27 yet will I not *make a
full e.* 5:18 ; 30:11 ; 46:28
5:10 but make not *a. f. e.*
Ezek. 11:13 ah L. wilt *m. a. f. e.* *f*

To the END.
Ex. 8:22 *to the e.* thou mayest
kno. I am the L. *Ezek.* 20:26
Deut. 17:20 *to the e.* that he may
prolong his days
Ps. 19:4 words *to e.* of world
30:12 *to the e.* my glo. may sing
119:112 perf. statutes *to the e.*
Ec. 3:11 find out from beg. *to e.*
7:14 *to the e.* man shou. find no,
Is. 48:20 *to the e.* of earth
49:6 my salvation *to e.* of earth
Jer. 3:5 keep anger *to the e.* *f*
Dan. 4:22 dominion *to the e.*
Mat. 10:22 endur. *to the e.* shall
be saved, 24:13 ; *Mark* 13:13
Acts 7:19 *to the e.* might not live
Rom. 1:11 *to the e.* you be estab.
4:16 *to the e.* promise be sure
2 *Cor.* 1:13 acknowledge *to the e.*
3:13 look *to e.* of that abolished
1 *Thes.* 3:13 *to the e.* he may est.
1 *Pet.* 1:13 and hope *to the e.*

Unto the END.
Job 34:36 Job be tried *unto e.*
Ps. 46:9 wars cease *unto e.*
119:33 I shall keep it *unto the e.*
Is. 62:11 proclaimed *u. e.* of earth
Dan. 6:26 his dominion be *u. e.*
Mat. 28:20 I am with you *u. e.*
John 13:1 loved them *u. the e.*
1 *Cor.* 1:8 confirm you *unto the e.*
Heb. 3:6 hold fast confidence *u. e.*
14 if hold begin. steadfast *u. e.*
6:11 assurance of hope *unto e.*
Rev. 2:26 keepeth my works *u. e.*

ENDAMAGE.
Ezr. 4:13 *e.* the revenue of kings

ENDANGER, ED.
Ec. 10:9 cleav. wood shall be *e.*
Dan. 1:10 *e.* my head to the king

ENDED, ETH, ING.
Gen. 2:2 seventh day G. *e.* work
2 *Sam.* 20:18 so they *e.* the mat.
Job 31:40 the words of Job are *e.*
Ps. 72:20 prayers of David are *e.*
Is. 24:8 noise of them rejoice *e.*
60:20 days of mourn. shall be *e.*
Jer. 8:20 the summer is *e.*
Mat. 7:28 when Jesus *e.* sayings
Luke 4:2 forty days *e.* he hunger.
13 devil had *e.* all temptation
John 13:2 supper being *e.*
Rev. 1:8 the beginning and *e.*

ENDLESS.
1 *Tim.* 1:4 heed to *e.* genealogies
Heb. 7:16 after power of an *e.* life

ENDEAVOR, ED, ING.
Acts 16:10 *e.* to go into Macedo.
Eph. 4:3 *e.* to keep unity of spir.
1 *Thes.* 2:17 we *e.* to see your f.
2 *Pet.* 1:15 will *e.* ye may be able

ENDEAVORS.
Ps. 28:4 accord. to wicked. of *e.*

EN-DOR.
Jos. 17:11 E. and her t. *Ps.* 83:10
1 *Sam.* 28:7 woman at E. hath s.

ENDOW.
Ex. 22:16 *e.* her to be his wife

ENDS.
Deut. 33:17 push peo. to *e.* of *e.*
1 *Sam.* 2:10 shall judge *e.* of *e.*
Job 28:24 looketh to *e.* of the *e.*
37:3 lightning unto *e.* of earth
38:13 take hold of *e.* of earth
Ps. 19:6 his circuit to the *e.* of it
22:27 *e.* of world shall remember
48:10 so is thy praise to the *e.* of
59:13 G. ruleth in Jacob to the *e.*
65:5 confidence of *e.* of the *e.*
67:7 *e.* of the earth sh. fear him
98:3 *e.* of earth seen salvation
135:7 vapors to ascend from the
e. of earth, *Jer.* 10:13 ; 51:16

Prov. 17:24 eyes of fool are in *e.*
30:4 established *e.* of the earth ?
Is. 40:28 Creator of *e.* of the earth
41:5 *e.* of the earth were afraid
9 taken from *e.* of the earth
43:6 daughters from *e.* of earth
45:22 be saved, all the *e.*
52:10 all *e.* see salvation of God
Jer. 16:19 shall come from the *e.*
25:31 a noise to *e.* of the earth
Ezek. 15:4 fire devoureth both *e.*
Mic.. 5:4 shall he be great to *e.*
Zec. 9:10 his dominion to *e.* of
Acts 13:47 be for salvation to *e.*
Rom. 10:18 words to *e.* of world
1 *Cor.* 10:11 *e.* of world are come

ENDUED.

Gen. 30:20 *e.* me with good dow.
2 *Chr.* 2:12 son *e.* with prudence
13 cunning man *e.* with under.
Luke 24:49 ye be *e.* with power
Jam. 3:13 *e.* with knowledge

ENDURE.

Gen. 33:14 children be able to *e.*
Ex. 18:23 thou shalt be able to *e.*
Est. 8 6 can I *e.* to see the evil
Job 8:15 fast, but it shall not *e.*
31:23 I could not *e.*
Ps. 9:7 the Lord shall *e.* for ever,
102:12, 26 ; 104:31
30:5 weeping may *e.* for a night
72:5 fear thee as long as sun *e.*
17 his name shall *e.* as the sun
89:29 his seed to *e.* for ever, 36
Prov. 27:24 crown *e.* to every *g.*
Ezek. 22:14 can thy heart *e.*
Mat. 24:13 he that shall *e.* to the
end, *Mark* 13:13
Mark 4:17 so *e.* but for a time
2 *Thes.* 1:4 tribulations that ye *e.*
2 *Tim.* 2:3 therefore *e.* hardness
10 *e.* all things for elect's sake
4:3 will not *e.* sound doctrine
5 in all things, *e.* afflictions
Heb. 12:7 if ye *e.* chastening, God
Heb. 12:20 not *e.* what was com.
Jam. 5:11 count them hap. w. *e.*
1 *Pet.* 2:19 for conscience *e.* grief

ENDURED.

Ps. 81:15 should have *e.* for ever
Rom. 9:22 God *e.* with long-suff.
2 *Tim.* 3:11 what persecut. I *e.*
Heb. 6:15 after he had patient. *e.*
10:32 *e.* great fight of afflictions
11:27 *e.* as seeing him invisible
12:2 *e.* cross ; 3 *e.* such contrad.

ENDURETH.

Ps. 30:5 anger *e.* but a moment
52:1 goodness of G. *e.* continu.
72:7 peace, so long as moon *e.*
100:5 truth *e.* to all generations
145:13 dominion *e.* through all
Mat. 10:22 *e.* to the end be saved
John 6:27 meat which *e.* unto life
1 *Cor.* 13:7 charity *e.* all things
Jam. 1:12 bless. that *e.* tempta.

ENDURETH for ever.

1 *Chr.* 16:34 his mercy *e. for ever*,
41 ; 2 *Chr.* 5:13 ; 7:3, 6 ; 20:21 ;
Ezr. 3:11 ; *Ps.* 106:1 ; 107:1 ;
118:1-4 ; 136:1-3, etc. ; 138:8 ;
Jer. 33:11
Ps. 111:3 righte. *e. f. e.* 112:3, 9
10 his praise *e. for ever*
117:2 his truth *e. for ever*
119:160 thy judgments *e. for e.*
135:13 thy name, O L. *e. for e.*
1 *Pet.* 1:25 word of the L. *e. f. e.*

ENDURING.

Ps. 19:9 fear of Lord clean, *e.*
2 *Cor.* 1:6 effectual in *e.* same
Heb. 10:34 in heaven *e.* substance

ENEAS. *Acts* 9:34
EN-EGLAIM. *Ezek.* 47:10

ENEMY.

Ex. 15:6 right hand dashed the *e.*
9 the *e.* said, I will pursue
23:22 I will be *e.* to thine en.
Num. 10:9 if go to war against *e.*
35:23 and was not his *e.*
Deut. 32:27 feared wrath of the *e.*
42 beginning of revenges on *e.*
33:27 he shall thrust out the *e.*
Jud. 16:23 God delivered our *e.*
1 *Sam.* 2:32 *e.* in my habitation
18:29 Saul became David's *e.*
24:19 his *e.* will he let him go?
1 *K.* 8:33 when thy people he
smitten before *e.* 2 *Chr.* 6:24
46 if sin, and thou deliver to *e.*
2 *Chr.* 25:8 make thee fall bef. *e.*
Est. 7:4 *e.* not counterv. damage
6 the *e.* is this wicked Haman
Job 33:10 counteth me for his *e.*
Ps. 7:5 let the *e.* persecute
8:2 mightest still *e.* and avenger
9:6 O thou *e.* destructions are
42:9 mourning bec. of *e.* ? 43:2
44:10 makest us to turn from *e.*
55:3 I mourn bec. of voice of *e.*
12 not an *e.* that reproached
61:3 a strong tower from the *e.*
64:1 preserve life from fear of *e.*
74:3 all that *e.* hath done
10 *e.* blaspheme thy name ?
18 remember *e.* hath reproach.
78:42 he delivered from *e.* 61
89:22 the *e.* not exact upon him
143:3 *e.* hath persecuted
Prov. 27:6 kisses of *e.* are deceit.
Is. 59:19 *e.* come in like a flood
63:10 was turned to be their *e.*
Jer. 6:25 sword of *e.* is on ev. side
15:11 cause *e.* to entreat thee
18:17 scatter them before *e.*
30:14 with wound of an *e.*
Lam. 1:9 *e.* hath magnified
16 because *e.* prevailed
2:3 drawn back hand bef. the *e.*
4 hath bent his bow like an *e.*
5 the Lord was as an *e.*
4:12 *e.* should have entered
Ezek. 36:2 the *e.* had said, Aha
Hos. 8:3 Is. *e.* shall pursue him
Mic. 2:8 my people risen up as *e.*
Nah. 3:11 seek strength bec. of *e.*
Mat. 13:25 his *e.* sowed tares
28 said, An *e.* hath done this
39 *e.* that sowed is the devil
Luke 10:19 all power of the *e.*
Acts 13:10 thou *e.* of all righte.
1 *Cor.* 15:26 the last *e.* is death
Gal. 4:16 am I become your *e.*
2 *Thes.* 3:15 not as an *e.*
Jam. 4:4 friend of world *e.* of G.

Hand of the ENEMY.

Lev. 26:25 shall be delivered into
the *hand of the e.* *Neh.* 9:27
Ps. 31:8 me up into *h. of e.*
78:61 he deliv. his glory in. *e. h.*
Ps. 106:10 red. from *h. of e.* 107:2
Lam. 1:7 people fell into *h. of e.*

Mine ENEMY.

1 *Sam.* 19:17 sent away mine *e.* ?
2 *Sam.* 22:18 mine *e.* *Ps.* 18:17
1 *K.* 21:20 found me, O mine *e.* ?
Job 16:9 mine *e.* sharpe. his eyes
27:7 let mine *e.* be as wicked
Ps. 7:4 I deliv. him th. is mine *e.*
13:2 how long mine *e.* be exalt.
4 lest mine *e.* say, I have prev.
41:11 mine *e.* not triumph
Lam. 2:22 I swaddled, mine *e.*
Mic. 7:8 rej. not aga. me, O m. *e.*
10 she that is m. *e.* shall see it

Thine ENEMY.

Deut. 28:57 thine *e.* shall distress
1 *Sam.* 24:4 deliver thine *e.* 26:8
28:16 Lord is become thine *e.*
2 *Sam.* 4:8 the head of thine *e.*

Job 13:24 holdest me for *thine e.*
Prov. 24:17 rej. not when *t. e.* fall
25:21 if *t. e.* hunger, *Rom.* 12:20
Lam. 2:17 thine *e.* to rejoice
Zep. 3:15 the L. cast out thine *e.*
Mat. 5:43 Thou shalt hate th. *e.*
Rom. 12:20 if *th. e.* hung. feed h.

ENEMIES.

1 *Sam.* 18:25 avenged of king's *e.*
20:15 when Lord cut off *e.* of D.
16 req. it at hand of David's *e.*
2 *Sam.* 12:14 occasion to *e.* to bl.
18:32 *e.* as that young man
2 *Chr.* 20:29 Lord fought aga. *e.*
Ps. 17:9 hide me from deadly *e.*
37:20 *e.* of L. be as fat of lambs
45:5 arrows sharp in king's *e.*
127:5 shall speak with *e.* in gate
Jer. 12:7 belov. into hand of h. *e.*
48:5 *e.* heard cry of destruction
Lam. 1:2 friends are become *e.*
5 her *e.* prosper
Mic. 7:6 *e.* are of own house
Rom. 5:10 when *e.* we were rec.
11:28 as con. gospel, they are *e.*
1 *Cor.* 15:25 put all *e.* under feet
Phil. 3:18 *e.* of the cross of Chr.
Col. 1:21 *e.* in your mind

His ENEMIES.

Gen. 22:16 possess gate of *his e.*
Num. 24:8 the nations *his e.*
32:21 he hath driven out *his e.*
Deut. 33:7 be a help from *his e.*
2 *Sam.* 7:1 rest from *his e.*
18:19 Lord avenged of *his e.*
22:1 out of the hand of all *his e.*
1 *Chr.* 22:9 give rest fr. all *h. e.*
Job 19:11 count. me one of *his e.*
Ps. 10:5 *his e.* he puffeth at them
41:2 not deliv. h. to will of *h. e.*
68:1 let *his e.* be scattered
21 G. shall wound head of *h. e.*
72:9 and *his e.* shall lick the d.
78:66 smote *his e.* in hinder pa.
89:42 hast made *his e.* to rejoice
97:3 a fire burneth up *his e.*
112:8 till he see des. upon *h. e.*
132:18 *his e.* clothe with shame
Prov. 16:7 *his e.* be at peace
Is. 9:11 shall join *his e.* together
42:13 he shall prevail ag. *his e.*
59:18 recompense to *his e.*
66:6 rendereth recomp. to *his e.*
14 indig. be known tow. *h. e.*
Jer. 44:30 Phar. into hand of *h. e.*
Nah. 1:2 reserveth wrath of *h. e.*
8 darkness shall pursue *his e.*
Heb. 10:13 h. *e.* made footstool

Mine ENEMIES.

Num. 23:11 curse mine *e.* 24:10
Deut. 32:41 vengeance to mine *e.*
1 *Sam.* 2:1 enlarged over m. *e.*
14:24 be avenged on mine *e.*
2 *Sam.* 5:20 L. hath broken forth
upon mine. *e.* 1 *Chr.* 14:11
22:4 saved from m. *e.* *Ps.* 18:3
38 pursued mine *e.* *Ps.* 18:37
41 necks of m. *e.* *Ps.* 18:40
49 bringeth me forth fr. m. *e.*
1 *Chr.* 12:17 betray me to mine *e.*
Ps. 3:7 hast smitten all mine *e.*
5:8 lead me, O L. bec. of m. *e.*
6:7 eye waxeth old bec. of m. *e.*
10 let all mine *e.* be ashamed
7:6 because of rage of mine *e.*
9:3 m. *e.* are turned
18:48 he deliv. me from mine. *e.*
23:5 in presence of mine *e.*
25:2 let not m. *e.* triumph, 35:19
19 consider m. *e.* they are ma.
27:2 m. *e.* came to eat my flesh
6 he lifted up above mine *e.*
11 because of mine *e.*
12 deliv. me n. to will of m. *e.*
31:11 I was a reproach am. m. *e.*
15 from hand of mine *e.*

Ps. 38:19 but *mine e.* are lively
41:5 *mine e.* speak evil of me
42:10 *m. e.* reproach me, 102:8
54:5 shall reward evil to *e.*
7 desire upon *mine e.* 59:10
56:2 *m. e.* would swal. me up
9 *m. e.* shall turn back
59:1 deliver me from *m. e.* 143:9
69:4 they being *mine e.*
18 deliver me, bec. of *mine e.*
71:10 *mine e.* speak against **me**
92:11 see desire on *mine e.*
119:98 wiser than *mine e.*
139 *m. e.* have forgotten
157 many are *mine e.*
138:7 forth thy hand ag. *m. e.*
139:22 I count them *mine e.*
143:12 cut off *mine e.*
Is. 1:24 avenge me of *mine e.*
Lam. 1:21 *m. e.* heard of my tro.
3:52 *m. e.* chased me like a bird
Luke 19:27 *m. e.* bring and slay

Our ENEMIES.
Ex. 1:10 they join also to *our e.*
Deut. 32:31 *our e.* being judges
1 *Sam.* 4:3 save us from *our e.*
12:10 but deliver us from *our e.*
2 *Sam.* 19:9 saved us fr. o. *e. Ps.* 44:7
Ps. 44:5 push down *our e.*
60:12 tread *our e.* 108:13
80:6 *our e.* laugh am. themselves
136:24 redeemed us from *our e.*
Lam. 3:46 o. e. op. their mouths
Luke 1:71 be saved from *our e.*
74 being delivered from *our e.*

Their ENEMIES.
Lev. 26:36 in land of *their e.*
Jos. 7:8 turn. backs before *t. e.* 12
21:44 stood not a man of *th. e.*
23:1 rest from *t. e. Est.* 9:16
Jud. 2:14 into the hand of *t. e.*
18 deliv. them from *t. e.* 8:34
2 *K.* 21:14 into the hand of *th. e.*
2 *Chr.* 6:36 ; 25:20 ; *Neh.* 9:27
Ps. 78:53 sea overwhelmed *t. e.*
81:14 should soon subdue *th. e.*
105:24 stronger than *their e.*
106:11 waters covered *their e.*
42 *their e.* oppressed them
Jer. 15:9 deliver to sw. bef. *t. e.*
19:7 fall before *their e.* 20:4
9 *their e.* shall straiten them
20:5 into the hands of *t. e.* 21:7 ;
34:20, 21 ; *Ezek.* 39:23
Ezek. 39:27 out of *their e.* hands
Amos 9:4 captivity before *th. e.*
Zec. 10:5 tread down *their e.*
Rev. 11:5 fire devoureth *their e.*
12 *their e.* beheld them

Thine ENEMIES.
Gen. 14:20 del. *t. e.* into thy hand
49:8 thy hand be in neck of *t. e.*
Ex. 23:22 an enemy to *thine e.*
27 make *thine e.* to turn
Num. 10:35 let *thine e.* be scat.
Deut. 6:19 cast out all *thine e.*
28:53 *t. e.* shall distress, 55:57
33:29 *thine e.* be found liars
Jos. 7:13 not stand bef. *t. e.*
Jud. 5:31 so let *t. e.* perish
11:36 veng. for thee of *thine e.*
1 *Sam.* 25:29 souls of *th. e.* sling
2 *Sam.* 7:9 cut off *t. e.* 1 *Chr.* 17:8
19:6 lov. *th. e.* hat. thy friends
24:13 three months before *t. e.*
1 *K.* 3:11 nor asked the life of *thine e.* 2 *Chr.* 1:11
Ps. 8:2 because of *thine e.*
21:8 thy hand find out all *th. e.*
66:3 thy power *thine e.* submit
68:23 dipped in blood of *thine e.*
74:4 *t. e.* roar ; 83:2 *t. e.* make t.
23 forget not the voice of *th. e.*
89:10 scat. *th. e.* with thy arm
51 wherewith *th. e.* reproached

92:9 *thine e.* O Lord, shall per.
110:1 *thine e.* thy footstool, *Mat* 22:44 ; *Mark* 12:36 ; *Luke* 20:43 ; *Heb.* 1:13
2 in the midst of *thine e.*
139:20 *th. e.* take thy name in v.
Is. 26:11 fire of *t. e.* devour them
62:8 no m. give corn to *th. e.*
Jer. 15:14 to pass with *thine e.*
Lam. 2:16 *th. e.* have opened m.
Dan. 4:19 interpreta. be to *th. e.*
Mic. 5:9 all *thine e.* shall be cut off
Nah. 3:13 gate be opened to *t. e.*
Luke 19:43 *t. e.* shall cast trench

Your ENEMIES.
Lev. 26:7 ye shall chase *your e.*
8 *your e.* fall bef. you by sword
15 sow in vain, *y. e.* shall eat it
17 shall be slain bef. *your e.*
Lev. 26:37 to stand before *your e.*
Num. 10:9 be saved from *your e.*
14:42 before *y. e. Deut.* 1:42
Deut. 20:4 L. goeth to fight *y. e.*
28:68 ye shall be sold to *y. e.*
Jos. 10:25 shall Lord do to *y. e.*
1 *Sam.* 12:11 L. delivered you out of hand of *y. e.* 2 *K.* 17:39
Mat. 5:44 love *y. e. Luke* 6:27, 35

ENGAGED.
Jer. 30:21 who is this *e.* his heart

EN-GEDI.
Jos. 15:62 wilder. of Judah E.
1 *Sam.* 23:29 D. dwelt at E. 24:1
2 *Chr.* 20:2 Jehoshap. are in E.

ENGINES.
2 *Chr.* 26:15 Uzziah made *e.*
Ezek. 26:9 set *e.* of war ag. walls

ENGRAFTED.
Jam. 1:21 with meekness *e.* wo.

ENGRAVE, EN.
Zec. 3:9 I will *e.* graving thereof
2 *Cor.* 3:7 ministration of dea. *e.*

ENGRAVER.
Ex. 28:11 work of an *e.* in stone
38:23 Aholiab, an *e.*

ENJOIN, ED.
Job 36:23 hath *e.* him his way
Phile. 8 to *e.* what is convenient
Heb. 9:20 blood which G. hath *e.*

ENJOY, ED.
Lev. 26:34 land *e.* her sab. 43
Num. 36:8 Is. may *e.* inheritance
Deut. 28:41 beget sons, not *e.* th.
Jos. 1:15 ret. to land, and *e.* it
2 *Chr.* 36:21 till land *e.* sabbaths
Ec. 2:1 e. pleasure, this is vanity
24 his soul *e.* good, 3:13 ; 5:18
Is. 65:22 elect long *e.* the work
Acts 24:2 we *e.* great quietness
1 *Tim.* 6:17 giv. all things to *e.*
Heb. 11:25 th. *e.* pleasures of sin

ENLARGE.
Gen. 9:27 God shall *e.* Japheth
Ex. 34:24 I will *e.* thy borders
1 *Chr.* 4:10 wouldst *e.* my coast
Ps. 119:32 shalt *e.* my heart
Is. 54:2 *e.* the place of thy tent
Amos 1:13 might *e.* their border
Mic. 1:16 *e.* thy baldness as eagle
Mat. 23:5 *e.* borders of garments

ENLARGED.
1 *Sam.* 2:1 mouth is *e.* over ene.
2 *Sam.* 22:37 *e.* steps, *Ps.* 18:36
Ps. 4:1 *e.* me when in distress
25:17 troubles of my heart are *e.*
Is. 5:14 hell hath *e.* herself
57:8 thou hast *e.* thy bed
60:5 heart shall fear and be *e.*
2 *Cor.* 6:11 O Cor. our heart is *e.*
13 for recompense, be ye also *e.*
10:15 that we shall be *e.* by you

Deut. 33:20 blessed be he *e.* Gad
Job 12:23 he *e.* the nations, and
Ezek. 41:7 and there was an *e.*
Hab. 2:5 who *e.* his desire as hell

ENLARGEMENT.
Est. 4:14 *e.* from another place

ENLIGHTEN, ED.
Ps. 18:28 L. will *e.* my darkness
1 *Sam.* 14:27 Jon.'s eyes were *e.*
Job 33:30 *e.* with light of living
Ps. 97:4 his lightnings *e.* world
Eph. 1:18 eyes of understand. *e.*
Heb. 6:4 impos. for those once *e.*

ENLIGHTENING.
Ps. 19:8 is pure, *e.* the eyes.

EN-MISHPAT.   *Gen.* 14:7

ENMITY.
Gen. 3:15 I will put *e.* betw. thee
Num. 35:22 he thrust without *e.*
Luke 23.12 before they were at *e.*
Rom. 8:7 carnal mind is *e.* ag. G.
Eph. 2:15 abolished in his flesh *e.*
16 having slain the *e.* thereby
Jam. 4.4 frriendship of world is *e.*

ENOCH.
Gen. 4:17 bare E. ; 5:18 begat E.
5:22 E. walked with God.
Luke 3:37 Mathus. was son of E.
Heb. 11.5 E. was translated
Jude 14 E. also prophesied

ENON.   *John* 3.23

ENOS.
Gen. 4:26 call. his son's name E.
Luke 3:38 Cainan was son of E.

ENOUGH.
Gen. 33:9 Esau said, I have *e.*
11 take my blessing, I have *e.*
34:21 land is large *e.* for them
Gen. 45:28 it is *e.* Jos. is yet alive
Ex. 9:28 entreat Lord, for it is *e.*
36:5 bring much more than *e.*
Jos. 17:16 hill is not *e.* for us
2 *Sam.* 24:16 it is *e.* 1 *K.* 19:4 ;
1 *Chr.* 21:15 ; *Mark* 14:41 ;
Luke 22:38
2 *Chr.* 31:10 we have had *e.* to *e.*
Prov. 30:15 things say not, It is *e.*
16 fire that saith not, It is *e.*
Is. 56:11 can never have *e.*
Jer. 49:9 will destroy till have *e.*
Hos. 4:10 eat, and not have *e.*
Hag. 1:6 ye eat, but have not *e.*
Mal. 3:10 not room *e.* to rec. it
Mat. 10:25 *e.* for disciple to be
25:9 be not *e.* for us and you
Luke 15:17 servants have bread *e.*

ENQUIRE.   *See* INQUIRE.

ENRICH, ED, EST.
1 *Sam.* 17:25 king will *e.* him
Ezek. 27:33 didst *e.* kings of earth
Ps. 65:9 *e.* it with river of God
1 *Cor.* 1:5 in everything ye are *e.*
2 *Cor.* 9:11 being *e.* in every th.

EN-ROGEL.
2 *Sam.* 17:17 Ahim. stayed by E.
1 *K.* 1:9 sheep and oxen by E.

ENSAMPLE.
Phil. 3:17 as ye have us for an *e.*
2 *Thes.* 3:9 to make oursel. an *e.*
2 *Pet.* 2:6 Sodom and Gomor. an *e.*

ENSAMPLES.
1 *Cor.* 10:11 hap. to them for *e.*
1 *Thes.* 1:7 so that ye w. *e.* to all
1 *Pet.* 5:3 but being *e.* to the flo.

ENSIGN, S.
Ps. 74:4 set up their *e.* for signs
Is. 5:26 he will lift up an *e.*
11:10 stand for an *e.* to people
12 set up an *e.* for the nations
18:3 when he lifteth up an *e.*
30:17 till ye be left as *e.* on hill
31:9 his princes be afraid of *e.*

Zec. 9:16 lifted as an *e.*

ENSNARED.

Job 34:30 lest people be *e.*

ENSUE.

1 *Pet.* 3:11 seek peace, and *e.* it

ENTANGLE, ED, ETH.

Ex. 14:3 they are *e.* in the land
Mat. 22:15 how they might *e.* him
Gal. 5:1 be not *e.* with yoke
2 *Tim.* 2:4 *e.* him affairs of life
2 *Pet.* 2:20 they are again *e.*

ENTER.

Deut. 23:8 children shall *e.* cong.
29:12 shouldest *e.* into covenant
2 *Sam.* 22:7 my cry did *e.* his *e.*
2 *K.* 7:4 if *e.* city, then famine
19:23 I will *e.* into the lodgings
   of his borders, *Is.* 37:24
2 *Chr.* 30:8 *e.* into his sanctuary
Job 22:4 will he *e.* into judgm. ?
34:23 *e.* into judgment with God
Ps. 37:15 sword *e.* their heart
45:15 shall *e.* into king's palace
100:4 *e.* into gates with thanks.
118:20 gate into which right. *e.*
Prov. 18:6 fool's lips *e.* content.
Is. 2:10 *e.* into the rock
3:14 *e.* into judg. with ancients
26:2 righteous nation may *e.* in
  20 *e.* thou into thy chambers
57:2 he shall *e.* into peace
Jer. 7:2 that *e.* gates, 17:20 ; 22:2
14:18 if I *e.* into the city, famine
17:25 shall *e.* gates, kings, 22:4
21:13 shall *e.* our habitations ?
42:15 if ye set faces to *e.* Egypt
Ezek. 7:22 robbers shall *e.* in. it
13:9 nor *e.* into land of Israel
26:10 as men *e.* into a city
37:5 cause breath to *e.* into you
44:2 gate shut, no man *e.* by it
  16 shall *e.* into my sanctuary
Dan. 11:7 shall *e.* into fortress
  24 he shall *e.* peaceably
  40 he shall *e.* into the countries
  41 he shall *e.* into glorious land
Joel 2:9 *e.* in at the windows
Amos 5:5 nor *e.* into Gilgal
Mat. 5:20 in no case *e.* into king.
6:6 prayest *e.* into thy closet
7:13 *e.* in at str. gate, *Luke* 13:24
  21 that saith, Lord, shall *e.* in
10:11 city ye *e. Luke* 10:8, 10
12:29 *e.* str. man's h. *Mark* 3:27
  45 *e.* in dwell there. *Luke* 11:26
18:8 it is better to *e.* into life
  halt, 9 ; *Mark* 9:43, 45, 47
19:17 if thou wilt *e.* into life
  24 rich man to *e.* into kingdom,
  Mark 10:25 ; *Luke* 18:25
Mat. 25:21 *e.* into joy of thy Lord
Mark 1:45 no more openly *e.* city
5:12 *e.* into swine, *Luke* 8:32
6:10 house ye *e. Luke* 9:4 ; 10:5
9:25 and *e.* no more into him
14:38 *e.* into tempt. *Luke* 22:46
Luke 8:16 which *e.* in may see
13:24 many will seek to *e.* in
24:26 and to *e.* into his glory ?
John 3:4 can he *e.* into womb
  5 he cannot *e.* into king. of G.
10:9 by me if any man *e.* in
Acts 14:22 through tribulation *e.*
20:29 grievous wolves shall *e.* in
Heb. 4:3 *e.* into rest, if *e.* rest, 5
  6 remaineth, some must *e.*
  11 let us labor to *e.* that rest
10:19 *e.* holiest by blood of Jes.
Rev. 15:8 no man able to *e.* tem.
21:27 in no wise *e.* that defileth
22:14 *e.* in thro. gates into city

ENTER not.

Ps. 143:2 *e.* not into judgment
Prov. 4:14 *e.* not path of wicked
23:10 *e.* not fields of fatherless
Jer. 16:5 *e.* not house of mourn.

Mat. 10:5 any city of Samar. *e. n.*
26:41 *e. n.* into temp. *Luke* 22:40

Not ENTER.

Num. 20:24 Aaron *not e.* into la.
2 *Chr.* 7:2 priests could *n. e.* ho.
Ps. 95:11 should *not e.* my rest
Is. 59:14 and equity *cannot e.*
Lam. 1:10 should *not e.* congreg.
Ezek. 20:38 they shall *not e.* land
44:9 nor uncircumcised *e.* sanct.
Hos. 11:9 *not e.* into the city
Mat. 18:3 *not e.* king. of heaven
Mark 10:15 *n. e.* ther. *Luke* 18:17
Heb. 3:11 *not e.* into my rest, 18
  19 *not e.* because of unbelief

See KINGDOM.

ENTERED.

2 *Chr.* 15:12 *e.* into co. to seek L.
27:2 Jotham *e.* not temple of L.
Job 38:16 *e.* into springs of sea ?
  22 *e.* into treas. of the snow ?
Jer. 2:7 but when ye *e.* ye defiled
9:21 death is *e.* into our palaces
34:10 which had *e.* into coven.
Lam. 1:10 heath. *e.* her sanctuary
4:12 enemy should have *e.* gates
Ezek. 2:2 spirit *e.* into me, 3:24
16:8 I *e.* into a cove. with thee
36:20 they *e.* unto heathen
44:2 God of Isr. hath *e.* in by it
Ob. 11 foreigners *e.* his gates
  13 shouldest not have *e.* gate
Hab. 3:16 rottenness *e.* my bones
Mat. 24:38 he *e.* the house of God
24:38 Noah *e.* ark, *Luke* 17:27
Mark 6:56 whith. he *e.* laid sick
Luke 1:40 Mary *e.* ho. of Zachar.
7:44 I *e.* thy house, thou gavest
9:34 they feared as they *e.* cloud
11:52 lawyers, ye *e.* not in your.
22:3 *e.* Satan into J. *John* 13:27
  10 arc *e.* 'city, there shall meet
John 4:38 are *e.* into their labors
18:1 a garden, into which he *e.*
  33 then Pilate *e.* judgment-hall
Acts 11:8 nothing uncl. *e.* mouth
28:8 to whom Paul *e.* in
Rom. 5:12 sin *e.* ; 20 the law *e.*
1 *Cor.* 2:9 not have *e.* heart of m.
Heb. 4:6 *e.* not bec. of unbelief
  10 for he that is *e.* into his rest
6:20 forerunner is for us *e.*
9:12 he *e.* once holy place, 24
Jam. 5:4 *e.* ears of L. of Sabaoth
2 *John* 7 many deceivers are *e.*
Rev. 11:11 S. of life *e.* into them

ENTERETH.

Prov. 2:10 when wisdom *e.* heart
17:10 a reproof *e.* more into wise
Mat. 15:17 whatsoever *e.* in at
  the mouth, *Mark* 7:18
Mark 5:40 *e.* where damsel was
Luke 22:10 fol. into house he *e.*
John 10:1 *e.* not by door into fold
  2 *e.* in by door, is the sheph.
Heb. 6:19 *e.* into that within veil
9:25 as high-priest *e.* every year

ENTERING.

Is. 23:1 there is no house, no *e.* in
Ezek. 44:5 mark *e.* in of the ho.
Mat. 23:13 neither suffer ye them
  e. to go in, *Luke* 11:52
Mark 4:19 the lusts *e.* in choke
  7:15 noth. without *e.* can defile
  16:5 and *e.* into the sepulchre
Luke 19:30 at your *e.* find colt
Acts 8:3 Saul *e.* into every house
1 *Thes.* 1:9 what manner of *e.*
Heb. 4:1 promise of *e.* into his
  rest

ENTERPRISE.

Job 5:12 hands cannot perform *e.*

ENTERTAIN.

Heb 13:2 not forgetful to *e.* stran.

ENTICE.

Ex. 22:16 if a man *e.* a maid
Deut. 13:6 wife *e.* thee secretly
Jud. 14:15 *e.* thy husband
  16:5 said to Delilah, *e.* him
2 *Chr.* 18:19 who shall *e.* Ahab ?
  20 I will *e.* him ; 21 sh. *e.* him
Prov. 1:10 if sinners *e.* cons. not

ENTICED, ETH.

Job 31:27 if heart been secretly *e.*
Prov. 16:29 a viol. man *e.* neigh.
Jer. 20:10 peradvent. he will be *e.*
Jam. 1:14 is tempted when *e.*

ENTICING words.

1 *Cor.* 2:4 preaching not w. *e. w.*
Col. 2:4 any beguile with *e. w.*

ENTIRE.

Jam. 1:4 that ye be per. and *e.*

ENTRANCE.

Jud. 1:24 show us *e.* into city
Ps. 119:130 *e.* of word giv. light
1 *Thes.* 2:1 yoursel. know our *e.*
2 *Pet.* 1:11 so an *e.* be ministered

ENTREAT.

Ex. 8:8 P. called for Moses, and
  said *e.* L. 28 ; 9:28 ; 10:17
  9 when shall I *e.* for thee
  29 I will *e.* Lord that swarms
Ruth 1:16 *e.* me not to leave thee
1 *Sam.* 2:25 man sin, who sh. *e.* ?
1 *K.* 13:6 *e.* the face of L. thy G.
Ps. 45:12 among people, *e.* favor
Prov. 19:6 many will *e.* favor of
Jer. 15:11 cause enemy *e.* thee
Acts 7:6 should *e.* them evil
1 *Cor.* 4:13 being defamed, we *e.*
Phil. 4:3 I *e.* thee also, y.-fellow
1 *Tim.* 5:1 but *e.* him as a father

ENTREATED.

Gen. 12:16 he *e.* Abraham well
25:21 I. *e.* for his wife, L. was *e.*
Ex. 5:22 why hast evil *e.* peo. ?
  8:30 Moses went and *e.* L. 10:18
Deut. 26:6 Egyptians evil *e.* us
2 *Sam.* 24:25 L. was *e.* for the la.
Ezr. 8:23 sought G. and was *e.*
Job 19:16 *e.* him with my mouth
  17 I *e.* for children's sake
Ps. 119:58 *e.* thy favor
Is. 19:22 he shall be *e.* of them
Mat. 22:6 *e.* spiteful. *Luke* 18:32
Luke 15:28 his father, *e.* him
20:11 *e.* him shamefully
Acts 7:19 same evil *e.* our fathers
1 *Thes.* 2:2 we were shameful. *e.*
Heb. 12:19 *e.* word not be spoken
Jam. 3:17 wisd. is easy to be *e.*

ENTREATETH.

Job 24:21 he evil *e.* the barren

ENTREATIES.

Prov. 18:23 poor useth *e.* but rich
2 *Cor.* 8:4 pray. us with much *e.*

ENTRY.

Prov. 8:3 wis. crieth at *e.* of city

ENVY, Substantive.

Job 5:2 *e.* slayeth the silly one
Prov. 14:30 *e.* is rotten. of bones
27:4 who able to stand bef. *e.* ?
Ec. 9:6 hatred and *e.* is perished
Is. 11:13 *e.* of Ephraim shall dep.
26:11 be ashamed for their *e.*
Ezek. 35:11 according to thine *e.*
Mat. 27:18 for *e. Mark* 15:10
Acts 7:9 patriarchs mov. with *e.*
13:45 Jews filled with *e.* spake
17:5 the Jews moved with *e.*
Rom. 1:19 full of *e.* murder
Phil. 1:15 prea. Christ even of *e.*
1 *Tim.* 6:4 whereof cometh *e.*
Tit. 3:3 living in malice and *e.*
Jam. 4:5 spirit in us lusteth to *e.*

ENVY, Verb.
Prov. 3:31 *e.* not the oppressor
23:17 let not heart *e.* sinners
Is. 11:13 Ephraim sh. not *e.* Jud.

ENVIED.
Gen. 26:14 Philistines *e.* Isaac
30:1 Rachel *e.* her sister
37:11 Joseph's brethren *e.* him
Ps. 106:16 they *e.* Moses also
Ec. 4:4 a man is *e.* of neighbor
Ezek. 31:9 trees in garden *e.* him

ENVIES.
1 *Pet.* 2:1 laying aside malice, *e.*

ENVIEST, ETH.
Num. 11:29 *e.* thou for my sake?
1 *Cor.* 13:4 charity *e.* not

ENVYING.
Rom. 13:13 let us walk, not in *e.*
1 *Cor.* 3:3 for whereas there is *e.*
Gal. 5:26 *e.* one another
Jam. 3:14 but if ye have bitter *e.*
16 where *e.* is, is confusion

ENVYINGS.
2 *Cor.* 12:20 I fear lest there be *e.*
Gal. 5:21 wor. of the flesh are *e.*

ENVIOUS.
Ps. 37:1 *e.* aga. workers of iniq.
73:3 for I was *e.* at the foolish
Prov. 24:1 be not *e.* ag. evil men
19 neither be *e.* at the wicked

ENVIRON.
Jos. 7:9 Canaanites *e.* us round

EPAPHRAS.
Col. 1:7 as ye learned of E. our
4:12 E. saluteth you, *Phile.* 23

EPAPHRODITUS.
Phil. 2:25 send to you E. 4:18

EPENETUS. *Rom.* 16:5

EPHAH.
Lev. 19:36 a just *e. Ezek.* 45:10
Is. 5:10 seed of homer yield an *e.*
Amos 8:5 making the *e.* small
Zec. 5:8 and he cast it into the *e.*

EPHAH. *Gen.* 25:4 ; 1 *Chr.* 1:33 ;
2:46, 47 ; *Is.* 60:6

EPHES-DAMMIM. 1 *Sam.* 17:1

EPHESIANS. *Acts* 19:28, 34, 35

EPHESUS.
Acts 18:19 P. came to E. 21 ; 19:17
1 *Cor.* 15:32 fought with be at E.
2 *Tim.* 1:18 minis. to me at E.
Rev. 1:11 to E. ; 2:1 angel at E.

EPHOD.
Ex. 28:4 they shall make an *e.* 6
Lev. 8:7 he put the *e.* upon him
Jud. 8:27 Gideon made an *e.*
17:5 the man Micah made an *e.*
1 *Sam.* 2:18 Samuel gird. with *e.*
23:9 David said, Bring *e.* 30:7
2 *Sam.* 6:14 D. was girded with
linen *e.* 1 *Chr.* 15:27
Hos. 3:4 many days without *e.*

EPHPHATHA. *Mark* 7:34

EPHRAIM, a place.
2 *Sam.* 13:23 sheep-sh. beside E.
2 *Chr.* 13:19 A. took E. and tow.
John 11:54 into city called E.

Mount EPHRAIM.
Jos. 17:15 if *mo. E.* be too narrow
Jud. 2:9 buried Joshua in *m. E.*
7:24 through *mount E.* 17:1, 8
1 *Sam.* 1:1 of *m. E.* 2 *Sam.* 20:21
9:4 Saul passed through *mo. E.*
2 *K.* 5:22 two men co. fr. *m. E.*
Jer. 31:6 upon *m. E.* 50:19

EPHRAIM, a person or people.
Gen. 41:52 Jos.'s s. son was E.
48:14 right hand on E. head, 20
Num. 1:10 the prince of E. 7:48
2:18 shall be the standard of E.
Deut. 33:17 ten thousands of E.

Jud. 5:14 out of E. was a root
12:4 Jephthah fought with E.
1 *Chr.* 7:22 E. their fath. mourn.
2 *Chr.* 17:2 garrisons in E. 25:10
30:18 E. not clea. ; 31:1 images
Ps. 80:2 before E. stir up stren.
Is. 7:5, 8, 9, 17 ; 9:9, 21 ; 11:13 ; 28:1
Jer. 7:15 cast out wh. seed of E.
Ezek. 37:16 stick of E. 19 ; 48:5
Hos. 5, 5, 9, 13, 14 ; 6:10 ; 7:1, 8
8:9 E. hired lov. ; 11 E. to sin,
9:3, 8 ; 10:6, 11 ; 11:3, 9, 12
14:8 E. say. Wh. to do with id. ?
Zec. 9:10 chariot from E. 13

EPHRAIM is.
Ps. 60:7 ; *Jer.* 31:9, 20 ; *Hos.* 4:17
Hos. 7:11 E. silly d. ; 10:11 heifer

EPHRAIM, with tribe.
Num. 1:33 nu. of E. 13:8 ; 33:24
Jos. 16:8 inheritance of E. 21:5
Ps. 78:67 chose not *tribe* of E.

EPHRAIMITE, S. *Jud.* 12:5, 6

EPHRATAH.
Ruth 4:11 worthily in E.
1 *Chr.* 2:50 first-born of E. 4:4
Ps. 132:6 we heard of it at E.
Mic. 5:2 Beth-lehem E. tho' little

EPHRATH. *Gen.* 35:16, 19 ;
48:7 ; 1 *Chr.* 2:19

EPHRATHITE, S. *Ruth* 1:2 ;
1 *Sam.* 1:1 ; 17:12 ; 1 *K.* 11:26

EPHRON. *Gen.* 23:8, 16 ; 25:9 ;
49:30 ; 50:13

EPICUREANS. *Acts* 17:18

EPISTLE.
Acts 15:30 they deliv. *e.* 23:33
Rom. 16:22 I Tert. who wrote *e.*
1 *Cor.* 5:9 I wrote to you in an *e.*
2 *Cor.* 3:2 ye are our *e.* written
3 declared to be *e.* of Christ
7:8 the same *e.* made you sorry
Col. 4:16 wh. this *e.* is read, likewise read *e.* from Laodicea
1 *Thes.* 5:27 this *e.* be read to all
2 *Thes.* 2:15 taught by word or *e.*
3:14 if obey not word by this *e.*
17 which is the tok. in every *e.*
2 *Pet.* 3:1 this sec. *e.* I now write

EPISTLES.
2 *Cor.* 3:1 or need *e.* of commen.
2 *Pet.* 3:16 as in all his *e.* speak.

EQUAL.
Ps. 17:2 eyes behold things *e.*
55:13 but it was thou. mine *e.*
Prov. 26:7 legs of lame are not *e.*
Is. 40:25 to wh. sh. I be *e. ?* 46:5
Lam. 2:13 *e.* to thee. O virgin
Ezek. 18:25 The way of the Lord
is not *e.* 29 ; 33:17, 20
29 O Isr. are not my ways *e. ?*
33:17 their way is not *e.*
Mat. 20:12 hast made them *e.*
Luke 20:36 are *e.* unto angels
John 5:18 himself *e.* with God
Phil. 2:6 not rob. to be *e.* with G.
Col. 4:1 gave servants what is *e.*
Rev. 21:16 breadth and height *e.*

EQUAL, Verb.
Job 28:17 gold and crystal not *e.*
19 topaz of Ethi. shall not *e.* it

EQUALITY.
2 *Cor.* 8:14 by an *e.* may be an *e.*

EQUALS.
Gal. 1:14 I profited above my *e.*

EQUITY.
Ps. 98:9 he shall judge with *e.*
99:4 thou dost establish *e.*
Prov. 1:3 to rec. instruction of *e.*
2:9 shalt thou understand *e.*
17:26 to strike princes for *e.*
Ec. 2:21 whose labor is in *e.*
Is. 11:4 repr. with *e.* for meek
59:14 and *e.* cannot enter

Mic. 3:9 ye that pervert all *e.*
Mal. 2:6 walked with me in *e.*

ER. *Gen.* 38:3. 7 ; 1 *Chr.* 2:3 ;
4:21 ; *Luke* 3:28

ERASTUS.
Acts 19:22 sent Timoth. and E.
2 *Tim.* 4:20 E. abode at Corinth

ERRAND.
Gen. 24:33 I have told mine *e.*
Jud. 3:19 I have a secret *e.*
2 *K.* 9:5 an *e.* to thee, O captain

ERR.
2 *Chr.* 33:9 M. made Judah to *e.*
Ps. 95:10 do *e.* in their heart
119:21 which do *e.* from thy
118 hast trodden them that *e.*
Prov. 14:22 not *e.* that dev. evil ?
19:27 instruc. that causeth to *e.*
Is. 3:12 they wh. lead thee cause
thee to *e.* 9:16
19:14 have caused Egypt to *e.*
28:7 they *e.* in vision
30:28 a bridle caus. them to *e.*
35:8 wayfaring men shall not *e.*
63:17 hast thou made us to *e.*
Jer. 23:13 the prophets caused
Israel to *e.* 32 ; *Mic.* 3:5
Hos. 4:12 whoredoms caused to *e.*
Amos 2:4 their lies caused to *e.*
Mat. 22:29 ye do *e.* not know. the
scriptures, *Mark.* 12:24, 27
Heb. 3:10 *e.* in their hearts
Jam. 1:16 do not *e.* my beloved
5:19 if any *e.* from the truth

ERRED.
Lev. 5:18 ignor. wherein he *e.*
1 *Sam.* 26:21 have *e.* exceedingly
Job 6:24 wherein I have *e.*
19:4 indeed that I have *e.*
Ps. 119:110 I *e.* not from thy pre.
Is. 28:7 have *e.* thro' wine, priest
and prophet have *e.*
27:24 that *e.* in spirit shall come
1 *Tim.* 6:10 have *e.* from the faith
21 some have *e.* concern. faith
2 *Tim.* 2:18 concern. tru. have *e.*

ERRETH.
Prov. 10:17 refuseth reproof *e.*
Ezek. 45:20 for every one that *e.*

ERROR.
2 *Sam.* 6:7 smote Uzzah for his *e.*
Job 19:4 *e.* remain. with myself
Ec. 5:6 neither say it was an *e.*
10:5 an evil I have seen as an *e.*
Is. 32:6 to utter *e.* against the L.
Dan. 6:4 nor was *e.* found in him
Mat. 27:64 last *e.* worse than first
Rom. 1:27 recompense of their *e.*
Jam. 5:20 from the *e.* of his way
2 *Pet.* 2:18 them who live in *e.*
3:17 led away with *e.* of wicked
1 *John* 4:6 know we spirit of *e.*
Jude 11 after the *e.* of Balaam

ERRORS.
Ps. 19:12 can understand his *e. ?*
Jer. 10:15 the work of *e.* 51:18
Heb. 9:7 he offer. for *e.* of people

ESAIAS. See ISAIAH.
ESAR-HADDON. 2 *K.* 19:37 ;
Ezr. 4:2 ; *Is.* 37:38

ESAU.
Gen. 25:25 his name E. 27, 29
27:11 E. is a hairy m. 21, 24, 42
32:3 sent messengers to E. 11, 18
33:4 E. ran to meet him, 9 ; 35:1
36:1 genera. of E. ; 43 fa. of E.
Deut. 2:5 mt. S. to E. *Jos.* 24:4
Jer. 49:10 I have made E. bare
Ob. 6 E. searched out, 18:21
Mal. 1:2 E.'s br. ? 3 ; *Rom.* 9:13
Heb. 11:20 Isaac blessed E.
12:16 profane person as E.

ESCAPE, Substantive.
Ps. 55:8 hasten my *e.* from storm

ESCAPE, Verb.

Gen. 19:17 *e.* to the mountain
20 Oh let me *e.* ; 22 *e.* thither
32:8 the other company shall *e.*
Jos. 8:22 they let none of them *e.*
1 *Sam.* 27:1 *e.* to land of Philist.
2 *Sam.* 15:14 let us flee, not else *e.*
1 *K.* 18:40 let none *e.* 2 *K.* 9:15
2 *K.* 10:24 if any of the men *e.*
19:31 *e.* out of Zion, *Is.* 37:32
Ezr. 9:8 to leave a remnant to *e.*
Est. 4:13 think not thou shalt *e.*
Job 11:20 the wicked shall not *e.*
Ps. 56:7 shall they *e.* by iniq. ?
71:2 and cause me to *e.*
141:10 wicked fall, whilst I *e.*
Prov. 19:5 speak. lies. shall not *e.*
Ec. 7:26 pleaseth God shall *e.*
Is. 20:6 and how shall we *e.*
66:19 those that *e.* to the nati.
Jer. 11:11 evil not be able to *e.*
25:35 nor princip. of the flock *e.*
32:4 Zed. not *e.* 34:3 ; 38:18, 23
42:17 go into Egypt *e.* 44:14
44:14 none return but such as *e.*
28 yet a small number that *e.*
46:6 let not mighty man *e.*
48:8 spoiler come, no city sh. *e.*
50:28 the voice of them that *e.*
29 let none *e.* recompense her
Ezek. 6:8 may have some shall *e.*
9 they that *e.* shall remem. me
7:16 shall *e.* and be like doves
17:15 *e.* that doeth such things ?
18 done these things, sh. not *e.*
Dan. 11:41 *e.* out of his hand
42 the land of Egypt sh. not *e.*
Joel 2:3 nothing shall *e.* them
Ob. 14 cut of those that did *e.*
Mat. 23:33 *e.* damnati. of hell ?
Luke 21:36 account. worthy to *e.*
Acts 27:42 kill prison. lest any *e.*
Rom. 2:3 shalt *e.* judg. of God ?
1 *Cor.* 10:13 will make a way to *e.*
1 *Thes.* 5:3 and they shall not *e.*
Heb. 2:3 how sh. *e.* if we neglect
12:25 much more shall not we *e.*

ESCAPED.

Gen. 14:13 there came one had *e.*
Num. 21:29 sons that *e.* into cap.
Deut. 23:15 not deliver servant *e.*
Jud. 3:29 *e.* not, 1 *Sam.* 30:17
21:17 inherit. for them that *e.*
1 *Sam.* 14:41 J. taken, but peo. *e.*
19:10 D. fled and *e.* that night
2 *Sam.* 1:3 out of the ca. am I *e.*
4:6 and Rachab and Baanah *e.*
1 *K.* 20:20 Ben-hadad the king *e.*
2 *K.* 19:30 remnant of Judah
shall take root, *Is.* 37:31
2 *Chr.* 16:7 is host of Syria *e.*
30:6 he will return to you that *e.*
Ezr. 9:15 for we remain yet *e.* as
Job 1:15 I only am *e.* 16, 17, 19
19:20 *e.* with the sk. of my teeth
Ps. 124:7 our soul is *e.* as a bird
Is. 4:2 be comely for them *e.*
10:20 and such as are *e.* of Jacob
45:20 draw near, ye that are *e.*
Jer. 51:50 have *e.* rem. L. afar off
Lam. 2:22 none *e.* nor remain
Ezek. 24:27 opened to him *e.*
33:21 one that had *e.* came
John 10:39 *e.* out of their hands
Acts 27:44 so they *e.* all safe
28:4 tho' he *e.* the sea. yet ven.
2 *Cor.* 11:33 I was let down and *e.*
Heb. 11:34 through faith *e.*
12:25 if *e.* not who refused him
2 *Pet.* 1:4 *e.* corruption in world
2:18 those that were clean *e.*
20 *e.* the pollutions of world

ESCAPETH.

1 *K.* 19:17 that *e.* swo. of Hazael
shall Jehu slay ; that *e.* Jehu
Is. 15:9 bring lions upon him *e.*
Jer. 48:19 ask her *e.* Wh. is done ?

Ezek. 24:26 *e.* sh. come unto thee
Amos 9:1 he that *e.* not be deliv.

ESCAPING.

Ezr. 9:14 there should be no *e.*

ESCHEW.

1 *Pet.* 3:11 let him *e.* evil, do good

ESCHEWED, ETH.

Job 1:1 feared God, *e.* evil, 8 ; 2:3

ESEK. *Gen.* 26:20

ESHCOL.

Gen. 14:13 M. brother of E. 24
Num. 13:24 place called brook E.
32:9 went up unto valley of E.

ESLI. *Luke* 3:25

ESPECIALLY.

Ps. 31:11 *e.* am. my neighbors
Acts 25:26 *e.* before thee, O king
Gal. 6:10 *e.* the househ. of faith
1 *Tim.* 4:10 *e.* of tho. that believe
5:8 prov. *s.* for them of his own
17 *e.* they who labor in word
2 *Tim.* 4:13 but *e.* the parchments
Phile. 16 a brother beloved *s.*

ESPOUSALS.

Cant. 3:11 crowned in day of *e.*
Jer. 2:2 I remem. love of thine *e.*

ESPOUSED.

2 *Sam.* 3:14 deliv. me Michal I *e.*
Mat. 1:18 when Mary was *e.* to J.
Luke 1:27 to a virgin *e.* to a man
2 *Cor.* 11:2 *e.* you to one husband

ESPY.

Jos. 14:7 Moses sent me to *e.*
See SPY, SPIED.

ESROM. *Mat.* 1:3 ; *Luke* 3:33

ESTABLISH.

Gen. 6:18 will I *e.* cov. 9:9 ; 17:7 ;
Lev. 26:9 ; *Ezek.* 16:62
17:19 I will *e.* my covenant, 21
Deut. 8:18 that he may *e.* his cov.
28:9 L. shall *e.* thee a holy peo.
29:13 he may *e.* thee for a peo.
1 *Sam.* 1:23 L. *e.* 2 *Sam.* 7:25
2 *Sam.* 7:12 in his kingdom, 13 ;
1 *Chr.* 17:11 ; 22:10 ; 28:7
1 *K.* 9:5 *e.* throne of thy kingdom
15:4 and to *e.* Jerusalem
1 *Chr.* 17:12 *e.* his throne for ever
2 *Chr.* 7:18 will I *e.* throne
9:8 God loved Israel to *e.* them.
Job 36:7 doth *e.* them for ever
Ps. 7:9 *e.* just ; 48:8 G. will *e.* it
87:5 the Highest shall *e.* her
89:2 faithfulness shalt *e.*
4 thy seed will I *e.* for ever
90:17 *e.* work of our hands, *e.* it
99:4 thou dost *e.* equity, thou
119:38 *s.* thy word to thy serv.
Prov. 15:25 *e.* border of the wid.
Is. 9:7 to *e.* it with judgment
49:8 for a cov. to *e.* the earth
62:7 till he *e.* and make Jerus.
Jer. 33:2 that formed it, to *e.* it
Ezek. 16:60 will *e.* an everla. cov.
Dan. 6:7 consult. to *e.* royal stat.
11:14 exalt thems. to *e.* vision
Amos 5:15 *e.* judgm. in the gate
Rom. 3:31 yea, we *e.* the law
10:3 going about to *e.* own
16:25 power to *e.* you
1 *Thes.* 3:2 sent Tim. to *e.* you
13 *s.* your hearts unblameable
2 *Thes.* 2:17 *s.* you in ev. g. word
3:3 Lord shall *s.* you, and keep
Heb. 10:9 that he may *e.* second
Jam. 5:8 patient, *s.* your hearts
1 *Pet.* 5:10 the God of all grace *e.*

ESTABLISHED.

Gen. 9:17 token of covenant I *e.*
41:32 because thin. is *e.* by God
Ezr. 6:4 I have also *e.* my cov.
Deut. 32:6 made and *e.* thee ?

1 *Sam.* 3:20 S. was *e.* a prophet
13:13 would L. *e.* thy kingdom
20:31 thou shalt not be *e.* nor
2 *Sam.* 5:12 perc. L. had *e.* him
7:25 let the house of thy servant
David be *e.* 1 *Chr.* 17:24
1 *K.* 2:12 king. was *e.* greatly
1 *Chr.* 17:23 let thing be *e.*
2 *Chr.* 1:9 L. let thy promise be *e.*
Job 21:8 seed is *e.* in their sight
Ps. 24:2 hath *e.* it on the floods
40:2 feet on rock, *e.* my goings
78:5 *e.* a testimony in Jacob
69 earth he *e.* for ever, 119:90
93:1 world *e.* ; 2 throne *e.* of old
112:8 his heart is *e.*
140:11 let not evil speaker be *e.*
148:6 *e.* the waters for ever and
Prov. 3:19 L. hath *e.* the heavens
4:26 let all thy ways be *e.*
8:28 he *e.* the clouds above
12:3 shall not be *e.* by wicked.
15:22 in multi. of counsell. *e.*
16:12 throne is *e.* by righteous.
20:18 ev. purp. is *e.* by counsel
24:3 by understand. is a house *e.*
30:4 hath *e.* ends of the earth
Is. 7:9 if not believe, not be *e.*
16:5 in mercy shall throne be *e.*
45:18 made earth, he hath *e.* it
Jer. 10:12 *e.* world, 51:15
Dan. 4:36 was *e.* in my kingdom
Hab. 1:12 *e.* them for correction
Mat. 18:16 of two witn. ev. w. *e.*
Acts 16:5 churches *e.* in the faith
Rom. 1:11 to the end you m. be *e.*
Col. 2:7 and *s.* in the faith
Heb. 8:6 *e.* upon better promises
13:9 that heart be *e.* with grace
2 *Pet.* 1:12 tho. *e.* in present tru.

Shall be ESTABLISHED.

Lev. 25:30 h. *s.* be *e.* 2 *Sam.* 7:16
Deut. 19:15 at mouth of two or t.
wit. *s.* matter be *e.* 2 *Cor.* 13:1
1 *Sam.* 24:20 kingd. *s.* be *e.* in h.
2 *Sam.* 7:16 thy house, kingdom,
throne shall be *e.* 1 *K.* 2:45
1 *Chr.* 17:14 his throne *shall be e.*
for evermore, *Ps.* 89:37
2 *Chr.* 20:20 believe in G. *s.* be *e.*
Job 22:28 shalt decree, it *s.* be *e.*
Ps. 89:21 my hand *shall be e.*
96:10 the world *shall be e.*
102:28 their seed *shall be e.*
Prov. 12:19 lip of truth *sh.* be *e.*
16:3 and thy thoughts *s.* be *e.*
25:5 throne *s.* be *e.* for e. 29:14
Is. 2:2 mount. of L. house *s.* be *e.*
16:5 in mercy *shall* throne be *e.*
54:14 in righteousn. *s.* thou be *e.*
Jer. 30:20 their congrega. *s.* be *e.*
Mic. 4:1 mount. of ho. of L. *s.* be *e.*
Zec. 5:11 a house, and it *s.* be *e.*

ESTABLISHETH.

Prov. 29:4 by judgment *e.* land
Dan. 6:15 no decree *e.* be chang.
Hab. 2:12 that *e.* a city by iniq.
2 *Cor.* 1:21 *e.* us with you in Ch.

ESTATE.

Gen. 43:7 man asked us of our *s.*
1 *Chr.* 17:17 *e.* of man of high d.
2 *Chr.* 24:13 house of G. in his *e.*
Est. 1:19 give her royal *e.* to an.
2:18 gifts according to *s.* of king
Ps. 39:5 man at best *s.* is vanity
136:23 remembered us in low *e.*
Prov. 27:23 to know *s.* of flocks
28:2 man of knowl. *s.* prolonged
Ec. 1:16 I am come to great *e.*
3:18 concern. *e.* of sons of men
Is. 22:19 thy *s.* pull thee down
Ezek. 16:55 S. return to former *e.*
Dan. 11:7 stand up in his *e.* 21
38 in his *e.* honor God of forces
Mat. 12:45 last *e.* of that man w.
than first, *Luke* 11:26
Luke 1:48 low *e.* of his handm.

Acts 22:5 *e.* of elders bear witn.
Rom. 12:16 con. to men of low *e.*
Phil. 2:19 when I know your *s.*
20 naturally care for your *s.*
4:11 whatso. *s.* I am to be cont.
Col. 4:7 all my *s.* shall Tychicus
8 that he might know your *e.*
Jude 6 ang. who kept not first *e.*

ESTATES.
Ezek. 36:11 settle you after old *e.*
Mark 6:21 a supper to his chief *e.*

ESTEEM.
Job 36:19 will he *e.* thy riches ?
Ps. 119:128 I *e.* all thy precepts
Is. 53:4 *e.* him smitten of God
Phil. 2:3 *e.* other better than th.
1 *Thes.* 5:13 *e.* highly for work's

ESTEEMED.
Deut. 32:15 lightly *e.* rock of sal.
1 *Sam.* 2:30 desp. me, be lightly *e.*
18:23 seeing I am lightly *e.*
Job 23:12 I *e.* words of his mouth
Prov. 17:28 *e.* a man of underst.
Is. 29:16 be *e.* as potter's clay
17 fruitful field be *e.* as a forest
53:3 and we *e.* him not
Lam. 4:2 *e.* as earthen pitchers
Luke 16:15 *e.* among men is abo.
1 *Cor.* 6:4 to judge who least *e.*

ESTEEMETH.
Job 41:26 he *e.* iron as straw
Rom. 14:5 *e.* one day ab. another
14 that *e.* any thing unclean

ESTEEMING.
Heb. 11:26 *e.* reproach of Christ

ESTIMATION.
Lev. 5:15 bring a ram with thy *e.*
27:2 thy *e.* 3, 5, 25 ; *Num.* 18:16

ESTRANGED.
Job 19:13 acquaintance are *e.*
Ps. 58:3 wicked *e.* from womb
78:30 they were not *e.* from lust
Jer. 19:4 they have *e.* this place
Ezek. 14:5 they are all *e.* from me

ETAM. *Jud.* 15:8, 11

ETERNAL.
Deut. 33:27 *e.* God is thy refuge
Is. 60:15 make thee *e.* excellency
Mark 3:29 in danger of *e.* damn.
Rom. 1:20 *e.* power and Godhead
2 *Cor.* 4:17 an *e.* weight of glory
18 which are not seen, are *e.*
5:1 a house *e.* in the heavens
Eph. 3:11 ac. to *e.* purpose in C.
1 *Tim.* 1:17 to king *e.* be honor
2 *Tim.* 2:10 obt. salv. with *e.* glo.
Heb. 5:9 author of *e.* salvation
6:2 the doctrine of *e.* judgment
9:12 obt. *e.* redemption for us
14 *e.* Spirit offered himself
15 promise of *e.* inheritance
1 *Pet.* 5:10 called us to his *e.* glo.
Jude 7 suff. vengeance of *e.* fire

ETERNAL life.
Mat. 19:16 that I may have *e. l. ?*
25:46 right. shall go into *life e.*
Mark 10:17 that I may inherit *e.
life ? Luke* 10:25 ; 18:18
30 rec. in world to come *e. life*
John 3:15 believe sh. have *e. l.*
4:36 gathereth fruit unto *life e.*
5:39 in them think ye have *e. l.*
6:54 drink. my blood, hath *e. l.*
68 thou hast the words of *e. l.*
10:28 give unto my sheep *e. life*
12:25 hateth life, keep it to *e. l.*
17:2 give *e. life* to as many
3 this is *l. e.* might know thee
Acts 13:48 were ordained to *e. l.*
Rom. 2:7 seek for glory, *e. life*
5:21 grace reign to *e. life*
6:23 but the gift of God is *e. l.*
1 *Tim.* 6:12 lay hold on *e. life*, 19
Tit. 1:2 in hope of *e. l.* which G.

3:7 accord. to hope of *e. life*
1 *John* 1:2 *e. l.* which was with F.
2:25 promise he promised, *e. l.*
3:15 no murderer hath *e. life*
5:11 that God given to us *e. life*
13 may know ye have *e. life*
20 the true God, and *e. life*
Jude 21 for mercy of L. to *e. life*

ETERNITY.
Is. 57:15 lofty One that inhab. *e.*

ETHAM.
Ex. 13:20 encamped in E. *Num.*
33:6, 8

ETHAN.
1 *K.* 4:31 Sol. was wiser than E.
1 *Chr.* 2:6 sons of Ze. Zim. and E.

ETHANIM. 1 *K.* 8:2
ETHBAAL. 1 *K.* 16:31

ETHIOPIA.
2 *K.* 19:9 king of E. *Is.* 37:9
Est. 1:1 from India to E. 8:9
Job 28:19 E. shall not equal it
Ps. 68:31 E. shall stretch hands
87:4 Philistia and Tyre with E.
Is. 20:3 ashamed of E.
43:3 for thy ransom E. for thee
45:14 merch. of E. *Nah.* 3:9
Acts 8:27 a man of E. an eunuch

ETHIOPIAN.
Num. 12:1 because of E. woman
2 *Chr.* 14:9 E. came out ag. Asa
Jer. 13:23 can E. change his skin?
38:6 Ebed-mel. E. 10, 12 ; 39:16

ETHIOPIANS.
2 *Chr.* 14:12 ; 16:8 ; 21:16 ; *Is.* 20:4
Dan. 11:43 E. sh. be at his steps
Amos 9:7 are ye not chil. of E. ?
Zep. 2:12 ye E. shall be slain by
Acts 8:27 under queen of E.

EUBULUS. 2 *Tim.* 4:21
EUNICE. 2 *Tim.* 1:5

EUNUCH, ∴
2 *K.* 9:32 there looked out *e.*
20:18 thy sons be *e.* in palace of
king of Babylon, *Is.* 39:7
Is. 56:3 *e.* say I am a dry tree
4 thus saith L. unto the *e.*
Jer. 29:2 after *e.* were departed
38:7 Ebed-melech one of the *e.*
Dan. 1:9 favor with prince of *e.*
Mat. 19:12 some *e.* so born, some
are made *e.* made themsel. *e.*
Acts 8:27 *e.* had come to worship
39 the *e.* saw Philip no more

EUODIAS. *Phil.* 4:2

EUPHRATES.
Gen. 2:14 the fourth river is E.
15:18 great river, the river E.
Deut. 1:7 go to river E. *Jos.* 1:4
2 *K.* 23:29 up to E. 2 *Chr.* 35:20
24:7 from Eg. to E. 1 *Chr.* 5:9
Jer. 13:4 go to E. 5, 7 ; 46:10
51:63 m. of E. *Rev.* 9:14 ; 16:12

EUROCLYDON.
Acts 27:14 arose a wind called *e.*

EUTYCHUS. *Acts* 20:9

EVANGELIST, S.
Acts 21:8 house of Philip the *e.*
Eph. 4:11 he gave some *e.*
2 *Tim.* 4:5 do the work of an *e.*

EVE.
Gen. 3:20 ; 4:1
2 *Cor.* 11:3 as serpent beguiled E.
1 *Tim.* 2:13 A. first form. then E.

EVEN, Substantive.
Ex. 18:14 people stand by thee
from morning to *e.*
Lev. 23:5 at *e.* is the L. passover,
Num. 9:3 ; *Deut.* 16:6
Deut. 28:67 would God it were *e.*
Jud. 20:23 they wept till *e.*
26 fasted till *e.* 2 *Sam.* 1:12

21:2 peo. abode till *e.* before G.
1 *Chr.* 23:30 praise the L. every *e.*
Ezek. 12:7 in *e.* I digged thro. w.
Mat. 8:16 when *e.* was come, 20:8 ;
26:20 ; 27:57 ; *Mark* 4:35 ;
6:47 ; 11:19 ; 15:42
Mark 1:32 at *e.* brought disease
13:35 at *e.* at midnight, or at
John 6:16 when *e.* was now come

EVEN, Adverb.
1 *K.* 1:48 mine eyes *e.* seeing it
Prov. 22:19 known *e.* to thee

EVEN, Adjective.
Job 31:6 be weighed in *e.* balance
Ps. 26:12 standeth in an *e.* place
Cant. 4:2 a flock of sheep *e.* shorn
Luke 19:44 lay thee *e.* with gro.

EVENING.
Ex. 12:6 Israel shall kill it in *e.*
Jud. 19:9 day drawch towards *e.*
1 *Sam.* 14:24 cursed eateth till *e.*
Ps. 59:6 they return at *e.* they
14 at *e.* let them return
90:6 in the *e.* it is cut down
104:23 goeth to labor until *e.*
Prov. 7:9 went to her house in *e.*
Ec. 11:6 in *e.* withhold not hand
Jer. 6:4 shadows of *e.* stretched
Ezek. 33:22 hand of L. on me in *e.*
Zep. 2:7 they lie down in *e.*
Mat. 14:23 *e.* he was there alone
16:2 when it is *e.* ye say, It will
Luke 24:29 for it is toward *e.*
John 20:19 same day at *e.* ca. J.

EVENING, with morning.
Gen. 1:5 *e.* and m. were first day
Ex. 18:13 stood by M. fr. m. to *e.*
1 *Sam.* 17:16 drew near m. and *e.*
Job 4:20 destroyed from m. to *e.*
Ps. 55:17 *e.* m. at noon w. I pray
65:8 outgoings of m. *e.* to rej.
Dan. 8:26 vision of *e.* and m.
Acts 28:23 persuad. from m. to *e.*

EVENING, Adjective.
Ezr. 9:4 astonished till *e.* sacri.
Ps. 141:2 prayer be as *e.* sacrifice
Dan. 9:21 touched me about *e.*
Hab. 1:8 mo. fierce than *e.* wolv.
Zep. 3:3 her judges are *e.* wolves
Zec. 14:7 at *e.* time it sh. be light

EVENINGS.
Jer. 5:6 wolf of the *e.* spoil them

EVENT.
Ec. 2:14 one *e.* to them all. 9:3
9:2 one *e.* to right. and wicked

EVEN- or EVENING-TIDE.
Gen. 24:63 to meditate at *e.-tide*
Is. 17:14 behold. at *e. t.* trouble
Mark 11:11 *e.-t.* Jesus went out
Acts 4:3 in hold. now *e.-t.*

EVER.
Num. 22:30 *e.* since I was thine
Deut. 4:33 did *e.* peo. hear voice
19:9 to walk *e.* in his ways
Job 4:7 who *e.* perished inno. ?
Ps. 5:11 let them *e.* shout for joy
25:6 tender mercies *e.* of old
Ps. 25:15 mine eyes are *e.* tow. L.
37:26 *e.* merciful, and lendeth
51:3 my sin is *e.* before me
90:2 *e.* formed earth, *Prov.* 8:23
111:5 *e.* be mindful of covenant
119:98 command. are *e.* with me
Cant. 6:12 or *e.* I was aware, my
Joel 2:2 hath not been *e.* the like
Mat. 24:21 no, nor *e.* shall be
Mark 15:8 to do as he had *e.*
Luke 15:31 thou art *e.* with me
John 4:29 told me all *e.* I did
8:35 but the Son abideth *e.*
1 *Thes.* 4:17 so *e.* be with the L.
5:15 *e.* follow that wh. is good
2 *Tim.* 3:7 *e.* learning, never able
Heb. 7:24 this man continueth *e.*
25 *e.* liveth to make interces.

Jude 25 be glory, now and *e.*
See ENDURETH.

For EVER.

Gen. 13:15 give it and to seed *f. e.*
43:9 bear blame *for e.* 44:32
Ex. 3:15 this is my name *for e.*
14:13 see them no more *for e.*
19:9 peo. may believe thee *f. e.*
21:6 he shall serve him *for e.*
Lev. 25:30 house established *f. e.*
46 be your bondmen *for e.*
Num. 18:19 a coven. of salt *f. e.*
Deut. 5:29 with them *for e.* 12:28
15:17 shall be thy servant *for e.*
23:6 not seek their peace *for e.*
29:29 revealed belong to us *f. e.*
Jos. 4:24 ye might fear L. *for e.*
1 *Sam.* 2:30 walk before me *f. e.*
20:15 not cut off kindness *for e.*
2 *Sam.* 7:24 confi. Is. to thee *f. e.*
26 thy name be magnified *f. e.*
29 that it may continue *for e.*
1 *K.* 10:9 L. loved Israel *f. e.*
11:39 afflict D. seed, not *for e.*
1 *Chr.* 17:22 make thine *for e.*
28:9 he will cast thee off *for e.*
29:18 O Lord, keep this *for e.*
2 *Chr.* 7:16 name be there *for e.*
33:4 Jerusalem name be *for e.*
Job 4:20 they perish *for e.*
14:20 prevailest *for e.* ag. him
20:7 perish *for e.* like his dung
23:7 deliv. *f. e.* from my judge
36:7 doth establish them *for e.*
Ps. 9:7 Lord shall endure *for e.*
18 exp. of poor not perish *f. e.*
12:7 shalt preserve them *for e.*
13:1 forget me, O Lord, *for e. ?*
19:9 fear clean, enduring *for e.*
21:6 made him most blessed *f. e.*
23:6 dwell in house of Lord *f. e.*
28:9 and lift them up *for e.*
29:10 Lord sitteth King *for e.*
30:12 give thanks *for e.* 79:13
33:11 counsel of L. standeth *f. e.*
37:18 their inheritance be *for e.*
28 his saints preserved *for e.*
29 righteous dwell in land *f. e.*
41:12 settest me before face *f. e.*
44:8 we praise thy name *for e.*
23 arise, cast us not off *for e.*
45:2 God hath blessed thee *f. e.*
49:8 red. of soul ceaseth *for e.*
11 houses shall continue *for e.*
52:5 likewise destroy thee *f. e.*
9 I will praise thee *for e.*
61:4 abide in tabernacle *for e.*
7 shall abide before God *for e.*
8 I will sing praise *for e.*
66:7 ruleth by his power *for e.*
68:16 Lord will dwell in it *for e.*
72:17 name shall endure *for e.*
19 bless. be glorious name *f. e.*
73:26 God is my portion *for e.*
74:1 why cast us off *for e. ?*
10 blaspheme thy name *for e. ?*
19 forget not con. of poor *f. e.*
75:9 I will declare *for e.* I will
77:7 will the Lord cast off *for e. ?*
8 his mercy clean gone *for e. ?*
79:5 wilt thou be angry *for e. ?*
81:15 their time sh. endure *f. e.*
83:17 them be confounded *f. e.*
85:5 wilt be angry with us *f. e. ?*
89:1 sing of mercies of L. *for e.*
2 mercy shall be built up *for e.*
29 his seed to endure *for e.* 36
46 wilt thou hide thyself *f. e. ?*
92:7 it is that be destroyed *f. e.*
93:5 holiness becom. house *f. e.*
103:9 neither keep anger *for e.*
105:8 remembered covenant *f. e.*
110:4 a priest *for e.* after order
Heb. 5:6 ; 6:20 ; 7:17, 21
111:9 commanded covenant *f. e.*
112:6 shall not be moved *for e.*

125:2 from henceforth even *f. e.*
131:3 ; *Is.* 9:7
133:14 this is my rest *for e.*
Ps. 146:6 L. keepeth truth *f. e.*
10 the Lord shall reign *for e.*
Prov. 27:24 riches are not *for e.*
Ec. 2:16 no rem. of wise *for e.*
3:14 God doeth, shall be *for e.*
9:6 nor any more a portion *f. e.*
Is. 26:4 trust ye in Lord *for e.*
32:17 quietness and assu. *for e.*
34:10 smoke thereof go up *f. e.*
17 they shall possess it *for e.*
40:8 word of G. shall stand *f. e.*
51:6 my salvation shall be *for e.*
8 my righteousness be *for e.*
57:16 I will not contend *for e.*
59:21 my words not depart *f. e.*
60:21 thy peo. inherit land *f. e.*
64:9 nor remember iniquity *f. e.*
65:18 be glad and rejoice *for e.*
Jer. 3:5 he reserve anger *for e.*
12 I will not keep anger *for e.*
17:4 fire which shall burn *for e.*
25 J. and this city remain *f. e.*
31:40 plucked up any more *f. e.*
32:39 they may fear me *for e.*
Lam. 3:31 will not cast off *for e.*
5:19 thou, O L. remainest *for e.*
20 wherefore forget us *for e. ?*
Ezek. 37:25 be their prince *for e.*
43:7 in midst of Israel *for e.* 9
Dan. 2:44 his kingdom stand *f. e.*
4:34 praised him that liveth *f. e.*
6:26 G. of Daniel, steadfast *f. e.*
7:18 saints possess kingdom *f. e.*
12:7 sw. by him that liveth *f. e.*
Joel 3:20 Judah shall dwell *for e.*
Ob. 10 shalt be cut off *for e.*
Mic. 2:9 tak. away my glory *f. e.*
4:7 Lord reign over them *for e.*
7:18 retaineth not anger *for e.*
Mal. 1:4 L. hath indignation *f. e.*
Mat. 6:13 power and glory *for e.*
Luke 1:33 reign over Jacob *for e.*
55 spake to Ab. and seed *f. e.*
John 8:35 serv. abideth not *f. e.*
12:34 that Christ abideth *for e.*
Rom. 1:25 Creator, blessed *for e.*
9:5 over all, God blessed *for e.*
11:36 be glory *for e.* 16:27
2 *Cor.* 9:9 righte. remaineth *f. e.*
Phile. 15 shouldst rec. him *for e.*
Heb. 10:12 *for e.* sat down
14 perfected *f. e.* them sancti.
13:8 J. C. same to-day and *f. e.*
1 *Pet.* 1:23 which liveth *for e.*
25 word of Lord endureth *f. e.*
2 *John* 2 be with us *for e.*

Live for EVER.

Gen. 3:22 tree of life and *l. for e.*
Deut. 32:40 and say, I *live for e.*
1 *K.* 1:31 let king David *l. for e.*
Ps. 22:26 heart shall *live for e.*
49:9 should still *live for e.*
Dan. 2:4 O king *live for e.* 3:9 ;
5:10 ; 6:6, 21
Zec. 1:5 prophets, do they *l. for e.*
John 6:51 if any man eat of this
bread, he shall *l. for e.* 58

For EVER and EVER.

Ex. 15:18 reign *for e. and e.*
1 *Chr.* 16:36 blessed be God *for*
e. and e. 29:10 ; *Dan.* 2:20
Neh. 9:5 bless your G. *for e. a. e.*
Ps. 9:5 thy name *for e. and e.*
10:16 Lord is king *for e. and e.*
21:4 length of days *for e. and e.*
45:6 thy throne, O G. is *for e. a.*
17 praise thee *for e. and e.*
48:14 this G. is our God *for e. a.*
52:8 I trust in mercy of G. *f. e. a.*
111:8 stand fast *for e. and e.*
119:44 I keep thy law *for e. a. e.*
145:1 bless thy name *for e. a. e.*
2 thy name *for e. and e.* 21
148:6 stablish. them *for e. and e.*

Is. 30:8 be for time to come *for e.*
64:10 none pass thro' it *for e. a.*
Jer. 7:7 land I gave *for e. and e.*
25:5 to you and fathers *for e. a. e.*
Dan. 7:18 pos. kingdom *f. e. a. e.*
12:3 as the stars *for e. and e.*
Mic. 4:5 in name of God *f. e. a. e.*
Gal. 1:5 glory *for e. and e. Phil.*
4:20 ; 1 *Tim.* 1:17 ; 2 *Tim.*
4:18 ; *Heb.* 13:21
Heb. 1:8 throne O G. is *for e. a. e.*
Rev. 4:9 who liveth *for e. a. e.* 10 ;
5:14 ; 10:6 ; 15:7
5:13 honor be to L. *for e. and e.*
7:12 power be to our G. *f. e. a. e.*
11:15 C. shall reign *for e. and e.*
20:10 be tormented *for e. and e.*
22:5 shall reign *for e. and e.*

EVERLASTING.

Gen. 17:8 an *e.* possession, 48:4
21:33 the *e.* God, *Is.* 40:28 ; *Rom.*
16:26

Gen. 49:26 bound of the *e.* hills
Ex. 40:15 *e.* priesth. *Num.* 25:13
Deut. 33:27 undern. are *e.* arms
Ps. 24:7 *e.* doors, 9; 100:5 mercy *e.*
112:6 righte. in *e.* remembrance
119:142 thy righteousn. is *e.* 144
139:24 lead me in the way *e.*
145:13 kingd. is an *e.* kingdom,
Dan. 4:3 ; 7:27 ; 2 *Pet.* 1:11
Prov. 10:25 an *e.* foundation
Is. 9:6 be called, the *e.* Father
26:4 in L. Jehov. is *e.* strength
33:14 dwell with *e.* burnings ?
35:10 with *e.* joy, 51:11 ; 61:7
45:17 *e.* salva. ; 54:8 an *e.* kindn.
55:13 *e.* sign ; 56:5 *e.* na. 63:12
60:19 L. be to thee an *e.* lig. 20
Jer. 10:10 *e.* king ; 20:11 *e.* confu.
23:40 bring an *e.* reproach on y.
31:3 loved thee with an *e.* love
Dan. 4:34 is an *e.* dominion, 7:14
Hab. 3:6 *e.* mountains scattered
Mat. 18:8 cast into *e.* fire, 25:41
25:46 go into *e.* punishment.
Luke 16:9 into *e.* habitations
2 *Thes.* 1:9 pun. with *e.* destruc.
2:16 hath given us *e.* consolation
1 *Tim.* 6:16 be honor and pow. *e.*
Jude 6 the angels res. in *e.* cha.
Rev. 14:6 the *e.* gospel to preach

See COVENANT.

From EVERLASTING.

Ps. 14:31 bles. be G. *f. e.* 106:48
90:2 *from e.* to *e.* thou art God
93:2 throne of old, thou art *f. e.*
103:17 mercy of the L. is *f. e.*
Prov. 8:23 I was set up *from e.*
Is. 63:16 O. L. thy name is *f. e.*
Mic. 5:2 whose goings forth *f. e.*
Hab. 1:12 art thou not *f. e.* O L.

EVERLASTING life.

Dan. 12:2 awake, some to *e. life*
Mat. 19:29 shall inherit *e. life*
Luke 18:30 world to come *e. life*
John 3:16 believeth, have *e. l.* 36
4:14 water springing up to *e. l.*
5:24 heareth my words hath *e. l.*
6:27 which endureth to *e. life*
40 the Son, may have *e. life*
47 believeth on me hath *e. life*
12:50 commandment is *life e.*
Acts 13:46 unworthy of *e. life*
Rom. 6:22 ye have the end, *e. l.*
Gal. 6:8 of the Sp. reap *l. e.*
1 *Tim.* 1:16 hereafter bel. to *l. e.*

EVERMORE.

2 *Sam.* 22:51 mercy unto Dav. *e.*
1 *Chr.* 17:14 throne be estab. *e.*
Ps. 16:11 are pleasures for *e.*
18:50 mercy to his seed for *e.*
37:27 do good, and dwell for *e.*
77:8 doth his promise fail for *e. ?*
86:12 will glorify thy na. for *e.*

89:28 mercy keep for him for *e*.
52 blessed be the L. for *e*. am.
92:8 Lord, art most high for *e*.
105:4 seek Lord, seek his face *e*.
106:31 counted for righte. for *e*.
113:2 blessed be na. of L. for *e*.
115:18 will bless the Lord for *e*.
121:8 L. preser. thy going out *e*.
132:12 sit upon thy throne for *e*.
133:3 Lord command. life for *e*.
John 6:34 *e*. give us this bread
2 *Cor.* 11:31 Father blessed for *e*.
1 *Thes.* 5:16 rejoice *e*.
Heb. 7:28 who is consecra. for *e*.
Rev. 1:18 behold, I am alive for *e*.

EVERY.

Gen. 6:5 *e*. imagination was evil
Ps. 119:101 refrained fr. *e*. evil
104 I hate *e*. false way, 128
Prov. 15:3 eyes of L. are in *e*. pl.
30:5 *e*. word of God is pure
Is. 45:23 *e*. knee, *Rom* 14:11
Mat. 4:4 by *e*. word that proc.
1 *Cor.* 4:17 as I teach *e*. wh. in *e*.
2 *Cor.* 10:5 into captiv. *e*. thoug.
Eph. 1:21 abo. *e*. name, *Phil.* 2:9
2 *Tim.* 2:21 prep. to *e*. good work
Heb. 12:1 lay aside *e*. weight
Jam. 1:17 *e*. good and perf. gift
1 *John* 4:1 believe not *e*. spirit

See BEAST, CITY, DAY, MAN,
MORNING, WAY, SIDE, THING.

EVERY one.

Num. 16:3 cong. are holy *e*. one
Deut. 4:4 ye are alive *e*. one of y.
1 *K.* 22:28 hearken *e*. one of you
2 *Chr.* 30:18 Lord pardon *e*. one
Ps. 71:18 thy power to *e*. one
115:8 *e*. one that trusteth, 135:18
Is. 43:7 *e*. o. called by my name
55:1 ho, *e*. o. that thirsteth
Jer. 25:5 turn *e*. o. from evil way
Dan. 12:1 *e*. o. found writ. in b.
Mat. 7:8 *e*. o. that ask. *Lu.* 11:10
Mark 7:14 hearken to me *e*. one
Luke 19:26 to *e*. one which hath
John 3:8 so is *e*. one born of Sp.
18:37 *e*. o. that is of truth,
Acts 17:27 not far from *e*. o.
Rom. 14:12 *e*. o. sh. give account
2 *Tim.* 2:19 *e*. o. that nameth

EVERY where.

1 *Chr.* 13:2 abroad to breth. *e. w*.
Mark 16:20 and preached *e. w*.
Luke 9:6 pre. gos. *e. w*. *Acts* 8:4
Acts 17:30 com. all *e. w*. to rep.
28:22 *e. w*. spoken against
1 *Cor.* 4:17 as I teach *e. where* in
Phil. 4:12 *e. w*. in all things
1 *Tim.* 2:8 that men pray *e. w*.

EVIDENCE.

Jer. 32:10 I subscribed the *e*. and
Heb. 11:1 *e*. of things not seen

EVIDENCES.

Jer. 32:44 buy fields, subscribe *e*.

EVIDENT.

Job 6:28 for it is *e*. to you if I lie
Gal. 3:11 justified by the law is *e*.
Phil. 1:28 *e*. token of perdition
Heb. 7:14 *e*. L. sprang out of J.
15 it is yet far more *e*. for that

EVIDENTLY.

Gal. 3:1 Jesus C. been *e*. set forth

EVIL.

Gen. 19:19 some *e*. take me, I die
44:5 ye have done *e*. in so doing
34 *e*. that shall come on my fa.
50:20 ye thought *e*. against me
Ex. 5:23 done *e*. to this people
10:10 look to it, *e*. is before you
32:14 the L. repented of the *e*.
2 *Sam.* 24:16 ; 1 *Chr.* 21:15
Deut. 19:20 com. no more such *e*.
29:21 Lord sh. sep. him unto *e*.
30:15 set bef. thee death and *e*.

31:29 *e*. befall you in latter days
Jos. 24:15 seem *e*. to serve Lord
Jud. 2:15 hand of L. ag. th. for *e*.
9:57 *e*. of Shechem did G. rend.
20:34 they knew not *e*. was near
1 *Sam.* 20:7 *e*. is determined
24:11 *e*. nor transg. in my hand
17 whereas I rewarded thee *e*.
25:17 *e*. is determ. aga. master
28 *e*. hath not been found
26:18 what *e*. is in my hand ?
29:6 I have not found *e*. in thee
2 *Sa.n.* 3:39 Lord rew. doer of *e*.
12:11 I will raise up *e*. ag. thee
19:7 worse than all *e*. that befell
1 *K.* 14:9 *e*. above all before thee
16:25 Omri wrought *e*. in eyes of
22:23 the L. hath spoken *e*. concerning thee, 2 *Chr.* 18:22
2 *K.* 21:12 bringing such *e*. on J.
22:20 eyes not see all the *e*.
1 *Chr.* 21:17 that have done *e*.
2 *Chr.* 20:9 if when *e*. cometh
Est. 7:7 he saw *e*. determined
Job. 1:1 and eschewed *e*. 8 ; 2:3
5:19 in seven no *e*. touch thee
31:29 lift up when *e*. found him
42:11 comforted him over all *e*.
Ps. 5:4 nor sh. *e*. dwell with thee
7:4 if I rewarded *e*. to him
15:3 nor doeth *e*. to his neighbor
21:11 intended *e*. against thee
23:4 I will fear no *e*. for thou art
34:21 *e*. shall slay the wicked
36:4 he abhorreth not *e*.
40:14 put to shame wish me *e*.
41:5 mine enemies speak *e*.
49:5 in days of *e*. ?
50:19 givest thy mouth to *e*.
54:5 reward *e*. to my enemies
56:5 thoughts aga. me for *e*.
90:15 years wherein we seen *e*.
91:10 *e*. befall thee, *Jer.* 23:17
97:10 that love the Lord, hate *e*.
109:20 that speak *e*. ag. my soul
140:11 *e*. shall hunt the viol. m.
Prov. 1:16 feet run to *e*. *Is.* 59:7
33 shall be quiet from fear of *e*.
3:29 devise not *e*. ag. neighbor
5:14 almost in all *e*. in midst
11:19 pursueth *e*. pur. it to dea.
12:20 in them that imagine *e*.
21 no *e*. happen to the just
13:21 *e*. pursueth sinners
14:22 they err that devise *e*. ?
16:4 wicked for the day of *e*.
27 ungodly man diggeth up. *e*
30 moving lips bringeth *e*.
19:23 shall not be visited with *e*.
20:8 scat. away *e*. with his eyes
22 say not, I will recompen. *e*.
21:10 soul of the wicked des. *e*.
22:3 pru. man foreseeth *e*. 27:12
Prov. 30:32 if thought *e*. lay thy
Ec. 2:21 is vanity, and a great *e*.
5:13 there is a sore *e*. which I, 16
6:1 *e*. which I have seen, 10:5
9:3 an *e*. am. things done, heart
of the sons of m. is full of *e*,
11:2 know. not what *e*. on earth
Is. 3:9 rewarded *e*. to themselves
13:11 punish the world for *e*.
33:15 shut. eyes from seeing *e*.
45:7 I make peace and create *e*.
47:11 theref. sh. *e*. come on thee
56:2 keepeth hand from doing *e*.
57:1 the righte. is taken from *e*.
Jer. 1:14 out of north an *e*. 6:1
2:3 *e*. shall come upon them,
4:4 because of *e*. of your doings,
23:2 ; 26:3 ; 44:22
5:12 neit. shall *e*. come upon us
7:30 chil. of Judah have done *e*
11:15 doest *e*. th. thou rejoicest
17 pronounced *e*. for *e*. of Isr.
15:11 entreat well in time of *e*.
17:17 my hope in the day of *e*.
18 bring on them the day of *e*.

18:8 turn from *e*. I will repent
of the *e*. 26:3 ; 13, 19 ; 42:10
11 I frame *e*. against you
19:15 bring *e*. I have pronounced
21:10 my face ag. this city for *e*.
25:32 *e*. go from nation
26:8 prophesied *e*. of *e*.
29:11 thoughts of peace not of *e*.
32:30 chil. of Jud. only done *e*.
35:17 the *e*. that I have pronounced against them, 36:31
38:9 these men have done *e*.
44:11 set my face ag. you for *e*.
17 had plenty, and saw no *e*.
27 watch over them for *e*.
29 words stand aga. you for *e*.
51:24 render to Bab. all the *e*.
60 wrote *e*. eho. come on Bab.
Ezek. 7:5 an *e*. an only *e*. is come
14:22 be comforted conc. the *e*.
Dan. 9:14 L. watched upon the *e*.
Joel 2:13 Lord repenteth of the *e*.
Amos 3:6 *e*. in city ?
9:10 *e*. shall not overtake us
Jon. 3:10 God repented of *e*. 4:2
Mic. 1:12 *e*. came down from L.
2:1 work *e*. upon their beds
3 do I devise an *e*.
3:11 Lord amo. us ? none *e*. can
Nah. 1:11 imagineth *e*. ag. L.
Hab. 1:13 eyes that behold *e*.
2:9 delivered from power of *e*.
Zep. 3:15 not see *e*. any more
Zec. 7:10 none imagine *e*. 8:17
Mal. 1:8 ye of. sick, is it not *e*. ?
2:17 every one that doeth *e*.
Mat. 5:11 all manner of *e*.
37 more than these, com. of *e*.
39 I say, that ye resist not *e*.
6:34 sufficient to the d. is the *e*.
9:4 why th. ye *e*. in your hearts?
27:23 What *e*. hath he done ?
Mark 15:14 ; *Luke* 23:22
Mark 9:39 lightly speak *e*. of
Luke 6:45 bring. forth what is *e*.
John 3:20 doeth *e*. hateth light
5:29 that have done *e*. to resur.
18:23 if spoken *e*. bear witness
Acts 9:13 much *e*. he hath done
23:9 we find no *e*. in this man
Rom. 2:9 every soul that doeth *e*.
7:19 *e*. I would not, that I do
12:9 abhor that which is *e*.
17 recomp. to no man *e*. for *e*.
21 be not overcome of *e*. but
13:4 exec. wrath on him doeth *e*.
14:20 *e*. for him who eateth evil.
16:19 simple concerning *e*.
1 *Cor.* 13:5 charity thinketh no *e*.
1 *Thes.* 5:15 none render *e*. for *e*.
22 abstain from appear. of *e*.
1 *Tim.* 6:10 money root of all *e*.
Tit. 3:2 to speak *e*. of no man
Jam. 3:8 tongue is an unruly *e*.
1 *Pet.* 3:9 not rendering *e*. for *e*.
3 *John* 11 doeth *e*. not seen God

Bring, brought EVIL.

Jos. 23:15 b. on you all *e*.
2 *Sam.* 15:14 lest A. b. *e*. on us
17:14 L. might b. *e*. upon Absa.
1 *K.* 14:10 b. *e*. on house of Jero.
17:20 also b. *e*. on the widow ?
21:29 not b. the *e*. in his days
2 *K.* 22:16 I will b. *e*. upon this
place, 2 *Chr.* 34:24
2 *Chr.* 34:28 eyes see *e*. I will b.
Is. 31:2 b. *e*. not call back word
Jer. 4:6 I will b. *e*. from the north
6:19 I will b. *e*. upon this people
11:11 I will b. *e*. upon them.
19:3 b. *e*. upon this place, 15
23:12 b. *e*. the year of visitation
Jer. 25:29 I begin to b. *e*. on the
35:17 b. on Judah all the *e*. 36:31
39:16 b. words on this city for *e*.
45:5 I will b. *e*. upon all flesh

See DID, DO.

EVIL, *joined with good.*
Gen. 2:9 tree of kno. *g.* and *e.* 17
3:5 as gods know. *g.* and *e.* 22
44:4 wheref. rewarded *e.* for *g.* ℙ
Deut. 1:39 no kno. *g.* and *e.*
1 Sam. 25:21 requit. me *e.* for *g.*
2 Sam. 19:35 disc. bet. *g.* and *e.* ℙ
1 K. 22:8 prophesy *g.* but *e.* 18
2 Chr. 18:7 nev. prophe. *g.* but *e.*
·17 not prophesy *good* but *e.*
Job 2:10 receive *g.* and not *e.* ℙ
30:26 I looked for *good, e.* came
Ps. 35:12 rew me *e.* for *g.* 109:5
38:20 render *e.* for *g.*
52:3 thou lovest *e.* more than *g.*
Prov. 15:3 behold. *e.* and the *g.*
17:13 rewardeth *e.* for *good*
31:12 will do him *good, e.* not *e.*
Is. 5:20 woe to th. call *e. g. g. e.*
7:15 refuse *e.* and choose *g.* 16
Jer. 18:20 *e.* be recomp. for *g.* ℙ
42:6 whe. *g.* or *e.* we will obey
Lam. 3:38 proceed. not *e.* and *g.*
Amos 5:14 seek *g.* and not *e.* that
9:4 eyes on them for *e.* not *g.*
Mic. 3:2 hate *good* and love *e.*
Rom. 7:21 do *g.* is. *e.* present
9:11 having done *good* or *e.*
Heb. 5:14 exerc. to disc. *g.* and *e.*
3 John 11 follow not *e.* but *good*
See GREAT.

From EVIL.
Gen. 48:16 redeemed me *f.* all *e.*
1 Sam. 25:39 kept his serv. *f. e.*
1 Chr. 4:10 keep me *from e.*
Job 28:28 to depart *f. e.*
Ps. 34:13 keep thy tongue *f. e.*
14 dep. *f. e.* 37:27; Prov. 3:7
121:7 preserve thee *f.* all *e.*
Prov. 4:27 remove thy foot *f. e.*
13:19 abomination to depart *f. e.*
14:16 a wise man departeth *f. e.*
16:6 men depart *from e.*
17 to depart *from e.*
Is. 59:15 *f. e.* makes himself
Jer. 9:3 they proceed *f. e.* to *e.*
23:22 should have turned *f. e.*
way, and *e.* of their doings
51:64 Bab. not rise *from* the *e.*
Mat. 6:13 del. us *f. e.* Luke 11:4
John 17:15 keep them *f. e.*
2 Thes. 3:3 and keep you *f. e.*
1 Pet. 3:10 refrain his tong. *f. e.*

Put away EVIL.
Deut. 13:5 p. the *e. a.* from *m.*
17:7 put the *e. a.* from am. 19:19;
21:21; 22:21, 24; 24:7
12 *put e. away* from Israel,
21:22; Jud. 20:13
Ec. 11:10 *put a. e.* from thy flesh
Is. 1:16 wash you *p. away e.*

EVIL in the sight of the Lord.
Num. 32:13 *e.* in *s. Jud.* 3:12
Jud. 2:11 Isr. did *e. in s. of the*
Lord, 3:7, 12; 4:1; 6:1; 10:6;
13:1; 1 K. 11:6; 14:22; 15:26,
34; 16:7, 30; 22:52; 2 K. 8:18,
27; 13:2, 11; 14:24; 15:9, 18,
24, 28; 17:2; 21:2, 20; 2 Chr.
22:4; 33:2, 22; 36:5, 9, 12
1 Sam. 15:19 didst *e. in s. of L.*
1 K. 16:19 in doing *e. in s. of L.*
21:20 sold to work *e. in s. of L.*
2 K. 3:2 wrought *e. in s. of L.*
17:17 to do *e. in s. of Lord*
21:16 in doing what was *e. in s.*
of Lord, 23:32, 37; 24:9, 19
1 Chr. 2:3 Er was *e. in s. of L.*
2 Chr. 33:6 Man. wro. *e. in s. of L.*

This EVIL.
Ex. 32:12 repent of *t. e.*
1 Sam. 6:9 hath done us *t.* gr. *e.*
12:19 added *t. e.* to ask a *k.*
2 Sam. 13:16 *t. e.* in send. away
1 K. 9:9 L. brought on th. *t. e.*
2 K. 6:33 behold *t. e.* is of Lord

2 Chr. 7:22 theref. brought *t. e.*
Neh. 13:18 our G. bring *this e.*
Job 2:11 J.'s friends heard of *t. e.*
Ps. 51:4 done *t. e.* in thy sight
Jer. 16:10 pronounced *t. e.* ag. us
32:23 thou hast caused all *t. e.*
42 as I brought *t. e.* on people
40:2 pronoun. *t. e.* on th. place
44:7 wheref. commit *t.* great *e.*
23 theref. *t. e.* is happen. to y.
Dan. 9:13 all *t. e.* is come on us
Jon. 1:7 for whose cause *t. e.* 8

EVIL, Adjective.
Gen. 6:5 thoughts only *e.* 8:21
Gen. 37:20 *e.* beast dev. him, 33
Ex. 5:19 did see were in. *e.* case
33:4 when heard these *e.* tidings
Num. 14:27 how long bear *e.* con.
20:5 bring us unto this *e.* place
Deut. 1:35 not one of this *e.* gen.
22:14 an *e.* name upon her, 19
28:54 his *e.* toward brother
56 her eye to *e.* toward husb.
1 Sam. 2:23 your *e.* dealings
1 K. 5:4 nor *e.* occurrent
Ezr. 9:13 come for our *e.* deeds
Ps. 41:8 *e.* disease cleav. to him
64:5 encourage in an *e.* matter
78:49 by sending *e.* angels
112:7 not be afraid of *e.* tidings
140:11 let not *e.* speaker be est.
Prov. 6:24 to keep from *e.* woman
14:19 the *e.* bow before the good
Ec. 5:14 perish by *e.* travel
6:2 end it is an *e.* disease
9:12 fishes taken in *e.* net
Is. 7:5 taken *e.* counsel aga. thee
32:7 instruments of churl are *e.*
Jer. 8:3 that remain of *e.* family
12:14 against mine *e.* neighbors
13:10 *e.* people refuse to hear
23:10 their course is *e.*
24:3 *e.* figs, very *e.* 8; 29:17
49:23 they have heard *e.* tidings
Ezek. 5:16 *e.* arrows of famine
17 will I send on you *e.* beasts
6:11 for all the *e.* abominations
34:25 cause *e.* beasts to cease
38:10 shalt think an *e.* thought
Hab. 2:9 coveteth an *e.* covetous.
Mat. 5:45 sun to rise on the *e.*
7:11 if being *e.* Luke 11:13
18 cannot bring forth *e.* fruit
12:34 how can ye being *e.* speak
39 an *e.* generation, Luke 11:29
15:19 out of the heart proceed
e. thoughts, Mark 7:21
24:48 if *e.* servant say in heart
Luke 6:22 cast out name as *e.*
35 kind to unthankful and *e.*
John 3:19 because deeds were *e.*
Acts 24:20 found *e.* doing in me
1 Cor. 15:33 *e.* communications
Gal. 1:4 deliver us from *e.* world
Eph. 4:31 *e.* speaking be put aw.
Phil. 3:2 beware of evil workers
Col. 3:5 mortify *e.* concupiscence
1 Tim. 6:4 cometh *e.* surmisings
Tit. 1:12 Cretians are *e.* beasts
Heb. 10:22 sprinkled from *e.*
Jam. 2:4 judges of *e.* thoughts
4:16 all such rejoicing is *e.*
1 Pet. 2:1 laying aside *e.* speak.
Rev. 2:2 canst not bear them *e.*

EVIL day or days.
Gen. 47:9 few and *e.* of life
Prov. 15:15 *d.* of afflicted are *e.*
Ec. 12:1 *e. days* come not
Amos 6:3 put far away *e. d.*
Eph. 5:16 because *days* are *e.*
6:13 able to withstand in *e. day*
Day of EVIL. See EVIL, Subst.

EVIL doer or doers.
Job 8:20 neither will he help *e. d.*
Ps. 26:5 hated congrega. of *e. d.*
37:1 fret not because of *e. d.*

9 *e. d.* shall be cut off, but
94:16 will rise up aga. *e. do.* ℙ
119:115 depart from me ye *e. d.*
Is. 1:4 sinful nation seed of *e. d.*
9:17 every one is an *e. d.*
14:20 seed of *e. d.*
31:2 will arise ag. house of *e. d.*
Jer. 20:13 deliv. poor from *e. d.*
23:14 strengthen hands of *e. d.*
2 Tim. 2:9 I suffer troub. as *e. d.*
1 Pet. 2:12 speak ag. you as *e. d.*
14 sent for punishment of *e. d.*
3:16 speak *e.* of you as of *e. d.*
4:15 let none suffer as an *e. d.*
See DOINGS, EYE.

EVIL heart.
Gen. 8:21 imagination of *h.* is *e.*
Jer. 3:17 after imagina. of *e. h.*
7:24 walked in imagina. of *e. h.*
11:8 every one in imagi. of *e. h.*
16:12 after imagination of *e. h.*
18:12 do imagination of *e. h.*
Heb. 3:12 be an *e. h.* of unbelief

EVIL man or men.
Job 35:12 bec. of pride of *e. men*
Ps. 10:15 break arm of *e. man*
140:1 deliver me from *e. man*
Prov. 2:12 deli. from way of *e. m.*
4:14 go not in way of *e. men*
12:12 wicked desir. net of *e. m.*
17:11 *e. man* seeketh only rebel.
24:1 be not envious aga. *e. men*
19 fret not because of *e. men*
20 shall be no reward to *e. m.*
Prov. 28:5 *e. m.* unders. not judg.
29:6 in transg. of *e. m.* is snare
Mat. 12:35 *e. m.* out of *e.* treasure, bring. *e.* th. Luke 6:45
2 Tim. 3:13 *e. m.* shall wax wor.
See REPORT.

EVIL spirit or spirits.
Jud. 9:23 *e. s.* betw. Abimelech
1 Sam. 16:14 *e. s.* troub. him, 15
16 when *e. spirit* is upon thee
23 *e. spirit* departed from him
18:10 *e. spirit* came on S. 19:9
Luke 7:21 cured many of *e. s.*
8:2 a woman healed of *e. spirits*
Acts 19:12 *e. s.* went out of them
15 *e. s.* said, Jesus, I know, Pa.

EVIL thing.
Neh. 13:17 what *e. t.* is th. ye do?
Ps. 141:4 incline not heart to *e. t.*
Ec. 8:3 stand not in an *e. thing*
5 keepeth com. sh. feel no *e. t.*
12:14 secret *t.* wheth. good or *e.*
Jer. 2:19 it is an *e.* th. and bitter
Tit. 2:8 no *e. t.* to say of you

EVIL things.
Jos. 23:15 bring on you all *e. t.*
Prov. 15:28 poureth out *e. t.*
Jer. 3:5 hast done *e. t.*
Mat. 12:35 *e.* man br. forth *e. t.*
Mark 7:23 *t. t.* come from within
Luke 16:25 likewise Lazarus *e. t.*
Rom. 1:30 inventors of *e. things*
1 Cor. 10:6 not lust after *e. t.*

EVIL time.
Ps. 37:19 not be ashamed in *e. t.*
Ec. 9:12 are snared in an *e. t.*
Amos 5:13 it is an *e. t.*
Mic. 2:3 nor go haughtily, *t.* is *e.*

EVIL way.
1 K. 13:33 J. ret. not from *e. w.*
Ps. 119:101 refrained fr. ev. *e. w.*
Prov. 8:13 fear of L. to hate *e. w.*
28:10 to go astray in *e. way*
Jer. 18:11 return ye from *e. w.*
25:5; 26:3; 35:15; 36:3, 7
23:22 turned them from *e. way*
Jon. 3:8 turn ev. one from *e. w.*
10 saw they turned from *e. w.*

EVIL ways.
2 K. 17:13 turn from your *e. ways,*
Ezek. 33:11

Ezek. 36:31 remember your *e. w.*
Zec. 1:4 turn ye now from *e. w.*

EVIL work *or* works.
Ec. 4:3 hath not seen *e. work*
8:11 sentence against an *e. work*
John 7:7 *works* thereof are *e.*
Rom. 13:3 terror to good but *e. w.*
2 Tim. 4:18 deliver me from *e. w.*
Jam. 3:16 and every *e. w.*
1 John 3:12 his own *w.* were *e*

EVIL, Adverb.
Ex. 5:22 *e.* entreated this peo. ?
Deut. 26:6 Egypt *e.* entreated us
1 Chr. 7:23 went *e.* with his ho.
Job 24:21 *e.* entreated the barren
John 18:23 spoken *e.* bear witn.
Acts 7:6 entreat *e.* 400 years
19 same *e.* entreated our fath.
14:2 *e.* affected against brethren
19:9 spake of *e.* that way before
23:5 not speak *e.* of ruler of peo.
Rom. 14:16 not good be *e.* spoken
1 Cor. 10:30 am I *e.* spoken of
Jam. 4:11 sp. not *e.* he that spe.
of brother, speaks *e.* of law
1 Pet. 3:16 whereas they speak *e.*
17 than suffer for *e.* doing
4:4 speaking *e.* of you
14 on their part *e.* spoken of
2 Pet. 2:2 way of truth *e.* spok. of
10 speak *e.* of dignities, *Jude* 8
12 speak *e.* of things they understand not, *Jude* 10

EVIL-MERODACH. *2 K.* 25:27;
Jer. 52:31

EVILS.
Deut. 31:17 *e.* shall befall them,
will say, Are not these *e.*
Ps. 40:12 innumer. *e.* comp. me
Jer. 2:13 have committed two *e.*
Ezek. 6:9 loathe themselves for *e.*
20:43 loathe yourselves for all *e.*
Luke 3:19 for all *e.* H. had done

EWE *or* EWES.
Gen. 21:28 Abraham set seven *e.*
31:38 thy *e.* not cast their young
Lev. 14:10 take one *e.* lamb
2 Sam. 12:3 nothing save *e.* lamb
Ps. 78:71 from following the *e.*

EXACT.
Deut 15:3 of foreigner may *e.* ag.
Neh. 5:10 I likewise might *e.*
Neh. 5:11 hundredth of mo. ye *e.*
Ps. 89:22 enemy not *e.* upon him
Is. 58:3 in fasts you *e.* all labors
Luke 3:13 *e.* no more than is app

EXACTED, ETH.
2 K. 15:20 Menahem *e.* of Israel
23:35 Jehoakim *e.* the gold
Job 11:6 G. *e.* less than iniquity

EXACTION, S.
Neh. 10:31 would leave *e.* of debt
Ezek. 45:9 take away your *e.*

EXACTORS.
Is. 60:17 make *e.* righteousness

EXALT.
Ex. 15:2 father's G. I will *e.*
1 Sam. 2:10 *e.* horn of anointed
Job 17:4 shalt thou not *e.* them
Ps. 34:3 let us *e.* his name
37:34 *e.* thee to inherit the land
66:7 let not rebellious *e.* thems.
92:10 my horn *e.* like the horn
99:5 *e.* ye the Lord our God, 9
107:32 let *e.* him in congregation
118:28 art my God, I will *e.* thee
140:8 lest wicked *e.* themselves
Prov. 4:8 *e.* her, she shall prom.
Is. 13:2 *e.* the voice unto them
14:13 I will *e.* throne above sta.
25:1 art my God, I will *e.* thee
Ezek. 21:26 *e.* him that is low
29:15 nor *e.* itself above nations
31:14 to the end none of trees *e.*

Dan. 11:14 robbers of thy peo. *e.*
36 *e.* himself above every god
Hos. 11:7 none would *e.* him
Ob. 4 tho' *e.* thyself as the eagle
Mat. 23:12 whoso shall *e.* himself
2 Cor. 11:20 if a man *e.* himself
1 Pet. 5:6 may *e.* you in time

EXALTED.
Num. 24:7 kingdom shall be *e.*
1 Sam. 2:1 said, My horn is *e.*
2 Sam. 5:12 he had *e.* kingdom
22:47 *e.* be the God of the rock
of my salvation, *Ps.* 18:46
1 K. 1:5 Adonijah *e.* himself
14:7 I *e.* thee from people, 16:2
2 K. 19:22 against whom hast
thou *e.* thy voice? *Is.* 37:23
1 Chr. 29:11 thou art *e.* as head
Neh. 9:5 is *e.* above all blessing
Job 5:11 mourn be *e.* to safety
24:24 are *e.* for a little while
36:7 establish, and they are *e.*
Ps. 12:8 when the vilest are *e.*
13:2 how long ene. *e.* over me?
21:13 be *e.* in thine own streng.
46:10 I will be *e.* am. heathen,
I will be *e.* in the earth
47:9 to God, he is greatly *e.*
57:5 be *e.* above heavens, 11
75:10 horns of right. shall be *e.*
89:16 thy right. sh. they be *e.*
17 in thy favor our horn be *e.*
19 *e.* one chosen out of people
24 in my name his horn be *e.*
97:9 art *e.* far above all gods
108:5 *e.* above the heavens
112:9 his horn be *e.* with honor
118:16 right hand of Lord is *e.*
Prov. 11:11 by blessing city is *e.*
Is. 2:2 mount. of Lord's house be
e. above the hills, *Mic.* 4:1
11 L. be *e.* 17 ; 5:16
12:4 mention that his name is *e.*
30:18 be *e.* that he have mercy
33:5 L. is *e.* ; 10 now will I be *e.*
40:4 every valley shall be *e.*
49:11 my highways shall be *e.*
52:13 my servant shall be *e.*
Ezek. 17:24 I the Lord *e.* low tr.
19:11 her stature was *e.* 31:5
Hos. 13:1 Ephraim *e.* himself
6 and their heart was *e.*
Mat. 11:23 *e.* to heav. *Luke* 10:15
23:12 humble himself shall be
e. Luke 14:11 ; 18:14
Luke 1:52 *e.* them of low degree
Acts 2:33 by right hand of God *e.*
5:31 him hath God *e.*
13:17 God of Israel *e.* the people
2 Cor. 11:7 that you might be *e.*
12:7 be *e.* above measure, 7
Phile. 20 be *e.* both high. *e.* him
Jam. 1:8 bro. rejoice that he is *e.*

EXALTEST, ETH.
Ex. 9:17 *e.* thyself against my
people
Job 36:22 God *e.* by his power
Ps. 148:14 *e.* horn of his people
Prov. 14:29 hasty of sp. *e.* folly
34 righteousness *e.* a nation
17:19 *e.* gate, seek. destruction
Luke 14:11 *e.* him, 18:14
2 Cor. 10:5 every thing that *e.*
2 Thes. 2:4 *e* him above all

EXAMINATION.
Acts 25:26 after *e.* had, I might

EXAMINE.
Ezr. 10:16 sat down to *e.* matter
Ps. 26:2 *e.* me O Lord
1 Cor. 9:3 answer to them that *e.*
11:28 let a man *e.* himself
2 Cor. 13:5 *e.* yourselves, prove

EXAMINED, ING.
Luke 23:14 I have *e.* him
Acts 4:9 if we be *e.* of good deed
12:19 Herod *e.* the keepers

22:24 should be *e.* by scourging
29 departed who should *e.* him
24:8 by *e.* of whom thou mayest
28:18 *e.* me, would ha. let me go

EXAMPLE, S.
Mat. 1:19 make her a public *e.*
John 13:15 have given you an *e.*
1 Cor. 10:6 were our *e.*
1 Tim. 4:12 *e.* of believers
Heb. 4:11 fall after same *e.*
8:5 serve unto *e.* of heavenly
Jam. 5:10 prophets for *e.* suffer.
1 Pet. 2:21 C. suff. leave. us an *e.*
Jude 7 for an *e.* suffering

See ENSAMPLE, S.

EXCEED.
Deut. 25:3 forty stripes and not
e. lest if he *e.* brother
Mat. 5:20 right. *e.* the scribes
2 Cor. 3:9 ministration *e.*

EXCEEDED.
1 Sam. 20:41 wept, till David *e.*
1 K. 10:23 Sol. *e.* all for riches

EXCEEDEST, ETH.
1 K. 10:7 wisdom *e.* the fame
2 Chr. 9:6 *e.* fame that I heard

EXCEEDING.
Gen. 15:1 thy *e.* great reward
17:6 make thee *e.* fruitful
27:34 E. cried with *e.* bitter cry
Ex. 1:7 Israel waxed *e.* mighty
19:16 the trumpet *e.* loud
Num. 14:7 land we passed is *e.*
1 Sam. 2:3 no more *e.* proudly
2 Sam. 8:8 D. took *e.* much brass
12:2 man had *e.* many flocks
1 K. 4:29 G. gave Sol. wisdom *e.*
1 Chr. 20:2 brought *e.* much spoil
22:5 must be *e.* magnifical
2 Chr. 11:12 cities *e.* strong
14:14 was *e.* much spoil in them
16:12 Asa, disease was *e.* great
32:27 Hez. had *e.* much riches
Ps. 21:6 hast made him *e.* glad
43:4 I go unto God, my *e.* joy
119:96 thy command. is *e.* broad
Prov. 30:24 four things are *e. w.*
Ec. 7:24 which is *e.* deep
Ezek. 9:9 iniq. of Is. is *e.* great
16:13 and wast *e.* beautiful
37:10 *e.* great army
47:10 fish of great sea *e.* many
Dan. 3:22 the furnace was *e.* hot
7:19 fourth beast was *e.* dreadful
8:9 horn, which waxed *e.* great
Jon. 3:3 was an *e.* great city
4:6 Jonah was *e.* glad
Mat. 2:10 rej. with *e.* great joy
16 Herod mocked, was *e.* wro.
4:8 taketh up into *e.* high moun.
5:12 rejoice and be *e.* glad
8:28 possess. with devils *e.* fier.
26:22 they were *e.* sorrowful
38 *e.* sorrowful, *Mark* 14:34
Mark 6:26 the king was *e.* sorry
9:3 his raiment *e.* white as snow
Acts 7:20 M. born, and was *e.* fa.
Rom. 7:13 sin become *e.* sinful
2 Cor. 4:17 work. *e.* weight glory
9:14 for *e.* grace of God in you
Eph. 1:19 *e.* greatness
2:7 might show *e.* riches of gra.
3:20 is able to do *e.* abundantly
1 Tim. 1:14 grace of L. *e.* abund.
1 Pet. 4:13 be glad al. with *e.* joy
2 Pet. 1:4 *e.* great promises
Jude 24 you faultless with *e.* joy
Rev. 16:21 the pla. was *e.* great

EXCEEDINGLY.
Gen. 7:19 the waters prevailed *e.*
13:13 men of S. were sinners *e.*
16:10 I will multiply thy seed *e.*
17:2 I will multiply thee *e.*
20 I will multiply Ishmael *e. e.*
27:33 and Isaac trembled very *e.*
30:43 Jacob increased *e.* 47:27

2 *Sam.* 13:15 Amnon hated her *e.*
2 *K.* 10:4 elders Samaria *e.* afraid
1 *Chr.* 29:25 L. magnified Solomon *e.* 2 *Chr.* 1:1
2 *Chr.* 17:12 Jch. waxed great *e.*
26:8 Uzziah strength. himself *e.*
Neh. 2:10 it grieved them *e.*
Est. 4:4 queen was *e.* grieved
Job 3:22 rejoice *e.* when they find
Ps. 68:3 the righteous *e.* rejoice
106:14 lusted *e.* in the wildern.
119:167 testim. I love them *e.*
123:3 *e.* filled with contempt, 4
Is. 24:19 the earth is moved *e.*
Dan. 7:7 a fourth beast strong *e.*
Jon. 1:10 men were *e.* afraid
16 the men feared the Lord *e.*
4:1 it displeased Jonah *e.*
Mat. 19:25 they were *e.* amazed
Mark 4:41 they feared *e.* and said
15:14 cried out the more *e.*
Acts 16:20 these men do *e.* trou.
26:11 being *e.* mad against them
27:18 *e.* tossed with a tempest
2 *Cor.* 7:13 and *e.* the more joyed
Gal. 1:14 *e.* zealous of the tradit.
1 *Thes.* 3:10 praying *e.*
2 *Thes.* 1:3 your faith groweth *e.*
Heb. 12:21 Moses said, I *e.* fear

EXCEL.
Gen. 49:4 unsta. as wa. sh. not *e.*
1 *Chr.* 15:21 with harps on Sh. *e.*
Ps. 103:20 that *e.* in strength
Is. 10:10 images did *e.* them
1 *Cor.* 14:12 seek that ye may *e.*

EXCELLED, EST.
1 *K.* 4:30 Sol's wisdom *e.* Egypt
Prov. 31:29 but thou *e.* them all

EXCELLETH.
Ec. 2:13 wis. *e.* folly. light *e.* da.
2 *Cor.* 3:10 reason of glory that *e.*

EXCELLENCY.
Gen. 49:3 *e.* of dignity, *e.* of pow.
Ex. 15:7 greatness of thine *e.*
Deut. 33:26 who rideth in his *e.*
29 who is the sword of thy *e.*
Job 4:21 their *e.* go away?
13:11 his *e.* make afraid?
20:6 *e.* mount up to the heavens
37:4 thunder. with voice of h. *e.*
40:10 deck with majesty and *e.*
Ps. 47:4 the *e.* of Jacob
62:4 cast him down from his *e.*
68:34 his *e.* is over Israel
Ec. 7:12 the *e.* of knowledge is
Is. 13:19 beauty of the Chald. *e.*
35:2 *e.* of Carmel, *e.* of our God
60:15 I make thee an eternal *e.*
Ezek. 24:21 the *e.* of your streng.
Amos 6:8 I abhor the *e.* of Jacob
8:7 L. hath sworn by *e.* of Jacob
Nah. 2:2 *e.* of Jacob, the *e.* of Is.
1 *Cor.* 2:1 not with *e.* speech
2 *Cor.* 4:7 that *e.* of pow. may be
Phile. 3:8 all things lost for *e.*

EXCELLENT.
Est. 1:4 showed *e.* majesty
Job 37:23 Almighty is *e.* in power
Ps. 8:1 how *e.* thy name! 9
16:3 *e.* in wh. is all my delight
36:7 how *e.* is thy loving-kind.
76:4 more *e.* than the mountains
141:5 it shall be an *e.* oil
148:13 Lord, his name alone is *e.*
150:2 accord. to his *e.* greatness
Prov. 8:6 will speak of *e.* things
12:26 righte. more *e.* th. neigh.
17:7 *e.* speech become. n. a fool
Cant. 5:15 countenance *e.*
Is. 4:2 fruit of earth shall be *e.*
12:5 L. hath done *e.* things
28:29 L. of hosts *e.* in working
Ezek. 16:7 come to *e.* ornaments
Dan. 2:31 whose brightn. was *e.*
4:36 *e.* majesty was added unto

5:12 *e.* spirit found in D. 6:3
14 *e.* wisdom is found in thee
Luke 1:3 most *e.* Theophilus
Acts 23:26 the *e.* governor Felix
Rom. 2:18 approvest things more *e. Phile.* 1:10
1 *Cor.* 12:31 show I a more *e.* way
Heb. 1:4 obtained a more *e.* name
8:6 obtained a more *e.* ministry
11:4 A. offered more *e.* sacrifice
2 *Pet.* 1:17 voice from the *e.* glo.

EXCEPT.
Gen. 32:26 not go *e.* thou bless
42:15 *e.* young. bro. come, 43:3, 5
Num. 16:13 *e.* make thyself a pr.
Deut. 32:30 *e.* their Rock had sold
Jos. 7:12 *e.* you destroy accursed
1 *Sam.* 25:34 *e.* thou hadst hasted
2 *Sam.* 3:13 *e.* thou first bring M.
5:6 *e.* thou take away the blind
2 *K.* 4:24 slack not riding. *e.*
Est. 2:14 *e.* king delighted.
4:11 *e.* king hold golden sceptre
Ps. 127:1 *e.* L. build, *e.* L. keep
Prov. 4:16 sleep not *e.* done mis.
Is. 1:9 *e.* L. left remn. *Rom.* 9:29
Dan. 3:28 nor wors. god, *e.* o. G.
Dan. 6:5 *e.* find it con. law of
Amos 3:3 two walk *e.* agreed?
Mat. 5:20 *e.* righteousness exc.
12:29 *e.* blind str. m. *Mark* 3:27
18:3 I say to you *e.* ye be conv.
19:9 put away wife *e.* for forni.
24:22 *e.* day be short, *Mark* 13:20
26:42 may not pass *e.* I drink
Mark 7:3 Phar. *e.* wash oft
Luke 9:13 *e.* we go and buy meat
13:2 *e.* ye repent, ye shall per. 5
John 3:2 *e.* G. be with him
3 *e.* a man be born again
3:5 *e.* a man be born of water
27 nothing *e.* it be given
4:48 *e.* ye see signs and wonders
6:44 *e.* the Father draw him
53 *e.* ye eat fle. of the S. of m.
65 *e.* it were given him
12:24 *e.* a corn of wheat fall into
15:4 ye cannot bear fruit *e.* ye
19:11 no power *e.* it were given
20:25 *e.* I see print of the nails
Acts 8:1 all scat. *e.* the apostles
31 *e.* some man guide me?
15:1 *e.* ye be circumcised
24:21 *e.* it be for this one voice
26:29 all as I am. *e.* these bonds
27:31 *e.* these abide in ship
Rom. 7:7 not known lust *e.* law
10:15 how preach *e.* they be sent
1 *Cor.* 14:5 with tongues *e.* he in.
6 *e.* I shall speak by revelation
7 *e.* they gave distinction
9 *e.* ye utter words easy under.
15:36 not quickened *e.* it die
2 *Cor.* 12:13 *e.* I was not burden.
13:5 *e.* ye be reprobates?
2 *Thes.* 2:3 *e.* come a falling aw.
2 *Tim.* 2:5 not crowned, *e.* he st.
Rev. 2:5 remove candle *e.* th. rep.
22 tribulation *e.* they repent

EXCEPTED.
1 *Cor.* 15:27 is *e.* who put things

EXCESS.
Mat. 23:25 within are full of *e.*
Eph. 5:18 wine, wherein is *e.*
1 *Pet.* 4:3 lusts, and *e.* of wine
4 ye run not to the same *e.*

EXCHANGE.
Gen. 47:17 Jos. gave bread in *e.*
Lev. 27:10 *e.* thereof shall be
Job 28:17 *e.* sh. not be for jewels
Mat. 16:26 wh. sh. a man give in *e.* for his soul? *Mark* 8:37

EXCHANGE, Verb.
Ezek. 48:14 nor *e.* first-fruits

EXCHANGERS.
Mat. 25:27 to put money to *e.*

EXCLUDE, D.
Rom. 3:27 boasting? it is *e.*
Gal. 4:17 they would *e.* you

EXCUSE.
Luke 14:18 began to make *e.*
Rom. 1:20 so they are without *e.*

EXCUSE, Verb.
2 *Cor.* 12:19 think you we *e.* our.

EXCUSED, ING.
Luke 14:18 have me *e.* 19
Rom. 2:15 thoughts accus. or *e.*

EXECRATION.
Jer. 42:18 and ye shall be an *e.*
44:12 an *e.* and reproach

EXECUTE.
Ex. 12:12 will *e.* judgment
Num. 5:30 priest shall *e.* upon
8:11 that they may *e.* service
Deut. 10:18 doth *e.* judg. of wid.
Ps. 119:84 when wilt thou *e.*
149:7 to *e.* venge. upon heathen
9 to *e.* the judgment written
Jer. 7:5 *e.* judg. between man and
21:12 *e.* judg. in the morning
22:3 *e.* judgm. and righteousn.
23:5 branch shall *e.* judg. 33:15
Ezek. 5:8 will *e.* judg. in thee, 10
15 when I shall *e.* judg. in thee
11:9 I will *e.* judg. among you
25:11 I will *e.* judg. upon Moab
17 I will *e.* venge. upon them
30:14 and *e.* judgments in No
19 thus I will *e.* judg. in Egypt
45:9 *e.* judgment and justice
Hos. 11:9 not *e.* the fierceness
Mic. 5:15 and I will *e.* vengeance
7:9 and *e.* judgment for me
Zec. 7:9 *e.* true judgment
8:16 *e.* the judgment of truth
John 5:27 given authority to *e.*
Rom. 13:4 minister of G. *e.* wrath
Jude 15 to *e.* judgment on all

EXECUTED.
Num. 33:4 on gods the L. *e.* judg.
Deut. 33:21 he *e.* justice of the L.
2 *Sam.* 8:15 D. *e.* ju. 1 *Chr.* 18:14
1 *Chr.* 6:10 *e.* the priest's office
24:2 E. and Ith. *e.* priest's office
Ezr. 7:26 let judg. be *e.* speedily
Ps. 106:30 Phinehas, and *e.* judg.
Ec. 8:11 sentence not *e.* speedily
Jer. 23:20 anger of the L. have *e.*
Ezek. 11:12 nei. *e.* my judg. 20:24
18:8 *e.* true judg. bet. man, 17
23:10 they had *e.* judg. upon her
28:22 I shall have *e.* judg. 26
39:21 shall see judg. I have *e.*
Luke 1:8 wh. Z. *e.* priest's office

EXECUTEDST.
1 *Sam.* 28:18 nor *e.* wrath on A.

EXECUTEST, ETH.
Ps. 9:16 is known by judg. he *e.*
99:4 thou *e.* judgment in Jacob
103:6 Lord *e.* right. and judgm.
146:7 L. *e.* judgm. for the oppr.
Is. 46:11 that *e.* my counsel
Jer. 5:1 if any *e.* judgment
Joel 3:13 he is str. that *e.* word

EXECUTING.
2 *Chr.* 11:14 Jero. cast off from *e.*
22:8 J. *e.* judg. on Ahab's house

EXECUTION, ER.
Est. 9:1 decree to be put in *e.*
Mark 6:27 king sent an *e.*

EXEMPTED.
1 *K.* 15:22 a procla. none was *e.*

EXERCISE.
1 *Tim.* 4:8 bodily *e.* profit. little

EXERCISE, Verb.
Ps. 131:1 nor do I *e.* things
Jer. 9:24 L. which *e.* loving-kind.

Mat. 20:25 princes of the Gen. *e.*
dominion, that are great *e.*
autho. *Mark* 10:42; *Lv.* 22:25
Acts 24:16 I *e.* mys. to have cons.
1 *Tim.* 4:7 *e.* thyself to godliness

EXERCISED, ETH.
Ec. 1:13 sore trav. to be *e.* 3:10
Ezek. 22:29 peo. of land *e.* robb.
Heb. 5:14 senses *e.* to disc. good
12:11 fruit of right. to them *e.*
2 *Pet.* 2:14 heart *e.* with covetous
Rev. 13:12 *e.* power of first beast

EXHORT.
Acts 2:40 many words did he *e.*
27: 22 I *e.* you to be of good ch.
1 *Thes.* 4:1 brethren, and *e.* you
5:14 now we *e.* you, warn unru.
2 *Thes.* 3:12 comm. and *e.* by C.
1 *Tim.* 2:1 I *e.* that first of all
6:2 these things teach and *e.*
2 *Tim.* 4:2 *e.* with long-suffering
Tit. 1:9 may be able to *e.* and co.
2:6 young men *e.* to be sober
9 *e.* servants to be obedient
15 speak, *e.* and rebuke
Heb. 3:13 *e.* one another daily
1 *Pet.* 5:1 the elders am. you I *e.*
Jude 3 for me to write and *e.*

EXHORTATION.
Luke 3:18 many things in *e.*
Acts 13:15 ye have word of *e.* say
20:2 when P. had given much *e.*
Rom. 12:8 exhort. let wait on *e.*
1 *Cor.* 14:3 speak. unto men to *e.*
2 *Cor.* 8:17 he accepted the *e.*
1 *Thes.* 2:3 *e.* was not of deceit
1 *Tim.* 4:13 give attendance to *e.*
Heb. 12:5 ye have forgot. the *e.*
13:22 suffer the word of *e.*

EXHORTED, ING.
Acts 11:23 B. *e.* to cleave to Lord
14:22 *e.* them to con. in fai.
15:32 *e.* brethren with m. words
18:27 breth. wrote *e.* disciples
Heb. 10:25 but *e.* one anoth. and
1 *Pet.* 5:12 by S. I have written *e.*
1 *Thes.* 2:11 you know how we *e.*

EXILE.
2 *Sam.* 15:19 a stranger and an *e.*
Is. 51:14 captive *e.* hasteneth

EXORCISTS.
Acts 19:13 vagabond Jews, *e.*

EXPECTATION.
Ps. 9:18 *e.* of poor shall not **per.**
62:5 wait on G. my *e.* from **him**
Prov. 10:28 *e.* of wicked, 11:7
11:23 *e.* of the wicked is **wrath**
23:18 *e.* sh. not be cut off, 24:14
Is. 20:5 be ashamed of their *e.*
6 behold, such is our *e.*
Zec. 9:5 her *e.* shall be ashamed
Luke 3:15 as peo. were in *e.* J.
Acts 12:11 delivered fr. *e.* of Jews
Rom. 8:19 *e.* of creature waiteth
Phil. 1:20 my earnest *e.*

EXPECTED, ING.
Jer. 29:11 to give an *e.* end
Acts 3:5 *e.* to receive something
Heb. 10:13 *e.* enemies be made

EXPEDIENT.
John 11:50 *e.* for us one man die
16:7 *e.* for you that I go away
18:14 *e.* that one man die for pe.
1 *Cor.* 6:12 all things not *e.* 10:23
2 *Cor.* 8:10 *e.* for you who begun
12:1 it is not *e.* for me to glory

EXPEL, LED.
Jos. 13:13 Is. *e.* not Geshurites
23:5 G. shall *e.* them before you
Jud. 1:20 he *e.* three sons of A.
11:7 ye *e.* me out of house?
2 *Sam.* 14:14 his banish. be not *e.*
Acts 13:50 *e.* them out of coasts

EXPENSES.
Ezr. 6:4 *e.* be given out
8 I decree that *e.* be given to

EXPERIENCE.
Gen. 30:27 by *e.* the Lord blessed
Ec. 1:16 my heart had *e.* of wis.
Rom. 5:4 worketh *e.* and *e.*

EXPERIMENT.
2 *Cor.* 9:13 by *e.* of this minist.

EXPERT.
1 *Chr.* 12:33 Zeb. 50.000 *e.* in war
35 Danites *e.* in war: 36 Asher
Cant. 3:8 hold swords, *e.* in war
Jer. 50:9 shall be as *e.* man
Acts 26:3 know thee *e.* in custo.

EXPIRED.
1 *Sam.* 18:26 the days were not *e.*
2 *Sam.* 11:1 y. was *e.* 1 *Chr.* 20:1
1 *Chr.* 17:11 come wh. days be *e.*
2 *Chr.* 36:10 when year *e.* Neb.
Est. 1:5 when days were *e.*
Ezek. 43:27 when days are *e.*
Acts 7:30 forty years were *e.*
Rev. 20:7 1000 years *e.* S. loosed

EXPLOITS.
Dan. 11:28 he shall do *e.*
32 shall be strong and do *e.*

EXPOUND, ED.
Jud. 14:14 could not *e.* riddle
14:19 garments to them who *e.*
Mark 4:34 when alone *e.* all th.
Luke 24:27 *e.* to them all script.
Acts 11:4 but Peter *e.* it by order
18:26 Aq. and Pris. *e.* to him
28:23 Paul *e.* the kingdom of G.

EXPRESS.
Heb. 1:3 being *e.* image of person

EXPRESS, ED.
Num. 1:17 took men *e.* by names
1 *Chr.* 12:31 M. 18,000 *e.* by name
16:41 who were *e.* by name
2 *Chr.* 28:15 men *e.* took captives
31:19 *e.* to give portions
Ezr. 8:20 Nethinim *e.* by name

EXPRESSLY.
1 *Sam.* 20:21 if I *e.* say to the lad
Ezek. 1:3 word came *e.* to Ezek.
1 *Tim.* 4:1 Spirit speak. *e.* some

EXTEND, ED.
Ezr. 7:28 *e.* mercy; 9:9 to us
Ps. 109:12 be none to *e.* mercy
Is. 66:12 will *e.* peace like river

EXTENDETH.
Ps. 16:2 goodness *e.* not to thee

EXTINCT.
Job 17:1 my days are *e.*
Is. 43:17 are *e.* they quenched

EXTOL, LED.
Ps. 30:1 I will *e.* thee, O Lord
66:17 he was *e.* with my tongue
68:4 *e.* him that rideth on heav.
145:1 I will *e.* thee, my God
Is. 52:13 my servant shall be *e.*
Dan. 4:37 I Nebuchad. *e.* King

EXTORTION, ER, ERS.
Ps. 109:11 *e.* catch all he hath
Is. 16:4 *e.* at an end, the spoiler
Ezek. 22:12 has gained by *e.*
Mat. 23:35 they are full of *e.*
Luke 18:11 not as other men, *e.*
1 *Cor.* 5:10 not altogether with *e.*
11 if any be drunkard, an *e.*
6:10 nor *e.* inherit kingd. of G.

EXTREME.
Deut. 28:22 L. smite with *e.* burn.

EXTREMITY.
Job 35:15 knoweth not in great *e.*

EYE.
Ex. 21:24 *e.* for *e.* *Lev.* 24:20;
Deut. 19:21; *Mat.* 5:38
26 if man smite *e.* of servant
Lev. 21:20 hath blemish in *e.*
Deut. 28:54 his *e.* shall be evil

56 *e.* shall be evil to. husband
32:10 as apple of his *e.*
34:7 his *e.* was not dim
Ezr. 5:5 *e.* of God was on elders
Job 7:8 *e.* that hath seen me
10:18 and no *e.* had seen me
20:9 *e.* wh. saw sh. see no more
24:15 *e.* of adulterer waiteth for
twil. saying, No *e.* shall see
29:11 wh. *e.* saw me, it gave wi.
Ps. 33:18 *e.* of Lord on them
35:19 nei. let them with *e.*
21 aha, aha, our *e.* hath seen it
94:9 formed *e.* sh. he not see?
Prov. 10:10 winketh with the *e.*
20:12 the seeing *e.* L. hath made
22:9 bountif. *e.* shall be blessed
30:17 *e.* that mocketh at father
Ec. 1:8 *e.* not satisfied
4:8 neither *e.* satis. with riches
Is. 13:18 *e.* shall not spare child.
52:8 for they shall see *e.* to *e.*
64:4 nei. hath *e.* seen, 1 *Cor.* 2:9
Lam. 2:4 slew all pleasant to *e.*
Ezek. 9:5 let not your *e.* spare
Mic. 4:11 let our *e.* look on Zion
Mat. 6:22 light of the body is the
e. *Luke* 11:34
7:3 mote in brother's *e.* beam in
thine own *e.* *Luke* 6:41, 42
18:9 if *e.* offend thee pluck out
19:24 camel go thro' *e.* of needle,
Mark 10:25 ; *Luke* 18:25
1 *Cor.* 12:16 bec. I am not the *e.*
17 the whole body were an *e.*
21 *e.* cannot say
15:52 in twinkling of an *e.*
Rev. 1:7 every *e.* shall see him

Evil EYE.
Prov. 23:6 bread of him hath *e.* *e.*
28:22 hast. to be rich hath *e.* *e.*
Mat. 6:23 if *e.* be *e.* *Luke* 11:34
20:15 is thine *e.* *e.*
Mark 7:22 of heart proceed. *e.* *e.*

Mine EYE.
1 *Sam.* 24:10 *mine e.* spared thee
Job 7:7 *m. e.* shall no more see
13:1 *mine e.* hath seen all this
16:20 *mine e.* pour. tears to God
17:7 *mine e.* is dim by sorrow
42:5 but *mine e.* seeth thee
Ps. 6:7 *m. e.* con. with grief, 31:9
32:8 guide thee with *mine e.*
54:7 *mine e.* hath seen his desire
88:9 *mine e.* mourn. by reason
92:11 *mine e.* sh. see my desire
Lam. 1:16 *m. e.* *m. e.* run. 3:48
3:49 *mine e.* trickleth down
51 *mine e.* affecteth my heart
Ezek. 5:11 neith. sh. *m. e.* spare,
7:4, 9; 8:18; 9:10; 20:17

Thine EYE.
Deut. 7:16 *thine e.* sh. not pity,
13:8; 19:13, 21; 25:12
15:9 *thine e.* be evil ag. brother
Mat. 6:22 *t. e.* be sing. *Lu.* 11:34
7:3 beam in *th.* own *e.* *Luke* 6:41
18:9 *t. e.* offend. *Mark* 9:47

See APPLE.

EYEBROWS.
Lev. 14:9 shall shave hair off *e.*

EYELIDS.
Job 16:16 on mine *e.* is shadow
41:18 eyes like *e.* of the morning
Ps. 11:4 his *e.* try child. of men
132:4 or slumber to mine *e.*
Prov. 4:25 let thine *e.* look
6:4 or slumber to thine *e.*
25 neither let her take with *e.*
30:13 their *e.* are lifted up
Jer. 9:18 *e.* may gush with wat.

Right EYE.
Zec. 11:17 on his *r. e.* his *r. e.*
shall be utterly darkened
Mat. 5:29 if *r. e.* off. pluck it out

EYE-SALVE.
Rev. 3:18 anoint eyes with *e.-s.*

EYE-SERVICE.
Eph. 6:6 not with *e.-s. Col.* 3:22

EYESIGHT.
2 *Sam.* 22:25 accor. to my cleanness in his *e. Ps.* 18:24

EYE-WITNESSES.
Luke 1:2 from beginning *e.-w.*
2 *Pet.* 1:16 were *e.-w.* of majesty

EYED.
1 *Sam.* 18:9 Saul *e.* David

Tender EYED.
Gen. 29:17 Leah was *tender e.*

EYES.
Gen. 3:6 and pleasant to the *e.*
  7 *e.* of them both were opened
16:4 mistress was despised in *e.*
  5 I was despised in her *e.*
20:16 is to thee a covering of *e.*
21:19 God opened Hagar's *e.*
39:7 wife cast her *e.* on Joseph
Gen. 48:10 *e.* of Israel were dim
Ex. 5:21 abhorred in *e.* of Phar.
Lev. 4:13 hid from *e.* of assembly
26:16 burning ague sh. cons. *e.*
Num. 10:31 instead of *e.*
20:12 to sanctify me in *e.* of Is.
22:31 Lord opened *e.* of Balaam
24:3 man whose *e.* are open, 15
Deut. 16:19 doth blind *e.* of wise
28:65 L. shall give failing of *e.*
Jud. 16:28 avenged for two *e.*
2 *Sam.* 6:20 uncov. in *e.* of hand.
24:3 that *e.* of king may see it
1 *K.* 1:20 *e.* of all Isr. upon thee
2 *K.* 6:17 L. open *e.* of young m.
  20 Lord, open *e.* of these men
25:7 out *e.* of Z. *Jer.* 39:7; 52:11
1 *Chr.* 13:4 right in *e.* of people
Job 10:4 hast thou *e.* of flesh?
11:20 *e.* of the wicked shall fail
17:5 *e.* of his children shall fail
28:21 hid from the *e.* of all liv.
29:15 I was *e.* to the blind
31:16 caused *e.* of widow to fail
39:29 and her *e.* behold afar off
Ps. 15:4 in whose *e.* vile person
19:8 commandment enlighten *e.*
115:5 *e.* have they, 135:16
123:2 *e.* of servant, *e.* of maiden
145:15 *e.* of all wait upon thee
146:8 L. openeth *e.* of the blind
Prov. 10:26 as smo. to *e.* so slug.
15:30 light of *e.* rejoiceth heart
17:8 precious stone in *e.* of him
  24 *e.* of fool in ends of earth
23:29 who hath redness of *e.?*
27:20 *e.* of man are never satis.
Ec. 2:14 wise man's *e.* in head
6:9 better the sight of *e.* than
11:7 pleasant for *e.* to behold
Cant. 1:15 thou hast doves' *e.* 4:1
Is. 3:8 to provoke *e.* of his glory
  16 daugh. of Z. with wanton *e.*
5:15 *e.* of lofty shall be humbled
29:18 *e.* of the blind shall see
32:3 *e.* of them that see
35:5 then *e.* of blind sh. be ope.
42:7 open the blind *e.* to bring
43:8 blind that have *e.*
52:10 made bare his arm in *e.* of
59:10 grope as if we had no *e.*
Jer. 5:21 ha. *e.* see not, *Ezek.* 12:2
Ezek. 1:18 rings were full of *e.*
10:12 the wheels were full of *e.*
38:23 be known in *e.* of nations
Dan. 7:8 in horn *e.* like *e.* of man
  20 that had *e.* and a mouth
Hab. 1:13 purer *e.* than beh. evil
Zec. 3:9 upon one stone seven *e.*
8:6 marvellous in *e.* of remnant
Mat. 18:9 rather than hav. two *e.*
  cast into hell fire, *Mark* 9:47
Mark 8:18 having *e.* see ye not?

Luke 4:20 *e.* of all fast. on him
10:23 blessed are *e.* which see
John 9:6 anoint. *e.* of blind man
  32 opened *e.* of one born blind
10:21 can devil open *e.* of blind
Acts 9:40 Dorcas opened her *e.*
Rom. 11:8 given *e.* should not see
Gal. 3:1 before *e.* Christ been set
Eph. 1:18 *e.* of your understand.
Heb. 4:13 all things naked to *e.*
2 *Pet.* 2:14 *e.* full of adultery
1 *John* 2:16 lust of the *e.* and pri.
Rev. 4:6 four beasts full of *e.*
  8 and were full of *e.* within
5:6 a Lamb having seven *e.*

His EYES.
Gen. 27:1 Isaac, his *e.* were dim
49:12 *h. e.* sh. be red with wine
Num. 24:4 having *his e.* open, 16
Jud. 16:21 Philist. put out *his e.*
1 *Sam.* 3:2 Eli. *his e.* dim, 4:15
14:27 *his e.* were enlightened
1 *K.* 14:4 Ahijah, *his e.* were set
2 *K.* 4:34 child, put *his e.* on *h. e.*
  35 child sneezed, opened *his e.*
6:17 open *his e.* that he may see
25:7 slew sons of Zedekiah bef.
  his e. Jer. 39:6; 52:10
1 *Chr.* 21:23 k. do good in *his e.*
Est. 8:5 and I pleasing in *his e.*
Job 16:9 enemy sharpeneth *his e.*
21:20 *his e.* shall see his destruc.
24:23 *his e.* are on their ways
27:19 the rich man open. *his e.*
34:21 *h. e.* are on the ways of m.
36:7 he withdraweth not *his e.*
40:24 he taketh it with *his e.*
41:18 *his e.* are like eyelids of m.
Ps. 10:8 *his e.* set against poor
11:4 *h. e.* behold child. of men
36:1 no fear of God before *his e.*
66:7 *his e.* behold the nations
Prov. 6:13 he winketh with *his e.*
Prov. 16:30 he shut. *his e.* to dev.
20:8 scattereth evil with *his e.*
21:10 find no favor in *h. e.*
28:27 hid. *his e.* sh. have curse
Ec. 8:16 sleep with *his e.*
Cant. 5:12 *his e.* are as eyes of d
8:10 in *h. e.* as one that found
Is. 11:3 after sight of *his e.*
17:7 *his e.* have res. to holy One
33:15 shutteth *his e.* from seeing
Jer. 32:4 *his e.* shall behold *his e.*
20:7 cast away abomin. of *his e.*
Dan. 8:5 horn between *his e.* 21
10:6 *his e.* were as lamps of fire
Mark 8:23 he had spit on *his e.*
  25 after he put hands on *his e.*
John 9:14 and opened *his e.*
  21 or who hath opened *his e.*
Acts 3:4 P. fastening *his e.* upon
9:8 when *his e.* were opened
  18 there fell from *his e.* scales
13:9 then Saul set *his e.* on him
1 *John* 2:11 dark. hath blind. *h. e.*
Rev. 1:14 *his e.* as a flame of fire,
  2:18; 19:12

Lift or lifted up EYES.
Gen. 13:10 Lot *lifted up* his *e.*
  14 *lift up* th. *e.* and look, 31:12;
    Deut. 3:27; 2 *K.* 19:22; *Is.*
    49:18; 60:4; *Jer.* 3:2; *Ezek.*
    8:5; *Zec.* 5:5
18:2 Abra. *lift up* his *e.* 22:4, 13
24:63 Isaac; 64 Reb. *l. up* their
31:10 Ja. 33:1; 43:29 Jo. *l. u. e.*
Ex. 14:10 *lift up* their *e.* Egypt.
Num. 24:2 Balaam *lift up* his *e.*
Deut. 4:19 *l. u. e.* to heaven
Jos. 5:13 Joshua *lifted up* his *e.*
Jud. 19:17 old man *lift up* his *e.*
1 *Sam.* 6:13 *lift up* e. and saw ark
2 *Sam.* 13:34 watch. *l. u. e.* 18:24
1 *Chr.* 21:16 D. *l. up e.* saw angel
Job 2:12 they *lift up e.*

Ps. 121:1 I will *lift up* mine *e.*
123:1 to thee *lift* I *up* mine *e.*
Is. 51:6 *lift up* your *e. Ezek.*
  33:25; *John* 4:35
Ezek. 18:6 nor *l. up e.* to idols, 15
  12 hath *lift up* his *e.* to idols
Dan. 4:34 I Neb. *l. up* mine *e.*
8:3 *lifted up* mine *e.* 10:5; *Zec.*
  1:18; 2:1; 5:1, 5, 9; 6:1
Mat. 17:8 *l. up e.* saw no man
Luke 6:20 Jesus *lifted up* his *e.*
  John 6:5; 11:41; 17:1
16:23 in hell he *lift up* his *e.*
18:13 not *l. up* so much as *e.*

EYES of the Lord.
Gen. 6:8 N. found gr. in *e. of L.*
Deut. 11:12 *e. of the L.* alw. on it
13:18 do what is right in *e. of L.*
1 *Sam.* 26:24 life set by in *e. of L.*
1 *K.* 15:5 D. did right in *e. of the*
  Lord, 11; 22:43; 2 *Chr.* 14:2
2 *Chr.* 16:9 the *e. of the Lord* run
  to and fro. *Zec.* 4:10
Ps. 34:15 *e. of the Lord* are on the
  righteous, 1 *Pet.* 3:12
Prov. 15:3 *e. of L.* in every place
22:12 *e. of the L.* preserve kno.
Is. 49:5 glorious in *e.of the L.*
Amos 9:8 *e. of L.* are on sin. kin.

Mine EYES.
Gen. 31:40 sleep depart. fr. *m. e.*
44:21 I may set *mine e.* on him
1 *Sam.* 13:3 before to blind *m. e.*
14:29 how *mine e.* enlightened
26:24 life much set by in *m. e.*
1 *K.* 1:48 one to sit, *m. e.* see. it
9:3 mine *e.* shall be there per-
  petually, 2 *Chr.* 7:16
10:7 until *m. e.* seen it, 2 *Chr.* 9:6
11:33 to do that which is right
  in *m. e.* 14:8; 2 *K.* 10:30
2 *Chr.* 7:15 now *m. e.* sh. be open
Job 4:16 an image was bef. *m. e.*
19:27 mine *e.* shall behold
31:1 a covenant with *mine e.*
31:7 heart walked after *m. e.*
Ps. 13:3 lighten *mine e.*
25:15 *m. e.* are ever toward the
26:3 lov.-kindness is before *m. e.*
38:10 light of *m. e.* it is gone
69:3 *m. e.* fail, whilst I wait for
77:4 thou holdest *mine e.* wak.
101:3 no evil thing before *m. e.*
  6 *mine e.* shall be on faithful
116:8 hast deliv. *m. e.* from tears
119:18 open *m. e.;* 37 turn *m. e.*
  82 *mine e.* fail for thy word
123 *m. e.* fail for thy salvation
136 rivers of wa. run down *m. e.*
148 *m. e.* prev. night-watches
131:1 nor *mine e.* lofty
132:4 not give sleep to *mine e.*
Ps. 141:8 *m. e.* are unto thee, O G.
Ec. 2:10 whatso. *m. e.* desired
Is. 1:15 hide *mine e.* from you
  16 away evil doings from *m. e.*
6:5 *mine e.* have seen the King
38:14 *mine e.* fail with looking
65:12 did evil before *mine e.* 66:4
Jer. 9:1 *m. e.* were foun. of tears
13:17 *mine e.* shall weep sore
14:17 *m. e.* run down with tears
16:17 *m. e.* are on their ways, nor
  their iniq. hid from *mine e.*
24:6 I will set *mine e.* on them
Lam. 2:11 *m. e.* do fail with tears
Hos. 13:14 repent. hid from *m. e.*
Amos 9:4 set *mine e.* on them
Mic. 7:10 *mine e.* shall behold
Zec. 8:6 marvellous in *mine e.*
12:4 open *mine e.* on house of J.
Luke 2:30 mine *e.* have seen
John 9:11 J. anointed *mine e.* 15
  30 yet he hath opened *mine e.*
Acts 11:6 when I had fast. *m. e.*

Our EYES.
Num. 11:6 manna before *our e.*

Deut. 6:22 signs before *our e.*
21:7 nor have *our e.* seen it
2 *Chr.* 20:12 *our e.* are upon thee
Ezr. 9:8 our God lighten *our e.*
Ps. 118:23 marvellous in *our e.*
   Mat. 21:42; *Mark* 12:11
123:2 *our e.* wait upon Lord
Jer. 9:18 *our e.* run with tears
Lam. 4:17 *our e.* as yet failed
5:17 for these things *o. e.* are dim
Joel 1:16 meat cut before *our e.*
Mat. 20:33 that *our e.* be opened
1 *John* 1:1 have seen with *our e.*

Own EYES.

Num. 15:39 seek not after *own e.*
Deut. 12:8 what is right in his
   own e. Jud. 17:6 ; 21:25
Neh. 6:16 ene. cast down in *o. e.*
Job 32:1 because righteous in *o. e.*
Ps. 36:2 he flattereth him. in *o. e.*
Prov. 3:7 be not wise in *own e.*
12:15 way of fools is right in *o. e.*
16:2 ways of man clean in *o. e.*
21:2 way of man is right in *o. e.*
30:12 generat. pure in their *o. e.*
Is. 5:21 woe to them wise in *o. e.*
Gal. 4:15 would have plucked *o.e.*

Their EYES.

Gen. 42:24 bound S. before *t. e.*
Ex. 8:26 abom. of E. before *t. e.*
Lev. 20:4 any ways hide *their e.*
Num. 20:8 speak to rock bef. *t. e.*
27:14 sanctify at water bef. *t. e.*
Ezr. 3:12 founda. laid before *t. e.*
Job 21:8 offspring before *their e.*
Ps. 17:11 they have set *their e.*
69:23 let *their e.* be darkened
73:7 *their e.* stand out
Prov. 29:13 L. lighten. both *t. e.*
30:13 O how lofty are *their e.*
Ec. 5:11 behold. them with *t. e.*
Is. 6:10 shut *t. e.* lest see with *t.*
   e. Mat. 13:15; *Acts* 28:27
44:18 for he hath shut *their e.*
Jer. 14:6 *their e.* did fail because
Ezek. 6:9 with *t. e.* wh. go whor.
21:6 bitterness sigh before *t. e.*
22:26 hid *t. e.* from my sabbaths
24:25 desire of *their e.*
36:23 be sanctified before *t. e.*
37:20 sticks in thy hand bef. *t. e.*
38:16 sanctified, O Gog, bef. *t. e.*
Zec. 14:12 and *t. e.* shall consume
Mat. 9:29 touched he *their e.*

   30 *their e.* were opened
13:15 *their e.* they have closed

20:34 Jesus touched *their e. th.*
   e. received sight
26:43 *t. e.* were heavy, *Mk.* 14:40
Luke 24:16 *their e.* were holden
31 *their e.* were opened
John 12:40 he hath blinded *t. e.*
Acts 26:18 to open *t. e.* and to
Rom. 3:18 no fear of G. bef. *t. e.*
11:10 let *their e.* be darkened
Rev. 7:17 all tears from *t. e.* 21:4

Thine EYES.

Gen. 30:27 found favor in *thine e.*
46:4 J. put his hand on *thine e.*
47:19 shalt we die before *thine e.*
Ex. 13:9 memorial between *t. e.*
   16 frontlets betw. *t. e. Deut.* 6:8
Deut. 3:21 *thine e.* have seen all
27 lift up *t. e.* behold it with *t. e.*
4:9 forget things wh. *t. e.* have
7:19 temptations *t. e.* saw, 29:3
10:21 things which *thine e.* seen
28:31 shall be slain before *t. e.*
32 *thine e.* shail look, and fail
34 for the sight of *thine e.* 67
34:4 to see with *thine e.*

Ruth 2:9 let *t. e.* be on the field
10 have I found grace in *t. e. ?*
1 *Sam.* 2:33 to consume *thine e.*
24:10 *t. e.* seen how L. delivered
25:8 men find favor in *thine e.*
26:21 soul precious in *thine e.*
27:5 found grace in *thine e.*
2 *Sam.* 12:11 thy wives be. *t. e.*
22:28 *t. e.* are on the haughty
1 *K.* 8:29 *t. e.* open toward this
   house, 52 ; 2 *Chr.* 6:20, 40
20:6 is pleasant in *thine e.*
2 *K.* 7:2 thou shalt see it with *t. e.*
10:5 what is good in *thine e.*
19:16 open Lord *t. e. Is.* 37:17
22:20 *t. e.* shall not see all evil
1 *Chr.* 17:17 small thing in *t. e.*
2 *Chr.* 34:28 nor shall *thine e.* see
Neh. 1:6 let *thine e.* open
Job 7:8 *thine e.* are upon me
11:4 I am clean in *thine e.*
14:3 dost thou open *t. e.* on such?
15:12 what do *t. e.* wink at?
Ps. 31:22 cut off from be. *t. e.*
50:21 set in order before *t. e.*
91:8 with *t. e.* shalt thou behold
139:16 *t. e.* did see my substance
Prov. 4:25 let *thine e.* look right
6:4 give not sleep to *thine e.*
20:13 open *thine e.* and thou
23:5 set *t. e.* on that wh. is not ?

26 let *thine e.* observe my ways
33 *t. e.* shall beh. strange wom.
25:7 prince whom *t. e.* have seen
Ec. 11:9 walk in sight of *thine e.*
Cant. 4:9 ravished heart with *t. e.*
6:5 turn away *thine e.* from me
7:4 *thine e.* like the fish-pools
Is. 30:20 *t. e.* shall see teachers
33:17 *thine e.* shall see king
20 *t. e.* see Jeru. quiet habitat.
Jer. 5:3 are not *t. e.* on truth ?
20:4 fall by sword *t. e.* behold it
22:17 *t. e.* are not but for covet.
31:16 refrain *thine e.* from tears
32:19 *t. e.* open on ways of men
34:3 *t. e.* behold king of Bab.
42:2 as *thine e.* do behold us
Lam. 2:18 let not apple of *t. e.*
Ezek. 23:40 for wh. paintedst *t. e.*
24:16 take fr. thee desire of *t. e.*
40:4 behold with *thine e.* 44:5
Dan. 9:18 open *t. e.* and behold
Luke 19:42 now hid from *thine e.*
John 9:10 were *t. e.* opened ? 26
17 he hath opened *thine e. ?*
Rev. 3:18 anoint *thine e.*

Your EYES.

Gen. 3:5 day eat *y. e.* be opened
19:8 them as is good in *your e.*
34:11 Let me find grace in *y. e.*
12 *y. e.* and eyes of brother
50:4 found grace in *your e.*
Num. 33:55 *ye* let remain shall
   be pricks in *y. e. Jos.* 23:13
Deut. 1:30 that he did before *y. e.*
   4:34 ; 29:2
4:3 *your e.* have seen what Lord
   did, 11:7 ; *Jos.* 24:7
9:17 I brake two tables bef. *y. e.*
11:18 as frontlets between *y. e.*
14:1 not make boldness bet. *y. e.*
1 *Sam.* 11:2 thrust out *y.* right *e.*
12:16 what Lord do before *y. e.*
2 *Chr.* 29:8 as see with *your e.*
Is. 29:10 Lord hath closed *y. e.*
40:26 lift up *y. e. Jer.* 13:20
Jer. 7:11 den of robbers in *y. e.*
29:21 slay them before *your e.*
Ezek. 24:21 the desire of *your e.*
Hag. 2:3 in *your e.* in comparison
Mal. 1:5 *your e.* shall see, the L.
Mat. 13:16 blessed are *your e.*

EZEKIEL.   *Ezek.* 24:24
EZEL.   1 *Sam.* 20:19
EZRA.   *Ezr.* 7:12, 25 ; 10:1 : *Neh.*
   8:2, 6 ; 12:13, 26, 36

F

FABLES.

1 *Tim.* 1:4 nor give heed to *f.*
4:7 but refuse old wives' *f.*
2 *Tim* 4:4 shall be turned unto *f.*
Tit. 1:14 not giving heed to *f.*
2 *Pet.* 1:16 cunningly devised *f.*

FACE.

Gen. 3:19 in sweat of *f.* shall eat
16:8 I flee from *f.* of mistress
24:47 I put ear-rings upon her *f.*
35:1 fleddest from *f.* of Esau, 7
36:6 E. went from *f.* of brot. J.
46:28 to direct his *f.* to Goshen
48:12 J. bowed with *f.* to earth
Ex. 2:15 Moses fled *f.* of Pharaoh
14:25 let us flee from *f.* of Israel
34:29 skin of his *f.* shone, 30, 35

Ex. 34:33 he put a veil on his *f.*
Lev. 13:41 hair fallen tow. his *f.*
19:32 shalt honor *f.* of old man
Num. 12:14 father had spit in *f.*
19:3 slay red heifer before *f.*
Deut. 1:17 not be af. of *f.* of man
8:20 nations L. destroyed bef. *f.*

25:2 wicked be beaten bef. his *f.*
9 and spit in his *f.* and say
28:31 ass sh. be taken bef. thy *f.*
Jos. 7:10 wheref. liest upon *f. ?*
1 *Sam.* 5:3 D. falleth on his *f.* 4
24:8 D. stooped with *f.* to earth
25:41 Abigail bowed on *f.*
28:14 stooped with *f.* to ground
2 *Sam.* 2:22 hold up my *f.* to J. ?
14:33 A. bowed on *f.* to ground
24:20 Araunah bowed himself
   bef. king on *f.* 1 *Chr.* 21:21
1 *K.* 1:23 Nathan bowed with *f.*
31 B.-sheba bowed with her *f.*
8:14 turned his *f.* 2 *Chr.* 6:3
18:42 E. put *f.* between knees
19:13 wrapped his *f.* in mantle
20:38 prophet disg. ashes on *f.*
21:4 Ahab turned away his *f.*
2 *K.* 4:29 lay staff on *f.* of child
31 G. laid his staff on *f.* of child
8:15 Hazael spread it on his *f.*
9:30 Jezebel painted her *f.*
32 J. lifted up his *f.* to window
13:14 Joash wept over his *f.*

20:2 H. turn. *f.* to wall, *Is.* 38:2
2 *Chr.* 6:42 turn not away the *f.*
   of thine anointed, *Ps.* 132:10
30:9 L. will not turn *f.* from you
32:21 returned with shame of *f.*
35:22 Jos. would not turn his *f.*
Ezr. 9:6 I blush to lift up my *f.*
7 confusion of *f. Dan.* 9:8
Job 1:11 will curse thee to *f.* 2:5
4:15 a spirit passed before my *f.*
11:15 lift up *f.* without spot
16:8 leanness beareth wit. to *f.*
16 my *f.* is foul with weeping
21:31 who declare his way to *f. ?*
22:26 lift up thy *f.* unto God
24:15 and disguiseth his *f.*
26:9 he holdeth back *f.* of throne
30:10 spare not to spit in my *f.*
41:13 who discover *f.* of garm. ?
14 can open doors of his *f. ?*
Ps. 5:8 way straight before my *f.*
17:15 I will beh. thy *f.* in right.
21:12 make ready arrows ag. *f.*
41:12 set. me before thy *f.*
84:9 look upon *f.* of th. anoint.

89:14 mercy and truth go bef. *f.*
Prov. 7:13 with an impudent *f.*
21:29 wicked man hard. his *f.*
Ec. 8:1 boldness of *f.* be chang.
Is. 16:4 the *f.* of the spoiler
25:7 will destroy *f.* of covering
28:25 made plain the *f.* thereof
29:22 nei. shall his *f.* wax pale
49:23 shall bow to thee with *f.*
65:3 that provoketh me to my *f.*
Jer. 2:27 turn. back, not *f.* 32:33
4:30 thou rentest *f.* with paint
13:26 thy skirts upon thy *f.* that
    shame may appear, *Nah.* 3:5
18:17 the back, and not the *f.*
22:25 whose *f.* thou fearest
Lam. 3:35 right of man before *f.*
Ezek. 1:10 *f.* of man, *f.* of lion, *f.*
    of an ox, the *f.* of an eagle
3:8 made thy *f.* strong ag. faces
7:22 my *f.* will I turn fr. them
10:14 *f.* of man, lion, eag. 41:19
14:3 stumbling-block before *f.*
38:18 fury shall come in my *f.*
Dan. 8:18 in a sleep on *f.* 10:9
10:6 *f.* as appear. of lightning
11:18 turn *f.* unto the isles
Hos. 5:5 Is. testifieth to *f.* 7:10
Joel 2:6 before *f.* people be pain.
20 will drive him with his *f.*
Nah. 2:1 hateth come before *f.*
Mat. 6:17 anoint head, wash *f.*
11:10 I send my messenger bef.
    thy *f. Mark* 1:2; *Luke* 7:27
18:10 angels behold *f.* of my F.
26:67 did they spit in his face
Luke 2:31 hast prepared bef. *f.*
9:52 messengers before *f.* 10:1
53 *f.* as tho' he would go to J.
22:64 they struck him on the *f.*
John 11:44 *f.* bound with napkin
Acts 2:25 I foresaw L. bef. my *f.*
7:45 G. drave before *f.* of fath.
1 *Cor.* 14:25 falling down on *f.*
2 *Cor.* 3:7 could not behold *f.*
13 M. who put a veil over *f.*
18 with open *f.* beholding
4:6 glory of God in *f.* of Jesus
11:20 if man smite you on *f.*
Gal. 1:22 unkn. by *f.* to churches
2:11 I withstood him to the *f.*
Jam. 1:23 natural *f.* in glass
Rev. 4:7 beast had *f.* as a man
10:1 *f.* was as it were the sun
12:14 nourished from *f.* of serp.
20:11 from whose *f.* heaven fled

See SEEK, SET, SHINE, SKY, WATERS, WILDERNESS, WORLD.

FACE, *with* **cover,** *or* **covered.**
Gen. 38:15 harlot bec. she c. *f.*
Ex. 10:5 locusts c. *f.* of earth, 15
Num. 22:5 *cover f.* of the earth
2 *Sam.* 19:4 c. his *f.* and cried
Est. 7:8 covered Haman's *f.*
Job 15:27 c. his *f.* with fatness
23:17 c. darkness from my *f.*
Ps. 44:15 shame of my *f.* hath c.
69:7 shame cov. my *f.*
Prov. 24:31 nettles had c. *f.*
Is. 6:2 with twain he c. *f.*
Ezek. 12:6 thou shalt c. thy *f.*
12 the prince shall c. his *f.*
Mark 14:65 to spit and c. his *f.*

FACE of the country.
2 *Sam.* 18:8 scattered over *f.* of c.

FACE of the deep.
Gen. 1:2 darkness upon *f.* of t. d.
Job 38:30 *f.* of the deep is frozen
Prov. 8:27 compass on *f.* of the d.

FACE of the earth.
Gen. 1:29 herb on *f.* of the earth
4:14 driven me from *f.* of the e.
6:1 multiply on *f.* of the earth
7:3 seed alive on *f.* of all the e.
4 destroy from *f.* of the e. *Deut.*
6:15; 1 *K.* 13:34; *Amos* 9:8

8:9 on the *f.* of the whole *earth*
11:4 we be scat. on *f.* of the e.
41:56 famine over the *f.* of the e.
Num. 12:3 abo. all on *f.* of the e.
Deut. 7:6 peo. on the *f.* of the e.
1 *Sam.* 20:15 off from *f.* of the e.
Ps. 104:30 renewest *f.* of the e.
Is. 23:17 kingd. on *f.* of the earth
Jer. 8:2 on the *f.* of the e. 16:4
Ezek. 38:20 all on *f.* of the earth
Dan. 8:5 came on *f.* of the earth
Amos 5:8 pour. on *f.* of the e. 9:6
Zec. 5:3 curse over *f.* of the earth
Luke 12:56 can discern *f.* of the e.
21:35 on the *f.* of the whole e.
Acts 17:26 to dwell on *f.* of the e.

Gen. 32:30 I have seen G. *f.* to *f.*
Ex. 33:11 L. spake to M. *f.* to *f.*
Num. 14:14 Lord art seen *f.* to *f.*
Deut. 5:4 talked with you *f.* to *f.*
34:10 M. whom L. knew *f.* to *f.*
Jud. 6:22 seen angel *f.* to *f.*
Prov. 27:19 *f.* answereth to *f.*
Ezek. 20:35 I will plead *f.* to *f.*
Acts 25:16 have accusers *f.* to *f.*
1 *Cor.* 13:12 a glass, but *f.* to *f.*
2 *John* 12 and speak *f.* to *f.*
3 *John* 14 and speak *f.* to *f.*

Fell on FACE, or FACES.
Gen. 50:1 J. *f.* on his father's *f.*
18 brethren *fell* b. before his *f.*
Lev. 9:24 they *fell* on their *f.*
Num. 14:5 A. *f.* on *f.* 16:22, 45
16:4 Moses; 22:31 B. *f.* flat on *f.*
Jos. 5:14 Joshua *f.* on his *f.* 7:6
Jud. 13:20 M. and wife *fell* on *f.*
1 *Sam.* 17:49 Gol.; 20:41 D. *f.* on *f.*
25:23 Abig.; 2 *Sam.* 9:6 Mephib.
2 *Sam.* 14:4 wo. of T. *f.* on her *f.*
22 Joab; 18:28 Ahimaaz *f.* on *f.*
1 *K.* 18:7 Obad.; 39 peo. *f.* on *f.*
Ezek. 1:28 *f.* on my *f.* 3:23; 9:8;
11:13; 43:3; 44:4; *Dan.* 8:17
Dan. 2:46 Nebuch. *f.* upon his *f.*
Mat. 17:6 disci.; 26:39 J. *f.* on *f.*
Luke 5:12 leper; 17:16 S. *f.* on *f.*
Rev. 11:16 24 elders *f.* on their *f.*

FACE of the field.
2 *K.* 9:37 Jez. dung on *f.* of the *f.*

FACE of the gate.
Ezek. 40:15 *f.* of the g. of entrance

FACE of the ground.
Gen. 2:6 mist watered *f.* of the g.
7:23 destr. that was on *f.* of the g.
8:8 abated from off *f.* of the g.
13 *f.* of the ground was dry

Hide, hideth, *or* **hid FACE.**
Gen. 4:14 from thy *f.* sh. I be *h.*
Ex. 3:6 and Moses *hid* his *f.*
Deut. 31:17 *hid* my *f.* 18; 32:20
Job 13:24 wherefore *hidest* thou
    thy *f. Ps.* 44:24; 88:14
Ps. 10:11 he *hideth* his *f.*
13:1 how long wilt *hide* thy *f.*
27:9 *h.* not *f.* 69:17; 102:2; 143:7
30:7 didst *hide* thy *f.* 104:29
51:9 *hide* thy *f.* from my sins
Is. 8:17 h. his *f.* from house of J.
Is. 50:6 I *hid* not my *f.* from sh.
54:8 in wrath I *hid* my *f.*
59:2 sins have *h.* his *f.* from you
64:7 thou hast *hid* thy *f.*
Jer. 16:17 not *hid* from my *f.*
33:5 *hid* my *f.* from city
Ezek. 39:23 *h.* I my *f.* fr. them, 24
29 nor will I *hide* my *f.*
Mic. 3:4 he will *h. f.* at that time
Rev. 6:16 *hide* us from *f.* of him

FACE of the house.
Ezek. 41:14 breadth of *f.* of house

FACE of the Lord.
Gen. 19:13 cry before *f.* of the L.
1 *Sam.* 26:20 blood before *f.* of L.
1 *K.* 13:6 entreat *f.* of the Lord

Ps. 34:16 *f.* of the Lord against
    them that do evil, 1 *Pet.* 3:12
Lam. 2:19 heart before *f.* of L.
Luke 1:76 go before *f.* of Lord

FACE of the porch.
Ezek. 40:15 *f.* of the p. 50 cubits
41:15 thick planks on *f.* of the p.

FACE, *with* **look, see, seen,**
Gen. 32:20 afterw. I will *s.* his *f.*
33:10 therefore have I *s.* thy *f.*
43:3 shall not *s.* my *f.* 5; 44:23
46:30 let me die since I have *s. f.*
48:11 not thought to *see* thy *f.*
Ex. 10:28 *see* my *f.* no more
29 Moses said, I will *see* thy *f.*
33:20 thou canst not *see* my *f.*
23 but my *f.* shall not be seen
34:35 children of Is. *s. f.* of M.
2 *Sam.* 14:28 two y.s. not king's *f.*
2 *K.* 14:8 let us *look* one another
    in the *f.* 2 *Chr.* 25:17
11 *looked* one another in the *f.*
Est. 1:14 7 princes w. *s.* king's *f.*
Acts 6:15 *saw* his *f.* as *f.* of angel
20:25 sh. *see* my *f.* no more, 38
Col. 2:1 as have not *seen* my *f.*
Rev. 22:4 they shall *see* his *f.*

Seek FACE.
1 *Chr.* 16:11 *seek* his *f. Ps.* 105:4
2 *Chr.* 7:14 if my people *s.* my *f.*
Ps. 24:6 that *seek* thy *f.* O Jacob
27:8 s. ye my *f.* thy *f.* L. will I *s.*
Prov. 7:15 I came to *seek* thy *f.*
Hos. 5:15 till they *seek* my *f.*

Set FACE.
Gen. 31:21 J. *set f.* to mount Gil.
Lev. 17:10 *set f.* against soul, 20:6
20:3 *set f.* ag. that m. 5; *Eze.* 14:8
26:17 *set* my *f.* aga. *Jer.* 44:11
Is. 50:7 have *set* my *f.* like flint
Jer. 21:10 *set* my *f.* ag. this city
Ezek. 4:3 *set* my *f.* against it
6:2 *set* thy *f.* tow. mountains
13:17 *set* thy *f.* ag. daughters
15:7 *set* my *f.* against them
20:46 *set* thy *f.* toward the south
21:2 *set* thy *f.* toward Jerusalem
16 whithersoever thy *f.* is *set*
28:21 *f.* ag. Zidon; 29:2 *f.* ag. P.
35:2 *f.* ag. mount S.; 38:2 *f.* a. G.
Dan. 9:3 I *set* my *f.* to Lord God
10:15 *set* my *f.* toward ground
11:17 he shall *set* his *f.* to enter
Luke 9:51 *set f.* to go to Jerusa.

FACE shine.
Num. 6:25 L. make *f.* to *s.* on thee
Ps. 31:16 make thy *f.* to *shine* on
    thy servant, 119:135
67:1 cause his *f.* to *shine* on us
80:3 cause thy *f.* to *shine*, 7, 19
104:15 to make his *f.* to *shine*
Ec. 8:1 maketh his *f.* to *shine*
Dan. 9:17 cause thy *f.* to *shine*
Mat. 17:2 his *f.* did *shine* as sun

FACE of the sky.
Mat. 16:3 disc. the *f. f. Luke* 12:56

FACE of the waters.
Gen. 1:2 S. of G. mov. *f.* of w.
7:18 ark went upon *f.* of the w.

FACE of the wilderness.
Ex. 16:14 on *f.* of the w. lay

FACE of the world.
Job 37:12 command. on *f.* of w.
Is. 14:21 nor fill *f.* of w.
27:6 Israel fill *f.* of w. with fruit

FACES.
Gen. 9:23 their *f.* were backward
Ex. 19:7 Moses laid before th. *f.*
20:20 his fear be before your *f.*
25:20 *f.* shall look one to anoth.
37:9 mercy-seat-ward *f.* of cher.
2 *Sam.* 19:5 shamed *f.* of serv.
1 *K.* 2:15 all Israel set *f.* on me
1 *Chr.* 12:8 *f.* were like *f.* of lions

2 *Chr.* 3:13 their *f.* were inward
Job 9:24 he covereth *f.* of judges
40:13 and bind their *f.* in secret
Ps. 34:5 *f.* were not ashamed
Is. 3:15 that ye grind *f.* of poor
13:8 their *f.* shall be as flames
25:8 will wipe tears from all *f.*
53:3 hid as it were our *f.* from
Jer. 1:8 be not afraid of their *f.*
5:3 their *f.* harder than a rock
30:6 all *f.* turned into paleness
42:15 set *f.* to enter, 17 ; 44:12
50:5 Zion, with *f.* thitherward
Lam. 5:12 *f.* of elders not hon.
Ezek. 1:6 ev. one four *f.* 10, 11, 15
7:18 shame shall be on their *f.*
8:16 with *f.* toward the east
14:6 turn *f.* from abominations
20:47 all *f.* shall be burnt
41:18 every cherub had two *f.*
Dan. 9:7 unto us confusion of *f.*
Joel 2:6 *f.* shall gather blackness
Hab. 1:9 *f.* shall sup up as east w.
Mal. 2:3 I will spread dung on *f.*
Mat. 6:16 hypocrites disfigure *f.*
Luke 24:5 have bowed *f.* to earth
Rev. 7:11 fell before throne on *f.*
9:7 *f.* of locusts as *f.* of men

See Fell on FACE, or FACES.

FADE.

2 *Sam.* 22:46 strangers shall *f.*
away, *Ps.* 18:45
Is. 64:6 and we all *f.* as a leaf
Jer. 8:13 and the leaf shall *f.*
Ezek. 47:12 who. leaf shall not *f.*
Jam. 1:11 rich man shall *f.* away

FADETH.

Is. 1:30 as an oak, whose leaf *f.*
24:4 and *f.* the world *f.*
40:7 grass withereth, flower *f.* 8
1 Pet. 1:4 inheritance *f.* not away
5:4 cro. of glory that *f.* not aw.

FADING.

Is. 28:1 glorious beauty *f.* flow.
4 beauty shall be *f.* flower

FAIL, Substantive.

Jos. 3:10 without *f.* drive Can.
Jud. 11:30 without *f.* deliver A.
Ezr. 6:9 day by day without *f.*

FAIL, Verb.

Gen. 47:16 cattle, if money *f.*
Deut. 28:32 eyes *f.* with longing
31:6 he will not *f.* thee, 8 ; *Jos.*
1:5 ; *1 Chr.* 28:20
1 Sam. 17:32 no man's heart *f.*
20:5 sho. not *f.* to sit with king
1 K. 2:4 shall not *f.* man on thron.
of Isr. 8:25 ; 9:5 ; *2 Chr.* 6:16
17:14 neith. sh. cruse of oil *f.* 16
Est. 6:10 let nothing *f.* of all
9:27 not *f.* keep days of P. 28
Job 11:20 eyes of wicked shall *f.*
14:11 as waters *f.* from the sea
17:5 eyes of his children sh. *f.*
31:16 caused eyes of wid. to *f.*
Ps. 12:1 faithful *f.* fr. am. men
69:3 mine eyes *f.* while I wait
77:8 doth his promise *f.* for ever
119:82 mine eyes *f.* for thy word
123 mine eyes *f.* for thy salva.
Prov. 22:8 rod of his anger sh. *f.*
Ec. 12:5 desire *f.* man goeth
Is. 19:5 wat. *f.* ; 21:16 gl. of K. *f.*
31:3 they all shall *f.* togeth
32:6 cause drink of thirsty to *f.*
10 for the vintage shall *f.*
34:16 no one of these shall *f.*
38:14 mine eyes *f.* with looking
42:4 not *f.* nor be discouraged
57:16 spirit should *f.* before me
58:11 spring whose waters *f.* not
Jer. 14:6 eyes did *f.* bec. no gra.
15:18 as waters that *f.* *f.*
48:33 wine to *f.* *Hos.* 9:2
Lam. 2:31 mine eyes *f.* with tea.
3:22 because compassions *f.* not

Hab. 3:17 labor of olive shall *f.*
Luke 16:9 ye *f.* they may receive
17 one tittle of the law to *f.*
22:32 that thy faith *f.* not
1 Cor. 13:8 prophecies they sh. *f.*
Heb. 1:12 thy years shall not *f.*
11:32 time would *f.* me to tell
12:15 any man *f.* of grace of G.

FAILED.

Gen. 42:28 their heart *f.* them
47:15 money *f.* in land of Egypt
Jos. 3:16 waters *f.* were cut off
21:45 *f.* not any good which L.
promised, 23:14 ; *1 K.* 8:56
Job 19:14 my kinsfolk have *f.*
Ps. 142:4 refuge *f.* no man cared
Cant. 5:6 soul *f.* when he spake
Lam. 4:17 our eyes as yet *f.*

FAILETH.

Gen. 47:15 who. we die ? money *f.*
Job 21:10 gendereth and *f.* not
Ps. 31:10 strength *f.* me, 38:10
40:12 my heart *f.* me, 73:26
71:9 forsake not when strength
109:24 my flesh *f.* of fatness
143:7 O Lord, my spirit *f.*
Ec. 10:3 wisdom *f.* him
Is. 15:6 grass *f.* no green thing
41:17 their tongue *f.* for thirst
44:12 hungry and his strength *f.*
Ezek. 12:22 and every vision *f.*
Luke 12:33 treas. in heaven *f.* not
1 Cor. 13:8 charity never *f.* but

FAILING.

Deut. 28:65 L. shall give *f.* of ey.
Luke 21:26 men's heart *f.* for fe.

FAIN.

Job 27:22 *f.* flee out of his hand
Luke 15:16 *f.* filled belly

FAINT, Adjective.

Gen. 25:29 E. and he was *f.* 30
Deut. 25:18 when thou wast *f.*
Jud. 8:4 *f.* yet pursuing them
1 Sam. 14:28 peo. were very *f.* 31
30:10 so *f.* could not go over, 21
2 Sam. 16:2 such as be *f.*
Is. 1:5 the whole heart is *f.*
13:7 shall all hands be *f.*
29:8 awaketh, behold he is *f.*
40:29 he giveth power to the *f.*
Jer. 8:18 my heart is *f.*
Lam. 5:17 for this our heart is *f*

FAINT, Verb.

Deut. 20:3 let not your hearts *f.*
8 lest his brethren's heart *f.*
Jos. 2:9 inhabitants of land *f.*
Prov. 24:10 *f.* in day of adversity
Is. 40:30 shall *f.* *Amos* 8:13
31 walk and not *f.*
Jer. 51:46 and lest your hearts *f.*
Lam. 2:19 young children *f.*
Ezek. 21:7 every spirit shall *f.*
15 their heart may *f.*
Mat. 15:32 fasting, lest they *f.*
Mark 8:3 away fasting, will *f.*
Luke 18:1 to pray, not to *f.*
2 Cor. 4:1 rec. mercy we *f.* not
16 for which cause we *f.* not
Gal. 6:9 shall reap, if we *f.* not
Eph. 3:13 *f.* not at my tribula.
5 nor *f.* when rebuked of him

FAINTED.

Gen. 45:26 Jacob's heart *f.*
Ps. 27:13 *f.* unl. I had believed
107:5 their soul *f.* in them
Is. 51:20 thy sons *f.* they lie
Jer. 45:3 I *f.* in my sighing
Ezek. 31:15 trees of field *f.*
Dan. 8:27 I Daniel *f.*
Jon. 2:7 soul *f.* I rememb. Lord
4:8 *f.* and wished in him. to die
Mat. 9:36 comp. on them bec. *f.*
Rev. 2:3 labored, and hast not *f.*

FAINTEST, ETH.

Job 4:5 upon thee, and thou
Ps. 84:2 soul *f.* for courts of L.
119:81 my soul *f.* for saivation
Is. 10:18 a standard-bearer *f.*
40:28 ends of earth *f.* not

FAINT-HEARTED.

Deut. 20:8 and *f.* let him return
Is. 7:4 nor be *f.* for the two tails
Jer. 49:23 H. and Arpad are *f.*

FAINTNESS.

Lev. 26:36 send *f.* into hearts

FAIR.

Gen. 6:2 daugh. of men were *f.*
12:11 Sar. *f.* 14 ; 24:16 R. 26:7
2 Sam. 13:1 Tamar was *f.* 14:27
1 K. 1:4 Abishag a *f.* damsel
Est. 1:11 Vashti *f.* ; 2:7 Est. *f.*
2:2 *f.* young virgins be sought
Job 37:22 *f.* weather cometh out
42:15 so *f.* as Job's daughters
Prov. 7:21 with *f.* speech
11:22 *f.* woman with. discretion
26:25 when he speaketh *f.*
Cant. 1:15 thou art *f.* 16 ; 4:1, 7
2:10 my love, my *f.* one, 13
4:10 *f.* is thy love, my *f.* sister
6:10 *f.* as moon ; 7:6 *f.* art thou
Is. 5:9 many houses great and *f.*
54:11 lay stones with *f.* colors
Jer. 11:16 and olive-tree *f.*
12:6 though they speak *f.* words
46:20 Egypt like a very *f.* heifer
Ezek. 16:17 hast taken *f.* jewels
39 shall take *f.* jewels, 23:26
31:3 cedar in L. with *f.* branches
7 *f.* in his greatness
9 made him *f.* by multitude
Dan. 4:12 leaves were *f.* 21
Amos 8:13 *f.* virgins shall faint
Zec. 3:5 let them set a *f.* mitre
Mat. 16:2 it will be *f.* weather
Acts 7:20 Moses was exceeding *f.*
Rom. 16:18 *f.* speeches deceive
Gal. 6:12 make *f.* show in flesh

FAIRER, EST.

Jud. 15:2 younger sist. *f.* than
Ps. 45:2 *f.* than child. of men
Cant. 1:8 O *f.* am. wo. 5:9 ; 6:1
Dan. 1:15 countenances app. *f.*

FAIR-HAVENS.

Acts 27:8 place called the *f.-h.*

FAIRS.

Ezek. 27:12 tra. in *f.* 14, 16, 19, 22
27 thy *f.* shall fall into the seas

FAITH.

Deut. 32:20 in whom is no *f.*
Mat. 6:30 O ye of little *f.* 8:26;
14:31 ; 16:8 ; *Luke* 12:28
8:10 great *f.* no not, *Luke* 7:9
17:20 *f.* as grain of mustard seed
23:23 judgment, mercy, and *f.*
Mark 4:40 ye have no *f.* ?
11:22 Jesus saith, Have *f.* in G.
Luke 17:5 Lord increase our *f.*
6 if ye had *f.* ye might say
18:8 wh. S. of man com. fi. *f.* ?
Acts 6:5 Ste. a man full of *f.* 8
7 priests were obedie. to the *f.*
11:24 Barnabas good, full of *f.*
13:8 seek. to turn deputy fr. *f.*
14:9 that he had *f.* to be healed
22 exhorting to continue in *f.*
27 opened door of *f.* to Genti.
16:5 churches established in *f.*
20:21 *f.* toward our L. Jesus C.
24:24 Felix heard P. concern. *f.*
Rom. 1:5 obedience to *f.*
17 righter. of G. rev. fr. *f.* to *f.*
3:3 make *f.* of God without ef.
27 excluded by law of *f.*
4:5 *f.* counted for righteous. 9
11 circum. seal of righte. of *f.*
12 steps of that *f.* of Abraham
13 through righteous. of *f.*

14 they of law be heirs *f*. is **v.**
16 of *f*. of the *f*. of Abraham
9:30 righte. which is of *f*. 10:6
10:8 word of *f*. which we prea.
17 so then *f*. cometh by hear.
12:3 God dealt measure of *f*.
6 according to proportion of *f*.'
14:22 hast thou *f*. ?
23 eat. not of *f*. not of *f*. is sin
16:26 for the obedience of *f*.
1 *Cor*. 12:9 another *f*. by same S.
13:2 though I have all *f*.
13 now abideth *f*. hope, charl.
Gal. 1:23 *f*. which once destroy.
3:2 or by the hearing of *f*. 5
7 they which are of *f*. 9
12 law is not of *f*. but man
23 before *f*. came; 25 *f*. is co.
5:6 *f*. which worketh by love
22 fruit of Sp. is love, joy, *f*.
6:10 are of the household of *f*.
Eph. 4:5 one L. one *f*. one bapt.
13 come in the unity of the *f*.
6:16 taking the shield of *f*.
Phil. 1:25 further. and joy of *f*.
27 striving tog. for *f*. of gospel
1 *Thes*. 1:3 rememb. work of *f*.
5:8 the breastplate of *f*.
2 *Thes*. 1:11 work of *f*. with pow.
3:2 for all men have not *f*.
1 *Tim*. 1:5 *f*. unfeigned
19 holding *f*. concerning *f*.
3:9 holding the mystery of *f*.
4:1 some shall depart fr. the *f*.
5:8 he hath denied the *f*. and is
12 have cast off their first *f*.
6:10 have erred from the *f*. 21
11 follow *f*.; 12 fight fight of *f*.
2 *Tim*. 1:5 unfeigned *f*. in thee
2:18 overthrow the *f*. of some
22 follow *f*.; 3:8 reprobate *f*.
3:10 thou hast fully known *f*.
4:7 have kept the *f*. henceforth
Tit. 1:1 the *f*. of God's elect
4 T. mine own son aft. com. *f*.
Phile. 5 hearing of thy *f*.
Heb. 4:2 not mixed with *f*.
6:1 not laying the foundat. of *f*.
10:22 in full assurance of *f*.
23 hold fast profession of *f*.
11:1 *f*. is substance of things
6 without *f*. impossi. to pl. G.
12:2 and finisher of our *f*.
13:7 whose *f*. follow, consider.
Jam. 2:1 *f*. with respect of pers.
14 he hath *f*. can *f*. save him ?
17 *f*. with. works is dead, 20, 26
18 hast *f*. and I have works
22 *f*. wrought with works, and
by works was *f*. made perf.
5:15 prayer of *f*. shall save sick
2 *Pet*. 1:1 obtained like prec. *f*.
1 *John* 5:4 overcome. wor. our *f*.
Jude 3 earnestly contend for *f*.
Jude 20 building yours. on h. *f*.
Rev. 2:13 hast not denied my *f*.
19 I know thy works and *f*.
13:10 patience and *f*. of saints
14:12 that keep the *f*. of Jesus

By FAITH.

Hab. 2:4 shall live *by f*. *Rom*.
1:17; *Gal*. 3:11; *Heb*. 10:38
Acts 15:9 purifying hearts *by f*.
26:18 sanctified *by f*.
Rom. 3:28 righteous. of G. *by f*.
28 justi. *b*. *f*. 5:1; *Gal*. 2:16; 3:24
30 justify circumcision *by f*.
5:2 we have access *by f*.
11:20 standest *by f*. 2 *Cor*. 1:24
2 *Cor* 5:7 walk *by f*. not by sight
Gal. 2:20 I live *by f*. of S. of God
8:22 promise *by f*. might be giv.
26 child. of G. *by f*. in Chr. J.
5:5 hope of righteousness *by f*.
Eph. 3:12 we have access *by f*.
17 C. may dwell in hearts *by f*.
Phil. 3:9 righteousn of G. *by f*.

Heb. 11:4 *by f*. Abel; 5 *by f*. En.
7 *by f*. Noah; 8 *by f*. Ara. 9, 17
20 *by f*. Isaac; 21 Jac. ; 22 Jos.
23 *by f*. Moses, 24:27; 31 Rah.
29 *by f*. passed through Red s.
30 *by f*. walls of Jer. fell down
Jam. 2:24 works justi. not *by f*.

In FAITH.

Rom. 4:19 being not weak *in f*.
20 but was strong *in f*.
14:1 him weak *in f*. receive you
1 *Cor*. 16:13 stand fast *in f*.
2 *Cor*. 13:5 exam. wh. ye be *in f*.
Col. 1:23 if ye continue *in* the *f*.
2:7 and stablished *in* the *f*.
1 *Tim*. 1:2 Tim. my own son *in f*.
4 godly edifying which is *in f*.
2:7 teacher of the Gentiles *in f*.
15 saved, if they continue *in f*.
3:13 they purchase boldn. *in f*.
4:12 example of believers *in f*.
2 *Tim*. 1:13 hold fast form *in f*.
Heb. 11:13 these all died *in f*.
Jam. 1:6 but let them ask *in f*.
2:5 poor of this world, rich *in f*.
1 *Pet*. 5:9 resist, steadfast *in f*.

Their FAITH.

Mat. 9:2 Jesus seeing their *f*.
Mark 2:5 ; *Luke* 5:20

Through FAITH.

Acts 3:16 *through f*. in his name
Rom. 3:25 propitiation *t. f*.
30 justify uncircumcision *t. f*.
31 do we make void law *t. f*. ?
Gal. 3:8 God justify heathen *t. f*.
14 promise of the Spirit *t. f*.
Eph. 2:8 are ye saved *t. f*.
Phil. 3:9 righteousn. wh. is *t. f*.
Col. 2:12 risen *t. f*. of ope. of G.
2 *Tim*. 3:15 wise to salvation *t. f*.
Heb. 6:12 *t. f*. inherit promises
11 *t. f*. S. received strength
28 *thro' f*. kept the passover
33 *thro' f*. subdued kingdoms
39 obtained a good report *t. f*.
1 *Pet*. 1:5 kept *t. f*. to salvation

Thy FAITH.

Mat. 9:2 *t. f*. hath made thee
whole, *Mark* 5:34; 10:52;
Luke 8:48; 17:19
15:28 O woman, great is *thy f*.
Luke 7:50 *t. f*. h. saved th. 18:42
22:32 prayed that *thy f*. fail not
Phile. 6 communication of *thy f*.
Jam. 2:18 show *t. f*. without w.

Your FAITH.

Mat. 9:29 according to *y. f*. be it
Luke 8:25 where is *your f*. ?
Rom. 1:8 *y. f*. is spoken
1 *Cor*. 2:5 *y. f*. not stand in wis.
15:14 *your f*. is also vain, 17
2 *Cor*. 1:24 dominion over *y. f*.
10:15 when *your f*. is increased
Eph. 1:15 after I heard of *y. f*.
Phil. 2:17 offer. on service of *y. f*.
Col. 1:4 since we heard of *y. f*.
2:5 steadfastness of *y. f*. in Ch.
1 *Thes*. 1:8 *your f*. to God-ward
3:5 I sent to know *your f*.
7 we were comforted by *y. f*.
10 what is lacking in *your f*.
2 *Thes*. 1:3 *y. f*. groweth exceed.
Jam. 1:3 trying of *y. f*. worketh
1 *Pet*. 1:7 trial of *y. f*. precious
9 end of *y. f*. even salvation
21 that *y. f*. might be in God
2 *Pet*. 1:5 add to *your f*. virtue

FAITHFUL.

Num. 12:7 Mo. *f*. *Heb*. 3:2, 5
Deut. 7:9 *f*. G. who keepeth cov.
1 *Sam*. 2:35 will raise up *f*. prie.
2 *Sam*. 20:19 *f*. in Israel
Neh. 13:13 *f*. to distribute
Ps. 12:1 the *f*. fail from am. men
31:23 the Lord preserveth the *f*.

89:37 as a *f*. witness in heaven
101:6 mine eyes shall be on *f*.
119:86 commandments are *f*.
138 thy testimonies very *f*.
Prov. 11:13 *f*. spirit conc. matter
13:17 a *f*. ambassador is health
14:5 a *f*. witness will not lie
20:6 a *f*. man who can find ?
27:6 *f*. the wounds of a friend
Is. 1:21 how is *f*. city become
26 shalt be called the *f*. city
8:2 I took unto me *f*. witness.
Jer. 42:5 L. be *f*. witness bet. us
Dan. 6:4 forasmuch as he was *f*.
Hos. 11:12 Ju. is *f*. with saints
Mat. 24:45 who then is *f*.
25:21 well done, good and *f*. se.
23 *f*. in a few th. *Luke* 19:17
Luke 12:42 who is *f*. and wise?
16:10 *f*. in least is *f*. in much
12 not *f*. in what is ano. man's
Acts 16:15 ye have judged me *f*.
1 *Cor*. 1:9 God is *f*. 10:13
4:2 stewards, that a man be *f*.
17 sent Timothy, *f*. in the L.
7:25 mercy of the Lord to be *f*.
Gal. 3:9 blessed with *f*. Abraham
Eph. 1:1 to saints and *f*. in C. J.
6:21 Tychicus a *f*. minister
Col. 1:2 saints and *f*. breth. in C.
7 Ep. for you *f*. minister, 4:7
4:9 Onesimus, a *f*. brother
1 *Thes*. 5:24 *f*. is he that calleth
2 *Thes*. 3:3 L. is *f*. who stablish
1 *Tim*. 1:12 Christ he counted *f*.
15 a *f*. saying, 4:9; *Tit*. 3:8
2 *Tim*. 2:2 same commit to *f*. m.
11 *f*. saying; 13 he abideth *f*.
Tit. 1:6 having *f*. children
9 holding fast the *f*. word
Heb. 2:17 he might be *f*.
3:2 *f*. to him that appointed h.
10:23 is *f*. that promised, 11:11
1 *Pet*. 4:19 souls as to a *f*. Crea.
1 *John* 1:9 he is *f*. to forgive us
Rev. 1:5 C. the *f*. witness, 3:14
2:10 be *f*. unto death
19:11 was called *f*.
21:5 words are true and *f*. 22:6

FAITHFULLY.

2 *K*. 12:15 for they dealt *f*. 22:7
2 *Chr*. 31:12 brought offerings *f*.
34:12 men did the work *f*.
Prov. 29:14 *f*. judgeth the poor
Jer. 23:28 speak my word *f*.

FAITHFULNESS.

1 *Sam*. 26:23 render to man his *f*.
Ps. 5:9 no *f*. in their mouth
36:5 thy *f*. reacheth unto clouds
40:10 I have declared thy *f*.
89:1 I will make known thy *f*.
2 thy *f*. shalt thou establish
5 thy *f*. also in the congrega.
8 to thy *f*. round about thee ?
24 *f*. and mercy be with thee
92:2 good to show *f*. every night
119:75 in *f*. hast afflicted me
90 thy *f*. is unto all genera.
143:1 in thy *f*. answer me
Is. 11:5 *f*. shall be girdle
25:1 thy counsels of old are *f*.
Lam. 3:23 great thy *f*.
Hos. 2:20 I will betroth thee in *f*.

FAITHLESS.

Mat. 17:17 O *f*. generation, *Mark*
9:19 ; *Luke* 9:41
John 20:27 not *f*. but believing

FALL, Substantive.

Prov. 16:18 haughty spirit bef. *f*.
29:16 righteous shall see their *f*.
Jer. 49:21 moved at noise of *f*.
Mat. 7:27 great was the *f*. of it
Luke 2:34 child set for *f*.
Rom. 11:11 thro' their *f*. salva-
tion is come to the Gentiles
12 if *f*. of them be riches

FALL, Verb.

Gen. 2:21 deep sleep to *f.* on A.
45:24 see that ye *f.* n. out by w.
49:17 his rider shall *f.* backw.
Lev. 19:29 land *f.* to whoredom
26:36 sh. *f.* when none pursue
37 shall *f.* one upon another
Num. 14:29 carc. sh. *f.* wild. 32
Jud. 15:12 ye will not *f.* me
18 *f.* into hand of uncircum.
Ruth 2:16 let *f.* some handfuls
1 *Sam.* 3:19 none of words *f.* gr.
14:45 not hair of head *f.* ground,
2 *Sam.* 14:11 ; 1 *K.* 1:52 ; *Acts* 27:34
22:17 would not *f.* on the pric.
1 *Sam.* 22:18 turn th. and *f.* on pr.
2 *Sam.* 1:15 *f.* on h. 1 *K.* 2:29, 31
24:14 *f.* in hand of G. not *f.* into
hand of man, 1 *Chr.* 21:13
2 *K.* 7:4 let us *f.* unto host of S.
10:10 *f.* nothing of word of L.
1 *Chr.* 12:19 he will *f.* to master
2 *Chr.* 21:15 till bowels *f.* out
25:8 G. *f.* before enemy
Est. 6:13 thou begun to *f.*
Job 13:11 his dread *f.* on yon
31:22 arm *f.* fr. shoulder-blade
Ps. 5:10 *f.* by own counsels
9:3 enemies sh. *f.* and perish
10:10 that the poor may *f.*
35:8 into destruction let him *f.*
37:24 he *f.* shall not be utterly
64:8 make their tongue to *f.* on
82:7 shall *f.* like one of princes
91:7 a thousand shall *f.*
118:13 thrust at me I might *f.*
140:10 burning coals *f.* on them
141:10 wicked *f.* into own nets
145:14 Lord upholdeth all th. *f.*
Prov. 10:8 a prating fool sh. *f.* 10
11:5 wicked shall *f.*
14 wh. no counsel is the peo. *f.*
28 trusteth in his riches sh. *f.*
22:14 abhor. of L. sh. *f.* therein
24:16 shall *f.* into mischief
26:27 whoso diggeth pit shall *f.*
28:14 that hardeneth heart sh. *f.*
18 perverse shall *f.* at once
Ec. 4:10 if they *f.* one lift fellow
11:3 if the tree *f.* tow. the south
Is. 10:4 they sh. *f.* under slain
34 Leb. shall *f.* by mighty one
22:25 nail fast. sure place sh. *f.*
24:18 shall *f.* into the pit.
20 earth shall *f.* and not rise
30:13 iniq. as breach ready to *f.*
40:30 young man sh. utterly *f.*
47:11 mischiefs sh. *f.* upon thee
Jer. 6:15 *f.* am. them that *f.* 8:12
21 fathers and sons shall *f.*
8:4 shall they *f.* and not arise ?
9:22 carcasses of men shall *f.*
15:8 I have caused him to *f.*
19 whirlwind *f.* on head, 23:23
25:27 drunken, and spue, and *f.*
37:14 I *f.* not away to Chaldeans
44:12 shall all *f.* in land of Eg.
46:6 they shall stumble and *f.*
48:44 that fleeth shall *f.* into pit
49:26 young men *f.* 50:30
50:32 most proud stumble and *f.*
51:4 slain *f.* in land of C. 47, 49
44 wall of Babylon shall *f.*
Lam. 1:14 made strength to *f.*
Ezek. 6:7 shall *f.* in the midst
13:11 it shall *f.* and ye, O great
hailstones, shall *f.*
24:6 piece by piece, let no lot *f.*
29:5 shalt *f.* on open fields, 39:5
30:6 they that uphold E. sh. *f.*
22 I will cause the sword to *f.*
32:12 will I cause multit. to *f.*
33:12 not *f.* thereby in the day
35:8 in all thy rivers shall th. *f.*
38:20 steep places *f.* ev. wall *f.*
39:3 arrows to *f.* ; 4 sh. *f.* mo.
44:12 caused Is. to *f.* into iniq.

Dan. 11:14 robbers of peo. sh. *f.*
19 but he shall stumble and *f.*
34 they shall *f.* ; 35 some *f.*
Hos. 4:5 shalt thou *f.* in the day,
the prophet also shall *f.*
5:5 Eph. shall *f.* Judah shall *f.*
10:8 shall say to hills *f.* on us
14:9 transgressors shall *f.*
Amos 3:5 can a bird *f.* in snare ?
14 horns of altar sh. *f.* to gro.
9:9 shall not least grain *f.*
Mic. 7:8 mine enemy, when I *f.*
Nah. 3:12 sh. *f.* into the mouth
Mat. 10:29 not one sparrow *f.*
12:11 if it *f.* into a pit on sab.
15:14 *f.* into ditch, *Luke* 6:39
27 crumbs wh. *f.* masters' tab.
21:44 whoso *f.* on this stone be
broken, *Luke* 20:18
24:29 stars shall *f.* from heaven,
Mark 13:25
Luke 10:18 I beheld S. as light. *f.*
23:30 say to mountains *f.* on us
John 12:24 except a corn *f.*
Acts 27:17 lest they *f.* into quic.
32 cut ropes and let her *f.* off
34 shall not a hair *f.* from he.
Rom. 11:11 stumbled that th. *f.*
14:13 to *f.* in brother's way
1 *Cor.* 10:12 take heed lest he *f.*
1 *Tim.* 3:6 *f.* into condemnation
7 lest *f.* into reproach
6:9 will be rich *f.* into tempt.
Heb. 4:11 lest any *f.* after same
10:31 fearful to *f.* into hands
Jam. 1:2 ye *f.* into temptations

FALL away.

Jam. 5:12 swear not, lest ye *f.*
2 *Pet.* 1:10 do th. things, ye n. *f.*
3:17 lest ye *f.* from steadfastn.
Rev. 6:16 mount. and ro. *f.* on us
9:1 I saw a star *f.* from heaven

FALL away.

Luke 8:13 in time of tempt. *f. a.*
Heb. 6:6 if they *f. a.* to renew

FALL down.

Deut. 22:4 thy brother's ass *f. d.*
Jos. 6:5 wall of city shall *f. d.*
1 *Sam.* 21:13 David let spit. *f. d.*
Ps. 72:11 all kings shall *f. down*
Is. 31:3 that is holp. shall *f. d.*
34:4 their host shall *f. d.*
44:19 sh. I *f. d.* to sto. of tree ?
45:14 the Sabeans shall *f. d.*
46:6 they *f. d.* yea, they worsh.
Ezek. 30:25 arms of Pha. sh. *f. d.*
Dan. 3:5 *f. d.* and wor. image, 10
15 if ye *f. d.* and worship im.
11:26 and many shall *f. down*
Mat. 4:9 *f. d.* and wor. *Luke* 4:7
Rev. 4:10 twenty-four elders *f. d.*

FALL, joined with sword.

Ex. 5:3 he *f.* with pest. or *s.*
Num. 14:3 to this land to *f.* by *s.*
43 and ye shall *f.* by the *sword*
2 *K.* 19:7 Senacherib *f.* by *swo.*
Ps. 63:10 sh. *f.* by *s. Ezek.* 6:11
Is. 3:25 thy men shall *f.* by *s.*
13:15 every one shall *f.* by the *s.*
37:7 I will cause him to *f.* by
the *s.* in h. own la. *Jer.* 19:7
Jer. 20:4 P.'s friends sh. *f.* by *s.*
Ezek. 5:12 third part sh. *f.* by *s.*
6:12 that is near shall *f.* by *s.*
11:10 ye shall *f.* by the *s.*
17:21 fugitives shall *f.* by the *s.*
23:25 remnant shall *f.* by the *s.*
25:13 they of D. sh. *f.* by the *s.*
30:5 men in league sh. *f.* by t. *s.*
22 I will cause the *sword* to *f.*
Dan. 11:33 underst. *f.* by the *s.*
Hos. 7:16 princes sh. *f.* by the *s.*
13:16 Samaria shall *f.* by the *s.*
Joel 2:8 they *f.* on the *sword*
Luke 21:24 shall *f.* by edge of *s.*

FALLEN.

Gen. 4:6 why is thy counte. *f.* ?

Lev. 13:41 hair *f.* off from head
25:35 thy brother be *f.* in decay
Jud. 3:25 their lord was *f.* dead
19:27 the woman was *f.* at door
1 *Sam.* 5:3 D. was *f.* upon his fa.
26:12 a deep sleep *f.* upon them
31:8 S. and h. sons *f.* 1 *Chr.* 10:8
3:38 a great man is *f.* this d.
2 *K.* 13:14 Elisha was *f.* sick
2 *Chr.* 20:24 dead bodies *f.*
29:9 our fathers have *f.*
Est. 7:8 Ham. was *f.* on the bed
Ps. 20:8 brought down and *f.*
36:12 the workers of iniquity *f.*
Is. 14:12 thou *f.* fr. heaven, O L.
Ezek. 32:22 all of them *f.* 23:24
Hos. 14:1 hast *f.* by iniquity
Luke 14:5 an ox *f.* into a pit ?
Acts 8:16 H. G. was *f.* on none
20:9 Eutychus *f.* into deep sl.
26:14 when we were all *f.*
27:29 lest they have *f.* dead
28:6 looked when P. sh. *f.* dead
Phile. 1:12 *f.* out to fur. of gospel
Rev. 2:5 rem. whence thou art *f.*

Are FALLEN.

2 *Sam.* 1:4 ma. of the peo. are *f.*
19 how are mighty *f.* ! 25:27
22:39 *a. f.* under feet, *Ps.* 18:38
Ps. 16:6 lines are *f.* to me
55:4 ter. of death are *f.* on me
69:9 reproaches of them are *f.*
Is. 9:10 the bricks are *f.* down
Jer. 38:19 Jews that are *f.* to C.
46:12 they are *f.* both togeth.
50:15 Bab.'s foundations are *f.*
Lam. 2:21 my virgins are *f.*
Ezek. 31:12 his branches are *f.*
Hos. 7:7 all their kings are *f.*
1 *Cor.* 15:6 some are *f.* asleep. 18
Gal. 5:4 law, ye are *f.* from grace
Rev. 17:10 seven kings, five *a. f.*

Is FALLEN.

Num. 32:19 lot is *f.* on th. side J.
Jos. 2:9 I know your terror is *f.*
Job 1:16 fire of G. is *f.* fr. heaven
Ps. 7:15 and is *f.* into the ditch
Is. 3:8 Jer. ruined, and Jud. is *f.*
21:9 B. is *f.* *Rev.* 14:8 ; 18:2
59:14 truth is *f.* in the streets
Jer. 48:32 spoil. is *f.* on sum. fr.
51:8 Babylon is suddenly *f.*
Lam. 5:16 crown is *f.* from our
heads
Ezek. 13:12 when the wall is *f.*
Amos 5:2 virgin of Israel is *f.*
Amos 9:11 raise up tab. th. is *f.*
Acts 15:16 taber. of D, wh. is *f.*

FALLEST, ETH.

Ex. 1:10 when *f.* out any war
2 *Sam.* 3:29 not fail one that *f.*
34 as a man *f.* bef. wick. men
17:12 as dew *f.* on ground
Job 4:13 deep sleep *f.* 33:15
Prov. 11:17 mess. *f.* into misch.
17:20 perv. tongue *f.* into mis.
24:16 just man *f.* seven times
17 rejoice not when enemy *f.*
Ec. 4:10 him alone when *f.*
11:3 wh. tree *f.* there shall it be
Is. 34:4 the leaf *f.* off the vine
44:15 image and *f.* down, 17
Jer. 37:13 thou *f.* away to Chald.
Dan. 3:6 whoso *f.* not down, 11
Mat. 17:15 ofttimes *f.* into fire
Luke 11:17 house div. ag. ho. *f.*
15:12 goods that *f.* to me
Rom. 14:4 master he stand. or *f.*
Jam. 1:11 flower th. *f.* 1 *Pet.* 1:24

FALLING.

Num. 24:4 *f.* into trance. 16
Job 4:4 upholden him that *f.*
14:18 mount *f.* cometh to nau.
Ps. 56:13 del. feet from *f.* 116:8
Prov. 25:26 righte. *f.* bef. wick.
Is. 34:4 as a *f.* fig from fig-tree

Luke 8:47 trembling *f.* down
22:44 drops of blood *f.* down
Acts 1:18 and Judas *f.* headlong
1 *Cor.* 14:25 *f.* he will worsh. G.
2 *Thes.* 2:3 except come a *f.* aw.
Jude 24 is able to keep from *f.*

FALLOW.

Jer. 4:3 *f.* ground, *Hos.* 10:12

FALSE.

Ex. 23:1 shalt not raise *f.* report
7 keep thee far from a *f.* mat.
2 *K.* 9:12 it is *f.* tell us now
Job 36:4 my words shall n. be *f.*
Ps. 119:104 I hate ev. *f.* way, 128
120:3 done thee, *f.* tongue
Prov. 11:1 *f.* balance is abomination
17:4 giveth heed to *f.* lips
20:23 a *f.* balance is not good
25:14 whoso boasteth of a *f.* gift
Jer. 14:14 prophesy a *f.* vision
23:32 prophesy *f.* dreams
37:14 it is *f.* I fall not away
Lam. 2:14 seen for thee *f.* burdens
Ezek. 21:23 shall be as a *f.* divin.
Zec. 8:17 evil, love no *f.* oath
10:2 divin. have told *f.* dreams
Mal. 3:5 witness ag. *f.* swearers
Mat. 24:24 shall arise *f.* Christs
and *f.* prophets, *Mark* 13:22
Luke 19:8 any thing by *f.* accusa.
2 *Cor.* 11:13 such are *f.* apostles
26 in perils among *f.* brethren
Gal. 2:4 because of *f.* brethren
Tit. 2:3 they be not *f.* accusers
2 *Pet.* 2:1 there sh. be *f.* teachers

See PROPHET.

FALSE prophets.

Mat. 7:15 *f. p.* in sheep's cloth.
24:11 many *f. p.* shall rise, 24
Mark 13:22 *f. p.* rise show signs
Luke 6:26 did fathers to the *f. p.*
2 *Pet.* 2:1 there were *f. p.* am. p.
1 *John* 4:1 *f. p.* gone out

FALSE witness, es.

Ex. 20:16 thou shalt not bear *f. wit. Deut.* 5:20; *Mat.* 19:18
Deut. 19:16 if a *f. witness* rise up
18 if the witness be a *f. witness*
Ps. 27:12 *f. witnesses* are risen
35:11 *f. w.* did rise
Prov. 6:19 a *f. w.* speaketh lies
12:17 a *f. w.* show. deceit, 14:5
19:5 *f. w.* not be unpunished, 9
21:28 *f. witness* shall perish
25:18 that beareth *f. w.*
Mat. 15:19 out of heart pro. *f. w.*
26:59 elders sought *f. w.* ag. Je.
60 many *f. witnesses* came, at
last came two *f. witnesses*
Mark 14:56 bear *f. w.* ag. him, 57
Acts 6:13 and set up *f. w.*
1 *Cor.* 15:15 we are found *f. w.*

FALSEHOOD.

2 *Sam.* 18:13 sh. have wroug. *f.*
Job 21:34 in answers remaineth *f.*
Ps. 7:14 he hath brought forth *f.*
119:118 for deceit is *f.*
144:8 a right hand of *f.* 11
Is. 28:15 under *f.* have we hid
57:4 seed of *f.* 59:13 words of *f.*
Jer. 10:14 image is *f.* 51:17
Hos. 7:1 for they commit *f.*
Mic. 2:11 walking in spirit and *f.*

FALSELY.

Gen. 21:23 thou wilt not deal *f.*
Lev. 6:3 lost, and sweareth *f.*
19:11 neither deal *f.* nor lie
12 not swear by my name *f.*
Deut. 19:18 witn. have testifi. *f.*
Ps. 44:17 nor have we dealt *f.*
Jer. 5:2 L. liveth, they swear *f.*
31 prophets prophesy *f.* 29:9
6:13 every one dealeth *f.* 8:10

7:9 ye steal, mur. and swear *f. ?*
40:16 for thou speakest *f.* of Is.
43:2 speakest *f.* L. hath not sent
Hos. 10:4 swe. *f.* in making cov.
Zec. 5:4 enter house swear *f.*
Mat. 5:11 say evil against you *f.*
Luke 3:14 nor accuse any *f.*
1 *Tim.* 6:20 opp. of science *f.*
1 *Pet.* 3:16 *f.* accuse good conv.

FALSIFYING.

Amos 8:5 *f.* balances by deceit

FAME.

Gen. 45:16 *f.* was heard in Phar.
Num. 14:15 have heard *f.* of thee
Jos. 6:27 Joshua's *f.* was noised
9:9 we heard the *f.* of God
1 *K.* 4:31 *f.* was in all nations
10:1 heard *f.* of Sol. 2 *Chr.* 9:1
7 wish. exceedeth *f.* 2 *Chr.* 9:6
1 *Chr.* 14:17 *f.* of D. was to all
Est. 9:4 Mordecai's *f.* thro' prov.
Job 28:22 we have heard *f.*
Is. 66:19 that have not heard *f.*
Jer. 6:24 we have heard the *f.*
Zep. 3:19 and I will get them *f.*
Mat. 4:24 *f.* of J. abroad, *Mark* 1:28; *Luke* 4:14, 37; 5:15
9:26 the *f.* thereof went abroad
31 they spread abroad his *f.*
14:1 Herod heard of *f.* of Jesus

FAMILIAR.

Job 19:14 my *f.* friends have for.
Ps. 41:9 my *f.* friend lift up heel

FAMILIAR spirit.

Lev. 20:27 man or wom. of a *f. s.*
1 *Sam.* 28:7 wo. that hath *f. s.* 8
2 *Chr.* 33:6 Man. dealt with *f. s.*
Is. 29:4 as one that hath a *f. s.*

FAMILIAR spirits.

Lev. 19:31 reg. not th. have *f. s.*
20:6 soul that turneth after *f. s.*
Deut. 18:11 nor consulter w. *f. s.*
1 *Sam.* 28:3 S. put away th. *f. s.* 9
2 *K.* 21:6 with *f. s.* ; 23:24 *f. s.*
Is. 8:19 seek *f. s.* ; 19:3 hath *f. s.*

FAMILIARS.

Jer. 20:10 *f.* watched for halting

FAMILY.

Lev. 20:5 I will set face ag. his *f.*
25:10 return ev. man to his *f.* 41
47 the stock of the strang. *f.*
Num. 36:6 *f.* of father's tribe, 12
Deut. 29:18 lest a *f.* turn from L.
Jos. 7:14 *f.* which Lord taketh
Jud. 1:25 go man and all his *f.*
6:15 my *f.* is poor in Manasseh
Jer. 3:14 one of a cit. two of a *f.*
Zec. 12:12 *f.* sh. mourn, 13, 14
Eph. 3:15 *f.* in heav. and earth

FAMILIES.

Gen. 10:5 Gentiles divided aft. *f.*
12:3 all *f.* of earth, 28:14
Ex. 12:21 take lamb ac. to yo. *f.*
Neh. 4:13 people after their *f.*
Job 31:34 did cont. of *f.* ter. me ?
Ps. 68:6 G. setteth solitary in *f.*
107:41 mak. him *f.* like a flock
Jer. 1:15 will call all *f.* of north
10:25 fury on *f.* call not name
25:9 will take all the *f.* of north
31:1 God of all the *f.* of Israel
33:24 *f.* which L. hath chosen
Ezek. 20:32 as *f.* of countries
Amos 3:2 you have I kn. of all *f.*
Nah. 3:4 selleth *f.* thro' witchr.
Zec. 12:14 *f.* that remain
14:17 will not come of all *f.*

FAMINE.

Gen. 12:10 *f.* was grievous in la.
26:1 *f.* in land, besides first *f.*
41:27 7 empty ears 7 years *f.*
30 *f.* shall consume the land
31 plenty not kn. by rea. of *f.*
56 *f.* was over all face of earth
47:13 fainted by reason of *f.*

Ruth 1:1 ruled there was *f.*
2 *Sam.* 21:1 *f.* in the days of D.
24:13 shall years of *f.* come ?
1 *K.* 8:37 in land *f.* 2 *Chr.* 20:9
18:2 *f.* in Samaria, 2 *K.* 6:25
2 *K.* 7:4 then the *f.* is in the city
8:1 the Lord hath call. for a *f.*
25:3 *f.* prevailed in J. no bread
2 *Chr.* 32:11 H. per. you to die *f.*
Job 5:20 in *f.* he shall red. thee *f.*
Job 5:22 at destruc. *f.* thou sh. la.
30:3 want and *f.* were solitary
Ps. 33:19 keep them alive in *f.*
37:19 in days of *f.*
105:16 he called for a *f.*
Is. 14:30 I will kill root with *f.*
51:19 destruction, *f.* and sword
Jer. 14:15 by *f.* sh. proph. be con.
18 them that are sick with *f.*
15:2 such for the *f.* to the *f.*
18:21 deliver up children to *f.*
21:7 deliver from the *f.* to Neb.
24:10 send *f.* am. them, 29:17
27:8 nation will I pun. with *f.*
34:17 liberty for you to the *f.*
42:16 the *f.* shall follow
52:6 the *f.* was sore in the city
Lam. 5:10 skin black, bec. of *f.*
Ezek. 5:12 part consumed with *f.*
16 evil arrows of *f.*
17 I send on you *f.* 14:13
7:15 *f.* within *f.* and pestilence
12:16 leave a few men from *f.*
36:29 will lay no *f.* upon you
Amos 8:11 I will send *f.*
Luke 4:25 great *f.* through land
15:14 a mighty *f.* in that land
Rom. 8:35 *f.* sep. fr. love C. ?
Rev. 18:8 in one day, death, *f.*

By the FAMINE.

Jer. 11:22 sons and d. die *by t. f.*
14:12 I will consume *by t. f.* 15
16:4 he con. *by t. f.* 44:12, 18, 27
21:9 abideth in city die *by t. f.*
38:2 shall die *by f. Ezek.* 6:12
42:17 they shall die *by the f.*
22 that ye shall die *by the f.*
44:13 I have punish. J. *by t. f.*
Ezek. 6:11 they shall fall *by the f.*

FAMINES.

Mat. 24:7 shall be *f.* pestilences,
Mark 13:8 ; *Luke* 21:11

FAMISH, ED.

Gen. 41:55 all land of Egypt *f.*
Prov. 10:3 not suffer right. to *f.*
Is. 5:13 their honor. men are *f.*
Zep. 2:11 will *f.* gods of earth

FAMOUS.

Num. 16:2 *f.* in congrega. 26:9
Ruth 4:11 be thou *f.* in Bethleh.
14 his name may be *f.* in Israel
1 *Chr.* 5:24 were *f.* men, 12:30
Ps. 74:5 was *f.* as he lifted axes
136:18 to him who slew *f.* kings
Ezek. 23:10 became *f.* am. wom.
32:18 daughters of *f.* nations

FAN, Substantive.

Is. 30:24 winnowed with *f.*
Jer. 15:7 I will fan with *f.*
Mat. 3:12 wh. *f.* is in h. *Luke* 3:17

FAN, Verb.

Is. 41:16 sh. *f.* them, winds sh.
Jer. 4:11 a dry wind not to *f.*
15:7 I will *f.* them with a fan
51:2 fanners that shall *f.* her

FAR.

Gen. 18:25 *f.* from thee to slay
Ex. 8:28 ye shall not go very *f.*
23:7 keep *f.* from false matter
Deut. 12:21 if the *f.* thee, 14:24
29:22 stranger from a *f.* land
Jos. 9:22 *f.* from you
Jud. 9:17 adventured life *f.*
19:11 day was *f.* spent
1 *Sam.* 20:9 J. said, *f.* be it from

2 *Chr.* 26:15 name spr. *f.* abroad
Neh. 4:19 separ. one *f.* from an.
Est. 9:20 Jews both nigh and *f.* ·
Job 5:4 his child. *f.* from safety
11:14 Iniquity *f.* away. 22:23
34:10 *f.* be it from God
Ps. 10:5 judg. are *f.* out of sight
22:1 why so *f.* from help. me ?
73:27 that are *f.* from thee
97:9 L. exalted *f.* above all gods
103:12 as *f.* as east fr. west. so *f.*
109:17 blessing be *f.* from him
119:155 salva. is *f.* from wicked
Prov. 4:24 and perver. lips put *f.*
15:29 Lord is *f.* from the wicked
22:15 rod of cor. sh. drive it *f.*
31:10 her price is *f.* above rub.
Ec. 2:13 *f.* as light excel. dark.
Is. 19:6 shall turn rivers *f.* away
46:12 hear ye that *f.* from right.
54:14 thou shalt be *f.* from opp.
59:9 is judgment *f.* from us
Jer. 51:64 thus *f.* are words of J.
Lam. 3:17 my soul *f.* from peace
Ezek. 11:15 get ye *f.* from the L.
Dan. 11:2 fourth king *f.* richer
Amos 6:3 put *f.* away evil day
Mat. 16:22 be it *f.* from thee, L.
Mark 6:35 day was now *f.* spent
12:34 not *f.* from kingd. of God

Mark 13:34 man taking a *f.* jour.
Luke 7:6 was not *f.* from house
22:51 Jesus said, Suf. ye thus *f.*
24:29 for the day is *f.* spent
50 out as *f.* as to Bethany
John 21:8 were not *f.* from land
Acts 17:27 not *f.* from every one
22:21 send thee *f.* hence to Gen.
28:15 meet us as *f.* as Ap.-forum
Rom. 13:12 the night is *f.* spent
2 *Cor.* 4:17 *f.* more ex. weight
Eph. 1:21 *f.* abo. all principality
4:10 ascended up *f.* above all
Phil. 1:23 with C. wh. is *f.* bet.
Heb. 7:15 it is yet *f.* more evid.

See COUNTRY, COUNTRIES.

FAR from me.

1 *Sam.* 2:30 Be it *f. from me*,
22:15 ; 2 *Sam.* 20:20 ; 23:17
Job 13:21 thy hand *f. from me*
19:13 hath put my bre. *f. f. me*
21:16 wicked is *f. f. m.* 22:18
30:10 they flee *f. from me*
Ps. 22:11 O Lord be not *f. f. me*,
19 ; 35:22 ; 38:21 ; 71:12
27:9 hide not thy face *f. fr. me*
88:8 mine acquaintance *f. f. me*
18 lover and friend *f. from me*
Prov. 30:8 remove *f. f. me* vanity
Ec. 7:23 but was *f. from me*
Is. 29:13 their heart *f. from me*
Jer. 2:5 they are gone *f. from me*
Lam. 1:16 comfort. is *f. from me*
Ezek. 44:10 Lev. are gone *f. f. me*
Mat. 15:8 is *f. f. me*, *Mark.* 7:6

From FAR.

Deut. 28:49 na. ag. *f. f. Jer.* 5:15
Job 36:3 fetch my know. *f. f.*
Is. 5:26 lift up ensign *f. f.*
10:3 desol. which sh. come *f. f.*
22:3 which are fled *from f.*
30:27 the name of L. com. *f. f.*
43:6 bring my sons *from f.* 60:9
49:1 hearken, ye people *from f.*
12 these shall come *from f.*
60:4 thy sons shall come *from f.*
Jer. 30:10 I will save thee *from f.*
Ezek. 23:40 for men to come *f. f.*
Mark 8:3 div. of them came *f. f.*

See AFAR.

FAR off.

Deut. 13:7 serve the gods *f. off*
20:15 thus do to cities very *f. off*
30:11 nor is com. *f. off*
2 *Sam.* 15:17 king tarried *f. off*
2 *Chr.* 6:36 captives to land *f. off*

Ps. 55:7 would I wander *f. off*
Prov. 27:10 than a brother *f. off*
Ec. 7:24 *f. off* who find out ?
Is. 17:13 they shall flee *f. off*
33:13 ye *f. off*, what I done
17 behold land that is *f. off*
46:13 my right. not be *f. off*
57:19 peace to him *f. off*
59:11 salvation, but it is *f. off*
Ezek. 6:12 *f. off* die of pestilence
8:6 *f. off* from my sanctuary ?
11:16 I have cast them *f. off*
12:27 prophesieth of times *f. off*
22:5 those that be *f. off* sh. mock
Dan. 9:7 confus. to Israel *f. off*
Joel 2:20 rem. *f. off* north. army
3:8 sell them to Sabeans *f. off*
Mic. 4:7 her cast *f. off*. a nation
Zec. 6:25 *f. off* come and build
Eph. 2:13 *f. off* are made nigh

FARE, ED.

1 *Sam.* 17:18 look how thy br. *f.*
Jon. 1:3 paid the *f.* thereof
Luke 16:19 rich man *f.* sumptu.

FAREWELL.

Luke 9:61 bid them *f.* at home
Acts 15:29 well, *f.* 18:21 ; 23:30
2 *Cor.* 13:11 finally brethren, *f.*

FARTHER. *See* FURTHER.

FARTHING, S.

Mat. 5:26 paid the uttermost *f.*
10:29 two sparrows sold for *f. ?*
Mark 12:42 threw two mites, a *f.*
Luke 12:6 five sparr. for two *f.*

FASHION.

Mark 2:12 never saw it on this *f.*
Luke 9:29 *f.* of his countenance
Acts 7:44 make tabernacle to *f.*
1 *Cor.* 7:31 *f.* world pass. away
Phil. 2:8 found in *f.* as a man
Jam. 1:11 the grace of *f.* perish.

FASHION, ED, ETH, ING.

Job 10:8 hands *f.* me, *Ps.* 119:73
31:15 not one *f.* us in the wo. ?
Ps. 33:15 he *f.* their hearts alike
139:16 in continuance were *f.*
Is. 22:11 nei. respect to him *f.* it
44:12 the smith *f.* it with ham.
Is. 45:9 clay say to him that *f.*
Ezek. 16:7 thy breasts are *f.*
Phil. 3:21 *f.* like to his glo. body
1 *Pet.* 1:14 not *f.* to former lusts

FAST, Adverb.

Jud. 15:13 we will bind thee *f.*
Ps. 65:6 strength set *f.* moun.
Prov. 4:13 *f.* hold of instruction
Jer. 48:16 afflic. of M. hasteth *f.*
59:33 took captiv. held them *f.*
Jon. 1:5 lay in ship, *f.* asleep

FAST, Substantive.

1 *K.* 21:9 pro. a *f.* 2 *Chr.* 20:3 ;
Ezr. 8:21 ; *Jer.* 36:9 ; *Jon.* 3:5
Is. 58:3 in *f.* you find pleasure
5 a *f.* wilt thou call this a *f. ?*
6 this the *f.* I have chosen ?
Joel 1:14 sanc. *f.* call assem. 2:15
Zec. 8:19 *f.* of 4th, 5th, 7th, 10th
month
Acts 27:9 *f.* was now already past

FAST, Verb.

2 *Sam.* 12:23 child dead, why *f.*
Is. 58:4 ye *f.* for strife. sh. not *f.*
Jer. 14:12 when *f.* I will not hear
Zec. 7:5 did ye at all *f.* unto me ?
Mat. 6:16 ye *f.* be not of sad
counten. that may ap. to *f.*
9:14 disc. *f.* not ? *Mark* 2:18
15 then *f.* *Mark* 2:20 ; *Lu.* 5:35
Mark 2:18 disc. of J. used to *f.*
19 children of bridechamber *f.*
Luke 5:33 discip. of J. *f.* often ?
18:12 I *f.* twice in the week

FASTED, EST.

Jud. 20:26 *f.* th. day, 1 *Sam.* 7:6

1 *Sam.* 31:13 *f.* 7 d. 1 *Chr.* 10:12
2 *Sam.* 1:12 *f.* for S. ; 1 *K.* 21:27 A.
Neh. 1:4 Neh. *f.* and pra. *Ez.* 8:23
Is. 58:3 why have we *f. ?*
Mat. 4:2 Jesus *f.* forty days
6:17 when thou *f.* anoint head
Acts 13:3 *f.* laid hands on them

FASTING, S.

Neh. 9:1 were assembled with *f.*
Est. 4:3 dec. came there was *f.*
Ps. 35:13 humbled soul with *f.*
69:10 chast. my soul with *f.*
109:24 knees weak through *f.*
Jer. 36:6 the words on *f.* day
Dan. 6:18 passed the night *f.*
9:3 D. set him. to seek by *f.*
Joel 2:12 turn ye with *f.*
Mat. 15:32 send them away *f.*
17:21 but by *f.* *Mark* 9:29
Mark 8:3 if I send them away *f.*
Luke 2:37 Anna served G. with *f.*
Acts 10:30 four days ago I was *f.*
14:23 and had prayed with *f.*
27:33 fourteenth day ye cont. *f.*
1 *Cor.* 7:5 give yourselves to *f.*
2 *Cor.* 6:5 approv. ourselves in *f.*
11:27 *f.* often, in cold and nak.

FASTEN, ED, ING.

Judg. 4:21 J. *f.* nail into ground
1 *Chr.* 10:10 *f.* head in temple
Job 38:6 wher. are foundations *f.*
Ec. 12:11 as nails *f.* by masters
Is. 22:23 I will *f.* him as a nail
25 nail *f.* in the sure place
41:7 he *f.* it, it sh. not be moved
Jer. 10:4 they *f.* it with nails
Luke 4:20 eyes of all *f.* on him
Acts 3:4 Peter *f.* his eyes on him
11:6 when I had *f.* my eyes
28:3 a viper *f.* on his hand

FAT.

Gen. 4:4 Abel brought *f.* of flock
Ex. 29:13 take the *f. Lev.* 3:3,
4, 9, 10 ; 4:8 ; 7:3, 4
Lev. 3:16 all the *f.* is the Lord's
4:26 burn his *f.* 6:12 ; 17:6
7:24 *f.* of beast that dieth
9:24 fire from Lord consumed *f.*
Deut. 32:14 *f.* of lambs, *f.* of kid
Jud. 3:22 *f.* closed on the blade
1 *Sam.* 2:15 before they burnt *f.*
15:22 hearken is better than *f.*
2 *Sam.* 1:22 from *f.* of mighty
2 *Chr.* 35:14 offer. *f.* until night
Job 15:27 collops of *f.* on flanks
Ps. 17:10 inclosed in th. own *f.*
Is. 1:11 full of *f.* of fed beasts
34:6 *f.* with the *f.* of kidneys
43:24 nor filled me with *f.*
Ezek. 44:7 ye offer *f.* and blood

Eat FAT.

Gen. 45:18 shall *eat f.* of land
Lev. 3:17 *eat* no *f.* 7:23
7:25 whoso *eateth f.* be cut off
Deut. 32:38 *eat f.* of sacrifices
Neh. 8:10 *eat f.* drink the sweet
Ezek. 34:3 ye *eat f.* and clothe
39:19 ye shall *eat f.* till full
Zec. 11:16 shall *eat* flesh of *f.*

FAT, Adjective.

Gen. 41:2 came up seven kine *f.*
49:20 out of A. his bread be *f.*
Num. 13:20 land is *f.* or lean
Deut. 31:20 when waxen *f.* then
32:15 Jeshurun waxed *f.* kicked
Jud. 3:17 Egl. was very *f.* man
1 *Sam.* 2:29 to make *f.* with off.
28:24 the woman had a *f.* calf
1 *Chr.* 4:40 they found *f.* pasture
Neh. 9:25 took a *f.* land bec. *f.*
Ps. 22:29 they *f.* on earth
37:20 enemies as *f.* of lambs
92:14 shall be *f.* and flourish.
119:70 heart is as *f.* as grease
Prov. 11:25 lib. soul be made *f.*
13:4 soul of diligent be made *f.*

15:30 good report mak. bones *f.*
28:25 trusteth in L. be made *f.*
Is. 5:17 of *f.* ones strangers eat
6:10 make the hea. of th. peo. *f.*
10:16 send am. *f.* ones leanness
25:6 feast of *f.* th. full of mar.
28:1 on head of the *f.* valleys, 4
30:23 bread be *f.* and plenteous
34:6 sword of the L. is made *f.*
7 dust shall be *f.* with fatness
58:11 L. shall make *f.* thy bones
Jer. 5:28 waxen *f.* they shine
50:11 ye are grown *f.* as heifer
Ezek. 34:14 in *f.* pasture sh. feed
16 I will destroy *f.* and strong
20 judge bet. *f.* cattle and lean
45:15 lamb out of *f.* pastures
Amos 5:22 nor reg. off. of *f.* bea.
Hab. 1:16 by them portion is *f.*

FATHER.

Gen. 17:4 be *f.* of many nations,
   5; *Rom.* 4:17, 18
44:19 have ye a *f. ?* 20 we have
45:8 made me a *f.* to Pharaoh
Lev. 24:10 *f.* was an Egyptian
Num. 11:12 as nursing *f.*
30:16 statutes betw. *f.* and dau.
Jud. 17:10 be to me a *f.*
18:19 be to us a *f.* and a priest
Est. 2:7 Esther had nei. *f.* nor
Job 29:16 I was a *f.* to the poor
31:18 with me as with a *f.*
38:28 hath the rain a *f.*
Ps. 68:5 a *f.* of fatherless is God
103:13 as a *f.* pitieth children
Prov. 3:12 correcteth, as *f.* son
4:1 hear the instruction of a *f.*
10:1 maketh a glad *f.* 15:20
17:21 *f.* of a fool hath no joy
23:24 *f.* of righteous sh. rejoice
Is. 9:6 called everlasting *f.*
22:21 Eliakim be *f.* to inhabit.
38:19 *f.* to child. make kn. truth
Jer. 31:9 for I am a *f.* to Israel
Ezek. 18:4 as soul of *f.* so of son
20 son shall not bear iniq. of *f.*
22:7 in thee they set light by *f.*
Mic. 7:6 son dishonoreth the *f.*
Mal. 1:6 a *f.* where mine honor?
2:10 have we not all one *f. ?*
Mat. 10:20 *f.* del. ch. *Mark* 13:12
37 that loveth *f.* more than me
11:25 Jesus said, I th. thee. *F.*
26 so *F. Lu.* 10:21; *John* 11:41
27 knoweth the Son but the *F.*
15:4 that curseth *f. Mark* 7:10
19:5 leave *f.* and cleave to wife
29 that hath forsaken *f.* for my
   name's sake. *Mark* 10:29
28:19 baptizing in name of *F.*
Mark 9:24 *f.* of child cried
13:32 knoweth no man but *F.*
14:36 Abba, *F.* all th. possible
Luke 10:22 who the *F.* is, but S.
11:11 if a son ask bread of a *f.*
12:53 *f.* be divided against the
   son and son against the *f.*
15:21 *f.* I have sinned aga. hea.
16:27 I pray thee *f.* send him
22:42 *F.* if willing, remove cup
23:34 *F.* forgive them, they
46 *F.* into thy hands I com.
John 1:14 only begotten of *F.*
18 Son who is in bosom of *F.*
3:35 *F.* loveth the Son, 5:20
4:11 nor at Jerusal. worship *F.*
23 shall worship *F.* in spirit
5:19 do noth. but what *F.* do
21 as *F.* rais. up dead, so Son
22 the *F.* judgeth no man, but
23 honor the Son even as *F.*
26 the *F.* hath life in himself
36 works *F.* hath giv. me bear
   witness *F.* hath sent me
37 *F.* which hath sent, 8:16;
   12:49; 14:24; 1 *John* 4:14
5:45 will ac. you to the *F.*

6:37 all the *F.* giveth me, shall
39 *F.* will that I lose nothing
42 Jesus whose *f.* we know?

John 6:44 exc. the *F.* draw him
45 learned of *F.* cometh to me
46 not any hath seen the *F.* he
57 se. me, and I live by the *F.*
8:16 am not alone, but I and *F.*
18 *F.* beareth witness of me
27 unders. not he spake of *F.*
29 *F.* hath not left me alone
41 we have one *F.* even God
44 devil is liar, and the *f.* of it
10:15 *F.* know. me, so I the *F.*
36 whom the *F.* hath sanctified
38 *F.* is in me, and I in him
12:27 *F.* save me from this hour
28 *F.* glorify thy name, then
50 as *F.* said to me, so I speak
13:1 should depart unto the *F.*
3 that *F.* had given all things
14:6 com. to the *F.* but by me
8 Lord, show us the *F.*
9 seen me, hath seen the *F.*
11 I in *F.* and *F.* in me, 17:21
13 *F.* may be glorified in Son
16 pray the *F.* for you, 16:26
31 I love the *F.* as *F.* gave co.
15:9 as the *F.* hath loved me, so
16 whatsoever ye ask *F.* 16:26
26 I will send Comfor. from *F.*
16:3 not known the *F.* nor me
15 all things *F.* hath, are mine
16 because I go to the *F.* 17
25 show you plainly of the *F.*
27 the *F.* loveth you, because
28 I came from *F.* and go to *F.*
32 am not alone, *F.* is with me
17:1 *F.* hour is come, glorify S.
5 O *F.* glorify thou me with
11 holy *F.* keep th. given me
24 *F.* I will they be where I am
25 O right. *F.* world hath not

Acts 1:4 wait for promise of *F.*
7 *F.* put in his own power
2:33 received of *F.* the promise

Rom. 4:11 be *f.* of them believe
12 *f.* of circumcision to them
16 Abraham, who is *f.* of us all
6:4 as Christ was raised by *F.*
8:15 whereby we cry, Abba, *F.*
11:28 are belov. for the *F.* sake
15:6 *F.* of our L. J. C. 2 *Cor.* 1:3;
   11:31; *Eph.* 1:3; 1 *Pet.* 1:3

1 *Cor.* 8:6 is but one God, the *F.*
15:24 deliv. up kingdom to *F.*
2 *Cor.* 1:3 *F.* of mercies
6:18 I will be a *F.* unto you
Gal. 1:3 peace from *F.* 2 *Tim.*
   1:2; *Tit.* 1:4
4 ac. to will of God and our *F.*
4:2 until time appointed of *F.*
6 Spirit crying, Abba, *F.*
Eph. 1:17 G. of Jesus *F.* of glory
2:18 access by one Spirit to *F.*
3:14 bow my knees unto the *F.*
4:6 one God and *F.* all
5:20 giving thanks to *F. Col.*
   1:3, 12; 3:17
6:23 love with faith from *F.*
Phil. 2:11 is Lord, to glory of *F.*
22 as a son with the *f.* he hath
Col. 1:19 it plea. *F.* that all fuln.
2:2 acknowl. of mystery of *F.*
1 *Thes.* 1:1 church in God the *F.*
3:11 charged you, as a *f.* doth
1 *Tim.* 5:1 entreat him as a *f.*
Heb. 1:5 I will be to him a *F.* he
7:3 Melchizedek without *f.*
12:7 what son *f.* chasten. not?
9 in subjection to *F.* of spirits
Jam. 1:17 com. from *F.* of lights
3:9 bless we God, even the *F.*
1 *Pet.* 1:2 foreknowl. of the *F.*
17 call on *F.* who judgeth
2 *Pet.* 1:17 receiv. from *F.* honor

1 *John* 1:2 life wh. was with *F.*
3 our fellow. is with *F.*
2:1 an advocate with the *F. J.*
13 because ye have known *F.*
15 love of the *F.* is not in him
16 pride of life is not of the *F.*
22 antichrist deni. *F.* and Son
23 whoso deni. S. hath not *F.*
3:1 what manner of love the *F.*
5:7 three bear record, the *F.*
2 *John* 3 mercy and peace fr. *F.*
4 we received a com. from *F.*
9 abideth in Christ hath *F.*
Jude 1 sanctified by God the *F.*
See ABRAHAM.

Her FATHER.

Gen. 19:33 fl.-born lay with *her f.*
29:12 he was her *f.* brother
Lev. 21:9 she profaneth *her f.*
Num. 12:14 if *h. f.* had but spit
Deut. 21:13 bewail *h. f.* a month
Jud. 15:6 Philistines burnt *h. f.*
Est. 2:7 *h. f.* and mother dead

His FATHER.

Gen. 2:24 shall a man leave *his f.*
   Mark 10:7; *Eph.* 5:31
28:7 Jacob obeyed *his f.* and his
31:53 J. sware by fear of *his f.*
37:1 *his f.* was a stranger
22 to deliver him to *his f.*
44:22 the lad cannot leave *his f.*
46:1 sacrifices to God of *his f.*
29 Joseph went to meet *his f.*
47:12 Joseph nourished *his f.*
Ex. 21:15 smit. *f.* be put to dea.
17 curseth *his f. Lev.* 20:9
Lev. 19:3 fear every man *his f.*
Deut. 21:18 will not obey *his f.*
27:16 setteth light by *his f.*
33:9 *his f.* I have not seen him
1 *Sam.* 14:1 Jona. told not *his f.*
19:4 spake good of D. to *his f.*
20:34 *h. f.* had done him shame
2 *Sam.* 7:14 will be *his f.* he son
10:2 as *his f.* showed kindness
   to me, 1 *Chr.* 19:2
1 *K.* 11:4 not perf. as David *h. f.*
6 as did Dav. *his f.* 15:11; 2 *K.*
   18:3; 2 *Chr.* 28:1; 29:2
33 not as *f.* 2 *K.* 14:3; 16:2
15:3 walked in all sins of *his f.*
26 way of *f.* 22:43; 2 *K.* 21:21
2 *K.* 3:2 did evil, but not like *f.*
1 *Chr.* 17:13 I will be *his f.* 28:6
2 *Chr.* 3:1 L. appeared to D. *his f.*
17:4 Jehos. sought God of *his f.*
34:2 in ways of David *his f.* 3
Prov. 13:1 hear. instruction of *f.*
15:5 despiseth *h. f.* instruction
17:25 foolish son a grief to *h. f.*
19:13 is the calamity of *his f.*
26 wasteth *his f.* caus. shame
20:20 curseth *h. f.* lamp put out
28:7 com. of riot. shameth *his f.*
24 whoso robbeth *his f.*
29:3 lov. wisdom rejoiceth *h. f.*
30:17 mocketh *f.* ravens pick
Is. 45:10 woe to him saith to *h. f.*
Ezek. 18:14 son seeth *h. f.* sins
17 not die for iniquity of *his f.*
Amos 2:7 *his f.* go in to maid
Zec. 13:3 *his f.* thrust him thro'
Mal. 1:6 a son honors *his f.*
Mat. 10:35 at variance ag. *his f.*
15:5 to *h. f.* it is gift, *Mark* 7:11
6 and honor not *his f.* be free
16:27 Son come in glory of *h. F.*
   Mark 8:38; *Luke* 9:26
21:31 whether did will of *h. f. ?*
Luke 1:32 give him thr. of *his f.*
59 called after name of *his f.*
62 they made signs unto *his f.*
9:42 J. delivered him to *his f.*
14:26 and hate not *his f.*
15:12 younger said to *his f.*
20 arose and came to *his f.*

John 5:18 said that G. was *his F.*
Acts 16:1 but *his f.* was a Greek
Heb. 7:10 in the loins of *his f.*
Rev. 1:6 kings and pr. to *his F.*
14:1 *his F.* name in foreheads

See HOUSE.

FATHER-IN-LAW.

Ex. 18:1 Moses' *f.-in-law*, 8, 14, 17; *Jud.* 1:16; 4:11
27 Moses let *f.-in-law* depart
Jud. 19:4 *f.-in-law* retained him
John 18:13 *f.-in-law* to Caiaphas

My FATHER.

Gen. 19:34 I lay yest. with *my f.*
20:12 the daughter of *my f.*
27:34 E. cried. Bless me. *my f.*
31:5 the God of *my f.* 42; 32:9;
Ex. 18:4
44:24 thy servant *my f.* 27:30
32 suret y for the lad to *my f.*
45:3 doth *my f.* yet live?
47:1 *my f.* and breth. are come
Deut. 26:5 a Syrian was *my f.*
Jos. 2:13 will save alive *my f.*
Jud. 9:17 *my f.* fought for you
14:16 I have not told it *my f.*
1 Sam. 14:29 *my f.* troub. the land
18:18 what is *my f.* family?
20:2 *my f.* will do nothing
13 L. be with thee as with *my f.*
22:3 let *my f.* be with you
2 Sam. 16:3 restore king, of *my f.*
1 K. 2:26 barest ark before *my f.*
in all wherein *my f.* was affl.
44 wickedness didst to D. *my f.*
3:6 showed to D. *my f.* mercy
7 made king instead of *my f.*
5:3 *my f.* could not build house
8:17 in heart of D. *my f.* to build
12:10 little finger be thicker th.
my f. loins, 2 *Chr.* 10:10
11 *my f.* lade you, 2 *Chr.* 10:11
14 *my f.* chastised, 2 *Chr.* 10:14

1 K. 15:19 lea. be. *my f.* 2 *Chr.* 16:3
19:20 kiss *my f.* and mother
2 K. 2:12 Elisha cried, *my f. my f.*
6:21 *my f.* shall I smite them?
13:14 Joash said, *my f. my f.*
1 Chr. 28:4 chose me bef. all. ho. of *my f.* and among sons
2 Chr. 2:3 didst deal with *my f.*
Job 17:14 I said to corrup. *my f.*
Ps. 27:10 *f.* and mother forsake
89:26 thou art *my F.* my God
Prov. 4:3 for I was *my f.* son
Is. 8:4 knowledge to cry *my f.*
Jer. 2:27 stock, thou art *my f.*
3:4 thou not cry, *my F. P* 19
20:15 brought tidings to *my f.*
Dan. 5:13 *my f.* brought out of J.
Mat. 7:21 doeth will of *F.* 12:50
8:21 go bury *my f.* Luke 9:59
10:32 him confess before *my f.*
33 him will I deny bef. *my f.*
11:27 delivered of *F.* Luke 10:22
15:13 *my f.* hath not planted
16:17 *my F.* in heaven revealed
18:10 angels beh. face of *my f.*
19 it shall be done of *my F.*
35 heavenly *F.* also do to you
20:23 it is prepared of *my F.*
24:36 that day know. but *my F.*
25:34 come, ye blessed of *my F.*
26:29 drink it new in *F.* kingd.
39 O *my F.* let this cup pass
42 *my F.* thy will be done
53 I cannot pray to *my F. ?*
Luke 2:49 about *my F.* business
15:18 I will arise and go to *my f.*
16:27 send him to *my f.* house
22:29 as *my F.* hath appointed
24:49 the promise of *my F.*
John 5:17 *my F.* worketh
30 but the will of *my F.*
43 I am come in *my F.* name
6:32 *my f.* giv. you true bread

65 except it be given of *my F.*
8:19 nei. know. me, nor *my F.*
28 as *my F.* hath taught
38 I have seen with *my F.*
49 I honor *my F.* ye dishonor
54 it is *my F.* that honor. me
10:17 doth *my F.* love me
18 this com. I recei. of *my F.*
25 works I do in *my F.* name
29 *my F.* is greater than all
30 I and *my F.* are one
32 good works from *my F.*
37 if I do not works of *my F.*
12:26 him will *my F.* honor
14:7 should have known *my F.*
12 because I go to *my F.* 16:10
20 shall know I am in *my F.*
21 shall be loved of *my F.* 23
28 *my F.* is greater than I
15:1 *my F.* is the husbandman
8 herein is *my F.* glorified
10 I kept *my F.* commandm.
15 all that I heard of *my F.*
23 hateth me hateth *my F.* 24
18:11 cup *my F.* hath given
20:17 to *my F.* and your *F.*
21 as *my F.* hath sent me, so
Rev. 2:27 as I received of *my F.*
3:5 confess his name bef. *my F.*

Our FATHER.

Gen. 19:31 *o. f.* old; 32 *o. f.* dri.
43:28 *our f.* is in good health
44:31 *o. f.* with sorrow to grave
Num. 27:3 *o. f.* died in wildern.
4 name of *our f.* done away?
1 Chr. 29:10 bless. be th. L. *o. F.*
Is. 63:16 thou art *our F.*
64:8 art *our F.* we are the clay
Jer. 35:6 *our f.* com. drink no w.
Mat. 6:9 *our F.* Luke 11:2
Mark 11:10 blessed king. of *o. f.*
Luke 3:8 have Abraham to *our f.*
John 4:12 greater than *o. f.? 8:53*
Acts 7:2 God appeared to *our f.*
Rom. 1:7 peace fr. G. *our F.* 1 *Cor.* 1:3; 2 *Cor.* 1:2; *Eph.* 1:2; *Phil.* 1:2; *Col.* 1:2; 1 *Thes.* 1:1; 2 *Thes.* 1:2; 1 *Tim.* 1:2; *Phile.* 3
9:10 even by *our f.* Isaac
Gal. 1:4 will of God and *our F.*
Phil. 4:20 to *our F.* be glory
1 Thes. 1:3 sight of G. and *o. F.*
3:11 *our F.* direct our way
13 stablish in holiness bef. *o. F.*
2 Thes. 1:1 church in God *our F.*
2:16 *our F.* comfort your hearts

Their FATHER.

Gen. 9:23 saw not naked. of *t. f.*
19:36 with child by *their f.*
Ex. 40:15 daist anoint *their f.*
1 Sam. 2:25 heark. not to *their f.*
10:12 one said, Who is *their f.*
1 Chr. 24:2 N. Abihu died bef. *t. f.*
2 Chr. 21:3 *t. f.* gave great gifts

Job 42:15 *t. f.* gave inheritance
Prov. 30:11 that curseth *their f.*
Jer. 16:7 con. to drink for *t. f.*
35:14 Jona. sons obeyed *t. f.* 16
Ezek. 22:10 disc. *t. f.* nakedness
Mat. 4:21 with Zebedee *their f.*
22 left *t. f.* and followed him

Thy FATHER.

Gen. 12:1 get from *thy f.* house
46:3 I am the God of *thy f.*
49:25 by the God of *thy f.*
26 blessings of *thy f.* prevailed
50:16 *t. f.* com. before he died
17 forgive serv. of G. of *t. f.*
Ex. 20:12 honor *t. f.* and mother, *Deut.* 5:16; *Mat.* 15:4; 19:19
Deut. 6:3 as G. of *t. f.* promised
32:6 is not he *t. f.* bought thee?
7 ask *thy f.* and he will show
Ruth 2:11 thou hast left *thy f.*
1 Sam. 20:6 if *thy f.* miss me
2 Sam. 6:21 chose me before *t. f.*

10:3 thinkest thou that D. doth honor *thy f.* 1 *Chr.* 19:3
16:19 served in *thy f.* presence
1 K. 11:12 for David *t. f.* sake
2 K. 3:13 get to prophets of *t. f.*
20:5 thus saith the G. of D. *t. f.*
2 Chr. 21:12; *Is.* 38:5
1 Chr. 28:9 son, know G. of *t. f.*
2 Chr. 7:17 if walk bef. me as *t. f.*
Job 15:10 much older than *thy f.*
Prov. 1:8 instruct. of *thy f.* 23:22
6:20 keep *thy f.* commandment
23:25 *t. f.* and mother sh. be gl.
27:10 *thy f.* friend forsake not
Is. 43:27 *thy f.* hath sinned
58:14 heritage of Jacob *thy f.*
Jer. 12:6 house of *t. f.* dealt trea.
22:15 did not *thy f.* eat, drink
Ezek. 16:3 *thy f.* was an Amorite
Dan. 5:11 in the days of *thy f.*
18 God gave *thy f.* a kingdom
Mat. 6:4 *t. F.* who seeth in sec.
6 pray to *t. F.* who is in secret
Mark 7:10 M. said, Honor *thy f.*
10:19; *Luke* 18:20; *Eph.* 6:2
Luke 2:48 *thy f.* and I sought
15:27 *thy f.* hath killed calf
John 8:19 Where is *thy f.?*

Your FATHER.

Gen. 31:7 *your f.* hath deceived
43:7 is *your f.* alive?
44:17 get up in peace to *your f.*
45:19 bring *your f.* and come
49:2 hearken unto Israel *your f.*
Jer. 35:18 obeyed Jonadab y. *f.*
Ezek. 16:45 *your f.* an Amorite
Mat. 5:16 glorify *your F.* in hea.
45 may be children of *your F.*
48 as *y. F.* in heaven is perfect
6:1 otherwise no reward of *y. F.*
8 *y. F.* knoweth what things ye have need of, 32; *Luke* 12:30
14 if ye forgive, *y. F.* will for.
15 nei. will *y. F.* forgive your trespasses, *Mark* 11:25, 26
10:29 sparrow fall without *y. F.*
18:14 not will of *y. F.* one perish
23:9 call no man *y. f.* on earth, for one is *your F.* in heaven
Luke 6:36 as *your F.* is merciful
12:32 *y. F.* pleas. to give kingd.
John 8:38 that seen with *your F.*
41 ye do the deeds of *your F.*
42 J. said, if God were *your F.*
44 ye are of *y. f.* the devil, and the lusts of *y. f.* ye will do
20:17 I asc. to *my F.* and *y. F.*

FATHERS.

Ex. 10:6 *thy f.* nor *thy f.*
20:5 visiting iniquity of *f.* 34:7;
Num. 14:18; *Deut.* 5:9
Deut. 24:16 *f.* not be put to death
for children, 2 *K.* 14:6
Job 30:1 *f.* I would ha. disdained
Prov. 19:14 inheritance of *f.*
Is. 49:23 kings be thy nursing *f.*
Jer. 6:21 *f.* and sons sh. fall, 13:14
7:18 *f.* kindle the fire
31:29 *f.* eaten sour grapes, *Ezek.* 18:2
32:18 recompensest iniq. of *f.*
47:3 *f.* not look back to child.
Ezek. 5:10 *f.* shall eat the sons
Mal. 4:6 turn *f.* to ch. *Luke* 1:17
John 7:22 of Moses, but of the *f.*
Acts 7:2 and *f.* hearken. 22:1
13:32 promise made to the *f.*
22:3 perf. manner of law of *f.*
Rom. 9:5 whose are the *f.*
1 Cor. 4:15 have ye not many *f.*
Eph. 6:4 *f.* prov. not, *Col.* 3:21
Heb. 1:1 in times past to *f.*
12:9 we had *f.* who corrected
2 Pet. 3:4 since the *f.* fell asleep
1 John 2:13 write unto you *f.* 14

See BURIED, CHIEF.

His FATHERS.

2 K. 15:9 did evil as *his f.* had
  21:22 fors. G. of *h. f.* 2 *Chr.*21:10
2 *Chr.* 21:19 like burning of *h. f.*
  28:25 A. provoked L. G. of *h. f.*
  30:19 to seek God of *his f.*
  33:12 humbled before G. of *h. f.*
Ps. 49:19 generation of *his f.*
  109:14 iniquity of *his f.*
Dan. 11:24 what *his f.* not done
  37 nor regard the God of *his f.*
  38 a god whom *his f.* knew not
Acts 13:36 Dav. was laid to *h. f.*

My FATHERS.

Gen. 47:9 not at. years of *my f.*
  30 I will lie with *my f.*
  48:16 name of *my f.* be named
  49:29 bury me with *my f.*
Ex. 15:2 he is *my f.* God
1 *K.* 19:4 no better than *my f.*
  21:3 inheritance of *my f.* 4.
2 *K.* 19:12 which *my f.* destroyed,
  2 *Chr.* 32:14 ; *Is.* 37:12
2 *Chr.* 32:13 I and *my f.* done
Ps. 39:12 soj. as *my f.* were
Dan. 2:23 O God of *my f.*
Acts 24:14 worship God of *my f.*
Gal. 1:14 traditions of *my f.*

Our FATHERS.

Gen. 46:34 we and also *o. f.* 47:3
Num. 20:15 our *f.* went down
Deut. 5:3 not covenant with *o. f.*
  6:23 he sware to *our f.* 26:3, 15
  26:7 cried to the God of *our f.*
Jos. 24:17 brought *o. f.* out of E.
Jud. 6:13 mirac. *o. f.* told us of?
1 *K.* 8:57 as he was with *our f.*
  58 statutes he commanded *o. f.*
2 *K.* 22:13 our *f.* not hearkened
1 *Chr.* 12:17 G. of *our f.* rebuke it
  29:15 as sojourners, as *our f.*
  18 O L. God of *our f.* keep for
    ever in the heart, 2 *Chr.* 20:6
2 *Chr.* 6:31 gavest *o. f.* Neh. 9:36
  29:6 for *our f.* have trespassed
  9 *o. f.* have fallen by the sword
  34:21 *our f.* have not kept word
Ezr. 5:12 after *o. f.* provoked G.
  7:27 blessed be the God of *o. f.*
  9:7 since *o. f.* in great trespass
Neh. 9:9 see affliction of *our f.*
  16 *our f.* dealt proudly
Ps. 22:4 *our f.* trusted in thee
  44:1 *o. f.* told what didst, 78:3
  106:6 we have sinned with *o. f.*
  7 *o. f.* understood not wonders
Is. 64:11 *our f.* praised thee
Jer. 3:24 devoured labor of *o. f.*
  25 *and our f.* not obeyed voice
  16:19 *our f.* have inherited lies
  44:17 as we have done, *our f.*
Lam. 5:7 *our f.* sinned
Dan. 9:8 confus. of face to *our f.*
  16 our sins and iniq. of *our f.*
Mic. 7:20 sworn to *o. f.* from old
Mal. 2:10 profaning cov. of *our f.*
Mat. 23:30 in days of *our f.*
Luke 1:55 as he spake to *our f.*
  72 mercy promised to *our f.*
John 4:20 *our f.* wors. in mount.
  6:31 *our f.* eat manna in desert
Acts 3:13 God of *o. f.* hath glori.
  25 cove. God made with *our f.*
  5:30 G. of *o. f.* raised up Jesus
  7:11 *our f.* found no sustenance
  15 Jacob died, he and *our f.*
  19 and evil entreated *our f.*
  38 he which spake with *our f.*
  39 whom *o. f.* would not obey
  13:17 God of Israel chose *our f.*
  15:10 yoke *o. f.* not able to bear
  26:6 promise made to *our f.*
  28:25 well spake by E. to *our f.*
1 *Cor.* 10:1 *o. f.* were under cloud

Slept with FATHERS.

1 *K.* 2:10 David *slept w. f.* 11:21
  43 Sol. *slept w. f.* 2 *Chr.* 9:31

---

2 *K.* 20:21 H. *s. w. f.* 2 *Chr.* 32:33
2 *Chr.* 26:23 Uzziah *slept with f.*

Their FATHERS.

Ex. 4:5 G. of *t. f.* hath appeared
Lev. 26:39 in iniquity of *their f.*
  26:40 confess iniq. of *their f.*
Num. 11:12 swarest to *t. f.* 14:23;
  Deut. 10:11; 31:20; *Jos.* 1:6;
  5:6; 21:43, 44; *Jer.* 32:22
Deut. 29:25 forsaken cov. of *t. f.*
Jos. 4:6 children ask *their f.* 21
  22:14 head of house of *their f.*
Jud. 2:10 gathered to *their f.*
  12 forsook the God of *their f.*
  17 out of way *t. f.* walked in
  19 corrupted more than *t. f.*
  20 covenant I commanded *t. f.*
Jud. 2:22 keep way of L. as *t. f.*
1 *K.* 8:34 land thou gavest to *t.
  f.* 48; 2 *Chr.* 6:25, 38
  9:9 brought *t. f.* out of Egypt
  14:15 he gave to *their f.* 2 *K.*
  21:8; *Jer.* 16:15; 24:10
  22 provok. above all *t. f.* done
1 *Chr.* 5:25 transgr. ag. God of *f.*
  29:20 blessed God of *their f.*
2 *Chr.* 7:22 for. G. of *f.* 24:24; 28:6
  11:16 sacrifice to God of *their f.*
  13:18 relied on God of *their f.*
  14:4 to seek God of *t. f.* 15:12
  19:4 back to the God of *their f.*
  20:33 prepa. hearts to G. of *t. f.*
  30:7 trespassed ag. God of *t. f.*
  22 confession to God of *their f.*
  34:33 following the God of *t. f.*
  36:15 G. of *t. f.* sent messengers
Neh. 9:2 confessed iniq. of *t. f.*
Job 8:8 prepare to search of *t. f.*
  15:18 wise men told from *t. f.*
Ps. 78:8 might not be as *their f.*
  12 marv. things in sight of *t. f.*
  57 dealt unfaithfully like *t. f.*
Prov. 17:6 glory of child. are *t. f.*
Is. 14:21 slaughter for iniq. of *f.*
Jer. 7:26 did worse than *their f.*
  9:14 Baalim, which *t. f.* taught
  16 nor *t. f.* have known, 19:4
  23:27 as *t. f.* forgotten my name
  31:32 not accord. to covenant I
    made with *t. f.* 11:10; *Heb.*8:9
  50:7 sinned ag. L. hope of *t. f.*
Ezek. 2:3 *t. f.* have transgressed
  5:10 and sons shall eat *their f.*
  20:4 cause know abom. of *t. f.*
Amos 2:4 after which *t. f.* walked
Mal. 4:6 heart of children to *t. f.*
Luke 6:23 like manner did *t. f.*
  26 so did *t. f.* to false prophets

Thy FATHERS.

Gen. 15:15 shalt go to *thy f.*
Ex. 13:5 sware to *thy f.* 11; *Deut.*
  6:10, 18; 7:12, 13; 8:18; 9:5;
  13:17; 19:8; 28:11; 29:13; 30:20
Deut. 4:31 not forget cov. of *t. f.*
  37 because he loved *thy f.*
  10:22 *thy f.* went with 70 persons
  12:1 land the G. of *thy f.* giveth
  19:8 land he prom. *thy f.* 27:3
  30:5 multipl. thee above *thy f.*
  9 as he rejoiced over *thy f.*
  31:16 with *thy f.* 2 *Sam.* 7:12
1 *K.* 13:22 not to sepulchre of *t. f.*
2 *K.* 20:17 *thy f.* laid up
  22:20 to *thy f.* 2 *Chr.* 34:28
1 *Chr.* 17:11 go to be with *thy f.*
Ps. 45:16 instead of *thy f.*
Jer. 34:5 the burnings of *thy f.*
Acts 7:32 I am the God of *thy f.*

Your FATHERS.

Gen. 48:21 bring to land of *y. f.*
Ex. 3:13 God of *your f.* sent me
  Deut. 1:11; 4:1; *Jos.* 18:3
  2 *Chr.* 28:9; 29:5
Num. 32:14 risen up in *y. f.* stead
Jos. 24:2 *your f.* dwell other side
  6 I brought *y. f.* out of Egypt

---

1 *Sam.* 12:7 acts L. did to *y. f.*
  8 *y. f.* cried, L. bro. forth *y. f.*
  15 hand of L. ag. you as *y. f.*
2 *Chr.* 13:12 not ag. God of *y. f.*
  30:7 not like *y. f.* 8; *Zec.* 1:4
Ezr. 10:11 confes. to G. of *y. f.*
Ps. 95:9 *your f.* tempted, *Heb.* 8:9
Is. 65:7 and iniquities of *your f.*
Jer. 2:5 iniq. *y. f.* found in me?
  11:7 I earnestly protested to *y. f.*
  16:11 *your f.* have forsaken me
  12 done worse than *your f.*
  34:14 *y. f.* heark. not unto me
  44:3 knew not, they nor *your f.*
  8 forgotten wickedn. of *y. f.*?
Ezek. 20:18 not in statutes of *y. f.*
  27 in this *your f.* blasphemed
  30 after manner of *your f.*
  36 as I pleaded with *your f.*?
  37:25 dwell in land *y. f.* dwelt
Hos. 9:10 I saw *y. f.* as first ripe
Joel 1:2 been in days of *your f.*
Zec. 1:2 L. displeased with *y. f.*
  4 be not as *your f.*
  5 *your f.* where are they ?
  6 words take hold of *your f.*
Mal. 3:7 days of *y. f.* ye are gone.
Mat. 23:32 fill up measure of *y. f.*
Luke 11:47 *your f.* killed them
  48 ye allow deeds of *your f.*
John 6:49 *your f.* did eat manna
  58 *your f.* eat, and are dead
Acts 7:51 resist Holy G. as *y. f.*
  52 have not *y. f.* persecuted ?
1 *Pet.* 1:18 by tradition from *y. f.*

FATHERLESS.

Ex. 22:22 not afflict *f.* child
Ex. 22:24 your children sh. be *f.*
Deut. 10:18 execute judgment of
  f. Ps. 82:3; *Is.* 1:17
Job 6:27 ye overwhelm the *f.*
  22:9 arms of *f.* been broken
  24:3 drive away ass of the *f.*
  9 pluck *f.* from the breast
  29:12 because I delivered the *f.*
  31:17 the *f.* not eaten thereof
  21 if I lifted up my hand ag. *f.*
Ps. 10:14 thou art helper of *f.*
  18 judge the *f.* and oppressed
  68:5 a father of the *f.*
  109:9 let his children be *f.*
  12 nor any favor his *f.* children
Prov. 23:10 enter not fields of *f.*
Is. 1:23 judge not *f.* Jer. 5:28
  9:17 not have mercy on their *f.*
  10:2 that they may rob the *f.*
Jer. 49:11 leave thy *f.* children
Lam. 5:3 we are orphans and *f.*
Ezek. 22:7 in thee have vexed *f.*
Hos. 14:3 in thee *f.* findeth mercy
Mal. 3:5 witness ag. those op. *f.*
Jam. 1:27 pure religion to visit *f.*

FATHERLESS, with stranger.

Deut. 14:29 *stra.* and *f.* shall eat,
  24:19, 20, 21; 26:12, 13
  16:11 *s.* and *f.* rejoice with thee
  24:17 not perv. jud. of *s.* nor *f.*
  27:19 perv. judg. of *s.* and *f.*
Ps. 94:6 slay *s.* and murder *f.*
  146:9 Lord preserveth *s.* and *f.*
Jer. 7:6 if ye oppress not the *st.*
  and *f.* 22:3 ; *Zec.* 7:10

FATHOMS.

Acts 27:28 found it twenty *f.*

FATLING, S.

1 *Sam.* 15:9 Saul spared best of *f.*
Ps. 66:15 burnt sacrifices of *f.*
Is. 11:6 lion, and the *f.* together
Ezek. 39:18 all of them *f.* of B.
Mat. 22:4 oxen and *f.* are killed

FATNESS.

Gen. 27:28 G. give thee of the *f.*
  39 dwelling be *f.* of the earth
Deut. 32:15 art covered with *f.*

FATNESS

Jud. 9:9 should I leave my *f.*
Job 15:27 cover. face with his *f.*
36:16 thy table sh. be full of *f.*
Ps. 36:8 satisfied with *f.*
63:5 my soul satisfied as with *f.*
65:11 all thy paths drop *f.*
73:7 eyes stand out with *f.*
109:24 my flesh faileth of *f.*
Is. 17:4 *f.* of his flesh wax lean
34:6 sword of Lord is fat wi. *f.*
7 their dust be made fat wi. *f.*
55:2 let soul delight itself in *f.*
Jer. 31:14 soul of priests with *f.*
Rom. 11:17 partak. of *f.* of olive

FATS.

Joel 2:24 *f.* shall overflow, 3:13

FATTED.

Jer. 46:21 men like *f.* bullocks
See CALF.

FATTEST.

Ps. 78:31 wrath of God slew *f.*
Dan. 11:24 enter on the *f.* places

FAULT, S.

Gen. 41:9 I remember *f.* this day
Ex. 5:16 *f.* is in thine own peo.
Deut. 25:2 beaten accord. to h. *f.*
1 *Sam.* 29:3 I found no *f.* in him
2 *Sam.* 3:8 chargest me with a *f.*
Ps. 19:12 cleanse from secret *f.*
59:4 they prepare without my *f.*
Dan. 6:4 could find no *f.* in him
Mat. 18:15 tresp. tell him his *f.*
Mark 7:2 unw. hands they *f.*
Luke 23:4 I find no *f.* in th. man,
14; *John* 18:38; 19:4, 6
Rom. 9:19 doth he yet find *f. f*
1 *Cor.* 6:7 utterly a *f.* among you
Gal. 6:1 man be overtaken in *f.*
Heb. 8:8 finding *f.* with them
Jam. 5:16 conf. *f.* one to another
1 *Pet.* 2:20 if when buffeted for *f.*
Rev. 14:5 without *f.* bef. throne

FAULTLESS.

Heb. 8:7 if first cov. had been *f.*
Jude 24 is able to present you *f.*

FAULTY.

2 *Sam.* 14:13 king speak as one *f.*
Hos. 10:2 shall they be found *f.*

FAVOR, Substantive.

Gen. 39:21 gave Jos. *f.* in sight
Ex. 3:21 give peop. *f.* in sight of
Egyptians, 11:3; 12:36
Deut. 28:50 not show *f.* to young
33:23 O Naph. satisfied with *f.*
Jos. 11:20 they might have no *f.*
Sam. 2:26 Samuel in *f.* with L.
Job 10:12 granted me life and *f.*
Ps. 5:12 with *f.* compass him
30:5 in his *f.* is life,
7 by *f.* made mountain to sta.
44:3 because hadst a *f.* to them
45:12 rich shall entreat thy *f.*
89:17 in thy *f.* our horn exalted
106:4 remember me with *f.* thou
112:5 a good man showeth *f.*
119:58 I entreated thy *f.*
Prov. 11:27 seek. good procur. *f.*
13:15 good understand. giv. *f.*
14:9 among righteous there is *f.*
35 king's *f.* toward wise serv.
16:15 his *f.* is as a cloud of rain
19:6 many entreat *f.* of prince
12 king's *f.* is as dew up. grass
21:10 his neighbor findeth no *f.*
22:1 lov. *f.* rather to be chosen
29:26 many seek the ruler's *f.*
31:30 *f.* is deceitful
Ec. 9:11 nor *f.* to men of skill
Is. 26:10 *f.* be showed to wicked
27:11 formed show them no *f.*
60:10 but in my *f.* I had mercy
Jer. 16:13 I will not show *f.*
Dan. 1:9 brought Daniel into *f.*
Luke 2:52 Jesus increased in *f.*
Acts 2:47 *f.* with all the people

7:10 God gave Moses *f.* in sight
25:3 high-priest desired *f.*

Find *or* found FAVOR.

Gen. 18:3 if I have *f. f.* 30:27:
Num. 11:15; 1 *Sam.* 20:29;
Neh. 2:5; *Est.* 5:8; 7:3; 8:5
Num. 11:11 why h. I not *f. f. f*
Deut. 24:1 that she *find* no *f.*
1 *Sam.* 16:22 David find *f.*
25:8 let the young men find *f.*
2 *Sam.* 15:25 if I *f. f.* in ey. of L.
Prov. 3:4 so *f. f.* in sight of God
28:23 *find* more *f.* than he flat.
Cant. 8:10 I was as one *found f.*
Luke 1:30 hast *f. f.* with God
Acts 7:46 who *f. f.* before God

Obtain, ed, eth FAVOR.

Est. 2:15 Esther ob. *f.* 17; 5:2
Prov. 8:35 findeth me shall ob. *f.*
12:2 good man ob. *f.* of Lord
18:22 findeth a wife, obtaineth *f.*

FAVOR, Verb.

1 *Sam.* 29:6 the lords *f.* thee not
Ps. 35:27 *f.* my righteous cause
102:13 set time to *f.* her is come
14 thy servants *f.* dust thereof
109:12 to *f.* fatherless children

FAVORABLE.

Jud. 21:22 be *f.* for our sakes
Job 33:26 God will *b. f.* unto him
Ps. 77:7 will L. be *f.* no more *f*
85:1 hast been *f.* to thy land

FAVORED, EST, ETH.

Gen. 29:17 Rachel was well-*f.*
39:6 Jos. well-*f.;* 41:2 kine, 18
41:3 il-*f.* kine, 4, 19, 21, 27
2 *Sam.* 20:11 *f.* Joab, go after ɔ.
Ps. 41:11 by this I know thou *f.*
Lam. 4:16 they *f.* not the elders
Dan. 1:4 children well-*f.* skilful
Nah. 3:4 whored. of well-*f.* har.
Luke 1:28 hail, thou highly *f.*

FEAR, Substantive.

Gen. 9:2 *f.* of you be on ev. beast
31:42 *f.* of Is. had been with me
53 Jacob sware by *f.* of Isaac
Ex. 15:16 *f.* sh. fall upon them
23:27 send my *f.* before thee
Deut. 2:25 *f.* of thee on nations
11:25 lay *f.* of you on land
1 *Chr.* 14:17 *f.* of him on nations
Ezr. 3:3 *f.* was on them because
Neh. 6:14 that put me in *f.* 19
Est. 8:17 *f.* of Jews fell on them
9:3 *f.* of Mordecai fell on them
Job 4:6 is not this thy *f.*
14 *f.* came on me and tremb.
6:14 forsaketh *f.* of Almighty
9:34 let not his *f.* terrify me
15:4 yea, thou castest off *f.* and
21:9 their houses are safe from *f.*
22:10 sudden *f.* troubleth thee
25:2 dominion and *f.* with him
39:22 he mocketh at *f.*
Ps. 5:7 in thy *f.* will I worship
9:20 put them in *f.* O Lord
14:5 there were they in great *f.*
31:11 I was a *f.* to acquaintance
13 *f.* was on every side
48:6 *f.* took hold upon them
53:5 were in *f.* where no *f.* was
64:1 pres. my life fr. *f.* of enemy
90:11 to thy *f.* so is thy wrath
105:38 *f.* of them fell upon them
119:38 thy serv. devot. to thy *f.*
Prov. 1:26 mock when *f.* cometh
27 when your *f.* cometh as d.

Prov. 1:33 be quiet from *f.* of evil
3:25 be not afraid of sudden *f.*
10:24 *f.* of wicked come on him
20:2 *f.* of king as roaring of lion
29:25 *f.* of man bringeth a snare
Cant. 3:8 sw. bec. of *f.* in night
Is. 7:25 not come the *f.* of briers
8:12 neither fear ye their *f.*
13 the Lord, let him be your *f.*

14:3 shall give thee rest from *f.*
21:4 night of pleasure into *f.*
24:17 *f.* and the pit upon thee
18 fleeth from *f.* *Jer.* 48:44
29:13 their *f.* is taught by men
63:17 hardened heart from thy *f.*
Jer. 2:19 that my *f.* is not in thee
6:25 *f.* is on ev. side, 20:10
30:5 we have heard a voice of *f.*
32:40 put my *f.* in their hearts
48:43 *f.* shall be on thee, O M.
49:5 I will bring a *f.* upon thee
24 *f.* hath seized on Damascus
29 shall cry. *f.* is on every side
Lam. 3:47 *f.* and snare is come
Ezek. 30:13 put a *f.* in land of E.
Mal. 1:6 where is my *f. f*
Luke 1:12 Z. saw him, *f.* fell on
65 *f.* ca. on all, 7:16; *Acts* 2:43;
5:5, 11; 19:17; *Rev.* 11:11
Rom. 13:7 *f.* to whom *f.* is due
1 *Cor.* 2:3 in weakness and *f.*
2 *Cor.* 7:11 what *f.* what vehem.
2 *Tim.* 1:7 not giv. us spirit of *f.*
Heb. 2:15 through *f.* of death
12:28 reverence and godly *f.*
1 *Pet.* 1:17 pass time of soj. in *f.*
3:15 with meekness and *f.*
1 *John* 4:18 no *f.* in l. cast out *f.*

For FEAR.

Deut. 28:67 *f.* the *f.* thou sh. fear
Jos. 22:24 done it *f. f.* of thing
1 *Sam.* 21:10 fled *f. f.* of S. 23:26
Job 22:4 reprove *f. f.* of thee ?
Is. 31:9 to his strong-hold *f. f.*
Jer. 46:5 *f. f.* was round about
50:16 *f. f.* of oppressing sword
Mal. 2:5 *f. f.* wherew. he feared
Mat. 14:26 discip. cried out *f. f.*
28:4 *f. f.* of him keepers shake
Luke 21:26 hearts failing for *f.*
John 7:13 spake openly *f. f.*
19:38 but secretly *f. f.* of Jews
20:19 assembled *f. f.* of the J.
Rev. 18:10 *f. f.* of torment, 15

Fear of GOD.

Gen. 20:11 *f.* of G. not in place
2 *Sam.* 23:3 ruling in *f.* of God
2 *Chr.* 20:29 *f.* of G. on all king.
Neh. 5:9 to walk in the *f. f.* G. ?
15 so did not L. bec. of *f.* of G.
Ps. 36:1 no *f.* of G. bef. his eyes
Rom. 3:18 no *f.* of G. bef. th. ey.
2 *Cor.* 7:1 holiness in *f.* of God
Eph. 5:21 submitting in *f.* of G.

Fear of the LORD.

1 *Sam.* 11:7 *f.* of L. 2 *Chr.* 17:10
2 *Chr.* 14:14 *f.* of L. ca. on them
19:7 *f.* of the L. be upon you
9 thus do in *f.* of the Lord
Job 28:28 *f.* of the L. is wisdom
Ps. 19:9 *f.* of the Lord is clean
34:11 I will teach you *f.* of L.
111:10 *f.* of L. begin. of wisdom
Prov. 1:7 *f.* of L. beg. of kn. 9:10
29 did not choose the *f.* of L.
2:5 shalt understand *f.* of the L.
8:3 *f.* of L. is to hate evil
10:27 *f.* of the L. prolong. days
14:26 in *f.* of Lord is str. confid.
27 *f.* of L. is a fountain of life
15:16 better is lit. with *f.* of L.
33 *f.* of L. is instruction
16:6 by *f.* of L. men dep. fr. evil
19:23 *f.* of the L. tendeth to life
22:4 by *f.* of L. are riches and h.
23:17 be in *f.* of Lord all day
Is. 2:10 hide in dust, for *f.* of L.
19 go into caves for *f.* of L.
21 go into clefts, for *f.* of Lord
11:2 spirit of know. and *f.* of L.
3 quick understand. in *f.* of L.
33:6 *f.* of L. is his treasure
Acts 9:31 walking in *f.* of the L.

With FEAR.

Ps. 2:11 serve the Lord *with f.*
Mat. 28:8 with *f.* and great joy
Luke 5:26 were all filled *with f.*
8:37 Gadarenes tak. *w.* great *f.*
2 *Cor.* 7:15 *with f.* received him
Eph. 6:5 obedience *w. f.* and tr.
Phil. 2:12 work out salva. *w. f.*
Heb. 11:7 N. *w. f.* prepared ark
1 *Pet.* 2:18 be subj. to mast. *w.f.*
3:2 chaste conv. coup. *w.f.*
Jude 23 and others save *with f.*

Without FEAR.

Job 39:16 her labor in vain *w. f.*
41:33 not his like, made *w. f.*
Luke 1:74 serve him *with f.*
1 *Cor.* 16:10 may be with *y. w. f.*
Phil. 1:14 bold to sp. word *w. f.*
Jude 12 feeding themselv. *w. f.*

FEARS.

Ps. 34:4 delivered me fr. all my *f.*
Ec. 12:5 when *f.* be in the way
Is. 66:4 bring their *f.* upon them
2 *Cor.* 7:5 within were *f.*

FEAR, Verb.

Lev. 19:3 *f.* every man his moth.
Num. 14:9 nei. *f.* people of land
Deut. 4:10 may learn to *f.* me
5:29 O that they would *f.* me
28:58 *f.* glori. name, the Lord
66 thou shalt *f.* day and night
67 fear wherewith thou sha. *f.*
Jud. 7:10 if thou *f.* to go down
1 *K.* 8:40 *f.* thee, 2 *Chr.* 6:31
43 name to *f.* thee, 2 *Chr.* 6:33
2 *K.* 17:38 neither *f.* other gods
39 the Lord your G. ye shall *f.*
1 *Chr.* 16:30 *f.* before him all the
earth, *Ps.* 96:9
Neh. 1:11 desire to *f.* thy name
Job 31:34 did I *f.* a great multi
Ps. 23:4 I will *f.* no evil,
27:1 whom shall I *f. ?*
31:19 goodness for them *f.* thee
40:3 many shall see it, and *f.*
49:5 I *f.* in days of evil *?*
52:6 righte. also shall see and *f.*
60:4 a banner to them that *f.*
61:5 herit. of those *f.* thy name
64:9 shall *f.* and declare work
72:5 *f.* thee as long as sun end.
86:11 unite my heart to *f.* name
102:15 so heath. shall *f.* thy n.
119:39 my reproach which I *f.*
63 compan. of them that *f.* th.
74 they that *f.* thee will be gl.
79 let those *f.* thee turn to me
Ec. 3:14 that men *f.* before him
Is. 8:12 neither *f.* ye their fear
19:16 Eg. shall be afraid and *f.*
25:3 city of ter. nations *f.* the
44:11 the workmen shall *f.*
50:10 so shall they *f.* name of L.
60:5 thy heart *f.* and be enlarg.
Jer. 10:7 who would not *f.* th. O
23:4 and they shall *f.* no more
32:39 one heart that they *f.* me
33:9 shall *f.* for the goodness
51:46 and lest ye *f.* for rumor
Dan. 6:26 *f.* before G. of Daniel
Hos. 10:5 inhab. of Samaria sh. *f.*
Mic. 7:17 and *f.* because of thee
Zep. 3:7 said, Surely wilt *f.* me
Hag. 1:12 people did *f.* before L.
Zec. 9:5 Ashk. shall see it, and *f.*
Mal 4:2 to you *f.* my name
Mat. 21:26 we say, Of men, we *f.*
Luke 12:5 whom ye shall *f.*
Rom. 8:15 spirit of bondage to *f.*
11:20 be not high-minded, but *f.*
2 *Cor.* 12:20 I *f.* lest not find you
1 *Tim.* 5:20 others also may *f.*
Heb. 4:1 let us *f.* lest a promise
12:21 M. said, I exceedingly *f.*
Rev. 2:10 *f.* none of those things
11:18 rew. to them *f.* thy name

FEAR God.

Gen. 42:18 and live, for I *f.* G.
Ex. 18:21 provide such as *f.* God
Lev. 19:14 shalt *f.* thy God, 32
25:17 thou sh. *f.* thy G. 36, 43
Job 1:9 doth J. *f.* G. for naught *?*
Ps. 66:16 all ye that *f.* God
Ec. 5:7 vanities, but *f.* thou God
8:12 well with them that *f.* G.
12:13 *f.* G. and keep his com.
Is. 29:23 they sh. *f.* G. of Israel
Luke 23:40 dost not thou *f.* G. *?*
Acts 13:16 *f.* God, give audience
1 *Pet.* 2:17 *f.* God, honor the k.
Rev. 14:7 *f.* God, and give glory

Hear and FEAR.

Deut. 13:11 Is. shall *h. a. f.* 21:21
17:13 all the peo. shall *h. a. f.*
19:20 who remain sh. *hear a. f.*

FEAR him.

Deut. 13:4 walk after G. and *f. h.*
2 *K.* 17:36 *him* shall ye *f.*
Job 37:24 men therefore *f. him*
Ps. 22:23 *f. him*, seed of Israel
25 before them that *f. him.*
25:14 secret of L. with th. *f. h.*
33:18 eye of L. on them *f. him*
34:7 encamp. about them *f. h.*
9 no want to them that *f. him*
67:7 ends of the earth shall *f. h.*
85:9 salva. is nigh them *f. him*
103:11 his mercy to them *f. h.*
Ps. 103:13 L. pit. th. that *f. him*
17 mercy of L. is on them *f. h.*
111:5 meat to them that *f. him*
145:19 desire of them *f. him*
147:11 pleas. in them that *f. h.*
Mat. 10:28 *f.* h. able *Luke* 12:5
Luke 1:50 mercy on them *f. him*
Rev. 19:5 praise God. ye that *f. h.*

Fear the LORD.

Deut. 6:2 mightest *f. t.* L. thy G.
13 shalt *f.* L. 10:20; 2 *K.* 17:39
24 to *f.* L. for our good always
10:12 *f. the* L. walk in his ways
14:23 to *f.* L. 17:19; 31:12, 13
Jos. 4:24 might *f.* Lord your G.
1 *Sam.* 12:14 if ye will *f. the* L.
24 *f.* L. serve him in truth
1 *K.* 18:12 but I *f.* L. 2 *K.* 4:1
2 *K.* 17:28 taught them how *f.* L.
Ps. 15:4 honoreth them *f.* Lord
22:23 ye that *f.* L. praise him
33:8 let all the earth *f. the* Lord
34:9 O *f. the* L. ye his saints
115:11 ye that *f.* L. trust in L.
13 he will bless them that *f.* L.
118:4 *f.* L. say, his mercy end.
135:20 ye that *f.* L. bless the L.
Prov. 3:7 *f.* L. depart from evil
24:21 *f. the* Lord, and the king
Jer. 5:24 nor say th. Let us *f.* L.
26:19 did he not *f. the* Lord
Hos. 3:5 afterwards sh. Is. *f.* L.
Jon. 1:9 I *f.* L. the G. of heaven

FEAR not.

Gen. 15:1 *f. not* Ab. I am shield
26:24 *f. no', I am with thee
35:17 midwife said to R. *f. n.*
43:23 Peace be to you, *f. not*
46:3 *f. not* to go down to Egypt
50:19 *f. not*, am I in place of G. *?*
Ex. 14:13 *f.* n. stand, see salva.
20:20 *f. not*, G. is come to prove
Num. 14:9 L. with us, *f.* them n.
21:34 L. saith to Mo. *f.* him *not*
Deut. 20:3 *f. not* your enemies
31:8 L. doth go before thee, *f.*
not, *Jos.* 8:1; 1 *Chr.* 28:20
Jud. 6:10 *f. not* gods of Amorites
23 peace. *f. not*, thou sh. not d.
1 *Sam.* 4:20 said to her, *f. not*
12:20 Sam. said to people, *f. not*
22:23 abide thou with me, *f. n.*
23:17 Jonathan said to D. *f. not*

2 *Sam.* 13:28 kill Amnon, *f. not*
1 *K.* 17:13 said to widow, *f. not*
2 *K.* 6:16 *f. no'*, more with us
17:34 to this day they *f. not* L.
25:24 *f. not* to serve Chaldees
2 *Chr.* 20:17 be with you, *f. n.*
Ps. 55:19 therefore they *f. not* G.
64:4 shoot at him, and *f. not*
Is. 7:4 *f. not* tails of firebrands
35:4 to them of fear. heart, *f. n.*
41:10 *f.* n. I am with thee, 43:5
13 hold thy hand, saying, *f. n.*
41:14 *f. not*, thou worm Jacob
43:1 *f.* n. I have redeemed thee
44:2 *f. not*, O Jacob my servant,
Jer. 30:10; 46:27, 28
8 *f.* ye *not*, ha. not I told th. *?*
51:7 *f. not* the reproach of men
54:4 *f.* n. thou shalt not be ash.
Jer. 5:22 *f.* ye *not* me *?*
Lam. 3:57 thou saidst, *f. not*
Dan. 10:12 *f. not*, Daniel, 19
Joel 2:21 *f. not*, O land, be glad
Zep. 3:16 be said to Jer. *f. not*
Hag. 2:5 Sp. rem. am. you, *f. not*
Zec. 8:13 sh. be a blessing, *f. not*
15 do well to Judah, *f.* ye *not*
Mal. 3:5 witness ag. them *f. not*
Mat. 1:20 *f.* n. to take to thee M.
10:26 *f.* them *not*, nothing, cov.
28 *f. not* them who kill body
28:5 angel said to women, *f. not*
Luke 1:13 *f.* nor Zach. ; 30 Mary
2:10 shepherds, *f.* n.; 5:10 Sim.
8:50 Jairus *f. not*, believe only
12:32 *f. not*, little flock
18:4 though I *f. not* God,
John 12:15 *f. not* daughter of S.
Acts 27:24 *f. no'*, Paul,
Rev. 1:17 *f. not*. I am the first

Not FEAR.

Ex. 9:30 ye will n. yet *f.* the L.
2 *K.* 17:35 not *f.* other gods, 37
Job 9:35 I speak, and *not f.* him
11:15 steadfast, thou shalt n. *f.*
Ps. 27:3 tho. host encamp, not *f.*
46:2 not *f.* though earth be rem.
56:4 n. *f.* wh. flesh can do, 118:6
Is. 54:14 from oppression, n. *f.*
Jer. 10:7 who would not *f.* thee
Amos 3:8 who will not *f. ?*
Luke 23:40 dost not thou *f.* God *?*

Heb. 13:6 not *f.* what man do
Rev. 15:4 who shall n. *f.* thee,

FEARED.

Gen. 26:7 *f.* to say, She is my w.
Ex. 9:20 he that *f.* word of Lord
Deut. 25:18 Amalek *f.* not God
32:17 to new gods fathers *f.* not
27 were it not I *f.* the wrath of
Jos. 4:14 *f.* Josh. as they did M.
1 *Sam.* 14:26 people *f.* the oath
15:24 because I *f.* the people
1 *K.* 3:28 and all Israel *f.* king
2 *K.* 17:25 they *f.* not the Lord
1 *Chr.* 16:25 to be *f.* above all
gods, *Ps.* 96:4
Ps. 76:7 art to be *f.*; 8 earth *f.*
11 pres. to him ought to be *f.*
78:53 led them safely, so *f.* not
130:4 forgiveness, mayest be *f.*
Is. 41:5 the isles saw it, and *f.*
51:13 hast *f.* continually
57:11 whom hast thou *f.*
Jer. 3:8 treach. sister Jud. *f.* not
42:16 sword my *f.* overtake you
44:10 nor have they *f.*
Ezek. 11:8 ye have *f.* the sword
Dan. 5:19 nations *f.* before him
Mal. 2:5 wherewith he *f.* me
Mat. 14:5 Herod *f.* multi. 21:46
Mark 4:41 they *f.* exceedingly
6:20 Herod *f.* John, knowing
11:18 and chief priests *f.* Jesus
32 *f.* the people, 12:12 ; *Luke*
20:19 ; 22:2 : *Ac'.* 5:26

FEARED

Luke 9:34 f. as th. entered cloud
45 f. to ask him of that saying
18:2 was a judge which f. not G.
19:21 I f. thee, art austere man
John 9:22 bec. they f. the Jews
Acts 16:38 magistrates f. when
Heb. 5:7 C. heard, in that he f.

FEARED God.
Ex. 1:17 but midwives f. God
Neh. 7:2 he f. God above many
Job 1:1 Job was one that f. God
Acts 10:2 Cornelius was one f. G.

FEARED greatly.
Jos. 10:2 Canaanites f. greatly
1 Sam. 12:18 the people g. f. L.
1 K. 18:3 now Obadiah f. Lord g.
Job 3:25 thing I g. f. is come
Ps. 89:7 God is g. to be f.
Mat. 27:54 centurion f. greatly

FEARED the Lord.
Ex. 14:31 f. L. believed Moses
2 K. 17:32 so they f. the L. 33, 41
Hos. 10:3 no king, bec. not f. L.
Jon. 1:16 man f. L. exceedingly
Mal. 3:16 that f. snake oft, a
book of remem. for th. f. L.

FEAREST.
Gen. 22:12 I know thou f. God
Is. 57:11 held peace thou f. not?
Jer. 22:25 hand of them thou f.

FEARETH.
Job 1:8 Job one that f. God, 2:3
Ps. 25:12 what man is he f. L.?
112:1 blessed is the man f. L.
128:1 blessed is every one f. L.
4 thus man be blessed f. Lord
Prov. 13:13 f. command. be rew.
14:2 walk, in uprightness f. L.
16 wise man f. and departeth
28:14 hap. is the man f. always
31:30 woman f. Lord be praised
Ec. 7:18 f. God come forth
8:13 because he f. not before G.
9:2 as he that f. an oath
Is. 50:10 who is am. you f. L.?
Acts 10:22 Cornelius one f. God
35 he that f. him is accepted
13:26 who. among you f. God
1 John 4:18 f. is not perf. in love

FEARFUL.
Ex. 15:11 like thee, f. in praises
Deut. 20:8 f. let return, Jud. 7:3
28:58 mayest fear this f. name
Is. 35:4 say to them of f. heart
Mat. 8:26 f. O ye of little faith?
Mark 4:40 why are ye so f.?
Luke 21:11 f. sights in div. pla.
Heb. 10:27 f. looking for of judg.
31 f. to fall into hands of God
Rev. 21:8 f. have part in the lake

FEARFULNESS.
Ps. 55:5 f. and trembling come
Is. 21:4 f. affrighted me
33:14 f. surprised the hypocrites

FEARFULLY.
Ps. 139:14 f. and wonderf. made

FEARING.
Jos. 22:25 children cease f. Lord
Mark 5:33 the woman f. came
Acts 23:10 the captain f. lest P.
Gal. 2:12 f. them of circumcision
Col. 3:22 singleness of heart f. G.
Heb. 11:27 not f. wrath of king

FEAST.
Gen. 19:3 L. made f. ; 21:8 Abr.
26:30 Isaac ; 29:22 Laban
40:20 Pharaoh made a f. to all
Ex. 5:1 hold a f. to me, 10:9
12:14 keep it a f. Lev. 23:39, 41
13:6 seventh day shall be a f.
23:14 three times keep f. in ye.
32:5 A. said, To-morrow is a f.
Num. 29:12 shall keep f. to L.
Deut. 16:14 shalt rejoice in thy f.

Jud. 14:10 Samson made a f.
1 Sam. 25:36 N. held f. like king
1 K. 8:2 all assembl. at the f.
12:32 Jeroboam ordained a f.
like the f. that is in Judah
2 Chr. 7:8 Sol. kept f. 7 days, 9 ;
30:22 ; Neh. 8:18 ; Ezek. 45:25
Est. 1:3 Ahasuerus made f. 2:18
9 Vashti made f. ; 8:17 Jews
Prov. 15:15 merry heart cont. f.
Ec. 10:19 f. is made for laughter
Is. 25:6 L. make to all peop. a f.
Ezek. 45:23 seven days of f. pre.
Dan. 5:1 Belshazzar made a f.
Mat. 27:15 at that f. wont to release a prisoner, Mark 15:6
Luke 2:42 after custom of f.
5:29 Leyi made him a great f.
14:13 makest a f. call the poor
23:17 must release one at the f.
John 2:8 bear to governor of f.
4:45 Galileans hav. seen all he
did at f. for they went to f.
5:1 after this was a f. of the J.
6:4 the passover f. of the J.
7:8 go up to this f. I go not up
10 went he also up to the f.
11 Jews sought him at the f.
14 midst of the f. Jesus taught
37 that great day of the f.
10:22 at the f. of dedication
11:56 he will not come to the f.?
12:12 much people come to f.
20 Greeks that came to the f.
13:29 buy what we need ag. f.
Acts 18:21 I must keep this f.
1 Cor. 5:8 f. not with old leaven
10:27 that believe not bid to f.

FEAST day or days.
Hos. 2:11 cause her f. d. to cease
9:5 what will ye do in day of f.
Amos 5:21 I despise your f. days
Mat. 26:5 not on f. d. Mark 14:2
John 2:23 in f. d. many believed

FEAST of the passover.
Mat. 26:2 f. of pass. Mark 14:1
Luke 2:41 every year at f. of pas.
John 13:1 before f. of p. J. knew

Solemn FEAST.
Deut. 16:15 seven days keep s. f.
Ps. 81:3 blow trumpet on s. f. d.
Lam. 2:7 noise as in sol. f. day
Hos. 12:9 dwell as in days of s. f.

FEAST of tabernacles.
Lev. 23:34 shall be the f. of tab.
Deut. 16:16 in f. 31:10 ; 2 Chr.
8:13
Zec. 14:16 even go up to keep f.
18 heathen that come not to f.
John 7:2 Jews' f. was at hand

FEAST of unleavened bread.
Ex. 12:17 ob. f. 23:15 ; 34:18
Lev. 23:6 on the 15th day is f.
Deut. 16:16 in f. 2 Chr. 8:13
2 Chr. 30:13 assembl. to keep f.
Mat. 26:17 f. of un. discip. came
Mark 14:1 was the f. Luke 22:1

FEAST of weeks.
Ex. 34:22 ob. f.- Deut. 16:10

FEAST, ED.
Job 1:4 sons f. in their houses
2 Pet. 2:13 sporting while they f.
Jude 12 when they f. with you

FEASTING.
Est. 9:17 made it a day of f. 18
Job 1:5 days of f. were gone
Ec. 7:2 go to the house of f.
Jer. 16:8 into the house of f.

FEASTS.
Lev. 23:2 these are my f. 4, 37, 44
Ps. 35:16 hypocr. mockers in f.
Is. 5:12 pipe and wine in their f.
Jer. 51:39 in heat I will make
their f.

Ezek. 45:17 to give offerings in f.
Amos 8:10 turn your f. into mo.
Zec. 8:19 shall be cheerful f.
Mat. 23:6 love. uppermost rooms
at f. Mark 12:39 ; Luke 20:46
Jude 12 are spots in f. of charity

Appointed FEASTS.
Is. 1:14 ap. f. my soul hateth

Set FEASTS.
Num. 29:39 these th. do in set f.

Solemn FEASTS.
2 Chr. 2:4 build a house for sol. f.
8:13 sol. f. three times in a ye.
Lam. 1:4 bec. none come to s. f.
2:6 caused s. f. to be forgotten
Ezek. 36:38 flock of Jer. in s. f.
46:9 when come bef. L. in sol. f.
Hos. 2:11 cause to cease her s. f.
Nah. 1:15 O Judah, keep thy s. f.
Mal. 2:3 even dung of your sol. f.

FEATHERED. See FOWL.

FEATHERS.
Job 39:13 gavest f. to ostrich?
Ps. 68:13 f. cov. with yel. gold
91:4 shall cover thee with his f.
Ezek. 17:3 an eagle full of f.
Dan. 4:33 hairs like eagles'.

FED.
Gen. 48:15 G. who f. me all my
Ex. 16:32 bread where. I f. you
Deut. 8:3 he f. thee with manna
16 f. thee in the wilderness
1 K. 18:4 f. them with bread, 13
Ps. 37:3 verily thou shalt be f.
78:72 f. them acc. to his integ.
81:16 f. them with finest of wh.
Is. 1:11 full of fat of f. beasts
Jer. 5:7 I f. them to the full
8 as f. horses in the morning
Ezek. 16:19 honey wherew. I f.
34:3 ye kill them that are f.
8 f. themselves, f. not my flo.
Dan. 4:12 all flesh was f. with it
5:21 f. Neb. with grass like ox.
Zec. 11:7 and I f. the flock
Mat. 25:37 hunger. and f. thee?
Mark 5:14 f. swine, Luke 8:34
Luke 16:21 to be f. with crumbs
1 Cor. 3:2 have f. you with milk

FEEBLE.
Deut. 25:18 Amalekites smote f.
1 Sam. 2:5 many children, is f.
2 Sam. 4:1 Ish-bosheth's han. f.
2 Chr. 28:15 car. the f. on asses
Neh. 4:2 what do these f. Jews?
Job 4:4 strengthen. the f. knees
Ps. 38:8 I am f. and sore broken
105:37 not one f. per. am. tribes
Prov. 30:26 conies are f. folk
Is. 16:14 remnant shall be f.
35:3 weak hands conf. f. knees
Jer. 6:24 our hands waxed f.
47:3 Damascus is waxed f.
50:43 the king's hands waxed f.
Ezek. 7:17 all ha. sh. be f. 21:7
Zec. 12:8 he that is f. be as Dav.
1 Cor. 12:22 memb. to be more f.
1 Thes. 5:14 comf. the f. minded
Heb. 12:12 lift up the f. knees

FEEBLENESS.
Jer. 47:3 fath. n. look back for f.

FEEBLER.
Gen. 30:42 the f. were Laban's

FEED.
Gen. 37:12 f. their father's flock
16 tell me, where they f. flocks
46:32 for their trade to f. cattle
Ex. 22:5. f. in another's field
34:3 nor flocks f. bef. that mo.
2 Sam. 5:2 shalt f. my people Is.
7:7 to f. Israel, 1 Chr. 17:6
1 K. 17:4 I com. ravens to f. thee
Job 24:2 take away flocks, and f.
20 worm sh. f. sweetly on him

Ps. 28:9 *f.* them, and lift them
49:14 death shall *f.* on them
78:71 he brought David to *f.* **J.**
Prov. 10:21 lips of right. *f.* many
Cant. 4:5 roses which *f.* am. lil.
6:2 belov. gone to *f.* in gardens
Is. 5:17 *f.* after their manner
11:7 the cow and the bear **sh. f.**
14:30 first-b. of the poor **sh. f.**
27:10 their calf *f.* and lie **down**
30:23 thy cattle *f.* in large **past.**
40:11 *f.* his flock as a shepherd
49.9 they shall *f.* in the ways
61:5 strangers **sh.** *f.* your flocks
65:25 wolf and lamb shall *f.* tog.
Jer. 3:15 **sh.** *f.* you with knowl.
6:3 sh. *f.* every one in his place
23:2 ag. pastors that *f.* my **peo.**
4 shepherds shall *f.* them
50:19 Israel shall *f.* on Carmel
Lam. 4:5 *f.* delicately are desol.
Ezek. 34:2 shepherds that *f.* th.
3 but ye *f.* not the flock
10 neither shepherds *f.* thems.
23 servant David shall *f.* them
Dan. 11:26 *f.* of his meat destroy
Hos. 4:16 Lord will *f.* them
Hos. 9:2 wine-press not *f.* them
Jon. 3:7 let them not *f.*
Mic. 5:4 *f.* in strength of Lord
Zep. 2:7 they shall *f.* thereupon
3:13 shall *f.* none make afraid
Zec. 11:9 I will not *f.* you
16 not *f.* that that standeth
Luke 15:15 sent him to *f.* swine
Acts 20:28 take heed to *f.* church
1 *Cor.* 13:3 I give all to *f.* poor
Rev. 7:17 L. **sh.** *f.* and lead them
12:6 sho. *f.* her there 1,260 days

FEED, *imperatively.*
Gen. 25:30 *f.* me with red pottage
29:7 water ye the sheep, *f.* them
1 *K.* 22:27 *f.* him with bread and
water of afflict. 2 *Chr.* 18:26
Prov. 30:8 *f.* me with food conv.
Cant. 1:8 *f.* thy kids beside tents
Mic. 7:14 *f.* thy people
Zec. 11:4 *f.* flock of the slaughter
John 21:15 *f.* my lambs
16 *f.* my sheep, 17
Rom. 12:20 if ene. hunger *f.* him
1 *Pet.* 5:2 *f.* flock of God

I will FEED.
Gen. 30:31 I *will* ag. *f.* thy flock
2 *Sam.* 19:33 I *will f.* thee
Is. 49:26 I *w. f.* them oppr. thee
58:14 I *w. f.* thee with heritage
Jer. 9:15 *f.* with wormw. 23:15
Ezek. 34:14 I *w. f.* them
16 I *will f.* the fat with judgm.
Zec. 11:7 I *w. f.* flock of slaught.

FEED, EST, ETH.
Ps. 80:5 *f.* with bread of tears
Prov. 15:14 the mouth of fools *f.*
Cant. 1:7 tell me where thou *f.*
2:16 *f.* among the lilies, 6:3
Is. 44:20 he *f.* on ashes
Hos. 12:1 Ephraim *f.* on wind
Mat. 6:26 heav. Father *f.* them
Luke 12:24 sow not, God *f.* them
1 *Cor.* 9:7 who *f.* a flock

FEEDING.
Gen. 37:2 Joseph was *f.* the flock
Job 1:14 ploughing, the asses *f.*
Ezek. 34:10 cause to cease *f.* flock
Nah. 2:11 where *f.* pl. of lions ?
Mat. 8:30 swi. *f. Mark* 5:11 ; *Luke* 8:32
Luke 17:7 a servant *f.* cattle
Jude 12 *f.* themsel. without fear

FEEL, ING.
Gen. 27:21 that I may *f.* thee
Jud. 16:26 I may *f.* the pillars
Job 20:20 shall not *f.* quietness
Ps. 58:9 bef. pots can *f.* thorns
Ec. 8:5 keep. comman. *f.* no evil

Acts 17:27 if haply might *f.* after
Eph. 4:19 who being past *f.*
Heb. 4:15 *f.* of our infirmities

FEET.
Gen. 49:10 from.between his *f.*
33 J. gathered up his *f.* in bed
Ex. 3:5 shoes off thy *f. Acts* 7:33
Deut. 2:28 pass thro' on my *f.*
28:57 young one from bet. *f.*
33:3 and they sat down at thy *f.*
Jos. 3:15 *f.* of priests in Jordan
10:24 *f.* on necks of these kings
14:9 land thy *f.* have trodden
Jud. 3:24 he covereth his *f.*
4:15 Sisera fled on his *f.* 17
5:27 at her *f.* he fell down dead
Ruth 3:8 a woman lay at his *f.*
1 *Sam.* 2:9 keep *f.* of his saints
24:3 Saul went in to cover his *f.*
2 *Sam.* 3:34 nor thy *f.* put in. fet.
4:4 lame of his *f.* 9:3, 13
12 cut off th. hands and th. *f.*
19:24 Mephib. not dressed his *f.*
22:34 maketh my *f.* like hinds'
f. Ps. 18:33 ; *Hab.* 3:19
37 *f.* did not slip. *Ps.* 18:36
1 *K.* 2:5 blo. of war in shoes on *f.*
14:6 A. heard the sound of h. *f.*
12 *f.* enter the city
15:23 A. diseased *f.* 2 *Chr.* 16:12
2 *K.* 4:27 she caught by the *f.*
6:32 sound of master's *f.* beh. ?
9:35 found no more than the *f.*
13:21 dead man stood on his *f.*
21:8 *f.* of Israel move any more
Neh. 9:21 their *f.* swelled not
Job 12:5 to slip with his *f.*
13:27 my *f.* in the stocks ; 33.11
a print on heels of my *f.*
18:8 cast into a net by own *f.*
11 terrors shall drive him to *f.*
29:15 *f.* was I to the lame
30:12 youth push away my *f.*
Ps. 22:16 pierced hands and *f.*
25:15 pluck my *f.* out of the net
31:8 set my *f.* in a large room
40:2 he set my *f.* on a rock, and

Ps. 56:13 del. my *f.* fr. falling ?
66:9 suff. not our *f.* to be moved
73:2 my *f.* were almost gone
74:3 lift up thy *f.* to desolations
105:18 whose *f.* hurt with fet.
115:7 *f.* have they but walk not
116:8 deliv. my *f.* from falling
119:59 turned my *f.* to testim.
101 refr. my *f.* from evil way
105 thy wo. is a lamp to my *f.*
122:2 *f.* stand within thy gates
Prov. 1:16 *f.* run to evil, 6:18 ;
Is. 59:7
4:26 ponder the path of thy *f.*
5:5 her *f.* go down to death, her
6:13 wicked man speak. with *f.*
28 go on coals, *f.* n. be burnt ?
7:11 her *f.* abide not in house
19:2 hasteth with his *f.* sinneth
26:6 cutteth off *f.* and drinketh
29:5 spreadeth a net for his *f.*
Cant. 7:1 beautiful are thy *f.*
Is. 3:18 a tinkling with their *f.*
18 ornaments about their *f.*
6:2 with twain he covered his *f.*
7:20 lord shall shave hair off *f.*
23:7 own *f.* shall carry her afar
26:6 *f.* of poor sh. tread it down
32:20 send forth the *f.* of ox
41:3 he had not gone with *f.*
49:23 sh. lick up dust of thy *f.*
52:7 *f.* of him bring. good tid.
60:13 place of my *f.* glorious
Jer. 13:16 before *f.* stumble on
mountain
14:10 have not refrained their *f.*
18:22 they hid snares for my *f.*
38:22 thy *f.* are sunk in mire
Lam. 1:13 spread a net for my *f.*
Ezek. 1:7 their *f.* were straight *f.*

2·2 Spirit set me on my *f.* 3:24
16:25 opened thy *f.* to every one
24:17 put thy shoes upon thy *f.*
25:6 beca. stamped with the *f.*
32:2 troubledst wat. with thy *f.*
34:18 foul residue with your *f.* ?
19 what ye have fouled with *f.*
37:10 and stood upon their *f.*
Dan. 2:33 his *f.* part of iron, 42
34 smote image upon his *f.*
7:7 stamped residue with *f.* 19
10:6 *f.* like br. *Rev.* 1:15 ; 2:18
Nah. 1:3 clouds are dust of his *f.*
15 *f.* of him bringeth good tid.
Zec. 14:4 *f.* stand on mount of O.
Mat. 10:14 shake off the dust of
your *f. Mark* 6:11 ; *Luke* 9:5
15:30 cast the lame at Jesus' *f.*
18:8 rather than having two *f.*
28:9 held by *f.* worshipped him
Luke 1:79 *f.* into way of peace
7:38 kissed his *f.* and anointed
8:35 found man at *f.* of Jesus
41 Jai. fell down at Jesus' *f.*
10:39 M. which sat at Jesus' *f.*
15:22 put shoes on his *f.*
24:39 beh. my hands and my *f.*
John 11:2 and wiped his *f.* 12:3
20:12 the other angel at the *f.*
Acts 3:7 his *f.* received strength
4:35 laid at apostles' *f.* 37 ; 5:2
5:9 the *f.* of them which buried
7:58 clothes at young man's *f.*
13:25 shoes of his *f.* not worthy
51 shook off dust of their *f.*
14:10 Stand upright on *f.*
16:24 their *f.* fast in the stocks
21:11 Agabus bound his own *f.*
22:3 brought up at *f.* of Gamal.
26:16 rise and stand upon thy *f.*
Rom. 3:15 *f.* swift to shed blood
10:15 *f.* of them preach gospel
1 *Cor.* 12:21 to *f.* I have no need
Eph. 6:15 *f.* shod with prepara.
Heb. 12:13 stra. paths for your *f.*
Rev. 3:9 worship before thy *f.*
10:1 his *f.* as pillars of fire
11:11 witnesses stood on th. *f.*
13:2 his *f.* as the *f.* of a bear
22:8 I fell to worship bef. his *f.*

At his FEET.
Jud. 4:10 with 10,000 *at his f.*
Hab. 3:5 burning coals *at his f.*
Mat. 18:29 fel. serv. fell *at his f.*
Mark 7:25 Syroph. fell *at his f.*
Luke 7:38 she stood *at his f.*
Acts 5:10 Sapphira fell *at his f.*
Rev. 1:17 I fell *at his f.* as dead
19:10 I fell *at his f.* to worship

FEET, *joined with* **sole, s.**
Deut. 11:24 *s.* of *f.* tread be yours
1 *K.* 5:3 wars, under *s.* of his *f.*
2 *K.* 19:24 *s.* of *f.* dried. *Is.* 37:25
Is. 60:14 bow down at *s.* of *f.*
Ezek. 1:7 *s.* of *f.* was like a calf's
43:7 *s.* of my *f.* no more defiled
Mal. 4:3 ashes under *s.* of your *f.*

Under FEET.
Ex. 24:10 *under* his *f.* sapphire
2 *Sam.* 22:10 dark. *u. f. Ps.* 18:9
39 they are fallen *under* my *f.*
Ps. 8:6 put all things *under* his
f. 1 *Cor.* 15:27 ; *Eph.* 1:22
47:3 subdue nations *u.* our *f.*
91:13 dragon shalt trample *u. f.*
Is. 14:19 a carcass trodden *u. f.*
28:3 drunkards be trodden *u. f.*
Lam. 3:34 *u.* his *f.* all prisoners
Mat. 7:6 trample *u.* their *f.*
Rom. 16:20 bruise Sat. *u.* your *f.*
1 *Cor.* 15:25 all enemies *u.* his *f.*
Heb. 2:8 in subjection *u.* his *f.*
Rev. 12:1 moon *under* her *f.*

FEET, *with* **wash, ed.**
Ex. 30:19 A. and his sons shall
wash their *f.* 21 ; 40:31

2 *Sam.* 11:8 Uriah, go *w.* thy *f.*
Ps. 58:10 *w. f.* in blood of wick.
Cant. 5:3 I have *washed* my *f.*
Luke 7:38 *wash* his *f.* with tears
John 13:5 *wash* the disciples' *f.*
6 Lord, dost thou *wash* my *f.?*
10 needeth not save to *w.* h. *f.*
14 if I your L. have *w.* your *f.*
1 *Tim.* 5:10 she ha. *w.* saints' *f.*

FEIGN, ED, EST.
1 *Sam.* 21:13 D. *f.* himself mad
2 *Sam.* 14:2 *f.* thyself a mourner
1 *K.* 14:5 *f.* herself another wom.
Neh. 6.8 thou *f.* them
Ps. 17:1 prayer not out *f.* lips
Luke 20:20 *f.* them. just men
Pet. 2:3 with *f.* words

FEIGNEDLY.
3:10 turn to me *f.* saith **L.**

FELIX. *Acts* 23:24; 24:3, 25; 25:14

FELL.
Gen. 4:5 Cain's countenance *f.*
44:14 Joseph's breth. *f.* bef. him
Jos. 22:20 wrath *f.* on congrega.
Jud. 7:13 smote tent that it *f.*
8:10 there *f.* 120,000 men
16:30 the house *f.* on the lords
1 *Sam.* 4:18 Eli *f.* from seat
11:7 fear of Lord *f.* on people
14:13 Philistines *f.* before Jon.
22:18 Doeg *f.* upon the priests
28:20 Saul *f.* straightway along
29:3 no fault since he *f.* to me
31:4 Saul took sw. and *f.* on it
2 *Sam.* 4:4 Mephibosheth *f.*
20:8 Joab's sword *f.* out, as he
21:9 they *f.* all seven together
1 *K.* 2:25 Benaiah *f.* on Adonijah
32 *f.* on two men more right.
34 Benaiah *f.* on J.; 46 Shimei
20:30 a wall *f.* on 27,000 men
2 *K.* 1:13 captain *f.* on his knees
2:13 mantle that *f.* from Elijah
4:8 it *f.* on a day, Elisha, 11,18
6:5 axe head *f.* into the water
1 *Chr.* 21:14 *f.* of Isr. 70,000 men
27:24 *f.* wrath for it against Isr.
2 *Chr.* 17:10 fear of L. *f.* on all
20:18 inhabitants *f.* before Lord
21:19 his bowels *f.* out by reas.
Ezr. 9:5 I *f.* on my knees, and
Est. 9:3 fear of Mor. *f.* on them
Job 1:15 Sabe. *f.* on the asses, 17
19 house *f.* on the young men
Ps. 27:2 eat up my flesh, they *f.*
78:64 their priests *f.* by sword
105:38 fear of Israel *f.* on Egypt
Jer. 39:9 *f.* away, *f.* to him, 52:15
46:16 one *f.* upon another
Lam. 1:7 her people *f.* into hand
5:13 children *f.* under the wood
Ezek. 8:1 ha. of L. *f.* on me, 11:5
39:23 so *f.* they all by the sw.
Dan. 4:31 *f.* a voice from heaven
7:20 before whom three *f.*
10:7 great quaking *f.* on them
Mat. 7:25 the house *f.* not
27 house *f.* Luke 6:49
13:4 seed *f.* by the wayside, *Mark* 4:4; *Luke* 8:5
Mark 9:20 he *f.* and wallowed
14:35 Jesus *f.* on the ground
Luke 1:12 fear *f.* upon Zacharias
10:30 *f.* among thieves, 36
13:4 on whom tower in Silo. *f.*
15:20 his father *f.* on his neck
16:21 crumbs wh. *f.* from table
John 18:6 went backward, and *f.*
Acts 1:25 Jud., by transgress. *f.*
26 the lot *f.* upon Matthias
7:60 had said this, he *f.* asleep
9:4 Saul *f.* and heard a voice
10:10 Peter *f.* into a trance
44 Holy Ghost *f.* on all, 11:15
12:7 chains *f.* off Peter's hands
13:11 there *f.* on him a mist

Acts 13:36 D. *f.* on sleep, saw cor.
19:17 fear *f.* on Jews at Ephesus
20:10 Paul *f.* on Eutychus
37 they all *f.* on Paul's neck
22:7 I *f.* unto the ground, and
Rom. 11:22 on them wh. *f.* sever.
15:3 reproached thee, *f.* on me
1 *Cor.* 10:8 *f.* in one day 23,000
Heb. 3:17 whose carcasses *f.*
2 *Pet.* 3:4 the fathers *f.* asleep
Rev. 1:17 I *f.* at his feet as dead
6:13 and the stars of heaven *f.*
8:10 *f.* great star from heaven
1:11 fear *f.* on them which saw
13 tenth of city *f.* by earthqua.
16:2 there *f.* a grievous sore
19 and the cities of nations *f.*
21 there *f.* on men a great hail
19:10 I *f.* at his feet to worship
See FACE, FACES.

FELL down.
Deut. 9:18 I *f. down* before L. **25**
Jos. 6:20 shouted, the wall *f. d.*
Jud. 5:27 he bowed, there *f. d.*
19:26 concubine *f. d.* at door
1 *Sam.* 31:1 *f. d.* in Gil. 1 *Chr.* 10:1
2 *Sam.* 2:16 so they *f. d.* together
23 Asahel *f. d.* there and died
19:18 Shimei *f. down*
2 *K.* 1:2 Ahaziah *f. d.* thro' latt.
1 *Chr.* 13:17 *f. d.* of Is. 500,000 m.
Job 1:20 Job *f. d.* on the ground
Ps. 107:12 *f. down* none to help
Dan. 3:7 all nations *f. d.* and w.
23 these three *f. d.* in furnace
Mat. 2:11 wise men *f. d.* and wo.
18:26 servant *f. d.* saying, 29
Mark 3:11 unclean spirits *f. d.*
Luke 5:8 P. *f. d.* at Jesus' knees
8:28 man which had devils *f. d.*
41 Jairus *f. d.*; 17:16 Samar.
Acts 5:5 Ananias *f. d.*; 10 Sapp.
10:25 Cornelius; 16:29 jailer
19:35 the image which *f. down*
20:9 Eutychus *f. d.*
Heb. 11:30 by faith the walls *f. d.*
Rev. 5:8 elders *f. d.* 14; 19:4
22:8 John *f. d.* before the angel

FELL, EST, ING.
2 *Sam.* 3:34 bef. wick. so *f.* thou
2 *K.* 3:19 shall *f.* every good tree
6:5 as one was *f.* a beam

FELLER.
Is. 14:8 no *f.* is come up. ag. us

FELLOW.
Gen. 19:9 this *f.* came in to soj.
Ex. 2:13 why smit. thou thy *f.?*
Jud. 7:22 the L. set every man's sword ag. his *f.* 1 *Sam.* 14:20
1 *Sam.* 21:15 brought this *f.* to play the madman, sh. this *f.*
25:21 kept all this *f.* hath
29:4 make this *f.* return
2 *Sam.* 2:16 caught ev. one his *f.*
1 *K.* 22:27 *f.* in pris. 2 *Chr.* 18:26
2 *K.* 9:11 why came this mad *f.*
Ec. 4:10 fall, one will lift his *f.*
Is. 34:14 satyr shall cry to his *f.*
Zec. 13:7 awake, O sword. agai. my Sh. and man th. is my *f.*
Mat. 26:71 *f.* also w. J. *Lu.* 22:59
Luke 23:2 this *f.* pervert. nation
John 9:29 for this *f.* we know not
11:16 Didymus said to *f.* dis.
Acts 18:13 *f.* pers. to worship G.
22:22 away with such a *f.* from
24:5 found this man a pestil. *f.*

FELLOW-CITIZENS.
Eph. 2:19 *f.*-citizens with saints

FELLOW-HEIRS.
Eph. 3:6 Gentiles sh. be *f.-heirs*

FELLOW-HELPER, S.
2 *Cor.* 8:23 Titus, my *f.-helper*
3 *John* 8 be *f.-h.* to the truth

FELLOW-LABORER, S.
1 *Thes.* 3:2 sent Tim. our *f.-lab.*
Phil. 4:3 with other *f.-laborers*
Phile. 1 Paul to Phile. our *f.-l.*
24 Marcus, Demas, Lucas, *f.-l.*

FELLOW-PRISONER, S.
Rom. 16:7 And. and Junia *f.-p.*
Col. 4:10 Aristarch. *f.-p.* saluteth
Phile. 23 Epaphras my *f.-p.* in C.

FELLOW-SERVANT, S.
Mat. 18:28 *f.-ser.* who owed him
29 *f.-s.* fell down at his feet
24:49 begin to smite his *f.-s.*
Col. 1:7 Epaphras our dear *f.-ser.*
4:7 Tychicus, who is a *f.-serv.*
Rev. 6:11 *f.-s.* should be fulfilled
19:10 I am thy *f.-servant,* 22:9

FELLOW-SOLDIER.
Phil. 2:25 Epaphroditus my *f.-s.*
Phile. 2 Paul to Archippus, *f.-s.*

FELLOW-WORKERS.
Col. 4:11 these only are my *f.-w.*

FELLOWS.
Jud. 18:25 angry *f.* run on thee
2 *Sam.* 6:20 as one of vain *f.*
Ps. 45:7 with the oil of gladness above thy *f. Heb.* 1:9
Is. 44:11 his *f.* shall be ashamed
Ezek. 37:19 tribes of Israel his *f.*
Dan. 2:13 D. and his *f.* to be sla.
7:20 look more stout than his *f.*
Zec. 3:8 thou and thy *f.* that sit
Mat. 11:16 calling to their *f.*
Acts 17:5 lewd *f.* of baser sort

FELLOWSHIP.
Lev. 6:2 to keep, or in *f.*
Ps. 94:20 iniq. have *f.* wi. thee?
Acts 2:42 contin. in apostles' *f.*
1 *Cor.* 1:9 called to *f.* of his Son
10:20 sh. have *f.* with devils
2 *Cor.* 6:14 what *f.* hath righte.
8:4 *f.* of ministering to saints
Gal. 2:9 the right hand of *f.*
Eph. 3:9 is *f.* of the mystery
5:11 no *f.* with works of darkn.
Phil. 1:5 your *f.* in the gospel
2:1 if there be any *f.* of the Sp.
3:10 know *f.* of his sufferings
1 *John* 1:3 have *f.* with us, our *f.* is with the Father
6 if we say we have *f.* with h.
7 walk in light, we have *f.*

FELT.
Gen. 27:22 and Isaac *f.* Jacob
Ex. 10:21 darkn. that may be *f.*
Prov. 23:35 beaten me, I *f.* it not
Mark 5:29 she *f.* she was healed
Acts 28:5 off beast and *f.* no harm

FEMALE.
Gen. 1:27 male and *f.* created, 5:2
6:19 two of ev. sort, male and *f.*
7:16 went in male and *f.*
Lev. 4:28 offering, a *f.* 32; 5:6
Num. 5:3 male and *f.* sh. ye put
Deut. 4:16 likeness of male or *f.*
7:14 not be male nor *f.* barren
Mat. 19:4 m. and *f. Mark* 10:6
Gal. 3:28 in Christ male nor *f.*

FENCE.
Ps. 62:3 ye sh. be as a tottering *f.*

FENCED, Verb.
Job 10:11 *f.* me with bones
19:8 he hath *f.* up my way
Is. 5:2 a vineyard, and he *f.* it

FENCED, Adjective.
Deut. 28:52 *f.* walls come down
2 *Sam.* 23:7 touch th. must be *f.*
2 *K.* 3:19 shall smite every *f.* city
17:9 from tower to *f.* city, 18:8
Is. 2:15 day of L. on ev. *f.* wall
Jer. 15:20 make thee a *f.* wall
Ezek. 36:35 ruined cities bec. *f.*

FENCED cities.

Num. 32:17 dwell in *f. c.*
Deut. 9:1 pos. *c. f.* up to heaven
Jos. 10:20 rest entered into *f. c.*
14:12 that the *cities* were *f.*
2 *Sam.* 20:6 lest he get *f. c.*
2 *K.* 19:25 should. lay waste *f. c.*
2 *Chr.* 8:5 Solomon built *f. cities*
12:4 Shishak took *f. c.* of Judah
Jer. 5:17 sh. impoverish thy *f. c.*
Dan. 11:15 shall take most *f. c.*
Hos. 8:14 Judah hath multi. *f. c.*
Zep. 1:16 day of alarm ag. *f. c.*

FENS.

Job 40:21 Behemoth in cov. of *f.*

FERRET.

Lev. 11:30 the *f.* unclean

FERRY-BOAT.

2 *Sam.* 19:18 *f -b.* for king's hou.

FERVENT, LY.

Acts 18:25 Apollos, *f.* in spirit
Rom. 12:11 *f.* in spirit, serv. L.
2 *Cor.* 7:7 your *f.* mind tow. me.
Col. 4:12 laboring *f.* in prayers
Jam. 5:16 *f.* pray. of a righteous
1 *Pet.* 1:22 ye love one another *f.*
4:8 above all th. have *f.* charity
2 *Pet.* 3:10 melt with *f.* heat, 12

FESTUS. *Acts* 24:27 ; 25:9,14,23 ;
26:25

FETCH.

Gen. 18:5 will *f.* morsel of bread
27:45 I will *f.* thee from thence
Num. 20:10 *f.* water out of rock ?
Deut. 30:4 thence will L. *f.* thee
Jud. 11:5 went to *f.* Jephthah
1 *Sam.* 4:3 *f.* ark of covenant
6:21 come and *f.* ark up to you
16:11 send and *f.* Saul, 20:31
2 *Sam.* 5:23 *f.* a compass behind
14:13 king doth not *f.* banished
2 *Sam.* 14:20 *f.* ab. this form of
1 *K.* 17:10 *f.* me a little water
2 *K.* 6:13 wh. that I may *f.* him
2 *Chr.* 18:8 *f.* quick. Micaiah son
Job 36:3 *f.* my knowl. from far
Is. 56:12 I will *f.* wine
Acts 16:37 come, and *f.* us out

FETCHED.

1 *Sam.* 7:1 *f.* up ark of the Lord
10:23 they *f.* Saul thence
2 *Sam.* 9:5 and *f.* Mephibosheth
11:27 *f.* Bath-sheba to his house
1 *K.* 9:28 they *f.* from Ophir gold
2 *K.* 11:4 Jehoiada *f.* rulers
Jer. 26:23 *f.* Urijah out of Egypt
Acts 28:13 thence we *f.* compass

FETTERS.

Jud. 16:21 bound Samson with *f.*
2 *Sam.* 3:34 nor thy feet put in *f.*
2 *K.* 25:7 bound Zedeki. with *f.*
2 *Chr.* 33:11 Mana. bound with *f.*
36:6 Jehoiakim bound with *f.*
Ps. 105:18 feet they hurt with *f.*
149:8 to bind nobles with *f.*
Mark 5:4 often with *f. Lu.* 8:29

FEVER.

Deut. 28:22 smite thee with a *f.*
Mat. 8:14 P. wife's mother sick
of *f. Mark* 1:30 ; *Luke* 4:38
John 4:52 at 7th hour *f.* left him
Acts 28:8 father of Pub. sick of *f.*

FEW.

Gen. 34:30 I being *f.* th. will slay
47:9 *f.* and evil have the days
Lev. 26:22 you *f. Deut.* 4:27 ; 28:62
Num. 13:18 the people wheth. *f.*
26:54 to *f.* give less inher. 35:8
56 divided betw. many and *f.*
Deut. 26:5 sojourned with a *f.*
33:6 let not Reuben's men be *f.*
1 *Sam.* 14:6 to save by many or *f.*
2 *Chr.* 29:34 the prie. were too *f.*
Neh. 7:4 city large, but people *f.*

Job 10:20 are not my days *f. ?*
14:1 man is of *f.* days
16:22 when a *f.* years are come
Ps. 109:8 let his days be *f.*
Ec. 5:2 let thy words be *f.*
9:14 a little city, and *f.* men
12:3 grinders cease, because *f.*
Is. 10:19 rest of trees shall be *f.*
24:6 are burned, and *f.* men left
Ezek. 5:3 also take a *f.* in numb.
12:16 leave a *f.* men from sword
Dan. 11:20 *f.* days be destroyed
Mat. 7:14 *f.* there be that find it
9:37 laborers are *f. Luke* 10:2
20:16 call. but *f.* chosen, 22:14
25:21 faithful in *f.* things, 23
Mark 6:5 hands on a *f.* sick folk
Luke 12:48 beaten with *f.* stripes
13:23 *f.* that be saved ?
Acts 24:4 wouldst hear *f.* words
Eph. 3:3 wrote afore in *f.* words
Heb. 12:10 for *f.* days chastened
13:22 I have written in *f.* words
1 *Pet.* 3:20 where. *f.* that is eight
Rev. 2:14 a *f.* things ag. thee, 20
3:4 a *f.* names even in Sardis

But a FEW.

Gen. 29:20 seemed *but a f.* days
Lev. 25:52 if remain b. a *f.* years
Jos. 7:3 men of Ai arc *but a f.*
1 *Chr.* 16:19 *but f. Ps.* 105:12
Jer. 42:2 for we are left *but a f.*

Not a FEW.

Is. 10:7 cut off nations *not a f.*
Jer. 30:19 multi. them, *not* be a *f.*
Acts 17:4 chief women *not a f.*

FEWER, EST.

Num. 33:54 to *f.* give less inher.
Deut. 7:7 ye were *f.* of all people

FEWNESS.

Lev. 25:16 accord. to *f.* of years

FIDELITY.

Tit. 2:10 serv. showing good *f.*

FIELD.

Gen. 23:20 *f.* and cave made sure
27:27 smell of son is as of a *f.*
31:4 Rachel and Leah to the *f.*
49:30 in *f.* Abra. bought, 50:13
Ex. 22:5 cause a *f.* to be eaten
6 so that the *f.* be consumed
Lev. 25:3 six years sh. sow thy *f.*
27:17 if he sanctify his *f.* 18
20 if he will not redeem the *f.*
Deut. 5:21 neith. sh. covet his *f.*
Jos. 15:18 ask a *f. Jud.* 1:14
Ruth 2:8 go not to gl. in ano. *f.*
4:5 day thou buyest *f.* of Naomi
2 *Sam.* 14:30 Joab's *f.* is near
31 why serv. set my *f.* on fire?
2 *K.* 18:17 in highway of fuller's
f. Is. 7:3 ; 36:2
Neh. 13:10 every one to his *f.*
Ps. 96:12 let the *f.* be joyful
Prov. 24:30 went by *f.* of slothful
27:26 goats are the price of *f.*
31:16 considereth a *f.* and buy.
Ec. 5:9 king is served by the *f.*
Is. 5:8 woe to them lay *f.* to *f.*
16:10 taken out of plentiful *f.*
Jer. 12:4 herbs of ev. *f.* wither ?
26:18 plou. like a *f. Mic.* 3:12
32:7 buy thee my *f.* 8:25
35:9 nei. have we vineyard. *f.*
48:33 gladn. is taken from the *f.*
Joel 1:10 the *f.* is wasted
Mat. 13:24 good seed in his *f.* 31
38 the *f.* is the world, the good
44 is like unto treas. hid in a *f.*
27:7 bought the potter's *f.* 10
8 the *f.* of blood, *Acts* 1:19
Luke 17:7 when come from the *f.*
Acts 1:18 this man purchas. a *f.*

Fruitful FIELD.

Is. 10:18 consume glory of *f. f.*
29:17 Leban. turned into a *f. f.*

32:15 wilderness be a *fruitful f.*
fruit. f. be counted a forest
16 righteous. in the *fruit. f.*
Ezek. 17:5 planted seed in a *f. f.*

In the FIELD

Gen. 4:8 when they were in *t. f.*
24:63 out to meditate in *the f.*
37:15 Joseph wander. in *the f.*
Ex. 9:19 all thou hast in *f.*
25 the hail smote all in *the f.*
16:25 to-day not find it in *the f.*
Deut. 21:1 slain, lying in *the f.*
28:3 bless. sh. thou be in *the f.*
16 cursed sh. thou be in *the f.*
Jud. 13:9 angel came to w. in *f.*
1 *Sam.* 19:3 beside fath. in *the f.*
30:11 found an Egypt. in *the f.*
2 *Sam.* 14:6 two strove in *the f.*
1 *K.* 11:29 two alone in *the f.*
14:11 dieth of Jerob. in *the f.*
21:24 that die. of Ahab in *the f.*
1 *Chr.* 19:9 kings were in *the f.*
Job 24:6 reap ev. one corn in *t. f.*
Ps. 78:12 marv. things in *t. f.* 43
Prov. 24:27 fit for thyself in *t. f.*
Jer. 14:5 hind also calved in *t. f.*
17:3 O my mountain in *the f.*
41:8 treasures in *the f.* of wheat
Ezek. 7:15 in *the f.* shall die
26:6 slay thy daughters in *t. f.* 8
Mic. 4:10 shall dwell in *the f.*
Zec. 10:1 to ev. one grass in *t. f.*
Mal. 3:11 vine cast fruit in *the f.*
Mat. 24:18 nor let him in *f.* ret.

Mark 13:16 ; *Luke* 17:31
40 two be in *the f. Luke* 17:36
Luke 2:8 sheph. abiding in *the f.*
12:28 clothe grass to day in *t. f.*
15:25 his elder son was in *the f.*

Into the FIELD.

Num. 22:23 ass went *into the f.*
Jud. 9:42 people went *into the f.*
1 *Sam.* 6:14 cart came *into the f.*
20:11 J. said. Let us go *into f.*
2 *Sam.* 20:12 removed Am. *into f.*
Cant. 7:11 let us go forth *in. t. f.*
Jer. 6:25 go not forth *into the f.*
14:18 if I go *into the f.*

Of the FIELD.

Gen. 2:5 every plant of *the f.*
34:7 sons of J. came out of *t. f.*
47:24 four parts for seed of *t. f.*
Lev. 26:4 trees of *f.* sh. yield fru.
27:28 no devoted thing of *the f.*
Deut. 20:19 tree of *the f.*
Jud. 5:4 marchedst out of *the f.*
19:16 man from work out of *f.*
2 *K.* 9:25 cast in portion of *the f.*
37 carc. as dung on face of *t. f.*
Job 5:23 in league with sto. of *f.*
Ps. 103:15 as flower of *f.* he flou.
Cant. 2:7 the roes of *the f.* 3:5
Is. 37:27 inhabit. as grass of *f.*
40:6 and as the flower of *the f.*
43:20 beast of *the f.* shall honor
55:12 trees of *the f.* sh. clap han.
Jer. 4:17 as keepers of *the f.*
18:14 snow from rock of *the f.*
Lam. 4:9 want of fruits of *the f.*
Ezek. 16:7 multiply as bud of *t. f.*
17:24 trees of *the f.* shall know
34:27 tree of *the f.* shall fruit
36:30 multiply increase of *the f.*
39:10 take no wood out of *f.*
Dan. 4:15 tender grass of *the f.*
Hos. 10:4 as hemlock in the *f.*
12:11 heaps in furrows of *the f.*
Joel 1:11 harv. of *the f.* is perish.
Mic. 1:6 Sama. as a heap of *t. f.*
Mat. 6:28 consider lilies of *the f.*
30 if G. so clothe grass of *t. f.*

See BEAST, BEASTS.

Open FIELD.

Lev. 14:7 liv. bird loose into *o. f.*
17:5 sacrifices in the *open f.*

Ezek. 16:5 cast out in the *o. f.*
32:4 cast thee on the *open f.*
33:27 that is in *o. f.* give to
39:5 shalt fall upon the *open f.*

FIELDS.

Lev. 25:31 counted as the *f.*
Num. 14:33 hast not given us *f.*
20:17 not pass through *f.* 21:22
Deut. 11:15 send grass into thy *f.*
32:13 eat increase of the *f.*
  32 as vine of the *f.* of Gomor.
Jos. 21:12 *f.* gave they to Caleb
1 *Sam.* 8:14 he will take your *f.*
22:7 will son of J. give you *f. ?*
25:15 a wall to us when in *f.*
1 *K.* 2:26 get thee to thi. own *f.*
1 *Chr.* 16:32 let *f.* rejoice and all
27:25 storehouses in *f.* cities
Job 5:10 sendeth waters on *f.*
Ps. 107:37 sow the *f.* and plant
132:6 found it in *f.* of the wood
Prov. 8:26 had not made the *f.*
23:10 enter not to *f.* of fatherl.
Is. 16:8 *f.* of Heshbon languish
Jer. 32:15 *f.* shall be possessed
  43 *f.* bought ; 44 men sh. buy *f.*
Ob. 19 sh. possess *f.* of Ephraim
Mic. 2:2 they covet *f.* and take
  4 he hath divided our *f.*
Hab. 3:17 altho. *f.* yield no meat
Mark 2:23 through *f. Luke* 6:1
John 4:35 up eyes, and look on *f.*
Jam. 5:4 which reaped your *f.*

Open FIELDS.

Lev. 14:53 let go liv. bird in *o. f.*
Num. 19:16 slain with sw. in *o. f.*
2 *Sam.* 11:11 encamped in *o. f.*
Ezek. 29:5 shalt fall upon the *o.f.*

FIERCE.

Gen. 49:7 anger, for it was *f.*
Deut. 28:50 nation of a *f.* count.
Job 4:10 voice of *f.* lion
  10:16 huntest me as *f.* lion
  28:8 nor hath *f.* lion passed by
  41:10 none so *f.* dare stir him
Is. 19:4 *f.* king shall rule over
  33:19 thou shalt not see a *f.* peo.
Dan. 8:23 a king of *f.* counten.
Hab. 1:8 horses more *f.* than wol.
Mat. 8:28 devils, exceeding *f.*
Luke 23:5 they were more *f.*
2 *Tim.* 3:3 inconti. *f.* despisers
Jam. 3:4 ships driven of *f.* winds

FIERCENESS.

Job 39:24 swallo. ground with *f.*
Jer. 25:38 land desolate *f.* of opp.

See ANGER, WRATH.

FIERCER.

2 *Sam.* 19:43 words *of* J. were *f.*

FIERY.

Num. 21:6 the L. sent *f.* serpents
  8 make thee a *f.* serpent
Deut. 8:15 wherein were *f.* serp.
33:2 from right hand went *f.* law
Ps. 21:9 make them as a *f.* oven
Is. 14:29 fruit be *f.* flying serp.
Dan. 3:6 into midst of *f.* furnace
  7:9 his throne was like *f.* flame
  10 a *f.* stream issued and came
Eph. 6:16 able to quench *f.* darts
Heb. 10:27 judgment and *f.* indi.
1 *Pet.* 4:12 not stran. con. *f.* trial

FIFTH.

2 *Sam.* 2:23 smote A. under *f.* rib
3:27 Ab. under *f.* ; 4:6 Ish-bosh.
20:10 J. smote Ama. under *f.* rib
Rev. 6:9 when he opened *f.* seal
9:1 the *f.* angel sounded
16:10 *f.* angel poured out vial

FIFTEEN.

John 11:18 Bethany *f.* furl. off J.
Acts 27:28 found it *f.* fathoms
Gal. 1:18 I abode with P. *f.* days

FIFTY.

Num. 4:3 from 30 y. old and upw.
  even to *f.* 23, 30, 35, 39
8:25 fr. age of *f.* serve no more
1 *K.* 18:4 hid them by *f.* in cave
2 *K.* 1:9 cap. of *f.* with his *f.* 11,13
  10 fire consume these all *f.* 12
Est. 5:14 gal. *f.* cubits high, 7:9
Luke 7:41 one 500 pence, other *f.*
16:6 sit down quickly, write *f.*
John 8:57 art not yet *f.* years old

FIFTY, *with* six.

Ezr. 2:22 men of Netop. *f.* and *s.*

FIFTY thousand.

Acts 19:19 price books burnt *f. t.*

FIFTIES.

Mark 6:40 sat d. by *f. Luke* 9:14

FIFTIETH.

Lev. 25:10 shall hallow *f.* year
  11 a jubilee shall that *f.* year be

FIG, S.

Gen. 3:7 *f.* leaves for aprons
1 *Sam.* 25:18 A. took 200 cakes *f.*
30:12 gave Egyptian cake of *f.*
2 *K.* 20:7 take lump *f. Is.* 38:21
Nah. 13:15 sab. some brought *f.*
Cant. 2:13 fig-t. put. for. green *f.*
Is. 34:4 fall *f.* from fig-tree
Jer. 8:13 shall be no *f.* on fig-tree
  24:1 two baskets *f.* one good, 2,3
  8 evil *f.* that cannot be eaten
  29:17 make them like vile *f.*
Nah. 3:12 fig-t. with first ripe *f.*
Mat. 7:16 do men gather *f.* of
  thistles? *Luke* 6:44
Jam. 3:12 fig bear. or vine *f. ?*
Rev. 6:13 fig-tree casteth unt. *f.*

FIG-TREE.

Jud. 9:10 trees said to *f.-t.* 11
1 *K.* 4:25 dw. under *f.-t. Mic.* 4:4
2 *K.* 18:31 eat ev. one *f.-t. Is.*36:16
Prov. 27:18 keepeth *f.-t.*
Hos. 9:10 first ripe in *f.-t.* thereof
Joel 1:7 he hath barked my *f.-t.*
  12 the *f.-t.* languisheth
Hab. 3:17 altho' *f.-t.* sh. not blo.
Zec. 3:10 call ev. man under *f.-t.*
Mat. 21:19 he saw *f.-t.* in way,
  Mark 11:13
  20 *f.-t.* withered, *Mark* 11:20,21
  24:32 parable of *f.-t. Mark* 13:28
Luke 13:6 man had *f.-t.* planted
  7 seeking fruit on this *f.-t.*
  21:29 behold the *f.-t.*
John 1:48 und. *f.-t.* I saw thee, 50

FIG-TREES.

Deut. 7:8 land of vines, and *f.-t.*
Ps. 105:33 smote vines and *f.-t.*
Jer. 5:17 eat thy vines and *f.-t.*
Hos. 2:12 I will destroy her *f.-t.*
Amos 4:9 when g. and *f.-t.* incr.
Nah. 3:12 strong-ho. be like *f.-t.*

FIGHT, Substantive.

1 *Sam.* 17:20 host was going to *f.*
1 *Tim.* 6:12 fight the good *f.*
2 *Tim.* 4:7 I have fought a good *f.*
Heb. 10:32 endured great *f.*
  11:34 waxed valiant in *f.*

FIGHT, Verb.

Deut. 1:41 we will go up and *f.*
  42 go not up, nor *f.* for I am
1 *Sam.* 4:9 quit like men, and *f.*
  17:10 give man that we may *f.*
2 *Sam.* 11:20 nigh when ye did *f.*
1 *K.* 22:31 *f.* not gr. 2 *Chr.* 18:30
2 *Chr.* 20:17 shall not need to *f.*
Ps. 144:1 teach. my fingers to *f.*
Jer. 51:30 men forborne to *f.*
Zec. 10:5 *f.* bec. L. is with them
  14:14 Judah shall *f.* at Jerusa.
John 18:36 then would my ser. *f.*
1 *Cor.* 9:26 *f.* I not as beateth air
Jam. 4:2 ye kill, ye *f.* and war

FIGHT against.

Ex. 1:10 join enemies and *f. a.*
Deut. 20:10 nigh to a city to *f. a.*
Jos. 19:47 Danites went *f. a.* Le.
Jud. 1:1 shall go up first *f. a. ?*
  11:8 Jephth. to *f. a.* Ammon, 9
  25 against Israel, or *f. a.* them ?
1 *Sam.* 15:18 *f. a.* A. consumed
23:1 Philistines *f. a.* Keilah
29:8 I may not *f. a.* enemies
1 *K.* 12:34 not *f. a.* 2 *Chr.* 11:4
  20:23 let us *f. a.* them, 25
  22:32 turned to *f. a.* Jehosh.
2 *K.* 3:21 kings were come to *f. a.*
2 *Chr.* 13:12 *f.* ye not *a.* the Lord
32:2 Sen. purposed to *f. a.* Jer.
35:20 Necho come to *f. a.* Car.
Neh. 4:8 come and *f. a.* Jerusa.
Ps. 35:1 *f. a.* them that *f. a.* me
56:2 they be many that *f. a.* me
Is. 19:2 sh. *f.* every one *a.* brot.
29:7 all nations that *f. a.* Ariel
  8 nations that *f. a.* mount Z.
Jer. 1:19 shall *f. a.* thee, 15:20
21:5 I myself will *f. against* you
32:24 Ch. *f. a.* 29 ; 34:22 ; 37:8
Zec. 14:3 L. *f. a.* those nations
Acts 5:39 ye be found *f. a.* God
23:9 let us not *f. against* God
Rev. 2:16 *f. a.* them with sword

FIGHT for.

Ex. 14:14 L. *f. for, Deut.*1:30; 3:22;
  20:4
2 *K.* 10:3 *f. for* master's house
Neh. 4:14 *f. for* your brethren
  20 our God shall *f. for* us
Is. 31:4 L. shall come to *f. for* Z.

FIGHT with.

Jud. 9:38 go out and *f. with* Ab.
Jud. 11:6 may *f. w.* chil. of Am.
1 *Sam.* 13:5 Phi. *f. w.* Israel, 28:1
  17:9 if he be able to *f. with* me
  32 thy ser. will go and *f. w,* P.
2 *Chr.* 35:22 Jo. disguised to *f. w.*
Is. 30:32 shaking will he *f. w.* us
Jer. 32:5 though ye *f. w.* Chald.
Dan. 10:20 return to *f. w.* prince
  11:11 king of south came *f. w.*

FIGHTETH, ING.

Ex. 14:25 L. *f.* for them ag. Eg.
Jos. 23:10 L. God that *f.* for you
1 *Sam.* 25:28 my lord *f.* battles
Ps. 56:1 O God, he *f.* oppresseth

FIGHTINGS.

2 *Cor.* 7:5 without *f.* within fears
Jam. 4:1 wh. come wars and *f. ?*

FIGURE.

Deut. 4:16 similitude of any *f.*
Is. 44:13 maketh after *f.* of man
Rom. 5:14 *f.* of him that was
1 *Cor.* 4:6 these I have in *f.* tra.
Heb. 9:9 which was a *f.* of time
  11:19 whence he rec. him in a *f.*
1 *Pet.* 3:21 like *f.* even baptism

FIGURES.

1 *K.* 6:29 with carved *f.* of cher.
Acts 7:43 *f.* wh. ye made to wor.
Heb. 9:24 are the *f.* of the true

FILE.

1 *Sam.* 13:21 a *f.* for mattocks

FILL, Substantive.

Lev. 25:19 ye shall eat your *f.*
Deut. 23:24 may. eat grapes thy *f.*
Prov. 7:18 take our *f.* of love

FILL, Verb.

Gen. 1:22 *f.* waters in the seas
42:25 Jos. com. to *f.* sacks, 44:1
Ex. 10:6 locusts shall *f.* houses
16:32 Mo. said, *f.* a homer of it
1 *Sam.* 16:1 *f.* thy horn with oil
18:33 *f.* four barrels with water
Job 18:21 *f.* mouth with laughing
15:2 sh. wise man *f.* his belly ?
20:23 when about to *f.* his belly

23:4 would *f.* mouth with argu.
38:39 or *f.* appe. of young lions
41:7 *f.* skin with barbed irons?
Ps. 81:10 mouth wide I will *f.*
83:16 *f.* their faces with shame
110:6 *f.* places with dead bodies
Prov. 1:13 we shall *f.* our houses
8:21 I will *f.* their treasures
Is. 8:8 sh. *f.* breadth of thy land
14:21 nor *f.* the face of world
27:6 Isr. shall *f.* face of world
56:12 will *f.* with strong drink
Jer. 13:13 I will *f.* inh. wi. drun.
23:24 I *f.* heaven and earth
51:14 I will *f.* thee with men
Ezek. 3:3 *f.* thy bowels
9:7 *f.* the courts with the slain
10:2 *f.* hands with coals of fire
24:4 *f.* it with the choice bones
30:11 shall *f.* land with slain
32:4 will *f.* beasts of whole earth
5 I will *f.* val. with thy height
35:8 I will *f.* mount. with slain
Zep. 1:9 who *f.* master's house
Hag. 2:7 will *f.* house with glory
Mat. 9:16 which is put in to *f.* it
15:33 wh. bread to *f.* multitude?
23:32 *f.* ye up then the measure
John 2:7 *f.* water-pots with water
Rom. 15:13 God of hope *f.* you
Eph. 4:10 he might *f.* all things
Col. 1:24 *f.* up what is behind
1 *Thes.* 2:16 to *f.* up their sins
Rev. 18:6 cup filled, *f.* double

FILLED.

Gen. 6:13 earth is *f.* with viol.
21:19 and *f.* bottle with water
24:16 Rebekah *f.* her pitcher
26:15 P. had *f.* wells with earth
Ex. 2:16 they *f.* troughs to water
28:3 I have *f.* with wisd. 35:35
31:3 I have *f.* with S. of G. 35:31
40:34 glory of L. *f.* tabern. 35
Jos. 9:13 bottles we *f.* were new
1 *K.* 8:10 cloud *f.* house of Lord
11 gl. *f.* house, 2 *Chr.* 5:14; 7:1,2
18:35 *f.* trench also with water
20:27 the Syrians *f.* the country
2 *K.* 21:16 *f.* Je. with blood, 24:4
23:14 J. *f.* their places wi. bones
Job 3:15 princes *f.* houses with
16:8 hast *f.* me with wrinkles
22:18 yet he *f.* houses with good
Ps. 38:7 loins *f.* with loath. dis.
71:8 my mouth be *f.* with praise
72:19 let earth be *f.* with glory
80:9 deep root, it *f.* the land
104:28 hand, are *f.* with good
123:3 we are *f.* with contempt
4 soul is exceedingly *f.* with

Prov. 5:10 strang. *f.* with wealth
25:16 lest thou be *f.* with honey
30:16 the earth not *f.* with water
22 a fool when *f.* with meat
Ec. 1:8 nor is ear *f.* with hearing
6:3 his soul be not *f.* with good
7 and yet the appetite is not *f.*
Cant. 5:2 my head is *f.* with dew
Is. 6:1 his train *f.* the temple
21:3 are my loins *f.* with pain
33:5 L. hath *f.* Zion with judg.
34:6 sword of L. is *f.* with blood
43:24 *f.* me with fat of sacrifices
Jer. 15:17 hast *f.* me with indig.
46:12 thy cry hath *f.* the land
51:34 he hath *f.* belly
Lam. 3:15 he hath *f.* with bitter.
30 he is *f.* full with reproach
Ezek. 8:17 *f.* land with violence
10:3 and cloud *f.* the inner court
11:6 ye have *f.* streets with slain
28:16 they *f.* midst with viol.
36:38 waste cities *f.* flocks of
43:5 glory of Lord *f.* house, 44:4
Dan. 2:35 stone cut *f.* whole earth
Nah. 2:12 lion *f.* holes with prey
Hab. 2:16 thou art *f.* with shame

Hag. 1:6 ye are not *f.* with drink
Zec. 9:13 I have *f.* bow with E.
Mat. 27:48 *f.* sponge with vinegar. *Mark* 15:36; *John* 19:29
Mark 2:21 new piece that *f.* it up
7:27 let the children first be *f.*
Luke 1:53 he hath *f.* the hungry
2:40 Jesus *f.* with wisdom
5:7 came and *f.* both the ships
14:23 compel that house be *f.*
15:16 would fain have *f.* belly
John 2:7 they *f.* them up to brim
6:13 *f.* twelve baskets with fra.
16:6 sorrow hath *f.* your heart
Acts 2:2 mighty wind *f.* house
4:8 Peter *f.* with the Holy Ghost
5:3 why hath Satan *f.* thy heart
28 have *f.* Jerus. with doctr.
9:17 be *f.* with the Holy Ghost
13:9 Paul *f.* with Holy Ghost
Rom. 1:29 *f.* with all unright.
15:14 *f.* with all knowledge
24 I be somewhat *f.* with
2 *Cor.* 7:4 I am *f.* with comfort
Eph. 3:19 be *f.* with all fulness
5:18 with wine, but *f.* with Sp.
Phil. 1:11 *f.* with fruits of right.
Col. 1:9 be *f.* with knowledge
2 *Tim.* 1:4 I may be *f.* with joy
Jam. 2:16 be ye warmed and *f.*
Rev. 8:5 angel *f.* censer with fire
15:1 is *f.* up the wrath of God
18:6 cup which she *f.* fill double

Shall be FILLED.

Ex. 16:12 in morning ye *s.* be *f.*
Num. 14:21 earth *s.* be *f.* with gl.
2 *K.* 3:17 val. *s.* be *f.* with water
Prov. 1:31 *s.* be *f.* with own dev.
3:10 so *shall* thy barns be *f.*
12:21 wicked *s.* be *f.* with misc.
14:14 backslider *shall* be *f.* with
20:17 mouth *s.* be *f.* with gravel
24:4 by knowl. *s.* chambers be *f.*
Jer. 13:12 bottle *s.* be *f.* with wine
Ezek. 23:33 *s.* be *f.* with drunk.
39:20 ye *shall be f.* at my table
Hab. 2:14 earth *s.* be *f.* with kn.
Zec. 9:15 *shall be f.* like bowls
Mat. 5:6 that hunger, they *s.* be *f.*
Luke 1:15 J. *s.* be *f.* with Holy G.
3:5 every valley *shall be f.*
6:21 blessed hunger, ye *sh.* be *f.*

Was FILLED.

Gen. 6:11 earth *was f.* with viol.
1 *K.* 7:14 Hiram *was f.* with wis.
2 *K.* 3:20 country *was f.* with wa.
2 *Chr.* 5:13 house *w. f.* with cloud
16:14 bed *w. f.* with sweet odors
Ps. 126:2 mouth *w. f.* with laug.
Is. 6:4 house *was f.* with smoke
Jer. 51:5 land *w. f.* with sin ag.
Ezek. 10:4 house *f.* with the cloud
Luke 1:41 Elis. *w. f.* with H. G.
67 Zacharias *was f.* with H. G.
John 12:3 house *was f.* with odor
Acts 19:29 city *w. f.* with confu.
Rev. 15:8 temple *w. f.* with smoke

Were FILLED.

Hos. 13:6 were *f.* and their heart
Luke 4:28 they *w. f.* with wrath
5:26 were *f.* with fear. saying
6:11 they were *f.* with madness
8:23 they were *f.* with water
John 6:12 when they were *f.*
26 eat of the loaves, and were *f.*
Acts 2:4 *w.* all *f.* with H. G. 4:31
3:10 they were *f.* with wonder
5:17 were *f.* with indignation
13:45 Jews were *f.* with envy

Acts 13:52 disciples were *f.* joy
Rev. 19:21 fowls *w. f.* with flesh
See EAT.

FILLEDST.

Deut. 6:11 houses full, thou *f.*

FILLEST.

Ps. 17:14 whose belly thou *f.*

FILLETH.

Job 9:18 he *f.* me with bitterness
Ps. 84:6 rain also *f.* the pools
107:9 he *f.* the hungry soul
129:7 where. mower *f.* not hand
147:14 *f.* thee with finest wheat
Eph. 1:23 fulness of him that *f.*

FILLET, S.

Ex. 27:10 their *f.* shall be of silver, 11; 38:10, 11, 12, 17, 19
36:38 overlaid chapiters and *f.*
Jer. 52:21 a *f.* of twelve cubits

FILLETED.

Ex. 27:17 be *f.* with silver, 38:17
38:28 overlaid chapiters and *f.*

FILLING.

Acts 14:17 *f.* our hearts with food

FILTH.

Is. 4:4 when L. washed *f.* of Z.
Nah. 3:6 will cast abominable *f.*
1 *Cor.* 4:13 as the *f.* of the world
1 *Pet.* 3:21 not put away *f.* of flesh

FILTHINESS.

2 *Chr.* 29:5 carry *f.* out of holy
Ezr. 6:21 sep. from *f.* of heathen
9:11 unclean with *f.* of people
Prov. 30:12 not washed from *f.*
Is. 28:8 full of vomit and *f.*
Lam. 1:9 her *f.* is in her skirts
Ezek. 22:15 I will consume thy *f.*
24:11 *f.* of it may be molten
13 in thy *f.* is lewdness
36:25 from all *f.* will I cleanse
2 *Cor.* 7:1 cleanse ours. from all *f.*
Eph. 5:4 nor let *f.* be once named
Jam. 1:21 wheref. lay apart all *f.*
Rev. 17:4 full of abomin. and *f.*

FILTHY.

Job 15:16 much more *f.* is man?
Ps. 14:3 altogether become *f.* 53:3
Is. 64:6 all our right. as *f.* rags
Zep. 3:1 woe to her that is *f.*
Zec. 3:3 J. clothed with *f.* garm.
4 take away the *f.* garments
Col. 3:8 you put off *f.* communi.
1 *Tim.* 3:3 not greedy of *f.* lucre,8
Tit. 1:7 not given to *f.* lucre
11 teaching for *f.* lu. 1 *Pet.* 5:2
2 *Pet.* 2:7 Lot vexed with *f.* con.
Jude 8 *f.* dreamers defile the flesh
Rev. 22:11 *f.* let him be *f.* still

FINALLY.

2 *Cor.* 13:11 *f.* farewell, *Eph.* 6:10
Phil. 3:1; 4:8; 2 *Thes.* 3:1;
1 *Pet.* 3:8

FIND.

Gen. 19:11 wearied to *f.* the door
Num. 32:23 sin shall *f.* you out
Deut. 22:25 man *f.* damsel, 28
Ruth 1:9 L. grant ye may *f.* rest
1 *Sam.* 20:21 go, *f.* out arrows, 36
24:19 *f.* enemy let him go?
1 *K.* 18:5 perad. we may *f.* grass
2 *Chr.* 2:14 *f.* out every device
Job 23:3 O where I might *f.* him
Ps. 10:15 seek wicked till *f.* none
Prov. 2:5 shalt *f.* knowl. of God
4:22 words life to those that *f.*
8:12 *f.* out know. of witty inv.
Ec. 7:27 one by one *f.* out acc.
12:10 to *f.* out acceptable words
Cant. 5:8 if *f.* my beloved
Is. 34:14 screechowl shall *f.* place
58:3 in day of fast you *f.* pleas.
Lam. 1:6 like harts that *f.* no
2:9 prophets also *f.* no vision
Dan. 6:4 sought to *f.* occasion ag.
Daniel but could *f.* none
5 except we *f.* it con. law of G.
Mat. 7:14 few there be that *f.* it
18:13 and if so be that he *f.* it

Mark 11:13 if haply he might *f.*
13:36 he *f.* you sleeping
Luke 6:7 might *f.* accusation
12:38 *f.* them so, blessed serv.
13:7 seeking fruit and *f.* none
15:4 that wh. is lost till he *f.* it
8 seek diligently till she *f.* it?
John 10:9 in and out, *f.* pasture
Acts 7:46 desired to *f.* tabernacle
17:27 feel after him and *f.* this man
23:9 we *f.* no evil in this man
Rom. 9:19 doth he yet *f.* fault?
2 *Cor.* 9:4 and *f.* you unprepared
2 *Tim.* 1:18 *f.* mercy of Lord
See FAVOR.

Can, or canst FIND.
Gen. 41:38 *can f.* such one
Ex. 5:11 get straw where c. *f.* it
Ezr. 7:16 silver and gold *can f.*
Job 3:22 glad when they *can f.*
11:7 c. thou by searching *f.* out
G. c. thou *f.* out Almighty?
Prov. 20:6 faith. man who c. *f.*?
31:10 who c. *f.* a virtuous wom.?
Ec. 3:11 c. *f.* out work G. maketh
7:24 exceed. deep, who c. *f.* it?
Jer. 5:1 if ye c. *f.* man seek. tru.

Cannot FIND.
1 *K.* 18:12 c. *f.* thee, will slay
Job 17:10 1 c. *f.* one wise man
37:23 Almighty, we c. *f.* him
Ec. 8:17 a man c. *f.* out work

FIND grace.
Gen. 32:5 1 may *f. grace* in thy
sight, *Ex.* 33:13
33:8 to *f. g.* in sight of my lord
15 let me *f. g.; Ruth* 34:11 1. me *f. g.*
47:25 let us *f. grace* in sight of
Ruth 2:2 in wh. sight I shall *f. g.*
1 *Sam.* 1:18 let thy handm. *f. g.*
2 *Sam.* 16:4 *f. grace* in thy sight
Heb. 4:16 we may *f. g.* to help

***I* FIND.**
Gen. 18:26 *I f.* in Sod. 50 righte.
28 if *I f.* 45; 30 if *I f.* 30 there
Ps. 132:5 *I f.* out place for L.
Ec. 7:26 *I f.* more bit. th. death
Cant. 8:1 when *I* sh. *f.* thee
Luke 23:4 *I f.* no fault in this
man, *John* 18:38; 19:4, 6
Rom. 7:18 th. wh. is good *I f.* not
21 *I f.* law, that wh. I do good

Not FIND, or FIND not.
Ex. 16:25 to-day ye shall *not f.*
2 *Sam.* 17:20 could *not f.* them
Prov. 1:28 but shall *not f.* me,
Hos. 5:6; *John* 7:34, 36
Ec. 7:28 soul seeketh, but *I f. n.*
Cant. 5:6 but I could *not f.* him
Is. 41:12 sh. *not f.* them, *Hos.* 2:7
Hos. 2:6 she shall *not f.* paths
Luke 5:19 *no f.* what way they
19:48 *not f.* what might do to J.
John 7:35 we shall *not f.* him
Rom. 7:18 how to do good, I *f. n.*
2 *Cor.* 12:20 I shall *not f.* you
Rev. 9:6 death, and shall *not f.* it

Shall, or shalt FIND.
Deut. 4:29 seek L. thou s. *f.* him
28:65 s. *f.* no ease am. nations
Jud. 9:33 as thou s. *f.* occasion
2 *Chr.* 20:16 s. *f.* at end of brook
30:9 children s. *f.* compassion
Ezr. 4:15 thou s. *f.* in book
Ps. 17:3 and s. *f.* nothing
21:8 thy hand s. *f.* out enemies
Prov. 8:17 they that seek me
early s. *f.* me, *Jer.* 29:13
Ec. 11:1 s. *f.* it after many days
Jer. 6:16 s. *f.* rest *Mat.* 11:29
Mat. 7:7 and ye s. *f. Luke* 11:9
10:39 los. life for my sake s. *f.* it
17:27 thou s. *f.* a piece of money
21:2 s. *f.* an ass tied, *Mark* 11:2
22:9 as many as ye *shall f.* bid

24:46 when cometh, s. *f.* so doing, *Luke* 12:37, 43
Luke 2:12 ye *shall f.* babe wrapt
18:8 *shall* he *f.* faith on earth?
Rev. 18:14 thou s. *f.* th. no more

FINDETH.
Gen. 4:14 that *f.* me sh. slay me
Job 33:10 he *f.* occasions aga. me
Ps. 119:162 I rej. as one *f.* spoil
Prov. 3:13 happy man *f.* wisdom
8:35 whoso *f.* me *f.* life,
14:6 seeketh wisdom *f.* it not
18:22 whoso *f.* wife *f.* good th.
21:10 his neighbor *f.* no favor
21 that followeth mercy *f.* life
Ec. 9:10 whats. thy hand *f.* to do
Lam. 1:3 am. heathen, *f.* no rest
Hos. 14:3 fatherless *f.* mercy
Mat. 7:8 seeketh *f. Luke* 11:10
10:39 that *f.* his life shall lose it
12:43 seeking rest, *f.* none
44 *f.* it empty, *Luke* 11:25
John 1:41 he first *f.* own brother
43 Jes. *f.* Philip; 45 Phi. *f.* N.

FINDING.
Gen. 4:15 lest any *f.* Cain
Job 9:10 doeth things past *f.* out
Is. 58:13 *f.* thine own pleasure
Luke 11:24 seeking rest *f.* none
Rom. 11:33 and his ways past *f.*
Heb. 8:8 for *f.* fault with them

FINE, Verb.
Job 28:1 place for gold where *f.*

FINE, Adjective.
Ezr. 8:27 ves. of *f.* cop. as gold
Is. 19:9 that work in *f.* flax
Rev. 1:15 feet like *f.* brass, 2:18

FINE flour or meal.
Gen. 18:6 three measures of *f. m.*
Lev. 2:1 offering be of *f. fl.* 24:5
4 cakes of *f. fl.* mingled wi. oil
5:7; 7:12; 14:10, 21; 23:13;
Num. 6:15; 7:13, 19, 25, 31,
37, 43, 49, 55, 61; 8:8
1 *K.* 4:22 30 measures of *f.* flour
2 *K.* 7:1 mea. *f. f.* for she. 16, 18
Ezek. 16:13 thou didst eat *f. fl.*
19 I gave thee *f.* flour, and oil
Rev. 18:13 merchandise of *f. fl.*

FINE gold.
2 *Chr.* 3:5 overlaid with *f. gold*
8 most holy overlaid with *f. g.*
Job 31:24 to *f. g.* Thou art confi.
Ps. 19:10 desired th. much *f. g.*
119:127 I love com. above *f. g.*
Prov. 3:14 gain of wisd. th. *f. g.*
8:19 better than gold, than *f. g.*
25:12 as ornament of *f. g.*
Cant. 5:11 head is as most *f. g.*
15 as pill. set on sock. of *f. g.*
Is. 13:12 more preci. than *f. g.*
Lam. 4:1 most *f. g.* changed
2 sons of Z. comparab. to *f. g.*
Dan. 2:32 image's head *f. gold*
10:5 girded with *f. g.* of Uphaz
Zec. 9:3 T. heaped *f. g.* as mire

FINE linen.
Ex. 25:4 ye shall take *f. linen*
26:1 curtains of *f.* twined *linen*
31 v. of *f. l.* 36:35; 2 *Chr.* 3:14
36 *f.* twined *linen* 27:9, 16, 18;
36:37; 38:9, 16, 18
28:5 they sh. take gold and *f. l.*
6 the ephod of *f. linen,* 39:2
8 girdle *f. l.* 39:5, 29; 39:8
35:35 all manner of work and *f.*
linen, 38:23; 2 *Chr.* 2:14
36:8 curtains of *f. linen*
39:27 coats of *f. l.* for Aaron
28 mitre of *f. l.* bonnets of *f. l.*
1 *Chr.* 15:27 clothed wi. robe *f. l.*
Est. 8:15 M. wi. garment of *f. l.*
Prov. 7:16 decked bed with *f. l.*
31:24 maketh . *l.* and selleth
Ezek. 27:7 *f. linen* from Egypt

Mark 15:46 Jose. bought *f. linen*
Luke 16:19 man in pur. and *f. l.*
Rev. 18:12 merchandise of *f. lin.*
19:8 granted to be arrayed *f. l.*
14 armies in heav. clot. in *f. l.*

FINER.
Prov. 25:4 come forth ves. for *f.*

FINEST.
Ps. 81:16 fed with *f.* of wheat
147:14 filleth thee with *f.* of wh.

FINING.
Prov. 17:3 *f.* pot is for sil. 27:21

FINGER.
Ex. 8:19 mag. said, This *f.* of G.
29:12 blood on altar with thy *f.*
31:18 tables written with the *f.*
of God, *Deut.* 9:10
Lev. 4:6 sh. dip *f.* in blood, 17,
25, 30, 34; 8:15; 9:9; 16:14, 19
14:16 priest dip right *f.* in oil, 27
1 *K.* 12:10 my little *f.* thicker,
2 *Chr.* 10:10
Is. 58:9 putting forth of the *f.*
Luke 11:20 with *f.* of G. cast out
16:24 may dip tip of *f.* in water
John 8:6 with *f.* wrote on g.
20:25 put my *f.* into the print
27 reach hither thy *f.* and beh.

FINGERS.
2 *Sam.* 21:20 on every hand six
f. 1 *Chr.* 20:6
Ps. 8:3 thy heav. work of thy *f.*
144:1 teacheth my *f.* to fight
Prov. 6:13 wicked teach. with *f.*
7:3 bind them on *f.* write them
Cant. 5:5 my *f.* wi. sweet myrrh
Is. 2:8 which own *f.* made, 17:8
Jer. 52:21 thick. of pillar four *f.*
Dan. 5.5 came forth *f.* of man's
Mat. 23:4 will not move with
one of their *f. Luke* 11:46
Mark 7:33 he put his *f.* into ears

FINISH.
Gen. 6:16 in cubit sh. *f.* it above
Dan. 9:24 *f.* transgression, make
Luke 14:28 whe. sufficient to *f.*
29 and is not able to *f.* it
John 4:34 to do his will, *f.* work
5:36 works F. given me to *f.*
Acts 20:24 I might *f.* my course
Rom. 9:28 he will *f.* the work
2 *Cor.* 8:6 should also *f.* in you

FINISHED.
Gen. 2:1 heav. and earth were *f.*
Ex. 39:32 all work *f.* 40:33
1 *K.* 6:9 Sol. built house and *f.*
it, 14, 22, 38; 2 *Chr.* 5:1; 7:11
7:1 Solomon *f.* all his house,
9:1, 25; 2 *Chr.* 8:16
1 *Chr.* 28:20 till thou hast *f.*
Ezr. 5:16 build. and yet not *f.*
6:14 eld. of J. built and *f.* it, 15
Neh. 6:15 wall *f.* in 52 days
Dan. 5:26 numbe. kingd. and *f.*
Mat. 13:53 when Jes. *f.* parables
19:1 Jesus had *f.* sayings, 26:1
John 17:4 *f.* work thou gavest
19:30 said, It is *f.* bowed head
2 *Tim.* 4:7 I have *f.* my course
Heb. 4:3 works *f.* from foundat.
Jam. 1:15 sin, wh. *f.* bring death
Rev. 10:7 mystery of G. sho. be *f.*
11:7 witnesses ha. *f.* testimony
20:5 till thousand years were *f.*

FINISHER.
Heb. 12:2 J. author and *f.* of faith

FINS.
Lev. 11:9 hath *f.* eat. *Deut.* 14:9
10 hath not *f.* be abomina. 12

FIRE,
Gen. 22:6 Abra. took *f.* in hand
7 father, behold *f.* and wood

Ex. 3:2 the bush burned with f.
9:23 Lord sent hail and f. ran
12:8 that night roast with f. 9
19:18 Lord on mount Sinai in f.
22:6 if f. break out, and catch
40:38 f. was on tabernacle by
night, Num. 9:16 ; Deut. 1:33
Lev. 1:7 s. of priest put f. on al.
8 upon wood in f. 12, 17 ; 3:5
2:14 ears of corn dried by f.
9:24 came f. out from before L.
10:1 sons of A. put f. in censers
2 out f. from L. and devoured
18:21 any seed pass th. f. Deut.
18:10 ; 2 K. 17:17 ; 23:10
Num. 6:18 and put it in the f.
11:2 M. prayed, f. was quenched
16:46 censer, and put f. therein
21:28 f. gone out from Heshbon
31:23 ev. thing th. may abide f.
Deut. 4:11 mount. burnt with f.
36 he showed thee his great f.
5:5 were afraid by reason of f.
Jos. 7:25 Isr. burned A. with f.
Jud. 6:21 rose up f. out of rock
9:15 let f. come out of bramble
16:9 th. of tow when touch. f.
1 K. 18:23 lay wood, put no f. 25
24 God that answereth by f.
38 f. of L. fell, 2 Chr. 7:1, 3
19:12 after earthquake f. but L.
not in f. after f. still small
2 K. 1:10 then let f. come down
2:11 a chariot and horses of f.
6:17: mount. full of char. of f.
16:3 A. made son pass thro' f.
19:18 have cast gods into f.
21:6 Manasseh made son pass
thro' f. 2 Chr. 33:6
1 Chr 21:26 ans. fr. heaven by f.
Job 1:16 the f. of God is fallen
18:5 spark of his f. shall not
41:19 and sparks of f. leap out
Ps. 39:3 I was musing f. burned
46:9 burneth chariot in the f.
66:12 went thro' f. and water
68:2 as wax melteth bef. f. so
74:7 have cast f. into sanctu.
78:14 with light of f. 105:39
83:14 as the f. burneth the wood
97:3 f. goeth before him,
118:12 quenched as f. of thorns
140:10 let them be cast into f.
148:8 f. and hail, stormy wind
Prov. 6:27 take f. in bosom ?
16:27 in his lips is as burning f.
26:20 no wood is, f. goeth out
30:16 and f. saith not enough
Is. 9:5 burning and fuel of f.
18 wickedness burneth as f.
19 people shall be as fuel of f.
10:16 burning like burn. of a f.
30:14 to take f. from hearth
33 the pile is f. and much wo.
31:9 saith Lord, whose f. is in Z.
37:19 kings of A. cast gods to f.
43:2 walk. thro' f. not be burnt
44:16 burneth part in the f. and
saith. Aha, I have seen f.
50:11 walk in the light of your f.
64:2 when melti. f. burneth, f.
causeth waters to boil
65:5 f. that burneth all the day
66:24 nei. their f. be quenched
Jer. 4:4 fury come forth like f.
5:14 my words in thy mouth f.
20:9 word as f. shut up in bones
21:12 lest my fury go out like f.

Jer. 22:7 choice cedars in the f.
29:22 king of Baby. roasted in f.
32:35 sons to pass thro' f. unto Mol. Ezek. 16:21 ; 20:26, 31
36:22 there was f. on hearth
23 roll. and cast it into the f.
Lam. 2:3 burned like flaming f.
4 he poured out his fury like f.
Ezek. 1:4 a f. infolding itself

13 f. bright. out of f. lightning
10:6 f. from between wheels
21:31 will blow thee in f. 22:21
22:20 blow f. upon it, to melt
24:9 even make pile for f. 12
36.5 in the f. of my jeal. 38:19
Dan. 3:27 upon bod. f. had no p.
7:9 wheels like burning f.
10:6 and his eyes as lamps of f.
Hos. 7:6 burneth as a flaming f.
Joel 2:30 f. pillars, Acts 2:19
Amos 5:6 lest he break like f.
7:4 God called to contend by f.
Ob. 18 house of J. shall be a f.
Mic. 1:4 molten as wax before f.
Nah. 1:6 fury poured out like f.
Hab. 2:13 sh. labor in very f.
Zec. 2:5 unto her a wall of f.
3:2 brand plucked out of the f. f
12:6 hearth of f. like torch of f.
13:9 bring third part thro' f.
Mal. 3:2 he is like a refiner's f.
Mat. 3:10 ev. tree that bringeth
not good fruit is cast into f.
7:19 ; Luke 3:9 ; John 15:6
11 baptize with Holy Ghost
and f. Luke 3:16
13:42 cast into furnace of f. 50
17:15 he falleth into f. Mar. 9:22
18:8 be cast into everlasting
f. Mark 9:43, 46
25:41 cursed. into everlasting f.
Mark 9:14 wh. f. is not quen. 45
14:54 P. warmed himself at f.
Luke 9:54 wilt thou that we c. f. f
17:29 the same day it rained f.
22:56 beh. him as he sat by f.
Acts 3:3 cloven tong. like as of f.
28:3 when Paul laid sticks on f.
5 he shook off the beast into f.
1 Cor. 3:13 sh. be. reveal. by f. 15
2 Thes. 1:8 in flamin. f. taking
Heb. 1:7 ministers a flame of f.
11:34 faith quench. violence f.
12:18 mount that burned with f.
Jam. 3:5 great mat. little f. kin.
6 tongue is a f. a world of ini.
5:3 eat your flesh as it were f.
1 Pet. 1:7 though tried with f.
2 Pet. 3:7 reserved unto f. ag. day
12 heav. being on f. sh. be dis.
Jude 7 the venge. of eternal f.
23 pulling them out of the f.
Rev. 3:18 buy gold tried in f.
4:5 seven lamps of f. burning
8:5 angel filled censer with f.
7 there followed hail and f.
8 great mount. burning with f.
9:17 out of mouths issued f. 11:5
13:13 maketh f. come down
14:18 angel had power over f.
15:2 sea of glass mingled w. f.
16:8 power to scorch men w. f.
20:9 f. came down from God
10 dev. was cast into lake of f.
14 dea. and hell cast lake of f.
21:8 in lake wh. burneth with f.

See BRIMSTONE, BURN or BURNT,
COALS, CONSUME, CONSUM-
ING, DEVOUR, DEVOURED,
DEVOURING, FLAME, HELL,
MIDST.

Kindle, or kindled FIRE.

Ex. 22:6 that a f. make restitu.
35:3 ye sh. k. no f. on the sab.
Deut. 32:22 for a f. is k. in my
anger, Jer. 15:14 ; 17:4
2 Sam. 22:13 coals of f. kindled
Ps. 78:21 f. was k. against Jacob
Is. 50:11 beh. all ye that k. a f.
Jer. 7:18 gather. wood. fath. k. f.
11:16 hath f. k. on green olive,
21:14 ; 43:12 ; 49:27 ; 50:32
Lam. 4:11 L. hath k. a f. in Z.
Ezek. 20:47 I will k. f. in forest
24:10 k. f. consume the flesh
Mal. 1:10 nor do ye k. f. on altar

Luke 12:49 f. what if already k. f
22:55 when had k. a f. in hall
Acts 28:2 barbarians kindled f.

Made by FIRE.

Ex. 29:18 an offering made by f.
25, 41 ; Lev. 1:9, 13, 17 ; 2:2, 9,
16 ; 3:3, 5, 9, 11, 14, 16 ; 7:5,
25 ; 8:21, 28 ; 21:6 ; 22:27 ; 23:8,
13, 18, 25, 27, 36, 37 ; 24:7;
Num. 15:3, 10, 13, 14 ; 18:17;
28:3
Lev. 2:3 offerings of Lord m. by f.
10 ; 3:3 ; 4:35 ; 5:12 ; 6:17, 18 ;
7:30, 35 ; 10:12, 15 ; 21:21 ; 24:9;
Deut. 18:1 ; 1 Sam. 2:28

Pillar of FIRE.

Ex. 14:24 L. looked thro' p. of f.
Rev. 10:1 and his feet as p. of f.

Send, or sent FIRE.

Lam. 1:13 from above he sent f.
Ezek. 39:6 I will s. f. on Magog
Amos 1:4 I will s. f. into h. of H.
7 I will s. f. on the wall of G.
10 I will s. f. on wall of Ty. 12
2:2 I will s. a f. on M. ; 5 Judah
Luke 12:49 come to s. f. on earth

Set FIRE.

Deut. 32:22 s. on f. foundations
Jos. 8:8 s. city of Ai on f. 19
Jud. 1:8 Judah had s. Jer. on f.
9:49 the people s. the hold on f.
15.5 had s. the brands on f.
2 Sam. 14:30 s. J.'s field on f. 31
2 K. 8:12 H. will s. holds on f.
Ps. 57:4 am. th. that are s. on f.
Is. 27:11 women set them on f.
42:25 he hath set him on f.
Jer. 6:1 s. up a sign of f. in Bet.
32:29 C. shall s. on f. this city
Ezek. 30:8 s. a f. in Egypt, 14, 16
39:9 s. on f. burn weapons of G.
Jam. 3:6 tongue s. on f. course
of nature, is set on f. of hell

Strange FIRE.

Lev. 10:1 N. and Abi. offered s. f.
Num. 3:4 died wh. off. s. f. 26:61

FIREBRAND, S.

Jud. 15:4 S. took f. put f. midst
Prov. 26:18 madman casteth f.
Is. 7:4 two tails of these smok. f.
Amos 4:11 f. plucked out of bur

FIRE-PANS.

Ex. 27:3 make basons and f.-p.
38:3 he made the f.-p. of brass
2 K. 25:15 f.-p. car. Jer. 52:19

FIRES.

Is. 24:15 glorify ye Lord in f.

FIRKINS.

John 2:6 containing two or th. f.

FIRM.

Jos. 3:17 pri. stood f. on gr. 4:3
Job 41:23 are f. in themselves
24 his heart is as f. as a stone
Ps. 73:4 no bands, but stre. is f.
Dan. 6:7 consulted to make f.
Heb. 3:6 rejoic. of hope f. to end

FIRMAMENT.

Gen. 1:6 f. in midst of waters
7 G. f. waters under and ab. f.
8 and God called the f. Heaven
14 let th. be lights in f. 15, 17
20 fowl that fly in open f.
Ps. 19:1 f. showeth handiwork
150:1 praise him in f. power
Ezek. 1:22 likeness of f. as cryst.
25 a voice from f. over heads
26 above f. likeness of throne
Dan. 12:3 shine as bright. of f.

FIR.

1 K. 5:8 concerning timber of f.
6:15 cov. floor with planks of f.
Cant. 1:17 cedar, our rafters of f.

FIR-TREE, S.

1 *K.* 5:10 H. gave Solo. *f.* 9:11
6:34 the two doors were of *f.-t.*
2 *K.* 19:23 cut tall *f.-t. Is.* 37:24
2 *Chr.* 2:8 send *f.-t.* ; *Is.* 14:8 *f.-t.*
3:5 house he ceiled with *f.-t.*
Ps. 104:17 for stork *f.-t.* are house
Is. 41:19 I set in the desert *f.-t.*
35:13 inst. of th. sh. come *f.-t.*
60:13 the *f.-t.* the pine-tree
Ezek. 27:5 ship-boards, *f.-t.*
Hos. 14:8 like *f.-t.* ; *Zec.* 11:2
Nah. 2:3 *f.-t.* sh. be terribly sha.

FIR-WOOD.

2 *Sam.* 6:5 instru. made of *f.-w.*

FIRST.

Gen. 25:25 *f.* came out red
38:28 said, This came out *f.*
Ex. 23:19 *f.* of fruits bring to L.
28:17 *f.* row sh. be sardius, 39:10
34:1 like to *f.* 4 ; *Deut.* 10:1, 3
Num. 2:9 J. these sh. *f.* set forth
24:20 Amalek was *f.* of nations
Deut. 11:14 give *f.* rain and lat.
17:7 hands of witn. shall be *f.*
1 *Sam.* 14:35 *f.* altar S. built L.
2 *Sam.* 23:19 attained not to *f.*
three, 23 ; 1 *Chr.* 11:21, 25
Ezr. 3:12 glory of the *f.* house
Job 15:7 art th. the *f.* man born ?
Prov. 18:17 is *f.* in own cause
Is. 43:27 *f.* father hath sinned
Dan. 6:2 Daniel was *f.* president
7:4 the *f.* beast was like a lion
Hag. 2:3 saw house in *f.* glory
Zec. 12:7 save tents of Judah *f.*
Mat. 5:24 *f.* be reconciled to bro.
6:33 seek ye *f.* kingdom of God
7:5 *f.* cast beam out of own eye,
Luke 6:42
8:21 *f.* to go and bury, *Luke* 9:59
12:45 worse than *f. Luke* 11:26
17:10 must *f.* come, *Mark* 9:12
27 take up fish that *f.* cometh
21:31 of twain ? They say, the
36 other servants more than *f.*
22:38 this *f.* com. *Mark* 12:28, 30
Mark 4:28 *f.* the blade, then ear
7:27 let the children *f.* be filled
9:35 desire to be *f.* shall be
13:10 gospel must *f.* be publish.
16:9 appeared *f.* to Mary Magd.
Luke 6:1 on second sab. after *f.*
11:38 that he had not *f.* washed
14:28 sit. not down *f.* and coun.
John 5:4 *f.* step. in made whole
8:7 with. sin, let him *f.* cast st.
Acts 3:26 to you *f.* God sent him
11:26 called Christ. *f.* in Antio.
12:10 passed *f.* and second ward
26:23 C. *f.* that sho. rise fr. dead
Rom. 2:9 of Jew *f.* also of G. 10
11:35 who hath *f.* given to him ?
1 *Cor.* 12:28 *f.* apostles, sec. pro.
14:30 let the *f.* hold his peace
15:46 *f.* man A. made liv. soul
47 *f.* man is of the earth, eart.
2 *Cor.* 8:5 *f.* gave selves to Lord
12 if there be *f.* a willing mind
Eph. 1:12 *f.* trusted in Christ
6:2 *f.* command. with promise
1 *Thes.* 4:16 dead in C. sh. rise *f.*
2 *Thes.* 2:3 exc. a falling away *f.*
1 *Tim.* 1:16 in me *f.* C. J. might
2:13 Ad. was *f.* formed, then E.
3:10 let these also *f.* be proved
5:12 have cast off their *f.* faith
2 *Tim.* 1:5 faith dwelt *f.* in gran.
2:6 husbandman must *f.* part.
4:16 at my *f.* ans. no man stood
Tit. 3:10 after *f.* and sec. admo.
Heb. 5:12 which be *f.* principles
7:27 offer *f.* for his own sins
8:7 *f.* covenant, 13 ; 9:1, 15, 18
9:8 *f.* tab. where. show-bre. 6, 8
10:9 taketh away *f.* that he may
Jam. 3:17 wisd. from above is *f.*

---

1 *John* 4:19 love him bec. he *f.*
Jude 6 angels who kept *f.* es.
Rev. 2:4 thou hast left thy *f.* love
5 do *f.* works, else I will come
13:12 the power of the *f.* beast
20:5 this is the *f.* resurrection
21:1 *f.* heaven and *f.* earth

At the FIRST.

Gen. 13:4 A. made altar *at t. f.*
43:20 came *at t. f.* to buy food
Deut. 9:18 I fell bef. L. as *at f.* 25
Is. 1:26 restore judges as *at the f.*
9:1 *at the f.* he lightly afflicted
Jer. 7:12 wh. I set my name *at f.*
John 19:39 at the *f.* came to Jes.
Acts 15:14 G. *at t. f.* did visit G.
Heb. 2:3 *at t. f.* beg. to be spoken

FIRST-BORN.

Gen. 19:31 *f.-b.* said to youn. 34
33 *f.-b.* went in lay with *f.* 37
27:19 said, I am Es. thy *f.-b.* 32
26:19 give younger bef. the *f.-b.*
43:33 *f.-b.* accord. to birthright
Ex. 4:22 Is. is my son, my *f.-b.*
23 will slay thy son, thy *f.-b.*
11:5 all *f.-b.* in land of E. shall
12:12 I will smite all *f.-b.*
29 smote all *f.-b.* in Egypt.
13:15
13:2 sanctify unto me all *f.-b.*
22:29 *f.-b.* of thy sons shalt
thou give
34:20 *f.-b.* sons red. *Num.* 18:15
Num. 3:12 instead of *f.-b.* 41, 45
13 bec. all *f.-b* of Is. are mine
Deut. 21:17 for the right of *f.-b.*
Jos. 6:26 lay foundation in *f.-b.*
1 *K.* 16:34 laid found. in Ab. *f.-b.*
Job 18:13 *f.-b.* of death shall dev.
Ps. 78:51 he smote all *f.-b.* in E.
105:36 ; 135:8 ; 136:10
89:27 my *f.-b.* higher th. kings
Is. 14:30 the *f.-b.* of poor sh. feed
Jer. 31:9 and Ephraim is my *f.-b.*
Mic. 6:7 give *f.-b.* for transgr. ?
Zec. 12:10 in bitterness for *f.-b.*
Ma. 1:25 bro. *f.-b. Luke* 2:7
Rom. 8:29 *f.-b.* am. many breth.
Col. 1:15 *f.-b.* of every creature
18 beginning, *f.-b.* from dead
Heb. 11:28 he that destroyed *f.-b.*
12:23 are come to church of *f.-b.*

FIRST-FRUIT, S.

Ex. 22:29 to offer the *f.* ripe *fr.*
23:16 *f.-f.* of thy labor thou hast
19 *f.-f.* of la. 34:26 ; *Deut.* 26:2
Lev. 2:12 oblat. of *f.-f.* ye shall
14 meat-offer. of *f.-f.* green ears
23:10 a sheaf of *f.-f.* 17:20
Num. 18:12 *f.-f.* of oil, wine
Deut. 18:4 the *f.-fruit* of thy corn
26:10 brought *f.-f* of land
2 *K.* 4:42 brought man of G. *f.-f.*
2 *Chr.* 31:5 in abundance the *f.-f.*
Neh. 10:35 *f.-fruits* of our ground
37 the *f.-fruits* of our dough
12:44 chambers for *f.-f.* 13:31
Prov. 3:9 honor L. with *f.-fruits*
Jer. 2:3 Israel *f.-f.* of his increase
Mic. 7:1 my soul desired *f.-fruit*
Rom. 8:23 have *f.-f.* of Spirit
11:16 if *f.-f.* be holy
16:5 *f.-f.* of Achaia, 1 *Cor.* 16:15
1 *Cor.* 15:20 C. *f.-f.* of them th. 23
Jam. 1:18 kind of *f.-fr.* of creat.
Rev. 14:4 being the *f.-f.* unto God

FIRSTLING, S.

Gen. 4:4 Abel brought *f.* of flock
Ex. 13:12 set apart rec. *f.* 34:19
13 *f.* of ass thou shalt red. 34:20
Lev. 27:26 L.'s *f.* no man sancti.
Num. 18:15 *f.* of uncl. beasts, 17
Deut. 12:6 ye sh. bring *f.* of her.
15:19 *f.* males sanctify to the L.
33:17 J.'s glory like *f.* of bullock

FISH.

Gen. 1:26 dom. over *f.* of sea, 28
Ex. 7:18 *f.* in river shall die, 21
Num. 11:22 all *f.* of sea be gath.
Deut. 4:18 liken. of any *f.* in wa.
Ps. 8:8 put the *f.* under his feet
105:29 waters into blood, slew *f.*
Is. 19:10 sluices and ponds for *f.*
50:2 their *f.* stinketh
Ezek. 29:4 *f.* to stick to thy scal.
5 and all the *f.* of thy rivers
47:10 *f.* sh. be as *f.* of great sea
Jon. 1:17 Lord prepared great *f.*
2:1 prayed to L. out of *f.'s* belly
10 L. spoke to *f.* it vomited J.
Mat. 7:10 if he ask *f.* will he give
17:27 take up *f.* that first com.
Luke 24:42 gave him piece br. *f.*
John 21:9 they saw *f.* laid, 10, 13

FISH, ING.

Jer. 16:16 fishers, and they sh. *f.*
John 21:3 S. Peter saith, I go a *f.*

FISH-GATE.

2 *Chr.* 33:14 M. built to ent. *f.-g.*
Neh. 3:5 *f.-g.* did sons of H. bui.
12:39 from above the *f.-gate*
Zep. 1:10 noise of cry from *f.-g.*

FISH-HOOKS.

Amos 4:2 will take poster. w. *f.*

FISH-POOLS.

Cant. 7:4 th. eyes like *f.-p.* of H.

FISH-SPEARS.

Job 41:7 fill head with *f.-s.*

FISHERMEN.

Luke 5:2 *f.* were gone out of th.

FISHER, S.

Is. 19:8 *f.* also shall mourn and
Jer. 16:16 send for many *f.* sa. L.
Ezek. 47:10 *f.* shall stand upon it
Mat. 4:18 they were *f. Mark* 1:16
19 *f.* of men, *Mark* 1:17
John 21:7 Peter girt *f.* coat to h.

FISHES.

Gen. 9:2 fear of you be on all *f.*
1 *K.* 4:33 of creeping thi. and *f.*
Job 12:8 *f.* of sea shall declare
Ec. 9:12 *f.* that are taken in evil
Hab. 1:14 mak. men as *f.* of sea
Mat. 14:17 five loaves and two *f.*
Mar. 6:38 ; *Lu.* 9:13 ; *John* 6:9
15:34 serv. loaves lit. *f. Mark* 8:7
Luke 5:6 multit. of *f. John* 21:6
5:9 astonished at draught of *f.*
John 21:11 P. drew net full gr. *f.*
1 *Cor.* 15:39 flesh of be. and of *f.*

FIST, S.

Ex. 21:18 one smite ano. with *f.*
Prov. 30:4 hath gath. wind in *f.* ?
Is. 58:4 smite with *f.* of wicked.

FIT.

Lev. 16:21 by hand of a *f.* man
1 *Chr.* 7:11 *f.* to go to war, 12:8
Job 34:18 *f.* to say king, Th. wic.?
Ezek. 15:5 made *f.* for no work
Luke 9:62 is *f.* for kingdom of G.
14:35 not *f.* for the land
Acts 22:22 not *f.* that he sh. live
Col. 3:18 wives, submit as *f.* in L.

FITS.

Is. 28:25 doth he not cast *f.* ?
Is. 28:7 *f.* not thresh. *f.* are bea.
Ezek. 4:9 wheat, barley, millet, *f.*

FITLY.

Prov. 25:11 word *f.* spok. appl. of
Eph. 2:21 the building *f.* framed
4:16 form wh. whole body *f.* jo.

FITTED, ETH.

1 *K.* 6:35 gold *f.* up. carved work
Is. 44:13 carpent. *f.* it with plan.
Rom. 9:22 ves. of wrath *f.* to des.

FIVE.

Gen. 14:9 of S. four kings with *f.*
18:28 destroy all for lack of *f. f.*

Jos. 13:3 *f.* lords of Ph. *Jud.* 3:3
Is. 19:18 *f.* cities speak lang. of C.
30:17 at rebuke of *f.* shall ye flee
Mat. 14:17 we have here but *f.*
loaves, *Mark* 6:38; *Luke* 9:13
25:2 *f.* of them wise, *f.* foolish
Luke 12:6 are not *f.* spar. sold ?
16:28 father's house I have *f.* b.
John 4:18 hast had *f.* husbands
5:2 a pool having *f.* porches
1 *Cor.* 14:19 I rath. speak *f.* wor.
2 *Cor.* 11:24 *f.* times rec. 40 strip.
Rev. 17:10 sev. kings *f.* are fallen

FIXED.

Ps. 57:7 heart is *f.* I w. sing, 108:1
112:7 heart *f.* trusting in Lord
Luke 16:26 betw. us is a gulf *f.*

FLAG, S.

Ex. 2:3 she laid the ark in the *f.*
5 when she saw ark am. the *f.*
Job 8:11 can *f.* grow with. water ?
Is. 19:6 reeds and *f.* shall wither

FLAGON, S.

2 *Sam.* 6:19 *f.* of wine, 1 *Chr.* 16:3
Cant. 2:5 stay me wi. *f.* com. me
Is. 22:24 even to all vessels of *f.*
Hos. 3:1 love *f.* of wine

FLAKES.

Job 41:23 *f.* of his flesh are join.

FLAME, S.

Ex. 3:2 in *f.* of fire. *Acts* 7:30
Num. 21:28 *f.* fr. city, *Jer.* 48:45
Jud. 13:20 *f.* w. up, angel in *f.*
Job 15:30 *f.* sh. dry up branches
41:21 *f.* goeth out of his mouth
Ps. 29:7 voice of L. div. *f.* of fire
106:18 *f.* burnt up the wicked
Cant. 8:6 coals wh. hath a veh. *f.*
Is. 5:24 *f.* consumeth the chaff
10:17 Holy One shall be for a *f.*
13:8 their faces shall be as *f.*
29:6 visited with *f.* of devo. fire
43:2 nei. sh. *f.* kindle upon thee
66:15 rebuke with *f.* of fire
Ezek. 20:47 *f.* sh. not be quench.
Dan. 7:9 throne was like fiery *f.*
11 till body given to burning *f.*
Joel 1:19 *f.* hath burnt trees
2:3 behind them a *f.* burneth
Ob. 18 house of Jos. shall be a *f.*
Luke 16:24 tormented in this *f.*
Heb. 1:7 mak. ministers *f.* of fire
Rev. 1:14 as *f.* of fire, 2:18; 19:12

FLAMING.

Gen. 3:24 at gard. of Eden *f.* sw.
Ezek. 20:47 *f.* flame not be quen.
Nah. 2:3 chariots be wi. *f.* torch.

FLANKS.

Lev. 3:4 the fat which is by the *f.* 10, 15; 4:9; 7:4
Job 15:27 mak. collops of fat on *f.*

FLASH.

Ezek. 1:14 appear. of *f.* of lightn.

FLAT.

Lev. 21:18 that hath *f.* nose
Num. 22:31 Baalam fell *f.* on face
Jos. 6:5 wall of city sh. fall *f.* 20

FLATTER, ETH.

Ps. 5:9 they *f.* with their tongue
36:2 he *f.* him. in his own eyes
78:36 did *f.* him with mouth
Prov. 2:16 stranger who *f.* 7:5
20:19 med. not with him that *f.*
28:23 more favor than he that *f.*
29:5 man that *f.* spreadeth a net

FLATTERING.

Job 32:21 nei. let me gi. *f.* tit. 22
Ps. 12:2 with *f.* lips
Prov. 7:21 with the *f.* of her lips
26:28 a *f.* mouth worketh ruin
Ezek. 12:24 shall be no more *f.*
1 *Thes.* 2:5 neither used *f.* words

FLATTERY, IES.

Job 17:5 speaketh *f.* to friends

Prov. 6:24 *f.* of strange woman
Dan. 11:21 he sh. obt. king. by *f.*
32 shall he corrupt by *f.*
34 many shall cleave with *f.*

FLAX.

Ex. 9:31 *f.* was smitten *f.* boiled
Jos. 2:6 she hid with stalks of *f.*
Jud. 15:14 cords became as *f.*
Prov. 31:13 she seeks wool and *f.*
Is. 19:9 work in fine *f.* confound.
42:3 the smoking *f.* he shall not
quench, *Mat.* 12:20
Hos. 2:5 lovers that give me *f.*

FLAY, ED.

Mic. 3:3 *f.* their skins
2 *Chr.* 35:11 blood, the Levites *f.*

FLEA.

1 *Sam.* 24:14 come after *f.* ? 26:20

FLED.

Gen. 14:10 kings of So. and G. *f.*
16:6 H. *f.* ; 31:22 ; J. *f. Hos.* 12:12
Ex. 2:15 M. *f.* fr. P. 4:3 ; *Acts* 7:29
14:5 told king of Egypt peop. *f.*
Ps. 31:11 did see me *f.* from me
114:3 the sea saw it and *f.* Jord.
Is. 22:3 thy rulers are *f.* tog.
Jer. 4:25 birds of the heavens *f.*
9:10 the fowl and beast are *f.*
Jon. 4:2 theref. I *f.* to Tarshish
Zec. 14:5 as ye *f.* before earthqu.
Mat. 8:33 they that kept them *f.*
26:56 forsook and *f. Mark* 14:50
Mark 16:8 *f.* from the sepulchre
Acts 16:27 supposing prisoners *f.*
Heb. 6:18 *f.* for ref. to lay hold
Rev. 12:6 wom. *f.* ; 16:20 ev. isl. *f.*
20:11 face earth and heaven *f.*

He FLED.

Gen. 35:7 wh. he *f.* from brother
39:12 he left ga. and *f.* 13, 15, 18
Num. 20:6 fr. whence he *f. Num.* 35:25
Jon. 1:10 he *f.* from pres. of L.
Mark 14:52 he *f.* left lin. clo. and *f.*

Is FLED.

Num. 35:32 no sat. for him th. *f.*
Is. 10:29 Gibeah of Saul is *f.*

They FLED.

Gen. 14:10 *t.* th. remained *f.* to
Jos. 10:11 as *t. f.* L. cast gr. ston.
1 *Sam.* 4:10 *f.* every man to tent, 2 *K.* 14:12
Ps. 104:7 at thy rebuke *they f.*
Is. 21:15 *they f.* from the swords
Lam. 4:15 when *t. f.* away
Dan. 10:7 *they f.* to save themse.
Hos. 7:13 woe for *they* have *f.*
Luke 8:34 saw what done *t. f.*
Acts 19:16 *they f.* out of house

FLEDDEST.

Gen. 35:1 when *f.* from face of E.
Ps. 114:5 wh. ailed O sea, th. *f.* ?

FLEECE.

Deut. 18:4 first of *f.* give Levites
Jud. 6:37 *f.* of wool in flo. 38, 39
Job 31:20 warm. with *f.* of sheep

FLEE.

Gen. 16:8 *f.* fr. face of mistress
19:20 this city is near to *f.* unto
Ex. 21:13 place whither he sh. *f.*
Lev. 26:17 *f.* when none purs. 36
Num. 10:35 hate thee *f. Ps.* 68:1
35:6 cities, that man-slayer may
f. 11, 15 ; *Deut.* 4:42 ; 19:3, 4,
5 ; *Jos.* 20:3, 4, 9
Deut. 28:7 and *f.* seven ways, 25
Jos. 8:5 as at first we will *f.* 6
20 had no power to *f.* this way
Jud. 20:32 let us *f.* and draw th.
2 *Sam.* 4:4 nurse haste to *f.* fell
2 4:13 wilt thou *f.* three months ?
2 *K.* 9:3 open door and *f.* tar. not
Neh. 6:11 should such a man *f.* ?

Job 20:24 he sh. *f.* from weapon
27:22 fain *f.* out of his hand
41:28 arrow cannot make him *f.*
Ps. 11:1 how say ye to my soul *f.*
68:12 kings of armies *f.* apace
139:7 whither sh. I *f.* fr. pres. ?
143:9 O Lord, I *f.* to thee
Prov. 28:1 wick. *f.* no man purs.
Is. 10:3 will ye *f.* for help ?
15:5 fugitives shall *f.* unto Zoar
30:16 for we will *f.* on horses
17 at rebuke of five shall ye *f.*
Jer. 4:29 city *f.* for noi. of horse.
48:6 *f.* save lives, be like heath
Amos 5:19 man did *f.* from lion
Jon. 1:3 Jon. rose up to *f.* to T.
Mat. 2:13 take young child and *f.*
3:7 to *f.* from wrath ? *Luke* 3:7
10:23 when perse. in this city *f.*
24:16 let them in J. *f.* to mountains. *Mark* 13:14 ; *Luke* 21:21
John 10:5 stranger not follow
but *f.*
1 *Cor.* 6:18 *f.* forni. ; 10:14 *f.* idol.
1 *Tim.* 6:11 man of G. *f.* th. thin.
2 *Tim.* 2:22 *f.* also youthful lusts
Jam. 4:7 res. the devil, he will *f.*
Rev. 9:6 death shall *f.* from them

FLEE away.

Gen. 31:27 didst *f. a.* secretly ?
Job 9:25 days *f. a.* th. see no good
20:8 he shall *f. away* as a dream
Ps. 64:8 all that see them sh. *f. a.*
Cant. 2:17 shadows *f. away*, 4:6
Is. 35:10 sighing sh. *f. a.* 51:11
Jer. 46:6 let not the swift *f. away*
Amos 7:12 seer, go *f. a.* into land
9:1 that fleeth shall not *f. away*
Nah. 2:8 Nineveh shall *f. away*
3:17 as grasshoppers they *f. a.*

FLEEING, ETH.

Lev. 26:36 sh. flee as *f.* from sw.
Deut. 4:42 *f.* to one of th. cities
19:11 *f.* into one of cities
Job 14:2 he *f.* also as a shadow
30:3 want and famine *f.* to wil.
Jer. 48:19 ask him that *f.*
Amos 9:1 that *f.* of them
John 10:12 a hireling *f.* 13

FLESH.

Gen. 2:21 G. closed up *f.* instead
24 and they shall be one *f.*
6:3 man, for he is *f.*
17:11 circum. *f.* of foresk. 14, 23
Ex. 4:7 hand turned as other *f.*
29:14 *f.* burn with fire, *Lev.* 9:11 ;
16:27 ; *Num.* 19:5
Lev. 6:27 wh. touch *f.* sh. be holy
8:31 boil *f.* at door of tabernacle
13:10 quick raw *f.* 14, 15, 16, 24
38 if in skin of *f.* 39
15:19 if issue in her *f.* be blood
21:5 nor sh. make cuttings in *f.*
Num. 11:33 *f.* was betw. teeth
Deut. 32:42 sword shall devour *f.*
Jud. 6:20 take *f.* and unl. cakes
21 fire out of rock consumed *f.*
1 *Sam.* 2:13 *f.* was in seething
15 give *f.* to roast for the prie.
1 *K.* 17:6 ravens brought bread *f.*
2 *K.* 4:34 *f.* of child waxed warm
2 *Chr.* 32:8 with him is arm of *f.*
Neh. 5:5 our *f.* is as *f.* of breth.
Job 10:4 hast thou eyes of *f.* ?
11 clothed me with skin and *f.*
Ps. 56:4 not fear what *f.* can do
78:20 can he provide *f.* for peo. ?
39 remembered th. were but *f.*
79:2 *f.* of saints given to beasts
Prov. 4:22 sayings health to *f.*
23:20 not am. riot. eaters of *f.*
Is. 31:3 horses are *f.* not spirit
49:26 feed them with own *f.*
Jer. 11:15 *f.* is passed from thee
17:5 cursed be man that mak. *f.*

Ezek. 4:14 nor came abomina. *f.*
11:3 city is caldron, and we *f.*
19 I will give heart of *f.* 36:26
23:20 whose *f.* is as *f.* of asses
24:10 consume the *f.* spice it
Dan. 2:11 gods, who. dw. not *f.*
7:5 Arise, devour much *f.*
10:3 neither *f.* nor wine
Hos. 8:13 sacrif. *f.* for sacrifices
Mic. 3:2 pluck *f.* from off bones
Zep. 1:17 *f.* shall be poured
Hag. 2:12 bear holy *f.* in skirt
Zec. 14:12 their *f.* shall consume
Mat. 16:17 *f.* and blood not rev.
19:5 sh. be one *f.* 6; *Mark* 10:8;
1 *Cor.* 6:16 ; *Eph.* 5:31
24:22 no *f.* be saved, *Mark* 13:20
26:41 sp. will. *f.* we. *Mark* 14:38
Luke 24:39 hath not *f.* and bones
John 1:14 the WORD was made *f.*
6:63 the *f.* profiteth nothing
Acts 2:30 seed of David according to *f.* Rom. 1:3
Rom. 3:20 shall no *f.* be justified
4:1 Abraham as pertaining to *f.*
7:25 with *f.* I serve law of sin
8:3 law was weak through *f.*
G. sent Son in like. of sin. *f.*
9:3 and kinsmen according to *f.*
5 concerning *f.* Christ came
13:14 not provision for the *f.*
1 *Cor.* 1:29 that no *f.* should glo.
15:39 one *f.* of men, ano. of bea.
50 *f.* and blood cannot inherit
2 *Cor.* 4:11 life of J. be manifest *f.*
7:5 *f.* had no rest but troubled
10:2 as if we walked accord. to *f.*
Gal. 1:16 confer not with *f.*
2:16 shall no *f.* be justified
3:3 made perfect by the *f.*
5:13 liberty for an occasion to *f.*
17 *f.* lusteth ag. Sp. Sp. ag. *f.*
24 that are C.'s crucified *f.*
Eph. 2:3 conv. in lusts of our *f.*
6:5 masters accord. to *f.* Col. 3:22
12 wrestle not ag. *f.* and blood
Heb. 2:14 child. are partak. of *f.*
12:9 fathers of *f.* who corrected
Jude 7 and going after strange *f.*
Jude 8 filthy dream. defile the *f.*
23 even garments spotted by *f.*
Rev. 19:18 *f.* of capt. *f.* of might.
21 all fowls were filled with *f.*

See EAT, EATETH.

After the FLESH.

John 8:15 ye judge *after the f.*
Rom. 8:1 walk not *after the f.* 4
5 are a *f.* mind things of *f.*
12 not debtors to live *after f.* 13
13 if ye live *aft. t. f.* ye sh. die
1 *Cor.* 1:26 not ma. wise m. *a. t. f.*
10:18 behold Israel *after the f.*
2 *Cor.* 5:16 we know no man *af.
the f.* have kn. Ch. *a. t. f.*
10:3 we do not war *after the f.*
11:18 that many glory *af. the f.*
Gal. 4:23 Ishm. born *af. t. f.* 29
2 *Pet.* 2:10 th. that walk *af. t. f.*

All FLESH.

Gen. 6:12 *a. f.* had corrupt. way
13 end of *all f.* is come bef. me
6:19 of *all f.* two of ev. sort, 7:15
7:21 *a. f.* died that moved, 8:17 ;
9:11, 15, 16, 17
Lev. 17:14 life of *a. f.* is the blood
Num. 8:7 let them shave *all f.*
16:22 G. of spirits of *all f.* 27:16
Job 34:15 *all f.* sh. perish togeth.
Ps. 65:2 to thee shall *all f.* come
136:25 who giveth food to *all f.*
145:21 let *all f.* bless holy name
Is. 40:5 *all f.* sh. see it together
6 *all f.* 's grass, 1 *Pet.* 1:24
49:26 *a. f.* know I am S. *Ez.* 21:5
66:16 will L. plead with *all f.*
23 *all f.* shall come to worship
24 they sh. be abhorr. to *all f.*

Jer. 25:31 will plead with *all f.*
32:27 I am the Lord God of *a. f.*
Ezek. 21:4 sword go against *a. f.*
Dan. 4:12 and *all f.* was fed of it
Joel 2:28 Spur S. on *a. f.* Acts 2:17
Zec. 2:13 silent *all f.* before Lord
Luke 3:6 *a. f.* sh. see salv. of G.
John 17:2 given power over *a. f.*
1 *Cor.* 15:39 *a. f.* is not same fl.

His FLESH.

Ex. 29:34 seethe *h. f.* in holy pl.
Lev. 4:11 burn all *h. f.* 8:17
6:10 linen breeches on *h. f.* 16:4
13:3 in skin of *his f.* 4, 11, 13
14:9 wash *h. f.* in water, 15:16 ;
16:24, 28 ; *Num.* 19:7
1 *K.* 21:27 Ah. put sack. on *h. f.*
2 *K.* 5:14 *his f.* came again as
6:30 Jor. had sackcloth on *his f.*
Job 2:5 touch bone and *his f.*
31:31 O that we had of *his f.*
33:25 *f.* sh. be fresh. than child's
41:23 flakes of *his f.* are joined
Prov. 11:17 that is cruel troub. *f.*
Ec. 4:5 foldeth hands eateth *f.*
Is. 17:4 fatness of *f.* sh. wax lean
John 6:52 this man give *f.* to eat?
Acts 2:31 nei. *his f.* did see cor.
Gal. 6:8 that soweth to *his f.*
Eph. 2:15 abolished in *his f.*
5:29 no man hated *his* own *f.*
30 memb. of his body, of *h. f.*
Col. 1:22 reconc. in body of *his f.*
Heb. 5:7 who in the days of *h. f.*
10:20 veil, that is to say, *his f.*

In the FLESH, *or* **in FLESH.**

Gen. 17:24 A. circum. *in t. f.* 25
Ezek. 44:7 uncircum. *in the f.* 9
Dan. 1:15 fairer and fatter *in t. f.*
Rom. 2:28 circ. outward *in the f.*
7:5 *in the f.* the motions of sin
8:3 sin condemned sin *in the f.*
8 that are *in t. f.* cannot pl. G.
9 are not *in t. f.* but in the Sp.
1 *Cor.* 7:28 sh. have trouble *in f.*
2 *Cor.* 10:3 tho' we walk *in the f.*
12:7 was given a thorn *in the f.*
Gal. 2:20 life wh. I now live *in f.*
6:12 to make fair show *in the f.*
Eph. 2:11 Gentiles *in the flesh*
Phil. 1:22 if I live *in the f.* this
24 abide *in t. f.* more needful
3:3 have no confidence *in the f.* 4
Col. 2:1 have not seen face *in t. f.*
1 *Tim.* 3:16 G. was manif. *in t. f.*
1 *Pet.* 3:18 put to death *in the f.*
4:1 Christ hath suffered *in the f.*
2 live rest of his time *in the f.*
6 according to men *in the f.*
1 *John* 4:2 den. C. come *in t. f.* 3
2 *John* 7 that C. come *in the f.*

My FLESH.

Job 4:15 hair of *my f.* stood up
6:12 or is *my f.* brass?
7:5 *my f.* is clothed with worms
13:14 take *my f.* in my teeth?
19:26 yet in *my f.* shall I see G.

Ps. 16:9 *my f.* shall rest in hope,
Acts 2:26
38:3 no soundness in *my f.* 7
63:1 *my f.* longeth for thee
73:26 *my f.* faileth
84:2 my heart and *my f.* crieth
109:24 *my f.* faileth of fatness
119:120 *my f.* trembleth for fear
Lam. 3:4 *my f.* hath he made
old
John 6:51 bread I give, is *my f.*
54 cat. *my f.* hath eter. life, 56
55 *my f.* is meat indeed
Rom. 7:18 in *my f.* dwel. no good
11:14 prov. them wh. are *my f.*
Gal. 4:14 tem. wh. was in *my f.*
Col. 1:24 afflict. of Ch. in *my f.*

See BONE.

Of the FLESH.

Ex. 29:34 aught *of t. f.* remain
Prov. 14:30 sound h. is life *of f.*
Ec. 12:12 much study is w. *of f.*
John 1:13 not of will *of the f.*
3:6 which is born *of f.* is flesh
Rom. 8:5 mind the things *of t. f.*
9:8 are the children *of t. f.*
1 *Cor.* 5:5 to S. for destruc. *of f.*
2 *Cor.* 7:1 fr. all filthiness *of t. f.*
Gal. 4:13 thro' infirmity *of t. f.*
5:16 shall not fulfil lusts *of t. f.*
19 works *of t. f.* are manifest
6:8 soweth to *f.* sh. *of t. f.* reap
Eph. 2:3 walked in lusts *of the f.*
Col. 2:11 the body of sins *of t. f.*
23 to the satisfying *of the f.*
Heb. 9:13 the purifying *of the f.*
1 *Pet.* 3:21 put. away filth *of t. f.*
2 *Pet.* 2:18 thro' the lusts *of t. f.*
1 *John* 2:16 lust *of t. f.*

Thy FLESH.

Gen. 40:19 birds shall eat *thy f.*
1 *Sam.* 17:44 give t. *f.* unto fowls
2 *Sam.* 5:1 bo. and t. *f.* 1 *Chr.* 11:1
2 *K.* 5:10 and t. *f.* shall come
Prov. 5:11 mourn wh. *t. f.* is con.
Ec. 5:6 to cause *t. f.* to sin
Is. 58:7 hide not from *thy* own *f.*
Ezek. 32:5 will lay *t. f.* on moun.

Your FLESH.

Lev. 19:28 not make cut. in *y. f.*
Jud. 8:7 then I will tear *y. f.*
Ezek. 36:26 heart out of *y. f.*
Rom. 6:19 infirmity of *your f.*
Gal. 6:13 they may glory in *y.*
Col. 2:13 dead in uncir. of *y. f.*
Jam. 5:3 rust shall eat *your f.*

FLESHED. *See* FAT, LEAN.

FLESH-HOOK, S.

Ex. 27:3 shalt make his *f.-h.*
38:3 the vessels and *f.-h.*
Num. 4:14 put on pur. cloth *f.-h.*
1 *Sam.* 2:13 servant with a *f.-h.*
14 all that *f.-h.* brought up
1 *Chr.* 28:17 pure gold for *f.-h.*
2 *Chr.* 4:16 pots and *f.-h.*

FLESHLY.

2 *Cor.* 1:12 not with *f.* wisdom
3:3 but in *f.* tables of the heart
Col. 2:18 puff. up by his *f.* mind
1 *Pet.* 2:11 abstain from *f.* lusts

FLESH-POTS.

Ex. 16:3 when we sat by *f.-p.*

FLEW.

1 *Sam.* 14:32 peo. *f.* upon the sp.
Is. 6:6 then *f.* one of seraphim

FLIES.

Ex. 8:21 send swarms of *f.* 31
Ps. 78:45 send divers sorts of *f.*
105:31 divers sorts of *f.*
Ec. 10:1 dead *f.* cause ointment

FLIETH.

Deut. 14:19 creeping thing *f.*
28:49 as swift as the eagle *f.*
Ps. 91:5 arrow that *f.* by day
Nah. 3:16 cank. spoileth and *f.*

FLIGHT.

Amos 2:14 *f.* sh. perish from sw
Mat. 24:20 pray *f.* be not in win
ter, *Mark* 13:18
Heb. 11:34 turned to *f.* armies

See PUT.

FLINT.

Deut. 8:15 water out of rock of *f.*
Ps. 114:8 turning *f.* into fount.
Is. 5:28 hoofs sh. be counted *f.*
50:7 have I set my face like *f.*
Ezek. 3:9 harder than *f.*

FLINTY.

Deut. 32:13 oil out of *f.* rock

FLOATS.

1 *K.* 5:9 I will conv. them by sea
in *f.* 2 *Chr.* 2:16

FLOCK.

Gen. 4:4 Ab. bro. firstlings of *f.*
37:2 J. was feeding *f.* with bre.
12 brethren went to feed *f.* 13
Ex. 2:16 troughs to wat. fath. *f.*
17 Moses helped, watered *f.* 19
3:1 Moses led *f.* back of desert
Lev. 5:18 a ram without blemish
out of *f.* 6:6; *Ezr.* 10:19;
Ezek. 43:23, 25
27:32 tithe of the herd or of *f.*
Deut. 15:19 first males of *f.*
1 *Sam.* 17:34 took lamb out of *f.*
Job 30:1 set with dogs of my *f.*
Cant. 1:7 makest *f.* to rest
8 by the footsteps of the *f.*
4:1 hair as a *f.* of goats, 6:5
2 teeth like a *f.* of sheep, 6:6
Is. 40:11 he sh. feed *f.* like shep.
Jer. 13:17 L. *f.* is carried captive
20 wh. is *f.* given thee beauti. ?
23:2 ye have scattered my *f.*
3 gather remnant of my *f.*
25:34 principal of the *f.* 35, 36
31:12 the young of the *f.*
49:20 least of *f.* sh. draw, 50:45
51:23 break shepherd and his *f.*
Ezek. 24:5 take the choice of *f.*
34:3 but ye feed not *f.*
6 *f.* scattered on face of earth
8 because my *f.* became a prey
10 I will require my *f.* I will
12 as a sheph. seek. out his *f.*
15 feed my *f.* ; 17 O my *f.*
22 therefore will I save my *f.*
31 *f.* of my pasture are men
Amos 7:15 as I followed *f.*
Jon. 3:7 let not herd nor *f.* taste
Mic. 4:8 thou, O tower of the *f.*
7:14 feed thy people, the *f.* of
Hab. 3:17 the *f.* shall be cut off
Zec. 9:16 save them as *f.* of peo.
11:4 will feed *f.* of slaughter, 7
7 poor of the *f.* that waited, 11
17 idle sheph. that leaveth *f.*
Mal. 1:14 deceiver wh. hath in *f.*
Mat. 26:31 sheep of *f.* sh. be scat.
Luke 2:8 keeping watch over *f.*
12:32 fear not, little *f.*
Acts 20:28 take heed to all the *f.*
29 griev. wolves not sparing *f.*
1 *Cor.* 9:7 who feedeth a *f.*
1 *Pet.* 5:2 feed *f.* of God am. you
3 being ensamples to the *f.*

Like a FLOCK.

Job 21:11 send little ones *l. a. f.*
Ps. 77:20 leddest people *l. a. f.*
80:1 thou th. leddest Jos. *l. a. f.*
107:41 mak. him families *l. a f.*
Ezek. 36:37 increase them *l. a. f.*

FLOCKS.

Gen. 29:2 three *f.* of sheep, 3, 8
30:38 J. set rod he pill. bef. *f.* 39
37:14 whether it be well with *f.*
47:4 have no pasture for *f.*
Lev. 1:10 if his offering be of *f.*
Num. 31:9 took spoil of their *f.*
Deut. 7:13 will also bless the *f.*
28:4 blessed be *f.* of thy sheep
18 cursed sh. be *f.* of thy sheep
Jud. 5:16 to hear bleating of *f.*
1 *K.* 20:27 two little *f.* of kids
Job 24:2 violently take away *f.*
Ps. 65:13 past. are clothed wi. *f.*
78:48 he gave *f.* to hot thunder.
Cant. 1:7 turn aside by *f.*
Is. 32:14 palaces sh. be pasture *f.*
60:7 *f.* of Kedar sh. be gathered
61:5 stand and feed *f.*
65:10 Sh. shall be a fold for *f.*
Jer. 33:12 sheph. causing *f.* to lie
13 *f.* sh. pass ag. under the rod
50:8 be as he-goats before the *f.*
Ezek. 34:2 sh. not sheph. feed *f.* ?
Joel 1:18 *f.* of sheep desolate
Mic. 5:8 lion among *f.* of sheep
Zep. 2:6 sea-coast folds for *f.* 14

FLOCKS, *with* herds.

Gen. 13:5 Lot also had *f.* and *h.*
24:35 L. hath given A. *f.* and *h.*
26:14 Isa. had poss. of *f.* and *h.*
50:8 *f.* and *h.* left in land of G.
Ex. 10:9 will go with *f.* and *h.*
12:32 your *f.* and *h.* and be gone
34:3 let *f.* nor *h.* feed bef. mount
Num. 11:22 sh. *f.* and *h.* be slain
Deut. 12:6 firstlings of *h.* and *f.*
17 ; 14:26 : *Neh.* 10:36
1 *Sam.* 30:20 David *f.* and *h.*
2 *Sam.* 12:2 had many *f.* and *h.*
Prov. 27:23 know *f.* look to *h.*
Jer. 3:24 shame devour. *f.* and *h.*
Hos. 5:6 shall go with *f.* and *h.*

FLOOD.

Gen. 6:17 bring a *f.* of water
7:6 *f.* of waters on earth, 7, 10
Gen. 7:17 *f.* was forty d. on earth
9:11 any more a *f.* to destroy
28 Noah lived after *f.* 350 years
10:1 were sons born after *f.* 32
Jos. 24:2 other side of *f.* 3, 14, 15
Job 14:11 *f.* decayeth and drieth
22:16 foun. overthrown with *f.*
28:4 *f.* breaketh from inhabitant
Ps. 29:10 Lord sitteth upon *f.*
66:6 went through *f.* on foot
69:15 let not water *f.* overflow
90:5 carriest away as with *f.*
Is. 59:19 enemy come in like *f.*
Jer. 46:7 who that cometh as *f.* ?
8 Egypt riseth up like a *f.*
Dan. 9:26 end shall be with a *f.*
11:22 arms of *f.* sh. be overflo.
Amos 8:8 rise up wholly as *f.* 9:5
9:5 drowned as by *f.* of Egypt
Nah. 1:8 an overrunning *f.*
Mat. 24:38 in days before *f.*
39 till *f.* came, *Luke* 17:27
Luke 6:48 *f.* arose stream beat
2 *Pet.* 2:5 bring. in *f.* on world
Rev. 12:15 poured water as *f.* 16

FLOODS.

Ex. 15:8 *f.* stood upright
2 *Sam.* 22:5 *f.* of ungodly made
me afraid, *Ps.* 18:4
Job 28:11 bindeth *f.* from overfl.
Ps. 24:2 hath establ. it upon *f.*
32:6 surely in *f.* of great waters
69:2 waters where *f.* overfl. me
78:44 turned their *f.* into blood
93:3 *f.* have lifted up, O Lord
98:8 let the *f.* clap their hands
Cant. 8:7 neither can *f.* drown
Is. 44:3 pour *f.* on dry ground
Jon. 2:3 *f.* compassed me about
Mat. 7:25 *f.* came, winds bl. 27

2 *Chr.* 34:11 timber to *f.* houses

FLOOR, Verb.

Gen. 50:10 to thresh. *f.* of A. 11
Num. 5:17 pri. sh. take dust in *f.*
15:20 thresh. *f.* 18:27, 30
Deut. 15:14 furnish out of *f.*
Jud. 6:37 a fleece of wool in *f.*
Ruth 3:2 he win. in threshing *f.*
2 *Sam.* 6:6 Nach. th. *f.* 1 *Chr.* 13:9
24:18 rear alt. in thresh. *f.* of A.
21 D. said, to buy threshing *f.*
1 *K.* 6:30 overlaid *f.* of house
2 *K.* 6:27 out of barn *f.*
2 *Chr.* 3:1 threshing *f.* of Ornan
Is. 21:10 and the corn of my *f.*
Jer. 51:33 dau. of B. like thre. *f.*
Dan. 2:35 chaff of sum. thres. *f.*
Hos. 9:1 reward on every corn *f.*
2 *f.* and wine-pr. not feed them
13:3 as chaff driven out of *f.*
Joel 2:24 *f.* shall be full of wheat
Mic. 4:12 gather as sheaves to *f.*
Mat. 3:12 thor. purge *f.* *Lu.* 3:17

FLOUR.

Ex. 29:2 wheat. *f.* sh. thou make

Lev. 2:2 handful of the *f.* 6:15
Num. 28:5 part of ephah of *f.* for
meat-of. 20, 28 ; 29:3, 9, 14
Jud. 6:19 ephah of *f.* ; 1 *Sam.* 1:24
1 *Sam.* 28:24 took *f.* and kneaded
it, 2 *Sam.* 13:8
2 *Sam.* 17:28 bro. *f.* parched corn
See DEAL, FINE.

FLOURISH.

Ps. 72:7 in his days sh. right. *f.*
16 they of city sh. *f.* like grass
92:7 when all workers of iniq. *f.*
13 righteous shall *f.*
13 shall *f.* in courts of our G.
132:18 upon himself sh. crown *f.*
Prov. 11:28 right. sh. *f.* as bran.
14:11 tabern. of upright shall *f.*
Ec. 12:5 almond-tree shall *f.*
Is. 17:11 thou sh. make seed *f.*
66:14 your bones shall *f.*
Ezek. 17:24 have made dry tree *f.*

FLOURISHED.

Cant. 6:11 went to see vine *f.*
Phil. 4:10 your care of me hath *f.*

FLOURISHETH, ING.

Ps. 90:6 in the morning it *f.*
92:14 they shall be fat and *f.*
103:15 as flower of field, he *f.*
Dan. 4:4 I was at rest, and *f.*

FLOW.

Job 20:28 his goods shall *f.* away
Ps. 147:18 wind blow, waters *f.*
Cant. 4:16 the spices may *f.* out
Is. 2:2 nations shall *f.* unto it
48:21 waters to *f.* out of rock
60:5 shalt see and *f.* together
64:1 mountains might *f.* down
Jer. 31:12 *f.* to goodness of L.
Jer. 51:44 nations sh. not *f.* tog.
Joel 3:18 hills shall *f.* with milk,
rivers of Jud. *f.* with waters
Mic. 4:1 peo. sh. *f.* to mou. of L.
John 7:38 out of belly sh. *f.* l. w.

FLOWED.

Jos. 4:18 Jordan *f.* over banks
Is. 64:3 mount. *f.* down at pres.
Lam. 3:54 waters *f.* over my head

FLOWETH.

Lev. 20:24 *f.* with milk and hon.
Num. 13:27 ; 14:8 ; 16:13, 14 ;
Deut. 6:3 ; 11:9 ; 26:15 ; 27:3 ;
31:20 ; *Jos.* 5:6

FLOWING.

Ex. 3:8 *f.* with milk and honey,
17 ; 13:5 ; 33:3 ; *Jer.* 11:5 ;
32:22 ; *Ezek.* 20:6, 15
Prov. 18:4 well-sp. of wis. as *f.*
Is. 66:12 glo. of G. like *f.* stream
Jer. 18:14 cold *f.* waters be firs. *f.*
49:4 gloriest thou in *f.* valley ?

FLOWER.

Ex. 25:33 *f.* in one branch, 37:19
1 *Sam.* 2:33 incr. die in *f.* of age
Job 14:2 forth as *f.* is cut down
15:33 he shall cast *f.* as olive
Ps. 103:15 as *f.* of field
Is. 18:5 sour grape is rip. in *f.*
28:1 glorious beauty is fad. *f.* 4
40:6 goodliness is as *f.* of field
7 *f.* fadeth, 8 ; *Neh.* 1:4 ; *Jam.*
1:10, 11 ; 1 *Pet.* 1:24
1 *Cor.* 7:36 she pass *f.* of her
age

FLOWERS.

Ex. 25:31 *f.* of the same, 37:17
37:20 almonds, knops, and his *f.*
Lev. 15:24 her *f.* be upon him, 33
1 *K.* 6:18 carved with knops and
open *f.* 29, 32, 35 ; 7:26, 49
2 *Chr.* 4:5 cup with *f.* of lilies, 21
Cant. 2:12 *f.* appear on earth
5:13 bed of spices, as sweet *f.*

FLUTE, S.

Dan. 3:5 hear sound of *f.* 7, 10, 15

FLUTTERETH.

Deut. 32:11 as eagle *f.* ov. young

FLUX.

Acts 28:8 lay sick of a *f.*

FLY.

Is. 7:18 sh. hiss for the *f.* in E.

FLY, Verb.

Gen. 1:20 fowl th. may *f.* earth
1 *Sam.* 15:19 didst *f.* on the spoil
2 *Sam.* 22:11 did *f.* on wings of wind, *Ps.* 18:10
Job 5:7 as sparks *f.* upward
39:26 doth hawk *f.* by thy wis.
Ps. 55:6 then would I *f.* away
90:10 cut off, and we *f.* away
Prov. 23:5 riches *f.* away
Is. 6:2 with two he did *f.*
11:14 *f.* on shoulders of Philist.
60:8 who are these that *f.*
Jer. 48:40 he shall *f.* as an eagle
Ezek. 13:20 hunt souls to make *f.*
Dan. 9:21 G. caused to *f.* swiftly
Hos. 9:11 sh. *f.* away like a bird
Hab. 1:8 they shall *f.* as eagle
Rev. 14:6 saw another angel *f.*
19:17 that *f.* midst of heaven

FLYING.

Lev. 11:21 eat of every *f.* thing
Ps. 148:10 all cattle and *f.* fowl
Prov. 26:2 as swallow by *f.*
Is. 14:29 shall be fiery *f.* serpent
31:5 birds *f.* so will L. defend J.
Zec. 5:1 and behold a *f.* roll, 2
Rev. 4:7 beast like a *f.* eagle
8:13 angel *f.* thro' midst of hea.

FOAL, S.

Gen. 32:15 J. took 20 asses, 10 *f.*
49:11 binding his *f.* to the vine
Zec. 9:9 colt *f.* of ass, *Mat.* 21:5

FOAM.

Hos. 10:7 king of S. cut off as *f.*

FOAMED, ING.

Mark 9:18 *f.* and gnasheth with his teeth, *Luke* 9:39
20 on ground and wallowed, *f.*
Jude 13 waves *f.* out own shame

FODDER.

Job 6:5 or loweth ox over his *f. f.*

FOES.

1 *Chr.* 21:12 destroyed before *f.*
Est. 9:16 Jews slew of *f.* 75,000
Ps. 27:2 mine enemies and *f.*
30:1 not made my *f.* to rejoice
89:23 I will beat down his *f.*
Mat. 10:36 man's *f.* be of house
Acts 2:35 I make *f.* footstool

FOLD

Heb. 1:12 as a vesture sh. thou *f.*

FOLD, Substantive.

Is. 13:20 sheph. make their *f.*
65:10 Sharon shall be *f.*
Ezek. 34:14 on mount. shall *f.*
Hab. 3:17 flock sh. be cut from *f.*
Mat. 13:8 bro. forth fruit, some thirty *f.* 23; *Mark* 4:8, 20
19:29 forsaken ho. receive 100 *f.*
John 10:16 sheep wh. not of this *f.* one *f.* and one shepherd

FOLDS.

Num. 32:24 build *f.* for sheep, 36
Ps. 50:9 take no he-goats of *f.*
Zep. 2:6 sea-coast be *f.* for flocks

FOLDEN.

Nah. 1:10 wh. they be *f.* together

FOLDETH, ING.

Prov. 6:10 *f.* of hands, 24:33
Ec. 4:5 *f.* his hands together

FOLK.

Prov. 30:26 conies but feeble *f.*
Jer. 51:58 *f.* shall labor in fire
Mark 6:5 hands on few sick *f.*
John 5:3 multitude of impotent *f.*
Acts 5:16 about, bringing sick *f.*

FOLLOW.

Gen. 24:8 not willing to *f.*
44:4 Jos. said, Up, *f.* after men
Ex. 14:4 harden P. he shall *f.*
21:22 no mischief *f.* 23
23:2 not *f.* multitude to do evil
Deut. 16:20 what just sh. thou *f.*
Jud. 9:3 hearts inclined to *f.* A.
1 *K.* 19:20 I will *f.* thee
Ps. 45:14 companions *f.* her
119:150 that *f.* after mischief
Is. 5:11 may *f.* strong drink
51:1 that *f.* after righteousness
Jer. 17:16 being pastor to *f.* thee
Ezek. 13:3 prophets *f.* own spirit
Hos. 6:3 we *f.* on to know the L.
Mat. 8:19 Master, I will *f.* thee, *Luke* 9:57, 61
Mark 16:17 signs *f.* them th. be.
John 10:5 stran. will they not *f.*
13:37 L. why cannot I *f.* thee?
Acts 3:24 prophets from S. that *f.*
Rom. 14:19 *f.* thi. th. make peace
1 *Cor.* 14:1 *f.* after charity, desire
Phil. 3:12 I *f.* after, if that I may
1 *Thes.* 5:15 *f.* that which is good
2 *Thes.* 3:9 ensample to you to *f.*
1 *Tim.* 5:24 men they *f.* after
6:11 man of God *f.* 2 *Tim.* 2:22
Heb. 12:14 *f.* peace with all men
13:7 whose faith *f.* considering
1 *Pet.* 1:11 testified glory sh. *f.*
2:21 example, that ye should *f.*
2 *Pet.* 2:2 shall *f.* pernicious ways
3 *John* 11 *f.* not that which is evil
Rev. 14:4 they that *f.* the Lamb
13 and their works do *f.* them

FOLLOW him.

1 *K.* 18:21 if Lord be God, *f.* him
Mark 5:37 suff. no man to *f.* him
Lu. 22:10 *f. h.* into ho. *Mark* 14:13
John 10:4 sheep *f. him*

FOLLOW me.

Gen. 24:5 woman not *f. me,* 39
2 *K.* 6:19 *f. me,* I will bring you
Ps. 23:6 goodn. and mercy *f. me*
Mat. 4:19 Jes. saith, *f. me,* 8:22; 9:9; *Mark* 2:14; *Luke* 5:27
16:24 take up cross *f. me, Mark* 8:34; 10:21; *Luke* 9:23
19:21 sell that thou hast, *f. me, Luke* 18:22
Luke 9:59 *f. me, John* 1:43; 21:22
John 10:27 sheep hear voi. *f. me*
12:26 if man serve, let him *f. me*
13:36 thou canst not *f. me* now
Acts 12:8 garm. about thee, *f. me*

FOLLOWED.

Gen. 24:61 R. and damsels *f.* m.
Num. 32:12 *f.* Lord, *Deut.* 1:36
Jos. 6:8 ark of covenant *f.* them
14:8 I wholly *f.* L. my God, 9, 14
Jud. 2:12 forsook L. *f.* oth. gods
1 *Sam.* 14:22 they *f.* hard after P.
31:2 Philistines *f.* Saul, 2 *Sam.* 1:6; 1 *Chr.* 10:2
2 *Sam.* 2:10 house of Judah *f.* D.
3:31 king David himself *f.* bier
17:23 Ahith. saw counsel not *f.*
1 *K.* 16:21 half of people *f.* Tibni, half *f.* Omri, 22
2 *K.* 17:15 *f.* vanity, became vain
Ps. 68:25 play. on instruments *f.*
Ezek. 10:11 head looked they *f.*
Amos 7:15 L. took me as I *f.* flock
Mat. 27:55 many wom. wh. *f.* J.
Mark 10:28 we left all and *f.* thee, *Luke* 18:28
Luke 22:54 and Peter *f.* afar off
Acts 13:43 relig. proselytes *f.* P.
16:17 the same *f.* Paul and us
Rom. 9:30 Gent. who *f.* not righ.
31 who *f.* after law of righteo.
1 *Cor.* 10:4 drank of rock that *f.*
1 *Tim.* 5:10 *f.* every good work
2 *Pet.* 1:16 not *f.* cun. dev. fables

FOLLOWED him.

Num. 16:25 M. elders of Is. *f. h.*
Jud. 9:4 light persons who *f. h.*
2 *Sam.* 11:8 *f. h.* a mess of meat
Mat. 4:20 they left their nets and *f. him, Mark* 1:18
22 left the ship and *f. him*
25 *f. him* great multitude, 8:1; 12:15; 19:2; 20:29; *Mark* 2:15; 5:24; *Luke* 23:27; *John* 6:2
8:23 disciples *f. him, Luke* 22:39
9:27 two blind men *f. him*
26:58 Peter *f. him, Mark* 14:54
Luke 5:11 forsook all, *f. him,* 28
Acts 12:9 P. went out and *f. him*
Rev. 19:14 armies *f. him*

FOLLOWED me.

Num. 14:24 servant C. hath *f. me*
1 *K.* 14:8 D. *f. me* with all heart
Mat. 19:28 *f. me* in regeneration

FOLLOWEDST.

Ruth 3:10 thou *f.* not young men

FOLLOWERS.

1 *Cor.* 4:16 *f.* of me, 11:1; *Phil.* 3:17
Eph. 5:1 be ye *f.* of God
1 *Thes.* 1:6 *f.* of us and of the L.
2:14 ye became *f.* of churches
Heb. 6:12 *f.* of them who thro' fa.
1 *Pet.* 3:13 be *f.* of that is good

FOLLOWETH.

Ps. 63:8 soul *f.* hard after thee
Prov. 12:11 *f.* vain persons, 28:19
15:9 loveth him *f.* righte. 21:21
Hos. 12:1 Eph. *f.* after east wind
Mat. 10:38 tak. not up cro. and *f.*
Mark 9:38 *f.* not us, *Luke* 9:49
John 8:12 *f.* me not walk in dar.

FOLLOWING.

Deut. 12:30 not snared by *f.* them
Jos. 22:16 from *f.* Lord, 18, 23, 29; 1 *Sam.* 12:20; 2 *K.* 17:21; 2 *Chr.* 25:27; 34:33
Jud. 2:19 in *f.* other gods
2 *Sam.* 2:19 Asahel turned not from *f.* Abner, 26, 30
7:8 I took thee from *f.* sheep, 1 *Chr.* 17:7; *Ps.* 78:71
1 *K.* 21:26 abominably in *f.* idols
Ps. 48:13 may tell to generat. *f.*
109:13 gen. *f.* let name be blot.
Mark 16:20 word with signs *f.*
Luke 13:33 to-morrow and day *f.*
John 1:43 day *f.* ; 6:22 the day
Acts 23:11 night *f.* Lord stood by
2 *Pet.* 2:15 *f.* way of Balaam

FOLLY.

Gen. 34:7 Sh. wrought *f.* in Isr.
Deut. 22:21 by playing whore
Jos. 7:15 Ach. wrought *f.* in Is.
Jud. 19:23 do not this *f.*
20:6 have committed *f.* in Israel
1 *Sam.* 25:25 Nab. *f.* is with him
2 *Sam.* 13:12 do not thou this *f.*
Job 4:18 angels he charg. with *f.*
24:12 God layeth not *f.* to them
42:8 lest I deal with you after *f.*
Ps. 49:13 their way is their *f.*
85:8 not turn again to *f.*
Prov. 5:23 in his *f.* he sh. go ast.
13:16 a fool layeth open his *f.*
14:8 the *f.* of fools is deceitful
18 the simple inherit *f.*
24 the foolishness of fools is *f.*
29 hasty of spirit exalteth *f.*
15:21 *f.* joy to him dest. of wis.
16:22 instruction of fools is *f.*
17:12 a fool in his *f.*
18:13 it is *f.* and shame
26:4 answer not fool accord. to *f.*
5 answer fool according to *f.*
11 so a fool returneth to his *f.*

Ec. 1:17 to know wisdom and *f.*
2:3 I sought to lay hold on *f.*
12 to behold *f.* ; 13 excelleth *f.*
7:25 to know wickedness of *f.*
10:1 so a little *f.* him in reput.
6 *f.* is set in dignity
Is. 9:17 every mouth speaketh *f.*
Jer. 23:13 seen *f.* in the prophets
2 *Cor.* 11:1 bear with me in my *f.*
2 *Tim.* 3:9 *f.* be made manifest

FOOD.
Gen. 2:9 every tree good for *f.*
3:6 saw the tree was good for *f.*
Gen. 6:21 take unto thee of all *f.*
41:35 gather *f.* of th. good years
42:7 came to buy *f.* 43:2 ; 44:25
33 take *f.* for famine
44:1 commanded fill sacks wi. *f.*
47:24 for *f.* for your little ones
Ex. 21:10 her *f.* not diminished
Lev. 3:11 the *f.* of the offering, 16
19:23 have planted trees for *f.*
22:7 holy things, it is his *f.*
Deut. 10:18 in giving stranger *f.*
1 *Sam.* 14:24 eateth *f.* till even
2 *Sam.* 9:10 master's son have *f.*
1 *K.* 5:9 in giving *f.* for my hous.
Job 23:12 words more than *f.*
24:5 wilderness yieldeth *f.*
38:41 provideth for raven *f.* ?
40:20 mount. bring him forth *f.*
Ps. 78:25 man did eat angels' *f.*
104:14 forth *f.* out of the earth
136:25 who giveth *f.* to all flesh
146:7 who giveth *f.* to hungry
147:9 giveth to the beast his *f.*
Prov. 6:8 ant gathereth *f.* in har.
13:23 much *f.* in tillage of poor
27:27 goats' milk eno. for thy *f.*
28:3 rain which leaveth no *f.*
30:8 feed me with *f.* convenient
31:14 bringeth her *f.* from afar
Ezek. 16:27 I dimin. ordinary *f.*
48:18 increase thereof be for *f.*
Acts 14:17 fill. our hearts with *f.*
2 *Cor.* 9:10 minister bread for *f.*
1 *Tim.* 6:8 hav. *f.* and raiment
Jam. 2:15 be destitute of daily *f.*

FOOL.
1 *Sam.* 26:21 have played the *f.*
Ps. 14:1 *f.* said in heart, 53:1
49:10 *f.* and brutish person
92:6 neither doth *f.* understand
Prov. 10:8 prating *f.* sh. fall, 10
23 sport to a *f.* to do mischief
11:29 *f.* be servant to the wise
12:15 way of *f.* right in own eyes
16 *f.* wrath is presently known
13:16 a *f.* layeth open his folly
14:16 *f.* rageth and is confident
15:5 *f.* despiseth father's instr.
17:7 excel. speech becom. not *f.*
10 than 100 stripes into a *f.*
12 a bear meet rather than *f.*
16 a price in hand of *f.*
21 he that begetteth a *f.*
28 *f.* when he hold. his peace
18:2 a *f.* no delight in underst.
6 *f.* lips enter into contention
7 *f.* mouth is his destruction
20:3 every *f.* will be meddling
26:4 answer not *f.* ; 5 answer *f.*
8 so is he giveth honor to a *f.*
26:10 God rewardeth *f.*
11 so a *f.* returneth to his folly
27:3 *f.* wrath heavier than both
22 tho' bray a *f.* in a mortar
29:11 a *f.* uttereth all his mind
Ec. 2:14 *f.* walketh in darkness
15 happeneth to *f.* even to me
16 np rem. of wise more than *f.*
19 whether he be wise or a *f.* ?
4:5 *f.* foldeth his hands together
5:3 *f.* voice known by multitude
6:8 what ha. wise more than *f.* ?
10:2 a *f.* heart is as his left hand
14 a *f.* also is full of words

Jer. 17:11 and at his end be a *f.*
Mat. 5:22 wh. shall say, Thou *f.*
Luke 12:20 *f.* this night thy soul
1 *Cor.* 3:18 *f.* that he may be wise
15:36 thou *f.* that thou sowest
2 *Cor.* 11:16 no man think me a *f.*
12:6 to glory, I shall not be a *f.*
11 am become a *f.* in glorying

As a FOOL.
2 *Sam.* 3:33 died Abner *as a f.?*
Prov. 7:22 *as a f.* to correction
Ec. 2:16 dieth wise man ? *as f.*
2 *Cor.* 11:16 *as a f.* receive me
23 ministers? I speak *as a f.*

For a FOOL.
Prov. 19:10 not seemly *for a f.*
24:7 wisdom is too high *for a f.*
26:1 honor not seemly *for a f.*
3 and a rod *for the f.* back
30:22 *for a f.* when he is filled

Is a FOOL.
Prov. 10:18 utter. slander *is a f.*
19:1 perverse in lips, and *is a f.*
28:26 trust. in own heart *is a f.*
Ec. 10:3 that *is a f.* walketh, he
saith to ev. one that he *is a f.*
Hos. 9:7 the prophet *is a f.*

Of a FOOL.
Prov. 12:15 way of *a f.* is right
17:21 father of *a f.* hath no joy
24 eyes of *a f.* are in ends of
23:9 speak not in the ears of *a f.*
Prov. 26:6 a me. by hand of *a f.* 29:20
12 more hope of *a f.* 29:20
Ec. 7:6 so is laughter of *a f.*
10:12 lips of *a f.* will swallow

FOOLS.
2 *Sam.* 13:13 be as one of the *f.*
Job 12:17 maketh the judges *f.*
30:8 they were children of *f.*
Ps. 75:4 to *f.* deal not foolishly
94:8 *f.* when will ye be wise ?
107:17 *f.* bec. of transgression
Prov. 1:7 *f.* despise wisdom
22 how long, ye *f.* will ye hate
32 prosperity of *f.* destr. them
3:35 shame sh. be promot. of *f.*
8:5 *f.* be ye of underst. heart
10:21 *f.* die for want of wisdom
12:23 heart of *f.* proclaim. fool.
13:19 to *f.* to depart from evil
20 companion of *f.* be destr.
14:8 folly of *f.* is deceit
9 *f.* make a mock at sin
24 the foolishness of *f.* is folly
33 midst of *f.* is made known
15:2 mouth of *f.* poureth foolis.
14 mouth of *f.* feedeth on fool.
16:22 instruction of *f.* is folly
19:29 stripes prep. for back of *f.*
26:7 parable in mouth of *f.* 9
Ec. 5:1 than give sacrifice of *f.*
4 he hath no pleasure in *f.*
7:4 heart of *f.* in house of mirth
5 than to hear the song of *f.*
9 anger resteth in bosom of *f.*
9:17 cry of him ruleth among *f.*
Is. 19:11 princes of Zoan *f.* 13
35:8 *f.* shall not err therein
*Mat.*23:17 *f.* and bl. 19; *Luke* 11:40
Luke 24:25 O *f.* slow to believe
Rom. 1:22 to be wise, became *f.*
1 *Cor.* 4:10 are *f.* for Christ's sake
2 *Cor.* 11:19 for ye suffer *f.* gladly
Eph. 5:15 see ye walk not as *f.*

FOOLISH.
Deut. 32:6 requite L. *f.* people?
21 provoke them to anger with
a *f.* nation, *Rom.* 10:19
Job 2:10 as one of *f.* women
5:2 for wrath killeth the *f.* man
3 I have seen the *f.* taking root
Ps. 5:5 *f.* not stand in thy sight
39:8 make me not reproach of *f.*
73:3 for I was envious at the *f.*

22 so *f.* was I and ignorant
74:18 *f.* people have blasphemed
22 *f.* reproacheth thee daily
Prov. 9:6 forsake the *f.* and live
13 a *f.* woman is clamorous
10:1 *f.* son heaviness of mother
14 mouth of *f.* near destruct.
14:1 the *f.* plucketh house down
3 mouth of *f.* is a rod of pride
7 go from presence of a *f.* man
15:7 heart of the *f.* doeth not so
20 *f.* man despiseth his mother
17:25 *f.* son is grief to his father
19:13 *f.* son calamity of father
21:20 a *f.* man spendeth a treas.
29:9 if wise contendeth with *f.*
Ec. 4:13 wise child than *f.* king
7:17 be not wicked, neither *f.*
10:15 labor of the *f.* wearieth
Is. 44:25 maketh knowledge *f.*
Jer. 4:22 for my people is *f.*
5:4 these are poor, they are *f.*
21 hear now this, O *f.* people
10:8 they are brutish and *f.*
Lam. 2:14 proph. seen *f.* things
Ezek. 13:3 woe to the *f.* prophets
Zec. 11:15 instru. of *f.* shepherds
Mat. 7:26 be likened to a *f.* man
25:2 five were wise and five *f.*
Rom. 1:21 *f.* heart was darkened
2:20 an instructor of the *f.*
1 *Cor.* 1:20 *f.* wis. of this world
Gal. 3:1 O *f.* Galatians
3 are ye so *f.* ? having begun
Eph. 5:4 filthiness, nor *f.* talking
1 *Tim.* 6:9 rich, fall into *f.* lusts
2 *Tim.* 2:23 *f.* questions, *Tit.* 3:9
Tit. 3:3 we were sometimes *f.*
1 *Pet.* 2:15 silence ignorance of *f.*

FOOLISHLY.
Gen. 31:28 thou hast now done
f. 1 *Sam.* 13:13 ; 2 *Chr.* 16:9
Num. 12:11 sin wherein done *f.*
2 *Sam.* 24:10 I have done very *f.*
Job 1:22 nor charged God *f.*
Ps. 75:4 to the fools, deal not *f.*
Prov. 14:17 soon angry dealeth *f.*
30:32 if *f.* in lifting up thyself
2 *Cor.* 11:17 I speak as it were *f.*
21 I speak *f.* I am bold also

FOOLISHNESS.
2 *Sam.* 15:31 counsel of A. into *f.*
Ps. 38:5 stink, because of my *f.*
Ps. 69:5 O G. thou knowest my *f.*
Prov. 12:23 heart of fools pro. *f.*
14:24 but the *f.* of fools is folly
15:2 mouth of fools pour. out *f.*
14 mouth of fools feedeth on *f.*
19:3 *f.* of man pervert. his way
22:15 *f.* bound in heart of child
24:9 the thought of *f.* is sin
27:22 yet will not his *f.* depart
Ec. 7:25 know wickedness of *f.*
10:13 beginning of words is *f.*
Mark 7:22 *f.* come from within
1 *Cor.* 1:18 to them that perish *f.*
21 by *f.* of preaching to save
23 preach Christ to Greeks *f.*
25 *f.* of God is wiser than men
2:14 things of Spirit *f.* unto him
3:19 wisdom of this world is *f.*

FOOT.
Gen. 41:44 without thee no man
shall lift up his *f.*
Ex. 21:24 *f.* for *f. Deut.* 19:21
Num. 22:25 crushed Balaam's *f.*
Deut. 8:4 nor did thy *f.* swell
11:10 wateredst it with thy *f.*
29:5 shoe is not waxen old on *f.*
32:35 *f.* shall slide in due time
33:24 let Asher dip his *f.* in oil
Jos. 1:3 every place *f.* sh. tread
5:15 loose shoe from off thy *f.*
Jud. 5:15 Barak was sent on *f.*
2 *Sam.* 2:18 Asa. was as light of *f.*
21:20 on *f.* six toes, 1 *Chr.* 20:6

2 K. 9:33 trod Jezebel under *f.*
2 Chr. 33:8 nor remove *f.* of Isr.
Job 23:11 *f.* hath held his steps
28:4 even waters forgotten of *f.*
31:5 if my *f.* hasted to deceit
39:15 forgetteth *f.* may crush
Ps. 9:15 they hid *f.* taken
26:12 *f.* standeth in even place
36:11 let not the *f.* of pride
38:16 *f.* slippeth, they magnify
66:6 went thro' the flood on *f.*
68:23 *f.* may be dipped in blood
91:12 lest thou dash *f.* against a
   stone, Mat. 4:6; Luke 4:11
94:18 I said, My *f.* slippeth
121:3 not suffer *f.* to be moved
Prov. 1:15 thy *f.* from their path
3:23 thy *f.* shall not stumble
26 keep thy *f.* fr. being taken
4:27 remove thy *f.* from evil
25:17 *f.* from neighbor's house
19 like a *f.* out of joint
Ec. 5:1 keep thy *f.* when goest
Is. 14:25 on mount. tread under *f.*
18:7 a nation trodden under *f.*
20:2 put off shoe from off thy *f.*
26:6 the *f.* shall tread it down
41:2 called righteous to his *f.*
58:13 turn *f.* from my sabbath
Jer. 2:25 thy *f.* fr. being unshod
12:10 my portion under *f.*
Lam. 1:15 Lord trodden under *f.*
Ezek. 6:11 stamp with thy *f.*
29:11 no *f.* of man, of beast
32:13 *f.* of man trouble them
Dan. 8:13 to be trodden under *f.*
Amos 2:15 swift of *f.* not deliver
Mat. 5:13 salt trodden under *f.*
14:13 people followed him on *f.*
18:8 if thy *f.* offend, Mark 9:45
22:13 bind him hand and *f.* and
   Mark 6:33 many ran a *f.* thither
John 11:44 bound hand and *f.*
Acts 7:5 so much as to set his *f.*
20:13 minding himself to go a *f.*
1 Cor. 12:15 if the *f.* say, Bec. I
Heb. 10:29 trodden under *f.* the S.
Rev. 1:13 clothed with garm. to *f.*
11:2 city shall tread under *f.*

Sole of FOOT.
Gen. 8:9 no rest for sole of *f.*
Deut. 28:56 not set *s.* of *f.* on gr.
65 nor shall sole of thy *f.* rest
Jos. 1:3 ev. place *s.* of *f.* tread on
2 Sam. 14:25 like Abs. fr. *s.* of *f.*
Is. 1:6 *s.* of *f.* to head
Ezek. 1:7 sole of *f.* like calf's

FOOT-BREADTH.
Deut. 2:5 not so much as *f.-br.*

Right FOOT, left FOOT.
Rev. 10:2 he set his *r. f.* upon the
   sea, and his *l. f.* on the earth
See TOE.

FOOTED.
Lev. 11:3 cloven *f.* that ye sh. eat
   7 though cloven *f.* unclean
21:19 broken *f.* not approach
Acts 10:12 of four *f.* beasts, 11:6
Rom. 1:23 like four *f.* beasts

FOOTMEN.
1 Sam. 22:17 to the *f.* Slay priests
Jer. 12:5 if thou hast run with *f.*

FOOTSTEPS.
Ps. 17:5 that my *f.* slip not
77:19 thy *f.* are not known
89:51 reproa. *f.* of anointed
Cant. 1:8 go by *f.* of the flock

FOOTSTOOL.
1 Chr. 28:2 house for *f.* of God
Ps. 99:5 worship at his *f.* 132:7
110:1 enem. thy *f.* Mat. 22:44 ;
   Mark 12:36 ; Luke 20:43 ; Acts
   2:35 ; Heb. 1:13
Is. 66:1 earth is my *f.* Acts 7:49
Lam. 2:1 remembered not his *f.*

Mat. 5:35 by the earth it is his *f.*
Heb. 10:13 till enemies be *f.*
Jam. 2:3 sit here under my *f.*

FORBADE.
Deut. 2:37 nor to whatso. L. *f.*
Mat. 3:14 John *f.* him, saying, I
Mark 9:38 we *f.* him, Luke 9:49
2 Pet. 2:16 ass *f.* madn. of proph.

FORBARE.
1 Sam. 23:13 Saul *f.* to go forth
Jer. 41:8 Ishmael *f.* and slew not

FORBEARANCE.
Rom. 2:4 or despis. riches of *f.* ?
3:25 remission of sins thro' *f.*

FORBEAR, ING.
Deut. 23:22 *f.* to vow it
1 K. 22:6 go or *f.* ? 2 Chr. 18:5
2 Chr. 25:16 *f.* why be smitten ?
35:21 *f.* thee from meddling
Neh. 9:30 many years didst *f.*
Job 16:6 I *f.* what am I eased ?
Prov. 24:11 if *f.* to deliver them
25:15 by long *f.* prince persuad.
Jer. 20:9 I was weary with *f.*
40:4 if it seem ill unto thee *f.*
Ezek. 2:5 will hear, or *f.* 7 ; 3:11
3:27 that forbeareth, let him *f.*
24:17 *f.* to cry, make no mourn.
Zec. 11:12 give price, if not *f.*
1 Cor. 9:6 power to *f.* working ?
2 Cor. 12:6 I *f.* lest any think
Eph. 4:2 *f.* in love, Col. 3:13
6:9 masters *f.* threatening
1 Thes. 3:1 could no longer *f.* 5

FORBID.
Num. 11:28 my lord M. *f.* them
Mark 9:39 *f.* him not, Luke 9:50
10:14 suffer little child. and *f.*
   them not, Luke 18:16
Luke 6:29 *f.* not to take coat also
Acts 10:47 can any man *f.* water
24:23 *f.* none of his acquaint.
1 Cor. 14:39 *f.* not sp. with tong.

God FORBID.
Gen. 44:7 God *f.* 17 ; Jos. 22:29 ;
   24:16 ; 1 Sam. 12:23 ; 14:45 ;
   20:2 ; Job 27:5 ; Luke 20:16 ;
   Rom. 3:4, 6, 31 ; 6:2, 15 ; 7:7,
   13 ; 9:14 ; 11:1, 11 ; 1 Cor. 6:15 ;
   Gal. 2:17 ; 3:21 ; 6:14

FORBIDDEN, ETH, ING.
Lev. 5:17 commit any of things *f.*
Deut. 4:23 the likeness of what *f.*
Luke 23:2 *f.* to give tribute to C.
Acts 16:6 were *f.* to preach in A.
28:31 preaching no man *f.* him
1 Thes. 2:16 *f.* us to speak to G.
1 Tim. 4:3 *f.* to marry and com.
3 John 10 *f.* them that would re.

FORBORNE.
Jer. 51:30 mighty men *f.* to fight

FORCE, Substantive.
Deut. 34:7 his natural *f.* abated
1 Sam. 2:16 I will take it by *f.*
Ezr. 4:23 made them cease by *f.*
Job 30:18 great *f.* of my disease
40:16 his *f.* in navel of his belly
Jer. 18:21 out blood by *f.* of swo.
23:10 is evil, their *f.* is not right
48:45 shadow because of *f.*
Ezek. 34:4 with *f.* ye ruled them
35:5 shed blood by *f.* of the sw.
Amos 2:14 stro. not strengthen *f.*
Mat. 11:12 violent take it by *f.*
John 6:15 would take him by *f.*
Acts 23:10 to take Paul by *f.*
Heb. 9:17 testament is of *f.* after

FORCE, ED.
Deut. 22:25 if the man *f.* her
Jud. 20:5 concubine have they *f.*
1 Sam. 13:12 I *f.* myself
2 Sam. 13:12 brother do not *f.*
   14 Amnon *f.* Tamar, 22, 32
Est. 7:8 will he *f.* the queen ?
Prov. 7:21 with flat. she *f.* him

FORCES.
Job 36:19 will not esteem the *f.*
Is. 60:5 *f.* of Gentiles shall come
   11 may bring *f.* of the Gentiles
Jer. 40:7 captains of *f.* 13 ; 41:11,
   13, 16 ; 42:1, 8 ; 43:4, 5
Dan. 11:10 assemble multi. of *f.*
   38 shall he honor the God of *f.*
Ob. 11 strangers carried away *f.*

FORCIBLE.
Job 6:25 how *f.* are right words

FORCING.
Deut. 20:19 *f.* an axe aga. them
Prov. 30:33 *f.* of wrath bringeth

FORDS.
Is. 16:2 daughters at *f.* of Arnon

FORECAST.
Dan. 11:24 sh. *f.* his devices, 25

FOREFATHERS.
Jer. 11:10 turn. to iniquities of *f.*
2 Tim. 1:3 whom I served from *f.*

FOREFRONT.
1 Sam. 17:49 stone sunk in his *f.*
2 Chr. 26:20 Uzziah leprous in *f.*
Jer. 3:3 thou hast a whore's *f.*
Ezek. 3:9 as adamant I made *f.*
16:12 and I put jewel on thy *f.*
Rev. 14:9 mark of beast in his *f.*
17:5 on her *f.* a name written

FOREHEADS.
Ezek. 3:8 strong against their *f.*
9:4 on the *f.* of them that sigh
Rev. 7:3 sealed serv. of God in *f.*
9:4 not seal of God in their *f.*
13:16 all to receive a mark in *f.*
14:1 Father's name in their *f.*
20:4 nor received his mark on *f.*
22:4 his name sh. be in their *f.*

FOREIGNER, S.
Ex. 12:45 a *f.* not eat thereof
Deut. 15:3 of a *f.* exact it again
Ob. 11 in the day *f.* entered gat.
Eph. 2:19 ye are no more *f.*

FOREKNEW, KNOW.
Rom. 8:29 whom he did *f.*
11:2 not cast away people he *f.*

FOREKNOWLEDGE.
Acts 2:23 delivered by *f.* of God
1 Pet. 1:2 according to *f.* of God

FOREORDAINED.
1 Pet. 1:20 who verily was *f.*

FOREPART.
Acts 27:41 *f.* of ship stuck fast

FORERUNNER.
Heb. 6:20 whither *f.* is for us

FORESAW.
Acts 2:25 *f.* Lord always before

FORESEETH, ING.
Prov. 22:3 man *f.* the evil, 27:12
Gal. 3:8 the scripture *f.* that God

FORESKIN, S.
Gen. 17:11 circumc. flesh of *f.* 23
Ex. 4:25 Zip. cut off *f.* of son
Lev. 12:3 flesh of his *f.* sh. be cir.
Deut. 10:16 circumcise *f.* of heart
Jos. 5:3 circumcised at hill of *f.*
1 Sam. 18:25 100 *f.* of Philistines
   27 D. brought *f.* and gave th.
2 Sam. 3:14 I espoused for 100 *f.*
Jer. 4:4 take away the *f.* of heart
Hab. 2:16 let thy *f.* be uncovered

FOREST, S.
1 Sam. 22:5 D. came to *f.* of H.
1 K. 7:2 Solomon built hou. of *f.*
2 K. 19:23 will enter into *f.* of
   his Carmel, Is. 37:24
2 Chr. 27:4 J. built castles in *f.*

Ps. 29:9 voice of L. discover. *f.*
50:10 ev. beast of the *f.* is mine
104:20 beasts of *f.* do creep forth
Is. 9:18 kindle in thickets of *f.*
10:18 consume glory of his *f.*
19 rest of trees of his *f.* be few
34 cut down the thickets of *f.*
21:13 in *f.* of Ara. shall ye lodge
22:8 didst look to armor of *f.*
29:17 esteemed as a *f.* 32:15
32:19 hail coming down on *f.*
44:14 cypress from am. trees *f.*
23 break forth into sing. O *f.*
56:9 yea, all ye beasts in the *f.*
Jer. 5:6 lion out of *f.* shall slay
10:3 one cutteth a tree out of *f.*
12:8 heritage, as a lion in *f.*
21:14 will kindle a fire in the *f.*
26:18 high places of *f. Mic.* 3:12
46:23 they shall cut down her *f.*
Ezek. 15:6 vine-tree am. trees *f.*
20:46 prophesy aga. *f.* of south
39:10 neither cut any out of *f.*
Hos. 2:12 I will make them a *f.*
Amos 3:4 will lion roar in the *f.*
Mic. 5:8 as a lion am. beasts of *f.*
Zec. 11:2 *f.* of vintage is come

FORETELL.
2 *Cor.* 13:2 I *f.* you as if present

FORETOLD.
Mark 13:23 I have *f.* you all
Acts 3:24 proph. *f.* of these days

FOREWARN, ED.
Luke 12:5 *f.* whom ye shall fear
1 *Thes.* 4:6 we also have *f.* you

FORFEITED.
Ezr. 10:8 substance should be *f.*

FORGAT.
Gen. 40:23 Joseph, but *f.* him
Jud. 3:7 children of Israel *f.* L.
1 *Sam.* 12:9 when they *f.* the L.
Ps. 78:11 and they *f.* his works
106:13 soon *f.* ; 21 *f.* God th. S.
Lam. 3:17 peace, I *f.* prosperity
Hos. 2:13 after lovers and *f.* me

FORGAVE, EST.
Ps. 32:5 *f.* iniquity of my sin
78:38 he *f.* their iniquity, and
99:8 wast a God that *f.* them
Mat. 18: 27 and *f.* him the debt
32 O wicked servant, I *f.* all
Luke 7:42 he frankly *f.* them
42 that he to whom he *f.* most
2 *Cor.* 2:10 if I *f.* any thing, for
your sakes *f.* I it
Col. 3:13 as Christ *f.* you

FORGED.
Ps. 119:69 proud have *f.* a lie

FORGERS.
Job 13:4 ye are *f.* of lies

FORGET.
Gen. 27:45 till thy brother *f.*
41:51 God made me *f.* my toil
Deut. 4:9 *f.* things eyes ha. seen
23 lest ye *f.* covenant of Lord
31 Lord will not *f.* the coven.
6:12 beware lest *f.* L. 8:11, 14, 19
9:7 *f.* not how provokedest Lord
25:19 blot out Amalek, not *f.*
1 *Sam.* 1:11 if not *f.* handmaid
2 *K.* 17:38 covenant shall not *f.*
Job 8:13 so paths of all that *f.* G.
9:27 I will *f.* my complaint
11:16 thou shalt *f.* thy misery
24:20 the womb shall *f.* him
Ps. 9:17 all nations that *f.* God
10:12 O Lord *f.* not the humble
13:1 how long wilt thou *f.* me?
45:10 *f.* thine own people, and
50:22 consider this ye that *f.* G.
59:11 lest my people *f.*
74:19 *f.* not congrega. of poor
23 *f.* not voice of thine enem.
78:7 might not *f.* works of God

102:4 that I *f.* to eat my bread
103:2 *f.* not all his benefits
119:16 I will not *f.* thy word
83 do I not *f.* statutes, 109, 141
93 I will never *f.* thy precepts
153 for I do not *f.* thy law
176 for I not *f.* thy command.
137:5 if I *f.* thee, O Jerusalem,
let right hand *f.* cunning
Prov. 3:1 my son *f.* not my law
4:5 get wisdom, *f.* it not
31:5 lest they drink and *f.* law
7 drink and *f.* his poverty
Is. 49:15 can a woman *f.* child?
54:4 shalt *f.* shame of thy youth
65:11 that *f.* my holy mountain
Jer. 2:32 maid *f.* her ornaments?
23:27 my people to *f.* my name
39 even I, will utterly *f.* you
Lam. 5:20 dost *f.* us for ever?
Hos. 4:6 also *f.* thy children
Amos 8:7 never *f.* any of works
Heb. 6:10 G. not unrighte. to *f.*
13:16 to communicate *f.* not

FORGETFUL, NESS.
Ps. 88:12 known in land of *f.* ?
Heb. 13:2 not *f.* to entertain str.
Jam. 1:25 a *f.* hearer, but a doer

FORGETTEST, ETH, ING.
Job 39:15 *f.* foot may crush them
Ps. 9:12 *f.* not cry of humble
44:24 why *f.* thou our affliction?
Prov. 2:17 *f.* covenant of her God
Is. 51:13 and *f.* Lord thy Maker
Phil. 3:13 *f.* those things behind
Jam. 1:24 he *f.* what manner of

FORGIVE.
Gen. 50:17 *f.* trespass of brethren
Ex. 10:17 *f.* my sin this once
32:32 yet now if wilt *f.* their sin
Num. 30:5 Lord shall *f.* her, 8, 12
Jos. 24:19 will not *f.* your sins
1 *Sam.* 25:28 pray *f.* the trespass
1 *K.* 8:30 hear. *f.* 39 ; 2 *Chr.* 6:21
34 hear and *f.* the sin of Israel
36 *f.* sin or servant. 2 *Chr.* 6:25
50 *f.* thy peo. that have sinned
2 *Chr.* 7:14 then will I hear and *f.*
Ps. 25:18 and *f.* all my sins
86:5 L. art good and ready to *f.*
Is. 2:9 therefore *f.* them not
Jer. 18:23 *f.* not their iniquity
31:34 for I will *f.* their iniquity
36:3 I may *f.* their iniquity and
Dan. 9:19 O Lord, hear, O L. *f.*
Amos 7:2 I said, *f.* I beseech th.
Mat. 6:12 *f.* us as we *f. Luke* 11:4
14 if ye *f.* men their trespasses
15 ye *f.* not, neither will your
9:6 hath power on earth to *f.*
sins, *Mark* 2:10 ; *Luke* 5:24
18:21 how oft sin, and I *f.* him?
35 if ye.from your hearts *f.* not
Mark 2:7 can *f.* sins, *Luke* 5:21
11:25 praying, *f.* that your
26 if not *f.* your F. will not *f.*
Luke 6:37 *f.* ye shall be forgiven
17:3 brother repent, *f.* him, 4
23:34 Father *f.* them
2 *Cor.* 2:7 ye ought rather to *f.*
10 to whom ye *f.* any, I *f.* also
12:13 to you, *f.* me this wrong
1 *John* 1:9 to *f.* us our sins

FORGIVEN.
Lev. 4:20 it sh. be *f.* 26, 31, 35 ;
5:10, 13, 16, 18 ; 6:7 ; 19:22 ;
Num. 15:25, 26, 28; *Deut.* 21:8
Num. 14:19 pardon, as *f.* from E.
Ps. 32:1 wh. trans. is *f. Rom.* 4:7
85:2 hast *f.* iniquity of thy peo.
Is. 33:24 people be *f.* their iniq.
Mat. 9:2 sins *f.* thee, 5 ; *Mark*
2:5, 9 ; *Luke* 5:20, 23 ; 7:48
12:31 all sin be *f.* but ag. Holy
G. 32 ; *Mark* 3:28 ; *Luke* 12:10
Mark 4:12 sin should be *f.* them

Luke 6:37 forgive and ye sh. be *f.*
7:47 her sins which are many
are *f.* to whom little is *f.*
Acts 8:22 thought of heart be *f.*
Eph. 4:32 for Christ's sake *f.* you
Col. 2:13 having *f.* all trespasses
Jam. 5:15 com. sins they sh. be *f.*
1 *John* 2:12 bec. your sins are *f.*

FORGIVETH, ING.
Ex. 34:7 *f.* iniq. *Num.* 14:18
Ps. 103:3 *f.* all thine iniquities
Luke 7:49 who is this *f.* sins?
Eph. 4:32 *f.* one ano. *Col.* 3:13

FORGIVENESS, ES.
Ps. 130:4 there is *f.* with thee
Dan. 9:9 the L. our G. belong *f.*
Mark 3:29 nev. *f.* but in danger
Acts 5:31 him G. exalt. to give *f.*
13:38 through him is preached *f.*
26:18 they may receive *f.* of sins
Eph. 1:7 have *f.* of sins, *Col.* 1:14

FORGOTTEN.
Gen. 41:30 the plenty shall be *f.*
Deut. 24:19 and hast *f.* a sheaf
26:13 neither have I *f.* them
31:21 this song shall not be *f.*
32:18 *f.* God that formed thee
Job 19:14 familiar friends *f.* me
28:4 even waters *f.* of the foot
Ps. 9:18 needy not always be *f.*
10:11 said in heart, God hath *f.*
31:12 I am *f.* as dead man
42:9 My rock, why hast *f.* me?
44:17 yet have we not *f.* thee
20 if we have *f.* name of our G.
77:9 hath G. *f.* to be gracious?
119:61 but I have not *f.* thy law
139 mine enemies *f.* thy words
Ec. 2:16 days to come all be *f.*
8:10 wicked were *f.* in the city
9:5 the memory of them is *f.*
Is. 17:10 *f.* God of thy salvation
23:15 Tyre shall be *f.* 70 years
16 take a harp, thou harlot *f.*
44:21 O Isr. thou shalt not be *f.*
49:14 Zion said, Lord hath *f.* me
65:16 the former troubles are *f.*
Jer. 2:32 peo. *f.* me, 13:25 ; 18:15
3:21 have *f.* the Lord their God
20:11 never be *f.* 23:40
23:27 forget as fathers have *f.*
30:14 all thy lovers have *f.* thee
44:9 *f.* wickedness of your fath.
50:5 join in cov. shall not be *f.*
6 have *f.* their resting-place
Lam. 2:6 sabbaths to be *f.* in Z.
Ezek. 22:12 hast *f.* me, saith L.
23:35 because thou hast *f.* me
Hos. 4:6 seeing thou hast *f.* law
8:14 Israel hath *f.* his Maker
13:6 therefore have they *f.* me
Mat. 16:5 *f.* bread, *Mark* 8:14
Luke 12:6 not one of them is *f.*
Heb. 12:5 ye have *f.* exhortation
2 *Pet.* 1:9 *f.* that he was purged

FORKS.
1 *Sam.* 13:21 they had a file for *f.*

FORM, Substantive.
Gen. 1:2 the earth was without *f.*
1 *Sam.* 28:14 what *f.* is he of?
2 *Sam.* 14:20 this *f.* of speech
Job 4:16 could not discern the *f.*
Is. 52:14 his *f.* more than sons
53:2 hath no *f.* nor comeliness
Jer. 4:23 lo, it was without *f.*
Ezek. 10:8 appeared *f.* of a hand
43:11 show them *f.* of the house
Dan. 3:19 *f.* of visage changed
25 *f.* of fourth like Son of God
Mark 16:12 he app. in another *f.*
Rom. 2:20 hast *f.* of knowledge
6:17 obeyed that *f.* of doctrine
Phil. 2:6 who being in *f.* of God
7 took upon him *f.* of a servant
2 *Tim.* 1:13 *f.* of sound words
3:5 having a *f.* of godliness

FORM, Verb.
Is. 45:7 I *f.* the light

FORMED.
Gen. 2:7 God *f.* man of the dust
19 out of ground G. *f.* ev. beast
Deut. 32:18 forgot. G, that *f.* thee
2 *K.* 19:25 that I *f.* it ? *Is.* 37:26
Job 26:5 things *f.* under water
13 his hand *f.* crooked serpent
33:6 am *f.* out of the clay
Ps. 90:2 or ever hadst *f.* earth
94:9 *f.* the eye, sh. he not see ?
95:5 his hands *f.* the dry land
Prov. 26:10 great God that *f.* all
Is. 27:11 *f.* them show no favor
43:1 he that *f.* thee, O Israel
7 I have *f.* him, yea, made him
10 before me was no god *f.*
21 this peo. have I *f.* for mys.
44:2 and *f.* thee from the womb
10 who hath *f.* a god or image
21 my servant, I have *f.* thee
24 thus saith he that *f.* thee
45:18 G. hath *f.* earth, he *f.* it
49:5 *f.* me to be his servant
54:17 no weapon *f.* against thee
Jer. 1:5 before I *f.* thee in belly
33:2 the L. that *f.* it to establish
Amos 7:1 he *f.* grasshoppers
Rom. 9:20 th. *f.* say to him *f.* it
Gal. 4:19 till Christ be *f.* in you
1 *Tim.* 2:13 Adam first *f.* then E.

FORMER.
1 *Sam.* 17:30 answer. after *f.* ma.
2 *K.* 17:34 do after *f.* manner, 40
Job 8:8 inquire, I pray, of *f.* age
30:3 wilderness in *f.* time waste
Ps. 79:8 O rem. not *f.* iniquities
89:49 *f.* loving-kindnesses ?
Ec. 1:11 no rem. of *f.* things
7:10 that *f.* days were better
Is. 41:22 show *f.* things, 43:9
42:9 *f.* things are come to pass
43:18 remember ye not *f.* things
46:9 remember *f.* things of old
48:3 I have declared *f.* things
61:4 shall raise up *f.* desolations
65:7 measure *f.* work into bos.
16 because *f.* troubles are forg.
17 the *f.* shall not be rememb.
Jer. 5:24 giveth *f.* and latter rain
Hos. 6:3 ; *Joel* 2:23
10:16 is *f.* of all things, 51:19
34:5 the *f.* kings before thee
36:28 write in it all *f.* words
Ezek. 16:55 return to *f.* estate
Dan. 11:29 shall not be as the *f.*
Hag. 2:9 great. than of *f.* house
Zec. 1:4 the *f.* prophets, 7:7, 12
8:11 I will not be as in *f.* days
14:8 waters, half toward *f.* sea
Mal. 3:4 pleasant as in *f.* years
Acts 1:1 *f.* treatise have I made
Eph. 4:22 concern. *f.* conversa.
1 *Pet.* 1:14 according to *f.* lusts
Rev. 21:4 *f.* things passed away

FORMETH.
Amos 4:13 that *f.* the mountains
Zec. 12:1 and *f.* spirit of man

FORNICATION.
Ezek. 16:29 multi. *f.* in Canaan
Mat. 5:32 saving for *f.* 19:9
John 8:41 we be not born of *f.*
Acts 15:20 abstain fr. *f.* 29 ; 21:25
Rom. 1:29 being filled with all *f.*
1 *Cor.* 5:1 *f.* among you, such *f.*
6:13 the body is not for *f.* but
18 flee *f.* ; 7:2 to avoid *f.*
2 *Cor.* 12:21 not repented of *f.*
Gal. 5:19 works of the flesh *f.*
Eph. 5:3 *f.* let it not be named
Col. 3:5 mortify therefore *f.*
1 *Thes.* 4:3 should abstain fr *f.*
Jude 7 giving themsel. over to *f.*
Rev. 2:21 to repent of her *f.*
9:21 nor repent of their *f.*
14:8 wine of wrath of *f.* 18:3

Rev. 17:2 dr. with wine of her *f.*
4 cup full of filthiness of her *f.*
19:2 corrupt earth with her *f.*

FORNICATIONS.
Ezek. 16:15 poured out thy *f.*
Mat. 15:19 proceed *f.* *Mark* 7:21
See COMMIT, COMMITTED.

FORNICATOR, S.
1 *Cor.* 5:9 not to comp. with *f.*
10 altogether with *f.* of world
11 called a brother be a *f.*
6:9 nor shall *f.* inherit kingdom
Heb. 12:16 lest there be any *f.* or

FORSAKE.
Deut. 31:16 this people will *f.* me
17 in that day I will *f.* them
Jos. 24:16 G. forbid we sh. *f.* L.
20 if ye *f.* the Lord, and serve
Jud. 9:11 sho. I *f.* my sweetness
2 *K.* 21:14 I will *f.* remnant
1 *Chr.* 28:9 if thou *f.* him, he wi.
2 *Chr.* 7:19 if ye *f.* my statutes
15:2 if ye *f.* him he will *f.* you
Ezr. 8:22 wrath ag. them *f.* him
Ps. 27:10 father and mother *f.*
37:8 cease from anger, *f.* wrath
89:30 if his children *f.* my law
94:14 will he *f.* his inheritance
119:53 bec. wicked *f.* thy law
Prov. 3:3 not mercy and truth *f.*
9:6 *f.* the foolish, and live
28:4 that *f.* law, praise wicked
Is. 1:28 that *f.* L. be consumed
55:7 let the wicked *f.* his way
65:11 ye are they that *f.* the L.
Jer. 17:13 *f.* L. shall be ashamed
23:33 I will even *f.* you, 39
51:9 *f.* Babylon, and let us go
Lam. 5:20 why dost *f.* us so long
Dan. 11:30 that *f.* holy covenant
Jon. 2:8 *f.* their own mercy
Acts 21:21 teachest to *f.* Moses

FORSAKE not.
Deut. 12:19 take heed *f. n.* Levite
Job 20:13 spare it and *f.* it *not*
Ps. 38:21 *f.* me *not*, 71:9, 18
119:8 O *f.* me *not* utterly
138:8 *f. not* works of thy hands
Prov. 1:8 *f. n.* law of moth. 6:20
4:2 doctrine, *f.* ye *not* my law
6 *f.* her *n.* she sh. preserve thee
27:10 and father's *f.* friend *f. not*

Not FORSAKE.
Deut. 4:31 he will *not f.* thee,
31:6, 8 ; 1 *Chr.* 28:20
14:27 thou shalt *not f.* Levite
Jos. 1:5 nor *f.* thee, *Heb.* 13:5
1 *Sam.* 12:22 *not f.* his people,
1 *K.* 6:13
1 *K.* 8:57 let him *not f.* us
Neh. 9:31 thou didst *not f.* them
10:39 *not f.* the ho. of our God
Ps. 27:9 neither *f.* me, O God
Is. 41:17 I will *not f.* them
42:16 will I do, and *not f.* them
Ezek. 20:8 nor did *f.* idols of Eg.

FORSAKEN.
2 *Chr.* 21:10 had *f.* L. 24:24 ; 28:6
Neh. 13:11 why is house of G. *f.* ?
Job 18:4 sh. earth be *f.* for thee ?
Ps. 37:25 not seen righteous *f.*
Is. 7:16 land be *f.* of both kings
17:2 the cities of Aroer are *f.*
9 shall be as a *f.* bough
27:10 the habitation sh. be *f.*
32:14 because palaces sh. be *f.*
54:6 called thee as a wom. *f.*
62:4 shalt no more be t. med *f.*
Jer. 4:29 every city shall be *f.*
18:14 wat. from ano. pl. be *f.* ?
Ezek. 36:4 saith Lord to cities *f.*
Amos 5:2 virgin of Israel is *f.*
Zep. 2:4 G. be *f.* and Ashkelon

Have, hast, hath FOR-SAKEN.
Deut. 28:20 whereby *f.* me
29:25 bec. *f.* Lord, *Jud.* 10:10
Jud. 10:13 yet ye *have f.* me and
10:13 now Lord *hath f.* us
1 *Sam.* 8:8 works wherewith *f.*
12:10 because we *h. f.* Lord
1 *K.* 11:33 because they *h. f.* me
18:18 ye *h. f.* commandm. of L.
19:10 Israel *h. f.* covenant, 14
2 *K.* 22:17 because they *h. f.* me,
2 *Chr.* 34:25 ; *Jer.* 16:11 ; 19:4
2 *Chr.* 12:5 he *have f.* me, and I
13:11 but ye *have f.* him
24:20 ye *have f.* L. he ha. *f.* you
29:6 our fathers have *f.* him
Ezr. 9:10 *h. f.* thy commandm.
Job 20:19 because he *hath f.* poor
Ps. 22:1 why *hast* thou *f.* me ?
Mat. 27:46 ; *Mark* 15:34
71:11 saying, God *hath f.* him
Is. 1:4 they *have f.* the Lord
49:14 Zion said, Lord *hath f.* me
54:7 for a moment *have* I *f.* thee
Jer. 1:16 who *have f.* me
2:13 *h. f.* me, fountain of waters
17 in that thou *hast f.* Lord, 19
5:7 thy children *have f.* me, 19
9:13 because they *h. f.* my law
19 confound. bec. we *h. f.* land
12:7 I *have f.* my house, I have
15:6 thou *hast f.* me, saith Lord
17:13 *h. f.* fount. of living wat.
22:9 they *h. f.* covenant of God
25:38 *hath f.* his covert
Ezek. 8:12 Lord *hath f.* earth, 9:9
Mat. 19:27 we *have f.* all
29 every one that *h. f.* houses
2 *Tim.* 4:10 Demas *hath f.* me
2 *Pet.* 2:15 which *h. f.* right way

Not FORSAKEN.
2 *Chr.* 13:10 the Lord is our God,
we have *not f.* him
Ezr. 9:9 *f.* us in our bondage
Ps. 9:10 *not f.* them seek thee
Is. 62:12 be called a city *not f.*
Jer. 51:5 Israel hath *not* been *f.*
2 *Cor.* 4:9 persecuted, but *not f.*

FORSAKETH, ING.
Job 6:14 he *f.* fear of Almighty
Ps. 37:28 Lord *f.* not his saints
Prov. 2:17 *f.* guide of her youth
15:10 griev. to him that *f.* way
28:13 whoso confesseth and *f.*
Luke 14:33 whoso *f.* not all hath
Heb. 10:25 not *f.* the assembling

FORSOOK, EST.
Deut. 32:15 *f.* G. that made him
Jud. 2:12 they *f.* Lord, 13 ; 10:6
1 *Sam.* 31:7 *f.* cities, 1 *Chr.* 10:7
1 *K.* 9:9 because *f.* Lord their G.
12:8 Rehoboam *f.* counsel of old
men, 13 ; 2 *Chr.* 10:8, 13
2 *K.* 21:22 Amon *f.* G. of fathers
2 *Chr.* 7:22 they *f.* God of fathers
12:1 Rehoboam *f.* law of Lord
Neh. 9:17 slow to anger, *f.* not
19 *f.* them not in wilderness
Ps. 78:60 *f.* tabernacle of Shiloh
119:87 but I *f.* not thy precepts
Is. 58:2 *f.* not ordinance of God
Jer. 14:5 hind calved, and *f.* it
Mat. 26:56 *f.* him, *Mark* 14:50
Mark 1:18 they *f.* their nets
Luke 5:11 *f.* all, followed him
2 *Tim.* 4:16 all men *f.* me
Heb. 11:27 by faith Moses *f.* E.

FORSWEAR.
Mat. 5:33 thou sh. not *f.* thyself

FORT, S.
2 *Sam.* 5:9 David dwelt in the *f.*
2 *K.* 25:1 build *f.* ag. J. *Jer.* 52:4

FORT

Is. 25:12 *f.* of walls bring down
29:3 I will raise *f.* against thee
32:14 the *f.* be for dens forever
Ezek. 4:2 a *f.* ag. it, 21:22 ; 26:8
17;17 building *f.* cut off many
21:22 divination to build a *f.*
26:8 shall make a *f.* against thee
33:27 they in the *f.* shall die
Dan. 11:19 tow. *f.* of own land

FORTH.

Ps. 113:2 blessed be Lord, from
this time *f.* 115:18 ; 121:8
Jer. 49:5 be driven out right *f.*
Mat. 16:21 that time *f.* began J.
22:46 that day *f.* ask questions
John 11:53 that day *f.*

FORTHWITH.

Mat. 13:5 and *f.* they sprung up
Mark 1:43 and *f.* sent him away
John 19:34 *f.* came out blood and
Acts 12:10 *f.* the angel departed

FORTUNATUS.   1 *Cor.* 16:17

FORTY.

Acts 23:13 more than *f.* consp. 21

FORTY stripes.

Deut. 25:3 *f. str.* he may give
2 *Cor.* 11:24 of the Jews rec. *f. s.*

FORTY years.

Ex. 16:35 man. *f. y.* Neh. 9:21
Num. 14:33 wander *f. y.* 32:13
34 bear your iniquities *f. y.*
Deut. 2:7 thy walking these *f. y.*
8:2 God led thee *f. years*, 29:5
Jos. 5:6 walked *f. y.* in wildern.
14:7 *f. years* old was I when M.
Jud. 3:11 rest *f. y.* 5:31 ; 8:28
13:1 Isr. into the hand of P. *f. y.*
2 *Sam.* 15:7 after *f. y.* Absa. said
Ps. 95:10 *f. y.* long was I grieved
Ezek. 29:11 nor be inhabited *f. y.*
13 end of *f. y.* will gather Eg.
Amos 2:10 I led you *f. y.*

Amos 5:25 sacrifi. *f. y. Acts* 7:42
Acts 4:22 was above *f. y.* old
7:23 M. *f. y.* old visited breth.
36 wonders in wilderness *f. y.*
13:18 *f. y.* suffered he
21 gave Saul by space of *f. y.*
Heb. 3:9 fathers saw works *f. y.*
17 with whom grieved *f. y.*

FORTY-TWO

2 *K.* 2:24 bears tear *f.-t.* children
Rev. 11:2 tread *f.-t.* months
13:5 to continue *f.-t.* months

FORTY-FIVE years.

Jos. 14:10 kept me alive *f.-f. y.*

FORTY-SIX years.

John 2:20 *f.-s. y.* temple build.

FORTY-NINE years.

Lev. 25:8 space be *f.-n. years*

FORTIFY, IED.

Jud. 9:31 *f.* city against thee
Neh. 4:2 Jews *f.* themselves ?
Is. 22:10 broken to *f.* wall
Jer. 51:53 she *f.* her strength
Mic. 7:12 come from *f.* cities
Nah. 2:1 *f.* thy power mightily
3:14 *f.* thy strong-holds

FORTRESS, ES.

2 *Sam.* 22:2 my *f. Ps.* 18:2 ; 31:3;
71:3 :91:2 ; 144:2
Is. 17:3 *f.* sh. cease from Ephra.
25:12 *f.* shall he bring down
34:13 nettles come up in the *f.*
Jer. 6:27 I have set thee for a *f.*
10:17 O inhabitant of the *f.*
16:19 O Lord, my *f.* in affliction
Dan. 11:7 *f.* of king of the north
10 be stirred up even to his *f.*
Hos. 10:14 thy *f.* shall be spoiled
Amos 5:9 spoiled sh. come ag. *f.*
Mic. 7:12 sh. come to thee fr. *f.*

FORWARD, NESS.

Jer. 7:24 and they went not *f.*
Zec. 1:15 helped *f.* the affliction
2 *Cor.* 8:8 occasion of *f.* of others
8:10 to be *f.* a year ago
17 more *f.* of his own accord
9:2 I know the *f.* of your mind
Gal. 2:10 same I also was *f.* to do
3 *John* 6 if bring *f.* on journey

See That DAY, GO, SET, WENT.

FOUGHT.

Jos. 10:14 L. *f.* for Isr. 42 ; 23:3
Jud. 1:5 *f.* against Adoni-bezek
8 Judah had *f.* ag. Jerusalem
5:19 kings *f.* kings of Canaan
20 they *f.* from heaven, stars *f.*
9:17 my father *f.* for you, and
39 Gaal *f.* with Abimelech
12:4 Gilead *f.* with Ephraim
1 *Sam.* 4:10 Philist. *f.* 1 *Chr.* 10:1
14:47 Saul *f.* ag. all his enemies
19:8 David *f.* Philistines, 23:5
2 *Sam.* 2:28 nor *f.* they any more
10:17 Syr. *f.* ag. D. 1 *Chr.* 19:17
2 *Chr.* 20:29 L. *f.* ag. enemies
Ps. 109:3 *f.* ag. me with. cause
Is. 20:1 Tartan *f.* ag. Ashdod
63:10 turned enemy *f.* ag. them
Jer. 34:1 peo. *f.* ag. Jerusalem, 7
Zec. 14:3 *f.* in the day of battle
12 L. smite these *f.* ag. Jerus.
1 *Cor.* 15:32 I have *f.* with beasts
2 *Tim.* 4:7 I have *f.* a good fight
Rev. 12:7 Michael *f.* ag. dragon

FOUL.

Job 16:16 my face is *f.* wi. weep.
Mat. 16:3 it will be *f.* weather
Mark 9:25 rebuked the *f.* spirit
Rev. 18:2 Bab. hold of ev. *f.* spi.

FOUL, ED, EDST.

Ezek. 32:2 and *f.* their rivers
34:18 ye must *f.* the residue
19 they drink what ye have *f.*

FOUND.

Gen. 8:9 the dove *f.* no rest for
26:19 Isaac's servants *f.* a well
27:20 how hast *f.* it so quickly ?
31:33 Laban *f.* not images
37:32 said, This coat have we *f.*
38:23 I sent kid, hast not *f.* her
44:16 G. hath *f.* out the iniquity
Lev. 6:3 have *f.* that was lost
Num. 15:32 *f.* man gather. sticks
Deut. 22:3 with what *f.* do likew.
14 I *f.* her not a maid, 17
27 *f.* her in field, damsel cried
24:1 *f.* some uncleanness in her
32:10 he *f.* him in a desert land
Jos. 2:22 pursuers *f.* them not
Jud. 14:18 had not *f.* out riddle
21:12 *f.* four hundred virgins
1 *Sam.* 9:4 they *f.* not the asses
11 *f.* maidens going to draw
19:5 not *f.* aught in my hand

1 *Sam.* 13:22 no sword *f.* in hand
25:28 evil not been *f.* with thee
29:3 I have *f.* no fault in him
30:11 *f.* an Egyptian in the field
31:8 *f.* S. and three sons fallen
2 *Sam.* 7:27 *f.* in his heart to
pray this prayer, 1 *Chr.* 17:25
1 *K.* 7:47 nor weight of brass *f.*
11:29 Ahijah *f.* Jerobo. in way
13:28 *f.* his carcase cast in way
18:10 took an oath *f.* thee not
20:36 lion *f.* him and slew him
21:20 *f.* me mine enemy ?
2 *K.* 2:17 Elijah, but *f.* him not
9:35 *f.* no more of her than skull
22:8 I *f.* law in house of the L.
25:19 took sixty men *f.* in city
1 *Chr.* 4:40 th. *f.* fat pasture and
2 *Chr.* 19:3 good th. *f.* in thee
Neh. 5:8 *f.* nothing to answer

Job 28:13 nor wisdom *f.* in land
31:29 when evil *f.* mine enemy
32:3 bec. they had *f.* to answer
13 We have *f.* wisdom
33:24 the pit, I have *f.* a ransom
42:15 *f.* so fair as daught. of Job
Ps. 69:20 comforters, but *f.* none
76:5 none have *f.* their hands
84:3 sparrow hath *f.* a house
89:20 I have *f.* Dav. my servant
107:4 and *f.* no city to dwell in
116:3 I *f.* trouble and sorrow
132:6 we *f.* it in the fields
Prov. 7:15 and I have *f.* thee
24:14 so wisdom be when *f.* it
25:16 hast *f.* honey ?
Ec. 7:28 I *f.* a woman not *f.*
29 I *f.* God made man upright
Cant. 3:1 but I *f.* him not, 2
3 the watchman *f.* me, 5:7
4 but I *f.* him my soul loveth
Is. 10:10 *f.* kingdoms of idols
14 my hand *f.* riches of people
22:3 all *f.* in thee are bound
57:10 hast *f.* the life of thy hand
65:1 *f.* of them sought me not
Jer. 2:5 iniquity fath. *f.* in me ?
34 in thy skirts is *f.* the blood
5:26 my people are *f.* wicked
15:16 words *f.* I did eat them
23:11 in my house *f.* wickedn.
41:8 *f.* that said, Slay us not
50:7 all that *f.* them dev. them
Lam. 2:16 this is day we have *f.*
Ezek. 22:30 for a man, I *f.* none
Dan. 5:12 ex. spirit *f.* in Daniel
27 art weighed and *f.* wanting
6:4 nor any fault *f.* in Daniel
11 these men *f.* Daniel praying
Hos. 9:10 I *f.* Israel like grapes
12:4 he *f.* him in Beth-el, and
8 I have *f.* me out substance
14:8 from me is thy fruit *f.*
Mic. 1:13 transg. of Is. *f.* in thee
Mat. 2:8 have *f.* him bring word
8:10 not *f.* so gr. faith, *Luke* 7:9
13:44 when a man *f.* he hideth
46 *f.* one pearl of great price
18:28 *f.* one of his fellow serv.
20:6 *f.* others standing idle
21:19 he *f.* nothing thereon,
Mark 11:13 ; *Luke* 13:6
22:10 gath. as many as they *f.*
26:43 he *f.* them asleep, *Mark*
14:40 ; *Luke* 22:45
60 sou. wit. *f.* none, *Mar.* 14:55
27:32 they *f.* a man of Cyrene
Mark 1:37 when they had *f.* him
7:2 eat with def. hands *f.* fault
30 she *f.* the devil gone out
11:4 *f.* colt tied by door without
Luke 2:16 *f.* babe ly. in a manger
46 after three days *f.* him
4:17 *f.* place where it was writ.
7:10 they *f.* the servant whole
8:35 *f.* the man clothed
15:6 for I have *f.* my sheep
9 when she hath *f.* the piece
17:18 none *f.* that ret. to give gl.
19:32 *f.* even as he said, 22:13
23:2 we *f.* perverting the nation
14 I have *f.* no fault
24:2 *f.* the stone rolled away
3 *f.* not body of the Lord Jesus
23 when they *f.* not his body
33 *f.* the eleven gath. together
John 1:41 we have *f.* Messias, 45
2:14 Jesus *f.* in the temp. those
Acts 5:10 came in, and *f.* her de.
22 officers *f.* them not in pris.
7:11 our fathers *f.* no sustena.
9:2 that if *f.* any of this way
10:27 P. *f.* many come together
12:19 when Herod *f.* not Peter
13:6 they *f.* a certain sorcerer
22 I have *f.* David a man after
17:23 I *f.* altar with inscription
24:5 *f.* this man a pestilent

Acts 24:20 if they *f.* any evil do.
25:25 I *f.* noth. worthy of death
28:14 Puteoli, wh. we *f.* breth.
Rom. 4:1 what Abraham *f.*
7:10 to life I *f.* to be unto death
1 *Cor.* 15:15 we are *f.* false witn.
2 *Cor.* 2:13 bec. I *f.* not Titus
Gal. 2:17 we also are *f.* sinners
Phil. 2:8 *f.* in fashion as a man
1 *Tim.* 3:10 being *f.* blameless
2 *Tim.* 1:17 Onesiphorus *f.* me
Heb. 12:17 *f.* no place of repent.
1 *Pet.* 1:7 faith be *f.* to praise
2 *John* 4 *f.* of thy children
Rev. 2:2 and hast *f.* them liars
3:2 not *f.* thy works perfect
12:8 nor their place *f.* in heaven
16:20 mountains were not *f.*

Be FOUND.

Gen. 18:29 peradvent. *be* forty *f.*
Ex. 21:16 a man if he *be f.*
22:2 if that *be f.* breaking up, 7
4 if the theft *be* certainly *f.*
1 *Sam.* 10:21 Saul could not *be f.*
2 *Sam.* 17:12 come on him where
he shall *be f.*
1 *K.* 1:52 if wickedness *be f.*
1 *Chr.* 28:9 seek him he will *be*
f. of thee, 2 *Chr.* 15:2
Job 20:8 fly away and not *be f.*
28:12 where shall wisdom *be f. ?*
Ps. 32:6 pray when may *be f.*
36:2 till his iniq. *be f.* hateful
37:36 but he could not *be f.*
Prov. 6:31 if he *be f.* he sh. rest.
16:31 if it *be f.* in way of right.
30:6 and thou *be f.* a liar
10 and thou *be f.* guilty
Is. 34:16 shall not *be f.* a sherd
35:9 nor any beast *be f.* there
51:3 joy and gladness *be f.*
55:6 seek L. while he may *be f.*
Jer. 29:14 I will *be f.* of you
50:20 sins of J. shall not *be f.*
Ezek. 26:21 shalt never *be f.*
Dan. 11:19 he sh. fall and n. *be f.*
12:1 ev. one that *be f.* written
Hos. 10:2 sh. they *be f.* faulty
Zep. 3:13 nor deceit. tongue *be f.*
Zec. 10:10 place not *be f.*
Acts 5:39 lest *be f.* to fight ag. G.
1 *Cor.* 4:2 a steward *be f.* faithful
2 *Cor.* 5:3 shall not *be f.* naked
11:12 may *be f.* even as we
12:20 *be f.* such as would not
Phil. 3:9 *be f.* in him
2 *Pet.* 3:14 *be f.* of him in peace
Rev. 18:21 Baby. *be f.* no more
22 no craftsman *be f.* in thee

See FAVOR.

FOUND grace.

Gen. 6:8 Noah *f.* in eyes of L.
19:19 servant *f. g.* in thy sight
33:10 if I have *f. g.* 47:29; 50:4
39:4 Joseph *f. grace* in his sight
Ex. 33:12 thou hast also *f. g.* 17
13 if I have *f. g.* 34:9; *Jud.*
6:17; 1 *Sam.* 27:5
16 known that I have *f. g. ?*
Num. 32:5 if we have *f. grace*
1 *Sam.* 20:3 father know I *f. g.*
Jer. 31:2 people *f. g.* in wildern.

Is FOUND.

Gen. 44:10 with whom cup *is f.*
1 *K.* 14:13 *is f.* some good thing
2 *K.* 22:13 this book that *is f.*
Ezr. 4:19 it *is f.* city been reb.
Job 19:28 root of the matter *is f.*
Prov. 10:13 in lips wisdom *is f.*
Is. 13:15 that *is* f. be thrust
65:8 new wine *is f.* in cluster
Jer. 2:26 the thief when he *is f.*
34 *is f.* the blood of innocents
11:9 a conspiracy *is f.* am. Jud.
Dan. 5:14 excel. wisdom *is f.* 12
Hos. 14:8 from me *is* thy fruit *f.*

Luke 15:24 was lost and *is f.* 32
2 *Cor.* 7:14 boasting *is f.* a truth

Was FOUND.

Gen. 44:12 cup *w. f.* in B. sack
1 *Sam.* 13:22 with S. and J. *w. f.*
2 *Chr.* 15:4 he *was f.* of them, 15
Ezr. 6:2 there *w. f.* at A. a roll
Ec. 9:15 *w. f.* in it poor wise m.
Jer. 48:27 *w.* he *f.* among thiev. ?
Ezek. 28:15 iniqui. *was f.* in thee
Dan. 1:19 none *w. f.* like Daniel
2:35 no place *was f.* for them
5:11 wisd. of gods *was f.* in him
6:22 innocency *was f.* in me
Mat. 1:18 *w. f.* wi. child of H. G.
Luke 9:36 Jesus *was f.* alone
Acts 8:40 Philip *was f.* at Azotus
Rom. 10:20 I *was f.* of them that
1 *Pet.* 2:22 nor *w.* guile *f.* in mou.
Rev. 5:4 *was f.* worthy to open
Rev. 14:5 in th. mo. *w. f.* no guile
18:24 in her *was f.* blood of pro.
20:11 any *f.* no place for them

Was not FOUND.

Mal. 2:6 iniq. *w. n. f.* in his lips
Heb. 11:5 Enoch *was not f.*
Rev. 20:15 *was not f.* written.

FOUNDATION.

Ex. 9:18 not been in Eg. since *f.*
Jos. 6:26 lay *f.* in his first-born
1 *K.* 5:17 hewn stones to lay *f.*
6:37 in fourth year was *f.* laid
7:9 of costly stones from the *f.*
16:34 laid *f.* of Jericho
2 *Chr.* 8:16 prepared to day of *f.*
31:7 began to lay *f.* of the heaps
Ezr. 3:10 when build. laid *f.* 12
5:16 Sheshbazzar laid the *f.*
Job 4:19 whose *f.* is in the dust
22:16 *f.* overflown with a flood
Ps. 87:1 *f.* is in holy mountains
102:25 of old thou hast laid *f.*
137:7 rase it, rase it, even to *f.*
Prov. 10:25 righteous is everl. *f.*
Is. 28:16 I lay in Zion for a *f.* a
44:28 thy *f.* shall be laid
48:13 my hand laid *f.* of earth
Ezek. 13:14 *f.* thereof be discov.
Hab. 3:13 discovering *f.* to neck
Hag. 2:18 day the *f.* was laid
Zec. 4:9 Zerubbabel hath laid *f.*
8:9 prophets when the *f.* was
laid
12:1 which lay. *f.* of the earth
Luke 6:48 laid the *f.* on a rock
49 without a *f.* built a house
14:29 after he hath laid the *f.*
Rom. 15:20 bui. on ano. man's *f.*
1 *Cor.* 3:10 master-build, laid *f.*
11 for other *f.* can no man lay
12 if any build on this *f.* gold
Eph. 2:20 on *f.* of the prophets
1 *Tim.* 6:19 laying up a good *f.*
2 *Tim.* 2:19 *f.* of G. standeth sure
Heb. 1:10 laid *f.* of the earth
6:1 not laying *f.* of repentance
Rev. 21:19 the first *f.* jasper

FOUNDATION of the world.

Mat. 13:35 secret from *f. of w.*
25:34 kingdom prep. fr. *f. of w.*
Luke 11:50 bl. shed from *f. of w.*
John 17:24 before *f. of w.*
Eph. 1:4 chosen us bef. *f. of w.*
Heb. 4:3 works finish. fr. *f. of w.*
9:26 suffered since *f. of w.*
1 *Pet.* 1:20 foreord. bef. *f. of w.*
Rev. 13:8 L. slain from *f. of w.*
17:8 names not writ. fr. *f. of w.*

FOUNDATIONS.

Deut. 32:22 set on fire *f.* of moun.
2 *Sam.* 22:8 *f.* of heaven moved
16 *f.* were discov. *Ps.* 18:7, 15
Ezr. 4:12 and joined the *f.*
6:3 let the *f.* be strongly laid
Job 38:4 when I laid *f.* of earth ?
6 whereupon are the *f.* fasten.

Ps. 11:3 if *f.* be destroyed, what
82:5 all the *f.* are out of course
104:5 who laid *f.* of earth
Prov. 8:29 appointed *f.* of earth
Is. 16:7 for *f.* of Kir-haresseth
24:18 *f.* of the earth do shake
40:21 not unders. from the *f.*
51:13 Lord that laid *f.* of earth
16 I may lay *f.* of the earth
54:11 lay *f.* with sapphires
58:12 raise up *f.* of many gener.
Jer. 31:37 if *f.* can be searched
50:15 her *f.* are fallen
51:26 not take of thee sto. for *f.*
Lam. 4:11 it hath devour. the *f.*
Ezek. 30:4 Egypt's *f.* brok. down
41:8 the *f.* of the side chambers
Mic. 1:6 will discover *f.* thereof
6:2 ye strong *f.* of the earth
Acts 16:26 *f.* of prison were shak.
Heb. 11:10 for a city that hath *f.*
Rev. 21:14 walls of city had 12 *f.*
19 *f.* garnished with precious
stones

FOUNDED.

Ps. 24:2 he hath *f.* it on the seas
89:11 fuln. thereof thou *f.* them
104:8 to place thou *f.* for them
119:152 testimonies, hast *f.* th.
Prov. 3:19 by wisdom hath *f.*
Is. 14:32 the Lord hath *f.* Zion
23:13 was not till Assyrian *f.* it
Amos 9:6 *f.* his troop in earth
Mat. 7:25 it fell not, *f.* on a rock
Luke 6:48 it was *f.* on a rock

FOUNDER.

Jud. 17:4 gave them to the *f.*
Jer. 6:29 the *f.* melteth in vain
10:9 work of the hands of the *f.*
14 *f.* conf. by graven im. 51:17

FOUNTAIN.

Gen. 16:7 found Hagar by a *f.*
Lev. 11:36 a *f.* wherein is water
20:18 he discovered her *f.* the *f.*
Deut. 33:28 *f.* of J. be on a land
Ps. 36:9 with thee is the *f.*
68:26 bless Lord from *f.* of Isr.
74:15 thou didst cleave the *f.*
114:8 flint into a *f.* of water
Prov. 5:18 let thy *f.* be blessed
13:14 law of wise is a *f.* of life
14:27 fear of Lord is a *f.* of life
25:26 is as a troubled *f.*
Ec. 12:6 pitcher be broken at *f.*
Cant. 4:12 *f.* sealed ; 15 *f.* of gar.
Jer. 2:13 *f.* of living wat. 17:13
6:7 as *f.* casteth out waters
9:1 Oh that mine eyes were a *f.*
Joel 3:18 a *f.* come forth
Zec. 13:1 that day a *f.* be opened
Mark 5:29 *f.* of her blo. dried up
Jam. 3:11 *f.* send forth sw. wat.
12 no *f.* can yield salt water
Rev. 21:6 I will give of *f.* of life

FOUNTAINS.

Gen. 7:11 *f.* of deep broken up
8:2 *f.* of the deep were stopped
Deut. 8:7 bringeth into land of *f.*
1 *K.* 18:5 go to all *f.* of water
2 *Chr.* 32:4 much pe. who stop. *f.*
Prov. 5:16 let thy *f.* be dispersed
8:24 no *f.* abonnding with wat.
28 he strengthened *f.* of deep
Is. 41:18 will open *f.* in valleys
Hos. 13:15 *f.* shall be dried up
Rev. 7:17 lead them to living *f.*
8:10 star fell on the *f.* of waters
14:7 worship him made the *f.*
16:4 angel poured his vial on *f.*

FOUR.

Gen. 2:10 river became *f.* heads
14:9 *f.* kings joined battle
47:24 *f.* parts be own, for seed

Er. 22:1 shall restore *f.* sheep
Lev. 11:20 fowls going on all *f.*
  27 go on all *f.* unclean. 42
Job 42:16 son's sons, even *f.*
Prov. 30:15 *f.* say not. It is eno.
  18 be *f.* things wh. I know not
  24 be *f.* things little on earth
  29 *f.* things are comely
Is. 17:6 *f.* or five in out. branch.
Jer. 15:3 app. over them *f.* kinds
Ezek. 1:5 *f.* living creatures
  14:21 *f.* sore judgments on Jer.
  37:9 from *f.* winds, O breath
Dan. 3:25 lo, I see *f.* men loose
  7:2 *f.* winds strove on sea
  17 these *f.* beasts are *f.* kings
  8:8 came *f.* notable horns
  22 *f.* kingdoms shall stand
  11:4 kingdom towards *f.* winds
Amos 1:3 for *f.* w. not turn away
  punish. 6, 9, 11, 13; 2:1, 4, 6
Zec. 1:18 and behold *f.* horns
Mat. 24:31 gather his elect from
  the *f.* winds, *Mark* 13:27
John 4:35 yet *f.* months, harvest
  11:17 Lazarus in grave *f.* days
  19:23 made *f.* parts of his garm.
Acts 10:30 *f.* days ago was fast.
  21:9 Philip had *f.* daughters
  23 we have *f.* men have a vow
Rev. 4:6 round throne *f.* beasts
  5:14 *f.* beasts said, Amen. 6:6
  9:14 *f.* angels who are bound
  14:3 a new song before *f.* beasts
  19:4 and the *f.* beasts fell down

See CORNERS, DAYS.

FOUR times.
Neh. 6:4 sent *f. t.* after this sort

FOURFOLD.
2 *Sam.* 12:6 restore the lamb *f.*
Luke 19:8 any thing, I restore *f.*

See FOOTED, TWENTY, HUN-
DRED, THOUSAND.

FOURSCORE.
Ex. 7:7 Moses was *f.* years old,
  when spake to Pharaoh
Jud. 3:30 land had rest *f.* years
2 *Sam.* 19:32 Barzillai was *f.* yea.
2 *K.* 6:25 ass's head for *f.* pieces
Ps. 90:10 and if be *f.* years
Cant. 6:18 and *f.* concubines
Luke 2:37 wid. *f.* and four years
  16:7 take thy bill and write *f.*

FOURSCORE and five.
Jos. 14:10 I am this day *f.* and *fl.*

FOURSQUARE.
Rev. 21:16 the city lieth *f.*

FOURTEEN.
Gen. 31:41 serv. *f.* years for dau.
Mat. 1:17 from Dav. to carrying
  away *f.* to Ch. *f.* generations
2 *Cor.* 12:2 man above *f.* years
Gal. 2:1 *f.* years after I went up

FOURTEENTH.
Acts 27:27 *f.* night was come

See DAY.

FOURTH.
Gen. 15:16 in *f.* gen. come hither
Ex. 20:5 iniq. to *f.* generation,
  34:7; *Num.* 14:18; *Deut.* 5:9
Lev. 19:24 in *f.* year fruit holy
2 *K.* 10:30 child. of *f.* gen. 15:12
Dan. 2:40 *f.* kingdom str. as iron
  3:25 *f.* is like the Son of God
  7:23 *f.* beast be the *f.* kingdom
  11:2 the *f.* shall be far richer
Mat. 14:25 *f.* J. came unto *f.* watch
Rev. 4:7 *f.* beast like flying eagle
  6:7 when opened the *f.* seal
  8:12 the *f.* angel sounded
  16:8 *f.* angel poured vial

See DAY, MONTH, PART.

FOWL.
Gen. 1:26 dominion over *f.* 28
  2:19 God formed every *f.* of air
  7:23 *f.* of heaven was destroyed
  8:17 bring forth of *f.* of cattle
  9:2 fear of you be on every *f.*
  10 establish covenant with *f.*
Deut. 4:17 likeness of winged *f.*
Job 28:7 a path no *f.* knoweth
Ps. 8:8 have dominion over *f.*
  148:10 flying *f.* praise the L.
Jer. 9:10 *f.* of heavens are fled
Ezek. 17:23 under it sh. dw. all *f.*
  39:17 speak to ev. feathered *f.*
  44:31 not eat torn *f.* or beast
Dan. 7:6 four wings of a *f.*

FOWLS.
Gen. 7:3 take of *f.* also by sevens
  15:11 when *f.* came on carcasses
Lev. 1:14 burnt sacrifice be of *f.*
  11:13 *f.* have in abomination
Deut. 14:20 of clean *f.* may eat
  28:26 carcass be meat to all *f.*
1 *Sam.* 17:44 thy flesh to the *f.* 46
1 *K.* 4:33 Solomon spake of *f.*
  14:11 dieth, *f.* eat, 16:4; 21:24
Neh. 5:18 *f.* were prepar. for me
Job 12:7 ask *f.* and they sh. tell
Ps. 50:11 I know all the *f.*
  78:27 rained *f.* as sand of sea
Is. 18:6 be left to *f.* of mountains,
  f. shall summer upon them
Dan. 4:14 *f.* get from his branch.
Mat. 6:26 the *f.* they sow not
  13:4 *f.* dev. *Mark* 4:4; *Lu.* 8:5
Mark 4:32 *f.* m. lodge, *Lu.* 13:19
Luke 12:24 are ye better than *f.* ?
Acts 10:12 wherein were *f.* 11:6
Rev. 19:17 an angel cried to all *f.*
  21 *f.* were filled with th. flesh

FOWLS of heaven.
Job 35:11 wiser than *f.* of heaven
Ps. 79:2 thy servants meat to *f.*
  104:12 *f.* of h. have their habit.
Jer. 7:33 carcasses of peo. meat
  for *f.* of h. 16:4; 19:7; 34:20
  15:3 appoint *f.* of hea. to destr.
Ezek. 29:5 Ph. for meat to *f.* of h.
  31:6 *f.* of h. made nests in Assy.
  13 on his ruin sh. *f.* of h. rem.
  32:4 *f.* of heaven to remain
  38:20 *f.* of h. shake at my pres.
Dan. 2:38 *f.* of h. to Nebuchad.
Hos. 2:18 covenant with *f.* of h.
  4:3 shall languish with *f.* of hea.
  7:12 bring them down as *f.* of h.
Zep. 1:3 will consume *f.* of hea.
Luke 13:19 *f.* of h. lodged in bra.

FOWLER, S.
Ps. 91:3 from the snare of the *f.*
  124:7 soul out of the snare of *f.*
Prov. 6:5 as a bird from the *f.*
Hos. 9:8 prophet is a snare of *f.*

FOX, ES.
Jud. 15:4 Samson caught 300 *f.*
Neh. 4:3 *f.* shall break stone-wa.
Ps. 63:10 shall be portion for *f.*
Cant. 2:15 take the *f.* the little *f.*
Lam. 5:18 the *f.* walk upon Zion
Ezek. 13:4 thy proph. are like *f.*
Mat. 8:20 *f.* ha. holes, *Luke* 9:58
Luke 13:32 go tell *f.* I cast out

FRAGMENTS.
Mat. 14:20 took up the *f. Mark*
  6:43; *Luke* 9:17; *John* 6:13
Mark 8:19 many baskets of *f.* ?
John 6:12 gather up the *f.*

FRAIL.
Ps. 39:4 may know how *f.* I am

FRAME.
Ps. 103:14 he knoweth our *f.* he
Ezek. 40:2 was as the *f.* of a city

FRAME, ED, ETH.
Jud. 12:6 not *f.* to pronounce it

Ps. 50:19 thy tongue *f.* deceit
  94:20 which *f.* mischi. by a law
Is. 29:16 *f.* say to him that *f.* it?
Jer. 18:11 I *f.* evil against you
Hos. 5:4 will not *f.* to turn to G.
Eph. 2:21 in whom the build *f.*
Heb. 11:3 worlds *f.* by word of G.

FRANKINCENSE.
Ex. 30:34 spices with pure *f.*
Lev. 2:1 put *f.* 5:11; 24:7 ; *Num.*
  5:15
  16 priest burn oil with *f.* 6:15
1 *Chr.* 9:29 appoint. to oversee *f.*
Neh. 13:5 where they laid the *f.*
Cant. 3:6 who this perf. with *f.* ?
  4:6 I will get me to the hill of *f.*
  14 cinnam. with all trees of *f.*
Mat. 2:11 they present. to him *f.*
Rev. 18:13 no man buy. their *f.*

FRANKLY.
Luke 7:42 *f.* forgave them both

FRAUD.
Ps. 10:7 his mouth is full of *f.*
Jam. 5:4 hire kept back by *f.*

FRAY.
Deut. 28:26 *f.* them, *Jer.* 7:33
Zec. 1:21 these are come to *f.*

FRECKLED.
Lev. 13:39 it is a *f.* spot groweth

FREE.
Ex. 21:2 in sev. year go out *f.*
  Deut. 15:12; *Jer.* 34:9, 14
  5 if servant say, I will not go
  out *f.*
  11 she go out *f.* with. money
  26 let him go *f.* for eye's sake
Lev. 19:20 not put to dea. not *f.*
Num. 5:19 be *f.* from bitter wat.
  28 if woman not defiled, be *f.*
Deut. 15:18 not hard wh. sen. *f.*
  24:5 sh. he *f.* at home one year
1 *Sam.* 17:25 father's house *f.*
2 *Chr.* 29:31 were of *f.* heart off.
Job 3:19 servant *f.* from master
  39:5 who sent out wild ass *f.* ?
Ps. 51:12 uphold me with *f.* Sp.
  88:5 *f.* am. the dead, likee slain
  105:20 the king let him go *f.*
Is. 58:6 to let the oppressed go *f.*
Jer. 34:9 each let servant go *f.*
  11 whom they let go *f.* to ret.
Mat. 15:6 honor not father, be *f.*
  17:26 then are the children *f.*
Mark 7:11 it is Corb. he sh. be *f.*
John 8:32 truth sh. make you *f.*
  33 sayest, Ye shall be made *f.*
  36 if Son make you *f.* *f.* indeed
Acts 22:28 but I was *f.* born
Rom. 5:15 not as offence, so *f.*
  16 *f.* gift is of many offences
  18 *f.* gift came upon all men
  6:18 being made *f.* from sin, 22
  20 were *f.* from righteousness
  7:3 husband be dead, she is *f.*
  8:2 life made me *f.* from death
1 *Cor.* 7:21 if mayest be made *f.*
  9:1 not an apostle, am I not *f.* ?
  19 though I be *f.* from all men
  12:13 by one Spirit, bond or *f.*
Gal. 3:28 bond nor *f.* *Col.* 3:11
  4:26 Jerus. which is above is *f.*
  31 but children of the *f.*
  5:1 liberty where. C. made us *f.*
Eph. 6:8 receive of L. bond or *f.*
2 *Thes.* 3:1 word have *f.* course
1 *Pet.* 2:16 as *f.* not using liberty
Rev. 13:16 *f.* and bond to receive
  19:18 flesh of both bond and *f.*

FREED.
Jos. 9:23 shall none of you be *f.*
Rom. 6:7 he dead, is *f.* from sin

FREEDOM.
Lev. 19:20 wom. not *f.* given her
Acts 22:28 with great sum this *f.*

FREELY.

Gen. 2:16 of every tree f. eat
Num. 11:5 the fish we did eat f.
1 Sam. 14:30 if people eaten f.
Ezr. 2:68 chief fathers offered f.
7:15 king hath offered f. to God
Ps. 54:6 will f. sacrifice to thee
Hos. 14:4 I will love them f.
Mat. 10:8 f. received, f. give
Acts 2:29 breth. let me f. speak
26:26 before whom I speak f.
Rom. 3:24 justified f. by grace
8:32 also f. give us all things
1 Cor. 2:12 the things f. given us
2 Cor. 11:7 preach. gospel of G. f.
Rev. 21:6 of fountain of life f.
22:17 whosoever will, let him take f.

FREEMAN.

1 Cor. 7:22 called, is the Lord's f.
Rev. 6:15 bond and f. hid them.

FREE offerings.

Ex. 36:3 f. offerings every morn
Amos 4:5 publish the f. offerings

FREQUENT.

2 Cor. 11:23 in prisons more f.

FREEWILL-OFFERING.

Lev. 22:21 a f.-off. sh. be perfect
Deut. 23:23 f.-off. shalt thou keep
Ezr. 3:5 willingly offered a f.-off.
7:16 silver canst find with f.-off.
8:28 silver and gold f.-offering

FREEWILL-OFFERINGS.

Deut. 12:6 thither bring f.-offer.
Ps. 119:108 accept f.-offerings

FREE-WOMAN.

Gal. 4:22 had two sons by f.-w.
23 but he of f. was by promise
31 not child. of bondw. of f.-w.

FRESH, ER.

Num. 11:8 taste of manna as f.
Job 29:20 my glory was f. in me
33:25 flesh be f. than a child's
Ps. 92:10 anointed with f. oil
Jam. 3:12 yield salt water and f.

FRET.

Lev. 13:55 burn it in fire, it is f.

FRET, TED, ETH, ING.

Lev. 13:51 is a f. leprosy, 14:44
1 Sam. 1:6 to make her f.
Ps. 37:1 f. not, 7, 8; Prov. 24:19
Prov. 19:3 his heart f. against L.
Is. 8:21 when hungry they sh. f.
Ezek. 16:43 f. me in these things

FRIEND.

Ex. 33:11 G. spake as man to f.
Deut. 13:6 if thy f. entice thee
Jud. 14:20 he used as his f.
2 Sam. 13:3 Amnon had a f. Jon.
15:37 Hushai, David's f. 16:16
16:17 is this thy kindness to f. ?
2 Chr. 20:7 to seed of Abr. thy f.
Job 6:14 pity be showed from f.
27 and you dig a pit for your f.
Ps. 35:14 as though been my f.
41:9 familiar f. lift up his heel
88:18 lover and f. far from me
Prov. 6:1 if be surety for thy f.
3 hand of f. make sure thy f.
17:17 a f. loveth at all times
18 surety in presence of his f.
18:24 a f. closer than a brother
19:6 is a f. to him giveth gifts
22:11 the king shall be his f.
27:6 faithful are wounds of a f.
9 man's f. by hearty counsel
10 own f. father's f. forsa. not
14 bless. his f. with loud voice
17 sharpeneth counten. of f.
Cant. 5:16 beloved, this is my f.
Is. 41:8 art seed of Abra. my f.
Jer. 6:21 the neighbor and his f.
19:9 eat every one flesh of his f.
Hos. 3:1 belo. of her f. adulteress

Mic. 7:5 trust ye not in a f.
Mat. 11:19 f. of public. Luke 7:34
20:13 f. I do thee no wrong
22:12 f. how camest in hither?
26:50 f. why art thou come?
Luke 11:5 shall have a f. and say, f. lend me three loaves
14:10 may say, f. go up higher
John 3:29 f. of bridegr. rejoiceth
11:11 our f. Lazarus sleepeth
19:12 thou art not Cesar's f.
Acts 12:20 made Blastus their f.
Jam. 2:23 Abraham call. f. of G.
4:4 f. of world, is enemy of G.

FRIENDLY.

Jud. 19:3 to speak f. to her
Ruth 2:13 spoken f. to handm.
Prov. 18:24 show himself f.

FRIENDS.

1 Sam. 30:26 D. sent spoil to f.
2 Sam. 3:8 kindness to Saul's f.
19:6 lovest enemies hatest f.
1 K. 16:11 left not one of his f.
Est. 5:10 Haman called for his f.
14 then said wife and f. to him
6:13 Haman told f. every thing
Job 2:11 when Job's three f. he.
16:20 my f. scorn me
17:5 speaketh flattery to his f.
19:14 my f. have forgotten me
19 my inward f. abhorred me
21 have pity on me, O ye f.
32:3 Elihu's wrath kind. ag. f.
42:7 kindled ag. Eliphaz and f.
10 when he prayed for his f.
Ps. 38:11 f. aloof from my sore
Prov. 14:20 the rich hath many f.
16:28 whisperer separat. chief f.
Prov. 17:9 repeat. matter, sep. f.
18:24 hath f. show him. friendly
19:4 wealth maketh many f.
7 more do f. go far from him
Cant. 5:1 eat, O f. drink, yea
Jer. 20:4 thee a terror to thy f.
6 buried there, thou and thy f.
38:22 thy f. have set thee on
Lam. 1:2 her f. have dealt treac.
Zec. 13:6 wounded in house of f.
Mark 3:21 when his f. heard of it
5:19 J. saith, Go home to thy f.
Luke 7:6 centurion sent f. to him
12:4 my f. be not afraid of them
14:12 a dinner, call not thy f.
15:6 he calleth together his f.
9 she calleth her f. saying
29 make merry with my f.
16:9 make f. of the mammon
21:16 ye shall be betrayed by f.
23:12 Pilate and Herod made f.
John 15:13 down his life for his f.
14 ye are my f. if ye do what I
15 but I have called you f.
Acts 10:24 Cornelius called his f.
19:31 who were f. sent to him
27:3 liberty to go to his f.
3 John 14 f. salute thee, greet f.

FRIENDSHIP.

Prov. 22:24 no f. with angry man
Jam. 4:4 f. of world is enmity

FRINGE, S.

Num. 15:38 make f. put on f. 39
Deut. 22:12 make thee f.

To and FRO.

Gen. 8:7 a raven, went to and f.
2 K. 4:35 Elisha walked to and f.
Job 1:7 said, Fr. going to a. f. 2:2
7:4 I am full of tossings to and f.
13:25 a leaf driven to and f. ?
Ps. 107:27 they reel to and f.
Prov. 21:6 vanity tossed to and f.
Is. 24:20 earth shall reel to a. f.
33:4 running to and f. of locusts
49:21 and removing to and f.
Ezek. 27:19 Dan going to and f.
Zec. 1:10 L. sent to walk to a. f.
11 we have walked to and f.

6:7 walk to a. f. so they walked to and f. through earth
Eph. 4:14 no more tossed to a. f
See RUN.

FROGS.

Ex. 8:2 all thy borders with f.
7 the magicians brought up f.
Ps. 78:45 he sent f. which destr.
105:30 the land brought forth f.
Rev. 16:13 unclean spirits like f.

FRONT.

2 Sam. 10:9 f. of battle ag. him

FRONTLETS.

Ex. 13:16 be for f. between eyes
Deut. 6:8 shall be as f. 11:18

FROST.

Gen. 31:40 f. consumed by night
Ex. 16:14 as small as the hoar f.
Job 37:10 by breath of G. f. given
38:29 f. of heaven, who hath
Ps. 78:47 dest. syca. trees with f.
147:16 he scattereth the hoar f.
Jer. 36:30 Jeh. body cast out to f.

FROWARD.

Deut. 32:20 a very f. generation
2 Sam. 22:27 with f. wilt show thyself f. Ps. 18:26
Job 5:13 counsel of f. carried he.
Ps. 101:4 a f. heart shall depart
Prov. 2:12 man speaketh f. thin.
15 ways crooked, f. in paths
3:32 f. is abomination to Lord
4:24 put away fr. thee f. mouth
6:12 walketh with a f. mouth
8:8 there is nothing f. in them
13 and the f. mouth do I hate
10:31 f. tongue shall be cut out
11:20 of a f. heart, are abomin.
16:28 a f. man soweth strife
30 shut. eyes to devise f. things
17:20 f. heart, findeth no good
21:8 the way of a man is f.
22:5 thorns are in way of the f.
1 Pet. 2:18 serv. be subject to f.

FROWARDLY.

Is. 57:17 he went on f. in way

FROWARDNESS.

Prov. 2:14 delight in f. of wicked
6:14 f. is in his heart
10:32 mouth of wicked speak. f.

FROZEN.

Job 38:30 face of the deep is f.

FRUIT.

Gen. 1:29 every tree wherein is f.
4:3 Cain brought of the f.
Gen. 30:2 hath with. f. of womb
Ex. 21:22 so that her f. depart
Lev. 19:23 count f. uncircumc.
24 fourth year f. shall be holy
25:3 six years shalt gather in f.
27:30 the tithe of f. is the Lord's
Num. 13:26 showed th. f. of land
Deut. 1:25 the f. in their hands
7:13 he will bless f. of thy land
22:9 lest f. of viney. be defiled
26:2 take of first of all the f.
28:4 blessed be f. of thy body
11 plent. in f. of thy body, 30:9
18 cursed be the f. of thy body
40 thine olive shall cast his f.
42 thy f. shall locust consume
Jud. 9:11 sho. I forsake my f. ?
2 Sam. 16:2 summer f. for young
Ps. 21:10 their f. shalt destroy
72:16 f. thereof shake like Leb.
104:13 earth is satisfied with f.
105:35 locusts devoured the f.
127:3 f. of womb is his reward
132:11 of f. of thy body
Prov. 8:19 my f. is bet. than gold
10:16 f. of wicked tendeth to sin
11:30 f. of righteous tree of life
12:14 satisfied by f. of mouth
13:2 satisfied with f. of mouth
18:20 satisfied with f. of mouth

31:16 with *f.* of her hand she
31 give her of *f.* of her hands
Cant. 2:3 his *f.* sweet to my taste
8:11 for the *f.* bring silver
12 that keep *f.* two hundred
Is. 3:10 sh. eat *f.* of their doings
4:2 *f.* of earth shall be excellent
10:12 punish *f.* of stout heart
13:18 no pity on *f.* of the womb
14:29 his *f.* be a fiery serpent
27:6 fill face of the world with *f.*
9 the *f.* to take away his sin
28:4 hasty *f.* before the summer
57:19 I create *f.* of lips, peace
65:21 and eat the *f.* of them
Jer. 6:19 will bring *f.* of thoug.
7:20 my fury be on *f.* of ground
11.16 olive-tree of goodly *f.*
19 let us destroy tree with *f.*
17:10 *f.* of doings, 21:14; 32:19
Ezek. 17:9 cut off the *f.* thereof
19:12 east wind dried up her *f.*
14 fire is gone, hath devour. *f.*
25:4 they shall eat thy *f.* and
36:30 I will multiply *f.* of tree
47:12 nor *f.* thereof be consum.
Dan. 4:12 *f.* thereof much, 21
14 and said thus, Scatter his *f.*
Hos. 10:13 have eaten *f.* of lies
14:8 from me is thy *f.* come
Amos 2:9 destroyed *f.* from ab.
6:12 *f.* of right. into hemlock
7:14 a gatherer of sycamore *f.*
8:1 a basket of summer *f.* 2
Mic. 6:7 bo. for sin of soul?
7:13 land deso. for *f.* of doings
Hab. 3:17 neither *f.* be in vines
Hag. 1:10 earth stayed fr. her *f.*
Zec. 8:12 vine shall give her *f.*
Mal. 1:12 table is pollut. and *f.*
3:11 nor your vine cast her *f.*
Mat. 12:33 and his *f.* good, for the
tree is known by his *f.*
21:19 let no *f.* grow on thee
34 when time of *f.* drew near
26:29 I will not drink of *f.* of the
vine. *Mark* 14:25
Mark 12:2 might rec. *f.* of vine.
Luke 1:42 bles. is *f.* of thy womb
13:6 sought *f.* and found none
7 I come seeking *f.* on fig-tree
20:10 should give him of the *f.*
John 4:36 gather. *f.* to life eter.
Acts 2:30 of *f.* of his loins raise
Rom. 1:13 I might have some *f.*
6:21 what *f.* had ye in th. thin.
22 have your *f.* unto holiness
15:28 sealed to them this *f.*
Gal. 5:22 *f.* of Spirit is love
Eph. 5:9 *f.* of Sp. is in all good.
Phil. 1:22 this is *f.* of my labor
4:17 desire *f.* that may abound
Heb. 13:15 offer *f.* of our lips
Jam. 3:18 *f.* of right. so. in peace
5:7 waiteth for the precious *f.*
Jude 12 *f.* withereth, without *f.*

See EAT.

Bear, *or* **beareth FRUIT.**
2 *K.* 19:30 *b. f.* upward, *Is.* 37:31
Ezek. 17:8 that it might *bear f.*
23 in height of Is. It shall *b. f.*
Hos. 9:16 they shall *bear* no *f.*
Joel 2:22 the tree *beareth* her *f.*
Mat. 13:23 is he who *beareth f.*
Luke 8:8 good ground, and *b. f.*
13:9 if it *bear f.* well
John 15:2 ev. branch in me that
beareth not *f.* that *beareth f.*
John 15:4 branch cannot *b. f.*
8 *b.* much *f.* so be my disciples

Bring, bringeth, *or* **brought
forth FRUIT.**
Lev. 25:21 *b. forth f.* three years
Num. 13:20 and *bring* of the *f.*
Neh. 10:35 *b. f.* of all trees, 37
Ps. 1:3 *bring. forth f.* in season
92:14 *bring forth f.* in old age

Jer. 12:2 wicked *bring forth f.*
Ezek. 36:11 they shall *bring f. f.*
47:12 sh. *b. f.* new *f.* for meat
Hos. 10:1 Is. *b. f. f.* to himself
Mat. 3:10 *bringeth* not *forth* good
f. 7:19; *Luke* 3:9
7:17 every good tree *b. f.* good *f.*
18 good tree cannot *b. f.* evil *f.*
13:26 when blade *brought f. f.*
Mark 4:20 hear word and *b. f. f.*
28 earth *b. forth f.* of herself
Luke 8:14 *b.* no *f.* to perfection
15 *bring forth f.* with patience
John 12:24 if it die, it *b. f.* much *f.*
15:2 it may *bring forth* more *f.*
6 abideth in me, *b. f.* much *f.*
16 I ordained that you sh. *b. f. f.*
Rom. 7:4 we should *b. f.* to G.
5 work to *b. f. f.* unto death
Col. 1:6 gospel *b. forth f.* in you
Jam. 5:18 E. prayed earth *b. f. f.*

See FIRST-FRUITS.

FRUIT-TREES.
Neh. 9:25 possessed *f.-t.* in abun.

**Yield, yieldeth, yielding
FRUIT.**
Gen. 1:11 fruit-tree *yielding f.*
Lev. 25:19 land shall *yield* her *f.*
26:4 trees of field shall *y.* their *f.*
Deut. 11:17 land *yield* not her *f.*
Prov. 12:12 root of righteous *y. f.*
Jer. 17:8 nor shall cease fr. *y. f.*
Ezek. 34:27 tree of field shall *y. f.*
36:8 *yield* your *f.* to my people
Mark 4:7 thorns chok. it, *y.* no *f.*
8 on good ground, and did *y. f.*
Heb. 12:11 *y.* peace. *f.* of righte.
Rev. 22:2 *y.* her *f.* every month

FRUITFUL.
Gen. 1:22 be *f.* 28; 8:17; 9:7; 35:11
17:6 I will make thee exceed. *f.*
20 Ishmael *f.*; 48:4 Jacob *f.*
26:22 made room, we shall be *f.*
28:3 God Almighty make thee *f.*
41:52 for God caused me to be *f.*
49:22 Joseph is a *f.* bough, even
Ex. 1:7 children of Israel were *f.*
Lev. 26:9 I will make you *f.*
Ps. 107:34 *f.* land into barrenness
128:3 thy wife shall be a *f.* vine
148:9 *f.* trees, praise the Lord
Is. 5:1 hath vineyard in a *f.* hill
17:6 in the outmost *f.* branches
32:12 shall lament for *f.* vine
Jer. 4:26 *f.* place was a wildern.
23:3 they sh. be *f.* and increase
Ezek. 19:10 she was *f.*
Hos. 13:15 though he be *f.*
Acts 14:17 gave rain and *f.*
Col. 1:10 *f.* in every good work

See FIELD.

FRUITS.
Gen. 43:11 take of the best *f.*
Ex. 22:29 to offer first of ripe *f.*
23:10 six years gather in the *f.*
Lev. 25:15 accor. to years of *f.* 10
22 till her *f.* come in, eat old
26:20 nor sh. trees yield their *f.*
Deut. 33:14 precious *f.* by sun
2 *Sam.* 9:10 thy sons bring in *f.*
2 *K.* 8:6 restore to her all the *f.*
19:29 plant vineyards, and eat *f.*
Job 31:39 if eaten *f.* with. money
Ps. 107:37 which may yield *f.*
Ec. 2:5 trees of all kind of *f.*
Cant. 4:13 orchard with pleas. *f.*
16 my beloved eat pleasant *f.*
6:11 I went to see *f.* of valley
7:13 at gates all manner of *f.*
Is. 33:9 B. and Car. shake off *f.*
Lam. 4:9 pine aw. for want of *f.*
Mal. 3:11 he shall not destroy *f.*
Mat. 3:8 *f.* meet for rep. *Luke* 3:8
7:16 ye sh. know them by *f.*, 20
21:34 they might receive the *f.*

41 render him *f.* in th. season
43 given to nation bringing *f.*
Luke 12:17 where to bestow *f.*
2 *Cor.* 9:10 increase *f.* of righte.
Phil. 1:11 filled with *f.* of right.
2 *Tim.* 2:6 first partaker of the *f.*
Jam. 3:17 wisdom full of good *f.*
Rev. 18:14 *f.* thy soul lusted after
22.2 bare twelve manner of *f.*

See FIRST.

Summer FRUITS.
2 *Sam.* 16:1 Ziba with 100 of *s. f.*
Is. 16:9 thy summer *f.* are fallen
Jer. 40:10 gather wine and *s. f.*
48:32 spoiler is fallen on *s. f.*
Mic. 7:1 as when gathered. *s. f.*

FRUSTRATE, ETH.
Ezr. 4:5 hired to *f.* their purpose
Is. 44:25 *f.* tokens of the liars
Gal. 2:21 I do not *f.* grace of G.

FRYING-PAN.
Lev. 2:7 meat-off. baken in *f.-p.*
7:9 dress. in *f.-p.* be the priest's

FUEL.
Is. 9:5 with burn. and *f.* of fire
19 people be as *f.* of the fire
Ezek. 15:4 vine-t. into fire for *f.* 6
21:32 shalt be for *f.* to fire

FUGITIVE.
Gen. 4:12 a *f.* shalt thou be
14 I sh. be a *f.* and a vagabond

FUGITIVES.
Jud. 12:4 ye Gileadites are *f.*
2 *K.* 25:11 *f.* that fell to king
Is. 15:5 Moab, his *f.* flee to Zoar
Ezek. 17:21 all his *f.* fall by swo.

FULFIL.
Gen. 29:27 *f.* her week, and we
Ex. 5:13 *f.* your daily tasks
23:26 num. of thy days I will *f.*
1 *K.* 2:27 he might *f.* word of L.
1 *Chr.* 22:13 takest heed to *f.*
2 *Chr.* 36:21 *f.* threescore and ten
Job 39:2 number months they *f.*?
Ps. 20:4 Lord *f.* all thy counsel
5 the Lord *f.* all thy petitions
145:19 *f.* desire of them fear him
Mat. 3:15 to *f.* all righteousness
5:17 not come to destr. but to *f.*
Acts 13:22 shall *f.* all my will
Rom. 2:27 uncircum. if it *f.* law
13:14 to *f.* the lusts thereof
Gal. 5:16 sh. not *f.* lusts of flesh
6:2 and so *f.* the law of Christ
Phil. 2:2 *f.* ye my joy, that ye be
Col. 1:25 to *f.* the word of God
4:17 taken heed thou *f.* ministry
2 *Thes.* 1:11 *f.* good pl. of his will
Jam. 2:8 if ye *f.* the royal law
Rev. 17:17 in hearts to *f.* his will

FULFILLED.
Gen. 25:24 when her days were *f.*
29:21 give me wife, days are *f.*
50:3 forty days were *f.* for so
Ex. 5:14 why not *f.* your task?
Lev. 12:4 till days of puri. be *f.* 6
Num. 6:13 days of separation *f.*
2 *Sam.* 7:12 when thy days be *f.*
1 *K.* 8:15 with his hand *f.* it
24 *f.* it with hand, 2 *Chr.* 6:15
2 *Chr.* 6:4 hath *f.* that he spake
Ezr. 1:1 word of L. might be *f.*
Job 36:17 hast *f.* judgment
Lam. 2:17 *f.* his word
4:18 our days are *f.* end come
Ezek. 5:2 when days of siege *f.*
Dan. 4:33 same hour was thi. *f.*
10:3 till three whole weeks *f.*
Mat. 1:22 that it might be *f.* 2:15
23; 8:17; 12:17; 13:35; 21:4;
27:35; *John* 12:38; 15:25; 17:12;
18:9, 32; 19:24, 28
2:17 was *f.* that spoken, 27:9
5:18 in no wise pass till all be *f.*
13:14 is *f.* prophecy of Esaias
24:34 shall not pass till all be *f.*

Mark 1:5 the time is *f.*
13:4 wh. sign when all sh. be *f. ?*
Luke 1:20 words wh. shall be *f.*
2:43 when they had *f.* the days
21:22 that all written may be *f.*
24 until times of Gentiles be *f.*
22:16 not eat till *f.* in kin. of G.
24:44 all must be *f.* spoken by M.
John 3:29 my joy therefore is *f.*
17:13 my joy *f.* in themselves
Acts 3:18 showed, he hath so *f.*
9:23 many days *f.* the Jews took
12:25 Paul and Bar. *f.* ministry
13:25 and as John *f.* his course
2:5 *f.* them in condemning him
29 when had *f.* all written
33 God hath *f.* the same to us
14:26 to grace for work they *f.*
Rom. 8:4 right. of law be *f.* in us
13:8 loveth another hath *f.* law
2 *Cor.* 10:6 when obedience is *f.*
Gal. 5:14 law is *f.* in one word
Rev. 6:11 killing of breth. be *f.*
15:8 till seven plagues were *f.*
17:17 till the words of God be *f.*
20:3 no more till 1,000 yrs. be *f.*
See SCRIPTURE.

FULFILLING.
Ps. 148:8 stormy wi. *f.* his word

Rom. 13:10 love is the *f.* of law
Eph. 2:3 *f.* desires of flesh

FULL.
Gen. 15:16 iniq. of A. not yet *f.*
25:8 Abra. old, and *f.* of years
35:29 Isa. being old, and *f.* days
41:7 thin ears dev. seven *f.* ears
Ex. 22:3 sh. make *f.* restitution
Num. 22:18 house *f.* of sil. 24:13
Jud. 6:38 bowl *f.* of water
Ruth 1:21 I went out *f.* and Lord
2:12 a *f.* reward be given thee
1 *Sam.* 18:27 in *f.* tale to king
2 *K.* 3:16 make val. *f.* of ditches
6:17 the mountain *f.* of horses
7:15 all the way *f.* of garments
10:21 house of Baal *f.*
1 *Chr.* 21:22 grant for *f.* price, 24
Job 5:26 come to grave in *f.* age
7:4 *f.* of tossings to and fro
10:15 I am *f.* of confusion, see
11:2 man *f.* of talk be justified ?
14:1 few days *f.* of trouble
20:11 bones *f.* of sins of youth
21:23 dieth in his *f.* strength
24 his breasts *f.* of milk
32:18 I am *f.* of matter
Ps. 17:14 *f.* of child. leave rest
69:20 I am *f.* of heaviness
73:10 waters of a *f.* cup wrung
74:20 *f.* of habitations of cruelty
78:25 sent them meat to the *f.*
104:16 trees of Lord are *f.* of sap
127:5 hath quiver *f.* of them
144:13 our garners may be *f.*
Prov. 17:1 house *f.* of sacrifices
27:7 *f.* soul loatheth honey-co.
20 hell and destruction never *f.*
30:9 lest I be *f.* and deny thee
Ec. 1:7 into sea, yet sea not *f.*
11:3 clouds *f.* of rain
Is. 1:11 *f.* of burnt offerings
15 your hands are *f.* of blood
11:9 earth sh. be *f.* of kno. of L.
25:6 a feast *f.* of marrow
28:8 for all table are *f.* of vomit
Jer. 6:11 I am *f.* of fury of the L.
Lam. 1:1 city that was *f.* of peo
Ezek. 1:18 rings were *f.* of eyes
10:12 wheels were *f.* of eyes
37:1 valley wh. was *f.* of bones
Joel 2:24 floors sh. be *f.* of wheat
Mic. 3:8 *f.* of power by spirit
Hab. 3:3 earth *f.* of his praise
Zec. 8:5 st. *f.* of boys and girls
Mat. 6:22 *f.* of light, *Luke* 11:36

14:20 of fragments twelve bask.
f. Mark 6:43
15:37 left seven baskets *f.*
23:25 within are *f.* of extortion
27 *f.* of dead men's bones, 28
Luke 1:57 now Eliz. *f.* time came
4:1 Jesus being *f.* of Holy Gh.
6:25 woe unto you *f.*
16:20 L. laid at gate *f.* of sores
John 1:14 among us *f.* of grace
7:8 my time is not yet *f.* come
15:11 your joy might be *f.* 16:24
Acts 2:13 men *f.* of new wine
6:3 look out men *f.* of Holy G. 5
9:36 Dorcas *f.* of good works
13:10 said, O *f.* of all subtilty
Rom. 1:29 *f.* of envy, murder
1 *Cor.* 4:8 now ye are *f.* now rich
Phil. 4:12 instructed to be *f.*
18 and abound, I am *f.*
2 *Tim.* 4:5 *f.* proof of ministry
Heb. 5:14 meat to them of *f.* age
Jam. 3:8 tongue *f.* of deadly poi.
1 *Pet.* 1:8 joy unspeak. *f.* of glo.
2 *Pet.* 2:14 eyes *f.* of adultery
1 *John* 1:4 your joy may be *f.*
Rev. 4:6 four beasts *f.* of eyes, 8
5:8 golden vials *f.* of odors
15:7 gold. vials *f.* of wrath of G.
17:3 *f.* of names of blasphemy
4 golden cup *f.* of abominat.
21:9 sev. vials *f.* of seven plag.

See ASSURANCE, COMPASSION.

Is FULL.
Ps. 10:7 mouth is *f. Rom.* 3:14
26:10 right hand is *f.* of bribes
29:4 voice of L. is *f.* of majesty
33:5 earth is *f.* of goodness of L.
65:9 river of G. wh. is *f.* of wat.
75:8 wine red, it is *f.* of mixture
104:24 earth is *f.* of thy riches
119:64 earth, O L. is *f.* of mercy
Ec. 10:14 a fool is *f.* of words
Is. 2:6 land is *f.* of silver, is *f.*
8 their land also is *f.* of idols
6:3 whole earth is *f.* of his glo.
Jer. 5:27 cage is *f.* of birds,
Ezek. 7:23 land is *f.* of crimes
9:9 land is *f.* of blood, city is *f.*
Nah. 3:1 sj all *f.* of lies and rob.
Luke 11:34 body is *f.* of light, is *f.*
39 inward part is *f.* of ravening

To the FULL.
Ex. 16:3 did eat bread *to the f.* 8
Lev. 26:5 shall eat bread *to the f.*

FULLER, S.
2 *K.* 18:17 in highway of the *f.*
field, *Is.* 7:3 ; 36:2
Mal. 3:2 like refiner's fire, *f.* soap
Mark 9:3 no *f.* on earth can wh.

FULLY.
Num. 14:24 C. that followed me *f.*
Ec. 8:11 heart of sons of m. is *f.*
Nah. 1:10 dev. as stubble *f.* dry
Acts 2:1 day of Pentec. was *f.* c.
Rom. 4:21 being *f.* persuaded,
14:5 let ev. man be *f.* persuaded
2 *Tim.* 3:10 hast *f.* kno. my doc.
Rev. 14:18 thrust sickle, grapes *f.*

FULLNESS.
1 *Chr.* 16:32 let sea roar and the
f. thereof, *Ps.* 96:11 ; 98:7
Ps. 16:11 in thy pres. is *f.* of joy
24:1 L.'s and *f.* 1 *Cor.* 10:26, 28
50:12 world mine, and *f.* 89:11
John 1:16 his *f.* have we received
Rom. 11:12 much more their *f. ?*
25 *f.* of the Gentiles be come
15:29 shall come in *f.* of gospel
Gal. 4:4 wh. *f.* of time was come
Eph. 1:10 in *f.* of times
23 *f.* of him that filleth

3:19 be filled with all *f.* of God
4:13 come to stature of *f.* of C.
Col. 1:19 in him sho. all *f.* dwell
2:9 in him dwelleth *f.* of God.

FURBISH, ED.
Jer. 46:4 *f.* spears, put on briga.
Ezek. 21:9 sword sharpened. *f.* 10
11 given to be *f.* ; 28 sword *f.*

FURIOUS.
Prov. 22:24 with *f.* man not go
29:22 *f.* man aboundeth in tran.
Ezek. 5:15 exec. judg. in *f.* 25:17
Dan. 2:12 Nebuchad. was very *f.*
Nah. 1:2 Lord revengeth and is *f.*

FURIOUSLY.
2 *K.* 9:20 like Jehu, he driveth *f.*

FURLONGS.
Luke 24:13 Emmaus from J. 60 *f.*
John 6:19 had rowed about 25 *f.*
11:18 Bethany nigh J. abo. 15 *f.*
Rev. 14:20 by space of 1,600 *f.*
21:16 he measured city, 12,000 *f.*

FURNACE, S.
Gen. 15:17 smoking *f.* burning
19:28 smoke went as smo. of *f.*
Ex. 9:8 handf. of ashes of *f.* 10
19:18 ascended as smoke of *f.*
Deut. 4:20 L. hath taken out of *f.*
1 *K.* 8:51 fr. midst of *f. Jer.* 11:4
Neh. 3:11 rep. tower of *f.* 12:38
Ps. 12:6 silver tried in *f.* of earth
Prov. 17:3 *f.* for gold, 27:21
Is. 31:9 fire in Zion, *f.* in Jerusa.
48:10 chosen in *f.* of affliction
Ezek. 22:18 Is. dross in mid. of *f.*
20 as tin in the midst of *f.* 22
Dan. 3:6 in midst of fiery *f.* 11
Mat. 13:42 cast into *f.* of fire, 50
Rev. 1:15 feet as if burned in a *f.*
9:2 as the smoke of a great *f.*

FURNISH.
Deut. 15:14 thou shalt *f.* him
Ps. 78:19 G. *f.* table in wilder. ?
Is. 65:11 *f.* the drink-offering
Jer. 46:19 *f.* to go into captivity

FURNISHED.
1 *K.* 9:11 Hiram *f.* Sol. with ced.
Prov. 9:2 hath also *f.* her table
Mat. 22:10 wed. *f.* with guests
Mark 14:15 a room *f. Luke* 22:12
2 *Tim.* 3:17 *f.* unto all good wor.

FURNITURE.
Gen. 31:34 Rachel put in cam. *f.*
Ex. 31:7 and his *f.* 39:33
35:14 the candlestick and his *f.*
Nah. 2:9 end of all pleasant *f.*

FURROW, S.
Job 31:38 or *f.* thereof complain
39:10 canst bind unicorn in *f. ?*
Ps. 65:10 thou settlest *f.* thereof
129:3 plough. made long their *f.*
Ezek. 17:7 might water it by *f.*
10 it shall wither in the *f.*
Hos. 10:4 hemlock in *f.* of field
12:11 their altars as heaps in *f.*

FURTHER.
Job 38:11 hither. come, but no *f.*
40:5 but I will proceed no *f.*
Ec. 12:12 *f.* my son, be admon.
Mat. 26:65 what *f.* need of wit. ?
Mark 14:63 ; *Luke* 22:71

Luke 24:28 tho' he would gone *f.*
Acts 4:17 spread no *f.* am. people
24:4 be not *f.* tedious unto thee
27:28 gone a little *f.* th. sounded
2 *Tim.* 3:9 shall proceed no *f.*
Heb. 7:11 what *f.* need an. priest

FURTHER, ED, Verb.

Ezr. 8:36 *f.* peo. and house of G.
Ps. 140:8 O L. *f.* not wicked dev.

FURTHERANCE.

Phil. 1:12 rather to *f.* of gospel
25 sh. abide with you for yo. *f.*

FURTHERMORE.

Ex. 4:6 Lord said *f.* to Moses
Ezek. 8:6 Lord said *f.* to Ezekiel

FURY.

Gen. 27:44 thy brother's *f.* turn
Job 20:23 God cast *f.* of wrath
Is. 27:4 *f.* is not in me
34:2 his *f.* is upon their armies
51:13 bec. of *f.* of oppressor;
and where is *f.* of oppressor?

17 *Jer.* wh. has drunk cup of *f.*
20 are full of *f.* of the Lord
22 even dregs of cup of my *f.*
59:18 repay *f.* to adversaries
63:3 trample them in my *f.*
5 my *f.* it upheld me, 6
Jer. 4:4 lest my *f.* come like fire
6:11 I am full of *f.* of the Lord
21:5 will fight against you in *f.*
12 lest my *f.* go out like fire
23:19 gone forth in *f.* 30:23
25:15 the wine-cup of this *f.*
36:7 great *f.* L. hath pronounced
Lam. 4:11 L. hath accomplish. *f.*
Ezek. 5:13 cause my *f.* to rest
6:12 will I accomplish my *f.*

8:18 therefore will I deal in *f.*
13:13 stormy wind in my *f.*
16:38 I will give thee blood in *f.*
19:12 she was plucked up in *f.*
20:33 with *f.* pou. out will I rule
21:17 I will cause my *f.* to rest
24:8 it might cause *f.* to rest
13 till I have caused *f.* to rest
38:18 that my *f.* shall come up
Dan. 3:13 Nebuchadnez. in *f.* 19
8:6 ran unto him in the *f.*
9:16 let thy *f.* be turned away
11:44 shall go forth with great *f.*
Mic. 5:15 execute *f.* on heathen
Zec. 8:2 jealous with great *f.*
See POUR, POURED.

G

GAAL. *Jud.* 9:41
GABBATHA. *John* 19:13
GABRIEL. *Dan.* 8:16; 9:21;
Luke 1:19, 26

GAD.

Gen. 30:11 she called his name G.
35:26 sons of Zilp. G. and Asher
46:16 the sons of G. *Num.* 1:24;
26:15, 18
49:19 G. a troop shall overcome
Num. 1:14 prin. of G. 2:14; 7:42
32:1 ch. of G. had cat. 2, 29, 33
Deut. 27:13 mount E. to curse G.
Jos. 4:12 children of G. passed
over
22:9 chil. of G. returned fr. Shi.
2 *Sam.* 24:11 G. D.'s seer, 1 *Chr.*
29:9
1 *Chr.* 29:29 in book of G. 12:14
Ezek. 48:27 a portion for G. 34

Tribe of GAD.

Num. 1:25 of *t.* of G. 45,650, 2:14
Jos. 20:8 out of the *tribe of* G.
Rev. 7:5 *tribe of* G. sealed 12,000

GADARENES. *Mark* 5:1; *Luke*
8:26, 37

GADDEST.

Jer. 2:36 why g. thou to change?

GADITE, S.

Deut. 3:12 land gave I unto G. 16
1 *Chr.* 12:8 G. separated, 26:32

GAIN, Substantive.

Jud. 5:19 kings of C. took no g.
Job 22:3 it g. to make way per. ?
Prov. 1:19 every one greedy of g.
3:14 g. is better than fine gold
15:27 is greedy of g. troubleth
28:8 by unjust g. increaseth
Is. 33:15 despis. g. of oppression
56:11 for his g. from quarter
Ezek. 22:13 smit. hand at dish. g.
27 princes wolves to get dis. g.
Dan. 11:39 divide land for g.
Mic. 4:13 I will consec. g. to L.
Acts 16:16 bro. masters much g.
19:24 no small g. to craftsmen
2 *Cor.* 12:17 did I make g. of y. ?
18 Titus make a g. of you?
Phil. 1:21 live is Christ, die is g.
3:7 what things were g. to me
1 *Tim.* 6:5 supposing g. is godli.
6 godliness with content. is g.
Jam. 4:13 buy, sell, and get g.

GAIN, Verb.

Dan. 2:8 that ye would g. time
Mat. 16:26 g. who. wor. and lose
soul, *Mark* 8:36; *Luke* 9:25
1 *Cor.* 9:19 I might g. the more
20 might g. Jews; 22 g. weak
21 might g. them without law

GAINED.

Job 27:8 wh. hope tho' hath g. ?
Ezek. 22:12 thou hast greedily g.

Mat. 18:15 hast g. thy brother
25:17 that received two g. 22
20 have g. besides five talents
Luke 19:15 how much ev. man g.
16 Lord, thy pound hath g. ten
18 Lord, thy pound hath g. five
Acts 27:21 to have g. this harm

GAINS.

Acts 16:19 hope of g. was gone

GAINSAY, ERS.

Luke 21:15 advers. not able to g.
Tit. 1:9 might be able to conv. g.

GAINSAYING.

Acts 10:29 came I to you with. g.
Rom. 10:21 hands to a g. people
Jude 11 perished in g. of Korah

GAIUS.

Acts 19:29 G. man of Macedonia
20:4 G. of Derbe accompan. P.
Rom. 16:23 G. host saluteth you
1 *Cor.* 1:14 I baptiz. none but G.
3 *John* 1 un. the well-beloved G.

GALATIA.

Acts 16:6; 1 *Cor.* 16:1; 2 *Tim.* 4:10
1 *Pet.* 1:1 scat. through Pont. G.

GALATIANS. *Gal.* 3:1
GALBANUM. *Ex.* 30:34
GALEED. *Jos.* 31:47, 48

GALILEE.

Jos. 20:7 G. for a city of refuge
1 *K.* 9:11 gave H. 20 cities in G.
Is. 9:1 did more afflict her in G.
Mat. 2:22 J. in the parts of G.
3:13 cometh J. fr. G. *Mark* 1:9
4:15 G. of Gent 21:11 Js. of G.
15:29 sea of G. 26:32; 27:55
Mark 1:39 throughout N. G. 15:41
Luke 4:14, 44; 23:5, 55; *John*
7:41, 52
Acts 1:11 men of G. ; 5:37 G. rose
9:31 churches rest through. G.
10:37 word began from G.
13:31 seen of them from G.

GALILEAN, S.

Mark 14:70 art a G. *Luke* 22:59
Luke 13:1 told him of the G.
23:6 asked whe. man were a G.
John 4:45 was come. G. rec. him
Acts 2:7 all these that speak, G. ?

GALL.

Deut. 29:18 a root that beareth g.
32:32 grapes are grapes of g.
Job 16:13 he poureth out my g.
20:14 his meat is the g. of asps
25 sword cometh out of his g.
Ps. 69:21 gave me g. for meat
Jer. 8:14 G. hath given water g.
9:15 will give water of g. 23:15
Lam. 3:5 compassed me with g.
19 remembering worm. and g.
Amos 6:12 turned judg. into g.
Mat. 27:34 vine. mingled with g,
Acts 8:23 art in g. of bitterness

GALLANT.

Is. 33:21 nor shall g. ship pass

GALLERY, IES.

Cant. 7:5 king is held in the g.
Ezek. 41:15 measured g. thereof
42:3 against pave. g. against g.

GALLEY.

Is. 33:21 wherein shall go no g.

GALLIM.

1 *Sam.* 25:44 Phal. of G. *Is.* 10:30

GALLIO. *Acts* 18:12, 17

GALLOWS.

Est. 6:4 to hang Mordecai on g.
7:10 hanged Haman on g. 8:7
9:13 ten sons be hanged on g. 25

GAMALIEL.

Num. 1:10; 2:20; 7:54, 59; 10:23
Acts 5:34 P. named G. ; 23:3 feet

GAMMADIM. *Ezek.* 27:11

GAP, S.

Ezek. 13:5 have not gone up to g.
22:30 that should stand in g.

GAPED.

Job 16:10 ha. g. on me. *Ps.* 22:13

GARDEN.

Gen. 2:15 and put him in the g.
3:23 Lord sent him forth from g.
13:10 as g. of Lord, *Is.* 51:3
Deut. 11:10 waterest it as g.
1 *K.* 21:2 may have it for g.
Job 8:16 branch shoot. in his g.
Cant. 4:12 g. enclosed is my sis.
16 blow on g. let him come g.
5:1 I am come into my g.
6:2 my beloved gone to his g. 11
Is. 1:8 daugh. of Z. as lodge in g.
30 as a g. which hath no water
58:11 shalt be like a watered g.
61:11 g. causeth things sown
Jer. 31:12 souls be as a watered g.
Lam. 2:6 taberna. as it were of g.
Ezek. 28:13 in Eden the g. of G.
31:8 cedars in g. of G. not hide
9 trees in g. of God envied him
36:35 desolate land like g. of E.
Joel 2:3 land as g. of Eden before
Luke 13:19 took and cast into g.
John 18:1 over Ced. where was g.
26 did not I see thee in the g. ?
19:41 a g. and in g. a sepulchre

GARDENS.

Num. 24:6 as g. by river side
Ec. 2:5 I made me g. and orch.
Cant. 4:15 a fountain of g.
6:2 feed in g. and gather lilies
8:13 thou that dwellest in the g.
Is. 1:29 sh. be confounded for g.
65:3 a peo. that sacrificeth in g.
66:17 purify themselves in g.
Jer. 29:5 plant g. eat fruit, 28
Amos 4:9 blasting, when g. incr.
9:14 they shall also make g.

GARDENER.

John 20:15 supposing he been *g.*

GARLANDS.

Acts 14:13 priest bro. oxen and *g.*

GARLICK.

Num. 11:5 we rem. *g.* eat in Eg.

GARMENT.

Gen. 9:23 Sh. and Japhet took *g*
25:25 first red, like a hairy *g.*
39:12 caught Joseph by his *g.*
15 he left his *g.* with me, 18
16 laid up his *g.* till lord came
Lev. 13:47 *g.* wh. plag. of lep. 49
51 if plague be spread in the *g*
59 plague of lep. in *g.* 14:55
15:17 *g.* whereon seed of copula.
19:19 *g.* mingled, *Deut.* 22:11
Deut. 22:5 man not put on w. *g*
Jos. 7:21 a goodly Babylonish *g.*
Jud. 8:25 spread *g.* and cast
1 *K.* 11:29 Jero. clad with new *g.*
Ezr. 9:5 rent *g.* and mantle
Est. 8:15 Mor. went *g.* of purple
Job 13:28 a *g.* that is moth-eaten
30:18 by force of dis. *g.* changed
38:9 I made the cloud the *g.*
41:13 can discover face of *g.* *?*
Ps. 69:11 I made sackcloth my *g.*
73:6 violence cover. them as *g.*
102:26 wax old like *g.* *Is.* 50:9;
51:6 ; *Heb.* 1:11
104:2 cov. with lights as with *g.*
6 cov. with the deep as with *g.*
109:18 clothed with cursing as *g.*
Prov. 20:16 *g.* is surety, 27:13
25:20 taketh *g.* in cold weather
30:4 hath bound waters in a *g.* *?*
31:5 moth sh. eat them like *g.*
61:3 *g.* of praise for spirit
Ezek. 18:7 cov. naked with *g.* 16
Dan. 7:9 *g.* was white as snow
Mic. 2:8 pull off robe with the *g.*
Hag. 2:12 holy flesh in skirt of *g.*
Zec. 13:4 nei. shall wear rough *g.*
Mal. 2:16 cover. violence with *g.*
Mat. 9:16 new cloth to old *g.*
Mark 2:21 ; *Luke* 5:36
20 touched hem of *g.* 21 ; 14:36 ;
Mark 5:27 ; *Luke* 8:44
22:11 had not wedding *g.* 12
Mark 13:16 not turn back take *g.*
Luke 22:36 let him sell *g.*
Acts 12:8 cast thy *g.* about thee
Jude 23 hating *g.* spotted by fle.
Rev. 1:13 clothed with *g.*

GARMENTS.

Gen. 35:2 clean, change your *g.*
38:14 Tamar put widow's *g.* off
49:11 washed his *g.* in wine
Ex. 28:3 Aaron's *g.* 20 consecrate
29:21 blood on A.'s *g.* *Lev.* 8:30
Lev. 6:11 *g.* on other *g.* 16:23, 24
Num. 15:38 fringes in bord. of *g.*
20:26 strip A. of *g.* put on E. 28
Jos. 9:5 Gibeonites brou. old *g.*
1 *Sam.* 18:4 J. gave David his *g.*
2 *Sam.* 10:4 cut off their *g.* in the
middle, 1 *Chr.* 19:4
2 *K.* 5:26 is it time to receive *g.*
7:15 all the way was full of *g.*
Ezr. 2:69 gave 100 priests' *g.*
Neh. 7:70 Tirsh. 530 priests' *g.*
72 the peo. gave 67 priests' *g.*
Job 37:17 *g.* warm, when quieteth
Ps. 2:18 part my *g.* among them
45:8 all thy *g.* smell of myrrh
133:2 ointm. went to skirt of *g.*
Ec. 9:8 let thy *g.* be alw. white
Cant. 4:11 smell of *g.* smell of L.
Is. 9:5 battle is *g.* rolled in blood
52:1 put on beautiful *g.* O Jer.
59:6 their webs sh. not beco. *g.*
17 put on the *g.* of vengeance.
61:10 clothed me with *g.* of sal.
63:1 cometh with dyed *g.* 3
Ezek. 16:18 took. thy broidered *g.*

42:14 there shall lay their *g.*
Dan. 3:21 in coats and other *g.*
Joel 2:13 rend heart, and not *g.*
Zec. 3:3 J. clothed wi. filthy *g.* 4
Mat. 21:8 spread *g.* *Mark* 11:8
23:5 they enlarge borders of *g.*
27:35 parted his *n.* *Mark* 15:24
Mark 10:50 Bartim. casting his *g.*
11:7 cast *g.* on colt, *Luke* 19:35
Luke 24:4 two men in shining *g.*
John 13:4 laid aside *g.* and took
Acts 9:39 coats and *g.* Dor. made
Jam. 5:2 your *g.* are moth-eaten
Rev. 3:4 few names not defiled *g.*
16:15 blessed that keepeth his *g.*

Holy GARMENTS.

Ex. 28:2 make *h. g.* for Aaron, 4
31:10 wisdom to make *holy g.*
Lev. 16:4 *h. g.* he sh. wash, 32

GARNER, S.

Ps. 144:13 our *g.* may be full
Joel 1:17 the *g.* are laid desolate
Mat. 3:12 wheat into *g.* *Lu.* 3:17

GARNISH, ED.

2 *Chr.* 3:6 he *g.* the house with
Job 26:13 by S. he *g.* heavens
Mat. 12:44 sw. and *g.* *Luke* 11:25
23:29 *g.* sepulchres of righteous
Rev. 21:19 foundations of wall *g.*

GARRISON, S.

1 *Sam.* 10:5 hill where *g.* of Phil.
13:3 Jonathan smote *g.* of Phil.
14:1 to the Philistines' *g.* 6
15 the *g.* and spoilers trembled
2 *Sam.* 8:6 David put *g.* in Syria,
1 *Chr.* 18:6
14 put *g.* in Ed. 1 *Chr.* 18:13
23:14 *g.* of Philistines was then
in Bethlehem, 1 *Chr.* 11:16
2 *Chr.* 17:2 Jehosh. set *g.* in Ju.
Ezek. 26:11 strong *g.* go down
2 *Cor.* 11:32 gov. kept city wi. *g.*

GAT.

2 *Sam.* 8:13 David *g.* him a name
1 *K.* 1:1 cov. him, but *g.* no heat
Ps. 116:3 pains of hell *g.* hold
Ec. 2:8 I *g.* men-singers
Lam. 5:9 *g.* our bread with peril

GATE.

Gen. 22:17 poss. *g.* of enem. 24:60
28:17 this is the *g.* of heaven
Ex. 32:27 go in and out *g.* to *g.*
Deut. 21:19 bring him to *g.*
Jud. 16:3 Sams. took doors of *g.*
Ruth 4:1 then went Boaz to *g.*
2 *Sam.* 23:15 water of Bethlehem
by *g.* 16 ; 1 *Chr.* 11:18
2 *K.* 7:17 lord have charge of *g.*
1 *Chr.* 26:13 cast lots for every *g.*
Neh. 13:19 commanded *g.* be shut
Est. 4:2 M. before king's *g.* 6:12
Ps. 118:20 his *g.* of the Lord
Is. 14:31 howl, O *g.* cry, O city
24:12 *g.* smit. with destruction
28:6 turn battle to the *g.*
Lam. 5:14 elders have ceased
from *g.*
Ezek. 11:1 at door of *g.* 25 men
43:4 glory of Lord by way of *g.*
44:2 this *g.* shall be shut, none
45:19 put blood on posts of *g.*
46:1 *g.* of inner court be shut, 2
48:31 one *g.* of R. one *g.* of Ju.
Mic. 1:9 come into *g.* of my peo.
Mat. 7:13 enter in at straight *g.*
wide is *g.* broad is way, 14 ;
Luke 13:24
Luke 7:12 came nigh *g.* of city
16:20 beggar Lazarus laid at *g.*
Acts 10:17 men fr. C. stood be. *g.*
12:10 the iron *g.* wh. opened.
14 Rhoda opened not *g.*
Heb. 13:12 J. suffered without *g.*
Rev. 21:21 several *g.* of one pearl

See ENTERING, ENTERETH.

His GATE.

Prov. 17:19 exalteth *h. g.*

At the GATE.

2 *K.* 11:6 at the *g.* of Sur. third
at the *g.* 2 *Chr.* 23:5
2 *Chr.* 24:8 at *g.* of house of L.
Est. 5:13 M. sitting at king's *g.*
Acts 3:2 daily at *g.* of temple
10 sat for alms at beautiful *g.*

High GATE.

2 *Chr.* 23:20 came thro. *high g.*
27:3 Joth. built *high g.* of house
Jer. 20:2 Jerem. in stocks in *h. g.*

In the GATE.

Gen. 19:1 Lot sat in the *g.* of So.
Ex. 32:26 M. stood in *g.* of camp
Jud. 16:2 laid wait for S. in *t. g.*
Ruth 4:11 peo. in *g.* said
2 *Sam.* 3:27 J. took Abner in *t. g.*
2 *K.* 7:20 peo. trod on him in *t. g.*
Est. 2:19 sat in *t.* king's *g.* 21
5:9 Ha. saw him in *t.* king's *g.*
Job 5:4 children crushed in *t. g.*
31:21 I saw my help in the *g.*
Ps. 69:12 sit in *t. g.*
127:5 speak with enemies in *g.*
Prov. 22:22 oppress afflic. in *t. g.*
Is. 29:21 snare for him rep. in *g.*
Jer. 7:2 in *t. g.* of Lord's house
38:7 king sitting in *t. g.* of B.
Dan. 2:49 Daniel sat in *t. g.*
Amos 5:10 him that rebuk. in *g.*
12 they turn aside poor in *t. g.*
15 establish judgment in the *g.*

Old GATE.

Neh. 3:6 *old g.* repaired Jehoiada
12:39 priests went above *old g.*

Prison GATE.

Neh. 12:39 th. stood still in *p. g.*

Sheep GATE.

Neh. 12:39 went even unto *s. g.*

Valley GATE.

2 *Chr.* 26:9 U. built tew. at *v. g.*
Neh. 2:13 went out by *g.* of *v.* 15
3:13 *valley g.* repaired Hanun

Water GATE.

Neh. 3:26 Nethin. dwelt ag. *w. g*
8:1 street before *water g.* 3, 16
12:37 priests went even to *w. g.*

GATES.

Deut. 12:12 rejoice with. your *g.*
Jos. 6:26 in youngest son set up
g. 1 *K.* 16:34
Jud. 5:8 new gods, war in *g.*
11 people of Lord shall go to *g.*
2 *Chr.* 31:2 A. app. to prai. in *g.*
Neh. 1:3 *g.* burnt, 2:3 13, 17
12:30 priests and Lev. purifi. *g.* 9
Ps. 9:14 thy praise in the *g.*
24:7 lift up your heads, O ye *g.*
87:2 Lord loveth the *g.* of Zion
100:4 enter into *g.* with thanks.
107:16 he hath broken *g.* of br.
118:19 open *g.* of righteousness
Prov. 1:21 in opening of *g.* 8:3
8:34 watching daily at my *g.*
14:19 wicked at *g.* of righteous
31:23 husband is known in *g.*
31 let own works praise in *g.*
Is. 3:26 and her *g.* shall lament
26:2 open *g.* righteous may ent.
38:10 I shall go to *g.* of grave
45:1 open bef. him two-leaved *g.*
2 I will break the *g.* of brass
62:10 go through, go through *g.*
Jer. 14:2 Jud. mourn. *g.* languish
15:7 fan them with fan in *g.*
17:21 no burden on sab. by *g.* 24
25 then shall enter into *g.* 22:4
22:19 cast forth beyond the *g.*
Lam. 1:4 Zion's *g.* are desolate
2:9 her *g.* are sunk into ground

Ezek. 21:15 point of sw. ag. th. *g.*
22 battering rams aga. the *g.*
26:2 broken that was *g.* of peo.
Ob. 11 foreigners entered *g.*
Nah. 2:6 *g.* of rivers sh. be open.
Zec. 8:16 truth and peace in *g.*
Mat. 16:18 *g.* of hell not prevail
Acts 9:24 they watched *g.*
Rev. 21:12 city had twelve *g.* at
g. twelve angels
13 east thr. *g.* on north thr. *g.*
21 twelve *g.* were twel. pearls
25 *g.* of it shall not be shut

See BARS, DEATH.

Thy GATES.
Ex. 20:10 str. wi. *t. g. Deut.* 5:14
Deut. 6:9 write them *t. g.* 11:20
12:15 eat flesh in *t. g.* 17, 18, 21
14:21 str. in *t. g.* ; 27 Le. in *t. g.*
28 tithe in *t. g.* ; 29 wid. in *t. g.*
16:5 passover in *thy g.* ; Levite
in *thy g.* 14 ; 26:12
31:12 gather peo. within *t. g.*
Ps. 122:2 feet stand wi. *t. g.* O J.
Is. 54:12 I will make *t. g.* of car.
60:11 *thy g.* sh. be open contin.
18 walls salvation, *thy g.* praise

GATH.
1 *Sam.* 5:8 ark be car. to G. 6:17
2 *Sam.* 1:20 tell it not in G.
21:22 to giant in G. 1 *Chr.* 20:8
2 *K.* 12:17 Hazael fought ag. G.
1 *Chr.* 18:1
Amos 6:2 to G. of Philistines
Mic. 1:10 declare ye it not at G.

GATHER.
Gen. 31:46 *g.* stones, th. took st.
41:35 *g.* all food of those years
Ex. 5:7 *g.* straw ; 12 *g.* stubble
9:19 *g.* cattle ; 16:4 *g.* cer. rate
16:5 *g.* twice as m. ; 26 six da. *g.*
23:10 six y. sow and *g. Lev.* 25:3
Lev. 19:9 sh. not *g.* glean. 23:22
10 thou sh. not *g.* every grape
Num. 10:4 trumpet, princes *g.*
11:16 *g.* seventy men of elders
19:9 man clean *g.* ashes
Deut. 28:30 vine. and not *g.* 39
38 much seed out, *g.* little in
30:3 *g.* from all nations, *Ezek.*
36:34
2 *K.* 4:39 went to field to *g.* her.
22:20 *g.* to fathers, 2 *Chr.* 34:28
2 *Chr.* 24:5 *g.* money to rep. ho.
Job 24:6 *g.* vintage of wicked
34:14 *g.* to himself his spirit
39:12 seed, and *g.* it into barn ?
Ps. 26:9 *g.* not soul wi. sinners
104:28 that givest them they *g.*
106:47 *g.* us from am. heathen
Prov. 28:8 *g.* for him pity poor
Ec. 2:26 travail to *g.* and heap
Is. 34:15 owl *g.* under shadow
40:11 shall *g.* lambs with arms
43:5 will *g.* thee from the west
54:7 with great mercies will I *g.*
62:10 highway, *g.* out the stones
66:18 will *g.* all nations
Jer. 6:1 *g.* to flee ; 7:18 chil. *g.* w.
9:22 none sh. *g.* ; 10:17 *g.* up w.
29:14 *g.* you from all nations
31:8 *g.* from coasts of earth,
32:37 ; *Ezek.* 20:34, 41 ; 34:13
31:10 scatter Israel will *g.* him
Ezek. 11:17 will *g.* you fr. people
16:37 I will *g.* all thy lovers
22:19 will *g.* you to midst of J.
20 as *g.* silver so I *g.* you, 21
24:4 *g.* pieces ; 29:13 will *g.* Eg.
Hos. 8:10 hired am. nat. I will *g.*
9:6 Egypt shall *g.* them up.
Joel 2:6 faces shall *g.* blackness
16 *g.* people, *g.* children
3:2 I will *g.* all nations
Mic. 2:12 I will *g.* remnant of Is.
4:6 *g.* her driven, *Zep.* 3:19

12 he shall *g.* them as sheaves
5:1 *g.* in troops, O da. of troops
Nah. 2:10 faces of all *g.* blackn.
Hab. 1:9 they shall *g.* captivity
15 and *g.* them in their drag.
Zep. 3:18 will *g.* th. are sorrow.
Zec. 10:8 I will hiss and *g.* 10
Mat. 3:12 *g.* wheat, *Luke* 3:17
6:26 nor do they *g.* into barns
7:16 *g.* grapes of th. ? *Luke* 6:44
13:28 wilt thou that we *g.* them
29 while ye *g.* up the tares
30 burn tares but *g.* the wheat
41 shall *g.* out of his kingdom
25:26 I *g.* wh. I have not strewed
Luke 13:34 as hen doth *g.* brood
John 6:12 *g.* fragments that rem.
15:6 men *g.* them and cast them
Rev. 14:8 *g.* clusters of vine
16:14 *g.* them to battle of that
day

GATHER together.
Gen. 34:30 few they shall *g.*
49:1 *g.* selves to. ye sons of J. 2
Lev. 8:3 *g.* congregation of Israel
together, Num. 8:9
Num. 21:16 *g.* people *together,*
Deut. 4:10 ; 31:12
2 *Sam.* 12:28 *g.* the rest *together*
1 *Chr.* 16:35 O God, and *g.* us *to.*
22:2 com. to *g.* stOp. strangers
Est. 2:3 *g. together* fair virgins
4:16 *g. tog.* Jews in Shushan
Job 11:10 if he *g. t.* who hinder
Ps. 50:5 *g.* saints *tog.* unto me
104:22 they *g.* themselves *tog.*
Ec. 3:5 a time to *g.* stones *tog.*
Is. 11:12 *g. to.* dispersed of Jud.
49:18 *g. to.* come to me, 60:4
Jer. 4:5 blow trumpet, cry *g. to.*
Zep. 2:1 *g. to.* yea, *g. to.* O nat.
Mat. 13:30 *g. together* first tares
24:31 *g. t.* his elect, *Mark* 13:27
John 11:52 *g. t.* in one, *Eph.* 1:10

Rev. 19:17 *g. to.* to supper of G.
20:8 to *g.* Gog and Magog *tog.*

GATHERED.
Gen. 25:8 Abr. was *g.* to his peo.
17 Ishmael *g.* ; 35:29 Isaac *g.*
49:29 J. was *g.* to his people, 33,
Ex. 16:18 he that *g.* much, he
that *g.* little 2 *Cor.* 8:15
Lev. 23:39 when ye have *g.*
Num. 11:32 *g.* qu. ? 15:32 *g.* stic.
20:24 Aaron be *g.* to people, 26
27:13 Moses *g.* to his people,
312 ; *Deut.* 32:50
Jud. 1:7 *g.* meat under table
3:13 Abiezer was *g.* after him
1 *Sam.* 5:8 th. *g.* lords of Philist.
22:2 ev. one in distress *g.* to D.
2 *Sam.* 14:14 wat. spilt can. be *g.*
2 *K.* 22:20 Josiah be *g.* to grave
in peace, 2 *Chr.* 34:28
Job 27:19 rich lie, but not be *g.*
Ps. 107:3 *g.* them out of lands
Prov. 27:25 herbs of mount. are *g.*
30:4 hath *g.* wind in fists?
Is. 5:2 and *g.* out the stones
10:14 gathereth eggs, have I *g.*
27:12 *g.* one by one, O Israel
34:15 vultures *g.* ; 16 Sp. *g.*
49:5 Is. not *g.* yet I be glorious
Jer. 3:17 all nations be *g.*
Ezek. 28:25 wh. I have *g.* hon. of
38:13 hast thou *g.* thy company
39:28 have *g.* them to own land
Mic. 7:1 wh. *g.* sum. of fruits
Mat. 13:40 as tares are *g.*
47 net cast and *g.* of every kind
25:32 bef. him be *g.* all nations
27:27 *g.* to him the whole band
John 11:47 *g.* chief priests and
Acts 28:3 Paul *g.* bundle of sticks
Rev. 14:19 angel *g.* vine of earth

GATHERED together.
Ex. 8:14 *g.* them *to.* on heaps
Num. 11:32 fish of sea be *g. tog.*
Jud. 20:1 congreg. *g. tog.* as one
man, 11 ; *Ezr.* 3:1 ; *Neh.* 8:1
Job 30:7 under nettles were *g. t.*
Ps. 47:9 princes of peo. are *g. t.*
102:22 people *g. tog.* to serve L.
Hos. 1:11 chil. of Judah be *g. t.*
Zec. 12:3 tho. all people be *g. t.*
Mat. 18:20 two or three are *g. t.*
23:37 how often would I have *g.*
children *to. Luke* 13:34
24:28 be *g. tog. Luke* 17:37
Mark 1:33 all the city was *g. t.*
Luke 15:13 younger son *g.* all *t.*
Acts 4:26 rulers *g. to.* against L.
12:12 many *g. together* praying
1 *Cor.* 5:4 *g. t.* and my spirit
Rev. 16:16 *g. t.* into pl. Armaged.
19:19 beast and army *g. t.*

GATHERER, s.
Jer. 6:9 hand as grape *g.* into
49:9 if grape *g.* come, *Ob.* 5
Amos 7:14 I was *g.* of sycamore

GATHERETH.
Num. 19:10 that *g.* ashes shall
Ps. 33:7 *g.* waters of sea together
41:6 heart *g.* iniquity to itself
147:2 *g.* outcasts of Is. *Is.* 56:8
Prov. 6:8 ant *g.* food in harvest
10:5 that *g.* in summer is wise
Is. 10:14 one *g.* eggs th. are left
17:5 when the harvest-man *g.*
Hab. 2:5 *g.* to him all nations
Mat. 12:30 *g.* not scat. *Luke* 11:23
23:37 as a hen *g.* her chickens
John 4:36 he that reapeth *g.* fruit

GATHERING, s.
Gen. 49:10 to him shall *g.* of peo.
Num. 15:33 found him *g.* sticks
1 *K.* 17:10 widow was *g.* sticks
Is. 33:4 spoil like *g.* of caterpil.
Mat. 25:24 *g.* where not strewed
Acts 16:10 assuredly *g.* L. called
1 *Cor.* 16:2 be no *g.* wh. I come

GAVE.
Gen. 2:20 Ad. *g.* names to cattle
3:12 woman *g.* me of the tree
14:20 *g.* tithes of all, *Heb.* 7:2, 4
Jos. 21:44 L. *g.* them rest, 2 *Chr.*
15:15 ; 20:30
1 *Sam.* 10:9 G. *g.* Saul ano. heart
Job 1:21 L. *g.* Lord hath taken
Ps. 18:13 Highest *g.* his voice
69:21 *g.* me gall, *g.* vinegar
Ec. 12:7 spir. return to G. th. *g.*
Is. 43:3 I *g.* Egypt for ransom
50:6 I *g.* my back to the smiters
Ezek. 20:12 I *g.* them my sab. 25
Hos. 13:11 I *g.* thee a king in
anger
Mat. 14:19 *g.* loaves to disciples,
15:36 ; 26:26 ; *Mark* 6:41 ; 8:6 ;
14:22 ; *Luke* 9:16 ; 22:19

Mat. 21:23 who *g.* thee authority ? *Mark* 11:28 ; *Luke* 20:2
25:35 ye *g.* me meat, *g.* drink
John 1:12 *g.* he power to bec. so.
3:16 G. so loved w. he *g.* Son
10:29 Fa. who *g.* them me is
14:31 as Father *g.* me command.
Acts 2:4 to speak as Sp. *g.* utter
1 *Cor.* 3:6 watered, but G. *g.* inc.
2 *Cor.* 8:5 but first *g.* selves to L.
Gal. 1:4 *g.* him for sins, *Tit.* 2:14
2:20 loved me, *g.* himself for me
Eph. 1:22 *g.* him to be head over
4:8 captive and *g.* gifts
11 he *g.* some apostles, some
5:25 loved church *g.* hims. for
1 *Tim.* 2:6 *g.* himself ransom
Rev. 13:2 dragon *g.* him power

GAVE up.
Gen. 25:8 Abraham *g. up* ghost
17 Ishmael ; 35:29 Isaac *g. up*

GAVE

Lam. 1:19 my elders *g. up* ghost
Mark 15:37 J *g. up* ghost, 39 ;
   Luke 23:46 ; *John* 19:30
Acts 5:5 An. *g. up* gh. ; 12:23 He.
Rev. 20:13 the sea *g. up* the dead

GAVEST.

Gen. 3:12 wom. whom thou *g.*
1 *K.* 8:34 land which thou *g.* to
   fathers, 40, 48 ; 2 *Cor.* 6:25,
   31, 38 ; *Neh.* 9:35
Neh. 9:20 *g.* Spirit, *g.* water for
   22 *g.* kingdoms ; 27 *g.* saviours
Ps. 21:4 he asked life, th. *g.* it
Luke 7:44 *g.* me no water, 45
John 17:4 I finis. work thou *g.*
   12 those thou *g.* I have kept
   22 the glory thou *g.* I have *g.*
18:9 thou *g.* me ha. I lost none

GAY.

Jam. 2:3 that weareth *g.* cloth.

GAZA.

Jud. 16:1 Samson went to G.
Jer. 47:1 Pharaoh smote G. 5
Amos 1:7 send fire on wall of G.
Zec. 9:5 king sh. perish from G.
Acts 8:26 goeth from Jeru. to G.

GAZE.

Ex. 19:21 break thro' to L. to *g.*

GAZING.

Nah. 3:6 I will set thee *g.* stock
Acts 1:11 why stand ye *g.* to h. ?
Heb. 10:33 were made *g.* stock

GEBA.

Jos. 21:17 G. with, 1 *Chr.* 6:60
1 *K.* 15:22 Asa b. G. 2 *Chr.* 16:6
Is. 10:29 taken lodging at G.
Zec. 14:10 be as plain from G.

GEBAL. *Ps.* 83:7 ; *Ezek.* 27:9
GEBIM. *Is.* 10:31

GEDALIAH.

2 *K.* 25:24 G. sware, *Jer.* 40:9
1 *Chr.* 25:3 G. and Z. *Ezr.* 10:18
Jer. 38:1 G. son of Pashur heard
   41:2 Ishmael smote G. 43:6
Zep. 1:1 son of Cushi, son of G.

GEHAZI. 2 *K.* 4:12, 27 ; 5:21,
   25 ; 8:4

GEMARIAH. *Jer.* 29:3 ; 36:25

GENDER.

Lev. 19:19 sh. not let cat. *g.* wi.
2 *Tim.* 2:23 knowing th. *g.* str.

GENDERED. ETH.

Job 21:10 bull *g.* and faileth not
   38:29 hoary frost. who *g.* it ?
Gal. 4:24 mount Sin. wh. *g.* to

GENEALOGY.

1 *Chr.* 5:1 *g.* not to be reckoned
Ezr. 2:62 sought *g. Neh.* 7:64
   8:1 *g.* of them that went up
Neh. 7:5 I found register of *g.*

GENEALOGIES.

1 *Chr.* 9:1 Israel reckoned by *g.*
2 *Chr.* 12:15 book of She. con. *g.*
   31:19 portions to all reck. by *g.*
1 *Tim.* 1:4 no heed to endless *g.*
Tit. 3:9 avoid fool. questions *g.*

GENERAL.

1 *Chr.* 27:34 *g.* king's army Joab
Heb. 12:23 *g.* assembly and chu.

GENERALLY.

2 *Sam.* 17:11 Is. be *g.* gathered
Jer. 48:38 lamenta. *g.* on house-t.

GENERATION.

Gen. 7:1 ha. I seen right. in *g.*
Ex. 17:16 war with Amal. fr. *g.*
Deut. 28:2 not enter to tenth *g.*
   3 Am. to tenth *g.* not enter
   8 Ed. and Eg. in third *g.* shall
   32:5 perverse and crooked *g.* 20
Jud. 2:10 that *g.* gath. to father
Ps. 12:7 preserve them from *g.*

Ps. 14:5 God is in *g.* of righte.
   22:30 accounted to Lord for a *g.*
   24:6 this *g.* of them that seek
   49:19 he shall go to *g.* of fathers
   73:15 I should offend ag. the *g.*
   78:4 show. to *g.* praise of Lord
   6 that *g.* to come might know
   8 a stubborn and rebellious *g.*
   95:10 grieved with *g. Heb.* 3:10
   109:13 *g.* fol. name be blotted
   112:2 *g.* of upright be blessed
   145:4 one *g.* praise thy works
Prov. 27:24 crown end. eve. *g. ?*
   30:11 a *g.* that curseth father
   12 there is *g.* pure in own eyes
   13 *g.* lofty ; 14 *g.* whose teeth
Ec. 1:4 one *g.* passeth, another *g.*
Is. 13:20 not dwelt in from *g.* to
    g. Jer. 50:39
   34:10 from *g.* to *g.* it shall lie, 17
   51:8 my salvat. be from *g.* to *g.*
   53:8 who decl. his *g. Acts* 8:33
Lam. 5:19 throne rem. fr. *g.* to *g.*
Dan. 4:3 his. dom. f. *g.* to *g.* 34
Mat. 1:1 book of *g.* of Jesus Ch.
   3:7 O *g.* of vipers, 12:34 ; 23:33 ;
    Luke 3:7
   11:16 shall liken *g. Luke* 7:31
   12:39 adulterous *g.* seeketh sign,
    16:4 ; *Mark* 8:12 ; *Luke* 11:29
   41 in jugdm. with *g. Luke* 11:32
   42 queen of S. wi. *g. Luke* 11:31
   17:17 O perverse *g. Mark* 9:19 ;
    Luke 9:41
   23:36 things come on this *g.*
   24:34 this *g.* not pass, *Mark*
    13:30 ; *Luke* 21:32
Mark 8:38 asha. of me in sin, *g.*
Luke 1:50 mercy on them *g.* to *g.*
   11:30 so sh. S. of man be to *g.*
   50 blood of proph. req. of *g.* 51
   16:8 child. of world in *g.* wiser
Acts 2:40 save from untoward *g.*
   13:36 David, after served own *g.*
1 *Pet.* 2:9 ye are a chosen *g.*

See FOURTH.

GENERATIONS.

Gen. 2:4 these are *g.* of heavens
   5:1 *g.* of Ad. ; 6:9 *g.* of N. 10:1
   6:9 Noah was perfect in his *g.*
   9:12 covenant for perpetual *g.*
   11:10 *g.* of Shem ; 27 *g.* of Te.
   17:12 every man-ch. in *g.* circ.
   25:12 *g.* of Ish. 13 ; 1 *Chr.* 1:29
   19 *g.* of Isaac ; 36:1 *g.* of E. 9
   37:2 these are the *g.* of Jacob
Ex. 3:15 memorial to all *g.*
   12:14 feast to Lord through. *g.*
   42 a night to be observed in *g.*
   16:32 homer to be kept for *g.* 33
   27:21 a statute forever to their
    g. 30:21 ; *Lev.* 3:17 ; 6:18 ;
    7:36 ; 10:9 ; 17:7 ; 23:14, 21,
    31, 41
   30:8 incense ; 31 oil through. *g.*
   31:13 sab. a sign through *g.* 16
   40:15 everlasting priest. throu' *g.*
Deut. 7:9 L. keepeth cov. 1,000 *g.*
   32:7 consider years of many *g.*
Jud. 3:2 *g.* of Israel might teach
Ruth 4:18 these are *g.* of Pharez
1 *Chr.* 16:15 word which he commanded to a 1,000 *g. Ps.* 105:8
Job 42:16 J. saw son's s. four *g.*
Ps. 33:11 thoughts of h. to all *g.*
   45:17 name remember. in all *g.*
   61:6 the king's years as many *g.*
   72:5 shall fear thee thro' all *g.*
   79:13 will show praise to all *g.*
   85:5 th. draw anger to all *g. ?*
   89:4 will build throne to all *g.*
   90:1 our dwelling-pla. in all *g.*
   100:5 his truth end. to all *g.*
   102:12 thy remem. to all *g.*
   24 thy years through all *g.*
   106:31 counted righte. to all *g.*
   119:90 thy faith. is to all *g.*

135:13 thy mem. through. all *g.*
145:13 thy dom. through. all *g.*
146:10 thy G. O Zion to all *g.*
Is. 41:4 calling *g.* from begin.
   51:9 awake, O arm of L. as in *g.*
   60:15 make thee joy of *g.*
   61:4 repair desolations of *g.*
Mat. 1:17 *g.* fr. Abr. to Dav. 14 *g.*
Luke 1:48 *g.* sh. call me blessed
Col. 1:26 mys. hid fr. ages and *g.*

GENNESARET. *Mat.* 14:34 ;
   Mark 6:53 ; *Luke* 5:1

GENTILE.

Rom. 2:9 Jew first, also of *g.* 10

GENTILES.

Gen. 10:5 isles of *g.* were divided
Is. 11:10 root of Jes. to it sh. *g.*
   42:1 judgm. to *g. Mat.* 12:18
Is. 42:6 light to *g.* 49:6 ; *Luke*
   2:32 ; *Acts* 13:47
   49:22 I will lift my hand to *g.*
   54:3 thy seed shall inherit the *g.*
   60:3 *g.* shall come to thy light
   5 forces of *g.* shall come, 11
   16 shalt suck the milk of *g.*
   61:6 ye shall eat the riches of *g.*
   9 seed sh. be known am. the *g.*
   62:2 *g.* sh. see thy righteousness
   66:12 glory of *g.* like flow. stre.
   19 declare my glory among *g.*
Jer. 4:7 destroyer of *g.* is on way
   14:22 vanities of *g.* cause rain ?
Lam. 2:9 king and princes am. *g.*
Ezek. 4:13 eat defil. bread am. *g.*
Joel 3:9 proclaim ye this am. *g.*
Mic. 5:8 remnant of Jacob am. *g.*
Zec. 1:21 to cast out horns of *g.*
Mal. 1:11 name sh. be gr. am. *g.*
Mat. 4:15 Galilee of the *g.*
   6:32 after all th. things *g.* seek
   10:5 go not into way of the *g.*
   18 testimony ag. them and *g.*
   12:21 in his name sh. the *g.* tru.
   20:19 shall deliver him to the *g.*
    Mark 10:33 ; *Luke* 18:32
   25 prin. of *g.* exer. *Luke* 22:25
Luke 21:24 Jerusal. trodden of *g.*
   till times of *g.* be fulfilled
John 7:35 to disp. am *g.* teach *g.*
Acts 7:45 with Je. into pos. of *g.*
   9:15 to bear my name before *g.*
   10:45 on the *g.* was poured gift
   11:1 *g.* received word of God
   18 hath G. to *g.* granted rep. ?
   13:42 *g.* besought words preach.
   46 P. and B. said, We turn to *g.*
   14:27 opened door of faith to *g.*
   15:3 declare the conversion of *g.*
   7 *g.* by my mou. sh. hear word
   12 wonders G. wrought am. *g.*
   14 God at first did visit *g.* 17
   19 them which from am. the *g.*
   23 greeting to breth. of the *g.*
   18:6 henceforth I will go to *g.*
   21:19 God wrought am. the *g.*
   21 teach. J. am. *g.* to forsake
   25 touch. the *g.* which believe
   22:21 I will send thee far to *g.*
   26:20 *g.* that they should repent
   23 Ch. sh. show light to the *g.*
   28:28 salvation of God sent to *g.*
Rom. 1:13 fruit, as am. other *g.*
   2:14 *g.* which have not the law
   24 God blasphemed am. the *g.*
   3:9 proved Jews and *g.* und. sin
   29 is he not of *g. ?* yes of *g.*
   9:24 not of Jews, but also of *g.*
   30 *g.* wh. follo. not after right.
   11:11 salvation come to the *g.*
   12 dimin. of them riches of *g.*
   13 to you *g.* as the apos. of *g.*
   25 till the fulness of *g.* be come
   15:9 that *g.* might glorify God ;
    I will confess among *g.*
   10 rejoice, ye *g.* with his peo.
   11 praise L. all *g.* and laud

GENTILES (cont.)

12 over *g.* in him shall *g.* trust
16 minist. of Jesus Christ to *g.*
  that offering up of the *g.* 18
27 if *g.* have been made parts.
16:4 all the churches of the *g.*
1 *Cor.* 5:1 not named among *g.*
10:20 thing *g.* sacrifice to devils
32 offence neither to J. nor *g.*
12:2 ye know ye were *g.* carried
13 whether we be Jews or *g.*
Gal. 2:12 he did eat with *g.*
14 man. of *g.* why compel. *g. ?*
15 Jews, and not sinners of *g.*
3:14 blessing of Abraham on *g.*
Eph. 2:11 in time past *g.* in flesh
3:1 prisoner of Jesus Ch. for *g.*
6 that *g.* should be fellow-heirs
8 preach am. *g.* unsea. riches
4:17 ye walk not as other *g.*
Col. 1:27 glory of mystery am. *g.*
1 *Thes.* 2:16 forbid. to spe. to *g.*
4:5 in lust of concupis. as the *g.*
1 *Tim.* 2:7 ordained teacher of *g.*
3:16 preached to the *g.*
2 *Tim.* 1:11 teacher of *g.*
1 *Pet.* 2:12 convers. honest am. *g.*
4:3 to have wrought will of *g.*
3 *John* 7 taking nothing of the *g.*
Rev. 11:2 the court is given to *g.*

GENTLE.

1 *Thes.* 2:7 were *g.* among you
2 *Tim.* 2:24 ser. of L. must be *g.*
Tit. 3:2 *g.* showing all meekness
Jam. 3:17 wisd. from ab. pure *g.*
1 *Pet.* 2:18 subject not only to *g.*

GENTLENESS.

2 *Sam.* 22:36 thy *g.* made me great, *Ps.* 18:35
2 *Cor.* 10:1 I bes. you by *g.* of **C.**
Gal. 5:22 fruit of the Spirit is *g.*

GENTLY.

2 *Sam.* 18:5 deal *g.* with Absalom
Is. 40:11 *g.* lead those wi. young

GERA.

Jud. 3:15 ; 2 *Sam.* 16:5
GERAHS. *Ex.* 30:13 ; *Lev.* 27:25 ; *Num.* 3:47 ; 18:16 ; *Eze.* 45:12
GERAR. *Gen.* 20:1, 2 ; 26:6, 20
GERGESENES. *Mat.* 8:28

GERIZIM.

Deut. 11:29 bles. on mt. G. **27**:12
Jos. 8:33 aga. mount G. *Jud.* 9:7

GERSHOM, GERSHON.

Gen. 46:11 G. Kohath and Merari
Ex. 6:16 ; *Num.* 3:17 ; 1 *Chr.* 6:1 ; 23:6
Ex. 2:22 name of Moses' son G.
Num. 3:21 G. family of Libnites
4:28 sons of G. 7:7 ; 10:17
Jos. 21:6 children of G. had, **27**
Ezr. 8:2 sons of Phinehas, G.

GESHUR.

2 *Sam.* 13:37 and went to G. **38**
14:23 Joab went to G. 32
15:8 servant vowed a vow at G.

GESHURITES.

Jos. 13:13 G. dw. among, 1 *Sam.* 27:8

GET.

Gen. 34:4 *g.* me damsel to wife
Ex. 14:17 will *g.* honour up. Pha.
Lev. 14:21 poor and cannot *g.* **22**
Deut. 8:18 power to *g.* wealth
Jud. 14:2 *g.* her me to wife, **3**
1 *K.* 1:2 that king may *g.* heat
Ps. 119:104 precepts I *g.* under.
Prov. 4:5 *g.* wisdom, *g.* under.
16:16 better *g.* wisd. than gold
17:16 in hand of fool to *g.* wis.
Ec. 3:6 there is a time to *g.*
Lam. 3:1 I cannot *g.* out
Ezek. 22:27 to *g.* dishonest gain
Dan. 4:14 beasts *g.* from under
Zep. 3:19 I will *g.* them praise
Luke 9:12 lodge and *g.* victuals

GET (cont.)

2 *Cor.* 2:11 lest Sat. *g.* advantage
Jam. 4:13 buy, sell, and *g.* gain

GET thee.

Gen. 12:1 *g. t.* out of co. *Acts* 7:3
Ex. 10:28 *g. thee* from me
11:8 *g. thee* out, and all people
19:24 Lord said to Moses, *g. th.* down, 32:7 ; *Deut.* 9:12
1 *K.* 17:3 *g. t.* hence ; 9 to Zarep.
18:41 Elijah said, *g. thee* up
2 *K.* 3:13 *g. t.* to prophets of fath.
Is. 40:9 O Z. *g. t.* to high mount.
47:5 and *g. thee* into darkness
Jer. 13:1 *g. thee* a linen girdle
Mat. 4:10 J. saith, *g. t.* hence, **5**.
16:23 said to Peter, *g. t.* behind me, **8**. *Mark* 8:33 ; *Luke* 4:8
Acts 10:20 arise, *g. thee* down
22:18 *g. t.* quickly out of Jerus.

GET ye.

Gen. 19:14 said, Up, *g. ye* out
Is. 30:11 *g. ye* out of way
Jer. 49:31 *g. ye* to wealthy nat.
Joel 3:13 *g. ye* down
Zec. 6:7 *g. ye* hence, walk to

GET you.

Gen. 34:10 *g. you* possessions
42:2 *g. you* down thither
Ex. 5:4 *g. you* to your burdens
11 *g. you* str. wh. you can find
Num. 16:24 *g. y.* up fr. tab. of K.
Jos. 2:16 *g. you* to the mountain
1 *Sam.* 25:5 *g. you* up to Carmel
Jer. 49:30 flee, *g. you* far off

GETHSEMANE.

Mat. 26:36 called G. *Mark* 14:32

GETTETH.

2 *Sam.* 5:8 whoso *g.* to gutter
Prov. 3:13 man that *g.* underst.
9:7 reproveth scorner *g.* shame, rebuketh wicked man *g.* blot
15:32 hear. reproof *g.* underst.
18:15 prudent *g.* knowledge
19:8 that *g.* wisdom loveth soul
Jer. 17:11 *g.* riches not by right
48:44 that *g.* out of pit

GETTING.

Gen. 31:18 J. carried cattle of *g.*
Prov. 4:7 with all thy *g.* get und.
21:6 *g.* of treas. by lying tongue

GHOST.

Gen. 49:33 J. yielded up the *g.*
Job 10:18 I had given up *g.*
11:20 hope as giving up of *g.*
14:10 man giveth up *g.*
Jer. 15:9 she hath given up *g.*
Mat. 27:50 J. cried, yielded up *g.*
Acts 5:10 Sapphira yielded up *g.*

See GAVE, GIVING UP, HOLY.

GIAH.

2 *Sam.* 2:24

GIANT.

2 *Sam.* 21:16 of *g.* 18 ; 1 *Chr.* 20:4
1 *Chr.* 20:6 son of *g.* ; **8** born to *g.*
Job 16:14 runneth on me like *g.*

GIANTS.

Gen. 6:4 there were *g.* in earth
Num. 13:33 we saw *g.* sons of A.
Deut. 2:11 Em. were counted *g.*
3:11 Og. of B. remained of rem-nant of *g.* *Jos.* 12:4 ; 13:12
13 Bash. called the land of *g.*
Jos. 15:8 lot of J. at valley of *g.*
17:15 get thee up to land of *g.*
18:16 Benj. came to valley of *g.*

GIBEAH.

Jud. 19:14 by G. 16 ; 20:9, 13
1 *Sam.* 10:26 home to G. 15:34
2 *Sam.* 21:6 serv. sons to L. in G.
Is. 10:29 afraid, G. of Saul is fled
Hos. 5:8 blow cornet in G. 9:9
10:9 sinned from days of G.

GIBEON.

Jos. 10:12 stand still upon G.

GIBEON (cont.)

2 *Sam.* 3:30 slain Asahel at G.
1 *K.* 3:5 in G. L. app. to Sol. 9:2
1 *Chr.* 8:29 at G. dw. father, 9:35
21:29 altar of b.-offering at G.
Is. 28:21 as in the valley of G.
GIBEONITES. 2 *Sam.* 21:1, 9

GIDEON.

Jud. 6:11, 24, 34 ; 7:1, 14, 18 ; 8:21
Heb. 11:32 wou. fail to tell of G.

GIDEONI. *Num.* 1:11 ; 2:22 ; 7:60,65

GIEREAGLE.

Lev. 11:18 abom. *g. Deut.* 14:17

GIFT.

Gen. 34:12 so much dowry and *g.*
Ex. 23:8 take no *g.* for *g.* blind-eth the wise, *Deut.* 16:19
Num. 8:19 given Lev. as *g.* 18:6
Ps. 45:12 daughter of T. with *g.*
Prov. 17:8 *g.* as precious stone
23 wicked tak. *g.* out of bosom
18:16 a man's *g.* maketh room
21:14 *g.* in secret pacifieth ang.
25:14 whoso boasteth of false *g.*
Ec. 3:13 it is the *g.* of G. 5:19
7:7 *g.* destroyeth the heart
Mat. 5:23 bring *g.* to the altar
24 leave *g.* before altar and go
8:4 offer *g.* that M. commanded
15:5 a *g.* by whatso. thou might-est be profited, *Mark* 7:11
23:18 whoso sweareth by *g.* 19
John 4:10 thou knewest *g.* of G.
Acts 2:38 sh. receive *g.* of H. G.
8:20 thought *g.* of G. be purch.
10:45 on Gentiles poured out *g.*
11:17 God gave them like *g.*
Rom. 1:11 impart spiritual *g.*
5:15 not as offence, so is free *g.*
16 *g.* free *g.* of many offences
17 which receive *g.* of righte.
18 the free *g.* came on all men
6:23 the *g.* of God is eternal life
1 *Cor.* 1:7 ye come behi. in no *g.*
7:7 ev. man hath pro. *g.* of God
13:2 tho' I have *g.* of prophecy
2 *Cor.* 8:4 that we would rec. *g.*
9:15 thanks to God for unsp. *g.*
Eph. 2:8 faith is the *g.* of God
4:7 accord. to meas. of *g.* of Ch.
Phil. 4:17 not bec. I desire a *g.*
1 *Tim.* 4:14 neglect not *g.* in thee
2 *Tim.* 1:6 stir up the *g.* in thee
Heb. 6:4 tasted of heavenly *g.*
Jam. 1:17 every good *g.* and per-fect *g.* is from above

GIFTS.

Gen. 25:6 Abra. gave *g.* to sons
Lev. 23:38 feasts, besides your *g.*
Num. 18:29 of all your *g.* offer
2 *Chr.* 19:7 with L. is no tak. *g.*
Est. 2:18 Ahasuerus gave *g.*
9:22 sending *g.* to the poor
Ps. 68:18 received *g.* for men
72:10 kings of Sheba offer *g.*
Prov. 6:35 though thou givest *g.*
15:27 that hateth *g.* shall live
19:6 man friend to him giv. *g.*
29:4 *g.* overthroweth judgment
Is. 1:23 every one loveth *g.*
Ezek. 16:33 *g.* to whor. *g.* to lov.
20:26 I polluted them in own *g.*
31 when ye offer *g.* ye pollute
39 pollute name no more wi. *g.*
22:12 in thee have they taken *g.*
Dan. 2:48 king gave Daniel *g.*
5:17 let thy *g.* be to thyself
Mat. 2:11 presented to him *g.*
Mat. 7:11 to gi. good *g. Lu.* 11:13
Luke 21:1 rich casting their *g.*
5 temple was adorned with *g.*
Rom. 11:29 *g.* of G. without rep.
12:6 *g.* differing accor. to grace
1 *Cor.* 12:1 concerning spirit. *g.*
4 there are diversities of *g.*
9 another *g.* of healing, **28**, 30

31 covet earnestly the best *g.*
14:1 and desire spiritual *g.*
Eph. 4:8 and gave *g.* to men
Heb. 2:4 God witness with *g.*
5:1 may offer *g.* and sacrifices
8:3 high-priced ord. to offer *g.*
4 there are priests that offer *g.*
9:9 offered, both *g.* and sacrif.
11:4 God testifying of Abel's *g.*
Rev. 11:10 dwell on earth send *g.*

GIHON.

Gen. 2:13 name of river is G.
1 *K.* 1:33 bring Sol. to G. 38, 45

GILBOA.

1 *Sam.* 31:1, 8; 2 *Sam.* 21:12;
1 *Chr.* 10:1, 8
2 *Sam.* 1:21 G. let th. be no dew

GILEAD.

Num. 32:1 G. place for cattle, 40
Ps. 60:7 G. mine, Man. 108:8
Cant. 4:1 hair as goats fr. G. 6:5
Jer. 8:22 there no balm in G. ?
22:6 art G. ; 46:11 go into G.
Hos. 6:8 G. is the city of them
12:11 is there iniquity in G. ?
GILEADITE, S. *Jud.* 10:3 ; 11:1;
12:4, 5; 2 *Sam.* 17:27

GILGAL.

Jos. 4:19 enc. in G. 9:6 ; 10:6
Jud. 2:1 angel came from G.
1 *Sam.* 7:16 S. went to G. 11:14
13:7 Saul in G. ; 8 Sam. 15:33
Amos 4:4 at G. multiply trans.
Mic. 6:5 him from Shittim to G.
GILONITE. 2 *Sam.* 15:12; 23:34

GIN, S.

Job 18:9 G. sh. take him by heel
Ps. 140:5; 141:9 ; *Is.* 8:14; *Am.* 3:5

GIRD.

Ex. 29:5 G. him with girdle, 9
Jud. 3:16 Ehud did *g.*
1 *Sam.* 25:13 *g.* on ev. man sword
Ps. 45:3 *g.* sword on thy thigh
Is. 8:9 *g.* yours. ye shall be br.
Ezek. 44:18 *g.* what caus. sweat
Joel 1:13 *g.* yours. and lament
Luke 12:37 sh. *g.* himself and
17:8 *g.* thyself and serve me
John 21:18 old, another *g.* thee
Acts 12:8 *g.* and bind on sandals
See LOINS, SACKCLOTH.

GIRDED.

Lev. 8:7 he *g.* him with girdle
1 *Sam.* 2:18 Sam. *g.* wi. linen ep.
2 *Sam.* 6:14 David *g.* with ephod
20:8 Joab's garment *g.* to him
22:40 *g.* with strength *Ps.* 18:39
1 *K.* 20:32 *g.* sackcloth on loins
Ps. 30:11 *g.* me with gladness
65:6 being *g.* with power
93:1 strength wherewith he *g.*
109:19 girdle wherewith he is *g.*
Is. 45:5 I *g.* thee, though thou
Lam. 2:10 elders of Zion *g.* with
Ezek. 16:10 I *g.* thee with fine li.
23:15 images *g.* with girdles
Joel 1:8 lament like a virgin *g.*
John 13:4 took towel and *g.* him.
5 towel wherewith he was *g.*
Rev. 15:6 breasts *g.* with girdle
See LOINS, SWORD.

GIRDEDST.

John 21:18 when young *g.* thys.

GIRDETH.

1 *K.* 20:11 him that *g.* his harn.
Job 12:18 and he *g.* their loins
Ps. 18:32 it is God that *g.* me
Prov. 31:17 she *g.* her loins

GIRDING.

Is. 3:24 inst. of stom. *g.* of sack.
22:12 L. did call to *g.* with sack.

GIRDLE.

Ex. 28:4 they shall make a *g.*
8 curious *g.* of ephod. 27, 28 ;
29:5 ; 39:5, 20 ; *Lev.* 8:7
39 thou make *g.* of needlework
39:29 *g.* of fine twined linen
1 *Sam.* 18:4 gave Da. bow and *g.*
1 *K.* 2:5 blood of war on his *g.*
2 *K.* 1:8 Elij. girt with *g.* of lea.
Job 12:18 loins of kings with *g.*
Ps. 109:19 *g.* wherewith he is
Is. 3:24 instead of a *g.* a rent
5:27 nor shall *g.* of loins be
Is. 11:5 righteous. be *g.* of loins
faithfulness *g.* of reins
22:21 strengthen Eliakim wi. *g.*
Jer. 13:1 get thee a linen *g.*
10 as this *g.* good for nothing
Mat. 3:4 J. had a l. *g. Mark* 1:6
Acts 21:11 took P.'s *g.* owneth *g.*
Rev. 1:13 gi. about paps gold. *g.*

GIRDLES.

Ex. 28:40 for Aaron's sons *g.*
29:9 Aaron and sons with *g.*
Prov. 31:24 deliver. *g.* to merch.
Ezek. 23:15 images of C. with *g.*
Rev. 15:6 angels *g.* wi. golden *g.*

GIRGASHITE, S.

Gen. 10:16 beg. the G. 1 *Chr.* 1:14
15:21 the land G. *Neh.* 9:8
Jos. 3:10 will drive out the G.

GIRL, S.

Joel 3:3 have sold *g.* for wine
Zec. 8:5 full of boys and *g.*

GIRT.

1 *Sam.* 2:4 that stumbled are *g.*
2 *K.* 1:8 *g.* with girdle of leather
John 21:7 S. Pet. *g.* fisher's coat
Eph. 6:14 loins *g.* with truth
Rev. 1:13 *g.* about paps golden *g.*
GITTITE. 2 *Sam.* 6:10 ; 15:19 ;
21:19

GIVE.

Gen. 15:2 what wilt *g.* me ?
23:11 the field I *g.* thee and
28:22 all thou *g.* me I will *g.*
Ex. 10:25 must *g.* us sacrifices
30:12 shall *g.* ev. man ransom
13 *g.* every one half a shekel
Num. 11:4 sh. *g.* flesh to eat? 18
22:18 if B. *g.* me house, 24:13
35:2 shall *g.* to Levites suburbs
Deut. 16:17 every man *g.* as he is
able, *Ezek.* 46:5, 11
25:3 forty stripes he may *g.*
1 *Sam.* 22:7 son of Jesse *g.* fields ?
2 *Sam.* 23:15 oh th. one *g.* me dr.
of well of Beth. 1 *Chr.* 11:17
1 *K.* 13:8 if thou wilt *g.* me.
2 *Chr.* 30:12 hand of G. to *g.* one
Ezr. 9:8 and to *g.* us a nail
9 to *g.* us a reviving in Judah
Job 2:4 man hath he *g.* for life
Ps. 2:8 I shall *g.* thee heathen
37:4 he shall *g.* thee desires
49:7 none can *g.* to God a rans.
51:16 not sac. else wo. I *g.* it
73:20 can he *g.* bread also ?
91:11 *g.* angels charge, *Mat.* 4:6
109:4 I *g.* myself unto prayer
Prov. 29:15 rod and reproof *g.*
17 he shall *g.* rest, *g.* delight
Ec. 2:26 he may *g.* to him good
Cant. 8:7 if man *g.* substance
Is. 30:23 then he shall *g.* rain
55:10 that it *g.* seed to sower
61:3 *g.* them beauty for ashes
Jer. 3:19 shall I *g.* pleas. land ?
17:10 *g.* man ac. to ways, 32:19
29:11 *g.* you an expected end
Ezek. 3:26 *g.* that I *g.* thee
3:3 till bowels with roll I *g.*
46:16 prince *g.* gift to sons, 17
Dan. 9:22 come to *g.* thee skill
Mic. 6:7 I *g.* first-born for tran. ?

Zec. 8:12 vine shall *g.* fruit, gro.
shall *g.* incre. heav. *g.* dew
Mat. 7:9 ask bread, will *g.* sto. ?
10 will he *g.* serp. ? *Luke* 11:11
11 how to *g.* gifts to child. so
F. to *g.* that ask, *Luke* 11:13
14:7 to *g.* what she would ask
16:26 *g.* in exchange for soul ?
Mark 8:37
19:7 *g.* writing of divorcement ?
26:15 what will ye *g.* me
Mark 6:25 *g.* me head of John
12:9 he will *g.* vineyard to oth.
Luke 4:6 to whom. I will, I *g.* it
6:38 good measure shall men *g.*
11:8 *g.* as many as he needeth
John 4:14 water I shall *g.* him
6:27 meat Son of man shall *g.*
52 can this man *g.* his flesh?
10:28 I *g.* to them eternal life
12:22 what thou ask G. will *g.*
13:29 that he should *g.* to poor
14:16 he shall *g.* you Comforter
27 my peace I *g.* to you : not as
world giveth, *g.* I unto you
15:16 what. ye ask he may *g.*
16:23 what. ye ask he will *g.*
17:2 he should *g.* eternal life
Acts 3:6 such as I have *g.* I thee
6:4 will *g.* ourselves to prayer
20:35 more blessed to *g.* than r.
Rom. 8:32 him also freely *g.*
Eph. 1:17 God may *g.* you spirit
4:28 have to *g.* to him needeth
2 *Tim.* 4:8 righte. Judge shall *g.*
Heb. 2:1 to *g.* more earnest heed
1 *John* 5:16 *g.* life for them that
Rev. 13:15 power to *g.* life to im.
16:19 to *g.* her cup of wine
22:12 *g.* every man ac. to work

See ACCOUNT, GLORY, SWARE.

GIVE, *imperatively.*

Gen. 14:21 *g.* me the persons
27:28 G. *g.* thee dew of heaven
29:21 *g.* me wife; 30:1 *g.* child.
Num. 6:26 Lord *g.* thee peace
Jos. 2:12 and *g.* me true token
15:19 *g.* bless. *g.* spr. *Jud.* 1:15
1 *Sam.* 8:6 *g.* us a king to judge
17:10 *g.* me man that we may
1 *K.* 3:9 *g.* servant understand.
26 *g.* her the living child, 27
2 *K.* 6:29 I said; *g.* thy son that
1 *Chr.* 16:28 *g.* to Lord glory and
strength, 29 ; *Ps.* 29:1 ; 96:7, 8
22:12 the Lord *g.* thee wisdom
2 *Chr.* 1:10 *g.* me now wisdom
23:21 nor let me *g.* flat. titles
Ps. 28:4 *g.* according to deeds
60:11 *g.* help fr. trouble, 108:12
86:16 *g.* strength to thy servant
119:34 *g.* me understanding, 73,
125, 144, 169
Prov. 9:9 *g.* instru. to wise man
23:26 my son, *g.* me thy heart
25:21 if enemy hunger, *g.* him
bread, *Rom.* 12:20
30:8 *g.* me neither poverty nor
15 two daughters, crying *g. g.*
Ec. 11:2 *g.* a portion to seven
Is. 62:7 *g.* no rest till establish J.
Jer. 18:19 *g.* heed to me, O Lord
Lam. 2:18 *g.* thyself no rest
3:65 *g.* them sorrow of heart
Ezek. 3:17 *g.* warning from me
Dan. 5:17 *g.* rewards to another
Hos. 4:18 rulers do love, *g.* ye
9:14 *g.* O Lord, what wilt *g.* ?
13:10 *g.* me a king and princes
Zec. 11:12 *g.* me my price
Mat. 5:42 *g.* to him that asketh
6:11 *g.* us our daily b. *Luke* 11:3
9:24 *g.* place ; 10:8 freely *g.*
14:16 *g.* them to eat, *Mark* 6:37;
Luke 9:13
17:27 and *g.* to them for me
19:21 *g.* to poor, *Mark* 10:21

20:8 and *g.* them their hire
25:8 *g.* us of your oil, lamps out
Luke 6:38 *g.* and it shall be giv.
11:41 *g.* alms of such, 12:33
14:9 say, *g.* this man place
15:12 give me portion of goods
John 4:7 J. saith, *g.* me drink, 10
6:34 L. everm. *g.* us this bread
9:24 *g.* God praise, man is sin.
Acts 8:19 S. said, *g.* me power
Rom. 12:19 *g.* place to wrath
1 *Cor.* 10:32 *g.* none offence
2 *Cor.* 9:7 let him *g.* not grudg.
Col. 4:1 *g.* servants that is just
1 *Tim.* 4:13 *g.* attend. to reading
15 *g.* thyself to them
Rev. 10:9 *g.* me the little book
18:7 torment and sorrow *g.* her

See CHARGE, EAR, GLORY, LIGHT.

I will GIVE.

Gen. 17:8 *I will g.* to thee land
wherein thou art a stranger,
48:4 ; *Deut.* 34:4
16 *I will g.* son ; 28:22 tenth to
Ex. 3:31 *I will g.* favor ; 33:14
Lev. 26:4 *I w. g.* rain, *Deut.* 11:14
6 *I will g.* peace in the land
1 *Sam.* 1:11 *I will g.* him to L.
2 *Sam.* 12:11 *I will g.* wives to
1 *K.* 11:13 *I will g.* one tribe
31 *I will g.* ten tribes to thee
13:7 *I will g.* reward ; 21:2
21:7 *I will g.* vineyard of Nab.
1 *Chr.* 22:9 *I will g.* rest, *I w. g.*
2 *Chr.* 1:12 *I will g.* thee riches
Ps. 30:12 O L. *I will g.* thanks
57:7 *I will* sing *g.* praise, 108:1
Prov. 3:28 to-morrow *I will g.*
Is. 3:4 *I w. g.* child. to be princ.
41:27 *I will g.* to Jerusalem one
that bringeth good tidings
42:6 *I will g.* thee for cove. 49:8
45:3 *I will g.* treas. ; 49:6 light
Jer. 3:15 *I will g.* you pastors
9:15 *I will g.* waters of gall to
14:13 *I will g.* peace in land
17:3 *I will g.* substance to spoil
24:7 *I will g.* heart to know me
32:39 *I w. g.* heart, *Ezek.* 11:19
Ezek. 7:21 *I will g.* to strangers
11:17 *I will g.* you land of Isr.
16:38 *I w. g.* thee blood in fury
39 *I w. g.* thee into their hand
Ezek. 16:61 *I will g.* them for dau.
21:27 whose right it is, *I will g.*
29:21 *I will g.* opening of mouth
36:26 *I will g.* you heart of flesh
Mat. 11:28 and *I will g.* you rest
16:19 *I will g.* to thee the keys
20:4 what. is right *I will g.* you
14 *I will g.* to last even as to
Mark 6:22 ask, *I will g.* it thee
Luke 21:15 *I w. g.* you a mouth
John 6:51 bread *I will g.* is my
Acts 13:34 *I will g.* mercies of D.
Rev. 2:10 *I will g.* thee a crown
17 *I will g.* him a white stone
23 *I w. g.* ev. one ac. to works
28 *I will g.* him the morn. star
11:3 *I will g.* power to my two
21:6 *I w. g.* him athirst w. of l.

Will I GIVE.

Gen. 12:7 to thy seed *w. I g.* this
land, 13:15 ; 24:7 ; 28:13 ; 35:12 ;
Ex. 32:13 ; 33:1
Deut. 1:36 to him *will I g.* land
1 *Sam.* 18:17 M. her *w. I g.* thee
Ps. 18:49 *will I g.* thanks to
Cant. 7:12 *will I g.* thee my
Is. 43:4 *will I g.* men for thee
Ezek. 36:36 new heart *w. I g.* you
Hag. 2:9 this place *will I g.* peace
Mat. 4:9 Th. things *will I g.*
Luke 4:6 this power *will I g.* thee
Rev. 2:7 over. *will I g.* 17, 26

Lord GIVE.

Ex. 12:25 to land which *L.* will
g. you, *Lev.* 14:34 ; 23:10 ; 25:2
Num. 15:2
16:8 *Lord* shall *g.* flesh to eat
Num. 22:13 *Lord* refuseth to *g.*
36:2 *L.* com. to *g.* land by lot
Deut. 1:25 land the *Lord* doth *g.*
28:65 *L.* shall *g.* tremb. heart
Jos. 17:4 *L.* com. to *g.* inherit.
1 *K.* 15:4 L. his God did *g.* lamp
2 *Chr.* 25:9 L. is able to *g.* much
Ps. 29:11 L. *g.* strength to peo.
84:11 L. will *g.* grace and glory
85:12 L. shall *g.* which is good
Is. 7:14 L. hims. shall *g.* a sign
14:3 the *Lord* shall *g.* thee rest
30:20 *Lord g.* you bread of adv.
Zec. 10:1 *L. g.* showers of rain
Luke 1:32 *L.* shall *g.* him throne
2 *Tim.* 1:16 *L. g.* mercy to house

Not GIVE, *or* GIVE not.

Ex. 5:10 I will *not g.* straw
30:15 rich *n. g.* more, poor *n.* l.
Lev. 25:37 shall *not g.* money on
Deut. 7:3 dau. shall *not g.* to son
Jud. 21:7 we will *not g.* wives
Ezr. 9:12 *g. not* your daughters,
Neh. 10:30 ; 13:25
Ps. 132:4 will *n. g.* sleep to eyes
Prov. 6:4 *g. not* sleep to eyes
31:3 *g. not* thy strength to wo.
Is. 13:10 constel. *not g.* light
42:8 glory *not g.* to anot. 48:11
62:8 I will *no* more *g.* thy corn
Ezek. 32:7 moon *sh. n. g.* her lig.
Mat. 24:29 ; *Mark* 13:24
Joel 2:17 *g. not* heritage to rep.
Mat. 7:6 *g. n.* that is holy to dog
Mark 12:15 sh. we *g.* or *not g.* ?
Eph. 4:27 neither *g.* place to de.
Jam. 2:16 *g. n.* things they need

GIVE thanks.

2 *Sam.* 22:50 I will *g. t.* to thee,
Ps. 18:49
1 *Chr.* 16:8 *g. t.* to the L. *Ps.* 105:1;
106:1 ; 107:1, 118:1 ; 136:1, 3
35 save us, that we may *g. th.*
to thy holy name, *Ps.* 106:47
25:3 with a harp to *g. thanks*
Ps. 6:5 in grave who shall *g. t.*
30:4 *g. th.* at the remembrance
of his holiness, 97:12
12 O Lord, I will *g. t.* for ever
35:18 I will *g. t.* in congregation
75:1 to thee, O God, do we *g. t.*
79:13 so we thy people will *g. t.*
92:1 good thing to *g. t.* to Lord
106:47 to *g. t.* to holy name
119:62 at midnight I will *g. t.*
122:4 tribes go up to *g. thanks*
136:2 *g. t.* to God of gods, 26
140:13 right. *g. t.* to thy name
Rom. 16:4 to whom I *g. thanks*
1 *Cor.* 10:30 that for which *I g. t.*
Eph. 1:16 I cease not to *g. t.* for
Col. 1:3 we *g. t.* to G. and Father
1 *Thes.* 1:2 we *g. thanks* to God
5:18 in everything *g. thanks*
2 *Thes.* 2:13 we are bound to *g. t.*
Rev. 11:17 we *g.* thee t. L. G. A.

GIVE up.

Deut. 23:14 Lord walketh to *g. up*
thine enemies, 31:5
1 *K.* 14:16 he shall *g.* Israel *up*
Job 3:11 why did not I *g. up* gh. ?
13:19 I shall *g. up* the ghost
Is. 43:6 I say to north, *g. up*
Hos. 11:8 how sh. I *g. up* Eph. ?

GIVEN.

Lev. 20:3 he hath *g.* seed to Mo.
Num. 18:6 *g.* as a gift for the L.
Ruth 2:12 reward *g.* thee of L.
2 *Sam.* 12:8 have *g.* such things
18:11 would have *g.* ten shekels
19:42 or hath king *g.* us gift ?

1 *K.* 13:5 sign man of G. had *g.*
1 *Chr.* 29:14 thine have we *g.*
Est. 3:11 silver is *g.* to thee
7:3 my life be *g.* at my petition
Job 3:20 light *g.* him in misery ?
Ps. 79:2 dead bodies *g.* to be m.
112:9 hath *g.* to poor, 2 *Cor.* 9:9
115:16 earth hath *g.* to *g.* of men
Prov. 19:17 hath *g.* will he pay
Ec. 8:8 wicked deliv. those *g.* it
12:11 which are *g.* fr. one shep.
Is. 9:6 Child born, Son is *g.*
Jer. 6:13 ev. one *g.* to cov. 8:10
Ezek. 11:15 to us is land *g.* 33:24
35:12 they are *g.* to consume
Dan. 2:38 fowls hath he *g.* into
7:4 lion, man's heart was *g.*
Mat. 13:11 *g.* you to know mys.
of king. *Mark* 4:11 ; *Lu.* 8:10
19:11 save they to whom it is *g.*
21:43 *g.* to nation bring. fruits
22:30 are *g.* in marriage, *Mark*
12:25 ; *Luke* 20:35
26:9 and *g.* to poor, *Mark* 14:5
28:18 power *g.* to me in heaven
Mark 4:24 that hear more be *g.*
Luke 12:48 much *g.* much req.
John 3:27 nothing, except it be *g.*
5:26 *g.* to the Son to have life
6:39 of all he hath *g.* me
65 no man come except *g.* him
19:11 except it were *g.* from
Acts 4:12 none other name *g.*
Rom. 5:5 H. Ghost which is *g.*
11:35 who hath first *g.* to him
15:15 grace that is *g.* me of God
1 *Cor.* 2:12 things freely *g.* of G.
Gal. 3:21 law *g.* could have *g.*
Eph. 3:2 is *g.* me to you-ward
8 me who am least is grace *g.*
5:2 C. loved and *g.* hims. for us
Phil. 1:29 you *g.* in behalf of C.
2:9 *g.* him a name above ev. n.
Heb. 4:8 if Jes. had *g.* them rest
1 *John* 3:24 Sp. wh. he hath *g.* us
4:13 bec. he hath *g.* us of Spirit
Rev. 6:11 white robes *g.* to every
13:5 power *g.* to con. 42 months
7 it was *g.* him to make war

God, *or* Lord hath, had GIVEN.

Gen. 24:35 L. *h. g.* Abrah. flocks
30:6 said, *God hath g.* me a son
18 *God hath g.* me my hire
43:23 *God hath g.* you treasure
Ex. 16:15 bread which *Lord h. g.*
29 *Lord h. g.* you the sabbath
Num. 22:7 going over to land wh.
Lord hath g. them, 9 ; *Deut.*
3:18 ; 28:52 ; *Jos.* 2:9, 14 ; 23:13,
15 ; *Jer.* 25:5
Jos. 6:16 shout, *Lord h. g.* city
1 *Sam.* 1:27 L. *h. g.* me my peti.
15:28 L. *h. g.* it to neigh. 28:17
2 *Chr.* 36:23 all kingd. of earth.
hath God g. me, *Ezr.* 1:2
Ec. 5:19 to who. *G. h. g.* riches
Is. 8:18 I and the children *Lord*
hath g. Heb. 2:13
50:4 *Lord h. g.* me tongue
Jer. 11:18 *L. hath g.* me knowl.
47:7 *Lord hath g.* it a charge
John 6:23 *Lord hath g.* thanks
Acts 27:24 *G. h. g.* thee all that
Rom. 11:8 *G. h. g.* spirit of slum.
2 *Cor.* 10:8 the *Lord h. g.* us for
edification, 13:10
1 *Thes.* 4:8 *G.* who *h. g.* Holy S.
1 *John* 5:11 record *G. hath g.* us

See REST.

I have, *or* have I GIVEN.

Gen. 27:37 bret. *h. I g.* for serv.
1 *K.* 3:13 *I h. g.* th. hast not asked
Is. 55:4 *I h. g.* him for witness
Ezek. 4:15 *I h. g.* thee cow's du.
Amos 4:6 *I h. g.* clean. of teeth.
9:15 no more out of land *I h. g.*

John 13:15 *I h. g.* an example
17:8 *I h. g.* words thou gave, 14
22 glory gavest me, *I h. g.* th.
1 *Cor.* 16:1 *I h. g.* order to chur.

Not GIVEN.

Deut. 26:14 I have *not g.* thereof
29:4 L. hath *not g.* you a heart
1 *Chr.* 22:18 hath he *n. g.* you rest
Job 22:7 hast *not g.* water
Ps. 78:63 maid. *n. g.* to marriage
Ezek. 3:20 hast *not g.* warning
Mat. 13:11 to them it is *not g.*
John 7:39 Holy G. was *not* yet *g.*
1 *Tim.* 3:3 bishop *not g.* to wine,
    no striker, *Tit.* 1:7
8 deacons *not g.* to much wine
2 *Tim.* 1:7 G. *n. g.* us sp. of fear
Tit. 2:3 aged wom. *n. g.* to wine

Shall be GIVEN.

Est. 5:3 *s. be g.* to half of kingd.
Ps. 72:15 *s. be g.* of gold of Sheba
120:3 what *shall be g.* thee
Is. 3:11 reward of hands *s. be g.*
33:16 bread *shall be g.* him
35:2 glory of Lebanon *s. be g.*
Ezek. 47:11 marshes, *shall be g.*
Dan. 7:25 saints *s. be g.* to hand
    27 kingdom *s. be g.* to saints
Mat. 7:7 it *shall be g. Luke* 11:9
10:19 *s. be g.* sa. hour, *Mark* 13:11
12:39 no sign *s. be g. Mark* 8:12;
    Luke 11:29
13:12 to him *shall be g.* 25:29 ;
    Mark 4:25; *Luke* 8:18
20:23 it *s. be g.* for whom prep.
21:43 kin. of G. *s. be g.* to nation
Luke 6:38 give, and it *shall be g.*
Phile. 22 thro' prayers I *s. be g.*
Jam. 1:5 ask of G. and it *s. be g.*

Thou hast, *or* hast thou GIVEN.

Gen. 15:3 to me *t. hast g.* no seed
Jos. 15:19 *thou hast g.* south land,
    Jud. 1:15
1 *Sam.* 22:13 *t. hast g.* him bread
2 *Sam.* 12:14 *thou hast g.* occasion
    22:36 *thou hast* also *g. Ps.* 18:35
    41 *t. h. g.* me necks of *e. Ps.* 18:40
Ezr. 9:13 *thou hast g.* us deliver.
Ps. 21:2 *thou h. g.* heart's desire
44:11 *thou hast g.* us like sheep
60:4 *thou h. g.* a banner to them
61:5 *thou h. g.* me the heritage
71:3 *thou h. g.* com. to save
John 17:2 *thou hast g.* him power
    7 all things *thou hast g.* me
    9 I pray for them *thou h. g.* me
    11 keep those *thou hast g.* me
Rev. 16:6 *t. h. g.* blood to drink

GIVER.

Is. 24:2 taker of usury, so with *g.*
2 *Cor.* 9:7 G. loveth a cheerful *g.*

GIVEST.

Deut. 15:9 *g.* him naught, 10
Job 35:7 if righteous, what *g. ?*
Ps. 50:19 *g.* thy mouth to evil
80:5 thou *g.* them tears'to drink
104:28 that *g.* them, tney gather
145:15 thou *g.* them their meat
Prov. 6:35 tho' thou *g.* many gifts
Ezek. 16:33 thou *g.* to thy lovers
    34 *g.* reward, none is given
1 *Cor.* 14:17 thou *g.* thanks well

GIVETH.

Ex. 16:29 *g.* on sixth day bread
20:12 days long in land which
    L. *g. Deut.* 4:40; 5:16; 25:15
25:2 ev. man that *g.* it willingly
Deut. 2:29 into land which L. G.
    g. thee, 4:1, 21; 11:17, 31; 12:1,
    10; 15:4, 7; 16:20; 17:14; 18:9;
    19:1, 2, 10, 14; 21:1, 23; 24:4;
    26:1, 2; 27:2, 3; 28:8; *Jos.*
    1:11, 15
8:18 he *g.* power to get wealth
9:6 *g.* not land for thy righteo.

13:1 if a prophet *g.* thee a sign
16:5 which L. *g.* thee, 18 ; 17:2
Job 5:10 who *g.* rain upon earth
33:13 he *g.* no account of ways
34:29 *g.* quiet; 35:10 *g.* songs
36:6 *g.* right; 31 *g.* meat
Ps. 18:50 deliv. *g.* he to king
68:35 God of Is. that *g.* strength
119:130 entr of words *g.* light
127:2 so he *g.* his beloved sleep
Prov. 2:6 L *g.* wisdom out of m.
3:34 *g.* grace to lowly, *Jam.* 4:6;
    1 *Pet.* 5:5
13:15 good understand. *g.* favor
21:26 right. *g.* spareth not, 22:9
28:27 that *g.* to poor sh. not lack
Ec. 2:26 God *g.* to good man wis-
    dom, to sinner *g.* travail
6:2 God *g.* him not power to eat
Is. 40:29 he *g.* power to the faint
42:5 he that *g.* breath to people
Jer. 5:24 *g.* rain ; 31:35 *g.* sun
Lam. 3:30 *g.* cheek to him smit.
Hab. 2:15 woe to him. *g.* neigh.
Mat. 5:15 it *g.* light to all in ho.
John 3:34 God *g.* not Spirit
6:32 Father *g.* you true bread

John 6:33 who *g.* life to the world
    37 all the Father *g.* me
10:11 good shepherd *g.* his life
14:27 not as the world *g.* give I
Acts 17:25 he *g.* to all life
Rom. 12:8 *g.* with simplicity
1 *Cor.* 3:7 G. that *g.* the increase
7:38 that *g.* in marriage
15:38 G. *g.* body as pleased him
    57 thanks to G. who *g.* victory
2 *Cor.* 3:6 letter killeth, sp. *g.* life
1 *Tim.* 6:17 *g.* richly all things
Jam. 1:5 ask of God that *g.* to all
4:6 *g.* more grace, God *g.* grace
1 *Pet.* 4:11 of ability that God *g.*
Rev. 22:5 L. God *g.* them light

GIVING.

Deut. 10:18 stranger in *g.* food
21:17 *g.* him a double portion
Ruth 1:6 visited peo. in *g.* bread
Job 11:20 hope as *g.* up of ghost
Mat. 24:38 and *g.* in marriage
Acts 8:9 *g.* out himself
    15:8 *g.* them the Holy Ghost
Rom. 4:20 st. in faith, *g.* G. glory
9:4 *g.* of law, service of God
1 *Cor.* 14:7 *g.* sou. ; 16 *g.* thanks
2 *Cor.* 6:3 *g.* no offence
Phil. 4:15 conc. *g.* and receiving
1 *Tim.* 4:1 *g.* heed to seducing sp.
1 *Pet.* 3:7 *g.* honor to the wife
2 *Pet.* 1:5 *g.* all diligence
Jude 7 *g.* thems. to fornication

See THANKS.

GLAD.

Ex. 4:14 he will be *g.* in heart
1 *K.* 8:66 w. to tents *g.* 2 *Chr.* 7:10
Est. 5:9 Haman *g.* ; 8:15 Sh. *g.*
Job 3:22 *g.* when find the grave
22:19 righte. see, *g. Ps.* 64:10
Ps. 16:9 my heart *g.* glory rejoi.
21:6 made him *g.* with count.
34:2 hear and be *g.* 69:32
45:8 have made thee *g.*
46:4 make *g.* city of God
67:4 the nations be *g.* and sing
90:15 make us *g.* ; 92:4 made *g.*
97:1 let isles be *g.*; 8 Z. was *g.*
104:15 wine that maketh *g.*
    34 be *g.* in Lord ; 105:38 Eg. *g.*
107:30 are they *g.* bec. quiet
122:1 *g.* when said, Let us go
126:3 things, whereof are *g.*
Prov. 10:1 a *g.* father, 15:20
12:25 a good word maketh it *g.*
17:5 that is *g.* at calamities
23:25 father and mother be *g.*
24:17 heart not be *g.*
27:11 make my heart *g.*

Is. 35:1 wilderness be *g.*
Jer. 20:15 child born, ma. him *g.*
Dan. 6:23 king exceeding *g.*
Jon. 4:6 Jonah *g.* bec. of gourd
Zec. 10:7 chil. see it and be *g.*
Mark 14:11 *g.* and prom. *Lu.* 22:5
Luke 1:19 to show these *g.* tid.
8:1 *g.* tidings of the kingdom
15:32 we make merry, be *g.*
John 8:56 saw my day, was *g.*
Acts 11:23 seen grace of G. was *g.*
13:48 Gentiles heard, were *g.*
Rom. 16:19 am *g.* on your behalf
1 *Cor.* 16:17 *g.* of coming of Step.
2 *Cor.* 2:2 that maketh me *g.?*
13:9 are *g.* when we are weak
1 *Pet.* 4:13 ye may be *g.* also

GLAD, *joined with* rejoice.

1 *Chr.* 16:31 let heav. be *g.* earth
    rej. Lord reigneth, *Ps.* 96:11
Ps. 9:2 I will be *g.* and rejoice
14:7 Jacob *rejoice* Is. be *g.* 53:6
31:7 be *g.* and *rejoice* in mercy
32:11 be *g.* and *re.* ye ri. 68:3
40:16 thee, be *g.* and *rej.* 70:4
48:11 Z. *re.* daugh. of J. be *g.*
90:14 we may be *g.* and *rejoice*
118:24 we will *r.* and be *g.* in it
Cant. 1:4 we will be *g.* and *rej.*
Is. 25:9 we will *rej.* and be *g.*
65:18 be you *g.* and *rej.* for ever
66:10 *rej.* y. with Jer. and be *g.*
Lam. 4:21 *re.* and be *g.* O dau.
Joel 2:21 O land, be *g.* and *rej.*
    23 be *g.* ye child. of Zion, *rej.*
Hab. 1:15 they *rejoice* and are *g.*
Zep. 3:14 be *g.* and *rej.* O dau.
Mat. 5:12 *r.* and be *g.* great re.
Acts 2:26 heart *r.* tongue was *g.*
Rev. 19:7 be *g.* and *r.* marriage

GLADLY.

Mark 12:37 people heard Ch. *g.*
Acts 2:41 *g.* re. words were bapt.
21:17 the breth. received us *g.*
2 *Cor.* 11:19 ye suffer fools *g.*
12:9 most *g.* will I rather glory
15 I will *g.* spend and be spent

GLADNESS.

Num. 10:10 in day of *g.* ye shall
2 *Sam.* 6:12 Da. br. ark with *g.*
1 *Chr.* 16:27 strength and *g.* in
2 *Chr.* 29:30 sang praises with *g.*
30:21 Israel kept feast with *g.*
    23 kept other seven days w. *g.*
Neh. 8:17 there was great *g.*
Est. 8:16 had light, and *g.* 17
9:17 day of feast, and *g.* 18, 19
Ps. 4:7 thou put *g.* in my heart
30:11 thou girded me with *g.*
45:7 anoi. with oil of *g. Heb.* 1:9
    15 with *g.* shall they be brou.
51:8 make me to hear joy and *g.*
97:11 *g.* is sown for the upright
100:2 serve the Lord with *g.*
105:43 brought chosen with *g.*
106:5 that I may rejoice in *g.*
Cant. 3:11 day of *g.* of his heart
Is. 22:13 joy and *g.* slay. oxen
30:29 have song and *g.* of heart
35:10 obtain joy and *g.* 51:11
51:3 joy and *g.* found therein
Jer. 7:34 voice of mirth and *g.*
    16:9 ; 25:10
31:7 sing with *g.* for Jacob
33:11 heard voice of joy and *g.*
48:33 joy and *g.* taken fr. field
Joel 1:16 joy and *g.* from h. of G.
Zec. 8:19 h. of Jud. joy and *g.*
Mark 4:16 who receive it with *g.*
Luke 1:14 shalt have joy and *g.*
Acts 2:46 eat meat w. *g.* of heart
12:14 she opened not gate for *g.*
14:17 fill. hea. with food and *g.*
Phil. 2:29 receive him with all *g.*

GLASS, ES.

Is. 3:23 Lord will take away *g.*

1 *Cor.* 13:12 we see through a *g.*
2 *Cor.* 3:18 beholding as in a *g.*
Jam. 1:23 man behold. face in *g.*
Rev. 4:6 sea of *g.* like unto crys.
15:2 sea of *g.* mingled with fire
21:18 city pure gold, like c. *g.* 21

See LOOKING.

GLEAN, ED.
Lev. 19:10 not *g.* v. *Deut.* 24:21
Ruth 2:2 let me go to field and *g.*
3 she came and *g.* after reapers
Jer. 6:9 they shall *g.* the remnant

GLEANING, S.
Lev. 19:9 not gath., *g.* of h. 23:22
Jud. 8:2 is not *g.* of gr. of Eph.
Is. 17:6 *g.* grapes shall be left
24:13 as *g.* grapes when vint.
Jer. 49:9 they not leave some *g.?*
Mic. 7:1 as grape *g.* of the vint.

GLEDE.
Deut. 14:13 shall not eat the *g.*

GLISTERING.
1 *Chr.* 29:2 I have pre. *g.* stones
Job 20:25 the *g.* sword cometh
Luke 9:29 his raim. white and *g.*

GLITTER, ING.
Deut. 32:41 if I whet. *g.* sword
Job 39:23 the *g.* spear rattleth
Ezek. 21:10 furb. that it may *g.*
28 furbished to cons. bec. of *g.*
Nah. 3:3 horseman lifteth *g.* sp.
Hab. 3:11 shining of thy *g.* spear

GLOOMINESS.
Joel 2:2 darkn. *g.* *Zep.* 1:15

GLORIFY.
Ps. 22:23 seed of Jacob *g.* him
50:15 and thou shalt *g.* me
86:9 nations shall come and *g.*
12 and I will *g.* thy name
Is. 24:15 *g.* ye Lord in the fires
25:3 the strong people *g.* thee
60:7 I will *g.* house of my glory
Jer. 30:19 I wil. also *g.* them
Mat. 5:16 *g.* Father in heaven
John 12:28 F. *g.* thy name
13:32 God sh. *g.* him in himself
16:14 he shall *g.* me
17:1 *g.* thy son, that thy Son *g.*
5 *g.* me with thine own self
21:19 what death he sho. *g.* G.
Rom. 15:6 mind and mouth *g.* G.
9 that Gentiles might *g.* God
1 *Cor.* 6:20 *g.* God in body and s.
2 *Cor.* 9:13 *g.* God for your subj.
1 *Pet.* 2:12 *g.* God in day of visi.
4:16 *g.* God on this behalf
Rev. 15:4 and *g.* thy name

GLORIFIED.
Lev. 10:3 bef. ail peo. I will be *g.*
Is. 26:15 increased nation, art *g.*
44:23 L. hath *g.* himself in Is.
49:3 O Is. in whom I will be *g.*
55:5 Holy One of Is. hath *g.* 60:9
60:21 that I may be *g.*
61:3 planting of L. that he be *g.*
Is. 66:5 said, Let the Lord be *g.*
Ezek. 28:22 I will be *g.* in midst
39:13 the day that I shall be *g.*
Dan. 5:23 God hast thou not *g.*
Mat. 9:8 marvelled, and *g.* God,
Mark 2:12; *Luke* 5:26
15:31 they *g.* the God of Israel
Luke 4:15 synagogues, being *g.*
7:16 and they *g.* God
13:13 made straight, and *g.* G.
17:15 leper *g.* G. ; 23:47 centur.
John 7:39 because Jes. not yet *g.*
11:4 Son of God might be *g.*
12:16 but when Jesus was *g.*
23 the Son of men should be *g.*
28 I have *g.* it, will glorify it
13:31 Son of man *g.* God is *g.*
32 if G. be *g.* in him G. sh. gl.
14:13 Father may be *g.* in Son

15:8 my Father *g.* ye bear fruit
17:4 I have *g.* thee on earth
10 and I am *g.* in them
Acts 3:13 G. of fathers hath *g.* S.
4:21 men *g.* God
11:18 held peace, and *g.* God
13:48 Gentiles *g.* word of Lord
21:20 they of Jerusalem *g.* Lord
Rom. 1:21 they *g.* him not as G.
8:17 that we may be also *g.*
30 wh. he justified, them he *g.*
Gal. 1:24 and they *g.* God in me
2 *Thes.* 1:10 wh. he come to be *g.*
12 name of Jesus may be *g.*
3:1 that word of Lord may be *g.*
Heb. 5:5 so Christ *g.* not himself
1 *Pet.* 4:11 G. in all things be *g.*
14 but on your part he is *g.*
Rev. 18:7 how much *g.* herself

GLORIFIETH, ING.
Ps. 50:23 whoso. offer. praise *g.*
Luke 2:20 sheph. returned, *g.* G.
5:25 departed to own ho. *g.* God
18:43 blind man followed, *g.* G.

GLORY, Substantive.
Gen. 31:1 father's gotten this *g.*
Ex. 28:2 garm. for A. for *g.* 40
1 *Sam.* 2:8 inherit throne of *g.*
4:21 *g.* is departed from Isr. 22
1 *Chr.* 22:5 ho. for L. must be *g.*
29:11 thine is greatness, power
and *g.* *Mat.* 6:13
Est. 5:11 H. told *g.* of riches
Job 39:20 *g.* of nostrils terrible
40:10 array thyself with *g.*
Ps. 24:7 King of *g.* sh. come in, 9
10 who is this King of *g.?*
29:3 the God of *g.* thundereth
49:16 *g.* of house is increased
73:24 afterward receive me to *g.*
79:9 O God, for *g.* of name
85:9 that *g.* may dwell in land
89:17 art *g.* of their strength
106:20 changed *g.* into similit.
145:11 *g.* of thy kingdom
149:5 the saints be joyful in *g.*
Prov. 3:35 wise shall inherit *g.*
17:6 *g.* of children are fathers
20:29 *g.* of young men is stren.
25:27 to search own *g.* is not *g.*
28:12 righteous rej. there is *g.*
Is. 2:10 hide for *g.* of maj. 19:21
4:5 the *g.* shall be a defence
5:14 *g.* and pomp desc. unto it
10:3 where will ye leave *g.?*
12 punish *g.* of high looks
18 consume *g.* of his forest
13:19 Babylon *g.* of kingdoms
14:18 all lie in *g.* each in house
16:14 *g.* of M. sh. be contemned
17:3 as *g.* of children of Israel
4 *g.* of Jacob sh. be made th.
20:5 ashamed of Egypt their *g.*
21:16 the *g.* of Kedar shall fail
22:24 on him *g.* of father's ho.
23:9 to stain pride of *g.*
24:16 songs, even *g.* to righte.
35:2 *g.* of Lebanon be given
61:6 their *g.* ye boast yourselv.
66:11 delighted wi. abund. of *g.*
12 *g.* of Gentiles as flowing st.
Jer. 2:11 people have changed *g.*
13:11 might be to me for a *g.*
18 crown of your *g.*
Ezek. 20:6 the *g.* of all lands, 15
24:25 from them joy of their *g.*
25:9 open *g.* of the country
26:20 *g.* in land of the living
31:18 art thou thus like in *g.?*
Dan. 2:37 power and *g.* 7:14
4:36 *g.* of kingdom returned
11:39 increase with *g.*
Hos. 4:7 change *g.* into shame
9:11 Ephraim, their *g.* fly away
10:5 priests rejoi. for *g.* thereof
Mic. 1:15 Adullam the *g.* of Isr.
Nah. 2:9 none end of store and *g.*

Hab. 2:16 filled wi. shame for *g.*
Hag. 2:3 saw house in first *g.?*
7 fill house with *g.* saith Lord
9 *g.* of latter house greater
Zec. 2:5 I will be *g.* in midst
8 after *g.* sent me to nations
6:13 build temple, he bear *g.*
11:3 their *g.* is spoiled
12:7 *g.* of house of Dav. *g.* of J.
Mat. 4:8 kingd. and *g.* of them
6:2 sound trumpet, have *g.*
16:27 in *g.* of Fa. *Mark* 8:38
24:30 S. coming with power and
g. *Mark* 13:26 ; *Luke* 21:27
Luke 2:14 *g.* to G. in high. 19:38
32 the *g.* of thy people Israel
4:6 power will I give th. and *g.*
9:31 in *g.* spake of his decease
John 17:5 *g.* wh. I had with thee
22 *g.* thou gavest me
Acts 7:2 G. of *g.* appeared
12:23 because he gave not G. *g.*
22:11 I could not see *g.* of light
Rom. 4:20 strong, giving *g.* to G.
6:4 raised by *g.* of the Father
8:18 not wor. be com. with *g.*
9:4 pertaineth *g.* and covenants
23 had afore prepared unto *g.*
11:36 *g.* for ev. *Gal.* 1:5 ; 2 *Tim.*
4:18 ; *Heb.* 13:21 ; 1 *Pet.* 5:11
16:27 to God be *g.* 1 *Tim.* 1:17
1 *Cor.* 2:7 God ordained to our *g.*
8 not crucified the Lord of *g.*
11:7 woman is the *g.* of the man
15 wo. ha. long hair, is *g.* to h.
15:40 *g.* of celestial, *g.* of terres.
41 one *g.* of sun, ano. *g.* of m.
43 sown in dishon. raised in *g.*
2 *Cor.* 3:7 *g.* of his countenance
9 if condemnation be *g.* righteousness exceed in *g.*
10 no *g.* by reason of *g.* th. ex.
18 all are changed from *g.* to *g.*
4:17 work. eternal weight of *g.*
8:19 administered, to *g.* of Lord
23 messengers, and *g.* of Christ
Eph. 1:6 praise of *g.* of his grace
17 Father of *g.* give you Spirit
18 know what is riches of *g.*
3:13 tribulations, wh. is your *g.*
21 *g.* in the church by Chr. J.
Phil. 1:11 fruits, by Christ to *g.*
3:19 whose *g.* is in their shame
4:19 according to his rich. in *g.*
20 God and our F. be *g.* for ev.
Col. 1:27 Christ the hope of *g.*
3:4 ye sh. appear with him in *g.*
1 *Thes.* 2:6 nor of men sought *g.*
12 called you to king. and *g.*
20 for ye are our *g.* and joy
2 *Thes.* 1:9 pun. from *g.* of power
2:14 obtaining of *g.* of our Lord
1 *Tim.* 3:16 received up unto *g.*
2 *Tim.* 1:10 Christ, with eter. *g.*
Heb. 2:10 bringing sons unto *g.*
3:3 man counted worthy mo. *g.*
9:5 cherubim of *g.* shadowing
Jam. 2:1 faith of Jesus, L. of *g.*
1 *Pet.* 1:8 rej. with joy full of *g.*
11 testified *g.* that sho. follow
21 God raised him, gave him *g.*
24 *g.* of man as flower of grass
2:20 what *g.* is it, when buffet.?
4:14 spirit of *g.* resteth on you
5:1 the *g.* that shall be revealed
10 called us to eternal *g.* by C.
2 *Pet.* 1:3 that hath called us to *g.*
17 voice to him from excel. *g.*
3:18 to him be *g.* ever, *Rev.* 1:6
Jude 25 only G. our Savio. be *g.*
Rev. 4:11 worthy to rec. *g.* 5:12
7:12 blessing and *g.* to our God
11:13 rem. affrighted, gave *g.*

See CROWN, HONOR, VAIN.

Give GLORY.
Jos. 7:19 my son, *give g.* to God

1 *Sam.* 6:5 shall *give g.* to God
1 *Chr.* 16:28 *g.* to L. *g.* 29 ; *Ps.*
    29:1, 2 ; 96:7, 8 ; *Jer.* 13:16
Ps. 84:11 L. will *g.* grace and *g.*
    115:1 to thy name *give g.*
Is. 42:12 let them *g. g.* unto L.
Mal. 2:2 to heart, to *give g.*
Luke 17:18 returned to *give g.*
Rev. 4:9 those beasts *give g.*
    14:7 fear God, *give g.* to him
    16:9 repented not to *give g.*

GLORY of God.

Ps. 19:1 heavens declare *g. of G.*
Prov. 25:2 *g. of God* to conceal
Ezek. 8:4 the *g. of G.* of Israel
    9:3 *g. of G.* gone up fr. cherub
    10:19 *g. of God* over th. 11:22
    43:2 *g. of God* came from east
John 11:4 sickness is for *g. of G.*
    40 shouldst see *g. of God*
Acts 7:55 S. looked, saw *g. of G.*
Rom. 3:23 short of *g. of God*
    5:2 rej. in hope of the *g. of God*
    15:7 as C. receiv. us, to *g. of G.*
1 *Cor.* 10:31 all to *g. of G.*
    11:7 man is image and *g. of God*
2 *Cor.* 4:6 lig. of kno. of *g. of G.*
    15 thanks. redound to *g. of G.*
Phil. 1:11 by Ch. to the *g. of God*
    2:11 J. is Lord to the *g. of God*
Rev. 15:8 filled w. sm. f. *g. of G.*
    21:11 Jerusa. having *g. of God*
    23 the *g. of God* did lighten it

His GLORY.

Deut. 5:24 L. hath showed *his g.*
    33:17 *his g.* firstling of bullock
1 *Chr.* 16:24 declare *his g.* among
    the heathen, *Ps.* 96:3
Ps. 21:5 *his g.* is great in salva.
    29:9 every one speak of *his g.*
    49:17 *his g.* shall not descend
    72:19 earth be filled with *his g.*
    78:61 deliv. *his g.* to enemy's h.
    89:44 hast made *h. g.* to cease
    97:6 and all the people see *h. g.*
    102:16 build J. appear in *his g.*
    113:4 *h. g.* above heav. 148:13
Is. 3:8 to provoke eyes of *his g.*
    6:3 whole earth full of *his g.*
    10:16 *his g.* kindle a burning
    59:19 *his g.* from rising of sun
    60:2 *his g.* shall be seen
Jer. 22:18 Ah L. or Ah *his g.*
Ezek. 43:2 earth shin. with *h. g.*
Dan. 5:20 took *h. g.* from him
Hab. 3:3 *his g.* covered heavens
Mat. 6:29 Sol. in *h. g. Luke* 12:27
    19:28 S. of m. sit in *h. g. Lu.* 9:26
Luke 9:32 wh. awake, saw *his g.*
    24:26 to enter into *his g.*
John 1:14 beheld *h. g. g.* of only
    2:11 J. manifested forth *his g.*
    12:41 said E. when saw *his g.*
Rom. 3:7 thro. my lie unto *h. g.*
    9:23 known riches of *his g.*
Eph. 1:12 the praise of *his g.* 14
    3:16 according to riches of *his g.*
Heb. 1:3 the brightness of *his g.*
1 *Pet.* 4:13 when *h. g.* be revealed
Jude 24 before presence of *h. g.*
Rev. 18:1 earth light. with *h. g.*

My GLORY.

Gen. 45:13 of all *my g.*
Ex. 29:43 sanctified by *my g.*
    33:22 whie m. *g.* passeth by
Num. 14:22 wh. have seen *m. g.*
Job 19:9 hath stript me of *my g.*
    29:20 *my g.* was fresh in me
Ps. 3:3 thou art m. *g.* and lifter
    4:2 long turn *m. g.* to shame?
    16:9 m. *g.* rej. ; 30:12 m. *g.* sing
    57:8 awake, m. *g.* ; 62:7 m. *g.*
    108:1 give praise with m. *g.*
Is. 42:8 m. *g.* not give, 48:11
    43:7 created him for *my g.*
    46:13 salvation for Israel *my g.*

60:7 will glorify house of *my g.*
66:18 shall come and see *my g.*
    19 seen m. *g.* declare m. *g.*
Ezek. 39:31 set *my g.* am. heath.
Mic. 2:9 from chil. taken *my g.*
John 8:50 I seek not *mi.* own *g.*
    17:24 they may behold *my g.*

GLORY of the Lord.

Ex. 16:7 ye shall see *g. of t. L.*
    10 *g. of t. L.* appear. *Lev.* 9:23 ;
    Num. 14:10 ; 16:19, 42 ; 20:6
    24:16 *g. of the Lord* abode on S.
    17 *g. of the L.* like devour. fire
    40:34 *g. of the L.* filled taber. 35
Lev. 9:6 *g. of the L.* shall appear
Num. 11:21 filled with *g. of L.*
1 *K.* 8:11 the *g. of the L.* filled
    tile house, 2 *Chr.* 5:14 ; 7:1,
    2, 3 ; *Ezek.* 43:5 ; 44:4
Ps. 104:31 *g. of the L.* sh. endure
    138:5 for great is the *g. of t. L.*
Is. 35:2 they shall see *g. of t. L.*
    40:5 *g. of the L.* shall be reveal.
    58:8 *g. of the L.* sh. be rearward
    60:1 *g. of the L.* is risen
Ezek. 1:28 likeness of *g. of t. L.*
    3:12 blessed be *g. of the Lord*
    23 *g. of the L.* stood there
    10:4 *g. of the L.* went fr. cherub
    18 *g. of L.* departed from thre.
    11:23 *g. of the L.* went from city
    43:4 *g. of t. L.* came into house
Hab. 2:14 filled wi. kn. of *g. of L.*
Luke 2:9 *g. of t. L.* shone round
2 *Cor.* 3:18 *g. of the Lord*

Thy GLORY.

Ex. 33:18 said, Show me *thy g.*
Ps. 8:1 *thy g.* above the heavens
    45:3 sword on thigh, with *thy g.*
    57:5 *thy g.* ab. earth, 11 ; 108:5
    63:2 see *thy* power and *g.*
Ps. 90:16 let *t. g.* app. unto chil.
    102:15 all kings of earth *thy g.*
Is. 22:18 chariots of *t. g.*
    60:19 God *thy g.* ; 62:2 see *thy g.*
    63:15 behold from habit. of *t. g.*
Jer. 14:21 nor dis. throne of *t. g.*
    48:18 come down from *thy g.*
Hab. 2:16 spewing sh. be on *t. g.*

GLORIOUS.

Ex. 15:6 right hand, O Lord, *g.*
    11 like Lord, *g.* in holiness
Deut. 28:58 fear this *g.* name
2 *Sam.* 8:20 *g.* was the k. of Isr.
1 *Chr.* 29:13 praise thy *g.* name
Neh. 9:5 blessed be thy *g.* name
Ps. 45:13 king's dau. *g.* within
    66:2 make his praise *g.*
    72:19 blessed be *g.* name
    66:4 more *g.* than mountains
    87:3 *g.* things spoken of thee
    111:3 work honorable and *g.*
    145:5 speak of *g.* honor of maj.
    12 make known *g.* majesty
Is. 4:2 branch of the Lord be *g.*
    11:10 root of Jesse, his rest *g.*
    22:23 for a *g.* throne to house
    28:1 *g.* beauty is fading flower
    4 *g.* beauty on head of valley
    33:21 *g.* L. be a place of streams
    49:5 I shall be *g.* in eyes of L.
    60:13 the place of my feet *g.*
    63:1 who is this, *g.* in apparel ?
    12 led them with his *g.* arm
    14 people to make *g.* name
Jer. 17:12 a *g.* high throne from
Ezek. 27:25 *g.* in midst of seas
Dan. 11:16 he sh. stand in *g.* land
    41 he shall enter into *g.* land
    45 between seas, in *g.* holy m.
Luke 13:17 rejoiced for *g.* things
Rom. 8:21 into *g.* liberty of chil.
2 *Cor.* 3:7 ministration engra. *g.*
    3:8 ministration of Sp. rather *g.*
    4:4 lest light of *g.* gospel shine
Eph. 5:27 present it a *g.* church

Phil. 3:21 fashioned like *g.* body
Col. 1:11 accord. to his *g.* power
1 *Tim.* 1:11 accord. to *g.* gospel
Tit. 2:13 looking for *g.* appearing

GLORIOUSLY.

Ex. 15:1 he hath triumphed *g.*
Is. 24:23 reign before ancients *g.*

GLORY, Verb.

Ex. 8:9 Moses said, *g.* over me
2 *K.* 14:10 *g.* of this, and tarry
1 *Chr.* 16:10 *g.* ye in his holy
    name, *Ps.* 105:3
    35 we may *g.* in thy praise
Ps. 63:11 swear. by him shall *g.*
    64:10 the upright in heart sh. *g.*
    106:5 I may *g.* with thy inheri.
Is. 41:16 shalt *g.* in Holy One
    45:25 in L. shall seed of Isr. *g.*
Jer. 4:2 and in him shall they *g.*
    9:23 let not wise, rich man *g.*
    24 *g.* in this, that he knoweth
Rom. 4:2 he hath whereof to *g.*
    5:3 we *g.* in tribulations also
    15:17 I have whereof I may *g.*
1 *Cor.* 1:29 no flesh *g.* in his pre.
    31 glor. *g.* in L. 2 *Cor.* 10:17
    3:21 let no man *g.* in men
    4:7 *g.* as if hadst not received ?
    9:16 nothing to *g.* of
2 *Cor.* 5:12 to *g.* on our behalf,
    who *g.* in apppearance
    11:12 wherein *g.* be found
    18 *g.* after the flesh, I will *g.*
    20 If *g.* I will *g.* of my infirmi.
    12:1 not expedient for me to *g.*
    5 of myself I will not *g.*
    6 I desire to *g.* not be a fool
    9 rather *g.* in my infirmities
Gal. 6:13 may *g.* in your flesh
    14 I should *g.* save in the cross
2 *Thes.* 1:4 so that we *g.* in you
Jam. 3:14 if ye have envy. *g.* not

GLORIEST, ETH.

Jer. 9:24 let him that *g.* 1 *Cor.*
    1:31 ; 2 *Cor.* 10:17
    49:4 why *g.* thou in valleys ?

GLORYING.

1 *Cor.* 5:6 your *g.* is not good
    9:15 than any sh. make *g.* void
2 *Cor.* 7:4 great is my *g.* of you
    12:11 I am become a fool in *g.*

GLUTTON.

Deut. 21:20 this our son is a *g.*
Prov. 23:21 *g.* sh. come to pover.

GLUTTONOUS.

Mat. 11:19 a man *g. Luke* 7:34

GNASH, ED, ED, ETH, ING.

Job 16:9 he *g.* on me, *Ps.* 37:12
Ps. 35:16 *g.* on me with teeth
Ps. 112:10 he shall *g. w.* his teeth
Lam. 2:16 hiss and *g.* the teeth
Mat. 8:12 *g.* of t. 13:42, 50 ; 23:13 ;
    24:51 ; 25:30 ; *Luke* 13:28
Mark 9:18 he foameth and *g.*
Acts 7:54 *g.* on him with teeth

GNAT.

Mat. 23:24 strain at *g.* sw. camel

GNAW, ED.

Zep. 3:3 they *g.* not the bones
Rev. 16:10 *g.* tongues for pain

GO.

Gen. 3:14 on thy belly shalt *g.*
    16:8 whither wilt thou *g.* ?
    24:42 prosper my way wh. I *g.*
    58 wilt thou *g.* with this man ?
    26:16 Ah! said to Is. *g.* from us
    28:20 if C. keep me in way I *g.*
    32:26 let me *g.* ; I will not let
    thee *g.* except thou bless me
    37:30 whither shall I *g.* ?
    43:8 send the lad, we will *g.*

Ex. 3:19 will not let you *g.* 4:21
21 when ye *g.* sh. not *g.* empty
4:23 let my son *g.* if thou refuse,
  8:2, 21; 9:2; 10:4
5:1 let my people *g.* 7:16; 8:1,
  20; 9:1, 13; 10:3
2 nor will I let Israel *g.*
8:8 I will let people *g.* 28; 9:28
32 nor would he let people *g.*
  7:14; 9:35; 10:26, 27
10:9 *g.* with our young and old
13:21 light to them *g. Neh.* 9:12, 19
14:5 that we have let Israel *g.*
17:5 *g.* on before the people
23:23 angel *g.* bef. thee, 32:34
32:23 to *g.* before us, *Acts* 7:40
33:14 my pres. sh. *g.* with thee
34:9 if found grace, *g.* am. us
Num. 22:13 L. refuse. leave to *g.*
20 if the men called thee, *g.*
24:14 now I *g.* unto my people
31:23 make it *g.* through fire
32:6 *g.* to war, and ye sit here?
17 but we will *g.* ready armed
Deut. 1:33 way ye should *g.*
4:5 ye *g.* 6:1; 11:8, 11; 30:18
40 that it *g.* well, 5:16; 19:13
11:28 if ye *g.* after gods, 28:14
31:6 he it is that doth *g.*
7 must *g.* with this people
8 he it is that doth *g.* bef. thee
16 whither they *g.* amongst
21 know imagina. they *g.* abo.
Jos. 1:16 whither sendest will *g.*
3:4 may know way we must *g.*
Jud. 1:25 let *g.* man and family
4:8 if thou wilt *g.* then I will *g.*
6:14 said *g.* in this thy might
7:4 this shall *g.* the same sh. *g.*
18:6 is way wherein ye *g.*
9 not slothful to *g.* to possess
19:25 day began, they let her *g.*
Ruth 1:18 steadf. minded to *g.*
1 *Sam.* 5:11 let it *g.* th. its place
6:6 did they not let people *g.?*
12:21 ye *g.* after vain things
16:2 how can I *g.?* if Saul hear
17:33 not able to *g.* ag. Philist.
18:2 let him *g.* no more home
23:13 D. went whither could *g.*
2 *Sam.* 12:23 I shall *g.* to him
13:13 whither cause shame to *g.*
15:20 seeing I *g.* whither I may
17:11 *g.* to battle in thy person
20:11 David, let him *g.* after J.
1 *K.* 2:2 I *g.* way of all the earth
11:22 let me *g.* in any wise
13:17 nor *g.* by way thou camest
20:42 let *g.* a man appointed
22:4 *g.* with me, 2 *Chr.* 18:3
2 *K.* 3:7 *g.* with me ag. Moab?
4:23 wilt thou *g.* to him to-day?
6:22 set bread that he may *g.*
10:24 he that letteth him *g.*
18:21 *g.* into hand, *Is.* 36:6
2 *Chr.* 14:11 in thy name we *g.*
25:7 let not army of Israel *g.*
8 if thou wilt *g.* do it, be stro.
Job 6:18 they *g.* to nothing
10:21 before I *g.* whence I shall
  not return, 16:22
20:26 it *g.* ill with him
21:29 not asked th. *g.* by way?
27:6 righteous. I will not let *g.*
Ps. 32:8 teach in way shalt *g.?*
39:13 before I *g.* hence, and be
42:9 why *g.* I mourning, 43:2
49:19 *g.* to generation of fathers
84:7 *g.* fr. strength to strength
85:13 right. shall *g.* before him
89:14 mercy and truth *g.* before
107:7 might *g.* to a city of habi.
132:7 we will *g.* into his taber.
139:7 whither *g.* from thy pres.
Prov. 2:19 none that *g.* return
3:28 *g.* and come ag. to-morrow
6:28 can one *g.* on hot coals
9:15 passengers who *g.* right on

14:7 *g.* from presence of foolish
15:12 neither scorner *g.* to wise
19:7 more do his friends *g.* far
22:6 train child in way he sh. *g.*
30:29 three things which *g.* well
Ec. 3:20 all *g.* unto one place
5:15 naked to *g.* as he came, 16
6:6 do not all *g.* to one place?
7:2 to *g.* to house of mourning
9:3 they *g.* to the dead
10:15 kn. not how to *g.* to city
12:5 mourners *g.* about streets
Cant. 3:4 I would not let him *g.*
Is. 3:16 and mincing as they *g.*
6:8 and who will *g.* for us?
9 *g.* tell his people, *Acts* 28:26
27:4 I would *g.* through them
28:13 they might *g.* and fall
45:13 shall let *g.* my captives
48:17 by way shouldest *g.*
58:8 righteousn. *g.* before thee
62:10 *g.* thro' *g.* thro' the gates
Jer. 1:7 shalt *g.* to all I send th.
9:2 I might *g.* from my people
31:22 how long *g.* about, O dau.
34:3 *g.* to Babylon, *Mic.* 4:10
40:4 good to *g.* there *g.* 5
42:22 die, whither ye des. to *g.*
46:22 voice shall *g.* like serpent
50:33 refused to let them *g.*
Ezek. 8:6 sho. *g.* far fr. sanctu.?
14:17 sword *g.* through the land
21:16 *g.* thee one way or other
Hos. 5:6 *g.* with floc. to seek L.
7:11 they *g.* to Assyria
12 when they *g.* I will spread
11:3 I taught Ephr. also to *g.*
Mic. 5:8 if he *g.* through tread.
Zec. 6:7 the bay sought to *g.*
8 these *g.* towards the north
8:21 inhab. of one city *g.* to an.
23 *g.* with you, we have heard
9:4 *g.* with whirlwinds of south
Mat. 2:22 Joseph was afraid to *g.*
5:41 *g.* mile, *g.* twain, *Luke* 7:8
8:7 and I say *g.* and he goeth
10:6 *g.* rath. to lost sheep of Is.
21:30 I *g.* sir, and went not
25:9 *g.* rather to them that sell
28:19 *g.* ye and teach all nations
Mark 6:38 *g.* see; 11:6 let th. *g.*
Luke 1:17 shall *g.* before him
9:51 set face to *g.* to Jerusalem
60 *g.* and preach kingd. of God
10:37 *g.* thou and do likewise
22:33 I am ready to *g.* to prison
68 not ans. me, nor let me *g.*
23:22 chastise him, let him *g.*
John 6:68 L. to whom sh. we *g.*
7:33 I *g.* unto him sent me
8:14 but I know whither I *g.*
21 I *g.* my way, whither I *g.*
13:36 whither I *g.* not follow
14:2 I *g.* to pre. place for you
4 whither I *g.* ye know
12 bec. I *g.* to Father, 16:10
28 I *g.* to Father, 16:17, 28
19:12 if thou let this man *g.*
Acts 1:25 *g.* to his own place
3:13 when deter. to let him *g.*
4:21 threatened, let them *g.*
23 being let *g.* went to comp.
5:40 sh. not speak, let them *g.*
16:35 saying, Let those men, *g.*
20:22 *g.* bound in spirit to Jer.
25:12 to Cesar shalt thou *g.*
26:18 examined me, let me *g.*
Rom. 15:25 now I *g.* to Jerusal.
1 *Cor.* 6:1 *g.* to law before unjust
10:27 and ye be disposed to *g.*
16:4 if meet I *g.* also, they sh. *g.*
2 *Cor.* 9:5 exhort breth. *g.* before
Phil. 2:23 how it will *g.* with me
Jam. 4:13 will *g.* un. such a city

See FREE.

GO aside,
Num. 5:12 11 any man's wi. *g. a.*

Deut. 28:14 shalt not *g. a.* from
Jer. 15:5 *g. a.* to ask how doest
Acts 4:15 commanded th. to *g. a.*

GO astray.
Deut. 22:1 not see h. ox *g. a.*
Ps. 58:3 *g. a.* as soon as born
Prov. 5:23 in great. of folly *g. a.*
7:25 *g.* not *a.* into her paths
28:10 causeth righteous to *g. a.*
Jer. 50:6 shepherds caused *g. a.*
Ezek. 14:11 Israel *g.* no more *a.*

GO away.
Ex. 8:28 not *g.* very far *away*
Deut. 15:16 say, I will not *g. a.*
1 *Sam.* 24:19 he let ene. *g. a.?*
Job 4:21 doth not excel. *g. a.?*
15:30 by breath of mouth *g. a.*
Jer. 51:40 escaped sword *g. a.*
Hos. 5:14 I will tear and *g. a.*
Mat. 25:46 *g. a.* to ever. punish.
John 6:67 will ye also *g. a.?*
14:28 how I said, I *g. a.* 16:7

GO their way
John 18:8 let these *g. their way*

GO thy way.
Dan. 12:13 *g. t. way* till the end
Acts 24:25 *g. thy w.* for this time

GO your way.
Mark 11:2 *g. your w.* into village
Luke 10:10 rec. you not, *g. y. w.*

GO back.
Ex. 14:21 caused sea to *g. back*
Jos. 23:12 ye in any wise *g. back*
Jud. 11:35 mouth, I cannot *g. b.*
2 *K.* 20:9 shall the shadow *g. b.*
Ps. 80:18 not *g. back* from thee
Jer. 40:5 *g. back* to Gedaliah, son
Ezek. 24:14 I will not *g. back*

GO down.
Gen. 46:3 fear not to *g. d.* to Eg.
Num. 16:30 *g.* d. into the pit
Deut. 24:15 nor sun *g. d.* on hire
Jos. 10:13 sun hasted not to *g. d.*
Jud. 7:10 fear to *g. d. g.* with P.
2 *Sam.* 11:8 *g. d.* to thy house.
15:30 make thee *g.* up and d.
2 *K.* 1:15 *g. down* with him
20:10 shadow to *g. d.* ten deg.
Ps. 28:1 in moment *g. d.* to gr.
Ps. 22:29 all that *g. d.* to dust
28:1 like th. *g. d.* to pit, 143:7
55:15 let *g. d.* quick into hell
107:23 that *g. d.* to sea in ships
115:17 any that *g. d.* into silence
Prov. 5:4 her feet *g. d.* to death
Is. 14:19 cast out, as those *g. d.*
30:2 woe to th. *g. d.* to Eg. 31:1
38:18 *g. d.* into pit cannot hope
60:20 sun sh. not *g. d.* nor moon
Jer. 50:27 let *g. d.* to slaughter
Ezek. 26:20 them that *g. d.* to
  the pit, 31:14; 32:18, 24, 25,
  29, 30
47:8 th. waters *g. d.* into desert
Amos 8:9 sun to *g. d.* at noon
Mic. 3:6 sun *g. d.* over prophets
Mark 13:15 him on ho. not *g. d.*
Acts 25:5 able to *g. d.* with me
Eph. 4:26 not sun *g. d.* on wrath

GO forth.
Gen. 8:16 *g. f.* of the ark, thou
42:15 not *g. f.* hence, except
2 *Sam.* 11:1 at time kings *g. f.*
18:2 I will *g. f.* with you myself
19:7 if thou *g.* not *f.* not tarry
1 *K.* 2:36 *g.* not *f.* any whither
22:22 he said, I will *g. forth*
2 *K.* 9:15 none *g. forth*
19:31 out of Jerusalem shall *g.*
  forth a remnant, *Is.* 37:32
Job 24:5 as wild asses *g.* they *f.*
Ps. 78:52 made his people to *g. f.*
108:11 wilt not *g. f.* with hosts?
Prov. 25:8 *g.* not *f.* hastily to st.
30:29 no king, *g. f.* by bands

Cant. 3:11 *g. f.* O dau. of Zion
7:11 let us *g. f.* into villages
Is. 2:3 out of Z. shall *g. f.* law,
    Mic. 4:2
42:13 L. sh. *g. f.* mighty man
48:20 *g. f.* Babylon, *Jer.* 50:8
49:9 say to prisoners, *g. f.*
    17 made these waste shall *g. f.*
62:1 till righteous. thereof *g. f.*
Jer. 6:25 *g.* not *forth* into field
14:18 if I *g. f.* into the field
15:2 whither shall we *g. forth* ?
25:32 evil *g. f.* from nation to
31:4 thou shalt *g. f.* in dances
    39 the measur. line shall *g. f.*
38:17 wilt *g. f.* to king of Baby.
43:12 he shall *g. f.* in peace
Ezek. 12:4 they that *g. f.* to capt.
30:9 in that day messen. sh. *g. f.*
Dan. 11:44 he sh. *g. f.* with fury
Joel 2:16 let bridegr. *g. f.* cham.
Hab. 1:4 judgment never *g. f.*
Zec. 6:5 four spirits wh. *g. f.*
    6 black horses *g. f.* to north
14:3 then sh. L. *g. f.* and fight
Mal. 4:2 ye sh. *g. f.* and grow
Mat. 24:26 is in desert., *g. f.*
Acts 16:3 would Paul have *g. f.*
Heb. 13:13 let us *y. forth* to him
Rev. 16:14 sp. of devils wh. *g. f.*

GO forward.

Ex. 14:15 speak to Is. they *g. f.*
2 *K.* 20:9 shadow *g. f.* ten deg.
Job 23:8 I *g. forw.* but he is not
    there

GO in, into, or not GO in.

Num. 4:19 A. and sons sh. *g. in*
    8:15 after that sh. Levites *g. in*
27:17 *g.* out and *g. in* before
32:9 should not *g. into* the land
Deut. 1:38 Josh. sh. *g. in* thither
4:1 and *g. in* and possess, 8:1
Ps. 26:4 not *g. in* with dissem.
118:19 open gates, I will *g. in*
119:35 *g. in* path of thy com.
132:7 we will *g. into* his tabern.
Prov. 27:10 nor *g. i.* brother's h.
Is. 2:19 *g.* into holes of rocks
Jer. 4:5 let us *g. into* def. cities
36:5 I cannot *g. into* house of L.
42:14 we will *g. into* land of E.
    19 L. said, *g.* ye not i. Egypt
Ezek. 46:10 when they *g. into*
Nah. 3:14 *g. into* clay, and tread
Zec. 6:10 *g. into* house of Josiah
Mat. 2:20 take child, *g. into* Isr.
7:13 many there be that *g. in*
20:4 *g. into* the vineyard, 7
21:2 *g. into* village, *Luke* 19:30
    31 harlots *g. into* king. of God
22:9 *g. into* highways, bid to
26:13 neither *g. in.* nor suffer
26:18 *g. into* city, *Mark* 14:13
Mark 6:36 may *g. into* country
8:26 nor *g. into* town, nor tell
16:15 *g. into* all the world
Luke 15:28 and would not *g. i.*
John 10:9 he shall *g. in* and out
Acts 1:11 ye see him *g. i.* heaven
Rev. 17:8 beast shall *g. i.* perdi.

See CAPTIVITY.

GO in.

Gen. 16:2 *g. in* unto my maid
19:34 make drink wine, *g. in*
30:3 my maid Bilhah, *g. in* to
38:8 *g. in* unto brother's wife
Deut. 21:13 thou *g. in* to her
    22:13 take a wife, *g. in* to her
25:5 husb. brother *g. in* to her
Jos. 23:12 make marriages, *g. in*
Jud. 15:1 will *g. in* to my wife
2 *Sam.* 16:21 *g. in* to fath. concu.
1 *K.* 11:2 ye sh. not *g. in* to them
Ezek. 23:44 as they *g. in* to wom.
Amos 2:7 man and father *g. in*

GO in peace.

Gen. 15:15 *g.* to thy fathers *in p.*
Ex. 4:18 J. said to Mos. *g. in p.*
18:23 people *g.* to place *in p.*
Jud. 18:6 said to Danites, *g. in p.*
1 *Sam.* 1:17 E. said to H. *g. in p.*
20:42 Jona. said to Dav. *g. in p.*
25:35 David said to Ab. *g. in p.*
29:7 Achish said to Da. *g. in p.*
2 *Sam.* 15:9 said to Abs. *g. in p.*
1 *K.* 2:6 let not head *g.* do. in p.
2 *K.* 5:19 Elisha said, *in peace*
Mark 5:34 *g. in p.* and be whole
Luke 7:50 saved thee, *g. in p.* 8:48
Acts 15:33 they were let *g. in p.*

Let us GO.

Gen. 37:17 let us *g.* to Dothan
Ex. 3:18 now *let us g.* three days'
    journey, 5:3
5:8 they say, *let us g.* sac. 17
13:15 Ph. would hardly *l. us g.*
Deut. 13:2 *l. us g.* aft. gods, 6:13
1 *Sam.* 9:9 *let us g.* to seer, 10
11:14 *let us g.* to Gilgal, and
14:1 *let us g.* to Philistines, 6
2 *K.* 6:2 *let us g.* to Jordan
Ps. 122:1 *let us g.* into h. of Lord
Is. 2:3 *let us g.* to mount. of L.
Jer. 4:5 *let us g.* into def. cities
6:5 *let us g.* destroy her palaces
35:11 *let us g.* to Jeru. for fear
46:16 *let us g.* to our people
51:9 *let us g.* ev. one to country
Mark 1:38 *let us g.* to next towns
14:42 *let us g.* he that betrayeth
Luke 2:15 *let us g.* to Bethlehem
John 11:7 *let us g.* to Judea
    15 *let us g.* to him ; 16 that we
14:31 arise, *let us g.* hence
Acts 15:36 *let us g.* visit brethren
Heb. 6:1 *let us g.* to perfection

I will GO.

Gen. 13:9 *I w. g.* right, *I w. g.* 1.
24:58 wilt *g.* with man ? *I. w. g.*
33:12 *I will g.* bef. thee, *Is.* 45:2
45:28 *I w. g.* see him bef. I die
Num. 20:19 *I will g.* on feet
23:3 stand by burnt-off. *I w. g.*
Deut. 2:27 *I will g.* along high.
Jud. 1:3 *I w. g.* with thee
    4:8 if thou *g.* with me, *I w. g.*
    9 I *will* surely *g.* with thee
16:20 *I w. g.* as at other times
Ruth 1:16 wh. thou goest. *I w. g.*
2 *K.* 6:3 he answered, *I will g.*
2 *Chr.* 18:29 said, *I w. g.* to battle
Ps. 43:4 then w. *I g.* to altar of G
66:13 *I will g.* into thy house
71:16 *I will g.* in strength of L.
118:19 open gates, *I will g.* in
Jer. 2:25 strangers, after *I will g.*
Ezek. 38:11 *I will g.* to them.
Hos. 2:5 said. *I w. g.* after lovers
    7 *I will g.* to my first husband
5:15 *I will g.* to my place, till
Mic. 1:8 *I w. g.* stript and naked
Zec. 8:21 seek the Lord, *I will g.*
Mat. 26:32 *I w. g.* before into
    Galilee, *Mark* 14:28
Luke 15:18 *I w.* arise and *g.* to
Acts 18:6 hence *I w. g.* to Gent.

GO near.

Deut. 5:27 *g. n.* hear all L. says
2 *Sam.* 1:15 *g. n.* fall upon him
Job 31:37 as a prince wou. I *g. n.*
Acts 8:29 *g. n.* join to chariot

GO not, or not GO.

Ex. 33:15 if thy presence *g. not*
Num. 10:30 Hob. said, I will *n. g.*
20:20 he said. Thou shalt *n. g.*
12:16 said to Bal. shalt *not g.*
    18 *n. g.* bey. word of L. 24:13
Deut. 3:27 shalt *n. g.* over Jordan
6:14 ye shall *n. g.* after other
    gods, 1 *K.* 11:10
24:19 thou sh. *n. g.* to fetch it

32:52 thou shalt *not g.* thither
Jos. 8:4 *g. n.* far from the city
Jud. 20:8 we will *n. g.* to tent
Ruth 3:17 *g. n.* empty to mother
1 *Sam.* 17:39 D. said, I *cannot g.*
29:8 I may not *g.* to fight enc.
2 *Sam.* 13:25 n. all *g.* would *n. g.*
2 *K.* 2:18 did I not say, *g. n.* ?
1 *Chr.* 21:30 David could *n. g.*
2 *Chr.* 25:13 soldiers should *n. g.*
Prov. 4:13 take instruc. let *n. g.*
    14 *g. n.* into way of evil men
22:24 with furious man sh. *n. g.*
Is. 52:12 shall *n. g.* with haste
Jer. 10:5 be borne, they *cann. g.*
16:8 sh. *n. g.* to house of feast.
25:6 *g. n.* after other gods, 35:15
27:18 vessels left *g. not* to Baby.
42:19 *g. not* into Egypt, 43:2
49:12 thou shalt *not g.* unpun.
Lam. 4:18 *cannot g.* in streets
Ezek. 42:14 priests sh. *not g.*
Mat. 10:5 *g. n.* into way of Gent.
Luke 10:7 *g. n.* fr. house to house
17:23 there, *g. n.* after, 21:8

GO over.

Deut. 3:25 let me *g. o.* see land
    28 Joshua sh. *g. o.* before, 31:3
4:14 land whither ye *g. over*, 26 ;
    31:13 ; 32:47
    22 I must not *g. o.* Jordan
24:20 shalt not *g. o.* the boughs
30:13 who shall *g. o.* sea for us
31:3 the Lord will *g. o.* before
34:4 thou shalt not *g. o.* thither
Jos. 1:2 arise, *g. over* this Jordan
Jud. 12:5 Eph. said, Let me *g. o.*
1 *Sam.* 13:1 let us *g. o.* to Ph. 6
30:10 so faint, could not *g. o.*
2 *Sam.* 16:9 let me *g. o.* and take
19:37 Chimham, let him *g. o.*
Is. 8:7 come and *g. over* banks
11:15 make men *g. o.* dry-shod
51:23 bow down, we may *g. o.*
54:9 waters of N. no more *g. o.*
Jer. 41:10 Ishm. departed to *g. o.*

GO out.

Gen. 9:10 all that *g. out* of ark
24:11 women *g. o.* to draw wat.
45:1 every man *g. o.* from me
Ex. 6:11 let child. of Isr. *g. out*
8:29 behold, I *g. out* from thee
11:8 after that I will *g. out*
    10 not let chil. of Israel *g. out*
12:22 none shall *g. out* at door
16:4 people *g. o.* and gather
    29 no man *g. o.* on sev. day
21:2 in sev. year he sh. *g. o.* free
    3 came by hims. *g. o.* by hims. ;
        if marr. wife *g. o.* with him
    4 he shall *g. out* by himself
    5 if serv. say, I will not *g. o.*
    7 maid-serv. not *g. o.* as men
    11 then shall she *g. o.* free
Lev. 6:13 fire on altar never *g. o.*
8:33 out *g. o.* of tab. in sev. days
10:7 not *g. o.* out at door, lest die
14:38 priest shall *g. o.* of house
15:16 if man's seed of corp. *g. o.*
16:18 sh. *g. o.* to altar before L.
21:12 nor *g. out* of sanctuary
25:28 in jubilee it sh. *g. o.* 31, 33
    54 sh. *g. o.* in jub. ; 54 sh. *g. o.*
Deut. 24:5 taken wife, *g. o.* one way
28:25 thou shalt *g. out* one way
Jos. 2:19 who *g. o.* blood on head
Jud. 9:38 *g. o.* and fight them
16:20 will *g. o.* as at oth. times
20:28 sh. I again *g. out* to battle
1 *Sam.* 19:3 *g. o.* stand bes. fath.
20:11 let us *g. out* into the field
28:1 Achish said, *g. o.* with me
2 *Sam.* 5:24 the L. sh. *g. o.* befo.
21:17 thou sh. *g.* no more *o.*
1 *K.* 15:17 not suf. any to *g. o.* or
    come in to Asa, 2 *Chr.* 16:1
20:31 ropes on our heads, *g. o.*

1 *Chr.* 20:1 kings *g. o.* to battle
2 *Chr.* 18:21 *g. o.* be a lying spirit
20:17 to-morrow *g. out* against
26:18 *g. o.* of sanctuary, hast. tr.
20 yea, himself hasted to *g. o.*
Job 15:13 words *g. o.* of mouth
Ps. 60:10 not *g. o.* with armies
Prov. 22:10 scorner, conten. *g. o.*
Ec. 8:3 not hasty to *g. o.* of sight
Is. 52:11 depart, *g. o.* fr. thence
12 ye sh. not *g. o.* with haste
55:12 ye shall *g. out* with joy
Jer. 21:12 lest fury *g. o.* like fire
51:45 *g.* ye *o.* of midst of her
Ezek. 15:7 shall *g. out* from fire
44:3 prince sh. *g. o.* same way
46:9 enter, by north, *g. o.* by s.
Amos 4:3 sh. *g. out* at breaches
Zec. 14:3 liv. waters *g. o.* fr. J.
Mat. 25:6 bridegr. cometh, *g. o.*
Luke 9:5 when ye *g. o.* of city
14:21 *g. o.* into streets and lanes
23 *g. o.* into high. and hedges
1 *Cor.* 5:10 must *g. o.* of world
Heb. 11:8 A. when he call. to *g. o.*
Rev. 3:12 over, *g.* no more *out*
20:8 sh. *g. o.* to deceive nations

GO to.
Gen. 11:3 *g. to*, let us make brick
4 *g. to*, let us build: 7
Ec. 2:1 *g. to* now now, I will prove
Is. 5:5 *g. to*, I tell what I will
Jam. 4:13 *g. to*, ye that say
5:1 *g. to* now, ye rich men

GO up.
Gen. 35:1 arise, *g. up* to Bethel, 3
44:33 let lad *g. up* with breth.
34 sh. I *g. up* to father? 45:9
50:6 Phar. said, *g. up*, bury fa.
Ex. 8:3 frogs *g. up* into house
19:12 *g.* not *up* into mount
20:26 nor sh. *g. up* by steps
24:2 neither sh. peo. *g. up* with
32:30 sinned a sin, I will *g. up*
33:1 *g. up*, thou and the people
3 I will not *g. up* in midst
34:24 not desire land, *g. up*
Lev. 19:16 thou shalt not *g. up*
and down as a tale-bearer
Num. 13:30 let *g. up* and pos. it
31 not able to *g. up* ag. people
14:42 *g.* not *up* ; 44 pres. to *g.*
Deut. 25:7 let bro.'s wife *g. up*
30:12 who sh. *g. up* to heaven
Jos. 7:3 *g. up*, 3000 *g. up*
22:33 not intend to *g. up* again.
Jud. 1:1 who *g. up* for us to fight
2 L. said, Judah sh. *g. up*, 20:18
2:1 I made you *g. up* out of Eg.
11:37 *g. up* and down on moun.
18:9 we may *g. up* against them
20:9 *g. up* by lot against Gibeah
18 which sh. *g. up* first to bat.
23 shall I *g. up* ? 2 *Sam.* 2:1
1 *Sam.* 1:22 not *g. up* till child
6:20 to whom sh. he *g. up* fr. us ?
9:13 find him before he *g. up*
14 Samuel to *g. up* to place, 19
14:9 say, Tarry, will not *g. up*
10 come unto us, we will *g. up*
2 *Sam.* 2:1 *g. up* to any cities of
Ju. ? L. said, *g. up* to Hebr.
5:19 shall I *g. up* aga. Philis. ?
15:20 I make thee *g. up* with us
19:34 how long have I to live,
that I should *g. up* ?
24:18 *g. up*, rear alt. 1 *Chr.* 21:18
1 *K.* 12:24 not *g. up*, 2 *Chr.* 11:4
27 people *g. up* to do sacrifice
28 too much to *g. up* to Jerus.
18:43 *g. up* look towards sea
22:6 *g. up*, for the Lord shall deliver it, 12 ; 2 *Chr.* 18:11, 14
20 *g. up* fall at Ram. 2 *Ch.* 18:19
2 *K.* 1:3 *g. up* meet messengers
2:23 *g. up*, thou bald head

3:7 wilt thou *g. up* ag. Moab ?
8 Which way sh. we *g. up* ?
12:17 Haz. set face to *g. up* to J.
18:25 *g. up* ag. land, *Is.* 36:10
20:5 on third day sh. *g. up*
8 sign that I *g. up* ? *Is.* 38:22
22:4 *g. up* to Hilkiah, high-pr.
1 *Chr.* 14:10 sh. I *g. up* ? 14 *g.* not
2 *Chr.* 18:5 sh. we *g. up* to Ram. ?
36:23 let him *g. up*, *Ezr.* 1:3

Ezr. 7:9 to *g. up* from Babylon
13 minded to *g. up*, go with me
Neh. 4:3 fox *g. up* he break down
Ps. 104:8 *g. up* by mountains
132:3 I will not *g. up* into bed
Cant. 6:6 sheep *g. up* from wash.
7:8 I will *g. up* to palm-tree
Is. 2:3 let us *g. up* to mountain
of Lord, *Mic.* 4:2
7:6 let us *g. up* against Judah
15:5 with weep. sh. they *g. up*
21:2 *g. up*, E. ; 34:10 smoke *g. up*
35:9 nor ravenous beast *g. up*
36:10 *g. up* against this land
Jer. 5:10 *g.* ye *up* upon her walls
6:4 and let us *g. up* at noon
21:2 Nebuchadnezzar may *g. up*
22:20 *g. up* to Lebanon, and cry
31:6 let us *g. up* to Z. to the L.
46:8 I will *g. up* and cov. earth
11 *g. up* into Gilead, take balm
48:5 continual weep. sh. *g. up*
49:28 *g. up* to Kedar, spoil
50:21 *g. up* aga. land of Merath.
Ezek. 38:11 *g. up* to unwalled v.
40:26 seven steps to *g. up* to it
Hos. 4:15 nei. *g. up* to Bethaven
Hag. 1:8 *g. up* to mount. bring
Zec. 14:16 *g. up* fr. year to year
Mat. 20:18 we *g. up* to Jerusal.
Mark 10:33 ; *Luke* 18:31
Luke 14:10 Friend, *g. up* higher
John 7:8 *g. up* to feast, I *g.* not
Acts 15:2 *g. up* to Jer. about qu.
21:4 Paul not *g. up* to Jerus. 12
25:9 wilt thou *g. up* to Jeru. ?

GO a whoring.
Ex. 34:15 *g. a whor.* after gods
16 sons, daughters *g. a whor.*
Lev. 20:5 cut off all that *g. a w.*
Num. 15:39 ye use to *g. a whor.*
Deut. 31:16 people will *g. a who.*
2 *Chr.* 21:13 Je. made Ju. *g. a w.*
Ps. 73:27 destroyed all *g. a who.*
Ezek. 6:9 *g. a whor.* after idols

GOEST.
Gen. 28:15 keep thee wh. thou *g.*
32:17 whi. *g.* thou ? *Jud.* 19:17 ;
Zec. 2:2 ; *John* 13:36 ; 16:5
Ex. 33:16 that thou *g.* with us
34:12 no cove. whither thou *g.*
Num. 14:14 *g.* bef. them by day
Deut. 11:10 thou *g.* is not as E.
12:29 cut off nations wh. thou *g.*
20:1 *g.* to battle, seest, 21:10
23:20 God bless thee whither
thou *g. Jos.* 1:7
28:6 blessed when thou *g.* out
19 cursed when thou *g.* out
21 pestilence whither thou *g.*
63 plucked land whi. thou *g.*
32:50 die in mount whither *g.*
Jos. 1:9 L. with thee whi. th. *g.*
Jud. 14:3 *g.* take a wife of Phil.
Ruth 1:16 whi. thou *g.* I will go
2 *Sam.* 15:19 where. *g.* with us ?
1 *K.* 2:37 day *g.* over brook, 42
Ps. 44:9 *g.* not forth with armies
Prov. 4:12 when *g.* steps not str.
6:22 when thou *g.* it shall lead
Ec. 5:1 keep thy foot, *g.* to hou.
9:10 wisdom in grave whith. *g.*
Jer. 45:5 for prey whith. thou *g.*
Mat. 8:19 I will follow whither-
soever thou *g. Luke* 9:57
Luke 12:58 thou wi. thine adver.

Ex. 7:15 he *g.* out into water
22:26 del. th. that sun *g.* down
28:29 Aaron bear when he *g.*
30 Aaron's heart when he *g.* in
35 sound heard when he *g.* in
Lev. 11:21 eat that *g.* on all four
14:46 that *g.* into house unclean
15:32 seed *g.* from him, 22:4
16:17 none in taber. when he *g.*
22:3 who *g.* to holy things unc
27:21 when it *g.* in jubilee
Num. 5:29 when wife *g.* aside
Deut. 1:30 L. which *g.* before
9:3 God is he that *g.* before you
20:4 Lord your G. *g.* with you
23:9 when host *g.* ag. enemies
24:13 deli. pledge when sun *g.*
Jud. 5:31 when *g.* in might
1 *Sam.* 22:14 Dav. who *g.* at bid.
30:24 his part is that *g.* to bat.
2 *K.* 5:18 *g.* to house of Rimmon
11:8 king as he *g.* 2 *Chr.* 23:7
Job 7:9 *g.* to grave, no more
9:11 he *g.* by me, I see him not
34:8 *g.* with workers of iniquity
37:2 sound *g.* out of mouth
39:21 he *g.* to meet armed **men**

Ps. 17:1 *g.* not out of feigned
lips
41:6 when he *g.* abroad, he tell.
68:21 such as *g.* on in trespass.
88:16 fierce wrath *g.* over me
97:3 a fire *g.* before him, burn.
104:23 man *g.* forth to work
126:6 he *g.* forth and weepeth
146:4 breath *g.* forth, he return.

Prov. 6:29 *g.* in to neigh. wife
11:10 when *g.* well with right.
16:18 pride *g.* befo. destruction
20:19 *g.* about as tale-bearer
26:9 thorn *g.* into hand
20 wh. no wood is, fire *g.* out
31:18 candle *g.* not out by night

Ec. 1:5 sun *g.* down, and hasteth
3:21 the spirit of man *g. up*, the
spirit of beast *g.* down
12:5 bec. man *g.* to long home

Is. 28:19 from time it *g.* forth
30:29 when one *g.* with a pipe
55:11 my word be that *g.* forth
59:8 *g.* therein sh. not know pe.
63:14 a beast *g.* down into val.

Jer. 5:6 *g.* out thence be torn
6:4 woe unto us, for day *g.*
21:9 *g.* out to Chal. sh. live, 38:2
22:10 weep for him that *g.*
30:23 whirlwind of Lord *g.* forth
44:17 do what *g.* out of mouth
49:17 *g.* by it be aston. 50:13
Ezek. 7:14 but none *g.* to battle
33:31 heart *g.* after covetousn.
44:27 in day he *g.* into sanct.
Hos. 6:4 good. as dew *g.* away
5 judgments as light that *g.*
Zec. 5:3 this the curse that *g.*
6 this is an ephah that *g.* forth

Mat. 8:9 Go. and he *g. Luke* 7:8
13:44 for joy *g.* and selleth all
15:11 what *g.* into mouth defil.
17:21 *g.* not out but by prayer
26:24 Son of man *g.* as it is wri.
Mark 14:21 ; *Luke* 22:22
28:7 *g.* bef. to Gall. *Mark* 16:7
John 3:8 canst not tell whi. it *g.*
7:20 *g.* about to kill thee ?
10:4 he *g.* before, sheep follow
11:31 she *g.* unto the grave
12:35 knoweth not whither he
g. 1 *John* 2:11
1 *Cor.* 6:6 bro. *g.* to law wi. bro.
9:7 *g.* a warf. at own charges ?
Jam. 1:24 beholdeth him. and *g.*

Rev. 14:4 follow Lamb whi. he *g.*
17:11 of the seven, *g.* into per⌐
19:15 out of mouth *g.* sharp sw.

GOING.

Ex. 17:12 to *g.* down of sun
23:4 if thine enc.'s ox *g.* astray
Num. 34:4 *g.* forth be from south
Deut. 16:6 pass. at *g.* down of sun
33:18 rejoice, Zebulun, in *g.* out
Jos. 7:5 smote them in *g.* down
10:11 in *g.* down to Bethoron
27 *g.* down of sun car. taken
23:14 *g.* the way of all the earth
Jud. 19:18 I am *g.* to house of L.
1 *Sam.* 10:3 3 men *g.* up to God
2 *Sam.* 2:19 in *g.* he turned not
5:24 sound of *g.* in, 1 *Chr.* 14:15
1 *K.* 17:11 she was *g.* to fetch it
22:36 proc. at *g.* down of sun
2 *K.* 2:23 *g.* by way, child. mock.
9:27 smote Ahaziah at *g.* to Gur
2 *Chr.* 18:34 sun *g.* down, he died
Job 1:7 from *g.* to and fro, 2:2
33:24 deliv. from *g.* down to pit
28 deliver soul from *g.* into pit
Ps. 19:6 *g.* from end of heaven
50:1 from rising of sun to *g.*
down, 113:3; *Mal.* 1:11
104:19 sun knoweth his *g.* down
Prov. 7:27 *g.* to chamb. of death
14:15 prudent looketh well to *g.*
30:29 yea, four are comely in *g.*
Is. 13:10 sun darkened in *g.*
Jer. 50:4 *g.* and weeping seek L.
Ezek. 40:31 *g.* up 8 steps, 34, 37
44:5 every *g.* forth of sanctuary
46:12 after *g.* forth, shut gate
Dan. 6:14 till *g.* down of sun
9:25 *g.* forth of commandment
Hos. 6:3 his *g.* forth is prepared
Mat. 26:46 let us be *g.* he is at h.
Luke 14:31 what king *g.* to war ?
John 8:59 *g.* thro. midst of them
Acts 20:5 *g.* before, tar. at Troas
Rom. 10:3 *g.* to estab. own right.
1 *Tim.* 5:24 sins *g.* bef. to judg.
Heb. 7:18 a disannul. of com. *g.*
Jude 7 *g.* after strange flesh, are

See COMING.

GOINGS.

Num. 33:2 Mos. wrote th. *g.* out
Num. 34:5 the *g.* out of their bor.
8, 9, 12; *Jos.* 15:4, 7, 11;
16:3, 8; 18:12, 14
Job 34:21 he seeth all his *g.*
Ps. 17:5 hold my *g.* in thy paths
40:2 and established my *g.*
68:24 seen thy *g.* even *g.* of God
140:4 purposed to overthrow *g.*
Prov. 5:21 he pondereth all his *g.*
20:24 man's *g.* are of the Lord
Is. 59:8 no judgment in their *g.*
Ezek. 42:11 *g.* out accord. to fas.
43:11 show them *g.* out thereof
Mic. 5:2 whose *g.* forth from

GOAD, S.

Jud. 3:31 slew 600 with ox *g.*
1 *Sam.* 13:21 had file to sharp. *g.*
Ec. 12:11 words of wise as *g.*

GOAT.

Lev. 3:12 if his offering be a *g.*
4:24 lay his hand on head of *g.*
7:23 eat no fat of ox, sheep, or *g.*
9:15 the *g.* which was sin-offer.
10:16 Moses sought *g.* sin-offer.
16:9 Aaron shall bring the *g.*
22 let go the *g.* in wilderness
17:3 whosoever killeth a *g.*
22:27 *g.* is brought forth 7 days
Num. 15:27 thro. ignor. bring *g.*
18:17 first. of *g.* sh. not redeem
28:22 one *g.* for a sin-offering,
29:22, 28, 31, 34, 38
Deut. 14:4 eat ox, sheep. and *g.*
Ezek. 43:25 prepa. every day a *g.*

Dan. 8:5 the *g.* had a nota. horn
21 rough *g.* is king of Grecia

He-GOAT.

Num. 7:17 five rams, five *he-g.* 23,
29, 35, 41, 47, 53, 59, 65, 71,
77, 83
88 *he-g.* sixty, the lambs sixty
Deut. 32:14 *he-g.* of breed of Bas.
2 *Chr.* 17:11 Arab. br. 7,700 *he-g.*
29:21 seven *he-g.* for sin-offering
Ezr. 6:17 at dedication 12 *he-g.*
8:35 children offered 12 *he-g.*
Ps. 50:9 I will take no *he-g.* out
Prov. 30:31 com. in going, a *he-g.*
Is. 1:11 not in the blood of *he-g.*
Jer. 50:8 as the *he-g.* before flocks
51:40 bring like rams with *he-g.*
Ezek. 34:17 betw. rams and *he-g.*
Dan. 8:5 behold, a *he-g.* fr. west
8 the *he-g.* waxed very great

Live GOAT.

Lev. 16:20 bring *l. g.* ; 21 lay ha.

Scape-GOAT.

Lev. 16:8 the other lot for *sca.-g.*
10 let him go for *sca.-g.* to wil.
26 that let go *scape-g.* shall

She-GOAT, S.

Gen. 15:9 heifer, a *she-g.* of 3 ye.
31:38 *she-g.* not cast th. young
32:14 200 *she-g.* and 20 he-goats

Wild GOAT.

Deut. 14:5 ye sh. eat the *wild g.*

GOATS.

Gen. 27:9 fetch two kids of *g.*
16 put skins of *g.* on his hands
30:32 spotted and speck. am. *g.*
33 speckled *g.* ; 35 removed *g.*
37:31 killed a kid of the *g.*
Ex. 12:5 take it fr. sheep or *g.*
Lev. 1:10 offering be sheep or *g.*
4:23 if sin come to knowl. shall
bring a kid of the *g.* 28 ; 5:6
9:3 kid of *g.* for a sin-offering
16:5 two kids of *g.* ; 7 two *g.* pr.
22:19 a male of the sheep or *g.*
23:19 kid of *g.* for a sin-offering,
Num. 7:16 ; 15:24
Num. 7:87 kids of *g.* for a sin-of.
1 *Sam.* 25:2 Nabal had a thou. *g.*
Ps. 50:13 or will I drink bl. of *g.*
66:15 I will offer bullo. with *g.*
Prov. 27:26 *g.* are price of field
27 thou sh. have *g.* milk enou.
Cant. 4:1 hair as flock of *g.* 6:5
Is. 34:6 sw. fat with blood of *g.*
Ezek. 27:21 Arabia occup. in *g.*
39:18 drink blood of la. and *g.*
43:22 second day offer kid of *g.*
45:23 kid of *g.* daily for sin-off.
Zec. 10:3 I punished the *g.*
Mat. 25:32 divid. sheep from *g.*
33 set the *g.* on his left hand
Heb. 9:12 entered by blood of *g.*
13 if the blood of *g.* sanctifieth
19 took blood of *g.* and sprink.
10:4 pos. blood of *g.* take sins

GOAT'S hair.

Ex. 25:4 offer. ye sh. take, *g. h.*
26:7 make curtains of *g. hair*
35:6 let him bring *g. hair*

Ex. 35:23 with wh. was fo. *g. h.*
26 all the women spun *g. hair*
36:14 curtains of *g. h.* for tent
Num. 31:20 purify work of *g. h.*
1 *Sam.* 19:13 pillow of *g. hair,* 16

GOAT-SKINS.

Heb. 11:37 wandered in *g.-skins*

Wild GOATS.

1 *Sam.* 24:2 Da. on rocks of *w. g.*
Job 39:1 when *wild g.* br. forth
Ps. 104:18 high hills ref. for *w. g.*

GOB. 2 *Sam.* 21:18

GOBLET.

Cant. 7:2 thy navel like round *g.*

GOD, *referred to man.*

Ex. 4:16 be to Aaron inst. of G.
7:1 made thee a G. to Pharaoh

GOD, *for idol.*

Jud. 6:31 if a *g.* let him plead
8:33 made Baal-berith their *g.*
9:27 went into house of their *g.*
11:24 which Chemo. thy *g.* giv.
16:23 Philis. *g.* was Dagon, 24
1 *Sam.* 5:7 hand is sore on our *g.*
1 *K.* 11:33 worship. *g.* of Moab
18:27 he is a *g.* either talking or
2 *K.* 1:2 B. the *g.* of Ekron, 16
19:37 wors. in house of Nisroch,
his *g.* 2 *Chr.* 32:21 ; *Is.* 37:38
Ps. 16:4 hasten after another *g.*
Is. 44:10 formed *g.* or molt. im. ?
15 maketh *g.* worship. it, 17
45:20 pray to a *g.* cannot save
46:6 maketh it a *g.* they wors.
Dan. 1:2 ves. to house of his *g.*
4:8 according to name of my *g.*
11:36 magnify him. above ev. *g.*
Amos 5:26 star of y. *g. Acts* 7:43
8:14 say, Thy *g.* O Dan, liveth
Jon. 1:5 cried ev. man to his *g.*
Mic. 4:5 walk in name of his *g.*
Hab. 1:11 imput. power to his *g.*
Acts 12:22 voice of a *g.* not a man

Any GOD.

Ex. 22:20 sac. to *a. g.* save L.
2 *Sam.* 7:22 is there *any g.* besides, 1 *Chr.* 17:20
Dan. 3:28 not worship *a. g.* exc.
6:7 petition of *a. g.* or man, 12
11:37 neither sh. he regard *a. g.*

Other GOD.

Ex. 34:14 shalt worship no *o. g.*
Dan. 3:29 no *other g.* can deliver
1 *Cor.* 8:4 is none *o. g.* but one

Strange GOD.

Deut. 32:12 no *s. g.* with them
Ps. 44:20 not hands to *strange g.*
81:9 no *strange g.* be in thee
Is. 43:12 no *s. g.* among them
Dan. 11:39 thus sh. do with *s. g.*

GOD.

Gen. 16:13 Lord, thou G. seest
17:7 a G. to thee and thy seed
31:13 I am the G. of Bethel
42:28 what is this G. done us ?
45:8 you sent me hither, but G.
48:21 I die, but G. be with you
Ex. 6:7 you to me, to you G.
18:19 and G. shall be with thee
Num. 23:23 what G. hath wro. ?
24:23 who live when G. do. this ?
Deut. 4:7 wh. nat. hath G. so ni. ?
29:13 he may be to thee a G.
1 *Sam.* 3:17 G. do so and more al.
14:44 ; 25:22 ; 2 *Sam.* 3:9, 35 ;
19:13 ; 1 *K.* 2:23 ; 2 *K.* 6:31
17:46 know there is a G. in Is.
22:3 know what G. will do
2 *Sam.* 22:32 who is G. save the
Lord ? *Ps.* 18:31
1 *K.* 18:21 if the L. be G. follow
39 the Lord, he is G. the Lord
19:15 thou art G. even thou
2 *Chr.* 20:6 O Lord G. art thou
not G. in heaven ?
Ezr. 1:3 his G. be with him
Neh. 9:17 a G. ready to pardon
Job 22:13 doth G. kn. ? *Ps.* 73:11
Ps. 5:4 not a G. hast pleasure in
52:7 made not G. his strength
86:10 th. art G. alone, *Is.* 37:16
Is. 12:2 behold, G. is my salvat.
44:8 is there a G. besides me ?
45:22 I am G. there is none else
46:9 I am G. th. is none like me
Jer. 31:33 I will be their G. 32:38

Ezek. 28:2 said, I sit in seat of G.
  9 thou sh. be a man, and no G.
Hos. 8:6 workm. made it, no G.
Mic. 7:18 who is a G. like thee?
Mat. 1:23 Immanuel, which is G.
  6:24 ye cannot serve G. and
    mammon, *Luke* 16:13
Mat. 19:17 there is none good but
  one, that is G. *Mark* 10:18;
    Luke 18:19
Mark 12:32 there is one G.
John 1:1 the Word was with G.
  3:2 do miracles, ex. G. with him
  8:41 have one Father, even G.
  42 I proceeded, came from G.
  17:3 know thee, only true G.
Acts 2:22 wonders which G. did
  5:29 obey G. rather than men
  7:9 sold Joseph, but G. wi. him
  10:34 no respecter of persons
Rom. 3:4 G. be true, man a liar
  8:31 if G. for us, who ag. us?
  15:5 G. of patience and consol.
1 *Cor.* 8:6 but one G. the Father
  15:28 that G. may be all in all
2 *Cor.* 1:21 he wh. an. us is G.
  4:4 *g.* of this world blinded
  13:11 G. of love and peace with
2 *Thes.* 2:4 above all called G.
1 *Tim.* 3:16 G. mani. in the flesh
Tit. 1:16 profess they know G.
Heb. 3:4 he that built all thi. is G.
  4:10 ceased from works, as G.
  8:10 to them a G. they a people
1 *John* 1:5 G. light, him no dark.
  4:12 no man seen G. any time
Rev. 21:3 G. hims. be with them
  4 G. shall wipe away all tears
  7 I will be his G. he be my son

Against GOD.

Gen. 39:9 wickedn. and sin a. G.
Num. 21:5 peo. sp. a. G. *Ps.* 78:19
1 *Chr.* 5:25 they transgr. *ag.* G.
2 *Chr.* 32:19 spake *ag.* G. of Jer.
Job 15:13 turn, thy spirit *ag.* G.
  25 stretch. out his hand *a,* G.
  34:37 multip. his words *a.* G.
Dan. 3:29 speak amiss *a.* G. of S.
  11:36 marv. things *a.* G. of gods
Hos. 13:16 hath rebelled *a.* G.
Acts 5:39 be found to fight *a.* G.
  6:11 spoken blas. words *a.* G.
  23:9 let us not fight *against* G.
Rom. 8:7 carnal mind en. *a.* G.
  9:20 who art thou repliest *a.* G. ?
Rev. 13:6 opened his mouth *a,* G.
See ALMIGHTY.

Before GOD.

Gen. 6:11 earth was corrupt *b.* G.
Ex. 18:12 eat wi. M. father *b.* G.
Jos. 24:1 presented thems. *b.* G.
Jud. 21:2 people abode *before* G.
1 *Chr.* 13:8 D. and Is. played *b.* G.
  10 and there Uzzah died *b.* G.
  16:1 offered burnt sacri. *bef.* G.
2 *Chr.* 33:12 Manasseh hum. *b.* G.
  34:27 Josiah's heart hum. *b.* G.
Ezr. 7:19 deliver *b,* G. of Jerus.
Job 15:4 restrainest prayer *b.* G.
Ps. 42:2 shall I appear *b.* G. ?
  56:13 *b.* G. in light of living
  61:7 he shall abide *b.* G. for ever
  68:3 let righteous rejoice *b.* G.
  84:7 ov. one in Zion appear *b.* G.
Ec. 2:26 give to him good *b.* G.
  5:2 heart hasty to utter *bef.* G.
  8:13 because he feareth not *b.* G.
Dan. 6:10 gave thanks *before* G.
  11 found making supplic. *b.* G.
  26 men tremble *b.* G. of Daniel
Luke 1:6 were both right. *b.* G.
  12:6 not one is forgotten *b.* G.
  24:19 a prophet mighty *bef.* G.
Acts 7:46 who found favor *b.* G.

10:4 come for a memorial *b.* G.
  33 all here present *before* G.
23:1 lived in good consci. *b.* G.
Rom. 2:13 not hearers just *b.* G.
  3:19 world may bec. guilty *b.* G.
  4:2 whereof to glory, not *b.* G.
  14:22 have faith to thyself *b.* G.
2 *Cor.* 12:19 speak *b.* G. in Chr.
Gal. 1:20 behold, *b.* G. I lie not
1 *Thes.* 3:13 estab. hearts *b.* G.
1 *Tim.* 5:4 good and accept. *b.* G.
  21 charge thee *b.* G. 2 *Tim.* 4:1
Jam. 1:27 pure religion *before* G.
Rev. 3:2 works not perfect *b.* G.
  9:13 voice from horns of al. *b.* G.
  12:10 accus. *b.* G. day and night
  16:19 Babylon in rememb. *b.* G.
  20:12 I saw dead stand *b.* G.

See CALLED, CHOSEN, COM-
MANDED.

Eternal GOD.

Deut. 33:27 the *e.* G. is thy refuge

Everlasting GOD.

Gen. 21:33 A. called name *e.* G.
Is. 40:28 the *e.* G. fainteth not
Rom. 16:26 command. of *e.* G.

See FATHER, FEAR, FORBID,
GAVE, GLORIFY.

High GOD.

Gen. 14:18 priest of the most *h.*
  G. *Heb.* 7:1
  19 blessed be Ab. of most *h.* G.
  20 blessed be the most *h.* G.
  22 lift up my hand to most *h.* G.
Ps. 57:2 cry unto G. most *high*
  78:35 the *h.* G. their Redeemer
  56 tempted the most *high* G.
Dan. 3:26 servants of most *h.* G.
  4:2 wonders *high* G. wrought
  5:18 *h.* G. gave Nebuch. king.
  21 he knew most *h.* G. ruled
Mic. 6:6 bow my. bef. most *h.* G.
Mark 5:7 Son of m. *h.* G. *Lu.* 8:28
Acts 16:17 serv. of most *high* G.

Holy GOD.

Jos. 24:19 he is a *holy* G. jealous
1 *Sam.* 6:20 who stand bef. *h.* G. ?
Ps. 99:9 the Lord our G. is *holy*
Is. 5:16 G. that is *h,* be sancti.

GOD of heaven.

2 *Chr.* 36:23 all kingdoms of earth
  hath G. *of h.* giv. me, *Ezr.* 1:2
Ezr. 5:11 servants of G. *of h.*
  12 our fath. provoked G. *of h.*
  6:9 burnt-offerings of G. *of h.*
  7:12 scribe of law of G. *of h.* 21
  23 commanded by G. *of h.*
Neh. 1:4 prayed bef. G. *of h.* 2:4
Ps. 136:26 give thanks to G. *of h.*
Dan. 2:18 desire mer. of G. *of h.*
  19 Daniel blessed the G. *of h.*
  44 G. *of h.* sh. set up kingdom
Jon. 1:9 I fear the L. G. *of h.*
Rev. 11:13 gave glory to G. *of h.*
  16:11 they blasphemed G. *of h.*

GOD of hosts.

Ps. 80:7 turn us, O G. *of h.* 19
  14 return, we beseech, G. *of h.*
Amos 5:27 wh. name is G. *of h.*

See LORD GOD.

GOD is.

Gen. 21:22 G. *is* with thee in all
  31:50 G. *is* witness betwixt
Ex. 20:30 fear not, G. *is* come
Num. 23:19 G. *is* not a man, that
Deut. 3:24 what G. *is* in heaven
  33:27 eternal G. *is* thy refuge
Jos. 24:19 G. *is* a j. G. *Nah.* 1:2
1 *Sam.* 4:7 G. *is* come into camp
  10:7 G. *is* with thee, 1 *Chr.* 17:2
  28:15 G. *is* departed from me
2 *Sam.* 22:33 G. *is* my strength
1 *Chr.* 14:15 G. *is* gone forth bef.
2 *Chr.* 13:12 G. himself *is* wi. us

Job 33:12 G. *is* greater than man
  36:5 G. *is* mighty, despis. not
  26 G. *is* great, we know him
Ps. 7:11 G. *is* angry with wicked
  10:4 G. *is* not in his thoughts
  14:5 G. *is* in generation of righ.
  33:12 whose G. *is* Lord, 144:15
  46:1 G. *is* refuge and str. 62:8
  5 G. *is* in midst of her
  47:5 G. *is* gone up ; 7 G. *is* king
  48:3 G. *is* known in her palaces
  50:6 G. *is* judge, Selah, 75:7
  54:4 Behold, G. *is* my helper
  56:9 I know, for G. *is* for me
  59:9 I wait, G. *is* my def. 17
  62:7 in G. *is* my salvat. *Is.* 12:2
  68:5 father of fatherless is G.
  73:1 truly G. *is* good to Israel
  26 G. *is* the str. of my heart
  74:12 G. *is* my king of old
  89:7 G *is* greatly to be feared
  116:5 Lord our G. *is* merciful
  118:27 G. *is* L. that showed light
Ec. 5:2 G. *is* in hea. thou on ear.
Is. 5:16 G. that *is* holy be sancti.
  8:10 G. *is* with us; 45:14 G. in
Zec. 8:23 heard G. *is* with you
Mat. 3:9 G. *is* able of these stones
  to raise, *Luke* 3:8
  22:32 G. *is* not of dead, but liv.
John 3:33 to seal that G. *is* true
  4:24 G. *is* a Spirit ; 13:31
Acts 10:34 G. *is* no resp. of per.
Rom. 1:9 G. *is* wit. wh. I serve
  11:23 G. *is* able to graff them
  14:4 G. *is* able to make him
1 *Cor.* 1:9 G. *is* faith. by wh. call.
  10:13 G. *is* faith. will not suffer
  14:25 report that G. *is* in you
  33 G. *is* not author of confusion
2 *Cor.* 1:18 G. *is* true, our word
  9:8 G. *is* able make grace
Gal. 3:20 G. one ; 6:7 not mocked
Eph. 2:4 G. who *is* rich in mercy
Phil. 1:8 G. *is* record, I long
  3:19 many walk, G. *is* th. belly
1 *Thes.* 2:5 nor cloak, G. *is* wit.
Heb. 6:10 G. *is* not unrighteous
  11:16 G. *is* not ash. to be called
  12:29 G. *is* a consuming fire
Heb. 13:16 with such sac. G. *is* pl.
1 *John* 1:5 G. *is* light; 4:8 *is* love,16
  3:20 G. *is* greater th. our heart

GOD of Israel.

Ex. 24:10 went, saw G. *of Israel*
Num. 16:9 G. *of Is.* separated you
Jos. 7:19 gl. to G. *of I.* 1 *Sam.* 6:5
  12:33 G. *of Is.* their inheritance
  22:16 what trespass ag. G. *of Is.?*
  24 what ye do with G. *of Is.?*
  24:23 incline heart to G. *of Is.*
Jud. 11:23 G. *of Is.* dispossessed
Ruth 2:12 reward of G. *of Is.*
1 *Sam.* 1:17 G. *of Is.* grant petit.
  5:11 send away ark of G. *of Is.*
1 *K.* 8:23 Lord G. *of Israel,* no
  god is like thee, 2 *Chr.* 6:14
  14:13 good thing tow. G. *of Is.*
1 *Chr.* 4:10 Ja. called on G. *of I.*
  17:24 Lord of hosts is G. *of Is.*
2 *Chr.* 15:13 not seek G. *of Is. ?*
Ezr. 7:15 freely offered G. *of Is.*
  9:4 tremb. at words of G. *of Is.*
Ps. 41:13 blessed be the L. G. *of*
  Is. from everlasting to ever.
  72:18 ; 106:48 ; *Luke* 1:68
Is. 41:17 G. *of Is.* will not fors.
  45:3 I which call am G. *of Is.*
  48:2 stay themselves on G. *of I.*
Ezek. 8:4 the glory of G. *of Is.*
Mat. 15:31 multitude glo. G. *of I.*

Living GOD.

Deut. 5:26 heard voice of *liv.* G.
Jos. 3:10 hereby know the *l.* G.
1 *Sam.* 17:26 defy arm. of *l.* G. 36
2 *K.* 19:4 king of Assyria sent to
  reproach *l.* G. 16 ; *Is.* 37:4,17

Ps. 42:2 my soul thirst. for *l.* G.
84:2 my heart crieth for *l.* G.
Jer. 10:10 the *l.* G. everlas. King
23:36 perverted words of *l.* G.
Dan. 6:26 steadfast for ever
Hos. 1:10 ye are sons of *living* G.
Mat. 16:16 art Christ, Son of *living* G. *John* 6:69
26:63 I adjure thee by *l.* G. tell
Acts 14:15 turn from van. to *l.* G.
Rom. 9:26 be called chil. of *l.* G.
2 *Cor.* 3:3 with the Spirit of *l.* G.
6:16 ye are the temple of *l.* G.
1 *Thes.* 1:9 fr. idols to serve *l.* G.
1 *Tim.* 3:15 church of the *l.* G.
4:10 we trust in the *l.* G. 6:17
Heb. 3:12 evil heart dep. fr. *l.* G.
9:14 purge cons. to serve *l.* G.
10:31 to fall into hands of *l.* G.
12:22 come to Zion, city of *l.* G.
Rev. 7:2 angel hav. seal of *l.* G.

Lord GOD, *Lord his* GOD,
Lord our, their, your GOD.
See these in the divisions of
the word LORD.

Merciful GOD.

Ex. 34:6 the Lord G. *m.* gracious
Deut. 4:31 L. thy G. is a *m.* G.
2 *Chr.* 30:9 L. your G. is *merciful*
Neh. 9:31 art a gracious, *m.* G.
Ps. 116:5 gracious is L. G. is *m.*
Jon. 4:2 I knew thou art a G. *m.*

Mighty GOD.

Gen. 49:24 hands of *m.* G. of Ja.
Deut. 7:21 Lord is among you, a *mighty* G. 10:17
Neh. 9:32 therefore our G. the *m.*
Job 36:5 G. is *m.* and despiseth
Ps. 50:1 the *m.* G. hath spoken
132:2 vowed to the *m.* G. of Jacob
5 till I find a habitat. for *m.* G.
Is. 9:6 name sh. be called *m.* G.
10:21 remnant sh. ret. to *m.* G.
Jer. 32:18 *m.* G. the L. of hosts
Hab. 1:12 O *m.* G. thou hast stab.

My GOD.

Gen. 28:21 then sh. L. be *my* G.
Ex. 15:2 he is *my* G. my father's
Ruth 1:16 people, thy G. *my* G.
2 *Sam.* 22:7 cried to *my* G. *Ps.*18:6
22 not dep. fr. *my* G. *Ps.* 18:21
30 *my* G. I leaped, *Ps.* 18:29
1 *Chr.* 28:20 *my* G. be with thee
2 *Chr.*18:13 what *my* G. saith
Neh. 5:19 on me, *my* G. 13:31
13:14 remember me, *my* G. 22
Ps. 22:1 *my* G. *my* G. why hast
thou forsaken me? *Mat.*27:46
10 *my* G. fr. my mother's belly
31:14 I said, Thou art *my* G.
38:21 O *my* G. be not far, 71:12
89:26 thou art my Fath. *my* G.
104:33 praise to *my* G. 146:2
118:28 *my* G. I will praise thee
145:1 I will extol thee, *my* G.
Prov. 30:9 name of *my* G. in vain
Is. 7:13 ye weary *my* G. also?
40:27 judg. passed from *my* G.
44:17 deliver me, thou art *my* G.

Is. 61:10 soul be joyful in *my* G.
Dan. 6:22 *my* G. sent his angel
Hos. 2:23 they shall say, Thou
art *my* G. *Zec.* 13:9
8:2 Is. cry, *my* G. we know thee
9:17 *my* G. will cast them away
Mic. 7:7 wait, *my* G. will hear
John 20:17 say, I ascend to *my* G.
28 Th. said, *my* Lord and *my* G.
Rom. 1:8 I thank *my* G. through
J. Christ, for you all, 1 *Cor.*
1:4 ; 14:18 ; *Phil.* 1:3 ; *Phile.* 4
2 *Cor.* 12:21 *my* G. will humble
Phil. 4:19 *my* G. supply need
Rev. 3:12 write name of *my* G.

See LORD *my God.*

No GOD.

Deut. 32:39 th. is *no* G. with me
1 *K.* 8:23 *no* G. like thee, 2 *Ch.*6:14
2 *K.* 1:16 is it bec. *no* G. in Is.
5:15 I know th. is *no* G. in earth
2 *Chr.* 32:15 *no* G. of any nation
Ps. 14:1 said, There is *no* G. 53:1
Is. 43:10 bef. me *no* G. formed
44:6 besides me there is *no* G. 8 ;
45, 5, 14, 21
Ezek. 28:9 shalt be a man, *no* G.
Hos. 13:4 sh. know *no* G. but me

O GOD.

Num. 12:13 heal her now, *O* G.
Jud. 16:28 strengthen me, *O* G.
Ps. 4:1 hear me, *O* G. of right.
25:22 redeem Is. *O* G. out of tr.
51:14 deliver from guilti. *O* G.
56:12 thy vows upon me, *O* G.
Is. 64:4 nor hath eye seen, *O* G.
Heb. 10:7 come to do will, *O* G. 9

Of GOD.

2 *Chr.* 10:15 the cause *of* G.
Ps. 7:10 my defence is *of* G.
Is. 53:4 esteem him smit. *of* G.
Mat. 16:23 savorest not things *of*
G. *Mark* 8:33
John 1:13 not will of man, *of* G.
6:46 he *of* G. seen the Father
7:17 know doc. whether *of* G.
8:47 he that is *of* G. heareth
9:16 this man not *of* G. ; 33
12:43 praise of men than *of* G.
Acts 5:39 if *of* G. ye cannot over.
Rom. 2:29 pr. not of men, *of* G.
9:16 but *of* G. that show. mercy
13:1 powers that be ord. *of* G.
1 *Cor.* 1:30 who *of* G. is made
6:19 have *of* G. not your own
11:12 things *of* G. 2 *Cor.* 5:18
2 *Cor.* 2:17 in sight *of* G. speak
3:5 our sufficiency is *of* G.
Phil. 1:28 salvation, that *of* G.
3:9 the right. which is *of* G.
Heb. 5:4 he called *of* G. as Aaron
1 *John* 3:10 doeth not righteousness, is not *of* G.
4:1 try the spirits whether *of* G.
3 con. not Chr. come, not *of* G.
6 we are *of* G. ; 5:19 we know
3 *John* 11 that doeth good is *of* G

See ANGEL, ARK, BORN, CHIL-
DREN, CHOSEN, CHURCH,
COUNSEL, FEAR, GLORY,
GRACE, HAND, HOUSE, KING-
DOM, KNOWLEDGE, LOVE,
MAN, PEOPLE, POWER, SER-
VANT, SIGHT, SON, SONS,
SPIRIT, WILL, WORDS, WORK,
WORKS, WORLD, WRATH.

Our GOD.

Ex. 5:8 let us sacri. to *our* G.
Deut. 31:17 *o.* G. not amongst us
32:3 ascribe great. unto *our* G.
Jos. 24:18 serve L. he is *our* G.
Jud. 10:10 have forsaken *our* G.
1 *Sam.* 2:2 nei. rock like *our* G.
2 *Sam.* 10:12 let us play the men
for cities of *o.* G. 1 *Chr.* 19:3
22:32 a rock save *o.* G. ? *Ps.*18:31
1 *Chr.* 29:13 *o.* G. we thank thee
2 *Chr.* 2:5 great is *o.* G. above all
14:11 O Lord, thou art *our* G.
20:7 *o.* G. who didst drive out
Ezr. 9:10 O *o.* G. what shalt we
Neh. 4:4 *our* G. ; 20 *our* G. fight
6:16 work wrought of *our* G.
9:32 *o.* G. the great, mighty G.
13:2 *o.* G. turned curse to bless.
Ps. 40:3 a new song, pr. to *o.* G.
48:14 God is *our* G. for ever
50:3 *our* G. sh. not keep silence
67:6 *o.* *our* G. shall bless us
68:20 *our* G. is the G. of salvat.
77:13 so great a G. as *our* G. ?
95:7 is *o.* G. ; 115:3 *o.* G. in hea.
116:5 gracious is L. G. is. merc.

Is. 25:9 this is *o.* G. we have wai.
55:7 *o.* G. will abund. pardon
59:13 departing from *our* G.
Is. 61:2 day of veng. of *our* G.
Dan. 3:17 *our* G. able to deliver
Zec. 9:7 remaineth be for *our* G.
1 *Cor.* 6:11 sancti. by Sp. of *o.* G.
Heb. 12:29 *o.* G. is a consum. fire
Rev. 5:10 made us to *o.* G. kings
7:10 salv. to *our* G. who sitteth
12 blessing and honor to *o.* G.

See PEACE, SAID, SAITH, SERVE,
SENT, SPEED, SPEAK, SPOKEN.

Their GOD.

Gen. 17:8 I will be *t.* G. *Ex.* 29:45 ;
Jer. 24:7 ; 31:33 ; 32:38 ; *Ezek.*
11:20 ; 34:24 ; 37:23, 27 ; *Zec.*
8:8 ; 2 *Cor.* 6:16 ; *Rev.* 21:3
Lev. 21:6 shall be holy to *t.* G.
26:45 might be *t.* G. *Ezek.* 14:11
2 *Sam.* 7:24 thou art become *their*
G. 1 *Chr.* 17:22
Ps. 5:5 eye of *t.* G. on elders
79:10 where *their* G. ? 115:2 ;
Joel 2:17
Is. 8:19 sh. not peo. seek *t.* G. ?
21 curse their king and *their* G.
58:2 forsook not ordin. of *t.* G.
Jer. 5:4 know not judg. of *t.* G.
Dan. 11:32 people that know *t.* G.
Hos. 4:12 gone a who. from *t.* G.
5:4 frame doings to turn to *t.* G.
Zec. 12:5 strength in Lord *t.* G.
Heb. 11:16 not ashamed to be *t.* G.

See LORD *their God.*

Thy GOD.

Lev. 19:14 fear thy G. 25:17, 43
Deut. 10:21 he is thy praise, *t.* G.
26:17 this day the L. to be *t.* G.
Ruth 1:16 peo. my pe. *t.* G. my G.
2 *K.* 19:10 let not *thy* G. deceive
thee, *Is.* 37:10
1 *Chr.* 12:18 *thy* G. helpeth thee
2 *Chr.* 9:8 because *t.* G. loved Is.
Ezr. 7:14 accord. to law of *thy* G.
25 after the wisdom of *thy* G.
Neh. 9:18 *t.* G. that brought thee
Ps. 42:3 say, Wh. is thy G. ? 10
45:7 *thy* G. anointed, *Heb.* 1:9
50:7 O Is. I am G. even *thy* G.
68:28 *t.* G. com. thy strength
147:12 praise *thy* G. O Zion
Is. 41:10 be not dism. I am *t.* G.
51:20 full of rebuke of *thy* G.
52:7 saith to Zion, *thy* G. reign.
60:19 *thy* G. shall be thy glory
62:5 só shall *t.* G. rej. over thee
Dan. 6:16 *thy* G. whom thou ser.
20 is *thy* G. able to deliver ?
10:12 chasten thyself bef. *t.* G.
Hos. 4:6 hast forgot. law of *t.* G.
9:1 gone a whoring from *thy* G.
12:6 turn to *t.* G. wait on *t.* G.
Amos 4:12 prepare to meet *thy* G.
Jon. 1:6 arise, call upon *t.* G.
Mic. 6:8 walk humbly with *t.* G.

See LORD *thy god.*

To, or unto GOD.

Gen. 40:8 interpreta. be. *to* G. ?
Ex. 2:23 their cry came *to* G.
Lev. 21:7 he is holy *unto* his G.
Deut. 32:17 sac. not *to* G. 1 *Cor.*
10:20
33:26 none like *to* G. of Jeshu.
Jud. 13:5 a Naz. *u.* G. 7 ; 16:17
1 *Sam.* 10:3 3 men go. up *to* G.
1 *Chr.* 26:32 matter perta. *to* G.
Job 22:2 can man be pr. *to* G. ?
34:31 is meet to be said *un.* G.
Ps. 62:11 power belongeth *to* G.
68:20 *to* G. be. issues fr. death
31 Ethio. stretch hands *to* G.
73:28 good to draw near *to* G.
77:1 I cried *un.* G. even *unto* G.
Ec. 12:7 spirit sh. return *unto* G.
Is. 58:2 delight in appr. *to* G.

Lam. 3:41 hearts wi. hands *to* G.
Mat. 22:21 render *u.* G. things
 which are G.'s, *Mark* 12:17 ;
 Luke 20:25
John 13:3 come from G. w. *to* G.
Acts 4:19 hearken than *unto* G.
5:4 not lied unto men, *unto* G.
26:18 fr. power of Satan *unto* G.
20 turn *to* G. and do works
Rom. 6:10 liveth *unto* G. ; 11
 13 yield yourselves *u.* G. alive
7:4 bring forth fruit *unto* G.
12:1 your bodies a liv. sac. *u.* G.
14:12 account of himself *to* G.
1 *Cor.* 14:2 speaketh *unto* G.
15:24 deliv. up kingdom *to* G.
Phil. 4:20 now *u.* G. our Father
Heb. 7:25 to save th. come *un.* G.
 11:6 that cometh *to* G. must be.
 12:23 are come *to* G. the Judge
Jam. 4:7 submit yourselves *to* G.
1 *Pet.* 3:18 Ch. suf. bring us *to* G.
4:6 live according *to* G. in spirit
Rev. 5:9 redeemed us *to* G. by b.
12:5 child caught up *unto* G.
14:4 first-fr. *unto* G. and Lamb

See TRUE.

With GOD.

Gen. 5:22 En. walked *w.* G. 24.
6:9 N. walked *w.* G. ; 32:28 Jac.
Ex. 19:17 br. peo. to meet *w.* G.
1 *Sam.* 14:45 wrought *w.* G.
2 *Sam.* 23:5 ho. be not so *w.* G.
2 *Chr.* 35:21 forbear med. *w.* G.
Job 9:2 sh. man be just *with* G.
 13:3 I desire to reason *with* G.
 16:21 plead for a man *with* G.
 25:4 can a man be just *w.* G. ?
 27:13 por. of wicked man *w.* G.
 34:9 sh. delight himself *w.* G.
 23 he enter into judg. *w.* G.
 37:22 *with* G. is ter. majesty
Ps. 78:8 spirit not stead. *w.* G.
Hos. 11:12 Judah yet ruleth *w.* G.
12:3 Jacob had power *with* G.
Mat. 19:26 *w.* G. all things possi.
 Mark 10:27 ; *Lu.* 1:37 ; 18:27
Luke 1:30 hast found favor *w.* G.
2:25 increased in favor *with* G.
John 1:1 the Word was *with* G.
5:18 him. equal *w.* G. *Phil.* 2:6
Rom. 2:11 no resp. of pers. *w.* G.
5:1 by faith, we have pe. *w.* G.
9:14 is there unright. *with* G. ?
1 *Cor.* 3:9 we are laborers *w.* G.
 19 wisdom of world fool. *w.* G.
7:24 ev. man therein abide *w.* G.
2 *Thes.* 1:16 a right. thing *with* G.
Jam. 4:4 friendsh. enmity *w.* G.
1 *Pet.* 2:20 is acceptable *w.* G.

Would GOD. *See* WOULD.

Your GOD.

Gen. 43:23 *y.* G. hath given trea.
Ex. 8:25 go ye, sacrifice to *y.* G.
Lev. 11:45 bringeth you out of
 Egypt be *your* G. 22:33 ;
 25:38 ; *Num.* 15:41
 26:12 I will be *your* God, ye
 my people, *Jer.* 7:23 ; 11:4 ;
 30:22 ; *Ezek.* 36:28
Num. 10:10 a memorial bef. *y.* G.
 15:40 my com. be holy to *y.* G.
Jos. 24:27 lest ye deny *your* G.
1 *Sam.* 10:19 have rejected *y.* G.
2 *Chr.* 32:14 that *y.* G. deliver y.
 15 much less sh. *y.* G. deliver ?
Is. 35:4 *y* G. come with veng.
 40:1 com. my people, saith *y.* G.
 9 cities of Judah, behold *y.* G.
 59:2 separ. bet. you and *y.* G.
Ezek. 34:1 I am *y.* G. saith Lord
Dan. 2:47 of a truth it is, *y.* G. is
Hos. 1:9 I will not be *your* G.
John 8:54 ye say that he is *y.* G.
20:17 ascend to my God, *y.* G.

See LORD *your* God.

GODDESS.

1 *K.* 11:5 Sol. went after the *g.*
 33 worshipped Ashtor. the *g.*
Acts 19:27 temple of gr. *g.* Diana
 35 Ephesians worshippers of *g.*
37 nor yet blasph. of your *g.*

GODHEAD.

Acts 17:29 nor think *g.* like gold
Rom. 1:20 his eter. power and *g.*
Col. 2:9 in him fulness of the *g.*

GODLY.

Ps. 4:3 L. set apart him that is *g.*
12:1 help, for the *g.* man ceas.
32:6 for this every one *g.* pray
Mal. 2:15 he might seek *g.* seed
2 *Cor.* 1:12 in *g.* sincer. our con.
7:9 sorry after a *g.* manner, 11
 10 for *g.* sorrow worketh rep.
 11:2 jeal. over you with *g.* jeal.
2 *Tim.* 3:12 all that live *g.* in C.
Tit. 2:12 that ye should live *g.*
Heb. 12:28 serve G. with *g.* fear
2 *Pet.* 2:9 how to deliver the *g.*
3 *John* 6 bring for after *g.* sort

GODLINESS.

1 *Tim.* 2:2 may lead a life in *g.*
 10 becometh women profes. *g.*
3:16 great is the mystery of *g.*
4:7 exer. thyself rather unto *g.*
 8 *g.* is profit. unto all things
6:3 the doctrine according to *g.*
 5 supposing that gain is *g.*
 6 *g.* with contentment is gain
 11 follow righteousness, *g.* fai.
Tim. 3:5 having a form of *g.*
Tit. 1:1 truth which is after *g.*
2 *Pet.* 1:3 things pertain to *g.*
 6 add to *g.* brotherly kind. 7.
3:11 persons ought to be in *g.*

GOD-WARD.

Ex. 18:19 be thou for peo. to G.
2 *Cor.* 3:4 have we thro. C. to G.
1 *Thes.* 1:8 faith to G. is spread.

GODS.

Gen. 3:5 ye shall be as *g.*
 31:30 where. hast stolen my *g.* ?
Ex. 12:12 ag. all *g.* of Egypt
 20:23 sh. not make *g.* of silver
 22:28 thou sh. not revile the *g.*
 23:24 shalt not bow to their *g.*
  32 make no cove. with their *g.*
 32:4 these be thy *g.* O Israel, 8
 31 they have made *g.* of gold
 34:15 go a whoring after their *g.*
 17 make no molt. *g. Lev.* 19:4
Num. 25:2 people to sac. of *g.*
 33:4 the Egyptians' *g.* L. exec.
  judgme. *Jer.* 43:12, 13 ; 46:25
Deut. 7:25 im. of their *g.* burn
 10:17 Lord your G. is God of *g.*
 12:3 hew down im. of their *g.*
 30 inquire not after their *g.*
 31 have done abomina. to their
 g. sons and dau. in fire to *g.*
 13:7 entice thee to *g.* of people
 20:18 not do as they to their *g.*
 32:37 sh. say, Where are th. *g.* ?
Jos. 22:22 Lord God of *g.* know.
 23:7 nor mention of their *g.*
Jud. 2:3 they chose new *g.*
 6:10 fear not *g.* of Amorites
 10:14 cry to *g.* ye have chosen
 17:5 Micah had a house of *g.*
 18:24 ye have taken my *g.*
Ruth 1:15 sister-in-law ba. to *g.*
1 *Sam.* 4:8 the *g.* smote Egypt.
 6:5 his hand from off your *g.*
 17:43 Phil. cursed Da. by his *g.*
 28:13 I saw *g.* as. out of earth
2 *Sam.* 7:23 redeem. from th. *g.*
1 *K.* 11:2 turn your heart after *g.*
 8 Solomon sacrificed to their *g.*
 12:28 behold thy *g.* O Israel
 18:24 call name of your *g.* 25
 19:2 let *g.* do so to me, 20:10
 20:23 their *g.* are *g.* of hills

2 *K.* 17:29 every nation made *g.*
 33 feared the L. served own *g.*
 18:33 hath *g.* delivered his land ?
 19:12 ; 2 *Chr.* 32:13, 14 ; *Is.*
 36:18 ; 37:12
 34 wh. are *g.* of H. ? *Is.* 36:19
 19:18 cast *g.* in. fire, were no *g.*
1 *Chr.* 5:25 went a whoring af. *g.*
 10:10 armor in house of their *g.*
 14:12 left their *g.* David burnt
2 *Chr.* 13:8 calv. Jero. ma. for *g.*
 9 a priest to th. that are no *g.*
 25:14 br. *g.* of Seir to be his *g.*
 28:23 Ahaz sacrificed to the *g.*
 32:17 *g.* of nations have not de.
Ezr. 1:7 vessels in house of *g.*
Ps. 82:1 he judg. among the *g.*
 6 said, Ye are *g. John* 10:34
 136:2 give thanks unto God of *g.*
 138:1 bef. the *g.* will I praise
Is. 21:9 Bab. fall her *g.* broken
 41:23 we may know ye are *g.*
 42:17 images, Ye are our *g.*
Jer. 2:11 changes *g.* are no *g.* ?
 28 where are thy *g.* thou made?
  to number of cit. are thy *g.*
 11:13
 5:7 sworn by th. that are no *g.*
 10:11 *g.* have not made heaven
 11:12 to *g.* they offer incense
 16:20 man make *g.* are no *g.* ?
 48:35 that burn. incense to *g.*
Dan. 2:11 can show it, except *g.*
 47 your God is a God of *g.*
 4:8 in whom is spirit of holy *g.*
 9 sp. of *g.* is in thee. 18 ; 5:14
 5:4 *g.* of gold and silver, 23
 11 like the wisdom of the *g.*
 11:8 carry into E. *g.* w. princes
 36 speak things ag. God of *g.*
Hos. 14:3 ne. say, Ye are our *g.*
Nah. 1:14 out of house of thy *g.*
John. 10:35 if he called them *g.*
Acts 14:11 the *g.* are come down
 19:26 be no *g.* made with hands
1 *Cor.* 8:5 called *g.* there be *g.*
Gal. 4:8 ser. to th. wh. are no *g.*

See SERVE.

All GODS.

Ex. 18:11 L. greater than *all g.*
1 *Chr.* 16:25 ab. *all g. Ps.* 96:4
 26 *all g.* of peo. idols, *Ps.* 96:5
2 *Chr.* 2:5 G. ab. *all g. Ps.* 135:5
Ps. 95:3 L. is a K. above *all g.*
 97:7 worship *all g.* ; 9 ab. *all g.*
Zep. 2:11 famish *all g.* of earth

Among the GODS.

Ex. 15:11 *am. t. g.* who like th. ?
2 *K.* 18:35 who *a. t. g.* could del.
 con.? 2 *Chr.* 32:14 ; *Is.* 36:20
Ps. 86:8 *a. t. g.* none like thee

Other GODS.

Ex. 20:3 no *other g.* before me,
 Deut. 5:7
 23:13 make no mention of *o. g.*
Deut. 6:14 ye shall not go after
 o. g. 11:28 ; 28:14 ; 1 *K.* 11:10;
 Jer. 25:6 ; 35:15
 7:4 turn thy son to serve *o. g.*
 8:19 if thou walk after *o. g.*
 13:2 let us go after *o. g.* 6:13
 17:3 hath gone and served *o. g.*
  29:26 ; *Jos.* 23:16 ; *Jud.* 10:13 ;
  1 *Sam.* 8:8 ; *Jer.* 11:10
 18:20 speak in name of *o. g.*
 30:17 *o. g.* and serve, *Jer.* 22:9
 31:18 that day turned to *o. g.*
 20 will they turn to *other g.*
Jud. 2:12 forsook L. fol. *other g.*
 17 went a whoring after *o. g.*
 19 follow. *other g.* to serve th.
1 *Sam.* 26:19 say. Go serve *o. g.*
1 *K.* 9:9 have taken hold upon
 other g. 2 *Chr.* 7:22
 11:4 wives turned heart af. *o. g.*
 14:9 hast gone and made *o. g.*

2 *K.* 5:17 not offer sacri. to *o. g.*
17:7 Is. sinned and feared *o. g.*
35 ye shall not fear *o. g.* 37, 38
22:17 and burnt incense to *oth.*
g. 2 *Chr.* 34:25; *Jer.* 1:16; 19:4
2 *Chr.* 28:25 Ahaz bur. in. to *o. g.*
Jer. 7:6 nor walk after *other g.*
9 *o. g.* wh. ye know not, 13:10
16:11 for. me, walked after *o. g.*
44:5 burn no incense to *other g.*
8 burning incense to *o. g.* 15
Hos. 3:1 look to *o. g.* love wine

See SERVE.

Strange GODS.
Gen. 35:2 put a. *s. g.* 1 *Sam.* 7:3
4 gave Jacob *s. g. Jos.* 24:23
Deut. 32:16 provoked with *s. g.*
Jos. 24:20 forsake L. serve *s. g.*
Jud. 10:16 put away their *s. g.*
2 *Chr.* 14:3 Asa took altar of *s. g.*
33:15 Josiah took away *s. g.*
Jer. 5:19 as ye served *strange g.*
Acts 17:18 a setter forth of *s. g.*

GOG
1 *Chr.* 5:4 ; *Ezek.* 38:2, 3, 16, 18 ;
39:11
Rev. 20:8 G. and Magog, to gath.

GOLD.
Gen. 2:11 land of Havilah, is *g*
12 the *g.* of that land is good
41:42 put chain of *g.* on Jos.
Ex. 20:23 sh. make gods of *g.*
25:12 shalt cast four rings of
for ark, 26 ; 26:29 ; 28:23, 26,
27 ; 37:3, 13
13 stav. of shittim-wood, overlay with *g.* 28; 26:29, 37;
30:5 ; 37:4, 15, 28
18 two cherubim of *g.* 37:7
26:8 fifty taches of *g.* 36:13
32 hooks sh. be of *g.* 37 ; 36:38
28:6 ephod *g.* ; 8 girdle; 15 b. p.
11 ouches of *g.* 13 ; 39:6, 13, 16
24 chains of *g.* ; 33 bells of *g.*
32:24 who hath *g.* let him br. it
31 have made them gods of *g.*
35:22 they brought jewels of *g.*
36:34 over. the boards with *g.*
38 over. chapiters, fillets w. *g.*
38:34 all the *g.* was occupied
39:3 beat *g.* into thin plates
40:5 set altar of *g.* before ark
Num. 7:14 ten shekels of *g.* 20
84 at dedication 11 spoons of *g.*
86 *g.* of spoons 120 shekels
31:50 captains' obla. *g.* chains
Jos. 7:21 a wedge of *g.* fifty shek.
24 took Ach. and wedge of *g.*
Jud. 8:26 ear-r. 1,700 shek. of *g.*
1 *Sam.* 6:8 jewels of *g.* in coffer
11 laid mice of *g.* on the cart
15 coffer with jewels of *g.*
2 *Sam.* 8:7 Dav. took shiel. of *g.*
1 *K.* 6:22 house he overlaid w. *g.*
28 overlaid cherub. with *g.*
2 *Chr.* 3:10
7:48 S. made altar and table *g.*
49 lamps and tongs *g.* ; 50 hin.
9:11 Hiram king of Tyre furnished *g.* and cedar, 10:11 ;
2 *Chr.* 9:10
10:2 queen of Sh. came with *g.*
14 wt. of *g.* in year, 2 *Chr.* 9:13
16 made 200 targ. of beaten *g.*
17 made 300 shields of *g.*
18 overlaid throne with best *g.*
12:28 Jerob. made calves of *g.*
22:48 Jehos. made sh. go for *g.*
2 *K.* 18:16 Hezek. cut *g.* fr. doors
1 *Chr.* 28:14 David gave *g.* for *g.*
2 *Chr.* 3:6 the *g.* was *g.* of Parv.
2 *Chr.* 4:7 cand'sticks of *g.* ; 8 ba.
22 snuffers, censers, spoons, *g.*
9:18 steps to throne, foots. *g.*
12:9 Shishak carried shield of *g.*
Ezr. 8:27 copper precious as *g.*

Neh. 7:70 Tirsh. gave 1,000 dr. *g.*
71 chief of fath. gave *g.* ; 72
Job 22:24 lay up as dust *g.* of O.
23:10 I shall come forth like *g.*
28:6 earth hath the dust of *g.*
15 cannot be gotten for *g.*
16 it cannot be valued with *g.*
17 *g.* and crys. cannot equal it
31:24 if I made *g.* my hope
36:19 he esteem riches? not *g.*
42:11 gave Job an ear-ring of *g.*
Ps. 19:10 more to be des. than *g.*
45:9 stand queen in *g.* of Ophir
72:15 him be given *g.* of Sheba
Prov. 11:22 je. of *g.* in swine's s.
16:16 better to get wis. than *g.*
20:15 *g.* and a multi. of rubies
Cant. 1:10 comely *g.* chains *g.*
5:14 his *g.* rings set with beryl
Is. 30:22 ornament of im. of *g.*
40:19 spreadeth it over with *g.*
60:17 for brass I will bring *g.*
Jer. 4:30 deckest with orna. of *g.*
Lam. 4:1 how is *g.* become dim
Ezek. 27:22 merchants oc. wi. *g.*
Dan. 2:38 head of *g.* ; 3:1 im. *g.*
5:23 hast praised the gods of *g.*
29 chain of *g.* about Dan. neck
Zec. 4:2 a candlestick all of *g.*
13:9 I will try th. as *g.* is tried
Mat. 2:11 they pres. to him *g.*
23:16 swear by *g.* of the temple
17 whe. greater, *g.* or temple?
1 *Tim.* 2:9 not adorned with *g.*
or pearls, 1 *Pet.* 3:3
Heb. 9:4 ark over. round with *g.*
Jam. 2:2 come man with *g.* ring
1 *Pet.* 1:7 faith more pre. than *g.*
Rev. 3:18 to buy of me *g.* tried
4:4 elders on heads crowns of *g.*
9:7 locusts on heads crowns *g.*
17:4 woman was decked with *g.*
18:16 great city decked with *g.*

See BEATEN, CROWN, FINE.

Pure GOLD
Ex. 25:11 overlay ark with *pure*
g. 24 ; 30:3 ; 37:2, 11, 26
17 a mercy-seat of p. *g.* 37:6
29 dishes, of pure *g.* 37:16, 23
31 candl. *p. g.* 37:17 ; 1 *K.* 7:49
38 snuff dishes *p. g.* 2 *Chr.* 4:22
28:14 chains of *p. g.* 22 ; 39:15
1 *K.* 6:20 oracle overlaid w. *p. g.*
10:21 ve. of Le. *p. g.* 2 *Chr.* 9:20
1 *Chr.* 28:17 *p. g.* for flesh-hooks
2 *Chr.* 3:4 over. porch with *p. g.*
9:17 over. throne with *pure g.*
Job 28:19 wisd. not val. wi. *p. g.*
Ps. 21:3 a crown of *p. g.* on head
Rev. 21:18 city *p. g.* ; 21 street

GOLD, with silver.
Gen. 13:2 Ab. rich in *s.* and *g.* 24
44:8 steal of lord's hou. *s.* or *g.*
Ex. 3:22 jewels of *silver* and *g.*
11:2 ; 12:35
25:3 this offering, take *s.* and *g.*
31:4 in *g. s.* and brass, 35:32
Num. 22:18 ho. fu. *s.* and *g.* 24:13
31:22 only *g.* and *s.* abide fire
Deut. 7:25 shalt not des. *s.* and *g.*
8:13 *s.* and *g.* is multiplied
17:17 sh. he multiply *s.* and *g.*
29:17 seen their idols, *s.* and *g.*
Jos. 6:19 *s.* and *g.* con. to L. 24
22:8 ret. to tents with *s.* and *g.*
2 *Sam.* 8:11 *silver* and *g.* David
dedicated, 1 *K.* 7:51
21:4 will have no *s.* or *g.* of Sa.
1 *K.* 15:15 Asa brought into hou
of L. *s.* and *g.* 2 *Chr.* 15:18
18 Asa took *s.* and *g.* 2 *Chr.*
16:2
19 a pr. of *s.* and *g.* 2 *Chr.* 16:3
20:3, *s.* and *g.* mine ; 5 *s.* and *g.*
1 *Chr.* 29:3 my to. of good, *g.* and *s.*
2 *Chr.* 1:15 *s.* and *g.* plenteous

Ezr. 1:4 help with *silver* and *g.*
2:69 gave *s.* and *g.* ; 7:15
8:25 weighed *silver* and *g.* 33
Est. 1:6 beds were of *g.* and *s.*
Job 28:1 vein for *s.* a place for *g.*
Ps. 68:13 with *s.* feathers w. *g.*
105:37 br. forth with *s.* and *g.*
115:4 idols are *s.* and *g.* 135:15
119:72 law better than *g.* and *s.*
Prov. 8:10 not *silver* receive
knowledge rather than *g.*
17:3 fining-pot for *s.* fur. for *g.*
27:21
22:1 favor rather than *s.* or *g.*
25:11 apples of *g.* in pict. or *s.*
Ec. 2:8 I gathered also *s.* and *g.*
Cant. 1:11 bord. of *g.* studs of *s.*
3:10 pillars of *s.* bottom of *g.*
Is. 2:7 the land full of *s.* and *g.*
20 cast idols of *s.* and *g.* 31:7
13:17 shall not regard *s.* or *g.*
46:6 lavish *g.* and weigh *silver*
60:9 bring th. *s.* and *g.* w. them
Jer. 10:4 deck it with *s.* and *g.*
Ezek. 7:19 cast away *s.* and *g. s.*
and *g.* not able del. *Zep.* 1:18
16:13 decked with *g.* and *silver*
Dan. 2:35 *s.* and *g.* broken, 45
5:4 praised gods of *s.* and *g.* 23
11:38 a god honor w. *g.* and *s.*
43 power over treas. of *g.* and *s.*
Hos. 2:8 I multi. her *s.* and *g.*
8:4 of *s.* and *g.* they made idols
Joel 3:5 have taken my *s.* and *g.*
Nah. 2:9 take spoil of *s.* and *g.*
Hab. 2:19 laid over with *s.* and *g.*
Hag. 2:8 the *s.* is mine, *g.* mine
Zec. 6:11 *s.* and *g.* make crowns
Mal. 3:3 purge them as *g.* and *s.*
Mat. 10:9 provide nei. *g.* nor *s.*
Acts 3:6 *s.* and *g.* have I none
17:29 think Godh. like *s.* and *g.*
20:33 I cov. no man's *s.* or *g.*
1 *Cor.* 3:12 build on found. *g. s.*
2 *Tim.* 2:20 essels of *s.* and *g.*
Jam. 5:3 your *g.* and *s.* cankered
1 *Pet.* 1:18 not red. w. *s.* and *g.*
Rev. 9:20 rep. not of idols of *s. g.*

Talent and talents of GOLD.
Ex. 25:39 a *t.* of *g.* sh. he make
37:24 of a *tal.* of pure *g.* made
2 *Sam.* 12:30 weight of crown a
talent of *g.* 1 *Chr.* 20:2
1 *K.* 9:14 Hir. sent Sol. 120 *t. of g.*
28 sent from Ophir 420 *t. of g.*
10:10 she gave Solomon 120 *talents of g.* 2 *Chr.* 9:9
14 in 1 yr. came to S. 666 *t. of g.*
2 *K.* 23:33 put the land to a *talent of g.* 2 *Chr.* 36:3
1 *Chr.* 22:14 D. pre. 100,000 *t. of g.*
29:4 my own good 3,000 *t. of g.*
7 chief of fa. gave 5,000 *t. of g.*
2 *Chr.* 8:18 took fr. O. 450 *t. of g.*
Ezr. 8:26 weigh. *of g.* ves. 100 *t.*

Vessels of GOLD.
2 *Sam.* 8:10 Toi sent to David
vessels of *g.* 1 *Chr.* 18:10
1 *K.* 10:21 Solomon's drinking
v. were *of g.* 2 *Chr.* 9:20
25 broke *v. of g.* 2 *Chr.* 9:24
2 *K.* 12:13 for house of L. *v. of g.*
24:13 Neb. cut in pieces *v. of g.*
2 *Chr.* 24:14 money made *v. of g.*
Ezr. 1:11 *v. of g.* and silver 5,400
5:14 the *v. of g.* Cyrus delivered
8:26 weighed of *v. of g.* 100 tal.
Est. 1:7 gave drink in *v. of g.*
Dan. 11:8 carry into E. *v. of g.*
2 *Tim.* 2:20 not only *v. of g.*

GOLDEN.
Ex. 25:25 a *g.* crown to border
28:34 a *g.* bell ; 30:4 rings, 39:20
32:2 Aar. said, Break *g.* ear-r.
Lev. 8:9 on forefront put *g.* plate
Num. 7:26 *g.* spoon of 10 shekels

Jud. 8:24 had *g.* ear-rings
26 the weight of *g.* ear-rings
1 *Sam.* 6:4 emer. *g.* mice, 17, 18
2 *K.* 10:29 departed not fr. *g.* ca.
1 *Chr.* 28:17 for *g.* basins gave
2 *Chr.* 13:8 are with you *g.* calv.
Ezr. 6:5 let *g.* ves. be restored
Est. 4:11 the king shall hold out
a *g.* sceptre, 5:2 ; 8:4
Ec. 12:6 the *g.* bowl be broken
Is. 13:12 more prec. than *g.* w.
14:4 hath the *g.* city ceased
Jer. 51:7 Baby. hath been *g.* cup
Dan. 3:5 worship *g.* image, 12
5:2 Bel. commanded bring. *g.*
vessels
3 they brought the *g.* vessels
Zec. 4:12 *g.* pipes empty *g.* oil
Heb. 9:4 *g.* censer and ark. *g.* pot
Rev. 1:12 I saw 7 *g.* candlesticks
13 girt ab. paps with *g.* girdle
20 mystery of 7 *g.* candlesticks
2:1 in midst of *g.* candlesticks
5:8 *g.* vials, 15:7 ; 8:3 *g.* censer
14:14 on head *g.* cr. ; 17:4 *g.* cup
21:15 a *g.* reed to measure city
See ALTAR.

GOLDSMITH, S.

Neh. 3:8 Uzziel of the *g.* repaired
31 the *g.* son ; 32 *g.* and mer.
Is. 40:19 *g.* spread. it with gold
41:7 carpenter encourag. the *g.*
46:6 hire a *g.* and mak. it a god

GOLGOTHA. *Mat.* 27:33 ; *Mark* 15:22 ; *John* 19:17

GOLIATH.

1 *Sam.* 17:4 G. of G. went out, 23
21:9 sword of G. is here, 22:10
2 *Sam.* 21:19 brother of G. 1 *Chr.* 20:5

GOMER.

Gen. 10:2 Japheth, G. 1 *Chr.* 1:5
Ezek. 38:6 G. and all his bands
Hos. 1:3 he took G. the daughter

GOMORRAH.

Gen. 13:10 ; 14:11 ; 18:20 ; 19:24, 28
Deut. 29:28 ; *Is.* 1:9 ; 13:19 ; *Jer.* 23:14 ; 49:18 ; 50:40 ; *Amos* 4:11 ; *Rom.* 9:29 ; 2 *Pet.* 2:6 ; *Jude* 7
32:32 vine is of the fields of G.
Is. 1:10 ye peo. of G. *Zep.* 2:9
Mat. 10:15 toler. for G. *Mark* 6:11

GONE.

Gen. 34:17 take daugh. we be *g.*
42:33 take food, and be *g.*
Ex. 12:32 take flocks, and be *g.*
Deut. 32:36 seeth their pow. is *g.*
1 *Sam.* 14:3 knew not Jo. was *g.*
17 see who is *g.* from us
15:20 g. the way the Lord sent
20:41 as soon as the lad was *g.*
2 *Sam.* 3:7 g. into fath. concub.
24 quite *g.* ; 13:15 arise, be *g.*
1 *K.* 2:41 Shimei *g.* from Jerusa.
13:24 when *g.* a lion met him
18:12 soon as *g.* Spirit sh. carry
20:40 as I was busy, he was *g.*
1 *Chr.* 17:5 g. from tent to tent
Job 7:4 sh. I rise, and night be *g.*
19:10 destroyed me, and I am *g.*
24:24 exalted for a while, but *g.*
28:4 they are dried up and *g.*
Ps. 38:10 light of mine eyes is *g.*
42:4 I had *g.* with multitude
73:2 my feet were almost *g.*
77:8 is his mercy *g.* for ever?
103:16 wind pass. over it, is *g.*
109:23 I am *g.* like the shadow
Prov. 20:14 *g.* his way, boasting
Ec. 8:10 who had come and *g.*
Cant. 2:11 the rain is over and *g.*
5:6 beloved had withd. and *g.*
6:1 whither is thy beloved *g.?*

Is. 5:13 my people *g.* into capti.
24:11 the mirth of the land is *g.*
41:3 by the way he had not *g.*
Jer. 2:5 iniquity that th. are *g.?*
23 say, I have not *g.* after B. ?
5:23 people are revolted and *g.*
9:10 beasts *g.* ; 14:18 thou art *g.*
44:14 none *g.* into E. sh. escape
28 remnant that are *g.* sh. kn.
50:6 *g.* from mountain to hill
Lam. 1:3 Ju. *g.* ; 5 Zion's ch. *g.*
6 *g.* with. strength ; 18 virg. *g.*
Ezek. 37:21 from heathen whi. *g.*
Dan. 2:5 the thing is *g.* fr. me, 8
Hos. 9:6 *g.* bec. of destruction
Amos 8:5 when will moon be *g.?*
Luke 2:15 angels *g.* from them
24:28 made as would *g.* further
John 4:8 disciples were *g.* to buy
12:19 the world is *g.* after him
Acts 16:19 saw hope of gains *g.*
20:25 *g.* preaching kingd. of G.
1 *Pet.* 3:22 who is *g.* into heaven
Jude 11 have *g.* in way of Cain

GONE about.

1 *Sam.* 15:12 Saul is *g. a.* and
Job 1:5 days of feast, were *g. a.*
Is. 15:8 *g. a.* borders of Moab
Acts 24:6 *g. a.* to profane temple

GONE aside.

Num. 5:19 not *g. a.* to unclean.
20 if thou hast *g. a.* to another
Ps. 14:3 they are all *g. a.* filthy
Acts 26:31 when they were *g. a.*

GONE astray.

Ps. 119:176 have *g. a.* like sheep
Is. 53:6 we like sheep have *g. a.*
Mat. 18:12 if a man have 100
sheep, one be *g. a.* he seeketh that *g. a.*
2 *Pet.* 2:15 forsak. way, and *g. a.*

GONE away.

2 *Sam.* 3:22 Ab. *g. a.* in peace, 23
23:9 the men of Israel were *g. a.*
Job 28:4 wat. were *g. a.* from m.
Is. 1:4 they are *g. a.* backward
Ezek. 44:10 Levites *g. a.* from me
Mal. 3:7 *g. a.* fr. my ordinances
John 6:22 his disciples *g. a.* alo.

GONE back.

Ruth 1:15 thy sister-in-law *g. b.*
Job 23:12 nor have I *g. back*
Ps. 53:3 every one is *g. b.* none
Jer. 40:5 while he was not *g. b.*

GONE down.

1 *Sam.* 15:12 Saul is *g. d.* to Gil.

1 *K.* 1:25 Adonijah is *g. down*
21:18 Ahab *g. d.* to possess vin.
2 *K.* 20:11 the shadow had *g. d.*
in dial of Ahaz, *Is.* 38:8
Cant. 6:2 my beloved is *g. d. down*
Jer. 15:9 sun is *g. d.* while day
48:15 his young men are *g. d.*
Ezek. 31:12 peo. *g. d.* from shad.
32:21 strong *g. d.* slain by swo.
24 Elam *g. d.* ; 27 Tubal ; 30 Z.
Jon. 1:5 Jonah *g. d.* sides of ship

GONE forth.

Ex. 19:1 when Israel was *g. f.*
2 *K.* 6:15 when servant was *g. f.*
1 *Chr.* 14:15 God is *g. f.* before
Is. 51:5 my salvation is *g. f.*
Jer. 4:7 *g. f.* to make land desol.
10:20 my children are *g. f.*
23:15 profaneness *g. f.* into land
19 whirlwind of Lord is *g. f.*
29:16 brethren that are not *g. f.*
Ezek. 7:10 day come, morn. *g. f.*
36:20 people of Lord are *g. f.*
Dan. 2:14 *g. f.* to slay wise men
10:20 when I am *g. f.* pre. come
Mark 10:17 when he *g. f.* one

GONE out.

Ex. 9:29 as soon as I am *g. o.*
Num. 16:46 wrath *g. o.* from L.

Deut. 13:13 certain men *g. out*
23:23 which is *g. o.* of thy lips
Jud. 14:18 not the Lord *g. out*
Ruth 1:13 hand of the L. is *g. o.*
1 *Sam.* 25:37 wine *g. o.* of Nabal
2 *K.* 5:2 Syrians *g. o.* by comp.
7:12 we hungry, there. they *g. o.*
20:4 Isaiah was *g. o.* to court
Ps. 19:4 *g. o.* through the earth
89:34 the thing that is *g. out*
Is. 45:23 word *g. o.* of my mouth
Ezek. 24:6 whose scum not *g. out*
Mat. 12:43 when unclean spirit
is *g. out, Luke* 11:24
25:8 give us oil, our lamps *g. o.*
Mark 5:30 virtue *g. o. Luke* 8:46
7:29 devil is *g. out* of daughter,
30 ; *Luke* 11:14
John 13:31 when *g. o.* Jesus said
Rom. 3:12 they are all *g. o.*
1 *John* 4:1 many false prop. *g. o.*

GONE over.

2 *Sam.* 17:20 they be *g. o.* brook
Ps. 38:4 mine iniquities *g. o.*
42:7 waves and billows are *g. o.*
124:4 stream *g. over* our soul
5 waters had *g. over* our soul
Is. 10:29 they are *g. o.* passage
16:8 are *g. o.* the sea, *Jer.* 48:32
Mat. 10:23 *g. o.* cities of Israel

GONE up.

Gen. 49:9 my son, thou art *g. up*
2 *K.* 1:4 not come off bed so
which *g. up.* 6, 16
Ps. 47:5 G. is *g. up* with a shout
Is. 15:2 he is *g. up* to Bajith
57:8 discov. to another, art *g. up*
Jer. 3:6 she is *g. up* on mount.
14:2 the cry of Jerusa. is *g. up*
34:21 king's army wh. are *g. up*
48:15 Moab is *g. up* out of cities
Ezek. 9:3 glory of G. of Isr. *g. up*
13:5 have not *g. up* into gaps
Hos. 8:9 they are *g. up* to Assy.
John 7:10 his breth. were *g. up*
Acts 18:22 *g. up* and saluted chu.

GONE a whoring.

Lev. 17:7 whom th. have *g. a w.*
Ezek. 23:30 bec. thou hast *g. a w.*
Hos. 4:12 *g. a w.* fr. under th. G.
9:1 thou hast *g. a w.* from God

GOOD, Substantive

Gen. 32:12 I will do thee *g.*
45:18 *g.* of the land of Goshen
20 *g.* of land of Egypt is yours
50:20 God meant it unto *g.*
Num. 10:29 Lord hath spoken *g*
Jos. 24:20 consume you, after he
hath done you *g.*
1 *Sam.* 20:12 there be *g.* tow. D.
24:17 rewarded me *g.* for evil
19 wheref. Lord rew. thee *g.*
25:30 according to *g.* spoken
2 *Sam.* 14:32 *g.* for me to been
16:12 L. will requite *g.* for curs.
1 *K.* 22:13 words of prophets declare *g.* to king, 2 *Chr.* 18:12
1 *Chr.* 29:3 I prepared of my *g.*
2 *Chr.* 24:16 had done *g.* in Isr.
Ezr. 9:12 eat the *g.* of the land
Est. 7:9 spoken *g.* for the king
Job 2:10 rec. *g.* at hand of God?
5:27 know thou it for thy *g.*
7:7 mine eye sh. no more see *g.*
9:25 days flee, they see no *g.*
15:3 with speeches can do no *g.*
21:16 their *g.* is not in th. hand
Job 22:21 peace, *g.* sh. co. to th.
24:21 he doeth not *g.* to widow
Ps. 4:6 who will show us *g.?*
14:1 do *g.* 3 ; 53:1 ; *Rom.* 3:12
34:12 loveth days, he may see *g.*
39:2 I h. my peace, even from *g.*
104:28 they are filled with *g.*
106:5 see the *g.* of thy choice
122:9 Lord, I will seek thy *g.*
128:5 shall see *g.* of Jerusalem

Prov. 3:27 with. not *g.* from **th.**
11:17 doeth *g.* to his own **soul**
27 he that diligently seek. *g.*
12:14 a man satisfied with *g.*
13:2 eat *g.* by fruit of his mouth
21 to righteous *g.* sh. be repaid
14:22 truth to them that dev. *g.*
16:20 hand. matter wisely fl. *g.*
17:20 froward heart find. no *g.*
22 a merry heart doeth *g.*
19:8 keep understand. find *g.*
Ec. 2:24 soul en. *g.* 3:13 ; 5:18
3:12 there is no *g.* in them
4:8 I labor. bereave soul of *g.* ?
5:11 what *g.* there to owners ?
6:3 his soul be not filled with *g.*
6 seen no *g.* all *g.* to one place
7:20 doeth *g.* and sinneth not
9:18 one sinner destro. much *g.*
Is. 1:19 ye sh. eat the *g.* of land
52:7 bringeth good tidings of *g.*
Jer. 8:15 no *g.* came, 14:19
17:6 sh. not see when *g.* cometh
18:10 if do evil, I will rep. of *g.*
20 I stood bef. thee to speak *g.*
29:32 neither sh. behold *g.* I do
32:42 I will bring thee *g.* I pro.
33:9 hear all the *g.* I do them
Ezek. 16:50 I took them I saw *g.*
Zec. 11:12 if *g.* give my price
Mat. 26:24 been *g.* not been born
John 5:29 done *g.* to resurrection
Acts 10:38 went about doing *g.*
14:17 he did *g.* and gave rain
Rom. 2:10 hon. ev. man. work. *g.*
1 *Thes.* 3:1 *g.* be left Athens
1 *John* 3:17 hath this world's *g.*

For GOOD.

Deut. 6:24 fear the L. for our *g.*
10:13 com. thee this day *for g.*
30:9 L.will rej. over thee *for g.*
Ezr. 8:22 God on them *for g.*
Neh. 5:19 O my G. *for g.* 13:31
Job 5:27 know thou it *for* thy *g.*
Ps. 86:17 show a token *for g.*
119:122 be surety for ser. *for g.*
Jer. 14:11 pray not *for* their *g.*
24:5 sent out of place *f.* their *g.*
6 set mine eyes on them *f. g.*
32:39 for fear, *for* the *g.* of them
Mic. 1:12 Maroth waited *for g.*
Rom. 8:28 all things work *for g.*
13:4 he is minister of God *for g.*
15:2 ev. one please neighb. *f. g.*

See BAD, EVIL.

GOOD, Adjective.

Gen. 24:12 send me *g.* speed
26:29 we have done noth. but *g*
27:46 what *g.* sh. my life do me ?
41:5 *g.* ears ; 26 *g.* kine ; 35 *g.* y.
43:28 our father is in *g.* health
46:29 Joseph wept a *g.* while
Deut. 33:16 for *g.* will of him
1 *Sam.* 2:24 it is no *g.* report
12:23 I will teach the *g.* way
25:15 men were very *g.* to us.
29:9 thou art *g.* in my sight
2 *Sam.* 15:3 see thy mat. are *g.*
19:18 what the king thought *g.*
1 *K.* 8:36 teach them the *g.* way
56 no word of *g.* promise fail.
12:7 speak *g.* words, 2 *Chr.* 10:7
2 *K.* 20:19 *g.* is word of L. *Is.* 39:8
2 *Chr.* 19:11 Lord sh. be with *g.*
30:18 the *g.* Lord pardon every
Ezr. 8:18 the *g.* hand of our God
Neh. 9:13 gave them *g.* statutes
20 thou gav. *g.* Spirit to them
Job 10:3 is it *g.* thou oppress ?
13:9 is it *g.* he search you out ?
39:4 their young in *g.* liking
Ps. 25:8 *g.* and upright is the L.
37:23 steps of *g.* man ord. by L.
45:1 my heart is inditing *g.*
86:5 thou, Lord, art *g.* 119:68
112:5 a *g.* man showeth favor

119:39 thy judgments are *g.*
66 teach *g.* judg. and knowl.
Prov. 2:9 shalt unders. ev. *g.* pa.
20 walk in way of *g.* men
12:25 *g.* word mak. heart glad
14:19 the evil bow before the *g.*
15:23 word in season, how *g.*
30 *g.* report maketh bones fat
20:18 with *g.* advice make war
22:1 *g.* name rather than riches
Ec. 4:9 *g.* reward for their labor
5:11 what *g.* to owners thereof ?
9:2 one event to *g.* and clean
11:6 wheth. they both alike be *g.*
Jer. 6:16 the *g.* way and walk
24:2 *g.* figs ; 3 very *g.* ; 5 *g.* figs
29:10 I will perform my *g.* word
Ezek. 17:8 planted in *g.* soil by
24:4 gather every *g.* piece, thigh
Dan. 4:2 I thought *g.* to show
Zec. 1:13 L. ans. with *g.* words
Mal. 2:13 receiv. it with *g.* will
Mat. 7:11 *g.* gifts, *Luke* 11:13
17 *g.* tree bringeth *g.* fruit, 18
9:22 be of *g.* comfort, *Luke* 8:48
13:8 in *g.* ground, 23 ; *Mark* 4:8,
20 ; *Luke* 8:8, 15
24 *g.* seed ; 9:16 *g.* Mas. *g.* th.
19:17 call. me *g.* ? none *g.* but
20:15 th. eye evil bec. I am *g.* ?
25:21 well done, thou *g.* servant
Luke 2:14 *g.* will toward men
6:38 *g.* measure, pressed down
10:42 Mary hath chosen *g.* part
12:32 your Fa.'s *g.* pleasure
John 2:10 thou hast kept *g.* wine
10:11 I *g.* shep. the *g.* shepherd
Acts 15:7 ye know that a *g.* whi.
Rom. 7:12 com. is holy, just, *g.*
12:2 *g.* and perfect will of God
1 *Cor.* 15:33 corrupt *g.* manners
1 *Thes.* 3:6 have *g.* remem. of us
2 *Tim.* 3:3 despis. of those are *g.*
Tit. 1:8 must be lover of *g.* men
Heb. 6:5 tasted the *g.* word of G.
Jam. 1:17 *g.* gift ; 2:3 sit in a *g.*
1 *Pet.* 2:18 only to *g.* and gentle
3:10 love life, and see *g.* days

See BAD, CHEER, CONSCIENCE,
COURAGE, DO, DAY, OLD
AGE.

GOOD heed.

Deut. 2:4 take *g.* heed, *Jos.* 23:11
Ec. 12:9 preacher gave *g.* heed

Is GOOD.

Gen. 2:12 gold of that land *is g.*
Deut. 1:14 thing thou spok. *is g.*
6:18 that which *is g.* in sight L.
1 *Sam.* 29:6 co. in with ho. *is g.*
1 *K.* 2:38 Shi. said, The say. *is g.*
42 the word I have heard *is g.*
22:13 speak that which *is g.*
2 *K.* 20:3 done wh. *is g.* *Is.* 38:3
1 *Chr.* 16:34 L. *is g.* 2 *Chr.* 5:13 ;
7:3 ; *Ezr.* 3:11 ; *Ps.* 100:5 ;
106:1 ; 107:1 ; 118:1, 29 ; 135:3 ;
136:1 ; 145:9 ; *Jer.* 33:11 ; *Lam.*
3:25 ; *Nah.* 1:7
19:13 which *is g.* in his sight
Job 34:4 am. ourselves wh. *is g.*
Ps. 34:8 and see the Lord *is g.*
69:16 thy loving kindness *is g.*
73:1 truly, God *is g.* to Israel
85:12 L. sh. give that wh. *is g.*
109:21 because thy mercy *is g.*
143:10 Spirit *is g.* lead into land
Prov. 11:23 desire of right. *is g.*
25:25 so *is g.* news from far co.
31:18 perce. her merchand. *is g.*
Ec. 2:26 giveth to a man that *is*
g. to him that *is g.* bef. God
6:12 know. what *is g.* for man ?
7:11 wisd. *is g.* with an inherit.
9:2 as *is* the *g.* so is the sinner
Is. 55:2 eat ye that which *is g.*
Jer. 13:10 this girdle *is g.* for no.

Hos. 4:13 shadow thereof *is g.*
Mic. 6:8 showed thee, what *is g.*
Mal. 2:17 ev. one doeth evil *is g.*
Mark 9:50 salt *is g.* *Luke* 14:34
Luke 6:45 bringeth that wh. *is g.*
18:19 none *is g.* save one
Rom. 7:13 wh. *is g.* made death
18 that *is g.* I find not
12:9 cleave to that which *is g.*
16:19 wise to what *is g.*
1 *Cor.* 7:26 this *is g.* for the pre.
Eph. 4:29 no com. but that *is g.*
1 *Thes.* 5:15 what *is g.* 3 *John* 11
21 hold fast that which *is g.*
1 *Tim.* 1:8 we know the law *is g.*
2:3 this *is g.* in the sight of G.
4:4 every creature of God *is g.*
5:4 for that *is g.* before God
1 *Pet.* 3:13 fol. of that which *is g.*

It is GOOD.

Ps. 52:9 name, for it *is g.* 54:6
73:28 *it is g.* to draw near to G.
92:1 *it is g.* thing to give than.
119:71 *it is g.* I have been afflic.
147:1 *it is g.* to sing praises
Prov. 24:13 eat honey, be. *it is g.*
Ec. 5:18 *it is g.* to eat and drink
7:18 *it is g.* that thou take hold
Lam. 3:26 *it is g.* bear yoke in
Mat. 5:13 *it is g.* for nothing.

Mat. 17:4 *it is g.* for us to be
here, *Mark* 9:5 ; *Luke* 9:33
Rom. 7:16 I con. to law, *it is g.*
14:21 *it is g.* nei. to eat flesh nor
1 *Cor.* 7:1 *it is g.* for a man not
to touch a woman, 8
26 I say *it is g.* for a man
Gal. 4:18 *it is g.* zeal. affected

GOOD land.

Ex. 3:8 come to *g. l.* *Deut.* 8:7
Num. 14:7 the land is a *g. land*
Deut. 1:25 a *g. l.* the L. doth give
35 none of that gener. see *g. l.*
3:25 let me go and see the *g. l.*
4:21 should not go unto *g. land*
22 ye shall possess that *g. land*
6:18 go in and possess *g. land* .
8:7 bringeth thee into a *g. land*
10 bless the L. for the *g. land*
9:6 giveth not *g. l.* for thy righ.
11:17 lest ye perish from off *g. l.*
Jos. 23:13 perish from *g. l.* 15
16 perish quickly from off *g. l.*
Jud. 18:9 seen the land very *g.*
1 *K.* 14:15 root Israel out of *g. l.*
2 *K.* 3:19 mar ev. *g.* piece of *l.* 25
1 *Chr.* 28:8 possess this *g. land*

GOOD man.

2 *Sam.* 18:27 Ahimaaz is a *g. m.*
Ps. 37:23 steps of a *g. man*
112:5 a *g. man* showeth favor
Prov. 7:19 *g. man* is not at home
12:2 a *g. man* obtaineth favor
13:22 *g. m.* leaveth an inherit.
14:14 a *g. m.* is satisfied, 12:14
Mic. 7:2 the *g. man* is perished
Mat. 12:35 a *g. man* out of good
treasure, *Luke* 6:45
20:11 murmured. ag. *g. m.*
24:43 *g. man* had kn. *Luke* 12:39
Luke 23:50 Joseph was a *g. man*
John 7:12 said, He is a *g. man*
Acts 11:24 Barnabas was a *g. m.*
Rom. 5:7 for a *g. m.* some w. die

Not GOOD.

Gen. 2:18 *not g.* man be alone
2 *Sam.* 17:7 counsel *not g.*
Ps. 36:4 in way that is *not g.*

Prov. 16:29 lead into way *not g.*
17:26 to punish just is *not g.*
18:5 is *not g.* to accept wicked
19:2 soul with. know. *n. g.*
20:23 a false balance is *not g.*
24:23 *n. g.* respect of per. 28:21
25:27 *not g.* to eat much honey
Is. 65:2 walketh in way *n. g.*
Ezek. 18:18 did that wh. is *n. g.*
20:25 I gave them statutes *n. g.*
36:31 your doings were *n. g.*
Mat. 19:10 it is *not g.* to marry
Acts 15:38 Paul thought *not g.*
1 *Cor.* 5:6 your glorying is *not g.*

Seem, seemed, seemeth GOOD.

Jos. 9:25 as it *seemeth g.* to do
    unto us, *Jud.* 10:15 : 1 *Sam.*
    14:36, 40; *Ezr.* 7:18; *Est.*
    3:11; *Jer.* 26:14; 40:4
Jud. 19:24 do what *s. g.*
1 *Sam.* 1:23 what *seemeth g.* 3:18;
    11:10; 24:4
2 *Sam.* 3:19 all that *seem g.* to Is.
    10:12 do that *s.* him *g.* 15:26
19:37 do to C. what *seem g.* 38
24:22 and offer up what *s. g.*
1 *K.* 21:2 if it *seem g.* to thee,
    Jer. 40:4
1 *Chr.* 13:2 if it *seem g.* to you
Ezr. 5:17 k. *g.* king, *Est.* 5:4
Jer. 18:4 as *seemed g.* to potter
Mat. 11:26 *s. g.* in sig. *Luke* 10:21
Luke 1:3 it *seemed g.* to me
Acts 15:25 it *seemed g.* unto us
    28 it *seemed g.* to the H. Ghost

GOOD, *with thing.*

Ex. 18:17 *thing* doest is not *g.*
Deut. 26:11 rejoice in every *g. t.*
Jos. 21:45 failed not any *g. t.*
1 *Sam.* 26:16 this *thing* is not *g.*
1 *K.* 14:13 him is fou. some *g. t.*
2 *K.* 8:9 took of ev. *g. t.* of Da.
Ps. 34:10 seek L. not want *g. t.*
38:20 I follow *thing* that *g.* is
84:11 no *g. th.* will he withhold
92:1 it is *g. t.* to give thanks
Prov. 18:22 a wife, findeth *g. th.*
Jer. 33:14 will perform *g. t.*
Hos. 8:3 cast off *thing* that is *g.*
Mat. 19:16 what *g. thing* sh. I do
John 1:46 any *g. t.* out of Naz. ?
Rom. 7:18 in my flesh dw. no *g. t.*
Gal. 4:18 zeal. affected in *g. t.*
Eph. 4:28 working *th.* which is *g.*
6:8 knowing *g. t.* man doeth
2 *Tim.* 1:14 *g. t.* commit to thee
Phile. 6 ack. every *g. th.* in you
Heb. 13:9 a *g. t.* heart be establ.

GOOD things.

Deut. 6:11 houses full of *g. t.*
Jos. 23:14 not one failed of *g. t.*
    15 that all *g. things* are come
Job 22:18 filled th. hous. wi. *g. t.*
Ps. 103:5 sat. thy mouth w. *g. t.*
Prov. 28:10 upright sh. have *g. t.*
Jer. 5:25 sins have withh. *g. t.*
Mat. 7:11 give *g. things* to them
12:34 being evil, speak *g. t.*
    35 a good man bringeth *g. th.*
Luke 1:53 filled hungry with *g. t.*
16:25 in lifetime receivedst *g. t.*
Rom. 10:15 glad tidings of *g. th.*
Gal. 6:6 communicate in all *g. t.*
Tit. 2:3 women teachers of *g. t.*
3:8 these *t.* are *g.* and profitable
Heb. 9:11 Christ high-pr. of *g. t.*
10:1 a shadow of *g. th.* to come

GOOD tidings.

2 *Sam.* 4:10 have brought *g. tid.*
18:27 cometh with *g. tidings*
1 *K.* 1:42 and bringest *g. tidings*
2 *K.* 7:9 a day of *g. tidings*
Is. 40:9 O Zion that bringest *g. t.*
41:27 give J. one bringeth *g. t.*
52:7 him that bringeth *g. t.*

61:1 anointed to preach *g. tid.*
Nah. 1:15 beh. him bringeth *g. t.*
Luke 2:10 I bring you *g. t.*
1 *Thes.* 3:6 *g. t.* of your faith

GOOD understanding.

1 *Sam.* 25:3 Abi. was wo. of *g. u.*
Ps. 111:10 *g. u.* have all that do
Prov. 3:4 find favor and *g. und.*
13:15 *g. understan.* giveth favor

Was GOOD.

Gen. 1:4 saw that it *w. g.* 10, 25
    31 G. saw ev. th. it *w.* very *g.*
3:6 the woman saw tree *was g.*
40:16 baker saw interpre. *w. g.*
41:37 thing *w. g.* in eyes of Phar.
49:15 Issachar saw rest *w. g.*
1 *Sam.* 15:9 S. spar. all that *w. g.*
2 *Chr.* 14:2 Asa did that wh. *w. g.*
31:20 Hezekiah wro. what *w. g.*
Ec. 2:3 see what *w.* that *g.*

GOOD work.

Neh. 2:18 strengthen for *g. w.*
Mat. 26:10 wro. *g. w. Mark* 14:6
John 10:33 for *g. w.* we stone not
2 *Cor.* 9:8 abound to every *g. w.*
Phil. 1:6 which hath begun *g. w.*
Col. 1:10 fruitful in every *g. w.*
2 *Thes.* 2:17 in every *g. w.*
1 *Tim.* 3:1 a bishop, desir. *g. w.*
5:10 diligently followed *g. w..*
2 *Tim.* 2:21 prepared to ev. *g. w.*
Tit. 1:16 to every *g. w.* reprobate
3:1 to be ready to every *g. w.*
Heb. 13:21 make perf. in ev. *g. w.*

GOOD works.

1 *Sam.* 19:4 *w.* to thee been *g.*
Mat. 5:16 may see your *g. w.*
John 10:32 *g. w.* I have showed
Acts 9:36 Dorcas full of *g. works*
Rom. 13:3 not a terror to *g. w.*
Eph. 2:10 created in Ch. to *g. w.*
1 *Tim.* 2:10 be adorned w. *g. w.*
5:10 well reported for *g. works*
    25 *g. w.* of some are manifest
6:18 that they be rich in *g. w.*
2 *Tim.* 3:17 furnished to all *g. w.*
Tit. 2:7 thyself a pattern in *g. w.*
    14 zealous of *g. works*
3:8 careful to maintain *g. w.* 14
Heb. 10:24 prov. to love and *g. w.*
1 *Pet.* 2:12 by *g. w.* glorify God

GOODLY.

Gen. 39:6 Joseph was a *g.* person
49:21 Nap. a hind, giv. *g.* words
Ex. 2:2 saw he was a *g.* child
39:28 made *g.* bonnets
Num. 24:5 *g.* are thy tents, O J.
Deut. 3:25 that *g.* mountain
6:10 *g.* cities which build. not
8:12 thou hast built *g.* houses
Jos. 7:21 a *g.* Babylon. garment
1 *Sam.* 9:2 S. a young man, and *g.*
16:12 David was *g.* to look to
2 *Sam.* 23:21 Ben. slew a *g.* man
1 *K.* 1:6 Adonijah was a *g.* man
Job 39:13 *g.* wings to peacocks
Ps. 16:6 I have a *g.* heritage
80:10 boughs were like *g.* cedars
Jer. 3:19 sh. I give thee *g.* heri. ?
11:16 olive-tree of *g.* fruit
Ezek. 17:8 it might be a *g.* vine
    23 bear fruit, and be a *g.* cedar
Hos. 10:1 have made *g.* images
Joel 3:5 your tem. my *g.* things
Zec. 10:3 made them as *g.* horse
11:13 a *g.* price I was prized at
Mat. 13:45 merch. seek. *g.* pearls
Luke 21:5 adorned with *g.* stones
Jam. 2:2 a man in *g.* apparel
Ren. 18:14 things dainty and *g.*

GOODLIER, EST.

1 *Sam.* 8:16 your *g.* young men
9:2 not in Israel a *g.* person
1 *K.* 20:3 child. even *g.* are mine

GOODNESS.

Ex. 18:9 rejo. for *g.* L. had done
33:19 make *g.* pass before thee
34:6 Lord God abundant in *g.*
Num. 10:32 wh. *g.* L. sh. do to us
2 *Sam.* 7:28 prom. *g.* 1 *Chr.* 17:26
1 *K.* 8:66 joyful for *g.* 2 *Chr.* 7:10
2 *Chr.* 6:41 saints rejoice in *g.*
32:32 Hezek. *g.* ; 35:26 Josiah *g.*
Neh. 9:25 delighted thems. in *g.*
    35 have not served thee in *g.*
Ps. 16:2 my *g.* ext. not to thee
21:3 prev. with blessings of *g.*
23:6 surely *g.* shall follow me
25:7 remem. me, for thy *g.* sake
27:13 I believed to see *g.* of L.
31:19 O how great is thy *g.*
33:5 earth is full of *g.* of Lord
52:1 *g.* of God endureth contin.
65:4 satis. with *g.* of thy house
    11 crownest the year with *g.*
68:10 prep. of thy *g.* for poor
107:8 pr. L. for his *g.* 15, 21, 31
    9 filleth hungry soul with *g.*
144:2 my *g.* and my fortress
145:7 utter memory of thy *g.*
Prov. 20:6 procla. ev. one his *g.*
Is. 63:7 *g.* toward the house of
    Israel
Jer. 2:7 bro. you to eat *g.* thereof
31:12 flow together to *g.* of L.
    14 people satisfied with my *g.*
33:9 shall tremble for all the *g.*
Hos. 3:5 fear the Lord and his *g.*
6:4 your *g.* is as a morn. cloud
10:1 according to *g.* of his land
Zec. 9:17 great is his *g.*
Rom. 2:4 *g.* of G. lead. to repent.
11:22 behold, the *g.* of G. towa.
    thee *g.* if thou continue in *g.*
15:14 that your are full of *g.*
Gal. 5:22 fru. of Sp. is *g. Eph.* 5:9
2 *Thes.* 1:11 fulfil *g.* ple. of his

GOODS.

Gen. 14:16 Abr. brought back *g.*
    21 take the *g.* to thyself
24:10 *g.* of master in his hand
31:18 J. carried away his *g.* 46:6
Ex. 22:8 hand to neighbor's *g.* 11
Num. 16:32 earth swall. their *g.*
31:9 spoil of Midian and their *g.*
35:3 for Levites' cattle and *g.*
Deut. 28:11 make plenteous in *g.*
2 *Chr.* 21:14 smite wives, thy *g.*
Ezr. 1:4 the men help him wi. *g.*
    6 strength. their hands with *g.*
6:8 king's *g.* expenses be given
7:26 banishm. or to confis. of *g.*
Neh. 9:25 poss. houses full of *g.*
Job 20:10 his hands eh. restore *g.*
    21 therefore no man look for *g.*
    28 his *g.* shall flow away
Ec. 5:11 when *g.* increase
Ezek. 38:12 have cattle and *g.*
    13 come to take cattle and *g.*
Zep. 1:13 *g.* shall bec. a booty
Mat. 12:29 enter str. man's hou.
    and take *g. ! Mark* 3:27
24:47 make him ruler over *g.*
25:14 deliver. unto them his *g.*
Luke 6:30 taketh away thy *g.*
11:21 his *g.* are in peace
12:18 there will I bestow my *g.*
    19 thou hast much *g.* laid up
15:12 give me the portion of *g.*
16:1 accused that he wasted *g.*
19:8 half of my *g.* give to poor
Acts 2:45 sold *g.* and parted th.
1 *Cor.* 13:3 I bestow all my *g.*
Heb. 10:34 spoiling of your *g.*
Rev. 3:17 and increased with *g.*

GOPHER wood.

Gen. 6:14 an ark of *g. w.*

GORE, ED.

Ex. 21:28 if ox *g.* man or woman
    31 whe. *g.* a son or daughter

GORGEOUS, LY.

Ezek. 23:12 Assyrians clothed *g.*
Luke 7:25 *g.* apparel. in king's
    23:11 H. arrayed Jesus in *g.*
    robe

GOSHEN.

Gen. 45:10 dwell in land of G.
    46:34; 47:4, 6, 27
Ex. 8:22; 9:26; *Jos.* 10:41; 11:16;
    15:51

GOSPEL.

Mark 1:1 beginning of *g.* of J. C.
    15 said, Repent and believe *g.*
    8:35 lose life for my sake and *g.*
    10:29 for my sake and *g.*
    13:10 the *g.* must be published
Acts 15:7 by my mouth hear *g.*
    20:24 the *g.* of the grace of God
Rom. 1:1 separat. to the *g.* of G.
    9 I serve with my spirit in *g.*
    16 not ashamed of *g.* of Christ
    2:16 judge secrets ac. to my *g.*
    10:16 have not all obeyed the *g.*
    11:28 concerning *g.* are enemies
    15:16 ministering the *g.* of God
    29 blessing of the *g.* of Christ
    16:25 estab. you according to *g.*
1 Cor. 4:15 begotten you thro' *g.*
    9:12 lest we hinder *g.* of Christ
    17 a dispensation of *g.* is com.
    18 I preach *g.* I may make *g.*
    of Christ with. charge; that
    I abuse not my po. in the *g.*
    23 this I do for the *g.* sake
2 Cor. 4:3 if *g.* hid, hid to them
    4 light of glor. *g.* should shine
    8:18 whose praise is in *g.*
    9:13 prof. subjection to the *g.*
    11:4 receive another *g. Gal.* 1:6
Gal. 1:7 would pervert *g.* of Chr.
    2:2 communicated *g.* I preach
    5 truth of *g.* might continue
    7 *g.* of uncir. committed to me
    14 according to truth of the *g.*
Eph. 1:13 *g.* of your salvation
    3:6 partake prom. in Chr. by *g.*
    6:15 preparation of *g.* of peace
    19 make known mystery of *g.*
Phil. 1:5 fellowship in the *g.*
    7 def. and confirmation of *g.* 17
    12 fallen out to furthera. of *g.*
    27 let your conversation be as
    beco. *g.* striv. for faith of *g.*
    2:22 hath served with me in *g.*
    4:3 help-women with me in *g.*
    15 in the beginning of the *g.*
Col. 1:5 heard bef. of truth of *g.*
    23 not moved from hope of *g.*
1 Thes. 1:5 *g.* came not in word
    2:2 bold to speak the *g.* of God
    4 to be put in trust with *g.*
    8 willing to impart not *g.* only
    3:2 Ti. our fellow-laborer in *g.*
2 Thes. 1:8 on them that obey
    not the *g. 1 Pet.* 4:17
    2:14 whereunto called you by *g.*
1 Tim. 1:11 according to *g.* of G.
2 Tim. 1:8 partaker of affli. of *g.*
    10 immortality to light thro' *g.*
    2:8 J. C. raised according to *g.*
Phile. 13 minist. in bonds of *g.*

GOSPEL, *with* preach, ed, ing.

Mat. 4:23 Jesus went *preaching*
    the *g.* 9:35; *Mark* 1:14
    11:5 poor have *g. p. Luke* 7:22
    24:14 *g.* be *p.* 26:13; *Mark* 14:9
Mark 16:15 *p. g.* to ev. creature
Luke 4:18 anointed me to *p. g.*
    9:6 *p.* the *g.* and healing
    20:1 he taught and *preached g.*
Acts 8:25 *pre. g.* to Samaritans
    16:10 L. had called us to *p. g.*
Rom. 1:15 I am ready to *p. g.*
    10:15 beautiful feet that *p. g.*
    15:19 I have fully *pre. g.* of Ch.
    20 so have I strived to *prea. g.*

---

1 Cor. 1:17 not to bapt. but *pr. g.*
    9:14 that *p. g.* should live of *g.*
    16 tho' I *p. g.* nothing to glory
    of, woe to me if I *pr.* not *g.*
    18 when I *p. g.* I may make *g.*
    15:1 I declare the *g.* which I *pr.*
2 Cor. 2:12 I came to T. to *pr. g.*
    10:14 as far as to you in *p. g.*
    11:7 I *pr.* to you freely the *g.*
Gal. 1:8 tho' we *pr.* any other *g.*
    11 *g. p.* of me not after man
    3:8 *prea.* before the *g.* to Abra.
    4:13 infirmity of flesh I *p. g.*
1 Thes. 2:9 we *p.* to you *g.* of G.
Heb. 4:2 to us was *g. preached*
1 Pet. 1:12 them that *pre.* the *g.*
    25 which by *g.* is *pr.* to you
    4:6 for this cause was the *g. pr.*
Rev. 14:6 having everl. *g.* to *p.*

GOT.

Gen. 39:12 Jos. *g.* him out, 15
Ps. 44:3 *g.* not land by sword
Ec. 2:7 I *g.* servan. and maidens

GOTTEN.

Gen. 4:1 I have *g.* a man

Ex. 14:18 when I have *g.* honor
Lev. 6:4 thing he hath deceit. *g.*
Deut. 8:17 hand hath *g.* wealth
2 Sam. 17:13 be *g.* into a city
Job 28:15 wisdom not *g.* for gold
    31:25 rejoic. bec. hand *g.* much
Ps. 98:1 arm hath *g.* victory
Prov. 13:11 wealth *g.* by vanity
    20:21 inheritance *g.* hastily
Ec. 1:16 *g.* more wisdom than all
Is. 15:7 abundance *g.* they carry
Ezek. 38:4 wisdom hast *g.* riches
Dan. 9:15 thou hast *g.* renown
Rev. 15:2 them that *g.* victory

GOVERN.

1 K. 21:7 dost *g.* kingdom of Is. ?
Job 34:17 shall he that hateth *g.* ?
Ps. 67:4 thou sh. *g.* the nations

GOVERNMENT, S.

Is. 9:6 *g.* shall be upon shoulder
    7 of incr. of his *g.* sh. be no end
    22:21 I commit *g.* to his hand
1 Cor. 12:28 *g.* divers. of tongues
2 Pet. 2:10 them that despise *g.*

GOVERNOR.

Gen. 42:6 Jos. *g.* over land, 45:26
1 K. 18:3 Ob. *g.* over Ahab's ho.
1 Chr. 29:22 anointed S. chief *g.*
Ezr. 5:14 C. deliv. vessels to *g.*
Neh. 5:14 not eaten bread of *g.*
    18 required not the bread of *g.*
Ps. 22:28 he is *g.* am. the nation.
Jer. 30:21 *g.* sh. proceed fr. them
    40:5 go back to Gedaliah the *g.*
    41:2 Ish. smote Gedaliah the *g.*
Hag. 1:14 L. stirred up Zerub. *g.*
    2:2 speak to Zerub. the *g.* 21
Zec. 9:7 sh. be as a *g.* in Judah
Mal. 1:8 offer it now to thy *g.*
    2:6 out of thee sh. come *g.*
    28:14 if this come to *g.'s* ears
John 2:8 bear to *g.* of the feast
Acts 24:1 informed *g.* against P.
2 Cor. 11:32 the *g.* under Aretas
Jam. 3:4 ships turned wh. *g.* lis.

GOVERNORS.

Jud. 5:9 my heart tow. *g.* of Isr.
    14 out of Machir came down *g.*
Ezr. 8:36 delivered com. to *g.*
Neh. 2:7 let letters be given to *g.*
    5:15 the *g.* chargeable to people
Dan. 2:48 made Dan. chief of *g.*
Zec. 12:5 *g.* of Judah shall say
    6 will make *g.* of J. like hearth
Mat. 10:18 sh. be brought bef. *g.*
Gal. 4:2 under tutors and *g.*
1 Pet. 2:14 submit yoursel. to *g.*

GOURD, S.

2 K. 4:39 one gathered wild *g.*

Jon. 4:6 God prepared *g.* J. glad
    7 a worm smote *g.* it withered
    10 thou hast had pity on the *g.*

GOZAN. *2 K.* 17:6; 18:11; 19:12;
    1 Chr. 5:26; *Is.* 37:12

GRACE.

Ezr. 9:8 little space *g.* showed
Est. 2:17 E. obtained *g.* in sight
Ps. 45:2 *g.* poured into lips
    84:11 Lord is a sun, will give *g.*
Prov. 1:9 an ornament of *g.*
    3:22 so shall they be life and *g.*
    34 giveth *g.* to lowly, *Jam.* 4:6
    4:9 to head ornament of *g.*
    22:11 for *g.* of lips king his fri.
Zec. 4:7 shoutings, crying, *g. g.*
    12:10 will pour the Sprit of *g.*
John 1:14 begotten of F. full of *g.*
    16 have all received *g.* for *g.*
    17 *g.* and truth came by J. C.
Acts 4:33 great *g.* was on them
    14:3 testimony to word of his *g.*
    18:27 which believed thro' *g.*
    20:32 com. you to word of *g.*
Rom. 1:5 by wh. we received *g.*
    7 *g.* and peace from G. our F.
    1 Cor. 1:3; *2 Cor.* 1:2; *Gal.*
    1:3; *Eph.* 1:2; *Phil.* 1:2; *Col.*
    1:2; *1 Thes.* 1:1; *2 Thes.* 1:2;
    Phile. 3
    3:24 justified freely by his *g.*
    4:4 reward is not reckoned of *g.*
    16 that it might be by *g.*
    5:2 we have access into this *g.*
    17 receive abundance of *g.*
    20 sin abounded, *g.* more
    21 *g.* reign thro' righteousness
    6:1 con. in sin, that *g.* abound?
    14 under *g.*, 15 bec. under *g.* ?
    11:5 according to election of *g.*
    6 if by *g.* no more of works
    12:3 through *g.* given unto me
    6 gifts differing according to *g.*
    15:15 the *g.* given to me of God
1 Cor. 10:30 if I by *g.* be partak.
    15:10 *g.* bestowed not in vain

2 Cor. 4:15 *g.* red. to glory of G.
    8:6 finish in you the same *g.*
    7 see that ye abound in this *g.*
    19 travel with us with this *g.*
    9:8 G. is able to make *g.* abound
    12:9 my *g.* is sufficient for thee
Gal. 1:6 who called you to *g.*
    15 G. who called me by his *g.*
    2:9 when James perceived *g.*
    5:4 justm. by law, fallen from *g.*
Eph. 1:6 praise of the glory of *g.*
    7 according to riches of *g.*
    2:5 by *g.* saved through faith, 8
    7 might show the riches of *g.*
    3:8 to me is this *g.* given
    4:7 to ev. one of us is given *g.*
    29 may minister *g.* to hearers
    6:24 *g.* with all that love L. J.
Phil. 1:7 are all partakers of *g.*
Col. 3:16 sing. with *g.* in hearts
    4:6 let speech be alway with *g.*
    18 *g.* be with you, *2 Tim.* 4:22 ;
    Tit. 3:15 ; *Heb.* 13:25
2 Thes. 2:16 hope through *g.*
1 Tim. 1:2 *g.* mercy, and peace
    from G. our Father, *2 Tim.*
    1:2; *Tit.* 1:4 ; *2 John* 3
    1:14 *g.* of Lord abundant
    6:21 *g.* be with thee. Amen
2 Tim. 1:9 called us accord. to *g.*
    2:1 be strong in the *g.* in Christ
Tit. 3:7 justified by *g.*
Heb. 4:16 boldly to throne of *g.*
    10:29 despite to the Spirit of *g.*
    12:28 let us have *g.* to serve G.
    13:9 the heart be estab. with *g.*
Jam. 1:11 *g.* of fashion perisheth
    4:6 giveth more *g.* to humble
1 Pet. 1:2 *g.* be multi. *2 Pet.* 1:2
    10 prophesied of *g.* to come

13 hope for *g.* 3:7 heirs of *g.*
5:5 God giveth *g.* to humble
10 G. of *g.* called us to glory
2 *Pet.* 3:18 grow in *g.* and in Ch.
Jude 4 turning *g.* of G. to lasciv.
Rev. 1:4 *g.* from him

See FIND, *or* FOUND.

GRACE of God.

Luke 2:40 *g. of God* upon him
Acts 11:23 he had seen *g. of God*
13:43 persua. to con. in *g. of G.*
14:26 recom. to *g. of G.* 15:40
20:24 the gospel of *g. of God*
Rom. 5:15 *g. of G.* hath abound.
1 *Cor.* 1:4 *g. of G.* given by J. C.
3:10 ac. to *g. of G.* given to me
15:10 by *g. of God* I am what I am, yet not I, but *g. of God*
2 *Cor.* 1:12 by *g. of G.* we had
6:1 rec. not the *g. of G.* in vain
8:1 *g of G.* bestow. on churches
9:14 the exceeding *g. of G.*
Gal. 2:21 not frustrate *g. of G.*
Eph. 3:2 dispensation of *g. of G.*
7 accor. to the gift of *g. of G.*
Col. 1:6 ye knew the *g. of G.*
2 *Thes.* 1:12 according to *g. of G.*
Tit. 2:11 *g. of G.* bringeth salv.
Heb. 2:9 by *g. of G.* taste death
12:15 any man fail of *g. of G.*
1 *Pet.* 4:10 stewards of *g. of G.*
5:12 this is the true *g. of God*

GRACE of our Lord Jesus.

Acts 15:11 *g. of L. J.* sh. be saved
Rom. 16:20 *g. of our Lord J.* be with you, 24; 1 *Cor.* 16:23; *Phil.* 4:23; 1 *Thes.* 5:28; 2 *Thes.* 3:18
2 *Cor.* 8:9 the *g. of our L. J. C.*
13:14 the *g. of our L. J. Christ*
Gal. 6:18 *g. of L. J.* wi. s. *Phi.* 25
Rev. 22:21 *g. of L. J.* be with you

GRACIOUS.

Gen. 43:29 God be *g.* to thee
Ex. 22:27 I will hear, I am *g.*
33:19 be *g.* to whom I be *g.*
34:6 the Lord God, *g.* 2 *Chr.* 30:9; *Ps.* 103:8; 116:5; 145:8; *Joel* 2:13
Num. 6:25 make face shine *g.*
2 *Sam.* 12:22 tell wh. G. will be *g.*
Neh. 9:17 a God *g.* merciful, 31
Job 33:24 then he is *g.* to him
Ps. 77:9 God forgotten to be *g. ?*
86:15 art God *g.* 111:4; 112:4
Prov. 11:16 *g.* wo. retain. honor
Ec. 10:12 words of wise man *g.*
Is. 30:18 L. wilt wait that he be *g.*
19 be *g.* to thee; 33:2 *g.* to us
Jer. 22:23 *g.* when pangs come
Amos 5:15 the Lord will be *g.*
Jon. 4:2 thou art a *g.* God
Mal. 1:9 beseech G. he will be *g.*
Luke 4:22 wondered at *g.* words
1 *Pet.* 2:3 if ye tasted the L. is *g.*

GRACIOUSLY.

Gen. 33:5 child. God *g.* given me
Gen. 33:11 G. hath dealt *g.* with
Ps. 119:29 grant me thy law *g.*
Hos. 14:2 receive us *g.*

GRAFT, ED.

Rom. 11:17 wild olive-t. wert *g.*
19 that I might be *g.* in
23 they sh. be *g.* G. is able to *g.*
24 cut out and *g.* these be *g.*

GRAIN, S.

Amos 9:9 not least *g.* fall on ear.
Mat. 13:31 kingdom of heaven is like a *g.* of mustard-seed, *Mark* 4:31; *Luke* 13:19
17:20 faith as a *g.* of mustard-s. ye shall say to this mount. remove, *Luke* 17:6
1 *Cor.* 15:37 *g.* wheat, or other *g.*

GRANDMOTHER.

2 *Tim.* 1:5 faith dwelt in thy *g.*

GRANT, Substantive.

Ezr. 3:7 accord. to *g.* of Cyrus

GRANT, Verb.

Lev. 25:24 *g.* a redemption
1 *Sam.* 1:17 God *g.* thee petition
1 *Chr.* 21:22 *g.* this threshing-fl.; thou shall *g.* it me
2 *Chr.* 12:7 I will *g.* them deliv.
Neh. 1:11 *g.* mercy in sight of
Est. 5:8 the king *g.* my petition
Job 6:8 G. *g.* the thing I long for
Ps. 20:4 *g.* thee to thine heart
85:7 O Lord, *g.* us salvation
119:29 *g.* me thy law graciously
140:8 *g.* not, O L. de. of wicked
Mat. 20:21 *g.* my two sons may sit, *Mark* 10:37
Luke 1:74 *g.* to us that we being
Acts 4:29 *g.* with boldness
Rom. 15:5 G. *g.* you to be like-m.
Eph. 3:16 *g.* you to be strength.
2 *Tim.* 1:18 L. *g.* he find mercy
Rev. 3:21 *g.* to sit in my throne

GRANTED.

1 *Chr.* 4:10 God *g.* what he requ.
2 *Chr.* 1:12 and knowl. is *g.* thee
Ezr. 7:6 king *g.* all his requests
Neh. 2:8 *g.* accord. to hand of G.
Est. 5:6 petit. sh. be *g.* 7:2; 9:12
9:13 let it be *g.* to Jews in Shu.
Job 10:12 hast *g.* life and favor
Prov. 10:24 desire of right. be *g.*
Acts 11:18 G. *g.* Gen. repentance
14:3 *g.* signs to be done by han.
Rev. 19:8 *g.* she sh. be arrayed

GRAPE.

Lev. 19:10 not gather *g.* of wine
Deut. 32:14 drink blood of *g.*
Job 15:33 shake off unripe *g.*
Cant. 2:13 *g.* give good smell
7:12 the tender *g.* appear
Is. 18:5 sour *g.* is ripening
Jer. 31:29 have eaten a sour *g.*
30 ev. man that eateth sour *g.*
Mic. 7:1 as *g.* gleanings of vint.

GRAPE-GATHERER.

Jer. 6:9 turn back hand as *g.-g.*
49:9 if *g.-g.* come, *Ob.* 5

GRAPES.

Gen. 40:10 clusters bro. ripe *g.*
49:11 washed clothes in bl. of *g.*
Lev. 25:5 nor gather *g.* undressed
11 in jubilee, nor ga. *g.* of vine
Num. 6:3 nor shall eat moist *g.*
13:20 time of the first ripe *g.*
23 cut a branch with clus. of *g.*
Deut. 23:24 mayest eat *g.* thy fill
24:21 wh. thou gatherest the *g.*
28:30 plant vine. not ga. *g.* 39
32:32 their *g.* are *g.* of gall
Jud. 8:2 gleaning of *g.* of Ephr.
Neh. 13:15 wine and *g.* on sab.
Cant. 2:15 vines have tender *g.*
7:7 breasts are like clust. of *g.*
Is. 5:2 it should bring forth *g.*
4 bring forth *g.* bro. wild *g. ?*
17:6 gleaning *g.* shall be left
24:13 *g.* when vintage is done
Jer. 8:13 there sh. be no *g.* on vi.
25:30 as they that tread *g.*
49:9 gleaning *g. Ob.* 5
Ezek. 18:2 have eaten sour *g.*
Hos. 9:10 like *g.* in wilderness
Amos 9:13 treader of *g.* ov. sower
Mat. 7:16 man ga. *g.* of thorns?
Luke 6:44 nor of brambles ga. *g.*
Rev. 14:18 her *g.* are fully ripe

GRASS.

Gen. 1:11 earth bring forth *g.*
12 the earth brought forth *g.*
Num. 22:4 licketh up *g.* of field
Deut. 11:15 send *g.* for thy cattle
29:23 any *g.* groweth therein
32:2 distil as showers upon *g.*
2 *Sam.* 23:4 the *g.* springing out

1 *K.* 18:5 find *g.* to save horses
2 *K.* 19:26 as *g.* of the field, as *g.* on the house-tops, *Is.* 37:27
Job 5:25 offspring as *g.* of earth
6:5 ass bray when he hath *g.*
40:15 behem. eateth *g.* as an ox
Ps. 37:2 sh. be cut down like *g.*
72:6 like rain upon mown *g.*
16 they shall flourish like *g.*
90:5 they are like *g.* wh. grow.
92:7 the wicked spring as *g.*
102:4 heart is withered like *g.*
11 a shadow, withered like *g.*
103:15 man, his days are as *g.*
104:14 causeth *g.* to grow
106:20 an ox that eateth *g.*
129:6 as *g.* upon the house-tops
147:8 *g.* to grow upon mount.
Prov. 19:12 as dew on *g.*
27:25 tender *g.* showeth itself
Is. 15:6 the *g.* faileth
35:7 in hab. of dragons sh. be *g.*
40:6 All flesh is *g.* 1 *Pet.* 1:24
7 *g.* wither. surely peo. is *g.* 8
44:4 eh. spring up as *g.* in wat.
Jer. 14:5 forsook it because no *g.*
50:11 grown fat as heifer at *g.*
Dan. 4:15 leave stump in *g.* 23
25 eat *g.* as oxen, 32, 33; 5:21
Mic. 5:7 as showers upon the *g.*
Zec. 10:1 L. shall give ev. one *g.*
Mat. 6:30 clothe *g. Luke* 12:28
14:19 sit down on *g. Mark* 6:39
John 6:10 there was much *g.*
Jam. 1:10 as *g.* he sh. pass away
11 sun risen, withereth the *g.*
Rev. 8:7 all green *g.* burnt up
9:4 should not hurt *g.* of earth

GRASSHOPPER, S.

Lev. 11:22 the *g.* after his kind
Num. 13:33 in our sight as *g.*
Jud. 6:5 as *g.* for multitude, 7:12
Job 39:20 afraid as a *g. ?*
Ec. 12:5 *g.* shall be a burden
Is. 40:22 inhabitants are as *g.*
Jer. 46:23 they are more than *g.*
Amos 7:1 formed *g.* in the begin.
Nah. 3:17 thy captains are as *g.*

GRATE. *See* BRAZEN.

GRAVE, Substantive.

Gen. 35:20 J. set a pillar on her *g.*
37:35 will go down to *g.*
42:38 with sorrow to *g.* 44:31
50:5 bury me in my *g.*
Num. 19:16 who touch. *g.* is unc.
1 *Sam.* 2:6 L. bring down to *g.*
2 *Sam.* 3:32 and peo. wept at *g.*
19:37 by the *g.* of my father
1 *K.* 2:6 not his head go to *g.*
9 bring to the *g.* with blood
14:13 Jeroboam shall come to *g.*
2 *K.* 22:20 to thy *g.* 2 *Chr.* 34:28
Job 3:22 when they find the *g.*
5:26 come to *g.* in full age
7:9 goeth to *g.* come up no more
10:19 carried from womb to *g.*
14:13 O that thou hide me in *g.*
17:13 the *g.* is my house
21:13 they go down to the *g.*
32 yet shall he be brought to *g.*
30:24 not stretch hand to the *g.*
33:22 soul draweth near to *g.*
Ps. 6:5 in *g.* who give thanks?
30:3 brought my soul from *g.*
31:17 wicked be silent in the *g.*
49:14 laid in *g.* consume *g.*
15 red. soul from power of *g.*
88:3 my life draweth nigh to *g.*
11 loving-kindness decl. in *g.*
89:48 del. soul from hand of *g.*
141:7 bones scat. at *g.'s* mouth
Prov. 1:12 swallow them as *g.*
30:13 *g.* and barren womb
Ec. 9:10 no wisdom in *g.*
Cant. 8:6 jealousy is cruel as *g.*

Is. 14:11 pomp is brought to *g.*
19 cast out of thy *g.* like a br.
38:10 shall go to the gates of *g.*
18 the *g.* cannot praise thee
53:9 made his *g.* with wicked
Jer. 20:17 mother might been *g.*
Ezek. 32:23 company round *g.*
Hos. 13:14 ransom from power of *g.* O *g.* I will be destruction
Nah. 1:14 make thy *g.*
John 11:17 had lain in *g.* 4 days
31 goeth to *g.* to weep there
12:17 called Lazarus out of *g.*
1 *Cor.* 15:55 *g.* wh. is thy victory?

GRAVE-CLOTHES.
John 11:44 Laz. bound with *g.-c.*

GRAVE, Adjective.
1 *Tim.* 3:8 deac. be *g.;* 11 wives *g.*
Tit. 2:2 aged men be sober, *g.*

GRAVE, Verb.
Ex. 28:9 sh. *g.* on onyx-stones
Ex. 29:36 pl. of pure gold, *g.* on
2 *Chr.* 2:7 send a man that can *g.*
14 sent a cunning man to *g.*

GRAVED.
1 *K.* 7:36 on borders of, cherubim
2 *Chr.* 3:7 *g.* cherubim on walls

GRAVEL.
Prov. 20:17 shall be filled with *g.*
Is. 48:19 offsp. of bowels like *g.*
Lam. 3:16 broken teeth with *g.*

GRAVEN, Verb.
Is. 49:16 *g.* thee on pa. of hands
Hab. 2:18 the maker hath *g.* it

GRAVEN.
Ex. 32:16 writing of God *g.*
39:6 signets *g.* with names of Is.
Job 19:24 were *g.* with iron pen
Jer. 17:1 is *g.* upon table of heart
Acts 17:29 Godhead is like gold *g.*

GRAVEN image.
Ex. 20:4 sh. not make unto thee
any *g. i. Lev.* 26:1; *Deut.* 5:8
Deut. 4:16 lest make a *g. im.* 25
27:15 cursed man maketh *g. i.*
Jud. 17:3 for son to make *g. im.*
18:30 Dan set up *g. image,* 31
2 *K.* 21:7 Manasseh set *g. image*
Is. 40:19 workmen melteth *g. i.*
20 workman to prepare *g. in .*
44:9 they that make *g. image*
10 who hath molten a *g. im.*
17 with residue he maketh *g. i.*
45:20 set up wood of their *g. i.*
48:5 my *g. i.* hath commanded
Jer. 10:14 conf. by *g. im.* 51:17
Nah. 1:14 I will cut off the *g. i.*
Hab. 2:18 what profit. the *g. i.?*

GRAVEN images.
Deut. 7:5 shall burn their *g. im.*
12:3 ye shall hew down *g. im.*
2 *K.* 17:41 feared L. served *g. i.*
2 *Chr.* 34:7 he had beaten *g. im.*
Ps. 78:58 moved to jeal. with *g. i.*
97:7 conf. all that serve *g. im.*
Is. 21:9 Bab. fallen, and *g. im.*
30:22 defile the cover. of *g. im.*
42:8 nei. give my praise to *g. i.*
17 ashamed that trust in *g. i.*
Jer. 8:19 prov. to anger with *g. i.*
50:38 it is the land of *g. images*
51:47 do judgment on *g. im.* 52
Hos. 11:2 burnt incense to *g. i.*
Mic. 1:7 *g. i.* be beaten to pieces
5:13 thy *g. images* will I cut off

GRAVES.
Ex. 14:11 were no *g.* in Egypt
2 *K.* 23:6 cast the powder on *g.*
2 *Chr.* 34:4 strewed it on the *g.*
Job 17:1 the *g.* are ready for me
Is. 65:4 which remain among *g.*
Jer. 8:1 bri. priests' bones out *g.*
Ezek. 32:22 *g.* about him, 23,25,26
37:12 open *g.* cause to come up

13 I have brought out of *g.*
39:11 give Gog place of *g.* in Is.
Mat. 27:52 the *g.* were opened
53 bod. of saints came out of *g.*
Luke 11:44 as *g.* wh. appear not
John 5:28 all in *g.* sh. hear voice
Rev. 11:9 not suffer bod. put in *g.*

GRAVETH.
Is. 22:16 he that *g.* a habitation

GRAVING.
Ex. 32:4 fash. *g.* calf with *g.* tool

GRAVING, S.
1 *K.* 7:31 upon mouth of laver *g.*
2 *Chr.* 2:14 any manner of *g.*
Zec. 3:9 engrave *g.* thereof

GRAVITY.
1 *Tim.* 3:4 chil. in subject. wi. *g.*
Tit. 2:7 in doctrine showing *g.*

GRAY. See HAIRS *and* HEAD.

GRAY-HEADED.
1 *Sam.* 12:2 I am old and *g.-h.*
Job 15:10 with us are the *g.-h.*
Ps. 71:18 wh. I am old and *g.-h.*

GREASE.
Ps. 119:70 heart is as fat as *g.*

GREAT.
Gen. 12:2 make name *g.*
39:9 how can I do this *g.* sin?
48:19 my son, he also shall be *g.*
Deut. 10:17 the Lord your God is
a *g.* God, 2 *Chr.* 2:5
11:7 have seen *g.* acts of the L.
18:16 nei. let me see this *g.* fire
29:24 what mean. this *g.* anger?
Jos. 7:9 what do unto *g.* name?
Jud. 5:15 *g.* thoughts of heart
2 *Sam.* 7:9 made thee *g.* name
22 thou art *g.* O Lord God
22:36 thy gentleness hath made
me *g. Ps.* 18:35
1 *K.* 8:42 h. of *g.* name, 2 *Chr.* 6:32
2 *K.* 4:8 Shunem, was *g.* woman
1 *Chr.* 16:25 *g.* is Lord, *Ps.* 48:1;
96:4; 135:5; 145:3
21:13 very *g.* are his mercies
29:12 in thy hand is to make *g.*
2 *Chr.* 2:5 house is *g. g.* is our G.
28:13 tresp., *g.* ; 34:21 *g.* wrath
Neh. 4:14 remember L. who is *g.*
9:32 our God the *g.* the mighty
Est. 1:20 published, for it is *g.*
Job 22:5 is not thy wickedn. *g.?*
36:18 a *g.* ransom ; 26 God is *g.*
39:11 wilt trust bec. strength *g.*
Ps. 14:5 they in *g.* fear, 53:5
19:11 keeping them *g.* reward
21:5 glory *g.* in thy salvation
25:11 pardon iniquity, it is *g.*
31:19 O how *g.* is thy goodness
86:10 art *g.* and doest wondrous
92:5 how *g.* are thy works
139:17 God, how *g.* is the sum
Ec. 9:13 wisdom seemed *g.* to me
Is. 5:9 houses even *g.* and fair
9:2 seen *g.* light, *Mat.* 4:46
12:6 *g.* is the Holy One of Israel
19:20 send a Saviour a *g.* one
53:12 a portion with *g.*
54:13 *g.* shall be peace of child.
Jer. 5:27 are become *g.* and rich
10:6 thy name is *g.* in might
32:18 *g.* the mighty G. is name
19 *g.* in counsel
Lam. 3:23 *g.* is thy faithfulness
Ezek. 17:3 *g.* eagle *g.* wings, 7
36:23 sanctify my *g.* name
Dan. 4:3 how *g.* his signs
Joel 3:13 their wickedness is *g.*
Zec. 9:17 how *g.* his goodness
Mal. 1:11 name *g.* among Gen. 11
Mat. 5:12 be glad, *g.* is reward in
heaven, *Luke* 6:23, 35
19 be called great in kingd. of
6:23 how *g.* is that darkness
13:46 *g.* price ; 15:28 *g.* faith

19:22 *g.* posses. *Mark* 10:42
20:25 they *g.* exercise authority
26 who *g.* am. you, *Mark* 10:43
22:36 which is *g.* commandm. ?
38 first and *g.* commandment
Luke 1:15 *g.* in sight of the Lord
9:48 least among you shall be *g.*
10:2 harvest *g.* the laborers few
16:26 bet. us and you *g.* gulf
Acts 8:9 that he was some *g.* one
19:28 *g.* is D. of Ephesians ! 34
2 *Cor.* 7:4 *g.* my boldn. *g.* glory
Col. 4:13 hath a *g.* zeal for you
1 *Tim.* 3:16 *g.* is mys. of godlin.
2 *Tim.* 2:20 in *g.* house
Tit. 2:13 appearing of the *g.* God
Jam. 3:5 *g.* matter little fire kin.
Rev. 16:19 *g.* Babylon came in
17:5 Babylon the *g.* 18:2

See CITY, COMPANY, CONGREGA-
TION, CRY, DAY, DESTRUC-
TION.

GREAT evil.
1 *Sam.* 6:9 hath done us this *g. e.*
Ec. 2:21 is vanity and a *g. evil*
Jer. 16:10 I L. pronounced this *g. e.*
32:42 brought *g. e.* upon people
44:7 why commit this *g. evil?*

See EXCEEDING, JOY.

GREAT King or kings.
Ps. 47:2 the Lord is a *g. King*
48:2 Zion, the city of the *g. K.*
95:3 L. is a *g. K.* above all gods
136:17 to him that smote *g. k.*
Ec. 9:14 there came a *g. k.* against
Jer. 25:14 *g.* sh. serve th. 27:7
Mal. 1:14 I am a *g. K.* saith the L.
Mat. 5:35 Jerus. is city of *g. K.*

GREAT men.
2 *Sam.* 7:9 like name of *g. men* in
earth, 1 *Chr.* 17:8
Job 32:9 *g. men* not always wise
Prov. 25:6 stand not in pl. of *g. m.*
Jer. 5:5 I will get me unto *g. m.*
Ezek. 21:14 it is the sw. of *g. m.*
Nah. 3:10 all her *g. m.* in chains
Rev. 6:15 *g. men* hid themselves
18:23 thy merchants were *g. m.*

GREAT multitude, s.
2 *Chr.* 13:8 ye be a *g. multitude*
20:15 not dis. by reason of *g. m.*
28:5 carried *g. m.* captive to D,
Job 31:34 did I fear *g. m.* or con.
Is. 16:14 *g. m.* sh. be contemned
Jer. 44:15 wo. stood by, a *g. m.*
Ezek. 47:9 a very *g. mul.* of fish
Dan. 11:11 k. of south set *g. m.*
Mat. 4:25 *g. mult.* followed him,
8:1; 12:15; 19:2; 20:29; *Mark*
3:7; *John* 6:2
Mat. 8:18 when J. saw *g. multi-*
tudes, 14:14 ; *Mark* 9:14
15:30 *g. multitudes* came
33 bread as fill so *g.* a *multit.*
21:8 a *g. m.* spread their garm .
26:47 *g. m.* with sw. *Mark* 14:43
Luke 5:6 inclus. a *g. m.* of fishes
Acts 14:1 a *g. m.* of J. believed
17:4 of devout Greeks a *g. m.*
Rev. 7:9 *g. m.* no man could nu.
19:6 the voice of a *g. multitude*

GREAT nation, s.
Gen. 12:2 I will make of thee a
g. n. 18:18 ; 46:3 ; *Ex.* 32:10
17:20 make Ishm. a *g. n.* 21:18
Deut. 26:5 he bec. there a *n. g.*
Ps. 135:10 smote *g. n.* slew kings
Jer. 6:22 a *g. n.* shall be raised
Ezek. 31:6 under shad. dwelt *g. n.*

GREAT people.
Deut. 2:10 Em. dwelt a *p. g.* 21
21 Zamzummim, a *people g.*
Jos. 7:14 seeing I am a *g. people*
15 be a *g. p. ;* 17 art a *g. people*

1 *K.* 3:9 this *g. p.* ? 2 *Chr.* 1:10
5:7 given wise son over *g. p.*
Is. 13:4 noise in moun. as of *g. p.*

GREAT power.

Ex. 32:11 out of Egypt with *g. p.*
2 *K.* 17:36; *Neh.* 1:10
Num. 14:17 *p.* of my lord be *g.*
Job 23:6 plead ag. me with *g. p.*
Is. 147:5 great Lord and of *g. p.*
Jer. 27:5 made the earth, man,
    and beast by my *g. p.* 32:17
Nah. 1:3 slow to anger, *g.* in *p.*
Mark 13:26 in clouds with *g. p.*
Acts 4:33 with *g. p.* gave apostles
8:10 this man is the *g. p.* of God
Rev. 11:17 hast taken thy *g. p.*

GREAT sea.

Num. 34:6 have *g. s.* for a border
Jos. 1:4 from wilder. to the *g. s.*
15:12 west border to *g. sea*
Ezek. 47:10 as a fish of the *g. sea*
15 border of land from the *g. s.*
Dan. 7:2 four winds upon *g. sea*

See SIX.

GREAT slaughter.

Jos. 10:10 slew them with *g. s.*
Jud. 11:33 Jeph. smote with *g. s.*
15:8 Samson smote with *g. s.*
1 *Sam.* 4:10 Ph. smote w. *g. s.* 17
6:19 smitten people with *g. s.*
19:8 D. slew with a *g. s.* 23:5
2 *Sam.* 18:7 a *g. s.* of 20,000
1 *K.* 20:21 Israel slew A. w. *g. s.*
2 *Chr.* 28:5 Is. smote Ah. w. *g. s.*
Is. 30:25 day of *g. slaughter*
34:6 L. hath *g. s.* in land of Id.

Small and GREAT.

Gen. 19:11 sm. w. blind. *s. and g.*
Deut. 1:17 hear *s.* as well as *g.*
25:13 divers weights, *g. and sm.*
1 *Sam.* 5:9 smote men *s. and g.*
20:2 will do noth. *g.* or *s.*
30:2 slew not any either *g.* or *s.*
2 *K.* 23:2 *s. and g.* went to house,
    2 *Chr.* 34:30
25:26 peo. *s. and g.* came to Eg.
1 *Chr.* 26:13 pint to death, *s.* or *g.*
2 *Chr.* 15:13 put to brethren, *g. and s.*
31:15 give to brethren, *g. and s.*
Est. 1:5 A. made a feast to *g. a. s.*
20 to husbands honor *g. and s.*
Job 3:19 *small and g.* are there
37:6 the *s.* rain *and g.* rain
Ps. 104:25 th. creeping, *s. and g.*
115:13 fear the L. *small and g.*
Ec. 2:7 pos. of *g. and s.* cattle
Jer. 16:6 *g. and s.* sh. die in land
Amos 8:5 ephah *s.* the shekel *g.*
Acts 26:22 witnessing to *s. and g.*
Rev. 11:18 that fear him, *s. a. g.*
13:16 *s. and g.* to receive mark
19:5 praise our G. *small and g.*
20:12 *s. and g.* stand before G.

So GREAT.

Ex. 32:21 bro. *so g.* sin on them
Deut. 4:7 nat. *so g.* hath G. ? 8
1 *K.* 3:9 *so g.* people, 2 *Chr.* 1:10
Ps. 77:13 *so g.* a God as our G. ?
103:11 *so g.* is his mercy
Mat. 8:10 not *so g.* faith, *Luke* 7:9
2 *Cor.* 1:10 deliv. from *so g.* death
Heb. 2:3 if we neglect *so g.* salv.
12:1 *so g.* a cloud of witnesses
Jam. 3:4 *so g.* turned with helm

GREAT stone, s.

Gen. 29:2 *g. s.* on well's mouth
Deut. 27:2 set up *g. s.*
Jos. 10:11 cast *g. s.* from heaven
24:26 Joshua took *g. s.*
1 *Sam.* 6:18 they set *g. s.* of Abel
14:33 roll a *g. stone* unto me
2 *Sam.* 20:8 were at *g. s.* in Gib.
1 *K.* 5:17 brought *g. s.* to lay
7:10 founda. of *g. s. Ezr.* 5:8
2 *Chr.* 26:15 engines to shoot *g. s.*

Ezr. 6:4 three rows of *g. s.*
Jer. 43:9 take *g. s.* and hide them
Mat. 27:60 rolled a *g. s.* to door

GREAT thing, s.

Deut. 10:21 God hath done *g. t.*
1 *Sam.* 12:16 this *g. t.* L. will do
2 *Sam.* 7:21 word's sa. done *g. t.*
    23 and to do for you *g. things*
2 *K.* 5:13 if prophet bid thee *g. t.*
8:4 the *g. t.* Elisha hath done
1 *Chr.* 17:19 making kn. th. *g. t.*
Job 5:9 doeth *g. t.* 9:10; 37:5
Ps. 71:19 done *g. things*
106:21 God who had done *g. t.*
126:2 L. had done *g. things,* 3
Jer. 33:3 show *g.* and mighty *t.*
45:5 seek. thou *g. t.* for thyself?
Dan. 7:8 speak *g. t.* 20 ; *Rev.* 13:5
Hos. 8:12 have written the *g. t.*
Joel 2:20 bec. he hath done *g. t.*
Mark 3:8 heard what *g. t.* he did
5:19 tell *g. t.* L. done, *Luke* 8:39
Luke 1:49 mighty hath done *g. t.*
8:39 published *g. t.* J. had done
Acts 9:16 *g. t.* he must suffer
1 *Cor.* 9:11 *g. t.* if we reap carnal?
2 *Cor.* 11:15 no *g. t.* if min. be tr.
Jam. 3:5 tongue boasteth *g. t.*

Very GREAT.

Ex. 11:3 Mos. was *v. g.* in land
Num. 13:28 walled and *v. g.*
2 *Sam.* 19:32 Barz. was a *v. g.* m.
1 *K.* 10:2 S. came *w. v. g.* train
1 *Chr.* 21:13 *v. g.* are his mercies
2 *Chr.* 16:14 a *v. g.* burning for A.
Job 2:13 saw his grief was *v. g.*
Ps. 104:1 my God, thou art *v. g.*
Mark 8:1 the multitude *v. g.*
16:4 sto. was away, it was *v. g.*

Was GREAT.

Gen. 6:5 wickedn. of man *w. g.*
13:6 their substance *w. g.*
Job 31:25 I rej. my wealth *w. g.*
Ec. 2:9 I *w. g.* and increased
Lam. 1:1 she *w. g.* am. nations
Dan. 4:10 the tree's height *w. g.*
Mat. 7:27 *g. w.* the fall, *Luke* 6:49

GREAT waters.

Ps. 32:6 in floods of *g. w.*
77:19 thy path in *g. waters*
107:23 that do business in *g. w.*
144:7 deliver me out of *g. w.*
Jer. 51:55 waves roar like *g. w.*
Ezek. 1:24 noi. of wings like *g. w.*
'7:5 placed the seed by *g. w.*
8 planted in good soil by *g. w.*
26:19 *g. w.* shall cover thee
27:26 brought thee to *g. w.*
31:7 for his root was by *g. w.*
15 the *g. waters* were stayed
Heb. 3:15 walk through *g. w.*

GREAT while.

2 *Sam.* 7:19 spoken of servant's
    house for *g. w.* 1 *Chr.* 17:17
Mark 1:35 rising a *g. w.* bef. day
Luke 10:13 a *g. w.* ago repented
Acts 28:6 barbar. looked a *g. w.*

GREAT work, s. .

Ex. 14:31 saw *g. w.* the L. did
Jud. 2:7 seen the *g. w.* of the L.
1 *Chr.* 29:1 and *w.* is *g.*
Neh. 4:19 *w.* is *g.* and we separ.
6:3 doing a *g. w.* I cannot come
Ps. 111:2 *w.* of L. *g. Rev.* 15:3

GREATER.

Gen. 1:16 *g.* light to rule the day
4:13 punish. *g.* than I can bear
41:40 only in throne will I be *g.*
Ex. 18:11 L. is *g.* than all gods
Num. 14:12 *g.* nation, *Deut.* 9:14
Deut. 1:28 *g.* and taller than we
4:38 drive nations *g.* than thou,
    7:1 ; 9:1 ; 11:23
1 *K.* 1:37 throne *g.* than Dav. 47
1 *Chr.* 11:9 Dav. waxed *g.* and *g.*

2 *Chr.* 3:5 *g.* house ceiled
Job 33:12 God is *g.* than man
Hag. 2:9 latter house *g.* than for.
Mat. 11:11 not risen a *g.* than J.
    Bapt. least *g. Luke* 7:28
12:6 is one *g.* than the temple
    41 a *g.* than S. here, *Luke* 11:32
    42 a *g.* than S. here, *Luke* 11:31
23:14 receive *g.* damnat. *Mark*
    12:40 ; *Luke* 20:47
    17 *g.* the gold, or the temple?
    19 is *g.* the gift, or the altar?
Luke 22:27 *g.* he that sit. or ser. ?
John 1:50 thou shalt see *g.*
    things, 5:20 ; 14:12
4:12 art *g.* than our father J. ?
John 5:36 *g.* witn. than that of J.
8:53 art *g.* than father Abrah. ?
10:29 Father *g.* than all, 14:28
13:16 ser. not *g.* th. lord, 15:20
15:13 *g.* love hath no man
19:11 that del. me hath *g.* sin
Acts 15:28 no *g.* burden
Heb. 6:13 could swear by no *g.*
    16 men verily swear by the *g.*
9:11 *g.* and more perfect tabern.
11:26 reproach of Ch. *g.* riches
Jam. 3:1 receive *g.* condemnat.
2 *Pet.* 2:11 angels are *g.* in power
1 *John* 3:20 G. is *g.* th. our heart
4:4 *g.* is he that is in you,
5:9 witness of G. is *g.*
3 *John* 4 no *g.* joy than to hear

GREATEST.

Job 1:3 this man was *g.* of all
Jer. 31:34 all know me from least
    to the *g. Heb.* 8:11
42:1 from least to *g.* came near
44:12 shall die, from least to *g.*
Jon. 3:5 sack. from *g.* to least
Mat. 13:32 it is *g.* am. herbs
18:1 who is *g.* in king. of heav. ?
    4 humble as child, same is *g.*
23:11 he that is *g.* be your serv.
Mark 9:34 should be *g. Luke* 9:46
Luke 22:24 a strife who sho. be *g.*
    26 he that is *g.* be as younger
1 *Cor.* 13:13 *g.* of these is charity

GREATLY.

Gen. 3:16 I will *g.* multiply sor.
Ex. 19:18 wh. mount quaked *g.*
Deut. 15:4 the Lord sh. *g.* bless
1 *Sam.* 12:18 peo. *g.* feared the L.
1 *K.* 18:3 Obadiah feared L. *g.*
1 *Chr.* 4:38 house of fath. inc. *g.*
16:25 the L. is *g.* to be praised,
    Ps. 48:1 ; 96:4 ; 145:3
2 *Chr.* 25:10 anger *g.* kindled
33:12 Manas. humbled himself *g.*
Job 8:7 latter end should *g.* inc.
Ps. 21:1 in thy salva. *g.* rejoice
28:7 heart *g.* rejoiceth
45:11 shall *g.* desire thy beauty
47:9 he is *g.* exalted
62:2 I shall not be *g.* moved
65:9 thou *g.* enrichest it
71:23 *g.* rejoice when I sing
78:59 wroth, and *g.* abhorred Is.
105:24 increased peo. *g.* 107:38
109:30 I will *g.* praise the Lord
112:1 delighteth *g.* in his com.
116:10 I was *g.* afflicted, I said
Prov. 23:24 father of righteous
    g. rejoice
Is. 42:17 *g.* ashamed th. trust
61:10 I will *g.* rejoice in the L.
Jer. 4:10 hast *g.* deceived people
Ezek. 20:13 sabbath *g.* polluted
Dan. 5:9 Belshazzar *g.* troubled
9:23 art *g.* beloved, 10:11, 19
Ob. 2 thou art *g.* despised
Zep. 1:14 day of L. hasteth *g.*
Zec. 9:9 rejoice *g.* daugh. of Z.
Mat. 27:14 governor marvelled *g.*
Mark 5:38 wept and wailed *g.*
9:15 they were amazed *g.*
12:27 ye therefore do *g.* err

John 3:29 rejoiceth *g.* because
Acts 6:7 disciples mult. in J. *g.*
1 *Cor.* 16:12 I *g.* desired Apollos
Phil. 1:8 *g.* I long after you all
1 *Thes.* 3:6 desiring *g.* to see us
2 *Tim.* 1:4 *g.* desiring to see thee
  4:15 *g.* withstood our words
1 *Pet.* 1:16 *g.* rejoiced tho. in he.
2 *John* 4 I rejoiced *g.* that I fou.
3 *John* 3 I rejoiced *g.* when bre.

See FEARED.

GREATNESS.

Ex. 15:7 *g.* of thy excellency
Num. 14:19 according to *g.*
Deut. 3:24 to show servant *g.*
  5:24 Lord hath showed his *g.*
  9:26 redeemed through thy *g.*
  11:2 chil. who have not seen *g.*
  32:3 ascribe ye *g.* unto our God
1 *Chr.* 17:21 make a name of *g.*
  29:11 thine, O Lord, is the *g.*
2 *Chr.* 9:6 half of *g.* not showed
Neh. 13:22 according to *g.*
Ps. 66:3 by *g.* of thy power
  71:21 thou shalt increase my *g.*
  79:11 accord. to *g.* power
  145:3 *g.* unsearch. ; 6 declare *g.*
  150:2 accord. to his excellent *g.*
Prov. 5:23 in *g.* of folly go astray
Is. 40:26 by *g.* of his might
  57:10 wearied in *g.* of thy way
  63:1 travelling in *g.* of strength
Jer. 13:22 *g.* of iniquity discove.
Ezek. 31:2 whom art like in *g. ?*
Dan. 4:22 *g.* reacheth heaven
Dan. 7:27 *g.* of king. given saints
Eph. 1:19 exceed. *g.* of his power

GREAVES.

1 *Sam.* 17:6 Gol. had *g.* of brass
GRECIA. *Dan.* 8:21 ; 10:20 ; 11:2

GRECIANS.

Joel 3:6 Judah have ye sold to G.
Acts 6:1 arose murmuring of G.
  9:29 Paul disputed ag. G. 11:20

GREECE.

Zec. 9:13 against thy sons, O G.
Acts 20:2 Paul came to G. and

GREEDY.

Ps. 17:12 a lion *g.* of prey
Prov. 1:19 every one *g.* of gain
  15:27 he that is *g.* troub. house
Is. 56:11 *g.* dogs never have en.
1 *Tim.* 3:3 not *g.* of filthy luc. 8

GREEDILY.

Prov. 21:26 coveteth *g.* all day
Ezek. 22:12 hast *g.* gained
Jude 11 ran *g.* after error of B.

GREEDINESS.

Eph. 4:19 uncleanness with *g.*

GREEK—*language*.
Luke 23:38 sup. in G. *John* 19:20
Acts 21:37 canst thou speak G. ?
Rev. 9:11 in G. tongue name A.

GREEK.

Rom. 1:16 to Jew first, also to G.
  10:12 no diff. betw. Jew and G.
Gal. 2:3 a G. 3:28 ; *Col.* 3:11

GREEKS.

John 12:20 cert. G. came to wor.
Acts 14:1 ; 17:4, 12 ; 18:4, 17
  19:10 the Jews and G. heard, 17
  20:21 testifying to Jews and G.
  21:28 brought G. into temple
Rom. 1:14 a debtor both to G.
1 *Cor.* 1:22 G. seek after, 23, 24

GREEN.

Gen. 1:30 *g.* herb for meat
  9:3 *g.* herb I have given you
Lev. 2:14 for first-fruits *g.* ears
  28:14 eat no *g.* ears, till ye have
Jud. 16:7 bind me with *g.* withs
  8 brought to her sev. *g.* withs

2 *K.* 19:26 inhabitants were as *g.*
  herbs, *Is.* 37:27
Job 8:16 he is *g.* before the sun
  15:32 his branch shall not be *g.*
  39:8 wild ass searcheth after *g.*
Ps. 23:2 lie down in *g.* pastures
  37:2 shall wither as the *g.* herb
  35 wicked spr. like *g.* bay-tree
Cant. 1:16 art fair, our bed *g.*
  2:13 fig-tr. putteth forth *g.* figs
Is. 15:6 there is no *g.* thing
Jer. 11:16 L. called name *g.* olive
  17:8 tree spreadeth, leaf be *g.*
Hos. 14:8 I am like a *g.* fir-tree
Mark 6:39 companies on *g.* grass
Rev. 8:7 all *g.* grass burnt up
  9:4 com. not to hurt any *g.*

GREEN tree.

Deut. 12:2 served gods under *g. t.*
1 *K.* 14:23 images under every *g.*
  tree, 2 *K.* 17:10
2 *K.* 16:4 Asa sacrificed under
  every *g. tree,* 2 *Chr.* 28:4
Ps. 52:8 *g.* olive *t.* in house of G.
Is. 57:5 infla. yours. under *g. t.*
Jer. 2:20 under *g. t.* thou wande.
  3:6 under *g. tree* played harlot
Ezek. 17:24 dried up the *g. tree*
  20:47 it shall devour every *g. t.*
Luke 23:31 do these things in *g. t.*

GREEN trees.

Jer. 17:2 remem. groves by *g. t.*

GREENISH.

Lev. 13:49 if plague *g.* on garm.
  14:37 plague be with strakes *g.*

GREENNESS.

Job 8:12 whilst it is yet in his *g.*

GREET.

1 *Sam.* 25:5 go to Na. and *g.* him
Rom. 16:3 *g.* Priscilla and Aquil.
  5 *g.* the church ; 6 *g.* Mary
  8 *g.* Amplias ; 11 *g.* household
1 *Cor.* 16:20 br. *g.* you, *Phil.* 4:21
  20 *g.* one another, 2 *Cor.* 13:12 ;
  1 *Pet.* 5:14
Col. 4:14 Luke and Demas *g.* you
1 *Thes.* 5:26 *g.* brethren
Tit. 3:15 *g.* them that love us
2 *John* 13 children of sister *g.* th.
3 *John* 14 *g.* the friends by name

GREETETH.

2 *Tim.* 4:21 Eubulus *g.* thee, P.

GREETING, S.

Mat. 23:7 *g.* in the markets, *Luke*
  11:43 ; 20:46
Acts 15:23 apostles, elders send *g.*
  23:26 Lysias to Felix sendeth *g.*
Jam. 1:1 to the 12 tribes abr. *g.*

GREW.

Gen. 2:5 L. made herb bef. it *g.*
  21:8 Is. *g.* 26:13 ; 21:20 Ishmael
  25:27 boys *g. ;* 47:27 Israel *g.*
Ex. 1:12 more afflicted, more *g.*
  2:10 M. *g. ; Jud.* 11:2 wife's so.
1 *Sam.* 2:21 child Samuel *g.* 26
2 *Sam.* 5:10 D. went on, *g.* great
  12:3 it *g.* up together with him
Ezek. 17:6 *g.* and bec. spreading
Dan. 4:11 tree *g.* and was strong
Mark 4:7 and the thorns *g.* up
Luke 1:80 *g.* and waxed, 2:40
  13:19 *g.* and waxed great tree
Acts 7:17 peo. *g.* and multiplied
  12:24 the word of God *g.* and
  19:20 mightily *g.* the word of

GREYHOUND.

Prov. 30:31 comely in goi' *g,* a *g.*

GRIEF, S.

Gen. 26:35 a *g.* unto Isaac and R.
1 *Sam.* 1:16 abundance of *g.*
2 *Chr.* 6:29 ev. one know own *g.*
Job 6:2 O that *g.* were weighed
  16:5 moving of lips assuage *g.*
  6 tho. I speak. *g.* not assuaged

Ps. 6:7 my eye is consumed because of *g.* 31:9
  31:10 my life is spent with *g.*
  69:26 to *g.* of those wounded
Prov. 17:25 fool. son *g.* to father
Ec. 1:18 in much wisd. much *g.*
  2:23 days are sorrows, travail *g.*
Is. 17:11 harv. a heap in day of *g.*
  53:3 a man acquainted with *g.*
  4 borne our *g.* carried sorrows
  10 pleased Lord put him to *g.*
Jer. 10:19 Truly this is a *g.*
  45:3 L. hath added *g.* to sorrow
Lam. 3:32 tho. he cause *g.*
Jon. 4:6 a gourd to del. from *g.*
2 *Cor.* 2:5 if caused *g.*
Heb. 13:17 do it with joy, not *g.*
1 *Pet.* 2:19 consc. to. G. endure *g.*

GRIEVANCE.

Hab. 1:3 why cause me to b. *g. ?*

GRIEVE.

1 *Sam.* 2:33 man to *g.* thy heart
1 *Chr.* 4:10 keep from evil, not *g.*
Ps. 78:40 oft did they *g.* him
Lam. 3:33 not willingly *g.* men
Eph. 4:30 *g.* not H. Spirit of God

GRIEVED.

Gen. 6:6 it repented L. that he
  had made man, it *g.* him
  45:5 be not *g.* that ye sold me
  49:23 archers have sorely *g.* him
Deut. 15:10 not *g.* wh. thou giv.
Jud. 10:16 *g.* for misery of Israel
1 *Sam.* 1:8 why is thy heart *g. ?*
  20:34 Jonathan was *g.* for David
  30:6 soul of all the peo. was *g.*
2 *Sam.* 19:2 king *g.* for his son
Neh. 13:8 it *g.* me sore,
Est. 4:4 queen exceedingly *g.*
Job 4:2 commune, wilt be *g. ?*
  30:25 my soul *g.* for the poor ?
Ps. 73:21 heart *g.* I was pricked
  95:10 forty years was I *g.*
  112:10 wicked see it, and be *g.*
  119:158 I beh. transgressors, *g.*
  139:21 am not I *g.* with those
Is. 54:6 L. called as a woman *g.*
Jer. 5:3 stricken, they not *g.*
Dan. 7:15 I Daniel was *g.*
  11:30 he shall be *g.* and return
Amos 6:6 not *g.* for affliction
Mark 3:5 *g.* for hardn. of hearts
  10:22 he went away *g.*
John 21:17 Peter was *g.*
Acts 4:2 *g.* that they taught peo.
  16:18 P. being *g.* said to spirit
Rom. 14:15 if brother *g.*
2 *Cor.* 2:4 not that ye be *g.*
  5 he hath not *g.* me
Heb. 3:10 I was *g.* with generati.
  17 with whom *g.* forty years ?

GRIEVETH.

Ruth 1:13 *g.* me for your sakes
Prov. 26:15 *g.* him to bring

GRIEVING.

Ezek. 28:24 no more a *g.* thorn

GRIEVOUS.

Gen. 12:10 famine was *g.*
  18:20 their sin is very *g.*
  41:31 famine shall be very *g.*
  50:11 *g.* mourning to the Egypt.
Ex. 8:24 a *g.* swarm of flies
  9:3 very *g.* murrain in Egypt
  8 to rain very *g.* hail, 24
  110:14 locusts were very *g.*
1 *K.* 2:8 Shim. cursed w. *g.* curse
  12:4 *g.* service, 2 *Chr.* 10:4
Ps. 10:5 his ways always *g.*
  31:18 speak *g.* things ag. right.
Prov. 15:1 *g.* words stir up anger
  10 correct. *g.* to him that fors.
Ec. 2:17 work wro. under sun *g.*
Is. 15:4 life shall be *g.* unto him
  21:2 *g.* vision is declared to me

GRIEVOUS

Jer. 6:28 are all *g.* revolters
10:19 my wound is *g.*
14:17 broken with very *g.* blow
16:4 they shall die of *g.* deaths
23:19 *g.* whirlwind shall fly
30:12 wound is *g. Nah.* 3:19
Mat. 23:4 burdens *g. Luke* 11:46
Acts 20:29 w. wolves enter am. y.
25:7 *g.* complaints against Paul
Phil. 3:1 to me indeed is not *g.*
Heb. 12:11 no chast. joyous but *g.*
1 *John* 5:3 commandments not *g.*
Rev. 16:2 a *g.* sore on men

GRIEVOUSLY

Is. 9:1 afterward did *g.* afflict
Lam. 1:8 Jerusa. hath *g.* sinned
20 heart is turned, I *g.* rebelled
Ezek. 14:13 sin. by trespassing *g.*
Mat. 8:6 servant *g.* tormented
15:22 my daughter is *g.* vexed

GRIEVOUSNESS

Is. 10:1 that write *g.* they presc.
21:15 fled from the *g.* of war

GRIND

Jud. 16:21 Sam. did *g.* in prison
Job 31:10 let my wife *g.* to anot.
Is. 3:15 mean ye to *g.* faces ?
47:2 millstones and *g.* meal
Lam. 13:5 took young men to *g.*
Mat. 21:44 *g.* him to p. *Lu.* 20:18

GRINDERS, ING.

Ec. 12:3 cease, bec. are few
4 when sound of *g.* is low
Mat. 24:41 two womb. *g. Lu.* 17:35

GRIZZLED

Gen. 31:10 speckled and *g.* 12
Zec. 6:3 in chariot we. *g.* horses
6 the *g.* go forth to. the south

GROAN

Job 24:12 men *g.* from out of city
Jer. 51:52 thro' land wounded *g.*
Joel 1:18 how do the beasts *g.*
Rom. 8:23 we ourselves *g.* within
2 *Cor.* 5:2 we *g.* des. to be cloth.
4 we in this tabernacle *g.*

GROANED, ETH.

John 11:33 he *g.* in spirit
Rom. 8:22 the whole creation *g.*

GROANING, S.

Ex. 2:24 God heard their *g.*
6:5 heard *g.* of Israel, *Acts* 7:34
Job 23:2 stroke is heavier than *g.*
Ps. 6:6 I am weary with *g.*
38:9 my *g.* is not hid from thee
102:5 *g.* bones cleave to skin
20 to hear the *g.* of prisoner
Ezek. 30:24 *g.* of wounded man
John 11:38 Jesus *g.* in himself
Rom. 8:26 *g.* that cannot be ut.

GROPE, ETH.

Deut. 28:29 *g.* at noon as blind *g.*
Job 5:14 *g.* in noonday
12:25 *g.* in dark without light
Is. 59:10 *g.* for wall like blind

GROSS

Is. 60:2 *g.* darkness cover people
Jer. 13:16 make it *g.* darkness
Mat. 13:15 waxed *g. Acts* 28:27

GROVE

Gen. 21:33 planted *g.* in Beer-sh.
Deut. 16:21 not plant *g.* near alt.
Jud. 6:25 cut down *g.* by it, 28
1 *K.* 15:13 made idol in *g.* 2 *Chr.*
15:16
16:33 A. made *g.* to provoke G.
2 *K.* 13:6 remained *g.* in Samar.
17:16 Israel made *g.* served Baal
21:3 reared up altars, made a *g.*
23:6 brought *g.* from ho. of L.
15 Josiah burnt high place
and *g.*

GROVES.

Ex. 34:13 cut down *g. Deut.* 7:5
Deut. 12:3 burn their *g.* with fire

Jud. 3:7 served *g.* 2 *Chr.* 24:18
1 *K.* 14:23 built *g.* on every high
hill, 2 *K.* 17:10
18:19 prophets of the *g.* 400
2 *K.* 18:4 Hezekiah cut down *g.*
23:14 Jos. cut *g.* 2 *Chr.* 34:3, 4
2 *Chr.* 14:3 brake images, cut *g.*
17:6 Jehos. took away the *g.*
33:3 M. made *g.*, 19 set up *g.*
34:3 purge Judah from the *g.*
Is. 17:8 neither sh. he respect *g.*
Jer. 17:2 remember altars and *g.*
Mic. 5:14 I will pluck up thy *g.*

GROUND, Verb.

Ex. 32:20 *g.* to powder, *Deut.* 9:21
Num. 11:8 the people *g.* manna

GROUND corn.

2 *Sam.* 17:19 *g.* c. on well's mou.

GROUND.

Gen. 2:5 not a man to till *g.*
7 God formed man of dust of *g.*
19 of *g.* the Lord formed every
3:17 cursed is *g.* for thy sake
4:2 Cain was a tiller of *g.*
10 blood crieth to me from *g.*
5:29 the *g.* the L. hath cursed
8:21 not again curse the *g.*
Ex. 3:5 stan. is holy *g. Acts* 7:33
Num. 16:31 *g.* clave asunder
Jud. 4:21 fastened nail into *g.*
1 *Sam.* 8:12 set them to ear his *g.*
2 *Sam.* 23:11 *g.* full of lentiles
2 *K.* 2:19 water naught. *g.* barren
9:26 cast him into the plat of *g.*
1 *Chr.* 11:13 *g.* full of barley
2 *Chr.* 4:17 cast them in clay *g.*
Neh. 10:35 first-fruits of our *g.*
Job 5:6 trouble spring out of *g.*
14:8 tho. stock thereof die in *g.*
18:10 snare is laid for him in *g.*
38:27 desolate and waste *g.*
39:24 swal. the *g.* with fiercen.
Ps. 105:35 dev. fruit of their *g.*
107:33 turn. springs into dry *g.*
35 turneth dry *g.* to water-spr.
Is. 28:24 break clods of his *g.*
29:4 shalt break out of the *g.*
30:23 thou shalt not sow the *g.*
24 asses that ear the *g.* sh. eat
35:7 parched *g.* shall bec. a pool
51:23 hast laid thy body as *g.*
Jer. 4:3 br. your fal. *g. Hos.* 10:12
14:4 because *g.* is chapt
Lam. 2:9 gates are sunk into *g.*
Ezek. 12:6 thou see not the *g.* 12
Dan. 8:5 came, touched not *g.*
Hos. 2:18 coven. for things of *g.*
Zec. 8:12 *g.* shall give increase
Mal. 3:11 not destroy fruit of *g.*
Mat. 13:8 into good *g. Luke* 8:8
23 send into good *g. Luke* 8:15
Mark 4:26 sho. cast seed into *g.*
Luke 12:16 *g.* of a certain man
13:7 why cumbereth it the *g. ?*
14:18 have bought a piece of *g.*
19:44 sh. lay thee with the *g.*
John 4:5 the parcel of *g.* J. gave
12:24 corn of wheat fall into *g.*

See DRY, FACE.

On, *or* **upon the GROUND.**

Gen. 38:9 On. spilled it *on the g.*
Ex. 4:3 cast rod *o. g.* cast *o. g.*
9:23 fire ran along *upon the g.*
14:16 go *on* dry *g.* thro' sea, 22
Deut. 22:6 bird's nest be *on t. g.*
Jud. 6:39 *u. t. g.* let there be dew
40 dew *upon* all the *g.*
1 *Sam.* 14:25 honey *u. the g.*
2 *Sam.* 14:14 water spilt *on t. g.*
17:12 as dew falleth *on t. g.*
2 *K.* 13:18 smite *u. t. g.* he smote
Job 1:20 Job fell *u. the g.*
2:13 sat down with him *u. t. g.*
16:13 pour. out my gall *u. g.*
Is. 3:26 desolate shall sit *on g.*
47:1 O daughter, sit *on the g.*

Jer. 25:33 shall be dung *u. the g.*
27:5 man and beast *u. the g.*
Lam. 2:10 dau. of Z. sit *on the g.*
21 young and old lie *on the g.*
Ezek. 24:7 poured it not *u. the g.*
26:16 princes shall sit *u. the g.*
Mat. 15:35 sit *on t. g. Mark* 8:6
Mark 4:5 so. fell *on* stony *g.* 16
8 *on* good *g.* 20; *Luke* 8:8, 15
9:20 fell *on the g.* and foaming
14:35 and fell *on g.* and prayed
John 8:6 he wrote *on the g.* 8
9:6 spat *on t. g.* and made clay

To, *or* **unto the GROUND.**

Gen. 3:19 till thou return *u. t. g.*
33:3 J. bowed himself *to the g.*
Jud. 20:21 dest. *to the g.* 22,000
25 dest. *to the g.* 18,000 men
Ruth 2:10 Ruth bowed *to the g.*
1 *Sam.* 3:19 his words *to the g.*
5:4 Dagon fallen on face *to g.*
25:23 Abigail bowed *to the g.*
28:14 S. stooped wi. face *to t. g.*
2 *Sam.* 14:4 fell on face *to the g.*
22 Joab fell *to the g.* on his fa.
33 Absalom bowed *to the g.*
20:10 Amasa's bowels *to t. g.*
1 *K.* 1:23 Nathan bowed *to the g.*
2 *K.* 2:15 sons of prophets, *to t. g.*
1 *Chr.* 21:21 Ornan bowed *to t. g.*
2 *Chr.* 7:3 Is. bow. with fa. *to g.*
Neh. 8:6 worship. Lo, faces *to g.*
Ps. 74:7 dwe. of thy name *to t. g.*
89:39 prof. crown, casting *to g.*
44 cast his throne down *to t. g.*
147:6 casteth the wicked *to t. g.*
Is. 14:12 cut down on face *to t. g. ?*
21:9 im. he hath brok. *to the g.*
25:12 bring *to the g.*
26:5 lofty city he layeth *to t. g.*
Jer. 14:2 languish, black *to t. g.*
Lam. 2:2 stron. of Judah, *to t. g.*
10 virgins hang heads *to t. g.*
Ezek. 19:12 mother cast *to the g.*
26:11 thy garrison sh. go *to t. g.*
Dan. 8:7 cast ram down *to t. g.*
10 hosts and stars *to the g.*
12 cast down the truth *to t. g.*
Amos 3:14 h. of altar fall *to t. g.*
Ob. 3 shall bring me *to the g.*
Mat. 10:29 shall not fall *to the g.*
Luke 22:44 dr. of blood fall. *to g.*
John 18:6 and fell *to the g.*
Acts 22:7 fell *to the g.*

GROUND.

1 *Tim.* 3:15 pillar and *g.* of truth

GROUNDED

Is. 30:32 *g.* staff shall pass
Eph. 3:17 rooted and *g.* in love
Col. 1:23 in faith, *g.* and settled

GROW.

Gen. 2:9 L. ma. ev. tree to *g.*
Num. 6:5 the locks of his hair *g.*
Jud. 16:22 hair of head be. to *g.*
2 *Sam.* 23:5 th. he make it not *g.*
2 *K.* 19:29 eat such things as *g.*
Job 8:11 can rush *g.* with. mire ?
14:19 things that *g.* out of dust
31:40 thistles *g.* inst. of wheat
39:4 they *g.* up with the corn
Ps. 92:12 *g.* like cedar in Leba.
104:14 grass to *g.* 147:8
Ec. 11:5 how the bones *g.*
Is. 11:1 br. sh. *g.* out of his roots
53:2 sh. *g.* up as a tender plant
Jer. 12:2 they *g.* yea, bring forth
33:15 branch of right. to *g.* to D.
Ezek. 44:20 nor suffer locks *g.* lo.
Hos. 14:5 he shall *g.* as the lily
7 shall revive, and *g.* as vine
Jon. 4:10 madest *g.* which came
Zec. 6:12 the BRANCH, he shall *g.*
Mal. 4:2 ye shall *g.* up as calves
Mat. 6:28 how they *g. Luke* 12:27
13:30 let both *g.* together
21:19 no fruit *g.* on thee hence.

Mark 4:27 seed g. kno. not how
Acts 5:24 doubted whereunto this g.
Eph. 4:15 may g. into him
1 Pet. 2:2 milk of word, th. ye g.
2 Pet. 3:18 g. in grace and kno.

GROWETH.
Ex. 10:5 locusts eat ev. tree g.
Lev. 13:39 spot that g. in skin
25:5 g. of its own accord, 11
Deut. 29:23 nor any grass g.
Jud. 19:9 the day g. to an end
Job 38:38 dust g. into hardness
Ps. 90:5 grass which g. up, 6
129:6 withereth afore it g. up
Is. 37:30 such as g. of itself
Mark 4:32 when it is sown it g.
Eph. 2:21 g. unto holy temple
2 Thes. 1:3 faith g. exceedingly

GROWN.
Gen. 38:11 Sh. be g. ; 14 was g.
Ex. 2:11 when Moses was g.
Deut. 32:15 thou art g. thick
Ruth 1:13 till they were g. ?
2 Sam. 10:5 tarry at Je. till your beards be g. 1 Chr. 19:5
2 K. 19:26 as corn blasted before it be g. Is. 37:27
Ezr. 9:6 tresp. g. up to heavens
Ps. 144:12 sons as plants g. up
Prov. 24:31 g. over with thorns
Jer. 50:11 ye are g. fat as heifer
Ezek. 16:7 bre. fashioned, hair g.
Dan. 4:22 g. strong, greatness g.
33 g. like eagles' feathers
Mat. 13:32 when g. greatest

GROWTH.
Amos 7:1 shooting up of lat. g.

GRUDGE.
Lev. 19:18 nor bear g. against pe.

GRUDGE, Verb.
Ps. 59:15 let them g. if not satis.
Jam. 5:9 g. not one ag. another

GRUDGING, LY.
2 Cor. 9:7 let him give, not g.
1 Pet. 4:9 hospitality without g.

GUARD.
Gen. 37:36 sold to capt. of g. 39:1
41:12 servant to captain of g.
1 K. 14:27 committed shields to chief of g. 2 Chr. 12:10
28 g. bro. them, 2 Chr. 12:11
2 K. 25:8 capt. of g. Jer. 52:12
10 cap. of g. b. walls, Jer. 52:14
11 captain of g. carried away
12 captain of g. left of poor

Neh. 4:22 in night may be a g.
23 nor men of g. put off clothes
Jer. 40:5 cap. of g. gave him vic.
52:30 cap. of g. took capt. 4,600
Ezek. 38:7 be thou a g. to them
Dan. 2:14 Dan. ans. capt. of g.
Acts 28:16 deli. pris. to cap. of g.

GUARD-CHAMBER.
1 K. 14:28 guard bare them to g.-c. 2 Chr. 12:11

GUEST.
Luke 19:7 to be g. with sinner

GUEST-CHAMBER.
Mark 14:14 whe. g.-c. ? Lu. 22:11

GUESTS.
1 K. 1:41 Adonijah and g. heard
Prov. 9:18 g. in depths of hell
Zep. 1:7 L. hath prep. and bid g.
Mat. 22:10 wed. furnished wi. g.
11 the king came in to see g.

GUIDE, S.
Ps. 48:14 our g. even to death
55:13 it was thou, a man, my g.
Prov. 2:17 forsak. g. of her youth
6:7 having no g. overseer, ruler
Jer. 3:4 thou art g. of my youth
Mic. 7:5 put not confidence in g.
Mat. 23:16 ye blind g. 24
Acts 1:16 g. to them that took J.
Rom. 2:19 thou art g. of blind

GUIDE.
Job 38:32 canst th. g. Arcturus ?
Ps. 25:9 meek will g. in judgm.
31:3 for thy name's sake g. me
32:8 I will teach and g. thee
73:24 shalt g. me with counsel
112:5 g. his affairs with discre.
Prov. 11:3 integrity of upright g.
Is. 49:10 by springs he sh. g. th.
51:18 there is none to g. her
58:11 L. shall g. thee continual.
Luke 1:79 g. feet into way of pe.
John 16:13 he will g. you
Acts 8:31 can I, ex. some g. me ?
1 Tim. 5:14 youn. women g. house

GUIDED, ING.
Gen. 48:14 g. hands wittingly
Ex. 15:13 g. them in strength
2 Chr. 32:22 Lord g. on ev. side
Job 31:18 g. her from mother's
Ps. 78:52 g. them in wilderness
72 g. them by skilful. of hands

GUILE.
Ex. 21:14 if a man slay with g.
Ps. 32:2 in whose spirit is no g.
34:13 lips from g. 1 Pet. 3:10
55:11 deceit and g. depart not

John 1:47 Israelite in wh. no g.
2 Cor. 12:16 I caught you with g.
1 Thes. 2:3 exhortation not in g.
1 Pet. 2:1 lay aside malice and g.
22 nor was g. found in his mo.
Rev. 14:5 in mo. was found no g.

GUILT.
Deut. 19:13 g. of inno. blood, 21:9

GUILTY.
Gen. 42:21 we are verily g.
Ex. 34:7 not clear g. Num. 14:18
Lev. 5:2 he shall be uncl. and g.
3 wh. he knoweth not, be g. 4
5 when g. he shall con. his sin
17 he wist it not, yet is he g.
6:4 he sinned and is g.
Num. 35:27 kill slayer not be g.
31 for a murderer g. of death
Jud. 21:22 not g. that sh. be g.
Prov. 30:10 lest curse, thou be g.
Ezek. 22:4 art become g. in blo.
Mat. 23:18 by gift on it, he g.
26:66 he is g. of death, **Mark** 14:64
Rom. 3:19 the world may bec. g.
1 Cor. 11:27 g. of body and blood
Jam. 2:10 offend in one, g. of all

GUILTINESS.
Gen. 26:10 shouldest have bro. g.
Ps. 51:14 del. me from blood-g.

GUILTLESS.
Ex. 20:7 hold him g. Deut. 25:1?
Num. 32:22 and be g. before L.
Jos. 2:19 blood on him, we be g.
1 Sam. 26:9 ag. L.'s anointed g.
2 Sam. 3:28 I and kingdom g. of blood
14:9 king and his throne be g.
1 K. 2:9 hold not g. for thou
Mat. 12:7 not have condemned g.

GULF.
Luke 16:26 bet. us and you a g.

GUR. 2 K. 9:27

GUSH, ED.
1 K. 18:28 till the blood g. out
Ps. 78:20 sm rock, waters g. out
105:41 open. rock, waters g. out
Is. 48:21 cl. rock, waters g. out
Jer. 9:18 eyelids g. out with wat.
Acts 1:18 burst as. bowels g. out

GUTTER, S.
Gen. 30:38 Jacob set rods in g.
41 laid rods bef. cat. in the g.
2 Sam. 5:8 getteth up to the g.

H

HA.
Job 39:25 saith am. trump. a, ha

HABERGEON.
Ex. 28:32 hole of a h. 39:23
Job 41:26 dart, h. cannot hold

HABERGEONS.
2 Chr. 26:14 h. Uzziah prepared
Neh. 4:16 half of servants held h.

HABITABLE.
Prov. 8:31 in the h. part of earth

HABITATION.
Ex. 15:2 I will prepare him a h.
Lev. 13:46 with. the camp his h.
1 Sam. 2:29 offering com. in h.
32 shalt see an enemy in my h.
2 Sam. 15:25 show me it and h.
2 Chr. 6:2 a house of h. for thee
29:6 turned from the h. of Lord
Ezr. 7:15 G. of Is. whose h. in J.
Job 5:3 but suddenly I cursed h.
24 shalt visit h. and sh. not sin

8:6 h. of righteousness prosper.
18:15 brimstone scat. upon h.
Ps. 26:8 loved h. of thy house
33:14 from place of h. looketh
69:25 let their h. be desolate
71:3 bc thou my strong h.
89:14 the h. of thy throne, 97:2
91:9 made the Most High thy h.
104:12 fowls of heaven have h.
107:7 might go to a city of h. 36
132:5 find a h. for God of Jacob
13 L. hath desired it for his h.
Prov. 3:33 blesseth the h. of just
Is. 22:16 graveth h. for himself
32:18 peo. dwell in peaceable h.
33:20 shall see Jerus. a quiet h.
34:13 it shall be a h. of dragons
35:7 h. of dragons sh. be grass
63:15 from the h. of thy holiness
Jer. 9:6 thy h. in midst of deceit
10:25 have made his h. desolate
25:30 L. sh. mightily roar on h.
31:23 L. bless, O h. of just, 50:7

41:17 dwelt in the h. of Chim.
49:19 not c. ag. h. of stro. 50:44
50:19 bri. Israel again to his h.
45 he sh. make their h. desol.
Ezek. 29:14 cause E. return to h.
Ob. 3 wh. h. high, saith in heart
Hab. 3:11 sun and moon st. in h.
Acts 1:20 let his h. bc desolate
17:26 determined bounds of h.
Eph. 2:22 h. of God thro' Spirit
Jude 6 angels wh. left their h.
Rev. 18:2 Baby. become h. of de.

Holy HABITATION.
Ex. 15:13 guided them to h. h.
Deut. 26:15 look down from h. h.
Ps. 68:5 Ju. of wid. is G. in h. h.
Jer. 25:30 utter voice from h. h.
Zec. 2:13 raised out of holy h.

HABITATIONS.
Gen. 49:5 instru. of cruelty in h.
Ex. 12:20 in h. eat unl. bread
35:3 kindle no fire thro' your h.

Ps. 74:20 dark places full of *h.*
Is 54:2 stretch forth curt. of *h.*
Jer. 9:10 *h.* of wild. lamentation
21:13 who sh. enter into our *h.?*
25:37 peaceable *h.* are cut down
49:20 sh. make their *h.* desolate
Lam. 2:2 L. swallowed *h.* of Jac.
Ezek. 6:14 *h.* make land desolate
Amos 1:2 *h.* of shepherds mourn
Luke 16:9 receive into everl. *h.*

HACHILAH.
1 *Sam.* 23:19 D. hid in H. 26:1

HAD.
Job 31:31 O that we *h.* of his fl. !
42:10 twice as much as he *h.*
Ps. 84:10 I *h.* rather be a door-k.
89:7 to be *h.* in reverence of all
Mat. 13:46 he sold all that he *h.*
22:28 of sev. for they all *h.* her
Mark 12:44 did cast in all she *h.*
John 4:18 hast *h.* five husbands
John 12:6 Judas *h.* the bag. and
15:22 *h.* not come they *h.* not *h.*
17:5 the glory I *h.* with thee
Acts 2:44 believed *h.* all common
Heb. 7:6 blessed him *h.* promises
1 *John* 2:7 com. *h.* fr. beginning
2 *John* 5 we *h.* from beginning.
See ALL, COMPASSION.

HADST.
Gen. 30:30 little *h.* bef. I came
Heb. 10:8 offer. for sin *h.* no ple.

HADADEZER, HADAR-
EZER.
2 *Sam.* 8:3, 5, 7, 8, 9, 10, 12; 10:16;
1 *K.* 11:23; 1 *Chr.* 18:3

HADADRIMMON. *Zec.* 12:11

HADORAM.
Gen. 10:27; 1 *Chr.* 1:21 ; 18:10
2 *Chr.* 10:18 Rehoboam sent H.

HADRACH. *Zec.* 9:1

HAFT.
Jud. 3:22 the *h.* also went in

HAGAR. *Gen.* 16:1, 3, 8, 16;
21:9, 14, 17; 25:12
HAGARENES. *Ps.* 83:6
HAGARITES. 1 *Chr.* 5:10, 19, 20

HAGGAI.
Ezr. 5:1 H. prophesied to J. 6:14
Hag. 1:1 L. by H. 3; 2:1, 10, 20
HAGGITH. 2 *Sam.* 3:4; 1 *K.*
1:5; 2:13; 1 *Chr.* 3:2

HAIL.
Ex. 9:18 cau. to rain grievous *h.*
23 Lord sent thunder and *h.*
26 children of Is. were, no *h.*
29 any more *h.;* 33 *h.* ceased
Job 38:22 seen treasures of the *h.?*
Ps. 78:47 destroyed vines wi. *h.*
48 gave cattle also to *h.*
105:32 he gave them *h.* for rain
148:8 fire, *h.* snow, and vapor
Is. 28:17 *h.* shall sweep away
Hag. 2:17 I smote you with *h.*
Rev. 8:7 there follow. *h.* and fire
11:19 temple opened, great *h.*
16:21 th. fell on men a great *h.*

HAIL, Verb.
Is. 32:19 people dwell, it shall *h.*

HAIL.
Mat. 26:49 Judas said, *h.* Master
27:29 *h.* king of the Jews, *Mark*
15:18 ; *John* 19:3
Luke 1:28 ang. came to M. said *h.*

HAILSTONES.
Jos. 10:11 which died with *h.*
Ps. 18:12 *h.* and coals of fire, 13
Is. 30:30 L. show indig. with *h.*
Ezek. 13:11 O great *h.* shall fall
13 shall be great *h.* in my fury
38:22 great *h.* fire, brimstone

HAIR.
Lev. 13:3 *h.* in plague tur. white
30 plague yellow *h.* ; 31 bl. *h.*
37 there is black *h.* grown
14:8 and shave off all his *h.* 9
Num. 6:19 *h.* of separa. shaven
Jud. 20:16 sling stones at *h.*
2 *Sam.* 14:26 bec. *h.* was heavy
1 *K.* 1:52 not a *h.* fall to earth
Neh. 13:25 I plucked off their *h.*
Job 4:15 *h.* of my flesh stood up
Cant. 4:1 *h.* as flock of goats, 6:5
Is. 3:4 instead of well-set *h.*
7:20 L. shave head, and *h.*
50:6 plucked off *h.*
Jer. 7:29 cut off thy *h.* O Jerus.
Ezek. 5:1 div. *h.* ; 16:7 *h.* grown
Mat. 3:4 camel's *h. Mark* 1:6
5:36 not make one *h.* wh. or bl.
John 11:2 wiped feet with *h.* 12:3
1 *Cor.* 11:14 if a man have long *h.*
15 woman have long *h.* glory
1 *Tim.* 2:9 not with broidered *h.*
1 *Pet.* 3:3 plaiting *h.* wear. gold
Rev. 6:12 black as sackcl. of *h.*
9:8 had *h.* as the *h.* of women
See GOATS, HEAD.

HAIRS.
Gen. 42:38 br. down *h.* 44:29, 31
Deut. 32:25 man of gray *h.*
Ps. 40:12 more than *h.* of h. 69:4
Is. 46:4 to hoar *h.* will I carry
Dan. 4:33 *h.* like eagles' feathers
Hos. 7:9 gray *h.* here and there
Mat. 10:30 the *h.* of your head
are numbered, *Luke* 12:7
Luke 7:38 wipe with *h.* of h. 44
Rev. 1:14 *h.* were white like wool

HAIRY.
Gen. 25:25 all over like *h.* garm.
27:11 Esau *h.* man ; 23 hands *h.*
2 *K.* 1:8 Elijah was a *h.* man
Ps. 68:21 *h.* scalp of such a one

HALE, ING.
Luke 12:58 advers. *h.* thee to ju.
Acts 8:3 Saul *h.* men and women

HALF.
Ex. 24:6 *h.* blood, *h.* sprinkled
Lev. 6:20 *h.* in morn. *h.* at night
1 *Sam.* 14:14 with *h.* acre of land
2 *Sam.* 10:4 shave off *h.* of beards
19:40 *h.* of Israel conducted D.
1 *K.* 3:25 *h.* child to one, *h.* oth.
10:7 *h.* was not told, 2 *Chr.* 9:6
13:8 whit give me *h.* thy house
16:21 *h.* followed Tibni, *h.* Omri
Neh. 13:24 *h.* in speech of Ashd.
Est. 5:3 to the *h.* of the kingdom, 7:2 ; *Mark* 6:23
Ps. 55:23 bl. men not live *h.* days
Dan. 12:7 and a *h. Rev.* 12:14
Zec. 14:2 *h.* of city into captivity
4 *h.* tow. south ; 8 *h.* tow. sea
Luke 10:30 leaving him *h.* dead
19:8 *h.* of goods I give to poor
Rev. 8:1 silence about *h.* an hour
11:9 bodies three days and *h.* 11
See SHEKEL, HIN, TRIBE.

HALL.
Mat. 27:27 sold. took Jes. into *h.*
Mark 15:16 soldiers led him to *h.*
Luke 22:55 kindled fire in the *h.*
See JUDGMENT.

HALLOW.
Ex. 29:1 *h.* them to minister
Lev. 22:32 I am the L. who *h.*
25:10 shall *h.* the fiftieth year
Num. 6:11 shall *h.* his head
1 *K.* 8:64 king *h.* court, 2 *Chr.* 7:7
Jer. 17:22 *h.* ye sabbath-d. 24, 27
Ezek. 20:20 and *h.* my sabbaths
44:24 keep laws *h.* my sabbaths

HALLOWED.
Ex. 20:11 bless. sabbath and *h.* it

29:21 Aaron be *h.* and his garm.
Lev. 12:4 shall touch no *h.* thing
22:32 be *h.* am. children of Isr.
Num. 3:13 *h.* to me first-b. in Is.
5:10 every man's *h.* things
16:37 censers, they are *h.* 38
Deut. 26:13 bro. away *h.* things
1 *Sam.* 21:4 there is *h.* bread, 6
1 *K.* 9:3 I have *h.* this house, 7
2 *Chr.* 36:14 pollu. hou. L. had *h.*
Mat. 6:9 be thy na. *Luke* 11:2

HALT.
Mat. 18:8 into life *h. Mark* 9:45
Luke 14:21 bring hither *h.*
John 5:3 *h.* wait. moving of wa.

HALT, ING.
1 *K.* 18:21 how long *h.* ye ?
Ps. 38:17 for I am ready to *h.*
Jer. 20:10 familiars watch. my *h.*

HALTED, ETH.
Gen. 32:31 J. passed, *h.* on thigh
Mic. 4:6 assemble her that *h.*
7 make her that *h.* a remnant
Zep. 3:19 I will save her that *h.*

HAM.
Gen. 5:32 ; 6:10 ; 9:18 ; 10:1 ; 1 *Chr.*
1:4
1 *Chr.* 4:40 they of H. dwelt
Ps. 105:23 la. of H. 27 ; 106:22

HAMAN.
See Book of Esther.

HAMATH.
Num. 34:8 Hor to entr. of H. *Jos.*
13:5 ; *Jud.* 3:3 ; 1 *K.* 8:65 ;
2 *K.* 14:25 ; 2 *Chr.* 7:8
2 *K.* 14:28 ; 18:34 ; 19:13 ; *Is.* 36:19
1 *Chr.* 13:5 D. sm. to H. 2 *Chr.* 8:4
Is. 10:9 H. as A. ? 11:11 ; *Jer.* 39:5 ;
49:23 ; 52:9 ; *Ezek.* 47:17
HAMMEDATHA. *Est.* 8:5 ; 9:10

HAMMER, S.
Jud. 4:21 J. took *h.* in her hand
5:26 with *h.* she smote Sisera
1 *K.* 6:7 neither *h.* nor axe heard
Ps. 74:6 br. carved work with *h.*
Is. 41:7 smootheth with the *h.*
44:12 smith fashioneth it wi. *h.*
Jer. 10:4 fast. it wi. nails and *h.*
23:29 like *h.* that breaketh rock
50:23 *h.* of wh. earth cut asund.

HAMON-GOG. *Ezek.* 39:11 15

HAMOR.
Gen. 33:19 H. Shechem's father,
Jos. 24:32
34:6 H. went out to Ja. 8, 24, 26
Jud. 9:28 serve the men of H.

HANAMEEL. *Jer.* 32:7, 8, 9, 12
HANANEEL. *Neh.* 3:1 ; 12:39 ;
Jer. 31:38 ; *Zec.* 14:10

HANANI.
1 *K.* 16:1 to Jehu son of H. 7
1 *Chr.* 25:4 H. son of Heman, 25
2 *Chr.* 16:7 H. seer, *Neh.* 1:2 ; 7:2
19:2 Jehu son of H. 20:34
Neh. 12:36 H. with musical inst.

HANANIAH.
1 *Chr.* 3:19 sons of Zerub. H.
Ezr. 10:28 H. Zab. stra. wives
Neh. 3:8 H. repaired, 7:2 ; 10:23 ;
12:12
Jer. 28:12 H. had broken J.'s, 17
37:13 son of H. took Jeremiah
Dan. 1:7 to H. name of S. 2:17

HAND.
Gen. 9:2 into *h.* are they deliv.
44:17 in whose *h.* cup found
Ex. 6:1 strong *h.* drive them out
13:3 strength of *h.* L. brought
14:8 Israel went out with a high
h. Num. 33:3
16 stretch out *h.* over the sea
19:13 there sh. not a *h.* touch it
21:24 *h.* for *h. Deut.* 19:21

34:29 tables of testi. in Mos. *h.*
38:15 on this *h.* and that *h.*
Deut. 15:9 *h.* of all the people
25:12 cut off her *h.*
Jos. 2:19 blo. on head *h.* on him
Jud. 1:35 *h.* of house of Joseph
4:9 sell Sisera into *h.* of a wom.
15:18 fall into *h.* of uncircum.
1 Sam. 12:3 who. *h.* rec. bribe?
13:22 nor spear fou. in *h.* of Is.
17:50 no sword in *h.* of David
20:19 when business was in *h.*
22:17 their *h.* also is with Dav.
2 Sam. 13:5 eat it at her *h.* 6
14:19 the *h.* of Joab in all this
21:20 had on every *h.* six fing.
1 Chr. 20:6
24:14 into *h.* of men, 1 Chr. 21:13
1 K. 2:46 established in *h.* of Sol.
13:6 king's *h.* was restored aga.
18:44 ariseth cloud like man's *h.*
22:6 L. sh. deliver it into king's
h. 12, 15 ; 2 Chr. 18:5 ; 28:5
2 K. 7:2 who. *h.* king leaned, 17
Ezr. 7:9 good *h.* of God on him
9:2 *h.* of princes chief in tresp.
Job 9:24 given into *h.* of wicked
12:6 into whose *h. G.* bringeth
10 in *h.* is soul of ev. liv. thing
20:22 *h.* of wicked come on him
21:16 good is not in their *h.*
34:20 mighty take. away wit. *h.*
37:7 sealeth up *h.* of ev. man
Ps. 31:8 not shut into *h.* of ene.
36:11 let not *h.* of wicked rem.
71:4 deliver me out of *h.* of
wicked, 82:4 ; 97:10
127:2 serv. look to *h.* of masters
127:4 in *h.* of mighty man
149:6 two-edged sword be in *h.*
Prov. 6:3 come into *h.* of friend
10:4 poor, dealeth slack *h.* but
h. of diligent maketh rich
11:21 *h.* join *h.* not unpun. 16:5
12:24 *h.* of diligent bear rule
17:16 in *h.* of fool get wisdom?
26:9 thorn goeth into *h.* of dru.
Is. 10:5 staff in *h.* my indigna.
13:2 shake *h.* may go into gates
19:4 into *h.* of cruel lord
28:2 cast down to earth wi, *h.*
Jer. 12:7 belo. into *h.* of enemies
18:4 vessel marred in *h.* of pot.
6 as clay in the potter's *h.*
21:5 outstretch. *h.* against you
26:24 *h.* of Ahikam with Jere.
not to give him into *h.* of pe.
Lam. 5:6 given *h.* to Egyptians
12 princes are hanged by the *h.*

Ezek. 2:9 a *h.* was sent me
8:3 put forth form of *h.* 10:8
16:49 nor. strength. *h.* of needy
28:9 no god in *h.* that slayeth
34:10 require flock at their *h.*
37:19 stick in *h.* of Ephraim
40:5 in man's *h.* a measur. reed

Dan. 5:5 came fing. of man's *h.*
23 G. in whose *h.* thy breath is
8:25 he shall be broken with *h.*
10:10 behold, a *h.* touched me

Joel 3:8 sons and dau. to *h.* Jud
Mat. 8:15 tou. *h.* ; 22:13 bind *h.*
Mark 3:1 withered *h.* 3; Lu. 6:8
14:41 is betrayed into *h.* of sin.
Luke 1:1 taken in *h.* to set forth
74 delivered out of *h.* of enem.
22:21 *h.* that betray. is with me
John 10:39 escaped out of th. *h.*
11:44 bound *h.* and foot
Acts 12:17 becko. to them wi. *h.*
1 Cor. 12:15 bec. I am not the *h.*
21 eye cannot say to *h.* no need
Gal. 3:19 by angels in *h.* of med.

Rev. 10:8 book in *h.* of angel
17:4 a golden cup in her *h.*
19:2 avenged blood of serv. at *h.*

At, *or* at the HAND.

Gen. 9:5 *at h.* of ev. beast, *at h.*
of man, *at h.* of man's brot.
33:19 J. bought *at h.* of children
Deut. 15:9 year of release is *at h.*
1 Sam. 20:16 *at h.* of D.'s enem.
2 K. 9:7 blood *at h.* of Jezebel
Is. 13:6 day of Lord *at h. Joel*
1:15 ; *Zep.* 1:7
Jer. 23:23 am I a God *at h.* ?
Ezek. 12:23 the days are *at h.*
33:6 blood req. *at* watchm.'s *h.*
Joel 2:1 day of Lord is nigh *at h.*
Mat. 3:2 heaven *at h.* 4:17 ; 10:7
26:18 ti. is *at h.* ; 45 hour *at h.*
46 *at h.* that bet. me, *Mar.* 14:42
Mark 1:15 kingdom of God is
at h. Luke 21:31
Luke 21:30 summer is nigh *at h.*
John 2:13 pass. was *at h.* 11:55
7:2 feast of tabernac. was *at h.*
19:42 sepulchre was nigh *at h.*
Rom. 13:12 night far sp. day *at h.*
Phil. 4:5 the Lord is *at h.*
2 Thes. 2:2 the day of Chs. is *at h.*
2 Tim. 4:6 time of depart. is *at h.*
1 Pet. 4:7 end of all things *at h.*
Rev. 1:3 the time is *at h.* 22:10

By the HAND.

Ex. 4:13 send *by the h.* of him
Lev. 8:36 Lord command. *by t. h.*
of Moses, 10:11 ; 26:46 ; *Num.*
4:37, 45, 49 ; 9:23 ; 10:13 ;
15:23 ; 16:40 ; 27:23 ; 36:13 ;
Jos. 14:2 ; 20:2 ; 21:2, 8 ; 22:9 ;
Jud. 3:4 ; 1 K. 8:53, 56 ;
2 Chr. 33:8 ; 35:6 ; Neh. 9:14 ;
Ps. 77:20
16:21 *by t. h.* of a fit man
Jos. 20:9 not die *by t. h.* of aven.
Jud. 16:26 to lad held *by t. h.*
1 Sam. 18:25 fall *by h.* of Philis.
27:1 one day perish *by t. h.* of 8
2 Sam. 3:18 *by h.* of my serv. D.
11:14 a letter, sent *by t. h.* of U.
12:25 sent *by h.* of Nathan
21:22 fell *by h.* of D. 1 Chr. 20:8
1 K. 2:25 sent *by h.* of Benaiah
14:18 he spake *by h.* of his serv.
2 K. 14:25 spake *by h.* of Jonah
27 saved them *by t. h.* of Jero.
2 Chr. 10:15 *by t. h.* of Ahijah
12:7 wrath *by t. h.* of Shishak
Prov. 26:6 message *by h.* of fool
Is. 51:18 that taketh *by the h.*
Jer. 27:3 yokes *by h.* of messeng.
31:32 took th. *by t. h. Heb.* 8:9
Ezek. 25:14 vengeance *by h.* of Is.
30:12 land waste *by h.* of strang.
Mat. 9:25 took her *by t. h. Mark*
1:31 ; 5:41 ; *Luke* 8:54
Mark 8:23 took blind man *by h.*
9:27 Jesus took him *by the h.*
Acts 7:35 a deliv. *by t. h.* of angel
9:8 but they led him *by the h.*
13:11 seek. some lead him *by h.*
Col. 4:18 salutation *by the h.*

See CHALDEANS, ENEMY.

HAND, *joined with* enemies.

1 Sam. 4:3 ark of coven. save out
h. of e. 12:10 ; 2 Sam. 3:18
12:11 deli. out of *h.* e. 2 K. 17:39
2 Sam. 19:9 out of *h.* of enemies
2 K. 21:14 will deliver them to *h.*
of e. 2 Chr. 25:20 ; Neh. 9:27
Neh. 9:28 left them in *h.* of th. e.
Ps. 31:15 deli. from *h.* of mine e.
Jer. 20:5 give this city into *h.* of
e. 21:7 ; 34:20, 21 ; Ezek. 39:23
44:30 give Phar. to *h.* of his e.
Mic. 4:10 red. thee from *h.* of e.
Luke 1:74 deli. out of *h.* of our e.

From the HAND.

Gen. 32:11 del. *f. t. h.* of brother
Deut. 7:8 redeemed *f. h.* of Pha.
Jud. 8:22 deliv. *f. h.* of Midian
1 Sam. 25:39 pleaded *f. h.* of N.

Job 5:15 saveth poor *f. h.* of mi.
6:23 redeem me *f. h.* of mighty
Ps. 89:48 del. soul *f. h.* of grave
106:10 sav. *f. h.* of him that hat.
redeemed *f. h.* of the enemy
144:7 del. *f. t. h.* of children, 11
Prov. 6:5 del. as roe *f. h.* of hun.
Jer. 20:13 deliv. poor *f. h.* of evil
31:11 *f. h.* of him stronger
Luke 1:71 *f. h.* of all that hate

HAND of God.

1 Sam. 5:11 *h.* of G. heavy
2 Chr. 30:12 *h.* of G. give heart
Ezr. 7:9 ac. to *h.* of G. Neh. 2:8
8:18 by good *h.* of God upon us
22 *h. of G.* is upon them
Neh. 2:18 told them of *h.* of G.
Job 2:10 re. good at the *h.* of G. ?
19:21 *h.* of God touched me
27:11 teach you by *h.* of G.
Ec. 2:24 from the *h.* of God
9:1 wise are in the *h.* of God
Is. 62:3 diadem in *h.* of God
Mark 16:19 and sat on right *h.* of
G. Rom. 8:34 ; Col. 3:1 ; Heb.
10:12 ; 1 Pet. 3:22
Acts 2:33 by right *h.* of God
7:55 stand. on right *h.* of G. 56
1 Pet. 5:6 under the *h.* of God

His HAND.

Gen. 3:22 forth *h. h.* take t. of life
16:12 *his h.* be agai. every man
41:42 Pharaoh took ring off *h. h.*
Ex. 4:4 *h. h.* became rod in *h. h.*
6 *his h.* was as leprous as snow
20 M. took rod of God in *his h.*
8:6 stretched *h. h.* over wat. 17
10:22 stretched *his h.* to heaven
17:11 held up *his h.* down *his h.*
21:16 fou. in *h. h.* ; 20 und. *h. h.*
22:4 if theft be found in *his h.*
8 hath put *his h.* to goods, 11
24:11 on nobles laid not *his h.*
32:15 tab. of testi. in *his h.* 34:4
Lev. 1:4 *h. h.* on head of burnt-o.
Num. 5:18 in *his h.* bitter water
22:23 sw. in *h. h.* 31 ; 1 Ch. 21:16
25:7 Phin. took a javelin in *h. h.*
Deut. 19:5 *his h.* fetch. a stroke
Jos. 5:13 with sword in *his h.*
8:26 drew not *his h.* till destroy.
Jud. 6:21 end of staff in *his h.*
7:14 to *h. h.* G. delivered Midian
1 Sam. 6:3 *his h.* not removed
9 it is not *his h.* that smote us
14:26 put *his h.* to his mouth
27 Jon. put *his h.* to his mouth
16:16 he shall play with *his h.*
23 played with *his h.* 18:10
17:40 his staff and sling in *h. h.*
57 head of Philistine in *his h.*
19:5 life in *h. h.* and slew Phil.
23:16 strengthened *his h.* in God
2 Sam. 6:6 *h. h.* to ark, 1 Ch. 13:10
1 K. 11:34 kingdom out of *his h.*
13:4 *his h.* he put forth ag. him
2 K. 5:11 call on L. strike *his h.*
10:15 and he gave him *his h.*
11:8 man with his weapon in
his h. 11 ; 2 Chr. 23:7
14:5 kingdom confirmed in *h. h.*
15:19 *his h.* might be with him
18:21 a man lean go into *his h.*
1 Chr. 28:19 understand by *his h.*
2 Chr. 26:19 a censer in *his h.*
Neh. 6:5 serv. with letter in *h. h.*
Job 6:9 let loose *h. h.* cut me off
15:23 day of dark. ready at *h. h.*
25 stretcheth out *h. h.* ag. God
26:13 *his h.* formed crooked ser.
27:22 fain flee out of *his h.*
28:9 putteth forth *his h.*
Ps. 37:24 L. uphold. him wi. *h. h.*
53 will not leave him in *h. h.*
78:42 remembered not *his h.*
89:25 set *his h.* also in the sea

95:4 in *his h.* are deep places
7 sheep of *his h.* to-day
106:26 lifted up *h. h.* ag. them
129:7 mower filleth not *his h.*
Prov. 19:24 a slothful man hideth
his h. 26:15
Ec. 5:14 a son, nothing in *his h.*
15 he may carry in *his h.*
Cant. 5:4 put in *his h.* by hole
Is. 5:25 *h. h.* is stretch. out still,
9:12, 17, 21; 10:4; 14:27
10:32 shake *h. h.* aga. mount Z.
11:11 set *h. h.* again the sec. ti.
15 shake *his h.* over the river
22:21 thy government into *h. h.*
28:4 while yet in *his h.*
31:3 L. shall stretch out *his h.*
37:20 O L. save us from *his h.*
40:12 waters in hollow of *his h.*
44:5 subscribe with *his h.*
49:2 in shad. of *his h.* he hid me
53:10 ple. of L. prosper in *h. h.*
56:2 keepeth *his h.* fr. doing ev.
Jer. 27:8 consumed th. by *his h.*
Lam. 1:14 transgression by *h. h.*
2:8 hath not withdrawn *his h.*
3:3 turneth *his h.* against me
Ezek. 8:11 with censer in *his h.*
9:1 destroying weapon *his h.*
17:18 lo, he had given *his h.*
30:24 put my sword in *his h.*
46:7 according as *h. h.* shall at.
Dan. 4:35 none can stay *his h.*
8:4 could deliver out of *his h.* 7
25 cause craft prosper in *his h.*
11:41 shall escape out of *his h.*
Hos. 7:5 he stretched out *his h.*
Hos. 12:7 bal. of dec. are in *his h.*
Hab. 3:4 horns com. out of *his h.*
Zep. 2:15 hiss and wag *his h.*
Zec. 8:4 man with staff in *his h.*
14:13 *h. h.* rise ag. hand of nei.
Mat. 3:12 fan is in *h. h.* *Lu.* 3:17
26:23 he that dippeth *h. h.*
Mark 3:5 *h. h.* resto. *Luke* 6:10
7:32 bes. to put *h. h.* upon him
John 3:35 given all th. into *h. h.*
18:22 struck with palm of *his h.*
Acts 7:25 God by *his h.* del. them
28:3 a viper fastened on *his h.*
4 saw the beast hang on *his h.*
Rev. 6:5 pair of balances in *h. h.*
10:2 had in *his h.* a little book
14:9 in his forehead, or in *his h.*
14 in *his h.* sharp sickle
20:1 angel with chain in *his h.*

HAND of the Lord, *or* **Lord's
HAND.**

Ex. 9:3 *h. of the L.* upon cattle
16:3 wo. had died by *h. of the L.*
Num. 11:23 *L.'s h.* waxed short?
Jos. 4:24 know *h. of L.* mighty
Jud. 2:15 *h. of Lord* ag. them
Ruth 1:13 *h. of the L.* is gone out
1 *Sam.* 5:6 *h. of Lord* heavy
7:13 *h. of the L.* ag. Philisttp.
12:15 then sh. *h. of L.* be ag. you
2 *Sam.* 24:14 *h. of L.* 1 *Chr.* 21:13
1 *K.* 18:46 *h. of L.* was on Elijah
2 *K.* 3:15 *h. of L.* came on Elisha
Ezr. 7:6 granted acc. to *h. of L.*
Job 12:9 *h. of L.* wro. this, *Is.*41:20
Ps. 75:8 in *h. of the L.* is a cup
Prov. 21:1 king's he. in *h. of L.*
Is. 19:16 shaking off *h.of the L.*
25:10 in moun. sh. *h. of L.* rest
40:2 rec. of the *L.'s h.* double
51:17 hast drunk at *h. of the L.*
59:1 *Lord's h.* is not shortened
62:3 crown of gl. in *h. of the L.*
66:14 *h. of L.* known tow. serv.
Jer. 25:17 took cup at the *L.'s h.*
51:7 Bab. golden cup in *L.'s h.*
Ezek. 1:3 *h. of the L.* upon him
3:14 *h. of L.* u. me, 22; 8:1; 37:1
33:22 *h. of L.* on me in evening
40:1 *h. of the L.* was with him

Luke 1:66 *h. of the L.* with him
Acts 11:21 *h. of the L.* with them
13:11 *h. of the L.* is upon thee
See LAY, *or* LAID.

Left HAND.

Gen. 13:9 if thou wilt take *left h.*
24:49 turn to the right *h.* or *left*
48:13 Joseph took Ephr. in his
right *h.* and Man. in his *left*
14 Is. laid *l. h.* on Manasseh's
Ex. 14:22 wall on right *h.* and *l.*
Lev. 14:15 pour oil into *left h.* 27
Num. 20:17 not turn to right *h.*
nor to *left*, *Deut.* 2:27; 5:32;
17:11, 20; 28:14
22:26 no way to turn, r. *h.* or *l.*
Jos. 1:7 to right *h.* or *left*, 23:6;
1 *Sam.* 6:12; *Prov.* 4:27
Jud. 3:21 E. put forth his *left h.*
7:20 held lamps in their *left h.*
2 *Sam.* 2:19 he turned not to *l. h.*
14:19 none turn to right *h.* or *l.*
1 *K.* 22:19 host of heaven on his
left h. 2 *Chr.* 18:18
2 *K.* 22:2 J. turn. not to r. *h.* or *l.*
1 *Chr.* 12:2 use both r. *h.* and *l.*
2 *Chr.* 3:17 name of that on *l. h.*
4:7 five candlest. on r. *h.* 5 on *l.*
Neh. 8:4 on his *l. h.* stood Ped.
Job 23:9 on *left h.* he doth work
Prov. 3:16 in her *left h.* riches
Ec. 10:2 fool's heart at his *l. h.*
Cant. 2:6 *l. h.* is under my head
8:3 his *left h.* under my head
Is. 9:20 he shall eat on *left h.*
30:21 when ye turn to *left h.*
54:3 break forth on r. *h.* and *l.*
Ezek. 16:46 dau. dwell at *left h.*
39:3 smite bow out of *left h.*
Dan. 12:7 he held up his *left h.*
Jon. 4:11 betw. right *h.* and *left*
Zec. 12:6 people on r. *h.* and *left*
Mat. 6:3 let not *l. h.* know what
20:21 one r. *h.* other *l. Mar.* 10:37
23 sit on r. *h.* and *l. Mark* 10:40
25:33 sheep on r. *h.* goats on *l.*
41 say to them on *l. h.* Depart
27:38 one on right *h.* other on
left, *Mark* 15:27; *Luke* 23:33
Acts 21:3 left Cyprus on *l. h.*
2 *Cor.* 6:7 armor on right *h.* and *l.*
See LIFT hand, *or* hands.

Mighty HAND.

Ex. 3:19 let go, not with *m. h.*
Deut. 3.24 show serv. thy *m. h.*
4:34 take him a nation by *m. h.*

Deut. 5:15 God bro. out of Eg. by
a *mighty h.* 6:21; 7:8, 19; 9:26;
11:2; 26:8; 34:12
2 *Chr.* 6:32 is come for thy *m. h.*
Ezek. 20:33 with a *m. h.* I rule
Dan. 9.15 out of Eg. with *m. h.*
1 *Pet.* 5:6 hum. under *m. h.* of G.

My HAND.

Gen. 14:22 lifted *my h.* to Lord
31:39 of *my h.* didst thou req. it
33:10 rec. my present at *my h.*
42:37 deliver him into *my h.*
43:9 of *my h.* shalt thou require
Ex. 7:17 smite with rod in *my h.*
15:9 *my h.* destroy; 17:9 in *my h.*
33:22 cover thee with *my h.*
Num. 22:29 a sword in *my h.*
Deut. 8:17 might of *my h.*
10:3 the two tables in *my h.*
32:39 del. out of *my h. Is.* 43:13
40 I lift up *my h.* to heaven
41 if *my h.* take hold on judg.
Jud. 6:36 save Is. by *my h.* 37
7:2 *My* own *h.* saved me
9:29 wo. peo. were under *my h.*
17:3 dedi. silv. to L. from *my h.*
1 *Sam.* 12:5 not fo. aught in *my h.*
17:46 L. will deliver into *my h.*
21:4 no com. bread under *my h.*

24:6 stretch *my h.* ag. L.'s ano.
11 no transgression in *my h.*
12 *my h.* shall not be upon, **13**
26:18 what evil is in *my h.* ?
23 Lord deliv. into *my h.* 24:10
28:21 put my life in *my h.*
2 *Sam.* 5:19 will deliver Philistines into *my h.* ? 1 *Chr.* 14:10
1 *K.* 13:6 that *my h.* may be rest.
2 *K.* 5:18 he leaneth on *my h.* in
2 *Chr.* 32:15 del. out of *my h.* ? 17
Job 13:14 wher. put life in *my h.* ?
29:20 bow was renewed in *my h.*
31:25 bec. *my h.* had gotten
27 mouth had kissed *my h.*
33:7 nei. shall *my h.* be heavy
Ps. 81:14 turned *my h.* ag. ene.
89:21 *my h.* shall be established
119:109 soul is contin. in *my h.*
Prov. 1:24 I have stretched *my h.*
Is. 1:25 turn *my h.* upon me
10:10 *my h.* hath found kingd.
13 by strength of *my h.*
14 *my h.* found riches of peo.
48:13 *my h.* laid foundation
50:2 *my h.* short. 11 this of *my h.*
51:16 cov. in shadow of *my h.*
66:2 *my h.* made, *Acts* 7:50
Jer. 6:12 I will stretch out *my h.*
15:6; 51:25
16:21 cause them to know *my h.*
25:15 wine-cup of fury at *my h.*
Ezek. 6:14 I stretch out *my h.*
12:7 dig. thro' wall with *my h.*
13:9 *my h.* shall be upon proph.
20:5 I lifted up *my h.* saying, I
am the Lord your God, 6:23,
28, 42; 36:7; 44:12; 47:14
22 I withdrew *my h.*
22:13 smitten *my h.* at thy dish.
Hos. 2:10 none del. out of *my h.*
Amos 9:2 shall *my h.* take them
Zec. 2:9 shake *my h.* on them
13:7 turn *my h.* upon little ones
John 10:28 nor pluck out of *my h.*
29 none pluck out of my F. *h.*
20:25 thrust *my h.* into his side
1 *Cor.* 16:21 salutation of me, P.
with my own h. 2 *Thes.* 3:17
Gal. 6:11 writ. wi. *my h. Phile.* 19

Our HAND.

Gen. 37:27 let not *our h.* be
Deut. 32:27 lest adv. say, *our h.*
Jud. 16:23 del. Samuel into o. *h.*
1 *Sam.* 14:10 into *our h.* 30:23
Jer. 11:21 thou die not by *our h.*
2 *Cor.* 10:16 made ready to *our h.*

Out of, *or* **out of the HAND.**

Gen. 48:22 took o. *of the h.* of A.
Num. 5:25 offering o. *of* wom. *h.*
11:15 kill me, I pray, *out of h.*
35:25 del. *out of h.* of avenger
1 *Sam.* 4:8 shall del. us *out of h.*
2 *Sam.* 12:7 *out of h.* of S. 22:1
23:21 spear *out of h.* of Egyptian's
1 *K.* 11:12 rend kingdom *out of h.*
Ps. 71:4 del. *out of h.* of wicked
82:4 rid them *out of h.* of wick.
97:10 del. *out of h.* of wicked
Jer. 15:21 deliver thee *out of h.*
21:12 *out of the h.* of oppr. 22:3
32:4 *out of h.* of Chal. 38:18, 23
Lam. 5:8 none del. *out of their h.*
Zec. 11:6 *out of* their *h.* not del.
John 10:39 escaped *out of* their *h.*
Acts 12:11 deliver *out of h.* of H.
Rev. 8:4 *out of* angel's *h.* 10:10

Right HAND.

Gen. 48:14 r. *h.* on Ephraim's
Ex. 15:6 thy r. *h.* O L. is glori.
29:20 blood on thumb of r. *h.*
Lev. 8:23, 24; 14:14, 17, 25, 28
Deut. 33:2 fr. r. *h.* went fiery law
Jud. 5:26 *right h.* to workman's
2 *Sam.* 20:9 J. took Am. w. r. *h.*
2 *K.* 23:13 on *right h.* of mount.

Job 23:9 hideth himself on *r. h.*
30:12 upon my *r. h.* rise youth
40:14 thine own *r. h.* can save
Ps. 16:8 he is at my *right h.*
11 at thy *r. h.* are pleasures
17:7 sav. by *r. h.* them that tru.
18:35 *r. h.* hath holden me up
20:6 saving strength of *right h.*
21:8 *r. h.* find those that hate
26:10 their *r. h.* is full of bribes
44:3 *r. h.* and arm saved them
45:4 thy *r. h.* shall teach ter. t.
9 on thy *right h.* the queen
48:10 thy *r. h.* full of righteous.
60:5 save with thy *right h.*
63:8 thy *right h.* upholdeth
73:23 holden me by my *r. h.*
74:11 why withdra. thy *r. h.?*
77:10 remember years of *r. h.*
78:54 mount. which *r. h.* purc.
80:15 vineyard wh. *r. h.* planted
17 hand be upon man of *r. h.*
89:25 I will set his *r. h.* in riv.
42 set up *r. h.* of adversaries
91:7 ten thousand fall at *r. h.*
98:1 his *r. h.* hath gotten victory
108:6 save me with thy *right h.*
109:6 let Satan stand at his *r. h.*
31 he shall stand at *r. h.* of poor
110:1 sit thou at my *r. h. Luke*
20:42; *Acts* 2:34; *Heb.* 1:13
5 L. at *right h.* shall strike
118:15 *r. h.* of L. doeth valiantly
16 *r. h.* of Lord is exalted
121:5 Lord is shade on thy *r. h.*
137:5 let *r. h.* forget cunning
138:7 thy *r. h.* shall save me
139:10 thy *r. h.* shall hold me
142:4 looked on my *r. h.* none
144:8 *r. h.* is *r. h.* of falseh. 11
Prov. 3:16 length of days in *r. h.*
27:16 ointm. of *r. h.* bewrayeth
Ec. 10:2 wi. man's heart at *r. h.*
Cant. 2:6 *r. h.* doth embrace me
8:3 *r. h.* should embrace me
Is. 41:10 uphold thee with *r. h.*
13 thy God will hold thy *r. h.*
44:20 is there not a lie in *r. h.?*
45:1 whose *r. h.* I have holden
48:13 *r. h.* hath spanned heav.
62:8 hath sworn by his *right h.*
63:12 led them by *r. h.* of Mos.
Jer. 22:24 signet on my *right h.*
Lam. 2:3 drawn back his *r. h.*
Ezek. 21:22 *r. h.* divinat. for Jer.
Hab. 2:16 cup of Lord's *right h.*
Zec. 3:1 Satan standing at *r. h.*
Mat. 5:30 if thy *r. h.* offend thee
6:3 let not left know *r. h.* doeth
Mark 14:62 see Son of man sit.
on *r. h.* of power, *Luke* 22:69
16:19 on *r. h.* of God, *Heb.* 1:3;
8:1; 10:12; 12:2; 1 *Pet.* 3:22
Luke 6:6 man whose *r. h.* with.
Acts 2:25 he is on my *right h.*
33 by *r. h.* of God exalted, 5:31
3:7 he took him by the *right h.*
7:55 Jesus standing on *r. h.* 56
Rom. 8:34 is even at *r. h.* of God
Eph. 1:20 set him at his *right h.*
Col. 3:1 Ch. sitteth on *r. h.* of G.
Rev. 1:16 in *r. h.* 7 stars, 20; 2:1
5:1 I saw in his *r. h.* a book, 7
13:16 receive mark in their *r. h.*

See **Left** HAND.

Right HANDS.
Gal. 2:9 gave Bar. *r. h.* of fellow.

Stretch forth, *or* **out HAND.**
Gen. 22:10 Abra. *s. f. h.* to slay
Ex. 3:20 I will *stretch out* my *h.*
on Egypt, 7:5; 9:15
14:16 *s. out h.* over sea, 26:7, 19
21 M. *stretch-o. h.* over sea, 27
1 *Sam.* 26:9 *s. forth h.* ag. Lord's
Prov. 31:20 *s. out h.* to the poor
Ezek. 14:9 *s. o. h.* on that prophet
25:13 *s. o.* my *h.* upon Edom, 16

Dan. 11:42 *s. f. h.* on countries
Zep. 1:4 on Judah ; 2:13 ag. Assy.

See STRONG.

Thy HAND.
Gen. 4:11 brother's blood fr. *t. h.*
16:6 thy maid is in *thy h.*
22:12 lay not *thy h.* upon the lad
24:2 *thy h.* under my thigh, 47:29
40:8 *thy h.* be in neck of enem.
Ex. 4:2 what is that in *thy h. ?*
Ex. 4:17 take rod in *t. h.* 7:15; 17:5
8:5 stretch forth *thy h.* 9:22;
10:12,21; *Mat.*12:13; *Mark* 3:5
Deut. 2:7 in works of *thy h.* 14:29;
15:10 ; 23:20; 28:8, 12, 20
24 have given into *thy h.* Sihon
3:2 del. Og and people into *t. h.*
13:9 thy *h.* shall be first on him
17 cleave nau. cursed th. to *t. h.*
14:25 bind up money in *thy h.*
15:7 shut *thy h.* fr. poor brother
8 open *thy h.* wide to brother
23:25 pluck the ears with *thy h.*
33:3 all his saints are in *thy h.*
Jos. 6:2 given into *thy h.* Jericho
9:25 we are in *thy h.* to do to us
10:6 slack not *thy h.* from serv.
Jud. 4:7 deliver Sisera into *t. h.*
8:15 Zeba and Zalmunna in *t. h.*
18:19 lay *thy h.* on thy mouth
1 *Sam.* 14:19 withdraw *thy h.*
2 *Sam.* 13:10 I may eat of *thy h.*
24:16 stay *thy h.* 1 *Chr.* 21:15
17 *thy h.* be ag. me, 1 *Chr.* 21:17
1 *K.* 17:11 morsel of bread in *t. h.*
20:42 let out of *thy h.* a man
2 *K.* 4:29 take my staff in *thy h.*
8:8 take a present in *thy h.*
9:1 take this box of oil in *thy h.*
13:16 put thy *h.* upon the bow
1 *Chr.* 4:10 *t. h.* might be with me
29:12 in *thy h.* power
16 cometh of *thy h.*
2 *Chr.* 20:6 in *t. h.* is th. not p. ?
Ezr. 7:14 law of God is in *thy h.*
25 wisdom of G. that is in *t. h.*
Job 1:11 but put forth *thy h.* 2:5
12 put not forth *thy h.*
2:6 he is in *thy h.* save his life
10:7 none can del. out of *thy h.*
11:14 iniq. in *thy h.* put away
13:21 with. *thy h.* far from me
35:7 what receiv. he of *thy h. ?*
Ps. 10:12 O God, lift up *thy h.*
14 to requite it with *thy h.*
17:14 from men which are *thy h.*
21:8 *thy h.* sh. find out all ene.
31:5 into *thy h.* I com. my spirit
15 my times are in *thy h.*
32:4 day and night *thy h.* heavy
38:2 *thy h.* press. ; 39:10 blow of
74:11 why withd. thou *thy h. ?*
80:17 *t. h.* on man of *t.* right *h.*
104:28 openest *thy h.* 145:16
119:173 *t. h.* help ; 139:5 *t. h.* on
139:10 there shall *t. h.* lead me
144:7 send *thy h.* from above
Prov. 3:27 in power of *thy h.*
6:1 stricken *thy h.* with a stra.
30:32 lay *t. h.* upon thy mouth
Ec. 7:18 withdraw not *thy h.*
9:10 whats. *thy h.* findeth to do
11:6 in evening with. not *thy h.*
Is. 26:11 when *thy h.* is lifted up
42:6 I the Lord will hold *thy h.*
47:6 given my inheritance into
thy h.
51:22 out of *thy h.* cup of trem.
57:10 th. hast found life of *t. h.*
64:8 we are the work of *thy h.*
Jer. 6:9 back *t. h.* as grape-gath.
15:17 I sat alone bec. of *thy h.*
25:28 refuse to take cup at *t. h.*
36:14 take in *thy h.* the roll
40:4 chains wh. were upon *t. h.*
Ezek. 3:18 his blood will I require at *thy h.* 20; 33:8

6:11 smite with *thy h.*
10:2 fill *thy h.* with coals of fire
23:31 give her cup into *thy h.*
37:17 shall become one in *thy h.*
38:12 turn *thy h.* on des. places
Dan. 2:38 fowls given into *thy h.*
Mic. 5:9 *thy h.* shall be lift up on
12 cut off witchc. out of *thy h.*
Mal. 18:8 if *thy h.* off. *Mark* 9:43
John 20:27 reach *t. h.* and thrust
Acts 4:28 to do whatever *thy h.*
30 stretch. forth *thy h.* to heal

Your HAND.
Gen. 43:12 double money in *y. h.*
Ex. 12:11 your staff in *your h.*
23:31 inhab. of land into *y. h.*
Deut. 12:7 rej. in all put *y. h.* to
Jos. 8:7 deliver it into *your h.* 20
24:8 gave Amorites into *y. h.*
Jud. 3:28 Moabites ; 7:15 Midi.
2 *Sam.* 4:11 not req. blood of *y. h.*
2 *Chr.* 28:9 G. deliv. them to *y. h.*
Is. 1:12 require this at *your h. ?*
Jer. 26:14 I am in *your h.*
44:25 and fulfilled with *your h.*
Mal. 1:10 nor accept offering at
your h.
13 sho. I accept this of *y. h. ?*
2:13 rec. with good will at *y. h.*

HANDED. *See* LEFT, WEAK.

HANDBREADTH.
Ex. 25:25 a *h.* round about, 37:12
1 *K.* 7:26 sea a *h.* thick, 2 *Chr.* 4:5
Ps. 39:5 made my days as a *h.*
Ezek. 40:5 six cubits long and a *h.*

HAND broad.
Ezek. 40:43 hooks a *h. b.* fastened

HANDFUL.
Lev. 2:2 take thereout *h.* flour,
5:12 ; 6:15 ; 9:17 ; *Num.* 5:26
1 *K.* 17:12 *h.* of meal in a barrel
Ps. 72:16 a *h.* of corn in earth
Ec. 4:6 better is *h.* with quietn.
Jer. 9:22 as *h.* after harvest-man

HANDFULS.
Gen. 41:47 brought forth by *h.*
Ex. 9:8 *h.* of ashes of furnace
Ruth 2:16 let fall also some *h.*
1 *K.* 20:10 dust of S. suffice for *h.*
Ezek. 13:19 pol. for *h.* of barley ?

HANDIWORK.
Ps. 19:1 firmament show. his *h.*

HANDKERCHIEFS.
Acts 19:12 from body to sick *h.*

HANDLE, S.
Gen. 4:21 J. father such as *h.* harp
Jud. 5:14 that *h.* pen of writer
1 *Chr.* 12:8 *h.* spear, 2 *Chr.* 25:5
Ps. 115:7 hands, but they *h.* not
Cant. 5:5 myrrh on *h.* of lock
Jer. 2:8 that *h.* law knew me not
46:9 Libyans that *h.* the shield
Ezek. 27:29 all that *h.* the oar
Luke 24:39 *h.* me ; *Col.* 2:21 *h.* not

HANDLED.
Ezek. 21:11 furbished, may be *h.*
Mark 12:4 away shamefully *h.*
1 *John* 1:1 have *h.* of word of life

HANDLETH, ING.
Prov. 16:20 that *h.* matter wisely
Jer. 50:16 him that *h.* sickle
Ezek. 38:4 all of them *h.* swords
Amos 2:15 stand that *h.* bow
2 *Cor.* 4:2 not *h.* word of God

HANDMAID.
Gen. 16:1 Sarai had a *h.* Hagar
29:24 Zilpah to be L.'s *h.* 35:26
29 Bil. Rachel's *h.* 30:4 ; 35:25
Ex. 23:12 son of *h.* be refreshed
Jud. 19:19 bread and wine for *h.*
Ruth 2:13 spoken friendly to *h.*
3:9 answer. I am Ruth, thy *h.*

1 Sam. 1:11 affliction of h.
16 count not thy h. dau. of Bel.
18 let h. find grace in thy sight
25:24 let h. speak ; 30:13 h.
41 let thy h. wash feet of serv.
2 Sam. 14:6 thy h. had two sons
1 K. 1:13 didst swear to thy h. ?
3:20 while thy h. slept
2 K. 4:2 thy h. hath not anything
16 do not lie to thy h.
Ps. 86:16 save the son of thy h.
116:6 servant, and son of h.
Prov. 30:23 a h. heir to mistress
Luke 1:38 behold the h. of the L.

HANDMAIDEN.
Luke 1:48 reg. low estate of h

HANDMAIDS.
Gen. 33:1 divided children to h.
2 put h. and children foremost
Ruth 2:13 not like to one of h.
2 Sam. 6:20 uncov. in eyes of h.
Joel 2:29 on h. I pour S. Acts 2:18

HANDS.
Gen. 27:22 the h. are the h. of E.
49:24 h. made strong by h. of G.
Ex. 17:12 but Moses' h. heavy
Lev. 8:27 A. h. on his son's h.
Num. 6:19 put on h. of Nazarite
Deut. 4:28 gods, work of men's h.
27:15 ; 2 K. 19:18 ; 2 Chr. 32:19
9:15 tables of cov. in two h.
17 I cast th. out of my two h.
17:7 h. of witnesses first on him
Jud. 8:6 h. of Zeba and Zalm. 15
34 delivered them out of h. of
enemies, 1 Sam. 14:48
19:27 h. were upon threshold
2 Sam. 2:7 h. be str. Zec. 8:9, 13
16:21 h. of all shall be strong
2 K. 3:11 water on h. of Elijah
9:35 fou. skull and palms of h.
1 Chr. 25:2 under the h. of Asaph
3 h. of Jedu. 6 h. of father
2 Chr. 15:7 let not h. be weak
Ezr. 4:4 weakened h. of people
Job 4:3 strengthened weak h.
16:11 turned me into h. of wick.
17:3 will strike h. with me ?
9 clean h. shall be stronger
Ps. 24:4 he that hath clean h.
26:10 h. is mis. 47:1 clap h.
58:2 weigh the viol. of your h.

Ps. 68:31 Ethiopia stretch out h.
115:4 their idols the work of
men's h. 135:15 ; Is. 37:19
7 they have h. but handle not
134:2 lift up h. in the sanctuary
140:4 keep me fr. h. of wicked
Prov. 6:10 folding of h. 24:33
17 hate the h. shed inno. blo.
12:14 recompense of man's h.
14:1 foolish plucketh it with h.
17:18 striketh h. becom. surety
22:26 be not one that strike h.
30:28 spider taketh hold wi. h.
31:13 work. willing. with her h.
19 layeth her h. to the spindle
31 give her of the fruit of h.
Ec. 4:6 both h. full with travel
7:26 h. as ba. 10:18 idlen. of h.
Cant. 7:1 work of h. of workm.
Is. 1:15 spread your h. hide my
eyes, your h. full of blood
2:8 worship work of th. own h.
13:7 theref. shall all h. be faint
35:3 strengthen ye weak h.
45:9 he hath no h.
59:3 h. are defiled with blood
Jer. 4:31 spr. h. say. Woe is me
10:3 work of h. of workmen
9 and of the h. of the founder
23:14 they strengthen also h. of
evil-doers, Ezek. 13:22
33:13 under h. of him that tell.
38:4 weaken h. of men of war
48:37 upon all h. h. be cuttings

Lam. 1:17 Zion spreadeth her h.
4:2 the work of h. of the potter
10 h. of pitiful women have s.
Ezek. 7:17 h. sh. be feeble, 21:7
Dan. 2:34 stone cut without h. 45
Mic. 7:3 may do evil wi. both h.
Nah. 3:19 shall clap h. over thee
Hag. 2:17 lab. of h. I smote you
Zac. 4:9 h. of Zer. laid founda.
Mat. 15:20 unwa. h. Mark 7:2, 5
17:22 betra. into h. of men,
26:45 ; Mark 9:31 ; Luke 9:44
18:8 two h. c. into fire, Mark 9:43
Mark 14:58 temple made with h.
Luke 22:53 stretched forth no h.
24:7 delivered to h. of sinful m.
Acts 2:23 wicked h. have crucifi.
5:12 h. of apostles wonders wr.
7:48 not in te. made w. h. 17:2
8:18 laying on of the apostles' h.
11:30 by h. of Barnabas and S.
17:25 nei. worship. wi. men's h.
19:26 no gods are made with h.
20:34 h. minis. to my necessities
2 Cor. 5:1 house not made with h.
Eph. 2:11 circum. in flesh by h.
Col. 2:11 circumcision without h.
1 Thes. 4:11 study to work w. h.
1 Tim. 2:8 lifting up holy h.
4:14 h. of the presby. Heb. 6:2
Heb. 9:11 taberna. not made w. h.
24 not ent. place made with h
10:31 fall in h. of the living G.
12:12 wherefore lift up the h.
Jam. 4:8 cleanse your h. sinners

See CLAP.

His HANDS.
Gen. 27:23 his h. hairy as brother
48:14 guiding his h. wittingly
Ex. 17:12 A. and H. stayed h. h.
32:19 M. cast tables out of h. h.
Lev. 15:11 not rinsed h. h. in w.
16:21 lay both h. h. upon head
Num. 24:10 Balak smote h. h. to.
Deut. 33:11 accept work of h. h.
34:9 M. laid his h. upon Joshua
Jud. 9:16 accord. to des. of h. h.
1 Sam. 5:4 palms of h. h. cut off
14:13 Jona. climbed up on h. h.
1 K. 8:22 S. spread h. h. tow.
heaven, 38:54 ; 2 Chr. 6:12,
13, 29
16:7 pro. him with work of h. h.
2 K. 4:34 and put h. h. upon h. h.
13:16 put h. h. up. king's hands
Job 1:10 blessed work of his h.
5:18 and his h. make whole
20:10 h. h. restore their goods
34:37 clappeth h. h. among us
Ps. 9:16 wicked snared in h. h.
28:5 regard not opera. of h. h.
78:72 guided by skilful. of h. h.
81:6 h. h. were deliv. from pots
95:5 his h. formed dry land
111:7 works of h. h. are verity
Prov. 21:25 his h. refuse to labor
Ec. 4:5 fool fold. his h. together
Cant. 5:14 h. h. are as gold rings
Is. 3:11 reward of h. h. be given
5:12 nor consider opera. of h. h.
17:8 altars, work of h. h.
25:11 L. shall spread forth his h.
33:15 shaketh his h.
Jer. 30:6 man w. h. h. on loins?
Hab. 3:10 lifted his h. on high
Mat. 19:13 h. h. on th. Mark 10:16
27:24 washed h. h. be. multitude
Mark 8:23 his h. on his eyes
Luke 24:40 show. h. h. John 20:20
50 lifted up h. h. blessed them
John 13:3 given all th. into his h.
20:25 see in h. h. print of nails
Acts 9:17 putting his h. on him
12:1 Herod stretched forth his h.
7 his chains fell off from h. h.
2 Cor. 11:33 by wall, escap. h. h.
Eph. 4:28 working with h. h.

See LAY, LAID.

My HANDS.
Gen. 20:5 in innocency of my h.
Jud. 12:3 I put my life in my h.
2 Sam. 22:21 according to cleanness of my h. Ps. 18:20, 24
35 he teacheth my h. to war,
Ps. 18:34 ; 144:1
Neh. 6:9 O God, strengthen my h.
Job 9:30 make my h. ne. so clean
16:17 any injustice in my h.
31:7 any blot cleaved to my h.
Ps. 7:3 if there be iniq. in my h.
22:16 pierced my h. and my feet
26:6 wash my h. in innocency
28:2 lift my h. tow. thy oracle
63:4 lift my h. in thy name
73:13 I have washed my h.
119:48 my h. will I lift
141:2 lifting up my h. as even.
143:6 stretch forth my h.
Is. 19:25 bless. the work of my h.
45:11 concerning work of my h.
12 my h. stretched out heavens
49:16 on palms of my h.
60:21 people the work of my h.
65:2 I have spread out my h.
Dan. 3:15 del. you out of my h.
10:10 on the palms of my h.
Luke 24:39 he. my h. John 20:27
John 13:9 also my h. and head
Rom. 10:21 I stretched my h.
2 Tim. 1:6 by putting on of m. h.

Our HANDS.
Gen. 5:29 concerning toil of o. h.
Deut. 21:7 o. h. have not shed b.
Jos. 2:24 delivered into our h.
Jud. 13:23 a meat-off. at our h.
1 Sam. 17:47 give you into o. h.
Ps. 44:20 stretched out our h.
90:17 establish work of our h.
Jer. 6:24 our h. wax feeble
Lam. 3:41 our heart with our h.
Hos. 14:3 work of our h.
1 Cor. 4:12 work. with our own h.
1 John 1:1 our h. hand. word of

Their HANDS.
Ex. 29:10 put t. h. on head
15 put t. h. on head of ram, 19
Num. 8:10 put their h. on Levit.
12 lay their h. on the bullock
Deut. 1:25 brought fruit in t. h.
21:6 wash t. h. over the heifer
2 Sam. 4:12 they cut off their h.
2 K. 11:12 they clapped their h.
22:17 prov. me. to anger with
works of their h. 2 Chr. 34:25
Ezr. 1:6 strengthened their h.
5:8 work prospereth in their h.
6:22 strengthen t. h. in work
Neh. 2:18 streng. t. h. for work
6:9 their h. shall be weakened
Job 5:12 t. h. cannot perf. enter.
30:2 whereto stre. t. h. profit ?
Ps. 76:5 m. of mi. not found t. h.
91:12 angels bear thee in t. h.
125:3 lest right. put t. h. to in.
Is. 25:11 tog. with spoils of t. h.
59:6 act of violence is in t. h.
65:22 elect enjoy work of t. h.
Jer. 1:16 worshipped works of t. h.
32:30 prov. with works of t. h.
Ezek. 10:12 t. h. and wings full
23:37 blood is in their h. 45
Jon. 3:8 turn from viol. in t. h.
Hag. 2:14 ev. work of t. h. uncl.
Mat. 4:6 in their h. they shall
bear thee up, Luke 4:11
15:2 wash not t. h. wh. they eat
26:67 others smote him with the
palms of t. h. Mark 14:65
Mark 7:3 exc. wash t. h. eat not
Luke 6:1 rubbing them in t. h.
John 19:3 smote him with their h.
Acts 14:3 won. to. be done by t. h.

Rev. 7:9 wh. robes, palms in t. *h.*
9:20 repented not of wor. of t. *h.*
20:4 nor had rec. mark in t. *h.*

Thy HANDS.

Deut. 16:15 Lord shall bless thee
  in all works of *thy h.* 24:19
Jud. 7:11 afterw. *thy h.* be stren.
2 *Sam.* 3:34 t. *h.* were not bound
Job 10:3 to despise work of *h. ?*
  8 *thy h.* made and fashion. me
  14:15 desire to work of *thy h.*
  22:30 deliv. by pureness of t. *h.*
Ps. 8:6 domin. over works of t. *h.*
  102:25 heavens work of *thy h.*
  119:73 *thy h.* have made me
  128:2 shalt eat labor of *thy h.*
  138:8 forsake not works of t. *h.*
  143:5 I muse on work of *thy h.*
Jer. 2:37 *thy h.* on thy head
Lam. 2:19 lift *thy h.* for thy chil.
Mic. 5:13 no more worship t. *h.*
Zec. 13:6 wh. are these in t. *h. ?*
Luke 23:46 to *thy h.* I com. my
John 21:18 shalt stretch *thy h.*
Heb. 1:10 heavens work of *thy h.*
  2:7 set him over works of *thy h.*

HANDSTAVES.

Ezek. 39:9 shall burn the *h.*

HANDWEAPON.

Num. 35:18 smite him with *h.*

HANDWRITING.

Col. 2:14 blotting out the *h.*

HANG.

Gen. 40:19 Pharaoh shall *h.* thee
Num. 25:4 *h.* them bef. the Lord
Deut. 21:22 if thou *h.* him
  28:66 thy life shall *h.* in doubt
Est. 6:4 speak to *h.* Mordecai
  7:9 king said, *h.* him thereon
Is. 22:24 they sh. *h.* on him glory
Lam. 2:10 virgins *h.* their heads
Ezek. 15:3 take pin to *h.* any ves.
Mat. 22:40 on th. two *h.* all law
Acts 28:4 ven. beast *h.* on hand
Heb. 12:12 up hands wh. *h.* down

HANGED.

Gen. 40:22 *h.* chief baker, 41:13
Deut. 21:23 that is *h.* is accursed
2 *Sam.* 17:23 Ahitho. *h.* ; 18:10 A.
  21:9 seven sons of Saul *h.* they
Est. 2:23 chamberlains were *h.*
  7:10 *h.* Ham. ; 9:14 *h.* ten sons
Ps. 137:2 *h.* harps on willows
Lam. 5:12 princes *h.* by hands
Ezek. 27:10 *h.* the shield, 11
Mat. 18:6 bet. millst. were *h.* ab.
  his neck, *Mark* 9:42; *Lu.* 17:2
  27:5 Judas went and *h.* himself
Luke 23:39 thieves who were *h.*
Acts 5:30 and *h.* on tree, 10:39

HANGETH.

Job 26:7 *h.* earth upon nothing
Gal. 3:13 cursed ev. one *h.* on tr.

HANGING.

Jos. 10:26 *h.* on trees till evening

HANGING, Substantive.

Ex. 26:36 make *h.* for door of tent
  37 make for the *h.* five pillars
27:16 *h.* for court-gate, 38:18 ;
  39:40 ; 40:8, 33
35:15 *h.* for door enter. tabernacle, 36:37 ; 39:38 ; 40:5, 28

HANGINGS.

Ex. 27:9 *h.* 100 cub. 11 ; 38:9, 11
  12 shall be *h.* of 50 cubits, 18
35:17 *h.* of court, 38:9, 16, 18 ;
  39:40 ; *Num.* 3:26 ; 4:25
2 *K.* 23:7 women wove *h.* for gr.

HANNAH. 1 *Sam.* 1:2; 2:21

HANOCH. *Gen.* 25:4; 46:9;
  Num. 26:5 ; 1 *Chr.* 1:33; 5:3

HANUN.

2 *Sam.* 10:1 H. reig. 1 *Chr.* 19:4

Neh. 3:13 H. repaired val. gate, 30

HAPLY.

Mark 11:13 if *h.* he mi. find fruit
Luke 14:29 lest *h.* after laid fou.
Acts 5:39 lest *h.* found fight a. G.
  17:27 if *h.* they might feel

HAPPEN.

Prov. 12:21 no evil *h.* to the just
Is. 41:22 show us what shall *h.*

HAPPENED.

2 *Sam.* 1:6 as I *h.* by chance on
Jer. 44:23 therefore evil is *h.*
Rom. 11:25 blindness is *h.* to Is.
1 *Cor.* 10:11 th. *h.* for ensamples
Phil. 1:12 things *h.* me fallen
1 *Pet.* 4:12 strange thing *h.* to y.
2 *Pet.* 2:22 *h.* according to prov.

HAPPENETH.

Ec. 2:14 one ev. *h.* to them all
  15 as it *h.* to fool, so it *h.* to me
  9:11 time and chance *h.* to all

HAPPY.

Deut. 33:29 *h.* art thou, O Israel
1 *K.* 10:8 *h.* thy men, *h.* thy servants, 2 *Chr.* 9:7
Job 5:17 *h.* is man. wh. G. correc.
Ps. 127:5 *h.* man hath quiver full
  137:8 *h.* he who reward. thee, 9
  144:15 *h.* people in such a case,
    h. peo. whose God is the L.
  146:5 *h.* is he that hath G. of J.
Prov. 3:13 *h.* man find. wisdom
  14:21 *h.* he hath mercy on poor
  16:20 whoso trust. in L. *h.* is he
  28:14 *h.* is man that fear. alway
  29:18 that keepeth law, *h.* is he
Jer. 12:1 why *h.* deal treacher. ?
Mal. 3:15 we call the proud *h.*
Jon. 13:17 kn. things, *h.* if do th.
Rom. 14:22 *h.* is he that condemn.
Jam. 5:11 them *h.* who endure
1 *Pet.* 3:14 suffer for righte. *h.* ye
  4:14 reproached for Ch. *h.* ye

HAPPIER.

1 *Cor.* 7:40 she is *h.* if she abide

HARAN, *a man.*

Gen. 11:26 T. begat H. 27, 28, 31

HARAN, *a place.*

Gen. 11;31 Terah came to H. 32
  12:4 Abram departed out of H.
  27:43 flee to H. 28:10 ; 29:4
2 *K.* 19:12 fath. destr. H. *Is.* 37:12

HARBONAH. *Est.* 1:10 ; 7:9

HARD.

Gen. 18:14 any th. too *h.* for L. ?
  35:16 Rachel had *h.* labor, 17
Ex. 1:14 lives bit. with *h.* bond.
Deut. 1:17 cause too *h.* bring me
  17:8 matter too *h.* in judgment
  26:6 Egypt laid on *h.* bondage
2 *Sam.* 3:39 sons of Zeruiah too *h.*
1 *K.* 10:1 to prove with *h.* ques-
  tions, 2 *Chr.* 9:1
2 *K.* 2:10 thou hast asked *h.* th.
Job 41:24 as *h.* as piece of millst.
Ps. 60:3 showed peo. *h.* things
  94:4 how long wick. spe. *h.* th.
Prov. 13:15 way of transgr. is *h.*
Jer. 32:17 nothing too *h.* 27
Ezek. 3:5 to people of *h.* lang. 6
Mat. 25:24 I knew thou art *h.*
Mark 10:24 *h.* for th. tru. in rich.
John 6:60 this is a *h.* saying
Acts 9:5 *h.* to kick ag. pri. 26:14
Heb. 5:11 and *h.* to be uttered
2 *Pet.* 3:16 thi. *h.* to be underst.
Jude 15 convince of *h.* speeches

HARD, Adjective.

Lev. 3:9 rump off *h.* backbone
1 *Chr.* 19:4 cut garm. *h.* by but.
Ps. 63:8 followeth *h.* after thee
Jon. 1:13 rowed *h.* to br. to land
Acts 18:7 joined *h.* to synagogue

HARDEN.

Ex. 4:21 I will *h.* Pharaoh's
  heart, 7:3 ; 14:4
  14:17 *h.* hearts of Egyptians
Deut. 15:7 shalt not *h.* thy heart
Jos. 11:20 L. to *h.* their hearts
Job 6:10 *h.* myself in sorrow
Ps. 95:8 *h.* not your hearts, *Heb.*
  3:8, 15 ; 4:7

HARDENED.

Ex. 7:13 L. *h.* Phar.'s heart, 9:12 ;
  10:1, 20, 27 ; 11:10 ; 14:8
  14 he *h.* ; 22 was *h.* 8:19 ; 9:7, 35
  8:15 he *h.* his heart, 32 ; 9:34
Deut. 2:30 G. *h.* his spirit
2 *K.* 17:14 they *h.* their necks
Neh. 9:16 *h.* th. necks, 17, 29
Job 9:4 who hath *h.* himself.
  39:16 *h.* against her young ones
Is. 63:17 why hast thou *h.* heart?
Jer. 7:26 but *h.* their neck
Dan. 5:20 his mind *h.* in pride
Mark 6:52 for their heart was *h.*
  8:17 have ye your heart yet *h. ?*
John 12:40 blinded eyes, *h.* heart
Acts 19:9 when divers were *h.*
Heb. 3:13 lest any of you be *h.*

HARDENETH.

Prov. 21:29 wicked man *h.* face
  28:14 *h.* heart fall into mischief
  29:1 being reproved *h.* his neck
Rom. 9:18 whom he will *h.*

HARD-HEARTED.

Ezek. 3:7 house of Israel are *h.-h.*

HARDER.

Prov. 18:19 *h.* to be won th. city
Jer. 5:3 made faces *h.* than rock
Ezek. 3:9 *h.* than flint made fore.

HARDLY.

Is. 8:21 shall pass through it *h.*
Mat. 19:23 rich m. *h.* ent. kingd.
  of G. *Mark* 10:23 ; *Luke* 18:24
Luke 9:39 *h.* departeth from him

HARDNESS.

Job 38:38 dust groweth into *h.*
Mat 19:8 *h.* of hearts, *Mark* 10:5
Mark 3:5 grieved for *h.* of heart
Mark 16:14 upb. with *h.* of heart
Rom. 2:5 *h.* and impenitent heart
2 *Tim.* 2:3 *h.* as soldier of J. C.

HARE.

Lev. 11:6 *h.* is uncl. *Deut.* 14:7

HARLOT.

Gen. 34:31 d. wi. sister as wi. *h.*
  38:15 he thought her to be a *h.*
Lev. 21:14 high-priest not take *h.*
Jos. 2:1 spies came to *h.'s* house
  6:17 only Rahab the *h.* sh. live
Jud. 16:1 Sam. saw there a *h.*
Prov. 7:10 woman wi. attire of *h.*
Is. 1:21 faithful city become a *h.*
  23:15 after 70 years T. sing as *h.*
Jer. 2:20 wanderest, playing *h.*
  3:1 thou hast played the *h.* 6, 8
Ezek. 16:15 playedst the *h.*
  16 playedst *h.* ; 28 played *h.*
  41 cause to cease from play. *h.*
  23:5 Aholah played the *h.*
Hos. 2:5 mother hath played *h.*
  4:15 though Israel play the *h.*
Joel 3:3 given a boy for a *h.*
Mic. 1:7 return to the hire of *h.*
Nah. 3:4 whored. of well fav. *h.*
1 *Cor.* 6:15 make th. mem. of *h.*
  16 is joined to a *h.* is one body
Heb. 11:31 *h.* Rahab perished not
Jam. 2:25 R. the *h.* just. by wor.

HARLOTS.

Prov. 29:3 keepeth comp. with *h.*
Jer. 5:7 assemble troops in *h. h.*
Hos. 4:14 sacrifice with *h.*
Mat. 21:31 *h.* go into king. of G.
  32 publicans and *h.* believed *h.*
Luke 15:30 devoured liv. with *h.*

Rev. 17:5 Babylon, mother of *h.*

HARM.

Lev. 5:16 amends for *h.* done
2 *K.* 4:41 was no *h.* in the pot
1 *Chr.* 16:22 pro. no *h.* Ps. 105:15
Prov. 3:30 if he have done no *h.*
Jer. 39:12 do him no *h.*
Acts 16:28 no *h.* ; 27:21 gained *h.*
28:5 felt no *h.* ; 6 saw no *h.* ; 21
    spake any *h.*

HARM, Verb.

1 *Pet.* 3:13 *h.* you, if ful. of good .

HARMLESS.

Mat. 10:16 serp. and *h.* as doves
Phil. 2:15 may be *h.* sons of G.
Heb. 7:26 holy, *h.* and undefiled

HARNESS, Substantive.

2 *K.* 20:11 girdeth on *h.* boast
22:34 joints of *h.* 2 *Chr.* 18:33
2 *Chr.* 9:24 brought every man *h.*

HARNESS, ED, Verb.

Ex. 13:18 Israel went up *h.*
Jer. 46:4 *h.* horses, up horsemen

HAROD. *Jud.* 7:1
HAROSHETH. *Jud.* 4:2

HARP.

Gen. 4:21 fa. of th. th. handle *h.*
1 *Sam.* 10:5 meet proph. with *h.*
16:16 cunning player on *h.*
1 *Chr.* 25:3 prophesied with *h.*
Job 21:12 the timbrel and *h.*
30:31 *h.* is turned to mourning
Ps. 33:2 praise L. with *h.* 150:3
43:4 on the *h.* will I praise thee
49:4 open dark saying upon *h.*
57:8 psaltery and *h.* 108:2
71:22 I will sing with *h.* 92:3 ;
    98:5 ; 147:7 ; 149:3
81:2 bring hither the pleasant *h.*
Is. 5:12 *h.* and viol in their feasts
16:11 bowels sound like a *h.*
Dan. 3:5 sound of *h.* 7, 10, 15
1 *Cor.* 14:7 whether pipe or *h.*

HARPS.

2 *Sam.* 6:5 D. and Is. played *h.*
1 *K.* 10:12 made of almug-trees *h.*
Ps. 137:2 hanged *h.* upon willows
Rev. 5:8 every one of them *h.*
14:2 harp. with *h.* ; 15:2 *h.* of G.

See CYMBAL.

HARPED.

1 *Cor.* 14:7 kn. what piped or *h.* ?

HARPERS.

Rev. 14:2 I heard the voice of *h.*
18:22 voice of *h.* heard no more

HARROW.

Job 39:10 will he *h.* valleys.

HARROWS.

2 *Sam.* 12:31 under *h.* of iron
1 *Chr.* 20:3 cut with saws and *h.*

HART, S.

Deut. 12:15 may eat flesh of the
    h. 14:5 ; 15:22
Ps. 42:1 as *h.* panteth after water
Is. 35:6 lame man leap as a *h.*

Lam. 1:6 princes become like *h.*

See YOUNG.

HARVEST.

Gen. 8:22 earth rem. *h.* not cease
45:6 shall nei. be earing nor *h.*
Ex. 23:16 the feast of *h.* 34:22
Lev. 25:5 accord of *h.* not reap
1 *Sam.* 6:13 men reaping their *h.*
12:17 is it not wheat-*h.* to-day ?
Job 5:5 whose *h.* hungry eateth
Prov. 6:8 ant gather food in *h.*
10:5 sleepeth in *h.* caus. shame
26:1 snow in sum. as rain in *h.*
Is. 9:3 according to joy in *h.*
16:9 shouting for *h.* is fallen
17:11 *h.* be heap in day of grief
18:4 cloud of dew in heat of *h.*
5 afore *h.* when bud is perfect

23:3 *h.* of the river is her reven.
Jer. 5:17 they shall eat up thy *h.*
24 reserveth to us weeks of *h.*
8:20 *h.* is past, sum. is ended
Joel 1:11 the *h.* of field perished
3:13 in sickle, for the *h.* is ripe
Amos 9:37 yet three months to *h.*
Mat. 9:37 the *h.* is plenteous
38 pray L. *h.* to send, *Luke* 10:2
13:30 grow together until *h.*
39 the *h.* is end of the world
Mark 4:29 put in sickle, *h.* come
Luke 10:2 said, The *h.* is great
John 4:35 fields are white to *h.*
Rev. 14:15 the *h.* of earth is ripe

HARVEST-MAN.

Is. 17:5 when *h.* m. gather. corn
Jer. 9:22 the handful after *h.-m.*

Time of HARVEST.

Jos. 3:15 Jord. overfloweth *t. h.*
Prov. 25:13 cold of snow *t. of h.*
Jer. 50:16 handleth sickle in *h.-t.*
51:33 the *t. of* her *h.* shall come
Mat. 13:20 *t. of* *h.* say to reapers

HAST.

Mat. 19:21 sell all thou *h.* *Mark*
    10:21 ; *Luke* 18:22
25:25 there thou *h.* that is thine
John 6:68 *h.* words of eternal life
7:20 thou *h.* a devil, 8:48, 52
Rom. 14:22 *h.* thou faith ?
1 *Cor.* 4:7 what *h.* thou that did.
Jam. 2:18 thou *h.* faith
Rev. 2:6 but this thou *h.*
8 *h.* a little strength, 3:1, 4
11 hold that fast which thou *h.*

HASTE, Substantive.

Ex. 12:11 ye shall eat in *h.*
33 out of land in *h.* *Deut.* 16:3
1 *Sam.* 21:8 king's business re-
    quired *h.*
Ps. 31:22 said in *h.* I am cut off
116:11 I said in *h.* All men liars
Is. 52:12 shall not go out with *h.*
Dan. 3:24 king rose in *h.*
6:19 went in *h.* to den of lions
Mark 6:25 came in *h.* to the king
Luke 1:39 went to hill-cou. w. *h.*

HASTE.

Gen. 19:22 *h.* thee, escape thither
1 *Sam.* 23:27 *h.* thee, for Philis.
Ps. 22:19 strength, *h.* to help me

See MAKE HASTE.

HASTED.

Gen. 18:7 and he *h.* to dress it
Jos. 4:10 people *h.* over Jordan
10:13 the sun *h.* not to go down
1 *Sam.* 17:48 David *h.* and ran to
25:23 Abigail saw Da. she *h.* 42
28:24 the witch at Endor *h.*
1 *K.* 20:41 prophet *h.* and took
2 *Chr.* 26:20 himself *h.* to go out
Est. 6:12 Haman *h.* to his house
14 they *h.* to bring Haman
Job 31:5 foot hath *h.* to deceit
Ps. 48:5 and *h.* away, 104:7
Acts 20:16 Paul *h.* to Jerusalem

HASTEN.

Ps. 16:4 *h.* after another god
55:8 I would *h.* my escape
Ec. 2:25 who can *h.* more than I ?
Is. 60:22 L. will *h.* in his time
Jer. 1:12 I will *h.* my word

HASTENED, ETH.

Est. 3:15 being *h.* by king, 8:14
Is. 51:14 the exile *h.* be loosed
Jer. 17:16 not *h.* fr. being pastor

HASTETH.

Job 9:26 as eagle that *h.* to prey
Prov. 7:23 as a bird *h.* to snare
19:2 he that *h.* wi. his feet sin.
28:22 *h.* to be rich, hath evil eye
Ec. 1:5 sun *h.* to where he arose
Hab. 1:8 fly as eagle that *h.*

Zep. 1:14 day of Lord *h.* greatly

HASTILY.

Jud. 2:23 without driving th. *h.*
Prov. 20:21 inheritance gotten *h.*
25:8 go not forth *h.* to strive
John 11:31 saw Mary she rose *h.*

HASTING.

Is. 16:5 and *h.* righteousness
2 *Pet.* 3:12 *h.* to day of the Lord

HASTY.

Prov. 14:29 *h.* of spirit exal. folly,
29:20 a man *h.* in words ?
Ec. 5:2 let not thy heart be *h.*
7:9 be not *h.* in thy spirit
8:3 not too *h.* to go out of sight
Is. 28:4 as *h.* fruit before summer
Dan. 2:15 why is decree so *h.* ;
Hab. 1:6 bitter and *h.* nation

HATCH, ETH.

Is. 34:15 owl shall *h.* and gather
59:5 they *h.* cockatrice's eggs
Jer. 17:11 as partridge on eggs *h.*

HATE.

Gen. 24:60 possess of those th. *h.*
Lev. 19:17 shalt not *h.* brother
26:17 th. *h.* you sh. reign over
Num. 10:35 let them that *h.* thee
Deut. 22:13 go unto her and *h.*
24:3 if the latter husband *h.* her
2 *Chr.* 19:2 love them that *h.* L.?
Job 8:22 *h.* thee clothed with sh.
Ps. 21:8 find those that *h.* thee
34:21 th. *h.* righteous sh. be des.
68:1 that *h.* him flee before him
83:2 *h.* thee have lifted up head
89:23 plague them that *h.* him
97:10 ye that love Lord *h.* evil
105:25 turned their heart to *h.*
129:5 let th. be turned that *h.* Z.
Prov. 1:22 fools. will ye *h.* know.
6:16 these six doth the Lord *h.*
8:13 fear of the Lord is to *h.* evil
9:8 rep. not scorner, lest *h.* thee
19:7 all brethren of poor *h.* him
29:10 bloodthirsty *h.* the uprig.
Ec. 3:8 time to l. and time to *h.*
Amos 5:10 they *h.* him that reb.
15 *h.* the evil, love the good
Mic. 3:2 *h.* good, and love evil
Mat. 5:43 love neigh. *h.* enemy
44 good to th. *h.* y. *Luke* 6:27
6:24 he will *h.* one, *Luke* 16:13
24:10 betray and *h.* one another
Luke 1:71 saved from hand th. *h.*
6:22 blessed are ye when men *h.*
14:26 *h.* not his father
John 7:7 the world cannot *h.* you
15:18 world *h.* you, 1 *John* 3:13
Rev. 17:16 these shall *h.* whore

I HATE.

1 *K.* 22:8 *I h.* him, 2 *Chr.* 18:7
Ps. 101:3 *I h.* work of them
119:104 *I h.* every false way, 128
113 *I h.* vain th. thy law I love
163 *I h.* and abhor lying
139:21 *I h.* them that hate thee ?
22 *I h.* them with perfect hatr.
Prov. 8:13 froward mouth do *I h.*
Is. 61:8 *I h.* robbery for burnt-off.
Jer. 44:4 do not this thing *I h.*
Amos 5:21 *I h.* your feast-days
Zec. 8:17 these are things *I h.*
Rom. 7:15 what *I h.* that do I
Rev. 2:6 deeds of Nicolait. *I h.* 15

HATE me.

Gen. 26:27 come, seeing *h. me* ?
Ex. 20:5 to third and fourth gen.
    of them that *h. me*, *Deut.* 5:9
Deut. 32:41 rew. them that *h. me*
2 *Sam.* 22:41 destroy them that
    h. me, *Ps.* 18:40
Ps. 9:13 suff. of them that *h. me*
25:19 *h. me* with cruel hatred
35:19 let them wink that *h. me*
38:19 *h. me* wrong. many, 69:4

41:7 all that *h. me* whisper tog.
69:14 deliv. fr. them that *h. me*
118:7 see desire on th. that *h. me*
Prov. 8:36 they that *h. me*

HATED.

Gen. 27:41 Esau *h.* Jacob
37:4 *h.* Joseph yet the more, 5, 8
49:23 shot at him and *h.* him
Deut. 1:27 bec. Lord *h.* us, 9:28
4:42 *h.* him n. 19:4, 6; *Jos.* 20:5
21:17 sh. acknowledge son of *h.*
Jud. 15:2 I thought thou *h.* her
2 *Sam.* 5:8 lame and blind are *h.*
Est. 9:1 rule them that *h.* them
Ps. 26:5 *h.* congreg. of evil-doers
31:6 I *h.* them that regard lying
44:7 put them to shame that *h.*
106:41 they that *h.* them ruled
Prov. 1:29 they *h.* knowledge
5:12 how have I *h.* instruction !
14:17 man of wicked dev. is *h.*

Prov. 14:20 poor is *h.* even of nei.
Ec. 2:17 *h.* life ; I *h.* labor
Is. 60:15 been forsaken and *h.*
Jer. 12:8 have I *h.* my heritage
Ezek. 16:37 gather them thou *h.*
35:6 since thou hast not *h.* blood
Hos. 9:15 *h.* them for wicked.
Mat. 1:3 I *h.* Esau, *Rom.* 9:13
Mat. 10:22 ye shall be *h.* *Mark*
13:13 ; *Luke* 21:17
24:9 ye shall be *h.* of all nations
Luke 19:14 his citizens *h.* him
John 15:18 it *h.* me bef. it *h.* you
24 seen and *h.* both me and F.
25 they *h.* me without a cause
17:14 the world hath *h.* them
Eph. 5:29 no man *h.* own flesh
Heb. 1:9 thou hast *h.* iniquity

HATEFUL, LY.

Ps. 36:2 iniq. be found to be *h.*
Ezek. 23:29 sh. deal with theo *h.*
Tit. 3:3 *h.* hating one another
Rev. 18:2 cage uncl. and *h.* bird

HATERS.

Ps. 81:15 *h.* of L. should submit
Rom. 1:30 backbiters, *h.* of God

HATEST.

2 *Sam.* 19:6 and *h.* thy friends
Ps. 5:5 *h.* workers of iniquity
45:7 lov. righte. *h.* wickedness
50:17 thou *h.* instruction
Rev. 2:6 *h.* deeds of Nicolaitans

HATETH.

Deut. 7:10 not slack to him *h.*
16:22 nor set up image Lord *h.*
Job 34:17 sh. he who *h.* right go.?
Ps. 11:5 loveth viol. his soul *h.*
120:6 dwelt him that *h.* peace
Prov. 11:15 *h.* suretyship is sure
12:1 he that *h.* reproof is brutish
13:5 a righteous man *h.* lying
24 he that spareth rod *h.* son
15:10 that *h.* reproof shall die
27 he that *h.* gifts shall live
26:24 that *h.* dissemb. with lips
28 lying tongue *h.* those afflic.
28:16 *h.* cove. sh. prolong days
29:24 partner with thief *h.* soul
Is. 1:14 appo. feasts my soul *h.*
Mal. 2:16 he *h.* putting away
John 3:20 ev. one doeth evil *h.* l.
7:7 me world *h.* bec. I testify
12:25 *h.* life in world sh. keep it
15:19 not of world, world *h.* you
23 *h.* me *h.* my Father also
1 *John* 2:9 *h.* bro. is in darkn. 11
3:15 *h.* his brother is murderer
4:20 I love G. *h.* brother, is liar

HATING.

Ex. 18:21 *h.* covetousness
Tit. 3:3 and *h.* one another
Jude 23 *h.* garm. spotted by flesh

HATH.

Prov. 23:29 who *h.* woe? who *h.*
sorrow? who *h.* wounds?
Is. 45:9 *h.* no ha. 50:10 no light
55:1 *h.* no money, buy and eat
Jer. 49:1 *h.* I. no sons? *h.* no heir?
Mat. 8:20 *h.* not where to lay his
head, *Luke* 9:58
11:15 he that *h.* ears to hear.
13:9, 43 ; *Mark* 4:9 ; *Luke* 8:8 ;
14:35 ; *Rev.* 2:7'
13:12 whoso. *h.* to him shall be
giv. who *h.* not, sh. be taken
that he *h.* 25:29 ; *Mark* 4:25 ;
Luke 8:18 ; 19:26
44 selleth all he *h.* buyeth field
1 *John* 5:12 he that *h.* the Son *h.*
life, *h.* not Son. *h.* not life
2 *John* 9 abideth not in Ch. *h.* not
G. abideth *h.* Father and S.

HATRED.

Num. 35:20 he thrust him of *h.*
Ps. 25:19 hate me with cruel *h.*
109:3 comp. me about with *h.*
5 rewarded me *h.* for my love
139:22 hate them with perf. *h.*
Prov. 10:12 *h.* stirreth up strifes
18 hideth *h.* with lying lips
15:17 than stalled ox and *h.*
Ec. 9:1 know. either love or *h.*
6 their *h.* and envy perished
Ezek. 25:15 destroy it for old *h.*
35:5 thou hast had perpetual *h.*
Hos. 9:8 proph. is *h.* in ho. of G.
Gal. 5:20 witchcraft, *h.* variance

HATS.

Dan. 3:21 bound in hosen and *h.*

HAUGHTY.

2 *Sam.* 22:28 th. eyes are upon *h.*
Ps. 131:1 L. my heart is not *h.*
Prov. 16:18 *h.* spirit before a fall
18:12 before destruction heart *h.*
21:24 *h.* scorner is his name
Is. 3:16 daughters of Zion are *h.*
24:4 the *h.* people of the earth
Zep. 3:11 no more *h.*

HAUGHTINESS.

Is. 2:11 *h.* of men bowed down
17 *h.* of men shall be made low
13:11 lay low the *h.* of wicked
16:6 heard *h.* of Moab, *Jer.* 48:29

HAUNT, Substantive.

1 *Sam.* 23:22 see where his *h.* is

HAUNT.

1 *Sam.* 30:31 where D. wont to *h.*
Ezek. 26:17 ter. be on all that *h.*

HAVE. See COMPASSION, DO-
MINION, *etc.*

HAVEN.

Gen. 49:13 Zebulun dwell at *h.*
Ps. 107:30 bringeth to desired *h.*
Acts 27:12 *h.* not commodious

HAVOC.

Acts 8:3 S. made *h.* of the church

HAWK.

Lev. 11:16 *h.* abom. *Deut.* 14:15
Job 39:26 doth *h.* fly by wisdom ?

HAY.

Prov. 27:25 *h.* appear. and grass
Is. 15:6 the *h.* is withered away
1 *Cor.* 3:12 buildeth on found. *h.*

HAZAEL.

1 *K.* 19:15 ano. H. to be king, 17
2 *K.* 8:9 H. went to meet Elisha
10:32 H. smote them, *Amos* 1:4
12:17 H. set face to go to Jeru.
13:3 Israel into the hand of H.

HAZEL.

Gen. 30:37 Jacob took rods of *h.*

HAZELELPONI. 1 *Chr.* 4:3
HAZEROTH. *Num.* 11:35 ; 12:16 ;
33:17

HAZOR.

Jos. 11:10 Joshua took H.
Jud. 4:2 ; 1 *K.* 9:15 ; 2 *K.* 15:29
Jer. 49:30 dwell deep, inh. of H.

HE.

Gen. 3:16 H. shall rule over thee
49:8 h. whom bret. shall praise
Deut. 32:39 I am h. and there is
no God with me. *Is.* 41:4 ;
43:10, 13 ; 46:4 ; 48:12
Mat. 24:26 h. is in desert
Mark 12:32 is none other but h.
Luke 24:6 said, h. is not here
John 1:15 h. of whom I spake, 30
7:11 wh. is h. ? 25 is not this h. ?
8:28 then shall ye kn. th. I am h.
9:9 is h. but h. said, I am h.
36 and said, Who is h. L. ? 37
1 *Cor.* 10:22 we stronger than h. ?

See BLESSED, DID, SAITH.

HEAD.

Gen. 3:15 it shall bruise thy h.
40:13 Ph. sh. lift up thy h. 19
49:26 blessings on head of Jos.
and on top of h. *Deut.* 33:16
Ex. 29:10 A. and sons put hands
on h. of bul. *Lev.* 4:4 ; 8:14
15 Aar. and sons put hands on
h. of ram, 19 ; *Lev.* 8:18, 22
Lev. 1:4 hand on h. of b.-offering
3:2 lay hand on h. of offering
4:29 hand on h. of s.-offering, 33
13:45 clothes rent, and his h. b.
19:32 shalt rise before hoary h.
21:5 not make bald. on their h.
Num. 5:18 priest uncov. wo. h.
6:5 no razor come on Nazar. h.
7 consecration of God on his h.
9 sh. shave h. 18 ; *Deut.* 21:12
Jud. 13:5 no razor come on h.
1 *Sam.* 17:57 Goliath's h. in hand
31:9 and they cut off Saul's h.
28:2 make the keeper of my h.
2 *Sam.* 1:2 earth upon h. 15:32
3:8 and said, Am a dog's h. ?
16:9 take off his h.
2 *K.* 2:3 master from h. to-day, 5
4:19 said to his fa. My h. my h.
6:31 h. of E. shall stand on him
19:21 dau. of Jeru. hath shaken
her h. at thee, *Is.* 37:22
2 *Chr.* 6:23 recompens. way on h.
Ezr. 9:6 iniq. increased over h.
Neh. 4:4 turn reproach on own h.
Est. 9:25 device ret. on own h.
Job 1:20 shaved h. and fell down
10:15 yet will I not lift up my h.
16:4 I could shake my h. at you
Ps. 3 the lifter up of my h.
7:16 mischief return on own h.
22:7 shoot out lip, shake the h.
23:5 anointest my h. with oil
27:6 now sh. my h. be lifted up
Ps. 38:4 iniq. gone over my h.
60:7 Ephr. strength of h. 108:8
68:21 G. shall wound h. of ene.
110:7 therefore sh. he lift up h.
140:9 h. of those that comp. me
141:5 which shall not break h.
Prov. 10:6 blessings on h. of just
11:26 blessing on h. selleth corn
25:22 of fire on h. *Rom.* 12:20
Ec. 2:14 wise man's eyes in h.
Cant. 2:6 hand under my h. 8:3
5:2 my h. is filled with dew
11 h. as fine gold ; 7:5 h. as C.
Is. 1:5 the whole h. is sick
51:11 everlasting joy on their h.
58:5 bow down h. as a bulrush ?
59:17 helmet of salvation on h.
Jer. 2:37 and thy hands on thy h.
9:1 O that my h. were waters
Ezek. 9:10 recompense way on h.
29:18 every h. was made bald
Dan. 2:38 thou art this h. of gold
Joel 3:4 recompense on your h. 7

Amos 2:7 dust on *h.* of the poor
8:10 bring baldness on every *h.*
9:1 he said, Cut them in the *h.*
Zec. 1:21 no man did lift up *h.*
6:11 set crowns on *h.* of Joshua
Mat. 5:36 neither swear by thy *h.*
27:30 sm. him on *h. Mark* 15:19
Mark 6:24 *h.* of John the Baptist
Luke 7:46 *h.* wi. oil didst not an.
John 13:9 also my hands and *h.*
1 *Cor.* 11:4 *h.* cov. dishonoreth
10 ought to ha. power on her *h.*
12:21 the *h.* to the feet
Eph. 1:22 gave him *h.* to church,
4:15 ; *Col.* 1:8
Col. 2:19 holding *h.* from body
Rev. 19:12 on *h.* many crowns

See BEARD, BALD, BOW, BOWED,
COVER, COVERED, CROWN.

Bed's HEAD.
Gen. 47:31 bowed himse. on *b. h.*

HEAD of the corner.
Mat. 21:42 beco. *h. Mark* 12:10 ;
Lu. 20:17 ; *Acts* 4:11 ; 1 *Pet.* 2:7

HEAD, for ruler, governor.
Num. 17:3 one rod *h.* of house
Deut. 28:13 L. will make thee *h.*
44 sh. be *h.* and thou the tail
Jud. 11:9 I your *h. ? * 11 him *h.*
2 *Sam.* 22:44 thou hast kept me
to be *h. Ps.* 18:43
Is. 7:8 *h.* of Damascus is Rezin, 9
9:14 cut off from Is. *h.* and tail
15 ancient and honorable is *h.*
Jer. 22:6 Gilead to me, *h.* of Leb.
Hos. 1:11 ap. themselves one *h.*
Hab. 3:13 *h.* out of ho. of wicked
14 strike through *h.* of villages
1 *Cor.* 11:3 *h.* of man is Ch. *h.* of
woman man, *h.* of Ch. is G.
Eph. 5:23 husband is *h.* of wife,
even as Christ is *h.* of church
Col. 2:10 who *h.* of principality

HEAD, for top, chief.
Is. 28:1 on *h.* of fat valleys, 4
51:20 lie at the *h.* of all streets
Ezek. 16:25 built places at *h.*
21:21 king stood at *h.* of 2 ways

HEAD, with hair, s.
Lev. 13:40 *h.* is fallen off *h.* 41
14:9 leper shave *hair* off his *h.*
Num. 6:5 locks of *h.* of *h.* grow
18 take *h.* of *h.* of his separat.
Jud. 16:22 of *h.* began to grow
1 *Sam.* 14:45 not *h.* of *h.* fall gr.
2 *Sam.* 14:26 *h.* of *h.* at 200 shek.
Ezr. 9:3 plucked off *h.* of my *h.*
Ps. 40:12 more than *h.* of *h.* 69:4
Cant. 7:5 *h.* of thy *h.* like purple
Dan. 3:27 nor *hair* of *h.* singed
7:9 *h.* of his *h.* like pure wool
Mat. 10:30 *h.* of your *h.* number.
Luke 12:7
Luke 7:38 wipe with *h.* of *h.* 44
21;18 shall not a *h.* of *h.* perish
Acts 27:34 nor a *hair* fall from *h.*
Rev. 1:14 his *h.* and *h.* were white

HEADBANDS.
Is. 3:20 take away *h.*

HEADLONG.
Job 5:13 counsel of frow. car. *h.*
Luke 4:29 cast him down *h.*
Acts 1:18 falling *h.* he burst asu.

Spear's HEAD.
1 *Sam.* 17:7 *spear's h.* weighed
600 shekels, 2 *Sam.* 21:16

HEADSTONE.
Ps. 118:22 be *h.* of corner
Zec. 4:7 bring *h.* with shoutings

HEADS.
Gen. 43:28 bowed th. *h. Ex.* 4:31
Lev. 10:6 uncover not your *h.*
1 *K.* 20:31 let us put ropes on *h.*
32 put ropes on their *h.*

2 *K.* 10:6 *h.* of your master's sons
8 brought the *h.* of king's sons
Ps. 24:7 lift your *h.* O ye gates, 9
66:12 men to ride over our *h.*
74:13 breakest the *h.* of dragon
14 brakest the *h.* of leviathan
109:25 shaked their *h.*
Is. 15:2 on their *h.* be baldness
35:10 everlasting joy on their *h.*
Jer. 14:3 they covered their *h.*
Ezek. 7:18 bald. sh. be on their *h.*
11:21 recomp. way on *h.* 22:31
32:27 laid swords under *h.*
44:18 linen bonnets on their *h.*
20 they shall poll their *h.*
Mat. 27:39 wag. *h. Mark* 15:29
Luke 21:28 and lift up your *h.*
Acts 18:6 yo. blood be on your *h.*
Rev. 9:7 their *h.* as it were cro.
13:1 a beast having seven *h.*
3 I saw one of his *h.* wounded
17:9 seven *h.* seven mountains
18:19 they cast dust on their *h.*

HEADS, for governors.
Ex. 18:25 made th. *h.* over peo.
Num. 25:4 take all the *h.* of peo.
Ps. 110:6 wound *h.* over countr.
Mic. 3:1 hear, O *h.* of Jacob, 9
11 *h.* thereof judge for reward

See FATHERS.

HEADY.
2 *Tim.* 3:4 men be *h.* high-mind.

HEAL.
Deut. 32:39 I kill, I wound, I *h.*
2 *K.* 20:5 *h.* thee, add to thy da.
2 *Chr.* 7:14 forgive sin. *h.* land
Ps. 6:2 *h.* me, for bones are vex.
41:4 *h.* my soul, I have sinned
60:2 *h.* the breaches thereof
Ex. 3:3 time to kill, time to *h.*
Is. 57:18 seen ways, and *h.* 19
Jer. 3:22 I will *h.* your backslid.
17:14 *h.* me, O Lord
30:17 I will *h.* thee of wounds
Lam. 2:13 br. great, who can *h. ?*
Hos. 6:1 ha. torn, and will *h.* us
14:4 I will *h.* their backslidings
Mat. 8:7 I will come and *h.* him
10:8 *h.* the sick, *Luke* 9:2 ; 10:9
12:10 *h.* on sab.-day *Luke* 14:3
13:15 be converted and I sho. *h.*
them, *John* 12:40 ; *Acts* 28:27
Mark 3:2 *h.* on sabbath, *Luke* 6:7
Luke 4:18 to *h.* broken-hearted
23 Physician, *h.* thyself
John 4:47 come down and *h.*
Acts 4:30 stretching hand to *h.*

HEALED.
Ex. 21:19 sh. cause him to be *h.*
Lev. 13:18 boil *h.* ; 37 scall is *h.*
14:3 plague of leprosy be *h.* 48
2 *K.* 2:21 *h.* waters ; 22 waters *h.*
2 *Chr.* 30:20 L. heark. and *h.* pe.
Ps. 30:2 cried to thee, thou *h.*
107:20 sent his word and *h.* th.
Is. 6:10 and convert, and be *h.*
53:5 with his stripes we are *h.*
Jer. 6:14 have *h.* the hurt, 8:11
17:14 and I shall be *h.*
51:9 we would have *h.* Babylon
Ezek. 34:4 neither have *h.* sick
47:8 the marshes shall be *h.* 9
11 the marshes shall not be *h.*
Hos. 7:1 when I would have *h.*
11:3 knew not that I *h.* them
Mat. 4:24 palsy, and he *h.* them
8:8 my serv. shall be *h. Lu.* 7:7
12:15 follow. he *h.* them, 14:14
Luke 8:43 nor could be *h.* of any
13:14 therefore come and be *h.*
17:15 saw he was *h.* turned ba.
22:51 touch. his ear and *h.* him
John 5:13 *h.* wist not who it was
Acts 4:14 beh. man who was *h.*
14:9 that he had faith to be *h.*
Heb. 12:13 but let it rather be *h.*

Jam. 5:16 pray that ye may be *h.*
1 *Pet.* 2:24 wh. stri. ye were *h.*
Rev. 13:3 deadly wo. was *h.* 12

HEALER.
Is. 3:7 saying, I will not be a *h.*

HEALETH.
Ex. 15:26 the L. that *h.* thee
Ps. 103:3 bless Lord who *h.* dis.
147:3 he *h.* the broken in heart
Is. 30:26 *h.* stroke of th. wound

HEALING, Substantive.
Jer. 14:19 there is no *h.* for us
Nah. 3:19 th. is no *h.* thy bruise
Mal. 4:2 with *h.* in his wings
Luke 9:11 healed them need *h.*
Acts 4:22 miracle of *h.* showed

1 *Cor.* 12:9 another gift of *h.* 28
30 have all the gifts of *h. ?*
Rev. 22:2 leaves for *h.* of nations

HEALING.
Jer. 30:13 thou hast no *h.* medic.
Mat. 4:23 *h.* all man. of sickness
Luke 9:6 preach. gos. *h.* everyw.
Acts 10:38 *h.* all oppressed

HEALTH.
Gen. 43:28 our father in good *h.*
2 *Sam.* 20:9 in *h.* my brother ?
Ps. 42:11 *h.* of my count. 43:5
67:2 saving *h.* may be known
Prov. 3:8 it sh. be *h.* to thy nav.
4:22 they are *h.* to their flesh
12:18 tongue of the wise is *h.*
13:17 a faithful ambassador is *h.*
16:24 sweet to soul, *h.* to bones
Is. 58:8 thy *h.* shall spring forth
Jer. 8:15 looked for a time of *h.*
22 not *h.* of my peo. recover. ?
30:17 I will restore *h.* unto thee
Acts 27:34 take meat, this is *h.*
3 *John* 2 mayest be in *h.*

HEAP, Substantive.
Gen. 31:46 a *h.* eat on the *h.*
52 this *h.* be witness
Ex. 15:8 floods stood as *h. Jos.*
3:13, 16 ; *Ps.* 33:7 ; 78:13
Deut. 13:16 shall be a *h.* for ever
Jos. 7:26 over him *h.* of stones
Ruth 3:7 lie down at *h.* of corn
2 *Sam.* 18:17 great *h.* on Absal.
Cant. 7:2 belly like *h.* of wheat
Is. 17:11 harvest shall be a *h.*
25:2 hast made of a city a *h.*
Jer. 30:18 city builded on own *h.*
Mic. 1:6 Samaria a *h.* of the field
Hab. 3:15 walk thro' *h.* of waters
Hag. 2:16 came to *h.* of 20 meas.

HEAP, Verb.
Deut. 32:23 *h.* misch. upon them
Job 16:4 *h.* up words against you
27:16 he *h.* up silver as the dust
36:13 hypocrites in heart *h.* wr.
Prov. 25:22 *h.* coals, *Rom.* 12:20
Ec. 2:26 to gather and to *h.* up
Ezek. 24:10 *h.* on wood, kindle
Hab. 1:10 sh. *h.* dust and take it
2 *Tim.* 4:3 *h.* to themsel. teach.

HEAPED, ETH.
Ps. 39:6 he *h.* up riches
Hab. 2:5 *h.* unto him all people
Jam. 5:3 have *h.* treasure toget.

HEAPS.
Jud. 15:16 jaw of ass, *h.* on *h.*
2 *K.* 10:8 lay ye them in two *h.*
2 *Chr.* 31:6 and laid them by *h.*
Job 15:28 houses ready to bec. *h.*
Ps. 79:1 laid Jerusalem on *h.*
Jer. 9:11 make Jerusal. *h.* 26:18
31:21 set thee up, make high *h.*
Hos. 12:11 their altars are as *h.*
Mic. 3:12 Jerus. shall become *h.*

HEAR.
Gen. 21:6 all that *h.* laugh
Ex. 32:18 them that sing do I *h.*

Num. 23:18 ri. up, Balak, and *h.*
30:4 *h.* her vow and her bond
Deut. 1:16 *h.* causes betw. breth.
  4:10 make them *h.* my words
  5:1 *h.* Is. the statutes, 6:3; 9:1;
    20:3; *Is.* 48:1; *Mark* 12:29
  27 *h.* all the L. our G. doth say
  12:28 *h.* these words, I com.
  13:12 shall *h.* say in one of cit.
  30:12 bring it that we may *h.*
  31:12 *h.* and fear L. 13 ; *Jer.* 6:10
Jos. 3:9 *h.* the words of the L.
Jud. 5:3 *h.* O ye kings, give ear
1 *Sam.* 2:23 *h.* your evil dealings
  15:14 low. of oxen which I *h.*
  16:2 if Saul *h.* it, he will kill me
2 *Sam.* 20:16 cr. out of city, *h. h.*
  22:45 soon as *h. Ps.* 18:44
1 *K.* 4:34 *h.* wisdom of Solomon,
  10:8, 24 ; 2 *Chr.* 9:7, 23 ; *Mat.*
  12:42 ; *Luke* 11:31
  8:30 *h.* in heaven and forg. 32,
    34, 36, 39, 43, 45, 49 ; 2 *Chr.* 6:21
  18:26 saying, O Baal, *h.* us
2 *K.* 7:6 *h.* a noise of chariots
  18:28 *h.* the word of the great
    King, *Is.* 36:13 ; 37:17
1 *Chr.* 14:15 wh. thou *h.* sound
Neh. 1:6 *h.* the prayer of servant
  4:4 *h.* O God, we are despised
  8:2 could *h.* with understand
Job 5:27, *h.* it, and know thou it
  13:17 *h.* dilig. my speech, 21:2
  27:9 *h.* his cry ? 34:2 *h.* words
  42:4 *h.* I beseech thee
Ps. 4:1 *h.* my prayer, O G. 39:12 ;
  54:2 ; 84:8 ; 102:1 ; 143:1
  20:1 *h.* thee in day of troub.
Ps. 20:9 let the king *h.* us
  27:7 *h.* O Lord, when I cry
  30:10 *h.* O L. and have mercy
  49:1 *h.* this all ye people
  50:7 *h.* peo. I will speak. 81:8
  51:8 make me *h.* joy and gladn
  59:7 who. say they, doth *h. ?*
  61:1 *h.* my cry, O God
  66:16 *h.* all ye that fear God
  102:20 *h.* groaning of prisoner
  138:4 *h.* words of thy mouth
  143:8 to *h.* thy loving-kindness
Prov. 1:8 *h.* instruction of father
  4:1 *h.* ye children, instruction
  10 *h.* and rec. sayings, 19:20
  8:6 *h.* I speak of excel. things
  33 *h.* instruction, and be wise
  19:27 cease to *h.* instruction
  22:17 *h.* the words of the wise
  23:19 *h.* thou, my son, be wise
Ec. 5:1 more ready to *h.* than
  7:5 better to *h.* rebuke of wise
  12:13 *h.* conclusion of matter
Cant. 8:13 cause me to *h.*
Is. 1:2 *h.* O heavens, give ear
  6:9 *h.* ye indeed, *Mark* 4:12
  18:3 bloweth a trumpet, *h.* ye
  33:13 *h.* ye that are afar off
  34:1 earth *h.* all that is therein
  42:18 *h.* ye deaf ; 23 will *h.*
  43:9 let them *h.* and say truth
  48:14 assemble yoursel. and *h.*
  55:3 *h.* soul sh. live, *John* 5:25
Jer. 6:18 *h.* ye nat. 19 O earth
  11:2 *h.* words of covenant, 6
  10 forefathers ref. to *h.* 13:10
  13:15 *h.* ye, give ear, L. spoken
  18:2 cause thee to *h.* my words
  23:22 cause my peo. to *h.* words
  38:25 princes *h.* that I have tal.
  49:20 *h.* counsel of Lord, 50:45
Lam. 1:18 *h.* I pray you, all peo.
Ezek. 2:8 *h.* wh. I say unto thee
  3:17 *h.* wo. at my mouth, 33:7
  27 he that heareth, let him *h.*
  33:31 *h.* words, not do them, 32
Dan. 9:17 *h.* prayer of thy serv.
  19 *h.* O Lord, forgive, hearken
Hos. 5:1 *h.* ye this, O priests
Joel 1:2 *h.* this, old men

Amos 3:1 *h.* this word L. hath
  spoken, 4:1 ; 5:1 ; 8:4
Mic. 1:2 *h.* all ye people
  3:1 *h.* I pray you, heads of J. 9
  6:2 *h.* O mountains ; *h.* ye rod
Nah. 3:19 all that *h.* bruit sh.
Mat. 11:4 show John that, *Luke 7:22*
  5 deaf *h. Mark* 7:37 ; *Luke 7:22*
  13:17 *h.* things ye *h. Luke* 10:24
  15:10 he said to multitude, *h.*
  17:5 bel. Son, *h.* him, *Mark* 9:7
  18:17 if he neglect to *h.* them
Mark 4:18 are such as *h.* the
  word, 20 ; *Luke* 8:12, 13
  24 heed wh. ye *h.* you that *h.*
Luke 5:1 pressed on him to *h.*
  15 multit. came together to *h.*
  6:17 came to *h.* him
  8:18 take heed there. how ye *h.*
  21 wh. *h.* word and do it, 11:28
  9:9 who is this of whom I *h. ?*
  16:2 how is it I *h.* this of thee ?
  29 Moses and prophets *h.* them
  19:48 peop. very attentive to *h.*
  21:38 come to temple to *h.* him
John 5:30 I *h.* I ju. 6:60 who *h. ?*
  7:1 judge man before it *h.* him
  9:27 wheref. wo. ye *h.* it aga. ?
  10:3 sheep *h.* voice
  12:47 if man *h.* words, bel. not
  14:24 word wh. ye *h.* is not mi.
Acts 2:8 *h.* ev. man in own tong.
  33 which ye now see and *h.*
  10:22 and to *h.* words of thee
  33 *h.* all things command. thee
  13:7 dearest to *h.* word of God
  44 whole city came to *h.* word
  15:7 Gen. by my mouth *h.* word
  17:21 *h.* some new thing
  22:1 *h.* ye my defence
  24:4 *h.* us of thy clemency
  25:22 I would *h.* man myself
  28:22 to *h.* what thou thinkest
1 *Cor.* 11:18 I *h.* th. be divisions
Phil. 1:27 may *h.* of your affairs
2 *Thes.* 3:11 we *h.* that some wa.
1 *Tim.* 4:16 and them that *h.* th.
2 *Tim.* 4:17 all Gentiles mig. *h.*
Jam. 1:19 eve. one be swift to *h.*
1 *John* 5:15 know that he *h.* us
3 *John* 4 *h.* children walk in tru.
Rev. 1:3 bless. *h.* words of prop.
9:20 neither see, nor *h.* nor wa.

See EAR, EARS, VOICE.

HEAR me.

Ex. 6:12 then shall Phar. *h. me ?*
1 *K.* 18:37 *h. me,* O Lord *h. me*
1 *Chr.* 28:2 *h. me,* my brethren
2 *Chr.* 13:4 *h. me,* thou Jeroboam
  15:2 *h. me,* Asa : 20:20 *h. me,* J.
  29:5 *h. me,* ye Levites, sanctify
Job 31:35 O that one wo. *h. me*
Ps. 4:1 *h. me* when I call, O God
  13:3 consider and *h. me,* O Lord
  17:6 thou wilt *h. me*
  33:16 for I said, *h. me,* lest they
  55:2 attend unto me, and *h. me*
  60:5 save with right hand, *h. me*
  69:13 in multit. of mercy, *h. me*
  17 *h. me* speedily, 143:7
Mic. 7:7 God will *h. me*
Acts 26:3 I beseech thee to *h. me*
  29 all *h. me,* were such as I am
1 *Cor.* 14:21 will they not *h. me ?*

HEAR not, *or* not HEAR.

1 *Sam.* 8:18 Lord will not *h.* you
Job 30:20 dost not *h.* me
  35:13 God will not *h.* vanity
Ps. 66:18 regard iniq. L. not *h.*
  94:9 planted ear, sh. he not *h. ?*
Is. 1:15 many prayers I will *not*
    h. Jer. 7:16 ; 11:14 ; 14:12 ;
    Ezek. 8:18 ; *Amos* 5:23
30:9 will not *h.* the law of Lord
59:1 ear heavy that it can not *h.*
  2 will n. *h.* ; 65:12 ye did n. *h.*
66:4 they did not *h. Zec.* 1:4

Jer. 5:21 have ears, and *h.* not,
  Ezek. 12:2 ; *Mark* 8:18
  13:17 will n. *h.* 22:5 ; *Mal.* 2:2
  17:23 mi. not *h.* 19:15 ; *Zec.* 7:11
  22:21 thou saidst, I will not *h.*
Dan. 5:23 praised gods of silver,
  wh. see *not* nor *h. Rev.* 9:20
Mic. 3:4 cry to L. he will not *h.*
Hab. 1:2 long cry, wilt not *h. ?*
Mat. 10:14 rec. you, nor *h.* wor.
  13:16 if he will *not h.* thee
  Luke 16:31 if he *h.* n. M. and pr.
John 8:43 bec. ye can not *h.* wo.
  47 ye therefore *h.* them *not*
  9:27 I told you, and ye did n. *h.*
  10:8 the sheep did not *h.* them
Acts 3:23 soul will n. *h.* destroy.
1 *Cor.* 14:21 will they not *h.* me
Gal. 4:21 do ye not *h.* the law ?

Would not HEAR.

Ex. 7:16 hitherto thou *w.* not *h.*
Deut. 1:43 Is. 3:26 ; 2 *K.* 17:14
2 *K.* 14:11 Amaziah, 2 *Chr.* 25:20
  18:12 Is. *Neh.* 9:29 ; *Zec.* 7:13
Jer. 13:11 they *w.* n. *h.* 29:19
  36:25 he *w.* n. *h. ; Zec.* 7:13
1 *w.* not *h.*

HEAR now, *or* now HEAR.

Num. 12:6 *h.* now my wor., 20:10
1 *Sam.* 22:7 said *h. now,* Benjam.
Job 13:6 *h.* now *h.* my reasoning
Prov. 5:7 *h.* me *now,* therefore
Is. 7:13 *h.* n. O house of David
  44:1 *h.* n. O Jacob, my servant
  47:8 *h.* now, thou given to pleas.
  51:21 *h. now* this, thou afflicted
Jer. 5:21 *h. now,* O foolish peop.
  28:15 *h. now,* Hananiah
  37:20 *h. now,* I pray thee
Mic. 6:1 *h.* ye *now* what L. saith
Zec. 3:8 *h.* n. Josh. high-priest
Acts 2:33 which ye n. see and *h.*
Phil. 1:30 saw in me, and *now h.*

Shall HEAR.

Ex. 15:14 *shall h.* be afraid, *Deut.*
  13:11 ; 17:13 ; 19:20 ; 21:21
Num. 14:13 Egyptians *shall h.* it
Deut. 4:6 *s. h.* all these statutes
1 *K.* 8:42 *s. h.* of thy great name
2 *K.* 19:7 *shall h.* rumor, *Is.* 37:7
Job 22:27 prayer to him, he *s. h.*
Ps. 34:2 humble *shall h.* thereof
  55:17 cry, and he *s. h.* my voice
  19 God *s. h.* and afflict them
  92:11 ears *s. h.* desire of wicked
  141:6 they *shall h.* my words
Is. 29:18 in that day *shall h.*
  30:19 *shall h.* he will answer
  21 thine ears *shall h.* a word
Jer. 33:9 a. h. all good that I do
Hos. 2:21 heaven *shall h.* earth
  22 earth *shall h.* corn and wine
Mat. 13:14 ye *shall h. Acts* 28:26
  18:15 *shall h.* thee
  24:6 ye *shall h.* of wars and ru-
    mors, *Mark* 13:7 ; *Luke* 21:9
John 5:25 the dead *shall h.* voice
  16:13 whatsoever he *shall h.*
Acts 3:22 him *shall* ye *h.* 7:37
  25:22 to-morrow thou *s. h.* him
Rom. 10:14 how *s.* they *h.* with.

Will HEAR.

Ex. 20:19 will *h. Deut.* 5:27
  22:23 cry, I will surely *h.* 27
Num. 9:8 will *h.* what L. com.
2 *K.* 19:4 God will *h.* the words
2 *Chr.* 7:14 w. *h.* fr. hea. *Ps.* 20:6
20:9 thou *w. h. Ps.* 38:15
Ps. 4:3 L. *will h.* ; 17:6 *w. h.* me
  85:8 *will h.* what God *will* speak
  145:19 he also *will h.* their cry
Prov. 1:5 *w. h.* and increase
Is. 41:17 the Lord *will h.* them
  65:24 are yet speaking, I *will h.*
Jer. 36:3 may be hou. of J. *w. h.*
Ezek. 2:5 whether *will h.* 7 ; 3:11
Hos. 2:21 I *will h.* the heavens

Mic. 7:7 wait for G. God *will h.*
Zec. 10:6 God *will h.* them, 13:9
Acts 17:32 we *will h.* thee again
21:22 *will h.* that thou art come
23:35 *will h.* thee wh. accusers
28:28 sal. sent Gentile, *will h.*

HEAR the word of the Lord.

1 *K.* 22:19 *h. the word of the Lo.*
  2 *Ch.* 18:18; *Jer.* 29:20; 42:15;
  Amos 7:16
2 *K.* 7:1 Elisha said, *h. word of*
  the Lord, Jer. 17:20; 21:11
20:16 Isa. said to Hezekiah, *h.*
  the word of the Lo. Is. 39:5
Is. 1:10 *h. w. of L.* rulers of So.
28:14 *h. w. of L.* scornful men
66:5 *h. w. of L.* ye that tremble
Jer. 2:4 *h. w. of L.* ho. of J. 10:1
7:2 *h. w. of Lord* all ye of h.
9:20 yet *h. w. of Lord,* O ye wo.
19:3 *h. w. of L.* kings of J. 22:2
22:29 O earth, *h. the w. of t. L.*
31:10 *h. w. of L.* O ye nations
34:4 *h. word of Lord,* O Zedek.
44:24 *h. word of Lord,* all J. 26
Ezek. 6:3 mountains of Is. 36:1
13:2 say to prophets, *h. w. of L.*
16:35 O harlot, *h. w. of the L.*
20:47 forest of south, *h. w. of L.*
34:7 shepherds, *h. w. of the L.* 9
Hos. 4:1 *h. w. of L.* child. of Isr.
Amos 7:16 Amaziah, *h. w. of L.*

HEARD.

Gen. 16:11 Lord *h.* thy affliction
21:26 neither yet *h.* I of it
Ex. 2:24 God *h.* their groaning
28:35 sound *h.* when goeth in
Lev. 24:14 that *h.* him
Num. 11:1 complained, L. *h.* it
12:2 spake ag. Moses, L. *h.* it
14:15 nations have *h.* fame
1 *Sam.* 7:9 cried, the L. *h.* him
1 *K.* 1:11 k. Adonijah doth reign
6:7 any tool of iron *h.* in house
2 *K.* 19:25 *h.* long ago, *Is.* 37:26
2 *Chr.* 5:13 one *h.* in praising
33:13 and *h.* his supplications
Ezr. 3:13 the noise was *h.* afar
Neh. 12:43 joy of Jerusa. *h.* afar
Job 15:8 hast *h.* secret of God ?
19:7 out of wrong, but not *h.*
26:14 how little a portion is *h.* ?
29:11 when the ear *h.* me
Ps. 6:9 L. hath *h.* my supplica.
10:17 *h.* desire of the humble
22:21 for thou hast *h.* me
  24 but when he cried he *h.*
  34:6; 40:1; 120:1
34:4 I sought the L. he *h.* me
38:13 I as a deaf man *h.* not
61:5 O God, hast *h.* my vows
66:19 verily God hath *h.* me
76:8 cause judgment to be *h.*
78:21 therefore the Lord *h.* this
  59 when God *h.* this
81:5 where I *h.* a language
97:8 Zion *h.* and was glad
118:21 for thou hast *h.* me
132:6 we *h.* of it at Ephratah
Prov. 21:13 cry hims. but not *h.*
Is. 10:30 cause it to be *h.* to L.
40:21 have ye not *h.* ?
  28 not *h.* everl. G. fainteth not
48:6 thou hast *h.* see all this
52:15 had not *h.* sh. they consi.
60:18 viol. no more *h.* in land
64:4 not *h.* what he prepared
65:19 weeping be no more *h.*
66:8 who hath *h.* such thing?
Jer. 4:19 *h.* sound of trumpet
6:7 wickedn. spoil, is *h.* in her
7:13 rising early, but ye *h.* not
8:6 I hearkened and *h.*
18:13 who hath *h.* such
  22 let cry be *h.* from houses
25:36 howling of flock sh. be *h.*

26:11 prophesied as ye have *h.*
34:10 *h.* man-servant sh. go free
35:17 but they have not *h.*
46:12 nations have *h.* of shame
50:46 cry is *h.* among nations
51:46 rumor shall be *h.* in land
Lam. 3:61 hast *h.* their reproach
Ezek. 26:13 shall be no more *h.*
Dan. 12:8 I *h.* but underst. not

Jon. 2:2 I cried to L. and he *h.*
Mic. 5:15 such as have not *h.*
Mal. 3:16 hearkened and *h.*
Mat. 5:21 ye h. it, 27, 33, 38, 43
6:7 shall be *h.* for much speak.
13:17 have not *h. Luke* 10:24
22:7 when the king *h.* thereof
26:65 have *h.* blas. *Mark* 14:64
Mark 4:15 they have *h.* Satan
14:11 they *h.* it they were glad
Luke 1:13 prayer is *h. Acts* 10:31
12:3 spoken, shall be *h.*
20:16 when they *h.* it, they said
John 3:32 he hath *h.* he testifieth
6:45 ev. man that hath *h.* of F.
8:6 wrote on ground as *h.* not
11:41 I thank thee thou hast *h.*
18:21 ask them which *h.* me
21:7 Simon P. *h.* it was the Lord
Acts 1:4 the promise ye *h.* of me
2:37 when *h.* this they were
4:4 many which *h.* the word be.
5:5 fear came on all that *h.*
13:48 when G. *h.* this were glad
14:9 the same *h.* Paul speak
16:14 woman worship. G. *h.* us
25 and the prisoners *h.* them
22:15 sh. witt. what seen and *h.*
24:24 *h.* concerning faith in C.
Rom. 10:14 they have not *h.*
  18 have they not *h.* ? yes, veri.
15:21 they that have not *h.*
1 *Cor.* 2:9 eye not seen, nor ear *h.*
Gal. 1:13 ye have *h.* of my conv.
Eph. 1:13 ye *h.* word of truth
  15 after I *h.* of your faith
4:21 if so be ye have *h.* him
Phil. 4:9 ye have *h.* and seen
Col. 1:4 we *h.* of your faith in C.
  6 ye *h.* of it, knew grace of G.
  9 we *h.* it, do not cease to pray
2 *Tim.* 2:2 things thou hast *h.*
Heb. 2:3 confirmed by them th. *h.*
3:16 when they had *h.*
4:2 with faith in them that *h.*
5:7 offered up prayers, was *h.*
Jam. 5:11 have *h.* of pati. of Job
1 *John* 2:18 ye *h.* antichrist, 4:3
  24 *h.* from begin. 3:11 ; 2 *John* 6
Rev. 3:3 remem. how th. hast *h.*
7:4 I *h.* number of them sealed
9:16 I *h.* number of horsemen
16:5 I *h.* the angel of waters
18:22 shall be *h.* no more
  23 voice of bride be *h.* no more
22:8 saw these things, *h.* them

I have HEARD.

Gen. 17:20 for Ishmael *I h. h.*
42:2 *I h. h.* there is corn Egypt
Ex. 3:7 *I h. h.* cry ; 6:5 *I h. h.* g.
16:12 *I h. h.* mur. *Num.* 14:27
1 *K.* 9:3 *I h. h.* thy prayer, 2 *K.*
  20:5 ; 2 *Chr.* 7:12 ; *Is.* 38:5
2 *K.* 19:20 hast prayed *I have h.*
22:19 *I h. h.* sa. L. 2 *Chr.* 34:27
Job 16:2 *I h. h.* many su. things
20:3 *I have h.* check of reproach
42:5 *I h. h.* by hearing of ear
Ps. 31:13 *I have h.* the slander
62:11 twice *I have h.* this
Is. 49:8 time *h.* I *h.* 2 *Cor.* 6:2
Jer. 23:25 *I h. h.* what prophets
31:18 *I h. h.* Ephraim bemoan.
49:14 *I h. h.* a rumor from Lord
Ezek. 35:12 *I h. h.* thy blasphe.
Hos. 14:8 *I have h.* and observed
Hab. 3:2 *I have h.* thy speech
John 8:26 those things *I have h.*

40 truth, which *I h. h.* of God
15:15 *I have h.* of my Father
Acts 7:34 *I have h.* their groaning
9:13 *I h. h.* by many of th. man

HEARD, with voice.

Gen. 3:8 they *h. voice* of the Lord
  10 I *h.* thy *voice,* and was afraid
21:17 God *h.* the *voice* of the lad
30:6 G. hath *h.* my *v.* and given
39:15 when he *h.* I lifted up *v.*
Num. 7:89 he *h.* the *v.* of one
20:16 we cried, he *h.* our *voice*
Deut. 1:34 L. *h.* the *v.* of words
4:12 similitude, only he *h.* a *v.*
  33 *v.* of God thou hast *h.* 5:26
5:23 ye *h.* the *v.* out of darkness
  24 *h.* his *voice* out of the fire
  28 L. *h.* the *v.* of your words
26:7 the L. *h.* our *v.* and looked
Jud. 18:25 let not *voice* be *h.*
1 *Sam.* 1:13 lips moved, *v.* not *h.*
1 *K.* 17:22 L. *h.* the *v.* of Elijah
2 *Chr.* 30:27 *v. h.* prayer came
Job 4:16 th. was silence, I *h.* a *v.*
33:8 *h.* the *v.* of thy words
37:4 not stay them when *v.* is *h.*
Ps. 3:4 L. with my *v.* he *h.* me
6:8 L. hath *h. v.* of my weeping
18:6 *h.* my *v.* out of his temple

Ps. 19:3 no speech where *v.* not *h.*
28:6 *h. v.* of my supplication
66:8 make *v.* of praise to be *h.*
116:1 I love L. he hath *h.* my *v.*
Cant. 2:12 *v.* of the turtle is *h.*
Is. 6:8 also I *h. v.* of the Lord
30:30 L. cause his gl. *v.* to be *h.*
42:2 *v.* to be *h.* in street
58:4 make your *voice* to be *h.*
65:19 *v.* of weeping no more *h.*
Jer. 3:21 a *v.* was *h.* upon high
4:31 have *h.* a *v.* as of a woman
9:19 *v.* of wailing is *h.* out of Z.
30:5 have *h.* a *v.* of trembling
31:15 *v.* was *h.* in R. *Mat.* 2:18
Lam. 3:56 thou hast *h.* my *voice*
Ezek. 1:28 I *h.* a *v.* of one that s.
3:12 I *h.* behind me *v.*
27:30 cause their *v.* to be *h.*
Dan. 8:16 *h.* a man's *v.* between
10:9 yet *h.* I the *v.* of his words
Nah. 2:13 *v.* of mes. no more *h.*
John 5:37 neither *h.* his *v.* at any
Acts 9:4 and *h.* a *voice* saying,
  Saul, Saul, 22:7 ; 26:14
11:7 *h.* a *v.* saying to me, Arise
22:9 *h.* not the *voice* of him
Heb. 12:19 wh. *voice* they that *h.*
2 *Pet.* 1:18 *v.* came fr. heav. we *h.*
Rev. 1:10 I *h.* a *v.* 16:1 ; 19:1 ;
  21:3
4:1 first *v.* I *h.* was as a trumpet
5:11 I *h.* the *v.* of many angels
6:6 I *h.* a *v.* in the midst
  7 I *h.* a *v.* of the fourth beast
9:13 *h.* a *v.* fr. the four horns
10:4 *h.* a *v.* from heaven 8 ; 14:2,
  13 ; 18:4
12:10 and I *h.* a loud *voice*
14:2 I *h.* the *v.* of harpers
19:6 I *h. v.* of multitude

We have HEARD.

Jos. 9:9 we have *h.* fame of him
2 *Sam.* 7:22 none like thee accor.
  to all we *h. h.* 1 *Chr.* 17:20
Ps. 44:1 we *h. h.* with our ears
48:8 as we *h. h.* so have we seen
78:3 sayings which we have *h.*
Is. 16:6 we *h. h.* of M. *Jer.* 48:29
24:16 we *h. h.* songs, glory to
Jer. 30:5 we *h. h.* voice of tremb.
51:51 confou. we *h. h.* reproach
Ob. 1 we *h. h.* a rumor from Lord
Zec. 8:23 for we have *h.* that God
Mark 14:58 we *have h.* him say
Luke 4:23 whatever *we have h.*
22:71 *we* ourselves *have h.*

John 4:42 believe, *we have h.*
12:34 we have *h.* out of the law
Acts 4:20 cannot but sp. *we h. h.*
6:11 *we have h.* him speak
14 *we have h.* him say, This J.
15:24 *we have h.* that certain
Heb. 2:1 heed to things *we have h.*
1 *John* 1:1 which *we have h.* 3
5 message which *we have h.*

HEARD, with word, s.

Num. 24:4 wh. *h. w.* of God, 16
Jos. 24:27 *h.* all the *w.* of Lord
1 *Sam.* 17:23 same *w.* D. *h.* them
31 wh. *w.* were *h.* David spake
1 *K.* 2:42 the *w.* that I *h.* is good
2 *K.* 6:30 king *h. w.* of woman
19:6 afraid of *w.* hast *h. Is.* 37:6
Job 33:8 I have *h.* voice of *words*
Ec. 9:16 poor man's *w.* not *h.*
17 *w.* of wise men are *h.*
Is. 37:4 the *w.* wh. God hath *h.*
Jer. 23:18 and *h.* his *words*
25:8 bec. ye have not *h.* my *w.*
26:21 princes *h.* his *word*
36:13 decl. all the *w.* he had *h.*
24 not afraid that *h.* these *w.*
38:1 Pashur *h.* the *w.* of Jerem.
Mat. 22:22 wh. they *h.* these *w.*
Mark 5:36 as Jesus *h.* the *word*
Luke 10:39 at Jes. feet, *h.* his *w.*
Acts 10:44 fell on them *h. word.*
2 *Cor.* 12:4 *h.* unspeakable *word*
Eph. 1:13 ye *h.* the *w.* of truth
Col. 1:5 ye *h. w.* of the gospel
1 *Thes.* 2:13 *w.* which ye *h.* of us
2 *Tim.* 1:13 sound *w.* hast *h.*
Heb. 12:19 that *h.* entre. that *w.*
1 *John* 2:7 *w.* ye ha. *h.* from beg.

HEARDEST.

Deut. 4:36 thou *h.* his words
2 *K.* 22:19 thou *h.* what I spake
ag. this place, 2 *Chr.* 34:27
Neh. 9:9 thou *h.* their cry
27 they cried, thou *h.* them, 28
Ps. 31:22 thou *h.* voice of sup.
119:26 I dec. my ways, thou *h.*
Is. 48:7 day when thou *h.* not
8 thou *h.* not, thou knew. not
Jon. 2:2 I cried, thou *h.*

HEARER, s.

Rom. 2:13 not *h.* of law are just.
Eph. 4:29 minister grace unto *h.*
2 *Tim.* 2:14 subverting of the *h.*
Jam. 1:22 doers of word, not *h.*
23 if any be a *h.* of the word
25 he being not a forgetful *h.*

HEAREST.

1 *Sam.* 24:9 *h.* thou m.'s words?
2 *Sam.* 5:24 *h.* sound in mulb.-t.
1 *K.* 8:30 *h.* forgive, 2 *Chr.* 6:21
Ps. 22:2 cry in daytime, *h.* not
65:2 thou that *h.* prayer
Mat. 21:16 *h.* thou what th. say?
27:13 *h.* thou not how many th.
John 3:8 and thou *h.* the sound
11:42 that thou *h.* me always

HEARETH.

Deut. 29:19 *h.* words of curse
1 *Sam.* 3:9 L. thy servant *h.* 10
Job 34:28 *h.* cry of the afflicted
Ps. 34:17 righte. cry, the Lord *h.*
38:14 as a man that *h.* not
69:33 L. *h.* poor, desp. not pris.
Prov. 8:34 blessed is man *h.* me
13:1 *h.* his father's instruction
8 but poor *h.* not rebuke
15:29 he *h.* prayer of righteous
31 that *h.* reproof of life, 32
18:13 answ. matter before *h.* it
21:28 the man that *h.* speaketh
25:10 that *h.* it put thee to sha.
29:24 *h.* cursing, bewrayeth not
42:20 open ears, but *h.* not
Ezek. 3:27 he that *h.* let him hear

Mat. 7:24 *h.* say. 26 ; *Luke* 6:47, 49
13:19 *h.* word of the kingdom
20 that *h.* the word, 22, 23
Luke 10:16 he that *h.* you *h.* me
John 3:29 standeth and *h.* him
5:24 *h.* my word, and believeth
8:47 that *is* of G. *h.* G.'s words
9:31 God *h.* not sinners
18:37 that is of truth, *h.* voice
2 *Cor.* 12:6 above th. he *h.* of me
1 *John* 4:5 the world *h.* them
6 he that knoweth God *h.* us
5:14 ask accord. to will, he *h.* us
Rev. 22:17 him that *h.* say, Come
18 to ev. man that *h.* the words

HEARING.

Deut. 31:11 read this law in th. *h.*
2 *Sam.* 18:12 our *h.* king charged
2 *K.* 4:31 neither voice nor *h.*
Job 33:8 hast spoken in my *h.*
42:5 I have heard of thee by *h.*
Is. 11:3 nor reprove af. *h.* of ears
21:3 bowed down at the *h.* of it
33:15 stoppeth ears fr. *h.* blood
Ezek. 9:5 said in my *h.* Go
10:13 cried unto them in my *h.*
Amos 8:11 *h.* word of the Lord
Acts 25:21 reserved to *h.* of Aug.
23 entered into the place of *h.*
Rom. 10:17 faith cometh by *h.*
1 *Cor.* 12:17 where were the *h.* ?
Gal. 3:2 or by the *h.* of faith, 5
Heb. 5:11 seeing ye are dull of *h.*

HEARING, Verb.

Prov. 20:12 h. ear, L. hath made
28:9 away ear from *h.* the law
Ec. 1:8 nor is ear filled with *h.*
Mat. 13:13 and *h.* they hear not
14 by *h.* ye shall hear
15 dull of *h. Acts* 28:27; *Heb.* 5:11
Mark 6:2 many *h.* were aston.
Luke 2:46 *h.* them and asking
Acts 5:5 Ananias *h.* these words
8:6 *h.* and seeing miracles
9:7 *h.* a voice, but seeing no m.
18:8 Corinthians *h.* believed
Phile. 5 *h.* of thy love and faith
2 *Pet.* 2:8 Lot in seeing and *h.*

HEARKEN.

Ex. 6:30 sh. Pharaoh *h.* to me ?
Deut. 7:12 *h.* to these judgments
11:13 *h.* dilig. to my commands
15:5 *h.* to voice of L. *Jer.* 17:24
18:15 to him ye shall *h.*
28:13 if thou *h.* to commandments, 1 *K.* 11:38
Jos. 1:17 so will we *h.* unto thee
1 *Sam.* 15:22 to *h.* th. fat of rams
30:24 who will *h.* to you in this ?
1 *K.* 8:28 have thou respect to *h.*
29 *h.* to prayer, 52; 2 *Chr.*
6:19, 20
Neh. 13:27 *h.* then to you ?
Ps. 81:8 if thou wilt *h.* unto me
Prov. 29:12 if a ruler *h.* to lies
Is. 32:3 ears of th. that hear *h.*
42:23 will *h.* for time to come ?
Jer. 26:3 will *h.* and turn fr. evil
5 *h.* to prophets whom I sent
29:12 pray to me. and I will *h.*
35:13 not rec. instruction to *h.*

Zec. 7:11 but they refused to *h.*
Acts 4:19 *h.* to you
12:13 a damsel came to *h.*

HEARKEN, imperatively.

Gen. 23:15 *h.* to me; 49:2 *h.* to Is.
Num. 23:18 *h.* to me, son of Zip.
Deut. 4:1 *h.* O Israel, to statutes
27:9 take heed, and *h.* O Israel
Jud. 9:7 *h.* to me, men of Shech.
1 *K.* 8:30 *h.* to the supplications,
2 *Chr.* 6:21
22:28 *h.* O peo. every one of you
2 *Chr.* 18:27 he said, *h.* all peop.
20:15 *h.* ye, all Judah, and Jer.

Job 13:6 *h.* to pleadings
32:10 I said *h.* to me, 33:31
33:1 I pray, *h.* to my words
34:10 *h.* unto me, men of under.
34 *w.* man *h.* 37:14 *h.* to this
Ps. 34:11 *h.* I will teach you
45:10 *h.* O daughter, and consid.
Prov. 7:24 *h.* to me, O chil. 8:32
Is. 28:23 *h.* and hear my speech
34:1 ye nations, *h.* ye peo. 49:1
46:3 *h.* unto me, O house of
Jacob, 48:12 ; *Hos.* 5:1
12 *h.* to me, stout-hearted
51:1 *h.* to me, th. fol. righteous.
4 *h.* unto me, my people
7 *h.* to me, ye th. know right.
55:2 *h.* diligently unto me
Dan. 9:19 O Lord, *h.* and do
Mic. 1:2 *h.* O earth, and all ther.
Mark 7:14 *h.* to me every one
Acts 2:14 *h.* to my words
7:2 brethren, and fathers, *h.*
15:13 men and brethren, *h.*
Jam. 2:5 my beloved brethren

See VOICE.

HEARKEN, with not.

Gen. 34:17 *not h.* to be circum.
Ex. 7:4 *not h.* to you, 22; 11:9
Deut. 13:3 *n. h.* to that dreamer
17:12 will *not h.* to the priest
18:19 will *not h.* to my words
21:18 he will *not h.* to them
23:5 *n. h.* to Bal. *Jos.* 24:10
Jos. 1:18 will *n. h.* to thy words
Jud. 2:17 would *not h.* to judges
1 *K.* 20:8 elders said, *h. n.* to him
2 *K.* 17:40 *n. h.* but after manner
18:31 *h. n.* to Hezek. *Is.* 36:16
2 *Chr.* 10:16 Rehob. would *not h.*
33:10 L. spake, they would *n. h.*
Job 33:33 if *n. h.* hold thy peace
Ps. 58:5 *n. h.* to voice of charm.
81:11 would *not h.* to my voice
Jer. 6:10 uncircumcised *cannot h.*
17 said, We will *not h.* 44:16
7:27 they will *not h.* unto thee
11:11 tho. they cry, I will *not h.*
16:12 they may not *h.* to me
17:27 if ye will *not h.* to me,
26:4 ; *Ezek.* 20:39
23:16 *h. not* to prophets, 27:9, 14,
16, 17 ; 29:8
38:15 wilt thou *not h.* to me ?
Ezek. 3:7 *n. h.* to thee, *n. h.* to me
20:8 and would *not h.* unto me
Hos. 9:17 did *n. h. Zec.* 1:4

HEARKENED.

Gen. 30:17 God *h.* unto Leah
22 God *h.* to Rachel and open.
34:24 to Hamor *h.* all that went
39:10 that Joseph *h.* not to her
Ex. 6:12 chil. of Is. not *h.* to me
7:13 Phar. *h.* not, 8:15, 19 ; 9:12
Deut. 9:19 Lord *h.* to me, 10:10
18:14 nations *h.* to obs. of times
34:9 Is. *h.* to Joshua, *Jos.* 1:17
1 *Sam.* 28:21 wom. of En. *h.* to S.
1 *K.* 12:15 king *h.* not to people,
16; 2 *Chr.* 10:15
24 they *h.* to word of the Lord
15:20 *h.* to king Asa, 2 *Chr.* 16:4
2 *K.* 13:4 the Lord *h.* to Jehoahaz
16:9 king of Assyria *h.* to Asa
20:13 Hezekiah *h.* to messengers
21:9 Judah *h.* not to the law
22:13 our fathers *h.* not to words
2 *Chr.* 24:17 J. *h.* to the princes
25:16 Amaz. *h.* not to the prop.
35:22 Josiah *h.* not to Pharaoh
Neh. 9:16 *h.* not to thy commandments, 29, 34; *Jer.* 34:14
Est. 3:4 Mordecai *h.* not to them
Ps. 81:13 O that my peo. had *h.*
Is. 21:7 and he *h.* diligently
48:18 O that thou hadst *h.*

Jer. 6:19 have not *h.* to my word,
7:24, 26; 25:3, 4, 7; 26:5;
29:19; 32:33; 34:17; 35:14, 15,
16; 36:31; 44:5
37:14 Irijah *h.* not to Jeremiah
Ezek. 3:6 would have *h.* not thee
Dan. 9:6 neither *h.* to thy serv
Mal. 3:16 the Lord *h. Jer.* 8.
Acts 27:21 should have *h.* to me
See VOICE.

HEARKENEDST.
Deut. 28:45 thou *h.* not to the L.

HEARKENETH, ING.
Ps. 103:20 angels *h.* to the voice
Prov. 1:33 *h.* to me sh. dw. safely
12:15 he that *h.* to coun. is wise

HEART, Noun.
Gen. 45:26 and Jacob's *h.* fainted
Ex. 23:9 know *h.* of a stranger
28:30 they shall be on Aaron's *h.*
35:35 hath filled with wisd. of *h.*
Lev. 26:16 and cause sorrow of *h.*
Num. 52:7 discourage *h.* of Is. ?
9 they discouraged the *h.* of Is.
Deut. 5:29 such a *h.* in t'em
28:28 smite wi. astonish. of *h.*
47 serv. not L. with glad. of *h.*
65 L. sh. give thee trembling *h.*
29:4 L. hath not given *h.* to per.
Jos. 14:8 made *h.* of people melt
Jud. 5:15 great thoughts of *h.*
16 were great searchings of *h.*
18:20 the priest's *h.* was glad.
1 *Sam.* 1:13 Han. spake in her *h.*
10:9 God gave him another *h.*
16:7 the Lord looketh on the *h.*
17:32 Let no man's *h.* fail
24:5 and David's *h.* smote him
25:31 offence of *h.* to my lord
36 and Nabal's *h.* was merry
2 *Sam.* 6:16 she despised him in
h. 1 *Chr.* 15:29
14:1 king's *h.* was tow. Absalom
18:14 darts thro. *h.* of Absalom
14 bowed *h.* of men of Judah
1 *K.* 3:9 an understanding *h.*
12 given thee understanding *h.*
8:66 glad of *h.* 2 *Chr.* 7:10
10:2 com. of all in *h.* 2 *Chr.* 9:1
11:4 perfect, as the *h.* of David
12:27 then sh. the *h.* of this peo.
2 *K.* 6:11 *h.* of king of As. troub.
12:4 into man's *h.* 2 *Chr.* 29:31
1 *Chr.* 12:33 not of double *h.*
16:10 let the *h.* rej. *Ps.* 105:3
29:17 triest *h.* 18; *Jer.* 11:20
2 *Chr.* 7:11 came into Solom.'s *h.*
Ezr. 6:22 turned *h.* of king
7:27 such as this in the king's *h.*
Neh. 2:2 noth. else but sor. of *h.*
Est. 1:10 *h.* of king merry
5:9 H. went forth with glad *h.*
Job 9:4 wise in *h.* and mighty
12:24 he taketh away *h.* of chief
29:13 caused widow's *h.* to sing
37:24 respecteth not wise of *h.*
38:36 given understanding to *h.*
Ps. 12:2 double *h.* they speak
19:8 sta. of L. right, rejoicing *h.*
34:18 nigh them of broken *h.*
44:21 knoweth secrets of the *h.*
45:5 arrows sharp in *h.* of ene.
58:2 *h.* ye work; 64:6 *h.* deep
73:7 more than *h.* could wish
101:4 froward *h.* shall depart
5 a proud *h.* will not I suffer
104:15 wine mak. glad the *h.*
bread strengthene. man's *h.*
Prov. 6:18 a *h.* that devis. wicked
7:10 a woman subtle of *h.*
8:5 be of an understanding *h.*
10:8 wise in *h.* will rec. comma.
12:8 he of perverse *h.*
20 deceit is in the *h.* of them
25 heaviness in *h.* of man
13:12 hope defer. maketh *h.* sick

14:10 *h.* knoweth own bittern.
13 in laughter *h.* is sorrowful
14 backslider in *h.* be filled
30 a sound *h.* is life of the flesh
33 wisdom resteth in *h.* of him
15:7 *h.* of foolish doeth not so
13 merry *h.* mak. cheer. coun.
by sorrow of *h.* sp. is broken
14 *h.* of him th. understandeth
15 a merry *h.* hath contin. feast
28 *h.* of righte. studieth to an.
30 light of eyes rejoiceth the *h.*
16:1 preparation of *h.* from L.·
5 proud *h.* abomination to L.
9 a man's *h.* deviseth his way
23 *h.* of wise teach. his mouth
17:16 price in hand, hath no *h.*
20 a froward *h.* find. no good
22 merry *h.* doeth good
18:12 bef. destruc. *h.* is haughty
15 *h.* of prudent getteth kno.
19:21 devices in a man's *h.*
20:5 counsel in *h.* like deep wa.
21:1 king's *h.* is in hand of L.
4 a high look and a proud *h.*
22:11 pureness of *h.* king his fr.
15 foolish, bound in *h.* of child

Prov. 24:12 pon. the *h.* cons. it ?
25:3 *h.* of k. is unsearchable
20 he that singeth to heavy *h.*
26:23 wicked *h.* is like potsherd
27:9 ointment and perf. rej. *h.*
19 *h.* of man answereth man
28:25 proud *h.* stirreth up strife
31:11 *h.* of her husb. doth trust
Ec. 7:3 sadn. of count. *h.* is bet.
4 *h.* of wise in house of mourn.
h. of fools in house of mirth
8:5 a wise man's *h.* discerneth
11 *h.* of men is set to do evil
9:3 the *h.* of men is full of evil
7 drink thy wine wi. merry *h.*
10:2 a wise man's *h.* at ri. hand,
but a fool's *h.* is at his left
Is. 6:10 make their *h.* fat, *Mat.*
13:15; *Acts* 28:27
10:12 I will punish the stout *h.*
13:7 every man's *h.* shall melt
30:29 shall have gladness of *h.*
32:4 *h.* of rash shall understand
35:4 say to them of fearful *h.*
44:20 dec. *h.* turned him aside
57:1 man layeth to *h. Jer.* 12:11
15 revive the *h.* of contrite on.
59:13 uttering from *h.* words
65:14 my serv. sing for joy of *h.*
but ye cry for sorrow of *h.*
Jer. 4:9 the *h.* of king shall perish
5:23 people hath a rebellious *h.*
9:26 Is. are uncircumcised in *h.*
11:20 that triest reins and *h.*
17:9 *h.* is deceitful ab. all things
10 I the Lord search *h.*
20:12 L. that seest reins and *h.*
24:7 I will give a *h.* to know me
Lam. 3:65 give them sorrow of *h.*
Ezek. 11:19 stony *h.* out of flesh
18:22 ye made *h.* of righte. sad
18:31 make a new *h.* and new s.
21:7 ev. *h.* sh. melt, all be feeble
25:15 veng. with despiteful *h.*
36:26 give you a *h.* of flesh
44:7 uncir. in *h.* 9; *Acts* 7:51
Dan. 4:16 a beast's *h.* be giv. him
7:4 and a man's *h.* was given it
Hos. 4:11 new wine take away *h.*
7:11 E. is like dove without *h.*
Nah. 2:10 *h.* melt. knees smite
Zep. 2:15 this city said in her *h.*
Mal. 2:2 ye do not lay it to *h.*
4:6 tho *h.* of fathers, to of child.
Mat. 11:29 meek and lowly in *h.*
12:34 of abund. of *h. Luke* 6:45
35 treasure of *h. Luke* 6:45
15:18 from the *h.* and defile man
19 out of *h.* evil th. *Mark* 7:21
Mark 16:14 upbra. with hard *h.*

Luke 2:19 M. pondered in her *h.*
51 moth. kept sayings in her *h.*
24:25 fools, slow of *h.* to believe
John 13:2 devil put into *h.* of J.
Acts 2:46 eat meat wi. singl. of *h.*
5:33 were cut to *h.* 7:54
11:23 purpose of *h.* they cl. to L.
Rom. 2:5 thy impeni. *h.* treas. up
29 circumcision of *h.* in the sp.
6:17 ye obeyed from *h.* that doc.
10:10 with the *h.* man believeth
1 *Cor.* 2:9 nei. enter. in *h.* of man
7:37 hath so decreed in his *h.*
2 *Cor.* 2:4 anguish of *h.* I wrote
3:3 written in fleshly tables of *h.*
8:16 earnest care into *h.* of Tit.
Eph. 6:6 doing will of G. from *h.*
Col. 3:22 in singl. of *h.* fear. God
1 *Thes.* 2:17 in presence, not in *h.*
Heb. 4:12 is a discerner of the *h.*
10:22 draw near with a true *h.*
13:9 good the *h.* be established
1 *Pet.* 3:4 let be hidden man of *h.*
2 *Pet.* 2:14 a *h.* ex. with covetous
Rev. 18:7 she saith in her *h.* I sit

HEART.
Ex. 15:8 congealed in *h.* of sea
Is. 19:1 *h.* of Egypt shall melt
Mat. 12:40 Son of man in *h.*

HEART, with all.
Deut. 11:13 with *all* your *h.* *Jos.*
22:5; 1 *Sam.* 12:20, 24
13:3 love the Lord with *all*
your *h.* 30:6; *Mat.* 22:37;
Mark 12:30, 33; *Luke* 10:27
26:16; do them with *all* thy *h.*
30:2 to L. *all h.* 10; *Joel* 2:12
Jud. 16:17 S. told *all* his *h.* 18
1 *K.* 2:4 walk before me with *all*
h. 8:23
8:48 return to thee with *all* th.
h. 2 *K.* 23:25; 2 *Chr.* 6:38
14:8 David fol. me wi. *all* his *h.*
2 *K.* 23:3 a covenant to walk with
all their *h.* 2 *Chr.* 34:31
2 *Chr.* 15:12 G. of fa. with *all h.*
15 had sworn with *all* their *h.*

2 *Chr.* 22:9 J. so. L. w. *all* his *h.*
31:21 did it with *all* his *h.*
Ps. 86:12 praise, O L. with *all h.*
Prov. 3:5 trust L. with *all* thy *h.*
Jer. 29:13 search me with *all h.*
Ezek. 36:5 joy of *all* their *h.*
Zep. 3:14 rejoice with *all* the *h.*
Acts 8:37 if thou beli. with *all h.*

See APPLY, BROKEN, CLEAN,
EVIL, HARDEN, HARDENED.

His HEART.
Gen. 6:5 imag. of *his h.* only evil
6 it grieved him at his *h.*
8:21 L. said in *h. h.*; 17:17 Abr.
27:41 E. said in *his h.* the days
Ex. 4:14 will be glad in *his h.*
7:23 neither did he set *his h.*
28:29 breastpl. of judg. on *h. h.*
35:34 he hath put in *his h.*
Deut. 2:30 L. made *his h.* obstin.
17:17 *his h.* turn not away
20 *his h.* be not lifted up above
19:6 aveng. pursue, *his h.* is hot
20:8 brethren's *h.* faint as *his h.*
24:15 poor, setteth *his h.* on it
29:19 blesseth himself in *his h.*
Ruth 3:7 his *h.* was merry
1 *Sam.* 4:13 *his h.* trem. for ark
25:37 it came that *his h.* died
27:1 D. in *his h.*; 28:5 *his h.* tre.
2 *Sam.* 7:27 thy servant found in
his h. 1 *Chr.* 17:25
13:33 let not Lord take to *his h.*
1 *K.* 10:24 which God had put in
his h. 2 *Chr.* 9:23
11:3 turned away *his h.* 4, 9
12:26 Jeroboam said in *his h.*
2 *K.* 9:24 arrow went out at *his h.*

2 *Chr.* 12:14 prepared not *his h.*
17:6 *his h.* was lift. up in ways
26:16 *his h.* was lifted up to des.
30:19 prepareth *his h.* to seek G.
32:25 for *his h.* was lifted up
26 hum. him. for pride of *his h.*
31 he might know all in *his h.*
Ezr. 7:10 Ezra prepared *his h.*
Neh. 9:8 foundest *his h.* faithful
Est. 6:6 H. thought in *his h.*
7:5 durst presume in *his h.*
Job 34:14 set *his h.* upon man
41:24 *his h.* is as firm as a stone
Ps. 10:3 boasteth of *his h.* desire
6 said in *his h.* 11, 13 ; 14:1 ; 53:1
15:2 speaketh truth in *his h.*
21:2 given him *his h.* desire
33:11 thoughts of *his h.*
37:31 law of his God in *his h.*
41:6 *his h.* gathereth iniquity
55:21 smooth, war in *his h.*
78:72 accor. to integrity of *h. h.*
112:7 *his h.* is fixed
8 *his h.* is established
Prov. 6:14 frowardis. is in *his h.*
18:2 *his h.* may discover itself
19:3 *his h.* fretteth ag. the Lord
23:7 as think. in *his h.* so is he:
but *his h.* is not with thee
28:14 that hardeneth *his h.* sh. f.
Ec. 2:23 *his h.* taketh no rest
5:20 God answer. in joy of *h. h.*
Cant. 3:11 day of gladn. of *h. h.*
Is. 7:2 *his h.* moved, h. of people
10:7 neither doth *his h.* think so
32:6 *his h.* will work iniquity
44:19 none considereth in *his h.*
57:17 frowardly in way of *h. h.*
Jer. 9:8 in *his h.* he layeth
30:21 *his h.* to approach to me
24 performed intents of *his h.*
48:29 heard haughtine. of *his h.*
Ezek. 14:4 set. up idols in *h. h.* 7
31:10 *his h.* lifted up, *Dan.* 5:20
Dan. 4:16 *h. h.* be changed, 5:21
11:12 *his h.* shall be lifted up
28 *his h.* be ag. the covenant
Mat. 5:28 com. adultery in *his h.*
13:19 was sown in *his h.*
24:48 say in *his h. Luke* 12:45
Mark 7:19 enter. not into *his h.*
11:23 not doubt in *h. h.* but bel.
Luke 6:45 good treasure of *h. h.*
Acts 7:23 came into *h. h.* to visit
1 *Cor.* 7:37 stand. stead. in *h. h.*
14:25 secrets of *h. h.* made man.
2 *Cor.* 9:7 purposeth in *his h.*

My HEART.
Deut. 29:19 in imagina. of *my h.*
Jos. 14:7 as it was in *my h.*
Jud. 5:9 *my h.* tow. governors
1 *Sam.* 2:1 *my h.* rejoiceth in L.
1 *K.* 9:3 *my h.* there, 2 *Chr.* 7:16
2 *K.* 5:26 went not *my h.* wi. th.
10:15 thy heart right as *my h. ?*
1 *Chr.* 12:17 *my h.* shall be knit
28:2 in *my h.* to build a house
2 *Chr.* 29:10 *my h.* to make a co.
Neh. 2:12 God put in *my h.* 7:5
Job 17:11 thoughts of *my h.*
23:16 God maketh *my h.* soft
27:6 *my h.* sh. not reproach me
31:7 *my h.* walk. af. mine eyes
9 *my h.* been dec. by a woman
27 *my h.* hath been se. enticed
33:3 words of uprightn. of *my h.*
37:1 *my h.* trembleth
Ps. 4:7 put gladness in *my h.*
13:2 sorrow in *my h.* daily
5 *my h.* sh. rejoice in thy salv.
16:9 *my h.* glad; 17:3 pro. *my h.*
19:14 medita. of *my h.* be accep.
22:14 *my h.* is like wax
26:2 try my reins, and *my h.*
25:17 troubles of *my h.* enlarged
27:3 *my h.* shall not fear
8 *my h.* said to thee, Thy face

28:7 *my h.* trust. *my h.* greatly
38:8 by reason of disq. of *my h.*
10 *my h.* panteth, *Is.* 21:4
39:3 *my h.* was hot within me
40:8 thy law is within *my h.*
10 not hid righteous. in *my h.*
12 therefore *my h.* faileth me
45:1 *my h.* is indi. good matter
Ps. 49:3 meditation of *my h.*
55:4 *my h.* is sore pained
57:7 *my h.* is fixed, 108:1
61:2 *my h.* is overwhelmed
66:18 if I regard iniq. in *my h.*
69:20 repro. hath broken *my h.*
73:13 cleansed *my h.* in vain
21 thus *my h.* was grieved
26 *my h.* faileth
84:2 *my h.* crieth out for liv. G.
86:11 unite *my h.* to fear
102:4 *my h.* is smitten and with.
109:22 *my h.* is wounded within
119:11 word have I hid in *my h.*
32 thou shalt enlarge *my h.*
36 incline *my h.* to thy testim.
80 *my h.* be sound in thy stat.
111 testim. the rejoic. of *my h.*
112 inclined *my h.* to thy stat.
131:1 L. *my h.* is not haughty
139:23 search me. know *my h.*
141:4 incline not *my h.* to evil
143:4 *my h.* within me is deso.
Prov. 5:12 *my h.* desp. reproof
20:9 say, I made *my h.* clean ?
23:15 be wise, *my h.* sh. rejoice
Ec. 1:13 I gave *my h.* to seek
16 *my h.* had great experience
17 gave *my h.* to know wisdom
2:1 *my h.* I will pro. 15 ; 3:17, 18
3 in *my h.* to give to wine
10 withheld not *my h.* from joy
20 to cause *my h.* to despair
7:25 ap. *my h.* to know, 8:9, 16
Cant. 4:9 thou ravished *my h.* 9
5:2 I sleep, but *my h.* waketh
Is. 63:4 day of veng. in *my h.*
Jer. 3:15 pastors accord. to *my h.*
4:19 pain. *my h. my h.* m. noise
7:31 neither came it into *my h.*
8:18 comf. myself, *my h.* is faint
12:3 seen me and tried *my h.*
15:16 joy and rejoicing of *my h.*
20:9 his word was in *my h.*
23:9 *my h.* broken ; 48:31 sh. m.
48:36 *my h.* shall sound for M.
Lam. 1:20 *my h.* is turned
22 *my h.* is faint
3:51 mine eye affecteth *my h.*
Hos. 11:8 *my h.* turned with. me
Acts 2:26 therefore did *my h.* rej.
21:13 to weep, and break *my h. ?*
Rom. 9:2 contin. sorrow in *my h.*
10:1 *my h.* desire to G. for Is. is
Phil. 1:7 bec. I have you in *my h.*

See APPLIED.

One HEART.
2 *Chr.* 30:12 to give *one h.*
Jer. 32:39 give *one h. Ezek.* 11:19
Acts 4:32 multitude were of *o. h.*

Our HEART.
Deut. 1:28 breth. have disc. *o. h.*
Ps. 33:21 for *our h.* shall rejoice
44:18 *our h.* is not turned back
Lam. 3:41 let us lift up *our h.*
5:15 joy of *o. h.* ; 17 *our h.* faint
Luke 24:32 did not *our h.* burn
2 *Cor.* 6:11 *our h.* is enlarged
1 *John* 3:20 if *our h.* cond. us, 21

Own HEART.
Num. 15:39 seek not after *own h.*
1 *Sam.* 13:14 m. after *o. h. Acts*
13:22

2 *Sam.* 7:21 accord. to thine *o. h.*
hast thou done, 1 *Chr.* 17:19
1 *K.* 8:38 the plague of his *o. h.*
Neh. 6:8 feignest th. out of *o. h.*

Ps. 4:4 commune with *own h.*
20:4 grant according to *own h.*

Ps. 37:15 sword sh. ent. th. *o. h.*
77:6 commune with mine *o. h.*
Prov. 28:26 trusteth his *own h.*
Ec. 1:16 I com. with *own h.*
7:22 *own h.* hast cursed others
Jer. 9:14 imagin. of *own h.* 23:17
23:16 a vision of their *own h.*
26 deceit of *o. h. Ezek.* 13:17
Jam. 1:26 deceiveth his *own h.*

Perfect HEART.
1 *K.* 8:61 h. be p. with the Lord
11:4 h. not p. with Lord, 15:3
15:14 nevertheless Asa's *h.* was
p. with Lord, 2 *Chr.* 15:17
2 *K.* 20:3 walked before thee
with a *perfect h. Is.* 38:3
1 *Chr.* 12:38 p. h. to make D. ki.
28:9 serve God with a *p. h.*
29:9 with *p. h.* they off. willing.
19 give to Sol. my son a *p. h.*
2 *Chr.* 16:9 them whose *h.* is *p.*
25:2 right, but not with a *p. h.*
Ps. 101:2 in my house with *p. h.*

Pure HEART.
Ps. 24:4 ascend ? that hath *p. h.*
Mat. 5:8 blessed are *pure* in *h.*
1 *Tim.* 1:5 charity out of *p. h.*
2 *Tim.* 2:22 call on L. out of *p. h.*
1 *Pet.* 1:22 love one an. with *p. h.*

Their HEART.
Gen. 42:28 *their h.* failed them
1 *Chr.* 29:18 prep. *t. h.* unto thee
Job 8:10 words out of *t. h. ?*
17:4 hid *t. h.* from understand.
Ps. 10:17 Lord wilt prepare *t. h.*
78:8 gen. that set not *t. h.* arig.
18 they tempted God in *t. h.*
37 *t. h.* was not right with him
95:10 peo. that do err in *t. h.*
105:25 turned *t. h.* to hate
107:12 he brought down *t. h.*
119:70 *t. h.* is as fat as grease
140:2 imagine mischiefs in *t. h.*
Prov. 24:2 *t. h.* stud. destruction
Ec. 3:11 hath set world in *t. h.*
9:3 madness is in *t. h.* while
Is. 6:10 understand with *t. h.*
Mat. 13:15 ; *Acts* 28:27
29:13 *t. h.* is far from me, *Mat.*
15:8 ; *Mark* 7:6
Jer. 13:10 walk in imag. of *t. h.*
14:14 proph. the deceit of *t. h.*
17:1 sin of Judah graven on *t. h.*
Lam. 2:18 *t. h.* cried to the Lord
Ezek. 14:3 set up idols in *t. h.*
20:16 *t. h.* went after idols
21:15 that *t. h.* may faint, ruins
33:31 *t. h.* goeth after covetous.
Hos. 4:8 they set *t. h.* on iniquity
7:6 made ready *t. h.* like an ov.
10:2 *t. h.* divided ; 13:6 *t. h.* exa.
13:8 will rend the caul of *t. h.*
Zec. 10:7 *t. h.* rejoice in the Lord
Mark 6:52 *t. h.* hard. *Rom.* 1:21
Luke 9:47 perce. thought of *t. h.*
John 12:40 he hath harden. *t. h.*
Acts 2:37 were pricked in *t. h.*
2 *Cor.* 3:15 M. read, vail on *t. h.*
Eph. 4:18 of the blindness of *t. h.*

Thy HEART.
Gen. 20:6 the integrity of *t. h.*
Lev. 19:17 not hate brot. in *t. h.*
Deut. 4:29 if seek him with *t. h.*
6:5 love the Lord with all *t. h.*
7:17 if thou shalt say in *t. h.*
these nations are more than
I. 8:17 ; 18:21 ; *Jer.* 13:22
8:14 *t. h.* be lifted, forget Lord
9:5 not for uprightness of *t. h.*
10:12 serve L. T. G. with all *t. h.*
15:9 not a thou. in *t. h.* wicked h.
10 *t. h.* shall not be grieved
28:67 for the fear of *thy h.*

30:6 circumc. *t. h.* and heart of
14 word is very nigh to *thy h.*
17 if *t. h.* turn, so that th. not
Jud. 19:6 let *t. h.* be merry, 9;
    1 *K.* 21:7
1 *Sam.* 2:33 man be to grieve *t. h.*
14:7 do all that is in *t. h. 2 Sam.*
    7:3 ; 1 *Chr.* 17:2
17:28 pride and naught. of *t. h.*
2 *Sam.* 3:21 over all *t. h.* desire.
3:1 in *t. h.* to build, 2 *Chr.*
    1:11 ; 6:8
2 *K.* 10:15 Jehu said, Is *t. h.* rig.
14:10 *t. h.* lifted, 2 *Chr.* 25:19
22:19 *t. h.* tender, 2 *Chr.* 34:27
2 *Chr.* 19:3 prep. *t. h.* to seek G.
Job 10:13 things hid in *t. h.*
11:13 prep. *t. h.* and stretch out
22:22 lay up his words in *t. h.*
Ps. 27:14 shall strengthen *t. h.*
37:4 give thee desires of *t. h.*
Prov. 2:2 apply *t. h.* to underst.
Prov. 2:10 when wisd. ent. *t. h.*
3:1 let *t. h.* keep my command.
    3 write them on ta. of *t. h.* 7:3
4:4 let *t. h.* ret. my words, 21
    23 keep *t. h.* with all diligence
6:21 bind continually upon *t. h.*
7:25 let not *t. h.* decline to ways
23:15 my son, if *t. h.* be wise
    17 let not *t. h.* envy sinners
    19 hear, my son, guide *t. h.* in
    26 give me *t. h.* let eyes obser.
    33 *t. h.* shall utter perverse th.
Ec. 5:2 not *t. h.* be hasty to utter
11:9 *t. h.* cheer, in ways of *t. h.*
    10 remove sorrow from *t. h.*
Is. 14:13 thou hast said in *t. h.*
33:18 *t. h.* shall meditate terror
47:7 not lay things to *t. h.* 57:11
    8 that sayest in *t. h.* I am, 10
Jer. 4:14 O Jerusalem wash *t. h.*
    18 bitter, bec. it reach. to *t. h.*
31:21 set *t. h.* toward high.
49:16 pride of *t. h.* decei. *Ob.* 3
Lam. 2:19 pour out *t. h.* bef. L.
Ezek. 3:10 my words received
    in *thy h.*
16:30 weak is *t. h.* saith L. G.
22:14 can *t. h.* endure in days
28:2 because *t. h.* is lifted up
    6 hast set *t. h.* as heart of G.
    17 *t. h.* was lifted up because
Dan. 2:30 know the thou. of *t. h.*
5:22 thou hast not humb. *t. h.*
Acts 5:3 why hath Satan fi. *t. h.* ?
    4 why conceived this in *t. h.* ?
8:21 *t. h.* not right in sight of G.
    22 thought of *t. h.* forgiven
Rom. 10:6 say not in *t. h.* who
    9 believe in *t. h.* that G. raised

Upright in HEART.

2 *Chr.* 29:34 Levites were *u. in h.*
Ps. 7:10 which saveth *u. in h.*
11:2 that they shoot at *u. in h.*
32:11 shout for joy ye *u. in h.*
36:10 contin. righte. to *u. in h.*
64:10 all *uprig. in h.* shall glory
94:15 *upri. in h.* shall follow it
97:11 gladness sown for *u. in h.*

Uprightness of HEART.

1 *K.* 3:6 walketh in *u. of h.* 9:4
Ps. 119:7 praise thee with *h.*

Whole HEART.

Ps. 9:1 I praise thee, O Lord, w.
    my *w. h.* 111:1 ; 138:1
119:2 seek him with the *w. h.*
    10 with my *w. h.* I sought
    34 I shall observe it with *w. h.*
    58 entreated favor with *w. h.*
    69 thy precepts with *w. h.*
    145 I cried with my *w. h.* O L.
Is. 1:5 head is sick. *w. h.* faint
Jer. 3:10 not turned with *w. h.*
24:7 return to me with *w. h.*
32:41 plant in land with *w. h.*

Whose HEART.

Ex. 35:26 women *w. h.* stirred
Deut. 29:18 *w. h.* turneth from L.
2 *Sam.* 17:10 *w. h.* is as *h.* of lion
1 *K.* 8:39 *w. h.* kn. 2 *Chr.* 6:30
2 *Chr.* 16:9 them *w. h.* is perfect
Ps. 84:5 in *w. h.* are ways of
Ec. 7:26 woman *w. h.* is snares
Is. 51:7 in *w. h.* is my law
Ezek. 11:21 *w. h.* walketh after
Acts 16:14 *w. h.* the L. opened

Your HEART.

Deut. 10:16 foresk. of *your h.*
    Jer. 4:4
11:16 that *y. h.* be not deceived
    18 lay up my words in *y. h.*
1 *K.* 11:2 will turn away *your h.*
1 *Chr.* 22:19 set *y. h.* to seek L.
Ps. 22:26 *y. h.* shall live for ever
31:24 he shall strengthen *y. h.*
62:8 pour out *y. h.* before him
    10 riches, set not *y. h.* on them
69:32 *y. h.* live that seek God
Is. 66:14 see this, *y. h.* shall rej.
Jer. 51:46 and lest *your h.* faint
Joel 2:13 rend *y. h.* not garments
Zec. 7:10 none imag. evil in *y. h.*
Mat. 6:21 *y. h.* be also, *Luke* 12:34
Mark 8:17 have ye *y. h.* hard. ?
10:5 for hard. of *y. h.* he wrote
John 14:1 not *y. h.* be troubl. 27
16:6 said this, sorrow filled *y. h.*
    22 I will see you, *y. h.* shall
Eph. 6:5 single. of *y. h.* as to C.

HEARTED.

Ex. 35:22 as were willing-*h.*
Deut. 20:8 what man is faint-*h.* ?
Ps. 76:5 the stout-*h.* are spoiled
Is. 24:7 all the merry-*h.* do sigh
61:1 sent me to bind up brok.-*h.*
Ezek. 3:7 house of Israel hard-*h.*

Tender-HEARTED.

2 *Chr.* 13:7 Reho. young and *t.-h.*
Eph. 4:32 kind one to ano. *t.-h.*

Wise-HEARTED.

Ex. 28:3 spe. to all th. are *w.-h.*
31:6 hearts of all that are *w.-h.*
35:10 *w.-h.* among you sh. come
    25 women that were *w -h.*
36:1 wro. every *w.-h.* man, 2, 8

HEARTH.

Gen. 18:6 make cakes upon *h.*
Ps. 102:3 bones are burnt as *h.*
Is. 30:14 sherd to take fire fr. *h.*
Jer. 36:22 a fire on the *h.* burni.
    23 roll into fire that was on *h.*
Zec. 12:6 governors of J. like *h.*

HEARTY, ILY.

Prov. 27:9 friend by *h.* counsel
Col. 3:23 do it *h.* as to the Lord

HEARTS.

Jos. 7:5 *h.* of the people melted
1 *Sam.* 10:26 *h.* G. had touched
2 *Sam.* 15:6 Absal. stole *h.* of Is.
1 *K.* 8:39 thou only knowest the
    h. 2 *Chr.* 6:30
1 *Chr.* 28:9 Lord searcheth all *h.*
Ps. 7:9 God trieth *h. Prov.* 17:3
Prov. 15:11 more then *h.* men
21:2 the Lord pondereth the *h.*
31:6 wine to those of heavy *h.*
Ezek. 32:9 also vex *h.* of people
Dan. 11:27 kings' *h.* to do misc.
Luke 1:17 turn *h.* of the fathers
    2:35 thoughts of *h.* be revealed
21:26 men's *h.* failing them
Acts 1:24 know. *h.* of men, 15:8
Rom. 8:27 he that searcheth *h.*
16:18 deceive *h.* of the simple
1 *Cor.* 4:5 manifest counsels of *h.*
Rev. 2:23 I am he searcheth *h.*

Our HEARTS.

Jos. 2:11 heard, *our h.* did melt
1 *K.* 8:58 incline *our h.* to him

Acts 14:17 filling *o. h.* with food
Rom. 5:5 love of G. abr. in *our h.*
2 *Cor.* 1:22 earnest of S. in *our h.*
3:2 our epistle written in *o. h.*
4:6 God hath shined in *our h.*
7:3 in *our h.* to die and live
1 *Thes.* 2:4 God, who trieth *o. h.*
Heb. 10:22 *our h.* fr. evil consci.
1 *John* 3:19 assure *o. h.* bef. him

Their HEARTS.

Lev. 26:36 a faintness into *t. h.*
Jud. 9:3 *t. h.* inclined to fol. A.
    19:22 making *their h.* merry
2 *Chr.* 6:14 be. thee with all *t. h.*
11:16 set *their h.* to seek the L.
20:33 not prep. *their h.* to God
Job 1:5 sons cursed G. in *their h.*
Ps. 28:3 mischief is in *their h.*
33:15 fashioneth *their h.* alike
35:25 let them not say in *t. h.*
81:12 gave up to *t.* own *h.* lust
125:4 that are upright in *t. h.*
Is. 44:18 hath shut *their h.* they
Jer. 31:33 law in *t. h. Heb.* 8:10
32:40 I will put my fear in *t. h.*
Ezek. 13:2 prop. out of *t.* own *h.*
    3:9 as an adamant
Mark 2:6 reasoning in *their h.*
    3:5 grieved for hardness of *t. h.*
    4:15 word sown in *t. h. Lu.* 8:12
Luke 1:51 imaginations of *t. h.*
    66 heard laid them up in *t. h.*
    3:15 all men mused in *their h.*
Acts 7:39 *t. h.* turned back to E.
Rom. 1:24 through lust of *th. h.*
    2:15 work of law written in *t. h.*
Col. 2:2 *t. h.* might be comforted
Heb. 3:10 always err in *their h.*
Rev. 17:17 G. hath put it in *t. h.*

Your HEARTS.

Gen. 18:5 comfort ye *your h.*
Deut. 20:3 O Is. let not *y. h.* faint
32:46 set *y. h.* to all the words
Jos. 24:23 incline *y. h.* to the L.
1 *Sam.* 6:6 do ye harden *your h.* ?
    7:3 return to L. with all *your h.*
    and prepa. *your h.* to the L.
Jer. 42:20 dissembled in *your h.*
Zec. 8:17 none imag. evil in *y. h.*
Mat. 9:4 think evil in *your h.* ?
18:35 if from *y. h.* forgive not
19:8 bec. of hardness of *y. h.*
Mark 2:8 why reas. th. in *y. h.* ?
Luke 5:22 reason ye in *your h.* ?
    16:15 God knoweth *your h.*
    21:14 settle in *y. h.* not to me.
    34 time *y. h.* be overcharged
24:38 do thoughts arise in *y. h.* ?
Gal. 4:6 sent S. of Son into *y. h.*
Eph. 3:17 Ch. may dwell in *y. h.*
5:19 mel. in *y. h.* to L. *Col.* 3:16
6:22 that he might comfort *y. h.*
Phil. 4:7 keep *y. h.* and minds
Col. 3:15 peace of G. rule in *y. h.*
    4:8 estate and comfort *y. h.*
1 *Thes.* 3:13 may stablish *y. h.*
2 *Thes.* 2:17 comfort *your h.*
    3:5 Lord direct *your h.* into love
Jam. 3:14 if ye ha. strife in *y. h.*
    4:8 pur. *y. h.* ye double-minded
5:5 ye have nourished *y. h.*
    8 be ye patient, stablish *y. h.*
1 *Pet.* 3:15 sanctify Lord in *y. h.*
2 *Pet.* 1:19 day-star arise in *y. h.*

HEAT.

Gen. 8:22 cold and *h.* summer
18:1 tent-door in *h.* of the day
Deut. 29:24 what meaneth the *h.*
1 *Sam.* 11:11 slew till *h.* of day
1 *K.* 1:1 gat no *h.* ; 2 Lord gat *h.*
Job 24:19 drought and *h.* consu.
30:30 bones are burnt with *h.*
Ps. 19:6 is nothing hid from *h.*
Ec. 4:11 toge. then they have *h.*

Is. 4:6 shad. in day from *h.* 25:4
18:4 clear *h.* on herbs, and like
cloud of dew in *h.* of harvest
25:5 as *h.* in a dry place, even *h.*
49:10 neither *h.* nor sun smite
Jer. 17:8 not see when *h.* cometh
36:30 dead body cast out to *h.*
51:39 in *h.* I will make feasts
Ezek. 3:14 I went in *h.* of spirit
Mat. 20:12 borne burden and *h.*
Luke 12:55 so. wind blow, be *h.*
Acts 28:3 came viper out of the *h.*
Jam. 1:11 sun risen with bur. *h.*
2 *Pet.* 3:10 elements melt with *h.*

HEATED.

Dan. 3:19 more th. wont to be *h.*
Hos. 7:4 as an oven *h.* by baker

HEATH.

Jer. 17:6 like *h.* in desert, 48:6

HEATHEN.

2 *Sam.* 22:44 kept me to be head
of *h. Ps.* 18:43
2 *K.* 16:3 abominat. of *h.* 17:15 ;
21:2 ; 2 *Chr.* 28:3 : 36:14
17:8 Is. walked in statutes of *h.*
1 *Chr.* 16:35 deliver us from *h.*
2 *Chr.* 20:6 rulest over king. of *h.*
33:9 Judah do worse than the *h.*
Ezr. 6:21 fr. filthiness of the *h.*
Neh. 5:8 redeem. Jews sold to *h.*
Ps. 2:1 do *h.* rage ? *Acts* 4:25
8 I give the *h.* for inheritance
9:5 thou hast rebuked the *h.*
15 the *h.* are sunk in the pit
19 let *h.* be judged in thy sight
10:16 the *h.* perish. out his land
33:10 counsel of *h.* to naught
44:2 how th. didst drive out *h.*
46:6 the *h.* raged, the kingdoms
47:8 God reigneth over the *h.*
59:5 theref. awake to visit all *h.*
8 have all the *h.* in derision
78:55 cast out the *h.* also, 80:8
79:1 *h.* are come into thine inh.
6 pour wrath on *h. Jer.* 10:25
10 *h.* say, Wh. their G. ? 115:2
94:10 he that chastiseth the *h.*
98:2 openly show in sight of *h.*
102:15 *h.* shall fear name of L.
106:41 gave them to hand of *h.*
111:6 give them heritage of *h.*
149:7 exe. vengeance upon *h.*
Is. 16:8 lords of *h.* broken down
Jer. 10:2 learn not way of *h.*
Lam. 1:10 seen that *h.* entered
Ezek. 11:12 after manners of *h.*
20:9 not be polluted be. *h.* 14:22
32 say, we will be as the *h.*
41 sanctified before *h.* 28:25
22:4 made thee a repr. to the *h.*
16 thine inheri. in sight of *h.*
23:30 gone a whoring after *h.*
25:7 deliver. thee for spoil to *h.*
8 house of Jud. is like to all *h.*
31:11 hand of mighty one of *h.*
34:29 neither bear shame of *h.*
36:3 possession to residue of *h.*
4 derision to the residue of *h.*
6 ye have borne shame of *h.*
23 *h.* know that I am the Lord,
36 ; 37:28 ; 38:16 ; 39:7
39:21 the *h.* shall see my judg.
Joel 2:17 *h.* sho. rule over them
3:11 come, all ye *h.* gather
12 let the *h.* be wakened
Amos 9:12 possess rem. of all *h.*
Ob. 15 day of L. is near on *h.*
16 so sh. *h.* drink continually
Mic. 5:15 exe. fury upon the *h.*
Hab. 3:12 didst thr. *h.* in anger
Zep. 2:11 isles of *h.* sh. worship
Hag. 2:22 destroy strength of *h.*
Zec. 1:15 displeased with *h.*
9:10 he sh. speak pea. to the *h.*

Zec. 14:14 wealth of *h.* shall be
Mat. 6:7 use not repeti. as *h.* do
18:17 let him be to thee as a *h.*
2 *Cor.* 11:26 in perils by the *h.*
Gal. 2:9 should go unto the *h.*
3:8 God would justify the *h.*

Among the HEATHEN.

Lev. 26:33 I will scat. you *a. t. h.*
Jer. 9:16 ; *Ezek.* 20:23 ; 22:15
38 ye shall perish *am. the h.*
2 *Sam.* 22:50 I will gi. thanks to
thee, O L. *a. t. h. Ps.* 18:49
1 *Chr.* 16:24 declare his glory
am. the h. Ps. 96:3
Ps. 44:11 thou scatter us *a. t. h.*
14 mak. us a by-word *a. the h.*
46:10 I will be exalted *a. t. h.*
96:10 say *a. t. h.* Lord reigneth
106:35 were mingled *a. the h.*
47 O L. gather us from *a. t. h.*
110:6 he shall judge *am. the h.*
126:2 *a.* L. ha. done great
Jer. 49:15 ma. thee small *a. t. h.*
Lam. 4:15 *a. h.* shall no more so.
20 under his shad. live *a. t. h.*
Ezek. 11:16 cast th. far off *a. t. h.*
12:16 declare abomina. *a. t. h.*
16:14 renown went forth *a. t. h.*
36:19 scatter them *am. the h.*
21 Isr. profaned *a. the h.* 22, 23
24 will take you fr. *a. h.* 37:21
39:21 will set my glory *a. t. h.*
Joel 2:19 no more a repro. *a. t. h.*
Ob. 1 an ambas. is sent *a. t. h.*
2 made thee small *a. the h.*
Hab. 1:5 behold ye *a. the h.*
Zec. 8:13 were a curse *a. t. h.*
Mal. 1:11 name be great *a. h.* 14
Gal. 1:16 preach him *a. the h.*

HEAVE, D.

Ex. 29:27 *h.* of ram of consecra.
Num. 15:20 offering so sh. ye *h.*
18:30 ye *h.* the best thereof, 32

See OFFERING, SHOULDER.

HEAVEN.

Gen. 1:1 G. created *h.* and earth
8 God called the firmament *h.*
14 lights in firmam. of *h.* 15
20 fowl that fly in firma. of *h.*
7:11 windows of *h.* were open.
8:2 windows of *h.* were stopped
14:19 pos. *h.* and earth, 22
19:24 rained fire from Lord of *h.*
27:28 G. give thee of d. of *h.* 39
28:17 This is the gate of *h.*
49:25 bless thee wi. bless. of *h.*
Ex. 20:11 Lord made *h.* 31:17
24:10 as it were the body of *h.*
Lev. 26:19 make your *h.* as iron
Deut. 4:11 burned to midst *h.*
26 I call *h.* and earth to witness, 30:19 ; 31:28
32 ask from side of *h.* to other
36 out of *h.* made th. hear voi.
10:14 *h.* and *h.* of *h. Ps.* 115:16
11:17 he shut up *h.* 1 *K.* 8:35 ;
2 *Chr.* 6:26 ; 7:13
28:12 open *h.* to give thee rain
23 *h.* over thy head shall be
30:4 utmost part of *h. Neh.* 1:9
33:13 the precious things of *h.*
26 God of *h.* rid. upon the *h.*
1 *Sam.* 2:10 out of *h.* sh. he thun.
2 *Sam.* 18:9 up bet. *h.* and earth
21:10 water dropped out of *h.*
22:8 the foundations of *h.* mov.
1 *K.* 8:27 *h.* and *h.* of heav. not
contain thee, 2 *Chr.* 2:6; 6:18
35 when *h.* is shut up no rain
2 *K.* 19:15 th. hast made *h.* and
earth, 2 *Chr.* 2:12; *Neh.* 9:6
1 *Chr.* 21:16 angel betw. *h.* and
Job 11:8 it is as high as *h.* ?
20:27 *h.* shall reveal his iniquity
22:12 is not G. in height of *h.* ?
14 walketh in the circuit of *h.*

26:11 the pillars of *h.* tremble
38:29 frost of *h.* who ha. ge. it ?
33 knowest thou ordin. of *h.* ?
37 who can stay bottles of *h.* ?
Ps. 19:6 going is from end of *h.*
69:34 *h.* and earth praise him
78:23 he opened the doors of *h.*
24 given them of corn of *h.*
89:29 th. to endure as days of *h.*
103:11 *h.* is high above earth
105:40 sat. them wi. bread of *h.*
115:15 L. who ma. *h.* and earth,
121:2 ; 124:8 ; 134:3 ; 146:6 ;
Is. 37:16 ; *Jer.* 32:17 ; *Acts*
4:24 ; 14:15 ; *Rev.* 14:7
147:8 covereth *h.* with clouds
148:13 gl. is above earth and *h.*
Prov. 25:3 *h.* for height, earth
Is. 40:12 hath meted out *h.* ?
66:1 *h.* is my throne, *Acts* 7:49

Jer. 7:18 cakes to queen of *h.*
10:2 be not dism. at signs of *h.*
23:24 do not I fill *h.* and earth ?
31:27 if *h.* above can be meas.
33:25 not appointed ordin. of *h.*
44:17 inc. to qu. of *h.* 18, 19, 25
51:15 hath stretched out the *h.*
Lam. 4:19 swifter th. eagles of *h.*
Ezek. 8:3 lift. me be. earth and *h.*
32:7 I will cover the *h.*
8 lights of *h.* will I make dark
Dan. 4:15 be wet with dew of *h.*
23, 25, 33 ; 5:21
35 doeth will in army of *h.*
5:23 lifted thyself ag. L. of *h.*
7:2 four winds of *h.* strove
13 man came with clouds of *h.*
8:8 toward four winds of *h.* 11:4
Amos 9:6 build his stories in *h.*
Hag. 1:10 *h.* is stayed from dew
Zec. 2:6 spr. you as winds of *h.*
Mal. 3:10 not open wind. of *h.*
Mat. 5:18 till *h.* and earth pass
34 nor swear by *h. Jam.* 5:12
11:25 thee, L. of *h. Luke* 10:21
23:22 swear by *h.* swear by G.
24:30 S. of man com. in clouds
of *h.* 26:64 ; *Mark* 14:62
31 elect from one end of *h.*
35 *h.* and earth sh. pass away,
Mark 13:31 ; *Luke* 21:33
36 not angels of *h.* but my F.
Mark 13:27 elect fr. ut. part of *h.*
Luke 3:21 J. praying, *h.* opened
4:25 when the *h.* was shut up
15:18 have sinned against *h.* 21
16:17 easier for *h.* and earth
21:26 powers of *h.* sh. be shaken
John 1:51 ye shall see *h.* open
Acts 3:21 wh. the *h.* must receive
10:11 saw *h.* opened, *Rev.* 19:11
Jam. 5:18 and the *h.* gave rain
Rev. 3:12 cometh down out of *h.*
6:14 *h.* departed as a scroll
8:13 angel flying thro' *h.* 14:6
10:6 created *h.* and the things
11:6 these have power to shut *h.*
16:17 a great voice out of *h.*
21 a great hail out of *h.*
18:20 rejoice over her, thou *h.*
19:17 to the fowls that fly in *h.*
20:9 fire came from G. out of *h.*
11 earth and *h.* fled away
21:1 I saw a new *h.* and earth
10 Jerus. descending out of *h.*

See FOWL, FOWLS.

From HEAVEN.

Ex. 16:4 rain bread *from h.*
20:22 talked with you *from h.*
Neh. 9:13
Deut. 26:15 look down *from h.*
Is. 63:15 ; *Lam.* 3:50
28:24 as dust *f. h.* shall it come
Jos. 10:11 L. cast great sto. *f. h.*
Jud. 5:20 fought *f. h.* the stars
2 *Sam.* 22:14 L. thundered *fr. h.*

2 *K.* 1:10 let fire come down *f. h.*
  th. came down fi. *f. h.* 12, 14
1 *Chr.* 21:26 answ. *f. h.* by fire
2 *Chr.* 6:21 hear *f. h.* 23, 27, 30
7:1 fire came down *from k.*
14 will I hear *f. h.* and forgive
Neh. 9:15 gav. them bread *f. h.*
Job 1:16 fire of G. fallen *from h.*
Ps. 14:2 L. look. down *f. h.* 53:2
33:13 the Lord looketh *from h.*
76:8 judment to be heard *f. h.*
80:14 O God, look down *f. h.*
85:11 right. shall look *from h.*
102:19 *f. h.* did the L. behold
Is. 14:12 how art thou fal. *f. h.*
55:10 as snow falleth *from h.*
Lam. 2:1 Lord cast down *f. h.*
Dan. 4:31 a voice *f. h. Mat.* 3:17;
    Luke 3:22 ; *John* 12:28
Mat. 16:1 show them sign *f. h.*
21:25 wh. was it ? *f. h.* or of
  men ? *Mark* 11:30; *Lu.* 20:4
28:2 for the angel descended *f.*
  h. Rev. 10:1 ; 18:1 ; 20:1
Mark 8:11 sign *f. h. Luke* 11:16
Luke 9:54 com. fire to come *f. h.*
10:18 behe. S. as lightning *f. h.*
17:29 fire and brimstone *f. h.*
21:11 great signs sh. the *f. h.*
22:43 angel *f. h.* strengthening
John 1:32 I saw S. descend. *f. h.*
3:13 came down *from h.* 6:33
27 exc. it be given him *fro. h.*
31 he that com. *f. h.* is above
6:31 he gave bread *from h.*
32 M. gave you not bread *f. h.*
38 I came *f. h.* not to do, 42
41 bread came *f. h.* 50, 51, 58
Acts 2:2 there came a sound *f. h.*
9:3 a light *f. h.* sh. 22:6 ; 26:13
11:5 a great sheet let down *f. h.*

Acts 14:17 and gave us rain *f. h.*
Rom. 1:18 wra. of G. is rev. *f. h.*
1 *Cor.* 15:47 se. man is Lord *f. h.*
2 *Cor.* 5:2 clothed with ho. *f. h.*
Gal. 1:8 angel *f. h.* preach
1 *Thes.* 1:10 wait for Son *from h.*
4:16 the L. shall descend *fr. h.*
2 *Thes.* 1:7 L. J. be revealed *f. h.*
Heb. 12:25 him that speak. *f. h.*
1 *Pet.* 1:12 with H. G. sent *f. h.*
Rev. 8:10 fell a great star *f. h.*
9:1 I saw a star fall *from h.*
10:4 I heard a voice *f. h.* saying,
  Seal things and write them
  not, 8; 11:12 ; 14:2, 13 ; 18:4
13:13 fire come down *from h.*

See GOD *of Heaven.*

Host, s of HEAVEN.
Deut. 4:19 *h. of h.* worship him
17:3 hath worship. the *h. of h.*
1 *K.* 22:19 saw L. sit on thr. and
  h. of h. sta. by, 2 *Chr.* 18:18
2 *K.* 17:16 Israel worshi. *h. of h.*
21:3 Manasseh worshipped all
  the *host of h.* 2 *Chr.* 33:3
5 alt. for *host of h.* 2 *Chr.* 33:5
23:4 bro. vessels for *host of h.* 5
Neh. 9:6 made *h. of h.* with their
  h. and *host of h.* worsh. thee
Is. 34:4 *h. of h.* sh. be dissolved
Jer. 8:2 spread them bef. *h. of h.*
19:13 burnt incense to *host of h.*
33:22 as *h. of h.* cannot be num.
Dan. 8:10 great, even to *h. of h.*
Zep. 1:5 off them worship. *h. of h.*
Acts 7:42 to worship *host of h.*

In HEAVEN.
Ex. 20:4 nor likeness of anything
  in *h. Deut.* 5:8
Deut. 3:24 what God in *h.* can
4:39 the Lord is G. *in h.* above
Jos. 2:11 he is God *in h.* above
1 *K.* 8:23 is no God like thee *in*
  h. 2 *Chr.* 6:14
30 hear thou *in h.* 32–49

2 *K.* 7:2 L. make wind. *in h.* 19
1 *Chr.* 29:11 all *in h.* and earth
Job 16:19 my witness is *in h.*
Ps. 11:4 Lord's throne is *in h.*
73:25 wh. have I *in h.* but thee
77:18 voice of thunder *in h.*
78:26 cast wind to blow *in h.*
89:6 who *in h.* can be co. to L. ?
  37 as faithful witnesses *in h.*
113:6 hum. him. to things *in h.*
119:89 thy word is settled *in h.*
Ec. 5:2 God *in h.* thou up. earth
Is. 34:5 sw. shall be bathed *in h.*
Dan. 2:28 G. *in h.* reveal. secrets
Amos 9:6 buildeth stories *in h.*
Mat. 5:12 great is your rew. *in h.*
16 glorify your Father *in h.*
45 chil. of your F. who is *in h.*
48 be perfect as your F. *in h.*
6:9 Our Father *in h. Luke* 11:2
10 on earth as *in h. Luke* 11:2
20 but lay up treasures *in h.*
7:11 F. *in h.* give good things
21 will of my F. *in h.* 12:50
10:32 confess bef. my F. *in h.*
33 him will I deny bef. F. *in h.*
16:17 F. wh. is *in h.* revealed it
19 shall be bound *in h.* 18:18
18:10 desp. not little ones *in h.*
19:21 treasure *in h. Luke* 18:22
22:30 angels *in h. Mark* 12:25
23:9 one is your F. who is *in h.*
24:30 sign of Son of man *in h.*
28:18 all power given me *in h.*
Mark 11:26 nor F. *in h.* forgive
13:25 powers *in h.* sh. be shak.
32 not angels which are *in h.*
Luke 6:23 your re. is great *in h.*
10:20 your names are writ. *in h.*
15:7 joy *in h.* over one sinner
19:38 peace *in h.* glory in high
John 3:13 even Son of man *in h.*
Acts 2:19 wonders *in h.* above
1 *Cor.* 8:5 whe. *in h.* or in earth
Eph. 1:10 gath. in one, thi. *in h.*
3:15 family *in h.* is named
6:9 your Master *in h. Col.* 4:1
Phil. 2:10 of things *in h.*
3:20 our conversation is *in h.*
Col. 1:5 hope wh. is laid up *in h.*
16 things created that are *in h.*
20 to reconcile all things *in h.*
Heb. 10:34 have *in h.* better sub.
12:23 first-born written *in h.*
1 *Pet.* 1:4 inherit. reserved *in h.*
1 *John* 5:7 three bear rec. *in h.*
Rev. 4:1 a door was opened *in h.*
  2 a throne was set *in h.*
5:13 every creature *in h.* saying
8:1 sil. *in h.*; 11:15 voices *in h.*
11:19 temple of G. opened *in h.*

Rev. 12:1 ap. great wonder *in h.* 3
7 there was war *in h.*
8 nor place fou. any more *in h.*
13:6 to blaspheme them *in h.*
14:17 came out of temple *in h.*
15:1 I saw another sign *in h.*
5 tabernacle of testimony *in h.*
19:14 the armies *in h.* followed

Into HEAVEN.
2 *K.* 2:1 L. wo. take Elijah *i. h.*
11 Eli. went by a whirlw. *i. h.*
Ps. 139:8 ascend *into h.* art there
Prov. 30:4 ascend. *i. h. Rom.* 10:6
Is. 14:13 I will ascend *into h.*
Mark 16:19 L. was received *i. h.*
Luke 2:15 angels gone away *i. h.*
24:51 was parted, carried *i. h.*
Acts 1:11 gazing *i. h.* taken *i. h.*
7:55 Stephen looked up *into h.*
10:16 vessel received *i. h.* 11:10
Heb. 9:24 but *into h.* itself
1 *Pet.* 3:22 gone *i. h.* on right h.

See KINGDOM.

HEAVEN, with stars.
Gen. 1:17 G. set *stars* in fir. of *h.*

22:17 will multiply thy seed as
  stars of *h.* 26:4 ; *Ex.* 32:13 ;
  1 *Chr.* 27:23 ; *Neh.* 9:23
Deut. 1:10 as are *stars* of *h.* 10:22
28:62 were as *s.* of *h.* for multi.
Is. 13:10 *s.* of *h.* sh. not give light
Ezek. 32:7 cover *h.* make *s.* dark
Nah. 3:16 multiplied as *s.* of *h.*
Mat. 24:29 *s.* fall fr. *h. Mark* 13:25
Rev. 6:13 *stars* of *h.* fell on earth
12:4 his tail drew third of *s.* of *h.*

To, or unto HEAVEN.
Gen. 11:4 tower may reach *u. h.*
28:12 top of it may reach *to h.*
Deut. 1:28 cities walled *to h.* 9:1
30:12 who sh. go up for us *to h.*
32:40 for I lift up my hand *to h.*
1 *Sam.* 5:12 cry of city w. up *to h.*
1 *K.* 8:54 with hands spread *to h.*
2 *Chr.* 28:9 a rage th. reach. *u. h.*
Ps. 107:26 they mount up *to h.*
Jer. 51:9 her judg. reacheth *u. h.*
Dan. 4:11 tree reached *to h.* 20
Amos 9:2 tho' they climb up *t. h.*
Mat. 11:23 Cap. art exalted *to h.*
14:19 look. up *to h.* he blessed,
  Mark 6:41; *Luke* 9:16
Mark 7:34 looking *to h.* he sighed
Luke 18:13 not lift his eyes *u. h.*
John 3:13 no man ascen. up *to h.*
17:1 Je. lifted up his eyes *to h.*
2 *Cor.* 12:2 caught up *to* third *h.*
Rev. 10:5 angel lifted hand *to h.*
11:12 ascend. up *to h.* in cloud
18:5 her sins have reached *u. h.*

Toward HEAVEN.
Gen. 15:5 look now *toward h.*
Ex. 10:22 stretch. his hand *t. h.*
Jud. 13:20 flame went up *t. h.*
1 *K.* 8:22 Solomon spread forth
  his hands *tow. h.* 2 *Chr.* 6:13
Job 2:12 dust on their heads *t. h.*
Prov. 23:5 fly aw. as eagle *t. h.*
Acts 1:10 looked steadfastly *t. h.*

Under HEAVEN.
Gen. 1:9 waters *under h.* be gat.
6:17 to destroy all flesh fr. *u. h.*
7:19 high hills *u.* the whole *h.*
Deut. 4:19 to all nations *u. h.*
7:24 dest. th. name fr. *u. h.* 9:14
29:20 L. blot out name fr. *u. h.*
2 *K.* 14:27 blot na. of Is. fr. *u. h.*
Job 28:24 G. seeth *u.* the whole *h.*
37:3 directeth it *u.* the whole *h.*
41:11 whatsoever is *u.* is mine
Ec. 1:13 search out all th. *u. h.*
2:3 that good they sho. do *u. h.*
3:1 a time to ev. purpose *u. h.*
Luke 17:24 lighte. one part *u. h.*
Acts 2:5 devout of ev. nation *u. h.*
4:12 none oth. name *u. h.* given
Col. 1:23 gospel to ev. creat. *u. h.*

HEAVENLY.
Mat. 6:14 h. Father will forgive
26 your *h.* Father feedeth them
32 *h.* F. knoweth ye have need
15:13 ev. plant *h.* F. hath not
18:35 so shall my *h.* Father do
Luke 2:13 the *h.* host praising G.
11:13 your *h.* F. sh. give the Sp.
John 3:12 I tell you of *h.* things
Acts 26:19 not disob. to *h.* vision
1 *Cor.* 15:48 as is the *h.* such are
  49 shall bear the image of the *h.*
Eph. 1:3 blessings in *h.* places
20 right hand in *h.* places, 2:6
3:10 the powers in *h.* places
2 *Tim.* 4:18 Lord pres. to *h.* king.
Heb. 3:1 partakers of *h.* calling
6:4 have tasted of the *h.* gift
Heb. 8:5 exa. and sh. of *h.* things
9:23 *h.* things with better sacri.
11:16 *h.* country ; 12:22 *h.* Jeru.

HEAVENS.

Gen. 2:1 *h.* and earth finished
4 generat. of the *h.* and earth
Deut. 32:1 O H. I will sp. *Is.* 1:2
33:28 his *h.* sh. drop down dew
Jud. 5:4 trembled, *h.* dropped
2 *Sam.* 22:10 bow. the *h. Ps.* 18:9
1 *K.* 8:27 *h.* cannot contain thee
1 *Chr.* 16:26 Lord made *h. Neh.*
9:6 ; *Ps.* 96:5 ; 102:25 ; 136:5
31 let the *h.* be glad, earth rej.
2 *Chr.* 6:25 hear fr. the *h.* 33,35,39
Job 14:12 till *h.* be no more
15:15 *h.* not clean in his sight
20:6 excellency mount up to *h.*
26:13 by Sp. he garnished the *h.*
35:5 look to the *h.* and see
Ps. 8:1 thy glory above *h.* 113:4
3 when I consider thy *h.*
19:1 *h.* declare the glory of God
33:6 by word of L. were *h.* made
50:4 sh. call to the *h.* from above
6 *h.* shall declare his righteou.
57:5 be thou exalted, O God,
above the *h.* 11 ; 108:5
10 mercy is great to *h.* 108:5
68:4 that rideth upon the *h.* 33
8 *h.* dropped at presence of G.
73:9 set their mouth ag. the *h.*
89:5 *h.* shall praise thy wonders
11 the *h.* are thine, earth also
96:11 the *h.* rejoice, *Rev.* 12:12
97:6 *h.* declare his righteousness
104:2 stretchest out *h. Is.* 40:22
108:4 mercy is great above *h.*
115:16 the *h.* are the Lord's
144:5 bow thy *h.* O L. and come
148:1 praise ye the Lord from *h.*
4 praise him hea. of *h.* and wa.
Prov. 3:19 he established the *h.*
8:27 when he prepared the *h.*
Is. 13:13 shake the *h. Hag.* 2:6,21
34:4 the *h.* shall be rolled toget.
44:23 sing, O ye *h.* for L. done it
24 stretch. forth the *h.* 45:12 ;
51:13 ; *Jer.* 10:12 ; *Zec.* 12:1
45:8 drop down, ye *h.* fr. above
48:13 my right hand spanned *h.*
49:13 sing. O *h.* be joy. O earth
50:3 I clothe *h.* with blackness
51:6 lift your eyes to *h.*
16 that I may plant the *h.*
55:9 as *h.* are higher than earth
64:1 rend the *h.* and come down
65:17 behold, I create new *h.*
66:22 new *h.* which I will make
Jer. 2:12 be astonished, O ye *h.*
4:23 I beh. *h.* they had no light
25 birds of *h.* were fled, 9:10
28 earth mourn, *h.* above black
10:11 gods not made *h.* sh. peri.
14:22 can the *h.* give showers ?
Ezek. 1:1 *h.* were open. *Mat.* 3:16
Dan. 4:26 known that *h.* do rule
Hos. 2:21 I will hear the *h.*
Joel 2:10 the *h.* shall tremble
Hab. 3:3 his glory covered the *h.*
Zec. 6:5 four spirits of the *h.*
8:12 the *h.* shall give their dew
Mat. 24:29 powers of *h.* shaken
Mark 1:10 he saw the *h.* opened
Acts 2:34 D. is not ascended to *h.*
7:56 behold, I see the *h.* opened
Heb. 1:10 *h.* work of thy hands
4:14 High-p. is passed into *h.*
7:26 H.-p. made higher than *h.*
2 *Pet.* 3:5 word of G. *h.* we. of old
7 *h.* wh. are now are kept in st.
10 *h.* sh. pass away with gr. no.
12 *h.* being on fire shall be dis.

In the HEAVENS.

Ps. 2:4 he that sitteth *in the h.*
18:13 L. also thundered *in the h.*
36:5 thy mercy, O L. is *in the h.*
89:2 faithfulness estab. *in the h.*
103:19 L. prep. his throne *in h.*
115:3 God is *in the h.*

123:1 O thou that dwell. *in t. h.*
Jer. 10:13 waters *in the h.* 51:16
Lam. 3:41 lift hearts to G. *in h.*
Joel 2:30 show wonders *in the h.*
Luke 12:33 a treasure *in the h.*
2 *Cor.* 5:1 not made w. hands,*in h.*
Heb. 8:1 thr. of Majesty *in t. h.*
9:23 patterns of things *in the h.*

HEAVY.

Ex. 17:12 Moses' hands were *h.*
18:18 this thing is too *h.*
Num. 11:14 not able, bec. too *h.*
1 *Sam.* 4:18 Eli was old man *h.*
2 *Sam.* 14:26 hair was *h.* on him
1 *K.* 12:4 father's *h.* yoke, 10, 11,
14 ; 2 *Chr.* 10:4, 10, 11, 14
1 *K.* 14:6 sent to thee with *h.* tid.
Neh. 5:18 bondage *h.* on people
Job 33:7 neither shall hand be *h.*
Ps. 32:4 thy hand was *h.* on me
38:4 *h.* burden, they are too *h.*
Prov. 25:20 songs to a *h.* heart
27:3 stone is *h.* sand weighty
31:6 wine to those of *h.* hearts
Is. 6:10 and make their ears *h.*
24:20 transgression shall be *h.*
30:27 the burden thereof is *h.*
46:1 carriages were *h.* loaden
58:6 to undo the *h.* burdens ?
59:1 nei. his ear *h.* that it cannot
Lam. 3:7 made chain *h.*
Mat. 11:28 ye that are *h.* laden
23:4 for they bind *h.* burdens
26:37 be sorrowful, and very *h.*
43 eyes were *h. Mark* 14:33, 40
Luke 9:32 were *h.* with sleep

HEAVIER.

Job 6:3 *h.* than sand of the sea
23:2 my stroke is *h.* than groan.
Prov. 27:3 a fool's wrath is *h.*

HEAVILY.

Ex. 14:25 that drave them *h.*
Ps. 35:14 bowed *h.* as one mour.
Is. 47:6 on ancient *h.* laid yoke.

HEAVINESS.

Ezr. 9:5 I rose from *h.*
Job 9:27 I will leave off my *h.*
Ps. 69:20 broken heart full of *h.*
119:28 my soul melteth for *h.*
Prov. 10:1 fool. son *h.* of mother
12:25 *h.* in heart mak. it stoop
14:13 end of that mirth is *h.*
Is. 61:3 garm. of praise for *h.*
Rom. 9:2 great *h.* and sorrow
3 *Cor.* 2:1 wou. not come ag. in *h.*
Phil. 2:26 brother was full of *h.*
Jam. 4:9 your joy be turned to *h.*
1 *Pet.* 1:6 if need be ye are in *h.*

HEBER.

Gen. 46:17 Beriah, H. 1 *Chr.* 7:31
Jud. 4:11 H. the Kenite, 17 ; 5:24
Luke 3:35 Phalec, was son of H.

HEBREW.

Gen. 14:13 Abra. the H. 39:14
41:12 a young man, a H.
Ex. 2:11 Egyptian smiting a H.
Jer. 34:9 should let a H. go free
Jon. 1:9 unto them I am a H.

HEBREWS.

Gen. 40:15 sto. out of land of H.
Ex. 2:6 this one of H. chil. 13 ;
3:18 ; 5:3 ; 7:16 ; 9:1 ; 10:3
1 *Sam.* 4:6 shout in camp of H. 9
13:3 let H. hear, 19 ; 14:11, 21
29:3 what do these H. hear ?
Acts 6:1 murmuring ag. the H.
2 *Cor.* 11:22 H. or Israelites ?
Phil. 3:5 of Benja. a Heb. of H.

HEBREW, language.

Luke 23:38 writ. in H. *John* 19:20
John 5:2 called in H. 19:13, 17
Acts 21:40 spake in H. 22:2 ; 26:14
Rev. 9:11 in H. Abaddon, 16:16

HEBREW man.

Deut. 15:12 if brother, a H. *man*

HEBREW servant.

Gen. 39:17 H. *s.* came, *Ex.* 21:2

HEBREW woman, women.

Ex. 1:16 midwife to H. *w.* 19
2:7 a nurse of the H. *women ?*
Deut. 15:12 if any H. *w.* be sold

HEBREWESS. *Jer.* 34:9

HEBRON, place.

Gen. 23:2 Sarah died in H. 35:27 ;
Jos. 14:15 ; 20:7 ; *Jud.* 1:10
37:14 Jacob sent Jos. out of H.
Num. 13:22 H. built before Zoan
2 *Sam.* 2:11 Dav. was king in H.
5:5 ; 1 *K.* 2:11 ; 1 *Chr.* 29:27
3:32 buried Abner in H. 4:12
5:3 in H. 1 *Chr.* 11:3 ; 12:38
15:7 Absalom vowed in H. 10
1 *Chr.* 12:38 perfect heart to H.

HEBRON, person.

Ex. 6:18 Kohath, H. *Num.* 3:19
1 *Chr.* 2:42, 43; 6:2, 18; 15:9; 23:12,
19 ; 24:23

HEDGE, S.

Job 1:10 not made a *h.* ab. him ?
Ps. 80:12 broken her *h. ?* 89:40
Prov. 15:19 way of sloth *h.* of th.
Ec. 10:8 breaketh *h.* serpent bite
Is. 5:5 take away the *h.* thereof
Jer. 49:3 run to and fro by the *h.*
Ezek. 13:5 nor made up *h.* 22:30
Mic. 7:4 sharper than a thorn *h.*
Nah. 3:17 as grasshoppers in *h.*
Mark 12:1 he set a *h.* about it
Luke 14:23 go to highways and *h.*

HEDGE, D.

Job 3:23 way is hid, whom G. *h.*
Lam. 3:7 he hath *h.* me about
Hos. 2:6 *h.* up thy way with tho.
Mat. 21:33 vineyard, *h.* it round

HEED.

2 *K.* 10:31 Jehu took no *h.*
Ps. 119:9 tak. *h.* ac. to thy word
Prov. 17:4 giveth *h.* to false lips
Ec. 12:9 preacher gave good *h.*
Jer. 18:18 not gi. *h.* to any words
19 give *h.* to me, O Lord
Acts 3:5 he gave *h.* unto them
8:6 people of Sam. gave *h.* to P.
10 gave *h.* to Simon least to
1 *Tim.* 1:4 *h.* to fables, *Tit.* 1:14
4:1 giving *h.* to seducing spirits
Heb. 2:1 we ought to give more *h.*

See TAKE.

HEEL, S.

Gen. 3:15 thou sh. bruise his *h.*
25:26 hold on E. *h. Hos.* 12:3
49:17 an adder biteth horse *h.*
Job 13:27 print on *h.* of my feet
18:9 gin shall take him by *h.*
Ps. 41:9 *h.* ag. me, *John* 13:18
49:5 iniq. of my *h.* compass me
Jer. 13:22 iniq. thy *h.* made bare

HEGE. *Est.* 2:3

HEIFER.

Num. 19:2 red *h.* ; 5 burn the *h.*
Deut. 21:3 the elders sh. take a *h.*
4 strike off the *h.* neck
6 shall wash hands over the *h.*
Jud. 14:18 not plou. with my *h.*
Is. 15:5 cry out for Moab as *h.*
Jer. 46:20 Egypt is like a fair *h.*
48:34 uttered their voice as a *h.*
50:11 grown fat as *h.* at grass
Hos. 4:16 Is. as a backsliding *h.*
10:11 Ephraim is as *h.* taught
Heb. 9:13 ashes of *h.* sp. unclean

HEIGHT, S.

Gen. 6:15 *h.* of ark sh. be 30 cu.
Ex. 25:10 ark of Shittim-wood, a
cu. and half *h.* 23 ; 37:1, 10

27:1 *h.* of altar, three cu. 38:1
18 *h.* of court, five cubits, 38:18
30:2 *h.* of altar of incense, 37:25
1 *Sam.* 16:7 look not on *h.* of sta.
17:4 Goliath's *h.* 6 cu. and a sp.
1 *K.* 6:2 *h.* of house of G. 30 cu.
20 oracle twenty cubits in *h.*
26 *h.* of cherub was ten cubits
7:2 *h.* of house of Leb. 30 cubits
16 *h.* of one chapiter 5 cubits
23 *h.* of molten sea five cubits
27 *h.* of one base three cubits
Ezr. 6:3 *h.* of God's house 60 cu.
Job 22:12 God in *h.* of heaven ?
Ps. 102:19 looked fr. *h.* of sanct.
148:1 praise the Lord in the *h.*
Prov. 25:3 the heaven for *h.*
Is. 7:11 ask it in the *h.* above
14:14 I will ascend above the *h.*
Jer. 49:16 O thou that holdest *h.*
51:53 fortify if. of her strength
Ezek. 17:23 in *h.* of Israel, 20:40
19:11 she appeared in her *h.*
31:5 therefore his *h.* was exalted
14 none of the trees exalt for *h.*
32:5 fill the valleys with thy *h.*
Dan. 3:1 image wh. *h.* was 60 cu.
4:11 *h.* reached unto heaven, 20
Amos 2:9 *h.* was like *h.* of cedars
Rom. 8:39 nor *h.* nor depth
Eph. 3:18 the *h.* of love of Ch. ?
Rev. 21:16 breadth and *h.* equal

HEINOUS.
Job 31:11 for this is a *h.* crime

HEIR, S.
Gen. 15:3 born in my house is *h.*
4 This shall not be thine *h.*
21:10 Ishmael shall not be *h.*
2 *Sam.* 14:7 we will destroy *h.*
Prov. 30:23 handmaid *h.* to mis.
Jer. 49:1 hath Is. no sons ? no *h. ?*
2 Is. *h.* to them that were his *h.*
Mic. 1:15 I will bring *h.* to thee
Mat. 21:38 this is the *h. Mark*
12:7 ; *Luke* 20:14
Rom. 4:13 should be *h.* of world
14 if they wh. are of law be *h.*
8:17 *h.* of G. joint *h.* with Ch.
Gal. 3:29 *h.* according to promise
4:1 *h.* as long as he is a child
7 an *h.* of God through Christ
30 son of bond-w. sh. not be *h.*
Eph. 3:6 Gent. sh. be fellow-*h.*
Tit. 3:7 *h.* according to the hope
Heb. 1:2 whom he appointed *h.*
14 who shall be *h.* of salvation
6:17 God willing to show to *h.*
11:7 became *h.* of righteousness
Jam. 2:5 *h.* of the kingdom

1 *Pet.* 3:7 as *h.* together of grace

HELAM. 2 *Sam.* 10:16
HELBON. *Ezek.* 27:18

HELD.
Ex. 17:11 wh. Moses *h.* up hand
Jud. 7:20 *h.* lamps in left hands
2 *Chr.* 4:5 sea *h.* 3,000 baths
Neh. 4:16 half *h.* both spears
17 other hand he *h.* a weapon
Est. 5:2 king *h.* out golden scep.
Job 23:11 my foot *h.* his steps
Ps. 32:9 wh. mouth must be *h.*
94:18 thy mercy, O L. *h.* me up
Cant. 3:4 I *h.* him, and wo. not
7:5 king is *h.* in the galleries
Jer. 50:33 took captives, *h.* them
Dan. 12:7 *h.* up his right hand
Mat. 12:14 *h.* a coun. *Mark* 15:1
Luke 22:63 men that *h.* Jesus
Acts 3:11 man was healed *h.* P.
14:4 part *h.* with J. part apostles
Rom. 7:6 wherein we were *h.*
Rev. 6:9 slain for testim. they *h.*

HELD peace.
Gen. 24:21 wondering *h.* his p.
Lev. 10:3 Aaron *h.* his *peace*

Num. 30:7 husband *h. p.* 11, 14
Neh. 5:8 th. p. found nothing
Job 29:10 nobles *h.* their *peace*
Ps. 39:2 I *h.* my p. from good
Is. 36:21 *h.* their *p. Mark* 3:4; 9:34
57:11 have not I *h.* my *peace ?*
Mat. 26:63 Jesus *h.* his *peace*
Luke 14:4 *h.* p. 20:26 ; *Acts* 11:18
Acts 15:13 *h.* their *p. Ja.* answer

HELDAI. *Zec.* 6:10
HELI. *Luke* 3:23
HELKATH-HAZZURIM. 2 *Sam.*
2:16

HELL.
Deut. 32:22 fire burn unto low. *h.*
2 *Sam.* 22:6 sorrows of *h.* compassed me, *Ps.* 18:5 ; 86:13
Job 11:8 deeper than *h.*
26:6 *h.* is naked before him
Ps. 9:17 wicked turned into *h.*
16:10 not le. soul in *h. Acts* 2:27
55:15 go down quick to *h.*
116:3 pains of *h.* gat hold on me
139:8 bed in *h.* thou art there
Prov. 5:5 steps take hold on *h.*
7:27 house way to *h.* going do.
9:18 guests are in depths of *h.*
15:11 *h.* and destruction bef. L.
24 he may depart from *h.*
23:14 deliver his soul from *h.*
27:20 *h.* and destruction ne. full
Is. 5:14 *h.* hath enlarged herself
14:9 *h.* from beneath is moved
15 shalt be brought down to *h.*
28:15 with *h.* are we at agreem.
18 agreem. with *h.* not stand
57:9 debase thyself even to *h.*
Ezek. 31:16 I cast him down to *h.*
17 went down to *h.* with him
32:21 speak to him out of *h.*
27 down to *h.* with weapons
Amos 9:2 tho' they dig into *h.*
Jon. 2:2 out of belly of *h.*
Hab. 2:5 enlargeth desire as *h.*
Mat. 5:22 in danger of *h.* fire
29 body be cast in *h.* 30
10:28 body in *h. Luke* 12:5
11:23 Capernaum brought down
to *h. Luke* 10:15
16:18 gates of *h.* sh. not prevail
18:9 having two eyes to be cast
into *h. Mark* 9:47
23:15 twofold more child of *h.*
33 can ye escape damna. of *h. ?*
Luke 16:23 in *h.* lifted up his eyes
Acts 2:31 soul was not left in *h.*
Jam. 3:6 tong. is set on fire of *h.*
2 *Pet.* 2:4 cast angels down to *h.*
Rev. 1:18 keys of *h.* and death
6:8 name Death, *h.* followed
20:13 death and *h.* del. up dead
14 death and *h.* cast in lake

HELM.
Jam. 3:4 turn. about wi. small *h.*

HELMET, S.
2 *Chr.* 26:14 Uzziah prepared *h.*
Is. 59:17 *h.* of salvation on head
Jer. 46:4 stand forth with your *h.*
Ezek. 23:24 ag. the shield and *h.*
27:10 shield and *h.* in thee
38:5 with shield and *h.*
Eph. 6:17 the *h.* of salvation
1 *Thes.* 5:8 *h.* hope of salvation

HELP, Substantive.
Gen. 2:18 a *h.* meet for him
20 not found a *h.* meet for him
Ex. 18:4 G. said he, was my *h.*
Deut. 33:7 *h.* to him fr. enemies
26 rideth on heaven in thy *h.*

Deut. 33:29 sa. by L. shi. of thy *h.*
Jud. 5:23 came not to *h.* of Lord
Job 6:13 is not my *h.* in me?
31:21 when I saw *h.* in the gate
Ps. 3:2 say of soul no *h.* for him
20:2 L. send *h.* from sanctuary

27:9 been my *h.* leave not, O
God
33:20 waits for L. he is our *h.*
35:2 stand up for my *h.* 44:26
40:17 my *h.* and my deliv. 70:5
42:5 praise for *h.* of countenance
46:1 God very present *h.*
60:11 *h.* vain *h.* of man, 108:12
63:7 bec. thou hast been my *h.*
71:12 God, make haste for my *h.*
89:19 *h.* on one that is mighty
94:17 unless L. had been my *h.*
115:9 their *h.* and shield, 10, 11
121:1 fr. whence cometh my *h.*
2 my *h.* cometh from the Lord
124:8 our *h.* is in name of Lord
146:3 tr. not man, in whom no *h.*
5 happy hath God of J. for *h.*
Is. 10:3 to wh. will ye flee for *h. ?*
30:5 nor be a *h.* nor profit
34:1 them that go to Eg. for *h.*
2 ag. *h.* of them that work ini.
Lam. 4:17 eyes failed for vain *h.*
Dan. 11:34 holpen with little *h.*
Hos. 13:9 in me is thy *h.*
Acts 26:22 obtained *h.* of God

HELP, Verb.
Gen. 49:25 God of fa. who sh. *h.*
Deut. 32:38 let them rise and *h.*
2 *Sam.* 10:11 be too hard for me,
I will *h.* thee, 1 *Chr.* 19:12
14:4 said, *h.* O king, 2 *K.* 6:26
2 *Chr.* 14:11 it is nothing with
thee to *h. h.* us, O Lord
19:2 should. thou *h.* the ungodly
20:9 thou wilt hear and *h.*
25:8 for God hath power to *h.*
26:13 power to *h.* the king
28:23 *h.* them that they may *h.*
32:8 with us is the L. to *h.* us
Job 8:20 nei. will he *h.* evil-doers
Ps. 12:1 *h.* L. ; 22:11 none to *h.*
22:19 haste thee to *h.* 38:22 ;
40:13 ; 70:1
37:40 L. *h.* them ; 46:5 G. *h.* her
59:4 awake to *h.* ; 79:9 *h.* us
107:12 was none to *h. Is.* 63:5
109:26 *h.* me, O Lord my God
118:7 my part with th. that *h.*
119:86 *h.* me ; 173 thy hand *h.*
175 let thy judgments *h.* me
Ec. 4:10 hath not another to *h.*
Is. 30:7 Egypt. shall *h.* in vain
41:10 will *h.* thee, 13, 14 ; 44:2
50:7 the Lord God will *h.* me, 9
Lam. 1:7 people fell, none did *h.*
Ezek. 32:21 speak out of hell with
them that *h.* him
Dan. 11:45 come to end, none *h.*
Mat. 15:25 saying, Lord, *h.* me
Mark 9:22 have compass. *h.* us
24 L. I believe, *h.* mine unbel.
Luke 5:7 they sh. come and *h.*
10:40 bid her therefore *h.* me
Acts 16:9 co. to Macedonia, *h.* us
21:28 crying out, M. of Israel, *h.*
Phil. 4:3 *h.* women wh. labored
Heb. 4:16 to *h.* in time of need

HELPED.
Ex. 2:17 Moses stood up and *h.*
1 *Sam.* 7:12 hitherto the L. *h.* us
1 *K.* 1:7 follow. Adonijah *h.* him
1 *Chr.* 15:26 God *h.* the Levites
2 *Chr.* 20:23 ev. one *h.* to destroy
26:15 was marvellously *h.*
Job 26:2 how hast thou *h.* him
Ps. 28:7 I am *h.* ; 118:13 L. *h.* me
116:6 brought low, he *h.* me
Is. 41:6 *h.* ev. one his neighbor
49:8 in day of salvation *h.* thee
Zec. 1:15 *h.* forw. the affliction
Acts 18:27 he *h.* them much
Rev. 12:16 earth *h.* the woman

HELPER.
2 *K.* 14:26 nor any *h.* for Israel
Job 30:13 mar my path, no *h.*

Ps. 10:14 art *h.* of fatherless
30:10 L. my *h.* ; 54:4 G. my *h.*
72:12 deliver him hath no *h.*
Jer. 47:4 Tyrus and Zidon ev. *h.*
Rom. 16:9 Urbane our *h.* in Ch.
Heb. 13:6 Lord is my *h.*

HELPERS.
1 *Chr.* 12:18 peace be to thy *h.*
Job 9:13 proud *h.* do stoop under
Ezek. 30.8 her *h.* sh. be destroyed
Nah. 3:9 Put and Lubim were *h.*
Rom. 16:3 Prisc. and Aq. my *h.*
2 *Cor.* 1:24 but are *h.* of your joy
3 *John* 8 be fellow-*h.* to the truth

HELPETH.
1 *Chr.* 12:18 for thy God *h.* thee
Is. 31:3 both he that *h.* shall fall
Rom. 8:26 Sp. also *h.* infirmities
1 *Cor.* 16:16 sub. to ev. one *h.* us

HELPING.
Ezr. 5:2 were prophets of G. *h.*
Ps. 22:1 why art so far from *h.*
2 *Cor.* 1:11 *h.* together by prayer

HELPS.
Acts 27:17 used *h.* undergi. ship
1 *Cor.* 12:28 healings, *h.* govern.

HELVE.
Deut. 19:5 head slippeth from *h.*

HEM, S.
Ex. 28:33 on *h.* thou shalt make
pomegran. 34; 39:24, 25, 26
Mat. 9:20 touch. *h.* of gar. 14:36

HEMAN.
1 *K.* 4:31 Sol. was wiser than H.
1 *Chr.* 2:6; 6:33; 15:17, 19; 16:42;
2 *Chr.* 5:12; 29:14; 35:15

HEMLOCK.
Hos. 10:4 judgment spr. up as *h.*
Amos 6:12 fruit of righte. to *h.*

HEN. *Zec.* 6:14

HEN.
Mat. 23:37 *h.* gath. ch. *Lu.* 13:34

HENCE.
Ex. 33:15 carry us not up *h.*
Ps. 39:13 bef. I go *h.* be no more
Mat. 17:20 remove *h.* to yon. pla.
Luke 4:9 cast thyself down fr. *h.*
16:26 pass from *h.* to you cannot
John 2:16 take these things *h.*
14:31 let us go *h.* ; 18:36 not *k.*
Acts 22:21 send thee *h.* to Gen.

HENCEFORTH.
Ps. 125:2 L. about people from *h.*
131:3 hope in the Lord from *h.*
Is. 9:7 estab. with justice fr. *h.*
52:1 *h.* there sh. no more come
59:21 thy seed's seed *h.*
Mic. 4:7 L. reign in Zion from *h.*
Mat. 23:39 ye shall not see me *h.*
Luke 5:10 fear not, from *h.* thou
12:52 *h.* sh. be five in one house
Acts 18:6 *h.* I will go to Gentiles
2 *Cor.* 5:15 not *h.* live to themsel.
Eph. 4:17 *h.* walk not as other
2 *Tim.* 4:8 *h.* laid up a crown
Rev. 14:13 blessed die in L. fr. *h.*

HENCEFORWARD.
Num. 15:23 *h.* am. generations
Mat. 21:19 no fruit gr. on thee *h.*

HEPHZI-BAH.
2 *K.* 21:1 Manasseh's mother, H.
Is. 62:4 thou shalt be called H.

HERALD.
Dan. 3:4 then a *h.* cried aloud

HERB.
Gen. 1:11 bring forth the *h.* 12
29 every *h.* bearing seed
2:5 made every *h.* ; 3:18 eat *h.*
9:3 *h.* I have given all things
Ex. 9:22 hail smote ev. *h.* 25
10:12 locusts eat every *h.* 15
Deut. 32:2 rain on tender *h.*

---

2 *K.* 19:26 as green *h.* *Is.* 37:27
Job 8:12 withereth bef. other *h.*
38:27 bud of tender *h.* to spring
Ps. 37:2 shall wither as green *h.*
104:14 causeth *h.* to grow
Is. 66:14 bones flourish like *h.*

HERBS.
Ex. 12:8 with bitter *h.* *Num.* 9:11
Deut. 11:10 as a garden of *h.*
1 *K.* 21:2 have it for gard. of *h.*
Ps. 105:35 did eat up all the *h.*
Prov. 15:17 better a dinner of *h.*
27:25 *h.* of mountains gathered
Is. 18:4 like a heat on *h.*
26:19 thy dew is as dew of *h.*
42:15 I will dry up all their *h.*
Jer. 12:4 *h.* of every field wither
Mat. 13:22 is greatest among all
h. Mark 4:32
Luke 11:42 all manner of *h.*
Rom. 14:2 who is weak, eat. *h.*
Heb. 6:7 and bringeth forth *h.*

HERD, S.
Ex. 10:9 with flocks and *h.*
Lev. 27:32 concerning tithe of *h.*
Deut. 12:21 shalt kill of thy *h.*
2 *Sam.* 12:4 spared to take of *h.*
1 *Chr.* 27:29 over the *h.* in Shar.
Is. 65:10 a place for *h.* to lie
Jer. 31:12 toge. for young of *h.*
Joel 1:18 *h.* of cattle perplexed
Jon. 3:7 let not *h.* taste any
thing
Hab. 3:17 shall be no *h.* in stalls
Mat. 8:30 a *h.* of swine feeding
Mark 5:11; *Luke* 8:32

See FLOCKS.

HERDMAN, MEN.
Gen. 13:7 strife betw. *h.* 26:20
1 *Sam.* 21:7 Doeg chiefest of *h.*
Amos 1:1 who was am. *h.* of Te.
7:14 I was no prophet, but a *h.*

HERE.
Deut. 5:3 who are all of us *h.*
Ps. 132:14 my rest, *h.* I dwell
Is. 28:10 *h.* a little, th. a little, 13
Hos. 7:9 gray hairs *h.* and there
Mat. 12:41 a greater than Jonas
is *h.* 42; *Luke* 11:31, 32
16:28 standing *h.* *Luke* 9:27
17:4 L. it is good for us to be *h.*
24:23 lo, *h.* is Ch. *Mark* 13:21
28:6 he is not *h.* he is risen,
Mark 16:6; *Luke* 24:6
Mark 13:1 what buildings are *h.*
John 11:21 if th. hadst been *h.* 32
Acts 9:10 behold, I am *h.* Lord
10:33 we are all *h.* before God
Heb. 13:14 *h.* have we no city

See STAND.

HEREAFTER.
Is. 41:23 things that come *h.*
Dan. 2:29 come to pass *h.* 45
Mat. 26:64 *h.* sh. ye see S. of m.
Mark 11:14 no man eat of thee *h.*
Luke 22:69 *h.* sh. Son of man sit
John 1:51 *h.* ye sh. see heaven
13:7 thou shalt know *h.*
14:30 *h.* I will not talk with you
1 *Tim.* 1:16 to them wh. *h.* beli.
Rev. 1:19 things which sh. be *h.*
4:1 show things wh. must be *h.*
9:12 come two woes more *h.*

HEREBY.
Jos. 3:10 *h.* know G. is am. you
1 *John* 2:3 *h.* we do know him
5 *h.* know that we are in him
3:16 *h.* perceive we love of God
19 *h.* know we are of the truth
24 *h.* we know he abideth in us
4:2 *h.* know ye Spirit of God
6 *h.* know we the Sp. of truth
13 *h.* know that we dw. in him

HEREIN.
1 *John* 4:10 *h.* is love, not that

HERESY, IES.
Acts 24:14 the way they call *h.*
1 *Cor.* 11:19 there be *h.* am. you
Gal. 5:20 works of flesh wrath, *h.*
2 *Pet.* 2:1 bring in damnable *h.*

HERETIC.
Tit. 3:10 *h.* after sec. admonition

HERETOFORE.
1 *Sam.* 4:7 been such a thing *h.*
2 *Cor.* 13:2 them which *h.* sinned

HEREUNTO.
1 *Pet.* 2:21 even *h.* were ye called

HEREWITH.
Mal. 3:10 and prove me now *h.*

HERITAGE, S.
Ex. 6:8 I will give it you for *h.*
Job 20:29 *h.* appointed by God
27:13 *h.* of oppressors they rec.
Ps. 16:6 yea, I have a goodly *h.*
61:5 *h.* of those fear thy name
94:5 break thy peo. afflict thy *h.*
111:6 give them *h.* of heathen
119:111 testimonies taken as *h.*
127:3 children are a *h.* of the L.
135:12 gave their land for a *h.*
136:21, 22
Is. 49:8 inherit the desolate *h.*
54:17 *h.* of servants of the Lord
58:14 feed thee with *h.* of Jacob
Jer. 2:7 my *h.* an abomination
3:19 sh. I give thee goodly *h.* ?
12:7 left *h.* ; 8 my *h.* is as lion
9 my *h.* is as speckled bird
15 bring ag. every man to his *h.*
17:4 thou shalt discont. from *h.*
50:11 O destroyers of my *h.*
Joel 2:17 give not *h.* to reproach
3:2 I will plead wi. them for *h.*
Mic. 2:2 oppress a man and *h.*
7:14 feed the flock of thy *h.*
18 passeth transgression of *h.*
Mal. 1:3 I laid Esau's *h.* waste
1 *Pet.* 5:3 being lords over G.'s *h.*

HERMAS, HERMES. *Ro.* 16:14
HERMOGENES. 2 *Tim.* 1:15

HERMON.
Jos. 13:11 all mt. H. Reuben had
Ps. 89:12 H. shall rejoice in thy
133:3 dew of H. that descended
Cant. 4:8 look from the top of H.

HERMONITES. *Ps.* 42:6

HEROD.
Mat. 2:12 not return to H. 15, 16
14:3 for H. had laid hold, 6
Mark 8:15 leaven of H. 6:17, 21
Luke 3:1 H. tetrarch of Galil. 19
9:7 H. heard of Jesus, 13:31
23:7 sent J. to H. 8, 11, 12, 15
Acts 4:27 H. and Pontius Pilate
12:1 H. vexed the chu. 6, 11, 21

HERODIANS.
Mat. 22:16 they sent th. disciples
with the *h. Mark* 12:13
Mark 3:6 P. took coun. with H.

HERODIAS.
Mat. 14:3 John in prison for H. 6
Mark 6:19 H. had quarrel, 17, 22
Luke 3:19 H. reprov. by J. for H.
HERODION. *Rom.* 16:11

HERON.
Lev. 11:19 *h.* uncl. *Deut.* 14:18
HERSELF. *See* SELF.

HESHBON.
Num. 21:28 fire go. out of H. 30
Jud. 11:26 Is. dw. in H. *Neh.* 9:22
Cant. 7:4 like fish-pools of H.
Is. 15:4 H. shall cry, *Jer.* 49:3
16:8 for field of H. languish, 9
Jer. 48:2 in H. they dev. evil, 45

HETH. *Gen.* 10:15; 23:7; 25:10;
27:46; 49:32; 1 *Chr.* 1:13

HEW, ED.
Ex. 34:1 *h.* 2 tables, *Deut.* 10:1
4 *h.* two tables, *Deut.* 10:3
Deut. 12:3 *h.* down grav. images
19:5 goeth with his neigh. to *h.*
1 *Sam.* 11:7 S. *h.* oxen in pieces
15:33 Samuel *h.* Agag in pieces
2 *Chr.* 2:2 Solo. told 80,000 to *h.*
Jer. 2:13 my peo. *h.* them cist.
Dan. 4:14 *h.* down the tree, 23
Hos. 6:5 I *h.* them by the proph.

HEWER, S.
Deut. 29:11 from *h.* of wood
Jos. 9:21 be *h.* of wood, 23
27 Jos. made them *h.* of wood
1 *K.* 5:15 80,000 *h.* in mountains,
2 *Chr.* 2:18
Jer. 46:22 ag. Eg. as *h.* of wood

HEWETH.
Is. 10:15 boast aga. him that *h.*
22:16 *h.* him out a sepulchre

HEWN.
Prov. 9:1 *h.* out seven pillars
Is. 10:33 high ones shall be *h.*
33:9 Leb. is asha. and *h.* down
51:1 rock whence ye are *h.*
Mat. 3:10 *h.* down and cast into
fire, 7:19; *Luke* 3:9
27:60 *h.* out of a rock, *Mark*
15:46; *Luke* 23:53

See STONE.

HEZEKIAH, *called* **EZE-
KIAS.**
2 *K.* 16:20 H. reign. in his stead.
18:15 H. gave all silver, 22, 31
19:1 H. hea. it, 15; 20:1, 3, 12, 21
2 *Chr.* 29:27 H. com. burnt-offerings, 30:18; 32:15, 33; 33:3
30:20 the Lord hearkened to H.
31:2 H. appoin. 32:8, 17, 22, 30
Is. 36:7, 14, 16; 37:1, 15; 38:1, 3;
39:1, 2, 8

HEZRON.
Gen. 46:9 Reuben, H. *Ex.* 6:14
Ruth 4:19 H. begat Ram
1 *Chr.* 2:9 sons of H. 18, 21, 25

HID.
Gen. 3:8 Adam and his wife *h.*
10 I was naked, and I *h.* myself
Ex. 2:2 *h.* Moses three months
12 M. *h.* the Egyptian in sand
3:6 and Moses *h.* his face
Jos. 2:4 Rahab *h.* the spies, 6
6:17 she *h.* the messengers, 25
1 *K.* 18:4 Obadiah *h.* prophets, 13
2 *K.* 4:27 the Lord *h.* it from me
11:2 they *h.* him and his nurse,
2 *Chr.* 22:11
Job 17:4 *h.* heart fr. understand.
29:8 saw me, and *h.* themselves
Ps. 9:15 in net which they *h.*
22:24 nei. *h.* his face from him
35:7 they *h.* for me their net
8 net he hath *h.* catch himself
119:11 word I *h.* in my heart
140:5 proud *h.* a snare for me
Is. 49:2 in quiver he *h.* me
50:6 I *h.* not my face fr. shame
53:3 we *h.* our faces from him
54:8 in little wrath I *h.* my face
57:17 I *h.* me and was wroth
59:2 *h.* his face from you
64:7 hast *h.* thy face from us
Jer. 13:5 and *h.* it by Euphrates
18:22 they *h.* snares for my feet
33:5 I *h.* my face from this city
36:26 but the Lord *h.* them
Ezek. 22:26 *h.* their eyes fr. sab.
39:23 therefore *h.* I my face, 24
Mat. 11:25 *h.* fr. wise, *Lu.* 10:21
13:33 *h.* in three meas. *Lu.* 13:21
25:18 and *h.* his lord's money
25 and *h.* thy talent in earth

Luke 1:24 Elizabeth *h.* herself
John 8:59 but Jesus *h.* himself
Rev. 6:15 bondm. and freem. *h.*

HID, Participle.
2 *Sam.* 18:13 no mat. *h.* fr. king,
1 *K.* 10:3; 2 *Chr.* 9:2
Job 3:21 more than for *h.* treas.
28:11 thing *h.* bringeth forth
21 *h.* from eyes of all living
38:30 wat. are *h.* as with a stone
Ps. 17:14 belly filled wi. *h.* treas.
19:6 nothing *h.* from the heat
Prov. 2:4 as for *h.* treasure
Is. 40:27 my way is *h.* from L.
42:22 are *h.* in prison-houses
Jer. 16:17 iniq. *h.* fr. mine eyes
Hos. 13:12 sin of Ephraim is *h.*
Mat. 10:26 noth. *h.* th. sh. not be
kn. *Mark* 4:22; *Lu.* 8:17; 12:2
Luke 9:45 saying was *h.* 18:34
19:42 are *h.* from thine eyes
Eph. 3:9 fr. begin. been *h.* in G.
Col. 1:26 been *h.* from ages
2:3 *h.* all the treas. of wisdom
3:3 your life is *h.* with Ch. in G.
Heb. 11:23 by faith Moses was *h.*

Be HID.
Gen. 4:14 from thy face sh. I *be h.*
Lev. 4:13 *be h.* fr. assembly, 5:3, 4
Job 20:26 sh. *be h.* in secret plac.
Is. 29:14 under. of pru. men *be h.*
Hos. 13:14 repentance shall *be h.*
Amos 9:3 they *be h.* fr. my sight
Nah. 3:11 thou shalt *be h.*
Zep. 2:3 ye shall *be h.*
2 *Cor.* 4:3 if our gospel *be h.*

Not be HID.
Mat. 5:14 city on hill *not be h.*
Mark 7:24 but he could *not be h.*
1 *Tim.* 5:25 otherwise *not be h.*

Not HID.
Ps. 32:5 mine iniq. have I *not h.*
38:9 my groaning is *not h.*
40:10 I have *n. h.* thy righteous.
69:5 my sins are *not h.* fr. thee
139:15 my substance was *not h.*
Jer. 16:17 are *not h.* fr. my face,
nor their ini. *h.* fr. mine eyes

HIDDEKEL.
Gen. 2:14 river is H. *Dan.* 10:4

HIDDEN.
Deut. 30:11 it is *not h.* from thee
Job 24:1 are *not h.* from thee
Ps. 51:6 in *h.* part make known
83:3 consulted ag. thy *h.* ones
Prov. 28:12 wicked rise, man *h.*
Is. 45:3 give thee *h.* riches
48:6 showed thee things, *h.* th.
Ob. 6 *h.* things sought up
Acts 26:26 none of these *h.*
1 *Cor.* 2:7 *h.* wisdom G. ordained
4:5 bring to light *h.* things
2 *Cor.* 4:2 renounced *h.* things
1 *Pet.* 3:4 the *h.* man of heart
Rev. 2:17 give to eat of *h.* manna

HIDE, Substantive.
Lev. 8:17 *h.* flesh be burnt, 9:11

HIDE, Verb.
Gen. 18:17 shall I *h.* from Abra. ?
1 *Sam.* 3:17 *h.* it not from me, if
thou *h.* 2 *Sam.* 14:18
Job 13:20 not *h.* myself from thee
14:13 wouldest *h.* me in grave
20:12 he *h.* it under his tongue
33:17 and *h.* pride from man
40:13 *h.* them in dust together
Ps. 17:8 *h.* me under thy wings
27:5 in time of tro. he sh. *h.* me,
in his tabern. sh. he *h.* me
31:20 sh. *h.* them in thy pres.
55:1 *h.* not thyself fr. my sup.
64:2 *h.* me fr. counsel of wick.
78:4 not *h.* them from their chi.
89:46 O L. wilt thou *h.* thyself

119:19 *h.* not thy commandm.
143:9 I flee to thee to *h.* me
Prov. 2:1 *h.* my com. with thee
Is. 1:15 I will *h.* mine eyes
2:10 and *h.* thee in the dust
3:9 *h.* not sin; 26:20 *h.* outcasts
26:20 *h.* thyself a little moment
58:7 *h.* not fr. thine own flesh
Jer. 36:19 *h.* thee and Jeremiah
Lam. 3:56 *h.* not ear at my brea.
Ezek. 28:3 no secret they can *h.*
31:8 cedars could not *h.* him
39:29 neither will I *h.* my face
Jam. 5:20 *h.* a multitude of sins
Rev. 6:16 *h.* us from him that

See FACE.

HIDE himself.
Jer. 23:24 *h. h.* in secret places
John 12:36 J. did *h. h.* fr. them

HIDE themselves.
2 *K.* 7:12 gone out to *h. t.* in fie.
Job 24:4 poor of the earth *h. t.*
34:22 where work. of iniq. *h. t.*
Ps. 56:6 *h. t.* mark my steps
Prov. 28:28 wick. rise, men *h. t.*
Amos 9:3 *h. t.* in top of Carmel

HIDEST.
Job 13:24 why *h.* thy face ? *Ps.*
44:24; 88:14
Ps. 10:1 why *h.* thy. in trouble ?
104:29 thou *h.* thy face
Is. 45:15 thou art G. th. *h.* thys.

HIDETH.
Job 23:9 *h.* himself on right hand
34:29 when he *h.* his face
42:3 who is he that *h.* counsel ?
Ps. 10:11 he *h.* face will nev. see
139:12 darkn. *h.* not from thee
Prov. 10:18 *h.* hated with lying
19:24 sloth. *h.* his hand, 26:15
22:3 pru. man *h.* himself, 27:12
27:16 whosoever *h.* her, *h.* wind
28:27 that *h.* eyes sh. ha. curse
Is. 8:17 L. that *h.* face from house of J.
Mal. 13:44 man hath found, he *h.*

HIDING.
Job 31:33 *h.* iniq. in my bosom
Ps. 32:7 art my *h.* place, 119:114
Is. 28:17 waters overflow *h.* pla.
32:2 as a *h.* place from the wind
Hab. 3:4 was *h.* of his power

HIEL. 1 *K.* 16:34
HIGGAION. *Ps.* 9:16

HIGH.
Gen. 29:7 Lo, it is yet *h.* day
Deut. 12:2 served gods on *h.* mo.
28:43 get up above the very *h.*
1 *Chr.* 17:17 state of man *h.* deg.
Job 11:8 *h.* as heaven
22:12 stars, how *h.* they are !
38:15 the *h.* arm sh. be broken
41:34 he beholdeth all *h.* things
Ps. 18:27 bring down *h.* looks
49:2 give ear, both low and *h.*
62:9 men of *h.* degree are a lie
71:19 thy righteous. O G. is *h.*
89:13 and *h.* is thy right hand
97:9 thou L. art *h.* above earth,
99:2; 113:4
101:5 him that hath a *h.* look
103:11 heaven is *h.* above earth
131:1 things too *h.* for me
138:6 L. be *h.* he hath respect
139:6 it is *h.* I cannot attain
149:6 let *h.* praises of God are
150:5 praise him on *h.* sounding
Prov. 18:11 as a *h.* wall in conceit
21:4 *h.* look, and proud heart
24:7 wisdom is too *h.* for a fool
Ec. 12:5 afraid of that wh. is *h.*

Is. 2:13 L. on cedars that *h.*
6:1 Lord on a throne, *h.* and
10:12 I will punish his *h.* looks
24:21 pun. *h.* ones that are on *h.*
30:13 as a breach in a *h.* wall
52:13 my servant sh. be very *h.*
57:15 the *h.* and lofty One
Jer. 17:12 a glorious *h.* throne
49:16 tho. thou make thy ne. *h.*
Ezek. 21:26 abase him is *h.*
Ob. 3 habitation is *h.* that saith
John 19:31 sabbath was a *h.* day
Acts 18:17 with a *h.* arm bro. he
Rom. 12:16 mind not *h.* things
13:11 it is *h.* time to awake
2 *Cor.* 10:5 cast. down ev. *h.* th.
Phil. 3:14 prize of the *h.* calling
Rev. 21:12 Jerusal. had a wall *h.*

See GATE, GOD, HILL, HILLS.

Most HIGH.

Num. 24:16 knowledge of M. H.
2 *Sam.* 22:14 M. H. ut. his voice
Ps. 7:17 sing praise to name of
   the Lord the M. H. 9:2; 92:1
46:4 tabernacles of the M. H.
47:2 the Lord M. H. is terrible
50:14 pay thy vows to the M. H.
56:2 fight aga. thee,.O M. H.
57:2 I will cry unto God M. H.
73:11 is there knowl. in M. H.
77:10 right hand of M. H.
78:17 provoking the M. H. 56
82:6 are the children of M. H.
83:18 art M. H. over all earth
Ps. 91:1 dwelleth in pl. of M. H.
9 made M. H. thy habitation
92:8 but thou, Lord, art *m. h.*
107:11 contem. counsel of M. H.
Is. 14:14 will be like the M. H.
Lam. 3:35 before face of M. H.
38 out of M. H. proc. not evil
Dan. 4:17 M. H. ruleth in kingd.
24 the decree of the M. H.
25 M. H. rules kingdom, 32
34 and I blessed the M. H.
7:18 saints of M. H. take king.
22 judg. given saints of M. H.
25 speak words against M. H.
27 saints of the M. H.
Hos. 7:16 return not to M. H.
11:7 called them to the M. H.
Acts 7:48 M. H. dwelleth not

See MOUNTAIN.

On HIGH.

Deut. 28:1 G. will set thee *on h.*
Job 5:11 set *on h.* th. that be low
16:19 and my record is *on h.*
39:18 she lifteth up herself *on h.*
27 eagle make her nest *on h.*
Ps. 7:7 for th. sakes return *on h.*
68:18 thou hast ascended *on h.*
69:29 O God, set me up *on h.*
91:14 I will set him *on h.*
93:4 L. *on h.* is mightier than
107:41 setteth he the poor *on h.*
Is. 26:5 bring. down them *on h.*
32:15 Sp. poured on us fr. *on h.*
40:26 lift up your eyes *on h.*
58:4 your voice heard *on h.*
Luke 1:78 day-spring from *on h.*
Eph. 4:8 he ascended up *on h.*

See PLACE, PLACES, PRIEST,
  TOWER.

HIGHER.

1 *Sam.* 9:2 S. *h.* than any of pe.
Job 35:5 clouds, which are *h.*
Ps. 61:2 lead to Rock that is *h.*
89:27 make him *h.* than kings
Ec. 5:8 there be *h.* than they
Is. 55:9 as hea. are *h.* than earth,
  so my ways *h.* th. your ways
Jer. 36:10 Bar. read in *h.* court
Dan. 8:3 one horn *h.* than other
Luke 14:10 may say, Go up *h.*
Rom. 13:1 subject to *h.* powers

Heb. 7:26 high-p. made *h.* than

HIGHEST.

Ps. 18:13 the H. gave his voice
87:5 H. himself shall establish
Prov. 8:26 nor *h.* part of dust
9:3 crieth on *h.* places of city
Ec. 5:8 higher than *h.* regard.
Ezek. 17:3 branch of cedar
Mat. 21:9 hosan. in *h. Mark* 11:10
Luke 1:32 called Son of the H.
35 power of H. overshad. thee
76 be called prophet of the H.
2:14 glory to G. in H. 19:38
6:35 ye shall be chil. of the H.
14:8 sit not down in *h.* room
20:46 love *h.* seats in synagog.

HIGHLY.

Luke 1:28 Thou art *h.* favored
16:15 *h.* esteemed among men
Rom. 12:3 think of him. more *h.*
Phil. 2:9 G. hath *h.* exalted him
1 *Thes.* 5:13 to est. them very *h.*

HIGH-MINDED.

Rom. 11:20 not *h.-m.* 1 *Tim.* 6:1
2 *Tim.* 3:4 traitors, heady, *h.-m.*

HIGHNESS.

Job 31:23 his *h.* I could not en.
Is. 13:3 that rejoice in my *h.*

HIGHWAY, S.

Jud. 5:6 days Jael *h.* unoccupied
Prov. 16:17 *h.* of upright
Is. 11:16 a *h.* for his people
19:23 a *h.* out of Eg. to Assyria
33:8 *h.* lie waste, way-faring
35:8 and a *h.* shall be there
40:3 make in desert a *h.* for G.
49:11 my *h.* shall be exalted
62:10 cast up *h.* gather stones
Jer. 31:21 thy heart towards *h.*
Amos 5:16 shall say in all *h.*
Mat. 22:9 go into *h. Luke* 14:23
Mark 10:46 Bartimeus sat by *h.*

HILKIAH.

2 *K.* 18:18 Eliak. son of H. 22:12
Neh. 8:4 on E.'s right, 12:7
Is. 22:20 s. of H. 2 *Chr.* 34:20, 22

HILL.

Jos. 24:33 Eleazar buried in *h.*
1 *Sam.* 7:1 come to *h.* of G. 10
Ps. 24:3 shall ascend to *h.* of L.
42:6 remember thee from *h.* M.
68:15 *h.* of G. is as *h.* of Bashan
16 A. G. desireth to dwell in
Cant. 4:6 get to *h.* of frankinc,
Is. 5:1 viney. in very fruitful *h.*
10:32 shake hand ag. *h.* of Jeru.
30:17 as an ensign on a *h.*
31:4 Lord shall fight for *h.*
40:4 mount. and *h.* be made low
Jer. 16:16 hunt them from ev. *h.*
31:39 measuring line on *h.* G.
49:16 holdest height of the *h.*
50:6 gone from mountain to *h.*
Mat. 5:14 city that is set on a *h.*
Luke 3:5 ev. *h.* be brought low
4:29 led him to brow of the *h.*
9:37 were come down from a *h.*
Acts 17:22 Paul stood in Mars *h.*

Hill-COUNTRY.

Jos. 13:6 inh. of *h.-c.* drive out
Luke 1:39 Mary went to *h.-c.*
65 nois. through all *h.-c.* of J.

High HILL.

Gen. 7:19 *h. h.* under heaven
1 *K.* 14:23 groves on every *high*
  h. 2 *K.* 17:10
Ps. 68:15 *high h.* as hill of B.
16 ye *high h. ?* this is the *h.*
Is. 30:25 on *high h.* rivers of wa.
Jer. 2:20 on *h. h.* thou wand. 33
17:2 remember groves on *h. h.*
Ezek. 6:13 sla. am. idols on *h. h.*
34:6 sheep wand. on every *h. h.*

Holy HILL.

Ps. 2:6 set my king on *h. h.* of
3:4 Lord heard me out of *h. h.*
15:1 who sh. dwell in thy *h. h.*
43:3 bring me to thy *h. h. ?*
99:9 worship at his *h. h.*

HILL, *with top.*

Ex. 17:9 will stand on *top* of *h.*
Num. 14:44 pres. to go to *h. t.*
Jud. 16:3 S. carried to *top* of *h.*
2 *K.* 1:9 Elijah sat on *top* of a *h.*

HILLS.

Gen. 49:26 ut. bound of everl. *h.*
Num. 23:9 fr. the *h.* I behold him
Deut. 8:7 spring out val. and *h.*
11:11 a land of *h.* and valleys
33:15 precious things of last. *h.*
1 *K.* 20:23 gods are gods of *h.* 28
22:17 saw all Is. scattered on *h.*
2 *K.* 16:4 burnt incense on the *h.*
2 *Chr.* 28:4
Job 15:7 wast thou made be. *h. ?*
Ps. 18:7 foundations of *h.* moved
50:10 cattle on thousand *h.*
65:12 little *h.* rejoice on ev. side
72:3 the little *h.* by righteousn.
80:10 *h.* covered with shadow
95:4 strength of the *h.* is his
97:5 *h.* melted like wax
98:8 the *h.* be joyful together
104:10 springs, which run am. *h.*
13 watereth *h.* from chambers
32 he touch. *h.* and they smo.
114:4 little *h.* skip. like lam. 6
121:1 will lift mine eyes to *h.*
148:9 mount. and *h.* praise Lord
Prov. 8:25 *h.* I brought forth
Cant. 2:8 he cometh skip. on *h.*
Is. 2:2 shall be exalted above *h.*
14 day of L. shall be on all *h.*
7:25 on all *h.* sh. not come fear
40:12 weighed *h.* in balance ?
41:15 shalt make *h.* as chaff
42:15 make waste moun. and *h.*
54:10 mount. depart, *h.* remov.
55:12 *h.* break forth into singi.
65:7 blasphemed me up. the *h.*
Jer. 3:23 salva. hoped for from *h.*
13:27 thy abominations on *h.*
Ezek. 6:3 thus saith L. to *h.* 36:4
36:6 to *h.* to rivers and valleys
Hos. 10:8 say to *h.* Fall on us
Joel 3:18 *h.* shall flow with milk
Mic. 4:1 be exalted above *h.*
6:1 let the *h.* hear thy voice
Nah. 1:5 *h.* melt. earth is burnt
Hab. 3:6 perpetual *h.* did bow
Luke 23:30 say to *h.* Cover us

HIM.

Rom. 11:36 of *h.* through *h.* and
  to *h.* are all things

HIN.

Ex. 29:40 fourth part of *h.* of oil
30:24 of oil-olive a *h.*
Lev. 19:36 a just *h.* shall ye have
23:13 the fourth part of a *h.* of
  oil, *Num.* 15:4 ; 28:14
Num. 15:5 fo. part of *h.* of wine
6 the third part of a *h.* of oil
9 mingled with half a *h.* of oil
Ezek. 4:11 sixth part of *h.* of wa.
45:24 *h.* of oil for ep. 46:5, 7, 11
46:14 a *h.* of oil to temper with

HIND, S.

Gen. 49:21 Naph. is a *h.* let loose
2 *Sam.* 22:34 my feet like *h.* feet,
  Ps. 18:33 ; *Hab.* 3:19
Job 39:1 mark when *h.* calve ?
Ps. 29:9 voice of L. mak. *h.* calve
Prov. 5:19 as loving *h.* and roe
Cant. 2:7 by *h.* of field, 3:5
Jer. 14:5 *h.* calved in the field

HINDER, Verb.

Gen. 24:56 *h.* me not, seeing L.
Neh. 4:8 and *h.* the building

Job 9:12 taketh away, who *h. ?*
11:10 shut up, who *h.* him ?
Acts 8:36 what *h.* me to be bap. ?
1 *Cor.* 9:12 lest we sho. *h.* gospel
Gal. 5:7 who did *h.* you ?

HINDERED, ETH.

Ezr. 6:8 exp. given, be not *h.*
Is. 14:6 is persecuted, none *h.*
Luke 11:52 entering in, ye *h.*
1 *Thes.* 2:18 wo. ha. come, S. *h.*
1 *Pet.* 3:7 your prayers be not *h.*

HINDER end, sea.

2 *Sam.* 2:23 smote with *h. e.* of
Zec. 14:8 half toward the *h. sea*

HINDERMOST, *or* HINDMOST.

Gen. 33:2 put Rachel and Jos. *h.*
Num. 2:31 go *h.* with standards
Deut. 25:18 and smote *h.* of thee
Jos. 10:19 and smite *h.* of them
Jer. 50:12 *h.* of nations wildern.

HINDER part, s.

1 *K.* 7:25 their *h. parts* were inward, 2 *Chr.* 4:4
Ps. 78:66 smote enemies in *h. p.*
Joel 2:20 *h. part* tow. utmost sea
Mark 4:38 J. was in *h. p.* of ship
Acts 27:41 *h. p.* broken with wa.

HINGES.

1 *K.* 7:50 the *h.* of gold for doors
Prov. 26:14 door turneth upon *h.*

HINNOM.

Jos. 15:8 border by valley of H.
2 *K.* 23:10 Tophet, in val. of H.
2 *Chr.* 28:3 incense in val. of H.
33:6 to pass through fire in H.
Jer. 19:2 valley of the son of H.
32:35 high places in valley of H.

HIP.

Jud. 15:8 sm. them *h.* and thigh

HIRAM.

2 *Sam.* 5:11 H. king, 1 *Chr.* 14:1
1 *K.* 5:1 H. sent his servants, 8
7:13 Sol. sent and fetched H.
9:12 H. came to see, 27 ; 10:11

HIRE, Substantive.

Gen. 31:8 ring-stra. sh. be thy *h.*
Ex. 22:15 hired thing ca. for *h.*
Deut. 23:18 not br. *h.* of a whore
1 *K.* 5:6 to thee will I give *h.*
Is. 23:17 she shall turn to her *h.*
18 her *h.* be holiness to Lord
Ezek. 16:31 not as harlot scor. *h.*
Mic. 1:7 the hires shall be burnt;
gathered of *h.* of harlot, return to the *h.* of a harlot
3:11 priests thereof teach for *h.*
Zec. 8:10 th. was no *h.* for man
Mat. 20:8 give them their *h.*
Luke 10:7 labor. worthy of his *h.*
Jam. 5:4 *h.* of laborers kept back

HIRE, EST.

Is. 46:6 *h.* goldsmith maketh god
Ezek. 16:33 *h.* them may come
Mat. 20:1 went out to *h.* labore.

HIRED.

Gen. 30:16 *h.* with son's mandr.
Lev. 19:13 wages of him *h.*
Deut. 23:4 they *h.* ag. thee Balaam, *Neh.* 13:2
Jud. 18:4 Micah *h.* me
2 *K.* 7:6 king of Israel *h.* ag. us
2 *Chr.* 24:12 *h.* masons and carp.
Ezr. 4:5 *h.* counsellors ag. them
Neh. 6:12 Sanballat had *h.* him
Is. 7:20 els with razor that is *h.*
Hos. 8:9 Ephraim hath *h.* lovers
10 they have *h.* am. nations
Mat. 20:7 bec. no man hath *h.* us
9 were *h.* about eleventh hour
Acts 28:30 P. two years in *h.* ho.

HIRED servant, s.

Ex. 12:45 a *h. servant* shall not eat thereof, *Lev.* 22:10
Lev. 25:6 sab. be meat for *h. s.*
40 as a *h. s.* sh. he be with th.
53 yearly *h. s.* shall he be with him
Deut. 15:18 worth double *h. ser.*
24:14 thou sh. not oppress *h. s.*
Mark 1:20 Zeb. in ship with *h. s.*
Luke 15:17 *h. s.* have bread, 19

HIRELING.

Job 7:1 days are like days of *h. ?*
2 a *h.* looketh for rew. of work
14:6 accomplish as a *h.*
Is. 16:14 years of *h.* 21:16
Mal. 3:5 against those oppress *h.*
John 10:12 a *h.* not the shepherd
13 *h.* fleeth, because he is a *h.*

HIS.

Cant. 2:16 bel. is mine, I am *h.*
Acts 16:33 baptized, he and all *h.*
2 *Tim.* 2:19 L. kno. them are *h.*

HISS.

1 *K.* 9:8 at house every one sh. *h.*
Job 27:23 *h.* him out of place
Is. 5:26 *h.* to them fr. end of ear.
7:18 Lord shall *h.* for fly in Eg.
Jer. 19:8 passeth thereby sh. *h.*
49:17 ; 50:13
Lam. 2:15 *h.* at daughter of Jer.
16 enemies *h.* and gnash teeth
Ezek. 27:36 merchants *h.* at thee
Zep. 2:15 ev. one passeth shall *h.*
Zec. 10:8 I will *h.* for them

HISSING.

2 *Chr.* 29:8 delivered them to *h.*
Jer. 18:16 make land perpet. *h.*
19:8 make our city des. and a *h.*
25:9 and I will make them a *h.*
18 ; 29:18
51:37 Babylon shall be a *h.*
Mic. 6:16 make inhabitants a *h.*

HIT.

1 *Sam.* 31:3 archers *h.* 1 *Chr.* 10:3

HITHER.

Gen. 45:8 not you sent me *h.*
Ex. 3:5 draw not nigh *h.*
2 *K.* 2:8 Jordan divided *h.* 14
Prov. 9:4 let turn in *h.* 16
Mat. 14:18 bring them *h.* to me
17:17 bring *h.* to me, *Luke* 9:41
22:12 friend, how camest th. *h.*
Luke 14:21 bring in *h.* the poor
15:23 bring *h.* the fatted calf
19:27 bring *h.* and slay them
John 20:27 reach *h.* thy finger
See COME.

HITHERTO.

Ex. 7:16 *h.* thou would. not hear
Jos. 17:14 L. hath blessed me *h.*
Jud. 16:13 *h.* thou hast mocked
1 *Sam.* 7:12 *h.* hath L. helped us
1 *Chr.* 9:18 *h.* waited in king's
12:29 *h.* greatest part kept war
Job 38:11 *h.* shalt thou come
John 5:17 my Father worketh *h.*
16:24 *h.* have ye asked nothing
1 *Cor.* 3:2 *h.* ye were not able

HITTITE.

Gen. 25:9 in field of Eph. the H.
49:30 bought of Eph. H. 50:13
Ex. 23:28 out H. 33:2 ; 34:11
2 *Sam.* 11:6 Send Uriah the H
Ezek. 16:3 thy mother a H. 45

HITTITES.

Gen. 15:20 hand of H. *Jos.* 1:4
Ex. 3:8, 17 ; 13:5 ; 23:23 ; *Deut.*
7:1 ; 20:17 ; *Jos.* 3:10 ; 12:8 ;
Jud. 3:5 ; 1 *K.* 10:29 ; *Neh.* 9:8
HIVITES, much in HITTITES.

HO.

Ruth 4:1 *h.* such a one, sit down

Is. 55:1 *h.* ev. one that thirsteth
Zec. 2:6 *h. h.* come forth

HOAR, HOARY. *See* FROST, HAIRS, HEAD.

HOARY.

Job 41:32 would think deep *h.*

HOBAB.

Num. 10:29 sa. to H. *Jud.* 4:11

HOISED.

Acts 27:40 they *h.* up mainsail

HOLD, S, Substantive.

Jud. 9:46 entered *h.* of god Ber.
49 put them to *h.* set *h.* on fire
1 *Sam.* 22:4 David in *h.* 24:22 ;
2 *Sam.* 5:17 ; 23:14
Jer. 51:30 remained in their *h.*
Ezek. 19:9 brought him into *h.*
Acts 4:3 in *h.* to next day
Rev. 18:2 the *h.* of ev. foul spirit
See STRONG.

HOLD.

Gen. 21:18 *h.* him in thy hand
Ex. 5:1 that they may *h.* feast
9:2 and wilt *h.* them still ?
10:9 we must *h.* a feast unto L.
20:7 L. not *h.* guiltl. *Deut.* 5:11
2 *Sam.* 22:2 *h.* my face to Joab
6:6 Uzziah put ha. to ark of G.
and took *h.* of it, 1 *Chr.* 13:9
1 *K.* 2:9 now *h.* him not guiltless
Est. 4:11 *h.* out golden sceptre
Job 6:24 and I will *h.* my tongue
9:28 wilt not *h.* me innocent
13:19 if I *h.* my tongue
17:9 right. shall *h.* on his way
Ps. 17:5 *h.* my goings in thy pa.
119:53 hor. hath taken *h.* on me
117 *h.* thou me up, I sh. be safe
139:10 thy right hand sh. *h.* me
Prov. 31:19 her hands *h.* distaff
Cant. 3:8 they all *h.* swords
Is. 41:13 L. *h.* thy right hand
42:6 and I will *h.* thy hand
Jer. 2:13 broken cist. *h.* no wat.
50:43 anguish took *h.* of him
Amos 6:10 he say, *h.* thy tongue
Zec. 11:5 *h.* themsel. not guilty
Mat. 6:24 *h.* to one, *Luke* 16:13
21:26 for all J. as a prophet
Mark 7:4 they received to *h.*
Rom. 1:18 *h.* truth in unrighte.
Phil. 2:29 *h.* such in reputation
2 *Thes.* 2:15 *h.* traditions ye have
Heb. 3:14 if we *h.* our confidence
Rev. 2:14 *h.* doctrine of Balaam
15 *h.* doctrine of Nicolaitans
See CAUGHT.

HOLD fast.

Job 8:15 he sh. *h.* it *f.* but not en.
27:6 my righteousness I *h. fast.*
Jer. 8:5 they *h. f.* deceit
1 *Thes.* 5:21 *h. fast* that is good
2 *Tim.* 1:13 *h. f.* form of so. wor.
Heb. 3:6 we *h. f.* the confidence
4:14 *h. f.* our profession, 10:23
Rev. 2:25 *h. f.* till I come
3:3 and *h. fast* and repent
11 *h.* that *f.* which thou hast

HOLD peace.

Ex. 14:14 ye shall *h.* your peace
Num. 30:4 if her father *h.* his *p.*
14 if her husband *h.* his *p.*
Jud. 18:19 *h. p.* lay hand on m.
2 *Sam.* 13:20 *h.* thy *p.* my sister
2 *K.* 2:3 *h.* you your peace, 5
Neh. 8:11 *h.* your *p.* day is holy
Job 11:3 lies make men *h. p. ?*
13:13 *h.* your *p.* let me alone
33:31 *h.* thy *p.* and I will speak
33 *h.* thy *p.* I will teach thee
Ps. 83:1 O. G. *h.* not thy *p.* 109:1
Is. 62:1 for Z 's sake not *h.* my *p.*
6 *h.* their *p.* day nor night
64:12 *h. peace* and afflict us ?

Jer. 4:19 cannot *h. peace*
Zep. 1:7 *h.* thy *p.* at pres. of L.
Mat. 20:31 reb. them bec. they
    sh. *h. p. Mark* 10:48; *Luke* 18:39
Mark 1:25 *h.* thy *p, Luke* 4:35
Luke 19:40 if they *h. p.* the sto.
Acts 12:17 beckoning to *h.* th. *p.*
18:9 be not afraid, *h.* not thy *p.*
1 *Cor.* 14;30 let the first *h.* his *p.*

See TAKE.

HOLDEN.

2 *K.* 23:22 not *h.* such a pass. 23
Job 36:8 *h.* in cords of affliction
Ps. 18:35 right hand hath *h.* me
71:6 by thee have I been *h.* up
73:23 *h.* me up by right hand
Prov. 5:22 *h.* with cords
Is. 45:1 wh. right hand I have *h.*
Luke 24:16 their eyes were *h.*
Acts 2:24 not possi. he sho. be *h.*
Rom. 14:4 yea, he shall be *h.* up

HOLDEST.

Est. 4:14 *h.* thy peace this time
Job 13:24 wherefore *h.* thou me
Ps. 77:4 thou *h.* my eyes waking
Jer. 49:16 O thou that *h.* height
Rev. 2:13 thou *h.* fast my name

HOLDETH.

Job 2:3 he *h.* fast his integrity
26:9 *h.* back face of his throne
Ps. 66:9 bless God who *h.* soul
Prov. 11:12 man of und. *h.* peace
17:28 a fool when he *h.* peace
Dan. 10:21 none *h.* w. me but M.
Rev. 2:1 *h.* stars in right hand

HOLDING.

Is. 33:15 shak. hands fr. *h.* bribes
Jer. 6:11 I am weary with *h.* in
Mark 7:3 *h.* tradition of elders
Phil. 2:16 *h.* forth word of life
Col. 2:19 and not *h.* the head
1 *Tim.* 1:19 *h.* faith
3:9 *h.* the mystery of faith
Tit. 1:9 *h.* fast faithful word
Rev. 7:1 four angels *h.* four win.

HOLE, S.

Ex. 28:32 a *h.* in the top of it
1 *Sam.* 14:11 Heb. come out of *h.*
2 *K.* 12:9 Jehoiada bored a *h.*
Cant. 5:4 in hand by *h.* of door
Is. 2:19 go into *h.* of rocks, 7:19
11:8 child sh. play on *h.* of asp.
42:22 they are all snared in *h.*
51:1 look to the *h.* of the pit
Jer. 16:16 hunt them out of *h.*
Ezek. 8:7 behold a *h.* in the wall
Nah. 2:12 filled his *h.* with prey
Hag. 1:6 put it in a bag with *h.*
Zec. 14:12 eyes consume in *h.*
Mat. 8:20 foxes ha. *h. Luke* 9:58

HOLIER, EST.

Is. 65:5 for I am *h.* than thou
Heb. 9:3 tabern. is called the *h.*
    8 way to *h.* not yet manifest
    10:19 to enter *h.* by blood of J.

HOLILY.

1 *Thes.* 2:10 how *h.* we behaved

HOLINESS.

Ex. 15:11 who like thee, in *h. ?*
28:36 *h.* to Lord, 39:30 ; *Zec.* 14:20, 21
1 *Chr.* 16:29 worship L. in beauty
    of *h. Ps.* 29:2 ; 96:9
2 *Chr.* 20:21 praise beauty of *h.*
31:18 sanctified themselv. in *h.*
Ps. 30:4 rememb. of his *h.* 97:12
47:8 God sitteth on throne of *h.*
48:1 praised in mount. of his *h.*
60:6 G. hath spoken in *h.* 108:7
89:35 sw. by my *h.* I will not lie
93:5 *h.* becom. thy house, O L.
110:3 willing, in beauties of *h.*
Is. 23:18 her hire sh. be *h.* to
35:8 sh. be called the way of *h.*

62:9 drink it in courts of my *h.*
63:15 from habitation of thy *h.*
    18 peo. of thy *h.* have posse. it
Jer. 2:3 Israel was *h.* to the Lord
31:23 O mountain of *h.*
Amos 4:2 hath sworn by his *h.*
Ob. 17 on mount Z. shall be *h.*
Mal. 2:11 Ju. hath prof. *h.* of L.
Luke 1:75 might serve him in *h.*
Acts 3:12 by *h.* made man walk
Rom. 1:4 according to spirit of *h.*
6:19 servants to righte. unto *h.*
    22 ye have your fruit unto *h.*
2 *Cor.* 7:1 perfect. *h.* in fear of G.
Eph. 4:24 new man created in *h.*
1 *Thes.* 3:13 stablish hearts in *h.*
4:7 not to uncleanness, but to *h.*
1 *Tim.* 2:15 conti. in faith and *h.*
Tit. 2:3 in behavior as becom. *h.*
Heb 12:10 be partakers of his *h.*
    14 peace with men, and *h.*

HOLLOW.

Gen. 32:25 *h.* of thigh, 32
Ex. 27:8 altar *h.* boards, 38:7
Jud. 15:19 God clave a *h.* place
Is. 40:12 waters in *h.* of hand

HOLPEN.

Ps. 83:8 have *h.* the chil. of Lot
86:17 bec. thou, L. hast *h.* me
Is. 31:3 he that is *h.* shall fall
Dan. 11:34 *h.* with a little help
Luke 1:54 hath *h.* his servant Is.

HOLY.

Ex. 3:5 pl. th. standest *h.* ground
16:23 to-morrow is *h.* sabbath
19:6 a *h.* nation, 1 *Pet.* 2:9
20:8 remember sabbath keep *h.*
28:38 hallow in all th. *h.* gifts
29:33 they are *h. ; / 34* bec. it is *h.*
30:25 an oil of *h.* ointment
    32 it is *h.* and sh. be *h.* unto y.
31:14 keep sabbath, it is *h.* 15
Lev. 8:9 put on A. the *h.* crown
10:10 difference bet. *h.* and unh.
16:4 put on the *h.* linen coat
    33 atonement for *h.* sanctua.
19:2 I the L. your G. am *h.* 21:8
20:7 be ye *h. ;* 21:7 he is *h.*
27:14 house to be *h.* to Lord
    30 tithe of the land is *h.* to L.
Num. 5:17 priest take *h.* water
15:40 remember and be *h.* to G.
16:3 all the congregation are *h.*
    5 show who are his, who is *h.*
18:17 not red. them, they are *h.*
1 *Sam.* 2:2 none *h.* as the Lord
21:5 ves. of young men are *h.*
2 *K.* 4:9 this is a *h.* man of God
1 *Chr.* 22:19 *h.* ves. to hon. of G.
2 *Chr.* 23:6 for they are *h.*
35:3 Levites which were *h.*
    13 *h.* offerings sod they in pots
Ezr. 8:28 ye are *h.* to the Lord
9:2 *h.* seed mingled themselves
Neh. 9:14 madest known *h.* sab.
Ps. 20:6 hear from his *h.* heaven
22:3 but thou art *h.* O thou that
28:2 lift hands tow. thy *h.* orac.
86:2 pres. my soul, for I am *h.*
98:1 his *h.* arm hath gotten vic.
99:5 worship at footst. he is *h.*
    9 exalt L. worship at his *h.* hill
Ps. 105:42 remembered *h.* prom.
145:17 L. is *h.* in all his works
Prov. 9:10 knowl. of *h.* is under
30:3 nor have I knowl. of the *h.*
Is. 4:3 Jerus. shall be called *h.*
6:3 *h. h.* is the Lord of Hosts
    13 *h.* seed substance thereof
27:13 worship in *h.* mountain
52:10 L. made bare his *h.* arm
58:13 call sabbath, *h.* of the L.
64:10 *h.* cities are a wilderness
    11 *h.* and beaut. house is burnt
Jer. 11:15 *h.* flesh passed fr. thee

Ezek. 22:26 no difference betwe.
    h. and profane
36:38 incr. them as the *h.* flock
42:13 *h.* chambers where priests
    14 their garments, they are *h.*
44:19 lay them in *h* chambers
    23 differ. betw. *h.* and profane
45:1 offer *h.* portion of land, 4
46:19 *h.* chambers of priests
48:10 for priests be *h.* oblation
    20 shall offer *h.* oblation, 21
Dan. 4:8 D. before me, in whom
    is spirit of *h.* gods, 9, 18; 5:11
11:28 heart against *h.* covenant
30 indignation ag. *h.* covenant
    intel. with forsakers of *h.* c.
Hag. 2:12 if one bear *h.* flesh,
    skirt touch br. sh. it be *h. ?*
Zec. 2:13 L. raised up *h.* habita.
Mat. 7:6 gi. not the. is *h.* to dogs
25:31 and *h.* angels with him
Mark 6:20 he was just and *h.*
    8:38 with *h.* angels, *Luke* 9:26
Luke 1:70 by the mouth of *h.*
    prophets, *Acts* 3:21
    72 remember his *h.* covenant
2:23 every male called *h.* to L.
John 17:11 *h.* Father keep those
Acts 4:27 against thy *h.* child J.
    30 won. done by name of *h.* ch.
7:32 place thou standest is *h.*
10:22 warned from G. by *h.* ang.
Rom. 1:2 prom. in *h.* scriptures
7:12 commandment is *h.* just
11:16 fir. fruit be *h.* if root be *h.*
12:1 bodies *h.* sacrifice to G.
16:16 salute with *h.* kiss, 1 *Cor.* 16:20 ; 2 *Cor.* 13:12 ; 1 *Thes.* 5:26 ; 1 *Pet.* 5:14
1 *Cor.* 3:17 temple of God is *h.*
    7:14 are *h. ; / 34* she may be *h.*
Eph. 1:4 be *h.* with. blame, 5:27
Col. 1:22 present *h.* and unblam.
    3:12 elect of G. *h.* and beloved
1 *Thes.* 5:27 to all *h.* brethren
1 *Tim.* 2:8 up *h.* hands
2 *Tim.* 1:9 called us with *h.* call.
    3:15 hast known *h.* scriptures
Tit. 1:8 bishop be sober, *h.* tem.
Heb. 3:1 *h.* brethren, partakers
7:26 high-pr. becu. us who is *h.*
1 *Pet.* 1:15 *h.* in conversation, 16
    2:5 *h.* priesth. offer up sacrifices
    3:5 *h.* women who trusted in G.
2 *Pet.* 1:18 with him in *h.* mount
    21 *h.* men spake mov. by H. G.
    2:21 turn fr. *h.* commandment
3:2 spoken before by *h.* prophe.
    11 persons to be in all *h.* conv.
Rev. 3:7 saith he that is *h.*
4:8 *h. h. h.* L. God Almighty
6:10 how long, O L. *h.* and true
14:10 in presence of *h.* angels
15:4 not fear thee ? thou art *h.*
18:20 *h.* apostles and prophets
20:6 *h.* who ha. part in first res.
21:10 showed me *h.* Jerusalem
22:6 Lord G. of the *h.* prophets
    11 he th. is *h.* let him be *h.* st.

See CONVOCATION.

HOLY day.

Ex. 35:2 seventh shall be *h. day*
Neh. 8:9 *d.* is *h.* unto L. 10, 11
10:31 not buy it on sab. or *h. d.*
Ps. 42:4 multi. that kept *h. d.*
Is. 58:13 doing plea. on my *h. d.*
Col. 2:16 no man judge of a *h. d.*

See GARMENTS.

HOLY Ghost.

Mat. 1:18 with child of H. G. 20
    3:11 with H. G. *Mark* 1:8 ; *Luke* 3:16 ; *John* 1:33 ; *Acts* 1:5
12:31 blasph. ag. H. G. not for-
    given, *Mark* 3:29 ; *Luke* 12:10
    32 whoso. speak. against H. G.
28:19 baptize in name of H. G.

Mark 12:36 David said by the H.
  Ghost, *Acts* 1:16
13:11 not ye speak, but H. G.
Luke 1:15 John filled with H. G.
  35 H. G. shall come upon thee
  41 Elizabeth filled with H. G.
  67 Zacharias filled with H. G.
Luke 2:25 Sim. H. G. upon him
  26 revealed unto him by H. G.
  3:22 H. G. desc. in bodily shape
  4:1 Jesus being full of H. G.
  12:12 H. G. shall teach you
John 7:39 H. G. not yet given
  14:26 Comforter, who is H. G.
  20:22 receive ye H. G. *Acts* 2:38
Acts 1:2 he thro. H. G. had given
  8 the H. G. is come on you
  2:4 all filled with H. G. 4:31
  33 promise of the H. G.
  4:8 filled with the H. Ghost
  5:3 S. filled he. to lie to H. G.?
  32 are witnesses, so is H. G.
  6:3 men full of the H. Ghost
  5 Stephen, man full of H. G.
  7:51 stiff-n. alw. resist H. G.
  55 Stephen full of H. Ghost
  8:15 prayed th. might re. H. G.
  17 hands on th. received H. G.
  18 when S. saw H. G. was giv.
  19 hands, they receive H. G.
  9:17 might. be filled with H. G.
  31 walking in comfort of H. G.
  10:38 G. anoint. J. with H. G.
  44 H. G. fell on all who heard
  45 on Gentiles was pou. H. G.
  47 received H. G. as well as we
  11:15 H. G. fell on them
  16 shall be baptized with H. G.
  24 Barnabas, full of H. G.
  13:4 being sent forth by H. G.
  9 filled with H. Ghost
  52 disciples filled with H. G.
  15:8 giving H. G. as he did
  28 it seemed good to the H. G.
  16:6 forbidden of H. G. to prea.
  19:2 received H. G. ? we have
    not heard there be H. G.
  6 hands on them, H. G. came
  20:23 save that the H. G. witn.
  28 H. G. made you overseers
  21:11 thus saith the H. Ghost
  28:25 spake H. G. by Esaias
Rom. 5:5 shed in hearts by H. G.
  9:1 consci. bear. wit. in H. G.
  14:17 kingd. of G. joy in H. G.
  15:13 through power of H. G.
  16 being sancti. by the H. G.
1 *Cor.* 2:13 words wh. H. G. tea.
  6:19 body is temple of H. G.
  12:3 Jesus is Lord, but by H. G.
2 *Cor.* 6:6 by the H. G. by love
  13:14 communion of H. G.
1 *Thes.* 1:5 gospel came in H. G.
  6 rec. word with joy of H. G.
2 *Tim.* 1:14 good th. k. by H. G.
Tit. 3:5 by renewing of H. G.
Heb. 2:4 with gifts of H. G.
  3:7 H. G. saith, To-day if ye h.
  6:4 made partakers of H. G.
'9:8 H. Ghost this signifying
  10:15 whereof H. G. is a witness
1 *Pet.* 1:12 H. G. sent fr. heaven
2 *Pet.* 1:21 as moved by H. G.
1 *John* 5:7 Fat. Word, and H. G.
Jude 20 beloved, pray. in H. G.
See GOD, HABITATION, HILL.

Most HOLY.

Ex. 26:33 betw. holy and *m. h.*
  29:37 an altar *most h.* 40:10
Lev. 2:3 remnant be Aaron's, it
  is *m. h.* 10 ; 6:17; 10:12
  6:25 sin-offering *m. h.* 29 ; 10:17
  7:1 tresp.-offering *m. h.* 6 ; 14:13
  21:22 both of *m. h.* and holy
  24:9 cakes of flour *m. h.* to him
Num. 4:4 about *m. h.* things
  19 approach *m. h.* things

18:9 offering to me shall be *m. h.*
  10 in *m. h.* place sh. thou eat it
1 *K.* 6:16 built th. for *m. h.* plac.
  7:50 made ves. for *m. h.* place
  8:6 brought the ark unto *most*
    h. place, 2 *Chr.* 5:7
1 *Chr.* 23:13 A. to sanctify *m. h.*
2 *Chr.* 3:8 Sol. *m. h.* house
  10 in *m. h.* house made cheru.
  4:22 inner doors for *m. h.* place
Ezr. 2:63 not eat of *most h.*
  things, *Neh.* 7:65
Ezek. 43:12 whole limit be *m. h.*
  44:13 not come near *m. h.* place
  45:3 sanctuary and *m. h.* place
Dan. 9:24 to anoint *most h.*
Jude 20 building on *m. h.* faith

HOLY mountain.

Ps. 87:1 foundation is in *h. m.*
Is. 11:9 nor dest. in *h. m.* 65:25
  56:7 will I bring to my *h. m.*
  57:13 he shall inherit my *h. m.*
  65:11 ye are th. forget my *h. m.*
Ezek. 20:40 in *h. m.* th. serve me
  28:14 wast upon *h. m.* of G.
Dan. 9:16 anger turned fr. *h. m.*
Dan. 9:20 pres. suppli. for *h. m.*
  11:45 plant tabernacles in *h. m.*
Joel 2:1 so. an alarm in my *h. m.*
  3:17 L. dwelling in Z. my *h. m.*
Ob. 16 drunk on my *h. m.*
Zec. 8:3 mount. of L. called *h. m.*

HOLY name.

Lev. 20:3 Molech, prof. my *h. n.*
  22:2 profane not my *h. n.* 32
1 *Chr.* 16:10 glory ye in his *h.*
  name, Ps. 105:3
  35 thanks to *h. n. Ps.* 106:47
  29:16 build a house for thy *h. n.*
  Ps. 33:21 trusted in his *h. name*
  99:3 praise terrible n. it is h.
  103:1 L. bless his *h. n.* 145:21
  111:9 h. and rev. his *n. Lw.* 1:49
Is. 57:15 lofty One, wh. *n.* is *h.*
Ezek. 20:39 pollute you my *h. n.*
  36:20 profaned my *h. n.*
  22 your sakes, for *h. n.'s* sake
  39:7 make known *h. n.* in Isr.
  25 be jealous for my *h. n.*
  43:7 my *h. n.* Is. no more defile
  8 defiled my *h. n.* by abomi.
Amos 2:7 to profane my *h. n.*

HOLY oil.

Ex. 30:25 h. anoint. *o.* 31 ; 37:29
Ps. 89:20 with *h. oil* I anoi. him

HOLY One.

Deut. 33:8 Thummim and Urim
  be with thy H. One.
Job 6:10 not con. words of H. O.
Ps. 16:10 nor suffer H. O. to see
  corruption, *Acts* 2:27 ; 13:35
  89:19 in vision to thy H. O.
Is. 10:17 H. O. sh. be for a flame
  29:23 sanctify H. O. of Jacob
  40:25 sh. I be equal? saith H. O.
  43:15 I am the Lord, your H. O.
  49:7 Redeemer of Is. his H. O.
Dan. 4:13 H. O. down fr. heaven
Hos. 11:9 H. O. in midst of thee
Hab. 1:12 from everl. my H. O.
  3:3 H. O. came from mount P.
Mark 1:24 I know th. who th. a.
  the H. O. of G. *Luke* 4:34
Acts 3:14 ye denied the H. One
1 *John* 2:20 unction from H. One

HOLY One of Israel.

2 *K.* 19:22 lifted thy eyes against
  the H. O. *of Israel, Is.* 37:23
Ps. 71:22 O thou H. O. *of Israel*
  78:41 limited the H. O. *of Is.*
  89:18 the H. O. *of Is.* is our ki.
Is. 1:4 provoked the H. O. *of Is.*
  5:19 coun of H. O. *of Israel*
  24 despised word of H. O. *of I.*
  12:6 great is H. O. *of Is.* in mid.

17:7 have respect to H. O. *of I.*
  29:19 rejoice in H. O. *of Israel*
  30:11 cause H. O. *of Is.* to cease
  12 saith the H. O. *of Is.* 15
  31:1 look not to the H. O. *of I.*
  41:14 saith thy Red. H. O. *of Is.*
  16 shalt glory in H. O. *of Is.*
  20 H. O. *of Is.* hath created it
  43:3 I am the L. the H. O. *of I.*
  45:11 the L. the H. O. *of Israel*
  47:4 L. is his name, H. O. *of Is.*
  48:17 Red. H. O. *of Israel*, 54:5
  49:7 Red. of *I.* and his H. O.
  55:5 nat. run to thee, H. O. *of I.*
  60:9 bring th. gold to H. O. *of I.*
  14 the Z. of the H. O. *of Is.*
Jer. 50:29 proud aga. H. O. *of I.*
  51:5 filled w. sin ag. H. O. *of I.*
Ezek. 39:7 I am the L. H. O. *of I.*

HOLY ones.

Dan. 4:17 dem. by word of *h. o.*

HOLY people.

Deut. 7:6 *h. p.* to the L. 14:2, 21
  26:19 thou may be *h. p.* to Lord
  28:9 L. shall establ. thee a *h. p.*
Is. 62:12 shall call them *h. p.*
Dan. 8:24 and destroy *h; p.*

HOLY place.

Ex. 28:29 goeth in unto *h. p.* 35
  43 to minister in *h. place,* 29:30
  29:31 seethe his flesh in the *h. p.*
  31:11 sweet incense for *h. p.*
  35:19 do service in *h. p.* 39:1, 41
  38:24 gold in all work of *h. p.*
Lev. 6:16 unlea. bread sh. be eat.
  in *h. p.* 26 ; 7:6 ; 10:13 : 24:9
  27 shalt wash that in the *h. p.*
  10:17 eaten sin-offer. in *h. p.?*
  18 blood not bro. within *h. p.*
  14:13 slay burnt-offering in *h. p.*
  16:2 come not at all tim. to *h. p.*
  16 atonement for *h. p.* 17, 27
  20 end of reconciling the *h. p.*
  24 shall wash his flesh in *h. p.*
Jos. 5:15 p. wh. thou stand is *h.*
1 *K.* 8:8 staves were seen in *h. p.*
2 *Chr.* 29:5 carry filth. out of *h. p.*
  30:27 prayer came to his *h. p.*
Ezr. 9:8 to give us a nail in *h. p.*
Ps. 24:3 sh. stand in his *h. p.?*
  46:4 streams make glad the *h. p.*
  68:17 Lord is am. them in *h. p.*
Ec. 8:10 had gone from *p.* of *h.*
Is. 57:15 I dw. in high and *h. p.*
Ezek. 41:4 this is the most *h. p.*
  42:13 *p.* is *h.* ; 14 out of *h. p.*
Mat. 24:15 abomination in *h. p.*
Acts 6:13 blasph. words ag. *h. p.*
  21:28 this man polluted *h. p.*
Heb. 9:12 Christ entered *h. p.*
  25 priest entered ev. year *h. p.*

HOLY places.

2 *Chr.* 8:11 bec. the *places* are *h.*
Ps. 68:35 terrible out of thy *h. p.*
Ezek. 21:2 drop thy word to. *h. p.*
Heb. 9:24 Ch. is not entered *h. p.*

Shall be HOLY.

Ex. 22:31 *s. be h.* men unto me
  29:37 what. touch. altar *s. be h.*
  30:32 it *shall be h.* unto you, 37
  40:9 anoint. tab. and it *s. be h.*
Lev. 11:44 ye *shall be h.* for I am
  holy, 45 ; 19:2 ; 20:26
  19:24 fruit *sh. be h.* to praise L.
  21:6 priests *s. be h.* unto th. G.
  23:20 they *shall be h.* to the L.
  25:12 jubilee, it *sh. be h.* to you
  27:9 man giveth to L. *s. be h.*
  10 exchange thereof *s. be h.* 33
  21 the jubilee, it *s. be h.* to L.
  32 the tenth *s. be h.* unto the L.
Num. 6:5 Nazarite *s. be h.* to L.
Deut. 23:14 theref. *s.* camp *be h.*
Ezek. 45:1 portion *s. be h.*
Joel 3:17 then *s.* Jerusalem *be h.*

HOLY Spirit.

Ps. 51:11 take not H. S. fr. me
Is. 63:10 rebel. and vexed H. S.
  11 put his H. S. within him?
Luke 11:13 heav. Fa. give H. S.
Eph. 1:13 sealed wi. H. S. of pro.
  4:30 grieve not the H. S. of God
1 *Thes.* 4:8 given us his H. S.

HOLY temple.

Ps. 5:7 worship tow. h. *t.* 138:2
  11:4 the Lord is in his *h. temple*
  65:4 satis. with goodness of *h. t.*
  79:1 *h. temple* have they defiled
Jon. 2:4 look again tow. thy *h. t.*
  7 my prayer came to thy *h. t.*
Mic. 1:2 L. from *h. t.* be witness
Hab. 2:20 the Lord is in his *h. t.*
Eph. 2:21 groweth to *h. t.*

HOLY thing.

Lev. 22:10 no stranger eat of *h. t.*
Num. 4:15 sh. not touch any *h. t.*
Ezek. 48:12 obla. to them. a *h. t.*
Luke 1:35 that *h. th.* born of thee

HOLY things.

Ex. 28:38 bear iniq. of *h. t.*
Lev. 5:15 thro. ignorance in *h. t.*
  22:2 sep. from the *h. t.* of Is.
  4 not eat of *h. t.* till clean, 6, 12
  7 shall afterward eat of *h. t.*
  15 shall not profane *h. t.* of Is.
  16 to bear iniq. when eat *h. t.*
Num. 4:20 not see, *h. t.* are cov.
  18:32 neither sh. ye pollute *h. t.*
Deut. 12:26 thy *h. t.* take and go
1 *Chr.* 23:28 office purifying *h. t.*
2 *Chr.* 31:6 bro. in tithe of *h. t.*
Neh. 10:33 ordinances for *h. t.*
  12:47 sanctified *h. t.* to Levites
Ezek. 22:8 thou despised my *h. t.*
  26 priests have profaned *h. t.*
  44:8 not kept charge of my *h. t.*
1 *Cor.* 9:13 minister about *h. t.*

HOME.

Gen. 43:16 bring these men *h.*
Ex. 9:19 not brought *h.* su. die
Deut. 21:12 br. her *h.* to thy hou.
  24:5 shall be free at *h.* one year
Ruth 1:21 L. hath brought me *h.*
1 *Sam.* 6:7 bring their calves *h.*
  10 men shut up th. calves at *h.*
  18:2 go no more *h.* to fath.'s ho.
2 *Sam.* 14:13 not fetch *h.* banish.
  17:23 Ahithophel gat him *h.*
1 *K.* 5:14 a month in L. two at *h.*
  13:7 come *h.* with me, 15
1 *Chr.* 13:12 bring ark of G. *h.* 13
2 *Chr.* 25:10 go *h.* they return *h.*
Est. 5:10 when Haman came *h.*
Job 39:12 will bring *h.* thy seed
Ps. 68:12 she that tarried at *h.*
Prov. 7:19 good man is not at *h.*
  20 come *h.* at day appointed
Ec. 12:5 man goeth to his long *h.*
Lam. 1:20 at *h.* there is as death
Hab. 2:5 neither keepeth at *h.*
Hag. 1:9 when ye brought it *h.*

Mat. 8:6 my serv. lieth at *h.* sick
Mark 5:19 go *h.* to thy friends
Luke 9:61 bid th. farewell at *h.*
John 19:27 took her to his own *h.*
  20:10 disc. went to their own *h.*
1 *Cor.* 14:35 hunger, eat at *h.*
  14:35 ask husbands at *h.*
2 *Cor.* 5:6 we are at *h.* in body
1 *Tim.* 5:4 to show piety at *h.*
Tit. 2:5 be discreet, keepers at *h.*

HOME-BORN.

Ex. 12:49 to him that is *h.-b.*
Lev. 18:9 whe. *b.* at *h.* or abroad
Jer. 2:14 is Israel a *h.-b.* slave?

HOMER.

Lev. 27:16 a *h.* of barley-seed
Is. 5:10 seed of a *h.* yield ephah
Ezek. 45:14 for ten baths are a *h.*
Hos. 3:2 bou. for *h.* and half *h.*

HONEST.

Luke 8:15 an *h.* and good heart
Acts 6:3 seven of *h.* report
Rom. 12:17 *h.* in sight of all
2 *Cor.* 8:21 *h.* th. in sight of L.
  13:7 do that which is *h.*
Phil. 4:8 whatso. things are *h.*
1 *Pet.* 2:12 having conversat. *h.*

HONESTLY.

Rom. 13:13 walk *h.* as in the day
1 *Thes.* 4:12 walk *h.* toward them
Heb. 13:18 in all things to live *h.*

HONESTY.

1 *Tim.* 2:2 lead life god. and *h.*

HONEY.

Gen. 43:11 carry a little *h.* spices
Ex. 16:31 wafers made with *h.*
Lev. 2:11 burn no leaven, nor *h.*
Deut. 8:8 a land of oil-olive and
    h. 2 *K.* 18:32
  32:13 he made him to suck *h.*
Jud. 14:8 *h.* in carcass of lion, 9
  18 what is sweeter than *h.?*
1 *Sam.* 14:25 was *h.* upon ground
  26 *h.* dropped; 29 I tasted *h.* 43
2 *Sam.* 17:29 bro. *h.* and butter
1 *K.* 14:3 take a cruse of *h.*
Job 20:17 sh. not see brooks of *h.*
Ps. 19:10 judgmt sweeter than
    h. 119:103
  81:16 *h.* out of rock sati. thee
Prov. 24:13 eat *h.* is good, 25:16
  25:27 not good to eat much *h.*
Cant. 4:11 *h.* and milk und. ton.
  5:1 honey-comb with my *h.*
Is. 7:15 butter and *h.* sh. he eat
  22 butter and *h.* sh. ev. one eat
Jer. 41:8 treasures of *h.* in field
Ezek. 3:3 in my mouth as *h.*
  27:17 Ju: traded in *h.* and balm
Mat. 3:4 J. Baptist's meat locus.
  and wild *h. Mark* 1:6
Rev. 10:9 thy mouth sweet as *h.*
  10 in my mouth sweet as *h.*
See FLOWETH, FLOWING.

HONEY-COMB.

1 *Sam.* 14:27 and dip. it in *h.-c.*
Ps. 19:10 sweeter than *h.-c.*
Prov. 5:3 lips of str. wo. as *h.-c.*
  16:24 pleasant words are as *h.-c.*
  24:13 eat *h.-c.* sweet to thy taste
  27:7 full soul loatheth a *h.-c.*
Cant. 4:11 thy lips drop as a *h.-c.*
  5:1 eaten my *h.-c.* with honey
Luke 24:42 gave piece of *h.-c.*

HONOR, S.

Gen. 49:6 h. be not thou united
Ex. 14:17 get me *h.* on Phar. 18
Num. 22:17 promote thee to *h.* 37
  24:11 L. hath kept thee from *h.*
Deut. 26:19 above nations in *h.*
Jud. 4:9 journey not be for th. *h.*
  13:17 pass. we may do thee *h.*
2 *Sam.* 6:22 shall I be had in *h.*
1 *K.* 3:13 given thee rich. and *h.*
1 *Chr.* 16:27 glory and *h.* are in
  29:12 riches and *h.* come of thee
  28 D. died, full of riches and *h.*
2 *Chr.* 1:11 not asked riches or *h.*
  12 riches, wealth, and *h.*
  26:18 nor shall it be for thy *h.*
  32:33 inhabit. of Jer. did him *h.*
Est. 1:4 *h.* of his excel. majesty
  20 wives shall give to husb. *h.*
  6:3 wh. *h.* ha. been done for th.?
  8:16 the Jews had joy and *h.*
Job 14:21 his sons come to *h.*
Ps. 7:5 ene. lay mine *h.* in dust
  8:5 crowned with *h. Heb.* 2:7, 9
  21:5 *h.* and maj. thou laid on him
  26:8 where thine *h.* dwelleth
  49:12 man being in *h.* abid. not
  20 in *h.* and understandeth
  66:2 sing forth *h.* of his name
  71:8 mouth filled with thy *h.*
  96:6 *h.* and majesty are bef. him

  104:1 thou art clothed with *h.*
  112:9 horn sh. be exalt. with *h.*
  145:5 speak of *h.* of thy majesty
  149:9 this *h.* have all his saints
Prov. 3:16 left hand riches and *h.*
  4:8 she shall bring thee to *h.*
  5:9 lest thou give th. *h.* to oth.
  8:18 riches and *h.* are with me
  11:16 gracious woman retain. *h.*
  14:28 the people is the king's *h.*
  15:33 bef. *h.* is humility, 18:12
  20:3 an *h.* to cease from strife
  21:21 follow. mercy, findeth *h.*
  22:4 fear of L. are riches and *h.*
  25:2 *h.* of kings to search
  26:1 *h.* is not seemly for a fool
  8 so is he that giv. *h.* to a fool
  29:23 *h.* shall uphold humble
  31:25 and *h.* are her clothing
Ec. 6:2 to wh. G. hath given *h.*
  10:1 that is in reputation for *h.*
Jer. 33:9 an *h.* before all nations
Dan. 2:6 receive rewards and *h.*
  4:30 built for *h.* of my majesty
  36 *h.* and brightness returned
  5:18 G. gave father glory and *h.*
  11:21 shall not give *h.* of king.
Mal. 1:6 where is mine *h.?*
Mat. 13:57 prophet not without
  h. Mark 6:4 : *John* 4:44
John 5:41 I rec. not *h.* from men
  44 receive *h.* one of another
  8:54 honor myself, *h.* is nothing
Acts 28:10 hon. us with many *h.*
Rom. 2:7 seek glory and *h.*
  10 *h.* to ev. man worketh good
  9:21 of same lump ma. ves. to *h.*
  12:10 in *h.* prefer. one another
  13:7 render *h.* to wh. *h.* is due
1 *Cor.* 12:23 bestow abund. *h.* 24
2 *Cor.* 6:8 by *h.* and dishonor
Col. 2:23 not in *h.* to satis. flesh
1 *Thes.* 4:4 to possess vessel in *h.*
1 *Tim.* 1:17 to G. be *h.* and glory
  5:17 elders worthy of double *h.*
  6:1 count masters worthy of *h.*
  16 to whom be *h.* and power
2 *Tim.* 2:20 some to *h.* 21
Heb. 3:3 more *h.* than house
  5:4 no man taketh *h.* to himself
1 *Pet.* 1:7 to praise, *h.* glory
  3:7 *h.* to wife as weaker vessel
2 *Pet.* 1:17 from G. the Father *h.*
Rev. 4:9 beasts give glory and *h.*
  11 to receive glory and *h.* 5:12
  5:13 *h.* power, and might, be to
    him, 7:12 : 19:1
  19:7 let us rejoice, give *h.*
  21:24 glory and *h.* to it, 26

HONOR, Verb.

Ex. 20:12 *h.* thy father and thy
  mother, *Deut.* 5:16 ; *Mat.*
  15:4 ; 19:19 ; *Mark* 7:10 ; 10:19 ;
  Luke 18:20 ; *Eph.* 6:2
Lev. 19:15 not *h.* per. of mighty
  32 shalt *h.* the face of old man
Jud. 9:9 by me they *h.* God
1 *Sam.* 2:30 th. th. *h.* me I will *h.*
  15:30 yet *h.* me now bef. elders
Est. 6:6 delighteth to *h.* 7, 9, 11
Ps. 91:15 deliver him and *h.* him
Prov. 3:9 *h.* L. with thy substa.
Is. 29:13 with lips do *h.* me
  43:20 beast of field shall *h.* me
  58:13 *h.* him, not doing own
Dan. 4:37 and *h.* King of heaven
  11:38 *h.* God of forces, a god
    whom fa. knew not sh. he *h.*
Mat. 15:6 *h.* not fath. or mother
John 5:23 all men *h.* Son as h. F.
  8:49 I *h.* Father, ye dishonor me
  54 if I *h.* myself, my *h.* is noth.
  12:26 him will Father *h.*
1 *Tim.* 5:3 *h.* wid. that are wid.
1 *Pet.* 2:17 *h.* all men, *h.* the king

HONORABLE.

Num. 22:15 sent princes more *h.*

1 *Sam.* 9:6 th. is in the city a man
of God, and he is an *h.* man
2 *Sam.* 23:19 was he not most *h.*
of three? 1 *Chr.* 11:21
23 was more *h.* than the thirty
2 *K.* 5:1 Naaman *h.* with master
1 *Chr.* 4:9 more *h.* than brethren
Job 22:8 the *h.* man dwelt in it
Ps. 45:9 daughters am. *h.* women
111:3 his work is *h.* and glori.
Is. 3:3 doth take away *h.* man
5 base behave proudly ag. *h.*
5:13 their *h.* men are famished
9:15 ancient and *h.* he is head
23:8 traffickers are *h.* of earth
9 into contempt all *h.* of earth
42:21 magnify law, make it *h.*
43:4 been *h.* , 58:13 holy of L. *h.*
Nah. 3:10 cast lots for her *h.* men
Mark 15:43 Jos. an *h.* counsellor
Luke 14:8 lest more *h.* man be
Acts 13:50 J. stirred up *h.* wom.
17:12 *h.* women not few believe
1 *Cor.* 4:10 ye are stro. ye are *h.*
12:23 members we think less *h.*
Heb. 13:4 marriage *h.* bed unde.

HONORED.
Ex. 14:4 I will be *h.* on Pharaoh
Prov. 13:18 regard. reproof be *h.*
27:18 wait. on master sh. be *h.*
Is. 43:23 nor *h.* me wi. sacrifices
Lam. 1:8 all that *h.* her despise
5:12 faces of elders were not *h.*
Dan. 4:34 I praised and. *h.* him
1 *Cor.* 12:26 or one member be *h.*

HONOREST, ETH.
1 *Sam.* 2:29 *h.* thy sons above me
Ps. 15:4 *h.* them that fear Lord
Prov. 12:9 he that *h.* himself.
14:31 that *h.* him hath mercy
Mal. 1:6 son *h.* father
Mat. 15:8 *h.* me w. lips, *Mar.* 7:6
John 5:23 *h.* not Son, *h.* not Fa.
8:54 it is my Father that *h.* me

HOODS.
Is. 3:23 I will take away the *h.*

HOOF, S.
Ex. 10:26 shall not a *h.* be left
Lev. 11:3 whatever parteth *h.*
4 of them that divide the *h.*
5 divideth not *h.* 6; *Deut.* 14:7
7 swine, tho' div. *h. Deut.* 14:8
Jud. 5:22 were horse *h.* broken
Ps. 69:31 better than ox with *h.*
Is. 5:28 horses' *h.* shall be coun.
Jer. 47:3 noise of stamping of *h.*
Mic. 4:13 will make thy *h.* brass

HOOK, S.
Ex. 26:32 *h.* of gold, 37; 36:36
2 *K.* 19:28 *h.* in nose, *Is.* 37:29
Job 41:1 dr. leviathan wi. *h. ? 2*
Is. 2:4 sp. into prun. *h. Mic.* 4:3
18:5 cut off sprigs with prun. *h.*
Ezek. 29:4 put *h.* in thy jaw, 38:4
40:43 with. were *h.* hand broad
Joel 3:10 pruning *h.* into spears
Mat. 17:27 cast a *h.* take up fish

HOPE.
Ezr. 10:2 there is *h.* in Israel
Job 4:6 this thy fear, thy *h. ?*
5:16 poor hath *h.* iniq. stoppeth
7:6 my days spent without *h.*
8:13 hypocrite's *h.* sh. peri. 14
11:18 because there is *h.*
20 *h.* be as giving up of ghost
14:7 *h.* of tree if it be cut down
19 thou destroyest *h.* of man
27:8 what is *h.* of hypocrite?
Ps. 78:7 might set their *h.* in G.
146:5 happy he whose *h.* is in L.
Prov. 10:28 *h.* of righ. gladness
11:7 *h.* of unjust men perisheth
13:12 *h.* defer. mak. heart sick
14:32 the right. hath *h.* in death
19:18 chast. son wh. there is *h.*

26:12 *h.* of fool than him, 29:20
Ec. 9:4 joined to liv. there is *h.*
Is. 57:10 no *h. Jer.* 2:25; 18:12
Jer. 14:8 O the *h.* of Israel, 17:13
17:7 blessed man whose *h.* L. is
31:17 there is *h.* in end, saith L.
50:7 the Lord, *h.* of their faith.
Lam. 3:21 therefore have I *h.*
Ezek. 37:11 our bones dri. *h.* lost
Hos. 2:15 val. of Achor door of *h.*
Joel 3:16 L. will be *h.* of his peo.
Zec. 9:12 turn, ye prisoners of *h.*
Acts 16:19 *h.* of gains was gone
23:6 *h.* and resurrection of dead
24:15 *h.* tow. G. which th. allow
26:6 judged for *h.* of the prom.
27:20 all *h.* we should be saved
28:20 for *h.* of Israel I am bound
Rom. 5:4 patience, experien. *h.*
5 *h.* maketh not ashamed
8:24 as by *h.* but *h.* seen is not *h.*
15:4 thro' patien. might have *h.*
13 that ye may abound in *h.*
1 *Cor.* 9:10 be partaker of his *h.*
13:13 faith, *h.* charity, th. three
15:19 in this life only we ha. *h.*
2 *Cor.* 1:7 our *h.* of you is stead.
3:12 seeing that we have such *h.*
10:15 *h.* when faith is increased
Gal. 5:5 the Spirit wait for *h.*
Eph. 1:18 *h.* of his calling
2:12 no *h.* with. G. in world
4:4 as ye are called in one *h.*
Col. 1:5 *h.* laid up for you in hea.
23 not moved from *h.* of gospel
27 Christ in you, *h.* of glory
1 *Thes.* 1:3 patience of *h.* in Jes.
2:19 for what is our *h.* or joy ?
4:13 as others who have no *h.*
5:8 helmet the *h.* of salvation
2 *Thes.* 2:16 given us good *h.*
1 *Tim.* 1:1 Lord Jesus, is our *h.*
Tit. 2:13 for that blessed *h.*
3:7 accord. to *h.* of eternal life
Heb. 3:6 rejoice. of *h.* firm to end
6:11 full assurance of *h.* to end
18 to lay hold on *h.* before us
19 wh. *h.* we have as an anch.
7:19 bringing in of a better *h.*
1 *Pet.* 1:3 begot. us to a lively *h.*
21 faith and *h.* might be in G.
3:15 reason of *h.* that is in you
1 *John* 3:3 man that hath this *h.*

In HOPE.
Ps. 16:9 rest in *h. Acts* 2:26
Rom. 4:18 ag. hope believ. in *h.*
5:2 rejoice in *h.* of glory of God
8:20 subjected the same in *h.*
12:12 rejoicing in *h.* patient
15:13 that ye may abound in *h.*
1 *Cor.* 9:10 plougheth in *h.* thres.
Tit. 1:2 in *h.* of eternal life

My HOPE.
Job 17:15 where is now my *h. ?*
19:10 my *h.* hath he removed
31:24 if I have made gold my *h.*
Ps. 39:7 my *h.* is in thee
71:5 thou art my *h. Jer.* 17:17
119:116 asha. of my *h. Phil.* 1:20
Lam. 3:18 my *h.* perished

HOPE, Verb.
Job 6:11 stren. that I should *h.*
Ps. 22:9 didst make me *h.*
31:24 all that *h.* in the L.
33:18 *h.* in his mercy, 147:11
22 as we *h.* in thee
38:15 L. do I *h.* thou wilt hear
42:5 *h.* thou in God, 11; 43:5
71:14 but I will *h.* continually
119:49 hast caused me to *h.*
81 *h.* in thy word, 114; 130:5
130:7 let Israel *h.* in L. 131:3
Lam. 3:24 there. will I *h.* in him
26 that man both *h.* and wait
Luke 6:34 them of whom ye *h.*
Acts 26:7 our tribes *h.* to come

Rom. 8:24 why doth he *h.* for ?
25 if we *h.* for that we see not
Phil. 2:23 him I *h.* to send pres.
1 *Pet.* 1:13 be sober, and *h.* to end

HOPED.
Job 6:20 con. bec. they had *h.*
Ps. 119:43 have *h.* in thy judgm.
74 I have *h.* in thy word, 147
166 L. I have *h.* for thy salva.
Jer. 3:23 vain is salvation *h.* for
Luke 23:8 *h.* to have seen mirac.
Acts 24:26 *h.* money sho. be giv.
Heb. 11:1 substance of th. *h.* for

HOPING, ETH.
Luke 6:35 lend, *h.* for nothing ag.
1 *Cor.* 13:7 charity *h.* all things

HOPHNI. 1 *Sa.* 1:3; 2:34; 4:11, 17

HOREB.
Ex. 3:1 came to H. 1 *K.* 19:8
Deut. 1:6 spake to us in H. 4:15
Ps. 106:19 made a calf in H.
Mal. 4:4 commanded M. in H.
HOR-HAGIDGAD. *Num.* 33:32

HORMAH.
Num. 14:45 discomfi. to H. 21:3
1 *Sam.* 30:30 pre. to H. 1 *Chr.* 4:30

HORN.
Ex. 21:29 if ox push with *h.*
1 *Sam.* 2:1 my *h.* is exalted in L.
10 eh. exalt *h.* of his anointed
16:1 fill thy *h.* with oil, 13
2 *Sam.* 22:3 *h.* of my sal. *Ps.* 18:2
1 *K.* 1:39 Zadok took a *h.* of oil
Job 16:15 defiled my *h.* in dust
Ps. 75:4 wicked, lift not up *h.* 5
89:17 our *h.* shall be exalted
24 in my name sh. *h.* be exalted
92:10 my *h.* shalt thou exalt
112:9 his *h.* shall be exalted
132:17 make *h.* of David to bud
Lam. 2:3 cut off all the *h.* of Is.
17 set up *h.* of thine adversaries
Ezek. 29:21 cause *h.* of Is. to bud
Dan. 7:8 am. them a little *h.* 20
11 great words which *h.* spake
21 *h.* made war with saints
8:5 the goat had a notable *h.*
8 great *h.* was broken
9 came forth little *h.*
21 great *h.* that is betw. eyes
Mic. 4:13 I will make thy *h.* iron
Zec. 1:21 lift up *h.* over the land
Luke 1:69 raised up *h.* of salvat.

HORNS.
Gen. 22:13 caught in thic. by *h.*
Ex. 27:2 make *h.* of it on four
corners, his *h.* be of the
same, 30:2; 37:25; 38:2
Ex. 29:12 put off the bl. on *h.* of
the altar, *Lev.* 4:7, 18, 25, 30,
34; 8:15; 9:9; 16:18
30:3 pure gold overlay *h.* 37:26
Deut. 33:17 *h.* like *h.* of unicorns
1 *K.* 22:11 Zedekiah made *h.*
of iron, 2 *Chr.* 18:10
Ps. 22:21 from *h.* of unicorns
69:31 bullock that hath *h.*
75:10 *h.* of wicked will I cut off,
but *h.* of righ. sh. be exalted
118:27 bind sacrifice to *h.* of alt.
Ezek. 27:15 a present *h.* of ivory
34:21 pushed all diseased wi. *h.*
Dan. 7:7 fou. beast had ten *h.* 20
8 I consid. *h.* three *h.* pluc. up
24 ten *h.* ten kings
8:3 ram two *h.* two *h.* were high
6 he-goat ca. to ram had two *h.*
7 smote ram, brake his two *h.*
20 two *h.* kings of Me. and P.
Amos 6:13 not taken *h.* by stree. ?
Hab. 3:4 *h.* coming out of hand
Zec. 1:18 and behold, four *h.*
19 *h.* have scattered Judah, 21

Rev. 5:6 in midst L. having 7 *h.*
12:3 a red dragon, having ten *h.*
13:1 beast ten *h. h.* ten cro.
  11 beast had two *h.* like a lamb
17:3 scarlet-colored beast, ten *h.*
  7 beast seven heads and ten *h.*
12 ten *h.* thou saw. ten kin. 16
See RAMS.

HORNET, S.
Ex. 23:28 will send *h.* bef. thee
Deut. 7:20 L. send *h.* am. them
Jos. 24:12 I sent the *h.* bef. you

HORONAIM.   *Jer.* 48:3, 5, 34

HORRIBLE.
Ps. 11:6 on wicked rain *h.* temp.
40:2 brought me out of *h.* pit
Jer. 5:30 *h.* thing committed
18:13 virgin of Is. done *h.* thing
23:14 seen in proph. a *h.* thing
Hos. 6:10 seen a *h.* thing in Israel

HORRIBLY.
Jer. 2:12 be *h.* afraid, O ye heav.
Ezek. 32:10 kings sh. be *h.* afraid

HORROR.
Gen. 15:12 a *h.* of great darkness
Ps. 55:5 *h.* hath overwhelmed
119:53 *h.* hath taken hold on me

HORSE.
Gen. 49:17 adder biteth *h.* heels
Ex. 15:21 *h.* and rider thr. in sea
Jud. 5:22 were *h.* hoofs broken
1 *K.* 10:29 a *h.* for 150 shekels,
  2 *Chr.* 1:17
Est. 6:8 *h.* king rideth on, 9, 10
Job 39:18 scometh *h.* and rider
  19 hast thou giv. *h.* strength ?
Ps. 32:9 be not as the *h.* or mule
33:17 a *h.* vain thing for safety
76:6 char. and *h.* cast into sleep
147:10 del. not in strength of *h.*
Prov. 21:31 *h.* prep. ag. battle
26:3 a whip for *h.* a rod for fool
Is. 63:13 led thro' deep, as a *h.*
Jer. 8:6 *h.* rusheth into the battle
Amos 2:15 he th. rideth *h.* deliv.
Zec. 1:8 riding upon a red *h.*
9:10 cut off the *h.* from Jerus.
10:3 made them as goodly *h.*
12:4 smite every *h.* with blind.
14:15 shall be plague of the *h.*
Rev. 6:2 behold white *h.* 19:11
  4 red *h.* ; 5 black *h.* ; 8 a pale *h.*
14:20 blood came to *h.* bridles
19:19 war ag. him that sat on *h.*
21 slain wi. sw. of him sat on *h.*

HORSEBACK.
2 *K.* 9:18 on *h.* to meet Jehu, 19
Est. 6:9 on *h.* through city, 11
8:10 sent letters by posts on *h.*

HORSE-GATE.
2 *Chr.* 23:15 entering of *h.-g.*
Neh. 3:28 from above the *h.-g.*
Jer. 31:40 to corner of the *h.-g.*

HORSES.
Gen. 47:17 bread in exch. for *h.*
Ex. 9:3 hand of Lord is upon *h.*
Deut. 17:16 not multi. *h.* to himself, to end he sho. multi. *h.*
1 *K.* 10:28 Solomon had *h.* out of
  Egypt, 2 *Chr.* 1:16, 17; 9:28
18:5 grass to save *h.* and mules
22:4 my *h.* are as thy *h.* 2 *K.* 3:7
2 *K.* 2:11 there appeared *h.* of fire
5:9 Naaman came wi. *h.* and ch.
7:10 *h.* tied ; 13 take five of *h.*
9:33 *Jez.* blood sprinkled on *h.*
18:23 del. thee 2,000 *h. Is.* 36:8
23:11 took away *h.* given to son
Ec. 10:7 I have seen serv. on *h.*
Is. 2:7 th. land is also full of *h.*
5:28 their *h.* hoofs sh. be coun.
30:16 for we will flee upon *h.*
31:1 stay on *h.* trust in chariots
  3 th. *h.* are flesh and not spirit

Jer. 4:13 *h.* are swifter than eag.
5:8 were as fed *h.* in the morn.
8:16 snorting of his *h.* was heard
12:5 canst thou contend wi. *h.* ?
46:4 harness the *h.* and get up
47:3 stamping of hoof of his *h.*
51:27 cause *h.* come up as cater.
Ezek. 17:15 give him *h.* and peo.
23:6 horsemen riding on *h.* 12
  20 whose issue is like iss. of *h.*
23 all of th. riding on *h.* 38:15
27:14 traded in thy fairs with *h.*
Hos. 1:7 save th. by battle nor *h.*
14:3 we will not ride on *h.*
Joel 2:4 app. of *h.* and horsemen
Amos 6:12 sh. *h.* run upon rock ?
Hab. 1:8 their *h.* also are swifter
3:8 thou didst ride on thy *h.*
  15 didst walk thro' sea with *h.*
Hag. 2:22 overthrow *h.* and rid.
Zec. 1:8 behind him were red *h.*
6:2 first chariot red *h.* sec. black
  3 third white *h.* in fou. bay *h.*
10:5 riders on *h.* be confounded
14:20 that day upon bells of the
  h. Holiness to the Lord
Jam. 3:3 we put bits in *h.* mou.
Rev. 9:7 the locusts were like *h.*
17 I saw the *h.* the heads of *h.*
18:13 buyeth merchandise of *h.*
19:14 armies follow. on white *h.*
18 eat flesh of kings and *h.*
See CHARIOTS.

HORSELEECH.
Prov. 30:15 *h.* had two daugh.

HORSEMAN, MEN.
Gen. 50:9 with Jos. chariots, *h.*
Ex. 14:9 *h.* of Pharaoh pursued
  17 honor on Pharaoh and his *h.*
15:19 Pharaoh and *h.* went into
  sea, *Jos.* 24:6
1 *Sam.* 8:11 your sons to be *h.*
2 *Sam.* 1:6 *h.* followed after him
1 *K.* 4:26 Sol. had 12,000 *h.* 10:26
9:19 Solomon had cities for *h.*
  22 ; 2 *Chr.* 8:6, 9
2 *K.* 2:12 chariot of Is. *h.* thereof
13:14 O my father, the *h.* of Is.
18:24 put thy trust in Eg. for *h.*
2 *Chr.* 16:8 host with many *h.*
Ezr. 8:22 ashamed to ask *h.*
Neh. 2:9 sent captains and *h.*
Is. 21:7 saw a chariot with *h.* 9
22:7 *h.* shall set themselves
31:1 trust in *h.* bec. they strong
36:9 put thy trust on Eg. for *h.*
Jer. 4:29 shall flee for noise of *h.*
46:4 get up ye *h.* and stand
Ezek. 23:6 *h.* riding on horses, 12
26:10 walls shake at noise of *h.*
38:4 bring forth horses and *h.*
Dan. 11:40 the king of the north
  shall come with *h.*
Hos. 1:7 not save by horses nor *h.*
Joel 2:4 as *h.* so shall they run
Nah. 3:3 *h.* lifteth up bright sw.
Hab. 1:8 *h.* shall spread thems.
  and th. *h.* sh. come from far
Acts 23:23 ready *h.* threescore
Rev. 9:16 number of army of *h.*

HOSANNA.
Mat. 21:9 *h.* to the Son of D. 15
Mark 11:9 *h.* bles. is he that com.
  h. in highest, 10 ; *John* 12:13

HOSEN.
Dan. 3:21 men bound in their *h.*

HOSHEA.
Deut. 32:44 H. spake to people
2 *K.* 15:30 H. made, 17:1, 3 ; 18:10
1 *Chr.* 27:20 ruler of Ephraim, H.
Neh. 10:23 H. and Han. seal. co.

HOSPITALITY.
Rom. 12:13 giv. to *h.* 1 *Tim.* 3:2
Tit. 1:8 but a lover of *h.*
1 *Pet.* 4:9 use *h.* one to another

HOST.
Luke 10:35 and gave them to *h.*
Rom. 16:23 Gaius my *h.*

HOST.
Gen. 2:1 earth finish. all *h.* of th.
32:2 he said, This is God's *h.*
Ex. 14:4 I honored on his *h.* 17
  24 L. looked to *h.* of Egyptians
  28 waters covered *h.* of Phar.
16:13 dew lay round about *h.*
Num. 31:14 wroth with offi. of *h.*
  48 officers of *h.* came to Moses
Deut. 2:14 men of war wa. fr. *h.*
23:9 when the *h.* goeth forth ag.
Jos. 1:11 pass thro' *h.* and com.
Jos. 3:2 officers went thro' the *h.*
  5:14 as capt. of the *h.* of the L.
Jud. 4:2 captain of *h.* was Sisera
7:8 *h.* of Midian was beneath
  9 get thee down unto the *h.* 10
  13 cake of bre. tumbled into *h.*
8:11 Gideon smote the *h.* 12
1 *Sam.* 11:11 S. came into the *h.*
14:15 there was trembling in *h.*
  19 the noise of the *h.* went on
17:20 D. came as *h.* was going
28:5 S. saw the *h.* of Philistines
29:6 coming with me in *h.*
2 *Sam.* 20:23 Joab was over all *h.*
  1 *Chr.* 18:15
23:16 brake thro' *h.* 1 *Chr.* 11:18
1 *K.* 2:32 Abner captain of the *h.*
22:34 carry me out of the *h.*
2 *K.* 3:9 no water for the *h.*
  4:13 be spoken to capt. of *h.* ?
6:14 horses and *h.* to Dothan
7:4 let us fall to *h.* of the Syri.
  6 L. made *h.* to he. noise of *h.*
9:5 captains of *h.* were sitting
25:19 prin. scribe of *h. Jer.* 52:25
1 *Chr.* 9:19 fathers over *h.* of L.
12:22 a great *h.* like the *h.* of G.
2 *Chr.* 18:33 carry me out of *h.*
24:24 the L. delivered a great *h.*
Ps. 27:3 tho' a *h.* should encamp
33:6 all *h.* made by thy mouth
  16 no king saved by mul. of *h.*
Is. 13:4 L. muster. *h.* of battle
24:21 L. sh. pun. *h.* of high ones
40:26 bring. out *h.* by number
Jer. 51:3 destroy utterly all her *h.*
Ezek. 1:24 speech, as noise of *h.*
Dan. 8:10 cast down some of *h.*
  11 magni. hims. to prince of *h.*
  12 *h.* given him ag. daily sacr.
  13 *h.* to be trodden under foot
Ob. 20 the captivity of this *h.*
Luke 2:13 heavenly *h.* prais. G.
See HEAVEN.

HOSTAGES.
2 *K.* 14:14 Jehoash took *h.* and
  returned to Sam. 2 *Chr.* 25:24

HOSTS.
Ex. 12:41 *h.* of L. went out of E.
Ps. 103:21 bless L. all *h.*
  108:11 O G. go forth with our *h.* ?
148:2 praise ye him, all his *h.*
Jer. 3:19 heritage of *h.* of nations
See GOD, LORD.

HOT.
Ex. 16:21 when the sun waxed *h.*
Lev. 13:24 there is a *h.* burning
Deut. 19:6 anger and *h.* displeas.
19:6 while his heart is *h.*
Jos. 9:12 our bread we took *h.*
Jud. 2:14 L. was *h.* against Isr.
  20 ; 3:8 ; 10:7
  6:39 let not thine anger be *h.*
1 *Sam.* 11:9 by the time sun be *h.*
21:6 put *h.* bread when taken
Neh. 7:3 not open. till sun be *h.*
Job 6:17 when *h.* they are cons.
Ps. 6:1 neither chasten in thy *h.*
  displeasure, 38:1
39:3 my *h.* was *h.* within me
78:48 flocks to *h.* thunderbolts

Prov. 6:28 one go upon *h.* coals?
Ezek. 24:11 brass of it may be *h.*
Dan. 3:22 furnace was exceed. *h.*
Hos. 7:7 they are all *h.* as oven
1 *Tim.* 4:2 seared with *h.* iron
Rev. 3:15 neither cold nor *h.* I
  would thou wert cold or *h.* 16
See WAX, *Verb.*

HOTLY.
Gen. 31:36 th. hast so *h.* pursued

HOTTEST
2 *Sam.* 11:15 front of the *h.* bat.

HOUGH, ED.
Jos. 11:6 shall *h.* their horses
  9 *h.* horses, burnt chariots
2 *Sam.* 8:4 Da. *h.* chariot horses

HOUR.
Dan. 4:19 D. astonish. for one *h.*
Mat. 9:22 whole from that *h.*
  15:28 dau. whole from that *h.*
  17:18 ch. was cured from that *h.*
  20:3 went out about the third *h.*
  5 sixth and ninth *h.*; 6 elev. *h.*
  12 these have wro. but one *h.*
  24:36 that *h.* knoweth no man,
    42; *Mark* 13:32
  44 such an *h.* as ye think not,
    50; *Luke* 12:40, 46
  25:13 know neither day nor *h.*
  26:40 wa. one *h.?* *Mark* 14:37
  45 the *h.* is at hand, S. of man
  27:45 from sixth *h.* was darkness
    over the land to ninth *h.*
    Mark 15:33; *Luke* 23:44
Mat. 27:46 ninth *h.* Jesus cried,
  Mark 15:34
Mark 13:11 given you in that *h.*
  14:35 if pos. the *h.* might pass
  15:25 third *h.* they cruci. him
Luke 10:21 in that *h.* J. rejoiced
  12:39 what *h.* thief would come
  22:53 your *h.* and power of dar.
  59 about the space of one *h.*
John 2:4 mine *h.* is not yet come
  4:6 it was about sixth *h.* 19:14
  21 believe me, *h.* cometh, 23
  52 then inq. he the *h.* he began
    to amend, at sev. *h.* fev. left
  5:25 the *h.* is coming, 28; 16:32
  7:30 *h.* was not yet come, 8:20
  12:23 *h.* is come, Son be gl. 17:1
  27 Fa. save me from this *h.* for
    this cause came I to this *h.*
  13:1 Jes. knew his *h.* was come
  16:21 because her *h.* is come
  19:27 from that *h.* disciple took
Acts 2:15 it is third *h.* of day
  3:1 *h.* of prayer being ninth *h.*
  10:3 about ninth *h.* angel com.
  9 P. went to pray about 6th *h.*
  23:23 make ready at the third *h.*
1 *Cor.* 4:11 to this present *h.*
  15:30 in jeopardy every *h.?*
Gal. 2:5 gave place, not for an *h.*
Rev. 3:3 not know what *h.* I will
  10 from *h.* of temptation
  8:1 was silence about half an *h.*
  9:15 prepar. for an *h.* and a day
  14:7 *h.* of his judgment is come
  17:12 rec. power as kings one *h.*
  18:10 in one *h.* is thy jud. come
  17 in one *h.* great riches is co.
  19 city in one *h.* made desolate

Same HOUR.
Dan. 3:6 *s. h.* cast into furn. 15
  4:33 *same h.* was thing fulfilled
  5:5 in *s. h.* came forth fingers
Mat. 8:13 serv. was healed *s. h.*
  10:19 given you *s. h. Luke* 12:12
Luke 7:21 *same h.* cured many
  20:19 *s.* sou. to lay ha. on him
John 4:53 knew it was at *s. h.*
Acts 16:18 he came out *same h.*
  33 took them *s. h.* of the night
Rev. 11:13 *s. h.* was earthquake

HOURS.
John 11:9 twelve *h.* in day?
Acts 5:7 about three *h.* after
  19:34 all cried about two *h.*

HOUSE.
Gen. 19:4 men compassed the *h.*
  24:31 I have prepared *h.* room
  39:5 L. blessed Egyptian's *h.*
  45:2 the *h.* of Pharaoh heard
Ex. 8:3 frogs shall come into *h.*
  12:3 a lamb according to the *h.*
  30 not *h.* wh. was not one dead
  46 not carry flesh out of the *h.*
  13:3 out of the *h.* of bond. 14;
    Deut. 5:6; 6:12
  20:17 shalt not covet neighbor's
    h. Deut. 5:21
Lev. 14:36 priest sh. empty the *h.*
  38 priest shall go out of the
    h. and shut up *h.* 45, 46, 49
  25:30 *h.* sold in walled city
Deut. 7:8 red. out of *h.* of bond.
  8:14 brought you out of land of
    E. from *h.* of bondage, 13:5,
    10; *Jos.* 24:17; *Jud.* 6:8; *Jer.*
    34:13; *Mic.* 6:4
  25:10 *h.* of him hath shoe loosed
Jos. 9:15 *h.* was on town wall
Jud. 16:26 pillars wher. *h.* stand.
  27 *h.* full of men and women
  30 the *h.* fell upon the lords
  17:5 Micah had a *h.* of gods
  19:18 no man receiveth me to *h.*
  22 sons of Belial beset *h.* 20:5
1 *Sam.* 3:14 I have sw. to *h.* of E.
  5:2 brought ark into *h.* of Dag.
  7:1 bro. ark to *h.* of Abinadab
  9:18 tell me where seer's *h.* is
  25:28 L. make my lord sure *h.*
2 *Sam.* 3:1 war betw. *h.* of Saul
  8 show kindness to *h.* of Saul
  5:8 lame and blind not co. to *h.*
  6:11 L. blessed *h.* of Obed-edom.
    David brought ark from his
    h. 12; 1 *Cor.* 13:14
  7:6 not dw. in any *h.* 1 *Chr.* 17:5
  11 he will make thee a *h.*
  29 bless *h.* of serv. 1 *Chr.* 17:27
  12:8 I gave thee thy master's *h.*
1 *K.* 2:24 who made me a *h.*
  6:22 whole *h.* overlaid with gold
  9:25 so Solomon finished the *h.*
  12:31 and Jeroboam made a *h.*
  17:15 her *h.* did eat many days
  21:22 thy *h.* like *h.* of Jeroboam
2 *K.* 8:3 cry to the king for her *h.*
2 *K.* 8:18 as did the *h.* of Ahab,
    27; 2 *Chr.* 21:6; 22:4
  9:8 *h.* of Ahab shall perish
  10:5 fight for your master's *h.*
  21 and the *h.* of Baal was full
  27 the *h.* of Baal a draught *h.*
  20:13 Hez. showed *h.* of precio.
    things, *h.* of arm. *Is.* 39:2
  23:27 *h.* of wh. my name sh. be
  25:9 ev. great man's *h.* he burnt
2 *Chr.* 7:1 glory of the Lord filled
  12 chosen this place for *h.*
Ezr. 5:8 went to *h.* of great God
  6:3 at Jer. let the *h.* be builded
Est. 2:3 gather all virgins to *h.*
  8:1 give *h.* of Ha. to Esther, 7
Job 1:13 drink. in brother's *h.* 18
  19 wind came smote cor. of *h.*
  20:19 *h.* which he builded not
  21:28 where is *h.* of the prince?
  30:23 to *h.* appointed for all liv.
  38:20 know paths to the *h.*
  39:6 whose *h.* I made wildern.
Ps. 31:2 rock be *h.* of defence
  84:3 sparrow hath found a *h.*
  104:17 stork, fir-trees are her *h.*
Prov. 2:18 *h.* inclineth to death
  7:8 yo. man went way to her *h.*
  11 her feet abide not in her *h.*
  27 her *h.* is the way to hell

9:1 wisdom hath builded her *h.*
12:7 *h.* of righteous shall stand
14:11 *h.* of wicked overthrown
15:25 L. will destroy *h.* of proud
17:1 *h.* full of sacrifices
19:14 *h.* and riches are inherit,
21:9 dwell in *h.*-top, 25:24
  12 right. consider. *h.* of wicked
24:3 through wisdom is *h.* built
25:17 withdraw fr. neighbor's *h.*
27:10 brot. *h.* day of calamity
Ec. 7:2 to go to *h.* of mourning,
  than *h.* of feasting
10:18 thro' idleness *h.* droppeth
12:3 keepers of *h.* shall tremble
Cant. 1:17 beams of our *h.* cedar
2:4 brought me to banquet. *h.*
3:4 bro. him to my mother's *h.*
8:2 br. thee into my mother's *h.*
Is. 5:8 woe to them join *h.* to *h.*
6:4 *h.* was filled with smoke
14:17 open. not *h.* of prisoners
23:1 th. is no *h.*; 24:10 *h.* shut
31:2 against *h.* of evil-doers
60:7 I will glo. *h.* of my glory
64:11 holy and beaut. *h.* burnt
Jer. 16:5 enter not *h.* of mourn.
  8 sh. not go into *h.* of feasting
37:20 not return to *h.* of J. 38:26
Ezek. 2:5 they are a rebellious *h.*
  3:9, 26, 27; 12:3
  8 be not rebellious like that *h.*
12:2 dwellest in midst of reb. *h.*
17:12 say now to rebellious *h.*
24:3 utter parable to rebel. *h.*
43:11 show them the form of *h.*
  12 law of *h.* on top of mount.
Amos 3:15 sceptre from *h.* of E.
  3:15 winter *h.* with summer *h.*
5:19 or went into *h.*
6:11 smite great *h.* and little *h.*
7:16 not word ag. *h.* of Isaac
Ob. 18 *h.* of Es. be for stubble
Mic. 3:12 mountain of the
  shalt be as high places
4:2 let us go up to *h.* of God
Nah. 1:14 out of *h.* of thy gods
Zec. 5:4 enter into *h.* of thief,
  into *h.* of him that sweareth
  falsely
Mat. 7:25 and beat upon that *h.*
  27; *Luke* 6:48
  10:12 come into *h.* salute it
  13 if *h.* be worthy, let your
    peace come, *Luke* 10:5
  12:25 every *h.* divided ag. itself
  29 strong man's *h. Mark* 3:27
  20:11 murmured ag. man of *h.*
  23:38 your *h.* is left to you deso-
    late, *Luke* 13:35
  24:43 man of *h.* kn. what watch
    thief wou. come, *Luke* 12:39
Mark 3:25 *h.* divided ag. itself
  10:29 hath left *h.* or brethren
  14:14 good man of *h. Lu.* 22:11
Luke 10:7 in that *h.* remain
  15:8 light candle and sweep *h.*
John 12:3 *h.* was filled with odor
Acts 2:2 sound fr. heaven fill. *h.*
  46 breaking bread from *h.* to *h.*
  10:6 Simon, tanner, *h.* by seasi.
  17:5 Jews assaulted *h.* of Jason
  18:7 *h.* joined hard to synagog.
  19:16 fled out of that *h.* naked
  20:20 tau. publicly, from *h.* to *h.*
Rom. 16:5 greet church in th. *h.*
1 *Cor.* 1:11 are of the *h.* of Chloe
1 *Cor.* 16:15 the *h.* of Stephan. 19
2 *Cor.* 5:1 earthly *h.* be dissolved
  2 clothed with *h.* from heaven
1 *Tim.* 5:13 wander. from *h.* to *h.*
  14 younger women guide *h.*
2 *Tim.* 1:16 mercy to *h.* of Ones.
  2:20 in a great *h.* vessels of gold
Heb. 3:3 built *h.* more *h.* than *h.*
  4 every *h.* is built by some m.
  6 wh. *h.* are we, if we hold fast
2 *John* 10 receive him not into *h.*

See AARON, BORN, BUILD or
BUILT, CHIEF, DAVID, DOOR,
DWELL.

HOUSE, with father.
Gen. 12:1 get thee fr. father's h.
24:7 G. took me from father's h.
38 thou sh. go to my fa.'s h.
40 wife for my son of f.'s h.
31:14 portion for us in f.'s h.
38:11 remain widow at f.'s h.
41:51 God made me forget f.'s h.
46:31 breth. and f.'s h. are come
50:22 in Egypt, he and f.'s h.
Ex. 12:3 accord. to h. of fathers
Num. 1:2 sum of Israel by h. of
  their f. 18, 22, 24, 28
  4 every one head oi h. of his
  f. 44; Jos. 22:14
2:2 pitch with ensign of f.'s h.
3:15 children of Levi after h. of
  their fathers, 20; 4:46
17:2 accord. to h. of their f.'s, 3
18:1 thou and f.'s h. bear. iniq.
30:3 being in her father's h. 16
Deut. 22:21 play whore in f.'s h.
Jos. 2:12 show kindn. to f.'s h.
Jud. 6:15 least in my f.'s h.
9:18 risen against my f.'s h.
11:2 shalt not inherit in f.'s h.
14:15 we burn thee and f.'s h.
16:31 the h. of his f. buried him
1 Sam. 2:27 appear to h. of thy f.
  30 h. of thy f. should walk
17:25 will make his f.'s h. free
18:2 go no more home to f.'s h.
22:16 thou and all f.'s h. sh. die
24:21 not destr. name out f.'s h.
2 Sam. 3:29 rest on Joab and
  his father's h.
14:9 iniq. be on me, and f.'s h.
19:28 all of f.'s h. dead men
1 K. 2:31 innoc. blood fr. f.'s h.
18:18 thou and f.'s h. trou.
1 Chr. 28:4 God chose me bef.
  h. of f.
Ezr. 2:59 their f.'s h. Neh. 1:6
10:16 chief of the h. of f.
Neh. 1:6 I and f.'s h. have sinned
Est. 4:14 and f.'s h. be destroyed
Ps. 45:10 forget peo. and f.'s h.
Is. 3:6 hold of brother of h. of f.
7:17 bring on thy f.'s h. days
22:23 glorious throne to f.'s h.
  24 hang on him glory of f.'s h.
Jer. 12:6 h. of f. dealt treacher.
Luke 16:27 send him to f.'s h.
John 2:16 make not my F.'s h.
  a house of merchandise
14:2 in F.'s h. are many mans.
Acts 7:20 M nourished in f.'s h.

HOUSE of God.
Gen. 28:17 none oth. but h. of G.
  22 this sto. I set sh. be G.'s h.
Jos. 9:23 draw. water for h. of G.
Jud. 18:31 h. of G. was in Shiloh
20:26 came unto h. of G. 21:2
  31 high. goeth up to h. of G.
2 Chr. 5:14 gl. of L. fill. h. of G.
22:12 he was hid in h. of G.
24:13 set h. of G. in his state
33:7 Man. set image in h. of G.
36:19 they burnt the h. of G.
Ezr. 5:8 went to h. of great G.
  15 let h. of G. be builded. 6:7
7:23 let it be done for h. of G.
Neh. 6:10 let us meet in h. of G.
13:11 why is h. of G. forsaken?
Ps. 42:4 went to h. of G. 55:14
52:8 an olive-tree in h. of G.
84:10 door-keeper in h. of G.
•Ec. 5:1 when goest to h. of G.
Is. 2:3 come, let us go up to the
  h. of G. Mic. 4:2
Hos. 9:8 proph. hated in h. of G.
Joel 1:13 drink-offering withholden from h. of G.
  16 gladness cut off fr. h. of G.

Zec. 7:2 sent to h. of G. men
Mat. 12:4 entered h. of G. did
  eat shewbread, Mark 2:26;
  Luke 6:4
1 Tim. 3:15 beh. thy. in h. of G.
Heb. 10:21 High-p. over. h. of G.
1 Pet. 4:17 judg. begin at h. of G.

His HOUSE.
Gen. 12:17 L. plagu. P. and h. h.
Gen. 17:27 men of h. h. circumc.
39:4 overseer over h. h. 5
45:8 Lord of h. h. Acts 7:10
Lev. 16:16 atonement for h. h. 11
27:14 a man shall sanctify h. h.
Num. 22:18 if B. give h. h. full
  of silver and gold, 24:13
Deut. 20:5 return to h. h. 6, 7, 8
24:10 shalt not go into his h.
Jud. 8:27 bec. a snare to his h.
1 Sam. 3:12 spoken concer. h. h.
  13 I will judge h. h. for ever
7:17 to Ramah, there was h. h.
25:1 Is. buried Samuel in h. h.
2 Sam. 6:21 bef. thy fa. and h. h.
11:9 U. went not to h. h. 10, 13
  27 David fetched her to h. h.
19:11 bring king back to h. h.
21:1 for Saul and h. bloody h.
1 K. 2:33 on h. h. th. sh. be pea.
7:1 S. building, and finish. h. h.
12:24 return every man to h. h.
  22:17; 1 Chr. 16:43; 2 Chr.
  11:4; 18:16
13:19 did eat bread in h. h.
20:43 went to h. h. heavy, 21:4
2 K. 6:32 Elisha sat in his h.
20:13 nothing in h. h. Hezekiah
1 Chr. 10:6 all h. h. died togeth.
13:14 the ark remained in h. h.
2 Chr. 24:16 good toward God
  and h. h.
Ezr. 6:11 h. h. be made dunghill
Neh. 3:28 repaired over ag. h. h.
5:13 God shake ev. man fr. h. h.
Job 1:10 a hedge about his h. ?
8:15 he shall lean on his h.
20:28 increase of his h.
21:21 what plea. ha. he in h. h.?
27:18 he buildeth his h.
Ps. 49:16 get gl. of h. h. is increased
105:21 made him Lord of h. h.
112:3 wealth and riches in h. h.
Prov. 6:31 give the substance of
  his h. Cant. 8:7
17:13 evil shall not dep. fr. h. h.
Mic. 2:2 oppress a man and h. h.
Hab. 2:9 an evil covet. to h. h.
Mat. 12:29 then he will spoil h.
  h. Mark 3:27
24:17 an. out of h. h. Mark 13:15
  43 not suffered h. h. to be bro.
Luke 8:41 he wo. come to h. h.
18:14 man went down to h. h.
John 4:53 himself beli. and h. h.
Acts 10:2 feared G. with all h. h.
  22 to send for thee to his h.
11:13 had seen an angel in h. h.
16:34 jailer brou. into his h. be-
  lievi. in G. with all h. h. 18:8
Col. 4:15 salute church in h. h.
Heb. 3:2 M. faithful in h. h. 5
11:7 prep. ark for saving h. h.

HOUSE of Jacob.
Gen. 46:27 souls of h. of Jacob
Ps. 114:1 h. of J. from people
Is. 2:5 h. of Jacob walk in light
  6 forsaken thy people, h. of J.
8:17 hideth face from h. of J.
14:1 shall cleave to h. of J.
58:1 show h. of Jacob their sins
Jer. 2:4 hear word of L. h. of J.
5:20 declare this in h. of Jacob
Ezek. 20:5 lifted hand to h. of J.
Amos 9:8 not ut. destroy h. of J.
Ob. 17 h. of J. pos. possessions
18 h. of J. shall be a fire

Mic. 2:7 art named the h. of J.
3:9 ye heads of the h. of Jacob
Luke 1:33 reign over h. of Jacob
HOUSE of Joseph.
Gen. 43:17 bro. men into J.'s h.
Jos. 18:5 h. of J. abide in coast
Jud. 1:22 h. of J. went aga. B.
  35 hand of h. of Jos. prevailed
Amos 5:6 like fire in h. of Jos.
Ob. 18:1 h. of J. shall be a flame
Zec. 10:6 I will save the h. of J.
HOUSE of Israel.
Lev. 10:6 let h. of Israel bewail
17:3 what man th. be of h. of Is.
  kill. ox or lamb, 8:10; 22:18
1 Sam. 7:2 the h. of I. lamented
2 Sam. 6:5 h. of I. played bef. L.
12:8 I gave thee the h. of Israel
1 K. 20:31 kings of h. of I. merc.
Ps. 98:3 truth toward h. of I.
115:12 he will bless h. of Israel
135:19 O h. of Israel, bless Lord
Is. 5:7 vineyard of L. is h. of I.
14:2 h. of Israel possesses them
46:3 remn. of h. of I. hearken
63:7 goodness tow. the h. of I.
Jer. 2:26 so is h. of I. ashamed
3:18 h. of J. walk with h. of Is.
Jer. 3:20 dealt tr. O. h. of I. 5:11
79:26 all h. of I. uncircumcised
11:10 h. of I. broken covenant
17 evil for evil, of h. of Israel
13:11 cleave to me, h. of Israel
31:27 sow h. of I. wi. seed of m.
  31 make cov. with h. of I. 33
33:14 that I promised to h. of I.
48:13 h. of I. ashamed of Bethel
Ezek. 3:1 sp. to h. of Israel, 17:2,
  20:27, 30; 24:21; 33:10; 36:22
  7 h. of I. not hearken unto me,
  h. of I. impud. and hard-he.
17 watchman to h. of I. 33:7.
4:4 lay iniq. of h. of I. upon it
5 bear iniquity of h. of Israel
5:4 fire come forth into h. of I.
8:10 idols of h. of I. portrayed
9:9 iniq. of h. of I. is great
12:24 nor more divi. in h. of I.
13:5 nor made hedge for h. of I.
9 in the writing of h. of Israel
14:11 h. of I. go no more astray
18:6 eyes to idols of h. of I. 15
25 h. of I. is not my way eq. ?
  31 O h. of Israel ? 33:11
20:13 h. of I. rebelled ag. me
  39 for you, O h. of I. go ye
40 there shall h. of I. serve me
22:18 h. of I. is to me bec. dross
28:24 no more prick. br. h. of I.
29:6 a staff of reed to h. of I.
  16 no more confid. of h. of I.
1 cause horn of h. of I. to bud
36:10 multiply all the h. of I.
17 h. of I. dwelt in own land
21 my name wh. h. of I. prof.
32 be ashamed, O h. of Israel
37 I will be inq. of by h. of I.
37:11 bones are whole h. of I.
16 for the h. of I. his compan.
39:12 7 mo. h. of I. be burying
22 h. of I. sh. know I am the L.
23 h. of I. went into captivity
29 pour. out my Sp. on h. of I.
44:12 caused h. of Israel fall
22 maidens of seed of h. of I.
45:6 possession for who. h. of I.
8 rest of land give to h. of I.
17 reconciliation for h. of I.
Hos. 1:4 cease kingd. of h. of I.
6 no more ha. mer. on h. of I.
6:10 a horrible thing in h. of I.
11:12 h. of I. compasseth me
Amos 5:3 sh. leave ten to h. of I.
25 offered sacrifices, O h. of I.
7:10 consp. ag. thee in h. of I.
9:9 sift h. of I. am. all nations

Mic. 1:5 for sins of *h. of I.* is this
Zec. 8:13 were a curse, O *h. of I.*
Mat. 10:6 sheep of *h. of I.* 15:24
Acts 2:36 let all *h. of I.* know
7:42 O *h. of I.* have off. beasts?
Heb. 8:8 new cov. with *h. of I.* 10

HOUSE of Judah.

2 *Sam.* 2:4 anointed D. king ov.
  h. of J. 7, 11; 1 *Chr.* 28:4
12:8 I gave thee the *h. of Jud.*
2 *K.* 19:30 remnant escaped of
  the *h. of Judah, Is.* 37:31
Is. 22:21 be a father to *h. of J.*
Jer. 3:18 *h. of J.* walk with *h. I.*
5:11 *h. of J.* dealt treacherously
11:10 *h. of J.* broken covenant
12:14 pluck *h. of J.* fr. am. them
13:11 caused cle. to me *h. of J.*
31:27 sow *h. of J.* with seed
31 make new cov. with *h. of J.*
33:14 good I promised to *h. of J.*
36:3 *h. of J.* hear all the evil
Ezek. 4:6 bear iniq. of *h. of J.* 9:9
8:17 a light thing to *h. of J.?*
25:3 Am. said, Aha, ag. *h. of J.*
8 *h. of J.* like to all heathen
12 Edom hath dealt ag. *h. of J.*
Hos. 1:7 mercy upon *h. of J.*
5:12 be to *h. of J.* as rottenness
14 as a young lion to *h. of J.*
Zep. 2:7 for remnant of *h. of J.*
Zec. 8:13 a curse, O *h. of Judah*
15 to do well to *h. of Judah*
19 be to *h. of J.* joy and glad.
10:3 Lord hath visited *h. of J.*
6 I will strengthen the *h. of J.*
12:4 open m. eyes unto *h. of J.*
Heb. 8:8 a new cov. with *h. of J.*

King's HOUSE.

2 *Sam.* 11:2 wal. on roof of *k.'s h.*
1 *K.* 9:1 Sol. had finished *k.'s h.*
14:26 took away the treasure
  of *king's h.* 15:18; 2 *K.* 16:8;
  2 *Chr.* 12:9; 25:4
2 *K.* 7:11 told it to the *k.'s h.*
2 *Chr.* 23:5 third part be at *k.'s h.*
28:21 took a port. out of *h. of k.*
Ezr. 6:4 expe. given out *k.'s h.*
Est. 2:9 seven maid. out *k.'s h.*
Est. 4:13 think not esc. in *k.'s h.*
9:4 Mordecai was great in *k.'s h.*
Hos. 5:1 give ye ear, O *h. of k.*

HOUSE of Levi.

Num. 17:8 rod of A. for *h. of L.*
Ps. 135:20 bless the L. O *h. of L.*
Zec. 12:13 family of *h. of L.*

in the HOUSE.

Gen. 34:29 spoiled all *in the h.*
39:5 bless. of L. on all *in the h.*
  8 wot. not what is with me *in
  the h.*
46:16 fame was heard in P.'s *h.*
Ex. 12:46 in one *h.* passover
Lev. 14:34 put plague of leprosy
  in a h. 35, 43, 44, 47, 48
Jos. 2:19 with thee *in the h.*
Ruth 1:9 each *in h.* of husband
2:7 she tarried a little *in the h.*
1 *Sam.* 28:24 a fat calf *in the h.*
31:9 publ. it *in the h.* of their id.
10 put armor *in the h.* of Asht.
1 *K.* 3:17 I and this wom. dw. *in
  one h.* deli. of a child *in t. h.*
6:7 not any tool heard *in the h.*
14:13 found good *in the h.* if J.
2 *K.* 4:2 wh. hast thou *in t. h.?*
35 walked *in the h.* to and fro
5:18 I bow *in the h.* of Rimmon
19:37 as he was worshipping *in
  h.* of Nisroch, *Is.* 37:38
2 *Chr.* 36:17 slew yo. men *in t. h.*
Ezr. 1:7 *in the h.* of his gods
6:1 search made *in t. h.* of rolls
Est. 7:8 force queen *in the h.?*
9 gallows standeth *in h.* of Ha.
Ps. 119:54 *in the h.* of my pilg.

Prov. 3:33 curse of Lord *in h.*
5:10 be *in t. h.* of a stranger
7:11 her feet abide not *in h. h.*
15:6 *in the h.* of the righteous
Ec. 7:4 heart of wise is *in h.* of
  mourn. he of fools *in h. mi.*
Is. 44:13 mak. idol remain *in h.*
Jer. 7:30 abominations *in h.* 32:34
34:15 a covenant bef. me *in t. h.*
Amos 6:9 ten men *in one h.*
Mic. 6:10 wicked. *in h.* of wicked
Zec. 13:6 wounded *in h.* of frien.
Mat. 5:15 light to all are *in c. h.*
Mark 9:33 being *in the h.*
14:3 being *in t. h.* S. the leper
Luke 8:27 *in any h.* but tombs
John 8:35 abideth not *in the h.*
11:20 Mary sat still *in the h.*
Acts 9:11 inq. *in t. h.* of Judas
10:32 P. is lodged *in h.* of Sim.

HOUSE, with Lord.

Ex. 23:19 first fruits bring into *h.*
  of *L.* 34:26; *Neh.* 10:35
Deut. 23:18 pr. of dog to *h.* of *L.*
Jos. 6:24 put in treas. of *h.* of *L.*
1 *Sam.* 1:7 she went to *h.* of *L.*
24 Hannah bro. him to the
  h. of the *L.* 2 *K.* 12:4, 9, 13;
  22:4; 2 *Chr.* 34:14
1 *K.* 3:1 end of building *h.* of *L.*
6:37 the foundation of the *h.* of
  the *Lord* laid, 2 *Chr.* 8:16;
  Ezr. 3:11; *Zec.* 8:9
7:40 work made for *h.* of *Lord,*
  45:51; 2 *Chr.* 4:16; 5:1; 24:14
8:10 cloud filled *h.* of *L.* 11;
  2 *Chr.* 5:13; 7:2; *Ezek.* 44:4
63 so Israel dedicated *h.* of *L.*
2 *K.* 11:3 hid in *h.* of *L.* six yea.
4 took an oath in *h.* of the *L.*
15 let her not be slain in *h.* of
  Lord, 2 *Chr.* 23:14
12:10 money found in *h.* of the
  Lord, 14:14; 16:8; 18:15
11 oversight of the *h.* of the *L.*
16 press.-money not in *h.* of *L.*
20:5 third day sh. go to *h.* of *L.*
8 L. will heal me, that I shall
  go up to the *h.* of *L.* *Is.* 38:22
23:2 words found in *h.* of *Lord,*
  24; 2 *Chr.* 34:17, 30
7 Sodomites were by *h.* of *L.*
25:9 he burnt *h.* of *L.* *Jer.* 52:13
1 *Chr.* 6:31 service in the *h.* of *L.*
22:1 D. said, This is the *h.* of *L.*
11 build the *h.* of *L.* thy God
14 I have prepared for *h.* of *L.*
23:4 set forw. work of *h.* of *L.*
26:12 to minister in *h.* of the *L.*
2 *Chr.* 8:16 *h.* of *L.* was perfected
29:5 sanctify *h.* of the *Lord*
15 came to cleanse *h.* of *Lord*
33:15 M. took idol out *h.* of *L.*
34:15 book of law in *h.* of *L.*
36:14 priests polluted *h.* of *L.*
Ezr. 7:27 beautify *h.* of the *L.*
Ps. 23:6 dw. in *h.* of *L.* for ever
27:4 dwell in *h.* of *L.* all my life
92:13 be planted in *h.* of *Lord*
Ps. 116:19 pay my vows in *L.'s h.*
118:26 bless. you out of *h.* of *L.*
122:1 let us go into the *h.* of *L.*
9 bec. of *h.* of *L.* seek thy good
134:1 th. stand in *h.* of *L.* 135:2
Is. 2:2 *L.'s h.* be established in
  the top of mount. *Mic.* 4:1
Jer. 17:26 praise to *h.* of *L.*
26:2 come to worship in *L.'s h.*
36:5 I cannot go into *h.* of *L.*
6 in *L.'s h.* upon fasting day
51:51 come to sanctua. of *L.'s h.*
Lam. 2:7 made a noise in *h.* of *L.*
Hag. 1:2 time *L.'s h.* be built
See COURT, DOOR, GATE, TREAS-
  URES, VESSELS.

My HOUSE.

Gen. 15:2 stew. of *my h.* is Eliez.

3 one born in *my h.* is mi. heir
Num. 12:7 is faithful in all *m. h.*
Jos. 24:15 me and *m. h.* serve *L.*
Jud. 11:31 fo. of doors of *m. h.*
1 *Sam.* 21:15 fel. come to into *m. h.*
2 *Sam.* 7:18 O L. G. what is *my
  h.?* 1 *Chr.* 17:16
11:11 shall I then go into *m. h.?*
23:5 tho' *my h.* be not so wi. G.
1 *K.* 21:2 bec. it is near to *my h.*
1 *K.* 20:15 all things that are in
  my h. Is. 39:4
1 *Chr.* 17:14 settle him in *my h.*
Job 17:13 the grave is *my h.*
Ps. 101:2 in *my h.* wi. perf. heart
132:3 not come to tab. of *my h.*
Prov. 7:6 at window of *my h.*
Is. 3:7 in *my h.* is neither bread
56:5 I give in *my h.* a name
7 make them joyful in *my h.*
  of prayer, *my h.* sh. be called
  a *h.* of prayer, *Mat.* 21:13;
  Mark 11:17; *Luke* 19:46
Jer. 11:15 wh. bel. do in *my h.?*
12:7 I have forsaken *my h.*
23:11 in *my h.* I found wickedn.
Ezek. 8:1 as I sat in *my h.*
44:7 to pollute it, even *my h.*
Dan. 4:4 N. was at rest in *my h.*
Hag. 1:9 *my h.* that is waste
Zec. 3:7 shalt also judge *my h.*
9:8 I will encamp about *my h.*
Mal. 3:10 meat in *my h.*
Mat. 12:44 I will return into *my
  h. Luke* 11:24
Luke 9:61 bid farewell at *my h.*
14:23 that *my h.* may be filled
Acts 10:30 I pray. in *my h.*
16:15 come into *my h.*

Own HOUSE.

Gen. 14:14 serv. born in his *o. h.*
2 *Sam.* 4:11 person in his *o. h.*
12:11 ev. ag. thee out of th. *o. h.*
19:30 come in peace to *own h.*
1 *K.* 2:34 Joab buried in his *o. h.*
3:1 an end of building *own h.*
7:1 S. building his *o. h.* 13 years
12:16 now see to thine *own h.*
  David, 2 *Chr.* 10:16
1 *K.* 14:12 get thee into th. *o. h.*
2 *K.* 21:18 Man. was buried in
  garden of *o. h.* 2 *Chr.* 33:20
23 slew the king in his *own h.*
  2 *Chr.* 33:24
2 *Chr.* 7:11 in his heart in *o. h.*
Est. 1:22 man rule in his *o. h.*
Prov. 11:29 that troubleth *o. h.*
15:27 greedy troubleth *own h.*
Is. 14:18 in glory, ev. one *o. h.*
Mic. 7:6 enemies are of *o. h.*
Hag. 1:9 run ev. man to *own h.*
Mat. 13:57 proph. is not without
  honor, save in *o. h. Mark* 6:4
Luke 1:23 departed to *o. h.* 5:25
56 Mary returned to her *o. h.*
5:29 Levi made a feast in *o. h.*
8:39 return to thy *own h.*
John 7:53 ev. man went to *o. h.*
Acts 28:30 P. dw. 2 years in *o. h.*
1 *Tim.* 3:4 ruleth well his *o. h.*
5 know not how to rule *o. h.*
5:8 especially for those of *o. h.*
Heb. 3:6 Ch. as a Son over *o. h.*

This HOUSE.

Gen. 39:9 none gre. in *t. h.* th. 1
1 *K.* 6:12 *t. h.* thou art building
8:27 how much less *t. h.* I bu.?
29 eyes be opened toward *t. h.*
31 before thine altar in *this h.*
33 supplica. to thee in *t. h.* 42
38 spread his hands tow. *t. h.*
9:3 I have hallowed *this h.*
8 at *this h.* every one sh. hiss
2 *Chr.* 6:20 eyes be open on *t. h.*
22 oath come bef. altar in *t. h.*
24 make supplication in *t. h.*
32 if th. come and pray in *t. h.*
7:16 now have I sancti. *t. h.* 20

2 *Chr.* 7:21 and *t. h.* wh:ch is hi.
Ezr. 3:12 foundation of *this h.*
Jer. 7:10 stand before me in *t. h.*
11 is *t. h.* bec. a den of rob. ?
22:5 *t. h.* shall bec. a desolation
26:6 will I make *t. h.* like Shil.
9 *t. h.* shall be like Shiloh
Hag. 1:4 *this h.* lie waste ?
2:3 who is left saw *t. h.* first ?
7 I will fill *t. h.* with glory
9 glory of *t. h.* greater than
Luke 10:5 Peace be to *this h.*
19:9 this day salv. come to *t. h.*

Thy HOUSE.
Gen. 7:1 come thou and *t. h.*
Num. 18:11 is clean in *t. h.* 13
Deut. 6:7 talk of th. in *t. h.* 11:19
9 write on posts of *t. h.* 11:20
7:26 an abomination to *t. h.*
21:12 bring her home to *t. h.*
22:8 bring not blood upon *t. h.*
25:14 in *t. h.* divers measures
26:11 G. given to thee and *t. h.*
Jos. 2:3 men entered into *thy h.*
12:1 will burn *thy h.*
Ruth 4:11 woman come into *t. h.*
12 let *t. h.* be like house of P.
1 *Sam.* 2:30 *t. h.* sh. walk before
31 not be an old man in *t. h.*
33 *t. h.* sh. die in flower of age
36 every one in *thy h.* crouch
25:6 peace to *thy h.*
2 *Sam.* 7:16 *t. h.* estab. for ever
11:8 go to *thy h.* wash thy feet
12:10 sw. never depart fr. *t. h.*
1 *K.* 13:8 if thou give half *thy h.*
2 *K.* 20:1 *thy h.* in order, *Is.* 38:1
15 wh. seen in *thy h.* ? *Is.* 39:4
17 *thy h.* sh. be carri. *Is.* 39:6
Ps. 5:7 I will come into *thy h.*
26:8 loved habitation of *t. h.*
36:8 satisf. with fatness of *t. h.*
50:9 will take no bullock of *t. h.*
65:4 sati. with goodness of *t. h.*
66:13 go to *t. h.* with b.-offerin.
69:9 zeal of *t h.* hath eaten me
up, *John* 2:17
93:5 holiness becometh *thy h.*
128:3 as fruitful vine by *thy h.*
Is. 58:7 that are cast to *thy h.*
Jer. 38:17 thou sh. live, and *t. h.*
Ezek. 3:24 shut thyself wit. *t. h.*
44:30 blessing to rest in *thy h.*
Hab. 2:10 consulted sh. to *t. h.*
Mat. 9:6 arise, go to *t. h. Mark*
2:11 ; *Luke* 5:24
26:18 keep passover at *thy h.*
Luke 7:44 entered *thy h.*
19:5 to-day I must abide at *t. h.*
Acts 11:44 all *t. h.* saved, 16:31
Phile. 2 to the church in *thy h.*

See TOPS.

HOUSES.
Ex. 1:21 he made midwives' *h.*
12:7 upper door-posts of the *h.*
13 blood be for token on the *h.*
15 put away leaven out of y. *h.*
Lev. 25:31 *h.* of vill. be counted
Num. 16:32 swallowed their *h.*
32:18 will not return to our *h.*
Deut. 6:11 *h.* of good things
8:12 built goodly *h.* dw. therein
19:1 dw. in their *h. Neh.* 9:25
Jos. 9:12 hot provision out of *h.*
Jud. 18:14 know th. is in th. *h.*
1 *K.* 13:32 he cried against the *h.*
20:6 search *h.* of thy servants
2 *K.* 17:29 in the *h.* of high pla.
23:7 brake down *h.* of Sodomit.
19 *h.* of high pla. Josiah took
25:9 burnt *h.* of Jeru. *Jer.* 52:13
1 *Chr.* 15:1 David made *h.* in ci.
28:11 gave to Sol. pattern of *h.*
2 *Chr.* 34:11 buy timber to fi. *h.*
35:4 prepare yourselves by

Neh. 4:14 fight for wives and *h.*
5:3 we mortg. our lands and *h.*
7:4 peo. few and *h.* not builded
Job 1:4 feasted in their *h.*
3:15 filled their *h.* with silver.
4:19 that dwell in *h.* of clay
15:28 dw. in *h.* no man inhabit.
21:9 their *h.* arc safe from fear
22:18 filled their *h.* with good
24:16 they dig through *h.*
Ps. 49:11 *h.* sh. continue for ever
83:12 let us take the *h.* of God
Prov. 1:13 fill our *h.* with spoil
30:26 make they th. *h.* in rocks
Ec. 2:4 I builded me *h.*
Is. 3:14 spoil of poor in your *h.*
5:9 *h.* shall be desolate, 6:11
8:14 rock of offence to both *h.*
13:16 *h.* spoiled, wives ravished
21 *h.* full of doleful creatures
15:3 on tops of *h.* ev. one howl
Is. 22:10 *h.* ha. ye broken to for.
32:13 upon all the *h.* of joy
Jer. 5:7 by troops in harlot's *h.*
27 so are their *h.* full of deceit
29:5 build *h.* dwell in them, 28
32:15 *h.* and fields be possessed
29 *h.* on wh. roofs the „ offered
33:4 *h.* of this city, *h.* of kings
43:12 fire in *h.* of gods of Eg. 13
Lam. 5:2 our *h.* turned to aliens
Ezek. 7:24 heathen possess th. *h.*
16:41 they sh. burn thy *h.* 23:47
26:12 destroy thy pleasant *h.*
28:26 build *h.* plant vineyards
33:30 ag. thee in doors of the *h.*
Dan. 2:5 *h.* made a dunghill
3:29 *h.* sh. be made a dunghill
Joel 2:9 shall climb up upon *h.*
Amos 3:15 *h.* of ivory sh. perish
Mic. 1:14 *h.* of A. be lie to kings
2:2 covet *h.* take them away
9 women ye cast from their *h.*
Zep. 1:9 fill master's *h.* with vio.
13 their *h.* become a desolation
Hag. 1:4 dwell in your ceiled *h.* ?
Zec. 14:2 the *h.* shall be rifled
Mat. 11:8 soft cloth. kings' *h.*
19:29 hath forsaken *h.* or wife
23:14 for ye devour widows' *h.*
Mark 12:40 ; *Luke* 20:47
Mark 8:3 if send them fast. to *h.*
Luke 16:4 receive me into th. *h.*
Acts 4:34 possess. of *h.* sold th.
1 *Cor.* 11:22 ye not *h.* to eat in ?
1 *Tim.* 3:12 deacons rul. *h.* well
2 *Tim.* 3:6 which creep into *h.*
Tit. 1:11 subvert whole *h.*

HOUSEHOLD, S.
Gen. 18:19 will command his *h.*
35:2 J. said to his *h.* put away
45:11 th. and *h.* come to poverty
47:12 Jos. nourished his fa.'s *h.*
24 four par. be food for your *h.*
Ex. 1:1 ev. man and *h.* came
12:4 if *h.* be little for the lamb
Lev. 16:17 an atonement for *h.*
Num. 18:31 eat it, and your *h.*
Deut. 6:22 showed wonders on *h.*
11:6 swallowed them and *h.*
15:20 eat it bef. L. thou and *h.*
Jos. 2:18 bring thy father's *h.*
6:25 saved R. her father's *h.*
Jud. 18:25 with lives of thy *h.*
1 *Sam.* 25:17 evil determi. ag. *h.*
27:3 ev. man with his *h.* even
Da. with wives, **2** *Sam.* 2:3
2 *Sam.* 6:11 blessed him and *h.*
20 D. returned to bless his *h.*
16:2 asses be for king's *h.* to ri.
17:23 and put his *h.* in order
19:18 a boat to carry king's *h.*
1 *K.* 4:7 victuals for king and *h.*
5:11 S. gave Hiram wheat to *h.*
2 *K.* 8:1 go and thy *h.* sojourn
Job 1:3 3,000 camels great *h.*

Prov. 27:27 goat's milk for *h.*
31:15 riseth and giv. meat to *h.*
21 not afraid of snow for her *h.*
for all her *h.* are clothed
27 look. well to ways of her *h.*
Mat. 10:25 call them of his *h.*
36 man's foes *h.* be of own *h.*
24:45-ruler over *h. Luke* 12:42
Acts 16:15 baptized and her *h.*
1 *Cor.* 1:16 baptized *h.* of Steph.
Gal. 6:10 are of the *h.* of faith
Eph. 2:19 but of the *h.* of God
Phil. 4:22 that are of Cæsar's *h.*
2 *Tim.* 4:19 salute *h.* of Onesiph.

HOUSEHOLDER.
Mat. 13:27 servants of *h.* came
52 like a man that is a *h.* 20:1
21:33 a certain *h.* planted viney.

HOUSEHOLD-SERVANTS.
Acts 10:7 Cornel. called two *h.-s.*

HOUSEHOLD-STUFF.
Gen. 31:37 hast found of *h.-s.* ?
Neh. 13:8 cast out all *h.-s.* of T.

HOW long.
Num. 14:11 *h. l.* ere th. believe ?
2 *Sam.* 19:34 *h. l.* have I to live ?
1 *K.* 18:21 *h. l.* halt ye between ?
Job 8:2 *h. l.* wilt thou speak ? *h.*
l. sh. words be like st. wind ?
18:2 *h. l.* ere ma. end of words ?
Ps. 4:2 *h. l.* will ye turn my glo.
to shame ? *h. l.* love vanity ?
6:3 but thou. O Lord. *h. long?*
13:1 *h. l.* wilt forget me, O L. ?
2 *h. l.* take coun. in my soul ?
h. l. enemy be ex. over me ?
74:9 nor any am. us know *h. l.*
10 O G. *h. l.* advers. reproach ?
79:5 *h. l.* wilt be angry ? 80:4
82:2 *h. l.* will judge unjustly ?
89:46 *h. l.* L. wilt hide thyself ?
Ps. 90:13 return, O Lord, *h. lo.?*
94:3 *h. l.* shall wick triumph ?
4 *h. l.* sh. th. utter ha. things ?
Prov. 1:22 *h. l.* will love simplic.
Is. 6:11 then said I, Lord *h. l.?*
Jer. 4:21 *h. l.* sh. I see standard ?
12:4 *h. l.* sh. the land mourn ?
23:26 *h. l.* be in heart of prop. ?
47:6 O sw. of L. *h. l.* ere be qu. ?
Dan. 8:13 *h. l.* be vision of sac. ?
12:6 *h. l.* to end of wonders ?
Hab. 1:2 *h. long* shall I cry ?
Mat. 17:17 *h. l.* shall I be with
you ? *h. l.* suf. ? *Mark* 9:19 ;
Luke 9:41
Mark 9:21 *h. l.* since this came ?
John 10:24 *h. l.* make to doubt ?
Rev. 6:10 *h. l.* O L. holy and tr.

HOW many times.
1 *K.* 22:16 *h. many times* shall I
adjure thee ? 2 *Chr.* 18:15

HOW much.
2 *K.* 5:13 *h. much* rather he saith
Cant. 4:10 *h. m.* better thy love
Mat. 12:12 *h. m.* is man better
Luke 16:5 *h. m.* owest thou ? 7
Heb. 8:6 by *h. m.* he is Mediator
10:29 of *h. m.* sorer punishment
Rev. 18:7 *h. m.* she hath glorified

HOW much less.
1 *K.* 8:27 *h. much less* this house
wh. I have built, 2 *Chr.* 6:18
2 *Chr.* 32:15 *h. m. l.* sh. G. deliv.
Job 4:19 *h. m. l.* in houses of cl.

HOW much more.
Luke 12:24 *h. m. m.* are ye better
28 *h. m. m.* will he clothe you ?
Rom. 11:12 *h. m. m.* th. fullness ?
Phile. 16 bro. *h. m. m.* to thee ?

HOWL.

Is. 13:6 *h.* day of L. is at hand
14:31 *h.* O gate, cry O city
15:2 Moab sh. *h.* 3 ; 16:7
23:1 *h.* ye ships of Tarshish
  6 over to Tarsh. *h.* inhabitants
52:5 rule over make them *h.*
65:14 *h.* for vexation of spirit
Jer. 4:8 lament and *h.* 4:20
25:34 *h.* ye shepherds and cry
47:2 inhabitants of land shall *h.*
48:31 *h.* for M. ; 39 they shall *h.*
49:3 *h.* O Heshb. : 51:8 *h.* for B.
Ezek. 21:12 cry and *h.* son of m.
30:2 prophesy and say, *h.* ye
Joel 1:5 *h.* drinkers ; 11 *h.* v.-dre.
  13 *h.* ye ministers of the altar
Mic. 1:8 theref. I will wail and *h.*
Zep. 1:11 *h.* inhabit. of Maktesh
Zec. 11:2 *h.* fir-tree, *h.* O ye oaks
Jam. 5:1 ye rich m. weep and *h.*

HOWLED, ING.

Deut. 32:10 found him in was. *h.*
Hos. 7:14 they *h.* on their beds

HOWLING, S.

Is. 15:8 *h.* is gone to Eglaim
Jer. 25:36 *h.* of principal of flock
Amos 8:3 songs of tem. sh. be *h.*
Zep. 1:10 a *h.* from second gate
Zec. 11:3 voice of *h.* of shepher.

HUGE.

2 *Chr.* 16:8 Eth. and Lub. *h.* ho.

HUMBLE.

Job 22:29 he shall save *h.* person
Ps. 9:12 forgetteth not cry of *h.*
10:12 O Lord, forget not the *h.*
  17 L. hast heard desire of *h.*
34:2 the *h.* shall hear thereof
69:32 *h.* shall hear this and be
Prov. 16:19 better be of *h.* spirit
29:23 honor shall uphold the *h.*
Is. 57:15 with him of *h.* spirit, to
  revive spirit of *h.*
Jam. 4:6 giv. gra. to *h.* 1 *Pet.* 5:5

HUMBLE, Verb.

Ex. 10:3 wilt ref. to *h.* thyself
Deut. 8:2 *h.* thee and pr. thee, 16
Jud. 19:24 bring out, and *h.* th.
2 *Chr.* 7:14 shall *h.* themselves
34:27 didst *h.* thyself bef. God
Prov. 6:3 *h.* thyself, make sure
Jer. 13:18 *h.* yourselves, sit do.
Mat. 18:4 *h.* himself, 23:12
2 *Cor.* 12:21 my God will *h.* me
Jam. 4:10 *h.* your. in sight of L.
1 *Pet.* 5:6 *h.* yourselves under G.

HUMBLED.

Lev. 26:41 uncircum. hearts *h.*
Deut. 8:3 *h.* thee and suffered
21:14 hast *h.* her, 22:29
22:24 hath *h.* his neighbor's wi.
2 *K.* 22:19 *h.* thyself before L.
2 *Chr.* 12:6 princes and king *h.*
  7 L. saw they *h.* themselves
  12 he *h.* himself, wrath turned
2 *Chr.* 32:26 Heze. *h.* himself be
33:12 Manas. *h.* himself greatly
  19 set up images be. he was *h.*
  23 A. *h.* not himself before L.
  as Manas. his father *h.* him.
36:12 Zedekiah *h.* not himself
Ps. 35:13 I *h.* my soul with fast.
Is. 2:11 lofty looks of man be *h.*
  5:15 man be *h.* eyes of lof. be *h.*
10:33 the haughty shall be *h.*
Jer. 44:10 not *h.* even to this day
Lam. 3:20 soul in rem. and is *h.*
Ezek. 22:10 in thee have they *h.*
  11 another hath *h.* his sister
Dan. 5:22 his son not *h.* heart
Phil. 2:8 *h.* himself and became

HUMBLEDST, ETH.

1 *K.* 21:29 Ahab *h.* because he *h.*
2 *Chr.* 34:27 bec. thou *h.* thyself
Ps. 10:10 crouch, and *h.* himself

113:6 *h.* himself to behold thin.
Is. 2:9 the great man *h.* himself
Luke 14:11 *h.* hims. be ex. 18:14

HUMBLENESS.

Col. 3:12 put on *h.* of mind

HUMBLY.

2 *Sam.* 16:4 I *h.* beseech thee
Mic. 6:8 and to walk *h.* with G.

HUMILIATION.

Acts 8:33 in his *h.* his judgment

HUMILITY.

Prov. 15:33 bef. honor is *h.* 18:12
22:4 by *h.* are riches and honor
Acts 20:19 serving L. with *h.*
Col. 2:18 no man begu. you in *h.*
  23 in will-worship and *h.*
1 *Pet.* 5:5 and be clothed with *h.*

HUNDRED-FOLD. *See* FOLD.

HUNDRED.

Gen. 17:17 child be born to him
  h. ye. old ? 21:5 ; *Rom.* 4:19
Lev. 26:8 chase a. a *h.* to flight
Deut. 22:19 amerce in *h.* shekels
Jud. 20:10 ten of *h.* a *h.* of 1,000
1 *Sam.* 18:25 but a *h.* foreski.
  2 *Sam.* 3:14
25:18 a *h.* clusters, 2 *Sam.* 16:1
1 *K.* 4:23 Provision for *h.* sheep
18:4 Obad. took a *h.* proph. 13
2 *K.* 4:43 I set this bef. *h.* men ?
1 *Chr.* 12:14 least was over a *h.*
21:3 L. make his people *h.* tim
Ezr. 2:69 gave *h.* priests' garm.
  6:17 at dedication a *h.* bullocks
7:22 done to a. *h.* talents of sil
  h. measures of wheat and
  wine, and a *h.* baths of oil
Neh. 5:11 *h.* part of the money
Prov. 17:10 than *h.* strip. to fool
Ec. 6:3 if a man beget a *h.* child.
8:12 sinner do evil a *h.* times
Is. 65:20 the child shall die a *h.*
  ye. old, but the sinner being
  a *h.* years old sh. be accurs.
Ezek. 40:19 measured a *h.* cubits,
  23, 47 ; 41:13, 14, 15 ; 42:8
Amos 5:3 went out by a 1,000,
  sh. leave a *h.* that wh. went
  forth by a *h.* shall leave ten
Mat. 18:12 if a man have a *h.*
  sheep, *Luke* 15:4
  28 who owed him a *h.* pence
Luke 16:6 a *h.* measures of oil
  7 how much ow. thou ? *h.* me.
John 19:39 myrrh and aloes *h.*

One HUNDRED and twenty.

Gen. 6:3 his days be *h.* and *t.* y.
Deut. 31:2 a *h.* and *t.* years old
34:7 M. *h. t.* years when he died

One HUNDRED and twenty-seven.

Est. 1:1 Ahasu. reigned over *h.*
  twenty-s. prov. 8:9 ; 9:30

One HUNDRED and thirty.

Gen. 47:9 years of my pilgrimage
  are a *h.* and *thirty*

One HUNDRED and fifty.

Gen. 7:24 wa. prev. *h. f.* da. 8:3

One HUNDRED and fifty-three.

John 21:11 full of fishes a *h. f. t.*

One HUNDRED and eighty.

Est. 1:4 A. feast for *h. e.* days

A HUNDRED and forty-four thousand.

Rev. 7:4 *h. f.-f. t.* tribes of Israel
14:1 *h. f.-f. t.* having F.'s name
  3 no man le. song but *h. f.-f. t.*

A HUNDRED and eighty-five thousand.

2 *K.* 19:35 that night the angel
  of the L. smote the Assy.
  h. eighty-five th. *Is.* 37:36

Two HUNDRED.

John 6:7 *t. h.* penny. not suffi.

Three HUNDRED.

Jud. 7:6 number lap. *t. h.* men
15:4 Samson caught *t. h.* foxes
2 *Sam.* 21:16 sp. weigh. *t. h.* sh.
1 *K.* 11:3 S. had *t. h.* concubines
John 12:5 ointm. for *t. h.* pence

Four HUNDRED.

Gen. 15:13 afflict *f. h.* ye. *Acts* 7:6
1 *Sam.* 30:17 *f. h.* young men
1 *K.* 18:19 prop. of groves, *f. h.*
Acts 5:36 *f. h.* joined themselves

Four HUNDRED and thirty.

Ex. 12:40 in E. *f. h. t.* years
Gal. 3:17 law. wh. was *f. h. t.* y.

Four HUNDRED and fifty.

1 *K.* 18:19 pro. of Baal *f. h. f.* 22
Acts 13:20 judges about *f. h. f.*

Four HUNDRED and eighty.

1 *K.* 6:1 in *f. h. e.* years Solom.

Four HUNDRED thousand.

Jud. 20:2 Benjamin *f. h. t.* 17
2 *Chr.* 13:3 array wi. *f. h. t.* men

Four HUNDRED and seventy thousand.

1 *Chr.* 21:5 *f. h. s. t.* drew sword

Five HUNDRED.

Num. 31:28 one soul *f. h.* for L.
Luke 7:41 one owned *f. h.* pence
1 *Cor.* 15:6 *f. h.* brethren at once

Six HUNDRED.

Gen. 7:6 N. *s. h.* ye. flood ca. 11
Jud. 3:31 Shamgar slew *six h.*
1 *Sam.* 17:7 spear weigh. *s. h.* sh.
1 *K.* 10:16 *six h.* shekels of gold
  to one target, 2 *Chr.* 9:15

Six HUNDRED and sixty-six.

Rev. 13:18 num. be *six h. a. s.-s.*

Six HUNDRED thousand.

Num. 1:46 all numb. were *s. h. t.*

Seven HUNDRED.

1 *K.* 11:3 Sol. had *seven h.* wives

Nine HUNDRED and thirty.

Gen. 5:5 Adam lived *nine h. t.* y.

Nine HUNDRED sixty-nine.

Gen. 5:27 Methus. n. *h. s.-n.* ye.

HUNDREDS.

Ex. 18:21 rul. of *h.* 25 ; *Deut.* 1:15
Num. 31:14 wr. with capt. ov. *h.*
1 *Sam.* 22:7 J. make capts. of *h.*
2 *Sam.* 18:1 D. set captains of *h.*
  4 all the people came out by *h.*
2 *K.* 11:4 Jehoi. set rul. over *h.*
  10 to captains over *h.* did pri.
  give spears, 2 *Chr.* 23:9
1 *Chr.* 13:1 consu. wi. capt. of *h.*
28:1 D. assembled capt. over *h.*
29:6 captains of *h.* off. willingly
2 *Chr.* 23:1 Jeh. took capt. of *h.*
Mark 6:40 sat do. in ranks by *h.*

HUNGER, Substantive.

Ex. 16:3 kill this assembly wi. *h.*
Deut. 28:48 serve thine ene. in *h.*
32:24 shall be burnt with *h.*
Neh. 9:15 bread fr. heaven for *h.*
Ps. 34:10 do lack and suffer *h.*
Prov. 19:15 idle soul sh. suffer *h.*
Jer. 38:9 he is like to die for *h.*
42:14 see no war nor have *h.*
Lam. 2:19 faint for *h.*
  4:9 they that be slain with *h.*
Ezek. 34:29 no more con. with *h.*
Luke 15:17 and I perish with *h.*
2 *Cor.* 11:27 I have been in *h.*
Rev. 6:8 to kill with *h.*

HUNGER, Verb.

Deut. 8:3 he suffered thee to *h.*
Is. 49:10 shall not *h.* nor thirst
Mat. 5:6 blessed are they that *h.*
  after righteous. *Luke* 6:21

Luke 6:25 woe to full, ye shall *h.*
John 6:35 com. to me sh. never *h.*
Rom. 12:20 if enemy *h.* feed him
1 *Cor.* 4:11 we both *h.* and thirst
11:34 if any man *h.* let him eat
Rev. 7:16 they shall *h.* no more

HUNGER-BITTEN.

Job 18:12 his stron. sh. be *h.-b.*

HUNGERED.

Mat. 4:2 afterwards a *h. Luke* 4:2
12:1 his disciples were a *h.*
3 what David did when he was
  a *h. Mark* 2:25 ; *Luke* 6:3
21:18 as he returned to city he *h.*
25:35 I *h.* and ye gave me meat
37 when saw we thee a *h.* ? 44
42 I *h.* and ye gave me no meat

HUNGRY.

2 *Sam.* 17:29 the people is *h.*
2 *K.* 7:12 they kn. that we be *h.*
Job 5:5 whose harv. the *h.* eateth
22:7 withholden bread from *h.*
24:10 take the sheaf fr. the *h.*
Ps. 50:12 if *h.* I would not tell
107:5 *h.* and thirsty
9 filleth *h.* soul with goodness
36 there he maketh *h.* to dwell
146:7 Lord giveth food to the *h.*
Prov. 6:30 to satis. soul when *h.*
25:21 if enemy be *h.* give bread
27:7 to *h.* soul bitter th. is sw.
Is. 8:21 hardly bestead and *h.*
  when *h.* shall fret themselv.
9:20 snatch on right hand, be *h.*
29:8 when a *h.* man dreameth
32:6 to make empty soul of *h.*
44:12 is *h.* and strength faileth
58:7 not deal thy bread to *h.* ?
  10 draw out thy soul to the *h.*
65:13 serv. eat, but ye sh. be *h.*
Ezek. 18:7 giv. his bread to *h.* 16.
Mark 11:12 from Beth. he was *h.*
Luke 1:53 filled *h.* with good th.
Acts 10:10 Peter became very *h.*
1 *Cor.* 11:21 one *h.* another drun.
Phil. 4:12 to be full and be *h.*

HUNT.

Gen. 27:5 Es. went to *h.* venison
1 *Sam.* 26:20 as wh. one doth *h.*
Job 38:39 wilt *h.* prey for lion ?
Ps. 140:11 evil sh. *h.* violent man
Prov. 6:26 adulteress will *h.*
Jer. 16:16 *h.* them from ev. mou.
Lam. 4:18 they *h.* our steps
Ezek. 13:18 will ye *h.* souls ?
  20 wherewith ye there *h.* souls
Mic. 7:2 *h.* every man his broth.

HUNTED.

Ezek. 13:21 no more in y. hand *h.*

HUNTER, S.

Gen. 10:9 he was a mighty *h.* be.
  L. even as N. the mighty *h.*
25:27 Esau was a cunning *h.*
Prov. 6:5 as a roe fro. hand of *h.*
Jer. 16:16 and after I send for *h.*

HUNTEST, ETH.

Lev. 17:13 *h.* and catcheth beast
1 *Sam.* 24:11 yet thou *h.* my soul
Job 10:16 *h.* me as a fierce lion

HUNTING.

Gen. 27:30 E. brother came fr. *h.*
Prov. 12:27 roast. not took in *h.*

HUR.

Ex. 17:10 H. we. up, 12 ; 24:14
1 *Chr.* 2:19 which bare H. 20, 50

HURL, ETH, ING.

Num. 35:20 *h.* at him by lying
1 *Chr.* 12:2 ri. hand and left in *h.*
Job 27:21 as a stone *h.* him out

HURT, Substantive.

Gen. 4:23 slain yo. man to my *h.*
26:29 that thou wilt do us no *h.*
31:29 in power of hand to do *h.*

1 *Sam.* 20:21 peace to thee, no *h.*
24:9 behold, David seek. thy *h.*
2 *Sam.* 18:32 all that rise to do *h.*
2 *K.* 14:10 why shouldest thou
  med. to thy *h.* ? 2 *Chr.* 25:19
Ezr. 4:22 damage to *h.* of kings ?
Ps. 15:4 that sweareth to his *h.*
35:4 that devise my *h.* 70:2
  26 ashamed that rej. at my *h.*
38:12 seek my *h.* speak misch.
41:7 aga. me do they devise *h.*
71:13 cov. with reproach seek *h.*
  24 brought to sha. seek my *h.*
Ec. 5:13 riches for owners to *h.*
8:9 ruleth over another to his *h.*
Jer. 6:14 healed *h.* of peo. 8:11
7:6 neith. walk after gods to *h.*
8:21 for *h.* of my people am I *h.*
10:19 woe is me for my *h.*
25:6 and I will do you no *h.*
  7 ye provo. me to your own *h.*
38:4 not welfare of peo. but *h.*
Dan. 3:25 ha. no *h.* ; 6:22 do. no *h.*
  6:23 no manner of *h.* found
Acts 27:10 this voyage be with *h.*

HURT, Participle.

Ex. 22:10 if a beast be *h.* 14
1 *Sam.* 25:15 and we not *h.*
Ec. 10:9 remov. stones sh. be *h.*
Jer. 8:21 for *h.* of my peo. am I *h.*
Rev. 2:11 not be *h.* of sec. death

HURT, Verb.

Gen. 31:7 G. suf. hi. not to *h.* me
Ex. 21:22 *h.* woman with child
  35 if one man's ox *h.* another's
1 *Sam.* 25:7 shepherds we *h.* not
Job 35:8 wickedn. may *h.* a man
Ps. 105:18 wh. feet *h.* with fett.
Is. 11:9 shall not *h.* nor destroy
  in my holy mountain, 65:25
27:3 lest any *h.* it, I will keep it
Dan. 6:22 lions have not *h.* me
Mark 16:18 it shall not *h.* them
Luke 4:35 out of him, *h.* him not
Acts 18:10 set on thee to *h.*
Rev. 6:6 see thou *h.* not the oil
7:2 given to *h.* earth and sea
  3 *h.* not earth, neither sea
9:4 should not *h.* grass of earth
  10 their power was to *h.* men
  19 heads, with them they *h.*
11:5 if any *h.* them, fire proceed.

HURTFUL.

Ps. 144:10 deli. David fr. *h.* swo.
1 *Tim.* 6:9 rich fall into *h.* lusts

HURTING.

1 *Sam.* 25:34 Lord kept me fr. *h.*

HUSBAND.

Ex. 4:25 bloody *h.* art thou, 26
Lev. 19:20 lieth with woman betrothed to a *h. Deut.* 22:23
21:3 may be defiled for sister
  who had no *h. Ezek.* 44:25
Num. 30:6 if she had at all a *h.*
Deut. 22:22 woman married to *h.*
  24:3 if the latter *h.* hate her
  4 former *h.* may not take her
25:5 duty of a *h.* brother to her
28:56 eye sh. be evil to. *h.*
Ruth 1:12 I am too old to have *h.*
Jer. 6:11 *h.* with wife sh. be tak.
31:32 altho' I was a *h.* to them
Joel 1:8 girded with sackcl. for *h.*
Luke 2:36 lived wi. *h.* sev. years
John 4:17 have no *h.*
Rom. 7:2 *h.* dead she is loosed, 3
1 *Cor.* 7:3 *h.* render to wife due
  benevolence, like. wife to *h.*
  4 *h.* hath not power of own
  11 let not *h.* put away his wife
  14 unbeliev. is sanctified by
  wife, and wife sancti. by *h.*
2 *Cor.* 11:2 espoused to one *h.*
Gal. 4:27 more chil. than hath *h.*
Eph. 5:23 the *h.* is head of wife
1 *Tim.* 3:2 *h.* of one wi. *Tit.* 1:6

Her HUSBAND.

Gen. 3:6 eat fruit, gave to *h. h.*
Lev. 21:7 wo. put away fr. *h. h.*
Num. 5:20 to anoth. inst. of *h. h.*
  30:7 *h. h.* heard it, and held
  peace, 8, 10, 11, 12, 13, 14
Deut. 25:5 *h. h.* brot. go in unto
Ruth 1:9 in house of *h. h.*
2:1 Nao. had kinsman of *her h.*
1 *Sam.* 1:22 sa. to *h. h.* I will not
2:19 she came up with *her h.*
2 *Sam.* 11:26 wife of U. heard *h.*
  was dead, she mo. for *h. h.*
2 *K.* 4:14 hath no child, *h. h.* old
Prov. 12:4 virt. wife cro. to *h. h.*
31:11 heart of *h. h.* trust in her
  23 *her h.* is known in the gates
  28 *h. h.* riseth up and prai. her
Jer. 3:20 as wife depa. from *h. h.*
Ezek. 16:32 strangers inst. of *h. h.*
  45 loatheth *her h.* and children
Hos. 2:2 neither I *h. h.*
Mat. 1:19 Jos. *her h.* being just
Luke 16:18 mar. her aw. fr. *h. h.*
Acts 5:10 buried her by *her h.*
Rom. 7:2 bound by law to *h. h.*
  3 *her h.* dead she is free
1 *Cor.* 7:2 woman have *h.* own *h.*
  10 let not wife depart fr. *her h.*
  11 be reconciled to *her h.*
  34 how she may please *her h.*
  39 bound as long as *her h.*
Eph. 5:33 wife reverence *her h.*
Rev. 21:2 bride adorned for *her h.*

My HUSBAND.

Gen. 29:32 my *h.* will love me
  34 will my *h.* be joined to me
  30:18 given maiden to *my h.*
  20 now will *my h.* dw. wi. me
Deut. 25:7 *my h.* brother refuseth
2 *Sam.* 14:5 I am a widow, *my h.*
  dead, 2 *K.* 4:1
Hos. 2:7 and return to *my* first *h.*

Thy HUSBAND.

Gen. 3:16 desire shall be to *t. h.*
Num. 5:19 anoth. inst. of *t. h.* 20
Jud. 14:15 to wife, Entice *t. h.*
2 *K.* 4:26 is it well with *thy h.*
Is. 54:5 thy Maker is *thy h.*
Acts 5:9 that have buried *t. h.*
1 *Cor.* 7:16 thou shalt save *thy h.*

HUSBANDMAN.

Gen. 9:20 Noah began to be a *h.*
Jer. 51:23 break in pieces the *h.*
Amos 5:16 call *h.* to mourning
Zec. 13:5 no prophet, am a *h.*
John 15:1 I true vine, Fath. is *h.*
2 *Tim.* 2:6 the *h.* that laboreth
Jam. 5:7 *h.* waiteth for fruit of
  earth

HUSBANDMEN.

2 *K.* 25:12 he left of the poor to
  be *h. Jer.* 52:16
Jer. 31:24 shall dwell in Judah *h.*
Joel 1:11 be ashamed ye *h.* howl
Mat. 21:33 he let it out to *h.*
  Mark 12:2 ; *Luke* 20:9
  34 sent his servants to *h. Mark*
  12:2 ; *Luke* 20:10
  38 when *h.* saw the son, *Mark*
  12:7 ; *Luke* 20:14
  40 what will he do to those *h.* ?
  41 let out vineyard to other *h.*
Mark 12:2 might receive fr. *h.* 9

HUSBANDRY.

2 *Chr.* 26:10 Uzziah loved *h.*
1 *Cor.* 3:9 ye are God's *h.* ye are

HUSBANDS.

Ruth 1:11 they may be your *h.* ?
  13 stay for them fr. having *h.* ?
Est. 1:17 despise *h.* in their eyes
  20 wives give to their *h.* honor
Ezek. 16:45 loathed *h.* and child.
John 4:18 thou hast had five *h.*
1 *Cor.* 14:35 ask their *h.* at home

Eph. 5:22 wives submit to *h.* 24
  25 *h.* love your wives, *Col.* 3:19
Col. 3:18 wives, submit to own *h.*
1 *Tim.* 3:12 deac. *h.* of one wife
Tit. 2:4 teach women to love *h.*
  5 be obedient to their own *h.*
1 *Pet.* 3:1 in subjection to own *h.*
  7 ye *h.* dwell with them accor.

HUSHAI.
2 *Sam.* 15:32 H. to meet D. 17:5
1 *Chr.* 27:33 H. king's compani.

HUSK, S.
Num. 6:4 kernel even to the *h.*
2 *K.* 4:42 full ears of corn in *h.*
Luke 15:16 filled belly with *h.*

HUZZAB. *Nah.* 2:7

HYMENEUS.
1 *Tim.* 1:20 wh. is H. 2 *Tim.* 2:17

HYMN, S.
Mat. 26:30 when they had sung
  a *h. Mark* 14:26
Eph. 5:19 spea. in psalms and *h.*
Col. 3:16 admo. in psalms and *h.*

HYPOCRISY, IES.
Is. 32:6 iniquity, to practise *h.*
Mat. 23:28 within are full of *h.*
Mark 12:15 he knowing their *h.*
Luke 12:1 leaven of Pharisees *h.*
1 *Tim.* 4:2 speaking lies in *h.*
1 *Pet.* 2:1 aside all malice and *h.*
Jam. 3:17 wisdom pure witho. *h.*

HYPOCRITE.
Job 8:13 the *h.* hope shall perish
  13:16 *h.* shall not come bef. him
  17:8 innocent stir up against *h.*
  20:5 joy of *h.* but for a moment
  27:8 what is the hope of the *h.?*
  34:30 that the *h.* reign not, lest
Prov. 11:9 *h.* with mouth destroy
Is. 9:17 for every one is a *h.*
Mat. 7:5 *h.* first cast out beam
Luke 6:42 thou *h.* cast beam out
  13:15 *h.* doth not each loose ox?

HYPOCRITES.
Job 15:34 congrega. of *h.* desolate
  36:13 *h.* in heart heap up wrath
Is. 33:14 fearfulness surprised *h.*

IDOL.
1 *K.* 15:13 she made an *i.* in
  grove, 2 *Chr.* 15:16
2 *Chr.* 33:7 set *i.* in house of God
Is. 48:5 lest say, Mine *i.* hath
  66:3 inc. as if he blessed an *i.*
Jer. 22:28 is this C. a broken *i.?*
Acts 7:41 offered sacrifice to *i.*
1 *Cor.* 8:4 *i.* noth. in world, 10:19
  7 some with conscience of *i.*

IDOLS.
Lev. 19:4 turn not to *i.*; 26 no *i.*
  26:30 cast your carcasses on *i.*
Deut. 29:17 ye have seen their *i.*
1 *Sam.* 31:9 pub. it in house of *i.*
1 *K.* 15:12 Asa removed the *i.*
  21:26 A. did abomi. in follow. *i.*
2 *K.* 17:12 th. serv. *i.* 2 *Chr.* 24:18
  21:11 made Judah to sin with *i.*
  23:24 *i.* that were spied in land
1 *Chr.* 10:9 carry tidin. to their *i.*
  16:26 all gods of the peo. are *i.*
2 *Chr.* 15:8 Asa put *i.* out of Jud.
  34:7 Josiah cut down all *i.* in Is.
Ps. 96:5 all gods of nations are *i.*
  97:7 that boast themselves of *i.*
  106:36 and they served their *i.*
  115:4 *i.* are silv. and g. 135:15
Is. 2:8 land is full of *i.* worship
  18 *i.* he shall utterly abolish
  20 shall cast away his *i.* 31:7
  10:11 as I done to Samaria and
  her *i.* so do to Jer. and her *i.*
  19:1 *i.* of Egypt shall be moved
  8 seek to *i.* and to charmers
  45:16 mak. of *i.* go to confusion
  46:1 their *i.* were on the beasts
  57:5 inflam. yourselves with *i.*
Jer. 50:2 her *i.* are confounded
  38 they are mad upon their *i.*
Ezek. 6:6 your *i.* may be broken
  9 go a whoring after their *i.*
  13 did offer savor to their *i.*
  8:10 I saw all the *i.* of Israel
  14:3 set up their *i.* in heart, 4, 7
  6 turn yourselves from your *i.*
  16:36 wi. *i.* of thy abomination
  18:6 nor lift eyes to *i.* 12, 15
  20:7 defile not yourse. with *i.* 18
  16 heart after *i.*; 24 eyes af. *i.*
  31 ye pollute yourselves with
  your *i.* 22:4; 23:7, 30, 37
  39 pol. my name no more wi. *i.*
  22:3 the city maketh *i.*
  23:39 slain their chil. to their *i.*
  49 bear the sins of your *i.*
  30:13 I will destroy *i.*

Mat. 6:2 not sound trump. as *h.*
  5 thou shalt not be as *h.*
  16 when ye fast, be not as *h.*
  15:7 ye *h.* well did Esaias prophesy, *Mark* 7:6
  16:3 O *h.* ye discern face of sky,
  Luke 12:56
  22:18 Why tempt ye me, ye *h.*
  23:13 Phari. *h.* ye shut kingd.
  ag. men, 14, 15, 23, 25, 27, 29
  24:51 ap. him portion with *h.*
Luke 11:44 scribes and Phari. *h.*

HYPOCRITICAL.
Ps. 35:16 *h.* mockers in feasts
Is. 10:6 send him ag. *h.* nation

HYSSOP.
Ex. 12:22 bunch of *h.* and dip it
Lev. 14:4 scar. and *h.* 6, 49, 51, 52
Num. 19:6 cast *h.* into midst of
  18 take *h.* dip it in water
1 *K.* 4:33 cedar-tree, even unto *h.*
Ps. 51:7 purge with *h.* be clean
John 19:29 sponge put it on *h.*
Heb. 9:19 blood with *h.* sprinkl.

I

Ex. 3:14 I AM, THAT I AM.
Deut. 32:39 I, even I, am he
Is. 41:4 the Lord, the first, I am
  he, 43:11, 25
  10 I am with thee, I am thy G.
Mat. 26:22 Lord, is it I?
IBHAR. 2 *Sa.* 5:15; 1 *Chr.* 3:6; 14:5

ICE.
Job 6:16 blackish by reason of *i.*
  38:29 out of wh. womb came *i.?*
Ps. 147:17 he casteth forth his *i.*

ICHABOD. 1 *Sam.* 4:21; 14:3

ICONIUM.
Acts 13:51 Barnab. came unto I.
  14:1 in I. went into synago. 19
2 *Tim.* 3:11 afflictions came at I.

IDDO.
2 *Chr.* 9:29 I. seer, 12:15; 13:22
Ezr. 5:1 I. prophesied, *Zec.* 1:1, 7
Neh. 12:4 I. with priests went up

IDLE.
Ex. 5:8 be *i.* therefore they cry
  17 he said, Ye are *i.* ye are *i.*
Prov. 19:15 *i.* soul suffer hunger
Mat. 12:36 ev. *i.* word men speak
  20:3 standing *i.* in market-pl. 6
Luke 24:11 seemed as *i.* tales
1 *Tim.* 5:13 they learn to be *i.*

IDLENESS.
Prov. 31:27 eateth not bread of *i.*
Ec. 10:18 thro' *i.* house droppeth
Ezek. 16:49 abundan. of *i.* in her

IDOLATER, S.
1 *Cor.* 5:10 with the covet. or *i.*
  11 any called a brother be an *i.*
  6:9 *i.* not inherit kingdom of G.
  10:7 neither be *i.* as some were
Eph. 5:5 who is *i.* hath any inh.
Rev. 21:8 *i.* have part in the lake
  22:15 murderers and *i.* and liars

IDOLATROUS.
2 *K.* 23:5 Jos. put down *i.* priests

IDOLATRY, IES.
1 *Sam.* 15:23 is as iniquity and *i.*
Acts 17:16 city wholly given to *i.*
1 *Cor.* 10:14 beloved, flee from *i.*
Gal. 5:20 the works of the flesh *i.*
Col. 3:5 covetousness, which is *i.*
1 *Pet.* 4:3 walked in abomina. *i.*

IDOL, Adjective.
Zec. 11:17 woe to *i.* shepherd

Ezek. 36:25 fr. *i.* clea. you, 37:23
  44:10 went astray after *i.*
  12 ministered before their *i.*
Hos. 4:17 Ephra. is joined to *i.*
  8:4 of silver and gold made *i.*
  14:8 what have I to do with *i.*
Mic. 1:7 the *i.* will I lay desolate
Hab. 2:18 trust. to make dumb *i.*
Zec. 10:2 *i.* have spoken vanity
  13:2 I will cut off names of *i.*
Acts 15:20 abst. fr. polluti. of *i.*
  29 abst. fr. meats offer. *i.* 21:25
Rom. 2:22 thou that abhorrest *i.*
1 *Cor.* 8:1 touching th. offered to
  i. 4, 10; 10:19, 28; *Rev.* 2:14, 20
  12:2 Gentiles carried to dumb *i.*
2 *Cor.* 6:16 agree. of G. with *i.?*
1 *Thes.* 1:9 turned to God from *i.*
1 *John* 5:21 keep yoursel. from *i.*
Rev. 9:20 not wor. devils and *i.*

IDUMEA..
Is. 34:5 sword sh. come on I. 6
Ezek. 35:15 all I. shall be, 36:5
Mark 3:8 multi. followed from I.

IGNOMINY.
Prov. 18:3 and with *i.* reproach

IGNORANCE.
Lev. 4:2 if a soul sin thro' *i.*
  5:15; *Num.* 15:24, 27, 28, 29
  13 congre. sin thro' *i.*; 22 ruler
  27 if the people sin through *i.*
Num. 15:25 forgiv. them, it is *i.*
Acts 3:17 through *i.* ye did it
  17:30 times of *i.* God winked at
Eph. 4:18 alienated through *i.*
1 *Pet.* 1:14 according to lusts in *i.*
  2:15 put to silen. *i.* of fool. men

IGNORANT.
Ps. 73:22 and I. I was as a beast
Is. 56:10 all *i.* they are all dumb
  63:16 though Abram be *i.* of us
Acts 4:13 perceived they were *i.*
Rom. 1:13 I would not have you
  i. brethren, 1 *Cor.* 10:1; 12:1;
  2 *Cor.* 1:8; 1 *Thes.* 4:13
  10:3 being *i.* of God's righteous.
  11:25 sh. be *i.* of this mystery
1 *Cor.* 14:38 man *i.* let him be *i.*
2 *Cor.* 2:11 not *i.* of Satan's devi.
Heb. 5:2 have compassion on *i.*
2 *Pet.* 3:5 they willingly are *i.*
  8 be not *i.* of this one thing

IGNORANTLY.
Num. 15:28 soul sinneth *i.*
Deut. 19:4 wh. killeth neighbor *i.*

Acts 17:23 ye *i.* worship I declare
1 *Tim.* 1:13 because I did it *i.*

ILL.
Gen. 41:3 kine *i.*-fav. 4, 19, 20, 21
43:6 why dealt so i. with me?
Deut. 15:21 hath any *i.* blemish
Ps. 106:32 it went i. with Moses
Is. 3:11 woe to wicked, sh. be *i.*
Joel 2:20 *i.* savor shall come up
Rom. 13:10 love worketh no *i.*

ILL, *or evil-favoredness.*
Deut. 17:1 not sac. sheep wherein
is blemish or *e.-f.*

ILLUMINATED.
Heb. 10:32 after ye *i.* endur. fight

ILLYRICUM.
Rom. 15:19 round about unto I.

IMAGE.
Gen. 1:26 let us make man in our
i. 27 ; 9:6
5:3 in his own i. after his *i.*
Lev. 26:1 nor rear up a standing
i. *Deut.* 16:22
1 *Sam.* 19:13 Michal took an i.
2 *Chr.* 33:7 set car. i. in ho. of G.
Job 4:16 i. was before mine eyes
Ps. 73:20 shalt despise their *i.*
Ezek. 8:3 there was seat of i. 5
Dan. 2:31 great i. stood bef. thee
35 stone smote i. bec. mount.
3:1 Nebuchad. made i. of gold
6 worship the golden i. 10, 15
Hos. 3:4 sh. abioe without an i.
Mat. 22:20 said, Whose is this
i. ? *Mark* 12:16 ; *Luke* 20:24
Acts 19:35 i. which fell from Ju.
Rom. 1:23 changed gl. of G. to i.
8:29 be conformed to i. of Son
11:4 bowed the knee to i. of B.
1 *Cor.* 11:7 he is i. and gl. of G.
15:49 we have borne i. of earthy
2 *Cor.* 3:18 changed into same i.
4:4 Christ is i. of God, *Col.*, 1:15
Col. 3:10 i. of him that created
Heb. 1:3 express i. of his person
10:1 not the very i. of things
Rev. 13:14 make i. to .he beast
15 give life to the i. of beast
14:9 if any man worship i.
11 have no rest, who worsh. i.
Rev. 15:2 vic. ov. beast and his i.
16:2 sore fell on them wors. i.
19:20 he deceived them wors. i.
20:4 not worshipped bea. nor i.

See GRAVEN.

IMAGE-WORK.
2 *Chr.* 3:10 two cherubim i.-w.

Molten IMAGE.
Deut. 9:12 made them a m. i.
Ps. 106:19 worshipped *molten* i.
Jer. 10:14 his *m.* i. falseh. 51:17
Hab. 2:18 what profit. the *m.* i.

IMAGES.
Gen. 31:19 stolen fath.'s i. 34, 35
Ex. 23:24 sh. break their i. 34:13 ;
Deut. 7:5 ; *Num.* 33:52
Lev. 26:30 will cut down your i.
1 *Sam.* 6:5 i. of emerods, 11
1 *K.* 14:9 hast made i. to pro. me
23 high places, i. and groves
2 *K.* 10:26 they brought i. out
11:18 i. brake, 18:4 ; 23:14
17:10 set up i. ; 16 they made i.
23:24 Josiah put away i. in land
Is. 17:8 not look to groves or i.
27:9 groves and i. not stand up
30:22 ye shall defile orna. of i.
41:29 their molten i. are wind
Jer. 43:13 break i. of B.-shemesh
50:2 her i. are broken in pieces
Ezek. 6:4 your i. shall be broken
6 that your i. may be cut down
7:20 made i. of abominations
16:17 mad. to thyself i. of men
21:21 king of Bab. consulted i.

23:14 i. of Chaldeans portrayed
30:13 will cause their i. to cease
Hos. 10:1 have made goodly i.
2 break their alt. spoil their i.
13:2 they have made i. of silver
Amos 5:26 borne tab. of your i.
Mic. 5:13 standing i. will I cut off

IMAGERY.
Ezek. 8:12 in chamber of i.

IMAGINATION, S.
Gen. 6:5 i. of his heart was evil
8:21 i. of man's heart is evil
Deut. 29:19 though I walk in i.
31:21 for I know their i.
1 *Chr.* 28:9 understands all the i.
29:18 keep this in i. of heart
Prov. 6:18 heart th. devis. wic. i.
Jer. 23:17 ev. one walketh after i.
Lam. 3:60 hast seen i. ag. me
61 hast heard their i. ag. me
Luke 1:51 scattered proud in i.
Rom. 1:21 became vain in th. i.
2 *Cor.* 10:5 casting down i.

See IMAGE.

IMAGINE.
Job 6:26 ye i. to reprove words ?
21:27 devices wrong. i. ag. me
Ps. 2:1 do peo. i. vain thing?
38:12 and i. deceits all day long
62:3 how long will ye i. mischief
140:2 i. mischiefs in their heart
Prov. 12:20 deceit in them i. evil
Hos. 7:15 yet do they i. mischief
Nah. 1:9 what do ye i. ag. L. ?
Zec. 7:10 let none i. evil, 8:17
Acts 4:25 do peo. i. vain things?

IMAGINED, ETH.
Gen. 11:6 nothing rest. they i.
Ps. 10:2 taken in devices they i.
21:11 they i. mischievous device
Nah. 1:11 one i. evil ag. the L.

IMMEDIATELY.
Mat. 26:74 i. the cock crew, *Luke*
22:60 ; *John* 18:27
Mark 1:31 i. the fever left her
4:15 Satan cometh i. and taketh
Lu. 6:49 i. fell ; 8:44 i. stanched
19:11 kingdom of God i. appear
John 5:9 and i. man was whole
Acts 12:23 i. angel of L. smote
16:26 i. all doors were opened
Gal. 1:16 i. conferred not
Rev. 4:2 and i. was in the Spirit

IMMORTAL.
1 *Tim.* 1:17 K. eternal, i. invis.

IMMORTALITY.
Rom. 2:7 to them who seek for i.
1 *Cor.* 15:53 mortal must put on i.
54 mortal shall have put on i.
1 *Tim.* 6:16 i. dwelling in light
2 *Tim.* 1:10 brought i. to light

IMMUTABLE.
Heb. 6:18 that by two i. things

IMMUTABILITY.
Heb. 6:17 the i. of his counsel

IMPART, ED.
Job 39:17 nor i. to her underst.
Luke 3:11 him i. to him ha. none
Rom. 1:11 i. some spiritual gift
1 *Thes.* 2:8 willing to ha. i. souls

IMPEDIMENT.
Mark 7:32 had i. in his speech

IMPENITENT.
Rom. 2:5 thou, after thy i. heart

IMPERIOUS.
Ezek. 16:30 work of an i. woman

IMPLACABLE.
Rom. 1:31 without affection, i.

IMPLEAD.
Acts 19:38 let them i. one anoth.

IMPORTUNITY.
Luke 11:8 because of his i.

IMPOSE, ED.
Ezr. 7:24 not be lawful to i. toll
Heb. 9:10 carnal ordinances i. on

IMPOSSIBLE.
Mat. 17:20 nothing i. unto you
19:26 with men is i. *Mark* 10:27 ;
Luke 18:27
Luke 1:37 with G. noth. i. 18:27
17:1 i. but offences will come
Heb. 6:4 i. for those enlightened
18 it was i. for G. to lie
11:6 without faith i. to please G.

IMPOTENT.
John 5:3 a multitude of i. folk
Acts 4:9 good deed done i. man
14:8 man at Lystra, i. in feet

IMPOVERISH, ED.
Jud. 6:6 Israel was greatly
Is. 40:20 he that is so i.
Jer. 5:17 shall i. fenced cities
Mal. 1:4 Edom saith, We are i.

IMPRISONED.
Acts 22:19 i. and beat them

IMPRISONMENT, S.
Ezr. 7:26 banishment or i.
2 *Cor.* 6:5 approv. in stripes, in i.
Heb. 11:36 mockings, bonds, i.

IMPUDENT.
Prov. 7:13 with i. face she said
Ezek. 2:4 for they are i. children
3:7 house of Is. i. hard-hearted

IMPUTE, ED.
Lev. 7:18 nor sh. it be i. to him
17:4 blood sh. be i. to that man
1 *Sam.* 22:15 let not king i. any t.
2 *Sam.* 19:19 not my lord i. iniq.
Rom. 4:8 Lord will not i. sin
11 righteous. mi. be i. to them
22 therefore it was i. to him for
righteousness, 23 ; *Jam.* 2:23
24 to whom it shall be i.
5:13 sin not i. wh. th. is no law

IMPUTETH, ING.
Ps. 32:2 whom Lord i. not iniq.
Hab. 1:11 i. his power to his god
Rom. 4:6 to whom G. i. righte.
2 *Cor.* 5:19 not i. tresp. to them

INASMUCH.
Mat. 25:40 i. as ye have done it
45 i. as ye did it not to one

INCENSE.
Ex. 30:8 shall burn perpetual i.
9 ye shall offer no strange i.
37:29 pure i. of sweet spices
40:5 altar of gold for i. bef. ark
Lev. 10:1 took censer, put i.
16:13 put i. on fire before Lord
Num. 7:14 spoon full of i. 86
16:35 fire cons. 250 men offer. i.
46 Mo. said to Aar. Put on i.
47 put on i. and made atonem.
Deut. 33:10 shall put i. bef. thee
2 *Chr.* 30:14 altars of i.
34:25 burned i. to other gods
Ps. 66:15 offer to thee i.
141:2 prayer set bef. thee as i.
Is. 1:13 i. is an abomination
43:23 not wearied thee with i.
60:6 shall bring gold and i.
65:3 burn. i. on altars of brick
66:3 burneth i. as if he blessed
Jer. 6:20 why cometh i. from S. ?
11:17 prov. to anger, offering i.
41:5 offerings and i. in th. hand
48:35 him that burneth i. to g.
Ezek. 8:11 thick cloud of i. went
16:18 mine oil and i. before them
Mal. 1:11 ev. place i. be offered
Luke 1:10 without at time of i.
Rev. 8:3 given to him much i.
4 smoke of i. ascended bef. G.

See ALTAR, BURN, BURNT.

Sweet INCENSE.

Ex. 25:6 spices for *sweet i.* 35:8,
28; *Num.* 4:16
31:11 oil and *s. i.* for holy place
39:38 brought oil and *s. i.* to M.
Lev. 16:12 hands full of *sweet i.*

INCENSED.

Is. 41:11 *i.* ag. thee be ashamed
45:24 *i.* against him be ashamed

INCLINE.

Jos. 24:23 *i.* your heart to the L.
1 *K.* 8:58 he may *i.* our hearts
Ps. 78:1 *i.* your ears to words
119:36 *i.* my heart to thy testi.
141:4 *i.* not my heart to evil
See EAR.

INCLINED, ETH.

Jud. 9:3 hearts *i.* to follow A.
Ps. 40:1 Lord *i.* unto me, 116:2
119:112 *i.* my heart to thy stat.
Prov. 2:18 her house *i.* to death
5:13 nor *i.* mine ear to them
Jer. 7:24 nor *i.* ear, 26; 11:8;
17:23; 34:14
25:4 not *i.* y. ear, 35:15; 44:5

INCONTINENCY.

1 *Cor.* 7:5 tempt you not for y. *i.*

INCONTINENT.

2 *Tim.* 3:3 without affection, *i.*

INCORRUPTIBLE.

Rom. 1.23 changed glory of *i.* G.
1 *Cor.* 9:25 to obtain an *i.* crown
15:52 the dead shall be raised *i.*
1 *Pet.* 1:4 an inheri. *i.* undefiled
23 born of *i.* seed by word of G.

INCORRUPTION.

1 *Cor.* 15:42 cor. it is raised in *i.*
50 nei. doth corruption inh. *i.*
53 corruptible must put on *i.*
54 corrup. shall have put on *i.*

INCREASE, Substantive.

Lev. 25:36 no usury of him or *i.*
37 lend him victuals for *i.*
26:4 the land shall yield her *i.*
20 land shall not yield her *i.*
Num. 18:30 *i.* of threshing-floor
32:14 an *i.* of sinful men
Deut. 14:22 tithe all *i.* of seed
28 bring forth tithe of *i.*
28:18 cursed be *i.* of kine, 51
1 *Sam.* 2:33 *i.* of thy house sh. die
Job 20:28 *i.* of house shall depart
31:12 root out all mine *i.*
Ps. 67:6 earth shall yield her *i.*
78:46 gave their *i.* to caterpillar
85:12 our land shall yield her *i.*
Prov. 14:4 much *i.* by stre. of ox
18:20 with *i.* of lips sh. be filled
Ec. 5:10 not be satisfied with *i.*
Is. 9:7 *i.* of his gov. be no end
Jer. 2:3 *i.* was holiness to Lord
Ezek. 18:8 nor hath taken *i.* 17
13 on usury, taken *i.* 22:12
34:27 earth shall yield her *i.*
Zec. 8:12 ground sh. give her *i.*
1 *Cor.* 3:6 I planted, G. gave *i.* 7
Eph. 4:16 maketh *i.* of the body
Col. 2:19 body incr. wi. *i.* of G.

INCREASE, Verb.

Lev. 25:16 by years thou *i.* price
Deut. 6:3 ye may *i.* mightily
7:22 beasts of field *i.* on thee
1 *Chr.* 27:23 would *i.* Is. like stars
Job 8:7 thy latter end greatly *i.*
Ps. 44:12 dost not *i.* thy wealth
62:10 riches *i.* set not heart
73:12 in world, *i.* in riches
115:14 the L. shall *i.* you more
Prov. 1:5 wise man *i.* learn. 9:9
22:16 oppresseth poor to *i.* rich.
28:28 they perish, righteous *i.*
Ec. 5:11 goods *i.* increased eat
6:11 be many things that *i.*
Is. 29:19 meek *i.* their joy in L.

Ezek. 5:16 I will *i.* famine on you
36:29 *i.* it, lay no famine on you
37 *i.* them with men like a flock
Dan. 11:39 he shall *i.* with glory
Hos. 4:10 commit whored. not *i.*
Zec. 10:8 *i.* as they have increa.
Luke 17:5 said, Lord, *i.* our faith
John 3:30 must *i.* I must decrea.
2 *Cor.* 9:10 *i.* fruits of righteous.
1 *Thes.* 3:12 L. make y. *i.* in love
4:10 that ye *i.* more and more
2 *Tim.* 2:16 *i.* to more ungodli.

INCREASED.

Gen. 7:17 wat. *i.* bare up ark, 18
30:30 little hadst, it is now *i.*
43 Jacob *i.* ; *Ex.* 1:7 Israel *i.*
1 *Sam.* 14:19 noise went on and *i.*
1 *Chr.* 4:38 house of fa. *i.* greatly
Ezr. 9:6 iniq. *i.* over our head
Ps. 3:1 they *i.* that trouble me
4:7 their corn and wine *i.*
49:16 glory of his house is *i.*
Prov. 9:11 years of life sh. be *i.*
Ec. 2:9 I *i.* more than all bef. me
5:11 they are *i.* that eat them
Is. 9:3 multip. nation, not *i.* joy
26:15 thou hast *i.* nation, O L.
Jer. 5:6 their backslidings are *i.*
15:8 widows *i.* ab. sands of sea
30:14 bec. thy sins were *i.* 15
Ezek. 16:26 *i.* thy whored. 23:14
28:5 by wisdom hast thou *i.*
Dan. 12:4 knowledge shall be *i.*
Hos. 4:7 as they *i.* so th. sinned
10:1 accord. to fruit, he *i.* altars
Zec. 10:8 incr. as they have *i.*
Mark 4:8 that sprang up and *i.*
Luke 2:52 Jesus *i.* in wisdom
Acts 6:7 and the word of God *i.*
16:5 churches *i.* in number daily
2 *Cor.* 10:15 hope when faith is *i.*
Rev. 3:17 rich, and *i.* with goods

INCREASEST, ETH.

Job 10:16 afflic. *i.* ; 12:23 *i.* nati.
17 *i.* thine indig. upon me
Ps. 74:23 the tumult of those *i.*
Prov. 11:24 scattereth and yet *i.*
23:28 *i.* transgressors am. men
24:5 man of know. *i.* strength
28:8 unjust gain, *i.* substance
29:16 wicked multip. transg. *i.*
Ec. 1:18 *i.* knowledge, *i.* sorrow
Is. 40:29 he *i.* strength
Hos. 12:1 *i.* lies and desolation
Hab. 2:6 woe to him that *i.* that
Col. 2:19 body *i.* with inc. of G.

INCREASING.

Col. 1:10 *i.* in knowledge of God

INCREDIBLE.

Acts 26:8 *i.* G. should raise dead ?

INCURABLE.

2 *Chr.* 21:18 smote him wi. *i.* di.
Job 34:6 my wound is *i.* without
Jer. 15:18 why is my wound *i. ?*
30:12 bruise is *i.* ; sorrow is *i.*
Mic. 1:9 wound *i.* it is come to J.

INDEBTED.

Luke 11:4 forgive every one *i.*

INDEED.

Gen. 37:8 sh. thou *i.* reign ov. us ?
10 mother and breth. *i.* come ?
1 *K.* 8:27 but will God *i.* dwell on
earth ? 2 *Chr.* 6:18
1 *Chr.* 4:10 wouldest bless me *i.*
Job 19:4 be it *i.* that I have erred
Is. 6:9 hear ye *i.* see ye *i.* but
Mat. 3:11 I *i.* baptize, *Mark* 1:8;
John 3:16
Mark 11:32 he was a prophet *i.*
Luke 23:41 *i.* just ; 24:34 risen *i.*
John 1:47 behold an Israelite *i.*
4:42 that this is *i.* the Christ
6:55 flesh meat *i.* blood drink *i.*
7:26 do rulers know *i.* this is C. ?
8:36 Son make free, ye be free *i.*

Rom. 8:7 law, neither *i.* can be
1 *Tim.* 5:3 hon. widows are wi. *i.*
5 that is widow *i.* desolate, 16

See ENDEAVOR.

INDIGNATION.

2 *K.* 3:27 great *i.* against Israel
Job 10:17 increasest *i.* upon me
Ps. 69:24 pour out thy *i.* on them
78:49 cast on them wrath, *i.*
102:10 bec. of thine *i.* and wrath
Is. 10:5 staff in hand is mine *i.*
25 yet a little, the *i.* sh. cease
13:5 weapons of *i. Jer.* 50:25
26:20 till *i.* be overpast
30:27 his lips are full of *i.*
34:2 *i.* of Lord is on all nations
66:14 *i.* kno. towards enemies
Jer. 10:10 not able to abide *i.*
15:17 thou hast filled me with *i.*
Lam. 2:6 despised in *i.* of anger
Ezek. 21:31 pour mi. *i.* upon thee
22:24 not rained on day of his *i.*
31 poured out mine *i.* on them
Dan. 11:30 *i.* against holy cove.
Mic. 7:9 I will bear *i.* of Lord
Nah. 1:6 who can stand bef. *i. ?*
Hab. 3:12 march thro' land in *i.*
Zec. 1:12 had *i.* seventy years
Mal. 1:4 against whom L. hath *i.*
Mat. 20:24 moved wi. *i.* ag. two
26:8 had *i.* saying, To what
Luke 13:14 ruler answer. with *i.*
Acts 5:17 they were filled with *i.*
Rom. 2:8 obey unright. *i.* wrath
2 *Cor.* 7:11 yea, what *i. !*
Heb. 10:27 looking for of fiery *i.*
Rev. 14:10 poured out cup of *i.*

INDITING.

Ps. 45:1 heart is *i.* good matter

INDUSTRIOUS.

1 *K.* 11:28 young man was *i.*

INEXCUSABLE.

Rom. 2:1 therefore thou art *i.*

INFALLIBLE.

Acts 1:3 showed hims. by *i.* proo.

INFAMOUS.

Ezek. 22:5 mock thee wh. art *i.*

INFAMY.

Prov. 25:10 th. *i.* turn not away
Ezek. 36:3 are an *i.* of the people

INFANT, S.

1 *Sam.* 15:3 slay man, wo. and *i.*
Job 3:16 as *i.* wh. never saw light
Is. 65:20 no more an *i.* of days
Hos. 13:16 *i.* be dashed in pieces
Luke 18:15 they bro. *i.* to him

INFERIOR.

Job 12:3 understand. not *i.* 13:2
Dan. 2:33 another kingdom *i.*
2 *Cor.* 12:13 *i.* to other churches

INFIDEL.

2 *Cor.* 6:15 that believ. with *i. ?*
1 *Tim.* 5:8 is worse than an *i.*

INFINITE.

Job 22:5 are not th. iniquities *i. ?*
Ps. 147:5 his understanding is *i.*
Nah. 3:9 her strength, it was *i.*

INFIRMITY.

Lev. 12:2 days of separation for *i.*
Ps. 77:10 this is mine *i.*
Prov. 18:14 sp. of man sustain *i.*
Luke 13:11 woman which had *i.*
12 thou art loosed fr. thine *i.*
John 5:5 an *i.* thirty-eight years
Rom. 6:19 bec. of *i.* of your flesh
Gal. 4:13 through *i.* I preached
Heb. 5:2 himself comp. with *i.*
7:28 high-priests which have *i.*

INFIRMITIES.

Mat. 8:17 himself took our *i.*

INFIRMITIES

Luke 5:15 to be healed of *i.*
7:21 cured many of their *i.* 8:2
Rom. 8:26 Sp. also helpeth our *i.*
15:1 strong bear *i.* of the weak
2 *Cor.* 11:30 things conc. mine *i.*
12:5 I gl. not, but in mine *i.* 9
10 I take pleasure in mine *i.*
1 *Tim.* 5:23 use wine for thine *i.*
Heb. 4:15 touched with feel. of *i.*

INFLAME, ING.

Is. 5:11 conti. till wine *i.* them
57:5 *i.* yourselves with idols

INFLAMMATION.

Lev. 13:28 an *i.* of the burning
Deut. 28:22 L. smite thee with *i.*

INFLICTED.

2 *Cor.* 2:6 punishm. which was *i.*

INFLUENCES.

Job 38:31 bind *i.* of Pleiades?

INFOLDING.

Ezek. 1:4 *i.* itself, and a brightn.

INFORM, ED.

Deut. 17:10 accord. to all they *i.*
Dan. 9:22 *i.* me, talked with me
Acts 21:21 are *i.* thou teachest, 24
24:1 *i.* against Paul, 25:2, 15

INGATHERING.

Ex. 23:16 feast of *i.* end of year

INGRAFTED.

Jam. 1:21 rec. with meek *i.* word

INHABIT.

Num. 35:34 defile not land sh. *i.*
Prov. 10:30 wicked not *i.* earth
Is. 42:11 villages Kedar doth *i.*
65:21 sh. build houses and *i.* th.
22 sh. not build, and anoth. *i.*
Jer. 17:6 shall *i.* parched places
Ezek. 33:24 that *i.* wastes of Isr.
Amos 9:14 waste cities *i.* them
Zep. 1:13 build houses, not *i.*

INHABITANT.

Is. 5:9 houses great without *i.*
6:11 cities be wasted without *i.*
12:6 cry out and shout, *i.* of Zi.
20:6 the *i.* of this isle shall say
24:17 snare on thee, O *i.* of earth
33:24 *i.* shall not say, I am sick
Jer. 2:15 cities burned without *i.*
4:7 cities laid waste without *i.*
9:11 ; 26:9 ; 33:10 ; 34:22
44:22 land a curse without an *i.*
46:19 desolate, with. *i.* 51:29, 37
Amos 1:5 will cut off *i.* from A.
8 I will cut off *i.* from Ashdod
Mic. 1:12 the *i.* of Maroth waited
13 *i.* of Lachish, bind chariot
15 to thee, O *i.* of Mareshah
Zep. 2:5 destroy, th. sh. be no *i.*
3:6 cities destroyed, is none *i.*

INHABITANTS.

Gen. 19:25 overthrew *i.* of cities
Ex. 15:15 *i.* of Canaan melt away
Lev. 18:25 land vomiteth out *i.*
25:10 procl. liberty to *i.* thereof
Num. 13:32 land eateth up *i.*
Deut. 13:15 surely smite *i.* of city
Jos. 2:24 *i.* of country do faint
11:19 peace, save *i.* of Gibeon
17:12 could not drive out the *i.*
Jud. 1:19, 27
Jud. 5:7 *i.* of the villages ceased
23 curse ye bitterly *i.* thereof
Ruth 4:4 buy it before the *i.*
2 *K.* 19:26 *i.* were of small power
2 *Chr.* 20:23 aga. *i.* of mount Seir
Job 26:5 are formed from und. *i.*
Ps. 33:8 *i.* of world stand in awe
14 he looketh on all *i.* of earth
49:1 give ear, all ye *i.* of world
75:3 earth and *i.* thereof dissolv.
Is. 10:13 put down *i.* like a man
18:3 ye *i.* of the world, see ye
23:2 be still, ye *i.* of the isle, 6

24:1 and scattere. abroad the *i.*
5 earth defiled under *i.* thereof
6 the *i.* of the earth are burned
26:9 *i.* of world learn righteous.
18 nor have *i.* of the world fal.
38:11 no more with *i.* of world
40:22 *i.* thereof as grasshoppers
42:10 *i.* sing to Lord a new song
11 let *i.* of rock sing
49:19 land nar. by reason of *i.*
Jer. 13:13 fill *i.* wi. drunkenness
21:6 I will smite *i.* of this city
23:14 as Sodom, and *i.* thereof
25:29 sw. upon *i.* thereof, 50:35
26:15 bring innocent blood on *i.*
49:8 dwell deep, O *i.* of D. 30
50:34 L. disquiet *i.* of Babylon
51:35 blood upon *i.* of Chaldea
Lam. 4:12 *i.* of world not believ.
Dan. 4:35 *i.* of earth as nothing
Mic. 6:12 *i.* thereof spoken lies
16 I should make *i.* a hissing
Zec. 8:20 come *i.* of many cities
21 *i.* of one city go to another
Rev. 17:2 *i.* of earth made drunk
See JERUSALEM.

INHABITANTS of the land.

Gen. 34:30 stink away *i. of l.*
Ex. 34:12 lest ma. cov. *i. of l.* 15
Num. 32:17 because of *i. of l.*
Jos. 2:9 all the *i. of the l.* faint
7:9 *i. of l. land* shall hear of it
9:24 to destroy all *i. of the land*
Jer. 1:14 evil sh. break on *i. of l.*
10:18 I will fling out *i. of land*
47:2 all the *i. of l.* shall howl
Hos. 4:1 hath controv. with *i. of l*
Joel 2:1 let the *i. of the l.* tremble
Zec. 11:6 no more pity *i. of land*

INHABITED.

Ex. 16:35 till th. came to land *i.*
Lev. 16:22 iniqu. to a land not *i.*
Is. 13:20 it shall never be *i.*
44:26 saith to J. Thou shalt be *i.*
45:18 he formed earth to be *i.*
54:3 make desola. cities to be *i.*
Jer. 6:8 lest I make land not *i.*
17:6 in a salt land and not *i.*
22:6 make thee cities not *i.*
46:26 sh. be *i.* as in days of old
50:13 not be *i.* ; 39 no more *i.*
Ezek. 12:19 cities *i.* be laid waste
29:11 nor sh. it be *i.* forty years
36:10 cities *i.* and wastes build.
38:12 desolate places now *i.*
Zec. 2:4 Jerusal. be *i.* as towns
12:6 Jerusalem shall be *i.* again
14:10 lifted up, *i.* in her place
11 Jerusalem shall be safely *i.*

INHABITERS.

Rev. 8:13 woe, woe, to *i.* of earth
12:12 woe to *i.* of earth and sea

INHABITEST, ETH.

Job 15:28 in houses no man *i.*
Ps. 22:3 thou that *i.* prais. of Is.
Is. 57:15 lofty One that *i.* eterni.

INHABITING.

Ps. 74:14 meat to peo. *i.* wilder.

INHERIT.

Gen. 15:8 sh. I kn. th. I sh. *i.* it?
Ex. 32:13 they sh. *i.* it for ever
Num. 18:24 given it to Lev. to *i.*
32:19 not *i.* on yonder side Jor
Deut. 1:38 shall cause Is. to *i.* it
21:16 maketh his sons to *i.* wh
Jud. 11:2 not *i.* in fa.'s house
1 *Sam.* 2:8 *i.* the throne of glory
Ps. 25:13 his seed sh. *i.* the earth
37:9 wait on L. sh. *i.* the earth
11 meek sh. *i.* earth, *Mat.* 5:5
22 blessed of him shall *i.* earth
69:36 seed of his serv. shall *i.* it
82:8 O G. thou sh. *i.* all nations

Prov. 3:35 the wise shall *i.* glory
8:21 those who love me, *i.* sub.
11:29 troubl. own house, *i.* wi.
14:18 the simple *i.* folly
Is. 49:8 to *i.* desolate heritages
Is. 54:3 thy seed shall *i.* Gentiles
65:9 and mine elect shall *i.* it
Jer. 49:1 why doth th. ki. *i.* Gad?
Zec. 2:12 the L. shall *i.* Judah
Mat. 19:29 sh. *i.* everlasting life
25:34 come *i.* the kingdom pre.
Mark 10:17 that I may *i.* eternal
life, *Luke* 10:25 ; 18:18
1 *Cor.* 6:9 unrigh. not *i.* king. G.
10 nei. extortion. *i.* *Gal.* 5:21
15:50 flesh and blood cannot *i.*
kingd. of G. nor cor. *i.* inc.
Heb. 6:12 thro' faith *i.* promises
1 *Pet.* 3:9 promised *i.* blessing
Rev. 21:7 he overcom. *i.* things

INHERIT land.

Gen. 28:4 thou mayest *i. land*
Num. 34:13 this is *land* ye sh. *i.*
Deut. 2:31 thou mayest *i.* his *l.*
16:20 *i. l.* L. giveth thee, 19:3
Ps. 37:29 righteous shall *i.* the *l.*
34 he sh. exalt thee to *i.* the *l.*
Is. 60:21 shall *i.* the *l.* for ever

INHERITANCE.

Gen. 31:14 is there any *i.* ?
Ex. 15:17 plant th. in thine *i.*
Lev. 25:46 take them as *i.*
Num. 18:20 have no *i.* thine *i.*
27:8 cause his *i.* to pass
9 *i.* breth. 10 father's brethren
32:19 our *i.* is fallen on this
side, 32; 34:15
34:18 to divide the land by *i.*
36:3 put to the *i.* of the tribe, 4
9 nor *i.* remove from one tribe
Deut. 4:20 people of *i.* as ye are
9:26 destroy not *i.* 29 thy *i.*
32:9 Jacob is the lot of his *i.*
Jos. 13:14 sac. of L. their *i.* 18:7
33 the L. G. of Is. was their *i.*
24:28 people depart, every man
to his *i.* *Jud.* 2:6 ; 21:24
Ruth 4:6 not red. *i.* mar mine *i.*
1 *Sam.* 10:1 anointed thee over *i.*
26:19 from abiding in *i.* of Lord
2 *Sam.* 20:1 neither have we *i.*
in son of Jesse, 1 *K.* 12:16
21:3 ye may bless *i.* of the Lord
1 *K.* 8:51 be thy peo. and t. *i.* 53
Neh. 11:20 every one in his *i.*
Job 31:2 what *i.* of Almighty?
Ps. 16:5 the portion of mine *i.*
28:9 thine *i.* 33:12 cho. for *i.*
37:18 their *i.* shall be for ever
47:4 shall choose our *i.* for us
68:9 thou didst confirm thine *i.*
74:2 thine *i.* th. hast redeemed
78:62 was wroth with his *i.*
71 broug. him to feed Is. his *i.*
79:1 heathen come into thine *i.*
94:14 neither will he forsake *i.*
105:11 Canaan, lot of your *i.*
106:5 may glory with thine *i.*
40 that he abhorred his own *i.*
Prov. 13:22 good man leaveth *i.*
17:2 part of *i.* among brethren
19:14 hou. and riches *i.* of fath.
20:21 *i.* may be gotten hastily
Ec. 7:11 wisdom good with an *i.*
Is. 19:25 blessed be Is. mine *i.*
47:6 I have polluted mine *i.*
63:17 for serv. sake, tribes of *i.*
Jer. 10:16 Is. rod of his *i.* 51:19
32:8 for right of *i.* is thine
Lam. 5:2 *i.* turned to strangers
Ezek. 44:28 to them for *i.* I am *i.*
46:16 *i.* shall be his son's, 17
18 not take people's *i.*
Mat. 21:38 let us seize on his *i.*
Mark 12:7 *i.* be ours, *Luke* 20:14
Luke 12:13 he divide *i.* with me

Acts 20:32 *i.* among sanctified
26:18 *i.* am. them sancti. by fa.
Gal. 3:18 if the *i.* be of the law
Eph. 1:11 in whom obtained *i.*
14 the earnes. of our *i.*
18 riches of the glory of his *i.*
5:5 hath any *i.* in kingd. of Ch.
Col. 1:12 partakers of *i.* of saints
8:24 ye shall rec. the rew. of *i.*
Heb. 1:4 he hath by *i.* obtained
9:15 promise of eternal *i.*
Pet. 1:4 begot. *i.* incorruptible

For INHERITANCE.
Ex. 34:9 take us *for* thine *i.*
Num. 18:21 tenth in Isr. *f. i.* 26
26:53 land sh. be divided *f.* an *i.*
33:54 ; 34:2 ; 36:2 ; *Deut.* 4:21,
38 ; 15:4 ; 19:10 ; *Jos.* 13:6, 7,
32 ; 14:1 ; 19:49, 51 ; *Ezek.* 45:1;
47:22 ; 48:29
Deut. 20:16 the Lord doth give
thee *for* an *i.* 21:23 ; 24:4 ;
25:19 ; 26:1 ; *Jos.* 11:23 ; 13:6 ;
14:13 ; 1 *K.* 8:36 ; 2 *Chr.* 6:27 ;
Jer. 3:18
Ps. 2:8 give thee heathen *f. i.*
Ezek. 33:24 land is given us *f. i.*
47:14 land sh. fall to you *f.* an *i.*
Heb. 11:8 a place he sho. rec. *f. i.*

No, or None INHERITANCE.
Num. 18:20 sh. have *no i.* 23,
24 ; 26:62 ; *Deut.* 10:9 ; 14:27,
29 ; 18:1, 2 ; *Jos.* 13:14, 33 ; 14:3
2 *Chr.* 10:16 we have *no i.* in son
Acts 7:5 he gave him *none i.*

INHERITANCES.
Jos. 19:51 the *i.* Joshua divided

INHERITED, ETH.
Num. 32:18 not return till Is. *i.*
35:8 his inheriting which he *i.*
Ps. 105:44 *i.* labor of the people
Jer. 16:19 our fathers *i.* lies
Ezek. 33:24 Abraham *i.* the land
Heb. 12:17 would have *i.* blessing

INHERITOR.
Is. 65:9 out of Jud. *i.* of mount
See ENJOY, ENJOIN.

INIQUITY.
Gen. 15:16 *i.* of the Amorites
19:15 lest be consumed in *i.*
44:16 G. ha. found out *i.* of ser.
Ex. 20:5 visiting the *i.* of fathers
upon the children, 34:7 ;
Num. 14:18 ; *Deut.* 5:9
34:7 forgiving *i. Num.* 14:18
Lev. 18:25 therefore do I visit *i.*
Num. 5:15 bringing *i.* to rem.
31 the man be guiltless from *i.*
23:21 not beheld *i.* in Jacob
Deut. 32:4 God of truth with *i.*
Jos. 22:17 is *i.* of P. too little ?
1 *Sam.* 3:14 *i.* of Eli's not purged
15:23 and stubbornness is as *i.*
20:8 if th. be in me *i.* slay me
25:24 let *i.* be, 2 *Sam.* 14:9
2 *Sam.* 14:32 if there be *i.* in me
19:19 let not L. impute *i.* to me
24:10 to take away *i.* of thy servant, 1 *Chr.* 21:8
2 *Chr.* 19:7 there is no *i.* with L.
Job 4:8 they that plough *i.*
5:16 and *i.* stoppeth her mouth
6:29 I pray you, let it not be *i.*
30 is there *i.* in my tongue ?
11:6 G. exact. less th. *i.* deserv.
14 if *i.* be in thy hand
15:5 thy mouth uttereth thine *i.*
16 filthy is man wh. drink. *i.*
22:23 put away *i.* from thy tab.
31:11 *i.* to be punished, 28
33:9 nor is there *i.* in me
34:32 if I have done *i.*
36:21 take heed, regard not *i.*
23 who can say, Thou wro. *i. ?*

Ps. 7:3 if be *i.* in my hands
14 behold, he travaileth with *i.*
32:2 to whom L. imputeth not *i.*
5 thou forgavest *i.* of my sin
36:3 words of his mouth are *i.*
39:11 dost correct man for *i.*
41:6 his heart gather. *i.* to itse.
49:5 *i.* of my heels compass
51:5 behold, I was shapen in *i.*
53:1 have done abominable *i.*
55:3 for they cast *i.* upon me
56:7 shall they escape by *i. ?*
66:18 if I regard *i.* in my heart
85:2 forgiven *i.* of thy people
94:20 throne of *i.* have fellowsh.
107:42 *i.* shall stop her mouth
109:14 let *i.* of his fa.'s be rem.
119:3 do no *i.* walk in his ways
133 let not *i.* have dominion
125:3 let put forth hands to *i.*
Prov. 10:6 by truth *i.* is purged
19:28 mouth of wicked devou. *i.*
22:8 soweth *i.* shall reap vanity
Ec. 3:16 place of right. *i.* there
Is. 1:4 a people laden with *i.*
13 *i.* even the solemn meeting
5:18 woe to them that draw *i.*
6:7 thine *i.* is taken away
14:21 prepare for *i.* of fathers
22:14 *i.* not be purged from you
29:20 watch for *i.* are cut off
30:13 *i.* shall be as a breach
40:2 her *i.* is pardoned
53:6 L. laid on him *i.* of us all
57:17 for *i.* of covetousness
59:3 your fingers defiled with *i.*
4 bring forth *i.* 6 works of *i.* 7
64:9 nor remember *i.* for ever
Jer. 2:5 what *i.* have fa. fo. in me
22 thine *i.* is marked before me
3:13 only acknowledge thine *i.*
13:22 greatn. of *i.* are thy skirts
14:20 acknowledge *i.* of fathers
16:10 our *i.* 17 *i.* hid from eyes
30:14 multi. of *i.* 15 ; *Hos.* 9:7
32:18 recompensest *i.* of fathers
Lam. 2:14 not discovered thine *i.*

Lam. 4:22 punishm. of *i.* accom.
will visit *i.* O daug. of Edom
Ezek. 4:4 lay *i.* of house of Is. on
7:13 nor strength. himself in *i.*
18:17 not die for *i.* of his father
30 so *i.* shall not be your ruin
21:23 call to remembrance *i.* 24
25 *i.* sh. have an end, 29 ; 35:5
28:15 till *i.* found in thee
18 defiled sanctu. by *i.* of traf.
44:12 houses of Israel fall into *i.*
Dan. 9:24 reconciliation for *i.*

Hos. 7:1 *i.* of Ephraim discovered
10:9 children of *i.* 13 reaped *i.*
12:8 they shall find no *i.* in me
11 is there *i.* in Gilead ?
13:12 *i.* of Ephraim bound up
14:1 thou hast fallen by thine *i.*
2 take away *i.* rec. graciously
Mic. 2:1 woe to them that devise *i.*
3:10 build up Jerusalem with *i.*
7:18 G. like thee, pardoneth *i. ?*
Hab. 1:13 canst not look on *i.*
2:12 woe to him estab. city by *i.*
Zep. 3:5 just Lord, will not do *i.*
13 remnant of Israel not do *i.*
Zec. 3:4 caused *i.* pass from thee
9 remove *i.* of land in one day
Mal. 2:6 *i.* not found in his lips
Mat. 13:41 gather them wh. do *i.*
23:28 are full of hypocrisy and *i.*
24:12 because *i.* shall abound
Acts 1:18 field with reward of *i.*
8:23 thou art in bond of *i.*
Rom. 6:19 servants to *i.* unto *i.*
1 *Cor.* 13:6 rejoiceth not in *i.* but
2 *Thes.* 2:7 mystery of *i.* doth w.
2 *Tim.* 2:19 nameth C. dep. fr. *i.*
Tit. 2:14 might redeem us fr. *i.*
Heb. 1:9 and thou hast hated *i.*

Jam. 3:6 tong. is fire, world of *i.*
See BEAR, COMMIT, COMMITTED.

His INIQUITY.
Num. 15:31 his *i.* be upon him
Job 20:27 heavens revealed his *i.*
21:19 G. layeth up h. *i.* for chil.
Ps. 36:2 h. *i.* be found hateful
Jer. 31:30 die for *his i. Ezek.*
3:18, 19 ; 7:16 ; 18:26
Ezek. 14:7 stum.-block of h. *i.* 14
18:18 sh. die in h. *i.* 33:8, 9
33:6 he is taken away in *his i.*
2 *Pet.* 2:16 Bal. rebuked for *h. i.*

Mine INIQUITY.
1 *Sam.* 20:1 what is mine *i. ?*
2 *Sam.* 22:24 I kept myself from
mine *i. Ps.* 18:23
Job 7:21 not take away m. *i. ?*
10:6 thou inquirest after m. *i.*
14 not acquit me from *mine i.*
14:17 thou sewest up m. *i.*
31:33 hiding m. *i.* in my bosom
Ps. 25:11 pardon m. *i.* it is great
31:10 stre. faileth beca. of m. *i.*
32:5 mine *i.* have I not hid
38:18 for I will declare mine *i.*
51:2 wash me thoro. fr. m. *i.*

Their INIQUITY.
Lev. 26:39 pine away in *their i.*
40 if they confess th. *i.* 41, 43
Neh. 4:5 and cover not *their i.*
Ps. 69:27 add iniquity unto *t. i.*
78:38 forg. *t. i.* 89:32 visit *t. i.*
94:23 bring upon them *their i.*
106:43 were bro. low for *their i.*
Is. 13:11 punish wicked for *t. i.*
26:12 punish inhabitants for *t. i.*
33:24 peo. shall be forgiven *t. i.*
Jer. 14:10 will now remem. *th. i.*
16:18 he will recompense *th. i.*
18:23 forgive not *their i.*
25:12 punish nation for *their i.*
31:34 for I will forgive *their i.*
33:8 cleanse them from all *th. i.*
36:3 that I may forgive *their i.*
31 punish his servants for *t. i.*
Ezek. 4:5 laid on th. years of *t. i.*
17 may consume away for *t. i.*
7:19 stumbling-bl. of *t. i.* 14:3
14:10 bear punishment of *th. i.*
29:16 bringeth *t. i.* to remem.
39:23 Is. into captivity for *t. i.*
Hos. 4:8 set their heart on *th. i.*
5:5 shall Is. and Eph. fall in *t. i.*
9:9 he will remember *their i.*

Work INIQUITY.
Ps. 141:4 with men that *w. i.*
Is. 31:2 ag. help of them *w. i.*
32:6 *w. i.* to practise hypocrisy
Mat. 7:23 depart fr. me, ye *w. i.*

Workers of INIQUITY.
Job 31:3 punishment to *w. of i.*
34:8 go in comp. with *w. of i.*
22 *w. of i.* hide themselves
Ps. 5:5 hatest all *workers of i.*
6:8 all ye *w. of i.* Luke 13:27
Ps. 14:4 *w. of i.* no knowl. ? **53:4**
28:3 draw not away wi. *w. of i.*
36:12 the *w. of i.* fallen
37:1 nor be envious ag. *w. of i.*
59:2 deliver me from *w. of i.*
64:2 insurrection of the *w. of i.*
92:7 all the *w. of i.* do flourish
9 the *w. of i.* shall be scattered
94:4 *w. of i.* boast themselves
16 stand up for me aga. *w. of i.*
125:5 lead th. forth with *w. of i.*
141:9 keep me fr. gins of *w. of i.*
Prov. 10:29 dest. to *w. of i.* 21:15

INIQUITIES.
Lev. 16:21 confess over goat all *i.*
26:39 in *i.* of fa. sh. they pine
Ezr. 9:6 *i.* increased over head
13 punished less *i.* deserved
Neh. 9:2 Is. confessed *i.* of fath.

Job 13:23 how many are mine *i*
26 makest me to poss. *i.* of yo
22:5 wicked. great, *i.* infinite
Ps. 38:4 i. gone over my head
40:12 i. have taken hold on me
51:9 hide fa. fr. sins, blot out *i.*
64:6 search out *i.* 65:3 *i.* preva.
79:8 remember not ag. us *i.*
90:8 hast set our *i.* before
103:3 L. who forgiveth all *i.*
10 nor rewarded us accord. to *i.*
130:3 shou. mark *i.* who stand?
8 redeem Israel from all his *i.*
Prov. 5:22 own *i.* take wicked
Is. 43:24 wearied me with th. *i.*
53:5 he was bruised for our *i.*
59:12 our *i.* we know them
64:6 i. like wind taken us away
7 consum. us because of our *i.*
Jer. 11:10 to *i.* of forefathers
14:7 though our *i.* testify ag. us
Lam. 4:13 for *i.* of her priests
Ezek. 28:18 by multi. of thine *i.*
Dan. 4:27 break off thine *i.*
9:13 we might turn from our *i.*
Mic. 7:19 he will subdue our *i.*
Acts 3:26 turn. ev. one fr. his *i.*
Rom. 4:7 blessed they wh. *i.* for.
Rev. 18:5 God hath rememb. *i.*

Their INIQUITIES.
Lev. 16:22 goat bear on him *i.* *i.*
Ps. 107:17 fools bec. of *their i.*
Is. 53:11 he shall bear *their i.*
Jer. 33:8 I will pardon all *their i.*
Lam. 5:7 we have borne *i.*
Ezek. 32:27 *i.* i. be on their bones
Heb. 8:12 *i.* i. rem. no more, 10:17

Your INIQUITIES.
Num. 14:34 forty ye. ye bear *y. i.*
Is. 50:1 for *y.* i. ye sold yourself
59:2 *y.* i. separated you and G.
65:7 *your i.* I will recompense
Jer. 5:25 *y.* i. turned away fr. yo.
Ezek. 24:23 ye pine away for *y.* i.
36:31 loathe yourselves for *y.* i.
Amos 3:2 punish you for *y.* i.

INJURED.
Gal. 4:12 ye have not *i.* me at all

INJURIOUS.
1 *Tim.* 1:13 a persecutor and *i.*

INJUSTICE.
Job 16:17 not for *i.* in my hands

INK.
Jer. 36:18 wrote them with *i.*
2 *Cor.* 3:3 not with *i.* but the S.
2 *John* 12 not wr. wi. *i.* 3 *John* 13

INKHORN.
Ezek. 9:2 writer's *i.* by side, 3, 11

INN.
Gen. 42:27 ass proven. in the *i.*
43:21 came to *i.* opened sacks
Ex. 4:24 in the *i.* L. met him
Luke 2:7 no room for them in *i.*
10:34 brought him to an *i.*

INNER.
1 *K.* 6:27 cherubim in *i.* house
1 *Chr.* 28:11 patterns of *i.* parlors
Est. 4:11 to king into *i.* court
5:1 Esther stood in the *i.* court
Ezek. 10:3 cloud filled the *i.* cou.
42:15 end of measuring *i.* house
46:1 gate of *i.* court sh. six da.
Acts 16:24 thrust in into *i.* pris.
Eph. 3:16 strengthened in *i.* man
See CHAMBER.

INNERMOST.
Prov. 18:8 *i.* parts of belly, 26:22

INNOCENCY.
Gen. 20:5 in the *i.* of my hands
Ps. 26:6 wash my hands in *i.*
73:13 I washed hands in *i.*
Dan. 6:22 *i.* was found in me
Hos. 8:5 how long ere attain
to *i.* ?

INNOCENT, S.
Ex. 23:7 *i.* and right. slay not
Deut. 27:25 tak. reward to slay *i.*
Job 4:7 who ever perished be. *i.* ?
9:23 laugh at the trial of the *i.*
28 thou wilt not hold me *i.*
17:8 *i.* stir up against hypocrite
22:19 the *i.* laugh them to scorn
30 shall deliver island of the *i.*
27:17 *i.* shall divide the silver
33:9 I am *i.* nor is iniq. in me
Ps. 10:8 in sec. places murder *i.*
15:5 taketh reward against *i.*
19:13 *i.* fr. great transgression
Prov. 1:11 lurk privily for *i.*
28:20 haste to be rich not be *i.*
Jer. 2:34 found blood of poor *i.*
35 thou sayest, Because I am *i.*
19:4 filled place with blood of *i.*
Mat. 27:24 I am *i.* of the blood of
See BLOOD.

INNUMERABLE.
Job 21:33 there are *i.* before him
Ps. 40:12 *i.* evils comp. about
104:25 wherein things creep, *i.*
Jer. 46:23 grasshoppers, are *i.*
Luke 12:1 an *i.* mult. gathered
Heb. 11:12 sand by sea-shore *i.*
12:22 to *i.* company of angels

INORDINATE.
Ezek. 23:11 corrupt in *i.* love
Col. 3:5 fornication, *i.* affection

INQUIRE.
Gen. 24:57 we will *i.* at damsel
25:22 Rebekah went to *i.* of L.
Ex. 18:15 people come to *i.* of G.
Deut. 12:30 *i.* not after their gods
13:14 shalt *i.* and make search
Jud. 4:20 when any man doth *i.*
1 *Sam.* 22:15 th. begin to *i.* of G.
28:7 seek me a woman, that I *i.*
1 *K.* 22:5 *i.* at the word of the
Lord to-day, 2 *Chr.* 18:4
2 *K.* go, *i.* of Baal-zebub
16:15 bra. altar for me to *i.* by
22:13 *i.* of L. for me, 2 *Chr.* 34:21
1 *Chr.* 10:13 familiar spirit to *i.*
21:30 David not go bef. it to *i.*
Ezr. 7:14 sent to *i.* concerning J.
Job 8:8 for *i.* of the former age
Ps. 27:4 and to *i.* in his temple
Ec. 7:10 thou dost not *i.* wisely
Is. 21:12 if ye will *i.* ye
Jer. 21:2 *i.* of the Lord for us
37:7 that sent you to *i.* of me
Ezek. 14:7 cometh to proph. to *i.*
20:1 elders came to *i.* of Lord
Mat. 10:11 *i.* who is worthy
Luke 22:23 to *i.* among them-
selves, *John* 16:19
Acts 9:11 *i.* for Saul
19:39 if *i.* concerning other mat.
23:15 as tho' *i.* something, 20
2 *Cor* 8:23 any do *i.* of Titus

INQUIRED.
Jud. 20:27 children of Is. *i.* of L.
1 *Sam.* 22:10 Abimelech *i.* of L.
23:2 David *i.* of the Lord, 4;
30:8 ; 2 *Sam.* 2:1 ; 5:19, 23 ;
21:1 ; 1 *Chr.* 14:10, 14
28:6 Saul *i.* Lord answered not
2 *Sam.* 16:23 as if *i.* at oracle of
1 *Chr.* 10:14 Saul *i.* not of Lord
13:3 *i.* not at ark in days of S.
Ps. 78:34 and *i.* early after God
Ezek. 14:3 should I be *i.* of at all
20:3 as I live I will not be *i.* of
31 shall I be *i.* of by you, O Israel? I will not be *i.* of by
36:37 I will yet for this be *i.* of
Dan. 1:20 in all king *i.* of them
Zep. 1:6 have not *i.* for the Lord
Mat. 2:7 Herod *i.* of wise men, 16
John 4:52 *i.* hour began to ame.
2 *Cor.* 8:23 or our brethren be *i.*
1 *Pet.* 1:10 of wh. sal. prophets *i.*

INQUIREST.
Job 10:6 *i.* after mine iniquity

INQUIRY.
Prov. 20:25 after vows to make *i.*

INQUISITION.
Deut. 19:18 jud. sh. make dili. *i.*
Est. 2:23 *i.* was made of matter
Ps. 9:12 when mak. *i.* for blood

INSCRIPTION.
Acts 17:23 an altar with this *i.*

INSIDE.
1 *K.* 6:15 cov. walls *i.* with wood

INSPIRATION.
Job 32:8 *i.* Alm. giv. understan.
2 *Tim.* 3:16 scripture is by *i.* of

INSTANT, LY.
Is. 29:5 it sh. be at an *i.* sudden.
30:13 whose breaking com. at *i.*
Jer. 18:7 at what *i.* I speak, 9
Luke 2:38 com. th. *i.* gave than.
7:4 they besought him *i.*
Acts 26:7 twelve tribes *i.* serve
Rom. 12:12 continu. *i.* in prayer
2 *Tim.* 4:2 be *i.* in season, out of

INSTRUCT.
Deut. 4:36 hear, th. he mi. *i.* thee
Neh. 9:20 gavest thy S. to *i.* th.
Job 40:2 shall he that contend *i.*
Ps. 16:7 my reins also *i.* me
32:8 I will *i.* thee and teach th.
Cant. 8:2 who will *i.* me
Is. 28:26 God doth *i.* him
Dan. 11:33 underst. sh. *i.* many
1 *Cor.* 2:16 that he may *i.* him

INSTRUCTED.
Deut. 32:10 L. led him ab. *i.* him
Job 4:3 behold thou hast *i.* many
Ps. 2:10 be *i.* ye judges of earth
Prov. 5:13 mine ear to th. *i.* me
21:11 the wise is *i.* he receiveth
Is. 8:11 L. spake thus and *i.* me
40:14 *i.* him and taught him
Jer. 6:8 be *i.* O J. lest soul dep.
31:19 after *i.* I smote on thigh
Mat. 13:52 every scribe who is *i.*
14:8 being bef. *i.* of her mother
Luke 1:4 things th. hast been *i.*
Acts 18:25 was *i.* in way of Lord
Rom. 2:18 being *i.* out of law
Phil. 4:12 in all things, I am *i.*

INSTRUCTING.
2 *Tim.* 2:25 *i.* those that oppose

INSTRUCTION.
Job 33:16 open. ears, stealeth *i.*
Ps. 50:17 seeing thou hatest *i.*
Prov. 1:2 to know wisdom and *i.*
3 to receive the *i.* of wisdom
7 fools des. wisdom and *i.* 15:5
8 son, hear *i.* of thy father, 4:1
4:13 take hold of *i.*
5:12 say, How have I hated *i.*
23 die without *i.* go astray
6:23 reproofs of *i.* way of life
8:10 receive my *i.* ; 33 hear *i.*
9:9 give *i.* to a wise man
10:17 in way of life that keep. *i.*
12:1 loveth *i.* loveth knowledge
13:1 wise son heareth father's *i.*
18 shame to him that refus. *i.*
15:32 refus. *i.* despiseth his soul
33 fear of L. is the *i.* of wisd.
16:22 but the *i.* of fools is folly
19:20 hear counsel and rec. *i.*
27 cease to hear *i.*
23:12 apply thy heart to *i.*
23 buy also *i.* and understand.
Jer. 17:23 not hear nor rec. *i.*
32:33 not hearkened to rec. *i.*
Ezek. 5:15 a repro. a taunt, an *i.*
Zep. 3:7 surely thou wilt rec. *i.*
2 *Tim.* 3:16 scrip. is profitable *i.*

INSTRUCTOR, S.
Gen. 4:22 Tubal Cain an *i.*
Rom. 2:20 an *i.* of the foolish

1 *Cor.* 4:15 ye have 10,000 *i.*

INSTRUMENT.

Num. 35:16 smite him with *i.*
Ps. 33:2 wi. *i.* of ten strings, 92:3
144:9 sing new song, O G. on *i.*
Is. 28:27 not thr. with thresh. *i.*
41:15 make th. sharp thresh. *i.*
54:16 bringeth forth *i.* for work
Ezek. 33:2 song of one play on *i.*

INSTRUMENTS.

Gen. 49:5 *i.* of cruelty in habita.
Ex. 25:9 pattern of all the *i.*
Num. 3:8 all *i.* of tabernacle
7:1 sancti. all *i.* thereof, 31:6
1 *Sam.* 8:12 *i.* of war, of char.
18:6 meet S. with *i.* of music
1 *K.* 19:21 boiled th. flesh with *i.*
1 *Chr.* 9:29 oversee *i.* of sanctu.
16:42 make sou. with musical *i.*
Ps. 7:13 prepared *i.* of death
68:25 players on *i.* be thero
87:7 players on *i.* be there
150:4 with stringed *i.*
Ec. 2:8 musical *i.* of all sorts
Is. 32:7 *i.* also of the churl
Dan. 6:18 nor *i.* of music brou.
Amos 1:3 threshed G. with *i.* of
6:5 invent to themsel. *i.* of mu.
Hab. 3:19 singing on stringed *i.*
Zec. 11:15 *i.* of foolish shepherd
Rom. 6:13 nor y. mem. *i.* of un-
right. members as *i.* of righ.

INSURRECTION.

Ezr. 4:19 this city hath made *i.*
Ps. 64:2 *i.* of workers of iniquity
Mark 15:7 bound th. th. made *i.*
who had commit. mur. in *i.*
Acts 18:12 J. made *i.* one accord

INTEGRITY.

Gen. 20:5 *i.* of my heart, 6
Job 2:3 still he holdeth fast his *i.*
9 dost thou still retain th. *i.* ?
27:5 I will not remove my *i.*
31:6 that God may know my *i.*
Ps. 7:8 according to my *i.* in me
25:21 *i.* and uprightn. preserve
26:1 I have walked in mine *i.*
11 as for me, I will walk in *i.*
41:12 thou uphold. me in my *i.*
78:72 fed accord. to *i.* of heart
Prov. 11:3 *i.* of upright guide th.
19:1 poor that walketh in *i.*
20:7 just man walketh in his *i.*

INTELLIGENCE.

Dan. 11:30 *i.* with them forsake

INTEND.

2 *Chr.* 28:13 *i.* to add more to si.
Acts 5:28 *i.* to bring man's blood
35 what ye *i.* to do these men

INTENDED, EST.

Ex. 2:14 *i.* thou to kill me
Ps. 21:11 *i.* evil against thee

INTENDING.

Luke 14:28 wh. of you *i.* to build
Acts 12:4 *i.* after Easter to bring

INTENT, S.

2 *Chr.* 16:1 *i.* might let none go
Jer 30:24 performed *i.* of heart
John 11:15 not there to the *i.*
13:28 for what *i.* he spake
Acts 9:21 came hither for that *i.*
10:29 what *i.* ye ha. sent for me
1 *Cor.* 10:6 *i.* we should not lust
Eph. 3:10 *i.* that now to princi.
Heb. 4:12 discerner of *i.* of heart

INTERCESSION, S.

Is. 53:12 *i.* for transgressors
Jer. 7:16 ne. lift cry, nor make *i.*
27:18 let th. now make *i.* to L.
Rom. 8:26 Sp. maketh *i.* 27, 34
11:2 maketh *i.* to G. ag. Israel
*Heb.*7:25 liveth to make *i.*
1 *Tim.* 2:1 prayers and *i.* be ma.

INTERCESSOR.

Is. 59:16 wondered th. was no *i.*

INTERMEDDLE, ETH.

Prov. 14:10 stranger not *i.*
18:1 seeketh and *i.* with wisd.

INTERMISSION.

Lam. 3:49 ceaseth not without *i.*

INTERPRET.

Gen. 41:8 none could *i.* to Phar.
12 accord. to dream he did *i.*
1 *Cor.* 12:30 do all *i.* ; 14:5 exc. *i.*
14:13 he may *i.* ; 27 let one *i.*

INTERPRETATION.

Gen. 40:5 *i.* of dream, 41:11
12 Joseph said, This is the *i.*
of it, 18 ; *Dan.* 4:24 ; 5:26
Prov. 1:6 unders. proverb and *i.*
Dan. 2:4 we shall show *i.* 7, 36
45 dream is certain, and *i.* sure
4:19 *i.* thereof be to thine ene.
John 1:42 Cephas, is by *i.* a stone
9:7 pool of Siloam, is by *i.* sent
Acts 9:36 Tab. by *i.* called Dorc.
13:8 Elymas sorcerer, na. by *i.*
1 *Cor.* 12:10 another *i.* of tongues
14:26 every one of you ha. an *i.*
Heb. 7:2 by *i.* king of righteous.
2 *Pet.* 1:20 no prophecy of pri. *i.*

INTERPRETATIONS.

Gen. 40:8 do not *i.* belong to G. ?
Dan. 5:16 thou canst make *i.*

INTERPRETED.

Ezr. 4:7 and *i.* in Syrian tongue
Mat. 1:23 being *i.* is, G. with us
Mark 5:41 wh. is, being *i.* damsel
15:22 being *i.* place of a skull
34 *i.* my God, my God
John 1:38 *i.* master ; 41 *i.* Christ
Acts 4:36 *i.* son of consolation

INTERPRETER, S.

Gen. 40:8 and there is no *i.* of it
42:23 Joseph spake to th. by *i.*
Job 33:23 and *i.* one am. thous.
1 *Cor.* 14:28 if there be no *i.* keep

INTERPRETING.

Dan. 5:12 *i.* of dreams found in

INTREAT, ED, etc. *See* EN-
TREAT.

INTRUDING.

Col. 2:18 *i.* into things not seen

INVADE, ED.

1 *Sam.* 23:27 Philistines *i.* land
2 *K.* 13:20 Moabites *i.* land
2 *Chr.* 20:10 would. not let Is. *i.*
28:18 Philistines had *i.* cities
Hab. 3:16 will *i.* them with
troops

INVASION.

1 *Sam.* 30:14 made *i.* on the south

INVENT, ED.

2 *Chr.* 26:15 engines by cunni.
Amos 6:5 *i.* instruments of music

INVENTIONS.

Ps. 99:8 tookest veng. of their *i.*
106:29 prov. him to anger wi. *i.*
39 whoring with their own *i.*
Prov. 8:12 knowledge of witty *i.*
Ec. 7:29 sought out many *i.*

INVENTORS.

Rom. 1:30 *i.* of evil things

INVISIBLE.

Rom. 1:20 *i.* things clearly seen
Col. 1:15 image of the *i.* God
16 heaven and earth, vi. and *i.*
1 *Tim.* 1:17 to King immortal, *i.*
Heb. 11:27 seeing him who is *i.*

INVITED.

1 *Sam.* 9:24 I have *i.* the people
2 *Sam.* 13:23 Absa. *i.* king's son
Est. 5:12 to-morrow am I *i.*

INWARD.

Lev. 13:55 in fire, it is fret *i.*

1 *K.* 7:25 all hinder parts were *i.*
2 *Chr.* 8:13 and th. faces were *i.*
Job 19:19 my *i.* friends abhor. me
38:36 put wisdom in *i.* parts
Ps. 5:9 *i.* part is very wickedn.
49:11 *i.* thought is, that houses
51:6 desirest truth in the *i.* par.
64:6 *i.* thought of them is deep
Prov. 20:27 all *i.* parts of belly
30 stripes the *i.* parts of belly
Is. 16:11 *i.* parts sound for Ker-h.
Jer. 31:33 put my law in *i.* parts
Luke 11:39 *i.* part full of raven.
Rom. 7:22 law of G. after *i.* man
2 *Cor.* 4:16 the *i.* man is renew.
7:15 *i.* affection more abundant

INWARDLY.

Ps. 62:4 with mouths, curse *i.*
Mat. 7:15 but *i.* they are wolves
Rom. 2:29 a Jew who is one *i.*

INWARDS.

Ex. 29:13 covereth *i.* 22 ; *Lev.*
8:3, 9, 14 ; 4:8 ; 7:3 ; 9:19
17 thou shalt wash the *i.* *Lev.*
1:9, 13 ; 9:14
Lev. 4:11 *i.* and dung burn
8:16 fat on *i.* M. burnt on altar
21 he washed *i.* and legs

IRON, Substantive.

Num. 35:16 with instrument of *i.*
Deut. 3:11 Og's bedstead was *i.*
4:20 L. brought you out of the *i.*
furnace, 1 *K.* 8:51 ; *Jer.* 11:4
8:9 a land whose stones are *i.*
28:23 earth under. thee sh. be *i.*
48 yo. of *i.* on neck ; *Jer.* 28:14
Jos. 8:31 over wh. no man lift *i.*
17:16 chariots of *i.* *Jud.* 1:19
Jud. 4:3 900 chariots of *i.* 13
1 *Sam.* 17:7 spear's head weighed
609 shekels of *i.*
2 *Sam.* 12:31 under harrows of *i.*
axes of *i.* 1 *Chr.* 20:3
23:7 must be fenced with *i.*
1 *K.* 6:7 nor any tool of *i.* heard
22:11 horns of *i.* 2 *Chr.* 18:10
2 *K.* 6:6 and the *i.* did swim
1 *Chr.* 22:3 prep. *i.* in abundance
29:2 prep. *i.* for things of *i.* 7
Job 28:2 *i.* is taken out of earth
40:18 behemoth's bones like *i.*
41:27 he esteemeth *i.* as straw
Ps. 2:9 break them with rod of *i.*
105:18 hurt, he was laid in *i.*
107:10 bound in *i.* ; 16 bars of *i.*
149:8 bind nobles with fet. of *i.*
Prov. 27:17 *i.* sharpeneth *i.*
Ec. 10:10 if the *i.* be blunt
Is. 10:34 cut thic. of forest wi. *i.*
45:2 I will cut asunder bars of *i.*
60:17 for *i.* I will bring silver
Jer. 15:12 shall *i.* break north. *i.*
17:1 written with pen of *i.*
28:13 make for them yokes of *i.*
Ezek. 4:3 *i.* pan, set for wall of *i.*
27:12 Tarshish merchant with *i.*
Dan. 2:33 legs of *i.* feet part *i.*
35 the *i.* and clay broken
40 fourth kingdom strong as *i.*
7:19 whose teeth were of *i.*
Amos 1:3 Gil. with instru. of *i.*
Mic. 4:13 I will make thy horn *i.*
1 *Tim.* 4:2 consc. seared with *i.*
Rev. 2:27 rule th. with a rod of *i.*
12:5 ; 19:15
9:9 as it were breastplates of *i.*
See BRASS.

IRON.

Deut. 27:5 not lift up any *i.* tool
Jos. 17:18 they have *i.* chariots
Job 19:24 graven with *i.* pen
20:24 shall flee from *i.* weapon
Is. 48:4 thy neck is an *i.* sinew
Jer. 1:18 thee this day *i.* pillar
Ezek. 4:3 take unto thee *i.* pan
Dan. 7:7 it had great *i.* teeth

Acts 12:10 came to the *i.* gate

IRONS.
Job 41:7 fill skin with barbed *i.?*

IS.
Rev. 1:4 which *i.* was, and *i.* to
  come, 8; 4:8
17:8 that was, *i.* not, yet *i.*
  10 one *i.* the other *i.* not come

IS not.
Gen. 37:30 said, The child *i. not*
42:13 youn. with fa. one *i. n.* 32
42:36 Joseph *i. not,* Simeon *i. n.*
Rev. 17:8 beast was, and *i. n.* 11

ISAAC.
Gen. 17:19 his name I. 21:3, 12
21:10 heir with my son, even I.
22:2 take thine only son I. 9
24:4 take a wife for. I. 14
25:5 had unto I. 9, 11, 20, 26
26:1 I. went to Abimelech
28:1 I. called Jacob, blessed h.
31:42 fear of I. had been with
35:27 Jacob came to I, 29
48:15 God before wh. I. walked
Ex. 3:6 the God of I. 15, 16; 4:5;
  Gen. 32:9 ; 1 *K.* 18:36 ; 1 *Chr.*
  29:18; 2 *Chr.* 30:6; *Mat.* 22:32;
  Mark 12:26 ; *Luke* 20:37;
  Acts 3:13
Jos. 24:3 and gave him I.
1 *Chr.* 16:16 unto I. *Ps.* 105:9
Amos 7:9 high places of I.
Mat. 1:2 Abraham begat I. and I.
  begat J. *Luke* 3:34 ; *Acts* 7:8
8:11 many shall sit down with I.
Luke 13:28 see I. in kingd. of G.
Rom. 9:10 conceived by father I.
Gal. 4:28 we, as I. was, are of pro.
Heb. 11:9 in tabernacles with I.
  17 Abraham offered up I.
  20 I. blessed Jacob, *Jam.* 2:21

ISAIAH, or ESAIAS.
2 *K.* 19:2 Eliakim to I. *Is.* 37:2
20:1 I. came to him, *Is.* 38:1
2 *Chr.* 26:22 acts did I. wr. 32:32
Is. 20:3 my serv. I. hath walked
Mat. 3:3 pro. E. 4:14 ; 8:17 ; 12:17;
  13:14; *Luke* 3:4 ; *John* 1:23
15:7 E. proph. of you, *Mark* 7:6
Luke 4:17 book of prophet E.
John 12:39 bec. that E. said, 41
Acts 8:28 the eunuch read E. 30
28:25 spake the H. Ghost by E.
Rom. 9:27 E. crieth conc. Israel
10:16 E. saith, L. who hath? 20
15:12 E. saith, There shall be

ISCARIOT. *See* JUDAS.
ISH-BOSHETH.   2 *Sam.* 2:8 ;
  3:8, 14 ; 4:8, 12

ISHMAEL.
Gen. 16:11 call name I. 15, 16
17:18 O that I. mi. live, 20, 25
25:17 these are the years of I.
28:9 then went Esau unto I.
2 *K.* 25:23 I. came to, *Jer.* 40:8
Jer. 40:14 Ammon. sent I. 15, 16
41:6 I. went to meet th. 10, 15

ISHMAELITES.
Gen. 37:27 let us sell him to I.
39:1 Potiphar bought him of I.
Jud. 8:24 because they were I.
Ps. 83:6 I. confederate ag. thee

ISLAND.
Job 22:30 deliver *i.* of innocent
Is. 34:14 meet wild beasts of *i.*
Acts 27:16 running under cert. *i.*
  26 must be cast on certain *i.*

28:1 knew *i.* was called Melita
  7 possess. of chief man of *i.*
28:9 who had diseases in *i.*
Rev. 6:14 every *i.* was moved out
16:20 every *i.* fled away

ISLANDS.
Is. 11:11 receive people from *i.*
13:22 wild beasts of *i.* shall cry
41:1 keep silence bef. me, O *i.*
42:12 declare Lord's praise in *i.*
  15 make rivers *i.* dry up pools
59:18 the *i.* he will pay recomp.
Jer. 50:39 wild beasts of *i.* dwell

ISLE.
Is. 20:6 the inhabitants of the *i.*
23:2 be still, inhabitants of *i.*
  6 howl, ye inhabitants of the *i.*
Acts 13:6 through *i.* to Paphos
28:11 ship which wintered in *i.*
Rev. 1:9 was in *i.* called Patmos

ISLES.
Gen. 10:5 th. were *i.* of Gentiles
Est. 10:1 A. laid a tribute on *i.*
Ps. 72:10 kings of *i.* bring pres.
97:1 let multitudes of *i.* be glad
Is. 24:15 glorify Lord in the *i.*
40:15 tak. up *i.* as a little thing
41:5 the *i.* saw it and feared
42:4 the *i.* shall wait for his law
49:1 listen, O *i.* unto me
51:5 *i.* shall wait upon me and
  trust, 60:9
66:19 *i.* afar off not heard fame
Jer. 2:10 pass over *i.* of Chittim
25:22 kings of *i.* drink after th.
Ezek. 26:15 sh. not *i.* sh. at sou.?
  18 *i.* tremble, *i.* shall be troub.
27:3 merch. of peo. for many *i.*
  6 brought out of *i.* of Chittim
  7 blue and purple from *i.* of E.
  15 many *i.* were merchandise
35 inhabit. of *i.* be astonished
39:6 dwell carelessly in the *i.*
Dan. 11:18 eh. turn his face to *i.*
Zep. 2:11 *i.* of heathen worship

ISRAEL.
Gen. 32:28 na. no more J. but I.
35:10 I. sh. be name, 1 *K.* 18:31
47:31 I. bowed him. on bed's h.
48:20 in thee sh. I. bless, 49:24
Ex. 5:2 voice to let I. go, 14:5,30
Num. 10:29 good concerning I.
  36 return to I. 20:14 ; 21:2, 17
23:7 defy I. ; 24:17 out of I.
Deut. 33:28 I. dwell, 1 *K.* 4:25
1 *Chr.* 29:18 G. of I. 1 *K.* 18:36 ;
  2 *Chr.* 6:16 ; 30:6 ; *Jer.* 31:1
Ps. 14:7 I. shall be glad, 53:6
25:22 redeem I. out of all troub.
121:4 that keepeth I. nei. slum.
125:5 peace sh. be upon I. 128:6
Jer. 14:8 O Lord, hope of I. 17:13
50:20 iniquity of I. sought, 51:5
Hos. 11:1 I. a child, I loved him
  8 how deliver thee, I ? 12:12
Acts 28:20 for hope of I. Israel
Rom. 9:6 not all I. of I. 27, 31
10:1 prayer for I. they be saved
  19 did not I. know?
11:2 intercession ag. I. 7, 26
1 *Cor.* 10:18 behold I. after flesh
Gal. 6:16 peace upon the I. of G.

O ISRAEL.
Ex. 32:4 these be thy gods, O I.
Num. 24:5 thy tabernacles, O I.
Deut. 4:1 hearken, O I. 27:9
5:1 O I. 6:3, 4 ; 9:1 ; 20:3 ; *Ps.*
  50:7 ; *Is.* 44:1 ; 48:12
33:29 happy O I. *Mark* 12:29

2 *Sam.* 20:1 ev. man to his tents,
  O I. 1 *K.* 12:16 ; 2 *Chr.* 10:16

1 *K.* 12:28 behold thy gods, O I.
Ps. 115:9 O I. trust thou in Lord
Is. 40:27 why speak. thou, O I.?
43:1 O I. fear not, 22 ; *Jer.* 30:10
44:21 remember these, O I. 49:3
Jer. 4:1 return, O I. *Hos.* 14:1
Ezek. 13:4 O I. thy prophets
Hos. 9:1 rejoice not, O I. for joy
10:9 O I. thou hast sinned from
13:9 O I. thou hast destr. thys.

Amos 4:12 to meet thy God, O I.
Zep. 3:14 shout O I. be glad

ISRAELITE.
Num. 25:14 the I. that was slain
2 *Sam.* 17:25 son of Ithra, an I.
John 1:47 behold an I. indeed
Rom. 11:1 I also am an I.

ISRAELITES.
Ex. 9:7 not one of cattle of I.
Lev. 23:42 I. shall dwell in booths
Jos. 3:17 I. passed on dry ground
1 *Chr.* 9:2 first inhabit. were I.
Rom. 9:4 to whom pertaineth
2 *Cor.* 11:22 are they I. ? so am I.

ISRAELITISH.   *Lev.* 24:10, 11

ISSACHAR.
Gen. 30:18 I. called his name I.
35:23 L. son, I. 46:13 ; 1 *Chr.* 7:1
49:14 I. is a strong ass
Deut. 27:12 I. st. to bless, 33:18
1 *K.* 4:17 Jehosh. an officer in I.
1 *Chr.* 12:40 that were nigh to I.
26:5 I. seventh son of O.-edom
2 *Chr.* 30:18 I. had not cleansed
Ezek. 48:25 border of Simeon, I.

Tribe of ISSACHAR.
Num. 1:29 numbered of *t. of* I.
2:5 next Judah shall be *t. of* I.
34:26 prince of *t. of* I. Paltiel
Jos. 19:23 inheritance of *t. of* I.
  21:6 families of *tribe of* I. and
  Asher, 28 ; 1 *Chr* 6:62, 72
Rev. 7:7 *t. of* I. were seal. 12,000

ISSUE, Substantive.
Gen. 48:6 I. which th. begettest
Lev. 12:7 *i.* of blood, 15:25 ; *Mat.*
  9:20; *Mark* 5:25; *Luke* 8:43, 44
15:2 hath running *i.* 3 ; 22:4
  8 he that hath *i.* spit upon, 28
Is. 22:24 the offspring and I.
Ezek. 23:20 *i.* like the *i.* of horses
Mat. 22:25 having no *i.* left wife

ISSUE.
2 *K.* 20:18 sons that *i. Is.* 39:7
Ezek. 47:8 waters *i.* toward east

ISSUED.
Job 38:8 break forth as if it *i.*
Ezek. 47:1 waters *i.* from under
  12 waters *i.* out of sanctuary
Dan. 7:10 fiery str. *i.* came forth
Rev. 9:17 out of mouth *i.* fire 18

ISSUES.
Ps. 68:20 to God belong the *i.*
Prov. 4:23 out of heart are *i.*

ITALIAN.   *Acts* 10:1

ITALY.
Acts 18:2 cert. Jew come from I.
27:1 that we should sail into I.
Heb. 13:24 they of I. salute you

ITCH, ING.
Deut. 28:27 L. smite thee with *i.*
2 Tim. 4:3 teachers having *i.* ears

ITHAMAR.
Ex. 6:23 Abihu and I. 1 *Chr.* 6:3
Num. 4:28 under hand of I.

1 *Chr.* 24:3 Abimel. of sons of I.
Ezr. 8:2 of sons of I. Daniel

ITHIEL.
Neh. 11:7 I. son of Jes. *Prov.* 30:1
ITUREA. *Luke* 3:1

IVAH.
2 *K.* 18:34 gods of Hena and I. ?
19:13 wh. king of I. ? *Is.* 37:13

IVORY.
1 *K.* 10:18 throne of *i.* 2 *Chr.* 9:17

22 silver and *i.* 2 *Chr.* 9:21
22:39 *i.* house wh. Ahab made
Ps. 45:8 out of the *i.* palaces
Cant. 5:14 his belly as bright *i.*
7:4 thy neck is as a tower of *i.*
Ezek. 27:6 thy benches of *i.*
15 bro. for present horns of *i.*
Amos 3:15 houses of *i.* sh. perish
6:4 that lie upon beds of *i.*
Rev. 18:12 no man buy. ves. of *i.*

J

JAAZANIAH.
2 *K.* 25:23 J. came to Gedaliah
Jer. 35:3 J. of Rechab. *Ezek.* 8:11

JABAL. *Gen.* 4:20
JABBOK. *Gen.* 32:22; *Deut.* 2:37;
3:16; *Jos.* 12:2

JABESH.
1 *Sam.* 11:5 S. of men of J. 31:12
2 *K.* 15:10 the son of J. conspired

JABESH-GILEAD.
Jud. 21:8 none fr. J.-G. 10, 12, 14
1 *Sam.* 11:1 Naha. enc. ag. J.-G.
31:11 J.-G. heard Phi. had done,
1 *Chr.* 10:12
2 *Sam.* 2:4 men of J.-G. 21:12
JABEZ. 1 *Chr.* 2:55; 4:9, 10

JABIN.
Jos. 11:1 when J. king of Hazor
Jud. 4:2 sold into hand of J. 24
Ps. 83:9 do to them as unto J.

JACHIN.
1 *K.* 7:21 right h. J. 2 *Chr.* 3:17

JACINTH.
Rev. 9:17 breastplates of fire, *j.*
21:20 eleventh found. was a *j.*

JACOB.
Gen. 25:26 he was called J. 27
Num. 23:7 curse me, J. and defy
24:17 sh. come a Star out of J.
Deut. 33:28 of J. on land of corn
Ps. 20:1 God of J. 46:7; 75:9; 76:6;
81:1; 84:8; 94:7; 114:7; 132:2;
146:5
87:2 Z. more than dwell. of J.
105:23 J. sojourned in land of H.
135:4 L. chos. J. *Is.* 10:21; 14:1
Is. 2:3 of J. 41:21; *Mic.* 4:2; *Mat.*
22:32; *Mark* 12:26; *Luke* 20:37;
Acts 3:13; 7:32, 46
27:9 iniq. of J. purged, 48:20
41:14 thou worm J. *Jer.* 30:10
44:5 call himself by name J. 23
58:14 feed with heritage of J.
Amos 7:2 by whom sh. J. arise? 5
Mal. 1:2 I. yet I loved J. *Ro.* 9:13
3:6 sons of J. not consumed
Mat. 1:2 I. begat J.; 15 Matthan
8:11 J. in king. of G. *Luke* 13:28
John 4:6 J.'s well was there
Rom. 11:26 turn ungodl. from J.
Heb. 11:20 by faith Is. bles. J. 21

JAEL.
Jud. 4:17 fled to tent of J. 5:6
JAH. *Ps.* 68:4

JAHAZ.
Num. 21:23 fou. at J. *Deut.* 2:32
Is. 15:4 heard to J. *Jud.* 11:20

JAHAZAH.
Jos. 21:36 J. to Lev. *Jer.* 48:21

JAILER.
Acts 16:23 chargi..g *j.* to keep

JAIR.
Num. 32:41 J. took to. *Deut.* 3:14
Jud. 10:3 J. judged Is. 22 years
5 J. died; 1 *Chr.* 2:22 begat J.

JAIRUS.
Mark 5:22 J. a ruler, *Luke* 8:41
JAMBRES. 2 *Tim.* 3:8

JAMES.
Mat. 4:21 J. and John, *Mark* 1:19
10:2 J. son of Zeb. *Mark* 3:17
3 J. son, *Mark* 3:18; *Acts* 1:13
13:55 J. and Joses, *Mark* 6:3;
15:40; 16:1; *Luke* 24:10
17:1 Peter, J. and John, *Mark*
5:37; 9:2; 13:3; 14:33; *Luke*
8:51; *Acts* 1:13
Mark 10:41 displ. wi. J. *Lu.* 5:10
Acts 12:2 Herod killed J. wi. sw.
17 show to J. 15:13; 21:18
1 *Cor.* 15:7 after that seen of J.
Gal. 1:19 save J. Lord's brother
2:12 certain came from J. 9

JANGLING.
1 *Tim.* 1:6 turned aside to vain *j.*
JANNA. *Luke* 3:24
JANNES. 2 *Tim.* 3:8

JAPHETH.
Gen. 5:32 J. son of N. 6:10; 7:13
9:23 Shem and J. took garm. 18
27 God sh. enlarge J. 1 *Chr.* 1:4
10:1 unto J. sons born, 21

JAREB. *Hos.* 5:13; 10:6
JARED. *Gen.* 5:15; *Luke* 3:37
JASHER. *Jos.* 10:13; 2 *Sam.* 1:18

JASON.
Acts 17:5 house of J. *Rom.* 16:21

JASPER.
Ex. 28:20 onyx and *j.* 39:13
Ezek. 28:13 diamond and *j.* cov.
Rev. 4:3 to look upon like a *j.*
21:11 light was like to *j.* stone
18 build. of wall of city was *j.*
19 the first foundation was *j.*

JAVAN.
Gen. 10:2 sons of Jap. J. 1 *Chr.* 1:5
Is. 66:19 those that escape to J.
Ezek. 27:13 J. and Tubal thy, 19

JAVELIN.
Num. 25:7 took a *j.* in his hand
1 *Sam.* 18:10 *j.* in S. hand, 19:9
19:10 he smote the *j.* into wall

JAW, S.
Jud. 15:19 God clave place in *j.*
Job 29:17 I break *j.* of the wicked
41:2 bore *j.* thro'. with a thorn ?
Ps. 22:15 tongue cleaveth to *j.*
Is. 30:28 a bridle in *j.* of people
Hos. 11:4 take off yoke on their *j.*

JAWBONE.
Jud. 15:15 Samson found *j.* of ass
16 with *j.* of ass have I slain
17 cast away *j.* out of his hand

JAW-TEETH.
Prov. 30:14 their *j.-t.* as knives

JAZER.
Num. 32:1 land of J. 3; *Is.* 16:9

JEALOUS.
Ex. 20:5 I the Lord thy G. am a
j. God, 34:14; *Deut.* 4:24;
5:9; 6:15; *Jos.* 24:19
Num. 5:14 he *j.* of his wife
1 *K.* 19:10 have been *j.* for L. 14
Ezek. 39:25 *j.* for my holy name
Joel 2:18 then will the L. be *j.*
Nah. 1:2 God is *j.* and L. reven.
Zec. 1:14 *j.* for Jer.; 8:2 *j.* for Z.
2 *Cor.* 11:2 for I am *j.* over you

JEALOUSY.
Num. 5:14 sp. of *j.* come on him
15 it is an offering of *j.* 18, 25
29 this is the law of *j.*
25:11 consumed not Is. in my *j.*
Deut. 29:20 *j.* smoke ag. man
32:16 prov. him to *j.* 1 *K.* 14:22
21 moved me to *j.* them to *j.*
Ps. 78:58 mov. to *j.* with images
79:5 how long, L. sh. thy *j.* bu. ?
Prov. 6:34 *j.* is the rage of man
Cant. 8:6 *j.* is cruel sa the grave
Is. 42:13 stir up *j.* like man of w.
Ezek. 8:3 wh. seat image of *j.* *j.* 5
16:38 give blood in fury and *j.*
42 my *j.* shall depart from thee
23:25 I will set my *j.* ag. thee
36:5 in *j.* have I spok. 6; 38:19
Zep. 1:18 land dev. by *j.* 3:8
Zec. 1:14 jealous for Z. wi. *j.* 8:2
Rom. 10:19 will provoke you to *j.*
11:11 Gen. to provoke them to *j.*
1 *Cor.* 10:22 do we prov. L. to *j.* ?
2 *Cor.* 11:2 jealous with godly *j.*

JEBUSITE.
Gen. 10:16 Canaan begat the J.
Ex. 33:2 will drive out J. 34:11
2 *Sam.* 24:16, 18; 1 *Chr.* 1:14; 21:15

JEBUSITES.
Num. 13:29 J. dw. in mountains
Jos. 15:63 J. dw. with children
Jud. 1:21 driveth J. 19:11; 2 *Sam.*
5:8

JECONIAH. 1 *Chr.* 3:16, 17;
Jer. 24:1; 27:20; 28:4
JEDIDIAH. 2 *Sam.* 12:25
JEDUTHUN. 1 *Chr.* 16:41, 42;
25:6; 2 *Chr.* 29:14

JEGAR-SAHADUTHA.
Gen. 31:47 La. called heap J.-S.

JEHOAHAZ, *called Ahaziah.*
2 *K.* 10:35 J. son of Jehu reigned
13:1 J. son of J. began to reign
23:30 peo. took J. 2 *Chr.* 21:17

JEHOASH, *or* JOASH.
2 *K.* 11:21 J. seven years old
12:20 slew J. in house M. 13:10
14:8 messengers to J.; J. slept

JEHOIACHIN.

2 *K.* 24:8 J. 18 years old when he
25:27 lift head of J. *Jer.* 52:31
2 *Chr.* 36:9 J. eight years old

JEHOIADA.

2 *Sam.* 8:18 son of J. 20:23 ; 1 *Chr.*
11:22, 24 ; 1 *K.* 1:44 ; 4:4
2 *K.* 11:17 J. ma. cov. 2 *Chr.* 23:16
2 *Chr.* 24:2 all days of J. 17 ; 22
Jer. 29:26 thee pri. instead of J.

JEHOIAKIM.

2 *K.* 23:34 name to J. 2 *Chr.* 36:4
Jer. 22:18 concerning J. 26:22
36:28 J. burnt, 30 ; *Dan.* 1:2
52:2 did wh. was evil as J. had
JEHONADAB. 2 *K.* 10:15, 23

JEHORAM.

1 *K.* 22:50 J. son of Jeh. 2 *K.* 8:16
2 *K.* 1:17 J. reigned, 2 *Chr.* 17:8
2 *Chr.* 21:9 J. smote Edom. 16
22:5 went with J. ag. Hazael, 7

JEHOSHAPHAT.

2 *Sam.* 8:16 J. recorder, 20:24
1 *K.* 4:3, 17 ; 15:24 ; 1 *Chr.* 18:15
22:2 J. came to Ahab, 2 *K.* 3:14
1 *Chr.* 15:24 J. blew with trump.
2 *Chr.* 17:3 L. was with J. 18:9, 28
20:3 J. feared Lord, 21:12 ; 22:9
Joel 3:2 down to valley of J. 12

JEHOSHUA.

Num. 13:16 Oshea J. 1 *Chr.* 7:27

JEHOVAH.

Ex. 6:3 by J. was I not known
Ps. 83:18 wh. name alone is J.
Is. 12:2 Lord J. is my strength
26:4 the Lord J. is everlasting
JEHOVAH-JIREH. *Gen.* 22:14
JEHOVAH-NISSI. *Ex.* 17:15
JEHOVAH-SHALOM. *Jud.* 6:24

JEHU.

1 *K.* 16:1 J. son of H. 2 *Chr.* 20:34
19:16 J. son of Nimshi shalt
2 *K.* 9:2 look there J. 13, 14, 24
10:11 J. slew all remain. 18, 31
2 *Chr.* 19:2 J. to meet Jeh. 22:8
Hos. 1:4 blood of Jezreel on J.

JEOPARDED.

Jud. 5:18 peo. that *j.* their lives

JEOPARDY.

2 *Sam.* 23:17 men that went in *j.*
of their lives, 1 *Chr.* 11:19
1 *Chr.* 12:19 to *j.* of our heads
Luke 8:23 water, they were in *j.*
1 *Cor.* 15:30 why stand we in *j.*

JEPHTHAH.

Jud. 11:1 J. mighty, 3, 11, 40
12:7 J. judged Israel six years
1 *Sam.* 12:11 L. sent J. and del.
Heb. 11:32 would fail to tell of J.
JEPHUNNEH. *Num.* 13:6 ;
1 *Chr.* 7:38
JERAHMEEL. 1 *Chr.* 2:9, 33 ;
24:29 ; *Jer.* 36:26

JEREMIAH.

2 *K.* 23:31 ; 24:18 ; *Jer.* 52:1
2 *Chr.* 35:25 J. lamented for Jos.
36:12 humb. bef. J. 22 ; *Ezr.* 1:1
Neh. 10:2 J. sealed, 12:1, 12, 34
Jer. 1:1 words of J. son of Hilk.
51:64 thus far are words of J.
Mat. 2:17 was spoken by J. 27:9
16:14 others say thou art J.

JERICHO.

Jos. 2:1 view J. 3:16 ; 6:1 ; 24:11
6:26 cursed man that buildeth J.
1 *K.* 16:34 days did Hiel build J.
Luke 10:30 went down to J.
Heb. 11:30 walls of J. fell

JEROBOAM.

1 *K.* 11:28 J. mighty man of valor
40 Solomon sought to kill J.
13:1 J. st. by altar, 14:1, 6, 30

---

2 *K.* 10:31 ; 13:6, 13 ; 14:24
2 *Chr.* 11:14 J. cast off L. 13:8, 20
Amos 7:11 Am. saith, J. shall die
JEROBOAM, **with Nebat.**
1 *K.* 11:26 ; 12:15 ; 16:3, 26, 31 ;
21:22 ; 22:52 ; 2 *K.* 3:3 ; 9:9 ;
10:29 ; 13:2, 11 ; 14:24 ; 15:9,
18, 24, 28 ; 2 *Chr.* 10:15
JERUBBAAL. *Jud.* 6:32 ; 7:1 ;
8:29,35 ; 9:2,5,16,28 ; 1 *Sam.* 12:11
JERUBBESHETH. 2 *Sam.* 11:21

JERUSALEM.

Jos. 18:28 wh. is J. *Jud.* 19:10
2 *Sam.* 24:16 on J. 1 *Chr.* 21:15
1 *K.* 3:1 end of build. wall of J.
11:13 J. I have chosen, 2 *K.*
23:27 ; 2 *Chr.* 6:6
Ps. 51:18 build walls of J. 79:1, 3 ;
147:2
122:3 J. is builded as a city
6 pray for peace of J. 128:5
125:2 as mount. round about J.
137:6 pref. not J. abo. ch. joy, 7
Is. 31:5 defend J. 33:20
40:2 sp. comfortably to J. 52:9
62:1 for J.'s sake not rest till, 7
64:10 J. a desola. *Jer.* 2:2 ; 9:11
Jer. 39:8 walls of J. 44:2, 6
Joel 3:1 bring captivi. of J. 20 ;
Zec. 14:11
Zec. 1:17 choose J. 2:12 ; 8:3
Mal. 3:4 offering of J. sh. be ple.
Mat. 3:5 out to him J. *Mark* 1:5
16:21 how he must go to J.
Luke 2:22 parents bro. him to J.
13:4 above all dwelt in J. ?
33 prophet perish out of J.
21:20 J. comp. with armies, 24
24:49 tarry in J. ; 47 begin. at J.
John 4:20 in J. men are to wors.
12:12 heard Jesus coming to J.
Acts 9:2 bound unto J. 20:22
21:31 all J. in uproar, 22:18
Rom. 15:31 service for J. accept,
1 *Cor.* 16:3
Gal. 4:25 J. wh. now is ; 26 J. ab.
Rev. 3:12 the new J. 21:2, 10

O JERUSALEM.

Ps. 116:19 midst of thee, O J.
122:2 within thy gates, O J.
137:5 if I forget, O J. 147:12
Is. 40:9 O J. that bringest good
51:17 up, O J. ; 52:2 arise, O J.
52:1 put on thy garments, O J.
Jer. 4:14 O J. wash thy heart fr.
6:8 be thou instructed, O J.
7:29 cut off thy hair, O J. and
13:27 O J. wilt not be made cl.
15:5 pity upon thee, O J. ?
Mat. 23:37 O J. O J. *Luke* 13:34
JESHUA. *Ezr.* 2:2 ; 3:2

JESHURUN.

Deut. 32:15 J. wax. fat, 33:5, 26
Is. 44:2 fear not, thou J.

JESSE.

Ruth 4:17 O. fath. of J. *Mat.* 1:5
1 *Sam.* 16:1 J. the Beth-lehemite
9 sanctified J. and sons, 18, 19
20:31 as long as son of J. liveth
22:7 son of J. give fields ? 8, 9
25:10 who is David? son of J. ?
2 *Sam.* 20:1 son of J. 1 *K.* 12:16
1 *Chr.* 12:18 son of J. 2 *Chr.* 10:16
Is. 11:10 root of the stem of J.
10 a root of J. *Rom.* 15:12
Acts 13:22 found David son of J.

JESTING.

Eph. 5:4 nor *j.* not convenient
JESUITES. *Num.* 26:44

JESUS, *for Joshua.*
Acts 7:45 brought in with J. into
Heb. 4:8 if J. had given th. rest
JESUS, called *Justus.* *Col.* 4:11

JETHRO, *called Reuel.*

Ex. 3:1 kept flock of J. his fath.
4:18 Moses returned to J. his
18:1 when J. heard, 5, 6, 9, 12

JEW.

Est. 3:4 told them he was a J.
Rom. 1:16 to J. first, 2:9, 10
2:17 a J. and restest in law
28 he is not a J. 29
3:1 what advantage J. ? 10:12 ;
Gal. 3:28 ; *Col.* 3:11
1 *Cor.* 9:20 to J. a J. to gain J.
Gal. 2:14 a J. livest as Gentiles

JEWEL.

Prov. 11:22 J. of gold swine's sn.
20:15 lips of knowl. emotions *j.*
Ezek. 16:12 I put a *j.* on forehead

JEWELS.

Gen. 24:53 bro. forth *j.* of silver
Ex. 3:22 shall borrow *j.* of gold,
11:2 ; 12:35
35:22 they brought all *j.* of gold
Num. 31:51 took gold, even the *j.*
1 *Sam.* 6:8 *j.* of gold in coffer, 15
2 *Chr.* 20:25 riches and preci. *j.*
32:27 treasuries for all pleas. *j.*
Job 28:17 excha. of it not be for *j.*
Cant. 1:10 cheeks comely with *j.*
7:1 joints of thy thighs like *j.*
Is. 61:10 adorneth herself with *j.*
Ezek. 16:17 thy *j.* of my gold
39 shall take thy fair *j.* 23:26
Hos. 2:13 decked wi. ear. *j.* and *j.*
Mal. 3:17 when I make up my *j.*

King of the JEWS.

Mat. 2:2 born *K. of the J.* ?
27:11 art thou *K. of t. J.* ? *Mar.*
15:2 ; *Luke* 23:3 ; *John* 18:33
29 hail, *K. of the J. Mar.* 15:18 ;
John 19:3
37 this is *K. of the J. Mark*
15:26 ; *Luke* 23:38 ; *Jo.* 19:19
Mark 15:9 *K. of the J. John* 18:39
12 whom ye call *K. of the J.*
Luke 23:37 if thou be *K. of the J.*
John 19:21 I am *K. of the J.*
JEWESS. *Acts* 16:1 ; 24:24
JEWISH. *Tit.* 1:14
JEWRY. *Dan.* 5:13

JEZEBEL.

1 *K.* 16:31 took to wife J. 18:4
21:11 as J. had sent, 15, 23, 25
2 *K.* 9:7 at the hand of J. 10, 36
Rev. 2:20 sufferest that wom. J.

JEZREEL, *place and person.*

2 *Sam.* 2:9 Ish-bosh. king over J.
1 *K.* 18:45 Ahab went to J. 21:1
21:23 eat Jez. by J. 2 *K.* 9:10
2 *K.* 8:29 went to J. 2 *Chr.* 22:6
10:6 come to me to J. to-morrow
Hos. 1:4 avenge blood of J.
5 break bow in valley of J. 11
2:22 wine, and oil shall hear J.

JOAB.

2 *Sam.* 2:18 of Zeruiah, J. 22, 24
3:29 Ab. rest on J. 8:16 ; 20:23
11:7 demand. how J. did, 11, 14
14:3 J. put words in two, 19, 30
20:9 J. killed Amasa, 17
1 *K.* 1:7 Adonijah confer. with J.
2:28 J. fled to tabernacle of L.
1 *Chr.* 4:14 ; 11:6 ; 18:15 ; 27:34
Ezr. 2:6 of chil. of J. *Neh.* 7:11

JOAH.

2 *K.* 18:18 J. son of As. *Is.* 36:3
1 *Chr.* 6:21 J. son of Zim. 2 *K.* 26:4
JOANNA. *Luke* 3:27 ; 8:3

JOASH.

Jud. 6:11 to J. Abi-ezrite, 7:14

1 *K.* 22:26 back to J. king's son
2 *K.* 11:2 st. J. 2 *Chr.* 18:25 ; 24:22

JOB.
Gen. 46:13 sons of Issachar, J.
Job 1:1 man whose name was J.
42:17 J. died, being old
Ezek. 14:14 though D. and J. 20
Jam. 5:11 heard of patience of J.

JOEL.
1 *Sam.* 8:2 Samuel's first-born, J.
1 *Chr.* 15:11 David called J. 27:20
Joel 1:1 the word came to J.
Acts 2:16 spok. by the proph. J.

JOHANAN.
2. *K.* 25:23 J. ca. to G. *Jer.* 40:8
1 *Chr.* 3:15 sons of J. *J. Ezr.* 10:6
Jer. 41:11 wh. J. heard of all evil

JOHN, *son of Zacharias.*
Mat. 3:4 J. had raim *Mark* 1:6
Mat. 3:14 J. came, but J. for. him
14:10 behe. J. *Mark* 6:16 ; *Lu.* 9:9
21:26 hol. J. *Mar.* 11:32 ; *Lu.* 20:6
Luke 1:13 call his name J. 60
9:7 J. was risen from the dead
John 1:6 a man sent from God, J.
Acts 13:24 when J. first preached

JOHN, *the Apostle.*
Mat. 4:21 James and J. he called
th. 10:2 ; *Mark* 1:19 ; 3:17
Luke 22:8 Pet. and J. to prepare
Acts 3:1 Peter and J. went
12:2 Herod killed brother of J.
Rev. 1:1 signifi. it to serv. J. 4, 9
21:2 J. saw the new Jerusalem

JOHN. *Acts* 4:6
JOHN, surnamed *Mark. Acts*
12:12, 25 ; 13:5, 13 ; 15:37

JOIN.
Ez. 1:10 lest they J. enemies
Ezr. 9:14 J. in affinity with peo.
Prov. 11:21 hand J. in ha. 16:5
Is. 5:8 woe to them J. house
9:11 L. J. his enemies together
56:6 sons of stranger J. thems.
Jer. 50:5 let us J. ourselves to L.
Ezek. 37:17 J. th. one to another
Acts 5:13 no man J. himself
8:29 J. thyself to this chariot
9:26 Saul assayed to J. himself

JOINED.
Gen. 14:3 all these kings were J.
29:34 this time husb. be J. to me
2 *Chr.* 20:36 J. with Ahaziah, 37
Ezr. 4:12 up walls, J. foundatio.
Job 3:6 not be J. to days of year
41:17 leviathan's scales are J.
23 flakes of his flesh J. togeth.
Ps. 83:8 A. also is J. with them
Ec. 9:4 J. to all living is hope
Is. 13:15 every one J. them
14:1 strangers be J. with them
20 not J. with them in burial
56:3 nor him hath J. to L. speak
Ezek. 1:9 wings J. one to another
Hos. 4:17 Ephraim is J. to idols
Zec. 2:11 many nations J. to L.
Mat. 19:6 what G. J. *Mark* 10:9
Luke 15:15 J. himself to citizen
Acts 5:36 four hund. J. themsel.
18:7 house J. hard to synagogue
1 *Cor.* 1:10 perfect. J. in sa. mind
6:16 J. to a harlot is one body
17 J. to the Lord is one spirit
Eph. 4:16 whole body fitly J.
5:31 and shall be J. to his wife

See BAAL-PEOR.

JOINING.
1 *Chr.* 22:3 prepared iron for J.
2 *Chr.* 3:12 J. to wing of cherub

JOINT.
Gen. 32:25 Jac.'s thigh out of J.
Ps. 22:14 my bones are out of J.
Prov. 25:19 like foot out of J.
Eph. 4:16 wh. every J. supplieth

JOINTS.
1 *K.* 22:34 smote king of I. betw.
J. of harness, 2 *Chr.* 18:33
Cant. 7:1 J. of thighs like jewels
Dan. 5:6 J. of loins were loosed
Col. 2:19 body by J. knit togeth.
Heb. 4:12 divid. of J. and marrow

JOINT-HEIRS.
Rom. 8:17 and J. with Christ

JONADAB, *or* JEHONADAB.
2 *Sam.* 13:3 J. Amnon's friend
2 *K.* 10:15 J. came to meet Jehu
Jer. 35:6 J. commanded us, 18

JONAH, *or* JONAS.
2 *K.* 14:25 spake by his servant J.
Jon. 1:3 J. rose up, 7, 15, 17
4:6 the gourd to come over J.
Mat. 12:39, 41 ; 16:4 ; *Lu.* 11:29, 30
John 21:15 Simon son of J. 16, 17

JONATHAN.
Jud. 18:30 J. and his sons were
1 *Sam.* 13:2 men were with J. 22
14:13 J. climbed on hands
20:13 the Lord do so to J. 16, 37
2 *Sam.* 1:4 S. and J. are dead, 26
4:4 J. had a son was lame, 9:3
Jer. 40:8 J. came to Gedal. to M.

JOPPA.
2 *Chr.* 2:16 by sea to J. *Ezr.* 3:7
Jon. 1:3 Jonah went down to J.
Acts 9:36 at J. a disciple, 43
10:5 send to J. call for Sim. 32
11:5 in the city of J. praying

JORAM, *called* JEHORAM.
2 *Sam.* 8:10 sent J. his son, to
David
2 *K.* 8:16 J. of A. ; 28 wound. J.
9:14 Jehu conspired ag. J. 24

1 *Chr.* 26:25 Levites J. over tre.
2 *Chr.* 22:7 destr. by com. to J.

JORDAN.
Gen. 13:11 Lot chose plain of J.
Jos. 3:15 J. overfloweth banks
4:3 stones out of midst of J.
22:25 made J. a border betw. us
Jud. 3:28 fords of J. 7:24 ; 12:5
2 *Sam.* 19:15 king returned to J.
2 *K.* 2:13 Elisha stood by J.
5:10 saying, Wash in J. seven
Job 40:23 trust. can draw up J.
Ps. 42:6 remember fr. land of J.
114:3 J. was driven back, 5
Jer. 12:5 do in swelling of J. ?
49:19 from swelling of J. 50:44
Zec. 11:3 pride of J. is spoiled
Mat. 3:6 in J. *Mark* 1:5, 9

Beyond JORDAN.
Gen. 50:10 floor of Atad *bey.* J. 11
Deut. 3:25 good land *beyond* J.
Jos. 13:8 inherit. *beyond* J. 18:7
Is. 9:1 *bey.* J. in Galil. *Mat.* 4:15
John 1:28 Bethabara *bey.* J. 3:26

Over JORDAN.
Gen. 32:10 I passed over J.
Num. 32:5 br. us not o. J. 33:51
Deut. 3:27 not go o. J. 4:21 ; 31:2
9:1 to pass o. J. this day, 11:31
Jos. 1:2 go over J. 11
4:22 Israel came over J. 24:11
2 *Sam.* 2:29 passed o. J. 17:22 ;
19:15 ; 1 *Chr.* 12:15 ; 19:17

JORIM, JOSE. *Luke* 3:29

JOSEPH.
Gen. 30:24 she called his name J.
37:5 J. dreamed a dream
39:5 Egypt.'s house for J.'s sake
40:9 butler told his dream to J.
49:22 J. is a fruitful bough, 26
50:7 J. went up to bury father
Deut. 33:13 J. blessed be his land
1 *Chr.* 5:2 the birthright was J.
Ps. 80:1 leadest J. like a flock
105:17 J. who was sold for a ser.

Ezek. 37:16 for J. stick of Ephr.
47:13 J. shall have two portions
48:32 one gate of J. gate of B.
Amos 6:6 grieved for afflict. of J.
Acts 7:9 patriarchs sold J. 13, 14
Heb. 11:21 J. blessed sons of J. 22

JOSEPH, *husband of Mary.*
Mat. 1:16 ; 2:13 ; *Luke* 2:4 ; 3:23 ;
4:22 ; *John* 1:45 ; 6:42

JOSEPH, *name of divers men.*
Num. 13:7 of Igal, son of J.
Mat. 27:57 J. of Arim. 59 ; *Mark*
15:43, 45 ; *Lu.* 23:50 ; *Jo.* 19:38
Luke 3:24 was son of J. 26, 30
Acts 1:23 two, J. called Barsabas

JOSES.
Mat. 13:55 Ja. and J. *Mark* 6:3
27:56 moth. of J. *Mark* 15:40, 47
Acts 4:36 J. surnamed Barnabas

JOSHUA, JEHOSHUA, OSHEA.
Ex. 17:13 J. discomfited Amalek
24:13 Moses and his minister J.
Jos. 1:10 J. commanded officers,
2:1 to 24:31
1 *Sam.* 6:14 into field of J. 18
1 *K.* 16:34 wh. he spake by J.
Hag. 1:1 J. son of Josed. 12, 14
Zec. 3:1 showed me J. h.-priest
6:11 set crowns on head of J.

JOSIAH.
1 *K.* 13:2 child born, J. by name
2 *K.* 21:24 J. king, 2 *Chr.* 33:25
22:1 J. was eight years old
23:29 J. ag. Phar. 2 *Chr.* 35:22
2 *Chr.* 35:1 J. kept passo. 18–25
Jer. 1:2 in days of J. 3:6
Zep. 1:1 word came in days of J.
Mat. 1:10 Amon begat J. 11

JOT.
Mat. 5:18 one J. or tittle

JOTHAM.
Jud. 9:5 J. son of Jerubbaal, 21
2 *K.* 15:5 J. judged, 2 *Chr.* 26:21
1 *Chr.* 2:47 sons of Jahdai, J. 5:17
2 *Chr.* 27:6 J. became mighty
Is. 1:1 ; *Ho.* 1:1 ; *Mic.* 1:1 ; *Mat.* 1:9

JOURNEY.
Gen. 24:21 L. made J. prosperous
31:23 La. pursued him 7 days' J.
Ex. 13:20 took J. from Succoth
16:1 Israelites took J. from Elim
Num. 9:10 be in J. yet keep pass.
13 not in J. forbear. keep pass.
Deut. 1:2 eleven days J. from H.
10:11 take thy J. before people
Jos. 9:11 ta'. victuals for your J.
Jud. 4:9 J. thou takest not
1 *Sam.* 15:18 L. sent thee on a J.
1 *K.* 18:27 or he is in a J.
19:7 the J. is too great for thee
2 *K.* 3:9 compa. of seven days' J.
Neh. 2:6 how long sh. thy J. be?
Prov. 7:19 man gone a long J.
Mat. 10:10 nor scrip for your J.
Mark 6:8 nothing for J. *Luke* 9:3
Luke 11:6 a friend of mine in J.
15:13 took J. into a far country
John 4:6 Jesus wearied with J.
Rom. 1:10 have prosperous J.
15:24 I trust to see you in my J.
1 *Cor.* 16:6 bring me on my J.
Tit. 3:13 Zenas and Apollos on J.
3 *John* 6 whom bring forw. on J.

Day's JOURNEY.
Num. 11:31 quails fall a *day's* J.
1 *K.* 19:4 went *day's* J. to wild.
Jon. 3:4 to enter city J. *a* J.
Luke 2:44 a *d.'s* J. am. acquaint.
Acts 1:12 from Jerusal. a *day's* J.

See THREE DAYS.

JOURNEYED.

Gen. 12:9 Ab. *j.* going south, 20:1
13:11 Lot *j.* east ; 33:17 Jacob *j.*
35:5 Israel *j.* toward Beth-el
Ex. 40:37 th. *j.* not, *Num.* 9:21
Num. 9:17 children of Israel *j.* 18
19 kept charge of L. and *j.* not
Acts 9:3 as S. *j.* he came near Da.
7 men *j.* with him stood, 26:13

JOURNEYING, S.

Num. 10:28 *j.* of Israel's armies
29 we are *j.* to the place
Luke 13:22 as he was *j.* toward J.
2 *Cor.* 11:26 in *j.* often, in perils

JOURNEYS.

Gen. 13:3 Abram went on his *j.*
Ex. 17:1 *j.* according to comma.
40:36 went on in *j. Num.* 10:12
38 cloud on taber. thro' their *j.*
Num. 10:6 an alarm for their *j.*
33:1 these are the *j.* of Israel, 2

JOY, Substantive.

1 *Chr.* 12:40 there was *j.* in Israel
15:16 lift. up the voice with *j.*
25 went to bring the ark wi. *j.*
29:17 seen with *j.* the peo. offer
Ezr. 3:13 not discern the peo. of *j.*
6:16 ded. of hou. of God with *j.*
Neh. 8:10 *j.* of L. is your strength
12:43 *j.* of Jern. heard afar off
Est. 8:16 light, *j.* and honor
9:22 turned from sorrow to *j.*
make days of feasting and *j.*
Job 8:19 this is the *j.* of his way
20:5 *j.* of hypocrite but for mo.
21:3 caus. widow's hea. sing *j.*
33:26 will see his face with *j.*
41:22 sorrow turned to *j.*
Ps. 16:11 presence fulness of *j.*
27:6 offer in tabern. sacrifi. of *j.*
30:5 *j.* cometh in the morning
42:4 I went with the voice of *j.*
43:4 I go to G. my exceeding *j.*
48:2 *j.* of the earth is mount Z.
51:12 restore to me *j.* of salva.
67:4 be glad and sing for *j.*
105:43 bro. forth people with *j.*
126:5 sow in tears sh. reap in *j.*
137:6 prefer not Jer. to chief *j.*
Prov. 12:20 counsel. of peace is *j.*
14:10 stranger not intermed. *j.*
15:21 folly is *j.* desti. of wisdom
23 man hath *j.* by ans. of mou.
17:21 father of a fool hath no *j.*
21:15 *j.* to the just to do judg.
23:24 beget. wise child have *j.*
Ec. 2:10 with. not heart from *j.*
26 God giveth knowled. and *j.*
5:20 God ans. him in *j.* of heart
9:7 go thy way, eat bread wi. *j.*
Is. 9:3 increased *j.* accord. to *j*
17 L. sh. have no *j.* in yo. men
12:3 with *j.* shall ye draw water
16:10 *j.* taken out plentiful field
24:8 *j.* harp ceas. ; 11 *j.* is dark.
29:19 meek sh. incre. th. *j.* in L.
32:13 houses of *j.* ; 14 *j.* w. asses
35:2 rej. even with *j.* and sing.
10 everl. *j.* on their heads, 51:11
52:9 br. into *j.* ; 55:12 go with *j.*
60:15 a *j.* of many generations
61:3 give them oil of *j.*
7 everlasting *j.* sh. be to them
65:14 servants shall sing for *j.*
18 beho. I create her peo. a *j.*
66:5 he shall appear to your *j.*
10 rejoice for *j.* with her
Jer. 15:16 word was *j.* of my hea.
31:13 turn th. mourning into *j.*
33:9 it sh. be to me a name of *j.*
11 there sh. be heard voice of *j.*
48:27 thou skippedst for *j.*

Jer. 48:33 *j.* is tak. fr. plen. field
49:25 city of my *j.*
Lam. 2:15 the *j.* of whole earth
5:15 the *j.* of our heart is ceased

Ezek. 24:25 take fr. them *j.* of gl.
36:5 with the *j.* of all th. heart
Hos. 9:1 rejoice not, O Is. for *j.*
Joel 1:12 *j.* is withered from men
Zep. 3:17 rejo. over thee with *j.*
Mat. 13:20 anon with *j.* receiveth it, *Luke* 8:13
44 for *j.* thereof goeth and sell.
25:21 enter into *j.* of thy L. 23
Lu. 1:44 babe leaped in wo. for *j.*
6:23 rej. in that day, leap for *j.*
10:17 seventy returned with *j.*
15:7 *j.* in heav. over one sinner
10 there is *j.* in pres. of angels
24:41 they yet believed not for *j.*
John 3:29 my *j.* therefo. is fulfil.
15:11 that my *j.* might remain in you, th. your *j.* might be full
16:20 sorrow be turned to *j.*
21 for *j.* that a man is born
22 your *j.* no man tak. fr. you
24 that your *j.* be full
17:13 *j.* fulfilled in themselves
Acts 2:28 make me full of *j.*
13:52 discip. were filled with *j.*
20:24 finish my course with *j.*
Rom. 14:17 kingdom of God is *j.*
15:13 God filled you with *j.*
32 co. to you wi. *j.* by will of G.
2 *Cor.* 1:24 are helpers of your *j.*
2:3 that my *j.* is *j.* of you all
7:13 more joyed we for *j.* of T.
8:2 their *j.* abounded to riches
Gal. 5:22 Spirit is love, *j.* peace
Phil. 1:4 making request with *j.*
25 furtherance and *j.* of faith
2:2 my *j.* 4:1 *j.* and crown
1 *Thes.* 1:6 received word with *j.*
2:19 what is your hope or *j. ?*
20 for ye are our glory and *j.*
3:9 *j.* wherewith wo *j.* before G.
2 *Tim.* 1:4 I may be filled with *j.*
Phile. 20 let me have *j.* of thee
Heb. 12:2 for *j.* that was bef. him
13:17 do it with *j.* not with grief
Jam. 1:2 count it *j.* when ye fall
4:9 *j.* be turned into heaviness
1 *Pet.* 1:8 rej. with *j.* unspeakab.
4:13 glad also with exceeding *j.*
1 *John* 1:4 *j.* be full, 2 *John* 12
3 *John* 4 no greater *j.* than to h.
Jude 24 faultless with exceed. *j.*
See GLADNESS.

Great JOY.

1 *K.* 1:40 peo. rejoiced with *g. j.*
2 *Chr.* 30:26 *g. j.* in Jerusalem
Neh. 12:43 rejoice with *great j.*
Mat. 2:10 rejoiced with *great j.*
28:8 from sep. wi. fear and *g. j.*
Luke 2:10 br. tidings of *great j.*
24:52 returned to Jer. with *g. j.*
Acts 8:8 there was *g. j.* in th. city
15:3 caused *g. j.* to the brethren
Phile. 7 we have *g. j.* in thy love

Shout, or Shouted for JOY.

Ezr. 3:12 *shouted* aloud for *j.*
Job 38:7 sons of God *shouted* f. *j.*
Ps. 5:11 let them *sh.* f. *j.* 35:27
32:11 *s.* f. *j.* all th. are upright
65:13 the valleys *shout for j.*
132:9 let thy saints *s. for j.* 16

JOY, Verb.

Ps. 21:1 shall *j.* in thy strength
Is. 9:3 *j.* bef. thee accord. to joy
65:19 I rejoice and *j.* in my peo.
Hab. 3:18 I will *j.* in G. of salva.
Zep. 3:17 *j.* over thee with sing.
Rom. 5:11 but we also *j.* in God
Phil. 2:17 *j.* and rejoice wi. you
1 *Thes.* 3:9 joy wherewith ye *j.*

JOYED.

2 *Cor.* 7:13 more joy for joy of T.

JOYFUL.

1 *K.* 8:66 went to their tents *j.*
Ezr. 6:22 L. hath made them *j.*
Job 3:7 no *j.* voice come therein

Ps. 5:11 th. love thy name be *j.*
35:9 my soul be *j.* in the Lord
63:5 praise thee with *j.* lips
66:1 make a *j.* noise to God
81:1 make *j.* noise to G. of Jac.
89:15 blessed peo. know *j.* sound
95:1 make *j.* noise to rock of sa.
2 *j.* noise with psa. 98:4 ; 100:1
98:6 make a *j.* noise before L.
8 hills be *j.* together before L.
113:9 barren be *j.* mother of ch.
149:2 children of Zion *j.* in king
5 let the saints be *j.* in glory
Ec. 7:14 in day of prosper. be *j.*
Is. 49:13 sing heav. be *j.* earth
56:7 make *j.* in house of prayer

Is. 61:10 soul shall be *j.* in my G.
2 *Cor.* 7:4 *j.* in all our tribulat.

JOYFULLY.

Ec. 9:9 live *j.* wi. wife th. lovest
Luke 19:6 Zacch. received him *j.*
Heb. 10:34 took *j.* spoil. of goods

JOYFULNESS.

Deut. 28:47 servedst not L. w. *j.*
Col. 1:11 to long-suffering with *j.*

JOYING.

Col. 2:5 with you in the spirit, *j.*

JOYOUS.

Is. 22:2 art full of stirs, a *j.* city
23:7 is this your *j.* city, whose
32:13 all houses of joy in *j.* city
Heb. 12:11 no chastening seem. *j.*

JUBAL. *Gen.* 4:21

JUBILEE.

Lev. 25:9 trumpet of the *j.* 10:54
27:17 his field from year of *j.* 18
Num. 36:4 *j.* then th. inheritance

JUDAH.

Gen. 29:35 she called him name J.
35:23 the sons of Leah, J.
38:15 J. thought Tamar a harlot
46:12 sons of J. 28 ; *Num.* 26:19
49:8 J. he whom thy brethren
9 J. is a lion's whelp
10 sceptre not depart from J.
Ex. 1:2 sons of Israel, Levi, J.
Num. 2:3 camp of J. shall pitch
Deut. 33:7 blessing of J. 27:12
Jos. 7:17 bro. family of J. 18:5
Jud. 1:2 J. go first, 19 ; 10:9
1 *Sam.* 18:16 all J. loved David
2 *Sam.* 5:5 David reigned, 19:15
1 *K.* 14:22 J. did evil, 2 *K.* 17:19
2 *K.* 8:19 L. not destroy J. 14:10
21:11 ma. J. sin, 16 ; 2 *Chr.* 33:9
23:27 remove J. out of my sight
2 *Chr.* 12:12 in J. things w. well
Ps. 60:7 J. my lawgiver, 108:8
76:1 in J. God known, 114:2
Is. 1:1 vision conc. J. 3:1 ; 7:6
11:12 together dispersed of J. 13
22:8 discovered covering of J.
Jer. 17:1 sin of J. writ. with iron
33:7 captiv. of J. return, 42:15
50:20 sins of J. not found, 53:5
Joel 3:20 J. dw. for ever, Am. 2:4
Mic. 5:2 among thousands of J.
Zec. 2:12 L. inh. J. 12:7 ; 14:14
Mal. 2:11 J. dealt treacherously
3:4 offering of J. pleasant
Mat. 1:2 Ja. begat J. 3 J. begat
Luke 3:33 Phares was son of J.
Heb. 7:14 our L. sprang of J.

Land of JUDAH.

Deut. 34:2 showed him land of J.
Ruth 1:7 to return in land of J.
Is. 19:17 of J. a terror, 26:1
Mat. 2:6 Bethlehem, in l. of J.

Men of JUDAH.

Jud. 15:10 m. of J. why come
2 *Sam.* 2:4 m. of J. anointed D.
19:14 heart of J. 43 ; 20:2
24:9 men of J. 500,000
Ezr. 10:9 m. of J. gathered toget.

Is. 5:7 *m. of* J. his pleas. plant
Jer. 36:31 upon the *men of* J. all
43:9 in sight of *men of* J.
44:27 all *m. of* J. be consumed
Dan. 9:7 confusion to *men of* J.

Tribe of JUDAH.
Num. 1:27 numb. *of tribe of* J.
7:12 Nashon, prince of *t. of* J.
1 *K.* 12:20 *t. of* J. followed Dav.
2 *K.* 17:18 none left but *t. of* J.
Ps. 78:68 but he chose *t. of* J.
Rev. 5:5 L. of *t. of* J. prevailed
7:5 of *tribe of* J. sealed 12,000

JUDAS.
Mat. 13:55 brethren Sim. and J.
26:47 J. one of twelve. *Mark*
14:43; *Lu.* 22:47; *John* 18,5
27:3 J. repented, bro. 30 pieces
John 13:29 because J. had bag
14:22 J. saith, How is it
Acts 1:16 D. spake concern. J. 25
5:37 after this man rose up J.
9:11 inquire in the house of J.
15:22 J. surnamed Barsabas, 27

JUDAS Iscariot.
Mat. 10:4 J. I. who betra. *Mark*
3:19; *Luke* 6:16; *John* 6:71;
13:2
26:14 J. I. to chief p. *Mark* 14:10
Luke 22:3 enter. Satan into J. I.
John 13:26 he gave sop to J. I.

JUDEA.
Ezr. 5:8 went into prov. of J.
Mat. 24:16 them wh. be in J. flee,
Mark 13:14; *Luke* 21:21
John 4:3 left J. dep. to Galilee
7:3 and go into J. again, 11:7
Acts 1:8 in all J. ye sh. be witn.
9:31 church. rest thro. J. 10:37
Rom. 15:31 do not believe in J.
1 *Thes.* 2:14 churches which in J.

JUDGE, Substantive.
Gen. 18:25 J. of all the earth
19:9 this fel. ca. needs be a J.
Ex. 2:14 J. over us, *Acts* 7:27, 35
Deut. 17:9 come to the J. shall be
12 man will not hearken to J.
25:2 j. sh. cause him to lie down
Jud. 2:18 the Lord was with J.
11:27 L. the J. be j. this day
2 *Sam.* 15:4 O that I were ma. j.
Job 9:15 make supplica. to my J.
23:7 delivered for ever fr. my J.
31:28 iniq. be punished by J.
Ps. 50:6 for God is j. himself
68:5 j. of widows; 75:7 G. is j.
94:2 thou J. of the earth
Is. 3:2 take away fr. Jer. the j.
Amos 2:3 cut off j. from midst
Mic. 5:1 shall smite j. of Israel
7:3 the j. asketh for a reward
Mat. 5:25 adv. deliver thee to j.
the j. to officer, *Luke* 12:58
Luke 12:14 who made me j. ?
18:2 in city, a j. feared not G.
6 hear what unjust j. saith
Acts 10:42 j. of quick and dead
18:15 j. of no such matters
24:10 many years a j. of nation
2 *Tim.* 4:8 Lord the righteous j.
Heb. 12:23 G. the J. of all
Jam. 4:11 not do. of law, but a j.
5:9 J. standeth before the door

JUDGE, Verb, *applied to* GOD
and CHRIST.
Gen. 16:5 j. between me and
thee, 1 *Sam.* 24:12, 15
Ex. 5:21 L. look on you and j.
Deut. 32:36 L. sh. j. his people,
Ps. 50:4; 135:14; *Heb.* 10:30
1 *Sam.* 2:10 L. j. ends of earth
1 *K.* 8:32 j. servants, 2 *Chr.* 6:23
1 *Chr.* 16:33 cometh to j. the
earth, *Ps.* 96:13; 98:9

2 *Chr.* 20:12 wilt thou not j. ?
Job 22:13 j. through dark cloud ?
Ps. 7:8 the L. sh. j. the people
righteously, 9:8; 50:4; 96:10
10:18 j. fatherless and oppressed
26:1 j. me, O Lord, 7; 35:24;
43:1; 54:1; *Lam.* 3:59
82:8 arise, O God, j. the earth
96:13 j. the world with righteousness, 98:9; *Acts* 17:31
110:6 shall j. among the heathen
Ec. 3:17 God shall j. righteous
Is. 2:4 shall j. among nations
3:13 Lord standeth to j. people
11:3 not j. after sight of eyes, 4
51:5 mine arm shall j. people
Ezek. 7:3 will j. accord. to ways
34:17 I j. betw. cattle and cattle
Joel 3:12 will I sit to j. heathen
Mic. 4:3 shall j. among people
John 5:30 I j. my judg. is just
8:15 I j. no man ; 16 yet if I j.
26 things to say and to j.
12:47 I came not to j. world
Rom. 2:16 G. j. secrets of men
3:6 how sh. G. j. the world ?
2 *Tim.* 4:1 j. quick and dead,
1 *Pet.* 4:5
Heb. 13:4 adulterers God will j.
Rev. 6:10 dost thou not j.
19:11 in righteousness he doth j.

See, further, *I will* JUDGE.

JUDGE, *applied to* MAN, *or*
other things.
Gen. 31:37 j. betwixt us both
49:16 Dan shall j. his people
Ex. 18:13 Moses sat to j. people
16 I j. one and another
Lev. 19:15 in right. thou j. thy
neighbor, *Deut.* 1:16 ; 16:18
1 *Sam.* 2:25 man sin, judge j. hi.
8:5 make us a king to j. us, 6, 20
1 *K.* 3:9 underst. heart to j. who
is to j. this peo. 2 *Chr.* 1:10
2 *Chr.* 1:11 mayest j. my people
19:6 for ye j. not for man
Ezr. 7:25 which may j. people
Ps. 58:1 j. uprightly, sons of m.
72:2 j. people with righteousn.
4 j. poor of people, *Prov.* 31:9
82:2 how lo. will ye j. unjustly
Is. 1:17 j. fath. plead for widow
23 j. not fatherless, *Jer.* 5:28
5:3 j. betwixt me and my viney.
Ezek. 22:4 sh. j. thee, 45; 24:14
44:24 j. according to my judgm.
Ob. 21 saviors come to j.
Mic. 3:11 heads thereof j. for re.
Zec. 3:7 shalt also j. my house
Mat. 7:1 j. not that ye be not ju.
2 for with what judgment ye j.
Luke 6:37
Luke 12:57 why j. not what is r. ?
John 7:24 j. not accord. to appearance, but j. right. judg.
51 law j. man before it hear
8:15 j. after flesh ; 12:48 same j.
18:31 j. him accord. to your law
Acts 4:19 j. ye ; 13:46 j. yoursel.
23:3 sittest thou to j. me ?
Rom. 2:27 fulfil the law, j. thee
14:3 j. him eateth ; 10 j. brother
13 let us not j. one another
1 *Cor.* 4:3 j. not myself ; 5 j. not
5:12 what have I to do to j. wi.
do ye not j. them within ?
6:2 do not know saints j. world ?
3 know ye not we sh. j. angels ?
4 set to j. who are least estee.
5 able to j. between his breth.
10:15 j. wh. I say ; 11:13 j. your.
11:31 if we should j. ourselves
14:29 proph. speak, the oth. j.

2 *Cor.* 5:14 because we thus j.
Col. 2:16 let no man therefore j.
Jam. 4:11 but if thou j. the law

I will JUDGE.
1 *Sam.* 3:13 *I will* j. house
Ps. 75:2 *I will* j. uprightly
Ezek. 7:3 *I will* j. according to
thy ways, 8:27 ; 33:20
11:10 *I will* j. you in Israel, 11
16:38 *I will* j. thee as women
21:30 *I will* j. thee wh. th. wast
34:20 I, *even I w.* j. fat cattle, 22

Will I JUDGE.
Gen. 15:14 the nation they shall
serve *will I* j. *Acts* 7:7
Luke 19:22 out of mouth *w.* 1 j.

JUDGED.
Gen. 30:6 God hath j. me
Jud. 3:10 Oth. j. 4:4 Deborah
10:2 Tola j. 3 Jair ; 12:7 Jeph.
12:8 Ibzan j. 11 Elon ; 14 Abdon
15:20 Samson j. I. 20 y'rs, 16:31
1 *Sam.* 4:18 Eli j. 7:6 Sam. 15,
16, 17
Ps. 9:19 let heathen be j.
37:33 condemn him wh. he is j.
109:7 wh. j. let him be condem.
Jer. 22:16 he j. cause of the poor
Ezek. 16:38 women shed blood j.
28:23 wounded shall be j. in her
35:11 known, wh. I have j. thee
36:19 accord. to doings I j. them
Dan. 9:12 ag. judges that j. us
Mat. 7:1 jud. not, th. ye be not j.
2 ye shall be j. *Luke* 6:37
Luke 7:43 Thou hast rightly j.
John 16:11 pri. of this world is j.
Acts 16:15 j. me to be faithful
24:6 j. according to law
25:9 be j. of these things, 20
10 I stand, wh. I ought to be j.
26:6 am j. for hope of promise
Rom. 2:12 j. by law, *Jam.* 2:12
3:4 overcome when thou art j.
7 am I also j. as a sinner ?
1 *Cor.* 2:15 he himself j. no man
4:3 that I should be j. of you
5:3 I have j. already, as though
6:2 if the world sh. be j. by you
10:29 for why is my liberty j. of
11:31 judge we should not be j.
32 we are j. we are chastened
14:24 convinced, he is j. of all
Heb. 11:11 she j. him faithful
1 *Pet.* 4:6 be j. according to men
Rev. 11:18 that they should be j.
16:5 righteous bec. thou j. thus
19:2 he hath j. the great whore
20:12 dead j. out of those things
13 j. ev. man accord. to works

JUDGES.
Ex. 21:22 pay as j. determine
22:8 master sh. be brought to j.
9 cause of both sh. come bef. j.
Deut. 1:16 I charged your j.
16:18 j. sh. thou make in gates
19:18 j. sh. make diligent inqu.
21:2 elders and j. shall come to
32:31 even our enemies being j.
Jos. 23:2 J. called for the, 24:1
Jud. 2:16 Lord raised up j. 18
Ruth. 1:1 wh. j. ruled famine was
1 *Sam.* 8:1 made sons j. over I. 2
2 *Sam.* 7:11 com. j. over my peo.
1 *Chr.* 17:6 sp. a word to any j. 10
23:4 6,000 were officers and j.
2 *Chr.* 1:2 Solom. spake to the j.
19:5 set j. in land ; 6 said to j.
Ezr. 7:25 set j. may judge people
Job 9:24 he cover. the face of j.
12:17 he maketh the j. fools
31:11 iniq. to be punished by j.
Ps. 2:10 be instructed j. of earth
141:6 when j. are overthrown
148:11 princes, and j. of earth
Prov. 8:16 princes rule, and j.
Is. 1:26 I will restore thy j
40:23 mak. j. of earth as vanity

Dan. 9:12 words against our *j.*
Hos. 7:7 have devoured their *j.*
13:10 where are thy *j.* of whom
Zep. 3:3 *j.* are evening wolves
Mal. 12:8 for your *j. Luke* 11:19
Acts 13:20 he gave them *j.*
Jam. 2:4 become *j.* of evil thou.

JUDGEST.
Ps. 51:4 be clear when thou *j.*
Jer. 11:20 L. of hosts, *j.* righte.
Rom. 2:1 whoso. thou art that *j.*
3 O man, that *j.* them
14:4 that *j.* another man's ser. ?
Jam. 4:12 who art thou *j.* ano. ?

JUDGETH.
Job 21:22 *j.* those that were high
Ps. 7:11 God *j.* the righteous
58:11 a God that *j.* in earth
82:1 of mighty, he *j.* am. gods
Prov. 29:14 that faithfully *j.*
John 5:22 the Father *j.* no man
8:50 one that seeketh and *j.*
12:48 hath one that *j.* him
1 *Cor.* 2:15 he that is spirit. *j.* all
4:4 he that *j.* me is the Lord
5:13 th. that are without, G. *j.*
Jam. 4:11 that *j.* his brot. *j.* law
1 *Pet.* 1:17 with. respect of per. *j.*
2:23 com. himself to him that *j.*
Rev. 18:8 strong is the L. that *j.*

JUDGING.
2 *K.* 15:5 *j.* the people of the
2 *Chr.* 26:21
Ps. 9:4 sattest in the thr. *j.* right
Is. 16:5 sit *j.* and seeking judgm.
Mat. 19:28 *j.* 12 tribes, *Luke* 22:30

JUDGMENT.
Ex. 12:12 ag. the gods execute *j.*
21:31 accord. to this *j.* be it do.
23:2 after many, to wrest *j.* 6
28:15 make the breastplate of *j.*
Num. 27:11 Is. a stat. of *j.* 35:29
21 after *j.* of Urim before Lord
Deut. 1:17 not afraid of man, *j.*
10:18 execute *j.* of fatherless
16:10 judge people with just *j.*
19 not wrest *j.* 17:11 accord. *j.*
24:17 not pervert *j.* of stranger
27:19 cursed be that pervert. *j.*
32:4 for all his ways are *j.*
41 if my hand take hold on *j.*
1 *Sam.* 8:3 took bribes pervert. *j.*
2 *Sam.* 8:15 David executed *j.*
and justice, 1 *Chr.* 18:14
15:2 came to king for *j.* 6
1 *K.* 3:11 understan. to discer. *j.*
28 Israel heard of the *j.*
7:7 porch of *j.* 20:40 so thy *j.*
2 *K.* 25:6 took king and gave *j.*
2 *Chr.* 19:8 chief of fathers for *j*
20:9 cometh on us as sword, *j.*
Ezr. 7:26 let *j.* be executed
Est. 1:13 that knew law and *j.*
Job 8:3 doth God pervert *j.* ?
9:19 speak of *j.* 19:7 th. is no *j.*
19:29 ye may know there is a *j.*
32:9 neither do aged understt. *j.*
34:4 let us choose to us *j.*
12 nei. will Almighty pervert *j.*
35:14 yet *j.* is before him
36:17 thou fulfilled *j.* of wicked
j. and just. take hold on th.
Ps. 7:6 awake for me to the *j.*
9:7 prepared his throne for *j.*
8 minister *j.* to people in righ.
16 L. known by *j.* he execut.
33:5 loveth right. and *j.* 37:28
37:6 bring forth thy *j.*
30 his tongue talketh of *j.*
72:2 shall judge thy poor with *j.*
76:8 *j.* to be heard from heaven
9 G. arose to *j.* save the meek
89:14 justice and *j.* are hab. 97:2
94:15 *j.* sh. return to righteous.

99:4 the king's strength loveth
j. thou executest *j.* and rig.
101:1 sing of mercy and *j.*
103:6 L. execut. *j.* for op. 146:7
106:3 bless. are they th. keep *j.*
30 Phine. stood and execut. *j.*
111:7 works of his hands are *j.*
119:66 teach me *j.* and knowle.
121 I have done *j.* and justice
149 quicken me accord. to *j.*
122:5 there are set thrones of *j.*
149:9 exec. on them *j.* written
Prov. 1:3 instr. of wisdom and *j.*
2:8 he keep. the paths of *j.*
9 then shalt thou understand *j.*
8:20 in the midst of paths of *j.*
13:23 destroyed for want of *j.*
17:23 tak. gift to perv. ways *j.*
19:28 ungodly witness scorn. *j.*
20:8 that sitteth in throne *j.*
28:5 evil men understand not *j.*
29:4 king by *j.* establish. land
26 ev. man's *j.* cometh from L.
31:5 nor perv. *j.* of the afflicted
Ec. 3:16 under sun place of *j.*
5:8 seest violent perverting of *j.*
8:5 wise man disce. time and *j.*
6 to ev. purp. th. is time and *j.*
Is. 1:17 seek *j.* 21 full of *j.*
27 Z. shall be redeemed wi. *j.*
4:4 purged Jeru. by spirit of *j.*
5:7 looked for *j.* 16:5 seeking *j.*
9:7 and to establish it with *j.*
10:2 turn aside needy from *j.*
16:3 execute *j. Jer.* 21:12; 22:3;
Ezek. 18:8; 45:9; *Zec.* 7:9; 8:16
28:6 and for a spirit of *j.* to him
17 I will also lay *j.* to the line
30:18 mercy. for L. is God of *j.*
32:16 *j.* sh. dwell in wilderness
33:5 L. hath filled Zion with *j.*
34:5 on people of my curse to *j.*
40:14 taught him in path of *j.*
41:1 come near together to *j.*
42:1 bring forth *j.* to Gentiles
3 sh. bring forth *j.* unto truth
4 not fail, till he set *j.* in earth
53:8 taken from prison and fr. *j.*
56:1 *j.* and justice, *Hos.* 12:6
59:8 there is no *j.* in their goin.
9 therefore is *j.* far from us
11 we look for *j.* there is none
14 *j.* is turned away backwards
15 displeas. him th. was no *j.*
61:8 I the L. love *j.* hate robbe.
Jer. 5:1 if th. be any execute. *j.*
4 know not the *i.* of th. G. 8:7
5 they have known the *j.* of G.
7:5 if ye thoroughly execute *j.*
9:24 exer. *j.* and righteousness
10:24 correct me, but with *j.*
21:12 execute *j.* in the morning
23:5 execute *j.* in earth, 33:15
48:21 *j.* is come upon pl. count.
49:12 whose *j.* was not to drink
51:9 her *j.* reacheth to heaven
Ezek. 23:24 I will set *j.* bc. them
Dan. 4:37 all whose ways are *j.*
7:10 *j.* was set; 26 *j.* shalt sit
22 *j.* was given to the saints
Hos. 5:1 give ear, *j.* is tow. you
10:4 *j.* springeth as hemlock
Amos 5:7 turn *j.* to wormwood
15 and establish *j.* in the gate
24 let *j.* run down as waters
6:12 ye have turned *j.* into gall
Mic. 3:1 not to kn. *j.* ; 8 full of *j.*
9 that abhor *j.* ; 7:9 execute *j.*
Hab. 1:4 *j.* doth never go forth
7 *j.* sh. proceed of themselves
12 O L. thou ordain. th. for *j.*
Zep. 3:8 which wrought his *j.*
3:5 ev. morning bring *j.* to light
Mal. 2:17 say, Where is G. of *j.*
Mat. 5:21 in danger of the *j.* 22
7:2 with what *j.* ye judged
12:18 show *j.* to the Gentiles
20 he send forth *j.* unto victo.

23:23 have omitted *j.* mercy
Luke 11:42 pass over *j.* love of G.
John 5:22 committed all *j.* to S.
27 given him authori. to ex. *j.*
7:24 but judge righteous *j.*
9:39 for *j.* I am come into world
12:31 now is the *j.* of this world
16:8 reprove the world of *j.* 11
Acts 8:33 his *j.* was taken away
24:25 as he reasoned of *j.* Felix
Rom. 1:32 knowing the *j.* of God
2:2 *j.* of G. is according to truth
3 think. thou sh. escape *j.* of
5 revelation of righteous *j.* of
5:16 *j.* by one to condemnation
18 *j.* came to all to condemna.
1 *Cor.* 1:10 joined together in *j.*
4:3 I sh. be judged of man's *j.*
2 *Thes.* 1:5 token of the *j.* of G.
1 *Tim.* 5:24 open, going before
to *j.*
Heb. 6:2 eternal *j.* ; 9:27 after
this the *j.*
10:27 certain fearful look. for *j.*
Jam. 2:13 have *j.* without mercy, rejoiceth against *j.*
1 *Pet.* 4:17 *j.* begin at ho. of G.
2 *Pet.* 2:3 whose *j.* lingereth not
4 chains of darkness, reser. *j.*
Jude 6 to *j.* of the great day
15 to execute *j.* upon all
Rev. 14:7 hour of his *j.* is come
17:1 show *j.* of the great whore
Rev. 18:10 in one hour thy *j.* co.
20:4 and *j.* was given to them

See BEAR, DAY.

Do JUDGMENT.
Gen. 18:19 do justice and *j.* 1 *K.*
10:9 ; *Prov.* 21:3 ; *Jer.* 22:15
1 *K.* 3:28 wisdom of G. to do *j.*
2 *Chr.* 9:8 set over them to do *j.*
Prov. 21:7 they refuse to do *j.*
15 it is joy to the just to do *j.*
Jer. 51:47 do *j.* on gr. images, 52

JUDGMENT-HALL.
John 18:28 led Jesus to h. of *j.*
themselves we. not into *j.-h.*
33 Pilate entered *j.-h.* again
19:9 went into the *j.-h.*
Acts 23:35 kept in Herod's *j.-h.*

In JUDGMENT.
Lev. 19:15 no unright. in *j.* 35
Num. 35:12 bef. congrega. in *j.*
Deut. 1:17 not respect per. in *j.*
Jud. 5:10 ye that sit in *j.*
Job 9:32 come together in *j.*
37:23 excel. in power and in *j.*
Ps. 1:5 shall not stand in *j.*
25:9 meek will he guide in *j.*
Prov. 16:10 transgress. not in *j.*
18:5 overthrow righteous in *j.*
24:23 not good res. persons in *j.*
Is. 5:16 L. of hosts exalted in *j.*
28:6 sitteth in *j.* 7 stumble in *j.*
32:1 princes shall rule in *j.*
54:17 tongue rise ag. thee in *j.*
Jer. 4:2 in righteousn. and in *j.*
Ezek. 44:24 in contro. stand in *j.*
Hos. 8:19 betroth thee to me in *j.*
Mal. 3:5 come near to you in *j.*
Mat. 12:41 men of Nin. rise in *j.*
42 queen of south shall rise in
j. Luke 11:31, 32
Phil. 1:9 love may abound in *j.*

Into JUDGMENT.
Job 14:3 and bringest me into *j.*
34:23 enter into *j.* with God
Ps. 143:2 enter not *i. j.* wi. serv.
Ec. 11:9 will bring thee into *j.*
12:14 God bring ev. work into *j.*
Is. 3:14 Lord will enter into *j.*

My JUDGMENT.
Job 27:2 taken away my *j.* 34:5
29:14 my *j.* was as a robe
40:8 wilt thou disannul my *j.* ?

Ps. 35:23 awake to *my j.*
Is. 40:27 *my j.* is passed over
49:4 *my j.* is with the Lord
51:4 make *my j.* to rest
Ezek. 39:21 heathen sh. see *my j.*
John 5:30 *my j.* just; 8:16 *my j.*
1 *Cor.* 7:25 yet I give *my j.*
40 happier if she abi. in *my j.*

JUDGMENT-SEAT.

Mat. 27:19 set on *j.-s. John* 19:13
Acts 18:12 J. brought him to *j.-s.*
16 he drave them from the *j.-s.*
17 beat Sosthenes before *j.-s.*
25:10 I stand at Cesar's *j.-s.*
17 on morrow I sat on *j.-s.*
Rom. 14:10 sh. all stand before
j.-s of Christ, 2 *Cor.* 5:10
Jam. 2:6 draw you before *j.-s.*

JUDGMENTS.

Ex. 6:6 redeem you with *j* 7:4
21:1 *j.* thou sh. set before them
Num. 33:4 on gods L. executed *j.*
35:24 judge according to th. *j.*
Deut. 33:10 sh. teach Jac. thy *j.*
2 *Sam.* 22:23 his *j.* were before
me, *Ps.* 18:22
1 *Chr.* 16:12 *j.* of mou. *Ps.* 105:5
14 his *j.* in all earth, *Ps.* 105:7
Neh. 9:29 sinned against thy *j.*
Ps. 10:5 thy *j.* are out of sight
19:9 tho *j.* of the Lord are true
36:6 thy *j.* are a great deep
48:11 let Judah be glad of thy *j.*
72:1 give the king thy *j.* O God
97:8 because of thy *j.* O Lord
119:7 I learned thy righteous *j.*
13 lips declared *j.* of thy mo.
20 longing it hath unto thy *j.*
30 thy *j.* have I laid before me
39 reproach, for thy *j.* are good
43 for I have hoped in thy *j.*
52 I remember thy *j.* of old
62 because of thy right. *j.* 164
75 I know that thy *j.* are right
102 have not departed from *j.*
106 I will keep righteous *j.*
108 teach me *j.* 120 afraid of *j.*
137 right. upright are thy *j.*
156 quicken me accor. to thy *j.*
160 ev. one of thy righteou.
175 and let thy *j.* help me
147:20 his *j.* they have not kno.
Prov. 19:29 *j.* prep. for scorners
Is. 26:8 in way of thy *j.*
9 when thy *j.* are in the earth
Jer. 12:1 talk with thee of thy *j.*
Ezek. 5:7 accord. to *j.* of nations
8 execute *j.* in midst of thee,
10, 15; 11:9
16:41 exe. *j.* in sight of women
23:24 judge thee accord. to *j.*
28:26 executed *j.* on all those
34:16 I will feed them with *j.*
Dan. 9:5 departing from thy *j.*
Hos. 6:5 thy *j.* are as the light
Zep. 3:15 L. taken away thy *j.*
Rom. 11:33 unsearch. are his *j.*
1 *Cor.* 6:4 have *j.* of things of life
Rev. 15:4 *j.* are made manifest
16:7 righteous are thy *j.* 19:2

My JUDGMENTS.

Lev. 18:4 ye shall do *my j.*
5 ye shall keep *my j.* 25:18
26:15 if your soul abhor *my j.*
43 because they despised *my j.*
1 *Chr.* 28:7 constant to do *my j.*
Ps. 89:30 chil. walk not in *my j.*
Jer. 1:16 utter *my j.* ag. them
Ezek. 5:6 changed *my j.* to wick.
7 neither have kept *my j.*
14:21 send *my* four sore *j.* on J.
44:24 judge it accord to *my j.*

Statutes and JUDGMENTS.

Lev. 18:5 keep *my stat. and my
j.* 26; 20:22; *Deut.* 7:11; 11:1;
26:16, 17; 30:16; 1 *K.* 2:3;

8:58; 9:4; 11:33
19:37 ye sh. observe all *my
statutes a. my j. Deut.* 11:32;
12:1; 2 *Chr.* 7:17
Deut. 4:1 I hearken to *s. a. j.* 5:1
5 I have taught you *sta. and j.*
8 hath *sta. and j.* so righteous
14 te. *st. and j.* 6:1; *Ezr.* 7:10
5:31 *st. and j.* thou shalt teach
6:20 what mean *statutes and j.*
8:11 keeping *s. and j. Neh.* 1:7
1 *K.* 6:12 walk in *s.* execute *j.*
2 *Chr.* 19:10 between *s. and j.*
Neh. 9:13 gav. them right *s. a. j.*
10:29 to do all his *sta. and j.*
Ps. 147:19 showeth his *s. and j.*
Ezek. 5:6 ref. *my j. and my sta.*
11:12 not walked in my *s.* nor
executed my *j.* 20:13, 16, 21
18:9 walked in my *statutes and
j.* 17; 20:19; 37:24
20:11 gave them *s.* and sho. *j.*
18 not in *s.* of faith. nor th. *j.*
25 gave th. *sta.* not good, *a. j.*
Mal. 4:4 law of M. with *s. and j.*

JUICE.

Cant. 8:2 wine of *j.* of pomegra.

JULIA. *Rom.* 16:15

JULIUS. *Acts* 27:1

JUMPING.

Nah. 3:2 noise of the *j.* chariots

JUNIA. *Rom.* 16:7

JUNIPER.

1 *K.* 19:4 Elijah sat under *j.* 5
Job 30:4 cut *j.* roots for meat
Ps. 120:4 arrows, coals of *j.*

JUPITER.

Acts 14:12 called Barnabas J.
19:35 which fell down from J

JURISDICTION.

Luke 23:7 belong to Herod's *j.*

JUST.

Gen. 6:9 Noah was *j.* man
Lev. 19:36 *j.* balance, *j.* weights,
a *j.* ephah, and a *j.* hin, *Deut.*
25:15; *Ezek.* 45:10
Deut. 16:18 judge with *j.* judgm.
32:4 a God, *j.* and right is he
2 *Sam.* 23:3 rul. men must be *j.*
Neh. 9:33 *j.* in all brought on us
Job 4:17 man be more *j.* than G.
9:2 should man be *j.* with God
12:4 *j.* man is laughed to scorn
27:17 but the *j.* shall put it on
Ps. 7:9 wicked. end, establish *j.*
37:12 wicked plotteth against *j.*
Prov. 3:33 bless. habitation of *j.*
4:18 path of *j.* as shining light
9:9 teach a *j.* man, he will incr.
10:6 blessing upon he. of the *j.*
7 memory of the *j.* is blessed
20 tongue of *j.* is as choice sil.
31 mouth of *j.* bringeth wisd.
11:1 a *j.* weight is his delight
9 thro' knowledge *j.* delivered
12:13 *j.* sh. come out of trouble
21 sh. no evil happen to the *j.*
13:22 weal. of sin. laid up for *j.*
16:11 *j.* we. and balance Lord's
17:15 condemneth *j.* is abomin.

Prov. 17:26 to punish the *j.* is
18:17 first in own cause seem. *j.*
20:7 *j.* man walketh in integrity
21:15 joy to *j.* to do judgment
24:16 *j.* man falleth seven times
29:10 hate upright, *j.* seek soul
Ec. 7:15 a *j.* man that perisheth
20 not a *j.* man on earth
8:14 *j.* men to wh. it happeneth
Is. 26:7 way of *j.* is uprightness,
dost weigh path of *j.*
29:21 *j.* for thing of naught
45:21 a *j.* God, and a Saviour
Lam. 4:13 shed blood of *j.* in her

Ezek. 18:5 man be *j.* and do right
9 he is *j.* he shall surely live
Hos. 14:9 *j.* shall walk in them
Amos 5:12 they afflict the *j.*
Hab. 2:4 *j.* sh. live by faith, *Rom.*
1:17; *Gal.* 3:11; *Heb.* 10:38
Zep. 3:5 the *j.* Lord is in midst
Zec. 9:9 he is *j.* and hav. salva.
Mat. 1:19 Joseph, being a *j.* man
5:45 send. rain on *j.* and unjust
13:49 sever wicked from am. *j.*
27:19 nothing to do with *j.* man
24 innocent of blood of *j.* per.
Mark 6:20 know. he was *j.* man
Luke 1:17 disobed. to wisd. of *j.*
2:25 Simeon was *j.* and devout
14:14 at the resurrec. of the *j.*
15:7 ninety and nine *j.* persons
20:20 spies feign themselves *j.*
23:50 Jos. was good man and *j.*
John 5:30 and my judgment is *j.*
Acts 10:22 Cornelius, a *j.* man
24:15 resurrection of *j.* and unj.
Rom. 2:13 not hear. of law are *j.*
3:8 damnation *j.* 26 might be *j.*
7:12 the commandment holy, *j.*
Phil. 4:8 whatsoev. things are *j.*
Col. 4:1 give servants which is *j.*
Tit. 1:8 bishop must be *j.* holy
Heb. 2:2 received *j.* recompense
12:23 sp. of *j.* men made perfect
Jam. 5:6 condemned and kill. *j.*
1 *Pet.* 3:18 the *j.* for the unjust
2 *Pet.* 2:7 delivered *j.* Lot
1 *John* 1:9 he is *j.* to forgive sins
Rev. 15:3 *j.* and tr. are thy ways

Most JUST.

Job 34:17 condemn him is *m. j.* ?

JUST One.

Acts 3:14 ye denied the J. O.
7:52 show. bef. coming of J. O.
22:14 his will, and see that J. O.

JUSTICE.

Gen. 18:19 keep w. of L. to do *j.*
Deut. 33:21 execute. the *j.* of L.
2 *Sam.* 8:15 David executed *j.*
1 *Chr.* 18:14
15:4 made judge I would do *j.*
Job 8:3 doth Almigh. pervert *j.* ?
36:17 and *j.* take hold on thee
37:23 excellent in plenty of *j.*
Ps. 82:3 do *j.* to afflicted
89:14 *j.* and judgm. are habita.
119:121 have done judg. and *j.*
Prov. 1:3 to rec. instruction of *j.*
8:15 kings reign, princes dec. *j.*
Ec. 5:8 seest perverting of *j.*
Is. 9:7 to estab. his thro. with *j.*
56:1 and do *j.* for my salvation
58:2 ask of me ordinances of *j.*
59:4 none calleth for *j.* nor ple.
9 nor doth *j.* overtake us
14 *j.* standeth afar of
Jer. 23:5 execute judgm. and *j.*
31:23 L. bless thee, habita. of *j.*
Ezek. 45:9 O princes, execute *j.*

See Do JUDGMENT, *before.*

JUSTIFICATION.

Rom. 4:25 raised again for our *j.*
5:16 gift of many offences to *j.*
18 free gift ca. on all men to *j.*

JUSTIFY.

Ex. 23:7 I will not *j.* the wicked
Deut. 25:1 they sh. *j.* righteous
Job 9:20 if I *j.* myself
27:5 God forbid I should *j.* you
33:32 for I desire to *j.* thee
Is. 5:23 *j.* the wicked for reward
53:11 my right. servant *j.* many
Luke 10:29 willing to *j.* himself
16:15 *j.* yourselves before men
Rom. 3:30 God sh. *j.* circumcis.
Gal. 3:8 foreseeing God *j.* heath.

JUSTIFIED.

Job 11:2 man full of talk be j. ?
13:18 behold, I know I sh. be j.?
25:4 can man be j. with God?
32:2 j. himself rather than God
Ps. 51:4 that thou mightest be j.
143:2 no man living be j.
Is. 43:9 may be j. 26 thou be
Is. 45:25 L. all seed of Isr. be j.
Jer. 3:11 backsliding Is. j. hers.
Ezek. 16:51 j. sisters in abom. 52
Mat. 11:19 wisdom is j. of her
children, Luke 7:35
12:37 by thy words th. sh. be j
Luke 7:29 and publicans j. G.
18:14 this man went down j.
Acts 13:39 all that believe are j.
from wh. ye could not be j.
Rom. 2:13 doers of law sh. be j.

KAB.

2 K. 6:25 k. of doves' dung sold

KABZEEL. Jos. 15:21

KADESH.

Gen. 14:8 to Emish. which is K.
Num. 13:26 wilder. of Par. to K.
Deut. 1:46 ye abode in K. many
Ps. 29:8 shak. wilderness of K.

KADESH-BARNEA.

Num. 32:8 I sent them from K.
Deut. 9:23 ; Jos. 14:7
Jos. 10:41 smote from K. to Gaza

KAREAH, or CAREAH. 2 K.
25:23 ; Jer. 40:8, 13 ; 41:11 ;
43:4

KEDEMAH. Gen. 25:15
KEDEMOTH. Deut. 2:26

KEDAR.

Gen. 25:13 of Ish. K. 1 Chr. 1:29
Ps. 120:5 I dwell in tents of K.
Cant. 1:5 comely as tents of K.
Is. 21:16 glory of K. sh. fail, 17
42:11 vil. that K. doth inhabit
60:7 flocks of K. sh. be gather.
Jer. 2:10 see and send to K.
49:28 concerning K. thus saith
Ezek. 27:21 princes of K. occu.

KEEP.

Gen. 2:15 L. put him in E. to k.
18:19 shall k. the way of Lord
28:15 am with thee to k. thee, 20
41:35 let them k. food in ci:ies
Ex. 12:6 k. it till fourteenth day
14 ye sh. k. it a feast to L. 25 ;
23:15 ; 34:18 ; Lev. 23:31
47 congregation of Is. sh. k. it
20:8 remember sab.-day to k. it,
31:13, 14, 16 ; Deut. 5:12, 15
22:7 man deliver money to k. 10
23:7 k. thee from false matter
14 three times k. a feast
20 I send an angel to k. thee
Lev. 18:14 ye sh. k. my ordinances, 30 ; 24:9 ; Ezek. 11:20
19:3 ye sh. k. my sabbaths, 30 ;
26:2 ; Is. 56:4
23:39 k. a feast sev. 2 Chr. 30:13
25:18 k. my judg. and do them
Num. 6:24 L. bless thee and k.
9:3 in fourteenth day ye shall k.
29:12 k. feast to the L. sev. days
36:7 k. himself to inheritance, 9
Deut. 7:8 k. the oath
12 the L. sh. k. the covenant
Deut. 16:10 k. feast of weeks to
17:19 learn to k. words of law
29:9 k. words of this covenant
Jos. 6:18 k. from accursed thing
Jud. 2:22 whether k. way of L.
1 Sam. 2:9 k. feet of his saints

3:4 might. be j. in thy sayings
20 no flesh be j. in his sight
24 j. freely by his gra. Tit. 3:7
28 a man is j. by faith, 5:1 ;
Gal. 2:16 ; 3:24
4:2 if Abraham we. j. by works
5:1 j. by faith we have peace
9 j. by his blood, we shall be
8:30 whom he j. he also glorifi.
1 Cor. 4:4 yet am I not hereby j.
6:11 ye are j. in name of L. J.
Gal. 2:16 not j. by law, 3:11
5:4 whosoever are j. by law
1 Tim. 3:16 j. in spirit
Jam. 2:21 was not Abraham j.
24 see how by works man is j.
25 was not Rahab j. by works?

JUSTIFIER.

Rom. 3:26 j. of him who believ.

K

2 Sam. 18:18 no son to k. name
1 K. 8:25 k. with thy servant
David, 2 Chr. 6:16
1 Chr. 4:10 k. me from evil
12:33 50,000 could k. rank, 38
29:18 k. this forever in heart
2 Chr. 22:9 no power to k. still
30:23 counsel to k. other 7 days
Ezr. 8:29 watch and k. them
Neh. 12:27 k. ded. with gladness
Est. 3:8 nor k. they king's laws
Job 14:13 thou wouldest k. me
20:13 tho' he k. it still within
Ps. 12:7 sh. k. them, O L. 31:20
17:8 k. me as apple of eye
19:13 k. from presumptuous sins
25:20 O k. my soul, and deliver
34:13 k. thy tongue from evil
37:34 k. his way ; 39:1 k. mouth
89:28 my mercy wil. I k. for him
91:11 angels charge, to k. thee
103:9 nor will k. anger for ever
106:3 blessed are they k. judg.
113:9 barren women to k. house
119:2 blessed they th. k. his tes.
4 com. us to k. thy precepts
17 live and k. thy word, 101
33 teach me, I sh. k. it to end
63 compan. of them k. thy pr.
69 k. thy prec. with heart, 134
88 k. testimony of thy mouth
100 because I k. thy precepts
106 will k. thy righteous judg.
146 I shall k. thy testimonies
127:1 except Lord k. city
140:4 k. me fr. hands of wicked
141:3 O L. k. the door of my lips
Prov. 2:11 underst. shall k. thee
20 mayest k. paths of righteous
3:21 my son, k. sound wisdom
26 L. shall k. thy foot fr. being
4:6 love wisdom, she sh. k. thee
13 k. instructi. let her not go
21 k. my sayings in thy heart
23 k. thy heart wi. all diligen.
5:2 thy lips may k. knowledge
6:22 when sleepest it sh. k. thee
7:1 my son, k. my words
5 k. thee from strange woman
8:32 blessed they th. k. my ways
22:5 he that doth k. his soul, 18
28:4 such as k. the law contend
Ec. 3:6 time to k. and cast away
5:1 k. foot when goest to house
Is. 26:3 k. him in perfect peace
27:3 the L. do k. it, k. it night
42:6 I will k. thee
43:6 k. not back ; 56:1 k. judg.
Jer. 3:5 will k. anger to end? 12
31:10 k. him as shep. doth flock
42:4 I will k. nothing back
Ezek. 20:19 k. my judgm. 36:27
43:11 they may k. the wh. form

JUSTIFYING, ETH.

1 K. 8:32 and j. the righteous,
2 Chr. 6:23
Prov. 17:15 he that j. the wicked
Is. 50:8 he is near that j.
Rom. 5:5 him that j. ungodly
8:33 God's elect ? is G. that j.

JUSTLE.

Nah. 2:4 the chariots shall j.

JUSTLY.

Mic. 6:8 L. require but to do j.
Luke 23:41 indeed j. we receive
1 Thes. 2:10 holily and j. behav.

JUSTUS.

Acts 1:23 who was surnamed J.
18:7 ent. man's house named J.
Col. 4:11 Jesus who is called J.

Hos. 12:6 k. mercy and judgment
Mic. 7:5 k. the doors of thy mou.
Nah. 1:15 k. feasts ; 2:1 k. muni.
Zec. 13:5 taught me to k. cattle
Mal. 2:7 priests' lips sho. k. kno.
Mark 7:9 k. your own tradition
Luke 4:10 angels charge to k. th.
11:28 blessed th. hear word, k. it
19:43 thy enemies shall k. thee
John 8:51 k. my say. never see
55 know him, k. his saying
12:25 hateth life in world k. it
14:23 man love me k. my words
15:20 saying, they will k. yours
17:11 k. thy name ; 15 k. fr. evil
Acts 15:5 k. back part of price
10:28 that is a Jew to k. comp.
15:5 com. them to k. law of M.
29 from wh. if ye k. yourselves
16:4 deliver. them decrees to k.
Rom. 2:25 profiteth, if th. k. law
26 k. the righteousness of law
1 Cor. 5:8 therefore let us k. feast
11 writ. to you not k. company
7:37 decreed he will k. his virg.
9:22 I k. under my body
15:2 k. in mem. wh. I preached
2 Cor. 11:9 and so will I k. my.
Gal. 6:13 nei. do circum. k. law
Eph. 4:3 to k. the unity of Spirit
Phil. 4:7 peace of G. k. y. hearts
2 Thes. 3:3 estab. and k. from ev.
1 Tim. 5:22 k. thyself pure
6:20 k. that commit. to thy tru.
2 Tim. 1:12 k. that I com. to him
14 commit. to thee k. by H. G.
Jam. 1:27 to k. himself unspot.
1 John 5:21 k. yourselves fr. idols
Jude 21 k. yoursel. in love of G.
Jude 24 him that is ab. to k. you
Rev. 1:3 blessed th. that k. thin.
3:10 k. thee from hour of temp.
22:9 who k. sayings of this book

KEEP alive.

Gen. 6:19 into ark to k. th. a. 20
Num. 31:18 chil. k. a. for yours.
2 Sam. 8:2 one full line to k. a.
Ps. 22:29 no. can k. a. own soul
33:19 k. them alive in famine
41:2 Lord preser. and k. him a.

KEEP charge.

Num. 1:53 Levites k. c. of taber.
18:4 ; 31:30 ; 1 Chr. 23:32
3:8 k. c. of the children of Israel
32 k. c. of the sanctuary. 18:5
Ezek. 44:16 mini. to me. k. my c.
Zec. 3:7 if thou wilt k. my c.

KEEP commandments.

Ex. 16:28 refuse ye to k. my c.
20:6 mercy to th. that k. my c.
Deut. 5:10 ; 7:9 ; Dan. 9:4

Lev. 22:31 sh. ye *k.* my *c.* and do
   them, *Deut.* 4:40; 6:17; 7:11
26:3 *k.* my *com. Deut.* 11:22;
   19:9; 28:9; 30:10; 1 *K.* 3:14
Deut. 5:29 fear me and *k.* my *c.*
8:2 know whet. th. would. *k. c.*
26:17 avouched Lord to *k.* his *c.*
   18 that thou shouldest *k. c.*
Jos. 22:5 take heed to *k. com.*
1 *K.* 2:3 charge of Lord to *k. k. c.*
6:12 *k.* my *comman.* 2 *K.* 17:13;
   Prov. 4:4; 7:2
8:58 incline hearts to *k.* his *c.*
   61 heart be perfect to *k.* his *c.*
9:6 not *k. com.* I will cut off Is.
1 *Chr.* 29:19 Sol. perf. hea. to *k. c.*
Ps. 78:7 works of G. but *k.* his *c.*
119:60 delayed not to *k.* thy *c.*
   115 dep. evil-doers, I will *k. c.*
Prov. 3:1 let thy heart *k.* my *c.*
6:20 my son, *k.* thy father's *c.*
Ec. 8:2 coun. thee to *k.* king's *c.*
12:13 fear God and *k.* his *com.*
Mat. 19:17 enter life, *k.* the *c.*
John 14:15 if ye love me, *k.* my *c.*
1 *Tim.* 6:14 *k.* this *c.* witho. spot
1 *John* 2:3 we kn. him if we *k. c.*
3:22 ask we receive, bec. we *k. c.*
5:2 we love God and *k.* his *com.*
   3 love of God that we *k.* his *c.*
Rev. 12:17 war with seed wh. *k. c.*
14:12 they which *k.* the *c.* of G.

See COVENANT.

KEEP passover.

Ex. 12:48 stranger *k.* p. to Lord
Num. 9:2 chil. of Is. *k. p.* in its
   seas. 4; *Deut.* 16:1; 2 *K.* 23:21
2 *Chr.* 30:1 co. to *k.* the *p.* to G.
   35:18 nor did kings *k.* such a *p.*
Mat. 26:18 *k. p.* at thy house

KEEP silence.

Jud. 3:19 said, *k.* all went out
Ps. 35:22 *k.* not *silence,* 83:1
50:3 shall come, and sh. not *k. s.*
Ec. 3:7 time to *k. s.* time to spe.
Is. 41:1 *k. s.* bef. me, O islands
Lam. 2:10 elders of da. of Z. *k. s.*
Amos 5:13 the prudent shall *k. s.*
Hab. 2:20 L, in temp. earth *k. s.*
1 *Cor.* 14:28 let him *k. s.* in chur.
   34 let women *k. sil.* in church.

KEEP statutes.

Ex. 15:26 if th. wilt *k.* all his *s.*
Deut. 30:10; 1 *K.* 9:4; 11:38
Lev. 18:5 *k.* my *s.* and judg. 26;
   19:19; 20:8, 22; *Ezek.* 44:24
Deut. 6:2 fear Lord to *k.* his *stat.*
26:17 avouched Lord to *k.* his *s.*
1 *K.* 11:33 in my ways to *k. s.*
Ps. 119:5 ways directed to *k. s.*
   8 I will *k.* thy *s.* 145
Ezek. 18:21 wicked turn and *k. s.*

KEEPER.

Gen. 4:2 Abel was a *k.* of sheep
   9 am I my brother's *k. ?*
39:22 *k.* committed to Joseph
   33 *k.* looked not to any thing
1 *Sam.* 17:20 D. left sheep wi. *k.*
28:2 make thee *k.* of my head
2 *K.* 22:14 *k.* of the wardrobe,
   2 *Chr.* 34:22
Est. 2:3 Hege *k.* of women, 8, 15
Job 27:18 booth that *k.* maketh
Ps. 121:5 Lord thy *k.*
Cant. 1:6 made me *k.* of viney.
Acts 16:27 *k.* of prison awaking

KEEPERS.

Ec. 12:3 *k.* of house tremble
Cant. 5:7 *k.* took away my veil
8:11 Sol. let out vineyard to *k.*
Jer. 4:17 as *k.* of the field
Mat. 28:4 fear of him *k.* did sha.
Acts 5:23 *k.* standing bef. doors
Acts 12:6 *k.* kept pris.; 19 exa. *k.*
Tit. 2:5 chaste, *k.* at home
See DOOR.

KEEPEST.

1 *K.* 8:23 who *k.* covenant with
   serv. 2 *Chr.* 6:14 ; *Neh.* 9:32
Acts 21:24 orderly and *k.* the law

KEEPETH.

Ex. 21:18 die not, but *k.* his bed
Deut. 7:9 faithful God which *k.*
   covenant. *Neh.* 1:5
1 *Sam.* 16:11 behold, he *k.* sheep
Job 33:18 *k.* back soul from pit
Ps. 34:20 he *k.* all his bones
   121:3 that *k.* th. not slumber, 4
   146:6 L. which *k.* truth for ever
Prov. 2:8 *k.* paths of judgment
   10:17 in way of life *k.* instruct.
   13:3 *k.* his mouth *k.* life, 21:23
   6 righteousness *k.* him upright
   16:17 *k.* way preserv. soul, 19:16
   19:8 *k.* understanding find good
   24:12 *k.* soul, do. not he know ?
   27:18 *k.* fig-tree shall eat fruit
   28:7 whoso *k.* law is a wise son
   29:11 wise man *k.* it till afterw.
   18 that *k.* the law, happy is he
Ec. 8:5 *k.* command. feel no evil
Is. 26:2 nation *k.* truth
   56:2 *k.* sab. from polluting it, 6
Jer. 48:10 cursed be he *k.* back
Lam. 3:28 sitteth alone *k.* silen.
Hab. 2:5 proud, nei. *k.* at home
Luke 11:21 strong man *k.* palace
John 7:19 none of you *k.* law
   9:16 bec. he *k.* not sabbath
   14:21 hath com. and *k.* them
   24 *k.* not my sayings
1 *John* 2:4 know him, and *k.* not
   5 *k.* word, in him is love, 3:24
   5:18 is begot. of God *k.* himself
Rev. 2:26 overcom. and *k.* works
16:15 blessed he that *k.* garm.
22:7 blessed he that *k.* sayings

KEEPING.

Ex. 34:7 L. *k.* mercy for thous,
Deut. 8:11 not *k.* his commands
1 *Sam.* 25:16 with them *k.* sheep
Ps. 19:11 *k.* of them great rew.
Ezek. 17:14 by *k.* of his covenant
Dan. 9:4 great God *k.* covenant
Luke 2:8 shepherds *k.* watch
1 *Cor.* 7:19 *k.* commandm. of G.
1 *Pet.* 4:19 com. *k.* of souls to him

KEILAH.

Jos. 15:44 K. and Achzib
1 *Sam.* 23:1 Philist. fight aga. K.
Neh. 3:17 ruler of h. part of K. 18

KEMUEL   *Gen.* 22:21
KENEZ.   *Jos.* 15:17

KENITES.

Gen. 15:19 thy seed have I gi. K.
Num. 24:21 Balaam look. on K.
1 *Sam.* 15:6 S. said to K. Depart
27:10 road against south of K.

KEPT.

Gen. 26:5 Abrah. *k.* my charge
   29:9 came wi. sheep, she *k.* th.
Ex. 3:1 Moses *k.* flock of Jethro
   16:23 to be *k.* till the morning
   32 manna *k.* for genera. 33, 34
   21:29 owner not *k.* him in, 36
Num. 17:10 A.'s rod *k.* for token
   19:9 water *k.* for congregation
   24:11 Lord hath *k.* thee back
Deut. 32:10 *k.* them as ap. of eye
   33:9 observed word, *k.* covenant
Jos. 14:10 *k.* me alive 45 years
Ruth 2:23 *k.* by maidens of Boaz
1 *Sam.* 17:34 ser. *k.* fath.'s sheep
   21:4 *k.* themselves from women
   25:33 blessed thou who *k.* me
   26:15 why not *k.* lord the king ?
   16 ye have not *k.* your master
2 *Sam.* 13:34 young man *k.* watch
   22:22 I have kept the ways of
   the Lord, *Ps.* 18:21, 23
   24 have kept myself from iniq.
   44 *k.* me to be head of heathen

---

1 *K.* 2:43 not *k.* the oath of Lord
   8:24 hast *k.* with D. what thou
   promisedst him, 2 *Chr.* 6:15
   11:11 hast not *k.* my covenant
   13:21 man of G. not *k.* comman.
1 *Chr.* 10:13 word of L. S. *k.* not
   12:1 David *k.* himself close
2 *Chr.* 7:8 S. *k.* feast 7 days, 9
   30:21 *k.* feast of unleavened br.
   Ezr. 6:22
   35:18 no pass, like that *k.* in Is.
Ezr. 3:4 *k.* feast of tabernacles
   6:19 chil. of captiv. *k.* passover
Neh. 1:7 have not *k.* command.
   8:18 they *k.* the feast seven days
Job 23:11 his ways have I *k.*
Job 28:21 *k.* clo. from fowls of air
Ps. 17:4 *k.* fr. paths of destroyer
   30:3 *k.* me alive; 42:4 *k.* h. day
   78:10 *k.* not the covenant of G.
   99:7 they *k.* his testimonies
   119:22 for I *k.* thy testim. 167
   55 *k.* thy law ; 56 *k.* prec. 168
   67 *k.* word ; 158 *k.* not wo.
Ec. 2:10 eyes desired *k.* not from
   5:13 riches *k.* for owners thereof
Cant. 1:6 vineyard have I not *k.*
Is. 30:29 when solemnity is *k.*
Jer. 16:11 laws ; 35:18 *k.* prec.
Ezek. 5:7 nor *k.* my judgm. 20:21
   44:8 not *k.* charge of holy things
   15 *k.* charge of sanctuary, 48:11
Dan. 5:19 he *k.* alive, he set up
   7:28 I *k.* the matter in my heart
Hos. 12:12 serv. for wife, *k.* sheep
Amos 1:11 Ed. *k.* wrath for ever
Mal. 2:9 not *k.* my ways, 3:7
   3:14 profit have *k.* his ordinan.
Mat. 13:35 things been *k.* secret
   19:20 these have I *k.* from my
   youth, *Luke* 18:21
Mark 4:22 nor any thing *k.* secr.
   9:10 *k.* that saying. *Luke* 9:36
Luke 2:19 *k.* things in heart, 51
   8:29 was *k.* bound with chains
John 2:10 thou hast *k.* good wine
   15:10 I *k.* Father's commandm.
   20 if they have *k.* my saying
   17:6 and have *k.* thy word
   12 those thou gav. me I have *k.*
Acts 5:2 *k.* back part of the price
   7:53 received law, and not *k.* it
   12:5 P. *k.* in prison ; 6 *k.* prison
   20:20 *k.* back nothing profitable
   22:20 *k.* the raiment of them
   28:16 with soldier that *k.* him
Rom. 16:25 mystery *k.* secret
2 *Cor.* 11:9 I *k.* from being burd.
Gal. 3:23 we were *k.* under law
2 *Tim.* 4:7 course, I *k.* the faith
Heb. 11:28 Moses *k.* the passover
Jam. 5:4 hire is *k.* back by fraud
1 *Pet.* 1:5 are *k.* by power of God
2 *Pet.* 3:7 same word *k.* in store
Jude 6 angels *k.* not first estate
Rev. 3:8 *k.* word, not deni. name
   10 hast *k.* word of my patience

KEPT silence.

Job 29:21 men give ear, and *k. s.*
31:34 fear multi. that I *k. s. ?*
Ps. 32:3 I *k. s.* bones waxed old
50:21 things th. done, and I *k. s.*
Acts 15:12 all the multitude *k. s.*
22:2 spake Heb. *k.* the more *s.*

KERCHIEFS.

Ezek. 13:18 *k.* on head of stature
   21 your *k.* also will I tear

KEREN-HAPPUCH.   *Job* 42:14
KERIOTH. *Jer.* 48:24,41; *Am.* 2:2

KERNELS.

Num. 6:4 eat noth. from the *k.*

KETTLE.

1 *Sam.* 2:14 struck into *k.* or pot
KETURAH. *Gen.* 25:1, 4 ; 1 *Chr.*
   1:32, 33

KEY, S.

Jud. 3:25 took a *k.* and opened
Is. 22:22 *k.* of house of David
Mat. 16:19 *k.* of kingd. of heaven
Luke 11:52 tak. *k.* of knowledge
Rev. 1:18 *k.* of hell and of death
3:7 he that hath the *k.* of David
9:1 *k.* of bottomless pit, 20:1

KEZIA. *Job* 42:14
KEZIZ. *Jos.* 18:21
KIBROTH-HATTAAVAH. *Nu.*
11:34, 35

KICK, ED.

Deut. 32:15 J. waxed fat and *k.*
1 *Sam.* 2:29 *k.* ye at my sacrifice?
Acts 9:5 ha. to *k.* ag. pri. 26:14

KID.

Gen. 37:31 J.'s breth. killed a *k.*
Ex. 23:19 sh. not seethe the *k.*
34:26 ; *Deut.* 14:21
Lev. 4:23 offering, a *k.* of goats,
28 ; 9:3 ; *Ezek.* 43:22 ; 45:23
23:19 sacrifice one *k.* of goats,
Num. 7:16, 22, 28 ; 15:24 ;
28:15, 30 ; 29:5, 11, 16, 19, 25
Jud. 6:19 Gid. made ready a *k.*
14:6 Samson rent lion as a *k.*
Is. 11:6 leopard lie down with *k.*
Luke 15:29 thou never gavest a *k.*

KIDNEYS.

Ex. 29:13 thou shalt take two *k.*
and burn, 22 ; *Lev.* 3:4, 10, 15;
4:9 ; 7:4 ; 8:16, 25
Lev. 9:10 *k.* burnt on altar, 19
Deut. 32:14 fat of *k.* of wheat
Is. 34:6 with fat of *k.* of rams
KIDRON. 2 *Sam.* 15:23

KIDS.

Gen. 27:9 fetch me from th. 2 *k.*
16 put skins of *k.* on his hands
Lev. 16:5 two *k.* of the goats
1 *K.* 20:27 like two lit. floc. of *k.*
Cant. 1:8 feed thy *k.* bes. shep.'s

KILL.

Gen. 4:15 lest any find. C. *k.* him
12:12 th. wi. *k.* me, but save th.
27:42 purposing to *k.* thee
37:21 said, Let us not *k.* him
Ex. 1:16 if it be son, ye *k.* him
2:14 intend. to *k.* me? *Acts* 7:28
16:3 *k.* this assembly
17:3 *k.* us and chil. with thirst
20:13 thou shalt not *k.* *Deut.*
5:17 ; *Mat.* 5:21 ; *Rom.* 13:9
22:1 if man steal ox, and *k.* it
29:11 *k.* bullock before the L.
Lev. 1:5 ; 4:4
Lev. 1:11 *k.* it on side altar, 16:15
8:2 *k.* it at door of tabernacle
4:24 *k.* it in place where they *k.*
14:50 he shall *k.* one of the birds
20:4 seed to Moloch, *k.* him not
16 shalt *k.* woman and beast
Num. 11:15 if deal thus, *k.* me
14:15 if thou *k.* all this people
16:13 bro. us to *k.* us in wilder.
22:29 for now would I *k.* thee
31:17 *k.* ev. woman known man
Deut. 4:42 who *k.* his neighbor
12:15 mayest *k.* and eat flesh
13:9 thou shalt surely *k.* him
32:39 I *k.* and I make alive
Jud. 13:23 I. were plea. to *k.* us
16:2 wh. it is day, we sh. *k.* him
20:31 began to *k.* 39
1 *Sam.* 17:9 be able to *k.* me
19:2 Saul seeketh to *k.* thee, 17
30:15 swear thou wilt nei. *k.* me
2 *Sam.* 14:7 that we may *k.* him
32 let him *k.* me
21:4 nor for us sh. th. *k.* any m.
2 *K.* 5:7 am I God, to *k.* ?
7:4 if they *k.* us, we sh. but die
11:15 follow. her *k.* with sword
2 *Chr.* 35:6 *k.* the passover

KILLED.

Gen. 37:31 Joseph's coat, *k.* kid
Ex. 21:29 the ox hath *k.* a man
Lev. 6:25 place wh. burnt-offer.
is *k.* sin-off. be *k.* bef. the L.
8:19 ram he *k.* 14:5 bird be *k.*
14:6 dip them in blo. of bird *k.*
Num. 16:41 ye *k.* peo. of the L.
31:19 whoso. hath *k.* any person
1 *Sam.* 24:11 cut skirt, *k.* th. not
25:11 take my flesh I have *k.*
2 *Sam.* 12:9 thou hast *k.* Uriah
1 *K.* 21:19 *k.* and tak. possession ?
2 *Chr.* 25:3 slew th. that *k.* king
30:15 *k.* the passover, 35:1, 11 ;
Ezr. 6:20
Ps. 44:22 for thy sake are we *k.*
Prov. 9:2 she hath *k.* her beasts
Lam. 2:21 thou ha. *k.* not pitied
Mat. 16:21 *k.* and raised again,
Mark 8:31 ; 9:31
21:35 be. one, and *k.* *Mark* 12:5

Mat. 22:4 oxen and fatlin. are *k.*
23:31 chil. of them *k.* prophets
Mark 12:8 *k.* him cast him out
14:12 wh. they *k.* the passover
Luke 11:47 fathers *k.* them, 48
12:5 after he hath *k.* ha. power
15:27 fa. hath *k.* fatted calf, 30
22:7 day when pass. must be *k.*
Acts 3:15 *k.* the Prince of life
12:2 *k.* James, brother of John
16:27 would have *k.* himself
23:12 nor drink till they *k.* Paul
Rom. 8:36 for thy sake we are *k.*
11:3 L. they have *k.* thy proph.
2 *Cor.* 6:9 chastened and not *k.*
Thes. 2:15 *k.* the Lord Jesus
Jam. 5:6 condemned and *k.* just
Rev. 6:11 sh. be *k.* as they were
9:18 the third part of man *k.*
20 the rest which were not *k.*
11:5 if hurt him he must be *k.*
13:10 must be *k.* with sword
15 image of beast, should be *k.*

KILLEDST, EST.

Ex. 2:14 as thou *k.* Egyptian
Mat. 23:37 *k.* prophets, *Luke* 13:34

KILLETH.

Lev. 24:17 he that *k.* any man sh.
be put to dea. *Num.* 35:30
18 that *k.* a beast, 21

Num. 35:11 *k.* any unawares, 15 ;
Deut. 19:4 ; *Jos.* 20:3, 9
1 *Sam.* 2:6 L. *k.* and maketh alive
Job 5:2 wrath *k.* the foolish man
24:14 the murderer *k.* the poor
Prov. 21:25 des. of slothful *k.* him
Is. 66:3 he that *k.* an ox
John 16:2 who *k.* you do. G. ser.
2 *Cor.* 3:6 letter *k.* Sp. giveth life
Rev. 13:10 he that *k.* with sword
must be killed

KILLING.

2 *Chr.* 30:17 charge of *k.* passover
Is. 22:13 slaying oxen, *k.* sheep
Hos. 4:2 swearing, lying, and *k.*
Mark 12:5 beating some, *k.* some

KIN.

Lev. 18:6 none appro. to near *k.*
20:19 he uncovereth his near *k.*
25:25 *k.* come to redeem it, 49
Ruth 2:20 man is near *k.* to us
2 *Sam.* 19:42 king near *k.* to us

KIND.

2 *Chr.* 10:7 if thou be *k.* to people
Luke 6:35 G. is *k.* to unthankful
1 *Cor.* 13:4 charity suff. and is *k.*
Eph. 4:32 be *k.* one to another

KIND, Substantive.

Gen. 1:11 yield. fruit after *k.* 12
21 waters brought forth after *k.*
25 God made beast after his *k.*
6:20 fowls after th. *k.* cattle aft.
k. ev. creeping thing after *k.*
Lev. 11:14 hawk after his *k.* 15,
16, 19 ; *Deut.* 14:14
19:19 not let cattle with div. *k.*
Neh. 13:20 sellers of all *k.* ware
Ec. 2:5 I planted trees of all *k.*
Mat. 13:47 gathered of every *k.*
17:21 *k.* go. not out, *Mark* 9:29
1 *Cor.* 15:39 th. is one *k.* of flesh
Jam. 1:18 be a *k.* of first-fruits
3:7 every *k.* of beast and birds

KINDS.

Gen. 8:19 creepeth after their *k.*
2 *Chr.* 16:14 with divers *k.* spices
Jer. 15:3 appoint over th. four *k.*
1 *Cor.* 12:10 divers *k.* of tongues
14:10 are so many *k.* of voices

KINDLE.

Prov. 26:21 con. man to *k.* strife
Is. 9:18 shall *k.* in the thickets
10:16 *k.* a burning like a fire
30:33 breath of Lord doth *k.* it
43:2 nor sh. flame *k.* upon thee
Jer. 33:18 want man to *k.* m.-off.
Ob. 18 fire and flame *k.* in them

KINDLED.

Lev. 10:6 bewail burn. L. hath *k.*
Num. 11:33 wrath of the Lord
was *k.* *Deut.* 11:17 ; 2 *K.*
22:13, 17 ; *Ps.* 106:40
2 *Sam.* 22:9 coals *k.* *Ps.* 18:8
Job 19:11 he hath *k.* his wrath
32:2 then was *k.* wrath of Elihu
42:7 wrath is *k.* against thee
Ps. 2:12 wrath is *k.* but a little
124:3 their wrath *k.* against us
Is. 50:11 sparks that ye have *k.*
Jer. 44:6 wrath *k.* in cities of J.
Ezek. 20:48 I the Lord have *k.* it
Hos. 11:8 my repentings are *k.*
Luke 12:49 will I, if it be *k.* ?
See ANGER, FIRE.

KINDLETH.

Job 41:21 his breath *k.* coals
Is. 44:15 *k.* it, and baketh bread
Jam. 3:5 how great, a little fire *k.*

KINDLY.

Gen. 24:49 if you deal *k.* 47:29
34:3 Shech. spake *k.* to damsel
50:21 Joseph spake *k.* to breth.
Jos. 2:14 deal *k.* and truly
Ruth 1:8 the L. deal *k.* with you
1 *Sam.* 20:8 deal *k.* with thy ser.

Rom. 12:10 be *k.* one to another

KINDNESS.

Gen. 20:13 *k.* thou shalt show
21:23 the *k.* I have done to thee
24:12 O L. show *k.* tc my master
40:14 and show *k.* I pray thee
Jos. 2:12 *k.* to my fa.'s house
Jud. 8:35 nor showed *k.* to Jer.
Ruth 2:20 not left off *k.* to living
3:10 show. more *k.* in latter end
1 *Sam.* 15:6 ye showed *k.* to Isr.
20:14 show me the *k.* of the L.
2 *Sam.* 2:5 showed *k.* to your lord
6 I also will requite you this *k.*
9:3 that I may show *k.* to him
16:17 is this thy *k.* to friend?
1 *K.* 2:7 *k.* to sons of Barzillai
3:6 kept for David this great *k.*
2 *Chr.* 24:22 J. remember. not *k.*
Neh. 9:17 G. gracious, of great *k.*
Est. 2:9 maiden obt. *k.* of him
Ps. 31:21 showed me marvel. *k.*
117:2 for his merciful *k.* is great
119:76 merciful *k.* be my comf.
141:5 right. smite, it sh. be a *k.*
Prov. 19:22 desire of man is his *k.*
31:26 in her tongue is law of *k.*
Is. 54:8 with *k.* will I have mercy
10 *k.* shall not depart from thee
Jer. 2:2 I remem. *k.* of thy youth
Joel 2:13 he is of gr. *k. Jon.* 4:2
Acts 28:2 showed us no little *k.*
2 *Cor.* 6:6 by long-suffering by *k.*
Eph. 2:7 in his *k.* toward us
Col. 3:12 on *k.* humblen. of mind
Tit. 3:4 after the *k.* of G. our
2 *Pet.* 1:7 brotherly-*k.* to *k.* char.

Loving-KINDNESS.

Ps. 17:7 show thy *l.-k.* 92:2
26:3 thy *l.-k.* is before mine eyes
36:7 how excellent is thy *l.-k.*
10 O continue thy *l.-k.* to them
40:10 not concealed thy *l.-k.*
11 let thy *l.-k.* preserve me
42:8 Lord will command *l.-k.*
48:9 we thought of thy *l.-k.* O G.
51:1 have mercy accord. to *l.-k.*
63:3 thy *l.-k.* is better than life
69:16 for thy *l.-k.* is good
88:11 sh. *l.-k.* be declar. in grave?
89:33 *l.-k.* will I not take fr. him
92:2 to show forth *l.-k.* in morn.
103:4 crowneth thee with *l.-k.*
107:43 understand *l.-k.* of the L.
119:88 quicken me after *l.-k.* 159
138:2 praise thy name for *l.-k.*
143:8 cause me to hear thy *l.-k.*
Jer. 9:24 L. which exercise *l.-k.*
16:5 tak. away peace, even *l.-k.*
31:3 with *l.-k.* have I dr. thee
32:18 show. *l.-k.* unto thousands
Hos. 2:19 betro. th. to me in *l.-k.*

Loving-KINDNESSES.

Ps. 25:6 remem. mercies and *l.-k.*
89:49 where are thy former *l.-k.*
Is. 63:7 mention *l.-k.* of the Lord

KINDRED.

Gen. 12:1 get thee fr. *k. Acts* 7:3
24:4 go to *k.* and take wife, 38:40
31:3 return to thy *k.* 13; 32:9
43:7 asked us straitly of our *k.*
Num. 10:30 dep. to own la. and *k.*
Jos. 6:23 brought out all her *k.*
Ruth 2:3 of *k.* of Elimelech, 3:2
Est. 2:10 show. not peo. or *k.* 20
8:6 end. to see destruction of *k.*
Ezek. 11:15 men of thy *k.* said
Luke 1:61 none of *k.* called
Acts 4:6 were of *k.* of high-priest
7:13 Joseph's *k.* known to Pha.
19 dealt subtilely with our *k.*
Rev. 5:9 redeem'd us out of ev. *k.*
14:6 gospel to preach to ev. *k.*

KINDREDS.

1 *Chr.* 16:28 give to the Lord, ye *k. Ps.* 96:7
Ps. 22:27 *k.* of nations worship
Acts 3:25 all *k.* of earth. blessed
Rev. 1:7 all *k.* of earth shall wail
7:9 multitude of *k.* bef. throne
11:9 *k.* see dead bodies thr. days
13:7 pow. given him over all *k.*

KINE.

Gen. 32:15 forty *k.* ten bulls to E.
Gen. 41:2 seven well-favored *k.* 18
3 seven *k.* out of river, 4, 19, 20
26 seven good *k.* are sev. years
27 sev. ill-favored *k.* sev. years
Deut. 7:13 bless increa. of thy *k.*
28:4 blessed be incr. of thy *k.*
18 cursed be incr. of thy *k.*
32:14 butter of *k.* milk of sheep
1 *Sam.* 6:7 ta. two milch *k.* tie *k.*
10 took two *k.* 12 *k.* took way
2 *Sam.* 17:29 and cheese of *k.*
Amos 4:1 hear this, ye *k.* of Bas.

KING.

Gen. 14:18 M. *k.* of Sal. *Heb.* 7:1
Ex. 1:8 arose new *k.* over Egypt
Num. 23:21 shout of a *k.* am. th.
24:7 his *k.* be higher than Agag
Deut. 17:14 I will set *k.* over me
33:5 and he was *k.* in Jeshurun
Jud. 8:18 resem. child. of a *k.*
9:8 trees went to anoint a *k.*
17:6 in those days no *k.* in Isr.
18:1; 19:1; 21:25
1 *Sam.* 2:10 L. give strength to *k.*
8:5 go make us a *k.* to judge us
6 gi. a *k.* 9 show man. of *k.* 11
10 have a *k.* 22 make th. a *k.*
20 that our *k.* may judge us
10:19 nay, but set a *k.* over us
24 said, G. save the *k.* 2 *Sam.*
16:16; 2 *K.* 11:12; 2 *Chr.* 23:11
12:1 I have made a *k.* over you
2 the *k.* walketh before you
12 said, Nay, a *k.* sh. reign ov.
us, when God ·vas your *k.*
17 wicked. great in asking a *k.*
19 this evil, to ask a *k.*
25 conn. both you and your *k.*
15:1 to anoint thee to be *k.*
23 rej. thee from being *k.* 26
16:1 I have provided me a *k.*
20:5 not fail to sit with *k.*
22:15 let not *k.* imp. any thing
24:20 I know that thou sh. be *k.*
25:36 Nabal held feast like a *k.*
2 *Sam.* 5:12 estab. him *k.* over I.
11:8 a mess of meat from *k.*
12:7 I anointed thee *k.* over Is.
14:9 *k.* and his throne be guilt.
17 as an angel of God, so is my lord the *k.* 19:27
15:2 had controversy, ca. to *k.*
3 none deputed of *k.* to hear
16:9 sh. this dead dog curse *k.?*
17:2 I will smite the *k.* only
18:13 is no matter hid from *k.*
19:9 *k.* saved us out of hand of
11 speech of Israel come to *k.*
22 I know that I am *k.* over Is.
28 wh. right to cry more to *k.?*
43 we have ten parts in the *k.*
22:51 tower of salv. for his *k.*
1 *K.* 1:35 Solomon *k.* in my stead
3:7 servant *k.* instead of David
28 heard judg. the *k.* judged
8:62 *k.* and all Is. offer. sacrifice
10:3 not any thing hid from *k.*
11:37 thou shalt be *k.* over Isr.
14:2 who told me I should be *k.*
14 L. raise up a king over Is.
21:10 didst blaspheme G. and *k.*
12:13 prophets declare good to the *k.* 2 *Chr.* 18:12
47 no *k.* in E. a deputy was *k.*
2 *K.* 1:11 *k.* said, Come down, 9
4:13 wouldest be spok. for to *k.*

7:2 lord on whose hand *k.* lean.
8:3 to cry to the *k.* for her hou.
13 L. showed thou shalt be *k.*
20 E. made *k.* over themselves
11:8 be with *k.* as he goeth out
1 *Chr.* 4:23 they dwelt wi. the *k.*
29:20 worshipped Lord and *k.*
2 *Chr.* 2:11 he made thee *k.* 9:8
10:15 *k.* hearkened not to peop.
11:22 he thought to make him *k.*
24:21 stoned him at com. of *k.*
25:16 thou made of *k.* counsel?
Ezr. 4:12 be it kn. to *k.* 13; 5:8
6:10 pray for life of *k.* and sons
7:27 put in *k.* heart to beautify
8:22 req. of *k.* band of soldiers
Neh. 1:11 I was the *k.* cup-bearer
6:7 saying, There is a *k.* in Ju.
Est. 4:16 will go in unto the *k.*
6:6 the *k.* delighteth to honor, 9
7:8 word went out of *k.* mouth
Job 15:24 as a *k.* ready to battle
18:14 bring him to *k.* of terrors
29:25 dwelt as a *k.* in the army
34:18 say to *k.* thou art wick.?
41:34 a *k.* over children of pride
Ps. 2:6 set my *k.* upon holy hill
5:2 my *k.* and my God, 84:3
10:16 Lord is *k.* for ever, 29:10
18:50 deliverance giveth he to *k.*
20:9 let *k.* hear us when we call
Ps. 21:1 *k.* shall joy in thy stren.
7 the *k.* trusted in the Lord
24:7 *k.* of glory shall come in, 9
8 who is *k.* of glory? the Lord
10 L. of hosts, he is *k.* of glory
33:16 no *k.* saved by multitude
45:1 things I made touc. the *k.*
11 so shall the *k.* greatly desi.
14 brought to the *k.* in raim.
47:6 praises to *k.* 7 God is *k.*
61:6 prolong *k.* life and years
63:11 the *k.* shall rejoice in God
72:1 give the *k.* thy judgments
74:12 God is my *k.* of old
84:18 H. One of Israel is our *k.*
96:6 make a noise bef. L. the *k.*
99:4 *k.* also loveth judgment
149:2 children of Z. joyful in *k.*
Prov. 14:28 people is the *k.* hon.
35 *k.* favor toward wise serv.
20:28 mercy and truth pres. *k.*
22:11 the *k.* shall be his friend
24:21 fear the Lord and the *k.*
25:5 take wicked from bef. *k.*
30:27 the locusts have no *k.*
31 *k.* against wh. no rising up
Ec. 2:12 man do cometh after *k.*
5:9 *k.* hims. served by the field
8:4 where word of a *k.* is power
10:16 woe to thee, wh. *k.* is ch.
17 bles. wh. *k.* is son of nobles
20 curse not the *k.* in thought
Cant. 1:4 *k.* bro. me to chamber
12 while the *k.* sitteth at table
3:11 *k.* Solomon with the crown
Is. 6:5 mine eyes ha. seen the *k.*
8:21 curse their *k.* and their G.
23:15 according to days of one *k.*
30:33 for the *k.* it is prepared
32:1 *k.* shall reign in righteous.
33:17 thine eyes shall see the *k.*
22 L. is our *k.* he will save us
43:15 Creator of Israel your *k.*
57:9 wentest to *k.* with ointm.
Jer. 4:9 heart of *k.* shall perish
8:19 is not her *k.* in her?
10:10 true God, everlasting *k.*
23:5 a *k.* shall reign and prosper
38:25 wh. said to *k.* the *k.* to th.
46:18 *k.* whose name is the Lord of hosts, 48:15; 51:57
49:38 I will des. *k.* and princes
Lam. 2:6 L. despised *k.* and pri.
Ezek. 17:13 hath tak. of *k.* seed
16 *k.* dwell. that made him *k.*
26:7 I will bring a *k.* of kings
37:22 one *k.* be *k.* to them all, 24

Dan. 2:24 bring me in before the *k.* and I will show the *k.*
4:31 while word was in *k.* mou.
37 I honor *k.* of heaven
5:5 *k.* saw part of hand th. wro.
8:23 a *k.* of fierce countenance
11:3 a mighty *k.* shall stand up
36 *k.* sh. do accord. to his will
Hos. 3:4 Is. sh. abide without *k.*
5 Is. seek L. and Dav. their *k.*
7:3 make *k.* glad with wicked.
5 in day of our *k.* princes made
10:3 what then should a *k.* do ?
7 her *k.* is cut off, as the foam
13:10 will be thy *k.* give me *k.*
11 gave thee *k.* in mine anger
Amos 7:13 *k.* chapel, the *k.* court
Mic. 4:9 why cry, is there no *k.* ?
Zec. 9:9 *k.* cometh, *Mat.* 21:5
14:9 L. shall be *k.* over all earth
16 go up to worship *k.* 17
Mat. 18:23 likened to cert. *k.* 22:2
22:11 when the *k.* came in
Mark 6:25 came with haste to *k.*
Luke 14:31 what *k.* goeth to war
19:38 blessed be *k.* that cometh
23:2 that he himself is Ch. a *k.*
John 6:15 to make him *k.*
12:15 behold thy *k.* come on ass
18:37 Pil. said, Art thou a *k.* ?
19:12 whoso. maketh himself *k.*
14 Pilate saith, Behold your *k.*
15 shall I crucify your *k.* ?
Acts 7:18 till another *k.* arose
13:21 afterward they desir. a *k.*
17:7 th. is another *k.* one Jesus
1 *Tim.* 1:17 now to the *k.* etern.
6:15 K. of kings, and L. of lords
Heb. 11:23 not afraid of *k.* com.
1 *Pet.* 2:13 whe. to *k.* as supreme
17 fear God, honor the *k.*
Rev. 9:11 they had a *k.* over th.
15:3 just are thy ways, K. of sai.
17:14 L. of lords, K. of ki. 19:16

KING *of the Amorites.* See SIHON.

KING of Assyria.
2 *K.* 15:19 Pul *k. of A.* ag. land
20 exac. money to give *k. of A.*
17:6 Hosea *k. of A.* took Sama.
2 *K.* 18:11 *k. of A.* did car. I. to A.
33 deliv. out of hand of *k. of A.*
Ezr. 6:22 turned heart of *k. of A.*
Is. 7:17 L. bring upon *k. of Ass.*
20 shave by *k. of Assyr.* head
Jer. 50:17 *k. of A.* devoured him
Nah. 3:18 slumber, O *k. of Assy.*

See BASHAN, BABYLON, DAVID.

KING of Egypt.
Ex. 3:19 *k. of Egypt* not let you
2 *K.* 24:7 *k. of Egypt* came not
2 *Chr.* 12:2 *k. of E.* came ag. Jer.
33:6 *k. of E.* put him down at J.
4 *k. of E.* made Eliakim king
Is. 36:6 so is *k. of Egypt* to all

See PHARAOH, GREAT, HOUSE, JEWS.

KING of Israel.
1 *Sam.* 26:20 *k. of Israel* is come
2 *Sam.* 6:20 glorious was *k. of Is.*
1 *K.* 22:31 fight only wi. *k. of Is.*
32 it is *k. of Is.* 2 *Chr.* 18:31
2 *K.* 6:11 which of us for *k. of Is.*
16:7 out of hand of *k. of Israel*
2 *Chr.* 18:30 fight not, sa. wi. *k. I.*
Hos. 10:15 *k. of Israel* be cut off
Zep. 3:15 *k. of Israel* in midst
Mat. 27:42 if he be *k. of Israel* let
him descend, *Mark* 15:32
John 1:49 thou art *k. of Israel*
12:13 blessed is the *k. of Israel*

KING of Judah.
2 *K.* 22:18 *k. of J.* wh. sent you
2 *Chr.* 35:21 what have I to do
with thee, thou *k. of Judah*

Jer. 37:7 *k. of J.* who sent you ?

KING of Moab.
Num. 23:7 *k. of M.* brought fr. A.
Jos. 24:9 *k. of M.* warred ag. Is.
Jud. 3:14 Is. ser. *k. of M.* 18 yrs.
11:25 art thou bet. th. *k. of M.* ?
1 *Sam.* 12:9 sold them to *k. of M.*
22:4 Da. bro. father to *k. of M.*
2 *K.* 3:4 *k. of M.* a sheep-master
26 *k. of Moab* saw battle
Jer. 27:3 send yokes to *k. of M.*

O KING.
1 *Sam.* 17:55 O *k.* I cannot tell
26:17 lord, O *k.* 2 *Sam.* 14:9, 22 :
16:4 ; 19:26 ; 1 *K.* 1:13, 20, 24 ;
20:4 ; 2 *K.* 6:12, 26 ; 8:5
2 *Sam.* 14:4 wo. said, Help, O *k.*
2 *Chr.* 25:7 O *k.* let not ar. of Is.
Ps. 145:1 I will extol thee, O *k.*
Jer. 10:7 thee, O *k.* of nations ?
Dan. 2:4 O *k.* live for ever, 3:9 ;
5:10 ; 6:21
29 O *k.* thy thoughts came into
31 thou, O *k.* sawest an image
37 thou, O *k.* art a *k.* of kings
3:10 thou, O *k.* hast ma. a decr.
17 del. us out of thy hand, O *k.*
18 be it known to thee, O *k.*
24 they answered, True, O *k.*
4:22 it is thou, O *k.* that art gr.
27 O *k.* let counsel be accept.
6:7 ask peti. save of thee, O *k.*
8 now, O *k.* establish decree
22 O *k.* I have done no hurt
Acts 26:13 O *k.* I saw in way
19 O *k.* I was not disobedient

KING of Persia.
Ezr. 4:3 *k. of Persia* commanded
5 reign of Darius *k. of P.* 9:9
7 Bish. wrote unto *k. of P.* 6:14

See CYRUS.

KING of Syria.
1 *K.* 20:20 *k. of S.* esc. on horse
2 *K.* 5:1 capt. of host of *k. of S.*
8:7 *k. of S.* sick ; 9 *k. of S.* sent
13:4 bec. *k. of S.* oppress. them
16:7 out of hand of *k. of Syria*
2 *Chr.* 16:7 relied on *k. of Syria*

See BENHADAD, HAZAEL, REZIN.

KING of Tyre.
2 *Sam.* 5:11 H. *k. of T.* 1 *Chr.* 14:1
1 *K.* 5:1 *k. of T.* sent S. servants
2 *Chr.* 2:11 *k. of T.* ans. in writ.

KINGS.
Gen. 17:6 *k.* shall come out of
thee, 16 ; 35:11
36:31 *k.* that reigned in Edom
Jos. 10:5 five *k.* of Amorites tog.
24 put feet on necks of those *k.*
12:24 all these *k.* thirty and one
Jud. 1:7 seventy *k.* thu. cu off
2 *Sam.* 11:1 when *k.* go to battle
1 *K.* 3:13 not any ans. *k.* like thee,
10:23 ; 2 *Chr.* 1:12 ; 9:22
4:24 Solomon over all the *k.*
2 *K.* 3:10 called three *k.* together
23 the *k.* are surely slain
10:4 two *k.* stood not bef. him
1 *Chr.* 16:21 reprov. *k. Ps.* 105:14
2 *Chr.* 9:23 *k.* sought presence S.
21:20 the sepulchres of *k.* 24:25
26:23 field of burial belong. to *k.*
Ezr. 4:15 city being hurtful to *k.*
6:12 G. dest. *k.* alter this house
7:12 Artaxerxes king of *k.* to E.
Neh. 9:32 trou. little to us and *k.*
34 nor have our *k.* kept thy law
Job 3:14 had I been at rest wi. *k.*
12:18 he looseth the bond of *k.*
36:7 *k.* are they on the throne
Ps. 2:2 the *k.* of the ear. *Acts* 4:26
10 therefore, O *k.* be instruct.
45:9 *k.* daughters among women
48:4 lo, the *k.* were assembled
68:12 *k.* of armies did flee apace

14 the Almighty scat. *k.* in it
29 sh. *k.* bring presents to thee
72:11 *k.* shall fall down be. him
76:12 terrible to *k.* of the earth
89:27 higher than *k.* of the earth
102:15 *k.* of earth sh. fear thy g.
110:5 strike *k.* in day of wrath
119:46 speak of testim. befo. *k.*
135:10 smote nations, and sl. *k.*
136:17 which smote great *k.* 18
138:4 *k.* of earth praise th. 148:11
144:10 he that giveth salva. to *k.*
149:8 bind their *k.* with chains

Prov. 8:15 by me *k.* reign
16:12 abom. for *k.* commit wick.
13 right. lips are delight of *k.*
22:29 dilig. shall stand before *k.*
25:2 honor of *k.* to search mat.
3 heart of *k.* is unsearchable
30:28 the spider is in *k.* palaces
31:3 ways to that wh. destroy *k.*
4 it is not for *k.* to drink

Ec. 2:8 peculiar treasure of *k.*
Is. 7:16 land forsaken of both *k.*
10:8 are not princes altoge. *k.* ?
14:18 *k.* of nations lie in glory
19:11 I am the son of ancient *k.*
24:21 L. punish *k.* of the earth
41:2 who made him ruler over *k.*
45:1 I will loose the loins of *k.*
49:7 *k.* shall see and arise
23 *k.* sh. be thy nursing fathers
52:15 *k.* sh. shut mouths at him
60:3 *k.* to brightn. of thy rising
10 *k.* shall minister to thee
11 that their *k.* may be brong.
16 thou shalt suck breast of *k.*
62:2 all *k.* shall see thy glory
Jer. 2:26 *k.* and princes ashamed
13:13 *k.* that sit on David's thr.
22:4 *k.* sitting upon throne of D.
25:18 made Judah and *k.* drink
34:5 with burnings of former *k.*
41:17 *k.* and princes bu. incense
46:25 punish their *k.* and gods
49:3 their *k.* shall go to captivi.
50:41 many *k.* shall be raised up
Lam. 4:12 *k.* of earth not believ.
Ezek. 27:35 *k.* be sore afra. 32:10
28:17 I will lay thee before *k.*
43:7 *k.* no more defile my name
Dan. 2:21 removeth *k.* set. up *k.*
44 in the days of these *k.*
47 that your G. is a Lord of *k.*
7:17 four great beasts are four *k.*
24 the ten horns are ten *k.*
9:6 spake in thy name to our *k.*
8 to *k.* and princes belong con.
11:2 three *k.* 27 these *k.* hearts
Hos. 7:7 all their *k.* are fallen
8:4 they set up *k.* but not by me
Hab. 1:10 they shall scoff at *k.*
Mat. 10:18 bron. before *k.* for my
sake, *Mark* 13:9 ; *Luke* 21:12
11:8 wear soft cloth. in *k.* hous.
17:25 of wh. do *k.* of earth take ?
Luke 10:24 *k.* have desired to see
22:25 *k.* of Gentiles exercise
1 *Cor.* 4:8 ye have reigned as *k.*
1 *Tim.* 2:2 pray, be made for *k.*
6:15 King of *k.* and Lord of
lords, *Rev.* 17:14 ; 19:16
Heb. 7:1 returned from slang. *k.*
Rev. 1:5 J. Christ prince of *k.*
6 *k.* and priest unto God, 5:10
6:15 *k.* of earth hid themselves
10:11 must prophesy before *k.*
16:12 way of *k.* of east prepared
14 spirits which go forth to *k.*
Rev. 17:2 *k.* of earth commit. for.
10 seven *k.* five are fallen
12 ten *k.* w. receive pow. as *k.*
18 wh. reign. over *k.* of earth
18:3 *k.* of earth have committed
9 *k.* of earth who shall bewail
19:18 eat the flesh of *k.* and cap.
21:24 *k.* of the earth bring glory

KINGS of the Amorites.

Deut. 4:47 two *k. of the A.* 31:4;
  Jos. 2:10 ; 9:10 ; 24:12
Jos. 10:5 five *k. of A.* together. 6
See BOOK, GREAT.

KINGS of Israel.

1 *K.* 14:19 book of the Chronicles of the *k. of Is.* 15:31 ;
  16:5; 14, 20, 27; 22:39 ; 2 *K.*
  1:18; 10:34; 13:8, 12; 14:15
  28 ; 15:11, 15, 21, 26, 31
  16:33 prov. more th. all *k. of I.*
  20:31 *k. of I.* are merciful kings
2 *K.* 7:2 evil but not as *k. of I.*
  23:19 away horses *k. of I.* made
  22 a passo. in days of *k. of I.*
1 *Chr.* 9:1 written in book of *k.*
  of I. 2 *Chr.* 16:11 ; 25:26;
  27:7 ; 28:26 ; 32:32 ; 33:18
2 *Chr.* 20:34 in book of Jehu
  who is mentioned in book
  of the *k. of I.* 35:27 ; 36:8
  28:27 not into sepul. of *k. of I.*
Mic. 1:14 shall be a lie to *k. of I.*

KINGS of Judah.

1 *K.* 14:29 the book of the Chronicles of the *k. of Jud.* 15:7,
  23; 22:45 : 2 *K.* 8:23 ; 15:6,
  36; 16:19; 20:20; 21:17, 25;
  23:28 ; 24:5
2 *K.* 12:19 written in the book of
  the Chronicles of the *k. of.*
  J. 14:18 ; 2 *Chr.* 25:26; 28:26;
  32:32 ; 35:27 ; 36:8
  23:11 horses *k. of J.* had given
  12 down altars *k. of J.* made
  22 not pass. in days of *k. of J.*
2 *Chr.* 34:11 houses *k. of J.* des.
Jer. 1:18 made pillar ag. *k. of J.*
  8:1 bring out bones of *k. of J.*
  19:4 gods *k. of J.* ha. not known
  20:5 treas. of *k. of J.* to enemies
  44:9 forgot. wickedn. of *k. of J.*

See KINGS *of Israel.*

KINGDOM.

Ex. 19:6 ye sh. be a *k.* of priests
Deut. 3:4 took *k.* of Og in Bash.
1 *Sam.* 10:16 mat. of *k.* he told
  25 Sam. told manner of the *k.*
  11:14 renew k. th. 14:47 took *k.*
  15:28 Lord rent *k.* of Is. 28:17
  18:8 w. can he ha. more but *k.*
2 *Sam.* 3:10 translate *k.* from S.
  16:3 restore me *k.* of my father
1 *K.* 2:22 ask *k.* he is elder brot.
  11:11 will rend *k.* from th. 31:35
  13 will not rend away all *k.* 34
  12:21 to bring *k.* again to Rehoboam, 2 *Chr.* 11:1
  14:8 rent *k.* from house of Dav.
  18:10 no *k.* my lord ha. not sent
2 *K.* 14:5 soon as *k.* confirmed
1 *Chr.* 16:20 fr. one *k.* to another
  people, *Ps.* 105:13
  29:11 thine is the *k.* O Lord,
  Ps. 22:28 ; *Mat.* 6:13
2 *Chr.* 13:8 withstand *k.* of Lord
  22:9 no power to keep still *k.*
Neh. 9:35 not serv. thee in th. *k.*
Est. 1:14 pri. wh. sat first in *k.*
  4:14 come to *k.* for such a time
  5:3 be given to half of *k.* 6; 7:2
Is. 19:2 shall fight *k.* ag. *k. hat.*
  24:7 ; *Mark* 13:8 ; *Luke* 21:10
  60:12 *k.* not serve thee, *Jer.* 27:8
Jer. 18:7 I speak concerning a *k.*
Lam. 2:2 he hath polluted the *k.*
Ezek. 16:13 didst prosper into *k.*
  17:14 the *k.* might be base
  29:14 shall be there a base *k.*
Dan. 2:37 G. hath given thee *k.*
  44 sh. G. of heaven set up a *k.*
  4:17 ruleth in *k.* of men, 25, 32
  31 the *k.* is departed from thee
  6:4 against Dan. concerning *k.*
  7:18 saints take *k.* and pos. *k.*

22 time came saints posses. *k.*
27 whose *k.* is an everlasting *k.*
11:21 not give the honor of *k.*
Hos. 1:4 cause to cease *k.* of Isr.
Amos 9:8 eyes of L. upon sinf. *k.*
Ob. 21 *k.* shall be the Lord's
Mat. 4:23 gosp. of *k.* 9:35 ; 24:14
  8:12 child. of *k.* shall be cast
  12:25 *k.* divided is bro. to desolation. *Mark* 3:24 ; *Lu.* 11:17
  13:38 good seed are child. of *k.*
  43 shine as sun in *k.* of Father
  25:34 inherit *k.* prepared for you
  26:29 drink it new in Fath.'s *k.*
Mark 11:10 blessed be *k.* of fath.
Luke 12:32 F.'s pleas. to give *k.*
  19:12 nobleman went to rec. *k.*
  22:29 I appoint unto you a *k.*
Acts 1:6 restore *k.* again to Isr.?
1 *Cor.* 15:24 have delivered up *k.*
Col. 1:13 translated us into the *k.*
Heb. 12:28 *k.* th. cannot be mov.
Jam. 2:5 heirs of *k.* he promised
2 *Pet.* 1:11 entrance into everl. *k.*
Rev. 1:9 companion in *k.*
  17:12 which have received no *k.*
  17 and give their *k.* to the beast.

See THRONE, ESTABLISH, ESTAB-
  LISHED.

KINGDOM of God.

Mat. 6:33 but seek ye first the *k.*
  of *God, Luke* 12:31
  12:28 *k. of God* is come unto
  you, *Luke* 10:9, 11:20
  19:24 than for a rich man to enter into *k. of G. Mark* 10:23 ;
  Luke 18:24
  21:31 harlots go into *k. of God*
  43 *k. of G.* be taken from you
Mark 1:14 preaching *k. of God,*
  Acts 8:12 ; 20:25 ; 28:31
  15 the *k. of God* is at hand
  4:11 to know the mystery of *k.*
  of *God, Luke* 8:10
  9:1 till they have seen *k. of G.*
  47 better to enter into *k. of G.*
  10:14 such is *k. of G. Luke* 18:16
  15 whoso not receive *k. of G.*
  24 hard for th. trust in riches
  to enter *k. of G.* 25 ; *Lu.* 18:25
  12:34 art not far from *k. of God*
  14:25 I drink it new in *k. of G.*
  15:43 which waited for the *k. of*
  God, Luke 23:51
Luke 4:43 I must preach *k. of G.*
  6:20 for yours is the *k. of God*
  7:28 least in *k. of G.* greater th.
  9:2 sent th. to preach *k. of G.* 60
  27 not taste de. till see *k. of G.*
  62 lo. back, not fit for *k. of G.*
  13:28 see prophets in *k. of God*
  14:15 he eat bread in *k. of God*
  16:16 time *k. of God* preached
  17:20 *k. of God* cometh not
  21 *k. of God* is within you
  18:29 left child. for *k. of G.* sake
  19:11 tho. *k. of G.* sho. appear
  21:31 that *k. of G.* is at hand
  22:16 be fulfilled in *k. of God*
  18 not drink until *k. of G.* co.
John 3:3 bo. ag. can see *k. of G.*
  5 cannot enter into *k. of God*
Acts 1:3 things pertaining to *k.*
  of *God,* 8:12 ; 19:8
  14:22 thro' tribul. enter *k. of G.*
  28:23 expou. and testi. *k. of G.*
Rom. 14:17 *k. of G.* is not meat
1 *Cor.* 4:20 *k. of God* is not in w.
  6:9 unright. not inherit *k. of G.*
  10 nor extortioners inhe. *k. of*
  God, Gal. 5:21 ; *Eph.* 5:5
  15:50 flesh can. in. *k. of G.*
2 *Thes.* 1:5 worthy *k. of God*
Rev. 12:10 is come *k. of* our *God*

KINGDOM of heaven.

Mat. 3:2 repent, for *k. of heaven*
  is at hand, 4:17 ; 10:7

5:3 theirs is *k. of heaven,* 10
  19 least in *k. of h.* g. in *k. of h.*
  20 in no case ent. *k. of h.* 18:3
  7:21 saith, Lord, sh. ent. *k. of h.*
  8:11 sit with Abrah. in *k. of h.*
  11:11 least in *k. of h.* gre. th. he
  12 *k. of heaven* suffer. violence
  13:11 know mysteries of *k. of h.*
  16:19 give thee keys of *k. of h.*
  18:1 who is great. in *k. of h.* ? 4
  23:13 shut up *k. of h.* aga. men

His KINGDOM.

Gen. 10:10 begin. of *his k.* was B.
Num. 24:7 *his k.* shall be exalted
Deut. 17:18 sit. on throne of *h. k.*
1 *Chr.* 11:10 strengthened in *h. k.*
2 *Chr.* 1:1 S. strengthen. in *h. k.*
Ps. 103:19 *h. k.* ruleth over all
  145:12 glorious majesty of *h. k.*
Is. 9:7 *h. k.* to order and establi.
Dan. 4:3 *his k.* is an everl. king.
  34 *h. k.* fr. generat. 6:26 ; 7:14
  11:4 *h. k.* broken and pluck. up
Mat. 12:26 *h. k.* stand ? *Lu.* 11:18
  13:41 gather out of *his k.* all th.
  16:28 S. of man coming in *h. k.*
Luke 1:33 of *h. k.* sh. be no end
1 *Thes.* 2:12 called you to *h. k.*
2 *Tim.* 4:1 appearing and *his k.*
Rev. 16:10 *his k.* full of darkness

My KINGDOM.

Gen. 20:9 brou. on me and *m. k.*
2 *Sam.* 3:28 I and *m. k.* are guil.
Dan. 4:36 glo. of *my k.* in *my k.*
  6:26 in every dominion of *my k.*
Mark 6:23 to half of *my k.*
Luke 22:30 drink at *my* table in
  my k.
John 18:36 *my k.* not of th. world

Thy KINGDOM.

1 *Sam.* 13:14 t. *k.* sh. not contin.
Ps. 45:6 t. *k.* ri. sceptre, *Heb.* 1:8
  145:11 speak of glory of *thy k.*
  13 *thy k.* is everlasting kingd.
Dan. 4:26 t. *k.* shall be sure
  5:11 mau in *t. k.* 26 numb. *t. k.*
  28 *t. k.* divided to Med. and P.
Mat. 6:10 *t. k.* come, *Luke* 11:2
  20:21 the other on left in *t. k.*
Luke 23:42 thou comest to *t. k.*

KINGDOMS.

1 *Sam.* 10:18 out of hand of all *k.*
1 *K.* 4:21 Sol. reigned over all *k.*
2 *K.* 19:15 God of all *k.* of earth
2 *Chr.* 12:8 may know serv. of *k.*
  20:6 thou rulest over all the *k.*
  36:23 all *k.* hath the Lord given
  me, *Ezr.* 1:2
Ps. 46:6 heath. raged, *k.* moved
  79:6 wrath on *k.* have not called
  102:22 *k.* gathered to serve Lord
Is. 10:10 hand found *k.* of idols
  13:4 noise of *k.* of nations gath.
  14:16 is this man did shake *k.* ?
  23:11 shook *k.* 37:16 God of *k.*
Jer. 1:10 over *k.* I have set thee
  15:4 rem. to all *k.* 24:9 ; 34:17
  25:26 all *k.* of world shall drink
  29:18 make th. terror to all *k.*
  34:1 *k.* fought against Jerusal.
Ezek. 29:15 be the bas. of the *k.*
  37:22 nor be divided into two *k.*
Dan. 2:44 shall cons. all these *k.*
  7:23 shall be diverse from all *k.*
  8:22 four *k.* stand out of nation
Nah. 3:5 will show *k.* thy shame
Zep. 3:8 assemble the *k.* to pour
Hag. 2:22 overthrow throne of *k.*
Mat. 4:8 all *k.* of world, *Luke* 4:5
Heb. 11:33 thro' faith subdued *k.*
Rev. 11:15 *k.* of world are *k.* of L.

KINGLY.

Dan. 5:20 deposed from *k.* thro.

KINSFOLK, S.

1 *K.* 16:11 none of Baasha's *k.*

KINSFOLK

2 *K.* 10:11 Jehu slew Ahab's *k.*
Job 19:14 *k.* failed and forgot. me
Luke 2:44 sought Jesus among *k.*
21:16 betrayed by *k.* and friends

KINSMAN.

Num. 5:8 if the man have no *k.*
27:11 give his inheritance to *k.*
Ruth 3:9 near *k.* 12 *k.* nearer
13 perform to thee part of a *k.*
4:1 behold *k.* of whom B. spake
14 not left thee without a *k.*
John 18:26 *k.* whose ear P. cut off
Rom. 16:11 salute Herodi. my *k.*

KINSMEN.

Ruth 2:20 is one of our next *k.*
Ps. 38:11 lovers and *k.* stood off
Luke 14:12 call not breth. nor *k.*
Acts 10:24 Cornelius called his *k.*
Rom. 9:3 my *k.* according to flesh
16:7 salute *k.* 21 *k.* salute you

KINSWOMAN, MEN.

Lev. 18:12 is my father's near *k.*
13 she is thy mother's near *k.*
17 for they are her near *k.*
Prov. 7:4 call understand. thy *k.*

KIR.

2 *K.* 16:9 people captive to K.
Is. 15:1 K. of M. is laid waste
Amos 9:7 bro. Assyrians from K.

KIR-HARASETH.

2 *K.* 3:25 in K. left they stones
Is. 16:7 foundations of K. shall

KIRIATHAIM.

Gen. 14:5 smote E. in Shav. K.
Jer. 48:1 K. is confounded, 23

KIRJATH-ARBA.

Gen. 23:2 Sar. died in K. *Jos.*
14:15 ; 20:7 ; *Jud.* 1:10

KIRJATH-JEARIM.

Jos. 9:17 K. a city of Hivites
1 *Sam.* 7:1 men of K. fetched ark
1 *Chr.* 13:5 the ark of God fr. K.
2 *Chr.* 1:4 broug. the ark fr. K.
KIRJATH-SEPHER. *Jos.* 15:15,
49

KISH.

1 *Sam.* 9:1 man wh. na. K. 14:51
10:11 wh. is come to son of K. ?
2 *Sam.* 21:14 Sa. in sepulchre K.
Acts 13:21 G. gave the son of K.

KISS, ES.

Prov. 27:6 *k.* of an enemy deceit.
Cant. 1:2 *k.* me with *k.* of mouth
Luke 7:45 thou gavest me no *k.*
22:48 betra. Son of man wi. *k.?*
Rom. 16:16 salute with a holy *k.*
1 *Cor.* 16:20 gr. wi. *k.* 2 *Cor.* 13:12
1 *Thes.* 5:26 greet breth. w. h. *k.*
1 *Pet.* 5:14 greet with *k.* of chari.

KISS, Verb.

Gen. 27:26 come near and *k.* me
31:28 not suffered to *k.* my sons
2 *Sam.* 20:9 Ama. by beard to *k.*
1 *K.* 19:20 *k.* my father and mot.
Ps. 2:12 *k.* Son, lest he be angry
Prov. 24:26 every man *k.* his lips
Cant. 1:2 *k.* me with kisses of m.
8:1 I would *k.* thee, yet I should
Hos. 13:2 men sacrifi. *k.* the calv.
Mat. 26:48 whomsoever I *k.* hold
him fast, *Mark* 14:44
Luke 7:45 not ceased *k.* my feet
22:47 Judas drew near to J. to *k.*

KISSED.

Gen. 27:27 Ja. came and *k.* him
29:11 Jacob *k.* Rachel and wept
31:55 La. *k.* sons and daughters
45:15 J. *k.* all his brethren
48:10 J. *k.* Joseph's sons
50:1 Jos. fell on fa.'s face *k.* him
Ex. 4:27 met Moses and *k.* him
18:7 met father-in-law *k.* him
Ruth 1:9 Na. *k.* daughters-in-law

---

1 *Sam.* 10:1 poured oil and *k.* S.
20:41 Jonathan and David *k.*
2 *Sam.* 14:33 king *k.* Absalom
15:5 Absa. *k.* any man came ni.
1 *K.* 19:18 mouth hath not *k.*
Job 31:27 mouth hath *k.* hand
Ps. 85:10 and peace *k.* each other
Prov. 7:13 caught him *k.* him
Mat. 26:49 said, Hail, Master,
and *k.* him, *Mark* 14:45
Luke 7:38 M. *k.* feet and anointed
15:20 fell on his neck and *k.* him
Acts 20:37 fell on P.'s neck *k.* h.

KITE.

Lev. 11:14 *k.* uncl. *Deut.* 14:13
KITTIM. *Gen.* 10:4 ; 1 *Chr.* 1:7

KNEAD, ED.

Gen. 18:6 *k.* it and make cakes
1 *Sam.* 28:24 took flour and *k.* it
2 *Sam.* 13:8 Tamar took flour *k.*
Jer. 7:18 women *k.* their dough
Hos. 7:4 the baker *k.* the dough

KNEADING.

Ex. 8:3 frogs co. into *k.*-troughs
12:34 *k.*-troughs bound in cloth.

KNEE.

Gen. 41:43 they cried, Bow the *k.*
Is. 45:23 unto me every *k.* sh.
bow, *Rom.* 14:11 ; *Phil.* 2:10
Mat. 27:29 bowed the *k.* bef. him
Rom. 11:4 bowed the *k.* to Baal

KNEEL, ED.

Gen. 24:11 ma. his camels *k.* do.
2 *Chr.* 6:13 Solomon *k.* on knees
Ps. 95:6 let us *k.* before the L.
Dan. 6:10 D. *k.* three times a day
Luke 22:41 and Jesus *k.* down
Acts 7:60 Stephen *k.* and cried
9:40 Peter *k.* prayed ; 20:36 P.
21:5 we *k.* down on the shore

KNEELING.

1 *K.* 8:54 Solomon rose from *k.*
Mat. 17:14 a man *k.* to him, say-
ing, *Mark* 10:17
Mark 1:40 came a leper *k.*

KNEES.

Gen. 30:3 maid sh. bear on my *k.*
48:12 brou. them fr. between *k.*
50:23 brought up on Joseph's *k.*
Deut. 28:35 Lord smite thee in *k.*
Jud. 7:5 bowed down *k.* 6
16:19 made Sam. sleep on her *k.*
1 *K.* 8:54 arose fr. kneeling on *k.*
18:42 Elijah put face bet. his *k.*
19:18 *k.* have not bowed to Baal
2 *K.* 1:13 fell on *k.* before Elijah
4:20 sat on mother's *k.* till noon
2 *Chr.* 6:13 Sol. kneeled on his *k.*
Ezr. 9:5 I fell on my *k.*
Job 3:12 why did *k.* prevent me
4:4 strengthened the feeble *k.*
Ps. 109:24 *k.* weak thro' fasting
Is. 35:3 confirm the feeble *k.*
66:12 and be dandled on her *k.*
Ezek. 7:17 *k.* weak as water, 21:7
47:4 the waters were to the *k.*
Dan. 5:6 *k.* smo. one ag. another
6:10 kneeled on *k.* three times
10:10 a hand set me upon my *k.*
Nah. 2:10 the *k.* smite together
Mark 15:19 bowing *k.* worship.
Luke 5:8 Peter fell at Jesus' *k.*
Eph. 3:14 bow my *k.* to Father
Heb. 12:12 hands hang do. fc. *k.*

KNEW.

Gen. 4:1 Adam *k.* E. his wife, 25
17 Cain *k.* wife, she conceived
38:26 Jud. *k.* her again no more
Jud. 11:39 daughter *k.* no man
19:25 *k.* her and abused her
1 *K.* 1:4 but the king *k.* her not
Mat. 1:25 Joseph *k.* her not

KNEW.

Gen. 3:7 Adam and Eve *k.* that

9:24 Noah *k.* what son had done
38:9 O. *k.* seed should not be h.
42:7 Joseph saw and *k.* breth. 8
Num. 24:16 *k.* knowl. of M. H.
Deut. 34:10 wh. L. *k.* face to face
1 *Sam.* 3:20 *k.* Sam. was a prop.
18:28 Saul L. was with David
20:39 D. and Jonathan *k.* mat.
22:17 bec. they *k.* when he fled
26:17 Saul *k.* David's voice
2 *Sam.* 11:16 *k.* that valiant men
2 *Chr.* 33:13 Manas. *k.* L. was G.
Est. 1:13 that *k.* law and judgm.
Job 23:3 *k.* where I might find
Is. 48:4 I *k.* thou art obstinate
7 should. say, Behold, I *k.* th.
Jer. 1:5 formed thee, I *k.* thee
32:8 I *k.* this was word of Lord
41:4 slain Gedaliah, no man *k.*
44:15 *k.* wives burnt incense
Dan. 5:21 he *k.* Most High ruled
6:10 Daniel *k.* wri. was signed
Jon. 4:2 *k.* thou art a graci. God
Zec. 11:11 *k.* it was word of L.
Mat. 7:23 profess I never *k.* you
12:25 J. *k.* thoughts, *Luke* 6:8
25:24 I *k.* thee, thou art hard m.
Mark 1:34 because they *k.* him
Luke 4:41 they *k.* he was Christ
12:47 servant *k.* his lord's will
24:31 eyes opened, they *k.* him
John 2:24 because he *k.* all men
25 for he *k.* what was in man
6:6 himself *k.* what he would do
64 Jesus *k.* from the beginning
11:42 I *k.* that thou hearest me
57 if any man *k.* where he we.
13:1 Jesus *k.* his hour was co.
11 he *k.* who should betray h.
28 no man at the table *k.* for
18:2 Judas *k.* the place
Acts 12:14 Rhoda *k.* Peter's voi.
22:29 *k.* that he was a Roman
Rom. 1:21 bec. when they *k.* G.
1 *Cor.* 2:8 no. of princes of wo. *k.*
2 *Cor.* 5:21 sin, who *k.* no sin
12:2 I *k.* a man in Christ, 3
Col. 1:6 since ye *k.* grace of God
2:1 *k.* what great conflict I have
Jude 5 though ye once *k.* this
Rev. 19:12 name writ. no man *k.*

KNEW not.

Gen. 38:16 place, and *k.* it *not*
38:16 Judah *k. not* she was his
Ex. 1:8 king which *k. n.* Joseph
Num. 22:34 I *k. not* thou stood.
Deut. 8:16 thy fathers *k. not*
29:26 gods thy fath. *k. not,* 32:17
Jud. 2:10 generation *k. not* L.
14:4 *k. not* that it was of the L.
1 *Sam.* 2:12 sons of Eli *k. n.* L.
20:39 the lad *k. not* any thing
2 *Sam.* 11:20 *k.* ye n. th. would
18:29 but I *k. not* what it was
22:44 peop. I *k. n.* sh. serve me
Job 2:12 Job's friends *k.* him *not*
29:16 cause I *k. n.* I search. out
42:3 th. I *k. n.* wonder. for me
Ps. 35:11 charge things I *k. not*
Prov. 24:12 behold, we *k.* it *not*
Is. 42:16 blind by way they *k. n.*
25 set him on fire, yet he *k. n.*
55:5 nations that *k. not* thee
Jer. 2:8 that handle law, *k.* me *n.*
11:19 I *k. not* they had devised
44:3 serve gods whom they *k. n.*
Dan. 11:38 whom fathers *k. not*
Hos. 8:4 made prin. and I *k.* it *n.*
11:3 they *k. not* that I healed
Mat. 17:12 E. co. they *k.* him *n.*
24:39 *k. not* till the flood came
Luke 2:43 Jos. and mother *k. n.*
12:48 *k. not* and did commit th.
John 1:10 the world *k.* him *not*
31 and I *k.* him *not,* 33
20:9 they *k. not* the scriptures
14 *k. not* that it was J. 21:4

Acts 13:27 because they *k.* him *n.*
19:32 *k. n.* wherefore they came
27:39 when day, they *k. n.* land
1 *Cor.* 1:21 by wisdom *k. not* G.
Gal. 4:8 then when ye *k. n.* God
1 *John* 3:1 because it *k.* him *not*

KNEWEST.
Deut. 8:3 fed with manna, *k.* not
Ruth 2:11 to people thou *k.* not
Ps. 142:3 then thou *k.* my path
Is. 48:8 heardest not, thou *k.* not
Mat. 25:26 thou *k.* I reaped where
    I sowed not, *Luke* 19:22
Luke 19:44 *k.* not time of visit.
John 4:10 if thou *k.* gift of God

KNIFE.
Gen. 22:6 Abraham took *k.* 10
Jud. 19:29 took *k.* and laid hold
Prov. 23:2 put a *k.* to thy throat
Ezek. 5:1 take thee a sharp *k.* 2

KNIVES.
Jos. 5:2 make sharp *k.*
    3 Joshua made him sharp *k.*
1 *K.* 18:28 cut themselves with *k.*
Ezr. 1:9 nine and twenty *k.*
Prov. 30:14 teeth as *k.* dev. poor

KNIT.
Jud. 20:11 Is. were *k.* together
1 *Sam.* 18:1 Jonathan *k.* to Da.
1 *Chr.* 12:17 my heart be *k.* to y.
Acts 10:11 sheet *k.* at four corne.
Col. 2:2 hearts *k.* together in lo.
    19 body *k.* together increaseth

KNOCK, ED.
Mat. 7:7 *k.* it sh. be op. *Lu.* 11:9
Luke 13:25 begin to *k.* at door
Acts 12:13 as Peter *k.* at the door
Rev. 3:20 I stand at door and *k.*

KNOCKETH, ING.
Cant. 5:2 voice of beloved that *k.*
Mat. 7:8 him that *k.* shall be
    opened, *Luke* 11:10
Luke 12:36 when he *k.* they may
Acts 12:16 Peter continued *k.*

KNOP, S.
Ex. 25:31 his *k.* and his flowers,
    33, 34, 36 ; 37:17, 19, 20, 22
1 *K.* 6:18 cedar carved with *k.*
    7:24 *k.* compass. it, *k.* cast into

KNOW.
Gen. 3:5 God doth *k.* your eyes
    22 one of us, to *k.* good and e.
    18:21 I will go and see, I will *k.*
Ex. 18:16 *k.* the statutes of God
Num. 14:31 they shall *k.* the la.
Deut. 4:39 *k.* this day, 11:2
    8:2 *k.* what was in thy heart
    13:3 *k.* whether ye love the Lo.
Jos. 4:22 let your children *k.*
    22:22 and Israel he shall *k.*
Ruth 3:11 city of my peo. doth *k.*
    14 before one could *k.* another
1 *Sam.* 17:47 assembly shall *k.* L.
    21:2 let no man *k.* any thing
    24:11 *k.* there is no evil in me
    28:2 *k.* what thy servant can do
2 *Sam.* 3:25 thy going out, *k.* all
    19:20 serv. *k.* that I have sinned
1 *K.* 8:38 *k.* every man the
    plague, 2 *Chr.* 6:29
2 *K.* 5:8 sh. *k.* there is a prophet
    10:10 *k.* there shall fall nothing
1 *Chr.* 28:9 *k.* thou G. of thy fat.
2 *Chr.* 13:5 to *k.* that the L. gave
Est. 4:5 *k.* what it was, and why
Job 5:24 *k.* thy tabernacle
    25 *k.* that thy seed sh. be great
    27 and *k.* thou it for thy good
    7:10 nor shall his place *k.*
    8:9 but of yesterday, *k.* nothing
    11:6 *k.* that God exacteth less
    8 what canst thou *k.* ?
    13:23 make me *k.* my transgres.
    19:6 *k.* that G. hath overthrown
    21:19 G. reward. him, he sh. *k.*
    22:13 sayest, How doth God *k.* ?

24:1 they that *k.* him not see ?
    17 if one *k.* them, they are in
    34:4 *k.* am. oursel. what is good
    37:15 dost *k.* when God dispos.
    38:20 *k.* the paths to the house
Ps. 4:3 *k.* L. hath set apart godly
    9:10 that *k.* thy na. trust in thee
    39:4 L. make me to *k.* mine end
    46:10 still, and *k.* that I am G.
    51:6 in hid. part make me to *k.*
    59:13 let them *k.* that G. ruleth
    73:11 doth G. *k.* 16 thought to *k.*
    89:15 blessed are they that *k.*
    103:16 place shall *k.* it no more
    139:23 *k.* my heart, *k.* my thou.
    142:4 no man would *k.* me
    143:8 *k.* way wherein I should
Prov. 1:2 *k.* wisd. and instruct
    4:1 attend to *k.* understanding
    10:32 righteous *k.* wh. is accept.
    27:23 dilig. to *k.* state of flocks
Ec. 1:17 gave heart to *k.* wisd.
    7:25 applied heart to *k.* wisdom
    8:17 tho. a wise man think *to k.*
    9:5 the living *k.* they shall die
    11:9 *k.* that G. will bring to ju.
Is. 7:16 before the child shall *k.*
    19:21 Egyptians shall *k.* the L.
    41:20 that they may see and *k.*
    49:26 all flesh shall *k.* I am
    50:4 *k.* how to speak in season
    52:6 my people sh. *k.* my name
    58:2 and delight to *k.* my ways
    60:16 *k.* that I the L. am thy S.
Jer. 2:19 *k.* it is evil to forsake
Jer. 9:6 thro' deceit refuse to *k.*
    15:15 *k.* that for thy sake I suf.
    16:21 cause them to *k.* my hand,
    and they sh. *k.* my name is
    17:9 heart deceit. who can *k.* it ?
    24:7 give them a heart to *k.* me
    31:34 *k.* the Lord, for they shall
    all *k.* me, *Heb.* 8:11
    36:19 let no man *k.* where ye be
Ezek. 2:5 *k.* ha. been a pro. 33:33
    5:13 *k.* I the Lord have spoken
    25:14 they sh. *k.* my vengeance
    28:19 all that *k.* thee be aston.
    34:30 they *k.* I am with them
    37:28 heathen shall *k.* 39:23
Dan. 2:21 know. to them who *k.*
    4:25 *k.* that M. High ruleth, 32
    7:16 made me *k.* interpretation
    11:32 peo. that *k.* God be strong
Hos. 2:20 thou shalt *k.* the Lord
    9:7 Israel shall *k.* it
    13:4 thou sh. *k.* no God but me
    14:9 prudent, and he sh. *k.* th.
Mic. 3:1 for you to *k.* judgment
Zec. 2:11 *k.* the L. sent me, 4:9
Mal. 2:4 ye sh. *k.* I have sent th.
Mat. 6:3 let not thy left hand *k.*
    7:11 *k.* how to give, *Luke* 11:13
    9:30 see no man *k.* it: *Mark*
    5:43 ; 7:24 ; 9:30
    13:11 it is given to you to *k.*
    Mark 4:11 ; *Luke* 8:10
    24:33 *k.* desolation is near,
    Mark 13:29 ; *Luke* 21:20
John 4:42 we *k.* that this is Chr.
    7:17 he shall *k.* of the doctrine
    10:4 sheep fol. they *k.* his voice
    14 am good Shep. *k.* my sheep
    13:7 thou shalt *k.* hereafter
    35 men *k.* ye are my disciples
    18:21 behold, they *k.* what I sa.
Acts 1:7 not for you to *k.* times
    22:14 *k.* his will and see J. One
    26:4 from my youth *k.* all Jews
Rom. 7:1 speak to them that *k.*
    10:19 I say, Did not Israel *k.* ?
1 *Cor.* 2:14 neither can he *k.* th.
    8:2 know. noth. as ought to *k.*
Eph. 3:19 *k.* the love of Christ
1 *Thes.* 3:5 I sent to *k.* your faith
    4:4 ev. one sho. *k.* how to pos.
    5:12 *k.* them who labor among
1 *Tim.* 4:3 believe and *k.* truth

---

2 *Tim.* 3:1 *k.* also that in last da.
Tit. 1:16 profess that they *k.* G.,
Jam. 2:20 wilt thou *k.* O vain
Jude 10 what they *k.* naturally
Rev. 2:23 churches sh. *k.* I am he
    3:9 make them *k.* I have loved

See CERTAIN, CERTAINLY, CERTAINTY.

I KNOW.
Gen. 12:11 *I k.* thou art fair wo.
    15:8 *I k.* that I shall inherit?
    18:19 *I k.* he will com. his chil.
    22:12 *I k.* that thou fearest God
    48:19 *I k.* it, my son, *I k.* it
Ex. 3:7 said, *I k.* their sorrows
    4:14 brother ? *I k.* he can speak
    18:11 *I k.* L. grea. than all gods
    33:12 *I k.* thee by thy name, 17
Deut. 31:21 *I k.* th. imagination
    29 *I k.* that after my death
Jos. 2:9 *I k.* L. hath given you
Jud. 17:13 *k.* *I* L. will do good
1 *Sam.* 20:30 *I k.* cho. son of J. ?
    24:20 *I k.* thou shalt surely be
    29:9 *I k.* thou art good
2 *K.* 2:3 *I k.* it, hold peace, 5
    5:15 *I k.* there is no G. in earth
    19:27 *I k.* thy abode, *Is.* 37:28
1 *Chr.* 29:17 *I k.* thou triest heart
2 *Chr.* 25:16 *I k.* G. hath determ.
Job 9:28 *I k.* not hold-me innoc.
    13:2 ye know., the same do *I k.*
    18 *I k.* that I shall be justified
    19:25 *I k.* my Redeemer liveth
    21:27 *I k.* your thoughts
    30:23 *I k.* th. bring me to death
    42:2 *I k.* thou canst do every th.
Ps. 20:6 *I k.* L. sav. his anointed
    41:11 *I k.* thou favorest me
    50:11 *I k.* all fowls of mountain
    119:75 *I k.* O L. thy judg. right.
    135:5 *I k.* L. is greater above all
    140:12 *I k.* L. will maint. cause
Ec. 3:12 *I k.* th. no good in them
    8:12 *I k.* it shall be well with
Is. 47:8 nor shall *I k.* loss of chi.
    66:18 *I k.* works and thoughts
Jer. 10:23 *I k.* the way of man
    11:18 L. given me knowl. *I k.* it
    29:11 *I k.* the thoughts I think
    23 *I k.* and am witness, sai. L.
    48:30 *I k.* his wrath, saith L.
Ezek. 11:5 *I k.* things that come
Hos. 13:5 *I* did *k.* thee in wilder
Jon. 1:12 *I k.* for my sake temp.
Mat. 28:5 *I k.* that ye seek Jesus
Mark 1:24 *I k.* who thou art,
    Luke 4:34
Luke 1:18 whereby sh. *I k.* this
John 4:25 *I k.* that Messias com.
    8:37 *I k.* ye are Abraham's seed
    55 *I k.* him ; 9:25 one thi. *I k.*
    10:15 knoweth me, *I k.* Father
    27 *I k.* my sheep, they fol. me
    11:22 *I k.* that what thou ask G.
    24 *I k.* that he shall rise again
    18:18 *I k.* whom I have chosen
Acts 12:11 *I k.* for a surety Lord
    19:15 Jesus *I k.* and Paul *I k.*
    20:25 *I k.* ye see my fa. no more
Rom. 7:18 *I k.* in me dw. no good
1 *Cor.* 4:4 *I k.* nothing by myself
    13:12 *I k.* in part, then shall *I k.*
Phil. 1:19 *I k.* this shall turn
    25 *I k.* I shall abide with you
2 *Tim.* 1:12 *I k.* whom I believed
1 *John* 2:4 he that saith, *I k.* him
Rev. 2:2 *I k.* thy works, 13 ; 3:8

KNOW not, *or* not KNOW.
Gen. 4:9 where is Abel ? *I k. not*
    27:2 *I k. not* day of my death
Ex. 5:2 *I k. n.* L. nor will I let I.
1 *Sam.* 3:7 Sam. did not yet *k.* L.
1 *K.* 18:12 Sp. carry thee *I k. not*
2 *K.* 17:26 *k. n.* manner of God

Ezr. 7:25 teach ye th. that *k. not*
Job 9:21 would I *not k.* my soul
15:9 know. thou that we *k.* ?
21:29 do ye *not k.* their tokens ?
24:13 *k. not* the ways thereof
  16 dig in dark. they *k. n.* light
32:22 *k. not* to give flatter. titles
36:26 God great, we *k.* him *not*
Ps. 71:15 *k. n.* numbers thereof
82:5 *k. not* neither understand
94:10 teach man, shall *not*
  he *k.* ?
101:4 I will *n. k.* wicked person
Prov. 4:19 *k. n.* at what stumble
24:12 doth *not* he *k.* it, and sh.
30:18 four things which I *k. not*
Ec. 9:5 dead *k. not* anything
Is. 1:3 but Israel doth *not k.*
43:19 ye *n. k.* it ? 44:8 I *k. not*
47:11 *not k.* from wh. it ariseth
59:8 way of peace they *k. not*
Jer. 5:4 they *k. not* way of Lord
7:9 after gods, whom ye *k. n.* ?
8:7 my people *k. not* judgments
9:3 they *k. not* me, saith Lord
10:25 fury on heathen *k.* thee *n.*
Ezek. 38:14 shalt thou *not k.* it
Hos. 2:8 did *n. k.* I gave her corn
Amos 3:10 th. *k. not* to do right
Mic. 4:12 *k. not* thoughts of Lo.
Mat. 25:12 I say, I *k.* you *not*
26:70 I *k. not* what thou sayest
  72 saying, I *k. not* the man,
  74 ; *Mark* 14:68, 71

Mark 10:38 ye *k. not* what ye ask
12:24 because ye *k. n.* scriptures
Luke 1:34 seeing I *k. not* a man
13:25 I *k. n.* whence you are, 27
22:57 say. Woman, I *k.* him *not*
  60 I *k. not* what thou sayest
23:34 they *k. not* what they do
24:16 that they should *n. k.* him
John 1:26 one am. you ye *k. not*
8:55 say, I *k.* him *n.* should lie
9:21 hath opened eyes, we *k. n.*
  29 we *k. not* from whence he is
10:5 *k. not* voice of strangers
14:5 we *k. not* whith. thou goest
15:21 *k. not* him that sent me
Acts 21:34 could not *k.* certainty
Rom. 8:26 *k. n.* what should pray
1 *Cor.* 2:2 determined *not to k.*
  any thing
14:11 *k. not* meaning of voice
1 *Thes.* 4:5 Gentiles wh. *k. n.* G.
2 *Thes.* 1:8 vengeance on them
  k. not God
1 *Tim.* 3:5 man *k. n.* how to rule
Jude 10 evil of things they *k. n.*
Rev. 3:3 not *k.* what hour I come

See Ye KNOW.

KNOW that I am the Lord.

Ex. 6:7 ye shall *k. that I am the*
  L. 16:12 ; 1 *K.* 20:28 ; *Ezek.*
  6:7, 13 ; 7:4, 9 ; 11:10, 12 ;
  12:20 ; 13:9, 14, 21, 23 ; 14:8 ;
  15:7 ; 20:38, 42, 44 ; 23:49 ;
  24:24 ; 25:5 ; 35:9 ; 36:11 ;
  37:6, 13 ; *Joel* 3:17
7:5 Egyptians *k. that I am the*
  L. 14:4, 18
  17 shall *k. that I am the L.* 1 *K.*
  20:13 ; *Is.* 49:23 ; *Ezek.* 16:62 ;
  22:16 ; 25:7 ; 35:4, 12
Ex. 29:46 they shall *k. that I am*
  the L. Ezek. 6:10, 14 ; 7:27 ;
  12:15, 16 ; 24:27 ; 25:11, 17 ;
  26:6 ; 28:22, 23, 24, 26 ; 29:9,
  16:21 ; 30:8, 19, 25, 26 ; 32:15 ;
  33:26 ; 34:27 ; 35:15 ; 36:38;
  38:23 ; 39:6, 28
Jer. 24:7 heart to *k. t. I am t. L.*
Ezek. 20:12 might *k. t. I am L.*
36:23 heath. sh. *k. I am L.* 39:7
39:22 Is. shall *k. t. I am the L.*

May, mayest, *or* might KNOW.

Ex. 8:10 thou *mayest k.* there is
  none like God, 9:14
9:29 *m. k.* earth is the Lord's
11:7 *may k.* L. put a difference
33:13 show me way, th. I *m. k.*
Num. 22:19 *m. k.* wh. L. will say
Deut. 4:35 *m. k.* that L. he is G.
Jos. 3:4 *m. k.* way ye should go
4:24 people *m. k.* hand of the L.
1 *Sam.* 17:46 *m. k.* th. is a G. in
  Is. 1 *K.* 8:43, 60 ; 2 *K.* 19:19
2 *Sam.* 24:2 *m. k.* num. of peop.
1 *K.* 18:37 people *m. k.* th. art G.
2 *Chr.* 6:33 people *may k.* thy na.
Job 19:29 *m. k.* there is a judg.
31:6 that God *may k.* my integ.
37:7 all men *may k.* his work
Ps. 9:20 *m. k.* th. to be but men
39:4 that *may k.* how frail I am
83:18 *m. k.* thou art M. High
109:27 *m. k.* this is thy hand
119:125 that I *m. k.* thy testim.
Is. 5:19 draw nigh that we *m. k.*
7:15 he *may k.* to refuse the ev.
37:20 all *may k.* that thou art L.
41:23 ye *may k.* we are gods
43:10 ye *may k.* and believe me
45:3 thou *m. k.* I am G. of Isr.
  6 *may k.* from rising of sun
Ezek. 21:5 all flesh *may k.* I have
38:16 that heathen *may k.* me
Dan. 2:30 *m. k.* though. of heart
4:17 to intent that living *m. k.*
Mic. 6:5 *m. k.* righteousn. of L.
John 10:38 ye *may k.* and believe
14:31 the world *may k.* 17:23
17:3 *m. k.* thee the only true G.
Acts 17:19 *m. k.* wh. th. doctrine
1 *Cor.* 2:12 *m. k.* things given
2 *Cor.* 2:4 *m. k.* love I ha. to you
9 that I *m. k.* the proof of you
Eph. 1:18 ye *m. k.* hope of call.
6:22 ye *might k.* our affairs
Phil. 3:10 that I *may k.* him
Col. 4:6 ye *m. k.* how to answer
1 *Tim.* 3:15 *m. k.* how thou oug.
1 *John* 5:13 *m. k.* ye ha. eternal
  20 we *m. k.* him that is true

We KNOW, *or* KNOW we.

Gen. 29:5 they said, we *k.* him
Deut. 18:21 how shall we *k.* wo.
2 *Chr.* 20:12 nor *k. not* what to do
Job 36:26 G. is gr. we *k.* him not
Is. 59:12 our iniqui. we *k.* them
Hos. 6:3 then sh. we *k.* if we fol.
8:2 cry to me, My G. we *k.*
Mat. 22:16 we *k.* thou art true,
  Mark 12:14 ; *Luke* 20:21
John 3:11 we speak th. *we* do *k.*
4:22 we *k.* what we worship
6:42 wh. father and moth. we *k.*
7:27 we *k.* whence this man is
8:52 we *k.* that th. hast a devil
9:20 we *k.* that this is our son
  29 *we k.* that God spake to
  Moses
31 *we k.* God heareth not sin.
14:5 L. we *k.* not whi. th. goest
21:24 *we k.* his testimo. is true
Acts 17:20 we would *k.* wh. these
Rom. 7:14 we *k.* law is spiritual
8:28 we *k.* things work for good
1 *Cor.* 8:1 *we k.* we all ha. knowl.
4 *we k.* an idol is noth. in wor.
13:9 for *we k.* in part, and prop.
2 *Cor.* 5:1 *we k.* if our earthly h.
  16 *k.* we no man after the flesh
1 *Tim.* 1:8 *we k.* that law is good
Heb. 10:30 *we k.* him hath said
1 *John* 2:3 *we k.* that *we k.* him
  5 *k.* that *we* are in him
  18 *we k.* that it is the last time
3:2 *we k.* that wh. he sh. appear
14 *we k.* we ha. passed fr. dea.
19 *we k.* we are of the truth
24 *we k.* that he abideth in us

4:6 *k. we* sp. of truth and error
  13 *k. we* that we dwell in him
5:2 *we k.* we love child. of God
  15 *we k.* that he heareth us, *we*
  k. we have petitions
  19 *we k.* that we are of God
  20 that *we may k.* him that
  is true

Ye KNOW, *or* KNOW ye.

Gen. 29:5 he said, *k.* ye Laban ?
Ezr. 16:6 at even ye shall *k.*
23:9 ye *k.* the heart of stranger
Num. 14:34 ye *k.* breach of prom.
Jos. 3:10 ye shall *k.* the living G.
2 *K.* 9:11 ye *k.* man and his com.
Job 13:2 what ye *k.* same do I kn.
Ps. 100:3 *k.* ye that Lord he is G.
Is. 51:7 ye that *k.* righteousness
Jer. 48:17 all ye that *k.* his ways
Ezek. 17:21 ye *k.* I have spo. 37:14
Joel 2:27 ye sh. *k.* I am in midst
Zec. 2:9 ye sh. *k.* L. sent me, 6:15
Mat. 7:16 ye shall *k.* by fruits, 20
20:25 ye *k.* princes of the Gentiles, *Mark* 10:42
24:32 ye *k.* summer is nigh,
  Mark 13:28 ; *Luke* 21:30
25:13 ye *k.* neither day nor hour
Mark 4:13 *k.* ye not this parab. ?
Luke 21:31 *k.* ye king. of G. is ni.
John 7:28 ye both *k.* me, and kn.
8:28 then sh. ye. *k.* that I am he
  32 and ye shall *k.* the truth
11:49 C. said, *k.* ye nothing at all
13:12 *k.* ye what I have done?
  17 if ye *k.* these things, happy
14:4 wh. I go ye *k.* and way ye *k.*
  7 from henceforth ye *k.* him, 17
  20 ye shall *k.* I am in my Fath.
15:18 ye *k.* that it hated me
Acts 2:22 as ye yourselves also *k.*
19:25 ye *k.* that by this craft we
1 *Cor.* 15:58 ye *k.* lab. not in vain
2 *Cor.* 8:9 ye *k.* grace of our Lord
Gal. 3:7 *k.* ye they wh. are of fa.
Phil. 2:22 ye *k.* the proof of him
1 *Thes.* 1:5 ye *k.* wh. man. of men
2:2 shamefully entreat. as ye *k.*
  11 ye *k.* how we exhorted
2 *Thes.* 2:6 ye *k.* what witholdeth
Heb. 12:17 ye *k.* he wo. ha. inher.
1 *Pet.* 1:18 ye *k.* ye not redeemed
2 *Pet.* 3:17 ye *k.* these things bef.
1 *John* 2:20 and ye *k.* all things
  21 truth, but because ye *k.* it
  29 ye *k.* he is rig. ye *k.* ev. one
3:5 ye *k.* he manifested, 15
4:2 hereby *k.* ye Spirit of God
3 *John* 12 ye *k.* our record is true

Ye KNOW not, *or* KNOW ye not.

2 *Sam.* 3:38 *k.* ye not th. is a pri.
Job 21:29 do ye *not k.* th. tokens
Mat. 20:22 ye *k. not* what ye ask
24:42 ye *k. not* wh. hour L. come
Mark 4:13 *k.* ye *not* this parab. ?
12:24 bec. ye *k. not* scriptures
13:33 ye *k. not* when time is, 35
Luke 9:55 ye *k. not* what manner
John 1:26 whom ye *k. not.*
4:22 ye worship ye *k. not* what
  32 meat to me ye *k. not* of
7:28 sent me is true, wh. ye *k. n.*
8:19 ye neither *k.* me nor Father
9:30 ye *k. not* from whence he is
2 *Cor.* 13:5 *k.* ye *not* yourselves
Jam. 4:14 ye *k. not* wh. be on m.
1 *John* 2:21 ye *k. not* the truth

KNOWEST.

Gen. 30:26 thou *k.* service I done
47:6 *k.* any man of activ. among
Ex. 32:22 *k.* peo. set on mischief
Num. 20:14 *k.* travel hath befal.
Deut. 28:33 a nation thou *k. not*
Jos. 14:6 *k.* thing the Lord said

2 *Sam.* 2:26 *k.* thou not th. it w.
7:20 L. *k.* thy serv. 1 *Chr.* 17:18
17:8 said Huchai, thou *k.* father
1 *K.* 2:5 *k.* also what Joab did
9 *k.* what thou oughtest to do
44 *k.* all thou didst to David
8:39 whose heart thou *k.* thou
only *k.* 2 *Chr.* 6:30
2 *K.* 2:3 *k.* thou L. will take, 5
4:1 *k.* thy serv. did fear the L.
Job 10:7 thou *k.* I am not wicked
15:9 wh. *k.* th. th. we kn. not ?
20:4 *k.* thou not this of old
34:33 theref. speak what thou *k.*
38:5 who laid meas. if thou *k.* ?
21 *k.* thou it, because
39:1 *k.* when goats bri. forth, 2
Ps. 40:9 O L. thou *k.* *Jer.* 15:15
69:5 O God, thou *k.* my foolish
139:2 thou *k.* my down-sitting
4 O Lord, thou *k.* it altogether
Prov. 27:1 *k.* not what a day br.
Ec. 11:2 *k.* not what evil
5 *k.* not what is way of Spirit
6 thou *k.* not whc. sh. prosper
Is. 55:5 call a nation thou *k.* not
Jer. 5:15 nation wh. lang. *k.* not
12:3 but thou, O Lord, *k.* me
17:16 nor des. woful day, th. *k.*
18:23 thou *k.* their counsel
Jer. 33:3 show things thou *k.* not
Dan. 10:20 *k.* thou wheref. I co.
Zec. 4:5 *k.* not wh. these be, 13
Mark 10:19 *k.* com. *Luke* 18:20
Luke 22:34 thrice deny th. *k.* me
John 1:48 N. said, When. *k.* me ?
3:10 a master, *k.* not th. things ?
13:7 what I do, thou *k.* not now
16:30 thou *k.* all things, 21:17
21:15 L. thou *k.* I love thee, 16
Acts 1:24 *k.* the hearts of all men
Rom. 2:18 *k.* his will, and appr.
1 *Cor.* 7:16 what *k.* thou, O wife
2 *Tim.* 1:15 *k.* all they in Asia
Rev. 3:17 *k.* not th. art wretched
7:14 said unto him, Sir, thou *k.*

KNOWETH.

Gen. 33:13 *k.* children are tender
Deut. 2:7 *k.* thy walk. thro' wild.
34:6 no man *k.* Mos. sepulchre
Jos. 22:22 God of gods, he *k.* Is.
1 *Sam.* 20:3 father certainly *k.*
2 *Sam.* 14:22 serv. *k.* I found gr.
17:10 Is. *k.* thy father is mighty
Job 11:11 he *k.* vain men
15:23 *k.* day of darkness is ready
23:10 but he *k.* the way I take
28:7 there is a path no fowl *k.*
23 God understandeth and *k.*
34:25 therefore he *k.* their works
Ps. 1:6 Lord *k.* way of righteous
37:18 the L. *k.* days of the upri.
44:21 he *k.* the secrets of heart
74:9 nor is there any am. us *k.*
94:11 L. *k.* thou. of man vanity
103:14 he *k.* our frame
104:19 sun *k.* his going down
138:6 the proud he *k.* afar off
139:14 thy works, my soul *k.*
Ec. 6:8 *k.* to walk before living
7:22 thy heart *k.* th. hast cursed
9:1 no man *k.* eit. love or hatred
Is. 1:3 the ox *k.* his owner
Jer. 9:24 understandeth and *k.*
Dan. 2:22 he *k.* what is in darkn.
Nah. 1:7 L. *k.* them trust in him
Zep. 3:5 the unjust *k.* no shame
Mat. 6:8 Fa. *k.* what ye need
32 *k.* ye have need, *Luke* 12:30
11:27 no man *k.* Son but the
Father, nor any *k.* Father
save the Son, *Luke* 10:22
24:36 that day *k.* *Mark* 13:32
Luke 16:15 God *k.* your hearts
John 7:15 how *k.* this man let. ?
27 no man *k.* whence he is
10:15 Fa. *k.* me ; 14:17 nor *k.*
19:35 he *k.* that he saith true

Acts 15:8 God which *k.* hearts
Rom. 8:27 *k.* what is mind of S.
1 *Cor.* 2:11 what man *k.* th. of a
man, even th. of G. *k.* no m.
8:2 if any man think he *k.* any.
2 *Cor.* 11:11 love you not ? G. *k.*
31 God, Fa. of our L. *k.* a lie
12:2 I cannot tell, God *k.* 3
2 *Tim.* 2:19 L. *k.* th. that are his
Jam. 4:17 him that *k.* to do good
2 *Pet.* 2:9 L. *k.* how to de. godly
1 *John* 3:20 God is greater and *k.*
4:6 he that *k.* God heareth us
7 that lov. is born of God, *k.* G.
Rev. 2:17 name writ. no man *k.*
12:12 *k.* he hath but short time

Who KNOWETH, or not KNOWETH.

Est. 4:14 *w. k.* whe. th. art come
Job 12:9 *who k.* not in all these
14:21 come to honor, he *k.* it n.
18:21 place of him that *k.* n. G.
28:13 man *k.* not the price
Ps. 39:6 *k.* not who shall gather
90:11 *who k.* power of anger ?
92:6 a brutish man *k.* not
Prov. 7:23 *k.* not it is for his life
9:18 he *k.* not dead are there
24:22 *who k.* the ruin of them
Ec. 2:19 *w. k.* whe. he be wise
3:21 *who k.* the spirit of man
6:12 *who k.* what is good for m.
8:7 he *k.* not that wh. shall be
9:12 man also *k.* not his time
10:15 he *k.* not how to go to city
Is. 29:15 seeth us, *who k.* us ?
Hos. 7:9 gray hairs, yet *k. not*
Joel 2:14 *who k.* if he will return
Mark 4:27 gr. up, he *k. not* how
John 7:49 peo. *w. k.* n. the law
12:35 darkness, *k. n.* whither
15:15 serv. *k. n.* what lord doeth
1 *John* 2:11 walk. in dark. *k.* n.
3:1 therefore the world *k.* us *n.*
4:8 *k. not* God, for God is love

KNOWING.

Gen. 3:5 as gods *k.* good and evil
1 *K.* 2:32 my father David not *k.*
Mat. 9:4 *k.* their thoughts, *Luke* 11:17
22:29 ye err, not *k.* scriptures
Mark 5:30 Jesus *k.* in himself
33 woman *k.* what was done
6:20 *k.* that he was a just man
Luke 9:33 E. not *k.* what he said
John 13:3 Jesus *k.* Fa. had given
18:4 Jesus *k.* all that sho. come
19:28 J. *k.* all things were acco.
21:12 none ask him, *k.* it was L.
Acts 2:30 *k.* that God had sworn
5:7 wife not *k.* what was done
20:22 not *k.* things shall befall
Rom. 1:32 *k.* the judgment of G.
2:4 not *k.* goodness of God
13:11 *k.* time, now it is high ti.
2 *Cor.* 4:14 *k.* he wh. raised L. J.
5:6 *k.* that wh. we are at home
Eph. 6:8 *k.* what good any man
Col. 3:24 *k.* of L. ye rec. reward
1 *Tim.* 1:9 *k.* this, law is for la.
2 *Tim.* 3:14 *k.* of wh. thou learn.
Heb. 10:34 *k.* ye have in heaven
11:8 not *k.* whither he went
Jam. 1:3 *k.* this, trying of y. fai.
1 *Pet.* 3:9 *k.* ye are thereu. called
2 *Pet.* 1:14 *k.* shortly I must put

KNOWLEDGE.

Gen. 2:9 tree of *k.* good and ev. 17
Ex. 31:3 filled Bez. in *k.* 35:31
Lev. 4:23 if sin come to *k.* 28
Num. 24:16 *k.* of the Most High
Ruth 2:10 should. take *k.* of me
1 *Sam.* 2:3 the L. is a God of *k.*
1 *K.* 9:27 *k.* of sea ; 2 *Chr.* 8:18
2 *Chr.* 1:11 thou hast asked *k.*
12 wisdom and *k.* is granted

Neh. 10:28 every one having *k.*
Job 15:2 wise man ut. vain *k.* ?
21:14: desire not *k.* of thy ways
22 shall any teach God *k.* ?
33:3 my lips sh. utter *k.* clearly
36:3 I will fetch my *k.* from afar
4 per. in *k.* is with thee, 37:16
Ps. 19:2 night to night show. *k.*
73:11 is there *k.* in Most High ?
94:10 he that teacheth man *k.*
119:66 teach me judgm. and *k.*
139:6 such *k.* too wonder. for me
144:3 what is man thou takest *k.* of ?

Prov. 1:7 fear of Lord begi. of *k.*
22 fools hate *k.* 2:3 cri. after *k.*
29 they hated *k.* did not choose
2:6 out of his mouth cometh *k.*
10 *k.* is pleasant to thy soul
3:20 by *k.* depths are broken up
5:2 that thy lips may keep *k.*
8:10 *k.* rather than choice gold
12 and find out *k.* of inventions
9:10 *k.* of Holy is understanding
10:14 wise men lay up *k.*
11:9 thro' *k.* sh. just be deliver.
12:23 a prud. man concealeth *k.*
13:16 ev. prud. man deal. wi. *k.*
14:6 *k.* easy to him that unders.
7 perceiv. not in him lips of *k.*
18 prudent are crowned with *k.*
15:2 tongue of wise useth *k.*
7 lips of the wise disperse *k.*
14 hath understanding seek. *k.*
17:27 hath *k.* spareth his words
18:15 heart of prudent getteth *k.*
and ear of wise seeketh *k.*
19:25 and he will understand *k.*
27 cease to err from words of *k.*
20:15 lips of *k.* precious jewel
21:11 wise instructed, he rec. *k.*
22:12 eyes of the L. preserve *k.*
23:12 apply th. ear to words of *k.*
24:4 by *k.* sh. chambers be filled
5 a man of *k.* increas. strength
28:2 by man of *k.* state be pro.
30:3 nor have the *k.* of Holy

Ec. 1:16 had experience of *k.*
18 increaseth *k.* increaseth sor.
2:21 a man whose labor is in *k.*
26 God giveth a man *k.* and joy
7:12 excellency of *k.* is wisdom
9:10 nor *k.* in grave, whi. goest
Is. 11:2 *k.* and fear of the Lord
28:9 whom shall he teach *k.* ?
32:4 heart of rash sh. underst. *k.*
33:6 wisd. and *k.* shall be stabi.
40:14 judgment, and taught *k.*
44:19 neither is th. *k.* nor unde.
25 and maketh their *k.* foolish
47:10 thy *k.* hath perverted thee
53:11 by *k.* right. serv. justify

Jer. 3:15 shall feed you with *k.*
10:14 ev. man brutish in his *k.*
Dan. 12:4 shall be increased
Hos. 4:6 peo. destroyed for lack of *k.* thou reject. *k.* I rej th.
Hab. 2:14 earth fill. with *k.* of L.
Mal. 2:7 priest's lips sho. keep *k.*
Luke 1:77 to give *k.* of salvation
11:52 taken away key of *k.*
Acts 4:13 marvelled and took *k.*
24:22 more perfect *k.* of th. way
Rom. 1:28 not like to re. G. in *k.*
2:20 which hast the form of *k.*
3:20 for by law is the *k.* of sin
10:2 a zeal, not according to *k.*
15:14 are filled with all *k.*
1 *Cor.* 1:5 are enriched in all *k.*
8:1 we all have *k.* puffeth up
10 which hast *k.* at meat
11 thro' thy *k.* sh. brother per.
12:8 word of *k.* by same Spirit
13:2 underst. mysteries and *k.*
8 there be *k.* it sh. vanish away
14:6 speak by revelation or *k.*

2 Cor. 2:14 manif. savor of his k.
4:6 light of k. of the glory of G.
6:6 by k. by long-suffering
8:7 as ye abound in faith and k.
11:6 rude in speech, not in k.
Eph. 1:17 wisdom in k. of him
3:19 love of C. which passeth k.
4:13 unity of faith, and k. of S.
Phil. 1:9 may abound more in k.
8:8 all things loss for k. of Chr.
Col. 1:9 filled with k. of his will
2:3 hid treas. of wisdom and k.
3:10 new man renewed in k.
1 Tim. 2:4 come to k. of truth
2 Tim. 3:7 to come to k. of truth
Heb. 10:26 if we sin after rec. k.
Jam. 3:13 wise man, end. wi. k. ?
1 Pet. 3:7 dwell according to k.
2 Pet. 1:5 virtue k. k. temperance
1:8 nor unfruit. in k. of our L.
3:18 grow in k. of our Lord Jes.

KNOWLEDGE of God.
Prov. 2:5 thou shalt find k. of G.
Hos. 4:1 nor k. of G. in the land
6:6 k. of G. more than bu.-offer.
Rom.11:33 of wisd. and k. of G.
1 Cor. 15:34 have not k. of G.
2 Cor. 10:5 exalteth ng. k. of G.
Col. 1:10 increasing in k. of God
2 Pet. 1:2 peace, thro' k. of God

KNOWLEDGE of the Lord.
2 Chr. 30:22 taught good k. of L.
Is. 11:9 earth full of k. of the L.
2 Pet. 2:20 escaped thro' k. of L.

No KNOWLEDGE.
Deut. 1:39 child. that day no k.
Ps. 14:4 work. of iniq. no k. 53:4
Is. 5:13 because they have no k.
45:20 have no k. set up images
58:3 afflicted soul, takest no k.
Jer. 4:22 do good, th. have no k.

Without KNOWLEDGE.
Num. 15:24 with. k. of congrega.
Job 35:16 multipli. words w. k.
36:12 perish, and die with. k.
38:2 counsel by woor. wi. k. 42:3
Prov. 19:2 not good soul be w. k.

KNOWN.
Gen. 24:16 nor had any man k.
Ex. 2:14 surely this thing is k.
Lev. 4:14 they have sinned is k.
Num. 31:17 kill ev. wo. k. man
Deut. 1:13 k. among tribes, 15
Jos. 24:31 k. works of the Lord
1 K. 18:36 let it be k. thou art G.
Ps. 9:16 Lord is k. by judgment
31:7 k. my soul in adversities
48:3 God is k. in her palaces
67:2 thy way may be k. on earth
76:1 in Judah is God k. his na.
77:19 thy footsteps are not k.
79:10 let him be k. among heat.
88:12 shall wond. be k. in dark ?
91:14 bec. he hath k. my name
139:1 searched me, and k. me

Prov. 12:16 fool's wrath pres. k.
20:11 a child is k. by his doings
31:23 her husband is k. in gates
Ec. 5:3 fool's voice k. by multit.
Is. 61:9 seed k. among Gentiles
66:14 Lord to be k. to his servants
Jer. 5:5 have k. the way of the L.
Ezek. 36:32 saith L. G. be it k.
to you, Acts 4:10; 13:38; 28:28
38:23 k. in eyes of many nations
Dan. 4:26 sh. have k. heav. rule
Amos 3:2 you only have I k.
Zec. 14:7 a day shall be k. L.
Mat. 12:33 tree k. by fr. Luke 6:44
24:43 if g. man had k. Luke 12:39
Luke 19:42 k. in this thy day
24:35 k. in breaking of bread
John 7:4 himself seeketh to be k.
8:19 if ye had k. me ye should
have k. my Father also, 14:7
10:14 I know sheep, am k.
17:25 these have k. thou sent me
Acts 2:14 be this k. unto you
15:18 k. unto G. are all his wor.

Acts 22:30 k. the certainty, 23:28
Rom. 1:19 wh. may be k. of God
11:34 who hath k. the mind of
Lord, 1 Cor. 2:16
1 Cor. 13:12 even as I also am k.
14:7 k. what is piped or harped
2 Cor. 3:2 epistle known and read
5:16 have k. Christ after flesh
6:9 unknown, and yet well k.
Gal. 4:9 k. God or are k. of God
Eph. 3:10 might be k. by church
Phil. 4:5 moderation k. to all m.
2 Tim. 3:10 fully k. my doctrine
15 fr. a child k. holy scriptures
1 John 2:13 bec. ye ha. k. him, 14
2 John 1 them that have k. truth

Made, or madest KNOWN.
Gen. 45:1 Joseph m. himself k.
Neh. 9:14 m. k. thy holy sabbath
Ps. 98:2 Lord m. k. his salvation
103:7 m. k. his ways to Moses
Dan. 2:23 m. k. to us king's m.
Hos. 5:9 m. k. that which sh. be
Luke 2:17 m. k. abroad saying
John 15:15 all I heard, I m. k.
Acts 2:28 m. k. to me ways of life
7:13 Joseph m. k. to brethren
Rom. 16:26 m. k. to all nations
Eph. 1:9 m. k. to us mystery
3:3 he m. k. to me mystery
Phil. 4:6 requests be m. k. to G.
2 Pet. 1:16 m. k. coming of our L.

Make KNOWN.
Num. 12:6 I will m. myself k.
1 Chr. 16:8 m. k. his deeds amo.
people, Ps. 105:1
Ps. 89:1 m. k. thy faithfulness
106:8 m. k. his mighty power
145:12 to m. k. to sons of men
Prov. 1:23 make k. my words

Is. 38:19 father sh. m. k. truth
64:2 m. thy name k. to adversa.
Ezek. 35:11 m. myself k. among
them
39:7 m. my holy name k. in Isr.
Dan. 2:25 man will m. k. to king
28 Lord m. k. to the king, 29
Hab. 3:2 in midst of years m. k.
Rom. 9:22 God will. to m. po. k.
23 m. k. riches of his glory
Eph. 6:19 m. k. mystery of gosp.
Col. 1:27 to whom G. will m. k.

Not KNOWN.
Gen. 19:8 two dau. have not k.
man, Num. 31:18, 35; Jud.
21:12
41:21 n. be k. they had eaten
31 plenty shall n. be k. in land
Ex. 6:3 by name Jehovah I n. k.
Deut 11:2 chil. have n. k. 31:13
28 after gods ye k. n. 13:6, 13
Jud. 3:1 had not k. wars of Can.
16:9 so his strength was not k.
Ruth 3:14 not be k. wo. came in
1 K. 14:2 n. k. to be wife of Jer.
Ps. 18:43 peo. whom I have n. k.
77:19 thy footsteps are not k.
79:6 wra. on heathen ha. n. k.
95:10 n. k. my ways, Heb. 3:10
147:20 judgm. they have n. k.
Ec. 6:5 not seen sun n. k. any th.
Is. 42:16 paths they have not k.
44:18 have n. k. nor understood
45:4 tho' thou hast n. k. me, 5
Jer. 4:22 they have not k. me
Ezek. 32:9 count. thou hast n. k.
Dan. 2:5 will n. make k. drea 9
4:7 n. make k. interpreta. 5:8
Hos. 5:4 they have not k. the L.
Nah. 3:17 place n. k. w. they are
Mat. 10:26 is nothing hid that
shall n. be k. Luke 8:17; 12:2
John 8:55 ye have not k. him
14:9 yet hast thou not k. me
16:3 have not k. the Father nor
17:25 Fa. world hath n. k. thee
Rom. 3:17 way of pe. they not k.
7:7 I had not k. sin but by law
2 Pet. 2:21 not k. way of righte.
1 John 3:6 sinner not seen not k.
Rev. 2:24 not k. the depths of S.

KOHATH.
Gen. 46:11 ; Ex. 6:16 ; Num. 3:17,
30 ; 16:1 ; 1 Chr. 6:2, 22, 61
1 Chr. 15:5 of sons of K. Uriel

KOHATHITES. Num. 4:34 ;
Jos. 21:4 ; 2 Chr. 34:12

KORAH.
Gen. 36:5 Aholibamah bare K. 16
Ex. 6:21 sons of Iz. K. Num. 16:1
Num. 16:2 censers, K. 19, 40
26:9 Dathan str. in comp. of K.
27:3 father not in comp. of K.
1 Chr. 1:35 the sons of Esau, K.
Jude 11 perished in gains. of K.

L

LABAN.
Gen. 24:29 Reb. had a brother L.
30:36 Jac. fed rest of L.'s flocks
31:2 countenance of L. 12, 55
32:4 I have sojourned with L.

LABOR, Substantive.
Gen. 31:42 G. seen l. of my hands
35:16 Rachel had hard l. 17
Deut. 26:7 L. heard, looked on l.
Neh. 5:13 God sha. ev. man fr. l.
Job 39:11 with the. leave l. to him
Ps. 90:10 their strength l. sorrow
104:23 man goeth to l. till even.
105:44 inherited l. of the people

107:12 bro. down heart with l.
109:11 let stranger spoil his l.
128:2 sh. eat the l. of thy hands
Prov. 10:16 l. tendeth to life
13:11 gathereth by l. shall incr.
14:23 in all l. there is profit

Ec. 1:3 wh. profit hath man of l.
8 all things are full of l. man
2:10 rejoiced in my portion of l.
18 I hated all l. wh. I had tak.
19 shall he rule over all my l.
21 man whose l. is in wisdom
22 what hath man of all his l. ?
24 enjoy good in l. 3:13 ; 5:18

4:8 yet is th. no end of all his l.
9 they have a good rewa. for l.
5:15 nothing of l. he may carry
19 rejoice in l. this is gift of G.
6:7 l. of man is for his mouth
9:9 portion in thy l. under sun
10:15 l. of foolish wearieth
Is. 45:14 l. of Egypt come to thee
55:2 why spend your l. for that
Jer. 3:24 devoured l. of fathers
20:18 came I out of wo. to see l. ?
Ezek. 29:20 giv. land of Eg. for l.
Hab. 3:17 though l. of olive fail
Hag. 1:11 drought on l. of hands
John 4:38 reap wh. bestow. no l.

Rom. 16:6 bestow. much *l.* on us
1 *Cor.* 3:8 man rec. accord. to *l.*
15:58 know your *l.* is not in vain
Gal. 4:11 lest I bestow. *l.* in vain
Phil. 1:22 this is fruit of my *l.*
1 *Thes.* 1:3 remember. *l.* of love
2:9 remember our *l.* and travail
3:5 and our *l.* be in vain
2 *Thes.* 3:8 but wrought with *l.*
Heb. 6:10 not forget your *l.* of lo.
Rev. 2:2 I kn. thy *l.* and patience

LABOR, Verb.

Ex. 20:9 six days *l. Deut.* 5:13
Jos. 24:13 for wh. he did not *l.*
Neh. 4:22 guard us, and *l.* on day
Job 9:29 why then *l.* I in vain ?
Ps. 127:1 exc. L. build *l.* in vain
144:14 oxen may be strong to *l.*
Prov. 21:25 his hands refuse to *l.*
23:4 *l.* not to be rich, cease from
Ec. 4:8 saith, For whom do I *l. ?*
8:17 tho' a man *l.* to seek it out
Is. 22:4 weep, *l.* not to comfort
65:23 they shall not *l.* in vain
Jer. 51:58 the peop. sh. *l.* in vain
Lam. 5:5 under persecution we *l.*
Mic. 4:10 *l.* to bring forth, O Zi.
Hab. 2:13 people should *l.* in fire
Mat. 11:28 co. to me all ye th. *l.*
John 6:27 *l.* not for meat th. per.
Rom. 16:12 Tryphosa, who *l.*
1 *Cor.* 4:12 *l.* with our own hands
2 *Cor.* 5:9 we *l.* to be accepted
Eph. 4:28 rather *l.* wi. his hands
Col. 1:29 whereunto I *l.* striving
1 *Thes.* 5:12 know them which *l.*
1 *Tim.* 4:10 *l.* and suffer reproach
5:17 that *l.* in word and doctrine
Heb. 4:11 *l.* to enter into that rest

LABORED.

Neh. 4:21 so we *l.* in the work
Job 20:18 he *l.* for, sh. he restore
Ec. 2:11 looked on labor I *l.* to do
19 rule over my labor I have *l.*
5:16 wh. prof. ha. he th. *l.* wind ?
Is. 47:15 with whom thou hast *l.*
49:4 I said, I have *l.* in vain
62:8 not drink, for which thou *l.*
Dan. 6:14 king *l.* to deliv. Daniel
John 4:38 *l.* and ye are entered
Rom. 16:12 salute P. who *l.* in L.
1 *Cor.* 15:10 I *l.* more abundantly
Phil. 2:16 I have not *l.* in vain
4:3 help those that *l.* with me
Rev. 2:3 for my name's sake *l.*

LABORER, S.

Mat. 9:37 harvest plenteous, but
l. few, 38 ; *Luke* 10:2
20:1 went out early to hire *l.*
Luke 10:7 *l.* is worthy of his hire
1 *Cor.* 3:9 *l.* together with God
1 *Tim.* 5:18 *l.* is worthy of rewa.
Jam. 5:4 behold the hire of the *l.*

LABORETH.

Prov. 16:26 he that *l. l.* for hims.
Ec. 3:9 wh. profit in that he *l. ?*
1 *Cor.* 16:16 sub. to ev. one that *l.*
2 *Tim.* 2:6 the husbandm. that *l.*

LABORING.

Ec. 5:12 sleep of *l.* man sweet
Acts 20:35 *l.* you. to sup. weak
Col. 4:12 *l.* for you in prayer
1 *Thes.* 2:9 *l.* night and day

LABORS.

Ex. 23:16 first-fruits of thy *l.*
Deut. 28:33 thy *l.* sh. a nation eat
Prov. 5:10 *l.* be in ho. of stranger
Is. 58:3 in day of fast ye ex. all *l.*
Jer. 20:5 I will deliver all their *l.*
Hos. 12:8 in my *l.* sh. find no ini.
Hag. 2:17 smote you in all the *l.*
John 4:38 are entered in their *l.*
2 *Cor.* 6:5 in *l.* in watchings
10:15 boasting of other men's *l.*
11:23 *l.* more abundn. in stripes
Rev. 14:13 may rest from their *l.*

LACE.

Ex. 28:28 sh. bind the breastpla.
with *l.* 37 ; 39:31

LACHISH.

Jos. 10:32 the Lord delivered L.
2 *K.* 14:19 and he fled to L.
18:14 Hezek. sent to king to L.
2 *Chr.* 11:9 Rehoboam built L.
25:27 they sent to L. after him
Mic. 1:13 O inhabitant of L. bind

LACK, Substantive.

Gen. 18:28 wilt des. all for *l.* five ?
Ex. 16:18 that gathered little had
no *l.* 2 *Cor.* 8:15
Job 4:11 lion perish. for *l.* of prey
38:41 young wand. for *l.* of meat
Hos. 4:6 peo. destroyed for *l.* kn.
Phil. 2:30 life to supply *l.* of ser.
1 *Thes.* 4:12 that ye *l.* of nothing

LACK, Verb.

Gen. 18:28 if there shall *l.* five
Deut. 8:9 shall not *l.* anything
Ps. 34:10 the young lions do *l.*
Prov. 28:27 giv. to poor sh. not *l.*
Ec. 9:8 let thy head *l.* no-ointm.
Mat. 19:20 I kept, wh. I *l.* yet ?
Jam. 1:5 any *l.* wisd. ask of God

LACKED.

Deut. 2:7 thou hast *l.* nothing
1 *K.* 4:27 provid. victual, th. noth.
Neh. 9:21 sustain th. th. *l.* noth.
Luke 22:35 *l.* ye any thing ?
Acts 4:34 any amo. them that *l.*
1 *Cor.* 12:24 honor to which *l.*
Phil. 4:10 careful, *l.* opportunity

LACKEST.

Mark 10:21 but one thing thou *l.*
Luke 18:22

LACKETH.

Num. 31:49 there *l.* not one man
2 *Sam.* 3:29 not fail one *l.* bread
Prov. 6:32 adult. *l.* understand.
12:9 honor. himself and *l.* bread
2 *Pet.* 1:9 th. *l.* th. things is blind

LACKING.

Lev. 22:23 th. hath any thing *l.*
Jud. 21:3 th. sho. be one tribe *l.*
Jer. 23:4 no more, nor sh. be *l.*
1 *Cor.* 16:17 wh. was *l.* they sup.
2 *Cor.* 11:9 *l.* to me breth. sup.
1 *Thes.* 3:10 might perf. what is *l.*

LAD, S.

Gen. 21:17 God heard voice of *l.*
18 lift up *l.* 19 gave *l.* drink
20 G. was with *l.* and he grew
22:5 I and the *l.* will go yonder
12 lay not thy hand upon *l.*
44:22 *l.* cannot leave father, 30
33 abide inst. of *l.* let the *l.* go
34 his life is bound up in the *l.*
48:16 A. redeemed me, bless *l.*
1 *Sam.* 20:36 Jona. said to *l.* Run
John 6:9 *l.* ha. five barley loaves

LADDER.

Gen. 28:12 behold a *l.* set up

LADE, ED.

Gen. 42:26 *l.* asses wi. corn, 44:13
45:17 *l.* beasts, go to Canaan
1 *K.* 12:11 father did *l.* with yoke
Neh. 4:17 th. *l.* wrought in work
Luke 11:46 *l.* men with burdens
Acts 28:10 *l.* us wi. thi. necessary

LADEN.

Gen. 45:23 *l.* with good things
Is. 1:4 a people *l.* with iniquity
Mat. 11:28 all that are heavy *l.*
2 *Tim.* 3:6 women, *l.* with sins

LADETH, ING.

Neh. 13:15 some on sab. *l.* asses
Hab. 2:6 woe to him that *l.* him.
Acts 27:10 damage not only of *l.*

LADY.

Is. 47:5 no more be called a *l.*
7 saidst, I shall be a *l.* for ever
2 *John* 1 the elder to the elect *l.*
5 *l.* that we love one another

LADIES.

Jud. 5:29 wise *l.* answered her
Est. 1:18 likew. shall *l.* of Persia

LAID. See after LAY.
LAISH. *Jud.* 18:14 ; 1 *Sam.* 25:44;
2 *Sam.* 3:15 ; *Is.* 10:30

LAKE.

Luke 5:1 Jesus stood by *l.* of G.
2 two ships standing by the *l.*
8:23 a storm of wind on the *l.*
33 herd ran violently into *l.*
Rev. 19:20 both cast in *l.* fire
20:10 devil cast into *l.* of fire
14 death and hell cast in *l.*
15 not in bo. of life, cast into *l.*
21:8 murderers have part in *l.*

LAMB.

Gen. 22:7 *l.* for a burnt offering ?
8 God will provide himself a *l.*
Ex. 12:3 they shall take a *l.* 21
5 *l.* shall be without blemish
13:13 sh. redeem with a *l.* 34:20
29:39 one *l.* th. sh. offer in morn.
other *l.* at even, 41 ; *Nu.* 28:4
40 a *l.* a tenth deal of flour,
Num. 28:21 ; 29:4, 10, 15
Lev. 9:3 take a *l.* of first year,
14:10 ; *Num.* 6:12 ; 7:15, 21
14:12 the priest shall take *l.*
23:12 sh. offer a *l.* with. blemish
Num. 6:14 ewe-*l.* of first year
15:5 with the sacrifice for one *l.*
1 *Sam.* 7:9 Samuel off. sucking *l.*
2 *Sam.* 12:4 took poor man's *l.*
Is. 11:6 wolf shall dwell with *l.*
16:1 send ye *l.* to ruler of land
53:7 he was brought as a *l.* to
the slaughter, *Jer.* 11:19
65:25 wolf and *l.* sh. feed toget.
66:3 sacrificeth a *l.* as if he cut
Ezek. 45:15 one *l.* out of a flock
Hos. 4:16 L. will feed them as *l.*
John 1:29 behold the L. of G. 36
Acts 8:32 a *l.* dumb bef. shearer
1 *Pet.* 1:19 as a *l.* without blem.
Rev. 5:6 midst of eld. stood a L.
8 four beasts fell down bef. L.
12 worthy the L. that was slain
6:16 hide us from wrath of L.
7:10 salvation to our G. and L.
14 made white in blood of L.
17 L. shall feed and lead
12:11 overc. him by blood of L.
13:8 L. sl. from found. of world
11 he had two horns like a *l.*
14:1 L. stood on the mount Si.
4 these are they that follow L.
10 tormented in presence of L.
15:3 song of M. and song of L.
17:14 war with L. and L. overc.
19:7 for marriage of L. is come
21:9 show thee bride, L. wife
14 twelve apostles of L.
22 God Alm. and L. are temple
23 the L. is the light thereof
27 writ. in the L. book of life
22:1 out of thr. of God and L. 3

LAMBS.

Gen. 30:40 J. did separate the *l.*
Num. 7:87 *l.* of first year twelve
Deut. 32:14 with fat of *l.*
1 *Sam.* 15:9 S. spared the best *l.*
2 *K.* 3:4 Moab rendered 100,000 *l.*
1 *Chr.* 29:21 offered to L. 1,000 *l.*
2 *Chr.* 29:22 priests killed *l.* 32
Ezr. 7:17 thou mayest buy *l.*
Ps. 37:20 wick. sh. be as fat of *l.*
114:4 little hills skip. like *l.* 6
Prov. 27:26 *l.* for thy clothing

Is. 1:11 I deli. not in blood of *l.*
5:17 *l.* feed after their manner
34:6 sword of L. with blood of *l.*
40:11 gather the *l.* with his arm
Jer. 51:40 like *l.* to slaughter
Ezek. 39:18 shall drink blo. of *L.*
46:4 in sab. L. 6 new moons *l.*
Amos 6:4 and eat *l.* out of flock
Luke 10:3 as *l.* among wolves
John 21:15 Jes. saith, Feed my *l.*

Seven LAMBS.

Gen. 21:28 Abrah. set *sev.* ewe-*l.*
Lev. 23:18 offer with bread *sev. l.*
Num. 28:11 ye shall offer *s. l.* of
first year, 19, 27; 29:2, 8, 36
2 *Chr.* 29:21 brought *s. l.* for offering

Two LAMBS.

Ex. 29:38 *two l.* of the first year
offer, *Num.* 28:3
Lev. 14:10 on 8th day take *two l.*
Num. 28:9 and on sabbath *two l.*

LAME.

Lev. 21:18 *l.* man sh. not appro.
Deut. 15:21 if *l.* shalt not sacrifi.
2 *Sam.* 4:4 Jon. had son, *l.* 9:3. 13
5:6 exc. take away blind and *l.*
19:26 because thy servant is *l.*
Job 29:15 eyes to blind, feet to *l.*
Prov. 26:7 legs of *l.* are not equal
Is. 33:23 the *l.* take the prey
35:6 *l.* man leap as a hart
Jer. 31:8 bring with them the *l.*
Mal. 1:8 ye offer *l.* for sacrifice ?
Mat. 11:5 the *l.* walk, 15:31 ; 21:14;
Luke 7:22
Luke 14:13 call poor, *l.* and blind
Acts 3:2 a man, *l.* fr. womb, car.
8:7 many th. were *l.* we. healed
Heb. 12:13 *l.* be turn. out of way

LAMECH. *Gen.* 4:18, 19 ; 5:25 ;
1 *Chr.* 1:3 ; *Luke* 3:36

LAMENT.

Jud. 11:40 dau. of Is. went to *l.*
Is. 19:8 fishers also mourn and *l.*
32:12 they shall *l.* for the teats
Jer. 16:5 neither go to *l.* them, 6
22:18 they shall not *l.* for him
34:5 *l.* thee, saying, Ah, L.
Ezek. 32:16 daugh. of nations *l.*
Joel 1:8 *l.* like virgin with sackc.
13 gird yourselves, *l.* ye priests
Mic. 2:4 *l.* with doleful lamenta.
John 16:20 Ye shall weep and *l.*
Rev. 18:9 kings of earth shall *l.*

LAMENTED.

1 *Sam.* 6:19 people *l.* because L.
25:1 Israelites *l.* Samuel, 28:3
2 *Sam.* 1:17 David *l.* over Saul
3:33 the king *l.* over Abner
2 *Chr.* 35:25 Jeremiah *l.* for Josi.
Jer. 16:4 die and not be *l.* 25:33
Mat. 11:17 but ye have not *l.*
Luke 23:27 a great company *l.*

LAMENTABLE.

Dan. 6:20 king cried wi. *l.* voice

LAMENTATION.

Gen. 50:10 mourned with sore *l.*
2 *Sam.* 1:17 D. lamented with *l.*
Ps. 78:64 widows made no *l.*
Jer. 7:29 *l.* on high places
9:10 habitations of wildern. a *l.*
31:15 in Ramah *l. Mat.* 2:18
48:38 there shall be *l.* generally
Lam. 2:5 Lord hath increased *l.*
Ezek. 19:1 take up a *l.* for princ.
14 this is a *l.* and sh. be for a *l.*
28:12 take up *l.* on king of Tyr.
32:2 take up a *l.* for Pharaoh, 16
Amos 5:16 such as are skilf. of *l.*
8:10 turn all your songs into *l.*
Acts 8:2 great *l.* over Stephen

LAMENTATIONS.

2 *Chr.* 35:25 of Josiah in their *l.*
Ezek. 2:10 was written therein *l.*

LAMP.

Gen. 15:17 burning *l.* that passed
Ex. 27:20 cause the *l.* to burn
1 *Sam.* 3:3 ere *l.* went out
2 *Sam.* 22:29 thou art my *l.* O L.
1 *K.* 15:4 G. gave him a *l.* in Je.
Job 12:5 as a *l.* despised in him
Ps. 119:105 thy word is *l.* to feet
132:17 ordained *l.* for mine ano.
Prov. 6:23 commandment is a *l.*
13:9 *l.* of wicked sh. be put out
20:20 curs. father, *l.* be put out
Is. 62:1 salva. as *l.* that burneth
Rev. 8:10 burning as it were *l.*

LAMPS.

Ex. 25:37 light *l.* thereof, 40:4
30:7 dress. *l.* burn incense on it
35:14 his *l.* with oil for the light
40:25 lighted the *l.* before the
Lord, *Num.* 8:2, 3
Lev. 24:2 *l.* to burn 2 *Chr.* 13:11
Jud. 7:16 put *l.* within pitchers
20 held the *l.* in their left hand
1 *K.* 7:49 *l.* of gold, 2 *Chr.* 4:21
Job 41:19 out of mou. go burn. *l.*
Ezek. 1:13 like appearance of *l.*
Dan. 10:6 his eyes as *l.* of fire
Mat. 25:1 ten virgins took *l.* 3, 4
7 virgins arose, trimmed th. *l.*
8 give us oil, our *l.* are go. out

Seven LAMPS.

Ex. 37:23 *s. l.* of pure gold
Zec. 4:2 candlestick and *seven l.*
Rev. 4:5 *seven l.* of fire burning

LANCE.

Jer. 50:42 they that hold *l.* cruel

LANCETS.

1 *K.* 18:28 cut themselves with *l.*

LAND.

Gen. 2:12 gold of that *l.* is good
10:11 out of that *l.* went Ashur
12:1 into *l.* I show thee, *Acts* 7:3
13:6 *l.* not able to bear them
17:8 I will give unto thee and
thy seed the *l.* 28:13 ; 35:12
20:15 behold, my *l.* is before th.
24:37 Canaanite, in wh. *l.* I dw.
47:20 brought *l.* so *l.* beca. Ph.
22 *l.* of priests he bought not
Ex. 10:15 the *l.* was darkened
20:12 days may be long upon *l.*
Lev. 16:22 goat bear iniquit. to *l.*
18:28 *l.* spue not you out, 20:22
25:2 *l.* keep a sabbath, 26:34
23 *l.* not be sold, the *l.* is mine
26:4 *l.* sh. yield increase, 25:19
38 *l.* of your enem. eat you up
Num. 13:32 *l.* is a *l.* eateth inha.
14:24 serv. Cal. I will bring to *l.*
15:2 wh. come into *l.* of habita.
18 ; *Deut.* 17:14 ; 18:9 ; 26:1
32:4 country L. em. *l.* for cattle
33:53 for blood defileth the *l.*
Deut. 2:20 counted *l.* of gia. 3:13
8:9 *l.* whose stones are iron
11:12 a *l.* which L. careth for
29:23 wh. *l.* brimstone and salt
32:10 found him in a desert *l.*
43 he will be merciful to his *l.*
33:13 blessed of the L. be his *l.*
34:1 Lord showed him all the *l.*
Jos. 2:1 sent men, say. View *l.*
11:16 Joshua took all that *l.* 23
14:15 the *l.* had rest from war
24:13 a *l.* for wh. ye did not lab.
Jud. 3:11 *l.* rest forty years, 5:31
30 *l.* had rest fourscore years
18:10 ye shall come to a large *l.*
1 *Sam.* 14:29 father troubled *l.*
2 *Sam.* 3:12 say. Whose is the *l.*?
9:7 I restore thee all the *l.* of S.
21:14 God entreated for *l.* 24:25
2 *K.* 8:3 to cry to king for her *l.*
17:26 manner of G. of the *l.* 27
18:33 delivered his *l. Is.* 36:18

21:8 move any more out of the
l. 2 *Chr.* 33:8
25:12 left poor of *l. Jer.* 52:16
1 *Chr.* 4:40 and the *l.* was wide
2 *Chr.* 7:20 pluck them out of *l.*
34:8 when he had purged the *l.*
Ezr. 9:12 eat good of *l. Is.* 1:19
Neh. 5:16 nor bought we any *l.*
Job 31:38 my *l.* cry against me
37:13 correct. or his *l.* or mercy
39:6 the barren *l.* his dwellings

Ps. 10:16 heathen peri. out of *l.*
42:6 remember thee fr. *l.* of Jor.
44:3 got not *l.* in possession
52:5 root thee out of *l.* of living
80:9 deep root, and it filled *l.*
101:6 mine eyes on faithful of *l.*
8 I will destroy wick. of the *l.*
105:16 he called for famine on *l.*
106:24 they despised pleasant *l.*
38 *l.* was polluted with blood
107:34 turn. fruitful *l.* into bar.
143:6 thi. after thee as thirsty *l.*
10 lead me into *l.* of uprightn.
Prov. 12:11 tilleth *l.* 28:19
28:2 for transgression of *l.*
Ec. 11:9 O *l.* wh. king is child
17 blessed, O *l.* wh. king is son

Is. 5:30 look unto *l.* behold sor.
7:16 *l.* thou abhorrest be forsa.
9:19 wrath of Lord *l.* darkened
18:1 woe to the *l.* shadowing
19:24 a blessing in midst of *l.*
21:1 com. from desert, terrible *l.*
24:3 *l.* shall be utterly emptied
11 the mirth of the *l.* is gone
30:6 *l.* of trouble and anguish
32:2 shadow of rock in weary *l.*
13 on *l.* of peo. sh. come thor.
33:17 *l.* that is very far off
35:7 thirsty *l.* springs of water
49:19 *l.* of destruction too nar.
53:8 cut off out of *l.* of living
Jer. 2:2 a *l.* that was not sown
6 led us through a *l.* of deserts
7 entered, ye defiled my *l.* 3:9
15 young lions made *l.* waste
3:19 shall I give thee plea. *l.* ?
4:20 the whole *l.* is spoiled
5:19 in a *l.* that is not yours
6:8 make thee *l.* not inhabited
8:16 whole *l.* trembled
9:12 *l.* perisheth and is burnt
11:19 cut him off from *l.* of liv.
12:4 how long shall *l.* mourn ?
15 I will bring ev. man to his *l.*
16:15 bro. fr. *l.* of north, 31:16
18 bec. they have defiled my *l.*

Jer. 22:27 *l.* whereu. they desire
23:15 profanen. gone forth to *l.*
46:12 thy cry hath filled the *l.*
50:18 punish king of Bab. and *l.*
38 it is the *l.* of graven images
51:43 *l.* wherein no man dwell.
Ezek. 7:23 *l.* full of bloody crimes
8:17 have filled *l.* with violence
9:9 and the land is full of blood
14:17 sword on *l.* 19 pestilence
17:5 he took also of seed of the *l.*
13 hath taken mighty of the *l.*
22:24 the *l.* is not cleansed
30 stand in gap before me for *l.*
32:4 then I leave thee up. the *l.*
33:2 when I bring sw. upon *l.*
24 *l.* given us for inheritance
36:5 appointed *l.* into possess.
13 thou *l.* devourest up men
38:9 a cloud to cover the *l.* 16
11 to *l.* of unwalled villages
39:12 they may cleanse the *l.*
Dan. 11:16 stand in glorious *l.* 41
Hos. 4:3 therefore shall *l.* mourn
Joel 1:6 a nation come upon *l.*
2:3 the *l.* as garden of Eden
18 then will L. be jealous for *l.*
21 O *l.* be glad ; 3:2 parted *l.*

Amos 5:2 forsaken upon her *l.*
7:10 *l.* not able to bear words
8:4 make poor of the *l.* to fail
  8 shall not *l.* tremble for this?
Zep. 3:19 and fame in every *l.*
Zec. 3:9 remove iniq. of that *l.*
12:12 *l.* shall mourn, ev. family
13:2 unclean spirit pass out of *l.*
Mal. 3:12 shall be delightsome *l.*
Mat. 9:26 fame went abr. into ?.
10:15 tolerable for *l.* of S. 11:24
27:45 was darkn. over all the *l.*
      Mark 15:33
Mark 6:47 and he alone on the *l.*
Luke 14:35 neither fit for the *l.*
John 6:21 immed. ship was at *l.*
Acts 4:37 Barn. having *l.* sold it
5:8 tell me whether ye sold *l.*
27:39 was day, they knew not *l.*
43 into the sea, and get to *l.* 44

See BENJAMIN, CHALDEANS, CA-
NAAN, DARKNESS, DESO-
LATE, DIVIDE, DIVIDED.

Dry LAND.

Gen. 1:9 and let the d. *l.* appear
10 God called the *dry l.* earth
7:22 all that was in *dry l.* died
Ex. 4:9 pour water on *dry l.*
14:21 Lord made the sea *dry l.*
  29 Israel walked on *dry l.*
15:19 on *d. l.* mi. of sea, *Neh.* 9:11
Jos. 4:18 priests' lifted on *d. l.*
  22 Is. came over Jord. on *d. l.*
Ps. 63:1 long. for thee in a *d. l.*
66:6 turned the sea into *dry l.*
68:6 rebellious dwell in *dry l.*
95:5 his hands formed the *d. l.*
Is. 41:18 make *dry l.* springs
Jer. 50:12 hindermost shall be a
    dry l.
51:43 cities are *d. l.* and wilder.
Hos. 2:3 lest I set her as a *d. l.*
Jon. 1:9 who made sea and *d. l.*
Hag. 2:6 shake sea and *dry l.*
Heb. 11:29 pass. R. sea as by *d. l.*

See DWELL, EGYPT, GOOD.

In the LAND.

Gen. 13:7 Canaanite dw. *in the l.*
41:31 plenty not be kn. *in the l.*
47:4 to sojourn *in the l.* come
Ex. 8:27 sacrifice to G. *in the l.*
9:5 L. sh. do this thing *in the l.*
Lev. 26:6 I will give peace *in the l.*
Deut. 5:16 go well wi. thee *in l.*
11:9 that you may prolong your
  days *in the l.* 21; 25:15
25:19 given thee rest *in the l.*
31:13 as long as live *in the l.*
Jud. 18:7 no magistr. *in the l.*
2 *Sam.* 15:4 that I we. judge *in l.*
2 *Chr.* 6:31 fear th. so long as *in l.*
33:31 that was done *in the l.*
Job 28:13 nor is it found *in the l.*
Ps. 27:13 good. of the L. *in the l.*
116:9 walk before L. *in the l.*
142:5 thou art my port. *in the l.*
Is. 7:22 sh. every one eat *in the l.*
26:10 *in the l.* of uprightness
38:11 not see Lord *in the l.*
Ezek. 26:20 set glory *in the l.*
32:23 terror *in the l.* 24:32
37:22 make them one nat. *in l.*
45:8 *in the l.* sh. be his posses.
Hos. 4:1 there is no truth *in the l.*
Luke 21:23 great distress *in the l.*
Heb. 11:9 by faith he soj. *in the l.*

See INHABITANTS, INHERIT, IS-
RAEL, JUDAH.

Our LAND.

Gen. 47:19 buy us and *our l.*
Ps. 85:12 and *o. l.* sh. yield incr.
Mic. 5:5 Assyrian sh. come to *o. l.*

Own LAND.

Ex. 18:27 Jethro went into his *o.*
  l. Num. 10:30
1 *K.* 10:6 he. in my *o. l.* 2 *Chr.* 9:5

---

2 *K.* 18:32 take you to a land like
  your *own l. Is.* 36:17
2 *Chr.* 32:21 retur. wi. sha. to *o. l.*
Is. 13:14 flee ev. one to his *o. l.*
14:1 set them in their *own l.*
37:7 fall by sword in his *own l.*
Jer. 23:8 dw. in their *o. l.* 27:11
37:7 *Eg.* into their *own l.* 42:12
Ezek. 34:13 bring them to their
  o. l. 36:24; 37:14, 21; 39:28
Amos 7:11 led capt. out their *o. l.*

See PEOPLE, POSSESS, POSSES-
SION, STRANGE.

Their LAND, S.

Gen. 47:22 priests sold not *t. l.*
Num. 18:20 A. had no inh. in *t. l.*
Deut. 2:5 not give you of *t. l.* 9
29:28 L. rooted them out of *t. l.*
1 *K.* 8:48 pray to thee tow. *t. l.*
2 *Chr.* 7:14 forg. sin and heal *t. l.*
Ps. 105:32 flaming fire in *t. l.*
135:12 gave *t. l.* for inher. 136:21
Is. 2:7 *their l.* is full of silver
  8 *their l.* also is full of idols
Jer. 12:14 pluck them out *their l.*
16:15 I will bri. them ag. to *t. l.*
51:5 *their l.* was filled with sin
Ezek. 34:27 they sh. be safe in *their l.*
39:26 dwelt safely in *their l.*
Amos 9:15 plant them on *t. l.*

This LAND.

Gen. 12:7 L. said, Unto thy seed
  will I give *this l.* 15:18; 24:7;
  48:4; *Ex.* 32:13
31:13 get thee out from *this l.*
50:24 G. will bri. you out of *t. l.*
Num. 14:3 L. bro. us unto *this l.*
32:5 let *t. l.* be given to thy ser.
  22 *this l.* sh. be your possess.
Deut. 4:22 I must die in *this l.*
29:24 the Lord done thus to
  this l.? 27; 1 *K.* 9:8; 2 *Chr.*
  7:21
Jud. 2:2 no league wi. inh. of *t. l.*
2 *Chr.* 30:9 shall come into *t. l.*
Jer. 14:15 sw. sh. not be in *t. l.*
16:3 fathers that begot in *this l.*
22:12 he shall see *t. l.* no more
24:6 I will bring them ag. to *t. l.*
25:9 bring them against *this l.*
11 *t.* whole *l.* sh. be a desolat.
32:41 I will plant them in *t. l.*
36:29 king of Bab. destroy *t. l.*
42:10 ye will abide in *this l.* 13
45:4 I will pluck up *t.* whole *l.*
Ezek. 11:15 to us is *this l.* given
47:14 *t. l.* sh. fall to you for inh.
Acts 7:4 removed him into *t. l.*

Thy LAND.

Ex. 23:10 six years sh. sow *t. l.*
26 noth. sh. cast young in *t. l.*
34:24 nor sh. any man desire *t. l.*
Deut. 7:13 will bless fruit of *t. l.*
21:23 that *thy l.* be not defiled
28:12 to give the rain to *thy l.*
16 cursed be fruit of *thy l.* 42
2 *Sam.* 24:13 sh. fam. come to *t. l.*
Ps. 85:1 been favorable to *thy l.*
Is. 8:8 wings fill breadth of *t. l.*
60:18 viol. no more heard in *t. l.*
62:4 nor sh. *t. l.* be termed des.
  L. delight. in thee, and *t. l.*
Ezek. 32:8 set darkness on *thy l.*
Amos 7:17 *thy l.* shall be divided
Nah. 3:13 gates of *t. l.* sh. be wi.

Your LAND.

Gen. 47:23 I bought you and *y. l.*
Lev. 19:9 harvest of *y. l. 23:22*
26:25 and dwell in *y. l.* safely
  6 nor shall we. go through *y. l.*
20 *y. l.* sh. not yield her inc.
Deut. 11:14 give you rain of *y. l.*
1 *Sam.* 6:5 light. hand fr. off *y. l.*
Jer. 5:19 serv. stran. gods in *y. l.*
27:10 remove you far from *y. l.*
44:22 theref. is *y. l.* a desolation

LANDED, ING.

Acts 18:22 when we *l.* at Cesarea
21:3 sailed to Syria and *l.* at T.
28:12 *l.* at Syracuse three days

LANDMARK, S.

Deut. 19:14 not remo. thy neigh
  bor's *l. Prov.* 22:28; 23:10
27:17 cursed that removeth *l.*
Job 24:2 some remove the *l.*

LANDS.

Gen. 41:54 dearth in all *l.* 57
47:18 not left but bodies and *l.*
Jud. 11:13 restore those *l.* again
1 *Chr.* 14:17 fame of D. went all *l.*
2 *Chr.* 17:10 fear fell on all the *l.*
32:17 gods of other *l.* have not
Ezr. 9:1 not separ. fr. peo. of *l.*
Neh. 5:3 have mortgaged our *l.*
  5 for other men have our *l.*
  11 restore, I pray you, their *l.*
Ps. 49:11 th. *l.* after own names
66:1 make noise all ye *l.* 100:1
105:44 give them *l.* of heathen
106:27 to scatter them in *l.*
107:3 gathered them out of *l.*
Jer. 27:6 these *l.* to Nebuchadn.
Ezek. 20:6 wh. is glory of all *l.* 15
39:27 gather out of enemies' *l.*
Mat. 19:29 hath forsaken houses,
  l. Mark 10:29
Mark 10:30 rec. hundred-fold, *l.*
Acts 4:34 were possessors of *l.*

LANES.

Luke 14:21 go quickly into the *l.*

LANGUAGE, S.

Gen. 11:1 wh. earth was of one *l.*
  6 people is one, have all one *l.*
  7 and there confound their *l.* 9
2 *K.* 18:26 speak in the Syrian *l.*
  Is. 36:11, 13
Neh. 13:24 chil. not speak Jews'
  l. but accord. to *l.* of people
Ps. 19:3 no *l.* wh. voice is heard
81:5 heard a *l.* I understood not
114:1 from a people of strange *l.*
Is. 19:18 five cities speak *l.* Can.
Jer. 5:15 wh. *l.* thou know. not
Ezek. 3:5 to a people of hard *l.* 6
Dan. 3:4 people, nations and *l.*
  7 all *l.* fell down and worship.
  29 every *l.* that speaketh amiss
4:1 Neb. all *l.* 6:25 D. to all *l.*
5:19 all *l.* trembled and feared
7:14 nations, and *l.* sho. serve
Zep. 3:9 turn to people a pure *l.*
Zec. 8:23 ten men out of all *l.*
Acts 2:6 heard th. speak in all *l.*

LANGUISH.

Is. 16:8 the fields of Heshbon *l.*
19:8 spread nets on wat. sh. *l.*
24:4 haughty people of earth *l.*
Jer. 14:2 the gates of Judah *l.*
Hos. 4:3 every one therein sh. *l.*

LANGUISHED, ETH.

Is. 24:4 world *l.* and fad. away
  7 the vine *l.* 33:9 the earth *l.*
Jer. 15:9 that hath borne seven *l.*
Lam. 2:8 wall lament, *l.* together
Joel 1:10 the oil *l.* 12 fig-tree *l.*
Nah. 1:4 Bashan *l.* and Carmel *l.*

LANGUISHING.

Ps. 41:3 L. strength. on bed of *l.*

LANTERNS.

John 18:3 Judas cometh with *l.*

LAODICEA.

Col. 2:1 for them at L. 4:13,15,16

LAODICEANS.

Col. 4:16 in church of L. *Rev.* 3:14

LAP.

2 *K.* 4:39 gathered gourds, *l.* full
Neh. 5:13 I shook my *l.* and said
Prov. 16:33 lot is cast into the *l.*

LAPPED, ETH.

Jud. 7:5 that *l.* water as a dog
6 number *l.* were three hund.
7 by them th. *l.* I will save you

LAPWING. See BAT.

LARGE.

Ex. 3:8 into a good and *l.* land
2 *Sam.* 22:20 he brought me into
a *l.* place, *Ps.* 18:19
Neh. 4:19 the work is gre. and *l.*
9:35 not served thee in *l.* land
Ps. 31:8 set my feet in a *l.* room
118:5 Lord set me in a *l.* place
Is. 22:18 toss thee in a *l.* country
30:23 cattle feed in *l.* past. 33
Jer. 22:14 I will build *l.* chamb.
Ezek. 23:32 sist. cup deep and *l.*
Hos. 4:16 L. feed them in a *l.* pl.
Mat. 28:12 gave *l.* money to sol.
Mark 14:15 and he will show you
a *l.* upper room, *Luke* 22:12
Gal. 6:11 *l.* letter I have written
Rev. 21:16 length as *l.* as breadth

LARGENESS.

1 *K.* 4:29 God gave S. *l.* of heart

LASCIVIOUSNESS.

Mark 7:22 out of heart proceed *l.*
2 *Cor.* 12:21 not repented of the *l.*
Gal. 5:19 works of flesh manif. *l.*
Eph. 4:19 given themselves to *l.*
1 *Pet.* 4:3 when we walked in *l.*
Jude 4 turning grace of G. into *l.*

LAST.

Gen. 49:19 Gad sh. overcome at *l.*
Num. 23:10 my *l.* end be like his
2 *Sam.* 23:1 *l.* words of David
1 *Chr.* 23:27 by *l.* words of David
Neh. 8:18 from first day to the *l.*
Prov. 5:11 thou mourn at the *l.*
Is. 41:4 I Lord, first and *l.* 44:6;
48:12; *Rev.* 1:11, 17; 2:8;
22:13
Lam. 1:9 remembereth not *l.* end
Dan. 8:3 the higher came up *l.*
Amos 9:1 will slay the *l.* of them
Mat. 12:45 *l.* state of that man is
worse than first., *Luke* 11:26
19:30 first shall be *l.* and *l.* first.
20:16; *Mark* 10:31; *Luke* 13:30
20:12 *l.* have wrought one hour
14 give to *l.* even as unto thee
27:64 *l.* error worse than the fi.
Mark 9:35 first, same sh. be *l.*
Luke 12:59 till *l.* hast paid *l.* m.
1 *Cor.* 4:9 set forth us apostles *l.*
15:8 *l.* of all he was seen of me
26 *l.* enemy is death; 45 *l.* Ad.
Rev. 2:19 *l.* works be more th. fi.

LAST day, s.

Gen. 49:1 befall you in *l.* days
John 6:39 should raise it up ag.
at the *l.* d. 40, 44, 54
7:37 in *l.* d. great day of feast
11:24 he shall rise again at *l.* d.
2 *Tim.* 3:1 *l.* day perilous times
Heb. 1:2 spoken in *l.* d. by his S.
Jam. 5:3 heaped treasure for *l.* d.
2 *Pet.* 3:3 come in *l.* d. scoffers

LAST time, s.

1 *Pet.* 1:5 to be revealed in *l.* t.
20 manifest in these *l.* times
1 *John* 2:18 children, it is the *l.* t.
Jude 18 should be mockers in *l.* t.

LASTED, ING.

Deut. 33:15 precious th. of *l.* hills
Jud. 14:17 wept whilst feast *l.*

LATCHET.

Is. 5:27 *l.* of their shoes broken
Mark 1:7 *l.* of wh. shoes, *Lu.* 3:16

LATE, LY.

Ps. 127:2 vain for you to sit up *l.*
Mic. 2:8 of *l.* my people risen up
Acts 18:2 Aquila *l.* come from I.

LATIN.

Luke 23:38 writ. in L. *John* 19:20

LATTER.

Deut. 11:14 give first and *l.* rain
Job 19:25 Redeemer, st. at *l.* day
29:23 open. mouth, as for *l.* rain
Prov. 16:15 as cloud of *l.* rain
19:20 mayest be wise in *l.* end
Jer. 3:3 there ha. been no *l.* rain
5:24 form. and *l.* rain in season
Dan. 8:23 *l.* time of their kingd.
Hos. 6:3 as *l.* and former rain
Joel 2:23 *l.* rain in first month
Amos 7:1 in beginning of *l.* grow.
Hag. 2:9 glory of *l.* house greater
Zec. 10:1 rain in time of *l.* rain
1 *Tim.* 4:1 in *l.* times some dep.

See DAYS, END.

LATTICE.

Jud. 5:28 cried through the *l.*
2 *K.* 1:2 Ahaziah fell through *l.*
Cant. 2:9 show. himself thro' *l.*

LAUD.

Rom. 15:11 praise L. and *l.* him

LAUGH.

Gen. 18:13 wheref. did Sarah *l.* ?
21:6 G. made me to *l.* all will *l.*
Job 5:22 at famine thou shalt *l.*
9:23 will *l.* at trial of innocent
22:19 innocent *l.* them to scorn
Ps. 2:4 sitteth in heavens sh. *l.*
22:7 that see me *l.* me to scorn
37:13 the Lord shall *l.* at him
52:6 righteous also sh. *l.* at him
59:8 thou, O L. shall *l.* at them
80:6 enemies *l.* am. themselves
Prov. 1:26 *l.* at your calamity
29:9 rage or *l.* there is no rest
Ec. 3:4 time to weep, time to *l.*
Luke 6:21 ye that weep, ye sh. *l.*
25 woe unto you that *l.* now

LAUGHED.

Gen. 17:17 Abra. *l.* 18:12 Sarah
18:15 S. denied, saying, I *l.* not
2 *K.* 19:21 daughter of Zion hath
l. *Is.* 37:22
2 *Chr.* 30:10 they *l.* them to sco.
Neh. 2:19 they *l.* us to scorn
Job 12:4 upright man *l.* to scorn
29:24 *l.* on them, they beli. not

Ezek. 23:32 shalt be *l.* to scorn
Mat. 9:24 they *l.* him to scorn,
Mark 5:40; *Luke* 8:53

LAUGHETH, ING.

Job 8:21 he fill thy mouth with *l.*
41:29 he *l.* at shaking of a spear

LAUGHTER.

Ps. 126:2 mouth filled with *l.*
Prov. 14:13 in *l.* heart sorrowful
Ec. 2:2 I said of *l.* It is mad
7:3 sorrow is better than *l.*
6 thorns, so is the *l.* of fool
Jam. 4:9 *l.* turned to mourning

LAUNCH, ED.

Luke 5:4 Sim. *l.* out into deep
8:22 go over, and they *l.* forth
Acts 21:1 after had *l.* 27:2, 4

LAVER, S.

Ex. 30:18 make a *l.* of brass
28 *l.* and fo. 31:9; 35:16; 39:39
38:8 he made the *l.* of brass
40:7 thou shalt set the *l.* 30
Lev. 8:11 anoint. both *l.* and foot
1 *K.* 7:30 under *l.* were unders.
38 made ten *l.* of brass; one *l.*
40 baths; and ev. *l.* 4 cubits
40 and H. made the *l.*
43 and the ten *l.* on the bases,
2 *Chr.* 4:6, 14
2 *K.* 16:17 king A. removed *l.*

LAVISH.

Is. 46:6 they *l.* gold out of bag

LAW.

Gen. 47:26 made it a *l.* over land
Ex. 12:49 *l.* to him home-born
Lev. 24:22; *Num.* 15:16, 29
Deut. 17:11 to sentence of the *l.*
33:2 fr. right hand went fiery *l.*
4 Moses commanded us a *l.*
Jos. 8:32 wrote copy of *l.* to M.
22:5 take heed to the *l.* 2 *K.*
17:13, 37; 21:8
2 *K.* 17:34 nor do after the *l.*
1 *Chr.* 22:12 mayest keep *l.* of G.
2 *Chr.* 19:10 between *l.* and com.
30:16 place according to *l.* of M.
Ezr. 7:6 scribe in *l.* 12, 21
14 according to *l.* of thy God
26 not do *l.* of G. and *l.* of king
Neh. 8:7 cause people underst. *l.*
9 wh. they heard the wo. of *l.*
10:29 made oath to walk in G. *l.*
12:44 gather them portions of *l.*
Est. 1:8 drinking according to *l.*
4:11 *l.* of his to put him to dea.
16 which is not according to *l.*
Job 22:22 rec. *l.* from his mouth
Ps. 1:2 in his *l.* he meditates
37:31 *l.* of his G. is in his heart
78:5 for he appointed a *l.* in Is.
10 refused to walk in his *l.*
81:4 was a *l.* of the G. of Jacob
105:10 confirm. same to J. for *l.*
119:72 *l.* of mouth bet. than gold
Prov. 1:8 forsake not the *l.* of thy
mother, 6:20
6:23 command. lamp, *l.* is light
13:14 *l.* of wise is fount. of life
28:4 forsake *l.* praise wick. such
as keep *l.* contend with them
7 keepeth the *l.* is a wise son
29:18 that keep. *l.* happy is he
31:5 lest drink and forget the *l.*
26 in her tongue is *l.* of kindn.
Is. 2:3 out of Zion shall go forth
the *l.* *Mic.* 4:2
8:16 seal *l.* 20 to *l.* and testim.
42:4 the isles sh. wait for his *l.*
21 Lord will magnify the *l.*
51:4 a *l.* shall proceed from me
Jer. 2:8 they that handle the *l.*
18:18 *l.* not perish from priest
44:23 not obey. nor walk. in *l.*
Lam. 2:9 the *l.* is no more
Ezek. 7:26 *l.* perish from priests
Dan. 6:5 concerning *l.* of his G.
12 according to *l.* of Medes, 15
Hos. 4:6 has forgotten *l.* of God
Hab. 1:4 theref. the *l.* is slacked
Zep. 3:4 priests done viol. to *l.*
Mal. 2:6 *l.* of truth was in mouth
7 sh. seek the *l.* at his mouth
9 have been partial in the *l.*
Mat. 5:17 not to come to dest. *l.*
18 sh. in no wise pass fr. the *l.*
40 if any man sue th. at the *l.*
11:13 *l.* pro. till Jo. *Luke* 16:16
22:36 great commandment in *l.*
40 on two command. hang *l.*
23:23 omitted weigh. mat. of *l.*
Luke 2:27 do after custom of *l.*
5:17 were doctors of *l.* sitting
16:17 one tittle of the *l.* to fail
John 1:17 *l.* was given by Moses
7:19 did not Moses give you *l.* ?
23 *l.* of Moses should not be
John 7:49 who know. not the *l.*
51 doth *l.* judge before it be ?
10:34 written in *l.* Ye are gods ?
12:34 heard out of *l.* that Christ
18:31 judge him according to *l.*
19:7 by our *l.* he ought to die
Acts 6:13 blasphe. words aga. *l.*
7:53 have received *l.* by angels
13:15 reading of *l.* and prophets
39 not justified by *l.* of Moses
15:5 command to keep *l.* of Mo.
24 circumcised and keep the *l.*
18:15 a question of *l.* look to it
19:38 *l.* is open ; 21:20 zeal. of *l.*

21:28 this man teach. against *l*.
22:12 devout man accord. to *l*.
23:3 sittest thou to jud. after *l*.
25:8 nor against *l*. of the Jews
28:23 persua. them out of the *l*.

Rom. 2:12 sin. in *l*. judged by *l*.
13 not hearers of the *l*. are just
14 Gentiles have not *l*. to do
    things contained in *l*. these
    hav. not *l*. are a *l*. unto the.
17 called a Jew, and rest. in *l*.
20 the form of truth in the *l*.
23 that makest thy boast of
    the *l*. through break. the *l*.
3:20 by deeds of *l*. no flesh be
    justified. for by the *l*. is
    knowl. of sin, 28 ; *Gal.* 2:16
21 righ. of God witnessed by *l*.
27 by what *l*. excluded ? by *l*.
31 do we ˉmake void the *l*. ?
4:14 they which are of *l*. be hei.
15 *l*. worketh wrath wh. no *l*.
5:13 until *l*. sin was in world,
    but sin not im. wh. is no *l*.
20 *l*. entered. offence might
7:1 speak to them wh. know *l*.
2 wo. bound by *l*. to husband
4 ye also become dead to the *l*.
7 is *l*. sin, I had not kno. sin,
    but by *l*. nor lust, ex. *l*. said
8 without *l*. sin was dead
12 the *l*. is holy, and comman.
14 know th. the *l*. is spiritual
16 *l*. that is good 1 *Tim.* 1:8
22 I delight in the *l*. of God
23 I see another *l*. warring ag.
    the *l*. of my mind, to *l*. of
25 with mind I serve *l*. of God
8:2 the *l*. of life made me free
3 for what the *l*. could not do
4 righteousness of the *l*. fulfil.
7 carnal mind not subject to *l*.
9:31 Israel followed *l*. of righte.
10:4 Christ is the end of the *l*.
13:8 loveth another. fulfilled *l*.
10 love is the fulfilli. of the *l*.

1 *Cor.* 6:1 dare any of you to *l*. ?
6 brother goeth to *l*. with bro.
7:39 wife is bound by the *l*.
15:56 strength of sin is the *l*.

Gal. 2:16 not just. by works of *l*.
19 I thro' the *l*. am de. to the *l*.
21 if righteousness come by *l*.
3:2 received ye Spirit by the *l*. ?
5 miracles, doeth he it by *l*. ?
11 no man is justified by the *l*.
12 and the *l*. is not of faith
13 C. redeem. us fr. curse of *l*.
19 wheref. then serveth the *l*. ?
21 is the *l*. aga. the promises ?
    righteous. had been by the *l*.
24 *l*. was our schoolmaster
5:3 is a debtor to do the who. *l*.
4 whosoever are just. by the *l*.
14 all the *l*. is fulfil. in one w.
23 tempera. ag. such is no *l*.
6:2 so fulfil the *l*. of Christ. 13

Eph. 2:15 abolished in his fle. *l*.
Phil. 3:6 touching righ. in the *l*.
9 mine own righteou. of the *l*.
1 *Tim.* 1:7 to be teache. of the *l*.
9 *l*. is not made for right. man
Tit. 3:9 avoid content. about *l*.
Heb. 7:5 take tithes accord. to *l*.
12 made of nece. a change of *l*.
16 not after the *l*. of a carnal
19 for the *l*. made noth. perfect
28 *l*. make. men high-priests
8:4 offer gifts accord. to the *l*.
9:22 all things are by the *l*.
10:1 *l*. hav. shadow of good th.
28 he that desp. Moses' *l*. died
Jam. 1:25 looketh into perfect *l*.
2:8 fulfil the royal *l*. ye do well
9 convinced of *l*. as transgres.
12 they th. be judged by the *l*.
4:11 that speaketh evil of the *l*.

1 *John* 3:4 whosoever committeth sin transgres. also the *l*.

See BOOK.

LAW of the Lord.
Ex. 13:9 *L's l*. be in thy mouth
2 *K.* 10:31 no heed to wa. in *l. L.*
2 *Chr.* 12:1 R. forsook *l. of t. L.*
31:4 encouraged in *l. of the L.*
Ezr. 7:10 heart to seek *l. of t. L.*
Ps. 1:2 delight in *l. of the L.*
19:7 the *l. of the L.* is perfect
119:1 blessed th. walk in *l. of L.*
Is. 5:24 cast away the *l. of L.*
30:9 children not hear *l. of L.*
Jer. 8:8 say, *l. of L.* is with us
Amos 2:4 they have des. *l. of L.*

My LAW.
Ex. 16:4 whether walk in *my l.*
2 *Chr.* 6:16 childr. walk in *my l.*
Ps. 78:1 my peo. to *my l.* incline
Prov. 3:1 my son, forg. not *my l.*
4:2 fors. not *my l.* 7:2 keep *my l.*
Is. 51:7 peo. in wh. heart is *my l.*
Jer. 6:19 not hearken. unto *my l.*
16:11 forsa. me, not kept *my l.*
31:33 put *my l.* in their parts
44:10 nor walked in *my l.*
Ezek. 22:26 priests ha. vio. *my l.*
Hos. 8:1 they trespass ag. *my l.*
12 writ. to him things of *my l.*

This LAW.
Num. 5:30 priests shall exe. *t. l.*
Deut. 1:5 Moses to declare *this l*
17:18 write him a copy of *t. l.*
28:58 if th. wilt not observe *t. l.*
31:9 M. wrote *t. l.* 11 read *t. l.*
24 wri. words of *t. l.* in a book

This is the LAW.
Ezek. 43:12 *this is the l.* of house
Mat. 7:12 *this is the l.* and prop.

Thy LAW.
Deut. 33:10 shall teach Isr. *thy l.*
Neh. 9:26 cast *t. l.* behind backs
34 nor our princes kept *thy l.*
Ps. 40:8 *t. l.* is within my heart
94:12 teachest him out of *thy l.*
119:18 wondr. things art of *t. l.*
29 and grant *t. l.* graciously
34 and I shall keep *thy l.*
44 so shall keep *t. l.* continu.
51 have I not declined fr. *t. l.*
55 I rememb. and kept *thy l.*
61 I have not forgotten *thy l.*
70 but I delight in *thy l.*
77 for *t. l.* is my delight, 92, 174
85 pits, wh. are not after *t. l.*
97 love *t. l.* 109 not forget *t. l.*
113 *t. l.* I love, 163 ; 126 ma. vo.
136 because they keep not *t. l.*
142 *t. l.* is truth ; 150 far fr. *t. l.*
165 peace have they love *t. l.*
Jer. 32:23 nor walk in *t. l.*
Dan. 9:11 have transgressed *t. l.*

Under the LAW.
Rom. 6:14 ye are not *under t. l.*
15 sho. we sin bec. not *u. l.* ?
1 *Cor.* 9:20 as *u. t. l.* that I might
    gain them th. that are *u. t. l.*
21 not without law to G. *u. l.*
Gal. 3:23 kept *u. l.* 4:4 made *u. l.*
4:5 sent Son to red. them *un. l.*
5:18 led by Sp. are not *u. t. l.*

Without LAW.
2 *Chr.* 15:3 Is. hath been *with. l.*
Rom. 2:12 many as sinned *w. l.*
3:21 righteousness of God *w. l.*
7:8 *w. l.* sin dead ; 9 I was alive
1 *Cor.* 9:21 *w. l.* not *w. l.* to God

Written in the LAW.
1 *K.* 2:3 as it is *written in the l.*
    of Moses, 2 *Chr.* 23:18 ; 25:4 ;
    31:3 ; *Ezr.* 3:2 ; *Neh.* 10:34,
    36 ; *Dan.* 9:13 ; *Luke* 2:23
Dan. 9:11 oath is *w. in t. l.* of
    Moses

Luke 10:26 what is *wri. in t. l.* ?
24:44 all must be ful. *w. in t. l.*
Acts 24:14 belie. things *w. in t. l.*

LAWS.
Gen. 26:5 Abraham kept my *l.* ?
Ex. 16:28 how long ref. my *l.* ?
18:16 make them know *l.* of G.
20 teach th. ordinances and *l.*
Neh. 9:13 thou gavest th. true *l.*
Est. 1:19 among *l.* of Persians
3:8 their *l.* are div. from all peo.
    nei. keep they the king's *l.*
Is. 24:5 th. have transgressed *l.*
Dan. 7:25 to change times and *l.*
9:10 nor obeyed to walk in *l.*
Heb. 8:10 put my *l.* into th. mind
10:16 put my *l.* in their hearts

LAWFUL.
Is. 49:24 sh. *l.* captive be deliv. ?
Ezek. 18:5 do that which is *l.* 21,
    27 ; 33:14, 19
19 son ha. done that is *l.* 33:16
Mat. 12:2 do what is not *l. Mark*
    2:24 ; *Luke* 6:2
4 was not *l.* for him to eat,
    Mark 2:26 ; *Luke* 6:4

Mat. 12:10 is it *l.* to heal on sab. ?
    12 ; *Mark* 3:4 ; 6:9 ; 14:3
14:4 it is not *l.* for thee to have
    her, *Mark* 6:18
19:3 *l.* to put aw. wife? *Mar.* 10:2
John 5:10 not *l.* to carry thy bed
    18:31 not *l.* to put man to death
Acts 19:39 determ. in *l.* assembly
    22:25 is it *l.* to scourge a Rom. ?
1 *Cor.* 6:12 all things *l.* 10:23
2 *Cor.* 12:4 not *l.* for man to utter

LAWFULLY.
1 *Tim.* 1:8 go. if a man use it *l.*
2 *Tim.* 2:5 not crown. except *l.*

LAWGIVER.
Gen. 49:10 *l.* from betw. his feet
Num. 21:18 digged by direc. of *l.*
Deut. 33:21 in a portion of the *l.*
Ps. 60:7 Judah is my *l.* 108:8
Is. 33:22 *l.* is our *l.* and king
Jam. 4:12 one *l.* is able to save

LAWLESS.
1 *Tim.* 1:9 law for *l.* disobedient

LAWYER, S.
Mat. 22:35 a *l.* asked, *Luke* 10:25
Luke 7:30 *l.* reject. counsel of G.
11:46 woe to you *l.* 52 ; 14:3 J.

LAY.
Ex. 5:8 tale of bricks ye shall *l.*
16:13 *l.* round about host, 14
22:25 neither sh. thou *l.* on him
Lev. 1:7 *l.* the wood on the fire
8 priests sh. *l.* parts in ord. 12
Num. 12:11 L. *l.* not sin upon us
Deut. 7:15 *l.* on them that hate
11:25 *l.* fear of you upon land
21:8 *l.* not innoc. blood to peop.
Jud. 16:3 Sam. *l.* till midnight
Ruth 3:8 a woman *l.* at his feet
1 *Sam.* 3:15 Samuel *l.* till morn.
26:5 Saul *l.* in the trench, 7
2 *Sam.* 4:5 who *l.* on bed at noon
12:3 ewe-lamb *l.* in his bosom
16 D. *l.* all night on earth, 13:31
1 *K.* 13:31 *l.* my bones beside his
18:23 *l.* it on wood put no fire
2 *K.* 4:34 went and *l.* on the chi.
2 *Chr.* 36:21 long as she *l.* desol.
Est. 4:3 *l.* in sackcloth and ashes
Job 29:19 dew *l.* all ni. on branch
34:23 not *l.* on man more than
Ps. 7:5 *l.* mine honor in the dust
38:12 seek life, *l.* snares for me
84:3 a nest, where she *l.* young
Ec. 7:2 living will *l.* it to heart

Is. 5:8 woe to them that *l.* field
13:9 *l.* land desolate, *Ezek.* 33:28
11 will *l.* low hau. of terrible
22:22 house of D. *l.* on shoulder
25:12 the fortress shall be *l.* low
28:16 I will *l.* in Z. a tried stone
17 judgment will I *l.* to the li.
29:21 *l.* a snare for him that re.
34:15 there sh. the great owl *l.*
38:21 and *l.* it for a plaster
54:11 *l.* thy stones with colors
Jer. 6:21 will *l.* stumbling-blocks
before this peop. *Ezek.* 3:20
Ezek. 4:1 take a tile and *l.* it be.
4 *l.* iniquity of house of Israel
25:14 *l.* vengeance on Edom, 17
32:5 will *l.* thy flesh on mount
36:29 I will *l.* no famine upon
34 land be tilled, it *l.* desolate
37:6 I will *l.* sinews upon you
Jon. 1:14 *l.* not on us inno. blood
Mic. 1:7 idols will I *l.* desolate
Mal. 2:2 if ye will not *l.* it to he.
Mat. 8:20 hath not where to *l.*
his head, *Luke* 9:58
28:6 see place where the Lord *l.*
Mark 2:4 bed wh. sick of palsy *l.*
Luke 19:44 *l.* thee with ground
Acts 7:60 L. *l.* not this sin to th.
15:28 *l.* on you no grea. burden
Rom. 8:33 *l.* any thing to God's
9:33 I *l.* in Zion a stumbling-st
1 *Cor.* 16:2 every one *l.* by him
Heb. 12:1 let us *l.* aside ev. weig.
Jam. 1:21 *l.* apart all filthiness
1 *Pet.* 2:6 *l.* in Zion a chief cor.

See FOUNDATION.

LAY down.

Gen. 19:33 L. per. not she *l. d.* 35
28:11 Jacob *l. d.* in place to sl.
Num. 24:9 he *l. d.* as a lion
Jud. 5:27 he *l. down* at her feet
Ruth 3:4 uncov. feet, *l.* thee *d.*
1 *Sam.* 19:24 Saul *l. down* naked
Job 17:3 *l. d.* put me in surety
Ps. 4:8 I will *l.* me *d.* in peace
104:22 young lions *l. d.* in dens
Ezek. 19:2 mother *l. d.* am. lions
Amos 2:8 *l.* thems. *d.* on clothes
John 10:15 *l. d.* life for sheep, 17
John 10:18 I. it *down* of myself
13:37 *l.* my li. for thy sake, 38
15:13 *l. d.* his life for his friends
1 *John* 3:16 *l. d.* lives for breth.

LAY hand.

Gen. 22:12 *l.* n. thy *h.* on the lad
37:22 no blood, *l.* no *h.* on Jos.
Ex. 7:4 I may *l.* my *h.* on Egypt
Lev. 3:2 *l. h.* on head of offer. 8
4:4 sh. *l. h.* on bullock's he. 15
29 sh. *l. h.* on sin-offering, 33
Num. 27:18 L. said, *l. h.* on Jos.
Jud. 18:19 *l. h.* on thy mouth
Job 9:33 any days-man to *l. h.*
21:5 mark me, *l. h.* on mouth
40:4 will *l.* my *h.* on my mouth
41:8 *l. h.* on him, remem. battle
Prov. 30:32 tho' evil, *l. h.* mouth
Is. 11:14 *l.* their *h.* on Edom
Mic. 7:16 sh. *l. h.* on their mou.
Mat. 9:18 come, *l.* thy *h.* on her

LAY hands.

Lev. 16:21 A. sh. *l.* bo. *h.* on goat
Num. 8:12 Lev. *l. h.* on bullocks
Neh. 13:21 again, *l. h.* on you
Mat. 21:46 they sought to *l. h.*
on him, *Luke* 20:19
Mark 5:23 come *l.* thy *h.* on her
16:18 *l. h.* on sick, they recover
Luke 21:12 they shall *l. h.* on you
1 *Tim.* 5:22 *l. h.* suddenly on no

LAY hold.

Prov. 3:18 tree of life to th. *l. h.*
Ec. 2:3 I sought to *l. h.* on folly
Is. 5:29 roar, and *l. h.* on prey
Jer. 6:23 *l. h.* on bow and spear

Zec. 14:13 ev. one *l. h.* on neigh.
Mark 3:21 friends went to *l. h.*
12:12 sought to *l. hold* on him
1 *Tim.* 6:12 *l. h.* on eter. life, 19
Heb. 6:18 *l. h.* on hope set be. us

LAY up.

Gen. 41:35 *l. up* corn under Pha.
Ex. 16:23 *l. up* manna till morn.
33 *l. up* a pot of manna
Num. 17:4 sh. *l.* them *up* in tab.
Deut. 11:18 *l. up* my words
Job 22:22 *l. up* his words in heart
24 then shalt *l. up* gold as dust
Prov. 7:1 *l. up* my commandm.
10:14 wise men *l. up* knowledge
Mat. 6:19 *l.* not *up* for you treas.
20 *l. up* treasures in heaven
2 *Cor.* 12:14 children not to *l. up*

LAY wait.

Ezr. 8:31 del. fr. such as *l.* in *w.*
Ps. 71:10 *l.* wait for my soul
Prov. 1:11 let us *l. wait* for blood
18 they *l. w.* for their own bl.
24:15 *l.* not *w.* against righte.
Jer. 5:26 *l. w.* as he that setteth

LAY waste.

Is. 5:6 I will *l.* it *w.* it shall not
Ezek. 35:4 I will *l.* thy cities *w.*

LAY with.

Gen. 19:33 *l. w.* her father 34, 35
30:16 Jacob *l. w.* L. that night
34:2 Shechem *l. with* Dinah
35:22 Reuben *l. with* Bilhah
Deut. 22:22 man that *l. w.* wom.
25 man that *l. w.* her shall die
29 that *l. w.* her give 50 shek.
1 *Sam.* 2:22 Eli's sons *l. w.* wom.
2 *Sam.* 13:14 forc. T. and *l. w.*
Ezek. 23:8 in her youth *l. w.* her

LAID.

Gen. 22:6 wood, and *l.* it on Isa.
30:41 Jacob *l.* rods before cattle
48:14 *l.* it on Ephraim's head
Ex. 2:3 *l.* it on flags by river
Deut. 26:6 Egy. *l.* on us bondage
Jos. 7:23 they *l.* them bef. the L.
Ruth 4:16 and *l.* it in her bosom
2 *Sam.* 18:17 *l.* heap of stones on
1 *K.* 3:20 *l.* it in her bosom, and
l. her dead child in my bos.
13:29 prophet *l.* carcase on ass
17:19 and *l.* him on his own bed
2 *K.* 9:25 *l.* this burden on him
20:7 they *l.* it on the boil
Job 6:2 calamity *l.* in balances
18:10 snares *l.* for him in ground
38:6 or who *l.* the corner-stone
Ps. 21:5 majesty hast *l.* on him
31:4 out of the net they *l.* for me
49:14 they are *l.* in the grave
62:9 to be *l.* in the balance
79:1 they have *l.* Jeru. on heaps
88:6 hast *l.* me in the lowest pit
89:19 *l.* help on one mighty
105:18 fetters, he was *l.* in iron
119:30 judg. have I *l.* before me
110 *l.* a snare for me, 141:9
142:3 privily *l.* a snare for me
Is. 43:25 *l.* it not to heart, 57:11

Is. 47:6 thou has heavily *l.* yoke
53:6 L. *l.* on him iniq. of us all
Jer. 50:24 *l.* a snare for thee
Ezek. 32:19 *l.* wi. the uncircum.
35:12 saying, They are *l.* desol.
Hos. 11:4 I *l.* meat unto them
Ob. 7 *l.* a wound under thee
Mic. 5:1 hath *l.* siege against us
Hab. 2:19 it is *l.* over with gold
Hag. 2:15 before a stone was *l.*
Zec. 3:9 behold stone I have *l.*
Mat. 3:10 axe *l.* to root, *Luke* 3:9
27:60 *l.* it in his own new tomb
Mark 7:30 her daughter *l.* on bed
15:47 M. beheld where he was *l.*
16:6 behold where they *l.* him

Luke 2:7 first-born *l.* in manger
16:20 Lazarus was *l.* at his gate
23:53 wherein never man before
was *l. John* 19:41
John 11:34 wh. have ye *l.* him ?
20:2 know not wh. th. *l.* him, 13
Acts 3:2 *l.* at gate of temple
4:37 *l.* money at apostles' f. 5:2
9:37 *l.* her in an upper chamber
13:36 David *l.* to his fathers
25:7 *l.* compla. could not prove
1 *Cor.* 9:16 necessity *l.* upon me
2 *Tim.* 4:16 not *l.* to their charge

See FOUNDATION.

LAID down.

Jos. 2:8 bef. they were *l. down*
1 *Sam.* 3:2 Eli *l. d.* in his place
3 and Samuel was *l. d.* to sleep
2 *Sam.* 13:8 Amnon was *l. down*
1 *K.* 19:6 and *l.* him *down* again
21:4 Ahab came and *l.* him *d.*
Ps. 3:5 I *l.* me *d.* and slept
Luke 19:22 tak. up th. I *l.* not *d.*
Acts 4:35 *l.* th. *d.* at apostles' fe.
7:58 *l. d.* their clothes at young
Rom. 16:4 for my life *l. d.* necks
1 *John* 3:16 he *l. d.* his life for us

LAID hand.

Ex. 24:11 on the nobles *l.* not *h.*
2 *Sam.* 13:19 Tamar *l. h.* on head
Est. 9:10 *l.* not *h.* on sp. 15, 16
Job 29:9 princes *l. h.* on th. mo.
Ps. 139:5 hast *l.* thy *h.* upon me
Rev. 1:17 *l.* his right *h.* upon me

LAID hands.

Lev. 8:14 A. a. h. sons *l. h.* 18, 22
Num. 27:23 and Moses *l.* his *ha.*
on Joshua, *Deut.* 34:9
Ob. 13 nor *l. h.* on th. substance
Mat. 18:28 *l. h.* took him by thr.
Mark 6:5 *l. h.* on a few sick folk
Luke 4:40 *l. h.* on ev. one of th.
13:13 he *l. his h.* on her
John 7:30 but no man *l. hands*
on him, 44 ; 8:20
Acts 4:3 *l. h.* on apostles, 5:18
6:6 they *l. h.* on the deacons
13:3 *l. h.* on Paul and Barnabas
19:6 Paul *l.* his *h.* on them

LAID hold.

Gen. 19:16 *l. h.* on Lot's hand
1 *Sam.* 15:27 S. *l. h.* on Sam. sk.
2 *Chr.* 7:22 *l. hold* on other gods
Mat. 14:3 *l. h.* on J. *Mark* 6:17
Luke 23:26 *l. h.* on one Simon
Rev. 20:2 *l. hold* on the dragon

LAID up.

Gen. 41:48 Jos. *l. up* food in cit.
Ex. 16:34 A. *l. up* pot of manna
Num. 17:7 M. *l. up* rods befo. L.
1 *Sam.* 10:25 S. *l.* it *up* before L.
21:12 David *l. up.* words in he.
Ezr. 6:1 treasures *l. up* in Baby.
Ps. 31:19 hast *l. up* for them
Prov. 13:22 wealth of sin. *l. up*
Cant. 7:13 fruits I have *l. up*
Is. 15:7 that *l. up* sh. they carry
23:18 hire not treasured or *l. up*
39:6 which fathers *l. up*
Luke 1:66 all *l.* them *up* in hearts
12:19 thou hast mu. goods *l. up*
Col. 1:5 hope wh. is *l. up* for you
2 *Tim.* 4:8 is *l. up* for me a crown

LAID wait.

Job 31:9 *l. w.* at neighbor's door
Lam. 4:19 *l. w.* for us in wilder.
Acts 20:3 Jews *l. w.* for hi. 23:30

LAID waste.

Ps. 79:7 *l. w.* his dwelling-place
Is. 15:1 Kir *l. w.* 23:1 T. is *l. w.*
23:14 ships, your strength *l. w.*
37:18 kings of Assy. *l. w.* nati
64:11 pleasant things are *l. w.*
Jer. 4:7 thy cities sh. be *l. w.*
without an inhabita. *Ezek.*
6:6 ; 12:20 ; 19:7 ; 29:12

Ezek. 26:2 sh. be repl. now *l. w.*
Amos 7:9 sanctuaries of Is. *l. w.*
Nah. 3:7 and say, Ninev. is *l. w*

LAIDEST.

Ps. 66:11 *l.* affliction on loins
Luke 19:21 th. takest up th. th. *l.*

LAIN.

Gen. 26:10 have *l.* with thy wife
Jud. 21:11 destroy wom. th. *l.*
Job 3:13 now should I have *l.* st.
Ps. 68:13 ye have *l.* am. the pots
John 20:12 where body of Jes. *l.*

LAYEST, ETH.

Num. 11:11 *l.* burden of people
1 *Sam.* 28:9 *l.* a snare for my life?
Job 21:19 G. *l.* up his iniquity
24:12 God *l.* not folly to them
41:26 sword of him that *l.* at h.
Ps. 104:3 *l.* beams of chambers
Prov. 2:7 *l.* up wisd. for righte.
26:24 *l.* up deceit within him
Is. 26:5 the lofty city he *l.* low
56:2 blessed is man that *l.* hold
57:1 and no man *l.* it to heart
Jer. 9:8 *l.* wait ; 12:11 *l.* to heart
Zec. 12:1 *l.* foundation of earth
Luke 12:21 that *l.* up treasure
15:5 he *l.* it on his shoulders

LAYING.

Num. 35:20 *l.* wait, th. he die, 22
Ps. 64:5 commune of *l.* snares
Mark 7:8 *l.* aside commandment
Luke 11:54 *l.* wait for him
Acts 8:18 *l.* on of apostles' hands
9:24 *l.* wait was known of Saul
23:16 kinsmen heard of th. *l. w.*
25:3 *l.* wait in the way to kill
1 *Tim.* 4:14 with *l.* on of hands
6:19 *l.* up in store good founda.
Heb. 6:1 not *l.* again foundation
2 aud of *l.* on of hands
1 *Pet.* 2:1 *l.* aside all malice

LAZARUS.

Luke 16:20 beggar named L.
John 11:2 Mary whose broth. L.
12:2 L. one that sat at table, 17

LEAD.

Ex. 15:10 sank as *l.* in waters
Num. 31:22 *l.* that may abide fire
Job 19:24 graven with iron and *l.*
Jer. 6:29 *l.* is consumed of the fi.
Ezek. 22:18 *l.* in midst of furnace
20 as th. gather *l.* I gather you
27:12 and *l.* Tarshish traded
Zec. 5:7 lifted up a talent of *l.*
8 weight of *l.* on mouth there.

LEAD.

Gen. 33:14 *l.* on softly as cattle
Ex. 13:21 pillar of cloud *l.* them
32:34 *l.* the people to the place
Deut. 32:12 Lord alone did *l.* hi.
Jud. 5:12 *l.* thy captivity captive
Neh. 9:19 pil. of cloud to *l.* them
Ps. 5:8 *l.* me in thy righteousne.
25:5 *l.* in truth ; 27:11 *l.* in plain
31:3 for thy name's sake *l.* me
43:3 light and truth, let them *l.*
60:9 *l.* me into Edom ? 108:10
61:2 *l.* to rock higher than I
125:5 *l.* th. with workers of ini.
139:10 there sh. thy hand *l.* me
24 *l.* me in the way of everlas.
143:10 *l.* me to land of upright.
Prov. 8:20 *l.* in way of righteou.
Cant. 8:2 *l.* thee to mother's ho.
Is. 3:12 that *l.* thee cause to err
11:6 a little child shall *l.* them
40:11 gently *l.* those with young
42:16 *l.* th. in paths not known
49:10 hath mercy on them, *l.* th.
57:18 I will *l.* him and restore
63:14 so didst thou *l.* thy people
Jer. 31:9 with supplica. I *l.* them
Nah. 2:7 her maids *l.* her

Mat. 6:13 *l.* us not into temptat.
Luke 11:4
15:14 if blind *l.* blind, *Lu.* 6:39
Luke 13:15 and *l.* him to wateri.
Acts 13:11 seeking some to *l.* hi.
1 *Cor.* 9:5 not power to *l.* sister ?
1 *Tim.* 2:2 we may *l.* a quiet life
Heb. 8:9 *l.* them out of Egypt
Rev. 7:17 Lamb feed and *l.* them

LEADER, S.

1 *Chr.* 12:27 Jehoi. *l.* of Aaronit.
13:1 David consulted with ev. *l.*
2 *Chr.* 32:21 angel whi. cut off *l.*
Is. 9:16 *l.* of people cause to err
55:4 given him a *l.* to the peop.
Mat. 15:14 be blind *l.* of the blin.

LEADEST.

Ps. 80:1 *l.* Joseph like a flock

LEADETH.

Job 12:17 he *l.* counsellors away
19 he *l.* princes away spoiled
Ps. 23:2 *l.* me beside still waters
3 *l.* me in paths of righteouen.
Prov. 16:29 *l.* him into way
Is. 48:17 thy God which *l.* thee
Mal. 7:13 wide is way *l.* to destr.
14 narrow is way that *l.* to life
John 10:3 calleth sheep and *l.* th.
Rom. 2:4 goodn. of God *l.* to rep.
Rev. 13:10 *l.* th. go into captivity

LEAF.

Gen. 8:11 in her mou. was oli. *l.*
Lev. 26:36 sound of a shaken *l.*
Job 13:25 break *l.* dr. to and fro ?
Ps. 1:3 his *l.* shall not wither
Is. 1:30 be as oak whose *l.* fadeth
34:4 host fall as *l.* 64:6 fade as *l.*
Jer. 17:8 neit her *l.* shall be green
Ezek. 47:12 the *l.* shall not fade

LEAVES.

Gen. 3:7 sew. fig *l.* made aprons
Jer. 36:23 when Je. read 3 or 4 *l.*
Ezek. 17:9 sh. wither in all the *l.*
Mat. 21:19 nothing thereon but *l.*
Mark 11:13
24:32 put. forth *l. Mark* 13:28
Rev. 22:2 *l.* for healing of nations

LEAVES, *for doors.*

1 *K.* 6:34 two *l.* of the one door
Ezek. 41:24 doors had two *l.* api.

LEAGUE.

Jos. 9:15 made *l.* wi. Gibeon. 16
Jud. 2:2 make no *l.* wi. inhabit.
1 *Sam.* 22:8 made *l.* with David
2 *Sam.* 5:3 David made *l.* wi. th.
1 *K.* 5:12 Hiram and Sol. made *l.*
15:19 a *l.* between me and thee
2 *Chr.* 16:3 break *l.* with Baasha
Job 5:23 in *l.* with stones of field
Ezek. 30:5 men that is in *l.* sh. f.
Dan. 11:23 after *l.* he work dece.

LEAH.

Gen. 29:16 daughter was L. 30:19
Ruth 4:11 L. make wom. like L.

LEAN, ED.

Jud. 16:26 I may *l.* on pillars
2 *K.* 18:21 on which if a man *l.*
go into hand, *Is.* 36:6
Job 8:15 *l.* on house, it not stand
Prov. 3:5 *l.* not to own underst.
Amos 5:19 *l.* his hand on wall
Mic. 3:11 yet they *l.* on the Lord
John 21:20 *l.* on his breast at su.

LEANETH, ING.

2 *Sam.* 3:29 one *l.* on a staff
2 *K.* 5:18 *l.* on my hand in house
Cant. 8:5 cometh up *l.* on belov.
John 13:23 was *l.* on Jesus' bos.
Heb. 11:21 Jacob *l.* on top of sta.

LEAN, NESS.

Gen. 41:3 out of river *l.*-flesh. 19
4 *l.*-fleshed eat up sev. fat, 20
2 *Sam.* 13:4 being king's son *l.*
Ps. 106:15 sent *l.* into their soul

Is. 10:16 L. send am. fat ones *l.*
17:4 fatness of flesh sh. wax *l.*
24:16 I said, My *l.* my *l.* woe
Ezek. 34:20 judge betw. fat and *l.*

LEAP.

Gen. 31:12 rams wh. *l.* on cattle
Lev. 11:21 have legs to *l.* withal
Deut. 33:22 Dan sh. *l.* from Bash.
Job 41:19 sparks of fire *l.* out
Ps. 68:16 why *l.* ye, ye high hills
Is. 35:6 then shall lame man *l.*
Joel 2:5 like chariots sh. they *l.*
Luke 6:23 rejoice ye, *l.* for joy

LEAPED.

Gen. 31:10 rams wh. *l.* upon cat.
2 *Sam.* 22:30 *l.* over wa. *Ps.* 18:29
Luke 1:41 babe *l.* in womb, 44
Acts 14:10 and he *l.* and walked
19:16 evil spirit was, *l.* on them

LEAPING.

2 *Sam.* 6:16 Michal saw David *l.*
Cant. 2:8 behold, he cometh *l.*
Acts 3:8 and he *l.* up and walked

LEARN.

Deut. 4:10 may *l.* to fear, 14:23
5:1 may *l.* and keep, and do th.
17:19 read that he may *l.* to fear
31:12 hear, and *l.* and fear the L.
13 children may *l.* to fe. the L.
Ps. 119:71 might *l.* statutes, 73
Prov. 22:25 lest thou *l.* his ways
Is. 1:17 *l.* to do well, seek judg.
2:4 *l.* war any more, *Mic.* 4:3
26:9 inhabitants *l.* righteousne.
10 will not wicked *l.* righteou.
29:24 that murmured *l.* doctrine
Jer. 10:2 *l.* not way of heathen
12:16 diligently *l.* ways of peop.
Mat. 9:13 go *l.* what th. meneth
11:29 *l.* of me, for I am meek
1 *Cor.* 14:35 *l.* anythi. let th. ask
1 *Tim.* 2:11 let wom. *l.* in silence
5:4 *l.* first to sh. piety at home
Tit. 3:14 *l.* to maint. good works
Rev. 14:3 no man could *l.* song

LEARNED.

Gen. 30:27 have *l.* by experience
Ps. 106:35 heathen, and *l.* works
119:7 I have *l.* righteous judg.
Prov. 30:3 I neith. *l.* wisdom nor
Is. 29:11 deliver to one that is *l.*
50:4 God given me tongue of *l.*
he waken. ear to hear as *l.*
John 6:45 man that hath *l.* of F.
7:15 man letters, hav. never *l.*
Acts 7:22 Moses *l.* wisdom of E.
Eph. 4:20 ye have not so *l.* Chr.
Phil. 4:11 *l.* in ev. state to be co.
2 *Tim.* 3:14 contin. in thing thou
l. knowing of wh. th. *l.* th.
Heb. 5:8 yet *l.* by obedience

LEARNING.

Prov. 1:5 wise man will incre. *l.*
9:9 just man, he will incre. in *l.*
16:21 sweetn. of lips increas. *l.*
23 he. of wise addeth *l.* to lips
Dan. 1:17 G. gave them skill in *l.*
Acts 26:24 *l.* doth make thee mad
Rom. 15:4 things writ. for our *l.*
2 *Tim.* 3:7 ever *l.* and never able

LEASING.

Ps. 4:2 how long seek after *l. ?*
5:6 shalt destroy them speak *l.*

LEAST.

Gen. 32:10 not worthy *l.* of merc.
Jud. 6:15 *l.* in my father's house
Mat. 2:6 not *l.* among the princ.
1:11 *l.* in kingdom of heaven
is greater than he, *Luke* 7:28
1 *Cor.* 15:9 I am least of the apo.
Eph. 3:8 less than *l.* of all saints

See GREATEST.

At LEAST.

1 *Sam.* 21:4 kept *at l.* from wom.
Luke 19:42 kno. *at l.* in thy day

LEATHER.
2 K. 1:8 girt with a girdle of *l.*

LEATHERN.
Mat. 3:4 John had *l.* girdle about

LEAVE, Substantive.
Num. 22:13 L. refuseth to give *l.*
1 *Sam.* 20:6 Da. asked *l.* of me, 28
Neh. 13:6 obtained I *l.* of king
Mark 5:13 Jesus gave them *l.*
John 19:38 *l.* to take away body
Acts 18:18 Paul took *l.* of breth.
21:6 taken our *l.* one of another
2 *Cor.* 2:13 taking . I went to M.

LEAVE.
Gen. 2:24 *l.* father and mother,
  Mat. 19:5; *Mark* 10:7; *Eph.*
  5:31
33:15 *l.* wi. thee some of the fo.
44:22 the lad cannot *l.* his fath.
Ex. 16:19 let no man *l.* manna
23:11 *l.* beasts of field shall eat
Lev. 7:15 not *l.* peace-offer. 22:30
16:23 off garm. and *l.* them the.
19:10 *l.* them for the poor, 23:22
Num. 9:12 *l.* none of the passov.
32:15 again *l.* them in wildern.
Deut. 28:51 shall not *l.* thee corn
54 remnant of chil. he shall *l.*
Jud. 9:9 should I *l.* my fatness
13 said, Should I *l.* my wine
Ruth 1:16 entreat me not to *l.*
1 *Sam.* 9:5 fa. *l.* caring for asses
2 *Sam.* 14:7 not *l.* husb. a name
2 *K.* 4:43 shall eat and *l.* thereof
13:7 nor did he *l.* of the people
Ezr. 9:8 *l.* us remnant to escape
12 *l.* it for inheritance to chil.
Neh. 6:3 work cease whi. I *l.* it?
10:31 would *l.* the seventh year
Job 39:11 wilt *l.* labor to him?
Ps. 16:10 thou wilt not *l.* my
  soul in hell, *Acts* 2:27
17:14 *l.* substance to their babes
27:9 my help, *l.* me not, 119:121
49:10 *l.* their wealth to others
141:8 O God, *l.* not my soul des.
Prov. 2:13 *l.* paths of uprightne.
Ec. 2:18 *l.* it to man after me
10:4 ruler ag. thee, *l.* not place
Is. 10:3 where will ye *l.* glory?
65:15 *l.* your name for a curse
Jer. 9:2 I might *l.* my people
14:9 call. by thy name, *l.* us not
17:11 *l.* th. in midst of his days
48:28 *l.* cities and dwell in rocks
49:9 not *l.* some glean. grapes?
11 *l.* chil. I will preserve them
Ezek. 16:39 *l.* thee naked, 23:29
Hos. 12:14 *l.* his blood upon him
Joel 2:14 *l.* blessing behind him
Amos 5:3 shall *l.* ten to Israel
7 *l.* off righteousness in earth
Mal. 4:1 *l.* neit. root nor branch
Mat. 5:24 *l.* thy gift bef. the alt.
18:12 *l.* ninety and nine, *Luke*
  15:4
23:23 and not to *l.* other undone
Luke 19:44 not *l.* in th. one stone
John 14:27 my peace I *l.* wi. you
16:28 I *l.* world and go to Fath.
32 *l.* me alone, yet I am not al.
Acts 6:2 we should *l.* the word
1 *Cor.* 7:13 let her not *l.* him.
Heb. 13:5 I will never *l.* thee

I will, or will I LEAVE.
Job 9:27 *I will l.* off my heavine.
10:1 *I will l.* complaint on mys.
Ezek. 6:8 *I will l.* a remnant
12:16 but *I will l.* a few men
29:5 *I w. l.* thee into wilderness
Zep. 3:12 *I w. l.* in midst of thee

I will not LEAVE.
2 *K.* 2:2 *I will not l.* thee, 4:30
John 14:18 *I w. n. l.* you comfort.

LEAVED.
Is. 45:1 open thee two-*l.* gates

LEAVETH.
Prov. 13:22 good man *l.* inherit.
28:3 sweeping rain wh. *l.* no fo.
Mat. 4:11 then the devil *l.* him

LEAVEN.
Ex. 12:15 away *l.* seven days, 19
13:7 nei. *l.* seen in thy quarters
34:25 not offer the blood with *l.*
Lev. 2:11 no meat-off. made wi. *l.*
10:12 eat meat-offeri. without *l.*
Amos 4:5 offer a sacrifice with *l.*
Mat. 13:33 kingdom of heaven is
  like *l. Luke* 13:21
16:6 beware of *l.* Phar. and Sad.
  11; *Mark* 8:15; *Luke* 12:1
12 th. not beware of *l.* of bread
1 *Cor.* 5:6 little *l.* leaveneth wh.
  lump, *Gal.* 5:9
7 purge out therefore the old *l.*
8 keep the feast, not wi. old *l.*

LEAVENED.
Ex. 12:15 wh. eateth *l.* bread, 19
20 eat nothing *l.* in habitations
Mat. 13:33 till whole was *l. Luke*
  13:21
See BREAD.

LEAVENETH.
1 *Cor.* 5:6 little leaven *l.* lump,
  Gal. 5:9

LEAVING.
Rom. 1:27 *l.* natural use of wom.
Heb. 6:1 *l.* principles of Christ
1 *Pet.* 2:21 suffered, *l.* an examp.

LEBANON.
Deut. 3:25 goodly mount. and L.
Jud. 3:3 Hiv. dwelt in mount L.
1 *K.* 5:14 ten tho. a month to L.
2 *K.* 19:23 sides of L. *Is.* 37:24
Ps. 29:6 L. like young unicorn
72:16 fruit shake like L. 92:12
Cant. 4:8 L. my spou. 11, 15; 5:15
7:4 thy nose is as tower of L.
Is. 10:34 L. shall fall, 33:9
29:17 L. turned into fruitf. field
35:2 glory of L. be given unto it
40:16 L. not sufficient to burn
60:13 glory of L. sh. come to th.
Jer. 18:14 leave the snow of L. ?
22:6 thou art head of L. to me
Ezek. 31:15 I caused L. to mourn
Hos. 14:5 forth roots as L. 6, 7
Nah. 1:4 flower of L. languisheth
Hab. 2:17 violence of L. sh. cov.
Zec. 10:10 them into land of L.
11:1 open thy doors, O L.

LEBBEUS. *Mat.* 10:3

LED.
Gen. 24:27 being in way, L. *l.* me
48 who hath *l.* me in right
Ex. 3:1 Moses *l.* flock to back of
13:17 *l.* not thro' land of Philis.
18 God *l.* them through wilde.
15:13 in mercy *l.* forth the peo.
Deut. 8:2 L. *l.* thee forty years
29:5 *l.* you forty years in wilde.
1 *K.* 8:48 *l.* them away captive
Ps. 78:14 *l.* them with a cloud
53 *l.* them safely, th. fear. not
106:9 *l.* th. thro' depths as thro'
  wilderness, 136:16 ; *Is.* 63:13
107:7 *l.* them by the right way
Prov. 4:11 *l.* thee in right paths
Is. 9:16 *l.* of them are destroyed
48:21 thirsted not wh. th. *l.* th.
55:12 shall be *l.* forth with pea.
63:12 *l.* them by right hand
Jer. 2:6 L. *l.* us thro' wilderness
17 when he *l.* thee by the way
22:12 die in place whi. th. *l.* him
23:8 L. which *l.* house of Israel
Lam. 3:2 hath *l.* me into darkn.
Ezek. 39:28 to be *l.* into captivi.
Amos 2:10 *l.* 40 years thro' wild.
Mat. 4:1 Jes. *l.* of Spirit, *Lu.* 4:1

Luke 4:29 *l.* Jesus to brow of hill
21:24 shall be *l.* away captive
24:50 *l.* them out as far as Beth.
Acts 8:32 *l.* as sheep to slaughter
Rom. 8:14 *l.* by Spirit of God
1 *Cor.* 12:2 even as ye were *l.*
Gal. 5:18 if ye be *l.* by the Spirit
2 *Tim.* 3:6 *l.* away with div. lus.

LEDDEST.
2 *Sam.* 5:2 *l.* out Is. 1 *Chr.* 11:2
Neh. 9:12 *l.* th. by a cloudy pillar
Ps. 77:20 *l.* thy peo. like a flock

LEDGES.
1 *K.* 7:28 borders between the *l.*
35 *l.* and borders were the sa.
36 plates of *l.* graved cherubim

LEEKS.
Num. 11:5 rememb. *l.* and onio.

LEES.
Is. 25:6 feast of wine on the *l.*
Jer. 48:11 M. hath set. on his *l.*
Zep. 1:12 pun. men settled on *l.*

LEFT.
Gen. 29:35 Judah, *l.* bear. 30:9
30:12 *l.* gar. in hand, 13, 15, 18
41:49 gathe. till he *l.* numberin.
47:18 not aught *l.* but bodies
50:8 little ones *l.* th. in Goshen
Ex. 2:20 why have ye *l.* man?
10:12 all that the hail *l.* 15
16:20 some *l.* of it till morning
34:25 nor sacrifice be *l.* till mor.
Lev. 2:10 which is *l.* of meat-off.
26:39 are *l.* of you sh. pine away
43 land also shall be *l.* of them
Num. 26:65 not *l.* a man, *Jos.*
  8:17 ; *Jud.* 4:16 ; *Hos.* 9:12
Deut. 2:34 *l.* none to remain, *Jos.*
  10:33, 37, 39, 40 ; 11:8, 11, 14
4:27 ye shall be *l.* few in numb.
28:62 ; *Is.* 24:6 ; *Jer.* 42:2
32:36 there is none shut up or *l.*
Jos. 8:17 they *l.* the city open
11:15 *l.* nothing undone of all
22:3 have not *l.* your brethren
Jud. 2:23 L. *l.* those nations, 3:1
Ruth 1:3 was *l.* and her 2 sons, 5
18 then she *l.* speaking to her
2:11 *l.* thy father and mother
4:14 L. not *l.* thee this day
1 *Sam.* 2:36 every one *l.* in house
9:24 which is *l.* set it bef. thee
10:2 father *l.* care of the asses
17:20 *l.* the sheep with a keeper
2 *Sam.* 5:21 there they *l.* ima.es
9:1 is any *l.* of house of Saul?
13:30 there is not one of them *l.*
15:16 *l.* ten concubines, 16:21
17:12 not be *l.* so much as one
1 *K.* 9:21 children *l.* 2 *Chr.* 8:8
14:10 cut off him *l.* 2 *K.* 9:8
19:3 *l.* servant there ; 10 *l.* on. *l.*
18 have *l.* me 7,000 ; 20 *l.* ox.
2 *K.* 4:44 did eat and *l.* thereof
7:7 *l.* tents ; 13 all that are *l.*
8:6 since day she *l.* the land
10:11 he *l.* him none remaining
14:26 not any *l.* nor any helper
17:16 *l.* commandments of Lord
19:4 remn. that are *l. Is.* 37:4
20:17 nothing *l.* saith the Lord
25:12 *l.* of the poor of the land,
  Jer. 39:10 ; 52:16
2 *Chr.* 11:14 Levites *l.* suburbs
21:17 th. was never a son *l.* him
24:18 they *l.* house of the Lord
31:10 had enough, have *l.* plen.
32:31 God *l.* him to try him
34:21 inq. for them *l.* in Israel
Neh. 1:2 concern. Jews wh. had *l.*
8 remnant *l.* in great affliction
Job 20:21 none of his meat be *l.*
26 ill with him *l.* in tabernacle
Ps. 106:11 not one of them *l.*
Prov. 29:15 a child *l.* to himself

Is. 1:9 L. *l.* us a rem. *Rom.* 9:29
4:3 *l.* in Zion shall be call. holy
11:16 remnant that shall be *l.*
24:12 in the city is *l.* desolation
39:6 nothing be *l.* saith the L.
Jer. 12:7 *l.* heritage; 31:2 *l.* swo.
49:25 city of prai. not *l.* c. of joy
50:26 let nothing of her be *l.*
Ezek. 14:22 shall be *l.* a remnant
31:12 cut him off and ha. *l.* him
Dan. 2:44 not be *l.* to other peo.
Hag. 2:3 who is *l.* saw h. in glo. ?
Zec. 13:8 third part be *l.* therein
Mat. 4:20 *l.* nets ; 22 *l.* their ships
15:37 took up of meat that was
    l. Mark 8:8
22:25 *l.* wife to bro. *Mark* 12:20
Mat. 23:38 your house is *l.* desol.
24:2 sh. not be *l.* one stone upon
    anoth. *Mark* 13:2 ; *Luke* 21:6
40 one shall be tak. the oth. *l.*
    41 ; *Luke* 17:34, 35, 36
26:44 Jesus *l.* them and prayed
Mark 10:28 *l.* all and followed
29 hath *l.* house, *Luke* 18:28, 29
11:22 seven had her, *l.* no seed
Luke 5:28 *l.* all and followed him
10:40 sister *l.* me to serve alone
John 4:52 scv. hour fever *l.* him
Acts 2:31 soul was not *l.* in hell
14:17 he *l.* not without witness
21:32 they *l.* beating of Paul
2 *Tim.* 4:20 I *l.* sick at Miletum
Tit. 1:5 for this cause I *l.* thee
Heb. 2:8 he *l.* nothing that is not
Jude 6 angels *l.* their own habit.
Rev. 2:4 thou hast *l.* thy first lo.
See ALONE.

LEFT off.
Gen. 17:22 *l. off* talking with him
Ruth 2:20 hath not *l. off* kindn.
Job 32:15 no more, th. *l. off* spe.
Ps. 36:3 he hath *l. off* to be wise
Jer. 38:27 *l. off* speaking wi. him
44:18 we *l. off* to burn incense
Hos. 4:10 they *l. off* to take heed

LEFT corner.
2 *K.* 11:11 guard stood to the *l. c.*
See HAND.

LEFT-HANDED.
Jud. 3:15 Benjam. a man *l.-h.*
20:16 were 700 chosen men *l.-h.*

LEFT pillar.
1 *K.* 7:21 he set up the *l. pillar*

LEFT side.
2 *Chr.* 23:10 weapon fr. ri. to *l. s.*
Ezek. 1:10 face of an ox on *l. side*
4:4 lie also on thy *l. s.* lay iniq.
Zec. 4:3 olive tree upon *l. s.* 11

LEG, S.
Ex. 12:9 roast wi. fire head and *l.*
29:17 inwards and *l.* wa. *Lev.* 9:14
Lev. 4:11 head, and his *l.* burn
8:21 washed the inwards and *l.*
11:21 wh. have *l.* above th. feet
Deut. 28:35 smite thee in the *l.*
1 *Sam.* 17:6 greaves of brass on *l.*
Ps. 147:10 taketh no pleas. in *l.*
Prov. 26:7 *l.* of lame not equal
Cant. 5:15 *l.* are as pil. of marble
Is. 3:20 L. take ornaments of *l.*
47:2 make bare *l.* uncov. thigh
Dan. 2:33 his *l.* of iron
Amos 3:12 mouth of lion two *l.*
John 19:31 besought *l.* mi. he br.
32 soldi. came and brake the *l.*
33 they brake not his *l.*

LEGION.
Mark 5:9 name is L. *Luke* 8:30
LEGIONS. *Mat.* 26:53

LEISURE.
Mark 6:31 they had no *l.* to eat
LEMUEL. *Prov.* 31:1, 4

LEND.
Ex. 22:25 if thou *l.* money
Lev. 25:37 not *l.* him thy victuals
Deut. 15:6 sh. *l.* to many nations
8 thou sh. *l.* him suffi. for need
23:19 sh. not *l.* on usury to bro.
20 to stranger may *l.* on usury
28:12 *l.* to many nations
44 *l.* thou sh. not *l.* to him
Luke 6:34 if *l.* them of whom ye
    hope to rece. sin. also *l.* sin.
35 love enemies, do good and *l.*
11:5 say, Friend, *l.* me 3 loaves.

LENDER.
Prov. 22:7 borrower servant to *l.*
Is. 24:2 as with *l.* so wi. borrow.

LENDETH.
Ps. 37:26 merciful, *l.* seed bless.
112:5 good man show. fav. and *l.*
Prov. 19:17 pity on poor, *l.* to L.

LENGTH.
Deut. 30:20 and the *l.* of thy days
Job 12:12 *l.* of days, understand.
Ps. 21:4 even *l.* of days for ever
Prov. 3:2 *l.* of days sh. they add
16 *l.* of days is in her right ha.
Eph. 3:18 compre. *l.* of love of C.
Rev. 21:16 *l.* as large as breadth

At LENGTH.
Prov. 29:21 become his son *at l.*
Rom. 1:10 *at l.* may ha. journey

LENGTHEN, ED.
Deut. 25:15 thy days may be *l.*
1 *K.* 3:14 then will I *l.* thy days
Is. 54:2 *l.* thy cords, strengthen
    stakes

LENGTHENING.
Dan. 4:27 a *l.* of thy tranquillity

LENT.
Ex. 12:36 *l.* them as th. required
1 *Sam.* 1:28 I *l.* him to the Lord
2:20 loan which is *l.* to the L.
Jer. 15:10 I have not *l.* on usury

LENTILES.
Gen. 25:34 Jacob gave Esau of *l.*
2 *Sam.* 23:11 piece ground full *l.*
See BEANS.

LEOPARD, S.
Cant. 4:8 fr. mountains of the *l.*
Is. 11:6 *l.* sh. lie down with kid
Jer. 5:6 *l.* shall watch over cities
13:23 can *l.* change his spots?
Dan. 7:6 and lo, another like a *l.*
Hos. 13:7 I will be to them as a *l.*
Hab. 1:8 horses swifter than *l.*
Rev. 13:2 beast was like to a *l.*

LEPER.
Lev. 13:45 *l.* in whom the plague
14:3 if leprosy be healed in *l.*
22:4 the seed of Aaron is a *l.*
Num. 5:2 put out of camp ev. *l.*
2 *Sam.* 3:29 Joab, one that is a *l.*
2 *K.* 5:1 Naaman was a *l.*
11 strike his hand, and reco. *l.*
27 went from his presence a *l.*
15:5 Azari. was a *l.* to his death
2 *Chr.* 26:21 Uz. the ki. was a *l.*
23 for they said, He is a *l.*
Mat. 8:2 th. came a *l. Mark* 1:40
26:6 house of Sim. *l. Mark* 14:3

LEPERS.
2 *K.* 7:8 *l.* came to utterm. part
Mat. 10:8 cleanse *l.* raise dead
11:5 *l.* are cleansed, *Luke* 7:22
Luke 4:27 many *l.* were in Israel
17:12 ten men that were *l.*

LEPROSY.
Lev. 13:2 in skin like plague of *l.*
3 it is a plague of *l.*, 8:49
12 if a *l.* break out in the skin
13:13 if the *l.* covered his flesh
59 law of plague of *l.* 14:54, 57
14:3 if plague of *l.* be healed
7 him to be cleansed from *l.*

Deut. 24:8 heed in plague of *l.*
2 *K.* 5:6 recover him of his *l.*
27 *l.* of Naaman clea. unto thee
2 *Chr.* 26:19 *l.* rose in his foreh.
Mat. 8:3 his *l.* was cleansed,
    Mark 1:42 ; *Luke* 5:13
Luke 5:12 man full of *l.* besought
See FRETTING.

LEPROUS.
Ex. 4:6 hand was *l.* as snow
Lev. 13:44 is a *l.* man, unclean
Num. 12:10 Miriam became *l.*
2 *K.* 7:3 four *l.* men at the gate
2 *Chr.* 26:20 and Uzziah was *l.*

LESS.
Ex. 30:15 not *l.* than half shekel
Num. 22:18 bey. word of L. do *l.*
Mark 4:31 when it is sown it is *l.*
15:40 M. mother of James the *l.*
2 *Cor.* 12:15 more I love, *l.* am lo.
Eph. 3:8 am *l.* than the least
Heb. 7:7 *l.* is blessed of better

LESSER.
Gen. 1:16 *l.* light to rule night
Is. 7:25 for treading of *l.* cattle

LET.
Gen. 49:21 Napht. a hind *l.* loose
Ex. 3:19 king of Eg. will not *l.*
    you go, 4:21 ; 7:14 ; 8:32 ; 9:7,
    17, 35 ; 10:20, 27 ; 11:10
5:1 *l.* my people go, 7:16 : 8:1, 20;
    9:1, 13 ; 10:3
8:28 I will *l.* you go, 9:28 ; 13:7
18:27 M. *l.* father-in-law depart
21:26 *l.* him go free for eye, 27
Deut. 15:12 thou sh. *l.* him go fr.
18 not *l.* him go away empty
2 *Sam.* 11:12 to-m. *l.* thee depart
1 *K.* 18:40 *l.* none of them escape
Job 6:9 would *l.* loose his hand
27:6 righte. I will not *l.* it go
Ps. 69:6 *l.* not those be ashamed
109:6 *l.* Sa. stand at right hand
Cant. 3:4 would not *l.* him go
8:11 *l.* out vineyard to keepers
Is. 43:13 and who shall *l.* it?
Jer. 27:11 those will I *l.* remain
Mat. 21:33 planted a vineyard
    and *l.* it out to husbandmen,
    Mark 12:1 ; *Luke* 20:9
Luke 22:68 not answer nor *l.* go
John 19:12 if thou *l.* this man go
Acts 27:15 not bear up, *l.* her dr.
Rom. 1:13 but was *l.* hitherto
2 *Thes.* 2:7 now letteth, will *l.*
Heb. 2:1 lest we sh. *l.* them sleep
See ALONE.

LET down.
Ex. 17:11 wh. he *l. d.* his hands
2 *K.* 13:21 wh. the man was *l. d.*
Jer. 38:6 *l. d.* Jeremiah wi. cords
Ezek. 1:24 th. *l. d.* th. wings, 25
Mark 2:4 they *l. d.* bed wherein
    sick of palsy lay, *Luke* 5:19
Luke 5:4 *l. d.* your nets for drau.
Acts 9:25 *l.* him *d.* in a basket,
    2 *Cor.* 11:33
10:11 four corners, *l. d.* to earth
27:30 *l. down* boat into the sea

LETTER.
2 *Sam.* 11:14 Dav. wrote a *l.* to J.
2 *K.* 5:5 send *l.* to king of Israel
10:2 soon as *l.* cometh to thee
19:14 Hez. received *l.* 37:14
Ezr. 4:7 *l.* was writ. in Syrian
8 wrote a *l.* against Jerusalem
Neh. 2:8 *l.* to As. keeper of forest
Est. 9:29 wrote to confirm this *l.*
Jer. 29:1 words of *l.* Jerem. sent
Acts 23:25 Claud. wrote *l.* to Fel.
34 when governor had read *l.*
Rom. 2:27 by *l.* transgress law
29 circumcis. of heart, not in *l.*
7:6 not in the oldness of the *l.*

2 Cor. 3:6 not of l. but of Spirit
 7:8 sorry with l. I do not repent
Gal. 6:11 large a l. I have written
2 Thes. 2:2 be not shaken by l.
Heb. 13:22 I have written l.

LETTERS.

1 K. 21:8 Jezebel wrote l. 9
2 K. 10:1 Jehu wrote l. and sent
 20:12 king of Babylon sent l.
2 Chr. 30:1 Hez. wrote l. to Eph.
 6 posts went with l. from king
 32:17 wrote l. to rail on G. of Is.
Neh. 2:7 l. be given to governors
 6:17 sent l. to Tob. and l. came
Est. 1:22 Ahasuerus sent l.
 3:13 l. were sent by post, 8:10
 9:20 Mordecai sent l. to Jews, 30
Jer. 29:25 hast l. in thy name
Luke 23:38 writ. in l. of Hebrew
John 7:15 how know. this man l.
Acts 9:2 desired l. to Damascus
 15:23 the apostles wrote l.
 22:5 fr. whom also I received l.
 28:21 neither received l. out Ju.
1 Cor. 16:3 sh. approve by your l.
2 Cor. 3:1 nor need we l. of com.
 10:9 I would terrify you by l.
 10 l. are weighty and powerf.
 11 in word, by l. when absent

LETTEST.

Job 15:13 l. su. words out mouth
 41:1 with a cord thou l. down ?
Luke 2:29 L. l. thou thy ser. dep.

LETTETH.

2 K. 10:24 he that l. him go
Prov. 17:14 as when one l. water
2 Thes. 2:7 only he that now l.

LEVI.

Gen. 29:34 called L. Ex. 6:16;
 Num. 3:17
Num. 16:7 you, ye sons of L.
Deut. 10:9 L. hath no part
1 K. 12:31 priests were not of L.
1 Chr. 21:6 but L. count. he not
Ps. 135:20 bless L. O house of L.
Ezek. 40:46 among the sons of L.
Zec. 12:13 the house of L. apart
Mal. 2:4 cov. be with L. 8 ; 3:3
Mark 2:14 L. the son of Alpheus
Luke 3:24 Matthat son of L. 29
 5:27 a publican named L.
Heb. 7:9 L. payed tithes in Abr.

Tribe of LEVI.

Num. 1:49 not num. t. of L.
Deut. 10:8 separat. t. of L. 18:1
1 Chr. 23:14 we. named of t. of L.
Rev. 7:7 t. of L. sealed 12,000

LEVIATHAN.

Job 41:1 canst thou draw out l.
Ps. 74:14 breakest the heads of l.
 104:26 is that l. thou hast made
Is. 27:1 shall punish l. even l.

LEVITE.

Ex. 4:14 Aaron the L. thy brot. ?
Deut. 12:12 rej.bef. the Lord and
 the L. 18: 16:11, 14 ; 26:11, 13
Jud. 17:7 a young man a L. 9
 10 thy victuals, so the L. went
 12 Micah consecrated the L.
 13 I have a L. to my priest
 8:3 knew the voice of the L.
 19:1 a certain L. sojourning
2 Chr. 20:14 Jahaziel the L. came
 31:12 Conon. the L. over things
 14 Kore the L. over fr. will off.
Luke 10:32 likewise a L. came
Acts 4:36 Barnabas a L. hav. land

LEVITES.

Ex. 38:21 counted for serv. of L.
Lev. 25:32 cit. of L. may L. rede.
Num. 1:50 sh. appoint L. ov. tab.
 51 the L. shall take it down
 53 the L. shall pitch round abo.
 3:9 shall give L. unto Aaron
 12 I have taken L. the L. mine

---

 41 take the L. for me, 45 ; 8:14
 7:5 thou sh. give wago. unto L.
 8:6 take L. fr. Is. and cleanse
 11 Aaron sh. offer L. bef. the L.
 18:6 taken L. to do service, 23
 24 tithes I have given to the L.
 35:2 give unto the L. cities, 8
Jos. 14:3 to L. he gave none inh.
 21:3 Is. gave these cities to L. 8
 41 cities of L. were forty-eight
1 Sam. 6:15 L. took down ark
1 Chr. 15:15 child. of L. bare ark
 26 G. helped L. that bare ark
2 Chr. 5:12 L. were singers, 7:6
 19:11 also the L. shall be officers
 23:6 L. shall comp. the king, 7
 29:5 ye L. sanctify yourselves
 34:13 of the L. there were scrib.
 35:14 L. prep. for themselves, 15
Ezr. 6:18 set L. in their courses
Neh. 8:7 L. caused peo. to under.
 11 the L. stilled the people
 12:27 at dedica. th. sought L.
 13:10 L. were fled every one
 29 defiled priesthood of the L.
Jer. 33:22 I will multiply the L.
Ezek. 44:10 L. are gone bear ini.
 48:11 not astray wh. L. went

Priests and LEVITES.

Deut. 17:9 come to pries. and L.
Jos. 3:3 see p. a. L. bearing ark
1 K. 8:4 p. a. L. brought ark
2 Chr. 23:2 p. a. L. sh. be porters
 29:34 pri. and L. more upright
 30:15 pri. and L. were ashamed
 21 L. and pries. praised the L.
 27 p. and L. blessed the peop.
 31:9 Hez. questioned wi. p. a. L.
 35:8 princes gave to pr. and L.
Ezr. 6:20 pr. and L. were purif.
 9:1 p. a. L. have not separated
1) 5 Ezra made pr. a. L. to sw.
Neh. 9:38 our princes, L. and p.
 10:34 we cast lots amo. p. a. L.
 12:30 p. a. L. purified themselv.
Is. 66:21 take of th. for p. and L.
Jer. 33:18 p. a. L. not want a man
 21 the L. the p. my ministers
John 1:19 Jews sent p. and L.

LEVITICAL.

Heb. 7:11 were by l. priesthood

LEVY, Substantive.

1 K. 5:13 Sol. raised l. of 300,000
 14 Adoniram was over the l.
 9:15 reason of l. Solomon raised
Num. 31:28 l. a tribute to the L.
1 K. 9:21 on those did Solom. l.

LEVY, Verb.

Ezek. 16:27 asham. of thy l. way
 22:11 l. defiled thy daughter
 23:44 went in, unto the l. wom.
Acts 17:5 Jews took l. fellows

LEWDNESS.

Jud. 20:6 hn. have committed l.
Jer. 11:15 wrought l. with many
 13:27 seen l. of thy whoredom
Ezek. 16:43 sh. not commit this l.
 58 thou hast borne l. and abo.
 22:9 midst of thee th. commit l.
 23:21 remembr. l. of thy youth
 27 I make thy l. to cease, 48
 29 both thy l. and whoredom
 35 theref. bear thou also thy l.
 49 shall recompense your l.
 24:13 in thy filthiness is l.
Hos. 2:10 will I discover her l.
 6:9 priests murder. commit l.
Acts 18:14 matter of wrong.or l.

LIAR.

Job 24:25 who will make me a l. ?
Prov. 17:4 l. giv. ear to naughty
 19:22 poor man better than a l.
 30:6 and thou be found l.
Jer. 15:18 wilt th. be to me as l. ?

John 8:44 l. and the father of it
 55 say, I know him not, be l.
Rom. 3:4 God true, ev. man a l.
1 John 1:10 sinned, make him l.
 2:4 keepeth not com. is l. 4:20
 22 is a l. but he that denieth
 5:10 believ. not G. made him l.

LIARS.

Deut. 33:29 enemies found l.
Ps. 116:11 haste, all men are l.
Is. 44:25 frustrateth tokens of l.
Jer. 50:36 a sword is upon the l.
1 Tim. 1:10 law is made for l.
Tit. 1:12 Cretians are always l.
Rev. 2:2 and hast found them l.
 21:8 all l. have th. part in lake

LIBERAL, LY.

Deut. 15:14 shalt furnish him l.
Prov. 11:25 l. soul sh. be made fat
Is. 32:5 vile sh. not be called l.
 8 the l. deviseth l. things
2 Cor. 9:13 your l. distribution
Jam. 1:5 God giveth all men l.

LIBERALITY.

1 Cor. 16:3 bring your l. to Jeru.
2 Cor. 8:2 the riches of their l.

LIBERTINES.

Acts 6:9 called synagogue of l.

LIBERTY.

Lev. 25:10 proclaim l. thro' land
Ps. 119:45 and I will walk at l.
Is. 61:1 proclaim l. to captives
Jer. 34:8 covenant to proclaim l.
 15 done right, in proclaim. l.
 17 not heark. to me proclaiming l. I proclaim a l. for you
Ezek. 46:17 his to the year of l.
Luke 4:18 set at l. them bruised
Acts 24:23 keep P. let him have l.
 26:32 man might been set at l.
 27:3 gave l. to go to his friends
Rom. 8:21 from bondage into l.
1 Cor. 7:39 she is at l. to marry
 8:9 take heed lest th. l. of yours
 10:29 my l. judged of another
2 Cor. 3:17 Sp. of L. is, there is l.
Gal. 5:1 stand fast in the l. wherew.
 13 ye have been called to l.
Heb. 13:23 brother Tim. set at l.
Jam. 1:25 whoso look. to law of l.
 2:12 be judged by the law of l.
1 Pet. 2:16 not using l. for a cloak
2 Pet. 2:19 they promise them l.

LIBNAH.

Num. 33:20 pitched in L. 21
Jos. 10:29 passed to L. 21:13
2 K. 8:22 L. revolted, 2 Chr. 21:10

LIBYA. Ezek. 30:5 ; Acts 2:10
LIBYANS. Jer. 46:9 ; Dan. 11:43

LICE.

Ex. 8:16 dust became l. 17, 18
Ps. 105:31 l. in all their coasts

LICENSE.

Acts 21:40 when he had giv. P. l.
 25:16 accused have l. to answer

LICK.

Num. 22:4 this company l. up all
1 K. 21:19 shall dogs l. thy blood
Ps. 72:9 enemies sh. l. the dust
Is. 49:23 l. up dust of thy feet
Mic. 7:17 sh. l. dust like a serp.

LICKED, ETH.

Num. 22:4 as all, as ox l. grass
1 K. 18:38 l. up water in trench
 21:19 dogs l. blood of Naboth
 22:38 the dogs l. up his blood
Luke 16:21 dogs ca. and l. sores

LID.

2 K. 12:9 bored a hole in the l.

LIE, falsehood.

Ps. 62:9 men of hi. degree are a l.
 119:69 proud forged a l. ag. me

Is. 44:20 is not a *l.* in rig. hand?
Jer. 27:10 prophesy a *l.* to you to
  rem. you fr. land, 14, 15; 16
28:15 mak. peo. to trust in a *l.*
29:31 caused you to trust in a *l.*
Ezek. 21:29 divine a *l.* to thee
Mic. 1:14 shall be a *l.* to kings
Zec. 10:2 diviners have seen a *l.*
John 8:44 speaketh *l.* he speak.
Rom. 1:25 changed truth unto *l.*
3:7 through my *l.* to his glory
2 *Thes.* 2:11 they sh. believe a *l.*
1 *John* 2:21 no *l.* is of the truth
  27 of all things, and is no *l.*
Rev. 21:27 whatso. maketh a *l.*
22:15 whoso. lov. and maketh *l.*

LIES.

Jud. 16:10 th. hast told me *l.* 13
Job 11:3 *l.* make men hold peace?
13:4 ye are forgers of *l.*
Ps. 40:4 such as turn aside to *l.*
58:3 wicked go astray, speak. *l.*
62:4 delight in *l.* curse inwardly
63:11 mouth speak. *l.* be stopp.
101:7 tell. *l.* not tarry in my si.
Prov. 6:19 hates witness speak. *l.*
14:5 a false witness will utter *l.*
25 deceitful witness speak. *l.*
19:5 speaketh *l.* shall not escape
9 he that speaketh *l.* sh. perish
Prov. 29:12 if a ruler heark. to *l.*
30:8 remove fr. me vanity and *l.*
Is. 9:15 prophet that teacheth *l.*
28:15 have made *l.* our refuge
17 sweep away the refuge of *l.*
59:3 your lips have spoken *l.*
4 trust in vanity, and speak *l.*
Jer. 9:3 bend like th. bow for *l.*
5 tau. their tongue to speak *l.*
14:14 proph. prophe. *l.* 23:25, 26
16:19 our fathers have inher. *l.*
20:6 hast prophesied *l.* vanity
23:14 commit adult. walk in *l.*
32 cause peo. to err by their *l.*
48:30 his *l.* shall not so effect it
Ezek. 13:8 spoken vanity, seen *l.*
9 upon prophets that divine *l.*
22 with *l.* ye made right. sad
22:28 divining *l.* unto them
24:12 she wearied herself with *l.*
Dan. 11:27 speak *l.* at one table
Hos. 7:3 princes glad with *l.*
13 have spoken *l.* against me
10:13 ye have eaten fruit of *l.*
11:12 Ephr. comp. about wi. *l.*
12:1 he increaseth *l.* and desol.
Amos 2:4 *l.* caused them to err
Mic. 6:12 inhabi. have spoken *l.*
Nah. 3:1 city, it is full of *l.*
Hab. 2:18 and a teacher of *l.*
Zep. 3:13 Israel sh. not speak *l.*
Zec. 13:3 speak. *l.* in name of L.
1 *Tim.* 4:2 speak. *l.* in hypocrisy

LIE, Verb.

Lev. 6:2 if a soul *l.* to his neigh.
19:11 steal, nor *l.* one to another
Num. 23:19 man, that he sho. *l.*
1 *Sam.* 15:29 Str. of Is. will not *l.*
2 *K.* 4:16 do not *l.* to handmaid
Job 6:28 it is evident to you if I *l.*
34:6 should I *l.* against my right
Ps. 89:35 I will not *l.* to David
Prov. 14:5 faith. witn. will not *l.*
Is. 63:8 my peo. that will not *l.*
Mic. 2:11 walk. in falsehood do *l.*
Hab. 2:3 it shall speak and not *l.*
Acts 5:3 hath S. filled heart to *l.*?
Rom. 9:1 I say truth in Christ, I
  l. not, 1 *Tim.* 2:7
2 *Cor.* 11:31 L. knoweth, I *l.* not
Gal. 1:20 I wrote, behold I *l.* not
Col. 3:9 *l.* not one to another
Tit. 1:2 life, God that cannot *l.*
  promised. *Heb.* 6:18
Jam. 3:14 *l.* not against the truth
1 *John* 1:6 we *l.* and do not truth
Rev. 3:9 they are Jews, but do *l.*

LIED, ETH.

Lev. 6:3 lost, and *l.* concerning
1 *K.* 13:18 but he *l.* unto him
Ps. 78:36 *l.* unto him wi. tongues
Is. 57:11 been afraid, thou hast *l.*
Acts 5:4 th. hast not *l.* unto men

LIE, *to recline.*

Gen. 47:30 I will *l.* with my fat.
Ex. 23:11 let the ground *l.* still
Deut. 29:20 curses in book *l.* on h.
Jud. 19:20 thy wants *l.* on me
Ruth 3:4 mark the place he eh. *l.*
1 *K.* 1:2 let her *l.* in thy bosom
Ps. 57:4 I *l.* among them on fire
88:5 like slain that *l.* in grave
Ec. 4:11 two *l.* together ha. heat
Is. 13:21 wild beasts sh. *l.* there
14:18 kings of nations *l.* in glory
51:20 sons *l.* at head of streets
Lam. 2:21 young and old *l.* gro.
Ezek. 4:4 *l.* also upon thy left side
6 *l.* again on thy right side
9 thou sh. lie on thy side 390 d.
31:18 *l.* in midst of uncircumc.
32:21 they *l.* uncircumcised, 30
27 they shall not *l.* wi. mighty
34:14 shall they *l.* in a good fold
John 5:6 when Jesus saw him *l.*

LIE, ETH down.

Lev. 18:23 to *l.* thereto, 20:16
26:6 *l.* d. and none make afraid
Num. 23:24 not *l.* d. till he eat
Deut. 25:2 cause him to *l. down*
Ruth 3:7 B. went to *l. d.* at heap
1 *Sam.* 3:5 I call. not, *l. d.* ag. 6:9
2 *Sam.* 11:13 went to *l. d.* on bed
Job 7:4 wh. I *l. d.* I say, Sh. I ri.
11:19 *l. d.* none make thee afra.
14:12 so man *l. d.* and ris. not
20:11 *l. d.* with him in the dust
21:26 shall *l. d.* alike in the dust
27:19 rich man shall *l. down*
Ps. 23:2 *l. d.* in green pastures
Prov. 3:24 *l. d.* thy sleep be sweet
23:34 *l. d.* in the midst of sea
Is. 14:30 shall *l. d.* in safety
17:2 be for flocks which sh. *l. d.*
27:10 sh. the calf feed and *l. d.*
43:17 army and power sh. *l. d.*
Is. 50:11 shall *l. down* in sorrow
65:10 place for the herds to *l. d.*
Jer. 3:25 *l. d.* in shame and conf.
33:12 shep. causing flocks *l. d.*
Ezek. 34:15 I will cause them *l. d.*
Hos. 2:18 make them *l. d.* safely
Zep. 2:7 sh. *l. d.* in the evening
14 flocks sh. *l. d.* 15 beasts *l. d.*
3:13 remnant of Israel shall *l. d.*

LIE, ETH in wait.

Ex. 21:13 if a man *l.* not *in wait*
Deut. 19:11 hate neighbor, *l. w.*
Jos. 8:4 sh. *l. in w.* against city
Jud. 9:32 *l. in wait* in the field
21:20 *l. in w.* in the vineyards
1 *Sam.* 22:8 my ser. to *l. in w.* 13
Ps. 10:9 *l. in w.* secretly as a lion
59:3 they *l. in w.* for my soul
Prov. 7:12 *l. in w.* at ev. corner
12:6 wicked are to *l. in wait*
23:28 she *l. in w.* as for a prey
Mic. 7:2 they all *l. in w.* for bl.
Acts 23:21 *l. in wait* for him
Eph. 4:14 *l. in w.* to deceive me

LIE, ETH waste.

Neh. 2:3 fathers' sepulchres *l. w.*
17 see how Jerusalem *l. waste*
Is. 33:8 the highways *l. waste*
34:10 it sh. *l. w.* none sh. pass
Hag. 1:4 and this house *l. waste*

LIE, ETH with.

Gen. 19:32 and we will *l. w.* him
30:15 he shall *l. w.* thee to-night
39:7 *l. w.* me, 12; 2 *Sam.* 13:11
Ex. 22:16 if a man *l. w.* a maid
19 whoso *l. with* beast

Lev. 15:18 *w.* whom man shall *l.*
15:24 if any man *l. with* her at
18:20 not *l.* carnally *w.* neighb.
22 shall not *l. with* mankind
23 neither sh. thou *l. w.* beast
19:20 *l.* carnally *with* bondmaid
20:11 man *l. w.* his father's wife
12 if a man *l. with* daugh.-in-l.
13 mankind as *l. w.* woman
15 if a man *l. w.* a beast
18 if man *l. w.* wom. ha. sick.
Num. 5:13 if a man *l. with* her
Deut. 22:23 find her, and *l. with*
25 man force her, and *l. w.* her
27:20 that *l. with* father's wife
21 *l. w.* beast; 22 sist. 23 mot.
28:30 betroth a wife, ano. *l. w.*
2 *Sam.* 11:11 go to *l. w.* my wife?
Cant. 1:13 sh. *l.* all night betwixt
Mic. 7:5 mouth from her that *l.*

LIERS in wait.

Jos. 8:14 wist not th. were *l. i. w.*
Jud. 9:25 men of Sh. set *l. in w.*
16:12 *l. in w.* abid. in chamber
20:33 the *l. in wait* came forth
37 *l. in w.* hasted and rushed

LIEST.

Gen. 28:13 land whereon thou *l.*
Deut. 6:7 wh. thou *l.* down, 11:19
Jos. 7:10 wheref. *l.* on thy face?
Prov. 3:24 *l.* down sh. not be af.

LIETH.

Gen. 4:7 not well. sin *l.* at door
49:25 blessings of deep *l.* under
Lev. 14:47 that *l.* in house
15:4 bed whereon he *l.* is uncl.
20 th. she *l.* on is unclean, 26
24 bed whereon he *l.* be unc. 33
26:34 S. as long as *l.* desolate
Jud. 16:5 where his strength *l.*
Job 40:21 he *l.* under shady tree
Ps. 41:8 he *l.* he sh. rise no more
88:7 thy wrath *l.* hard on me
Mat. 8:6 servant *l.* at home sick
Mark 5:23 *l.* at point of death
Rom. 12:18 as much as *l.* in you
1 *John* 5:19 world *l.* in wickedn

LIEUTENANTS.

Ezr. 8:36 king's commis. to *l.*
Est. 3:12 commanded king's *l.*
8:9 Mord. had commanded to
9:3 rulers and *l.* helped Jews

LIFE.

Gen. 1:20 mov. creature hath *l.*
2:7 G. breathed the breath of *l.*
9 tree of *l.* in garden, 3:22
3:24 keep the way of tree of *l.*
6:17 dest. all wherein is *l.* 7:22
9:4 flesh with the *l.* shall ye not
  eat, *Lev.* 17:14
5 of man will I req. *l.* of man
18:10 return accord. to time of *l.*
42:15 by the *l.* of Pharaoh, 16
45:5 G. did send me to preser. *l.*
47:9 not attained to years of *l.*
Ex. 21:23 gi. *l.* for *l. Deut.* 19:21
Lev. 17:11 *l.* of flesh in the blood
18:18 besides the other in *l.* ti.
Deut. 12:23 blood is *l.* not eat *l.*
Deut. 20:19 tree of fic. is man's *l.*
24:6 taketh man's *l.* to pledge
30:15 I have set before thee,
  this day, *l.* 19; *Jer.* 21:8
32:47 not vain thi. bec. your *l.*
Jos. 2:14 answ. our *l.* for yours
1 *Sam.* 26:29 bo. up in bun. of *l.*
2 *Sam.* 15:21 whet. in death or *l.*
1 *K.* 3:11 not asked for thyself
  long *l.* 2 *Chr.* 1:11
2 *K.* 4:16 time of *l.* embrace, 17
7:7 left camp, fled for their *l.*
Ezr. 6:10 pray for *l.* of king
Est. 8:11 Jews to stand for *l.*

Job 3:20 why *l.* given to bit. soul?
10:12 thou hast granted me *l.*
24:22 riseth, no man sure of *l.*
33:4 breath of Al. given me *l.*
36:6 preserveth not *l.* of wicked
14 their *l.* is among the uncl.
Ps. 16:11 wilt show me path of *l.*
21:4 asked *l.* of thee, thou gav.
30:5 in his favor is *l.*
34:12 wh. man is he th. desi. *l.?*
36:9 with thee is fountain of *l.*
61:6 wilt prolong the king's *l.*
63:3 loving-kin. is better th. *l.*
66:9 bless G. who hold. soul in *l.*
78:50 gave *l.* over to pestilence
91:16 with long *l.* will I satisfy
133:3 blessing, even *l.* for ever
Prov. 1:19 which taketh away *l.*
2:19 take they hold of paths of *l.*
3:2 long *l.* and peace shall they
18 she is a tree of *l.* to them
22 so sh. they be *l.* to thy soul
4:22 *l.* to those that find them
23 out of heart are issues of *l.*
5:6 lest thou pon. the path of *l.*
6:23 reproofs are the way of *l.*
8:35 whoso findeth me findeth *l.*
10:11 mou. of right. is well of *l.*
11:30 fruit of right. is tree of *l.*
12:10 right. regardeth *l.* of bea.
28 in way of righteousness is *l.*
13:8 ran. of man's *l.* are riches
12 desire com. it is a tree of *l.*
14 law of wise is a fount. of *l.*
14:27 fear of L. is a fount. of *l.*
30 a sound heart is *l.* of flesh
15:4 wholes. tongue is tree of *l.*
24 way of *l.* is above to wise
31 heareth reproof of *l.* abideth
16:15 in king's countenance is *l.*
18:21 death *l.* in power of tong.
21:21 followeth mercy, find. *l.*
22:4 by humil. are riches and *l.*
Ec. 7:12 wisdom giveth *l.*
Is. 38:16 in all th. things is the *l.*
20 sing songs all days of our *l.*
57:10 hast found *l.* of thy hand
Jer. 8:3 death chos. rather th. *l.*
21:8 set bef. you the way of *l.*
Lam. 2:19 lift up thy hands for *l.*
Ezek. 13:22 not return by prom. *l.*
33:15 wicked walk in stat. of *l.*
Jon. 1:14 not perish for man's *l.*
Mal. 2:5 covenant with him of *l.*
Mat. 2:20 dead wh. sou. child's *l.*
6:25 take no thought for your *l.*
Luke 12:22
18:8 enter into *l.* halt or maim.
Mark 9:43
9 better to enter into *l.* with
one eye, *Mark* 9:45
9:17 enter into *l.* keep com.
Mark 3:4 is it lawful to save *l.* or
to kill? *Luke* 6:9
Luke 1:75 holiness all days of *l.*
12:15 *l.* consist. not in abund.
23 *l.* more than meat, the body
John 1:4 in him w. *l.* and *l.* w. ll.
3:36 believeth not S. not see *l.*
5:26 as Fat. hath *l.* in himself,
so hath he given to the S. *l.*
29 to resurrection of *l.*
40 will not come to me that
might have *l.* 10:10
6:33 giveth *l.* unto the world
35 I am the bread of *l.* 48
51 which I will give for the *l.*
53 blood, ye have no *l.* in you
63 words I speak to you, are *l.*
8:12 shall have the light of *l.*
11:25 the resurrec. and *l.* 14:6
20:31 believing ye might have *l.*
Acts 2:28 known to me ways of *l.*
17:25 seeing he giveth to all *l.*
27:22 no loss of any man's *l.*
Rom. 5:17 sh. reign in *l.* by one
18 all men to justification of *l.*
6:4 sho. walk in newness of *l.*

8:2 Spirit of *l.* in Christ Jesus
6 to be spiritually minded is *l.*
10 Sp. is *l.* bec. of righteousn.
11:15 but *l.* from the dead
1 *Cor.* 3:22 *l.* or death all yours
14:7 things with. *l.* giv. sound
2 *Cor.* 1:8 we despaired even of *l.*
2:16 to the other the savor of *l.*
3:6 letter killeth, Sp. giveth *l.*
4:10 *l.* of Jesus be manifested
12 death worketh in us, *l.* in y.
5:4 mortality swallowed up of *l.*
Gal. 2:20 *l.* wh. I now live in fle.
3:21 which could have given *l.*
Eph. 4:18 alienated fr. the *l.* of G.
Phil. 1:20 wheth. by *l.* or death
2:16 holding forth word of *l.*
Col. 3:3 your *l.* is hid wi. C. in G.
4 when Christ our *l.* sh. appear
1 *Tim.* 2:2 may lead a peacea. *l.*
4:8 having the promise of the *l.*
2 *Tim.* 1:1 accord. to prom. of *l.*
10 brought *l.* to light by gospel
3:10 known my manner of *l.*
Heb. 7:3 nei. days, nor end of *l.*
16 after power of endless *l.*
Jam. 1:12 sh. receive crown of *l.*
4:14 for what is your *l.?* a vap.
1 *Pet.* 3:7 heirs of the grace of *l.*
10 will love *l.* and see good d.
2 *Pet.* 1:3 things pertaining to *l.*
1 *John* 1:1 handled of word of *l.*
2 for the *l.* was manifested
2:16 pride of *l.* is not of the Fa.
5:12 he that hath the S. hath *l.*
he that hath not S. of G. n. *l.*
16 he sh. give him *l.* for them
Rev. 2:7 I give to eat of tree of *l.*
10 I will give thee a crown of *l.*
11:11 Sp. of *l.* from G. entered
13:15 power to give *l.* to beast
21:6 I will give to the thirsty *l.*
22:1 a pure river of water of *l.*
2 tree of *l.* bare 12 man. of fr.
14 have right to the tree of *l.*
17 let him take the water of *l.*
See BOOK, ETERNAL, EVERLAST-
ING.

His LIFE.
Gen. 44:30 *his l.* is bound up
Ex. 21:30 give for ransom of *h. l.*
Jud. 9:17 father adventur. *h. l.*
16:30 which he slew in *his l.*
1 *Sam.* 19:5 put *h. l.* in his hand
1 *K.* 20:39 thy life be for *his l.* 42
2 *K.* 10:24 *h. l.* be for life of him
Job 2:4 hath will he give for *h. l.*
6 in thy hand, but save *his l.*
33:18 and *his l.* from perishing
20 *h. l.* abhor. 22 *h. l.* to destr.
28 and *his l.* shall see the light
Prov. 7:23 kno. not, for it is *h. l.*
13:3 keepeth mou. keepeth *h. l.*
Ec. 7:15 wicked man prol. *his l.*
Is. 15:4 *his l.* shall be grievous
Jer. 21:9 *h. l.* to him for pr. 38:2
Ezek. 3:18 to warn, to save *his l.*
7:13 nor stren. in iniq. of *h. l.*
32:10 every man for *his l.*
Mat. 10:39 he that find. *h. l.* sh.
lose it; he that loseth *his l.*
sh. find it, 16:25; *Mark* 8:35;
Luke 9:24; 17:33; *John* 12:25
20:28 to give *his l.* a ransom for
many, *Mark* 10:45
Luke 14:26 hate not *his* own *l.*
John 10:11 good Shep. give. *h. l.*
15:13 lay down *h. l.* for friends
Acts 8:33 *his l.* is taken fr. earth
20:10 yourselves, *h. l.* is in him
Rom. 5:10 sh. be saved by *his l.*
Phil. 2:30 not regarding *his l.*
1 *John* 3:16 he laid down *his l.*

See DAYS.

My LIFE.
Gen. 19:19 mercy in saving *my l.*
27:46 I am weary of *my l.*

32:30 seen G. and *my l.* is pres.
48:15 G. which fed me all *my l.*
Jud. 12:3 *my l.* in my hands
1 *Sam.* 18:18 what is *my l.?*
20:1 that he seeketh *my l.?*
22:23 that seeketh *my l.* seeketh
28:9 layest a snare for *my l.?*
21 I put *my l.* in my hand
2 *Sam.* 1:9 *my l.* is yet whole
16:11 my son seeketh *my l.*
1 *K.* 19:4 now, take away *my l.*
2 *K.* 1:13 let *my l.* be precious, 14
Est. 7:3 let *my l.* be given me
Job 6:11 that I sho. prolong. *m. l.*
7:7 remem. *my l.* is but win *l.*
15 choosest death than *m ̤ l.*
9:21 yet I would despise *m̤y l.*
10:1 my soul is weary of *my l.*
13:14 put *my l.* in my hand?
Ps. 7:5 tread down *my l.*
23:6 mercy sh. fol. me all *my l.*
26:9 not *my l.* with bloody men
27:1 the L. is strength of *my l.*
4 in ho. of L. all days of *my l.*
31:10 *my l.* is spent with grief
Ps. 38:12 seek after *my l.*
42:8 prayer to God of *my l.*
64:1 preserve *my l.* from enemy
88:3 *my l.* draw. nigh to grave
143:3 smitten *my l.* to ground
Lam. 3:53 cut off *my l.* in dung.
58 L. thou hast redeemed *my l.*
Jon. 2:6 bro. *my l.* from corrupt.
4:3 O Lord, take *my l.* from me
John 10:15 lay down *my l.*
17 because I lay down *my l.*
13:37 lay do. *my l.* for thy sake
Acts 20:24 nor count I *my l.* dear

This LIFE.
Ps. 17:14 have portion in *this l.*
Ec. 6:12 is good for man in *t. l.?*
Acts 5:20 speak all words of *t. l.*
1 *Cor.* 6:3 thi. that pertain to *t. l.*
4 of things pertaining to *t. l.*
15:19 if in *t. l.* only we ha. hope
1 *John* 5:11 and *l.* is in his Son

Thy LIFE.
Gen. 19:17 escape for thy *l.*
Ex. 4:19 men dead wh. sou. *t. l.*
Deut. 28:66 *thy l.* hang in doubt
Jud. 18:25 and thou lose *thy l.*
Ruth 4:15 be a restorer of *thy l.*
1 *Sam.* 19:11 save not *thy l.*
26:24 as *thy l.* was much set by
2 *Sam.* 4:8 enemy sought *thy l.*
1 *K.* 1:12 thou mayest save *t. l.*
20:31 peradv. he will save *t. l.*
39 *thy l.* for his life, 42
Ps. 103:4 redeem. *t. l.* fr. destru.
Prov. 4:10 years of *thy l.* 9:11
13 keep her, for she is *thy l.*
9:11 years of thy *l.* be increased
Is. 43:4 will I give peo. for *t. l.*
Jer. 4:30 they will seek *thy l.*
11:21 of the men that seek *thy*
l. 22:25; 38:16
39:18 *thy l.* for a prey, 45:5
Luke 12:25 in *t. l.* rec. good thi.
John 13:38 lay down *t. l.* for my

To LIFE.
2 *K.* 8:1 son he restored *to l.* 5
Prov. 10:16 right. tendeth *to l.*
11:19 righteousn. tendeth *to l.*
19:23 fear of Lord tendeth *to l.*
Mat. 7:14 narrow way lead. *to l.*
John 5:24 but is passed fr. death
to l. 1 *John* 3:14
Rom. 7:10 com. ordained *to l.*
Heb. 11:35 their dead raised *to l.*

LIFT.
Gen. 7:17 ark was *l.* up above
21:18 *l.* up the lad, hold him
40:13 Pha. sh. *l.* up thy head, 19
Ex. 7:20 *l.* rod, smote wat. 14:16
20:25 if thou *l.* up a tool on it

Num. 6:26 L. *l.* up his counten.
23:24 *l.* up hims. as a young lion
Deut. 27:5 not *l.* up an iron tool
  on them, *Jos.* 8:31
Jos. 4:18 soles of priests' feet *l.*
2 *Sam.* 23:8 *l.* up spear agai. 800
  18 *l.* up sp. ag. 300, 1 *Chr.* 11:11
2 *K.* 9:32 *l.* up face to window
19:4 *l.* up thy pr. for rem. *Is.* 37:4
Ezr. 9:6 I blush to *l.* up my face
Job 10:15 will I not *l.* up head
  11:15 thou *l.* up thy face, 22:26
Ps. 4:6 *l.* up light of countenance
  7:6 in thine anger, *l.* up thyself
  24:7 *l.* up your heads, ye gate. 9
  25:1 to thee I *l.* soul, 86:4 ; 143:8
  28:2 hear voice wh. I *l.* up han.
  9 feed them and *l.* th. up for e.
  41:9 hath *l.* up his heel ag. me,
    John 13:18
  74:3 *l.* up feet to perpet. desola.
  75:4 to wicked, *l.* not up horn, 5
  93:3 floods have *l.* up their wav.
  94:2 *l.* up thyself, judge of earth
  110:7 theref. shall he *l.* up head
Ec. 4:10 will *l.* up his fellow
Is. 2:4 nation sh. not *l.* up swo.
  against nation, *Mic.* 4:3
  10:15 if staff should *l.* up itself
  24 shall *l.* up staff against thee
  13:2 *l.* up banner upon mounta.
  33:10 now will I *l.* up myself
  59:19 Lord shall *l.* up standard
  62:10 *l.* up standard for the peo.
Jer. 7:16 nor *l.* prayer, 11:14
  51:14 *l.* up a shout against thee
Lam. 3:41 let us *l.* up our hearts
Ezek. 8:3 Spirit *l.* me up, 11:1
  26:8 shall *l.* up buckler ag. thee
Zec. 1:21 no man did *l.* up head
Mat. 12:11 will he not *l.* out
Mark 1:31 took by hand, and *l.*
Luke 13:11 no wise *l.* up herself
  21:28 *l.* up heads, your redemp.
Jam. 4:10 and he shall *l.* you up

See EYES.

LIFT hand, s.

Gen. 14:22 *l.* up my *h.* to Lord
Deut. 32:40 I *l.* up my *h.* and say
Ps. 10:12 *l.* up thy *h.* forget not
  28:2 *l.* up my *h.* toward oracle
  63:4 I *l.* up my *h.* in thy name
  119:48 *h.* I *l.* up to command.
  134:2 *l.* up *hands* in sanctuary
Is. 49:22 *l.* up my *h.* to Gentiles
Lam. 2:19 *l.* up *h.* towards him
Heb. 12:12 *l.* up *h.* that hang

LIFT voice.

Job 38:34 canst *l.* up *voice to*
  clouds ?
Is. 24:14 shall *l.* up *v.* shall sing
  40:9 *l.* up thy *v.* with strength
  42:2 he shall not cry nor *l.* up *v.*
  11 wilderness and cit. *l.* up *v.*
  52:8 thy watchmen shall *l.* up *v.*
  58:1 *l.* up thy *v.* like a trumpet
Ezek. 21:22 *l.* up *v.* with shout.

LIFTED.

Gen. 40:20 *l.* up head of butler
Lev. 9:22 Aaron *l.* up hand
Num. 20:11 *l.* up hand, sm. rock
Deut. 8:14 heart *l.* up thou forget
  17:20 heart not *l.* above brethr.
1 *Sam.* 24:16 *l.* up voice and we.
  30:4 David and peo. *l.* up voice,
    2 *Sam.* 3:22
2 *Sam.* 20:21 *l.* up hand aga. ki.
  22:49 thou hast *l.* me up on high
1 *K.* 11:26 Jeroboam *l.* up hand
  against king, 27
2 *K.* 14:10 heart hath *l.* thee up
1 *Chr.* 14:2 kingd. was *l.* on high
2 *Chr.* 17:6 *l.* up in ways of Lord
  26:16 *l.* up to destruction, 32:25
Job 31:21 *l.* up hand ag. fatherl.
  29 or *l.* up myself when evil

Ps. 24:4 not *l.* up soul unto van.
  27:6 now shall my head be *l.* up
  30:1 thou hast *l.* me up, 102:10
  83:2 hate thee have *l.* up head·
  93:3 floods have *l.* up their voi.
  106:26 *l.* up his hand ag. them
Prov. 30:13 their eyelids are *l.* up
Is. 2:12 on ev. one that is *l.* up
  6:1 sit. on throne high and *l.* up
  26:11 when thy hand is *l.* up
Jer. 51:9 judgment *l.* up to skies
Ezek. 1:19 creatures *l.* up fr. ear.
  3:14 so the Spirit *l.* me up
  10:16 *l.* up. wings, 19 ; 11:22
  20:5 *l.* up hand to seed of J. 6
  28 land for wh. I *l.* up my hand
  to give them, 42 ; 47:14
  28:2 thy heart *l.* up, 5:17 ; 31:10
Dan. 5:20 heart *l.* up and hard.
  23 *l.* up thyself against the L.
  7:4 first beast was *l.* up fr. earth
Mic. 5:9 hand *l.* up on adversari.
Hab. 2:4 soul *l.* up is not upright
  3:10 *l.* up his hands on high
Zec. 5:7 *l.* up a talent of lead
  9:16 as stones of a crown, *l.* up
  14:10 sh. be *l.* up and inhabited
Mark 9:27 but Jesus *l.* him up
Luke 6:20 *l.* up eyes on his disc.
  24:50 *l.* up hands and blessed
John 3:14 as Moses *l.* up serpent
  8:28 ye have *l.* up Son of man
  12:32 I, if I be *l.* up, will draw
  34 Son of man must be *l.* up
Acts 4:24 *l.* up their voice to G.
  14:11 *l.* voice in speech of Lyc.
1 *Tim.* 3:6 *l.* up with pride he f.
Rev. 10:5 angel *l.* up hand

LIFTER.

Ps. 3:3 the *l.* up of my head

LIFTEST.

Job 30:22 thou *l.* me up
Ps. 9:13 me fr. gates of death
  18:48 *l.* above those rise ag. me
Prov. 2:3 *l.* up voice for unders.

LIFTETH.

1 *Sam.* 2:7 bringeth low, *l.* up, 8
2 *Chr.* 25:19 heart *l.* up to boast
Ps. 107:25 wind wh. *l.* up wave
  113:7 he *l.* needy out of dunghill
  147:6 the Lord *l.* up the meek
Is. 18:3 see wh. he *l.* up ensign
Nah. 3:3 horseman *l.* up sword

LIFTING.

1 *Chr.* 15:16 *l.* up voice with joy
Neh. 8:6 amen, with *l.* up hands
Ps. 141:2 *l.* up of my hands
Prov. 30:32 foolishly in *l.* up. th.
Is. 9:18 like *l.* up of smoke
  33:3 *l.* up of thyself nations are
1 *Tim.* 2:8 pray, *l.* up holy hands

LIGHT.

Gen. 44:3 soon as morning was *l.*
Ps. 139:11 even the night sh. be *l.*
Mic. 2:1 morn. *l.* they practice it
Zec. 14:7 even. time it shall be *l.*

LIGHT.

Num. 21:5 soul loatheth *l.* bread
Deut. 27:16 cursed set. *l.* by fath.
Jud. 9:4 vain and *l.* persons
2 *Sam.* 2:18 Asahel was *l.* of foot
Ezek. 22:7 set *l.* by fath. and mo.
Zep. 3:4 prophets *l.* and treach.
Mat. 11:30 yoke easy, burden *l.*
  22:5 *l.* of it and went their ways
2 *Cor.* 4:17 *l.* affliction worketh

LIGHT thing.

1 *Sam.* 18:23 seemeth it a *l.* th. ?
2 *K.* 20:10 *l.* *t.* shadow go down
Is. 49:6 *l.* *t.* that should. be serv.

LIGHT, Substantive.

Gen. 1:3 God said, Let there be *l.*
  4 God saw *l.* 5 G. called *l.* day
  16 the lesser *l.* to rule the nig.
Ex. 10:23 Is. had *l.* in dwellings

  14:20 the pillar gave *l.* by night
Num. 4:16 pertaineth oil for *l.*
2 *Sam.* 21:17 quench not *l.* of Is.
  23:4 shall be as *l.* of morning
1 *K.* 7:4 *l.* was against *l.*
  11:36 David my serv. may ha. *l.*
Neh. 9:19 pillar of fire to show *l.*
Est. 8:16 J. had *l.* and gladness
Job 3:4 neit. let *l.* shine upon it·
  9 let it look for *l.* but have no.
  8:20 *l.* given him in misery, 23
  10:22 where the *l.* is as darkness
  12:22 bring. to *l.* shadow of de.
  18:5 *l.* of wicked sh. be put out
  6 *l.* shall be dark in his taber.
  22:28 *l.* shall shine on thy ways
  24:13 those that rebel ag. the *l.*
  14 murderer rising with *l.*
  16 they know not the *l.*
  25:3 upon wh. doth not *l.* arise ?
  28:11 thing hid bringeth he to *l.*
  33:28 his life shall see the *l.*
  30 enlightened with *l.* of living
  36:30 spreadeth his *l.* upon it
  32 with clouds he covereth *l.*
  37:15 caused *l.* of cloud to shine
  21 see not bright *l.* in clouds
  38:15 fr. wicked *l.* is withholden
  19 wh. is way where *l.* dwel. ?
  24 by what way is *l.* parted ?
Ps. 4:6 lift up *l.* of countenance
  27:1 Lord is my *l.* and salvation
  37:6 bring forth righteous. as *l.*
  38:10 *l.* of mine eyes, it is gone
  49:19 they shall never see the *l.*
  74:16 prepared the *l.* and sun
  78:14 all the night with a *l.*
  97:11 *l.* is sown for the righte.
  104:2 coverest thyself with *l.*
  118:27 L. who hath showed us *l.*
  119:105 and a *l.* to my paths
  130 entra. of thy words giv. *l.*
  139:12 darkn. and *l.* alike to th.
Prov. 4:18 path of just as shin. *l.*
  6:23 commandm. lamp, law is *l.*
  13:9 *l.* of righteous rejoiceth
  15:30 *l.* of eyes rejoiceth heart
Ec. 11:7 *l.* is sweet and pleasant
  12:2 or the *l.* be not darkened
Is. 5:20 darkness for *l.* *l.* darkn.
  30 *l.* is darkened in heavens
  8:20 because there is no *l.* in th.
  9:2 great *l.* on th. hath *l.* shined
  10:17 *l.* of Is. shall be for a fire
  13:10 moon sh. not cause her *l.*
  to shine, *Mat.* 24:29 ; *Mark*
    13:24
  30:26 *l.* of moon as *l.* of sun. *l.*
  of sun as the *l.* of seven days
  51:4 judgment rest for *l.* to peo.
  59:9 wait for *l.* but behold obs.
  60:19 L. be to thee everlast. *l.*
Jer. 4:23 beheld heav. had no *l.*
  25:10 take from them *l.* of cand.
  31:35 L. giv. sun for *l.* by day,
  moon and stars for *l.* by nig.
Dan. 2:22 *l.* dwelleth with him
Hos. 6:5 judgm. as *l.* goeth forth
Mic. 7:9 L. bring me forth to *l.*
Hab. 3:4 his brightness was as *l.*
  11 at *l.* of thine arrows
Zep. 3:5 morn. bring judgm. to *l.*
Zec. 14:6 in that day *l.* not be cl.
Mat. 4:16 in death, *l.* sprung up
  5:14 *l.* of world ; 15 it giveth *l.*
  16 let your *l.* so shine be. men
  6:22 the *l.* of the body is the
  eye, *Luke* 11:34, 36
  17:2 his raiment white as the *l.*
Luke 2:32 *l.* to lighten Gentiles
  8:16 enter in may see *l.* 11:33
  16:8 wiser than children of *l.*
John 1:4 life was the *l.* of men
  7 came to bear witness of *l.* 8
  9 true *l.* wh. lighteth every m.
  3:19 *l.* is come into the world
  20 ev. one doeth evil hateth *l.*
  21 that doeth truth com. to *l.*

John 5:35 was a burn. and shi. *l.*
8:12 I am *l.* of world, he that
fol. me sh. have *l.* of life, 9:5
11:9 because he seeth the *l.*
10 because th. is no *l.* in him
12:35 a little wh. is *l.* with you
36 wh. ye have *l.* believe in *l.*
46 am come a *l.* into world
Acts 9:3 shined about him a *l.*
12:7 a *l.* shined in the prison
13:47 to be a *l.* to the Gentiles
16:29 called for a *l.* and sprang
22:6 there shone a great *l.* round
9 they with me saw indeed *l.*
26:13 midday I saw in way a *l.*
23 *l.* to people and to Gentiles
Rom. 2:19 *l.* of them are in dark.
13:12 put on the armor of *l.*
1 *Cor.* 4:5 bring to *l.* hid. things
2 *Cor.* 4:4 lest *l.* of gospel shine
6 commanded *l.* to shine out
11:14 transf. into an angel of *l.*
Eph. 5:8 are *l.* walk as chil. o *l.*
13 all things made mani. by *l.*
whatso. doth manifest is *l.*
Col. 1:12 inherit. of saints in *l.*
1 *Thes.* 5:5 are all children of *l.*
1 *Tim.* 6:16 dwelling in *l.* no man
2 *Tim.* 1:10 who brought life to *l.*
1 *Pet.* 2:9 called you to marvel. *l.*
2 *Pet* 1:19 a *l.* shin. in dark place
1 *John* 1:5 G. is *l.* in him no da.
Rev. 18:23 *l.* of candle sh. no mo.
21:11 *l.* like a stone most preci.
23 the Lamb is the *l.* thereof
22:5 they need no *l.* of the sun
See COUNTENANCE, DARKNESS.

Give LIGHT.
Gen. 1:15 let them be to g. *l.*
Ex. 13:21 pillar of fire to *give l.*
2 *K.* 8:19 *give* him a *l.* 2 *Chr.* 21:7
Neh. 9:12 *g.* them *l.* in the way
Ps. 105:39 fire to *g. l.* in night
Is. 13:10 stars of heaven not *g. l.*
42:6 *g.* for a *l.* to Gentiles, 49:6
60:19 moon *g. l. Ezek.* 32:7
Mat. 5:15 *g. l.* to all, *Luke* 11:36
2 *Cor.* 4:6 *g. l.* of knowle. of G.
Eph. 5:14 Christ shall *g.* thee *l.*

In the LIGHT.
Ps. 56:13 may walk *in the l.*
Is. 2:5 let us walk *in the l.* of L.
50:11 walk *in the l.* of your fire
John 12:36 light, believe *in t. l.*
1 *John* 1:7 *in t. l.* as he is *in l.*
2:9 he that saith he is *in the l.*
10 lov. brother, abideth *in t. l.*
Rev. 21:24 nations sh. walk *i. t. l.*

Thy LIGHT.
Ps. 36:9 in *thy l.* sh. we see light
43:3 send out *t. l.* and thy truth
Is. 58:8 then sh. *t. l.* break forth
10 then sh. *t. l.* rise in obscuri.
60:1 shine, for *thy l.* is come
3 Gentiles shall come to *thy l.*
19 the sun sh. be no more *t. l.*
20 L. shall be *t.* everlasting *l.*

LIGHT, ED.
Ex. 25:37 sh. *l.* the lamps, 40:4
Ps. 18:28 thou wilt *l.* my candle
Mat. 5:15 nor do men *l.* a candle
Luke 8:16 hath *l.* candle, 11:33
15:8 doth not *l.* a candle
Rev. 7:16 nor sh. sun *l.* on them

LIGHT on.
Ruth 2:3 to *l.* on part of B.'s fie.
2 *Sam.* 17:12 will *l.* on him

Gen. 24:64 saw I. she *l.* off camel
Jos. 15:18 *l.* off ass, *Jud.* 1:14
Jud. 4:15 Sisera *l.* off his chariot
1 *Sam.* 25:23 Abigail *l.* off the ass
2 *K.* 5:21 Naaman *l.* from chari.

LIGHTED, ETH on.
Gen. 28:11 J. *l.* on certain place

Deut. 19:5 slip. and *l.* on neigh.
Is. 9:8 word to Jacob it *l.* on Isr.

LIGHTEN, *to illumine.*
2 *Sam.* 22:29 L. will *l.* my dark.
Ezr. 9:8 our God may *l.* our eyes
Ps. 13:3 *l.* mine eyes. lest I sleep
Luke 2:32 a light to *l.* Gentiles
Rev. 21:23 the glory of G. did *l.* it

LIGHTEN, ETH.
Ps. 34:5 looked to him and we. *l.*
77:18 the lightnings *l.* the world
Prov. 29:13 L. *l.* both their eyes
Luke 17:24 lightn. *l.* out one part
Rev. 18:1 earth *l.* with his glory
See ENLIGHTENED.

LIGHTEN, ED.
1 *Sam.* 6:5 he will *l.* his hand
Jon. 1:5 cast wares into sea to *l.*
Acts 27:18 next day th. *l.* sh. 38

LIGHTER.
1 *K.* 12:4 make thou our yoke *l.*
9, 10 ; 2 *Chr.* 10:10
Ps. 62:9 altogether *l.* than vanity

LIGHTEST, ETH.
Ex. 30:8 Aaron *l.* lamps at even
Num. 8:2 when thou *l.* lamps
John 1:9 true light *l.* every man

LIGHTING.
Is. 30:30 L. show *l.* down of arm
Mat. 3:16 a dove, and *l.* on him

LIGHTLY.
Gen. 26:10 might *l.* have lain
Is. 9:1 he *l.* afflicted the land
Jer. 4:24 all the hills moved *l.*
Mark 9:39 *l.* speak evil of me
See ESTEEMED.

LIGHTNESS.
Jer. 3:9 thro' *l.* of her whoredo.
23:32 cause peo. to err by the. *l.*
2 *Cor.* 1:17 minded, did I use *l. ?*

LIGHTNING.
2 *Sam.* 22:15 sent *l.* and discom.
Job 28:26 made way for *l.* of thu.
37:3 directeth *l.* to ends of earth
38:25 divided a way for the *l.*
Ps. 144:6 cast forth *l.* scatter th.
Ezek. 1:14 ran as appearance of *l.*
Dan. 10:6 face as appearance *l.*
Zec. 9:14 his arrow go forth as *l.*
Mat. 24:27 as *l.* cometh out of
the east, *Luke* 17:24
28:3 his countenance was as *l.*
Luke 10:18 as *l.* fall from heaven

LIGHTNINGS.
Ex. 19:16 thunders, *l.* and cloud
20:18 all the people saw the *l.*
Job 38:35 send *l.* th. may go ?
Ps. 18:14 *l.* and discomfited th.
77:18 *l.* lighted the world, 97:4
135:7 he maketh *l.* for the rain
Jer. 10:13 mak. *l.* wi. rain, 51:16
Nah. 2:4 chariots shall run like *l.*
Rev. 4:5 out of throne proceed. *l.*
8:5 thunderings and *l.* 11:19
16:18 *l.* and a great earthquake

LIGHTS.
Gen. 1:14 let there be *l.* in firma.
16 God made two great *l.*
1 *K.* 6:4 windows of narrow *l.*
Ps. 136:7 made great *l.*
Ezek. 32:8 bri. *l.* will I make d.
Luke 12:35 loins girded, *l.* burn.
Acts 20:8 *l.* in upper chamber
Phil. 2:15 ye shine as *l.* in world
Jam. 1:17 down from Father of *l.*

LIGN-ALOES.
Num. 24:6 trees of *l.-a.* L. plant.

LIGURE.
Ex. 28:19 third row a *l.* 39:12

LIKE.
Ex. 15:11 who is *l.* unto thee ?
Deut. 33:29 ; 1 *K.* 8:23 ; 2 *Chr.*
6:14 ; *Ps.* 35:10 ; 71:19

Is. 57:20 wicked *l.* troubled sea
64:6 iniquities *l.* wind have tak.
Jer. 11:19 *l.* a lamb bro. to slau.
23:29 is not my word *l.* fire ?
Ezek. 18:10 doeth *l.* any of these
25:8 house of Ju. *l.* to heathen
31:2 whom art th. *l.* in great. 18
Dan. 3:25 fourth is *l.* Son of God
7:13 one *l.* the Son of man came
Hos. 4:9 sh. be *l.* people. *l.* priest
6:7 *l.* men have transgressed
Mat. 13:31 *l.* to a grain of mustard-seed, *Mark* 4:31 ; *Luke*
13:19
44 *l.* a treasure ; 45 *l.* a merch.
47 *l.* a net ; 52 *l.* household. 20:1
22:2 heav. is *l.* to a certain king
Acts 14:15 are men of *l.* passions
Heb. 2:17 made *l.* his brethren
7:3 made *l.* to the Son of God
Jam. 1:6 that waver. is *l.* a wave
23 *l.* a man beholding his face
5:17 E. was subject to *l.* passio.
2 *Pet.* 1:1 obtain. *l.* precious faith
1 *John* 3:2 we shall be *l.* him
Rev. 1:13 *l.* the Son of man, 14:14

LIKE manner.
Ex. 7:11 in *l. m.* with enchantm.
Luke 6:23 in *l. m.* did th. fathers
20:31 in *l. m.* did the seventh
Acts 1:11 in *l. m.* as have seen

LIKE-MINDED.
Rom. 15:5 G. gra. you to be *l.-m.*
Phil. 2:2 *l.-m.* 20 no man *l.-m.*

None LIKE.
Ex. 8:10 there is *n.-l.* the L. our
God, 9:14 ; *Deut.* 33:26 ; 2 *Sa.*
7:22 ; 1 *Chr.* 17:20
11:6 *n. l.* cry of land of Egypt
1 *Sam.* 10:24 *n. l.* S. among peo.
1 *K.* 3:12 there was *n. l.* Solomon
21:25 there was *n. l.* to Ahab.
2 *K.* 18:5 there was *n. l.* Hezekí.
Ps. 86:8 among the gods *n. l.* to
thee, *Jer.* 10:6, 7
Is. 46:9 am G. there is *n. l.* me
Jer. 30:7 day *l.* great, *n. l.* it
Dan. 1:19 among all *n. l.* Daniel

Such LIKE.
Mark 7:8 *s. l.* things ye do, 13
Gal. 5:21 drunkenness, and *s. l.*

LIKE, ED.
Deut. 25:7 *l.* not to take her, 8
1 *Chr.* 28:4 sons of my fat. *l.* me
Rom. 1:28 did not *l.* to retain G.

LIKEN.
Is. 40:18 to whom *l.* G. ? 25 ; 46:5
Lam. 2:13 what sh. I *l.* to thee ?
Mat. 7:24 I will *l.* him to a man
11:16 whereunto *l.* this genera-
tion ? *Luke* 7:31
Mark 4:30 *l.* kingd. ? *Luke* 13:20

LIKENED.
Ps. 89:6 who am. sons *l.* to L. ?
Jer. 6:2 I *l.* the daughter of Zion
Mat. 7:26 sh. be *l.* to foolish m.
13:24 heaven is *l.* 18:23 ; 25:1

LIKENESS.
Gen. 1:26 make man after *l.* 5:1
5:3 A. begat a son in his own *l.*
Ex. 20:4 not make *l.* of anything
Deut. 4:16 the *l.* of male or fe-
male, 17, 18, 23, 25 ; 5:8
Ps. 17:15 wh. awake with thy *l.*
Is. 40:18 what *l.* comp. to him ?
Ezek. 1:5 *l.* of four liv. creatures
28 *l.* of the glory of the Lord
10:21 *l.* of the hands of man
Acts 14:11 gods come in *l.* of men
Rom. 6:5 in *l.* of his death, we
shall be in *l.* of resurrection
8:3 G. sending Son in *l.* of flesh
Phil. 2:7 was made in *l.* of men

LIKETH.
Deut. 23:16 dwell where it *l.* him

Amos 4:5 this *l.* you, O child. of

LIKING.

Job 39:4 young on. are in good *l.*
Dan. 1:10 why see faces worse *l.*

LIKEWISE.

Ps. 49:10 *l.* brut. person perish
52:5 God shall *l.* destroy thee
Ec. 7:22 *l.* hast cursed others
Mat. 20:5 abo. sixth hour, did *l.*
21:36 and they did unto them *l.*
Luke 6:31 do ye also to them *l.*
13:3 ye shall all *l.* perish, 5
16:25 *l.* Laz. received evil thin.
22:20 *l.* also cup after supper
John 5:19 these doeth the Son *l.*
1 *Cor.* 7:3 *l.* the wife to husband
Heb. 2:14 he himself *l.* took part
1 *Pet.* 4:1 arm yourselves *l.*
Jude 8 *l.* these filthy dreamers
Rev. 8:12 day shone not, night *l.*

LILY.

Cant. 2:1 I am the *l.* of the val.
2 as *l.* am. thorns, so my love
Hos. 14:5 Is. shall grow as the *l.*

LILIES.

Cant. 2:16 belov. feed. am. *l.* 6:3
4:5 like two roses among the *l.*
5:13 lips like *l.* dropping myrrh
7:2 belly like wheat set with *l.*
Mat. 6:28 consider the *l.* how
they grow, *Luke* 12:27

LILY-WORK.

1 *K.* 7:19 chapiters were of *l.-w.*
22 on top of pillars was *l.-w.*

LIME.

Is. 33:12 peo. be as burnings of *l.*
Amos 2:1 bon. of king of E. to *l.*

LIMIT, ED, ETH.

Ps. 78:41 *l.* Holy One of Israel
Ezek. 43:12 *l.* thereof shall be ho.
Heb. 4:7 he *l.* a certain day

LINE, S.

2 *K.* 21:13 over *J. l.* of Samaria
Job 38:5 stretched *l.* on earth?
Ps. 16:6 *l.* fallen in pleas. places
19:4 their *l.* is gone thro' earth
78:55 divided inheritance by *l.*
Is. 28:10 *l.* must be upon *l.* 13
17 judgm. also will I lay to *l.*
34:11 stretch on it *l.* of confus.
Amos 7:17 land be divided by *l.*
Zec. 1:16 *l.* be stretched on Jeru.
2 *Cor.* 10:16 in another man's *l.*

LINEAGE.

Luke 2:4 he was of *l.* of David

LINEN.

Ex. 28:42 make them *l.* breeches
Lev. 6:10 put on *l.* garment, 16:4
1 Sam. 2:18 minis. with *l.* ephod
22:18 slew 85 that did we. *l.* ep.
2 *Sam.* 6:14 D. girded wi. *l.* eph.
1 *K.* 10:28 Solomon had *l.* yarn
brought, 2 *Chr.* 1:16
Jer. 13:1 get thee a *l.* girdle
Mat. 27:59 he wrapped it in a
clean *l.* cloth, *John* 19:40
Mark 14:51 *l.* cloth about his bo.
52 left *l.* cloth and fled naked
Luke 24:12 *l.* cl. laid by
themselves, *John* 20:6
John 20:5 John saw the *l.* clothes

LINEN.

Lev. 19:19 nor shall a garment
mingled of *l.* and woollen
co. upon thee. *Deut.* 22:11
1 *Chr.* 15:27 D. had on eph. of *l.*
Mark 15:46 wrap. in *l. Luke* 23:53
Rev. 15:6 angels clothed in *l.*

See FINE.

LINGERED, ETH.

Gen. 19:16 Lot *l.* men laid hold
43:10 except *l.* we had returned
2 *Pet.* 2:3 judg. of a long time *l.*

LINTEL, S.

Ex. 12:22 strike *l.* and two posts
t *K.* 6:31 *l.* and posts a fifth part
Amos 9:1 smite *l.* posts shake
Zep. 2:14 bittern lodge in upper *l.*

LINUS. 2 *Tim.* 4:21

Gen. 49:9 Judah couched as a *l.*
Num. 24:9 Israel lay down as a *l.*
Deut. 33:20 Gad dwelleth as a *l.*
Jud. 14:8 turned to see carc. of *l.*
bees and honey in carc. of *l.*
1 Sam. 17:34 ca. a *l.* and took la.
2 *Sam.* 17:10 heart as hea. of a *l.*
23:20 slew *l.* in pit, 1 *Chr.* 11:22
1 *K.* 13:24 a *l.* met him by way
and slew him, *l.* also stood
20:36 a *l.* sh. slay thee; a *l.* fou.
Job 4:10 roaring of *l.* voice of *l.*
10:16 huntest me as a fierce *l.*
28:8 nor the fierce *l.* passed by
38:39 wilt th. hunt prey for *l.?*
Ps. 7:2 lest tear my soul like *l.*
10:9 lieth in wait secretly as a *l.*
17:12 like a *l.* greedy of his prey
22:13 they gaped on me as a *l.*
91:13 thou shalt tread on the *l.*
Prov. 19:12 king's wra. is as a *l.*
20:2 fear of king is as roar. of *l.*
22:13 saith, There is a *l.* in way.
26:13 *l.* in way, a *l.* in the street
28:1 righteous are bold as a *l.*
30:30 a *l.* strongest am. beasts
Ec. 9:4 liv. dog better th. dead *l.*
Is. 5:29 th. roaring sh. be like *l.*
11:7 *l.* sh. eat str. like ox, 65:25
21:8 he cried, A *l.* my lord
35:9 no *l.* there, nor ravenous
38:13 as *l.* so will he bre. bones
Jer. 2:30 devour. prophets like *l.*
4:7 *l.* is come from his thicket
5:6 a *l.* out of forest sh. slay th.
12:8 my heritage is to me as a *l.*
25:38 forsak. his covert as the *l.*
49:19 shall come up like *l.* 50:44
Lam. 3:10 he was to me as a *l.*
Ezek. 1:10 face of *l.* on right side
10:14 third was the face of a *l.*
22:25 a conspir. like a roaring *l.*
Dan. 7:4 first like a *l.* had wings
Hos. 5:14 I will be to Eph. as a *l.*
11:10 he shall roar like a *l.*,
13:7 to them as *l.* 8 will devour
Joel 1:6 teeth of a *l.* cheek-teeth
Amos 3:4 *l.* roar hath no prey?
8 *l.* roared, who will not fear?
12 taketh out of mouth of *l.*
Mic. 5:8 rem. of Jac. sh. be as *l.*
Nah. 2:12 *l.* tear in pieces
2 *Tim.* 4:17 de. out of mouth of *l.*
1 *Pet.* 5:8 devil as a *l.* walk. abo.
Rev. 4:7 first beast was like a *l.*
5:5 the *l.* of the tribe of Judah
10:3 a loud voice as a *l.* roareth
13:2 his mouth was as mo. of *l.*

See BEAR.

LION-LIKE.

2 *Sam.* 23:20 slew two *l.-l.* men
of Moab 1 *Chr.* 11:22

Old LION.

Is. 30:6 whence come the old *l.?*
Nah. 2:11 even the old *l.* walked

Young LION.

Is. 11:6 calf and y. *l.* lie down
31:4 like as the young *l.* roaring
Ezek. 19:3 it became a young *l.* 6
32:2 like a y. *l.* of the nations
41:19 face of y. *l.* toward tree

LIONESS, ES.

Ezek. 19:2 wh. is thy moth. ? a *l.*
Nah. 2:12 lion strangled for his *l.*

LIONS.

2 *Sam.* 1:28 S. and Jon. strong. *l.*
1 *K.* 10:19 two *l.* stood beside
the stays, 2 *Chr.* 9:18

2 *K.* 17:25 L. sent *l.* among them
1 *Chr.* 12:8 faces like faces of *l.*
Ps. 22:21 save me from *l.* mouth
35:17 rescue my darling from *l.*
57:4 my soul is among *l.* I lie
Cant. 4:8 top of Am. from *l.* dens
Is. 15:9 *l.* upon him that escap.
Jer. 50:17 *l.* driven Israel away
51:38 shall roar together like *l.*
Ezek. 19:2 she lay down amo. *l.*
Dan. 6:27 D. from power of *l.*
Nah. 2:11 wh. is dwelling of *l.?*
Zep. 3:3 princes are roaring *l.*
Heb. 11:33 faith sto. mouths of *l.*
Rev. 9:8 teeth as the teeth of *l.*
17 heads of horses as hea. of *l.*

See DEN.

LION'S whelp, s.

Gen. 49:9 Judah is *l.'s w.* from
Deut. 33:22 Dan is *l.'s w.* from
Job 4:11 *l.'s w.* scattered abroad
28:8 *l.'s w.* have not trodden it
Jer. 51:38 sh. yell as *l.'s whelps*

Young LIONS.

Ps. 34:10 y. *l.* suffer hunger
58:6 break out gr. teeth of y. *l.*
104:21 y. *l.* roar after their prey
Jer. 2:15 y. *l.* roared upon him
Ezek. 19:2 nourished among y. *l.*
38:13 the y. *l.* shall say to thee
Zec. 2:3 voice of roaring of y. *l.*

LIP.

Lev. 13:45 a covering on his *l.*
Ps. 22:7 they shoot out the *l.*
Prov. 12:19 *l.* of truth establish.

LIPS.

Ex. 6:12 of uncircumcised *l.* 30
1 Sam. 1:13 only her *l.* moved
Ps. 12:2 flat *l.* do they speak
4 *l.* own, who is lord over us?
17:1 goeth not out of feigned *l.*
31:18 lying *l.* be put to silence
59:7 behold, swords are in th. *l.*
12 words of their *l.* be taken
63:5 praise thee with joyful *l.*
120:2 deli. my soul from lying *l.*
140:3 poison is under their *l.*
9 let mischief of own *l.* cover
Prov. 4:24 perverse *l.* put fr. th.
5:3 *l.* of a strange woman drop
7:21 flatter. of *l.* she forced him
10:13 in *l.* of him that hath un.
21 *l.* of righteous feed many
32 *l.* of righteous know
12:22 lying *l.* abomination to L.
14:3 *l.* of wise sh. preserve them
7 not in him *l.* of knowledge
23 talk of *l.* tendeth to penury
15:7 *l.* of wise disperse knowl.
16:13 righte. *l.* delight of kings
21 sweet. of *l.* increaseth learn.
17:4 wicked giv. heed to false *l.*
7 less do lying *l.* bec. a prince
18:6 fools *l.* enter into conten.
20:15 *l.* of knowl. are a jewel
24:2 their *l.* talk of mischief
26:23 burning *l.* like a potsherd
Ec. 10:12 *l.* of fool swal. himself
Cant. 7:9 causing *l.* of th. asleep
Is. 6:5 a man of uncle. *l.* I dwell
in midst of people of uncl. *l.*
28:11 stammer. *l.* will he speak
29:13 peo. with *l.* do honor me
57:19 I create the fruit of the *l.*
59:3 your *l.* have spoken lies
Ezek. 36:3 tak. up in *l.* of talkers
Hos. 14:2 render calves of our *l.*
Mic. 3:7 they shall cover their *l.*
Mal. 2:7 priest's *l.* keep knowl.
Mat. 15:8 that honoreth me with
their *l. Mark* 7:6
Rom. 3:13 poison is under th. *l.*
1 *Cor.* 14:21 other *l.* I speak to
Heb. 13:15 fruit of *l.* giv. thanks

His LIPS.

Job 2:10 did not J. sin with *his l.*
11:5 G. open *his l.* against thee
23:12 back fr. comman. of *his l.*
Ps. 21:2 withholden req. of *his l.*
106:33 spake unadvis. with *h. l.*
Prov. 10:19 refrain *his l.* is wise
12:13 spared by transg. of *his l.*
16:27 *his l.* as a burning fire
30 *his l.* bringeth evil to pass
17:28 shutteth *his l.* as a man of
18:7 *his l.* are snare of his soul
19:1 that is perverse in *his l.*
20:19 that flattereth with *his l.*
Prov. 22:11 for grace of *his l.* the
24:26 kiss *his l.* gives ri. answer
Cant. 5:13 *his l.* like lilies drop.
Is. 11:4 breath of *h. l.* slay wick.
30:27 *his l.* full of indignation
Mal. 2:6 iniq. not found in *his l.*
1 *Pet.* 3:10 *his l.* speak no guile

My LIPS.

Ps. 16:4 their names into *my l.*
40:9 not refrained *my l.* O Lord
51:15 O Lord, open thou *my l.*
63:3 *my l.* shall praise thee
66:14 vows, which *my l.* uttered
89:34 thing gone out of *my l.*
119:13 wi. *my l.* have I declared
171 *my l.* shall utter thy praise
141:3 Lord, keep door of *my l.*
Prov. 8:6 the opening of *my l.* 7
Jer. 17:16 came out of *my l.* was
Dan. 10:16 sons of men tou. *my l.*

Thy LIPS.

2 *K.* 19:28 I will put my bridle
in *thy l. Is.* 37:29
Job 8:21 fill *thy l.* with rejoicing
15:6 *l.* own *l.* testify aga. thee
Ps. 17:4 word of *t. l.* I have kept
34:13 keep *l.* fr. from spea. guile
45:2 grace is poured into *thy l.*
Prov. 5:2 *thy l.* may keep know.
22:18 they shall be fitted in *t. l.*
23:16 when *thy l.* speak right
24:28 deceive not with *thy l.*
27:2 praise thee, not *t.* own *l.*
Cant. 4:3 *thy l.* are like scarlet
11 *thy l.* drop as honey-comb
Is. 6:7 this hath touched *thy l.*
Ezek. 24:17 cover not *thy l.*

LIQUOR, S.

Ex. 22:29 offer the first of thy *l.*
Num. 6:3 nor drink any *l.* of gr.
Cant. 7:2 goblet wh. want. not *l.*

LISTED.

Mat. 17:12 done to him whatsoever they *l. Mark* 9:13

LISTEN.

Is. 49:1 *l.* O isles, unto me

LISTETH.

John 3:8 wind blow. where it *l.*
Jam. 3:4 whithersoever gover. *l.*

LITTERS.

Is. 66:20 bring your breth. in *l.*

LITTLE.

Gen. 30:30 but *l.* thou hadst
Ex. 12:4 househ. too *l.* for lamb
16:18 that gathered *l.* had no
lack, 2 *Cor.* 8:15
23:30 by *l.* and *l.* drive them
out, *Deut.* 7:22
Deut. 28:38 and gather but *l.* in
Jos. 22:17 is iniq. in Peor too *l.* ?
1 *Sam.* 15:17 *l.* in th. own sight
1 *K.* 12:10 my *l.* finger thicker
than, 2 *Chr.* 10:10
17:12 *l.* oil in cruse ; 13 *l.* cake
18:44 *l.* cloud like a man's hand
20:27 Is. pitch. like two *l.* flocks
2 *K.* 5:2 brought captive *l.* maid
Ezr. 9:8 give us a *l.* reviving
Neh. 9:32 let not trouble seem *l.*
Job 4:12 ear received a *l.* thereof
26:14 *l.* portion heard of him

Ps. 2:12 wrath kindled but a *l.*
8:5 made him a *l.* lower than
the angels, *Heb.* 2:7
37:16 *l.* that a right. man hath
65:12 *l.* hills rejoice on ev. side
68:27 *l.* Benjamin, with th. rul.
72:3 *l.* hills by righteousness
114:4 *l.* hills skip. like lambs, 6
Prov. 6:10 a *l.* sleep, *l.* slumber,
a *l.* folding, 24:33
10:20 heart of wicked is *l.* worth
15:16 better is *l.* with fear of L.
16:8 better is *l.* with righteous.
30:24 four things *l.* on earth
Ec. 5:12 whether eat *l.* or much
9:14 a *l.* city and few men in it
10:1 *l.* folly him is in reputation
Cant. 8:8 we have a *l.* sister
Is. 26:20 hide thy. for *l.* moment
28:10 here a *l.* and there a *l.* 13
40:15 tak. up isles as a *l.* thing
54:8 in a *l.* wrath I hid my face
Ezek. 11:16 to them a *l.* sanctu.
16:47 as if that were very *l.* th.
Dan. 7:8 up another *l.* horn. 8:9
11:34 be holpen with a *l.* help
Hos. 8:10 sorrow a *l.* for burden
Amos 6:11 smite *l.* house
Mic. 5:2 tho' *l.* among thousands
Hag. 1:6 sown much, bring in *l.*
9 looked for much, it ca. to *l.*
Zec. 1:15 was but a *l.* displeased
Mat. 14:31 O thou of *l.* faith
15:34 seven, and a few *l.* fishes

Mat. 26:39 he went a *l.* further,
Mark 1:19 ; 14:35
Mark 5:23 my *l.* daughter lieth
Luke 7:47 to whom *l.* is forgiven
12:32 *l.* flock ; 19:3 *l.* of stature
19:17 been fulfilled in a very *l.*
John 6:7 every one may take a *l.*
Acts 5:34 apostles forth a *l.* space
28:2 showed us *l.* kindness
1 *Cor.* 5:6 *l.* leaven leav. *Gal.* 5:9
2 *Cor.* 11:1 bear with me a *l.*
16 that I may boast myself a *l.*
1 *Tim.* 4:8 bodily ex. profiteth *l.*
5:23 use *l.* wine for stomach's
Heb. 2:9 a *l.* lower than angels
Jam. 3:5 tongue is a *l.* member
4:14 vapor appeareth for *l.* time
Rev. 3:8 thou hast a *l.* strength
6:11 should rest for a *l.* season
20:3 be loosed a *l.* season

See BOOK, CHAMBERS, CHILD,
CHILDREN.

LITTLE one, s.

Gen. 19:20 Lot said, It is a *l. one*
44:20 have a *l. one*, broth. dead
Ex. 10:10 go and your *l. ones*, 24
Jos. 8:35 before women and *l. o.*
2 *Chr.* 20:13 before Lord and *l. o.*
Ezr. 8:21 seek right way for *l. o.*
Ps. 137:9 dasheth *l. o.* ag. stones
Is. 60:22 *l. one* bec. a thousand
Zec. 13:7 turn my hand on *l. o.*
Mat. 10:42 dri. to one of th. *l. o.*
18:6 offend one of these *l. ones*,
Mark 9:42 ; *Luke* 17:2
10 despise not one of th. *l. o.*
14 one of these *l. o.* sho. perish

LITTLE while.

Job 24:24 exalted for a *l. while*
Ps. 37:10 a *l. w.* and the wicked
Is. 10:25 *l. w.* indignation cease
63:18 possessed it but a *l. w.*
Jer. 51:33 a *l. w.* harvest sh. co.
Hos. 1:4 a *l. while* I will avenge
Hag. 2:6 a *l. w.* I will sh. heaven
John 7:33 *l. w.* I am with, 13:33
12:35 a *l. w.* is light with you
14:19 *l. w.* world seeth me no
16:16 *l. w.* ye sh. see me, 17, 19
18 a *l. while* ye cannot tell
Heb. 10:37 *l. w.* he that sh. come

LIVE.

Is. 6:6 hav. a *l.* coal in his hand
See GOAT.

LIVE.

Gen. 3:22 tree of life *l.* for ever
19:20 and my soul shall *l.*
20:7 pray for thee, thou shalt *l.*
27:40 by the sword shalt thou *l.*
31:32 fin. thy go. let him not *l.*
42:18 this do, and *l.* for I fear G.
Ex. 33:20 no man see me and *l.*
Lev. 18:5 he shall *l.* in them,
Neh. 9:29 ; *Ezek.* 20:11, 13, 21
Num. 21:8 looketh on ser. sh. *l.*
24:23 shall *l.* when G. doeth
Deut. 4:10 fear me all days th. *l.*
33 hear, as thou hast, and *l.* ?
8:3 by ev. wo. of L. doth man *l.*
19:5 flee to one of th. cit. and *l.*
33:6 let Reuben *l.* and not die
Job 14:14 man die, sh. he *l.* ag. ?
21:7 do wicked *l.* become old ?
Ps. 22:26 your heart *l.* for ever
49:9 *l.* and not see corruption
63:4 will I bless thee while I *l.*
69:32 hearts sh. *l.* that seek G.
72:15 shall *l.* 118:17 not die, *l.*
119:144 understand. and I sh. *l.*
175 let soul *l.* it sh. praise thee
146:2 while I *l.* will I praise L.
Prov. 4:4 keep my com. *l.* 7:2
9:6 forsake foolish and *l.*
15:27 he that hateth gifts sh. *l.*
Ec. 6:3 many years, 6 ; 11:8
9:9 *l.* joyfully wi. wife th. lovest
Is. 26:19 dead men. sh. *l.* togeth.
38:16 L. by these things men *l.*
55:3 hear, and your soul shall *l.*
Jer. 38:20 and thy soul shall *l.*
Lam. 4:20 under shad. we sh. *l.*
Ezek. 3:21 he shall surely *l.* 18:9,
17 ; 33:13, 15, 16
16:6 when thou wast in blood *l.*
18:19 kept my statutes shall *l.*
21, 22 ; 20:11, 25
24 wicked man doeth sh. he *l.*
32 turn yourselves and *l.* 33:11
33:10 sins on us, how sh. we *l.* ?
19 do that wh. is law. he sh. *l.*
37:3 can these bones *l.* ?
47:9 ev. thing liveth and mov
eth sh. *l.* everything shall *l.*
Hos. 6:2 he will rev. us, we sh. *l.*
Amos 5:4 seek me, and ye sh. *l.* 6
Jon. 4:3 bet. to die than to *l.* 8

Hab. 2:4 just sh. *l.* by his faith,
Rom. 1:17
Mat. 4:4 not *l.* by bread, *Lu.* 4:4
9:18 she shall *l. Mark* 5:23
Luke 10:28 this do, and th. sh. *l.*
20:38 not G. of dead, all *l.* unto
John 5:25 hear voice of S. and *l.*
6:57 I l. by F. so he that eateth
me, even he shall *l.* by me
11:25 tho' he were de. yet sh. *l.*
14:19 because I *l.* ye sh. *l.* also
Acts 17:28 in him we *l.* and move
22:22 it is not fit that he sho. *l.*
Rom. 6:2 *l.* any longer therein ?
8 we believe we sh. *l.* with him
8:12 debtors not to *l.* after flesh
13 if ye *l.* after flesh, ye sh. die,
if thro' Sp. mortify bo. ye *l.*
10:5 doeth these things shall *l.*
by them, *Gal.* 3:12
12:18 *l.* peaceably with all men
14:8 whether we *l.* we *l.* to Lo.
whe. we *l.* or die we are L.'s
1 *Cor.* 9:13 *l.* of things of temple
14 preach gospel sho. *l.* of gos.
2 *Cor.* 4:11 *l.* are deliv. to death
6:9 behold, we *l.* as chastened
7:3 to die and *l.* with you
13:4 *l.* with him by power of G.
Gal. 2:14 Gentiles to *l.* as Jews
19 that I might *l.* unto God

20 I *l.* yet not I, life I now *l.* in
flesh, I *l.* by faith of S. of G.
3:11 just *l.* by faith, *Heb.* 10:38
5:25 if we *l.* in the Spirit
Phil. 1:21 for me to *l.* is Christ
22 if I *l.* in the flesh
1 *Thes.* 3:8 we *l.* if sta. fast in L.
5:10 died that we sh. *l.* wi. him
2 *Tim.* 2:11 we sh. also *l.* with
3:12 all *l.* godly suf. persecution
Tit. 2:12 we should *l.* soberly
Heb. 12:9 to F. of spirits and *l.*
13:18 willing to *l.* honestly
Jam. 4:15 if Lord will we sh. *l.*
1 *Pet.* 2:24 we *l.* to righteousness
4:2 no longer should I *l.* in flesh
6 *l.* according to God in Spirit
2 *Pet.* 2:6 to those that *l.* ungodly
18 escaped from them *l.* in err.
1 *John* 4:9 we might *l.* thro' him
Rev. 13:14 beast had wound did *l.*

See FOR EVER.

As I LIVE.

Num. 14:21 *as I l.* earth be fill. 28
Job 27:6 so long as *I l. Ps.* 104:33;
116:2
Is. 49:18 *as I l.* saith the Lord;
Jer. 22:24; *Ezek.* 5:11; 14:16,
18, 20; 16:48; 17:16, 19; 18:3;
20:3, 33; 33:11, 27; 34:8; 35:6,
11; *Zep.* 2:9; *Rom.* 14:11
Jer. 46:18 *as I l.* saith the king

May, might, *or* mayest LIVE.

Deut. 4:1 do to them, ye *m. l.*
5:33; 8:1; 30:6, 16
42 flee, to one of th. citi. *m. l.*
16:20 what is just fol. that *m. l.*
3o:19 thou and thy seed *m. l.*
Ps. 119:17 bountif. that I *m. l.*
77 mer. come to me, that I *m. l.*
116 uphold me, that I *may l*
Jer. 35:7 that ye *m.* many days
Ezek. 37:9 slain, that they *m. l.*
Amos 5:14 seek good, th. ye *m. l.*
Eph. 6:3 *mayest l.* long on earth

Not LIVE.

Ex. 19:13 touch mountain *not l.*
Deut. 8:3 man doth *n. l.* by bread
only, *Mat.* 4:4; *Luke* 4:4
2 *K.* 10:19 wanting he shall *not l.*
20:1 thou shalt *not l. Is.* 38:1
Job 7:16 I would *not l.* always
Ps. 55:23 wick. *n. l.* half th. days
Is. 26:14 are dead, they sh. *not l.*
Ezek. 13:19 souls that should *n. l.*
18:13 he shall *not l.*
Zec. 13:3 say, Thou shalt *not l.*
Acts 7:19 to the end they mi. *n. l.*
25:24 ought *not* to *l.* any longer
28:4 vengeance suffereth *n.* to *l.*
2 *Cor.* 5:15 sho. *n. l.* to themsel.

LIVED.

Gen. 25:6 from Isaac, while he *l.*
Num. 14:38 Joshua and C. *l.* still
21:9 beheld serp. of brass he *l.*
Deut. 5:26 heard voice of G. and *l.*
2 *Sam.* 19:6 if Absalom had *l.*
Ps. 49:18 while he *l.* blessed soul
Ezek. 37:10 into them, and th. *l.*
Acts 23:1 *l.* in good conscience
Col. 3:7 sometime, wh. *l.* in th.
Jam. 5:5 *l.* in pleasure on earth
Rev. 18:7 hath *l.* deliciously, 9
20:4 *l.* with Christ; 5 *l.* not ag.

LIVELY.

Ex. 1:19 Hebrew women are *l.*
Ps. 38:19 but my enemies are *l.*
Acts 7:38 who received *l.* oracles
1 *Pet.* 1:3 begot. us ag. to *l.* hope
2:5 ye, as *l.* stones, are built

LIVER.

Ex. 29:13 the caul above the *l.*
22; *Lev.* 3:4, 10, 15; 4:9; 7:4;
8:16, 25; 9:10, 19
Prov. 7:23 dart strike through *l.*

Lam. 2:11 *l.* poured upon earth
Ezek. 21:21 he looked in the *l.*

See CAUL.

LIVES.

Ex. 1:14 they made th. *l.* bitter
Jos. 2:13 deliver our *l.* fr. death
Jud. 5:18 peo. jeoparded their *l.*
2 *Sam.* 1:23 were lovely in th. *l.*
23:17 that went in jeopardy of
their *l.* 1 *Chr.* 11:19
Prov. 1:18 lurk privily for own *l.*
Jer. 19:7 which seek th. *l.* 46:26
9 seek their *l.* sh. strait. them
Lam. 5:9 gat bread wi. peril of *l.*
Dan. 7:12 *l.* prolon. for a season
Luke 9:56 to destroy men's *l.*
Acts 15:26 men have hazarded *l.*
27:10 voy. be with damage of *l.*
1 *John* 3:16 lay down *l.* for breth.
Rev. 12:11 they loved not their *l.*

LIVEST.

Gal. 2:14 a Jew *l.* after manner
Rev. 3:1 that thou *l.* and art dead

LIVETH.

Gen. 9:3 every thing *l.* be meat
Deut. 5:24 G. talk with man, he *l.*
1 *Sam.* 1:28 to L. as long as he *l.*
20:31 as son of Jesse *l.* on grou.
2 *Sam.* 2:27 as God *l.* unless th.
22:47 the Lord *l.* blessed be my
rock, *Ps.* 18:46
1 *K.* 17:23 Elijah said, Thy son *l.*
Job 19:25 I know my Redeemer *l.*
27:2 as G. *l.* who ha. taken away
Ps. 89:48 what man *l.* not see de.?
Jer. 4:2 the Lord *l.* in truth
5:2 Lord *l.* they swear falsely
12:16 my name, the Lord *l.*
16:14 the Lord *l.* 15; 23:7, 8
44:26 Egypt, saying, The L. *l.*
Ezek. 47:9 every thing that *l.*
Hos. 4:15 nor swear, the Lord *l.*
Amos 8:14 say, Thy G. O Dan, *l.*
and the manner of Beersh. *l.*
John 4:50 thy way, son *l.* 51, 53
11:26 whosoever *l.* and believ.
Rom. 6:10 in that he *l.* he *l.* to G.
7:1 over man as long as he *l.* 2
3 while husb. *l.* she be married
14:7 *l.* or dieth to himself
1 *Cor.* 7:39 as long as her husb. *l.*
2 *Cor.* 13:4 *l.* by the power of G.
Gal. 2:20 I live, but Ch. *l.* in me
1 *Tim.* 5:6 *l.* in pleasure is dead
Heb. 7:8 it is witnessed that he *l.*
25 ever *l.* to make intercession
9:17 no strength while testa. *l.*
Rev. 1:18 he that *l.* and was dead

See FOR EVER.

As the Lord LIVETH.

Jud. 8:19 *as the L. l.* if ye have
1 *Sam.* 14:39 *as the L. l.* 45; 19:6;
20:21; 25:26; 26:10, 16; 28:10;
29:6; 2 *Sam.* 4:9; 12:5; 14:11;
1 *K.* 1:29
20:3 *as t.* L. *l.* there is but a step
25:34 God of Is. *l.* whi. kept me
2 *Sam.* 15:21 *as* L. *l.* as my lord
1 *K.* 2:24 *as the Lord l.* 3 *K.* 5:20;
2 *Chr.* 18:13; *Jer.* 38:16
17:1 *as Lord* God of Is. *l.* 18:15
12 *as the Lord* thy God *l.* 18:10
2 *K.* 3:14 *as Lord* of hosts *l.* 5:16

As thy soul LIVETH.

1 *Sam.* 1:26 *as s. l.* I am the wom.
17:55 Abner said, *As thy soul l.*
25:26 *as soul l.* seeing Lord hath
2 *Sam.* 11:11 *as t. s. l.* will not do

LIVING.

Gen. 1:28 dominion over *l.* thing
2:7 and man became a *l.* soul
3:20 she was mother of all *l.*
6:19 every *l.* thing of all flesh
7:4 ev. *l.* substance will I destr.
8:1 Noah and every *l.* thing

Lev. 11:10 any *l.* thing in water
Num. 16:48 stood bet. dead and *l.*
1 *K.* 3:22 the *l.* is my son, 23
25 divide the *l.* child into two
Job 12:10 in his hand ev. *l.* thing
28:13 nor found in land of the *l.*
21 it is hid from eyes of all *l.*
30:23 house appointed for all *l.*
Job 33:30 enlight. wi. light of *l.*
Ps. 27:13 good. of L. in land of *l.*
52:5 root thee out of land of *l.*
56:13 walk in the light of the *l.*
58:9 sh. take th. away, both *l.*
69:28 blotted out of book of *l.*
116:9 walk bef. L. in land of *l.*
142:5 my portion in land of *l.*
143:2 in thy sight no man *l.*
145:16 satisfiest every *l.* thing
Ec. 4:2 more than *l.* are alive
15 I considered all *l.* wh. walk
6:8 knoweth to walk before *l.*
7:2 the *l.* will lay it to heart
9:4 that is joined to all the *l.*
5 the *l.* know that they sh. die
Cant. 4:15 a well of *l.* water
Is. 4:3 written among *l.* in Jer.
8:19 seek to their God for the *l.*
38:11 not see L. in land of the *l.*
19 the *l.* he sh. prai. thee
53:8 cut off out of the land of *l.*
Jer. 2:13 forsaken *l.* waters, 17:13
11:19 cut him off fr. land of *l.*
Lam. 3:39 wheref. doth *l.* comp.
Ezek. 26:20 set glory in land of *l.*
32:23 terror in land of *l.* 24-32
Dan. 4:17 that the *l.* may know
Zec. 14:8 *l.* waters shall go out
Mat. 22:32 God is the God of *l.*
Mark 12:27; *Luke* 20:38
Mark 12:44 cast in even all her *l.*
Luke 8:43 spent *l.* on physicians
15:12 he divided to them his *l.*
13 wasted subs. with riot. *l.* 30
24:5 why seek ye *l.* among dead
John 4:10 given thee *l.* water
11 fr. whence hast thou *l.* wat.
6:51 I am the *l.* bread wh. came
57 the *l.* Father hath sent me
7:38 sh. flow rivers of *l.* water
Rom. 12:1 bodies a *l.* sacrifice
14:9 Lord both of dead and *l.*
1 *Cor.* 15:45 A. was made *l.* soul
Col. 2:20 *l.* in world are subject
Heb. 10:20 by a new and *l.* way
1 *Pet.* 2:4 coming as to a *l.* stone
Rev. 7:17 Lamb lead to *l.* fount.
16:3 every *l.* soul died in the sea

See BIRD, CREATURE, GOD.

LIZARD.

Lev. 11:30 *l.* snail, mole, unclean

LO.

Job 9:19 strength, *l.* he is strong
Ps. 37:36 pas. away, *l.* he was not
40:7 I. I come ; 132:6 *l.* heard
52:7 *l.* the man that made not G.
73:27 *l.* they th. are far sh. peri.
92:9 *l.* thine enemies sh. perish
Cant. 2:11 *l.* the winter is past
Is. 25:9 *l.* this is our God
Jer. 4:23 *l.* it was without form
25 and *l.* there was no man
Hag. 1:9 and *l.* it came to little
Mat. 24:23 *l.* here is Chr. *l.* there
28:20 *l.* I am with you always
Acts 13:46 *l.* we turn to Gentiles
Heb. 10:7 *l.* I co. to do thy will, 9

LOADEN.

Is. 46:1 carriages were heavy *l.*

LOADETH.

Ps. 68:19 daily *l.* us wi. benefits

LOAF.

Ex. 29:23 one *l.* of bread
1 *Chr.* 16:3 D. dealt to ev. one a *l.*
Mark 8:14 nei. had more th. one *l.*

LO-AMMI. *Hos.* 1:9

LOAN.

1 *Sam.* 2:20 *l.* which is lent to L.

LOATHE.

Ex. 7:18 Egypt. shall *l.* to drink
Job 7:16 I *l.* it, I would not live
Ezek. 6:9 *l.* themselves for evils
20:43 *l.* yourselves in own sight
36:31 *l.* yourselves for iniquities

LOATHED.

Jer. 14:19 hath thy soul *l.* Zion ?
Zec. 11:8 my soul *l.* them

LOATHETH.

Num. 21:5 soul *l.* this light bread
Prov. 27:7 full soul *l.* honey-co.
Ezek. 16:45 *l.* husb. and children

LOATHING.

Ezek. 16:5 cast out to *l.* of person

LOATHSOME.

Num. 11:20 till it be *l.* to you
Job 7:5 my skin is broken and *l.*
Ps. 38:7 loins filled with a *l.* dis.
Prov. 13:5 a wicked man is *l.*

LOAVES.

Lev. 23:17 two *l.* of two tent'l
1 *Sam.* 25:18 Abigail took 200 *l.*
1 *K.* 14:3 take with thee ten *l.*
2 *K.* 4:42 brought man of G. 20 *l.*
Mat. 14:17 we have here but 5 *l.*
  19 and he took five *l. Mark*
    6:38 ; *Luke* 9:13
  15:34 how many *l.* have ye ?
  36 took the seven *l. Mark* 8:6
  16:9 nor remem. five *l.* of 5,000
  10 nor the seven *l.* of the 4,000
Mark 6:44 eat of *l.* were 5,000
  52 consider. not miracles of *l.*
Luke 11:5 say, Fri. lend me 3 *l.*
John 6:9 lad here hath 5 barley *l.*
  11 Jesus took *l.* and distribut.
  13 fragments of five barley *l.*
  26 because ye did eat of five *l.*

See BREAD.

LOCK, S.

Num. 6:5 let *l.* of the hair grow
Jud. 16:13 weavest the seven *l.*
Neh. 3:3 set up doors, and *l.*
  thereof. 6, 13. 14, 15
Cant. 4:1 doves' eyes with. thy *l.*
  5:2 my *l.* are filled with drops
  5 myrrh on handles of the *l.*
  11 his *l.* are bushy, and black
  6:7 thy temples within thy *l.*
Is. 47:2 uncov. thy *l.* make bare
Ezek. 8:3 he took me by *l.* of he.
  44:20 nor suffer *l.* to grow long

See BARS.

LOCUST.

Ex. 10:4 to-morrow I will bri. *l.*
Deut. 28:38 *l.* shall consume it
Ps. 105:34 he spake, and *l.* came
Prov. 30:27 the *l.* have no king
Is. 33:4 running to and fro of *l.*
Nah. 3:15 make thyself ma. as *l.*
Mat. 3:4 his meat was *l.* and wild
  honey, *Mark* 1:6
Rev. 9:3 th. came out of smoke *l.*
  7 shapes of *l.* we. like to hors.

LODGE.

Is. 1:8 daughter of Z. left as a *l.*

LODGE, Verb.

Gen. 24:23 is th. room for us to *l.?*
Num. 22:8 *l.* here this night
Jos. 4:3 place where ye shall *l.*
Jud. 19:9 *l.* here, that thy heart
Neh. 4:22 let every one *l.* in Jer.
  13:21 why *l.* ye about the wall ?

Job 24:7 naked *l.* without cloth.
  31:32 stran. did not *l.* in street
Cant. 7:11 let us *l.* in the villages
Is. 21:13 forest in Ara. sh. ye *l.*
  65:4 and *l.* in monuments
Jer. 4:14 how long vain thoug. *l.*
Zep. 2:14 beasts sh. *l.* in lintels
Mat. 13:32 birds *l.* in branches,
  Mark 4:32 ; *Luke* 13:19
Acts 21:16 with wh. we should *l.*

LODGED.

Gen. 32:13 J. *l.* there that night
  21 *l.* that night in company
Jos. 2:1 a harlot's house, and *l.*
  4:8 carried them, where they *l.*
Jud. 19:4 eat and drink, *l.* there
1 *K.* 19:9 came into a cave and *l.*
1 *Chr.* 9:27 *l.* round house of God
Neh. 13:20 *l.* without Jerusalem
Is. 1:21 righteousness *l.* in it
Mat. 21:17 went to Betha. and *l.*
Acts 10:18 whether Simon *l.* th.
  28:7 *l.* us three days courteous.
1 *Tim.* 5:10 if she have *l.* strang.

LODGEST.

Ruth 1:16 wh. th. *l.* I will lodge

LODGETH.

Acts 10:6 *l.* with one Si. a tanner

LODGING, S.

Jos. 4:3 leave them in the *l.*
2 *K.* 19:23 enter *l.* of his borders
Is. 10:29 taken up their *l.* at G.
Acts 28:23 came to him into *l.*
Phile. 22 withal prepare me a *l.*

LOFT, Y.

1 *K.* 17:19 carried him into a *l.*
Ps. 131:1 not haugh. nor eyes *l.*
Prov. 30:13 L. how *l.* are th. eyes
Is. 2:11 *l.* looks be humbled, 5:15
  26:5 the *l.* city he layeth low
  57:7 on *l.* mountain hast set bed
  15 thus sai. the high and *l.* one
Acts 20:9 Euty. fell from third *l.*

LOFTILY.

Ps. 73:8 corrupt, they speak *l.*

LOFTINESS.

Is. 2:17 *l.* of man shall be bowed
Jer. 48:29 the pride of Moab,
  his *l.*

LOG.

Lev. 14:10 priest take a *l.* 12, 24

LOINS.

Gen. 35:11 kings co. out of thy *l.*
  37:34 J. put sackcloth on his *l.*
  46:26 souls out of his *l. Ex.* 1:5
Ex. 12:11 eat it, with *l.* girded
  28:42 breeches reach from the *l.*
Deut. 33:11 smite thro' *l.* of them
1 *K.* 2:5 blood in girdle about *l.*
  8:19 son shall come forth of thy
    l. 2 *Chr.* 6:9
  12:10 thicker than my father's
    l. 2 *Chr.* 10:10
  20:31 put sackcloth on our *l.*
2 *K.* 1:8 girdle of leather about
  his *l. Mat.* 3:4 ; *Mark* 1:6
  4:29 gird up thy *l.* 9:1 ; *Job* 38:3 ;
    40:7 ; *Jer.* 1:17
Job 31:20 if his *l.* ha. not blessed
  40:16 lo, his strength is in his *l.*
Ps. 38:7 my *l.* filled wi. disease
  66:11 laid affliction upon our *l.*
  69:23 their *l.* continually shake
Is. 5:27 neither girdle of *l.* loosed
  11:5 righteousn. girdle of his *l.*
  20:2 loose sackcloth from thy *l.*
  21:3 are my *l.* filled with pain
  32:11 gird sackcl. upon your *l.*
Jer. 13:1 a linen girdle put on *l.*
  30:6 ev. man with hands on *l.*
  48:37 upon *l.* shall be sackcloth
Ezek. 1:27 fr. appearance of his *l.*
  8:2 from his *l.* downward, fire
  21:6 with the breaking of thy *l.*

23:15 with girdles upon their *l.*
44:18 have linen breeches on *l.*
47:4 the waters were to the *l.*
Dan. 5:6 joints of *l.* were loosed
  10:5 I. were gird. with fine gold
Amos 8:10 bring sack. on your *l.*
Nah. 2:1 make thy *l.* strong
  10 and much pain is in all *l.*
Luke 12:35 let your *l.* be girded
Acts 2:30 of his *l.* he wo. raise C.
Eph. 6:14 hav. your *l.* girt about
Heb. 7:5 came out of *l.* of Abrah.
  10 he was yet in *l.* of his father
1 *Pet.* 1:13 wheref. gird *l.* of mind

LOIS. 2 *Tim.* 1:5

LONG.

Ex. 19:13 trumpet sound. *l.* 19
  20:12 that thy days may be *l.*
Num. 9:19 the cloud tarried *l.*
Deut. 1:6 ye dwelt *l.* enough, 2:3
  19:6 overtake him, way is *l.*
Jos. 6:5 they make a *l.* blast
1 *K.* 3:11 not asked *l.* 2 *Chr.* 1:11
2 *Chr.* 15:3 for a *l.* season Israel
Ps. 91:16 wi. *l.* life will I satisfy
  95:10 forty years *l.* was I grieved
  120:6 my soul hath *l.* dwelt
  129:3 ploughers made *l.* furrows
  143:3 that have been *l.* dead
Prov. 3:2 *l.* life sh. th. add to thee
  7:19 good man is gone a *l.* jour.
  23:30 they that tarry *l.* at wine
  25:15 *l.* forbearing is a prince
Ec. 12:5 man go. to his *l.* home
Is. 65:22 elect *l.* enjoy the work
Jer. 29:28 this captivity is *l.*
Lam. 2:20 wo. eat child span *l.?*
Ezek. 17:3 great eagle *l.* winged
  44:20 nor suffer locks to grow *l.*
Dan. 10:1 time appointed was *l.*
Hos. 13:13 not stay *l.* in the place
Mat. 11:21 repented *l.* ago
  23:14 for pretence make *l.* pray.
    Mark 12:40 ; *Luke* 20:47
Mark 12:38 who go in *l.* clothing,
    Luke 20:46
  16:5 clothed in a *l.* white garm.
Luke 18:7 tho' he bear *l.* with th.
  23:8 to see him of a *l.* season
Acts 20:9 Paul was *l.* preaching
1 *Cor.* 11:14 if a man have *l.* hair
  15 wom. have *l.* hair, it is glo.
Eph. 6:3 mayest live *l.* on earth
1 *Tim.* 3:15 if I tarry *l.* that thou
Jam. 5:7 husbandm. ha. *l.* pati.

See AGO.

As LONG as.

Lev. 26:34 as *l.* as it lieth des. 35
Num. 9:18 as *l.* as cloud abode
Deut. 31:13 as *l.* as you live
1 *Sam.* 1:28 lent to L. as *l.* as liv.
  20:31 as *l.* as son of Jesse liveth
2 *Chr.* 26:5 as *l.* as he sought L.
  36:21 as *l.* as she lay desolate
Ps. 72:5 *l.* as sun and m. endure
  17 name continued as *l.* as sun
  104:33 sing to L. as *l.* as I live
  116:2 call up. him as *l.* as I live
Ezek. 42:11 as *l.* as they, as broad
Mat. 9:15 as *l.* as bridegroom is
  with them, *Mark* 2:19
John 9:5 as *l.* as I am in world
Rom. 7:1 over man as *l.* as he liv.
1 *Cor.* 7:39 bound as *l.* as husba.
Gal. 4:1 heir as *l.* as he is a child
1 *Pet.* 3:6 daught. as *l.* as do well
2 *Pet.* 1:13 as *l.* as I am in taber.

See CUBITS, DAY, HOUR.

So LONG.

Jud. 5:28 chariot so *l.* in coming
2 *Chr.* 6:31 fear thee so *l.* as live
Est. 5:13 so *l.* as I see Mordecai
Job 27:6 not repro. so *l.* as I live
Ps. 72:7 so *l.* as moon endureth
Luke 1:21 marvel. he tarried so *l.*

Rom. 7:2 her husb. *so l.* as liveth
Heb. 4:7 after *so l.* a time

LONG time.
Gen. 26:8 had been there a *l. t.*
Num. 20:15 dwelt in Egypt *l. t.*
Deut. 20:19 besiege a city a *l. t.*
Jos. 11:18 Josh. made war a *l. t.*
23:1 a *l. t.* after Josh. wax. old
1 *Sam.* 7:2 wh. ark abode *l.* was *l.*
Is. 42:14 have *l. t.* holden peace
Lam. 5:20 forsake us so *l. time*
Mat. 25:19 after a *l. t.* the lord of
those serv. come. *Luke* 20:9
Luke 8:27 man had devils a *l. t.*
20:9 went to far country for *l. t.*
John 5:6 a *l. time* in that case
14:9 have I been so *l. t.* wi. you
Acts 14:3 *l. time* abode with disciples. 28
2 *Pet.* 2:3 judgm. of *l. t.* lingereth

LONG while.
Acts 20:11 a *l. w.* till bre. of day

LONG, Verb.
Job 3:21 *l.* for death, but com. not
6:8 grant me thing that I *l.* for
Rom. 1:11 for I *l.* to see you
2 *Cor.* 9:14 prayer wh. *l.* after you
Phil. 1:8 greatly I *l.* after you all

LONGED.
2 *Sam.* 13:39 David *l.* to go forth
23:15 David *l.* and said, O that
one. 1 *Chr.* 11:17
Ps. 119:40 I *l.* after thy precepts
131 I *l.* for thy commandments
174 I have *l.* for thy salvation
Phil. 2:26 for he *l.* after you all
4:1 dearly beloved and *l.* for

LONGEST.
Gen. 31:30 *l.* after father's house

LONGER.
Ex. 9:28 and ye shall stay no *l.*
Jud. 2:14 could not any *l.* stand
2 *K.* 6:33 should I wait for L. *l. ?*
Job 11:9 measure is *l.* than earth
Jer. 44:22 the L. could no *l.* bear
Luke 16:2 may. be no *l.* steward
Acts 18:20 desired him to tarry *l.*
25:24 he ought not to live any *l.*
Rom. 6:2 how live any *l.* therein
2 *Thes.* 3:1 we could no *l.* forb. 5
1 *Pet.* 4:2 *l.* live rest of his time.
Rev. 10:6 there sho. be time no *l*

LONGETH.
Gen. 34:8 my son *l.* for your dau.
Deut. 12:20 thy soul *l.* to eat flesh
Ps. 63:1 flesh *l.* for thee
84:2 my soul *l.* for courts of L.

LONGING.
Deut. 28:32 eyes sh. fail *l.* for th.
Ps. 107:9 he satisfieth the *l.* soul
119:20 soul break. for *l.* it hath

LONG-SUFFERING.
Ex. 34:6 Lo. G. *l.-s. Num.* 14:18;
Ps. 86:15; 2 *Pet.* 8:9
Jer. 15:15 me not aw. in thy *l.-s.*
Rom. 2:4 despi. riches of his *l.-s.*
9:22 endured with much *l.-s.*
2 Cor. 6:6 by *l.-s.* by kindness
Gal. 5:22 fruit of Sp. is love, *l.-s.*
Eph. 4:2 with *l.-s.* forbearing
Col. 1:11 strengthened to all *l.-s.*
3:12 elect of G. meekness, *l.-s.*
1 *Tim.* 1:16. might show *l.-s.*
2 *Tim.* 3:10 kno. my faith, *l.-s.*
4:2 with all *l.-s.* and doctrine
1 *Pet.* 3:20 *l.-s.* of God waited
2 *Pet.* 3:15 *l.-s.* of L. is salvation

LOOK, b.
Ps. 18:27 bring down high *l.*
101:5 a high *l.* I will not suffer
Prov. 6:17 Lord hateth a proud *l.*
21:4 high *l.* and proud heart
Is. 2:11 lofty *l.* of man humbled
10:12 punish glory of his high *l.*

Ezek. 2:6 nor dismayed at *l.* 3:9
Dan. 7:20 *l.* more stout than fel.

LOOK.
Gen. 15:5 *l.* now towards heaven
19:17 for life, *l.* not behind thee
41:33 let Pharaoh *l.* out a man
42:1 why *l.* one upon another?
Ex. 25:20 faces *l.* one to another
Deut. 9:27 *l.* not to stubbornness
28:32 thine eyes shall *l.* and fail
1 *Sam.* 16:12 Dav. goodly to *l.* to
2 *K.* 14:8 *l.* one another in face
1 *Chr.* 12:17 G. of fat. *l.* thereon
Job 3:9 *l.* for light, have none
20:21 sh. no man *l.* for his goods
35:5 *l.* to the heavens and see
Ps. 5:3 prayer to thee and *l.* up
40:12 that I am not able to *l.* up
123:2 eyes of serv. *l.* to masters
Prov. 27:23 and *l.* well to herds
Ec. 12:3 that *l.* out at windows
Cant. 4:8 *l.* from top of Amana
Is. 5:30 if one *l.* unto the land
8:21 curse king, and *l.* upward
22 they shall *l.* unto the earth
17:7 shall a man *l.* to his maker
22:4 *l.* away fr. me, I will weep
31:1 they *l.* not to H. One of Is.
42:18 *l.* ye blind, th. ye may see
45:22 *l.* unto me, and be saved
51:1 *l.* to rock whence are hewn
56:11 all *l.* to their own way
69:11 *l.* for judgment, but none
66:2 but to this man will I *l.*
Jer. 13:16 while ye *l.* for light
39:12 take and *l.* well to him
40:4 and I will *l.* well to thee
46:5 mighty fled, and *l.* not back
47:3 fathers not *l.* back to chil.
Hos. 3:1 who *l.* to other gods
Jon. 2:4 *l.* toward holy temple
Mic. 7:7 therefore I *l.* to the Lord
Nah. 2:8 but none shall *l.* back
Mat. 11:3 *l.* for ano. ? *Luke* 7:19,20
Mark 8:25 and made him *l.* up
Luke 21:28 thin. begin, then *l.* up
John 7:52 *l.* for out of Galilee
Acts 6:3 *l.* ye out seven men
18:15 quest. of words, *l.* ye to it
2 *Cor.* 3:13 steadfastly *l.* to end
4:18 we *l.* at things wh. are seen
Phil. 3:20 we *l.* for the Saviour
Heb. 9:28 to them th. *l.* sh. he ap.
1 *Pet.* 1:12 angels desire to *l.* in.
2 *Pet.* 3:13 we *l.* for new heav.
14 seeing ye *l.* for such things
2 *John* 8 *l.* to yourselves
Rev. 5:3 no man able to *l.* there.
4 to read book nor *l.* thereon

LOOK down.
Deut. 26:15 *l. d.* from holy habi.
Ps. 80:14 *l. d.* and visit this vine
85:11 right. *l. d.* from heaven
Is. 63:15 *l. down* from heaven
Lam. 3:50 till L. *l. d.* and behold

LOOK on, or upon.
Gen. 12:11 a fair woman to *l. on*
24:16 Rebekah fair to *l. on*, 26:7
Ex. 3:6 Moses afraid to *l. on* G.
39:43 Moses did *l. upon* all work
Lev. 13:3 priest *l. u.* the plague
Num. 15:39 that ye may *l. u.* it
2 *Sam.* 9:8 *l. u.* such a dead dog
16:12 L. will *l. u.* my affliction
2 *Chr.* 24:22 L. *l. u.* and require
Job 6:28 be content, *l. upon* me
40:12 *l. u.* ev. one that is proud
Ps. 22:17 bones stare and *l. upon*
25:18 *l. upon* mine affliction
35:17 how long wilt thou *l. u. ?*
84:9 *l. u.* face of thine anointed
119:132 *l. u.* me, and be merciful
Prov. 4:25 let th. eyes *l.* right *on*
23:31 *l.* not *on* wine wh. it is red
Cant. 1:6 *l.* not *on* me
6:13 that we may *l. upon* thee

Is. 33:20 *l. upon* Zion, the city
51:6 *l. upon* the earth beneath
Mic. 4:11 let our eye *l. u.* Zion
Nah. 3:7 that *l. u.* thee, shall flee
Hab. 1:13 purer eyes *l. u.* iniq.
2:15 mayest *l. u.* their nakedn.
Zec. 12:10 *l. u.* me they pierced
Luke 9:38 master, *l. u.* my son
John 4:35 lift eyes, *l. upon* fields
19:37 *l. u.* him they have pierced
Acts 3:4 P. and J. said, *l. u.* us, 12
Phil. 2:4 *l.* not *on* his own things
Rev. 4:3 was to *l. u.* like a jasper

LOOKED.
Gen. 6:12 God *l.* on the earth
19:26 his wife *l.* back fr. behind
26:8 *l.* out at a window
Ex. 2:12 *l.* this way and th. way
4:31 *l.* on their afflic. *Deut.* 26:7
14:24 the Lord *l.* on the host
33:8 the people *l.* after Moses
Num. 24:20 when he *l.* on Amal.
Jud. 5:28 *l.* out at window
6:14 the Lord *l.* upon him
1 *Sam.* 6:19 they had *l.* into ark
2 *Sam.* 6:16 Michal *l.* thro' win.
22:42 *l.* but th. was none to save
1 *K.* 18:43 serv. went up and *l.*
2 *K.* 2:24 El. turned back and *l.*
9:30 Jezebel *l.* out at a window
14:11 *l.* one another in the face
Ps. 14:2 L. *l.* if any did underst.
34:5 *l.* to him, and were light.
53:2 G. *l.* down on chil. of men
102:19 *l.* down fr. his sanctuary
109:25 when they *l.* they shaked
their heads
Cant. 1:6 bec. son hath *l.* on me
Is. 5:2 *l.* it sho. br. forth grapes
7 *l.* for judg. behold oppress.
22:11 ye have not *l.* to maker
Jer. 8:15 we *l.* for peace, 14:19
Ezek. 10:11 whither the head *l.*
21:21 consulted, he *l.* in liver
Hag. 1:9 *l.* for much, came to lit.
Mark 6:41 he *l.* up to heaven
8:24 he *l.* and said, I see men
Luke 1:25 *l.* on me to take away
2:38 all that *l.* for redemption
10:32 a Lev. came and *l.* on him
22:61 Lord turn. *l.* upon Peter
John 13:22 disc. *l.* one on anoth.
Acts 1:10 *l.* steadfastly to heaven
28:6 after they *l.* a great while
Heb. 11:10 *l.* for city hath found.
1 *John* 1:1 which we have *l.* upon

I LOOKED.
Job 80:26 *l.* for good, evil came
Ps. 69:20 *I l.* for some to take
142:4 *I l.* on my right hand
Prov. 7:6 *I l.* thro' my casement
24:32 *I l.* on it, received instr.
Ec. 2:11 *I l.* on works my hands
Is. 5:4 *I l.* it sho. br. forth grapes
63:5 *I l.* there was none to help
Acts 22:13 same hour *I l.* upon
Rev. 4:1 *I l.* and beh. a door was
opened, 6:8; 14:1, 14; 15:5

LOOKEST.
Job 13:27 *l.* narrowly to paths
Hab. 1:13 *l.* on them deal treach.

LOOKETH.
Num. 21:8 when he *l.* on it
20 *l.* toward Jeshimon, 23:28
1 *Sam.* 16:7 *l.* on outw. appear.
Job 7:2 a hireling *l.* for reward
28:24 he *l.* to ends of the earth
33:27 he *l.* on men, and if any
Ps. 33:13 Lord *l.* from heaven
14 he *l.* on inhab. of the world
104:32 *l.* on earth, it trembleth
Prov. 31:27 *l.* well to household
Cant. 6:10 who is she th. *l.* forth
Is. 28:4 when he that *l.* upon it

Mat. 5:28 who *l.* on wom. to lust
24:50 lord shall come when he *l.*
    not for him, *Luke* 12:46
Jam. 1:25 whoso *l.* into perf. law

LOOKING.

1 *Chr.* 15:29 Michal *l.* out window
Is. 38:14 mine eyes fail with *l.*
Mat. 14:19 *l.* up to hea. *Luke* 9:16
Mark 7:31 and *l.* up to heaven
    15:40 there were also women *l.*
Luke 6:10 *l.* round about th. all
    9:62 *l.* back, fit for kingd. of G.
    21:26 hearts failing for *l.* after
Acts 6:15 *l.* steadfastly on him
    23:21 *l.* for a promise from thee
Tit. 2:13 *l.* for that blessed hope
Heb. 10:27 fearful *l.* for of judgm.
    12:2 *l.* unto Jesus the author
    15 *l.* diligently, lest any fail
2 *Pet.* 3:12 *l.* for the coming of G.
Jude 21 *l.* for mercy of our L. J.

LOOKING-GLASS, ES.

Ex. 38:8 laver and foot of *l.-g.*
Job 37:18 spre. out sky as *l.-g.*

LOOPS.

Ex. 26:4 shalt make *l.* of blue, 5
    36:11 made *l.* of blue on curtain

LOOSE.

Gen. 49:21 Naph. is a hind let *l.*
Lev. 14:7 let the living bird *l.*
Job 6:9 he would let *l.* his hand
    30:11 they have let *l.* the bridle
Dan. 3:25 lo, I see four men *l.*

LOOSE, Verb.

Jos. 5:15 *l.* thy shoe fr. off foot
Job 38:31 canst thou *i.* the bands
Ps. 102:20 *l.* th. appoin. to death
Is. 20:2 *l.* sackcloth fr. thy loins
    45:1 I will *l.* the loins of kings
    52:2 O. J. *l.* thyself from bands
    58:6 *l.* the bands of wickedness
Jer. 40:4 behold, I *l.* thee this day
Mat. 16:19 ye *l.* on earth, 18:18
Mat. 21:2 *l.* and bring them to
    me, *Mark* 11:2, 4 ; *Luke* 19:30
Luke 19:31 why do ye *l.* him ? 33
John 11:44 *l.* him and let him go
Acts 13:25 I am not worthy to *l.*
    24:26 money given, he might *l.*
Rev. 5:2 who is worthy to *l.* seals
    5 prevailed to *l.* the 7 seals
    9:14 *l.* four angels wh. are bou.

LOOSED.

Deut. 25:10 that hath his shoe *l.*
Job 30:11 bec. he hath *l.* my cord
    39:5 who ha. *l.* bands of w. ass ?
Ps. 105:20 king sent and *l.* him
    116:16 thou hast *l.* my bands
Ec. 12:6 or ever silver cord be *l.*
Is. 5:27 nor girdle of loins be *l.*
    51:14 hasten. that he may be *l.*
Dan. 5:6 joints of his lo. were *l.*
Mat. 16:19 be *l.* in heaven, 18:18
    18:27 compassion, and *l.* him
Mark 7:35 string of his tongue
    was *l. Luke* 1:64
Luke 13:12 woman art *l.* fr. infir.
    16 ought not daughter to be *l.*
Acts 2:24 having *l.* pains of death
    13:13 when Paul and company *l.*
    16:26 every one's bands were *l.*
    22:30 he *l.* him from his bands
    27:21 and have not *l.* from Crete
Rom. 7:2 husb. be dead, she is *l.*
    1 *Cor.* 7:27 art thou *l.* fr. wife ?
Rev. 15 the four angels were *l.*
    20:3 after that he must be *l.* 7

LOOSETH.

Job 12:18 he *l.* the bond of kings
Ps. 146:7 Lord *l.* the prisoners

LOOSING.

Mark 11:5 what do you *l.* colt ?
Luke 19:33 they were *l.* the colt
Acts 16:11 therefore *l.* from Tro.

LOP.

Is. 10:33 the L. sh. *l.* the bough

LORD, 'S.

Gen. 18:14 any th. too har. for L. ?
    28:21 then sh. the L. be my G.
Ex. 5:2 who is L. I sho. obey ?
    9:29 know that the earth is the
    L.'s, *Ps.* 24:1 ; 1 *Cor.* 10:26
    13:12 the males shall be the L.'s
    32:26 who is on the L.'s side
Lev. 16:8 Aaron shall cast one lot
    for the L. 25:4 ; 27:2
Num. 14:14 that th. L. art seen
    18:6 given as a gift for the L.
    23:26 all the L. speak. must I do
Deut. 4:35 know that the L. he
    is God, 39 ; 1 *K.* 18:39
    5:5 I stood bet. the L. and you
    10:17 and L. of lords a great G.
    29:2 have seen all that the L. did
    32:6 do ye thus requite the L.
    33:29 O people, saved by the L.
Jos. 22:22 swear unto me by the
    L. 1 *Sam.* 24:21
Jud. 1:19 the L. was with Judah
    2:10 generat. wh. knew not L.
    6:13 if L. with us, why is this ?
    11:31 shall surely be L.'s
Ruth 1:17 L. do so to me, and
    more, 1 *Sam.* 20:13
1 *Sam.* 2:2 th. is none holy as L.
    3:18 L. do what seemeth good,
    2 *Sam.* 10:12 ; 1 *Chr.* 19:13 ;
    John 21:7
    19 the L. was with him, 18:12,
    14 ; 2 *K.* 18:7 ; 1 *Chr.* 9:20
    20:23 L. betw. thee and me, 42
2 *Sam.* 7:24 L. art become their
    God, 1 *Chr.* 17:22
1 *K.* 18:21 if L. be G. follow him
1 *Chr.* 16:25 for great is the L.
    Ps. 48:1 ; 145:3
    17:26 and now, L. thou art God
    21:24 not take wh. is th. for L.
2 *Chr.* 19:6 ju. not for man, but L.
    11 the L. sh. be with the good
    33:13 Manasseh knew L. was G.
Neh. 9:6 thou art L. alo. *Is.* 37:20
Ps. 4:3 L. hath set apart godly
    33:12 nation, whose G. is the L.
    45:11 thy L. worship thou him
    66:18 regard iniq. L. not hear
    92:8 L. art most high, 97:9
    100:3 know ye that L. is he G.
    109:21 for me, O G. the L. 140:7
    116:5 gracious is L. and righte.
    118:23 this is the L.'s doing
    27 God is L. wh. hath showed
    134:1 if it had not been the L. 2
    130:8 if thou, L. sh. mark iniq.
    132:5 find out a place for the L.
Prov. 24:18 lest L. see it, disple.
    30:9 and say, Who is the L. ?
Is. 42:24 did not L. be ag. whom
    52:12 the L. will go before you
Jer. 5:10 for they are not the L.'s
    23:6 L. our righteousness, 33:16
    31:34 saying, Know L. *Heb.* 8:11
Ezek. 35:10 whereas L. was there
Dan. 2:47 God is L. of kings
    9:17 face to shine, for L.'s sake
Hos. 12:14 reproach sh. L. return
Joel 2:21 L. will do great things
Amos 3:6 evil in city L. not done
Ob. 21 kingdom shall be L.'s
Mic. 2:13 the L. on head of them
    3:11 lean on L. say. Is not L.
    6:8 what doth L. req. of thee ?
Zec. 1:5 swear by L. and Malch.
Zec. 14:3 then shall L. go forth
    9 in that day sh. th. be one L.
Mat. 7:21 not ev. one that saith,
    L. L. shall enter the kingd.
    22 ; *Luke* 13:25
    15:27 truth L. 25:11 L. L. open
    21:3 L. hath need, *Mark* 11:3 ;
    Luke 19:31, 34

    22:43 how doth D. call him L. ?
    45 ; *Mark* 12:37 ; *Luke* 20:44
    24:42 know not wh. hour L. co.
    46 whom his L. shall find so
    doing, *Luke* 12:43, 46
    50 L. of that servant sh. come
    25:21 enter into joy of thy L.
    37 L. wh. saw we th. hun. ? 44
    26:22 began to say, L. is it I ?
    28:6 the place where the L. lay
Mark 2:28 L. of Sab. *Luke* 6:5
    5:19 great things L. hath done
    10:51 L. that I may rece. sight,
    Mat. 20:23
    16:20 L. working with them
Luke 1:17 ready a peo. for the L.
    6:46 call me L. L. and do not
    14:21 show. his L. these things
    17:5 said unto L. Incr. our faith
    37 wh. L. ? 23:42 L. rem. me
    24:34 saying, the L. is risen
John 6:68 L. to whom sh. we go
    9:36 who is he. L. that I might
    13:13 ye call me Master and L.
    25 L. who is it ? 20:25 seen L.
    20:2 taken L. out of sepulchre
    21:12 knowing it was L.
Acts 2:36 cruci. both L. and Ch.
    9:5 Who art thou, L. 26:15
    10:4 and said, What is it, L. ?
    14 Peter said, Not so, L. 11:8
    36 Jesus Christ, he is L. of all
    22:10 What shall I do, L. ?
Rom. 10:12 the same L. over all
    14:9 might be L. of dead and liv.
1 *Cor.* 2:8 not cruci. L. of glory
    3:5 as L. gave to every man
    44 he that judgeth me is the L.
    19 if the L. will, *Jam.* 4:15
    6:13 for L. 7:10 not L. but L.
    15:47 sec. man is L. fr. heaven
2 *Cor.* 5:8 present with the L.
    11:17 I speak it not after the L.
Eph. 4:5 one L. one faith
    5:29 even as the L. the church
Phil. 2:11 confess Jesus C. is L.
    4:5 be known, L. is at hand
1 *Thes.* 4:17 we ever be with L.
1 *Tim.* 6:15 K. of kings, L. of l.
2 *Tim.* 3:11 out of all L. deliv.
Heb. 2:3 began to be spok. by L.
    8:11 know L. for all shall know
Jam. 5:15 L. shall raise sick up
2 *Pet.* 3:8 day is with L. as thou.
Jude 9 M. said, L. rebuke thee
Rev. 11:15 bec. kingdoms of L.
    17:14 for he is L. of lords, 19:16

Against the LORD.

1 *Sam.* 2:25 if a man sin *a. t.* L.
    12:23 sin *a.* L. in ceas. to pray
Prov. 21:30 nor counsel *a. t.* L.
Is. 3:8 their doings are *a. the* L.
    32:6 utter error *against the* L.
Jer. 48:26 magni. himself *a.* L. 42
Dan. 5:23 lift. up thyself *a. t.* L.
Nah. 1:9 what do ye imag. *a.* L. ?

    See LIVETH, ANOINTED, AP-
    PEARED.

Before the LORD.

Gen. 18:22 Abra. stood *b. the* L.
Ex. 16:9 say, Come near *b. t.* L.
    33 lay up *b. the* L. 1 *Sam.* 10:25
    23:17 three times in ye. ap. *b.* L.
    34:24 ; *Deut.* 16:16 ; 1 *Sam.* 1:21
    27:21 order lamps *b. t.* L. 40:25
    28:12 A. bear their names *b.* L.
Lev. 4:6 sprinkle seven times *be.*
    the L. 17 ; 14:16, 27
    9:24 came a fire out fr. *b. the* L.
    10:2 they died *b.* L. *Num.* 3:4
Num. 5:16 set her *b.* L. 18:30
    10:9 he remem. *b.* L. your God
    25:4 hang them up *before the* L.
Num. 27:5 Moses brought cause
    b. the L.

Deut. 9:18 I fell down *b. the* L.
12:18 must eat them *b. the* L.
18:7 his breth. stand there *b.* L.
19:17 controv. sh. stand *b.* L.
Jud. 18:6 *b. the* L. is your way
1 *Sam.* 21:7 day detained *b.* L.
2 *Sam.* 21:9 hang. th. in hill *b.* L.
2 *K.* 19:14 Hezekiah spread it *b. the* L. *Is.* 37:14
Ps. 96:13 *b.* L. com. to jud. 98:8
109:15 be *b. the* L. continually
116:9 walk *b.* L. in land of liv.
Prov. 15:11 hell and destr. *b.* L.
Is. 23:18 them that dwell *b.* L.
Mic. 6:6 where. sh. I come *b.* L. ?
Zec. 2:13 be sil. all flesh *b. t.* L.
Mal. 3:14 walked mournf. *b. t.* L.
2 *Tim.* 2:14 charg. them *b. t.* L.
2 *Pet.* 2:11 no railing accus. *b.* L.
See BLESS, BLESSED, CALLED, CAST *out*, CHOSEN, CHOOSE, COMMANDED, FEAR, FEARED, REJOICE.

From the LORD.
Gen. 4:1 have gotten man *f.* L.
19:24 fire *f. t.* L. out of heaven
24:50 the thing proceed. *f. t.* L.
Num. 11:31 we. forth wind *f.* L
16:35 th. came out a fire *f. t.* L.
46 wrath gone out *from the* L.
1 *Sam.* 16:14 ev. sp. *f. t.* L. 19:9
26:12 sleep *f. t.* L. fallen on th.
1 *K.* 2:15 it was his *from the* L.
33 peace for ever *from the* L.
Ps. 24:5 sh. rec. blessing *f. t.* L.
109:20 reward mine adver. *f.* L.
121:2 my help cometh *f. the* L.
Prov. 16:1 ans. of tongue is *f.* L.
19:14 a prudent wife is *f. t.* L.
29:26 man's judgm. cometh *f.* L.
Is. 39:15 to hide counsel *f. t.* L.
40:27 sayest, My way hid *f.* L.
Jer. 7:1 word that came to Jere. *from the* L. 11:1 ; 18:1 ; 21:1 ; 26:1 ; 27:1 ; 30:1 ; 32:1 ; 34:1, 8, 12 ; 35:1 ; 36:1 ; 40:1
17:5 cursed wh. heart dep. *f.* L.
37:17 is there any word *f. t.* L. ?
49:14 I have heard a rumor *f.* L.
Lam. 2:9 pro. find no vision *f.* L.
3:18 strength is perished *f.* L.
Ezek. 11:15 get you far *f. the* L.
33:30 hear what word com. *f.* L.
Hos. 1:2 whored. departing *f.* L.
Ob. 1 have heard a rumor *f. t.* L.
Mic. 1:12 evil came down *f. t.* L.
5:7 remnant sh. be as dew *f.* L.
Zec. 14:13 tumult *f.* L. am. them
Luke 1:45 things told her *f. t.* L.
2 *Cor.* 5:6 we are absent *f. t.* L.

See GIVE, GIVEN.

LORD God.
Gen. 24:27 blessed be L. G. of A.
Ex. 34:6 L. G. merciful and gra.
Jos. 22:22 the L. G. of gods
24:2 the L. G. of Isr. *Jud.* 4:6 ; 1 *Sam.* 2:30 ; 1 *K.* 1:30 ; 1 *Chr.* 23:25 ; 24:19
1 *Sam.* 6:20 to stand before L. G.
2 *Sam.* 7:18 who am I, O L. G.
2 *K.* 2:14 wh. is L. G. of Elijah ?
Ezek. 36:23 I am the L. sa. L. G.
39:5 I have spoken it, saith the L. G. 23:34 ; 26:14 ; 28:10
Dan. 9:3 I set my face unto L. G.
Hos. 12:5 L. G. is his memorial
Amos 3:7 L. G. will do nothing
8 the L. G. hath spoken
Hab. 3:19 L. G. is my strength
1 *Pet.* 3:15 sanctify L. G. in hea.
Rev. 4:8 holy, holy, L. God Almighty, 11:17 ; 16:7
18:8 strong is L. G. who judge.
19:6 L. G. omnipotent reigneth
21:22 the L. G. and the Lamb
22:5 the L. G. giveth them light

See AH, FATHERS.

LORD his God.
Num. 23:21 L. *h. G.* is with him
1 *Sam.* 30:6 David encouraged himself in the L. *his God* .
1 *K.* 5:3 hou. to name of L. *h. G.*
11:4 not perfect with L. *h.* God 15:3
15:4 did L. *h. G.* give him lamp
2 *K.* 16:2 right in sig. of L. *h. G.*
2 *Chr.* 1:1 L. *h. G.* was with him
14:11 Asa cried unto the L. *h. G.*
31:20 wrou. right before L. *h. G.*
Ezr. 7:6 acco. to hand of L. *h. G.*
Mic. 5:4 in the name of L. *h. G.*

LORD my God.
1 *K.* 5:4 L. *my G.* given me rest
1 *K.* 5:5 build house unto name of L. *my G.* 1 *Chr.* 22:7 ; 2 *Chr.* 2:4
Ezr. 7:28 hand of L. *my God*
9:5 I spr. out hands to L. *my G.*
Jer. 31:18 thou art the L. *my G.*
Dan. 9:4 prayed unto L. *m. G.* 23

LORD our God.
Deut. 4:7 L. *o. G.* in all things
5:24 L. *o. G.* showed us glory
6:4 O Israel, the L. *our God* is one Lord, *Mark* 12:29
Jos. 22:19 altar of L. *o. G.* 29.
24:17 L. *o. G.* bro. us out of E.
1 *Sam.* 7:8 to cry to L. *our God.*
Ps. 20:7 remem. name of L. *o. G.*
90:17 beauty of L. *o. G.* be on us
99:5 exalt ye the L. *our God,* 9
8 O L. *our God* thou forg. th
9 for the L. *our God* is holy
105:7 for he is the L. *our God*
122:9 bec. of house of L. *o. G.*
123:2 eyes wait on L. *our God*
Jer. 3:22 thou art the L. *our G*
Dan. 9:9 to L. *our G.* be. merc.
Mic. 4:5 in name of L. *our God*
Acts 2:39 as many as L. *o. G.* call
Rev. 19:1 hon. and po. to L. *o. G.*

LORD their God.
2 *K.* 17:9 not right ag. L. *t.* God
19 kept not com. of L. *t.* G
Luke 1:16 shall turn to L. *t. G.*

LORD thy God.
Ex. 20:2 the L. *t.* G. *Ps.* 81:10
Deut. 4:24 L. *t.* G. is consum. fire
31 L. *t.* G. is a merciful God
7:9 the L. *thy God*, he is God
8:5 so L. *thy G.* chasteneth thee
19:31 not do so to L. *thy God*
28:58 fearful name, the L. *t.* G.
Jos. 1:9 L. *t.* G. is with thee
2 *Sam.* 14:17 L. *t.* G. be wi. thee
24:23 the L. *t.* G. accept thee
Is. 42:3 I am the L. *thy God*
Jer. 42:2 pray for us to L. *t.* God
Mic. 7:10 said, Where L. *t.* G. ?
Mat. 4:7 thou shalt not tempt the L. *thy God*, *Luke* 4:12

LORD your God.
Lev. 19:2 I the L. *y. G.* am holy
Deut. 10:17 L. *y. G.* of go.
Acts 3:22 pro. L. *y. G.* raise, 7:37

LORD of hosts.
2 *Sam.* 6:2 by name of L. *of h,*
7:26 the L. *of h.* over Isr.
Ps. 24:10 L. *of h.* king of glory
46:7. L. *of hosts* is with us, 11
48:8 seen in the city of L. *of h.*
Is. 6:3 holy, holy, is L. *of h.*
8:13 sanctify the L. *of hosts*
47:4 L. *of h.* his name, 48:2 ; 51:15 ; 54:5 ; *Jer.* 10:16 ; 31:35 ; 32:18 ; 50:34 ; 51:19
Jer. 46:18 name is L. *of h.* 48:15
Hab. 2:13 is it not of L. *of hosts*
Zec. 2:9 L. *of h.* sent 11 ; 4:9

See Saith the LORD.

I the LORD.
Lev. 19:2 for *I the* L. your God, am holy, 20:26 ; 21:8
Num. 14:35 *I the* L. have said it, I will do it, *Ezek.* 21:17
Is. 27:3 *I the* L. do keep it
45:7 *I the* L. do all these things
8 *I the* L. have created it
19 *I the* L. speak righteousness
60:22 *I the* L. will hasten it
Jer. 17:10 *I the* L. search hearts
Ezek. 14:9 *I t.* L. have dec. prop.
34:24 *I the* L. will be their God

I am the LORD.
Gen. 15:7 *I am the* L. th. brong.
Ex. 6:2 *I am t.* L. 6, 8, 29 ; 12:12 ; *Lev.* 18:5, 6, 21 ; *Num.* 3:13 ; *Is.* 43:11, 15
20:2 *I am t.* L. thy G. who bro.
Lev. 22:32 *I am the* L. wh. hal.
Is. 42:8 *I am t.* L. that is name
44:5 one shall say, *I am the* L.'s
Jer. 9:24 knoweth that *I a. t.* L.
32:27 *I am t.* L. the G. of all fl.
Mal. 3:6 *I am t.* L. I change not

See KNOW.

LORD Jesus. *See* JESUS.

In the LORD.
Gen. 15:6 he believed *in the* L.
1 *Sam.* 2:1 heart rejoiceth *in t.* L.
Ps. 4:5 put your trust *in the* L.
11:1 *in the* L. put I my trust, 26:1 ; 31:6 ; 73:28
31:24 all ye that hope *in the* L.
32:11 be glad *in the* L. and rej.
34:2 my soul shall boast *in t.* L.
35:9 my soul be joy. *in the* L.
Ps. 37:4 delight thyself *in the* L. *Is.* 58:14
7 rest *in the* L. and wait
56:10 *in t.* L. will I praise his
64:10 the righteous shall be gl. *in the* L. 104:34
Prov. 3:5 trust *in the* L. wi. hea.
Is. 26:4 *in t.* L. Jehovah is ever.
45:24 *in the* L. have I righteous.
25 *in the* L. seed of Is. justifi.
Zep. 3:2 trusted not *in the* L.
Acts 9:42 many believed *in t.* L.
14:3 speaking boldly *in the* L.
Rom. 16:2 ye receive her *in t.* L.
8 Amplias, my belov. *in t.* L.
12 who labored much *in t.* L.
13 Rufus chosen *in the* L.
22 Tertius, salute you *in t.* L.
1 *Cor.* 1:31 glorieth, let him glo. *in the* L. 2 *Cor.* 10:17
4:17 faith. *in* L. 7:22 call. *in* L.
7:39 be married, only *in the* L.
9:1 my work *in the* L. ?
2 apostleship are ye *in t.* L.
11:11 nor woman wi. man *in t.* L.
15:58 labor not in vain *in t.* L.
Eph. 2:21 a holy temple *in t.* L.
4:17 therefore, testify *in the* L.
5:8 now are ye light *in the* L.
6:1 obey your parents *in the* L.
10 brethren, be strong *in t.* L.
21 a faithful minister *in the* L.
Phil. 1:14 brethren *in the* L.
2:29 receive him theret. *in t.* L.
4:1 sta. fast *in t.* L. 1 *Thes.* 3:8
2 be of the same mind *in t.* L.
10 I rejoiced *in the* L. greatly
Col. 3:18 submit to husb. *in t.* L.
4:7 Tychicus fellow-ser. *in t.* L.
17 minist. th. received *in t.* L.
1 *Thes.* 5:12 th. over you *in t.* L.
2 *Thes.* 3:4 have confidence *in* L.
Phile. 16 the bond and *in t.* L.
20 let me have joy of thee *in t.* L. refr. my bowels *in t.* L.
Rev. 14:13 bless. are dead *in t.* L.

See REJOICE, TRUST.

LORD is.

Gen. 28:16 the L. *is* in this place
Ex. 9:27 the L. *is* righteous, I wicked, 2 *Chr.* 12:6
15:2 the L. *is* my strength
3 L. *is* man of war, L. *is* name
Num. 14:9 the L. *is* with us
18 the L. *is* long-suffering, of great, *Nah.* 1:3
42 for the L. *is* not among you
1 K. 8:60 know that the L. *is* G.
2 Chr. 13:10 the L. *is* our God
15:2 L. *is* wi. you wh. ye for h.
Ps. 10:16 the L. *is* king for ever
34:8 O taste and see L. *is* good
89:18 L. *is* our defence and king
92:15 show that L. *is* upright
93:1 L. *is* clothed with strength
94:22 L. *is* my defence and rock
95:3 the L. *is* a great G. 96:4; 99:2; 135:5
100:5 L. *is* g. 135:3; 145:9; *Jer.* 33:11; *Lam.* 3:25; *Nah.* 1:7
103:8 L. *is* merciful and gracious. 111:4; 145:8
113:4 L. *is* high ab. all nations
118:6 the L. *is* on my side
121:5 L. *is* keeper, L. *is* shade
125:2 the L. *is* round about
129:4 L. *is* righteous, 145:17: *Lam.* 1:18; *Dan.* 9:14
145:18 L. *is* nigh to all that call
Prov. 15:29 L. *is* far from wicked
Is. 30:18 L. *is* God of judgment
Jer. 10:10 the L. *is* the true God
17:7 trust in L. who. hope L. *is*
20:11 L. *is* with me as terri. one
Lam. 3:24 the L. *is* my portion
Ezek. 48:35 name of city, L. *is* t.
Amos 5:8 the L. *is* his name, 9:6
Zep. 3:5 just L. *is* in midst, 15
Luke 24:34 the L. *is* risen indeed
2 Cor. 3:17 the L. *is* that Spirit
Phil. 4:5 the L. *is* at hand
Heb. 13:6 the L. *is* my helper
1 Pet. 2:3 tasted the L. *is* graci.
See MADE.

My LORD.

Gen. 19:18 said, not so, *my* L.
Jud. 6:13 *my* L. if L. be wi. us
15 O *my* L. shall I save Israel
Ps. 16:2 said, Thou art *my* L.
35:23 stir up thyself, *my* God and *my* L. *John* 20:28
110:1 Lord said to *my* L. *Mat.* 22:44; *Mark* 12:36; *Luke* 20:42; *Acts* 2:34
Is. 21:8 *my* L. I stand on tower
Dan. 10:17 serv. of *my* L. talk ?
Zec. 1:9 O *my* L. wh. are these ?
4:4; 6:4; 4:5 no, *my* L. 13
Mat. 24:48 *my* L. delayeth his coming, *Luke* 12:45
Luke 1:43 mother of *my* L. come
John 20:13 taken away *my* L.
Phil. 3:8 knowledge of Ch. Jes.
my L.

Name of the LORD.

Gen. 12:8 A. called on *n. of t.* L.
26:25 Isaac called on *n. of t.* L.
Ex. 20:7 shalt not take *name of the* L. in vain, *Deut.* 5:11
33:19 proclaim *n. of the* L.
34:5 L. proclaimed *n. of the* L.
Lev. 24:11 blasphe. *n. of the* L. 16
Deut. 18:5 minister in *n. of t.* L. 7
22 prophet speak, in *n. of the* L.
28:10 called by the *n. of the* L.
32:3 I will publish *n. of the* L.
Jos. 9:9 serv. come of *n. of t.* L.
1 Sam. 17:45 come in *n. of t.* L.
20:42 sw. both of us in *n. of* L.
2 Sam. 6:2 called by *n. of the* L.
1 K. 22:16 that which is true in *name of the* L. 2 *Chr.* 18:15
Job 1:21 blessed be the *name of the* L. *Ps.* 113:2

Ps. 20:7 will remember *n. of t.* L.
102:15 heathen fear *n. of the* L.
21 to declare *n of* L. in Zion
113:1 praise the *name of t.* L. 135:1; 148:5, 13; *Joel* 2:26
116:4 then called I on *n. of* L.
118:26 cometh in *n. of the* L.
122:4 give thanks to *n. of t.* L.
124:8 our help is in *n. of t.* L.
129:8 we bless you in *n. of t.* L.
Prov. 18:10 *n. of* L. strong tower
Is. 18:7 to place of *n. of the* L.
24:15 glorify the *n. of t.* L.
30:27 *n. of t.* L. cometh fr. far
56:6 and to love the *n. of the* L.
59:19 so sh. they fear *n. of t.* L.
Jer. 3:17 nations gath. to *n. of* L.
Mic. 4:5 walk in *name of the* L.
5:4 in majesty of *n. of the* L.
Zep. 3:12 sh. trust in *n. of t.* L.
Mat. 21:9 cometh in *n. of the* L. 23:39; *Mark* 11:9, 10; *Luke* 13:35; 19:38; *John* 12:13
Acts 9:29 spake boldly in *n. of* L.
10:48 baptized in *n. of the* L.
19:13 call over them *n. of t.* L.
21:13 ready to die for *n. of t.* L.

O LORD.

Ex. 15:11 who like thee, *O* L. ?
2 Sam. 23:17 far from thee, *O* L.
1 Chr. 17:20 *O* L. none like thee
Ps. 6:3 but thou, *O* L. how long
8:1 *O* L. our Lord, how excel.
22:19 not far fr. me *O* L. 35:22
115:1 not unto us, *O* L.
Rev. 6:10 how long, *O* L. holy

Of the LORD.

2 K. 6:33 beh. this evil is *of* L.
Prov. 20:24 man's goings *of t.* L.
21:31 battle, safety is *of t.* L.
Acts 21:14 will *of t.* L. be done
1 Cor. 11:23 received *of the* L.
Jam. 5:11 seen the end *of the* L.

See ANGER, ANGEL, COMMAND-MENT, CONGREGATION, COUN-SEL, DAY, EYES, FACE, FEAR, FEAST, GLORY, HAND, HOUSE, KNOWLEDGE, LAW, OFFER-INGS, PRAISE.

Saith the LORD.

Num. 24:13 what the L. *s.*
1 K. 22:14 L. *s.* that will I speak

See LIVE, SAVED.

LORD, *with* seek.

1 Chr. 16:10 heart rejoice that *s.* L. *Ps.* 105:3, 4
11 *seek* the L. and his strength
22:19 set your heart to *seek* the L. 2 *Chr.* 11:16
2 Chr. 12:14 pr. not heart to *s.* L.
14:4 commanded Jud. to *s.* L.
15:13 whoso. would not *seek* L.
20:3 Jehosh. set himself to *s.* L.
4 cities of J. they came to *s.* L.
Ezr. 6:21 were come to *seek* L.
Ps. 32:26 praise L. that *s.* him
34:10 that *s.* L. shall not want
Prov. 28:5 th. *s.* L. understand
Is. 31:1; *Hos.* 7:10
51:1 ye that *seek* the L.
55:6 *s.* L. wh. he may be found
Jer. 50:4 go and *s.* the L. God
Hos. 3:5 return and *seek* the L.
5:6 go with herds to *s.* the L.
10:12 it is time to *seek* the L.
Amos 5:6 *s.* L. and ye shall live
Zep. 2:3 *s.* the L. meek of earth
Zec. 8:21 let us go and *s.* the L.
22 many people come and *s.* L.
Mal. 3:1 L. wh. ye *s.* sud. come
Acts 15:17 residue might *s.* the L.
17:27 ther should *s* the L.

LORD, *with* sent.

Ex. 7:16 L. of Hebrews *s.* me

Jer. 28:9 L. hath truly *sent* him
15 Hananiah, L. hath not *s.*
Acts 9:17 L. Jesus *s.* me to thee
12:11 know L. hath *sent* angel

Serve the LORD.

Ex. 10:7 that they may *s. t.* L.
22:25 ye shall *s. t.* L. your God
Deut. 10:12 to *s. t.* L. thy God
Jos. 24:14 fear and *s.* ye the L.
15 seem evil un. you to *s. t.* L.
18 therefore will we *s.* L. 21, 24
1 Sam. 12:20 *s.* L. with your hea.
2 Sam. 15:8 then I will *s.* L.
2 Chr. 30:8 *s.* L. your God, 35:3
33:16 com. Judah to *s.* L. 34:33
Ps. 2:11 *s.* L. wi. fear, rejoice
100:2 *serve t.* L. with gladness
102:22 kingdoms gather. to *s.* L.
Col. 3:24 ye *serve t.* L. Christ

Servant, *s* of the LORD.

Deut. 34:5 Moses, the *s. of t.* L.
Jos. 1:1 death of Moses *s. of* L.
13 Moses the *servant of the* L. commanded, 8:31, 33; 11:12; 22:2, 5; 2 *K.* 18:12
15 Moses, *s. of the* L. gave you, 12:6; 13:8; 18:7; 22:4
24:29 Joshua, son of Nun, *s. of the* L. *Jud.* 2:8
Ps. 113:1 praise the L. praise, O ye *servants of the* L. 135:1
134:1 O ye *servants of the* L.
Is. 42:19 blind or deaf as L.'s *s.*
54:17 heritage of *s. of the* L.
2 Tim. 2:24 *s. of the* L. not strive

See SHOWED.

Sight of the LORD.

Gen. 38:7 Er wicked in *s. of the* L.
Lev. 10:19 accepted in *s. of t.* L.
Deut. 6:18 good in *s. of* L. 12:28
12:25 do what is right in *s. of the* L. 21:9; 2 *K.* 12:2; 14:3; 15:3, 24; 18:3; 22:2; 2 *Chr.* 20:32; 24:2; 25:2; 26:4; 27:2; 29:2; 34:2
1 Sam. 12:17 wicked. ha. done in *s. of* L. 1 *K.* 11:25; 2 *K.* 21:6
2 K. 3:18 light thing in *s. of* L.
16:2 did not what was right in *s. of the* L. 2 *Chr.* 28:1
Ps. 116:15 precious in *s. of t.* L.
Mal. 2:17 good in *s. of the* L.
Luke 1:15 be great in *s. of t.* L.
2 Cor. 8:21 not only in *s. of t.* L.
Jam. 4:10 humble in *s. of the* L.

See EVIL, SMITE.

Spirit of the LORD.

Jud. 3:10 *S. of the* L. came on O.
6:34 *S. of the* L. came on Gid.
11:29 *S. of the* L. came on Jep.
13:25 *S. of the* L. began to move Samson, 14:6, 19; 15:14
1 Sam. 10:6 *S. of the* L. ca. on S.
16:13 *S. of the* L. came on Day.
14 *S. of the* L. depart. from S.
2 Sam. 23:2 *S. of the* L. spake
1 K. 18:12 *S. of* L. sh. carry thee
22:24 which way went *S. of the* L. 2 *Chr.* 18:23
2 K. 2:16 lest *S. of* L. taken him
2 Chr. 20:14 on Ja. came *S. of* L.
Is. 11:2 *S. of* L. sh. rest upon him
40:7 bec. *S. of* L. bloweth on it
13 hath directed *S. of the* L.
59:19 *S. of* L. sh. lift up stand.
61:1 *S. of* L. up. me, *Luke* 4:18
63:14 *S. of* L. caused him rest
Ezek. 11:5 *S. of* L. fell upon me
37:1 carried me in *S. of the* L.
Mic. 2:7 is the *S. of* L. straitened
3:8 full of power by *S. of* L.
Acts 5:9 to tempt *S. of* L.
8:39 *S. of* L. caught away Philip
2 Cor. 3:17 wh. *S. of t.* L. liberty
18 even as by *S. of the* L.

LORD, with spoken.
Ex. 19:8 all L. hath *s.* will we do
34:32 in command. all L. had *s.*
Num. 10:29 the L. hath *s.* good
12:2 hath L. indeed *s.* by Moses
Jos. 21:45 failed not L. had *s.*
1 *Sam.* 3:18 do it, the L. hath *s.*
2 *Sam.* 3:18 do it, the L. hath *s.*
7:29 continue, thou, L. ha. *s.* it
1 *K.* 13:3 sign which L. hath *s.*
Ps. 50:1 L. hath *s.* and called
Jer. 23:35 what hath the L. *s.* 37
48:8 destroyed, as the L. hath *s.*
Ezek. 22:28 when L. hath not *s.*
26:5 for I have *s.* it, saith the
L. 28:10 ; 39:5
Amos 3:8 L. God hath *spoken*
Mat. 1:22 wh. was *s.* of L. 2:15
Mark 16:19 after L. had *spoken*
Acts 9:27 seen L. and he had *s.*
Heb. 2:3 began to be *s.* by the L.

Temple of the LORD.
2 *Chr.* 26:16 U. went in. *t.* of L.
Jer. 7:4 *t.* of the L. are these
Ezek. 8:16 at door of *t.* of L. 25
men, with backs to. *t.* of L.
Hag. 2:15 bef. sto. laid in *t.* of L.
Zec. 6:12 build *t.* of L. 13:15
14 for memorial in *t.* of the L.
Luke 1:9 Z. went into *t.* of L.

Voice of the LORD.
Ps. 29:3 v. of L. is upon waters
106:25 heark. not to *v.* of *t.* L.
Is. 6:8 I heard *v.* of the L.
Acts 7:31 v. of the L. came to M.

Way of the LORD.
Gen. 18:19 house. keep *w.* of L.
Jud. 2:22 will keep *way* of *t.* L.
Ps. 119:1 blessed walk *w.* of L.
Prov. 10:29 *way* of L. is streng.
Is. 40:3 prepare ye *w.* of the L.
Mat. 3:4 ; *Mark* 1:3 ; *Lu.* 3:4
Jer. 5:4 know not *w.* of the L.
John 1:23 make stra. *w.* of the L.
Acts 18:25 Apollos in. in *w.* of L.

Ways of the LORD.
2 *Sam.* 22:22 for I have kept the
w. of the L. *Ps.* 18:21
2 *Chr.* 17:6 lifted up in *w.* of L.
Ps. 138:5 sing in the *w.* of L.
Hos. 14:9 the *w.* of L. are right
Acts 13:10 cease perv. *w.* of *t.* L.

Word of the LORD.
Num. 22:18 can. go bey. *w.* of L.
Deut. 5:5 show you *w.* of L.
2 *Sam.* 22:31 *w.* tried, *Ps.* 18:30
1 *K.* 13:1 came man by *w.* of L.
2 cried ag. altar in *word* of L.
17:24 *w.* of L. in my mouth
2 *K.* 10:10 earth noth. of *w.* of L.
20:19 good is *w.* of L. *Is.* 39:8
Ps. 33:4 the *word* of L. is right
6 by *w.* of L. heavens made
105:19 *w.* of L. tried him
Is. 2:3 the *word* of the L. from
Jerusalem, *Mic.* 4:2
Jer. 2:31 see ye the *w.* of the L.
Amos 8:12 to seek *w.* of L.
Zep. 2:5 *w.* of L. against you
Zec. 4:6 *w.* of L. to Zerubbabel
1 *Thes.* 1:8 sounded out *w.* of L.
4:15 say unto you by *w.* of L.
2 *Thes.* 3:1 *w.* of L. ha. free cou.
1 *Pet.* 1:25 *w.* of L. endu. for. ev.

Words of the LORD.
Ex. 24:3 M. told people all *w.* of
the L. *Num.* 11:24
4 Moses wrote all *w.* of the L.
2 *Chr.* 29:15 came by *w.* of the L.
Ps. 12:6 *w.* of the L. pure words
Jer. 36:4 Bar. wrote all *w.* of L.
Amos 8:11 fam. of hear. *w.* of L.

See CAME, HEAR.

Work of the LORD.
Ex. 34:10 people see *w.* of the L.

Is. 5:12 regard not *w.* of the L.
Jer. 48:10 cursed doth *w.* of L.
50:25 this is the *work* of the L.
51:10 declare in Z. the *w.* of L.
1 *Cor.* 15:58 abound in *w.* of L.
16:10 worketh the *w.* of the L.

Works of the LORD.
Jos. 24:31 known all *w.* of L.
Jud. 2:7 seen all great *w.* of L.
Ps. 28:5 regard not *w.* of L.
46:8 behold great *w.* of the L.
77:11 I will remember *w.* of L.
107:24 these see the *w.* of the L.
111:2 *works* of the L. are great
118:17 declare the *w.* of the L.

Wrath of the LORD.
Num. 11:33 *w.* of the L. kindled
Deut. 11:17 *w.* of L. kindle aga.
2 *K.* 22:13 for great is the *wrath*
of the L. 2 *Chr.* 34:21
2 *Chr.* 12:12 *wrath* of L. turned
29:8 *w.* of the L. upon Judah
32:26 *w.* of L. came not on them
36:16 until *wrath* of L. arose
Ps. 106:40 *w.* of the L. kindled
Is. 9:19 thro' *w.* of L. land dark.
13:13 earth rem. in *w.* of the L.
Jer. 50:13 because of *w.* of the L.
Ezek. 7:19 gold not deliver them
in day of *w.* of *t.* L. *Zep.* 1:18

LORD, as applied to man.
Gen. 18:12 I am old, L. being old
27:29 be *l.* over thy brethren
37 I have made him thy *l.*
32:4 thus shall ye speak to my *l.*
18 it is a pres. sent to my *l.* E.
42:10 nay, my *l.* but to buy food
30 man who is *l.* of the land, 33
45:8 made me *l.* of all his house
9 God made me *l.* of all Egypt
Num. 12:11 my *l.* I beseech thee
36:2 the Lord commanded my *l.*
Jud. 4:18 turn in, my *l.* turn in
19:26 woman fell wh. her *l.* was
Ruth 2:13 fav. in thy sight, my *l.*
1 *Sam.* 1:26 my *l.* as thy soul liv.
26:17 my voice, my *l.* O king
2 *Sam.* 14:17 so is my *l.* the king
19 turn fr. aught *l.* hath spok.
1 *K.* 1:37 Lord been with my *l.*
2 *K.* 5:3 would God my *l.* were
6:26 saying, Help, my *l.* O king
7:2 *l.* on which hand king le. 17
8:5 my *l.* O king, this is woman
Ps. 12:4 who is *l.* over us?
Jer. 22:18 saying, Ah *l.* 34:5
37:20 now, I pray thee, my *l.*
38:9 my *l.* the king, these men
Dan. 2:10 no *l.* asked such thin.
4:24 come saying of *l.* the king.
Mat. 10:24 nor is serv. above *l.*
25 enough that ser. be as his *l.*
18:26 *l.* have patience with me
31 told their *l.* all that was do.
24:48 my *l.* delayeth, *Lu.* 12:45
Luke 12:36 men wait for their *l.*
16:3 *l.* taketh away stewardship
5 called *l.'s* debtors to him,
How mu. ow. thou to my *l.*?
John 15:15 know not what *l.* do.
20 serv. not greater than his *l.*
Acts 25:26 noth. to write to my *l.*
Gal. 4:1 fr. servant, tho' *l.* of all
1 *Pet.* 3:6 Abraham. call. him *l.*

LORDS.
Gen. 19:2 behold, now, my *l.*
Num. 21:28 consumed *l.* of high
Deut. 10:17 is Lord of *l.* 1 *Tim.*
6:15 ; *Rev.* 17:14
Jud. 16:5 *l.* of Philistines ca. up
30 the house fell upon the *l.*
1 *Sam.* 5:8 gathered *l.* of Phil. 11
7:7 *l.* of Philistines went ag. Is.
Ezr. 8:25 offering which *l.* offer.
Is. 16:8 *l.* of heathen bro. plants
26:13 other *l.* have dominion

Jer. 2:31 say my peop. we are *l.*
Dan. 5:1 feast to thous. of his *l.*
23 and thy *l.* have drunk wine
6:17 sealed with signet of *l.*
Mark 6:21 H. make supper to *l.*
1 *Cor.* 8:5 gods many, and. *l.* ma.
1 *Pet.* 5:3 ne. being *l.* over God's

LORDSHIP.
Mark 10:42 they rule over Gentiles exercise *l.* *Luke* 22:25

LO-RUHAMAH. *Hos.* 1:6, 8

LOSE, ETH.
Job 31:39 the owners *l.* their life
Prov. 23:8 and *l.* thy sweet wor.
Ec. 3:6 time to get, time to *l.*
Mat. 10:39 he that findeth his
life shall *l.* it, 16:25 ; *Mark*
8:35 ; *Luke* 9:24
39 he that *l.* his life for my sa.
42 no wise *l.* reward, *Mark* 9:41
16:26 and *l.* his own soul, *Mark*
8:36 ; *Luke* 9:25
Luke 15:4 if he *l.* one sheep
8 ten pieces of silver, if she *l.*
17:33 who shall *l.* his life prese.
John 6:39 I should *l.* nothing
12:25 that lov. his life shall *l.* it
2 *John* 8 look that we *l.* none

LOSS.
Ex. 21:19 sh. pay for *l.* of time
Acts 27:21 gain. this harm and *l.*
22 sh. be no *l.* of any man's li.
1 *Cor.* 3:15 burned, he sh. suf. *l.*
Phil. 3:7 those I counted *l.* for C.
8 I counted all things *l.* for C.
for wh. I suffered the *l.* of all

LOST, passively.
Ex. 22:9 any manner of *l.* thing,
Deut. 24:3
Lev. 6:3 found that which was *l.*
4 restore *l.* th. wh. he found
Num. 6:12 days th. were sh. be *l.*
1 *Sam.* 9:3 asses of Kish were *l.*
20 asses that were *l.* are found
Ps. 119:176 astray like *l.* sheep
Jer. 50:6 peo. hath been *l.* sheep
Ezek. 19:5 saw that hope was *l.*
34:4 nor sought that wh. was *l.*
16 I will seek that which was *l.*
37:11 they say, Our hope is *l.*
Mat. 10:6 rather to the *l.* sheep
15:24 not sent but to *l.* sheep
18:11 Son is come to save what
was *l.* *Luke* 19:10
Luke 15:4 go after that wh. is *l.*
6 I found my sheep which is *l.*
24 son was *l.* 32 brother was *l.*
John 6:12 fragments, noth. be *l.*
17:12 none is *l.* but son of perd.
2 *Cor.* 4:3 gospel hid to th. that *l.*

LOST, actively.
Deut. 22:3 thy brother's he ha. *l.*
1 *K.* 20:25 army like that thou *l.*
Is. 49:20 after thou hast *l.* other
21 seeing I have *l.* my children
Mat. 5:13 if salt *l.* savor, *Mark*
9:50 ; *Luke* 14:34
Luke 15:9 I found piece wh. I *l.*
John 18:9 gav. me, I have *l.* none

LOT.
Gen. 11:27 Haran begat L. 31
13:5 L. had flocks, 7, 11 ; 14:12
19:1 L. sat in gate of Sod. 10, 36
Ps. 83:8 holpen children of L.
Luke 17:32 remember L. wife
2 *Pet.* 2:7 deliver just L. vexed

LOT.
Lev. 16:8 one *l.* for the L. 9, 10
Num. 26:55 land shall be divided
by *l.* *Ezek.* 48:29
33:54 he sh. divide the land by
l. 36:2 ; *Jos.* 13:6 ; *Ezek.* 47:22
34:13 the land ye sh. inhe. by *l.*
Deut. 32:9 J. is *l.* of inheritance

Jos. 15:1 the *l.* of tribe of Judah
16:1 *l.* of Joseph ; 17:1 Manas.
17:14 hast given me but one *l. ?*
18:11 the *l.* of tribe of Benjamin
19:1 second *l.* came forth to Si.
10 third *l.* came for Zebulon
17 fourth *l.* came out to Issac.
19:24 fifth *l.* to tribe of Asher
32 and the sixth *l.* to Napthali
40 sev. *l.* came for tribe of Dan
21:4 *l.* for Kohath. 1 *Chr.* 6:54
Jud. 1:3 come up with me into
my *l.* to fight ag. Canaanites
20:9 we will go up by *l.* aga. it
1 *Sam.* 14:41 G. give me perfe. *l.*
1 *Chr.* 16:18 Canaan, *l.* of your
inheritance, *Ps.* 105:11
24:5 they were divided by *l.*
Ps. 16:5 thou maintainest my *l.*
125:3 not rest on *l.* of righteous
Prov. 1:14 cast in *l.* among us
16:33 the *l.* is cast into the lap
18:18 *l.* caus. contentions cease
Is. 17:14 *l.* of them that rob us
34:17 hast cast the *l.* for them
57:6 sm. stones of stream thy *l.*
Jer. 13:25 this is thy *l.* from me
Ezek. 24:6 let no *l.* fall upon it
Dan. 12:13 shall stand in thy *l.*
Mic. 2:5 none th. cast cord by *l.*
Luke 1:9 his *l.* was to burn ince.
Acts 1:26 the *l.* fell on Matthias
8:21 thou hast no *l.* in matter
13:19 he divided their land by *l.*

LOTS.

1 *Sam.* 14:42 cast *l.* bet. me and
1 *Chr.* 24:31 cast *l.* ag. brethren
Mat. 27:35 casting *l. Mark* 15:24
Acts 1:26 they gave forth their *l.*

See CAST.

LOTHE. See LOATHE.

LOUD.

Ps. 33:3 play skillf. wi. *l.* noise
98:4 make a *l.* noise and rejoice
150:5 praise him on *l.* cymbals

LOUD, *with voice, s.*

Gen. 39:14 I cried with a *l. voice*
Ex. 19:16 *v.* of trump. exceed. *l.*
Deut. 27:14 Lev. speak with *l. v.*
1 *Sam.* 15:23 wept with *l. v.*
1 *K.* 8:55 he blessed with a *l. v.*
Prov. 27:14 bles. friend with *l. v.*
Ezek. 8:18 they cry with a *l. voi.*
9:1 he cried with a *l. voice*
Luke 1:42 spake out with a *l. v.*
8:28 sp. cried with *l. v. Acts* 8:7
17:15 with a *l. v.* glorified God
23:23 were instant with *l. voices*
Acts 14:10 said with a *l. v.* Stand
26:24 Festus said with a *l. v.* P.
Rev. 5:2 angel proclaim. wi. *l. v.*
12 angels saying with a *l. v.*
8:13 angel saying with a *l. voice,*
Woe, woe 14:7, 9, 15
12:10 I heard a *l. v.* in heaven

LOUDER.

Ex. 19:19 trumpet wax. *l.* and *l.*

LOVE.

2 *Sam.* 1:26 passing *l.* of women
13:15 hatred greater than *l.*
Prov. 5:19 be ravish. with her *l.*
7:18 let us take our fill of *l.*
10:12 up strifes, *l.* covereth sins
15:17 a dinner of herbs wh. *l.* is
17:9 covereth transg. seeketh *l.*
27:5 rebuke better than secret *l.*
Ec. 9:1 no man knoweth *l.*
6 their *l.* and hatred is perish.
Cant. 2:4 and his banner was *l.*
5 comf. me, I am sick of *l.* 5:8
3:10 midst being paved with *l.*
7:6 how pleas. O *l.* for delights !
8:6 *l.* is strong as death, jealous.
7 many waters cannot quen. *l.*
Jer. 2:2 the *l.* of thy espousals

33 why trim. way to seek *l. ?*
31:3 loved thee with everlast. *l.*
Ezek. 16:8 thy time was ti. of *l.*
23:11 corrupt in her inordin. *l.*
17 B. came to her to bed of *l.*
33:31 mouth they show much *l.*
Dan. 1:9 bro. Daniel to tender *l.*
Hos. 3:1 according to the *l.* of L.
11:4 I drew them wi. ban. of *l.*
Mal. 24:12 *l.* of many wax cold
John 13:35 have *l.* one to anoth.
15:13 greater *l.* hath no man
17:26 *l.* wherewith th. loved me
Rom. 8:35 separate from *l.* of C. ?
12:9 *l.* be without dissimulation
10 affectioned with brother. *l.*
13:10 *l.* work. no ill, *l.* is fulfil.
15:30 I beseech you for *l.* of Sp.
2 *Cor.* 2:4 that you may know *l.*
8 confirm your *l.* toward him
5:14 *l.* of Christ constraineth us
6:6 Holy Ghost, by *l.* unfeigned
8:8 prove the sincerity of yo. *l.*
24 show the proof of your *l.*
13:11 God of *l.* shall be with you
Gal. 5:6 faith which work. by *l.*
13 by *l.* serve one another
22 the fruit of the Spirit is *l.*
Eph. 1:15 after I heard of your *l.*
3:19 to know the *l.* of Christ
6:23 and *l.* with faith from God
Phil. 1:9 th. your *l.* may abound
17 the other of *l.* doth preach
2:1 if there be any comfort of *l.*
2 like-minded, have the same *l.*
Col. 1:4 *l.* wh. ye have to saints
8 declared to us your *l.* in Spi.
1 *Thes.* 1:3 rememb. labor of *l.*
4:9 as touching brotherly *l.*
5:8 on breastpla. of faith and *l.*
2 *Thes* 2:10 receiv. not *l.* of tru.
1 *Tim.* 1:14 abun. wi. faith and *l.*
6:10 *l.* of money is root of all e.
11 fol. righteousn. *l.* patience
2 *Tim.* 1:7 not spi. of fear, but *l.*
Phile. 9 for *l.* sake I beseech thee
Heb. 6:10 work and labor of *l.*
10:24 unto *l.* and to good works
13:1 let brotherly *l.* continue
1 *Pet.* 1:22 unfeigned *l.* of breth.
1 *John* 2:15 *l.* of F. is not in him
3:1 behold what *l.* Father ha.
4:7 love one another, *l.* is of G.
8 God is *l.* 10 herein is *l.*
15 known the *l.* God hath to
17 herein is our *l.* made perfect
18 there is no fear in *l.* perf. *l.*
2 *John* 6 this is *l.* that we walk
Jude 2 peace and *l.* be multiplied
Rev. 2:4 thou hast left thy first *l.*

LOVE of God.

Luke 11:42 judgm. and *l.* of G.
John 5:42 ye have not *l.* of G.
Rom. 5:5 *l. of G.* is shed in hea.
8:39 to separa. us fr. the *l. of G.*
2 *Cor.* 13:14 *l. of G.* be with you
2 *Thes.* 3:5 dir. hearts to *l. of G.*
Tit. 3:4 kindness and *l. of G.*
1 *John* 2:5 in him veri. is *l. of G.*
3:16 hereby perceive we *l. of G.*
17 how dwell. *l. of G.* in him ?
4:9 manifest. *l. of G.* toward us
5:3 the *l. of G.* that we keep
Jude 21 keep yoursel. in *l. of G.*

His LOVE.

Deut. 7:7 L. did not set *h. l.* on
Ps. 91:14 hath set *h. l.* upon me
Is. 63:9 in *h. l.* and pity he red.
Zep. 3:17 he will rest in *his l.*
John 15:10 abide in *his l.*
Rom. 5:8 G. commended *h. l.*
1 *John* 4:12 *his l.* perfected in us

In LOVE.

1 *K.* 11:2 Sol. clave to these *in l.*
Is. 38:17 *in l.* to my soul deliver.
1 *Cor.* 4:21 I co. wi. rod or *in l. ?*

2 *Cor.* 8:7 as ye abound *in l.* to
Eph. 1:4 with bla. bef. him *in l.*
3:17 rooted and grounded *in l.*
4:2 forbearing one another *in l.*
15 but speaking the truth *in l.*
Eph. 4:16 edifying of itself *in l.*
5:2 walk *in l.* as C. hath loved
Col. 2:2 being knit together *in l.*
1 *Thes.* 3:12 make you incr. *in l.*
5:13 esteem them *in l.* for wor.
2 *Tim.* 1:13 *in* faith and *l.* in Ch.
1 *John* 4:16 dwe. *in l.* dwel. in G.
18 there is no fear *in l.*
2 *John* 3 Son of F. *in* tru. and *l.*

My LOVE.

Ps. 109:4 for *my l.* th. are adver.
5 reward. me hatred for *my l.*
Cant. 1:9 com. O *my l.* to horses
15 behold, th. art fair, *my l.* 4:1
2:2 as lily, so is *my l.* am. daug.
7 not awake *my l.* my fair one, 13
10 rise up, *my l.* my fair one, 13
4:7 *my l.* there is no spot in thee
5:2 open to *my l.* my dove
6:4 beautiful, O *my l.* as Tirzah
John 15:9 continue ye in *my l.*
10 ye shall abide in *my l.*
1 *Cor.* 16:24 *my l.* be with you all

Thy LOVE.

Cant. 1:2 *t. l.* bet. th. wine, 4:10
4 remem. *t. l.* more than wine
4:10 how fair is *thy l.* my sister
Phile. 5 hearing of *t. l.* and faith
7 joy and consolation in *thy l.*
Rev. 2:4 thou hast left *thy* first *l.*

LOVE. Verb.

Lev. 19:18 thou shalt *l.* thy
neighbor as thyself, 34 ; *Mat.*
19:19 ; 22:39 ; *Mark* 12:31
Deut. 6:5 thou shalt *l.* the L. thy
G. with all thy heart, 10:12 ;
11:1, 13, 22 ; 19:9 ; 30:6
7:9 faithful G. keepeth covenant
with th. th. *l.* him, *Dan.* 9:4
13 he will *l.* thee, bless
10:15 delight in fathers to *l.* th.
19 *l.* therefore the stranger
13:3 to know whether ye *l.* L.
30:16 I command thee to *l.* L.
20 that thou mayest *l.* the L.
Jos. 22:5 take heed to *l.* L. 23:11
Jud. 5:31 them that *l.* him
1 *Sam.* 18:22 king's serv. *l.* thee
2 *Chr.* 19:2 shoul. thou *l.* them?
Neh. 1:5 mercy for th. th. *l.* him
Ps. 4:2 how *l.* will ye *l.* vanity?
5:11 them that *l.* thy name
18:1 I will *l.* thee, O Lord
31:23 O *l.* the Lord, all ye saints
40:16 such as *l.* thy salvat. 70:4
69:36 they that *l.* his name shall
97:10 ye that *l.* the L. hate evil
119:132 to those that *l.* thy na.
165 peace have they who *l.* thy
122:6 they prosper that *l.* thee
145:20 L. pres. them that *l.* him
Prov. 1:22 simple, will ye *l.* sim.
4:6 *l.* wisdom, she sh. keep thee
8:36 they that hate me, *l.* death
9:8 reb. wise man he will *l.* thee
16:13 kings *l.* him speak. right
18:21 they that *l.* it sh. eat fruit
Ec. 3:8 time to *l.* time to hate
Cant. 1:3 do the virgins *l.* thee
4 more th. wine, upright *l.* th.
Is. 56:6 serve and *l.* name of L.
61:8 I the Lord *l.* judgment
66:10 be glad all ye that *l.* her
Jer. 5:31 my peo. *l.* to have it so
Hos. 3:1 L. woman belov. flagons
4:18 her rulers with shame do *l.*
9:15 I will *l.* them no more
14:4 I will *l.* them freely
Amos 5:15 hate evil and *l.* good
Mic. 3:2 who hate good and *l. e.*
6:8 *l.* mercy and do walk hum.

Zec. 8:17 and *l.* no false oath
19 therefore *l.* truth and peace
Mat. 5:43 said, *l.* thy neighbor
44 but I say, *l.* your enemies,
   Luke 6:27, 32, 35
46 if ye *l.* them which *l.* you
6:5 *l.* to pray, in synagogues
24 hate one *l.* other, *Luke* 16:13
22:37 th. shall *l.* L. thy G. *Mark*
   12:30, 33 ; *Luke* 10:27
23:6 *l.* upper rooms at feasts
Mark 12:38 *l.* to go in long cloth.
Luke 7:42 wh. will *l.* him most ?
11:43 *l.* greet. in markets, 20:46
John 14:21 I *l.* him mani. myself
23 if a man *l.* me, Fath. *l.* him
15:12 that ye *l.* one another, 17
19 the world would *l.* his own
Rom. 8:28 good to them th. *l.* G.
13:8 any thing, but to *l.* one an.
9 thou shalt *l.* thy neighbor as
   thyself, *Gal.* 5:14 ; *Jam.* 2:8
1 *Cor.* 2:9 G. for them that *l.* him
8:3 if any man *l.* G. same
   known
Eph. 5:25 husb. *l.* your wives as
   C. loved ch. 28, 33 ; *Col.* 3:19
6:24 grace be with th. *l.* our L.
1 *Thes.* 4:9 taught to *l.* one ano.
2 *Tim.* 4:8 them that *l.* his ap.
Tit. 2:4 young women to *l.* hus.
3:15 greet them that *l.* us in fa.
Jam. 1:12 them that *l.* him, 2:5
1 *Pet.* 1:8 whom not seen, ye *l.*
22 *l.* one ano. with pure heart
2:17 honor men, *l.* brotherhood
3:8 as *l.* brethren ; 10 that *l.* life
1 *John* 2:15 *l.* not the world
3:11 fr. begin. that we should *l.*
   one anoth. 4:7, 11 ; 2 *John* 5
14 because we *l.* the brethren
23 *l.* one another, as he gave
4:12 if we *l.* one another
19 *l.* him bec. he first loved us
20 can he *l.* G. hath not seen
21 loveth God *l.* his brother al.
5:2 we *l.* the children of God

I LOVE

Ex. 21:5 sh. say, *I l.* my master
Jud. 16:15 canst thou say, *I l.*
2 *Sam.* 13:4 *I l.* Tamar, my broth.
Ps. 116:1 *I l.* L. bec. he heard
119:97 O how *I l.* thy law
   113 but thy law do *I l.* 163
119 theref. *I l.* thy testimonies
127 *I l.* thy commands ab. gold
159 consi. how *I l.* thy precepts
167 thy testimonies *I l.* exce.
Prov. 8:17 *I l.* them that *l.* me
John 14:31 know th. *I l.* the Fa.
21:15 L. knowest *I l.* thee, 16, 17
2 *Cor.* 12:15 tho' the more *I l.* you
1 *John* 4:20 if a man say, *I l.* God
2 *John* 1 *I l.* in the truth, 3 *John* 1
Rev. 3:19 as many as *I l.* I rebuke

LOVE me.

Gen. 29:32 my husb. will *l.* me
Ex. 20:6 showing mercy to them
   that *l.* me, *Deut.* 5:10
Prov. 8:17 I love them that *l.* me
21 that *l.* me to inh. substance
John 8:42 G. your F. ye wo. *l.* me
10:17 theref. doth Father *l.* me
14:15 if ye *l.* me, keep my com.
23 man *l.* me, keep my words

LOVE not.

Prov. 20:13 *l.* not sleep
1 *Cor.* 16:22 if any man *l.* not L.
2 *Cor.* 11:11 because I *l.* you not ?
1 *John* 3:15 *l.* not the world
3:18 n. *l.* in word nor tongue

LOVED.

Gen. 24:67 took Rebe. and *l.* her
25:28 *l.* Esau, Rebekah *l.* Jacob
27:14 made such as his father *l.*
29:18 Jacob *l.* Rachel more, 30

34:3 Shechem *l.* Dinah
37:3 Israel *l.* Joseph more. 4
Deut. 4:37 bec. he *l.* thy fathers
7:8 because L. *l.* you, 23:5 ; 33:3
Jud. 16:4 Samson *l.* a woman
1 *Sam.* 1:5 Elkanah *l.* Hannah
16:21 and Saul *l.* David
18:1 Jonathan *l.* David, 3 ; 20:17
16 Israel and Judah *l.* David
20 Michal Saul's daught. *l.* D.
2 *Sam.* 12:24 the L. *l.* Solomon
13:1 Amnon son of David *l.* Ta.
15 love wherewith he *l.* her
1 *K.* 3:3 Solomon *l.* the Lord
10:9 the Lord *l.* Israel, 2 *Chr.* 9:8
11:1 Solomon *l.* many women
2 *Chr.* 2:11 and the Lord *l.* his
   people, *Is.* 48:14
11:21 Rehoboam *l.* Maachah
26:10 Uzziah *l.* husbandry
Est. 2:17 king *l.* Esther abo. all
Job 19:19 they whom I *l.* turned
Ps. 47:4 excellency of Jacob he *l.*
78:68 mount of Zion which he *l.*
109:17 *l.* cursing, so let it come
Jer. 8:2 host of heaven they *l.*
14:10 thus ha. they *l.* to wander
Ezek. 16:37 gather th. thou ha. *l.*
Hos. 9:1 thou hast *l.* a reward
10 abomina. according as th. *l.*
11:1 when Is. was child, I *l.* him
Mal. 1:2 wherein hast th. *l.* us ?
2:11 profaned holin. of L. he *l.*
Mark 10:21 J. beholding *l.* him
Luke 7:47 sins forgiven, *l.* much
John 3:16 God so *l.* the world
19 *l.* darkness rather th. light
11:5 Jesus *l.* Martha, and sister
36 said Jews, Behold how he *l.*
12:43 they *l.* the praise of men
13:1 hav. *l.* his own, he *l.* them
23 discip. whom Jesus *l.* 19:26 ;
   20:2 ; 21:7, 20
14:21 her that lov. me shall be *l.*
28 if ye *l.* me, ye would rejoice
15:9 as F. *l.* me, so I *l.* you
16:27 Father lov. you, ye *l.* me
17:23 hast *l.* them, as thou *l.* me
26 love wh. thou hast *l.*
Rom. 8:37 conquer. thro' him *l.*
2 *Cor.* 12:15 love you, less I be *l.*
Gal. 2:20 who *l.* me, gave hims.
Eph. 2:4 love wherewith he *l.* us
5:2 as Christ also hath *l.* us
   25 even as Christ *l.* the church
2 *Thes.* 2:16 God our F. ha. *l.* us
2 *Tim.* 4:10 Demas *l.* this world
Heb. 1:9 thou hast *l.* righteousn.
2 *Pet.* 2:15 Balaam *l.* the wages
1 *John* 4:10 not that we *l.* God
11 if God so *l.* us
19 love him, bec. he first *l.* us
Rev. 1:5 to him that *l.* us
12:11 *l.* not their lives to death

I have LOVED.

Ps. 26:8 *I have l.* thy house
119:47 commands wh. *I h.* .. 48
Is. 43:4 *I have l.* thee, therefore
Jer. 2:25 *I have l.* strangers
31:3 *I h. l.* with everlasting love
Mal. 1:2 *I have l.* you, say ye say
John 13:34 as *I ha. l.* you, 15:12
15:9 Father I. me so *I h. l.* you
Rom. 9:13 Jacob *I h. l.* but E.
Rev. 3:9 make them know *I h. l.*

LOVEDST.

Is. 57:8 thou *l.* their bed where
John 17:24 *l.* me bef. foundation

LOVELY.

2 *Sam.* 1:23 S. and Jo. *l.* in lives
Cant. 5:16 he is altogether *l.*
Ezek. 33:32 art to them as *l.* song
Phil. 4:8 whatsoev. things are *l.*

LOVER.

1 *K.* 5:1 Hiram was *l.* of David
Ps. 88:18 *l.* and friend hast put
Tit. 1:8 *l.* of hospitali. *l.* of men

LOVERS.

Ps. 38:11 *l.* and friends stand
Jer. 3:1 played harlot with ma. *l.*
4:30 thy *l.* will despise thee
22:20 for all thy *l.* are destroyed
22 thy *l.* shall go into captiv.
30:14 all thy *l.* have forgot. thee
Lam. 1:2 all her *l.* none to comf.
19 called for *l.* they deceiv. me
Ezek. 16:33 giv. gifts to all thy *l.*
36 nakedn. discover. wi. thy *l.*
23:22 raise up thy *l.* again. thee
Hos. 2:5 go after *l.* 7 follow *l.*
10 discover lewd. in sight of *l.*
12 rewards my *l.* ha. given me
8:9 Ephraim hath hired *l.*
2 *Tim.* 3:2 men be *l.* of own selves
4 *l.* of pleas. more than *l.* of G.

LOVES.

Prov. 7:18 solace ourselves wi. *l.*
Cant. 7:12 there I give thee my *l.*

LOVEST.

Jud. 14:16 hate me, and *l.* not
2 *Sam.* 19:6 thou *l.* thine enemies
Ps. 45:7 thou *l.* righteousness
52:3 thon *l.* evil more than good
4 thou *l.* all devouring words
Ec. 9:9 live with wife thou *l.*
John 11:3 he whom th. *l.* is sick
21:15 son of Zo. *l.* th. me ? 16:17

LOVETH.

Gen. 44:20 and his father *l.* him
Deut. 10:18 Lord *l.* the stranger
Ps. 11:5 him that *l.* violence
7 Lord *l.* righteousness, 33:5
34:12 man that *l.* many days ?
37:28 Lord *l.* judgment, 99:4
87:2 the Lord *l.* gates of Zion
119:140 word is pure, thy ser. *l.*
146:8 the Lord *l.* the righteous
Prov. 3:12 whom L. *l.* he correct.
12:1 *l.* instruction, *l.* knowledge
13:24 that *l.* him, chasten. him
15:9 *l.* him followeth aft. right.
12 scorner *l.* not one th. repro.
17:17 a friend *l.* at all times
19 *l.* transgres. that *l.* strife
19:8 getteth wisdom *l.* own soul
21:17 he that *l.* wine and oil
22:11 that *l.* pureness of heart
29:3 *l.* wisdom rejoiceth father
Ec. 5:10 th. *l.* silver, th. *l.* abun.
Cant. 1:7 O thou wh. my soul *l.*
3:2 seek him my soul *l.* 3, 4
Is. 1:23 every one *l.* gifts
Mat. 10:37 that *l.* fath. or mother
Luke 7:5 for he *l.* our nation
47 little is forgiven, *l.* little
John 3:35 Father *l.* Son, 5:20
12:25 that *l.* his life sh. lose it
14:21 hath com. he it is *l.* me,
   he that *l.* me be loved of Fa.
24 *l.* me not, keep. not sayings
John 16:27 the Fath. hims. *l.* you
Rom. 13:8 that *l.* another
Eph. 5:28 that *l.* wife *l.* himself
Heb. 12:6 whom L. *l.* he chasten.
1 *John* 2:10 he that *l.* his brother
3:10 he that *l.* not his brother
14 *l.* not broth. abideth 4:8, 20
4:7 ev. one that *l.* is born of G.
21 he who *l.* God, *l.* his brother
5:1 *l.* him begat, *l.* him begot.
Rev. 22:15 *l.* and maketh a lie

LOVING.

Prov. 5:19 let her be as *l.* hind
22:1 *l.* favor rather than silver
Is. 56:10 sleeping, *l.* to slumber

See KINDNESS, KINDNESSES.

LOW.

Deut. 28:43 sh. co. down very *l.*
1 *Sam.* 2:7 the Lord bringeth *l.*
2 *Chr.* 26:10 cattle in *l.* country
28:18 invaded cities of *l.* count.

Job 5:11 set on high th. that be *l.*
40:12 look on proud bring him *l.*
Ps. 49:2 high and *l.* rich and poor
62:9 men of *l.* degree are vanity
136:23 remember. us in *l.* estate
Prov. 29:23 man's pride br. him *l.*
Ec. 10:6 the rich sit in *l.* place
Is. 25:12 high walls sh. he lay *l.*
26:5 lofty city he layeth it *l.*
29:4 speech *l.* out of the dust
32:19 city sh. be *l.* in a *l.* place
Lam. 3:55 name out of *l.* dunge.
Ezek. 17:6 vine of *l.* stature
24 know I have exalted *l.* tree
21:26 exalt him that is *l.*
26:20 set th. in *l.* parts of earth
Luke 1:48 he regardeth *l.* estate
52 exalted them of *l.* degrec
Rom. 12:16 to men of *l.* estate
Jam. 1:9 brother of *l.* degree
10 rich in that he is made *l.*

See BROUGHT.

LOWER.
Lev. 13:20 ris. be in sight *l.* than
Neh. 4:13 set in *l.* places the peo.
Ps. 8:5 thou hast made him *l.* than the angels. *Heb.* 2:7, 9
63:9 go into *l.* parts of the earth
Prov. 25:7 *l.* in presen. of prince
Is. 22:9 gathered wat. of *l.* pool
44:23 shout ye *l.* parts of earth
Eph. 4:9 descended into *l.* parts

LOWERING.
Mat. 16:3 the sky is red and *l.*

LOWEST.
Deut. 32:22 shall burn to *l.* hell
1 *K.* 12:31 made priests of *l.* of people, 13:33 ; 2 *K.* 17:32
Ps. 86:13 deliv. soul from *l.* hell
88:6 thou hast laid me in *l.* pit
Luke 14:9 begin to take *l.* room
10 and sit down in the *l.* room

LOWETH, ING.
1 *Sam.* 15:14 kine went along *l.*
15:14 what meaneth *l.* of oxen ?
Job 6:5 *l.* the ox over his fodder ?

LOWLY.
Ps. 138:6 hath he respect to *l.*
Prov. 3:34 he giveth grace to *l.*
11:2 but with *l.* is wisdom
16:19 be of humble spirit wi. *l.*
Zec. 9:9 *l.* and riding on an ass
Mat. 11:29 for I am meek and *l.*

LOWLINESS.
Eph. 4:2 walk with *l.* and meek.
Phil. 2:3 in *l.* of mind, esteem

LUCAS. *Phile.* 24
LUCIFER. *Is.* 14:12
LUCIUS. *Acts* 13:1 ; *Rom.* 16:2

LUCRE.
1 *Sam.* 8:3 8. sons turned after *l.*
1 *Tim.* 3:3 bishop not greedy of *l.* 8
Tit. 1:7 not given to filthy *l.*
11 teach. things not for filthy *l.*
1 *Pet.* 5:2 flock not for filthy *l.*

LUKE. *Col.* 4:14 ; 2 *Tim.* 4:11

LUKEWARM.
Rev. 3:16 because thou art *l.*

LUMP.
2 *K.* 20:7 take *l.* of figs, *Is.* 38:21
Rom. 9:21 of same *l.* one vessel
11:16 first-fruit holy *l.* is holy
1 *Cor.* 5:6 leav. whole *l. Gal.* 5:9
7 old leav. that ye be a new *l.*

LUNATIC.
Mat. 4:24 those were *l.* he healed
17:15 mercy on my son, he *l.*

LURK.
Prov. 1:11 come, let us *l.* privily
18 they *l.* privily for own lives

LURKING.
1 *Sam.* 23:23 knowl. of *l.* places
Ps. 10:8 in *l.* places of villages
17:12 yo. lion *l.* in secret places

LUST.
Ex. 15:9 my *l.* shall be satisfied
Ps. 78:18 asking meat for th. *l.*
30 not estranged from their *l.*
81:12 up to their own hearts' *l.*
Rom. 1:27 burned in their *l.* one
7:7 had not known *l.* except law
Gal. 5:16 not fulfil *l.* of flesh
Jam. 1:14 when drawn of his *l.*
15 when *l.* hath conceived
2 *Pet.* 1:4 corrup. in world thro' *l.*
2:10 after flesh in *l.* of unclean.
1 *John* 2:16 *l.* of flesh, *l.* of eye
17 passeth away, and *l.* thereof

LUST, Verb.
Prov. 6:25 *l.* not after beauty
Mat. 5:28 look. on woman to *l.*
1 *Cor.* 10:6 not *l.* after evil things
Jam. 4:2 ye *l.* and have not

LUSTED, ETH.
Num. 11:34 buried people that *l.*
Deut. 12:15 what thy soul *l.* after, 20, 21 ; 14:26
Ps. 106:14 they *l.* exceedingly
1 *Cor.* 10:6 not lust as th. also *l.*
Gal. 5:17 flesh *l.* against the Sp.
Jam. 4:5 spirit in us *l.* to envy
Rev. 18:14 fruits thy soul *l.* after

LUSTING.
Num. 11:4 mixed multit. fell a *l.*

LUSTS.
Mark 4:19 *l.* of things cho. word
John 8:44 *l.* of father ye will do
Rom. 6:12 sho. obey in *l.* thereof
13:14 no provision, to fulfil *l.*
Gal. 5:24 crucified flesh with *l.*
Eph. 2:3 conversa. in *l.* of flesh
4:22 corrupt accord. to deceit. *l.*
1 *Tim.* 6:9 foolish and hurtful *l.*
2 *Tim.* 2:22 flee youthful *l.*
4:3 after own *l.* heap teachers
Tit. 2:12 that denying worldly *l.*
3:3 divers *l.* and pleasures
Jam. 4:1 hence, even of your *l. ?*
3 may consume it on your *l.*
1 *Pet.* 1:14 according to former *l.*
2:11 you abstain fr. fleshly *l.*
4:2 no longer live to *l.* of men

2 *Pet.* 2:18 allure thro' *l.* of flesh
Jude 16 complain. walk. after *l.*
18 walk after their ungodly *l.*

LUSTY.
Jud. 3:29 slew 10,000 men, all *l.*
LUZ. *Gen.* 28:19 ; 48:3 ; *Jud.* 1:23
LYCAONIA. *Acts* 14:6, 11
LYDDA. *Acts* 9:32. 35, 38
LYDIA. *Ezek.* 30:5 ; *Acts* 16:14,40

LYING.
Ps. 31:6 I have hated them that regard *l.* vanities.
18 let *l.* lips be put to silence
52:3 lovest *l.* rather than right.
59:12 cursing and *l.* they speak
109:2 spoken with *l.* tongue
119:29 remove fr. me way of *l.*
163 I hate and abhor *l.* but thy
120:2 deliver my soul fr. *l.* lips
Prov. 6:17 proud look, a *l.* tong.
10:18 hatred with *l.* lips is fool
12:19 *l.* tongue is for a moment
22 *l.* lips abomination to the L.
13:5 a righteous man hateth *l.*
17:7 do *l.* lips become a prince
21:6 treas. by *l.* tongue vanity
26:28 *l.* tongue hat. those afflict
Is. 30:9 rebellious peo. *l.* childr.
32:7 wicked devices, *l.* words
59:13 in *l.* against the Lord
Jer. 7:4 trust ye not in *l.* words
8 behold, ye trust in *l.* words
29:23 spo. *l.* words in my name
Ezek. 13:6 vanity and *l.* divina.
19 *l.* to my peo. that hear lies
Dan. 2:9 ye have prep. *l.* words
Hos. 4:2 swearing, *l.* and killing
Jon. 2:8 observe *l.* vanities forsa.
Eph. 4:25 put. away *l.* sp. truth
2 *Thes.* 2:9 whose coming is wi. *l.*

LYING.
Ex. 23:5 ass of him hateth th. *l.*
Ps. 139:3 my path and *l.* down
Is. 56:10 *l.* down, lov. to slumber
Luke 2:12 babe *l.* in manger, 16
John 13:25 *l.* on Jesus' breast
20:5 he saw the linen clothes *l.*
7 napkin not *l.* wi. lin. clothes

LYING spirit.
1 *K.* 22:22 a *l.* spi. in the mouth of prophets, 2 *Chr.* 18:21
23 Lord hath put a *l. spirit* in prophets, 2 *Chr.* 18:22

LYING in wait.
Jud. 16:9 th. were men *l.* in-w.
Lam. 3:10 as a bear *l.* in wait
Acts 20:19 by *l.* in wait of Jews
23:16 heard of their *l.* in wait

LYING with.
Gen. 34:7 *l.* with Jacob's daugh.
Num. 31:17 known man by *l. w.*
18 not kn. *l.* 35 ; *Jud.* 21:12
Deut. 22:22 man found *l. w.* wom.

LYSANIAS. *Luke* 3:1
LYSIAS. *Acts* 23:26
LYSTRA. *Acts* 14:6, 8 ; 16:1, 2 ; 2 *Tim.* 3:11

M

MAACHAH. *Gen.* 22:24 ; 2 *Sam.* 3:3 ; 1 *Chr.* 3:2
MAASEIAH.
2 *Chr.* 28:7 Zic. slew M. *Jer.* 21:1
MAATH. *Luke* 3:26
MACEDONIA.
Acts 16:9 into M. 18:5 ; 19:21
Rom. 15:26 pleased them of M.
2 *Cor.* 7:5 were come into M.
8:1 grace of God churches of M.
9:2 I boast of you to them of M.
11:9 brethren from M. supplied

1 *Thes.* 1:7 that believe in M. 8
4:10 brethren that are in M.
MACHIR. *Gen.* 50:23 ; *Nu.* 26:29; 27:1 ; 32:39 ; 36:1 ; *Jos.* 17:1 ; *Jud.* 5:14 ; 2 *Sam.* 9:4 ; 17:27
MACHPELAH. *Gen.* 23:9, 17, 19, 25:9 ; 49:30 ; 50:13

MAD.
Deut. 28:34 m. for sight of eyes
1 *Sam.* 21:13 feigned himself m.
2 *K.* 9:11 this m. fellow to thee
Ps. 102:8 they th. are m. ag. me

Ec. 2:2 it is m. of mirth
7:7 oppres. maketh wise man m.
Is. 44:25 maketh diviners m.
Jer. 25:16 be moved and be m.
29:26 man is m. put in prison
50:38 they are m. upon idols
51:7 theref. the nations are m.
Hos. 9:7 the spiritual man is m.
John 10:20 he hath devil, is m.
Acts 12:15 said to Rh. Th. art m.
26:11 being exceed. m. ag. th.
24 much learn. make thee m.
25 I am not m. most noble F.

1 *Cor.* 14:23 not say ye are *m. ?*

MADE, *meant of God, Lord, Christ.*

Gen. 1:31 G. saw ev. thing he *m.*
5:1 in liken. of G. *m.* he him, 9:6
6:6 repent. he had *m.* man, 7

I have MADE.

Gen. 7:4 destroy liv. sub. *I h. m.*

MADE haste.

Gen. 24:46 Rebekah *m. haste*
Jud. 13:10 Manoah's wife *m. h.*
2 *Sam.* 4:4 Mephib.'s nurse *m. h.*
Ps. 119:60 I *m. h.* delayed not
Luke 19:6 Zaccheus *m. h.*

See ISRAEL, SIN, KNOWN.

MADE manifest.

Luke 8:17 shall not be *m. m.*
John 1:31 that he sho. be *m. m.*
3:21 his deeds may be *m. m.*
9:3 works of God sho. be *m. m.*
Rom. 10:20 I was *m. m.* to them
16:26 now is *m. m.* to nations
1 *Cor.* 3:13 work shall be *m. m.*
11:19 approved may be *m. m.*
14:25 secrets of his heart *m. m.*
2 *Cor.* 4:10 J. should be *m. m.* 11
11:6 we have been thoro. *m. m.*
Eph. 5:13 approved are *m. m.*
Col. 1:26 *m. m.* to his saints
2 *Tim.* 1:10 now *m. m.* by Christ
Heb. 9:8 holiest not yet *m. m.*
1 *John* 2:19 they might be *m. m.*
Rev. 15:4 thy judgm. are *m. m.*

MADE peace.

Jos. 9:15 Joshua *m. p.* 10:1, 4
11:19 not a city *m. p.* with Isr.
2 *Sam.* 10:19 when the servants
of Hadarezer were smit. th.
m. p. with Isr. 1 *Chr.* 19:19
1 *K.* 22:44 Jehoshaphat *m. peace*

MADE ready.

Gen. 43:25 they *m. r.* present
46:29 Joseph *m. ready* chariot
Ex. 14:6 Pharaoh *m. r.* chariot
Jud. 6:19 G. went and *m. r.* kid
1 *Chr.* 28:2 had *m. r.* for building
Ps. 7:12 bent his bow and *m. r.*
Hos. 7:6 have *m. ready* their
heart
Mat. 26:19 discip. *m. r.* passov.
Mark 14:16; *Luke* 22:13
2 *Cor.* 10:16 boast of things *m. r.*
Rev. 19:7 wife hath *m.* herself *r.*

MADE void.

Num. 30:12 her husb. hath *m. v.*
Ps. 89:39 hast *m. v.* covenant
119:126 they have *m. v.* thy law
Rom. 4:14 law heirs, faith *m. v.*

MADE, *passively.*

John 1:3 all things *m.* by him,
without him not any th. *m.*
10 the world was *m.* by him
14 the Word was *m.* flesh
5:6 be *m.* whole ? 14 *m.* whole
8:33 be *m.* free; 9:39 *m.* blind

MADEST.

Jon. 4:10 neither *m.* it grow
Heb. 2:7 *m.* him low. th. angels

MAD man, men.

1 *Sam.* 21:15 ha. I need of *m. m.*
Prov. 26:18 *m. m.* casteth firebr.
Jer. 48:2 O *m. m.* sw. sh. pursue

**MADMANNAH, MADMENAH,
MADMEN,** *Jos.* 15:31; *Is.*
10:31; *Jer.* 48:2

MADNESS.

Deut. 28:28 smite thee with *m.*
Ec. 1:17 to know wisd. and *m.*
2:12 I turned myself to beh. *m.*
7:25 wickedness of folly and *m.*
9:3 *m.* is in heart, wh. they live
10:13 his talk is mischievous *m.*
Zec. 12:4 sm. horse and rider *m.*

Luke 6:11 they were filled w. *m.*
2 *Pet.* 2:16 dumb as forbade *m.*

MAGDALA. *Mat.* 15:39

MAGICIAN, S.

Gen. 41:8 Pharaoh called for *m.*
Ex. 7:11 the *m.* of Egypt did so
in like manner, 22 ; 8:7, 18
9:11 *m.* could not stand bef. M.
Dan. 1:20 ten times ber. than *m.*
2:2 king commanded to call *m.*
10 asked such things at any *m.*
4:7 then came in the *m.*
9 O Belteshazzar, master of *m.*
5:11 father made master of *m.*

MAGISTRATE, S.

Jud. 18:7 no *m.* in the land
Ezr. 7:25 Ezra set *m.* and judges
Luke 12:11 they bring you to *m.*
58 when thou goest to the *m.*
Acts 16:20 Paul and Silas to *m.*
22 *m.* commanded to beat them
35 the *m.* sent the serjeants, 36
Tit. 3:1 put th. in mi. to obey *m.*

MAGNIFICAL.

1 *Chr.* 22:5 the house must be *m.*

MAGNIFICENCE.

Acts 19:27 her *m.* sh. be destro.

MAGNIFY.

Jos. 3:7 will I begin to *m.*
Job 7:17 what is man that thou
shouldest *m.* him ?
19:5 if ye will *m.* yourselves
36:24 remember thou *m.* work
Ps. 34:3 O *m.* the Lord with me
35:26 cloth. with shame that *m.*
38:16 th. *m.* themselves ag. me
55:12 did *m.* himself against me
69:30 did *m.* him with thanksg.
Is. 10:15 saw *m.* itself ag. him ?
42:21 he will *m.* the law
Ezek. 38:23 thus will I *m.* myself
Dan. 8:25 *m.* himself in his heart
11:36 the king shall *m.* himself
Zec. 12:7 not *m.* thems. ag. Jud.
Luke 1:46 my soul doth *m.* the L.
Acts 10:46 sp. wi. tongues, *m.* G.
Rom. 11:13 apostle, I *m.* office

MAGNIFIED.

Gen. 19:19 hast *m.* thy mercy
2 *Sam.* 7:26 and let thy name be
m. 1 *Chr.* 17:24
1 *Chr.* 29:25 m. Solo. 2 *Chr.* 1:1
Ps. 35:27 let the Lord be *m.*
40:16 say contin. L. be *m.* 70:4
138:2 thou hast *m.* thy word
Jer. 48:26 *m.* hims. 42 ; *Dan.* 8:11
Lam. 1:9 enemy hath *m.* hims.
Zep. 2:8 *m.* against their border
Mal. 1:5 L. will be *m.* from Isr.
Acts 5:13 the people *m.* them
19:17 name of the L. J. was *m.*
Phil. 1:20 Ch. be *m.* in my body

MAGOG.

Gen. 10:2 ; 1 *Chr.* 1:5 ; *Ezek.* 38:2
Rev. 20:8 gather G. and M. battle

MAHALATH. 2 *Chr.* 11:18

MAHANAIM.

Gen. 32:2 J. called the place M.
1 *K.* 2:8 when I went to M.

**MAHER-SHALAL-HASH-
BAZ.**

Is. 8:1 write concerning M.

MAHLAH. *Num.* 26:33

MAHLON. *Ruth* 1:2, 5 ; 4:9,10

MAID.

Gen. 16:2 go in to my *m.*
6 behold, thy *m.* is in thy hand
30:3 behold, my *m.* Bilhah
Ex. 2:5 she sent her *m.*
8 *m.* went and called mother
21:20 if a man smite his *m.*
22:16 if man entice *m.* not betr.
Deut. 22:14 fou. her not a *m.* 17
2 *K.* 5:2 bro. captive little *m.*

Est. 2:7 *m.* fair and beautiful
Job 31:1 why sho. I think on *m. ?*
Prov. 30:19 way of man with *m.*
Is. 24:2 be as with *m.* with mist.
Jer. 2:32 can *m.* forget ornam. ?
51:22 break young man and *m.*
Amos 2:7 and fa. go to same *m.*
Mat. 9:24 *m.* is not dead
26:71 another *m.* saw him, *Mark*
14:69 ; *Luke* 22:56
Luke 8:54 called, saying, *m.* arise

MAID-CHILD.

Lev. 12:5 if she bear a *m.-c.* unc.

MAIDEN.

Gen. 30:18 given *m.* to my husb.
Jud. 19:24 my daughter, a *m.*
2 *Chr.* 36:17 comp. on young *m.*
Ps. 123:2 eyes of *m.* to mistress
Luke 8:51 father and moth. of *m.*

MAIDENS.

Ex. 2:5 *m.* walk. along by river
Ruth 2:8 abide fast by my *m.*
22 good thou go out with *m.*
1 *Sam.* 9:11 *m.* going to dr. wat.
Est. 4:16 I and my *m.* will fast
Job 41:5 bind him for thy *m. ?*
Ps. 78:63 *m.* not giv. to marri.
148:12 y. men and *m.* praise L.
Prov. 9:3 hath sent forth her *m.*
31:15 she giveth a portion to *m.*
Ec. 2:7 I got me serv. and *m.*
Ezek. 44:22 take *m.* of seed of Is.
Luke 12:45 ser. begin to beat *m.*

MAIDS.

Est. 2:9 preferred her and *m.*
Job 19:15 *m.* count me stranger
Lam. 5:11 ravished *m.* in cities
Ezek. 9:6 slay both *m.* and chil.
Nah. 2:7 her *m.* shall lead her
Zec. 9:17 cheerful, new wine *m.*

MAID-SERVANT.

Ex. 11:5 first-born of *m.-s.*
20:10 thy *m.-s.* sh. do no work
17 not covet neighbor's *m.-s.*
21:7 sell daughter to be *m.-s.*
27 if he smite out *m.-s.'s* tooth
Deut. 5:14 that thy *m.-s.* rest
21 nei. desire neighbor's *m.-s.*
15:17 to thy *m.-s.* do likewise
Jud. 9:18 Abimel. son of *m.-s.*
Job 31:13 if I did desp. my *m.-s.*
Jer. 34:9 man-s. and *m.-s.* go, 10

MAID-SERVANTS.

Gen. 20:17 Ab. wife and *m.-s.*
31:33 L. entered two *m.-s.* tents
Deut. 12:12 rejoice, ye and *m.-s.*
1 *Sam.* 8:16 sh. take your *m.-s.*
2 *Sam.* 6:22 of the *m.-s.* sh. I be
2 *K.* 5:26 time to receive *m.-s. ?*

MAIL.

1 *Sam.* 17:5 with coat of *m.* 38

MAIMED.

Lev. 22:22 blind or *m.* shall not
Mat. 15:30 those that were *m.*
18:8 bet. enter life *m. Mark* 9:43
Luke 14:13 mak. feast, call *m.* 21

MAINSAIL.

Acts 27:40 hoised up *m.* to wind

MAINTAIN.

1 *K.* 8:45 then hear and *m.* their
cause, 49, 59 ; 2 *Chr.* 6:35, 39
1 *Chr.* 26:27 to *m.* house of the L.
Job 13:15 *m.* mine own ways
Ps. 140:12 L. will *m.* afflicted
Tit. 3:8 to *m.* good works, 14

MAINTAINED, EST.

Ps. 9:4 thou hast *m.* my right
16:5 L. is my portion. *m.* my lot

MAINTENANCE.

Ezr. 4:14 we have *m.* from king
Prov. 27:27 *m.* for thy maidens

MAJESTY.

1 *Chr.* 29:11 thine, O Lord, is *m.*
    25 bestowed on him royal *m.*
Est. 1:4 showed honor of his *m.*
Job 37:22 with G. is terrible *m.*
    40:10 deck thyself now with *m.*
Ps. 21:5 honor and *m.* hast thou
    29:4 voice of the L. is full of *m.*
    45:3 glory and *m.* 4 in *m.* ride
    93:1 Lord is clothed with *m.*
    96:6 honor and *m.* are bef. him
    104:1 thou art clothed with *m.*
    145:5 speak of honor of thy *m.*
    12 glorious *m.* of his kingdom
Is. 2:10 glory of his *m.* 19, 21
    24:14 shall sing for *m.* of the L.
    26:10 not behold the *m.* of Lord
Ezek. 7:20 ornament, he set in *m.*
Dan. 4:30 built for honor of *m.*
    36 excellent *m.* added to me
    5:18 G. gave Nebuchadnez. *m.*
Mic. 5:4 feed in *m.* of name of L.
Heb. 1:3 on right hand of *m.* 8:1
2 *Pet.* 1:16 eye-witnes. of his *m.*
Jude 25 to God be glory and *m.*

MAKE.

Gen. 1:26 *m.* man ; 2:18 *m.* him
    3:6 tree desired to *m.* one wise
    12:2 will *m.* thee a great nation,
    21:18 ; 46:3 ; *Ex.* 32:10
2 *Sam.* 7:11 will *m.* thee a house
Ps. 39:4 L. *m.* me to kn. mi. end
    90:15 *m.* us glad accord. to days
Is. 46:5 to wh. will ye *m.* equal
Zec. 13:2 w. Jerusalem a cup
Mal. 2:15 did.not he *m.* one ?
Mat. 27:65 *m.* it sure as ye can
Mark 5:39 why *m.* ye this ado ?
John 10:24 long *m.* us to doubt ?
Eph. 2:15 to *m.* in himself of tw.
Rev. 21:5 I *m.* all things new

See AFRAID, ATONEMENT, COVE-
NANT, DESOLATE, DESOLA-
TION, END, FIRE, GOOD.

MAKE haste.

Deut. 32:35 come on them *m. h.*
2 *Chr.* 35:21 G. comman. to *m. h.*
Est. 5:5 cause Haman *m. h.* 6:10
Job 20:2 for this I *m. haste*
Ps. 38:22 *m. haste* to help me, O
    Lord, 40:13 ; 70:1 ; 71:12
    70:5 needy, *m. h.* to me, 141:1
Prov. 1:16 *m. h.* shed b. *Is.* 59:7
Cant. 8:14 *m. haste*, my beloved
Is. 28:16 believeth sh. not *m. h.*
    49:17 thy children sh. *m. haste*
Jer. 9:18 *m. h.* take up wailing
Nah. 2:5 *m. haste* to wall thereof
Acts 22:18 *m. h.* out of Jerusalem
See KNOWN.

MAKE manifest.

1 *Cor.* 4:5 *m. m.* counsels of hea.
Eph. 5:13 wh. doth *m. m.* is light
Col. 4:4 may *m.* it *m.* as I ought

See MENTION, NOISE.

MAKE ready.

Ps. 11:2 they *m. r.* their arrow
    21:12 when shalt *m. r.* thine ar.
Ezek. 7:14 blown trump. to *m. r.*
Mark 14:15 *m. r. Luke* 22:12
Luke 1:17 *m. r.* a peo. prepared
    17:8 rather say, *m. r.* wherew.

MAKE speed.

2 *Sam.* 15:14 *m. speed* to depart
Is. 5:19 let him *m. s.* and hasten

MAKE waste.

Lev. 26:31 I will *m.* your cit. *w.*
Is. 42:15 I will *m. w.* mountains
Ezek. 5:14 I will *m.* Jerusa. *w.*
    29:10 *m.* land of Egypt *w.* 30:12

MAKER.

Job 4:17 more pure than his M. ?
    32:22 my M. will soon take me
    35:10 where is God my M. ?
    36:3 ascribe righteou. to my M.

Ps. 95:6 kneel before L. our M.
Prov. 14:31 reproacheth his M.
    17:5 mock. poor, reproach. M.
    22:2 rich and poor, L. M. of all
Is. 1:31 the *m.* of it as a spark
    17:7 shall man look to his M.
    22:11 have not looked to the *m.*
    45:9 woe to him striv. with M.
    16 go to confusion *m.* of idols
    51:13 forgettest the L. thy M.
    54:5 thy M. is thy husband
Jer. 33:2 thus saith the L. the M.
Hos. 8:14 Is. hath forgot. his M.
Hab. 2:18 what profiteth graven
    image that *m.* hath graven ?
Heb. 11:10 builder and *m.* is God

MAKEST.

Is. 45:9 shall the clay say to him
    that fash. it, What *m.* thou ?
John 8:53 whom *m.* thou thys. ?
    10:33 being a man *m.* thyself G.

MAKETH.

Deut. 29:12 oath which the L. *m.*
1 *Sam.* 2:6 L. killeth and *m.* alive
    7 the L. *m.* poor and *m.* rich
Is. 44:24 I am L. th. *m.* all thin.
Acts 9:34 Jesus C. *m.* thee whole
1 *Cor.* 4:7 who *m.* thee to differ ?
2 *Cor.* 2:2 who is he th. *m.* glad ?
Rev. 21:27 what. *m.* a lie, 22:15

MAKETH haste.

Prov. 28:20 *m. haste* to be rich

MAKING.

Ps. 19:7 the testimony of the L.
    is sure, *m.* wise simple
Ec. 12:12 of *m.* books no end
Mark 7:13 *m.* word of G. none eff.
John 5:18 *m.* hims. equal wi. G.
2 *Cor.* 6:10 yet *m.* many rich
Eph. 1:16 *m.* mention of you,
    1 *Thes.* 1:2 ; *Phile.* 4
Phil. 1:4 prayer for you, *m.* req.
Jude 22 have compassion, *m.* dif.

MAKING, Noun.

Ezek. 27:16 wares of thy *m.* 18

MAKKEDAH. *Jos.* 10:10, 16, 20, 28

MALCHAM. *Zep.* 1:5

MALCHUS. *John* 18:10

MALE.

Gen. 1:27 ев *m.* circ. 34:15, 22, 24
Ex. 13:12 the *m.* shall be Lord's,
    34:19 ; *Luke* 2:23
Lev. 1:3 a *m.* without blemish,
    10 ; 4:23 ; 22:19
    7:6 every *m.* am. priests sh. eat
Num. 1:2 every *m.* by their polls
    3:15 every *m.* from a month old
    31:17 kill ev. *m.* am. little ones
Deut. 20:13 shalt smite every *m.*
Jud. 21:11 ye sh. destroy ev. *m.*
1 *K.* 11:15 smitten every *m.* 16
Mal. 1:14 wh. hath in flock a *m.*

See FEMALE.

MALE-CHILDREN.

Jos. 17:2 were *m.-c.* of Manas.

MALEFACTOR, S.

Luke 23:32 two *m.* led with him
    33 they crucified him, and *m.*
John 18:30 if he were not a *m.*

MALES.

Gen. 34:25 Si. and Levi slew *m.*
Ex. 12:48 be circumcised
    13:15 sacri. to L. all being *m.*
    23:17 thy *m.* shall appear before
    the Lord God, *Deut.* 16:16
Num. 31:7 Midianites, slew *m.*
Deut. 15:19 firstling *m.* sanctify
Jos. 5:4 *m.* came out of Egypt
2 *Chr.* 31:19 gi. portions to all *m.*

MALICE.

1 *Cor.* 5:8 not with leaven of *m.*
    14:20 howbeit in *m.* be ye chil.
Eph. 4:31 put away fr. you all *m.*

Col. 3:8 also put off all these, *m.*
Tit. 3:3 sometimes living in *m.*
1 *Pet.* 2:1 laying aside all *m.*

MALICIOUS.

3 *John* 10 ag. us with *m.* words

MALICIOUSNESS.

Rom. 1:29 with unrighteous. *m.*
1 *Pet.* 2:16 for a cloak of *m.*

MALIGNITY.

Rom. 1:29 full of envy, mur. *m.*

MALLOWS.

Job 30:4 cut up *m.* by bushes

MAMMON.

Mat. 6:24 G. and *m. Luke* 16:13
Luke 16:9 friends of *m.* of unr. 11

MAMRE.

Gen. 13:18 A. dwelt in M. 14:13
    14:24 Eshcol, M. let th. portion
    23:17 bef. M. 19; 49:30; 50:13

MAN.

Gen. 1:26 God said, Let us make
    m. in our image, 27; 9:6
2 *L.* G. formed *m.* of the dust
    18 is not good *m.* sho. be alone
    25 both naked, *m.* and his wife
    3:22 the *m.* is bec. as one of us
    6:3 Sp. shall not strive with *m.*
    19:8 I have two daughters wh.
    have not kn. *m. Num.* 31:35
    24:65 what *m.* is this walketh ?
Deut. 4:32 since day G. creat. *m.*
    5:24 God doth talk with *m.*
    8:3 *m.* doth not live by bread
    only. *Mat.* 4:4 ; *Luke* 4:4
    20:19 tree of the field is *m.* life
Jos. 7:14 come *m.* by *m.* 17, 18
Jud. 8:21 as *m.* is, so strength
    9:13 wine cheereth G. and *m.*
    16:7 weak as another *m.* 11, 17
1 *Sam.* 9:6 *m.* of G. honorable *m.*
    16:7 Lord seeth not as *m.* seeth
2 *Sam.* 12:7 said, Th. art the *m.*
    16:7 come out, thou bloody *m.* 8
2 *K.* 9:11 ye know the *m.*

2 *Chr.* 19:6 ye judge not for *m.*
Job 4:17 sh. *m.* be mo. just th. G.
    7:17 what is *m.* that thou sho. ?
    magnify him ? 15:14 ; *Ps.* 8:4 ;
    144:3 : *Heb.* 2:6
    9:2 how sh. *m.* be just wi. G. ?
    10:4 or seest thou as *m.* seeth ?
    5 are thy days as days of *m.* ?
    11:12 vain *m.* would be wise
    15:7 art thou first *m.* born ?
    14 wh. is *m.* th. he sh. be cle. ?
    25:6 much less *m.* that is worm
    32:13 G. thrusteth down, not *m.*
    33:12 God is greater than *m.*
Ps. 56:11 not afr. wh. *m.* can do
    78:25 *m.* did eat angels' food
    80:17 thy hand be on the *m.*
    104:23 *m.* goeth forth to work
    118:6 not fear wh. *m.* can do
Prov. 20:24 *m.'s* goings are of L.
Ec. 6:11 what is *m.* the better ?
    12 kno. what is good for *m.* ?
Hos. 11:9 I am God, and not *m.*
Mic. 6:8 show. O *m.* wh. is good
Zec. 13:7 ag. *m.* that is my fellow
Mat. 19:6 what G. ha. joined, let
    not *m.* put asun. *Mark* 10:9
    26:72 I do not know the *m.* 74
Mark 2:27 sab. was made for *m.*
Luke 5:20 *m.* thy sins forgiven
    18:4 fear not G. nor regard *m.*
    22:58 Peter said, *m.* I am not
    60 *m.* I kn. not what thou say.
    23:53 laid in sepulchre wherein
    nev. *m.* was laid, *John* 19:41
John 2:25 knew what was in *m.*
    19:5 Pilate said, Behold the *m.*
1 *Cor.* 2:11 what *m.* knoweth the
    things of a *m.* ?
    10:13 tempta. as is com. to *m.*
    11:3 head of the woman is *m.*
    8 the *m.* is not of the woman

9 but the woman for the *m.*
11 nor is the *m.* with. the wo.
nor woman without the *m.*
12 even so is *m.* by woman
15:21 by *m.* came death, by *m.*
45 first *m.* Adam was made
47 first *m.* is of the earth ; the
second *m.* is the L. fr. hea.
2 *Cor.* 4:16 tho' our outward *m.*
perish, inward *m.* is renew.
Gal. 1:1 not of men, nei. by *m.*
11 I preached not after *m.*
Eph. 2:15 ma. of tw. one new *m.*
3:16 by his Sp. in the inner *m.*
4:24 ye have put on new *m.*
Col. 3:10 put on new *m.* renewed
1 *Thes.* 4:8 despi. not *m.* but G.
1 *Tim.* 2:5 one Mediator bet. G.
and men, the *m.* Chr. Jesus
1 *Pet.* 3:4 hidden *m.* of the heart

A MAN.

Gen. 4:23 for I have slain a *m.*
19:31 not *a m.* to come in unto
41:38 a *m.* in whom Sp. of G. is
49:6 in their anger slew *a m.*
1 *Sam.* 13:14 L. sought him *a m.*
14:36 let us not leave *a m.*
16:17 provide me *a m.* can play
17:8 choose you *a m.* for you
10 give me *a m.* we may fight
25:17 *a m.* cannot speak to him
30:17 there escaped not *a m.*
2 *Sam.* 3:34 as *a m.* falleth before
20:1 there happened to be *a m.*
1 *K.* 2:2 and show thyself *a m.*
4 not fail *a m.* on throne, 8:25
20:39 behold, *a m.* turned aside
2 *K.* 10:21 th. was not *a m.* left
1 *Chr.* 22:9 shall be *a m.* of rest
2 *Chr.* 6:16 not fail th. *a m.* 7:18
Neh. 6:11 sho. such *a m.* flee?
Job 2:4 all *a m.* ha. give for life
3:23 why is light given to *a m.*
4:17 *a m.* be more pure th. M. ?
9:32 he is not *a m.* as I am
12:14 behold, he shut. up *a m.*
14:14 if *a m.* die, sh. he live ag. ?
16:21 O that one mi. plead for *a
m.* with G. as *a m.* pleadeth
22:2 can *a m.* be profit. to God ?
34:29 whet. ag. nation or *a m.*
35:8 thy wicked. may hurt *a m.*
37:20 if *a m.* speak
38:3 gird loins like *a m.* 40:7
Ps. 38:14 as *a m.* heareth not
55:13 it was thou, *a m.* equal
88:4 *a m.* th. hath no strength
105:17 he sent *a m.* before them
147:10 not pleas. in legs of *a m.*
Prov. 3:30 strive not with *a m.*
14:12 seem. right to *a m.* 16:25
16:2 all ways of *a m.* are clean
7 when *a m.'s* ways please L.
27:21 so is *a m.* to his praise
28:12 wicked rise *a m.* hidden
Prov. 28:23 he that rebuketh *a m.*
29:20 seest th. *a m.* th. is hasty ?
Ec. 2:26 God giv. to *a m.* good
4:4 *a m.* is envied of neighbor
6:2 *a m.* wh. G. ha. given rich.
12 who tell *a m.* what sh. be ?
10:14 *a m.* cannot tell wh. sh.
Cant. 8:7 if *a m.* would give all
Is. 6:5 *a m.* of unclean lips
13:12 make *a m.* more prec.
17:7 at that day shall *a m.* look
28:20 *a m.* can stretch himself
29:21 make *a m.* an offender
32:2 *a m.* shall be a hiding pl.
47:3 I will not meet th. as *a m.*
53:3 he is *a m.* of sorrows
58:5 day for *a m.* to afflict soul ?
Jer. 4:29 not *a m.* dwell therein
5:1 seek if ye can find *a m.*
15:10 borne me *a m.* of strife
16:20 shall *a m.* make gods ?
22:30 *a m.* that shall not prosp.

23:9 *a m.* wine hath overcome
30:6 whether *a m.* doth travail ?
31:22 woman sh. compass *a m.*
33:17 D. shall never want *a m.*
18 nor shall priest want *a m.*
35:19 Jon. shall not want *a m.*
50:42 array like *a m.* to battle
Lam. 3:26 it is good for *a m.*
27 good for *a m.* he bear yoke
39 *a m.* for punishment of sins
Ezek. 22:30 I sought for *a m.*
28:2 thou art *a m.* and not G. 9
32:2 if people of land take *a m.*
Dan. 2:10 not *a m.* on earth can
7:4 st. as *a m.* and *a m.'s* heart
10:11 O Daniel, *a m.* beloved
Hos. 9:12 shall not be *a m.* left
11:4 drew th. wi. cords of *a m.*
Amos 2:7 *a m.* and fa. go to maid
5:19 as if *a m.* did flee fr. lion
Mic. 2:2 oppress *a m.* and house
7:6 *a m.'s* enemies the men of
his own house, *Mat.* 10:36
Mal. 3:17 as *a m.* spareth his son
Mat. 8:9 am *a m.* und. au. *Lu.* 7:8
10:35 to set *a m.* at variance
12:12 is *a m.* better than sheep ?
15:11 out of mouth defileth *a m.*
19:3 is it lawful for *a m.* to put
away wife ? *Mark* 10:2
22:24 if *a m.* die, having no ch.
26:18 go into city, to such *a
m. Mark* 14:3 ; *Luke* 22:10
Luke 1:34 seeing I kn. not *a m.*
5:8 for I am *a m.* sinful O Lord
John 1:6 *a m.* sent from God
30 *a m.* who is pref. before me
3:3 exc. *a m.* be born again, 5
4 can *a m.* be born when old ?
27 *a m.* can receive nothing
4:29 come, see *a m.* which told
7:23 because I made *a m.*
8:40 *a m.* that hath told you
9:11 *a m.* called Jes. made clay
16 can *a m.* do such miracles ?
10:33 being *a m.* mak. thyself G.
14:23 if *a m.* love me
16:21 for joy that *a m.* is born
Acts 2:22 J. *a m.* approved of G.
10:26 I myself am also *a m.*
13:22 D. *a m.* after my heart
41 though *a m.* declare to you
16:9 there stood *a m.* of Maced.
21:39 I am *a m.* who am a Jew
Rom. 2:21 *a m.* sh. not steal
22 *a m.* sho. not commit adul.
3:5 I sp. as *a m.* 7:1 dominion
1 *Cor.* 9:8 say I th. thin. as *a m.*
11:7 *a m.* ought not cover head
28 let *a m.* examine himself
13:11 wh. *a m.* put away child.
2 *Cor.* 2:6 sufficient to such *a m.*
8:12 according to that *a m.* ha.
12:2 I knew *a m.* in Christ, 3
4 not lawful for *a m.* to utter
Gal. 2:16 *a m.* not justified
6:1 *a m.* be overtaken in fault
3 if *a m.* think himself some
Phil. 2:8 found in fash. as *a m.*
1 *Tim.* 1:8 if *a m.* use it lawfully
3:1 if *a m.* desire office of bish.
5 if *a m.* know not how to rule
2 *Tim.* 2:5 if *a m.* strive
21 if *a m.* theref. purge himse.
Jam. 1:23 like *a m.* beholding
2:2 if th. come *a m.* with ring
14 thou. *a m.* say, he hath fai.
18 *a m.* say, Thou hast faith
24 by works *a m.* is justified
1 *Pet.* 2:19 if *a m.* for conscience
2 *Pet.* 2:19 of wh. *a m.* is overc.
1 *John* 4:20 if *a m.* say, I love G.
Rev. 4:7 beast had a face as *a m.*

Any MAN.

Gen. 24:16 nor had *a. m.* kn. her
Ex. 24:14 if *a. m.* have matters
34:3 nor let *a. m.* be seen thro'

24 nor shall *any m.* desire land
Num. 6:9 if *any m.* die suddenly
21:9 if serpent had bitten *a. m.*
Deut. 19:11 if *any m.* hate neigh.
22:8 if *any m.* fall from thence
Jos. 1:5 not *a. m.* be able to sta.
Jud. 4:20 if *any m.* inquire, Is
there *any m.* here ?
16:17 and be like *a. other m.*
18:7 no business with *a. m.* 28
1 *Sam.* 2:16 *a. m.* said, Fail not
2 *Sam.* 15:5 wh. *a. m.* came nigh
19:22 sh. *a. m.* be put to death
21:4 nor for us sh. th. kill *a. m.*
1 *K.* 8:38 if supplication be made
by *any m.* 2 *Chr.* 6:29
2 *K.* 4:29 meet *a. m.* salute h. n.
2 *Chr.* 6:5 nor chose I *any m.*
Neh. 2:12 nor told I *a. m.* wh. G.
Job 32:21 not accept *any m.*
Prov. 30:2 more brutish th. *a.-m.*
Is. 52:14 more marred th. *a. m.*
Jer. 44:26 in mouth of *any m.*
Ezek. 9:6 come not near *any m.*
Dan. 6:7 ask petition of *a. m.* 12
Mat. 5:40 if *any m.* sue thee
11:27 nor know. *a. m.* the Fat.
12:19 nor sh. *a. m.* hear voice
16:24 if *any m.* will come after
me, *Luke* 9:23
21:3 if *a. m.* say aught to you
Mark 11:3 ; *Luke* 19:31
22:16 nor carest thou for *a. m.*
46 nor durst *any m.* fr. th. day
24:23 if *any m.* say, Lo here is
Christ, *Mark* 13:21
Mark 1:44 say nothing to *a. m.*
4:23 if *a. m.* hath ears to hear,
7:16 ; *Rev.* 13:9
5:4 neit. could *a. m.* tame him
9:30 not that *a. m.* sho. know it
Luke 14:26 if *a. m.* come to me
19:8 taken any thing from *a. m.*
John 4:33 hath *a. m.* bro. aught
6:46 not th. *a. m.* hath seen F.
51 if *any m.* eat of this bread
7:17 if *a. m.* do his will know
37 *a. m.* thirst, let him come
10:9 by me if *any m.* enter in
11:57 if *a. m.* knew wh. he were
12:26 if *any m.* serve me
47 if *any m.* hear my words
16:30 not that *a. m.* should ask
Acts 19:38 a matter ag. *any m.*
27:22 be no loss of *a. m.'s* life
Rom. 8:9 if *a. m.* ha. not S. of C.
1 *Cor.* 3:12 if *a. m.* build on fou.
14 *a. m.* work ; 15 work burnt
18 if *a. m.* am. you seem. wise
8:2 if *a. m.* among you think
3 *a. m.* love God, 11:34 hunger
10:28 if *a. m.* say this is offered
16:22 if *a. m.* love not the L. J.
2 *Cor.* 5:17 if *any m.* be in Chr.
10:7 if *any m.* trust to himself
12:6 lest *a. m.* sho. think of me
Gal. 1:9 if *a. m.* pre. other gosp.
Eph. 2:9 lest *any m.* should boa.
1 *Thes.* 5:15 for evil to *any m.*
2 *Thes.* 3:8 nor eat *a. m.'s* bread
Heb. 4:11 *a. m.* fall after same
10:38 but if *any m.* draw back
12:15 *a. m.* fail of grace of God
Jam. 1:13 nor tempteth *any m.*
1 *Pet.* 4:11 if *any m.* speak
1 *John* 2:1 if *a. m.* sin, ha. advo.
15 if *any m.* love the world
27 need not that *any m.* teach
Rev. 3:20 if *a. m.* hear my voice
22:18 if *a. m.* add to these thin.
19 if *any m.* take away words

See BEAST, BLESSED, CURSED.

MAN-CHILD.

Gen. 17:10 *m.-c.* be circumc. 12
14 uncircumc. *m.-c.* be cut off
Lev. 12:2 if wom. ha. borne *m.-c.*
1 *Sam.* 1:11 give to handm. *m.-c.*

Job 3:3 it was said, There is a
  m.-c. conceived, *Jer.* 20:15
Is. 66:7 deliv. of *m.-c. Rev.* 12:5
Rev. 12:13 wom. bro. forth *m.-c.*

See EACH.

Every MAN.

Gen. 16:12 his hand be ag. *e. m.*
  45:1 cause *e. m.* to go out
Deut. 16:17 *e. m.* give as able
2 *Sam.* 13:9 they went out *e. m.*
Phil. 2:4 look not *e. m.* on his

See EVIL, FOOLISH.

MAN of God.

Deut. 33:1 M. *m. of G. Jos.* 14:6
Jud. 13:6 *m. of G.* came to me
1 *Sam.* 2:27 a *m. of G.* to Eli
  9:6 there is in city a *m. of G.*

1 *Sam.* 9:7 not a pr. to br. *m. of G.*
1 *K.* 12:22 Shem. the *m. of G.*
  13:1 came *m. of G.* out Judah
  26 *m. of G.* who was disobed.
  17:18 do with thee, O *m. of G. ?*
  24 that thou art *m. of G. ?*
  20:28 there came a *m. of God*
2 *K.* 1:9 *m. of G.* king said, 11
  13 O *m. of G.* let my life be
  4:16 thou *m. of God,* do not lie
  40 O *m. of G.* death in pot
  42 brought *m. of God* bread
  5:14 accord. to saying *m. of G.*
  6:10 to place *m. of G.* told him
  7:2 lord answered *m. of G.* 19
  17 people trod on *m. of G.* 18
  8:2 after the saying of *m. of G.*
  7 *m. of God ; m. of God* wept
  8 and go meet the *m. of God*
  13:19 *m. of G.* wroth with him
  23:16 to word which *m. of God*
  17 it is sepulchre of *m. of God*
1 *Chr.* 23:14 concern. M. the *m.*
  of G. 2 *Chr.* 30:16 ; *Ezr.* 3:2
2 *Chr.* 8:14 D. the *m. of G.* Neh.
  12:24, 36
  25:7 came a *m. of G.* to Amaz.
  9 *m. of G.* answered, the Lord
Jer. 35:4 son of Igda. a *m. of G.*
1 *Tim.* 6:11 O *m. of G.* flee these
2 *Tim.* 3:17 *m. of G.* be perfect.

See GOOD.

Mighty MAN.

Jud. 6:12 L. is with thee, *m. m.*
  11:1 Jephthah was a *m. m.*
Ruth 2:1 N. had kinsman *m. m.*
1 *Sam.* 9:1 Kish a Benj. *m. m.*
  16:18 David *m. m.* 2 *Sam.* 17:10
1 *K.* 11:28 Jeroboam was *m. m.*
2 *K.* 5:1 Naaman was a *m. m.*
1 *Chr.* 12:4 Ismaiah a *m. m.* 30
2 *Chr.* 17:17 Eliada *m. m.* of val.
  28:7 Zichri, *m. m.* of Ephraim
Job 22:8 as *m. m.* he had earth
Ps. 33:16 *m. m.* not deliv. by str.
  52:1 boast. in mischief, *m. m.*
  78:65 L. awaked like a *m. m.*
  127:4 arrows in hand of *m. m.*
Is. 3:2 L. doth take away *m. m.*
  5:15 *m. m.* shall be humbled
  31:8 fall wi. sw. not of a *m. m.*
  42:13 L. go forth as a *m. m.*
Jer. 9:23 nor let the *m. m.* glory
  14:9 shouldest be as a *m. m.*
  46:6 *m. m.* escape ; 12 stumbled
Zep. 1:14 *m. m.* shall cry bitterly
Zec. 9:13 as sword of a *m. m.*
  10:7 Eph. shall be like a *m. m.*

No MAN.

Gen. 31:50 no *m.* is with us
  41:44 with. thee *no m.* lift hand
Ex. 16:19 let *no m.* leave of it
  29 let *no m.* go out of his place
  22:10 driv. away, *no m.* seeing
  33:20 *no m.* sh. see me and live
  34:3 *no m.* sh. come up wi. thee
Num. 5:19 if *no m.* ha. lain with
Deut. 7:24 *no m.* able to st. 11:25

  34:6 *no m.* know. his sepulchre
Jos. 23:9 *no m.* hath been able
Jud. 11:39 J. daugh. knew *no m.*
  21:12 virgins th. had kno. *no m.*
1 *Sam.* 2:9 by stre. *no m.* prevail
  26:12 *no m.* saw nor knew it
1 *K.* 8:46 for there is *no m.* that
  sinneth not, 2 *Chr.* 6:36
2 *K.* 7:5 was *no m.* in camp, 10
  23:18 let *no m.* move his bones
1 *Chr.* 16:21 he suffered *no m.* to
  do them wrong, *Ps.* 105:14
Est. 5:12 queen let *no m.* come
  8:8 *no m.* reverse ; 9:2 withstand
Job 11:3 *no m.* make thee asha. ?
  20:21 *no m.* look for his goods
  24:22 *no m.* is sure of his life
  38:26 wh. *no m.* is, wher. *no m.*
Ps. 22:6 I am worm, and *no m.*
  142:4 there was *no m. Is.* 41:28 ;
  59:16 ; *Jer.* 4:25
Prov. 1:24 and *no m.* regarded
Ec. 8:8 *no m.* ha. power over sp.
  9:1 *no m.* know. love or hatred
Is. 9:19 *no m.* shall spare bro.
  24:10 *no m.* come ; 33:8 regard.
  50:2 when I came, was th. *no m.*
  57:1 and *no m.* layeth it to hea.
  Jer. 12:11
  60:15 *no m.* went through thee
Jer. 2:6 *no m.* dwelt ; 8:6 repent
  22:30 *no m.* of his seed sh. pros.
  30:17 Zion, whom *no m.* seeketh
  36:19 let *no m.* know wh. ye be
  38:24 *no m.* know these words
  40:15 *no m.* know ; 41:4 knew it
  44:2 *no m.* dwell. therein, 51:43
  49:18 *no m.* abide, 33 ; 50:40
Lam. 4:4 *no m.* breaketh it
Ezek. 14:15 *no m.* pass through
  44:2 *no m.* sh. enter in by gate
Hos. 4:4 let *no m.* reprove anoth.
Zep. 3:6 so that there is *no m.*
Zec. 1:21 *no m.* did lift his head
  7:14 that *no m.* passed through
Mat. 6:24 *no m.* can serve two
  masters, *Luke* 16:13
  8:4 tell *no m.* 16:20 ; *Mark* 7:36 ;
  9:14 ; 9:21
  9:30 *no m.* know it, *Mark* 5:43 ;
  7:24 ; 8:30 ; 9:9
  11:27 *no m.* knoweth the Son
  but the Father, *Luke* 10:22
  17:8 they saw *no m.* save Jesus
  22:46 *no m.* was able to answer
  23:9 call *no m.* father on earth
  24:36 that day and hour know.
  no m. Mark 13:32
Mark 10:29 *no m.* that hath left
  house, *Luke* 18:29
  11:14 *no m.* eat fruit of thee
  12:14 know thou care, for *no m.*
Luke 3:14 vio. to *no m.* 10:4 sal.
John 1:18 *no m.* hath seen God,
  1 *John* 4:12
  5:22 the Father judgeth *no m.*
  6:44 *no m.* can come to me, 65
  7:30 *no m.* laid hands, 44 ; 8:20
  8:11 *no m.* L. 15 I judge *no m.*
  9:4 night com. *no m.* can work
  10:18 *no m.* taketh it from me
  29 *no m.* able to pluck th. out
  13:28 *no m.* at table knew why
  14:6 *no m.* com. to F. but by me
Acts 4:17 that th. speak to *no m.*
  5:13 durst *no m.* join himself
  23 we found *no m.* within
  9:7 hear. voice, seeing *no m.*
  18:10 *no m.* shall set on thee
Rom. 13:8 owe *no m.* any thing
  14:7 and *no m.* dieth to himself
1 *Cor.* 2:11 thi. of G. know. *no m.*
  15 he himself judged of *no m.*
  3:11 other found. can *no m.* lay
  18 let *no m.* deceive himself, 21
  10:24 let *no m.* seek his own
2 *Cor.* 5:16 know *no m.* after fle.
  7:2 wrong. *no m.* corrupt. *no m.*

Gal. 3:11 *no m.* justified by law
Eph. 5:6 *no m.* decei. 2 *Thes.* 2:3
  29 *no m.* ever hated own flesh
2 *Tim.* 4:16 first ans. *no m.* stood
Tit. 3:2 to speak evil of *no m.*
Heb. 5:4 *no m.* taketh this honor
  12:14 without whi. *no m.* see L.
Jam. 3:8 tongue can *no m.* tame
Rev. 2:17 a name *no m.* knoweth
  3:7 shutteth, and *no m.* openeth
  8 *no m.* shut it ; 11 take crown
  5:3 *no m.* able to open book, 4
  13:17 *no m.* might buy or sell
  14:3 *no m.* could learn that song
  15:8 *no m.* able to enter temple
  19:12 a name writ. *no m.* knew

Of MAN.

2 *Sam.* 7:19 is th. manner *of m. ?*
Prov. 30:19 way of *m.* wi. maid
Ec. 12:13 whole duty *of m.*
Rev. 13:18 the number *of* a *m.*
  21:17 according to meas. *of* a *m.*

See OLD.

One MAN.

Gen. 42:11 are all *o. m.* sons, 13
Num. 14:15 tho. kill peo. as *o. m.*
  31:49 there lacketh not *one m.*
Jos. 23:10 *o. m.* chase thous.
Jud. 20:1 cong. gather. as *o. m.*
  8 all the people arose as *o. m.*
2 *Sam.* 19:14 as heart of *o. m.*
Ec. 7:28 *o. m.* am. a thousand
Is. 4:1 sev. wom. take hold *o. m.*
John 11:50 *o. m.* die for peo. 18:14
Rom. 5:12 by *o. m.* sin ent. wor.
  15 which is by *one m.* Jesus
  17 by *o. m.* offence death reig.
  19 as by *one m.* disobedience
  14:5 *one m.* esteemeth one day
1 *Tim.* 5:9 hav. been wi. of *o. m.*

See POOR, RICH, RIGHTEOUS.

MAN-SERVANT.

Ex. 20:10 not do work, thy *m.-s.*
  Deut. 5:14
  17 neighbor's *m.-s. Deut.* 5:21
  21:27 smite out *m.-s.'s* tooth
  32 if the ox shall push a *m.-s.*
Deut. 12:18 thou and thy *m.-s.* 14
  16:11 rejoice, thou and *m.-s.* 14
Job 31:13 if I did desp. my *m.-s.*
Jer. 34:9 let his *m.-s.* go free

MAN-SLAYER, S.

Num. 35:6 six cities for *m.-s.*
  12 that the *m.-s.* die not
1 *Tim.* 1:9 law was ma. for *m.-s.*

Son of MAN.

Num. 23:19 nor *s. of m.* repent
Job 25:6 *s. of m.* which is worm
Ps. 8:4 and the *s. of m.* that thou
  visitest him, *Heb.* 2:6
  80:17 *s. of m.* th. madest strong
  144:3 *s. of m.* makest account
  146:3 put not trust in *s. of m.*
Is. 51:12 not afraid of *son of m.*
  56:2 blessed is *s. of m.* lay. hold
Jer. 49:18 nor shall the *son of m.*
  dwell in it, 33 ; 50:40
  51:43 nei. doth any *s. of m.* pass
Ezek. 8:15 seen, O *s. of m. ?* 17
  21:6 sigh, *s. of m.* with bittern.
Dan. 7:13 one like the *Son of m.*
  Rev. 1:13 ; 14:14
Mat. 8:20 *S. of m.* ha. not where
  to lay his head, *Luke* 9:58
  9:6 *S. of m.* ha. power to forgi.
  sins, *Mark* 2:10 ; *Luke* 5:24
  10:23 not gone, *S. of m.* come
  11:19 *S. of m.* came, *Luke* 7:34
  12:8 *S. of m.* is Lord even of
  sab. *Mark* 2:28 ; *Luke* 6:5
  32 whosoever speaketh against
  Son of m. Luke 12:10
  40 *S. of m.* 3 days and nights
  13:37 sow. good seed is *S. of m.*
  41 *S. of m.* send forth angels

16:18 say that I, *S. of m.* am ?
17:9 *S. of m.* be risen, *Mark* 9:9
22 *S. of m.* shall be betrayed,
   20:18 ; 26:2, 45 ; *Mark* 14:41 ;
   Luke 9:44
24:27 so shall coming of *S. of m.*
   be, 37, 39 ; *Luke* 17:26
30 shall see *Son of m.* coming,
   Mark 13:26 ; *Luke* 21:27
44 in such hour as ye think not
   S. of m. cometh, *Luke* 12:40
25:31 *S. of m.* come in glory
26:24 the *Son of m.* goeth, *Mark*
   14:21 ; *Luke* 22:22
Mark 8:38 of him shall *S. of m.*
   be ashamed when he come.
9:12 it is written of *Son of m.*
31 the *S. of m.* is delivered,
   10:33 ; *Luke* 24:7
13:34 *S. of m.* as man taking
Luke 6:22 repr. you for *S. of m.*
9:22 *Son of m.* must suffer, 26
56 *S. of m.* not come to destr.
11:30 so shall *Son of m.* be, 17:24
12:8 him shall *S. of m.* confess
17:22 to see day of *S. of m.*
18:8 when *Son of m.* cometh
19:10 *S. of m.* come to save lost
21:36 to stand before *S. of m.*
22:48 betray. *S. of m.* wi. kiss ?
John 1:51 descending on *S. of m.*
3:13 even *Son of m.* in heaven
14 so must *Son of m.* be lifted
5:27 because he is the *S. of m.*
6:27 *S. of m.* sh. give unto you
53 exc. ye eat flesh of *S. of m.*
62 shall see *S. of m.* ascend
8:28 ye have lift up *S. of m.*
12:23 *S. of m.* should be glorifi.
34 the *S. of m.* must be lifted
   up, who is this *S. of m.* ?
13:31 now is *S. of m.* glorified
Acts 7:56 *S. of m.* on right hand

See SON.

That MAN.
Lev. 17:9 *t. m.* be cut off from p.
20:3 I will set my face against
   that m. 5 ; *Ezek.* 14:8
Num. 9:13 not offer. *t. m.* bear
Deut. 17:5 stone *that m.* 12
22:18 take *t. m.* chastise him
25:9 so sh. it be done to *that m.*
29:20 jealousy smoke aga. *t. m.*
Jos. 22:20 *t. m.* perished not al.
Ps. 37:37 end of *t. m.* is peace
87:5 this and *t. m.* born in her
Acts 17:31 *t. m.* he hath ordained
2 *Thes.* 2:3 *t. m.* be revealed
3:14 note *t. m.* have no comp.
Jam. 1:7 let not *that m.* think

This MAN.
Gen. 24:58 wilt go with *t. m.* ?
26:11 he that toucheth *this m.*
Ex. 10:7 how lo. *t. m.* be snare ?
Deut. 22:16 gave my dau. to *t. m.*
Jud. 19:23 *t. m.* come to house
   24 to *t. m.* do not so vile a th.
1 *Sam.* 1:3 *t. m.* went yearly
10:27 said, How sh. *t. m.* save ?
17:25 seen *this m.* come up ?
25:25 let not my lord reg. *t. m.*
1 *K.* 20:7 *t. m.* seeketh mischief
   39 and said, Keep *this m.*
2 *K.* 5:7 *this m.* sends to recover
Neh. 1:11 mercy in sight of *t. m.*
Est. 9:4 *t. m.* M. waxed greater
Job 1:3 *t. m.* greatest of men
Ps. 87:4 *this m.* born there, 5, 6
Is. 66:2 to *this m.* will I look
Jer. 22:30 write *this m.* childless
26:11 *t. m.* is worthy to die, 16
38:4 *t. m.* seeketh not welfare
Dan. 8:16 *t. m.* understand vision
Jon. 1:14 nor per. for *t. m.'s* life
Mic. 6:5 *this m.* shall be peace
Mat. 8:9 I say to *this m.* Go

13:54 whence had *this m.* this
   wisdom ? *Mark* 6:2
27:47 this m. calleth for Elias
Mark 14:71 I know not *this m.*
15:39 *this m.* was Son of God
Luke 14:9 thee, Give *t. m.* place
22:56 *t. m.* was also with him
23:4 I find no fault in *t. m.* 14
   18 saying, Away with *this m.*
John 7:27 we know *this m.*
   46 never man spake like *t. m.*
18:17 one of *this m.'s* disciples ?
   40 not *this m.* but Barabbas
19:12 if thou let *this m.* go
21:21 and what shall *this m.* do ?
Acts 3:12 made *t. m.* to walk, 16
4:10 by him doth *t. m.* stand
8:10 *this m.* is great power of G.
13:23 of *t. m.* God raised Jesus
   38 *this m.* is preached to you
Heb. 7:24 *t. m.* continueth ever
8:3 *t. m.* have somewhat to offer
10:12 *t. m.* offered one sacrifice

See UNDERSTANDING.

MAN of war.
Ex. 15:3 the Lord is a *m. of w.*
Jos. 17:1 Machir was a *m. of w.*
1 *Sam.* 16:18 David a *m. of w.*
   2 *Sam.* 17:8 ; 1 *Chr.* 28:3
17:33 Goliath *m. of w.* fr. youth
Is. 3:2 L. take away *m. of war*
42:13 stir up jeal. like *m. of war*

Wicked MAN.
Deut. 25:2 *w. m.* worthy to be
Job 15:20 *w. m.* travail. with pa.
20:29 portion of *w. m.* 27:13
Ps. 109:6 set thou a *w. m.* over
Prov. 6:12 a *wicked m.* walketh
9:7 rebuketh *w. m.* getteth blot
11:7 when a *wicked m.* dieth
13:5 a *wicked m.* loathsome
17:23 *w. m.* tak. gift out bosom
21:29 *w. m.* hardeneth his face
24:15 lay not wait, O *wicked m.*
Ec. 7:15 *w. m.* prolongeth days
Ezek. 3:18 *w. m.* shall die in ini.
18:24 doeth that wh. *w. m.* do.
   27 *w. m.* turneth from wicked.
33:8 O *w. m.* th. shalt surely die,
   that *w. m.* shall die in his

Wise MAN.
Gen. 41:33 look out *m.* discre. *w.*
1 *K.* 2:9 Solomon was a *wise m.*
1 *Chr.* 27:32 D.'s uncle a *w. m.*
Job 15:2 *w. m.* utter vain know. ?
17:10 I cannot find one *w. m.*
34:34 let *w. m.* hearken to me
Prov. 1:5 a *w. m.* hear and incr.
9:8 rebuke *w. m.* he will love
9 give instruction to *wise m.*
14:16 *w. m.* feareth, and depart.
16:14 a *w. m.* pacify wr. of king
17:10 reproof enter. into a *w. m.*
21:22 *wise m.* scaleth the city
26:12 *w. m.* in own conceit ?
29:9 if *w. m.* contend. w. foolish
   11 but a *wise m.* keepeth it in
Ec. 2:14 *w. m.'s* eyes in head
   16 how dieth *wise m.* ? as fool
   19 wheth. he be *wise m.* or fool
7:7 oppression mak. *w. m.* mad
8:1 who is as *wise m.* who kno.
5 a *wise m.'s* heart discerneth
   17 tho' a *w. m.* think to know
9:15 found in it a poor *wise m.*
10:2 *w. m.'s* heart at right hand
   12 words of a *wise m.* gracious
Jer. 9:12 *w. m.* they may unde. ?
   23 let not *wise m.* gl. in wisd.
Mat. 7:24 liken him to a *w. m.*
1 *Cor.* 6:5 not a *w. m.* am. you
Jam. 3:13 who is a *w. m.* endued

MAN, with woman.
Gen. 3:12 *m.* said, The *woman*
20:3 dead *m.* for *w.* is *m.'s* wife
Ex. 36:6 let no *m.* nor *w.* work

Lev. 15:18 *w.* with wh. *m.* shall
   33 an issue of the *m.* and *w.*
20:27 *m.* or *w.* hath familiar sp.
Num. 6:2 *m.* or *w.* separate
31:17 kill *woman* that hath kno.
   m. Jud. 21:11
Deut. 17:5 bring *m.* or *w.* st. th.
22:5 *m.* not wear that pertain.
   to *m.* nor *m.* put on *w.'s*
   garment
Deut. 22:22 *m.* found lying with
   w. both *m.* th. lay with the
   w. and *w.*
1 *Sam.* 15:3 slay both *m.* and *w.*
27:9 left neither *m.* nor *w.* alive
1 *Chr.* 16:3 dealt to *m.* and *w.*
2 *Chr.* 15:13 not seek L. *m.* or *w.*
Jer. 44:7 cut off *m. w.* and child.
51:22 break in pieces *m.* and *w.*
1 *Cor.* 11:3 head of the *w.* is *m.*
   7 *woman* is the glory of the *m.*
   8 *m.* is not of *w.* but *w.* of *m.*
   11 nor is *m.* without *w.* in L.
   12 as *w.* is of *m.* so is *m.* by *w.*
1 *Tim.* 5:16 any *m.* or *w.* ha. wi.

Young MAN.
Gen. 4:23 slain *y. m.* to my hurt
18:7 Abraham gave it to a *y. m.*
41:12 there was with us a *y. m.*
Num. 11:27 ran *y. m.* and to. M.
Deut. 32:25 des. *y. m.* and virgin
Jud. 17:12 *y. m.* bec. his priest
1 *Sam.* 9:2 S. was a choice *y. m.*
17:58 whose son art thou, *y. m.*
30:13 I am *young m.* of Egypt
2 *Sam.* 1:5 said to *young m.* 13
14:21 bring *y. m.* Absal. again
18:5 deal gently with the *y. m.*
   29 is *y. m.* Absalom safe ? 32
32 enemies of lord be as *y. m.*
1 *K.* 11:28 Solomon seeing *y. m.*
2 *K.* 6:17 L. opened eyes of *y. m.*
9:4 the *y. m.* went to Ramoth
1 *Chr.* 12:28 Zadok, a *young m.*
2 *Chr.* 36:17 no compas. on *y. m.*
Ps. 119:9 sh. *y. m.* cleanse way ?
Prov. 1:4 to *y. m.* knowledge
7:7 *y. m.* void of understanding
Ec. 11:9 rej. O *y. m.* in youth
Is. 62:5 as *y. m.* marrieth virgin
Jer. 51:22 break *y. m.* and maid
Mat. 19:20 *young m.* said
Mark 14:51 follow. certain *y. m.*
16:5 *y. m.* sitting on right side
Luke 7:14 *y. m.* I say to thee
Acts 7:58 clothes at *y. m.'s* feet
20:9 there sat in window a *y. m.*
23:17 bring *y. m.* to captain, 18
   22 captain let the *y. m.* depart

MANAEN. *Acts* 13:1

MANASSEH.
Gen. 41:51 called first-born M.
48:5 two sons M. and Eph. 20
2 *K.* 20:21 M. reign. 2 *Chr.* 32:33
21:9 M. seduced th. to do ev. 16
24:3 sins of M. this came upon
2 *Chr.* 33:11 M. among thorns
   13 M. knew that Lord was G.
Ps. 60:7 M. mine, 80:2 ; 108:8
Is. 9:21 M. shall eat Ephraim

Tribe of MANASSEH.
Num. 1:35 of *tribe of* M. 32,200
Jos. 4:12 the half *t. of* M. passed
13:7 and half *tribe of* M.
17:1 lot for M. 20:8 ; 22:10
1 *Chr.* 5:18 half *t.* M. 6:70 ; 12:31
26:32 G. half *tribe of* M. 27:21
Rev. 7:6 *t. of* M. sealed 12,000

MANDRAKES.
Gen. 30:14 Reuben found *m.*
   15 wouldest take my son's *m.* ?
   he sh. lie wi. thee for's *m.*
   16 hired thee with my son's *m.*
Cant. 7:13 *m.* give a smell

MANEH. *Ezek.* 45:12

MANGER.

Luke 2:7 and laid him in a *m.*
  12 shall find him lying in *m.*
  16 found the babe lying in *m.*

MANIFEST.

Ec. 3:18 with that God might *m.*
  them
John 14:21 *m.* myself to him
  22 *m.* thyself to us
Acts 4:16 miracle *m.* to all at J.
Rom. 1:19 kn. of G. is *m,* in th.
1 *Cor.* 4:5 *m.* counsels of hearts
  15:27 it is *m.* he is excepted
2 *Cor.* 2:14 makes *m.* the savor
Gal. 5:19 works of flesh are *m.*
Phil. 1:13 bonds in Christ are *m.*
Col. 4:4 that I may make it *m.*
1 Thes. 1:5 a *m.* token of righte.
1 *Tim.* 3:16 God was *m.* in flesh
  5:25 good works of some are *m.*
2 *Tim.* 3:9 body be *m.* to all m.
Heb. 4:13 no creat. that is not *m.*
1 *Pet.* 1:20 was *m.* in these times
1 *John* 3:10 children of G. are *m.*

See MADE.

MANIFESTATION.

Rom. 8:19 for *m.* of sons of God
1 *Cor.* 12:7 *m.* of S. giv. to man
2 *Cor.* 4:2 *m.* of truth commend.

MANIFESTED.

Mark 4:22 hid wh. sh. not be *m.*
John 2:11 and *m.* forth his glory
  17:6 *m.* thy name unto men
Rom. 3:21 righteous. of G. is *m.*
Tit. 1:3 in due time *m.* his word
1 *John* 1:2 life *m.* we have seen
  3:5 *m.* to take away our sins
  8 for this purp. was S. of G. *m.*
  4:9 in this was *m.* love of God

MANIFESTLY.

2 *Cor.* 3:3 *m.* declared to be epi.

MANIFOLD.

Neh. 9:19 in *m.* mercies forsook.
  27 *m.* mercies gavest them
Ps. 104:24 how *m.* are works
Amos 5:12 I know your *m.* transg.
Luke 18:30 not receive *m.* more
Eph. 3:10 known *m.* wisd. of G.
1 *Pet.* 1:6 through *m.* temptatio.
  4:10 stewards of *m.* grace of G.

MANKIND.

Lev. 18:22 shall not lie with *m.*
  20:13 man lie with *m.* as wom.
Job 12:10 in hand breath of *m.*
1 *Tim.* 1:10 law of them defile *m.*
Jam. 3:7 hath been tamed of *m.*

MANNA.

Ex. 16:15 they said, It is *m.*
  35 Israel did eat *m.* 40 years
Num. 11:6 noth. besides this *m.*
  7 *m.* was as coriander-seed
  9 fell on camp, *m.* fell on it
Deut. 8:3 fed thee with *m.* 16 ;
  Neh. 9:20 ; *Ps.* 78:24
Jos. 5:12 *m.* ceased, no more
John 6:31 fathers did eat *m.* 49
  58 not as fathers did eat *m.*
Heb. 9:4 golden pot that had *m.*
Rev. 2:17 to eat of hidden *m.*

MANNER.

Gen. 25:23 two *m.* of peo. sepa.
Ex. 1:14 bitter in *m.* of service
  12:16 no *m.* of work done in th.
  22:9 *m.* of trespass, *m.* of lost
  31:3 *m.* of workmansh. 5 ; 35:31,
  33, 35 ; 36:1 ; 1 *Chr.* 28:21
Lev. 5:10 offer. ac. to *m. Nu.* 9:14
  23:31 ye shall do no *m.* of work
  24:22 one *m.* of law *Num.* 15:6
Num. 5:13 she be taken with *m.*
  28:18 do no *m.* of servile work
Deut. 4:15 no *m.* of similitude
  15:2 this is *m.* of the release
  27:21 lieth wi. any *m.* of beast
Ruth 4:7 this *m.* in former time

---

1 *Sam.* 8:9 show *m.* of king, 11
  10:25 Samuel told *m.* of kingd.
  21:5 bread is in a *m.* common
2 *Sam.* 7:19 is this *m.* of man ?
2 *K.* 1:7 what *m.* of man ?
  11:14 stood by pillar, as *m.* was
  17:26 know not *m.* of G. of land
1 *Chr.* 23:29 for all *m.* of meas.
Est. 1:13 king's *m.* towards all
Ps. 107:18 abhor. all *m.* of meat
Cant. 7:13 all *m.* of pleas. fruits
Is. 5:17 lambs feed after their *m.*
Jer. 22:21 this hath been thy *m.*
Dan. 6:23 no *m.* of hurt found
Mat. 4:23 heal. all *m.* sickn. 10:1
  5:11 say all *m.* of evil ag. you
  8:27 what *m.* of man is this,
    Mark 4:41 ; *Luke* 8:25
  12:31 all *m.* of sin forg. to men
Mark 13:1 see what *m.* of ston.
Luke 1:29 what *m.* of salutation
  66 what *m.* of child sh. th. be ?
  7:39 what *m.* of woman this
  9:55 know not wh. *m.* of spirit
  24:17 what *m.* of communicat. ?
John 19:40 as *m.* of J. is to bury
Acts 17:2 Paul, as his *m.* was
  20:18 know wh. *m.* I have been
  22:3 according to perfect *m.*
  25:16 it is not *m.* of Romans
  26:4 my *m.* of life from youth
2 *Cor.* 7:9 sorry after godly *m.*
1 *Thes.* 1:5 ye kn. what *m.* of *m.*
  9 what *m.* of entering in we
2 *Tim.* 3:10 known my *m.* of life
Heb. 10:25 as the *m.* of some is
Jam. 1:24 forge. what *m.* of man
1 *Pet.* 1:11 wh. *m.* of time the S.
  15 holy in all *m.* of conversa.
2 *Pet.* 3:11 what *m.* of persons
1 *John* 3:1 behold what *m.* of love
Rev. 11:5 in this *m.* be killed
  22:2 which bare 12 *m.* of fruits

After the MANNER.

Gen. 18:11 with S. a. *m.* of wom.
  19:31 come in unto us a. t. *m.*
Jud. 18:7 a. the *m.* of Zidonians
Is. 10:24 a. *m.* of E. 26 ; *Am.* 4:10
Ezek. 20:30 polluted a. *m.* of fat.
  23:15 a. *the m.* of Babylonians
Ezek. 23:45 a. the *m.* of adulter.
John 2:6 a. the *m.* of purifying J.
Acts 15:1 circumcised a. t. *m.* M.
Rom. 6:19 I speak a. t. *m.* of
  men, 1 *Cor.* 15:32 ; *Gal.* 3:15
1 *Cor.* 11:25 a. same *m.* he took
Gal. 2:14 a. the *m.* of Gentiles

After this MANNER.

Mat. 6:9 *after this m.* pray ye
1 *Cor.* 7:7 one a. *this m.* and an.

See LIKE.

MANNERS.

Lev. 20:23 not walk in *m.* of nat.
2 *K.* 17:34 do after former *m.*
Ezek. 11:12 after *m.* of heathens
Acts 13:18 40 years suff. their *m.*
1 *Cor.* 15:33 ev. com. co. good *m.*
Heb. 1:1 God in divers *m.* spake
MANOAH. *Jud.* 13:8, 21 ; 16:31

MANSIONS.

John 14:2 in Fa.'s ho. many *m.*

MANTLE, S.

Jud. 4:18 Jael cov. Sis. with *m.*
1 *Sam.* 28:14 covered with a *m.*
1 *K.* 19:13 Elijah wrapped in *m.*
  19 Eli. cast his *m.* upon Elisha
2 *K.* 2:8 Elijah took *m.* smote
  13 Elisha took Elijah's *m.* 14
Ezr. 9:3 I he. this, I rent my *m.* 5
Job 1:20 Job arose and rent *m.*
  2:12 they rent every one his *m.*
Ps. 109:29 confusion, as with *m.*
Is. 3:22 I will take away the *m.*

MANY.

Gen. 17:4 thou sh. be a father of
  m. nations, 5 ; *Rom.* 4:17, 18
  37:3 a coat of *m.* colors, 23, 32
Ex. 19:21 gaze, and *m.* perish
Num. 13:18 wheth. be few or *m.*
  26:56 pos. divided between *m.*
  35:8 from them have *m.* cities
Deut. 15:6 to *m.* nations, 28:12
31:17 *m.* evils shall befall, 21
1 *Sam.* 14:6 save by *m.* or few
1 *K.* 4:20 Judah and Is. were *m.*
  7:47 they were exceeding *m.*
2 *Chr.* 14:11 no. to help with *m.*
Neh. 7:2 he feared God above *m.*
  13:26 among *m.* nations no king
Ps. 3:1 *m.* are they that rise up
  2 be *m.* that say of my soul, 4:6
  25:19 mine enemies are *m.* 56:2
  32:10 *m.* sor. shall be to wicked
  34:19 *m.* are afflictions of right.
  40:3 *m.* sh. see it and fear
  55:18 for there were *m.* with me
Prov. 4:10 years of thy life be *m.*
  10:21 lips of righteous feed *m.*
  14:20 the rich hath *m.* friends
  19:4 wealth maketh *m.* friends
Ec. 11:8 days of darkness be *m.*
Is. 53:12 he bare the sin of *m.*
Jer. 42:3 are left but few of *m.*
  46:16 he made *m.* to fall
Lam. 1:22 for my sighs are *m.*
Ezek. 33:24 we are *m.* land given
Dan. 12:4 *m.* sh. run to and fro
Mat. 7:13 *m.* there be that go
  22 *m.* will say in that day, L.
  8:11 *m.* sh. come from east and
  13:58 did not *m.* mighty works
  19:30 *m.* first be last, *Mark* 10:31
  20:16 *m.* called, few chos. 22:14
  24:5 *m.* sh. co. in my name and
    sh. dec. *m. Mark* 13:6 ; *Luke*
    21:8
  12 love of *m.* shall wax cold
  26:28 my blood shed for *m.*
Luke 1:16 *m.* sh. he turn to Lord
  2:34 fall and ris. of *m.* in Israel
  4:25 *m.* widows ; 27 *m.* lepers
  7:47 her sins are *m.* are forgiven
John 6:9 are they among so *m.* ?
  60 *m.* of his disciples said, 66
  21:11 for all so *m.* net not brok.
Acts 9:13 I have heard by *m.*
  19:19 *m.* bro. books and burnt
  26:10 *m.* of saints did I shut up
Rom. 5:15 off. of one *m.* be dead
  19 *m.* made sin. *m.* made righ.
  12:5 be. *m.* are one body in Ch.
1 *Cor.* 1:26 not *m.* wise, not *m.*
  4:15 yet have ye not *m.* fathers
  8:5 there be gods *m.* lords *m.*
  10:5 with *m.* G. was not pleased
  17 we being *m.* are one bread
  33 profit of *m.* that they be sa.
  11:30 for this cause *m.* weak
  12:14 not one member, but *m.*
2 *Cor.* 1:11 thanks be giv. by *m.*
  6:10 as poor, yet mak. *m.* rich
Gal. 1:14 and profited above *m.*
  3:16 and to seeds, as of *m.*
Phil. 3:18 *m.* walk of wh. I told
Heb. 2:10 bring *m.* sons to glory
Heb. 7:23 they truly were *m.* pr.
  9:28 Christ once bear sins of *m.*
  11:12 sprang of one so *m.* stars
Jam. 3:1 my brethren, be not *m.*

After MANY.

Ex. 23:2 speak in a cause to decline *after m.*

As MANY as.

Jud. 3:1 as *m.* as had not known
2 *Sam.* 2:23 as *m. as* came to pl.
2 *Chr.* 29:31 as *m. as* of free hea.
Mat. 22:9 as *m. as* ye find bid
Mark 6:56 as *m. as* touched him
Luke 11:8 as *m. as* he needeth
John 1:12 as *m. as* received him

Acts 2:39 to *as m. as* L. shall call
3:24 *as m. as* ha. spoken foreto.
5:11 fear ca. on *as m. as* heard
36 *as m. as* obeyed him, 37
13:48 *as m. as* ordained to life
Rom. 2:12 *as m. as* have sinned
8:14 *as m. as* are led by Sp. of
Gal. 3:10 *as m. as* are of works
6:12 *as m. as* desire to make
16 *as m. as* walk to this rule
Phil. 3:15 let *as m. as* be perfect
Col. 2:1 *as m. as* not seen my fa.
1 *Tim.* 6:1 *as m.* servants *as* are
Rev. 2:24 *as m. as* have not this
3:19 *as m. as* I love I rebuke
13:15 *as m. as* wo. not worship

See BELIEVED, DAYS, HOW.

MANY people.

Ex. 5:5 *p.* of the land are m
Deut. 2:21 *p.* great and m.
Jud. 7:2 *p.* too m. for; 4 too m.
2 *Sam.* 1:4 m. of the *p.* are fallen
Ezr. 10:13 *p.* are m. time of rain
Est. 8:17 m. *p.* of land bec. Jews
Is. 2:3 m. *people* shall go
17:12 woe to multitude of m. *p.*
Ezek. 3:6 not to m. *p.* of strange
17:9 wither with. m. *p.* to pluck
32:9 I will vex hearts of m. *p.*
10 I will make m. *p.* amazed
38:9 and m. *p.* with thee, 15
Mic. 4:3 he shall judge am. m. *p.*
13 shalt beat in pieces m. *p.*
5:7 remnant of J. amidst m. *p.*
Zec. 8:22 m. *p.* come and seck L
Rev. 10:11 must prop. bef. m. *p.*

MANY things.

Job 23:14 m. such *t.* are wi. him
Ec. 6:11 m. *t.* that incr. vanity
Is. 42:20 seeing m. *t.* but observ.
Mat. 13:3 spake m. *t.* in parables
16:21 and suffer m. *things*, *Mark*
8:31; 9:12; *Luke* 9:22; 17:25
25:21 ruler over m. *things*
27:19 I have suffered m. *things*
Mark 6:20 he did m. *t.* and heard
Luke 10:41 troubled about m. *t.*
John 8:26 have m. *t.* to say, 16:12
21:25 m. other *t.* wh. Jesus did
Acts 26:9 that I ought to do m. *t.*
Gal. 3:4 suffer. so m. *t.* in vain ?
Heb. 5:11 we have m. *t.* to say
Jam. 3:2 in m. *t.* we offend all
2 *John* 12 having m. *things* to
write to you, 3 *John* 13

MANY a time, s.

1 *K.* 22:16 how m. *t.* I adj. thee ?
Neh. 9:28 m. *times* didst thou deliver them, *Ps.* 106:43
Ps. 78:38 m. a *t.* turned anger
129:1 m. a *t.* they afflicted me, 2

See WATERS.

MANY years.

Lev. 25:51 if th. be m. *y.* behind
Ezr. 5:11 house builded m. *y.*
Neh. 9:30 m. *years* didst forbear
Ec. 6:3 if a man live m. *years*
11:8 if a man live m. *y.* and rej.
Is. 32:10 m. days and *y.* troubled
Ezek. 38:17 wh. prophesied m. *y.*
Zec. 7:3 weep as I done th. m. *y.*
Luke 12:19 goods laid up m. *y.*
15:29 these m. *y.* do I serve
Acts 24:10 been m. *y.* a judge
17 after m. *y.* I came to bring
Rom. 15:23 desire m. *y.* to come

MAR.

Lev. 19:27 nor m. corn. of beard
Ruth 4:6 lest I m. own inherit.
1 *Sam.* 6:5 mice that m. the land
2 *K.* 3:19 m. good piece of land
Job 30:13 they m. my path, they
Jer. 13:9 thus I m. pride of Jud.

MARRED.

Is. 52:14 his visage was so m.

Jer. 13:7 girdle m. 18:4 ves. m.
Nah. 2:2 and m. vine branches
Mark 2:22 the bottles will be m.

MARA. *Ruth* 1:20

MARAH.

Ex. 15:23 drink of wat. of M.
Num. 33:8 3 days, pitched in M.

MARAN-ATHA.

1 *Cor.* 16:22 him be anath. m.

MARBLE.

1 *Chr.* 29:2 prepared m. in abun.
Est. 1:6 silver rings, pill. of m.
Cant. 5:15 his legs as pill. of m.
Rev. 18:12 ves. of m. no man buy.

MARCH.

Ps. 68:7 didst m. thro' wildern.
Jer. 46:22 shall m. with army
Joel 2:7 shall m. ev. one his ways
Hab. 1:6 m. thro' breadth of land
3:12 thou didst m. through land

MARCHED, ST.

Ex. 14:10 Egypt. m. after them
Jud. 5:4 thou m. earth trembled

MARCUS.

Col. 4:10 M. sister's son to Barn.
Phile. 24 M. saluteth, 1 *Pet.* 5:13

MARK.

Acts 12:12 John, surnam. M.
15:39 took M. sailed to Cyprus
2 *Tim.* 4:11 take M. bring him

MARK, Substantive.

Gen. 4:15 L. set a m. upon Cain
1 *Sam.* 20:20 as tho' I shot at m.
Job 7:20 why set me as a m. ag.
thee ? 16:12 ; *Lam.* 3:12
Ezek. 9:4 a m. on men that sigh
Phil. 3:14 press tow. m. for prize
Rev. 13:16 caused all to rec. a m.
17 none buy, save that had m.
14:9 any man rec. m. in foreh.
11 whosoever receiveth his m.
15:2 over image, and over his m.
16:2 on them had m. of beast
19:20 deceived them that rec. m.
20:4 nor his m. they liv. wi. Ch.

MARK, Verb.

Ruth 3:4 thou shalt m. the place
1 *K.* 20:7 m. how this man seek.
22 m. and see what thou doest
Job 18:2 m. and we will speak
21:5 m. me and be astonished
33:31 m. well, O J. heark. to me
Ps. 37:37 m. the perfect man
48:13 m. well her bulwarks
56:6 they m. my steps
130:3 if thou shouldest m. iniq.
Ezek. 44:5 m. entering of house
Rom. 16:17 m. th. who cause div.
Phil. 3:17 m. them who walk so

MARKED.

1 *Sam.* 1:12 Eli m. her mouth
Job 22:15 hast thou m. old way ?
24:16 they had m. in daytime
Jer. 2:22 iniquity is m. befo. me
23:18 m. his word and heard it
Luke 14:7 m. how they ch. rooms

MARKS.

Lev. 19:28 not print any m.
Gal. 6:17 I bear in body m. of L.

MARKEST, ETH.

Job 10:14 if I sin, then thou m.
33:11 stocks, he m. all my paths
Is. 44:13 m. it out with compass

MARKET, S.

Ezek. 27:13 traded in m. 17, 19, 25
Mat. 11:16 children sitting in m.
20:3 others standing idle in m.
23:7 love greetings in the m.
Luke 11:43 ; 20:46
Mark 7:4 when they come fr. m.
12:38 love salutations in m.
Luke 7:32 child. sitting in m.-pl.
John 5:2 a pool by the sheep-m.
Acts 16:19 drew them into m.-p.

17:17 disputed in the m. daily.

MARRIAGE.

Ex. 21:10 duty of m. sh. he not
Ps. 78:63 maid, not given to m.
Mat. 22:2 king made m. for son
4 ready, come unto the m.
9 all ye find, bid to the m.
30 in resurrection not given in
m. *Mark* 12:25 ; *Luke* 20:35
24:38 given in m. until day N.
25:10 ready went wi. him to m.
Luke 17:27 given in m. 20:34
John 2:1 a m. in Cana of Galilee
1 *Cor.* 7:38 giveth her in m.
Heb. 13:4 m. is honorable in all
Rev. 19:7 m. of Lamb is come
9 called to m. supper of Lamb

MARRIAGES.

Gen. 34:9 make ye m. with us
Deut. 7:3 nei. shalt thou make m.
Jos. 23:12 if ye make m.

MARRY.

Gen. 38:8 go to bro. wife, m. her
Num. 36:6 only to family of th.
father's tribe shall they m.
Deut. 25:5 wife of dead sh. not m.
Is. 62:5 so shall thy sons m.
Mat. 5:32 m. her that is divorced
19:9 ; *Mark* 10:11
19:10 be so, it is not good to m.
22:24 brother shall m. his wife
30 nei. m. nor given in marri.
Mark 12:25 ; *Luke* 20:35
1 *Cor.* 7:9 cannot cont. let them
m. better to m. than to burn
36 he sinneth not, let them m.
1 *Tim.* 4:3 forbidding to m. and
5:11 wax wanton, they will m.
14 younger wom. m. bear chil.

MARRIED.

Gen. 19:14 to them th. m. daugh.
Ex. 21:3 m. wife go out wi. him
Lev. 22:12 if m. to a stranger
Num. 12:1 E. whom he had m.
36:3 if m. to sons of other tribes
Deut. 22:22 lying with wom. m.
1 *Chr.* 2:21 m. wh. sixty years old
Neh. 13:23 m. wives of Ashdod
Prov. 30:23 odious wh. she is m.
Is. 54:1 more of desolate than m.
62:4 thy land shall be m.
Jer. 3:14 turn, for I am m. to you
Mal. 2:11 m. dau. of strange god
Mat. 22:25 first when he had m.
Mark 6:17 for he had m. her
10:12 m. another com. adultery
Luke 14:20 m. a wife, can. come
17:27 they drank, they m. wives
Rom. 7:3 husband liv. she be m.
1 *Cor.* 7:10 to the m. I command
33 but he that is m. careth for
34 she that is m. car. for thin.
39 to be m. to whom she will

MARRIETH.

Is. 62:5 as young man m. virgin
Mat. 19:9 m. her is put away,
doth com. adult. *Luke* 16:18

MARRYING.

Neh. 13:27 in m. strange wives
Mat. 24:38 m. giving in marriage

MARINERS.

Ezek. 27:8 inha. of Zidon thy m.
9 ships of sea with their m.
27 m. fall into midst of seas
29 m. come down fr. th. ships
Jon. 1:5 the m. were afraid

MARROW.

Job 21:24 bones moisten. with m.
Ps. 63:5 soul satisfied as wi. m.
Prov. 3:8 health and m. to bones
Is. 25:6 feast of things full of m.
Heb. 4:12 divi. asun. of j. and m.

MARSHES.

Ezek. 47:11 miry places and m.

MARS-HILL. *Acts* 17:22

MART.

Is. 23:3 she is a *m.* of nations

MARTHA.

Luke 10:38 a woman named M.
40 M. was cumbered, 41
John 11:1 town of M. 5, 30; 12:2

MARTYR, S.

Acts 22:20 blood of thy *m.* Step.
Rev. 2:13 Anti. was faithful *m.*
17:6 drunken with blood of *m.*

MARVEL, S.

Ex. 34:10 *m.* as have not been
2 *Cor.* 11:14 no *m.* Satan transf.

MARVEL.

Ec. 5:8 *m.* not at the matter
Mark 5:20 and all men did *m.*
John 5:20 that ye may *m.*
  28 *m.* not at this, hour is com.
7:21 done one work, and ye *m.*
Acts 3:12 Is. why *m.* ye at this?
Gal. 1:6 I *m.* that ye are so soon
1 *John* 3:13 *m.* not if world hate
Rev. 17:7 wheref. didst thou *m.?*

MARVELLED.

Gen. 43:33 men *m.* one at anoth.
Ps. 48:5 saw it, and so they *m.*
Mat. 8:10 Jesus heard it, he *m.*
  27 but the men *m.* saying
9:8 *m.* and glorified God, 33
22:22 they *m.* at him, *Mark*
  12:17; *Luke* 20:26
27:14 govern. *m. Mark* 15:5, 44
Mark 6:6 *m.* because of unbelief
Luke 1:21 *m.* he tarried so long
  63 name is John, they *m.* all
2:33 Joseph and his mother *m.*
7:9 when J. heard, he *m.* at him
John 4:27 *m.* he talked wi. wom.
7:15 Jews *m.* how knoweth this
Acts 2:7 *m.* are not th. Galileans?
4:13 *m.* took knowled. of them

MARVELLOUS.

Job 5:9 who doeth *m.* things
10:16 thou showest thyself *m.*
Ps. 17:7 show *m.* loving-kindn.
31:21 showed me *m.* kindness
78:12 *m.* things did he in sight
98:1 he hath done *m.* things
118:23 it is *m.* in our eyes, *Mat.*
  21:42; *Mark* 12:11
Dan. 11:36 speak *m.* things
Mic. 7:15 show unto him *m.* thi.
Zec. 8:6 be *m.* in mine eyes?
John 9:30 herein is a *m.* thing
1 *Pet.* 2:9 called you into *m.* light
Rev. 15:1 ano. sign great and *m.*

MARVELLOUS work, s.

1 *Chr.* 16:12 reme. his *m. works,*
  Ps. 105:5
  24 declare *m. w.* amo. nations
Ps. 9:1 show forth thy *m. w.*
139:14 great and *m.* are thy *w.*
  Rev. 15:3
Is. 29:14 I proceed to do *m. w.*

MARVELLOUSLY.

2 *Chr.* 26:15 he was *m.* helped
Job 37:5 thunder. *m.* with voice
Hab. 1:5 beh. regard, wonder *m.*

MARY.

Mat. 1:16 Joseph husband of M.
13:55 called M. *Mark* 6:3; 16:1
Luke 1:27 virgin's name was M.
2:5 w*i*th M. his wife, 16, 19
10:42 M. hath cho. *John* 11:1, 20
John 12:3 M. took pound of oint.
19:25 M. stood by cross, 20:16
Acts 1:14 conti. in prayer. wi. M.
12:12 Peter came to house of M.
Rom. 16:6 greet M. besto. labor

MARY Magdalene.

Mat. 27:56 amo. wh. were M. M.
  61; *Mark* 15:40; *John* 19:25
28:1 came M. M. *John* 20:1
Mark 16:1 M. M. brought spices,
  Luke 24:10

John 20:18 M. M. told disciples

MASONS.

2 *Sam.* 5:11 Hiram sent to David
  m. 1 *Chr.* 14:1
2 *K.* 12:12 gave money to *m.* and
  hew. of stone, 22:6 ; *Ezr.* 3:7
1 *Chr.* 22:2 set *m.* to hew stones
2 *Chr.* 24:12 hired *m.* to rep. hou.

MASSAH.

Ex. 17:7 place M. *Deut.* 33:8
Deut. 6:16 tempted in M. 9:22

MAST, S.

Prov. 23:34 lieth on top of a *m.*
Is. 33:23 could not strength. *m.*
Ezek. 27:5 cedars to make *m.*

. MASTER.

Gen. 39:20 *m.* put Jos. in prison
Ex. 21:8 she pleased not her *m.*
22:8 *m.* of the house be brought
Jud. 19:22 spake to *m.* of house
  23 *m.* of house went out to th.
1 *Sam.* 25:17 determined ag. *m.*
26:16 you have not kept your *m.*
2 *Sam.* 2:7 your *m.* Saul is dead
1 *K.* 22:17 the Lord said, These
  have no *m.* 2 *Chr.* 18:16
2 *K.* 6:5 alas *m.* it was borrowed
22 drink, and go to their *m.*
10:2 seeing your *m.* sons
  6 take heads of your *m.* sons
19:6 say to your *m. Is.* 37:6
1 *Chr.* 15:27 Chenan. *m.* of song
Is. 24:2 as with serv. so with *m.*
Dan. 1:3 king spake to the *m.*
4:9 O B. *m.* of magicians, 5:11
Mal. 1:6 if I be *m.* wh. fear?
2:12 the Lord will cut off *m.*
Mat. 8:19 *m.* I will follow thee
9:11 why eat. your *m.* wi. pub.?
10:25 if they have called *m.* Be.
12:58 *m.* we would see sign ˙
17:24 doth not your *m.* pay tri.?
22:16 *m.* we know that thou art
  true, *Mark* 12:14
23:8 one is your *m.* even Ch. 10
26:18 *m.* saith, Time is at hand
  25 Judas said, *m.* is it I?
  49 hail *m.* kissed, *Mark* 14:45
Mark 5:35 why troubl. thou *m.?*
9:5 *m.* it is good for us to be
  here, *Luke* 9:33
10:17 good *m.* what shall I do?
  Luke 10:25
13:35 ye know not wh. *m.* com.
Luke 7:40 *m.* say ; 8:24 perish
8:49 daugh. dead. troub. not *m.*
13:25 when *m.* of house is risen
John 3:10 art thou a *m.* of Isr.?
11:28 *m.* is come and call. for th.
13:13 ye call me *m.* ye say well
14 I your *m.* washed your feet
Acts 27:11 centurion believed *m.*
Eph. 6:9 *m.* is in heaven, *Col.* 4:1

His MASTER.

Gen. 24:9 hand un thigh of *h. m.*
39:2 Jos. was in house of *his m.*
Ex. 21:4 if *h. m.* given him wife
Deut. 23:15 thou sh. not deliv. to
  his m. serv. escaped fr. *h. m.*
Jud. 19:11 servant said to *h. m.*
1 *Sam.* 25:10 serv. break fr. *h. m.*
29:4 reconcile himself to *his m.*
2 *K.* 5:1 Naaman great wi. *h. m.*
6:32 sound of *h. m.* feet behind?
9:31 had Zi. peace, slew *h. m.?*
19:4 *his m.* hath sent to reproach God, *Is.* 37:4
1 *Chr.* 12:19 he will fall to *h. m.*
Job 3:19 servant free from *h. m.*
Prov. 27:18 that waiteth on *h. m.*
30:10 accuse not a serv. to *h. m.*
Is. 1:3 ass knoweth *his m.* crib
Mal. 1:6 a serv. honoreth *his m.*
Mat. 10:24 disciple is not above
  his m. Luke 6:40
  25 that disciple be as *h. m.*

Luke 6:40 ev. one perf. as *h. m.*
Rom. 14:4 to *h. m.* he standeth

My MASTER.

Gen. 24:12 my *m.* Abrah. 14:65
39:8 my *m.* wotteth not what is
Ex. 21:5 ser. say, I love *my m.*
1 *Sam.* 24:6 God forbid I do this
  to *my m.*
30:13 my *m.* left me bec. I fell
2 *K.* 5:18 *my m.* goeth into house
  20 my *m.* hath spared Naaman
6:15 my *m.* how shall we do?
10:9 I conspired against *my m.*
  27 hath *my m.* sent me to thy
    master? *Is.* 36:12
Is. 36:8 give pledges to *my m.*

Thy MASTER.

Gen. 24:51 be *thy m.* son's wife
1 *Sam.* 29:10 rise early wi. *t. m.*
2 *Sam.* 9:9 I give *t. m.* all that S.
12:8 *t. m.* house, *t. m.* wives
16:3 where is *thy m.* son?
2 *K.* 2:3 will take away *t. m.* 5
9:7 shalt smite house of *t. m.*
18:27 master sent me to *thy m.*

MASTER-BUILDER.

1 *Cor.* 3:10 as wise *m.-b.* I have

MASTERS.

Ex. 21:4 children sh. be her *m.*
Ps. 123:2 eyes of serv. look to *m.*
Prov. 25:13 refresheth soul of *m.*
Amos 4:1 say to *m.* let us drink
Zep. 1:9 fill *m.* houses with viol.
Mat. 6:24 no man can serve two
  m. Luke 16:13
23:10 neither be ye called *m.*
Acts 16:16 brought *m.* much gain
Eph. 6:5 be obedient to *m. Col.*
  3:22. *Tit.* 2:9 ; 1 *Pet.* 2:18
  9 ye, *m.* do the same things
    unto them, *Col.* 4:1
1 *Tim.* 6:1 count their *m.* worthy
  2 believ. *m.* let th. not despise
Jam. 3:1 not many *m.* knowing

MASTERY, IES.

Ex. 32:18 them that shout for *m.*
Dan. 6:24 lions had *m.* of them
1 *Cor.* 9:25 that striv. for the *m.*
2 *Tim.* 2:5 if a man strive for *m.*

MATE.

Is. 34:15 every vult. with her *m.*
  16 none shall want her *m.*

MATRIX.

Ex. 13:12 all that open *m.* 15
34:19 all that open. *m.* is mine
Num. 3:12 inst. of first-b. op. *m.*
18:15 ev. thing th. open *m.* thi.
MATTAN. 2 *K.* 11:18; 2 *Chr.*
  23:17
MATTATHIAS. *Luke* 3:25

MATTER.

Gen. 24:9 sware concerning *m.*
30:15 is it small *m.* th. ha. tak.
Ex. 18:16 have *m.* come to me
  22 ev. great *m.* they shall bring
  26 ev. small *m.* judged thems.
23:7 keep thee far fr. false *m.*
Num. 16:49 died about *m.* of K.
25:18 beguiled you in *m.* of P.
31:16 com. trespass in *m.* of P.
Deut. 17:8 if th. arise *m.* too hard
Ruth 3:18 know how *m.* will fall
1 *Sam.* 10:16 of the *m.* of kingd.
20:23 *m.* thou and I spoken of
2 *Sam.* 1:4 how went the *m.?*
18:13 no *m.* hid from king
20:18 ended *m.* 21 *m.* not so
1 *K.* 8:59 as the *m.* shall require
2 *Chr.* 26:32 every *m.* pert. to G.
1 *Chr.* 27:1 served king in any *m.*
1 *Chr.* 8:15 departed not from
  any *m.*
24:5 the *m.* they hastened not
Ezr. 5:5 till *m.* came to Darius
Neh. 6:13 have *m.* for evil report

Est. 2:23 inquisition made of *m.*
Job 19:28 seeing root of the *m.*
32:18 answer, I am full of *m.*
Ps. 45:1 heart inditing good *m.*
64:5 encourage them. in evil *m.*
Prov. 11:13 spirit concealeth *m.*
16:20 that handleth a *m.* wisely
17:9 repeat. *m.* separateth frien.
18:13 answereth *m.* bef. heareth
25:2 honor of kings to search *m.*
Ec. 10:20 hath wings tell *m.*
12:13 hear conclusion of *m.*
Jer. 38:27 *m.* was not perceived
Dan. 2:10 not a man can sh. *m.*
7:28 hitherto is the end of *m.*
9:23 understand *m.* and consid.
Mark 10:10 disci. asked same *m.*
Acts 15:6 elders consider this *m.*
18:14 said, If it were *m.* of wro.
19:38 if Demetrius have a *m.*
24:22 I will know utterm. of *m.*
1 *Cor.* 6:1 dare any having a *m.*
2 *Cor.* 9:5 as a *m.* of bounty
Gal. 2:6 maketh no *m.* to me
Jam. 3:5 how gr. a *m.* little fire

This MATTER.

Deut. 3:26 speak no more of *t. m.*
22:26 slay. neighbor so is *th. m.*
1 *Sam.* 30:24 hearken in *this m.*
2 *Sam.* 19:42 angry for *this m.?*
Ezr. 5:5 concerning *this m.*
10:4 *this m.* belongeth to thee
9 people trembling bec. of *t. m.*
Est. 9:26 concerning *this m.*
Dan. 1:14 M. consented in *t. m.*
3:16 not careful to ans. in *t. m.*
Acts 8:21 nei. part nor lot in *t. m.*
17:32 hear thee again of *this m.*
2 *Cor.* 7:11 yoursel. clear in *t. m.*

MATTERS.

Ex. 24:14 if any have *m.*
1 *Sam.* 16:18 prudent in *m.*
2 *Sam.* 11:19 end of telling *m.*
15:3 see *m.* are good and right
19:29 speakest any more of *m.?*
2 *Chr.* 19:11 Ama. over you in *m.*
Neh. 11:24 all *m.* concerning peo.
Est. 3:4 Mord.'s *m.* would stand
9:31 the *m.* of the fastings, 32
Job 33:13 giv. not account of *m.*
Ps. 35:20 deceitful *m.* ag. them
131:1 nor exercise myself in *m.*
Dan. 1:20 in *m.* of wisd. he found
7:1 and told the sum of the *m.*
Mat. 23:23 omitted weightier *m.*
Acts 18:15 no judge of such *m.*
19:39 any thing conc. other *m.*
25:20 be judged of these *m.*
1 *Cor.* 6:2 judge the smallest *m.*
1 *Pet.* 4:15 busybody in men's *m.*

MATTHEW. *Mat.* 9:9; 10:3;
Mark 3:18; *Luke* 6:15; *Acts*
1:13

MATTHIAS. *Acts* 1:23, 26

MATTOCK, S.

1 *Sam.* 13:20 sharpen axe and *m.*
21 they had a file for the *m.*
2 *Chr.* 34:6 did Josiah with th. *m.*
Is. 7:25 hills be digged with *m.*

MAUL.

Prov. 25:18 false witness, is a *m.*

MAW.

Deut. 18:3 to priest 2 ch. and *m.*

MAZZAROTH. *Job* 38:32

MEADOW, S.

Gen. 41:2 and they fed in a *m.*
Jud. 20:33 out of *m.* of Gibeah

MEAL.

Num. 5:15 ephah of barley *m.*
2 *K.* 4:41 *m.* cast it into pot
1 *Chr.* 12:40 nigh brought *m.*
Is. 47:2 millstones, grind *m.*
Hos. 8:7 bud shall yield no *m.*
See BARREL, MEASURES.

MEAL-TIME.

Ruth 2:14 at *m.-t.* come hither

MEAN, Verb.

Ex. 12:26 *m.* ye by this service?
Deut. 6:20 what *m.* testimonies?
Jos. 4:6 what *m.* th. stones? 21
Is. 3:15 what *m.* ye that ye beat
Ezek. 17:12 what these thi. *m.?*
18:2 what *m.* that use prov.?
Mark 9:10 wh. ris. fr. dead *m.?*
Acts 10:17 what vision sho. *m.*
17:20 know what th. things *m.*
21:13 what *m.* ye to weep and
2 *Cor.* 8:13 I *m.* not that oth. men

MEAN, Adjective.

Prov. 22:29 not stand bef. *m.* men
Is. 2:9 *m.* man boweth down
5:15 *m.* man shall be bro. down
31:8 sw. not of *m.* man devour

MEAN time.

Luke 12:1 *m.* t. gath. multitude

MEAN while.

1 *K.* 18:45 *m. w.* heaven black
John 4:31 *m. w.* disciples prayed
Rom. 2:15 thoughts *m. w.* accus.

MEANEST, ETH.

Gen. 33:8 what *m.* thou by this?
Deut. 29:24 what *m.* this anger?
1 *Sam.* 4:6 wh. *m.* this shout? 14
15:14 what *m.* this bleating?
2 *Sam.* 16:2 what *m.* thou by
these? *Ezek.* 37:18
Is. 10:7 howbeit he *m.* not so
Jon. 1:6 wh. *m.* thou, O sleep.?
Mat. 9:13 learn what that *m.*
12:7 if ye had kn. what this *m.*
Acts 2:12 saying, What *m.* this?

MEANING, Substantive.

Dan. 8:15 D. had sought for *m.*
1 *Cor.* 14:11 if I know not the *m.*

MEANING.

Acts 27:2 *m.* to sail by coa. of A.

MEANS.

Ex. 34:7 will by no means clear
the guilty, *Num.* 14:18
Jud. 5:22 broken by *m.* of pran.
16:5 by what *m.* may prevail
2 *Sam.* 14:14 doth he devise *m.*
1 *K.* 20:39 if by any *m.* be miss.
Jer. 5:31 priests bear rule by *m.*
Mal. 1:9 hath been by your *m.*
Mat. 5:26 by no *m.* come out
Luke 5:18 sought *m.* to bring
10:19 nothing by any *m.* hurt
John 9:21 by what *m.* he seeth
Acts 4:9 by what *m.* he is whole
18:21 must by all *m.* keep feast
Rom. 1:10 any *m.* I mi. journey
1 *Cor.* 8:9 by any *m.* this liberty
9:22 I might by all *m.* save
27 by any *m.* when I preached
2 *Cor.* 1:11 by *m.* of many
11:3 lest by any *m.* as serpent
Gal. 2:2 lest by any *m.* I sho. run
1 *Thes.* 3:5 lest by some *m.*
2 *Thes.* 2:3 no man dec. by any *m.*
3:16 peace always by all *m.*
Heb. 9:15 by *m.* of death called

MEANT.

Gen. 50:20 God *m.* it unto good
Luke 15:26 asked what these *m.*
18:36 passed, asked what it *m.*

MEASURE.

Ex. 26:2 curtains sh. ha. one *m.* 8
Lev. 19:35 not do unright. in *m.*
Deut. 25:15 just *m.* sh. th. have
1 *K.* 6:25 cub. one *m.* 7:37 bases
2 *K.* 7:1 a *m.* of fine flour, 16, 18
Job 11:9 the *m.* thereof is longer
28:25 weigheth the waters by *m.*
Ps. 39:4 to know *m.* of my days
80:5 tears to drink in great *m.*
Is. 5:14 hell opened without *m.*
27:8 in *m.* when it shoot. forth
40:12 com. dust of earth in *m.*

Jer. 30:11 cor. thee in *m.* 46:28
51:13 *m.* of thy covetousness
Ezek. 4:11 drink water by *m.* 16
Mic. 6:10 scant *m.* abominable
Mat. 7:2 with what *m.* you mete,
Mark 4:24; *Luke* 6:38
23:32 fill ye up *m.* of your fath.
Mark 6:51 amazed beyond *m.*
Luke 6:38 good *m.* pressed down
John 3:34 G. giveth not Sp. by *m.*
Rom. 12:3 dealt to every man *m.*
2 *Cor.* 1:8 were pressed out of *m.*
10:13 not boast of things with.
our *m.* but acco. to *m.* 14, 15
11:23 in stripes above *m.*
12:7 lest I be exalted above *m.*
Gal. 1:13 beyond *m.* I persecuted
Eph. 4:7 according to *m.* of Ch.
13 to the *m.* of the stature
16 working in *m.* of every part
Rev. 6:6 *m.* of wheat for penny
21:17 according to *m.* of a man

MEASURE, Verb.

Num. 35:5 *m.* from without city
Deut. 21:2 they shall *m.* to cities
Is. 65:7 I will *m.* their for. work
Ezek. 43:10 let them *m.* pattern
Rev. 11:1 and *m.* temple of God
21:15 a golden reed to *m.* city

MEASURED.

Ruth 3:15 *m.* six meas. of barley
2 *Sam.* 8:2 *m.* with a line
Is. 40:42 who *m.* wat, in hand?
Jer. 31:37 heaven ab. can be *m.*
33:22 sand of sea cannot be *m.*
Ezek. 40:5 he *m.* the breadth of
building, 6, 8, 9, 11, 13 24
41:5 he *m.* wall; 13 *m.* house
15 *m.* the length of building
42:16 he *m.* east with a measu.
17 *m.* north ; 18 south ; 19 west
Hos. 1:10 sand of sea not be *m.*
Hab. 3:6 he stood and *m.* earth
Rev. 21:16 *m.* city ; 17 *m.* wall

MEASURES.

Gen. 18:6 three *m.* of fine meal
Deut. 25:14 not have divers *m.*
1 *K.* 4:22 Solo.'s provision 30 *m.*
of flour, and 60 *m.* of meal
5:11 gave Hir. 20,000 *m.* wheat,
20 *m.* of pure oil, 2 *Chr.* 2:10
18:32 would contain 2 *m.* seed
1 *Chr.* 23:29 for all manner of *m.*
Ezr. 7:22 hundred *m.* of wheat
Job 38:5 hath laid *m.* thereof?
Prov. 20:10 divers *m.* abo. to L.
Jer. 13:25 is portion of thy *m.*
Ezek. 40:24 accord. to these *m.* 29
28 gate according to th. *m.* 32
Hag. 2:16 a heap of twenty *m.*
Mat. 13:33 like unto leaven hid
in three *m.* meal, *Luke* 13:21
Luke 16:6 a hundred *m.* of oil
7 he said, A hundred *m.* wheat
See BARLEY.

MEASURING.

Jer. 31:39 *m.* line shall go forth
Ezek. 40:3 man with *m.* reed, 5
42:16 with *m.* reed, 17, 18, 19
Zec. 2:1 with *m.* line in hand
2 *Cor.* 10:12 *m.* thems. by them.

MEAT.

Gen. 1:29 to you it sh. be for *m.*
30 I have given ev. herb for *m.*
9:3 ev. moving thing sh. be *m.*
27:31 E. also made savory *m.*
Lev. 22:11 he that is born in his
house shall eat of his *m.*
25:6 land shall be *m.* for you, 7
Deut. 2:6 ye sh. buy *m.* of them
28 shalt sell me *m.* for money
20:20 destroy trees not for *m.*
Jud. 1:7 kings gathered their *m.*
14:14 of eater came forth *m.*
1 *Sam.* 20:5 not fail to sit at *m.*

2 *Sam.* 11:8 follow. a mess of *m.*
12:3 it did eat of his own *m.*
1 *K.* 10.5 she saw the *m.* of his
table, 2 *Chr.* 9:4
19:8 he went in strength of *m.*
1 *Chr.* 12:40 were nigh bro. *m.*
Ezr. 3:7 gave *m.* and drink
Job 6:7 ref. are as sorrowful *m.*
12:11 doth not mouth taste *m. ?*
20:14 *m.* in bowels is turned
33:20 soul abhorreth dainty *m.*
34:3 as the mouth tasteth *m.*
36:31 giveth *m.* in abundance
38:41 wander for lack of *m.*

Ps. 42:3 tears have been my *m.*
44:11 given us like sheep for *m.*
59:15 wand. up and down for *m.*
69:21 gave me gall for my *m.*
74:14 gavest him to be *m.* to p.
78:18 tempted G. by asking *m.*
25 he sent them *m.* to the full
30 while *m.* was in mouths
104:21 yo. lions seek *m.* fr. God
27 mayest give them their *m.*
107:18 soul abhorreth all *m.*
111:5 given *m.* to them that fear
145:15 givest them *m.* in season
Prov. 6:8 ant provideth her *m.*
30:22 a fool when filled with *m.*
25 they prepare th. *m.* in sum.
31:15 giveth *m.* to household
Is. 62:8 no more gi. *m.* to enem.
Lam. 1:11 pleasant things for *m.*
19 elders died whi. they sou. *m.*
Ezek. 4:10 *m.* shall be by weight
16:19 my *m.* which I gave thee
29:5 I have given thee for *m.* to
beasts, 34:5, 8
34:10 may not be *m.* for them
47:12 trees for *m.* fruit for *m.*

Dan. 1:8 not defile hims. with *m.*
4:12 in it was *m.* for all, 21
11:26 th. feed of *m.* sh. destroy
Hos. 11:4 I laid *m.* unto them
Joel 1:16 is not the *m.* cut off ?
Hab. 1:16 portion is fat, *m.* plen.
3:17 the fields shall yield no *m.*
Hag. 2:12 if one touch any *m.*
Mal. 3:10 that there may be *m.*
Mat. 3:4 and his *m.* was locusts
6:25 life more th. *m. ? Lu.* 12:23
9:10 as Jesus sat at *m.* in house,
26:7 ; *Mark* 2:15 ; 14:3 ; 16:14 ;
Luke 24:30
Mat. 10:10 wor. worthy of his *m.*
15:37 the broken *m. Mark* 8:8
24:45 *m.* in due seas. *Luke* 12:42
25:35 hungered, ye gave me *m.*
42 hungered, gave me no *m.*
Luke 3:11 he that hath *m.*
8:55 commanded to give her *m.*
14:10 worship in presence of th.
that sit at *m.*
17:7 will say, Sit down to *m.*
22:27 greater, he that sit. at *m.*
24:41 here any *m. ? John* 21:5
John 4:8 disci. gone to buy *m.*
32 I have *m.* to eat ye know
34 my *m.* is to do will of him
6:27 labor not for the *m.* which
perisheth, but for that *m.*
55 for my flesh is *m.* indeed
Acts 2:46 eat their *m.* with glad.
9:19 when he had received *m.*
27:33 besou. them to take *m.* 34
Rom. 14:15 grie. wi. thy *m.* dest.
not with *m.* for wh. C. died
17 kingdom of God not *m.*
20 for *m.* dest. not work of G.
1 *Cor.* 3:2 with milk, not wi. *m.*
8:8 *m.* commend. us not to G.
10 if any man see thee sit at *m.*
13 if *m.* make brother offend
10:3 did eat same spiritual *m*
Col. 2:16 no man judge you in *m.*
Heb. 5:12 milk, not strong *m.*
14 strong *m.* belongeth to th.

12:16 for *m.* sold his birthright
See FOWLS.

MEAT-OFFERING.

Ex. 29:41 according to *m.-o.*
Lev. 2:1 offer a *m.-o.* 4, 5, 7, 14
6:14 this is law of *m.-o.* 7:37
Num. 4:16 to Eleazar daily *m.-o.*
15:6 for *m.-o.* two tenth deals of
flour, 28:9, 12
Jos. 22:23 altar to offer *m.-o.*
Jud. 13:19 took kid with *m.-o.*
1 *Chr.* 21:23 wheat for the *m.-o.*
Is. 57:6 hast thou offered a *m.-o.*
Ezek. 42:13 there they lay *m.-o.*
44:29 they shall eat the *m.-o.*
46:5 *m.-o.* an ephah for ram
7 *m.-o.* an eph. for bullock, 11
Joel 1:9 the *m.-o.* is cut off
13 the *m.-o.* is withholden
2:14 even a *m.-o.* to our God

MEAT-OFFERINGS.

Jos. 22:29 build altar for *m.-o.*
1 *K.* 8:64 Solomon offered *m.-o.*
Ezr. 7:17 buy lambs with *m.-o.*
Neh. 13:5 where they laid *m.-o.*
Jer. 33:18 not want kindle *m.-o.*
Ezek. 45:17 prin. part give *m.-o.*
Amos 5:22 though ye offer *m.-o.*

MEATS.

Prov. 23:6 nei. desire dainty *m.*
Acts 15:29 abstain fr. *m.* offered
1 *Cor.* 6:13 *m.* for belly, belly *m.*
1 *Tim.* 4:3 to abstain from *m.*
Heb. 9:10 which stood only in *m.*
13:9 estab. with grace, not *m.*
MEDAD. *Num.* 11:26
MEDAN. *Gen.* 25:2

MEDDLE.

Deut. 2:5 *m.* not that of mount S.
19 *m.* not with child. of Am.
2 *K.* 14:10 why *m.* to thy hurt ?
2 *Chr.* 25:19
Prov. 20:19 *m.* not with him
24:21 *m.* not th. given to change

MEDDLED, ETH.

Prov. 17:14 contention bef. it *m.*
26:17 *m.* strife not belonging

MEDDLING.

2 *Chr.* 35:21 forbear fr. *m.* with G.
Prov. 20:3 every fool will be *m.*

MEDE, S.

2 *K.* 17:6 in cities of M. 18:11
Ezr. 6:2 in province of M.
Est. 1:19 among laws of M.
Is. 13:17 will stir M. *Jer.* 51:11
Dan. 5:28 kingd. is given to M.
6:8 law of M. 12 ; 9:1 ; 11:1

MEDIA.

Est. 1:3 of Persia and M. 14, 18
10:2 book of kings of M.
Is. 21:2 O M. all sighing ceaseth
Dan. 8:20 two horns kings of M.

MEDIATOR.

Gal. 3:19 angels in hand of *m.*
20 a *m.* is not a *m.* of one
1 *Tim.* 2:5 is but one *m.* Jesus
Heb. 8:6 *m.* of a better covenant
9:15 he is *m.* of New Testament
12:24 J. *m.* of the new covenant

MEDICINE.

Prov. 17:22 doeth good like a *m.*
Jer. 30:13 thou hast no heal. *m.*
46:11 in vain thou use many *m.*
Ezek. 47:12 the leaf sh. be for *m.*

MEDITATE.

Gen. 24:63 Isaac went out to *m.*
Jos. 1:8 *m.* therein day and nig.
Ps. 1:2 doth *m.* day and night
63:6 *m.* on th. in night watches
77:12 I will *m.* of all thy work
119:15 I *m.* in thy precepts, 78
23 serv. *m.* in thy statutes, 48
148 I might *m.* in thy word
143:5 I *m.* on all thy works

Is. 33:18 thy heart sh. *m.* terror
Luke 21:14 settle it not to *m.*
1 *Tim.* 4:15 *m.* upon these things

MEDITATION.

Ps. 5:1 give ear, consider my *m.*
19:14 let *m.* of heart be accept.
49:3 *m.* of heart sh. be of under.
104:34 *m.* of him shall be sweet
119:97 love thy law, it is my *m.*
99 thy testimonies are my *m.*

MEEK.

Num. 12:3 Moses was very *m.*
Ps. 22:26 *m.* sh. eat and be satis.
25:9 *m.* will he guide in judgm.
37:11 *m.* shall inherit the earth
76:9 God arose to save all *m.*
147:6 the Lord lifted up the *m.*
149:4 beautify *m.* with salvation
Is. 11:4 for the *m.* of earth
29:19 *m.* shall increase their joy
61:1 good tidings to the *m.*
Amos 2:7 turn aside way of *m.*
Zep. 2:3 seek L. ye *m.* of earth
Mat. 5:5 blessed are the *m.*
11:29 for I am *m.* and lowly
21:5 thy king cometh to thee *m.*
1 *Pet.* 3:4 ornament of a *m.* spirit

MEEKNESS.

Ps. 45:4 because of truth and *m.*
Zep. 2:3 seek *m.* ye shall be hid
1 *Cor.* 4:21 sh. I come in sp. of *m.?*
2 *Cor.* 10:1 beseech by *m.* of Chr.
Gal. 5:23 fruit of the Spirit is *m.*
6:1 restore in the spirit of *m.*
Eph. 4:2 with lowliness and *m,*
Col. 3:12 put on *m.* long-suffer.
1 *Tim.* 6:11 love, patience, *m.*
2 *Tim.* 2:25 in *m.* instruct. those
Tit. 3:2 showing *m.* to all men
Jam. 1:21 receive with *m.* word
3:13 works with *m.* of wisdom
1 *Pet.* 3:15 reason of hope wi. *m.*

MEET, Adjective.

Gen. 2:18 make a help *m.* for him
20 not found help *m.* for Adam
Ex. 8:26 it is not *m.* so to do
Deut. 3:18 all that are *m.* for war
Jud. 5:30 *m.* for necks of them
Job 34:31 it is *m.* to be said to G.
Prov. 11:24 withhol. more th. *m.*
Jer. 26:14 do wi. me as seem. *m.*
27:5 to whom it seemed *m.*
Ezek. 15:4 is it *m.* for any work
5 less shall it be *m.* for work
Mat. 3:8 fruits *m.* for repentance
15:26 not *m.* to take children's
bread, *Mark* 7:27
Acts 26:20 works *m.* for repent.
Rom. 1:27 recomp. wh. was *m.*
1 *Cor.* 15:9 not *m.* to be called
16:4 if it be *m.* that I go also
Col. 1:12 made us *m.* to be part.
2 *Thes.* 1:3 thank God, as it is *m.*
Heb. 6:7 herbs *m.* for them
2 *Pet.* 1:13 think *m.* to stir you

MEETEST.

2 *K.* 10:3 look out the *m.* of

MEET, Verb.

Gen. 24:65 walketh to *m.* us ?
32:6 E. cometh to *m.* thee, 33:4
46:29 Joseph went up to *m.* Is.
Ex. 4:14 Aaron com. to *m.* thee
27 go into wildern. to *m.* Mos.
18:7 M. went to *m.* fath.-in-law
19:17 bro. people to *m.* with G.
25:22 there I will *m.* with thee,
29:42, 43 ; 30:6, 36 ; *Num.* 17:4
Num. 23:15 while I *m.* Lord
Jos. 2:16 lest pursuers *m.* you
9:11 take victuals, go *m.* them
Jud. 11:31 out doors to *m.* me
34 daughter came to *m.* him
1 *Sam.* 10:3 shall *m.* thee 3 men
5 shalt *m.* company of proph.
18:6 women came to *m.* Saul
25:32 Lord sent thee to *m.* me

2 *Sam.* 6:20 Michal came to *m.* D.
1 *K.* 2:8 Shimei came down to *m.*
18:16 Obadiah went to meet A.
21:18 go down to *m.* Ahab
2 *K.* 1:3 go up to *m.* messengers
7 man came up to *m.* you?
2 *K.* 2:15 sons of prop. came to *m.*
4:26 run, I pray thee, to *m.* her
29 if *m.* any man, sal. him not
8:8 and go, *m.* the man of God
9 so Hazael went to *m.* him
9:17 take horseman, send to *m.*
Neh. 6:2 let us *m.* together, 10
Job 5:14 *m.* darkness in daytime
39:21 goeth to *m.* armed men
Prov. 7:15 came I forth to *m.*
17:12 bear robbed of whelps *m.*
22:2 rich and poor *m.* together
29:13 the po.r and deceit. man
m. toge..er
Is. 7:3 go fo rth to *m.* Ahaz
14:9 hell is moved to *m.* thee
34:14 beasts of desert shall *m.*
47:3 I will not *m.* thee
Jer. 51:31 one post run to *m.* an.
Amos 4:12 prepare to *m.* thy G.
Zec. 2:3 angel went out to *m.*
Mat. 8:34 city came to *m.* Jesus
25:1 went forth to *m.* bridegro.
6 bridegro. com. go to *m.* him
Mark 14:13 there shall *m.* you a
man, *Luke* 22:10
Luke 14:31 ten thou. to *m.* him
Acts 28:15 came to *m.* us as far
1 *Thes.* 4:17 in clouds to *m.* Lord

MEETEST, ETH, ING.

Gen. 32:17 E. my brother *m.* thee
Num. 35:19 when he *m.* him, 21
1 *Sam.* 21:1 afraid at *m.* of Dav.
Is. 1:13 iniq. even solemn *m.*
64:5 thou *m.* him that rejoiceth

MEGIDDO.

Jud. 5:19 fought by wat. of M.
1 *K.* 9:15 raised a levy build M.
2 *K.* 9:27; 23:30; 2 *Chr.* 35:22

MEGIDDON. *Zec.* 12:11
MEHETABEL. *Gen.* 36:39
MEHUJAEL. *Gen.* 4:18
MELCHI. *Luke* 3:24

MELCHISEDEK.

Gen. 14:18 M. bro. forth bread
Ps. 110:4 order of M. *Heb.* 5:10
Heb. 7:1 M. priest of God, 10, 21

MELITA. *Acts* 28:1

MELODY.

Is. 23:16 make sweet *m.* sing
51:3 found therein, voice of *m.*
Amos 5:23 not hear *m.* of viols
Eph. 5:19 making *m.* to Lord

MELONS.

Num. 11:5 we remember the *m.*

MELT.

Ex. 15:15 inhabit. of Canaan *m.*
Jos. 2:11 our hearts did *m.*
14:8 bret. made heart of peo. *m.*
2 *Sam.* 17:10 heart of lion, ut. *m.*
Ps. 58:7 let them *m.* away
Is. 13:7 every man's heart shall
m. Ezek. 21:7
19:1 heart of Egypt shall *m.*
Jer. 9:7 behold, I will *m.* them
Ezek. 22:20 to *m.* it I will leave
Amos 9:5 touch. land, it shall *m.*
13 the hills shall *m. Nah.* 1:5
2 *Pet.* 3:10 elem. *m.* with heat, 12

MELTED.

Ex. 16:21 sun waxed hot it *m.*
Jos. 5:1 heard that th. hearts *m.*
7:5 the hearts of the people *m.*
Jud. 5:5 mountains *m.* bef. Lord
1 *Sam.* 14:16 multitude *m.* away
Ps. 22:14 heart *m.* in midst
46:6 uttered voice, the earth *m.*
97:5 the hills *m.* like wax
107:26 soul *m.* bec. of trouble

Is. 34:3 mountains *m.* wi. blood
Ezek. 22:21 *m.* in midst thereof
22 as silver is *m.* in. furnace

MELTETH.

Ps. 58:8 as a snail which *m.* let
68:2 wax *m.* so let wicked peri.
119:28 my soul *m.* for heaviness
147:18 sendeth out word *m.* th.
Jer. 6:29 the founder *m.* in vain
Nah. 2:10 heart of Nineveh *m.*

MELTING.

Jam. 64:2 as when *m.* fire burne.

MEMBER.

Deut. 23:1 his privy *m.* cut off
1 *Cor.* 12:14 body is not one *m.*
19 all one *m.* where were bo. ?
26 one *m.* suffer, one *m.* honor.
Jam. 3:5 the tongue is a little *m.*

MEMBERS.

Job 17:7 my *m.* are as a shadow
Ps. 139:16 in book all *m.* written
Mat. 5:29 one of *m.* sh. perish, 30
Rom. 6:13 nei. your *m.* instrum.
7:5 sins did work in our *m.*
Rom. 7:23 see ano. law in *m.* wa.
12:4 many *m.* in one body
5 every one *m.* one of another
1 *Cor.* 6:15 your bodies *m.* of C.
12:12 the body hath many *m.*
18 but now hath G. set the *m.*
20 but now are they many *m.*
26 all the *m.* suffer with it
27 are the body of Ch. and *m.*
Eph. 4:25 are *m.* one of another
5:30 we are *m.* of his body
Col. 3:5 mortify your *m.* on ear.
Jam. 3:6 tongue one of our *m.*
4:1 lusts that war in your *m.*

MEMORIAL.

Ex. 3:15 *m.* unto all generations
17:14 wri. this for a *m.* in book
28:12 for stones of *m.* to Israel
29 for a *m.* before the L. 39:7
30:16 money may be for a *m.*
Lev. 23:24 a *m.* of blowing trumpets, *Num.* 10:10
24:7 frankinc. on bread for *m.*
Num. 5:15 it is an offering of *m.*
18 offering of *m.* in her hands
16:40 brazen censers a *m.* to Is.
31:54 gold of captains for *m.*
Jos. 4:7 th. stones sh. be for *m.*
Neh. 2:20 have no portion nor *m.*
Est. 9:28 nor *m.* of them perish
Ps. 9:6 th. *m.* perished with th.
135:13 *m.* through. all generat.
Hos. 12:5 L. of hosts; L. is his *m.*
Zec. 6:14 the crowns be for a *m.*
Mat. 26:13 this be told for a *m.*
of her, *Mark* 14:9
Acts 10:4 prayers come up for *m.*

MEMORY.

Ps. 109:15 cut off *m.* of them
145:7 utter *m.* of thy goodness
Prov. 10:7 *m.* of the just blessed
Ec. 9:5 *m.* of them is forgotten
Is. 26:14 made their *m.* to perish
1 *Cor.* 15:2 keep in *m.* I preach.

MEMUCAN. *Est.* 1:14, 16, 21
MEMPHIS. *Hos.* 9:6

MEN.

Gen. 4:26 began *m.* to call on L.
6:1 when *m.* began to multiply
18:2 lo, three *m.* stood by him
19:4 *m.* of the city, *m.* of Sodom
32:28 power with God and *m.*
34:21 these *m.* are peaceable
42:11 true *m.* 31; 43:16 bring
46:32 *m.* are shepherds
Ex. 1:17 saved *m.* children, 18
10:11 ye th. *m.* serve the Lord
34:23 thrice in year *m.* children
Num. 13:32 *m.* of great stature
16:14 put out eyes of these *m.*
29 these *m.* die the death of all

Deut. 1:35 not one of these *m.*
shall see good land
33:6 let R. let not his *m.* be few
Jud. 6:27 he feared *m.* of city
9:54 *m.* say not of me, A woman
1 *Sam.* 2:26 favor with L. and *m.*
2 *Sam.* 3:39 these *m.* sons of Zer.
10:12 play the *m.* for our people
19:28 dead *m.* before the king
23:3 ruleth over *m.* must be just
20 slew two lion-like *m.* of
Moab, 1 *Chr.* 11:22
2 *Chr.* 6:18 will God dw. wi. *m.* ?
Ps. 9:20 kn. thems. to be but *m.*
17:14 from *m.* wh. are thy hand
82:7 but ye shall die like *m.*
Is. 7:13 sm. thing to weary *m.* ?
31:3 now the Egyptians are *m.*
38:16 O L. by th. things *m.* live
43:4 there. will I gi. *m.* for thee
46:8 rememb. show yoursel. *m.*
Mic. 7:6 man's enemies are *m.*
Hab. 1:14 makest *m.* as fishes
Zec. 3:8 they are *m.* wondered at
Mat. 7:12 whatsoe. ye would *m.*
should do to you, *Luke* 6:31
10:32 conf. me bef. *m. Luke* 12:8
13:25 *m.* slept, enemy came
16:13 *m.* say I am? *Mark* 8:27
Mark 8:24 *m.* as trees walking
10:27 Jesus saith, With *m.* it is
impossible, *Luke* 18:27
Luke 2:14 good will toward *m.*
5:10 hencef. thou shalt catch *m.*
12:48 to wh. *m.* have commit.
18:11 I am not as other *m.* are
Acts 2:13 these *m.* full of wine
5:4 thou hast not lied unto *m.*
29 to obey God rather than *m.*
10:19 behold three *m.* seek thee
14:15 we are *m.* of like passions
24:16 void of off. to God and *m.*
Rom. 1:27 *m.* with *m.* working
1 *Cor.* 4:9 spe. to angels and *m.*
14:2 for he speaketh not to *m.*
1 *Cor.* 14:21 with *m.* of other to.
2 *Cor.* 8:13 not that other *m.* be
Eph. 6:7 L. not to *m. Col.* 3:23
1 *Thes.* 2:4 speak not as plea. *m.*
Heb. 6:16 for *m.* verily swear
7:8 *m.* that die receive tithes
9:27 is appointed to *m.* once to
12:23 spir. of just *m.* made perf.
Jam. 3:9 therewith curse we *m.*
1 *Pet.* 4:6 judged according to *m.*
2 *Pet.* 1:21 holy *m.* of G. spake
Rev. 9:4 only those *m.* wh. have
21:3 tabernacle of G. is with *m.*

All MEN.

Ps. 89:47 made all *m.* in vain
116:11 I sa. in haste, *a. m.* liars
Ex. 7:2 that is the end of *all m.*
Zec. 8:10 set *a. m.* ag. neighbor
Luke 6:26 woe wh. *a. m.* speak
John 5:23 *all m.* sh. honor the S.
12:32 will draw *all m.* unto me
Rom. 5:12 death pas. upon *a. m.*
18 judgment came on *all m.* to
condemnation, the free gift
came on *all m.* to justificat.
12:17 honest in sight of *all m.*
18 live peaceably with *all m.*
1 *Cor.* 7:7 I would *all m.* were as
9:19 for tho' I be free fr. *all m.*
15:19 we are of *all m.* most mis.
2 *Cor.* 3:2 kn. and read of *all m.*
Gal. 6:10 let us do good to *all m.*
1 *Thes.* 2:15 contrary to *all m.*
5:15 follow wh. is good to *all m.*
2 *Thes.* 3:2 *all m.* have not faith
1 *Tim.* 2:1 giving tha. for *a. m.*
4 will have *all m.* to be saved
4:10 trust in God, Sa. of *all m.*
2 *Tim.* 2:24 be gentle to *all m.*
4:16 no man stood, *all m.* forso.
Tit. 2:11 grace of G. ap. to *all m.*
Heb. 12:14 fol. peace with *all m.*
Jam. 1:5 ask of G. th. giv. *all m.*

1 *Pet.* 2:17 honor *all m.* love bro.
3 *John* 12 D. good rep. of *all m.*

See BRETHREN, CHIEF, CHIL-
DREN, CHOSEN, EVIL, GREAT.

In MEN.

1 *Cor.* 3:21 no man glory *in m.*

See ISRAEL, JUDAH.

Like MEN.

1 *Sam.* 4:9 your *. l. m.* 1 *Cor.* 16:13
Ps. 82:7 ye shall die *like m.*
Hos. 6:7 they *l. m.* transg. cove.
Luke 12:36 *l. m.* that wait for L.

Mighty MEN.

Gen. 6:4 *m. m.* whi. were of old
Jos' 1:14 *m. m.* of valor sh. pass
8:3 Joshua ch. out 30,000 *m. m.*
1 *Sam.* 2:4 bows of *m. m.* broken
2 *Sam.* 16:6 *m. m.* on his right
17:8 *m.* that they may be *m.*
23:8 these be names of *m. m.*
16 *mighty m.* brake host, *m.*
1 *K.* 1:8 *m. m.* not with Adonij.
10 *m. m.* and Sol. he called not
2 *K.* 15:20 exact. *m. m.* of wealth
24:14 carri. away *m. m.* of valor
1 *Chr.* 5:24 and were *m. m.* of
valor, 7:7, 9, 11, 40
12:1 they were among the *m. m.*
29:24 *m. m.* submitted to Solo.
2 *Chr.* 13:3 J. set battle against
Abijah, being *mighty m.* of
valor, 14:8 ; 17:13, 14, 16
25:6 Amaz. hired 100,000 *m. m.*
32:3 H. took counsel with *m. m.*
21 angel cut off all the *m. m.*
Neh. 11:14 their brethren *m. m.*
Job 34:24 break in pieces *m. m.*
Ec. 7:19 wisdom strength. *m. m.*
Cant. 4:4 shields of *mighty m.*
Is. 21:17 *m. m.* sh. be diminish.
Jer. 5:16 they are all *mighty m.*
46:9 *m. m.* come ; 48:14 we are
48:41 the hearts of *m. m.* of M.
49:22 heart of *mighty m.* of Ed.
50:36 a sword is upon her *m. m.*
51:30 *m. m.* of Babylon forbor.
56 her *m. m.* are taken
57 drunk captains and *m. m.*
Lam. 1:15 L. hath trodden *m. m.*
Ezek. 39:20 at table with *m. m.*
Dan. 3:20 commanded *m. m.*
Hos. 10:13 trust in *mighty m*
Joel 2:7 they sh. run like *m. m.*
3:9 prepare war, wake *m. m.*
Ob. 9 thy *m. m.* O Teman
Nah. 2:3 shield of his *mighty m.*
Zec. 10:5 they shall be as *m. m.*
Rev. 6:15 *m. m.* hide themselves
19:18 ye may eat flesh of *m. m.*

MEN-PLEASERS.

Eph. 6:6 eye-servants as *m.-p.*
Col. 3:22

Sons of MEN.

Ps. 4:2 O ye *s. of m.* how 1. 58:1
31:19 trust in thee bef. *s. of m.*
33:13 Lord beholdeth *s. of m.*
57:4 I lie among the *sons of m.*
145:12 to make kno. to *s. of m.*
Prov. 8:31 del. were wi. *s. of m.*
Ec. 1:13 hath given to *s. of m.*
2:3 delights of the *sons of m.*
3:10 God hath given to *s. of m.*
18 concerning estate of *s. of m.*
8:11 *s. of m.* to do evil
9:3 heart of *s. of m.* full of evil
12 so are *s. of m.* snared in ev.
Is. 52:14 form more th. *s. of m.*
Jer. 32:19 eyes are upon *s. of m.*
Dan. 5:21 driven from *s. of m.*
10:16 like simil. of *s. of m.*
Joel 1:12 joy withered fr. *s. of m.*
Mic. 5:7 nor waiteth for *s. of m.*
Mark 3:28 sins be forgi. *s. of m.*
Eph. 3:5 not made kn. to *s. of m.*

See OLD, RICH, RIGHTEOUS, SING-
ING.

MEN-SERVANTS.

Gen. 12:16 Abram had *m.-s.*
20:14 Abimelech gave *m.-s.*
30:43 J. had *m.-s.* camels, 32:5
Ex. 21:7 not go out as *m.-s.*
Deut. 12:12 bef. L. ye and *m.-s.*
1 *Sam.* 8:16 will take you *m.-s.*
2 *K.* 5:26 is time to rec. *m.-s. ?*
Luke 12:45 begin to beat *m.-s.*

MEN-STEALERS.

1 *Tim.* 1:10 law is made for *m.-s.*

See TWO.

MEN of war.

Num. 31:49 sum of *m. of war*
Deut. 2:14 till generation of *m.*
of w. came out, 16 ; *Jos.* 5:6
1 *K.* 9:22 they were *m. of w.* and
his captains, 2 *Chr.* 8:9
2 *K.* 25:4 *m. of w.* fled. *Jer.* 52:7
Jer. 38:4 weak. hands of *m. of w.*
49:26 *m. of w.* be cut off, 50:30
51:32 *m. of war* are affrighted
Ezek. 27:10 P. were thy *m. of w.*
27 thy *m. of war* shall fall
Joel 2:7 climb wall like *m. of w.*
3:9 let all *m. of war* draw near
Luke 23:11 H. with his *m. of w.*

MEN, with wicked.

Gen. 13:13 *m.* of Sodom were *w.*
Num. 16:26 de. fr. tents of *w. m.*
2 *Sam.* 3:34 man fall. bef. *w. m.*
4:11 more wh. sc. *m.* have slain
Job 22:15 old way *w. m.* ha. tro.
34:8 which walketh with *w. m.*
26 striketh them as *wicked m.*
36 because of answers of *w. m.*
Ec. 8:14 *w. m.* to wh. it happen.
Jer. 5:26 am. my peo. fou. *w. m.*
Mat. 21:41 miser. destroy *w. m.*
2 *Thes.* 3:2 delivered from *w. m.*

Wise MEN.

Gen. 41:8 Ph. call. *w. m. Ex.* 7:11
Ex. 36:4 *w. m.* wrought work
Deut. 1:13 take ye *wise m.* and
Job 15:18 which *w. m.* have told
34:2 hear my words, O ye *w. m.*
Ps. 49:10 seeth that *wise m.* die
Prov. 10:14 *w. m.* lay up knowl.
13:20 walketh with *w. m.*
29:8 *w. m.* turn away wrath
Ec. 9:17 words of *w. m.* heard
Is. 19:12 where are thy *wise m.*
29:14 wisd. of *w. m.* shall perish
44:25 turneth *w. m.* backward
Jer. 8:9 the *wise m.* are ashamed
10:7 the *wise m.* of the nations
51:57 make drunken her *w. m.*
Ezek. 27:8 thy *wise m.* O Tyrus
9 the *w. m.* were thy calkers
Dan. 2:12 to destroy all *wise m.*
4:6 decree to bring in all *w. m.*
Ob. 8 destroy *w. m.* out of Edom
Mat. 2:1 came *w. m.* from east
1 *Cor.* 1:26 not many *wise m.*
10:15 I speak as to *w. m.*

MEN, with women.

Deut. 2:34 utterly destroyed the
m. and *women, Jos.* 8:25
Jud. 9:49 about 1,000 *m.* and *w.*
16:27 house full of *m.* and *w.*
2 *Sam.* 6:19 dealt to the *w.* as *m.*
Acts 5:14 added to L. *m.* and *w.*
8:3 Saul, haling *m.* and *women*
12 baptized, both *m.* and *w.*
9:2 *m.* or *w.* bring them bound
22:4 into prisons both *m.* and *w.*

MEN, *women, and children. See*
CHILDREN.

Ye MEN.

Job 34:10 heark. *ye m.* of under.
Acts 1:11 *ye m.* of G. 2:14 of Jud.
5:35 *ye m.* of Is. 17:22 of Athens
13:15 *ye m.* and brethren, if ye
19:35 *ye m.* of Ephesus

Young MEN.

Gen. 14:24 wh. *y. m.* have eaten
Ex. 24:5 *y. m.* which offer. burn.
Jos. 6:23 *y. m.* that were spies
Jud. 14:10 so used *y. m.* to do
Ruth 3:10 followedst not *y. m.*
1 *Sam.* 2:17 sin of *y. m.* very gr.
8:16 take your goodliest *y. m.*
21:4 if *y. m.* kept from women
25:8 ask *y. m.* they will show
25 thy handmaid saw not *y. m.*
30:17 400 *y. m.* wh. rode on ca.
2 *Sam.* 2:14 *y. m.* arise and play
13:32 sup. they slain all *y. m.*
18:15 ten *y. m.* bare J.'s armor
1 *K.* 12:8 Re. consult. with *y. m.*
14 counsel of *y. m.* 2 *Chr.* 10:8
20:14 *young m.* of the princes
2 *K.* 5:22 two *y. m.* of prophets
8:12 their *y. m.* wilt thou slay
Job 1:19 fell on *y. m.* are dead
29:8 *y. m.* saw me, hid themsel.
Ps. 78:63 fire consum. their *y. m.*
148:12 praise L. *y. m.* and maid.
Prov. 20:29 gl. of *y. m.* strength
Is. 9:17 L. no joy in their *y. m.*
13:18 bows dash *y. m.* to pieces
23:4 nei. do I nourish up *y. m.*
31:8 his *y. m.* shall be disconft.
40:30 the *y. m.* shall utterly fall
Jer. 6:11 fury on assem. of *y. m.*
9:21 cut off *y. m.* from streets
11:22 *y. m.* sh. die by the sword
15:8 brought ag. moth. of *y. m.*
18:21 let *y. m.* be slain by swo.
31:13 both *y. m.* and old rejoice
48:15 chosen *young m.* gone to
slaughter
49:26 *y. m.* shall fall in streets
50:30 theref. *y. m.* fall in streets
51:3 spare not *y. m.* des. utterly
Lam. 1:15 assem. to crush *y. m.*
18 virgins and *y. m.* into capt.
2:21 *y. m.* and old lie on ground
5:13 they took *y. m.* to grind
14 *y. m.* ceased fr. their music
Ezek. 23:6 desirable *y. m.* 12, 23
Joel 2:28 *y. m.* see vis. *Acts* 2:17
Amos 2:11 *y. m.* for Nazarites
4:10 *y. m.* slain with the sword
8:13 your *y. m.* faint for thirst
Zec. 9:17 make *y. m.* cheerful
Mark 14:51 *y. m.* laid hold
Acts 5:6 *y. m.* arose, wound him
Tit. 2:6 *y. m.* exhort to be sober
1 *John* 2:13 I wr. to you, *y. m.* 14

MENAHEM. 2 *K.* 15:14, 16

MEND, ING.

2 *Chr.* 24:12 brass to m. ho. of L.
34:10 workmen to *m.* house
Mat. 4:21 Z. *m.* nets, *Mark* 1:19

MENE. *Dan.* 5:25

MENSTRUOUS.

Is. 30:22 cast away as *m.* cloth
Lam. 1:17 Jeru. is as *m.* woman
Ezek. 18:6 come near to *m.* wo.

MENTION, Substantive

Gen. 40:14 *m.* of me unto Phar.
Ex. 23:13 make no *m.* of other
gods, 23:7
1 *Sam.* 4:18 made *m.* of ark of G.
Ps. 71:16 make *m.* of thy righte.
87:4 I will make *m.* of Rahab
Is. 12:4 *m.* th. his name is exalt.
19:17 make *m.* thereof be afraid
26:13 will make *m.* of thy name
48:1 make *m.* of the God of Isr.
49:1 he made *m.* of my name
62:6 ye that make *m.* of the L.
Jer. 4:16 make ye *m.* to nations
20:9 I will not make *m.* of him
Amos 6:10 not *m.* name of Lord
Rom. 1:9 *m.* you alw. in my pra.
Eph. 1:16 ; 1 *Thes.* 1:2
Phile. 4 *m.* of thee in my praye.
Heb. 11:22 *m.* of departing of Is.

MENTION, Verb.

Is. 63:7 *m.* loving-kindn. of Lord
Jer. 23:36 bur. of L. *m.* no more

MENTIONED.

1 *Chr.* 4:38 th. *m.* were princes
2 *Chr.* 20:34 J. *m.* in b. of kings
Ezek. 16:56 Sodom was not *m.*
  18:22 his transgres. not be *m.*
  24 his righteous. sh. not be *m.*
  33:16 none of his sin sh. be *m.*

MEPHIBOSHETH

2 *Sam.* 4:4 name was M. 9:10
21:7 but the king spared M.

MERAB.   1 *Sam.* 14:49 ; 18:19

MERARI.

Gen. 46:11 ; *Ex.* 6:16 ; *Num.* 3:17;
   1 *Chr.* 6:1, 16 ; 23:6
Num. 4:42 numbered of M. 10:17
Jos. 21:7 M. 40 ; 1 *Chr.* 6:63, 77

MERCHANDISE.

Deut. 21:14 not make *m.* of her
  24:7 broth. maketh *m.* of him
Prov. 3:14 *m.* bet. than *m.* of go.
  31:18 perceiveth her *m.* is good
Is. 23:18 her *m.* sh. be holiness
  45:14 *m.* of Ethio. come to thee
Ezek. 26:12 a prey of thy *m.*
  27:9 ships in thee to occupy *m.*
  15 isles were *m.* of hands
  28:16 multit. of *m.* have filled
Mat. 22:5 farm, another to *m.*
John 2:16 F.'s house hou. of *m.*
2 *Pet.* 2:3 words make *m.* of you
Rev. 18:11 no man buyeth th. *m.*

MERCHANT.

Gen. 23:16 cur. money with *m.*
  37:28 passed by Midian. *m.*-m.
1 *K.* 10:15 he had of *m.*-men
Prov. 31:14 like the *m.*-ships
  24 delivereth girdles to the *m.*
Cant. 3:6 perfume. powders of *m.*
Is. 23:11 command. ag. *m.* city
Ezek. 27:3 art a *m.* of pe. for isles
  12 Tarshish was thy *m.*
  16 Syria ; 18 Damas. ; 20 Dedan
Hos. 12:7 a *m.* balances of deceit
Zep. 1:11 *m.* peo. are cut down
Mal. 13:45 like a *m.*-man seeking

MERCHANTS.

1 *K.* 10:15 of traffic of spice *m.*
  28 the king's *m.* receiv. linen
  yarn, 2 *Chr.* 1:16
Neh. 3:32 goldsmiths and the *m.*
  13:20 *m.* lodged without Jerus.
Job 41:6 shall part him am. *m.* ?
Is. 23:2 *m.* of Zidon replenished
  8 city, whose *m.* are princes
  47:15 even thy *m.* sh. wander
Ezek. 17:4 set it in a city of *m.*
  27:13 Javan ; Tubal ; Mesh. *m.*
  15 Dedan ; 17 Judah and Israel
  thy *m.*
  21 in these were they thy *m.*
  22 *m.* of Sheba and Raam. 23
  36 the *m.* shall hiss at thee
  38:13 and the *m.* of Tarshish
Nah. 3:16 multip. *m.* above stars
Rev. 18:3 *m.* of earth waxen rich
  11 *m.* of earth weep over her
  23 *m.* were great *m.* of earth

MERCURIUS. *Acts* 14:12

MERCY.

Gen. 24:27 destitute master of *m.*
  43:14 God give you *m.* before
Ex. 34:7 keeping *m.* for thousands, *Dan.* 9:4
Num. 14:18 the Lord is of great
  m. Ps. 103:11; 145:3
Deut. 7:9 keep coven. and *m.* 12
2 *Sam.* 7:15 *m.* not depart from
  him, 1 *Chr.* 17:13 ; *Ps.* 89:24
  20 and truth be with thee
1 *K.* 8:23 keepest covenant and
  m. with serv. *Neh.* 1:5 ; 9:32

---

1 *Chr.* 16:34 his *m.* endureth for
  ever, 41 ; 2 *Chr.* 5:13 ; 7:3, 6 ;
  20:21 ; *Ezr.* 3:11 ; *Ps.* 106:1 ;
  107:1 ; 118:1 ; 136:1-26 ; *Jer.*
  33:11

Ezr. 7:28 extended *m.* to me
  9:9 extend. *m.* to us in sight of
Neh. 1:11 *m.* in sight of man
Job 37:13 for correction or for *m.*

Ps. 21:7 thro' *m.* of Most High
  23:6 goodness and *m.* follow me
  25:10 paths of the Lord are *m.*
  32:10 *m.* shall comp. him about
  33:18 them that hope in his *m.*
  52:8 I trust in the *m.* of God
  57:3 send forth *m.* and truth
  59:10 God of *m.* sh. prev. me, 17
  61:7 O prepare *m.* and truth
  62:12 unto thee belongeth *m.*
  66:20 not turned *m.* from me
  77:8 is his *m.* cl. gone for ever ?
  85:10 *m.* and truth m. together
  86:5 plenteous in *m.* 15 ; 103:8
  89:2 *m.* sh. be built up for ever
  14 *m.* and truth go be. thy face
  28 my *m.* will I keep for him
  98:3 remembered *m.* toward Is.
  100:5 L. is good, his *m.* is everl.
  101:1 will sing *m.* and judgm.
  103:17 *m.* of Lord is everlasting
  109:12 none extend *m.* to him
  130:7 with the Lord there is *m.*
  147:11 pleas. in those hope *m.*

Prov. 3:3 let not *m.* forsake thee
  14:21 he that hath *m.* on poor
  22 *m.* and truth sh. be to them
Prov. 14:31 he that hon. G. ha. *m.*
  16:6 by *m.* iniquity is purged
  20:28 *m.* and truth preserve the
  king, and his throne is upholden by *m.: Is.* 16:5
  21:21 followeth after *m.* find. life
Is. 49:10 that hath *m.* on them
  54:10 Lord that hath *m.* on thee
  60:10 my favor had *m.* on thee
Jer. 6:23 cruel, and have no *m.*
Hos. 4:1 there is no *m.* in land
  6:6 I desired *m.* and not sacrif.
  10:12 reap in *m.* 12:6 keep *m.*
  14:3 in thee the fatherl. find *m.*

Jon. 2:8 forsake their own *m.*
Mic. 6:8 do justly, and love *m.*
  7:18 because he delight. in *m.*
  20 wilt perform *m.* to Abraham
Hab. 3:2 L. in wrath remem. *m.*
Mat. 5:7 merciful, sh. obtain *m.*
  23:23 omitted judgment and *m.*
Luke 1:50 *m.* on them fear him
  54 Is. in remembran. of his *m.*
  72 to perform the *m.* promised
  78 through tender *m.* of God
Rom. 9:23 glory on vessels of *m.*
  11:30 obtained *m.* thro' unbelief
  31 your *m.* th. also may ob. *m.*
  15:9 might glorify God for *m.*
1 *Cor.* 7:25 obtai. *m.* to be faith.
2 *Cor.* 4:1 as we have received *m.*
Gal. 6:16 peace and *m.* on Israel
Eph. 2:4 God who is rich in *m.*
Phil. 2:27 God had *m.* on him
1 *Tim.* 1:2 *m.* and peace fr. G.
  2 *Tim.* 1:2 ; *Tit.* 1:4 ; 2 *John* 3
  13 I obtained *m.* because,
2 *Tim.* 1:16 Lord give *m.* to hou.
  18 he may find *m.* of the Lord
Tit. 3:5 according to *m.* he saved
Heb. 4:16 that we may obtain *m.*
  10:28 desp. law died without *m.*
Jam. 2:13 judgm. without *m.* th.
  showed no *m. m.* rejoiceth
  3:17 wisd. from above full of *m.*
  5:11 pitiful and of tender *m.*
1 *Pet.* 1:3 according to abund. *m.*
  2:10 *m.* now have obtained *m.*
Jude 2 *m.* to you, peace, and love
  21 looking for *m.* of Lord Jes.

Have MERCY.

Ps. 4:1 *have m.* upon me, 6:2;
  9:13 ; 25:16 ; 27:7 ; 30:10 ; 31:9;
  51:1 ; 86:16
  102:13 *h. m.* on Z. 123:2 on us, 3
Prov. 28:13 forsak. sins sh. *h. m.*
Is. 9:17 nei. *h. m.* on fatherless
  14:1 Lord will *have m.* on Jac.
  27:11 th. made th. will not *h. m.*
  30:18 that he may *have m.*
  49:13 God will *h. m.* on afflicted
  54:8 with kindness will I *h. m.*
  55:7 return, and he will *have m.*
Jer. 13:14 nor *have m.* 21:7
  30:18 I will *have m.* on dwelling
  31:20 I will surely *h. m.* 33:26;
  Ezek. 39:25 ; *Hos.* 1:7 ; 2:23
  42:12 that he may *h. m.* on you
Hos. 1:6 no more *h. m.* on Is. 2:4
Zec. 1:12 long wilt th. not *h. m.*
  10:6 for I *have m.* upon them
Mat. 9:13 I will *have m.* 12:7
  27 thou son of David, *h. m.* on
  me, 15:22 ; 20:30, 31 ; *Mark*
  10:47, 48 ; *Luke* 18:38, 39
Luke 16:24 Abraham, *h. m.* en m.
  17:13 Jesus, Master, *h. m.* on us
Rom. 9:15 I will *have m.* on wh.
  I will *have m.* 18
  11:32 that he might *h. m.* on all

MERCY-SEAT.

Ex. 25:17 make a *m.-s.* of gold
  22 from above *m.-s.* bet. cherubim, *Lev.* 16:2 ; *Num.* 7:89
  26:34 put *m.-s.* on ark, 40:20
Lev. 16:13 incense cover *m.-s.*

MERCY, *with* show, ed, eth, ing.

Gen. 39:21 Lord was with Josep.
  and *showed* him *m.*
Ex. 20:6 *showing m.* to thousan.
  Deut. 5:10
  33:19 *s. m.* on wh. I will *s. m.*
Deut. 7:2 no covenant, nor *s. m.*
Jud. 1:24 and we will *s.* thee *m.*
2 *Sam.* 22:51 *s. m.* to his anoint.
  Ps. 18:50
1 *K.* 3:6 hast *showed* to D. my
  father, great *m.* 2 *Chr.* 1:8
2 *Chr.* 6:14 *s. m.* to thy servants
Ps. 37:21 the righteous *s. m.*
  85:7 *s.* us thy *m.* O Lord
  109:16 remembered not to *s. m.*
Is. 47:6 didst *show* them no *m.*
Jer. 50:42 and will not *s. m.*
Dan. 4:27 break off sins, *s. m.*
Zec. 7:9 execute judgm. *s. m.*
Luke 1:58 L. *s.* great *m.* on her
  10:37 that *showed m.* on him
Rom. 9:16 but of God that *s. m*
Jam. 2:13 that hath *s.* no *m.*

Thy MERCY.

Gen. 19:19 hast magnified *t. m.*
Ex. 15:13 in *t. m.* led forth peo.
Num. 14:19 greatness of *thy m.*
Neh. 13:22 according to *thy m.*
Ps. 5:7 in multitude of *thy m.*
  6:4 return, O Lord, save me for
  thy m.'s sake. 31:16
  13:5 I have trusted in *thy m.*
  25:7 accor. to *thy m.* remem. me
  31:7 I will rejoice in *thy m.*
  33:22 let my *m.* O L. be upon us
  36:5 *t. m.* O L. is in the heavens
  44:26 redeem us for *t. m.'s* sake
  57:10 *thy m.* is great to heavens
  59:16 I will sing aloud of *thy m.*
  69:13 in multitude of *thy m.*
  85:7 show us *t. m.* 86:13 great
  90:14 O satisfy us with *thy m.*
  94:18 *t. m.* O Lord, held me up
  108:4 *thy m.* is great above hea.
  109:21 because *thy m.* is good
  26 according to *thy m.*
  115:1 for *t. m.* and truth's sake
  119:64 earth is full of *thy m.*
  124 deal wi. servant ac. to *t. m.*

138:8 *thy m.* endureth for ever
143:12 of *t. m.* cut off mine ene.

MERCIES.

Gen. 32:10 not worthy of thy *m.*
2 *Sam.* 24:14 for his *m.* are great,
1 *Chr.* 21:13
2 *Chr.* 6:42 remember *m.* of Dav.
Neh. 9:19 in *m.* forsook. th. not
27 accord. to thy *m.* thou gav.
31 *m.* didst not consume them
Ps. 51:1 thy *m.* blot out transg.
69:13 in multitude of thy *m.*
16 according to thy tender *m.*
89:1 I will sing of the *m.* of L.
106:7 remembered not thy *m.*
45 repented accord. to his *m.*
119:41 let thy *m.* also come
Is. 54:7 with *m.* will I gather
55:3 sure *m.* of D. *Acts* 13:34
63:15 where is thy *m.* tow. me?
Jer. 16:5 taken away my *m.*
42:12 I will show *m.* unto you
Lam. 3:22 of L.'s *m.* we are not
22 compassion according to *m.*
Dan. 2:18 *m.* concerning this
9:9 to the L. our God belong *m.*
18 not for righteousn. but *m.*
Hos. 2:19 I will betr. thee in *m.*
Zec. 1:16 am returned with *m.*
Rom. 12:1 I bes. you by *m.* of G.
2 *Cor.* 1:3 Father of *m.* and God
Phil. 2:1 if there be any fellowship, *m.*
Col. 3:12 put on bowels of *m.*

Tender MERCIES.

Ps. 25:6 remem. thy *t. m.* 51:1
40:11 withhold not thy *ten. m.*
77:9 in anger shut up his *t. m.*
79:8 thy *tender m.* prevent us
103:4 L. crown. thee with *t. m.*
119:77 thy *t. m.* come unto me
156 great are thy *ten. m.* O L.
145:9 *t. m.* over all his works
Prov. 12:10 *t. m.* of wicked cruel

MERCIFUL.

Gen. 19:16 Lord being *m.* to Lot
Ex. 34:6 L. G. *m.* and gracious
Deut. 21:8 be *m.* O L. to Israel
32:43 and will be *m.* to his land
2 *Sam.* 22:26 with *m.* thou wilt
show thyself *m. Ps.* 18:25
1 *K.* 20:31 kings of Is. *m.* kings
2 *Chr.* 30:9 L. G. gracious and *m.*
Neh. 9:17 ready to pardon and *m.*
Ps. 26:11 redeem me, and be *m.*
to me, 41:4, 10; 56:1; 57:1;
86:3; 119:58, 132
37:26 the righteous is ever *m.*
59:5 be not *m.* to any wicked
67:1 G. be *m.* to us, and bl. us
103:8 Lord is *m.* and gracious
117:2 his *m.* kindness is great
119:76 *m.* kindness for my com.
Prov. 11:17 *m.* man doeth good
Is. 57:1 *m.* men are taken away
Jer. 3:12 I am *m.* saith the Lord
Joel 2:13 he is gracious and *m.*
Jon. 4:2 knew thou art a *m.* G.
Mat. 5:7 *m.* shall obtain mercy
Luke 6:36 be *m.* as your F. is *m.*
18:13 God be *m.* to me a sinner
Heb. 2:17 be a *m.* high-priest
8:12 be *m.* to their unright.

MERIBAH.

Ex. 17:7 called name of place M.
Num. 20:13, 24; *Deut.* 32:51; 33:8
Ps. 81:7 proved thee at wat. M.

MERODACH. *Jer.* 50:2
MERODACH-BALADAN. *Is.*
39:1
MEROM. *Jos.* 11:5, 7
MEROZ. *Jud.* 5:23

MERRY.

Gen. 43:34 drank and were *m.*
Jud. 9:27 trode grapes, made *m.*

16:25 their hearts were *m.*
19:6 and let thy heart be *m.*
Ruth 3:7 Boaz's heart was *m.*
1 *Sam.* 25:36 Nabal's heart *m.*
2 *Sam.* 13:28 when Amnon is *m*
1 *K.* 4:20 Judah and Isr. were *m.*
21:7 and let his heart be *m.*
2 *Chr.* 7:10 sent people away *m.*
Est. 1:10 heart of king was *m.*
Prov. 15:13 *m.* heart ma. cheerf.
15 *m.* heart ha. continual feast
17:22 a *m.* heart doeth good
Ec. 8:15 better to eat and be *m.*
9:7 drink wine with a *m.* heart
10:19 laughter, wine maketh *m.*
Is. 24:7 the *m.* hearted do sigh
Jer. 30:19 voi. of th. th. make *m.*
31:4 dances of th. that make *m.*
Luke 12:19 ease, eat and be *m.*
15:23 and be *m.* 24; 29 I might
32 it was meet we should be *m.*
Jam. 5:13 is any *m.?* sing psal.
Rev. 11:10 rejoice and make *m.*

MERRILY.

Est. 5:14 go in *m.* with king

MESHECH.

Gen. 10:2 M. son of Japheth,
1 *Chr.* 1:5, 17
Ps. 120:5 I sojourn in M.
Ezek. 39:1 ag. chief prince of M.

MESOPOTAMIA.

Gen. 24:10 Eliezer went to M.
Deut. 23:4 Bal. of M. *Jud.* 3:8
1 *Chr.* 19:6 hire chari. out of M.
Acts 2:9 dwellers in M. we hear
7:2 G. appeared to Abra. in M.

MESS, ES.

Gen. 43:34 sent *m.* to them, Benjamin's *m.*
2 *Sam.* 11:8 Uriah a *m.* from king

MESSAGE.

Jud. 3:20 I have *m.* from God
1 *K.* 20:12 Benhad. heard this *m.*
Prov. 26:6 sendeth *m.* by fool
Hag. 1:13 spake Hag. in L.'s *m.*
Luke 19:14 citiz. sent *m.* aft. him
1 *John* 1:5 *m.* we ha. heard, 3:11

MESSENGER.

Gen. 50:16 sent a *m.* to Joseph
1 *K.* 19:2 Jezebel sent *m.* to Elij.
22:13 the *m.* went to call Micaiah, 2 *Chr.* 18:12
2 *K.* 6:32 ere the *m.* came to him
9:18 the *m.* came to them, but
Job 1:11 there came a *m.* to Job
33:23 if there be *m.* interpreter
Prov. 13:17 *m.* fall. into mischief
17:11 cruel *m.* shall be sent
25:13 faithful *m.* to them
Is. 42:19 as my *m.* that I sent?
Jer. 51:31 one *m.* run to meet
Ezek. 23:40 to wh. a *m.* was sent
Hag. 1:13 Haggai, the Lord's *m.*
Mal. 2:7 he is *m.* of L. of hosts
3:1 send *m.* of covenant, *Mat.*
11:10 ; *Mark* 1:2 ; *Luke* 7:27
2 *Cor.* 12:7 *m.* of Satan to buffet
Phil. 2:25 companion, your *m.*

MESSENGERS.

Gen. 32:3 Jacob sent *m.* to Esau
Num. 22:5 Balak sent *m.* to Bal.
Jos. 6:17 Rahab hid the *m.* 25
1 *Sam.* 19:11 Saul sent *m.* to
David, 14, 15, 20, 21
25:14 David sent *m.* to salute
2 *Sam.* 2:5 sent *m.* to Jabesh-gil.
3:12 sent *m.* to D. on his behalf
5:11 H. sent *m.* to D. 1 *Chr.* 14:1
11:4 Dav. sent *m.* to Bathsheba
12:27 Joab sent *m.* to David
2 *K.* 1:3 meet the *m.* of Ahaziah
17:4 Hoshea had sent *m.* to So
19:23 *m.* th. hast reproached L.
1 *Chr.* 19:2 *m.* to comfort Hanun
2 *Chr.* 36:15 L. sent them by *m.*

16 they mocked the *m.* of God
Prov. 16:14 wrath of king as *m.*
Is. 14:32 answer of *m.* of nation?
18:2 go ye swift *m.* to a nation
37:14 letter from *m.* and read it
44:26 performeth counsel of *m.*
57:9 didst send thy *m.* afar off
Jer. 27:3 send by hand of the *m.*
Ezek. 23:16 sent *m.* into Chaldea
Ezek. 30:9 *m.* go forth from me
Nah. 2:13 voice of *m.* no more
Luke 7:24 *m.* of John were gone
9:52 and sent *m.* before his face
2 *Cor.* 8:23 *m.* of the churches
Jam. 2:25 Rahab had receiv. *m.*

MESSIAH.

Dan. 9:25 from commandment
to build Jerus. unto the M.
the Prince shall be 7 weeks
26 after 62 weeks M. be cut off
John 1:41 found M. wh. is Christ
4:25 I know that M. cometh

MET.

Gen. 32:1 angel of God *m.* him
33:8 by this drove I *m.?*
Ex. 3:18 God of the Hebrews *m.*
with us, 5:3
4:24 L. in him, sought to kill
27 Aaron went and *m.* Moses
5:20 they *m.* Moses and Aaron
Num. 23:4 God *m.* Balaam, 16
1 *Sam.* 10:10 prophets *m.* Saul
1 *K.* 13:24 was gone, lion *m.* him
Ps. 85:10 mercy and tru. *m.* tog.
Prov. 7:10 *m.* him a woman
Amos 5:19 and a bear *m.* him
Mat. 8:28 *m.* him two devils
Mark 1:14 place wh. two ways *m.*
Luke 9:37 much people *m.* him,
John 12:18
17:12 *m.* him ten men lepers
John 11:20 Martha *m.* him, 30
Acts 10:25 Cornelius *m.* him and
27:41 a place where two seas *m.*
Heb. 7:1 *m.* Abraham returning

METE, D.

Ex. 16:18 *m.* it with a homer
Ps. 60:6 *m.* valley of Suc. 108:7
Is. 18:2 go to a nation *m.* out, 7
40:12 *m.* out heaven with span
Mat. 7:2 measure ye *m.* be meas.
to you, *Mark* 4:24 ; *Luke* 6:38

METEYARD.

Lev. 19:35 no unrighteous. in *m.*

METHEG-AMMAH. 2 *Sam.* 8:1

METHUSELAH.

Gen. 5:27 days of M. 969 years
1 *Chr.* 1:3 M. Lamech, *Luke* 3:37

MICAH.

Jud. 17:1 mount Eph. called M.
Jer. 26:18 M. prophes. *Mic.* 1:1

MICAIAH. 1 *K.* 22:8, 24 ; 2 *Chr.*
18:8, 23, 25

MICE.

1 *Sam.* 6:4 five golden *m.* accord.
5 sh. make images of your *m.*

MICHAEL.

Dan. 10:13 M. ch. prince, 21; 12:1
Jude 9 M. contending with dev.
Rev. 12:7 M. fought ag. dragon

MICHAIAH.

2 *Chr.* 17:7 Jehoshaphat sent M.
Neh. 12:35 son of M. give thanks
Jer. 36:11 M. heard Baruch, 13

MICHAL.

1 *Sam.* 14:49 S.'s yr. daughter M.
19:13 M. took an image and
2 *Sam.* 3:13 ex. first bring M. 14
6:16 M. looked thro', 1 *Chr.* 15:29

MICHMASH. 1 *Sam.* 13:2 ; *Is.*
10:28

MID-DAY.

1 *K.* 18:29 when *m.-d.* was past

Neh. 8:3 from morning to *m.-d.*
Acts 26:13 *m.-d.* I saw in way

MIDDLE.

Jud. 16:29 hold of two *m.* pillars
1 *K.* 8:64 the king did hallow
   m. court, 2 *Chr.* 7:7
2 *K.* 20:4 Isaiah gone to *m.* court
Jer. 39:3 princes sat in *m.* gate
Eph. 2:14 broken down *m.* wall

MIDDLEMOST.

Ezek. 42:5 higher than the *m.* 6

MIDIAN.

Ex. 2:15 dwelt in land of M.
Num. 22:4 M. said to elders of M.
  25:15 dau. of chief house of M.
  31:3 avenge the L. of M. 8, 9
Jud. 6:1 delivered them to M. 2
  7:14 into hand G. delivered M.
  8:22 deliv. from M. 28; 9:17
Is. 9:4 bro. yoke, as in day of M.
  10:26 accord. to slaughter of M.
  60:6 dromedaries of M. cover
Hab. 3:7 curtains of M. tremble

MIDIANITES.

Gen. 37:28 M. merchantmen, 36
Num. 25:17 vex the M. 31:2
Jud. 6:7 Is. cried because of M.
  7:25 two princes of the M. 8:1

Ps. 83:9 do to them as to M.

MIDIANITISH. *Num.* 25:6, 16

MIDNIGHT.

Ex. 11:4 M. I will go into Egypt
  12:29 at *m.* L. smote first-born
Jud. 16:3 Samson lay till *m.*
Ruth 3:8 at *m.* man was afraid
1 *K.* 3:20 she arose at *m.* and
Job 34:20 peo. be troubled at *m.*
Ps. 119:62 at *m.* I will give than.
Mat. 25:6 at *m.* there was a cry
Mark 13:35 come at even or *m.*
Luke 11:5 shall go to him at *m.*
Acts 16:25 at *m.* Paul prayed
  20:7 P. continued speech till *m.*

MIDST.

Ex. 14:16 sh. go on dry ground
  through *m.* of sea, *Num.*
  33:8; *Neh.* 9:11; *Ps.* 136:14
Deut. 13:5 put evil away from *m.*
3 *Chr.* 32:4 ran thr. *m.* of land
Cant. 3:10 *m.* paved with love
Is. 58:9 from *m.* of thee the yoke
Jer. 30:21 proceed fr. *m.* of them
Ezek. 9:4 go through *m.* of city
  14:8 cut him off from *m.* of pe. 9
  15:4 *m.* burnt, is it meet
  28:16 filled *m.* of thee with viol.
  18 bring forth fire from *m.*
Dan. 3:26 ca. forth of *m.* of fire
Luke 4:30 passing thro' *m.* of th.
John 7:14 about the *m.* of feast
  8:59 going through *m.* of them
Rev. 8:13 flying thro' *m.* of heav.

In the MIDST.

Gen. 2:9 tr. of life *in t. m.* 3:3
  15:10 A. divided them *in t. m.*
Ex. 8:22 I am L. *in t. m.* of earth
  14:29 dry land *in m.* 15:19
  33:3 I will not go up *in m.*
Num. 2:17 tabern. *in m.* of camp
  35:5 shall be *in m. Ezek.* 48:15
Deut. 11:3 acts he did *in m.* of E.
  23:14 God walketh *in t. m.*
Jos. 3:17 *in m.* of Jordan, 4:10
  7:21 hid *in the m.* of my tent
2 *Sam.* 18:14 *in the m.* of oak
2 *K.* 6:20 were *in m.* of Samaria
1 *Chr.* 19:4 garments *in the m.*
Neh. 4:11 till we come *in the m.*
Ps. 22:14 *in the m.* of bowels
  22 *in t. m.* of the congregation
  will I praise thee, *Heb.* 2:12
  46:5 God is *in the m.* of her
  102:24 take not away *in m.* of d.
  110:2 rule *in m.* of enemies
  138:7 I walk *in m.* of trouble

Prov. 4:21 keep th. *in m.* heart
  5:14 all evil *in m.* of congrega.
  8:20 *in the m.* of paths of judg.
  14:33 is *in m.* of fools is folly
  23:34 lieth down *in m.* of sea
Is. 6:5 *in m.* of a people
  7:6 set a king *in the m.* 17
  12:6 great is the Holy One *in the*
  m. of thee, *Hos.* 11:9
  19:24 blessing *in t. m.* of land
Jer. 14:9 Lord, art *in the m.* of us
  17:11 *in m.* of his days
Lam. 4:13 blood of just *in m.*
Ezek. 5:5 set *in m.* of nations
  6:7 shall fall *in m.* of you, 11:7
  17:16 *in m.* of Babylon shall die
  23:39 *in m.* of my house
  43:7 I will dw. *in t. m.* of Is. 9
Dan. 3:25 walking *in m.* of fire
Joel 2:27 I am *in the m.* of Israel
Mic. 6:14 cast. down shall *in m.*
Nah. 3:13 *in m.* of thee are wo.
Hab. 3:2 *in the m.* of the years
Zep. 3:5 L. is *in the m.* thereof
  12 leave *in the m.* a poor people
  15 Lord is *in the m.* of thee, 17
Zec. 2:5 glory *in the m.* of her
  10 will dwell *in m.* of thee, 11
  8:3 dwell *in the mi* of Jerusa. 8
Mat. 10:16 sheep *in m.* of wolves
  14:24 ship was *in the m.* of the
  sea, *Mark* 6:47
  18:2 little child *in m. Mark* 9:36
  20 there am I *in the m.* of them
Luke 23:45 temple was rent *in m.*
  24:36 Jesus himself stood *in the*
  m. John 20:19, 26
John 19:18 and Jesus *in the m.*
Rev. 4:6 *in m.* of thr. four beasts
  5:6 *in m.* of throne Lamb, 7:17

Into the MIDST.

Ex. 24:18 Moses went *into t. m.*
  33:5 I will come *into the m.*
Ps. 57:6 *i. m.* whereof they are
Jer. 21:4 assemble th. *i. m.* of ci.
  51:63 cast it *into the m.* of river
Ezek. 5:4 cast them *i. m.* of fire
  22:19 I will gather you *into m.*
  of Jerusalem

Out of the MIDST.

Ex. 3:4 *o. of m.* of bush, 24:16
Deut. 4:12 L. spake *out of the m.*
  of fire, 15:33, 36; 5:4, 22, 24
  34 take nation *out of m.* of an.
Jos. 4:3 *out of m.* of Jordan, 8
Is. 24:18 cometh *out of m.* of pit
  52:11 depart, go *out of the m.* of
  her, *Jer.* 50:8; 51:6, 45
Ezek. 11:7 forth *out of m.* of it
  29:4 br. thee *out of m.* of rivers
  32:21 sp. to him *o. of m.* of hell
Zep. 3:11 away *out of m.* of thee

MIDWIFE, VES.

Gen. 35:17 *m.* said unto Rachel
  38:28 *m.* bound on hand thread
Ex. 1:16 when ye do the office of
  a *m.* 17, 19, 20, 21

MIGHT, Substantive.

Gen. 49:3 Re. first-born, my *m.*
Num. 14:13 this people in thy *m.*
Deut. 3:24 do according to thy *m.*
  6:5 love thy God with all thy *m.*
  8:17 *m.* of my hand gotten weal.
  28:32 be no *m.* in thy hand
Jud. 5:31 sun goeth forth in *m.*
  6:14 go in thy *m.* 16:30 bowed
2 *Sam.* 6:14 D. danced with all *m.*
2 *K.* 23:25 J. turned to L. wi. *m.*
  24:16 king bro. cap. men of *m.*
1 *Chr.* 12:8 men of *m.* came to D.
  29:2 I prepared house with *m.*
  12 in thy hand is power and *m.*
  2 *Chr.* 20:6
2 *Chr.* 20:12 have no *m.* ag. this
Est. 10:2 Ahasue. power and *m.*
Ps. 76:5 none of the men of *m.*

  145:6 speak of *m.* of thy acts
Ec. 9:10 find. do it with thy *m.*
Is. 11:2 *m.* shall rest on him
  33:13 ye that acknow. my *m.*
  40:26 call. them by great. of *m.*
  29 to them that have no *m.*
Jer. 9:23 nor let man glory in *m.*
  10:6 thy name is great in *m.*
  16:21 cause th. to know my *m.*
  49:35 break chief of their *m.*
  51:30 their *m.* hath failed
Ezek. 32:30 ashamed of their *m.*
Dan. 2:20 wisdom and *m.* are his
  23 O G. who hast given me *m.*
  4:30 built by *m.* of my power
Mic. 3:8 full of judgment and *m.*
  7:16 nations confound. at th. *m.*
Zec. 4:6 not by *m.* nor by power
Eph. 1:21 far above all *m.* power
  3:16 to be strengthened with *m.*
  Col. 1:11
  6:10 L. and in power of his *m.*
2 *Pet.* 2:11 angels greater in *m.*
Rev. 7:12 glo. and *m.* be unto G.

See FULFILLED.

MIGHTY.

Gen. 10:9 *m.* hunter before L.
  18:18 Abraham bec. a *m.* nation
  23:6 thou art a *m.* prince
Ex. 1:7 children of Israel. *m.* 20
  9:28 be no more *m.* thunderings
  10:19 L. turned a *m.* west wind
  15:10 sank as lead in *m.* water
Lev. 19:15 nor honor person of *m.*
Num. 22:6 this people are too *m.*
Deut. 4:37 he bro. thee out with
  m. power, 9:29
  26:5 a nation, *m.* and populous
Jud. 5:13 have dominion over *m.*
  23 came not to help L. ag. *m.*
1 *Sam.* 4:8 out of hand of *m.* gods
2 *Sam.* 1:19 how are *m.* fallen ! 25
  21 shield of the *m.* is cast aw.
2 *K.* 24:15 *m.* of the land captive
1 *Chr.* 1:10 Nim. *m.* 12:28 Zadok
2 *Chr.* 26:13 made war with *m.*
  27:6 so Jotham became *m.*
Ezr. 4:20 been *m.* king over Jer.
  7:28 mercy to me bef. *m.* princes
Neh. 3:16 N. repaired to the *m.*
  9:11 threw. stone in *m.* waters
Job 5:15 he saveth poor from *m.*
  6:23 redeem me fr. hand of *m.* ?
  9:4 wise in heart, *m.* in streng.
  12:19 he overthroweth the *m.*
  21 weakeneth strength of *m.*
  21:7 wherefore are wicked *m.* ?
  24:22 draweth *m.* wi. his power
  34:20 *m.* shall be taken away
  35:9 by reason of arm of *m.*
  41:25 raiseth himself, *m.* afraid
Ps. 24:8 strong and *m.* in battle
  29:1 give to the L. O ye *m.* glo.
  45:3 gird thy sword, O most *m.*
  59:3 *m.* are gathered against me
  68:33 send out voice, *m.* voice
  74:15 thou driedst up *m.* rivers
  82:1 God in congrega. of the *m.*
  89:6 who am, sons *m*, like to L. ?
Ps. 89:13 thou hast a *m.* arm
  19 I have laid help upon one *m.*
  93:4 L. mightier than *m.* waves
  106:8 make *m.* power known
  112:2 seed shall be *m.* on earth
  135:10 smote nat. slew *m.* kings
Prov. 16:32 better than the *m.*
  18:18 lot parteth betwe. the *m.*
  23:11 their Redeemer is *m.*
Is. 3:25 thy *m.* sh. fall in war
  5:22 woe to them that are *m.*
  11:15 wi. *m.* wind sh. his hand
  22:17 carry thee aw. wi. *m.* cap.
  49:24 shall prey be taken fr. *m.* ?
  63:1 in righteousn. *m.* to save
Jer. 5:15 *m.* and ancient nation
  32:19 gr. in counsel, *m.* in work
  33:3 I will show thee *m.* things

Ezek. 17:13 hath taken *m.* of land
32:12 swords of *m.* make th. fall
21 strong among *m.* sh. speak
27 not lie wi. *m.* that are fallen
38:15 come with a *m.* army
39:18 ye shall eat flesh of *m.*
Dan. 4:3 *m.* are his wonders !
8:24 his power shall be *m.*
11:3 a *m.* king shall stand up
Amos 2:14 nei. shall *m.* deliver
16 courageous am. *m.* sh. flee
5:12 *m.* sins ; 24 *m.* stream
Jon. 1:4 there was a *m.* tempest
Zec. 11:2 howl, *m.* are spoiled
Mat. 11:20 most of *m.* works
21 if *m.* works which were, 23
13:54 hath this man *m.* works ?
58 he did not many *m.* works
there, *Mark* 6:5
14:2 John the Bap. therefore *m.*
works do show, *Mark* 6:14
Mark 6:2 *m.* works by his hand
Luke 1:49 *m.* hath done great th.
52 he hath put down the *m.*
9:43 amazed at *m.* power of G.
19:37 praised God for *m.* works
24:19 was a prophet *m.* in deed
Acts 7:22 Moses was *m.* in words
18:24 Apol. was *m.* in script.
Rom. 15:19 obed. thro' *m.* signs
1 *Cor.* 1:26 not many *m.*
27 chos. weak, to confound *m.*
2 *Cor.* 10:4 warfare *m.* thro' God
13:3 is not weak, but *m.* in you
Gal. 2:8 the same was *m.* in me
Eph. 1:19 working of *m.* power
2 *Thes.* 1:7 J. with his *m.* angels
Rev. 6:13 when shak. of *m.* wind
10:1 I saw ano. *m.* angel, 18:21
18:10 *m.* city ; 19:6 *m.* thunder.

See ACTS, GOD, HAND, MAN, MEN.

MIGHTY one.
Gen. 10:8 N. began to be a *m. o.*
Is. 1:24 Lord of hosts, the *m. O.*
of Is. 30:29 ; 49:26 ; 60:16
10:34 Leb. shall fall by a *m. o.*
28:2 L. hath a *m.* and strong *o.*
Jer. 20:11 L. is wi. me as a *m. o.*
Ezek. 31:11 deliver. him to *m. o.*

MIGHTY ones.
Jud. 5:22 broken by their *m. o.*
Is. 13:3 have called my *m. ones*
Jer. 46:5 their *m. o.* are beaten
Joel 3:11 cause *m. o.* to come

MIGHTIER.
Gen. 26:16 thou art *m.* than we
Ex. 1:9 child. of Is. *m.* than we
Num. 14:12 and *m.* than they,
Deut. 4:38 ; 7:1 ; 9:1, 14 ; 11:23
Ps. 93:4 L. is *m.* than many wa.
Ec. 6:10 nei. content with *m.*
Mat. 3:11 that com. aft. me is *m.*
than I, *Mark* 1:7 ; *Luke* 3:16

MIGHTIES.
1 *Chr.* 11:12 Ele. was one of 3 *m.*
19 these thi. did these three *m.*
24 B. had a name am. three *m.*

MIGHTILY.
Deut. 6:3 ye may increase *m.*
Jud. 4:3 Jabin *m.* oppressed Is.
14:6 Sp. of the L. came *m.* 15:14
Jer. 25:30 the Lord shall *m.* roar
Jon. 3:8 man and beast cry *m.*
Nah. 2:1 fortify thy power *m.*
Acts 18:28 *m.* convinced Jews
19:20 so *m.* grew word of God
Col. 1:29 worketh in me *m.*
Rev. 18:2 cried *m.* saying, Bab.

MILCAH.
Gen. 11:29 M. daught. of Haran,
22:20 ; 24:15 ; *Num.* 26:33

MILCH.
Gen. 32:15 thirty *m.* camels
1 *Sam.* 6:7 take two *m.* kine, 10

MILCOM.   1 *K.* 11:5, 33 ; 2 *K.*
23:13
MILDEW. *See* BLASTING.

MILE.
Mat. 5:41 compel thee to go a *m.*
MILETUM.   2 *Tim.* 4:20
MILETUS.   *Acts* 20:15, 17

MILK, Substantive.
Gen. 18:8 A. took butter and *m.*
49:12 his teeth be white wi. *m.*
Deut. 32:14 kine, *m.* of sheep
Jud. 4:19 J. opened bottle of *m.*
5:25 asked water, she gave *m.*
Job 10:10 not pou. me out as *m.* ?
21:24 his breasts are full of *m.*
Prov. 27:27 shalt have goats' *m.*
30:33 churning *m.* bring. butter
Cant. 4:11 *m.* under thy tongue
5:1 drunk wine with my *m.*
12 his eyes washed with *m.*
Is. 7:22 abund. of *m.* shall give
28:9 that are weaned from *m.*
55:1 wi. and *m.* without money
60:16 thou sh. suck *m.* of Gent.
Lam. 4:7 Nazar. whiter than *m.*
Ezek. 25:4 eat fruit, and drink *m.*
Joel 3:18 hills shall flow with *m.*
1 *Cor.* 3:2 I have fed you with *m.*
9:7 who eateth not of the *m.* ?
Heb. 5:12 as have need of *m.* ?
13 ev. one useth *m.* is a babe
1 *Pet.* 2:2 new-born babes des. *m.*

See FLOWING.

MILK.
Is. 66:11 that ye may *m.* out

MILL, S.
Ex. 11:5 *m.*-servant behind *m.*
Num. 11:8 ground manna in *m.*
Mat. 24:41 two wom. grind. at *m.*

MILLET.
Ezek. 4:9 take *m.* and make bre.

MILLIONS.
Gen. 24:60 mother of thous. *m.*

MILLO.
Jud. 9:6 house of M. gather. 20
2 *Sam.* 5:9 round about from M.
1 *K.* 9:24 Solo. build M. 11:27
2 *K.* 12:20 slew Joash in M.

MILLSTONE, S.
Deut. 24:6 no man take *m.* pled.
Jud. 9:53 a woman cast a piece
of *m.* 2 *Sam.* 11:21
Job 41:24 heart as hard as a *m.*
Is. 47:2 take *m.* and grind meal
Jer. 25:10 take away sound of *m.*
Mat. 18:6 a *m.* hanged about his
neck, *Mark* 9:42 ; *Luke* 17:2
Rev. 18:21 an angel took up a
stone like a great *m.*

MINCING.
Is. 3:16 walk. and *m.* as they go

MIND, Substantive.
Gen. 26:35 a grief of *m.* to Isaac
Lev. 24:12 *m.* of L. showed them
Deut. 18:6 come wi. desire of *m.*
28:65 L. sh. give thee sor. of *m.*
30:1 call th. to *m.* am. nations
1 *Chr.* 28:9 serve with willing *m.*
Neh. 4:6 peo. had a *m.* to work
Job 23:13 one *m.* who turn him ?
Ps. 31:12 a dead man out of *m.*
Prov. 21:27 bring. it wi. wic. *m.*
29:11 a fool uttereth all his *m.*
Is. 26:3 wh. *m.* is stayed on thee
46:8 again to *m.* O transgress.
65:17 former sh. not come to *m.*
Jer. 3:16 ark sh. not come to *m.*
44:21 came it not into his *m.* ?
Dan. 5:20 *m.* hardened in pride
Hab. 1:11 then sh. his *m.* change
Mark 5:15 his right *m. Luke* 8:35
14:72 P. called to *m.* words of J.
Luke 12:29 nei. be of doubtful *m.*
Acts 17:11 all readiness of *m.*

20:19 serv. L. with humi. of *m.*
Rom. 1:28 ga. up to reprobate *m.*
7:25 with *m.* I serve law of God
8:7 carnal *m.* enmity against G.
27 knoweth what is *m.* of Sp.
11:34 who hath kno. *m.* of L. ?
12:16 same *m.* one tow. another
14:5 persuaded in his own *m.*
15:6 may with one *m.* glori. G.
1 *Cor.* 1:10 joined in the same *m.*
2:16 known *m.* of L. to instruct
him ? we have *m.* of Christ
2 *Cor.* 7:7 fervent *m.* toward me
8:12 if a willing *m.* it is accept.
13:11 brethr. be of one *m. Phil.*
1:27 ; 2:2
Eph. 2:3 desires of flesh and *m.*
4:17 Gent. walk in vanity of *m.*
Phil. 2:3 in lowli. of *m.* let each
5 let this *m.* be in you wh. was
4:2 be of the same *m.* in the L.
Col. 2:18 puffed up by fleshly *m.*
3:12 humbleness of *m.* meekn.

2 *Thes.* 2:2 not soon shaken in *m.*
2 *Tim.* 1:7 spirit of sound *m.*
Tit. 1:15 *m.* and conscience defi.
3:1 put them in *m.* to be subj.
Heb. 8:10 my laws into th. *m.*
1 *Pet.* 3:8 be ye all of same *m.*
4:1 arm yours. like. wi. one *m.*
5:2 filthy lucre, but of ready *m.*
Rev. 17:9 *m.* which hath wisdom
13 these have one *m.* and shall

See ALIENATED.

Mine, *or* my MIND.
Num. 16:28 done th. of *m.* own *m.*
24:13 good or bad of *m.* own *m.*
1 *Sam.* 2:35 that wh. is in *m. m.*
1 *Chr.* 22:7 in *m. m.* to build ho.
Jer. 15:1 my *m.* could not be
19:5 nei. came it to my *m.* 32:35
Lam. 3:21 this I recall to my *m.*
Rom. 7:23 war. ag. law of my *m.*

Thy MIND.
1 *Sam.* 9:20 set not *t. m.* on asses
Job 34:33 should it be according
to *thy m.* ?
Ezek. 38:10 thi. came into *t. m.*
Dan. 2:29 thou. came into *t. m.*
Mat. 22:37 love L. the G. wi. all
t. m. Mark 12:30 ; *Luke* 10:27
Phile. 14 without *thy m.*

Your MIND.
Gen. 23:8 if y. *m.* I should bury
Jer. 51:50 Jer. come into *your m.*
Ezek. 11:5 things come into *y. m.*
20:32 that wh. cometh into *y. m.*
Rom. 12:2 by renewing of *y. m.*
2 *Cor.* 8:19 declar. of *y.* ready m.
9:2 I know forwardness of *y. m.*
Eph. 4:23 renewed in sp. of *y. m.*
Col. 1:21 enemies in *your m.*
1 *Pet.* 1:13 loins of *y. m.* be sober

MIND, Verb.
Rom. 8:5 *m.* things of the flesh
12:16 *m.* not high things, but
Phil. 3:16 let us *m.* same thing
19 who *m.* earthly things

MINDED.
Ruth 1:18 she was steadfastly *m.*
2 *Chr.* 24:4 *m.* to repair house
Ezr. 7:13 of th. own free will
Mat. 1:19 *m.* to put her away
Rom. 8:6 to be carn. *m.* is death,
to be spiritually *m.* is life
11:20 be not high-*m.* but fear
15:5 grant you to be like-*m.*
2 *Cor.* 1:15 I was *m.* to come
17 thus *m.* did I use lightness
Gal. 5:10 be no otherwise *m.*
Phil. 2:2 that ye be like-*m.*
20 no man like-*m.* will care
3:15 as many as be perf. be thus
m. if ye be otherwise *m.*
1 *Thes.* 5:14 comf. the feeble-*m.*
1 *Tim.* 6:17 rich be not high-*m.*

2 *Tim.* 3:4 men heady, high-*m.*
Tit. 2:6 exhort to be sober-*m.*
Jam. 1:8 double-*m.* man unstab.
4:8 purify hearts ye double-*m.*

MINDFUL.

1 *Chr.* 16:15 be *m.* of covenant
Neh. 9:17 fathers were not *m.*
Ps. 8:4 what is man, that thou
    art *m.* of him ? *Heb.* 2:6
111:5 ever be *m.* of covenant
115:12 L. hath been *m.* of us
Is. 17:10 not been *m.* of rock
2 *Tim.* 1:4 being *m.* of thy tears
Heb. 11:15 been *m.* of that coun.
2 *Pet.* 3:2 be *m.* of words spoken

MINDING.

Acts 20:13 P. *m.* himself to go

MINDS.

Jud. 19:30 consider, speak yo. *m.*
2 *Sam.* 17:8 be chafed in their *m.*
2 *K.* 9:15 if it be your *m.*
Ezek. 24:25 they set their *m.*
36:5 with despiteful *m.* to cast
Acts 14:2 their *m.* evil affected
28:6 they changed their *m.* and
    said he was a god
2 *Cor.* 3:14 their *m.* were blind
4:4 god of th. world ha. blin. *m.*
11:3 so your *m.* sho. be corrup.
Phil. 4:7 peace of G. keep yo. *m.*
1 *Tim.* 6:5 corrupt *m.* 2 *Tim.* 3:8
Heb. 10:16 in *m.* will I write
12:3 wear. and faint in your *m.*
2 *Pet.* 3:1 I stir up your pure *m.*

MINE.

Gen. 31:43 all that thou seest *m.*
48:5 *m.* as Reuben and S. be *m.*
Ex. 19:5 for all the earth is *m.*
    Ps. 50:12
Ps. 60:7 Gilead *m.* Man. *m.* 108:8
Ezek. 23:4 were *m.* 5 she was
    29:9 river *m.* 35:10 count. *m.*
Hag. 2:8 silver is *m.* gold is *m.*
Mal. 3:17 they sh. be *m.* saith L.
Mat. 20:23 not *m. Mark* 10:40
John 17:10 *m.* are thine, thine *m.*

MINGLE.

Is. 5:22 men *m.* strong drink
Dan. 2:43 *m.* with seed of men

MINGLED.

Ex. 9:24 fire *m.* with the hail
Lev. 19:19 not s. field wi. *m.* seed
Ezr. 9:2 holy seed *m.* themsel.
Ps. 102:9 *m.* drink wi. weeping
106:35 were *m.* among heathen
Prov. 9:2 she hath *m.* her wine
5 drink of wine wh. I have *m.*
Is. 19:14 L. *m.* a perverse spirit
Jer. 25:20 cup to all *m.* peo. 24
50:37 sw. on *m.* peo. *Ezek.* 30:5
Luke 13:1 blood Pilat had *m.*
Rev. 8:7 hail and fire *m.* with bl.

MINISH, ED.

Ex. 5:19 not *m.* aught of task
Ps. 107:39 again they are *m.*

MINISTER.

Ex. 24:13 Moses and his *m.* Jos.
Jos. 1:1 spake to Joshua, M. *m.*
Mat. 20:26 your *m. Mark* 10:43
Luke 4:20 gave book again to *m.*
Acts 13:5 had also J. to their *m.*
26:16 make th. a *m.* and witn.
Rom. 13:4 is *m.* of G. to thee, 6
15:8 Ch. was *m.* of circumcision
16 be *m.* of Jesus to Gentiles
Gal. 2:17 is Ch. the *m.* of sin ?
Eph. 3:7 whereof I was made a
    m. Col. 1:23, 25
6:21 Ty. a faithful *m. Col.* 4:7
Col. 1:7 Epaphras, a faithful *m.*
1 *Thes.* 3:2 brother and *m.* of G.
1 *Tim.* 4:6 a good *m.* of Christ
Heb. 8:2 a *m.* of the sanctuary

MINISTER, Verb.

Ex. 28:1 that he may *m.* to me in
    the priest's office, 3, 4, 41;
    29:1, 44; 30:30; 31:10; 35:19;
    39:41; 40:13, 15
85 it shall be upon Aar. to *m.*
29:44 sanctify Aar. to *m.* to me
Lev. 7:35 presented them to *m.*
Num. 8:26 wi. their brethren
Deut. 10:8 tribe of L. to *m.* to h.
21:5 God hath chos. them to *m.*
1 *Sam.* 2:11 child did *m.* to Lord
1 *K.* 8:11 priest could not stand
    to *m.* 2 *Chr.* 5:14
1 *Chr.* 15:2 chosen to *m.* bef. hi.
23:13 to *m.* to the Lord and to
    give thanks, 2 *Chr.* 31:2
2 *Chr.* 13:10 pries. *m.* sons of A.
Ps. 9:8 *m.* judgment to people
Is. 60:7 rams of Nebaioth *m.*
    10 their kings shall *m.* to thee
Jer. 33:22 multi. Levites that *m.*
Ezek. 40:46 near to *m.* 44:15, 16
44:11 stand before them to *m.*
Mat. 20:28 to be ministered to,
    but to *m. Mark* 10:45
25:44 and did not *m.* to thee ?
Acts 24:23 acquaint. to *m.* to him
Rom. 15:25 I go to *m.* to saints
    27 *m.* to them in carnal things
1 *Cor.* 9:13 *m.* about holy things
2 *Cor.* 9:10 *m.* bread for your fo.
Eph. 4:29 *m.* grace to hearers
1 *Tim.* 1:4 which *m.* questions
Heb. 1:14 *m.* to heirs of salvation
6:10 minis. to saints, and do *m.*
1 *Pet.* 1:12 but to us they did *m.*
4:10 *m.* the same one to another
    11 if any man *m.* let him do it

MINISTERED.

Num. 3:4 E. and I. *m. Deut.* 10:6
1 *Sam.* 2:18 Samuel *m.* bef. L. 3:1
2 *Sam.* 13:17 his servant that *m.*
1 *K.* 1:4 Abishag *m.* to David, 15
19:21 Elijah, and *m.* to him
Ezek. 44:12 *m.* before their idols
Dan. 7:10 thousands *m.* unto him
Mat. 4:11 angels came and *m.* to
    him, *Mark* 1:13
8:15 she rose and *m. Mark* 1:31
Luke 8:3 *m.* to him of substance
Acts 13:2 as they *m.* and fasted
20:34 have *m.* to my necessities
2 *Cor.* 3:3 epistle of Ch. *m.* by us
Phil. 2:25 that *m.* to my wants
Col. 2:19 having nourishment *m.*
2 *Tim.* 1:18 many th. *m.* unto me
Phile. 13 he might have *m.*
Heb. 6:10 have *m.* to the saints
2 *Pet.* 1:11 entrance be *m.* to you

MINISTERETH.

2 *Cor.* 9:10 *m.* seed to the sower
Gal. 3:5 that *m.* to you the Spi.

MINISTERING.

1 *Chr.* 9:28 charge of *m.* vessels
Ezek. 44:11 house, *m.* to house
Mat. 27:55 followed J. *m.* to him
Rom. 12:7 w. on *m.* 15:16 *m.* gos.
2 *Cor.* 8:4 and take on us the *m.*
9:1 for as touching *m.* to saints
Heb. 1:14 are they not *m.* spirits
10:11 every priest standeth *m.*

MINISTERS.

1 *K.* 10:5 atten. of his *m.* 2 *Chr.* 9:4
Ezr. 7:24 not lawful, toll on *m.*
8:17 they sho. bring un. us *m.*
Ps. 103:21 *m.* that do his plea.
104:4 *m.* a flaming fire, *Heb.* 1:7
Is. 61:6 shall call you *m.* of God
Jer. 33:21 covenant be broken
    with David and my *m.*
Ezek. 45:4 holy port. for the *m.*
Joel 1:9 L.'s *m.* mourn ; 13 howl
2:17 *m.* weep between the porch
Luke 1:2 from beginni. were *m.*
Rom. 13:6 *m.* attend. continually

1 *Cor.* 3:5 *m.* by whom ye belie.
4:1 so account of us as of the *m.*
2 *Cor.* 3:6 who made us able *m.*
6:4 approv. ourselv. as *m.* of G.
11:15 his *m.* also be transformed
    as the *m.* of righteousness
23 are they *m.* of Christ ? I am

MINISTRATION.

Luke 1:23 days of *m.* were ended
Acts 6:1 widows neglected in *m.*
2 *Cor.* 3:7 if *m.* of death glorious
    8 *m.* of Spirit be glorious ? 9
9:13 the experiment of this *m.*

MINISTRY.

Num. 4:12 instruments of *m.*
2 *Chr.* 7:6 D. praised by their *m.*
Hos. 12:10 used similitud. by *m.*
Acts 1:17 his obtain. part of *m.*
    25 that he may take part of *m.*
6:4 will give ourselves to *m.*
12:25 when they fulfilled th. *m.*
20:24 finish my course, and *m.*
21:19 things G. wro. by his *m.*
Rom. 12:7 *m.* let us wait on our
1 *Cor.* 16:15 addicted to *m.* of sa.
2 *Cor.* 4:1 seeing we have this *m.*
5:18 giv. us *m.* of reconciliation
6:3 that the *m.* be not blamed
Eph. 4:12 work of *m.* for edifyi.
Col. 4:17 take heed to the *m.*
Tim. 1:12 putting me into *m.*
2 *Tim.* 4:5 full proof of thy *m.*
    11 profitable to me for the *m.*
Heb. 8:6 obtained a more ex. *m.*
9:21 sprinkled the vessels of *m.*

MINNI. *Jer.* 51:27
MINNITH. *Jud.* 11:33

MINSTREL, S.

2 *K.* 3:15 but now bring me a *m.*
Mat. 9:23 when Jesus saw the *m.*

MINT.

Mat. 23:23 ye pay tithe of *m.*
Luke 11:42 ye tithe *m.* all herbs

MIRACLE.

Ex. 7:9 P. sh. speak, Show a *m.*
Mark 6:52 consid. not *m.* of loa.
9:39 no man which shall do *m.*
Luke 23:8 hoped to have seen *m.*
John 4:54 second *m.* Jesus did
10:41 many said, Jo. did no *m.*
Acts 4:16 a notable *m.* been done
    22 on wh. this *m.* was wroug.

MIRACLES.

Num. 14:22 which have seen *m.*
Deut. 11:3 have not seen his *m.*
29:3 th. eyes have seen those *m.*
Jud. 6:13 where be all his *m.*
John 2:11 beginning of *m.* did J.
    23 many beli. wh. they saw *m.*
3:2 no man can do th. *m.* ex. G.
6:26 not because ye saw the *m.*
7:31 will he do more *m.* th. this
9:16 can a sinner do such *m.* ?
11:47 this man doeth many *m.*
12:37 he had done so many *m.*
Acts 2:22 approved of God by *m.*
6:8 Stephen did great *m.*
8:6 hearing and seeing the *m.*
    13 wondered, beholding the *m.*
15:12 what *m.* G. had wrought
19:11 G. wrought spec. *m.* by P.
1 *Cor.* 12:10 to the working of *m.*
    28 teachers ; after that *m.*
    29 are all workers of *m.* ?
Gal. 3:5 he that worketh *m.*
Heb. 2:4 G. bearing witn. wi. *m.*
Rev. 13:14 decei. by means of *m.*
16:14 spirits of devils work. *m.*
19:20 false prophet tha. wro. *m.*

MIRE.

2 *Sam.* 22:43 stamp them as *m.*
    of street, *Is.* 10:6 ; *Mic.* 7:10
Job 8:11 can rush grow wit. *m.* ?
30:19 he hath cast me into *m.*
41:30 spread. things on the *m.*

Ps. 69:2 I sink in deep *m.* where
14 deliver me out of the *m.*
Is. 57:20 whose wat. cast up *m.*
Jer. 38:6 in dung. no wat. but *m.*
22 thy feet are sunk in the *m.*
Zec. 9:3 gold as *m.* of streets
10:5 tread th. enemies in the *m.*
2 Pet. 2:22 sow wallowing in *m.*

MIRY.
Ps. 40:2 bro. me out of *m.* clay
Ezek. 47:11 *m.* pla. not be healed
Dan. 2:41 iron mixed with *m.* 43

MIRIAM.
Ex. 15:20 M. took a timbrel in
Num. 12:1 M. and Aaron, 10, 15
Deut. 24:9 what God did to M.
Mic. 6:4 I sent before thee M.

MIRTH.
Gen. 31:27 sent th. away wi. *m.*
Neh. 8:12 peo. went to make *m.*
Ps. 137:3 that wasted us des. *m.*
Prov. 14:13 end of *m.* heaviness
Ec. 2:1 I will prove th. with *m.*
2 I said of *m.* what doeth it ?
7:4 heart of fools is in ho. of *m.*
8:15 then I commended *m.*
Is. 24:8 *m.* of tabrets
11 the *m.* of the land is gone
Jer. 7:34 I will cause to cease
the voice of *m.* from Judah,
16:9 ; 25:10 ; *Hos.* 2:11
Ezek. 21:10 she wi. th. make *m.* ?

MISCARRYING.
Hos. 9:14 give them a *m.* womb

MISCHIEF.
Gen. 42:4 lest some *m.* bef. him
38 if *m.* befall him, 44:29
Ex. 21:22 and yet no *m.* follow
32:12 for *m.* did he bring them
22 knowest peo. that are on *m.*
1 Sam. 23:9 Saul practised *m.*
2 Sam. 16:8 art taken in thy *m.*
1 K. 11:25 the *m.* that Hadad did
20:7 this man seeketh *m.*
2 K. 7:9 some *m.* will befall us
Neh. 6:2 thought to do me *m.*
Est. 8:3 E. sou. to put away *m.*
Job 15:35 conceive *m.* and vanity
Ps. 7:14 m. bro. forth falsehood
16 his *m.* shall ret. on his head
10:7 under his tongue is *m.*
14 thou beholdest *m.* and spite
26:10 in whose hands is *m.*
28:3 but *m.* is in their hearts
36:4 wicked dev. on his bed
52:1 why boast. thyself in *m.* ?
55:10 *m.* and sorrow in midst
62:3 how long will ye ima. *m.* ?
94:20 frameth *m.* by a law
119:150 draw nigh that fol. *m.*
140:9 *m.* of own lips cover them
Prov. 4:16 ex. they ha. done *m.*
6:14 he deviseth *m.* continually
18 feet swift in running to *m.*
10:23 is sport to a fool to do *m.*
11:27 that seek. *m.* it shall co.
12:21 wicked be filled with *m.*
13:17 wicked mes. falleth in *m.*
17:20 a perv. tongue fall. in *m.*
24:2 their heart studieth *m.*
16 wicked fall into *m.* 28:14
Is. 47:11 *m.* sh. fall upon thee
59:4 trust in vanity, conc. *m.*
Ezek. 7:26 *m.* sh. come upon *m.*
11:2 men that devise *m.*
Dan. 11:27 king's hearts to do *m.*
Hos. 7:15 do they imagine *m.*
Acts 13:10 full of all *m.* th. child

MISCHIEFS.
Deut. 32:23 heap *m.* on them
Ps. 52:2 thy tongue deviseth *m.*
140:2 imagine *m.* in their heart

MISCHIEVOUS.
Ps. 21:11 imagined a *m.* device
38:12 seek my hurt, speak *m.* t.

Prov. 24:8 be called *m.* person
Ec. 10:13 end of his talk is *m.*
Mic. 7:3 man utter. his *m.* desire

MISERABLE, LY.
Job 16:2 Job said, *m.* comforters
Mat. 21:41 *m.* destroy wicked *m.*
1 Cor. 15:19 are of all most *m.*
Rev. 3:17 know. not thou art *m.*

MISERY, IES.
Jud. 10:16 soul grieved for *m.*
Job 3:20 given to him in *m.*
11:16 thou shalt forget thy *m.*
Prov. 31:7 rem. his *m.* no more
Ec. 8:6 the *m.* of a man is great
Lam. 1:7 Jerusal. in days of *m.*
3:19 re, mine affliction and *m.*
Rom. 3:16 *m.* are in their ways
Jam. 5:1 howl for your *m.*

MISHAEL.
Ex. 6:22 ; *Lev.* 10:4 ; *Neh.* 8:4
Dan. 1:6 of childr. of Judah, M.

MISS.
Jud. 20:16 sling at, and not *m.*
1 Sam. 25:15 if thy fath. at all *m.*

MISSED, ING.
1 Sam. 20:18 thou shalt be *m.*
25:7 neither was there aught *m.*
15 neith. *m.* any thing as long
21 nothing was *m.* of all
1 K. 20:39 any means he be *m.*

MIST.
Gen. 2:6 th. went a *m.* fr. earth
Acts 13:11 there fell on him a *m.*
2 Pet. 2:17 *m.* of darkn. reserved

MISTRESS.
Gen. 16:4 Sarah her *m.* despised
8 flee fr. my *m.* S. 9 return to
1 K. 17:17 son of *m.* fell sick
2 K. 5:3 said to her *m.* would G.
Ps. 123:2 eyes of maiden to *m.*
Prov. 30:23 that is heir to her *m.*
Is. 24:2 as with maid so with *m.*
Nah. 3:4 the *m.* of witchcrafts

MISUSED.
2 Chr. 36:16 they *m.* his prophe.

MITE, S.
Mark 12:42 a certain poor widow
threw in two *m. Luke* 21:2
Luke 12:59 thou hast paid last *m.*

MITRE.
Ex. 28:4 make a *m.* 39 ; 39:28
29:6 put the *m.* upon his head
Lev. 8:9 put holy crown on *m.*
16:4 wi. lin. *m.* sh. he be attired
Zec. 3:5 set fair *m.* on his head

MIXED.
Ex. 12:38 *m.* multitude went up
Num. 11:4 *m.* multi. fell a lusti.
Neh. 13:3 separated fr. *m.* multi.
Prov. 23:30 go to seek *m.* wine
Is. 1:22 thy wine *m.* with water
Dan. 2:41 thou saw. the iron *m.*
Hos. 7:8 Ephraim *m.* am. people
Heb. 4:2 not being *m.* with faith

MIXTURE.
Ps. 75:8 there is a cup full of *m.*
John 19:39 Nicodemus, and bro.
a *m.* of myrrh and aloes
Rev. 14:10 poured out without *m.*

MIZAR. *Ps.* 42:6

MIZPAH.
Gen. 31:49 hea. of heap called M.
1 K. 15:22 Ge. and M. *2 Chr.* 16:6
2 K. 25:23 to Ged. to M. *Jer.* 41:1
Neh. 3:7 men of Gibeon and M.
Jer. 40:10 I will dwell at M.
41:3 slew all J. that were at M.
Hos. 5:1 have been a snare on M.

MIZPEH.
Jos. 15:38 Dilean and M.
Jud. 10:17 in M. 11:11 ; 21:5
20:1 Israel was gathered in M.
1 Sam. 7:5 all Isr. to M. 6 ; 22:3

10:17 Samuel called peo. to M.
MIZRAIM. *Gen.* 10:6
MNASON. *Acts* 21:16

MOAB.
Gen. 19:37 daugh.'s son was M.
Ex. 15:15 tremb. on men of M.
Num. 21:29 ; 22:3 ; 24:17 ; 25:1
Deut. 2:18 pass thro' coast of M.
34:5 Moses died in land of M.
Jud. 3:29 they slew of M. about
10:6 Israel serv. the gods of M.
11:15 took not away land of M.
Ruth 1:2 ca. into country of M.
1 Sam. 14:47 Saul fought ag. M.
2 Sam. 8:2 David smote M. ; 3:20
1 K. 11:7 the abomination of M.
2 K. 1:1 then M. rebelled, 3:7, 23
1 Chr. 4:22 dominion in M. 18:11
2 Chr. 20:1 M. came ag. Jeh. 10
Neh. 13:23 J. married wiv. of M.
Ps. 60:8 M. my washpot, 108:9
83:6 M. is confederate ag. thee
Is. 11:14 lay the hand upon M.
15:1 burden of M. 16:13 ; *Jer.*
48:1 ; *Ezek.* 25:8 ; *Amos* 2:2
16:6 heard of pride of M. 11,
14 ; *Jer.* 48:29
25:10 M. shall be trodden down
Jer. 9:26 Egypt, Judah, and M.
25:21 made M. to drink of cup
48:2 prai. of M. 9, 11, 20, 26, 47
Amos 2:2 send a fire upon M.
Zep. 2:9 M. shall be as Sodom

MOABITE.
Deut. 23:3 M. sh. not, *Neh.* 13:1
1 Chr. 11:46 Ithma the M. a val.

MOABITES.
Gen. 19:37 the father of the M.
Deut. 2:9 said, Distress not M.
Jud. 3:28 L. hath delivered M.
2 Sam. 8:2 M. beca. 1 *Chr.* 18:2
1 K. 11:1 loved women of the M.
2 K. 3:18 he will deli. the M. 24
13:20 bands of M. invaded, 24:2
Ezr. 9:1 to abominations of M.

MOCK, Substantive.
Prov. 14:9 fools make a *m.* at sin

MOCK.
Gen. 39:14 bro. Heb. to *m.* us, 17
Job 13:9 mocketh, do ye *m.* him
21:3 after I have spoken, *m.* on
Prov. 1:26 *m.* wh. your fear com.
Jer. 38:19 and thy *m.* me
Lam. 1:7 did *m.* at her sabbaths
Ezek. 22:5 shall *m.* thee who art
Mat. 20:19 deliver to G. to *m.* h.
Mark 10:34 *m.* him and scourge
Luke 14:29 begin to *m.* him

MOCKED.
Gen. 19:14 one that *m.* to sons
Num. 22:29 bec. thou hast *m.* me
Jud. 16:10 *m.* me, 13, 15
1 K. 18:27 at noon, Elijah *m.* th.
2 K. 2:23 little child. *m.* Elisha
2 Chr. 30:10 lau. to scorn and *m.*
36:16 *m.* the messengers of God
Neh. 4:1 Sanballat *m.* the Jews
Job 12:4 one *m.* of his neighbor
Mat. 2:16 H. saw that he was *m.*
27:29 they bowed the knee and
m. 31 ; *Mark* 15:20
Luke 18:32 *m.* spitef. entreated
22:63 men that held J. *m.* him
23:11 Herod *m.* 36 soldiers *m.*
Acts 17:32 resurrection, some *m.*
Gal. 6:7 not deceiv. G. is not *m.*

MOCKER, S.
Job 17:2 are th. not *m.* with me ?
Ps. 35:16 hypocrit. *m.* in feasts
Prov. 20:1 wine is a *m.* st. drink
Is. 28:22 be not *m.* lest bands be
Jer. 15:17 sat not in assem. of *m.*
Jude 18 sh. be *m.* latter times

MOCKEST, ETH.
Job 11:3 when thou *m.* sh. no *m.*

13:9 as one *m.* anoth. do ye so
39:22 *m.* at fear, not affrighted
Prov. 17:5 m. poor repro. Maker
30:17 that *m.* at his father
Jer. 20:7 derision, ev. one *m.* me

MOCKING.

Gen. 21:9 saw son of Hagar *m.*
Mat. 27:41 priests *m. Mark* 15:31
Acts 2:13 oth. *m.* said, These *m.*

MOCKING, S.

Ezek. 22:4 made thee a *m.* to all
Heb. 11:36 had trial of cruel *m.*

MODERATION.

Phil. 4:5 let your *m.* be known

MODERATELY.

Joel 2:23 gi. you former rain *m.*

MODEST.

1 *Tim.* 2:9 adorn in *m.* apparel

MOIST.

Num. 6:3 nor shall he eat *m.* gr.

MOISTENED.

Job 21:24 bones *m.* with marrow

MOISTURE.

Ps. 32:4 *m.* turned to drought
Luke 8:6 because it lacked *m.*

MOLADAH. *Jos.* 15:26

MOLE.

Lev. 11:30 snail and *m.* are uncl.

MOLES. *See* BATS.

MOLECH.

Lev. 18:21 pass thro. fire to M.
20:2 of his seed to M. *Jer.* 32:35
1 *K.* 11:7 a high place for M.
2 *K.* 23:10 son pass thro' to M.

Is. 1:6 nor *m.* with ointment

MOLOCH. *Amos* 5:26 ; *Acts* 7:43

MOLTEN.

Ex. 32:4 he had made a *m.* calf,
8 ; *Deut.* 9:12, 16 ; *Neh.* 9:18
34:17 no *m..*gods, *Lev.* 19:4
1 *K.* 7:16 chapiters of *m.* brass
23 a *m.* sea ; 30 underset. *m.*
Job 28:2 brass is *m.* out of stone
37:18 sky as a *m.* looking-glass
Ezek. 24:11 filthiness be *m.* in it
Mic. 1:4 mountains shall be *m.*

See IMAGE.

MOMENT.

Ex. 33:5 midst of thee in a *m.*
Num. 16:21 consume th. in a *m.*
Job 7:18 shouldest try him e. *m.*
20:5 joy of hypoc. but for a *m.*
21:13 in a *m.* go down to grave
34:20 in a *m.* shall they die
Ps. 30:5 his anger end. but a *m.*
73:19 into desolation as in a *m.*
Prov. 12:19 ly. tong. but for a *m.*
Is. 26:20 as it were for a *m.*
27:3 I will water it every *m.*
47:9 things shall come in a *m.*
54:7 for a small *m.* have I forsa.
8 I hid my face fr. th. for a *m.*
Jer. 4:20 my curtains in a *m.*
Lam. 4:6 Sodom overth. in a *m.*
Ezek. 26:16 tremble ev. *m.* 32:10
Luke 4:5 king. of world in a *m.*
1 *Cor.* 15:52 be changed in a *m.*
2 *Cor.* 4:17 which is but for a *m.*

MONEY.

Gen. 23:9 as much *m.* as worth
13 I will give thee *m.* for field
31:15 quite devoured our *m.*
42:25 to restore every man's *m.*
27 espied *m.* 28 *m.* restored
43:12 double *m.* in hand, 15
44:1 ev. man's *m.* in sack's mo.
47:14 gathered all *m.* in Egypt
15 *m.* faileth ; 18 our *m.* spent
Ex. 21:11 go out free without *m.*
21 he is his *m.* 35 divide *m.*
30 be laid on him a sum of *m.*

22:7 man deliver *m.* to neighbor
25 lend *m.* to any of my people
30:16 take atonement *m.* of Isr.
Lev. 25:37 not give him *m.* on
usury, *Deut.* 23:19
Num. 3:49 Mos. took redemp. *m.*
Deut. 2:6 and water for *m.* 28
14:25 turn into *m.* 26 bestow *m.*
21:14 not sell her at all for *m.*
Jud. 5:19 took no gain of *m.*
16:18 lords bro. *m.* to Delilah
17:4 restored *m.* to his mother
1 *K.* 21:2 give worth of it in *m.*
2 *K.* 5:26 is it a time to rec. *m.?*
12:4 the *m.* of dedicated things
7 now receive no more *m.* 8
10 *m.* in chest, 2 *Chr.* 24:11
16 and sin *m.* was not brought
15:20 exacted the *m.* of Israel
23:35 Jehoakim gave *m.* to Ph.
Ezr. 3:7 gave *m.* also to masons
7:17 buy speedily with this *m.*
Neh. 5:4 borrowed *m.* for king
10 my servants exact of th. *m.*
Est. 4:7 sum of *m.* H. promised
Job 31:39 eaten fruits without *m.*
42:11 ev. man also gave him *m.*
Ps. 15:5 putteth not *m.* to usury
Prov. 7:20 taken bag of *m.*
Ec. 7:12 wisd. and *m.* a defence
10:19 but *m.* answers all things
Is. 52:3 be redeemed without *m.*
55:1 he that hath no *m.* come
2 wheref. spend ye *m.* for that
Jer. 32:9 weigh. *m.* 17 shekels 10
44 men shall buy fields for *m.*
Lam. 5:4 drunk. our wa. for *m.*
Mic. 3:11 prophets divine for *m.*
Mat. 17:24 received trib. *m.* ca.
27 thou shalt find a place of *m.*
22:19 show me the tribute *m.*
25:18 earth, hid his lord's *m.*
27 *m.* to exchang. *Luke* 19:23
28:12 large *m.* to soldiers, 15
Mark 6:8 they took no *m.* in
their purse, *Luke* 9:3
12:41 people cast *m.* into treas.
14:11 and promised to give him
m. Luke 22:5
Acts 4:37 brought *m.* and laid it
8:18 Simon offered them *m.*
20 P. said, *m.* perish with thee
24:26 hoped *m.* sho. been given
1 *Tim.* 6:10 love of *m..*root of all

See BOUGHT.

MONEY-CHANGERS.

Mat. 21:12 Jesus overthrew tables of *m.-c. Mark* 11:15
John 2:14 found in temple *m.-c.*

MONSTERS.

Lam. 4:3 sea *m.* draw out breast

MONTH.

Gen. 29:14 wi. La. space of a *m.*
Ex. 13:4 came ye out in *m.* Ab.
23:15 keep feast in the *m.* Abib
34:18 in *m.* Abib thou ca. fr. E.
Deut. 16:1 ; *Jos.* 5:10
Lev. 27:6 from a *m.* old to 5 years
Num. 3:15 ev. male fr. a *m.* old,
22, 28, 34, 39, 40, 43 ; 26:62
9:22 *m.* or year cloud tarried
11:20 eat flesh, even a wh. *m.* 21
18:16 from a *m.* old shalt thou
28:14 burnt-offer. every *m.* 29:6
Deut. 21:13 in house full *m.*
1 *K.* 4:7 his *m.* made provis. 27
5:14 *m.* they were in Lebanon
Est. 9:22 *m.* turned fr. sorrow
Jer. 2:24 her *m.* they shall find
Hos. 5:7 *m.* devour th. with por.
Zec. 11:8 I cut off in one *m.*
Rev. 9:15 prep. for a day and *m.*
22:2 yielded her fruit every *m.*

See FIRST.

Second MONTH.

Gen. 7:11 *s. m.* fount. broken up

8:14 in *s. m.* was earth dried
Ex. 16:1 came to sin in *sec. m.*
Num. 1:1 in *s. m.* take sum of
9:11 on *s. m.* shall keep passover, 2 *Chr.* 30:2
10:11 on *s. m.* cloud was taken

Third MONTH.

Ex. 19:1 in *t. m.* came into Sin.
2 *Chr.* 31:7 *t. m.* began to lay fo.
Ezek. 31:1 in *t. m.* word of Lord

Fourth MONTH.

2 *K.* 25:3 *f. m.* famine prevailed
Jer. 39:2 *f. m.* city broken up
52:6 *f. m.* famine sore in city
Zec. 8:19 fast of *f. m.* be joy

See FIFTH.

Sixth MONTH.

Hag. 1:1 in *s. m.* word of L. ca.
15 in *s. m.* did work in hou. of
Luke 1:26 in *s. m.* angel sent
36 *s. m.* with her called barren

See SEVENTH.

Eighth MONTH.

Zec. 1:1 *e. m.* came word to Ze.

Ninth MONTH.

Ezr. 10:9 *n. m.* peo. sat tremb.
Jer. 36:22 sat in house in *n. m.*
Hag. 2:10 in *n. m.* came word of L.
Zec. 7:1 word came to Z. in *n. m.*

Tenth MONTH.

Gen. 8:5 decreased until *tenth m.*
Ezr. 10:16 sat down in *tenth m.*
Est. 2:16 taken to king in *t. m.*

Eleventh MONTH.

Deut. 1:3 *e. m.* Moses spake to
Zec. 1:7 *e. m.* came word to Zec.

Twelfth MONTH.

Est. 3:7 cast lots to *twelfth m.*
Ezek. 32:1 *t. m.* word of L. came

This MONTH.

Ex. 12:2 *t. m.* sh. be beginning
3 *t. m.* take every man a lamb
Neh. 9:1 *t. m.* Israel assembled

MONTHLY.

Is. 47:13 the *m.* prognosticators

MONTHS.

Num. 10:10 in begin. of your *m.*
28:11 in beginnings of *m.* offer
Jud. 11:37 let me alone two *m.*
1 *Sam.* 6:1 ark in country 7 *m.*
2 *Sam.* 2:11 D. reign. seven years
and six *m.* 5:5 ; 1 *Chr.* 3:4
6:11 ark was with O.-edom 3 *m.*
1 *K.* 5:14 two *m.* were at home
1 *Chr.* 27:1 thro' the *m.* of year
Est. 2:12 after she had been 12
m. purified, six *m.* with oil
of myrrh, six *m.* with odors
Job 3:6 not come to numb. of *m.*
7:3 made to possess *m.* of vani.
14:5 number of his *m.* wi. thee
21:21 number of his *m.* cut off
29:2 O that I were as in *m.* past
39:2 canst thou number the *m.?*
Ezek. 39:14 after end of seven *m.*
47:12 new fruit according to *m.*
Dan. 4:29 at the end of twel. *m.*
Luke 1:24 and hid herself five *m.*
4:25 when heaven was shut up
3 ye. and 6 *m. Jam.* 5:17
John 4:35 yet four *m.* then harv.
Acts 18:11 P. abode year and 6 *m.*
Gal. 4:10 observed days and *m.*
Rev. 9:5 be tormented five *m.* 10
11:2 tread under foot 42 *m.*
13:5 power given to con. 42 *m.*

See THREE.

MONUMENTS.

Is. 65:4 peo. which lodge in *m.*

MOON.

Deut. 33:14 precious thin. by *m.*
Jos. 10:12 *m.* in valley of Aijalon
Job 25:5 behold *m.* it shine. not

Ps. 8:3 when I consider the *m.*
72:7 so long as *m.* endureth
89:37 establ. forever at the *m.*
104:19 appointed *m.* for seasons
Ec. 12:2 while sun, *m.* or stars
Cant. 6:10 fair as *m.* clear as sun
Is. 3:18 round tires like the *m.*

See SUN.

New MOON.

1 *Sam.* 20:5 to-mor. is *new m.* 18
2 *K.* 4:23 neither *new m.* nor sa.
Ps. 81:3 blow trumpet in *n. m.*
Is. 66:23 fr. one *new m.* to anoth.
Ezek. 46:1 in *n. m.* sh. be opened
6 in *n. m.* offer young bullock
Amos 8:5 will *n. m.* be gone?
Col. 2:16 judge you of the *n. m.*

New MOONS.

1 *Chr.* 23:31 offer burnt sacri. in
n. m. 2 *Chr.* 2:4; 31:3: *Ezr.*
3:5: *Neh.* 10:33; *Ezek.* 46:3
Is. 1:13 *new m.* and sabbaths
14 *n. m.* and feasts my soul ha.
Ezek. 45:17 drink-off. in *new m.*
Hos. 2:11 cause *new m.* to cease

MORDECAI.

Ezr. 2:2 M. came up, *Neh.* 7:7
Est. 2:5 a Jew, name was M.
10:3 M. was next to Ahasuerus

MORE.

Ex. 1:12 the *m.* they afflicted
them, the *m.* they grew.
16:17 gath. some *m.* some less
30:15 the rich shall not give *m.*
1 *Sam.* 3:17 G. do so to th. *a. m.*
Ps. 19:10 m. to be des. than gold
71:14 I will praise th. *m.* and *m.*
Mat. 18:16 take with th. 1 or 2 *m.*
John 21:15 lovest thou me *m. f*
Heb. 12:26 once *m.* I shake, *27*

See ABUNDANTLY.

Any MORE.

Gen. 8:12 dove ret. not *any m.*
21 not curse ground *a. m.* 9:11
17:5 nor name *a. m.* be call. Ab.
35:10 nor *a. m.* be called Jacob
Ex. 8:29 not deal deceitful. *a. m.*
11:6 nor a cry be like it *any m.*
Jos. 7:12 nei. be with you *a. m.*
Ezek. 5:9 I will not do *any m. f*
Hos. 14:8 what have I *any m. f*
Luke 22:16 I will not eat *any m.*

Much MORE.

Ex. 36:5 the people bring *m. m.*
Mat. 6:30 sh. he not *m. m.* clo. *f*
Luke 7:26 *m. m.* than a prophet
Rom. 5:9 *m. m.* be. now justified
10 *much m.* being reconciled
17 *m. m.* they that receive
20 when sin abund. gra. *m. m.*
2 *Cor.* 3:11 *m. m.* wh. remaineth

No MORE.

Est. 2:14 came *no m.* to king
Job 7:8 see me *no m.* 9 come up
10 shall return *no m.* to house
Rev. 21:1 *no m.* sea; 4 death;
22:3 curse

MOREOVER.

Ps. 19:11 *m.* by th. serv. warned
Is. 39:8 *m.* there shall be peace
Heb. 11:36 *m.* of bonds and imp.

MORIAH.

Gen. 22:2 get th. into land of M.
2 *Chr.* 3:1 Sol. built house in M.

MORNING.

Gen. 19:15 when the *m.* arose
24:54 Abra. rose up in the *m.*
26:31 rose betimes in the *m.*
29:25 in the *m.* behold it was L.
40:6 Jos. came into them in *m.*
49:27 in *m.* he sh. devour prey
Ex. 7:15 get thee to Phar. in *m.*
10:13 *m.* east wind bro. locusts
14:27 sea returned to stre. in *m.*

16:7 in *m.* ye sh. see glory of L
8 give you in the *m.* bread, 12
13 in the *m.* the dew lay round
29:39 one lamb in *m. Num.* 28:4
34:2 be ready in the *m.*
25 nor shall pass. be left to *m.*
Lev. 6:9 burning all night to *m.*
Lom. 9:21 cloud taken up in *m.*
Deut. 28:67 in *m.* would it were
Jud. 6:31 put to death whilst *m.*
16:2 in the *m.* when it is day
19:37 rose in *m.* opened doors
20:19 chil. of Israel rose in *m.*
2 *Sam.* 23:4 and he shall be **as**
the *m.* when the sun riseth,
even a *m.* without clouds
24:11 when D. was up in the *m.*
1 *K.* 3:21 when I consid. it in *m.*
18:26 called on B. fr. *m.* to noon
Neh. 4:21 some labored from *m.*
8:3 read from *m.* until mid-day
Job 7:21 thou shalt seek me in *m.*
11:17 shine forth, be as the *m.*
24:17 *m.* to th. as sha. of death
38:12 hast thou commanded *m.*
41:18 his eyes like eyelids of *m.*
Ps. 5:3 my voice shalt thou **hear**
in the *m.* O Lord, in *m.*
Ps. 30:5 but joy cometh in the *m.*
49:14 dominion over them in *m.*
59:16 will sing thy mercy in *m.*
88:13 in the *m.* shall my prayer
90:5 the *m.* they are like grass
6 in the *m.* it flourisheth up
119:147 I prevented dawn. of *m.*
130:6 they that watch for *m.*
139:9 if I take wings of the *m.*
143:8 thy loving-kindness in *m.*
Ec. 10:16 princes eat in the *m.*
11:6 in the *m.* sow thy seed
Cant. 6:10 she looketh like *m.*
Is. 14:12 O Lucifer, son of *m.*
17:14 before the *m.* he is not
21:12 watchman said, *m.* com.
28:19 mo. by *m.* sh. it pass over
50:4 he wakeneth *m.* by *m.*
58:8 thy light break forth as *m.*
Jer. 5:8 were as fed horses in *m.*
20:16 hear the cry in the *m.*
21:12 execute judgm. in the *m.*
Ezek. 7:7 the *m.* is come on thee
10 the *m.* is gone forth, the rod
12:8 in the *m.* came word of L.
24:18 I spake to the peo. in the
m. at even my wife died, I
did in the *m.* as commanded
33:22 it came to me in the *m.*
Hos. 6:3 his going forth is as *m.*
4 your goodness is as *m.* cloud
7:6 in the *m.* it burneth as fire
10:15 in a *m.* sh. king be cut off
Joel 2:2 as *m.* spread on mount.
Amos 4:13 maketh the *m.* dark.
5:8 turn shad. of death into *m.*
Jon. 4:7 God prepared a worm
when the *m.* rose
Mic. 2:1 when the *m.* is light
Mat. 16:3 in the *m.* it will be fo.
27:1 when the *m.* was come
Mark 11:20 in *m.* as they passed
13:35 at cock-crowing, or in *m.*

Early in the MORNING.

Gen. 19:27 Abraham gat up *e. in
the m.* 21:14 ; 22:3
28:18 Jacob rose up *e. in the m.*
31:55 Laban rose *e. in the m.*
Ex. 8:20 said, Rise *e. in m.* 9:13
24:4 Moses rose *early in m.* 34:4
Jos. 3:1 Joshua rose *early in the
m.* 6:12 ; 7:16 ; 8:10
Jud. 6:28 men of city r. *e. in m.*
1 *Sam.* 1:19 they rose up *e. in t.
m.* 29:11 ; 2 *K.* 3:22 ; 19:35 ;
2 *Chr.* 20:20 ; *Is.* 37:36
15:12 Sa. rose *e. in m.* 17:20 D
29:10 wherefore rise *e. in the m.*
Job 1:5 Job rose up *e. in the m.*

Prov. 27:14 rising *early in the m.*
Is. 5:11 woe to th. th. rise *e. in m.*
37:36 arose *e. in t. m.* all dead
Dan. 6:19 Darius rose *e. in t. m.*
Mat. 20:1 went *early in the m.*
Mark 16:2 *early in the m.* came
to sepulchre, *Luke* 24:1
Luke 21:38 came *e. i. m. John* 8:2
Acts 5:21 entered temple *e. in m.*

See EVENING.

Every MORNING.

Ex. 16:21 gath. manna *every m.*
30:7 burn sweet incense *e. m.*
Lev. 6:12 priest burn wood *e. m.*
1 *Chr.* 9:27 *e. m.* pertain. to por.
2 *Chr.* 13:11 burn to Lord *e. m.*
Job 7:18 shouldest visit him *e. m.*
Ps. 73:14 have been chaste. *e. m.*
Is. 33:2 be thou our arm *e. m.*
Lam. 3:23 L.'s mercies new *e. m.*
Ezek. 46:13 prepare a lamb *e. m.*
Amos 4:4 bring sacrifices *e. m.*
Zep. 3:5 *e. m.* doth bring judgm.

MORNING light.

1 *Sam.* 14:36 spoil th. until *m. l.*
25:22 pertain to him by *m. l.*
36 Abi. told nothing until *m. l.*
2 *Sam.* 17:22 passed *T.* by *m. l.*
2 *K.* 7:9 if we tarry until *m. li.*

See CLOUD.

MORNING star, s.

Job 38:7 wh. *m. s.* sang together
Rev. 2:28 I will give him *m. s.*
22:16 I, Jesus, am bright *m. s.*

Until the MORNING.

Ex. 12:10 let noth. of it remain
u. the m. 16:19 ; 23:18 ; 29:34 ;
Lev. 7:15 ; *Num.* 9:12
16:20 some of th. left *u. t. m.*
23 lay up for you *until the m.*
Lev. 19:13 not abide *u. t. m.*
Deut. 16:4 any flesh rem. *u. the m.*
Jud. 19:25 abused her *u. t. m.*
Ruth 3:13 dawn *u. m.* 14 lay
1 *Sam.* 3:15 Samuel lay *u. t. m.*
19:2 take heed to thyself *u. t. m.*
2 *K.* 10:8 heads of kings *u. t. m.*
Prov. 7:18 our fill of love *u. m.*
Is. 38:13 I reckoned *until the m.*

MORNING watch.

Ex. 14:24 in *m. w.* L. said to M.
1 *Sam.* 11:11 mi. of host in *m. w.*

MORROW.

Ex. 8:23 to-*m.* shall this sign be
9:5 to-*m.* the L. sh. do this thi.
6 L. did thing, on *m.* cattle di.
16:23 to-*m.* is rest of holy sab.
19:10 sanc. them to-day and *m.*
32:5 to-*m.* is a feast to the Lord
Lev. 7:16 on *m.* remain. cat. 19:6
22:30 leave none of it till *m.*
23:15 ye shall count from *m.*
Num. 11:18 sanctify yourselves
against to-*m. Jos.* 7:13
16:16 they and A. to-*m.* bef. L.
41 on *m.* congreg. murmured
Jos. 3:5 to-*m.* L. will do wond.
5:12 manna ceased on the *m.*
22:18 to-*m.* wroth wi. congreg.
Jud. 19:9 to-*m.* get early on way
20:28 to-*m.* I will deliver them
1 *Sam.* 11:9 to-*m.* by ti. sun hot
20:5 to-*m.* is the new moon, 18
28:19 to-*m.* shalt thou and sons
1 *K.* 20:6 send her to-*m.*
2 *K.* 6:28 will eat my son, to-*m.*
8:15 on *m.* he took a thick cloth
2 *Chr.* 20:16 to-*m.* go ye down, 17
Est. 5:8 to-*m.* as king hath said
12 to-*m.* am I invited to her
Prov. 3:28 to-*m.* I will give
27:1 boast not thyself to-*m.*
Is. 22:13 let us eat, for to-*m.* we
die, 1 *Cor.* 15:32
56:12 to-*m.* shall be as this day

Zep. 3:3 gn. not bones till to-*m.*
Mat. 6:30 to -*m.* is cast into the oven, *Luke* 12:28
34 take no thought for *m.* for *m.* sh. take thought for itself
Luke 12:32 to-day, and to-*m.*
33 walk to-day and to-*m.*
Acts 20:7 P. rea. to depart on *m.*
25:22 to-*m.* thou shalt hear him
Jam. 4:13 to-day or to-*m.* will go
14 know not what sh. be on *m.*

MORSEL.
Gen. 18:5 fetch a *m.* of bread
Jud. 19:5 comf. heart with *m.*
Ruth 2:14 dip thy *m.* in vinegar
Job 31:17 eaten my *m.* myself
Prov. 17:1 bet. dry *m.* and quiet
23:8 *m.* hast eaten shall vomit
Heb. 12:16 E. for *m.* sold birthri.

See BREAD.

MORSELS.
Ps. 147:17 cast. forth ice like *m.*

MORTAL.
Job 4:17 *m.* man mo. just th. G. ?
Rom. 6:12 sin reign in *m.* body
8:11 quicken *m.* bodies by Spi.
1 *Cor.* 15:53 *m.* on immortal. 54
2 *Cor.* 4:11 J. manifest, in *m.* fle.

MORTALITY.
2 *Cor.* 5:4 *m.* swallow. up of life

MORTALLY.
Deut. 19:11 smite neighbor *m.*

MORTAR.
Gen. 11:3 slime had they for *m.*
Ex. 1:14 serve in *m.* and brick
Lev. 14:42 take *m.* and plast. ho.
45 break down *m.* of the house
Is. 41:25 upon princes as up. *m.*
Ezek. 13:10 daubed it with untempered *m.* 11, 14, 15 ; 22:28
Nah. 3:14 clay, and tread the *m.*

MORTAR.
Num. 11:8 or beat it in a *m.*
Prov. 27:22 bray fool in *m.*

MORTGAGED.
Neh. 5:3 we have *m.* our lands

MORTIFY.
Rom. 8.13 ye *m.* deeds of body
Col. 3:5 *m.* your members

MOSEROTH. *Num.* 33:30

MOSES.
Ex. 2:10 called his name M.
Jos. 1:5 as I was with M. 3:7
Ps. 103:7 made kn. ways to M.
105:26 he sent M. and Aaron
106:16 envied M. in camp, 32
Is. 63:12 by right hand of M.
Jer. 15:1 though M. stood be. me
Mal. 4:4 remember law of M.
Mat. 17:3 there appeared M. and Elias, *Mark* 9:4 ; *Luke* 9:30
19:7 why did M. command. ?
23:2 Pharisees sit in M.'s seat
Mark 10:3 what did M. com. ?
Mark 12:19 M. wrote, *Luke* 20:28
Luke 16:29 M. and prophets
20:37 M. showed at the bush
24:27 beginning at M. and pro.
John 1:17 law given by M. 45
3:14 as M. lifted serpent
5:45 M. accuseth ; 46 believed M.
6:32 M. ga. you not that bread
7:19 M. give you law ? 22, 23
9:28 M. disciples ; 29 G. spake
Acts 3:22 M. said, A prophet
6:11 blas. words against M. 14
7:20 M. born, 32, 35, 37
13:39 not justified by law of M.
15:1 circumcised after M. 5
21 M. hath in every city them
21:21 teachest to forsake M.
26:22 things M. did say, 28:23
2 *Cor.* 3:13 not as M. who, 15
2 *Tim.* 3:8 as Jan. withstood M.

Heb. 3:2 M. faithful, 8, 5, 16
9:19 M. spoken every precept
10:28 despised M. law
11:23 by faith M. was hid three
12:21 M. said, I fear and quake
Jude 9 disput. about body of M.
Rev. 15:3 sing the song of M.

MOST.
Prov. 20:6 *m.* men proclaim
Luke 7:42 wh. will love him *m.* ?
43 he to whom he forgave *m.*
Acts 20:38 sorrowing of. of all for
1 *Cor.* 14:27 two, or at *m.* three

MOTE.
Mat. 7:3 *m.* in brother's eye, *Luke* 6:41
4 let me pull *m.* out of th. eye
5 then th. see clear. to cast *m.* out of broth.'s eye, *Luke* 6:42

MOTH.
Job 4:19 crushed before the *m.*
27:18 buildeth his house as a *m.*
Ps. 39:11 beauty consu. like *m.*
Is. 50:9 *m.* shall eat them, 51:8
Hos. 5:12 I be to Ephr. as a *m.*
Mat. 6:19 wh. *m.* and rust corru.
20 nei. *m.* nor rust, *Luke* 12:33

MOTH-EATEN.
Job 13:28 as garm. that is *m.-e.*
Jam. 5:2 your garments are *m.-e.*

MOTHER.
Gen. 3:20 was *m.* of all living
17:16 shall be a *m.* of nations
24:60 *m.* thousands of millions
32:11 lest he smite *m.* with chi.
Ex. 2:8 and called child's *m.*
Lev. 20:14 her *m.* is wickedness
Jud. 5:7 Deb. arose a *m.* in Isr.
28 *m.* of Sisera looked out
Ruth 1:8 ret. each to *m.'s* house
2 *Sam.* 17:25 Zeruiah, Joab's *m.*
20:19 to destroy a *m.* in Israel
1 *K.* 2:19 a seat for the king's *m.*
3:27 child, she is the *m.* thereof
2 *K.* 24:15 carried away king's *m.*
Ps. 113:9 be a joyful *m.* of child.
Prov. 30:11 generat. not bless *m.*
Cant. 6:9 only one of her *m.*
Is. 50:1 whe. bill of *m.* divorce ?
Jer. 50:12 *m.* be sore confounded
Ex. 16:44 as is *m.* so is daughter
45 your *m.* was a Hittite
23:2 two, daughters of one *m.*
Hos. 2:2 plead with your *m.*
5 th. *m.* hath played the harlot
10:14 *m.* was dashed in pieces
Mic. 7:6 daughter riseth up ag. her *m.* *Mat.* 10:35 ; *Lu.* 12:53
Mat. 8:14 P.'s wife's *m.* *Lu.* 4:38
14:8 before instructed of her *m.*
19:12 so born from *m.'s* womb
20:20 *m.* of Zebedee's children
Luke 1:43 *m.* of L. come to me ?
John 2:1 *m.* of J. there, *Acts* 1:14
Acts 12:12 hou. of Mary, *m.* of J.
Gal. 4:26 Jerusalem *m.* of us all
Rev. 17:5 the *m.* of harlots and

See FATHER.

His MOTHER.
Gen. 21:21 *h. m.* took him a wife
24:67 comf. after death of *h. m.*
27:14 Jacob bro. them to *his m.*
43:29 brother Benj. *h. m.'s* son
44:20 he alone is left of *his m.*
Ex. 23:19 not seethe kid in *his m.'s* milk, 34:26 ; *Deut.* 14:21
Lev. 20:17 man take *h. m.'s* daug.
Num. 12:12 out of *his m.'s* womb
Deut. 27:22 lieth with *h. m.'s* da.
Jud. 9:1 went to *h. m.'s* brethr.
1 *Sam.* 2:19 *h. m.* made a lit. co.
1 *K.* 15:13 *his m.* he removed
17:23 Elijah deliv. him to *h. m.*
22:52 walked in way of *h. m.*
2 *K.* 4:19 lad, Carry him to *h. m.*

1 *Chr.* 4:9 *h. m.* called name Ja.
2 *Chr.* 22:3 *his m.* was his coun.
Ps. 35:14 as one mourn. for *h. m.*
109:14 not sin of *his m.* blotted
131:2 child weaned of *h. m.*
Prov. 10:1 son is heavi. of *h. m.*
15:20 foolish man despis. *h. m.*
29:15 left bringeth *h. m.* to sh.
31:1 prophecy *h. m.* taught him
Ec. 5:15 came forth of *h. m.'s w.*
Cant. 3:11 *his m.* crowned him
Is. 66:13 wh. *h. m.* comforteth
Mat. 1:18 *h. m.* was espoused
2:13 young child and *h. m.* 20
12:46 *h. m.* stood with. *Mark* 3:31 ; *Luke* 8:19
13:55 is not *h. m.* called Mary ?
Luke 1:15 Holy G. fr. *h. m.'s* wo.
60 *h. m.* said, He sh. be call. J.
2:51 *h. m.* kept these sayings
7:12 only son of *h. m.* a widow
15 he delivered him to *h. m.*
John 3:4 sec. time into *h. m.'s w.*
19:25 *h. m.* stood by cross of J.
26 when J. saw *h. m.*
Acts 3:2 lame fr. *h. m.* wo. 14:8
Rom. 16:13 salute R. and *his m.*

MOTHER-IN-LAW.
Deut. 27:23 curs. lieth wi. *m.-i.-l.*
Ruth 1:14 Or. kissed her *m.-i.-l.*
2:23 R. dwelt with her *m.-i.-l.*
3:17 go not empty to thy *m.-i.-l.*
Mic. 7:6 dau.-in-law ag. *m.-i.-l.*
Mat. 10:35 ; *Luke* 12:53

My MOTHER.
Gen. 20:12 not daughter of *m. m.*
Jud. 8:19 the sons of *my m.*
16:17 Nazar. from *my m.'s* wo.
1 *K.* 2:20 to her, Ask on, *my m.*
Job 1:21 naked out of *my m.'s w.*
3:10 sh. not doors of *my m.'s w.*
17:14 to worm, Thou art *m. m.*
31:18 guid. her fr. *m. m.'s* wo.
Ps. 22:9 wh. on *m. m.'s* breasts
10 my God from *m. m.'s* belly
51:5 in sin did *m. m.* conce. me
69:8 alien to *m. m.'s* children
71:6 out of *m. m.'s* bowels
139:13 cov. me in *my m.'s* womb
Prov. 4:3 bel. in sight of *my m.*
Cant. 1:16 *my m.'s* children ang.
3:4 brou. him to *my m.'s* house
8:1 sucked the breasts of *my m.*
2 bring th. into *my m.'s* house
Is. 49:1 from bowels of *my m.*
Jer. 15:10 woe is me, *my m.*
20:14 day wherein *my m.* bare
17 *my m.* might been my grave
Mat. 12:48 Jesus said, Who is *my m.* ? *Mark* 3:33
49 behold *my m.* and brethren, *Mark* 3:34 ; *Luke* 8:21
Gal. 1:15 separat. fr. *my m.'s w.*

Thy MOTHER.
Gen. 27:29 let *thy m.'s* sons bow
37:10 I and *thy m.* bow to thee ?
Lev. 18:7 nakedness of *thy m.*
Deut. 13:6 son of *thy m.* ent. th.
1 *Sam.* 15:33 *thy m.* be childless
20:30 confus. of *t. m.'s* nakedn.
2 *K.* 9:22 whoredoms of *thy m.*
Ps. 50:20 slander. *t. own m.'s* son
Prov. 1:8 the law of *thy m.* 6:20
23:22 and despise not *thy m.*
Cant. 8:5 *thy m.* brou. thee forth
Jer. 22:26 *thy m.* that bare thee
Ezek. 16:3 fa. Amorite, *t. m.* Hit.
45 thou art *thy m.'s* daughter
19:2 say, What is *thy m.* ?
10 *thy m.* is like a vine
Hos. 4:5 I will destroy *thy m.*
Mat. 12:47 beh. *t. m.* and breth. *Mark* 3:32 ; *Luke* 8:20 ; *John* 19:27
2 *Tim.* 1:5 which dwelt in *t. m.*

MOTHERS.
Is. 49:23 queens be thy nurs. *m.*

Jer. 16:3 saith the L. concern. *m.*
Lam. 2:12 say to their *m.* where
　is corn and wine? soul was
　poured to their *m.* bosom.
5:3 fatherless, our *m.* as widows
Mark 10:30 hun.-fold. sisters. *m.*
1 *Tim.* 1:9 law for murder. of *m.*
5:2 entreat elder women as *m.*

MOTIONS.

Rom. 7:5 the *m.* of sins did work

MOULDY.

Jos. 9:5 provision dry and *m.* 12

MOUNT, 'ING.

Job 20:6 excel. *m.* to heavens
39:27 do. eagle *m.* at thy com.?
Ps. 107:26 they *m.* up to heaven
Is. 9:18 *m.* as lift. up of smoke
15:5 by *m.* up of Luhith they go
Is. 40:31 shall *m.* up with wings
Jer. 51:53 tho. Babylon sho. *m.*
Ezek. 10:16 cherub. lift *m.* 19

MOUNT.

Gen. 31:54 J. offered sacri. on *m.*
Ex. 18:5 encamped at *m.* of G.
19:12 whoso toucheth the *m.*
　14 Moses went down from the
　m. 32:15 ; 34:29
16 thick cloud upon *m.* 24:15
18 *m.* Si. was altoget. on smo.
23 set bounds about the *m.*
24:16 glory of Lord upon *m.* Si.
17 devouring fire on top of *m.*
31:18 L. gave Mos. on *m.* Sinai
32:19 M. brake them beneath *m.*
34:2 and come up to *m.* Sinai
　3 nor let man be seen thro' *m.*
Num. 10:33 they departed fr. *m.*
20:28 Aaron died in *m.* Hor
Deut. 1:6 dw. long enough in *m.*
　7 turn you, go to *m.* of Amor.
9:15 the *m.* burned with fire
27:13 these shall stand on *m.* E.
33:2 L. shined forth from *m.* P.
Jud. 4:6 draw towards *m.* Tabor
2 *Sam.* 15:30 D. went by the *m.*
　32 *m.* where he worshipped G.
1 *K.* 19:8 Elijah went to *m.* of G.
11 stand on the *m.* bef. the L.
2 *K.* 23:13 the *m.* of corruption
Neh. 9:13 thou camest on *m.* Si.
Cant. 4:1 flock of goats fr. *m.* G.
Is. 10:32 *m.* of dau. of Zion, 16:1
14:13 I will sit on *m.* of congre.
27:13 worship in holy *m.* at J.
29:3 siege ag. thee with a *m.*
Jer. 6:6 cast a *m.* against Jerusa.
　Ezek. 4:2 ; 21:22 ; 26:8
Dan. 11:15 k. of north cast up *m.*
Ob. 8 destroy unders. out *m.* E.
21 saviors sh. come to judge *m.*
Hab. 3:3 H. One from *m.* Paran
Acts 7:30 in wilderness of *m.* S.
Gal. 4:24 one from the *m.* Sinai
25 Agar is *m.* Sinai in Arabia
Heb. 12:18 not come to the *m.*

See CARMEL, GERIZIM.

Before the MOUNT.

Ex. 19:2 Israel camped *b. t. m.*
34:3 nei. let flocks feed *b. t. m.*

See EPHRAIM.

In, *or* into the MOUNT.

Gen. 22:14 *in t. m.* of L. be seen
31:54 tarried all night *in t. m.*
Ex. 4:27 met him *in t. m.* of God
19:12 take heed, go not up *i. m.*
24:12 come *i. t. m.* Deut. 10:1
13 went *in t. m.* of G. 15, 18
18 M. was *in t. m.* 40 days and
40 nights, *Deut.* 9:9 ; 10:10
25:40 after pat. showed thee *in
　t. m.* 26:30 ; 27:8 ; *Heb.* 8:5
Num. 27:12 get thee *into m.* A.
Deut. 32:50 die *in m.* as A. died
Jos. 8:30 altar to L. *in m.* Ebal
2 *K.* 28:16 spied sepulchres *in m.*

---

2 *Chr.* 3:1 house of L. *in m.* Mo.
Is. 28:21 L. rise up as *in m.* P.
Acts 7:38 angel spake *in m.* Sin.
2 *Pet.* 1:18 we were *in* holy *m.*

See GILBOA.

MOUNT of Olives.

Zec. 14:4 his feet shall stand on
　m. of O. *m.* of O. shall clea.
Mat. 21:1 they were come to the
　m. of Olives, *Luke* 19:29
24:3 upon *m.* of O. *Mark* 13:3
26:30 they went out into *m.* of
　O. *Mark* 14:26 ; *Luke* 22:39
Luke 19:37 at descent of *m.* of O.
21:37 and abode in *m.* of O.
Acts 1:12 returned fr. *m.* of O.

See SEIR, ZION.

MOUNTS.

Jer. 32:24 *m.* are come to city
33:4 houses thrown down by *m.*
Ezek. 17:17 for him, by cast. *m.*

MOUNTAIN.

Gen. 14:10 they th. re. fled to *m.*
19:17 escape to the *m.* of G.
Ex. 3:1 came to the *m.* of G.
12 peo. sh. serve God on th. *m.*
19:3 L. called to him out of *m.*
20:18 people saw *m.* smoking
Num. 14:40 gat th. into top of *m.*
Deut. 2:8 ye have compassed *m.*
3:25 let me see that goodly *m.*
4:11 *m.* burnt with fire, 5:23
Jos. 2:16 get ye to *m.* and hide
11:16 Jos. took the plain and *m.*
14:12 give me *m.* 17:18 *m.* thine
Jud. 1:19 drave out inhabitants
　of *m.*

1 *Sam.* 17:3 Philistines stood on
　a *m.* on one side, and Israel
　stood on a *m.* on the oth. si.
23:26 Saul went on this side of
　m. and David on th. si.
2 *K.* 2:16 S. cast him on some *m.*
6:17 *m.* full of horses and char.
Job 14:18 *m.* fall. com. to naught
Ps. 11:1 flee as bird to your *m.* ?
30:7 hast made my *m.* to stand
78:54 bro. to *m.* his right hand
Is. 2:2 *m.* of L.'s house, *Mic.* 4:1
3 let us go to *m.* of L. *Mic.* 4:2
30:17 as a beacon on top of *m.*
29 one goeth with pipe to *m.*
40:4 every *m.* and hill sh. be
　made low, *Luke* 3:5
Jer. 16:16 hunt them fr. every *m.*
17:3 O my *m.* in the field
26:18 *m.* of the house as high
　places of forest, *Mic.* 3:12
50:6 people gone fr. *m.* to hill
51:25 O destroying *m.* saith L.
　I will make thee a burnt *m.*
Lam. 5:18 because of *m.* of Zion
Ezek. 11:23 gl. of L. stood on *m.*
28:16 cast thee out of *m.* of God
43:12 law of house on top of *m.*
Dan. 2:35 stone became great *m.*
45 the stone was cut out of *m.*
Mic. 7:12 co. to thee *m.* to *m.*
Hag. 1:8 go up to *m.* bring wood
Zec. 4:7 who art th. O great *m.*
8:3 be called the *m.* of the Lord
14:4 half of the *m.* shall remove
Mat. 5:1 he went up into a *m.*
　14:23 ; 15:29 ; *Mark* 3:13 ; 6:46 ;
　Luke 6:12 ; 9:28 ; *John* 6:3, 15
17:1 bringeth them into high *m.*
9 and as they came down from
　the *m. Mark* 9:9
20 have faith, say to this *m.*
　Remove, 21:21 ; *Mark* 11:23
28:16 *m.* where Jesus appointed
Luke 8:32 swine feeding on *m.*
Heb. 12:20 much as beast tou. *m.*
Rev. 6:14 every *m.* and isl. rem.
8:8 a great *m.* burning with fire

High MOUNTAIN.

Is. 13:2 lift up banner up. *h. m.*
30:25 shall be upon every *h. m.*
40:9 get thee up into the *h. m.*
57:7 on *h. m.* hast th. set thy b.
Jer. 3:6 gone up upon ev. *h. m.*
Ezek. 17:22 plant it on a *high m.*
40:2 set me on a very *high m.*
Mat. 4:8 devil taken him up into
　an exceeding *h. m. Luke* 4:5
17:1 Jesus taketh P., James and
　John into a *h. m. Mark* 9:2
Rev. 21:10 car. me in Sp. to *h. m.*

See HOLY.

In the, *or* in this MOUNTAIN.

Gen. 19:30 went and dwelt in *m.*
Ex. 15:17 plant them *in the m.*
Num. 13:17 said, Go up *in t. m.*
Deut. 32:49 get thee up *in t. m.*
Ps. 48:1 G. praised *in m.* of holi.
Is. 25:6 *in this m.* L. make feast
　7 destroy *in t. m.* face of cov.
10 *in this m.* hand of L. rest
Ezek. 17:23 *in the m.* of Israel
Amos 4:1 *in the m.* of Samaria
6:1 woe to th. trust *in m.* of S,
John 4:20 fath. worship. *in t. m.*
21 nei. *in this m.* nor Jerusal.

MOUNTAINS.

Gen. 7:20 the *m.* were covered
8:4 the ark rested upon the *m.*
5 tenth month tops of *m.* seen
Num. 33:48 departed from the *m.*
Deut. 12:2 destroy pla. on hi. *m.*
Jos. 11:21 cut off Anakim fr. *m.*
Jud. 5:5 *m.* melted from bef. L.
11:37 go up and down on *m.*
2 *Sam.* 1:21 *m.* of Gilboa
1 *K.* 19:11 a strong wind rent *m.*
1 *Chr.* 12:8 swift as roes on *m.*
2 *Chr.* 18:16 Israel scatter. on *m.*
Job 9:5 which removeth the *m.*
28:9 overturneth *m.* by roots
40:20 *m.* bring him forth food
Ps. 36:6 thy right. like great *m.*
46:2 though the *m.* be carried
3 tho' *m.* shake with swelling
65:6 his strength setteth fast *m.*
72:3 *m.* bring peace to the peo.
76:4 more glori. than *m.* of prey
83:14 flame setteth *m.* on fire
90:2 before *m.* we. brought for.
104:6 waters stood above *m.*
　8 up by the *m.* down by valle.
114:4 *m.* skipped like rams, 6
125:2 as *m.* round about Jerusa.
133:3 dew that descended on *m.*
144:5 touch *m.* they shall smoke
Ps. 147:8 mak. gr. to grow on *m.*
148:9 *m.* and hills praise the L-
Prov. 8:25 before *m.* were settled
Cant. 2:8 cometh leaping on *m.*
17 be like a roe on the *m.* 8:14
4:8 look from *m.* of the leopards
Is. 2:14 day of L. be on high *m.*
14:25 *m.* tread him under foot
18:3 lifteth up ensign on the *m.*
34:3 *m.* melted with their blood
40:12 hath weighed *m.* in scales
41:15 thou shalt thresh the *m.*
42:15 make waste *m.* and hills
44:23 into singing, ye *m.* 49:13
49:11 make all my *m.* a way
52:7 how beautiful on the *m.* are
　the feet, *Nah.* 1:15
54:10 for the *m.* shall depart
55:12 *m.* shall break forth befo.
64:1 *m.* flow down at presen. 3
65:7 have burned incense on *m.*
Jer. 4:24 beh. *m.* and th. tremb.
9:10 for *m.* will I take up weep.
13:16 feet stumble on dark *m.*
17:26 from *m.* bringing offerin.
31:5 plant vines on *m.* of Sama.
46:18 as Tabor among the *m.*
50:6 turned them away on *m.*
Lam. 4:19 pursued us on the *m.*

Ezek. 6:2 set face toward *m.* of I.
7:16 sh. be on the *m.* like doves
18:6 not eaten upon *m.* 11, 15
19:9 voice no more heard on *m.*
22:9 they eat upon the *m.*
31:12 upon *m.* branches fallen
32:5 I will lay thy flesh on *m.*
33:28 *m.* of Is. shall be desolate
34:6 sheep wander. through *m.*
13 feed them on *m.* of Israel. 14
35:8 fill his *m.* with slain men
36:1 prophesy unto *m.* Is. 4
8 *m.* of Is. shoot forth branch
37:22 one nation on *m.* of Israel
38:8 gathered ag. *m.* of Is.
20 *m.* shall be thrown down
21 sw. against him thro' all *m.*
39:2 bring thee on *m.* of Israel
4 shall fall on the *m.* of Israel
17 great sacrifice on *m.* of Isr.
Joel 2:2 morn. spread upon *m.*
3:18 *m.* sh. drop down new wine
Amos 3:9 assemble on *m.* of Sa.
4:13 formeth *m.* L. is his name
9:13 *m.* shall drop sweet wine
Mic. 1:4 the *m.* shall be molten
6:1 contend thou before the *m.*
2 O ye *m.* the L.'s controversy
Nah. 1:5 the *m.* quake at him
3:18 people scattered on the *m.*
Hab. 3:6 everlasting *m.* scattered
10 *m.* saw thee, and trembled
Hag. 1:11 for a drought on *m.*
Zec. 6:1 chariots bet. *m.* of brass
Mal. 1:3 and laid his *m.* waste
Mat. 18:12 goeth into the *m.*
24:16 let them in Jud. flee to *m.*
1 *Cor.* 13:2 that I could remo. *m.*
Rev. 16:20 *m.* were not found
17:9 seven heads are seven *m.*

In the MOUNTAINS.
Ex. 32:12 to slay them *in t. m.*
Num. 33:47 pitched *in t. m.* of A.
Deut. 2:37 cam. not to cit. *in m.*
Jos. 10:6 kings that dw. *in t. m.*
Jud. 6:2 Is. made dens *in t. m.*
1 *K.* 5:15 80,000 hewers *in t. m.*
2 *Chr.* 21:11 high places *in t. m.*
Is. 13:4 noise of multi. *in t. m.*
Mark 5:5 ni. and day was *in m.*
Heb. 11:38 wandered in the *m.*

Of the MOUNTAINS.
Gen. 8:5 tops of *t. m.* were seen
22:2 offer him on one of *the m.*
Num. 23:7 out of *the m.* of east
Deut. 32:22 foundations of *t. m.*
33:15 chief thin. *of t.* ancient *m.*
Jud. 9:25 for him in top *of t. m.*
36 peo. down from top of *t. m.*
seest shadow of *the m.*
2 *K.* 19:23 to hei. of *t. m. Is.* 37:24
Job 24:8 showers of *the m.*
39:8 range of *t. m.* his pasture
Ps. 50:11 all fowls of *t. m.*
72:16 handful corn on top of *t. m.*
Prov. 27:25 herbs of *t. m.* gath.
Is. 2:2 in top of *the m. Mic.* 4:1
42:11 shout from top of *the m.*
Jer. 3:23 fr. multitude of *the m.*
32:44 witness. in cities of *t. m.*
36:13 in cities of *the m.*
Ezek. 6:13 slain in tops of *the m.*
7:7 the sounding ag. of *the m.*
Hos. 4:13 sacri. on tops of *the m.*
Joel 2:5 char. on tops of *the m.*
Jon. 2:6 down to bot. of *the m.*
Zec. 14:5 flee to valley of *the m.*
Rev. 6:15 hid in rocks of *the m.*

To the MOUNTAINS.
Cant. 4:6 *to the m.* of myrrh
Is. 22:5 trou. and crying *to t. m.*
Ezek. 6:3 saith L. *to the m.* 36:4
32:6 water with blood *to the m.*
36:1 prophesy *to the m.* of Is. 6
Hos. 10:8 sh. say *to the m.* Cover
Mark 13:14 that be in Judea flee
to the m. Luke 21:21
Luke 23:30 *to m.* Fall, *Rev.* 6:16

MOURN.
Gen. 23:2 Ab. came to *m.* Sarah
1 *Sam.* 16:1 how long *m.* for S. ?
2 *Sam.* 3:31 and *m.* before Abner
1 *K.* 13:29 old proph. came to *m.*
14:13 all Israel sh. *m.* for him
Neh. 8:9 this day is holy, *m.* not
Job 2:11 appointm. to *m.* wi. hi.
5:11 those wh. *m.* may be exal.
14:22 soul within him shall *m.*
Ps. 55:2 I *m.* in my complaint
Prov. 5:11 and th. *m.* at the last
29:2 wicked rule, the people *m.*
Ec. 3:4 time to *m.* time to dance
Is. 3:26 gates sh. lament and *m.*
16:7 for Kir-hareseth shall ye *m.*
19:8 fishers *m.* 38:14 I did *m.*
59:11 we *m.* sore like doves
61:2 sent me to comf. all that *m.*
3 to appoint them that *m.* in Z.
66:10 rejoice all ye that *m.*
Jer. 4:28 for this earth shall *m.*
12:4 how long sh. the land *m. ?*
48:31 *m.* for the men of Kir-her.
Lam. 1:4 the ways of Zion do *m.*
Ezek. 7:12 let not the seller *m.*
27 king shall *m.* and the prin.
24:16 nei. sh. thou *m.* nor weep
23 shall pine away and *m.*
31:15 caused Leb. to *m.* for him
Hos. 4:3 theref. sh. the land *m. ?*
10:5 peo. shall *m.* over Samaria
Joel 1:9 the Lord's ministers *m.*
Amos 1:2 habita. of shepher. *m.*
8:8 every one *m.* therein, 9:5
Zec. 12:10 and shall *m.* for him
12 land *m.* every family apart
Mat. 5:4 blessed are they that *m.*
9:15 child. of bride-chamb. *m. ?*
24:30 all the tribes of earth *m.*
Luke 6:25 laugh, for ye sh. *m.*
Jam. 4:9 afflicted, *m.* and weep
Rev. 18:11 merch. weep and *m.*

MOURNED.
Gen. 37:34 Jacob *m.* for his son
50:3 Egyptians *m.* for Jacob, 10
Ex. 33:4 heard th. evil tidings,
they *m. Num.* 14:39
Num. 20:29 congrega. *m.* for A.
1 *Sam.* 15:35 Samuel *m.* for Saul
2 *Sam.* 1:12 *m.* for Saul and Jon.
11:26 Bath-sheba *m.* for Uriah
13:27 David *m.* for his son Abs.
14:2 one that had *m.* for dead
1 *K.* 13:30 they *m.* over man of G.
14:18 Is. *m.* for Jeroboam's son
1 *Chr.* 7:22 Ephr. their father *m.*
2 *Chr.* 35:24 Judah *m.* for Josiah
Ezr. 10:6 *m.* for transgression
Neh. 1:4 sat and *m.* certain days
Zec. 7:5 when ye *m.* and fasted
Mat. 11:17 we have *m.* unto you,
Luke 7:32
Mark 16:10 as they *m.* and wept
1 *Cor.* 5:2 and have not rather *m.*

MOURNER, S.
2 *Sam.* 14:2 feign thyself a *m.*
Job 29:25 one that comforteth *m.*
Ec. 12:5 *m.* go about the streets
Is. 57:18 restore comf. to his *m.*
Hos. 9:4 sacrifi. be as bread of *m.*

MOURNETH.
2 *Sam.* 19:1 king *m.* for Absalom
Ps. 35:14 I bowed as one that *m.*
88:9 mine eye *m.* by affliction
Is. 24:4 earth *m.* and fad. 33:9
7 new wine *m.* vine languish.
Jer. 12:11 viney. being desol. *m.*
14:2 Jud. *m.* and gates languish
23:10 bec. of swearing land *m.*
Joel 1:10 land *m.* corn is wasted
Zec. 12:10 one that *m.* first-born

MOURNFULLY.
Mal. 3:14 we have walked *m.*

MOURNING.
Gen. 27:41 days of *m.* at hand
50:10 made a *m.* for his father
11 saw *m.* this is a grievous *m*
Deut. 26:14 not eaten in *m.*
34:8 days of *m.* for Mo. ended
2 *Sam.* 11:27 when *m.* was past
19:2 victory was turned to *m.*
Est. 4:3 there was *m.* am. Jews
9:22 was turned to them fr. *m.*
Job 3:8 ready to raise their *m.*
Job 30:31 harp also is turn. to *m.*
Ps. 30:11 turned *m.* to dancing
Ec. 7:2 better go to house of *m.*
4 heart of wise in house of *m.*
Is. 22:12 Lord did call to *m.*
61:11 sor. and *m.* shall flee away
60:20 days of *m.* shall be ended
61:3 give them oil of joy for *m.*
Jer. 6:26 *m.* as for an only son
16:5 enter not into house of *m.*
31:13 turn their *m.* into joy
Lam. 2:5 daughter of Judah *m.*
5:15 our dance is turned into *m.*
Ezek. 2:10 lamentations, *m.* woe
24:17 no *m.* for dead ; 31:15 I cau.
Joel 2:12 with weeping and *m.*
Amos 5:16 call husbandm. to *m.*
8:10 feasts into *m.* I will make
it as the *m.* of an only son
Mic. 1:11 came not forth in *m.*
Zec. 12:11 in *m.* in Jerusalem as *m.*
of Hadadrimmon
Mat. 2:18 great *m.* Rachel weep.
2 *Cor.* 7:7 he told us your *m.*
Jam. 4:9 laugh. be turned to *m.*
Rev. 18:8 one day death and *m.*

MOURNING.
Gen. 37:35 go down to grave *m.*
2 *Sam.* 14:2 put on *m.* apparel
Est. 6:12 H. hasted to house *m.*
Job 30:28 I went *m.* without sun
Ps. 38:6 I go *m.* all day long
42:9 why go I *m.* because of op-
pression of enemy ? 43:2
Jer. 9:17 call for the *m.* women
16:7 *m.* to comf. them for dead
Ezek. 7:16 *m.* for their iniquities
Dan. 10:2 D. was *m.* three weeks
Mic. 1:8 will make a *m.* as owls

MOUSE.
Lev. 11:29 weasel and *m.* be unc.
Is. 66:17 eating abomin. and *m.*

MOUTH.
Gen. 8:11 in her *m.* was olive lc.
24:57 damsel, inquire at her *m.*
29:2 great stone on well's *m.*
3 rolled stone fr. well's *m.* 10
42:27 his money was in sack's
m. 43:12, 21
Ex. 4:11 who made man's *m. ?*
16 he shall be to thee in. of *m.*
Num. 12:8 him speak *m.* to *m.*
16:30 earth open her *m.* and sw.
23:5 L. put a word in Bal.'s *m.*
35:30 put to death by *m.* of witnesses, *Deut.* 17:6 ; 19:15
Jos. 10:18 sto. to *m.* of cave, 27
22 open *m.* of cave, bring out
1 *Sam.* 1:12 Eli marked her *m.*
2 *Sam.* 14:3 J. put words in *m.* 19
17:19 a covering over well's *m.*
1 *K.* 19:18 every *m.* not kissed
22:13 the prophets declare good
to the king with one *m.*
22 lying spirit in *m.* of his
prophets, 23 ; 2 *Chr.* 18:21, 22
2 *Chr.* 35:22 hea. not to *m.* of G.
36:21 fulfil word of Lord by *m.*
of Jeremiah, 22 ; *Ezr.* 1:1
Est. 7:8 word we. out king's *m.*
Job 5:16 iniquity stop. her *m.*
12:11 doth *m.* taste meat ? 34:3
32:5 there was no answer in *m.*

Ps. 8:2 out of *m.* of babes
22:21 save me from the lion's *m.*
32:9 *m.* must be held with brid.
37:30 *m.* of right. speak. wisd.
38:14 in wh. *m.* are no reproofs
63:11 but *m.* that speaketh lies
69:15 let not the pit shut her *m.*
107:42 iniquity shall stop her *m.*
109:2 *m.* of wick. *m.* of deceitf.
126:2 *m.* filled with laughter
141:7 bones scat. at grave's *m.*
144:8 whose *m.* speak. vanit. 11
Prov. 4:24 put away froward *m.*
5:3 her *m.* is smoother than oil
6:12 walketh wi. frow. *m.* 10:32
8:13 the froward *m.* do I hate
10:6 violence cov. *m.* of wic. 11
14 *m.* of fool. near destruction
31 *m.* of just bringeth wisdom
11:11 city over. by *m.* of wicked
12:6 *m.* of upright deliver them
14:3 in *m.* of fool. is rod of pride
15:2 *m.* of fools poureth foolish.
14 *m.* of fools feed. on foolish.
28 *m.* of wicked pour. out evil
18:4 words of a man's *m.* deep
7 a fool's *m.* is his destruction
19:28 *m.* of wicked devour iniq.
22:14 *m.* of a strange woman
26:7 parable in *m.* of fools. 9
28 flattering *m.* worketh ruin
30:20 eateth and wipeth her *m.*
Ec. 10:12 words of a w. man's *m.*
Is. 9:12 devour Is. with open *m.*
17 and every *m.* speaketh folly
57:4 ag. wh. make ye wide *m.?*
59:21 Sp. not depart out of *m.*
Jer. 32:4 speak *m.* to *m.* 34:3
36:4 Baruch wrote from *m.* of
Jeremiah, 27, 32; 45:1
44:17 goeth forth out of *m.*
26 no more named in *m.*
Lam. 3:38 out of *m.* of Most H.
Ezek. 21:22 open *m.* in slaughter
29:21 will give thee open. of *m.*
Dan. 4:31 word was in king's *m.*
6:17 stone laid on *m.* of the den
7:5 it had three ribs in *m.* of it
8 a *m.* speaking gr. things, 20
Hos. 2:17 names of B. out her *m.*
Amos 3:12 as shep. tak. ort of *m.*
Nah. 3:12 fall into *m.* of eater
Zec. 5:8 weight of lead on *m.*
Mat. 4:4 proceed. out of *m.* of G.
12:34 of the heart *m.* speaketh
15:11 what go. in *m.* defil. not
18:16 in *m.* of two or three witness. every word, 2 *Cor.* 13:1
21:16 out *m.* of babes ha. praise
Luke 1:70 spake by *m.* of proph.
21:15 I will give you a *m.*
Acts 1:16 the Holy Ghost spake
by *m.* of David, 4:25
3:18 showed by *m.* of proph. 21
15:27 tell you same things by *m.*
23:2 commanded to smite on *m.*
Rom. 3:14 wh. *m.* is full of curs.
19 every *m.* may be stopped
10:10 with *m.* confes. is made
15:6 ye may with one *m.* glo. G.
1 *Cor.* 9:9 not muzzle *m.* of ox
2 *Tim.* 4:17 deliv. out *m.* of lion
Jam. 3:10 out of *m.* proceed bles.
Rev. 13:2 a *m.* speaking blasph.
16:13 spirits out of *m.* of dragon

His MOUTH.

Ex. 4:15 and put words in *his m.*
and I will be with *his m.*
Num. 23:16 G. put word in *h. m.*
Deut. 18:18 put words in *h. m.*
1 *Sam.* 14:26 put hand to *h. m.* 27
17:35 delivered it out of *his m.*
2 *Sam.* 18:25 there is tid. in *h. m.*
22:9 fire out of *his m. Ps.* 18:8
1 *K.* 8:15 wi. *h. m.* to D. 2 *Chr.* 6:4
2 *K.* 4:34 he put *his m.* on *his m.*
1 *Chr.* 16:12 judgments of *his m.*

Job 15:30 by breath of *his m.*
20:12 wicked. be sweet in *h. m.*
13 keep it still within *h. m.*
22:22 receive law from *his m.*
23:12 esteemed words of *his m.*
37:2 sound goeth out of *his m.*
40:23 draw up Jord. into *his m.*
41:19 out of *his m.* go bu. lamps
21 a flame goeth out of *his m.*
Ps. 10:7 *h. m.* is full of cursing
33:6 made by breath of *h. m.*
36:3 words of *his m.* are iniq.
38:13 dumb man open. not *h. m.*
55:21 words of *his m.* smoother
105:5 rem. judgments of *his m.*
Prov. 2:6 out of *h. m.* knowledge
11:9 *his m.* destroyeth neighb.
12:14 good by fruit of *his m.*
13:2 eat good by fruit of *his m.*
3 keepeth *his m.* keep. his life
15:23 hath joy by ans. of *h. m.*
16:10 *his m.* transgres. not judg.
23 heart of wise teacheth *h. m.*
26 for *his m.* craveth it of him
18:6 *his m.* calleth for strokes
20 satisfied with fruit of *his m.*
19:24 not bring it to *h. m.* 26:15
26:17 *his m.* filled with gravel
21:23 keepeth *h. m.* keep. soul
Ec. 6:7 labor of man is for *h. m.*
10:13 words of *his m.* is foolish.
Cant. 1:2 kiss wi. kisses of *h. m.*
5:16 *h. m.* is sweet, is my belo.
Is. 11:4 earth with rod of *h. m.*
53:9 neither any deceit in *h. m.*
Jer. 9:8 speak. peace. with *h. m.*
20 receive the word of *his m.*
36:17 write all th. words at *h. m.*
51:44 bring out of *h. m.* that wh.
Lam. 3:29 putteth *his m.* in dust
4:4 tong. cleav. to roof of *h. m.*
Zec. 9:7 take blood out of *his m.*
Mal. 2:6 law of truth in *his m.*
7 should seek the law at *h. m.*
Luke 1:64 and *his m.* was opened
4:22 gracious words out of *h. m.*
6:45 abund. of heart *h. m.* speak
11:54 catch somew. out of *h. m.*
22:71 have heard of *his* own *m.*
John 19:29 and put it to *his m.*
2 *Thes.* 2:8 consume with sp. of
his m.
1 *Pet.* 2:22 neither guile in *h. m.*
Rev. 1:16 out of *his m.* went a
sharp sword, 19:15, 21
12:15 cast out of *his m.* water
13:2 *his m.* was as mou. of lion
See LORD.

My MOUTH.

Gen. 45:12 *my m.* speak to you
Num. 22:38 put. in *my m.* 23:12
Deut. 32:1 hear words of *my m.*
1 *Sam.* 2:1 *my m.* is enlarg. over
Job 7:11 I will not refrain *my m.*
9:20 *my* own *m.* shall cond. me
16:5 strengthen you with *my m.*
19:16 entreated serv. wi. *my m.*
23:4 fill *my m.* with arguments
31:27 *my m.* kissed my hand
30 neither suffer. *my m.* to sin
33:2 tongue ha. spok. in *my m.*
40:4 I lay my hand upon *my m.*
Ps. 17:3 *my m.* shall not transgr.
19:14 words of *my m.* be accept.
34:1 praise continual. in *my m.*
39:1 keep *my m.* with a bridle
40:3 put a new song in *my m.*
49:3 *my m.* shall speak of wisd.
51:15 *my m.* sh. forth thy praise
54:2 give ear to words of *my m.*
63:5 *my m.* shall praise thee
66:14 *my m.* hath spoken when I
17 I cried to him with *my m.*
71:8 *my m.* be filled with praise
15 *my m.* show forth righteou.
78:1 incl. ears to wor. of *my m.*
2 I will open *my m.* in a para.

89:1 with *my m.* will I make kn.
109:30 praise the L. with *my m.*
119:43 word of tr. out of *my m.*
103 sweet, th. honey to *my m.*
108 freewill-offerings of *my m.*
137:6 tongue cl. to roof of *my m.*
141:3 set a watch before *my m.*
145:21 *my m.* sh. speak praise
Prov. 4:5 fr. words of *my m.* 5:7
7:24 attend to words of *my m.*
8:7 for *my m.* shall speak truth
8 words of *my m.* in righteous.
Is. 6:7 he laid the coal on *my m.*
30:2 have not asked at *my m.*
34:16 *my m.* it hath commanded
45:23 word is gone out of *my m.*
48:3 things forth out of *my m.*
49:2 made *my m.* like sharp
55:11 word that go. out *my m.*
Jer. 1:9 Lord touched *my m.*
15:19 thou shalt be as *my m.*
36:6 hast written from *my m.*
Ezek. 3:3 in *my m.* like honey
17 hear word at *my m.* 33:7
4:14 abomin. flesh into *my m.*
Dan. 10:3 fle. nor wine in *my m.*
Hos. 6:5 slain by words of *my m.*
Mat. 13:35 open *my m.* in parab.
Acts 11:8 any time enter. *my m.*
15:7 Gentiles by *my m.* sh. hear
Eph. 6:19 open *my m.* boldly
Rev. 2:16 fight with sw. of *my m.*
3:16 spew thee out of *my m.*
10:10 book in *my m.* sweet

MOUTH, *with* opened.

Gen. 4:11 earth *opened* her *m.*
Num. 16:32 carth *op.* her *m.* and
swal. them. 26:10; *Deut.* 11:6
22:28 Lord *opened m.* of the ass
Jud. 11:35 *o. my m.* to Lord, 36
Job 3:1 *op.* Job his *m.* and curs.
29:23 *opened* their *m. Ps.* 35:21
33:2 beh. now, I have *op. my m.*
Ps. 39:9 I *o.* not *my m.* because
109:2 *m.* of deceitful *o.* ag. me
119:131 I *o. my m.* and panted
Is. 5:14 hath *opened* her *m.*
10:14 there was none that *o. m.*
53:7 yet he *opened* not his *m.*
Ezek. 3:2 I *o. my m.* he caused
24:27 thy *m.* be *opened,* 33:22
Dan. 10:16 I *o. my m.* and spake
Mat. 5:2 he *o.* his *m.* and taught
17:27 when thou hast *o.* his *m.*
Luke 1:64 *m.* was *o.* immediately
Acts 8:32 so he *open.* not his *m.*
35 Philip *o. m.* 10:34 P. *o. m.*
2 *Cor.* 6:11 our *m.* is *ope.* to you
Rev. 12:16 earth *opened* her *m.*
13:6 he *o.* his *m.* in blasphemy

MOUTH, *with* openeth.

Ps. 38:13 dumb man *o.* not his *m.*
Prov. 24:7 fool *o.* not his *m.* in g.
31:26 she *o.* her *m.* with wisdom

Their MOUTH.

Jud. 7:6 put. their hand to *t. m.*
Neh. 9:20 not thy manna fr. *t. m.*
Job 5:15 saveth poor from *t. m.*
16:10 gaped upon me with *t. m.*
29:9 princes laid hand on *t. m.*
10 tongue clea. to roof of *t. m.*
Ps. 5:9 no faithfulness in *t. m.*
17:10 with *their m.* they spe.
proudly
58:6 bre. teeth, O God, in *t. m.*
59:7 they belch out with *t. m.*
12 sin of *t. m.* and words of ll.
62:4 bless with *t. m.* curse inw.
73:9 set *t. m.* aga. the heavens
78:36 did flatter him with *t. m.*
149:6 praises of God be in *t. m.*
Is. 29:13 peo. draw near wi. *t. m.*
Jer. 7:28 truth cut off from *t. m.*
12:2 thou art near in *their m.*
Lam. 2:16 enemies opened *t. m.*
Ezek. 33:31 with *t. m.* they show
34:10 deliver my flock from *t. m.*

Mic. 6:12 tongue deceitf. in *t. m.*
7:16 sh. lay their hand on *t. m.*
Zep. 3:13 deceit. tongue in *t. m.*
Zec. 14:12 tongue cons. in *th. m.*
Mat. 15:8 draweth nigh wi. *t. m.*
Jude 16 *t. m.* speak. great words
Rev. 19 power is in *t. m.*
  11:5 fire proceedeth out of *t. m.*
  14:5 in *t. m.* was found no guile

Thy MOUTH.

Ex. 4:12 I will be with *thy m.* 15
13:9 Lord's law may be in *t. m.*
23:13 of other gods out of *t. m.*
Deut. 23:23 promised with *t. m.*
30:14 word is nigh to thee, in *thy m. Rom.* 10:8
Jos. 1:8 not depart out of *t. m.*
Jud. 9:38 where is now *thy m.* ?
11:36 opened *thy m.* to the Lord
18:19 h. upon *t. m. Prov.* 30:32
2 *Sam.* 1:16 *t. m.* testifi. ag. thee
1 *K.* 8:24 spa. wi. *t. m.* & 2 *Ch.* 6:15
17:24 word of L. in *t. m.* truth
Job 8:2 words of *t. m.* like wind
21 fill *thy m.* with laughing
15:5 *thy m.* uttereth thine iniq.
6 *th.* own *m.* condemneth thee
13 let. such words go out *t. m.*
Ps. 50:16 take my coven. in *t. m.*
19 thou givest *thy m.* to evil
81:10 open *t. m.* wide I will fill
103:5 satisfi. *t. m.* wi. good th.
119:13 the judgments of *thy m.*
72 law of *thy m.* is better to me
88 keep testimony of *thy m.*
138:4 hear the words of *thy m.*
Prov. 6:2 with words of *t. m.*
27:2 praise th. not *thine* own *m.*
31:8 open *thy m.* for the dumb
9 open *t. m.* judge righteously
Ec. 5:2 be not rash with *thy m.*
6 suff. not *t. m.* cause fle. to sin
Cant. 7:9 roof of *t. m.* like wine
Is. 51:16 words in *t. m. Jer.* 1:9
59:21 which I put in *thy m.*
Jer. 5:14 make words in *t. m.* fire
Ezek. 2:8 open *thy m.* and eat
3:26 tongue cle. to roof of *t. m.*
27 I will open *t. m.* and th. sh.
16:56 S. not mentioned by *t. m.*
Hos. 8:1 set trumpet to *thy m.*
Mic. 7:5 keep doors of *thy m.*
Luke 19:22 out of *thine* own *m.*
Rom. 10:9 confess with *thy m.*
Rev. 10:9 in *t. m.* sweet as honey

Your MOUTH.

Num. 32:24 proceed. out of *y. m.*
1 *Sam.* 2:3 come out of *your m.*
Job 21:5 lay your hand on *y. m.*
Ezek. 35:13 with *y. m.* boasted
Joel 1:5 wine is cut off from *y. m.*
Eph. 4:29 no corrupt communi-
    cation out of *your m. Col.* 3:8

MOUTHS.

Deut. 31:19 put it in their *m.*
21 forgotten out of *m.* of seed
Ps. 22:13 gap. on me with th. *m.*
78:30 meat was yet in their *m.*
115:5 have *m.* speak not, 135:16
135:17 nei. is any breath in *m.*
Is. 52:15 kings shut *m.* at him
Jer. 44:25 spoken with your *m.*
Lam. 3:46 enemies opened th. *m.*
Dan. 6:22 G. hath shut lions' *m.*
Mic. 3:5 putteth not into th. *m.*
Tit. 1:11 wh. *m.* must be stopped
Heb. 11:33 stop. the *m.* of lions
Jam. 3:3 put bits in horses' *m.*
Rev. 9:17 out of *m.* issued fire

MOVE.

Ex. 11:7 not a dog *m.* tongue
Lev. 11:10 all that *m.* in waters
Deut. 23:25 not *m.* a sickle
32:21 will *m.* them to jealousy
Jud. 13:25 Sp. of L. began to *m.*

2 *Sam.* 7:10 may dwell and *m.* no
  more, 2 *K.* 21:8
2 *K.* 23:18 let no man *m.* bones
Jer. 10:4 fasten it that it *m.* not
Mic. 7:17 sh. *m.* out their holes
Mat. 23:4 they will not *m.* them
Acts 17:28 live, *m.* ha. our being
20:24 none of th. things *m.* me

MOVEABLE.

Prov. 5:6 her ways are *m.*

MOVED.

Gen. 1:2 Sp. of God *m.* on waters
7:21 all flesh died that *m.*
Deut. 32:21 me to jealousy
Jos. 10:21 none *m.* his tongue
15:18 that she *m.* him to ask of
  father a field, *Jud.* 1:14
Ruth 1:19 city was *m.* ab. them
1 *Sam.* 1:13 only her lips *m.*
2 *Sam.* 18:33 king was much *m.*
22:8 foundations of heaven *m.*
24:1 he *m.* David against them
1 *Chr.* 16:30 world stable, that it
  be not *m. Ps.* 93:1; 96:10
17:9 and shall be *m.* no more
2 *Chr.* 18:31 G. *m.* them to depart
Ezr. 4:15 they have *m.* sedition
Est. 5:9 Mord. *m.* not for him
Job 37:1 at this my heart is *m.*
41:23 they cannot be *m.*
Ps. 10:6 I shall not be *m.* 16:8;
  30:6; 62:2, 6.
13:4 those rejoice when I am *m.*
15:5 doeth these sh. never be *m.*
18:7 foundations of the hills *m.*
21:7 trusteth in L. sh. not be *m.*
46:5 sh. not be *m.* God sh. help
6 heathen raged, kingdoms *m.*
55:22 never suff. right. to be *m.*
66:9 suffer. not our feet to be *m.*
68:8 S. was *m.* at presence of G.
78:58 they *m.* him to jealousy
99:1 L. reigneth, let earth be *m.*
112:6 surely he shall not be *m.*
121:3 not suffer thy foot to be *m.*
Prov. 12:3 root of the righteous
  shall not be *m.*
Cant. 5:4 my bowels *m.* for him
Is. 6:4 the posts of the door *m.*
7:2 heart was *m.* as trees are *m.*
10:14 there was none *m.*
14:9 hell fr. ben. is *m.* for thee
19:1 idols of Egypt shall be *m.*
24:19 earth brok. down and *m.*
40:20 im. that sh. not be *m.* 41:7
Jer. 4:24 all the hills *m.* lightly
25:16 they sh. drink and be *m.*
46:7 whose waters *m.* 8
49:21 the earth is *m.* at noise
50:46 at taking of Bab. earth *m.*
Dan. 8:7 he was *m.* with choler
11:11 king of south shall be *m.*
Mat. 9:36 he was *m.* with compassion on them, 14:14; 18:27;
  Mark 1:41; 6:34
20:24 were *m.* with indignation
21:10 all the city was *m.* saying
Mark 15:11 chief priests *m.* peo.
Acts 2:25 that I sho. not be *m.*
17:5 but the Jews *m.* with envy
21:30 city was *m.* and peo. ran
Col. 1:23 be not *m.* from gospel
1 *Thes.* 3:3 no man be *m.* by th.
Heb. 11:7 Noah, *m.* with fear
11:28 kingd. wh. cannot be *m.*
2 *Pet.* 1:21 as *m.* by the H. Ghost
Rev. 6:14 mount. and island *m.*

MOVEDST, ETH.

Gen. 1:21 created ev. crea. th. *m.*
9:2 fear sh. be upon all that *m.*
Lev. 11:46 every creature that *m.*
Job 2:3 thou *m.* against him
Ps. 69:34 every thing that *m.*
Prov. 23:31 not on wi. wh. it *m.*
Ezek. 47:9 that *m.* whithersoever

MOVER.

Acts 24:5 this fel. *m.* of sedition

MOVING.

Gen. 1:20 wat. bring forth *m.* cre.
9:3 every *m.* thing sh. be meat
Prov. 16:30 *m.* his lips

MOVING, Substantive.

Job 16:5 *m.* of my lips, assu. gri.
John 5:3 waiting for *m.* of water

MOWER.

Ps. 129:7 *m.* filleth not his hand

MOWINGS.

Amos 7:1 growth after king's *m.*

MOWN.

Ps. 72:6 like rain upon *m.* grass

MUCH.

Luke 12:48 to whom *m.* is given,
  of him shall *m.* be required

MUFFLERS.

Is. 3:19 I will take away the *m.*

MULBERRY-TREES.

2 *Sam.* 5:23 come upon th. over
  against the *m.-t.* 1 *Chr.* 14:14
24 sound in the tops of *m.-t.*

MULE.

2 *Sam.* 13:29 every man upon *m.*
18:9 Absalom rode upon a *m.*
1 *K.* 1:33 to ride on my *m.* 38:44
Ps. 32:9 be not as horse or *m.*
Zec. 14:15 plague of horse, of *m.*

MULES.

Gen. 36:24 found *m.* in wildern.
1 *K.* 10:25 brought *m.* a rate year
  by year, 2 *Chr.* 9:24
18:5 grass to save the *m.* alive
2 *K.* 5:17 given to serv. two *m.*
1 *Chr.* 12:40 on camels and *m.*
Ezr. 2:66 their *m.* were 245, *Neh.*
  7:68
Est. 8:10 sent letters by *m.* 14
Is. 66:20 bring your breth. on *m.*

MULTIPLY.

Gen. 1:22 be fruitful and *m.* 28;
  8:17; 9:7; 35:11
6:1 men began to *m.* on earth
16:10 I will *m.* Hag. seed, 17:20
17:2 *m.* thee exceedingly, 48:4
22:17 in multiplying I will *m.*
  thy seed, 26:4, 24; *Heb.* 6:14
28:3 G. Almighty bless and *m.*
Ex. 1:10 deal wisely, lest th. *m.*
7:3 I will *m.* my signs in Egypt
23:29 lest beast of the field *m.*
32:13 thou saidst, I will *m.* your
  seed, *Lev.* 26:9; *Deut.* 7:13;
  13:17; 28:63; 30:5
Deut. 17:16 shall not *m.* horses
17 neither shall he *m.* wives
1 *Chr.* 4:27 neither did family *m.*
Job 29:18 I shall *m.* my days
Jer. 30:19 I will *m.* them
33:22 so will I *m.* seed of David
Ezek. 16:7 I have caused th. to *m.*
36:10 will *m.* men; 11 *m.* man
30 I will *m.* fruit of the tree
37:26 I will place and *m.* them
Amos 4:4 at G. *m.* transgression
2 *Cor.* 9:10 *m.* your seed sown

MULTIPLIED.

Gen. 47:27 Israel *m. Ex.* 1:7, 20
Ex. 1:12 afflicted *m.* and grew
11:9 my wonders may be *m.*
Deut. 1:10 L. your G. ha. *m.* you
8:13 gold is *m.* all thou hast *m.*
11:21 that your days be *m.*
Jos. 24:3 I *m.* his seed
Job 27:14 children be *m.* for sw.
35:6 if thy transgres. be *m.* ?
Ps. 16:4 their sorrows sh. be *m.*
38:19 they that hate me are *m.*
107:38 bless. them, they are *m.*
Prov. 9:11 thy days shall be *m.*
29:16 when wicked are *m.*
Is. 9:3 thou hast *m.* the nation
59:12 our transgressions are *m.*
Jer. 3:16 when ye be *m.*

Ezek. 5:7 ye *m.* more than nati.
11:6 *m.* your slain in this city
16:25 hast *m.* whoredoms, 23:19
29 *m.* fornications; 51 *m.* abo.
21:15 heart may faint, ruins *m.*
31:5 boughs *m.* 35:13 *m.* words
Dan. 4:1 peace be *m.* 6:25 ; 1 *Pet.*
1:2 ; 2 *Pet.* 1:2 ; *Jude* 2
Hos. 2:8 not know I *m.* her silver
12:10 I have *m.* visions
Nah. 3:16 hast *m.* merchants
Acts 6:1 number of disciples *m.* 7
7:17 people grew and *m.* in Eg.
9:31 walk. in fear of L. were *m.*
12:24 word of G. grew and *m.*

MULTIPLIEDST.

Neh. 9:23 their children also *m.*

MULTIPLIETH.

Job 9:17 he *m.* my wounds
34:37 he *m.* his words ag. God
35:16 *m.* words without knowl.

MULTIPLYING.

Gen. 22:17 in *m. Heb.* 6:14

MULTITUDE.

Gen. 16:10 it shall not be numb.
for *m.* 32:12 ; 1 *K.* 3:8
28:3 G. Alm. make thee a *m.*
30:30 it is now incre. unto a *m.*
48:4 make of thee a *m.* 16, 19
Ex. 12:38 a mixed *m.* went up
23:2 not follow a *m.* to do evil
Num. 11:4 mixed *m.* fell lusting
Deut. 1:10 ye as the stars for *m.*
10:22 ; 28:62 ; *Heb.* 11:12
Jos. 11:4 as sand on sea-shore for
m. Jud. 7:12 ; 1 *Sam.* 13:5 ;
2 *Sam.* 17:11 ; 1 *K.* 4:20
1 *Sam.* 14:16 the *m.* melted away
2 *Sam.* 6:19 dealt among *m.* of I.
1 *K.* 8:5 oxen not be told for *m.*
2 *K.* 7:13 they are as all the *m.*
19:23 with *m.* of my chariots to
sides of Lebanon, *Is.* 37:24
2 *Chr.* 1:9 a peo. like dust for *m.*
14:11 in thy name go aga. *m.*
20:24 the *m.* were dead bodies
30:18 a *m.* not cleansed thems.
32:7 be not afraid of all the *m.*
Neh. 13:3 separated fr. mixed *m.*
Est. 5:11 Haman told of the *m.*
10:3 Mordecai accepted of *m.*
Job 11:2 sh. *m.* of words be ans. ?
32:7 *m.* of years sh. teach wisd.
35:9 by reason of *m.* of oppres.
39:7 he scorneth *m.* of the city
Ps. 5:7 come in *m.* of thy mercy
10 cast out in *m.* of transgres.
33:16 th. is no king saved by *m.*
42:4 gone with *m.* to hou. of G.
49:6 boast in *m.* of their riches
51:1 accord. to *m.* of thy merci.
68:30 rebuke the *m.* of bulls
69:13 O God, in *m.* of mercy
16 accor. to *m.* of thy mercies
74:19 deliver me not to the *m.*
94:19 *m.* of my thoughts within
106:7 rem. not *m.* of thy merc.
45 accor. to *m.* of his mercies
109:30 I will praise am. the *m.*
Prov. 10:19 in the *m.* of words
11:14 *m.* of counsellors, 24:6
14:28 in *m.* of peo. king's honor
15:22 *m.* of counsellors establ.
20:15 gold, and a *m.* of rubies
Ec. 5:3 through *m.* of business,
fool's voice by *m.* of words
7 in *m.* of dreams div. vanities
Is. 1:11 wh. purpose *m.* of sacri.
5:13 *m.* dried up with thirst
14 *m.* descend into hell
17:12 woe to *m.* of many people
29:8 *m.* of nations that fight Z.
31:4 when *m.* of shepherds
47:12 stand now with the *m.* 9
13 wearied in *m.* of counsels
60:6 *m.* of camels shall cover
63:7 *m.* of his loving-kindness.

Jer. 10:13 *m.* of waters, 51:16
12:6 called a *m.* after thee
30:14 wounded for *m.* of iniq.
46:25 I will punish the *m.*
Lam. 1:5 for *m.* of transgress.
3:32 accord. to *m.* of mercies
Ezek. 7:12 wrath is on the *m.* 14
13 vision touching whole *m.*
14:4 accord. to *m.* of his idols
27:12 by *m.* of riches, 18, 33
16 by the *m.* of the wares. 18
31:18 Phar. and all his *m.* 32:32
32:24 Elam and *m.* 26 Tubal
39:11 bury Gog, and all his *m.*
Dan. 10:6 like voice of a *m.*
11:13 k. of north set forth a *m.*
Hos. 9:7 recomp. for *m.* of iniq.
10:13 thou didst trust in *m.*
Nah. 3:3 there is a *m.* of slain
Mat. 14:5 he feared the *m.* 21:46
15:32 compas. on *m. Mark* 8:2
Mark 5:31 *m.* throng. *Luke* 8:45
Luke 2:13 th. was wi. angel a *m.*
12:1 gath. an innumerable *m.*
22:6 betr. him in absence of *m.*
47 while he yet sp. behold *m.*
23:1 whole *m.* of them arose
John 5:13 a *m.* being in that pl.
21:6 not able for *m.* of fishes
Acts 4:32 the *m.* that believed
6:5 saying pleased whole *m.*
16:22 *m.* rose up against them
21:22 *m.* must come together
Jam. 5:20 sh. save a soul fr. dea.
and shall hide a *m.* of sins
1 *Pet.* 4:8 charity cov. *m.* of sins
See GREAT.

MULTITUDES.

Ezek. 32:20 draw her and her *m.*
Joel 3:14 *m.* *m.* in val. of decis.
Mat. 9:33 and the *m.* marvelled
36 when he saw *m.* was mov.
21:9 *m.* cried, saying, Hosanna
Acts 5:14 *m.* of men and women
13:45 J. saw the *m.* were filled
Rev. 17:15 the waters are *m.*
See GREAT.

MUNITION, S.

Is. 29:7 fight ag. her and her *m.*
33:16 defence sh. be *m.* of rocks
Nah. 2:1 keep *m.* watch the way

MURDER.

Ps. 10:8 in secret doth *m.* inno.
94:6 slay widow, *m.* fatherless
Jer. 7:9 *m.* and com. adultery ?
Hos. 6:9 so priests *m.* in the way

MURDER, S.

Mat. 15:19 out of the heart pro-
ceed *m. Mark* 7:21
19:18 said, Thou shalt do no *m.*
Mark 15:7 Barab. committed *m.*
Luke 23:19 for *m.* cast in pri. 25
Rom. 1:29 envy, *m.* debate
Gal. 5:21 flesh are envyings, *m.*
Rev. 9:21 not repented of th. *m.*

MURDERER.

Num. 35:16 *m.* the *m.* sh. surely
be put to death, 17, 18, 21, 31
19 revenger of blood slay *m.* 21
31 no satisfac. for life of a *m.*
2 *K.* 6:32 see how th. son a *m.*
Job 24:14 *m.* rising with light
Hos. 9:13 Eph. bring chil. to *m.*
John 8:44 a *m.* from beginning
Acts 3:14 *m.* be granted to you
28:4 no doubt this man a *m.*
1 *Pet.* 4:15 let none suffer as *m.*
1 *John* 3:15 whoso hateth broth.
is a *m.* ye know that no *m.*

MURDERERS.

2 *K.* 14:6 child. of *m.* he slew
Is. 1:21 lodged in it, but now *m.*
Jer. 4:31 wearied, because of *m.*
Mat. 22:7 sent and destroyed *m.*
Acts 7:52 have been now the *m.*
21:38 4,000 men that were *m.*

1 *Tim.* 1:9 law made for *m.*
Rev. 21:8 *m.* shall have part
22:15 with. are whore. and *m.*

MURMUR.

Ex. 16:7 that ye *m.* against us ?
8 hear. your *m. Num.* 14:27
Num. 14:36 made congrega. *m.*
16:11 what is Aa. that ye *m.* ?
17:5 whereby they *m.* ag. you
John 6:43 *m.* not am. yourselves
1 *Cor.* 10:10 neither *m.* as some

MURMURED.

Ex. 15:24 *m.* against Moses, 17:3
16:2 whole congregation of Isr.
m. Num. 14:2 ; 16:41
Num. 14:29 20 y. old, wh. ha. *m.*
Deut. 1:27 ye *m.* in your tents
Jos. 9:18 congre. *m.* ag. princes
Ps. 106:25 but *m.* in their tents
Is. 29:24 that *m.* sh. learn doctr.
Mark 14:5 they *m.* against her
Luke 5:30 scribes and Phari. *m.*
15:2 they *m.* saying, This man
19:7 *m.* that he was going to be
John 6:41 the Jews *m.* at him
61 he knew his disciples *m.*
7:32 Pharisees heard people *m.*
1 *Cor.* 10:10 as some of them *m.*

MURMURERS.

Jude 16 these are *m.* complainers

MURMURING, S.

Ex. 16:7 he heareth your *m.* 8, 9,
12 ; *Num.* 14:27
8 your *m.* are not against us
Num. 17:5 make to cease *m.* of I.
10 take away their *m.* fr. me
John 7:12 much *m.* among peo.
Acts 6:1 a *m.* against Hebrews
Phil. 2:14 do all thi. without *m.*

MURRAIN.

Ex. 9:3 be a very grievous *m.*

MUSE, ED, ING.

Ps. 39:3 I was *m.* the fire burned
143:5 I *m.* on works of thy han.
Luke 3:15 all men *m.* in th. hear.
MUSHI. *Ex.* 6:13

MUSIC.

1 *Sam.* 18:6 meet Saul with *m.*
1 *Chr.* 15:16 instruments of *m.*
2 *Chr.* 5:13 ; 23:13 ; 34:12
2 *Chr.* 7:6 wi. instruments of *m.*
Ec. 12:4 dau. of *m.* bro. low
Lam. 3:63 rising ; I am their *m.*
Dan. 3:5 kinds of *m.* 7:10, 15
6:18 instruments of *m.* brought
Amos 6:5 inv. instruments of *m.*
Luke 15:25 elder son heard *m.*

MUSICAL.

1 *Chr.* 16:42 *m.* instrum. of God
Neh. 12:36 *m.* instru. of David
Ec. 2:8 as *m.* instruments.

MUSICIANS.

Rev. 18:22 vo. of *m.* heard no *m.*

MUST.

Gen. 29:26 it *m.* not be so done
30:16 thou *m.* come in to me
43:11 if it *m.* be so now, do this
Num. 23:12 *m.* I not take heed
26 Lord speaketh that I *m.* do
Deut. 4:22 I *m.* die in this land
1 *Sam.* 14:43 and lo I *m.* die
2 *Sam.* 23:3 rul. men *m.* be just
Ezr. 10:12 said, so *m.* we do
Mark 8:31 S. of man *m.* suff. 9:12
Luke 22:37 the things written *m.*
be accomplished, 24:44
24:7 Son of man *m.* be delivered
John 3:7 ye *m.* be born again
Acts 4:12 whereby we *m.* be sav.

Acts 9:6 told th. what th. *m.* do
Rom. 13:5 *m.* needs be subject
1 *Cor.* 5:10 then *m.* ye needs go
MUSTARD-SEED. *See* GRAIN.

MUSTERED, ETH.
2 *K.* 25:19 scribe *m. Jer.* 52:25
Jer. 13:4 Lord *m.* host of battle

MUTTER, ED.
Is. 8:19 wizards th. peep and *m.*
59:3 tongue hath *m.* perversen.

MUTUAL.
Rom. 1:12 comforted by *m.* faith

MUZZLE.
Deut. 25:4 not *m.* ox, 1 *Cor.* 9:9;
1 *Tim.* 5:18

MYRA. *Acts* 27:5

MYRRH.
Gen. 37:25 bearing balm and *m.*
43:11 carry man a pres. *m.* nuts
Ex. 30:23 pure *m.* 500 shekels
Est. 2:12 6 months wi. oil of *m.*
Ps. 45:8 *m.* aloes and cassia
Prov. 7:17 perf. my bed with *m.*
Cant. 1:13 bundle of *m.* is belov.

NAAMAN.
2 *K.* 5:1 N. was leper, 11, 20, 27
Luke 4:27 none cleansed, sav. N.

NAASHON, or NAHSHON.
Num. 1:7 pri. was N. 2:3; 10:14
7:12 he that off. first day was N.
Ruth 4:20 Amminadab begat N.
1 *Chr.* 2:10, 11; *Mat.* 1:4
Luke 3:32 Salmon was son of N.

NABAL.
1 *Sam.* 25:3 was N. 4, 25, 38, 39
27:3 A. N. wife, 30:5; 2 *Sam.* 2:2

NABOTH.
1 *K.* 21:1 N. had vineyard, 7:19
2 *K.* 9:21 in portion of N. 25, 26

NADAB.
Ex. 6:23 Aaron, N. *Lev.* 10:1
24:1 come up, N. and Abihu, 9
Num. 3:4 N. died before L. 26:61
1 *K.* 14:20 N. reigned, 15:25

NAGGE. *Luke* 3:25

NAHASH.
1 *Sam.* 11:1 N. came up, 12:12
2 *Sam.* 10:2 son of N. 1 *Chr.* 19:2

NAHOR.
Gen. 11:22 Se. begat N. 24, 26, 29
22:20 brother N. 23; 24:15, 24
24:10 servant went to city of N.
31:53 God of Abraham and N.

NAIL.
Jud. 4:21 Jael took a *n.* of tent
22 the *n.* was in his temples
Jud. 5:26 she put her h. to the *n.*
Ezr. 9:8 give us a *n.* in holy pl.
Is. 22:23 a *n.* in a sure place, 25
Zec. 10:4 out of him came the *n.*

NAILS.
Deut. 21:12 sh. head, pare her *n.*
1 *Chr.* 22:3 iron in abund. for *n.*
2 *Chr.* 3:9 weight of *n.* fifty she.
Ec. 12:11 *n.* fastened by masters
Is. 41:7 his idol with *n. Jer.* 10:4
Dan. 4:33 his *n.* like bird's claws
7:19 beast, wh. *n.* were of brass
John 20:25 finger into print of *n.*

NAILING.
Col. 2:14 he *n.* it to his cross

NAIN. *Luke* 7:11

NAIOTH.
1 *Sam.* 19:18 Da. dwelt at N. 20:1

NAKED.
Gen. 2:25 were *n.* not ashamed
3:7 knew they were *n.* 10, 11
Ex. 32:25 Moses saw peo. were
n. for Aa. had made them *n.*
1 *Sam.* 19:24 Saul lay down *n.*

3:6 perf. with *m.* and frankinc.
4:6 get to moun. of *m.* and aloes
14 *m.* and aloes with chief spi.
5:1 gath. my *m.* with my spice
5 my hands dropped with *m.*
13 dropping sweet-smelling *m.*
Mat. 2:11 presented gold and *m.*
Mark 15:23 mingled with *m.*
John 19:39 bro. a mixture of *m.*

MYRTLE.
Neh. 8:15 go forth and fetch *m.*
Is. 41:19 plant in wildern. the *m.*
55:13 inst. of brier come up *m.*

MYRTLE-TREES.
Zec. 1:8 stood am. *m.-t.* 10, 11

MYSIA. *Acts* 16:7, 8

MYSTERY.
Mark 4:11 given to know *m.*
Rom. 11:25 that ye be ign. of *m.*
16:25 according to revela. of *m.*
1 *Cor.* 2:7 speak wis. of G. in *m.*

2 *Chr.* 28:15 with spoil clothed *n.*
19 Ahaz made Judah *n.*
Job 1:21 *n.* came I out of womb,
and *n.* shall I return thither
22:6 stripped *n.* of their clothi.
24:7 cause *n.* to lodge with. 10
26:6 hell is *n.* before him
Ec. 5:15 *n.* shall he return
Is. 58:7 when thou seest the *n.*
Lam. 4:21 shalt make thyself *n.*
Ezek. 18:7 if he covered the *n.* 16
Hos. 2:3 lest I strip her *n.*
Amos 2:16 flee away *n.*
Mic. 1:8 I will go stripped and *n.*
11 having thy shame *n.*
Hab. 3:9 bow was made quite *n.*
Mat. 25:36 *n.* and ye clothed me
38 when saw we thee *n. ?* 44
Mark 14:51 cloth ab. his *n.* body
52 and fled from them *n.*
John 21:7 Peter was *n.* and cast
Acts 19:16 fled out o' house *n.*
1 *Cor.* 4:11 to this hour we are *n.*
2 *Cor.* 5:3 shall not be found *n.*
Heb. 4:13 but all things are *n.* to
Jam. 2:15 if brother or sis. be *n.*
Rev. 3:17 poor, and blind, and *n.*
16:15 garments, lest he walk *n.*
17:16 make her desolate and *n.*

See BARE.

NAKEDNESS.
Gen. 9:22 H. saw *n.* of father, 23
42:9 see the *n.* of the land, 12
Ex. 20:26 thy *n.* not discovered
Lev. 18:6 none sh. uncover th. *n.*
7 the *n.* of father or mother,
8, 11, 15 ; 20:11
9 *n.* of sister ; 10 of son's dau.
11 *n.* of father's wife's daugh.
12 not uncover *n.* of f.'s sister
13 *n.* of mother's sister, 20:19
14 not uncover *n.* of f.'s broth.
15 *n.* of daughter-in-law
16 *n.* of thy brother's wife
17 *n.* of a woman and daught.
19 *n.* of wo. put apart, 20:18
20:17 sister's *n.* she see his *n.*
20 ha. uncovered his uncle's *n.*
21 hath uncovered brother's *n.*
Deut. 28:48 serve thine ene. in *n.*
1 *Sam.* 20:30 confu. of moth.'s *n.*
Is. 47:3 thy *n.* sh. be uncovered
Lam. 1:8 they have seen her *n.*
Ezek. 16:8 I covered thy *n.* yea
36 thy *n.* discovered, 23:18
16:37 discover thy *n.* to them
22:10 discovered th. father's *n.*
23:10 discovered her *n.* slew her
Hos. 2:9 wool and flax to cov. *n.*

15:51 I show you a *m.*
Eph. 1:9 made known to us *m.*
3:3 made known to me the *m.*
4 knowledge in the *m.* of Ch.
9 all see fellowship of *m.*
5:32 this is a great *m.*
6:19 to make known *m.* of the
gospel, *Col.* 1:26, 27 ; 4:3
Col. 2:2 acknowledgment of *m.*
2 *Thes.* 2:7 *m.* of iniq. doth work
1 *Tim.* 3:9 holding *m.* of faith
16 great is the *m.* of godliness
Rev. 1:20 *m.* of the seven stars
10:7 *m.* of God. sho. be finished
17:5 *m.* Babylon ; 7 *m.* of wom.

MYSTERIES.
Mat. 13:11 *m.* of the kingdom, to
them not given, *Luke* 8:10
1 *Cor.* 4:1 stewards of the *m.* of God
13:2 tho' I understand all *m.*
14:2 in the Sp. he speaketh *m.*

N

NAME.
Gen. 2:19 that was *n.* thereof
5:2 and called their *n.* Adam
11:4 us a *n.* lest we be scattered
48:6 called after *n.* of breth.
Ex. 34:14 L. whose *n.* is Jealous
Lev. 18:21 nei. profane the *n.* of
thy G. 19:12 ; 21:6 ; 22:2, 32
Num. 17:2 write every man's *n.*
27:4 why should *n.* of our father
Deut. 7:24 destroy *n.* under hea.
9:14 blot out *n.* fr. under heav.
22:14 bring up an evil *n.* on her
19 he bro. up evil *n.* on virgin
25:6 succeed in *n.* of his broth.
7 raise his brother a *n.* in Isr.
26:19 high in *n.* and honor
Deut. 28:58 fear this gl. and fe. *n.*
Jos. 23:7 nor make mention of *n.*
Ruth 4:5 raise up *n.* of dead, 10
17 her neighbors gave it a *n.*
2 *Sam.* 6:2 *n.* called by *n.* of Lord
7:9 I have *n.* that gr. great *n.* like *n.*
of gre. men in earth, 1 *Chr.*
17:8
23 God redeemed to make him
a *n.* 1 *Chr.* 17:21
8:13 David gat him a *n.* when
14:7 not leave to my husb. a *n.*
23:18 Abishai had *n.* amo. three
22 the *n.* among three mighty
men, 1 *Chr.* 11:20, 24
1 *K.* 1:47 G. make *n.* of Solomon
better than thy *n.*
14:21 Lord did choose to put
his *n.* there, 2 *Chr.* 12:13
18:24 call on *n.* of your gods, 25
21:8 Jezebel wrote in Ahab's *n.*
2 *K.* 14:27 not blot out *n.* of Isr.
Ezr. 2:61 and was called after
their *n. Neh.* 7:63
5:1 prophesied in *n.* of G. of Is.
Neh. 9:10 didst thou get th. a *n.*
Est. 8:8 write for J. in king's *n.*
Job 18:17 he shall have no *n.*
Ps. 9:5 put out their *n.* for ever
20:1 the *n.* of the God of Jacob
5 in *n.* of G. set up our banne.
44:20 if we forgot, *n.* of our G.
69:30 I will praise the *n.* of God
83:4 the *n.* of Israel be no more
18 whose *n.* alone is Jehovah
99:3 let th. praise thy great *n.*
109:13 let th. *n.* be blotted out
113:3 the L.'s *n.* is to be praised

Prov. 10:7 *n.* of wicked shall rot
18:10 *n.* of Lord is strong tower
22:1 good *n.* rather than riches
30:9 lest I take *n.* of G. in vain
Ec. 7:1 good *n.* bet. than ointm.
Is. 14:22 cut off fr. Baby. the *n.*
55:13 it sh. be to the L. for a *n.*
56:5 give a *n.* an everlasting *n.*
57:15 *n.* is holy ; 62:2 by new
63:12 make himself everlast. *n.*
14 to make thyself a glori. *n.*
65:15 ye shall leave your *n.* for
a curse to my chosen, and
call his servants by anoth. *n.*
66:22 your seed and *n.* remain
Jer. 13:11 might be for *n.* 33:9
32:20 which hast made thee a *n.*
33:16 the *n.* she shall be called
46:18 King, whose *n.* is the
Lord of hosts, 48:15 ; 51:57
Ezek. 20:29 *n.* is called Bamah
24:2 son of man, write *n.*
48:35 the *n.* of the city shall be
Dan. 2:20 blessed be the *n.* of G.
4:8 according to the *n.* of my G.
Hos. 2:17 no more remem. by *n.*
Amos 5:27 whose *n.* is G. of hos.
Mic. 4:5 in the *n.* of his god, we
will walk in the *n.* of our G.
Zep. 1:4 I will cut off *n.* of Ch.
3:20 I will make you a *n.*
Zec. 6:12 whose *n.* is Branch
Mat. 10:41 receiv. prophet in the
n. of a prophet, a righteous
42 cup of wat. in *n.* of disciple
28:19 baptizing them in *n.* of F.
Luke 1:61 none of ki. call. by *n.*
63 saying, His *n.* is John
6:22 sh. cast out your *n.* as evil
John 1:6 fr. God, who. *n.* was J.
3:18 not believed in *n.* of only
5:43 am come in my Fath.'s *n.*
10:25 I do in my Father's *n.*
Acts 2:38 baptized in *n.* of L. J.
3:6 in *n.* of Jesus Christ rise up
4:7 by wh. *n.* ha. ye done this ?
12 none other *n.* under heaven
17 sp. to no man in this *n.* 18
30 wonders done by *n.* of Jes.
5:28 sh. not teach in this *n.* 40
8:12 concerning the *n.* of Jesus
9:21 destroy, them called on *n.*
27 preached boldly in *n.* of J.
15:26 hazarded lives for *n.* of J.
16:18 in *n.* of Jesus come out
19:5 baptized in *n.* of Jesus
26:9 to do contrary to *n.* of J.
Rom. 2:24 *n.* of God blasphemed
1 *Cor.* 1:13 baptized in *n.* of P. ?
5:4 in the *n.* of L. J. *Eph.* 5:20
6:11 justified in the *n.* of L. J.
Eph. 1:21 above every *n.* named
Phil. 2:9 giv. him a *n.* ab. ev. *n.*
10 at *n.* of J. ev. knee shall b.
Col. 3:17 do all in the *n.* of L. J.
1 *Tim.* 6:1 *n.* of G. be not blas.
2 *Tim.* 2:19 the *n.* of Ch. depart
Heb. 1:4 obtained a more exc. *n.*
Jam. 2:7 blasp. that worthy *n.* ?
1 *Pet.* 4:14 reproach. for *n.* of C.
1 *John* 3:23 be. on *n.* of Son, 5:13
Rev. 2:17 a *n.* no man knoweth
3:1 hast a *n.* that thou livest
12 I will write on him *n.* of G.
13:1 on his heads *n.* of blasph.
14:1 Father's *n.* in their forehe.
16:9 men blasph. the *n.* of God
17:5 on her forehead was a *n.*
19:12 a *n.* written no man knew
16 on his thigh a *n.* written

See CALLED.

By, *or* by the NAME.

Ex. 6:3 I appeared by *t. n.* of G.
33:12 I know thee *by n.* 17
Num. 4:32 *by n.* ye shall reckon
Jos. 21:9 th. cities menti. *by n.*
1 *Chr.* 4:41 these written *by n.*

12:31 wh. were expressed *by n.*
16:41 ; 2 *Chr.* 28:15 ; 31:19
Est. 2:14 exc. were called *by n.*
Is. 44:5 sh. call himself *by the n.*
of Jacob, and surname him
self *by the n.* of Israel, 48:1
45:8 I the Lord call these *by n.*
John 10:3 calleth his sheep *by n.*
Acts 4:10 *by ths n.* of J. this man
1 *Cor.* 1:10 I bes. you *by n.* of L.
3 *John* 14 greet friends *by n.*

See EXPRESSED.

His NAME.

Ex. 3:13 shall say, What is *his*
n. ? Prov. 30:4
15:3 the Lord is *his n. Jer.* 32:2 ;
Amos 5:8 ; 9:6
20:7 not guiltless that taketh
his n. in vain, *Deut.* 5:11
28:21 wi. *h. n.* sh. they be, 39:14
Deut. 6:13 shalt swear *by h. n.*
10:8 bless in *his n.* 1 *Chr.* 23:13
12:5 choose to put *his n.* there,
21 ; 1 *K.* 14:21 ; 2 *Chr.* 12:13
11 sh. cause *his n.* to dw. there
14:23 choose to place *his n.*
there, 24 ; 16:6, 11 ; 26:2
25:6 *his n.* be not put out of Isr.
10 *his n.* sh. be called in Israel
29:20 Lord shall blot out *his n.*
Jud. 13:6 neit. told he me *his n.*
Ruth 4:14 *his n.* be famous in Is.
1 *Sam.* 12:22 for *his n.'s* sake,
Ps. 23:3 ; 106:8 ; 1 *John* 2:12 ;
3 *John* 7
18:30 *his n.* was much set by
25:25 as *his n.* is, Nabal is *his n.*
1 *Chr.* 16:8 call up *h. n.* make
known his deeds, *Ps.* 105:1
Is. 12:4
29 gl. due to *h. n. Ps.* 29:2 ; 96:8
Ezr. 6:12 G. caused *his n.* dwell
*Ps.*34:3 let us exalt *his n.* 66:2
41:5 shall he die *h. n.* perish ?
68:4 rideth on heav. by *h. n.* J.
69:36 that love *his n.* dw. there.
72:17 *his n.* shall endure for ever
19 and blessed be *his glori. n.*
76:1 *his n.* is great in Israel
96:2 unto L. bless *his n.* 100:4
99:6 Samuel that call on *his n.*
111:9 holy and reverend is *h. n.*
135:3 praises to *h. n.* it is pleas.
148:13 praise *his n.* for *his n.*,
149:3 praise *his n.* in the dance
Prov. 21:24 haug. scorner is *h. n.*
Ec. 6:4 *his n.* cov. with darkness
Is. 7:14 *his n.* Imman. *Mat.* 1:23
9:6 *his n.* be called Wonderful
12:4 that *his n.* is exalted
47:4 the Lord of hosts is *his n.*
48:2 ; 51:15 ; 54:5 ; *Jer.* 10:16 ;
31:35 ; 32:18 ; 50:34 ; 51:19
48:19 *h. n.* should not have been
Jer. 11:19 *h. n.* no more remem.
20:9 not spea. any more in *h. n.*
23:6 this is *h. n.* he shall be ca.
Amos 4:13 L. God of hosts is *h. n.*
Zec. 10:12 up and down in *h. n.*
14:9 shall be one L. and *h. n.* o.
Mal. 3:16 them th. tho. on *h. n.*
Mat. 1:23 sh. call *h. n.* Emman.
25 *h. n.* Jesus, *Luke* 1:31 ; 2:21
12:21 in *h. n.* shall Gent. trust
Mark 6:14 *h. n.* was spread abr
Luke 1:13 thou sh. call *his n.* J.
24:47 remission of sins in *h. n.*
John 1:12 that believe on *his n.*
2:23 many believed in *his n.*
5:43 if ano. come in *his own n.*
20:31 might have life thro' *h. n.*
Acts 3:16 *h. n.* thro' faith in *h. n.*
5:41 worthy to suffer for *his n.*
10:43 thro' *his n.* remis. of sins
15:14 take out a peo. for *his n.*
Rom. 1:5 am. all nations for *h. n.*
Heb. 6:10 love ye show. to. *h. n.*
13:15 giving thanks to *h. n.*

Rev. 3:5 not blot out *his n.*
Rev. 6:8 *h. n.* sat on him was de.
13:6 ag. God to blaspheme *h. n.*
17 the number of *his n.* 15:2
14:11 receiveth mark of *h. n.*
22:4 *his n.* sh. be in th. forehea.

See HOLY, LORD.

My NAME.

Gen. 32:29 why ask after *my n. ?*
48:16 let *my n.* be named
Ex. 3:15 this is *my n.* for ever
9:16 that *my n.* may be declared
20:24 where I record *my n.*
23:21 prov. not, *my n.* is in him
Lev. 19:12 not swear by *my n.*
20:3 M. to profane *my holy n.*
Num. 6:27 put *my n.* on Israel
Deut. 18:19 speak in *my n.* 20
Jud. 13:18 why ask. after *my n. ?*
1 *Sam.* 24:21 not destroy *my n.*
2 *Sam.* 7:13 house for *my n.* 1 *K.*
5:5 ; 8:18, 19 ; 1 *Chr.* 22:10
12:28 city be called after *my n.*
18:18 no son to keep *my n.*
1 *K.* 8:16 *my n.* might be there.
29 ; 11:36 ; 2 *K.* 21:4, 7 ; 2 *Chr.*
6:5, 6 ; 7:16 ; 33:4, 7
9:7 house I hallowed for *my n.*
1 *Chr.* 22:8 house to *my n.* 28:3
2 *Chr.* 6:8 build house for *my n.*
7:20 house I ha. sanct. for *my n.*
Neh. 1:9 to set *my n. Jer.* 7:12
Ps. 89:24 in *my n.* sh. horn be
91:14 bec. he hath known *my n.*
Is. 29:23 shall sanctify *my n.*
41:25 ri. of sun call on *my n.*
42:8 I am the L. that is *my n.*
48:9 for *my n.'s* sake I defer
11 how sho. *my n.* be pollut. ?
49:1 he made mention of *my n.*
52:5 *my n.* ev. day is blasphem.
6 my people shall know *my n.*
66:5 cast out for *my n.'s* sake
Jer. 14:14 in *my n.* 15 ; 23:25
16:21 they sh. know *my n.* is L.
23:27 they th. to cause peo. forget *my n.* as fa. forgot *my n.*
27:15 lie in *my n.* 29:9, 21, 23
34:16 turned and polluted *my n.*
44:26 sworn by *my great n. my*
n. no more named.
Ezek. 20:9 wro. for *my n.* 22:44
36:23 will sanctify *my great n.*
Zec. 13:9 call on *my n.*
Mal. 1:6 priests th. despise *my n.*
11 *my n.* sh. be great am. Gen.
in ev. place incen. off. *my n.*
14 *my n.* dreadful am. heathen
2:2 to give glory unto *my n.*
5 and was afraid before *my n.*
4:2 you that fear *my n.* the sun
Mat. 10:22 hat. for *my n.'s* sake,
24:9 ; *Mark* 13:13 *Luke* 21:17
18:5 receive a child in *my n.*
Mark 9:37 ; *Luke* 9:48
20 two or three gath. in *my n.*
19:29 fors. houses for *my n.'s* sa.
24:5 many shall come in *my n.*
Mark 13:6 ; *Luke* 21:8
Mark 5:9 say. *My n.* is Legion
9:39 no man do miracle in *my n.*
41 give water to drink in *my n.*
16:17 in *my n.* sh. cast out dev.
Luke 21:12 rulers for *my n.'s* sa.
John 14:13 what. ye ask in *my n.*
14 ; 15:16 ; 16:23, 24, 26
26 Comf. he will send in *my n.*
15:21 these thi. do for *my n.'s*
Acts 9:15 cho. ves. to bear *my n.*
16 must suffer for *my n.'s* sake
15:17 on whom *my n.* is called
Rom. 9:17 that *my n.* be declared
1 *Cor.* 1:15 I bapt. in *mi. own n.*
Rev. 2:3 for *my n.'s* sake labored
3 holdest fast *my n.*
3:8 and hast not denied *my n.*

See CALLED.

Thy NAME.
Gen. 12:2 make thy n. great
17:5 t. n. Abram, but t. n. be A.
32:27 said, What is thy n. ? 29;
Jud. 13:17
28 thy n. be no more Jacob,
but Israel, 35:10 ; 1 K. 18:31
Ex. 5:23 to P. to speak in thy n.
Jos. 7:9 what do to t. great n. ?
2 Sam. 7:26 let t. n. be magnifi.
22:50 sing praise to t. n. Ps. 9:2 ;
18:49 ; 61:8 ; 66:4 ; 92:1
1 K. 1:47 Solom. better than t. n.
8:33 turn and confess thy n. and
pray, 2 Chr. 6:24, 26:32
41 but cometh for thy n.'s sake
42 they shall hear of t. great n.
43 that all peo. may know thy
n. this house is called by
thy n. 2 Chr. 6:33, 34, 48
1 K. 8:44 house I built for thy
n. 48
1 Chr. 17:24 thy n. may be mag.
29:13 and praise in t. n. Ps. 44:8
2 Chr. 6:20 wouldest put thy n.
14:11 in thy n. we go ag. multi.
20:8 built thee a sanctu. for t. n.
9 for thy n. is in this house
Neh. 1:11 servants who fear t. n.
9:5 blessed be t. glorious n.

Ps. 5:11 th. love t. n. be joyful
8:1 how excel. is t. n. in earth, 9
9:10 they that know t. n. trust
22:22 will declare t. n. Heb 2:12
25:11 for t. n.'s sake pardon
31:3 for t. n.'s sake lead me
44:5 thro' thy n. tread them
45:17 I will make thy n. be rem.
48:10 accor. to t. n. so is praise
52:9 wait on t. n. 54:1 save me
61:5 heritage of those fear t. n.
63:4 lift my hands in thy n.
74:7 defiled dwelling-pl. of t. n.
10 sh. enemy bla. t. n. for ev. ?
18 fool. peo. blasphemed t. n.
21 poor and needy praise t. n.
75:1 t. n. is near works declare
79:6 not call. on t. n. Jer. 10:25
9 help us, O God, for g. of t. n.
purge our sins for t. n.'s sa.
80:18 we will call upon thy n.
83:16 that they may seek thy n.
O Lord
86:9 all nations glorify t. n. 12
11 unite my heart to fear t. n.
89:12 Hermon sh. rej. in t. n. 16
109:21 O Lord, for t. n.'s sake
115:1 not to us, but to t. n.
119:55 I rememb. t. n. in night
132 to do to those love thy n.
135:13 t. n. O Lord, en. for ever
138:2 praise t. n. for lov.-kindn.
magnified word above t. n.
139:20 enemies take t. n. in vain
140:13 righ. give thanks to t. n.
142:7 out of pris. I praise t. n.
143:11 qui. me for t. n.'s sake
145:1 I will bless thy n. 2
2 I will praise t. n. Is. 25:1
Cant. 1:3 t. n. is as ointment
Is. 26:8 des. of our soul to thy n.
13 make mention of thy n.
63:16 O L. t. n. is from everlas.
64:2 make t. n. kn. to adversar.
7 there is none calleth on t. n.
Jer. 10:6 thy n. is great in might
11:16 L. called thy n. olive-tree
14:7 do thou it for thy n.'s sake
21 not abhor us for t. n.'s sake
29:25 sent letters in thy n. to J.
Lam. 3:55 called on thy n.
Dan. 9:6 proph. spake in thy n.
Mic. 5:0 man of wisd. see thy n.
Nah. 1:14 no more of t. n. be so.
Mal. 1:6 ha. we despised thy n. ?
Mat. 6:9 hal. be t. n. Luke 11:2
7:22 in t. n. have we cast out

Mark 5:9 wh. is t. n. ? Luke 8:30
9:38 out dev. in t. n. Luke 9:49
Luke 10:17 devils subj. thro' t. n.
John 12:28 Father, glorify t. n.
17:6 manifested t. n. to men, 26
11 F. keep thro' thi. own n. 12
Acts 9:14 all that call on thy n.
Rom. 15:9 conf. and sing to t. n.
Rev. 11:18 rew. th. that fear t. n.
15:4 who not fear and glo. t. n. ?
See CALLED.

NAME, Verb.
1 Sam. 16:3 anoi. to me him I n.
28:8 bring him up wh. I shall n.
Is. 62:2 mouth of Lord shall n.

NAMED, ETH.
Gen. 23:16 A. weigh. silver he n.
27:36 is he not rightly n. Jac. ?
48:16 let my name be n. on th.
2 K. 17:34 chil. of Jacob he n. I.
Ec. 6:10 what hath been, is n.
Is. 61:6 shall be n. priests of L.
Jer. 44:26 shall no more be n.
Amos 6:1 n. chief of the nations
Mic. 2:7 O thou that art n. of J.
Luke 2:21 J. was n. of the angel
Rom. 15:20 not where Ch. was n.
1 Cor. 5:1 forni. not n. am. Gen.
Eph. 1:21 ab. ev. name that is n.
3:15 fam. in heav. and earth n.
5:3 covetousn. let it not be n.
2 Tim. 2:19 every one that n. C.

NAMELY.
Ec. 5:13 evil, n. riches kept
Is. 7:20 L. shave, n. by Assyria
Mark 12:31 n. this, shalt love

NAMES.
Gen. 2:20 Adam gave n. to cattle
26:18 called n. after n. f. called
Ex. 23:13 make no mention of n.
of other gods, Deut. 12:3
28:9 grave n. of child. of Isr. 21
12 Aaron bear n. before L. 29
Num. 1:2 numb. of n. by th. poll
Ezr. 5:14 what n. make building
Ph. 16:4 nor take n. in my lips
49:11 call lands after own n.
147:4 stars call. by n. Is. 46:26
Hos. 2:17 take away n. of Baalim
Zec. 13:2 cut off the n. of idols
Luke 10:20 n. written in heaven
Acts 1:15 number of n. were 120
18:15 if it be question of n.
Phil. 4:3 wh. n. are in book of li.
Rev. 3:4 hast a few n. in Sardis
13:8 whose n. not written, 17:8
17:3 woman full of n. of blasph.
21:12 n. written, n. of 12 tribes
14 in them the n. of 12 apostl.

NAOMI.
Ruth 1:2 Elimelech's wife, N. 20
2:1 N. had a kinsman of husb.
4:5 buy. field of hand of N. 9, 17

NAPKIN.
Luke 19:20 I have kept in n.
John 11:44 face bound with a n.
20:7 n. that was about his head

NAPHTALI.
Gen. 30:8 Rachel called name N.
35:25 Rachel's handmaid, N.
46:24 s. of N. Nu. 1:42 ; 1Ch. 7:13
49:21 N. is a hind let loose
Deut. 27:13 E. to curse ; Dan, N.
33:23 said, O N. satisfied with
Jos. 19:32 sixth lot came to N.
Jud. 1:33 nor did N. drive out
4:10 Barak called N. to Kedesh
5:18 Zebulun and N. jeoparded
6:35 Gid. sent messengers to N.
7:23 themselves tog. out of N.
1 K. 15:20 smote N. 2 Chr. 16:4
2 K. 15:29 carried N. cap. to As.
Ps. 68:27 there the princes of N.
Is. 9:1 he afflicted the land of N.
Ezek. 48:3 a portion for N. 34

Mat. 4:13 dw. in borders of N. 15

Tribe of NAPHTALI.
Num. 1:43 of N. 53,400
Jos. 19:39 inheritance of t. of N.
1 K. 7:14 widow's son of t. of N.
Rev. 7:6 of t. of N. sealed 12,000

NARROW.
Num. 22:26 angel of L. sto. in n.
Jos. 17:15 if Ephraim be too n.
1 K. 6:4 windows of n. light
Prov. 23:27 stra. woma:: is n. pit
Is. 49:19 land of destruct. too n.
Mat. 7:14 is way lead. to life

NARROWED, ER.
1 K. 6:6 in wall made n. rests
Is. 28:20 n. than he can wrap

NARROWLY.
Job 13:27 lookest n. to my paths
Is. 14:16 shall n. look upon thee

NATHAN.
2 Sam. 5:14 son of David, N. 7:2
7:17 so did N. speak, 12:1, 25
1 K. 1:10 N. called not, 22, 34
4:5 son of N. was over officers
1 Chr. 29:29 writ. in book of N.
2 Chr. 9:29 Sol. in book of N.
Ezr. 8:16 I sent fr. Ahava for N.
Zec. 12:12 family of house of N.
Luke 3:31 Matthata, son of N.

NATHANAEL.
John 1:45 Philip findeth N. 21:2

NATION.
Gen. 15:14 n. th. serve will I jud.
20:4 wilt slay a righteous n. ?
21:13 bondwoman I make n. ?
35:11 a n. kings come of thee
Ex. 9:24 N. E. since it became n.
19:6 shall be a holy n. 1 Pet. 2:9
21:8 to sell her to a strange n.
33:13 this n. is thy people
Lev. 18:26 nor n. commit abomi.
20:23 not walk in manners of n.
Num. 14:12 I will make of thee a
n. Deut. 9:14
Deut. 4:34 ha. G. assayed to take
a n. fr. midst of another n. ?
28:33 fruit of land shall n. eat
36 bring thee and king to a n.
49 bring n. ag. thee from far
50 a n. of fierce countenance
32:28 are a n. void of counsel
2 Sam. 7:23 what n. like thy
people ? 1 Chr. 17:21
1 K. 18:10 no n. my lord ha. not
se. to seek th. took oath of n.
2 K. 17:29 every n. made gods
1 Chr. 16:20 went from n. to n.
2 Chr. 15:6 was destroyed of n.
2 Chr. 32:15 god of any n. was able
Job 34:29 done ag. a n. or man
Ps. 33:12 bless. is n. wh. G. is L.
43:1 O G. plead ag. ungodly n.
83:4 cut off from being a n.
105:13 went from one n. to anot
106:5 rejoice in gladness of n.
147:20 not dealt so with any n.
Prov. 14:34 righteous. exalt. n.
Is. 1:4 sinful n. laden with iniq.
2:4 n. sh. not lift sword against
n. Mic. 4:3
9:3 thou hast multiplied the n.
10:6 send him aga. hypocrit. n.
14:32 what ans. messeng. of n. ?
18:2 messengers to a n. scatter.
and peeled, a n. meted, 7
26:2 open that righ. n. may en.
15 thou increas. n. O L. the n.
49:7 sai. L. to him h. abhorreth
55:5 shalt call n. thou know. not
58:2 seek me as a n. that did ri.
60:12 n. not serve thee perish
22 small one beco. a strong n.
65:1 a n. not called by my name
66:8 or shall n. be born at once ?

Jer. 2:11 hath a *n.* chang. gods ?
  5:9 my soul be avenged on such
    a *n.* 29 ; 9:9
  15 I will bring a *n.* on you fr.
    afar, a mighty *n.* ancient *n*
  7:28 a *n.* that obey. not the L.
  12:17 I will utt. destroy that *n.*
  18:7 concern. a *n.* pluck it up, 9
  8 *n.* ag. whom I pronounced
  25:12 punish *n.* for iniq. 27:8
  32 evil sh. go forth fr. *n.* to *n.*
  31:36 Israel cease being *n.* 33:24
  49:31 get you up to wealthy *n.*
  36 no *n.* whith. E. sh. not come
  50:3 out of north cometh *n.* ag.
Lam. 4:17 have watched for a *n.*
Ezek. 2:3 send thee to Is. rebe. *n*
  37:22 I will make them one *n.*
Dan. 8:22 four kingd. out of *n.*
  12:1 trou. nev. was since was *n.*
Joel 1:6 a *n.* come upon my land
Amos 6:14 will raise ag. you a *n.*
Mic. 4:7 will make her strong *n.*
Hab. 1:6 Ch. bitter and hasty *r.*
Zep. 2:1 gather together, O *n.*
  5 woe to the *n.* of Cherethites
Hag. 2:14 this peo. and *n.* before
Mal. 3:9 this *n.* have robbed me
Mat. 21:43 king. of G. given to *n.*
  24:7 *n.* sh. rise against *n.* *Mark*
  13:8 ; *Luke* 21:10
Luke 7:5 loveth our *n.* built us
John 11:48 R. shall take our *n.*
  50 one man die, *n.* perish not
  51 prophesied, Jesus die for *n.*
  52 not for that *n.* only, but th.
  18:35 thine own *n.* hath deliver.
Acts 2:5 devout men out of ev. *n.*
  7:7 *n.* to whom they be in bond
  10:22 good rep. am. *n.* of Jews
  28 to come to one of anoth. *n.*
  35 in every *n.* he that feareth
  24:2 worthy deeds done to th. *n.*
  10 thou hast been judge to *n.*
Gal. 1:14 profit. ab. equals in *n.*
Phil. 2:15 midst of perverse *n.*
Rev. 5:9 redee. us out of every *n.*
  14:6 gospel to preach to ev. *n*

See FOOLISH.

NATIONS.

Gen. 10:32 by th. were *n.* divided
  14:1 Ti. king of *n.* made war, 9
  17:4 shalt be a father of many
    n. 5 ; 48:19 ; *Rom.* 4:17, 18
  6 I will make *n.* of thee, 35:11
  16 Sarah sh. be a mother of *n.*
  25:23 L. said, Two *n.* in thy wo.
  27:29 let *n.* bow down to thee
Ex. 34:24 I will cast out the *n.*
    before thee, *Deut.* 4:38 ; 7:22 ;
    8:20
Lev. 18:24 the *n.* are defiled
  28 as it spued out the *n.*
Num. 23:9 not be reckon. am. *n.*
  24:8 Israel shall eat up the *n.*
  20 Amalek was first of the *n.*
Deut. 2:25 I will put fear on *n.*
  4:27 L. shall scatter you among
    the *n.* *Neh.* 1:8
  7:1 Lord hath cast out many *n.*
  9:1 *n.* great. than thyself, 11:23
  12:29 God shall cut off *n.* 19:1
  15:6 shalt lend to many *n.* 28:12
  28:1 L. will set thee abo. all *n.*
  32:8 Most High divid. to the *n.*
  43 rejoice, O ye *n.* with his pe.
Jud. 2:23 the Lord left those *n.*
  1 *K.* 11:2 of *n.* which the L. said
  2 *K.* 17:33 ser. gods aft. man. of *n.*
  2 *K.* 18:33 gods of *n.* deli. 19:12 ;
    2 *Chr.* 32:13, 14 ; *Is.* 36:18
  1 *Chr.* 16:31 say am. *n.* L. reign.
  17:21 driving out *n.* bef. people
Neh. 13:26 am. many *n.* no king
Job 12:23 the *n.* he enlargeth *n.*

Ps. 9:20 *n.* know themselves
  22:27 kindreds of *n.* worsh. thee
  28 Lord is governor am. the *n.*
  47:3 shall subdue *n.* under feet
  57:9 sing to thee am. *n.* 108:3
  66:7 his eyes behold the *n.*
  67:4 let the *n.* be glad
  96:5 all gods of the *n.* are idols
  106:27 overthrow seed among *n.*
  34 did not destroy *n.* L. com.
Prov. 24:24 *n.* shall abhor him
Is. 2:4 he sh. judge amo. the *n.*
  5:26 will lift up an ensign to *n.*
  10:7 in his heart to cut off *n.*
  11:12 shall set up ensign for *n.*
  14:6 ruled the *n.* in anger
  12 wh. didst weak. the *n.* 23:3
  18 kings of the *n.* lie in glory
  33:3 at lifting up *n.* were scat.
  34:1 come near, ye *n.* *Jer.* 31:10
  40:15 *n.* are as a drop of bucket
  52:15 so sh. he sprinkle many *n.*
  55:5 *n.* that knew not thee, run
  60:12 those *n.* shall be wasted
  64:2 *n.* tremble at thy presence
  66:19 send th. that escape to *n.*
Jer. 4:5 ordai. thee prophet to *n.*
  10 I have set thee over the *n.*
  4:2 *n.* shall bless themselves
  10:7 not fear thee, King of *n.* ?
  10 *n.* not able to abide his ind.
  22:8 many *n.* sh. pass this city
  25:14 *n.* shall serve, 27:7
  31 L. had a controver. with *n.*
  46:12 *n.* heard of thy shame
  50:12 hindermost of *n.* a wilder.
  46 cry is heard among the *n.*
  51:7 *n.* have drunken, *n.* mad
  20 wi. thee will I break *n.*
  27 prepare the *n.* against her
  41 Bab. an astonishm. am. *n.*
  44 *n.* shall not flow together
Lam. 1:1 city that was gr. am. *n.*
Ezek. 5:6 wickedn. more than *n.*
  14 make thee a reproach am. *n.*
  6:8 remnant shall escape am. *n.*
  9 remember me among *n.*
  12:15 I shall scatter th. am. *n.*
  19:4 the *n.* also heard of him
  8 *n.* set ag. him on every side
  20:3 many *n.* come against thee
  5 it shall become a spoil to *n.*
  28:7 bring upon thee the terri-
    ble of the *n.* 30:11 ; 31:12
  29:12 scatter Egypt am. *n.* 30:23
  15 sh. no more rule over the *n.*
  31:16 I made *n.* shake at sound
  32:2 thou art like lion of the *n.*
  16 daughters of *n.* lament, 18
  35:10 these two *n.* shall be mine
  36:13 land hast bereaved thy *n.*
  37:22 shall be no more two *n.*
  38:8 brought forth out of *n.* 12
  23 be known in eyes of *n.*
  39:27 sancti. in sight of many *n.*
Hos. 8:10 have hired among *n.*
  9:17 shall be wanderers amo. *n.*
Joel 3:2 they scattered among *n.*
Amos 6:1 woe to ch. chief of *n.*
Mic. 4:2 *n.* shall say, Let us go
  3 he shall rebuke strong *n.*
  11 many *n.* gathered ag. thee
  7:16 *n.* shall see, be confounded
Nah. 3:4 selleth *n.* thro' whored.
  5 I will show *n.* thy nakedness
Hab. 1:17 sh. not spare to slay *n.*
  2:8 thou hast spoiled many *n.*
  3:6 he drove asunder the *n.*
Zep. 3:6 I have cut off the *n.*
  8 my determin. is to gather *n.*
Zec. 2:11 many *n.* joined to Lord
  8:22 strong *n.* come to seek L.
  23 out of all languages of *n.*
Luke 12:30 these do *n.* seek after
  21:25 upon earth distress of *n.*
Acts 13:19 he dest. seven *n.* in C.
Rev. 2:26 I give power over *n.*
  10:11 must prophesy before *n.*

  11:9 *n.* shall see dead bodies
  18 *n.* were angry, thy wrath
  13:7 power given him over all *n.*
  16:19 the cities of the *n.* fell
  17:15 waters are *n.* and tongues
  20:3 should deceive *n.* no more
  21:24 *n.* wh. are saved sh. walk
  26 shall bring honor of *n.* to it
  22:2 leaves were for heal. of *n.*

See GREAT.

All NATIONS.

Deut. 4:19 hath divided to *all n.*
  28:37 become by word am. *all n.*
  1 *K.* 4:31 his fame was in *all n.*
  1 *Chr.* 16:24 decl. works am. *a. n.*
  2 *Chr.* 32:23 mag. in sight of *a. n.*
Ps. 67:2 saving health am. *all n.*
  72:11 *all n.* shall serve him
  17 *all n.* shall call him blessed
  82:8 for thou shalt inherit *all n.*
  86:9 *all n.* shall worsh. bef. thee
  113:4 L. is high above *all n.*
  117:1 praise Lord *all* ye *n.*
  118:10 *all n.* compassed me ab.
Is. 2:2 *all n.* shall flow unto it
  25:7 destroy the vail over *all n.*
  34:2 indignation of L. on *all n.*
  40:17 *all n.* before him as noth.
  66:18 gather *all n.* *Joel* 3:2
  20 br. your breth. out of *all n.*
Jer. 27:7 *all n.* serve, *Dan.* 7:14
Amos 9:9 house of Is. am. *all n.*
Hab. 2:5 gathereth to him *all n.*
Hag. 2:7 I will shake *all n.* and
    desire of *all n.* shall come
Zec. 14:2 I will gather *a. n.* ag. J.
  9 punish. of *all n.* come not
Mal. 3:12 *all n.* call you blessed
Mat. 24:9 hat. of *a. n.* for my sa.
  14 gospel of kingd. preached
    to *all n.* *Mark* 12:10 ; *Luke*
    24:47 ; *Rom.* 16:26
  25:32 bef. him sh. be gath. *all n.*
  28:19 go ye, and teach *all n.*
Mark 11:17 called of *all n.*
Luke 21:24 led captive into *all n.*
Acts 14:16 suffered *all n.* to walk
  17:26 made of one blood *all n.*
Rom. 1:5 obed. to faith am. *all n.*
  16:26 made known to *all n.*
Gal. 3:8 shall *all n.* be blessed
Rev. 7:9 a multitude of *all n.*
  12:5 to rule *all n.* with a rod
  14:8 she made *all n.* drink, 18:3
  15:4 *all n.* sh. come and worsh.
  18:23 by thy sor. *all n.* deceived

All the NATIONS.

Gen. 18:18 *all the n.* of the earth
    be blessed, 22:18 ; 26:4
Deut. 14:2 ab. *all the n.* on earth
  17:14 set a king over me, as *all*
    the n. 1 *Sam.* 8:5, 20
  30:1 call them to mind am. *all n.*
  3 L. gather thee from *all t. n.*
Ps. 9:17 *all t. n.* that forget G.
Is. 14:26 hand stretch. on *a. t. n.*
  29:7 multitude of *all the n.* 8
  37:18 laid waste *all the n.*
  43:9 let *all the n.* be gathered
  52:10 bare arm in eyes of *all n.*
  61:11 spring forth bef. *all the n.*
Jer. 3:17 *all the n.* shall be gath.
  25:15 *a. n.* drink ; 17 made *a. n.*
  26:6 this city a curse to *all t. n.*
  29:14 gather you from *all t. n.*
  18 a reproach am. *all t. n.* 44:8
  33:9 joy and honor bef. *all t. n.*
  46:28 make full end of *all the n.*
Zec. 7:14 scat. them am. *all t. n.*
  12:9 destroy *all the n.* that come
  14:16 left of *all the n.* that came
    These NATIONS.
Deut. 7:17 *th. n.* are more than I
  9:4 for wickedness of *these n.* 5
  11:23 the Lord drive out *all t. n.*
  12:30 did *t. n.* serve th. gods ?
  18:14 *t. n.* heark. to observers

28:65 am. *t. n.* shalt find no ease
29:18 lest any serve gods of *t. n.*
31:3 Lord will destroy *these n.*
Jos. 23:3 what L. done *these n.*
4 divided to you by lot *th. n.*
12 if ye cleave to remn. of *t. n.*
13 will no more drive out *t. n.*
Jud. 3:1 *t. n.* L. left to prove Is.
2 *K.* 17:41 so *these n.* feared Lord
Jer. 25:9 bring them against *t. n.*
28:14 I put yoke of iron on *t. n.*

NATIVE.
Jer. 22:10 no more see *n.* country

NATIVITY.
Gen. 11:28 Hu. died in land of *n.*
Ruth 2:11 hast left land of *n.*
Jer. 46:16 let us go to land of *n.*
Ezek. 16:3 thy *n.* is land of Ca.
4 thy *n.* in day th. wast born
21:30 judge thee in land of *n.*
23:15 Chaldea, land of their *n.*

NATURE.
Rom. 1:26 change th. against *n.*
2:14 do by *n.* things in the law
27 uncircu. by *n.* judge thee ?
11:24 olive-tr. wh. is wild by *n.*
were grafted contrary to *n.*
1 *Cor.* 11:14 doth not *n.* tea. you?
Gal. 2:15 Jews by *n.* not sinners
4:8 which by *n.* are no gods
Eph. 2:3 by *n.* children of wrath
Heb. 2:16 took not *n.* of angels
Jam. 3:6 set. on fire course of *n.*
2 *Pet.* 1:4 partakers of divine *n.*

NATURAL.
Deut. 34:7 nor his *n.* force abat.
Rom. 1:26 women change *n.* use
27 men leaving *n.* use of wom.
31 without *n.* affec. 2 *Tim.* 3:3
11:21 G. spared not *n.* bran. 23
1 *Cor.* 2:14 *n.* man rece. not Sp.
15:44 sown *n.* body, is *n.* body
46 that which is *n.* was first
Jam. 1:23 a man behold. *n.* face
2 *Pet.* 2:12 th. as *n.* brute beasts

NATURALLY.
Phil. 2:20 *n.* care for your state
Jude 10 but what they know *n.*

NAUGHT.
Gen. 29:15 sho. serve me for *n. ?*
Deut. 13:17 cle. *n.* cursed thing
15:9 brother, thou givest him *n.*
28:63 L. rej. to bring you to *n.*
2 *K.* 2:19 city pleasant, water *n.*
Neh. 4:15 God bro. counsel to *n.*
Job 1:9 doth Job fear G. for *n. ?*
8:22 place of wick. come to *n.*
14:18 mount. fall. cometh to *n.*
22:6 pledge fr. thy broth. for *n.*
Ps. 33:10 counsel of heath. to *n.*
44:12 sellest thy people for *n.*
Prov. 1:25 set at *n.* all counsel
20:14 it is *n.* it is *n.* saith buyer
Is. 8:10 take counsel, come to *n.*
29:20 terrible one is brok. to *n.*
21 turn aside just for thi. of *n.*
41:12 nothing, as a thing of *n.*
24 nothing, and your work *n.*
49:4 spent my strength for *n.*
52:3 sold yourselves for *n.*
5 people is taken away for *n.*
Jer. 14:14 vision, a thing of *n.*
Amos 5:5 Beth-el sh. come to *n.*
6:13 which rejoice in thing of *n.*
Mal. 1:10 shut doors for *n. ?* nei.
kindle fire on mi. altar for *n.*
Mark 9:12 set at *n. Luke* 23:11
Acts 4:11 this is stone set at *n.*
5:36 scattered and brought to *n.*
38 if work of men, come to *n.*
19:27 craft in danger set at *n.*
Rom. 14:10 set at *n.* thy broth. ?
1 *Cor.* 1:28 to bring to *n.* things
2:6 wisd. of th. world com. to *n.*
2 *Thes.* 3:8 man's bread for *n.*
Rev. 18:17 riches come to *n.*

NAUGHTY.
Prov. 6:12 a *n.* person walketh
17:4 liar giveth ear to *n.* tongue
Jer. 24:2 basket had very *n.* figs

NAUGHTINESS.
1 *Sam.* 17:28 the *n.* of thy heart
Prov. 11:6 taken in their own *n.*
Jam. 1:21 all superfluity of *n.*
NAUM. *Luke* 3:25

NAVEL.
Job 40:16 force is in *n.* of belly
Prov. 3:8 sh. be health to thy *n.*
Cant. 7:2 thy *n.* is like a goblet
Ezek. 16:4 thy *n.* was not cut

NAVES.
1 *K.* 7:33 *n.* and spokes molten

NAVY.
1 *K.* 9:26 Solo. made *n.* of ships
27 Hir. sent in *n.* his servants
10:11 the *n.* of Hiram bro. gold
22 Solomon had at sea a *n.*

NAY.
1 *K.* 2:17 he will not say thee *n.*
20 say not *n.* will not say th. *n.*
Mat. 5:37 let your communicati.
be yea, yea, *n. n. Jam.* 5:12
Luke 13:3 *n.* except ye repent, 5
16:30 he said, *n.* fath. Abraham
Acts 16:27 *n.* verily, but let th.
Rom. 3:37 *n.* but by law of faith
9:20 *n.* but O man
2 *Cor.* 1:17 be yea, yea, *n. n.*
18 word was not yea and *n.*
29 Jesus Christ was not yea
and *n.*

NAZARENE. *Mat.* 2:23
NAZARENES. *Acts* 24:5

NAZARETH.
Mat. 2:23 dw. in a city called N.
21:11 Jesus of N. *Mark* 1:24 ;
10:47 ; *Lu.* 4:34 ; 18:37 ; 24:19
Mark 14:67 wast wi. Jesus of N.
Luke 1:26 Gabriel was sent to N.
2:51 Jesus came to N. 4:16
John 1:45 J. of N. 18, 5, 7 ; 19:19 ;
Acts 22:2 ; 4:10 ; 6:14 ; 22:8
Acts 3:6 in name of Jesus of N.
10:38 God anointed Jesus of N.
26:9 contra. to name of Jesus
of N.

NAZARITE.
Num. 6:2 a vow of a N. to sepa-
rate themselves, 18, 19, 20
Jud. 13:5 shall be a N. 7 ; 16:17

NAZARITES.
Lam. 4:7 her N. purer than snow
Amos 2:11 raised yo. men for N.
12 ye gave N. wine to drink
NEAPOLIS. *Acts* 16:11

NEAR.
Gen. 19:20 city is *n.* to flee to
45:10 thou shalt be *n.* to me
48:10 bro. them *n.* and kissed
Lev. 18:6 not appr. any *n.* of kin
Num. 16:9 br. you *n.* to him. 10
Deut. 5:27 go th. *n.* and hear G.
Jud. 20:34 knew not evil was *n.*
2 *Sam.* 19:42 the king is *n.* of kin
Job 41:16 one is so *n.* another
Ps. 22:11 trou. is *n.* 75:1 name is
119:151 thou art *n.* O Lord
Is. 45:21 and bring them *n.*
55:6 call upon L. while he is *n.*
57:19 peace be to him that is *n.*
Ezek. 22:5 those that be *n.* mock
Ob. 15 day of L. is *n. Zec.* 1:14
Mat. 24:33 it is *n.* even at doors
See CAME, COME, DRAW, DREW.

NEARER.
Ruth 3:12 is a kinsman *n.* than I
Rom. 13:11 our salvation *n.* than

NEBAIOTH.
Gen. 25:13 Ish. N. 1 *Chr.* 1:29

Is. 60:7 rams of N. sh. minister

NEBO.
Num. 32:3 N. is a land for cattle
Deut. 32:49 unto mount N. 34:1
1 *Chr.* 5:8 even unto N. *Ezr.*
2:29 ; 10:43
Neh. 7:33 of the other N. fifty-t.
Is. 15:2 Moab shall howl over N.
46:1 N. stoopeth, *Jer.* 48:1
Jer. 48:22 judgm. come upon N.

**NEBUCHADNEZZAR, NE-
BUCHADREZZAR.**
2 *K.* 24:11 N. came against Jerus.
25:1 ; 2 *Chr.* 36:6 ; *Jer.* 39:1
25:22 peo. N. left, 1 *Chr.* 6:15 ;
Jer. 24:1 ; 29:1 ; 52:28
Ezr. 1:7 ves. N. taken, 5:14, 6:5
Jer. 27:8 not serve N. 28:11, 14
29:21 them into the hand of N.
32:28 this city into hand of N.
Ezek. 26:7 I will br. on Tyrus N.
Dan. 2:1 N. dreamed 4:37
3:1 N. ma. image of gold, 19, 24
4:28 this came upon king N. 33
5:18 high G. gave N. a kingdom

NEBUZAR-ADAN.
2 *K.* 25:8 N. came to Jerusalem
Jer. 39:10 N. left of poor of the

NECESSARY.
Job 23:12 his words more th. *n.*
Acts 13:46 *n.* the word be spoken
15:28 no burden than th. *n.* thi.
28:10 laded us with things *n.*
1 *Cor.* 12:22 memb. feeble are *n.*
2 *Cor.* 9:5 thought it *n.* to exhort
Phil. 2:25 supposed it *n.* to send
Tit. 3:14 good works for *n.* uses
Heb. 9:23 *n.* patterns sh. be puri.

NECESSITY.
Luke 23:17 of *n.* he must release
Rom. 12:13 distr. to *n.* of saints
1 *Cor.* 7:37 having no *n.* and **ha.**
9:16 for *n.* is laid upon me
2 *Cor.* 9:7 give not grud. or of *n.*
Phil. 4:16 once and ag. to my *n.*
Phile. 14 not be as it were of *n.*
Heb. 7:12 there is of *n.* a change
8:3 it is of *n.* this man have
9:16 there must of *n.* be death

NECESSITIES.
Acts 20:34 hands minis. to my *n.*
2 *Cor.* 6:4 as ministers of G. in *n.*
12:10 I take pleasure in *n.*
NECHO. 2 *K.* 23:29

NECK.
Gen. 27:16 skins on smooth of *n.*
40 break yoke from off thy *n.*
33:4 E. fell on his *n.* and kissed
41:42 gold chain ab. Joseph's *n.*
Ezek. 16:11 ; *Dan.* 5:7, 16, 29
45:14 Jos. fell on Benjamin's *n.*
46:29 he fell on Jacob's *n.*
49:8 hand be on *n.* of enemies
Ex. 13:13 if not, br. his *n.* 34:20
Lev. 5:8 wring off his head fr. *n.*
Deut. 21:4 strike off heifer's *n.*
28:48 a yoke of iron on thy *n.*
1 *Sam.* 4:18 his *n.* brake, and di.
2 *Chr.* 36:13 Zed. stiffened his *n.*
Neh. 9:29 they hardened their **n.**

Job 15:26 on him, even on his *n.*
16:12 hath taken me by the *n.*
39:19 clothed *n.* with thunder ?
41:22 in his *n.* remain. strength
Ps. 75:5 speak not with a stiff *n.*
Prov. 1:9 sh. be chains ab. thy *n.*
3:3 bind them about thy *n.* 6:21
22 life and grace to thy *n.*
Cant. 1:10 thy *n.* is comely
4:4 thy *n.* is like the tow. of D.
9 ravi. wi. one chain of thy *n.*
7:4 thy *n.* is a tower of ivory

Is. 8:8 sh. reach even to the *n.*
10:27 yoke be taken from thy *n.*
30:28 reach to midst of the *n.*
48:4 thy *n.* is an iron sinew
52:2 loose thyself fr. bands of *n.*
66:3 as if he cut off a dog's *n.*
Jer. 17:23 they made their *n.* stiff
27:2 yok. and put th. on thy *n.*
8 put *n.* under yoke of king, 11
28:10 took yoke from Jer. *n.* 12
14 put a yoke on *n.* of nations
30:8 break his yoke from off *n.*
Lam. 1:14 transgr. are on my *n.*
Hos. 10:11 passed over on her *n.*
Hab. 3:13 foundation to the *n.*
Mat. 18:6 a millstone hanged ab.
his *n.*, *Mark* 9:42; *Luke* 17:2
Luke 15:20 father fell on his *n.*
Acts 15:10 yoke on *n.* of disciples
26:37 fell on P.'s *n.* kissed him

See HARDEN.

NECKS.
Jos. 10:24 feet on *n.* of th. kings
Jud. 5:30 *n.* of them take spoil
8:21 ornaments on camels' *n.* 26
2 *Sam.* 22:41 given me *n.* of ene-
mies, *Ps.* 18:40
Neh. 3:5 put not *n.* to the work
Is. 3:16 with stretched-forth *n.*
Jer. 27:12 br. your *n.* under yoke
Lam. 5:5 *n.* under persecution
Ezek. 21:29 br. thee on *n.* of slain
Mic. 2:3 shall not remove your *n.*
Rom. 16:4 laid down th. own *n.*

NECROMANCER.
Deut. 18:11 not be am. you a *n.*

NEED.
Deut. 15:8 sufficient for his *n.*
1 *Sam.* 21:15 ha. I *n.* of madmen
2 *Chr.* 2:16 as much as shalt *n.*
20:17 shall not *n.* to fight in bat.
Ezr. 6:9 let wh. they *n.* be given
Prov. 31:11 sh. have no *n.* of sp.
Mat. 3:14 I have *n.* to be baptiz.
6:8 your F. knoweth what thin.
ye have *n.* of, 32 ; *Lu.* 12:30
9:12 that be whole *n.* not a physician, *Mark* 2:17; *Luke* 5:31
14:16 they *n.* not depart, give
21:3 the L. hath *n.* of th. *Mark*
11:3 ; *Luke* 19:31, 34
26:65 what further *n.* have we ?
Mark 14:63 ; *Luke* 22:71
Mark 2:25 D. did when he had *n.*
Luke 9:11 healed th. that had *n.*
15:7 just persons *n.* no repent.
John 13:29 things we have *n.* of
Acts 2:45 as ev. man had *n.* 4:35
Rom. 16:2 assist in what she *n.*
1 *Cor.* 7:36 *n.* so require, let him
12:21 not say, I have no *n.*
24 our comely parts have no *n.*
2 *Cor.* 3:1 or *n.* we epistles ?
Phil. 4:19 I kn. how to suffer *n.*
19 God sh. supply all your *n.*
1 *Thes.* 1:8 that we *n.* not speak
4:9 brotherly love, *n.* not write
5:1 of the times ye have no *n.*
Heb. 4:16 to help in time of *n.*
5:12 *n.* one teach you ; *n.* milk
7:11 what *n.* th. another priest
10:36 ye have *n.* of patience
1 *Pet.* 1:6 *n.* be, ye are in heavi.
1 *John* 2:27 *n.* not any man teach
3:17 see his brother have *n.*
Rev. 3:17 I have *n.* of nothing
21:23 city no *n.* of sun or moon
22:5 *n.* no candle, nor light

NEEDED.
John 2:25 *n.* not any sho. testify
Acts 17:25 tho' he *n.* anything

NEEDEST, ETH.
Gen. 33:15 Jacob said, What *n.*
Luke 11:8 as many as he *n.*
John 13:10 *n.* not save to wash
16:30 and *n.* not that any man

Eph. 4:28 to give him that *n.*
2 *Tim.* 2:15 workm. *n.* not to be
Heb. 7:27 who *n.* not offer sacrif.

NEEDFUL.
Ezr. 7:20 *n.* for house of thy G.
Luke 10:42 but one thing is *n.*
Acts 15:5 *n.* to circumcise them
Phil. 1:24 abide in flesh more *n.*
Jam. 2:16 things *n.* for the body
Jude 3 it was *n.* for me to write

NEEDLE.
Mat. 19:24 to go thro' eye of a *n.*
Mark 10:25 ; *Luke* 18:25

NEEDLE-WORK.
Ex. 26:36 hanging wrought with
n.-w. 27:16; 36:37; 38:18
28:39 ma. girdle of *n.-w.* 39:29
Jud. 5:30 divers colors of *n.-w.*
Ps. 45:14 bro. raiment of *n.-w.*

NEEDS.
Gen. 17:13 must *n.* be circumci.
19:9 this fel. will *n.* be a judge
24:5 must I *n.* bri. thy son ag. ?
2 *Sam.* 14:14 for we must *n.* die
Jer. 10:5 must *n.* be born, beca.
Mat. 18:7 *n.* be that offen. come
Mark 13:7 such things must *n.*
Luke 14:18 I must *n.* go and see
John 4:4 must *n.* go thro' Sama.
Acts 17:3 Christ must *n.* have
21:22 multitude must *n.* come
Rom. 13:5 ye must *n.* be subject
1 *Cor.* 5:10 must ye *n.* go out
2 *Cor.* 11:30 if I must *n.* glory

NEEDY.
Deut. 15:11 open thy hand to *n.*
24:14 servant that is poor and *n.*
Job 24:4 they turn *n.* out of way
14 murderer kill. poor and *n.*
Ps. 9:18 *n.* not alway be forgot.
12:5 the sighing of *n.* will arise
35:10 del. poor and *n.* 72:4, 13
37:14 bent bow to cast down *n.*
40:17 I am poor and *n.* 70:5
72:12 he sh. deliver the *n.* 82:4
13 he sh. spare the poor and *n.*
74:21 poor and *n.* praise thy na.
82:3 justice to afflicted and *n.*
4 del. poor and *n.* from wicked
86:1 I am poor and *n.* 109:22
109:16 persecuted poor and *n.*
113:7 lifteth *n.* out of dunghill
Prov. 30:14 de. *n.* from am. men
31:9 plead cause of poor and *n.*
20 reacheth forth hands to *n.*
Is. 10:2 turn aside *n.* fr. judgm.
14:30 *n.* shall lie down in safety
25:4 been a strength to the *n.*
26:6 steps of *n.* shall tread it do.
32:7 even when the *n.* speaketh
41:17 poor and *n.* seek water
Jer. 5:28 right of *n.* do they not
22:16 judg. cause of poor and *n.*
Ezek. 16:49 strength. hands of *n.*
18:12 oppressed the poor and *n.*
22:29 people vexed poor and *n.*
Amos 4:1 kine of Bash. crush *n.*
8:4 O ye that swallow up the *n.*
6 buy the *n.* for a pair of shoes

NEESINGS.
Job 41:18 by his *n.* light doth sh.

NEGLECT.
Mat. 18:17 if he shall *n.* to hear
them ; *n.* to hear the church
1 *Tim.* 4:14 *n.* not gift in thee
Heb. 2:3 how escape, if *n.* salv. ?

NEGLECTED, ING.
Acts 6:1 widows *n.* in ministra.
Col. 2:23 *n.* body, not in honor

NEGLIGENT.
2 *Chr.* 29:11 be not *n.* for the L.
2 *Pet.* 1:12 not be *n.* to put you

NEHEMIAH.
Ezr. 2:2 N. came with, *Neh.* 7:7

Neh. 1:1 the words of N. son of
3:16 N. son of Azbuk, repaired
8:9 N. wh. is the Tirsha. 10:1
12:47 Israel in days of N. gave

NEHUSHTAN.   **2** *K.* 18:4

NEIGHBOR.
Ex. 3:22 wom. borrow of *n.* 11:2
1 *Sam.* 15:28 hath given it to a *n.*
Prov. 27:10 better is a *n.* that is
Jer. 6:21 *n.* and friends sh. peri.
9:20 and teach every one her *n.*
Luke 10:36 *n.* to him am. thieves

NEIGHBOR, Adjective.
Jer. 49:18 overthrow of Sod. and
the *n.* cities thereof, 50:40

His NEIGHBOR.
Ex. 12:4 him and *h. n.* take lamb
22:8 put ha. to *h. n.'s* goods, 11
14 borrow ought of *his n.*
22:27 go slay every man *his n.*
Lev. 20:10 with *his n.'s* wife sh.
be put to death, *Deut.* 22:24
24:19 man cause blemish in *h. n.*
Deut. 4:42 kill his *n.* unaw. 19:4
15:2 creditor that lend to *his n.*
19:11 if any hate *his n.*
Deut. 22:26 a man ris. ag. *his n.*
27:24 curs. he th. smiteth *h. n.*
Ruth 4:7 his shoe, gave to *his n.*
1 *K.* 8:31 if man trespa. ag. *h. n.*
2 *Chr.* 6:22 if a man sin ag. *h. n.*
Job 12:4 as one mocked of *h. n.*
16:21 a man pleadeth for *h. n.*
Ps. 12:2 sp. vanity each wi. *h. n.*
15:3 nor doeth evil to *his n.*
101:5 whoso slandereth *his n.*
Prov. 6:29 goeth to *h. n.'s* wife
11:9 a hypocrite destroy. *h. n.*
12 void of wis. desp. *h. n.* 14:21
12:26 right. more ex. than *h. n.*
14:20 poor is hated even of *h. n.*
16:29 a vio. man enticeth *his n.*
18:17 *his n.* cometh and search.
19:4 poor is separated fr. *his n.*
21:10 *his n.* findeth no favor
25:18 bear false witn. ag. *his n.*
26:19 man that deceiveth *his n.*
29:5 flattereth *h. n.* spreadeth
Ec. 4:4 a man envied of *his n.*
Is. 3:5 oppressed ev. one by *h. n.*
19:2 fight ev. one against *h. n.*
41:6 helped every one *his n.*
Jer. 5:8 neighed after *h. n.'s* wife
7:5 judgm. bet. man and *his n.*
9:4 take ye heed ev. one of *h. n.*
5 th. will deceive ev. one *h. n.*
8 speak peaceably to *his n.*
22:8 say ev. man to *his n.* 23:35
13 useth *his n.'s* service
23:27 drea. tell ev. one to *h. n.*
30 steal words, ev. one fr. *h. n.*
31:34 teach no more every man
his n. *Heb.* 8:11
34:15 proclaiming li. to *h. n.* 17
Ezek. 18:6 nei. defi. *h. n.'s* wi. 15
11 defiled *h. n.* 22:11 ; 33:26
Hab. 2:15 giveth *h. n.* drink
Zec. 3:10 call every man *his n.*
8:10 I set men ev. one ag. *h. n.*
16 speak ev. man truth to *h. n.*
17 let none imag. evil ag. *h. n.*
Mark 12:33 love *h. n.* as himself
Acts 7:27 he that did *his n.* wro.
Rom. 13:10 work. no evil to *h. n.*
15:2 let every one please *his n.*
Eph. 4:25 speak truth with *h. n.*

My NEIGHBOR.
Job 31:9 I laid wait at *my n.'s* d.
Luke 10:29 to Je. Who is *my n.* ?

Thy NEIGHBOR.
Ex. 20:16 thou sh. not bear false
witness ag. *thy n. Deut.* 5:20
Lev. 18:20 not lie wi *t. n.'s* wife
19:13 thou sh. not defraud *t. n.*
15 in righte. shalt judge *thy n.*
16 nor stand ag. blood of *t. n.*

NEIGHBOR

17 in any wise rebuke *thy n.*
18 thou sh. love *t. n.* as thyself
Deut. 5:21 nor desire *t. n.'s* wife
19:14 not rem. *t. n.'s* landmark
1 *Sam.* 28:17 given it to *thy n.*
Prov. 3:28 say not to *thy n.* Go
29 devise not evil against *t. n.*
24:28 be not witness ag. *thy n.*
25:9 debate thy cause with *t. n.*
17 with. foot fr. *t. n.'s* house
Mat. 5:43 shalt love *thy n.* 19:19;
22:39 *Mark* 12:31; *Luke*
10:27 *Rom.* 13:9; *Gal.* 5:14;
Jam. 2:8

NEIGHBORS.

Jos. 9:16 heard th. were their *n.*
Ruth 4:17 her *n.* gave it a name
2 *K.* 4:3 borrow vessels of thy *n.*
Ps. 28:3 speak peace to their *n.*
31:11 I was reproach am. my *n.*
44:13 makest us repro. to our *n.*
79:4 are become reproach to *n.*
12 render to our *n.* seven-fold
80:6 makest us a strife to our *n.*
89:41 he is a reproach to his *n.*
Jer. 12:14 saith L. ag. all evil *n.*
Ezek. 22:12 gained of *n.* by exto.
Luke 1:58 her *n.* heard how Lord
14:12 make sup. call not rich *n.*
15:6 he called together his *n.*
John 9:8 *n.* who had seen him

NEIGHED.

Jer. 5:8 one *n.* after neigh. wife

NEIGHING, S.

Jer. 8:16 tremble at *n.* of strong
13:27 I have seen adult. and *n.*

NEPHEW, S.

Jud. 12:14 A. had 40 sons, 30 *n.*
Job 18:19 neither have son nor *n.*
Is. 14:22 I will cut off son and *n.*
1 *Tim.* 5:4 if widow have children or *n.*

NER. 1 *Chr.* 8:33 ; 9:36, 39
NEREUS. *Rom.* 16:15
NERGAL. 2 *K.* 17:30

NEST.

Num. 24:21 put. thy *n.* in a rock
Deut. 22:6 if a *n.* be before thee
32:11 eagle stirreth up her *n.*
Job 29:18 I shall die in my *n.*
39:27 eagle make *n.* on high
Ps. 84:3 swal. found *n.* for herse
Prov. 27:8 bird that wand. fr. *n.*
Is. 10:14 ha. found as *n.* riches
16:2 wander. bird cast out of *n.*
34:15 great owl make *n.*
Jer. 22:23 make. thy *n.* in cedars
48:28 dove makes *n.* in holes
49:16 make *n.* as high as eagle
Ob. 4 set thy *n.* among stars
Hab. 2:9 he may set *n.* on high.

NESTS.

Ps. 104:17 wh. birds make th. *n.*
Ezek. 31:6 all fowls made their *n.*
Mat. 8:20 birds of air *n.* *Lu.* 9:58

NET.

Job 18:8 cast into *n.* by own feet
19:6 God comp. me with his *n.*
Ps. 9:15 in *n.* they hid
25:15 plu. my feet out of *n.* 31:4
35:7 hid for me their *n.* in a pit
8 his *n.* he hid catch himself
57:6 prepared *n.* for my steps
66:11 thou broughtest us into *n.*
140:5 spread a *n.* by wayside
Prov. 1:17 in vain *n.* is spread
12:12 wick. desir. *n.* of evil men
29:5 man that flatter. spread. *n.*
Ec. 9:12 fishes taken in evil *n.*
Is. 51:20 as a wild bull in a *n.*
Lam. 1:13 spr. a *n.* for my feet
Ezek. 12:13 *n.* will I spread, 17:20
19:8 nations shall spread *n.*
32:3 spread my *n.* over thee
Hos. 5:1 ye have been *n.* on Ta.

7:12 spread my *n.* on them
Mic. 7:2 hunt brother with a *n.*
Hab. 1:15 catch them in their *n.*
16 they sacrifice to their *n.*
17 shall they empty their *n.*
Mat. 4:18 cast *n.* into, *Mark* 1:16
13:47 kingd. of heaven is like *n.*
Luke 5:5 I will let down the *n.*
6 multitude of fishes, *n.* brake
John 21:6 cast *n.* on right side
11 *n.* to land · not *n.* broken

NETS.

1 *K.* 7:17 *n.* of checker work
Ps. 140:10 wick. fall into own *n.*
Ec. 7:26 wom. whose heart is *n.*
Is. 19:8 they that sp. *n.* languish
Ezek. 26:5 spreading of *n.* in sea
14 place to spread *n.* on, 47:10
Mat. 4:21 James and J. mending
their *n.* *Mark* 1:19 ; *Lu.* 5:2
Mark 1:18 forsook *n.* follow. him
Luke 5:4 down *n.* for a draught

NETHANEEL.

Num. 1:8 N. the son of Zuar
2:5 N. the son of Zuar, shall be
captain, 7:18, 23 ; 10:15
1 *Chr.* 2:14 N. fourth son of Jes.
15:24 N. and Amasai blew with
24:6 the son of N. the scribe
26:4 sons of Obed-e. J. and N.
2 *Chr.* 17:7 Jehoshaphat sent N.
Ezr. 10:22 N. prie. *Neh.* 12:21, 36

NETHANIAH.

2 *K.* 25:23 son of N. 25 ; *Jer.* 40:8
1 *Chr.* 25:2 son of Asaph, N. 12
2 *Chr.* 17:8 Le. to teach, even N.
Jer. 36:14 princes sent son of N.
41:2 Ishmael, son of N. 15

NETHER.

Ex. 19:17 they stood at *n.* part
Deut. 24:6 no man take *n.* millet.
Jos. 15:19 gave her upper springs
and *n.* springs, *Jud.* 1:15
Job 41:24 heart hard as *n.* millst.
Ezek. 31:14 del. to death *n.* parts
16 comf. in *n.* parts of earth
18 down to *n.* parts of earth
32:18 cast do. to *n.* parts of ear.
24 E. gone down to *n.* pa. of e.

NETHERMOST.

1 *K.* 6:6 *n.* chamb. 5 cub. broad

NETHINIM.

1 *Chr.* 9:2 first inhabitants N.
Ezr. 2:43 N. went with Zerub.
58 the N. were 392, *Neh.* 7:60
7:7 some of N. went to Jer. 24
8:17 Iddo and breth. the N. 20
Neh. 3:26 N. dwelt in Op. 11:21
10:28 N. separated from people
11:21 Zi. and Gispa over the N.

NETTLES.

Job 30:7 under *n.* th. were gath.
Prov. 24:31 n. had covered face
Is. 34:13 *n.* and bram. in fortres
Hos. 9:6 *n.* possess pleas. places
Zep. 2:9 M. shall be breeding *n.*

NETWORK, S.

Ex. 27:4 grate of *n.* brass, 38:4
1 *K.* 7:18 two rows round *n.* 42
41 two *n.* upon the chapiters
42 400 pomegranates for two *n.*
Is. 19:9 weave *n.* be confounded
Jer. 52:22 with *n.* on chapiters
23 pomegranates on *n.* we. 100

NEVER.

Mat. 9:33 it was *n.* so seen in Is.
27:14 answered him to *n.* a word

NEW.

Ex. 1:8 arose a *n.* king over Eg.
Lev. 26:10 br. forth old, bec. of *n.*
Num. 16:30 Lord make *n.* thing
Deut. 20:5 built *n.* house, 22:8
24:5 taken a *n.* wife, not go
32:17 sacri. to devils, to *n.* gods

Jos. 9:13 bottles of wine were *n.*
Jud. 5:8 they chose *n.* gods
1 *Sam.* 6:7 make a *n.* cart
2 *Sam.* 6:3 on *n.* cart, 1 *Chr.* 13:7
21:16 being girded with *n.* sw.
1 *K.* 11:29 J. clad with *n.* gar. 30
Job 32:19 to burst like *n.* bottles
Ps. 33:3 sing *n.* song, 96:1 ; 98:1 ;
144:9 ; 149:1 ; *Is.* 42:10
40:3 put *n.* song in my mouth
Ec. 1:9 no *n.* thing under sun
10 may be said, This is *n.* ?
Cant. 7:13 pleas. frui. *n.* and old
Is. 42:9 *n.* things I declare, 48:6
43:19 I will do a *n.* thing
62:2 be called by a *n.* name
65:17 *n.* heavens, *n.* earth, 66:22
Jer. 26:10 *n.* gate of L.'s ho. 36:10
31:22 Lord hath creat. *n.* thing
Lam. 3:23 Lord's mercies are *n.*
Ezek. 11:19 a *n.* spirit, 36:26
18:31 make *n.* heart and *n.* spi.
47:12 trees bring forth *n.* fruit
Mat. 9:16 *n.* cloth to an old gar.
Mark 2:21 ; *Luke* 5:36
17 put *n.* wine into *n.* bottles,
Mark 2:22 ; *Luke* 5:38
13:52 bring. out things *n.* and o.
26:28 is my blood of *n.* testament, *Mark* 14:24, *Lu.* 22:20;
1 *Cor.* 11:25
29 drink it *n.* with, *Mark* 14:25
27:60 Jos. laid body in *n.* tomb
Mark 1:27 what *n.* doct. is this?
16:17 speak with *n.* tongues
John 13:34 *n.* com. I give you
Acts 17:19 what this *n.* doct. is?
21 tell or hear some *n.* thing
1 *Cor.* 5:7 ye may be a *n.* lump
2 *Cor.* 3:6 able minist. of *n.* test.
5:17 in Ch. he is a *n.* creature;
all things are become *n.*
Gal. 6:15 but a *n.* creature
Eph. 2:15 of twain, one *n.* man
4:24 ye put on *n.* man, *Col.* 3:10
Heb. 9:15 Media. of *n.* testament
10:20 by *n.* and living way
1 *Pet.* 2:2 as *n.* born babes desi.
2 *Pet.* 3:13 *n.* heavens, *n.* earth
1 *John* 2:7 write no *n.* comman.
8 *n.* commandment I write
2 *John* 5 not as though I wrote
n. commandment
Rev. 2:17 *n.* name written
3:12 name is *n.* Jerusalem; I will
write my *n.* name, 21:2
5:9 they sung a *n.* song, 14:3
21:1 I saw *n.* heaven and *n.* ear.
5 behold, I make all things *n.*

See COVENANT, MOON.

NEW wine.

Neh. 10:39 bring off. of *n. wine*
13:5 chamber where *n. w.* laid
12 bro. tithe of *n. w.* to treas.
Prov. 3:10 presses burst wi. *n. w.*
Is. 24:7 the *n. w.* mourneth
65:8 as *n. w.* is found in cluster
Hos. 4:11 *n. w.* take away heart
9:2 the *n. wine* shall fail in her
Joel 1:5 *n. w.* cut off ; 10 dried up
3:18 mountains shall drop *n. w.*
Hag. 1:11 call. for drou. on *n. w.*
Zec. 9:17 *n. w.* ma. maids cheer.
Mat. 9:17 *n. w.* into old bottles,
but *n. wine* into new, *Mark*
2:22 ; *Luke* 5:37
Acts 2:13 these men full of *n. w.*

NEWLY.

Deut. 32:17 to gods *n.* came up
Jud. 7:19 they had *n.* set watch

NEWNESS.

Rom. 6:4 shall walk in *n.* of life
7:6 should serve in *n.* of spirit

NEWS.

Prov. 25:25 so good *n.* from a far

NEXT.

Gen. 17:21 bear at set time *n.* ye.
Ex. 12:4 let him *n.* take lamb
Deut. 21:3 city. whi. is *n.* slain
  6 elders of city *n.* to slain man
1 *Sam.* 23:17 I shall be *n.* to th.
  30:17 Dav. smote to ev. of *n.* day
Est. 10:3 Mordecai was *n.* to A.
Mat. 27:62 *n.* day that followed
Mark 1:38 go into *n.* towns
John 1:29 *n.* day John see. Jes.
Acts 4:3 put th. in hold to *n.* day
  13:42 words preached *n.* sab. 44

NICANOR. *Acts* 6:5

NICODEMUS.

John 3:1 N. a ruler of the Jews
  7:50 N. came to Jesus, 19:39

NICOLAITANS. *Rev.* 2:6, 15
NICOPOLIS. *Tit.* 3:12
NIGER. *Acts* 13:1

NIGH.

Lev. 21:3 virgin that is *n.* to him
Num. 24:17 beh. him, not *n.* star
Deut. 4:7 hath G. so *n.* them ?
  22:2 if bro. be not *n.* unto thee
  30:14 is *n.* to thee, *Rom.* 10:8
2 *Sam.* 11:20 wh. appr. so *n.* ? 21
1 *K.* 8:59 let my words be *n.*
Ps. 34:18 is *n.* them of bro. hea.
  85:9 salva. *n.* them that fear him
  145:18 L. is *n.* to all that call
Joel 2:1 day of L. is *n.* at hand
Mat. 24:32 sum. is *n.* *Luke* 21:30
Mark 13:29 know that it is *n.*
Luke 21:20 kn. that desola. is *n.*
  31 know that king. of G. is *n.*
John 6:4 and the passover was *n.*
  11:55 the Jews' passover was *n.*
Eph. 2:13 made *n.* by blood of C.
  17 preach. to th. that were *n.*
Phil. 2:27 sick, *n.* unto death, 30
Heb. 6:8 is rejected, *n.* to cursing

See CAME, DRAW.

NIGHT.

Gen. 1:5 the darkness he call. *n.*
  14 lights, to divide day from *n.*
  1:16 lesser light to rule *n.*
  19:2 tarry all *n.* *Num.* 22:19 ;
    Jud. 19:6, 9
  33 drink wine that *n.* 34, 35
  24:54 tarried all *n.* 28:11 ; 31:54 ;
    32:13, 21
  30:15 shall lie with thee to *n.* 16
  46:2 G. spake to Is. in vis. of *n.*
  49:27 at *n.* he shall divide spoil
Ex. 12:8 eat the flesh in that *n.*
  42 is a *n.* to be observed to L.
  14:20 not near other all *n.*
Lev. 6:9 burning on altar all *n.*
  19:13 not abide with thee all *n.*
Num. 14:1 people wept that *n.*
  22:8 said, Lodge here this *n.* 19
Deut. 16:4 l. bread remain all *n.*
  21:23 body not remain all *n.*
Jud. 6:40 God did so that *n.*
  19:25 and abused her all the *n.*
Ruth 1:12 if I have a husb. to-*n.*
1 *Sam.* 15:11 S. cried to L. all *n.*
  19:11 if thou save not life to-*n.*
  28:25 Saul went away that *n.*
2 *Sam.* 2:29 Abner walked all *n.*
  32 J. and his men went all *n.*
  12:16 David lay all *n.* on earth
  17:1 will pursue after D. this *n.*
  16 lodge not this *n.* in plain
2 *K.* 19:35 th. *n.* the angel smote
2 *Chr.* 1:7 that *n.* did G. ap. to S.
Est. 6:1 that *n.* cou. not king sl.
Job 3:3 let *n.* perish in which
  7 let that *n.* be solitary
  4:13 the visions of the *n.*
  7:4 when shall the *n.* be gone?
  29:19 dew lay all *n.* on my bra.
  36:20 desire not *n.* peo. cut-off
Ps. 6:6 all *n.* make I my bed
  19:2 *n.* unto *n.* showeth knowl.

  30:5 weep. may endure for a *n.*
  78:14 led them all *n.* with light
  92:2 show forth faithful. ev.,*n.*
  104:20 maketh darkn. it is *n.*
  139:11 even the *n.* sh. be light
Prov. 7:9 passing in the dark *n.*
  31:15 ariseth while it is yet *n.*
Cant. 1:13 lie all *n.* betw. breas.
  5:2 my locks with drops of *n.*
Is. 5:11 continue until *n.*
  16:3 make thy shadow as the *n.*
  21:4 *n.* of pleas. turn. into fear
  11 watchman, what of the *n.* ?
  12 morning cometh, also the *n.*
  29:7 shall be as a dream of *n.*
Jer. 14:8 turneth aside for a *n.*
Dan. 2:19 secret revealed in *n.*
  5:30 that *n.* was Belshaz. slain
  6:18 king passed the *n.* fasting
Hos. 7:6 their baker sleep, all *n.*
Joel 1:13 lie all *n.* in sackcloth
Amos 5:8 mak. day dark with *n.*
Jon. 4:10 ca. up in *n.* perish. in *n.*
Mic. 3:6 *n.* shall be to you
Mat. 26:31 sh. be offended beca.
  of me this *n.* *Mark* 14:27
  34 this *n.* thou shalt deny me
Luke 5:5 toiled all *n.* taking not.
  6:12 he continued all *n.* in pray.
  12:20 this *n.* thy soul be requi.
  17:34 that *n.* two sh. be in one
John 9:4 *n.* com. no man work
  13:30 he went out, it was *n.*
  21:3 that *n.* they caught noth.
Acts 12:6 same *n.* Pe. was sleep.
  16:33 took them same hour of *n.*
  23:11 *n.* follow. Lord stood by
  27:23 stood by me this *n.* angel
Rom. 13:12 *n.* is spent
1 *Cor.* 11:23 *n.* he was betrayed
1 *Thes.* 5:5 we are not of the *n.*
Rev. 21:25 be no *n.* there, 22:5

By NIGHT.

Gen. 20:3 to Ab. in dream *by n.*
  31:24 G. ca. to La. in dre. *by n.*
  39 whet. stolen by day or *by n.*
  40 dron. consu. me, frost *by n.*
Ex. 12:31 called M. and A. *by n.*
  13:21 *by n.* in pillar of fire, 22 ;
    14:20 ; 40:38 ; *Neh.* 9:12
Num. 9:16 appear. of fire *by n.*
  21 taken up by day or *by n.*
Deut. 1:33 fire *by n.* to show way
  23:10 unclean. chanceth *by n.*
1 *Sam.* 14:36 go after Phili. *by n.*
  28:8 Saul came to woman *by n.*
2 *Sam.* 21:10 nor the beasts *by n.*
1 *K.* 3:5 Lord appeared to Solomon *by n.* 2 *Chr.* 7:12
2 *K.* 6:14 came *by n.* compassed
  25:4 fled *by n.* *Jer.* 52:7
Ps. 91:5 not be afraid *by n.*
  121:6 nor moon smite thee *by n.*
  134:1 *by n.* stand in house of L.
  136:9 moon rule by *n.* *Jer.* 31:35
Prov. 31:18 goeth not out *by n.*
Cant. 3:1 *by n.* I sought him
Is. 4:5 shining of a fire *by n.*
Jer. 6:5 let us go *by n.* destroy
  39:4 went forth out of city *by n.*
  49:9 if thieves *by n.* will destr.
Dan. 7:2 I saw in my vision *by n.*
Ob. 5 if thieves, if robbers *by n.*
Mat. 2:14 took chi. and mo. *by n.*
  27:64 disciples come *by n.* 28:13
Luke 2:8 watch over flock *by n.*
John 3:2 Nicod. came *by n.* 19:39
Acts 5:19 angel *by n.* open. pris.
  9:25 took P. *by n.* let him down

See DAY.

In the NIGHT.

1 *K.* 3:19 wom. child died *i. t. n.*
Neh. 2:12 arose *i. t. n.* 15 I went
  4:22 *in t. n.* they may guard us
  6:10 *in t. n.* will they slay thee
Job 5:14 in noonday as *in the n.*
  24:14 *in t. n.* murder. is as thief

  27:20 tempest steal. him *in t. n.*
  34:25 overturneth them *in the n.*
  35:10 who giv. songs *in the n.* ?
Ps. 16:7 my reins inst. me *i. t. n.*
  17:3 hast visited me *in the n.*
  22:2 I cry *in the n.* season
  42:8 *in t. n.* his song sh. be wi.
  77:2 sore ran *in t. n.* ceased not
  6 call to rem. my song *in t. n.*
  90:4 1,000 years as watch *in t. n.*
  105:39 a fire to give light *i. t. n.*
  119:55 remem. thy name *in t. n.*
Ec. 2:23 taketh not rest *in the n.*
Cant. 3:8 sw. bec. of fear *in t. n.*
Is. 15:1 *in t. n.* M. is laid waste
  26:9 soul desired thee *in the n.*
  30:29 have a song as *in the n.*
  59:10 at noonday as *in the n.*
Jer. 36:30 be cast out *in the n.*
Lam. 1:2 weepeth sore *in the n.*
  2:19 arise, cry out *in the n.*
Hos. 4:5 shall fall *in the n.*
John 11:10 man walk *in the n.*
Acts 16:9 vision to P. *in t. n.* 18:9
1 *Thes.* 5:2 day cometh as thief
  in the n. 2 *Pet.* 3:10
  7 sleep *in t. n.* drunk *in the n.*

NIGHTS.

Gen. 7:4 rain 40 days, 40 *n.* 12
Job 7:3 wearisome *n.* appointed
Is. 21:8 set in ward whole *n.*

See DAYS.

NIGHTHAWK.

Lev. 11:16 *n.* not eat, *Deut.* 14:15

NIGHT-WATCHES.

Ps. 63:6 I medi. on thee in *n.-w.*
  119:148 prevent *n.-w.* to medit.

NIMRIM. *Is.* 15:6

NIMROD.

Gen. 10:8 C. begat N. 1 *Chr.* 1:10
Mic. 5:6 land of Assyria and N.

NINE.

Deut. 3:11 Og's bedst. *n.* cubits
Neh. 11:1 *n.* parts dw. in oth. cit.
Luke 17:17 where are the *n.* ?

See HUNDRED.

NINETEEN.

2 *Sam.* 2:30 lacked of D. serv. *n.*

NINETEENTH.

2 *K.* 25:8 in the *n.* year of Nebuchadnezzar the house of the
  Lord was burnt, *Jer.* 52:12

NINETY.

Gen. 5:9 Enos lived *n.* years
  17:17 Sa. that is *n.* y. old, bear ?

NINETY-SIX.

Ezr. 8:35 offer. for Is. 1 *n.-s.* rams

NINETY-EIGHT.

1 *Sam.* 4:15 Eli was *n.-e.* yc. old

NINETY-NINE.

Gen. 17:1 Ab. was *n.-n.* years old
  24 *n.-n.* years old when circu.
Mat. 18:12 do. he not le. the *n.-n.*
  and seek. ? 13 ; *Luke* 15:4, 7

NINEVEH.

Gen. 10:11 Asher builded N.
2 *K.* 19:36 Sen. at N. *Is.* 37:37
Jon. 1:2 go to N. 3:2, 3 ; 4:11
Nah. 1:1 the burden of N.
  3:7 N. is waste, who will bem. ?
Zep. 2:13 make N. a desolation
Mat. 12:41 men of N. *Luke* 11:32

NINEVITES. *Luke* 11:30

NINTH.

Lev. 25:22 eat old fruit till *n.* ye.
1 *Chr.* 12:12 Elzabad, *n.* captain
  27:12 *n.* captain for *n.* month
Mat. 20:5 went out ab. *n.* hour
  27:45 darkness over all the land
    unto *n.* hour, *Mark* 15:33
  46 *n.* hour Jesus gave up ghost

Acts 3:1 hour of prayer, being *n.*
10:3 C. saw. vis. ab. *n.* hour, 30
Rev. 21:20 *n.* founda. was topaz
See DAY, MONTH.

NISAN.
Neh. 2:1 in the month N.
Est. 3:7 first month N.

NISROCH. 2 *K.* 19:37; *Is.* 37:38

NITRE.
Prov. 25:20 as vinegar upon *n.*
Jer. 2:22 tho' thou wash with *n.*

NO.
Jer. 46:25 pun. N. *Ezek.* 30:14, 16
Nah. 3:8 better th. populous N.

NOADIAH.
Ezr. 8:33 N. the son of Binnui
Neh. 6:14 think on prophet. N.

NOAH, NOE.
Gen. 5:29 called his name N. 30
6:8 N. found grace in eyes of L.
9 gen. of N. 10:1, 32 ; 1 *Cor.* 1:4
7:23 N. only remained alive
8:1 God remembered N. 6:20
9:24 N. awoke fr. his wine, 29
Is. 54:9 this is as waters of N.
Ezek. 14:14 N. Daniel, Job, 20
Mat. 24:37 days of N. *Luke* 17:26
Heb. 11:7 by faith N. be. warned
1 *Pet.* 3:20 waited in days of N.
2 *Pet.* 2:5 old world, but saved N.
NOAH. *Num.* 26:33 ; 27:1 ; 36:11 ;
Jos. 17:3

NOB.
1 *Sam.* 21:1 David came to N. to
22:9 son of J. com. to N. 11, 19
Neh. 11:32 chi. of Ben. dw. at N.
Is. 10:32 shall he remain at N.

NOBLE.
Ezr. 4:10 n. Asnapper brought
Est. 6:9 one of king's *n.* princes.
Jer. 2:21 I planted thee a *n.* vine
Luke 19:12 *n.* man went to far
John 4:46 *n.* man whose son
    49 *n.* man saith, Come ere chi.
Acts 17:11 Bere. more *n.* than T.
24:3 we accept it, *n.* Felix, 26:25
1 *Cor.* 1:26 not many *n.* are call.

NOBLES.
Ex. 24:11 on *n.* of Israel laid not
Num. 21:18 the *n.* of peo. digged
Jud. 5:13 dominion over the *n.*
1 *K.* 21:8 Jez. sent letter to *n.*
2 *Chr.* 23:20 Jehoiada took the *n.*
Neh. 2:16 nor had I told it to *n.*
3:5 *n.* not put necks to work
5:7 I rebuked the *n.* and rulers
6:17 *n.* of Judah sent letters
Neh. 7:5 G. put in hea. to gath. *n.*
10:29 they clave to brethren, *n.*
13:17 I contended with *n.* of J
Job 29:10 the *n.* held their peace
Ps. 83:11 make their *n.* like Oreb
149:8 bind *n.* with fet. of iron
Prov. 8:16 princes rule, *n.* judg
Ec. 10:17 wh. king is son of *n.*
Is. 13:2 go into gates of the *n.*
34:12 shall call *n.* to kingdom
43:14 brought down all their *n.*
Jer. 14:3 *n.* sent their little ones
27:20 Nebuc. carried captive *n.*
30:21 *n.* shall be of themselves
39:6 king slew all *n.* of Judah
Jon. 3:7 decree of king and *n.*
Nah. 3:18 thy *n.* dwell in dust

NOD. *Gen.* 4:16

NOISE.
Ex. 20:18 heard *n.* of trumpet
32:17 th. is a *n.* of war in camp
    18 *n.* of them that sing I hear
Jos. 6:10 not shout nor make *n.*
Jud. 5:11 deliv. fr. *n.* of archers
1 *Sam.* 4:6 what meaneth *n.* ? 14
1 *K.* 1:41 wherefore is this *n.* ?

---

45 this is the *n.* ye have heard
2 *K.* 7:6 *n.* of char. *n.* of horses
11:13 Athali. heard *n.* of guard,
    2 *Chr.* 23:12
1 *Chr.* 15:28 making *n.* with psal.
Ezr. 3:13 *n.* of joy fr. *n.* of weep.
Job 36:29 understand *n.* of taber.
    33 *n.* thereof showeth concern.
37:2 hear attentive. *n.* of voice
Ps. 33:3 play skilf. with loud *n.*
42:7 call. at *n.* of water-spouts
55:2 I mourn and make a *n.*
59:6 make a *n.* like a dog, 14
65:7 stilleth the *n.* of the seas
66:1 make a joyful *n.* to God,
    all ye lands, 81:1 ; 95:1, 2 ;
    98:4, 6 ; 100:1
93:4 L. mightier than *n.* of wat.
Is. 9:5 ev. battle is wi. confu. *n.*
13:4 *n.* of a multitude in moun-
    tains, a tumult. *n.* of kingd.
14:11 *n.* of thy viols is down
17:12 a *n.* like *n.* of the seas
24:8 *n.* of them that rej. endeth
    18 he who fleeth from the *n.*
25:5 shalt bring *n.* of strangers
29:6 visited of L. with great *n.*
31:4 nor abase himself for *n.*
33:3 at *n.* of tumult people fled
66:6 a voice of *n.* from the city
Jer. 4:19 my heart maketh *n.*
    29 the city shall flee for the *n.*
10:22 the *n.* of the bruit is come
11:16 *n.* of gr. tumult he kindl.
25:31 *n.* sh. co. to ends of earth
46:17 P. king of Egypt is but *n.*
47:3 at *n.* of stamping of horses
49:21 earth is moved at the *n.*
    of their fall, at the cry the *n.*
50:46 at *n.* of taking of Babylon
51:55 *n.* of th. voice is uttered
Lam. 2:7 made *n.* in house of L.
Ezek. 1:24 *n.* of their wings, like
    the *n.* of great waters, 43:2
3:13 *n.* of wheels, *n.* of rushing
19:7 land was desolate by *n.*
26:10 thy walls sh. shake at *n.*
    13 cause *n.* of songs to cease
37:7 as I prophesied, th. was *n.*
Joel 2:5 like *n.* of char. *n.* of fire
Amos 5:23 take fr. me *n.* of songs
Mic. 2:12 they sh. make great *n.*
Nah. 3:2 *n.* of whip, *n.* of wheels
Zep. 1:10 *n.* of cry fr. fish-gate
Zec. 9:15 drink and make a *n.*
Mat. 9:23 saw peo. making a *n.*
2 *Pet.* 3:10 hea. past away wi. *n.*
Rev. 6:1 I heard the *n.* of thund.

NOISED.
Jos. 6:27 Joshua, fame was *n.*
Mark 2:1 *n.* he was in the house
Luke 1:65 th. sayings *n.* abroad
Acts 2:6 when this was *n.* abroad

NOISOME.
Ps. 91:3 deli. thee fr. *n.* pestilen.
Ezek. 14:21 send sw. and *n.* bea.
Rev. 16:2 fell a *n.* grievous sore

There was NONE.
Num. 21:35 *t. w. n.* left him alive
2 *Sam.* 22:42 they looked, but *th.
    was n.* to save, *Ps.* 18:41
Ps. 139:16 yet *t. w. n.* of them

NOON.
Gen. 43:16 sh. dine with me at *n.*
    25 present ag. Jos. came at *n.*
Jud. 19:8 tarried until after *n.*
2 *Sam.* 4:5 who lay on bed at *n.*
1 *K.* 18:26 called on Ba. until *n.*
    27 at *n.* Elijah mocked them
20:16 and they went out at *n.*
2 *K.* 4:20 sat on her knees till *n.*
Ps. 55:17 at *n.* will I pray
Cant. 1:7 mak. flock to rest at *n.*
Jer. 6:4 arise, let us go up at *n.*
Amos 8:9 cau. sun go down at *n.*
Acts 22:6 about *n.* th. shone lig.

NOONDAY.
Deut. 28:29 thou sh. grope at *n.*
Job 5:14 they grope in the *n.*
    11:17 th. age be clearer than *n.*
Ps. 37:6 bring forth judgm. as *n.*
    91:6 destruction that wast. at *n.*
Is. 16:3 as night, in midst of *n.*
58:10 thy darkness sh. be as *n.*
59:10 we stumble at *n.* as night
Jer. 15:8 I have a spoiler at *n.*
Zep. 2:4 drive out Ashdod at *n.*

NOONTIDE.
Jer. 20:16 hear the shouting at *n.*

NOPH.
Is. 19:13 princes of N. deceived
Jer. 2:16 the children of N. have
    46:14 publish in N. 19 N. shall
Ezek. 30:13 ima. cease out N. 16

NORTH.
Gen. 28:14 thou sh. spread to *n.*
1 *K.* 7:25 three oxen looking
    toward *n.* 2 *Chr.* 4:4
1 *Chr.* 9:24 porters were tow. *n.*
Job 26:7 he stretched out the *n.*
37:9 cold cometh out of the *n.*
    22 fair weather com. out of *n.*
Ps. 48:2 on sides of *n.* the city
89:12 *n.* and south, thou created
Ec. 1:6 wind turneth about to *n.*
    11:3 if the tree fall toward the *n.*
Is. 14:13 I will sit in sides of *n.*
43:6 I will say to the *n.* G. up
Jer. 1:13 pot's face toward the *n.*
    14 out of the *n.* an evil break
    forth, 4:6 ; 46:20
15 families of kingdoms of *n.*
3:11 proclaim th. words tow. *n.*
18 come together out of the *n.*
6:1 evil appeareth out of the *n.*
23:8 which led Is. out of *n.* 31:8
25:9 take all the families of *n.*
26 the kings of *n.* far and near
46:6 they shall fall toward *n.*
10 L. hath a sacrifice in the *n.*
24 delivered to people of the *n.*
47:2 waters rise up out of the *n.*
50:3 out of *n.* cometh a nation
Ezek. 1:4 whirlw. came out of *n.*
8:5 I lifted mine eyes toward *n.*
20:47 all faces from south to *n.*
21:4 all flesh from south to *n.*
32:30 princes of *n.* all of
40:44 prospect toward the *n.* 46
41:11 one door toward *n.* 42:4
42:1 and building toward *n.*
    4 doors *n.* 11 chambers *n.* 13
46:19 holy chamb. looked to *n.*
48:10 holy oblation toward *n.*
Dan. 11:6 come to king of the *n.*
8 more years than king of *n.*
    11 fight wi. the king of the *n.*
13 the king of *n.* shall return
15 k. of the *n.* cast up a m. 40
44 tidings of *n.* sh. trouble hi.
Zep. 2:13 stretch hand ag. *n.*
Zec. 6:6 black horses go into *n.*
    8 have quieted my spirit in *n.*
14:4 mount. sh. remove tow. *n.*
Rev. 21:13 on *n.* were three gates

NORTH border.
Num. 34:7 this sh. be your *n. b.* 9

From the NORTH.
Ps. 107:3 gathered *from the n.*
    and the south, *Is.* 49:12 ; *Jer.*
    16:15 ; 23:8
Is. 14:31 come *f. t. n.* a smoke
41:25 I raised up one *from t. n.*
Jer. 4:6 I will bring evil *f. the n.*
    6:22 ; 10:22 ; 50:9, 41 ; 51:48
Ezek. 26:7 king of kings *f. t. n.*
39:2 will cause th. to come *f. n.*
Amos 8:12 wander *f. t. n.* to east
Zec. 2:6 flee *f.* the land of *t. n.*
Luke 13:29 come *f. t. n.* sit down

NORTH quarter.
Jos. 15:5 Judah's border in *n. q.*

NORTH side.

Ex. 26:20 tabernacle on *n. s.*
  35 thou shalt put table on *n. s.*
Num. 2:25 camp of Dan on *n. s.*
Jud. 21:19 feast *n. s.* Beth-el
2 *K.* 16:14 brazen altar on *n. s.*
Ezek. 42:17 he measured the *n. s.*
  48:30 goings out of city on *n. s.*

NORTHERN.

Jer. 15:12 break *n.* iron, and ste.
Joel 2:20 I will remove *n.* army

NORTHWARD.

Gen. 13:14 look *n.* Deut. 3:27
Ex. 40:22 tabernacle *n.* without
Lev. 1:11 on side of altar *n.*
Deut. 2:3 ye mount. turn you *n.*
1 *Sam.* 14:5 front of one rock *n.*
1 *Chr.* 26:14 Zechar.'s lot ca. *n.*
  17 *n.* were four Levites a day

NOSE.

Lev. 21:18 a flat *n.* sh. not offer
2 *K.* 19:28 hook in thy *n. Is.* 37:29
Job 40:24 his *n.* pierceth through
  41:2 canst thou put hook in *n. ?*
Prov. 30:33 wringing of the *n.*
Cant. 7:4 thy *n.* is as tower of L.
  8 smell of thy *n.* like apples
Is. 65:5 th. are a smoke in my *n.*
Ezek. 8:17 put branch to their *n.*
  23:25 take away thy *n.* and ears

NOSES.

Ps. 115:6 *n.* have they, smell not
Ezek. 39:11 stop *n.* of passengers

NOSE-JEWELS.

Is. 3:21 L. take away their *n. j.*

NOSTRILS.

Gen. 2:7 G. breath. into m.'s *n.*
  7:22 in wh. *n.* was breath of life
Ex. 15:8 wi. blast of thy *n.* wat.
Num. 11:20 eat till it come out *n.*
2 *Sam.* 22:9 went a smoke out of
  his *n. Ps.* 18:8, 15
  16 blast of the breath of his *n.*
Job 4:9 breath of *n.* consumed
  27:3 Spirit of God is in my *n.*
  39:20 glory of his *n.* is terrible
  41:20 out of his *n.* goeth smoke
Is. 2:22 whose breath is in his *n.*
Lam. 4:20 brea. of *n.* was taken
Amos 4:10 sti. of camps unto *n.*

NOTABLE.

Dan. 8:5 the goat had a *n.* horn
  8 for it came up four *n.* ones
Mat. 27:16 had then *n.* prisoner
Acts 2:20 before *n.* day of L. co.
  4:16 *n.* miracle hath been done

NOTE, ED.

Is. 30:8 write it, *n.* in book
Dan. 10:21 *n.* in scripture of tru.
2 *Thes.* 3:14 *n.* that man

NOTE.

Rom. 16:7 are of *n.* am. apostles

NOTHING.

Gen. 11:6 *n.* will be restrained
  19:8 only unto these men do *n.*
Ex. 12:10 let *n.* of it remain
  16:18 had *n.* over, 2 *Cor.* 8:15
  22:3 have *n.* then he sh. be sold
Deut. 22:26 damsel thou sh. do *n.*
Jud. 14:6 had *n.* in his hand
2 *Sam.* 24:24 wh. doth cost me *n.*
1 *K.* 8:9 there was *n.* in the ark
  11:22 answered *n. Luke* 22:35
Job 6:18 they go to *n.* and perish
  21 for now ye are *n.* ye see
  8:9 of yesterday, and know *n.*
  24:25 make speech *n.* worth
  26:7 hangeth the earth upon *n.*
  34:9 it profiteth-a man *n.*
Ps. 17:3 tried me and sh. find *n.*
  39:5 mine age is as *n.* bef. thee
  49:17 he shall carry *n.* away
  119:165 and *n.* sh. offend them
Prov. 9:13 and knoweth *n.*
  13:4 desir. and hath *n.* 20:4

---

7 mak. himself rich, yet ha. *n.*
  22:27 if thou hast *n.* to pay
Ec. 3:14 *n.* can be put to it
  5:15 he sh. take *n.* of his labor
  6:2 he wanteth *n.* for his soul
  7:14 should find *n.* after him
Is. 34:12 her princes shall be *n.*
  40:17 nations bef. him are as *n.*
  are to him less than *n.* 41:29
  23 bring. princes to *n.* 41:11, 12
Jer. 10:24 lest th. bring me to *n.*
  38:14 ask a thing, hide *n.* fr. me
  39:10 left of poor which had *n.*
  50:26 let *n.* of her be left
Lam. 1:12 is it *n.* to you ?
Ezek. 13:3 prop. that ha. seen *n.*
Dan. 4:35 inhabit. of earth as *n.*
Amos 3:4 lion cry if taken *n.*
  5 taken up snare, and taken *n.*
  7 surely Lord God will do *n.*
Hag. 2:3 in comp. of it as *n. ?*
Mat. 17:20 *n.* shall be impossible
  to you, *Luke* 1:37
  26:62 answerest thou *n. ?*
  27:12 he answer. *n. Mark* 14:60,
  61 ; 15:3, 4, 5
  19 ha. *n.* to do with just man
Mark 5:26 and was *n.* bettered
  9:29 forth by *n.* but by prayer
Luke 5:5 have toiled all night
  and taken *n. John* 21:3
  7:42 they had *n.* to pay
  10:19 *n.* sh. by any means hurt
Luke 11:6 I ha. *n.* to set bef. him
  23:41 this man hath done *n.*
John 3:27 man can receive *n.*
  5:19 S. can do *n.* of himself, **30**
  6:12 gather, that *n.* be lost
  39 given me, I should lose *n.*
  63 the flesh profiteth *n.*
  7:26 they say *n.* 8:28 I do *n.*
  9:33 could do *n.* 11:49 know *n.*
  12:19 perc. how ye prevail *n. ?*
  14:30 prince of world hath *n.*
  15:5 without me ye can do *n.*
  16:23 that day ye sh. ask me *n.*
  24 ye asked *n.* in my name
  18:20 in secret have I said *n.*
Acts 10:20 doubting *n.* 11:12
  19:36 quiet, and do *n.* rashly
  20:20 kept back *n.* profitable
  23:14 eat *n.* until we ha. slain P.
  27:33 fasting, having taken *n.*
1 *Cor.* 1:19 bring to *n.* understa.
  4:4 I know *n.* by myself
  5 judge *n.* before the time
  8:2 knoweth *n.* yet as he ought
  9:16 I have *n.* to glory of
  13:2 charity, am *n.* 2 *Cor.* 12:11
  3 not charity, it profit. me *n.*
2 *Cor.* 6:10 having *n.* yet posses.
  13:8 can do *n.* against the truth
Gal. 5:2 Ch. shall profit you *n.*
Phil. 2:3 let *n.* be done thro' str.
1 *Tim.* 4:4 good, *n.* to be refused
  5:21 doing *n.* by partiality
  6:4 he is proud, knowing *n.*
  7 we brought *n.* carry *n.* out
Tit. 3:13 that *n.* be wanting
Phile. 14 thy mind wou. I do *n.*
Heb. 2:8 left *n.* that is not put
  7:19 for the law made *n.* perfect
Jam. 1:4 and entire, wanting *n.*
  6 him ask in faith, *n.* wavering
3 *John* 7 taking *n.* of the Gentil.

For NOTHING.

Ex. 21:2 seventh go free *for n.*
Luke 6:35 lend, hoping *for n.* ag.
Phil. 4:6 be careful *for n.* but

In NOTHING.

Acts 17:21 A. spent time *in n.*
2 *Cor.* 12:11 *in n.* am I behind
Phil. 1:20 *in n.* I shall be asha.
  28 *in n.* terrified by adversari.

Is NOTHING.

Num. 11:6 *is n.* besides manna
Jud. 7:14 *is n.* else save sword

---

1 *Sam.* 27:1 there *is n.* bet. than
1 *K.* 18:43 and said, There *is n.*
2 *K.* 20:15 there *is n.* among my
  treasure, *Is.* 39:4
2 *Chr.* 14:11 *is n.* with th. to help
Neh. 2:2 *is n.* else but sorrow
Est. 6:3 th. *is n.* done for him
Ps. 19:6 th. *is n.* fr. heat thereof
Prov. 8:8 there *is n.* froward or
Ec. 2:24 *is n.* bet. for man, 3:22
  5:14 and there *is n.* in his hand
Jer. 32:17 *is n.* too hard for thee
Mat. 10:26 *is n.* that sh. not be
  revea. *Mark* 4:22 ; *Luke* 12:2
  23:16 swear by temple, it *is n.*
  18 shall swear by altar, it *is n.*
Mark 7:15 th. *is n.* from without
John 8:54 my honor *n.*
Rom. 14:14 there *is n.* unclean
1 *Cor.* 7:19 circumcision *is n.*
  8:4 an idol *is n.* in the world
Gal. 6:3 *is n.* he deceiv. himself
Tit. 1:15 that are defiled *is n.*

Of NOTHING.

Is. 41:24 behold, ye are *of n.*
1 *Thes.* 4:12 may have lack *of n.*
Rev. 3:17 increa. have need *of n.*

NOTWITHSTANDING.

Luke 10:11 *n.* be sure of this
  20 *n.* in this rejoice not
1 *Tim.* 2:15 *n.* shall be saved

NOUGHT. See NAUGHT.

NOURISH.

Gen. 45:11 will I *n.* thee, 50:21
Is. 7:21 man sh. *n.* young cow
  23:4 nor do I *n.* up young men
  44:14 an ash, the rain doth *n.* it

NOURISHED.

Gen. 47:12 Joseph *n.* his father
2 *Sam.* 12:3 lamb he bought *n.*
Is. 1:2 *n.* and brought up child.
Ezek. 19:2 she *n.* her whelps
Acts 7:20 *n.* in his father's house
  21 Pharaoh's daughter *n.* him
  12:20 *n.* by the king's country
1 *Tim.* 4:6 *n.* up in words of fai.
Jam. 5:5 have *n.* your hearts as
Rev. 12:14 *n.* for a time, times

NOURISHER, MENT.

Ruth 4:15 shall be *n.* of old age
Col. 2:19 and bands having *n.*

NOURISHETH, ING.

Dan. 1:5 so *n.* them three years
Eph. 5:29 but *n.* his flesh.

NOVICE.

1 *Tim.* 3:6 not *n.* lest lifted

NOWADAYS.

1 *Sam.* 25:10 many servants *n.*

NUMBER, Substantive.

Gen. 34:30 I being few in *n.*
  41:49 for it was without *n.*
Ex. 12:4 according to *n.* of souls
  16:16 according to *n.* of pers.
  23:26 *n.* of thy days I will fulfil
Lev. 25:15 *n.* of years after jubil.
  n. of years of fruit, 16, 50
  26:22 shall make you few in *n.*
Num. 1:2 *n.* of names, 18, 22
  3:22 *n.* of males a mo. old, 28–43
  48 odd *n.* to be redeemed
  14:29 *n.* from twenty years old
  15:12 according to *n.* prep. do to
  cv. one according to their *n.*
  23:10 who can count *n.* of Isr. ?
  31:36 half of portion was in *n.*
Deut. 4:27 *n.* am. heathen, 28:62
  7:7 more in *n.* than any people
  25:2 to be beaten by a certa. *n.*
  32:8 according to the *n.* of Isra.
Jos. 4:5 a stone according to *n.* 8
Jud. 6:5 camels without *n.* 7:12
  7:6 *n.* that lapped were 300 men
1 *Sam.* 6:4 *n.* of lords of Philist.
  18 *n.* of cities of the Philistin.

2 Sam. 2:15 and went over by *n.*
24:2 may know *n.* of the peo.
9 gave up sum of *n.* of people
1 *K.* 18:31 12 stones accord. to *n.*
1 *Chr.* 7:2 *n.* was in days of Dav.
  9 *n.* of th. after genealogy, 40
11:11 *n.* of mighty men D. had
22:16 gold and silver th. is no *n.*
23:3 their *n.* by their polls
25:7 the *n.* that were instruct.
27:23 David took not *n.* of them
2 Chr. 12:3 people were with. *n.*
26:12 *n.* of chief of the fathers
30:24 *n.* of priests sanctified th.
Ezr. 1:9 this is *n.* of the vessels
  2:2 the *n.* of the people of Isra.
3:4 daily burnt-offerings by *n.*
6:17 according to th. *n.* of trib.
8:34 by *n.* and by weight ev. o.
Job 1:5 according to *n.* of them
3:6 not come into *n.* of months
5:9 things without *n.* 9:10
14:5 *n.* of months are with thee
15:20 *n.* of years hid. to oppres.
25:3 is th. any *n.* of his armies?
31:37 dec. to him *n.* of my steps
34:24 mighty men without *n.*
36:26 *n.* of his years he search.
38:21 the *n.* of thy days is great
Ps. 105:12 but a few men in *n.*
  34 caterpillars, and without *n.*
139:18 more in *n.* than the sand
147:4 he telleth *n.* of the stars
Cant. 6:8 and virgins without *n.*
Is. 21:17 residue of *n.* of archers
40:26 bring. out their host by *n.*
65:11 drink-offering to that *n.*
Jer. 2:28 *n.* of cities are thy gods
  32 forgotten me days with. *n.*
11:13 accord. to *n.* of thy cities
44:28 small *n.* that escape sword
Ezek. 5:3 shalt take a few in *n.*
Dan. 9:2 I understood *n.* of years
Hos. 1:10 *n.* of Israel, *Rom.* 9:27
Joel 1:6 nation come up with. *n.*
Nah. 3:3 there is great *n.* of car.
Luke 22:3 Judas, being of the *n.*
John 6:10 sat, in *n.* 5,000, *Acts* 4:4
Acts 1:15 *n.* of names were 120
  5:36 to The. a *n.* of men joined
6:1 *n.* of discip. was multipl. 7
11:21 great *n.* bel. and turned
16:5 churches were incre. in *n.*
2 Cor. 10:12 not make ours. of *n.*
1 *Tim.* 5:9 let not wid. be in *n.*
Rev. 5:11 *n.* was 10,000 ti. 10,000
7:4 I heard the *n.* of them which

9:16 *n.* the army of horsemen
13:17 *n.* of name; 18 count *n.*
18 *n.* of a man, it is 666
15:2 had victory over *n.* of bea.
20:8 *n.* of Gog is as sand of sea

NUMBER, Verb.

Gen. 13:16 if a man can *n.* dust
15:5 stars, if able to *n.* them
Lev. 15:13 *n.* 7 days for cleansing
  28 shall *n.* to herself 7 days
23:16 after 7th sab. sh. *n.* 50 days
25:8 sh. *n.* 7 sabbaths of years
Num. 1:3 Aaron shall *n.* them
  49 thou shalt not *n.* tribe of L.
3:40 *n.* all first-born males of I.
4:23 until fifty years old *n.* th. 30
Deut. 16:9 seven weeks shalt
  thou *n.* begin to *n.*
1 *Sam.* 14:17 *n.* see who is gone
2 Sam. 24:1 go *n.* Is. and Judah
  2 go *n.* people, 4; 1 *Chr.* 21:2
1 *K.* 20:25 *n.* thee an army like
1 *Chr.* 21:1 provok. Dav. to *n.* I.
27:24 J. began to *n.* finished *n.*
Job 38:37 who can *n.* the clouds?
39:2 canst thou *n.* the months?
Ps. 90:12 teach us to *n.* our days
Is. 65:12 will I *n.* you to the sw.
Rev. 7:9 multi. no man could *n.*

NUMBERED.

Gen. 13:16 shall thy seed be *n.*
16:10 not be *n.* for multi. 32:12
Ex. 38:25 *n.* of congregation, 26
Num. 1:21 those th. were *n.* of
  them, 23, 44, 46; 2:4, 13, 15,
  19, 21, 23, 26, 28, 30
  47 Levites were not *n.* 2:33
2:9 were *n.* in camp of Judah
16 were *n.* in camp of Reuben
24 *n.* of Ephraim; 31 *n.* of Dan
3:16 and Moses *n.* them, 42
39 *n.* of Levites were 22,000
4:34 *n.* sons of Kohathites, 37
38 were *n.* of Gershonites, 41
42 *n. n.* of sons of Merari, 45
7:2 princes over th. that we *n.*
14:29 whisper. all that were *n.*
26:51 these were *n.* of chil. of I.
Jos. 8:10 Joshua *n.* the people
1 *Sam.* 15:4 *n.* peo. in Telaim
2 Sam. 18:1 David *n.* the people
24:10 heart sm. him after he *n.*
1 *K.* 3:8 people that cannot be *n.*
8:5 sheep and oxen that could
  not be *n.* 2 *Chr.* 5:6
20:15 *n.* princes of provinces

O

27 Is. were *n.* like two flocks
2 *K.* 3:6 Jehoram *n.* all Israel
1 *Chr.* 21:17 com. people to be *n.*
23:3 Lev. were *n.* fr. 30 years, 27
2 *Chr.* 2:17 Solo. *n.* all strangers
25:5 *n.* them from 20 years old
Ezr. 1:8 Cyrus *n.* the vessels to
Ps. 40:5 more than can be *n.*
Ec. 1:15 wanting cannot be *n.*
Is. 22:10 ye have *n.* the houses
53:12 *n.* with trans. *Mark* 15:28
Jer. 33:22 host of hea. can. be *n.*
Dan. 5:26 God hath *n.* thy king.
Hos. 1:10 sand of sea, can. be *n.*
Mat. 10:30 hairs of your head are
  all *n. Luke* 12:7
Acts 1:17 for he was *n.* with us
  26 Matthias *n.* wi. 11 apostles

NUMBEREST.

Ex. 30:12 a ransom, wh. thou *n.*
  that be no plague wh. *n.* them
Job 14:16 now thou *n.* my steps

NUMBERING.

Gen. 41:49 corn until he left *n.*
2 *Chr.* 2:17 after *n.* wherewith D.

NUMBERS.

1 *Chr.* 12:23 these are *n.* of bands
2 *Chr.* 17:14 these are *n.* of them
Ps. 71:15 I know not *n.* thereof

NURSE.

Gen. 24:59 sent away Re. and *n.*
35:8 Deborah, Rebek.'s *n.* died
Ex. 2:7 sh. I call to thee a *n.?*
Ruth 4:16 Naomi became *n.*
2 *Sam.* 4:4 *n.* took him up
2 *K.* 11:2 they hid him and his *n.*
  2 *Chr.* 22:11
1 *Thes.* 2:7 as *n.* cherish. her ch.

NURSE, ED.

Ex. 2:7 she may *n.* the child
  9 take this child and *n.* it, and
  the wo. took the ch. and *n.*
Is. 60:4 dau. sh. be *n.* at thy side

NURSING.

Num. 11:12 carry th. as *n.* father
Is. 49:23 kings be *n.* fathers, and
  queens thy *n.* mothers

NURTURE.

Eph. 6:4 bring th. up in *n.* of L.

NUTS.

Gen. 43:11 pres. *n.* and almonds
Cant. 6:11 down into gard. of *n.*

NYMPHAS. *Col.* 4:15

OAK.

Gen. 35:4 Jacob hid gods und. *o.*
  8 nurse was buried und. an *o.*
Jos. 24:26 set it up under an *o.*
Jud. 6:11 angel of L. sat und. *o.*
2 *Sam.* 18:9 went under an *o.*
  10 Absalom hanged in an *o.*
  14 was alive in midst of the *o.*
1 *K.* 13:14 found man of G. un. *o.*
1 *Chr.* 10:12 buried bones un. *o.*
Is. 1:30 be as *o.* whose leaf. fad.
6:13 as teil-tree, or *o.* whose
44:14 cyp. and *o.* to make a god
Ezek. 6:13 idols under every *o.*

OAKS.

Is. 1:29 shall be asham. of the *o.*
2:13 day of Lord on all the *o.*
Ezek. 27:6 of *o.* they made oars
Hos. 4:13 burn incense under *o.*
Amos 2:9 Amorite strong as *o.*
Zec. 11:2 O ye *o.* of Bashan

OAR, S.

Is. 33:21 sh. go no galley with *o.*
Ezek. 27:6 of oaks of Ba. made *o.*

29 all that handle *o.* shall cry

OATH.

Gen. 24:8 be clear from my *o.* 41
26:3 I will perform the *o.* which
  I sware to Abraham, *Deut.*
  7:8; *Ps.* 105:9; *Jer.* 11:5
  28 let there be an *o.* betw. us
50:25 J. took *o.* of childr. of Is.
Ex. 22:11 *o.* of Lord be betw. us
Lev. 5:4 pronounce with an *o.*
Num. 5:19 priest char. her by *o.*
  21 L. make thee an *o.* am. peo.
30:2 if a man swear an *o.* 10
  13 ev. binding *o.* to afflict soul
Deut. 29:12 his *o.* wh. L. maketh
  14 you only do I make this *o.*
Jos. 2:17 blameless of thine *o.*
9:20 wrath be on us beca. of *o.*
Jud. 21:5 Israel made a great *o.*
1 *Sam.* 14:26 people feared the *o.*
  27 S. charged them with *o.* 28
2 *Sam.* 21:7 spared M. bec. of *o.*
1 *K.* 2:43 why hast not kept *o.?*
8:31 *o.* be laid on him, *o.* come
  before thine alt. 2 *Chr.* 6:22

18:10 he took an *o.* of kingdom
2 *K.* 11:4 Jehoiada took *o.*
1 *Chr.* 16:16 mindful of *o.* to Isa.
2 *Chr.* 15:15 Judah rejoiced at *o.*
Neh. 5:12 Neh. took *o.* of priests
10:29 an *o.* to walk in God's law
Ec. 8:2 in regard of *o.* of God
9:2 as he that feareth an *o.*
Ezek. 16:59 despised *o.* 17:18, 19
17:13 hath taken an *o.* of him
  16 king, whose *o.* he despised
Dan. 9:11 and *o.* written in law
Zec. 8:17 love no false *o.*
Mat. 14:7 promised with *o.*
  9 for the *o.'s* sake, *Mark* 6:26
26:72 deni. with *o.* I do not kn.
Luke 1:73 the *o.* which he sware
Acts 2:30 God hath swo. with *o.*
23:21 bound themselves with *o.*
Heb. 6:16 an *o.* for confirmation
  17 God confirmed it by an *o.*
7:20 as not without an *o.* 21
  28 *o.* which was since the law
Jam. 5:12 sw. not by any oth. *o.*

OATHS.

Ezek. 21:23 that have sworn *o.*
Hab. 3:9 naked, according to *o.*
Mat. 5:33 perform to L. thine *o.*

OBADIAH.

1 K. 18:3 Ahab called O. 4, 7, 16
2 Chr. 17:7 sent to O. 34:12
Ezr. 8:9 O. son of Jeh. went up
Neh. 10:5 O. seal. 12:25 O. was
Ob. 1 vision of O. thus saith

OBED.

Ruth 4:17 called his name O.
21 Boaz begat O. 1 *Chr.* 2:12 ;
  Mat. 1:5
1 Chr. 11:47 O. one of D.'s val. m.
2 Chr. 23:1 son of O. into coven.
Luke 3:32 Jes. wh. was son of O.

OBED-EDOM.

2 Sam. 6:10 carried the ark into
  the house of O. 11, 12 ; 1 *Chr.*
  13:13, 14 ; 15:25
1 Chr. 15:18 O. a porter, 21, 24

OBEDIENCE.

Rom. 1:5 o. to faith among all
5:19 by *o.* of one many be made
6:16 or of *o.* unto righteousness
16:19 your *o.* is come abroad
26 made known for *o.* to faith
1 Cor. 14:34 women to be und. *o.*
2 Cor. 7:15 remembereth *o.* of all
10:5 ev. thought to *o.* of Christ
6 disobed. when *o.* is fulfilled
Phile. 21 confidence in thy *o.*
Heb. 5:8 learned *o.* by things suf.
1 Pet. 1:2 sanctifica. of Sp. to *o.*

OBEDIENT.

Ex. 24:7 Lord hath said, Be *o.*
Num. 27:30 that Israel may be *o.*
Deut. 4:30 be *o.* to his voice
Deut. 8:20 bec. ye wo. not be *o.*
2 Sam. 22:45 strangers shall be *o.*
Prov. 25:12 reprover on *o.* ear
Is. 1:19 if *o.* ye shall eat good
42:24 nei. were th. *o.* to his law
Acts 6:7 priests were *o.* to faith
Rom. 15:18 make Ge. *o.* by word
2 Cor. 2:9 know whether ye be *o.*
Eph. 6:5 servants be *o.* *Tit.* 2:9
Phil. 2:8 Ch. became *o.* to death
Tit. 2:5 wives, be *o.* to husbands
1 Pet. 1:14 be as *o.* children

OBEY.

Gen. 27:8 son, *o.* my voice, 13, 43
Ex. 5:2 who is Lord that I *o.*
19:5 now if ye will *o.* my voice
23:21 *o.* his voice ; 22 indeed *o.*
Deut. 11:27 a blessing if ye *o.* L.
13:4 *o.* his voice, 27:10 ; 30:2, 8 ;
  1 *Sam.* 12:14
30:20 thou mayest *o.* his voice
Jos. 24:24 L.'s voice will we *o.*
1 *Sam.* 8:19 peo. refused to *o.* S.
15:22 to *o.* is bet. than sacrifice
Neh. 9:17 and refused to *o.*
Job 36:11 if they *o.* and serve
Ps. 18:44 as th. hear, they sh. *o.*
Prov. 30:17 despis. to *o.* mother
Is. 11:14 childr. of Am. *o.* them
Jer. 7:23 *o.* my voice, 11:4, 7
26:13 amend your ways, *o.* voice
  of the Lord your God, 38:20 ;
  Zec. 6:15
35:14 Rechab. *o.* their father's
42:6 we will *o.* the voice of the
  L. our God, that it may be
  well with us wh. we *o.* the L.
Dan. 7:27 shall serve and *o.* him
Mat. 8:27 winds and sea *o.* him. ?
  Mark 4:41 ; *Luke* 8:25
Mark 1:27 unclean spirits *o.* him
Luke 17:6 plucked up, it shall *o.*
Acts 5:29 *o.* G. rather than men
32 God hath given to them *o.*
Rom. 2:8 them that *o.* unright.
6:12 that ye sho. *o.* it in lusts

16 servants to *o.* his servants
ye are to whom ye *o.*
Eph. 6:1 *o.* parents. *Col.* 3:20
Col. 3:22 servants *o.* masters
Tit. 3:1 put them in mind to *o.*
Heb. 5:9 salvation to all that *o.*
13:17 *o.* them that have the rule
Jam. 3:3 put bits that th. may *o.*

Not OBEY, OBEY net.

Deut. 11:28 curse, if ye will **not**
  o. 28:62 ; 1 *Sam.* 12:12 ; *Job*
  36:12 ; *Jer.* 12:17 ; 18:10
21:18 *not o.* voice of his father
1 *Sam.* 15:19 wh. didst thou *n. o.?*
Jer. 42:13 we will *not o.* the L.
Dan. 9:11 might *n. o.* thy voice
Acts 7:39 our fathers would *n. o.*
Rom. 2:8 and do *not o.* the truth
Gal. 3:1 who bewitched you, th.
  you should *not o. ?* 5:7
2 *Thes.* 1:8 ven. on th. that *o. n.*
3:14 if any man *o. n.* our word
1 Pet. 3:1 if any man *o. not* word
4:17 them that *o. not* gospel ?

OBEYED.

Gen. 22:18 bec. thou hast *o.* 26:5
28:7 Ja. *o.* his father and moth.
Jos. 22:2 have *o.* my voice
1 *Sam.* 15:20 I have *o.* voice of L.
24 I feared peo. and *o.* th. voice
28:21 handmaid *o.* thy voice
1 *Chr.* 29:23 Israel *o.* Solomon
2 *Chr.* 11:4 they *o.* words of L.
Jer. 34:10 they *o.* and let th. go
35:8 we *o.* voice of Jonadab, 10
18 *o.* the comm. of your father
Dan. 9:10 nei. have we *o.* the L.
Hag. 1:12 people *o.* voice of L.
Acts 5:36 many as *o.* Theud. 37
Rom. 6:17 *o.* from heart th. doc.
Phil. 2:12 ye *o.* not in my pres.
Heb. 11:8 by faith Abraham *o.*
1 Pet. 3:6 Sarah *o.* Abraham

Not OBEYED.

Jos. 5:6 consumed, they *o. n.*
Jud. 2:2 *n. o.* my voice, 6:10
1 *K.* 20:36 hast *n. o.* voice of L.
2 *K.* 18:12 they *o. not* voice of L.
Prov. 5:13 *not o.* voice of teach.
Jer. 3:13 ye have *n. o.* my voice,
  25 ; 42:21 ; 43:4, 7 ; 44:23
9:13 *n. o.* my voice, 11:8 ; 17:23 ;
  32:23 ; 40:3 ; *Dan.* 9:10, 14
Zep. 3:2 she *o. not* the voice
Rom. 10:16 have *n.* all *o.* gospel

OBEYEDST, ETH.

1 *Sam.* 28:18 *o.* not voice of L.
Is. 50:10 who *o.* voice of serv. ?
Jer. 7:28 a nation that *o.* not
  the Lord
Jer. 11:3 cur. be man that *o.* not
22:21 that thou *o.* not my voice

OBEYING.

Jud. 2:17 fa. *o.* they did not so
1 *Sam.* 15:22 as in *o.* voice of L.
1 Pet. 1:22 puri. souls in *o.* truth

OBEISANCE.

Gen. 37:7 your sheaves made *o.*
9 sun, moon, 11 stars made *o.*
43:28 they made *o.* to Joseph
Ex. 18:7 Moses did *o.* to father
2 *Sam.* 1:2 Amalek. did *o.* to D.
14:4 woman of Tekoah did *o.*
15:5 when any man ca. to do *o.*
1 *K.* 1:16 Bath-sheba did *o.* to D.
2 *Chr.* 24:17 princes of J. made *o.*

OBJECT.

Acts 24:19 *o.* if th. had aught ag.

OBLATION.

Lev. 2:4 *o.* of a meat-off. 5, 7, 13
12 as for *o.* of first-fruits offer
3:1 if his *o.* be a sacri. of peace
22:18 offer his *o.* for his vows
Num. 18:9 *o.* of theirs be holy
31:50 we have bro. an *o.* for L.

Is. 19:21 Egypt. sh. do *o.* to L.
40:20 impoverish, he hath no *o.*
66:3 offereth *o.* as swine's flesh
Jer. 14:12 when they offer an *o.*
Ezek. 44:30 ev. *o.* be priest's
45:1 when ye divide land, offer
  13 *o.* ye shall offer, 48:9, 20, 21
  16 give this *o.* for prince in Is.
Dan. 2:46 sho. offer an *o.* to Da.
9:21 time of *o.* 27 *o.* to cease

OBLATIONS.

Lev. 7:38 com. Israel to offer *o.*
2 *Chr.* 31:14 distribute *o.* of Lord
Is. 1:13 bring no more vain *o*
Ezek. 20:40 require first-fru. of *o.*

OBSCURE.

Prov. 20:20 lamp put in *o.* dark.

OBSCURITY.

Is. 29:18 blind see out of *o.*
58:10 shall thy light rise in *o.*
59:9 wait for light, but beho. *o.*

OBSERVATION.

Luke 17:20 king. of G. not wi. *o.*

OBSERVE.

Ex. 12:17 ye shall *o.* feast of unleav. bread, 24 ; *Deut.* 16:1
31:16 *o.* sabbath ; 34:22 *o.* feast
34:11 *o.* that wh. I comm. thee
  this day, *Deut.* 12:28 ; 24:8
Lev. 19:26 nor enchant. *o.* times
37 ye sh. *o.* all my statutes,
  2 *Chr.* 7:17 ; *Neh.* 1:5 ; *Ps.*
  105:45 ; *Ezek.* 37:24
Num. 28:2 sacrifice shall ye *o.*
Deut. 16:13 *o.* feast of tabernac.
1 *K.* 20:33 men did diligently *o.*
Ps. 107:43 will *o.* these things
119:34 *o.* with my whole heart
Prov. 23:26 let thine eyes *o.* ways
Jer. 8:7 the crane and swallow *o.*
Ezek. 20:18 neither *o.* judgments
Hos. 13:7 as a leop. will I *o.* th.
Jon. 2:8 that *o.* lying vanities
Mat. 28:20 teaching them to *o.*
Acts 16:21 custo. not lawful to *o.*
21:25 Gentiles *o.* no such thing
Gal. 4:10 ye *o.* days, and months
1 *Tim.* 5:21 then *o.* these things

See DO.

OBSERVED.

Gen. 37:11 his father *o.* saying
Ex. 12:42 it is a night to be *o.*
Num. 15:22 not *o.* commandm.
Deut. 33:9 for Levi *o.* thy word
2 *Sam.* 11:16 when J. *o.* the city
2 *K.* 21:6 Manasseh *o.* the times,
  2 Chr. 33:6
Hos. 14:8 I heard him, *o.* nim
Mark 6:20 He. feared and *o.* him
10:20 these I *o.* from my youth

OBSERVER, S.

Deut. 18:10 th. shall not be an *o.*
14 these nations hearken. to *o.*

OBSERVEST, ETH.

Ec. 11:4 he that *o.* the wind
Is. 42:20 seeing things, *o.* not

OBSTINATE.

Deut. 2:30 L. G. made his hea. *o.*
Is. 48:4 I knew that thou art *o.*

OBTAIN.

Gen. 16:2 may be I may *o.* chil.
Prov. 8:35 *o.* favor of the Lord
Is. 35:10 they shall *o.* joy, 51:11
Dan. 11:21 shall *o.* the kingdom
Luke 20:35 worthy to *o.* th. world
Rom. 11:31 thro' mercy *o.* mercy
1 *Cor.* 9:24 so run, that ye may *o.*
1 *Cor.* 9:25 do it to *o.* corrupt. cro.
1 *Thes.* 5:9 to *o.* salvation by L.
2 *Tim.* 2:10 *o.* salvation in C. J.
Heb. 4:16 that we may *o.* mercy
11:35 might *o.* bet. resurrection
Jam. 4:2 ye kill and cannot *o.*

OBTAINED.

Neh. 13:6 I *o*. leave of the king
Est. 2:9 Esth. *o*. kindn. 17 she *o*.
Hos. 2:23 that had not *o*. mercy
Acts 1:17 had *o*. part of ministry
22:28 great sum *o*. I freedom
26:22 having *o*. the help of God
27:13 suppos. they *o*. th. purpo.
Rom. 11:7 Is. not *o*. what he seek.
    for, but the elect. hath *o*. it
30 *o*. mercy thro' their unbelief
1 *Cor.* 7:25 one that hath *o*. mer.
Eph. 1:11 we have *o*. inheritance
1 *Tim.* 1:13 I *o*. mercy, bec. ig. 16
Heb. 1:4 *o*. more excellent name
6:15 endured, he *o*. the promis.
8:6 he *o*. a more excel. ministry
9:12 hav. *o*. eternal redemption
11:2 the elders *o*. good report, 39
4 Abel *o*. witness he was righ.
33 *o*. promises, stop. mouths
1 *Pet.* 2:10 *o*. mercy, now have *o*.
2 *Pet.* 1:1 *o*. like precious faith

See FAVOR.

OBTAINING.

2 *Thes.* 2:14 *o*. the glory of our L.

OCCASION.

Gen. 43:18 he may seek *o*. ag. us
Jud. 9:33 as find *o*. 1 *Sam.* 10:7
14:4 Samson sought *o*. ag. Phil.
2 *Sam.* 12:14 given *o*. to enemies
Ezr. 7:20 thou shalt have *o*.
Jer. 2:24 in her *o*. who can turn?
Ezek. 18:3 not have *o*. any more
Dan. 6:4 sought to find *o*. could
    find none *o*.
Rom. 7:8 *o*. by commandment, 11
14:13 put not *o*. to fall in way
2 *Cor.* 5:12 we give you *o*. to glo.
8:8 I speak by *o*. of forwardness
11:12 that I may cut off *o*. them
    which desire *o*.
Gal. 5:13 use not liberty for an *o*.
1 *Tim.* 5:14 younger give none *o*.
1 *John* 2:10 none *o*. of stumbling

OCCASIONED.

1 *Sam.* 22:22 have *o*. death of all

OCCASIONS.

Deut. 22:14 *o*. of speech aga. 17
Job 33:10 findeth *o*. against me

OCCUPATION.

Gen. 46:33 wh. *o*.? 47:3; *Jon* 1:8
Acts 18:3 by *o*. were tent-makers
19:25 workmen of like *o*.

OCCUPY.

Ezek. 27:9 marin. *o*. merchandise
Luke 19:13 servan. *o*. till I come

OCCUPIED, ETH.

Ex. 38:24 gold was *o*. for work
Jud. 16:11 ropes th. never we. *o*.
Ezek. 27:16 Syria *o*. 19 Javan *o*.
21 Arabia *o*. 22 Sh. *o*. in fairs
1 *Cor.* 14:16 *o*. room of unlearned
Heb. 13:9 profited th. that ha. *o*.

OCCUPIERS.

Ezek. 27:27 *o*. of merchandi. fall

OCCURRENT.

1 *K.* 5:4 adversary nor evil *o*.

ODD.

Num. 3:48 *o*. num. to be redeem.

ODED.

2 *Chr.* 15:1 on Azariah son of O.
28:9 prophet was th. called O.

ODIOUS.

1 *Chr.* 19:6 made themselv. *o*.
Prov. 30:23 for an *o*. woman

ODOR, S.

Lev. 26:31 not smell sav. of sw. *o*.
2 *Chr.* 16:14 in bed of sweet *o*.
Est. 2:12 oil of myrrh sweet *o*.
Jer. 34:5 sh. they burn *o*. for th.
Dan. 2:46 offer sweet *o*. to Daniel
John 12:3 filled with *o*. of ointm.

Phil. 4:18 an *o*. of a sweet smell
Rev. 5:8 golden vials full of *o*.
18:13 no man buyeth their *o*.

OFFENCE.

1 *Sam.* 25:31 this shall be no *o*.
Is. 8:14 *o*. to both houses of Is.
Hos. 5:15 they acknowl. their *o*.
Mat. 16:23 Sa. thou art *o*. to me
18:7 woe to man by wh. *o*. com.
Acts 24:16 a conscience void of *o*.
Rom. 5:15 not as *o*. so is free gift,
    for thro' *o*. of one m. dead. 18
17 by one man s *o*. death reig.
Rom. 5:20 that the *o*. might abo.
9:33 stumbling-stone, rock of *o*.
14:20 man who eateth with *o*.
1 *Cor.* 10:32 give no. *o*. 2 *Cor.* 6:3
2 *Cor.* 11:7 have I committed *o*.
Gal. 5:11 *o*. of cross ceased
Phil. 1:10 with. *o*. till day of Ch.
1 *Pet.* 2:8 *o*. to them wh. stumble

OFFENCES.

Ec. 10:4 yielding pacifi. great *o*.
Mat. 18:7 beca. of *o*. for it must
    needs be that *o*. *Luke* 17:1
Rom. 4:25 was deliver. for our *o*.
5:16 the free gift of many *o*.
16:17 mark them which cause *o*.

OFFEND.

Job 34:31 I will not *o*. any more
Ps. 73:15 I sho. *o*. ag. generation
119:165 nothing shall *o*. them
Jer. 2:3 that devour him shall *o*.
50:7 adversaries said, We *o*. not
Hab. 1:11 shall pass over and *o*.
Mat. 5:29 if thy right eye *o*. thee
    30 if thy right hand *o*. thee,
    18:8, 9; *Mark* 9:43, 45, 47
13:41 gather all things that *o*.
17:27 lest we should *o*. them
18:6 whoso *o*. one of these,
    Mark 9:42; *Luke* 17:2
John 6:61 said, Doth this *o*. you?
1 *Cor.* 8:13 brother *o*. lest he *o*.
Jam. 2:10 yet *o*. in one point
3:2 in many things we *o*. all

OFFENDED.

Gen. 20:9 ha. I *o*. thee? *Jer.* 37:18
40:1 butler and baker had *o*.
2 *K.* 18:14 have *o*. return fr. me
2 *Chr.* 28:13 have *o*. against L.
Prov. 18:19 a brother *o*. is harder
Ezek. 25:12 Edom hath greatly *o*.
Hos. 13:1 when Ephraim *o*. in B.
Mat. 11:6 blessed is he who shall
    not be *o*. *Luke* 7:23
13:21 when persecution aris. by
    and by he is *o*. *Mark* 4:17
57 were *o*. in him, *Mark* 6:3
15:12 Pharis. *o*. after they heard
24:10 then shall many be *o*.
26:31 *o*. becau. of me this night
    33 tho' all men shall be *o*. yet
    will I never be *o*. *Mark* 14:29
John 16:1 ye should not be *o*.
Acts 25:8 nor ag. Cesar ha. I *o*.
Rom. 14:21 whereby brother is *o*.
2 *Cor.* 11:29 is *o*. and I burn not?

OFFENDER, S.

1 *K.* 1:21 I and my son counted *o*.
Is. 29:21 man *o*. for a word
Acts 25:11 if I be an *o*. or have

OFFER.

Ex. 22:29 to *o*. the first-fruits
23:18 shalt not *o*. blood, 34:25
29:39 one lamb *o*. in morning,
    other at even, 41; *Nu.* 28:4,8
30:9 *o*. no strange inc. thereon
Lev. 1:3 *o*. male without blemish,
    3:6; 22:19, 20
2:13 with offerings thou shalt *o*.
3:1 if he *o*. peace-offering, *o*. it
    without blem. 6; 9:2; 19:5
12 goat he shall *o*. before Lord

5:8 *o*. for sin-offering first, 9:7
6:14 sons of A. *o*. before L. 22;
    14:19; 15:15, 30; *Num.* 6:11
7:3 *o*. of it all the fat thereof
12 *o*. it for a thanksgiv. 22:29
38 *o*. their oblations to the L.
17:7 no more *o*. sacri. to devils
9 to the door to *o*. it to Lord
19:6 eaten same day ye *o*. it
21:6 bread of their G. they do *o*.
21 hath blemish, not come too.
Num. 7:11 they *o*. their offerings
8:11 Aaron *o*. Levites, 13, 15
9:7 that we may not *o*.
15:7 *o*. th. part of a hin of wine
    19 shall *o*. a heave-offer. 18:24,
    26, 28, 29
16:40 no stranger come to *o*. in.
28:24 ye shall *o*. daily the meat
Deut. 12:14 L. sh. choose, there *o*.
18:3 priest's due fr. them th. *o*.
33:19 shall *o*. sacrifices of right-
    eousness. *Ps.* 4:5
Jud. 3:18 made an end to *o*. pre.
1 *Sam.* 1:21 went up to *o*. to L.
2:19 with her husb. to *o*. sacri.
28 him my priest, to *o*. on alt.
2 *Sam.* 24:12 *o*. thee three things,
    1 *Chr.* 21:10
1 *K.* 13:2 *o*. priests of high places
1 *Chr.* 29:14 to *o*. so willingly, 17
2 *Chr.* 24:14 made vessels to *o*.
Ezr. 6:10 *o*. sacrifices to God
Ps. 16:4 of blood will I not *o*.
Ps. 27:6 therefore I *o*. in tabern.
50:14 *o*. to God thanksgiving
51:19 then sh. they *o*. bullocks
66:15 will *o*. to thee burnt sacr.
72:10 kings of Sheba sh. *o*. gifts
116:17 *o*. sacrifice of thanksgiv.
Is. 57:7 wentest up to *o*. sacrifice
Jer. 11:12 gods to wh. th. *o*. inc.
Ezek. 20:31 when ye *o*. your gifts
44:7 when ye *o*. my bread
    15 they shall *o*. to me the fat
45:1 ye shall *o*. an oblation to
    the Lord, 13; 48:9
Dan. 2:46 *o*. an oblation to Dan.
Hos. 9:4 not *o*. wine-off. to Lord
Amos 4:5 *o*. sacrifice of thanksg.
Hag. 2:14 th. *o*. there is unclean
Mal. 1:7 ye *o*. polluted bread
    8 *o*. it now to thy governor
3:3 *o*. to the Lord an offering in
Mat. 5:24 then come and *o*. gift
8:4 *o*. gift Moses commanded,
    Mark 1:44; *Luke* 5:14
Luke 6:29 cheek, *o*. also other
11:12 will he *o*. him scorpion?
Heb. 5:1 *o*. gifts and sacrifices
    3 ought for hims. to *o*. for sins
7:27 needeth not to *o*. sacrifice
8:3 h.-priest ordained to *o*. this
    man ha. somewhat also to *o*.
9:25 he should *o*. himself often
13:15 by him let us *o*. sacrifice
1 *Pet.* 2:5 by J. C. to *o*. sacrifice
Rev. 8:3 should *o*. with prayers

See BURNT-OFFERINGS.

OFFERED.

Gen. 31:54 Ja. *o*. sacrifice, 46:1
Ex. 35:22 every man *o*. offering
Lev. 9:15 slew goat, *o*. it for sin
10:1 Nadab and Abi. *o*. strange
    fire, 16:1; *Num.* 3:4; 26:61
Num. 7:2 *o*. for the dedicat. 10
8:21 Aaron *o*. them as offering
22:40 Balak *o*. oxen and sheep,
    23:2, 4, 14, 30
Jud. 5:2 willingly *o*. themselv. 9
13:19 took a kid and *o*.
1 *Sam.* 1:4 time that Elkanah *o*.
2 *Sam.* 6:17 *o*. peace-offer. 24:25
1 *K.* 8:62 Solomon and Is. *o*. 63
12:32 Jeroboam *o*. in Beth-el, 33
22:43 peo. *o*. yet in high places

2 K. 3:20 meat-offering was *o.*
16:12 A. approached altar and *o.*
1 Chr. 29:9 that they *o.* willingly
2 Chr. 15:11 Asa *o.* to the Lord
17:16 Amaziah willingly *o.*
Ezr. 1:6 that was willingly *o.*
2:68 some of fathers *o.* freely
6:17 *o.* at dedic. of house of God
7:15 freely *o.* to the G. of Israel
10:19 they *o.* a ram of the flock
Neh. 11:2 willingly *o.* themselves
12:43 that day th. *o.* great sacri.
Is. 57:6 hast *o.* a meat-offering
66:3 as if he *o.* swine's blood
Jer. 32:29 have *o.* incense to Ba.
Ezek. 20:28 *o.* there th. sacrifices
Dan. 11:18 reproach *o.* to cease
Amos 5:25 have ye *o.* me sacri. ?
Jon. 1:16 and *o.* sacrifice to Lord
Mal. 1:11 inc. be *o.* to my name
Acts 8:18 Simon *o.* them money
15:29 meats *o.* to idols, 21:25
21:26 an offering should be *o.*
1 Cor. 8 1 things *o.* to idols, 4, 7, 10; 10:19, 28
Phil. 2:17 if I be *o.* on the service
2 Tim. 4:6 I am ready to be *o.*
Heb. 5:7 he had *o.* up prayers
7:27 when he *o.* up himself
9:7 blood, wh. he *o.* for himself
9 *o.* gifts; 14 *o.* himself to G.
28 C. *o.* to bear sins of many
11:4 by faith Abel *o.* to God
17 Ab. when tried, *o.* up Isaac
Jam. 2:21 A. justified when he *o.*

OFFERETH.

Ler. 6:26 priest that *o.* it for sin
7:18 imputed to him that *o.* it
21:8 he *o.* the bread of thy God
Ps. 50:23 *o.* praise glorifieth me
Is. 66:3 he that *o.* oblation as if

OFFERING, Substantive.

Gen. 4:3 Cain brought *o.* unto L.
4 L. had respect to Abel and *o.*
Ex. 25:2 bring me *o.* of ev. man
30:13 half shekel be *o.* of Lord
15 *o.* to Lord make atonement
Lev. 1:2 bring your *o.* of cattle
14 *o.* of fowls; 2:1 fine flour
2:11 no meat-*o.* made with leav.
3:2 lay his hand on head of *o.* 9
6:20 *o.* of Aaron and sons
7:16 if *o.* be vow, or volunt. *o.*
Num. 5:15 *o.* of jeal. *o.* of mem.
Num. 7:10 princes off. *o.* bef. alt.
8:11 offer Levites for an *o.* 21
9:13 *o.* of L. in appointed seas.
16:15 said, Respect not their *o.*
1 Sam. 2:29 wher. kick at mi. *o. ?*
3:14 shall not be purged with *o.*
26:19 if Lord have stirred thee
up ag. me, let him accept *o.*
1 K. 18:29 prophesied till *o.* of
evening sacrifice
1 Chr. 16:29 *o.* come, Ps. 96:8
Neh. 10:39 Is. sh. bring *o.* of corn
Is. 43:23 nor caus. th. serv. wi. *o.*
53:10 make his soul *o.* for sin
66:20 bring your breth. for an *o.*
Ezek. 20:28 provocat. of their *o.*
Zep. 3:10 daughter bring my *o.*
Mal. 1:10 nor accept *o.* at hand
13 bro. *o.* should I accept this ?
2:13 regardeth not *o.* any more
3:3 offer. to Lord an *o.* in right.
Rom. 15:16 *o.* of Gent. be accept.
Eph. 5:2 an *o.* to God for us
Heb. 10:5 *o.* thou wouldest not, 8
10 through *o.* of body of Jesus
14 by one *o.* he hath perfected
18 there is no more *o.* for sin

See BURNT, DRINK, FREE.

OFFERING, Participle.

1 Sam. 7:10 as S. was *o.* burnt-*o.*
2 Chr. 8:13 *o.* according to com.
29:29 made end of *o.* the king

30:22 seven days, *o.* peace-off.
35:14 sons of Aa. were busied *o.*
Ezr. 7:16 priests *o.* willingly for
Jer. 11:17 provoke me *o.* to Baal
Luke 23:36 and *o.* him vinegar
Heb. 10:11 ev. priest *o.* sacrifices

Heave-OFFERING.

Ex. 29:27 sanctify the *h.-o.*
Lev. 7:14 oblation for a *heave-o.*
Num. 15:19 sh. offer up *h.-o.* 20
21 of first dough gi. *h.-o.* to L.
18:24 tithes they offer as a *h.-o.*
28 give the Lord's *h.-o.* to Aa.
31:29 give to Eleazar for *h.-o.*
41 tribute wh. was the L. *h.-o.*

See MADE, MAKE, FIRE, BURNT-*offering.*

Peace-OFFERING.

Lev. 3:1 sacrifice of *p.-o.* 3, 6, 9

Sin-OFFERING.

Ex. 29:14 the flesh of bullock sh.
thou burn, it is a *s.-o. Lev.*
4:21, 21; 5:9, 11, 12
30:10 bl. of *s.-o.* of atonements
Lev. 4:3 let him bring a young
bullock without blemish, for
a *s.-o.* 16:3, 27 ; Num. 8:8
25 priest take blood of *s.-o.* 5:9
29 lay hand on head of *s.-o.* 33
32 bri. lamb for *s.-o. Num.* 6:14
5:6 lamb or kid of goats for *s.-o.*
9:3 ; 16:5, 15, 27 ; 23:19
8 priest shall offer the *s.-o.* fir.
6:25 this is the law of *s.-o.* 7:37
7:7 as *s.-o.* so is trespass, 14:13
9:2 take a young calf for a *s.-o.*
10:16 Moses sought goat of *s.-o.*
17 why have ye not eaten *s.-o.*
12:6 bring turtledove for a *s.-o.*
16:25 fat of *s.-o.* shall be burnt
Num. 7:16 kid of goats for *s.-o.*
22, 28 ; 15:24 ; 28:15 ; 29:5
2 Chr. 29:24 *s.-o.* made for Israel
Ezr. 8:35 12 he-goats for *s.-o.*
Ps. 40:6 *s.-o.* hast not required
Ezek. 43:19 priest bull. for *s.-o.*
25 every day a goat for a *s.-o.*
44:27 sanctuary, shall offer *s.-o.*
29 they shall eat the *sin-o.*
46:20 place wh. priests boil *s.-o.*

Trespass-OFFERING.

Lev. 5:6 he sh. bring *t.-o.* to L.
15 lambs without ble. for *t.-o.*
6:5 shall give it in day of *t.-o.*
14:12 take one he-lamb for *t.-o.*
21, 24, 25 ; Num. 6:12
1 Sam. 6:3 any wise return *t.-o.*
4 what shall be the *t.-o. ?* 8, 17
Ezek. 40:39 to slay *t.-o.* 42:13
44:29 eat *t.-o.* and ev. dedicated
46:20 where priests sh. boil *t.-o.*

Wave-OFFERING.

Ex. 29:24 for a *w.-o.* 26 ; Lev. 7:30 ;
8:27, 29 ; 9:21 ; 10:15 ; 14:12,
24 ; 23:20 ; Num. 6:20
27 sanctify breast of *w.-o.*
Lev. 23:15 bro. sheaf of *wave-o.*

Wood-OFFERING.

Neh. 10:34 cast lots for *wood-o.*
13:31 *w.-o.* at times appointed

OFFERINGS.

Lev. 1:10 if his *o.* be of the flocks
Lev. 2:13 with all thy *o.* shalt
offer salt
1 Sam. 2:29 fat with chief of *o.*
2 Sam. 1:21 let th. be no fie. of *o.*
2 Chr. 31:12 people brought in *o.*
35:8 gave priests for passo. *o.* 9
13 holy *o.* sod they in pots
Neh. 10:37 first-fruits of *o.* 12:44
Ps. 20:3 L. remember all thy *o.*
Jer. 41:5 *o.* and incense in hands
Ezek. 20:40 there will I requi. *o.*
Hos. 8:13 sacrifice flesh for *o.*
Amos 5:25 ye off. me *o.* 40 yrs. ?

Mal. 3:4 *o.* of Judah be pleasant
8 robbed thee ? in tithes and *o.*
Luke 21:4 of abund. cast in to *o.*
Acts 24:17 to bring alms and *o.*

See BURNT, DRINK, FREE.
Made by FIRE.

Heave-OFFERINGS.

Num. 18:8 given charge of *h.-o.*
Deut. 12:6 ye shall bring *heave-o.*

OFFERINGS of the Lord.

1 Sam. 2:17 men abhor. *o.* of *t. L.*

See MEAT.

Peace-OFFERINGS.

Ex. 24:5 sacrifice *p-o.* of oxen
29:28 a heave-offering of *p.-o.*
32:6 people brought *peace-o.*
Lev. 4:26 shall burn as fat of *p.-o.*
31, 35 ; 6:12
7:11 law of sacri. of *p.-o.* 13, 37
17:5 offer them for *p.-o.* 23:19
Num. 6:14 lamb *p.-o.* 17 a ram
7:17 sacri. of *p.-o.* two oxen, five
lambs, 23, 29, 35, 41 ; 29:39
10:10 blow over sacrifice of *p.-o.*
Jos. 8:31 Joshua sacrificed *p.-o.*
22:23 if offer *p.-o.* let L. req. it
Jud. 20:26 Is. offered *p.-o.* 21:4
1 Sam. 10:8 offer *peace-o.* 11:15
2 Sam. 6:17 D. offered *p.-o.* 24:25 ;
1 Chr. 21:26
1 K. 3:15 Sol. offered *p.-o.* 8:63
9:25 thrice a year S. offer. *p.-o.*
2 Chr. 31:2 appo. priests for *p.-o.*
33:16 Manasseh offered *p.-o.*
Prov. 7:14 I have *p.-o.* with me
Ezek. 45:15 *p.-o.* to make rec. 17
46:2 priest prepare his *p.-o.* and
12 prince prep. voluntary *p.-o.*
Amos 5:22 not regard *p.-o.* of fat

Sin-OFFERINGS.

Neh. 10:33 *sin-o.* to make atone.

Thank-OFFERINGS.

2 Chr. 29:31 bring *t.-o.* to house
33:16 altar, and sacrificed *t.-o.*

Wave-OFFERINGS.

Num. 18:11 *w.-o.* I have given

Wine-OFFERINGS.

Hos. 9:4 not off. *w.-o.* pleas. to G.

OFFICE.

Gen. 41:13 me he restored to *o.*
Ex. 1:16 wh. ye do *o.* of midwife
1 Chr. 6:32 they waited on th. *o.*
9:22 David did ordain in set *o.*
2 Chr. 24:11 chest Lro. to king's *o.*
31:18 in th. set *o.* they sancti.
Neh. 13:13 their *o.* was to distri.
Ps. 109:8 let another take his *o.*
Ezek. 44:13 sh. not do *o.* of priest
Rom. 11:13 I magnify my *o.*
12:4 all mem. have not same *o.*
1 Tim. 3:1 if a man desire *o.*
10 let them use *o.* of deacon, 13
Heb. 7:5 receive *o.* of priesthood

Priest's OFFICE.

Ex. 28:1 minister to me in the
p.'s o. 3, 4, 41 ; 29:1, 44 ; 30:30 ;
35:19 ; 40:13, 15 ; Lev. 7:35 ;
16:32 ; Num. 3:3
29:9 *p.'s o.* shall be theirs
31:10 minister in *p.'s o.* 39:41
Num. 3:4 Itha. minis. in *p.'s o.*
18:7 thou and sons keep *p.'s o.*
Deut. 10:6 Elea. min. in *p.'s o.*
1 Chr. 6:10 Aza. executed *p.'s o.*
2 Chr. 11:14 cast off fr. *p.'s o.*
Luke 1:8 Zacharias exec. *p.'s o.*

OFFICER.

Gen. 37:36 Poti. *o.* of Phar. 39:1
Jud. 9:28 is not Zebul his *o. ?*
1 K. 4:5 Zabud was principal *o.*
19 Geber was only *o.* in land
22:9 Ahab called an *o.* and said
2 K. 8:6 king appointed *o.*
25:19 Nebuzaradan took *o.*

OFFICER

Mat. 5:25 deliv. thee to *o.* and *o.*
cast into prison, 12:58

OFFICERS.

Gen. 40:2 Pha. wroth with two *o.*
41:34 let P. appoint *o.* over land
Ex. 5:15 *o.* of Israel cried to Ph.
Ex. 5:19 *o.* did see th. we. in ev.
Num. 11:16 gather unto me the
o. Deut. 31:28
Deut. 1:15 made th. *o.* am. tribes
16:18 judges and *o.* sh. th. make
20:5 *o.* shall speak to people, 8
1 *Sam.* 8:15 viney. give to his *o.*
1 *K.* 4:5 Azariah over the *o.*
7 Solomon had 12 *o.* over Isr.
2 *K.* 11:15 Jehoiada comman. *o.*
18 appointed *o.* over the house,
2 *Chr.* 23:18
24:12 Jehoia. went out with *o.*
15 *o.* and mighty car. he away
1 *Chr.* 23:4 6,000 were *o.* and jud.
26:29 Chenaniah and sons for *o.*
2 *Chr.* 8:10 Solomon's *o.* 250 bare
19:11 Levites shall be *o.* bef. y.
Est. 9:3 *o.* of kings helped Jews
Is. 60:17 I will make th. *o.* peace
Jer. 29:26 be *o.* in house of Lord
John 7:32 priests sent *o.* to take
46 *o.* answ. Never man spake
18:3 Judas having received *o.*
12 *o.* took Je. 22 *o.* struck Jes.
Acts 5:22 the *o.* found them not

OFFICES.

1 *Sam.* 2:36 put me into prie. *o.*
1 *Chr.* 24:3 dis. priests acc. to *o.*
2 *Chr.* 7:6 priests waited on th. *o.*
Neh. 13:14 not good deeds for *o.*

OFFSCOURING.

Lam. 3:45 hast made us as *o.*
1 *Cor.* 4:13 *o.* of all things

OFFSPRING.

Job 5:25 thy *o.* as grass of earth
21:8 *o.* is estab. bef. their eyes
27:14 *o.* not satisfied with bread
31:8 let my *o.* be rooted out
Is. 22:24 sh. hang on him, the *o.*
44:3 pour blessing on thine *o.*
48:19 *o.* of bowels like gravel
61:9 their *o.* shall be known
65:23 seed of the blessed, and *o.*
Acts 17:28 we are also his *o.* 29
Rev. 22:16 I am the *o.* of David

OFT.

2 *K.* 4:8 as *o.* as he passed by
Mat. 9:14 w. do we and P. fast *o. ?*
17:15 ofttimes he fall. into fire,
and *o.* into water, *Mark* 9:22
18:21 how *o.* sh. my broth. sin ?
Mark 7:3 exc. th. wash *o.* eat not
1 *Cor.* 11:25 as *o.* as ye drink
2 *Cor.* 11:23 prisons, in deaths *o.*

OFTEN, ER.

Prov. 29:1 that being *o.* reproved
Mal. 3:16 feared the L. spake *o.*
Mark 5:4 *o.* bound with fetters
Luke 5:33 why do dis. of J. f. *o. ?*
Acts 24:26 Felix sent for him *o.*
1 *Cor.* 11:26 as *o.* as ye eat bread
2 *Cor.* 11:26 in journeyings *o.*
27 I have been in watchings *o.*
1 *Tim.* 5:23 use wine for *o.* infir.
Heb. 9:25 nor yet offer himself *o.*
26 he must *o.* have suffered
Rev. 11:6 smite earth as *o.* as wi.

OFTENTIMES.

Job 33:29 th. things work. G. *o.*
Ec. 7:22 *o.* thy heart knoweth
Luke 8:29 *o.* it had caught him
John 18:2 Je. *o.* resorted thither
Rom. 1:13 *o.* I purposed to come
2 *Cor.* 8:22 have *o.* proved dilig.
Heb. 10:11 *o.* off. same sacrifices

OG.

Deut. 31:4 as he did to O.
Jos. 2:10 you did to O. 13:31

---

1 *K.* 4:19 was in the count. of O.

OIL.

Gen. 28:18 Jacob poured *o.* on the
top of it, 35:14
Ex. 25:6 take *o.* for the light,
35:14 : 39:37
29:2 cakes tempered with *o.* 40
30:25 make it *o.* for holy ointm.
Lev. 2:1 shall pour *o.* upon it, 6
4 cakes of fine flour mingled
with *o.* 5 ; 14:10, 21 ; 23:13 ;
Num. 6:15 ; 7:13, 19, 25, 31,
37, 43, 49, 55, 61, 67, 73, 79 ;
8:8 ; 28:13 ; 29:3, 9, 14
15 thy meat-offering, put *o.*
upon it, 6:21
16 priest shall burn part of *o.*
5:11 he shall put no *o.* upon it,
Num. 5:15
7:10 meat-offering mingled with
o. 9:4 ; 14:10
12 mingled with *o. Num.* 6:15
14:16 priest dip right finger in *o.*
17 rest of *o.* in his hand, 18, 29
Num. 11:8 as the taste of fresh *o.*
28:12 *o.* for bullock, *o.* for ram
Deut. 28:40 sh. not anoint thys.
wi. *o.* 2 *Sam.* 14:2 ; *Mic.* 6:15
32:13 suck *o.* out of rock
33:24 let Asher dip his foot in *o.*
1 *Sam.* 10:1 Sa. took a vial of *o.*
16:1 fill thy horn with *o.* 13
1 *K.* 1:39 Z. took horn of *o.*
5:11 gave Hir. 20 measures of *o.*
17:12 *o.* in cr. 14 nor cr. of *o.* 16
2 *K.* 4:2 nothing in house save *o.*
6 *o.* stayed ; 7 go sell the *o.*
9:1 take this box of *o.* to Ra. 3
6 he poured the *o.* on his head
1 *Chr.* 27:28 over the cellars of *o.*
Ezr. 3:7 *o.* to them of Zidon
Est. 2:12 with *o.* of myrrh
Job 24:11 *o.* within their walls
29:6 poured me out rivers of *o.*
Ps. 23:5 anoint my head with *o.*
55:21 words were softer than *o.*
104:15 *o.* to make face to shine
109:118 come like *o.* into bones
141:5 be a kindness, an excel. *o.*
Prov. 5:3 mouth smoother th. *o.*
21:20 *o.* in dwelling of the wise
Is. 61:3 give *o.* of joy for mourn.
Jer. 41:8 we have treasures of *o.*
Ezek. 16:13 thou didst eat *o.* 19
18 set mine *o.* and incense
27:17 Ju. traded in honey and *o.*
32:14 cause rivers to run like *o.*
45:14 ordinance of *o.* bath of *o.*
24 a hin of *o.* for an ephah
Hos. 2:5 lovers that give me *o.*
12:1 *o.* is carried into Egypt
Mic. 6:7 with 10,000 rivers of *o. ?*
Zec. 4:12 empty the golden *o.*
Mat. 25:3 the foolish took no *o.*
4 wise took *o.* 8 give us *o.*
Luke 7:46 with *o.* didst not ano.
16:6 a hundred measures of *o.*
See ANOINTED, ANOINTING,
BEATEN, LOG.

OIL, with wine.

Num. 18:12 best of *o.* and *w.* off.
Deut. 7:13 L. will bless w. and *o.*
11:14 mayest gather *w.* and *o.*
12:17 not eat the tithe of thy *w.*
and *o.* 14:23
18:4 first-fr. *w.* and *o.* 2 *Chr.* 31:5
28:51 leave th. ei. *w.* or *o.*
1 *Chr.* 9:29 oversee the *w.* and *o.*
12:40 were nigh bro. *w.* and *o.*
2 *Chr.* 2:10 baths *w.* and *o.* 15
41:11 Rehob. put in *o.* and *w.*
35:28 H. storehou. for *w.* and *o.*
Ezr. 6:9 give *w. o.* according
7:22 100 baths *w.* 100 baths *o.*
Neh. 5:11 restore *wine* and *o.*
10:37 first-fruits of *w.* and *o.*
39 offer. of corn, new *w.* and *o.*

13:5 tithes of corn, *w.* and *o.* 12
Prov. 21:17 loveth *wine* and *o.*
Jer. 31:12 flow to L. for *w.* and *o.*
40:10 gather ye *w.* fruits and *o.*
Hag. 1:11 drought on *w.* and *o.*
2:12 *w.* or *o.* shall it be holy ?
Luke 10:34 pouring in *o.* and *w.*
Rev. 6:6 see hurt not *w.* and *o.*
18:13 no man buy. th. *w.* and *o.*

OILED.

Ex. 29:23 one cake of *o.* bread.
Lev. 8:26

OIL-OLIVE.

Ex. 27:20 *o.-o.* beaten for light
30:24 take thou of *o.-o.* a hin
Lev. 24:2 br. unto thee pure *o.-o.*
Deut. 8:8 land of *o.-o.* 2 *K.* 18:32

OIL-TREE.

Is. 41:19 plant in wild. the *o.-t.*

OINTMENT.

Ex. 30:25 make oil of holy *o.*
2 *K.* 20:13 Hezek. showed them
precious *o. Is.* 39:2
1 *Chr.* 9:30 the prie. made the *o.*
Job 41:31 maketh sea boil like *o.*
Ps. 133:2 it is like precious *o.*
Prov. 27:9 *o.* and perfu. rej. hea.
16 *o.* of right hand bewrayeth
Ec. 7:1 good name bet. than *o.*
9:8 and let thy head lack no *o.*
10:1 dead flies cause *o.* to stink
Cant. 1:3 name is as *o.* poured
Is. 1:6 nor mollified with *o.*
57:9 wentest to king with *o.*
Mat. 26:7 box of precious *o.*
Mark 14:3 ; *Luke* 7:37
9 *o.* might been sold, *John* 12:5
12 hath poured *o.* on my body
Mark 14:4 why this waste of *o. ?*
Luke 7:38 anoin. feet with *o.* 46
John 11:2 M. anoin. the L. wi. *o.*
12:3 Mary took pound of *o.*
house was filled with odor
of the *o.*

OINTMENTS.

Cant. 1:3 because of thy good *o.*
4:10 smell of thine *o.* is better
Amos 6:6 anoi. them. wi. chief *o.*
Luke 23:56 prepared spices and *o.*
Rev. 18:13 no man buyeth th. *o.*

OLD.

Gen. 17:12 he th. is eight days *o.*
17 a child to him 100 years *o.*
19:4 comp. house, *o.* and young
Deut. 8:4 thy raiment waxed not
o. 29:5 ; *Neh.* 9:21
28:50 not regard the person of *o.*
Jos. 5:11 did eat *o.* corn, 12
9:4 took *o.* sacks ; 5 *o.* shoes 13
13:1 Jos. was *o.* in years, 23:1, 2
14:7 forty years *o.* was I
Ruth 1:12 too *o.* to have a husb.
1 *Sam.* 2:22 now Eli was very *o.*
1 *K.* 1:1 now king David was *o.*
15 ; 1 *Chr.* 23:1
11:4 when S. was *o.* wives turn.
13:11 dwelt *o.* proph. in Beth-el
2 *K.* 4:14 and her husband is *o.*
Est. 3:13 dest. J. *o.* and young
Job 21:7 wicked live, become *o. ?*
32:6 I am young, ye are very *o.*
Ps. 32:3 my bones waxed *o.*
37:25 have been young, now *o.*
71:18 now when I am *o.* O God
Prov. 22:6 wh. *o.* will not depart
23:10 removed not *o.* land-mark
22 desp. not. moth. when *o.*
Ec. 4:13 wise child th. *o.* king
Cant. 7:13 pleas. frui. new and *o.*
Is. 15:5 heifer 3 ye. *o. Jer.* 48:34
20:4 captives, young and *o.*
50:9 they shall wax *o.* as garm.
58:12 build *o.* waste places, 61:4
65:20 child sh. die 100 years *o.*
but sinner being 100 years *o.*

Jer. 6:16 see and ask for *o.* paths
38:11 took *o.* clouts, *o.* rags, 12
51:22 I will break young and old
Lam. 2:21 young and *o.* lie grou.
3:4 flesh and skin he made *o.*
Ezek. 9:6 slay utterly *o.* and you.
23:43 that was *o.* in adulteries
25:15 vengeau. to destroy for *o.*
36:11 will settle your *o.* estates
Mic. 6:6 with calv. of a *year o.?*
Mat. 2:16 H. slew chil. two ye. *o.*
9:16 new cloth to an *o.* garment
17 new wine in *o.* bot. *Mark*
2:21, 22; *Luke* 5:36, 37
13:52 bringeth treas. new and *o.*
Luke 4:22 J. 12 years *o.* went to
5:39 saith, The *o.* wine is better
9:8 one of *o.* prophets is risen
John 3:4 man be born when *o.?*
8:57 art not yet fifty years *o.?*
21:18 when thou shalt be *o.*
Acts 4:22 was above 40 years *o.*
21:16 brou. Mnason *o.* disciple
1 *Cor.* 5:7 purge out the *o.* leaven
8 keep feast, not wi. *o.* leaven
2 *Cor.* 3:14 read of *o.* testament
5:17 *o.* things are passed away
1 *Tim.* 4:7 refuse *o.* wives' fables
5:9 not taken under 60 years *o.*
Heb. 8:13 he hath made first *o.*
what wax. *o.* is ready to van.
2 *Pet.* 1:9 purged from his *o.* sins
2:5 if God spared not *o.* world
1 *John* 2:7 *o.* commandm. is word
Rev. 12:9 *o.* serpent the devil
20:2 hold on dragon that *o.* ser.

OLD age.

Gen. 15:15 buried in a good *o. a.*
21:2 Abra. a son of his *o. age,* 7
25:8 Abra. died in a good *o. age*
37:3 Jo. son of his *o. age,* 44:20
Jud. 8:32 Gid. died in good *o. a.*
Ruth 4:15 nourisher in th. *o. a.*
1 *K.* 15:23 Asa in *o. a.* diseased
1 *Chr.* 29:28 D. died in good *o. a.*
Job 30:2 in whom *o. age* perish.
Ps. 71:9 cast not off in *o. age*
92:14 bring forth fruit in *o. age*
Is. 46:4 even to your *o. a.* I am
Luke 1:36 conceived son in *o. a.*

Days of OLD. *See of* OLD.
OLD *gate. See* GATE.

OLD man.

Gen. 25:8 Abra. died an *o. man*
43:27 *o. man* of whom ye spake
44:20 we have a father, an *o. m.*
Lev. 19:32 honor face of *o. man*
Jud. 19:16 came an *o. m.* fr. wor.
1 *Sam.* 2:31 not *o. m.* in hou. 32
4:18 Eli *o. man ;* 17:12 J. *o. man*
28:14 *o. m.* cometh up. covered
2 *Chr.* 36:17 no compas. on *o. m.*
Is. 65:20 *o. m.* that hath not
Luke 1:18 I am an *o. man*
Rom. 6:6 our *o. man* is crucified
Eph. 4:22 off *o. m.* wh. is corrupt
Col. 3:9 put off *o. m.* with deeds

OLD men.

1 *K.* 12:6 consulted with *o. m.*
8 forsook counsel of *o. men,* 13;
2 *Chr.* 10:6, 8, 13
Ps. 148:12 *o. m.* praise the Lord
Prov. 17:6 child. crown of *o. m.*
20:29 beauty of *o. m.* gray head
Jer. 31:13 rej. young *men* and *o.*
Joel 1:2 hear this ye *o. men*
2:28 *o. m.* sh. dream, *Acts* 2:17
Zec. 8:4 *o. m.* dw ll in streets

Of OLD.

Gen. 6:4 *cf o.* men of renown
Neh. 12:46 *of o.* chief of singers
Job 20:4 kno. thou not this *of o.*
Ps. 25:6 tender me. ha. been *of o.*
44:1 work didst in times *of o.*
68:33 heavens which were *of o.*
74:2 which hast purchased *of o.*

12 for God is my king *of o.*
77:5 I considered the days *of o.*
11 will rem. thy wonders *of o.*
78:2 utter dark sayings *of o.*
93:2 throne is established *of o.*
102:25 *of o.* hast laid foundation
119:52 remembered judgm. *of o.*
152 testimonies I have k. *of o.*
143:5 I rem. days *of o. Is.* 63:11
Prov. 8:22 before his works *of o.*
Is. 25:1 thy counsels *of o.* are
30:33 Tophet is ordained *of o.*
46:9 remem. former things *of o.*
51:9 awake as in genera. *of o.*
57:11 I held peace *of o. ?*
63:9 carried them all days *of o.*
Jer. 28:8 bef. me and thee *of o.*
31:3 L. hath appeared *of o.*
46:26 inhabited as in days *of o.*
Lam. 1:7 she had in days *of o.*
2:17 commanded in days *of o.*
3:6 as they that be dead *of o.*
5:21 L. renew our days as *of o.*
Ezek. 26:20 places desolate *of o.*
Amos 9:11 as in days *of o.*
Mic. 5:2 goings have been f. *of o.*
7:14 feed in Ba. as in days *of o.*
20 sw. to fath. from days *of o.*
Nah. 2:8 Nineveh is *of o.* like a
Mal. 3:4 the L. as in days *of o.*
2 *Pet.* 3:5 the heavens were *of o.*
Jude 4 were *of o.* ordained

OLD time.

Deut. 2:20 giants dw. th. in *o. t.*
Jos. 24:2 dw. on oth. side in *o. t.*
2 *Sam.* 20:18 to speak in *o. t.*
Ezr. 4:15 moved sedition of *o. t.*
Jer. 2:20 of *o. t.* I have broken
Ezek. 26:20 down wi. peo. of *o. t.*
Mat. 5:21 by them of *o. t.* 27, 33
Acts 15:21 Mo. of *o. time* hath in
1 *Pet.* 3:5 in *o. t.* women adorned
2 *Pet.* 1:21 came not in *o. t.*

See WAX.

OLD way.

Job 22:15 *o. w.* wh. wicked men

OLDNESS.

Rom. 7:6 not serve in *o.* of letter

OLIVE.

Gen. 8:11 in mouth was *o.* leaf
Deut. 28:40 thine *o.* cast fruit
Neh. 8:15 and fetch *o.* branches
Job 15:33 cast off his flowers as *o.*
Ps. 128:3 children like *o.* plants
Hab. 3:17 althou. labor of *o.* fail
Zec. 4:12 these two *o.* branches
Jam. 3:12 fig-tree bear *o.* berries?

See OIL.

OLIVES.

Jud. 15:5 bu. vineyards and *o.*
Mic. 6:15 shalt tread the *o.* but

See MOUNT.

OLIVET.

2 *Sam.* 15:30 ascent to mount O.
Acts 1:12 from mount called O.

OLIVE-TREE.

Deut. 24:20 beatest thine *o.-t.*
Jud. 9:8 they said to the *o.-t.*
1 *K.* 6:23 two cherubim of *o.-t.*
31 two doors were of *o.-t.* 32
33 made for door-posts of *o.-t.*
Ps. 52:8 like a green *o.-t.*
Is. 17:6 shaking of *o.-t.* 24:13
Jer. 11:16 name a green *o.-t.*
Hos. 14:6 beauty be as the *o.-t.*
Hag. 2:19 *o.-t.* hath not brought
Rom. 11:17 the fatness of *o.-t.*
24 graffed in a good *o.-t.*

OLIVE-TREES.

Deut. 6:11 *o.-t.* thou plantest not
28:40 thou shalt have *o.-t.* but
1 *Chr.* 27:28 over *o.-t.* Baal-hanan
Amos 4:9 *o.-t.* increa. worm dev.

Zec. 4:3 two *o.-t.* by it on right
Rev. 11:4 the two *o.-t.* standing

Wild OLIVE-TREE.

Rom. 11:17 thou being *wild o.-t.*

OLIVE-YARD.

Ex. 23:11 thus do wi. thy *o.-y.*
Jos. 24:13 of vineyards and *o.-y.*
ye planted not, *Neh.* 9:25
1 *Sam.* 8:14 king take your *o.-y.*
2 *K.* 5:26 recei. money and *o.-y.*
Neh. 5:11 resto. to th. their *o.-y.*

OLYMPAS. *Rom.* 16:15
OMEGA. *Rev.* 1:8, 11; 21:6; 22:13

OMITTED.

Mat. 23:23 *o.* matters of the law

OMNIPOTENT.

Rev. 19:6 Lord God *o.* reigneth

OMRI.

1 *K.* 16:16 ma. O. king, 21, 25, 30
2 *K.* 8:26 daugh. of O. 2 *Chr.* 22:2
Mic. 6:16 statutes of O. are kept

ON. *Gen.* 41:45, 50; 46:10;
Num. 46:1

ONAN.

Gen. 38:4 called his name O. 9
46:12 of Ju. Er, O. *Num.* 26:19

ONCE.

Gen. 18:32 will speak but this *o.*
Ex. 10:17 forgive only this *o.*
30:10 atonement of incense *o.* a
ye. *Lev.* 16:34; *Heb.* 9:7, 12
Jos. 6:3 go round city *o.* 11, 14
Jud. 6:39 I will spe. but this *o.*
2 *K.* 6:10 saved himself not *o.*
Neh. 13:20 lodged without Jer. *o.*
Job 33:14 God speak. *o.* yea twi.
40:5 *o.* have I spoken, but
Ps. 62:11 God hath spoken *o.*
89:35 *o.* have I sworn
Prov. 28:18 perv. shall fall at *o.*
Is. 42:14 destroy and dev. at *o.*
66:8 or sh. a nati. be born at *o.*
Jer. 10:18 sling out inhabit. at *o.*
13:27 clean, wh. shall it *o.* be ?
16:21 I will this *o.* cause them
Hag. 2:6 *o.* it is a little while,
Heb. 12:26
Luke 23:18 they cried all at *o.*
Rom. 6:10 he died unto sin *o.*
7:9 I was alive without law *o.*
1 *Cor.* 15:6 seen of 500 bret. at *o.*
2 *Cor.* 11:25 thr. beaten, *o.* ston.
Gal. 1:23 'prea. faith he *o.* destr.
Eph. 5:3 let it not be *o.* named
Phil. 4:16 ye sent *o.* and again
1 *Thes.* 2:18 would have come *o.*
Heb. 7:27 for this he did *o.* when
9:26 but now *o.* in end of world
27 appointed to men *o.* to die
28 *o.* offered to bear sins, 10:10
10:2 the worshippers *o.* purged
12:27 yet *o.* more, signifieth
1 *Pet.* 3:18 Ch. suffered *o.* for sins
20 *o.* long-suffering of God
Jude 3 contend for faith *o.* deliv.
5 though ye *o.* knew this.

ONE.

Gen. 2:24 shall be *o.* flesh, *Mat.*
19:5; *Mark* 10:8 ; 1 *Cor.* 6:16
27:38 hast thou but *o.* blessing?
42:13 with father, *o.* is not, 32
44:28 the *o.* went out from me
Ex. 11:1 I will bring *o.* plague
12:46 in *o.* sh. it be eaten
49 *o.* law to him is home-born
Lev. 24:22 ; *Num.* 15:16, 29
23:29 not drive th. out in *o.* ye.
Num. 16:15 take *o.* as from them
36:8 of tribe shall be wife to *o.*
Deut. 4:42 fleeing to *o.* of these
cities, 19:5, 11
32:30 should *o.* chase a thousa.
Jud. 9:2 bet. that *o.* reign over ?
21:8 what *o.* is there of tribes

1 *Sam.* 18:21 son-in-law in *o.* of
2 *Sam.* 7:23 wh. *o.* nat. like peo. ?
19:7 will not tarry *o.* with thee
1 *K.* 1:48 given me *o.* to sit on
Job 9:3 answer him *o.* of a thou.
21:23 *o.* dieth in full strength
23:13 *o.* mind, who turn him ?
33:23 interpreter *o.* am. thous.
Ps. 49:16 not afr. when *o.* is rich
89:19 help on *o.* that is mighty
Ec. 3:20 all go unto *o.* place, 6:6
4:9 two are better than *o.*
11 how can *o.* be warm alone?
12 if *o.* prevail against him
7:27 counting *o.* by *o.* to find
Cant. 6:9 my undefiled is but *o.*
Is. 23:15 acc. to days of *o.* king
27:12 shall be gathered *o.* by *o.*
30:17 *o.* thou. flee at reb. of *o.*
Is. 34:16 no . of these shall fail
41:25 rais d up *o.* from north
44:5 *o.* shall say, I am Lord's
45:24 *o.* say, In L. have I right.
Dan. 7:13 *o.* like Son, 10:16, 18
Amos. 4:8 wandered to *o.* city
6:9 remain ten men in *o.* house
Zec. 3:9 on *o.* stone be seven eyes
14:9 *o.* Lord, and his name *o.*
Mal. 2:15 make *o.* ? wheref. *o.* ?
Mat. 5:18 *o.* jot or *o.* tit. not pass
17:4 thr. tabernacles, *o.* for thee,
o. for Mo. and *o.* for Elias,
Mark 9:5 ; *Luke* 9:33
18:16 take with thee *o.* or two.
19:17 none good but *o. Mark*
10:18 ; *Luke* 18:19
25:45 ye did it not to *o.* of least
Mark 14:19 say *o.* by *o.* is it I ?
Luke 7:8 to *o.* go, and he goeth
16:30 if *o.* went from dead, 31
17:22 to see *o.* of the days of S.
John 10:30 I and my Fa. are *o.*
17:11 be *o.* as we are, 21, 22
Acts 17:7 another king, *o.* Jesus
Eph. 2:14 both *o.* 15 *o.* new m.
4:5 *o.* faith, *o.* L. *o.* bapt. 6 *o.* G.
1 *John* 5:7 three *o.* 8 agree in *o.*

See ACCORD, ANOTHER, MAN, GOD.

As ONE.

Gen. 3:22 behold, man is *as o.*
Ec. 3:19 *as o.* dieth, so dieth
Cant. 1:7 be *as o.* turneth aside?

See DAY, HEART, EVERY.

Is ONE.

Gen. 11:6 peo. *is o.* 41:25 drea. **26**
Deut. 6:4 the Lord our God *is o.*
L. *Mark* 12:29
Gal. 3:20 med. of one, but G. *is o.*

See LITTLE, MAN.

Not ONE.

Gen. 24:41 if they give *n.* thee *o.*
Ex. 8:31 remained *not o.* 10:19
12:30 not house wh. *not o.* dead
Deut. 2:36 *not o.* city too strong
2 *Sam.* 13:30 is *n. o.* of them left
Rom. 3:10 is none right. *not o.*

See MIGHTY.

ONE, with other.

Gen. 13:11 separated, *o.* from *o.*
Ex. 14:20 *o.* came not near *o.*
17:12 stayed han. *o.* side, and *o.*
Deut. 4:32 *o.* side of heav. to *o.*
13:7 *o.* end of earth to *o.* 28:64
Jud. 16:29 hold of *o.* pill. and *o.*
1 *K.* 3:23 *o.* sai. This my son, *o.*
25 give half to *o.* and half to *o.*
Ec. 3:19 as *o.* dieth, so dieth *o.*
7:14 God hath set the *o.* over *o.*
Mat. 6:24 hate the *o.* and love the
other, or hold to the *o.* and
despise the *o. Luke* 16:13
24:40 *o.* taken, the *other* left,
41 ; *Luke* 17:34, 35, 36
Luke 6:29 if sm. on *o.* che. off. *o.*
Gal. 5:17 are contrary, *o.* to *oth.*

Rev. 17:10 *o.* is, *oth.* is not come
See PEOPLE.

There is ONE.

Ec. 4:8 *th. is one* alone, not seco.
Mark 12:32 the truth ; *th. is o.* G.
1 *Tim.* 2:5 ; *Jam.* 2:19

ONE of them.

Ex. 14·28 remained not *o. of th.*
Mat. 26:73 surely thou art *o. of t.*
Mark 14:69, 70
John 6:7 ev. *o. of t.* take a little

ONE thing.

Job 9:22 this is *o. t.* theref. I said
Mat. 21:24 I will ask you *o. thi.*
Luke 6:9 ; 20:3
Mark 10:21 *o. t.* lack. *Luke* 18:22
Luke 10:42 *o. thing* is needful
Acts 19:32 some cried *o. t.* 21:34
Phil. 3:13 but this *o. thing* I do

Wicked ONE.

Mat. 13:19 then cometh *w. o.*
38 tares are children of *w. o.*
1 *John* 2:13 overcome *w. o.* 14
3:12 not as C. who was of *w. o.*
5:18 *w. o.* toucheth him not

ONESIMUS.

Col. 4:9 O. a faithful brother
Phile. 10 beseech for my son O.

ONESIPHORUS.

2 *Tim.* 1:16 mercy to house of O.
4:19 salute the household of O.

ONLY.

Gen. 19:8 *o.* to these men do no.
22:2 take now thine *o.* son, Isa.
12 not withheld thine *o.* son, 16
2 *K.* 19:19 L. even thou *o. Is.*37:20
Job 34:29 ag. nation, or man *o.*
Ps. 51:4 ag. thee *o.* have I sinned
Cant. 6:9 she is *o.* one of mother
Luke 7:12 dead man, *o.* son of m.
8:42 one *o.* dau. 9:38 *o.* child
Rom. 5:3 and not *o.* so, 11
8:23 not *o.* they, but ourselves
13:27 to God *o.* wise, be glory,
1 *Tim.* 1:17 ; *Jude* 25
1 *Cor.* 7:39 *o.* in the Lord
2 *Tim.* 4:8 not to me *o.* but to all
See BEGOTTEN.

ONIONS.

Num 11:5 remem. *o.* and garlic

ONWARD.

Ex. 40:36 cloud up, Is. went *o.*

ONYCHA.

Ex. 30:34 take the spices, *o*

ONYX.

Ex. 28·20 4th row an *o.* 39:13
Job 28:16 wisdom not val. wi. *o.*
Ezek. 28:13 *o.* was thy covering
See STONES.

OPEN, Adjective.

Gen. 1:20 fowl fly in *o.* firma.
38:14 Tamar sat in *o.* place
Num. 19:15 ev. *o.* vessel is uncl.
24:3 man whose eyes are *o.* 4, 15
1 *Sam.* 3:1 word of L. no *o.* visi.
1 *K.* 6:18 cedar carved with *o.*
flowers, 29:32, 35
8:29 eyes be *o.* tow. this house,
52 ; 2 *Chr.* 6:20, 40 ; 7:15
Neh. 1:6 let thine eyes be *o.*
6:5 Sanb. wi. *o.* letter sent serv.
Job 34:26 wicked men in *o.* sight
Ps. 5:9 their throat is an *o.* sepulchre, *Rom.* 3:13
34:15 his ears are *o.* to their cry
Prov. 13:16 fool lay. *o.* his folly
27:5 *o.* rebuke bet. th. secret lo.
Is. 9:12 devour Is. with *o.* mouth
24:18 window from on high *o.*
60:11 thy gates sh. be *o.* contin.
Jer. 5:16 quiver is an *o.* sepulch.
32:11 what was sealed and *o.*
19 th. eyes *o.* on ways of men

Ezek. 37:2 many bones in *o.* val,
Dan. 6:10 windows *o.* in chamb.
Neh. 3:13 gates of land wide *o*
John 1:51 ye shall see heaven *o.*
Acts 16:27 prison doors *o.* drew
19:38 law *o.* there are deputies
2 *Cor.* 3:18 wee, wi. *o.* face behol.
6:11 our mouth is *o.* to you, our
1 *Tim.* 5:24 some men's sins *o.*
Heb. 6:6 put him to *o.* shame
1 *Pet.* 3:12 ears are *o.* to prayers
Rev. 3:8 set bef. thee an *o.* door
10:2 had in his hand a book *o.* 8

See FIELD, FIELDS.

OPEN, Verb.

Ex. 21:33 if a man shall *o.* a pit
Num. 8:16 inst. of such as *o.* wo.
16:30 if earth *o.* mouth and swa.
Deut. 15:8 thou shalt *o.* hand, 11
20:11 make aus. of peace and *o.*
28:12 L. sh. *o.* to thee his treas.
2 *K.* 9:3 then *o.* door, and flee
13:17 *o.* the window eastward
Job 11:5 O that G. wo. *o.* his lips
32:20 I will *o.* my lips and ans.
35:16 doth Job *o.* mouth in vain
41:14 who can *o.* doors of face?
Ps. 49:4 *o.* my dark saying
78:2 I will *o.* mouth in parable
81:10 *o.* thy mouth I will fill it
118:19 *o.* to me gates of righte.
Prov. 31:8 *o.* thy mouth for du.
9 *o.* thy mouth, judge righte.
Cant. 5:2 *o.* to me, my sister
5 I rose up too *o.* to my beloved
Is. 22:22 *o.* none shut, sh. none *o.*
26:2 *o.* gates, righte. may enter
28:24 do. he *o.* clods of ground ?
41:18 *o.* rivers in high places
42:7 *o.* blind eyes, bring out pr.
45:1 to *o.* before him the gates
8 let earth *o.* bring forth salv.
Jer. 13:19 cities shut up, none *o.*
50:26 *o.* her storehouses, cast h.
Ezek. 2:8 *o.* thy mouth and eat
3:27 when I speak I will *o.* thy
16:63 conf. and never *o.* mouth
21:22 to *o.* mouth in slaughter
25:9 I will *o.* side of M. fr. cities
37:12 I will *o.* your graves
46:12 one shall *o.* gate tow. east
Zec. 11:1 *o.* thy doors, O Leban.
Mal. 3:10 if I will not *o.* heaven
Mat. 13:35 *o.* mouth in parables
25:11 Lord, *o.* to us, *Luke* 13:25
Luke 12:36 when knock. may *o.*
Acts 18:14 P. was about to *o.* mo.
Eph. 6:19 that I may *o.* mouth
Col. 4:3 G. would *o.* door of utte.
Rev. 5:2 wort. to *o.* book? 3, 5, 9

See EYES.

OPENED.

Gen. 7:11 wind. of heav. were *o.*
29:31 the Lord *o.* Leah's womb
30:22 God *o.* Rachel's womb
41:56 Joseph *o.* all storehouses
42:27 one *o.* sack, 43:21 ; 44:11
Ex. 2:6 wh. she *o.* ark, saw child
Num. 16:32 earth *o.* mou. swallowed up Korah, *Ps.* 106:17
Jud. 3:25 he *o.* not doors, they *o.*
4:19 she *o.* a bottle of milk, and
19:27 her lord *o.* doors, went out
2 *K.* 9:10 Elisha *o.* door and fled
15:16 *o.* not to him, he smote
2 *Chr.* 29:3 Hezekiah *o.* doors of
Neh. 7:3 let not gates of J. be *o.*
8:5 E. *o.* book, when he *o.* peop.
13:19 gates not *o.* till after sab.
Job 31:32 *o.* my doors to traveller
38:17 gates of death been *o.* ?
Ps. 40:6 mine ears hast thou *o.*
78:23 tho' he *o.* doors of heaven
105:41 he *o.* rock, waters gushed
Cant. 5:6 I *o.* to my beloved, but

OPENED

Is. 14:17 *o.* not house of prison.
48:8 time that th. ear was not *o.*
50:5 Lord God hath *o.* mine ear
Jer. 20:12 to thee have I *o.* cause
50:25 Lord hath *o.* his armory
Ezek. 1:1 hea. *o.* Mat. 3:16; *Mar.*
1:10; *Luke* 3:21; *Acts* 7:56
16:25 hast *o.* thy feet to ev. one
37:13 I have *o.* your graves
44:2 gate shall not be *o.*
46:1 on sabbath it shall be *o.*
Dan. 7:10 judgment set, books *o.*
Nah. 2:6 gates of rivers sh. be *o.*
Zec. 13:1 fountain *o.* to David
Mat. 2:11 when they *o.* treasures
7:7 it shall be *o. Luke* 11:9, 10
27:52 graves were *o.* bodies aro.
Mark 7:34 be *o.* 35 ears were *o.*
Luke 4:17 *o.* book, found place
24:32 wh. he *o.* to us scriptures
45 *o.* he their understanding
Acts 5:19 angel by night *o.* pris.
10:11 Peter saw heaven *o.*
12:10 iron gates *o.* 14 *o.* not gate
14:27 how he *o.* door to Gentiles
16:14 Lydia, whose heart L. *o.*
26 the prison doors were *o.*
1 *Cor.* 16:9 a gr. door and effect.
is *o.* unto me, 2 *Cor.* 2:12
Heb. 4:13 all things are *o.* to him
Rev. 4:1 a door was *o.* in heaven
6:1 when Lamb *o.* one seal
3 *o.* second; 5 third; 7 fourth
9 *o.* fifth; 12 sixth; 8:1 seventh
9:2 *o.* the bottomless pit and
heaven *o.* and white horse
20:12 books *o.* book of life *o.*

See DAYS, MOUTH.

OPENEST.

Ps. 104:28 thou *o.* thy hand
145:16 thou *o.* thy hand

OPENETH.

Ex. 13:2 sanctify to me what *o.*
12 all *o.* matrix, 15; 34:19; *Nu.*
3:12; 18:15; *Luke* 2:23
Job 27:19 rich man *o.* his eyes
33:16 he *o.* ears of men
36:10 *o.* their ear to discipline
15 he *o.* their ears in oppressi.
Ps. 38:13 dumb man *o.* not mou.
Prov. 13:3 that *o.* wide his lips
24:7 *o.* not his mouth in gate
31:26 she *o.* mouth with wisdom
Is. 53:7 so he *o.* not his mouth
Ezek. 20:26 all that *o.* the womb
John 10:3 to him the porter *o.*
Rev. 3:7 *o.* and no man shutteth,
shutteth and no man *o.*

OPENING.

Is. 42:20 *o.* ears, but heareth not
Acts 17:3 *o.* and alleging Christ

OPENING, S.

1 *Chr.* 9:27 *o.* of house of God
Job 12:14 shutteth, there be no *o.*
Prov. 1:21 in the *o.* of the gates
8:6 *o.* of my lips shall be right
Is. 61:1 proclaim *o.* of the prison
Ezek. 29:21 give thee *o.* of mouth

OPENLY.

Gal. 3:8:21 wh. harlot th. was *o. ?*
Ps. 98:2 righteous. he *o.* showed
Mat. 6:4 F. reward thee *o.* 6, 18
Mark 8:32 spake that saying *o.*
John 7:4 seeketh to be known *o.*
10 we. he to feast, not *o.* secre.
13 no man spake of him *o.*
11:54 Jesus walked no more *o.*
13:20 J. said, I spake *o.* to wor.
Acts 10:40 God showed him *o.*
16:37 they have beaten us *o.*
Col. 2:15 made a show of them *o.*

OPERATION, S.

Ps. 28:5 regard not *o.* of his
Is. 5:12 nor consid. *o.* of hands
1 *Cor.* 12:6 th. are diversity of *o.*
Col. 2:12 risen thro' *o.* of faith

OPHEL.

2 *Chr.* 27:3 on wall of O. 33:14
Neh. 3:26 Nethin. in O. 27; 11:21

OPHIR.

Gen. 10:29 J. be. O. 1 *Chr.* 1:23
1 *K.* 9:28 came to O. 2 *Chr.* 8:18
10:11 bro. from O. great plenty
22:48 made ships go to O.
1 *Chr.* 29:4 3,000 ta. of gold of O.
Job 22:24 lay up the gold of O.
28:16 not valued wi. gold of O.
Ps. 45:9 the queen in gold of O.
Is. 13:12 prec. than wedge of O.

OPINION, S.

1 *K.* 18:21 h. long halt bet. 2 *o. ?*
Job 32:6 durst not show mine *o.*
10 I also will show mine *o.* 17

OPPORTUNITY.

Mat. 26:16 *o.* to bet. *Luke* 22:6
Gal. 6:10 as we have *o.* do good
Phil. 4:10 careful, ye lacked *o.*
Heb. 11:15 *o.* to have returned

OPPOSE, ED.

Acts 18:6 *o.* thems. and blasph.
2 *Tim.* 2:25 instructing th. th. *o.*

OPPOSEST, ETH.

Job 30:21 wi. strong hand *o.* thy.
2 *Thes.* 2.4 *o.* and exalt. himself

OPPOSITIONS.

1 *Tim.* 6:20 avoiding *o.* of science

OPPRESS.

Ex. 3:9 the Egyptians *o.* them
22:21 neither *o.* stranger, 23:9
Lev. 25:14 sh. not *o.* one and. 17
Deut. 23:16 shalt not *o.* servant
24:14 shalt not *o.* a hired serv.
Jud. 10:12 Moabites did *o.* you
Job 10:3 is it good thou shou. *o. ?*
Ps. 10:18 m. of earth no more *o.*
17:9 hide me fr. wicked that *o.*
119:122 let not the proud *o.* me
Prov. 22:22 nor *o.* the afflicted
Is. 49:26 feed them that *o.* thee
Jer. 7:6 if ye *o.* not the stranger
30:20 punish all that *o.* them
Ezek. 45:8 princes sh. no more *o.*
Hos. 12:7 merchant loveth to *o.*
Amos 4:1 kine of Bashan *o.* poor
Mic. 2:2 *o.* a man and his house
Zec. 7:10 *o.* not widow nor fath.
Mal. 3:5 witness ag. those that *o.*
Jam. 2:6 do not ri. men *o.* you ?

OPPRESSED.

Deut. 28:29 shalt be only *o.* 33
Jud. 2:18 by reason of th. that *o.*
4:3 Jabin *o.* Israel; 10:8 Phil. *o.*
6:9 out of the hand of all that *o.*
you, 1 *Sam.* 10:18
1 *Sam.* 12:3 whom have I *o. ?*
4 hast not defrauded nor *o.* us
2 *K.* 13:4 Assyria *o.* 22 king of
2 *Chr.* 16:10 Asa *o.* some of peo.
Job 20:19 *o.* and forsaken poor
35:9 they make the *o.* to cry
Ps. 9:9 Lord be a refuge for *o.*
10:18 judge the *o.* 103:6; 146:7
74:21 let not *o.* return ashamed
106:42 their enemies *o.* them
Ec. 4:1 tears of such as were *o.*
Is. 1:17 seek judgm. relieve *o.*
3:5 people shall be *o.* every one
23:12 O thou, *o.* virgin, daught.
38:14 I am *o.* undertake for me
52:4 Assy. *o.* them without cau.
53:7 he was *o.* and afflicted
58:6 fast? to let the *o.* go free
Jer. 50:33 Is. and Judah were *o.*
Ezek. 18:7 hath not *o.* any. 16
12 he hath *o.* 18 he cruelly *o.*
22:29 *o.* stranger wrongfully
Hos. 5:11 Ephr. is *o.* and broken
Amos 3:9 behold thee *o.* in midst
Acts 7:24 Moses avenged him *o.*
10:38 J. healed all that were *o.*

OPPRESSETH.

Num. 10:9 go to war ag. him *o.*
Ps. 56:1 he fighting daily *o.* me
Prov. 14:31 he that *o.* poor, 22:16
28:3 a poor man that *o.* the poor

OPPRESSING.

Jer. 46:16 let us go from *o.* swo.
50:16 for fear of the *o.* sword
Zep. 3:1 woe to the *o.* city

OPPRESSION.

Ex. 3:9 *o.* wherewith Egyptians
Deut. 26:7 L. looked on our *o.*
2 *K.* 13:4 Lord saw *o.* of Israel
Job 36:15 openeth their ears in *o.*
Ps. 12:5 for *o.* of poor will I arise
42:9 *o.* of the enemy. 43:2; 55:3
44:24 forget. our *o.* 62:10 trust
73:8 speak wickedly concern. *o.*
107:39 are brought low thro' *o.*
119:134 deliver me fr. *o.* of man
Ec. 5:8 if thou seest *o.* of poor
7:7 *o.* maketh a wise man mad
Is. 5:7 behold *o.* 30:12 trust *o.*
54:14 thou shalt be far from *o.*
59:13 from our G. speaking *o.*
Jer. 6:6 wholly *o.* in midst of h.
22:17 th. eyes and heart for *o.*
Ezek. 22:7 by *o.* with stranger
29 people of the land used *o.*
46:18 sh. not take inherit. by *o.*

OPPRESSIONS.

Job 35:9 by the multitude of *o.*
Ec. 4:1 I considered the *o.* done
Is. 33:15 despiseth the gain of *o.*

OPPRESSOR.

Job 3:18 they hear not voice of *o.*
15:20 number of years hid. to *o.*
Ps. 72:4 shall break in pieces *o.*
Prov. 3:31 envy not *o.* cho. none
28:16 want. understanding is *o.*
Is. 9:4 hast broken rod of his *o.*
14:4 say, How hath *o.* ceased !
51:13 hast feared fury of the *o.*
Jer. 21:12 out of hand of *o.* 22:3
25:38 because of fierceness of *o.*
Zec. 9:8 no *o.* shall pass through
10:4 out of him came every *o.*

OPPRESSORS.

Job 27:13 this is the herita. of *o.*
Ps. 54:3 *o.* seek after my soul
119:121 leave me not to mine *o.*
Ec. 4:1 side of *o.* th. was power
Is. 3:12 children are their *o.*
14:2 they shall rule over their *o.*
16:4 *o.* consumed out of the land
19:20 cry to Lord because of *o.*

ORACLE.

2 *Sam.* 16:23 inquired at *o.* of G.
1 *K.* 6:16 be built them for the *o.*
8:6 priests bro. ark of L. into *o.*
2 *Chr.* 4:20 should burn be. the *o.*
Ps. 28:2 lift up hands to. holy *o.*

ORACLES.

Acts 7:38 received the lively *o.*
Rom. 3:2 to them were com. *o.*
Heb. 5:12 first princip. of *o.* of G.
1 *Pet.* 4:11 speak of the *o.* of God

ORATION.

Acts 12:21 Herod made *o.* to th.

ORATOR.

Is. 3:3 from Ju. the eloquent *o.*
Acts 24:1 *o.* named Tertullus

ORCHARD, S.

Cant. 4:13 an *o.* of pomegranates
Ec. 2:5 I made me gard. and *o.*

ORDAIN.

1 *Chr.* 9:22 S. did *o.* in their offi.
17:9 I will *o.* a place for my pe.
Is. 26:12 L. that wilt *o.* peace
1 *Cor.* 7:17 so *o.* I in all churches
Tit. 1:5 thou shouldest *o.* elders

ORDAINED, ETH.

Num. 28:6 offering that was *o.*

1 *K.* 12:32 Jerobo. *o.* a feast, 33
2 *K.* 23:5 put down id. priests *o.*
2 *Chr.* 11:15 Jeroboam *o.* priests
  29:**27** instruments *o.* by David
Est. 9:27 Jews *o.* feast of Purim
Ps. 7:13 *o.* arrows ag. persecut.
  8:2 out of mouth of babes *o.*
  3 moon and stars thou hast *o.*
  81:5 *o.* in Joseph for testimony
  132:17 I have *o.* a lamp for mine
Is. 30:33 Tophet is *o.* of old
Jer. 1:5 I *o.* thee to be a prophet
Dan. 2:24 king *o.* to destroy men
Hab. 1:1**2** O L. thou hast *o.* them
Mark 3:14 Jesus *o.* 12 to be with
John 15:16 I *o.* ye sho. bri. fruit
Acts 1:22 *o.* to be witness with
  10:42 *o.* of God to be judge
  13:48 as were *o.* to eternal life
  14:23 when they *o.* them elders
  16:4 decrees were *o.* of apostles
  17:31 judge by man he hath *o.*
Rom. 7:10 command. *o.* to life
  13:1 powers that be, are *o.* of G
1 *Cor.* 2:7 hidden wisdom God *o.*
  9:14 Lord *o.* that they which pr.
Gal. 3:19 law was *o.* by angels
Eph. 2:10 wh. God hath before *o.*
1 *Tim.* 2:7 I am *o.* a preacher to G
Heb. 5:1 ev. high-priest is *o.* 8:3
  9:6 when these things were *o.*
Jude 4 *o.* to this condemnation

ORDER, Substantive.

2 *K.* 23:4 comp. priests of sec. *o.*
1 *Chr.* 6:32 waited accord. to *o.*
  15:13 sought him not aft. due *o.*
  23:31 *o.* commanded them be. L.
  25:2 acc. to *o.* of D. 6 ; 2 *Ch.* 8:14
Job 10:22 land of dark. without *o.*
Ps. 110:4 pri. after *o.* of M. *Heb.*
  5:6, 10 ; 6:20 ; 7:11, 17, 21
1 *Cor.* 16:1 have gi. *o.* to church.
Col. 2:5 beholding your *o.*
Heb. 7:11 not called after *o.* of A.

In ORDER.

Gen. 22:9 Abr. laid wood *in o.*
Ex. 40:4 thou sh. set *in o.* thin.
  that are to be set *in o.* Lev.
  1:7, 8, 12 ; 6:12 ; 24:8
  23 he set bread *in o.* upon it
2 *Sam.* 17:23 put his house *in o.*
1 *K.* 18:33 Elijah put wood *in o.*
2 *K.* 20:1 set house *in o.* *Is.* 38:1
2 *Chr.* 13:11 show-bread set *in o.*
  29:35 service of house of L. *in o.*
Job 33:5 set words *in o.* bef. me
Ps. 50:21 th. *in o.* bef. thine eyes
Ec. 12:9 the preacher set *in o.*
Is. 44:7 set it *in o.* before me
Ezek. 41:6 chambers were 30 *in o.*
Luke 1:1 hand to set forth *in o.* 3
  8 served before God *in* his *o.*
Acts 18:23 country of Phry. *in o.*
1 *Cor.* 11:34 rest will I set *in o.*
  15:23 ev. man shall rise *in* his *o.*
Tit. 1:5 I left thee to set *in o.*

ORDER, Verb.

Ex. 27:21 Aa. *o.* it, *Lev.* 24:3, 4
Jud. 13:12 how sh. we *o.* child ?
1 *K.* 20:14 who shall *o.* battle?
Job 23:4 *o.* my cause before him
  37:19 we cannot *o.* our speech
Ps. 119:133 *o.* steps in thy word
Is. 9:7 upon his kingdom to *o.* it
Jer. 46:3 *o.* ye buckler and shield

ORDERED, ETH.

Jud. 6:26 build altar *in o.* place
2 *Sam.* 23:5 covenant *o.* and sure
Job 13:18 I have *o.* my cause, I
Ps. 37:23 steps of good man are *o.*
  50:23 who *o.* conversation arig.

ORDERINGS.

1 *Chr.* 24:19 these were their *o.*

ORDERLY.

Acts 21:21 walkest *o.* keepest law

ORDINANCE.

Ex. 12:14 feast of passover for an
  o. forever, 24, 43 ; 13:10
  15:25 made a statute and an *o.*
Num. 9:14 according to *o.* of
  passover, 2 *Chr.* 35:13
  10:8 to be you for an *o.* for e.
  18:8 and to thy sons by an *o.*
  for ever, 2 *Chr.* 2:4
  19:2 *o.* of L. commanded, 31:21
Jos. 24:25 set them *o.* in Shech.
1 *Sam.* 30:2**5** made it *o.* for ever
2 *Chr.* 35:25 made them *o.* in Is.
Ezr. 3:10 after the *o.* of David
Is. 24:5 the law changed the *o.*
  58:2 forsook not *o.* of their God
Ezek. 46:14 offering by perpet. *o.*
Mal. 3:14 what pro. we kept *o.* ?
Rom. 13:2 power resists *o.* of G.
1 *Pet.* 2:13 submit to every *o.* of

ORDINANCES.

Ex. 18:20 shalt teach them *o.*
Lev. 18:3 neither walk in their *o.*
  4 ye sh. keep mine *o.* 30 ; 22:9 ;
  2 *Chr.* 33:8 ; *Ezek.* 11:20 ;
  43:11 ; 1 *Cor.* 11:2
Num. 9:12 to *o.* of passover, 14
2 *K.* 17:37 *o.* he wrote for you
Neh. 10:32 made *o.* made for us
Job 38:33 knowest thou the *o.* of
  heaven ? *Jer.* 31:35 ; 33:25
Ps. 99:7 kept *o.* he gave them
  119:91 continue according to *o.*
Is. 58:2 ask of me *o.* of justice
Jer. 31:36 if *o.* depart before me
Ezek. 43:18 these are *o.* of altar
  44:5 *o.* of the house of the Lord
Mal. 3:7 gone away fr. mine *o.*
Luke 1:6 commandments and *o.*
  of Lord
Eph. 2:15 commandment con-
  tained in *o.*
Col. 2:14 out handwriting of *o.*
  20 are ye subject to *o.* ?
Heb. 9:1 had *o.* of divine service
  10 carnal *o.* imposed on them

ORDINARY.

Ezek. 16:27 diminished *o.* food

OREB.

Jud. 7:25 of Mid. Zeeb, O. 8:3
Ps. 83:11 their nobles like O.
Is. 10:26 of Midian at rock of O.

ORGAN, S.

Gen. 4:21 of such as handle *o.*
Job 21:12 rejoice at sound of *o.*
  30:31 my *o.* turned into voice
Ps. 150:4 praised him with *o.*

ORION.

Job 9:9 maketh O. *Amos* 5:8
  38:31 loose the bands of O. ?

ORNAMENT.

Prov. 1:9 *o.* of grace to thy head
  4:9 give to head an *o.* of grace
  25:1**2** as an *o.* of fine gold, so is
Is. 30:22 defile *o.* of molten ima.
  49:18 clothe thee as with an *o.*
Ezek. 7:20 the beauty of his *o.*
1 *Pet.* 3:4 *o.* of meek, quiet spirit

ORNAMENTS.

Ex. 33:4 no man put on him *o.*
  5 put off thy *o.* from thee, 6
Jud. 8:21 *o.* on camels' neck
2 *Sam.* 1:24 S. who put *o.* on you
Is. 3:18 tinkling *o.* about feet
  61:10 decketh himself with *o.*
Jer. 2:32 can a maid forget her *o.*
  4:30 deckest thee wi. *o.* of gold
Ezek. 16:7 come to excellent *o.*
  11 decked thee with *o.* put
  23:40 deckedst thyself with *o.*

ORNAN.

1 *Chr.* 21:15 floor of O. 18, 28
  20 O. turned back, saw angel
  25 Da. gave to O. 600 shekels

ORPAH.

Ruth 1:4 name of one O. other R.
  14 O. kissed Naomi, but Ruth

ORPHANS.

Lam. 5:3 are *o.* our mothers wid.
OSPREY, OSSIFRAGE.
Lev. 11:13 *o.* and *o. Deut.* 14:12

OSTRICH, ES.

Job 39:13 wings and feath. to *o.*?
Lam. 4:3 like *o.* in the wildern.

OTHER.

Gen. 28:17 none *o.* but ho. of G.
Jud. 13:10 came to me *o.* day
  16:17 and be like any *o.* man
  20 go out, as at *o.* times before
1 *Sam.* L. called as at *o.* ti.
  20:25 S. sat on seat as at *o.* tim.
  21:9 there is no *o.* save th. here
Mat. 12:13 restored whole as *o.*
  Mark 3:5 ; *Luke* 6:10
Mark 7:4 many *o.* thin. th. be, 8
  12:32 and there is none *o.* but he
Luke 14:32 *o.* is yet a gr. way off
  18:11 that I am not as *o.* men
John 15:24 works no. *o.* man did
  21:25 there are many *o.* things
Acts 4:12 nei. is salva. in any *o.*
  8:34 himself, or of some *o.* man ?

See GOD, GODS, ONE, SIDE.

OTHERS.

Mat. 5:47 wh. do ye more th. *o.*?
Mark 15:31 saved *o.* *Luke* 23:35
Phil. 2:4 also on the things of *o.*
1 *Thes.* 2:6 not yet of *o.* sought

OTHERWISE.

2 *Chr.* 30:18 they eat passover *o.*
Ps. 38:16 *o.* should rej. over me
Rom. 11:6 *o.* grace no mo. grace ;
  o. work is no more work
Gal. 5:10 will be none *o.* minded
Phil. 3:15 any thing you be *o.*
1 *Tim.* 6:3 if any man teach *o.*

OTHNIEL.

Jos. 15:17 O. took it, *Jud.* 1:13
Jud. 3:9 raised deliverer, O. 11

OUCHES.

Ex. 28:11 *o.* of gold, 39:6, 13
  13 thou shalt make *o.* of gold
  14 fasten chains to the *o.* 39:18
  25 thou shalt fasten in two *o.*

OUGHT, *or rather* AUGHT.

Gen. 39:6 he knew not *o.* he had
  47:18 there is not *o.* left
Ex. 12:46 not car. forth *o.* flesh
Lev. 11:25 whoso beareth *o.* car.
  19:6 if *o.* remain unto third day
  25:14 sellest *o.* or buyest *o.*
Num. 15:24 if *o.* be committed
  30:6 or uttered *o.* out of her lips
Deut. 4:2 not add *o.* or diminish *o.*
  26:14 nei. have I taken *o.* in my
  mourn. nor given *o.* for dead
Jos. 21:45 there failed not *o.*
Ruth 1:17 if *o.* but death part
1 *Sam.* 12:4 nor hast th. taken *o.*
  5 have not found *o.* in my ha.
  25:7 neither was th. *o.* missing
  30:22 he will not give them *o.*
2 *Sam.* 3:35 if I taste bread or *o.*
  14:10 whoso saith *o.* to thee
2 *Sam.* 14:19 can turn fr. *o.* my lo.
Mat. 5:23 brother hath *o.* ag. th.
  21:3 if any man say *o.* to you
Mark 7:12 suf. him no more do *o.*
  8:23 and asked him if he saw *o.*
  11:25 forgive, if ye have *o.* ag.
John 4:33 brought him *o.* to eat?
Acts 4:32 nei. said *o.* was his own
  24:19 if they had *o.* against me
  28:19 had *o.* to ac. my nation of
Phile. 18 if he oweth thee *o.*

OUGHT.

Gen. 20:9 *o.* not be done, 34:7 :
Lev. 4:2, 27

OUGHT

2 Sam. 13:12 no such th. *o.* to be
1 Chr. 12:32 kn. what Is. *o.* to do
Mat. 23:23 *o.* ha. done, *Lu.* 11:42
Acts 24:19 who *o.* to have been
Rom. 8:26 to pray for as we *o.*
1 Tim. 5:13 speak. th. they *o.* not
Tit. 1:11 teach. thi. they *o.* not
Jam. 3:10 these thi. *o.* not to be
4:15 that ye *o.* to say, If the L.
2 Pet. 3:11 what pers. *o.* ye to be
3 John 8 we therefore *o.* to rece.

OUGHTEST

1 K. 2:9 wh. thou *o.* to do to him
Mat. 25:27 *o.* to put my money
Acts 10:6 tell thee what thou *o.*
1 Tim. 3:15 how th. *o.* to behave

OUR. *See* BROTHER, FATHER.
LORD.

OURS.

Gen. 31:16 hath taken that is *o.*
34:23 shall not ev. beast be *o. ?*
Mark 12:7 the inheritance shall
be *o. Luke* 20:14
1 Cor. 1:2 Jesus, both th. and *o.*
2 Cor. 1:14 ye are *o.* in day of L.

OUTCAST.

Ps. 147:2 gathereth *o.* of Israel
Is. 11:12 shall assemble *o.* 56:8
16:3 hide *o.* 4 let my *o.* dwell
27:13 *o.* in land of Eg. worship
Jer. 30:17 bec. they called thee *o.*
49:36 *o.* of Elam shall not come

OUTER.

Ezek. 46:21 broug. me to *o.* court
Mat. 8:12 *o.* darkn. 22:13 ; 25:30

OUTGOINGS.

Jos. 17:9 *o.* of it at sea, 19:29
18 and the *o.* it shall be thine
18:19 *o.* of the border at north
19:14 *o.* thereof are in the valley
22 *o.* of border at the Jord. 33
Ps. 65:8 makest *o.* of morning

OUTLANDISH.

Neh. 13:26 *o.* women caused Sol.

OUTLIVED.

Jud. 2:7 elders that *o.* Joshua

OUTRAGEOUS.

Prov. 27:4 wrath is cruel, ang. *o.*

OUTRUN.

John 20:4 other disciple *o.* Peter

OUTSIDE.

Jud. 7:11 Gideon went to the *o.*
1 K. 7:9 *o.* towards great court
Ezek. 40:5 beho. a wall on the *o.*
Mat. 23:25 *o.* of cup, *Luke* 11:39
26 that *o.* of them be clean also

OUTSTRETCHED.

Deut. 26:8 us out with an *o.* arm
Jer. 21:5 fight you with *o.* arm
27:5 made earth by my *o.* arm

OUTWARD.

1 Sam. 16:7 looketh on *o.* appear.
1 Chr. 26:29 for the *o.* business
Neh. 11:16 Levites for *o.* business
Est. 6:4 Ham. come to *o.* court
Ezek. 40:17 brought into *o.* court
Mat. 23:27 appear beautiful *o.*
Rom. 2:28 which is *o.* in flesh
2 Cor. 4:16 tho' our *o.* man perish
10:7 things after *o.* appearance ?
1 Pet. 3:3 not that *o.* adorning

OUTWARDLY.

Mat. 23:28 *o.* appear righteous
Rom. 2:28 not a Jew wh. is one *o.*

OUTWENT.

Mark 6:33 ran afoot, and *o.* them

OVEN.

Lev. 2:4 offering baken in *o.* 7:9
11:35 whether it be *o.* or ranges
26:26 bake your bread in one *o.*
Ps. 21:9 make them as a fiery *o.*
Lam. 5:10 skin was black like *o.*
Hos. 7:4 as an *o.* heated by baker

6 made ready heart like an *o.* 7
Mal. 4:1 that shall burn as an *o.*
Mat. 6:30 cast into *o. Luke* 12:28

OVENS.

Ex. 8:3 frogs come into thine *o.*

OVER.

Num. 27:16 set man *o.* congrega.
Cant. 2:11 winter past, rain is *o.*

OVER against.

Num. 8:2 lamps gi. light *o. a.* 3
2 Sam. 5:23 come on them *o. ag.*
mulberry-trees, 1 *Chr.* 14:14
1 K. 20:29 pitched one *o. a.* other
Neh. 7:3 ev. one to be *o. a.* house
Ec. 7:14 God set one *o. a.* other
Jer. 31:39 line go forth *o. ag.* it

See ALL, HIM, JORDAN, ISRAEL,
ME, THEE, THEM, US, YOU.

OVERCAME.

Acts 19:16 evil spi. was, *o.* then
Rev. 3:21 even as I also *o.*
12:11 *o.* him by blood of Lamb

OVERCHARGE, D.

Luke 21:34 lest your hearts be *o.*
2 Cor. 2:5 that I may not *o.* you

OVERCOME.

Gen. 49:19 troop shall *o.* him
Ex. 32:18 that cry for being *o.*
Num. 13:30 are well able to *o.* it
22:11 peradventure I sh. *o.* them
2 K. 16:5 Ahaz, could not *o.* him
Cant. 6:5 eyes, they have *o.* me
Is. 28:1 head of them that are *o.*
Jer. 23:9 man whom wine hath *o.*
Luke 11:22 stronger shall *o.* him
John 16:33 I have *o.* the world
Rom. 3:4 *o.* wh. thou art judged
12:21 be not *o.* of evil, *o.* evil
2 Pet. 2:19 of whom man is *o.*
20 ag. entangled therein and *o.*
1 John 2:13 *o.* wicked one, 14
4:4 are of God, have *o.* them
Rev. 11:7 beast sh. *o.* witnesses
13:7 war with saints, *o.* them
17:14 and Lamb shall *o.* them

OVERCOMETH.

1 John 5:4 born of God *o.* world,
victory *o.* world, 5
Rev. 2:7 *o.* will I give tree of life
11 he that *o.* shall not be hurt
17 him that *o.* will I gi. to eat
26 him that *o.* will I give pow.
3:5 he that *o.* shall be clothed
12 him that *o.* will I make pil.
21 that *o.* will I grant to sit
21:7 that *o.* shall inh. all things

OVERDRIVE.

Gen. 33:13 if men sho. *o.* them

OVERFLOW.

Deut. 11:4 water of Red sea *o.*
Ps. 62:2 come where floods *o.*
15 let not waterfloods *o.* me
Is. 8:8 thro' Jud. *o.* and go over
10:22 consumpti. decreed sh. *o.*
28:17 waters *o.* the hiding-place
43:2 rivers they sh. not *o.* thee
Jer. 47:2 waters of north *o.* land
Dan. 11:10 certai. come, *o.* 26, 40
Joel 2:24 fats *o.* with wine, 3:13

OVERFLOWED, ETH.

Jos. 3:15 in harvest Jor. *o.* banks
Ps. 78:20 smote rock, streams *o.*
2 Pet. 3:6 world *o.* with water

OVERFLOWING.

Job 28:11 bindeth floods from *o.*
38:25 watercourse for *o.* of wat.
Is. 28:2 flood of mighty wat. *o.*
15 when *o.* scourge pass, 18
30:28 his breath as *o.* stream
Jer. 47:2 north sh. be an *o.* flood
Ezek. 13:11 be an *o.* shower, 13
38:22 rain *o.* rain and hailstones
Hab. 3:10 the *o.* of the water

OVERFLOWN.

1 Chr. 12:15 Jor. when it had *o.*
Job 22:16 wh. foundation was *o.*
Dan. 11:22 with flood they be *o.*

OVERLAY.

Ex. 25:11 *o.* ark, 24 ; 30:3
27:2 *o.* altar with brass, 38:2

OVERLAID.

Ex. 26:32 pillars *o.* with gold
38:6 *o.* staves of shittim-wood
1 K. 3:19 died, because she *o.* it
2 Chr. 4:9 he *o.* doors with brass
Cant. 5:14 belly as bri. ivory *o.*

See GOLD.

OVERLAYING.

Ex. 38:17 the *o.* of chapiters, 19

OVERLIVED.

Jos. 24:31 days of elders th. *o.* J.

OVERMUCH.

Ec. 7:16 righte. *o.* 17 be not *o.*
2 Cor. 2:7 swallow. with *o.* sor.

OVERPASS.

Jer. 5:28 they *o.* deeds of wicked

OVERPAST.

Ps. 57:1 refuge until calam. be *o.*
Is. 26:20 hide until indign. be *o.*

OVERPLUS.

Lev. 25:27 let him restore the *o.*

OVERRAN, RUNNING.

2 Sam. 18:23 Ahimaaz *o.* Cushi
Nah. 1:8 an *o.* flood will he make

OVERSEE.

1 Chr. 9:29 appointed to *o.* vess.
2 Chr. 2:2 3,600 to *o.* them

OVERSEER.

Gen. 39:4 made *o.* over house, 5
Neh. 11:9 Joel th. *o.* 14 Zabd. *o.*
22 *o.* of Levites ; 12:42 Jez. *o.*
Prov. 6:7 the ant having no *o.*

OVERSEERS.

Gen. 41:34 let Pharaoh appoint *o.*
2 Chr. 2:18 Solomon set 3,600 *o.*
31:13 *o.* under hand of Cononiah
34:12 *o.* of all that wrought, 13
17 deliv. mon. into hand of *o.*
Acts 20:28 H. Ghost made you *o.*

OVERSHADOW, ED.

Mat. 17:5 bright cloud *o.* them,
Mark 9:7 ; *Luke* 9:34
Luke 1:35 power of High. *o.* thee
Acts 5:15 shadow of P. *o.* them

OVERSIGHT.

Gen. 43:12 peradv. it was an *o.*
Num. 3:32 *o.* of them that keep
4:16 the *o.* of all the tabernacle
2 K. 12:11 that had *o.* of house of
L. 22:5, 9 ; *2 Chr.* 34:10
1 Chr. 9:23 had the *o.* of the gates
Neh. 11:16 had the *o.* of business
13:4 the *o.* of the house of God
1 Pet. 5:2 taking *o.* not by const.

OVERSPREAD, ING.

Gen. 9:19 of th. whole earth was *o.*
Dan. 9:27 the *o.* of abominations

OVERTAKE.

Gen. 44:4 when thou dost *o.* th.
Ex. 15:9 I will pursue, I will *o.*
Deut. 19:6 lest avenger *o.* slayer
28:2 blessings come and *o.* thee
15 these curses shall *o.* thee, 45
Jos. 2:5 for ye shall *o.* them
1 Sam. 30:8 thou sh. surely *o.* th.
2 Sam. 15:14 lest Absalom *o.* us
Is. 59:9 bec. of dark. *o.* us
Jer. 42:16 sw. ye feared sh. *o.* you
Hos. 2:7 shall not *o.* her lovers
10:9 the battle did not *o.* them
Amos 9:10 evil shall not *o.* us
13 ploughman sh. *o.* the reaper
1 Thes. 5:4 should *o.* you as thief

OVERTAKEN, ETH.

1 Chr. 21:12 flee till sword *o.* th.

Ps. 18:37 purs. enemies *o.* them
Gal. 6:1 if a man be *o.* in a fault

OVERTHREW.

Gen. 19:25 God *o.* these cities, 29
Ex. 14:27 L. *o.* Eg. *Ps.* 136:15
Deut. 29:23 which L. *o.* in anger
Is. 13:19 when G. *o.* Sodom and
Gomo. *Jer.* 50:40 ; *Amos* 4:11
Jer. 20:16 he as cities the Lord *o.*
Mat. 21:12 J. *o.* tables of money-
chang. *Mark* 11:15 ; *John* 2:15

OVERTHROW, Substantive.

Gen. 19:29 G. sent Lot out of *o.*
Deut. 29:23 *o.* of Sod. *Jer.* 49:18
2 *Pet.* 2:6 condem. cities with *o.*

OVERTHROW, Verb.

Gen. 19:21 I will not *o.* this city
Ex. 23:24 thou sh. *o.* their gods
Deut. 12:3 ye shall *o.* their altars
2 *Sam.* 10:3 D. sent to spy and *o.*
11:25 make battle strong, *o.* it
1 *Chr.* 19:3 David sent to *o.* land
Ps. 106:26 to *o.* them in wildern.
27 to *o.* their seed am. nations
140:4 have pur. to *o.* my goings
11 evil hunt vio. man to *o.* him
Prov. 18:5 not good to *o.* righte.
Hag. 2:22 I will *o.* the throne of
kingd. I will *o.* the chariots
Acts 5:39 if it be of G. ye can. *o.*
2 *Tim.* 2:18 *o.* the faith of some

OVERTHROWETH.

Job 12:19 lead. princes, *o.* mighty
Prov. 13:6 wickedness *o.* sinner
21:12 G. *o.* wicked for wickedn.
22:12 *o.* words of transgressor
29:4 he that receiv. gifts *o.* land

OVERTHROWN.

Ex. 15:7 hast *o.* them that rose
Jud. 9:40 and many were *o.*
2 *Sam.* 17:9 some of them be *o.*
2 *Chr.* 14:13 Ethiopians were *o.*
Job 19:6 know th. G. hath *o.* me
Ps. 141:6 their judges are *o.*
Prov. 11:11 city is *o.* by wicked
12:7 wicked *o.* 14:11 ho. of wic.
Is. 1:7 your land is desolate as *o.*
Jer. 18:23 let them be *o.* bef. th.
Lam. 4:6 S. was *o.* as in moment
Dan. 11:41 many countries be *o.*
Amos 4:11 I have *o.* some of you
Jon. 3:4 40 days Ninev. sh. be *o.*
1 *Cor.* 10:5 were *o.* in wilderness

OVERTOOK.

Gen. 31:23 *o.* Jacob in mount
25 Lab. *o.* Jacob ; 44:6 steward
Jud. 18:22 Micah *o.* chil. of Dan
20:42 battle *o.* men of Benjamin
2 *K.* 25:5 army of Chaldeans *o.*
Zedekiah, *Jer.* 39:5 ; 52:8
Lam. 1:3 her persecuters *o.* her

OVERTURN.

Job 12:15 waters, they *o.* earth
Ezek. 21:27 I will *o. o.* it

OVERTURNED, ETH.

Jud. 7:13 the tent fell and *o.* it
Job 9:5 which *o.* the mountains
28:9 *o.* mountains by the roots
34:25 know th. works and *o.*

OVERWHELM, ED.

Job 6:27 yea, ye *o.* fatherless
Ps. 55:5 and horror hath *o.* me
61:2 when my heart is *o.*
77:3 my spirit *o.* 142:3 ; 143:4
78:53 the sea *o.* their enemies
124:4 then the waters had *o.* us

OVERWISE.

Ec. 7:16 nor make thyself *o.*

OWE.

Rom. 13:8 *o.* no man any thing

OWED.

Mat. 18:24 one *o.* him 10,000 tal.
28 one which *o.* him a 100 pen.
Luke 7:41 the one *o.* 500 pence

OWEST, ETH.

Mat. 18:28 pay me that thou *o.*
Luke 16:5 how much *o.* thou ? 7
Phile. 18 thee, or *o.* thee aught
19 *o.* to me even thine own

OWL.

Lev. 11:16 *o.* and cuckoo, *Deut.*
14:15, 16 : *Is.* 34:11, 15
17 the little *o.* and cormorant
Ps. 102:6 I am like *o.* of desert

OWLS.

Job 30:29 I am companion to *o.*
Is. 13:21 *o.* shall dwell there,
34:13 ; *Jer.* 50:39
43:20 dragons and *o.* honor me
Mic. 1:8 make a mourning as *o.*

OWN.

1 *Chr.* 29:14 *o.* have we giv. thee
16 we prepared, is all thine *o.*
Mat. 20:15 do wh. I will wi. *o.* ?
Luke 16:12 you that which is *o.* ?
John 1:11 came to his *o. o.* rece.
13:1 loved his *o.* that were
15:19 world would love his *o.*
Acts 5:4 was it not in th. *o.* pow.?
1 *Cor.* 6:19 ye are not your *o.*
10:24 let no man seek his *o.*
29 cons. not th. *o.* but of oth.
13:5 charity seeketh not her *o.*
Phil. 2:21 seek their *o.* things
1 *Tim.* 5:8 provide not for his *o.*

See COUNSEL, COUNTRY, EYES,
HEART, HOUSE, LAND,
PEOPLE, SELF, SELVES, SOUL,
WAY, WAYS, WILL.

OWNER.

Ex. 21:28 *o.* of ox shall be quit
34 *o.* of pit sh. make it good
36 his *o.* hath not kept him in
22:11 *o.* of it sh. accept thereof
12 make restitution to *o.*
15 but if *o.* thereof be with it
1 *K.* 16:24 Shemer, *o.* of the hill
Is. 1:3 the ox knoweth his *o.*
Acts 27:11 believed *o.* of the ship

OWNERS.

Job 31:39 caused *o.* to lose lives
Prov. 1:19 taketh away life of *o.*
Ec. 5:11 what good is there to *o.*
13 riches kept for *o.* to th. hurt
Luke 19:33 *o.* said, Why loose ye

OWNETH.

Lev. 14:35 he that *o.* the house
Acts 21:11 bind man *o.* th. girdle

OX.

Ex. 20:17 not covet. *o. Deut.* 5:21
21:28 if *o.* gore, be stoned, 29–36
22:1 if man steal *o.* or sheep
4 whether it be *o.* or ass, he
23:4 if thou meet th. enemy's *o.*
12 thine *o.* and thine ass rest
Ex. 34:19 firstl. of *o.* or sheep mi.
Lev. 7:23 eat no fat of *o.*
Num. 7:3 for each of princes *o.*
22:4 as the *o.* licketh up grass

Deut. 5:14 *o.* do no work on sab.
14:4 *o.* sheep, and goat may eat
22:1 not see bro.'s *o.* go astray
10 not plough with *o.* and ass
25:4 not muzzle *o.* treadeth out
corn, 1 *Cor.* 9:9 ; 1 *Tim.* 5:18
Jos. 6:21 they destroy *o.* and
sheep, 1 *Sam.* 15:15
Jud. 3:31 slew 600 with *o.*-goad
6:4 left neither sheep nor *o.*
1 *Sam.* 12:3 wh. *o.* have I taken ?
14:34 bring ev. man *o.* and sheep
Neh. 5:18 for me daily one *o.*
Job 6:5 loweth *o.* over fodder ?
24:3 take widow's *o.* for pledge
40:15 Behemoth eat. grass as *o.*
Ps. 69:31 please L. better than *o.*
106:20 glory into similitu. of *o.*
Prov. 7:22 *o.* goeth to slaughter
14:4 incre. by strength of the *o.*
15:17 better than a stalled *o.*
Is. 1:3 the *o.* knoweth his owner
11:7 lion shall eat straw like *o.*
32:20 send for. the feet of the *o.*
66:3 killeth *o.* as if he slew man
Jer. 11:19 was like a lamb or an *o.*
Ezek. 1:10 four had face of an *o.*
Luke 13:15 each loose *o.* on sab.
14:5 an *o.* or ass fallen into **a pit**

Wild OX.

Deut. 14:5 *wild o.* ye may **eat**

OXEN.

Gen. 12:16 Ab. had *o.* and **asses**
32:5 J. said, I have *o.* and **asses**
34:28 sons of J. took Shech. *o.*
Ex. 9:3 hand of Lord is upon *o.*
22:1 restore five *o.* for one ox
Num. 7:3 princes bro. twelve *o.*
22:40 Balak offered *o.* and sheep
23:1 prepare me here seven *o.*
Deut. 14:26 bestow money for *o.*
1 *Sam.* 11:7 hewed yoke of *o.*
14:14 yoke of *o.* might plough
32 took sheep *o.* and slew
15:9 Agag and the best of the *o.*
14 what meaneth lowing of *o.* ?
15 spared best of sheep and *o.*
27:9 David took away the *o.*
2 *Sam.* 6:6 hold of it, *o.* shook it
13 Da. sacrificed *o.* and fatlings
24:24 bought thres.-floor and *o.*
1 *K.* 1:9 Adonijah slew *o.* 19, 25
4:23 daily provision, ten fat *o.*
7:25 one sea, twelve *o.* under it,
44 ; 2 *Chr.* 4:4, 15
8:63 S. off. sacrifice to L. 22,000
o. 120,000 sheep, 2 *Chr.* 7:5
19:19 El. was ploughing with *o.*
20 Elisha left *o.* ran after Elij.
21 took yoke of *o.* slew them
2 *K.* 5:26 is it a time to rec. *o.* ?
2 *Chr.* 15:11 offered of spoil 700 *o.*
18:2 Ahab killed sheep and *o.*
29:33 consecrated things 600 *o.*
31:6 they brought in tithes of *o.*
35:8 for passo. three hundred *o.*
Job 1:3 his substance was 500 *o.*
14 *o.* ploughing, asses feeding
42:12 gave him 1,000 yoke of *o.*
Ps. 8:7 to have dominion over *o.*
144:14 that our *o.* may be strong
Prov. 14:4 wh. no *o.* crib is clean
Is. 7:25 for sending forth of *o.*
22:13 joy and gladn. slaying *o.*
30:24 *o.* and asses eat cl. prov.
Jer. 51:23 I break husb. and *o.*
Dan. 4:25 eat gr. as *o.* 33 ; 5:21
Amos 6:12 plough there with *o.* ?
Mat. 22:4 *o.* and fatlings killed
Luke 14:19 bought 5 yoke of *o.*
John 2:14 those in temple sold *o.*
Acts 14:13 priest of Jup. bro. *o.*
1 *Cor.* 9:9 doth G. ta. care for *o.* ?

OZEM. 1 *Chr.* 2:15
OZIAS. *Mat.* 1:8, 9

P

PAARAI. *2 Sam.* 23:35

PACES.

2 Sam. 6:13 when gone six *p.* he

PACIFY, ED, ETH.

Est. 7:10 then king's wrath *p.*
Prov. 16:14 a wise man *p.* wrath
21:14 a gift in secret *p.* anger
Ec. 10:4 yielding *p.* gr. offences
Ezek. 16:63 when I am *p.* toward

PADAN-ARAM.

Gen. 25:20 dau. of Bethuel of P.
28:6 Isa. sent Jacob away to P.
7 his father, and was gone to P.
31:18 had gotten in P.
Gen. 35:9 J. when he came fr. P.
26 sons born to him in P. 46:15

PADDLE.

Deut. 23:13 have *p.* on weapon

PAGIEL.

Num. 1:13 P. son of Ocran, 7:72

PAID. *See after* PAY.

PAIN.

Job 14:22 flesh on him sh. have *p.*
15:20 wicked travaileth with *p.*
33:19 is chastened also with *p.*
Ps. 25:18 mine affliction and *p.*
48:6 *p.* as a woman in travail,
Is. 13:8; 26:17
Is. 21:3 my loins filled with *p.*
26:18 child, we have been in *p.*
66:7 bef. her *p.* came, she was
Jer. 6:24 *p.* as wo. in trav. 22:23
12:13 put themselves to *p.* but
15:18 why is my *p.* perpetual
30:23 with *p.* on head of wicked
51:8 Babylon, take balm for *p.*
Ezek. 30:4 great *p.* in Ethiopia, 9
16 Sin shall have great *p.*
Mic. 4:10 *p.* and labor to bring
Nah. 2:10 much *p.* is in all loins
Rom. 8:22 creation travail. in *p.*
Rev. 12:2 and *p.* to be delivered
21:4 nor shall th. be any more *p.*
See PANGS.

PAINED.

Ps. 55:4 my heart is sore *p.*
Is. 23:5 they shall be sorely *p.*
Jer. 4:19 I am *p.* at very heart
Joel 2:6 people shall be much *p.*
Rev. 12:2 and *p.* to be delivered

PAINS.

1 Sam. 4:19 *p.* came upon her
Ps. 116:3 *p.* of hell gat hold
Acts 2:24 hav. loosed *p.* of death
Rev. 16:11 blasphem. bec. of *p.*

PAINFUL, NESS.

Ps. 73:16 it was too *p.* for me
2 Cor. 11:27 and *p.* in watchings

PAINTED, ST.

2 K. 9:30 Jezebel *p.* her face
Jer. 22:14 and *p.* with vermilion
Ezek. 23:40 thou *p.* thy eyes

PAINTING.

Jer. 4:30 thou rentest face wi. *p.*

PAIR.

Luke 2:24 offer *p.* of turtle-doves
Rev. 6:5 a *p.* of balances in hand

PALACE.

1 K. 16:18 Zimri burnt king's *p.*
21:1 Naboth had vine. by *p.*
2 K. 15:25 smote Pekaiah in *p.*
20:18 eunuchs in *p.* of king
1 Chr. 29:1 the *p.* is not for man
19 perfect heart to build the *p.*
Ezr. 4:14 maintenance fr. the *p.*
Neh. 1:1 was in Shushan the *p.*

7:2 ruler of *p.* charge over Jer.
Est. 3:15 in Shushan the *p.* 8:14
9:12 destroyed 500 men in the *p.*
Ps. 45:15 enter into king's *p.*
144:12 after similitude of a *p.*
Cant. 8:9 build a *p.* of silver
Is. 25:2 made *p.* of strangers
Dan. 4:4 flourishing in my *p.*
6:18 king went to *p.* pas. night
11:45 he shall plant *p.* between
     seas
Amos 4:3 shall cast into *p.*
Nah. 2:6 opened, *p.* dissolved
Mat. 26:58 Pe. followed Jesus to
   high-priest's *p. Mark* 14:54
Luke 11:21 a strong man keep. *p.*
Phil. 1:13 bonds manifest in *p.*

PALACES.

2 Chr. 36:19 and burnt all the *p.*
Ps. 45:8 myrrh, out of ivory *p.*
48:3 G. is known in *p.* for refu.
13 mark bulwarks, consider *p.*
78:69 sanctuary like high *p.*
122:7 prosperity within thy *p.*
Prov. 30:28 spider is in king's *p.*
Is. 13:22 dragons sh. cry in thy *p.*
32:14 the *p.* shall be forsaken
34:13 thorns come up in her *p.*
Jer. 6:5 let us destroy her *p.*
9:21 death is entered into our *p.*
17:27 fire shall devour *p.* of Jer.
49:27 consume *p.* of Benhadad
Lam. 2:5 hath swallowed her *p.*
Ezek. 19:7 knew their desol. *p.*
25:4 shall set their *p.* in thee
Amos 3:9 publish in *p.* at Ash-
   hod, in *p.* of Egypt
10 store up robbery in their *p.*
11 *p.* be spoiled; 6:8 hate *p.*
Mic. 5:5 he shall tread in our *p.*
See DEVOUR.

PALE, NESS.

Is. 29:22 nei. shall face wax *p.*
Jer. 30:6 all faces turned into *p.*
Rev. 6:8 looked, behold *p.* horse

PALESTINA.

Ex. 15:14 hold on men of P.
Is. 14:29 rej. not thou, whole P.
31 cry, O city, thou, whole P.

PALM.

Lev. 14:15 pour into *p.* 26
John 18:22 struck Jesus with *p.*

PALM branches.

Neh. 8:15 to mount and fet. *p. b.*

PALMER-WORM.

Joel 1:4 what *p.-w.* left, loc. eat.
2:25 restore years *p.-w.* eaten
Amos 4:9 fig-trees, the *p.-w.* dev.

PALMS.

1 Sam. 5:4 *p.* of hands cut off
2 K. 9:35 they found skull and *p.*
Is. 49:16 grav. thee on *p.* of han.
Dan. 10:10 set me on *p.* of hands
Mat. 26:67 others smote him wi.
   p. of their hands, *Mark* 14:65
Rev. 7:9 white robes, *p.* in han.

PALM-TREE.

Jud. 4:5 dwelt under *p.-t.* of D.
Ps. 92:12 right. flour like *p.-t.*
Cant. 7:7 stature is like to a *p.-t.*
8 I will go up to the *p.-t.*
Jer. 10:5 are upright as the *p.-t.*
Ezek. 41:19 face of man tow. *p.-t.*
Joel 1:12 *p.-t.* and apple-tree

PALM-TREES.

Ex. 15:27 El. wh. were 70 *p.-t.*
Lev. 23:40 take branches of *p.-t.*
Deut. 34:3 show. him city of *p.-t.*
Jud. 1:16 out of city of *p.-t.*

3:13 M. possessed city of *p.-t.*
1 K. 6:29 wi. figures of *p.-t.* 32,35;
   7:36; *2 Chr.* 3:5; *Ezek.* 40:16
2 Chr. 28:15 bro. th. to ci. of *p.-t.*
John 12:13 took branches of *p.-t.*

PALSY, IES.

Mat. 4:24 had *p.* he healed them,
   Mark 2:3; *Luke* 5:18
8:6 ser. lieth at home sick of *p.*
9:2 Je. said to sick of *p.* S. thy
   sins be forgiven, *Mark* 2:5
Mark 2:10 sick of *p. Luke* 5:24
Acts 8:7 many taken with *p.* and
9:33 Eneas, who was sick of *p.*

PAMPHYLIA.

Acts 13:13 P. came to Perga in P.
15:38 departed from them fr. P.
27:5 had sailed over sea of P.

PAN.

Lev. 2:5 meat-offer. baken in *p.*
6:21 in a *p.* it shall be made
7:9 dressed in *p.* shall be pries.
1 Sam. 2:14 serv. stuck it into *p.*
2 Sam. 13:9 Tam. took *p.* poured
Ezek. 4:3 take unto thee iron *p.*

PANS.

Ex. 27:3 make *p.* to rec. ashes
Num. 11:8 baked manna in *p.*
1 Chr. 9:31 thi. made in *p.* 23:29
2 Chr. 35:13 offer. sod they in *p.*

PANGS.

Is. 13:8 *p.* sh. take hold of them
21:3 *p.* take hold me as *p.* of w.
26:17 wom. crieth out in her *p.*
Jer. 22:23 gracious when *p.* come
48:41 heart of wom. in *p.* 49:22
50:43 *p.* as of a wom. *Mic.* 4:9

PANNAG.

Ezek. 27:17 traded in market, P.

PANT, ED, ETH.

Ps. 38:10 my heart *p.* stren. fail.
42:1 as hart *p.* so *p.* my soul
119:131 open. my mouth and *p.*
Is. 21:4 at the vision my heart *p.*
Amos 2:7 that *p.* after the dust

PAPER.

Is. 19:7 *p.* reeds shall wither
2 John 12 would not write wi. *p.*

PAPHOS. *Acts* 13:6

PAPS.

Ezek. 23:21 for the *p.* of thy you.
Luke 11:27 bles. are *p.* th. suck.
23:29 blessed *p.* never gave suck
Rev. 1:13 girt *p.* with gold. gird.

PARABLE.

Num. 23:7 Balaam took up *p.* and
   said, 24:3, 15, 20, 21, 23
Job 27:1 J. continued his *p.* 29:1
Ps. 49:4 I will incline ear to a *p.*
78:2 mouth, in a *p.* will I utter
Prov. 26:7 *p.* in mouth of fools, 9
Ezek. 17:2 speak a *p.* to Israel.
24:3 utter *p.* to rebellious house
Mic. 2:4 take up a *p.* against you
Hab. 2:6 these take up *p.* ag. you
Mat. 13:18 hear *p.* of the sower
24 ano. *p.* put he, 31, 33; 21:33
34 with. *p.* sp. not, *Mark* 4:34
24:32 learn a *p.* of the fig-tree,
   Mark 13:28; *Luke* 21:29
Mark 4:10 asked him of *p.* 7:17;
   Luke 8:9
12:12 spoken *p.* ag. th. *Lu.* 20:19
Luke 5:36 he spake a *p.* to them,
   6:39; 8:4; 12:16; 13:6; 14:7;
   15:3; 18:1, 9; 19:11; 20:9;
   21:29; *John* 10:6
12:41 L. spak. thou this *p.* to us?

PARABLES.

Ezek. 20:49 doth he not speak *p. ?*
Mat. 13:3 spake many things to
them in *p.* 13:34; 22:1; *Mark*
3:23; 4:2, 13, 33; 12:1
Mark 4:13 how will ye kn. all *p. ?*
Luke 8:10 *p.* seeing might not see

PARADISE.

Luke 23:43 to-day with me in *p.*
2 *Cor.* 12:4 was caught up into *p.*
Rev. 2:7 in the midst of *p.* of G.

PARAMOURS.

Ezek. 23:20 doted upon their *p.*

PARAN.

Gen. 21:21 wil. of P. *Num.* 10:12;
12:16; 13:3, 26; 1 *Sam.* 25:1
Deut. 33:2 forth from mount P.
Hab. 3:3 Holy One came from P.

PARBAR. 1 *Chr.* 26:18

PARCEL.

Gen. 33:19 J. bought *p.* of a field,
Jos. 24:32; *John* 4:5
Ruth 4:3 Na. selleth a *p.* of land
1 *Chr.* 11:13 *p.* of gr. full of bar. 14

PARCHED.

Is. 35:7 *p.* ground become pool
Jer. 17:6 shall inhabit *p.* places

See CORN.

PARCHMENTS.

2 *Tim.* 4:13 bri. especially the *p.*

PARDON.

Ex. 23:21 not *p.* your trangres.
34:9 *p.* our iniq. *Num.* 14:19
1 *Sam.* 15:25 *p.* my sins
2 *K.* 5:18 Lord, *p.* thy servant
24:4 which Lord would not *p.*
2 *Chr.* 30:18 good L. *p.* ev. one
Neh. 9:17 G. ready to *p.* gracious
Job 7:21 why not *p.* my transg. ?
Ps. 25:11 for name's sake *p.* ini.
Is. 55:7 he will abundantly *p.*
Jer. 5:1 I will *p.* it; 7 shall I *p.*
33:8 I will *p.* all their iniquities
50:20 I will *p.* whom I reserve

PARDONED, ETH.

Num. 14:20 I have *p.* ac. to word
Is. 40:2 tell her that iniq. is *p.*
Lam. 3:42 thou hast not *p.*
Mic. 7:18 G. like thee, *p.* iniq. ?

PARE.

Deut. 21:12 shave head, *p.* nails

PARENTS.

Mat. 10:21 children shall rise up
against their *p. Mark* 13:12
Luke 2:27 *p.* brought in child Je.
8:56 her *p.* were astonished, but
18:29 is no man that hath left *p.*
21:16 ye shall be betrayed by *p.*
John 9:2 who did sin, man or *p. ?*
22 these words spake *p.* 23
Rom. 1:30 diso. to *p.* 2 *Tim.* 3:2
2 *Cor.* 12:14 chil. not lay up for *p.*
Eph. 6:1 chil. obey *p. Col.* 3:20
1 *Tim.* 5:4 learn to requite th. *p.*
Heb. 11:23 Mo. was hid of his *p.*

PARLOR, S.

Jud. 3:20 Eg. was sitting in *p.*
23 Ehud shut doors of the *p.*
1 *Sam.* 9:22 S. bro. them to *p.*
1 *Chr.* 28:11 gave S. pattern of *p.*

PARMENAS. *Acts* 6:5

PART.

Ex. 19:17 at nether *p.* of mount.
Lev. 2:16 *p.* of beaten corn, *p.* oil
Num. 18:20 nei. have *p.* am. th.
Deut. 10:9; 12:12; 14:27, 29;
18:1; *Jos.* 14:4; 18:7; I am
thy *p.* and inherit. in Israel
22:41 utmost *p.* of people, 23:13
Jos. 22:25 ye have no *p.* in L. 27
Ruth 2:3 to light on *p.* of field
3:13 perf. to thee *p.* of kinsman

---

1 *Sam.* 23:20 our *p.* sh. be to del.
30:24 his *p.* is that goeth to bat.
2 *Sam.* 20:1 we have no *p.* in D.
2 *K.* 18:23 if able on thy *p.* to set
riders, *Is.* 36:8
1 *Chr.* 12:29 greatest *p.* kept ho.
2 *Chr.* 29:16 prie. we. to inner *p.*
Neh. 1:9 cast out to uttermost *p.*
5:11 rest. hundredth *p.* of mon.
Job 32:17 I will answer my *p.*
Ps. 5:9 inward *p.* is wickedness
51:6 in hidden *p.* know wisdom
118:7 L. takes my *p.* with them
Prov. 8:26 nor highest *p.* of dust
31 rejoic. in habitable *p.* of ear.
17:2 *p.* of inherit. amo. breth.
Is. 7:18 hiss for fly in utmost *p.*
24:16 fr. utmost *p.* heard songs
44:16 he burneth *p.* in fire, 19
Ezek. 45:17 prince's *p.* to give
Dan. 2:33 p. iron, *p.* clay, 41, 42
5:5 king saw *p.* of the hand, 24
11:31 arms shall stand on his *p.*
Amos. 7:4 it dev. deep, eat up *p.*
Mark 4:38 in hinder *p.* of ship
9:40 not against us, is on our *p.*
Luke 10:42 M. hath chos. good *p.*
17:24 lightning lighteneth one
p. shining to other *p.*
John 13:8 wash th. not, ha. no *p.*
19:23 four parts, ev. soldier a *p.*
Acts 1:17 obtained *p.* of ministry
25 may take *p.* of this minist.
5:2 Ananias kept *p.* of price, 3
8:21 thou hast neith. *p.* nor lot
14:4 *p.* wi. Jews. *p.* wi. apostles
19:32 *p.* knew not wheref. came
23:6 the one *p.* were Sadducees
27:12 more *p.* advised to depart
1 *Cor.* 12:24 honor to that *p.*
15:6 greater *p.* rem. to this day
16:17 was lacking on your *p.*
2 *Cor.* 6:15 *p.* he that believ. wi. infidel ?
Tit. 2:8 that he of the contr. *p.*
Heb. 2:14 himself took *p.* of same
1 *Pet.* 4:14 on th. *p.* he is evil spo.
of. on your *p.* glorified
Rev. 20:6 *p.* in first resurrection
21:8 liars sh. have *p.* in lake
22:19 G. shall take away his *p.*

PART, Verb.

Lev. 2:6 shalt *p.* meat-offering
Ruth 1:17 if aught but death *p.*
1 *Sam.* 30:24 they shall *p.* alike
2 *Sam.* 14:6 th. was none to *p.*
Job 41:6 shall they *p.* him among
the merchants ?
Ps. 22:18 they *p.* my garments

In PART.

Rom. 11:25 blindness *in p.* to Is.
1 *Cor.* 13:9 we know *in p.* and we
prophecy *in p.*
10 that *in p.* sh. be done away
12 I know *in p.* but then sh. I
2 *Cor.* 1:14 acknowledged us *in p.*
2:5 not grieved me but *in p.*

Third PART.

2 *K.* 11:5 a t. *p.* enter on Sabba.
2 *Chr.* 23:4 *t. p.* of you be port.
Neh. 10:32 charge ours. wi. *t. p.*
Ezek. 5:2 burn with fire a *t. p.* a
t. p. smite about it, a *third*
p. scatter in the wind, 12
Zec. 13:8 a *third p.* shall be left
9 I will bring the *t. p.* thro' fire
Rev. 8:7 *t. p.* of trees was burnt
8 *t. p.* of sea became blood
9 *t. p.* of creat. died, *t. p.* ships
11 *t. p.* of wat. bec. wormwood
12 *t. p.* of sun, moon, and stars
9:15 prep. to slay *t. p.* of men
12:4 his tail drew *t. p.* of stars

Fourth PART.

1 *Sam.* 9:8 have *f.* part of shekel
1 *K.* 6:33 posts of olive-tree *f. p.*
2 *K.* 6:25 *f. p.* cab of doves' dung

Neh. 9:3 read one *f. p.* ano. *f. p.*
Rev. 6:8 power given over *f. p.*

Fifth PART.

Gen. 41:34 take up *f. p.* of land
47:24 give *f. p.* to Pharaoh, 26
Lev. 5:16 add *f. p.* thereto, 6:5;
22:14; 27:13,19,27,31; *Num.* 5:7

Tenth PART.

Ex. 16:36 homer is the *tenth p.*
Lev. 5:11 *tenth p.* of an ephah of
fine flour, 6:20; *Num.* 28:5
Num. 5:15 *t. p.* of ephah of meal
18:26 ye shall offer even *t. p.*
Ezek. 45:11 ephah may cont. *t. p.*
Heb. 7:2 Abra. gave a *t. p.* of all
Rev. 11:13 the *t. p.* of city fell

PARTS.

Gen. 47:24 four *p.* sh. be yo. own
Lev. 22:23 any thing lack. in *p.*
Num. 31:27 div. prey into two *p.*
Deut. 19:3 divide land into 3 *p.*
Jos. 18:5 divide into seven *p.* 6, 9
1 *Sam.* 5:9 emer. in th. secret *p.*
2 *Sam.* 19:43 have ten *p.* in king
1 *K.* 16:21 Is. divided into two *p.*
2 *K.* 11:7 two *p.* watch ab. king
Neh. 11:1 9 *p.* dw. in other cities
Job 26:14 th. are *p.* of his ways
41:12 I will not conceal his *p.*
Ps. 2:8 uttermost *p.* of earth
63:9 go into lower *p.* of earth
65:8 dwell in utmost *p.* afraid
139:9 dwell in utmost *p.* of sea
Prov. 18:8 go to innerm. *p.* 26:22
Is. 3:17 Lord will disc. secret *p.*
44:23 shout, ye lower *p.* of earth
Jer. 34:18 between *p.* thereof, 19
Ezek. 26:20 in the low *p.* of earth
31:14 to nether *p.* of earth, 18
16 comforted in the nether *p.*
of earth, 32:18, 24
37:11 we are cut off for our *p.*
38:15 place out of north *p.* 39:2
Mat. 12:42 she came from uttermost *p. Luke* 11:31
John 19:23 garments made 4 *p.*
Rom. 15:23 no more place in *p.*
1 *Cor.* 12:24 comely *p.* no need
Eph. 4:9 descended into low. *p.*
Rev. 16:19 city divided into 3 *p.*

See BACK, HINDER, INWARD.

PARTED.

Gen. 2:10 river *p.* into four heads
2 *K.* 2:11 chariot *p.* both asunder
14 waters *p.* hither and thither
Job 38:24 what way is light *p.* ?
Joel 3:2 scatter. and *p.* my land
Mat. 27:35 *p.* his garmen. *Mark*
5:24; *Luke* 23:34; *John* 19:24
Luke 24:51 blessed them, was *p.*
Acts 2:45 *p.* them to all men

PARTETH.

Rev. 11:3 *p.* hoof, *Deut.* 14:6
Prov. 18:18 lot *p.* betw. mighty

PARTAKER.

Is. 50:18 been *p.* with adulterers
Cor. 9:10 sho. be *p.* of his hope
23 I be *p.* thereof with you
10:30 *p.* why am I evil spok. of ?
1 *Tim.* 5:22 *p.* of oth. men's sins
2 *Tim.* 1:8 be thou *p.* of afflicti.
2:6 husbandman be *p.* of fruits
1 *Pet.* 5:1 I am also *p.* of the gl.
2 *John* 11 biddeth G. speed is *p.*

PARTAKERS.

Mat. 23:30 not been *p.* in blood
Rom. 15:27 if Gentiles have been
p. of their spiritual things
1 *Cor.* 9:13 are *p.* with the altar
10:17 we are all *p.* of that bread
18 are not they which eat *p. ?*
21 cannot be *p.* of Lord's table
2 *Cor.* 1:7 you are *p.* of sufferings
Eph. 3:6 *p.* of his promise in Ch.
5:7 be not ye there. *p.* wi. them

Phil. 1:7 all are *p.* of my grace
Col. 1:12 to be *p.* of inheritance
1 *Tim.* 6:2 they are *p.* of benefit
Heb. 2:14 children *p.* of flesh
    and blood
    3:1 *p.* of the heavenly calling
    14 for we are made *p.* of Christ
    6:4 made *p.* of the Holy Ghost
    12:8 chastise. where. all are *p.*
    10 that we be *p.* of his holiness
1 *Pet.* 4:13 *p.* of Christ's suffer.
2 *Pet.* 1:4 *p.* of the divine nature
Rev. 18:4 that ye be not *p.* of her

PARTAKEST.
Rom. 11:17 with them *p.* of root

PARTHIANS. *Acts* 2:9

PARTIAL, ITY.
Mal. 2:9 but have been *p.* in law
1 *Tim.* 5:21 doing nothing by *p.*
Jam. 2:4 are ye not *p.* yoursel. ?
    3:17 without *p.* and hypocrisy

PARTICULAR, LY.
Acts 21:19 P. declared *p.* things
1 *Cor.* 12:27 of C. members in *p.*
Eph. 5:33 ev. one in *p.* love wife
Heb. 9:5 we cannot now speak *p.*

PARTIES.
Ex. 22:9 both *p.* come bef. judg.

PARTING.
Ezek. 21:21 king of B. stood at *p.*

PARTITION.
1 *K.* 6:21 he made a *p.* of gold
Eph. 2:14 bro. middle wall of *p.*

PARTLY.
Dan. 2:42 be *p.* strong, *p.* broken
1 *Cor.* 11:18 divisions, I *p.* belie.
Heb. 10:33 *p.* gaz.-stock, *p.* com.

PARTNER, S.
Prov. 29:24 whoso is *p.* with a
    thief
2 *Cor.* 8:23 Titus, he is my *p.*
Phile. 17 if count me a *p.* receive
Luke 5:7 they beckoned to th. *p.*
    10 James and John were *p.*

PARTRIDGE.
1 *Sam.* 26:20 when one hunt a *p.*
Jer. 17:11 as *p.* sitteth on eggs

PASHUR.
Neh. 10:3 P. sealed, *Jer.* 20:6
Jer. 20:1 P. son of Im. smote, 2
    3 L. call. not thy name P.
    21:1 Zedekiah sent unto him P.
    38:1 Gedal. the son of P. and P.

PASS.
Gen. 18:5 after that ye shall *p.*
    41:32 will shortly bring it to *p.*
Ex. 33:19 will make my good *p.*
Num. 27:7 inherit. of fa. to *p.* 8
Jos. 1:14 ye shall *p.* before breth.
1 *Sam.* 16:10 Jesse made 7 sons *p.*
Neh. 2:14 no place for beast to *p.*
Job 6:15 as stream they *p.* away
    11:16 rem. it as waters that *p.*
    34:20 peo. be troubled, *p.* away
Prov. 16:30 he bringeth evil to *p.*
    22:3 and the simple *p.* on, 27:12
Is. 30:32 grounded staff shall *p.*
    33:21 no gallant ship shall *p.*
    37:26 have I brought it to *p.*
Jer. 8:13 th. I have given shall *p.*
    15:14 make th. *p.* with enemies
    33:13 flocks sh. *p.* under hands
    51:43 nor doth son of man *p.*
Ezek. 20:37 I will cause you to *p.*
    32:19 wh. dost th. *p.* in beauty?
Amos 6:2 *p.* ye unto Calneh
Mic. 1:11 *p.* ye away, inhabit. of
    2:13 their king shall *p.* before
Zep. 2:2 decree br. forth, day *p.*
Zec. 3:4 have caused iniqu. to *p.*
Mat. 5:18 heav. and earth sh. *p.*
    26:39 cup *p.* fr. me, *Mark* 14:35
Luke 16:26 wh. would *p.* fr. hen.
    nor can they *p.* fr. us to you

19:4 he was to *p.* that way
1 *Cor.* 7:36 if she *p.* flower of age
2 *Pet.* 3:10 heavens sh. *p.* away

PASS by.
Ex. 33:22 cover thee whi. I *p. by*
Ps. 80:12 all they that *p. by*
    89:41 all that *p. by* way spoil
Jer. 22:8 many nations sh. *p. by*
Lam. 1:12 ye that *p. by* behold
    2:15 all that *p. by* clap th. hands
Ezek. 5:14 sight of all that *p. by*
    37:2 caused me to *p. by* them
Amos 7:8 I will not *p. by* th. 8:2
Mic. 2,8 garm. of them that *p. by*
Mat. 8:28 no man might *p. by*
Luke 18:36 hearing multit. *p. by*

See **CAME, COME.**

Not PASS.
Num. 20:17 will *n. p.* thro fields
    18 Edom said, Thou shalt *n. p.*
Job 14:5 his bounds he *cannot p.*
    19:8 fenced my way, *cannot p.*
Ps. 148:6 a decree wh. shall *n. p.*
Prov. 8:29 waters should *not p.*
Jer. 5:22 decree that it *cannot p.*
Mat. 24:34 this gene. shall *not p.*
    away, *Mark* 13:30 ; *Luke*
    21:32
    35 heaven and earth shall pass
    away, but my word sh. *n. p.*
    away, *Mark* 13:31 ; *Lu.* 21:33

PASS not.
Gen. 18:3 *p. not* away from serv.
2 *K.* 6:9 thou *p. not* such a place
Prov. 4:15 avoid it, *p. not* by it
Amos 5:5 we *p. not* to Beer-sheba

PASS over.
Gen. 8:1 God made wind *p. o.*
    31:52 I will not *p. o.* this heap
    32:16 *p. o.* bef. me, put a space
    33:14 lord *p. o.* bef. thy servant
Ex. 12:13 I will *p. over* you, 23
    15:16 till thy people *p. over*
Num. 32:27 serv. will *p. o.* 29:32
    30 not *p. o.* with you armed
Deut 2:18 *p. o.* thro' Ar this day
    3:18 shall *p. over* armed before
    9:1 *p. o.* Jordan, 11:31 ; 27:2 ;
    Jos. 1:11 ; 3:6, 14 ; 4:5
Jos. 22:19 *p. o.* into the land
Jud. 3:28 suff. not a man to *p. o.*
1 *Sam.* 14:8 will *p. o.* to th. men
2 *Sam.* 17:16 but speedily *p. over*
Ps. 104:9 that they may not *p. o.*
Prov. 19:11 to *p. o.* a transgres.
Is. 23:6 *p. over* to Tarshish
    31:9 *p. over* to his stronghold
    35:8 unclean shall not *p. over*
    51:10 way for ransomed to *p. o.*
Jer. 5:22 yet can they not *p. o.*
Ezek. 47:5 river I could not *p. o.*
Dan. 4:16 seven times *p. o.* 25
    11:40 king of north shall *p. o.*
Hab. 1:11 change, he shall *p. o.*
Luke 11:42 *p. over* judgment

PASS through.
Gen. 30:32 *p. t.* thy flock to-day
Ex. 12:12 *p. t.* Eg. this night
Lev. 18:21 any of thy seed *p. t.*
    fire. *Deut.* 18:10 ; 2 *K.* 17:17
Num. 20:17 *p. t.* thy country
    21:23 Sihon would not suffer Is.
    to *p. thro'* *Jud.* 11:20
Deut. 2:4 *p. thr.* coasts of Edom
    28 I will *p. thro'* on my feet
Jos. 1:11 *p. t.* host and command
2 *Sam.* 12:31 *p. t.* brick kiln
1 *K.* 18:6 divided land to *p. t.* it
2 *K.* 16:3 to *p. t.* the fire, 21:6 ;
    23:10 ; 2 *Chr.* 33:6 ; *Jer.*
    32:35 ; *Ezek.* 20:26, 31
Ps. 78:13 caused to *p. t.* 136:14
Is. 8:8 sh. *p. through* Judah
    23:10 *thro'* thy land as a river
    34:10 none sh. *p. t.* it for ever
Jer. 9:10 so that none can *p. t.*

Lam. 3:44 prayers sho. not *p. t.*
    4:21 cup shall also *p. t.* to thee
Ezek. 14:15 noi. beasts *p. t.* land,
    no man *p. t.* 29:11 ; 33:28
    39:15 passengers that *p. t.* land
Dan. 11:10 *p. t.* and overflow
Joel 3:17 shall *p. t.* her any more
Amos 5:17 I will *p. thro'* thee
Nah. 1:12 cut down, wh. he *p. t.*
    15 wicked no more *p. t.* thee
Zec. 9:8 no oppressor *p. t.* them
1 *Cor.* 16:5 shall *p. t.* Macedonia

PASSAGE, S.
Num. 20:21 Edom refused Is. *p.*
Jos. 22:11 an altar at *p.* of Isr'el
Jud. 12:6 and slew him at *p.*
1 *Sam.* 13:23 Ph. went out to *p.*
    14:4 betw. *p.* were sharp rocks
Is. 10:29 are gone over the *p.*
Jer. 22:20 lift thy voice, cry fr. *p.*
    51:32 show Bab. *p.* are stopped

PASSED.
Gen. 15:17 a lamp that *p.* betw.
Num. 26:17 have *p.* thy border
Jos. 3:4 have not *p.* this way
1 *Sam.* 15:12 gone about and *p.*
    29:2 Philist. *p.* on by hundreds
2 *Sam.* 15:18 servants *p.* on
2 *K.* 4:8 Elisha *p.* to Shunem
2 *Chr.* 9:22 Solomon *p.* all kings
Job 4:15 spirit *p.* before my face
    9:26 my days are *p.* away
    15:19 no stranger *p.* am. them
Ps. 18:12 his thick clouds *p.*
    37:36 yet he *p.* away, and lo
    90:9 all our days are *p.* away
Cant. 3:4 little that I *p.* fr. them
Is. 41:3 pursued, and *p.* safely
Jer. 11:15 holy flesh *p.* from thee
    46:17 hath *p.* time appointed
Dan. 3:27 smell of fire *p.* on th.
    6:18 went and *p.* night fasting
Nah. 3:19 wicked *p.* continually
Mark 6:35 now the time is far *p.*
John 5:24 but is *p.* from death to
    life, 1 *John* 3:14
Rom. 5:12 death *p.* on all men
Heb. 4:14 High-pri. *p.* into heav.
Rev. 21:1 first earth were *p.* aw.
    4 former things are *p.* away

PASSED by.
Ex. 34:6 Lord *p. by* before him
1 *K.* 13:25 *p. by* and saw the lion
    19:11 Lord *p. by* ; 19 Elijah *p. by*
2 *K.* 4:8 as he *p. by* he turned in
    6:30 the king *p. by* on the wall
Job 28:8 nor hath fierce lion *p. by*
Ps. 48:4 the kings *p. by* together
Ezek. 16:6 I *p. by* and saw thee, 8
    36:34 in sight of all that *p. by*
Hab. 3:10 overfl. of waters *p. by*
Mat. 20:30 heard that Jesus *p. by*
Mark 6:48 would have *p. by* them
Luke 10:31 *p. by* on other side, 32
John 8:59 midst of them, so *p. by*
Acts 17:23 as I *p. by* and beheld

PASSED over.
Gen. 31:21 and *p. over* the river
    32:10 with staff I *p. over* Jordan
Ex. 12:27 *p. over* houses of Isr.
Jos. 3:17 all *p. o.* on dry ground
    4:10 people hasted and *p. over*
    11 the ark of the Lord *p. over*
1 *Sam.* 14:23 *p. o.* to Bethaven
2 *Sam.* 15:23 king and peo. *p. o.*
Is. 40:27 judgment *p. o.* from G.
Ezek. 47:5 river could not be *p. o.*
Hos. 19:11 *p. o.* upon fair neck
Jon. 2:3 billows and waves *p. o.*

PASSED through.
Gen. 12:6 Abram *p. t.* the land
Num. 14:7 land which we *p. t.*
2 *Chr.* 30:10 posts *p. t.* country
Mic. 2:13 they *p. t.* thro' the gate
Zec. 7:14 that no man *p. thro'*
Acts 12:10 and *p. thro'* one street

1 *Cor.* 10:1 our fathers *p. t.* sea
Heb. 11:29 they *p. thro'* Red sea

PASSEDST.

Jud. 12:1 why *p.* thou over

PASSENGERS.

Prov. 9:15 she standeth to call *p.*
Ezek. 39:11 will give G. val. of *p.*
  14 bury with *p.* those that re.
  15 when *p.* see a man's bone

PASSEST.

Deut. 30:18 on land whi. thou *p.*
2 *Sam.* 15:33 if *p.* on, thou sh. be
1 *K.* 2:37 day thou *p.* over brook
Is. 43:2 when *p.* through waters

PASSETH.

Ex. 30:13 every one that *p.* 14
33:22 while my glory *p.* by
Jos. 3:11 Lord *p.* over before you
2 *K.* 4:9 man of G. wh. *p.* by us
12:4 money of every one that *p.*
Job 9:11 he *p.* on also, but I
14:20 against him, and he *p.*
37:21 wind *p.* and clean, them
Ps. 8:8 whatever *p.* thro' the sea
78:39 are a wind that *p.* away
103:16 for the wind *p.* over it
144:4 as a shadow that *p.* away
Prov. 10:25 as whirlwind *p.* so is
26:17 he th. *p.* by and meddleth
Ec. 1:4 one generation *p.* away
Is. 29:5 as chaff that *p.* away
Jer. 2:6 no man *p.* through, 9:12
18:16 every one that *p.* 19:8
Ezek. 35:7 from it him that *p.*
Hos. 13:3 early dew that *p.* away
Mic. 7:18 G. that *p.* by transgr.
Zep. 2:15 ev. one that *p.* by her
3:6 streets waste, none *p.* by
Zec. 9:8 bec. of him that *p.* by
Luke 18:37 told him th. J. *p.* by
1 *Cor.* 7:31 fashion of this world
  p. away, 1 *John* 2:17
Eph. 3:19 love of C. *p.* knowled.
Phil. 4:7 peace of G. *p.* underst.

PASSING.

2 *Sam.* 1:26 to me *p.* love of wo.
Ps. 84:6 *p.* through valley
Prov. 7:8 *p.* thro' street near co.
Is. 31:5 *p.* over, preserve Jerus.
Ezek. 39:14 *p.* thro' land to bury
Luke 4:30 *p.* through midst
Acts 5:15 shadow of Peter *p.* by

PASSION.

Acts 1:3 sho. hims. alive after *p.*

PASSIONS.

Acts 14:15 we are men of like *p.*
Jam. 5:17 Elias subject to like *p.*

PASSOVER.

Ex. 12:11 it is L.'s *p.* ye sh. eat,
  27; *Lev.* 23:5; *Num.* 28:16
  43 this is the ordinance of *p.*
Num. 9:5 kept *p. Jos.* 5:10
Deut. 16:2 sacrifice *p.* to Lord, 6
2 *K.* 23:22 not holden such a *p.*
2 *Chr.* 30:15 kill. *p.* in se. month,
  35:1, 11; *Ezr.* 6:20; *Mark*
  14:12 ; *Luke* 22:7
  18 eat *p.* otherw. than written
35:1 Jo. kept *p.* 17, 19 ; *Ezr.*6:19
  13 they roasted *p.* with fire
Ezek. 45:21 shall have *p.* of 7 da.
Mat. 26:17 wh. wilt we eat *p. ?*
  Mark 14:12 ; *Luke* 22:8, 11
Luke 22:5 have desired to eat *p.*
John 2:13 Jews' *p.* at hand, 11:55
  23 when he was in Jer. at *p.*
11:55 many went to J. before *p.*
12:1 J. came six days before *p.*
18:28 that they might eat *p.*
  39 sho. release to you one at *p.*
19:14 it was preparation of *p.*
1 *Cor.* 5:7 Ch. our *p.* is sacrificed
Heb. 11:28 thro' faith he kept *p.*

See FEAST, KEEP.

PASSOVERS.

2 *Chr.* 30:17 Le. had charge of *p.*

PAST.

Gen. 50:4 mourn. *p.* 2 *Sam.* 11:27
Num. 21:22 until we be *p.* bord.
Deut. 2:10 E. dwelt in times *p.*
14:32 ask now of days wh. are *p.*
1 *Sam.* 15:32 bitter. of death is *p.*
2 *Sam.* 3:17 so. David in time *p.*
16:1 D. was a little *p.* top of hill
1 *K.* 18:29 midday *p.* no voice
1 *Chr.* 9:20 Phin. ruler in time *p.*
Job 9:10 doeth things *p.* finding
14:13 keep me, until wrath *p.*
17:11 days are *p.* my purpose
29:2 O th. I we. as in months *p.*
Ec. 3:15 requireth that wh. is *p.*
Mat. 14:15 time is now *p.* send
Mark 16:1 when sab. was *p.* Ma.
Luke 9:36 voice *p.* J was alone
Acts 14:16 times *p* suff. all nati.
Rom. 11:30 in times *p.* not belie.
  33 his ways are *p.* finding out
2 *Cor.* 5:17 old things *p.* away
Gal. 1:13 conversation in time *p.*
5:21 as I told you in time *p.*
Eph. 2:2 in time *p.* ye walked
4:19 being *p.* feeling have given
Phile. 11 in time *p.* unprofitable
Heb. 1:1 spake in time *p.* to fath.
11:11 conceive, when she was *p.*
1 *Pet.* 2:10 in time *p.* were not
4:3 time *p.* of our life suffice
1 *John* 2:8 darkness *p.* light shi.
Rev. 9:12 one woe *p.* 11:14 woe *p.*

PASTOR, S.

Jer. 2:8 *p.* transgr. against me
3:15 *p.* according to my heart
10:21 for *p.* are become brutish
12:10 *p.* have destroy. vineyard
17:16 not hastened fr. being a *p.*
22:22 wind shall eat up thy *p.*
23:1 woe to *p.* that destr. sheep
  2 against *p.* that feed my sheep
Eph. 4:11 gave *p.* and teachers

PASTURE.

Gen. 47:4 thy servants ha. no *p.*
1 *Chr.* 4:39 they went to seek *p.*
  40 they found fat *p.* and good
  41 there was *p.* for their flocks
Job 39:8 range of moun. in his *p.*
Ps. 74:1 anger am. ag. sheep of *p.*
79:13 sheep of thy *p.* give than.
95:7 we are peo. of his *p.* 100:3
Is. 32:14 joy of asses, *p.* of flocks
Jer. 23:1 scatter sheep of my *p.*
25:36 Lord hath spoiled their *p.*
Lam. 1:6 like harts find no *p.*
Ezek. 34:14 feed in good *p.* fat *p.*
  18 small th. to ha. eat. good *p.*
  31 flock of my *p.* are men, I G.
Hos. 13:6 ac. to their *p.* so filled
Joel 1:18 beasts groan, ha. no *p.*
John 10:9 go in and out, find *p.*

PASTURES.

1 *K.* 4:23 S. had 20 ox. out of *p.*
Ps. 23:2 maketh me lie green *p.*
65:12 drop upon *p.* of wildern.
  13 *p.* are clothed with flocks
Is. 30:23 cat. sh. feed in large *p.*
49:9 *p.* shall be in high places
Ezek. 34:18 tread down your *p.*
45:15 lamb out of flock of fat *p.*
Joel 1:19 fire hath devour. *p.* 20
2:22 *p.* of wilderness do spring

PATARA.

Acts 21:1 from thence unto P.

PATE.

Ps. 7:16 sh. come do. on own *p.*

PATH.

Gen. 49:17 D. be an adder in *p.*
Num. 22:24 angel of L. st. in *p.*
Job 28:7 *p.* which no fowl know.
30:13 mar my *p.* set forward
41:32 he maketh a *p.* to shine

Ps. 16:11 show me the *p.* of life
27:11 lead me in a plain *p.*
77:19 way in sea, *p.* in great wa.
119:35 make me to go in *p.*
  105 thy word a light to my *p.*
139:3 thou compassest my *p.*
142:3 then thou knewest my *p.*
Prov. 1:15 refrain foot fr. their *p.*
2:9 sh. understand every good *p.*
4:15 enter not into *p.* of wicked
  18 *p.* of just is as shining light
  26 ponder the *p.* of thy feet
5:6 lest thou ponder *p.* of life
Is. 26:7 dost weigh *p.* of just
30:11 out of way, turn out of *p.*
40:14 taught him in *p.* of judgm.
43:16 maketh *p.* in mighty wat.
Joel 2:8 walk, every one in his *p.*

PATHROS. *Is.* 11:11; *Ezek.*
  29:14 ; 30:14

PATHWAY.

Prov. 12:28 in *p.* thereof no dea.

PATHS.

Job 6:18 *p.* of way turned aside
8:13 *p.* of all that forget God
13:27 lookest narrowly to my *p.*
19:8 hath set darkness in my *p.*
24:13 nei. abide in *p.* thereof
33:11 feet in stocks, mar. my *p.*
38:20 thou sh. keep *p.* of house
Ps. 8:8 passeth thro' *p.* of seas
17:4 kept me fr. *p.* of destroyer
  5 hold my goings in *p.* slip not
23:3 leadeth me in *p.* of righte.
25:4 O Lord, teach me thy *p.*
  10 *p.* of L. are mercy and truth
65:11 *p.* drop fatness on pasture
Prov. 2:8 keep. *p.* of judgment
Prov. 2:13 leave *p.* of uprightn.
  15 and they froward in their *p.*
  18 her *p.* incline unto the dead
  19 nei. take hold of *p.* of life
  20 keep *p.* of the righteous
3:6 direct *p.* 17 *p.* are peace
4:11 I have led thee in right *p.*
7:25 go not astray in her *p.*
8:2 standeth in places of *p.*
  20 I lead in *p.* of judgment
Is. 2:3 walk in his *p. Mic.* 4:2
3:12 they destroy way of thy *p.*
42:16 lead th. in *p.* not known
58:12 called, the restorer of *p.*
59:7 destruction are in their *p.*
  8 have made them crooked *p.*
Jer. 6:16 in way, ask for old *p.*
18:15 ancient *p.* to walk in *p.*
Lam. 3:9 he made my *p.* crooked
Hos. 2:6 she shall not find *p.*
Mat. 3:3 make his *p.* straight,
  Mark 1:3 ; *Luke* 3:4
Heb. 12:13 made strai. *p.* for feet

PATIENCE.

Mat. 18:26 have *p.* with me, and
  I will pay thee all, 29
Luke 8:15 br. forth fruit with *p.*
21:19 in *p.* possess ye your souls
Rom. 5:3 tribulation worketh *p.*
  4 *p.* experience, experi. hope
8:25 do we with *p.* wait for it
15:4 we thro' *p.* might ha. hope
5 G. *p.* grant you be like-min.
2 *Cor.* 6:4 ministers of God in *p.*
12:12 signs we. am. you in all *p.*
Col. 1:11 strengthened to all *p.*
1 *Thes.* 1:3 remem. your *p.* in J.
2 *Thes.* 1:4 gl. in you for your *p.*
1 *Tim.* 6:11 follow after love, *p.*
2 *Tim.* 3:10 hast known my *p.*
Tit. 2:2 be found in faith, *p.*
Heb. 6:12 thro' *p.* inh. promises
10:36 ye have need of *p.*
12:1 run with *p.* race before us
Jam. 1:3 trying of faith work. *p.*
  4 let *p.* have her perfect work
5:7 husbandman hath long *p.*
  10 an example of *p.* 11 *p.* of J.

2 *Pet.* 1:6 add to temper. *p.* to *p.*
Rev. 1:9 compan. in *p.* of Jesus
2:2 I know thy *p.* 19 ; 3 hast *p.*
3:10 hast kept word of my *p.*
13:10 here is *p.* of saints, 14:12

PATIENT.

Ec. 7:8 *p.* in sp. better than pro.
Rom. 2:7 *p.* continu. in well-do.
12:12 in hope, *p.* in tribulation
1 *Thes.* 5:14 be *p.* toward all men
2 *Thes.* 3:5 *p.* waiting for Christ
1 *Tim.* 3:3 luc. but *p.* 2 *Tim.* 2:24
Jam. 5:7 be *p.* breth. 8 ye also *p.*

PATIENTLY.

Ps. 37:7 rest in L. and wait *p.*
40:1 I waited *p.* for the Lord
Acts 26:3 I bes. thee hear me *p.*
Heb. 6:15 after he had *p.* endured
1 *Pet.* 2:20 if ye be buff. take it *p.*
    if ye do well and su. ta. it *p.*

PATMOS.

Rev. 1:9 in the isle called P.

PATRIARCH, S.

Acts 2:29 freely speak of *p.* Dav.
7:8 Jacob begat the twelve *p.*
9 *p.* sold Joseph into Egypt
Heb. 7:4 *p.* Abraham paid tithes

PATRIMONY.

Deut. 18:8 cometh of sale of *p.*

PATROBAS. *Rom.* 16:14

PATTERN, S.

Ex. 25:9 *p.* of all instruments
    40 make them after their *p.*
Jos. 22:28 the *p.* of altar of Lord
2 *K.* 16:10 Ahaz sent *p.* of altar
1 *Chr.* 28:11 D. g. S. *p.* 12, 18, 19
Ezek. 43:10 let them measure *p.*
1 *Tim.* 1:16 in me C. mig. sh. *p.*
Tit. 2:7 show. thyself *p.* of good
Heb. 8:5 accord. to *p.* I showed
9:23 necessary that *p.* of things

PAUL.

Acts 13:9 then Saul, called P.
28:16 but P. was suffered to
    (*Vide* Acts *passim.*)
1 *Cor.* 1:12 I am of P. 13 : 3:4, 5
3:22 whether P. or Apollos. or
16:21 saluta. of me P. *Col.* 4:18
1 *Thes.* 2:18 ev. I P. 2 *Thes.* 3:17
Phile. 9 such a one as P.
2 *Pet.* 3:15 as our belov. P. wrote

PAULUS.

Acts 13:7 the deputy Sergius P.

PAVED.

Ex. 24:10 under feet *p.* work
Cant. 3:10 being *p.* with love

PAVEMENT.

2 *K.* 16:17 put sea on *p.* of stones
2 *Chr.* 7:3 all Isr. bowed upon *p.*
Est. 1:6 beds were on *p.* of red
Ezek. 40:17 chambers and a *p.*
    18 *p.* by side of gates lower *p.*
42:3 over against *p.* was gallery
John 19:13 Pil. sat in pla. call. P.

PAVILION, S.

2 *Sam.* 22:12 ma. dar. *p. Ps.* 18:11
1 *K.* 20:12 Ben. drinking in *p.* 16
Ps. 27:5 he shall hide me in *p.*
31:20 keep them secretly in a *p.*
Jer. 43:10 Nebuch. spread his *p.*

PAW, S.

Lev. 11:27 goeth on *p.* unclean
1 *Sam.* 17:37 de. me out of *p.* of

PAWETH.

Job 39:21 horse *p.* in the valley

PAY.

Ex. 21:19 sh. *p.* for loss of time
    36 he shall surely *p.* ox for ox
22:7 thief be found, *p.* double, 9
Num. 20:19 if I drink I will *p.*
Deut. 23:21 shall not slack to *p.*
2 *Sam.* 15:7 let me go *p.* my vow
1 *K.* 20:39 thou shalt *p.* a talent

2 *K.* 4:7 sell oil, and *p.* thy debt
2 *Chr.* 8:8 them did S. make to *p.*
Ezr. 4:13 will they not *p.* toll
Est. 3:9 I will *p.* 10,000 tal. 4:7
Job 22:27 and shalt pay thy vows
Ps. 22:25 *p.* vows, 66:13 ; 116:14, 18
50:14 *p.* thy vows to Most High
76:11 vow, and *p.* to the Lord
Prov. 19:17 giv. will he *p.* again
22:27 if hast nothing to *p.*
Ec. 5:4 defer not to *p.* it, *p.* that
    5 not vow, than vow and not *p.*
Jon. 2:9 I will *p.* that I vowed
Mat. 17:24 doth not mas. *p.* tri. ?
    18:25 had not to *p. Luke* 7:42
    26 *p.* thee all ; 28 *p.* th. owest
    30 cast into prison, fill he *p.*
    34 till he *p.* all that was due
23:23 ye *p.* tithe of mint, anise
Rom. 13:6 for this cause *p.* trib.

PAID, PAYETH.

Ezr. 4:20 toll and custom *p.* th.
Ps. 37:21 wicked borrow. *p.* not
Prov. 7:14 this day ha. I *p.* vows
Jon. 1:3 *p.* fare thereof
Mat. 5:26 *p.* utter. far. *Luke* 12:59
Heb. 7:9 Levi *p.* tithes in Abrah.

PAYMENT.

Mat. 18:25 all sold, *p.* to be made

PEACE.

Mark 4:39 said to sea, *p.* be still

PEACE.

Gen. 41:16 G. give P. answ. of *p.*
Lev. 26:6 I will give *p.* in land
Num. 6:26 L. give thee *p.*
25:12 I give him my cov. of *p.*
Deut. 2:26 sent to Sihon with *p.*
20:10 come nigh city, procl. *p.*
    11 if it make th. answ. of *p.* 12
23:6 thou sh. not seek their *p.*
29:19 I shall have *p.* tho. walk
Jud. 4:17 *p.* betw. Jab. and Heb.
1 *Sam.* 7:14 *p.* betw. Is. and A.
20:7 servant shall have *p.*
    21 there is *p.* to thee
1 *K.* 2:33 on his thro. sha. be *p.*
4:24 Solom. had *p.* on all sides
5:12 *p.* betw. Hiram and Solo.
20:18 come for *p.* take th. alive
2 *K.* 9:17 say, Is it *p. Jehu* ? 18
    19 wh. hast th. to do wi. *p. ?* 22
    22 what *p.* so long as witchc. ?
    31 had Z. *p.* who slew mast. ?
20:19 *p.* in my days ? *Is.* 39:8
1 *Chr.* 22:9 I will give *p.* to Isr.
2 *Chr.* 15:5 th. tim. th. was no *p.*
Ezr. 4:17 rest bey. the river, *p.*
5:7 unto Darius, *p.* 7:12 unto E.
9:12 not seek their *p.* or wealth
Est. 9:30 Mord. sent words of *p.*
10:3 Mord. speaking *p.* to all
Job 5:23 beasts of field be at *p.*
22:21 acqu. thyself, and be at *p.*
25:2 maketh *p.* in high places
Ps. 7:4 evil to him th. was at *p.*
28:3 which speak *p.* to neigh.
29:11 bless his people with *p.*
34:14 good, seek *p.* 1 *Pet.* 3:11
35:20 speak not *p.* but devise
37:11 delight in abund. of *p.*
    37 end of the upright man is *p.*
55:20 put ag. such as be at *p.*
72:3 mountains shall bring *p.*
    7 of *p.* so long as moon endur.
85:8 he will speak *p.* to his peo.
    10 righteousness and *p.* kissed
119:165 gr. *p.* have they which
120:6 dw. with him th. hateth *p.*
Ps. 120:7 I am for *p.* they for war
122:6 pray for *p.* of Jerusalem
125:5 but *p.* sh. be upon Israel
128:6 thou shalt see *p.* upon Is.
147:14 maketh *p.* in thy borders
Prov. 3:17 pleasantness, paths *p.*
12:20 to counsellors of *p.* is joy
16:7 maketh enemies to be at *p.*

Ec. 3:8 time of war, time of *p.*
Is. 9:6 Prince of *p.* 7 increase *p.*
26:12 Lord thou wilt ordain *p.*
27:5 *p.* with me, he shall ma. *p.*
32:17 work of righteo. sh. be *p.*
33:7 ambassadors of *p.* sh. weep
38:17 or *p.* I had great bittern.
45:7 make *p.* and create evil
48:18 had thy *p.* been as river
    22 th. is no *p.* to wicked, 57:21
52:7 publisheth *p. Nah.* 1:15
53:5 chastisem. of our *p.* on him
54:10 nor coven. of *p.* be remov.
    13 great shall be *p.* of thy chil.
55:12 with joy, led forth with *p.*
57:2 enter into *p.* rest in beds
    19 fruit of lips, *p.* *p.* to him
59:8 way of *p.* kn. not, *Rom.* 3:17
60:17 make thine officers *p.*
66:12 I will extend *p.* to her
Jer. 4:10 ye sh. have *p.* whereas
6:14 *p. p.* when th. is no *p.* 8:11
8:15 for *p.* no good came, 14:19
12:5 if in land of *p.* they weari.
    12 sw. devour, no flesh have *p.*
14:13 I will give you assured *p.*
16:5 I have taken away my *p.*
28:9 prophet wh. prophesied *p.*
29:7 seek *p.* of city I caused
    11 I think tow. you thou. of *p.*
30:5 a voice of fear, not of *p.*
33:6 reveal to them abund. of *p.*
Lam. 3:17 rem. my soul from *p.*
Ezek. 7:25 seek *p.* th. shall be n.
13:10 *p.* and there was no *p.* 16
34:25 make a covena. of *p.* 37:26
Dan. 8:25 by *p.* he shall destroy
Ob. 7 men at *p.* deceived thee
Mic. 3:5 bite with teeth, cry *p.*
5:5 this man sh. be *p.* when A.
Hag. 2:9 this place I will give *p.*
Zec. 6:13 counsel of *p.* betw th.
8:10 nor was th. any *p.* to him.
    16 execute judgment and *p.*
    19 therefore love truth and *p.*
9:10 he sh. speak *p.* to heathen
Mal. 2:5 covenant of life and *p.*
Mat. 10:13 worthy, let *p.* come
    34 th. not I am come to send *p.*
Mark 9:50 have *p.* one with ano.
Luke 1:79 guide feet to way of *p.*
2:14 on earth *p.* good will tow.
10:6 if son of *p.* th. your *p.* rest
12:51 I am come to give *p.* ?
19:38 *p.* in heaven, gl. in highe.
    42 things belong to thy *p.*
John 14:27 *p.* I lea. you, *p.* I give
16:33 in me you might have *p.*
Acts 10:36 preaching *p.* by Jesus
Rom. 1:7 *p.* from God the Fath.
1 *Cor.* 1:3 ; 2 *Cor.* 1:2 ; *Gal.*
    1:3 ; *Eph.* 1:2 ; *Phil.* 1:2
2:10 *p.* to every man work. good
5:1 justified, we have *p.* with G.
8:6 to be spiritually mind. is *p.*
10:15 that preach gospel of *p.*
14:17 the kingdom of God is *p.*
    19 fol. things that make for *p.*
15:13 fill you with all joy and *p.*
1 *Cor.* 7:15 G. hath call. us to *p.*
14:33 author of *p.* as in church.
Gal. 5:22 Spirit is love, joy, *p.*
Eph. 2:14 is our *p.* 15 making *p.*
    17 Christ came and preach. *p.*
4:3 unity of Spirit in bond of *p.*
6:15 preparation of gospel of *p.*
Phil. 4:7 *p.* of God passeth und.
Col. 1:2 grace and *p.* from G. our
    Father, 1 *Thes.* 1:1 ; 2 *Thes.*
    1:2 ; 1 *Tim.* 1:2 ; 2 *Tim.* 1:2 ;
    Tit. 1:4 ; *Phile.* 3 ; 2 *John* 3
3:15 *p.* of God rule in your hea.
1 *Thes.* 5:3 when they sh. say *p.*
    13 be at *p.* among yourselves
2 *Thes.* 3:16 L. of *p.* give you *p.*
2 *Tim.* 2:22 follow *p. Heb.* 12:14
Heb. 7:2 king of Salem is k. of *p.*
11:31 Rahab received spies in *p.*

Jam. 3:18 p. of them th. ma. p. !
Rev. 1:4 p. from him that is. was
    6:4 power giv. to him to take p.

PEACE be.

Jud. 6:23 L. said, p. be to thee
1 *Sam.* 25:6 p. be to thee—house
1 *Chr.* 12:18 p. be to thee, p. be to
Ps. 122:7 p. be within thy walls
    8 now say, p. be within thee
Dan. 4:1 p. be multiplied, 6:25;
    1 *Pet.* 1:2; 2 *Pet.* 1:2; *Jude* 2
Dan. 10:19 p. be to thee, be stro.
Luke 10:5 p. be to this house
    24:36 he saith unto them, p. be
    to you, *John* 20:19, 21, 26
Gal. 6:16 p. be on them
Eph. 6:23 p. be to brethren, love
1 *Pet.* 5:14 p. be with all in Chr.
3 *John* 14 p. be to thee, our frie.

God of PEACE.

Rom. 15:33 God of p. be wi. you
    16:20 God of p. sh. bruise Satan
2 *Cor.* 13:11 the God of p. shall
    be with you, *Phil.* 4:9
1 *Thes.* 5:23 God of p. sanctify
Heb. 13:20 God of p. make you
    perfect

See HELD, HOLD.

In PEACE.

Gen. 26:29 sent thee away *in p.*
    28:21 I come to fa.'s house *in p.*
Jud. 11:31 when I return *in p.*
2 *Sam.* 15:27 return to city *in p.*
    19:30 king is come again *in p.*
1 *K.* 2:5 Joab shed blood *in p.*
    22:17 man *in p.* 2 *Chr.* 18:16, 26
    27 in prison, until I come *in p.*
2 *Chr.* 19:1 Jehosh. return. *in p.*
Job 5:24 thy taber. shall be *in p.*
Ps. 4:8 I will lay me down *in p.*
    55:18 he delivered my soul *in p.*
Is. 26:3 wilt keep him in perf. p.
Jer. 29:7 *in p.* sh. ye have peace
    34:5 but thou shalt die *in p.*
Mal. 2:6 walked with me *in p.*
Luke 2:29 let. serv. depart *in p.*
1 *Cor.* 16:11 cond. him forth *in p.*
2 *Cor.* 13:11 one mind, live *in p.*
Jam. 2:16 depart *in p.* be warm.
    3:18 righteousness is sown *in p.*
2 *Pet.* 3:14 be found of him *in p.*

See GO, MADE, OFFERINGS.

PEACEABLE.

Gen. 34:21 these men p. with us
2 *Sam.* 20:19 one of them th. p.
1 *Chr.* 4:40 land was wi. and p.
Is. 32:18 peo. dwell in p. habita.
Jer. 25:37 p. habitations are cut
1 *Tim.* 2:2 lead a quiet and p. li.
Heb. 12:11 yieldeth the p. fruit
Jam. 3:17 wisd. is pure, p. gent.

PEACEABLY.

Gen. 37:4 could not speak p.
Jud. 11:13 restore those lands p.
    21:13 send some p. to Benjam.
1 *Sam.* 16:4 said, Comest thou p.
    5 p. I am come, 1 *K.* 2:13
1 *Chr.* 12:17 if ye be come p.
Jer. 9:8 speaketh p. to neighbor
Dan. 11:21 shall come in p. 24
Rom. 12:18 live p. with all men

PEACEMAKERS.

Mat. 5:9 blessed are the p.

PEACOCKS.

1 *K.* 10:22 the navy came, bring-
    ing p. 2 *Chr.* 9:21
Job 39:13 gav. goodly win. to p. ?

PEARL.

Mat. 13:46 found p. of great price
Rev. 21:21 ev. gate. was of one p.

PEARLS.

Job 28:18 no menti. of coral or p.
Mat. 7:6 neither cast p. bef. sw.
    13:45 like merchant seeking p.

---

1 *Tim.* 2:9 not with p. or costly
Rev. 17:4 woman decked with p.
    18:12 no man buy. merc. of p. 16
    21:21 twelve gates were twe. p.

PECULIAR.

Ex. 19:5 sh. be p. treasure to me
Deut. 14:2 be a p. people unto
    himself, 26:18 ; 1 *Pet.* 2:9
Ps. 135:4 chosen Is. for p. treas.
Ec. 2:8 I gath. p. treas. of kings
Tit. 2:14 purify to himself p.
    people

PEDIGREES.

Num. 1:18 they declared their p.

PEELED.

Is. 18:2 nation scatter. and p. 7
Ezek. 29:18 every shoulder was p.

PEEP, ED.

Is. 8:19 wizards that p. and mut.
    10:14 none opened mouth or p.

PEKAH.

2 *K.* 15:25 P. conspired again. 29
    30 conspiracy against P. 16:5
2 *Chr.* 28:6 P. slew in Judah
Is. 7:1 Rezin and P. went towa.

PEKAHIAH. 2 *K.* 15:22, 23

PELATIAH.

1 *Chr.* 3:21 son of Hananiah P.
    4:42 ; *Neh.* 10:22 ; *Ezek.* 11:13

PELICAN.

Lev. 11:18 p. uncl. *Deut.* 14:17
Ps. 102:6 I am like p. of wildern

PEN.

Jud. 5:14 they that handle p.
Job 19:24 graven with an iron p.
Ps. 45:1 tongue is p. of writer
Is. 8:1 write it with a man's p.
Jer. 8:8 p. of scribes is in vain
    17:1 sin of Jud. written with
3 *John* 13 not with ink and p.

PENCE.

Mat. 18:28 one who owed 100 p.
Mark 14:5 have been sold for
    more than 300 p. *John* 12:5
Luke 7:41 the one owed 500 p.
    10:35 on mo. he took out two p.

PENIEL. *Gen.* 32:30

PENKNIFE.

Jer. 36:23 Jehu. cut roll with p.

PENNY.

Mat. 20:2 ag. with laborers for p.
    9 received every man a p. 13
    22:19 they brought unto him p.
Mark 12:15 bring p. *Luke* 20:24
Rev. 6:6 meas. of wheat for a p.
    three meas. of barley for a p.

PENNYWORTH.

Mark 6:37 buy 200 p. of bread
John 6:7 200 p. is not sufficient

PENTECOST.

Acts 2:1 wh. day of P. was come
    20:16 hasted to Jerus. day of P.
1 *Cor.* 16:8 tarry at Eph. until P.

PENUEL.

Gen. 32:31 as Ja. passed over P.
Jud. 8:8 Gid. went up to P. 17
1 *K.* 12:25 went and built P.

PENURY.

Prov. 14:23 talk of lips ten. to p.
Luke 21:4 she of her p. cast all

PEOPLE.

Gen. 27:29 let p. serve thee
    48:19 he sh. become a p. great
Ex. 6:7 take you for a p. *Deut.*
    4:20 ; 2 *Sam.* 7:24 ; *Jer.* 13:11
Lev. 20:24 separ. you from other
    p. 26
Num 22:5 p. come out fr. Eg. 11
Deut. 4:33 did p. hear vol. of G. ?
    7:6 G. ha. chosen thee special p.
    14:2 Lord hath cho. thee pec. p.

20:1 p. more than thou, be not
    28:32 sons given to another p.
    29:13 estab. thee for p. to hims.
    32:21 move them wi. th. not a p.
    33:29 who is like p. saved by L.?
1 *Sam.* 2:24 make L.'s p. transg.
    5:10 to slay us and our p. 11
2 *Sam.* 7:23 wh. G. redeem for p.
    22:28 afflicted p. thou wilt save,
    Ps. 18:27
    44 p. I kn. not, serve, *Ps.* 18:43
1 *K.* 22:28 hearken, O p. ev. one
2 *K.* 11:17 be L.'s p. 2 *Chr.* 23:16
1 *Chr.* 16:20 went from one kin.
    • to another p. *Ps.* 105:13
2 *Chr.* 1:9 made me king over p.
Est. 2:10 E. had not showed p.
    3:8 a certain p. scattered abroad
Job 36:20 when p. are cut off
Ps. 62:8 p. pour out your hearts
    66:8 bless God, p. 95:10 p. err
    114:1 went out fr. p. of strange
    144:15 happy p. 148:14 p. near
Prov. 14:34 sin is repro. to any p.
    28:15 wicked ruler over poor p.
    30:25 ants are a p. not strong
Is. 1:4 a p. laden with iniquity
    10 give ear to law, p. of Gomo.
    7:8 Ephraim broken, be not a p.
    8:19 sho. not p. seek their God ?
    27:11 a p. of no understanding
    30:9 this is a rebellious p. 65:3
    43:4 I will give p. for thy life
    8 bring forth blind p. ha. eyes
    65:3 a p. that provoketh me
    18 Jerus. rejoicing, her p. a joy
Jer. 6:22 p. com. fr. north, 50:41
    48:42 M. destroyed fr. being p.
Lam. 1:7 p. fell into hand of ene.
Hos. 4:9 sh. be like p. like priest
    9:1 rejoice not, O Is. as other p.
Jon. 1:8 of what p. art thou ?
Mic. 4:1 p. shall flow unto it
Zec. 8:20 there shall come p.
Luke 1:17 ready p. prep. for L.
Acts 15:14 take out of them a p.
Rom. 10:19 them that are no p.
Tit. 2:14 purify to hims. pecu. p.
Heb. 8:10 shall be to me a p.
1 *Pet.* 2:9 ye are a peculiar p.
    10 p. of G. in ti. past w. not p.
Rev. 5:9 redeem. us out of ev. p.

All PEOPLE.

Ex. 19:5 treas. above all p. *Deut.*
    7:6, 14 ; 10:15 ; *Ps.* 99:2
Deut. 7:7 were fewest of all p.
1 *K.* 4:34 came of all p. to hear S.
    8:43 all p. know name, 2 *Chr.*
    6:33
Est. 9:2 fear of th. fell on all p.
Ps. 96:3 declare wond. am. all p.
    117:1 praise L. all ye p. for his
    kindness, 148:11 ; *Rom.* 15:11
Is. 25:6 L. make to all p. a feast
    56:7 house of prayer for all p.
Lam. 1:11 all her p. seek bread
    18 hear, a p. behold, *Mic.* 1:2
Dan. 5:19 all p. feared bef. him
    7:14 all p. and nati. serve him
Mic. 4:5 all p. walk, ea. in name
Zep. 3:20 praise among all p.
Luke 2:10 tidings of joy to all p.
    31 prepared before face of a. p.

All the PEOPLE.

Ex. 18:14 all t. p. stand by thee
    19:8 a. t. p. answ. togeth. 24:3
    11 L. come down in si. of a. t. p.
Lev. 10:3 bef. a. t. p. I will be glo.
Num. 11:29 a. t. L.'s p. prophets
Deut. 13:9 hand of all t. p. 17:7
    27:15 all t. p. say, Amen, 16-21
    28:10 all t. p. sh. see that thou
Jos. 3:24 all the p. might know
    6:5 all the p. shall shout with
    7:3 said, Let not all t. p. go up
Jud. 20:8 all the p. arose

1Sa. 10:24 none li. him am. a. t. p.
11:4 all t. p. wept; 12:18 feared
30:6 soul of all the p. grieved
2 Sam. 2:28. a. t. p. stood, pursu.
17:3 br. back all the p. unto th.
19:9 all the p. were at strife
20:22 woman were at strife
1 K. 8:53 separate th. fr. all t. p.
60 a. t. p. of earth may know
2 K. 23:3 a. t. p. stood to coven.
1 Chr. 16:36 a. t. p. said, Amen
2 Chr. 7:4 a. t. p. offer. sacrifices
Ezr. 7:25 wh. may judge a. t. p.
Neh. 8:5 in sight of all the p.
Ps. 67:3 let a. t. p. praise thee, 5
97:6 and all the p. see his glory
106:48 all the p. say, Amen
Ec. 4:16 th. is no end of all t. p.
Jer. 34:8 made cov. wi. a. t. p. 10
43:4 all the p. obeyed not the L.
Ezek. 31:12 all the p. are gone
Dan. 3:7 when all t. p. heard
Zec. 11:10 bre. cov. with a. t. p.
14:12 Lord will smite all the p.
Mal. 2:9 ma. you base bef. a. t. p.
Luke 13:17 a. t. p. rejoiced
18:43 all the p. gave praise to G.
20:6 all the p. will stone us
Acts 10:41 not a. t. p. but witn.
21:27 stirred up all the p.

Among the PEOPLE.
Lev. 18:29 cut off from a. t. p.
Ezek. 28:19 that know thee a. p.
Dan. 11:33 that unders. a. the p.
Joel 2:17 sho. they say am. t. p.
Zec. 10:9 sow them a. the p.
John 7:43 a division am. the p.
Acts 3:23 destroyed from a. t. p.
4:17 spread no further a. t. p.
14:14 Barnab. and P. ran a. t. p.

See COMMON, FOOLISH.

PEOPLE of God.
Jud. 20:2 assembly of p. of God
2 Sam. 14:13 such th. ag. p. of G.
Ps. 47:9 even p. of G. of Abrah.
Heb. 4:9 remain. rest to p. of God
11:25 suf. affliction wi. p. of God
1 Pet. 2:10 but now p. of God

See GREAT.

His PEOPLE.
Gen. 17:14 cnt off from his p. Ex.
30:33, 38; 31:14; Lev. 7:20,
21, 25, 27; 17:4, 9; 19:8;
23:29; Num. 9:13; 15:30
49:16 Dan shall judge his p. 33
Ex. 18:1 for Moses and Is. his p.
Lev. 17:10 I will cut him off from
among his p. 20:3, 6; 23:30
Deut. 26:18 L. avouch. thee h. p.
32:9 the Lord's portion is his p.
36 sh. judge his p. Ps. 135:14
43 rej. O ye nations, wi. his p.
he will be merci. Rom. 15:10
33:7 L. and bring Jud. to his p.
Ruth 1:6 the Lord visited his p.
1 Sam. 12:22 L. not forsake h. p.
pleased L. to make you h. p.
15:1 anoint the king over h. p.
2 Sam. 8:15 David executed just.
to all his p. 1 Chr. 18:14
1 K. 20:42 thy pe. sh. go for h. p.
1 Chr. 21:3 make h. p. 100 times
1 Chr. 22:18 subt. bef. L. and h. p.
23:25 G. of Is. given rest to h. p.
2 Chr. 31:1 L. hath loved his p.
31:10 Lord hath blessed his p.
32:14 who could deliv. h. p.? 15
36:15 had compassion on his p.
16 wrath of L. rose ag. his p.
23 who of all his p. Ezr. 1:3
Job 18:19 not have son am. h. p.
Ps. 14:7 captivity of his p. 53:6
29:11 strength to his p. L. will
bl. his p. with peace. 68:35
50:4 that he may judge his p.
73:10 theref. his p. return hither

78:20 can he pro. flesh for h. p.?
62 he gave his p. over to swo.
71 bro. him to feed Jacob h. p.
85:8 will speak peace to his p.
94:14 Lord will not cast off h. p.
100:3 are h. p. 105:43 brought
105:24 increased his p. greatly
111:6 he showed his p. power
9 he sent redemption to his p.
113:8 with princes of his p.
116:14 in presence of all his p.
125:2 so is L. round about h. p.
136:16 who led his p. thro' wild.
Is. 3:14 with ancients of his p.
7:2 moved, and heart of his p.
14:32 poor of his p. trust in him
25:8 rebuke of his p. sh. he take
30:26 L. bind. up breach of h. p.
49:13 hath comforted h. p. 52:9
51:22 God plead. cause of h. p.
56:3 L. separated me fr. his p.
63:11 remem. Moses and his p.
Jer. 27:12 serve him and his p.
50:16 return every one to his p.
Ezek. 18:18 did not good am. h. p.
30:11 he and h. p. sh. brought
Joel 2:18 L. jealous and pity h. p.
19 answer and say to his p.
3:16 Lord will be hope of h. p.
Zec. 9:16 L. save them as his p.
Mat. 1:21 he shall save his p.
Luke 1:68 and redeemed h. p.
7:16 that God hath visited h. p.
Rom. 11:1 ha. G. cast away h. p.?
2 God hath not cast away h. p.?
Heb. 10:30 the L. sh. judge h. p.
Rev. 21:3 and they shall be h. p.

See HOLY, ISRAEL, MANY, MEN.

PEOPLE of the land.
Gen. 23:7 A. bow. to p. of t. l. 12
Ex. 5:5 the p. of t. l. are many
Lev. 20:2 p. of t. l. sh. stone him
4 if p. of the l. hide their eyes
Num. 14:9 nei. fear ye p. of t. l.
2 K. 11:14 all p. of t. l. rejoiced, 20
15:5 Joth. judged p. 2 Chr. 26:21
21:24 p. made J. ki. 2 Chr. 33:25
23:30 p. of the l. took Jehoahaz
his son, 2 Chr. 36:1
25:3 no free. for p. of t. Jer. 52:6
1 Chr. 5:25 after gods of p. of t. l.
Ezr. 10:2 stra. wives of p. of t. l.
11 separate from p. of the land
Neh. 10:30 not gi. dau. to p. of t. l.
31 if the p. of the l. bring ware
Est. 8:17 many p. of t. l. bec. J.
Jer. 34:19 p. of t. l. which passed
Ezek. 7:27 p. of t. l. be troubled
22:29 p. of t. l. used oppression
33:2 if p. of the l. take man
39:13 p. of t. l. shall bury them
45:16 p. of t. l. shall give obla.
22 sh. prince prepa. for p. of l.
46:3 p. of t. l. shall worship
9 p. of t. l. come in feasts
Dan. 9:6 proph. spa. to p. of t. l.
Hag. 2:4 be strong, ye p. of t. l.
Zec. 7:5 speak to all p. of the l.

Much PEOPLE.
Num. 20:20 E. came with m. p.
Jos. 11:4 they went with m. p.
2 Chr. 32:4 gath. m. p. together
Ps. 35:18 praise thee am. m. p.
Mark 5:21 m. p. gath. unto him
24 and much p. followed him
John 12:9 m. p. of Jews knew
Acts 5:37 drew away m. p. af. him
11:24 m. p. was added unto L.
18:10 I have m. p. in this city
19:26 P. hath turned away m. p.
Rev. 19:1 I heard a voice of m. p.

My PEOPLE.
Gen. 23:11 in presence of my p.
41:40 to thy word sh. all my p.
49:29 to be gathered to my p.

Ex. 3:7 I have seen affliction of
my p. Acts 7:34
5:1 saith L. God, Let my p. go,
7:16 : 8:1, 20 ; 9:1, 13 ; 10:3
8:22 land in wh. my p. are, 23
9:17 exalteat thyself ag. my p.
Ex. 9:27 L. righ. I and my p. wic.
12:31 get forth from am. my p.
22:25 if th. lend money to my p.
Lev. 26:12 and you sh. be my p.
Jer. 11:4; 30:22
Num. 24:14 I go unto my p.
Jud. 12:2 I and my p. at strife
14:3 never a wom. am. my p.?
Ruth 1:16 thy peo. shall be my p.
3:11 the city of my p. doth kn.
1 Sam. 9:16 to be cap. over my p.
2 Sam. 3:18 by D. wi. I save my p.
7:8 ruler over my p. 2 Chr. 6:5
1 K. 22:4 my p. as thy people,
2 K. 3:7; 2 Chr. 18:3
1 Chr. 17:6 I com. to feed my p.
28:2 Da. said, Hear me, my p.
29:14 and what my p.?
2 Chr. 1:11 mayest judge my p.
6:5 since day I bro. forth my p.
7:14 if my p. humb. themselves
Est. 7:3 let my p. be given me
4 I and my p. to be destroyed
Ps. 14:4 eat my p. as bread, 53:4
50:7 O my p. I will speak, 81:8
59:11 slay not, lest my p. forget
68:22 I will bring my p. fr. Bas.
78:1 give ear, O my p. to law
81:11 my p. would not hearken
142:subdueth my p. under me
Is. 1:3 my p. doth not consider
3:12 my p. child. are oppressors
15 that ye beat my p.?
10:2 take right fr. poor of my p.
24 O my p. that dwellest in Z.
19:25 blessed be Egypt, my p.
32:18 my p. sh. dwell in peace.
40:1 comfort ye, my p. saith G.
43:20 give drink to my p.
47:6 I was wroth with my p.
51:16 say to Z. Thou art my p.
52:4 my p. went down into Eg.
5 my p. is taken away
6 my p. shall know my name
58:1 show my p. th. transgres.
63:8 surely they are my p. chil.
65:10 Sharon a fold for my p.
19 rejoice in Jer. joy in my p.
22 as a tree, are days of my p.
Jer. 2:13 my p. have commit. ev.
31 say my p. we are lords?
32 my p. have forgot. me, 18:15
4:22 my p. is foolish, not kn. me
5:26 am. my p. are wicked men
31 my p. love, wh. will ye do?
7:23 obey my voice, be my p.
8:7 my p. kn. not judgm. of L.
9:2 that I might leave my p.
12:16 dilig. learn ways of my p.
15:7 destroy my p. th. retu. not
23:2 pastors that feed my p.
22 if they had caused my p.
27 think to cause my p. forget
24:7 they shall be my p. 31:1, 33;
32:38; Ezek. 11:20; 36:28;
37:23, 27; Zec. 8:8
29:32 nor good I will do my p.
31:14 my p. shall be satisfied
33:24 they have despised my p.
50:6 my p. hath been lost sheep
51:45 my p. go ye out of midst
of her, Rev. 18:4
Ezek. 13:9 not in assem. of my p.
19 ye pollute me among my p.
by lying to my p.
21 deliver my p. out of hand, 23
14:8 cut him off fr. midst my p.
11 but that they may be my p.
21:12 the sw. sh. be upon my p.
34:30 ev. house of Is. are my p.
37:12 O m. p. I will open gra. 13

38:16 thou shalt come ag. *my p.*
46:18 that *my p.* be not scatter.
Hos. 1:9 ye are not *my p.* 10
2:23 to them wh. were not *my p.*
4:6 *my p.* are destroyed for lack
    8 they eat up the sin of *my p.*
6:11 return. captivity of *my p.*
Joel 2:26 *my p.* nev. be asha. 27
3:2 plead with them for *my p.*
    3 they have cast lots for *my p.*
Amos 9:10 sinn. of *my p.* sh. die
Ob. 13 not enter. gate of *my p.*
Mic. 1:9 come to gate of *my p.*
2:8 *my p.* is risen as enemy
    9 women of *my p.* ye cast out
3:3 who also eat flesh of *my p.*
    5 proph. that make *my p.* err
6:3 O *my p.* wh. have I done? 5
16 shall bear reproach of *my p.*
Zep. 2:8 they reproached *my p.*
Zec. 2:11 many nations shall be
    my p.
8:7 save *my p.* from the east
13:9 it is *my p.* they shall say
Rom. 9:25 call them *my p.* which
    were not *my p.*
were as said, Ye are not *my p.*

2 *Cor.* 6:16 they shall be *my p.*

See DAUGHTER.

Of the PEOPLE.

Gen. 25:23 manner of *p.* be sep.
49:10 to him sh. gather. of *p.* be
Num. 26:4 take sum of *t. p.* fr. 20
Jos. 4:2 take 12 men of *the p.*
1 *Sam.* 9:2 higher than any of
    the p. 10:23
14:24 none of *the p.* tasted food
26:15 ca. one of *t. p.* destr. king
2 *K.* 13:7 nor did he leave of *t. p.*
Ezr. 3:3 of *the p.* of th. countries
Neh. 5:1 th. was a gre. cry of *t. p.*
7:73 some of *the p.* dw. in cities
Ps. 72:4 sh. judge poor of *the p.*
89:19 exalted one out of *the p.*
Is. 51:4 judg. for a light of *t. p.*
63:3 of *the p.* there was none
John 7:31 many of *t. p.* believed
11:42 bec. of *t. p.* that stand by
Acts 4:21 punish, beca. of *the p.*
Heb. 9:7 hims. and errors of *t. p.*
Rev. 11:9 they of *p.* see dead bod.

See EARS, ELDERS.

One PEOPLE.

Gen. 25:23 one *p.* sh. be stronger
34:16 dwell wi. you, bec. *one p.*
22 dwell with us, to be *one p.*

Own PEOPLE.

Ex. 5:16 the fault is in thi. *o. p.*
1 *Chr.* 17:21 went to redeem *o. p.*
2 *Chr.* 25:15 could not deli. *o. p.*
Ps. 45:10 forget also thy *own p.*
78:52 made his *o. p.* to go forth
Is. 13:14 ev. man turn to his *o. p.*
Jer. 46:16 let us go ag. to our *o. p.*

The PEOPLE.

Gen. 11:6 L. said, Behold *the p.*
Ex. 5:4 why let *t. p.* from work?
    5 *the p.* of land now are many
12:27 and *t. p.* bowed the head
14:31 *the p.* feared L. believed
15:14 *the p.* sh. hear and be afr.
16 *the p.* pass over wh. th. hast
24 *the p.* murmured, saying
16:30 *the p.* rest. on seventh day
17:1 th. was no water for *the p.*
    2 *t. p.* did chide Mo. *Num.* 20:3
6 water out of it, *the p.* drink
18:19 be th. for *the p.* God-ward
19:9 *t. p.* may hear when I spe.
17 Moses brought forth *the p.*
20:18 when *the p.* saw it afar, 21
24:8 Moses sprinkled it on *t. p.*
Lev. 9:7 ato. for thyself and *t. p.*
15 sin-offer. for *the p.* 18; 16:15
Num. 11:2 *the p.* cried to Moses

13:18 see *the p.* that dwelleth
14:1 *the p.* wept; 39 *t. p.* mour.
21:5 *the p.* spake against God
23:9 lo, *the p.* shall dwell alone
24 *the p.* rise up as a great lion
Deut. 4:10 said, Gather me *the p.*
18:3 the priest's due from *t. p.*
33:3 loved *the p.* 17 push *the p.*
19 they shall call *t. p.* to moun.
Jos. 4:10 and *the p.* hasted over
6:20 *t. p.* shout. 24:28 *t. p.* dep.
Jud. 7:2 *t. p.* are with thee, 4
1 *Sam.* 2:13 priest's cust. wi. *t. p.*
4:4 *t. p.* sent to Sh. to bring ark
8:19 *the p.* ref. to obey Samuel
14:45 *the p.* said, Sh. Jonathan
    die? so *the p.* rescued Jona.
15:15 *the p.* spared best of sheep
21 *the p.* took of the spoil oxen
30:6 *t. p.* spake of stoning him
2 *Sam.* 1:4 *t. p.* fled from battle
15:12 *the p.* incre. with Absalom
1 *K.* 1:40 *the p.* piped with pipes
16:22 *the p.* that followed Omri
    prevailed against *the p.*
2 *K.* 4:41 pour out for *the p.*
43 give *t. p.* that they may eat
11:17 coven. be. king and *t. p.*
18:36 but *the p.* held their peace
22:13 inquire of Lord for *the p.*
2 *Chr.* 12:3 *the p.* without numb.
20:33 *the p.* had not prepa. 30:3
27:2 and *the p.* did yet corruptly
30:20 and the Lord healed *the p.*
32:8 *the p.* rest. on words of H.
36:14 *the p.* transgr. very much
Ezr. 10:13 but *the p.* are many
Neh. 4:6 *t. p.* had mind to work
5:13 *the p.* did accord. to prom.
7:4 but *the p.* were few therein
8:16 *the p.* bro. palm branches
11:2 *t. p.* blessed all that offered
Est. 3:6 showed him *t. p.* of Mo.
4:11 *the p.* of king's provinces
Job 12:2 no doubt but ye are *t. p.*
34:30 lest *the p.* be ensnared
Ps. 2:1 why do *t. p.* im. vain th.?

Ps. 33:12 bles. *t. p.* he hath cho.
44:2 how thou didst afflict *t. p.*
45:17 *the p.* praise thee for ever
56:7 in th. anger cast down *t. p.*
67:3 let *the p.* praise thee, O G. 5
89:15 blessed is *t. p.* that know
95:7 we are *t. p.* of his pasture
96:13 he sh. judge *t. p.* with tru.
98:9 he sh. judge *t. p.* with eq.
99:1 L. reign. let *the p.* tremble
105:1 make kno. deeds am. *t. p.*
Prov. 11:14 no coun. is, *t. p.* fall
29:2 *the p.* rejoiced, *t. p.* mourn
18 wh. is no vision, *t. p.* perish

Is. 9:2 *t. p.* that walked in dark.
13 *t. p.* turneth not to him sm.
14:2 and *the p.* shall take them
24:2 be with *t. p.* so with priest
30:19 *the p.* shall dwell in Zion
33:24 *t. p.* be forgiven th. iniq.
34:5 my sword sh. come on *t. p.*
40:7 *t. p.* is grass, grass wither
51:7 *the p.* in wh. heart is my law
63:6 will tread *t. p.* in mi. anger
18 *t. p.* of thy holi. possess. it
Jer. 31:2 *t. p.* left of sw. found gr.
37:4 Jeremiah went amo. *the p.*
39:14 so he dwelt among *the p.*
40:5 go back and dw. with *t. p.* 6
51:58 *the p.* shall labor in vain
Ezek. 11:17 gather you from *t. p.*
20:34 br. you out from *t. p.* 34:13
25:7 I will cut thee off fr. *the p.*
26:20 bring thee down with *t. p.*
33:31 come to thee as *t. p.* com.
36:20 these are *the p.* of Lord
39:4 thou shalt fall, and *the p.*
42:14 approa. th. things for *t. p.*
44:19 shall not sanctify *the p.*
Dan. 9:26 *the p.* of the prince

11:32 *the p.* that know their G.
Hos. 4:14 *t. p.* doth not underst.
10:5 *the p.* thereof shall mourn
10 *t. p.* sh. be gath. aga. them
Joel 2:6 *the p.* sh. be much pain.
Amos 3:6 sh. *t. p.* not be afraid?
Jon. 3:5 *t. p.* of Nin. believ. God
Hab. 2:13 *t. p.* shall labor in fire,
    the p. shall weary themselv.
Zep. 2:10 magnifi. ag. *t. p.* of L.
Hag. 1:12 *t. p.* did fear the Lord
Mal. 1:4 *the p.* against whom L.
Mat. 4:16 *t. p.* in dark. saw light
21:26 we fear *t. p. Mark* 11:32
Luke 1:21 *t. p.* waited for Zacha.
3:15 as *the p.* were in expecta.
4:42 *the p.* sou. 5:1 *t. p.* pressed
8:40 *the p.* gladly received him
9:18 whom say *t. p.* that I am?
20:19 feared *t. p.* 22:2; 23:5 stir.
23:14 one that perverteth *t. p.*
John 7:12 he deceiveth *the p.*
11:50 man sho. die for *t. p.* 18:14
Acts 5:13 *the p.* magnified them
8:6 *t. p.* wi. one accord ga. heed
14:11 *t. p.* saw wh. P. had done
19 persuaded *t. p.* and ston. P.
26:17 delivering thee from *t. p.*
Heb. 5:3 as for *t. p.* so hims. 7:27
7:11 under it *t. p.* received law
13:12 he might sanctify *the p.*
Jude 5 Lord having saved *the p.*

This PEOPLE.

Ex. 3:21 I will give *t. p.* favor
5:22 why hast evil entrea. *t. p.?*
17:4 cried, Wh. sh. I do to *t. p.?*
18:18 wear away, thou and *t. p.*
32:9 seen *t. p.* 21 what did *t. p.*
31 *t. p.* have sinned a great sin
33:12 sayest, Bring up *this p.*
Num. 11:11 burden of all *t. p.*
14 I am not able to bear all *t. p.*
14:11 how long will *t. p.* prov. ?
15 if thou kill *t. p.* as one man
16 not able to br. *t. p.* into land
19 pardon *t. p.* hast forg. *t. p.*
22:6 I pray thee, curse *t. p.* 17
24:14 *th. p.* shall do to thy peo.
Deut. 5:28 heard voice of *this p.*
9:13 saying, I have seen *this p.*
27 look not to stubborn. of *t.p.*
31:7 for thou must go with *t. p.*
16 *t. p.* will go whor. after gods
Jud. 2:20 *t. p.* have transgressed
9:29 would to G. *t. p.* were und.
38 is not *this* the *p.* thou des.?
2 *Sam.* 16:18 wh. L. and *t. p.* ch.
1 *K.* 12:6 that I may answer *this*
    p. 9; 2 *Chr.* 10:6, 9
27 if *t. p.* do sacrifice at Jeru-
    salem
14:2 I should be king over *t. p.*
18:37 that *this p.* may know
2 *K.* 6:18 smite *t. p.* wi. blindn.
2 *Chr.* 1:10 come in before *th. p.*
Neh. 5:19 all I have done for *t. p.*
Is. 6:9 go and tell *t. p.* hear ye
Is. 6:10 make the heart of *t. p.*
    fat, *Mat.* 13:15; *Acts* 28:26, 27
9:16 leaders of *t. p.* cause th. err
23:13 *t. p.* was not till A. found
28:14 scornful men that rule *t. p.*
29:13 *t. p.* dr. near me wi. mou.
14 a marv. work among *t. p.*
43:21 *t. p.* ha. I form. for myself
Jer. 4:10 thou hast deceived *t. p.*
5:14 my words fire, *t. p.* wood
6:19 I will bring evil on *this p.*
    it stumbling-blo. bef. *this p.*
7:16 therefore pray not thou for
    this p. 11:14; 14:11
8:5 why is *this p.* slidden back?
13:10 *t.* evil *p.* who ref. to hear
15:1 my mind co. not be to. *t. p.*
16:5 tak. away my peace fr. *t. p.*
19:11 even so will I break *t. p.*
23:32 they shall not profit *t. p.*

PEOPLE

28:15 makest *t. p.* trust in a lie
29:32 a man to dwell amo. *t. p.*
32:42 bro. great evil upon *t. p.*
33:24 not what *t. p.* have spok.
35:16 *t. p.* have not hearkened
36:7 anger pronounced ag. *t. p.*
37:18 what have I offend. *t. p.?*
Mic. 2:11 sh. be prophet of *t. p.*
Hag. 2:14 so is *this p.* before me
Zec. 8:6 in eyes of remn. of *t. p.*
   11 I will not be to *this p.*
   12 cause rem. of *t. p.* possess
Mat. 15:8 *t. p.* draweth nigh
Mark 7:6 *t. p.* hon. me with lips
Luke 9:13 sho. buy meat for *t. p.*
   21:23 th. sh. be wrath upon *t. p.*
John 7:49 *t. p.* knoweth not law
Acts 13:17 G. of *t. p.* chose our
1 Cor. 14:21 I will speak to *t. p.*

Thy PEOPLE.

Ex. 5:23 neither delivered *t. p.*
   15:16 till *t. p.* pass over, O Lord
   22:28 ca. ruler of *t. p.* Acts 23:5
   23:11 poor of *thy p.* may eat
   33:13 consider this nation *t. p.*
   16 I and *t. p.* have found grace
Num. 5:21 make thee a curse
   and oath among *thy p.*
   27:13 shalt be gathered to *thy p.*
   31:2; Deut. 32:50
Deut. 9:12 *t. p.* corrupted thems.
   26 O Lord, destroy not *thy p.*
   29 yet are they *t. p.* Neh. 1:10
Ruth 1:10 return wi. thee to *t. p.*
   16 *thy p.* shall be my people
2 Sam. 7:23 and what nation is
   like *thy p.? 1* Chr. 17:21
   23 bef. *t. p.* who thou redeeme.
1 K. 3:8 serv. is in midst of *t. p.*
   8:44 if *thy p.* go out to battle
   50 forgive *t. p.* 2 Chr. 6:34, 39
   51 they be *t. p.* 2 Chr. 6:34, 39
   22:4 my people as *t. p.* 2 K. 3:7
1 Chr. 21:17 not hand be on *t. p.*
   29:18 thoughts of heart of *t. p.*
Ps. 3:8 blessing is upon *thy p.*
   28:9 save *t. p.* bless, Jer. 31:7
   44:12 sellest *thy p.* for naught
   60:3 showed *thy p.* hard things
   68:7 thou wentest before *thy p.*
   72:2 judge *t. p.* with righteous.
   77:20 leddest *thy p.* as flock
   79:13 *thy p.* will give thee than.
   80:4 angry aga. prayer of *t. p.?*
   83:3 crafty counsel against *t. p.*
   85:2 forgiven iniquity of *thy p.*
   6 that *t. p.* may rejoice in thee
   94:5 they break in pieces *t. p.*
   106:4 favor th. thou bearest *t. p.*
   110:3 *thy p.* shall be willing
Is. 2:6 thou hast forsaken *thy p.*
   7:17 L. bring on thee and *t. p.*
   14:20 destroyed land and *thy p.*
   60:21 *t. p.* shall be all righteous
   63:14 lead *t. p.* 64:9 are *thy p.*
Jer. 22:2 thou and *t. p.* that ent.
   27:13 die, thou and *t. p.* by sw.?
Ezek. 3:11 get to *t. p.* and speak
   13:17 against daughters of *t. p.*
   26:11 he sh. slay *t. p.* by sword
   33:2 speak to child. of *t. p.* 12
   17 yet the children of *t. p.* say
   30 chil. of *t. p.* still are talking
   37:18 chil. of *t. p.* shall speak
Dan. 9:16 *thy p.* bec. a reproach
   19 and *thy p.* are called by na.
   12:1 standeth for chil. of *thy p.*
   at that time *t. p.* sh. be deli.
Hos. 4:4 *t. p.* as they that strive
   10:14 a tumult arise among *t. p.*
Joel 2:17 spare *t. p.* O Lord
Mic. 7:14 feed *t. p.* with thy rod
Nah 3:13 *thy p.* in midst of thee
   18 *t. p.* scattered on mountain
Hab. 3:13 for salvation of *thy p.*

To, or unto the PEOPLE.

Ex. 4:16 be spokesman *to t. p.*

Ex. 19:10 go to *t. p.* 12 bounds
   to p.
Deut. 20:2 priest speak *to the p.*
   5 officers shall speak *to the p.*
Jud. 8:5 loaves of bread *to the p.*
Ruth 2:11 to *t. p.* th. knowest not
1 Sam. 26:7 Abishai came *to t. p.*
2 Sam. 24:3 L. thy G. add *to t. p.*
1 K. 12:15 king heark. not *to p.*
2 K. 4:42 give *to p.* they may eat
1 Chr. 10:9 carry tidings *to t. p.*
2 Chr. 35:8 gave willingly *to t. p.*
Neh. 4:22 said I *to the p.* lodge
   5:15 govern. chargeable *to t. p.*
   8:1 shall bring peace *to the p.*
Ps. 78:1 giveth breath *to the p.*
   49:22 set up my standard *to t. p.*
   55:4 given him for witness *to t.
   p.* a leader and com. *to t. p.*
Ezek. 24:18 spake *to t. p.* in morn.
Dan. 7:27 kingdom given *to t. p.*
Joel 3:8 sell them *to t. p.* afar off
Hab. 3:16 cometh *to t. p.* will in.
Zep. 3:9 turn *to t. p.* pure langu.
Mat. 12:46 yet talked *to the p.*
Acts 5:20 speak in temple *to t. p.*
   10:2 which gave alms *to the p.*
   42 comma. us to preach *to t. p.*
   13:31 seen of witnesses *to the p.*
   17:5 J. sought to bring *to the p.*
   19:33 made his defence *to the p.*
   21:39 suffer me to speak *to the p.*
   26:23 Christ show light *to the p.*

PEOPLES.

Rev. 10:11 prophesy bef. many *p.*
   17:15 waters thou sawest are *p.*

PEOR. Num. 23:28; 25:18; Jos.
   22:17

PERADVENTURE.

Gen. 18:24 *p.* there be 50 righte.
   28 *p.* there lack five of the fifty
   29 *p.* forty; 30 *p.* thirty; 31 *p.*
   twenty
   32 this once, *p.* ten shall be
   24:5 *p.* wom. not be willing, 39
   27:12 my father *p.* will feel me
   31:31 *p.* take by force thy daug.
   32:20 *p.* he will accept of me
   42:4 lest *p.* mischief befall him
   43:12 *p.* it was an oversight
   44:34 *p.* evil come on my father
   50:15 Joseph will *p.* hate us
Ex. 13:17 lest *p.* people repent
   32:30 *p.* I shall make atonement
Num. 22:6 *p.* I shall prevail, 11
   23:3 *p.* L. will come to meet me
   27 *p.* it please God thou curse
Jos. 9:7 *p.* ye dwell among us
1 Sam. 6:5 *p.* he will lighten ha.
   9:6 *p.* he can show us our way
1 K. 18:5 *p.* we may find grass
   27 *p.* sleep. must be awaked
   20:31 *p.* he will save thy life
2 K. 2:16 *p.* Spirit hath cast him
Jer. 20:10 *p.* he will be enticed
Rom. 5:7 *p.* for good men so. die
2 Tim. 2:25 *p.* G. give them rep.

PERCEIVE.

Deut. 29:4 not given heart to *p.*
Jos. 22:31 we *p.* Lord is am. us
1 Sam. 12:17 *p.* your wickedness
2 Sam. 19:6 I *p.* if A. had lived
2 K. 4:9 I *p.* this is a holy man
Job 9:11 *p.* not; 23:8 cannot *p.*
Prov. 1:2 *p.* words of understan.
Ec. 3:22 *p.* there is noth. better
Is. 6:9 see ye indeed, but *p.* not
   33:19 deeper speech th. canst *p.*
Mat. 13:14 shall see, and sh. not
   p. Mark 4:12; Acts 28:26
Mark 7:18 do ye not *p.* whatsoe.
   8:17 *p.* not, neither unders. ?
Luke 8:46 I *p.* virtue out of me
John 4:19 I *p.* thou art a prophet
   12:19 *p.* ye how pre. nothing ?

Acts 8:23 *p.* art in gall of bitter.
   10:34 *p.* G. is no respect. of per.
   17:22 I *p.* ye are too superstitio.
2 Cor. 7:8 I *p.* ep. made you sor.
1 John 3:16 here. *p.* we love of G.

PERCEIVED.

Gen. 19:33 *p.* not wh. she lay, 35
1 Sam. 28:14 S. *p.* it was Samuel
2 Sam. 5:12 D. *p.* Lord establish.
   him king over Is. 1 Chr. 14:2
1 K. 22:33 when captains *p.* it
   was not king. 2 Chr. 18:32
Neh. 6:12 *p.* G. had not sent him
   16 *p.* this work was wro. of G.
   13:10 *p.* portion of L. not given
Job 38:18 *p.* breadth of earth ?
Ec. 1:17 I *p.* this also is vexat.
   2:14 I *p.* one event happeneth
Is. 64:4 nor *p.* what God prep.
Jer. 23:18 who hath *p.* his word

Jer. 38:27 for matter was not *p.*
Mat. 21:45 *p.* he spa. Luke 20:19
   22:18 Jesus *p.* their wickedness
Mark 2:8 Jesus *p.* they reasoned
Luke 1:22 *p.* he had seen vision
   5:22 when Jesus *p.* th. thoughts
   9:45 saying hid, they *p.* it not
   20:23 but he *p.* their craftiness
John 6:15 J. *p.* would make him
Acts 4:13 *p.* they were unlearned
   23:6 Paul *p.* part were Pharise.
Gal. 2:9 James *p.* grace giv. me

PERCEIVEST, ETH.

Job 14:21 low, but he *p.* it not
   33:14 G. speaketh, man *p.* it not
Prov. 14:7 *p.* not in him knowl.
   31:18 *p.* her merchandi. is good
Luke 6:41 *p.* not beam in own eye

PERCEIVING.

Mark 12:28 *p.* he answered well
Luke 9:47 Jesus *p.* the thought
Acts 14:9 *p.* he had faith to be

PERDITION.

John 17:12 no. lost but son of *p.*
Phil. 1:28 to them a token of *p.*
2 Thes. 2:3 be revealed, son of *p.*
1 Tim. 6:9 wh. drown men in *p.*
Heb. 10:39 who draw back to *p.*
2 Pet. 3:7 and *p.* of ungodly men
Rev. 17:8 beast goeth into *p.*
   11 beast is eighth, goeth in. *p.*

PERFECT, Adjective.

Gen. 6:9 N. *p.* 17:1 be thou *p.*
Lev. 22:21 freewill-offering be *p.*
Deut. 18:13 thou shalt be *p.* with
   25:15 have *p.* weight, *p.* measu.
1 Sam. 14:41 S. said, Give *p.* lot
2 Sam. 22:33 he maketh my way
   p. Ps. 18:32
Ezr. 7:12 Artax. to E. *p.* peace
Job 1:1 that man was *p.* 8; 2:3
   8:20 G. not cast away a *p.* man
   9:20 I am *p.* 21 tho' I were *p.*
   22 he destroyeth *p.* and wicked
   22:3 thou makest thy ways *p. ?*
Ps. 37:37 *p.* man, end is peace
   64:4 may shoot in secret at *p.*
   101:2 behave myself in a *p.* way
   6 he that walketh in a *p.* way
   139:22 I hate th. with *p.* hatred
Prov. 2:21 *p.* shall remain in it
   4:18 path of just shin. to *p.* day
   11:5 righteousn. of *p.* sh. direct
Is. 26:3 keep him in *p.* peace
Ezek. 16:14 *p.* thro' my comelin.
   27:3 thou said, I am of *p.* beauty
   11 made thy beauty *p.* 28:12
   28:15 thou was *p.* in thy ways
Mat. 5:48 be *p.* even as Fa. is *p.*
   19:21 if thou wilt be *p.* go sell
Luke 1:3 hav. had *p.* understan.
John 17:23 be made *p.* in one
Acts 3:16 given him *p.* soundn.
   22:3 taught accor. to *p.* manner
   24:22 having more *p.* knowledge
Rom. 12:2 what is *p.* will of God

1 *Cor.* 2:6 among th. that are *p.*
2 *Cor.* 12:9 strength *p.* in weakn.
13:11 be *p.* be of good comfort
Gal. 3:3 are ye made *p.* by flesh ?
Eph. 4:13 till we come to *p.* man
Phil. 3:12 not as tho' already *p.*
15 as many as be *p.*
Col. 1:28 present every man *p.* in
4:12 stand *p.* in will of God
1 *Thes.* 3:10 *p.* which is lacking
2 *Tim.* 3:17 man of G. may be *p.*
Heb. 2:10 Captain of salvation *p.*
5:9 being made *p.* beca. Author
7:19 for law made nothing *p.*
9:9 not make him did service *p.*
11 greater and more *p.* tabern.
10:1 law never make comers *p.*
11:40 without us not made *p.*
12:23 spirits of just men made *p.*
13:21 G. make you *p.* in every
Jam. 1:4 let patience have her *p.*
work, that ye may be *p.*
17 every *p.* gift is from above
25 looketh into *p.* law of liber.
2:22 by works was faith ma. *p.*
3:2 offend not, same is *p.* man
1 *Pet.* 5:10 after suffer. make *p.*
1 *John* 4:17 herein is love made *p.*
18 *p.* love casteth out fear, he
that feareth is not *p.* in love

See HEART.

Is PERFECT.

Deut. 32:4 his work is *p.*
2 *Sam.* 23:31 way *is p. Ps.* 18:30
Job 36:4 he that *is p.* in kn. 37:16
Ps. 19:7 law of L. *is p.* convert.
Is. 18:5 harvest when bud *is p.*
42:19 blind as he that *is p.*
Mat. 5:48 as Father in heaven
is p.
Luke 6:40 every one that *is p.*
1 *Cor.* 13:10 that wh. *is p.* is co.

PERFECT, Verb.

Ps. 138:8 L. will *p.* wh. concern.

PERFECTED.

2 *Chr.* 8:16 so house of G. was *p.*
24.13 and work was *p.* by them
Ezek. 27:4 builders have *p.* bea.
Mat. 21:16 thou hast *p.* praise
Luke 13:32 third day I shall be *p.*
Heb. 10:14 by one offer he ha. *p.*
1 *John* 2:5 in him is love of G. *p.*
4:12 love one ano. his love is *p.*

PERFECTING.

2 *Cor.* 7:1 *p.* holin. in fear of G.
Eph. 4:12 for *p.* of the saints

PERFECTION.

Job 11:7 find Almighty to *p. ?*
15:29 nor shall he prolong *p.*
28:3 he searcheth out all *p.*
Ps. 50:2 out of Zion, *p.* of beauty
119:96 I have seen an end of *p.*
Is. 47:9 come upon thee in th. *p.*
Lam. 2:15 men call *p.* of beauty
Luke 8:14 bring no fruit to *p.*
2 *Cor.* 13:9 we wish, even your *p.*
Heb. 6:1 let us go on to *p.*
7:11 if *p.* were by Levit. priest.

PERFECTLY, NESS.

Jer. 23:20 lat. days consider it *p.*
Mat. 14:36 touch. made *p.* whole
Acts 18:26 expound. way of G. *p.*
23:15 inq. something more *p.* 20
1 *Cor.* 1:10 be *p.* joined together
Col. 3:14 charity is the bond of *p.*
1 *Thes.* 5:2 know *p.* that day of

PERFORMANCE.

Luke 1:45 shall be *p.* of th. thin.
2 *Cor.* 8:11 *p.* out of that ye have

PERFORM.

Gen. 26:3 I will *p.* oath, I sware
to Ab. *Deut.* 9:5 ; *Luke* 1:72
Ex. 18:18 not able to *p.* it thys.
Num. 4:23 that enter to *p.* serv.
Deut. 4:13 commanded you to *p*

23:23 gone out of thy lips sh. *p.*
25:7 not *p.* duty of husband's
brother
Ruth 3:13 *p.* part of kinsman
1 *Sam.* 3:12 I will *p.* against Eli
2 *Sam.* 14:15 king will *p.* requ.
1 *K.* 6:12 then I will *p.* my word
2 *K.* 23:3 to *p.* the words of this
covenant. 24 ; 2 *Chr.* 34:31
Est. 5:8 if please king to *p.* req.
Job 5:12 cannot *p.* enterprise
Ps. 21:11 a device not able to *p.*
61:8 that I may daily *p.* vows
119:106 have sworn, I will *p.* it
112 inclined heart to *p.* statut.
Is. 9:7 zeal of Lord will *p.* this
19:21 pay a vow to L. and *p.* it
Jer. 1:12 for I will hasten to *p.* it
11:5 *p.* oath which I have sworn
28:6 L. *p.* words thou hast pro.
29:10 I will *p.* good word, 33:14
44:25 will surely *p.* your vows
Ezek. 12:25 word, and will *p.* it
Mic. 7:20 wilt *p.* truth to Jacob
Nah. 1:15 keep feasts, *p.* vows
Mat. 5:33 *p.* to Lord thine oaths
Rom. 4:21 prom. able also to *p.*
7:18 how to *p.* that wh. is good
2 *Cor.* 8:11 now *p.* the doing of
Phil. 1:6 *p.* it until day of J. Ch.

PERFORMED.

1 *Sam.* 15:11 S. hath not *p.* com.
13 I have *p.* commandm. of L.
2 *Sam.* 21:14 *p.* all th. king com.
1 *K.* 6:12 Lord hath *p.* his word,
2 *Chr.* 6:10 ; *Neh.* 9:8
Est. 1:15 Vashti not *p.* comma.
5:6 half of kingdom be *p.* 7:2
Ps. 65:1 unto thee sh. vow be *p.*
Is. 10:12 when L. hath *p.* work
Jer. 23:20 till *p.* thoughts, 30:24
34:18 not *p.* words of covenant
35:14 words of Jonad. are *p.* 16
51:29 purpose of Lord sh. be *p.*
Ezek. 37:14 spo. and *p.* it, saith
Lord
Luke 1:20 these things be *p.*
2:39 wh. they had *p.* all things
Rom. 15:28 wh. I have *p.* all this

PERFORMER, ING.

Num. 15:3 offering in *p.* vow, 8
Neh. 5:13 man *p.* not th. promise
Job 23:14 he *p.* thing appointed
Ps. 57:2 cry to G. that *p.* all thi.
Is. 44:26 *p.* counsel of messeng.

PERFUME, S.

Ex. 30:35 shalt make it a *p.* 37
Prov. 27:9 *p.* rejoice the heart
Is. 57:9 didst increase thy *p.*

PERFUMED.

Prov. 7:17 *p.* bed with myrrh
Cant. 3:6 who is this cometh *p. ?*

PERGA. *Acts* 13:13 ; 14:25
PERGAMOS. *Rev.* 1:11 ; 2:12

PERHAPS.

Phile. 15 *p.* he depart. for season

PERIL, S.

Lam. 5:9 get our bread with *p.*
Rom. 8:35 shall *p.* separate us ?
2 *Cor.* 11:26 *p.* of waters, of rob.

PERILOUS.

2 *Tim.* 3:1 *p.* times shall come

PERISH.

Gen. 41:36 *p.* not thro' famine
Ex. 19:21 and many of them *p.*
Num. 17:12 die, we *p.* we all *p.*
24:20 latter end be had *p.*
Deut. 11:17 lest ye *p.* quickly
26:5 ready to *p.* was my father
28:20 thou *p.* quick. 22 ; *Jo.* 23:13
Jud. 5:31 let enemies *p.* O Lord
1 *Sam.* 26:10 into battle and *p*
Est. 3:13 cause to *p.* all J. 7:4
4:16 if I *p.* I *p.* 8:11 *p.* power
9:28 nor memorial *p.* fr. th. seed

Job 3:3 let the day *p.* I was born
4:9 by the blast of God they *p.*
20 *p.* for ever, without any
6:18 paths go to nothing and *p.*
29:13 bless. of him ready to *p.*
31:19 *p.* for want of clothing
Ps. 2:12 lest he be angry, ye *p.*
9:18 expectation of poor not *p.*
49:10 fool and brutish person *p.*
12 like beasts that *p.* 20
68:2 let wicked *p.* 83:17
80:16 *p.* at the rebuke of thy
146:4 very day his thoughts *p.*
Prov. 11:10 wh. wicked *p.* 28:28
29:18 there is no vision, peo. *p.*
31:6 drink to him ready to *p.*
Ec. 5:14 those riches *p.* by evil
Is. 26:14 made th. memory to *p.*
27:13 which were ready to *p.*
Jer. 18:18 the law shall not *p.*
27:10 drive you out, ye *p.* 15
40:15 remnant in Judah sho. *p.*
Ezek. 25:7 I will cause thee to *p.*
Dan. 2:18 that D. should not *p.*
Jon. 1:6 that we *p.* not, 3:9
14 not *p.* for this man's life
Mat. 5:29 one of thy mem. *p.* 30
8:25 L. save us, we *p. Luke* 8:24
9:17 wine runneth out, bot. *p.*
18:14 one of little ones sho. *p.*
Mark 4:38 carest th. not we *p. ?*
Luke 13:33 prophet *p.* out of J.
15:17 bread eno. I *p.* wf. hunger
21:18 not a hair of your head *p.*
John 3:15 whoso belie. not, *p.* 16
11:50 that whole nation *p.* not
Acts 8:20 thy money *p.* with th.
13:41 despisers, wonder and *p.*
2 *Cor.* 2:15 savor of C. in them *p.*
4:16 tho' outward man *p.* inwa.
Col. 2:22 which all are to *p.*
2 *Thes.* 2:10 unrig. in th. that *p.*
2 *Pet.* 3:9 not willing any sho. *p.*

Shall PERISH.

Lev. 26:38 ye *s. p.* among heath.
Deut. 4:26 ye *s.* soon utterly *p.*
8:19, 20 ; 30:18 ; *Jos.* 23:16
1 *Sam.* 27:1 I *s.* one day *p.* by S.
2 *K.* 9:8 whole house of A. *s. p.*
Job 8:13 hypocrite's hope *s. p.*
18:17 remem. *s. p.* 20:7 ; 36:12
34:15 all flesh *shall p.* together
Ps. 1:6 way of ungodly *shall p.*
37:20 wick. *s. p.* 92:9 enemies *p.*
73:27 that are far from thee *s. p.*
102:96 they *s. p.* thou endure
112:10 desire of wicked *shall p.*
Prov. 10:28 ex. of wick. *s. p.* 11:7
19:9 he that speaketh lies *s. p.*
21:28 a false witness *shall p.*
Is. 29:14 wisd. of wise men *s. p.*
41:11 that strive with thee *s. p.*
60:12 king. not serve thee *s. p.*
Jer. 4:9 heart of the king *s. p.*
6:21 neighbor and friend *s. p.*
10:11 the gods *s. p.* 15 ; 51:18
48:8 valley also *s. p.* and plain
Ezek. 7:26 law *s. p.* from priest
Amos 1:8 remnant of Phil. *s. p.*
2:14 therefore the flight *s. p.*
3:15 houses of ivory *shall p.*
Zec. 9:5 king *s. p.* from Gaza.
Mat. 26:52 *shall p.* with sword
Luke 5:37 wine spil. bottles *s. p.*
13:3 ye *shall* all likewise *p.* 5
John 10:28 the sheep *s.* never *p.* 5
Rom. 2:12 sinned with. law. *s. p.*
1 *Cor.* 8:11 *shall* weak brother *p.*
Heb. 1:11 they *s. p.* thou remai.
2 *Pet.* 2:12 *shall p.* in their cor.

PERISHED.

Num. 16:33 they *p.* fr. congreg.
Jos. 22:20 that man *p.* not alone
2 *Sam.* 1:27 weapons of war *p. !*
Job 4:7 who ev. *p.* being innoc.
30:2 in whom old age was *p.*

Ps. 9:6 memorial is *p.* with them
10:16 heathen are *p.* out of land
119:92 I sho. have *p.* in afflict.
Ec. 9:6 envy is *p. Jer.* 7:28 truth
Jer. 48:36 riches he hath got. *p.*
49:7 in counsel *p.* from prudent
Lam. 3:18 strength and hope *p.*
Joel 1:11 the harvest of field is *p.*
Jon. 4:10 which came up and *p.*
Mic. 4:9 why cry? is couns. *p. ?*
7:2 good man is *p.* out of earth
Mat. 8:32 h. of swine ran and *p.*
Lu. 11:51 *p.* bet. altar and temp.
Acts 5:37 he also *p.* and as many
1 *Cor.* 15:18 fallen asleep in C. *p.*
Heb. 11:31 harlot Rahab *p.* not
2 *Pet.* 3:6 overflo. with water *p.*
Jude 11 *p.* in gainsaying of C.

PERISHETH.

Job 4:11 lion *p.* for lack of prey
Prov. 11:7 hope of unjust men *p.*
Ec. 7:15 th. is a just man that *p.*
Is. 57:1 righteous *p.* and no man
Jer. 9:12 land *p.* and is burnt up
John 6:27 labor not for meat *p.*
Jam. 1:11 grace of fashion of it *p.*
1 *Pet.* 1:7 more prec. than gold *p.*

PERISHING.

Job 33:18 his life fr. *p.* by sword

PERIZZITE.   *Gen.* 13:7;   *Ex.*
33:2; 34:11;   *Jos.* 9:1; 11:3

PERIZZITES.   *Gen.* 15:20;   *Ex.*
3:8, 17;   23:23;   *Jud.* 1:4, 5;
3:5; 2 *Chr.* 8:7; *Ezr.* 9:1

PERJURED.

1 *Tim.* 1:10 for liars *p.* persons

PERMISSION.

1 *Cor.* 7:6 I speak this by *p.*

PERMIT.

1 *Cor.* 16:7 tarry awhile, if L. *p.*
Heb. 6:3 this will we do, if G. *p.*

PERMITTED.

Acts 26:1 thou art *p.* to speak
1 *Cor.* 14:34 not *p.* wo. to speak

PERNICIOUS.

2 *Pet.* 2:2 shall fol. their *p.* ways

PERPETUAL.

Gen. 9:12 cov. for *p.* generations
Ex. 29:9 priest's office be for *p.*
31:16 keep sab. for *p.* covenant
Lev. 3:17 a *p.* stat. not to eat fat
24:9 be Aaron's by a *p.* statute
25:34 it is their *p.* possession
Num. 19:21 a *p.* statute
Ps. 9:6 destruc. come to *p.* end
74:3 lift up feet to *p.* desolation
78:66 put them to a *p.* reproach
Jer. 5:22 by a decree, it cannot
8:5 slid. back by *p.* backsliding?
15:18 why is my pain *p.* and my
18:16 land desolate, *p.* hissing
23:40 bring upon you *p.* shame
25:9 make them *p.* desolat. 12
49:13 cities thereof be *p.* wastes
50:5 join Lord in a *p.* covenant
51:39 may sleep a *p.* sleep, 57
Ezek. 35:5 hast had a *p.* hatred
9 *p.* desolations, *Zep.* 2:9
46:14 *p.* ordinance to the Lord
Hab. 3:6 and the *p.* hills did bow

PERPETUALLY.

1 *K.* 9:3 be there *p.* 2 *Chr.* 7:16
Amos 1:11 his anger did tear *p.*

PERPLEXED.

Est. 3:15 city Shushan was *p.*
Joel 1:18 herds of cattle are *p.*
Luke 9:7 H. was *p.* 24:4 they were
2 *Cor.* 4:8 *p.* but not in despair

PERPLEXITY.

Is. 22:5 it is a day of *p.* by Lord
Mic. 7:4 now shall be their *p.*
Luke 21:25 distress of nation, *p.*

PERSECUTE.

Job 19:22 why do ye *p.* me as G.

28 *p.* him, seeing root in me?
Ps. 7:1 save me fr. them that *p.*
5 let the enemy *p.* my soul
10:2 wicked in his pride doth *p.*
31:15 del. me from them that *p.*
35:3 stop way ag. them that *p.*
6 let angel of Lord *p.* them
69:26 they *p.* him thou hast sm.
71:11 *p.* and take him
83:15 so *p.* them with thy tem.
119:84 judgm. on them that *p.*
86 they *p.* me wrongfully, help
Jer. 17:18 confounded that *p.* me

Jer. 29:18 I will *p.* them wi. sw.
Lam. 3:66 *p.* and destroy them
Mat. 5:11 bles. when men *p.* you
44 pray for them which *p.* you
10:23 when they *p.* you in one
23:34 *p.* them from city to city
Luke 11:49 they shall *p.* 21:12
John 5:16 the Jews *p.* Jesus
15:20 they will also *p.* you
Rom. 12:14 bless them which *p.*

PERSECUTED.

Deut. 30:7 curses on them th. *p.*
Ps. 109:16 because he *p.* the poor
119:161 princes *p.* me wi. cause
143:3 enemy hath *p.* my soul
Is. 14:6 rul. nations in anger *p.*
Lam. 3:43 with anger, and *p.* us
Mat. 5:10 blessed which are *p.*
12 so *p.* they prophets bef. you
John 15:20 if they have *p.* me
Acts 7:52 have not your fath. *p.*
22:4 I *p.* this way unto death
26:11 I *p.* them to strange cities
1 *Cor.* 4:12 being *p.* we suffer it
15:9 I *p.* church of G. *Gal.* 1:13
2 *Cor.* 4:9 we are *p.* not forsaken
Gal. 1:23 *p.* us in times past
4:29 born after flesh *p.* him
1 *Thes.* 2:15 killed L. and *p.* us
Rev. 12:13 dragon *p.* woman that

PERSECUTEST, ING.

Acts 9:4 Saul, Saul, why *p.* thou
me? 22:7; 26:14
5 I am Jesus, whom thou *p.*
22:8; 26:15
Phil. 3:6 concern. zeal, *p.* church

PERSECUTION.

Lam. 5:5 under *p.* have no rest
Mat. 13:21 wh. *p.* ari. *Mark* 4:17
Acts 8:1 great *p.* against church
11:19 were scatter. abroad on *p.*
13:50 and raised *p.* against Pa.
Rom. 8:35 sh. *p.* sep. us fr. C. ?
Gal. 5:11 why do I yet suffer *p. ?*
6:12 lest they should suffer *p.*
2 *Tim.* 3:12 godly shall suffer *p.*

PERSECUTIONS.

Mark 10:30 have lands with *p.*
2 *Cor.* 12:10 I take pleasure in *p.*
2 *Thes.* 1:4 faith in all your *p.*
2 *Tim.* 3:11 kn. my *p.* at Antioch

PERSECUTOR, S.

Neh. 9:11 their *p.* thou threwest
Ps. 7:13 ordaineth arrows ag. *p.*
119:157 many *p.* 142:6 del. from
Jer. 15:15 revenge me of my *p.*
20:11 theref. my *p.* sh. stumble
Lam. 1:3 all her *p.* overtook her
4:19 *p.* are swifter than eagles
1 *Tim.* 1:13 who was before a *p.*

PERSEVERANCE.

Eph. 6:18 watching with all *p.*

PERSIA.

2 *Chr.* 36:20 reign of king. of P.
Est. 1:3 to power of P. 14, 18
Ezek. 27:10 P. and Lud, 38:5
Dan. 8:20; 10:13, 20; 11:2
PERSIS.   *Rom.* 16:12

PERSON.

Lev. 19:15 nor honor *p.* of mighty

Num. 35:30 one witness sh. not
testify against any *p.*
Deut. 15:22 unc. and clean *p.* eat
27:25 reward to slay innocent *p.*
28:50 shall not regard *p.* of old
1 *Sam.* 16:18 David a comely *p.*
25:35 and have accepted thy *p.*
2 *Sam.* 4:11 have slain a righ. *p.*
14:14 nei. doth G. respect any *p.*
17:11 to battle in thine own *p.*
Job 22:29 shall save humble *p.*
Ps. 15:4 a vile *p.* is contemned
49:10 fool and brutish *p.* perish
101:4 I will not kn. a wicked *p.*
105:37 feeble *p.* am. their tribes
Prov. 28:17 to the blood of any *p.*
Is. 32:5 vile *p.* shall be no more
6 the vile *p.* will speak villany
Jer. 43:6 Johanan took ev. *p.* left
52:25 took seven near king's *p.*
Ezek. 16:5 to loathing of thy *p.*
33:6 if the sword take any *p.*
44:25 priests come at no dead *p.*
Dan. 11:21 sh. stand up a vi. *p.*
Mat. 22:16 regardest not *p.* of
men, *Mark* 12:14

1 *Cor.* 5:13 put away wicked *p.*
2 *Cor.* 2:10 forgave I it in *p.* of C.
Heb. 1:3 express image of his *p.*
12:16 or profane *p.* as Esau
2 *Pet.* 2:5 saved Noah, eighth *p.*

PERSONS.

Gen. 14:21 give me *p.* take goods
Lev. 27:2 *p.* shall be for the L.
Num. 19:18 sh. sprinkle it up. *p.*
Deut. 10:17 regardeth not *p.*
22 fat. went into Eg. wi. 70 *p.*
Jud. 9:2 sons of J. were 70 *p.*
5 slew threescore and ten *p.* 18
1 *Sam.* 9:22 wh. were about 30 *p.*
25:18 Dog slew eighty-five *p.*
22 occasion, death of all the *p.*
2 *K.* 10:6 king's sons being 70 *p.*
7 took king's sons, slew 70 *p.*
Ps. 26:4 ha. not sat with vain *p.*
Prov. 12:11 follow. vain *p.* 28:19
Jer. 52:29 carried from J. 832 *p.*
30 carried away of Jews 745 *p.*
Ezek. 17:17 to cut off many *p.*
27:13 traded the *p.* of men
Jon. 4:11 more than 120,000 *p.*
Zep. 3:4 her prophets treach. *p.*
Luke 15:7 ninety-nine just *p.*
Acts 17:17 disp. with devout *p.*
2 *Cor.* 1:11 by means of many *p.*
1 *Tim.* 1:10 law made for perj. *p.*
2 *Pet.* 3:11 what *p.* oug. ye to be
Jude 16 hav. men's *p.* in admir.

See RESPECT.

PERSUADE.

1 *K.* 22:20 who shall *p.* Ahab
21 I will *p.* him; 22 thou sh. *p.*
2 *Chr.* 32:11 doth not Hezek. *p.*
Is. 36:18 bew. lest Heze. *p.* you
Mat. 28:14 we will *p.* him, and
2 *Cor.* 5:11 terrors of L. *p.* men
Gal. 1:10 do I now *p.* men?

PERSUADED.

2 *Chr.* 18:2 Ahab *p.* Jehosaphat
Prov. 25:15 forbea. is a prince *p.*
Mat. 27:20 priests *p.* the multi.
Luke 16:31 will not be *p.* of one
20:6 be *p.* John was a prophet
Acts 13:43 *p.* them to continue
14:19 who *p.* the people
18:4 Paul *p.* Jews and Greeks
19:26 Paul hath *p.* much people
21:14 when he would not be *p.*
26:26 I am *p.* none of th. things
Rom. 4:21 *p.* that what he had
8:38 I am *p.* that nothing can
14:5 let every man be fully *p.*
14 I know and am *p.*
15:14 I myself also am *p.* of you
2 *Tim.* 1:5 I am *p.* that in thee

12 I am *p.* he is able to keep
Heb. 6:9 are *p.* bet. things of you
11:13 hav. seen afar off, were *p.*

PERSUADETH, EST.

2 *K.* 18:32 when Hezekiah *p.* you
Acts 18:13 P. *p.* men to worship
26:28 almost thou *p.* me to be

PERSUADING.

Acts 19:8 *p.* things concerning
28:23 *p.* them concerning Jesus

PERSUASION.

Gal. 5:8 *p.* cometh not of him

PERTAIN.

Lev. 7:20 peace-offerings *p.* to L.
1 *Sam.* 25:22 all that *p.* to him
Rom. 15:17 things which *p.* to G.
1 *Cor.* 6:3 things *p.* to this life
1 *Pet.* 1:3 all things that *p.* to life

PERTAINED.

Num. 31:43 half that *p.* to thee
Jud. 6:11 under oak that *p.* to J.
1 *Sam.* 25:21 of all that *p.* to N.
2 *Sam.* 2:15 which *p.* to Ish-bos.
6:12 G. blessed all that *p.* to O.
9:9 given all that *p.* to Saul
16:4 thine are all that *p.* to M.
1 *K.* 7:48 S. made vessels that *p.*
2 *K.* 24:7 that *p.* to king of E.
1 *Chr.* 9:27 opening ev. morn. *p.*
2 *Chr.* 12:4 took the cities wh. *p.*
34:33 Josiah took away abo. *p.*

PERTAINETH.

Lev. 14:32 that wh. *p.* to cleans.
Num. 4:16 office of Eleaz. *p.* oil
Deut. 22:5 wo. not wear what *p.*
2 *Chr.* 26:18 it *p.* not to Uzziah
Rom. 9:4 to whom *p.* adoption
Heb. 7:13 he *p.* to another tribe

PERTAINING.

1 *Chr.* 26:32 rulers *p.* to God
Acts 1:3 things *p.* to kingd. of G.
1 *Cor.* 6:4 judgm. of thi. *p.* to life
Heb. 2:17 H.-priest in thi. *p.* to G.
5:1 ordained in things *p.* to G.
9:9 not perf. as *p.* to conscience

PERVERSE.

Num. 22:32 thy way is *p.* bef. me
Deut. 32:5 they are a *p.* generat.
1 *Sam.* 20:30 son of *p.* woman
Job 6:30 cannot disc. *p.* things?
9:20 my mouth sh. prove me *p.*
Prov. 4:24 *p.* lips put from thee
Prov. 8:8 noth. fro. or *p.* in them
12:8 he of a *p.* heart sh. be desp.
14:2 he that is *p.* despiseth him
17:20 hath a *p.* tongue falleth
19:1 he that is *p.* in his lips
23:33 heart shall utter *p.* things
28:6 he that is *p.* in his ways
18 he that is *p.* in ways sh. fall
Is. 19:14 L. mingled a *p.* spirit
Mat. 17:17 O *p.* genera. *Luke* 9:41
Acts 20:30 men arise speaking *p.*
Phil. 2:15 blameless in *p.* nation
1 *Tim.* 6:5 *p.* disputings of men

PERVERSELY.

2 *Sam.* 19:19 what servant did *p.*
1 *K.* 8:47 have sin. and done *p.*
Ps. 119:78 they dealt *p.* with me

PERVERSENESS.

Num. 23:21 neither seen *p.* in Is.
Prov. 11:3 *p.* of trans. shall des.
15:4 *p.* therein as a breach in
Is. 30:12 ye trust in *p.* and stay
59:3 your tongues muttered *p.*
Ezek. 9:9 and the ci. is full of *p.*

PERVERT.

Deut. 16:19 a gift doth *p.* words
24:17 thou shalt not *p.* judgm.
Job 8:3 doth God *p.* judgment or
34:12 nor will the Al. *p.* judgm.
Prov. 17:23 to *p.* ways of judgm.
31:5 and *p.* the judgment of any
Mic. 3:9 hear this, ye that *p.* eq.

Acts 13:10 not cease to *p.* right
Gal. 1:7 would *p.* the gos. of C.

PERVERTED.

1 *Sam.* 8:3 Sa.'s sons *p.* judgm.
Job 33:27 have *p.* what was right
Is. 47:10 thy wisdom, it hath *p.*
Jer. 3:21 they have *p.* their way
23:36 ye have *p.* the words of G.

PERVERTETH.

Ex. 23:8 gift *p.* the righteous
Deut. 27:19 cursed be he that *p.*
Prov. 10:9 he that *p.* his ways
19:3 foolishness of a man *p.* way
Luke 23:14 man that *p.* people

PERVERTING.

Ec. 5:8 violent *p.* of judgment
Luke 23:2 this fellow *p.* nation

PESTILENCE.

Ex. 5:3 lest he fall on us wi. *p.*
9:15 I may smite thee with *p.*
Lev. 26:25 I will send *p.* among
Num. 14:12 will sm. th. with *p.*
Deut. 28:21 L. shall make *p.* cle.
2 *Sam.* 24:13 3 days' *p.* 1 *Chr.*21:12
15 the Lord sent a *p.* on Israel,
1 *Chr.* 21:14
1 *K.* 8:37 if there be famine, *p.*
2 *Chr.* 6:28 ; 7:13 ; 20:9
Ps. 78:50 gave th. life over to *p.*
91:3 deli. thee from noisome *p.*
6 nor *p.* that walketh in dark.
Jer. 14:12 I will consume them
by *p.* 24:10 ; 27:8
21:6 inhabitants shall die by *p.*
9 abideth in city die by *p.* 38:2
27:13 why will ye die by *p.* ?
28:8 prophets of old prop. of *p.*
29:17 I will send upon th. *p.* 18
32:24 city is given bec. of *p.* 36
34:17 liberty for you to the *p.*
42:17 go to E. shall die by *p.* 22
44:13 as I punished Jeru. by *p.*
Ezek. 5:12 a third *p.* die with *p.*
17 *p.* and blood pass thro' thee
6:11 by sword, famine, and *p.*
7:15 sword without, *p.* within
12:16 I will leave a few from *p.*
14:19 if I send *p.* into land, 21
28:23 will send her *p.* and blood
33:27 be in caves shall die of *p.*
38:22 I will plead ag. him wi. *p.*
Amos 4:10 I have sent am. you *p.*
Hab. 3:5 before him went *p.* and

PESTILENCES.

Mat. 24:7 shall be *p.* *Luke* 21:11

PESTILENT.

Acts 24:5 found this man a *p.* fel.

PESTLE.

Prov. 27:22 bray a fool with a *p.*

PETER.

Mat. 14:29 when P. was come
16:18 I say to thee thou art P.
23 said to P. get th. *Mark* 8:33
17:1 taketh P. James and John,
26:27 ; *Mark* 5:37 ; 9:2 ; 14:33 ;
Luke 8:51 ; 9:28
24 they rec. tribute, came to P.
26:58 P. follow. to H. P. palace
75 P. re. *Mark* 14:72 : *Lu.* 22:61
Mark 16:7 disci. and P. *John* 1:44
John 18:26 ear P. cut off, 21:17
Acts 1:15 in those days P. stood
Acts 3:3 see. P. and John, 4:8, 13
5:15 shadow of P. 8:14 ; 9:40
10:13 P. kill and eat, 44 ; 11:7
12:3 to take P. also, 6, 7, 13, 18
Gal. 1:18 went to see P. 2:7, 8, 14

Simon PETER.

Mat. 4:18 Jesus saw S. called P.
10:2 the first S. who is called P.
Mark 3:16 S. he surnamed P.
Luke 5:8 S. P. fell at Jes. knees
6:14 Simon whom he named P.
John 13:6 cometh to S. P. 20:2
21:15 Jesus saith to Simon P.

Acts 10:5 call for one S. whose
surname is P. 32 ; 11:13

PETITION, S.

1 *Sam.* 1:17 G. gr. thee thy *p.* 27
1 *K.* 2:16 ask one *p.* deny me not
20 I desire one small *p.* of thee
Est. 5:6 what is *p.* ? 7:2 ; 9:12
8 if it please king to grant *p.*
7:3 let my life be given at my *p.*
Ps. 20:5 Lord fulfil all thy *p.*
Dan. 6:7 whoso. ask *p.* of any, 12
13 maketh *p.* three times a day
1 *John* 5:15 we have *p.* we desired

PHALEC.

Luke 3:35 Ragau was son of P.

PHARAOH.

Gen. 12:17 the Lord plagued P.
40:2 P. wroth against. 13, 14
41:1 P. dream. 4, 7, 16, 34, 55
Ex. 5:2 P. said, who is the L. ?
14:4 will be honored upon P. **17**
1 *K.* 3:1 made affinity with P.
7:8 Solo. made a house for P.
2 *K.* 17:7 br. th. out fr. under P.
18:21 P. to that trust, *Is.* 36:6
23:35 accor. to command. of P.
Neh. 9:10 wond. on P. *Ps.* 135:9
Ps. 136:15 overthrew P. in R. sea
Is. 19:11 say ye to P. 30:2, 3
Jer. 25:19 made P. drink, 37:11
46:17 P. a noise ; 47:1 smote G.
Ezek. 29:2 face ag. P. 3 ; 30:22
30:21 brok. arm of P. 25 ; 31:18
Acts 7:13 kindred known to P. 21
Rom. 9:17 scripture saith to P.
Heb. 11:24 to be called son of P.

PHARAOH-HOPHRA. *Jer.*
44:30

PHARAOH-NECHO.

2 *K.* 23:29 P. N. went up, 33-35
Jer. 46:2 word came ag. P.-N.

PHAREZ.

Gen. 38:29 name was called P.
46:12 sons of Ju. P. 1 *Chr.* 2:4 ;
Mat. 1:3 ; *Luke* 3:33 ; the
sons of P. *Num.* 26:20, 21 ;
Ruth 4:18 ; 1 *Chr.* 2:5 ; 9:4
Ruth 4:12 be like the house of P.

PHARISEE.

Mat. 23:26 thou blind P. cleanse
Luke 11:37 P. beso. him to dine
18:10 went to pray, one a P.
Acts 23:6 I am a P. son of a P.
26:5 after strict. sect I lived a P.
Phil. 3:5 touching the law a P.

PHARISEES.

Mat. 5:20 exceed righteou. of P.
9:14 why do P. fast ? *Mark* 2:18
34 P. said, He cast. out devils
15:12 thou P. were offended
16:6 beware of leaven of the P.
11 ; *Mark* 8:15 ; *Luke* 12:1
19:3 P. also came to him
23:2 scribes and P. sit in M. seat
13 woe to scr. and P. 14, 15, 23,
25, 27, 29 ; *Luke* 11:42, 43, 44
Luke 5:30 P. murmured, 15:2
6:7 scribes and P. watched him
7:30 P. rejected counsel of God
11:39 P. make cl. outside of cup
16:14 P. who were covet. heard
John 1:24 were sent were of P.
3:1 a man of the P. named Nic.
7:32 P. sent officers to take him
48 any P. believed on him ?
11:47 then P. gathered a council
57 P. had given a commandn.
Acts 15:5 rose certain sect of P.
23:7 dissension bet. P. and Sad.
8 no resur. P. but confess both

PHARPAR.

2 *K.* 5:12 Abana and P. better

PHEBE.

Rom. 16:1 I com. unto you P.

PHENICE.

Acts 11:19 travelled as far as P.
15:3 Paul and Barnabas passed
through P.
21:2 find. ship sailing over to P.
27:12 they might attain to P.

PHILADELPHIA.

Rev. 1:11 write and send it to P.
3:7 angel of the church in P.

PHILIP.

Mat. 10:3 P. and Barthol. *Mark*
3:18 ; *Luke* 6:14 ; *Acts* 1:13
14:3 for his brother P. wife,
Mark 6:17 ; *Luke* 3:19
Luke 3:1 his brother P. tetrarch
John 1:43 Jesus findeth P. 44, 45
12:21 the same came to P. 22
14:9 hast thou not kn. me, P. ?
Acts 6:5 P. the deacon, 8:29
8:5 P. preached, 6, 12, 13, 30, 39
21:8 we enter. into house of P.

PHILIPPI.

Acts 16:12 Neapo. we came to P.
20:6 we sailed away from P.
1 *Thes.* 2:2 shamef. entreat at P.

PHILISTIA.

Ps. 60:8 P. triumph thou
87:4 Behold P. and Tyre, this
108:9 over P. will I triumph

PHILISTIM.

Gen. 10:14 came P. 1 *Chr.* 1:12

PHILISTINE.

1 *Sam.* 17:8 not I a P. 32, 43, 49
21:9 sw. of Goliath the P. 22:10
2 *Sam.* 21:17 Abishai smo. the P

PHILISTINES.

Gen. 21:34 Abraham in P. land
26:14 Isaac had flocks, P. env.
15 P. stopped wells Abrah. 18
Ex. 13:17 led th. not through P.
Ps. 83:7 the P. with the
Is. 2:6 soothsayers like the P.
9:12 before, and the P. behind
11:14 fly on shoulders of the P.
Zep. 2:5 land of P. I will destroy
Zec. 9:6 will cut off pride of P.

PHILOLOGUS.

Rom. 16:15 salute P. Julia, and

PHILOSOPHY.

Col. 2:8 lest any spoil you th. p.

PHILOSOPHERS.

Acts 17:18 cer. p. encounte. him

PHINEHAS.

Ex. 6:25 Eleazer's wife bare P.
Num. 25:11 P. hath turned wra.
Jos. 22:13 Israel sent P. 24:33
Jud. 20:28 P. stood before the
1 *Sam.* 1:3 Hophni and P. the
2:34 Hophni and P. sh. both die
4:17 Hophni and P. are dead, 19
14:3 the son of P. the Lord's
Ezr. 7:5 Abishua son of P. the
8:2 of the sons of P. Gersho. 33
Ps. 106:30 then stood up P.

PHLEGON.

Rom. 16:14 salute Asyncritus, P.

PHRYGIA.

Acts 16:6 had gone througho. P.
18:23 went over all count. of P.

PHURAH.

Jud. 7:11 he went down with P.

PHYLACTERIES.

Mat. 23:5 th. make broad th. p.

PHYSICIAN.

Jer. 8:22 is there no p. there?
Mat. 9:12 th. that be wh. need
not a p. *Mark* 2:17 ; *Luke* 5:31
Luke 4:23 proverb, p. heal thys.
Col. 4:14 Luke, the beloved p.

PHYSICIANS.

Gen. 50:2 Joseph com. p. to embalm father ; p. embalm. Is.

---

2 *Chr.* 16:12 Asa sou. not L. b. p.
Job 13:4 ye are all p. of no value
Mark 5:26 suffer many things of
p. *Luke* 8:43

PICK.

Prov. 30:17 ravens shall p. it out

PICTURES.

Num. 33:52 shall destroy all p.
Prov. 25:11 apples of gold in p.
Is. 2:16 day of L. on pleasant p.

PIECE.

Gen. 15:10 one p. ag. another
Num. 10:2 trumpets of whole p.
1 *Sam.* 2:36 crouch to him for p.
2 *Sam.* 6:19 to every one a good
p. of flesh, 1 *Chr.* 16:3
23:11 p. of grou. full of lentiles
2 *K.* 3:19 mar good p. of land, 25
Neh. 3:11 Has. repaired other p.
Job 41:24 hard as p. of millstone
42:11 ev. man gave p. of money
Prov. 6:26 brou. to a p. of bread
28:21 for p. bread man transgre.
Cant. 4:3 tem. p. of pomeg. 6:7
Jer. 37:21 give him daily p. bre.
Ezek. 24:4 every good p. the thi.
6 bring it out p. by p. let no
Amos 3:12 mouth of lion p. of e.
4:7 one p. was rained on, and p.
Mat. 9:16 no man putt. p. of new
cloth, *Mark* 2:21 ; *Luke* 5:36
17:27 thou sh. find p. of money
Luke 14:18 I bought p. of groun.
15:8 lose one p. doth li. a cand.
24:42 ga. him p. of broiled fish

PIECES.

Gen. 15:17 lamp passed betw. p.
20:16 given bro. 1,000 p. of silv.
33:19 bou. for 100 p. *Jos.* 24:32
37:28 sold Jos. for 20 p. of silver
33 Joseph is rent in p. 44:28
45:22 gave to Benjamin thirty p.
Ex. 22:13 if it be torn in p.
Lev. 2:6 part meat-offering in p.
9:13 presented burnt-of. with p.
Jud. 9:4 gave A. 70 p. of silver
16:5 give thee 1,100 p. of silver
19:29 div. concubine into 12 p.
1 *Sam.* 11:7 8. hewed oxen in p.
15:33 Samuel hewed Agag in p.
1 *K.* 11:30 Ahij. rent garm. in p.
19:11 wind brake in p. the rocks
2 *K.* 2:12 Eli. rent clothes in p.
5:5 Nam. took 6,000 p. of gold
6:25 ass's head sold for eigh. p.
18:4 brake in p. brazen serpent
2 *Chr.* 23:17 brake the images in
p. 31:1 ; 34:4 ; *Mic.* 1:7
Job 16:12 hath shaken me in p.
40:18 his bones are as p. of brass
Ps. 7:2 rending in p. none deliv.
50:22 lest I tear you in p.
68:30 till ev. one submit with p.
74:14 breakest heads of L. in p.
Cant. 8:11 for fruit bring 1,000 p.
Is. 3:15 beat my people to p. ?
Jer. 5:6 goeth out be torn in p. ?
23:29 hammer break. rock in p.
Lam. 3:11 he hath pull. me in p.
Ezek. 4:14 not eat. th. torn in p.
13:19 pollute me for p. of bread?
24:4 gather p. thereof into pot
Dan. 2:34 brake image in p. 45
6:24 lions brake th. bones in p.
7:7 iron teeth, and bra. in p. 19
Hos. 3:2 bought her for fifteen p.
Mic. 3:3 chop my people in p.
4:13 sh. beat in p. many people
5:8 as a lion teareth in p.
Nah. 2:12 lion did tear in p.
Zec. 11:12 th. weighed thirty p.
13 I took the 30 p. *Mat.* 27:6, 9
Luke 15:8 woman having ten p.
Acts 19:19 found price 50,000 p.
23:10 lest P. sho. be pulled in p.

27:44 and some on p. of the ship

See BREAK, BROKEN, CUT, DASH,
DASHED.

PIERCE.

Num. 24:8 p. them with arrows
2 *K.* 18:21 hand, p. it, *Is.* 36:6
Luke 2:35 sword sh. p. thro' soul

PIERCED.

Job 30:17 my bones are p.
Ps. 22:16 p. my hands and feet
Zec. 12:10 they sh. look on me
wh. they have p. *John* 19:37
John 19:34 one of soldiers p. side
1 *Tim.* 6:10 p. th. with sorrows
Rev. 1:7 they also which p. him

PIERCETH, ING.

Job 40:24 Behemoth's nose p.
Is. 27:1 L. shall punish p. serp.
Heb. 4:12 word of G. quick p.

PIERCINGS.

Prov. 12:18 speaketh like p. of a

PIETY.

1 *Tim.* 5:4 learn to show p.
PIGEON. *See* YOUNG.

PILATE.

Mat. 27:2 they delivered him to
Pontius P. 24 ; *Mark* 15:1
Mark 15:5 so that P. marvel. 44
Luke 3:1 Pon. P. being governor
23:12 same day P. and Her. 52
John 18:33 P. entered judg. hall
19:8 when P. heard, 12, 19, 38
Acts 13:13 pres. of P. 4:27 ; 13:28
1 *Tim.* 6:13 before P. witnessed

PILE.

Is. 30:33 p. of it fire and wood
Ezek. 24:9 make p. for fire great

PILGRIMAGE.

Gen. 47:9 days of my p. 130 yea.
not attain. to years of th. p.
Ex. 6:4 gi. them land of their p.
Ps. 119:54 my songs in the house
of my p.

PILGRIMS.

Heb. 11:13 we. strangers and p.
1 *Pet.* 2:11 as p. abs. from lusts

PILLAR.

Gen. 19:26 became a p. of salt
28:18 J. set it for p. 22 ; 35:14
31:13 where thou anointedst p.
51 behold this p. 52 p. witn.
35:20 Jacob set p. on R.'s grave
Ex. 33:9 cloudy p. descended 10
Jud. 9:6 A. king by plain of p.
20:40 flame arose with p.
2 *Sam.* 18:18 Absa. reared up a p.
1 *K.* 7:21 set up right p. left p.
2 *K.* 11:14 the king stood by a p.
23:3 ; 2 *Chr.* 23:13
Neh. 9:12 led. them by cloudy p.
Ps. 99:7 spake to th. in cloud. p.
Is. 19:19 and a p. at the border
Jer. 1:18 have made thee iron p.
52:21 p. was eighteen cubits
1 *Tim.* 3:15 p. and grou. of truth
Rev. 3:12 overcom. I make a p.

See CLOUD, FIRE.

PILLARS.

Ex. 24:4 M. built alt. and 12 p.
26:32 hang veil upon four p.
27:10 p. thereof brass hooks of
p. 11 ; 38:10, 11, 12, 17
16 p. four ; 38:17 sockets for p.
Jud. 16:25 Samson between p.
1 *Sam.* 2:8 p. of earth are Lord's
1 *K.* 7:15 he cast two p. of brass
10:12 made of almug-trees p.
2 *K.* 18:16 Hez. cut gold from p.
25:13 Chaldees brake in pieces
p. 16 ; *Jer.* 52:17, 20
Est. 1:6 fast. to rings and p
Job 9:6 the p. tremble, 26:11

Ps. 75:3 I bear up the *p.* of it
Prov. 9:1 hath hewn her sev. *p.*
Cant. 3:6 com. like *p.* of smo.
10 make *p.* thereof of silver
5:15 *p.* of marble set on gold
Joel 2:30 will show *p.* of smoke
Gal. 2:9 J. and Cephas to be *p.*
Rev. 10:1 feet were as *p.* of fire

PILLED.

Gen. 30:37 J. *p.* whi. strakes, 38

PILLOW, S.

Gen. 28:11 Jac. put stones for *p.*
18 Jacob took the stone, his *p.*
1 *Sam.* 19:13 *p.* of goats'hair, 16
Ezek. 13:18 woe to women sew *p.*
20 behold, I am again. your *p.*
Mark 4:38 J. was asleep on a *p.*

PILOTS.

Ezek. 27:8 wise men were thy *p.*
28 shake at the sound of thy *p.*

PIN.

Jud. 16:14 Delil. fast. with a *p.*
Ezek. 15:3 take *p.* of vine-tree?

PINE, ETH, ING.

Lev. 26:39 shall *p.* away, in iniq.
of their fathers shall they *p.*
Is. 38:12 cut me off with *p.* sick.
Lam. 4:9 these *p.* away, stricken
Ezek. 24:23 *p.* away for iniqu.
33:10 sins on us, we *p.* away
Mark 9:18 gnash. teeth, *p.* away

PINE.

Neh. 8:15 olive and *p.* branches

PINE-TREE.

Is. 41:19 plant *p.-t.* and box
60:13 *p.-t.* and box-trees sh. co.

PINNACLE.

Mat. 4:5 *p.* of temple, *Luke* 4:9

PINS.

Ex. 27:19 make *p.* of tabernacle,
35:18 : 38:20, 31 ; 39:40
Num. 3:37 under Merari, *p.* 4:32

PIPE, S.

1 *Sam.* 10:5 com. of proph. wi. *p.*
1 *K.* 1:40 the people piped wi. *p.*
Is. 5:12 the *p.* are in their feasts
30:29 when one goeth with a *p.*
Jer. 48:36 heart sh. sound like *p.*
Ezek. 28:13 workmanship of *p.*
Zec. 4:2 seven *p.* to seven lamps
12 which through the gold. *p.*
1 *Cor.* 14:7 whether *p.* or harp

PIPED.

1 *K.* 1:40 people *p.* with pipes
Mat. 11:17 *p.* unto you, *Luke* 7:32
1 *Cor.* 14:7 how kno. wh. is *p.* ?

PIPERS.

Rev. 18:22 voice of *p.* he. no mo.

PISGAH.

Num. 23:14 Balaam to top of P.
Deut. 3:27 up into top of P. 34:1
4:49 under the springs of P.

PISIDIA.

Acts 13:14 came to Antioch in P.
14:24 had passed throughout P.

PISS.

2 *K.* 18:27 drink own *p. Is.* 36:12
PISSETH. *See* WALL.

PIT, S.

Gen. 14:10 Siddim full of slime *p.*
37:20 cast him into some *p.* 24
Ex. 21:34 owner of *p.* ma. good
Lev. 11:36 a *p.* wherein is water
Num. 16:30 go down into *p.* 33
1 *Sam.* 13:6 Israelites hide in *p.*
2 *Sam.* 17:9 is now hid in so. *p.*
18:17 cast Absalom in great *p.*
23:20 sl. lion in *p.* 1 *Chr.* 11:22
2 *K.* 10:14 Jehu slew them at *p.*
Job 17:16 go down to bars of *p.*

33:18 keep. back soul from *p.* 30
24 deliver him from the *p.* 28
Ps. 9:15 heathen sunk into *p.*
28:1 I like them that go into *p.*
30:3 I should not go down to *p.*
9 what profit in my blood,
when I go down to the *p.* ?
35:7 hid for me their net in *p.* ?
40:2 br. me out of horrible *p.*
55:23 br. them to *p* of destruct.
69:15 let not *p.* shut her mouth
88:4 counted wi. th. go to *p.*
6 thou laid me in the lowest *p.*
119:85 proud digged *p.* for me
140:10 let th. be cast in. deep *p.*
143:7 go down to *p. Prov.* 1:12
Prov. 22:14 mouth of wo. deep *p.*
23:27 strange wo. is narrow *p.*
28:10 fall himself into own *p.*
17 he shall flee to the *p.*
Is. 14:15 brought to sides of *p.*
19 that go down to stones of *p.*
24:17 *p.* and snare are on thee
18 he that cometh out of midst
of the *p. Jer.* 48:43, 44
22 prisoners are gathered in *p.*
30:14 water withal out of the *p.*
38:17 deli. from *p.* of corruption
18 go down to *p.* cannot hope
51:14 he should not die in the *p.*
Jer. 2:6 L. led us thro' a la. of *p.*
14:3 came to *p.* found no water
41:7 cast them into midst of *p.*
9 *p.* which Asa made for fear
Lam. 4:20 anoi. of L. taken in *p.*
Ezek. 19:4 he was taken in *p.* 8
26:20 descend into *p.* 28:8 ;
31:14, 16 ; 32:18, 24, 25, 29, 30
32:23 graves set in the side of *p.*
Zep. 2:9 of nettles and salt *p.*
Zec. 9:11 sent prisoners out of *p.*
Mat. 12:11 if it fall into a *p.* on
the sabbath, *Luke* 14:5

See BOTTOMLESS, DIG, DIGGED.

PITCH, Substantive.

Gen. 6:14 pitch it within with *p.*
Ex. 2:3 she daubed it with *p.*
Is. 34:9 streams be turned to *p.*
and the land bec. burning *p.*

PITCH, Verb.

Num. 1:52 Is. sh. by his camp
53 L. shall *p.* round tabernacle
2:2 ev. man shall *p.* by standard
Deut. 1:33 search out place to *p.*
Jos. 4:20 Joshua did *p.* 12 stones
Is. 13:20 neither sh. Arabian *p.*
Jer. 6:3 shepherds shall *p.* tents

PITCHED.

Gen. 12:8 Abram *p.* his tent, and
13:12 Lot *p.* his tent toward S.
26:17 I. *p.* in valley of Gerar, 25
31:25 Jacob *p.* tent in mount,
Laban *p.* in Gilead
33:18 Jacob *p.* his tent before
Ex. 17:1 Israel *p.* in Rephidim
19:2 and had *p.* in wilderness
33:7 M. took tabernacle and *p.*
Num. 1:51 when tabernacle is *p.*
2:34 they *p.* by their standards
12:16 the peo. *p.* in wilderness
21:10 and Israel *p.* in Oboth
11 and *p.* in Ije-abarim, in the
33:5 and Israel *p.* in Succoth
6 *p.* in Etham, which is in the
Jos. 8:11 ambush *p.* on north
2 *Sam.* 17:26 Is. and Absalom *p.*
2 *K.* 25:1 Neb. *p.* ag. it, *Jer.* 52:4
1 *Chr.* 15:1 David prepared place
for ark, *p.* tent, 16:1 ; 2 *Chr.*
1:4
Heb. 8:2 tabernacle which L. *p.*

PITCHER, S.

Gen. 24:14 let down *p.* I pray th.
15 Rebekah came with *p.* 45
Jud. 7:16 empty *p.* lamps in *p.*
19 brake *p.* that were in, 20

Ec. 12:6 or the *p.* be broken at
Lam. 4:2 esteemed as earthen *p.*
Mark 14:13 bear. a *p. Luke* 22:10
PITHOM. *Ex.* 1:11

PITY, Substantive.

Deut. 7:16 eye shall have no *p.*
2 *Sam.* 12:6 because he had no *p.*
Job 6:14 to the afflicted *p.* should
19:21 have *p.* on me, *p.* on me, O
Ps. 69:20 looked for some to *p.*
Prov. 19:17 that hath *p.* on poor
Is. 13:18 they shall have no *p.* on
63:9 in his *p.* he redeemed
Jer. 15:5 shall have *p.* on thee
21:7 shall not spare, nor have *p.*
Ezek. 5:11 nor will I have *p.* 7:4,
9 ; 8:18 ; 9:10
9:5 eye spare, neither have *p.*
36:21 but I had *p.* for my holy
Amos 1:11 Ed. did cast off all *p.*
Jon. 4:10 thou hast had *p.*
Mat. 18:33 as I had *p.* on thee

PITY, Verb.

Deut. 13:8 nor shall thine eye *p.*
him, 19:13, 21
25:12 thine eye shall not *p.*
Prov. 28:8 him that will *p.* poor
Jer. 13:14 I will not *p.* nor spare
Joel 2:18 then the Lord will *p.*
Zec. 11:5 th. sheph. *p.* them not
6 I will no more *p.* inhabitants

PITIED, ETH.

Ps. 103:13 as a father *p.* his chil.
so L. *p.* them th. fear him
106:46 he made them to be *p.*
Lam. 2:2 ha. not *p.* 17, 21 ; 3:43
Ezek. 16:5 none eye *p.* thee
24:21 profane what your soul *p.*

PITIFUL.

Lam. 4:10 hands of *p.* women
Jam. 5:11 that the L. is very *p.*
1 *Pet.* 3:8 love as brethren, be *p.*

PLACE, Substantive.

Gen. 13:14 L. said, Look from *p.*
18:24 destroy, and not spare *p.*
20:13 kindness show at every *p.*
22:4 third day Abraham saw *p.*
30:25 I may go to my own *p.*
Ex. 3:5 p. where thou standest
is holy, *Jos.* 5:15
18:23 go to their *p.* in peace
23:20 to bring thee into the *p.*
Lev. 1:16 shall cast it by the *p.*
Num. 10:14 in first *p.* went out
Deut. 11:24 ev. *p.* whereon your
feet tread, *Jos.* 1:3
12:5 *p.* L. sh. choose, 14 ; 16:16
21 if *p.* be too far from, 14:24
Jud. 11:19 pass land to my *p.*
20:36 men of Israel gave *p.* to
Ruth 3:4 mark *p.* where he lieth
1 *Sam.* 20:25 Da.'s *p.* empty, 27
2 *Sam.* 2:23 died in the same *p.*
15:21 what *p.* my lord the king
17:9 hid in some pit, or other *p.*
18:18 it is called Absalom's *p.*
1 *K.* 8:29 eyes be open toward *p.*
2 *K.* 5:11 strike hand over the *p.*
6:1 *p.* wh. we dwell is too strait
1 *Chr.* 21:25 Dav. gave for the *p.*
2 *Chr.* 30:16 pri. stood in *p.* 35:10
35:15 sons of Asaph, in their *p.*
Neh. 2:3 *p.* of my father's sepul.
14 there was no *p.* for beast
13:11 I set singers in their *p.*
Est. 2:9 Est. and maids best *p.*
4:14 deliverance fr. anoth. *p.*
Job 6:17 consumed out of the. *p.*
9:6 shake the earth out of *p.*
16:18 let my cry have no *p.*
28:12 where is *p.* of underst. 20
23 he knoweth the *p.* thereof
36:20 peo. are cut off in their *p.*
38:19 where is *p.* thereof?
40:12 tread wicked in their *p.*

Ps. 26:8 *p.* where thine honor
12 my foot standeth in even *p.*
32:7 art my hiding *p.* 119:114
33:14 the *p.* of his habitation
103:16 *p.* thereof shall know it
Ec. 3:16 the *p.* of judgment, the
p. of righteousness
20 all go to one *p.* all are, 6:6
Is. 5:8 lay field, till th. be no *p.*
13:13 earth remove out of *p.*
14:2 and bring them to their *p.*
28:8 so that there is no *p.* clean
49:20 the *p.* is too strait for me
54:2 enlarge the *p.* of thy tent
60:13 will make *p.* of my feet
66:1 where is the *p.* of my rest ?
Jer. 7:12 go to my *p.* in Shil. 32
17:12 glorious throne is the *p.*
18:14 waters come from anot. *p.*
19:11 till there be no *p.* to bury
Ezek. 6:13 th. slain be on the *p.*
43:7 *p.* of my throne shall Israel
Dan. 2:35 no *p.* was found for
8:11 the *p.* of his sanctuary was
Hos. 5:15 I will return to my *p.*
Amos 8:3 dead bodies in ev. *p.*
Nah. 3:17 their *p.* is not known
Zec. 10:10 *p.* shall not be found
12:6 inhabit. ag. in her *p.* 14:10
Mal. 1:11 inc. be offered in ev. *p.*
Mat. 28:6 see the *p.* where the
Lord lay, *Mark* 16:6
Mark 6:10 in what *p.* soever ye
Luke 4:17 found the *p.* where it
10:1 sent two and two un. ev. *p.*
32 when he was at the *p.* pass.
14:9 and say, Give this man *p.*
John 4:20 Jerusalem is *p.* where
8:37 my word hath no *p.* in you
11:6 abode two days in same *p.*
48 Rom. shall take away our *p.*
18:2 Judas wh. betrayed, kn. *p.*
Acts 1:25 with one acco. in one *p.*
4:31 prayed, the *p.* was shaken
7:33 *p.* whereon thou standest
49 or what is the *p.* of my rest
8:32 the *p.* of scripture wh. he
Rom. 12:19 rather gi. *p.* to wrath
15:23 hav. no more *p.* in these
1 *Cor.* 1:2 in every *p.* call on J.
11:20 come together into one *p.*
14:23 church come into one *p.*
2 *Cor.* 2:14 knowledge in ev. *p.*
Gal. 2:5 to whom gave *p.* by sub.
Eph. 4:27 neither give *p.* to the
1 *Thes.* 1:8 in every *p.* your faith
Heb. 5:6 he saith also in ano. *p.*
8:7 no *p.* sho. have been sought
12:17 he found no *p.* of repent.
Jam. 3:11 at same *p.* sweet wat.
Rev. 12:8 nor was there *p.* found
20:11 for them was found no *p.*

PLACE, Verb.
Ex. 18:21 *p.* such to be rulers
Deut. 14:23 *p.* his name there,
16:2, 6, 11 ; 26:2
Ezr. 6:5 *p.* them in house of G.
Is. 46:13 I will *p.* salvation in Z.
Ezek. 37:14 *p.* you in yo. land, 26
Dan. 11:31 they sh. *p.* abomina.
Hos. 11:11 *p.* them in houses
Zec. 10:6 will bring them to *p.*

A PLACE.
Ex. 21:13 will appoint thee *a p.*
33:21 behold, th. is *a p.* by me
Num. 32:1 the place was *a p.* for
Deut. 23:12 thou shalt have *a p.*
Jos. 20:4 give him *a p.* in city
Jud. 18:10 *a p.* where is no want
1 *Sam.* 15:12 Saul set him up *a p.*
27:5 let them give me *a p.*
2 *Sam.* 7:10 I will appoint *a p.*
1 *K.* 8:21 I set there *a p.* for ark
2 *K.* 6:2 let us make *a p.* where
8 in such and such *a p.* sh. be
9 bew. thou pass not such *a p.*
1 *Chr.* 15:1 David prepared *a p.*

2 *Chr.* 6:2 I have built *a p.*
Job 28:1 there is *a p.* for gold
Ps. 132:5 until I find out *a p.*
Prov. 14:26 his childr. have *a p.*
Is. 4:6 shall be for *a p.* of refuge
33:21 the Lord will be to us *a p.*
34:14 find for herself *a p.* of rest
56:5 and within my walls *a p.*
65:10 Achor *a p.* for the herds
Ezek. 26:5 *a p.* for spread. nets, 14
Zep. 2:15 become *a p.* for beasts
Mat. 27:33 that is, *a p.* of a skull
John 14:2 I go to prepare *a p.* 3
19:17 into *a p.* called Golgotha
Heb. 2:6 one in *a* certain *p.* testi.
4:4 he spake in *a* certain *p.*
11:8 called to go out into *a p.*
Rev. 12:6 *a p.* prepared of God
16:16 *a p.* called Armageddon

See CHOOSE, DWELLING.

High PLACE.
Num. 23:3 Bal. went up to *a h. p.*
1 *Sam.* 9:12 sacri. to-day in *h. p.*
10:5 prophets coming from *h. p.*
1 *K.* 3:4 great *h. p.* 1 *Chr.* 16:39
11:7 Solomon built a *high p.*
2 *K.* 23:15 *high p.* that Jeroboam
made, Josi. brake down the
h. p. and burnt the *h. p.*
2 *Chr.* 1:3 Solomon went to *h. p.*
13 from his journey to *high p.*
Is. 16:12 Moab is weary on *h. p.*
Ezek. 16:24 *h. p.* in street, 25, 31
20:29 what is *h. p.* wher. ye go ?

His PLACE.
Gen. 18:33 Ab. returned to *h. p.*
31:55 Laban returned to *his p.*
Ex. 10:23 neither rose from *h. p.*
16:29 abide every man in *his p.*
none go out of *his p.*
Num. 2:17 in *his p.* by th. stan.
Deut. 21:19 br. him to gate of *h. p.*
Ruth 4:10 not cut off from *his p.*
1 *Sam.* 3:2 Eli was laid in *his p.*
9 Sam. went and lay in *his p.*
5:3 set Dagon in *his p.* again
23:22 *his p.* where his haunt is
2 *Sam.* 6:17 set ark of L. in *h. p.*
1 *K.* 8:6 the priests brought ark
to *his p.* 2 *Chr.* 5:7
1 *Chr.* 15:3 br. ark of L. to *his p.*
16:27 and gladness are in *his p.*
2 *Chr.* 24:11 carried chest to *h. p.*
34:31 king stood in *his p.*
Ezr. 1:4 let men of *his p.* help
2:68 for the house of God set it
in *his p.* 5:15 ; 6:7
Job 2:11 ev. one from *his* own *p.*
7:10 nei. shall *his p.* know him
8:18 if he destroy him fr. *his p.*
14:18 rock is remo. out of *his p.*
18:4 sh. rock be re. out of *h. p.?*
20:9 nor *h. p.* any more behold
27:21 hurleth him out of *his p.*
23 shall hiss him out of *his p.*
37:1 heart is remo. out of *his p.*
38:12 day-spring to know *h. p.*
Ps. 37:10 diligen. consider *his p.*
Prov. 27:8 wandereth from *his p.*
Ec. 1:5 sun hasteneth to *his p.*
Is. 36:21 Lord com. out of *his p.*
46:7 they set him in *his p.* from
h. p. shall he not remove
Jer. 4:7 he is gone from *his p.*
6:3 feed every one from *his p.*
Ezek. 3:12 glory of L. from *h. p.*
Mic. 1:3 L. cometh out of *his p.*
Zep. 2:11 wors. ev. one fr. *his p.*
Zec. 6:12 shall grow out of *h. p.*
Mat. 26:52 put thy sw. into *h. p.*
Acts 1:25 might go to *his* own *p.*

See HOLY, *Most* HOLY.

In the PLACE.
Gen 50:19 I am *in the p.* of God
Ex. 15:17 plant them *in the p.*
Jos. 4:9 J. set 12 stones *in the p.*

1 *K.* 21:19 *in the p.* where dogs
2 *Chr.* 3:1 *in t. p.* D. had prepar.
Prov. 25:6 stand not *in t. p.*
Ec. 11:3 *in the p.* where tree
Jer. 22:12 die *in t. p.* 38:9 ; 42:22
Ezek. 17:16 *in the p.* where king
Hos. 13:13 not stay long *in the p.*
John 19:41 *in the p.* wh. crucified

Of the PLACE.
Gen. 26:7 men *of the p.* ask. him,
lest men *of the p.* kill me
29:22 La. gathered men *of the p.*
32:30 name *of the p.* Peniel
2 *Sam.* 6:8 name *of t. p.* Perez-uz.
1 *Chr.* 28:11 *of t. p.* of mer.-seat
Ezek. 41:11 brea. *of the p.* 5 cub.
Joel 3:7 raise them out *of t. p.*
Nah. 1:8 make utter end *of t. p.*

That PLACE.
Deut. 12:3 dest. names out *th. p.*
17:10 sentence they of *that p.*
Mat. 14:35 men of *that p.* had kn.
Mark 6:10 ye depart from *th. p.*
John 5:13 a multit. being in *t. p.*
11:30 in *t. p.* Martha met him
Acts 21:12 we and they of *th. p.*

This PLACE.
Gen. 19:12 bri. them out of *th. p.*
13 destroy *t. p.* 14 get out *t. p.*
20:11 fear of G. is not in *this p.*
28:16 L. is in *t. p.* 17 dreadful
38:21 no harlot in *this p.* 22
Ex. 13:3 L. brought you fr. *t. p.*
Num. 20:5 bri. us unto *t. p.*
Deut. 1:31 God bare thee till ye
came to *this p.* 9:7 ; 11:5
Jud. 18:3 wh. mak. thou in *t. p.?*
1 *K.* 8:29 heark. to. *this p.* 30:35 ;
2 *Chr.* 6:20, 21, 26, 40 ; 7:15
2 *K.* 18:25 without L. ag. *this p.*
2 *Chr.* 7:12 chosen *t. p.* to myself
Job 18:21 *t. p.* of him knows not
Jer. 7:6 shed not in. blo. in *t. p.*
20 fury shall be poured on *t. p.*
14:13 give you peace in *this p.*
16:2 nei. sons nor daug. in *t. p.*
9 cause to cease out of *this p.*
19:3 bring evil upon *this p.*
12 thus will I do to *t. p.* 40:2
27:22 restore th. to *this p.* 32:37
28:3 bring to *t. p.* all vessels, 6
29:10 caus. you to return to *t. p.*
33:10 be heard in *this p.* joy
42:18 shall see *this p.* no more
44:29 I will punish you in *th. p.*
51:62 L. thou hast spo. ag. *t. p.*
Zep. 1:4 cut off remn. from *t. p.*
Hag. 2:9 in *t. p.* will I give peace
Mat. 12:6 in *this p.* one greater
Luke 16:28 lest come into *this p.*
Acts 6:14 J. shall destroy *th. p.*

Acts 7:7 shall serve me in *th. p.*
21:28 teacheth ag. law in *th. p.*
Heb. 4:5 and in *this p.* again

Thy PLACE.
Gen. 40:13 Pharaoh restore *t. p.*
Num. 24:11 flee thou to *thy p.*
2 *Sam.* 15:19 return to *thy p.*
Ec. 10:4 ag. thee, leave not *t. p.*
Ezek. 12:3 remo. from *t. p.* 38:15

To, *or* unto the PLACE.
Ex. 3:8 bring you *u. p.* of Cana.
32:34 lead people *unto the p.*
Num. 10:29 journeying *to the p.*
1 *Sam.* 20:19 *to the p.* wh. th. hide
2 *Sam.* 2:23 many came *to t. p.*
1 *Chr.* 15:12 bring ark *to the p.*
Neh. 1:9 I will bring th. *to the p.*
Ps. 104:8 *to the p.* thou founded
Is. 18:7 present brought *to t. p.*
Jer. 7:14 *to the p.* wh. I gave you
29:14 will bring you ag. *to t. p.*
Acts 25:23 ent. *into p.* of hearing

PLACED.
1 *K.* 12:32 Jeroboam *p.* priests

2 *K.* 17:6 and *p.* them in Halah
24 *p.* them in Samaria, 26
2 *Chr.* 1:14 wh. he *p.* in chariot
17:2 he *p.* forces in fenced cities
Job 20:4 si. man was *p.* on earth
Ps. 78:60 tent which he had *p.*
Is. 5:8 they may be *p.* alone
Jer. 5:22 wh. *p.* sand for bound
Ezek. 17:5 eagle *p.* it by waters

PLACES.

Gen. 28:15 keep thee in all *p.*
Ex. 20:24 *p.* wh. I rec. my name
Jas. 5:8 in *p.* till th. were whole
Jud. 5:11 deliv. from noise in *p.*
1 *Sam.* 7:16 judged Isr. in th. *p.*
30:31 Da. sent presents to all *p.*
2 *K.* 23:5 put down priests in *p.*
14 filled their *p.* with bones
Neh. 4:12 from *p.* whe. ye return
13 I set the people in lower *p.*
and on higher *p.*
Job 21:28 dwelling *p.* of wicked
37:8 beasts remain in their *p.*
Ps. 10:8 he sitteth in lurking *p.*
16:6 lines are fallen in pleas. *p.*
18:45 afraid out of their close *p.*
73:18 set them in slippery *p.*
74:20 dark *p.* of earth are full
103:22 bless the Lord in all *p.*
105:41 they ran in the dry *p.*
110:6 shall fill the *p.* with dead
Prov. 8:2 she standeth in *p.*
Cant. 2:14 art in the secret *p.*
Is. 32:18 dw. in quiet resting *p.*
40:4 and rough *p.* plain
45:2 make crooked *p.* straight
Jer. 4:12 wind fr. those *p.* sh. co.
6:3 all *p.* whither driven, 29:14
17:26 come from *p.* about Jeru.
24:9 a taunt and curse in all *p.*
32:44 witnesses in *p.* about Jer.
40:12 Jews return. out of all *p.*
45:5 thy life for a prey in all *p.*
Lam. 2:6 he hath destroy. his *p.*
Ezek. 34:12 deliver th. out of *p.*
26 will make *p.* round my hill
47:11 miry *p.* sh. not be healed
Amos 4:6 want of bread in yo. *p.*
Zec. 3:7 give thee *p.* to walk
Mat. 12:43 thro' dry *p. Lu.* 11:24
13:5 some fell on stony *p.* 20
Acts 24:3 we accept it in all *p.*
Eph. 1:3 blessed us in heaven. *p.*
20 at right hand in heavenly *p.*
2:6 sit together in heavenly *p.*
3:10 to powers in heavenly *p.*
Phil. 1:13 bonds manif. in all *p.*
Rev. 6:14 island moved out th. *p.*
See DESOLATE, HOLY.

High PLACES.

Lev. 26:30 I will dest. your *h. p.*
Num. 21:28 consu. lords of *h. p.*
33:52 pluck down all their *h. p.*
Deut. 32:13 ma. him ride on *h. p.*
33:29 shalt tread on their *h. p.*
Jud. 5:18 jeop. lives in *high p.*
1 *Sam.* 13:6 people hide in *h. p.*
2 *Sam.* 1:19 Israel slain in *h. p.*
25 thou wast slain in thy *h. p.*
22:34 and setteth me on my
high p. Ps. 18:33
1 *K.* 3:2 people sacrified in *h. p.*
2 *K.* 17:32; 2 *Chr.* 33:17
3 burnt inc. in *h. p.* 22:43; 2 *K.*
12:3; 15:4, 35; 16:4; 17:11
12:31 Jerob. made house of *h. p.*
32 Beth-el priests of *high p.*
13:2 shall offer priests of *h. p.*
32 cried against houses of *h. p.*
33 Jeroboam made of the peo.
priests of *h. p.* 2 *K.* 17:32
1 *K.* 15:14 *h. p.* were not remov.
22:43; 2 *K.* 12:3; 14:4; 15:4, 35
2 *K.* 17:29 gods in houses of *h. p.*
18:4 Hezekiah removed *h. p.* 22
23:8 defiled *h. p.* brake *p.* 13;
2 *Chr.* 31:1; 32:12; *Is.* 36:7

20 slew all the priests of *h. p.*
2 *Chr.* 11:15 ord. priests for *h. p.*
14:3 Asa took away *high p.* 5
15:17 *h. p.* not ta. away, 20:33
17:6 Jehosha. took away *h. p.*
21:11 J. made *h. p.* 28:25 Ahaz
34:3 purge Jerusalem from *h. p.*
Job 25:2 he maketh peace in *h. p.*
Ps. 78:58 provok. him with *h. p.*
Prov. 8:2 stand. on top of *h. p.*
9:14 sitteth on a seat in the *h. p.*
Is. 15:2 he is gone up to *h. p.*
41:18 I will open rivers in *h. p.*
49:9 pastures shall be in *h. p.*
58:14 cause thee to ride on *h. p.*
Jer. 3:2 lift up thine eyes to *h. p.*
21 a voice heard on *high p.*
4:11 dry wind in *h. p.* of wilder.
7:29 take up a lamenta. in *h. p.*
12:12 spoilers come on all *h. p.*
14:6 wild asses did stand in *h. p.*
17:3 I will give thy *h. p.* for sin
26:18 mountain shall become as
h. p. of the forest, *Mic.* 3:12
48:35 him that offereth in *h. p.*
Ezek. 6:3 I will destroy your *h. p.*
16:16 deckedst *h. p.* divers colo.
39 shall break down thy *h. p.*
36:2 ancient *high p.* are ours
Hos. 10:8 *h. p.* of Aven destroyed
Amos 4:13 and treadeth upon the
h. p. of the earth, *Mic.* 1:3
7:9 *h. p.* of Isaac sh. be desolate
Mic. 1:5 what are *h. p.* of Judah?
Hab. 3:19 make me walk on *h. p.*
Eph. 6:12 spiritual wick. in *h. p.*
See BUILT.

Waste PLACES.

Is. 5:17 *waste p.* of fat ones
51:3 L. will comfort her *w. p.*
52:9 ye *waste p.* of Jerusalem
58:12 shall build the old *w. p.*

PLAGUE, Substantive.

Ex. 11:1 bri. one *p.* on Pharaoh
12:13 the *p.* shall not be on you
Lev. 13:3 hair in *p.* turned wh. 17
5 if *p.* spr. not in skin, 6; 14:48
30 if man or wo. hath *p.* iest
see *p.* 31, 32, 50, 51, 55; 4:37
44 lepr. man, *p.* is in his head
50 shut up it that hath the *p.*
58 if *p.* be departed from them
14:35 there is as it were a *p.* in
Num. 8:19 be no *p.* among Israel
11:33 L. smote people with a *p.*
16:46 wrath is out, *p.* begun, 47
48 the *p.* was stayed, 50; 25:8
Deut. 28:61 every *p.* not written
Jos. 22:17 although there was *p.*
1 *Sam.* 6:4 one *p.* was on you all
2 *Sam.* 24:21 that the *p.* may be
stayed, 1 *Chr.* 21:22
1 *K.* 8:38 kn. ev. man *p.* of heart
2 *Chr.* 21:14 wi. *p.* will L. smite
Ps. 91:10 nor any *p.* come nigh
106:29 the *p.* brake upon them
30 judgm. so the *p.* was stayed
Zec. 14:12 be *p.* L. will smite, 18
Mark 5:29 she was healed of *p.*
Rev. 16:21 blasphemed *p.* of hail

PLAGUE, Verb.

Ps. 89:23 *p.* them that hate him

PLAGUED.

Gen. 12:17 the Lord *p.* Pharaoh
Ex. 32:35 the Lord *p.* the people
Jos. 24:5 and *p.* Egypt
1 *Chr.* 21:17 that *th.* should be *p.*
Ps. 73:5 nor are *p.* like oth. men
14 all the day have I been *p.*

PLAGUES.

Gen. 12:17 L. plagued Ph. wi. *p.*
Ex. 9:14 I will send all my *p.*
Lev. 26:21 bring 7 times more *p.*
Deut. 28:59 L. will make thy *p.*
1 *Sam.* 4:8 gods smote Eg. wi. *p.*

Jer. 19:8 beca. of *p.* 49:17; 50:13
Hos. 13:14 I will be thy *p.*
Mark 3:10 as many as had *p.*
Luke 7:21 cured many of their *p.*
Rev. 9:20 rest not killed by th. *p.*
11:6 to smite earth with *p.*
16:9 G. hath power over th. *p.*
18:4 that ye recei. not of her *p.*
8 therefo. shall her *p.* come in
22:18 God sh. add to him the *p.*

See SEVEN.

PLAIN, Adjective.

Gen. 25:27 Jacob was a *p.* man
Ps. 27:11 lead me in a *p.* path
Prov. 8:9 th. are *p.* to him that
15:19 the way of righteous is *p.*
Is. 28:25 he made *p.* the face
40:4 and rough places made *p.*
Jer. 48:21 judgment come on *p.*
Hab. 2:2 make it *p.* upon tables
Mark 7:35 loosed, he spake *p.*

PLAIN, Substantive.

Gen. 11:2 *p.* in land of Shinar
13:10 Lot beheld all the *p.* 11
12 Lot dwelled in cities of *p.*
19:17 nor stay thou in all the *p.*
25 he overthr. cities in the *p.*
Jos. 11:16 Jos. took valley and *p.*
Jud. 9:6 made Ab. king by *p.*
1 *Sam.* 10:3 come to *p.* of Tabor
2 *Sam.* 2:29 Abner walked thr' *p.*
15:28 I will tarry in the *p.* until
18:23 Ahimaaz ran by the *p.*
1 *K.* 7:46 in *p.* of Jord. did king
20:23 fight ag. them in the *p.* 25
2 *K.* 25:4 went to *p.* Jer. 52:7
Neh. 3:22 after him priests of *p.*
Jer. 17:26 shall come from the *p.*
21:13 against thee, O rock of *p.*
48:8 *p.* shall be destroyed
Ezek. 3:22 go forth in the *p.* 23
8:4 the vision that I saw in *p.*

PLAINS.

Gen. 18:1 L. appeared in the *p.*
Num. 22:1 Is. pitched in *p.* 33:48
26:63 numbered Israel in the *p.*
31:12 spoil to camp in the *p.*
36:13 L. commanded in the *p.*
Deut. 34:1 Mo. went from the *p.*
2 *Sam.* 17:16 lodge not in the *p.*
2 *K.* 25:5 Chaldees overtook him
in the *p. Jer.* 39:5; 52:8
1 *Chr.* 27:28 over trees in low *p.*
2 *Chr.* 9:27 cedar in lower *p.*
26:10 Uzziah had cattle in *p.*

PLAINLY.

Ex. 21:5 if the servant *p.* say
Deut. 27:8 write this law very *p.*
1 *Sam.* 2:27 *p.* appear to house
10:16 told us *p.* that the asses
Ezr. 4:18 let. hath been *p.* read
Is. 32:4 stammerer sh. speak *p.*
John 10:24 if thou be C. tell us *p.*
11:14 Jesus said to them *p.*
16:25 I shall show you *p.*
29 now speakest thou *p.* and
Heb. 11:14 such things declare *p.*

PLAINNESS.

2 *Cor.* 3:12 we use gr. *p.* of speech

PLAITING.

1 *Pet.* 3:3 let it not be *p.* of hair

PLANES.

Is. 44:13 fitteth image with *p.*

PLANETS.

2 *K.* 23:5 burnt incen. to sun, *p.*

PLANKS.

1 *K.* 6:15 covered floor with *p.*
Ezek. 41:25 were thick *p.* on face
26 side of house, and thick *p.*

PLANT, Substantive.

Gen. 2:5 God made every *p.*
Job 14:9 bring forth like the *p.*
Is. 5:7 men of Jud. his pleas. *p.*
17:11 shalt make thy *p.* grow
53:2 shall grow as a tender *p.*

PLANT

Jer. 2:21 turned into degener. *p.*
Ezek. 34:29 raise for them a *p.*
Mat. 15:13 every *p.* my Father

PLANTS.

1 *Chr.* 4:23 that dwell among *p.*
Ps. 128:3 thy children like *p.*
144:12 our sons may be as *p.*
Cant. 4:13 thy *p.* as an orchard
Is. 16:8 have broken down *p.*
17:10 shalt thou plant pleas. *p.*
Jer. 48:32 thy *p.* are gone over
Ezek. 31:4 riv. run. about his *p.*

PLANT, Verb.

Ex. 15:17 *p.* them in mount of
Deut. 16:21 thou shalt not *p.*
28:30 thou shall *p.* a viney. 39
2 *Sam.* 7:10 I will *p.* 1 *Chr.* 17:9
2 *K.* 19:29 *p.* vineyards, *Is.* 37:30
Ps. 107:37 sow the fields, and *p.*
Is. 17:10 thou shalt *p.* pleas.
41:19 I will *p.* in wilderness
51:16 that I may *p.* heavens
65:21 they shall *p.* vineyards
22 they sh. not *p.* and another
Jer. 1:10 to build and to *p.*
18:9 a kingdom, to build to *p.*
24:6 *p.* and not pluck, 42:10
29:5 *p.* gardens, and eat fruit
31:5 shall *p.* vines on mount.
28 I watch them to bu. and *p.*
32:41 I will *p.* them in this land
35:7 nor shall you sow, nor *p.*
Ezek. 17:22 *p.* it on a high, 23
28:26 they shall *p.* vineyards
36:36 L. build and *p.* that
Dan. 11:45 he sh. *p.* tabernacles
Amos 9:14 they sh. *p.* vineyards
15 I will *p.* them upon th. land
Zep. 1:13 they sh. *p.* vineyards

PLANTATION.

Ezek. 17:7 water it by fur. of *p.*

PLANTED.

Gen. 2:8 God *p.* a garden eastw.
9:20 Noah *p.* vine; 21:33 A. *p.*
Num. 24:6 trees which L. hath *p.*
Jos. 24:13 olive-yards ye *p.* not
Ps. 1:3 like a tree *p.* Jer. 17:8
80:8 cast out heathen, and *p.*
92:13 those that be *p.* in house
94:9 *p.* ear shall he not hear?
104:16 cedars which he hath *p.*
Ec. 2:4 I *p.* vine. 5 I *p.* trees
3:2 pluck up that which is *p.*
Is. 5:2 *p.* it with the choicest
40:24 yea, they shall not be *p.*
Jer. 2:21 I had *p.* thee a noble
11:17 Lord of hosts that *p.* thee
12:2 thou hast *p.* them, they
45:4 what I have *p.* I will pluck
Ezek. 17:5 *p.* it in a fruitful, 8
10 being *p.* shall it prosper?
19:10 *p.* by the waters, she was
Hos. 9:13 Ephr. is *p.* in a place
Amos 5:11 ye have *p.* vineyards
Mat. 15:13 heavenly Fath. not *p.*
21:33 householder *p.* Mark 12:1;
Luke 20:9

Luke 17:6 and be thou *p.* in sea
28 they sold, they *p.* builded
Rom. 6:5 have been *p.* together
1 *Cor.* 3:6 have *p.* Apollos water.

PLANTEDST, ETH.

Deut. 6:11 trees which thou *p.*
Ps. 44:2 drive out heath. and *p.*
Prov. 31:16 fruit she *p.* vineyard
Is. 44:14 he *p.* ash, and the rain
1 *Cor.* 3:7 neither is he that *p.*
8 he that *p.* and he that wat.
9:7 who *p.* a viney. and eateth

PLANTERS.

Jer. 31:5 *p.* shall plant and eat

PLANTING, S.

Is. 60:21 branch of my *p.*
61:3 called the *p.* of the Lord
Mic. 1:6 make Samaria as *p.*

PLASTER.

Is. 38:21 lay it for a *p.* on boil

PLASTER, ED.

Lev. 14:42 and shall *p.* the house
48 plague, after house was *p.*
Deut. 27:2 *p.* them with *p.* 4
Dan. 5:5 wrote on *p.* of palace

PLAT.

2 *K.* 9:26 requite thee in this *p.*
cast him into the *p.* of

PLATE.

Ex. 28:36 sh. make a *p.* of pure
39:30 they made the *p.* of holy
Lev. 8:9 on his forefront put *p.*

PLATES.

Ex. 39:3 beat gold into thin *p.*
Num. 16:38 ma. of censers *p.* 39
1 *K.* 7:30 every base had *p.* of
Jer. 10:9 silver spread into *p.* is

PLATTED.

Mat. 27:29 *p.* crown of thorns,
Mark 15:17; *John* 19:2

PLATTER.

Mat. 23:25 cl. outs. *p. Luke* 11:39

PLAY.

Ex. 32:6 rose to *p.* 1 *Cor.* 10:7
Deut. 22:21 *p.* whore in fa. house
1 *Sam.* 16:16 that he shall *p.* wi.
17 now a man that can *p.* well
2 *Sam.* 2:14 y. men arise and *p.*
6:21 therefore will I *p.* bef. L.
10:12 and let us *p.* the men for
Job 40:20 where beasts of field *p.*
41:5 wilt thou *p.* with him
Ps. 33:3 *p.* skilfully with a loud
104:26 whom thou made to *p.*
Is. 11:8 sucking child shall *p.*
Ezek. 33:32 and can *p.* well on

PLAYED.

Jud. 19:2 concubine *p.* whore
1 *Sam.* 16:23 Da. *p.* 18:10; 19:9
26:21 I have *p.* fool, and have
2 *Sam.* 6:5 all Is. *p.* 1 *Chr.* 13:8
2 *K.* 3:15 when the minstrel *p.*
Ezek. 16:28 *p.* whore with Assy.
See HARLOT.

PLAYER, S.

1 *Sam.* 16:16 who is a cunning *p.*
Ps. 68:25 the *p.* on instruments
87:7 as well the singers as *p.* on

PLAYETH, ING.

1 *Sam.* 16:18 Jesse, cunning in *p.*
1 *Chr.* 15:29 Da. dancing and *p.*
Ps. 68:25 am. them damsels *p.*
Ezek. 33:44 as to woman that *p.*
Zec. 8:5 boys and girls *p.* in the

PLEA.

Deut. 17:8 hard betw. *p.* and *p.*

PLEAD.

Jud. 6:31 will ye *p.* for Baal?
Job 9:19 shall set me a time to *p.*
13:19 who is he that will *p.* wi.
16:21 O that one might *p.* for a
19:5 if he will *p.* against me my
23:6 will he *p.* against me pow.
Is. 1:17 judgment, *p.* for widow
3:13 Lord stand up to *p.* and
43:26 let us *p.* together, declare
66:16 by fire will the Lord *p.*
Jer. 2:9 will yet *p.* with you, 35
29 wheref. will ye *p.* with me?
12:1 righteous, when I *p.* with
25:31 Lord will *p.* with all flesh
Ezek. 17:20 I will *p.* with him
35 and will I *p.* with you
38:22 I will *p.* against him with
Hos. 2:2 *p.* with your mother,
Joel 3:2 and I will *p.* with them
Mic. 6:2 and the Lord will *p.*
See CAUSE.

PLEADED, ETH.

1 *Sam.* 25:39 blessed be L. th. *p.*
Job 16:21 as a man *p.* for neigh.

PLEADING.

Job 13:6 hearken to the *p.* of my

PLEASANT.

Gen. 2:9 ev. tree grow that is *p.*
3:6 *p.* to the eyes and a tree
49:15 Issachar saw that it was *p.*
2 *Sam.* 1:23 S. and Jon. were *p.*
26 *p.* hast thou been to me
1 *K.* 20:6 whatever is *p.* they
2 *K.* 2:19 situation of city is *p.*
Ps. 16:6 lines fallen in *p.* places
106:24 they despised *p.* land
133:1 how *p.* for breth. to dwell
135:3 sing praises, it is *p.* 147:1
Prov. 2:10 knowledge is *p.*
5:19 the loving hind and *p.* roe
9:17 bread eaten in secret is *p.*
15:26 words of the pure are *p.*
16:24 *p.* words as honey-comb
22:18 for it is *p.* if thou keep
24:4 chambers filled with all *p.*
Ec. 11:7 *p.* it is for the eyes to
Cant. 1:16 thou art fair, yea, *p.*
4:16 come and eat his *p.* fruits
7:6 how fair and *p.* art thou, O
13 at our gates are all *p.* fruits
Is. 5:7 men of Ju. his *p.* plant
13:22 dragons shall cry in th. *p.*
17:10 shalt thou plant *p.* plants
32:12 they lament for *p.* fields
54:12 thy borders of *p.* stones
64:11 and all our *p.* things are
Jer. 3:19 sh. I give th. a *p.* land?
12:10 made my *p.* portion a des.
23:10 *p.* places of wilderness
25:34 shall fall like a *p.* vessel
31:20 Ephr. is he a *p.* child?
Lam. 1:7 remembered all her *p.*
10 spread his hand on her *p.*
11 have given their *p.* things
2:4 slew all that were *p.* to eye
Ezek. 26:12 shall destroy thy *p.*
33:32 song of one that hath *p.*
Dan. 8:9 great toward *v.* land
10:3 I ate no *p.* bread
11:38 honor a god wi. *p.* things
Hos. 9:13 Ephr. is in a *p.* place
Amos 5:11 planted *p.* vineyards
Mic. 2:9 cast out from *p.* houses
Nah. 2:9 gl. out of *p.* furniture
Zec. 7:14 laid *p.* land desolate
Mal. 3:4 offering of J. be *p.* L.

PLEASANTNESS.

Prov. 3:17 her ways are w. of *p.*

PLEASE.

Ex. 21:8 if she *p.* not master
Num. 23:27 peradvent. it will *p.*
2 *Sam.* 7:29 let it *p.* 1 *Chr.* 17:27
Job 6:9 even *p.* G. to destroy me
20:10 shall seek to *p.* the poor
Ps. 69:31 this also shall *p.* Lord
Prov. 16:7 man's ways *p.* Lord
Cant. 2:7 love till he *p.* 3:5; 8:4
Is. 2:6 *p.* themselves in children
55:11 accomplish that wh. I *p.*
56:4 choose things that *p.* me
John 8:29 I do th. things that *p.*
Rom. 8:8 they in flesh cannot *p.*
15:1 bear and not *p.* ourselves
2 let every one *p.* his neighbor
Cor. 7:32 car. how he may *p.* L.
33 *p.* his wife; 34 she may *p.*
10:33 even as I *p.* all men
Gal. 1:10 do I seek to *p.* men?
1 *Thes.* 2:15 they *p.* not G.
4:1 ought to walk and to *p.* G.
2 *Tim.* 2:4 that ye may *p.* him
Tit. 2:9 to *p.* them well in all
Heb. 11:6 with. faith impos. *p.* G.

PLEASED.

Gen. 28:8 daugh. of Ca. *p.* not I.

45:16 it p. Pharaoh well
Num. 24:1 Balaam saw it p. L.
Jud. 13:23 if the Lord were p.
14:7 and she p. Samson well
1 *Sam.* 12:22 it p. L. to make you
18:26 it p. D. to be the king's
2 *Sam.* 3:36 what the king did p.
19:6 if we had died, it had p.
1 *K.* 8:10 Solomon's speech p. L.
2 *Chr.* 30:4 thing p. the king,
Neh. 2:6 ; *Est.* 1:21 ; 2:4
Est. 2:9 the maiden p. the king
5:14 the thing p. Haman, he
Ps. 40:13 be p. O Lord, to deliver
51:19 then shalt thou be p. with
115:3 G. hath done whatsoever
he p. 135:6; *Jon.* 1:14
Is. 53:10 it p. the Lord to bruise
Mic. 6:7 will the Lord be p. with
Mal. 1:8 will he be p. with thee?
Acts 6:5 saying p. the multitude
12:3 bec. Herod saw it p. Jews
Rom. 15:3 for even Christ p. not
26 for it hath p. them of, 27
1 *Cor.* 1:21 it p. G. by foolishness
7:12 she p. to dwell with him
12:18 God set members as it p.
15:38 G. giveth a body as it p.
Gal. 1:10 for if I yet p. men, I
15 it p. God to reveal his Son
Col. 1:19 p. Father that in him
Heb. 11:5 had testimony he p. G.

Well PLEASED.
Is. 42:21 Lord is *well* p. for his
Mat. 3:17 in whom I am *well* p.
12:18; 17:5; *Mark* 1:11; *Luke*
3:22; 2 *Pet.* 1:17
1 *Cor.* 10:5 God was not *well* p.
Heb. 13:16 such sacri. G. is *w.* p.

Men-PLEASERS.
Eph. 6:6 eye-s. as *m.-p. Col.* 3:22

PLEASETH.
Gen. 16:6 do to her as it p. thee
Jud. 14:3 get her for me, she p.
Est. 2:4 maiden which p. king
Ec. 7:26 whoso p. G. sh. escape
8:3 he doeth whatsoever p. him

PLEASING.
Est. 8:5 if I be p. in his eyes
Hos. 9:4 neither shall they be p.
Col. 1:10 worthy of L. to all p.
1 *Thes.* 2:4 so we speak, not as p.
1 *John* 3:22 do things that are p.

Well-PLEASING.
Phil. 4:18 acceptable, *well-*p. to
God
Col. 3:20 for this is *well-*p. to L.
Heb. 13:21 work. what is *well-*p.

PLEASURE.
Gen. 18:12 old, shall I have p.?
1 *Chr.* 29:17 I know thou hast p.
Ezr. 5:17 let king send his p.
Neh. 9:37 dom. over cattle at p.
Est. 1:8 drink to every man's p.
Job 21:21 what p. hath he in ho.?
25 and never eateth with p.
22:3 is it any p. to Almighty
Ps. 5:4 not a God that hath p.
35:27 which hath p. in prosper.
51:18 do good in good p. to Z.
102:14 servants take p. in her
103:21 bless L. ye that do his p.
105:22 bind his princes at his p.
111:2 sou. out of all that have p.
147:10 taketh not p. in the legs
11 the Lord taketh p. in them
149:4 the Lord taketh p. in his
Prov. 21:17 he that loveth p.
Ec. 2:1 enjoy p. 5:4 no p. in fools
12:1 say, I have no p. in them
Is. 21:4 night of my p. turned
44:28 Cyrus shall perform my p.
46:10 stand, I will do all my p.
48:14 will do his p. on Babylon
53:10 and p. of the Lord shall
58:3 in day of your fast find p.
13 doing thy p. not finding p.

Jer. 2:24 snuffeth wind at her p.
34:16 set at liberty at their p.
48:38 a vessel wherein is no p.
Ezek. 16:37 wh. thou hast tak. p.
18:23 have I any p. that
wicked should die, 32; 33:11
Hos. 8:8 Is. vessel wherein no p.
Hag. 1:8 and I will take p. in it
Mal. 1:10 I have no p. in you
Luke 12:32 Father's good p. to
Acts 24:27 to do the Jews a p.
25:9 Festus to do the Jews a p.
Rom. 1:32 but have p. in them
2 *Cor.* 12:10 therefore I take p. in
Eph. 1:5 according to good p. 9
Phil. 2:13 to will and do his p.
2 *Thes.* 1:11 fulfil good p. of his
2:12 had p. in unrighteousness
1 *Tim.* 5:6 that liv. in p. is dead
Heb. 10:6 in sac. thou ha. no p. 8
38 my soul shall have no p. in
12:10 chastened us after own p.
Jam. 5:5 ye have lived in p. on
2 *Pet.* 2:13 as th. that count it p.
Rev. 4:11 for thy p. they are and

PLEASURES.
Job 36:11 spend their years in p.
Ps. 16:11 at thy right hand p.
36:8 drink of the river of thy p.
Is. 47:8 thou that art given to p.
Luke 8:14 are choked with the p.
2 *Tim.* 3:4 lovers of p. more than
Tit. 3:3 serv. divers lusts and p.
Heb. 11:25 enjoy the p. of sin

PLEDGE.
Gen. 38:17 wilt thou give p.?
18 what p.? 20 sent to rec. p.
Ex. 22:26 take raiment to p.
Deut. 24:6 no man take mil1st. to
p. he taketh a man's life to p.
12 shalt not sleep with p. 13
17 not take widow's raim. to p.
1 *Sam.* 17:18 fare, take their p.
Job 22:6 tak. p. from thy broth.
24:3 take a widow's ox for a p.
9 and they take a p. of the poor
Prov. 20:16 take a p. of him for
a strange woman, 27:13
Ezek. 18:7 to debtor his p. 12, 16
33:15 if wicked restore the p. he
Amos 2:8 on clothes laid to p. by

PLEDGES.
2 *K.* 18:23 give p. to, *Is.* 36:8

PLEIADES.
Job 9:9 wh. maketh Orion and P.
38:31 bind the influences of P.?

PLENTEOUS.
Gen. 41:34 fifth part in p. year
Deut. 28:11 L. make thee p. 30:9
2 *Chr.* 1:15 Solo. made gold p.
Ps. 86:5 art p. in mercy, 15
103:8 Lord is merciful, and p. in
130:7 with him is p. redemption
Is. 30:23 bread shall be fat and p.
Hab. 1:16 fat, and their meat p.
Mat. 9:37 the harvest truly is p.

PLENTEOUSNESS.
Gen. 41:53 seven years p. ended
Prov. 21:5 of diligent tend to p.

PLENTIFUL.
Ps. 68:9 thou didst send p. rain
Is. 16:10 joy is taken out of p.
Jer. 2:7 and I brought you to p.
48:33 gladness is taken from p.

PLENTIFULLY.
Job 26:3 hast p. declared thing
Ps. 31:23 p. rewardeth the proud
Luke 12:16 ground bro. forth p.

PLENTY.
Gen. 27:28 God give thee p. of
41:29 seven years of great p.
31 p. shall not be kno. in land
Lev. 11:36 wherein there is p.
2 *Chr.* 31:10 to eat have left p.
Job 22:25 shalt have p. of silver

37:23 in power and p. of justice
Prov. 3:10 barns be filled with p.
28:19 he that tilleth shall ha. p.
Jer. 44:17 then had we p. of vict.
Joel 2:26 sh. eat in p. and praise

PLOTTETH.
Ps. 37:12 wicked p. against just

PLOUGH.
Luke 9:62 having put hand to p.

PLOUGH.
Deut. 22:10 shalt not p. with ox
1 *Sam.* 14:14 yoke oxen might p.
Job 4:8 they that p. iniquity
Prov. 20:4 sluggard will not p.
Is. 28:24 doth the ploughman p.
Hos. 10:11 Judah sh. p. Jacob
Amos 6:12 will one p. there with
1 *Cor.* 9:10 he plougheth sho. p.

PLOUGHED, ETH.
Jud. 14:18 if ye had not p.
Ps. 129:3 ploughers p. on back
Jer. 26:18 shall be p. *Mic.* 3:12
Hos. 10:13 have p. wickedness
1 *Cor.* 9:10 that p. sh. pl. in hope

PLOUGHING.
1 *K.* 19:19 Elisha, who was p.
Job 1:14 oxen were p. and the
Prov. 21:4 the p. of the wicked
Luke 17:7 having a servant p.

PLOUGHMAN, MEN.
Is. 28:24 doth p. plough all day
61:5 sons of alien sh. be your p.
Jer. 14:4 the p. were ashamed
Amos 9:13 the p. shall overtake

PLOUGHSHARES.
Is. 2:4 beat sw. into p. *Mic.* 4:3
Joel 3:10 beat your p. into swo.

PLUCK.
Lev. 1:16 shall p. away his crop
Num. 33:52 p. down their high
Deut. 23:25 thou mayest p. ears
2 *Chr.* 7:20 then will I p. them up
Job 24:9 they p. fatherless from
Ps. 25:15 shall p. my feet out
52:5 p. thee out of thy place
74:11 thy right hand, p. it out
80:12 they which pass by p.
Ec. 3:2 and a time to p. up
Jer. 12:14 p. the house of Judah
17 utterly p. up and destroy
18:7 a kingdom, p. it up
22:24 would I p. thee thence
24:6 plant, and not p. 42:10
31:28 watched over th. to p. up
45:4 wh. I planted I will p. up
Ezek. 17:9 people, p. up by roots
23:34 thou sh. p. off thine own
Mic. 3:2 p. off the skin from
5:14 I will p. up thy groves
Mat. 5:29 if right eye offend thee
p. it out, 18:9; *Mark* 9:47
12:1 beg. to p. corn, *Mark* 2:23
John 10:28 nor sh. any p. them
29 no man is able to p. them

PLUCKED.
Gen. 8:11 was an olive leaf p. off
Ex. 4:7 and he p. his hand out
Deut. 28:63 shall be p. from land
Ruth 4:7 a man p. off his shoe
2 *Sam.* 23:21 p. the spear out of
Egyptian's hand, 1 *Chr.* 11:23
Ezr. 9:3 p. off hair of my head
Neh. 13:25 and p. off their hair
Job 29:17 p. spoil out of his teeth
Is. 50:6 them that p. off hair
Jer. 6:29 wicked are not p. away
12:15 after I have p. them out
31:40 it shall not be p. up
Ezek. 19:12 she was p. up in fury
Dan. 7:4 I beh. till wings we. p.
8 three of the first horns p. up
11:4 his kingdom sh. be p. up
Amos 4:11 as a firebrand p. out
Zec. 3:2 not this p. out of fire?

Mark 5:4 chains *p*, asunder
Luke 6:1 disciples *p*. ears of corn
17:6 be thou *p*. up by the root
Gal. 4:15 *p*. out your own eyes
Jude 12 twice dead, *p*. up by ro.

PLUCKETH.

Prov. 14:1 the foolish *p*. it down

PLUMB-LINE.

Amos. 7:7 L. stood on wall made
by a *p.-l*. wi. *p.-l*. in hand, 8

PLUMMET.

2 *K.* 21:13 stretch over Jerus. *p*.
Is. 28:17 lay righteousness to *p*.
Zec. 4:10 shall see *p*. in hand

PLUNGE.

Job 9:31 sh. thou *p*. me in ditch

POETS.

Acts 17:28 certain of your own *p*.

POINT, S.

Gen. 25:32 I am at the *p*. to die
Ec. 5:16 in all *p*. as he came
Jer. 17:1 writ. with *p*. of diamo.
Mark 5:23 daught. at *p*. of death
John 4:47 was at the *p*. of death
Heb. 4:15 was in all *p*. tempted
Jam. 2:10 offend in one *p*. is gu.

POINT.

Num. 34:7 *p*. out for you mount

POINTED.

Job 41:30 spread. sharp *p*. things

POISON.

Deut. 32:24 with *p*. of serpents
33 their wine is *p*. of dragons
Job 6:4 *p*. drinketh up my spirit
20:16 he shall suck *p*. of asps
Ps. 58:4 their *p*. like *p*. of serp.
140:3 adders' *p*. under their lips
Rom. 3:13 *p*. of asps under lips
Jam. 3:8 tongue is evil, full of *p*.

POLE.

Num. 21:8 set on *p*, 9 M. put it

POLICY.

Dan. 8:25 *p*. cause craft to pros.

POLISHED.

Ps. 144:12 *p*. after sim. of palace
Is. 49:2 hath made me *p*. shaft
Dan. 10:6 his feet like to *p*. brass

POLISHING.

Lam. 4:7 their *p*. was of sapph.

POLL, S.

Num. 1:2 every male by their *p*.
18:20, 22 ; 1 *Chr.* 23:3, 24
3:47 five shek. a piece by th. *p*.

POLL, ED.

2 *Sam.* 14:26 *p*. head, ye. end *p*.
Ezek. 44:20 they sh. *p*. th. heads
Mic. 1:16 and *p*. thee for children

POLLUTE.

Num. 18:32 neither *p*. holy thin.
35:33 so shall ye not *p*. the land
Jer. 7:30 in the house to *p*. it
Ezek. 7:21 *p*. my secret place, 22
13:19 will ye *p*. am. my people
20:31 ye *p*. yourselves with your
idols, 23:30 ; 36:18
39 *p*. holy name no more, 39:7
44:7 in my sanctuary to *p*. it
Dan. 11:31 they sh. *p*. sanctuary

POLLUTED.

Ex. 20:25 lift tool. thou hast *p*.
2 *K.* 23:16 Josiah *p*. the altar
Ps. 106:38 land *p*. with blood
Is. 47:6 I have *p*. mine inherit.
48:11 how sho. my name be *p*.
Jer. 2:23 canst say, I am not *p*. ?
3:1 not land be greatly *p*. ? 2
34:16 ye turned and *p*. my name
Lam. 2:2 he hath *p*. the kingdom
4:14 *p*. themselves with blood
Ezek. 4:14 soul hath not been *p*.
14:11 nor be *p*. with transgres.
16:6 I saw thee *p*. in own bl. 22
20:9 it should not be *p*. 14, 22

---

13 sabbaths greatly *p*. 16, 21, 24
26 I *p*. them in their own gifts
30 are ye *p*. after your fath. ?
23:17 was *p*. with Babylonians
Hos. 6:8 Gilead a city that is *p*.
9:4 all that eat thereof sh. be *p*.
Amos 7:17 thou sh. die in *p*. land
Mic. 2:10 not rest, because it is *p*.
Zep. 3:1 woe to her that is *p*.
4 her priests have *p*. sanctuary
Mal. 1:7 offered *p*. bread on altar
12 say, The ta. of the L. is *p*.
Acts 21:28 hath *p*. this holy place

POLLUTING.

Is. 56:2 keepeth sab. fr. *p*. it. 6

POLLUTION, S.

Ezek. 22:10 that was apart for *p*.
Acts 15:20 that they abs. from *p*.
2 *Pet.* 2:20 after having escap. *p*.

POLLUX.   *Acts* 28:11

POMEGRANATE.

Ex. 28:34 gold. bell and *p*. 39:26
1 *Sam.* 14:2 S. tarried under a *p*.
Cant. 4:3 temp. like piece *p*. 6:7
8:2 cause th. to drink juice of *p*.
Joel 1:12 the *p*. trees are wither.
Hag. 2:19 *p*. hath not bro. forth

POMEGRANATES.

Ex. 28:33 make *p*. 39:24, 25
Num. 13:23 they brought of *p*.
20:5 no pla. of seed, vines, or *p*.
Deut. 8:8 into land of *p*. oil-olive
1 *K.* 7:18 chapiters with *p*. 2 *K.*
25:17 ; 2 *Chr.* 3:16 ; *Jer.* 52:22
Cant. 4:13 orch. of *p*. with fruits
6:11 see wheth. *p*. budded, 7:12

POMMELS.

2 *Chr.* 4:12 *p*. of the chapiters

POMP.

Is. 5:14 *p*. shall descend to hell
14:11 *p*. is brought to the grave
Ezek. 7:24 make *p*. of strong ce.
30:18 *p*. of strength cease, 33:28
32:12 shall spoil the *p*. of Egypt
Acts 25:23 A. and B. come wi. *p*.

PONDER, ED, ETH.

Prov. 4:26 *p*. the path of thy feet
5:6 lest thou *p*. the path of life
21 the Lord *p*. all his goings
21:2 L. *p*. heart ; 24:12 he that
Luke 2:19 Mary *p*. them in her
heart

PONDS.

Ex. 7:19 stretch hand on *p*. 8:5
Is. 19:10 purposes, that make *p*.

PONTUS.   *Acts* 2:9 ;   18:2 ;
1 *Pet.* 1:1

POOL.

2 *Sam.* 2:13 on one side of the *p*.
4:12 they hanged them over *p*.
2 *K.* 18:17 by the conduit of the
upper *p*. *Is.* 7:3 ; 36:2
Neh. 2:14 I went to the king's *p*.
Is. 22:9 waters of the lower *p*.
11 a ditch for wa. of the old *p*.
35:7 parched ground bec. a *p*.
41:18 I will make wilderness *p*.
Nah. 2:8 Nin. of old is like a *p*.
John 5:2 there is at Jerusal. a *p*.
7 no man to put me into *p*.
9:7 wash in *p*. of Siloam, 11

POOLS.

Ex. 7:19 stretch thy hand on *p*.
Ps. 84:6 rain also filleth the *p*.
Ec. 2:6 I made me *p*. of water
Is. 14:23 I will make it for *p*.
42:15 I will dry up *p*. and herbs

POOR.

Ex. 23:11 *p*. of thy people eat
30:15 the *p*. shall not give less
Lev. 14:21 if he be *p*. and cannot
19:10 shalt leave them for the *p*.
15 shalt not resp. person of *p*.
25:25 if brother be *p*. 35, 39, 47

Deut. 15:4 when there be no *p*.
11 the *p*. shall never cease out
Ruth 3:10 young men, *p*. or rich
1 *Sam.* 2:7 L. make. *p*. and rich
8 raiseth up the *p*. *Ps.* 113:7
2 *Sam.* 12:1 one rich, the oth. *p*.
2 *K.* 25:12 captain of guard left
p. *Jer.* 39:10 ; 40:7 ; 52:15, 16
Job 5:15 he saveth *p*. from sword
16 *p*. hath hope, iniq. stoppeth
20:10 chil. sh. seek to please *p*.
19 because he oppressed the *p*.
24:4 *p*. of earth hide themselves
9 they take a pledge of the *p*.
14 murderer kill. *p*. and needy
29:12 because I delivered the *p*.
30:25 my soul grieved for *p*. ?
31:16 if I withheld *p*. fr. desire
19 have seen *p*. without cover.
34:19 nor reg. rich more than *p*.
28 they cause cry of *p*. to come
36:15 deliver *p*. *Ps.* 72:12
Ps. 9:18 expecta. of *p*. not perish
10:2 wicked in pride do pers. *p*.
8 his eyes are set against *p*.
9 he lieth in wait to catch *p*.
10 *p*. may fall by strong ones
14 *p*. commit. himself to thee
12:5 for the oppression of the *p*.
14:6 shamed the counsel of *p*.
35:10 deliverest the *p*. from him
37:14 bent bow to cast down *p*.
40:17 but I am *p*, 69:29 ; 70:5 ;
86:1 ; 109:22
41:1 he that considereth *p*.
49:2 low and high, rich and *p*.
68:10 prepared goodness for *p*.
69:33 L. heareth *p*. and despis.
72:4 he shall judge *p*. of people
13 spare the *p*. 82:3 defend *p*.
74:21 let the *p*. praise thy name
82:4 deliver the *p*. and needy
107:41 yet setteth he *p*. on high
109:31 stand at right hand of *p*.
132:15 satisfy her *p*. with bread
140:12 maintain right of the *p*.
Prov. 10:4 becometh *p*. dealeth
15 destruction of *p*. is poverty
13:7 mak. himself *p*. hath riches
8 the *p*. heareth not rebuke
23 much food is in tillage of *p*.
14:20 *p*. is hated of neighbor
21 hath mercy on *p*. happy
31 oppres. *p*. reproach. Maker
17:5 mock. *p*. reproach. Maker
18:23 the *p*. useth entreaties
19:4 *p*. is separ. from neighbor
7 brethren of *p*. do hate him
21:13 stoppeth ears at cry of *p*.
22:2 rich and *p*. meet together
7 the rich ruleth over the *p*.
16 he that oppresseth the *p*.
28:8 for him that will pity *p*.
11 *p*. that hath understanding
15 so is wicked ruler over *p*.
29:7 considereth cause of *p*. 13
14 king faithfully judgeth *p*.
30:9 lest I be *p*. and steal
14 teeth as swords, to dev. *p*.
31:9 plead the cause of the *p*.
Ec. 4:14 his kingdom becom. *p*.
5:8 seest oppression of the *p*.
6:8 what hath the *p*. that kno.
Is. 3:14 the spoil of the *p*. is in
15 grind the faces of the *p*. ?
10:2 take the right from the *p*.
30 to Laish, O *p*. Anathoth
11:4 with righ. sh. he judge *p*.
14:30 the first-born of the *p*.
32 *p*. of his people shall trust
26:6 feet of the *p*. shall tread
29:19 even *p*. among men shall
32:7 destroy the *p*. with lying
41:17 the *p*. and needy seek
58:7 that thou bring the *p*.
Jer. 2:34 blood of *p*. innocents
5:4 I said, Surely these are *p*.
20:13 delivered soul of the *p*.

22:16 judge the cause of the *p.*
Ezek. 16:49 strength. hand of *p.*
18:12 oppressed *p.* and needy
17 taken off his hand fr. the *p.*
22:29 they have vexed the *p.*
Amos 2:6 sold the *p.* for shoes
7 dust on the head of the *p.*
4:1 oppress the *p.* and crush
5:11 your treading is on the *p.*
12 turn aside the *p.* in gate
8:4 make *p.* of the land to fail
6 we may buy *p.* for silver
Hab. 3:14 rejoicing to devour *p.*
Zep. 3:12 the *p.* shall trust in L.
Zec. 7:10 oppress not the *p.*
11:7 I will feed even you, O *p.*
11 *p.* of the flock waited on me
Mat. 5:3 blessed are *p.* in spirit
11:5 the *p.* have gospel preach.
26:11 ye have the *p.* always,
Mark 14:7 ; *John* 12:8
Mark 12:43 *p.* widow, *Luke* 21:3
Luke 6:20 blessed be ye *p.* yours
14:13 call the *p.* the maimed, 21
John 12:6 not that he car. for *p.*
Rom. 15:26 make contribu. for *p.*
2 *Cor.* 6:10 as *p.* yet making rich
8:9 for your sakes he became *p.*
Gal. 2:10 should remem. the *p.*
Jam. 2:5 hath not G. chos. the *p.*
6 but ye have despised the *p.*
Rev. 3:17 knowest not th. art *p.*
13:16 he causeth rich and *p.* to

Is POOR.

Ex. 22:25 of my peo. that is *p.*
Deut. 24:14 op. servant that is *p.*
15 for he is *p.* and setteth his
Jud. 6:15 my family is *p.*
Prov. 19:1 better is the *p.* 28:6
22:22 rob not poor bec. he is *p.*
Ec. 4:13 better is a *p.* and wise
Is. 66:2 to him that is *p.*

POOR man.

Ex. 23:3 nor countenance *p. m.*
Deut. 15:7 is a *p. m.* harden not
24:12 if a *p. man,* sleep not wi.
1 *Sam.* 18:23 seeing I am a *p. m.*
2 *Sam.* 12:3 *p. man* had nothing
Ps. 34:6 this *p. m.* cried, and the
109:16 persecu. *p.* and needy *m.*
Prov. 19:22 a *p. man* is better
21:17 loveth pleas. sh. be *p. m.*
28:3 a *p. man* that oppresseth
29:13 *p.* and deceitful *m.* meet
Ec. 9:15 found in it *p.* wise *man*
16 *p. man's* wisdom is despis.
Jam. 2:2 there come in a *p. man*

To the POOR.

Lev. 23:22 leave them *to the p.*
Est. 9:22 sending gifts *to the p.*
Job 29:16 I was a father *to the p.*
36:6 he giveth right *to the p.*
Ps. 112:9 giv. *to t. p.* 2 *Cor.* 9:9
Prov. 22:9 giveth bread *to the p.*
28:27 he that giveth *to the p.*
31:20 stretcheth hand *to the p.*
Is. 25:4 been a strength *to the p.*
Dan. 4:27 show. mercy *to the p.*
Mat. 19:21 gi. *to t. p. Mark* 10:21
Luke 4:18 preach *to the p.* 7:22
19:8 half of goods I give *to t. p.*
John 13:29 give somet. *to the p.*
1 *Cor.* 13:3 my goods *to feed t. p.*
Jam. 2:3 and say *to t. p.* Stand

Thy POOR.

Ex. 23:6 wrest judgment of *t. p.*
Deut. 15:7 hand fr. *thy p.* brother
11 open thy hand wide *to t. p.*
Ps. 72:2 he shall judge *thy p.*
74:19 forget not *thy p.* forever

POORER, EST.

Lev. 27:8 if he be *p.* than thy
2 *K.* 24:14 none remained save *p.*

POPLAR, S.

Gen. 30:37 Jacob took rods of *p.*
Hos. 4:13 burn incense under *p.*

POPULOUS.

Deut. 26:5 bec. a nation great, *p.*
Nah. 3:8 art thou better than *p.*

PORCH.

Jud. 3:23 Ehud went through *p.*
1 *Chr.* 28:11 D. gave So. patt. *p.*
2 *Chr.* 29:7 shut doors of the *p.*
Ezek. 8:16 between *p.* and altar
Joel 2:17 priests weep between *p.*
Mat. 26:71 was gone out into *p.*
Mark 14:68 into the *p.* the cock
John 10:23 Je. walked in S.'s *p.*
Acts 3:11 toget. in Solomon's *p.*
5:12 with one accord in S.'s *p.*

PORCHES.

Ezek. 41:15 with temple and *p.*
John 5:2 Bethesda, having fi. *p.*

PORCIUS.

Acts 24:27 P. Festus came into

PORTER, S.

2 *Sam.* 18:26 watch. called to *p.*
2 *K.* 7:10 lepers called to the *p.*
1 *Chr.* 9:17 the *p.* were Shallum
23:5 four thousand were *p.*
2 *Chr.* 8:14 p. by their courses
35:15 the *p.* waited at ev. gate
Ezr. 7:7 and Nethinim went
Neh. 7:73 Levites and *p.* dwelt
Mark 13:34 commanded the *p.* to
John 10:3 to him the *p.* openeth

PORTION.

Gen. 14:24 let them take their *p.*
31:14 is there yet any *p.* for us?
48:22 given thee *p.* above breth.
Lev. 6:17 given them it for *p.*
Num. 31:47 M. took one *p.* of 50
Deut. 21:17 giv. him double *p.*
32:9 the Lord's *p.* is his people
33:21 in a *p.* of the lawgiver
Jos. 17:14 given me but one *p.*
1 *Sam.* 1:5 to Hannah he gave *p.*
1 *K.* 12:16 what *p.* have we in
David ? 2 *Chr.* 10:16
2 *K.* 2:9 let a double *p.* of thy
9:10 eat Jez. in *p.* of Jez. 36, 37
21 Joram met him in *p.* of Na.
25 cast him in *p.* of Na.'s field
2 *Chr.* 28:21 Ahaz took *p.* out of
31:4 to give *p.* of the priests, 16
Ezr. 4:16 shalt have no *p.*
Neh. 2:20 no *p.* nor right in Jer.
11:23 a certain *p.* should be
Job 20:29 this is *p.* of a wicked
24:18 their *p.* is cursed in earth
26:14 lit. a *p.* is heard ? 27:13
31:2 what *p.* of G. is fr. above?
Ps. 11:6 this shall be the *p.* of
16:5 L. is the *p.* of mine inher.
17:14 who have *p.* in this life
63:10 shall be a *p.* for foxes
73:26 God is my *p.* for ever
119:57 thou art my *p.* 142:5
Prov. 31:15 giv. a *p.* to maidens
Ec. 2:10 and this was my *p.*
21 shall he leave it for his *p.*
3:22 for that is his *p.* 5:18 ; 9:9
5:19 G. given power to take *p.*
9:6 nor have they any more *p.*
11:2 give a *p.* to seven, and also
Is. 17:14 this is the *p.* of them
53:12 I will divide him a *p.*
57:6 stones of stream is thy *p.*
61:7 they sh. rejoice in their *p.*
Jer. 10:16 the *p.* of Jacob, 51:19
12:10 they have tro. my *p.* made
my *p.* a desolate wilderness
13:25 this is *p.* of thy measures
52:34 every day a *p.* until death
Lam. 3:24 the Lord is my *p.*
Ezek. 45:1 shall offer a holy *p.* 4
Dan. 1:8 with *p.* of king's meat
4:15 let his *p.* be with beasts, 23
11:26 feed of the *p.* of his meat
Mic. 2:4 changed *p.* of my people
Hab. 1:16 by them their *p.* is fat
Zec. 2:12 Lord inherit Ju. his *p.*
Mat. 24:51 appoint him his *p.*

Luke 12:42 to give them their *p.*
46 his *p.* with unbelievers
15:12 give me the *p.* of goods

PORTIONS.

Deut. 18:8 they shall have like *p.*
Jos. 17:5 fell ten *p.* to Manasseh
1 *Sam.* 1:4 gave her daughters *p.*
2 *Chr.* 31:19 give *p.* to all males
Neh. 8:10 send *p.* to them, 12
12:44 *p.* priests; 47 *p.* of sing.
Est. 9:19 a day of sending *p.* 22
Ezek. 47:13 Jos. shall ha. two *p.*
Hos. 5:7 month shall de. their *p.*

PORTRAY, ED.

Ezek. 4:1 *p.* upon it city Jerusal.
8:10 all the idols of Israel *p.*
23:14 images of Chaldeans *p.*

POSSESS.

Gen. 22:17 seed *p.* gate, 24:60
Num. 13:30 and *p. Deut.* 1:21
27:11 next kinsman shall *p.* it
Deut. 1:39 they shall *p.* it
2:31 to *p.* that thou mayest
11:23 shall *p.* greater nations,
12:2, 29 ; 18:14 ; 31:3
Jos. 24:3 E. mount Seir to *p.* it
Jud. 11:23 shouldest thou *p.* it ?
24 wilt not thou *p.* what Che.
1 *K.* 21:18 he is gone down to *p.*
Job 7:3 to *p.* months of vanity
13:26 make. me to *p.* iniquities
Is. 34:11 bittern shall *p.* it, 17
Ezek. 7:24 they shall *p.* houses
35:10 be mine, we will *p.*
36:12 I will cause Is. to *p.* thee
Dan. 7:18 the saints shall *p.* the
Hos. 9:6 silver, nettles shall *p.*
Amos 9:12 they may *p.* Edom
Ob. 17 house of Jacob shall *p.*
19 sh. *p.* Esau, and Benj. *p.* G.
Hab. 1:6 Chaldeans to *p.* that is
Zep. 2:9 remnant shall *p.* them
Zec. 8:12 I will cause rem. to *p.*
Luke 18:12 give tithe of all I *p.*
21:19 in patience *p.* your souls
1 *Thes.* 4:4 know how to *p.* ves.

POSSESS, with land.

Lev. 20:24 give *l.* to *p. Nu.* 33:53;
Deut. 3:18 ; 5:31 ; 17:14
Num. 14:24 thy seed shall *p.* it, I
will bring them into this *l.*
Deut. 1:8 go in and *p.* the *land,*
4:1 ; 6:18 ; 8:1 ; 9:5, 23 ; 10:11;
11:31 ; *Jos.* 1:11
4:5 *land* whither ye go to *p.* it,
14, 26 ; 5:33 ; 6:1 ; 7:1 ; 11:10,
11, 29 ; 23:20
9:4 Lord brought me to *p.* th. *l.*
6 gives not this *l.* to *p.* for thy
11:8 be strong, and *p.* the *land*
28:21 consum. off *la.* goest to *p.*
63 plucked off the *l.* goest to *p.*
Jos. 23:5 ye shall *p.* their *land*
24:8 that ye might *p.* their *land*
Jud. 18:9 enter to *p.* the *land*
1 *Chr.* 28:8 ye may *p.* this good *l.*
Ezr. 9:11 ye go to *p.* an uncl. *l.*
Neh. 9:15 they should *p.* the *l.*
Is. 14:2 Is. sh. *p.* them in *l.* of L.
57:13 put. trust in me. shall *p. l.*
61:7 their *l.* sh. they *p.* double
Jer. 30:3 return to *l.* and *p.* it
Ezek. 33:25 shall ye *p. l. l.* ? 26
Amos 2:10 I bro. you to *p. land*

POSSESSED.

Num. 21:24 Is. *p.* Sihon's land
Deut. 30:5 to land thy fathers *p.*
Jos. 13:1 much land to be *p.*
21:43 *p.* it and dw. therein, 22:9
Jud. 3:13 Eg. king of M. *p.* city
11:21 Is. *p.* land of Amorites, 22
2 *K.* 17:24 men of Ava *p.* Sam.
Ps. 139:13 thou hast *p.* my reins
Prov. 8:22 L. *p.* me in beginning
Is. 63:18 peo. of holiness hath *p.*

Jer. 32:15 vineyards shall be *p.*
23 and they came in and *p.* it
Dan. 7:22 saints *p.* the kingdom
Luke 8:36 he that was *p.* cured
Acts 4:32 none said aught he *p.*
16:16 a damsel *p.* with a spirit
1 *Cor.* 7:30 buy as tho' th. *p.* not
See DEVILS.

POSSESSEST; ETH; ING.
Deut. 26:1 come into land and *p.*
Num. 36:8 ev. daughter that *p.*
Luke 12:15 a man's life consists
not in things which he *p.*
2 *Cor.* 6:16 noth. yet *p.* in all th.

POSSESSION.
Gen. 17:8 I will give land of Can.
for everlasting *p.* 48:4
26:14 Isaac had *p.* of flocks
47:11 gave them *p.* in land of E.
Lev. 14:34 wh. I give to you for *p.*
25:25 if bro. sold some of his *p.*
33 the Levites' *p.* shall go out
45 strangers sh. be your *p.* 46
27:16 if man sanc. some of his *p.*
24 return to wh. *p.* did belong
Num. 24:18 Edom be *p.* S. be a *p.*
27:4 give us a *p.* among breth.
32:5 given to thy serv. for *p.*
22 this land shall be your *p.*
35:2 give to Levites their *p.* 8
28 slayer shall return to his *p.*
Deut. 2:5 mount Seir to E. for *p.*
9 have given Ar to L. for *p.* 19
12 as Isra. did in land of his *p.*
11:6 earth swallow. all in th. *p.*
32:49 which I gave Israel for *p.*
Jos. 12:6 Moses gave it for a *p.*
22:4 get ye unto land of your *p.*
19 if *p.* be unclean, take *p.*
1 *K.* 21:15 take *p.* of vineyard
19 hast thou killed, taken *p.* ?
2 *Chr.* 20:11 cast us out of thy *p.*
Neh. 11:3 Jr. dwelt ev. one in *p.*
Ps. 2:8 utterm. parts for thy *p.*
44:3 got not land in *p.* by sword
69:35 dwell and have it in *p.*
83:12 take houses of God in *p.*
Prov. 28:10 upri. have good in *p.*
Is. 14:23 I will make it a *p.* for
Ezek. 11:15 this land given in *p.*
25:4 I will deliver thee for *p.*
36:2 high places are ours in *p.*
44:28 give them no *p.* in Israel
46:18 inherit. out of his own *p.*

Acts 5:1 An. with Sap. sold a *p.*
7:5 would give it to him for a *p.*
45 with Jesus into *p.* of Gent.
Eph. 1:14 redemption of the *p.*

POSSESSIONS.
Gen. 34:10 and get you *p.* therein
47:27 and Israel had *p.* therein
Num. 32:30 they shall have *p.*
Jos. 22:4 get to land of your *p.*
1 *Sam.* 25:2 whose *p.* were in C.
1 *Chr.* 9:2 inhabitants dw. in *p.*
2 *Chr.* 11:14 Levites left their *p.*
32:29 Hezeki. prov. *p.* of flocks
Ec. 2:7 I had great *p.* of great
Ob. 17 Jacob shall pos. their *p.*
Mat. 19:22 had *p. Mark* 10:22
Acts 2:45 sold *p.* and part. them
28:7 same quart. were *p.* of P.

POSSESSOR, S.
Gen. 14:19 high G. *p.* heaven, 22
Zec. 11:5 whose *p.* slay them
Acts 4:34 many as were *p.* lands

POSSIBLE.
Mat. 19:26 G. all *p. Mark* 10:27
24:24 if *p.* dec. elect, *Mar.* 13:22
26:39 if *p.* let this cup pass fr.
me, *Mark* 14:35
Mark 9:23 all things *p.* to him
14:36 all things *p. Luke* 18:27
Acts 2:24 not *p.* he sho. be hold.
20:16 if *p.* at Jerusal. day of P.

Rom. 12:18 if *p.* live peaceably
Gal. 4:15 if *p.* ye would have
Heb. 10:4 not *p.* blood of bulls

POST, S.
2 *Chr.* 30:6 *p.* went with letters,
Est. 3:13, 15 ; 8:10
Est. 8:14 *p.* rode on mules
Job 9:25 days are swifter than *p.*
Jer. 51:31 one *p.* run to meet an.

POST.
1 *Sam.* 1:9 E. sat on seat by a *p.*
Ezek. 40:16 on each *p.* palm-trees

POSTS.
Deut. 6:9 shalt write them on *p.*
Jud. 16:3 Samson took two *p.*
1 *K.* 7:5 doors and *p.* were square
Prov. 8:34 waiting at *p.* of doors
Is. 6:4 the *p.* of the door moved
57:8 behind the *p.* thou set up
Ezek. 40:10 *p.* had one measure
43:8 setting of their *p.* by my *p.*
Amos 9:1 that the *p.* may shake
See DOOR.

Side-POSTS.
Ex. 12:7 stri. blood on 2 *s.-p.* 22
1 *K.* 6:31 *s.-p.* were a fifth part

POSTERITY.
Gen. 45:7 preserve you a *p.*
Num. 9:10 any of yo. *p.* be uncl.
1 *K.* 16:3 take the *p.* of Baasha
21:21 take away the *p.* of Ahab
Ps. 49:13 *p.* approve th. sayings
109:13 let his *p.* be cut off
Dan. 11:4 not be divid. to his *p.*
Amos 4:2 your *p.* with fish-hooks

POT.
Ex. 16:33 take a *p.* put manna
Jud. 6:19 Gid. put broth in a *p.*
2 *K.* 4:2 not any thing, save a *p.*
38 on great *p.* 40 death in *p.*
Job 41:20 as out of a seething *p.*
31 maketh deep to boil like *p.*
Prov. 17:3 fining *p.* for sil. 27:21
Jer. 1:13 I see a seething *p.*
Ezek. 24:3 saith L. Set on a *p.*
6 woe to *p.* wh. scum is ther.
Mic. 3:3 chop in pieces, as for *p.*
Zec. 14:21 every *p.* in Jerusalem
Heb. 9:4 golden *p.* with manna

Water-POT, S.
John 2:6 there was set six *w.-p.*
4:28 woman then left her *w.-p.*

POTS.
Ex. 38:3 Bezaleel made the *p.*
Lev. 11:35 oven, or ranges for *p.*
1 *K.* 7:45 *p.* of brass, 2 *Chr.* 4:16
2 *Chr.* 4:11 Huram made the *p.*
Ps. 58:9 before your *p.* can feel
68:13 ye have lain among the *p.*
81:6 hands deliver. from the *p.*
Jer. 35:5 before Rech. *p.* of wine
Mark 7:4 wash. of cups and *p.*
See FLESH.

POTENTATE.
1 *Tim.* 6:15 blessed and only P.

POTIPHAR.
Gen. 37:36 sold Joseph to P. 39:1

POTI-PHERAH.
Gen. 41:45 the daughter of P. 50

POTSHERD, S.
Job 2:8 took *p.* to scrape himself
Ps. 22:15 stren. dried up like a *p.*
Prov. 26:23 are like a *p.* covered
Is. 45:9 let *p.* strive with the *p.*

POTTAGE.
Gen. 25:29 Jacob sod *p.* and Esau
30 feed me with *p.* 34 J. gave
2 *K.* 4:38 seethe *p.* for sons, 40
Hag. 2:12 if one touch bre. or *p.*

POTTER, S.
1 *Chr.* 4:23 these were the *p.*
Ps. 2:9 dash in pieces like *p.'s*

Is. 30:14 as breaking of a *p.'s*
vessel, *Jer.* 19:11 ; *Rev.* 2:27
Jer. 18:2 go down to *p.'s* house
19:1 get a *p.'s* earthen bottle
Lam. 4:2 work of han. of the *p.*
Zec. 11:13 said, Cast it unto *p.*
Mat. 27:10 gave th. for *p.'s* field
See CLAY.

POUND, S.
1 *K.* 10:17 three *p.* of gold went
Ezr. 2:69 treas. 5,000 *p.* of silver
Neh. 7:71 treas. 2,200 *p.* of silver
72 rest gave 2,000 *p.* of silver
Luke 19:13 delivered to his servants ten *p.* 16, 18, 24
John 12:3 M. took *p.* of ointment
19:39 and of aloes about 100 *p.*

POUR.
Ex. 4:9 *p.* water on dry land
29:7 *p.* anointing oil on head
12 *p.* blood of bullock beside
altar, *Lev.* 4:7, 18, 25, 30, 34
Lev. 2:1 *p.* oil on meat-offer. 6
14:15 *p.* it into palm of hand, 26
41 they shall *p.* out the dust
17:13 shall *p.* out blood thereof
Num. 24:7 he shall *p.* water out
Deut. 12:16 *p.* blood, 24 ; 15:23
1 *K.* 18:33 *p.* water on sacrifice
2 *K.* 4:4 *p.* oil into those vessels
41 *p.* out for the people
Job 36:27 *p.* rain accord. to vapor
Ps. 42:4 when I *p.* out my soul
62:8 *p.* out your heart bef. him
69:24 *p.* out thine indignation
79:6 *p.* out wrath on heathen
Prov. 1:23 will *p.* out my Sp. *Is.*
44:3; *Joel* 2:28, 29; *Ac.* 2:17,18
Is. 44:3 I will *p.* water on him
45:8 skies *p.* down righteousn.
Jer. 6:11 I will *p.* on children
7:18 to *p.* out drink-offerings
10:25 *p.* out fury on heathen
14:16 I will *p.* their wickedness
18:21 *p.* out their blood by swo.
44:17 *p.* out drink-off. 18, 19, 25
Lam. 2:19 *p.* out heart like wat.
Ezek. 7:8 now will I *p.* out fury,
14:19; 20:8, 13, 21 ; 30:15
21:31 *p.* out indignati. *Zep.* 3:8
24:3 set on pot and *p.* water in
Hos. 5:10 will *p.* out my wrath
Mic. 1:6 I will *p.* down stones
Zec. 12:10 *p.* on house of D.
Mal. 3:10 if I will not *p.* out
Rev. 16:1 *p.* out vials of wrath

POURED.
Gen. 28:18 Jacob *p.* oil on stone
35:14 Jacob *p.* a drink-offering
Ex. 9:33 rain not *p.* on earth
Lev. 4:12 ashes *p.* he sh. be burnt
8:12 Mo. *p.* oil on Aaron's head
21:10 on whose head oil was *p.*
Num. 28:7 *p.* to L. for drink-off.
Deut. 12:27 sacrifi. sh. be *p.* out
1 *Sam.* 1:15 I have *p.* out my soul
7:6 water, *p.* it out before Lord
10:1 Samuel *p.* oil on S.'s head
2 Sam. 23:16 Da. would not dri.
but *p.* it, 1 *Chr.* 11:18
1 *K.* 13:3 and ashes *p.* out, 5
2 *K.* 3:11 *p.* wat. on hands of E.
4:5 ves. to her, and she *p.* out
16:13 Ahaz *p.* his drink-offering
2 *Chr.* 12:7 wrath not *p.* out on J.
34:21 wrath of Lord *p.* on us
25 there. wrath shall be *p.* out
Job 3:24 my roarings are *p.* out
10:10 thou *p.* me out as milk
29:6 rock *p.* me out rivers of oil
30:16 now my soul is *p.* out
Ps. 22:14 I am *p.* out like water
45:2 grace is *p.* into thy lips
77:17 clouds *p.* out water, skies
142:2 I *p.* out my complaint
Cant. 1:3 name is as ointment *p.*

Is. 26:16 *p.* out a prayer, when
29:10 Lord hath *p.* on you sleep
32:15 the Spirit be *p.* out on us
42:25 he hath *p.* on him the fury
53:12 *p.* out his soul to death
57:6 hast *p.* out a drink-offering
Jer. 7:20 my fury shall be *p.* out
19:13 *p.* out offerings, 32:29
Jer. 42:18 as fury, so sh. it be *p.*
44:6 mine anger was *p.* forth
19 wh. we *p.* drink-offerings
Lam. 2:4 *p.* fury like fire, 4:11
11 my liver is *p.* 12 soul *p.*
4:1 stones of sanctuary *p.* out
Ezek. 16:36 thy filthiness was *p.*
20:28 *p.* out their drink-offering
33 with fury *p.* out I rule, 34
22:22 I the Lord *p.* out my fury
31 therefore, I *p.* indignation
23:8 they *p.* their whoredom on
24:7 she *p.* it not on the ground
36:18 wherefore I *p.* out my fury
39:29 I *p.* out my Spirit on Isr.
Dan. 9:11 there. curse is *p.* on us
27 determ. sh. be *p.* on desol.
Mic. 1:4 waters *p.* down a steep
Nah. 1:6 fury is *p.* out like fire
Zep. 1:17 their blood be *p.* out
Mat. 26:7 *p.* oint. 12 ; *Mark* 14:3
John 2:15 he *p.* out the money
Acts 10:45 on Gentil. was *p.* gift
Rev. 14:10 wine of wrath of G. *p.*
16:2 *p.* out vial, 3, 4, 8, 10, 12

POUREDST, ETH.

Job 12:21 *p.* contempt on prin-
  ces, *Ps.* 107:40
16:13 he *p.* out my gall on gro.
20 mine eye *p.* tears unto God
Ps. 75:8 wine is red, he *p.* out
Prov. 15:2 fools *p.* out foolishn.
28 the wicked *p.* out evil thi.
Ezek. 16:15 *p.* out thy fornicati.
Amos 5:8 *p.* out wat. on earth, 9:6.
John 13:5 *p.* water into a bason

POURING.

Ezek. 9:8 destroy all in *p.* fury
Luke 10:34 his wounds, *p.* in oil

POVERTY.

Gen. 45:11 all th. hast come to *p.*
Prov. 6:11 *p.* co. as armed, 24:34
10:15 destruction of *p.* is th. *p.*
11:24 withhold. but tend. to *p.*
13:18 *p.* be to him that refuseth
20:13 not sleep, lest come to *p.*
23:21 drun. and glut. come to *p.*
28:19 vain persons, sh. have *p.*
22 considereth not *p.* sh. come
30:8 give me neit. *p.* nor riches
31:7 drink and forget his *p.*
2 *Cor.* 8:2 their deep *p.* abounded
9 ye thro' his *p.* might be rich
Rev. 2:9 I kn. thy works and *p.*

POWDER, S.

Ex. 32:20 Moses burnt calf to *p.*
Deut. 28:24 make rain of land *p.*
2 *K.* 23:6 stamped the grove to *p.*
15 stamp. alt. to *p.* 2 *Chr.* 34:7
Cant. 3:6 perfumed wi. all the *p.*
Mat. 21:44 grind to *p.* *Luke* 20:18

POWER.

Gen. 32:28 as a prince hast th. *p.*
49:3 dignity, excellency of *p.*
Lev. 26:19 I will break your *p.*
Num. 22:38 have I *p.* to say ?
Deut. 4:37 bro. thee with his *p.*
8:18 it is he that giveth thee *p.*
32:36 wh. see their *p.* gone
2 *Sam.* 22:33 my strength and *p.*
2 *K.* 19:26 inhabitan. of small *p.*
1 *Chr.* 20:1 Joab led forth the *p.*
29:11 thine is the *p.* *Mat.* 6:13
12 in thy hand is *p.* 2 *Chr.* 20:6
2 *Chr.* 25:8 God hath *p.* to help
32:9 and all his *p.* with him
Ezr. 4:23 made th. cease by *p.*
8:22 his *p.* ag. all that forsake

Neh. 5:5 nor is it in our *p.* to red.
Est. 1:3 feast to *p.* of Persia
8:11 cause to perish *p.* of people
9:1 the Jews hoped to have *p.*
Job 5:20 redeem in war from *p.*
21:22 draweth mighty with *p.*
26:2 him that is without *p.* ?
12 divided the sea with his *p.*
14 his *p.* who can understand ?
36:22 God exalteth by his *p.*
41:12 I will not conceal his *p.*
Ps. 22:20 darling from *p.* of dog
40:15 redeem soul fr. *p.* of grave
62:11 *p.* belongeth unto God
65:6 setteth fast mount. with *p.*
66:7 ruleth by his *p.* for ever
68:35 he giveth *p.* to his people
78:26 by *p.* he bro. south wind
90:11 who know. *p.* of th. ang. ?
106:8 his mighty *p.* be known
111:6 showed people *p.* of works
150:1 praise in firma. of his *p.*
Ec. 4:1 side of oppressors was *p.*
5:19 hath given him *p.* to eat
6:2 God giveth him not *p.* to eat
8:4 word of a king is, there is *p.*
8 no man hath *p.* over spirit
Is. 37:27 inhabitants of small *p.*
Is. 40:29 he giv. *p.* to the faint
43:17 bring. forth army and *p.*
47:14 not deliver fr.*p.* of flame
Jer. 10:12 earth by his *p.* 51:15
Ezek. 22:6 their *p.* to shed blood
30:6 pride of her *p.* come down
Dan. 2:37 God hath given thee *p.*
6:27 delivered D. fr. *p.* of lions
8:6 fury of his *p.* 22 not in *p.*
24 his *p.* be mighty, not by *p.*
11:6 sh. not retain *p.* of his arm
25 shall stir up his *p.*
43 have *p.* over treas. of gold
12:7 scatter *p.* of the holy peop.
Hos. 12:3 by stren. had *p.* wi. G.
4 yea, he had *p.* over the angel
13:14 ransom th. from *p.* of gra.
Mic. 2:1 it is in *p.* of their hand
3:8 I am full of *p.* by the Spirit
Hab. 1:11 impu. his *p.* to his god
2:9 delivered from the *p.* of evil
3:4 there was hiding of his *p.*
Zec. 4:6 nor by *p.* but my Spirit
9:4 L. will smite her *p.* in sea
Mat. 9:6 hath *p.* to forgive sins,
  Mark 2:10 ; *Luke* 5:24
8 had given such *p.* to men
10:1 *p.* ag. uncl. spir. *Luke* 9:1
24:30 clouds with *p.* *Luke* 21:27
26:64 ri. hand of *p.* *Mark* 14:62
28:18 all *p.* is given me in heav.
Mark 3:15 *p.* to heal sickness.
9:1 kingd. of God come with *p.*
Luke 1:35 *p.* of Highest oversha.
4:6 said. All this *p.* will I give
32 for his word was with *p.*
36 with *p.* he command. spirits
5:17 *p.* of the Lord was present
10:19 I give you *p.* to tread on
  serp. and over *p.* of enemy
12:5 fear him that ha. *p.* to cast
20:20 deli. him to *p.* of governor
22:53 this is the *p.* of darkness
24:49 until ye be endued with *p.*
John 1:12 to them gave he *p.*
10:18 *p.* to lay it down, and *p.*
17:2 given him *p.* over all flesh
19:10 *p.* to crucify. *p.* to release
Acts 1:7 Fa. hath put in own *p.*
8 receive *p.* after Holy Ghost
3:12 by our own *p.* or holiness
4:7 by what *p.* ha. ye done this ?
5:4 was it not in thine own *p.* ?
6:8 Stephen full of faith and *p.*
8:19 say. Give me also this *p.*
10:38 anointed Jesus with *p.*
26:18 turn them fr. *p.* of Satan
Rom. 1:4 to be Son of G. wi. *p.*
20 his eternal *p.* and Godhead
9:21 hath not pot. *p.* over clay ?

13:2 whosoever resisteth the *p.*
3 wilt thou not be afraid of *p.?*
15:13 through *p.* of Holy Ghost
19 by the *p.* of the Spi. of God
16:25 now to him that is of *p.*
1 *Cor.* 2:4 in demonstration of *p.*
4:19 not kn. speech, but the *p.*
5:4 with *p.* of our L. J. Christ
6:12 not be bro. under *p.* of any
14 raise us up by his own *p.*
7:4 wife and husb. have not *p.*
9:4 ha. we not *p.* to eat and dr.?
5 have not we *p.* to lead wife ?
12 if oth. be partak. of this *p.*
  over you, we ha. not used *p.*
11:10 wom. ought to have *p.*
15:24 put down author. and *p.*
2 *Cor.* 4:7 excel. of *p.* be of God
8:3 to *p.* yea, beyond their *p.*
12:9 that the *p.* of Ch. may rest
13:10 according to *p.* G. given
Eph. 1:19 exceeding greatness of
  his *p.* work. of his mighty *p.*
21 above princi. *p.* and might
2:2 accord. to prince of *p.* of air
3:7 the effectual work of his *p.*
20 accord. to *p.* that worketh
Phil. 3:10 know the *p.* of resur.
Col. 1:11 accord. to his glori. *p.*
13 deliv. us from *p.* of darkn.
2:10 head of all princi. and *p.*
2 *Thes.* 1:9 pun. fr. glory of his *p.*
11 fulfil work of faith with *p.*
2:9 working of Satan wi. all *p.*
3:9 not because we have not *p.*
1 *Tim.* 6:16 wh. he honor and *p.*
2 *Tim.* 1:7 G. hath giv. sp. of *p.*
3:5 hav. godliness, denying *p.*
Heb. 1:3 by word of his *p.*
2:14 destroy him that had *p.*
7:16 after *p.* of an endless life
2 *Pet.* 1:3 *p.* given all things
16 made known *p.* of our **Lord**
Jude 25 to our Sav. glory and *p.*
Rev. 2:26 give *p.* over nations
4:11 worthy to receive *p.* 5:12
5:13 honor and *p.* be to him
6:4 *p.* was given to him
Rev. 6:8 *p.* giv. th. over 4th part
7:12 *p.* and might be giv. to G.
9:3 to them was given *p.*
10 their *p.* was to hurt men
19 their *p.* is in their mouth
11:3 give *p.* to my 2 witnesses
6 *p.* to shut heav. *p.* over wat.
12:10 now is *p.* of his Ch. come
13:2 the dragon gave him *p.* 4
5 *p.* was given to continue, 7
12 he exercis. *p.* of first beast
15 *p.* give life ; 14:18 *p.* ov. fire
15:8 filled with smoke from *p.*
16:8 *p.* giv. him to scorch men
9 blasphemed G. who hath *p.*
17:12 receive *p.* as kings
13 give their *p.* and strength
19:1 glory, honor, and *p.* to L.

POWER of God.

Mat. 22:29 know. scriptures
  nor *p.* of God, *Mark* 12:24
Luke 9:43 amazed at *p.* of God
22:69 sit on right of *p.* of God
Acts 8:10 man is great *p.* of God
Rom. 1:16 gospel is the *p.* of God
1 *Cor.* 1:18 saved, it is *p.* of God
24 Christ the *p.* of God
2:5 not stand but by *p.* of God
2 *Cor.* 6:7 of truth, by *p.* of God
13:4 he liveth by *p.* of God, we
  sh. live with him by *p.* of G.
2 *Tim.* 1:8 according to *p.* of G.
1 *Pet.* 1:5 by *p.* of G. thro' faith
See GREAT.

In POWER.

Gen. 31:29 in *p.* of my hand
Ex. 15:6 ri. hand glorious in *p.*
Job 21:7 why are wick. mi. in *p.?*
37:23 excellent in *p.* and judg.

Prov. 3:27 it is *in p.* of thy hand
18:21 and life *in p.* of tongue
Is. 40:26 that he is strong *in p.*
Nah. 1:3 slow to anger, gr. *in p.*
Luke 1:17 go before him *in p.*
4:14 Jesus returned *in p.* of Sp.
1 Cor. 4:20 not in word, but *in p.*
15:43 sown in weakn. rai. *in p.*
Eph. 6:10 strong *in* Lord and *p.*
1 Thes 1:5 in word and *in p.*
2 Pet. 2:11 angels greater *in p.*

My POWER.

Gen. 31:6 wi. all *my p.* I served
Ex. 9:16 to show in thee *my p.*
Deut. 8:17 *my p.* got. me wealth
Dan. 4:30 Babyl. built by *my p.*
Rom. 9:17 might show *my p.*
1 Cor. 9:18 I abuse not *my p.*

No POWER.

Ex. 21:8 he shall have *no p.*
Lev. 26:37 have *no p.* to stand
1 Sam. 30:4 had *no p.* to weep
2 Chr. 14:11 help them ha. *no p.*
22:9 house of Ahaziah had *no p.*
Is. 50:2 have I *no p.* to deliver?
Dan. 3:27 on bodi. fire had *no p.*
8:7 there was *no p.* in the ram
John 19:11 ha. *no p.* against me
Rom. 13:1 th. is *no p.* but of God
Rev. 20:6 second death hath *no p.*

Thy POWER.

Deut. 9:29 brought. out by *thy p.*
Job 1:12 all th. he hath is in *t. p.*
Ps. 21:13 sing, and praise *thy p.*
59:11 scat. by *t. p.* 16 sing *t. p.*
63:2 to see *t. p.* and thy glory
66:5 through greatness of *thy p.*
71:18 *t. p.* to ev. one is to come
79:11 accord. to greatn. of *t. p.*
110:3 be willing in day of *t. p.*
145:11 they shall talk of *thy p.*
Nah. 2:1 fortify *thy p.* mightily

POWERFUL.

Ps. 29:4 the voice of tho L. is *p.*
2 Cor. 10:10 for his letters are *p.*
Heb. 4:12 word of G. is quick, *p.*

POWERS.

Mat. 24:29 p. of heaven shall be
sh. *Mark* 13:25 ; *Luke* 21:26
Luke 12:11 when brought bef. *p.*
Rom. 8:38 nor *p.* can sepa. fr. G.
13:1 *p* that be ordained of God
Eph. 3:10 *p.* in heavenly places
6:12 against principalit. and *p.*
Col. 1:16 *p.* were created by him
2:15 hav. spoiled *p.* made show
Tit. 3:1 to be subject to *p.*
Heb. 6:5 tasted *p.* of the world
1 Pet. 3:22 right hand of God *p.*

PRACTICES.

2 Pet. 2:14 exercised with cov. *p.*

PRACTISE.

Ps. 141:4 not to *p.* wicked works
Is. 32:6 the vile sh. *p.* hypocrisy
Dan. 8:24 shall destroy, and *p.*
Mic. 2:1 morning is light they *p.*

PRACTISED.

1 Sam. 23:9 S. secretly *p.* misc.
Dan. 8:12 lit. horn *p.* and prosp.

PRAISE, Substantive.

Deut. 10:21 thy *p.* and thy God
26:19 to make thee high in *p.*
Jud. 5:3 I will sing *p.* to the L.
God of Israel, *Ps.* 7:17 ; 9:2 ;
57:7 ; 61:8 ; 104:33
1 Chr. 16:35 may glory in thy *p.*
2 Chr. 23:13 taught to sing *p.*
Neh. 9:5 who is exalted above *p.*
12:46 days of D. we. songs of *p.*
Ps. 9:14 I may show all thy *p.*
22:25 my *p.* shall be of thee
30:12 glory may sing *p.* to thee
33:1 for *p.* is comely for upright
34:1 his *p.* shall be in my mou.
35:28 shall speak of thy *p.*

40:3 *p.* to God, 42:4 voice of *p.*
48:10 thy *p.* to ends of earth
50:23 whoso offereth *p.* glorifie.
51:15 my mouth sh. show thy *p.*
65:1 *p.* waiteth for thee, O God
66:2 and make his *p.* glorious
8 make voice of his *p.* be hea.
71:6 my *p.* shall be continually
8 mouth be filled with thy *p.*
79:13 show thy *p.* 98:4 sing *p.*
100:4 enter his courts with *p.*
102:21 dec. his *p.* in Jerusalem
106:2 who can show all his *p.*?
12 sang *p.* 47 triumph in *p.*
108:1 I will sing, and give *p.*
100:1 G. of my *p.* 111:10 *p.* end.
119:171 my lips shall utter *p.*
138:1 before gods will I sing *p.*
145:21 mouth sh. speak *p.* of L.
147:1 *p.* is comely ; 7 sing *p.* on
148:14 exalteth the *p.* of saints
149:1 sing his *p.* in congregati.
Prov. 27:21 so is man to *p.*
Is. 42:8 not give *p.* to images
10 sing his *p.* from end of car.
12 declare his *p.* in the islands
43:21 they sh. show forth my *p.*
48:9 and for my *p.* will I refrain
60:18 thou shalt call thy gat. P.
61:3 garment of *p.* for heaviness
11 L. will cause *p.* to sp. forth
62:7 make Jerusa. a *p.* in earth
Jer. 13:11 might be to me a *p.*
17:14 O Lord, thou art my *p.*
26 bring. sacrifices of *p.* 33:11
33:9 shall be to me a joy, a *p.*
48:2 shall be no more *p.* of Mo.
51:41 how is *p.* of earth surpr. ?
Hab. 3:3 earth was full of his *p.*
Zep. 3:19 get them *p.* and fame
20 make you a *p.* am. all peo.
Mat. 21:16 thou hast perfect. *p.*
Luke 18:43 they saw it, gave *p.*
John 9:24 give G. the *p.*
12:43 *p.* of men more than G.
Rom. 2:29 whose *p.* is not of m.
13:3 thou shalt have *p.* of same
1 Cor. 4:5 ev. man have *p.* of G.
2 Cor. 8:18 whose *p.* is in gospel
Eph. 1:6 predestinat. to *p.* of gl.
12 *p.* of gl. who trusted in Ch. 14
Phil. 1:11 J. C. to *p.* and gl. of G.
4:8 if any *p.* think on th. things
Heb. 2:12 in church will I sing *p.*
13:15 let us offer sacrifice of *p.*
1 Pet. 1:7 might be found to *p.*
2:14 for *p.* of them that do well
4:11 to whom be *p.* for ever

PRAISE, Verb.

Gen. 49:8 he whom breth. sh. *p.*
Lev. 19:24 fruit holy to *p.* Lord
1 Chr. 29:13 *p.* thy glorious name
2 Chr. 8:14 Lev. to *p.* bef. prie.
20:21 sho. *p.* beauty of holiness
31:2 *p.* in gates of tents of L.
Ps. 21:13 so will we sing and *p.*
22:23 ye that fear Lord *p.* him
30:9 shall the dust *p.* thee?
42:5 I shall yet *p.* him, 11 ; 43:5
44:8 in G. we boast, *p.* name
45:17 there. shall people *p.* thee
49:18 men *p.* thee, wh. doest w.
63:3 lips sh. *p.* thee ; 5 mou. *p.*
67:3 let peop. praise th. 5 pe. *p.*
69:34 heaven and earth *p.* him
71:14 I will yet *p.* thee more
74:21 poor and needy *p.* name
76:10 wrath of man sh. *p.* thee
88:10 sh. dead arise and *p.* th. ?
89:5 heavens sh. *p.* thy wonders
99:3 let them *p.* thy great name
107:32 *p.* him in assem. of elders
113:1 *p.* him, O serv. of L. 135:1
115:17 dead *p.* not the Lord
119:164 seven ti. a day I *p.* thee
175 let my soul live, it sh. *p.*
138:2 I will *p.* thy name for thy

4 kings of earth shall *p.* thee
Ps. 142:7 br. out of pris. that I *p.*
145:4 genera. sh. *p.* thy works
10 thy works shall *p.* thee, O
147:12 *p.* L. Jeru. *p.* G. O Zion
148:1 *p.* ye L. *p.* him in heights
2 *p.* him, angels, *p.* him, host
3 *p.* sun and moon, *p.* ye stars
4 *p.* him, ye heaven of heavens
149:3 let them *p.* name in dance
150:1 *p.* G. in sanctu. *p.* him in
2 *p.* him for his acts, *p.* him
3 *p.* with trump ; 4 *p.* timbrel
5 *p.* him on sounding cymbals
Prov. 27:2 let anot. man *p.* thee
28:4 forsake the law *p.* wicked
31:31 let her own works *p.* her
Is. 38:18 grave cannot *p.* thee
19 the living he shall *p.* thee
Jer. 31:7 *p.* ye and say, O Lord
Dan. 2:23 I thank and *p.* thee
4:37 I *p.* and extol K. of heaven
Joel 2:26 *p.* the name of the Lord
Luke 19:37 disci. began to *p.* G.
1 Cor. 11:2 *p.* you, that ye reme.
17 in this I *p.* you not, 22
Rev. 19:5 saying, *p.* our God

I will, or will I PRAISE.

Gen. 29:35 Leah said, *I will p.*
Ps. 7:17 *I will p.* the Lord
9:1 *I w. p.* thee, 111:1 ; 138:1
22:22 in congrega. *w. I p.* thee
28:7 with my song *w. I p.* him
35:18 *I w. p.* am. much people,
57:9 ; 108:3 ; 109:30
43:4 on harp *will I p.* thee, O G.
52:9 *I will p.* thee for ever
54:6 *I w. p.* thy name, O Lord
56:4 in G. *w. I p.* his word, 10
69:30 *I w. p.* the name of God
71:22 *I w. p.* thee with psaltery
86:12 *I w. p.* thee, O L. my God
118:19 *I w.* go into them, *p.* L.
21 *I w. p.* thee, thou heard me
28 thou art my God, *I w. p.* th.
119:7 *I w. p.* thee with uprigh.
139:14 *I w. p.* thee I am wond.
145:2 *I w. p.* thy name for ever
Is. 12:1 *I w. p.* thee though thou
25:1 *I w. p.* thy name

PRAISE ye the Lord, or PRAISE the Lord.

Jud. 5:2 *p.* ye t. L. for aven. Isr.
1 Chr. 16:4 appoi. Lev. to *p. t. L.*
25:3 with a harp to *p. the L.*
2 Chr. 20:21 *p. t. L.* for his mer.
Ezr. 3:10 cymbals to *p. t. L.*
Ps. 22:26 sh. *p. t. L.* seek him
32:2 *p. t. L.* with harp
102:18 peo. created shall *p. t. L.*
104:35 *p. ye the* L. 166:1. 48 ;
111:1 ; 112:1 ; 113:1. 9 ; 115:18 ;
116:19 ; 117:2 ; 135:1 ; 146:1.
10 ; 147:20 ; 148:1. 14 ; 149:1,
9 ; 150:1. 6 ; *Jer.* 20:13
107:8 O that men would *p. t. L.*
15, 21, 31
109:30 I will greatly *p. t. Lord*
118:19 I will *p. L.* 135:3 *p. Lord*
146:2 while I live will *p. t. L.*
147:1 *p. ye the L.* for it is good
12 *p. t. L.* O Jerus. praise God
148:7 *p. t. L.* from the earth
Is. 12:4 *p. t. L.* call upon name
62:9 shall eat it, and *p. t. L.*
Jer. 33:11 *p. the Lord* of hosts
Rom. 15:11 *p. t. L.* all ye Gentil.

PRAISED.

Jud. 16:24 people *p.* Dagon
2 Sam. 14:25 none to be so m. *p.*
22:4 worthy to be *p. Ps.* 18:3
1 Chr. 16:25 L. is greatly to be *p.*
Ps. 48:1 ; 96:4 ; 145:3
36 all the people *p.* the Lord
23:5 four thousand *p.* the Lord,
2 Chr. 7:3 ; *Neh.* 5:13

2 *Chr.* 5:13 with instrum. *p.* L.
7:6 David *p.* by their ministry
30:21 Levites and priests *p.* L.
Ezr. 3:11 shout when th. *p.* L.
Ps. 72:15 daily shall he be *p.*
113:3 from rising of sun L. be *p.*
Prov. 31:30 feareth L. sh. be *p.*
Ec. 4:2 I *p.* dead more than liv.
Cant. 6:9 queens and concu. *p.*
Is. 64:11 wh. our fathers *p.* thee
Dan. 4:34 I *p.* and honored him
5:4 they *p.* the gods of gold, 23
Luke 1:64 and Zacharias *p.* God

PRAISES.
Ex. 15:11 who is like in. in *p.* ?
2 *Sam.* 22:50 sing *p.* to thy name,
Ps. 18:49; 92:1; 135:3
2 *Chr.* 29:30 commanded Lev. to
sing *p.* to Lord, they sang *p.*
Ps. 9:11 sing *p.* to the Lord in Z.
22:3 O thou that inhabitest *p.*
Ps. 27:6 yea, I will sing *p.* to G.
47:6; 68:32; 75:9; 108:3
47:7 sing *p.* with understanding
56:12 render *p.* to thee, 144:9
68:4 sing to G. *p.* to his name
78:4 to genera. to come *p.* of L.
146:2 I will sing *p.* to my God
147:1 good to sing *p.* to our G
149:3 sing *p.* to him with timb.
6 let *p.* of God be in mouths
Is. 60:6 show forth *p.* of the L.
63:7 I will mention *p.* of Lord
Acts 16:25 Paul and Silas sang *p*
1 *Pet.* 2:9 show forth *p.* of him

PRAISETH.
Prov. 31:28 her husb. also, *p.* her

PRAISING.
2 *Chr.* 5:13 sound heard in *p.* L.
23:12 Athaliah heard people *p.*
Ezr. 3:11 they sang in *p.* Lord
Ps. 84:4 will be still *p.* thee
Luke 2:13 heavenly host *p.* God
20 shepherds returned *p.* God
24:53 contin. in temple *p.* God
Acts 2:47 eat with gladn. *p.* G.
3:8 and leaping, and *p.* God, 9

PRANCING, S.
Jud. 5:22 broken by means of *p.*
Nah. 3:2 the noise of *p.* horses

PRATING.
Prov. 10:8 a *p.* fool shall fall. 10
3 *John* 10 *p.* ag. us with malicio.

PRAY.
Gen. 20:7 he shall *p.* for thee
1 *Sam.* 7:5 S. said, I will *p.* for y.
12:19 *p.* for thy servants to L.
23 I should sin in ceasing to *p.*
2 *Sam.* 7:27 in his heart to *p.*
1 *K.* 8:30 when they *p.* 35, 42, 44,
48; 2 *Chr.* 6:26, 34, 38
13:6 *p.* th. my hand be restored
2 *Chr.* 6:24 *p.* make supplica. 32
37 *p.* in land of their captivity
7:14 if my people shall *p.*
Ezr. 6:10 *p.* for life of the king
Neh. 1:6 hear prayer which I *p.*
Job 21:15 profit if we *p.* to him?
33:26 *p.* to G. he will be favor.
42:8 serv. Job shall *p.* for you
Ps. 5:2 my God, to thee will I *p.*
55:17 morn. and noon will I *p.*
122:6 *p.* for peace of Jerusalem
Is. 16:12 come to sanctuary to *p.*
45:20 *p.* to a god cannot save
Jer. 7:16 therefore *p.* not thou
for this people, 11:14; 14:11
29:7 peace of city, *p.* to Lord
12 *p.* to me, and I will hearken
37:3 *p.* now to the L. your God
42:4 *p.* to the L. your God
Zec. 7:2 sent men to *p.* before L.
8:21 speedily *p.* before Lord, 22
Mat. 5:44 *p.* for them which de-
spitefully use, *Luke* 6:27

6:5 for they love to *p.* standing
6 *p.* to Father which is in sec.
9 after this manner *p.* ye
9:38 *p.* L. of harvest, *Luke* 10:2
14:23 he went to a mount. to *p.*
Mark 6:46 ; *Luke* 6:12; 9:28
19:13 put hands on them and *p.*
24:20 *p.* your flight be not in
winter, *Mark* 13:18
26:36 go *p.* yonder, *Mark* 14:32
41 watch and *p.* *Mark* 13:33.
14:38; *Luke* 21:36 ; 22:40, 46
53 think. thou that I cannot *p.*
Mark 5:17 and they began to *p.*
11:24 what ye desire when ye *p.*
Luke 11:1 Lord. teach us to *p.*
2 he said to them. When ye *p.*
18:1 men ought always to *p.*
10 two men went to tem. to *p.*
John 14:16 I will *p.* Fath. 16:26
17:9 I *p.* for th. *p.* not for world
15 I *p.* not that thou take them
20 nor *p.* I for these alone
Acts 8:22 *p.* God if perh. thought
24 Simon said, *p.* ye to the L.
10:9 P. went on house-top to *p.*
Rom. 8:26 kn. not what we *p.* for
1 *Cor.* 11:13 wom. *p.* uncovered ?
14:3 let him *p.* that he interpr.
14 if I *p.* in unknown tongue
15 *p.* with sp. *p.* with underst.
2 *Cor.* 5:20 ambassa. for C. we *p.*
13:7 I *p.* to G. that ye do no ev.
Phil. 1:9 this I *p.* that your love
Col. 1:9 we do not cease to *p.*
1 *Thes.* 5:17 *p.* without ceasing
23 I *p.* G. your sp. be preserv.
25 brethren, *p.* for us, 2 *Thes.*
3:1 ; *Heb.* 13:18
2 *Thes* 1:1 ; we *p.* always for you
1 *Tim.* 2:8 I will that men *p.*
1 *Tim.* 4:16 I *p.* God it be not l.
Jam. 5:13 any afflicted ? let hi. *p.*
14 and let them *p.* over him
16 confess your faults, and *p.*
1 *John* 5:16 I do not say he sh. *p.*

PRAYED.
Gen. 20:17 Abraham *p.* to
Num. 11:2 Mo. *p.* fire quenched
21:7 M. *p.* for people, *Deut.* 9:26
Deut. 9:20 I *p.* for Aa. same time
1 *Sam.* 1:10 Hannah *p.* to L. 21
27 for this child I *p.* 8:6 Sam.
2 *K.* 4:33 Elisha *p.* 6:17, 18
19:15 Hezekiah *p.* before Lord
20:2 ; 2 *Chr.* 30:18 ; 32:24
2 *Chr.* 32:20 Isaiah *p.* 33:13 Ma.
Job 42:10 captivity when Job *p.*
Jer. 32:16 Jeremiah *p.* unto L.
Dan. 6:10 D. *p.* 3 ti. a day, 9:4
Jon. 2:1 Jonah *p.* to L. 4:2
Mat. 26:39 he fell and *p.* 42:44;
Mark 14:35, 39 ; *Luke* 22:41
Mark 1:35 solitary place and *p.*
Luke 5:3 Jesus *p.* him he would
16 withdrew into wilde. and *p.*
9:29 as he *p.* countenance alter.
18:11 the Pharisee stood and *p.*
22:32 I *p.* that thy faith fail not
44 agony he *p.* more earnestly
John 4:31 his disciples *p.* him
Acts 1:24 the disciples *p.* and sa.
4:31 when they had *p.* the place
8:15 Peter and John *p.* for them
9:40 Peter *p.* 10:2 Cornel. *p.* 30
10:48 then they *p.* him to tarry
13:3 had fasted and *p.* 14:23
16:9 *p.* him, saying, Come to M.
25 at midnight Paul and S. *p.*
20:36 Paul kneeled down and *p.*
21:5 we kneeled on shore and *p.*
22:17 while I *p.* in the temple
28:8 to whom P. entered and *p.*
Jam. 5:17 E. *p.* it mi. not rain, 18

PRAYER.
2 *Sam.* 7:27 pray this *p.* to thee
1 *K.* 8:28 respect *p.* of thy serv.

45 hear thou in heaven their *p.*
49 ; 2 *Chr.* 6:35, 39, 40
54 made end of praying this *p.*
2 *K.* 19:4 *p.* for remnant, *Is.* 37:4
2 *Chr.* 7:15 ears be attent to *p.*
30:27 their *p.* came to dwelling
33:18 Manasseh's *p.* how G. 19
Neh. 1:6 thou mayest hear the *p.*
4:9 nevertheless we made our *p.*
Job 15:4 yea, thou restrainest *p.*
22:27 shalt make thy *p.* to him
Ps. 65:2 O thou that hearest *p.*
72:15 *p.* shall be made for him
80:4 how long be angry ag. *p.*?
102:17 he will regard *p.* of desti.
109:4 but I gave myself unto *p.*
7 and let his *p.* become sin
Prov. 15:8 *p.* of upri. is delight
29 heareth the *p.* of righteous
28:9 his *p.* shall be abomination
Is. 26:16 poured out a *p*
56:7 joyfully in my house of *p.*
for my house shall be called
a house of *p.* *Mat.* 21:13;
Mark 11:17 ; *Luke* 19:46
Jer. 7:16 lift up cry nor *p.* 11:14
Lam. 3:44 *p.* should not pass
Dan. 9:3 set face to L. seek by *p.*
17 God, hear *p.* of thy servant
Hab. 3:1 a *p.* of Ha. the prophet
Mat. 17:21 not out but by *p.* and
fasting, *Mark* 9:29
Luke 1:13 Zacharias, thy *p.* hea.
Acts 3:1 temple at hour of *p.*
6:4 we will give ourselves to *p.*
10:31 Cornelius, thy *p.* is heard
12:5 *p.* made without ceasing
16:13 *p.* was wont be made
1 *Cor.* 7:5 give yourselves to *p.*
2 *Cor.* 1:11 helping by *p.* for us
9:14 by their *p.* for you, which
Eph. 6:18 praying with all *p.*
Phil. 1:4 in every *p.* of mine
19 turn to my salvat. thro' *p.*
4:6 by *p.* let requests be known
1 *Tim.* 4:5 it is sanctified by *p.*
Jam. 5:15 *p.* of faith shall save
16 *p.* of a righteous man avail.
1 *Pet.* 4:7 be sober, watch un. *v.*

See **HEARD.**

In PRAYER.
Neh. 11:17 Mattan. began *in p.*
Dan. 9:21 I was speaking *in p.*
Mat. 21:22 whate. ye ask *in p.*
Luke 6:12 contin. all night *in p.*
Acts 1:14 they continued *in p.*
Rom. 12:12 contin. instant *in p.*
Col. 4:2 continue *in p.* watch

My PRAYER.
Job 16:17 in mine hands: also
my p. is pure
Ps. 4:1 have mercy, hear *my p.*
17:1 ; 39:12 ; 54:2
5:3 in morn. will I direct *my p.*
6:9 the Lord will receive *my p.*
35:13 *my p.* returned to bosom
42:8 *my p.* to God of my life
55:1 give ear unto *my p.* O God
61:1 attend to *my p.* 64:1 ; 84:8 ;
86:6 ; 102:1 ; 143:1
66:19 attended to voice of *my p.*
20 God hath not turned *my p.*
69:13 *my p.* is to thee
88:2 let *my p.* come before th.
13 in morn. sh. *my p.* prev. th.
141:2 let *my p.* be set bef. thee
5 *my p.* shall be in their calam.
Lam. 3:8 he shutteth out *my p.*
Jon. 2:7 *my p.* came to thee
Rom. 10:1 *my p.* to G. for Is. is

PRAYERS.
Ps. 72:20 *p.* of David are ended
Is. 1:15 when ye make many *p.*
Mat. 23:14 for pretence making
long *p.* *Mark* 12:40 ; *Luke*
20:47

PRAYERS

Luke 2:37 Anna continued in *p.*
5:33 disciples of John make *p. ?*
Acts 2:42 breaking bread, and *p.*
10:4 thy *p.* are come up bef. G.
Rom. 1:9 I make mention of you
  in my *p. Eph.* 1:16 ; 1 *Thes.*
  1:2 ; 2 *Tim.* 1:3 ; *Phile.* 4.
15:30 strive with me in your *p.*
Col. 4:12 Epaphras labor. in *p.*
1 *Tim.* 2:1 I exh. that *p.* be made
5:5 widow indeed continu. in *p.*
Phile. 22 thro' your *p.* be given
Heb. 5:7 when he had offered *p.*
1 *Pet.* 3:7 that your *p.* be not
  12 his ear is open to their *p.*
Rev. 5:8 which are *p.* of saints
  8:3 offer it with *p.* of saints, 4

PRAYEST.

Mat. 6:5 when thou *p.* be not, 6.

PRAYETH, ING.

1 *Sam.* 1:12 as Hannah contin. *p.*
1 *K.* 8:28 hearken to prayer wh.
  thy servant *p.* 2 *Chr.* 6:19, 20
Is. 44:17 he worshippeth it, *p.*
Dan. 6:11 these found Daniel *p.*
9:20 I was speaking, and *p.*
Mark 11:25 when ye stand *p.*
Luke 1:10 people were *p.* with.
3:21 Jes. *p.* the heaven opened
9:18 as he was alone *p.*
  11:1 he was *p.* in certain place
Acts 9:11 beh. he *p.* 11:5 I was *p.*
12:12 many were together *p.*
1 *Cor.* 11:4 every man *p.* with his
  14:14 my spirit *p.* but my und.
Eph. 6:18 *p.* always in the Spirit
Col. 1:3 *p.* for you ; 4:3 *p.* for us
1 *Thes.* 3:10 night and day *p.*
Jude 20 ye *p.* in the Holy Ghost

PREACH.

Neh. 6:7 appoint. prophets to *p.*
Is. 61:1 hath anointed me to *p.*
Jon. 3:2 *p.* to it preaching I bid
Mat. 4:17 Jr. that Je. began to *p.*
10:27 what ye hear, that *p.* upon
  11:1 he departed thence to *p.*
Mark 1:4 John did *p.* baptism
3:14 send th. forth to *p. Luke* 9:2
Luke 4:18 to *p.* deliverance, 19
9:60 go and *p.* kingdom of God
Acts 5:42 ceased not to *p.* J. C.
10:42 he commanded us to *p.*
15:21 in every city them that *p.*
16:6 forbidden by H. Ghost to *p.*
17:3 Je. whom I *p.* to you is C.
Rom. 10:8 word of faith wh. we *p.*
  15 how shall they *p.* exc. sent ?
1 *Cor.* 1:23 we *p.* Christ crucified
9:16 tho' I *p.* the gospel, I have
  noth. to glory, woe if I *p.* not
15:11 so we *p.* so ye believed
2 *Cor.* 4:5 we *p.* not ourselves
Gal. 2:2 the gospel which I *p.*
5:11 breth. if I yet *p.* circumci.
Eph. 3:8 I should *p.* am. Gent.
Phil. 1:15 some indeed *p.* Christ
  16 one *p.* Christ of contention
Col. 1:28 we *p.* warning every
2 *Tim.* 4:2 *p.* the word, be inst.

PREACHED.

Ps. 40:9 I have *p.* righteousness
Mat. 11:5 poor have the gospel *p.*
Mark 1:7 John *p.* saying, There
  39 he *p.* in their synagogues
2:2 he *p.* the word to them
6:12 *p.* that men should repent
16:20 went and *p.* every where
Luke 3:18 many others thi. *p.* he
16:16 the kingdom of God is *p.*
24:47 remission of sin sho. be *p.*
Acts 3:20 J. C. who before was *p.*
4:2 *p.* thro' J. the resurrection
8:5 *p.* C. to Samaria ; 35 *p.* Jes.
  25 *p.* the word of L. *p.* ospel
40 Philip *p.* in all cities till he
9:20 Saul *p.* C. in synagogues

10:37 baptism which John *p.*
13:5 they *p.* the word of God
  24 when John had first *p.* bef.
38 *p.* to you forgiveness of sins
  42 that th. words might be *p.*
15:36 let us visit wh. we ha. *p.*
17:13 word of G. was *p.* of Paul
  18 he *p.* J. and the resurrect.
20:7 Paul *p.* ready to depart
1 *Cor.* 9:27 lest wh. I *p.* to others
15:2 keep in memory what I *p.*
  12 if C. be *p.* that he rose
2 *Cor.* 1:19 J. who was *p.* am. you
11:4 Jes. whom we have not *p.*
Gal. 1:8 oth. gospel th. we ha. *p.*
Eph. 2:17 and *p.* peace to you
Phil. 1:18 Christ is *p.* I rejoice
Col. 1:23 was *p.* to every creature
1 *Tim.* 3:1 *p.* unto the Gentiles
Heb. 4:2 word *p.* did not profit
  6 they to whom it was first *p.*
1 *Pet.* 3:19 *p.* to spirits in prison

See GOSPEL.

PREACHER.

Ec. 1:1 words of *p.* son of David
  12 I the *p.* was king over Isr.
12:9 because *p.* was wise
  10 the *p.* sought to find words
Rom. 10:14 hear without a *p. ?*
1 *Tim.* 2:7 ord. a *p.* 2 *Tim.* 1:11
2 *Pet.* 2:5 Noah, *p.* of righteous.

PREACHEST, ETH, ING.

Jon. 3:2 preach to it the *p.* I bid
Mat. 3:1 came John *p. Luke* 3:3
12:41 at *p.* of Jonas, *Luke* 11:32
Luke 8:1 *p.* and showing tidings
9:6 through towns *p.* the gospel
Acts 8:4 went every where *p.*
  12 *p.* concern. kingdom of G.
10:36 *p.* peace by Jesus Christ
11:19 *p.* word to none but Jews
19:13 by Jesus, whom Paul *p.*
20:9 as P. was long *p.* Eutychus
25 among wh. I have gone *p.*
28:31 *p.* the kingdom of God
Rom. 2:21 *p.* a man sho. not steal
16:25 according to *p.* of Jesus
1 *Cor.* 1:18 *p.* of cross is foolish.
  21 by foolishness of *p.* to save
2:4 my *p.* was not with enticing
15:14 if C. not risen, our *p.* vain
2 *Cor.* 10:14 come to you *p.* gos.
11:4 cometh *p.* another Jesus
Gal. 1:23 he *p.* faith he destroyed
2 *Tim.* 4:17 by me *p.* might be
Tit. 1:3 manif. his word thro' *v.*

PRECEPT, S.

Neh. 9:14 commandedst them *p.*
Ps. 119:4 com. us to keep thy *p.*
  15 I will meditate in thy *p.* 78
27 make me to understand *p.*
40 I have longed after thy *p.*
45 seek *p.* 87 forsook not *p.*
56 bec. I kept thy *p.* 100, 168
63 I will keep thy *p.* 69, 134
93 I will never forget thy *p*
94 I have sought thy *p.*
104 thro' thy *p.* I get underst.
110 yet I erred not from thy *p.*
128 theref. I esteem all thy *p.*
141 yet do not I forget thy *p.*
159 consider how I love thy *p.*
173 I have chosen thy *p.*
Is. 28:10 *p.* upon *p.* on *p.* 13
29:13 fear taught by *p.* of men
Jer. 35:18 ye kept all Jonad. *p.*
Dan. 9:5 rebelled, dep. fr. thy *p.*
Mark 10:5 he wrote you this *p.*
Heb. 9:19 Moses had spok. ev. *p.*

PRECIOUS.

Gen. 24:53 to R.'s mother *p.* thi.
Deut. 33:13 for *p.* things of heav.
  14 for *p.* fruits brought forth
15 for the *p.* things of the hills
16 for *p.* things of the earth
1 *Sam.* 3:1 word of Lord was *p.*

26:21 my soul *p.* in thine eyes
2 *K.* 1:13 let my life be *p.* 14
20:13 Hezekiah showed them *p.*
  things, *Is.* 39:2
2 *Chr.* 20:25 and *p.* jewels, which
21:3 Jehoshaphat gave *p.* thin
Ezr. 1:6 streng. with *p.* things
Job 28:10 seeth every *p.* thing
  16 cannot be val. with *p.* onyx
Ps. 49:8 redemption of soul is *p.*
72:14 and *p.* shall their blood be
116:15 *p.* in sight of L. is death
120:6 goeth forth bear. *p.* seed
133:2 it is like the *v.* ointment
Ps. 139:17 how *p.* thy thoughts
Prov. 1:13 sh. find *p.* substance
3:15 wis. is more *p.* than rubies
6:26 adulteress hunt for *p.* life
12:27 subst. of a dili. man is *p.*
20:15 lips of knowl. a *p.* jewel
24:4 cham. filled with *p.* riches
Ec. 7:1 a g. name bet. th. *p.* oin.
Is. 13:12 man more *p.* than gold
28:16 I lay in Zion a *p.* corner-
  stone, 1 *Pet.* 2:6
43:4 thou wast *p.* in my sight
Jer. 15:19 take *p.* from the vile
20:5 I will deliver the *p.* things
Lam. 4:2 the *p.* sons of Zion
Ezek. 22:25 ha. taken *p.* things
27:20 merchant in *p.* clothes
Dan. 11:8 carry away th. *p.* ves.
43 power over all *p.* things
Jam. 5:7 waiteth for the *p.* fruit
1 *Pet.* 1:7 more *p.* than gold
  19 but with *p.* blood of Christ
2:4 stone chosen of God, and *p.*
  7 to you which believe he is *p.*
2 *Pet.* 1:1 obtained like *p.* fruit.
  4 exceed. great and *p.* prom.
Rev. 18:12 no man buyeth *p.* ves.
21:11 light was like a stone *p.*

PREDESTINATE, ED.

Rom. 8:29 did foreknow. did *p.*
  30 wh. he did *p.* them he call.
Eph. 1:5 hav. *p.* us to adoption
  11 *p.* according to purpose

PRE-EMINENCE.

Ec. 3:19 man hath no *p.* above
Col. 1:18 that he might have *p.*
3 *John* 9 Diot. loveth to have *p.*

PREFER, ED, ING.

Est. 2:9 *p.* her and her maidens
Ps. 137:6 if I *p.* not J. above joy
Dan. 6:3 Daniel was *p.* ab. pres.
John 1:15 com. after me is *p.* 27
  30 who is *p.* before me
Rom. 12:10 in honor *p.* one ano.
1 *Tim.* 5:21 without *p.* one bef.

PREMEDITATE.

Mark 13:11 neither *p.* whatsoev.

PREPARATION, S.

1 *Chr.* 22:5 I will make *p.* for it
Prov. 16:1 *p.* of heart of man
Nah. 2:3 torches in day of *p.*
Mat. 27:62 day that followed the
  day of *p. Mark* 15:42 ; *Luke*
  23:54 ; *John* 19:14, 31, 42
Eph. 6:15 shod with *p.* of gospel

PREPARE

Ex. 15:2 I will *p.* him a habitat.
Num. 15:5 a drink-offering *p.*
  12 accor. to number ye sh. *p.*
23:1 B. said, *p.* me seven oxen
  29 build altars, *p.* 7 bullocks
Deut. 19:3 shalt *p.* thee a way
Jos. 1:11 *p.* your victuals
22:26 let us *p.* to build altar
1 *Sam.* 7:3 *p.* your hearts to L.
1 *Chr.* 9:32 to *p.* show-bread
29:18 O L. God, *p.* their heart
2 *Chr.* 2:9 *p.* timber in abund.
35:6 sanctify yourselves, and *p.*
Job 8:8 *p.* thyself to the search
11:13 *p.* thy heart toward him
27:16 *p.* raiment ; 17 may *p.* it

Ps. 10:17 thou wilt *p.* their heart
59:4 *p.* themselves with. fault
61:7 O *p.* mercy and truth
107:36 that they may *p.* a city
Prov. 24:27 *p.* thy work without
30:25 *p.* their meat in summer
Is. 14:21 *p.* slaugh. for children
21:5 *p.* table, watch in tower
40:3 *p.* ye the way of the Lord;
   Mal. 3:1; *Mat.* 3:3; *Mark*
   1:2, 3; *Luke* 1:76
20 workman to *p.* grav. image
57:14 say, Cast ye up, *p.* way
62:10 *p.* ye way of the people
65:11 *p.* a table for that troop
Jer. 6:4 *p.* ye war against her
12:3 *p.* them for day of slaugh.
22:7 I will *p.* destroyers
46:14 say ye, Stand fast and *p.*
51:12 set watchm. *p.* ambushes
Ezek. 4:15 th. shalt *p.* thy bread
12:3 *p.* thee stuff for removing
35:6 I will *p.* thee to blood
38:7 *p.* for thyself, thou and all
45:17 prince sh. *p.* sin-offering
   24 *p.* a meat-offering, 46:7, 14
46:15 *p.* lamb and meat-offering
Joel 3:9 *p.* war; *Amos* 4:12 *p.* meet
Mic. 3:5 they *p.* war against him
Mat. 11:10 shall *p.* way bef. thee
26:17 where wilt thou th. we *p.*
   Mark 14:12; *Luke* 22:8, 9
Luke 3:4 *p.* ye way of L. 7:27
John 14:2 I go to *p.* place, **3**
1 *Cor.* 14:8 who shall *p.* to bat. ?
Phile. 22 *p.* me also a lodging

PREPARED.

Gen. 24:31 I *p.* house and room
Ex. 12:39 neither *p.* any victual
23:20 br. thee to place I have *p.*
Num. 23:4 I have *p.* seven altars
2 *Sam.* 15:1 Absalom *p.* chariots
1 *K.* 6:19 the oracle he *p.* in ho.
1 *Chr.* 15:1 Da. *p.* a place for ark
   of God, 3, 12; 2 *Chr.* 1:4; 3:1
22:3 David *p.* iron in abundance
5 Dav. *p.* abund. bef. 14; 29:2
2 *Cor.* 8:16 work of Solo. was *p.*
12:14 Reho. *p.* not his heart
19:3 Jehoshaphat *p.* his heart
20:33 peo. had not *p.* th. heart
26:14 Uz. *p.* shields and spears
27:6 Jotham *p.* his ways bef. L.
29:19 vessels A. cast away we *p.*
   36 rejoiced G. had *p.* the peo.
31:11 *p.* chamb. in house of L.
35:20 when Josiah had *p.* tem.
Ezr. 7:10 Ezra had *p.* his heart
Neh. 5:18 which was *p.* for me
8:10 them for wh. nothing is *p.*
Est. 5:4 banq. I have *p.* 12; 6:14
6:4 Mordecai on gallows *p.* 7:10
Job 28:27 he *p.* it and searched it
29:7 when I *p.* my seat in street
Ps. 7:13 he *p.* instrum. of death
9:7 hath *p.* his throne for judg.
57:6 they *p.* a net for my steps
68:10 thou hast *p.* good. for poor
74:16 thou hast *p.* light and sun
103:19 the L. hath *p.* his throne
Prov. 8:27 when he *p.* heavens
19:29 judg. are *p.* for scorners
21:31 horse *p.* ag. day of battle
Is. 30:33 Tophet, for king it is *p.*
64:4 nelt. eye seen what he *p.*
Ezek. 23:41 a table *p.* before it
28:13 workmanship of pipes *p.*
38:7 be thou *p.* and pre. thyself
Dan. 2:9 ye have *p.* lying words
Hos. 2:8 silver and gold they *p.*
6:3 going forth *p.* as morning
Jon. 1:17 the L. *p.* great fish
4:6 God *p.* a gourd; 7 *p.* worm
8 God *p.* a vehement east wind
Nah. 2:3 the defence shall he *p.*
Zep. 1:7 Lord hath *p.* a sacrifice
Mat. 20:23 it sh. be given to th.
   for whom it is *p. Mark* 10:40

22:4 I have *p.* my dinner
25:34 kingdom *p.* 41 into fire *p.*
Mark 14:15 a large upp. room *p.*
Luke 1:17 people *p.* for the Lord
2:31 *p.* before face of all people
12:47 knew L.'s will, but *p.* not
23:56 they *p.* spices, 24:1
Rom. 9:23 ves. of mercy afore *p.*
1 *Cor.* 2:9 things God *p.* for them
2 *Tim.* 2:21 *p.* to ev. good work
Heb. 10:5 a body hast thou *p.* me
11:7 Noah *p.* ark to the saving
16 he hath *p.* for them a city
Rev. 8:6 seven angels *p.* to sound
9:7 locusts like hors. *p.* for bat.
15 which were *p.* for an hour
12:6 the woman hath a place *p.*
16:12 kings of east may be *p.*
21:2 holy city *p.* as a bride

PREPAREDST.

Ps. 80:9 thou *p.* room before it

PREPAREST, ETH.

Num. 15:8 wh. thou *p.* a bullock
2 *Chr.* 30:19 *p.* heart to seek G.
Job 15:35 their belly *p.* deceit
Ps. 23:5 *p.* a table before me
65:9 thou *p.* them corn for it
147:8 who *p.* rain for the earth

PREPARING.

Neh. 13:7 *p.* him a chamber
1 *Pet.* 3:20 Noah, wh. ark was *p.*

PRESBYTERY.

1 *Tim.* 4:14 laying on hands of *p.*

PRESCRIBED, ING.

Ezr. 7:22 and salt without *p.*
Is. 10:1 grievous. they have *p.*

PRESENCE.

Gen. 3:8 hid from *p.* of the Lord
4:16 Cain went from *p.* of Lord
27:30 Jacob was scarce from *p.*
45:3 Joseph's bret. troub. at *p.*
47:15 why sho. we die in thy *p.*
Ex. 10:11 driven from Phar. *p.*
33:14 my *p.* sh. go with thee, 15
35:20 Israel depart. fr. *p.* of M.
Lev. 22:3 shall be cut off fr. my *p.*
Num. 20:6 Moses went from *p.*
1 *Sam.* 18:11 David avoided *p.*
19:10 he slipped out of Saul's *p.*
2 *Sam.* 16:19 in thy father's *p.* so
   will I be in thy *p.*
1 *K.* 12:2 Jer. fled fr. *p.* of Solo.
2 *K.* 3:14 regard *p.* of Jehoshap.
5:27 and he went out fr. his *p.*
13:23 nei. cast he them fr. his *p.*
24:20 cast them out from his *p.*
1 *Chr.* 16:27 glory and honor in *p.*
   33 shall tress sing at *p.* of G.
2 *Chr.* 9:23 kings sought *p.* of S.
20:9 stand bef. house in thy *p.*
Neh. 2:1 not been sad in his *p.*
Est. 7:6 Haman was afraid at *p.*
Job 1:12 Sa. went fr. *p.* of L. 2:7
23:15 I am troubled at his *p.*
Ps. 9:3 shall perish at thy *p.*
16:11 in thy *p.* fulness of joy
17:2 sentence come from thy *p.*
31:20 hide th. in secret of thy *p.*
51:11 cast me not away fr. thy *p.*
68:2 wicked perish at *p.* of G.
   8 Sinai moved at the *p.* of G.
95:2 come bef. *p.* with thanks.
97:5 hills melted at the *p.* of G.
100:2 come bef. *p.* with singing
114:7 tremble at *p.* of the Lord
139:7 whither flee from thy *p.* ?
140:13 upright sh. dw. in thy *p.*
Prov. 14:7 go fr. *p.* of a fool. man
Is. 1:7 strangers dev. land in *p.*
19:1 idols of Eg. be moved at *p.*
63:9 angel of his *p.* saved them
64:1 moun. might flow at thy *p.*
2 nations tremble at thy *p.*
3 mountains flowed at thy *p.*

Jer. 4:26 cities broken at *p.* of L.
5:22 will ye not tremble at *p.*
23:39 cast out of my *p.* 52:3
Ezek. 38:20 shall shake at my *p.*
Jon. 1:3 Jonah rose to flee fr. *p.*
   10 men knew he fled fr. *p.* of L.
Nah. 1:5 earth is burnt at his *p.*
Zep. 1:7 hold peace at *p.* of Lord
Luke 13:26 eat. and drunk in *p.*
Acts 3:19 refreshing come fr. *p.*
5:41 departed from *p.* of council
1 *Chr.* 1:29 no flesh sho. gl. in *p.*
2 *Cor.* 10:1 who in *p.* am base
10 but his bodily *p.* is weak
Phil. 2:12 not as in my *p.* only
1 *Thes.* 2:17 taken from you in *p.*
2 *Thes.* 1:9 destruct. fr. *p.* of L.
Jude 24 faultless before *p.*

In the PRESENCE.

Gen. 16:12 dwell *in t. p.* of bret.
23:11 *in the p.* of my people
25:18 Ish. died in *t. p.* of breth.
2 *Sam.* 16:19 I not serve *in the p.*
1 *K.* 8:22 Solomon stood *in the p.*
1 *Chr.* 24:31 cast lots in *t. p.* of D.
Ps. 23:5 a table in *t. p.* of enem.
116:14 in *the p.* of all his peo. 18
Prov. 17:18 *in the p.* of friend
25:6 put not thyself *in the p.*
Jer. 28:1 Hanan. spake *in the p.*
Luke 1:19 stand *in the p.* of God
14:10 worship *in the p.* of them
15:10 joy *in the p.* of ang. of G.
John 20:30 signs did J. *in the p.*
Acts 3:13 deni. him *in t. p.* of P.
   16 given him soundness *in p.*
27:35 gave thanks to G. *in t. p.*
1 *Thes.* 2:19 are not ye *in the p.*
Heb. 9:24 appear *in the p.* of G.
Rev. 14:10 *in p.* of ang. *in p.* of G.

PRESENT, Substantive.

Gen. 32:13 he took a *p.* for E. 18
   21 so went *p.* over before him
33:10 receive my *p.* at my hand
43:11 said, Carry the man a *p.*
   26 brought him the *p.* in hand
Jud. 3:15 Is. sent a *p.* to Eglon
6:18 depart not till I bring *p.*
1 *Sam.* 9:7 th. is not *p.* for man
30:26 a *p.* of spoil of enemies
1 *K.* 9:16 for a *p.* to his daughter
10:25 bro. ev. man *p.* 2 *Chr.* 9:24
15:19 I have sent thee a *p.*
2 *K.* 8:8 the king said, Take a *p.*
17:4 bro. no *p.* to king of Assyr.
18:31 agreem. by a *p. Is.* 36:16
20:12 sent a *p.* to Hez. *Is.* 39:1
Is. 18:7 a *p.* brought to the Lord
Ezek. 27:15 brought a *p.* horns
Hos. 10:6 for a *p.* to king Jareb

PRESENT, Adjective.

1 *Sam.* 13:15 S. numb. people *p.*
2 *Sam.* 20:4 and be thou here *p.*
1 *K.* 20:27 Israel numbered all *p.*
1 *Chr.* 29:17 seen thy people *p.*
2 *Chr.* 30:21 Israel *p.* at Jerusal.
34:32 caused all *p.* to stand to it
Ezr. 8:25 all Israel *p.* offered
Est. 4:16 gather all the Jews *p.*
Ps. 46:1 G. is *p.* help in trouble
Luke 5:17 power of the L. was *p.*
13:1 were *p.* at that season
18:30 rec. more in this *p.* life
John 14:25 I have spok. being *p.*
Acts 10:33 are we all *p.* bef. God
21:18 all the elders were *p.*
Rom. 7:18 to will is *p.* with me
   21 do good, evil is *p.* with me
8:18 sufferings of this *p.* time
   38 nor things *p.* able to separ.
11:5 even at this *p.* time
1 *Cor.* 3:22 things *p.* or to come
4:11 to this *p.* hour we thirst
5:3 *p.* in spirit, as tho' I were *p.*
7:26 this is good for *p.* distress
15:6 greater part rem. to this *p.*

2 *Cor.* 5:8 willing to be *p.* wi. L.
9 that whether *p.* or absent
10:2 I may not be bold when *p.*
11:9 when I was *p.* with you
13:2 if I were *p.* second time
10 I write, lest being *p.*
Gal. 1:4 deliver us fr. *p.* world
4:18 not only when I am *p.*
20 I desire to be *p.* with you
2 *Tim.* 4:10 hav. loved *p.* world
Tit. 2:12 live godly in *p.* world
Heb. 9:9 figure for time then *p.*
12:11 no chastening for the *p.*
2 *Pet.* 1:12 establish. in *p.* truth

PRESENT, ED.

Gen. 46:29 Jos. *p.* himself to fa.
47:2 *p.* 5 brethren to Pharaoh
Ex. 34:2 and *p.* thyself there
Lev. 2:8 when it is *p.* to priest
9:12 Aaron's sons *p.* blood, 18
14:11 priest shall *p.* the man
16:10 the scape-goat shall be *p.*
27:8 bef. priest shall *p.* himself
Num. 3:6 and *p.* the tribe of Le.
Deut. 31:14 *p.* yours. before tab.
Jos. 24:1 *p.* themselves bef. God
Jud. 6:19 Gid. brought and *p.* it
20:2 tribes of Is. *p.* themselves
1 *Sam.* 10:19 *p.* yourselves be. L.
17:16 Goliath the Phil. *p.* hims.
Job 1:6 sons of G. ca. to *p.* them.
2:1 Satan came to *p.* himself
Jer. 36:7 will *p.* their supplicat.
38:26 I *p.* supplication bef. king
42:9 ye sent to *p.* your supplic.
Ezek. 20:28 they *p.* provocation
Dan. 9:18 we do not *p.* supplica.
Mat. 2:11 they *p.* to him gifts
Luke 2:22 bro. him to *p.* to Lord
Acts 9:41 call. saints, *p.* her alive
Rom. 12:1 that ye *p.* your bodies
2 *Cor.* 4:14 raise by Jesus, *p.* us
11:2 that I may *p.* you to Christ
Eph. 5:27 might *p.* it to himself
Col. 1:22 *p.* you holy unblamable
28 ye may *p.* ev. man perfect
Jude 24 him that is able to *p.* y.

PRESENTING.

Dan. 9:20 *p.* my supplica. be. L.

PRESENTLY.

1 *Sam.* 2:16 not fa. to burn fat *p.*
Prov. 12:16 fool's wrath *p.* kno.
Mat. 21:19 *p.* fig-tree withered
26:53 *p.* give more than 12 legi.
Phil. 2:23 him I hope to send *p.*

PRESENTS.

1 *Sam.* 10:27 brought him no *p.*
1 *K.* 4:21 they brought *p.* and
2 *K.* 17:3 Hos. gave Shalman. *p.*
Ps. 68:29 kings shall bring *p.*
72:10 and the isles shall bri. *p.*
76:11 let all bring *p.* to him
Mic. 1:14 give *p.* to Morsheth-g.

PRESERVE.

Gen. 19:32 we may *p.* seed, 34
45:5 send me before you to *p.*
7 G. sent to *p.* you a posterity
Deut. 6:24 he might *p.* us alive
Ps. 12:7 thou shalt *p.* them
16:1 *p.* me, O G. in thee I trust
25:21 let uprightness *p.* me
32:7 shalt *p.* me from trouble
40:11 let thy loving-kind. *p.* me
41:2 L. will *p.* and keep alive
61:7 prepare truth which may *p.*
64:1 hear me, *p.* my life fr. fear
79:11 *p.* th. those th. are to die
86:2 *p.* my soul, for I am holy
121:7 L. *p.* thee, he sh. *p.* soul
8 Lord shall *p.* thy going out
140:1 O L. *p.* me fr. vio. man, 4
Prov. 2:11 discretion shall *p.* th.
4:6 forsake her not, shall *p.* th.
14:3 lips of wise shall *p.* them
20:28 mercy and truth *p.* king
22:12 eyes of Lord *p.* knowledge

Is. 31:5 he will *p.* Jerusalem
49:8 I will *p.* thee and gi. thee
Jer. 49:11 child, I will *p.* alive
Luke 17:33 lose his life sh. *p.* it
2 *Tim.* 4:18 L. will *p.* to his king

PRESERVED, ETH.

Gen. 32:30 God and my life is *p.*
Jos. 24:17 and *p.* us in the way
1 *Sam.* 30:23 Lord who hath *p.*
2 *Sam.* 8:6 L. *p.* D. 1 *Ch.* 18:6, 13
Job 10:12 visitation *p.* my spirit
29:2 in days when God *p.* me
36:6 he *p.* not the life of wicked
Ps. 31:23 the Lord *p.* the faithful
37:28 his saints are *p.* forever
97:10 he *p.* the soul of his saints
116:6 the Lord *p.* the simple
145:20 L. *p.* them that love him
146:9 the Lord *p.* the strangers
Prov. 2:8 he *p.* way of his saints
16:17 keep. his way *p.* his soul
Is. 49:6 to restore the *p.* of Israel
Hos. 12:13 by a proph. was he *p.*
Mat. 9:17 both are *p.* Luke 5:38
1 *Thes.* 5:23 sp. soul. and body *p.*
Jude 1 sanctified, and *p.* in J. C.

PRESERVER.

Job 7:20 O thou P. of men?

PRESERVEST.

Neh. 9:6 L. made and *p.* them all
Ps. 36:6 O L. *p.* man and beast

PRESIDENTS.

Dan. 6:2 over three *p.* Dan. first
3 Daniel was prefer. above *p.*
6 *p.* and princes assembled, 7

PRESS.

Mark 2:4 could not come nigh
for the *p. Luke* 8:19
5:27 came in the *p.* behind him
30 Jesus turn. about in the *p.*
Luke 19:3 Zacch. not see J. for *p.*

PRESS, ES.

Prov. 3:10 *p.* burst with wine
Is. 16:10 tread no wine in th. *p.*
Joel 3:13 for the *p.* is full
Hag. 2:16 fifty vessels out of *p.*
See WINE.

PRESS-FAT.

Hag. 2:16 came to *p.* to draw

PRESS, ED, ETH.

Gen. 19:3 Lot *p.* on two angels
9 they *p.* sore on Lot, near do.
40:11 I took grapes and *p.* them
Jud. 16:16 Delilah *p.* wi. words
2 *Sam.* 13:25 Absalom *p.* him, 27
Est. 8:14 posts *p.* on by com.
Ps. 38:2 thy hand *p.* me sore
Ezek. 23:3 their breasts *p.* bruis.
Amos 2:13 I am *p.* as a cart is *p.*
Mark 3:10 *p.* on to touch him
Luke 5:1 as the people *p.* to hear
6:38 good measure *p.* down
8:45 multit. throng and *p.* thee
16:16 every man *p.* into it
Acts 18:5 Paul was *p.* in spirit
2 *Cor.* 1:8 were *p.* above measure
Phil. 3:14 I *p.* toward the mark

PRESUME, ED.

Deut. 18:20 prophet who shall *p.*
Est. 7:5 is he that durst *p.*
Num. 14:44 but they *p.* to go up

PRESUMPTUOUS.

Ps. 19:13 keep. serv. fr. *p.* sins
2 *Pet.* 2:10 *p.* are they, self-will.

PRESUMPTUOUSLY.

Ex. 21:14 if a man come *p.*
Num. 15:30 aught *p. Deut.* 17:12
Deut. 1:43 went *p.* up into hill
17:13 hear and do no more *p.*
18:22 prophet hath spoken it *p.*

PRETENCE.

Mat. 23:14 for a *p.* make long
prayers, *Mark* 12:40
Phil. 1:18 whether in *p.* or truth

PREVAIL.

Gen. 7:20 15 cubits did waters *p.*
Num. 22:6 peradventure I sh. *p.*
Jud. 16:5 by what means we *p.*
1 *Sam.* 2:9 by str. sh. no man *p.*
17:9 if I *p.* against him
26:25 great things and still *p.*
1 *K.* 22:22 *p.* also, 2 *Chr.* 18:21
Est. 6:13 shalt not *p.* ag. him
Job 15:24 they shall *p.* ag. him
18:9 robber shall *p.* against him
Ps. 9:19 O L. let not man *p.*
12:4 wi. our tongues will *we p.*
65:3 iniquities *p.* against me
Ec. 4:12 if one *p.* against him
Is. 7:1 could not *p.* against it
16:12 M. shall come, but not *p.*
42:13 shall *p.* against enemies
47:12 if so be thou mayest *p.*
Jer. 1:19 they sh. not *p.* ag. thee,
saith the Lord, 15:20 ; 20:11
5:22 waves toss, can they not *p.*
20:10 we shall *p.* against him
Dan. 11:7 deal ag. him and *p.*
Mat. 16:18 gates of hell sh. not *p.*
Mat. 27:24 Pi. saw he could *p.*
John 12:19 perceive ye how ye *p.*

PREVAILED.

Gen. 7:18 waters *p.* and inc. 19
24 waters *p.* on earth 150 days
30:8 I have wrestled and *p.*
32:25 when he saw he *p.* not
28 po. wi. G. and men, hast *p.*
47:20 the famine *p.* over them
49:26 bless. of thy fath. hath *p.*
Ex. 17:11 Israel *p.* Amalek *p.*
Jud. 1:35 hand of house of J. *p.*
2 *Sam.* 11:23 men *p.* against us
24:4 king's word *p.* against J.
2 *K.* 25:3 the famine *p.* in the ci.
1 *Chr.* 5:2 Judah *p.* above breth.
2 *Chr.* 13:18 J. *p.* bec. th. relied
Ps. 13:4 I have *p.* against thee
129:2 have not *p.* against me
Jer. 20:7 stronger than I, and *p.*
38:22 friends *p.* against thee
Lam. 1:16 weep bec. enemy *p.*
Dan. 7:21 sa. horn *p.* ag. saints
Hos. 12:4 power over angel *p.*
Ob. 7 men deceived thee and *p.*
Luke 23:23 voices of chief pr. *p.*
Acts 19:16 in whom evil spirit *p.*
20 mig. grew word of G. and *p.*
Rev. 5:5 root of David hath *p.*
12:8 dragon and his angels *p.*

PREVAILEST, ETH.

Job 14:20 *p.* for ever against him
Lam. 1:13 fire in bones, and it *p.*

PREVENT.

Job 3:12 why did knees *p.* me?
Ps. 59:10 G. of mercy shall *p.* me
79:8 let thy tender mercies *p.*
88:13 in morn. sh. my prayer *p.*
119:148 mine eyes *p.* ni.-watches
Amos 9:10 evil shall not *p.* us
1 *Thes.* 4:15 shall not *p.* them

PREVENTED, EST.

2 *Sam.* 22:6 the snares of death
p. me, *Ps.* 18:5
19 *p.* me in day of ca. *Ps.* 18:18
Job 30:27 days of afflict. *p.* me
41:11 who *p.* that I sho. repay?
Ps. 21:3 *p.* him with blessings
119:147 I *p.* dawning of morn.
Is. 21:14 they *p.* with. th. bread
Mat. 17:25 Jesus *p.* him, saying,
Simon

PREY.

Gen. 49:9 from the *p.* my son
27 in morning he shall dev. *p.*
Num. 14:3 our wives and childr.
sh. be a *p.* ? 31 ; *Deut.* 1:39
23:24 not lie down till eat of *p.*
31:12 captives and *p.* to Moses
27 divide the *p.* in two parts

Deut. 2:35 cattle we took for a *p.*
   3:7 ; *Jos.* 8:2, 27 ; 11:14
Jud. 5:30 div. *p.* a *p.* of divers
   8:24 give me the ear-rings of his *p.*
2 *K.* 21:14 Judah sh. become a *p.*
Neh. 4:4 give them for a *p.*
Est. 3:13 spoil of th. for *p.* 8:11
   9:15 on *p.* laid not hand, 16
Job 4:11 lion peris. for lack of *p.*
   9:26 as eagle that hasteth to *p.*
   24:5 as wild asses rising for *p.*
   38:39 wilt th. hunt *p.* for lion ?
   39:29 from thence she seek. *p.*
Ps. 17:12 a lion greedy of *p.*
   76:4 more ex. than mount. of *p.*
   104:21 young lions roar after *p.*
   124:6 hath not given us for *p.*
Prov. 23:28 *F* oth in wait as for *p.*
Is. 5:29 roar and lay hold of *p.*
   6 take *p.* of a hypocrit. nation
   31:4 young lion roaring on *p.*
   33:23 the *p.* of a great spoil
   42:22 for a *p.* none delivereth
   49:24 sh. *p.* be taken fr. mighty ?
   59:15 from evil mak. hims. a *p.*
Jer. 21:9 his life shall be to him
   for a *p.* 38:2 ; 39:18 ; 45:5
   30:16 and all that *p.* on thee will I give for a *p.*
Ezek. 7:21 give to stran. for a *p.*
   19:3 yo. lion, learned to catch *p.*
   22:27 princes like wol. raven. *p.*
   26:12 make a *p.* of merchandise
   29:19 shall take her spoil and *p.*
   34:8 bec. my flock became a *p.*
   22 flock sh. no more be a *p.* 28
   36:4 to the cities that bec. a *p.*
   38:12 go take spoil and *p.* 13
Dan. 11:24 scatter am. them *p.*
Amos 3:4 lion roar hath no *p.* ?
Nah. 2:12 lions filled holes wi. *p.*
   13 I will cut off thy *p.* fr. earth
   3:1 bloody city, *p.* departeth not
Zep. 3:8 till day I rise up to *p.*

PRICE, S.
Lev. 25:16 according to years in.
   p. to fewness, diminish *p.* 50
   52 shall give him again the *p.*
Deut. 23:18 not bring *p.* of a d.
2 *Sam.* 24:24 I will buy it of thee
   at a *p.* 1 *Chr.* 21:22, 24
Job 28:13 man knoweth not *p.* 15
   18 *p.* of wisdom is above rubi.
Ps. 44:12 not incr. wealth by *p.*
Prov. 17:16 *p.* in hand of fool ?
   27:26 goats are the *p.* of field
   31:10 her *p.* is far above rubies
Is. 45:13 shall let go not for *p.*
   55:1 wine and milk without *p.*
Zec. 11:12 give me *p.* weighed
   13 a goodly *p.* I was prized at
Mat. 13:46 found one pearl of *p.*
   27:6 beca. it is the *p.* of blood
Acts 4:34 brought *p.* of the thin.
   5:2 kept back part of the *p.* 3
   19:19 counted *p.* of books burnt
1 *Cor.* 6:20 bought with a *p.* 7:23
1 *Pet.* 3:4 meek spirit of great *p.*

PRICKED, ING.
Ps. 73:21 I was *p.* in my reins
Ezek. 28:24 be no more a *p.* briar
Acts 2:37 th. were *p.* in th. heart

PRICKS.
Num. 33:55 th. that remain be *p.*
Acts 9:5 kick against the *p.* 26:14

PRIDE.
Lev. 26:19 break *p.* of your pow.
1 *Sam.* 17:28 *p.* and naughtiness
2 *Chr.* 32:26 Hez. humbled for *p.*
Job 33:17 he may hide *p.* fr. man
   35:12 because of *p.* of evil men
   41:15 scales are his *p.* shut up
   34 king over all children of *p.*

Ps. 10:2 wicked in *p.* doth pers.
   4 thro' *p.* of his countenance
   31:20 hide them from *p.* of man
   36:11 let not the foot of *p.* come
   59:12 taken in their *p.*
   73:6 theref. *p.* compasseth them
Prov. 8:13 *p.* I hate ; 11:2 *p.* com.
   13:10 by *p.* cometh contention
   14:3 mouth of fool. is rod of *p.*
   16:18 *p.* goeth before destructi.
   29:23 a man's *p.* bring him low
Is. 9:9 say in *p.* of their hearts
   16:6 have heard of *p.* of M. his
   haughtiness and *p. Jer.* 48:29
   23:9 to stain *p.* of glory
   25:11 shall bring down their *p.*
   28:1 woe to the crown of *p.* 3
Jer. 13:9 I will mar *p.* of Judah
   17 shall weep for your *p.*
   49:16 *p.* of thy heart received
Ezek. 7:10 rod blos. *p.* budded
   16:49 iniqu. of thy sister Sod. *p.*
   56 not mentioned in day of *p.*
   30:6 *p.* of power sh. come down
Dan. 4:37 those that walk in *p.*
   5:20 mind was hardened in *p.*
Hos. 5:15 *p.* of Israel testify, 7:10
Ob. 3 *p.* of thy heart deceived
Zep. 2:10 shall they have for *p.*
   3:11 take away th. rejoice in *p.*
Zec. 9:6 cut off *p.* of Philistines
   10:11 *p.* of Assyria bro. down
   11:3 the *p.* of Jordan is spoiled
Mark 7:22 out of heart proce. *p.*
1 *Tim.* 3:6 being lifted up wi. *p.*
1 *John* 2:16 *p.* of life, not of Fa.

PRIEST.
Gen. 14:18 *p.* of M. High, *Heb.* 7:1
Ex. 2:16 *p.* of M. had seven dau.
Lev. 1:9 *p.* sh. burn it all on the
   altar, 13, 17 ; 2:2, 9, 16 ; 3:11,
   16 ; 4:10 ; 31:35 ; 7:5, 31
   4:6 the *p.* shall dip his finger, 17
   20 *p.* shall make atonement for
   them, 26 ; 5:6 ; 6:7 ; 12:8 ;
   15:15, 30 ; 61:30 ; 19:22
   7:8 *p.* shall have skin of offering
   13:3 *p.* sh. look on plague, 5, 6,
   17, 26, 21, 25, 26, 27, 30, 31, 32
   14:16 *p.* dip his right finger in
   21:9 if daughter of a *p.* profane
   22:11 if *p.* buy any soul
   23:11 *p.* shall wave it before L.
   27:8 *p.* shall value him, accord.
Num. 5:8 tres. recompensed to *p.*
   30 *p.* execute on her this law
   35:32 not dw. till death of h.-*p.*
Deut. 20:2 the *p.* shall approach
Jud. 17:5 one of sons became *p.*
   13 I have Levite to my *p.*
   18:4 Micah hired me, am his *p.*
1 *Sam.* 2:14 the *p.* took himself
   28 did I choose him to be *p.* ?
   35 raise me up a faithful *p.*
   14:36 then said *p.* Draw to God
   21:4 the *p.* answered, no bread
1 *Sam.* 21:6 *p.* gave him h. bread
1 *K.* 2:27 Abiathar from being *p.*
2 *Chr.* 13:9 the same may be a *p.*
   15:3 Israel without teaching *p.*
Ezr. 2:63 stood up *p. Neh.* 7:65
Ps. 110:4 a *p.* for ever after order
   of Melch. *Heb.* 5:6 ; 7:17, 21
Is. 8:2 I took witnesses, Uriah *p.*
   24:2 as with people, so with *p.*
   28:7 the *p.* and prophet erred
Jer. 6:13 to the *p.* every one
   dealeth falsely, 8:10
   14:18 *p.* go to a land they k. not
   18:18 law sh. not perish from *p.*
   23:11 prophet and *p.* are profa.
   33 when a *p.* sh. ask thee, 34
   29:26 Lord made thee *p.*
Lam. 2:6 despis. the king and *p.*
   20 the *p.* and prophet be slain
Ezek. 7:26 law shall perish fr. *p.*
   44:21 nor sh. any *p.* drink wine
   31 *p.* sh. not eat any thing to.

Hos. 4:4 they that strive with *p.*
   6 thou shalt be no *p.* to me
   9 shall be like people like *p.*
Amos 7:10 the *p.* of Bethel sent
Zec. 6:13 shall be *p.* on throne
Mal. 2:7 *p.* lips sho. keep knowl.
Mat. 8:4 go. show thyself to the
   p. Mark 1:44 ; *Luke* 5:14
Luke 1:5 a certain *p.* Zacharias
   10:31 came down a certain *p.*
Acts 14:13 *p.* of Jupiter br. oxen
Heb. 7:3 abideth a *p.* continually
   11 what need another *p.* rise
   15 after Melchizedek aris. a *p.*
   20 without an oath was ma. *p.*
   8:4 he should not be a *p.*
   10:11 ev. *p.* standeth minister.
See CHIEF.

High-PRIEST.
Lev. 21:10 *h.-p.* not uncover head
Num. 35:25 in city of refuge till
   death of *h.-p. Jos.* 20:6
2 *K.* 12:10 money in chest, *h.-p.*
   put it in bags, 2 *Chr.* 24:11
Zec. 3:1 Joshua *h.-p.* 8 ; 6:11
Mal. 26:3 pal. of *h.-p. Luke* 22:54
   57 led him to Caiaphas, the
   h.-p. John 18:24
   26:65 *h.-p.* rent clothes, *Mark* 14:63
Mark 2:26 days of Abiathar, *h.-p.*
John 11:49 Caia. *h.-p.* 51 ; 18:13
   18:15 disciple was kn. to *h.-p.*
Acts 4:6 were of kindred of *h.-p.*
   9:1 Saul went to the *h.-p.*
   22:5 also the *h.-p.* doth witness
   23:4 revilest thou God's *h.-p.* ?
Heb. 2:17 be a faithful *h.-p.*
   3:1 consider apostle *h.-p.*
   4:14 have great *h.-p.* in heaven
   15 *h.-p.* wh. cannot be touched
   5:1 *h.-p.* taken from amo. men
   5 C. glo. not himself to be *h.-p.*
   10 called a *h.-p.* after Me. 6:20
   7:26 such a *h.-p.* became us
   8:1 we have such a *h.-p.* on thr.
   3 every *h.-p.* ordained to offer
   9:7 second, went *h.-p.* alone
   11 a *h.-p.* of good things
   25 the *h.-p.* entereth holy place
   10:21 having a *h.-p.* over house
   13:11 bro. into sanctu. by *h.-p*
See OFFICE.

PRIESTS.
Gen. 47:22 land of *p.* bought not
   26 except land of the *p.* only
Ex. 19:6 to me a kingdom of *p.*
Lev. 1:11 *p.* sprinkle blood, 3:2
   22:10 a sojourner of the *p.*
   23:20 holy to the Lord for the *p.*
Deut. 18:3 this shall be *p.* due
Jos. 3:17 *p.* that bare the ark
   6:4 *p.* bare seven trumpets, 13
Jud. 18:30 he and sons were *p.*
1 *Sam.* 5:5 nor the *p.* of Dagon
   6:2 Philistines called for the *p.*
   22:17 turn and slay *p.* of Lord
   18 turn thou, and fall on the *p.*
1 *K.* 8:3 and *p.* took up the ark
   12:31 Jeroboam made *p.* 13:33
   13:2 on thee sh. he offer the *p.*
2 *K.* 10:11 Jehu slew Ahab's *p.*
   19 call me all Baal's *p.*
   12:6 *p.* had not repaired breach.
   23:5 he put down idolatrous *p.*
2 *Chr.* 4:6 the sea was for the *p.*
   5:12 120 *p.* sounding trumpets
   14 *p.* could not min. for cloud
   6:41 let *p.* be clothed with salv.
   8:14 appointed courses of the *p.*
   13:9 not cast out *p.* of Lord ?
   12 *p.* with trump. to cry alarm
   23:6 came to house of L. save *p.*
   26:19 Uzziah was wroth with *p.*
2 *Chr.* 29:34 but the *p.* were too
   30:3 *p.* had not sancti. themsel.
   34:5 Josiah burnt bones of *p.*
   35:8 gave it to *p.* for offerings

Ezr. 6:18 set *p.* in divisions
20 *p.* killed the passover for *p.*
9:7 *p.* been delivered to kings
Neh. 2:16 nor had I told it to *p.*
3:22 after him repaired the *p.*
9:32 trouble that come on *p.*
34 we nor our *p.* kept thy law
Ps. 78:64 their *p.* fell by sword
99:6 Moses and Aaron among *p.*
132:9 let thy *p.* be clothed with
16 clothe her *p.* with salvation
Is. 37:2 he sent elders of *p.*
61:6 named the *p.* of the Lord
Jer. 1:18 against the *p.* thereof
2:8 *p.* said not, Where is Lord?
26 *p.* ashamed ; 4:9 *p.* aston..
5:31 *p.* bare rule by th. means
8:1 bones of *p.* they shall bring
13:13 fill *p.* with drunkenness
31:14 satiate souls of *p.*
32:32 provoke to anger, their *p.*
48:7 into captivity with *p.* 49:3
Lam. 1:4 her *p.* sigh, her virgins
19 my *p.* gave up the ghost
4:13 iniq. of her *p.* shed blood
16 they respected not the *p.*
Ezek. 22:26 her *p.* viola. my law
40:45 this chamber is for *p.*
Hos. 5:1 hear this, O *p.* hearken
6:9 comp. of *p.* murder in way
Joel 1:9 the *p.* mourn, 13; 2:17
Mic. 3:11 the *p.* teach for hire
Zep. 1:4 cut off names of the *p.*
3:4 *p.* polluted the sanctuary
Hag. 2:11 as *p.* concerning law
Mal. 1:6 you, O *p.* that despise
2:1 *p.* this command. is for you
Mat. 12:4 lawf. only for *p.* to eat
5 *p.* profane sabbath, *Mark*
2:26 ; *Luke* 6:4
Mark 2:26 is not lawful but for *p.*
Luke 17:14 show yourselves to *p.*
Acts 4:1 the *p.* came upon them
6:7 a comp. of *p.* were obedient
Heb. 7:21 *p.* made without oath
23 *p.* not suffered to continue
8:4 seeing there are *p.* that offer
9:6 *p.* went into first tabernacle
Rev. 1:6 made us *p.* to God, 5:10
20:6 sh. be *p.* of God and Christ

See CHIEF, LEVITES, OFFICE.

High-PRIESTS.
Luke 3:2 An. and Ca. were *h.-p.*
Heb. 7:27 not daily as *h.-p.*
28 the law maketh men *h.-p.*

PRIESTHOOD.
Ex. 40:15 everl. *p.* throughout
generations, *Num.* 25:13
Num. 16:10 and seek ye the *p.*
18:1 shall bear iniquity of *p.*
Jos. 18:7 *p.* of L. is their inherit.
Ezr. 2:62 pollu. fr. *p. Neh.* 7:64
Neh. 13:29 defiled *p.* coven. of *p.*
Heb. 7:5 Levi, who receive the *p.*
11 if perfection were by Le. *p.*
12 for the *p.* being changed
14 M. spake nothing conc. **p.**
24 hath an unchangeable *p.*
1 *Pet.* 2:5 a holy *p.* 9 a royal *p.*

PRINCE.
Gen. 23:6 thou art a mighty *p.*
32:28 as *p.* hast thou po. wi. G.
34:2 wh. Shechem *p.* of country
Ex. 2:14 who made thee a *p.*
Num. 16:13 make thyself *p.*
17:6 for each *p.* a rod, twelve
34:18 take one *p.* of every tribe
Jos. 22:14 each chief house a *p.*
2 *Sam.* 3:38 kn. a *p.* not fallen?
1 *K.* 11:34 his days make him *p.*
14:7 made thee *p.* over peo. 16:2
Job 21:28 where is house of *p.* ?
31:37 as a *p.* wo. I go near him
Prov. 14:28 want is dest. of a *p.*
17:7 less do lying lips bec. a *p.*
25:7 lower in presence of the *p.*
15 forbearing is a *p.* persuaded

28:16 *p.* that want. understand.
Cant. 7:1 beautif. thy feet, O *p.*
Is. 9:6 called the P. of peace
Jer. 51:59 Seraiah was a quiet *p.*
Ezek. 7:27 the *p.* shall be clothed
12:10 concerneth *p.* in Jerusal.
12 and *p.* shall bear on should.
21:25 profane, wicked *p.* of Is.
28:2 say to the *p.* of Tyrus
30:13 be no more a *p.* of Egypt
34:24 my servant David, a *p.*
37:25 David sh. be th. *p.* for ev.
38:2 the *p.* of Meshech, 3; 39:1
44:3 gate for *p. p.* shall sit in it
45:17 it sh. be the *p.* part to give
Ezek. 46:2 the *p.* sh. enter by por.
4 offering that the *p.* shall offer
12 when *p.* prepares an offeri.
16 if *p.* give a gift to any sons
18 *p.* shall not take people's in.
48:21 residue shall be for the *p.*
Dan. 1:7 to whom *p.* gave names
8 he requested of *p.* of eunuchs
9 Daniel in favor with the *p.*
6:11 magnifi. himself even to *p.*
8:25 shall stand up against the *p.*
9:25 build unto Messiah the P.
26 people of *p.* that shall come
10:13 the *p.* of Persia withstood
20 *p.* of Persia, *p.* of Gre. come
21 none hold. but Michael *p.*
11:18 but a *p.* for his own beha.
22 also the *p.* of the covenant
12:1 Michael stand up, great *p.*
Hos. 3:4 shall abide without a *p.*
Mic. 7:3 *p.* and judge ask reward
Mat. 9:34 casteth out dev. by *p.*
of devils, 12:24; *Mark* 3:22
John 12:31 the *p.* of this world
14:30 for the *p.* of world cometh
16:11 *p.* of this world is judged
Acts 3:15 killed the P. of life
5:31 him God exalted to be a P.
Eph. 2:2 according to *p.* of air
Rev. 1:5 Jesus Christ P. of kings

PRINCES.
Gen. 12:15 *p.* also of Pharaoh
17:20 *p.* shall Ishm. beget, 25:16
Num. 7:3 for two *p.* 10 *p.* offer.
16:2 rose up 250 *p.* 21:18 *p.* dig.
22:8 and *p.* abode with Balaam
15 Ba. sent *p.* more honorable
Jos. 9:15 *p.* of congrega. sware
13:21 M. smote with *p.* of Mid.
22:14 P. ten *p.* sent to Reuben
Jud. 5:3 give ear, O ye *p.*
15 *p.* of Issachar were with D.
7:25 two *p.* of the Midianites
1 *Sam.* 2:8 to set them among *p.*
29:4 *p.* of Philisti. were wroth
1 *K.* 20:14 by young men of *p.*
1 *Chr.* 4:38 these *p.* in families
28:21 *p.* will be at thy command
2 *Chr.* 28:14 left spoil before *p.*
30:12 do commandments of *p.*
35:8 *p.* gave willingly to people
36:18 treas. of his *p.* to Babylon
Ezr. 7:28 bef. king's mighty *p.*
9:2 hand of *p.* hath been chief
10:8 according to counsel of *p.*
Neh. 9:34 nei. have *p.* kept law
Est. 1:3 feast to all his *p.* 2:18
6:9 of one of the king's noble *p.*
Job 3:15 had been at rest with *p.*
12:19 leadeth *p.* away spoiled
21 he poureth contempt on *p.*
29:9 the *p.* refrained talking
34:18 say to *p.* ye are ungodly ?
19 him that accepteth not *p.*
Ps. 45:16 *p.* in all the earth
47:9 *p.* of people are gathered
68:27 *p.* of Zebulon, *p.* of Nap.
31 *p.* shall come out of Egypt
76:12 he shall cut off spirit of *p.*
82:7 and fall like one of the *p.*
105:22 bind his *p.* at his pleas.
107:40 poureth contempt on *p.*

113:8 set him wi. *p.* even wi. *p.*
118:9 tru. in L. than confi. in *p.*
119:23 *p.* also did speak ag. me
161 *p.* perse. me without cause
146:3 put not your trust in *p.*
148:11 *p.* and judges of earth
Prov. 8:15 *p.* decree; 16 *p.* rule
17:26 it is not good to strike *p.*
19:10 much less a ser. to rule *p.*
28:2 many are the *p.* thereof
31:4 not for *p.* to drink strong
Ec. 10:7 *p.* walking as servants
16 when thy *p.* eat in the mor.
17 blessed art thou, wh. *p.* eat
Is. 1:23 thy *p.* are rebellious
3:4 I will give children to th. *p.*
14 L. enter into judgm. wi. *p.*
10:8 are not my *p.* alto. kings ?
19:11 *p.* of Zoan, *p.* of Noph, 13
21:5 ye *p.* anoint the shield
23:8 whose merchants are *p.*
30:4 his *p.* were at Zoan, amba.
31:9 *p.* shall be afraid of ensign
32:1 *p.* shall rule in judgment
34:12 all her *p.* shall be nothing
40:23 that bringeth *p.* to nothi.
41:25 and he shall come upon *p.*
43:28 I profaned *p.* of sanctuary
49:7 *p.* shall worship bec. of L.
Jer. 1:18 brazen walls ag. the *p.*
2:26 th. kings and *p.* ashamed
4:9 heart of *p.* sh. be astonish.
8:1 shall bring out bones of *p.*
17:25 *p.* sitting on throne of D.
26:16 *p.* said, This man is not
Jer. 32:32 kings and *p.* pro. me
34:21 *p.* I will give to enemies
38:17 if thou go to k. of B. *p.*
48:7 Ch. and *p.* go to capt. 49:3
40:38 I will destroy from the *p.*
50:35 sword on *p.* and wise men
51:57 I will make drunk her *p.*
Lam. 1:6 *p.* become like harts
2:9 kings and *p.* am. Gentiles
5:12 *p.* are hanged by th. hand
Ezek. 22:27 v. like wolves raven.
23:15 dyed attire, all of them *p.*
32:29 Edom and her *p.*
30 the *p.* of the north
39:18 ye shall drink blood of *p.*
45:8 my *p.* no more opp. people
Dan. 3:2 king sent to gather *p.*
6:1 to set over kingdom, 120 *p.*
4 *p.* sought occasion ag. Dani.
8:25 stand ag. the Prince of *p.*
9:8 confusion of face to our *p.*
10:13 Michael one of *p.* came
11:5 one of his *p.* sh. be strong
Hos. 7:3 they make *p.* glad
5 the *p.* have made him sick
16 their *p.* shall fall by sword
8:4 made *p.* and I knew it not
10 shall sorrow for king of *p.*
9:15 all their *p.* are revolters
13:10 Give me a king and *p.*
Amos. 1:15 into captiv. he and *p.*
Mic. 3:1 hear, *p.* of house of Is. 9
Hab. 1:10 the *p.* shall be a scorn
Zep. 1:8 I will punish the *p.*
3:3 *p.* within her are roar. lions
Mat. 20:25 *p.* of Gent. exercise
1 *Cor.* 2:6 nor wisdom of the *p.*
8 none of *p.* of this world

All the PRINCES.
2 *K.* 24:14 carried away *all the p.*
1 *Chr.* 29:24 *all p.* submit. them.
2 *Chr.* 24:23 destroyed *all the p.*
Est. 1:16 done wro. to *all the p.*
3:1 set his seat above *all the p.*
Ps. 83:11 *all* th. *p.* as Zebah and
Jer. 36:21 it in ears of *all the p.*
Ezek. 26:16 *all the p.* of the sea
Amos 2:3 will slay *all the p.*

See ISRAEL.

PRINCES of Judah.
Neh. 12:31 I brought up *p.* of Ju.
Ps. 68:27 there is *p.* of Judah

Jer. 52:10 slew all the *p.* of *Jud.*
Mat. 2:6 not least am. *p. of Jud.*

PRINCESS, ES.
1 *K.* 11:3 Solom. had 700 wiv. *p.*
Lam. 1:1 *p.* among provinces

PRINCIPAL.
Ex. 30:23 take th. also *p.* spices
Lev. 6:5 shall restore it in the *p.*
Num. 5:7 recomp. tresp. with *p.*
1 *K.* 4:5 son of Nathan *p.* officer
2 *K.* 25:19 the *p.* scribe of the host, *Jer.* 52:25
1 *Chr.* 24:6 one *p.* household
31 even *p.* fathers cast lots
Neh. 11:17 Mattaniah *p.* to begin
Prov. 4:7 wisdom is the *p.* thing
Is. 16:8 broken down *p.* plants
28:25 cast in *p.* wheat and barl.
Jer. 25:34 in ashes, ye. of flock
35 nor the *p.* of the flock escape
Mic. 5:5 raise ag. him 8 *p.* me.
Acts 25:23 *p.* of the city entered

PRINCIPALITY, IES.
Jer. 13:18 your *p.* sh. come down
Rom. 8:38 *p.* nor powers able
Eph. 1:21 far above all *p.* power
3:10 to *p.* might be kn. wisdom
6:12 wrestle ag. *p.* and power
Col. 1:16 *p.* were created by him
2:10 head of all *p.* and power
15 having spoiled *p.* he made
Tit. 3:1 mind to be subject to *p.*

PRINCIPLES.
Heb. 5:12 one teach you first *p.*
6:1 *p.* of the doctrine of Chr.

PRINT, ED.
Lev. 19:28 shall not *p.* any mar.
Job 19:23 O that my words were *p.* in a book

PRINT.
Job 13:27 settest a *p.* on heels
John 20:25 exc. I see *p.* of nails, and put my finger into *p.*

PRISCA. 2 *Tim.* 4:19
PRISCILLA. *Acts* 18:2, 26; *Rom.* 16:3; 1 *Cor.* 16:19

PRISON.
Gen. 39:20 Potiph. put Jos. in *p.*
40:3 put butler and baker in *p.*
42:19 bound in house of your *p.*
1 *K.* 22:27 put this fellow in *p.* 2 *Chr.* 18:26
2 *K.* 17:4 bound Hoshea in *p.*
25:29 changed his *p.* garment, *Jer.* 52:31, 33
Neh. 3:25 Palal repaired by *p.*
Ps. 142:7 bring my soul out of *p.*
Ec. 4:14 for out of *p.* he cometh
Is. 24:22 they sh. be shut up in *p.*
42:7 bring out prisoners from *p.*
22 all of them hid in *p.*
53:8 he was taken from *p.*
61:1 proclaim opening of the *p.*
Jer. 32:2 Jeremiah was shut in *p.*
12 before Jews in court of *p.*
33:1 word came to Jerem. while in *p.* 37:21; 38:6, 28; 39:15
37:4 had not put him into *p.*
15 put him in *p.* in Jon. house
39:14 took Jeremiah out of *p.*
52:11 put Zedekiah in *p.*
Mat. 4:12 John was cast into *p.*
5:25 be cast into *p. Luke* 12:58
11:2 J. heard in *p.* works of C.
14:3 Herod put him in *p.*
18:30 he cast him into *p.*
25:36 I was in *p.* ye came to me
39 when saw we thee in *p. ?* 44
Mark 1:14 after J. was put in *p.*
6:17 Her. had bound John in *p.*
Luke 3:20 he shut up John in *p.*
22:33 go with thee both into *p.*
23:19 for murder cast in *p.* 25
John 3:24 John not yet cast in *p.*
Acts 5:18 put apostles in com. *p.*

19 angel by night op. *p.* doors
8:3 men and women, com. to *p.*
12:4 Peter in *p.* 5 kept in *p.*
7 light in *p.* 17 L. br. out of *p.*
16:23 Paul and Silas cast in *p.*
24 inner *p.* 27 *p.* doors open
26:10 saints did I shut in *p.*
1 *Pet.* 3:19 preach. to spirits in *p.*
Rev. 2:10 shall cast some into *p.*
20:7 S. shall be loosed out his *p.*

See GATE.

PRISON-HOUSE.
Jud. 16:21 S. did grind in *p.-h.*
2 *Chr.* 16:10 Asa put H. in *p.-h.*
Is. 42:7 in darkness out of *p.-h.*

PRISONER.
Ps. 79:11 let sighing of *p.* come
102:20 hear groaning of the *p.*
Mat. 27:15 release to people a *p.*
Acts 23:18 P. called me to him
25:27 unreasonable to send a *p.*
28:17 yet was I delivered *p.*
Eph. 3:1 I P. the *p.* of Jesus, 4:1; *Phile.* 1:9
2 *Tim.* 1:8 not ashamed of his *p.*

See FELLOW.

PRISONERS.
Gen. 39:20 where king's *p.* were
Num. 21:1 took some of Israel *p.*
Job 3:18 there the *p.* rest toge.
Ps. 69:33 L. despiseth not his *p.*
146:7 the Lord looseth the *p.*
Is. 10:4 bow down under the *p.*
14:17 opened not house of *p.*
20:4 Assyria shall lead Egyp. *p.*
24:22 be gathered together as *p.*
42:7 bring out *p.* from prison
49:9 mayest say to *p.* Go forth
Lam. 3:34 crush under feet the *p.*
Zec. 9:11 have sent forth thy *p.*
12 turn to str.-hold, *p.* of hope
Acts 16:25 praises, *p.* heard them
27 supposing *p.* had been fled
27:1 delivered Paul and other *p.*
42 soldiers' coun. was to kill *p.*

PRISONS.
Luke 21:12 delivering you in. *p.*
Acts 22:4 del. in *p.* men and wo.
2 *Cor.* 11:23 in *p.* more frequent

PRIVATE, LY.
Mat. 24:3 disciples came to C. *p.*
Mark 6:32 Jesus went into a ship *p. Luke* 9:10
9:28 J. and And. ask him *p.* 13:3
Luke 10:23 turned to disciples *p.*
Acts 23:19 with Paul's kinsm. *p.*
Gal. 2:2 p. to them of reputation
2 *Pet.* 1:20 any *p.* interpretation

PRIVILY.
Jud. 9:31 he sent messengers *p.*
1 *Sam.* 24:4 Da. cut Saul's sk. *p.*
Ps. 10:8 eyes *p.* set against poor
11:2 may *p.* shoot at upright
31:4 out of net laid *p.* 142:3
64:5 commune of lay. snares *p.*
101:5 whoso *p.* slanders neighb.
Prov. 1:11 lurk *p.* for innocent
18 lurk *p.* for their own lives
Mat. 1:19 to put her away *p.*
2:7 Her. when he had *p.* called
Acts 16:37 now do they thrust us out *p. ?*
Gal. 2:4 came in *p.* to spy out
2 *Pet.* 2:1 *p.* bring damna. here.

PRIVY.
Deut. 23:1 *p.* member cut off
1 *K.* 2:44 wickedness heart *p.* to
Ezek. 21:14 enters *p.* chamber
Acts 5:2 wife also being *p.* to it

PRIZE.
1 *Cor.* 9:24 but one receiveth *p.*
Phil. 3:14 I press toward the *p.*

PRIZED.
Zec. 11:13 price that I was *p.* at

PROCEED.
Jos. 6:10 word *p.* out of mouth
2 *Sam.* 7:12 seed wh. shall *p.*
Job 40:5 but I will *p.* no further
Is. 29:14 *I p.* to do marvel. work
51:4 for a law shall *p.* from me
Jer. 9:3 they *p.* from evil to evil
30:21 governor shall *p.* fr. midst
Hab. 1:7 judgm. and dign. sh. *p.*
Mat. 15:18 *p.* out of mouth defile
19 heart *p.* murders, *Mark* 7:21
Eph. 4:29 no corrupt commu. *p.*
2 *Tim.* 3:9 they shall *p.* no furt.

PROCEEDED.
Num. 30:12 what. *p.* out of lips
Jud. 11:36 do that which *p.* out
Job 36:1 Elihu also *p.* and said
Luke 4:22 gracious words wh. *p.*
John 8:42 for I *p.* forth from God
Acts 12:3 he *p.* to take Peter also
Rev. 19:21 sword *p.* out of mouth

PROCEEDETH, ING.
Gen. 24:50 thing *p.* from the L.
Num. 30:2 according to all th. *p.*
Deut. 8:3 by every word that *p.* out of mouth of G. *Mat.* 4:4
1 *Sam.* 24:13 wick. *p.* fr. wicked
Ex. 10:5 error which *p.* fr. ruler
Lam. 3:38 out of M. High *p.* not
Hab. 1:4 wrong judgment *p.*
John 15:26 Spi. of truth *p.* fr. F.
Jam. 3:10 out of the same mo. *p.*
Rev. 11:5 fire *p.* out of th. mouth
22:1 water of life *p.* out of thr

PROCESS.
Gen. 4:3 in *p.* of time C. brought
38:12 in *p.* of time Shuah died
Ex. 2:23 in *p.* of time ki. of Eg.
Jud. 11:4 in *p.* chil. of Ammon
2 *Chr.* 21:19 in *p.* Jehor.'s bowe.

PROCHORUS. *Acts* 6:5

PROCLAIM.
Ex. 33:19 I will *p.* name of Lord
Lev. 23:2 feast of L. 4, 21, 37
25:10 *p.* lib. *Deut.* 20:10 *p.* peace
Jud. 7:3 to *p.* in ears of people
1 *K.* 21:9 *p.* a fast, set Naboth on
2 *K.* 10:20 Jehu said, *p.* assemb.
Neh. 8:15 *p.* they fetch branches
Est. 6:9 *p.* before him, Thus sh.
Prov. 20:6 men *p.* own goodness
Is. 61:1 he sent me to *p.* liberty
2 *p.* the acceptable year of L.
Jer. 3:12 *p.* th. words, 11:6; 19:2
7:2 stand in gate of L. *p.* there
34:8 made a coven. to *p.* liberty
17 I *p.* a liberty for you to sw.
Joel 3:9 *p.* this among the Gent.
Amos 4:5 *p.* the free-offerings

PROCLAIMED.
Ex. 34:5 *p.* name of Lord, 6
36:6 they caused it to be *p.*
1 *K.* 21:12 they *p.* a fast, set
2 *K.* 10:20 solemn assem. and *p.*
23:16 man of G. who *p.* 17
2 *Chr.* 20:3 Jehoshaphat *p.* a fast
Ezr. 8:21 *p.* a fast at Ahava
Est. 6:11 Haman *p.* before him
Is. 62:11 hath *p.* Thy salvation
Jer. 36:9 they *p.* a fast before L.
Jon. 3:5 *p.* a fast, put on sackc.
7 caused it to be *p.* thro' Nine.
Luke 12:3 be *p.* on house-tops

PROCLAIMETH, ING.
Prov. 12:23 heart of fools *p.*
Jer. 34:15 *p.* liberty ev. man, 17
Rev. 5:2 I saw a strong angel *p.*

PROCLAMATION.
Ex. 32:5 Aaron made *p.*
1 *K.* 15:22 king Asa made a *p.*
22:36 went *p.* throughout host
2 *Chr.* 24:9 J. made a *p.* through
36:22 Cyrus made *p.* *Ezr.* 1:1
Ezr. 10:7 E. made *p.* thro' Judah
Dan. 5:29 Belshazzar made *p.*

PROCURE, ED, ETH.

Prov. 11:27 seek. good *p.* favor
Jer. 2:17 hast thou not *p.* this
  4:18 thy doings *p.* th. things
  26:19 might we *p.* great evil
  33:9 for all posterity I *p.* to it

PRODUCE.

Is. 41:21 *p.* your cause, saith L.

PROFANE, Adjective.

Lev. 21:7 not ta. wife th. is *p.* 14
Jer. 23:11 proph. and priests *p.*
Ezek. 21:25 thus *p.* prince of I
  28:16 cast as *p.* out of mount
  42:20 sanctuary and *p.* place
  44:23 differe. betw. holy and *p.*
  48:15 sh. be a *p.* place for city
1 *Tim.* 1:9 law is made for *p.*
  4:7 ref. *p.* and old wives' fables
  6:20 avoid *p.* babbl. 2 *Tim.* 2:16
Heb. 12:16 lest th. be any *p.* per.

PROFANE, Verb.

Lev. 18:21 neit. shalt thou *p.* G.
  19:12 ; 20:3 ; 21:6 ; 22:2, 32
  21:12 shall not *p.* sanctuary, 23
  15 nor shall *p.* his seed among
  22:9 if they *p.* my ordinance
  15 shall not *p.* holy things
Neh. 13:17 evil do, *p.* sabbath
Ezek. 23:39 came to sanctu. to *p.*
  24:21 I will *p.* my sanctuary
Amos 2:7 to *p.* my holy name
Mat. 12:5 priests in temple *p.*
Acts 24:6 gone about to *p.* temp.

PROFANED.

Lev. 19:8 he *p.* hallowed things
Ps. 89:39 thou hast *p.* his crown
Is. 43:28 I have *p.* the princes of
Ezek. 22:8 thou *p.* my sab. 23:38
  26 *p.* my holy things, I am *p.*
  25:3 sanctuary when it was *p*
  36:20 they *p.* my holy name
  21 my name Is. had *p.* 22, 23
Mal. 1:12 ye have *p.* it, ye say
  2:11 Jud. hath *p.* holiness of L.

PROFANENESS.

Jer. 23:15 prophets of Jeru. is *p.*

PROFANETH, ING.

Lev. 21:9 she *p.* her father, sab.
Neh. 13:18 bring wrath by *p.* sab.
Mal. 2:10 by *p.* covenant of fath.

PROFESS.

Rom. 1:22 *p.* this day to the L.
Mat. 7:23 I *p.* I never knew you
Tit. 1:16 they *p.* they know God

PROFESSED, ING.'

Rom. 1:22 themsel. to be wise
2 *Cor.* 9:13 glori. God for your *p.*
1 *Tim.* 2:10 becometh women *p.*
  6:12 hast *p.* a good profession
  21 some *p.* have erred

PROFESSION.

1 *Tim.* 6:12 professed a good *p*
Heb. 3:1 the High-priest of our *p.*
  4:14 let us hold fast our *p.* 10:23

PROFIT, Substantive.

Gen. 25:32 what *p.* sh. birthright
  37:26 what *p.* if we slay broth. ?
Est. 3:8 it is not for king's *p.*
Job 21:15 what *p.* if we pray
  30:2 whereto strength *p.* me ?
  35:3 what *p.* if I be cleansed
Ps. 30:9 what *p.* is in my blood ?
Prov. 14:23 in all labor th. is *p.*
Ec. 1:3 what *p.* hath a man of all
  his labor? 3:9 ; 5:16
  2:11 there was no *p.* under sun
  5:9 the *p.* of the earth is for all
  7:11 by wisdom there is *p.* to
Is. 30:5 help nor *p.* but shame
Jer. 16:19 things where. is no *p.*
Mal. 3:14 what *p.* that we kept
Rom. 3:1 what *p.* of circumcis. ?
1 *Cor.* 7:35 I sp. for your own *p.*
  10:33 not seeking mine own *p.*

2 *Tim.* 2:14 about words to no *p.*
Heb. 12:10 chasteneth us for *p.*

PROFIT, Verb.

1 *Sam.* 12:21 thi. wh. cannot *p.*
Job 35:8 thy righteousn. may *p.*
Prov. 10:2 wickedness *p.* nothing
  11:4 riches *p.* not in day of wra.
Is. 30:5 peo. that could not *p.* 6
  44:9 delectable things sh. not *p.*
  47:12 thou shalt be able to *p.*
  57:12 works, shall not *p.* thee
Jer. 2:8 things that do not *p.*
  11 for that which doth not *p.*
  7:8 lying words that cannot *p.*
  12:13 put to pain, but sh. not *p.*
  23:32 they sh. not *p.* this peop.
Mark 8:36 what *p.* if gain world
1 *Cor.* 12:7 ev. man to *p.* withal
  14:6 what shall I *p.* you ?
Gal. 5:2 Ch. shall *p.* you nothing
Heb. 4:2 word preach. did not *p.*
Jam. 2:14 what doth it *p.* breth.
  16 give not thi. needf. wh. *p.* ?

PROFITABLE.

Job 22:2 can a man be *p.* to God ?
Ec. 10:10 wisdom is *p.* to direct
Is. 44:10 image is *p.* for nothing
Jer. 13:7 girdle was *p.* for noth.
Mat. 5:29 *p.* members perish, 30
Acts 20:20 I kept noth. *p.* to you
1 *Tim.* 4:8 godliness is *p.* to all
2 *Tim.* 3:16 all Scripture is *p.*
  4:11 M. is *p.* to me for ministry
Tit. 3:8 th. things are *p.* to men
Phile. 11 but now *p.* to thee

PROFITED, ETH.

Job 33:27 I have sinned, it *p.* not
  34:9 it *p.* noth. to delight in G.
Hab. 2:18 what *p.* graven image
Mat. 15:5 it is a gift whatever
  thou might. be *p.* Mark 7:11
  16:26 what is man *p.* if he gain
John 6:63 quicken. flesh *p.* noth.
Rom. 2:25 circumcision *p.* if th.
1 *Cor.* 13:3 not char. it *p.* noth.
Gal. 1:14 I *p.* in Jews' religion
1 *Tim.* 4:8 bodily exerci. *p.* little
Heb. 13:9 not *p.* them that occu.

PROFITING.

1 *Tim.* 4:15 thy *p.* may appear

PROFOUND.

Hos. 5:2 the revolters are *p.*

PROGENITORS.

Gen. 49:26 above bless. of my *p.*

PROGNOSTICATORS.

Is. 47:13 let monthly *p.* stand up

PROLONG, ED

Deut. 4:26 not *p.* your days, 30:18
  40 that thou mayest *p.* days on
  earth, 5:16, 33 ; 6:2 ; 11:9 ;
  17:20 ; 22:7
  32:47 ye shall *p.* your days
Job 6:11 that I should *p.* life ?
  15:29 wicked sh. not *p.* perfect.
Ps. 61:6 thou wilt *p.* king's life
Prov. 28:2 by knowl. shall be *p.*
  16 he that hateth covet. sh. *p.*
Ec. 8:12 a sinner's days be *p.*
  13 neit. shall wicked *p.* his days
Is. 13:22 her days shall not be *p.*
  53:10 seed, he shall *p.* his days
Ezek. 12:22 the days are *p.* and
  25 to pass, it sh. be no more *p.*
  28 none of my words be *p.* more
Dan. 7:12 their lives were *p.* for

PROLONGETH.

Prov. 10:27 fear of Lord *p.* days

PROMISE, Substantive.

Num. 14:34 kn. my breach of *p.*
1 *K.* 8:56 not failed of good *p.*
2 *Chr.* 1:9 let *p.* to David be esta.
Neh. 5:12 do according to this *p.*
  13 perform. not *p.* accor. to *p.*

Ps. 77:8 doth *p.* fail evermore ?
  105:42 remembered his holy *p.*
Luke 24:49 send *p.* of my Fath
Acts 1:4 wait for *p.* of the Father
  2:33 received *p.* of Holy Ghost
  39 the *p.* is to you and children
  7:17 time of the *p.* drew nigh
  13:23 his *p.* ha. raised a Saviour
  32 *p.* made to fathers
  23:21 looking for a *p.* from thee
  26:6 hope of the *p.* made of G. 7
Rom. 4:13 *p.* that he sh. be heir
  14 the *p.* is made of none effect
  16 the *p.* might be sure to seed
  20 he staggered not at the *p.*
  9:8 chil. of *p.* counted for seed
  9 this is word of *p.* I will come
Gal. 3:14 receive *p.* of the Spirit
  17 sho. make *p.* of none effect
  18 it is no more of *p.* but God
  gave it to Abraham by *p.*
  19 to whom the *p.* was made
  22 that the *p.* by faith of J. C.
  29 ye are heirs according to *p.*
  4:23 he of free woman was by *p.*
  28 we, as Isaac, children of *p.*
Eph. 1:13 with Holy Spirit of *p.*
  2:12 strangers from coven. of *p.*
  3:6 partakers of his *p.* in Christ
  6:2 first commandment with *p.*
1 *Tim.* 4:8 hav. the *p.* of the life
2 *Tim.* 1:1 according to *p.* of life
Heb. 4:1 fear, lest a *p.* being left
  6:13 God made *p.* to Abraham
  15 after he endured he obtai. *p.*
  17 will. to show to heirs of *p.*
  9:15 *p.* of eternal life, 10:36
  11:9 sojourned in land of *p.*
  heirs wi. him of the same *p.*
  39 these all received not the *p.*
2 *Pet.* 3:4 wh. is *p.* of his coming
  9 Lord not slack concer. his *p.*
  13 according to his *p.* we look
1 *John* 2:25 this is the *p.* he hath

PROMISE, Verb.

2 *Pet.* 2:19 while they *p.* liberty,
  they servants of corruption

PROMISED.

Ex. 12:25 give according as he *p.*
Num. 14:40 go to place Lord *p.*
Deut. 1:11 L. bless as he *p.* 15:6
  6:3 increase as the Lord *p.* thee
  10:9 L. is his inherit. as he *p.*
  12:20 L. enlarge border, as he *p.*
  19:8 give thee land he *p.* 27:3
  26:18 to be his people as he *p.*
Jos. 23:5 possess th. land as L. *p.*
2 *Sam.* 7:28 *p.* goodness to serv.
1 *K.* 2:24 made me house he *p.*
  5:12 L. gave S. wisdom as he *p.*
  8:20 I sit on thro. of Is. as L. *p.*
  56 given rest to people as he *p.*
  9:5 as I *p.* to David, thy father
2 *K.* 8:19 *p.* to gi. light, 2 Chr. 21:7
1 *Chr.* 17:26 th. hast *p.* goodness
2 *Chr.* 6:10 set on throne as L. *p.*
Neh. 9:23 concern. whi. thou *p.*
Jer. 32:43 all good I *p.* 33:14
Mat. 14:7 Herod *p.* with oath
Mark 14:11 *p.* to give money
Luke 1:72 mercy *p.* to our fath.
  22:6 he *p.* to betray him
Acts 7:5 he *p.* to give it to him
Rom. 1:2 gospel wh. he had *p.*
  4:21 what he *p.* he was able
Tit. 1:2 *p.* before world began
Heb. 10:23 he is faithful that *p.*
  11:11 him faithful that had *p.*
  12:26 hath *p.* saying, Yet once
Jam. 1:12 L. *p.* to them love, 2:5
1 *John* 2:25 hath *p.* us eter. life

PROMISEDST.

1 *K.* 8:24 David that thou *p.* 25
Neh. 9:15 *p.* they sho. go to land

PROMISES.

Rom. 9:4 to whom pertain *p.*
  15:8 to confirm *p.* made to fath.

2 *Cor.* 1:20 all *p.* of God in him
7:1 having therefore these *p.*
Gal. 3:16 to Abra. were *p.* made
21 is law against *p.* of God?
Heb. 6:12 thro' faith inherit *p.*
7:6 M. blessed him that had *p.*
8:6 established upon better *p.*
11:13 not having received *p.*
17 he that received *p.* off. son
33 through faith obtained *p.*
2 *Pet.* 1:4 given to us precious *p.*

PROMISING.

Ezek. 13:22 wick. way by *p.* life

PROMOTE, ED.

Num. 22:17 *p.* to honor, 24:11
37 am I not able to *p.* thee to
Jud. 9:9 go to be *p.* over, 11, 13
Est. 5:11 where. king had *p.* him
Prov. 4:8 exalt her, she sh. *p.* th.
Dan. 3:30 the king *p.* Shadrach

PROMOTION.

Ps. 75:6 *p.* cometh not from east
Prov. 3:35 shame be *p.* of fools

PRONOUNCE.

Lev. 5:4 man sh. *p.* with an oath
59 this is the law, *p.* it clean
Jud. 12:6 not frame to *p.* right

PRONOUNCED.

Neh. 6:12 he *p.* this prophecy
Jer. 11:17 the Lord hath *p.* evil
16:10 *p.* this great evil agai. us ?
19:15 ; 35:17 ; 40:2
26:13 Lord will rep. of evil he *p.*
19 Lord repented of evil he *p.*
34:5 for I have *p.* the word
36:7 L. hath *p.* ag. this people

PRONOUNCING.

Lev. 5:4 if a soul sware, *p.* to do

PROOF, S.

Acts 1:3 hims. alive by many *p.*
2 *Cor.* 2:9 might know the *p.*
8:24 show to them the *p.* of love
13:3 since ye seek a *p.* of Christ
Phil. 2:22 ye know the *p.* of him
2 *Tim.* 4:5 *p.* of thy ministry

PROPER.

1 *Chr.* 29:3 mine own *p.* good
Acts 1:19 in *p.* tongue, Aceldama
1 *Cor.* 7:7 every man hath *p.* gift
Heb. 11:23 saw he was a *p.* child

PROPHECY.

2 *Chr.* 9:29 Sol.'s acts in *p.* of A.
15:8 when Asa heard *p.* of Oded
Neh. 6:12 he pronounced this *p.*
Prov. 30:1 *p.* man spake to Ithiel
31:1 *p.* that his mother tau. him
Mat. 13:14 fulfilled *p.* of Esaias
1 *Cor.* 12:10 ano. *p.* by same Sp.
13:2 though I have the gift of *p.*
1 *Tim.* 4:14 gift given thee by *p.*
2 *Pet.* 1:19 a more sure word of *p.*
20 no *p.* of script. is of private
21 *p.* came not by will of man
Rev. 1:3 bless. they that hear *p.*
Rev. 11:6 rain not in da. of *p.*
19:10 testimony of J. is sp. of *p*
22:7 blessed that keepeth th. *p.*
10 seal not the say. of the *p.*
19 if any man take from this *p.*

PROPHECIES.

1 *Cor.* 13:8 whether *p.* they cease
1 *Tim.* 1:18 according to *p.* befo.

PROPHESY, Verb.

Num. 11:27 Eldad and Me. do *p.*
1 *K.* 22:8 he doth not *p.* good
18 not *p.* good, 2 *Chr.* 18:17
1 *Chr.* 25:1 should *p.* with harps
Is. 30:10 *p.* not right, *p.* deceits
Jer. 5:31 the prophets *p.* falsely
11:21 *p.* not in name of the L.
14:14 prophets *p.* lies, *p.* false
16 people to whom they *p.* cast
23:16 heark. not to proph. th. *p.*

25 *p.* lies in my name, 26, 32 ;
27:10, 14, 15, 16 ; 29:9, 21
25:30 *p.* against inhab. of earth
26:12 Lord sent me to *p.* against
Ezek. 4:7 *p.* against Jerusalem
6:2 *p.* ag. mount. of Israel, 36:1
11:4 *p.* against Jaaz. and Pel. *p.*
13:2 *p.* against proph. that *p.* 17
20:46 *p.* aga. the forest of south
21:2 *p.* against Israel ; 9 Jerusa.
14 Son of man *p.* smite hands
28 *p.* concerning Ammon. 25:2
28:21 Son of man *p.* against Zid.
29:2 *p.* aga. Pharaoh, king Eg.
30:2 *p.* against Egypt and king
34:2 *p.* against shepherds of Is.
35:2 *p.* against mount Seir
36:6 *p.* concerning land of Isra.
37:4 *p.* on th. bones ; 9 *p.* wind
38:2 *p.* against Gog, 14 ; 39:1
Joel 2:28 sons sh. *p. Acts* 2:17, 18
Amos 2:12 say. *p.* not, *Mic.* 2:6
3:8 L. spoken, who can but *p.*?
7:12 eat bread, and *p.* there
13 *p.* not any more at Beth-el
15 L. said, Go, *p.* to my pe. Is.
16 *p.* not against house of Isa.
Mic. 2:11 I will *p.* to thee of wine
Zec. 13:3 when any sh. *p.* then
Mat. 15:7 well did Es. *p.* of you
26:68 *p.* unto us, thou Ch. *Mark*
14:65 ; *Luke* 22:64
Acts 21:9 had virgins wh. did *p.*
Rom. 12:6 whether *p.* let us *p.* to
1 *Cor.* 13:9 part. and *p.* in part
14:1 rather *p.* 39 covet to *p.*
24 if all *p.* 31 we may all *p.*
Rev. 10:11 thou must *p.* before
11:3 witnesses sh. *p.* 1,260 days

PROPHESIED.

Num. 11:25 they *p.* did not cease
1 *Sam.* 10:10 Spirit of God came
on Saul, and he did *p.* 11;
18:10 ; 19:23, 24
1 *K.* 18:29 they *p.* until evening
22:10 prophets *p.* 12 ; 2 *Chr.* 18:9
1 *Chr.* 25:2 the sons of Asaph *p.*
2 *Chr.* 20:37 Eliezer *p.* against J.
Ezr. 5:1 Zechariah *p.* to the J.
Jer. 2:8 the prophets *p.* by Baal
20:1 Pashur heard that Jere. *p.*
23:13 the prophets of Samar. *p.*
21 I have not spok. yet they *p.*
26:9 why hast thou *p.* in name
18 Micah *p.* in days of Hezek.
20 Urijah *p.* 28:8 *p.* against
29:31 Shem. hath *p.* to you a lie
37:19 where prophets which *p.*?
Ezek. 11:13 when I *p.* Pelat. died
37:7 I *p.* as I was com. I *p.* 10
38:17 who *p.* I would bring thee
Zec. 13:4 proph. asha. when *p.*
Mat. 7:22 Lord, have we not *p.*
11:13 the proph. *p.* until John
Mark 7:6 well hath Es. *p.* of you
Luke 1:67 his father Zacharias *p.*
John 11:51 Caiaphas *p.* that Jes.
Acts 19:6 sp. with tongues and *p.*
1 *Cor.* 14:5 I would rather ye *p.*
Jude 14 Enoch *p.* of these things

PROPHESIETH.

2 *Chr.* 18:7 he nev. *p.* good to me
Jer. 28:9 prophet wh. *p.* of peace
Ezek. 12:27 he *p.* of times far off
Zec. 13:3 thrust him when he *p.*
1 *Cor.* 11:5 *p.* with head uncov.
14:3 he that *p.* speak. unto men
4 he that *p.* edifieth church
5 greater he that *p.* than he

PROPHESYING, S.

1 *Sam.* 10:13 made an end of *p.*
19:20 saw comp. of prophets *p.*
Ezr. 6:14 they prospered thro' *p.*
1 *Cor.* 11:4 *p.* having head cover.
14:6 exce. I speak to you by *p.*
22 but *p.* serveth not for them
1 *Thes.* 5:20 desp. not *p.* prove all

PROPHET.

Ex. 7:1 Aaron shall be thy *p.*
1 *Sam.* 22:5 the *p.* Gad said to D.
1 *K.* 1:32 call me Nathan the *p.*
11:29 Ahijah the *p.* found Jero.
13:11 dwelt an old *p.* in B. 25
29 *p.* took up car. of man of G.
the old *p.* came to bury him
18:36 Elij. the *p.* came and said
2 *K.* 5:3 would G. my lord wi. *p.*
13 if *p.* had bid do some great
6:12 Elisha the *p.* telleth what
23:18 with bones of *p.* that came
2 *Chr.* 12:5 came Shemai. the *p.*
13:22 written in story of the *p.*
15:8 wh. Asa heard proph. of *p.*
21:12 a writing from Eli. the *p.*
32:20 *p.* Isaiah prayed to heaven
35:18 from days of Samu. the *p.*
36:12 humbl. not himself bef. *p.*
Ezr. 6:14 prophesying of Ha. *p.*
Ps. 74:9 there is no *p.* amo. you
Is. 3:2 Lord doth away the *p.*
9:15 the *p.* that teacheth lies
28:7 *p.* erred thro' strong drink
Jer. 6:13 from *p.* to priests, 8:10
18:18 nor sh. word perish fr. *p.*
23:11 *p.* and priests are profane
28 the *p.* that hath a dream
28:6 the *p.* Jeremi. said, Amen
9 *p.* wh. prophesieth of peace,
word of *p.* co. to pass *p.* kn.
17 Hananiah *p.* died same year
37:2 nor servants hearken to *p.*
Lam. 2:20 shall *p.* be slain ?
Ezek. 7:26 then seek a vis. of *p.*
14:4 come. to *p.* I will ans. him
9 if *p.* be deceived, I have dec.
10 punishm. of *p.* sh. be even
Hos. 4:5 the *p.* sh. fall with thee
9:7 the *p.* is a fool : 8 *p.* a snare
Amos 7:14 I was no *p.* nor *p.* son
Zec. 13:5 I am no *p.* husbandman
Mal. 4:5 I will send Elijah the *p.*
Mat. 1:22 which was spoken by
the *p.* Isaiah, 2:15 : 3:3 ; 4:14
8:17 ; 21:4 ; *Luke* 3:4 ; *John*
1:23 ; 12:38 ; *Acts* 28:25
2:5 for thus it is written by *p.*.
17 spoken by Jeremy *p.* 27:9
12:39 the sign of the *p.* Jonas,
Luke 11:29
13:35 spoken by the *p.* Da. 27:35
21:11 this is Jesus *p.* of Nazar.
24:15 sp. of by D. *p. Mark* 13:14
Luke 1:76 thou child be called *p.*
4:17 delivered book of *p.* Esai.
24 no *p.* is accept. in his coun.
7:28 not a greater *p.* than John
John 7:40 of a truth this is the *p.*
52 out of Galilee ariseth no *p.*
Acts 2:16 spoken by the *p.* Joel
8:28 he read Esaias the *p.* 30
34 of whom speaketh *p.* this ?
13:20 gave judges until Sam. *p.*
2 *Pet.* 2:16 ass forb. madness of *p.*

See PRIEST.

A PROPHET.

Gen. 20:7 restore wife, he is a *p.*
Deut. 13:1 if there arise a *p.* or
18:15 I will raise a *p.* from am.
brethren, 18 ; *Acts* 3:22 ; 7:37
34:10 arose not a *p.* in Israel
Jud. 6:8 L. sent a *p.* to children
1 *Sam.* 3:20 Sam. esta. to be a *p.*
9:9 now called a *p.* called seer
1 *K.* 13:18 I am a *p.* as thou art
18:22 I only remain a *p.* of L.
22:7 is there not here a *p.* of
Lord ? 2 *K.* 3:11 : 2 *Chr.* 18:6
2 *K.* 5:8 know there is a *p.* in Is.
2 *Chr.* 25:15 L. sent a *p.* to Amaz.
28:9 a *p.* of the Lord was there
Jer. 1:5 I ordained thee a *p.*
29:26 maketh himself a *p.* 27
Ezek. 2:5 a *p.* among them, 33:33
14:7 cometh to a *p.* to inq. abo.

Hos. 12:13 by *a p.* L. brought Is.
    out of Eg. by *a p.* preserved
Mic. 2:11 be *a p.* of his people
Mat. 10:41 he. that receiv. *a p.* in
    name of *a p.* rec. *a p.* reward
    11:9 what went ye to see ? *a p.*
    13:57 *a p.* is not without honor,
    Mark 6:4 ; *John* 4:44
    14:5 accounted him *a p.* 21:26 ;
    Mark 11:32 ; *Luke* 20:6
    21:46 multi. took him for *a p.*
Mark 6:15 *a p.* or as one of pro.
Luke 7:16 *a* great *p.* among us
    39 if he were *a p.* would have
    13:33 it cannot be *a p.* perish
    24:19 Je. who was *a p.* mighty
John 4:19 I perceive th. art *a p.*
    9:17 blind man said, He is *a p.*
Acts 2:30 David *a p.* knowing G.
    21:10 *a* cert. *p.* named Agabus
1 Cor. 14:37 man think to be *a p.*
Tit. 1:12 *a p.* of their own land

False PROPHET.

Acts 13:6 *f. p.* a Jew named Bar.
Rev. 16:13 like frogs out of *f. p.*
    19:20 beast taken. wi. him *f. p.*
    20:10 cast wh. beast and *f. p.* are
    See LORD.

That PROPHET.

Deut. 13:5 *t. p.* shall die, 18:20
Ezek. 14:9 I the L. deceived *t. p.*
John 1:21 ask, Art thou *t. p. ?* 25
    6:14 this is of a truth *that p.*
Acts 3:23 wh. will not hear *t. p.*

PROPHETS.

Num. 11:29 L.'s people were *p.*
1 Sam. 10:5 meet a company of *p.*
    12 is Saul among the *p. ? ?* 19:24
    28:6 L. answ. him not by *p.* 15
1 K. 18:4 Obad. hid 100 *p.* by 50
    13 slew *p.* 19 *p.* of Baal 450, 22
    40 take *p.* of B. let none esca.
    19:10 Is. slain. *p.* 14 ; *Neh.* 9:26
    22:22 lying spirit, in *p.* 2 *Chr.*
    18:21
2 K. 3:13 *p.* of father, *p.* of mot.
2 Chr. 20:20 believe *p.* ye sh. pr.
    24:19 sent *p.* 36:16 misused *p.*
Ezr. 5:2 with th. were *p.* of God
Neh. 6:7 appointed *p.* to preach
    9:30 testifiedst by thy Spi. in *p.*
    32 trouble that ha. come on *p.*
Is. 29:10 *p.* proph. not, *Amos* 2:12
    30:10 *p.* proph. not, *Amos* 2:12
Jer. 2:8 *p.* prophesied by Baal
    30 your sword devoured yo. *p.*
    4:9 *p.* wonder ; 5:13 *p.* bec. wind
    5:31 *p.* prophesy falsely
    8:1 bring out the bones of *p.*
    13:13 fill *p.* with drunkenness
    14:14 *p.* proph. lies in my name
    15 by sword and famine sh. *p.*
    23:13 I have seen folly in the *p.*
    14 I have seen in *p.* horri. thi.
    15 from *p.* is profaneness gone
    21 I have not sent these *p.* yet
    26 *p.* of deceit of th. own heart
    30 I am against *p.* that steal, 31
    26:11 then spake *p.* This man is
    27:9 hearken not to your *p.* 16
    18 *p.* and word of L. with the.
    28:8 *p.* that have been before
    29:1 letter Jeremiah sent to *p.*
    8 let not your *p.* deceive you
    15 the Lord hath rais. us up *p.*
    32:32 and their *p.* provoke me
    37:19 where are now your *p.*
Lam. 2:9 *p.* find no vision fr. L.
    14 thy *p.* have seen vain thin.
    4:13 sins of her *p.* th. shed blood
Ezek. 13:2 prophesy agai. the *p.*
    3 saith L. Woe unto foolish *p.*
    4 O Israel, thy *p.* are like fox.
    9 my hand shall be upon the *p.*
    22:25 a conspiracy of her *p.*
    28 *p.* daubed them with mort.

Hos. 6:5 I have hewed th. by *p.*
    12:10 spoken by *p.* multiplied
Amos 2:11 raised of your sons *p.*
Mic. 3:6 sun sh. go down over *p.*
    11 and the *p.* divine for money
Zep. 3:4 her *p.* are light persons
Zec. 1:5 *p.* do they live for ever ?
    7:7 L. hath cried by former *p.*
    12 L. sent in Sp. by former *p.*
Mat. 5:12 persecuted *p.* Lu. 6:23
    17 think not I came to dest. *p.*
    7:12 this is the law and the *p.*
    13:17 *p.* desired to see, *Lu.* 10:24
    22:40 on these hang law and *p.*
    23:31 children of them killed *p.*
    34 send unto you *p. Lu.* 11:49
    37 O Jeru. thou that killest *p.*
Mark 1:2 as it is writ. in *p. Luke*
    18:31 • 24:25 ; *John* 6:45
Luke 1:70 spake by *p.* 2 *Pet.* 3:2
    16:16 law and *p.* were until J.
    29 said, They ha. M. and *p.* 31
    24:25 slow to beli. wh. *p.* spok.
John 1:45 him of wh. *p.* did wri.
    8:52 Abraham and *p.* dead. 53
Acts 3:18 showed by mo. of *p.* 21
    11:27 *p.* came from Jerusalem
    13:1 in church at Antioch cer. *p.*
    15 reading of the law and *p.*
    15:32 Judas and Silas being *p.*
    24:14 believing all written in *p.*
    26:22 none other th. than *p.* say
    27 Agrippa, believ. thou *p. ?*
Rom. 1:2 promis. afore by his *p.*
    3:21 witness. by the law and *p.*
    11:3 L. they have killed *p.*
1 Cor. 12:28 secondarily, *p.* thir.
    29 are all *p. ? ?* 14:29 let *p.* speak
Eph. 2:20 on the foundation of *p.*
    3:5 as now revealed to his *p.*
    4:11 gave some *p.* and teachers
1 Thes. 2:15 killed L. and the *p.*
Heb. 1:1 spake to fathers by *p.*
Jam. 5:10 take *p.* who have spo.
1 Pet. 1:10 of salvation *p.* inquir.
Rev. 11:10 th. *p.* tormented them
    18:20 rejoice. ye apostles and *p.*
    24 in her was found blood of *p.*
    22:9 I am of thy brethren the *p.*

All the PROPHETS.

1 K. 19:1 how he had sla.. *a. t. p.*
    22:10 and *all the p.* prophesied,
    12 ; 2 *Chr.* 18:9, 11
2 K. 10:19 call to me *a. t. p.* of B.
    17:13 testified ag. Is. by *a. t. p.*
Mat. 11:13 *a. the p.* prophesied
Luke 11:50 blood of *a. t. p.* req.
    13:28 wh. ye see *a. t. p.* in king.
    24:27 and beginning at *a. t. p.*
Acts 3:24 *all the p.* from Samuel
    10:43 to him give *all t. p.* witn.

False PROPHETS.

Mat. 7:15 beware of *false p.*
    24:11 many *false p.* shall rise,
    24 ; *Mark* 13:22
Luke 6:26 so did th. fath. to *f. p.*
2 Pet. 2:1 were *f. p.* among them
1 John 4:1 many *f. p.* gone out

My PROPHETS.

1 Chr. 16:22 do *my p.* no harm,
    Ps. 105:15

Of the PROPHETS.

1 Sam. 10:10 comp. *of p.* met h.
1 K. 20:35 cert. men of sons *of p.*
    41 king discern. he was *of t. p.*
    22:13 words *of t. p.* decla. good.
    2 *Chr.* 18:12
2 K. 2:3 sons *of t. p.* at Beth-el,
    5 the sons *of t. p.* at Jericho
    15 sons *of t. p.* said, spirit of E.
    4:38 pottage for sons *of the p.*
Neh. 6:14 thi. th. of rest *of t. p.*
Jer. 23:9 bec. *of the p.* bones sh.

    16 hea. not to words *of p.* 27:14
    26 sh. this be in heart *of t. p. ?*
Hos. 12:10 simil. by minist. *of p.*
Zec. 8:9 hear by mouth *of the p.*
Mat. 14:5 Elias or one *of the p.*
    Mark 6:15 ; 8:28
    23:29 tombs *of t. p. Luke* 11:47
    30 partakers in blood *of t. p.*
    26:56 scrip. *of t. p.* be fulfilled
Luke 9:8 one *of the p.* risen, 19
Acts 3:25 ye are children *of t. p.*
    7:52 wh. *of t. p.* not persecut. ?
    13:15 reading *of law* and *t. p.*
    27 they know not voice *of t. p.*
    15:15 to th. agree words *of t. p.*
    28:23 persuad. them out *of t. p.*
Rom. 16:26 manif. by scrip. *of p.*
1 Cor. 14:32 spirits *of t. p.* subj.
Eph. 2:20 built on founda. *of p.*
Heb. 11:32 fail me to tell *of t. p.*
Rev. 16:6 shed the blood *of t. p.*
    22:6 L. God *of t. p.* sent angel

Servants the PROPHETS.

2 K. 9:7 avenge blood of *s. t. p.*
    17:13 law I sent by my *s. the p.*
    23 Lord had said by his *s. t. p.*
    21:10 L. spa. by his *s. t. p.* 24:2
Ezr. 9:11 commanded by *s. t. p.*
Jer. 7:25 sent you my *serv. the*
    p. 25:4 ; 29:19 ; 35:15
Ezek. 38:17 in old tim. by *s. t. p.*
Dan. 9:6 nei. hearken. to *s. t. p.*
    10 laws sent be. us by his *s. t. p.*
Amos 3:7 reveal. secret to *s. t. p.*
Zec. 1:6 commanded my *s. t. p.*
Rev. 10:7 declared to his *s. t. p.*
    11:18 give reward to *s. the p.*

PROPHETESS.

Ex. 15:20 Miriam *p.* took timb.
Jud. 4:4 Deborah a *p.* judged Is.
2 K. 22:14 went to Huldah a *n.*
    2 *Chr.* 34:22
Neh. 6:14 think on *p.* Noadiah
Is. 8:3 went to *p.* she conceived
Luke 2:36 th. was one Anna a *p.*
Rev. 2:20 Jez. called herself a *p.*

PROPITIATION.

Rom. 3:25 God set to be a *p.*
1 John 2:2 *p.* for our sins, 4:10

PROPORTION.

1 K. 7:36 to the *p.* of every one
Job 41:12 not conceal comely *p.*
Rom. 12:6 accord. to *p.* of faith

PROSELYTE.

Mat. 23:15 sea and la. to ma. *p.*
Acts 2:10 Jews and *p.* we hear
    6:5 Nicholas a *p.* of Antioch
    13:43 Jews and religious *p.* fol-
    lowed Paul and Barnabas

PROSPECT.

Ezek. 40:44 *p.* was to the south
    46 *p.* north ; 42:15 *p.* east, 43:4

PROSPER.

Gen. 24:40 G. send angel, *p.* thee
    42 if now thou do *p.* my way
    39:3 Lord made Joseph to *p.* 23
Num. 14:41 transgress. not *p.*
Deut. 28:29 shn. not *p.* in thy wa.
    29:9 that ye may *p.* in all ye do.
    Jos. 1:7 ; 1 *K.* 2:3
1 K. 22:12 go to Ramoth-gilead
    and *p.* 15 ; 2 *Chr.* 18:11, 14
1 Chr. 22:11 my son, L. *p.* thee
    13 shalt *p.* if thou takest heed
2 Chr. 13:12 fight not, sh. not *p.*
    20:20 believe proph. so sh. ye *p.*
    24:20 why transg. ye can. *p. ?*
    26:5 Lord God made him to *p.*
Neh. 1:11 *p.* I pray thee, thy ser.
    2:20 G. of heaven, he will *p.* us
Job 12:6 tabernac. of robbers *p.*
Ps. 1:3 what. he doeth shall *p.*
    73:12 ungodly *p.* in the world
    122:6 they sh. *p.* that love thee
Prov. 28:13 cover. his sins not *p.*

Ec. 11:6 know. not whether *p.*
Is. 53:10 pleas. of L. *p.* in hands
54:17 no weapon ag. thee sh. *p.*
55:11 it shall *p.* in thing I sent
Jer. 2:37 thou sh. not *p.* in them
5:28 th. *p.* 10:21 not *p.* 20:11
12:1 doth way of wicked *p. ?*
22:30 man that sh. not *p.* in his
  days, man of his seed sh. *p.*
23:5 a king shall reign and *p.*
32:5 tho' ye fight, ye sh. not *p.*
Lam. 1:5 adversa. enemies *p.*
Ezek. 16:13 and thou didst *p.*
17:9 saith Lord, Shall it *p. ? 10*
15 shall he *p. ?* sh. he escape ?
Dan. 8:24 he sh. destroy and *p.*
25 he shall cause craft to *p.*
11:27 speak lies, sh. not *p.* 36
3 *John* 2 I wish th. thou may *p.*

PROSPERED, ETH.

Gen. 24:56 seeing L. *p.* my way
Jud. 4:24 hand of Is. *p.* ag. Jab.
2 *Sam.* 11:7 deman. how war *p.*
2 *K.* 18:7 Hezek. *p.* 2 *Chr.* 31:21 ;
  32:30 ; 2 *Chr.* 14:7 Asa *p.*
1 *Chr.* 29:23 Solomon *p.*
Ezr. 5:8 work *p.* in their hands
6:14 *p.* thro' prophesying of H.
Job 9:4 harden. ag. him and *p. ?*
Ps. 37:7 because of him that *p.*
Prov. 17:8 whi. it turneth it *p.*
Dan. 6:28 Dan. *p.* in reign of D.
8:12 cast down truth. and it *p.*
1 *Cor.* 16:2 as God hath *p.* him
3 *John* 2 in health, ev. as soul *p.*

PROSPERITY.

Deut. 23:6 th. sh. not seek th. *p.*
1 *Sam.* 25:6 say to him liv. in *p.*
1 *K.* 10:7 thy wisdom and *p.*
Job 15:21 in *p.* destr. shall come
36:11 sh. spend their days in *p.*
Ps. 30:6 in my *p.* I said
35:27 L. hath plea. in *p.* of ser.
73:3 I saw the *p.* of the wicked
118:25 O L. I bes. thee, send *p.*
122:7 peace wi. walls, *p.* in pal.
Prov. 1:32 *p.* of fools destroy th.
Ec. 7:14 in day of *p.* be joyful
Jer. 22:21 I spake to th. in thy *p.*
33:9 the *p.* that I procure to it
Lam. 3:17 fr. peace, I forgat *p.*
Zec. 1:17 cit. thro' *p.* be spread
7:7 J. was inhabited and in *p.*

PROSPEROUS, LY.

Gen. 24:21 L. made his journ. *p.*
39:2 L. was with Jo. a *p.* man
Jos. 1:8 thou make thy way *p.*
Jud. 18:5 way we go sh. be *p.*
2 *Chr.* 7:11 Solomon *p.* effected
Ps. 45:4 in thy majesty ride *p.*
Job 8:6 habitation of righte. *p.*
Is. 48:15 shall make his way *p.*
Zec. 8:12 the seed shall be *p.*
Rom. 1:10 I mi. have *p.* journey

PROSTITUTE.

Lev. 19:29 do not *p.* thy daught.

PROTECTION.

Deut. 32:38 rise up and be yo. *p.*

PROTEST, ED, ING.

Gen. 43:3 man did solemnly *p.*
1 *Sam.* 8:9 *p.* solemnly unto th.
1 *K.* 2:42 and I *p.* unto thee
Jer. 11:7 I *p.* to your fathers, ris.
  early and *p.* saying, Obey
Zec. 3:6 the angel of the L. *p.*
1 *Cor.* 15:31 I *p.* by rejoic. in C.

PROUD.

Job 9:13 the *p.* helpers do stoop
26:12 smiteth through the *p.*

Job 38:11 thy *p.* waves be stayed
40:11 behold every one th. is *p.*
  12 look on every one that is *p.*
Ps. 12:3 tongue speak *p.* things
31:23 and rewardeth the *p.* doer
40:4 blessed. respecteth not *p.*

86:14 *p.* are risen against me
94:2 render a reward to the *p.*
101:5 him that hath a *p.* heart
119:21 thou hast rebuked the *p.*
  51 *p.* have had me in derision
69 *p.* have forged a lie ag. me
78 let *p.* be ashamed, they de.
85 the *p.* digged pits for me
122 let not the *p.* oppress me
123:4 filled with contempt of *p.*
124:5 *p.* waters had gone over
138:6 the *p.* he knoweth afar off
140:5 *p.* have hid a snare for me
Prov. 6:17 Lord hateth a *p.* look
15:25 L. will destroy house of *p.*
16:5 *p.* in heart abomina. to L.
19 to divide spoil with the *p.*
21:4 a *p.* heart is sin
24 *p.* scorner, deals in *p.* wra.
28:25 *p.* heart stirreth up strife
Ec. 7:8 better than *p.* in spirit
Is. 2:12 day of L. on ev. one *p.*
13:11 arrogancy of *p.* to cease
16:6 we heard of M. he is ve. *p.*
Jer. 13:15 be not *p.* L. hath spo.
43:2 all *p.* men answ. Jeremiah
48:29 pride of Moab exceed. *p.*
50:29 hath been *p.* 31 O most *p.*
32 most *p.* sh. stumble and fa.
Hab. 2:5 he is a *p.* man, neither
Mat. 3:15 *p.* happy ; 4:1 *p.* stub.
Luke 1:51 hath scattered the *p.*
Rom. 1:30 unrighte. *p.* boasters
1 *Tim.* 6:4 he is *p.* know. noth.
2 *Tim.* 3:2 lov. of themselves, *p.*
Jam. 4:6 G. resisteth *p.* 1 *Pet.* 5:5

PROUDLY.

Ex. 18:11 *p.* he was above them
1 *Sam.* 2:3 talk no more so *p.*
Neh. 9:10 they dealt *p.* 16:29
Ps. 17:10 with mouth speak *p.*
  31:18 speak grievous things *p.*
Is. 3:5 shall behave himself *p.*
Ob. 12 neither have spoken *p.*

PROVE.

Ex. 16:4 I may *p.* th. *Deut.* 8:16
20:20 for God is come to *p.* you
Deut. 8:2 humble thee, *p.* thee
33:8 holy one, wh. thou didst *p.*
Jud. 2:22 I may *p.* Isr. 3:1, 4
6:39 let me *p.* thee but th. once
1 *K.* 10:1 came to *p.* S. 2 *Chr.* 9:1
Job 9:20 it shall *p.* me perverse
Ps. 26:2 exam. me, O L. *p.* me
Ec. 2:1 I will *p.* th. with mirth
Dan. 1:12 *p.* thy serv. I beseech
Mal. 3:10 *p.* me now herewith
Luke 14:19 oxen, I go to *p.* them
John 6:6 this he said to *p.* him
Acts 24:13 nei. can they *p.* 25:7
Rom. 12:2 *p.* what is that good
2 *Cor.* 8:8 to *p.* sincerity of love
13:5 *p.* your own selves, know
Gal. 6:4 let ev. man *p.* his work
1 *Thes.* 5:21 *p.* all things

PROVED.

Gen. 42:15 sh. be *p.* by life of Ph.
  26 that your words may be *p.*
Ex. 15:25 made stat. and *p.* them
1 *Sam.* 17:39 I have not *p.* them
Ps. 17:3 thou hast *p.* my heart
66:10 thou, O God, hast *p.* us
81:7 I *p.* thee at waters of M.
95:9 when your fathers *p.* me
Ec. 7:23 this have I *p.* by wisd.
Dan. 1:14 and *p.* them ten days
Rom. 3:9 we *p.* Jews and Genti.
2 *Cor.* 8:22 wh. we have often *p.*
1 *Tim.* 3:10 let th. also be first *p.*
Heb. 3:9 your fathers *p.* me

PROVETH, ING.

Deut. 13:3 Lord your G. *p.* you
Acts 9:22 Saul *p.* that this is Ch.
Eph. 5:10 *p.* what is accept. to L.

PROVENDER.

Gen. 24:25 we have straw and *p.*

---

32 gave straw and *p.* to cam.
42:27 opened sack to give ass *p.*
43:24 men gave their asses *p.*
Jud. 19:19 th. is straw and *p.* 21
Is. 30:24 asses shall eat clean *p.*

PROVERB.

Deut. 28:37 and ye shall be a *p.*
1 *Sam.* 10:12 *p.* is Saul am. prop.
24:13 as saith *p.* of the ancients
1 *K.* 9:7 Israel shall be a *p.*
2 *Chr.* 7:20 house will I ma. a *p.*
Ps. 69:11 I became a *p.* to them
Prov. 1:6 to understand a *p.* and
Is. 14:4 *p.* ag. king of Babylon
Jer. 24:9 to be a *p.* and a curse
Ezek. 12:23 I will make *p.* cease,
  no more use *p.* in Is. 18:2, 3
14:8 make him a sign and *p.*
Hab. 2:6 take up a *p.* ag. him
Luke 4:23 *p.* phys. heal thyself
John 16:29 spea. plain. and no *p.*
2 *Pet.* 2:22 happ. according to *p.*

PROVERBS.

Num. 21:27 they that speak in *p.*
1 *K.* 4:32 Solomon spake 3,000 *p.*
Prov. 1:1 *p.* of Solo. 10:1 ; 25:1
Ec. 12:9 preacher set in order *p.*
Ezek. 16:44 ev. one that useth *p.*
John 16:25 sp. in *p.* no more in *p.*

PROVIDE.

Gen. 22:8 G. will *p.* hims. lamb
30:30 shall I *p.* for own house ?
Ex. 18:21 thou sh. *p.* able men
1 *Sam.* 16:17 *p.* me man can play
2 *Chr.* 2:7 men whom Da. did *p.*
Ps. 78:20 can he *p.* flesh for pe. ?
Mat. 10:9 *p.* nei. gold nor silver
Luke 12:33 *p.* bags wax not old
Acts 23:24 *p.* beasts to set P. on
Rom. 12:17 *p.* things honest
1 *Tim.* 5:8 any *p.* not for house

PROVIDED.

Deut. 33:21 *p.* first part himself
1 *Sam.* 16:1 I have *p.* me a king
2 *Sam.* 19:32 *p.* king of susten.
1 *K.* 4:7 *p.* victuals for king, 27
Ps. 65:9 when thou hast *p.*
Luke 12:20 things th. hast *p. ?*
Heb. 11:40 having *p.* bet. things

PROVIDENCE.

Acts 24:2 done to nation by *p.*

PROVIDETH, ING.

Job 38:41 *p.* for the raven food
Prov. 6:8 *p.* meat in summer
2 *Cor.* 8:21 *p.* for honest things

PROVINCE, S.

1 *K.* 20:14 princes of *p.* 15, 17, 19
Ezr. 4:15 this city hurtful to *p.*
6:2 found in *p.* of the Medes
7:16 gold thou canst find in *p.*
Neh. 11:3 the. are chief of the *p.*
Est. 1:1 Ahasu. reigned 127 *p.*
  16 wrong to peo. in *p.* 22
2:3 king appoint officers in *p.*
3:8 people scattered in all *p.*
4:11 all peo. of king's *p.* know
9:4 Mord.'s fame went thro' *p.*
  28 these days sh. be kept in *p.*
Ec. 2:8 I gathered treas. of *p.*
5:8 if thou seest oppres. in a *p.*
Lam. 1:1 she was princess am. *p.*
Ezek. 19:8 against him from *p.*
Dan. 2:48 made D. ruler over *p.*
3:30 promoted Shad. in the *p.*
8:2 Shushan, in *p.* of Elam
11:24 enter fattest places of *p.*
Acts 23:34 he asked of what *p.*
25:1 when Fes. was come to *p.*

PROVISION.

Gen. 42:25 give them *p.* for way
45:21 Jos. gave them *p.* for way
Jos. 9:5 bread of th. *p.* was dry
  12 bread we took hot for our *p.*
1 *K.* 4:7 in his month made *p.*
  22 Solomon's *p.* was 30 meas.

2 *K.* 6:23 he prepared great *p.*
1 *Chr.* 29:19 for which I made *p.*
Ps. 132:15 I will bless her *p.*
Dan. 1:5 king appoint. daily *p.*
Rom. 13:14 ma. not *p.* for flesh

PROVOCATION.

1 *K.* 15:30 Jer. made Is. sin by *p.*
21:22 for the *p.* wherewith Ah.
2 *K.* 23:26 bec. of *p.* Manasseh
Neh. 9:18 wrought great *p.* 26
Job 17:2 eye continue in th. *p. ?*
Ps. 95:8 harden not your hearts
as in *p. Heb.* 3:8, 15
Jer. 32:31 this city ha. been a *p.*
Ezek. 20:28 th. they presented *p.*

PROVOKE.

Ex. 23:21 obey and *p.* him not
Num. 14:11 how long people *p. ?*
Deut. 31:20 if ye *p.* and break
Job 12:6 that *p.* God are secure
Ps. 78:40 how oft did th. *p.* him
Is. 3:8 doings against L. to *p.*
Jer. 7:19 they *p.* me to anger ?
44:8 in that ye *p.* me to wrath
Luke 11:53 began to urge and *p.*
Rom. 10:19 I will *p.* to jealousy
11:11 to *p.* them to jealousy, 14
1 *Cor.* 10:22 do we *p.* L. to jeal. ?
Eph. 6:4 *p.* not your chil. to wr.
Heb. 8:16 wh. they heard, did *p.*
10:24 *p.* to love and good works

PROVOKED.

Num. 14:23 nor sh. any that *p.*
Num. 16:30 these men have *p.* L.
Deut. 9:8 in Horeb ye *p.* the L.
22 at Tab. and Massah ye *p.* L.
1 *Sam.* 1:6 adversaries *p.* sore
7 so she *p.* her, theref. she we.
1 *K.* 14:22 Judah *p.* to jealousy
2 *K.* 23:26 Manasseh had *p.* him
1 *Chr.* 21:1 Satan *p.* David
Ezr. 5:12 our fathers had *p.* God
Ps. 78:56 tempted and *p.* God
106:7 but *p.* him at the sea
29 they *p.* him with invent.
33 they *p.* spirit of Moses, 43
Zec. 8:14 your fathers *p.* me
1 *Cor.* 13:5 char. is not easily *p.*
2 *Cor.* 9:2 your zeal *p.* very many

PROVOKEDST, ETH.

Deut. 9:7 forget not how *p.* Lord
Prov. 20:2 whoso *p.* him to ang.
Is. 65:3 peo. that *p.* me to anger
Ezek. 8:3 image which *p.* jeal.

See ANGER.

PROVOKING.

Deut. 32:19 because of *p.* sons
1 *K.* 14:15 made groves, *p.* Lord
16:7 ag. Baasha in *p.* Lord, 13
Ps. 78:17 by *p.* the Most H.
Gal. 5:26 vain glory, *p.* one ano.

PRUDENCE.

2 *Chr.* 2:12 son endued with *p.*
Prov. 8:12 I wisd. dwell with *p.*
Eph. 1:8 abound. in wisd. and *p.*

PRUDENT.

1 *Sam.* 16:18 Dav. *p.* in matters
Prov. 12:16 *p.* man cover. shame
23 a *p.* man conceal. knowl.
13:16 every *p.* man dealeth with
14:8 wisdom of *p.* to understand
15 the *p.* looketh to his goings
18 *p.* are crowned with knowl.
15:5 he that regar. *p.* repr. is *p.*
16:21 the wise shall be called *p.*
18:15 heart of *p.* getteth knowl.
19:14 a *p.* wife is from the Lord
22:3 a *p.* man foresec. evil, 27:12
Is. 3:2 take away *p.* and ancient
5:21 woe to *p.* in their own sig.
10:13 I have done it, for I am *p.*
29:14 understanding of *p.* men
Jer. 49:7 is counsel perish. fr. *p. ?*
Hos. 14:9 who is *p.* and he shall ?
Amos 5:13 *p.* shall keep silence

Mat. 11:25 hid these things from
the wise and *p. Luke* 10:21
Acts 13:7 Serg. Paulus, a *p.* man
1 *Cor.* 1:19 understanding of *p.*

PRUDENTLY.

Is. 52:13 my servant sh. deal *p.*

PRUNE, ED.

Lev. 25:3 six years shalt thou *p.*
4 eev. year not sow field nor *p.*
Is. 5:6 it shall not be *p.*

PRUNING.

Is. 2:4 beat spears into *p.* hooks
18:5 cut off sprigs with *p.* hooks
Joel 3:10 beat *p.* hooks into spe.
Mic. 4:3 beat spears into *p.* hoo.

PSALM.

1 *Chr.* 16:7 David deliver. this *p.*
Ps. 81:2 take *p.* 98:5 voice of *p.*
Acts 13:33 as writ. in second *p.*
35 saith in ano. *p.* Thou shalt
1 *Cor.* 14:26 every one hath a *p. ?*

PSALMIST.

2 *Sam.* 23:1 David sweet *p.* of Is

PSALMS.

1 *Chr.* 16:9 sing *p. Ps.* 105:2
Ps. 95:2 joyful noise with *p.*
Luke 20:42 D. saith in book of *p.*
24:44 which were written in *p.*
Acts 1:20 written in book of P.
Eph. 5:19 speak. to yours. in *p.*
Col. 3:16 admonish. other in *p.*
Jam. 5:13 is any merry ? sing *p.*

PSALTERY.

1 *Sam.* 10:5 meet prop. with a *p.*
Ps. 33:2 sing with the *p.* 144:9
57:8 awake *p.* and harp, 108:2
71:22 I will praise with *p.* 92:3
81:2 bring hither harp with *p.*
150:3 praise him with *p.* harp
Dan. 3:5 sound of *p.* 7, 10, 15

PSALTERIES. *See* CYMBALS.

PUBLIC, LY.

Mat. 1:19 make her a *p.* example
Acts 18:28 *p.* convinced the Jews
20:20 but have taught you *p.*

PUBLICAN, S.

Mat. 5:46 do not *p.* same ? 47
9:10 many *p.* sat with him,
Mark 2:15 ; *Luke* 5:29
11 why eat. your master wi. *p.*
10:3 Thomas, and Matthew *p.*
Mat. 11:19 a friend of *p. Lu.* 7:34
18:17 let him be as hea. and *p.*
21:31 *p.* go into kingdom of G.
32 *p.* and harlots beli. on him
Luke 3:12 came *p.* to be baptized
5:27 he saw a *p.* named Levi
7:29 *p.* justi. G. being baptized
15:1 then drew near to him *p.*
18:10 the one Pharisee, other *p.*
11 God, I thank thee, not as *p.*
13 *p.* standing afar off, said
19:2 Zaccheus chief among *p.*

PUBLISH.

Deut. 32:3 I will *p.* name of L.
1 *Sam.* 31:9 *p.* it in house of idols
2 *Sam.* 1:20 *p.* it not in Askelon
Neh. 8:15 *p.* that they bring time
Ps. 26:7 may *p.* with the voice
Jer. 4:5 *p.* in Jeru. 16 *p.* against
5:20 declare this, *p.* it in Judah
31:7 *p.* ye and say, O Lord save
46:14 *p.* in Migdol, *p.* in Noph
50:2 *p.* and conceal not
Amos 3:9 *p.* in palaces of Ashdod
4:5 proclaim and *p.* fr. offerings
Mark 1:45 he began to *p.* it, 5:20

PUBLISHED.

Est. 1:20 dec. *p.* thro' empire, 22
3:14 Haman's decree *p.* 8:13
Ps. 68:11 great company *p.* it
Jon. 3:7 he caused it to be *p.*
Mark 7:36 more a gre. deal th. *p.*
13:10 the gospel must first be *p.*

Luke 8:39 *p.* through whole city
Acts 10:37 that word wh. was *p.*
13:49 word of the Lord was *p.*

PUBLISHETH.

Is. 52:7 that *p.* peace, *p.* salvat.
Jer. 4:15 voice *p.* affliction
Nah. 1:15 feet of him *p.* peace

PUBLIUS.

Acts 28:8 the father of P. lay sick

PUDENS.

2 *Tim.* 4:21 greeteth thee and P.

PUFFED up.

1 *Cor.* 4:6 no one of you be *p. up*
18 some are *p. up,* as thou gh.I
19 not speech of th. are *p. up*
5:2 are *p. up* and not mourned
13:4 charity is not *p. up*
Col. 2:18 vainly *p. up*

PUFFETH at, up.

Ps. 10:5 enemies, he *p. at* them
12:5 safety fr. him th. *p. at* him
1 *Cor.* 8:1 knowl. *p. up,* charity

PUL.

2 *K.* 15:19 P. king of Assyria
1 *Chr.* 5:26 stirred up spirit of P.
Is. 66:19 those that escape to P.

PULL, ED.

Gen. 8:9 Noah *p.* the dove to him
19:10 the men *p.* Lot into house
1 *K.* 13:4 Jerob. could not *p.* it
Ezr. 6:11 let timber be *p.* down
Ps. 31:4 *p.* me out of net
Is. 22:19 fr. thy state *p.* th. down
Jer. 1:10 set th. to *p.* down, 18:7
12:3 *p.* them like sheep for sla.
24:6 build, not *p.* down, 42:10
Lam. 3:11 *p.* me in pieces
Ezek. 17:9 sh. he not *p.* up roots ?
Amos 9:15 shall no more be *p.* up
Mic. 2:8 *p.* off robe with garm.
Zec. 7:11 *p.* away shoulder
Mat. 7:4 *p.* out mote, *Luke* 6:42
Luke 12:18 *p.* down my barns
14:5 not *p.* him out on sab. ?
Acts 23:10 lest Paul sho. been *p.*

PULLING.

2 *Cor.* 10:4 mighty to *p.* down
Jude 23 with fear *p.* out of fire

PULPIT.

Neh. 8:4 Ezra stood upon a *p.*

PULSE.

2 *Sam.* 17:28 and parched *p.*
Dan. 1:12 let them give *p.*

PUNISH.

Lev. 26:18 *p.* you sev. times, 24
Prov. 17:26 to *p.* just not good
Is. 10:12 *p.* stout heart of king
13:11 I will *p.* world for evil
24:21 Lord shall *p.* the host
26:21 L. cometh to *p.* inhabit.
27:1 L. with strong sw. sh. *p.*
Jer. 9:25 *p.* them are circumcised
11:22 *p.* men of Anathoth
13:21 what say when he sh. *p. ?*
21:14 *p.* accord. to your doings
23:34 I will *p.* man ; 25:12 *p.*
king, 50:18
27:8 *p.* nation ; 29:32 *p.* Shem.
30:20 I will *p.* all th. oppress th.
36:31 I will *p.* Jehoiakim
Jer. 44:13 *p.* them in E. as I *p.* J.
29 a sign that I will *p.* you
46:25 I will *p.* the multitude
51:44 I will *p.* Bel in Babylon
Hos. 4:9 *p.* them for their ways
14 I will not *p.* your daughters
12:2 *p.* J. according to his ways
Amos 3:2 I will *p.* you for iniq.
Zep. 1:8 in day I will *p.* princes
9 I will *p.* all those that leap
12 *p.* men that are settled
Zec. 8:14 as I thoug. to *p.* them
Acts 4:21 how th. might *p.* them

PUNISHED.

Ex. 21:20 shall surely be *p.* 22
21 not be *p.* he is his money
Ezr. 9:13 *p.* less than iniq. des.
Job 31:11 it is iniq. to be *p.* 28
Prov. 21:11 when scorner is *p.*
22:3 simple are *p.* 27:12
Jer. 44:13 as I have *p.* Jerusa.
50:18 punish as I have *p.* king
Zep. 3:7 not cut off, how I *p.*
Zec. 10:3 shepherds, I *p.* goats
Acts 22:5 br. them bou. to be *p.*
26:11 I *p.* them in every synag.
2 Thes. 1:9 *p.* with destruction
2 Pet. 2:9 day of judgm. to be *p.*

PUNISHMENT.

Gen. 4:13 *p.* great. th. I can bear
Lev. 26:41 accept *p.* of iniq. 43
1 Sam. 28:10 no *p.* shall hap. th.
Job 31:3 a strange *p.* to workers
Prov. 19:19 man of wrath suf. *p.*
Lam. 3:39 for *p.* of his sins
4:6 *p.* of my people is greater
than the *p.* of Sodom
22 *p.* of thine iniq. is accomp.
Ezek. 14:10 bear *p.* of their iniq.
p. of prophets as *p.* of him
Amos 1:3 I will not turn away *p.*
thereof, 6, 9, 11, 13; 2:1, 4, 6
Zec. 14:19 this shall be *p.* of Eg.
Mat. 25:46 go into everlasting *p.*
2 Cor. 2:6 such a man is this *p.*
Heb. 10:29 how much sorer *p.*
1 Pet. 2:14 for *p.* of evil-doers

PUNISHMENTS.

Job 19:29 bringeth *p.* of sword
Ps. 149:7 execute *p.* upon people
PUNON *Num.* 33:42, 43

PUR.

Est. 3:7 cast P. that is, the lot
9:24 for Haman had cast P.
26 Purim, after the name of P.
See PURIM.

PURCHASE, Substantive.

Gen. 49:32 *p.* of field and cave
Jer. 32:11 I took evidence of *p.*
12 I gave evidence of *p.* 14, 16

PURCHASE, ED.

Gen. 25:10 Abra. *p.* of sons of H.
Ex. 15:16 over wh. thou hast *p.*
Lev. 25:33 if a man *p.* of Levites
Ruth 4:10 R. I *p.* to be my wife
Ps. 74:2 congregati. thou hast *p.*
78:54 wh. his right hand had *p.*
Acts 1:18 this man *p.* a field
8:20 gift of God may be *p.*
20:28 *p.* with his own blood
Eph. 1:14 redemption of *p.* pos.
1 Tim. 3:13 office of dea. well, *p.*

PURE.

Ex. 27:20 br. *p.* oil, *Lev.* 24:2
31:8 *p.* candles. 39:37; *Lev.* 24:4
Deut. 32:14 *p.* blood of grape
2 Sam. 22:27 with *p.* thou wilt
show thyself *p.* *Ps.* 18:26
Ezr. 6:20 all *p.* killed passover
Job 4:17 shall a man be more *p. ?*
8:6 thou wert *p.* and upright
11:4 thou said, My doctrine is *p.*
16:17 injustice, my prayer is *p.*
25:5 stars are not *p.* in his sight
Ps. 12:6 words of the Lord are *p.*
19:8 commandment of L. is *p.*
119:140 thy word is very *p.*
Prov. 15:26 words of *p.* are plea.
20:9 who can say, I am *p.* fr. sin ?
11 whether his work be *p.*
21:8 as for *p.* his work is right
30:5 every word of God is *p.*
12 a generation *p.* in own eyes
Dan. 7:9 hair of head like *p.* wool
Mic. 6:11 shall I count them *p. ?*
Zep. 3:9 turn to people *p.* langu.
Mal. 1:11 in ev. place a *p.* offer.
Acts 20:26 *p.* from blood of men

Rom. 14:20 all th. indeed are *p.*
Phil. 4:8 whatsoev. things are *p.*
1 Tim. 3:9 faith in a *p.* consci.
5:22 partak. of sins, keep thy. *p.*
2 Tim. 1:3 with *p.* conscience
Tit. 1:15 to the *p.* all thi. are *p.*
to the defiled nothing is *p.*
Heb. 10:22 bodies washed with *p.*
Jam. 1:27 *p.* relig. and undefiled
3:17 wisdom fr. above is first *p.*
2 Pet. 3:1 I stir up your *p.* minds
1 John 3:3 purifieth as he is *p.*
Rev. 15:6 ang. clothed in *p.* linen
22:1 showed a *p.* river of water

See HEART, GOLD.

PURELY.

Is. 1:25 I will *p.* purge away

PURENESS.

Job 22:30 deliv. by *p.* of hands
Prov. 22:11 he loved *p.* of heart
2 Cor. 6:6 appro. ourselves by *p.*

PURER.

Lam. 4:7 Nazarites *p.* than snow
Hab. 1:13 thou art of *p.* eyes

PURGE, ETH.

2 Chr. 34:3 Josiah began to *p.* J.
Ps. 51:7 *p.* me with hyssop
65:3 transgressions thou sh. *p.*
Is. 1:25 *p.* away thy dross
Ezek. 20:38 I will *p.* fr. am. you
43:26 seven days shall they *p.*
Dan. 11:35 some of th. *p.* them
Mal. 3:3 *p.* as gold and silver
Mat. 3:12 *p.* his floor, *Luke* 3:17
John 15:2 branch that bea. he *p.*
1 Cor. 5:7 *p.* out the old leaven
2 Tim. 2:21 if a man *p.* himself
Heb. 9:14 *p.* your conscience

PURGED.

1 Sam. 3:14 Eli's house not be *p.*
2 Chr. 34:8 when he had *p.* land
Prov. 16:6 by mercy iniq. is *p.*
Is. 4:4 *p.* blood of Jerusalem
6:7 iniq. taken away, sin is *p.*
22:14 this iniq. shall not be *p.*
27:9 by this iniq. of Jacob be *p.*
Ezek. 24:13 beca. I have *p.* thee,
and thou was not *p.*
Heb. 1:3 when he had *p.* our sins
9:22 almost all thi. are by law *p.*
10:2 bec. worshippers once *p.*
2 Pet. 1:9 forgotten he was *p.*

PURGING.

Mark 7:19 the draught, *p.* meats

PURIFICATION, S.

Num. 19:9 it is a *p.* for sin
17 ashes of burnt heifer *p.*
2 Chr. 30:19 *p.* of the sanctuary
Neh. 12:45 port. kept ward of *p.*
Est. 2:3 the things of their *p.*
12 so were the days of their *p.*
Luke 2:22 days of her *p.*
Acts 21:26 accomp. of days of *p.*

PURIFY.

Num. 19:12 shall *p.* himself, 19
20 unclean, and not *p.* himself
31:19 *p.* yourselves third day
20 *p.* all your raiment
Job 41:25 by rea. of break. th. *p.*
Is. 66:17 *p.* themselves in garden
Ezek. 43:26 seven days *p.* altar
Mal. 3:3 he shall *p.* sons of Levi
John 11:55 went to Jerus. to *p.*
Acts 21:24 take and *p.* thyself
Tit. 2:14 *p.* a peculiar people
Jam. 4:8 *p.* your hearts

PURIFIED, ETH.

Lev. 8:15 and *p.* the altar
Num. 8:21 Le. were *p.* *Ezek.* 6:20
19:13 touch dead body, *p.* not
31:23 *p.* with water of separat.
2 Sam. 11:4 Bathsheba was *p.*
Ps. 12:6 pure words, as silver *p.*
Dan. 12:10 many shall be *p.*

Acts 24:18 certain J. found me *p.*
Heb. 9:23 things in heavens *p.*
1 Pet. 1:22 ye *p.* your souls
1 John 3:3 this hope *p.* himself

PURIFIER.

Mal. 2:3 he shall sit as a *p.*

PURIFYING.

Lev. 12:4 continue in blood of *p.*
Num. 8:7 sprinkle water of *p.*
1 Chr. 23:28 in *p.* holy things
Est. 2:12 things for *p.* of women
John 2:6 manner of *p.* of Jews
3:25 th. arose question about *p.*
Acts 15:9 *p.* their hearts by faith
21:26 the next day *p.* himself
Heb. 9:13 sanctifi. to *p.* of flesh

PURIM.

Est. 9:26 called these days P.
28 days of P. sho. not fail, 29, 31
32 decree of Esther confirm. P.

PURITY.

1 Tim. 4:12 exam. in faith, in *p.*
5:2 rebuke younger with all *p.*

PURLOINING.

Tit. 2:10 not *p.* showing fidelity

PURPLE.

Ex. 25:4 the offering, *p.* 26:1
39:3 gold cut to work in the *p.*
Num. 4:13 take ashes, spread *p.*
Jud. 8:26 *p.* raiment on kings
2 Chr. 2:7 a man to work *p.* 14
3:14 made veil of blue, and *p.*
Est. 1:6 fast. with cords of *p.*
8:15 Mord. went with gar. of *p.*
Prov. 31:22 clothing is silk, *p.*
Cant. 3:10 made covering of *p.*
7:5 the hair of thy head like *p.*
Jer. 10:9 and *p.* is their clothin
Ezek. 27:7 *p.* which covered the
16 Syria colour. fairs with *p.*
Mark 15:17 clothed him with *p.*
20 they took off the *p.* fr. him
Luke 16:19 a rich man clo. in *p.*
John 19:2 soldiers put on him *p.*
5 then came Jesus, wearing *p.*
Acts 16:14 Lydia, a seller of *p.*
Rev. 17:4 woman arrayed in *p.*
18:12 buyeth merchandise of *p.*
16 great city, clothed in *p.*

PURPOSE.

Ruth 2:16 handfuls of *p.* for her
Ezr. 4:5 counsellors to frustr. *p.*
Neh. 8:4 a pulpit made for the *p.*
Job 33:17 withd. man from his *p.*
Prov. 20:18 ev. *p.* is established
Ec. 3:1 time to ev. *p.* 17; 8:6
Is. 1:11 to what *p.* sacrifices ?
14:26 this is *p.* that is purposed
30:7 Egypti. shall help to no *p.*
Jer. 49:30 Nebu. conceived a *p.*
51:29 ev. *p.* of L. be performed
Dan. 6:17 that *p.* be not chang.
Acts 11:23 that with *p.* of heart
27:13 suppos. obtained their *p.*
43 centurion kept them fr. *p.*
Rom. 8:28 called according to *p.*
9:11 that the *p.* of God stand
17 for this *p.* I raised thee up
Eph. 1:11 according to *p.* of him
3:11 accord. to eternal *p.* in C.
6:22 for same *p.* *Col.* 4:8
2 Tim. 1:9 called us accor. to *p.*
3:10 hast fully known my *p.*
1 John 3:8 for this *p.* Son of God

PURPOSES.

Job 17:11 days past, *p.* broken
Prov. 15:22 with. counsel *p.* are
Is. 19:10 shall be broken in *p.*
Jer. 49:20 counsel of L. *p.* 50:45

PURPOSE, ED.

1 K. 5:5 I *p.* to build house to L.
2 Chr. 28:10 *p.* to keep under Ju.
32:2 Sennacherib *p.* to fight J.
Ps. 17:3 *p.* mouth sh. not trans.
140:4 who have *p.* to overthrow

Is. 14:24 I ha. *p.* so sh. it stand
26 the purpose *p.* on earth
27 L. hath *p.* who disannul it?
28:9 Lord hath *p.* to stain pride
46:11 I have *p.* it, will do it
Jer. 4:28 I *p.* it, will not repent
36:3 repent me of evil wh. I *p.*
36:3 will hear all evil wh. I *p.*
49:20 purposes that he *p.* 50:45
Lam. 2:8 Lord *p.* to destroy wall
Dan. 1:8 Daniel *p.* not to defile
Acts 19:21 Paul *p.* to go to Jeru.
20:3 Paul *p.* to return thro' M.
Rom. 1:13 oftent. I *p.* to come
2 *Cor.* 1:17 I *p.* accord. to flesh?
Eph. 1:9 his will wh. he hath *p.*
3:11 purp. which he *p.* in C. J.

PURPOSETH, ING.
Gen. 27:42 Esau *p.* to kill thee
2 *Cor.* 9:7 as he *p.* in heart

PURSE, S.
Prov. 1:14 let us have one *p.*
Mat. 10:9 silver nor brass in *p.*
Mark 6:8 no money in their *p.*
Luke 10:4 neither *p.* nor scrip
22:25 I sent you without *p.*
36 he that hath a *p.* let him

PURSUE.
Gen. 35:5 did not *p.* sons of J.
Ex. 15:9 enemy said, I will *p.*
Deut. 19:6 avenger *p. Jos.* 20:5
Jos. 2:5 *p.* them quickly, 10:19
1 *Sam.* 25:29 a man is risen to *p.*
30:8 shall I *p. ?* he answered,
2 *Sam.* 17:1 arise and *p.* after D.
20:6 servants, *p.* after Sheba, 7
24:13 flee while enemies *p. ?*
Job 13:25 wilt thou *p.* dry stub. ?
30:15 ter. *p.* my soul as wind
Ps. 34:14 seek peace, and *p.* it
Is. 30:16 they that *p.* be swift
Jer. 48:2 Madmen, sword sh. *p.*
Ezek. 35:6 blood shall *p.* thee
Hos. 8:3 Israel, enemy shall *p.*
Amos 1:11 E. did *p.* his brother
Nah. 1:8 darkness *p.* his enemi.

PURSUED.
Gen. 14:14 Abram *p.* to Dan, 15
31:23 and Laban *p.* Jacob, 36
Ex. 14:8 Pharaoh *p.* Israel, 9, 23;
Deut. 11:4; *Jos.* 24:6
Jud. 1:6 *p.* after Adoni-bezek
7:23 Gideon *p.* Mid. 25; 8:12
1 *Sam.* 7:11 Israel *p.* Phil. 17:52
2 *Sam.* 2:19 Asahel *p.* Abner
22:38 I *p.* enemies, *Ps.* 18:37
1 *K.* 20:20 Syrians fled, Israel *p.*
2 *K.* 25:5 army of Chaldees *p.*
the king, *Jer.* 39:5; 52:8
2 *Chr.* 14:13 Asa *p.* Ethiop. to G.
Is. 41:3 he *p.* them and passed
Lam. 4:19 they *p.* us on mount.

PURSUER, S.
Jos. 2:16 mount. lest *p.* meet
8:20 people turned upon the *p.*
Lam. 1:6 are gone before the *p.*

PURSUETH, ING.
Lev. 26:17 shall flee wh. none *p.*
36 shall fall when none *p.* 37
Jud. 8:4 300 men, faint, yet *p.*
1 *Sam.* 23:28 S. returned from *p.*
2 *Sam.* 8:22 J. came from *p.* tro.
18:16 people returned from *p.* L.
1 *K.* 18:27 your god *p.* on jour.
Prov. 11:19 he th. *p.* evil, *p.* dea.
13:21 evil *p.* sinners, to righte.
19:7 he *p.* them with words
28:1 wick. flee when no man *p.*

PURTENANCE.
Ex. 12:9 roast wi. fire legs and *p.*

PUSH.
Ex. 21:29 if ox were to *p.* 36
Deut. 33:17 with them he shall *p.*
1 *K.* 22:11 with these shalt thou
p. the Syrians, 2 *Chr.* 18:10
Job 30:12 they *p.* away my feet

Ps. 44:5 thro' thee we *p.* enem.
Dan. 11:40 shall king *p.* at him

PUSHED, ING.
Ezek. 34:21 *p.* diseased with hor.
Dan. 8:4 I saw ram *p.* westward

PUT.
Gen. 2:8 there G. *p.* the man, 15
3:15 I will *p.* enmity bet. thee
27:15 *p.* th. upon Jacob her son
29:3 *p.* stone ag. on well's mou.
30:42 feeble, he *p.* not the rods
32:16 *p.* space between drove
39:4 all he *p.* into Joseph's ha.
40:15 should *p.* me into dunge.
42:17 he *p.* altogether in ward
46:4 Joseph *p.* hand on th. eyes
48:18 *p.* right hand upon head
Ex. 3:22 shall *p.* them on sons
4:6 L. said, *p.* thy hand in bos.
15 *p.* words in his mouth
8:23 I will *p.* division bet. my
15:26 I will *p.* none of diseases
22:5 *p.* beast in ano. man's field
11 oath he hath not *p.* his ha.
23:1 *p.* not thy hand wi. wicked
29:24 shall *p.* all in hands of A.
33:5 now *p.* off thy ornaments
Lev. 8:27 he *p.* all on A.'s hands
26:8 *p.* 10,000 to fli. *Deut.* 32:30
Num. 6:27 sh. *p.* my name on Is.
11:17 spirit on thee, *p.* on them
29 L. would *p.* his Spi. on th.
23:5 L. *p.* word in Ba.'s mouth
Deut. 10:2 shalt *p.* them in ark
5 I *p.* tables in the ark I made
12:5 place he sh. *p.* his name, 21
7 rej. in all ye *p.* your hand to
18:18 *p.* my words in his mouth
Jud. 12:3 I *p.* my life in my ha.
1 *Sam.* 2:36 *p.* me in priest's offi.
14:26 no man *p.* hand to his m.
17:39 David *p.* them off him
19:5 did *p.* his life in his hand
28:21 I *p.* my life in my hand
1 *K.* 7:8 to *p.* my name there,
11:36; 14:21
12:29 other calves *p.* he in Dan
18:23 on wood, *p.* no fire under
22:27 king *p.* fellow in prison
2 *K.* 4:34 *p.* mouth upon mouth
11:12 they *p.* the crown on him
13:16 *p.* hand on bow, he *p.* ha.
21:7 in Jer. will I *p.* my name,
2 *Chr.* 6:20; 12:13; 33:7
1 *Chr.* 11:19 *p.* lives in jeopardy
13:10 because he *p.* hand to ark
2 *Chr.* 6:11 in house I *p.* the ark
Ezr. 7:27 *p.* thin. in king's heart
Neh. 2:12 what G. *p.* in my heart
3:5 nobles *p.* not necks to work
4:23 that every one *p.* them off
6:14 T. would *p.* me in fear, 19
Job 4:18 he *p.* no trust in his ser.
13:14 I *p.* my life in my hand?
19:13 *p.* my brethren far fr. me
23:6 he would *p.* strength in me
Job 41:2 can. *p.* hook in. his no. ?
Ps. 4:7 *p.* gladness in my heart
8:6 thou hast *p.* all things under his feet, 1 *Cor.* 15:25, 27;
Eph. 1:22; *Heb.* 2:8
9:20 *p.* in fear, O L. that nation
31:18 let lying lips be *p.* to sile.
40:3 *p.* new song in my mouth
14 let them be *p.* to shame that
wish me evil, 44:7; 53:5
44:9 thou hast *p.* us to shame
78:66 *p.* them to perp. reproach
88:18 lover and friend *p.* fr. me
118:8 tr. L. than *p.* con. in man
9 tr. L. than put confi. in prin.
119:31 O L. *p.* me not to shame
Prov. 25:8 nel. *p.* thee to shame
10 heareth it *p.* thee to shame
Ec. 10:10 *p.* to more strength
Cant. 5:3 *p.* off coat, how *p.* on ?
Is. 5:20 that *p.* darkn. for light

10:13 I ha. *p.* down inhabitants
42:1 I have *p.* my Spirit upon
him, *Mat.* 12:18
47:11 not be able to *p.* it off
51:16 *p.* words in mou. *Jer.* 1:9
23 *p.* into hand that afflict th.
53:10 he hath *p.* him to grief
59:21 words I *p.* in thy mouth
63:11 where is he that *p.* his H.
Spirit within him?
Jer. 3:19 how shall I *p.* thee am.
8:14 Lord our G. *p.* us to silence
12:13 they *p.* themselves to pain
31:33 *p.* my law in inward parts
32:40 will *p.* my fear in hearts
Ezek. 8:17 *p.* branch to th. nose
11:19 I will put a new spirit
within you, 36:26, 27; 37:14
16:14 comel. I had *p.* upon thee
29:4 *p.* hooks in thy jaws, 38:4
30:13 *p.* a fear in land of Egypt
37:6 *p.* breath in you, ye shall
Dan. 5:19 and whom he *p.* down
Mic. 3:5 *p.* not into their mouths
7:5 *p.* not confidence in a guide
Zep. 3:19 ha. been *p.* to shame
Mat. 5:15 candle *p.* under bushel
19:6 no man *p.* asun. *Mark* 10:9
26:52 *p.* up thy swo. *John* 18:11
Mark 10:16 *p.* his hands on them
Luke 1:52 hath *p.* down mighty
15:22 *p.* it on him and *p.* a ring
John 5:7 none to *p.* me into pool
Acts 1:7 Fa. *p.* in his own power
4:3 they *p.* the apostles in hold
5:25 men whom ye *p.* in prison
13:46 *p.* word of God from you
15:9 *p.* no difference between us
1 *Cor.* 15:24 *p.* down authority
25 *p.* his enemies under his fe.
2 *Cor.* 8:16 G. *p.* same care in T.
Eph. 4:22 *p.* off old man, *Col.* 3:9
Col. 3:8 ye also *p.* off these, ang.
2 *Tim.* 1:6 I *p.* thee in remembr.
Tit. 3:1 *p.* them in mind to be
subject
Phile. 18 *p.* that on my account
Heb. 2:5 hath he not *p.* in subj.
6:6 *p.* him to an open shame
8:10 I will *p.* my laws in mind
10:16 *p.* my laws into th. hearts
Jam. 3:3 *p.* bits in horses' mou.
1 *Pet.* 2:15 *p.* to silence ignoran.
2 *Pet.* 1:14 I must *p.* off this tab.
Jude 5 will *p.* you in remembr.
Rev. 2:24 *p.* on you none other
17:17 God hath *p.* in th. hearts

PUT away.
Gen. 35:2 *p. away* strange gods
Lev. 21:7 nor take a woman *p. a.*
Deut. 19:13 *p. a.* guilt of in. 21:9
22:19 he may not *p.* her *a.* 29
Jos. 24:14 *p. a.* strange gods,
23; *Jud.* 10:16 ; 1 *Sam.* 7:3
1 *Sam.* 1:14 Eli said, *p. a.* wine
2 *Sam.* 7:15 Saul whom I *p. a.*
12:13 Lord hath *p. a.* thy sin
2 *Chr.* 15:8 Asa *p. a.* abom. idols
Rev. 10:3 a cove. to *p. a.* wives
19 gave hands to *p. a.* wives
Ps. 18:22 I did not *p. away* his
statutes
27:9 *p.* not thy serv. *a.* in anger
Prov. 4:24 *p. a.* a froward mou.
Is. 50:1 whom I have *p. away*
Jer. 3:1 if a man *p. a.* his wife
8 *p. a.* given her a bill of div.
Ezek. 44:22 nor pr. take her *p. a.*
Hos. 2:2 let her *p. a.* whoredoms
Amos 6:3 that *p.* far *a.* evil day
Mat. 1:19 J. minded to *p.* her *a.*
Mark 10:2 lawful to *p. a.* wife?
12 if a woman *p. a.* her husb.
1 *Cor.* 5:13 *p. a.* a wicked person
7:11 let not husb. *p. a.* wife, 12
Eph. 4:31 evil speaking be *p. a.*
1 *Tim.* 1:19 some having *p. aw.*

Heb. 9:26 *p. a.* sin by sacrifice
See DEATH, EVIL.

PUT forth.
Gen. 3:22 lest he *p. f.* take tree
8:9 N. *p. f.* his hand and took
19:10 men *p. forth* their hand
Ex. 4:4 *p. f.* thy hand and take
Deut. 33:14 precious things *p. f.*
Jud. 15:15 Samson *p. f.* took
1 *Sam.* 14:27 Jonathan *p. f.* rod
22:17 servants not *p. f.* to slay
24:10 not *p. f.* my hand ag. L.
2 *Sam.* 6:6 Uzziah *p. forth* his hand to ark, 1 *Chr.* 13:9
18:12 not *p. f.* my hand against
1 *K.* 13:4 Jeroboam *p. f.* his ha.
Job 1:11 *p. f.* hand and tou. 2:5
12 on himself *p.* not *f.* hand
Ps. 55:20 *p. f.* his hands ag. his
125:3 lest righteous *p. f.* hands
Prov. 8:1 understan. *p. f.* voice?
25:6 not *f.* thyself in presen.
Jer. 1:9 Lord *p. f.* his hand
Ezek. 8:3 he *p. f.* form of a hand
Mat. 9:25 when peop. were *p. f.*
13:24 para. *p.* he *f.* 31; *Lu.* 14:7
Acts 5:34 to *p.* the apostles *forth*
9:40 but Peter *p.* them all *forth*

PUT on.
Gen. 28:20 raiment to *p. on*
Lev. 6:10 priest sh. *p. on* linen
11 he sh. *p. on* other garments
16:4 shall *p. on* holy linen coat
Deut. 22:5 nor man *p. on* wom.'s
2 *Sam.* 1:24 S. *p. on* ornaments
14:2 *p. on* mourning apparel
1 *K.* 22:30 but *p.* thou *on* thy robes, 2 *Chr.* 18:29
2 *K.* 3:21 all able to *p. on* armor
Job 27:17 the just shall *p. it on*
Cant. 5:3 how shall I *p. it on?*
Is. 51:9 *p. on* strength, 52:1
Jer. 13:1 take girdle, *p. it on*, 2
Ezek. 24:17 and *p. on* thy shoes
42:14 *p. on* other garm. 44:19
Mat. 6:25 nor what ye shall *p. on*, *Luke* 12:22
21:7 *p.* on the ass their clothes
Mark 6:9 not *p. on* two coats
Luke 15:22 *p. on* him best robe
Rom. 13:14 *p.* ye *on* the L. J. C.
Gal. 3:27 baptized, have *p. on* C.

Eph. 4:24 *p. on* new m. *Col.* 3:10
Col. 3:12 *p. on* bowels of mercies
14 *p. on* charity, which is bo.

PUT out.
Gen. 38:28 one *p. out* his hand
Lev. 6:12 fire of altar not be *p. o.*
Num. 5:2 *p. out* of camp leper, 4
3 male and fem. shall ye *p. o.*
16:14 wilt thou *p. out* the eyes?
Deut. 7:22 L. will *p. o.* tho. nati.
25:6 that his name be not *p. o.*
Jud. 16:21 Philis. *p. o.* S.'s eyes
2 *Chr.* 29:7 have *p. o.* lamps
Job 18:5 light of wicked be *p. o.*
6 his candle be *p. out,* 21:17 ;
Prov. 13:9 ; 20:20 ; 24:20
Ps. 31:5 *p. o.* their name for ever
Ezek. 32:7 when I *p.* thee *out*
Mark 5:40 when he had *p.* them all *out, Luke* 8:54
John 9:22 be *p. o.* of synagogues
16:2 *p.* you *out* of synagogues

PUT trust.
Jud. 9:15 *p. t.* in my shadow
2 *K.* 18:24 *p. t.* on Eg. *Is.* 36:9
1 *Chr.* 5:20 they *p.* th. *t.* in him
Ps. 4:5 *p.* your *trust* in the Lord
5:11 all that *p. t.* in thee rejoice
7:1 O L. God in thee I *p. trust,*
16:1 ; 25:20 ; 71:1
9:10 know thy name, *p. trust* in them
11:1 in L. *p.* I my *t.* 31:1 ; 71:1
17:7 which *p.* their *t.* in thee
36:7 *p.* their *t.* under thy wings
56:4 in God I have *p.* my *trust*
73:28 I have *p.* my *t.* in the L.
146:3 *p.* not your *t.* in princes
Prov. 30:5 *p.* their *trust* in him
Jer. 39:18 hast *p.* thy *t.* in thee
1 *Thes.* 2:4 *p.* in *t.* with gospel
Heb. 2:13 I will *p.* my *t.* in him

PUT, Participle.
Lev. 11:38 if water be *p.* on seed
15:19 shall be *p.* apart sev. days
18:19 not as long as she is *p.*
1 *K.* 22:10 kings *p.* on their rob.
2 *K.* 14:12 Judah was *p.* to worse
1 *Chr.* 19:16 Syri. *p.* to worse, 19
2 *Chr.* 2:14 ev. device shall be *p.*
6:24 if Israel be *p.* to the worse
25:22 Jud. was *p.* to worse

Ps. 35:4 be *p.* to shame, 83:17
71:1 let me never be *p.* to con.
Prov. 25:7 shouldest be *p.* lower
Ec. 3:14 nothing can be *p.* to it
Is. 54:4 shalt not be *p.* to shame
Jer. 50:42 every one *p.* in array
Zep. 3:19 have been *p.* to shame
Mat. 14:3 for that *p.* in to fill up
Mark 1:14 John was *p.* in prison
John 13:2 devil *p.* into hea. of J.
Heb. 2:8 noth. not *p.* under him
Rev. 11:9 not bo. be *p.* in graves

PUTEOLI.
Acts 28:13 came next day to P.

PUTIEL.   *Ex.* 6:25

PUTTEST.
Deut. 12:18 *p.* thy hands, 15:10
2 *K.* 18:14 that thou *p.* on me
Ps. 119:119 thou *p.* away wicked

PUTTETH.
Ex. 30:33 *p.* any on a stranger
Num. 22:38 God *p.* in my mouth
Deut. 25:11 woman *p.* forth hand
Job 15:15 he *p.* no trust in saints
28:9 *p.* for. his hand upon rock
33:11 he *p.* my feet in the stoc.
Ps. 15:5 he that *p.* not his money
75:7 *p.* down one and set. up
Prov. 28:25 *p.* his trust in Lord
29:25 *p.* his trust in L. be safe
Is. 57:13 *p.* trust in me pos. land
Lam. 3:29 *p.* his mouth in dust
Mic. 3:5 *p.* not into their mouths
Mat. 9:16 *p.* new cloth, *Lu.* 5:36
Luke 8:16 no man *p.* ligh. candle
16:18 whoso *p.* away his wife
John 10:4 *p.* forth his own sheep

PUTTING.
Lev. 16:21 *p.* them upon head
Jud. 7:6 *p.* their hand to mouth
Is. 58:9 *p.* forth of the finger
Mat. 2:16 God hateth *p.* away
Acts 9:12 Anan. *p.* his hand, 17
19:33 Alex. J. *p.* him forward
Rom. 15:15 sort, as *p.* in mind
Eph. 4:25 *p.* away lying
Col. 2:11 in *p.* off body of sins
1 *Tim.* 1:12 *p.* me into ministry
2 *Tim.* 1:6 by *p.* on my hands
1 *Pet.* 3:21 not *p. a.* filth of flesh

PUTREFYING.
Is. 1:6 wounds, bruises, *p.* sores

Q

QUAILS.
Ex. 16:13 at even *q.* came up.
Num. 11:31 a wind fr. L. bro. *q.*
32 the people stood, gather. *q.*
Ps. 105:40 asked, he brought *q.*

QUAKE, ED.
Ex. 19:18 the mount *q.* greatly
1 *Sam.* 14:15 trembled, earth *q.*
Joel 2:10 earth shall *q.* bef. them
Nah. 1:5 the mountains *q.* at hi.
Mat. 27:51 earth *q.* the rocks re.
Heb. 12:21 M. said, I fear and *q.*

QUAKING.
Ezek. 12:18 eat thy bread with *q.*
Dan. 10:7 great *q.* fell on them

QUANTITY.
Is. 22:24 hang vessels of small *q.*

QUARREL.
Lev. 26:25 a sword sh. avenge *q.*
2 *K.* 5:7 see how he seeketh a *q.*
Mark 6:19 Her. had *q.* ag. John
Col. 3:13 if any have *q.* ag. any

QUARRIES.
Jud. 3:19 Ehud turned from *q.*
26 Ehud escaped beyond the *q.*

QUARTER.
Gen. 19:4 peo. from ev. *q.* to Lo.

Jos. 18:14 Kirjath-jearim, we. *q.*
Is. 47:15 merchants wander to *q.*
56:11 every one for gain from *q.*
Mark 1:45 came to him fr. ev. *q.*
See SOUTH.

QUARTERS.
Ex. 13:7 no leav. seen in thy *q.*
Deut. 22:12 fringes on four *q.*
1 *Chr.* 9:24 in four *q.* were port.
Jer. 49:36 from four *q.* of heaven
Acts 9:32 Peter passed thr. all *q.*
16:3 Jews which were in th. *q.*
28:7 in same *q.* were possessio.
Rev. 20:8 nations in 4 *q.* of earth

QUATERNIONS.
Acts 12:4 deliv. Peter to four *q.*

QUARTUS.
Rom. 16:23 Q. a brother, salute.

QUEEN.
1 *K.* 10:1 *q.* of Sheba heard of fame of Solomon, 2 *Chr.* 9:1
1 *K.* 10:4 wh. *q.* saw Solom.'s w.
10 spices *q.* of She. gave to S.
13 Solomon gave *q.* of Sheba all her desire, 2 *Chr.* 9:3, 12

11:19 gave Hadad sister of *q.*
15:13 Asa removed Maachah from being *q.* 2 *Chr.* 15:16
2 *K.* 10:13 salute children of *q.*
Neh. 2:6 king said, *q.* sitting by
Est. 1:9 Vashti *q.* made feast
11 bring the *q.* 12 *q.* refused
15 wh. sh. we do to *q.* Vashti?
16 the *q.* hath not done wrong
17 deed of *q.* sh. come abroad
2:4 maiden that pleaseth be *q.*
17 made Esther *q.* ins. of Vas.
4:4 *q.* grieved: 5:3 wilt, *q.* Est.
5:12 *q.* let no man to banquet
7:2 what is thy petition, *q.* Es. ?
7 Haman made request to *q.*
8 will he force the *q.* befo. me
8:1 house of Haman to Esth. *q.*
9:31 Mordecai and Esth. the *q.*
Ps. 45:9 the *q.* in gold of Ophir
Jer. 13:18 say to king and *q.*
44:17 burn inc. to *q.* of heaven
25 vowed to burn incense to *q.*
Dan. 5:10 *q.* came to banq. house
Mat. 12:42 *q.* of south shall rise up in judgment, *Luke* 11:31
Acts 8:27 Candace, *q.* of Ethiop.
Rev. 18:7 I sit *q.* am no widow

QUEENS.

Cant. 6:8 there are threesc. q. 9
Is. 49:23 their q. nursing moth.

QUENCH.

2 *Sam.* 14:7 they shall q. my coal
21:17 thou q. not light of Israel
Ps. 104:11 wild asses q. thirst
Cant. 8:7 waters cannot q. love
Is. 1:31 both burn, none q. them
42:3 shall he not q. *Mat.* 12:20
Jer. 4:4 burn, none q. it, 21:12
Amos 5:6 none to q. it in Beth-el
Eph. 6:16 to q. darts of wicked
1 *Thes.* 5:19 q. not the Spirit

QUENCHED.

Num. 11:2 fire q. 2 *Chr.* 34:25
2 *K.* 22:17 wrath shall not be q.
Ps. 118:12 they are q. as thorns
Is. 34:10 not be q. night nor day
43:17 they are q. as tow
66:24 nor shall their fire be q.
Jer. 7:20 shall not be q. 17:27
Ezek. 20:47 fla. sh. not be q. 48
Mark 9:43 fire never be q. 45
44 where fire is not q. 46, 48
Heb. 11:34 q. the violence of fire

QUESTION, Substantive.

Mat. 22:35 lawyer asked him q.
Mark 11:29 I ask one q. ans. me
12:34 durst ask q. *Luke* 20:40
John 3:25 arose q. bet disciples
Acts 15:2 came to apos. about q.
18:15 if it be a q. of words
19:40 danger to be called in q.
23:6 of resur. called in q. 24:21
Cor. 10:25 asking no q. for, 27

QUESTION, Verb.

Mark 8:11 Phar. began to q. him
9:16 What q. ye with them?

QUESTIONED, ING.

2 *Chr.* 31:9 Heze. q. with priests
Mark 1:27 q. among themselves
9:10 q. what rising from dead
14 and scribes q. with them
Luke 23:9 Pilate q. with him

QUESTIONS.

1 *K.* 10:1 queen came to prove q.
3 Sol. told her q. 2 *Chr.* 9:1, 2
Mat. 22:46 nei. ask him more q.
Luke 2:46 hearing and asking q.
Acts 23:29 accused of q. of law.
25:19 certain q. against him
20 doubted such manner of q.
26:3 kn. thee to be expert in q.
1 *Tim.* 1:4 minister q. than edi.
6:4 doting about q. and strifes
2 *Tim.* 2:23 unlearned q. *Tit.* 3:9

QUICK.

Lev. 13:10 there be q. raw flesh
24 the q. flesh that burneth
Num. 16:30 go down q. into pit
Ps. 55:15 go down q. into hell
124:3 had swallowed us up q.
Is. 11:3 make him of q. underst.
Acts 10:42 orda. to be judge of q.

---

2 *Tim.* 4:1 sh. judge q. and dead
Heb. 4:12 the word of God is q.
1 *Pet.* 4:5 to judge q. and dead

QUICKEN.

Ps. 71:20 thou shalt q. me again
80:18 q. us, we will call on name
119:25 q. me according, 107, 154
37 q. me in thy way

Ps. 119:40 q. me in thy righteou.
88 q. me after thy kindn. 159
149 q. me accord. to judgment
143:11 q. me, L. for name's sake
Rom. 8:11 shall q. mortal bodies

QUICKENED.

Ps. 119:50 thy word hath q. me
93 with precepts th. hast q. me
1 *Cor.* 15:36 thou sowest is not q.
Eph. 2:1 you he q. who were de.
5 q. us toge. with C. *Col.* 2:13
1 *Pet.* 3:18 death in flesh, q. by S.

QUICKENETH.

John 5:21 Father q. them, Son q.
6:63 Sp. q. flesh profit. nothing
Rom. 4:17 God, who q. dead
1 *Tim.* 6:13 God, who q. all thi.

QUICKENING.

1 *Cor.* 15:45 Adam made q. spir.

QUICKLY.

Gen. 18:6 make ready q. meas.
27:20 hast thou found it so q.
Ex. 32:8 turned q. out of way,
Deut. 9:12, 16; *Jud.* 2:17
Num. 16:46 go q. to congregation
Deut. 9:12 down q. 11:17 per. q.
28:20 perish q. because of doin.
Jos. 2:5 pursue q. overtake them
10:6 come up to us q. save us
23:16 ye shall perish q. off land
1 *Sam.* 20:19 thou sh. go down q.
2 *Sam.* 17:16 send q. and tell D.
18 went both of them away q.
21 arise, pass q. over the wat.
2 *K.* 1:11 said. Come down q.
Ec. 4:12 threef. cord not q. bro.
Mat. 5:25 agree with adversa. q.
28:7 go q. tell discip. he is risen
8 they departed q. *Mark* 16:8
Luke 16:6 sit down q. write fifty
John 11:29 M. arose q. came to J.
13:27 J. That thou doest do q.
Acts 12:7 saying, Arise up q. P.
22:18 get thee q. out of Jerusal.
Rev. 2:5 repent, else I come q. 16
8:11 behold, I come q. 22:7, 12
11:14 third woe cometh q.
22:20 I come q. even so come

QUICKSANDS.

Acts 27:17 they should fall into q.

QUIET.

Jud. 16:2 Phil. laid wait were q.
18:7 after Zidonians, q. secure
2 *K.* 11:20 city q. 2 *Chr.* 23:21
1 *Chr.* 4:40 land was wide and q.
2 *Chr.* 14:1 in his days land q.
5 the kingdom was q. 20:30

Job 3:13 now sho. I have been q.
26 neit. was I q. trouble came
21:23 dieth, being at ease, q.
Ps. 35:20 devise ag. q. in land
107:30 glad, because they be q.
Prov. 1:33 whoso hearken. be q.
Ec. 9:17 wor. of wise heard in q.
Is. 7:4 take heed, and be q. fear
14:7 the earth is at rest, and q.
32:18 my peo. shall dwell in q.
33:20 see Jerusal. q. habitation
Jer. 30:10 Jacob return, be in q.
47:6 how long ere thou be q.?
7 be q. seeing L. given charge
49:23 sorrow on sea, can. be q.
51:59 Seraiah was a q. prince
Ezek. 16:42 fury rest, I will be q.
Nah. 1:12 though q. be cut down
Acts 19:36 ye ought to be q.
1 *Thes.* 4:11 that ye stu. to be q.
1 *Tim.* 2:2 we may lead a q. life
1 *Pet.* 3:4 ornament of a q. spirit

QUIETED, ETH.

Job 37:17 q. earth by south wind
Ps. 131:2 q. myself as a child
Zec. 6:8 q. my spirit in north

QUIETLY.

2 *Sam.* 3:27 Joab took Abner q.
Lam. 3:26 q. wait for salva. of L.

QUIETNESS.

Jud. 8:28 the country was in q.
1 *Chr.* 22:9 I will give q. to Isr.
Job 20:20 sh. not feel q. in belly
34:29 q. who can make trouble?
Prov. 17:1 bet. dry morsel and q.
Ec. 4:6 better is handful with q.
Is. 30:15 in q. be your strength
32:17 righte. q. and assurance
Acts 24:2 we enjoy great q.
2 *Thes.* 3:12 we ex. that with q.

QUIT.

Ex. 21:19 smote him be q. 28
Jos. 2:20 we will be q. of oath
1 *Sam.* 4:9 q. like men, 1 *Cor.* 16:13

QUITE.

Gen. 31:15 q. devoured our mon.
Ex. 23:24 q. break down images
Num. 17:10 q. take away murm.
33:52 q. pluck down high places
2 *Sam.* 3:24 Abner away, q. gone
Job 6:13 is wisdom q. from me?
Hab. 3:9 thy bow made q. naked

QUIVER.

Gen. 27:3 take thy q. and bow
Job 39:23 q. rattleth against him
Ps. 127:5 man that hath q. full
Is. 22:6 E. bare q. with chariots
49:2 polished shaft in his q.
Jer. 5:16 q. is as open sepulchre
Lam. 3:13 arrows of q. ent. reins

QUIVERED.

Hab. 3:16 my lips q. at the voice

R

RABBAH, or RABBATH.

Deut. 3:11 is it not in R. of chil.
2 *Sam.* 11:1 J. besieged R. 12:26
17:27 Shobi R. brought beds
1 *Chr.* 20:1 Joab smote R. and
Jer. 49:2 alarm heard in R. 3
Ezek. 21:20 sw. may come to R.
25:5 I will make R. a stable
Amos 1:14 a fire in wall of R.

RABBI.

Mat. 23:7 called of men, r. r.
8 be not ye called r. for one is
John 1:38 R. wh. dwellest thou?
49 R. thou art the Son of God

3:2 R. we know thou art teach.
26 R. he that was with thee
6:25 R. when cam. thou hither?

RABBONI.

John 20:16 M. turn. and saith, R.

RAB-SHAKEH.

2 *K.* 18:17 Assy. sent R. *Is.* 36:2
37 told words of R. *Is.* 36:22
19:4 hear words of R. 37:4

RACA.

Mat. 5:22 say r. sh. be in danger

RACE.

Ps. 19:5 strong man to run a r.

Ec. 9:11 r. is not to the swift
1 *Cor.* 9:24 they wh. run in a r.
Heb. 12:1 run with patience r.

RACHEL.

Gen. 29:12 Jacob told R. that he
30:1 R. bare no chil. R. 2, 22
2 anger was kindled ag. R. 22
31:19 R. had stolen imag. 34
35:19 R. died, 24; 46:22; 48:7
Ruth 4:11 make woman like R.
1 *Sam.* 10:2 men by R. sepulch.
Jer. 31:15 R. weeping, *Mat.* 2:18

RAFTERS.

Cant. 1:17 beams cedar r. of fir

RAGAU.
Luke 3:35 Saruch, the son of R.

RAGE, Substantive.
2 *K.* 5:12 Naaman turned in a *r.*
19:27 I know thy *r. Is.* 37:28
2 *Chr.* 16:10 A. in a *r.* with seer
28:9 ye have slain them in a *r.*
Job 39:24 swallow. ground wi. *r.*
40:11 cast abroad *r.* of wrath
Ps. 7:6 lift up thyself bec. of *r.*
Prov. 6:34 jeal. is *r.* of a man
Dan. 3:13 Neb. commanded in *r.*
Hos. 7:16 fall for *r.* of th. tongue

RAGE, Verb.
Ps. 2:1 heathen *r. ? Acts* 4:25
Prov. 29:9 wheth. he *r.* or laugh
Jer. 46:9 come up *r.* ye chariots
Nah. 2:4 chariots sh. *r.* in stree.

RAGED, ETH.
Ps. 46:6 heath. *r.* kingd. moved
Prov. 14:16 fool *r.* is confident

RAGGED.
Is. 2:21 go into tops of *r.* rocks

RAGING.
Ps. 89:9 thou rulest *r.* of sea
Prov. 20:1 strong drink *r.*
Jon. 1:16 sea ceased from *r.*
Luke 8:24 rebuked *r.* of water
Jude 13 *r.* of waves of sea foam.

RAGS.
Prov. 23:21 clothe man with *r.*
Is. 64:6 righte. are as filthy *r.*
Jer. 38:11 Ebed. took rotten *r.*
12 *r.* under thine armholes

RAHAB.
Jos. 2:1 house of R. 6:17, 25
Ps. 87:4 I make mention of R.
89:10 thou hast broken R. in
Is. 51:9 not it that hath cut R.
Mat. 1:5 Salmon begat B. of R
Heb. 11:31 by faith harlot R
Jam. 2:25 was not R. justified ?

RAIL, ED.
1 *Sam.* 25:14 Nabal *r.* on David's
2 *Chr.* 32:17 Sen. wrote let. to *r.*
Mark. 15:29 that passed *r.* on J.
Luke 23:39 one of malefactors *r.*

RAILER.
1 *Cor.* 5:11 keep not com. wi. *r.*

RAILING.
1 *Tim.* 6:4 whereof co. strife, *r.*
1 *Pet.* 3:9 not rendering *r.* for *r.*
2 *Pet.* 2:11 angels br. not *r.* accu.
Jude 9 durst not bring *r.* accus.

RAIMENT.
Gen. 24:53 serv. gave *r.* to Reb.
27:15 Rebekah took goodly *r.*
27 Isaac smelled *r.* and blessed
28:20 if L. give me *r.* to put on
41:14 Joseph shaved, chang. *r.*
45:22 each man changes of *r.*
Ex. 3:22 borrow of Eg. *r.* 12:35
21:10 her *r.* sh. he not diminish
22:9 trespass for sheep, for *r.*
26 thou take neighbor's *r.* 27
Lev. 11:32 uncl. beasts fall on *r.*
Num. 31:20 purify all your *r.*
Deut. 8:4 thy *r.* waxed not old
10:18 L. loveth stranger, giv. *r.*
21:13 put *r.* of captivity fr. her
22:3 lost *r.* restore
24:13 he may sleep in his *r.*
17 shalt not take a widow's *r.*
Jos. 22:8 return with much *r.*
Jud. 3:16 E. a dagger under *r.*
8:26 purple *r.* was on kings
Ruth 3:3 and put thy *r.* on thee
1 *Sam.* 28:8 Saul disg. put on *r.*
2 *K.* 5:5 Naam. took chang. of *r.*
2 *Chr.* 9:24 Solomon, gold, and *r.*
Est. 4:4 sent *r.* to clothe Morde.
Job 27:16 tho' he prep. *r.* as clay
Ps. 45:11 brought to king in *r.*
Is. 14:19 cast out as *r.* of slain

63:3 and I will stain all my *r.*
Ezek. 16:13 *r.* was of fine linen
Zec. 3:4 clothe thee with *r.*
Mat. 3:4 J. had *r.* of camel's hair
6:25 body more th. *r. Luke* 12:23
28 why take ye thought for *r. ?*
11:8 clothed in soft *r. Lu.* 7:25
17:2 his *r.* white as light, *Mark*
9:3 ; *Luke* 9:29
27:31 put his own *r.* on him
28:3 and his *r.* white as snow
Luke 10:30 thieves stri. him of *r.*
23:34 parted his *r. John* 19:24
Acts 18:6 Paul shook his *r.*
22:20 I kept *r.* of them that sle.
1 *Tim.* 6:8 having food and *r.*
Jam. 2:2 a poor man in vile *r.*
Rev. 3:5 be clothed in white *r.*
18 buy white *r.* that thou ma.
4:4 I saw 24 elders in white *r.*

RAIN, Substantive.
Gen. 7:12 *r.* was upon earth
8:2 *r.* from heaven was restrain.
Ex. 9:33 the *r.* was not poured
34 Pharaoh saw the *r.* ceased
Lev. 26:4 will give you *r.* in due
season, *Deut.* 11:14 ; 28:12
Deut. 11 drink. of *r.* of heaven
17 shut heaven that th. be no
r. 1 *K.* 8:35 ; 2 *Chr.* 6:26 ; 7:13
28:24 Lord shall make *r.* of land
32:2 my doctrine sh. drop as *r.*
1 *Sam.* 12:17 call on L. to send *r.*
18 Lord sent thunder and *r.*
2 *Sam.* 1:21 let there be no *r.*
23:4 by clear shining after *r.*
1 *K.* 8:36 hear, give *r.* 2 *Chr.* 6:27
17:1 th. shall be no dew nor *r.* 7
14 till day that Lord send *r.*
18:1 I will send *r.* upon earth
41 a sound of abundance of *r.*
44 *r.* stop thee not ; 45 great *r.*
2 *K.* 3:17 not see wind, nor see *r.*
Ezr. 10:9 trembling for great *r.*
13 and it is a time of much *r.*
Job 5:10 giveth *r.* upon the earth
28:26 he made a decree for *r.*
29:23 waited for me as for the *r.*
36:27 clou. pour down *r.* accord.
37:6 to small *r.* and to great *r.*
38:28 hath *r.* a father?
Ps. 68:9 didst send plentiful *r.*
72:6 he shall come down like *r.*
84:6 the *r.* also filleth the pools
105:32 he gave them hail for *r.*
135:7 maketh lightnings for *r.*
147:8 L. prepareth *r.* for earth
Prov. 25:14 like clouds with *r.*
23 north wind driveth away *r.*
26:1 snow in summer, and *r.* in
28:3 oppresseth poor is like a *r*
Ec. 11:3 if clouds be full of *r.*
12:2 nor clouds return after *r.*
Cant. 2:11 the *r.* is over and go.
Is. 4:6 covert from storm and *r.*
5:6 com. clouds they rain no *r.*
30:23 then shall he give the *r.*
44:14 an ash, *r.* doth nourish it
55:10 as *r.* cometh from heaven
Jer. 5:24 let us fear L. giveth *r.*
10:13 maketh lightn. wi. *r.* 51:16
14:4 ground chapt, th. was no *r.*
22 vanities of G. can cause *r. ?*
Ezek. 1:28 as bow in cloud in *r.*
38:22 I will *r.* an overflowing *r.*
Hos. 6:3 shall make us as the *r.*
Joel 2:23 cause to come down *r.*
Amos 4:7 I have withholden *r.*
Zec. 14:17 upon th. be no *r.*
18 go not up, that have no *r.*
Mat. 5:45 he sendeth *r.* on just
7:25 and the *r.* descended, 27
Acts 14:17 did good, and gave *r.*
28:2 because of the present *r.*
Heb. 6:7 earth drinketh in the *r.*
Jam. 5:18 and the heav. gave *r.*

See LATTER.

RAIN, Verb.
Gen. 2:5 L. not caused it to *r.*
7:4 cause to *r.* 40 days a. nights
Ex. 9:18 to-morrow cause I *r.*
16:4 I will *r.* bread from heaven
Job 20:23 G. shall *r.* his fury
38:26 cause it to *r.* on the earth
Ps. 11:6 on wicked he shall *r.*
Is. 5:6 that they *r.* no rain on it
Ezek. 38:22 I will *r.* overflow. rn.
Hos. 10:12 come and *r.* righteou.
Amos. 4:7 I caused it to *r.* on city
Jam. 5:17 E. pray it mig. not *r.*
Rev. 11:6 *r.* not in days of prop.

RAINBOW.
Rev. 4:3 th. was a *r.* round about
10:1 and a *r.* was upon his head

RAINED.
Gen. 19:24 L. *r.* upon S. and G.
Ex. 9:23 the L. *r.* hail on Egypt
Ps. 78:24 *r.* down manna, 27
Ezek. 22:24 the land not *r.* upon
Amos 4:7 one piece was *r.* upon
Luke 17:29 it *r.* fire from heaven
Jam. 5:17 it *r.* not for 3 y.'s 6 m.

RAINY.
Prov. 27:15 dropping in a *r.* day

RAISE.
Gen. 38:8 *r.* up seed to brother ?
Ex. 23:1 shalt not *r.* false report
Deut. 18:15 L. thy God *r.* up a
prophet, 18 ; *Acts* 3:22 ; 7:37
25:7 refuseth to *r.* up to brother
Jos. 8:29 *r.* ther. a heap stones
Ruth 4:5 *r.* up name of dead, 10
1 *Sam.* 2:35 *r.* faithful priest
2 *Sam.* 12:11 *r.* evil against thee
17 went to *r.* him from earth
1 *K.* 14:14 L. shall *r.* king in Is.
1 *Chr.* 17:11 I will *r.* up thy seed
Job 3:8 ready to *r.* up mourning
19:12 his troops *r.* up ag. thee
30:12 *r.* ways of destruction
Ps. 41:10 L. be merciful, *r.* me
Is. 15:5 *r.* cry of destruction
29:3 I will *r.* forts against thee
44:26 will *r.* up decayed places
49:6 servant to *r.* tribes of Jacob
58:12 *r.* foundations of genera.
61:4 sh. *r.* up former desolations
Jer. 23:5 will *r.* to Dav. a branch
50:9 *r.* ag. Babylon assembly
32 none *r.* him ; 51:1 *r.* wind
Ezek. 23:22 will *r.* lovers ag. th.
34:29 will *r.* up plant of renown
Hos. 6:2 in third day he will *r.*
Joel 3:7 *r.* them whither ye driv.
Amos 5:2 virgin of Is. none to *r.*
6:14 I will *r.* a nation aga. you
9:11 I will *r.* tabernacle of Dav.
Mic. 5:5 *r.* against him 7 sheph.
Hab. 1:3 th. are that *r.* up strife
6 I will *r.* up Chaldeans
Zec. 11:16 *r.* shepherd in land
Mat. 3:9 *r.* children to A. *Lu.* 3:8
22:24 *r.* up seed to his brother,
Mark 12:19 ; *Luke* 20:28
John 2:19 three days I will *r.* it
6:39 *r.* it at last day, 40, 44, 54
Acts 2:30 he *r.* C. to sit on thro.
26:8 why incredible G. *r.* dead ?
1 *Cor.* 6:14 sh. *r.* up us by power
2 *Cor.* 4:14 sh. *r.* up us by Jesus
Heb. 11:19 God able to *r.* him.
Jam. 5:15 L. shall *r.* him up

RAISED.
Ex. 9:16 I *r.* thee up to show my
power, *Rom.* 9:17
Jos. 5:7 chil. he *r.* up in stead
7:26 *r.* over him heap of stones
Jud. 2:16 L. *r.* up judges, 18
3:9 *r.* a deliverer to Israel, 15
2 *Sam.* 23:1 who was *r.* on high
1 *K.* 5:13 Sol. *r.* a levy of Is. 9:15
Ezr. 1:5 all whose spirit God *r.*
Job 14:12 nor *r.* out of their sleep

RAISED

Cant. 8:5 r. th. under apple-tree
Is. 14:9 it r. up kings of nations
23:13 Assyrians r. palaces of C.
41:2 r. righteous man from eat
25 I r. up one from the north
45:13 I r. him up in righteous.
Jer. 6:22 great nation r. fr. earth
29:15 L. r. proph. in Babylon
50:41 kings shall be r. fr. earth
51:11 L. r. spirit of kings of M.
Dan. 7:5 bear r. up on one side
Amos 2:11 I r. up sons for prop.
Zec. 2:13 r. out of holy habitati.
9:13 when I r. thy sons, O Zion
Mat. 11:5 dead r. up, *Luke* 7:22
16:21 r. again, 17:23; *Luke* 9:22
Luke 1:69 r. up horn of salvation
20:37 dead are r. Moses showed
John 12:1 Laz. whom he r. 9, 17
Acts 2:24 whom God hath r. up,
32 ; 3:15, 26 ; 4:10; 5:30; 10:40;
13:30, 33, 34, 17:31; *Rom.*
10:9 ; 1 *Cor.* 6:14; 2 *Cor.*
12:7 angel r. Peter; 13:22 r. Da.
13:23 G. r. Israel a Saviour J.
Rom. 4:24 bel. on him that r. J.
25 r. again for our justification
6:4 C. was r. fr. dead by Father
9 Ch. r. fr. dead, dieth no mo.
7:4 to him who is r. from dead
8:11 if Sp. of him that r. Jesus
1 *Cor.* 15:15 r. up C. wh. he r. n.
16 dead rise not, C. is not r.
17 if C. be not r. faith is vain
35 men say, How are dead r. ?
42 sown in cor. r. in incorru. 52
43 it is r. in glory, r. in power
44 sown natu. body, r. spirit.
Eph. 2:6 r. us together in Ch. J.
Col. 2:12 through G. who r. him
1 *Thes.* he r. from dead.
2 *Tim.* 2:8 Je. seed of Da. was r.
Heb. 11:35 wom. received dead r.
1 *Pet.* 1:21 bel. in G. that r. him

RAISER.
Dan. 11:20 stand up r. of taxes

RAISETH.
1 *Sam.* 2:8 he r. poor, *Ps.* 113:7
Job 41:25 r. himself, mighty
Ps. 107:25 commands, r. winds
145:14 he r. those bowed, 146:8
John 5:21 the Father r. up dead
2 *Cor.* 1:9 trust in G. wh. r. dead

RAISING.
Hos. 7:4 baker who ceaseth fr. r.
Acts 24:12 found me r. up people

RAISINS.
1 *Sam.* 25:18 Ab. took 100 clus. r.
30:12 gave Egyp. two clusters r.
2 *Sam.* 16:1 met D. 100 bunch. r.
1 *Chr.* 12:40 brought bunch. of r.

RAM.
Ruth 4:19 ; 1 *Chr.* 2:9, 10, 25, 27
Job 32:2 Elihu of kindred of R.

RAM.
Gen. 15:9 take a r. 3 years old
22:13 a r. caught in a thicket
Ex. 29:15 take one r. 16 slay r.
29 r. of conse. 27, 31 ; *Lev.* 8:22
Lev. 9:2 take r. for burnt-offeri.
4 r. peace-offer. 19:21 trespass
Num. 5:8 besi. r. for atonement
Ezr. 10:19 they offered r.
Ezek. 43:23 they sh. offer a r. 25
45:24 ephah for a r. 46:5, 7, 11
46:6 in day of new moon a r.
Dan. 8:3 I saw r. had two horns
4 I saw r. pushing westward
6 goat ran to r. had two horns
7 no power in r. to deliver r.

RAMS.
Gen. 31:10 r. leaped ring-stre. 12
38 r. of flock have I not eaten
32:14 Jacob sent Esau twenty r.
Deut. 32:14 with r. breed of Bas.

1 *Sam.* 15:22 hearken th. fat of r.
2 *K.* 3:4 Moab rendered 100,000 r.
1 *Chr.* 29:21 sacrifi. to L. 1,000 r.
2 *Chr.* 17:11 Ar. brought 7,700 r.
Ezr. 6:17 off. at dedication 200 r.
7:17 buy with this money r.
8:35 offered ninety-six r. for sin
Ps. 66:15 with fat of r. *Is.* 34:6
114:4 mount. skipped like r. 6
Is. 1:11 full of burnt-offeri. of r.
34:6 filled with fat of kidn. of r.
60:7 r. of Nebaioth sh. minister
Jer. 51:40 br. to slaughter like r.
Ezek. 27:21 Kedar occupied in r.
34:17 I judge betw. r. and goats
Ezek. 39:18 ye sh. dr. blood of r.
Mic. 6:7 L. be pleased with r. ?
See BATTERING, SEVEN.

RAMS' horns.
Jos. 6:4 seven priests shall bear
before ark r. horns, 5, 6, 8, 13

RAMS' skins.
Ex. 25:5 r. sk. dyed red, 26:14;
35:7; 36:19; 39:34

RAMAH, RAMA.
Jos. 18:25 R. a city of tribe of
Jud. 4:5 Deborah dwelt betw. R.
1 *Sam.* 1:19 his house in R. 2:11
7:17 return to R. 15:34; 16:13
8:4 elders came to S. unto R.
19:18 Dav. came to Sa. to R. 22
25:1 buried in house at R. 28:3
1 *K.* 15:17 built R. 2 *Chr.* 16:1
2 *K.* 8:29 woun. at R. 2 *Chr.* 22:6
Neh. 11:33 chil. of B. dwell at R.
Is. 10:29 R. is afraid, Gibeah of
Jer. 31:15 heard in R. *Mat.* 2:18
Ezek. 27:22 the merchants of R.
Hos. 5:8 blow ye trumpet in R.

RAMOTH-GILEAD.
Deut. 4:43 ; *Jos.* 20:8 ; 21:38
1 *K.* 4:13 Geber officer in R.
22:3 that R. is ours, 4, 6, 12, 15
2 *K.* 8:28 against Hazael in R.
9:1 take box of oil, go to R. 14
2 *Chr.* 18:3, 11, 14 ; 22:5

RAMPART.
Lam. 2:8 he made r. to lament
Nah. 3:8 whose r. was the sea

RAN.
Gen. 18:2 Abr. r. from tent-door
7 r. to herd; 24:17 r. meet R.
24:20 Rebek. r. to well to draw
29:12 Rachel r. and told father
13 Laban r. to meet Jacob
33:4 Esau r. and embraced him
Ex. 9:23 fire r. along the ground
Num. 11:27 r. man and told Mo.
16:47 Aaron r. into congregat.
Jos. 7:22 messen. r. to A.'s tent
Jud. 7:21 host of Midian r. fled
13:10 Manoah's wife r. showed
1 *Sam.* 3:5 Samuel r. to Eli, said
10:23 they r. and fetched Saul
17:22 D. r. and saluted brethren
51 D. r. stood upon Philistine
20:36 as lad r. he shot an arrow
2 *Sam.* 18:23 Ahimaaz r. by plain
1 *K.* 2:39 serv. of Shimei r. away
18:35 water r. about the altar
46 Elijah r. before Ahab to Je.
19:20 Elisha r. after Elijah
22:35 blood r. in midst of char.
Ps. 77:2 my sore r. in the night
105:41 waters r. in dry places
133:2 ointment r. down on bea.
Jer. 23:21 I have not sent, they r.
47:2 th. r. out waters on ri. side
Dan. 8:6 the goat r. to the ram
Mat. 8:32 herd of swine r. into
sea, *Mark* 5:13 ; *Luke* 8:33
Mark 6:33 and r. afoot thither
Luke 15:20 father r. fell on neck
19:4 Zacch. r. and climbed tree
John 20:4 they r. both together

Acts 3:11 the people r. unto th.
7:57 they r. upon Stephen with
8:30 Philip r. to the chariot and
12:14 know Peter's voice she r.
14:14 Paul and Barnabas r. in
21:30 people r. and took Paul
32 captain took soldiers and r.
27:41 they r. the ship aground
Jude 11 r. after error of Balaam

RANG.
1 *Sam.* 4:5 shouted, the earth r.
1 *K.* 1:45 Is. shouted, the city r.

RANGE.
Job 39:8 r. of mountains pasture

RANGES.
Lev. 11:35 r. for pots, be broken
2 *K.* 11:8 cometh in r. be slain
15 ha. her forth, r. 2 *Chr.* 23:14

RANGING.
Prov. 28:15 roar. lion and r. bear

RANK.
Gen. 41:5 on one stock, r. good
7 seven thin ears dev. r. ears
Num. 2:16 set forth in second r.
24 shall go forward in third r.
1 *Chr.* 12:33 of Ze. 50,000 keep r.
38 men that keep r. came to H.

RANKS.
1 *K.* 7:4 against light three r. 5
Joel 2:7 shall not break their r.
Mark 6:40 sat down in r. by
hundreds.

RANSOM, Substantive.
Ex. 21:30 shall give for r. of life
30:12 give ev. man r. for his so.
Job 33:24 del. from pit, I found r.
36:18 great r. cannot deliv. thee
Ps. 49:7 nor can they give G. a r.
Prov. 6:35 will not regard any r.
13:8 r. of man's life are riches
21:18 wicked be r. for righteous
Is. 43:3 I gave Egypt for thy r.
Mat. 20:28 even as the Son of
man ga. life a r. *Mark* 10:45
1 *Tim.* 2:6 who gave himself r.

RANSOM.
Hos. 13:14 will r. them fr. grave

RANSOMED.
Is. 35:10 r. of the L. shall return
51:10 made sea a way for the r.
Jer. 31:11 L. redeemed J. and r.

RAPHA and RAPHU.
Num. 13:9 Benj. Palti, son of R.
1 *Chr.* 8:37 R. Eleasah, Azel

RARE.
Dan. 2:11 r. thing king requireth

RASE.
Ps. 137:7 r. it, r. it to foundat.

RASH, Ly.
Ec. 5:2 be not r. with mouth
Acts 19:36 be quiet, do nothi. r.

RATE.
Ex. 16:4 peo. gather certain r.
1 *K.* 10:25 mules at r. 2 *Chr.* 9:24
2 *K.* 25:30 daily r. for every day
2 *Chr.* 8:13 even after a certain r.

RATHER.
Jos. 22:24 we have not r. done
2 *K.* 5:13 r. when he saith to th.
Mat. 25:9 go ye r. to th. th. sell
Mark. 5:26 but r. grew worse
Rom. 8:34 yea, r. that is risen a.
1 *Cor.* 7:21 be made free, use it r.
Gal. 4:9 or r. known of God
Heb. 13:19 I beseech you r. do

RATTLETH.
Job 39:23 quiver r. against him

RATTLING.
Nah. 3:2 noise of r. of wheels

RAVEN, S.
Gen. 8:7 Noah sent forth a r.
Lev. 11:15 r. unclean, *Deut.* 14:14

RAVEN

1 *K.* 17:4 comma. *r.* to feed thee
6 the *r.* brought Elijah bread
Job 38:41 prov. *r.* food. *Ps.* 147:9
Prov. 30:17 *r.* of val. shall pick
Cant. 5:11 bushy, black as *r.*
Is. 34:11 the *r.* shall dwell in it
Luke 12:24 consider *r.* nei. sow

RAVENING.

Ps. 22:13 gaped as *r.* lion
Ezek. 22:25 like a roaring lion *r.*
27 princes are like wolves *r.*
Mat. 7:15 they are *r.* wolves
Luke 11:39 inw. part is full of *r.*

RAVENOUS.

Ps. 35:9 nor any *r.* beast sh. go
46:11 calling a *r.* bird from east
Ezek. 39:4 give thee to *r.* birds

RAVIN, Verb.

Gen. 49:27 Benjamin *r.* as wolf

RAVIN.

Nah. 2:12 lion filled dens with *r.*

RAVISHED.

Prov. 5:19 be thou *r.* with love
20 why be *r.* with st. woman ?
Cant. 4:9 thou hast *r.* my heart
Is. 13:16 wives of Bab. sh. be *r.*
Lam. 5:11 *r.* the women in Zion
Zec. 14:2 women in Jerus. be *r.*

RAW.

Ex. 12:9 eat not it *r.* nor sodden
Lev. 13:10 if th. be quick *r.* flesh
15 priest see *r.* flesh, *r.* flesh
1 *Sam.* 2:15 not sod. flesh, but *r.*

RAZOR.

Num. 6:5 nor *r.* upon head, *Jud.*
13:5 ; 16:17 ; 1 *Sam.* 1:11
Ps. 52:2 tongue like a sharp *r.*
Is. 7:20 Lord shave with a *r.*
Ezek. 5:1 take thee a barber's *r.*

REACH.

Gen. 11:4 tower *r.* to heaven
Ex. 28:42 breeches *r.* to thighs
Lev. 26:5 threshing *r.* to vintage
Num. 34:11 border shall *r.* to sea
Job 20:6 his head *r.* unto clouds
Is. 8:8 he shall *r.* even to neck
30:28 breath *r.* to midst of neck
Jer. 48:32 thy plants *r.* to sea
Zec. 14:5 mountains sh. *r.* to A.
John 20:27 *r.* hither thy finger
2 *Cor.* 10:13 mea. to *r.* unto you

REACHED.

Gen. 28:12 ladder's top *r.* to hea.
Ruth 2:14 he *r.* her parched corn
Dan. 4:11 height *r.* to heaven, 20
2 *Cor.* 10:14 tho' we *r.* not to you
Rev. 18:5 Babyl.'s sins *r.* heaven

REACHETH.

2 *Chr.* 28:9 rage that *r.* to heav.
Ps. 36:5 faithfulness *r.* clouds
108:4 thy truth *r.* to the clouds
Prov. 31:20 *r.* hands to needy
Jer. 4:10 the sword *r.* to the soul
18 because it *r.* to thy heart
51:9 Bab.'s judgm. *r.* to heaven
Dan. 4:22 thy greatness *r.* heav.

REACHING.

Phil. 3:13 *r.* forth to th. things

READ (*short e*).

Ex. 24:7 *r.* in audience of people
Jos. 8:34 *r.* words of the law, 10
2 *K.* 5:7 king of Isr. *r.* the letter
22:8 Shaphan *r.* book of law, 10
23:2 Josiah *r.* in their ears book
of the covenant, 2 *Chr.* 34:30
2 *Chr.* 34:24 bri. all the curses *r.*
Ezr. 4:18 letter been plainly *r.*
Neh. 8:3 he *r.* before all the book
of the law, 8 ; 13:1
9:3 stood in their place and *r.*
Est. 6:1 book of records was *r.*
Is. 37:14 received let. and *r.* it
Jer. 29:29 Zephani. the priest *r.*
36:10 then *r.* Bar. words of Jer.

21 Jehudi *r.* it in ears of king
23 he *r.* three or four leaves
Mat. 12:3 have ye not *r.* ? 19:4 ;
21:16 ; 22:31 ; *Mark* 2:25 ;
12:10. 26 ; *Luke* 6:3
John 19:20 this *r.* many of Jews
Acts 8:28 eunuch *r.* Esaias prop.
32 place of scripture wh. he *r.*
13:27 prophets *r.* ev. sab. 15:21
23:34 Governor had *r.* the letter
2 *Cor.* 3:2 epistle known and *r.*
15 when M. is *r.* the veil is on
Col. 4:16 when this epistle is *r.*
1 *Thes.* 5:27 that this epistle be *r.*

READ (*long e*).

Deut. 17:19 king shall *r.* therein
31:11 thou sh. *r.* this low before
Is. 29:11 *r.* this, I pray thee, 12
34:16 seek out book of L. and *r.*
Jer. 36:6 go and *r.* in the roll
15 sit do. and *r.* it in our ears
51:61 cometh to Babylon and *r.*
Dan. 5:7 whosoever shall *r.* this
17 gifts be to thyself, I will *r.*
Mat. 21:42 did ye never *r.* in sc. ?
Luke 4:16 Jesus went in for to *r.*
Acts 8:30 Philip heard him *r.* E.
2 *Cor.* 1:13 we write none other
things than what ye *r.*
Eph. 3:4 wh. ye *r.* ye may und.
Col. 4:16 *r.* epistle fr. Laodicea.
Rev. 5:4 none worthy to *r.* book

READEST.

Luke 10:26 in law, how *r.* thou?
Acts 8:30 un. thou what thou *r.* ?

READETH.

Hab. 2:2 he may run that *r.* it
Mat. 24:15 whoso *r.* let him un-
derstand, *Mark* 13:14
Rev. 1:3 blessed is he that *r.*

READING.

Neh. 8:8 caused to understand *r.*
Jer. 36:8 *r.* in the book of the L.
51:63 wh. hast ma. an end of *r.*
Acts 13:15 after the *r.* of the law
2 *Cor.* 3:14 untaken away in *r.*
1 *Tim.* 4:13 give attendance to *r.*

READINESS.

Acts 17:11 received word in *r.*
2 *Cor.* 8:11 as there was a *r.*
10:6 *r.* to revenge disobedience

READY.

Ex. 17:4 people *r.* to stone me
19:11 *r.* against third day, 15
34:2 *r.* in morning, and come
Num. 32:17 we will go *r.* armed
Deut. 26:5 a Syrian *r.* to perish
2 *Sam.* 15:15 thy servants are *r.*
18:22 hast no tidings *r.* ?
Ezr. 7:6 Ezra was a *r.* scribe
Neh. 9:17 art a God *r.* to pardon
Est. 3:14 they should be *r.* 8:13
Job 3:8 *r.* to raise their mourning
15:23 day of darkn. is *r.* at hand
24 prevail as a king *r.* to battle
28 in houses *r.* to become hea.
18:12 destruction *r.* at his side
29:13 blessing of him *r.* to peri.
Ps. 38:17 for I am *r.* to halt
45:1 tongue pen of a *r.* writer
86:5 Lord art good, *r.* to forgive
88:15 *r.* to die from my youth
Prov. 24:11 those *r.* to be slain
31:6 stro. drink to him *r.* to pe.
Ec. 5:1 *r.* to hear th. give sacrif.
Is. 27:13 who were *r.* to perish
30:13 iniq. as breach *r.* to fall
32:4 tongue of stam. *r.* to speak
38:20 the L. was *r.* to save me
51:13 as if he were *r.* to destroy
Dan. 3:15 if ye be *r.* to worship
Mat. 22:4 fatlings killed, all *r.*
8 the wedding is *r. Luke* 14:17
24:44 be ye also *r. Luke* 12:40
25:10 they that were *r.* went in
Mark 14:38 spirit is *r.* flesh weak

REASON, Substantive.

Luke 7:2 servant sick, *r.* to die
22:33 L. I am *r.* to go with thee
John 7:6 your time is always *r.*
Acts 21:13 I am *r.* not to be bou.
23:21 are *r.* looking for promise
Rom. 1:15 I am *r.* to preach gos.
2 *Cor.* 8:19 declaration of *r.* mind
9:2 Achaia was *r.* a year ago
3 that, as I said, ye might be *r.*
5 that the same might be *r.*
12:14 third time I am *r.* to come
1 *Tim.* 6:18 ye be *r.* to distribute
2 *Tim.* 4:6 now *r.* to be offered
Tit. 3:1 be *r.* to every good work
Heb. 8:13 is *r.* to vanish away
1 *Pet.* 1:5 *r.* to be revealed
3:15 be *r.* always to give answer
4:5 give account to him th. is *r.*
5:2 not for lucre, of a *r.* mind
Rev. 3:2 things that are *r.* to die
12:4 wo. was *r.* to be delivered

See MADE, MAKE.

REALM.

2 *Chr.* 20:30 the *r.* of Jehoshaph.
Ezr. 7:13 they of my *r.* who go
23 why be wrath against *r.* ?
Dan. 1:20 better th. all in his *r.*
6:3 king tho. to set him over *r.*
9:1 Darius, king over *r.* of Chal.
11:2 stir up all ag. *r.* of Grecia

REAP.

Lev. 19:9 when ye *r.* 23:10, 22
25:5 growth of itself sh. not *r.*
11 ye shall neither sow nor *r.*
Ruth 2:9 eyes be on field they *r.*
1 *Sam.* 8:12 set your serva. to *r.*
2 *K.* 19:29 in the third year sow
and *r. Is.* 37:30
Job 4:8 sow wickedness *r.* same
24:6 they *r.* every one his corn
Ps. 126:5 sow in tears *r.* in joy
Prov. 22:8 soweth iniq. *r.* vanity
Ec. 11:4 regard clouds sh. not *r.*
Jer. 12:13 sown wheat, *r.* thorns
Hos. 8:7 sown wind, *r.* whirlwind
10:12 sow in righte. *r.* in mercy
Mic. 6:15 sh. sow, but not *r.*
Mat. 6:26 fowls of the air *r.* not
25:26 I *r.* where I sowed not
John 4:38 to *r.* whereon no labor
1 *Cor.* 9:11 if we *r.* carnal things
2 *Cor.* 9:6 sow. sparingly *r.* spar.
Gal. 6:7 man sow. that sh. he *r.*
8 soweth to flesh shall *r.* cor.
9 we shall *r.* if faint not
Rev. 14:15 thrust in sickle and *r.*

REAPED.

Hos. 10:13 wickedness *r.* iniquity
Jam. 5:4 laborers which *r.* fields
Rev. 44:16 his sickle, ear. was *r.*

REAPER, S.

Ruth 2:3 Ruth gleaned after *r.*
7 I pray, let me glean after *r.*
2 *K.* 4:18 he went out to the *r.*
Amos 9:13 ploughm. overtake *r.*
Mat. 13:30 say to *r.* gather tares
39 enemy is devil, *r.* are angels

REAPEST.

Lev. 23:22 not cl. riddance wh. *r.*
Luke 19:21 thou *r.* didst not sow

REAPETH.

Is. 17:5 the harvest-man *r.* ears
John 4:36 he that *r.* recei. wages
37 one soweth, another *r.*

REAPING.

1 *Sam.* 6:13 Beth-shem. were *r.*
Mat. 25:24 man, *r. Luke* 19:22

REARWARD. *See* REREWARD.

REASON, Substantive.

1 *K.* 9:15 the *r.* of the levy
Prov. 26:16 seven men render *r.*
Ec. 7:25 I applied to search *r.*
Dan. 4:36 at time my *r.* returned
Acts 6:2 not *r.* we leave word
18:14 O J. *r.* would I sho. bear

1 *Pet.* 3:15 ask. you a *r.* of hope

By REASON.

Gen. 41:31 plenty not kno. *by r.*
Ex. 2:23 Isr. sighed *by r.* bonda.
3:7 cry *by r.* of their taskmasr.
Num. 9:10 uncl. *by r.* dead body
18:8 things given *by r.* of anoi.
Deut. 5:5 afraid *by r.* of the fire
1 *K.* 14:4 Ahijah's eyes *by r.* age
2 *Chr.* 5:14 not minister *by r.*
20:15 not afraid *by r.* of multit.
Job 17:7 eye dim *by r.* of sorrow
31:23 *by r.* of highness not end.
37:19 speech *by r.* of darkness
41:25 *by r.* of break. they purify
Ps. 78:65 man shout. *by r.* wine
90:10 if *by r.* of str. be fourscore
Is. 49:19 too nar. *by r.* of inhabi.
Ezek. 19:10 branches *by r.* of wa.
Dan. 8:12 given *by r.* of transgr.
Jon. 2:2 I cried *by r.* of affliction
John 12:11 *by r.* many beli. on J.
Rom. 8:20 *by r.* of him who subj.
Heb. 5:3 *by r.* hereof, off. for sins
7:23 not continue *by r.* death
2 *Pet.* 2:2 *by r.* of whom truth

REASON, Verb.

1 *Sam.* 12:7 I may *r.* with you
Job 9:14 ch. words to *r.* with God
13:3 and desire to *r.* with God
15:3 sh. he *r.* with unpro. talk?
Is. 1:18 now, let us *r.* together
Mat. 16:8 J. said, Why *r.* among
yourselves, *Mark* 2:8; 8:17
Luke 5:21 scr. and Pha. began *r.*
22 what *r.* ye in your hearts?

REASONABLE.

Rom. 12:1 sacrifice, your *r.* serv.

REASONED.

Mat. 16:7 r. am. themselv. 21:15;
Mark 8:16; 11:31; *Luke* 20:5
Mark 2:8 J. perceived they so *r.*
Luke 20:14 the husbandmen *r.*
24:15 while they *r.* J. drew near
Acts 17:2 three sabbaths Paul *r.*
18:4 he *r.* in synagogue ev. sab.
19 Paul *r.* with J. at Ephesus
24:25 as he *r.* of righteousness

REASONING.

Job 13:6 hear my *r.* and hearken
Mark 2:6 scribes *r.* in th. hearts
12:28 having heard them *r.* tog.
Luke 9:46 arose *r.* among them
Acts 28:29 J. departed, and had *r.*

REASONS.

Job 32:11 gave ear to your *r.*
Is. 41:21 br. *r.* saith king of Jac.

REBEKAH.

Gen. 22:23 Bethuel begat R.
24:15 R. ca. out. 51, 59, 60, 67
25:28 R. loved Jacob, 20
26:7 should kill me for R. 35
27:42 words of Es. were told R.
29:12 that he was R. son, 35:8
49:31 they buried Isaac and R.
Rom. 9:10 when R. conceived

REBEL.

Num. 14:9 only *r.* not aga. Lord
Jos. 1:18 whosoever *r.* shall die
22:16 builded altar ye might *r.*
19 *r.* not agai. L. *r.* not ag. us
29 God forbid we *r.* against L.
1 *Sam.* 12:14 ye obey and not *r.*
15 if ye will not obey L. but *r.*
Neh. 2:19 will ye *r.* aga. king?
6:6 thou and Jews think to *r.*
Job 24:13 those that *r.* aga. light
Is. 1:20 if ye *r.* ye sh. be devour.
Hos. 7:14 assemble for corn, *r.*

REBELLED.

Gen. 14:4 thirteenth year they *r.*
Num. 20:24 because ye *r.* ag. my
word at Meribah, 27:14;
Deut. 1:26, 43; 9:23

1 *K.* 12:19 Rehobo. fled. so Is. *r.*
ag. house of Da. 2 *Chr.* 10:19
2 *K.* 1:1 Moab *r.* ag. Israel, 3, 5, 7
18:7 Hezek. *r.* ag. Assyria
24:1 Jehoiakim *r.* against Neb.
20 Ze. *r.* 2 *Chr.* 36:13; *Jer.* 52:3
2 *Chr.* 13:6 Jerob. *r.* ag. his lord
Neh. 9:26 disobe. and *r.* ag. thee
Ps. 5:10 for they *r.* against thee
105:28 they *r.* not against word
107:11 they *r.* ag. words of God
Is. 1:2 nourish. children, they *r.*
63:10 *r.* and vexed Holy Spirit
Lam. 1:18 have *r.* 20 griev. *r.*
3:42 we have *r.* has not pardon.
Ezek. 2:3 send th. to nation th. *r.*
17:15 he *r.* in sending to Egypt
20:8 they *r.* against me, 13, 21
Dan. 9:5 *r.* by departing fr. thee
9 to God mercy, though we
have *r.*
Hos. 13:16 Samaria *r.* against G.

REBELLEST.

2 *K.* 18:20 on whom dost thou
trust, that thou *r.*? *Is.* 36:5

REBELLION.

Deut. 31:27 know thy *r.* and stiff
Jos. 22:22 sh. know if it be in *r.*
1 *Sam.* 15:23 *r.* is as witchcraft
Ezr. 4:19 that *r.* made therein
Neh. 9:17 in *r.* appointed a capt.
Job 34:37 addeth *r.* unto his sin
Prov. 17:11 evil man seeketh *r.*
Jer. 28:16 hast taught *r.* 29:32

REBELLIOUS.

Deut. 9:7 *r.* against L. 24; 31:27
21:18 a stubborn and *r.* son
1 *Sam.* 20:30 son of the *r.* woman
Ezr. 4:12 building the *r.* city, 15
Ps. 66:7 let not *r.* exalt themsel.
68:6 the *r.* dwell in a dry land
18 for *r.* 78:8 *r.* generation
Is. 1:23 princes *r.* companions
30:1 woe to *r.* chil. saith Lord
9 a *r.* people; 50:5 I was not *r.*
65:2 spread hands to a *r.* people
Jer. 4:17 she ha. been *r.* saith L.
5:23 this people hath a *r.* heart
Ezek. 2:3 send thee to a *r.* nation
5 they are a *r.* house, 6, 7; 3:9,
26, 27; 12:2, 3
8 be not *r.* like that *r.* house
12:2 dwell. in midst of *r.* house
17:12 say to *r.* house, 44:6
24:3 utter parable to *r.* house

REBELS.

Num. 17:10 A. rod token ag. *r.*
20:10 M. and A. said, Hear, *r.*
Ezek. 20:38 I will purge out *r.*

REBUKE, Substantive.

Deut. 28:20 Lord send on thee *r.*
2 *K.* 19:3 this is day of *r. Is.* 37:3
Ps. 18:15 at thy *r.* blast of nost.
76:6 at *r.* horse cast into sleep
80:16 per. at *r.* of countenance
104:7 at thy *r.* they fled away
Prov. 13:1 a scorner hear. not *r.*
8 but the poor heareth not *r.*
27:5 open *r.* bet. than secret love
Ec. 7:5 better to hear *r.* of wise
Is. 25:8 *r.* of his peo. take away
30:17 thousand flee at *r.* of one
at the *r.* of five shall ye flee
50:2 at thy *r.* I dry up the sea
51:20 thy sons lie full of *r.* of G.
66:15 render his *r.* with flames
Jer. 15:15 for thy sake I suff. *r.*
Hos. 5:9 Ep. sh. be des. day of *r.*
Phil. 2:15 without *r.* in per. nat.

REBUKE, Verb.

Lev. 19:17 in any wise *r.* neigh.
Ruth 2:16 glean them, *r.* her not
1 *Chr.* 12:17 God look thereon, *r.*
Ps. 6:1 O Lord, *r.* me not, 38:1
68:30 *r.* the spearmen, the bulls
Prov. 9:8 *r.* wise man

24:25 them that *r.* him
Is. 2:4 shall *r.* nations, *Mic.* 4:3
17:13 nations rush, G. *r.* them
54:9 I ·vou. not be wroth, nor *r.*
Zec. 3:2 Lord *r.* thee, even Lord
that hath chosen Jer. *r.* thee
Mal. 3:11 *r.* devo. for your sakes
Mat. 16:22 P. *r.* him, *Mark* 8:32
Luke 17:3 if brot. trespass *r.* him
19:39 said, Master, *r.* thy disc.
1 *Tim.* 5:1 *r.* not elder, entreat
20 them that sin, *r.* before all
2 *Tim.* 4:2 *r.* with long-suffering
Tit. 1:13 wheref. *r.* sharply, 2:15
Jude 9 Mich. said, The L. *r.* thee
Rev. 3:19 as many as I love I *r.*

REBUKED.

Gen. 31:42 hath seen and *r.* thee
37:10 his father *r.* him, and said
Neh. 5:7 I *r.* the nobles and rul.
Ps. 9:5 hast *r.* the heathen, hast
106:9 he *r.* Red sea, it was dry
119:21 thou hast *r.* the proud
Mat. 8:26 he *r.* the wind and the
sea, *Mark* 4:39; *Luke* 8:24
17:18 J. *r.* devil, and he depart.
19:13 his disci. *r.* them, *Mark*
10:13; *Luke* 18:15
20:31 multitude *r.* blind men
Mark 1:25 he *r.* the devil, 9:25;
Luke 4:35; 9:42
8:33 Jesus *r.* Peter, Get behind
Luke 4:39 stood, and *r.* the fever
9:55 J. turned, *r.* James and J.
18:39 went before, *r.* blind man
23:40 thief answering, *r.* him
Heb. 12:5 nor faint wh. *r.* of him
2 *Pet.* 2:16 Balaam was *r.* for ini.

REBUKER.

Hos. 5:2 I have been a *r.* of all

REBUKES.

Ps. 39:11 with *r.* dost cor. man
Ezek. 5:15 execute judgment in
r. 25:17

REBUKETH, ING.

2 *Sam.* 22:16 discover. at *r.* of L.
Prov. 9:7 he that *r.* wicked man
28:23 he that *r.* shall find favor
Amos 5:10 hate him that *r.* in
Nah. 1:4 he *r.* sea, and maketh
Luke 4:41 he *r.* th. suffered not

RECALL.

Lam. 3:21 this I *r.* to mind

RECEIPT.

Mat. 9:9 Mat. sitting at the *r.* of
custom, *Mark* 2:14; *Lu.* 5:27

RECEIVE.

Deut. 33:3 ev. one *r.* thy words
1 *Sam.* 10:4 thou *r.* of their han.
Job 2:10 *r.* good at hand of G.?
27:13 shall *r.* of the Almighty
Ps. 6:9 Lord will *r.* my prayer
24:5 he shall *r.* blessing from L.
49:15 G. red. soul, he sh. *r.* me
73:24 afterward *r.* me to glory
75:2 when I *r.* congregation
Prov. 2:1 if th. wilt *r.* my words
10:8 wise will *r.* commandm.
Is. 57:6 sho. I *r.* comfort in these
Ezek. 16:61 asha. wh. *r.* sisters
Dan. 2:6 ye shall *r.* of me gifts
Mic. 1:11 shall *r.* of you standing
Zep. 3:7 thou wilt *r.* instruction
Mat. 10:41 *r.* a prophet's reward
11:5 the blind *r.* their sight
14 if ye *r.* it, this is E. to come
19:11 all men cannot *r.* saying
20:7 whatsoever is right that *r.*
21:22 believing, ye shall *r.*
34 that they might *r.* fruits
Mark 4:16 *r.* the word with gladness, *Luke* 8:13
20 hear the word, and *r.* it
10:51 Lord, that I might *r.* my
sight, *Luke* 18:41
11:24 wh. ye pray, believe ye *r.*

Luke 10:8 city ye enter, they *r.*
16:9 *r.* into everlasting habita.
23:41 we *r.* reward of our deeds
John 5:43 own name, him ye *r.*
44 can ye believe, wh. *r.* honor
7:39 they that believe, *r.* H. **G.**
14:3 come again, and *r.* you
16:14 he shall *r.* of mine
24 ask and ye shall *r.*
Acts 1:8 but ye shall *r.* power
2:38 ye shall *r.* gift of Holy **G.**
8:15 pray. they might *r.* H. **G.**
19 on who. I lay hands may *r.*
9:12 that he might *r.* his sight
17 J. sent me, thou *r.* thy sig.
10:43 believeth, *r.* remis. of sins
26:18 may *r.* forgiveness of sins
Rom. 5:17 *r.* abundance of grace
16:2 that ye *r.* her in the Lord
1 *Cor.* 3:8 ev. man *r.* his reward
14 work abide, he *r.* reward
4:7 didst *r.* it, why glory ?
2 *Cor.* 5:10 every one *r.* things
6:17 unclean thing, I will *r.* you
8:4 praying, we would *r.* gift
11:4 or if ye *r.* another spirit
Gal. 3:14 might *r.* promise of **S.**
Eph. 6:8 same shall he *r.* of L.
Col. 3:24 shall *r.* reward of inh.
25 he shall *r.* for wrong done
Phile. 15 should. *r.* him for ever
Heb. 7:8 men that die *r.* tithes
9:15 might *r.* promise, 10:36
Jam. 1:7 think he *r.* any thing
3:1 sh. *r.* greater condemnation
5:7 he *r.* early and latter rain
1 *Pet.* 5:4 shall *r.* crown of glory
1 *John* 3:22 whatso. we ask we *r.*
5:9 if we *r.* witness of men
2 *John* 8 that we *r.* a full re*ward*
Rev. 14:9 if any man *r.* mark
17:12 *r.* powers as kings

RECEIVE, *imperatively.*
Gen. 33:10 *r.* pres. at my hand
Job 22:22 *r.* law from his mouth
Prov. 4:10 and *r.* my sayings
Jer. 9:20 let your ear *r.* the word
Ezek. 3:10 *r.* all my words
Hos. 14:2 say, *r.* us graciously
Mat. 19:12 is able let him *r.* it
Luke 18:42 *r.* sight, *Acts* 22:13
John 20:22 he saith, *r.* Holy Gh.
Acts 7:59 L. Jesus, *r.* my spirit
Rom. 14:1 him weak in faith *r.*
15:7 *r.* one ano. as Ch. received
2 *Cor.* 7:2 *r.* us, wronged no man
11:16 as a fool *r.* me, I boast
Phil. 2:29 *r.* him in L. with glad.
Col. 4:10 Mar. if he come, *r.* him
Phile. 12 *r.* him th. is mine own
17 count me partner, *r.* him

RECEIVE, *negatively.*
2 *K.* 5:16 Elisha said, I *r.* none
Job 2:10 we *r.* good, not *r.* evil?
Jer. 35:13 will ye not *r.* instruc.
Ezek. 36:30 ye shall *r.* no more
Mark 10:15 whosoever sh. not *r.*
kingdom of G. *Luke* 18:17
Luke 9:53 they did not *r.* him
10:10 they *r.* you not, go into
18:30 who shall not *r.* manifold
John 3:11 ye *r.* not our witness
27 a man can *r.* noth. except
5:41 I *r.* not honor from men
43 come in F.'s na. ye *r.* me not
14:17 Sp. whom world cannot *r.*
Acts 22:18 will not *r.* testimony
1 *Cor.* 4:7 wh. hast thou, not *r.* ?
2 *Cor.* 6:1 *r.* not grace of G. in v.
Jam. 4:3 ye ask and *r.* not
2 *John* 10 *r.* him not into house
3 *John* 10 nei. doth he *r.* breth.

RECEIVE, *infinitively.*
Gen. 4:11 earth op. mouth to *r.*
Deut. 9:9 gone up to *r.* tables
1 *K.* 8:64 braz. altar was too little
to *r.* burnt-offer. 2 *Chr.* 7:7

2 *K.* 5:26 time to *r.* money, to *r.*
12:8 priest to *r.* no more money
Prov. 1:3 *r.* instruction of wisd.
Jer. 5:3 refused to *r.* correction
Mal. 3:10 not room enough to *r.*
Mat. 19:12 to *r.* it, let him *r.* it
Mark 2:2 no room to *r.* them
Luke 6:34 of whom ye hope to *r.*
Acts 8:27 ex. disciples to *r.* him
20:35 more bles. to give than *r.*
3 *John* 8 we ought to *r.* such
Rev. 4:11 thou worthy to *r.* glo.
5:12 worthy is L. to *r.* power
13:16 causeth to *r.* mark in ha.

RECEIVED.
Gen. 26:12 Isaac *r.* hundred-fold
Ex. 32:4 Aaron *r.* at th. hand
Num. 12:14 let Miriam be *r.* in
23:20 I *r.* commandm. to bless
Jos. 13:8 Gadites *r.* inheritance
1 *Sam.* 12:3 of wh. hand ha. I *r.*
2 *K.* 19:14 Hezekiah *r.* the letter,
Is. 37:14
1 *Chr.* 12:18 David *r.* them
Job 4:12 mine ear *r.* little thereof
Ps. 68:18 hast *r.* gifts for men
Prov. 24:32 I looked and *r.* inst.
Is. 40:2 she hath *r.* of L.'s hand
Ezek. 18:17 hath not *r.* usury nor
Zep. 3:2 she *r.* not correction
Mat. 10:8 freely ye *r.* freely give
13:20 *r.* into stony gr. 22 thorns
23 *r.* seed into good ground
20:9 *r.* every man a penny, 10
34 immedi. their eyes *r.* sight
Mark 7:4 many things they *r.*
10:52 he immediately *r.* sight,
Luke 18:43 ; *Acts* 9:18
16:19 was *r.* into heav. *Acts* 1:9
Luke 6:24 ye have *r.* consolation
8:40 the people gladly *r.* him
9:11 *r.* them, spake of kingdom
51 time come he sho. be *r.* up
10:38 Martha *r.* him into house
15:27 *r.* him safe and sound
19:6 Zaccheus *r.* him joyfully
15 returned, having *r.* kingd.
John 1:11 ca. to his own, own *r.*
12 as many as *r.* him he gave
16 of fulness *r.* grace for grace
3:33 he that hath *r.* testimony
4:45 when come, Galil. *r.* him
6:21 willingly *r.* him in ship
9:11 washed, and I *r.* sight
15 Pharis. asked how *r.* sight
10:18 comman. *r.* of my Father
17:8 given thy words, *r.* them
18:3 Ju. having *r.* band of men
Acts 1:9 cloud *r.* him out of sig.
2:33 hav. *r.* of Father promise
41 they *r.* word were baptized
7:53 who have *r.* law by angels
8:14 Samaria *r.* word of God
17 hands on them *r.* Holy Gh.
9:19 *r.* meat was strengthened
10:47 which have *r.* Holy Gh.
11:1 heard Genti. *r.* word of G.
15:4 they were *r.* of the church
17:7 whom Jason hath *r.*
11 Bereans *r.* word with readi.
19:2 have ye *r.* the Holy Ghost ?
20:24 ministry which I *r.* of L.
21:17 the brethren *r.* us gladly
22:5 from whom I *r.* letters to
28:7 Publius *r.* us ; Paul *r.* all
21 nei. *r.* letters out of Judea
Rom. 1:5 by whom we *r.* grace
5:11 by whom we *r.* atonement
8:15 have not *r.* spirit of bond.
14:3 him that eateth, G. *r.* him
15:7 rec. one another as C. *r.* us
1 *Cor.* 2:12 *r.* not spirit of world
4:7 glory, as if thou hadst not *r.*
11:23 I *r.* of Lord that which

1 *Cor.* 15:1 which ye *r.* 3 wh. I *r.*
2 *Cor.* 4:1 as we *r.* mercy
11:4 spirit which ye have not *r.*

Gal. 1:9 anot. gospel than ye *r.*
12 I *r.* it not of man, neither
3:2 *r.* ye Sp. by works of law ?
4:14 *r.* me as an angel of God
Phil. 4:9 thi. ye have *r.* and seen
Col. 2:6 as ye *r.* Christ, so walk
4:10 whom ye *r.* commandm.
17 take heed to minis. thou *r.*
1 *Thes.* 1:6 *r.* word in affliction
2:13 when ye *r.* the word, ye *r.*
4:1 as ye *r.* of us how to walk
2 *Thes.* 2:10 they *r.* not the truth
1 *Tim.* 3:16 believed, *r.* into gl.
4:3 meats God created to be *r.*
4 crea. good, if *r.* with thanks.
Heb. 7:11 under it people *r.* law
10:26 if sin after *r.* knowledge
11:13 not having *r.* promises
17 *r.* promises offered only son
19 whence he *r.* him in a figure
35 women *r.* dead raised to life
39 these *r.* not the promise
1 *Pet.* 4:10 every one hath *r.* gift
2 *Pet.* 1:17 he *r.* from God honor
2 *John* 4 we have *r.* a command
Rev. 2:27 power, as *r.* of Father
3:3 remember how thou hast *r.*
19:20 that had *r.* mark of beast
20:4 nor *r.* mark reigned wi. C.

RECEIVEDST.
Luke 16:25 in lifetime *r.* good th.

RECEIVER.
Is. 33:18 scribe? where is *r.* ?

RECEIVETH.
Jud. 19:18 no man *r.* to house
Job 35:7 what *r.* he of thy hand ?
Prov. 21:11 when wise *r.* know.
29:4 he that *r.* gifts, overthr.
Jer. 7:28 nation *r.* not correction
Mal. 2:13 *r.* offer. with good-will
Mat. 7:8 that asketh *r. Luke* 11:10
10:40 that *r.* you, *r.* me ; *r.* me,
r. him sent me, *John* 13:20
41 he that *r.* a prophet, right.
13:20 heareth word, anon *r.* it
18:5 one such little child, *r.* me
Mark 9:37 *r.* not me, but him
that sent me, *Luke* 9:48
Luke 15:2 this man *r.* sinners
John 3:32 no man *r.* his testim.
12:48 he that *r.* not my words
1 *Cor.* 9:24 run all, one *r.* prize
Heb. 6:7 earth *r.* blessing fr. God
7:9 L. who *r.* tithes, paid tithes
Rev. 2:17 know. saving he *r.* it
14:11 whoso. *r.* mark of name

RECEIVETH not.
1 *Cor.* 2:14 *r. not* things of God
3 *John* 9 but Diotrephes *r.* us *n,*

RECEIVING.
2 *K.* 5:20 in not *r.* at his hands
Acts 17:15 *r.* a comman. to Silas
Rom. 11:15 wh. sh. *r.* of th. be ?
Phil. 4:15 concern. giving and *r.*
Heb. 12:28 wheref. we *r.* a king.
1 *Pet.* 1:9 *r.* the end of your faith

RECHAB.
2 *K.* 10:15 Jehonadab son of R.
1 *Chr.* 2:55 father of house of R.
Jer. 35:6 Jonadab the son of R.

RECHABITES.
Jer. 35:2 go to house of the R.

RECKON, ETH.
Lev. 25:50 he shall *r.* with him
27:18 priest shall *r.* to him, 23
Num. 4:32 by name *r.* instrum.
Ezek. 44:26 shall *r.* to him 7 days
Mat. 18:24 when he began to *r.*
25:19 lord of those servants *r.*
Rom. 6:11 *r.* yours. to be dead
8:18 I *r.* suffer. of present time

RECKONED.
Num. 23:9 people shall not be *r.*
2 *Sam.* 4:2 Beeroth *r.* to Benj.
2 *K.* 12:15 they *r.* not with men

1 *Chr.* 5:1 not be *r.* by birthrig.
7 genealogy of generations *r.*
17 *r.* by genealogies, 7:5, 7; 9:1,
22; 2 *Chr.* 31:19; *Ezr.* 2:62;
8:3; *Neh.* 7:5, 64
Ps. 40:5 thy tho' cannot be *r.*
Is. 38:13 I *r.* till morning
Luke 22:37 *r.* am. transgressors
Rom. 4:4 reward is not *r.* of gra.
9 *r.* to Abra. 10 how was it *r.?*

RECKONING.

2 *K.* 22:7 there was no *r.* made
1 *Chr.* 23:11 they were in one *r.*

RECOMMENDED.

Acts 14:26 whe. they had been *r.*
15:40 being *r.* to grace of God

RECOMPENSE.

Deut. 32:35 belong. veng. and *r.*
Job 15:31 vanity shall be his *r.*
Prov. 12:14 *r.* shall be rendered
Is. 35:4 God will come with a *r.*
59:18 repay *r.* to his enemies
66:6 voice of L. that render. *r.*
Jer. 51:6 will render to her a *r.*
Lam. 3:64 render to them a *r.*
Hos. 9:7 the days of *r.* are come
Joel 3:4 will ye render me *r.?*
7 I will return *r.* on your head
Luke 14:12 a *r.* be made thee
Rom. 1:27 rec. *r.* of their error
11:9 let their table be made a *r.*
2 *Cor.* 6:13 for a *r.* in the same
Heb. 2:2 trangr. received a *r.*
10:35 hath great *r.* of reward
11:26 he had respect to the *r.*

RECOMPENSES.

Is. 34:8 a year of *r.* for Zion
Jer. 51:56 L. God of *r.* shu. requ.

RECOMPENSE, Verb.

Num. 5:7 he shall *r.* his trespass
8 if he have no kinsman to *r.*
Ruth 2:12 the Lord *r.* thy work
2 *Sam.* 19:36 sho. king *r.* me?
Job 34:33 *r.* it whe. thou refuse
Prov. 20:22 say not, I wi. *r.* evil
Is. 65:6 I will *r.* into th. bosom
Jer. 16:18 I will *r.* their iniquity
25:14 I will *r.* them, *Hos.* 12:2
50:29 *r.* her according to work
Ezek. 7:3 will *r.* abominations, 8
4 will *r.* thy ways upon thee,
9; 9:10; 11:21; 16:43
17:19 my covenant I will *r.*
23:49 shall *r.* your lewdness
Joel 3:4 if ye *r.* me, will I return
Luke 14:14 they cannot *r.* thee
Rom. 12:17 *r.* no man evil for evil
2 *Thes.* 1:6 *r.* tribulation to them
Heb. 10:30 hath said, I will *r.*

RECOMPENSED.

Num. 5:8 let trespass be *r.* to L.
2 *Sam.* 23:21 accord. to cleanness
hath he *r.* 25; *Ps.* 18:20, 24
Prov. 11:31 righteous shall be *r.*
Jer. 18:20 sh. evil be *r.* for good?
Ezek. 22:31 th. own way ha. I *r.*
Luke 14:14 be *r.* at resurrection
Rom. 11:35 it shall be *r.* to him

RECOMPENSEST, ING.

2 *Chr.* 6:23 *r.* way upon his head
Jer. 32:18 *r.* iniquity of fathers

RECONCILE.

Lev. 6:30 blood is brought to *r.*
1 *Sam.* 29:4 wherew. he *r.* hims.
Ezek. 45:20 so shall he *r.* house
Eph. 2:16 he might *r.* both to G.
Col. 1:20 to *r.* all things to him.

RECONCILED.

Mat. 5:24 first be *r.* to brother
Rom. 5:10 when enem. *r.* to God
1 *Cor.* 7:11 let her be *r.* to husb.
2 *Cor.* 5:18 hath *r.* us to himself
20 in Ch. stead, be ye *r.* to God
Col. 1:21 were enemies, yet he *r.*

RECONCILIATION.

Lev. 8:15 to make a *r.* upon it
2 *Chr.* 29:24 made *r.* with blood
Ezek. 45:15 make *r.* for them, 17
Dan. 9:24 to make *r.* for iniquity
2 *Cor.* 5:18 given us minist. of *r.*
19 committed to us word of *r.*
Heb. 2:17 *r.* for the sins of people

RECONCILING.

Lev. 16:20 he made end of *r.*
Rom. 11:15 if casting away be *r.*
2 *Cor.* 5:19 God in Chr. *r.* world

RECORD, Substantive.

Ezr. 6:2 therein was *r.* written
Job 16:19 behold, *r.* is on high
John 1:19 this is the *r.* of John
32 John bare *r.* saying, 34
8:13 thou bearest *r.* of thyself,
thy *r.* is not true, 14
12:17 the peo. with him, bare *r.*
19:35 he saw bare *r.* his *r.* true
Rom. 10:2 bear *r.* they have zeal
2 *Cor.* 1:23 I call God for a *r.*
8:3 to their power I bear *r.*
Gal. 4:15 I bear you *r.*
Phil. 1:8 God is my *r.*
Col. 4:13 I bear *r.* he hath zeal
1 *John* 5:7 th. are 3 that bear *r.*
10 *r.* God gave of his Son, 11
3 *John* 12 we bear *r.* our *r.* is true
Rev. 1:2 who bare *r.* of word of G.

RECORDS.

Ezr. 4:15 search be made in *r.*
Est. 6:1 command. to bring *r.*

RECORD, Verb.

Ex. 20:24 where I *r.* my name
Deut. 30:19 I call heaven and
earth to *r.* 31:28
1 *Chr.* 16:4 appoint. Levites to *r.*
Is. 8:2 took faithful witnes. to *r.*
Acts 20:26 I take you to *r.*

RECORDED.

Neh. 12:22 Levites were *r.* chief

RECORDER.

2 *Sam.* 8:16 Jehosh. was *r.* 20:24;
1 *K.* 4:3; 1 *Chr.* 18:15
2 *K.* 18:18 and Joah the son of
Asaph *r. Is.* 36:3, 22
2 *Chr.* 34:8 Joah son of Joahaz *r.*

RECOUNT.

Nah. 2:5 he shall *r.* his worthies

RECOVER.

Jud. 11:26 did ye not *r.* them
1 *Sam.* 30:8 shalt without fail *r.*
2 *Sam.* 8:3 went to *r.* his border
2 *K.* 1:2 inquire whether I sh. *r.*
5:3 the prophet would *r.* him
11 strike his hand, and *r.* leper
8:8 shall I *r.* of this disease? 9
2 *Chr.* 13:20 nor did Jeroboam *r.*
14:13 could not *r.* themselves
Ps. 39:13 that I may *r.* strength
Is. 11:11 *r.* remn. of his people
38:16 *r.* me and make me live
21 for a plaster, and he shall *r.*
Hos. 2:9 and I will *r.* my wool
Mark 16:18 hands on sick, th. *r.*
3 *Tim.* 2:26 may *r.* themselves

RECOVERED.

1 *Sam.* 30:18 *r.* all Am. took, 19
22 not give aught of spoil we *r.*
2 *K.* 13:25 and *r.* cities of Israel
14:28 warred, and *r.* Damascus
16:6 Rez. king of Syria *r.* Elath
20:7 laid it on the boil, he *r.*
Is. 38:9 Hezekiah sick, *r.* 39:1
Jer. 8:22 why is not my peo. *r.?*
41:16 Johanan took people he *r.*

RECOVERING.

Luke 4:18 *r.* of sight to the blind

RED.

Gen. 25:25 came out *r.* all over
30 feed me with that *r.* pottage
49:12 eyes shall be *r.* with wine

Ex. 25:5 rams' skins dyed *r.*
26:14; 35:7; 36:19; 39:34
35:23 wi. wh. was found *r.* skins
Num. 19:2 bring thee a *r.* heifer
2 *K.* 3:22 Moabites saw water *r.*
Est. 1:6 a pavement of *r.* blue
Ps. 75:8 wine is *r.* full of mixtu.
Prov. 23:31 look not on wine *r.*
Is. 1:18 though your sins be *r.*
27:2 sing, a vineyard of *r.* wine
63:2 art thou *r.* in apparel?
Nah. 2:3 shield of mighty men *r.*
Zec. 1:8 a man on a *r.* horse
6:2 in first chariot we. *r.* horses
Mat. 16:2 fair weather, sky *r.* 3
Rev. 6:4 anot. horse that was *r.*
12:3 great *r.* dragon, sev. heads

RED sea.

Ex. 10:19 cast locusts into *R. s.*
13:18 G. led them by the *R. sea*
15:4 captains drowned in *R. s.*
22 Moses bro. Israel from *R. s.*
23:31 set thy bounds from *R. s.*
Num. 14:25 into wilder. by *R. s.*
21:14 what he did in the *R. s.?*
Deut. 1:40 take journey by *R. s.*
11:4 he made *R. sea* overflow
Jos. 2:10 the L. dried up *R. sea*
4:23 as L. your G. did to *R. sea*
24:6 Egypt. pursu. after to *R. s.*
Neh. 9:9 heard. their cry by *R. s.*
Ps. 106:7 provoked him at *R. s.*
9 rebuked *R. s.* it was dried up
22 done terrible things by *R. sea*
136:13 him who divided *R. sea*
15 overthrew Pharaoh in *R. s.*
Jer. 49:21 noise was heard in *R. s.*
Acts 7:36 showed wond. in *R. sea*
Heb. 11:29 by faith passed *R. s.*

REDDISH.

Lev. 13:19 somewhat *r.* 24, 43
42 a white *r.* sore, a leprosy
49 if plague be *r.* in garment
14:37 if plag. be with streaks, *r.*

REDEEM.

Ex. 6:6 I will *r.* you with arm
13:13 firstl. of ass shalt *r.* 34:20
15 first-b. of my chil. *r.* 34:20
Lev. 25:25 if any of his kin *r.* it
32 the cities may the Levit. *r.*
49 or any of kin may *r.* him
27:15 house will *r.* it, 19, 20, 31
Num. 18:15 first-born sh. thou *r.*
17 firstling of a goat sh. not *r.*
Ruth 4:4 *r.* it, if not, I will *r.* 11
6 I cannot *r.* it for mys. *r.* th.
3 *Sam.* 7:23 wh. nation is like Is.
God went to *r.?* 1 *Chr.* 17:21
Neh. 5:5 is it in our power to *r.*
Job 5:20 in famine he sh. *r.* thee
6:23 *r.* me from hand of mighty
Ps. 25:22 *r.* Is. O G. out of troub.
26:11 *r.* me and be merciful
44:26 *r.* us for thy mercies' sake
49:7 none of th. can *r.* his brot.
15 G. will *r.* my soul fr. grave
69:18 draw ni. to my soul, *r.* it
72:14 *r.* their soul from deceit
130:8 *r.* Isr. from all iniquities
Is. 50:2 short. that it cannot *r.?*
Jer. 15:21 I will *r.* thee
Hos. 13:14 I will *r.* them fr. death
Mic. 4:10 L. sh. *r.* thee fr. Baby.
Gal. 4:5 *r.* them were under law
Tit. 2:14 he might *r.* us fr. iniq.

REDEEMED.

Gen. 48:16 the angel which *r.* me
Ex. 15:13 people whom thou *r.*
21:8 then shall he let her be *r.*
Lev. 19:20 with bondmaid not *r.*
25:30 if house in city be not *r.*
48 broth. sold may be *r.* again
54 if he be not *r.* then go out
27:20 sold field, it sh. not be *r.*
27 an uncl. beast not *r.* be sold
28 no devot. thing sh. be *r.* 29
33 tithe and change not be *r.*

Num. 3:46 those *r.* more th. Lev.
Deut. 7:8 L. hath *r.* you fr. king
  of Egypt, 15:15; 24:18
9:26 thy people thou hast *r.*
13:5 L. *r.* you out of bondage
21:8 merciful to Is. thou hast *r.*
2 *Sam.* 4:9 L. *r.* soul, 1 K. 1:29
1 *Chr.* 17:21 whom thou *r.* out of
  Egypt, *Neh.* 1:10; *Ps.* 77:15
Neh. 5:8 we have *r.* the Jews
Ps. 31:5 thou hast *r.* me, O L. G.
71:23 my soul rejo. thou hast *r.*
74:2 thine inherit. thou hast *r.*
106:10 he *r.* them from enemy
107:2 let *r.* of the Lord say so
136:24 hath *r.* us from enemies
Is. 1;27 Zion be *r.* with judgm.
29:22 saith L. who *r.* Abraham
35:9 but the *r.* shall walk there
43:1 fear not, I have *r.* thee
44:22 ret. to me, I have *r.* thee
  23 Lord *r.* J. 48:20; *Jer.* 31:11
51:11 *r.* of the L. shall return
52:3 ye sh. be *r.* without money
  9 *r.* Jer. 62:12 holy people *r.*
63:4 *r.* is come; 9 he *r.* them
Lam. 3:58 thou hast *r.* my life
Hos. 7:13 tho' I *r.* them, yet they
Mic. 6.4 I *r.* thee out of house
Zec. 10:8 hiss, I have *r.* them
Luke 1:68 visited and *r.* his peo.
24:21 who should have *r.* Israel
Gal. 3:13 Christ *r.* us from curse
1 *Pet.* 1:18 not *r.* with corrupti.
Rev. 5:9 thou hast *r.* us to God
14:3 the 144,000 which were *r.*
  4 these were *r.* from am. men

REDEEMEDST.
2 *Sam.* 7:23 *r.* to thee from Egy.

REDEEMER.
Job 19:25 I know that my R. liv.
Ps. 19:14 O L. my stren. and R.
  78:35 the high G. was their R.
Prov. 23:11 their R. is mighty
Is. 41:14 thy R. Holy One, 54:5
43:14 saith L. your R. H. One
44:6 saith L. his R. L. of hosts
  24 sai. thy R. 48:17; 49:7; 54:8
47:4 as for our R. Lord of hosts
49:26 I the L. am thy R. 60:16
59:20 the R. shall come to Zion
63:16 art our Father, our R.
Jer. 50:34 their R. is strong

REDEEMETH.
Ps. 34:22 L. *r.* souls of his serv.
103:4 who *r.* life fr. destruction

REDEEMING.
Ruth 4:7 manner in Isr. conc. *r.*
Eph. 5:16 *r.* the time, *Col.* 4:5

REDEMPTION.
Lev. 25:24 ye shall grant a *r.*
  51 he sh. give price of his *r.* 52
Num. 3:49 Moses took *r.* money
Ps. 49:8 *r.* of their soul is prec.
111:9 he sent *r.* to his people
130:7 with L. th. is plenteo. *r.*
Jer. 32:7 right of *r.* is thine, 8
Luke 2:38 that looked for *r.*
21:28 your *r.* draweth nigh
Rom. 3:24 justified thro' *r.* in
8:23 for adoption, *r.* of our body
1 *Cor.* 1:30 Chr. is made to us *r.*
Eph. 1:7 in whom we have *r.*
  thro' his blood, *Col.* 1:14

Eph. 1:14 *r.* of purchased poss.
4:30 sealed unto the day of *r.*
Heb. 9:12 obtai. eternal *r.* for us
  15 the *r.* of the transgressions

REDNESS.
Prov. 23:29 who hath *r.* of eyes?

REDOUND.
2 *Cor.* 4:15 grace *r.* to glo. of G.

REED.
1 *K.* 14:15 L. sh. smite Isr. as *r.*

---

2 *K.* 18:21 thou trustest upon the
  staff of bruised *r. Is.* 36:6
Is. 42:3 a bruised *r.* shall he not
  break, *Mat.* 12:20
Ezek. 29:6 been staff of a *r.* to Is.
  40:3 a man with a measuring *r.*
Mat. 11:7 a *r.* shaken *Luke* 7:24
27:29 put a *r.* in his right hand
  30 sm. him with *r. Mark* 15:19
48 sponge on a *r. Mark* 15:36
Rev. 11:1 there was giv. me a *r.*
21:15 golden *r.* to meas. city, 16

REEDS.
Job 40:21 lieth in the covert of *r.*
Is. 19:6 *r.* and flags sh. wither, 7
35:7 in habita. of dragons be *r.*
Jer. 51:32 the *r.* they have burnt
Ezek. 42:16 measured east side,
  five hundred *r.* 17, 18, 19
45:1 shall be length of 25,000 *r.*

REEL.
Ps. 107:27 *r.* to and fro, and stag.
Is. 24:20 earth shall *r.* to and fro

REFINE.
Zec. 13:9 I will *r.* them as silver

REFINED.
1 *Chr.* 28:18 for the altar *r.* gold
29:4 7,000 talents of *r.* silver
Is. 25:6 wines on lees well *r.*
48:10 I have *r.* th. not with silv.
Zec. 13:9 refine th. as silver is *r.*

REFINER.
Mal. 3:2 for he is like a *r.'s* fire
  3 he sh. sit as a *r.* and purifier

REFORMATION.
Heb. 9:10 on th. until time of *r.*

REFORMED.
Lev. 26:23 if ye will not be *r.*

REFRAIN.
Gen. 45:1 J. could not *r.* himself
Job 7:11 I will not *r.* my mouth
Prov. 1:15 *r.* thy foot from path
Ec. 3:5 a time to *r.* fr. embracing
Is. 48:9 for my praise I will *r.*
  64:12 wilt thou *r.* thyself, O L.?
Jer. 31:16 *r.* voice from weeping
Acts 5:38 I say, *r.* from th. men
1 *Pet.* 3:10 *r.* his tong. from evil

REFRAINED.
Gen. 43:31 and Joseph *r.* himself
Est. 5:10 Haman *r.* himself
Job 29:9 the princes *r.* talking
Ps. 40:9 I have not *r.* my lips
119:101 I have *r.* my feet fr. evil
Is. 42:14 been still, *r.* myself
Jer. 14:10 have not *r.* their feet

REFRAINETH.
Prov. 10:19 that *r.* lips is wise

REFRESH.
1 *K.* 13:7 come home *r.* thyself
Acts 27:3 J. suffered P. to *r.* him.
Phile. 20 *r.* my bowels in the L.

REFRESHED, ETH.
Ex. 23:12 stranger may be *r.*
31:17 sev. day rested and was *r.*
1 *Sam.* 16:23 so Saul was *r.*
2 *Sam.* 16:14 David and people *r.*
Job 32:20 speak that I may be *r.*
Prov. 25:13 he *r.* soul of masters
Rom. 15:32 I may with you be *r.*
1 *Cor.* 16:18 *r.* my spi. and yours
2 *Cor.* 7:13 Titus, his spir. was *r.*
2 *Tim.* 1:16 for he often *r.* me
Phile. 7 bow. of saints *r.* by th.

REFRESHING.
Is. 28:12 *r.* yet they wo. not hear
Acts 3:19 times of *r.* shall come

REFUGE.
Num. 35:13 six cit. ha. for *r.* 15
Deut. 33:27 eternal God is thy *r.*
Jos. 20:3 *r.* from aveng. of blood
2 *Sam.* 22:3 my high tower and *r.*

Ps. 9:9 L. be a *r.* for oppressed
14:6 because the Lord is his *r.*
46:1 G. is *r.* 7, 11; 48:3 G. know
57:1 thy wings will make my *r.*
59:16 my *r.* in day of trouble
62:7 my *r.* is God; 8 God is *r.*
71:7 thou art strong *r.* 142:5
91:2 is my *r.* 9; 94:22 G. is my
104:18 hills *r.* for wild goats
142:4 *r.* failed; 5 thou art my *r.*
Prov. 14:26 chil. have place of *r.*
Is. 4:6 place of *r.* 25:4 needy *r.*
28:15 we have made lies our *r.*
  17 hail shall sweep away *r.*
Jer. 16:19 O L. my *r.* in affliction
Heb. 6:18 who have fled for *r.*

REFUSE.
1 *Sam.* 15:9 ev. thing that was *r.*
Lam. 3:45 hast made us as *r.*
Amos 8:6 may sell *r.* of wheat

REFUSE, Verb.
Ex. 4:23 if thou *r.* to let them
  go, 8:2; 9:2; 10:4
10:3 how long *r.* to humble thy.
16:28 *r.* ye to keep my com. ?
22:17 if her father utterly *r.*
Job 34:33 whe. thou *r.* or choose
Prov. 8:33 be wise, and *r.* it not
21:7 because they *r.* to do judg.
  25 his hands *r.* to labor
Is. 1:20 if ye *r.* sh. be devoured
  7:15 he may know to *r.* evil, 16
Jer. 8:5 *r.* to return ; 9:6 *r.* to kn.
13:10 peo. *r.* to hear my words
25:28 if they *r.* to take the cup
38:21 if thou *r.* to go forth
Acts 25:11 if offen. I *r.* not to die
1 *Tim.* 4:7 but *r.* profane fables
5:11 but the younger widows *r.*
Heb. 12:25 *r.* not him that speak.

REFUSED.
Gen. 37:35 Ja. *r.* to be comforted
39:8 J. *r.* to lie wi. master's wi.
48:19 Jacob *r.* to remove hand
Num. 20:21 Edom *r.* Is. passage
1 *Sam.* 8:19 people *r.* to obey S.
16:7 look not on him, I *r.* him
28:23 Saul *r.* said, I will not eat
2 *Sam.* 2:23 Asa. *r.* to turn aside
13:9 she poured, Amn. *r.* to eat
1 *K.* 20:35 man *r.* to smite him
21:15 vineyard he *r.* to give th.
2 *K.* 5:16 Naaman urged, he *r.*
Neh. 9:17 our fathers *r.* to obey
Est. 1:12 qu. Vashti *r.* to come
Job 6:7 things that my soul *r.*
Ps. 77:2 soul *r.* to be comforted
78:10 they *r.* to walk in his law
  67 he *r.* tabernacle of Joseph
118:22 stone which builders *r.*
Prov. 1:24 I have called, ye *r.*
Is. 54:6 thou wast *r.* saith thy G.
Jer. 5:3 *r.* to receive correction
11:10 fath. *r.* to hear my words
31:15 Rachel *r.* to be comforted
50:33 took them *r.* to let th. go
Ezek. 5:6 they *r.* my judgments
Hos. 11:5 beca. they *r.* to return
Zec. 7:11 but they *r.* to hearken
Acts 7:35 Moses whom they *r.*
1 *Tim.* 4:4 and nothing to be *r.*
Heb. 11:24 Mo. *r.* to be called son
12:25 *r.* him th. spake on earth

REFUSEDST.
Jer. 3:3 thou *r.* to be ashamed

REFUSETH.
Ex. 7:14 Pharaoh *r.* to let people
Num. 22:13 L. *r.* to give me lea.
Deut. 25:7 bro. *r.* to raise name
Prov. 10:17 he that *r.* reproof
13:18 sha. to him that *r.* instru.
15:32 that *r.* instruction despis.
Is. 8:6 people *r.* wat. of Shiloah
Jer. 15:18 wound *r.* to be healed

REGARD.
Ec. 8:2 in *r.* of the oath of God

Acts 8:11 and to him they had *r.*

REGARD, Verb.

Gen. 45:20 *r.* not your stuff, for
Ex. 5:9 let not *r.* vain words
Lev. 19:31 *r.* not familiar spirits
Deut. 28:50 not *r.* person of aged
1 *Sam.* 25:25 *r.* not man of Belial
2 *Sam.* 13:20 *r.* not, he is broth.
2 *K.* 3:14 that I *r.* Jehoshaphat
Job 3:4 let not G. *r.* it fr. above
35:13 nor will Almighty *r.* it
36:21 take heed, *r.* not iniquity
Ps. 28:5 they *r.* not works of L.
31:6 hated that *r.* lying vanities
66:18 if I *r.* iniq. in my heart
94:7 neit. shall G. of Jacob *r.* it
102:17 will *r.* prayer of destitu.
Prov. 5:2 mayest *r.* discretion
6:35 he will not *r.* any ransom
Is. 5:12 they *r.* not work of L.
13:17 M. who will not *r.* silver
Lam. 4:16 L. will no more *r.* th.
Dan. 11:37 *r.* God, nor *r.* any god
Amos 5:22 nor *r.* peace-offerings
Hab. 1:5 *r.* wonder marvellously
Mal. 1:9 will he *r.* yo. persons?
Luke 18:4 fear not God nor *r.* man
Rom. 14:6 Lord he doth not *r.*

REGARDED.

Ex. 9:21 *r.* not the word of Lord
1 *K.* 18:29 no voice, nor any *r.*
1 *Chr.* 17:17 thou hast *r.* me
Ps. 106:44 he *r.* their affliction
Prov. 1:24 stret. hand, no man *r.*
Dan. 3:12 O king, have not *r.*
Luke 1:48 he *r.* his handmaid
18:2 feared not G. nei. *r.* man
Heb. 8:9 I *r.* them not, saith L.

REGARDEST.

2 *Sam.* 19:6 thou *r.* not princes
Job 30:20 I stand up, *r.* me not
Mat. 22:16 thou *r.* not the persons of men, *Mark* 12:14

REGARDETH.

Deut. 10:17 *r.* not persons
Job 34:19 nor *r.* rich mo. th. poor
39:7 neither *r.* crying of driver
Prov. 12:10 right. *r.* life of beast
13:18 that *r.* reproof be honored
15:5 that *r.* reproof is prudent
29:7 wicked *r.* not cause of poor
Ec. 5:8 higher than highest *r.*
11:4 he that *r.* clouds not reap
Is. 33:8 desp. cities, *r.* no man
Dan. 6:13 David *r.* not thee
Mal. 2:13 *r.* not offer. any more
Rom. 14:6 that *r.* day, *r.* it to L.

REGARDING.

Job 4:20 perish without any *r.* it
Phil. 2:30 not *r.* life to sup. lack

REGEM-MELECH. *Zec.* 7:2

REGENERATION.

Mat. 19:28 wh. followed me in *r.*
Tit. 3:5 saved us by wash. of *r.*

REGION.

Deut. 3:4 all the *r.* of Argob, 13
1 *K.* 4:24 dominion over all the *r.*
Mat. 3:5 went to him *r.* round J.
4:16 which sat in *r.* of death
Mark 1:28 fame spread throughout *r.* of G. *Luke* 4:14; 7:17
6:55 ran thro' whole *r.* round
Acts 13:49 word of L. pub. thro' *r.*
14:6 they fled to *r.* round about
16:6 gone thro' the *r.* of Galatia

REGIONS.

Acts 8:1 scattered thro' *r.* of Ju.
2 *Cor.* 10:16 preach in *r.* beyond
11:10 stop me in *r.* of Achaia
Gal. 1:21 I came into *r.* of Syria

REGISTER.

Ezr. 2:62 sought *r.* Neh. 7:64
Neh. 7:5 found a *r.* of genealogy

REHABIAH. 1 *Chr.* 23:17

REHEARSE, ED.

Ex. 17:14 *r.* in ears of Joshua
Jud. 5:11 *r.* righteous acts of L.
1 *Sam.* 8:21 he *r.* in ears of Lord
17 31 *r.* David's words bef. Saul
Acts 11:4 Peter *r.* the matter
11:27 *r.* all G. done with them

REHOBOAM.

1 *K.* 11:43 R. son of Solo. 14:21
12:6 R. consulted men, 17, 21, 27
14:30 was war between R. 15:6
2 *Chr.* 9:31; 10:6, 17; 11:1
11:17 made R. strong, 21, 22
*'*3:7 against R. when R. was

REHOBOTH.

Gen. 10:11 builded Nin. and R.
26:22 Isaac called the well R.
36:37 S. of R. reigned, 1 *Chr.* 1:48

REHUM.

Ezr. 2:2 R. came with, *Neh.* 12:3
4:8 R. the chancellor, 17, 23
Neh. 3:17 R. the son of Bani
10:25 R. of chief of the people

REIGN, Substantive.

1 *K.* 6:1 Solomon's *r.* over Israel
1 *Chr.* 4:31 cities to *r.* of David
29:30 David's acts with *r.* writ.
2 *Chr.* 36:20 *r.* of king. Persia
Luke 3:1 year of *r.* of Tiberius

REIGN, Verb.

Gen. 37:8 shalt thou *r.* over us?
Ex. 15:18 the Lord shall *r.* for ever, *Ps.* 146:10
Lev. 26:17 they that hate shall *r.*
Deut. 15:6 *r.* over many nations
Jud. 9:2 seventy *r.* over you
8 *r.* thou over us, 10, 12, 14
1 *Sam.* 8:9 k. that shall *r.* 11
9:17 this same *r.* over my peop.
11:12 said, Shall S. *r.* over us?
12:12 a king shall *r.* over us
2 *Sam.* 3:21 thou mayest *r.* over
1 *K.* 1:11 heard th. Adonijah *r.?*
13 Sol. shall *r.* after me, 17, 30
2:15 set faces on me, I shou. *r.*
16:15 Zimri *r.* 7 days in Tirzah
2 *Chr.* 1:8 made me *r.* in his ste.
23:3 said, The king's son sh. *r.*
Job 34:30 the hypocrite *r.* not
Prov. 8:15 by me kings *r.*
Ec. 4:14 out prison he com. to *r.*
Is. 24:23 L. of hosts shall *r.* in Z.
32:1 king shall *r.* in righteous.
Jer. 22:15 shalt thou *r.* bec. thou
23:5 a king shall *r.* and prosper
33:21 D. sho. not have son to *r.*
Mic. 4:7 L. shall *r.* over th. in Z.
Mat. 2:22 heard Archelaus did *r.*
Luke 1:33 he shall *r.* over Jacob
19:14 not have this man to *r.*
27 enemies would not I sho. *r.*
Rom. 5:17 sh. *r.* in life by J. C.
21 so might grace *r.* by J. C.
6:12 let not sin *r.* in yo. bodies
15:12 shall rise to *r.* over Genti.
2 *Tim.* 2:12 if we suff. we sh. *r.*
Rev. 5:10 we shall *r.* on earth
11:15 he shall *r.* for ever
20:6 sh. *r.* wi. him 1,000 years
22:5 shall *r.* for ever and ever

See BEGAN.

REIGNED.

Gen. 36:31 the kings that *r.* in land of Edom, 1 *Chr.* 1:43
1 *Sam.* 13:1 Saul *r.* one yr. he *r.*
2 *Sam.* 2:10 Ish-bosh. *r.* two yea.
5:4 David *r.* 40 years over Jud.
5 Da. *r.* seven yea. in Hebron, thirty-three in Jerusa. 1 *K.* 2:11; 1 *Chr.* 3:4; 29:27
10:1 Ha. *r.* in stead, 1 *Chr.* 19:1
1 *K.* 4:21 and Solomon *r.* over all the kingd. 11:42; 1 *Chr.* 29:28; 2 *Chr.* 9:26, 30

Est. 1:1 Ahasuerus *r.* from Ind.
Jer. 22:11 Shall. *r.* instead of Jo.
Rom. 5:14 death *r.* fr. Ad. to M.
17 by one man's off. death *r.*
21 as sin *r.* to death, grace *r.*
1 *Cor.* 4:8 *r.* as kings without us
Rev. 11:17 great power and *r.*
20:4 *r.* with Ch. a thousand y.

REIGNEST.

1 *Chr.* 29:12 thou *r.* over all, and

REIGNETH.

1 *Sam.* 12:14 king that *r.* over y.
2 *Sam.* 15:10 Absalom *r.* in Heb.
1 *K.* 1:18 behold Adonijah *r.*
1 *Chr.* 16:31 the L. *r.* *Ps.* 96:10; 97:1; 99:1
Ps. 47:8 God *r.* over heathen
93:1 L. *r.* he is clothed wi. maj.
Prov. 30:22 a servant when he *r.*
Is. 52:7 saith unto Z. Thy G. *r.*
Rev. 17:18 *r.* over kings of earth
19:6 Lord God omnipotent *r.*

REIGNING.

1 *Sam.* 16:1 I rejected him fro. *r.*

REINS.

Job 16:13 he cleaveth my *r.* asu.
19:27 tho. my *r.* be consumed
Ps. 7:9 God trieth heart and *r.*
16:7 my *r.* also instr. me in ni.
26:2 O L. try my *r.* my heart
73:21 was I pricked in my *r.*
139:13 thou hast possess. my *r.*
Prov. 23:16 my *r.* shall rejoice
Is. 11:5 faithfuln. girdle of his *r.*
Jer. 11:20 O L. that triest the *r.*
12:2 thou art far from their *r.*
17:10 I try my *r.* 20:12 seest *r.*
Lam. 3:13 arrows to enter my *r.*
Rev. 2:23 he who searcheth *r.*

REJECT, ETH.

Hos. 4:6 I will *r.* thee
Mark 6:26 oath's sake wo. not *r.*
7:9 *r.* commandment of G.
John 12:48 he that *r.* me, receiv.
Tit. 3:10 after second admoni. *r.*

REJECTED.

1 *Sam.* 8:7 they have not *r.* thee, but they have *r.* me
10:19 ye have this day *r.* your G.
15:23 thou hast *r.* word of L. he also *r.* thee fr. being kin. 26
16:1 I *r.* him from being king
2 *K.* 17:15 they *r.* his statutes
20 Lord *r.* all the seed of Isra.
Is. 53:3 he is despised, *r.* of men
Jer. 2:37 Lord *r.* thy confidence
6:19 *r.* my law; 30 L. *r.* them
7:29 Lord hath *r.* generation of
8:9 they have *r.* word of Lord
14:19 hast thou utterly *r.* Jud.?
Lam. 5:22 thou hast utterly *r.* us
Hos. 4:6 thou hast *r.* knowledge
Mat. 21:42 stone which builders *r.* *Mark* 12:10; *Luke* 20:17
Mark 8:31 and he shall be *r.* of the elders, *Luke* 9:22
Luke 7:30 law. *r.* counsel of God
Luke 17:25 be *r.* of this generat.
Gal. 4:14 tempt. in flesh *r.* not
Heb. 6:8 that beareth thorns is *r.*
12:17 when *r.* would inherit. bless. was *r.*

REJOICE.

Deut. 12:7 ye sh. *r.* in all, 14:26
16:14 thou shalt *r.* in thy feast
15 God sh. bless thee, th. sh. *r.*
26:11 shalt *r.* in ev. good thing
28:63 L. will *r.* over you, 30:9
32:43 *r.* O nations, with his pe.
33:18 he said, *r.* Zebulun
Jud. 9:19 *r.* ye in Abimelech
1 *Sam.* 2:1 bec. I *r.* in thy salva.
19:5 thou sawest it, and didst *r.*
1 *Chr.* 16:10 let the heart of them *r.* that seek the L. *Ps.* 105:3
32 let fields *r.* and all therein

2 *Chr.* 6:41 and let thy saints *r.*
20:27 L. made th. *r. Neh.* 12:43
Job 20:18 he shall not *r.* therein
Ps. 2:11 serve L. *r.* with tremb.
5:11 all that put trust in thee *r.*
9:14 I will *r.* in thy salvation
13:4 those that trouble me *r.*
5 my heart shall *r.* in thy salv.
14:7 Ja. shall *r.* and Is. be glad
20:5 we will *r.* in thy salvation
21:1 in thy salvation shall he *r.*
30:1 made foes to *r.* over me
32:21 our heart shall *r.* in him
35:9 my soul sh. *r.* in his salva.
19 let not mine enemies *r.* ov.
21 O Lord, let them not *r.* over
26 let them be ashamed that *r.*
38:16 lest they sho. *r.* over me
48:11 let Zion *r.* let Jud. be glad
51:8 bones th. hast brok. may *r.*
58:10 righteous *r.* wh. he seeth
60:6 G. ha. spok. I will *r.* 108:7
63:7 in shad. of thy wings I *r.*
11 but the king shall *r.* in God
65:12 hills *r.* 66:6 did we *r.*
68:3 let righteous *r.* exceed. *r.*
4 *r.* bef. him ; 71:23 lips sh. *r.*
85:6 that thy people may *r.*
86:4 *r.* the soul of thy servant
89:12 Tabor and Hermon sh. *r.*
16 in thy name shall they *r.*
42 hast made enemies to *r.*
96:11 let heavens *r.* 12 trees *r.*
97:1 let earth *r.* isles be glad
98:4 make noise, *r.* sing praise
104:31 L. shall *r.* in his works
106:5 that I may *r.* in gladness
107:42 righte. shall see it and *r.*
109:28 be ashamed, let serva. *r.*
119:162 I *r.* at thy word
149:2 let Is. *r.* in him that made
Prov. 2:14 who *r.* to do evil
5:18 *r.* wife of thy youth
23:15 my heart shall *r.*
16 yea, my reins shall *r.*
24 father of righteous shall *r.*
25 she that bare thee shall *r.*
24:17 *r.* not wh. enemy falleth
28:12 wh. righteous men do *r.*
29:2 right. in authority, peo. *r.*
6 righteous doth sing and *r.*
31:25 shall *r.* in time to come
Ec. 3:12 a man to *r.* do good
22 that a man should *r.* 5:19
4:16 that come after shall not *r.*
11:8 live many years, and *r.*
9 *r.* O you, man, in thy youth
Is. 8:6 *r.* in Rezin and R.'s son
9:3 as men *r.* when divide spoil
13:3 that *r.* in my highness
14:29 *r.* not thou, whole Pales.
23:12 thou shalt no more *r.*
24:8 noise of them that *r.*
29:19 poor among them shall *r.*
35:1 desert sh. *r.* 2 blosso. and *r.*
61:7 for confusion they shall *r.*
65:13 behold, my ser. shall *r.*
19 I will *r.* in Jerusalem
6:1:10 *r.* with Jerusalem
14 when ye see this, heart *r.*
Jer. 31:13 then shall virgin *r.*
32:41 will *r.* over them
51:39 they may *r.* and sleep
Lam. 2:17 caused enemy to *r.*
Ezek. 7:12 let not the buyer *r.*
35:15 *r.* at inheritance of Israel
Hos. 9:1 *r.* not, O Israel, for joy
Amos 6:13 ye wh. *r.* in naught
Mic. 7:8 *r.* not ag. me, O enemy
Zep. 3:11 take away th. that *r.*
17 the Lord will *r.* over thee
Zec. 2:10 sing and *r.* O daughter
9:9 *r.* greatly, O daughter of Z.
10:7 and their heart shall *r.*
Luke 1:14 shall *r.* at his birth
6:23 *r.* ye in that day, and leap
10:20 in this *r.* not, rather *r.*
15:6 *r.* with me. I have found

19:37 the disciples began to *r.*
John 4:36 he that reapeth may *r.*
5:35 willing for a sea. to *r.*
14:28 if ye loved me, ye wou. *r.*
16:20 weep, the world shall *r.*
22 see you, your heart shall *r.*
Acts 2:26 theref. did my heart *r.*
Rom. 5:2 *r.* in hope of gl. of God
12:15 *r.* with them that do *r.*
15:10 he saith, *r.* ye Gentiles
1 *Cor.* 7:30 *r.* as tho' they rej. n.
12:26 all the members *r.* with it
2 *Cor.* 2:3 of whom I ought to *r.*
7:9 I *r.* not that ye were sorry
16 I *r.* I have confidence in you
Gal. 4:27 *r.* barren that bear. not
Phil. 1:18 I do *r.* yea, and will *r.*
2:16 I may *r.* in day of Christ
17 I joy and *r.* with you all
18 for the same cause do ye *r.*
28 when see him ag. ye may *r.*
3:3 we worship God, *r.* in C. J
Col. 1:24 *r.* in my suffer. for you
1 *Thes.* 5:16 *r.* evermore, pray
Jam. 1:9 let broth. of low deg. *r.*
4:16 ye *r.* in your boastings
1 *Pet.* 1:6 wherein ye greatly *r.*
8 ye *r.* with joy unspeakable
4:13 *r.* inasm. as ye are partak.
Rev. 11:10 th. that dw. on ear. *r.*
12:12 therefore *r.* ye heavens.
18:20 *r.* over her, thou heaven

See GLAD.

REJOICE before the Lord.
Lev. 23:40 *r. bef. t.* Lord 7 days
Deut. 12:12 *r. bef. t. L.* your God
18 and thou shalt *r. before the*
L. thy God, 16:11 ; 27:7

REJOICE in the Lord.
Ps. 33:1 *r. in the L.* righte. 97:12
Is. 41:16 *r. in L.* glory in H. One
61:10 I will greatly *r. in the L.*
Joel 2:23 chil. of Zion, *r. in t. L.*
Hab. 3:18 I will *r. in the Lord*
Zec. 10:7 heart shall *r. in the L.*
Phil. 3:1 brethren *r. in the Lord*
4:4 *r. in the Lord* alway

REJOICED.
Ex. 18:9 Jethro *r.* for goodness
Deut. 28:63 as Lord *r.* over you
30:9 as he *r.* over thy fathers
1 *Sam.* 11:15 S. and men of Is. *r.*
1 *K.* 1:40 people *r.* so earth rent
2 *K.* 11:14 the people *r.* and blew
1 *Chr.* 29:9 people *r.* and Dav. *r.*
2 *Chr.* 15:15 all Judah *r.* at oath
24:10 all princes and people *r.*
29:36 Hezekiah *r.* and all peop.
30:25 strangers of Is. and Ju. *r.*
Neh. 12:43 and *r.* the wives also,
and the children *r.*
Est. 8:15 the city of Shushan *r.*
Job 31:25 if I *r.* bec. my wealth
29 if I *r.* at destruction of him
Ps. 35:15 in mine advers. they *r.*
97:8 the daughters of Judah *r.*
119:14 ha. *r.* in way of thy test.
Ec. 2:10 my heart *r.* in labor
Jer. 15:17 I *r.* not in assembly
50:11 ye *r.* O destroyers of my
Ezek. 25:6 Ammon. *r.* ag. Israel
Hos. 10:5 priests that *r.* mourn
Ob. 12 nor should. thou have *r.*
Mat. 2:10 saw star, they *r.*
Luke 1:47 my sp. hath *r.* in God
10:21 in that hour J. *r.* in spir.
13:17 people *r.* for the things
John 8:56 your father Abrah. *r.*
Acts 7:41 *r.* in works of th. hands
15:31 they *r.* for the consolation
16:34 jailer *r.* believing in God
1 *Cor.* 7:30 as though they *r.* not
2 *Cor.* 7:7 told us, so I *r.* the mo.
Phil. 4:10 I *r.* in the Lord great.
2 *John* 4 I *r.* greatly, 3 *John* 3

REJOICETH.
1 *Sam.* 2:1 Han. said, My hea. *r.*
Job 39:21 horse *r.* in strength
Ps. 16:9 heart is glad, glory *r.*
19:5 which *r.* as a strong man
28:7 theref. my heart greatly *r.*
Prov. 11:10 well wi. right. city *r.*
13:9 the light of the righteo. *r.*
15:30 light of the eyes *r.* heart
29:3 whoso loveth wisdom *r.*
Is. 5:14 he that *r.* shall descend
62:5 as bridegroom *r.* over bride
64:5 thou meetest him that *r.*
Ezek. 35:14 when whole earth *r.*
Mat. 18:13 *r.* more of that sheep
John 3:29 friend of bridegroom *r.*
1 *Cor.* 13:6 *r.* not in ini. *r.* in tr.
Jam. 2:13 mercy *r.* against judg.

REJOICEST.
Jer. 11:15 when thou doest evil,
then thou *r.*

REJOICING.
1 *K.* 1:45 come up from thence *r.*
2 *Chr.* 23:18 burnt-offer. with *r.*
Job 8:21 he fill thy lips with *r.*
Ps. 19:8 statutes right, *r.* heart
45:15 with *r.* sh. they be broug.
107:22 declare his works with *r.*
118:15 voice of *r.* is in tabern.
119:111 they are *r.* of my heart
126:6 sh. come again with *r.*
Prov. 8:30 *r.* always before him
31 *r.* in habitable part of earth
Is. 65:18 I create Jerusalem a *r.*
Jer. 15:16 thy word was to me *r.*
Hab. 3:14 their *r.* was to devour
Zep. 2:15 this is *r.* city th. said
Luke 15:5 layeth it on should. *r.*
Acts 5:41 *r.* counted worthy to s.
8:39 eunuch went on his way *r.*
Rom. 12:12 *r.* in hope, patient in
1 *Cor.* 15:31 I protest by your *r.*
2 *Cor.* 1:12 our *r.* is testimony of
14 we are your *r.* ye are ours
6:10 as sorrowful, yet always *r.*
Gal. 6:4 sh. he have *r.* in himself
Phil. 1:26 your *r.* be more abun.
1 *Thes.* 2:19 wh. our crown of *r.*
Heb. 3:6 *r.* of hope firm to end
Jam. 4:16 boastings, such *r.* evil

RELEASE:
Deut. 15:1 end of 7 years make *r.*
9 the year of *r.* is at hand
31:10 solemnity of year of *r.*
Est. 2:18 he made a *r.* to prov.

RELEASE, Verb.
Deut. 15:2 creditor that lend. *r.*
Mat. 27:15 gover. was wont to *r.*
pris. *Luke* 23:17 ; *John* 18:39
17 w. will ye I *r.* 21 ; *Mark* 15:9
Mark 15:11 moved people, sho.
rather *r.* Barab. *Lu.* 23:18
Luke 23:16 I will chastise and *r.*
20 Pilate willing to *r.* Jesus
John 19:10 I have power to *r.* 12

RELEASED.
Mat. 27:26 then *r.* he Barabbas
Mark 15:15 ; *Luke* 23:25
Mark 15:6 at feast he *r.* prisoner

RELIEF.
Acts 11:29 determined to send *r.*

RELIEVE.
Lev. 25:35 if brother poor, *r.* him
Is. 1:17 and *r.* the oppressed
Lam. 1:11 thi. for meat to *r.* soul
16 comforter that should *r.* far
19 they sought meat to *r.* souls
1 *Tim.* 5:16 if any have wido. *r.*

RELIEVED, ETH.
Ps. 146:9 he *r.* fatherless, widow
1 *Tim.* 5:10 if she have *r.* afflict.

RELIGION.
Acts 26:5 straitest sect of our *r.*
Gal. 1:13 conversati. in Jews' *r.*
14 profited in the Jews' *r.*

Jam. 1:26 this man's *r.* is vain
  27 pure *r.* and undefiled bef. **G.**

RELIGIOUS.

Acts 13:43 *r.* proselytes follow. **P.**
Jam. 1:26 if any am. you seem *r.*

RELY, IED.

2 *Chr.* 13:18 becau. they *r.* on **L.**
  16:7 *r.* on Syr. hast not *r.* on **L.**
  8 because thou didst *r.* on **L.**

REMAIN.

Ex. 12:10 let noth. *r.* till morn.
  23:18 fat of sacri. *r.* till morni.
Lev. 19:6 if aught *r.* till 3d day
  27:18 according to years that *r.*
Num. 33:55 those ye let *r.*
Deut. 2:34 destroyed all, none *r.*
  16:4 nor any flesh *r.* till morn.
  19:20 those which *r.* shall hear
  21:23 his body sh. not *r.* on tree
Jos. 1:14 your little ones shall *r.*
  8:22 let none of th. *r.* 10:28, **30**
  23:4 I divided nations that *r.*
Jud. 5:17 did Dan *r.* in ships?
  21:7 wives for them that *r.* 16
1 *K.* 18:22 I only *r.* a proph. of **L.**
Ezr. 9:15 for we *r.* yet escaped
Job 21:32 shall he *r.* in the tomb
  27:15 those that *r.* sh. be buried
Ps. 55:7 would I *r.* in wilderness
Prov. 2:21 perfect sh. *r.* in land
  21:16 shall *r.* in congregation
Is. 10:32 yet shall he *r.* at Nob
  32:16 righteousn. shall *r.* in fie.
  65:4 which *r.* among the graves
  66:22 heavens and new earth *r.*
Jer. 8:3 residue that *r.* of family
  17:25 this city shall *r.* for ever
  27:11 th. will I let *r.* in own la.
  30:18 the palace shall *r.*
  38:4 weak. hands of men that *r.*
Jer. 42:17 no. of th. *r.* 44:14 ; 51:62
  44:7 com. evil, leave none to *r.*
Ezek. 7:11 violence risen. no. *r.*
  17:21 they that *r.* shall be scat.
  39:14 men to bury those that *r.*
Amos 6:9 if there *r.* ten men
Ob. 14 delivered those that *r.*
Zec. 12:14 families that *r.*
Luke 10:7 in same house *r.* eat.
John 6:12 gather fragm. that *r.*
  15:11 my joy might *r.* in you
  16 chosen that your fruit sh. *r.*
  19:31 bodies sho. not *r.* on cross
1 *Cor.* 15:6 of wh. greater part *r.*
1 *Thes.* 4:15 *r.* till coming of **L.**
  17 we which are alive and *r.*
Heb. 12:27 cannot be shaken *r.*
1 *John* 2:24 that ye have heard *r.*
Rev. 3:2 strengthen things wh. *r.*

REMAINDER.

Ex. 29:34 thou shalt burn the *r.*
Lev. 6:16 the *r.* shall Aaron eat
  7:17 *r.* on third day sh. be bur.
2 *Sam.* 14:7 leave nei. name, *r.*
Ps. 76:10 *r.* of wrath sh. restrain

REMAINED.

Gen. 7:23 Noah only *r.* alive
  14:10 they that *r.* fled to moun.
Ex. 14:28 th. *r.* not one chariot
Sam. 11:26 there *r.* two men
  35:28 he should *r.* in city of ref.
  36:12 inh. *r.* in house of father
Deut. 3:11 king of Bas. *r.* giants
Jos. 10:20 rest *r.* entered cities
  11:22 in Ashdod there *r.* Anak.
  18:2 there *r.* of Is. seven tribes
Jud. 7:3 there *r.* with G. 10,000
1 *Sam.* 11:11 they which *r.* scat.
2 *K.* 10:11 Jehu slew all that *r.* 17
  25:22 people *r.* set G. over them
1 *Chr.* 13:14 ark *r.* in fami. of O.
Ec. 2:9 my wisdom *r.* with me
Jer. 37:10 there *r.* wounded men
  21 *r.* in court of prison, 33:13
  41:10 Ishm. carried capt. that *r.*
  48:11 his taste *r.* in him

Lam. 51:30 mighty men *r.* in th. holds
Lam. 2:22 L.'s anger none *r.*
Dan. 10:8 *r.* no stren. in me, 17
  13 I *r.* there with kings of Pe.
Mat. 11:23 done in S. it would *r.*
  14:20 took up fragments that *r.*
  Luke 9:17 ; *John* 6:13
Luke 1:22 beckoned, *r.* speechl.
Acts 5:4 wh. it *r.* was it not thi.

REMAINEST.

Lam. 5:19 thou O L. *r. Heb.* 1:11

REMAINETH.

Gen. 8:22 while earth *r.* seed-ti.
  and harvest shall not cease
Ex. 12:10 which *r.* ye shall burn
Lev. 8:32 *r.* of flesh and bread
  16:16 so do for taberna. that *r.*
Num. 24:19 destroy him that *r.*
Jos. 8:29 heap of stones that *r.*
  13:1 there *r.* land to be possess.
Jud. 5:13 him that *r.* have dom.
1 *Sam.* 6:18 stone *r.* to this day
  16:11 J. said, There *r.* youngest
Job 19:4 my error *r.* with myself
  41:22 in his neck *r.* strength
Is. 4:3 he that *r.* in J. call. holy
Jer. 38:2 he that *r.* in city sh. die
Ezek. 6:12 he that *r.* besieged die
Hag. 2:5 so my Sp. *r.* am. them
Zec. 9:7 he that *r.* shall be for G.
John 9:41 therefore your sin *r.*
1 *Cor.* 7:29 it *r.* they that ha. wi.
2 *Cor.* 3:11 that which *r.* glorio.
  9:9 his righteousness *r.* for ev.
Heb. 4:6 it *r.* some must enter in
  9 there *r.* a rest to peop. of G.
  10:26 there *r.* no sacrifice for sin
1 *John* 3:9 for seed *r.* in him

REMAINING.

Num. 9:22 cloud *r.* on tabernacle
Deut. 3:3 till none was left *r.*
Jos. 10:33 and he left none *r.* 37, 39, 40 ; 11:8
2 *Sam.* 21:5 dest. fr. *r.* coasts
2 *K.* 10:11 Jehu left Ahab no. *r.*
1 *Chr.* 9:33 who *r.* in chambers
Job 18:19 nor any *r.* in dwelling
Ob. 18 shall not be any *r.* of Esau
John 1:33 on wh. shall see Sp. *r.*

REMALIAH.

Is. 7:4 anger of son of R. 5, 9
  8:6 rejoice in Rezin and R. son

REMEDY.

2 *Chr.* 36:16 wrath arose, no *r.*
Prov. 6:15 be broken without *r.*
  29:1 be destroyed, without *r.*

REMEMBER.

Gen. 40:23 did not butler *r.* Jos.
Ex. 13:3 Moses said to people *r.*
Ex. 20:8 *r.* sab.-day to keep holy
Num. 11:5 we *r.* fish eat in Egypt
  15:39 *r.* all commandm. of Lord
Deut. 5:15 *r.* thou wast a serv. in
  Eg. 15:15 ; 16:12 ; 24:18, 22
  7:18 *r.* what L. did to Pharaoh
  8:18 *r.* L. gi. pow. to get wealth
  9:7 *r.* thou provokest L. thy G.
  16:3 *r.* day camest out of Egypt
  24:9 *r.* what Lord did to Miriam
  25:17 *r.* what Amal. did to thee
  32:7 *r.* days of old, consider
Jos. 1:13 *r.* word wh. Moses com.
Jud. 9:2 *r.* I am your bone
1 *Sam.* 25:31 Ab. said, *r.* handm.
2 *Sam.* 14:11 let the king *r.* Lord
2 *K.* 9:25 *r.* when I rode after A.
  20:3 *r.* I walk. bef. thee, *Is.* 38:3
1 *Chr.* 16:12 *r.* works, *Ps.* 105:5
2 *Chr.* 6:42 *r.* mercies of David
Neh. 1:8 *r.* word thou com. Mos.
  4:14 *r.* L. wh. is great and terri
  13:29 *r.* th. that defiled priesth.
Job 4:7 who perished
  7:7 O *r.* my life is wind
  10:9 *r.* thou hast made me
  11:16 *r.* it as waters that pass

  36:24 *r.* thou magnify his work
  41:8 hand upon him, *r.* battle
Ps. 20:3 *r.* thy offerings, accept
  7 we will *r.* name of the Lord
  22:27 ends of world *r.* turn to L.
  25:6 *r.* thy mercies ever of old
  7 *r.* not sins of my you..*r.* me
  74:2 *r.* congreg. thou purchased
  18 *r.* this, enemy reproached
  22 *r.* how foolish man reproa.
  79:8 O *r.* not former iniquities
  89:47 *r.* how short my time is
  50 *r.* L. reproach of thy serv.
  103:18 th. that *r.* his command.
  119:49 *r.* word unto thy servant
  132:1 L. *r.* D. and his afflictions
  137:7 *r.* O Lord, child. of Edom
Prov. 31:7 *r.* misery no more
Ec. 5:20 he sh. not *r.* days of life
  11:8 let him *r.* days of darkness
  12:1 *r.* Creator in days of youth
Cant. 1:4 *r.* love more than wine
Is. 43:18 *r.* not former th. ? 46:9
  25 I will not *r.* sins
  44:21 *r.* these, O Jacob, and Is.
  46:8 *r.* this, show yoursel. men
  47:7 neither didst *r.* latter end
  54:4 not *r.* reproach of widowh.
  64:5 meetest those that *r.* thee
  9 neither *r.* iniquity for ever
Jam. 3:16 neither shall they *r.* it
  14:10 he will now *r.* their iniq.
  21 *r.* break not thy covenant
  17:2 their children *r.* their altars
  18:20 *r.* I stood to speak good
  31:20 I do earnestly *r.* him still
  44:21 did not the Lord *r.* them?
  51:50 ye that have escaped, *r.* L.
Lam. 5:1 *r.* O L. what is come
Ezek. 16:61 then sh. *r.* thy ways, 20:43 ; 36:31
  23:27 thou shalt not *r.* Egypt
Hos. 8:13 now will he *r.* th. iniq.
  9:9 therefore he will *r.* iniquity
Mic. 6:5 *r.* now what Ba. consul.
Hab. 3:2 O L. in wrath *r.* mercy
Mal. 4:4 *r.* the law of Moses
Mat. 16:9 *r.* loaves, *Mark* 8:18
Luke 1:72 *r.* his holy covenant
  16:25 *r.* that th. in thy lifetime
  17:32 *r.* Lot's wife ; 24:6 *r.* how
John 15:20 *r.* word that I said
  16:4 time shall come, ye may *r.*
Acts 20:31 *r.* that by three years
  35 *r.* words of the Lord Jesus
Gal. 2:10 we should *r.* the poor
Eph. 2:11 *r.* that in time past
Col. 4:18 *r.* my bonds
1 *Thes.* 2:9 ye *r.* breth. our labor
2 *Thes.* 2:5 *r.* ye not I told you ?
2 *Tim.* 2:8 *r.* that J. Ch. raised
Heb. 13:3 *r.* them are in bonds
  7 *r.* them which have the rule
Jude 17 *r.* words spoken of apos.
Rev. 2:5 *r.* fr. wh. thou art fallen
  3:3 *r.* how thou hast received

I REMEMBER.

Gen. 41:9 I do *r.* my faults
1 *Sam.* 15:2 I *r.* that which Am.
Job 21:6 when I *r.* I am afraid
Ps. 42:4 when I *r.* these, I pour
  63:6 wh. I *r.* thee upon my bed
  137:6 if I do not *r.* thee, let my
  143:5 I *r.* the days of old
Jer. 2:2 I *r.* thee, the kindness
Hos. 7:2 consider not that I *r.* all

I will REMEMBER.

Gen. 9:15 I will *r.* my coven. 16
Lev. 26:42 I w. *r.* coven. with A.
  45 I w. for their sakes *r.* cove.
Ps. 42:6 therefore will I *r.* thee
  77:10 I will *r.* the years of, 11
Jer. 31:34 I will *r.* their sin no more, *Heb.* 8:12 ; 10:17
Ezek. 16:60 I will *r.* my covenant
3 *John* 10 I will *r.* deeds he doeth

REMEMBER me.
Jud. 16:28 *r. me* that I may be
1 *Sam.* 1:11 look on hand. *r. me*
Neh. 13:14 *r. me*, O God, 22, 31
Job 14:13 appoint me, and *r. me*
Ps. 25:7 *r. me*, for thy sake, O L.
106:4 *r. me* with the favor that
Jer. 15:15 O L. thou know. *r. me*
Ezek. 6:9 escape of you sh. *r. me*
Zec. 10:9 sh. *r. me* in far countr.
Luke 23:42 L. *r. me* when comest
1 *Cor.* 11:2 ye *r. me* in all things

REMEMBERED.
Gen. 8:1 G. *r.* Noah ; 19:29 Abr.
30:22 G. *r.* Rachel ; 49:2 Jose. *r.*
Ex. 2:24 God *r.* his covenant, 6:5
Num. 10:9 ye shall be *r.* bef. L.
Jud. 8:34 child. of Isr. *r.* not L.
1 *Sam.* 1:19 the Lord *r.* Hannah
Est. 9:28 days of Pur. sho. be *r.*
Job 24:20 sin. shall be no more *r.*
Ps. 45:17 make thy name be *r.*
77:3 I *r.* God and was troubled
78:35 they *r.* G. was their Sav.
39 *r.* that they were but flesh
42 they *r.* not his hand, when
98:3 he *r.* his mercy tow. house
105:8 *r.* his covenant for ever
42 for he *r.* his holy promise
106:7 they *r.* not the multitude
45 he *r.* for them his covenant
109:14 iniq. of his fathers be *r.*
16 he *r.* not to show mercy
111:4 wonderful works to be *r.*
119:52 I *r.* thy judgments of old
55 I have *r.* thy name, O Lord
136:23 *r.* us in our low estate
137:1 we wept, when we *r.* Zion
Ec. 9:15 no man *r.* poor man
Is. 23:16 thou mayest be *r.*
57:11 thou hast not *r.* me
63:11 then he *r.* days of old
65:17 former heav. sh. not be *r.*
Jer. 11:19 may be no more *r.*
Lam. 1:7 Jerusalem *r.* in days
2:1 *r.* not his footstool in anger
Ezek. 3:20 his righteousness sh.
not be *r.* 33:13
16:22 not *r.* days of youth, 43
21:24 made your iniq. to be *r.*
25:10 Ammonites may not be *r.*
Hos. 2:17 no more *r.* *Zec.* 13:2
Amos 1:9 *r.* not the covenant
Jon. 2:7 soul fainted I *r.* Lord
Mal. 26:75 Peter *r.* the words of
Jesus, *Luke* 22:61
Luke 24:8 they *r.* his words
John 2:17 disciples *r.* it was wr.
22 when he was risen they *r.*
12:16 wh. J. was glorified th. *r.*
Acts 11:16 then *r.* I word of L.
Rev. 18:5 God hath *r.* her iniqui.

REMEMBEREST, ETH.
Ps. 9:12 mak. inquisition, he *r.*
88:5 like slain whom thou *r.*
103:14 he *r.* we are but dust
Lam. 1:9 she *r.* not her last end
Mat. 5:23 th. *r.* that thy brother
John 16:21 *r.* no more anguish
2 *Cor.* 7:15 whi. he *r.* obedience

REMEMBERING.
Lam. 3:19 *r.* mine affliction and
1 *Thes.* 1:3 *r.* your work of faith

REMEMBRANCE.
Ex. 17:14 put out *r.* of Amalek
Num. 5:15 bring iniquity to *r.*
Dan. 25:19 blot out *r.* of Amalek
32:26 make *r.* of them cease
2 *Sam.* 18:18 no son to keep *r.*
1 *K.* 17:18 to call my sin to *r.*?
Job 18:17 his *r.* perish fr. earth
Ps. 6:5 in death there is no *r.*
30:4 thanks at *r.* of holi. 97:12
34:16 to cut off the *r.* of them
38:1 psalm of Da. br. to *r.* 70:1
77:6 call to *r.* my song in night
83:4 Israel be no more in *r.*

102:12 *r.* unto all generations
112:6 righteous shall be in *r.*
Ec. 1:11 is no *r.* of former things
2:16 there is no *r.* of the wise
Is. 26:8 des. of our soul *r.* of thee
43:26 put me in *r.* let us plead
57:8 behind doors set up thy *r.*
Lam. 3:20 my soul hath th. in *r.*
Ezek. 21:23 call to *r.* the iniquity
24 bec. that ye are come to *r.*
23:19 to *r.* days of her youth, 21
29:16 bringeth their iniq. to *r.*
Mal. 3:16 book of *r.* was written
Mark 11:21 Peter calling to *r.*
Luke 1:54 hath holpen Is. in *r.*
22:19 do in *r.* of me, 1 *Cor.* 11:24
John 14:26 bring things to yo. *r.*
Acts 10:31 thine alms had in *r.*
1 *Cor.* 4:17 sh. bring you into *r.*
11:25 as ye dri. of it, in *r.* of me
Phil. 1:3 I thank God upon ev. *r.*
1 *Thes.* 3:6 that ye have good *r.*
1 *Tim.* 4:6 if thou put breth. in *r.*
2 *Tim.* 1:3 that I have *r.* of thee
5 I call to *r.* unfeigned faith
6 wherefore I put thee in *r.*
2:14 of th. things put them in *r.*
Heb. 10:3 there is a *r.* of sins
32 call to *r.* the former days
2 *Pet.* 1:12 always in *r.* *Jude* 5
13 putting you in *r.*
15 have th. things always in *r.*
3:1 pure minds by way of *r.*
Rev. 16:19 Babylon came in *r.*

REMEMBRANCES.
Job 13:12 your *r.* like to ashes

REMISSION.
Mat. 26:28 blo. shed for *r.* of sins
Mark 1:4 baptism of repentance
for *r.* *Luke* 3:3
Luke 1:57 salvation by *r.* of sins
24:47 that *r.* should be preached
Acts 2:38 baptized for *r.* of sins
10:43 whoso belie. sh. receive *r.*
Rom. 3:25 *r.* of sins th. are past
Heb. 9:22 without shed bl. no *r.*
10:18 where *r.* is, th. is no offe.

REMIT, TED.
John 20:23 sins ye *r.* they are *r.*

REMNANT.
Lev. 2:3 the *r.* of meat-offering
5:13 *r.* sh. be priest's as offering
14:18 *r.* of oil in priest's hand
Deut. 28:54 eye evil toward the *r.*
Jos. 23:12 if ye cleave to the *r.*
2 *Sam.* 21:2 Gibeonites *r.* of Am.
1 *K.* 14:10 I will take away the *r.*
2 *K.* 19:4 lift up thy prayer for
the *r.* *Is.* 37:4, 31, 32
30 *r.* escaped shall take root
31 out of Je. shall go forth a *r.*
21:14 forsa. *r.* of mine inherita.
25:11 *r.* did Nebuzar-adan carry
2 *Chr.* 30:6 retu. to the *r.* of you
Ezr. 3:8 the *r.* of their brethren
9:8 grace fr. L. to leave us a *r.*
14 so that there should be no *r.*
Neh. 1:3 *r.* left of the captivity
Job 22:20 *r.* of th. fire consumed
Is. 1:9 unless L. left us small *r.*
11:11 to recover *r.* of his people
16 there sh. be a highway for *r.*
14:22 cut off fr. Babylon the *r.*
30 kill thy root, he sh. sl. thy *r.*
15:9 I will bring lions on the *r.*
16:14 the *r.* shall be very small
17:3 kingdom shall cease from *r.*
46:3 hearken *r.* of house of Isr.
Jer. 6:9 they sh. glean *r.* of Isr.
11:23 there sh. be no *r.* of them
15:11 it shall be well with thy *r.*
23:3 I will gather *r.* of my flock
25:20 the *r.* of Ashdod did drink
31:7 O L. save thy peo. *r.* of Is.
40:11 king of Babylon left a *r.*
15 Jews scat. *r.* of Judah peri.

41:16 Joha. took *r.* of peo. 43:5
42:15 hear the Lord, ye *r.* of Ju.
19 O ye *r.* of Judah, go ye not
44:12 I will take the *r.* of Judah
28 *r.* sh. kn. wh. words stand
47:4 Lord will spoil *r.* of count.
Ezek. 5:10 whole *r.* will scatter
6:8 yet will I leave a *r.* that ye
11:13 L. wilt make end of *r.*?
14:22 behold, therein sh. be a *r.*
23:25 *r.* shall fall by the sword
25:16 destroy the *r.* of sea-coast
Joel 2:32 *r.* whom the L. sh. call
Amos 1:8 *r.* of Philist. sh. perish
5:15 God will be gracious to *r.*
9:12 that they may possess *r.*
Mic. 2:12 I will gather *r.* of Isra.
4:7 make her that halted, a *r.*
5:3 *r.* of brethren return to Isr.
7 *r.* of Ja. in midst of people, 8
7:18 transgres. of *r.* of heritage
Hab. 2:8 all the *r.* of the people
Zep. 1:4 I will cut off *r.* of Baal
2:7 coast for *r.* of house of Jud.
9 *r.* of people possess them
3:13 *r.* of Is. sh. not do iniquity
Hag. 1:12 *r.* of people obeyed L.
14 Lord stirred up spirit of *r.*
Zec. 8:6 marvellous in eyes of *r.*
12 I will cause *r.* of peo. to po.
Mat. 22:6 the *r.* took his servan.
Rom. 9:27 Es. crieth, *r.* be saved
Rom. 11:5 at present time there
is a *r.*
Rev. 11:13 the *r.* were affrighted
12:17 dragon we. to war with *r.*
19:21 *r.* were slain with sword

REMOVE.
Gen. 48:17 father's hand to *r.* it
Num. 36:7 inheritance of Is. *r.* 9
Deut. 19:14 not *r.* neigh's. land.
Jos. 3:3 ye shall *r.* from your place
2 *Sam.* 6:10 Da. would not *r.* ark
2 *K.* 23:27 L. said, I will *r.* Judah
24:3 Ju. to *r.* them out of sight
2 *Chr.* 33:8 neither will I *r.* Isr.
Job 24:2 some *r.* landmarks, they
27:5 I will not *r.* mine integrity
Ps. 36:11 let not wicked *r.* me
39:10 *r.* thy stroke away fr. me
119:22 *r.* from me reproach and
29 *r.* from me the way of lying
Prov. 4:27 *r.* thy foot from evil
5:8 *r.* thy way far from her
22:28 *r.* not the landmarks, 23:10
30:8 *r.* from me vanity and lies
Ec. 11:10 *r.* sorrow from heart
Is. 13:13 earth *r.* out of her place
46:7 from his place sh. he not *r.*
Jer. 4:1 return, thou shalt not *r.*
27:10 prophesy lie, *r.* from land
50:3 they shall *r.* shall depart
8 *r.* out of the midst of Babyl.
Ezek. 12:3 *r.* by day, thou sh. *r.*
45:9 O princes, *r.* violence and
Hos. 5:10 like them that *r.* bound
Joel 2:20 I will *r.* northern army
3:6 ye might *r.* them from bor.
Mic. 2:3 fr. wh. sh. not *r.* necks
Zec. 3:9 I will *r.* iniquity of land
14:4 mountain *r.* toward north
Mat. 17:20 say, *r.* hence, sh. be *r.*
Luke 22:42 if willing, *r.* this cup
1 *Cor.* 13:2 that I could *r.* mount.
Rev. 2:5 else I will *r.* candlestick

REMOVED.
Gen. 8:13 Noah *r.* covering of ark
47:21 Joseph *r.* people to cities
Ex. 14:19 angel of God *r.* and
20:18 people saw it and *r.* afar
Num. 21:12 *r.* pitched, 33:7-21
Deut. 28:25 *r.* into all kingdoms
Jos. 3:1 they *r.* from Shittim
1 *Sam.* 6:3 why his ha. is not *r.*
2 *Sam.* 20:12 he *r.* Amasa out of

1 *K.* 15:12 Asa *r.* the idols
13 *r.* fr. bei. queen, *2 Chr.* 15:16
14 high pla. not *r.* 2 *K.* 15:4, 35
2 *K.* 17:18 the Lord *r.* Israel out
of his sight, 23 ; 23:27
26 nations wh. th. *r.* know not
18:4 Hezekiah *r.* the high places
2 *Chr.* 35:12 th. *r.* burnt-offerings
Job 14:18 rock is *r.* out of place
18:4 sh. rock be *r.* out of place ?
19:10 hope hath he *r.* like a tree
36:16 would have *r.* out of stra.
Ps. 46:2 not fear tho' earth be *r.*
81:6 *r.* his shoulder from burden
103:12 so far he *r.* transgressions
104:5 earth, it should not be *r.*
125:1 as Zion which cannot be *r.*
Prov. 10:30 righteous never be *r.*
Is. 6:12 till L. *r.*ath *r.* men away
10:13 I have *r.* bounds of people
31 Madmenah is *r.* inhabitants
22:25 the sure place shall be *r.*
24:20 earth sh. be *r.* like cottage
26:15 hast *r.* it to ends of earth
29:13 *r.* their heart from me
30:20 yet sh. not teachers be *r.*
33:20 not one of stakes be *r.*
38:12 mine age *r.* fr. me as tent
54:10 the hills shall be *r.* coven.
of my peace shall not be *r.*
Jer. 15:4 cause to be *r.* to kingd.
24:9 deliv. to be *r.* 29:18 ; 34:17
Lam. 1:8 Jerusalem sinned, is *r.*
3:17 thou hast *r.* my soul
Ezek. 7:19 their gold shall be *r.*
23:46 I will give them to be *r.*
36:17 way uncl. of a *r.* woman
Amos 6:7 banq. of them sh. be *r.*
Mic. 2:4 how hath he *r.* it fr. me
7:11 in that day sh. decree be *r.*
Mat. 21:21 Be *r.* *Mark* 11:23
Acts 7:4 he *r.* Abraham into land
13:22 he *r.* Saul, raised David
Gal. 1:6 marvel ye are so soon *r.*

REMOVETH.
Deut. 27:17 cursed, th. *r.* landm.
Job 9:5 wh. *r.* the mountains
12:20 he *r.* speech of the trusty
Ec. 10:9 whoso *r.* stones be hurt
Dan. 2:21 chan. seasons, *r.* kings

REMOVING.
Gen. 30:32 *r.* from flock speckled
Is. 49:21 I am a captive *r.* to and
Ezek. 12:3 prepare stuff for *r.* 4
Heb. 12:27 signifieth *r.* of things

REMPHAN.
Acts 7:43 the star of your god R.

REND.
Ex. 39:23 ephod should not *r.*
Lev. 10:6 neither *r.* your clothes
13:56 priest *r.* plague out of gar.
1 *K.* 11:11 I will *r.* kingd. 12, 31
13 I will not *r.* away kingdom
2 *Chr.* 24:27 didst *r.* clothes, we.
Ec. 3:7 a time to *r.* time to sew
Is. 64:1 thou wouldest *r.* heavens
Ezek. 13:11 stormy wind *r.* it, 13
29:7 and *r.* all their shoulder
Hos. 13:8 I will *r.* caul of heart
Joel 2:13 *r.* your heart, not gar.
Mat. 7:6 lest they turn and *r.*
John 19:24 not *r.* it, but cast lots

RENDER.
Num. 18:9 offering they *r.* holy
Deut. 32:41 I will *r.* vengeance
43 *r.* vengeance to adversaries
Jud. 9:57 evil of men of S. G. *r.*
1 *Sam.* 26:23 L. *r.* to man faithf.
2 *Chr.* 6:30 *r.* to ev. man accord.
Job 33:26 will *r.* to man righte.
34:11 work of a man shall he *r.*
Ps. 28:24 *r.* to them their desert
38:20 they that *r.* evil for good
56:12 O God, I will *r.* praises to
79:12 *r.* to neighbor sevenfold
94:2 *r.* a word to the proud

116:12 what shall I *r.* to the L. ?
Prov. 24:12 shall not he *r.* to ev.
man ac. to words? *Rom.* 2:6
29 *r.* to man according to wo.
26:16 seven men can *r.* reason
Is. 66:15 Lord come to *r.* anger
Jer. 51:6 *r.* to Bab. recompen. 24
Lam. 3:64 *r.* to them recompense
Hos. 14:2 we *r.* calves of our lips
Joel 3:4 ye *r.* me a recompense ?
Zec. 9:12 will *r.* double to thee
Mat. 21:41 *r.* him fruits in season
22:21 *r.* unto Cesar things are
C.'s, *Mark* 12:17 ; *Luke* 20:25
Rom. 13:7 *r.* to all their dues
1 *Cor.* 7:3 husb. *r.* to wife bene.
1 *Thes.* 3:9 what thanks can we *r.*
5:15 see that none *r.* evil for ev.

RENDERED.
Jud. 9:56 G. *r.* wickedness of A.
2 *K.* 3:4 king of M. *r.* king of Is.
2 *Chr.* 32:25 Heze. *r.* not accord.
Prov. 12:14 rec. of man's ha. *r.*

RENDEREST, ETH, ING.
Ps. 62:12 *r.* to man acc. to work
Is. 66:6 voice of L. *r.* recomp.
1 *Pet* 3:9 not *r.* evil for evil

RENDEST, ING.
Ps. 7:2 my soul *r.* it in pieces
Jer. 4:30 *r.* face with painting

RENEW.
1 *Sam.* 11:14 go to G. *r.* kingd.
Ps. 51:10 *r.* right sp. within me
Is. 40:31 wait on L. *r.* strength
41:1 let people *r.* their stren.
Lam. 5:21 turn us, O L. *r.* days
Heb. 6:6 if fall, *r.* to repentance

RENEWED, EST.
2 *Chr.* 15:8 Asa *r.* altar of Lord
Job 10:17 *r.* witnesses ag. me
29:20 my bow was *r.* in my ha.
Ps. 103:5 youth is *r.* like eagle's
104:30 thou *r.* face of the earth
2 *Cor.* 4:16 inw. man *r.* day by d.
Eph. 4:23 be *r.* in spirit of minds
Col. 3:10 man wh. is *r.* in know.

RENEWING.
Rom. 12:2 transform. by *r.* mind
Tit. 3:5 he sav. us by *r.* of H. G.

RENOUNCED.
2 *Cor.* 4:2 have *r.* hidden things

RENOWN.
Gen. 6:4 giants of old, men of *r.*
Num. 16:2 fa. in cong. men of *r.*
Ezek. 16:14 *r.* went forth among
15 playedst harlot bec. of thy *r.*
34:29 raise for them a plant of *r.*
39:13 shall be to them *r.* sai. L.
Dan. 9:15 gotten thee *r.*

RENOWNED.
Num. 1:16 these *r.* of congrega.
Is. 14:20 evil-doers never *r.*
Ezek. 23:23 captai. lords, and *r.*
26:17 *r.* city was strong in sea

RENT, Substantive.
Is. 3:24 instead of girdle be a *r.*
Mat. 9:16 *r.* ma. worse, *Mar.* 2:21
Luke 5:36 then new maketh a *r.*

RENT, Participle.
Gen. 37:33 Joseph is *r.* in pieces
Jos. 9:4 wine bot. old and *r.* 13
2 *Sam.* 15:32 H. with his coat *r.*
1 *K.* 13:3 altar be *r.* 5 altar *r.*
Ezr. 9:5 having *r.* my garment
Mat. 27:51 veil of temple *r.* in
tw. *Mark* 15:28 ; *Luke* 23:45

See CLOTHES.

RENT, Verb.
Jud. 14:6 Samson *r.* lion as he *r.*
1 *Sam.* 15:27 Saul *r.* Sam. man.
28 L. hath *r.* kingdom, 28:17
2 *Sam.* 13:19 Tamar *r.* her garm.
1 *K.* 1:40 earth *r.* with the sou.

11:30 Ahijah *r.* Jerob. garment
19:11 strong wind *r.* mountains
2 *K.* 17:21 he *r.* Israel from Dav.
Ezr. 9:3 when I heard I *r.* garm.
Job 1:20 Job arose, and *r.* mantle
2:12 Job's fr. *r.* ev. one mantle
26:8 cloud is not *r.* under them
Jer. 36:24 nor *r.* their garments
Ezek. 30:16 Sin have pain, No *r.*
Mat. 27:51 veil was *r.* rocks *r.*
Mark 9:26 epi. cried, and *r.* him

REPAID.
Prov. 13:21 to right. good be *r.*

REPAIR.
2 *K.* 12:5 let priests *r.* breaches
of the house of God, 22:5, 6 ;
2 *Chr.* 24:4 ; 34:8, 10
7 why *r.* ye not house? 22:5, 6
2 *Chr.* 24:5 money to *r.* house
12 carpenters to *r.* house of L.
Ezr. 9:9 give reviv. to *r.* house
Is. 61:4 they shall *r.* waste cities

REPAIRED.
Jud. 21:23 Benjamin *r.* cities
1 *K.* 11:27 Solomon *r.* breaches
18:30 Elijah *r.* altar of the Lord
2 *K.* 12:6 the priests had not *r.*
14 and *r.* the house of the L.
1 *Chr.* 11:8 Joab *r.* rest of the ci.
2 *Chr.* 29:3 Hezek. *r.* the doors
32:5 Hezekiah *r.* Millo in city
33:16 Manasseh *r.* altar of Lord
Neh. 3:4 next to them *r.* 5–19
6 and after him *r.* 17–24

REPAIRER, ING.
2 *Chr.* 24:27 the *r.* of the house
Is. 58:12 shalt be called the *r.*

REPAY.
Deut. 7:10 will *r.* him to his face
Job 21:31 *r.* him what ha. done?
41:11 that I should *r.* him?
Is. 59:18 accord. to their deeds *r.*
fury, to islands *r.* recomp.
Luke 10:35 come again I will *r.*
Rom. 12:19 I will *r.* saith the L.
Phile. 19 I Paul, will *r.* it

REPAYETH.
Deut. 7:10 *r.* them that hate him

REPEATETH.
Prov. 17:9 but he that *r.* a mat.

REPENT.
Ex. 13:17 lest peradv. people *r.*
32:12 turn from thy wrath, *r.*
Num. 23:19 nei. son of man, *r.*
Deut. 32:36 Lord *r.* for his serv.
1 *Sam.* 15:29 Strength of I. not *r.*
1 *K.* 8:47 if they *r.* in the land
Job 42:6 and *r.* in dust and ashes
Ps. 90:13 let it *r.* thee concern.
110:4 Lord will not *r.* *Heb.* 7:21
135:14 he will *r.* himself conc.
Jer. 4:28 I purp. it, will not *r.*
18:8 nation turn, *r.* of ev. 26:13
10 then I will *r.* of the good
26:3 that I may *r.* 42:10 for I *r.*
Ezek. 14:6 *r.* and turn yourselves,
18:30
24:14 neither spare, nei. will *r.*
Joel 2:14 if he will return and *r.*
Jon. 3:9
Mat. 3:2 preach. saying *r.* 4:17
Mark 1:15 *r.* ye, and believe
6:12 preach. that men should *r.*
Luke 13:3 except ye *r.* perish, 5
16:30 if one we. fr. dead will *r.*
17:3 if thy brother *r.* forgive, 4
Acts 2:38 *r.* and be baptized ev.
3:19 *r.* ye theref. be converted
8:22 *r.* of this thy wickedness
17:30 commandeth all men to *r.*
26:20 they should *r.* turn to G.
2 *Cor.* 7:8 I do not *r.* tho' I did *r.*
Rev. 2:5 and *r.* except thou *r.*
16 *r.* else I will come unto th.
21 I gave her space to *r.* of her

3:3 how thou hast rec. and *r.*
19 be zealous therefore and *r.*

REPENTANCE.

Hos. 13:14 *r.* sh. be hid fr. eyes
Mat. 3:8 fru. meet for *r.* *Luke* 3:8
  11 I indeed bapti. you unto *r.*
Mat. 9:13 to call sinners to *r.*
  Mark 2:17; *Luke* 5:32
Mark 1:4 John did prea. bap. of
  r. Luke 3:3; *Acts* 13:24; 19:4
Luke 15:7 ninety-nine need no *r.*
  24:47 *r.* and remission of sins
Acts 5:31 God exalted to give *r.*
  11:18 to Gentiles granted *r.*
  20:21 testifying to Greeks *r.*
  26:20 works meet for *r.*
Rom. 2:4 good. of God lead. to *r.*
  11:29 gifts of God without *r.*
2 *Cor.* 7:9 I rej. ye sorrowed to *r.*
  10 godly sorrow worketh *r.*
2 *Tim.* 2:25 if G. will give th. *r.*
Heb. 6:1 laying again foun. of *r.*
  6 to renew them again to *r.*
  12:17 he found no place of *r.*
2 *Pet.* 3:9 perish, all come to *r.*

REPENTED.

Gen. 6:6 it *r.* Lord he made man
Ex. 32:14 *r.* of evil, 2 *Sam.* 24:16;
  1 *Chr.* 21:15; *Jer.* 26:19
Jud. 2:18 it *r.* L. because of th.
  21:6 the children of Israel, *r.* 15
1 *Sam.* 15:35 L. *r.* he made Saul
Ps. 106:45 L. *r.* acc. to mercies
Jer. 8:6 no man *r.* him of wick.
  20:16 cities I. overthrew *r.* not
  31:19 after I was turned, I *r.*
Amos 7:3 the Lord *r.* for this, 6
Jon. 3:10 God *r.* of the evil
Zec. 8:14 punish you, I *r.* not
Mat. 11:20 cities bec. they *r.* not
  21 would have *r. Luke* 10:13
  12:41 men of Nin. *r. Luke* 11:32
  21:29 afterward he *r.* and went
  32 when ye had seen it, *r.* not
  27:3 Ju. *r.* himself, bro't silver
2 *Cor.* 7:10 repent. not to be *r.*
  12:21 many that have not *r.*
Rev. 2:21 to repent, she *r.* not
  9:20 were not killed, yet *r.* not
  16:9 blasphemed G. *r.* not, 11

REPENTEST, ETH.

Gen. 6:7 it *r.* me I made them
1 *Sam.* 15:11 it *r.* me I set up S.
Jon. 4:2 gracious God *r.* of evil
Joel 2:13 slow to anger, *r.* him
Luke 15:7 one sinner *r.* 10

REPENTING, S.

Jer. 15:6 I am weary with *r.*
Hos. 11:8 *r.* are kindled together

REPETITIONS.

Mat. 6:7 use not vain *r.* as hea.

REPHAIM.

Gen. 14:5 smote R. in Ashteroth
  15:20 have I given land of R.
2 *Sam.* 5:18 in valley of R. 22;
  23:13; 1 *Chr.* 11:15; 14:9
Is. 17:5 gather. ears in val. of R.

REPHIDIM.

Ex. 17:1 pitch. in R. *Num.* 33:14
  8 and fought with Israel in R.
  19:2 dep. from R. *Num.* 33:15

REPLENISH, ED.

Gen. 1:28 mult. and *r.* earth, 9:1
Is. 2:6 bec. they be *r.* from east
  23:2 merchants of Zidon have *r.*
Jer. 31:25 and I have *r.* every
Ezek. 26:2 I sh. be *r.* in waste pl.
  27:25 thou wast *r.* made glori.

REPLIEST.

Rom. 9:20 thou that *r.* ag. God?

REPORT, Substantive.

Gen. 37:2 Jos. brought their *r.*
Ex. 23:1 shalt not raise false *r.*
Num. 13:32 brought up evil *r.*
  14:37 men that bring up evil *r.*

Deut. 2:25 nations shall hear *r.*
1 *Sam.* 2:24 no good *r.* I hear
1 *K.* 10:6 it was true *r.* 2 *Chr.* 9:5
Neh. 6:13 matter for an evil *r.*
Prov. 15:30 a good *r.* maketh fat
Is. 23:5 at *r.* concerning Egypt,
  so at the *r.* of Tyre
  28:19 vexation only to under. *r.*
  53:1 who hath believed our *r.?*
  John 12:38; *Rom.* 10:16
Jer. 50:43 Babylon heard the *r.*
Acts 6:3 seven men of honest *r.*
  10:22 Cornelius was of good *r.*
  22:12 Ananias having a good *r.*
2 *Cor.* 6:8 by evil *r.* and good *r.*
Phil. 4:8 what. thinge of good *r.*
1 *Tim.* 3:7 bishop have good *r.*
Heb. 11:2 elders obt. a good *r.*
  39 having obtained a good *r.*
2 *John* 12 Demetrius ha. good *r.*

REPORT, Verb.

Jer. 20:10 *r.* say they, will *r.* it
1 *Cor.* 14:25 will *r.* that God is in

REPORTED.

Neh. 6:6 it is *r.* among heathen
Neh. 6:7 sh. it be *r.* to king acc.
  19 *r.* his good deeds before
Est. 1:17 husb. when it sh. be *r.*
Ezek. 9:11 man had inkhorn *r.*
Mat. 28:15 saying commonly *r.*
Acts 4:23 *r.* all chief priests said
  16:2 Timotheus was well *r.*
Rom. 3:8 we be slanderously *r.*
1 *Cor.* 5:1 *r.* there is fornication
1 *Tim.* 5:10 *r.* for good works
1 *Pet.* 1:12 minis. things now *r.*

REPROACH.

Jos. 5:9 I rolled away *r.* of Eg.
1 *Sam.* 17:26 taketh away the *r.*
Neh. 1:3 remn. are afflic. and *r.*
  4:4 and turn their *r.* upon head
  5:9 because of the *r.* of heathen
Ps. 57:3 shall save me from *r.*
  69:7 for thy sake I ha. borne *r.*
  20 *r.* hath broken my heart
  71:13 let them be cover. with *r.*
  78:66 put them to perpetual *r.*
  79:12 their *r.* wherewith they
  89:50 remember *r.* of servants,
  I bear in my bosom the *r.*
  119:22 remove from me *r.* and
Prov. 6:33 *r.* shall not be wiped
  18:3 with ignominy cometh *r.*
  19:26 that caus. shame and *r.*
  22:10 strife and *r.* shall cease
Is. 4:1 name to take away our *r.*
  51:7 fear ye not the *r.* of men
  54:4 not remember the *r.* of thy
Jer. 23:40 I bring an everlast. *r.*
  31:19 because I did bear the *r.*
  51:51 confounded bec. heard *r.*
Lam. 3:30 he is fill. full with *r.*
  61 thou hast heard their *r.* O L.
  5:1 Lord consider and behold *r.*
Ezek. 16:57 discovered, time of *r.*
  21:28 concerning *r.* of Ammon.
  36:15 nor shalt thou bear *r.*
  30 ye shall receive no more *r.*
Dan. 11:18 cause *r.* cease, his *r.*
Hos. 12:14 his *r.* shall L. return
Joel 2:17 give not heritage to *r.*
Mic. 6:16 ye shall bear *r.* of peo.
Zep. 2:8 I heard the *r.* of Moab
  3:18 the *r.* of it was a burden
2 *Cor.* 11:21 I speak concern. *r.*
1 *Tim.* 3:7 report, lest fall into *r.*
  4:10 we both labour and suffer *r.*
Heb. 11:26 esteeming *r.* of Christ
  13:13 without camp, bearing *r.*

A REPROACH.

Gen. 34:14 do this, that were a *r.*
1 *Sam.* 11:2 lay it for a *r.* upon
Neh. 2:17 that be no more a *r.*
Ps. 15:3 not upon a *r.* ag. neigh.
  22:6 a *r.* of men, and despised
  31:11 I was a *r.* among enemies

39:8 make me not *r.* of foolish
44:13 thou makest us a *r.* to our
79:4 become a *r.* to neighbors
89:41 he is a *r.* to his neighbors
109:25 I became a *r.* to them
Prov. 14:34 sin is a *r.* to any pe.
Is. 30:5 a people that were a *r.*
Jer. 6:10 word of L. to them a *r.*
  20:8 word of L. was made a *r.*
  24:9 deliver for hurt to be a *r.*
  29:18; 42:18; 44:8, 12
  49:13 Bozrah shall become a *r.*
Ezek. 5:14 I will make thee a *r.*
  15 Jeru. sh. be a *r.* and taunt
  22:4 I made a *r.* unto heathen
Dan. 9:16 thy people become a *r.*
Joel 2:19 no more make you a *r.*

My REPROACH.

Gen. 30:23 God hath taken *my r.*
1 *Sam.* 25:39 ple. cause of *my r.*
Job 19:5 if plead ag. me *my r.*
  20:3 I have heard check of *my r.*
Ps. 69:10 I wept, that was *my r.*
  19 thou hast known *my r.*
  119:39 turn away *my r.*
Luke 1:25 *my r.* among men

REPROACH, Verb.

Ruth 2:15 let her glean, *r.* not
2 *K.* 19:4 whom' king of Assyria
  sent to *r.* G. 16; *Is.* 37:4, 17
Neh. 6:13 matter they might *r.*
Job 27:6 not *r.* long as I live
Ps. 42:10 mine enemies *r.* me
  74:10 how long advers. *r.* me?
  102:8 enemies' *r.* me all day
Luke 6:22 *r.* you for my sake

REPROACHED.

2 *K.* 19:22 whom th. *r.? Is.* 37:23
  23 messenger hast *r. Is.* 37:24
Job 19:3 ten times have ye *r.* me
Ps. 55:12 was not enemy that *r.*
  69:9 they that *r.* thee are fallen
  upon me, *Rom.* 15:3
  74:18 remember enemy hath *r.*
  79:12 wherewith they *r.* thee
Ps. 89:51 wherew. thine enem. *r.*
  have *r.* footsteps of anointed
Zep. 2:8 whereby they *r.* people
  10 bec. they *r.* and magnified
1 *Pet.* 4:14 if *r.* for C. hap. are ye

REPROACHES.

Ps. 69:9 the *r.* of them that repr.
  thee, *Rom.* 15:3
Is. 43:28 I have given Israel to *r.*
2 *Cor.* 12:10 pleas. in *r.* C.'s sake
Heb. 10:33 gazing-stock by *r.*

REPROACHEST, ETH.

Num. 15:30 doeth presump. *r.* L.
Ps. 44:16 voice of him that *r.*
  74:22 remem. foolish man *r.* th.
  119:42 to answer him that *r.* me,
  Prov. 27:11
Prov. 14:31 poor, *r.* Maker, 17:5
Luke 11:45 Master, thou *r.* us

REPROACHFULLY.

Job 16:10 smitten me on cheek *r.*
1 *Tim.* 5:14 none occa. to spe. *r.*

REPROBATE.

Jer. 6:30 *r.* silver men call them
Rom. 1:28 G. gave them to *r.*
2 *Tim.* 3:8 men *r.* concern. faith
Tit. 1:16 to every good work *r.*

REPROBATES.

2 *Cor.* 13:5 Chri. is in you, ex. *r.*
  6 shall know that we are not *r.*
  7 do that wh. is honest, tho' *r.*

REPROOF.

Job 26:11 they are astonish. at *r.*
Prov. 1:23 turn you at my *r.*
  25 none of my *r.* 30 despised *r.*
  5:11 and my heart despised *r.*
  10:17 he that refuseth *r.* erreth
  12:1 he that hateth *r.* is brutish
  13:18 he that regardeth *r.*

REPROOF

15:5 he that regard. *r.* is prud.
10 he that hateth *r.* shall die
31 heareth of *r.* of life am. wise
32 he that hear. *r.* get. under.
17:10 a *r.* enter. more into wise
29:15 rod and *r.* give wisdom
2 *Tim.* 3:16 scri. profitable for *r.*

REPROOFS

Ps. 38:14 in whose mouth no *r.*
Prov. 6:23 *r.* of instruc. are life

REPROVE

2 *K.* 19:4 *r.* Rabshakeh, *Is.* 37:4
Job 6:25 doth your arguing *r. ?*
26 do ye imagine to *r.* words
13:10 he will *r.* if ye accept
22:4 will he *r.* for fear of thee ?
Ps. 50:8 will not *r.* for burnt-off.
21 I will *r.* thee, set in order
141:5 let him *r.* me, it sh. be oil
Prov. 9:8 *r.* not scorner
19:25 *r.* one that hath underst.
30:6 lest he *r.* thee, found liar
Is. 11:3 neit. *r.* hearing of ears
4 *r.* with equity for meek
37:4 will *r.* words wh. L. heard
Jer. 2:19 backslidings sh. *r.* thee
Hos. 4:4 let no man *r.* another
John 16:8 he will *r.* world of sin
Eph. 5:11 no fellowship, rather *r.*
2 *Tim.* 4:2 *r.* rebuke, exhort

REPROVED

Gen. 20:16 thus she was *r.*
21:25 Abraham *r.* Abimelech
1 *Chr.* 16:21 yea, he *r.* kings for
their sakes, *Ps.* 105:14
Prov. 29:1 often *r.* harden. neck
Jer. 29:27 why hast not *r.* Jer. ?
Hab. 2:1 what answer, when *r. ?*
Luke 3:19 Herod being *r.* by J.
John 3:20 lest deeds be *r.*
Eph. 5:13 things *r.* made manif.

REPROVER

Prov. 25:12 so is a wise *r.* upon
Ezek. 3:26 not be to them a *r.*

REPROVETH

Job 40:2 he that *r.* God
Prov. 9:7 *r.* scorner get. shame
15:12 scorner loveth not one *r.*
Is. 29:21 lay snare for him *r.*

REPUTATION

Ec. 10:1 him in *r.* for wisdom
Acts 5:34 Gamaliel in *r.* am. peo.
Gal. 2:2 privately to them of *r.*
Phil. 2:7 made himself of no *r.*
29 receive him, hold such in *r.*

REPUTED

Job 18:3 *r.* vile in your sight ?
Dan. 4:35 inhab. *r.* as nothing

REQUEST, S.

Jud. 8:24 Gid. said, I desire a *r.*
2 *Sam.* 14:15 king sh. perform *r.*
22 king hath fulfilled *r.* of ser.
Ezr. 7:6 granted him all his *r.*
Neh. 2:4 for wh. dost th. make *r.*
Est. 4:8 to king to make *r.*
5:3 what is thy *r.* 6 ; 7:2 ; 9:12
7:3 life given me, peo. at my *r.*
7 Haman stood up to *r.* for life
Job 6:8 I might have my *r. ?*
Ps. 21:2 not withholden *r.*
106:15 gave th. *r.* sent leanness
Rom. 1:10 *r.* for prosper. journey
Phil. 1:4 in ev. prayer making *r.*
4:6 let your *r.* be known to God

REQUESTED

Jud. 8:26 wei. of ear-rings he *r.*
1 *K.* 19:4 Elijah *r.* he might die
1 *Chr.* 4:10 G. granted Jab. he *r.*
Dan. 1:8 he *r.* of prince of eunu.
2:49 Dan. *r.* of king, he set Sh.

REQUIRE.

Gen. 9:5 blood I *r.* of every beast
31:39 my hand didst thou *r.* it
43:9 of my hand sh. thou *r.* him
Deut. 10:12 doth L. *r. ?* *Mic.* 6:8

18:19 whoso not hear. I will *r.*
23:21 L. will surely *r.* it of thee
Jos. 22:23 let L. *r.* it, 1 *Sam.* 20:16
2 *Sam.* 3:13 one thing I *r.* of thee
4:11 shall I not *r.* his blood at ?
19:38 thou sh. *r.* that will I do
1 *K.* 8:59 maintain as matter *r.*
1 *Chr.* 21:3 why doth my lord *r.*
2 *Chr.* 24:22 L. look on it, *r.* it
Ezr. 7:21 whatso. Ezra *r.* of you
8:22 asham. to *r.* of king a band
Neh. 5:12 restore, and *r.* nothing
Ps. 10:13 said, Thou wilt not *r.*
Ezek. 3:18 his blood will I *r.* at
thy hand, 20 ; 33:6, 8
20:40 there will I *r.* your offer.
34:10 I will *r.* my flock at hand
1 *Cor.* 1:22 for the Jews *r.* a sign
7:36 *r.* let him do what he will

REQUIRED.

Gen. 42:22 behold, his blood is *r.*
Ex. 12:36 lent things as they *r.*
2 *Sam.* 12:20 he *r.* they set bread
1 *Chr.* 16:37 every day's work *r.*
2 *Chr.* 8:14 as the duty of every
day *r. Ezr.* 3:4
Neh. 5:18 *r.* not I bread of gover.
Est. 2:15 *r.* nothing but what
Ps. 40:6 sin-offer. hast th. not *r.*
137:3 they that wasted *r.* mirth
Prov. 30:7 two things have I *r.*
Is. 1:12 who *r.* this at your hand
Luke 11:50 *r.* of this generati. 51
12:20 this night thy soul *r.*
48 much given, of him be m. *r.*
19:23 I might have *r.* mine own
23:24 gave sentence sho. be as *r.*
1 *Cor.* 4:2 *r.* of stew. be faithful

REQUIREST, ETH, ING.

Ruth 3:11 do all that thou *r.*
Ec. 3:15 God *r.* that whi. is past
Dan. 2:11 a rare thing king *r.*
Luke 23:23 *r.* he might be cruci.

REQUITE.

Gen. 50:15 Jos. will *r.* us the evil
Deut. 32:6 do ye thus *r.* Lord?
2 *Sam.* 2:6 I will *r.* you this kin.
16:12 L. will *r.* me good for this
2 *K.* 9:26 I will *r.* thee in plat
Ps. 10:14 behold. to *r.* with hand
41:10 that I may *r.* them
Jer. 51:56 G. of recomp. shall *r.*
1 *Tim.* 5:4 learn to *r.* th. parents

REQUITED, ING.

Jud. 1:7 as I done, so God *r.* me
1 *Sam.* 25:21 *r.* me evil for good
2 *Chr.* 6:23 judge serv. by *r.* wic.

REREWARD, or REAR-WARD.

Num. 10:25 stand. of Dan was *r.*
Jos. 6:9 *r.* came after ark, 13 .
1 *Sam.* 29:2 D. and men pass. *r.*
Is. 52:12 G. of Is. will be your *r.*
58:8 glory of Lord sh. be thy *r.*

RESCUE, ETH.

Deut. 28:31 shalt have none to *r.*
Ps. 35:17 *r.* my soul fr. destruc.
Dan. 6:27 he delivereth and *r.*
Hos. 5:14 I take, none shall *r.*

RESCUED

1 *Sam.* 14:45 people *r.* Jonathan
30:18 David *r.* his two wives
Acts 23:27 came I with army, *r.*

RESEMBLANCE.

Zec. 5:6 their *r.* thro' all earth

RESEMBLE, ED.

Jud. 8:18 each *r.* childr. of king
Luke 13:18 shall *r.* kingd. of God
RESEN. *Gen.* 10:12

RESERVE.

Jer. 3:5 will he *r.* anger for ever ?
50:20 I will pardon whom I *r.*
2 *Pet.* 2:9 *r.* unj. to day of judg.

RESERVED.

Gen. 27:36 hast thou not *r.* bles.

Num. 18:9 most holy things *r.*
Jud. 21:22 *r.* not each his wife
Ruth 2:18 gave moth. that she *r.*
2 *Sam.* 8:4 but *r.* for one hundred chariots, 1 *Chr.* 18:4
Job 21:30 wicked *r.* for destruc.
38:23 I *r.* agai. time of trouble
Acts 25:21 Paul appealed to be *r.*
Rom. 11:4 I have *r.* 7,000 men
1 *Pet.* 1:4 inheritance *r.* in heav.
2 *Pet.* 2:4 deliv. to be *r.* to judg.
17 mist of darkn. is *r.* for ever
3:7 heav. and earth *r.* unto fire
Jude 6 he hath *r.* in chains
13 to wh. is *r.* blackn. of dark.

RESERVETH.

Jer. 5:24 *r.* to us weeks of harv.
Nah. 1:2 L. *r.* wrath for enemi.

RESIDUE.

Ex. 10:5 locusts shall eat the *r.*
Neh. 11:20 *r.* of Is. were in cities
Is. 28:5 L. diadem to *r.* of people
38:10 deprived of *r.* of years
44:17 the *r.* he maketh a god
Jer. 8:3 chosen, by all the *r.* of
15:9 *r.* I deliver to the sword
29:1 Jeremiah sent to *r.* of eld.
39:3 *r.* of princes of Babylon
41:10 Ishm. carri. captive the *r.*
Ezek. 9:8 destroy the *r.* of Isr. ?
23:25 thy *r.* shall be devoured
34:18 must tread *r.* of pastures
36:3 possession of *r.* to heathen
4 derision to *r.* of the heathen
5 have I spoken ag. *r.* of hea.
48:18 *r.* in length ag. oblation
21 the *r.* shall be for the prin.
Dan. 7:7 stamped *r.* with feet, 19
Zep. 2:9 *r.* of people shall spoil
Hag. 2:2 speak to Joshua and *r.*
Zec. 8:11 I will not be to the *r.*
14:2 *r.* of the people shall not
Mal. 2:15 had the *r.* of the Spir.
Mark 16:13 went and told it to *r.*
Acts 15:17 *r.* might seek the L.

RESIST.

Zec. 3:1 Satan at right hand to *r.*
Mat. 5:39 that ye *r.* not evil
Luke 21:15 adver. not able to *r.*
Acts 6:10 not able to *r.* wisdom
7:51 ye do always *r.* Holy Ghost
Rom. 13:2 *r.* shall receive damn.
2 *Tim.* 3:8 these also *r.* the truth
Jam. 4:7 *r.* devil and he will flee
5:6 killed just, doth not *r.* you
1 *Pet.* 5:9 wh. *r.* steadfast in fai.

RESISTED, ETH.

Rom. 9:19 who hath *r.* his will ?
13:2 whoso *r.* power, *r.* ordin.
Heb. 12:4 have not *r.* unto blood
Jam. 4:6 God *r.* proud, 1 *Pet.* 5:5

RESOLVED.

Luke 16:4 I am *r.* what to do

RESORT.

Neh. 4:20 *r.* ye thither to us
Ps. 71:3 whereunto I may *r.*
Mark 10:1 the people *r.* to him
John 18:20 whi. Jews always *r.*

RESORTED.

2 *Chr.* 11:13 priests and Levit. *r.*
Mark 2:13 multitude *r.* to him
John 10:41 and many *r.* to him
18:2 Jesus ofttimes *r.* thither
Acts 16:13 spake to wom. who *r.*

RESPECT.

Gen. 4:4 the Lord had *r.* to Abel
Ex. 2:25 God looked and had *r.*
Lev. 26:9 I will have *r.* unto you
1 *K.* 8:28 have thou *r.* to prayer
of thy servant, 2 *Chr.* 6:19
2 *K.* 13:23 the L. had *r.* to them
2 *Chr.* 19:7 *r.* of pers. with God,
Rom. 2:11; *Eph.* 6:9; *Col.* 3:25
Ps. 74:20 have *r.* unto covenant

119:6 I have r. to all thy com.
15 I will have r. unto thy ways
117 have r. to thy statutes
138:6 hath he r. to the lowly
Prov. 24:23 not good to have r.
of persons in judgm. 28:21
Is. 17:7 sh. have r. to Holy One
22:11 nor had r. to him that
2 *Cor.* 3:10 had no glory in th. r.
Phil. 4:11 I speak in r. of want
Col. 2:16 let none judge in r. of
Heb. 11:26 Mo. had r. to recomp
Jam. 2:1 not faith with r. of per.
3 have r. to him that weareth
9 if ye have r. to persons
1 *Pet.* 1:17 without r. of persons

RESPECT, Verb.
Lev. 19:15 thou sh. not r. person
Num. 16:15 Moses said, r. not
Deut. 1:17 not r. persons, 16:19
2 *Sam.* 14:14 neither doth God r.
Is. 17:8 nor shall r. that which

RESPECT, ETH.
Job 37:24 he r. not wise of heart
Ps. 40:4 blessed is man that r.
Lam. 4:16 r. not pers. of priest

RESPECTER.
Acts 10:34 God is no r. of persons

RESPITE.
Ex. 8:15 Phar. saw there was r.
1 *Sam.* 11:3 said, Give 7 days r.

REST, Substantive.
Gen. 49:15 Issa. saw r. was good
Ex. 16:23 to-morrow r. of sabb.
31:15 sev. is sabbath of r. 35:2;
Lev. 16:31; 23:3, 32; 25:4
33:14 and I will give thee r.
Lev. 25:5 a year of r. to land
Deut. 3:20 L. given r. *Jos.* 1:13
12:9 ye are not yet come to r.
25:19 God hath given thee r.
28:65 neither sh. sole of foot r.
Jos. 1:15 L. hath given breth. r.
14:15 land had r. fr. war, *Jud.*
3:11; 5:31
21:44 the Lord gave them r.
22:4 God given r. 23:1 L. giv. r.
Jud. 3:30 land had r. 80 years
Ruth 1:9 L. grant you may find r.
3:18 the man will not be in r.
2 *Sam.* 7:1 L. had giv. him r. 1 *K.*
5:4; 8:56; 2 *Chr.* 14:6, 7
1 *Chr.* 6:31 after that ark had r.
22:9 man of r. I will gi. him r.
23:25 God hath given r. to peo.
28:2 I had to build house of r.
2 *Chr.* 15:15 L. gave them r.
20:30 G. gave him r. round ab.
Neh. 9:28 after they had r.
Est. 9:16 J. had r. from enemies
Job 3:13 slept, had been at r.
17 there the weary be at r.
26 not in safety, nei. had I r.
11:18 shalt take thy r. in safety
17:16 our r. together is in dust
Ps. 38:3 neither is there any r.
55:6 then wo. I fly and be at r.
94:13 thou mayest give him r.
116:7 ret. to thy r. O my soul
132:8 arise, O Lord, into thy r.
14 this is my r. for ever
Prov. 29:17 cor. son, he give r.
Ec. 2:23 his heart taketh not r.
6:5 this hath more r. than other
Is. 11:10 Gent. seek, r. be glor.
14:3 the Lord shall give thee r.
7 the earth is at r. *Zec.* 1:11
18:4 L. said, I will take my r.
28:12 this is r. wherew. weary r.
30:15 retur. and r. sh. ye be sav.
34:14 find for herself a pl. of r.
66:1 where is place of my r. ?
Jer. 6:16 ye shall find r. for souls
30:10 Jacob shall be in r. 46:27
Ezek. 38:11 to them that are at r.
Dan. 4:4 I Nebuchad. was at r.

Mic. 2:10 this is not your r.
Zec. 9:1 Damascus shall be r.
Mat. 11:28 co. unto me, I give r.
29 ye sh. find r. to your souls
12:43 seek r. *Luke* 11:24
26:45 take your r. *Mark* 14:41
John 11:13 had spoken of tak. r.
Acts 7:49 what is place of my r.?
9:31 then had the churches r.
2 *Thes.* 1:7 are troub. r. with us
Heb. 3:11 not enter into r. 18
4:1 prom. left us of ent. into r.
3 wh. believed do enter into r.
8 if Jesus had given them r.
9 th. remaineth r. to peo. of G.
11 labor therefore to enter r.

See NO.

RESTS.
1 *K.* 6:6 he made narrowed r.

REST, Adjective.
Ex. 28:10 names of r. on stone
Num. 31:8 r. of them were slain
Deut. 3:13 the r. of Gilead gave I
Jud. 7:6 the r. bowed to drink
2 *K.* 4:7 live and childr. of the r.
1 *Chr.* 11:8 Joab repair. r. of city
2 *Chr.* 24:14 brought r. of money
Neh. 6:1 r. of enem. heard I built
11:1 r. of people also cast lots
Est. 9:12 wh. done in r. of prov.?
Ps. 17:14 leave r. to their babes
Is. 10:19 the r. of trees be few
Dan. 2:18 D. sh. not per. with r.
Zec. 11:9 r. eat flesh of another
Luke 12:26 why take tho. for r.?
24:9 told eleven and all the r.
Acts 2:37 to Pet. and r. of apost.

Acts 27:44 the r. esc. safe to land
1 *Cor.* 7:12 to the r. speak I
11:34 the r. will I set in order
1 *Pet.* 4:2 not live r. of his time
Rev. 2:24 to the r. in Thyatira
20:5 r. of dead lived not again

See ACTS.

REST, Verb.
Gen. 18:4 wash feet, r. und. tree
Ex. 5:5 make th. r. fr. burdens
23:11 in seventh year let it r.
12 seventh day shalt r. 34:21
34:21 in harvest thou shalt r.
Lev. 26:35 nor r. in sabbaths
Deut. 5:14 maid-serv. r. as thou
Jos. 3:13 feet of priests shall r.
2 *Sam.* 3:29 let it r. on head of J.
21:10 birds r. on them by day
2 *K.* 2:15 sp. of Elijah r. on Elis.
2 *Chr.* 14:11 we r. on thee
Job 3:18 the prisoners r. togeth.
14:6 may r. till he accomplish
Ps. 16:9 r. in hope, *Acts* 2:26
37:7 r. in the Lord, wait for him
125:3 rod of wick. not r. on rig.
Prov. 6:35 nor will he r. content
Cant. 1:7 makest flock r. at noon
Is. 7:19 shall r. in deso. valleys
11:2 Sp. of the Lord r. upon him
25:10 in moun. sh. hand of L. r.
28:12 ye cause the weary to r.
51:4 I will make judgment to r.
57:2 they shall r. in their beds
20 are like the sea, it cannot r.
62:1 for Jer.'s sake I will not r.
63:14 Sp. of L. caused him to r.
Jer. 31:2 to cause him to r.
Ezek. 5:13 my fury to r. upon th.
16:42; 21:17; 24:13
44:30 may cause blessing to r.
Dan. 12:13 th. shalt r. and stand
Hab. 3:16 I mi. r. day of trouble
Zep. 3:17 he will r. in love
Mark 6:31 come to desert and r.
Luke 10:6 your peace shall r.
2 *Cor.* 12:9 power of Chr. may r.
Heb. 4:4 God did r. seventh day
Rev. 4:8 r. not day and night

6:11 they should r. for a season
14:13 they may r. from labors

RESTED.
Gen. 2:2 he r. on seventh day,
3; *Ex.* 20:11; 31:17
8:4 the ark r. in seventh month
Ex. 10:14 locusts r. in Egypt
16:30 people r. on seventh day
Num. 9:18 as cloud ab. they r. 23
10:12 cloud r. in wild. of Paran
36 when it r. he said, Ret. O L.
11:25 Spirit r. upon them, 26
Jos. 11:23 the land r. from war
1 *K.* 6:10 chambers r. on house
2 *Chr.* 32:8 r. on words of Hez.
Est. 9:17 on 14th day r. 18
Job 30:27 bow. boiled and r. not
Luke 23:56 they r. sabbath-day

RESTEST, ETH.
Job 24:23 in safety, where, he r.
Prov. 14:33 wisdom r. in heart
Ec. 7:9 anger r. in bos. of fools
Rom. 2:17 thou art a J. r. in law
1 *Pet.* 4:14 Sp. of G. r. upon you

RESTING-PLACE, S.
Num. 10:33 to search out a r.-pl.
2 *Chr.* 6:41 O Lord, into thy r.-p.
Prov. 24:15 spoil not his r.-place
Is. 32:18 my peo. dwell in r.-pl.
Jer. 50:6 forgotten their r.-place

RESTITUTION.
Ex. 22:3 make full r. 5, 6, 12
Job 20:18 according to subs. r. be
Acts 3:21 until the times of r.

RESTORE.
Gen. 20:7 r. the man his wife
40:13 Ph. will r. thee thy place
42:25 to r. every man's money
Ex. 22:1 r. five oxen for an ox
4 theft be found, he shall r.
Lev. 6:5 shall r. it in principal
24:21 killeth a beast, he sh. r. it
25:27 r. overpl. to wh. he sold it
Num. 35:25 congregation r. him
Deut. 22:2 things strayed r. aga.
Jud. 11:13 theref. r. those lands
17:3 I will r. it unto thee, 1 *Sam.*
12:3; 1 *K.* 20:34
2 *Sam.* 9:7 r. thee all land of Sa.
12:6 he shall r. lamb fourfold
16:3 to-day house of Isr. r. me
2 *K.* 8:6 r. all that was hers
Neh. 5:11 r. I pray you; 12 will r.
Job 20:10 his han. r. their goods
18 which he labored for. sh. r.
Ps. 51:12 r. to me joy of salvati.
Prov. 6:31 he shall r. sevenfold
Is. 1:26 I will r. thy judges
42:22 for spoil. and none sai. r.
49:6 to r. the preserved of Isr.
57:18 will r. comforts unto him
Jer. 27:22 r. them to this place
30:17 r. health to thee
Ezek. 33:15 if wicked r. pledge
Dan. 9:25 command to r. Jerus.
Joel 2:25 I will r. you the years
Mal. 17:11 Elias sh. r. all things
Luke 19:8 I r. him fourfold
Acts 1:6 Lord, wilt thou r. king-
dom ?
Gal. 6:1 r. such a one in meek.

RESTORED.
Gen. 20:14 Abimelech r. Sarah
40:21 r. butler to his butlership
41:13 me he r. to mine office
42:28 money is r. in my sack
Deut. 28:31 thine ass sh. not be r.
Jud. 17:3 r. the 1,100 shekels, 4
1 *Sam.* 7:14 cities taken were r.
1 *K.* 13:6 the king's hand was r.
2 *K.* 8:1 whose son he r. 5
14:22 r. Elath to Jud. 2 *Chr.* 26:2
2 *Chr.* 8:2 the citi. Huram had r.
Ezr. 6:5 the vessels brought be r.
Ps. 69:4 I r. that which I took

Ezek. 18:7 *r.* to debtor his pledge
12 hath not *r.* pledge
Mat. 12:13 *r.* whole like as the
other, *Mark* 3:5; *Luke* 6:10
Mark 8:25 sight *r.* saw clearly
Heb. 13:19 that I may be *r.*

RESTORER.
Ruth 4:15 shall be to thee a *r.*
Is. 58:12 sh. be called *r.* of paths

RESTORETH.
Ps. 23:3 he *r.* my soul
Mark 9:12 El. cometh first and *r.*

RESTRAIN.
Job 15:8 dost thou *r.* wisdom?
Ps. 76:10 the wrath shalt thou *r.*

RESTRAINED.
Gen. 8:2 rain from heaven was *r.*
11:6 nothing will be *r.* fr. them
16:2 Lord *r.* me from bearing
Ex. 36:6 peo. were *r.* fr. bring.
1 *Sam.* 3:13 Eli's sons vile, *r.* not
Is. 63:15 mercies, are they *r.?*
Ezek. 31:15 I *r.* the floods there.
Acts 14:18 sayings scarce *r.* peo.

RESTRAINEST.
Job 15:4 thou *r.* prayer before G.

RESTRAINT.
1 *Sam.* 14:6 there is no *r.* to L.

RESURRECTION.
Mat. 22:23 th. is no *r. Mark* 12:18;
Acts 23:8; 1 *Cor.* 15:12
28 in *r.* whose wife sh. she be?
Mark 12:23; *Luke* 20:33
30 in *r.* they neither marry, 31
27:53 came out of graves aft. *r.*
Luke 14:14 be recompensed at *r.*
20:27 deny any *r.* 36 child. of *r.*
John 5:29 done good, to *r.* of life,
none evil, to *r.* of damnati.
11:25 J. said, I am the *r.* and life
Acts 1:22 witn. with us of his *r.*
2:31 David spake of *r.* of Christ
4:2 they preached thro' Jesus *r.*
33 witness of *r.* of Lord Jesus
17:18 preached Jesus and the *r.*
32 when they heard of the *r.*
23:6 of hope and *r.* I am called
24:15 there shall be a *r.* of dead
21 touching *r.* of the dead
Rom. 1:4 by *r.* from the dead
6:5 shall be in likeness of his *r.*
1 *Cor.* 15:13 but if there be no *r.*
21 by man came *r.* 42 so is *r.*
Phil. 3:10 know power of his *r.*
11 might attain to *r.* of dead
2 *Tim.* 2:18 *r.* is past already
Heb. 6:2 of *r.* from the dead
11:35 might obtain a better *r.*
1 *Pet.* 1:3 by *r.* of Jesus fr. dead
3:21 save us, by *r.* of Je. Christ
Rev. 20:5 this is the first *r.*
6 hath part in first *r.*

RETAIN.
Job 2:9 dost still *r.* integrity?
Prov. 4:4 thy heart *r.* my words
11:16 strong men *r.* riches
Ec. 8:8 no man power to *r.*
Dan. 11:6 she sh. not *r.* power
John 20:23 wh. soever sins ye *r.*
Rom. 1:28 did not like to *r.* God

RETAINED.
Jud. 7:8 Gideon *r.* those 300 men
19:4 damsel's father *r.* him
Dan. 10:8 I *r.* no strength, 16
John 20:23 sins ret. they are *r.*
Phile. 13 whom I would have *r.*

RETAINETH.
Prov. 3:18 happy ev. one *r.* **her**
11:16 a graci. woman *r.* honor
Mic. 7:18 *r.* not anger for ever

RETIRE.
2 *Sam.* 11:15 set in battle, and *r.*
Jer. 4:6 set up stand. *r.* **stay not**

RETIRED.
Jud. 20:39 when men of Israel *r.*
2 *Sam.* 20:22 they *r.* from city

RETURN, Substantive.
Gen. 14:17 meet Abram after *r.*
1 *Sam.* 7:17 Sam.'s *r.* was to Ra.
1 *K.* 20:22 at *r.* of the year the
king of Syria will come, 26

RETURN, Verb.
Gen. 3:19 dust th. art, to dust *r.*
16:9 *r.* to mistress and submit
18:10 I will cert. *r.* to thee, 14
31:3 *r.* to land of kindred, 13
32:9 Lord which saidst to me, *r.*
Ex. 4:18 let me *r.* to breth. 19
13:17 people repent, *r.* to Egypt
Lev. 25:10 *r.* to posses. 13, 27, 28
41 shall *r.* unto his own family
27:24 the field shall *r.* unto him
Num. 10:36 *r.* L. to many of Is.
14:4 let us make a capt. and *r.*
23:5 L. said, *r.* unto Balak
35:28 slayer shall *r. Jos.* 20:6
Deut. 3:20 then shall ye *r.* every
man to his posses. *Jos.* 1:15
17:16 nor cause people *r.* to Eg.
20:5 and *r.* to his house, 6, 7, 8
30:3 the Lord thy God will *r.*
8 thou shalt *r.* and obey the L.
Jos. 22:8 *r.* with much riches
Jud. 7:3 whos. afraid, let him *r.*
11:31 when I *r.* from children
Ruth 1:6 that she might *r.* fr. M.
8 go *r.* to her mother's house
15 *r.* thou after sister-in-law
1 *Sam.* 6:3 in any wise *r.* him
9:5 Saul said, Come, let us *r.*
26:21 then said Saul, I sinned, *r.*
29:4 said, Make this fellow *r.* 7
2 *Sam.* 2:26 ere thou bid peo. *r.?*
3:16 then said A. to him, Go, *r.*
10:5 beards grown, *r.* 1 *Chr.* 19:5
15:19 goest thou with us? *r.*
20 I go whither I may, *r.* thou
24:13 see what answer I sh. *r.*
1 *K.* 2:32 L. shall *r.* his blood, 33
44 Lord sh. *r.* thy wickedness
8:48 *r.* to thee with all th. heart
12:24 *r.* every man to his house
26 now shall kingd. *r.* to Dav.
19:15 *r.* on thy way to wildern.
22:17 *r.* every man to his house
in peace, 2 *Chr.* 11:4; 18:16
28 if *r.* in peace, 2 *Chr.* 18:27
2 *K.* 18:14 I offended, *r.* from me
19:7 king of Assyria sh. *r.* to his
own land, 33; *Is.* 37:7, 34
20:10 let shadow *r.* backward
2 *Chr.* 6:24 *r.* confess thy name
10:9 may *r.* answer to this peo.
18:26 fellow in prison until I *r.*
30:6 *r.* to you; 9 ye *r.* unto him
Neh. 2:6 said, When wilt th. *r.?*
4:12 whence ye shall *r.* to us
Est. 9:25 device of Haman sh. *r.*
Job 1:21 naked shall I *r.* thither
6:29 *r.* yea, *r.* ag. my righteous.
7:10 sh. *r.* no more to his house
15:22 believeth not he shall *r.*
17:10 but as for ye all, do ye *r.*
22:23 if thou *r.* to Almighty
33:25 shall *r.* to days of youth
36:10 that they *r.* from iniquity
Ps. 6:4 *r.* O L. deliver my soul
10 let mine enemies *r.* asham.
7:7 for their sakes therefore *r.*
16 mischief *r.* upon own head
59:6 *r.* at even. 14 let them *r.*
73:10 theref. his people *r.* hith.
74:21 let not oppress. *r.* asham.
80:14 *r.* we beseech thee, O G.
90:3 sayest, *r.* ye child. of men
13 *r.* O Lord? how long?
94:15 judgment *r.* to righteous.
104:29 they die, *r.* to their dust
116:7 *r.* to thy rest, O my soul
Prov. 2:19 no. th. go unto her *r.*

26:27 rolleth a stone, it will *r.*
Ec. 1:7 riv. come, thither they *r.*
5:15 naked sh. *r.* to go as he ca.
12:2 nor clouds *r.* after the rain
7 dust shall *r.* spirit *r.* to God
Cant. 6:13 *r. r.* O Shulami. *r.*
Is. 6:13 yet in it a tenth shall *r.*
10:21 remnant of Jacob sh. *r.* 22
21:12 if ye will, inqu. ye, *r.* co.
35:10 ransomed of L. sh. *r.* 51:11
44:22 *r.* unto me, I redeem. thee
63:17 *r.* for thy servant's **sake**

Jer. 3:1 shall he *r.* ag. ? yet *r.* to
22 *r.* ye backsliding children
4:1 if thou *r.* saith L. *r.* unto
12:15 I will *r.* and have compa.
15:19 if thou wilt *r.* let them *r.*
unto thee, *r.* not unto them
18:11 *r.* ev. one fr. evil way, 35:15
24:7 shall *r.* with whole heart
30:10 Jacob shall *r.* 46:27
31:8 great comp. shall *r.* thither
36:3 *r.* every man from evil way
7 will *r.* ev. one from evil way
44:14 should *r.* into land of Ju.
50:9 none shall *r.* in vain
Ezek. 16:55 they desire to *r.* th.
thou and thy daugh. shall *r.*
18:23 wicked *r.* fr. ways and live
Dan. 10:20 will *r.* to fight Persia
11:9 *r.* into his own land, 10, 28
13 the king of the north sh. *r.*
29 time appointed he shall *r.*
30 he shall be grieved, and *r.*
Hos. 2:7 and *r.* to first husband
9 I will *r.* take corn and wine
3:5 afterward chil. of Israel *r.*
7:16 they *r.* but not to M. High
8:13 they shall *r.* to Egypt, 9:3
12:14 reproach shall L. *r.* to hi.
14:7 they under shadow shall *r.*
Joel 2:14 know. he will *r.* repent
3:4 will *r.* recomp. on head, 7
Ob. 15 reward *r.* upon thy head
Mic. 5:3 remn. of brethren sh. *r.*
Mal. 1:4 Edom saith, We will *r.*
3:7 *r.* to me, and I will *r.* to y.
18 *r.* and discern between rig.
Mat. 10:13 let your peace *r.*
12:44 *r.* into house, *Luke* 11:24
24:18 nor let him in field *r.*
Luke 8:39 *r.* to thine own house
Acts 15:16 I will *r.* and build
18:21 I will *r.* to you, if G. will

To RETURN.
Num. 14:3 not better to *r.* to Eg.
Deut. 17:16 cause peo. to *r.* to E.
Ruth 1:16 not to leave th. or to *r.*
1 *Sam.* 29:11 David rose ear. to *r.*
2 *Chr.* 10:6 coun. give ye to *r.* 9
Neh. 9:17 captain to *r.* to bondage
Jer. 5:3 they have refused to *r.*
8:5; *Hos.* 11:5
22:27 they desire to *r.* 44:14
29:10 in causing you to *r.* to th.
place, 30:3; 32:44; 33:7, 11,
26; 34:22; 42:12
34:11 caused servants to *r.* 16
Ezek. 21:30 cause to *r.* to sheath?
47:6 caused me to *r.* to the river
Hos. 11:5 bec. they refused to *r.*
Luke 19:12 rec. kingd. and to *r.*
Acts 13:34 no more to *r.* to corr.
20:3 pur. to *r.* thro' Macedonia

RETURN to, or unto t. Lord.
1 *Sam.* 7:3 *r.* u. t. L. wi. hea.
Is. 19:22 they shall *r.* unto t. L.
55:7 let him *r.* u. t. L. mercy
Hos. 6:1 let us *r.* unto the Lord
7:10 they do not *r.* unto the L.
14:1 O Is. *r.* u. t. L. hast fallen

Not RETURN.
Num. 32:18 will *not r.* to houses
1 *Sam.* 15:26 S. said, I will *not r.*
2 *Sam.* 12:23 go, he sh. *n. r.* to
1 *K.* 13:16 I may *not r.* with thee

Job 10:21 whe. I shall *not r.* 16:22
39:4 and *r. not* unto them
Is. 45:23 word gone out, sh. *n. r.*
55:11 it shall *not r.* to me void
Jer. 5:3 turn away, and *not r.* ?
15:7 destroy, since they *r. not*
22:11 shall *not r.* any more, 27
23:20 anger of L. sh. *not r.* 30:24
Ezek. 7:13 for seller shall *not r.*
13:22 sho. *n. r.* fr. wicked ways
21:5 sw. shall *not r.* into sheath
35:9 thy cities shall *not r.*
46:9 he sh. *not r.* by way he ca.
Hos. 7:10 they do *not r.* to Lord
11:5 he sh. *not r.* to land of Eg.
9 I will *not r.* to destroy Ephr.
Mat. 2:12 warned sh. *not r.* to H.
Luke 16:31 let him likewise *n. r.*

RETURNED.

Gen. 8:3 waters *r.* from off earth
9 dove *r.* to him ; 12 *r.* not ag.
43:18 because money *r.* in sacks
Ex. 14:27 sea *r.* to strength, 28
19:8 M. *r.* words of people to L.
Lev. 22:13 if she is *r.* to father's
Num. 24:25 Bal. rose, *r.* to place
Jos. 2:16 hide till pursu. be *r.* 22
4:18 waters of Jor. *r.* to th. pla.
Jud. 2:19 judge was dead th. *r.*
5:29 she *r.* answer to herself
11:39 Gid.'s daugh. *r.* to father
Ruth 1:22 so Naomi and Ruth *r.*
1 *Sam.* 17:57 D. *r.* from slaughter
25:39 Lord *r.* wickedness of Na.
2 *Sam.* 1:22 sw. of S. *r.* not emp.
3:16 said Ab. Return, and he *r.*
6:20 Da. *r.* to bless his househ.
16:8 L. *r.* on the blood of house
19:15 king *r.* and came to Jord.
23:10 peo. *r.* after him to spoil
1 *K.* 13:10 *r.* not by way he came
33 after this Jer. *r.* not fr. evil
2 *K.* 4:35 Elisha *r.* and walked
2 *Chr.* 25:10 *r.* home in anger
32:21 Senn. *r.* with shame face
Neh. 9:28 when they *r.* and cried
Ps. 35:13 prayer *r.* into bosom
78:34 they *r.* inquired after G.
Is. 38:8 the sun *r.* ten degrees
Jer. 3:7 turn to me, she *r.* not
14:3 they *r.* wi. vessels empty
40:12 the Jews *r.* out of place
Ezek. 1:14 living creatures ran, *r.*
8:17 *r.* to provoke me to anger
47:7 I *r.* lo, at bank of river
Dan. 4:34 understanding *r.* 36
Hos. 6:11 I *r.* captivity of people
Amos 4:6 yet not *r.* to me, 8, 11
Zec. 1:6 they *r.* and said, As L.
16 I am *r.* to Jer. with mercies
7:14 no man passed thro' nor *r.*
8:3 I am *r.* to Zion, will dwell
Mat. 21:18 as he *r.* into city
Mark 14:40 *r.* found them asleep
Luke 2:20 sheph. *r.* glorifying G.
4:14 Jesus *r.* in power of Spirit
8:37 went into ship, and *r.* back
17:18 that *r.* to give glory to G.
19:15 *r.* having received kingd.
23:48 smote breasts, and *r.*
24:9 *r.* fr. sepulchre and told all
52 worshipped, *r.* to Jerusal.
Acts 8:25 apostles *r.* to Jerusal.
13:13 and John *r.* to Jerusalem
21:6 took ship, they *r.* home
Gal. 1:17 I *r.* ag. unto Damascus
Heb. 11:15 opportunity to have *r.*
1 *Pet.* 2:25 *r.* to Sheph. of souls

RETURNETH.

Ps. 146:4 breath goeth, *r.* to ear.
Prov. 26:11 as dog *r.* so a fool *r.*
Ec. 1:6 wind *r.* accord. to circu.
Is. 55:10 rain *r.* not thither, but
Ezek. 35:7 that *r.* I will cut off
Zec. 9:8 encamp bec. of him *r.*

RETURNING.

Is. 30:15 in *r.* rest ye be saved

Luke 7:10 *r.* found servant whole
Acts 8:28 *r.* sitting in chariot
Heb. 7:1 Abra. *r.* from slaughter

REUBEN.

Gen. 29:32 called his name R.
30:14 R. went in the days of
35:22 R. went and lay with Bil.
23 sons of Leah, R. Ja.'s 46:8 ;
49:3 ; *Num.* 26:5 ; 1 *Chr.* 5:1
37:22 R. said, Shed no blood, 29
46:9 sons of R. *Ex.* 6:14 ; *Num.*
16:1 ; 32:1, 37 ; *Deut.* 11:6 ;
Jos. 4:12 ; 1 *Chr.* 5:3, 18
Num. 2:10 of camp of R. 10:18
7:30 prince of children of R.
32:33 child. of R. *Jos.* 13:23
Deut. 27:13 mount E. to curse, R.
33:6 let R. live, and let not his
Jos. 15:6 Boh. son of R. 18:17
22:13 Is. sent to children of R.
Jud. 5:15 divisions of R. 16
Ezek. 48:6 a portion for R. 31

Tribe of REUBEN.

Num. 1:5 of *t. of* R. Elizur, 21
13:4 of *tribe of* R. Shammua
34:14 *tribe of* R. have received
Jos. 20:8 ; 21:36 ; 1 *Chr.* 6:63, 78
Rev. 7:5 *tribe of* R. sealed 12,000

REUBENITES.

Num. 26:7 are the families of R.
Deut. 3:12, 16 ; 29:8 ; *Jos.* 12:6 ;
13:8
Jos. 1:12 Josh. spake to R. 22:1
2 *K.* 10:33 Hazael smote the R.

REVEAL.

Job 20:27 heaven sh. *r.* iniquity
Jer. 33:6 *r.* them abund. of peace
Dan. 2:47 couldest *r.* this secret
Mat. 11:27 he to whomsoever
Son will *r.* him, *Lu.* 10:22
Gal. 1:16 called by grace to *r.* S.
Phil. 3:15 God sh. *r.* this unto y.

REVEALED.

Deut. 29:29 things *r.* to us
1 *Sam.* 3:7 word of Lord *r.* to h.
21 L. *r.* himself to Sam. in Sh.
2 *Sam.* 7:27 hast *r.* to thy serv.
Is. 22:14 *r.* in mine ears by L.
23:1 fr. Chittim it is *r.* to them
40:5 glory of the Lord sh. be *r.*
Is. 53:1 arm of L. *r.* ? *John* 12:38
56:1 righteousness near to be *r.*
Jer. 11:20 unto thee I *r.* my cau.
Dan. 2:19 th. was secret *r.* to D.
10:1 a thing was *r.* to Daniel
Mat. 10:26 nothing covered that
shall not be *r. Luke* 12:2
11:25 *r.* th. to babes, *Luke* 10:21
16:17 flesh and blood hath not *r.*
Luke 2:26 *r.* to Simeon by H. G.
35 thoughts of many hearts *r.*
17:30 day when Son of man is *r.*
Rom. 1:17 therein right. of G. *r.*
18 wrath of God is *r.* fr. heav.
8:18 glory which sh. be *r.* in us
1 *Cor.* 2:10 God *r.* them to us
3:13 bec. it shall be *r.* by fire
14:30 if any thing be *r.* to ano.
Gal. 3:23 faith whi. should be *r.*
Eph. 3:5 now *r.* to holy apostles
2 *Thes.* 1:7 when L. J. shall be *r.*
2:3 and that man of sin be *r.*
6 he might be *r.* in his time
8 wick. one *r.* whom L. cons.
1 *Pet.* 1:5 to be *r.* in last time
12 unto whom it was *r.*
4:13 when his glory shall be *r.*
5:1 partaker of g. that sh. be *r.*

REVEALER.

Dan. 2:47 G. of gods, *r.* of secrets

REVEALETH.

Prov. 11:13 talebea. *r.* sec. 20:19
Dan. 2:22 *r.* deep and secret th.
28 G. in heaven that *r.* secrets
29 *r.* secrets maketh known

Amos 3:7 *r.* secrets to prophets

REVELATION.

Rom. 2:5 *r.* of judgment of God
16:25 according to *r.* of mystery
1 *Cor.* 14:6 sh. speak to you by *r.*
26 every one of you hath a *r.*
Gal. 1:12 by *r.* of Jesus Christ
2:2 went up by *r.* and commu.
Eph. 1:17 may give you sp. of *r.*
3:3 by *r.* he made known to me
1 *Pet.* 1:13 grace br. at *r.* of J. C.
Rev. 1:1 *r.* of J. C. wh. God gave

REVELATIONS.

2 *Cor.* 12:1 come to visions and *r.*
7 exalted thro. abundance of *r.*

REVELLINGS.

Gal. 5:21 works of the fle. are *r.*
1 *Pet.* 4:3 ye walked in lusts, *r.*

REVENGE, ED, ETH.

Jer. 20:10 we shall take *r.* on h.
Ezek. 25:12 Ed. *r.* himself on th.
15 Philistines have dealt by *r.*
Nah. 1:2 the Lord *r.* the Lord *r.*
2 *Cor.* 7:11 what *r.* is wr. in you

REVENGER, S.

Num. 35:19 *r.* sh. slay murde. 21
24 judge between slayer and *r.*
27 if *r.* find him and *r.* kill
2 *Sam.* 14:11 wouldest not suf. *r.*
Rom. 13:4 minister of God, a *r.*

REVENGING.

Ps. 79:10 by the *r.* of the blood

REVENUE.

Ezr. 4:13 thou sh. endamage *r.*
Prov. 8:19 my *r.* better than sil.
Is. 23:3 harvest of river is her *r.*

REVENUES.

Prov. 15:6 in *r.* of wick. is trou.
16:8 a little is better than gr. *r.*
Jer. 12:13 be ashamed of your *r.*

REVERENCE, Verb.

Lev. 19:30 *r.* sanct. I am L. 26:2
Est. 3:2 king's serv. *r.* Haman
Mat. 21:37 they will *r.* my son,
Mark 12:6 ; *Luke* 20:13
Eph. 5:33 wife that she *r.* husb.

REVERENCE.

2 *Sam.* 9:6 Mephibosh. did *r.* Da.
1 *K.* 1:31 Bathsheba did *r.* king
Est. 3:2 Mord. did him not *r.* 5
Ps. 89:7 to be had in *r.* of all
Heb. 12:9 and we gave them *r.*
28 we may serve God with *r.*

REVEREND.

Ps. 111:9 holy and *r.* is his name

REVERSE.

Num. 23:20 he blessed, I can. *r.*
Est. 8:5 let it be written to *r.*
8 with king's ring, no man *r.*

REVILE.

Ex. 22:28 thou shalt not *r.* gods
Mat. 5:11 blessed when men *r.*

REVILED.

Mat. 27:39 that passed by *r.* him
Mark 15:32 that were crucified *r.*
John 9:28 they *r.* him, and said
1 *Cor.* 4:12 being *r.* we bless
1 *Pet.* 2:23 when he was *r.* not

REVILERS.

1 *Cor.* 6:10 nor *r.* inh. king. of G.

REVILEST.

Acts 23:4 *r.* God's high-priest

REVILINGS.

Is. 51:7 neither afraid of their *r.*
Zep. 2:8 *r.* of child. of Ammon

REVIVE.

Neh. 4:2 will they *r.* the stones ?
Ps. 85:6 wilt th. not *r.* us again
138:7 thou wilt *r.* me, th. shalt
Is. 57:15 *r.* spirit and to *r.* heart
of contrite ones
Hos. 6:2 after days will he *r.* us
14:7 they shall *r.* as corn

Hab. 3:2 O Lord, *r.* thy work in

REVIVED.

Gen. 45:27 the spirit of Jacob *r.*
Jud. 15:19 spirit came ag. he *r.*
1 *K.* 17:22 soul of child ca. he *r.*
2 *K.* 13:21 touch. bones of Eli. *r.*
Rom. 7:9 command. came. sin *r.*
14:9 Ch. both died, rose, and *r.*

REVIVING

Ezr. 9:8 to give us a little *r.* 9

REVOLT.

Is. 59:13 speaking oppres. and *r.*

REVOLT, Verb.

2 *Chr.* 21:10 same time did Li. *r.*
Is. 1:5 ye will *r.* more and more

REVOLTED.

2 *K.* 8:20 Edom *r.* 22 : 2 *Chr.* 21:8
22 Libnah *r.* at the same time
Is. 31:6 Israel have deeply *r.*
Jer. 5:23 people are *r.* and gone

REVOLTERS.

Jer. 6:28 all grievous *r.* walking
Hos. 5:2 *r.* are profound to make
9:15 love no more, princes *r.*

REVOLTING.

Jer. 5:23 this peo. hath a *r.* hea.

REWARD, Substantive.

Gen. 15:1 Ab. I am thy great *r.*
Num. 18:31 it is your *r.* for serv.
Deut. 10:17 G. who taketh not *r.*
27:25 cursed that tak. *r.* to slay
Ruth 2:12 a full *r.* be given of L.
2 *Sam.* 4:10 wd. have giv. him *r.*
19:36 king recompense such a *r.*
1 *K.* 13:7 I will give thee a *r.*
Job 6:22 Bring me or give a *r.*
7:2 hireling look. for *r.* of work
Ps. 15:5 nor taketh *r.* ag. innoc.
19:11 keeping of them is gre. *r.*
40:15 let them be desolate for *r.*
58:11 there is a *r.* for righteous
70:3 let th. be turned back for *r.*
91:8 shalt see the *r.* of wicked
94:2 render a *r.* to the proud
119:20 let this be *r.* of adversa.
127:3 fruit of womb is his *r.*
Prov. 11:18 righteousn. a sure *r.*
21:14 a *r.* in bosom st. wrath
24:14 then there shall be a *r.*
20 shall be no *r.* to evil **man**
Ec. 4:9 they have a good *r.*
9:5 nei. have they any more *r.*
Is. 3:11 the *r.* of hands be given
5:23 which justify wicked for *r.*
40:10 his *r.* is with him, 62:11
45:13 go my captives, not for *r.*
Jer. 40:5 capt. gave Jeremiah *r.*
Ezek. 16:34 givest *r.* no *r.* given
Hos. 9:1 thou hast loved a *r.*
Ob. 15 thy *r.* shall return upon
Mic. 3:11 judge for *r.* priests
7:3 and judge asketh for a *r.*
Mat. 5:12 *r.* in heaven, *Luke* 6:23
46 love you, what *r.* have ye ?
6:1 ye have no *r.* of your Father
2 they have their *r.* 5, 16
10:41 sh. receive a prophet's *r.*
sh. receive a right. man's *r.*
42 no wise lose *r.* *Mark* 9:41
Luke 6:35 your *r.* shall be great
23:41 we receive due *r.* of deeds
Acts 1:18 field with *r.* of iniqui.
Rom 4:4 to him that work. is *r.*
1 *Cor.* 3:8 man sh. receive his *r.*
14 abide, he shall receive a *r.*
9:17 if willingly, I have a *r.* 18
Col. 2:18 no man beg. you of *r.*
3:24 ye sh. receive *r.* of inherit.
1 *Tim.* 5:18 laborer worthy of *r.*
Heb. 2:2 recei. just recomp. of *r.*
10:35 great recompense of *r.*
11:26 he had respect to the *r.*
2 *Pet.* 2:13 shall receive the *r.* of
2 *John* 8 that we receive a full *r.*
Jude 11 after error of Bal. for *r.*

Rev. 11:18 thou shouldest give *r.*
22:12 I come quickly, my *r.* is

REWARD, Verb.

Deut. 32:41 and I will *r.* **them**
1 *Sam.* 24:19 Lord *r.* thee good
2 *Sam.* 3:39 L. sh. *r.* doer of evil
2 *Chr.* 20:11 behold how th. *r.* us
Ps. 54:5 shall *r.* evil to enemies
Prov. 25:22 the L. shall *r.* thee
Hos. 4:9 and I will *r.* them their
Mat. 6:4 Father sh. *r.* thee, 6:18
16:27 he shall *r.* every man
2 *Tim.* 4:14 Lord *r.* him accord.
Rev. 18:6 *r.* her, even as she rew.

REWARDED.

Gen. 44:4 wheref. have ye *r.* evil
1 *Sam.* 24:17 th. *r.* good, I *r.* evil
2 *Sam.* 22:21 L. *r.* me ac. *Ps.* 18:20
2 *Chr.* 15:7 your work shall be *r.*
Ps. 7:4 if I have *r.* evil to him
35:12 th. *r.* evil for good, 109:5
103:10 nor *r.* us accord. to iniq.
Prov. 13:13 feareth com. be *r.*
Is. 3:9 they have *r.* evil to them.
Jer. 31:16 work sh. be *r.* saith L.
Rev. 18:6 even as she *r.* you

REWARDER.

Heb. 11:6 a *r.* of them that seek

REWARDETH.

Job 21:19 he *r.* him, sh. know it
Ps. 31:23 plentifully *r.* proud
137:8 happy he that *r.* thee, as
Prov. 17:13 whoso *r.* evil for go.
6:10 both *r.* fool and *r.* transgr.

REWARDS.

Num. 22:7 with *r.* divination
Is. 1:23 every one followeth *r.*
Dan. 2:6 rec. of me gifts, and *r.*
5:17 said, give thy *r.* to another
Hos. 2:12 these are my *r.*

REZIN.

2 *K.* 15:37 R. the king, 16:5 ;
Is. 7:1
16:6 R. recovered Elath to, 9
Ezr. 2:48 childr. of R. *Neh.* 7:50
Is. 7:4 the fierce anger of R. 8
8:6 as this people rejoice in R.
9:11 set up the adversaries of R.

RHEGIUM.

Acts 28:13 comp. and came to R.

RHESA.

Luke 3:27 who was the son of R.

RHODA.

Acts 12:13 to hearken named R.

RHODES.

Acts 21:1 we came unto R.

RIB, S.

Gen. 2:21 God took one of his *r.*
22 the *r.* which God had taken
2 *Sam.* 3:23 sm. A. under fifth *r.*
3:27 J. smote Ab. under fifth *r.*
4:6 smote Ishbosh. under fifth *r.*
20:10 J. smote Ama. un. fifth *r.*
Dan. 7:5 beast had *r.* in mouth

RIBBAND.

Num. 15:38 on fring. of bord. a *r.*

RICH.

Gen. 13:2 Abram was *r.* in cattle
14:23 lest say, I ha. made A. *r.*
Ex. 30:15 *r.* shall not give more
Lev. 25:47 if a stranger wax *r.*
Ruth 3:10 fol. not men poor or *r.*
1 *Sam.* 2:7 L. maketh poor and *r.*
2 *Sam.* 12:1 two men in city, 1 *r.*
Job 15:29 he shall not be *r.* nei.
34:19 nor regardeth the *r.* more
Ps. 45:12 *r.* shall entreat favor
49:2 hear this, both *r.* and poor
16 be not afraid when one is *r.*
Prov. 10:4 hand of dilig. mak. *r.*
22 blessing of Lord, maketh *r.*
13:7 there is that mak. hims. *r.*
14:20 the *r.* hath many friends
18:23 the *r.* answereth roughly

21:17 lov. wine and oil not *r.*
22:2 *r.* and poor meet together
7 the *r.* ruleth over the poor
16 giveth to *r.* shall come to
23:4 labor not to be *r.* cease
28:6 perverse, though he be *r.*
20 he maketh haste to be *r.* 22
Ec. 5:12 abund. of *r.* not suffer
10:6 and the *r.* sit in low place
20 curse not *r.* in thy bedcham.
Is. 53:9 and with *r.* in his death
Jer. 5:27 are great and waxen *r.*
Hos. 12:8 Ephraim said, I am *r.*
Zec. 11:5 bless. be L. for I am *r.*
Mark 12:41 many that were *r.*
Luke 1:53 the *r.* he sent away
6:24 woe unto you that are *r.*
12:21 that is not *r.* toward God
14:12 call not thy *r.* neighbors
16:23 sorrowful, he was very *r.*
Rom. 10:12 same Lord is *r.* to all
1 *Cor.* 4:8 are full. now ye are *r.*
2 *Cor.* 6:10 yet making many *r.*
8:9 *r.* yet poor, ye might be *r.*
Eph. 2:4 God who is *r.* in mercy
1 *Tim.* 6:9 they th. will be *r.* fall
17 charge th. that are *r.* in this
18 and be *r.* in good works
Jam. 1:10 let the *r.* rejoice in th.
2:5 G. chosen poor, *r.* in faith ?
Rev. 2:9 I know poor. thou art *r.*
3:17 bec. thou sayest I am *r.* and
13:16 he causeth the *r.* and poor
18:19 made *r.* all that had ships

RICH man, or men.

2 *Sam.* 12:2 *r.* *man* had many fl.
Job 27:19 *r.* *man* shall lie down
Prov. 10:15 *r.* *man's* wealth is
his strong city, 18:11
28:11 *r.* man is wise in his own
Jer. 9:23 let not the *r.* man glory
Mic. 6:12 *r.* men thereof are full
Mat. 19:23 *r.* m. sh. hardly enter
24 than a *r.* m. to enter kingd.
of God, *Mark* 10:25; *Lu.* 18:25
27:57 a *r.* man of Arimathea
Luke 12:16 ground of *r.* man bro.
16:1 a certain *r.* m. had a stew.
19 a *r.* man was clo. in purple
21:1 and saw the *r.* man casting
Jam. 1:11 so shall the *r.* m. fade
2:6 do not *r.* men oppress you ?
5:1 ye *r.* men, weep and howl
Rev. 6:15 *r.* men hid themselves

RICHER.

Dan. 11:2 the fourth sh. be far *r.*

RICHES.

Gen. 31:16 the *r.* G. hath taken
36:7 *r.* more than they might
Jos. 22:8 return with much *r.*
1 *Sam.* 17:25 enrich with great *r.*
1 *K.* 3:11 neither hast asked *r.*
2 *Chr.* 1:11
13 giv. thee both *r.* and honor
10:23 Solom. exceeded all kings
of earth for *r.* 2 *Chr.* 9:22
1 *Chr.* 29:12 *r.* and honor come
28 David died full of days, *r.*
2 *Chr.* 17:5 *r.* and honor, 18:1
20:25 found *r.* with dead bodies
32:27 Hezek. had exceeding *r.*
Est. 1:4 showed *r.* of kingdom
5:11 Haman told them of his *r.*
Job 20:15 he swallowed down *r.*
36:19 will he esteem thy *r.* ?
Ps. 37:16 bet. than *r.* of wicked
39:6 heapeth up *r.* knoweth not
49:6 boast themselves in th. *r.*
52:7 trusted in abund. of his *r.*
62:10 if *r.* increase, set not heart
73:12 ungodly prosper, incr. *r.*
104:24 O Lord, earth is full of *r.*
112:3 wealth and *r.* in his house
119:14 rejo. as much as in all *r.*
Prov. 3:16 in her left hand *r.*
8:18 *r.* and honor are with me

11:4 *r.* profit not in day of wra.
16 wom. honor, strong men *r.*
28 he that trust. in *r.* shall fall
13:7 himself poor, hath great *r.*
8 ransom of man's life his *r.*
14:24 crown of wise is their *r.*
19:14 *r.* are inheritance of fath.
22:1 good name rather than *r.*
4 by the fear of the Lord are *r.*
16 oppres. poor to increase *r.*
23:5 for *r.* make themselves wi.
24:4 cham. be filled with all *r.*
27:24 for *r.* are not for ever
30:8 gi. me nei. poverty nor *r.*
Ec. 4:8 nor his eyes sati. with *r.*
5:13 even *r.* kept for owners
19 man whom G. given *r.* 6:2
9:11 nor yet *r.* to men of under.
Is. 8:4 *r.* of Damasc. taken away
10:14 hand found as a nest *r.*
30:6 carry their *r.* on yo. asses
45:3 I will give thee hidden *r.*
61:6 ye shall eat *r.* of Gentiles
Jer. 9:23 let not rich man gl. in *r.*
17:11 he that get. *r.* not by rig.
48:36 *r.* he hath gotten perished
Ezek. 26:12 make a spoil of thy *r.*
28:4 with understanding got. *r.*
5 by thy traffic increased *r.*
Dan. 11:2 thro' his *r.* sh. stir up
24 scat. am. prey, spoil and *r.*
28 then shall he return with *r.*
Mat. 13:22 deceitful. of *r.* choke
word, *Mark* 4:19; *Luke* 8:14
Mark 10:23 hardly th. that ha. *r.*
24 them that trust in *r.* to enter. *Luke* 18:24
Luke 16:11 who will commit *r.* ?
Rom. 2:4 or despiseth thou *r.* ?
9:23 make kn. *r.* of his glory
11:12 if fall of them be the *r.*
33 O the *r.* of the wisd. of God
2 *Cor.* 8:2 to *r.* of their liberality
Eph. 1:7 redemption accor. to *r.*
Eph. 1:18 *r.* of glory of inherita.
2:7 exceeding *r.* of his grace
3:8 I should preach unsearch. *r.*
16 grant you accord. to the *r.*
Phil. 4:19 accord. to *r.* in glory
Col. 1:27 what *r.* of the glory
1 *Tim.* 6:17 nor trust in uncer. *r.*
Heb. 11:26 repro. of C. greater *r.*
Jam. 5:2 your *r.* are corrupted
Rev. 5:12 worthy Lamb to rec. *r.*
18:17 great *r.* come to naught

RICHLY

Col. 3:16 let word of C. dwell *r.*
1 *Tim.* 6:17 God who giveth *r.*

RID

Gen. 37:22 that he might *r.* him
Ex. 6:6 *r.* you out of bondage
Lev. 26:6 *r.* evil beasts out land
Ps. 82:4 *r.* them out of wicked
144:7 *r.* me, and deliver me, 11

RIDDANCE

Lev. 23:22 th. shalt not make *r.*
Zep. 1:18 shall make speedy *r.*

RIDDEN

Num. 22:30 ass, wh. thou ha. *r.* ?

RIDDLE

Jud. 14:12 Sam. said, I will now
put forth a *r.* to you, 13–19
Ezek. 17:2 put forth a *r.* speak.

RIDE

Gen. 41:43 made him *r.* in char.
Deut. 32:13 made him *r.* on high
Jud. 5:10 that *r.* on white asses
2 *Sam.* 16:2 king's hous. to *r.* on
19:26 saddle ass that I may *r.*
1 *K.* 1:33 cause Solo. to *r.* 38, 44
2 *K.* 10:16 so th. made him to *r.*
Job 30:22 thou causest me to *r.*
Ps. 45:4 and in thy majesty *r.*
66:12 thou hast caused me to *r.*
Is. 30:16 we will *r.* upon swift
58:14 I will cause thee to *r.*

Jer. 6:23 *r.* on horses, 50:42
Hos. 10:11 will make Eph. to *r.*
14:3 we will not *r.* upon horses
Hab. 3:8 didst *r.* upon thy horses
Hag. 2:22 overthrow those th. *r.*

RIDER.

Gen. 49:17 so that *r.* shall fall
Ex. 15:1 horse and *r.* thrown, 21
Job 39:18 scorneth horse and *r.*
Jer. 51:21 *r.* break in pieces cha.
Zec. 12:4 smite *r.* with madness

RIDERS.

2 *K.* 18:23 if thou be able to set
on them, *Is.* 36:8
Est. 8:10 he sent letters by *r.*
Hag. 2:22 horses and *r.* co. down
Zec. 10:5 *r.* shall be confounded

RIDETH.

Deut. 33:26 who *r.* upon heaven
Est. 6:8 horse king *r.* upon
Ps. 68:4 extol him that *r.* 23
Is. 19:1 the L*r*. on a swift cloud
Amos 2:15 neither shall he that *r.*

RIDING.

2 *K.* 4:24 slack not thy *r.* for me
Jer. 17:25 kings enter *r.* 22:4
Ezek. 23:6 horsem. *r.* on hors. 12
23 all of them *r.* upon horses
38:15 thou and many people *r.*
Zec. 1:8 a man *r.* on a red horse
9:9 thy king com. unto thee *r.*

RIDGES.

Ps. 65:10 thou waterest *r.* thereof

RIFLED.

Zec. 14:2 houses *r.* wom. ravish.

RIGHT, Substantive.

Gen. 18:25 shall not the Judge
of all the earth do *r.* ?
Deut. 21:17 *r.* of first-born is his
Ruth 4:6 redeem thou my *r.*
2 *Sam.* 19:43 we ha. also more *r.*
Neh. 9:33 for thou hast done *r.*
Job 34:6 should I lie ag. my *r.* ?
17 sh. he th. hateth *r.* govern ?
36:6 he giveth *r.* to the poor
Ps. 9:4 hast maintained my *r.*
17:1 hear *r.* O Lo. attend to cry
140:12 L. maintain *r.* of poor
Prov. 16:8 great reve. without *r.*
13 they love him that speak. *r.*
Is. 10:2 to take away *r.* from
32:7 dest. when needy speak. *r.*
Jer. 5:28 *r.* of needy do not jud.
17:11 getteth riches not by *r.*
32:7 *r.* of redemption is thi. 8
Lam. 3:35 turn aside *r.* of man
Ezek. 21:27 he come whose *r.* it
Amos 5:12 turn poor from th. *r.*
Mal. 3:5 turn strang. from his *r.*
Heb. 13:10 they have no *r.* to eat
Rev. 22:14 have *r.* to tree of life

RIGHT, Adjective.

Gen. 24:48 L. led me in *r.* way
Deut. 32:4 G. of truth, just and *r.*
1 *Sam.* 12:23 teach you *r.* way
2 *Sam.* 15:3 matter good and *r.*
2 *K.* 10:15 is thy heart *r.* as my ?
Ezr. 8:21 seek of him a *r.* way
Neh. 9:13 then gavest *r.* judgm.
Job 6:25 how forc. are *r.* words !
34:23 not lay on man mo. th. *r.*
35:2 thinkest thou th. to be *r.* ?
Ps. 19:8 stat. of the Lord are *r.*
45:6 sceptre of thy king. *r.* sce.
51:10 O G. renew a *r.* sp. in me
107:7 led them forth by *r.* way
119:75 judgm. *r.* 128 precepts
Prov. 4:11 led thee in *r.* paths
8:6 opening of my lips sh. be *r.*
9 *r.* to them that find knowle.
12:5 thoughts of righteous are *r.*
14:12 way wh. seemeth *r.* 16:25
20:11 whether his work be *r.*
24:26 that giveth a *r.* answer
Ec. 4:4 I consid. every *r.* work

Is. 30:10 proph. not to us *r.* thin.
45:19 L. dec. things that are *r.*
Jer. 2:21 planted thee *r.* seed
23:10 and their force is not *r.*
34:15 had done *r.* in my sight
Hos. 14:9 ways of the Lord are *r.*
Amos 3:10 th. know not to do *r.*
Mark 5:15 his *r.* mind, *Luke* 8:35
Acts 4:19 whe. *r.* in sight of God
8:21 heart is not *r.* in sig. of G.
13:10 not cease to perv. *r.* ways

Is RIGHT.

Ex. 15:26 do that which is *r.*
Deut. 6:18 thou shalt do that is
r. 12:25; 21:9
12:8 what is *r.* in own eyes
1 *K.* 11:33 walked to do that *r.* 38
2 *K.* 10:30 that is *r.* in my eyes
Job 42:7 not spoken that is *r.* 8
Ps. 33:4 word of the Lord is *r.*
Prov. 12:15 way of the fool is *r.*
21:2 way of man is *r.* in his eyes
8 for pure, his work is *r.*
Ezek. 18:5 if a man do that is *r.*
19 done that is *r.* and kept
my stat. 21:27; 33:14, 16, 19
Mat. 20:4 what. is *r.* I will gi. 7.
Luke 12:57 judge ye not wh. *r.* ?
Eph. 6:1 obey par. in L. this is *r.*

Was RIGHT.

Jud. 17:6 ev. man did that which
was *r.* in own eyes, 21:25
1 *K.* 15:11 Asa did *r.* 2 *Chr.* 14:2
22:43 Jehos. did *r.* 2 *Chr.* 20:32
2 *K.* 12:2 Jeh. did *r.* 2 *Chr.* 24:2
14:3 Amaziah did *r.* 2 *Chr.* 25:2
15:3 Azariah did *r.* 2 *Chr.* 26:4
34 Jotham did *r.* 2 *Chr.* 27:2
16:2 A. did not *r.* in sight of L.
18:3 Hezekiah did *r.* 2 *Chr.* 29:2
22:2 Josiah did *r.* 2 *Chr.* 34:2
1 *Chr.* 13:4 was *r.* in eyes of peo.
Job 32:2 pervert. that wh. w. *r.*
Ps. 78:37 heart was not *r.*
Jer. 17:16 came out of lips w. *r.*

RIGHT.

Jos. 3:16 people passed *r.* ag. J.

RIGHT corner.

2 *K.* 11:11 guard stood rou. *r.* c.

See FOOT, HAND.

RIGHT, HAND.

RIGHT forth.

Jer. 49:5 be driven eve. man *r. f.*

RIGHT well.

Ps. 139:14 soul knoweth *r.* well

RIGHTEOUS.

Gen. 7:1 thee ha. I seen *r.* be. me
18:23 wilt destroy *r.* with wic. ?
24 if th. be 50 *r.* wilt thou ? 26
25 be far from thee to slay *r.*
20:4 L. wilt thou slay a *r.* nati.
38:26 said, She more *r.* than I
Ezr. 23:7 innocent and *r.* sl. not
Num. 23:10 let me die death of *r.*
Deut. 4:8 nation ha. judg. so *r.*
25:1 shall justify *r.* 2 *Chr.* 6:23
Jud. 5:11 *r.* acts, 1 *Sam.* 12:7
1 *Sam.* 24:17 thou more *r.* than I
2 *Sam.* 4:11 wick. slain *r.* person
1 *K.* 2:32 fell on two men more *r.*
8:32 justifying *r.* to give him
2 *K.* 10:9 Jehu said to peo. Be *r.*
Ezr. 9:15 G. of Israel *r.* *Neh.* 9:8
Job 4:7 where were *r.* cut off ?
9:15 tho' I we. *r.* would not an.
10:15 if I be *r.* not lift up head
15:14 what is man, he be *r.* ?
17:9 *r.* also sh. hold on his w.
22:3 is it pleas. to A. th. art *r.* ?
19 *r.* see it, glad, *Ps.* 107:42
23:7 *r.* might dispute with him
32:1 he was *r.* in his own eyes

Job 34:5 Job hath said, I am *r.*
35:7 if thou be *r.* what giv. thou
36:7 wit. not eyes fr. *r.* *Ps.* 34:15
40:8 cond. me that thou be *r.*

Ps. 1:5 nor sinners in cong. of *r.*
6 Lord knoweth way of the *r.*
5:12 wilt bless *r.* with favor
7:9 *r.* G. trieth hearts and reins
11 G. judg. *r.* angry wi. wicked
11:3 what can *r.* do? 5 L. tri. *r.*
14:5 God is in generation of *r.*
19:9 judgments of L. are true
    and *r.* 119:7, 62, 106, 160, 164
31:18 lips speak against the *r.*
32:11 be glad in Lord, rej. ye *r.*
33:1 rejoice in L. O ye *r.* 97:12
34:17 *r.* cry, L. heareth them
19 ma. are the afflictions of *r.*
21 that hate *r.* sh. be desolate
35:27 glad that favor *r.* cause
37:17 but Lord upholdeth the *r.*
21 but the *r.* showeth mercy
25 have I not seen *r.* forsaken
30 mouth of *r.* speaketh wisd.
32 wicked watch *r.* to slay him
39 salvation of the *r.* is of Lo.
52:6 *r.* also shall see, fear, laugh
55:22 never suff. *r.* to be moved
58:10 *r.* rejoice, he seeth veng.
11 there is a reward for the *r.*
64:10 *r.* shall be glad in the L.
68:3 let *r.* be glad, let them rej.
69:28 let them not be wri. wi. *r.*
72:7 in his days sh. *r.* flourish
94:21 gather against soul of *r.*
112:4 L. full of compas. *r.* 116:5
6 *r.* be in everl. remembrance
118:15 rejoicing in tabern. of *r.*
20 gate, into which *r.* sh. ent.
119:106 keep thy *r.* judgments
137 *r.* art thou, O L. *Jer.* 12:1
138 thy testimonials are *r.*
125:3 rod of wicked sh. not rest
    on *r.* lest *r.* put forth hands
140:13 *r.* give thanks to thy na.
141:5 let *r.* smite, kindness
142:7 *r.* shall compass me about
145:17 Lord *r.* in all his ways
146:8 Lord loveth *r.* preserveth
Prov. 2:7 layeth up wisd. for *r.*
20 mayest keep paths of *r.*
10:3 will not suffer *r.* to famish
16 labor of *r.* tendeth to life
21 the lips of the *r.* feed many
24 desire of *r.* shall be granted
25 *r.* is an everlasting founda.
28 hope of *r.* sh. be gladness
30 *r.* shall never be removed
32 lips of *r.* kn. what is accep.
11:8 *r.* is deliv. out of trouble.
10 well with *r.* city rejoiceth
21 seed of *r.* shall be delivered
23 desire of the *r.* is only good
28 *r.* shall flourish as a branch
31 *r.* be recompensed in earth
12:3 root of *r.* sh. not be moved
5 thoughts of the *r.* are right
7 house of the *r.* shall stand
12 root of the *r.* yieldeth fruit
26 *r.* is more excel. than neigh.
13:9 light of the *r.* rejoiceth
21 to *r.* good shall be repaid
25 *r.* eat. to satisfying of soul
14:9 among the *r.* there is favor
32 the *r.* hath hope in his dea.
15:6 in house of *r.* is much tre.
19 way of the *r.* is made plain
28 heart of *r.* studieth to ans.
29 he heareth the prayer of *r.*
18:5 not good to overthrow *r.*
10 *r.* runneth into it, is safe
21:18 shall be ransom for *r.*
26 *r.* giveth and spareth not
23:24 fath. of *r.* greatly rejoice
24:15 lay not wait ag. dwe. of *r.*
24 saith to wicked, Thou art *r.*
28:1 wicked flee, but *r.* bold
10 causeth *r.* to go astray
28 when wicked perish, *r.* inc.
29:2 *r.* in authority peo. rejoice
6 the *r.* doth sing and rejoice
7 *r.* considereth cause of poor

16 the *r.* shall see their fall
Ec. 3:17 G. judge *r.* and wicked
7:16 be not *r.* overmuch
9:1 *r.* and wise in hand of God
2 one event to *r.* and wicked
Is. 3:10 say to *r.* it be well
24:16 heard songs, glory to *r.*
26:2 open ye, that *r.* may enter
41:26 declared, we say, He is *r.*
53:11 *r.* serv. shall justify many
57:1 *r.* peri. *r.* taken from evil
60:21 people also shall be all *r.*
Jer. 12:1 *r.* art thou, O L. I plead
20:12 O Lord of hosts triest *r.*
Ezek. 13:22 with lies made *r.* sad
21:3 cut off *r.* and wicked, 4
Ezek. 21:13 wh. I say to *r.* he sh.
Amos 2:6 they sold *r.* for silver
Hab. 1:4 wicked comp. about *r.*
13 wicked devou. him more *r.*
Mal. 3:18 discern between *r.* and
Mat. 9:13 not come to call the *r.*

Mark 2:17; *Luke* 5:32
13:43 *r.* shine forth as sun
23:28 outwardly ap. *r.* to men
25:46 *r.* sh. go into life eternal
Luke 1:6 they were both *r.* bef. G.
18:9 trusted they were *r.*
John 7:24 judge not by ap. but *r.*
17:25 O *r.* F. world not known
Rom. 2:5 revel. of *r.* judg. of G.
3:10 there is none *r.* no not one
5:19 obed. of one, many made *r.*
2 *Tim.* 4:8 *r.* Judge shall give
Heb. 11:4 obt. witness he was *r.*
1 *Pet.* 3:12 eyes of L. are over *r.*
4:18 if *r.* scarcely be saved
2 *Pet.* 2:8 Lot vexed his *r.* soul
1 *John* 2:29 if ye know he is *r.*
3:7 doeth right. is *r.* as he is *r.*
12 his works evil, brother's *r.*
Rev. 16:5 angel say, Thou *r.*

7 O L. true and *r.* thy judgm.
22:11 that is *r.* let him be *r.* still

See LORD *is.*

RIGHTEOUS man, *or* men.

Ps. 37:16 lit. *r. m.* hath is better
Prov. 10:11 mo. of *r. m.* is a well
13:5 a *r. man* hateth lying
21:12 *r. m.* wisely consi. house
25:26 a *r. m.* falling bef. wicked
28:12 when *r. m.* rejoice, glory
Is. 41:2 raised *r. m.* from east
Ezek. 3:20 *r. m.* doth turn, 18:26
23:45 *r. m.* they sh. judge them
Mat. 10:41 that receiveth a *r. m.*
    in name of *r. m.* rec. *r. m.'s*
13:17 *r. men* desi. to see things
Luke 23:47 cert. this was a *r. m.*
Rom. 5:7 for *r. m.* will one die
1 *Tim.* 1:9 law not made for *r. m.*
2 *Pet.* 2:8 *r. m.* dwelling am. th.

RIGHTEOUSLY.

Deut. 1:16 judge *r. Prov.* 31:9
Ps. 67:4 sh. judge peo. *r.* 96:10
Is. 33:15 walk. *r.* sh. dwell high
Jer. 11:20 O Lord that judgest *r.*
Tit. 2:12 should live soberly, *r.*
1 *Pet.* 2:23 to him that judgeth *r.*

RIGHTEOUSNESS.

Deut. 6:25 it shall be our *r.*
24:13 shall be *r.* to thee bef. L.
33:19 shall offer sacrifices of *r.*
Job 29:14 I put on *r.* clothed me
36:3 ascribe *r.* to my Maker
Ps. 4:5 offer the sacrifices of *r.*
11:7 right. Lord loveth *r.* 33:5
15:2 worketh *r.* never be moved
23:3 leadeth me in paths of *r.*
24:5 *r.* fr. God of his salvation
40:9 I preached *r.* in congrega.
45:4 bec. of truth, meekness, *r.*
7 lovest *r.* hatest, *Heb.* 1:9
48:10 *r.* hand, O G. is full of *r.*
51:19 pleased with sacrifi. of *r.*
52:3 lying, rather than speak *r.*
58:1 speak *r.* O congregation?

72:2 shall judge people with *r.*
3 moun. bring peace, hills *r.*
85:10 *r.* and peace kis. each oth.
13 *r.* go before him
94:15 judgment shall ret. unto *r.*
96:13 he judge world wi. *r.* 98:9
97:2 *r.* habitation of his throne
99:4 executest *r.* J. 103:6
106:3 blessed is he that doeth *r.*
118:19 open to me gates of *r.*
119:144 *r.* of thy testimonies
172 all thy commandm. are *r.*
132:9 priests be clothed with *r.*
Prov. 2:9 sh. thou understand *r.*
8:18 durable riches, *r.* with me
20 I lead in the way of *r.*
10:2 *r.* deliver. from death, 11:4
11:5 *r.* of perfect direct his way
6 *r.* of upright shall del. them
18 to him that soweth *r.* rew.
19 as *r.* tend. to life, so he that
12:17 speaketh truth, show. *r.*
28 the way of *r.* life, in path.
13:6 *r.* keepeth him that is upr.
14:34 *r.* exalteth a nation, sin
15:9 he loveth him that fol. *r.*
16:8 bet. is a little with *r.* than
12 throne is established by *r.*
31 glory. if found in way of *r.*
21:21 followeth *r.* find. life, *r.*
Ec. 3:16 place of *r.* iniq. there
Is. 1:21 *r.* lodged in it
26 city of *r.* 27 converts wi. *r.*
32:1 take away *r.* of righteous
10:22 consum. overflow with *r.*
11:4 with *r.* shall he judge poor
Is. 11:5 *r.* be the girdle of his lo.
16:5 judgment, and hasting *r.*
26:9 inhab. of world will learn *r.*
10 showed, he will not learn *r.*
28:17 *r.* will I lay to plummet
32:16 *r.* shall remain in fruitful
17 work of *r.* peace; of *r.* quie.
33:5 the Lord filled Zion with *r.*
45:8 skies pour *r.* let *r.* spring
19 I the L. speak *r.* I declare
24 in the Lord have I *r.*
46:12 ye that are far from *r.*
51:1 follow *r.* 7 ye that know *r.*
54:17 their *r.* is of me, saith L.
58:2 seek me as a nation did *r.*
59:17 he put on *r.* as breastpl.
60:17 officers peace, exactors *r.*
61:3 might be called trees of *r.*
10 covered me with robe of *r.*
11 Lord will cause *r.* and pra.
63:1 until the *r.* thereof go forth
64:5 rejoiceth and worketh *r.*
Jer. 9:24 I Lord wh. exercise *r.*
22:3 execute ye judgm. and *r.*
23:6 name, Lord our *r.* 33:16
33:15 branch of *r.* to execute *r.*
51:10 Lord brought forth our *r.*
Ezek. 14:14 deliver souls by *r.* 20
18:20 *r.* of the righteous sh. be
33:12 *r.* of right. sh. not deliver
Dan. 4:27 break off thy sins by *r.*
9:7 O Lord *r.* belongeth to thee
24 bring in everlasting *r.*
12:3 they that turn many to *r.*
Hos. 10:12 he come and rain *r.*
Amos 5:7 who will leave off *r.* in
24 let *r.* run down as a stream
6:12 have turned fruit of *r.* to
Mic. 6:5 may know the *r.* of L.
Zep. 2:3 meek of earth seek *r.*
Mal. 4:2 shall Sun of *r.* arise
Mat. 3:15 becometh us to fulfil *r.*
5:6 hunger and thirst after *r.*
20 except *r.* exc. *r.* of scribes
21:32 John came in way of *r.*
Luke 1:75 in *r.* bef. him all days
John 16:8 rep. world of sin and *r.*
Acts 10:35 he that worketh *r.* is
13:10 enemy of all *r.* wilt th.?
24:25 reasoned of *r.* and judgm.
Rom. 1:17 therein is the *r.* of G.
2:26 uncircum. keep *r.* of law

3:5 unright. commend *r.* of G.
21 *r.* of God without the law
22 even the *r.* of God which is
4:6 to whom God imputed *r.*
11 seal of *r.* of the faith, that
r. might be imputed to them
13 promise was thro' *r.* of faith
5:17 which receive gift of *r.*
18 so by *r.* of one the free gift
21 grace reign thro' *r.* to eter.
6:13 instruments of *r.* to God
16 sin to death, obed. unto *r.*
18 ye became the servants of *r.*
19 yield memb. servants to *r.*
20 were serv. of sin, free fr. *r.*
8:4 *r.* of law might be fulfilled
10 Spirit is life because of *r.*
9:30 have attained to *r.* even *r.*
31 Israel fol'owed after *r.* hath
not atta'. ed to the law of *r.*
10:3 establ. sh their own *r.* have
not submitted to the *r.* of G.
5 Moses desc. the *r.* of law
6 *r.* which is of faith speaketh
10 with heart man believ. to *r.*
14:17 not meat and drink, *r.*
1 *Cor.* 1:30 of God who is made *r.*
15:34 awake to *r.* and sin not
2 *Cor.* 3:9 much more minis. of *r.*
5:21 might be made *r.* of God
6:7 armor of *r.* on right hand
14 what fellowship hath *r.* wi.
9:10 increase fruits of your *r.*
11:15 transformed as mini. of *r.*
Gal. 2:21 if *r.* come by law, Ch.
3:21 *r.* should have been by law
5:5 we thro' Spirit wait for *r.*
Eph. 5:9 fruit of Sp. is *r.* and tr.
6:14 having the breastplate of *r.*
Phil. 1:11 filled with fruits of *r.*
3:6 touching *r.* which is in law
9 the *r.* which is of G. by faith
1 *Tim.* 6:11 fol. aft. *r.* 2 *Tim.* 2:22
2 *Tim.* 4:8 laid up a crown of *r.*
Tit. 3:5 not by works of *r.*
Heb. 1:8 sceptre of *r.* is sceptre
5:13 is unskilful in word of *r.*
7:2 by interpretation king of *r.*
11:7 became heir of *r.* by faith
33 subdued kingd. wrought *r.*
12:11 yieldeth peace. fruit of *r.*
Jam. 1:20 worketh not *r.* of God
3:18 fruit of *r.* is sown in peace
1 *Pet.* 2:24 dead to sin live to *r.*
2 *Pet.* 1:1 faith through *r.* of God
2:5 save Noe a preacher of *r.*
2 *Pet.* 2:21 bet. not kn. way of *r.*
3:13 new earth, wherein dw. *r.*
1 *John* 2:29 doeth *r.* born of God
3:7 he that doeth *r.* is righteous
10 doeth not *r.* is not of God
Rev. 19:8 fine linen *r.* of saints

For RIGHTEOUSNESS.
Gen. 15:6 Ab. believ. L. counted
to him *r.* fr. Ps. 106:31; Rom.
4:3
Ps. 143:11 for thy *r.* sake bring
Is. 5:7 looked *for r.* but behold
Mat. 5:10 wh. are persecuted *f. r.*
Rom. 4:5 counted *f. r.* Gal. 3:6
9 reckoned to Abraham for *r.*
22 imp. to him *f. r. Jam.* 2:23
10:4 Ch. is the end of law *f. r.*
1 *Pet.* 3:14 if ye suffer *for r.* sake

His RIGHTEOUSNESS.
1 *Sam.* 26:23 L. render ev. *his r.*
1 *K.* 8:32 acc. to *h. r.* 2 Chr. 6:23
Job 33:26 will render man *his r.*
Ps. 7:17 praise L. acc. to *his r.*
22:31 they shall declare *his r.*
50:6 the heav. declare *his r.* 97:6
98:2 *his r.* hath openly showed
103:17 *h. r.* to children's child.
111:3 *h. r.* end. for ever, 112:3, 9
Ec. 7:15 just man perish in *his r.*
Is. 42:21 pleased for *his r.* sake
59:16 and *his r.* sustained him

Ezek. 3:20 turn fr. *h. r.* 18:24, 26
18:22 *his r.* that he hath done
33:12 not able to live for *his r.*
13 if he trust *his* own *r.* and
commit iniq. *his r.* not rem.
Mic. 7:9 and I shall behold *his r.*
Mat. 6:33 seek king. of G. *h. r.*
Rom. 3:25 to declare *his r.* 26
2 *Cor.* 9:9 given to poor *his r.*

In RIGHTEOUSNESS.
Lev. 19:15 in *r.* shalt thou judge
1 *K.* 3:6 walk. in truth and in *r.*
Ps. 9:8 he shall judge world *in r.*
17:15 I will beh. thy face *in r.*
65:5 terrible things *in r.* wilt
Prov. 8:8 words of mouth *in r.*
25:5 throne shall be estab. *in r.*
Is. 5:16 G. shall be sanct. *in r.*
32:1 a king shall reign *in r.*
42:6 I the L. callde thee *in r.*
45:13 I have raised him *in r.*
23 word gone out of mou. *in r.*
48:1 mention G. of Isr. not *in r.*
54:14 *in r.* shalt thou be estab.
63:1 speak *in r.* mighty to save
Jer. 4:2 the Lord liveth *in r.*
Hos. 2:19 I will betroth thee *in r.*
10:12 sow *in r.* reap in mercy
Zec. 8:8 I will be their God *in r.*
Mal. 3:3 offer an offering *in r.*
Acts 17:31 will judge world *in r.*
Rom. 9:28 will cut it short *in r.*
Eph. 4:24 God is created *in r.*
2 *Tim.* 3:16 scrip. for instr. *in r.*
Rev. 19:11 *in r.* he doth judge

My RIGHTEOUSNESS.
Gen. 30:33 my *r.* answer for me
Deut. 9:4 for *my r.* Lord bro. me
2 *Sam.* 22:21 reward me accord.
to *my r.* 25; Ps. 18:20, 24
Job 6:29 return ag. *my r.* is in it
27:6 *my r.* I hold fast
35:2 *my r.* more than God's
Ps. 4:1 I call, O God of *my r.*
7:8 judge me, O L. ac. to *my r.*
Is. 41:10 uph. with hand *my r.*
46:13 I bring *my r.* 51:5 *my r.* is
51:6 *my r.* sh. not be abolished
8 but *my r.* shall be for ever
56:1 come, *my r.* to be revealed
Phil. 3:9 not having *mine* own *r.*

Thy RIGHTEOUSNESS.
Deut. 9:5 for *thy r.* or upright. 6
Job 8:6 habi. of *t. r.* prosperous
35:8 *thy r.* may profit son of
Ps. 5:8 lead me, O Lord, in *t. r.*
31:1 deliver me in *thy r.* 71:2
35:24 judge me, O L. ac. to *t. r.*
28 shall speak of *thy r.* 71:24
36:6 *thy r.* is like great mount.
10 continue *thy r.* to upright
37:6 he shall bring forth *thy r.*
40:10 I have not hid *thy r.*
51:14 tongue shall sing of *thy r.*
69:27 let th. not come into *t. r.*
71:15 my mouth sh. show *thy r.*
16 I will make ment. of *thy r.*
19 *thy r.* O God, is very high
72:1 give *thy r.* unto king's son
88:12 *thy r.* be known in land
89:16 in *t. r.* sh. they be exalted
119:40 quicken *t. r.* 123 *thy r.*
142 *thy r.* is an everlast. right.
143:1 answer me, and in *thy r.*
11 for *t. r.* sake bring my soul
Ps. 145:7 they sh. sing of *thy r.*
Is. 48:18 *thy r.* as waves of sea
57:12 I will declare *thy r.*
58:8 *thy r.* shall go before thee
62:2 the Gentiles shall see *t. r.*
Dan. 9:16 O Lord, accord. to *t. r.*

RIGHTEOUSNESSES.
Is. 64:6 our *r.* are as filthy rags
Ezek. 33:13 his *r.* sh. not be rem.
Dan. 9:18 not for our *r.* but thy

RIGHTLY.
Gen. 27:36 is not he *r.* nam. J. ?
Luke 7:43 Thou hast *r.* judged
20:21 we know thou teachest *r.*
2 *Tim.* 2:15 *r.* divid. word of tru.

RIGOR.
Ex. 1:13 made Is. serve wi. *r.* 14
Lev. 25:43 not *r.* with *r.* 46, 53

RIMMON.
Jos. 15:32 Ain, and R. cities of
Jud. 20:45 rock R. 47; 21:13
2 *Sam.* 4:2 Rec. sons of R. 5, 9
2 *K.* 5:18 goeth into house of R.
1 *Chr.* 4:32 villages of Simeon R.
6:77 was given to Merari, R.
Zec. 14:10 turn. as a plain to R.

RING.
Gen. 41:42 Phar. took off his *r.*
Ex. 26:24 coup. to one *r.* 36:29
Est. 3:10 Ahasuerus took his *r.*
8:2 the king took off *r.* gave it
Luke 15:22 said, Put a *r.* on hand
Jam. 2:2 came man with gold *r.*

RINGLEADER.
Acts 24:5 *r.* of sect of Nazarenes

RINGS.
Ex. 25:12 cast four *r.* of gold
14 put staves into the *r.* 15;
27:7; 37:5; 38:7
26:29 and make their *r.* of gold,
28:23, 26, 27; 30:4; 36:34;
37:3, 13; 39:16, 19, 20
Est. 1:6 hangings fastened to *r.*
Cant. 5:14 hands are as gold *r.*
Is. 3:21 take away *r.* jewels
Ezek. 1:18 *r.* so high were dread.
r. were full of eyes

RING-STREAKED.
Gen. 30:35 he-goats were *r.-s.*
31:8 *r.-s.* sh. be thy hire, 10:12

RINSED.
Lev. 6:28 pot both scoured and *r.*
15:11 and hath not *r.* his hands
12 ev. vessel of wood sh. be *r.*

RIOT, Substantive.
Tit. 1:6 children not accus. of *r.*
1 *Pet.* 4:4 that you run not to *r.*

RIOT, ING.
Rom. 13:13 walk not in *r.*
2 *Pet.* 2:13 count it pleasure to *r.*

RIOTOUS.
Prov. 23:20 be not am. *r.* eaters
28:7 he that is companion of *r.*
Luke 15:13 wasted with *r.* living

RIP, PED.
2 *K.* 8:12 *r.* up women with chi.
15:16 women wi. child he *r.* up
Hos. 13:16 wo. wi. child be *r.* up
Amos 1:13 have *r.* up the women

RIPE.
Gen. 40:10 bro. forth *r.* grapes
Ex. 22:29 to offer thy *r.* fruits
Num. 13:20 time of first *r.* grap.
18:13 whatso. is first *r.* in land
Jer. 24:2 like figs that are first *r.*
Hos. 9:10; *Nah.* 3:12
Joel 3:13 sickle, for harvest is *r.*
Mic. 7:1 my soul-desired *r.* fruit
Rev. 14:15 harvest of earth is *r.*
18 gath. clusters, grapes are *r.*

RIPENING.
Is. 18:5 and the sour grape is *r.*

RIPHATH. *Gen.* 10:3

RISE.
Num. 24:17 sceptre *r.* out of Is.
Deut. 33:11 smite them that *r.*
that they *r.* not again
Jud. 8:21 they said, *r.* thou
1 *Sam.* 24:7 suff. them not to *r.*
2 *Sam.* 12:21 child dead, didst *r.*
Job 30:12 upon my right hand *r.*

RISE

Ps. 18:38 were not able to *r.*
27:3 tho. war sho. *r.* against me
36:12 shall not th. *r.* up again
140:10 that th. *r.* not up again
Prov. 28:12 when wicked *r.* 28
Cant. 3:2 *r.* now and go about
Is. 24:20 earth sh. fall and not *r.*
33:10 now will I *r.* saith the L.
43:17 lie together, shall not *r.*
Amos 5:2 virgin of Isr. no mo. *r.*
7:9 *r.* against house of Jerob.
Mat. 5:45 he maketh sun to *r.*
20:19 he shall *r.* ag. *Mark* 9:31;
    10:34; *Luke* 18:33; 24:7
24:11 many false proph. shall *r.*
    Mark 13:22
27:63 3 day I will *r. Mark* 8:31
Mark 12:23 when they shall *r.* 25
Luke 11:7 I cannot *r.* and give
John 5:8 J. saith, *r.* take up bed
11:23 J. saith, Thy bro. sh. *r.*
Acts 10:13 came a voice, *r.* Peter
26:23 that should *r.* from dead
Rom. 15:12 he that sh. *r.* to reign
1 *Cor.* 15:15 dead *r.* not, 16, 29, 32
1 *Thes.* 4:16 dead in Christ sh. *r.*

RISE up.

Ex. 8:20 *r. up.* bef. Phar. 9:13
Num. 10:35 *r. up* L. let enemies
23:24 people shall *r. up* as lion'
Deut. 19:15 one witness not *r. up*
28:7 L. cause enemies that *r. up*
31:16 this people will *r. up*
Neh. 2:18 let us *r. up* and build
Job 20:27 the earth shall *r. up*
Ps. 3:1 many are they *r. up*
17:7 save from those that *r. up*
18:48 liftest above th. that *r. up*
41:8 he shall *r. up* no more
44:5 tread them under th. *r. up*
92:11 desire of wicked *r. up*
94:16 who will *r. up* for me?
127:2 it is vain to *r. up* early
Ec. 12:4 *r. up* at voice of bird
Cant. 2:10 beloved said, *r. up*
Is. 5:11 woe unto them *r. up*
14:22 I will *r. up* against them
28:21 L. shall *r. up* as in Peraz.
Jer. 47:2 wat. *r. up* out of north
51:1 them that *r. up* against me
Amos 8:14 fall, never *r. up* again
Ob. 1 let us *r. up* against Edom
Zep. 3:8 until day that I *r. up*
Zec. 14:13 *r. up* against neighbor
Mat. 12:41 men of Nine. sh. *r. up*
    42 qu. of so. *r. up*, *Lu.* 11:31, 32
Mark 3:26 Sat. *r. up* ag. himself
Luke 5:23 easier to say, *r. up*
Acts 3:6 in name of Jesus *r. up*

RISEN.

Num. 32:14 *r.* up in fath. stead
1 *Sam.* 25:29 man *r.* to pursue
1 *K.* 8:20 I am *r.* up in room of
    David, 2 *Chr.* 6:10
Ps. 20:8 we are *r.* and stand
54:3 strangers are *r.* against me
86:14 O G. proud are *r.* ag. me
Is. 60:1 glory of the Lord is *r.*
Mic. 2:8 of late my peo. is *r.* up
Mat. 11:11 not *r.* a greater th. J.
14:2 John the Baptist *r.* fr. dead,
    Mark 6:14, 16; *Luke* 9:7
17:9 Son of man be *r. Mark* 9:9
26:32 *r.* I will go bef. *Mark* 14:28
28:6 is *r.* as he said, *Mark* 16:6
Mark 16:9 J. *r.* early first day
Luke 7:16 a great prophet is *r.*
9:8 one of prophets was *r.* 19
24:34 the Lord is *r.* indeed
Acts 17:3 C. must needs have *r.*
Rom. 8:34 yea rather that is *r.*
1 *Cor.* 15:13 then is Christ not *r.*
Col. 3:1 if ye be *r.* with Christ

RISEST.

Deut. 6:7 talk of th. when thou *r.*

RISETH.

Deut. 22:26 man *r.* against neigh.

Job 9:7 com. sun and it *r.* not
14:12 man lieth down, *r.* not
24:22 *r.* up and no man is sure
27:7 he that *r.* up against me
31:14 wh. sh. I do wh. G. *r.* up?
Prov. 24:16 man fall. and *r.* ag.
Is. 47:11 know fr. whence it *r.*

RISING, Substantive.

Lev. 13:2 in skin of his flesh a *r.*
    or bright spot, 10, 19, 28, 43
14:56 this is the law for a *r.*
Prov. 30:31 ag. whom is no *r.*
Is. 60:3 to brightness of thy *r.*
Mark 9:10 what the *r.* from dead
Luke 2:34 fall and *r.* of many

Sun-RISING.

Num. 2:3 toward *r.* of the *sun*
21:11 bef. Moab tow. *s.-r.* 34:15;
    Deut. 4:41, 47; *Jos.* 12:1;
    13:5; 19:12, 27, 34
Ps. 50:1 called earth fr. *r.* of *sun*
113:3 *r.* of *s.* L.'s name praised
Is. 41:25 fr. *r.* of *s.* shall he call
45:6 know from *r.* of the *sun*
59:19 fear his glory fr. *r.* of *sun*
Mal. 1:11 from *r.* of *sun* my name
Mark 16:2 to sepulc. at *r.* of *sun*

RITES.

Num. 9:3 keep it according to *r.*

RIVER.

Gen. 31:21 Jacob passed over *r.*
41:1 behold, he stood by the *r.*
Ex. 1:22 every son cast into *r.*
2:5 daughter of Phar. came to *r.*
4:9 water of *r.* sh. become blood
8:3 the *r.* shall bring forth frogs
Deut. 2:24 journey, pass over *r.*
Jos. 13:9 the city in the midst of
    the *r.* 2 *Sam.* 24:5
Jud. 5:21 *r.* Kis. that ancient *r.*
2 *Sam.* 17:13 draw city into *r.*
1 *K.* 4:21 Solomon reigned fr. *r.*
Ezr. 4:10 rest on this side the *r.*
    8:15 I gathered them to *r.*
Job 40:23 he drinketh up *r.*
Ps. 36:8 make them drink of *r.*
46:4 a *r.* streams sh. make glad
65:9 enrichest it with *r.* of God
72:8 have dominion from the *r.*
80:11 sent out branches unto *r.*
105:41 wat. ran in places like *r.*
Is. 8:7 bring. upon them the *r.*
11:15 shake his hand over the *r.*
19:5 and the *r.* shall be wasted
23:10 pass thro' thy land as a *r.*
48:18 had thy peace been as *r.*
66:12 ext. peace to her like a *r.*
Jer. 2:18 drink waters of the *r.*
17:8 spread. out her roots by *r.*
Lam. 2:18 tears run down like *r.*
Ezek. 29:3 My *r.* is my own, 9
47:5 it was a *r.* I could not pass
Amos 6:14 *r.* of the wilderness
Mic. 7:12 come from fortr. to *r.*
Zec. 9:10 his dominion from *r.*
10:11 deeps of *r.* shall dry up
Mark 1:5 baptized in *r.* Jordan
Acts 16:13 on sab. we went by *r.*
Rev. 22:1 showed me a pure *r.*

See BANK, BRINK, BEYOND,
    CHEBAR, EUPHRATES.

RIVERS.

Ex. 7:19 thy hand on the *r.* 8:5
Lev. 11:9 whatso. hath fins in *r.*
Deut. 10:7 a land of *r.* of waters
2 *K.* 5:12 are not *r.* of Damascus
19:24 I have dried up all the *r.*
Job 20:17 shall not see *r.* of hon.
28:10 cutteth out *r.* amo. rocks
29:6 rock poured me out *r.* of oil
Ps. 1:3 like a tree planted by *r.*
74:15 thou driedst up mighty *r.*
78:16 caused wat. to run like *r.*
89:25 set his right hand in *r.*
107:33 turneth *r.* into wildern.
119:136 *r.* of wat. run down eyes
137:1 by *r.* of Babylon we wept
Prov. 5:16 *r.* of waters in streets
21:1 in the hand of Lord, as *r.*
Ec. 1:7 all *r.* run into the sea
Cant. 5:12 as eyes of doves by *r.*
Is. 18:2 whose land *r.* spoiled, 7
19:6 they shall turn *r.* far away
30:25 on every high hill *r.*
32:2 be as *r.* in a dry place
33:21 L. be to us place of br. *r.*
37:25 all *r.* of besieged places
41:18 open *r.* in high places
42:15 I will make *r.* islands
43:2 passest thro' *r.* not overfl.
19 I will make *r.* in desert, 20
44:27 deep be dry, I wil. dry up *r.*
50:2 I make *r.* a wilderness
Jer. 31:9 I cau. th. to walk by *r.*
46:7 waters are moved as *r.* 8
Lam. 3:48 eye runneth *r.* of wat.
Ezek. 6:3 said L. to hills and *r.*
29:4 cause fish of thy *r.* to stick
10 I am against thee, again. *r.*
32:12 I will make *r.* dry
31:4 deep set him up with her *r.*
12 his boughs are broken by *r.*
32:2 camest forth with thy *r.*
14 cause their *r.* to run like oil
34:13 feed th. on mount. by *r.*
35:8 in *r.* sh. fall that are slain
36:6 say to hills, *r.* valleys
47:9 whithersoever *r.* sh. come
Joel 1:20 *r.* of waters dried up
3:18 *r.* of Jud. sh. flow wi. wat.
Mic. 6:7 pleased with 10,000 *r.*
Nah. 1:4 rebuk. sea, drieth up *r.*
Nah. 2:6 gates of *r.* sh. be open.
Hab. 3:8 was L. displeas. ag. *r.?*
9 thou didst clea. earth wi. *r.*
John 7:38 out of belly sh. flow *r.*
Rev. 8:10 fell on third part of *r.*

RIZPAH.

2 *Sam.* 3:7 concub. name was R.
21:8 delivered two sons of R. 10

ROAD.

1 *Sam.* 27:10 ye made *r.* to-day

ROAR.

1 *Chr.* 16:32 sea *r. Ps.* 96:11; 98:7
Ps. 46:3 not fear, though wat. *r.*
74:4 enemies *r.* in thy congre.
104:21 young lions *r.* after prey
Is. 5:29 they sh. *r.* like lions, 30
42:13 L. sh. *r.* prevail ag. enem.
59:11 we *r.* all like bears, mou.
Jer. 5:22 they *r.* yet not pass ov.
25:30 Lord shall *r.* from on high
31:35 divideth sea, wh. waves *r.*
50:42 their voice sh. *r.* like sea
51:38 shall *r.* together like lions
55 her waves *r.* like great wat.
Hos. 11:10 *r.* like lion. wh. he *r.*
Joel 3:16 L. out of Z. *Amos* 1:2
Amos 3:4 will lion *r.* if no prey?

ROARED.

Jud. 14:5 lion *r.* against Samson
Is. 51:15 divided sea, waves *r.*
Jer. 2:15 young lions *r.* upon him
Amos 3:8 *r.* who will not fear?

ROARETH.

Job 37:4 after a voice *r.* thunder.
Jer. 6:23 their voice *r.* like sea

ROARING, Substantive.

Rev. 10:3 angel cried, as a lion *r.*

Job 4:10 *r.* teeth of lions broken
Ps. 22:1 why so far from my *r.* ?
32:3 bones waxed old thr' my *r.*
Prov. 19:12 king's *r.* as *r.* of lion
20:2 fear of king is as *r.* of lion
Is. 5:29 their *r.* sh. be like a lion
30 shall roar like *r.* of the sea
Ezek. 19:7 land desol. noise of *r.*
Zec. 11:3 *r.* of young lions

ROARING, Adjective.

Ps. 22:13 gaped up. me as *r.* lion
Prov. 28:15 *r.* lion, so is wicked
Is. 31:4 as young lion *r.* on prey
Zep. 3:3 her princes are *r.* lions
Luke 21:25 sea and waves *r.*
1 *Pet.* 5:8 devil as a *r.* lion walk.

ROARINGS.

Job 3:24 my *r.* poured like wat.

ROAST, ED, ETH.

Ex. 12:8 eat in that night flesh *r.* with fire, *Deut.* 16:7
1 *Sam.* 2:15 flesh to *r.* for priest
2 *Chr.* 35:13 they *r.* passover
Prov. 12:27 slothful man, *r.* not
Is. 44:16 roasteth *r.* is satisfied
Jer. 29:22 whom king of Bab. *r.*

ROB, BETH.

Lev. 19:13 shalt not *r.* neighbor
26:22 beasts shall *r.* you of chil.
1 *Sam.* 23:1 they *r.* thresh.-floors
Prov. 22:22 *r.* not poor
28:24 whoso *r.* his fath. or mot.
Is. 10:2 that they may *r.* fatherl.
17:14 this is lot of th. that *r.* us
Ezek. 39:10 spoil and *r.* those th.
Mal. 3:8 will a man *r.* God?

ROBBED.

Jud. 9:25 *r.* all came by them
2 *Sam.* 17:8 chafed as a bear *r.*
Ps. 119:61 bands of wick. *r.* me
Prov. 17:12 a bear *r.* of whelps
Is. 10:13 I have *r.* their treasures
42:22 a people *r.* and spoiled
Jer. 50:37 sword on treas. be *r.*
Ezek. 33:15 if wick. give th. he *r.*
39:10 rob those that *r.* them
Mal. 3:8 *r.* me, wh. have we *r.* ?
2 *Cor.* 11:8 *r.* other churches

ROBBER.

Job 5:5 *r.* swallow. th. substance
18:9 *r.* shall prevail against him
Ezek. 18:10 beget son that is a *r.*
John 18:40 Barabbas was a *r.*

ROBBERS.

Job 12:6 tabernacles of *r.* prosp.
Is. 42:24 who gave Is. to the *r.* ?
Jer. 7:11 house bec. den of *r.* ?
Ezek. 7:22 *r.* sh. enter and defile
Dan. 11:14 *r.* of peo. exalt them-
Hos. 6:9 troops of *r.* wait for a man

7:1 troop of *r.* spoileth without
Ob. 5 if *r.* by night, would they
John 10:8 all came bef. me are *r.*
Acts 19:37 not *r.* of churches
2 *Cor.* 11:26 perils of water, of *r.*

ROBBERY.

Ps. 62:10 become not vain in *r.*
Prov. 21:7 *r.* of wick. dest. them
Is. 61:8 I hate *r.* for burnt-offer.
Ezek. 22:29 exerc. *r.* vexed poor
Amos 3:10 store *r.* in palaces
Nah. 3:1 city full of lies, *r.*
Phil. 2:6 thou. no *r.* to be equal

ROBE.

Ex. 28:4 make an ephod and *r.*
29:5 put on Aa. coat, *r. Lev.* 8:7
1 *Sam.* 18:4 Jona. stripped of *r.*
24:11 skirt of thy *r.* in my hand
1 *Chr.* 15:27 David clothed wi. *r.*
Job 29:14 my judgment was a *r.*
Is. 22:21 will clothe him with *r.*

61:10 cov. me with *r.* of righte.
Jon. 3:6 arose and laid *r.* fr. him
Mic. 2:8 ye pull off *r.* with garm.
Mat. 27:28 put on J. a scarlet *r.*
Luke 15:22 bri. best *r.* put it on
23:11 arrayed him in gorgeo. *r.*
John 19:2 put on Jes. a purple *r.*

ROBES.

2 *Sam.* 13:18 such *r.* we. virgins
1 *K.* 22:30 put thou on thy *r.*
Ezek. 26:16 princes lay :.way *r.*
Luke 20:46 scri. walk in long *r.*
Rev. 6:11 white *r.* given them
7:9 Lamb, clothed wi. white *r.*
13 in white *r.* ? 14 washed th. *r.*

ROCK.

Ex. 17:6 will stand bef. thee on *r.*
33:21 L. Thou stand upon a *r.*
Num. 20:8 sp. to *r.* bef. th. eyes
11 Mo. with rod smote *r.* twice
24:21 puttest thy nest in a *r.*
Deut. 8:15 brought wat. out of *r.*
32:4 he is *r.* his work is perfect
15 lightly esteemed *r.* of salv.
18 *r.* begat thee art unmindful
30 except the *r.* had sold them
31 their *r.* is not as our *r.*
37 where *r.* wh. they trusted ?
Jud. 6:21 fire of *r.* consu. flesh
7:25 slew Oreb on the *r.* Oreb
15:8 Sams. dwelt in top of *r.* E.
20:45 Benj. turned to *r.* of Rim.
1 *Sam.* 2:2 nei. any *r.* like our G.
14:4 sharp *r.* one side, sharp *r.*
2 *Sam.* 22:2 he said, Lord is my *r.*
Ps. 18:2 ; 92:15

3 G. of my *r.* in wh. I will tru.
32 a *r.* save our G. ? *Ps.* 18:31
47 blessed be my *r.* exalted be
G. of *r.* of salvati. *Ps.* 18:46
23:3 God of Israel said, R. of Is.
1 *Chr.* 11:15 captains went to *r.*
2 *Chr.* 25:12 cast down fr. top of *r.*
Neh. 9:15 wat. out of *r.* for their thirst, *Ps.* 78:16 ; 105:41
Job 14:18 *r.* is remo. out of place
18:4 sh. *r.* be remo. out of pla. ?
19:24 were graven in *r.* for ever
24:8 embr. *r.* for want of shelter
28:9 putteth forth hand upon *r.*
29:6 *r.* poured out rivers of oil
39:1 wild goats of *r.* bri. forth ?
28 dwelleth on *r.* on crag of *r.*
Ps. 27:5 shall set me on *r.* 40:2
28:1 unto thee I cry, O L. my *r.*
31:2 be thou my strong *r.*
3 thou art my *r.* and fort. 71:3
42:9 my *r.* why ha. thou forg. ?
61:2 lead me to *r.* higher than I
62:2 God is my *r.* 6 ; 7 *r.* of str.
78:20 smote *r.* waters gushed
89:26 *r.* of salva. 94:22 *r.* of ref.
95:1 joyful noise to *r.* of salva.
114:8 turned *r.* into stand. wat.
Cant. 2:14 art in clefts of *r.*
Is. 2:10 enter *r.* hide in. in dust
8:14 *r.* of offence to both houses
10:26 slaughter at *r.* of Oreb
17:10 not mindful of *r.* of stren.
22:16 habita. for himself in a *r.*
32:2 man be as shad. of great *r.*
42:11 let inhabitants of *r.* sing
48:21 caus. wat. to flow out of *r.*
51:1 look to *r.* ye are hewn
Jer. 5:3 made faces harder th. *r.*
18:14 snow which cometh fr. *r.*
21:13 I am ag. thee, inhab. of *r.*
23:29 hammer that breaketh *r.*
48:28 dwell in *r.* like the dove
49:16 thou dwell. in clefts of *r.*
Ezek. 24:7 set it upon top of *r.*
8 set her blood upon top of *r.*
26:4 make her like top of *r.* 14
Amos 6:12 ha. hors. run. upon *r.*?
Ob. 3 thou dwell. in clefts of *r.*
Mat. 7:24 built house upon *r.*
16:18 upon th. *r.* I build church

27:60 new tomb wh. he had hewn out in the *r. Mar.* 15:46
Luke 8:6 some fell on *r.* 13 on *r.*
Rom. 9:33 I lay in Si. a stumb.-stone, *r.* of offence, 1 *Pet.* 2:8
1 *Cor.* 10:4 drank of spiritual *r.*

ROCKS.

Num. 23:9 top of *r.* I see him
1 *Sam.* 13:6 hid themselves in *r.*
1 *K.* 19:11 strong wind break *r.*
Job 28:10 cutteth rivers amo. *r.*
30:6 dwell in caves of earth, *r.*
Ps. 78:15 he clave *r.* in wildern.
104:18 *r.* are a refuge for conies
Prov. 30:26 make th. houses in *r.*
Is. 2:19 shall go into holes of *r.*
7:19 they sh. rest in holes of *r.*
57:5 slaying children under *r.*
Jer. 4:29 whole city climb on *r.*
16:16 hunt th. out of holes of *r.*
51:25 I will roll thee from the *r.*
Nah. 1:6 the *r.* are thrown down
Mat. 27:51 earth quake, *r.* rent
Acts 27:29 lest they sho. fal. on *r.*
Rev. 6:16 said to *r.* Fall on us

ROD.

Ex. 4:4 became a *r.* in his hand
20 Moses took *r.* of God, 17:9
7:9 say to Aa. Take th. *r.* 19
20 lifted up *r.* and smote, 14:16
21:20 man smite servant with *r.*
Lev. 27:32 whatso. pass. und. *r.*
Num. 17:2 wri. man's name on *r.*
8 *r.* of Aaron budded, *Heb.* 9:4
20:11 with his *r.* he smote rock
1 *Sam.* 14:27 Jona. put end of *r.*
2 *Sam.* 7:14 I will chasten with *r.*
Job 9:34 let him take his *r.* away
21:9 neither is *r.* of God upon
Ps. 2:9 shalt break them with *r.*
23:4 thy *r.* and staff comfort me
74:2 remem. *r.* of thine inherit.
89:32 I will visit transg. with *r.*
110:2 the Lord shall send the *r.*
125:3 *r.* of wicked shall not rest
Prov. 10:13 a *r.* for back of fools, 26:3

13:24 he that spar. *r.* hateth son
14:3 mouth of foolish is a *r.* of
22:8 *r.* of his anger shall fail
15 *r.* of correction shall drive
23:13 thou sh. beat him wi. *r.* 14
29:15 *r.* and reproof give wisd.
Is. 9:4 hast broken *r.* of oppres.
10:5 O Assyr. *r.* of mine anger
15 as if the *r.* sho. shake itself
24 he shall smite with a *r.* and
26 as his *r.* was on the sea, so
11:1 *r.* out of the stem of Jesse
4 shall smite earth with the *r.*
14:29 *r.* that smote is broken
30:31 Assyr. beat. smote with *r.*
Jer. 10:16 Is. the *r.* of his, 51:19
48:17 how is beauti. *r.* broken !
Lam. 3:1 affliction by *r.* of wra.
Ezek. 7:11 viol. is risen into a *r.*
19:14 fire is gone out of a *r.*
20:37 cause to pass under the *r.*
21:10 contemn. *r.* of my son, 13
Mic. 5:1 smite judge of Is. wi. *r.*
6:9 hear the *r.* who appoint. it
7:14 feed thy people with thy *r.*
1 *Cor.* 4:21 sh. I come with a *r.* ?
Rev. 2:27 rule with *r.* of ir. 19:15
12:5 rule nations with *r.* of iron

RODE.

Gen. 24:61 Rebe. and damsels *r.*
Jud. 10:4 he had 30 sons that *r.*
1 *Sam.* 25:20 Abig. *r.* on ass, 42
30:17 400 which *r.* on camels
2 *Sam.* 22:11 he *r.* on a cherub, and did fly, *Ps.* 18:10
1 *K.* 13:13 old prophet *r.* on ass
2 *K.* 9:16 Jehu *r.* in a chariot
25 when I and thou *r.* togeth.
Neh. 2:12 beast that I *r.* upon
Est. 8:14 posts that *r.* on mules

RODS.

Gen. 30:37 Jac. took r. of poplar
Ex. 7:12 Aaron's rod swall. th. r.
Num. 17:6 princes ga. him 12 r.
Ezek. 19:11 she had strong r. for
12 her strong r. were broken
2 Cor. 11:25 thrice beaten wi. r.

ROE, S.

1 Chr. 12:8 swift as r. on mount.
Prov. 5:19 hind and pleasant r.
6:5 deli. thyself as r. fr. hunter
Cant. 2:7 I charge you by r. 3:5
9 my beloved is like a r. or a
17 be thou like r. or hart, 8:14
Is. 13:14 shall be as chased r.

See YOUNG.

Wild ROE.

2 Sam. 2:18 Asahel was as a w. r.

ROEBUCK, S.

Deut. 12:15 eat of the r. 22 ; 14:5 ;
15:22
1 K. 4:23 besides harts and r.

ROLL, Substantive.

Ezr. 6:1 sea. made in house of r.
2 was found at Achmetha a r.
Is. 8:1 take thee a great r. and
Jer. 36:2 take thee a r. of a book
23 till all the r. was consumed
29 saith L. Th. hast burnt th. r.
Ezek. 2:9 hand sent, and lo, a r.
3:1 eat this r. 2 caused me eat
Zec. 5:1 behold, a flying r. 2

ROLL, Verb.

Gen. 29:8 till they r. away
Jos. 10:18 Joshua said, r. stones
1 Sam. 14:33 r. a great stone
Jer. 51:25 I will r. thee down
Mic. 1:10 Aph. r. thyself in dust
Mark 16:3 who r. us away stone ?

ROLLED.

Gen. 29:3 r. stone from well, 10
Jos. 5:9 I ha. r. away reproach
Job 30:14 r. themselves on me
Is. 9:5 garments r. in blood
34:4 heavens r. toget. Rev. 6:14
Mat. 27:60 he r. a great stone to
door of sepulch. Mark 15:46
28:2 angel came r. back stone
Mark 16:4 stone was r. away
Luke 24:2 found stone r. away

ROLLER.

Ezek. 30:21 to put a r. to bind it

ROLLETH.

Prov. 26:27 he that r. a stone

ROLLING.

Is. 17:13 nations flee like r. thi.

ROMAN.

Acts 22:25 is a R. 26, 27, 29
23:27 unders. that he was a R.

ROMANS.

John 11:48 the R. shall come
Acts 16:21 obser. being R. 37, 38
28:17 prison. into hands of R.

ROME.

Acts 2:10 strangers of R. we do
18:2 Jews to depart from R.
19:21 there, I must also see R.
23:11 bear witness also as R.
28:16 when we came to R.
Rom. 1:7 all that be in R. 15
2 Tim. 1:17 when he was in R.

ROOF, S.

Gen. 19:8 under shadow of r.
Deut. 22:8 a battlement for r.
Jos. 2:6 brought them to the r.
Jud. 16:27 on r. were 3000 men
2 Sam. 11:2 David walked on r.
18:24 watchman went up to r.
Jer. 19:13 on wh. r. they, 32:29
Ezek. 40:13 measured gate fr. r.
Mat. 8:8 not worthy fh. should.
come under my r. Luke 7:6
Mark 2:4 they uncovered the r.

ROOF, with mouth.

Job 29:10 tongue clea. to r. of m.
Ps. 137:6 tong. cleave to r. of m.
Cant. 7:9 r. of m. like best wine
Lam. 4:4 cleaveth to r. of his m.
Ezek. 3:26 tong. clea. to r. of m.

ROOM.

Gen. 24:23 r. in father's house ?
25 have straw, and r. to lodge
31 I have prepa. r. for camels
26:22 Lord hath made r. for us
1 K. 2:35 king put Benaiah in
J.'s r. put Zad. in r. of Abi.
5:5 son wh. I will set in thy r.
8:20 I am risen in r. of David,
2 Chr. 6:10
19:16 Elis. shalt thou anoi. in r.
Ps. 31:8 set my feet in large r
80:9 thou preparedst r. before it
Prov. 18:16 a man's gift make. r.
Mal. 3:10 shall not be r. enough
Mark 2:2 no r. to receive them
14:15 a large up. r. Luke 22:12
Luke 2:7 because th. was no r.
12:17 I have no r. to bestow
14:8 sit not down in highest r.
10 sit down in the lowest r.
22 it is done, and yet th. is r
Acts 1:13 went up to an upper r.
24:27 Festus came in Felix's r.
1 Cor. 14:16 he that occupieth r.

ROOMS.

Gen. 6:14 r. sh. thou make in ark
1 K. 20:24 put captains in th. r.
1 Chr. 4:41 dwelt in their r.
Mat. 23:6 uppermost r. at feasts,
Mark 12:39 ; Luke 20:46
Luke 14:7 those chief r.

ROOT, Substantive.

Deut. 29:18 among you a r. that
Jud. 5:14 out of Eph. was a r.
2 K. 19:30 Judah shall take r.
Job 5:3 I have seen foolish ta. r.
14:8 though the r. thereof wax
19:28 seeing the r. of the matter
29:19 my r. spread out by wate.
Ps. 80:9 didst cause vine take r
Prov. 12:3 r. of the righteous
12 r. of the righteous yieldeth
Is. 5:24 their r. shall be rotten.
11:10 a r. of Jesse, Rom. 15:12
14:30 I will kill thy r. with fam.
27:6 come of Jacob take r. 37:31
40:24 their stock sh. not take r.
53:2 he shall grow up as a r. out
Jer. 12:2 they have taken r. they
Ezek. 31:7 his r. was by waters
Dan. 11:7 out of branch of her r.
Hos. 9:16 Eph. is smit. their r.
Mal. 4:1 sh. leave neither r. nor
Mat. 3:10 axe laid to r. Luke 3:9
13:6 because they had not r. 21 ;
Mark 4:6, 17 ; Luke 8:13
Luke 17:6 plucked up by the r.
Rom. 11:16 if the r. be holy
18 bearest not the r. but r. th.
1 Tim. 6:10 money is r. of all ev.
Heb. 12:15 lest any r. of bittern.
Rev. 5:5 r. of Da. hath prevailed
22:16 I am the r. of David

ROOT, Verb.

1 K. 14:15 he shall r. up Israel
Job 31:12 would r. all mine incr.
Ps. 52:5 and r. thee out of land
Jer. 1:10 I have set thee to r. out
Mat. 13:29 lest ye r. up wheat

ROOTED.

Deut 29:28 the Lord r. them out
Job 18:14 confidence sh. be r. out
31:8 let my offspring be r. out
Prov. 2:22 transgressors sh. be r.
Zep. 2:4 Ekron shall be r. up
Mat. 15:13 Fa. not planted, r. up
Eph. 3:17 being r. and grounded
Col. 2:7 r. and built up in him

ROOTS.

2 Chr. 7:20 pluck them up by r.
Job 8:17 his r. are wrapped about
18:16 his r. shall be dried up
28:9 overturn. mountains by r.
30:4 cut juniper r. for meat
Is. 11:1 bra. shall grow out of r.
Jer. 17:8 spreadeth out her r.
Ezek. 17:7 vine did bend her r.
Dan. 4:15 stump of his r. 23, 26
7:8 horns plucked up by the r.
Hos. 14:5 shall cast forth his r.
Amos 2:9 I destroyed his r. from
Mark 11:20 fig-tree dried from r.
Jude 12 trees, plucked up by r.

ROPES.

Jud. 16:11 bi. me wi. new r. 12
2 Sam. 17:13 Isr. bring r. to city
1 K. 20:31 put r. on heads, 32
Acts 27:32 soldiers cut off the r.

ROSE, Substantive.

Cant. 2:1 I am r. of Sharon
Is. 35:1 desert sh. blossom as r

ROSE, Verb.

Gen. 4:8 Cain r. up against Abel
32:31 sun r. upon him
Ex. 10:23 nor r. any from place
12:30 Pharaoh r. up in night
33:10 and all the people r. up
Num. 25:7 Phinehas r. up from
Deut. 33:2 Lord r. up from Seir
Jos. 3:16 waters stood and r. up
Jud. 6:21 r. up fire out of rock
1 K. 2:19 king r. up to meet her
Ps. 124:2 on our side men r. up
Cant. 5:5 I r. up to open to my
Lam. 3:62 the lips of those th. r.
Dan. 8:27 I r. up did king's bus.
Zep. 3:7 r. early and corrupted
Luke 5:28 r. up and followed him
16:31 not be persua. tho' one r.
22:45 when he r. from prayer
Acts 5:36 bef. th. days r. Theud.
10:41 drink with him after he r.
Rom. 14:9 Christ bo. died and r.
1 Cor. 10:7 eat, and r. up to play
15:4 he was buried and r. again
2 Cor. 5:15 him who died and r. ʃ
1 Thes. 4:14 J. died and r. again

See MORNING.

ROT.

Num. 5:21 Lord ma. thigh r.
22, 27
Prov. 10:7 name of wicked sh. r.
Is. 40:20 choos. a tree will not r.

ROTTEN.

Job 13:28 and he, as a r. thing
41:27 esteemeth brass as r. wo.
Jer. 38:12 put these r. rags und.
Joel 1:17 seed is r. under their
clods.

ROTTENNESS.

Prov. 12:4 maketh asha. is as r.
14:30 envy is r. of the bones
Is. 5:24 so their root sh. be as r
Hos. 5:12 be to house of Ju. as r
Hab. 3:16 wh. I heard r. entered

ROUGH.

Deut. 21:4 bring heifer to r. val.
Is. 27:8 he stayeth his r. wind
40:4 r. places sh. be made plain
Jer. 51:27 come as r. caterpillars
Zec. 13:4 neither wear r. garm.
Luke 3:5 r. ways be ma. smooth

ROUGHLY.

Gen. 42:7 Joseph spake r. 30
1 Sam. 20:10 fa. answer thee r. ?
1 K. 12:13 the king answered
the people r. 2 Chr. 10:13
Prov. 18:23 the rich answere. r.

ROUND, Verb.

Lev. 19:27 ye shall not r. corners

ROUND.

Ex. 16:14 there lay a r. thing

1 *K.* 7:35 *r.* comp. 10:19 throne
Is. 3:18 L. take away th. *r.* tires
Luke 19:43 enemies comp. thee *r.*

ROUND about.

Num. 16:34 all Is. *r. a.* them fled
Jos. 6:3 ye shall go *r. about* city
Job 37:12 turn. *r. a.* by counsels
Ps. 3:6 and set agai. me *r. about*
48:12 walk about Zion, go *r. a.*
59:6 and go *r. about* the city, 14
88:17 they came *r. ab.* me daily
Rom. 15:19 *r. about* to Illyricum

See CAMP.

ROUSE.

Gen. 49:9 who shall *r.* him up?

ROVERS.

1 *Chr.* 12:21 helped Da. agai. *r.*

ROW, S.

Ex. 28:17 four *r.* stones, 39:10
Lev. 24:6 six on a *r.* on table
1 *K.* 6:36 inner court wi. three *r.*
7:2 four *r.* of pillars; 3 flft. in *r.*
12 the great court with th. *r.*
2 *Chr.* 4:3 two *r.* of oxen cast
Cant. 1:10 with *r.* of jewels
Ezek. 46:23 boiling places und. *r.*

ROWED, ING.

Jon. 1:13 men *r.* hard to bring it
Mark 6:48 saw them toiling in *r.*
John 6:19 had *r.* 25 or 30 furlon.

ROWERS.

Ezek. 27:26 *r.* bro' thee into wa.

ROYAL.

Gen. 49:20 Ash. yield *r.* dainties
Jos. 10:2 Gib. as one of *r.* cities
1 *Sam.* 27:5 I dwell in *r.* city?
2 *Sam.* 12:26 Joab took the *r.* ci.
1 *K.* 10:13 Sol. gave of *r.* bounty
2 *K.* 11:1 Athaliah destroyed all
the seed *r.* 2 *Chr.* 22:10
1 *Chr.* 29:25 on Solomon *r.* maj.
Est. 1:7 gave them *r.* wine
11 bring Vashti with crown *r.*
2:16 Es. taken into house *r.*, 17
5:1 Esther put on *r.* apparel
6:8 let *r.* apparel be brought,
and the crown *r.*
8:15 Mord. went in *r.* apparel
Is. 62:3 *r.* diadem in hand of G.
Dan. 6:7 to establish *r.* statute
Acts 12:21 Herod in *r.* apparel
Jam. 2:8 if ye fulfil the *r.* law
1 *Pet.* 2:9 ye are a *r.* priesthood

RUBBING.

Luke 6:1 *r.* them in their hands

RUBBISH.

Neh. 4:2 revive stones out of *r.*
10 decayed and th. is much *r.*

RUBY, IES.

Job 28:18 price of wisdom is ab.
r. Prov. 8:11
Prov. 3:15 more precious than *r.*
20:15 and a multitude of *r.*
31:10 her price is far above *r.*
Lam. 4:7 N. more ruddy than *r.*

RUDDER-BANDS.

Acts 27:40 and loosed the *r.-b.*

RUDDY.

1 *Sam.* 16:12 David was *r.* 17:42
Cant. 5:10 beloved white and *r.*
Lam. 4:7 her Naz. were more *r.*

RUDE.

2 *Cor.* 11:6 tho' I be *r.* in speech

RUDIMENTS.

Col. 2:8 any spoil you after *r.*
20 if dead with Ch. from the *r.*

RUE.

Luke 11:42 mint, *r.* and herbs

RUFUS.

Mark 15:21 fa. of Alex. and R.
Rom. 16:13 salute R. chosen

RUHAMAH.

Hos. 2:1 say to your sisters, R.

RUIN.

2 *Chr.* 28:23 they were *r.* of him
Ps. 89:40 thought his holds to *r.*
Prov. 24:22 who knoweth the *r. ?*
26:28 flatter. mouth worketh *r.*
Is. 3:6 let *r.* be under thy hand
23:13 land of Chaldeans to *r.*
25:2 made of a defen. city, a *r.*
Ezek. 18:30 iniq. not be your *r.*
27:27 comp. fall in day of thy *r.*
31:13 on his *r.* sha. fowls rema.
Luke 6:49 *r.* of that house great

RUINS.

Ezek. 21:15 *r.* may be multiplied
Amos 9:11 in day will I raise *r.*
Acts 15:16 build ag. the *r.* there.

RUINED.

Is. 3:8 Jerusalem is *r.* and Jud.
Ezek. 36:35 *r.* cities bec. fenced
36 I the L. build the *r.* places

RUINOUS.

2 *K.* 19:25 lay waste fenced cities
into *r.* heaps, *Is.* 37:26
Is. 17:1 Damascus sh. be *r.* heap

RULE, Substantive.

1 *K.* 22:31 *r.* over Ahab's chario.
Est. 9:1 Jews had *r.* over them
Prov. 17:2 wise serv. *r.* over son
19:10 serv. have *r.* over princes
25:28 hath no *r.* ov. his own sp.
Ec. 2:19 yet shall he *r.* over all
Is. 44:13 as carpenter stretch. *r.*
63:19 never barest *r.* over th.
1 *Cor.* 15:24 have put down all *r.*
2 *Cor.* 10:13 to measure of the *r.*
15 enlarged according to our *r.*
Gal. 6:16 walk accord. to this *r.*
Phil. 3:16 let us walk by same *r.*
Heb. 13:7 that have *r.* over you
17 obey them that have *r.* 24

See BARE, BEAR.

RULE, Verb.

Gen. 1:16 greater light to *r.* day,
lesser light to *r.* night, 18
3:16 thy husb. shall *r.* over thee
4:7 desire, th. shalt *r.* over him
Lev. 25:43 not *r.* wi. rigor, 46, 53
Jud. 8:22 *r.* thou over us, thou
23 I will not *r.* over you, nor
shall my son *r.*
Ps. 110:2 *r.* in midst of enemies
136:8 sun to *r.* by day
Prov. 8:16 princes *r.* and nobles
Is. 3:4 babes shall *r.* over them
12 as for my peo. wom. *r.* over
14:2 sh. *r.* over their oppressors
19:4 fierce king sh. *r.* over them
28:14 *r.* this peo. in Jerusalem
32:1 princes sh. *r.* in judgment
40:10 his arm shall *r.* for him
41:2 made the righteous man *r.*
52:5 they that *r.* make th. howl
Ezek. 19:14 no strong rod to *r.*
20:33 wi. fury will I *r.* over you
29:15 no more *r.* over nations
Dan. 4:26 known that heavens *r.*
11:3 mighty kings that shall *r.*
Joel 2:17 heathen sho. *r.* over th.
Zec. 6:13 sit and *r.* on his throne
Mat. 2:6 a governor that shall *r.*
Mark 10:42 are accounted to *r.*
Col. 3:15 peace of G. *r.* in hearts
1 *Tim.* 3:5 kn. not how to *r.* ho.
5:17 elders that *r.* well, worthy
Rev. 2:27 *r.* with a rod of iron,
12:5 ; 19:15

RULED.

Gen. 24:2 his eld. servant that *r.*
41:40 at thy word my peo. be *r.*
1 *K.* 5:16 3,000 *r.* over the people
Ezr. 4:20 wh. *r.* over countries
Ps. 106:41 they that hated th. *r.*

Is. 14:6 that *r.* nations in anger
Lam. 5:8 servants ha. *r.* over us
Ezek. 34:4 wi. cruelty have ye *r.*
Dan. 5:21 till he knew that G. *r.*

RULER.

Gen. 41:43 Pharaoh made Joseph
r. 45:8 ; *Ps.* 105:21
Ex. 22:28 thou shalt not curse *r.*
Num. 13:2 ev. one a *r.* am. them
1 *Sam.* 25:30 appointed thee *r.*
over my peo. Is. 2 *Sam.* 6:21;
7:8 ; 1 *Chr.* 11:2 ; 17:7
2 *Sam.* 7:8 I took thee from fol.
sheep to be *r.* 1 *Chr.* 17:7
1 *K.* 1:35 I appointed Solomon *r.*
1 *Chr.* 5:2 Jud. came the chief *r.*
9:11 A. *r.* of h. of G. 2 *Chr.* 31:13
2 *Chr.* 7:18 not fail a m. to be *r.*
Ps. 68:27 little Benja. wi. their *r.*
105:20 even the *r.* of the people
Prov. 23:1 sittest to eat with a *r.*
28:15 so is a wicked *r.* over poor
29:12 if a *r.* hearken to lies
26 many seek *r.* favor
Ec. 10:4 if spirit of the *r.* rise
5 error proceedeth from the *r.*
Is. 3:6 our *r.* 7 make me not *r.*
16:1 send ye the lamb to the *r.*
Jer. 51:46 viol. in land, *r.* ag. *r.*
Dan. 2:10 no *r.* ask. such things
5:7 third *r.* in kingdom, 16:29
Mic. 5:2 out of thee shall come *r.*
Mat. 9:18 there came a certain *r.*
24:45 hath made *r. Luke* 12:42
25:21 I will make thee *r.* ov. 23
Luke 13:14 *r.* of synagogue ans.
John 2:9 when *r.* of feast tasted
3:1 Nicodemus, a *r.* of the Jews
Acts 7:27 who made thee a *r. ? 35
35 same did G. send to be a *r.*
18:17 Greeks beat Sosthenes *r.*
23:5 shalt not spe. evil of the *r.*

RULERS.

Gen. 47:6 make th. *r.* over cattle
Ex. 18:21 *r.* of thou. *r.* of hun. 25
34:31 Moses called *r.* of congre.
Deut. 1:13 I will make them *r.*
2 *Sam.* 8:18 David's sons were *r.*
1 *K.* 9:22 were *r.* of his chariots
2 *K.* 11:4 Jehoiada set *r.* over, 19
1 *Chr.* 27:31 these were *r.* of sub.
2 *Chr.* 35:8 *r.* of the house of G.
Ezr. 9:2 hand of *r.* chief in this
Neh. 4:16 *r.* were behind house
12:40 half of the *r.* with me
13:11 then contended I with *r.*
Est. 9:3 of provinces helped
Ps. 2:2 *r.* take counsel ag. Lord
Is. 1:10 hear word of L. *r.* of S.
14:5 L. hath broken scept. of *r.*
22:3 all thy *r.* are fled together
29:10 your *r.* hath he covered
49:7 servant of *r.* kings sh. see
Jer. 33:26 not take of seed be *r.*
51:28 against *r.* 57 prince *r.*
Ezek. 23:6 lov. were capts. and *r.*
23 I will raise up *r.* against th.
Dan. 3:3 all the *r.* were gather.
Hos. 4:18 *r.* with shame do love
Mark 5:22 one of *r.* of synagogue
13:9 brought bef. *r. Luke* 21:12
Luke 23:35 *r.* also derided him
24:20 priest and *r.* deliver. him
John 7:26 do the *r.* know Chri.?
48 have any *r.* believ. on him?
12:42 chief *r.* believed on him
Acts 3:17 ye did it, as also did *r.*
4:26 *r.* gathered against Lord
13:15 *r.* of synagogue sent to P.
14:5 assault of Jews, with th. *r.*
16:19 damsel's mast. drew to *r.*
17:8 troubled the people and *r.*
Rom. 13:3 *r.* not a terror to good
Eph. 6:12 against *r.* of darkness

RULEST

2 *Chr.* 20:6 *r.* thou over kingdo.

RULEST

Ps. 89:9 thou *r.* raging of sea

RULETH.

2 Sam. 23:3 that *r.* over men
Ps. 59:13 know that G. *r.* in Ja.
66:7 he *r.* by his power for ever
103:19 his kingdom over all
Prov. 16:32 that *r.* his sp. is bet.
22:7 rich *r.* over the poor
Ec. 8:9 one man *r.* over another
9:17 when *r.* among fools
Dan. 4:17 Most High *r.* 25, 32
Hos. 11:12 Judah yet *r.* with G.
Rom. 12:8 he that *r.* with dilig.
1 *Tim.* 3:4 one that *r.* his house

RULING.

2 Sam. 23:3 just, *r.* in fear of G.
Jer. 22:30 *r.* any more in Judah
1 *Tim.* 3:12 *r.* th. chil. and hou.

RUMBLING.

Jer. 47:3 at *r.* of his wheels

RUMOR, S.

2 K. 19:7 he shall hear *r. Is.* 37:7
Jer. 49:14 I have heard *r.* from L.
51:46 lest ye fear for *r.* in land,
a *r.* sh. co. one yea. ano. a *r.*
Ezek. 7:26 *r.* shall be upon *r.*
Ob. 1 we heard a *r.* from Lord
Mat. 24:6 wars and *r.* of wars
Mark 13:7 of wars and *r.* of wars
Luke 7:17 *r.* of him went forth

RUMP.

Ex. 29:22 the fat and the *r. Lev.*
3:9; 7:3; 8:25; 9:19

RUN.

Gen. 49:22 branches *r.* over wall
Jud. 18:25 angry fellows *r.* upon
1 *Sam.* 8:11 some shall *r.* before
20:36 *r.* find out now the arrows
2 *Sam.* 18:19 let me now *r.* 22, 23
22:30 ha. *r.* thro' troop, *Ps.* 18:29
2 *K.* 4:22 that I may *r.* to man
5:20 I will *r.* after Naaman
2 *Chr.* 16:9 ey. of L. *r.* to and fr.
Ps. 19:5 strong man to *r.* race
58:7 wat. which *r.* continually
59:4 they *r.* and prep. themsel.

RUNNEST.

Prov. 4:12 wh. thou *r.* thou shalt

RUNNETH.

Job 15:26 he *r.* upon him
16:14 *r.* upon me like a giant
Ps. 23:5 anoi. head, cup *r.* over
147:15 his word *r.* very swiftly
Prov. 18:18 righteous *r.* into it
Lam. 1:16 eyes *r.* do. wat. 3:48
John 20:2 *r.* and cometh to Sim.
Rom. 9:16 nor of him that *r.*

---

*78:16 caused waters to *r.* down
104:10 springs which *r.* am. hil.
119:32 I will *r.* way of thy com.
136 riv. of waters *r.* down mine
Prov. 1:16 *r.* to evil, *Is.* 59:7
Ec. 1:7 all the rivers *r.* to sea
Cant. 1:4 we will *r.* after thee
Is. 40:31 shall *r.* not be weary
55:5 nations shall *r.* to thee
Jer. 5:1 *r.* to and fro thro' streets
9:18 eyes *r.* down with tears
12:5 thou hast *r.* wi. footmen
13:17 eyes *r.* do. wi. tears, 14:17
49:3 lament, and *r.* to and fro
19 I will make him *r.* 50:44
51:31 one port *r.* to meet anoth.
Lam. 2:18 let tears *r.* down
Ezek. 24:16 nei. shall thy tears *r.*
32:14 cause rivers to *r.* like oil
Dan. 12:4 many sh. *r.* to and fro
Joel 2:7 shall *r.* like mighty
9 shall *r.* in city, sh. *r.* on wall
Amos 5:24 let judgm. *r.* down
6:21 shall horses *r.* upon rock?
8:12 sh. *r.* to and fro to seek L.
Hab. 2:2 he may *r.* that readeth
Hag. 1:9 and ye *r.* every man to
Zec. 4:10 eyes of L. *r.* to and fro
Mat. 28:8 *r.* to bring disciples
1 *Cor.* 9:24 which *r.* in a race *r.*
all, so *r.* that ye may obtain
26 I theref. so *r.* not uncertain.
Gal. 2:2 I should *r.* or h..d *r.* in
5:7 did *r.* well, who did hinder
Phil. 2:16 I have not *r* in vain
Heb. 12:1 let us *r.* with patience
1 *Pet.* 4:4 that ye *r.* not to excess

RUNNING.

Lev. 14:5 kill. over *r.* wat. 6, 50
15:2 man hath a *r.* issue, 22:4
Num. 19:17 person take *r.* water
2 *Sam.* 18:24 a man *r.* alone, 26
27 *r.* of forem. is like *r.* of Ah.
2 *K.* 5:21 Naaman saw him *r.*
2 *Chr.* 23:12 Athal. heard peo. *r.*
Prov. 5:15 *r.* waters out of well
6:18 swift in *r.* to mischief
Is. 33:4 *r.* to and fro of locusts
Ezek. 31:4 her rivers *r.* about
Mark 9:25 Jesus saw people *r.*
10:17 there came one *r.*
Luke 6:38 good meas. and *r.* ov.
Rev. 9:9 sound of char. *r.* to bat.

RUSH, Substantive.

Job 8:11 can *r.* grow with. mire?
Is. 9:14 will cut off branch and *r.*
19:15 whi. branch or *r.* may do

RUSH, ETH.

Is. 17:13 nations sh. *r.* like rush.
Jer. 8:6 as horse *r.* into battle

RUSHED.

Jud. 9:44 Abimelech *r.* forward
20:37 liers in wait *r.* upon Gib.
Acts 18:29 *r.* with one accord

RUSHES.

Is. 35:7 dragons lay shall be *r.*

RUSHING.

Is. 17:12 woe to.multitude and *r.*
of nations, *r.* like *r.* of wat.
Jer. 47:3 at *r.* of chariots fathers
Ezek. 3:12 I heard a great *r.* 13
Acts 2:2 sound as of *r.* mighty
wind

RUST.

Mat. 6:19 moth and *r.* corrupt, 20
Jam. 5:3 *r.* of th. sh. be witness

RUTH.

Ruth 1:4 name of other R. 14
4:5 must buy it also of R. 10
Mat. 1:5 Booz beg. of Obed of R.

RYE.

Ex. 9:32 wheat and *r.* not smit,
Is. 28:25 barley and *r.* in place

S

SABAOTH.

Rom. 9:29 except L. of *s.* had left
Jam. 5:4 into ears of the L. of *s.*

SABBATH.

Ex. 16:23 to-morrow is holy *s.*
25 to-day is a *s.* to the Lord
20:10 sev. day is a *s.* of L. 31:15;
35:2; *Lev.* 23:3; *Deut.* 5:14
31:14 ye shall keep the *s.* 16
Lev. 16:31 a *s.* of rest, 23:3, 32
23:11 after *s.* priest sh. wave it
16 after sev. *s.* shall ye number
24 first of month sh. ye number
32 from even to even your *s.*
39 first day a *s.* on eighth a *s.*
25:2 then sh. land keep a *s.* 4, 6
Num. 28:10 burnt-offering of *s.*
2 *K.* 4:23 neith. new moon nor *s.*
16:18 covert for *s.* turned Ahaz
1 *Chr.* 9:32 prep. show-br. ev. *s.*
2 *Chr.* 36:21 desolate she kept *s.*
Neh. 9:14 madest kn. thy holy *s.*
10:31 would not buy on the *s.*
13:15 tread wine-presses on *s.*
16 men of Tyre sold on the *s.*
21 came they no more on the *s.*
Is. 56:2 bles. man that keep *s.* 6
58:13 turn foot from *s.* call *s.*
66:23 from one *s.* to another
Ezek. 46:1 on *s.* it shall be open.
Amos 8:5 when will *s.* be gone?
Mat. 28:1 in end of *s.* came Mary

Mark 2:27 *s.* for m. not m. for *s.*
28 Son of m. is L. of *s. Lu.* 6:5
16:1 when *s.* was past M. Mag.
Luke 6:1 on second *s.* after first
13:15 doth not each on *s.* loose?
23:54 preparation, *s.* drew on
John 5:18 not only had bro. *s.*
Acts 13:42 preached to th. next *s.*
16:13 on *s.* we went out of city
18:4 reasoned in syna. every *s.*

See DAY, DAYS.

SABBATHS.

Ex. 31:13 my *s.* ye shall keep,
Lev. 19:3, 30; 26:2
Lev. 23:15 seven *s.* sh. be compl.
25:8 thou shalt number seven *s.*
26:34 then shall land enjoy *s.* 35,
43; 2 *Chr.* 36:21
1 *Chr.* 23:21 burnt-sa. in *s.* 2 *Chr.*
2:4; 8:13; 31:3; *Neh.* 10:33
Is. 1:13 new moons and *s.* I can.
56:4 eunuchs that keep my *s.*
Lam. 1:7 advers. did mock at *s.*
2:6 L. caused *s.* to be forgotten
Ezek. 20:12 I gave *s.* to be sign
13 my *s.* they polluted, 16, 24
22:8 hast profaned my *s.* 23:38
26 priests hid eyes from my *s.*
44:24 keep my laws, hallow *s.*
46:3 worship at this gate in *s.*
Hos. 2:11 make to cease her *s.*

SABEANS.

Job 1:15 the S. fell on the oxen
Is. 45:14 merchandise of the S.
Ezek. 23:42 common sort were S.
Joel 3:8 shall sell them to the S.

SACK.

Gen. 42:25 every man's money
into *s.* 35; 43:21; 44:1
44:2 silver cup in *s.* mouth
12 cup was found in Benj.'s *s.*
Lev. 11:32 *s.* of uncle. put in wa.

SACKBUT.

Dan. 3:5 sound of *s.* 7, 10, 15

SACKCLOTH.

Gen. 37:34 Jac. put *s.* upon loins
2 *Sam.* 3:31 gird you with *s.*
21:10 Rizpah took *s.* and spread
1 *K.* 20:31 put *s.* on loins, 32
21:27 Ahab put *s.* on flesh, lay in *s.*
2 *K.* 6:30 looked, had *s.* within
19:1 H. cover. him wi. *s. Is.* 37:1
2 eld. of priests with *s. Is.* 37:2
1 *Chr.* 21:16 D. and elders clo. *s.*
Est. 4:2 none enter cloth. with *s.*
Job 16:15 sewed *s.* upon my skin
Ps. 30:11 put off *s.* girded with
35:13 sick, my clothing was *s.*
69:11 I made *s.* also my garm.
Is. 3:24 stomacher, girding of *s.*
15:3 in street gir. them. with *s.*
20:2 loose *s.* from off thy loins
22:12 day did L. call to girding *s.*

32:11 gird *s.* on loins, *Jer.* 4:8;
6:26; 48:37; 49:3
50:3 I make *s.* covering of hea.
Lam. 2:10 they girded themsel.
with *s. Ezek.* 7:18; 27:31
Dan. 9:3 seek L. with fast. and *s.*
Joel 1:8 lament like virgin wi. *s.*
13 lie all night in *s.*
Amos 8:10 I will bring *s.* on loins
Jon. 3:5 people of Nin. put on *s.*
6 king covered him with *s.*
8 man and beast be co. with *s.*
Rev. 6:12 sun became black as *c.*
11:3 proph. 1260 days, clo. in *s.*

SACKCLOTHES.
Neh. 9:1 Is. assembled with *s.* on

SACKS.
Gen. 42:25 fill *s.* with corn, 44:1
43:12 money brought again in *s.*
22 tell who put money in *s.*
Jos. 9:4 Gibeonites took old *s.*

SACRIFICE.
Gen. 31:54 J. offer. *s.* on mount
Ex. 5:17 let us do *s.* to Lord, 8:8
12:27 it is *s.* of Lord's passover
34:15 and thou eat of his *s.*
25 nor *s.* of passover be left
Lev. 7:12 shall offer *s.* of thanks.
16 if *s.* be vow, eaten same day
27:11 beast which they do not *s.*
Num. 15:3 *s.* in perform. vow, **8**
28:6 *s.* made by fire unto Lord,
8, 13, 19, 24; 29:6, 13, 36
Deut. 18:3 from them th. offer *s.*
Jud. 16:23 offer great *s.* to Dagon
1 *Sam.* 1:21 to offer yearly *s.* 2:19
2:29 kick ye at my *s.* and offer. *?*
3:14 E.'s house not purged wi. *s.*
9:12 *s.* of my people to-day
15:22 to obey is better than *s.*
16:3 call Jesse to the *s.* and I, **5**
20:6 is a yearly *s.* for family, **29**
1 *K.* 12:27 people do *s.* at Jerus.
18:29 prophesied till evening *s.*
36 at evening *s.* E. drew near
2 *K.* 5:17 not offer *s.* to other go.
10:19 I have great *s.* to do to B.
17:36 him sh. ye fear, and do *s.*
2 *Chr.* 7:5 S. offered *s.* 22,000 ox.
12 chosen place for house of *s.*
Ezr. 9:4 sat aston. till evening *s.*
5 at even. *s.* I arose fr. heavin.
Ps. 40:6 *s.* didst not desire, 51:16
50:5 made coven. with me by *s.*
116:17 I offer *s.* of thanksgiving
118:27 bind *s.* to horns of altar
141:2 lifting up hands as eve. *s.*
Prov. 15:8 *s.* of wicked abomina.
21:3 justice more accep. than *s.*
Ec. 5:1 than give *s.* of fools
Is. 19:21 Eg. sh. do *s.* and oblat.
34:6 L. hath a *s.* in Boz. and Id.
57:7 thi. wentest thou to offer *s.*
Jer. 33:11 that bring *s.* of praise
18 nor want man to do *s.*
46:10 God a *s.* in north country
Ezek. 39:17 gath. to my *s.* gre. *s.*
19 drink blood till drunk of *s.*
44:11 they shall slay *s.* for peo.
46:24 ministers boil *s.* of people
Dan. 8:11 daily *s.* 9:27; 11:31
12 host given him ag. daily *s.*
12:11 daily *s.* sh. be taken away
Hos. 3:4 Is. sh. abide witho. a *s.*
6:6 I desired mercy and not *s.*
Mat. 9:13; 12:7
Amos 4:5 offer a *s.* of thanksgiv.
Jon. 1:16 men offered a *s.* to L.
Zep. 1:7 L. hath prepared a *s.* 8
Mal. 1:8 if ye offer blind for *s.*
Mark 9:49 every *s.* sh. be salted
Luke 2:24 offer a *s.* accor. to law
Acts 7:41 in those days off. *s.* to
14:13 would have done *s.* with
Rom. 12:1 present your bodies *s.*
1 *Cor.* 8:4 off. in *s.* idols, 10:19, 28

Eph. 5:2 *s.* to G. for sweet savor
Phil. 2:17 off. on *s.* of your faith
4:18 *s.* accep. well-pleas. to God
Heb. 7:27 daily as those to offer *s.*
9:26 put away sin by *s.* of him
10:5 *s.* and off. thou wou. not, 8
12 had offered one *s.* for sins
26 remain. no more *s.* for sins
11:4 Abel offered more excel. *s.*
13:15 let us offer *s.* of praise

See BURNT, PEACE-OFFERING.

SACRIFICE, Verb.
Ex. 3:18 go, *s.* to L. 5:3, 8; 8:27;
10:25; 8:25 go ye *s.*
8:26 *s.* abomina. of Egyptians *?*
13:15 I *s.* to L. openeth matrix
20:24 thou shalt *s.* burnt-offer.
Deut. 15:21 blem. not *s.* it, 17:1
1 *Sam.* 1:3 Elkan. went up to *s.*
15:15 peo. spared best to *s.* to L.
16:2 I am come to *s.* to Lord, 5.
2 *K.* 14:4 as yet the people did *s.*
2 *Chr.* 33:17
17:35 nor shall *s.* to other gods
2 *Chr.* 11:16 came to J. to *s.* to L.
Ezr. 4:2 seek your God and do *s.*
Neh. 4:2 will they *s.* *?*
Ps. 54:6 I will freely *s.* to thee,
Ps. 107:22 *s.* sacrifices of thanks.
Ezek. 39:17 gath. to my *s.* I do *s.*
Hos. 4:13 *s.* on tops of mountains
14 they *s.* with harlots, there.
8:13 th. *s.* but L. accepteth not
12:11 they *s.* bullocks in Gilgal
13:2 let men that *s.* kiss calves
Jon. 2:9 I will *s.* with thanksgi.
Hab. 1:16 they *s.* unto their net
Zec. 14:21 they that *s.* sh. seethe
1 *Cor.* 10:20 Gentiles *s.* to devils

SACRIFICED.
Ex. 32:8 made calf, *s.* thereunto
Deut. 32:17 *s.* to devils, not to G.
Jos. 8:31 *s.* thereon peace-offer.
Jud. 2:5 they *s.* there unto Lord
1 *Sam.* 11:15 pe. went to G. to *s.*
2 *Sam.* 6:13 Dav. *s.* ox. and fatl.
1 *K.* 3:2 only the people *s.* in the
high places, 3; 2 *K.* 12:3;
15:4, 35; 16:4; 2 *Chr.* 28:4
11:8 strange wives, *s.* to th. go.
2 *K.* 17:32 lowest priests wh. *s.*
1 *Chr.* 21:28 L. answ. then he *s.*
2 *Chr.* 5:6 assc. be. ark, *s.* sheep
28:23 A. *s.* to gods of Damascus
33:16 Manasseh *s.* on altar of L.
34:4 on graves of th. that had *s.*
Ps. 106:37 they *s.* sons to devils.
38 they *s.* to idols of Canaan
Ezek. 39:19 sacri. which I have *s.*
Hos. 11:2 they *s.* to Baalim
1 *Cor.* 5:7 Ch. our Pass. is *s.* for
Rev. 2:14 things *s.* to idols, **20**

SACRIFICEDST.
Deut. 16:4 flesh *s.* rem. all night

SACRIFICES.
Gen. 46:1 Is. at Beer-sheba off. *s.*
Ex. 10:25 thou must give us *s.*
18:12 Jethro took *s.* for God
Lev. 10:13 *s.* of L. made by fire
17:7 sh. no more offer *s.* to dev.
Num. 25:2 called people to *s.*
28:2 *s.* observe to offer in season
Deut. 12:6 thither bring your *s.*
33:19 offer *s.* of righteousness
Jos. 13:14 *s.* of L. their inherita.
22:28 altar not for *s.* 29
1 *Sam.* 6:15 sacrificed *s.* to the L.
15:22 hath L. as great del. in *s.*
1 *Chr.* 29:21 sacrificed *s.* in abu.
2 *Chr.* 7:1 fire came and cons. *s.*
29:31 bring *s.* they brought in *s.*
Ezr. 6:3 place where he offer. *s.*
10 may offer *s.* to G. of heaven
Neh. 12:43 that day th. offered *s.*
Ps. 4:5 offer *s.* of righteousness
27:6 theref. will I offer *s.* of joy

50:8 not reprove thee for thy *s.*
51:17 *s.* of God are a broken sp.
19 pleased with *s.* of righteous.
106:28 joined to Baal-peor eat *s.*
107:22 sacrifice *s.* of thanksgivi.
Prov. 17:1 house full of *s.*
Is. 1:11 to what purpose your *s. ?*
29:1 year to year, let th. kill *s.*
43:23 nor honor. me with thy *s.*
24 nor fill. me with fat of thy *s.*
56:7 their *s.* shall be accepted
Jer. 6:20 nor are your *s.* sweet
7:21 burnt offerings to your *s.*
17:26 bringing *s.* of praise to L.
Ezek. 20:28 saw hill, and offer. *s.*
Hos. 4:19 be ashamed, bec. of *s.*
9:4 *s.* be as bread of mourners
Amos 4:4 bring your *s.* ev. morn.
5:25 have ye offer. unto me *s. ?*
Mark 12:33 love L. is more th. *s.*
Luke 13:1 blood Pi. mingl. wi. *s.*
Acts 7:42 offered *s.* forty years *?*
1 *Cor.* 10:18 eat *s.* partak. of altar
Heb. 5:1 offer gifts, *s.* for sins
8:3 high-pri. ordained to offer *s.*
9:9 were offered both gif. and *s.*
23 heav. things with better *s.*
10:3 in th. *s.* is a remembrance
11 off. same *s.* that never can
13:16 wi. such *s.* G. is well ple.
1 *Pet.* 2:5 priesthood to off. up *s.*

See BURNT.

SACRIFICETH.
Ex. 22:20 he that *s.* to any good
Ec. 9:2 that *s.* him that *s.* not
Is. 65:3 peo. that *s.* in gardens
66:3 he that *s.* a lamb
Mal. 1:14 and *s.* a corrupt thing

SACRIFICING.
1 *K.* 8:5 L. were wi. him *s.* sheep
12:32 *s.* to calves he had made

SACRILEGE.
Rom. 2:22 dost thou commit *s. ?*

SAD.
Gen. 40:6 J. looked, they were *s.*
1 *Sam.* 1:18 counten. no more *s.*
1 *K.* 21:5 why is thy spirit so *s. ?*
Neh. 2:2 why is thy counten. *s. ?*
Ezek. 13:22 made heart of righte.
s. whom I have not made *s.*
Mat. 6:16 be not of a *s.* counten.
Mark 10:22 he was *s.* at saying
Luke 24:17 as ye walk, and are *s.*

SADDLE.
Lev. 15:9 what *s.* he rideth upon

SADDLE, Verb.
2 *Sam.* 19:26 I will *s.* me an ass
1 *K.* 13:13 said, *s.* me the ass, **27**

SADDLED.
Gen. 22:3 Abrah. rose and *s.* ass
Num. 22:21 Balaam *s.* his ass
Jud. 19:10 with L. two asses *s.*
2 *Sam.* 16:1 met D. with asses *s.*
17:23 Ahithophel *s.* his ass
1 *K.* 2:40 Shimei *s.* and went
13:13 they *s.* him the ass, 23, **27**
2 *K.* 4:24 the woman *s.* an ass

SADDUCEES.
Mat. 3:7 wh. he saw the S. come
16:1 S. came tempting Jesus
6 beware of leaven of S. 11, **12**
22:23 the same day came the S.
34 he had put the S. to silence
Acts 4:1 the priests and S. came
5:17 S. laid hands on apostles
23:6 P. percei. one part were S.
8 S. say, There is no resurrect.

SADLY.
Gen. 40:7 why look ye so *s. ?*

SADNESS.
Ec. 7:3 by *s.* of countenance

SAFE.
1 *Sam.* 12:11 and ye dwelled *s.*

2 *Sam.* 18:29 is Absalom *s.* ? 32
Job 21:9 their houses *s.* from fear
Ps. 119:117 hold me up, I *sh.* be *s.*
Prov. 18:10 right. run in. are *s.*
29:25 whoso trusteth in L. be *s.*
Is. 5:29 carry the prey away *s.*
Ezek. 34:27 *sh.* be *s.* in th. land
Luke 15:27 had received him *s.*
Acts 23:24 may bring him *s.* to F.
27:44 they escaped all *s.* to land
Phil. 3:1 to write, for you it is *s.*

SAFEGUARD.
1 *Sam.* 22:23 thou shalt be in *s.*

SAFELY.
Ps. 78:53 he led them on *s.*
Prov. 1:33 hear. to me sh. dw. *s.*
3:23 shalt thou walk in way *s.*
31:11 husb. doth *s.* trust in her
Is. 41:3 pursued them, passed *s.*
Hos. 2:18 I will make them lie *s.*
Zec. 14:11 Jerusalem shall *s.*
Mark 14:44 and lead him away *s.*
Acts 16:23 jailer to keep them *s.*

See DWELL.

SAFETY.
Job 3:26 not in *s.* nor had I rest
5:4 his children are far from *s.*
11 that th. may be exalted to *s.*
11:18 shalt take thy rest in *s.*
24:23 given him to be in *s.*
Ps. 12:5 I will set him in *s.*
33:17 horse is vain thing for *s.*
Prov. 11:14 in counsel. is *s.* 24:6
21:31 horse for battle, *s.* is of L.
Is. 14:30 shall lie down in *s.*
Acts 5:23 prison shut with all *s.*
1 *Thes.* 5:3 sh. say, Peace and *s.*

See DWELL.

SAFFRON.
Cant. 4:14 *s.* calamus and cinna.

SAIL, Substantive.
Is. 33:23 could not spread the *s.*
Ezek. 27:7 spreadest to be thy *s.*
Acts 27:17 strake *s.* so were driv.
40 hoised up main *s.* to wind

SAIL.
Acts 20:3 as he was about to *s.*
16 Paul had determined to *s.*
27:1 when we sho. *s.* into Italy
24 G. hath given thee th. th. *s.*

SAILED.
Luke 8:23 as th. *s.* he fell asleep
Acts 27:7 when we had *s.* slowly

SAILING.
Acts 21:2 finding a ship *s.* over
27:6 centurion found a ship *s.*
9 when *s.* was now dangerous

SAILORS.
Rev. 18:17 and *s.* stood afar off

SAINT.
Ps. 106:16 they envied Aa. the *s.*
Dan. 8:13 I heard one *s.* speaking, another *s.* said to that *s.* which
Phil. 4:21 Salute every *s.* in C. J.

SAINTS.
Deut. 33:2 came with 10,000 of *s.*
3 all his *s.* are in thy hand
1 *Sam.* 2:9 keep the feet of his *s.*
2 *Chr.* 6:11 let thy *s.* rejoice
Job 5:1 wh. of *s.* wilt thou turn?
15:15 putteth no trust in his *s.*
Ps. 16:3 to *s.* that are in earth
30:4 sing to Lord, O ye *s.* of his
31:23 O love the L. all ye his *s.*
34:9 fear the Lord, ye his *s.*
37:28 Lord forsaketh not his *s.*
50:5 gather my *s.* together to
52:9 for it is good before thy *s.*
79:2 flesh of thy *s.* to beasts
89:5 faithfulness in congre. of *s.*
7 God is feared in assem. of *s.*
97:10 preserveth souls of his *s.*

116:15 prec. to L. is death of *s.*
132:9 let thy *s.* shout for joy
16 *s.* shall shout aloud for joy
145:10 and *s.* shall bless thee
148:14 exalt. praise of all his *s.*
149:1 praise in congrega. of *s.*
5 let *s.* be joyful in glory
9 this honor have all his *s.*
Prov. 2:8 preserv. way of his *s.*
Dan. 7:18 *s.* sh. take king. 22, 27
21 same horn made war wi. *s.*
25 wear out the *s.* of M. High
Hos. 11:12 Ju. is faithful with *s.*
Zec. 14:5 G. sh. come and all *s.*
Mat. 27:52 bodies of *s.* that slept
Acts 9:13 evil hath done to thy *s.*
32 Peter came down also to *s.*
41 when he had called the *s.*
26:10 many of *s.* did I shut up
Rom. 1:7 belov. of G. called to *s.*
8:27 maketh intercession for *s.*
12:13 distributing to neces. of *s.*
15:25 go to Jer. to minister to *s.*
26 a contribution for poor *s.*
31 serv. may be accepted of *s.*
16:2 receive her as becometh *s.*
15 salute all the *s.* *Heb.* 13:24
1 *Cor.* 1:2 sanctif. called to be *s.*
6:2 know th. *s.* sh. jud. world?
14:33 as in all churches of *s.*
16:1 concern. collection for *s.*
15 addicted to ministry of *s.*
2 *Cor.* 1:1 with all *s.* in Achaia
8:4 take on us ministering to *s.*
9:1 touching ministering to *s.*
12 not only suppli. want of *s.*
13:13 *s.* salute you, *Phil.* 4:22
Eph. 1:1 to the *s.* at Ephesus
15 heard of your love to all *s.*
18 glo. of his inheritance in *s.*
2:19 fellow-citizens with *s.*
3:8 am less than least of all *s.*
18 able to comprehend with *s.*
4:12 for perfecting of the *s.*
5:3 not be named as becom. *s.*
6:18 pray. with prayer for all *s.*
Phil. 1:1 to all the *s.* in C. Jesus
Col. 1:2 to all the *s.* and faithful
4 the love ye have to all the *s.*
12 partak. of inheritance of *s.*
26 mystery made manif. to *s.*
1 *Thes.* 3:13 coming of L. with *s.*
2 *Thes.* 1:10 glorified in his *s.*
1 *Tim.* 5:10 washed the *s.* feet
Phile. 5 love thou hast to all *s.*
7 bowels of the *s.* are refreshed
Heb. 6:10 ye have minis. to *s.*
Jude 3 faith once delivered to *s.*
14 L. com. with 10,000 of his *s.*
Rev. 5:8 the prayers of *s.* 8:3, 4
11:18 should. give reward to *s.*
13:7 to make war with the *s.*
10 patience and faith of the *s.*
14:12 here is patience of the *s.*
15:3 just are thy ways, K. of *s.*
16:6 they shed blood of the *s.*
17:6 drunken with blood of *s.*
18:24 in her was blood of the *s.*
19:8 linen is righteousness of *s.*
20:9 compassed camp of the *s.*

SAITH.
See JESUS, LORD, etc.

SAKE.
Gen. 8:21 not curse gr. for m. *s.*
12:16 entreated Abram for her *s.*
18:29 not do it for forty's *s.*
31 not for tw.'s *s.* 32 ten's *s.*
20:11 slay me for my wife's *s.*
26:24 mult. thy seed for Ab.'s *s.*
39:5 bles. house for Joseph's *s.*
Ex. 18:8 to Egypt for Israel's *s.*
21:26 for eye's *s.* 27 tooth's *s.*
Num. 11:29 env. thou for my *s.* ?
25:11 he was zealous for my *s.*
1 *Sam.* 12:22 fors. peo. for na. *s.*
23:10 destroy the city for my *s.*

2 *Sam.* 5:12 Lord exalted kingd. for Israel's *s.*
7:21 for word's *s.* 1 *Chr.* 17:19
2 *Sam.* 9:1 kindness for Jon. *s.* 7
18:5 deal gently for my *s.*
1 *K.* 8:41 cometh out far country for thy name's *s.* 2 *Chr.* 6:32
11:12 for Dav. thy father's *s.* 13, 32, 34 ; 15:4 ; 2 *K.* 8:19 ; 19:34 ; 20:6 ; *Ps.* 132:10
13 Jerusalem's *s.* I have chos.
Neh. 9:31 consume for mercies' *s.*
Job 19:17 entre. for children's *s.*
Ps. 6:4 save for mercies' *s.* 31:16
23:3 lead. me for name's *s.* !1:3
25:7 remem. me for goodn' *s.*'s
11 for name's *s.* pardon iniq.
44:26 redeem us for mercies' *s.*
69:6 not be confound. for my *s.*
79:9 purge sins for thy name' *s.*
106:8 saved th. for his name's *s.*
109:21 do for me, for name's *s.*
115:1 thy mercy and truth's *s.*
143:11 quick. me for name's *s.*
Is. 37:35 for own *s.* and Dav. *s.*
42:21 for righteousness' *s.*
43:14 for your *s.* sent to Baby.
25 our transgress. for own *s.*
45:4 for Jacob's *s.* I have called
48:9 for my name's *s.* I defer
11 for mine own *s.* will I do
62:1 for Zion's *s.* Jerusalem's *s.*
63:17 return for thy servant's *s.*
66:5 cast out for my name's *s.*
Jer. 14:7 do thou it for name's *s.*
21 do not abhor us for na. *s.*
Ezek. 20:9 but I wrought for my name's *s.* 14, 22, 44 ; 36:22
Dan. 9:17 shine on, for L.'s *s.*
19 defer not for th. own *s.* O G.
Jon. 1:12 for my *s.* tempest is
Mic. 3:12. Z. for your *s.* be ploug.
Mat. 5:11 evil ag. you for my *s.*
10:22 hat. for my name's *s.* 24:9 ;
Mark 13:13 ; *Luke* 21:17
39 he that loseth life for my *s.*
16:25 ; *Mark* 8:35 ; *Luke* 9:24
14:3 Herod had bound John for Herodias' *s.* *Mark* 6:17
19:12 eun. for kingd. heav.'s *s.*
29 left lands for my *s.* sh. rec.
Mark 10:29 ; *Luke* 18:29
Mark 4:17 persec. for word's *s.*
Luke 6:22 for Son of man's *s.*
John 12:9 came not for Jesus' *s.*
13:38 lay down life for my *s.* ?
14:11 believe me for works' *s.*
15:21 do to you for my name's *s.*
Acts 9:16 suffer for my name's *s.*
26:7 hope's *s.* I am acc. of Jews
Rom. 4:23 written for his *s.* alone
11:28 are enemies for your *s.*
15:30 Lord's *s.* strive in prayers
1 *Cor.* 4:10 we are fools for C. *s.*
9:23 this I do for the gospel's *s.*
2 *Cor.* 4:5 your serv. for Jesus' *s.*
11 delivered to death for J. *s.*
12:10 pleas. in distress. for C. *s.*
Eph. 4:32 G. for C. *s.* forg. you
Phil. 1:29 to suffer for his *s.*
Col. 1:24 for his body's *s.* church
3:6 things' *s.* wrath of G. com.
1 *Thes.* 1:5 we were for your *s.*
5:13 esteem for their work's *s.*
Phile. 9 for love's *s.* I beseech
1 *Pet.* 2:13 submit to every ordi. of man for Lord's *s.*
1 *John* 2:12 forgiv. for name's *s.*
2 *John* 2 for truth's *s.* that dwel.
3 *John* 7 for his name's *s.*
Rev. 2:3 for name's *s.* labored

Thy SAKE.
Gen. 3:17 cursed is gro. for *thy s.*
12:13 be well with me for *thy s.*
30:27 hath bless. me for *thy s.*
Ps. 44:22 for *t. s.* kill. *Rom.* 8:36
69:7 for *t. s.* I have borne repr.

Is. 54:15 shall fall for *thy s.*
Jer. 15:15 for *t. s.* I suff. rebuke
John 13:37 lay down life for *t. s.*

SAKES.
Gen. 18:26 spare place for th. *s.*
Lev. 26:45 for their *s.* rem. cov.
Deut. 1:37 Lord was angry with me for your *s.* 3:26; 4:21
Jud. 21:22 favorable for our *s.*
Ruth 1:13 grieveth me for your *s.*
1 *Chr.* 16:21 he reproved kings for their *s. Ps.* 105:14
Ps. 7:7 for th. *s.* return on high
106:32 went ill wi. Mo. for th. *s.*
Is. 65:8 so will I do for serv.'s *s.*
Ezek. 36:22 not for your *s.* Is. 32
Dan. 2:30 for th. *s.* make known
Mark 6:26 for their *s.* which sat
John 11:15 glad for your *s.*
12:30 this voice came for your *s.*
17:19 for their *s.* I sanct. myself
Rom. 11:28 belov. for fathers' *s.*
1 *Cor.* 9:10 saith he it for our *s. ?*
2 *Cor.* 4:15 all things for your *s.*
8:9 for your *s.* he became poor
1 *Thes.* 3:9 joy for your *s.* bef. G.
2 *Tim.* 2:10 end. all for elect's *s.*

SALAMIS. *Acts* 13:5

SALATHIEL.
1 *Chr.* 3:17 S. son of, *Mat.* 1:12
Luke 3:27 which was son of S.

SALE.
Lev. 25:27 count years of *s.*
50 price of *s.* according to yea.
Deut. 18:8 that wh. cometh of *s.*

SALEM.
Gen. 14:18 Melchiz. king of S.
Ps. 76:2 in S. also his tabernacle
Heb. 7:1 Melchiz. king of S. 2

SALMON.
Ruth 4:20, 21; 1 *Chr.* 2:11; *Mat.* 1:4, 5
Ps. 68:14 white as snow in S.
Luke 3:32 wh. was the son of S.

SALMONE.
Acts 27:7 Crete, over against S.

SALOME. *Mark* 15:40; 16:1

SALT.
Gen. 19:26 Lot's wife became *s.*
Lev. 2:13 wi. all thy off. offer *s.*
Deut. 29:23 wh. land thereof is *s.*
Jos. 15:62 chil. of J. had city of *s.*
Jud. 9:45 and sowed it with *s.*
2 *Sam.* 8:13 Syrians in val. of *s.*
2 *K.* 2:20 cruse, put *s.* therein
21 went to spring, cast *s.* in
14:7 Amazi. slew in valley of *s.* 10,000, 1 *Chr.* 18:12; 2 *Chr.* 25:11
Ezr. 6:9 have need of, wheat, *s.*
7:22 *s.* without pres. how much
Job 6:6 unsav. eaten without *s. ?*
Jer. 17:6 inh. places in a *s.* land
Ezek. 43:24 cast *s.* upon them
47:11 marshes shall be giv. to *s.*
Zep. 2:9 Moab shall be as *s.* pits
Mat. 5:13 ye are *s.* of earth, if *s.*
Mark 9:49 sacrifice salted wi. *s.*
50 *s.* is good, if *s.* have lost his saltness, ha. *s.* in yourselves
Luke 14:34 *s.* is good, but if *s.*
Col. 4:6 speech be season. wi. *s.*
Jam. 3:12 yield *s.* water and fre.

See COVENANT.

SALT sea.
Gen. 14:3 vale of Sid. wh. is *s. s.*
Num. 34:12 goings out be at *s. s.*
Deut. 3:17 *s.* sea under Ashdoth
Jos. 3:16 wat. came tow. *s. sea*
12:3 plain to *s. sea,* 15:2; 18:19

SALTED.
Ezek. 16:4 thou wast not *s.* at all
Mat. 5:13 wherew. shall it be *s. ?*

Mark 9:49 ev. one sh. be *s.* with fire, ev. sacri. be *s.* with salt.

SALTNESS.
Mark 9:50 if salt have lost his *s.*

SALUTATION, S.
Mark 12:38 scribes who love *s.*
Luke 1:29 what manner of *s.*
41 at *s.* of M. babe leaped, 44
1 *Cor.* 16:21 greet you, the *s.* of me, *Col.* 4:18; 2 *Thes.* 3:17

SALUTE.
1 *Sam.* 10:4 they will *s.* thee and
13:10 meet S. they migh' *s.* him
25:14 Da. sent to *s.* our Master
2 *Sam.* 8:10 sent his son to *s.* D.
2 *K.* 4:29 *s.* him not, if any *s.* th.
10:13 we go to *s.* child. of king
Mat. 5:47 if ye *s.* brethren only
10:12 wh. ye come in house *s.* it
Mark 15:18 and began to *s.* him
Luke 10:4 *s.* no man by the way
Acts 25:13 came to *s.* Festus
Rom. 16:5 *s.* well-beloved Epe.
7 *s.* Andronicus; 9 *s.* Urbane
10 *s.* Apelles, *s.* Aristo. house
11 *s.* Herodian; 12 *s.* Persis
13 *s.* Rufus chosen in Lord
16 *s.* wi. holy kiss, churches *s.*
22 I Tertius, *s.* you in Lord
1 *Cor.* 16:19 churches of A. *s.* you, Aquila and Priscilla *s.* you
2 *Cor.* 13:13 sai. *s.* you, *Phil.* 4:22
Phil. 4:21 *s.* every saint in C. J.
Col. 4:15 *s.* brethren in Laodicea
2 *Tim.* 4:19 *s.* household of One.
Tit. 3:15 all that are with me *s.*
Phile. 23 there *s.* thee Epaphras
Heb. 13:24 *s.* them that have rule over you, they of Italy *s.*
3 *John* 14 our friends *s.* thee

SALUTED.
Jud. 18:15 the Danites *s.* Micah
1 *Sam.* 17:22 David *s.* his breth.
1 *Sam.* 30:21 David came to peo. *s.* them
Mark 9:15 peo. run. to J. *s.* him
Luke 1:40 M. entered, *s.* Elisab.
Acts 18:22 P. when he *s.* church
21:7 we came and *s.* brethren
19 when Paul had *s.* James

SALUTETH.
Rom. 16:23 and Erastus, *s.* you
Col. 4:10 fellow-prisoner, *s.* you
12 a servant of Christ. *s.* you
1 *Pet.* 5:13 church at Bab. *s.* you

SALVATION.
Ex. 14:13 and see the *s.* of the Lord, 2 *Chr.* 20:17
Deut. 32:15 esteemed rock of *s.*
1 *Sam.* 11:13 L. wrought *s.* in Is.
14:45 Jona. who wro. great *s.*
19:5 L. wrought great *s.* for Is.
2 *Sam.* 22:51 tower of *s.* for king
1 *Chr.* 16:23 show fr. day to d. *s.*
35 save us, O God of our *s.*
2 *Chr.* 6:41 priests be clo. with *s.*
Ps. 3:8 *s.* belongeth to the Lord
14:7 O th. *s.* of Is. we. come, 53:6
24:5 righteous. from G. of his *s.*
35:9 soul shall rejoice in his *s.*
37:39 *s.* of the righteous is of L.
50:23 to him will I show *s.* of G.
65:5 answer us O G. of our *s.*
68:19 blessed be L. G. of our *s.*
20 he that is our G. is G. of *s.*
74:12 work. *s.* in midst of earth
78:22 they trusted not in his *s.*
79:9 help us, O God of our *s.*
85:4 turn us, O God of our *s.*
9 his *s.* nigh them th. fear him
95:1 joyf. noise to rock of our *s.*
96:2 show his *s.* fr. day to day
98:2 Lord hath made kn. his *s.*
3 ends of earth seen *s.* of God
116:13 I will take cup of *s.*

118:15 voice of *s.* in tabernacle
119:155 *s.* is far from wicked
132:16 clothe her priests with *s.*
144:10 he that giv. *s.* unto kings
149:4 will beautify meek with *s.*
Is. 12:3 water out wells of *s.*
25:9 be glad and rejoice in his *s.*
26:1 *s.* will G. appoint for walls
33:2 our *s.* in time of trouble
6 knowledge, and stren. of *s.*
45:8 earth open, let th. bring *s.*
17 Is. be saved with everlas. *s.*
46:13 place *s.* in Zion, for Israel
49:8 in a day of *s.* I helped thee
52:7 feet of him that publish. *s.*
10 ends of earth sh. see *s.* of G.
59:11 we look for *s.* far from us
16 therefore his arm bro. *s.*
17 put on helmet of *s.* on head
60:18 thy walls *s.* gates praise
61:10 clo. me wi. garments of *s.*
62:1 *s.* thereof as lamp burneth
63:5 mine own arm brought *s.*
Jer. 3:23 in vain is *s.* hoped for fr. hills, truly in L. is *s.* cf Ier.
Lam. 3:26 wait for *s.* of Lord
Jon. 2:9 that I vowed, *s.* of Lord
Hab. 3:8 didst ride on char. of *s.*
13 wentest for *s.* of thy people even for *s.* with th. anointed
Zec. 9:9 King, just, having *s.*
Luke 1:69 raised up horn of *s.*
77 to give knowl. of *s.* to peo.
3:6 all flesh shall see *s.* of God
19:9 *s.* is come to this house
John 4:22 worship, *s.* is of Jews
Acts 4:12 nei. is *s.* in any other
13:26 to you is word of *s.* sent
47 be for *s.* to ends of the earth
16:17 th. men show us way of *s.*
28:28 *s.* of G. is sent to Gentiles
Rom. 1:16 power of God to *s.*
10:10 confession is made to *s.*
11:11 *s.* is come to Gentiles
13:11 *s.* nearer th. wh. we beli.
2 *Cor.* 1:6 comfort. is for your *s.*
6:2 in day of *s.* I succored thee; now accepted time, day of *s.*
7:10 sorrow work. repent. to *s.*
Eph. 1:13 heard gospel of your *s.*
6:17 helmet of *s.* sword of Spirit
Phil. 1:28 evident token of *s.*
2:12 work out your *s.* with fear
1 *Thes.* 5:8 for a helm. hope of *s.*
9 appoi. us to obtain *s.* by L.
2 *Thes.* 2:13 G. chosen you to *s.*
2 *Tim.* 2:10 may obtain *s.* Christ
3:15 able to make wise to *s.*
Tit. 2:11 grace of G. bringeth *s.*
Heb. 1:14 who shall be heirs of *s.*
2:3 escape, if we neg. so great *s.*
10 Captain of their *s.* perfect
5:9 became Author of *s.* to all
6:9 things that accompany *s.*
9:28 sh. ap. without sin to *s.*
1 *Pet.* 1:5 kept thro' faith unto *s.*
9 your faith *s.* of your souls
10 of wh. *s.* prophets have inq.
2 *Pet.* 3:15 long-suffer. of L. is *s.*
Jude 3 to write to you of com. *s.*
Rev. 7:10 *s.* to G. 19:1 *s.* to Lord
12:10 now is come *s.* and stren.

My SALVATION.
Ex. 15:2 L. my song, bec. my *s.*
2 *Sam.* 22:3 shield, horn of my *s.*
47 be rock of my *s. Ps.* 18:46
23:5 all my *s.* all my desire
Job 13:16 he also shall be my *s.*
Ps. 25:5 thou art God of my *s.*
27:1 the Lord is my light and my *s.* 62:6; *Is.* 12:2
9 O God of my *s.* 51:14; 88:1
38:22 O L. my *s.* 62:2 is my *s.* 6
62:1 God, from him com. my *s.*
7 G. my *s.* 89:26 rock of my *s.*
91:16 and show him my *s.*
118:14 L. bec. my *s.* 21; *Is.* 12:2
140:7 Lord the strength of my *s.*

Is. 12:2 G. is *my s.* is bec. *my s.*
46:13 *my s.* shall not tarry
49:6 *my s.* to end of the earth
51:5 *my s.* gone for. 6 for ever
8 *my s.* it. generation to gene.
56:1 *my s.* is near to come
Mic. 7:7 wait for God of *my s.*
Heb. 3:18 joy in God of *my s.*
Phil. 1:19 I kn. this turn to *my s.*

Thy SALVATION.
Gen. 49:18 I waited for *thy s.*
1 *Sam.* 2:1 bec. I rejoice in *t. s.*
2 *Sam.* 22:36 hast also given me
   the shield of *thy s. Ps.* 18:35
Ps. 9:14 I will rejoice in *thy s.*
13:5 my heart shall rej. in *thy s.*
20:5 we will rejoice in *thy s.*
21:1 in *t. s.* how shall he rej. !
5 his glory is great in *thy s.*
35:3 say unto soul, I am *thy s.*
40:10 declared faithful. and *t. s.*
16 let such as love *thy s.* say
51:12 rest. to me joy of *t. s.* 70:4
69:13 hear me in truth of *thy s.*
29 let *thy s.* set me up on high
71:15 mouth sh. show forth *t. s.*
85:7 O Lord, grant us *thy s.*
106:4 remember me with *thy s.*
119:41 let *t. s.* come ac. to word
81 my soul fainteth for *thy s.*
123 mine eyes fail for *thy s.*
166 Lord, I have hoped for *t. s.*
174 I have longed for *t. s.* O L.
Is. 17:10 hast forgot. God of *t. s.*
62:11 say to Zion, *t. s.* cometh
Luke 2:30 mine eyes ha. seen *t. s.*

SAMARIA.
1 *K.* 16:24 Omri bought hill S.
Mic. 1:6 will make S. as a heap
Luke 17:11 through midst of S.
John 4:4 must needs go thro' S.
Acts 8:1 thro' regions of S. 5, 14

In SAMARIA.
1 *K.* 16:28 O. buried *in* S.'22:37
  29 Ahab reigned *in* S. 22:51
Amos 3:12 taken that dwell *in* S.
Acts 1:8 to me in Judea and *in* S.

SAMARITAN.
Luke 10:33 a certain S. came
17:16 giv. him thanks, was a S.
John 8:48 art a S. hast a devil

SAMARITANS.
2 *K.* 17:29 hi. places S. had made
Mat. 10:5 city of S. enter not
Luke 9:52 ent. into village of S.
John 4:9 J. have no deal. wi. S.
  39 many of S. of that city bel.
  40 the S. besought him to tarry
Acts 8:25 preached in vil. of S.

SAME.
Jud. 7:4 *s.* shall go, *s.* sh. not go
Ps. 102:27 but thou art the *s.*
113:3 to going do. of *s. Mal.* 1:11
Acts 24:20 or let these *s.* here say
Heb. 1:12 thou art *s.* thy years
2:14 he likewise took part of *s.*
13:8 J. Ch. *s.* yesterday, to-day

See DAY, HOUR.

SAMOS. *Acts* 20:15
SAMOTHRACIA. *Acts* 16:11

SAMSON.
Jud. 13:24 his name S. 16:29
Heb. 11:32 would fail to tell of S.

SAMUEL.
1 *Sam.* 1:20 son, called him S.
2:18 S. ministered bef. 21 ; 4:1
8:15 and S. feared to show Eli
10:1 S. took a vial of oil, 15, 25
15:11 it grieved S. 27, 33
16:13 S. took the horn of oil
19:18 Da. fied and came to S.

1 *Sam.* 28:11 wom. Bring me S.
2 *Chr.* 35:18 like that from S.
Ps. 99:6 S. among them that

Jer. 15:1 though Moses and S.
Acts 3:24 the prophets from S.
13:20 450 years till S. prophet
Heb. 11:32 would fail to tell of S.

SANBALLAT.
Neh. 2:10 when S. heard of it, 19
4:1 when S. heard we builded
6:2 S. and Ges. sent to me, 14
12 for Tobiah and S. had hired
13:28 Joiada son-in-law to S.

SANCTIFICATION.
1 *Cor.* 1:30 of G. is made to us *s.*
1 *Thes.* 4:3 will of G. even yo. *s.*
4 kn. how to possess ves. in *s.*
2 *Thes.* 2:13 *s.* of Sp. 1 *Pet.* 1:2

SANCTIFY.
Ex. 13:2 *s.* unto me first-born
19:10 go and *s.* them to-day
22 let the priests *s.* themselves
23 set bounds ab. mount, *s.* it
28:41 ano. and *s.* Aa. and sons,
  29:33 ; 40:13 ; *Lev.* 8:12 ; 21:8
29:36 shalt *s.* altar, 37 ; 40:10
44 I will *s.* taberna. and altar
30:29 thou shalt *s.* the taberna.
  40:10, 11 ; *Lev.* 8:11
31:13 I am L. that doth *s.* you,
  Lev. 20:8 ; 21:8 ; *Ezek.* 20:12
Lev. 11:44 ye shall *s.* yourselves,
  20:7 ; *Num.* 11:18 ; *Jos.* 3:5 ;
  7:13 ; 1 *Sam.* 16:5
21:15 seed, I the Lord do *s.* him
  23 I the L. do *s.* them, 22:9, 16
27:14 when a man sh. *s.* house
Num. 20:12 believed me not, to
  s. me, 27:14
Deut. 5:12 keep the sabbath, to
  s. it, *Neh.* 13:22
15:19 firstling males thou sh. *s.*
Jos. 7:13 *s.* people, *s.* yourselves
1 *Chr.* 15:12 said, *s.* yourselves,
  2 *Chr.* 29:5 ; 35:6
23:13 that he sho. *s.* holy things
2 *Chr.* 29:34 uprig. in heart'to *s.*
30:17 every one not clean to *s.*
Is. 8:13 *s.* Lord of hosts himself
29:23 they sh. *s.* H. O. of Jacob
66:17 *s.* themselves in gardens
Ezek. 36:23 I will *s.* my gr. name
37:28 I the Lord do *s.* Israel
38:23 I magnify myself, *s.* mys.
44:19 *s.* peo. with garm. 46:20
Joel 1:14 *s.* ye a fast, 2:15
2:16 *s.* congregation, assemble
John 17:17 *s.* them thro' thy tru.
19 for their sakes I *s.* myself
Eph. 5:26 *s.* and cleanse church
1 *Thes.* 5:23 God of peace *s.* you
Heb. 13:12 that he might *s.* peo.
1 *Pet.* 3:15 but *s.* the Lord God

SANCTIFIED.
Gen. 2:3 G. blessed sev. day *s.* it
Ex. 19:14 Moses *s.* the people
29:43 the tabernacle shall be *s.*
Lev. 8:10 *s.* the tabernacle
  15 *s.* the altar ; 30 *s.* Aaron
10:3 I will be *s.* in th. that come
27:15 if he that *s.* it will redeem
  19 if he that *s.* the field will
Num. 7:1 *s.* tabernacle instrum.
8:17 I *s.* the first-born of Isr.
Deut. 32:51 because ye *s.* me not
1 *Sam.* 7:1 and *s.* Eleazar his son
16:5 he *s.* Jesse and his sons
21:5 though it were *s.* this day
1 *Chr.* 15:14 priests and Levit. *s.*
2 *Chr.* 5:11 all the priests were *s.*
7:16 now I have *s.* this hou. 20
29:15 gather. and *s.* themselves
  17 *s.* house of L. in eight days
  19 all the vessels have we *s.*
30:3 priests had not *s.* themsel.
  15 Lev. ashamed, *s.* themselv.
17 many in congregation not *s.*
31:18 set office they *s.* themsel.
Neh. 3:1 built and *s.* sheep-gate

12:47 *s.* holy things to Levites
Job 1:5 Job *s.* sons and daught.
Is. 5:16 holy God shall be *s.*
13:3 I have commanded *s.* ones
Jer. 1:5 I *s.* thee, ordained thee
Ezek. 20:41 be *s.* in you, 36:23
28:22 when I shall be *s.* in her
  25 *s.* in sight of heathen, 39:27
38:16 when I shall be *s.* in thee
48:11 be for priests that are *s.*'
John 10:36 him, whom the Fa. *s.*
17:19 that they also might be *s.*
Acts 20:32 an inheritance among
  them which are *s.* 26:18
Rom. 15:16 being *s.* by H. Ghost
1 *Cor.* 1:2 them th. are *s.* in C. J.
6:11 ye are *s.* in name of Lord
1 *Cor.* 7:14 husband is *s.* wife is *s.*
1 *Tim.* 4:5 it is *s.* by word of G.
2 *Tim.* 2:21 vessel *s.* for Master's
Heb. 2:11 they who are *s.* are all
10:10 by which will we are *s.*
  14 he perfect. them that are *s.*
29 coven. wherewith he was *s.*
Jude 1 to them that are *s.* by G.

SANCTIFIETH.
Mat. 23:17 temple that *s.* gold ?
  19 or the altar that *s.* the gift ?
Heb. 2:11 he that *s.* and they
9:13 if blood of bulls *s.* to puri.

SANCTUARY.
Ex. 15:17 plant them in the *s.*
25:8 and let them make me a *s.*
30:13 give every one after the *s.*
36:1 all man. of work for *s.* 3, 4
38:24 shek. after sh. of *s.* 26, 27 ;
  Lev. 5:15 ; 27:3, 25 ; *Num.*
  3:47, 50 ; 7:13, 19, 25, 31, 37 ;
  18:16
Lev. 4:6 sprinkle blood before *s.*
10:4 carry brethren fr. before *s.*
12:4 nor come into *s.* till her
16:33 make atonem. for holy *s.*
19:30 ye shall rever. my *s.* 26:2
21:12 nei. shall he go out of the
  s. nor prof. the *s.* of his God
Num. 3:28 keeping charge of *s.*
4:12 wherewith minister in *s.*
10:21 set forward, bearing the *s.*
18:1 bear the iniquity of the *s.*
3 not come nigh vessels of *s.*
5 ye shall keep charge of the *s.*
19:20 he hath defiled *s.* of the L.
Jos. 24:26 set up a stone by *s.*
1 *Chr.* 9:29 oversee instrum. of *s.*
22:19 build ye the *s.* of the Lord
24:5 divided for governors of *s.*
28:10 to build a house for the *s.*
2 *Chr.* 20:8 built thee a *s.* therein
26:18 go out of *s.* for thou hast
29:21 for a sin-offering for the *s.*
30:8 yield to L. enter into his *s.*
  19 accord. to purification of *s.*
36:17 king of Bab. sl. men in *s.*
Neh. 10:39 where are vessels of *s.*
Ps. 20:2 L. send thee help fr. *s.*
63:2 I have seen thee in the *s.*
68:24 seen thy goings in the *s.*
73:17 till I went into *s.* of God
74:3 enemy done wickedly in *s.*
  7 they have cast fire into thy *s.*
77:13 thy way, O G. is in the *s.*
78:54 brou. them to border of *s.*
69 built his *s.* like high palaces
96:6 stren. and beauty in his *s.*
102:19 looked fr. height of his *s.*
114:2 Jud. his *s.* Is. his domin.
134:2 lift up your hands in *s.*
150:1 praise L. praise God in *s.*
Is. 8:14 L. of hosts, sh. be for *s.*
16:12 he shall come to his *s.*
43:28 I have prof. princes of *s.*
60:13 beautify the place of my *s.*
63:18 our adversaries trodden *s.*
Jer. 17:12 from begin. is our *s.*
Lam. 1:10 heathen enter. her *s.*

2:7 the Lord hath abhor. his *s.*
20 shall prophet be slain in *s.?*
4:1 stones of *s.* are poured out
Ezek. 5:11 thou hast defil. my *s.*
11:16 be to them as a little *s.*
23:38 defiled my *s.* in same day
42:20 between *s.* and prof. place
44:5 with every going forth of *s.*
27 in day he goeth into *s.*
45:3 the *s.* and most holy place
47:12 their wat. issued out of *s.*
48:8 *s.* shall be in midst, 10, 21
Dan. 8:11 place of *s.* cast down
13 give *s.* to be trod. und. foot
14 then shall the *s.* be cleansed
9:17 cause face to shi. on thy *s.*
26 peo. shall destr. city and *s.*
11:31 sh. pollute *s.* of strength
Zep. 3:4 her priests polluted *s.*
Heb. 8:2 a minister of *s.* tabern.
9:1 first coven. had a worldly *s.*
2 tabernacle which is called *s.*
13:11 whose blood is bro. into *s.*

SANCTUARIES.

Lev. 21:23 that he prof. not my *s.*
26:31 I bring your *s.* to desolat.
Jer. 51:51 stran. are come into *s.*
Ezek. 28:18 defiled *s.* by iniqui.
Amos 7:9 *s.* of Is. sh. be laid wa.

SAND.

Gen. 22:17 multi. seed as *s.* 32:12
41:49 Joseph gathered corn as *s.*
Ex. 2:12 hid the Egyptian in *s.*
Deut. 33:19 suck of trea. hid in *s.*
Jos. 11:4 went much people as *s*
Jud. 7:12 their camels were as *s*
1 *Sam.* 13:5 P. gath. to fight as *s*
2 Sam. 17:11 all Is. be gath. as *s.*
1 *K.* 4:20 J. and Isr. are ma. as *s.*
29 G. gave S. larg. of hea. as *s.*
Job 6:3 it would be heavier th. *s.*
29:18 I shall mul. my days as *s.*
Ps. 78:27 feath. fowls like as *s.*
139:18 more in number than *s.*
Prov. 27:3 sto. heavy, *s.* weighty
Is. 10:22 tho' thy peo. Is. be as *s.*
48:19 seed also had been as *s.*
Jer. 5:22 plac. *s.* for bound of sea
15:8 widows increased above *s.*
33:22 *s.* of sea cannot be meas.
Hos. 1:10 Is. as *s.* Rom. 9:27
Hab. 1:9 gather captivity as *s.*
Mat. 7:26 man built house on *s.*
Heb. 11:12 spr. of one many as *s.*
Rev. 13:1 I stood upon *s.* of sea
20:8 number of whom is as *s.*

SANDALS.

Mark 6:9 but be shod with *s.* put
Acts 12:8 gird thyself, bind thy *s.*

SANG.

Ex. 15:1 then *s.* Moses this song
Num. 21:17 Isr. *s.* Spring O well
Jud. 5:1 then *s.* Debor. and Bar.
1 *Sam.* 29:5 not D. of wh. th. *s.?*
2 Chr. 29:28 singers *s.* trumpet
30 they *s.* praises with gladn.
Neh. 12:42 the singers *s.* aloud
Job 38:7 morning stars *s.* togeth.
Ps. 106:12 belie. words *s.* praise
Acts 16:25 Pa. and Sil. *s.* praises

SANK.

Ex. 15:5 *s.* into the bottom
10 *s.* as lead in mighty waters

SAP.

Ps. 104:16 trees of L. full of *s.*

SAPHIR.

Mic. 1:11 thou inhabitant of S.

SAPPHIRA.

Acts 5:1 Ananias, with S. wife

SAPPHIRE.

Ex. 24:10 paved work of *s.* stone
28:18 second row a *s.* 39:11
Job 28:16 cannot be val. with *s.*
Lam. 4:7 th. polishing was of *s.*

Ezek. 1:26 thro. appearance of *s,*
10:1 over them as it were a *s.*
28:13 *s.* and emerald thy cover.
Rev. 21:19 founda. of wall was *s.*

SAPPHIRES.

Job 28:6 stones of it place of *s.*
Cant. 5:14 ivory, overlaid with *s.*
Is. 54:11 lay foundations with *s.*

SARAH.

Gen. 17:15 not Sar. but S. shall
18:9 where is S. 11, 12, 13, 14
20:2 Abraham said of S. She is
14 Abimelech restored S.
21:1 the Lord did unto S. as he
23:2 S. died in Kirjath-arba, 19
24:67 brought her into S. tent
25:10 Abra. buried and S. 49:31
Num. 26:46 daugh. of Asher S.
Is. 51:2 look to S. that bare you
Rom. 4:19 deadness of S. womb
9:9 will come, S. sh. have a son
Heb. 11:11 thro' faith S. receiv.
1 *Pet.* 3:6 as S. obeyed Abraham

SARAI.

Gen. 11:29 Ab.'s wife S. 30; 16:1
12:17 plagu. Pharaoh bec. of S.
16:6 S. dealt hardly with Ha. 8

SARDINE.

Rev. 4:3 to look upon like a *s.* sto.

SARDIS.

Rev. 1:11 write and send it to S.
3:1 to the angel in S. write, 4

SARDIUS.

Ex. 28:17 first row be *s.* 39:10
Ezek. 28:13 *s.* and diam. thy cov.
Rev. 21:20 sixth founda. was *s.*

SARDONYX.

Rev. 21:20 fifth foundat. was a *s.*

SAREPTA.

Luke 4:26 S. a city of, 1 K. 17:9
SARGON. *Is.* 20:1

SARON.

Acts 9:35 all at S. saw him

SARUCH.

Luke 3:35 which was son of S.

SAT.

Gen. 31:34 Ra. *s.* upon images
Ex. 12:29 Pha. that *s.* on throne
18:13 Moses *s.* to judge people
Jud. 20:26 wept, and *s.* before L.
1 *Sam.* 1:9 E. *s.* by post of temp.
4:13 Eli *s.* by wayside
1 *K.* 16:11 soon as he *s.* on thro.
21:13 chil. of Belial *s.* before N.
1 *K.* 22:10 two kings *s.* on thro.
2 *K.* 6:32 Elisha *s.* in his house
1 *Chr.* 17:1 as Da. *s.* in his house
Job 29:25 I chose way, *s.* chief
Ps. 26:4 not *s.* with vain persons
Jer. 3:2 ways hast thou *s.* for th.
15:17 I *s.* not in assem. of mock.
36:22 king *s.* in winter-house
Ezek. 3:15 I *s.* where they *s.*
8:1 *s.* in my house, elders *s.* bef.
20:1 came to inqui. of L. and *s.*
Dan. 2:49 Da. *s.* in gate of king
Mat. 4:16 people who *s.* in dark.
14:9 wh. *s.* with him, Mark 6:26
26:55 I *s.* daily with you
58 Peter *s.* with servants
Mark 16:19 *s.* on right hand of G.
Luke 7:15 he that was dead *s.* up
10:39 Mary *s.* at Jesus' feet
19:30 a colt wher. never man *s.*
John 4:6 Je. wearied, *s.* on well
Acts 3:10 *s.* for alms at beau. gate
Rev. 4:3 he that *s.* on throne
14:14 one *s.* like Son of man
19:11 *s.* upon him called Faith.
19 war with him *s.* on horse

SAT down.

Ex. 32:6 people *s. down* to eat
Deut. 33:3 they *s. d.* at thy feet

Ezr. 9:3 *s. down* astonished
10:16 *s. down* to examine mat.
Neh. 1:4 I *s. d.* mourn. cer. days
Est. 3:15 king and Ham. *s. down*
Job 2:8 Job *s. down* am. the ash.
Ps. 137:1 we *s. down,* yea, wept
Cant. 2:3 I *s. down* under shad.
Mat. 9:10 sinners came, *s. down*
26:20 *s. d.* with 12, Luke 22:14
Luke 4:20 gave book to min. *s. d.*
5:3 *s. d.* taught peo. out of ship
John 8:2 *s. d.* and taught them
Acts 13:14 went into synag. *s. d.*
16:13 *s. d.* and spake to women
Heb. 1:3 *s. d.* ri. hand of G. 10:12

SATAN.

1 *Chr.* 21:1 S. provoked David to
Job 1:6 S. came among them, 2:1
12 S. went from presence of L.
Ps. 109:6 S. stand at his hand
Zec. 3:1 S. stand. at right hand
2 L. said to S. L. reb. thee, O S.
Mat. 4:10 Get thee hence, S.
12:26 if S. cast out S. Mark 3:23,
26; Luke 11:18
16:23 get thee behind me, S.
Mark 8:33; Luke 4:8
Mark 4:15 S. taketh away word
Luke 10:18 beheld S. as lightning
13:16 S. hath bound eight. years
22:3 then entered S. into Ju. Is.
31 Simon, S. desired to ha. you
John 13:27 S. entered him
Acts 5:3 hath S. filled thy heart
26:18 turn fr. power of S. to God
Rom. 16:20 G. bruise S. und. feet
1 *Cor.* 5:5 deli. such an one to S.
7:5 S. tempt not for incontin.
2 *Cor.* 2:11 lest S. get advantage
11:14 S. transf. into angel of li.
12:7 messeng. of S. to buffet me
1 *Thes.* 2:18 come, but S. hinder.
2 *Thes.* 2:9 com. after work. of S.
1 *Tim.* 1:20 whom I deliv. to S.
5:15 some already turned aft. S.
Rev. 2:9 not J. but synag. of S.
13 Satan's seat where S. dwel.
24 have not kno. depths of S.
3:9 make th. of synagogue of S.
12:9 dragon cast out, called S.
20:2 laid hold on drag. wh. is S.
7 S. shall be loosed out of pris.

SATIATE, ED.

Jer. 31:14 *s.* soul of priests
25 I have *s.* weary soul
46:10 sw. shall be *s.* with blood

SATISFACTION.

Num. 35:31 no *s.* for life of mur.
32 no *s.* for him fled for refuge

SATISFY.

Job 38:27 *s.* deso. and waste gro.
Ps. 90:14 *s.* us early with mercy
91:16 wi. long life will I *s.* him
132:15 I will *s.* poor with bread
Prov. 5:19 let her breast *s.* thee
6:30 steal to *s.* soul wh. hungry
Is. 58:10 thou *s.* afflicted soul
11 L. sh. guide and *s.* thy soul
Ezek. 7:19 shall not *s.* their souls
Mark 8:4 man *s.* these wi. bread

SATISFIED.

Ex. 15:9 lust be *s.* upon them
Lev. 26:26 ye shall eat, not be *s.*
Deut. 14:29 fatherl. eat and be *s.*
33:23 O Naphtali, *s.* with favor
Job 19:22 are ye not *s.* wi. flesh?
Job 27:14 offsp. not be *s.* with br.
31:31 we cannot be *s.*
Ps. 17:15 be *s.* with thy likeness
22:26 meek shall eat and be *s.*
36:8 they sh. be *s.* with fatness
37:19 days of fam. they sh. be *s.*
59:15 let them grudge if not *s.*
63:5 my soul be *s.* with marrow
65:4 *s.* with goodn. of thy house

81:16 honey out of rock I *s.* thee
104:13 earth is *s.* with fruit
105:40 *s.* th. wi. bread of heaven
Prov. 12:11 tilleth land sh. be *s.*
14 man be *s.* wi. good by fruit
14:14 good man be *s.* fr. himas.
18:20 a man's belly be *s.*
19:23 he th. hath it sh. abide *s.*
20:13 open eyes, thou sh. be *s.*
30:15 three th. that are never *s.*
Ec. 1:8 eye is not *s.* wi. seeing
4:8 nei. is his eye *s.* with rich.
5:10 loveth silver shall not be *s.*
Is. 9:20 not be *s. Mic.* 6:14
44:16 he roasteth roast, and is *s.*
53:11 see of travail of soul, be *s.*
66:11 *s.* with breasts of consola.
Jer. 31:14 peo. be *s.* with goodn.
50:10 all th. spoil Chaldea be *s.*
19 soul be *s.* on mount Ephra.
Lam. 5:6 giv. hand to E. to be *s.*
Ezek. 16:28 couldest not be *s.* 29
Amos 4:8 drink wat. were not *s.*
Hab. 2:5 as death, cannot be *s.*

SATISFIEST, EST.
Ps. 103:5 *s.* mouth with good th.
107:9 he *s.* longing soul
145:16 and thou *s.* every thing
Is. 55:2 labor for that wh. *s.* not

SATISFYING.
Prov. 13:25 eateth to *s.* of soul
Col. 2:23 honor to the *s.* of flesh

SATTEST.
Ps. 9:4 th. *s.* in throne judging
Ezek. 23:41 *s.* upon stately bed

SATYR, S.
Is. 13:21 owls dwell, *s.* dance
34:14 *s.* shall cry to his fellow

SAUL.
Gen. 36:37 S. of Rehoboth, 38
1 *Sam.* 9:2 name was S. 14:51
17 when Samuel saw S. 18
10:11 is S. also among, 12; 19:24
21:11 S. hath sl. his thousands
Is. 10:29 Gibeah of S. is fled
Acts 7:58 man's feet name was S.
8:1 and S. was consenting to, 3
9:4 S. S. why perse. 22:7; 26:14
11 and inquire for one call. S.
17 S. the Lord hath sent, 22:13
22 but S. increased in strength
24 laying wait was kno. of S.
26 when S. was come to Jeru.
11:25 went to Tarsus to seek S.
30 by hands of Barnab. and S.
13:1 prophets brought up wi. S.
2 separate me Barnabas and S.
7 called for Barnabas and S.
9 S. set his eyes on him
21 G. gave unto th. S. son of C.

SAVE, *for except.*
2 *Sam.* 22:32 *s.* the L.? *Ps.* 18:31
Mat. 11:27 nor knoweth any the
F. *s.* Son
17:8 no man, *s.* J. *Mark* 9:8
Luke 18:19 none good, *s.* one, G.
John 6:46 seen Fa. *s.* he of God

SAVE.
Gen. 45:7 G. sent me to *s.* lives
Deut. 20:4 the Lord goeth to *s.*
22:27 there was none to *s.* her
28:29 and no man shall *s.* thee
Jud. 6:14 thou shalt *s.* Israel
15 wherewith shall I *s.* Israel?
31 plead for B.? will ye *s.* him
36 if thou *s.* Israel by my hand
37 I know thou wilt *s.* Israel
1 *Sam.* 9:16 th. he may *s.* my peo.
10:24 God *s.* king, 2 *Sam.* 16:16;
2 *K.* 11:12; 2 *Chr.* 23:11
14:6 no restraint, to *s.* by many
19:11 if thou *s.* not thy. this ni.
2 *Sam.* 3:18 by hand of Da. *s. Is.*
22:28 affli. peo. wilt *s. Ps.* 18:27
42 none to *s.* them, *Ps.* 18:41

---

1 *K.* 1:12 mayest *s.* thi. own life
25 say, God *s.* king Adonijah
34 God *s.* king Solomon, 39
20:31 peradvent. will *s.* thy life
2 *K.* 19:34 I will defend this city
to *s.* it, *Is.* 37:35
Neh. 6:11 would go to *s.* his life
Job 2:6 in thy hand, *s.* his life
20.20 not *s.* that wh. he desired
22:29 he shall *s.* humble person
40:14 thine ri. hand can *s.* thee
Ps. 20:9 *s.* L. let king hear us
28:9 *s.* thy people, *Jer.* 31:7
37:40 he shall *s.* them
44:3 neit. did their arm *s.* them
60:5 *s.* with right hand, 108:6
69:35 God will *s.* Z. build Judah
72:4 he shall *s.* child. of needy
13 he shall *s.* souls of needy
76:9 when God arose to *s.* meek
86:2 O my God, *s.* thy servant
16 *s.* the son of thy handmaid
109:31 *s.* him fr. those that con.
118:25 *s.* I beseech thee, O Lord
145:19 hear their cry, *s.* them
Prov. 20:22 wait on L. sh. *s.* thee
Is. 35:4 your God will *s.* you
45:20 pray unto a god cannot *s.*
46:7 he cannot ans. nor *s.* him
47:15 none shall *s.* thee
49:25 saith L. I will *s.* thy chil.
59:1 not shortened, it cannot *s.*
63:1 in righteousn. mighty to *s.*
Jer. 2:28 arise, if th. can *s.* thee
11:12 not *s.* them at all
14:9 a migh. man that cannot *s.*
15:20 I am with thee to *s.* thee,
saith L. 30:11; 42:11; 46:27
30:10 O Israel, I will *s.* thee
48:6 flee, *s.* your lives, be like
Ezek. 3:18 warn wicked, *s.* life
34:22 theref. will I *s.* my flock
36:29 will *s.* you ; 37:23 *s.* them
Hos. 1:7 I will *s.* them by the L.
and will not *s.* th. by sword
13:10 is there any may *s.* thee?
Hab. 1:2 cry to thee, wilt not *s.*
Zep. 3:17 he will *s.* will rejoice
19 I will *s.* her that halteth
Zec. 8:7 *s.* my people from east
9:16 L. their God shall *s.* them
10:6 I will *s.* house of Joseph
12:7 the Lord sh. *s.* tents of Ju.
Mat. 1:21 Je. shall *s.* his people
16:25 whosoever will *s.* his life,
Mark 8:35 ; *Luke* 9:24 ; 17:33
18:11 Son of man come to *s.* th.
wh. was lost, *Luke* 19:10
27:42 saved others, himself he
cannot *s. Mark* 15:31
49 whether E. will come to *s.*
Mark 3:4 is it lawful to *s.* or
kill ? *Luke* 6:9
Luke 9:56 not to destroy, but *s.*
23:35 *s.* himself, if he be Christ
37 *s.* thyself; 39 if Ch. *s.* thys.
John 12:47 not to judge, to *s.*
Acts 2:40 *s.* yourselves fr. gener.
27:43 centurion, willing to *s.* P.
Rom. 11:14 if I might *s.* some of
them, 1 *Cor.* 9:22
1 *Cor.* 1:21 preaching to *s.* them
7:16 shalt *s.* husband, *s.* wife
1 *Tim.* 1:15 Ch. came to *s.* sinn.
4:16 in doing this sh. *s.* thyself
Heb. 5:7 him that was able to *s.*
7:25 he is able also to *s.* them
Jam. 1:21 able to *s.* your souls
2:14 can faith *s.* him
4:12 able to *s.* and destroy
5:15 prayer of faith shall *s.* sick
20 shall *s.* a soul from death
Jude 23 and others *s.* with fear

See ALIVE.

SAVE me.
2 *K.* 16:7 *s. me* out of hand of k.

Ps. 3:7 arise, O L. *s. me*, O. G.
6:4 *s. me* for thy mercies' sake,
31:16 ; 109:26
7:1 *s. me* from them that perse.
31:2 house of defence to *s. me*
44:6 nor shall my sword *s. me*
54:1 *s. me*, O G. by thy name
55:16 and the Lord shall *s. me*
57:3 send from heav. and *s. me*
59:2 *s. me* from bloody men
69:1 *s. me*, for waters are come
71:2 incline thine ear, *s. me*
3 given commandment to *s. me*
119:94 *s. me*, I sou. thy precepts
146 I cried unto thee, *s. me*
138:7 thy right hand sh. *s. me*
Is. 38:20 L. was ready to *s. me*
Jer. 17:14 O Lord, *s. me*
Mat. 14:30 saying, Lord, *s. me*
John 12:27 Fa. *s. me* fr. this hour

SAVE us.
Jos. 10:6 come quickly, *s. us*
1 *Sam.* 4:3 may *s. us* fr. enemies
7:8 cry to the L. he will *s. us*
10:27 how shall this man *s. us*
11:3 if there be no man to *s. us*
2 *K.* 19:19 *s.* thou *us* out of his
hand, *Is.* 37:20
1 *Chr.* 16:35 *s. us*, O God
Ps. 80:2 stir up strength, *s. us*
106:47 *s. us*, O Lord our God
Is. 25:9 wait. for him, will *s. us*
33:22 Lord is our king, will *s. us*
Jer. 2:27 in trouble say, *s. us*
Lam. 4:17 nation could not *s. us*
Hos. 14:3 Asshur shall not *s. us*
Mat. 8:25 awoke, saying, L. *s. us*
1 *Pet.* 3:21 bapt. doth also *s. us*

SAVED.
Gen. 47:25 hast *s.* our lives
Ex. 1:17 *s.* men-children, 18
Num. 22:33 *s.* her alive
31:15 have ye *s.* women alive ?
Jud. 7:2 own hand hath *s.* me
8:19 if he had *s.* them alive
1 *Sam.* 27:11 Da. *s.* neither man
2 *Sam.* 19:5 serv. have *s.* thy life
2 *K.* 6:10 and *s.* himself there
Neh. 9:27 gavest saviors, who *s.*
Ps. 33:16 no king is *s.* by multi.
44:7 thou hast *s.* us fr. enemies
106:8 *s.* them for name's sake
10 *s.* fr. him that hated them
Is. 43:12 and have *s.* and showed
45:22 *s.* all ends of the earth
Jer. 4:14 wash heart may. be *s.*
8:20 summer ended, are not *s.*
Mat. 19:25 who then can be *s.* ?
Mark 10:26 ; *Luke* 18:26
24:22 no flesh be *s. Mark* 13:20
27:42 he *s.* others, *Mark* 15:31 ;
Luke 23:35
Luke 1:71 *s.* from our enemies
7:50 faith hath *s.* thee, 18:42
8:12 lest they believe and be *s.*
13:23 L. are th. few that be *s.* ?
John 3:17 that world might be *s.*
5:34 I say, that ye might be *s.*
Acts 2:47 L. ad. such as sh. be *s.*
4:12 no other na. whereby be *s.*
16:30 what must I do to be *s.* ?
27:31 ex. abide in ship, not be *s.*
Rom. 8:24 we are *s.* by hope
10:1 for Is. that they may be *s.*
1 *Cor.* 1:18 t*o* us who are *s.* of G.
5:5 that the spirit may be *s.*
10:33 that they may be *s.*
15:2 by which also ye are *s.*
2 *Cor.* 2:15 sweet savor in them *s.*
Eph. 2:5 by grace ye are *s.* 8
1 *Thes.* 2:16 Gent. that they be *s.*
2 *Thes.* 2:10 love of truth. th. be *s.*
1 *Tim.* 2:4 have all men to be *s.*
Tit. 3:5 accord. to mercy he *s. us*
1 *Pet.* 3:20 wherein 8 souls we. *s.*
4:18 if righteous scarcely be *s.*
2 *Pet.* 2:5 *s.* Noah, eighth person

Rev. 31:24 natio. *s.* walk in light
God, *or* **Lord SAVED.**
Ex. 14:30 L. *s.* Is. 1 *Sam.* 14:23
Deut. 33:29 who like th. *s.* by *L. ?*
1 *Sam.* 10:19 reject. *G.* who *s.* y.
2 *K.* 14:27 *L. s.* them by Jerobo.
1 *Chr.* 11:14 *L. s.* them by deliv.
2 *Chr.* 32:22 thus *L. s.* Hezekiah
Ps. 34:6 *L. s.* him out of troubl.
107:13 *L. s.* them out of distres.
Is. 63:9 angel *s.* th. in his love
2 *Tim.* 1:9 *God* who hath *s.* us
Jude 5 the *L.* having *s.* people

Shall, *or* **shalt be SAVED.**
Num. 10:9 ye *s. be s.* fr. enemies
2 *Sam.* 22:4 I *sh. be s.* from mine
enemies. *Ps.* 18:3
Ps. 80:3 face to shi. we *s. be s.*
Prov. 28:18 walk. uprigh. *s. be s.*
Is. 30:15 in returning *s.* ye *be s.*
45:17 but Israel *s. be s.* in Lord
Jer. 17:14 L. save me, I *s. be s.*
23:6 days Jud. *s. be s.* 33:16
30:7 Jacob's trouble, he *s. be s.*
Mat. 10:22 that endureth to end
s. be s. 24:13 ; *Mark* 13:13
Mark 16:16 he that believ. *s. be s.*
John 10:9 by me he *shall be s.*
Acts 2:21 whosoever shall call on
Lord, *s. be s. Rom.* 10:13
11:14 th. and thy house *s. be s.*
15:11 thro' grace we *shall be s.*
16:31 believe on L. Je. *sh. be s.*
Rom. 5:9 we *sh. be s.* from wrath
10 we *shall be s.* by his life
9:27 Is. as sand, remnant *s. be s.*
10:9 bel. God raised him, *s. be s.*
11:26 so all Israel *shall be s.*
1 *Cor.* 3:15 but he himself *s. be s.*
1 *Tim.* 2:15 *s. be s.* in child-bear.

SAVEST.
2 *Sam.* 22:3 th. *s.* me fr. violence
Job 26:2 how *s.* thou the arm ?
Ps. 17:7 O thou that *s.* right hand

SAVETH.
1 *Sam.* 14:39 liveth, who *s.* Isra.
17:47 the L. *s.* not with sword
Job 5:15 *s.* poor from the sword
Ps. 7:10 God, who *s.* the upright
20:6 the Lord *s.* his anointed
Ps. 34:18 *s.*such as he of cont. sp.
107:19 he *s.* th. out of distresses

SAVING.
Gen. 19:19 mercy in *s.* my life
Neh. 4:23 *s.* that ev. one put off
Ps. 20:6 *s.* strength of ri. hand
28:8 *s.* strength of his anointed
67:2 *s.* health among all nations
Ec. 5:11 *s.* beholding of them
Amos 9:8 *s.* I will not destroy J.
Mat. 5:32 *s.* for cause of fornica.
Luke 4:27 none cleansed, *s.* Naa.
Heb. 10:39 believe to *s.* of soul
11:7 Noah prepared an ark to *s.*
Rev. 2:17 *s.* he that receiveth it

SAVIOUR.
2 *Sam.* 22:3 my refuge, my S.
2 *K.* 13:5 the L. gave Israel a *s.*
Ps. 106:21 forgat God their S.
Is. 19:20 shall send them a S.
43:3 I am H. O. of Is. thy S.
11 I am L. beside th. is no S.
45:15 hidest thyself, O God, S.
21 a just G. and a S. th. is no.
60:16 know I the L. am thy S.
63:8 my peo. so he was their S.
Jer. 14:8 S. of Israel in trouble
Hos. 13:4 th. is no S. beside me
Luke 1:47 sp. rejoic. in G. my S.
2:11 born in city of Da. a S.
John 4:42 this is Ch. S. of world
Acts 5:31 God exalted to be S.
13:23 God raised to Israel a S.
Eph. 5:23 Chr. is S. of the body
Phil. 3:20 whence we look for S.
1 *Tim.* 1:1 comm. of G. our S.

2:3 accept. in sight of G. our S.
4:10 trust in God who is S.
2 *Tim.* 1:10 appearing of our S.
Tit. 1:3 according to God our S.
4 peace from L. Jes. C. our S.
2:10 adorn doctr. of God our S.
13 glorious appearing of our S.
3:4 after kind. of G. S. appear.
6 shed on us through C. our S.
2 *Pet.* 1:1 righteous. of G. our S.
11 kingdom of our Lord and S.
2:20 knowledge of our L. and S.
3:2 apostles of the Lord and S.
18 grow in knowledge of our S.
1 *John* 4:14 Fa. sent Son to be S.
Jude 25 to only wise God our S.

SAVIORS.
Neh. 9:27 thou gavest them *s.*
Ob. 21 *s.* shall come up on Zion

SAVOR.
Ex. 5:21 made our *s.* be abhor.
Lev. 26:31 not *s.* of sweet odors
Ec. 10:1 ointm. send stinking *s.*
Cant. 1:3 *s.* of good ointment
Joel 2:20 his stink and his ill *s.*
Mat. 5:13 salt lost *s. Luke* 14:34
2 *Cor.* 2:14 maketh manifest *s.*
16 *s.* of death unto de. *s.* of life

Sweet SAVOR.
Gen. 8:21 Lord smelled a *sw. s.*
Ex. 29:18 it is *s. s. Lev.* 1:9, 13,
17 ; 2:9 ; 3:5 ; 8:21 ; *Num.*
15:14 ; 18:17 ; 28:8
25 for a *s. s.* an offer. to L. 41 ;
Lev. 2:12 ; 3:16 ; 4:31 ; 6:15,
21 ; 8:28 ; 17:6 ; 23:13 ; *Num.*
15:7, 24 ; 18:17 ; 28:13, 27 ; 29:2,
6, 8 ; *Ezek.* 16:19
Lev. 23:18 for a *sweet s.* unto the
L. *Num.* 28:24 ; 29:13, 36
Num. 15:3 make a *s. s.* unto L.
28:13 offering of a *s. s.* to Lord
Ezek. 6:13 wh. they did offer *s. s.*
20:28 there th. made their *s. s.*
41 accept you with your *s. s.*
2 *Cor.* 2:15 we are to God a *s. s.*
Eph. 5:2 a sacrifice to God for a
sweet smelling *s.*

Sweet SAVORS.
Ezr. 6:10 sacrifices of *s. s.* to G.

SAVOREST.
Mat. 16:23 th. *s.* not the things
that be of God, *Mark* 8:33

SAVORY.
Gen. 27:4 ma. me *s.* meat, 7, 14
31 Esau had made *s.* meat

SAW.
Gen. 6:2 sons of G. *s.* daugh. of
9:23 they *s.* not ; 22:4 Abrah. *s.*
26:28 we *s.* Lord was with thee
Ex. 2:12 he *s.* th. was no man
10:23 they *s.* not one ano. 3 days
24:10 they *s.* the G. of Isra. 11
Num. 25:7 when Phinehas *s.* it.
Jud. 19:30 all that *s.* it said, No
1 *Sam.* 10:14 *s.* they were no wh.
17:24 Is. when they *s.* the man
1 *K.* 19:3 wh. he *s.* that, he arose
2 *K.* 2:12 Elisha *s.* it, he *s.* him
2 *K.* 4:25 when man of God *s.* her
2 *Chr.* 15:9 *s.* Lord was with him
25:21 *s.* one another in the face
Neh. 6:16 when they *s.* th. thin.
Job 20:9 the eye which *s.* him
29:8 the young men *s.* me
11 when the eye *s.* me, it gave
Ps. 114:3 sea *s.* it, and fled,
Cant. 3:3 *s.* ye him my soul lo. ?
Ezek. 8:10 so I went in, and *s.*
Hag. 2:3 who am. you *s.* house ?
Mat. 2:9 the star which they *s.*
12:22 dumb both spake and *s.*
17:8 they *s.* no man, save Jesus
Mark 8:23 asked him, if he *s.*
Luke 8:34 they *s.* what was done
47 when the woman *s.* that she

9:32 awake, they *s.* his glory
24:24 even so, him they *s.* not
John 8:56 Abraham *s.* my day
12:41 Esaias, when he *s.* his gl.
19:35 he that *s.* it, bare record
Acts 9:8 eyes opened, *s.* no man
12:3 he *s.* it pleased the Jews

SAW, *with* **Lord** *or* **God.**
Gen. 1:4 *G. s.* light it was good
10 called dry land, *G. s.*
it was good, 12, 18, 21, 25, 31
Ex. 3:4 *L. s.* that he turn. aside
2 *K.* 14:26 *L. s.* affliction of Isr.
2 *Chr.* 12:7 *L. s.* they humbled
Is. 59:15 *L. s.* it, it displeas. him
16 *L. s.* that there was no man
Jon. 3:10 God *s.* their works

I SAW.
Gen. 41:19 such as *I* never *s.*
44:28 and I *s.* him not since
Jud. 13:23 *I s.* he deliv. me not
1 *Sam.* 28:13 *I s.* gods ascending
1 *K.* 22:19 *I s.* the Lord on his
throne, 2 *Chr.* 18:18
Job 31:21 when *I s.* my help
Prov. 24:32 *I s.* and considered it
Ec. 2:24 this *I s.* fr. hand of God
8:10 *I s.* the wicked buried
Ezek. 16:50 th. away as *I s.* good
Hos. 9:10 *I s.* your fath. as first
13 Ephraim, as *I s.* Tyrus
John 1:32 *I s.* Spirit descending
48 under the fig-tree, *I s.* thee
Acts 26:13 *I s.* a light fr. heaven
Gal. 1:19 other apostles *s. I* no.
2:14 when *I s.* that they walked
Rev. 1:17 when *I s.* him, I fell at

SAW, S.
2 *Sam.* 12:31 he put Ammonites
under *s.* 1 *Chr.* 20:3
Is. 10:15 sh. *s.* magnify ag. him ?

SAWED, N.
1 *K.* 7:9 costly stones *s.* wi. sta.
Heb. 11:37 they were *s.* asunder

SAWEST.
Gen. 20:10 *s.* th. done this thing ?
1 *Sam.* 19:5 *s.* it and didst rejoice
28:13 be not afraid, for what *s.*
2 *Sam.* 18:11 J. said, thou *s.* him
Dan. 2:34 thou *s.* till a stone, 45

SAY.
Gen. 34:11 what ye *s.* to me, 12
37:20 *s.* some beast devour. him
44:16 what sh. we *s.* to my lord
Num. 22:19 know what L. will *s.*
Deut. 31:17 will *s.* in that day
Jos. 22:28 when they should *s.*
Jud. 7:11 sh. hear what they *s.*
2 *Sam.* 21:4 what you shall *s.*
1 *K.* 1:36 the L. G. of my lord *s.*
2:17 for he will not *s.* thee nay
Ezr. 9:10 O G. wh. shall we *s. ?*
Job 9:12 who will *s.* to him,
What doest thou ? *Ec.* 8:4
37:19 teach us what we shall *s.*
Is. 44:5 one shall *s.* I am Lord's
58:9 and he shall *s.* Here I am
Jer. 14:17 therefore thou shalt *s.*
23:7 *s.* no more, The Lord liveth
39:12 as he shall *s.* unto thee
42:20 according to all L. shall *s.*
Ezek. 13:7 ye *s.* The L. saith it
Mic. 3:11 *s.* Is not Lord am. us ?
Zec. 11:5 they *s.* I am rich
Mat. 3:9 think not to *s.* in yourselves, *Luke* 3:8
13:51 underst. ? they *s.* Yea, L.
16:15 but wh. *s.* ye that I am ?
Mark 8:29 ; *Luke* 9:20
21:3 *s.* aug. to you, ye eh. *s.*
16 him, Hearest what these *s. ?*
26 if we shall *s.* Of men, *Mark*
11:32 ; *Luke* 20:6
22:3 for they *s.* and do not
Mark 1:44 see thou *s.* nothi. to

John 8:26 many thi. to *s.* 16:12
54 whom ye *s.* he is your God
Acts 21:23 this that we *s.* to thee
23:18 something to *s.* unto thee
Acts 26:22 none but wh. M. did *s.*
1 *Thes.* 4:15 we *s.* to you by L.
Heb. 5:11 have many things to *s.*
Jam. 4:15 for that ye ought to *s.*

See BEGAN.

SAY, imperatively.

Is. 43:9 or hear, and *s.* it is truth
Zec. 1:3 *s.* unto them, Turn ye
Mat. 21:3 *s.* The Lord hath need
of them, *Mark* 11:3
Luke 7:7 *s.* in a word, my serv.

I SAY.

Ex. 3:13 what sh. *I s.* to them ?
4:23 *I s.* unto th. Let my son go
6:29 sp. all that *I s. Ezek.* 44:5
Jud. 7:4 *I s.* this shall go with
Is. 38:15 what shall *I s. ?*
Ezek. 2:8 hear wh. *I s.* unto thee
Mat. 8:9 *I s.* to th. man, *Lu.* 7:8
Luke 6:46 do not things wh. *I s.*
1 *Cor.* 9:8 *s. I* these thi. as man ?
15:50 *I s.* brethren, 2 *Cor.* 9:6 ;
Gal. 3:17 ; 5:16 ; *Eph.* 4:17 ;
Col. 2:4
Gal. 1:9 before, so *s. I* now again
Heb. 11:32 what shall *I* more *s. ?*

I SAY unto you.

2 *K.* 2:18 did *I* not *s. u. y.* go not
Mark 13:37 what *I. s. u. y.* I say
Rev. 2:24 *u. y. I s.* and to rest

SAYEST.

Ex. 33:12 *s.* to me, Bring people
Num. 22:17 do whatsoever th. *s.*
Ruth 3:5 all that thou *s.* unto me
1 *K.* 18:11 and now thou *s.* go, 14
Neh. 6:8 no such things as th. *s.*
Job 22:13 *s.* how doth G. know ?
Prov. 24:12 if thou *s.* behold
Is. 40:27 why *s.* thou, O Jacob
47:8 that *s.* in thy heart, I am
Mat. 27:11 *J.* said unto him, th.
s. Mark 15:2 ; *Luke* 23:3 ;
John 18:37
John 1:22 what *s.* th. of thyself ?

SAYING, Participle.

Mat. 26:44 prayed 3d time *s.* sa.
Acts 26:22 *s.* none other things

SAYING, Substantive.

Deut. 1:23 the *s.* pleased me well
1 *Sam.* 18:8 the *s.* displeased S.
2 *Sam.* 17:4 *s.* pleased Absalom
6 shall we do after his *s. ?*
24:19 Da. accord. to *s.* of God
1 *K.* 2:38 Shimei said, *s.* is good
12:15 might perf. his *s.* by Ahij.
13:4 J. heard *s.* of man of God
15:29 acc. to *s.* of L. 2 *K.* 10:17
17:15 acc. to *s.* of Elij. 2 *K.* 4:2
2 *K.* 5:14 accor. to *s.* of man, 8:2
Est. 1:21 *s.* pleased the king
Ps. 49:4 open dark *s.* on harp
Jon. 4:2 my *s.* wh. in country
Mat. 15:12 offended after this *s.*
19:11 all men cannot rec. this *s.*
Mark 7:29 for this *s.* go thy way
9:10 kept that *s.* with themselv.
32 but they understood not
that *s. Luke* 3:50 ; 9:45
10:22 he was sad at that *s.*
Luke 1:29 was troubled at his *s.*
2:17 they made known abroa. *s.*
9:45 feared to ask him of that *s.*
18:34 this *s.* was hid from them
John 4:37 herein is. true, one so.
39 many beli. for *s.* of wom. 42
6:60 hard *s.* who can hear ?
7:36 what manner of *s.* he said ?
8:51 if a man keep my *s.* 52
55 I know him, keep his *s.*
12:38 *s.* of Esaias be fulfilled
15:20 kept my *s.* will keep yours

18:9 *s.* of Je. might be fulfill. 32
19:8 Pilate heard *s.* was afraid
21:23 went *s.* abroad am. breth.
Acts 6:5 *s.* pleased the multitude
16:36 keeper told this *s.* to Paul
Rom. 13:9 comprehend. in this *s.*
1 *Cor.* 15:54 be brought to pass *s.*
1 *Tim.* 1:15 this is a faithful *s.*
4:9 ; 2 *Tim.* 2:11 ; *Tit.* 3:8
3:1 this is true *s.* if man desire

SAYINGS.

Num. 14:39 Mo. told th. *s.* to pe.
2 *Chr.* 13:22 Ahijah's *s.* are writ.
33:19 written am. *s.* of the seers
Ps. 78:2 I will utter dark *s.*
Prov. 1:6 underst. dark *s.* of wi.
4:10 O my son, receive my *s.*
20 incline thine ear to my *s.*
Mat. 7:24 whoso heareth these
s. 26 ; *Luke* 6:47
Luke 1:65 these *s.* noised abroad
2:51 mother kept th. *s.* in heart
9:44 let th. *s.* sink into your ea.
John 14:24 lov. not, keep. not *s.*

Acts 14:18 *s.* scarce restrained
19:28 heard *s.* full of wrath
Rom. 3:4 might. be justi. in *s.*
Rev. 22:6 *s.* faithful and true
7 blessed that keep. *s.* of book
10 seal not *s.* of prophecy of
this book

SCAB.

Lev. 13:2 in skin of flesh a *s.*
6 it is but a *s.* 7 if *s.* spread
14:56 this is the law for a *s.*
Deut. 28:27 L. smite thee with *s.*
Is. 3:17 L. will sm. thee wi. a *s.*

SCABBARD.

Jer. 47:6 put up thys. into thy *s.*

SCABBED.

Lev. 21:20 scurvy or *s.* not appr.
22:22 or *s.* he sh. not offer to L.

SCAFFOLD.

2 *Chr.* 6:13 S. had made braz. *s.*

SCALES.

Lev. 11:9 whatsoever have *s.* eat,
Deut. 14:9
10 that have no *s.* not eat, 12 ;
Deut. 14:10
Job 41:15 his *s.* are his pride
Is. 40:12 weighed mount. in *s.*
Ezek. 29:4 cause fish to stick to *s.*
Acts 9:18 fell from eyes as it had
been *s.*

SCALETH.

Prov. 21:22 a wise man *s.* city

SCALL.

Lev. 13:30 it is a dry *s.* a lepr.
31 plague of *s.* not deeper than
skin, shut him up th. h. *s.* 33
33 shav. but *s.* sh. be not shave
14:54 law of all leprosy and *s.*

SCALP.

Ps. 68:21 G. sh. wound hairy *s.*

SCANT.

Mic. 6:10 *s.* meas. is abominable

SCAPE-GOAT. *See* GOAT.

SCARCE.

Gen. 27:30 Ja. *s.* gone fr. father
Acts 14:18 sayings *s.* restrai. peo

SCARCELY.

Rom. 5:7 *s.* for right. man 1 die
1 *Pet.* 4:18 if righte. *s.* be saved

SCARCENESS.

Deut. 8:9 sh. eat bread witho. *s.*

SCAREST.

Job 7:14 thou *s.* me with dreams

SCARLET.

Gen. 38:38 bound a *s.* thread, 30
Ex. 25:4 and purple and *s.* 26:1,
31, 36 ; 27:16 ; 28:5, 6, 8, 15 ;
35:6, 23, 25 ; 38:18, 23

Num. 4:8 spr. on them cloth of *s.*
Jos. 2:18 bind *s.* thr. in window
2 *Sam.* 1:24 S. who clo. you in *s.*
Prov. 31:21 house. clothed wi. *s.*
Cant. 4:3 lips like a thread of *s.*
Is. 1:18 tho' your sins be as *s.*
Lam. 4:5 that were bro. up in *s.*
Dan. 5:7 clothed with *s.* 16, 29
Nah. 2:3 valiant men are in *s.*
Mat. 27:28 put on Jes. a *s.* robe
Heb. 9:19 took water, and *s.* wool
Rev. 17:3 woman sit on *s.* beast
18:12 no man buy. merch. of *s.*
16 great city that was cl. wi. *s.*

SCATTER.

Gen. 11:9 thence did L. *s.* them
49:7 divide in Ja. *s.* them in Is
Lev. 26:33 I will *s.* you am. heat.
Num. 16:37 take censers, *s.* fire
Deut. 4:27 sh. *s.* you among hea.
28:64 ; *Jer.* 9:16 ; *Ezek.* 12:15
32:26 I would *s.* th. into corners
1 *K.* 14:15 *s.* them beyond river
Neh. 1:8 if ye transgress, I will *s.*
Ps. 59:11 *s.* by thy power, O L.
68:30 *s.* peo. that delight in war
106:27 lifted up hand to *s.* them
144:6 cast lightning, *s.* them
Is. 28:25 cast fitches, *s.* cummin
41:16 whirlwind shall *s.* them
Jer. 13:24 I will *s.* th. as stubble
18:17 I will *s.* th. as with wind
23:1 woe to pastors that *s.* sheep
49:32 I will *s.* them into all
winds, 36 ; *Ezek.* 5:10, 12
Ezek. 5:2 third part thou shalt *s.*
6:5 *s.* your bones about altars
10:2 *s.* the coals over the city
12:14 *s.* tow. wind all that help
20:23 I would *s.* them am. heat.
29:12 I *s.* Egyptians, 30:23, 26
Dan. 4:14 hew down tree. *s.* fruit
11:24 he shall *s.* am. them prey
12:7 to *s.* power of holy people
Hab. 3:14 came as whirlw. to *s.*
Zec. 1:21 lift horn over Ju. *s.* it

SCATTERED.

Gen. 11:4 lest be *s.* upon earth
Ex. 5:12 peo. *s.* to gath. stubble
Num. 10:35 let all thine enemies
be *s. Ps.* 68:1
Deut. 30:3 whither L. hath *s.* th.
1 *Sam.* 11:11 Ammonites were *s.*
13:8 people were *s.* from Saul
2 *Sam.* 18:8 bat. *s.* over country
22:15 and *s.* them, *Ps.* 18:14
1 *K.* 22:17 saw Is. *s.* 2 *Chr.* 18:16
2 *K.* 25:5 his army *s. Jer.* 52:8
Est. 3:8 certain people *s.* abroad
Job 4:11 stout lions' whe. are *s.*
18:15 brimstone be *s.* on habit.
Ps. 44:11 *s.* us am. heathen, 60:1
53:5 G. *s.* bones of him th. enc.
68:14 when Almighty *s.* kings
89:10 thou hast *s.* thine enemies
92:9 workers of iniqu. sh. be *s.*
141:7 bones *s.* at grave's mouth
Is. 18:2 go ye to a nation *s.*
7 present be brought of peo. *s.*
33:3 lifting thy. nations were *s.*
Jer. 3:13 *s.* ways to strangers
10:21 all their flocks shall be *s.*
23:2 ye have *s.* my flock, away
30:11 end of nations wh. I *s.* th.
31:10 he that *s.* Is. will gather
40:15 that Jews should be *s.*
50:17 Israel is a *s.* sheep, driven
Ezek. 6:8 ye be *s.* thro' countries
11:16 though I *s.* them
17:21 th. that remain shall be *s.*
29:13 Egyptians gath. whith. *s.*
34:5 flock *s.* because no sheph.
6 flock was *s.* on face of earth
12 have been *s.* in cloudy day
21 push. diseased till ye *s.* th.
36:19 I *s.* them among heathen
46:18 that my people be not *s.*

Joel 3:2 plead for pe. wh. they *s.*
Nah. 3:18 people is *s.* on mount.
Hab. 3:6 everlast. mountains *s.*
Zec. 1:19 horns wh. ha. *s.* Ju. 21
7:14 I *s.* them with whirlwind
13:7 smite Shepherd, the sheep
  be *s. Mat.* 26:31 ; *Mark* 14:27
Mat. 9:36 *s.* as sheep hav. no sh.
Luke 1:51 *s.* proud in imaginat.
John 11:52 gath. children were *s.*
16:32 hour cometh ye sh. be *s.*
Acts 5:36 obey. Theudas were *s.*
8:1 were *s.* thro' regions of Ju.
4 were *s.* went preaching, 11:19
Jam. 1:1 twelve tribes that are *s.*
1 *Pet.* 1:1 strangers sh. thro' Pon.

SCATTERETH.
Job 37:11 the thick cloud he *s.*
38:24 wh. *s.* east wind on earth
Ps. 147:16 he *s.* the hoarfrost
Prov. 11:24 that *s.* yet increaseth
20:8 king *s.* away evil with eyes
26 a wise king *s.* the wicked
Is. 24:1 *s.* inhabitants of earth
Mat. 12:30 he that gath. not. wi.
  me, *s.* abroad, *Luke* 11:23
John 10:12 wolf catche. *s.* sheep

SCATTERING.
Is. 30:30 L. sh. show anger wi. *s.*

SCENT.
Job 14:9 through *s.* of water
Jer. 48:11 his *s.* is not changed
Hos. 14:7 *s.* thereof as wine of L.

SCEPTRE.
Gen. 49:10 *s.* not depart from Ju.
Num. 24:17 *s.* shall rise out of Is.
Est. 4:11 king shall hold out *s.*
5:2 held out to *s.* Es. golden *s.*
Ps. 45:6 *s.* of kingdom is right *s.*
Is. 14:5 Lord hath broken *s.*
Ezek. 19:11 had strong rods for *s.*
14 hath no strong rod to be *s.*
Amos 1:5 cut off him that hold. *s.*
8 him that holdeth *s.* from A.
Zec. 10:11 the *s.* of Egypt shall
Heb. 1:8 *s.* of righteous. is the *s.*

SCEVA.
Acts 19:14 seven sons of one S.

SCHISM.
Cor. 12:25 there should be no *s.*

SCHOLAR.
1 *Chr.* 25:8 the teacher as the *s.*
Mal. 2:12 L. cut off master and *s.*

SCHOOL.
Acts 19:9 disputing in *s.* of one

SCHOOLMASTER.
Gal. 3:24 the law was our *s.*
25 we are no longer under a *s.*

SCIENCE.
Dan. 1:4 in wisd. understand. *s.*
1 *Tim.* 6:20 avoi. babblings of *s.*

SCOFF.
Hab. 1:10 they sh. *s.* at kings

SCOFFERS.
2 *Pet.* 3:3 in last days *s.* walking

SCORCH, ED.
Mat. 13:6 they were *s. Mark* 4:6
Rev. 16:8 power was given to *s.*
9 men were *s.* with great heat

SCORN, Substantive.
Est. 3:6 *s.* to lay hands on Mord.
Ps. 44:13 makest us a *s.* 79:4
Hab. 1:10 princes shall be a *s.*
See LAUGHED.

SCORN, Verb.
Job 16:20 my friends *s.* me

SCORNER.
Prov. 9:7 that reproveth a *s.*
8 reprove not a *s.* lest he hate
13:1 but a *s.* heareth not rebuke
14:6 *s.* seeketh wis. findeth not
15:12 *s.* loveth not that reprov.

19:25 smite *s.* the simple will
21:11 when *s.* is punish. simple
24 *s.* is name, deal. in wra.
22:10 cast out *s.* and contention
24:9 *s.* is abomination to men
Is. 29:20 the *s.* is consumed

SCORNERS.
Prov. 1:22 how long will *s.* deli.
3:34 surely he scorneth the *s.*
19:29 judgm. are prepared for *s.*
Hos. 7:5 stretched hand with *s.*

SCORNEST, ETH.
Job 39:7 he *s.* multitude of city
18 she *s.* horse and his rider
Prov. 3:34 surely he *s.* scorner
9:12 if *s.* thou alone sh. bear it.
19:28 ungodly witness *s.* judg.
Ezek. 16:31 harlot, in th. thou *s.*

SCORNFUL.
Ps. 1:1 nor sitteth in seat of *s.*
Prov. 29:8 *s.* bri. city into snare
Is. 28:14 hear word of Lord, ye *s.*

SCORNING.
Job 34:7 drinks *s.* like water ?
Ps. 123:4 filled wi. *s.* of those at
Prov. 1:22 scorners delight in *s.*

SCORPION.
Luke 11:12 will he off. him a *s.* ?
Rev. 9:5 torment was as of *s.*

SCORPIONS.
Deut. 8:15 thro' wilder. where *s.*
1 *K.* 12:11 I will chastise you
  with *s.* 14 ; 2 *Chr.* 10:11, 14
Ezek. 2:6 among *s.* be not afraid
Luke 10:19 power to tread on *s.*
Rev. 9:3 power, as *s.* have power
10 had tails like *s.* and stings

SCOURED.
Lev. 6:28 brazen pot, it sh. be *s.*

SCOURGE, S.
Jos. 23:13 *s.* in your sides
Job 5:21 thou sh. be hid from *s.*
9:23 if the *s.* slay suddenly
Is. 10:26 Lord shall stir up a *s.*
28:15 overflow. *s.* shall pass, 18
John 2:15 made *s.* of small cords

SCOURGE, Verb.
Mat. 10:17 they will *s.* in th. syn.
20:19 shall *s.* him, *Mark* 10:34 ;
  Luke 18:33
23:34 some of them ye shall *s.*
Acts 22:25 is it lawful to *s.* Ro. ?

SCOURGED, ETH
Lev. 19:20 maid, she shall be *s.*
Mat. 27:26 wh. he had *s.* Jesus,
  Mark 15:15 ; *John* 19:1
Heb. 12:6 the Lord *s.* every son

SCOURGING, S.
Acts 22:24 sh. be examined by *s.*
Heb. 11:36 others had trial of *s.*

SCRABBLED.
1 *Sam.* 21:13 Da. feigned mad, *s.*

SCRAPE, D.
Lev. 14:41 cause house to be *s.*
  sh. pour out dust they *s.* off
43 if plague came after he *s.*
Job 2:8 Job took a potsherd to *s.*
Ezek. 26:4 I will also *s.* her dust

SCREECHOWL.
Is. 34:14 *s.* also shall rest there

SCRIBE.
2 *Sam.* 8:17 Seraiah was the *s.*
20:25 Sheva was *s.* and Zadok
2 *K.* 18:18 Shebna the *s.* 37 ; 19:2;
  Is. 36:3, 22 ; 37:2
22:3 Sha. the *s.* 8, 9, 10, 12; 2 *Ch.*
  34:15, 18, 20 ; *Jer.* 36:10
25:15 princ. *s.* of host, *Jer.* 52:25
1 *Chr.* 24:6 Shemaiah *s.* wrote
27:32 Jona. a wise man and a *s.*
Ezr. 4:8 Shimshai the *s.* wrote a
  letter, 9, 17, 23
7:6 Ezra, a ready *s.* 11, 12 ; *Neh.*
  8:4, 9, 13 ; 12:26, 36

Neh. 8:4 Ezra, *s.* stood on pulpit
Is. 33:18 where is the *s.* ?
Jer. 36:12 Elishama the *s.* 20, 21
26 take Baruch the *s.* and Jer.
37:15 house of Jonath. the *s.* 20
Mat. 8:19 a *s.* said, Master, I will
13:52 *s.* instructed unto kingd.
Mark 12:32 *s.* said unto him
1 *Cor.* 1:20 where is the *s.* ?

SCRIBES.
1 *Chr.* 2:55 the families of the *s.*
2 *Chr.* 34:13 of Lev. there were *s.*
Est. 3:12 king's *s.* called, 8:9
Jer. 8:8 pen of the *s.* is in vain
Mat. 5:20 ex. righteousness of *s.*
7:29 not as the *s. Mark* 1:22
16:21 suffer many things of *s.*
17:10 say *s.* E. must, *Mark* 9:11
20:18 betrayed to *s. Mark* 10:33
21:15 when the *s.* saw, they we.
23:2 *s.* and Phari. sit in M. seat
13 woe to y. *s.* 14:29 ; *Lu.* 11:44
Mark 2:6 went certain *s.* reason.
16 when the *s.* saw him eat wi.
8:31 be rejected of *s. Luke* 9:22
9:14 *s.* questioning with discip.
11:18 *s.* and c.-priests, *Lu.* 19:47
12:35 *s.* say Christ is son of D. ?
38 said, Bew. of *s. Luke* 20:46
14:1 the *s.* sought to take him
Luke 5:30 *s.* and Pharisees, 15:2
6:7 *s.* and Pharis. watched him
11:23 *s.* began to urge vehem.
20:1 *s.* came upon him, elders
19 priests and *s.* sought to lay
22:2 and *s.* sought to kill him
23:10 *s.* stood and accused him
John 8:3 the *s.* brought a woman
Acts 4:5 *s.* gathered ag. apostles
6:12 *s.* brou. Stephen to council
23:9 *s.* of Pharisees' part arose

SCRIP.
1 *Sam.* 17:40 D. put stones in *s.*
Mat. 10:10 nor *s.* for your journ.
Mark 6:8 ; *Luke* 9:3 ; 10:4
Luke 22:35 I sent you without *s.*
36 let him take his purse and *s.*

SCRIPTURE.
Dan. 10:21 what is noted in *s.*
Mark 12:10 ha. ye not read this *s.*
15:28 *s.* was fulfilled which saith
Luke 4:21 this day is *s.* fulfilled
John 2:22 they believed the *s.*
7:42 hath not *s.* said, Ch. com. ?
10:35 the *s.* cannot be broken
19:35 another *s.* saith, They sh.
Acts 1:16 this *s.* must needs have
8:32 place of *s.* which he read
35 Philip began at the same *s.*
Rom. 4:3 what saith *s.* ? 11:2 ;
  Gal. 4:30
9:17 *s.* saith, 10:11 ; 1 *Tim.* 5:18
Gal. 3:8 the *s.* foreseeing that G.
22 the *s.* hath concluded all
2 *Tim.* 3:16 *s.* is by inspi. of G.
Jam. 4:5 think *s.* saith in vain ?
1 *Pet.* 2:6 it is contained in *s.*
2 *Pet.* 1:20 no *s.* is of priv. inter.

SCRIPTURES.
Mat. 21:42 ha. ye nev. read in *s.*
22:29 not know. *s. Mark* 12:24
26:54 how shall *s.* be fulfilled ?
Mark 14:49 *s.* must be fulfilled
Luke 24:27 he expounded in all *s.*
32 while he opened to us the *s.*
45 that they mi. understand *s.*
John 5:39 search *s.* for in them
Acts 17:2 he reasoned out of *s.*
11 and searched the *s.* daily
18:24 Apollos, mighty in the *s.*
28 showing by *s.* Jesus was C.
Rom. 1:2 afore by prop. in ho. *s.*
15:4 thro' comf. of *s.* have hope
16:26 by the *s.* made known
1 *Cor.* 15:3 Christ died acc. to *s.*
4 Christ rose accordi. to the *s.*
2 *Tim.* 3:15 from child hast kn. *s.*

2 *Pet.* 3:16 as they do also oth. *s.*

SCROLL.

Is. 34:4 heav. sh. be rolled as *s.*
Rev. 6:14 heaven departed as a *s.*

SCUM.

Ezek. 24:6 woe to the pot wh. *s.*
11 that the *s.* may be consum.
12 her *s.* went out, her *s.*
in fire

SCURVY.

Lev. 21:20 none sh. ap. that is *s.*
22:22 *s.* or scabbed sh. not offer

SCYTHIAN.

Col. 3:11 is neither barbarian, S.

SEA.

Ex. 14:16 stretch hand over *s.* 27
21 Lord caused the *s.* to go
back, made the *s.* dry
15:10 blow, the *s.* covered them
20:11 L. made the *s. Ps.* 95:5:
Jon. 1:9; *Acts* 4:24; 14:15
Deut. 30:13 nor is it beyond *s.*
Jos. 24:7 brought *s.* upon them
1 *K.* 7:23 a molten *s.* 2 *Chr.* 4:2
39 set *s.* on right side of house
10:22 king had at *s.* a navy
18:43 go up, look toward the *s.*
2 *K.* 14:25 he restored coast to *s.*
16:17 Ahaz took down the *s.*
25:13 *s.* did Chaldees break, 16
1 *Chr.* 16:32 let the *s.* roar, *Ps.*
96:11; 98:7
2 *Chr.* 4:6 *s.* for priests to wash
20:2 multit. against beyond *s.*
Neh. 9:11 thou didst div. *s.* went
thro' the *s. Job* 26:12; *Ps.*
74:13; 78:13; *Jer.* 31:35
Job 7:12 am I a *s. ?* 38:8 shut *s. ?*
11:9 measure is broader than *s.*
14:11 as the waters fail from *s.*
28:14 *s.* saith, It is not with me
41:31 maketh the *s.* like a pot
Ps. 66:6 he turned *s.* to dry land
72:8 have dominion from *s.* to *s.*
78:53 *s.* overwhelmed th. enem.
104:25 this great and wide *s.*
107:23 go down to *s.* in ships
114:3 the *s.* saw it; 5 O thou *s.*
Prov. 8:29 gave to *s.* his decree
Is. 11:9 wat. cover *s. Hab.* 2:14
16:8 branches stretched over *s.*
19:5 waters shall fail from *s.*
23:2 merch. of Zid. pass over *s.*
4 be ashamed, *s.* hath spoken
11 he stretched his hand ov. *s.*
24:14 they shall cry aloud fr. *s.*
42:10 sing to L. ye that go to *s.*
50:2 at my rebuke I dry up *s.*
51:10 art thou w. hath dried *s. ?*
57:20 wicked are like troubled *s.*
Jer. 6:23 their voice roar. like *s.*
27:19 saith L. the pillars and *s.*
48:32 plants are gone over *s.*
50:42 their voice sh. roar like *s.*
51:36 I will dry up her *s.*
42 *s.* is come up upon Babylon
Lam. 2:13 breach is great like *s.*
Ezek. 26:3 *s.* causeth his waves
Dan. 7:3 great beasts came fr. *s.*
Amos 8:12 wander from *s.* to *s.*
Jon. 1:11 that *s.* may be calm?
Mic. 7:12 shall come from *s.* to *s.*
Nah. 1:4 he rebuketh the *s.* and
Hab. 3:8 wrath ag. *s.* that didst
15 thou didst walk through *s.*
Hag. 2:6 I shake heav. earth, *s.*
Zec. 9:10 his domin. from *s.* to *s.*
10:11 he shall pass through *s.*
Mat. 8:26 he arose and rebuk. *s.*
27 *s.* obey him, *Mark* 4:39, 41
23:15 ye compass *s.* and land
Luke 21:25 *s.* and waves roaring
Acts 27:40 commit. themsel. to *s.*
28:4 tho' he hath escaped the *s.*
1 *Cor.* 10:1 fathers passed thro' *s.*
Rev. 4:6 before throne was *s.* of

7:2 given to hurt earth and *s.*
10:6 created *s.* things therein
14:7 worship him that made *s.*
15:2 I saw a *s.* of glass, mingled
20:13 the *s.* gave up the dead.
21:1 and there was no more *s.*

By the SEA.

Ex. 14:9 them encampi. *by t. s.*
2 *Sam.* 17:11 Is. as sand *by the s.*
1 *K.* 5:9 I will convey them *by*
the *s.* 2 *Chr.* 2:16
Is. 18:2 sendeth ambassad. *by s.*
Jer. 46:18 as Carmel *by the s.*
Mark 4:1 multitude was *by the s.*
Rev. 18:17 many as trade *by t. s.*

See COAST, GREAT.

In, *and* into the SEA.

Ex. 15:1 horse and rider *into t. s.*
4 Pha.'s host he cast *into the s.*
Ps. 77:19 thy way *in the s.*
89:25 I will set his hand *in t. s.*
Ec. 1:7 all rivers run *into the s.*
Is. 43:16 L. mak. way *in the s.*
Ezek. 26:17 city strong *in the s.*
18 isles that are *in the s.*
47:8 waters go *into the s.* which
brought forth *into the s.*
Jon. 1:4 a mighty tempest *in t. s.*
12 and cast me *into the s.* 15
Zec. 9:4 smite her power *in t. s.*
10:11 smite waves *in the s.*
Mat. 8:24 arose a temp. *in the s.*
13:47 kingdom of heaven is like
a net cast *into the s.*
Mat. 21:21 cast *into the s. Mark*
11:23
Mark 9:42 we. cast *i. s. Lu.* 17:2
Luke 17:6 be thou plant. *in t. s.*
John 21:7 Pe. cast himself *i. t. s.*
Acts 27:38 cast out wheat *i. t. s.*
43 cast themselves *into the s.*
2 *Cor.* 11:26 in perils *in the s.*
Jam. 3:7 beasts and thi. *in the s.*
Rev. 5:13 ev. creature *in the s.*
16:3 ev. living soul died *in t. s.*
18:19 all that had ships *in t. s.*

Of the SEA.

Gen. 1:26 have dominion over
the fish *of the s.* 28; *Ps.* 8:8
9:2 fear upon fishes *of the s.*
32:12 seed as sand *of the s.*
49:13 Z. dwell at haven *of t. s.*
Ex. 15:19 bro. ag. waters *of t. s.*
Num. 11:22 shall fish *of the s.* be
2 *Sam.* 22:16 channels *of t. s.* ap.
4 *K.* 18:44 aris. cloud out *of t. s.*
Job 6:3 heavier than sand *of t. s.*
9:8 tread. upon waves *of the s.*
12:8 fishes *of the s.* sh. declare
36:30 he covereth bot. *of the s.*
38:16 enter into springs *of t. s.*
Ps. 33:7 gathereth waters *of t. s.*
68:22 people fr. depths *of the s.*
89:9 rulest the raging *of the s.*
93:4 mightier th. waves *of t. s.*
139:9 dwell in utte. parts *of t. s.*
Is. 5:30 like roaring *of the s.*
9:1 afflict her by way *of the s.*
10:22 Is. be as sand *of t. s. Hos.*
1:10; *Rom.* 9:27
23:4 even strength *of the s*
51:10 made depths *of the s.*
60:5 abundance *of the s.* sh. be
63:11 bro. them up out *of the s.*
Jer. 5:22 sand for bound *of the s.*
33:22 nei. sand *of t. s.* be meas.
Ezek. 26:16 princes *of the s.*
27:3 Tyrus, at entry *of the s.*
9 ships *of the s.* were in thee
38:20 fishes *of the s.* sh. shake
Hos. 4:3 fishes *of the s.* be taken
Amos 5:8 call waters *of t. s.* 9:6
9:3 hid from sight in bot. *of t. s.*
Mic. 7:19 cast sins in. dep. *of t. s.*
Hab. 1:14 men as fishes *of the s.*
Zep. 1:3 I will con. fishes *of s.*

Mat. 4:15 by way *of the s.* bey. J.
18:6 drowned in depth *of the s.*
Jam. 1:6 wav. is like wave *of s.*
Jude 13 raging waves *of the s.*
Rev. 8:8 third part *of the s.* bec.
13:1 beast rise out *of the s.*
20:8 number is as sand *of the s.*

See MIDST.

On, *or* upon the SEA.

Ps. 65:5 afar off *upon the s.*
Jer. 49:23 faint-hearted, sor. *on s.*
Mat. 14:35 J. to them walking *on*
the *s. Mark* 6:48; *John* 6:19
Rev. 7:1 wind sho. not blow *o. s.*
10:2 set his right foot *upon t. s.*
15:2 saw th. stand *o. t. s.* of gla.
16:3 poured out vial *upon t. s.*

SEAFARING.

Ezek. 26:17 was inhab. of *s.* men

SEA-MONSTERS.

Lam. 4:3 even the *s.-m.* draw out

See RED, SALT, SAND.

SEA-SHORE.

Gen. 22:17 seed as sand on *s.-s.*
Ex. 14:30 Egyp. dead upon *s.-s.*
Jos. 11:4 as sand upon *s.-s.*
Jud. 5:17 Asher contin. on *s.-s.*
1 *Sam.* 13:5 Phil. as sand on *s.-s.*
1 *K.* 4:29 heart as sand on *s.-s.*
Jer. 47:7 a charge against *s.-s.*
Heb. 11:12 as sand by *s.-s.*

SEASIDE.

Deut. 1:7 turn ye, and go by *s.*
Jud. 7:12 Midi. lay as sand by *s.*
2 *Chr.* 8:17 Solomon went to *s.*
Mat. 13:1 Jesus sat by the *s.*
Mark 2:13 he went again by *s.*
4:1 he began to teach by the *s.*
Acts 10:6 Sim. house is by *s.* 32

SEAS.

Gen. 1:10 gath. of wat. called *s.*
22 and fill the waters in the *s.*
Deut. 33:19 suck of abund. of *s.*
Neh. 9:6 thou hast made the *s.*
Ps. 8:8 passeth thro' paths of *s.*
24:2 he founded it upon the *s.*
65:7 stilleth the noise of the *s.*
69:34 let the *s.* praise him
135:6 Lord pleased, did he in *s.*
Is. 17:12 a noise like noise of *s.*
Jer. 15:8 wid. are abo. sand of *s.*
Ezek. 27:4 bor. are in midst of *s.*
25 made glorious in midst of *s.*
Ezek. 27:26 in the midst of *s.* 34
28:2 in seat of G. in midst of *s.*
8 slain in the midst of the *s.*
Dan. 11:45 taber. of palace bet. *s.*
Jon. 2:3 cast me into midst of *s.*
Acts 27:41 place wh. two *s.* met

SEAL, Substantive.

1 *K.* 21:8 Jez. sealed wi. Ah. *s.*
Job 38:14 turned as clay to the *s.*
41:15 scales shut with a close *s.*
Cant. 8:6 *s.* on heart, *s.* on arm
John 3:33 his *s.* that God is true
Rom. 4:11 circum. as *s.* of right.
1 *Cor.* 9:2 *s.* of mine apostleship
2 *Tim.* 2:19 hav. this *s.* the Lord
Rev. 6:3 the sec. *s.* 5 the third *s.*
7 the fourth *s.* 9 the fifth *s.*
12 when he opened the sixth *s.*
7:2 having *s.* of the living God
8:1 when he opened seventh *s.*
9:4 hurt those that have not *s.*
20:3 shut him up, set a *s.* upon

SEALS.

Rev. 5:1 book sealed with 7 *s.*
5 lion of J. prevail. to loose *s.*
9 thou art worthy to open *s.*
6:1 the Lamb opened one of *s.*

SEAL, Verb.

Neh. 9:38 prin. and priests *s.* 10:1
Is. 8:16 *s.* law am. my disciples
Jer. 32:44 subs. evidences, *s.* th.

Dan. 9:24 70 weeks to *s.* vision
12:4 D. shut up words, *s.* book
Rev. 10:4 *s.* th. things 7 thunders
22:10 *s.* not sayings of prophecy

SEALED.

Deut. 32:34 is not this *s.* among ?
1 *K.* 21:8 letters were *s.* wi. Ah.
Est. 3:12 *s.* wi. king's ring, 8:8
Job 14:17 transgres. *s.* in a bag
Cant. 4:12 my spouse is foun. *s.*
Is. 29:11 vis. as words of book *s.*
Jer. 32:10 I subscri. and *s.* evid.
Dan. 6:17 king *s.* it with a sign.
12:9 words are closed up, and *s.*
John 6:27 him hath G. the Fa. *s.*
Rom. 15:28 when I have *s.* to th.
2 *Cor.* 1:22 who hath *s.* and giv.
Eph. 1:13 ye were *s.* with H. Sp.
4:30 whereby ye are *s.* to-day
Rev. 5:1 book *s.* with sev. seals
7:3 hurt not earth, till *s.* serv.
4 I heard number of them *s.*
5 of Jud. were *s.* 12,000, 6, 7, 8

SEALEST, ETH, ING.

Job 9:7 sun, and *s.* up the stars
33:16 and *s.* their instruction
37:7 he *s.* up hand of ev. man
Ezek. 28:12 thou *s.* sum of wisd.
Mat. 27:66 *s.* stone and setting

SEAM.

John 19:23 coat was without *s.*

SEARCH, Substantive.

Deut. 13:14 inquire and make *s.*
Ezr. 4:15 that *s.* be made, 5:17
19 *s.* hath been ma. found, 6:1
Job 8:8 prepare thyself to the *s.*
38:16 hast th. walked in the *s. ?*
Ps. 64:6 accomplish a diligent *s.*
77:6 my spirit made diligent *s.*
Jer. 2:34 not found it by secret *s.*

SEARCH, Verb.

Lev. 27:33 he sh. not *s.* whether
Num. 10:33 to *s.* out a resting-p.
13:2 that they may *s.* the land
14:7 land we passed to *s.* is good
Deut. 1:22 send men, they sh. *s.*
Jos. 2:2 men to *s.* country, 3
Jud. 18:2 Danites sent men to *s.*
1 *Sam.* 23:23 I will *s.* him out
2 *Sam.* 10:3 sent to *s.* 1 *Chr.* 19:3
1 *K.* 20:6 servants, they shall *s.*
2 *K.* 10:23 *s.* that none of serv.
Job 13:9 good that he should *s. ?*
Ps. 44:21 sh. not G. *s.* this out ?
139:23 *s.* me, O G. kn. my heart
Prov. 25:2 honor of kings to *s.*
27 men to *s.* their own glory
Ec. 1:13 heart to *s.* by wisd. 7:25
Jer. 17:10 I the Lord *s.* heart
29:13 shall *s.* for me with heart
Lam. 3:40 let us *s.* our ways
Ezek. 34:6 none did *s.* nor seek
8 neither did my shepherds *s.*
11 I will both *s.* my sheep
39:14 end of 7 months sh. they *s.*
Amos 9:3 will *s.* and take them
Zep. 1:12 *s.* Jerus. with candles
Mat. 2:8 *s.* dilig. for young child
John 5:39 *s.* scrip. they testify
7:52 *s.* out of G. aris. no proph.

SEARCHED.

Gen. 31:34 Lab. *s.* found not, 35
Num. 13:21 went up, and *s.* land
32 bro. evil report of land, *s.*

Num. 14:34 after number of days
s. land
Deut. 1:24 came to Eshcol, *s.* it
Job 5:27 *s.* it, know it for good
28:27 he prepared it, *s.* it out
29:16 cause I knew not I *s.* out
32:11 whi. ye *s.* out what to say
36:26 number of his years *s.* out
Ps. 139:1 O L. thou hast *s.* me
Jer. 31:37 founda. of earth *s.* out
46:23 forest, tho' it cannot be *s.*
Ob. 6 how things of Esau *s.* out

Acts 17:11 Bereans *s.* scriptures
1 *Pet.* 1:10 prophets *s.* diligently

SEARCHEST, ETH.

1 *Chr.* 28:9 the Lord *s.* all hearts
Job 10:6 th. thou *s.* after my sin
28:3 and he *s.* out all perfection
39:8 he *s.* after ev. green thing
Prov. 2:4 if thou *s.* for treas.
18:17 neighbor cometh, *s.* him
28:11 poor th. hath under. *s.* out
Rom. 8:27 *s.* knows mind of Sp.
1 *Cor.* 2:10 Spirit *s.* all things
Rev. 2:23 I am he wh. *s.* reins

SEARCHING, S.

Num. 13:25 ret. from *s.* of land
Jud. 5:16 divisions of Reuben *s.*
Job 11:7 canst thou by *s.* find G. ?
Prov. 20:27 *s.* inw. parts of belly
Is. 40:28 no *s.* of his understand.
1 *Pet.* 1:11 *s.* what time Sp. of C.

SEARED.

1 *Tim.* 4:2 consc. *s.* wi. hot iron

SEASON, Substantive.

Gen. 40:4 continued a *s.* in ward
Ex. 13:10 keep ordin. in his *s.*
Deut. 16:6 *s.* th. comest out of E.
28:12 give rain to land in *s.*
Jos. 24:7 dw. in wildern. long *s.*
2 *K.* 4:16 this *s.* embrace a son
1 *Chr.* 21:29 altar at that *s.* in G.
2 *Chr.* 15:3 for *s.* been with. God
Job 5:26 as corn cometh in his *s.*
38:32 bri. forth Mazzaroth in *s.*
Ps. 1:3 bringeth fruit in his *s.*
22:2 I cry in night *s.* not silent
Prov. 15:23 word in *s.* how good ?
Ec. 3:1 to every thing th. is a *s.*
Is. 50:4 to speak a word in *s.*
Jer. 5:24 former and lat. rain in *s.*
33:20 not be day and ni. in th. *s.*
Dan. 7:12 lives prolong. for a *s.*
Hos. 2:9 take my wine in *s.*
Mark 12:2 at *s.* he sent to husb.
Luke 1:20 words fulfilled in *s.*
4:13 devil dep. from him for *s.*
13:1 present at that *s.* some
20:10 at the *s.* he sent servant
23:8 desir. to see him a long *s.*
John 5:4 angel went down at *s.*
35 willing for a *s.* to rejoice
Acts 13:11 not seeing sun for *s.*
19:22 himself stayed in A. a *s.*
24:25 convenient *s.* I will call
2 *Cor.* 7:8 though but for a *s.*
2 *Tim.* 4:2 instant in *s.* out of *s.*
Phile. 15 therefore departed a *s.*
Heb. 11:25 pleas. of sin for a *s.*
1 *Pet.* 1:6 tho' for a *s.* if need be
Rev. 6:11 sho. rest yet a little *s.*
20:3 after that loosed a little *s.*

See APPOINTED, DUE.

SEASONS.

Gen. 1:14 lights be for signs, *s.*
Ex. 18:22 judge peo. at all *s.* 26
Lev. 23:4 feasts proc. in their *s.*
Ps. 16:7 reins instr. in night *s.*
104:19 appointeth moon for *s.*
Dan. 2:21 changeth times and *s.*
Mat. 21:41 render fruits in th. *s.*
Acts 1:7 not for you to know *s.*
14:17 gave us rain and fruitful *s.*
20:18 I been with you at all *s.*
1 *Thes.* 5:1 of *s.* have no need

SEASON, ED.

Lev. 2:13 shalt thou *s.* with salt
Mark 9:50 wherew. will *s.* it ?
Luke 14:34 wherew. sh. it be *s. ?*
Col. 4:6 speech be with grace, *s.*

SEAT.

Jud. 3:20 Eg. rose out of his *s.*
1 *Sam.* 1:9 Eli sat upon *s.* 4:13
4:18 he fell from off *s.* backw.
20:18 bec. thy *s.* will be empty
25 sat on *s.* on a *s.* by wall
2 *Sam.* 23:8 Tachmon. sat in *s.*

1 *K.* 2:19 a *s.* for king's mother
Est. 3:1 Ha.'s *s.* above princes
Job. 23:3 O that I mi. come to *s.*
29:7 I prepared my *s.* in street
Ps. 1:1 sitteth in *s.* of scornful
Prov. 9:14 woman sitteth on *s.*
Ezek. 8:3 *s.* of image of jealousy
28:2 I sit on *s.* of God in midst
Amos 6:3 cause *s.* of viol. **come**
Mat. 23:2 Phar. sit in Moses' *s.*
Rev. 2:13 dwel. where Satan's *s.*

See JUDGMENT, MERCY.

SEATED.

Deut. 33:21 lawgiver was he *s.*

SEATS.

Mat. 21:12 *s.* of them that sold
doves, *Mark* 11:15
23:6 chief *s.* in syn. *Mark* 12:39
Luke 1:52 put mighty fr. their *s.*
11:43 ye love uppermost *s.* 20:46
Rev. 4:4 four and twenty *s.* upon
th. twenty-four elders
11:16 elders sat before G. on *s.*

SEBA.

Gen. 10:7 sons of Cush, S. and
Ps. 72:10 kings of Sheba and S.
Is. 43:3 I gave Ethiopia and S.

SEBAT.   *Zec.* 1:7

SECOND.

Ex. 26:4 the coupling of the *s.*
5:10 ; 36:11, 12, 17
28:18 *s.* row be emerald, 39:11
Lev. 5:10 offer *s.* for burnt offer.
Num. 2:16 set forth in *s.* rank
2 *K.* 9:19 he sent *s.* on horseback
1 *Chr.* 15:18 brethren of *s.* degree
Ec. 4:8 one alone, th. is not a *s.*
15 *s.* child stand up in stead
Ezek. 10:14 *s.* face was face of m.
Dan. 7:5 beast, *s.* like to a bear
Mat. 21:30 to *s.* said likewise
22:26 likewise the *s.* had her,
Mark 12:21 ; *Luke* 20:30
Luke 19:18 *s.* came saying, Lord
John 4:54 *s.* miracle Jesus did
Acts 12:10 were past *s.* ward
1 *Cor.* 15:47 *s.* man L. fr. heaven
Heb. 10:9 aw. first, may estab. *s.*
2 *Pet.* 3:1 *s.* epistle I write you
Rev. 2:11 not hurt of *s.* dea. 20:6
20:14 hell, this is *s.* death, 21:8

See DAY, MONTH.

SECOND time.

Gen. 43:10 had returned *s. time*
Lev. 13:58 washed the *s. time*
1 *Sam.* 26:8 I will not smite *s. t.*
1 *K.* 18:34 do it *s. t.* did it *s. t.*
2 *K.* 10:6 Jehu wrote letter *s. t.*
Is. 11:11 L. set his hand *s. time*
Jer. 1:13 word of Lord came to
me a *s. time*, 13:3 ; 33:1
Jon. 3:1 word came to Jon. *s. t.*
Mat. 26:42 he went *s. t.* prayed
Mark 14:72 *s. t.* the cock crew
John 3:4 enter *s. time* into womb
21:16 Jesus saith to Pe. *s. time*
Acts 10:15 voice spake to P. *s. t.*
2 *Cor.* 13:2 if I were present *s. t.*
Heb. 9:28 he shall appear *s. time*

SECOND year.

Gen. 47:18 they came the *s. y.* to
Joseph, and said, *Num.* 1:1
Num. 9:1 first month of *s. y.* L.
10:11 *s. y.* cloud was taken up
2 *K.* 19:29 ye shall eat in *s. year*,
springeth of same, *Is.* 37:30

SECONDARILY.

1 *Cor.* 12:28 God set *s.* prophets

SECRET, Substantive.

Gen. 49:6 come not into their *s.*
Job 15:8 hast th. heard *s.* of G. ?
29:4 wh. *s.* of G. was upon tab.
40:13 and bind their faces in *s.*

Ps. 25:14 *s.* of Lord with them
27:5 in *s.* of tabernacle, 31:20
64:4 may shoot in *s.* at perfect
139:15 when I was made in *s.*
Prov. 3:32 *s.* is with righteous
9:17 bread eaten in *s.* pleasant
21:14 a gift in *s.* pacifieth anger
25:9 discover not a *s.* to another
Is. 45:19 not spoken in *s.* 48:16
Ezek. 28:3 no *s.* that th. can hide
Dan. 2:18 mercies of G. conc. *s.*
19 then was *s.* revealed to D.
30 *s.* not revealed to me
4:9 I know no *s.* troubleth thee
Amos 3:7 revealeth *s.* to his ser.
Mat. 6:4 alms may be in *s.* thy
Father who seeth in *s.* 6, 18
6 pray to Father who is in *s.*
18 appear to Fath. in *s.*
John 7:4 doeth any thing in *s.*
10 went to feast as it were in *s.*
18:20 openly, in *s.* I said noth.
Eph. 5:12 thi. done of them in *s.*

SECRET, Adjective.

Deut. 27:15 put. idol in *s.* place
29:29 *s.* things belong unto L.
Jud. 3:19 I have *s.* errand
13:18 askest my name, it is *s.*
1 *Sam.* 5:9 emerods in *s.* parts
1 *Sam.* 19:2 abide in *s.* place
Job 14:13 th. thou keep me in *s.*
15:11 is any *s.* thing with thee?
20:26 darkness be hid in *s.* pla.
Ps. 10:8 in *s.* places doth murder
17:12 lion lurking in *s.* places
18:11 made darkn. his *s.* place
19:12 clc. thou me from *s.* faults
64:2 hide me fr. *s.* counsel of wic.
81:7 I answered thee in *s.* place
90:8 *s.* sins in light of counten.
91:1 dwel. in *s.* place of Most H.
Prov. 27:5 rebuke bet. th. *s.* love
Ec. 12:14 to judgment ev. *s.* thi.
Cant. 2:14 that art in *s.* places
Is. 3:17 L. will discover *s.* parts
45:3 riches of *s.* places
Jer. 2:34 not found by *s.* search
13:17 soul sh. weep in *s.* places
23:24 hide himself in *s.* places
49:10 I have uncovered *s.* places
Lam. 3:10 as lion in *s.* places
Ezek. 7:22 pollute my *s.* place
Dan. 2:22 reveal. deep *s.* things
Mat. 13:35 kept *s.* from founda-
tion of world, *Rom.* 16:25
24:26 behold, he is in *s.* chamb.
Mark 4:22 nor was any thi. kept
s. Luke 8:17
Luke 11:33 put. candle in *s.* place

SECRETS.

Deut. 25:11 wife tak. him by *s.*
Job 11:6 shew thee *s.* of wisdom
Ps. 44:21 he knoweth *s.* of heart
Prov. 11:13 talebearer reveal. *s.*
20:19 as a talebearer, reveal. *s.*
Dan. 2:28 a God that revealeth *s.*
29 that revealeth *s.* make. kn.
47 your God is a revealer of *s.*
Rom. 2:16 God shall judge the *s.*
1 *Cor.* 14:25 thus are *s.* of heart

SECRETLY.

Gen. 31:27 wheref. didst flee *s.?*
Deut. 13:6 if bro. entice thee *s.*
27:24 smiteth his neighbor *s.*
28:57 eat for want of things *s.*
Jos. 2:1 sent two men to spy *s.*
1 *Sam.* 18:22 comm. with Dav. *s.*
23:9 Saul *s.* practised mischief
2 *Sam.* 12:12 for thou didst it *s.*
2 *K.* 17:9 did *s.* things not right
Job 4:12 a thing was *s.* bro. me
13:10 reprove, if you *s.* accept
31:27 heart hath been *s.* enticed
Ps. 10:9 lieth in wait *s.* as a lion
31:20 keep them *s.* in pavilion
Jer. 37:17 Zedekiah asked him *s.*

Hab. 3:14 to devour the poor *s.*
John 11:28 called M. her sister *s.*
19:38 Joseph was a disciple, *s.*

SECT.

Acts 5:17 wh. is *s.* of Sadducees
15:5 the *s.* of Pharisees believed
24:5 of the *s.* of the Nazarenes
26:5 straitest *s.* of our religion
28:22 *s.* everywhere spo. against

SECURE.

Jud. 8:11 smote host, it was *s.*
18:7 after manner of Zidoni. *s.*
Job 11:18 thou shalt be *s.*
12:6 they that provoke G. are *s.*
Mat. 28:14 persuade him, *s.* you

SECURELY.

Prov. 3:29 seeing he dwelleth *s.*
Mic. 2:8 them that pass by *s.*

SECURITY.

Acts 17:9 when they had taken *s.*

SEDITION, S.

Ezr. 4:15 moved *s.* in city, 19
Luke 23:19 for *s.* in prison, 25
Acts 24:5 this man mover of *s.*
Gal. 5:20 works of flesh are *s.*

SEDUCE, ED.

2 *K.* 21:9 Manasseh *s.* them to do
Is. 19:13 they have also *s.* Egypt
Ezek. 13:10 they have *s.* my peo.
Mark 13:22 signs and wonders *s.*
1 *John* 2:26 concern. them that *s.*
Rev. 2:20 Jezebel to *s.* my serv.

SEDUCERS.

2 *Tim.* 3:13 *s.* shall wax worse

SEDUCETH, ING.

Prov. 12:26 way of wicked *s.*
1 *Tim.* 4:1 giving heed to *s.* spi.

SEE.

Gen. 2:19 to *s.* what he won. call
11:5 Lord came down to *s.* city
44:23 shall *s.* my face no more
45:12 your eyes *s.* the eyes of
28 will go and *s.* Joseph bef.
48:11 I had not tho. to *s.* face
Ex. 3:3 *s.* this great sight, 4
5:19 officers *s.* th. were in evil
6:1 shalt *s.* what I will do to P.
Ex. 10:5 cannot be able to *s.* ear.
28 ta. heed, *s.* my face no mo.
12:13 when I *s.* blood
33:20 no man *s.* me and live
23 thou shalt *s.* my back parts
34:10 people shall *s.* work of L.
Lev. 13:19 priest shall *s.* him, 17
Num. 22:41 thence he might *s.*
23:9 from top of rocks I *s.* him
13 whe. mayest *s.* them, sh. *s.*
24:17 I sh. *s.* him, but not now
32:11 none that came out of Eg.
shall *s.* the land, *Deut.* 1:35
Deut. 1:36 save C. he sh. *s.* land
3:25 I pray thee, let me *s.* land
28:34 eyes wh. thou shalt *s.* 67
68 thou shalt *s.* it no more
29:4 hath not given eyes to *s.*
32:20 *s.* what their end will be
39 *s.* now, I, even I, am he.
52 thou shalt *s.* land bef. thee
34:4 I have caused thee to *s.*
Jos. 22:10 built great altar to *s.*
1 *Sam.* 15:35 came no more to *s.*
19:3 what I *s.* that I will tell
2 *Sam.* 13:5 when fath. com. to *s.*
14:32 let me *s.* the king's face
1 *K.* 12:16 now *s.* to thine own
house, David, 2 *Chr.* 10:16
22:25 *s.* that day, 2 *Chr.* 18:24
2 *K.* 2:10 *s.* when I am taken
6:17 open his eyes th. he may *s.*
20 open eyes that they may *s.*
7:2 shalt *s.* it with th. eyes, 19
13 send and *s.* 14 go and *s.*
10:16 *s.* my zeal for the Lord
19:16 open, Lord, thine eyes,
and *s. Is.* 37:17

23:17 what title is that that I *s.*
2 *Chr.* 25:17 let us *s.* one another
Job 7:7 mine eye no more *s.* good
8 eye th. ha. seen me, *s.* no m.
9:25 days flee away, *s.* no good
17:15 my hope, who shall *s.* it?
19:26 in my flesh shall I *s.* God
27 whom I shall *s.* for myself
20:9 eye shall *s.* him no more
24:1 why do th. not *s.* his days?
15 adulterer sai. No eye sh. *s.*
31:4 doth not he *s.* my ways?
33:28 his life shall *s.* the light
36:25 every man may *s.* it
Ps. 10:11 God will never *s.* it
14:2 G. looked to *s.* if any, 53:2
31:11 they that did *s.* me
34:8 O taste and *s.* Lord is good
12 many days, he may *s.* good
37:34 wicked cut off, sh. *s.* it
40:3 shall *s.* it and trust in Lord
41:6 *s.* me, he speaketh vanity
49:19 they shall never *s.* light
64:5 say, Who shall *s.* them?
8 all that *s.* th. shall flee away
66:5 come and *s.* works of God
86:17 they wh. hate me may *s.*
112:8 *s.* his desire upon enemi.
10 wicked *s.* it and be grieved
119:74 be glad when they *s.* me
128:5 shalt *s.* the good of Jerus.
Ec. 1:10 be said, *s.* this is new
2:3 till I might *s.* wh. was good
3:22 to *s.* what sh. be after him
Is. 6:10 lest *s.* with their eyes
26:11 they shall *s.* and be asha.
30:20 th. eyes sh. *s.* thy teachers
32:3 the eyes of them that *s.*
33:17 thine eyes sh. *s.* the king
41:20 that th. may *s.* and know
48:6 *s.* this; 49:7 kings shall *s.*
52:8 for they shall *s.* eye to eye
15 not been told them sh. th. *s.*
53:2 when we shall *s.* him
10 he shall *s.* his seed
60:5 thou sh. *s.* and flow toget.
61:9 all that *s.* them acknowl.
64:9 behold, *s.* we beseech
Jer. 1:11 I *s.* rod; 13 *s.* seeth. pot
2:10 *s.* if there be such a thing
19 *s.* that it is an evil thing
23 *s.* thy way in the valley
3:2 *s.* where thou hast not been
5:1 *s.* now and know, and seek
6:16 stand ye in the ways and *s.*
7:12 go and *s.* what I did to it
51:61 and shalt *s.* and shalt read
Ezek. 39:21 all the heath. shall *s.*
Dan. 3:25 lo, I *s.* four men loose
Joel 2:28 your young men sh. *s.*
visions, *Acts* 2:17
Amos 6:2 pass ye to Cal. and *s.*
Mic. 7:10 mine enemy shall *s.* it
Hab. 2:1 *s.* what he will say
Zec. 5:2 answer. I *s.* flying roll
5 lift your eyes, *s.* what is this
9:5 Ashkelon sh. *s.* it, and fear
10:7 their children shall *s.* it
Mal. 1:5 and your eyes shall *s.*
Mat. 5:8 pure in heart, sh. *s.* G.
Mat. 8:4 *s.* thou tell no man,
9:30; *Mark* 1:44; *Acts* 23:22
11:4 tell John th. ye hear and *s.*
12:38 would *s.* a sign from thee
13:14 seeing ye shall *s. Mark*
4:12; *Acts* 28:36
15 lest at any time they should
s. with their eyes, *Acts* 28:27
16 bless. are your eyes, they *s.*
17 to *s.* those things wh. ye *s.*
15:31 when they saw the blind
to *s. Luke* 7:22
16:28 *s.* Son of man coming
22:11 king came in to *s.* guests
24:6 wars, *s.* ye be not troubled
27:4 *s.* thou to that; 24 *s.* to it
28:6 come *s.* place where L. lay
10 Galilee, there shall *s.* me

Mark 5:14 to *s*. what was done
32 *s*. her had done this thing
6:38 go and *s*. 8:24 *s*. men
Luke 2:15 go to Bethleh. and *s*.
3:6 all flesh sh. *s*. salv. of God
8:16 who enter may *s*. 11:33
9:9 he desired to *s*. him, 23:8
27 not taste of death till th. *s*.
14:18 grou. I must go and *s*. it
17:22 when ye shall desire to *s*.
23 *s*. here, or *s*. there
19:3 Zaccheus sought to *s*. Jes.
John 1:39 come and *s*. 46; 11:34;
    Rev. 6:1, 3, 5, 7
50 thou shalt *s*. greater things
8:51 sayings, sh. never *s*. death
56 Abra. rejoiced to *s*. my day
9:15 do *s*. 25 blind, now I *s*.
39 th. who *s*. not might *s*. and
   th. who *s*. mi. be blind
12:21 saying, Sir, we would *s*. J.
16:22 but I will *s*. you again
Acts 20:25 *s*. my face no more, 38
22:14 know and *s*. that Just One
28:20 I called you, to *s*. you
Rom. 15:21 sp. of, they sh. *s*.
1 *Cor*. 8:10 if any man *s*. thee
Phil. 1:27 whether I come and *s*.
2:23 soon as I *s*. how it will go
1 *Thes*. 2:17 to *s*. your face with
3:6 desir. to *s*. us, we to *s*. you
1 *Tim*. 6:16 hath seen, nor can *s*.
Heb. 12:14 witho. holi. no man *s*.
13:23 come shortly, will *s*. you
1 *Pet*. 3:10 that will *s*. good days
1 *John* 5:16 if any man *s*. brother
3 *John* 14 I shall shortly *s*. thee
Rev. 1:7 every eye shall *s*. him
16:15 naked, they *s*. his shame
19:10 *s*. thou do it not, 22:9
22:4 and they shall *s*. his face

SEE not, or not SEE.

Gen. 21:16 not *s*. death of child
27:1 Is. old, that he could *not s*.
43:3 ye shall *not s*. my face, 5
44:26 we may *not s*. man's face
48:10 eyes of Is. dim, could *n. s*.
Ex. 33:20 canst *not s*. my face
Num. 14:23 they shall *not s*.
23:13 utmost part, shall *not s*.
1 *Sam*. 3:2 Eli could *not s*. 4:15
2 *Sam*. 3:13 *not s*. my face, exce.
14:24 let *not* Absal. *s*. my face
1 *K*. 14:4 Ahijah could *not s*.
2 *K*. 3:17 n. *s*. wind, nor sh. ye *s*.
22:20 thine eyes shall *n. s*. evil
Job 3:11 goeth by me, I *s*. him *n*.
20:17 *not s*. rivers of honey and
23:9 hideth that I cannot *s*. him
34:32 wh. I *s*. not teach thou me
35:14 thou shalt *not s*. him
37:21 men *s*. *not* bright light
Ps. 58:8 pass away, *not s*. sun
74:9 we *s*. *not* our signs, there is
89:48 liveth, shall *not s*. death
94:7 say, The Lord shall *not s*.
9 formed eye, shall he *not s*. ?
115:5 eyes, they *s*. not, 135:16
Is. 26:11 is lifted up, will *not s*.
33:19 th. shalt *not s*. a fierce peo.
38:11 I shall *not s*. the Lord
44:9 they *s*. not, they be asha.
18 shut eyes, that th. cannot *s*.
Jer. 5:21 eyes, *s*. not, *Ezek*. 12:12
12:4 he shall *not s*. our last end
14:13 ye shall *not s*. the sword
17:6 shall *not s*. when good com.
6 sh. *not s*. when heat cometh
23:24 that I shall *not s*. him ?
Ezek. 12:6 thou *s*. *not* ground, 12
13 shall he *not s*. it, tho' he die
Dan. 5:23 gods of gold, wh. *s*. *n*.
Zep. 3:15 thou shalt *not s*. evil
Mal. 13:15 seeing, *s*. not
23:39 shall *not s*. me, *Lu*. 13:35
24:2 *s*. ye *not* all these things ?
Mark 8:18 hav. eyes, *s*. ye *not* ?

Luke 2:26 *n*. *s*. dea. bef. seen C.
8:10 seeing, they might *not s*.
Luke 17:22 desi. to *s*. ye sh. *not s*.
John 3:3 cannot *s*. kingd. of G.
36 shall *not s*. life, wrath abid.
9:39 they who *s*. *not* might *s*.
12:40 that they should *not s*.
16:16 ye shall *not s*. me, 17, 19
18:26 did I *not s*. thee in gard. ?
Acts 22:11 I could *not s*. for glory
Rom. 11:8 th. they should *not s*.
10 darkened that may *not s*.
1 *Cor*. 16:7 for I will *not s*. you
Heb. 2:8 we *s*. *not* yet all things
11:5 that he should *not s*. death
1 *Pet*. 1:8 tho' now ye *s*. him *not*
2 *Pet*. 1:9 blind, can *not s*. a far

We SEE.

Ps. 36:9 in thy light shall *we s*.
Mark 15:32 *we* may *s*. *John* 6:30
John 9:41 *we s*. your sin remain.
1 *Cor*. 13:12 *we s*. thro' a glass
1 *Thes*. 3:10 pray, *we* might *s*.
1 *John* 3:2 for *we* shall *s*. him

Ye SEE, or SEE ye.

Ex. 14:13 *ye* sh. *s*. them no more
16:7 *ye* shall *s*. glory of Lord
Jos. 3:3 when *ye s*. ark of coven.
1 *Sam*. 10:24 *s*. *ye* him L. chos. ?
Cant. 6:13 what will *ye s*. in Sh.
Is. 6:9 *s*. *ye* indeed, perceive
42:18 blind, that *ye* may *s*.
66:14 wh. *ye s*. your hearts shall
Jer. 2:31 O generati. *s*. *ye* word
42:18 *ye* sh. *s*. the place no more
Ezek. 13:23 *ye* sh. *s*. no more va.
14:22 *ye* shall *s*. their way
Dan. 2:8 *ye s*. thing is gone
Mat. 13:17 have desired to **see**
   th. things *s*. *Luke* 10:23
24:33 when *ye* shall *s*. these th.
   Mark 13:29 ; *Luke* 21:31
26:64 hereafter shall *ye s*. **Son**
   of man, *Mark* 14:62
27:24 *s*. *ye* to it, *Mark* 15:36
28:7 in Ga. shall *ye s*. *Mark* 16:7
John 14:19 but *ye s*. 16:10 *ye s*.
16:16 a lit. *ye* shall *s*. me, 17, 19
Acts 2:33 wh. *ye* now *s*. and hear
25:24 *ye s*. this man, about wh.
1 *Pet*. 1:8 tho' now *ye s*. him not

SEEING.

Ex. 4:11 maketh *s*. or blind ?
22:10 driven away, no man *s*.
Num. 35:23 *s*. him not
1 *K*. 1:48 mine eyes even *s*. it
Prov. 20:12 Lord maketh *s*. eye
Ec. 1:8 eye not satisfied with *s*.
Is. 33:15 dismayed at the *s*. of it
33:15 shut. his eyes from *s*. evil
42:20 *s*. many things, but thou
Mat. 13:13 beca. they *s*. see not
14 *s*. ye shall see and shall not
   perc. *Mark* 4:12 ; *Acts* 28:26
John 9:7 washed and came *s*.
Acts 13:11 not *s*. sun for a season
2 *Pet*. 2:8 *s*. and hearing, vexed

SEED.

Gen. 1:11 herbs yield. *s*. 12, 29
47:19 give us *s*. 23 here is *s*.
24 four parts sh. be own for *s*.
Lev. 19:19 not sow with ming. *s*.
26:16 shall sow your *s*. in vain
27:16 estima. shall be acc. to *s*.
30 tithe of *s*. of land is Lord's
Num. 20:5 it is no place of *s*.
Deut. 11:10 Eg. where sowedst *s*.
28:38 carr *s*. much *s*. into field
1 *Sam*. 8:15 king take tenth of *s*.
1 *K*. 18:32 conta. 2 measures of *s*.
Ps. 126:6 bearing precious *s*.
Ec. 11:6 in morning sow thy *s*.
Is. 5:10 *s*. of homer sh. yield ep.
17:11 make thy *s*. to flourish
55:10 it may give *s*. to sower
Jer. 35:7 sow *s*. nor plant viney

Ezek. 17:5 he took of *s*. of land
Joel 1:17 *s*. is rotten under clods
Amos 9:13 overtake that sow. *s*.
Hag. 2:19 is the *s*. yet in barn ?
Zec. 8:12 *s*. shall be prosperous
Mal. 2:3 I will corrupt your *s*.
Mat. 13:19 *s*. by way-side, 20, **22**
23 receiv. *s*. into good ground
24 man sowed good *s*. in field
37 soweth good *s*. is S. of **man**
38 good *s*. are the children of
Mark 4:26 cast *s*. into ground
Luke 8:11 *s*. is the word of God
1 *Cor*. 15:38 ev. *s*. his own body
2 *Cor*. 9:10 minister. *s*. to **sower**
1 *Pet*. 1:23 born, not of corrup. *s*.
1 *John* 3:9 his *s*. remain. in **him**
See COPULATION.

SEED, for posterity.

Gen. 4:25 G. appoint. me ano. *s*.
7:3 keep *s*. alive on fa. of **earth**
15:3 Ab. said, To me giv. no *s*.
Gen. 19:32 preser. *s*. of father, **34**
38:8 raise *s*. to bro. *Mat*. 22:24 ;
   Mark 12:19 ; *Luke* 30:28
Lev. 21:21 a blemish of *s*. of As.
Num. 16:40 which is not *s*. of A.
Deut. 1:8 give it to their *s*. 11:9
4:37 chose *s*. after them, 10:15
31:21 out of mouths of their *s*.
Ruth 4:12 *s*. the Lord shall give
1 *Sam*. 2:20 L. give *s*. of this wo.
24:21 th. wilt not cut off my *s*.
1 *K*. 11:39 I will afflict *s*. of Dav.
2 *K*. 11:1 Athaliah destroyed all
   the *s*. royal, 2 *Chr*. 22:10
17:20 Lord rejected *s*. of Israel
25:25 Ishm. of *s*. royal, *Jer*. 41:1
1 *Chr*. 16:13 O ye *s*. of Israel
Ezr. 2:59 not show *s*. *Neh*. 7:61
9:2 holy *s*. have mingled them
Neh. 9:2 *s*. of Israel separated
Est. 9:27 J. took them and *s*. 31
Job 21:8 their *s*. is established in
Ps. 21:10 their *s*. sh. thou destr.
22:23 praise them, all ye *s*. of
   Jacob, all ye the *s*. of Israel
30 a *s*. shall serve him
37:28 *s*. of wicked shall be cut
69:36 the *s*. of his servants shall
102:28 their *s*. sh. be establish.
106:27 overthrow their *s*. among
Prov. 11:21 *s*. of righteous sh. be
Is. 1:4 nation, a *s*. of evil-doers
6:13 holy *s*. shall be substance
14:20 *s*. of evil-doers sh. never
45:19 I said not unto *s*. of Jacob
25 in L. all *s*. of Is. be justified
57:3 *s*. of adulterer and whore
4 transgres. a *s*. of falsehood
61:9 th. *s*. shall be among Gent.
65:9 I will bring a *s*. out of Ja.
23 *s*. of the blessed of the Lord
Jer. 2:21 I planted thee a right *s*.
7:15 I will cast out *s*. of Ephra.
31:27 *s*. of man and *s*. of beast
36 then *s*. of Is. also sh. cease
37 I cast off all *s*. of Is. 33:26
33:22 will I multiply *s*. of David
Ezek. 20:5 I lift. hand to *s*. of Ja.
43:19 give to be of *s*. of Zadok
Dan. 2:43 mingle with *s*. of men
9:1 Darius of *s*. of the Medes
Mal. 2:15 might seek a godly *s*.
Mark 12:20 left no *s*. 21, **22**
John 7:42 Ch. cometh of *s*. of D.
Acts 13:23 of man's *s*. G. rais. J.
Rom. 1:3 of *s*. of D. 2 *Tim*. 2:8
4:16 promise might be to his *s*.
9:8 chil. of prom. counted for *s*.
29 except Lord had left us a *s*.
Gal. 3:19 was added, till *s*. come
Rev. 12:17 war with remn. of *s*.
See ABRAHAM.

His SEED.

Gen. 17:19 cov. wi. Is. and h. *s*.
48:19 *his s*. sh. become nations

Lev. 20:2 any of *his s.* to Mol. 3, 4
21:15 nor profane *his s.* am. pe.
Num. 14:24 Caleb and *his s.*
24:7 *h. s.* sh. be in many waters
Jos. 24:3 I multiplied *his s.*
2 *Sam.* 4:8 aveng. of S. and *h. s.*
Neh. 9:8 a coven. to give it *h. s.*
Est. 10:3 speaking peace to *h. s.*
Ps. 25:13 *his s.* sh. inherit earth
37:25 nor seen *his s.* beg. bread
26 merciful, *his s.* is blessed
89:29 *his s.* I make to end. 36
112:2 *his s.* shall be mighty
Is. 53:10 *his s.* sh. prolong days
Jer. 22:28 cast out, he and *his s.*
30 no man of *his s.* sh. prosper
33:26 not take of *h. s.* to be rul.
49:10 Esau, *his s.* is spoiled
Acts 7:5 give it to him and *his s.*

Thy SEED.

Gen. 3:15 enmi. bet. *t. s.* and her
12:7 to *t. s.* will I give th. land,
13:15; 15:18; 17:8; 24:7; 26:3;
28:4, 13; 35:12; 48:4; *Ex.*
33:1; *Deut.* 34:4
13:16 *thy s.* dust, 16:10; 28:14
15:5 so sh. *thy s.* be, *Rom.* 4:18
13 *thy s.* be a stranger in land
17:12 not of *t. s.* sh. be circum.
21:12 in Is. *t. s.* call. *Heb.* 11:18
13 Ish. a nation, bec. he is *t. s.*
22:17 *thy s.* possess gate, 24:60
18 in *thy s.* all nations be bles.
26:4; 28:14; *Acts* 3:25
26:24 mult. *thy s.* for Abraham's
32:12 I will make *thy s.* as sand
48:11 G. hath showed me *thy s.*
Lev. 18:21 not of *t. s.* pass thro'
Deut. 28:46 for a sign on *thy s.*
30:19 thou and *thy s.* may live
1 *Sam.* 20:42 bet. my *s.* and *t. s.*

2 *Sam.* 7:12 set up *t. s.* 1 *Ch.* 17:11
Job 5:25 shalt know that *thy s.*
Ps. 89:4 *thy s.* will I establish
Is. 43:5 I bring *thy s.* from east
44:3 I pour my Spirit on *thy s.*
48:19 *thy s.* had been as sand
54:3 *thy s.* sh. inherit Gentiles
59:21 Sp. not depart out of the
mouth of *t. s.* nor *t.* seed's *s.*
Jer. 30:10 *t. s.* from land, 46:27
Gal. 3:16 to *t. s.* which is Christ

Your SEED.

Ex. 32:13 land I give to *y. s.*
Lev. 22:3 whoso. of *your s.* goeth
Is. 66:22 so *y. s.* and name rem.

SEED-TIME.

Gen. 8:22 *s.-t.* and harv. sh. not

SEEDS.

Deut. 22:9 not sow with divers *s.*
Mat. 13:4 so. *s.* fell by way-side
32 wh. is least of *s. Mark* 4:31
Gal. 3:16 saith not *s.* as of many

SEEK.

Gen. 37:16 I *s.* my brethren
43:18 that he may *s.* occasion
Deut. 4:29 *s.* him with thy heart
1 *Sam.* 9:3 said to S. Go *s.* asses
23:15 Saul come to *s.* his life,
25; 24:2; 26:2
25:26 th. that *s.* evil to my lord
29 risen to pursue and *s.* soul
27:1 Saul shall despair to *s.* me
1 *K.* 2:40 Shimei went to *s.* serv.
18:10 hath not sent to *s.* thee
19:10 *s.* my life to take it, 14
2 *K.* 2:16 go, and *s.* thy master
6:19 bring ye to man wh. ye *s.*
1 *Chr.* 28:8 *s.* commandm. of L.
9 if thou *s.* him, he will be
found, 2 *Chr.* 15:2
2 *Chr.* 19:3 prep. heart to *s.* God
30:19 prep. his heart to *s.* God
31:21 to *s.* his God, he did it
34:3 Josiah began to *s.* after G.

Ezr. 4:2 we *s.* your God as ye do
7:10 prepared his heart to *s.*
8:21 to *s.* him right way for us
22 G. is on them for good th. *s.*
Neh. 2:10 to *s.* welfare of Israel
Job 5:8 I would *s.* unto God
7:21 shalt *s.* me in the morning
8:5 if thou wouldst *s.* unto God
20:10 children shall *s.* to please
Ps. 4:2 vanity, *s.* after leasing
9:10 not forsaken th. that *s.* th.
10:15 *s.* out his wickedness
14:2 any that did *s.* God, 53:2
24:6 genera. of them that *s.* him
27:4 desired, that will I *s.* after
8 *s.* my face, thy fa. L. will I *s.*
34:14 *s.* peace, 1 *Pet.* 3:11
35:4 put to shame *s.* my soul
38:12 that *s.* my life, th. *s.* hurt
40:14 *s.* after my soul, 70:2
54:3 oppressors *s.* after my soul
63:1 my God, early will I *s.* th.
9 those that *s.* my soul go into
69:6 let not those that *s.* thee
32 heart shall live that *s.* God
70:4 let those that *s.* thee rejo.
71:13 with dishonor *s.* my hurt
24 bro. unto shame *s.* my hurt
83:16 they may *s.* thy name
104:21 yo. lions *s.* meat from G.
109:10 let his child. *s.* th. bread
119:2 *s.* him wi. th. whole heart
45 at liberty, for I *s.* thy prec.
176 as a sheep, *s.* thy servant
122:9 of God, I will *s.* thy good
Prov. 1:28 *s.* me, sh. not find me
8:17 and those that *s.* me early
23:35 I will *s.* it yet again
29:10 upright, just *s.* his soul
26 many *s.* the ruler's favor
Ec. 1:13 I gave my heart to *s.*
7:25 my heart to *s.* out wisdom
8:17 though man labor to *s.* it
Cant. 3:2 *s.* him my soul loveth
6:1 we may *s.* him with thee
Is. 1:17 *s.* judgment, relieve opp.
8:19 sho. not a people *s.* unto G.
11:10 to it shall Gentiles *s.*
26:9 wit. me will I *s.* thee early
34:16 *s.* ye out of book of Lord
41:12 thou shalt *s.* them
17 when the needy *s.* water
45:19 not to Ja. *s.* ye me in vain
58:2 yet they *s.* me daily, and
Jer. 2:24 *s.* her, in her mouth
4:30 thy lovers will *s.* thy life
11:21 men of Anath. *s.* thy life
19:7 th. that *s.* their lives, 21:7
9 that *s.* their lives sh. strait.
22:25 that *s.* thy life, 38:16
29:7 *s.* the peace of the city
13 shall *s.* me, and find me.
Jer. 34:20 them that *s.* th. life, 21
44:30 give Phar. to them that *s.*
46:26 Egyptians to those th. *s.*
49:37 dismayed bef. them th. *s.*
Lam. 1:11 people sigh, *s.* bread
Ezek. 7:25 they shall *s.* peace
26 then shall they *s.* a vision
34:11 sheep; and *s.* them out
12 so will I *s.* out my sheep
16 I will *s.* that wh. was lost
Dan. 9:3 God, to *s.* by prayer
Hos. 2:7 shall *s.* them, not find
Amos 5:4 saith the Lord, *s.* me
14 *s.* good and not evil
8:12 to *s.* the word of the Lord
Nah. 3:7 wh. sh. I *s.* comfort. ?
11 thou shalt *s.* strength
Zep. 2:3 *s.* ye the Lord
Zec. 11:16 a sheph. shall not *s.*
12:9 in th. day I will *s.* to destr.
Mal. 2:7 they should *s.* the law
15 he might *s.* a godly seed
Mat. 6:32 th. things do Gent. *s.*
33 *s.* ye first the kingdom of
God, *Luke* 12:31
7:7 *s.* and ye sh. find, *Lu.* 11:9

28:5 know ye *s.* J. *Mark* 16:6
Mark 1:37 All men *s.* for thee
3:32 thy brethren *s.* for thee
Luke 12:30 these thi. nations *s.*
13:24 many will *s.* to enter in
15:8 doth she not *s.* diligently ?
17:33 whos. shall *s.* to save life
19:10 Son of man is come to *s.*
24:5 why *s.* living among dead ?
John 1:38 Je. saith, What *s.* ye ?
6:26 ye *s.* me, not beca. ye saw
7:25 he whom they *s.* to kill ?
34 shall *s.* me, not find me, 36
8:21 ye shall *s.* me, die in sins
37 seed, but ye *s.* to kill me, 40
13:33 ye sh. *s.* me, whither I go
18:4 Jesus said, Whom *s.* ye ? 7
8 ye *s.* me, let th. go their way
Acts 10:19 behold, 3 men *s.* thee
21 P. said, I am he whom ye *s.*
Rom. 2:7 to th. who *s.* for glory
11:3 I am alone, they *s.* my life
1 *Cor.* 10:24 let no man *s.* his own
Gal. 1:10 do I *s.* to please men ?
Phil. 2:21 all *s.* their own things
Col. 3:1 *s.* those thi. that are ab.
Heb. 11:14 that they *s.* a country
13:14 have no city, we *s.* one
Rev. 9:6 in th. days men *s.* death

See FACE, LORD.

Not SEEK, or SEEK not.

Num. 15:39 *s. n.* after your heart
Deut. 23:6 thou shalt not *s.* their
peace, *Ezr.* 9:12
Ruth 3:1 shall I *not s.* rest ?
Ps. 10:4 wicked *not s.* after God
119:155 wicked *s. not* thy statu.
Jer. 30:14 lovers, they *s.* thee *n.*
45:5 great things ? *s.* them *not*
Amos 5:5 but *s. not* Beth-el
Zec. 11:16 a shepherd shall *not s.*
Luke 12:29 *s. n.* what ye sh. eat
John 5:30 bec. I *s. not* mine own
8:50 I *s. not* mine own glory
1 *Cor.* 7:27 *s. n.* loosed, *s. n.* wife
2 *Cor.* 12:14 for I *s. not* yours

SEEKEST.

Gen. 37:15 asked, What *s.* thou ?
Jud. 4:22 show thee man thou *s.*
2 *Sam.* 17:3 the man thou *s.*
20:19 *s.* to destroy a mother
1 *K.* 11:22 *s.* to go to thy country
Jer. 45:5 *s.* thou great things ?
John 4:27 said, What *s.* thou ?
20:15 saith, Woman, whom *s.*
thou ?

SEEKETH.

1 *Sam.* 19:2 Saul *s.* to kill thee
20:1 my sin, that he *s.* my life ?
22:23 that *s.* my life, *s.* thy life
24:9 saying, David *s.* thy hurt ?
Job 39:29 fr. thence she *s.* prey
Ps. 37:32 watch. *s.* to slay him
Prov. 11:27 *s.* good procur. favor,
but he that *s.* mischief
14:6 scorner *s.* wisdom
18:1 separated himself, *s.* wisd.
15 the ear of wise *s.* knowledge
Ec. 7:28 which yet my soul *s.*
Jer. 5:1 any that *s.* the truth
30:17 Z. whom no man *s.* after
Lam. 3:25 L. good to soul *s.* him
Ezek. 34:12 shepherd *s.* out flock
Mat. 7:8 *s.* findeth, *Luke* 11:10
18:12 and *s.* that gone astray
John 4:23 Fa. *s.* such to worship
7:4 and *s.* to be known openly
18 *s.* his own glory; *s.* his glo.
8:50 there is one that *s.* and ju.
Rom. 3:11 none that *s.* after God
Rom. 11:7 Isr. not obt. that he *s.*
1 *Cor.* 13:5 charity *s.* not her own

SEEKING.

Mat. 12:43 *s.* rest, and findeth
none, *Luke* 11:24

Mark 8:11 *s.* a sign from heaven
Luke 2:45 turned back *s.* him
11:54 *s.* to catch something
13:7 behold, I come *s.* fruit
John 6:24 to Capern. *s.* for Jesus
Acts 13:11 went *s.* some to lead
1 *Cor.* 10:33 not *s.* mine own pro.
1 *Pet.* 5:8 *s.* whom he may dev.

SEEM.

Gen. 27:12 I sh. *s.* as a deceiver
Deut. 15:18 not *s.* hard, wh. thou
25:3 thy brother should *s.* vile
Jos. 24:15 if it *s.* evil unto you
Neh. 9:32 let not trouble *s.* little
Est. 8:5 *s.* right before the king
1 *Cor.* 12:22 those members wh. *s.*
Heb. 4:1 lest any of you sho. *s.*
Jam. 1:26 if any *s.* to be religi.

See GOOD.

SEEMED.

Gen. 19:14 *s.* as one that mocked
29:20 *s.* to him but a few days
Jer. 27:5 unto whom it *s.* meet
Luke 24:11 th. words *s.* idle tales
Gal. 2:6 these who *s.* somewhat

SEEMETH.

Num. 16:9 *s.* it but a small thi. ?
Prov. 14:12 which *s.* right, 16:25
18:17 first in own cause *s.* just
Ezek. 34:18 *s.* it a small thing
Luke 8:18 what he *s.* to have
1 *Cor.* 3:18 If *s.* to be wise

See GOOD.

SEEMLY.

Prov. 19:10 deli. is not *s.* for fool
26:1 so honor is not *s.* for a fool

SEEN.

Num. 14:22 have *s.* my glory
27:13 when thou hast *s.* it, thou
Deut. 1:28 we have *s.* sons of A.
31 *s.* how Lord bare thee
3:21 eyes have *s.* all Lord done
4:9 forget things eyes hath *s.*
5:24 *s.* th. G. doth talk wi. man
11:7 your eyes have *s.* acts of L.
21:7 nor have our eyes *s.* it
33:9 said, I have not *s.* him
Jos. 24:7 *s.* what I have done
Jud. 2:7 eld. who *s.* great works
13:22 because we have *s.* God
18:9 we have *s.* land, very good
1 *Sam.* 23:22 hath *s.* me there
24:10 this day thine eyes have *s.*
2 *Sam.* 18:21 tell king thou hast *s.*
1 *K.* 10:7 I came, mine eyes *s.*
13:12 *s.* way man of God went
20:13 *s.* this great multitude ?
2 *K.* 20:15 what ha. they *s.* ? all
in house ha. they *s. Is.* 39:4
23:29 slew J. wh. he had *s.* him
Ezr. 3:12 had *s.* first house
Est. 9:26 that they had *s.* conc.
Job 7:8 eye ha. *s.* me, see no mo.
8:18 pla. say, I have not *s.* thee
10:18 and no eye had *s.* me
13:1 mine eye hath *s.* all this
20:7 have *s.* him say, Wh. is he ?
Ps. 10:14 thou hast *s.* it
35:21 eye *s.* it ; 22 hast *s.* it
48:8 so have we *s.* city of Lord
68:24 have *s.* thy goings, O G.
Prov. 25:7 thine eyes have *s.*
Ec. 4:3 not *s.* evil work that is
6:5 not *s.* nor known any
6 I live, yet hath he *s.* no good
Is. 6:5 mine eyes have *s.* Lord
64:4 nor eye *s.* what he prepared
66:8 who hath *s.* such things ?
Jer. 1:12 said L. thou hast well *s.*
3:6 *s.* what backsl. Isr. done ?
12:3 hast *s.* me, tried heart
Lam. 2:14 prop. have *s.* vain thi.
have *s.* false burdens
16 enemies say, We have *s.* it
3:59 O L. thou hast *s.* my wrong

Ezek. 8:12 *s.* what ancients do
15 hast thou *s.* this? 17 ; 47:6
13:7 have ye not *s.* vain vision
Mat. 13:17 proph. desired to see
th. thi. not *s.* them, *Lu.* 10:24
21:32 ye had *s.* it, repented not
Mark 9:1 have *s.* kingd. of God
9 tell no man what they had *s.*
16:14 beli. not wh. had *s.* him
Luke 1:22 that he had *s.* a vision
2:20 praising G. for thi. had *s.*
26 death, bef. he had *s.* L.'s C.
5:26 we have *s.* strange things
9:36 told things wh. they had *s.*
19:37 mighty works they had *s.*
Luke 24:23 had *s.* vision of ang.
37 supposed they had *s.* a spirit
John 1:18 no man hath *s.* God at
any time, 1 *John* 4:12
3:11 we testify that we have *s.*
32 what he hath *s.* and heard
4:45 Galileans had *s.* all he did
5:37 not at any time *s.* shape
6:46 not that any man *s.* Father
8:57 hast thou *s.* Abraham ?
9:8 neighbors which had *s.* him
37 hast *s.* it is he that talketh
11:45 had seen what J. did, bel.
14:9 *s.* me hath *s.* the Father
15:24 *s.* and hated both me
20:18 she had *s.* L. 25 *s.* Lord
29 bec. thou hast *s.* believed
Acts 4:20 speak things we ha. *s.*
9:27 declared how he had *s.* L.
10:17 vision he had *s.* sho. mean
11:23 he had *s.* grace of God
16:10 after he had *s.* vision
40 *s.* brethren, comforted them
1 *Cor.* 2:9 eye hath not *s.* nor ear
9:1 have I not *s.* Je. Ch. our L. ?
Phil. 4:9 things ye heard and *s.*
Col. 2:1 many as have not *s.* face
1 *Tim.* 6:16 wh. no man hath *s.*
1 *John* 1:1 we have *s.* with eyes
3 have *s.* declare we unto you
3:6 whoso. sin. hath not *s.* him
4:14 we have *s.* and do testify
20 brot. whom he hath *s.* how
can he love G. he ha. not *s.* ?
3 *John* 11 do. evil, hath not *s.* G.
Rev. 1:19 write thi. thou hast *s.*
22:8 heard and *s.* I fell down

HAVE I seen.

Gen. 7:1 thee *h. I s.* righteous
1 *Chr.* 29:17 now *h. I s.* people
Ec. 8:9 this *h. I s.* and applied
Jer. 46:5 wheref. *h. I s.* dismayed
Zec. 9:8 *h. I. s.* with mine eyes

I have SEEN.

Gen. 32:30 *I h. s.* G. face to face
33:10 *I have s.* thy face, 46:30
Ex. 3:9 *I h. s.* oppression, 16
32:9 *I h. s.* people, *Deut.* 9:13
Jud. 6:22 bec. *I h. s.* an angel
2 *K.* 20:5 thus saith the Lord, *I
have s.* thy tears, *Is.* 38:5
Job 15:17 that wh. *I h. s.* I decl.
31:19 if *I have s.* any perish
Ps. 37:35 *I h. s.* wicked in power
Ec. 1:14 *I h. s.* works under sun
5:13 evil wh. *I h. s.* under sun
18 that wh. *I h. s.* good to eat
6:1 evil which *I have s.* 10:5
Is. 57:18 *I have s.* his ways
Jer. 7:11 behold, *I h. s.* it, sai. L.
Dan. 2:26 make kn. dream *I h. s.*
John 8:38 I speak that *I have s.*
Acts 7:34 *I h. s.* affliction of peo.

Ye have SEEN.

Ex. 14:13 Egypt. wh. *ye have s.*
19:4 *ye h. s.* what I did to Egy.
20:22 *ye have s.* that I talked
Deut. 29:2 *ye have s.* all, *Jos.* 23:3
Jud. 9:48 what *ye have s.* me do
1 *Sam.* 17:25 *have ye s.* this man
Job 27:12 *ye yourselves h. s.* it
Luke 7:22 tell J. what *ye have s.*

John 6:36 *ye have s.* believe not
8:38 ye do that *ye h. s.* with fa.
14:7 *ye* know him, *have s.* him
Acts 1:11 come as *ye h. s.* him go
Jam. 5:11 *ye have s.* end of Lord

SEEN, passively.

Gen. 22:14 mount of L. sh. be *s.*
Ex. 33:23 my face sh. not be *s.*
34:3 any man be *s.* thro' mount
Num. 14:14 Lord *s.* face to face
Jud. 19:30 no deed done nor *s.*
2 *Sam.* 17:17 might not be *s.*
Is. 60:2 gl. shall be *s.* upon thee
Zec. 9:14 L. sh. be *s.* over them
Mat. 9:33 it was never so *s.* in I.
23:5 works do to be *s.* of men
Mark 16:11 he had been *s.* of her
Acts 1:3 *s.* of them 40 days, 13:31
Rom. 1:20 invis. things clearly *s.*
8:24 hope that is *s.* is not hope
1 *Cor.* 15:5 he was *s.* of Cephas
6 was *s.* of above 500 brethren
7 *s.* of James ; 8 was *s.* of me
2 *Cor.* 4:18 look not at things *s.*
Heb. 11:1 evid. of things not *s.*
3 things which are *s.* not made
7 N. warned of G. things not *s.*
13 hav. *s.* them were persuad.
1 *Pet.* 1:8 having not *s.* ye love

SEER.

1 *Sam.* 9:9 let us go to *s.* proph.
was beforetime called a *s.*
11 is *s.* here ? 18 where *s.* hou.
19 Samuel answer. I am the *s.*
2 *Sam.* 15:27 Art thou not a *s.* ?
24:11 word came to Gad, D.'s *s.*
1 *Chr.* 9:22 Samuel the *s.* did ord.
25:5 Heman, king's *s.* in word
26:28 Samuel the *s.* had dedica.
29:29 acts of Da. writ. in book
of Sam. in book of Gad, *s.*
2 *Chr.* 9:29 in visions of Iddo, *s.*
12:15 Rehob. in book of Iddo, *s.*
16:7 Hanani the *s.* came to Asa
10 then Asa was wroth with *s.*
19:2 Je. son of *s.* went to meet
29:25 commandment of Gad, *s.*
30 words of Da. and Asaph, *s.*
35:15 command. of Jeduthun, *s.*
Amos 7:12 O thou *s.* flee away

SEERS.

2 *K.* 17:13 against Is. and J. by *s.*
2 *Chr.* 33:18 words of *s.* th. spake
19 written am. the sayings of *s.*
Is. 29:10 the *s.* hath he covered
30:10 who say to the *s.* see not
Mic. 3:7 then sh. *s.* be ashamed

SEEST.

Gen. 16:13 spake, Thou G. *s.* me
31:43 La. said, All thou *s.* is mi.
Ex. 10:28 day thou *s.* my face
Deut. 12:13 ev. place that thou *s.*
Jud. 9:36 *s.* shadow of mount.
1 *K.* 21:29 *s.* how Ahab humbleth
Job 10:4 *s.* thou as man seeth ?
Is. 58:3 we fasted, thou *s.* not ?
7 when *s.* naked, cover him
Jer. 1:11 word came to Jeremi.
What *s.* thou ? 13 ; 24:3 ; *Amos*
7:8 ; 8:2 ; *Zec.* 4:9 ; 5:2
7:17 *s.* th. not what th. do in J.
32:24 come to pass, beh. th. *s.* it
Ezek. 8:6 *s.* thou what they do ?
40:4 declare all thou *s.* to Israel
Dan. 1:13 as thou *s.* deal wi. ser.
Luke 7:44 Simon *s.* thou wom. ?
Jam. 2:22 *s.* thou how faith wro.
Rev. 1:11 what *s.* write in a book

SEETH.

Gen. 16:13 looked after him *s.* ?
Ex. 4:14 wh. he *s.* thee, be glad
1 *Sam.* 16:7 L. *s.* not as man *s.*
2 *K.* 2:19 city pleasant, as lord *s.*
Job 28:10 eye *s.* precious thing
24 he *s.* under whole heaven
34:21 eyes on man, *s.* all goings
42:5 but now mine eyes *s.* thee

Ps. 37:13 he *s.* his day is coming
40:10 he *s.* that wise men die
Ec. 8:16 day nor night *s.* sleep
Is. 28:4 that looked upon it, *s.* it
29:15 who *s.* us? 47:10 none *s.*
Ezek. 8:12 the Lord *s.* us not, 9:9
12:27 vision he *s.* for many days
18:14 son that *s.* father's sins
Mat. 6:4 Fa. who *s.* in sec. 6, 18
John 1:29 next day John *s.* Jesus
5:19 but what he *s.* Father do
6:40 who *s.* Son, and believeth
9:21 wh. means he *s.* we kn. not
12:45 *s.* me *s.* him sent me
14:18 because it *s.* him not, nor
19 world *s.* me no more
Rom. 8:34 what a man *s.*
2 *Cor.* 12:6 above what he *s.* me
1 *John* 3:17 *s.* brother have need

SEETHE.

Ex. 16:23 to-day *s.* that ye will *s.*
23:19 sh. not *s.* a kid in mother's
milk, 34:26; *Deut.* 14:21
29:31 *s.* his flesh in holy place
2 *K.* 4:38 *s.* pottage for sons of
Ezek. 24:5 let them *s.* bones
Zec. 14:21 come and *s.* therein

SEETHING.

1 *Sam.* 2:13 while flesh was *s.*
Job 41:20 smoke as out of *s.* pot
Jer. 1:13 what seest thou? *s.* pot

SEGUB. 1 *K.* 16:34

SEIR.

Gen. 32:3 to the land of S. the
33:14 I come to my Lord to S.
36:20 sons of S. 21; 1 *Chr.* 1:38
Num. 24:18 S. sh. be a possessi.
Deut. 1:44 destroyed you in S.
33:2 Sinal and rose up from S.
Jud. 5:4 thou wentest out of S.
2 *Chr.* 20:23 of inhabitants of S.
25:11 smote of children of S.
14 the gods of the child. of S.
Is. 21:11 calleth to me out of S.
Ezek. 25:8 because Moab and S.

Mount SEIR.

Gen. 14:6 Horites in their *m.* S.
36:8 dwelt Esau in *mount* S. 9
Deut. 2:1 compassed mount S.
5 *mount* S. to Esau. *Jos.* 24:4
1 *Chr.* 4:42 500 went to *mount* S.
2 *Chr.* 20:10 children of *mount* S.
2 *Chr.* 20:22 ambushm. ag. *m.* S.
23 stood up against *mount* S.
Ezek. 35:2 thy face ag. mount S.
3 say to it, Behold, O *mount* S.
7 thus will I make *mount* S.

SEIZE, ED.

Jos. 8:7 rise up and *s.* upon city
Job 3:6 let darkness *s.* upon it
Ps. 55:15 let death *s.* upon them
Jer. 49:24 Damas. fear *s.* on her
Mat. 21:38 kill him, *s.* inherit.

SELAH.

Ps. 3:2 no help for him in God, *s.*
4 L. heard out of holy hill, *s.*
8 thy blessing upon people, *s.*
32:5 forgavest iniq. of my sin, *s.*
See Ps. 4:2, 4; 7:5; 9:16, 20; 20:3;
21:2; 24:6, 10; 32:4, 7; 39:5, 11;
44:8; 46:3, 7, 11; 47:4; 48:8;
49:13, 15; 50:6; 52:3, 5; 54:3;
55:7, 19; 57:3, 6; 59:5, 13; 60:4;
61:4; 62:4, 8; 66:4, 7, 15; 67:1,
4; 68:7, 19, 32; 75:3; 76:3, 9;
77:3, 9, 15; 81:7; 82:2; 83:8;
84:4, 8; 85:2; 87:3, 6; 88:7, 10;
89:4, 37, 45, 48; 140:3, 5, 8;
143:6; *Hab.* 3:3, 9, 13

SELEUCIA.

Acts 13:4 they departed unto S.

Own SELF.

Ex. 32:13 swarest by thine *o.* S.
John 5:30 can of *o. s.* do nothing
17:5 glorify me with thine *o. s.*

1 *Cor.* 4:3 I judge not mine *o. s.*
Phile. 19 even thine *own s.*
1 *Pet.* 2:24 his *o. s.* bare our sins

SELFSAME.

Mat. 8:13 servant healed *s.* hour
1 *Cor.* 12:11 worketh one *s.* Spirit
2 *Cor.* 5:5 wrought us for *s.* thing
7:11 *s.* thing, ye sorrowed after
See Same DAY.

SELF-WILL.

Gen. 49:6 in *s.-w.* dig. down wall
See FRET, HIDE.

SELF-WILLED.

Tit. 1:7 bishop must not be *s.-w.*
2 *Pet.* 2:10 presumptuous, *s.-w.*

SELL.

Gen. 25:31 *s.* me thy birthright
37:27 let us *s.* him to Ishmael.
Ex. 21:7 if a man *s.* his daughter
35 *s.* live ox, and divide money
22:1 if man steal ox, kill, or *s.*
Lev. 25:14 if thou *s.* to neighbor
29 if a man *s.* dwelling-house
47 if bro. *s.* himself to stranger
Deut. 2:28 sh. *s.* meat for money
14:21 *s.* that wh. dieth to alien
21:14 sh. not *s.* her for money
Jud. 4:9 *s.* Sisera into hand of
1 *K.* 21:25 Ahab did *s.* himself to
2 *K.* 4:7 go, *s.* oil, pay thy debt
Neh. 5:8 will ye *s.* your breth.?
10:31 victuals on sab.-day to *s.*
Prov. 23:23 buy truth, *s.* it not
Ezek. 30:12 *s.* land into hand of
48:14 not *s.* first-fruits of land
Joel 3:8 I will *s.* your sons and
daugh. *s.* them to Sabeans
Amos 8:5 that we may *s.* corn
6 and *s.* refuse of the wheat
Zec. 11:5 that *s.* say, I am rich
Mat. 19:21 and *s.* that hast, *Mark*
10:21; *Luke* 12:33; 18:22
25:9 go ye to them that *s.* buy
Luke 22:36 *s.* garm. buy sword
Jam. 4:13 we will buy and *s.*
Rev. 13:17 no man mi. buy or *s.*

SELLER, S.

Is. 24:2 with buyer, so with *s.*
Ezek. 7:12 rejoice, nor *s.* mourn
13 *s.* not return to that sold
Neh. 13:20 *s.* lodged without Je.
Acts 16:14 Lydia, a *s.* of purple

SELLEST, ETH.

Ex. 21:16 he that stealeth a man
and *s.* him, *Deut.* 24:7
Ruth 4:3 Naomi *s.* part of land
Ps. 44:12 *s.* thy peo. for naught
Prov. 11:26 blessing on him *s.*
31:24 maketh fine linen, *s.* it
Nah. 3:4 *s.* nations thro' whore.
Mat. 13:44 he *s.* all, buyeth field

SELVEDGE.

Ex. 26:4 fr. *s.* in coupling, 36:11

Own SELVES.

Acts 20:30 of *o. s.* shall men rise
2 *Cor.* 8:5 gave their *own s.* to L.
13:5 your *o. s.* know not *o. s.*
2 *Tim.* 3:2 lovers of their *own s.*
Jam. 1:22 deceiving your *own s.*
See ASSEMBLE, ED.

SEMEI.

Luke 3:26 Mattathias son of S.

SENATE.

Acts 5:21 called *s.* of Is. together

SENATORS.

Ps. 105:22 teach his *s.* wisdom

SEND.

Gen. 24:7 G. shall *s.* angel bef. 40
12 *s.* me good speed this day
54 *s.* me away unto master, 56
43:4 if thou wilt *s.* our brother
45:5 God did *s.* me to pres. life
Ex. 4:13 *s.* by him thou wilt *s.*
7:2 *s.* children of Is. out of land

12:33 *s.* them out in haste
33:12 know whom thou wilt *s.*
Lev. 16:21 *s.* him away
Num. 12:2 men to search land
31:4 every tribe *s.* thous. to war
Deut. 1:22 *s.* men bef. to search
19:12 elders *s.* fetch him thence
28:20 L. sh. *s.* upon thee cursing
48 enemies L. shall *s.* ag. thee
Jud. 13:8 man of God didst *s.*
1 *Sam.* 5:11 *s.* away ark, 6:8
6:3 *s.* ark, *s.* it not empty.
9:26 that I may *s.* thee away
11:3 that we may *s.* messengers
16:11 said to Jesse. *s.* fetch Da.
19 Saul said, *s.* me D. thy son
25:25 saw not men thou didst *s.*
2 *Sam.* 11:6 *s.* me U. the Hittite
14:32 that I may *s.* thee to king
15:36 ye sh. *s.* me every thing
17:16 now therefore *s.* quickly
1 *K.* 20:9 thou didst *s.* for serva.
2 *K.* 2:16 shall not *s.* 17 said *s.*
6:13 I may *s.* and fetch him
7:13 let us *s.* 9:17 *s.* meet Jehu
15:37 L. began to *s.* ag. Judah
1 *Chr.* 13:2 *s.* abroad unto breth.
2 *Chr.* 6:27 *s.* rain upon land
28:16 A. did *s.* to king of Assy.
32:9 Sennacherib did *s.* to Hez.
Ezr. 5:17 *s.* his pleasure to us
Neh. 2:5 wouldest *s.* me to Jud.
6 it pleased the king to *s.* me
8:10 *s.* portions unto them, 12
Job 21:11 they *s.* forth little ones
38:35 canst thou *s.* lightnings?
Ps. 43:3 *s.* out thy light
57:3 he sh. *s.* from heaven, and
save fr. reproach; God sh. *s.*
68:3 he doth *s.* out his voice
110:2 *s.* rod of strength out of Z.
118:25 Lord, *s.* now prosperity
144:7 *s.* thy hand from above
Prov. 22:21 truth to them that *s.*
Is. 6:8 wh. shall I *s.?* I said *s.*
10:16 Lord shall *s.* am. fat ones
16:1 *s.* ye lamb to ruler of land
19:20 shall *s.* them a Saviour
32:20 *s.* the feet of ox and ass
57:9 didst *s.* thy messengers
Jer. 1:7 go to all that I shall *s.*
2:10 *s.* to Kedar; 9:17 *s.* women
29:31 *s.* to all them of captivity
42:5 the L. shall *s.* thee to us
6 obey L. to whom we *s.* thee
Mat. 9:38 pray ye the Lord will
s. forth laborers. *Luke* 10:2
10:34 thi. not I come to *s.* peace
13:41 Son of man shall *s.* his
angels, 24:31; *Mark* 13:27
15:23 *s.* her away, crieth after
21:3 he will *s.* them, *Mark* 11:3
Mark 3:14 *s.* to preach, 6:7
5:10 would not *s.* them away
12 saying, *s.* us into swine
Luke 16:24 *s.* Laz. 27 *s.* to house
John 14:26 Fa. will *s.* in name
17:8 belie. that thou didst *s.* me
Acts 3:20 he shall *s.* Jesus Christ
7:35 same did G. *s.* to be a ruler
10:5 *s.* men to Joppa, 32; 11:13
15:22 *s.* men of their compa. 25
25:3 would *s.* for him to Jerus.
Phil. 2:19 I trust to *s.* Timot. 23
25 necessary to *s.* Epaphrodit.
2 *Thes.* 2:11 G. shall *s.* delusions
Tit. 3:12 I shall *s.* Artemas unto
Jam. 3:11 fount. *s.* sweet water?
Rev. 1:11 and *s.* to sev. churches
11:10 *s.* gifts to one another

I SEND.

Ex. 23:20 behold. *I s.* an angel
Num. 22:37 did *I* not earne. *s.?*
1 *Sam.* 20:12 what *I s.* not to thee
Is. 6:8 saying, Whom shall I *s.?*
Jer. 25:15 all, to whom *I s.* thee
Ezek. 2:3 *I s.* thee to Israel. 4
14:21 *I s.* my four sore judgme.

Mat. 10:16 I *s.* you as sheep
11:10 behold, I *s.* my messenger,
Mark 1:2; *Luke* 7:27
23:34 behold I *s.* you prophets
Mark 8:3 if I *s.* them away fast.
Luke 10:3 I *s.* you forth as lambs
24:49 I *s.* the promise of Father
John 13:20 whom I *s.* receiv. me
20:21 sent me, even so *s.* I you
Acts 25:21 kept till I *s.* to Cesar
26:17 unto whom now I *s.* thee

I will SEND.
Gen. 27:45 I *w. s.* and fetch thee
37:13 come, and I *will s.* thee
Ex. 3:10 I *w. s.* to Pha. *Acts* 7:34
Lev. 26:22 I *will s.* wild beasts
1 *Sam.* 9:16 I *w. s.* man of Benj.
16:1 I *will s.* thee to Jesse the
20:13 I *will s.* show it thee, *s.*
1 *K.* 18:1 I *w. s.* rain upon earth
20:6 I *w. s.* my serv. unto thee
34 I *will s.* thee away with co.
Is. 66:19 I *will s.* th. that escape
Jer. 43:10 I *will s.* Nebuchadne.
51:2 I *w. s.* unto Baby. fanners
Ezek. 5:16 I *will s.* famine, 17;
14:13; *Amos* 8:11
7:3 I *will s.* mine anger upon
Mal. 2:2 I *w. s.* cn. 4:5 I *w. s.* E.
3:1 I *will s.* my messenger
Mat. 15:32 I *will* not *s.* them
Luke 11:49 I *will s.* them proph.
20:13 I *will s.* my beloved son
John 15:26 Comfort. I *w. s.* 16:7
Acts 22:21 I *w. s.* thee far hence
1 *Cor.* 16:3 you approve, I *will s.*
See FIRE.

SENDEST.
Deut. 15:13 when *s.* him out, 18
Jos. 1:16 whithersoever thou *s.*
2 *K.* 1:6 thou *s.* to Baal-zebub
Job 14:20 chang. his countenance
and *s.* him away
Ps. 104:30 thou *s.* thy Spirit

SENDETH.
Job 12:15 he *s.* them out
Ps. 147:15 *s.* forth his comm. 18
Mark 11:1 *s.* two disciples, 14:13
Luke 14:32 *s.* and desireth peace
Acts 23:26 Claud. Lys. to Felix *s.*

SENDING.
2 *Sam.* 13:16 evil in *s.* me away
2 *Chr.* 36:15 *s.* his messengers,
Jer. 7:25; 25:4; 26:5; 29:19
35:15; 44:4
Est. 9:19 and of *s.* portions, 22
Ps. 78:49 *s.* evil angels among
Is. 7:25 *s.* forth of lesser cattle
Rom. 8:3 God *s.* his Son in like.

SENNACHERIB.
2 *K.* 18:13 S. came up, *Is.* 36:1
19:16 the words of S. *Is.* 37:17
20 prayed against S. *Is.* 37:21
36 S. dwelt at Ninev. *Is.* 37:37
2 *Chr.* 32:22 Hezekiah from S.

SENSES.
Heb. 5:14 have their *s.* exercised

SENSUAL.
Jam. 3:15 wisd. earthly, *s.* devil.
Jude 19 th. be *s.* having not Spi.

SENT.
Gen. 38:25 Ta. *s.* to her father-in.
41:14 Pharaoh *s.* and called Jos.
42:4 Benjamin Jacob *s.* not with
45:8 not you that *s.* me hither
50:16 *s.* a messenger unto Jos.
Ex. 3:14 I AM ha. *s.* me to you
5:22 why is it thou hast *s.* me ?
Num. 13:16 men Moses *s.* 14:36
22:10 king of Moab hath *s.* to
Jos. 44:7 y.'s old Wh. M. *s.* me
Jud. 20:6 I *s.* her through Israel
1 *Sam.* 31:9 *s.* into land of Philis.
2 *Sam.* 24:13 ans. him that *s.* me
1 *K.* 18:10 my lord hath not *s.* to

21:11 elders did as Jez. *s.* them
2 *K.* 1:6 return unto king that *s.*
6:10 king of Israel *s.* to place
19:4 master *s.* to reproach God
22:15 th. *s.* you, 18; 2 *Chr.* 34:23
Ezr. 4:11 copy of letter they *s.*
Neh. 6:4 *s.* unto me four times
Is. 48:16 God and his Spirit *s.* me
Jer. 14:3 nobles ha. *s.* little ones
23:21 I ha. not *s.* these prophets
37:7 say unto king that *s.* you
Ezek. 23:40 ye have *s.* for men to
Dan. 3:28 who had *s.* his angel
Hos. 5:13 Eph. *s.* to king Jareb
Lev. 7:2 *s.* unto house of God
Mat. 21:1 then *s.* Je. two discip.
27:19 Pilate's wife *s.* unto him
Luke 7:20 J. Baptist *s.* us to thee
10:1 Jesus *s.* them two and two
14:17 *s.* his servant at supper
23:11 him again to Pilate
John 1:22 ans. to them that *s.* us
4:34 to do will of him th. *s.* me
5:23 honoreth not F. wh. *s.* me
John 5:24 believeth him that *s.*
me, 12:44
30 him who *s.* me, 6:38, 39, 40
33 ye *s.* un. John, and he bare
36 I bear witn. the Fath. hath
s. me, 37; 6:57; 8:16, 18
6:44 except Father which *s.* me
7:16 not mine, his that *s.* me
18 seeketh his glory th. *s.* him
32 Phari. and priests *s.* officers
9:4 work the wor. of him *s.* me
10:36 of him whom Fa. hath *s.*
11:42 believe thou hast *s.* me
12:45 seeth me, seeth him *s.* me
49 Fa. who *s.* me gave me com.
14:24 not mine, Fa.'s who *s.* me
15:21 know not him that *s.* me
16:5 I go my way to him *s.* me
17:3 to know J. whom thou *s.*
18 *s.* me into the world, so I *s.*
21 may believe thou *s.* me
23 world may kn. thou *s.* me
25 these have kn. thou *s.* me
20:21 as my Father hath *s.* me
Acts 5:21 *s.* to prison to have
15:27 we have *s.* Jud. and Silas
19:31 Paul's friends *s.* unto him
2 *Cor.* 8:18 *s.* with him broth. 22
Phil. 4:16 *s.* in Thessalonica ye *s.*
1 *John* 4:14 testify Father *s.* Son

SENT away.
Gen. 12:20 Phara. *s. a.* Abraham
21:14 Abr. *s.* Ishm. and Hag. *a.*
25:6 Abr. *s.* Keturah's child. *a.*
26:27 hate me and hath *s.* me *a.*
29 we have *s.* thee *a.* in peace
28:6 Isaac blessed Ja. *s.* him *a.*
45:24 he *s.* his brethren *away*
Deut. 24:4 *s.* her *a.* not take her
1 *Sam.* 10:25 Samuel *s.* people *a.*
19:17 hast *s. a.* my enemy ?
2 *Sam.* 3:21 Dav. *s.* Abner *away*
24 why is it th. hast *s.* him *a. ?*
1 *Chr.* 12:19 Philistines *s.* Da. *a.*
Luke 8:38 Jesus *s.* him *away*
Acts 13:3 them, they *s.* them *a.*

God SENT.
Gen. 45:7 *God s.* me before you
Ex. 3:13 *G.* of your fathers *s.* me
15 *God* of Jacob hath *s.* me
Neh. 6:12 *God* had not *s.* him
Jer. 43:1 Lord their *God s.* him
2 *G.* hath not *s.* to thee to say
John 3:17 *G. s.* not Son to cond.
34 he whom *God* hath *s.* spea.
Acts 10:36 *G. s.* to child. of Israel
Gal. 4:4 *G. s.* Son made of wom.
6 *G. s.* forth Spirit of his Son
1 *John* 4:9 *G. s.* his only bego. S.
Rev. 22:6 *God s.* his angel

He SENT.
Gen. 45:23 *he s.* aft. this manner,
46:28 *he s.* Judah unto Joseph

Ex. 18:2 after *he* had *s.* her back
Jud. 11:28 Ammon hearkened
not to words *he s.*
2 *Sam.* 10:5 *he s.* to meet them,
1 *Chr.* 19:5
14:29 when *he s.* aga. he would
22:17 *he s.* from above, *Ps.* 18:16
1 *K.* 20:7 *he s.* to me for my wives
2 *Chr.* 25:15 *he s.* unto Amaziah
Ps. 105:17 *he s.* a man bef. them
107:20 *he s.* his word and healed
Is. 61:1 *he s.* me to bind up the
broken-hearted, *Luke* 4:18
Jer. 29:28 *he s.* unto us in Babyl.
42:21 *he* hath *s.* me unto you
Lam. 1:13 *he s.* fire into my bo.
Zec. 2:8 *he s.* me to nations
Mat. 21:36 ag. *he s.* other serva.
37 last of all *he s.* unto them
his son, *Mark* 12:4
John 5:38 for wh. *he* hath *s.* him
6:29 believe on him *he* hath *s.*
7:28 *he* that *s.* me is true, 8:26
29 I know him, *he* hath *s.* me
8:29 *he* that *s.* me is with me
42 neither came I myself, *he s.*
Acts 24:26 wheref. *he s.* for Paul

I SENT.
Gen. 32:5 I have *s.* to tell my lord
Ex. 3:12 a token I have *s.* thee
Num. 32:8 your fathers whom I *s.*
Jos. 24:5 I *s.* Moses, *Mic.* 6:4
Jud. 6:14 1a. have not I *s.* thee ?
2 *K.* 5:6 I *s.* Naaman my servant
17:13 the law which I *s.* to you
Is. 43:14 for your sake I have *s.*
55:11 sh. prosper whereto I *s.*
Jer. 7:25 I *s.* unto you all my
servants, 26:5; 35:15; 44:4
14:14 I *s.* them not, 15; 23:21,
32; 27:15; 29:9
29:31 I *s.* him not, caused you
Ezek. 3:6 surely had I *s.* thee
Dan. 10:11 O Dan. to thee am I *s.*
Joel 2:25 great army which I *s.*
Zec. 9:11 I *s.* forth thy prisoners
Mal. 2:4 ye know I have *s.* this
Luke 4:43 for therefore am I *s.*
John 17:18 I *s.* them into world
Acts 10:20 noth. I have *s.* them
1 *Cor.* 4:17 for this ha. I *s.* you T.
2 *Cor.* 12:17 did I make a gain of
you by any whom I *s.* ?
18 and with him I *s.* a brother
Eph. 6:22 whom I *s.* for same
purpose, *Col.* 4:8
Phil. 2:28 I *s.* him more carefully
1 *Thes.* 3:5 I *s.* to kn. your faith
Phile. 12 whom I have *s.* again
See LORD.

SENT forth.
Mat. 10:5 these twelve Jesus *s. f.*
22:3 *s. forth* his servants to call
Mark 6:17 Herod *s. f.* laid hold
Acts 9:30 brethren *s.* him *forth*
11:22 they *s. forth* Barnabas

SENT out.
Job 39:5 who *s. o.* wild ass free?
Jer. 24:5 I have *s. o.* of this place
Ezek. 31:4 *s. out* her little rivers
Acts 7:12 Jacob *s. out* our fathers
Jam. 2:25 Rahab had *s.* them *out*

SENT, passive.
Gen. 32:18 present *s.* to lord Es.
1 *K.* 14:6 *s.* with heavy tidings
Ezr. 7:14 forasm. as thou art *s.*
Ezek. 2:9 a hand was *s.* unto me
Dan. 5:24 part of hand *s.* fr. him
Mat. 15:24 *s.* to lost sheep of Isr.
23:37 stonest them *s. Luke* 13:34
Luke 1:19 am *s.* to speak to thee
4:26 unto none was Elias *s.*
John 1:6 a man *s.* from God
8 John was *s.* to bear witness
24 they *s.* were of the Pharis.
3:28 not Christ, but *s.* bef. him

9:7 which is by interpretati. *s.*
13:16 nor he that *s.* greater than
   he that *s.* him
Acts 10:17 men *s.* made inquiry
   29 came I as soon as *s.* for
13:4 *s.* forth by the Holy Ghost
   26 to you is word of salvat. *s.*
28:28 salvation of G. *s.* to Gent.
Rom. 10:15 how preach, exc. *s.* ?
Phil. 4:18 which were *s.* fr. you
1 *Pet.* 1:12 H. Ghost *s.* fr. heaven
Rev. 5:6 the seven spirits *s.* forth

SENTEST.
Ex. 15:7 *s.* forth thy wrath
Num. 13:27 whither thou *s.* us
1 *K.* 5:8 considered things th. *s.*

SENTENCE, S.
Deut. 17:9 they sh. show thee *s.*
   10 shalt do according to *s.* 11
Ps. 17:2 let my *s.* come forth
Prov. 16:10 *s.* in lips of king
Ec. 8:11 *s.* is not executed
Jer. 4:12 now also will I give *s.*
Dan. 5:12 hard *s.* found in Dan.
   8:23 a king understand. dark *s.*
Luke 23:34 Pilate gave *s.* that it
2 *Cor.* 1:9 we had the *s.* of death

SEPARATE, Verb.
Gen. 13:9 Abram said, *s.* thyself
   30:40 Jacob did *s.* the lambs
Lev. 15:31 sh. ye *s.* children of I.
   22:2 Aaron and sons that th. *s.*
Num. 6:2 when man or woman *s.*
   3 the Nazarite shall *s.* himself
   8:14 shall *s.* Levites from Israel
   16:21 *s.* from this congregation
Deut. 19:2 shalt *s.* three cities, 7
   29:21 Lord sh. *s.* him unto evil
1 *K.* 8:53 *s.* th. to be inheritance
Ezr. 10:11 *s.* yourselves fr. peop.
Jer. 37:12 Jerom. went to *s.* him.
Mal. 25:32 *s.* them as a shepherd
Luke 6:22 blessed when men *s.*
Acts 13:2 *s.* me Barnabas and S.
Rom. 8:35 who sh. *s.* us fr. C. ?
   39 noth. be able to *s.* us fr. G.
Jude 19 they who *s.* themselves

SEPARATE.
Gen. 49:26 him that was *s.* from
   his brethren, *Deut.* 33:16
Jos. 16:9 *s.* cities of Ephraim
Ezek. 41:12 build. before *s.* place
   13 measured house and *s.* pla.
   42:1 cham. ag. *s.* place, 10, 13
2 *Cor.* 6:17 Tr. among them, be *s.*
Heb. 7:26 undefiled, *s.* fr. sinners

SEPARATED.
Gen. 13:11 Abram and Lot *s.*
   25:23 two manner of peop. be *s.*
Ex. 33:16 so be *s.* from people
Lev. 20:24 I am L. who have *s.*
Lev. 20:25 I have *s.* from you as
Num. 16:9 God of Is. hath *s.* you
Deut. 10:8 Lord *s.* tribe of Levi
   32:8 when he *s.* sons of Adam
1 *Chr.* 12:8 Gadites *s.* unto David
   23:13 Aa. was *s.* that he should
Ezr. 6:21 such as had *s.* themse
   8:24 I *s.* twelve chief of priests
   9:1 priests and Lev. have not *s.*
   10:8 be *s.* from congregation
   16 all of th. by names were *s.*
Neh. 4:19 we are *s.* upon wall
   9:2 Is. *s.* themselves fr. strang.
   10:28 that *s.* clave to brethren
   13:3 *s.* fr. Israel the multitude
Prov. 18:1 a man hav. *s.* himself
   19:4 poor is *s.* from his neighb.
Is. 56:3 L. *s.* me from his people
   59:2 iniq. *s.* betw. you and God
Hos. 4:14 for themselves are *s.*
   9:10 went and *s.* themselves
Acts 19:9 Paul *s.* the disciples
Rom. 1:1 Paul *s.* to gospel of G.
Gal. 1:15 G. who *s.* me from my
   2:12 P. withdrew and *s.* himself

SEPARATETH.
Num. 6:5 fulfilled in which he *s.*
Prov. 16:28 a whisper. *s.* friends
   17:9 repeat. a matter *s.* friends
Ezek. 14:7 strang. wh. *s.* himself

SEPARATION.
Lev. 12:2 the *s.* for her infirmity
   5 uncl. two weeks, as in her *s.*
   15:20 bed she lieth up. in her *s.*
   26 be to her as the bed of h. *s.*
Num. 6:4 days of *s.* eat nothing
   8 days of *s.* is holy unto Lord
   12 because his *s.* was defiled
   18 Nazarite shave head of his
      s. and take the hair of his *s.*
   21 offering for *s.* after law of *s.*
   19:9 ashes be kept for wat. of *s.*
   13 water of *s.* not sprinkled, 20
   21 he that sprinkl. water of *s.*
      shall wash his clothes, that
      toucheth water of *s.* be unc.
   31:23 purified with water of *s.*
Ezek. 42:20 had a wall to make *s.*

SEPARATING.
Zec. 7:3 I weep in 5th month, *s.*

SEPHARVAIM.
2 *K.* 17:24 brought men from S.
   18:34 the gods of S. ? *Is.* 36:19
   19:13 king of S. ? *Is.* 37:13

SEPULCHRE.
Gen. 23:6 none with. thee his *s.*
Deut. 34:6 no man kno. of his *s.*
Jud. 8:32 buried in father's *s.*
1 *Sam.* 10:2 two men by R.'s *s.*
2 *Sam.* 2:32 As. in his father's *s.*
   4:12 Ishbosh. buried in Abn. *s.*
   17:23 Ahithophel in *s.* of father
   21:14 bones of Saul in *s.* of Kis.
1 *K.* 13:22 carcass not come to *s.*
   31 bury me in *s.* w. man of G.
2 *K.* 9:28 Ahaziah in the *s.*
   13:21 cast man into *s.* of Elisha
   21:26 Amon was buried in his *s.*
   23:17 it is *s.* of the man of God
   30 Josiah buried in his own *s.*
      2 *Chr.* 35:24
Ps. 5:9 throat open *s.* *Rom.* 3:13
   22:16 hewed out a *s.* here, as
      he that he. out a *s.* on high
Mat. 27:60 roll. stone to door of *s.*
   64 that the *s.* be made sure, 66
   28:1 other Mary came to see *s.*
Mark 15:46 laid him in a *s.* and
      rolled a stone to door of the
      s. Luke 23:53; *Acts* 13:29
   16:2 came to *s.* at rising of sun
   3 who sh. roll st. fr. door of *s.*
   5 entering *s.* 8 fled from *s.*
Luke 23:55 wom. also beheld *s.*
   24:1 in morning they came to *s.*
   2 stone rolled fr. *s. John* 20:1
   9 returned fr. *s.* 12 Peter ran
   22 women were early at the *s.*
John 19:41 in garden th. was a *s.*
   42 for the *s.* was nigh at hand
   20:1 com. Mary when dark to *s.*
   2 taken away L. out of the *s.*
   3 that disciple came to *s.* 4, ?
   6 cometh Peter, went into *s.*
   11 Mary stood at *s.* weeping
Acts 2:29 *s.* wi. us unto this day
   7:16 Jacob laid in *s.* Abraham

SEPULCHRES.
Gen. 23:6 in the choice of our *s.*
2 *K.* 23:16 Josiah spied the *s.* and
   took the bones out of the *s.*
2 *Chr.* 21:20 Jeh. not buried in *s.*
   24:25 Joash not ; 28:27 A. not *s.*
   32:33 Hezekiah buried in the *s.*
Neh. 2:3 place of my fathers' *s.*
   5 send me to city of fathers' *s.*
Neh. 3:16 rep. to place over ag. *s.*
Mat. 23:27 are like to whited *s.*
   29 because ye garnish the *s.*
Luke 11:47 *s.* of the prophets, 48

SERAIAH.
2 *Sam.* 8:17 S. was the scribe
2 *K.* 25:18 took S. *Jer.* 52:24
   23 to Gedaliah. S. *Jer.* 40:8
1 *Chr.* 4:14 S. begat Joab, 35
   6:14 Azariah begat S. and S.
Ezr. 7:1 E. son of S. *Neh.* 10:2
Neh. 11:11 S. was ruler of house
   12 S. the priest went up
   12 chief of the fathers of S.
Jer. 36:26 king commanded S.
   51:59 S. was a quiet prince
   61 Jeremiah said to S. when

SERAPHIM.
Is. 6:2 above it stood the *s.* each
   6 one of the *s.* hav. a live coal

SERGEANTS.
Acts 16:35 sent the *s.* saying
   38 *s.* told these words to mag.

SERGIUS PAULUS.
Acts 13:7 S. Paulus, a prudent

SERPENT.
Gen. 3:1 the *s.* was more subtle
   13 *s.* beguiled me, 2 *Cor.* 11:3
   49:17 Dan shall be a *s.* by way
Ex. 4:3 rod bec. a *s.* 7:9, 10, 15
Num. 21:8 said, Make thee a *s.*
   9 Moses made a *s.* of brass
Ex. 18:4 Hezek. brake brazen *s.*
Job 26:13 hand formed crooked *s.*
Ps. 58:4 th. poison like pois. of *s.*
   140:3 sharpen. tongues like a *s.*
Prov. 23:32 at last it bit. like a *s.*
   30:19 way of a *s.* upon a rock
Ec. 10:8 whoso break. a hedge *s.*
      shall bite him
   11 *s.* bite without enchantme.
Is. 14:29 of *s.* root come cocka-
      trice ; fruit be as fiery fly. *s.*
   27:1 L. sh. punish *s.* crooked *s.*
   30:6 viper and fiery flying *s.*
   65:25 dust shall be the *s.* meat
Jer. 46:22 voice sh. go like a *s.*
Amos 5:19 and a *s.* bite him
Mic. 7:17 lick the dust like a *s.*
Mat. 7:10 will he give him a *s.* ?
      Luke 11:11
John 3:14 as Moses lifted up *s.*
Rev. 12:9 old *s.* called devil, 20:2
   14 nourished fr. face of the *s.*
   15 the *s.* cast out of his mouth

SERPENTS.
Ex. 7:12 rods, they became *s.*
Num. 21:6 L. sent *s.* amo. them
   7 pray to L. he take away *s.*
Deut. 8:15 wherein were fiery *s.*
   32:24 send poi. of *s.* upon them
Jer. 8:17 I will send *s.* among y.
Mat. 10:16 be therefore wise as *s.*
   23:33 ye *s.* how can ye escape ?
Mark 16:18 they shall take up *s.*
Luke 10:19 power to tread on *s.*
1 *Cor.* 10:9 were destroyed of *s.*
Jam. 3:7 beasts and *s.* is tamed
Rev. 9:19 tails were like to *s.*
SERUG.   *Gen.* 11:20–22

SERVANT.
Gen. 9:25 Canaan, a *s.* of servan.
   24:34 said, I am Abraham's *s.*
   49:15 Issa. bowed and bec. a *s.*
Ex. 21:5 if the *s.* plainly say
Deut. 5:15 remem. thou wast a *s.*
   23:15 thou shalt not deliver *s.*
1 *Sam.* 2:13 priest's *s.* came, 15
   9:27 bid the *s.* pass on before us
   25:41 let thy handmaid be a *s.*
   29:3 is not David the *s.* of Saul ?
   30:13 I am *s.* to an Amalekite
2 *Sam.* 9:2 *s.* named Ziba, 19:17
   16:1 Ziba *s.* of Mephibosheth
   18:29 wh. Joab sent *s.* k.'s *s.*
1 *K.* 11:26 Jeroboam Solom.'s *s.*
   12:7 if thou wilt be a *s.* to peop.
Neh. 2:10 Tobi. *s.* Am. heard, 19

Job 3:19 there, and the *s.* is free
7:2 as a *s.* earne. desireth shad.
41:4 wilt take Leviathan for *s.?*
Ps. 105:17 Joseph, sold for a *s.*
Prov. 11:29 fool sh. be *s.* to wise
12:9 that is despi. and hath a *s.*
14:35 king's favor tow. a wise *s.*
17:2 wise *s.* shall rule over a son
19:10 much less a *s.* rule princes
22:7 the borrower is *s.* to lender
29:19 a *s.* not correct. with wor.
30:10 accuse not *s.* to master
22 not bear *s.* when reigneth
Is. 24:2 as with *s.* so with master
49:7 saith Lord to a *s.* of rulers
Jer. 2:14 is Israel a *s.?* a slave?
Dan. 6:20 O Daniel, *s.* of liv. G.
Dan. 10:17 can *s.* talk wi. my l. ?
Mal. 1:6 *s.* honoreth his master
Mat. 10:24 nor *s.* above his lord
25 enough for *s.* to be as his lo.
18:27 lord of that *s.* was moved
32 O thou wicked *s.* I forg. th.
20:27 be chief, let him be your
s. 23:11; *Mark* 10:44
24:45 is a faithful and wise *s.*
46 blessed is that *s. Luke* 12:43
48 evil *s.* shall say, *Luke* 12:45
50 lord of *s.* sh. come, *Lu.* 12:46
25:21 well done, th. good and
faithful *s.* 23; *Luke* 19:17
26 thou wicked and slothful *s.*
Luke 19:22
30 cast unprofit. *s.* into darkn.
26:51 P. struck *s.* of high-priest,
Mark 14:47; *John* 18:10
Mark 12:2 sent to husband. a *s.*
Luke 12:47 *s.* knew lord's will
14:21 so that *s.* showed his lord
17:7 which having a *s.* plowing
9 doth thank th. *s.?* I trow not
20:10 at season he sent a *s.* 11
John 8:34 commit. sin, *s.* of sin
35 the *s.* abideth not in house
13:16 *s.* is not greater, 15:20
15:15 *s.* knoweth not what lord
Rom. 1:1 Paul a *s.* of Je. Christ
14:4 who judgest ano. man's *s.?*
16:1 Phebe. a *s.* of the church
1 *Cor.* 7:21 art called being a *s.?*
22 being a *s.* is L.'s freeman
9:19 I made myself a *s.*
Gal. 1:10 I sho. not be *s.* of Chr.
4:1 child differeth noth. from *s.*
7 art no more a *s.* but a son
Phil. 2:7 he took the form of a *s.*
Col. 4:12 Epaphras, a *s.* of Christ
2 *Tim.* 2:24 *s.* of Lord not strive
Phile. 16 not as a *s.* above a *s.*
Heb. 3:5 Mo. was faithful as a *s.*
2 *Pet.* 1:1 Peter, a *s.* of J. Christ
Jude 1 Jude the *s.* of Jesus Chr.

See DAVID.

SERVANT, S. of God.

Gen. 50:17 forgive *s. of God*
1 *Chr.* 6:49 Moses the *s. of God*
2 *Chr.* 24:9 Moses *s. of God* laid
Neh. 10:29 by Moses *s. of God*
Dan. 6:20 O Daniel *s.* of liv. *God*
9:11 in law of Mo. the *s. of God*
Tit. 1:1 P. a *s. of God*, an apost.
Jam. 1:1 Ja. a *s. of G.* and of L.
1 *Pet.* 2:16 liberty, as a *s. of G.*
Rev. 7:3 sealed the *s.* of our *God*
15:3 song of Moses the *s. of G.*

See HIRED.

His SERVANT.

Gen. 9:26 Can. shall be *his s.* 27
Ex. 14:31 believed L. and *his s.*
21:20 if a man smite *his s.*
26 if smite eye of *his s.*
Jos. 5:14 what saith L. to *h. s.?*
9:24 God commanded *his s.* Mo.
Jud. 7:11 Gi. went wi. Ph. *his s.*
19:3 Levite went, having *his s.*
1 *Sam.* 19:4 let not the king sin
against *his s.*

12:15 let not king imp. to *his s.*
25:39 L. hath kept *h. s.* fr. evil
26:18 why doth my lo. pu. *h. s.?*
19 let lord hear words of *h. s.*
2 *Sam.* 9:11 my lord comm. *h. s.*
14:22 king fulfilled req. of *h. s.*
24:21 is my lord come to *h. s. ?*
1 *K.* 1:51 that will not slay *h. s.*
8:56 prom. by hand of Mo. *h. s.*
59 maintain cause of *h. s.* Isr.
14:18 spake by *h. s.* Ahi. 15:29
19:3 Eli. left *h. s.* at Beer-sheba
2 *K.* 9:36 word he spake by *h. s.*
14:25 word he spake by *h. s.* Jo.
17:3 Hoshea bec. *his s.* and gave
24:1 Jehoiakim became *his s.*
1 *Chr.* 16:13 O ye seed of Is. *h. s.*
2 *Chr.* 32:16 spake ag. *his s.* Hez
Neh. 4:22 let ev. one with *h. s.*
Ps. 35:27 L. hath pleas. of *his s.*
105:6 O ye seed of Abra. *his s.*
26 he sent Moses *his s.* and A.
42 remembered Abraham *his s.*
136:22 a heritage unto Is. *his s.*
Prov. 29:21 delicately bring. *h. s.*
Is. 44:26 confirm. word of *his s.*
48:20 Lord redeemed *h. s.* Jacob
49:5 from the womb to be *his s.*
50:10 obeyeth voice of *his s. ?*
Jer. 34:16 ev. man *h. s.* to return
Mat. 8:13 *his s.* was healed
Luke 1:54 hath holpen *his s.* Isr.
7:3 beseeching he wo. heal *h. s.*
14:17 sent *h. s.* at supper-time
Rev. 1:1 by his angel un. *h. s.* J.

See LORD, MAID.

Man-SERVANT.

Ex. 20:10 th. nor *m.-s. Deut.* 5:14
17 not cov. ne. *m.-s. Deut.* 5:21
21:27 smite out his *m.-s.* tooth
32 if the ox shall push a *m.-s.*
Deut. 12:18 eat, thou, and *m.-s.*
16:11 rejoice, th. and thy *m.-s.*
Job 31:13 if desp. cause of *m.-s.*
Jer. 34:9 let *m.-s.* go free, 10

My SERVANT.

Gen. 26:24 multi. seed for *my s.*
44:10 found he sh. be *my s.* 17
Num. 12:7 *my s.* Moses is not so
14:24 *my s.* Caleb had another
Jos. 1:2 Moses *my s.* is dead
1 *Sam.* 22:8 son stirred up *my s.*
27:12 he shall be *my s.* for ever
2 *Sam.* 19:26 O king, *my s.* decei.
2 *K.* 5:6 have sent Naaman *my s.*
21:8 according to law *my s.* M.
Job 1:8 consider. *my s.* Job ? 2:3
19:16 I called *my s.* he gave me
42:7 not spok. right, as *my s.* J.
8 go to *my s.* J. he shall pray
Is. 20:3 like as *my s.* Isa. hath
22:20 I will call *my s.* Eliakim
41:8 Israel, *my s.* fear not, 9
42:1 behold *my s.* wh. I uphold
19 who is blind but *my s.?*
43:10 are witnesses and *my s.*
44:1 O Ja. *my s.* 2 fear not, *m. s.*
21 for thou art *my s.* 49:3
45:4 for Ja. *my s.* sake, and Isr.
49:6 thou shouldest be *my s.*
52:13 *my s.* deal prudently
65:8 so will I do for *my s.* sake
Jer. 25:9 Nebuchadnezzar *my s.*
27:6 ; 43:10
30:10 O *my s.* Jacob, 46:27, 28
Ezek. 28:25 given *my s.* J. 37:25
Hag. 2:23 O Zerubbabel *my s.*
Zec. 3:8 *my s.* the BRANCH
Mal. 4:4 law of Moses, *my s.*
Mat. 8:8 *my s.* be healed, *Lu.* 7:7
8 to *my s.* do this, *Luke* 7:8
12:18 *my s.* whom I ha. chosen
John 12:26 th. shall also *my s.* be

Thy SERVANT.

Gen. 18:3 pass, I pray, fr. *thy s.*
19:19 *thy s.* found gra. *Neh.* 2:5

32:10 mercies showed to *thy s.*
18 say, They be *thy s.* Jacob's
33:5 chil. God hath given *thy s.*
44:31 grey hairs of *s.* our fa.
Ex. 4:10 spoken unto *thy s.*
Lev. 25:6 for thee, and for *thy s.*
Num. 11:11 where. hast affl. *t. s.*
Deut. 3:24 show *thy s.* thy great.
15:17 he shall be *thy s.* for ever
Jud. 7:10 go down with Ph. *t. s.*
1 *Sam.* 3:9 Lord *thy s.* heareth, 10
20:7 *thy s.* shall have peace
22:15 *thy s.* knew noth. of this
23:11 I beseech thee tell *thy s.*
28:2 sh. know what *t. s.* can do
2 *Sam.* 7:19 hast spoken of *thy s.*
20 thou, L. G. knowest thy *s.*
39 bless the house of *thy s.*
13:35 came, as thy *s.* said
15:21 even there will *thy s.* be
24:10 take away iniq. of *thy s.*
1 *K.* 1:26 even me, *t. s.* and Zad.
the priest, and *t. s.* Solomon
3:8 *thy s.* is in midst of thy peo.
9 give *thy s.* understand. heart
8:28 respect to prayer of *thy s.*
18:12 but I *thy s.* fear the Lord
20:40 as *thy s.* was busy here
2 *K.* 4:1 *thy s.* my husband dead.
thou know. *thy s.* did fear L.
5:18 L. pardon *t. s.* in this thing
25 Ge. said, *thy s.* went no wh.
8:13 is *t. s.* a dog? 16:7 am *t s.*
Neh. 1:11 prosp. I pray thee, *t. s.*
Ps. 19:11 by th. is *thy s.* warned
27:9 put not *thy s.* away
31:16 face to shine upon *thy s.*
69:17 hide not thy face fr. *thy s.*
86:2 O G. save *t. s.* that trusteth
16 give thy strength to *thy s.*
89:39 made void coven. of *thy s.*
116:16 am *t. s.* 119:125; 143:12
Ec. 7:21 hear *thy s.* curse thee
Is. 63:17 return, for *thy s.* sake
Dan. 9:17 hear prayer of *thy s.*
Luke 2:29 L. lettest *thy s.* depart

SERVANTS.

Gen. 9:25 a serv. of *s.* shall he be
27:37 breth. have I given for *s.*
Lev. 25:55 children of Is. are *s.*
1 *Sam.* 4:9 be not *s.* to Hebrews
7:8 Philist. and you *s.* of Saul
9 then will we be your *s.*
25:10 many *s.* break away from
41 wash feet of *s.* of my lord
2 *Sam.* 8:2 Moab. bec. David's *s.*
2 *Sam.* 8:6 Syrians bec. *s.* to D.
14 they of Edom be. David's *s.*
9:10 Ziba had 15 sons and 20 *s.*
11:11 *s.* of my lord are encamp.
1 *K.* 2:39 two *s.* of Shimei ran
2 *K.* 21:23 *s.* of Amon conspired
1 *Chr.* 21:3 are they not lord's *s.*
2 *Chr.* 8:9 of Israel S. made no *s.*
36:20 Babylon. wh. they were *s.*
Ezr. 5:11 we are the *s.* of God
Neh. 5:15 th. *s.* bare rule over p.
9:36 are *s.* this day, *s.* in land
Job 1:15 slain *s.* with sword, 17
Ps. 123:2 eyes of *s.* look to mast.
Ec. 2:7 I got me *s.* had *s.* born
10:7 I have seen *s.* on horses,
and princes walking as *s.*
Is. 14:2 Israel possess them for *s.*
Jer. 34:11 caused the *s.* they had
Lam. 5:8 *s.* have ruled over us
Dan. 3:26 *s.* of the m. high God
Joel 2:29 upon *s.* will I pour Sp.
Zec. 2:9 shall be a spoil to *s.*
Mat. 22:13 said to *s.* Bind him
25:19 the lord of those *s.* come.
Mark 14:65 the *s.* did strike Jes.
Luke 12:37 blessed are those *s.* 38
17:10 unprofitable *s.* have done
John 15:15 I call you not *s.* for
Acts 16:17 these men are *s.* of G.

Rom. 6:16 yield yoursel. *s.* to ob.
17 that ye were the *s.* of sin
18 became *s.* of righteousness
19 yielded your mem. *s.* to sin
20 *s.* of sin, were free fr. right.
22 free from sin. bec. *s.* to God
1 *Cor.* 7:23 be not ye *s.* of men
2 *Cor.* 4:5 oursel. your *s.* for Jes.
Eph. 6:5 *s.* obedi. to mast. *Col.*
3:22 ; *Tit.* 2:9 ; 1 *Pet.* 2:18
6 eye service, but as *s.* of Chr.
Phil. 1:1 Paul and Tim. *s.* of Ch.
Col. 4:1 give your *s.* what is just
1 *Tim.* 6:1 as many *s.* as are un.
1 *Pet.* 2:16 liberty, but as *s.* of G.
2 *Pet.* 2:19 themselves are *s.* of c.
Rev. 7:3 we have sealed *s.* of G.

See HIRED.

His SERVANTS.

Ex. 12:30 Phar. rose, and *his s.*
Num. 22:22 Bala. rid. and h. 2 *s.*
Deut. 32:36 L. sh. repent for h. *s.*
43 he will avenge blood of h. *s.*
1 *Sam.* 8:14 best, give to h. *s.* 15.
19:1 S. spake to h. *s.* to kill Da.
22:6 h. *s.* standing about him
2 *K.* 5:13 h. *s.* came near, spake
1 *Chr.* 19:3 h. *s.* come to search ?
2 *Chr.* 32:16 his *s.* spake ag. L.
Neh. 2:20 his *s.* will arise
Job 4:18 he put no trust in *his s.*
Ps. 69:36 seed of *his s.* inherit
135:14 repent himself conc. h. *s.*
Prov. 29:12 all *his s.* are wicked
Is. 56:6 love na. of L. to be h. *s.*
65:15 L. call h. *s.* by ano. name
66:14 L. be known toward *his s.*
Jer. 22:4 on horses, and *his s.*
36:31 punish him, seed, *his s.*
Ezek. 46:17 if p. give gift to h. *s.*
Dan. 3:28 deliver h. *s.* trusted
Mat. 18:23 king take acc. of h. *s.*
21:34 sent h. *s.* to husbandmen
Luke 19:13 he called *his* ten *s.*
Rom. 6:16 h. *s.* ye are wh. ye ob.
Rev. 1:1 h. *s.* things must come,
22:6
19:2 hath avenged blood of h. *s.*
5 praise God, ye h. *s.* fear him
22:3 and *his s.* shall serve him

See LORD, MAID, MEN.

My SERVANTS.

Lev. 25:42 my *s.* whom I bro. 55
1 *Sam.* 21:2 appoint. my *s.* a pl.
1 *K.* 5:6 my *s.* shall be with thy
servants, 2 *Chr.* 2:8
22:49 let my *s.* go with thy serv.
2 *K.* 9:7 aven. the blood of my *s.*
Neh. 4:23 nor my *s.* put off clo.
5:10 I and my *s.* mig. exact mo.
16 my *s.* were gather. to work
15:19 my *s.* set I at gates
Is. 65:9 my *s.* shall dwell there
13 my *s.* eat ; 14 my *s.* sing
Jer. 7:25 sent to you my *s.* 44:4
John 18:36 then wo. my *s.* fight
Acts 2:18 on my *s.* I will pour S.
Rev. 2:20 prophe. to seduce my *s.*

See PROPHETS.

Thy SERVANTS.

Gen. 44:16 G. found iniq. of t. *s.*
47:3 thy *s.* are shepherds
50:18 said, Behold, we be thy *s.*
Ex. 5:15 dealest thus with thy *s.*
11:8 these thy *s.* bow down
Ex. 32:13 remember Abraham,
Israel thy *s.* *Deut.* 9:27
Jos. 9:8 Gibeo. said, We are t. *s.*
10:6 slack not thy hand fr. t. *s.*
1 *Sam.* 12:19 pray for thy *s.* to L.
22:14 so faithf. am. t. *s.* as D. ?
2 *Sam.* 19:7 speak comf. to thy *s.*
1 *K.* 2:39 told Shimei, t. *s.* in G.
5:6 my servants shall be with
thy *s.* 2 *Chr.* 2:8

8:23 keepest mercy with thy *s.*
32 and judge t. *s.* 2 *Chr.* 6:23
10:8 happy th. t. *s.* 2 *Chr.* 9:7
12:7 thy *s.* for ever, 2 *Chr.* 10:7
2 *K.* 6:3 content, and go wi. t. *s.*
Neh. 1:10 these are thy *s.* and p.
11 attentive to prayer of thy *s.*
Ps. 79:2 bodies of thy *s.*
10 revenging of blood of t. *s.*
89:50 remem. reproach of thy *s.*
90:13 repent thee concern. t. *s.*
16 let thy work appear to t. *s.*
102:14 for thy *s.* take pleasure
28 child. of thy *s.* shall contin.
119:91 continue, for all are t. *s.*
Is. 37:24 by thy *s.* reproached L.
Dan. 1:12 prove thy *s.* ten days
13 as th. seest, deal with t. *s.*
Acts 4:29 grant unto thy *s.* that

See WOMEN.

SERVE.

Gen. 15:13 seed *s.* them 400 years
14 nation they *s.* I will judge
25:23 elder shall *s.* the younger
27:29 let people *s.* nations bow
40 by sw. live, and *s.* brother
29:18 I will *s.* 7 yrs. for Rachel
27 shalt *s.* seven other years
Ex. 1:13 made Is. *s.* with rigor
3:12 ye shall *s.* G. upon moun.
4:23 let my son go, he may *s.*
7:16 let my peo. go, that they
may *s.* 8:1, 20 ; 9:1, 13 ; 10:3
14:12 alone, that we *s.* Egypt
20:5 bow down nor *s.* *Deut.* 5:9
21:6 he shall *s.* him for ever
Lev. 25:40 *s.* thee to year of jub.
Num. 4:24 family of Gers. to *s.*
8:25 age of fifty, sh. *s.* no more
18:21 to Levi. for serv. they *s.*
Deut. 6:13 fear the Lord and *s.*
him, 10:12, 20 ; 11:13 ; 13:4 ;
Jos. 22:5 ; 24:14, 15 ; 1 *Sam.*
7:3 ; 12:14 ; 20, 24
15:12 bro. be sold, *s.* six years
28:48 shalt thou *s.* thine enem.
Jos. 24:15 cho. whom ye will *s.*
Jud. 9:38 Ab. that we *s.* him ?
1 *Sam.* 10:7 do as occasion sh. *s.*
11:1 make covenant, we will *s.*
12:10 deliver us, and we *s.* thee
17:9 be our servants, and *s.* us
2 *Sam.* 16:19 whom should I *s.* ?
should I not *s.* ?
22:44 people I knew not shall *s.*
me, *Ps.* 18:43
2 *K.* 10:18 but Jehu shall *s.* Baal
25:24 dwell in. the land and *s.*
the king of Babylon, *Jer.*
27:11, 12, 17 ; 28:14 ; 40:9
1 *Chr.* 28:9 *s.* him with perf. he.
2 *Chr.* 29:11 L. hath ch. you to *s.*
34:33 Josiah made all to *s.* Lord
Job 21:15 Almig. that we *s.* him ?
36:11 if they obey, and *s.* him
39:9 unicorn be will. to *s.* thee ?
Ps. 22:30 a seed shall *s.* him
72:11 all nations shall *s.* him
97:7 confounded that *s.* images
101:6 perfect way, he sh. *s.* me
Is. 14:3 bond. wast made to *s.*
19:23 Egyptians *s.* with Assyri.
43:23 ha. not caused thee to *s.*
24 made me to *s.* wi. thy sins
56:6 join themsel. to L. to *s.* h.
66:12 nation not *s.* thee sh. per.
Jer. 5:19 so shall ye *s.* strangers
17:4 cause thee to *s.* enemies
25:11 nations *s.* king of Babylon
14 nations *s.* themselves, 27:7
27:6 beasts have I given to *s.*
9 proph. say, Ye shall not *s.* 14
30:8 strang. no more *s.* themse.
34:9 none sho. *s.* himself of, 10
40:10 behold, I will *s.* Chaldea.
Ezek. 20:32 families to *s.* wood
39 *s.* ye every one his idols
40 all of th. in land sh. *s.* me

29:18 army *s.* against Tyrus
48:18 food to them that *s.* city
19 that *s.* city sh. *s.* of all trib.
Dan. 3:17 G. wh. we *s.* to deliver
28 not *s.* any, exc. th. own G.
7:27 dominions *s.* obey him
Zep. 3:9 *s.* him with consent
Mal. 3:14 it is in vain to *s.* God
Mat. 4:10 him only *s.* *Luke* 4:8
Mat. 6:24 no man can *s.* 2 mas.
cannot *s.* G. and M. *Lu.* 16:13
Luke 1:74 we deliv. might *s.* him
10:40 sister left me to *s.* alone
12:37 will come forth *s.* them
15:29 these many years I *s.* thee
17:8 gird thyself and *s.* me
22:26 chief, as he that doth *s.*
John 12:26 if any man *s.* me
Acts 6:2 lea. word of G. *s.* tables
7:7 come, *s.* me in this place
27:23 angel of God whom I *s.*
Rom. 1:9 G. my witness, wh. I *s.*
6:6 that we should not *s.* sin.
7:6 should *s.* in newness of spi.
25 with mind I *s.* law of God
9:12 said, elder shall *s.* younger
16:18 th. that are such *s.* not L.
Gal. 5:13 by love *s.* one another
Col. 3:24 reward, ye *s.* Lord Ch.
1 *Thes.* 1:9 turned fr. id. to *s.* G.
2 *Tim.* 1:3 I thank G. whom I *s.*
Heb. 8:5 *s.* to exam. of heavenly
9:14 purge fr. dead wo. to *s.* G.
12:28 may *s.* God acceptably
13:10 right to eat wh. *s.* tabern.
Rev. 7:15 *s.* him in his temple
22:3 his servants shall *s.* him

SERVED, with gods.

Ex. 23:24 sh. not *s.* th. *g.* *Deut.*
6:14 ; 28:14 ; *Jos.* 23:7 ; 2 *K.*
17:35 ; *Jer.* 25:6 ; 35:15
33 if thou *s.* th. *g.* it be a snare
Deut. 4:28 there ye shall *s.* *g.* the
work, 28:36, 64 ; *Jer.* 16:13
7:4 they may *s.* other *g.* 31:20
13:2 after, and *s.* other *g.* 6, 13
29:18 turneth from G. *s.* other *g.*
Jos. 24:16 (J. forb. we *s.* other *g.*
Jud. 2:19 corrupted themsel. to
s. other *g.* *Jer.* 11:10 ; 13:10
1 *Sam.* 26:19 saying, *s.* other *g.*
Jer. 44:3 prov. me, to *s.* other *g.*
Dan. 3:12 they *s.* not *g.* nor ima.
14 do ye not *s.* my *g.* ? 18

See LORD.

SERVED.

Gen. 14:4 they *s.* Chedorlaomer.
29:20 Ja. *s.* 7 yrs. for Rachel, 30
30:29 know. how I have *s.* thee
31:41 *s.* 14 years for thy daught.
Deut. 17:3 hath gone, *s.* other
gods, 29:26 ; *Jos.* 23:16
Jos. 24:2 fath. *s.* other gods, 15
31 Israel *s.* the Lord all the days
of Joshua, *Jud.* 2:7
Jud. 2:11 *s.* Baa. 13 ; 3:7 ; 10:6
3:6 daught. to sons, *s.* th. gods
14 Is. *s.* Eglon, eighteen years
8:1 why hast thou *s.* us thus ?
10:13 forsaken me, *s.* other gods
16 they put away th. gods, and
s. the Lord, 1 *Sam.* 7:4
2 *Sam.* 10:19 the Syrians *s.* Israel
16:19 *s.* in thy fath.'s presence
1 *K.* 4:21 presents, and *s.* Solom.
9:9 *s.* other gods, 2 *Chr.* 7:22
2 *K.* 10:18 Jehu said, Ah. *s.* Baal
21:3 Manasseh *s.* the host of
heaven, 2 *Chr.* 33:3
21 Amon *s.* idols, 2 *Chr.* 33:22
2 *Chr.* 24:18 princes of Ju. *s.* id.
Neh. 9:35 they have not *s.* thee
Ps. 106:36 and they *s.* their idols
137:8 reward. as thou hast *s.* us
Ec. 5:9 king him. is *s.* by field
Jer. 5:19 ye have *s.* strange gods
16:11 walk. after gods, *s.* them

34:14 *s.* six years, let him go
Ezek. 29:18 service he hath *s.* 20
34:27 out of hand of those th. *s.*
Hos. 12:12 Israel *s.* for wife
Luke 2:37 Anna *s.* G. in temple
John 12:2 ma. supper, Martha *s.*
Acts 13:36 Da. had *s.* generation
Rom. 1:25 worship. *s.* creature
Phil. 2:22 *s.* with me in gospel

SERVEDST.
Deut. 28:47 thou *s.* not the Lord

SERVEST, ETH.
Num. 3:36 under Mer. all that *s.*
Dan. 6:16 God thou *s.* wilt deli.
20 is God th. *s.* able to deliver?
Mal. 3:17 spareth son that *s.* him
18 him that *s.* G. him th. *s.* not
Luke 22:27 sit. at meat, or he
that *s.* ? I am as one that *s.*
14:18 in these things *s.* Ch.
1 *Cor.* 14:22 prophesying *s.* not
for them that believe not
Gal. 3:19 wherefore then *s.* law?

SERVICE.
Gen. 29:27 *s.* that th. shalt serve
Ex. 1:14 all *s.* in field ; their *s.*
12:26 wh. mean you by this *s.* ?
36:5 more than enough for *s.*
Num. 3:7 tribe of Levi to do *s.* 8
4:19 Aaron appoint them to *s.*
24 the *s.* of Gershonites, 27, 28
30 *s.* of the sons of Merari, 33, 43
8:11 Levites may execute *s.* of L.
25 50 years cease waiting on *s.*
16:9 small th. to bring you to *s.*
18:4 Levites be joined for all *s.*
1 *K.* 12:4 make grievous *s.* lighter
1 *Chr.* 6:31 whom Da. set over *s.*
9:13 men for work of *s.* 26:8
28:13 Levites for work of the *s.*
21 priests sh. be wi. thee for *s.*
29:5 who consecrate his *s.* to L. ?
7 for *s.* of house of God silver
2 *Chr.* 8:14 courses of priests to *s.*
12:8 know my *s.* and *s.* of kingd.
31:2 ev. man according to his *s.*
35:2 encouraged them to *s.* of L.
10 so *s.* of L. was prepared, 16
Ezr. 6:18 in courses for *s.* 7:19
Ps. 104:14 herb to grow *s.* of man
Jer. 22:13 that useth neighb.'s *s.*
Ezek. 29:18 cau. army to serve *s.*
44:14 keepers of house for the *s.*
John 16:2 kill. think doeth G. *s.*
Rom. 9:4 wh. pertaineth *s.* of G.
12:1 which is your reasonable *s.*
15:31 *s.* be accepted of saints
2 *Cor.* 9:12 adminstra. of this *s.*
11:8 taking wages to do you *s.*
Gal. 4:8 did *s.* to th. are no gods
Eph. 6:7 good-will doing *s.* to L.
Phil. 2:17 offered upon *s.* of faith
30 to supply your lack of *s.*
1 *Tim.* 6:2 do *s.* because beloved
Heb. 9:1 ordinances of divine *s.*
6 priests accomplish *s.* of God
9 make him that did *s.* perfect
Rev. 2:19 know thy works and *s.*

Bond-SERVICE.
1 *K.* 9:21 Sol. levy tribute of *b.-s.*

Eye-SERVICE.
Eph. 6:6 not *e.-s.* as men-pleasers

SERVILE.
Lev. 23:7 ye shall do no *s.* work,
8, 21, 25, 35, 36 ; *Num.* 28:18,
25, 26 ; 29:1, 12, 35.

SERVING.
Deut. 15:18 hired serv. in *s.*
Luke 10:40 M. cumbered about *s.*
Acts 20:19 *s.* Lord with humility
26:7 twelve tribes *s.* G. day and
Rom. 12:11 fervent in spirit, *s.* L.
Tit. 3:3 sometimes fool. *s.* lusts

SERVITOR.
2 *K.* 4:43 *s.* said, set this bef. 100 ?

SERVITUDE.
2 *Chr.* 10:4 griev. *s.* of thy father
Lam. 1:3 Jud. gone because of *s.*

SET.
Gen. 4:15 L. *s.* mark upon Cain
9:13 I *s.* my bow in cloud
41:33 let Phar. *s.* him over Eg.
43:9 if I bring not and *s.* him
48:20 J. *s.* Eph. before Manass.
Ex. 7:23 nor *s.* his heart to this
19:12 *s.* bounds ; 26:35 *s.* table
21:1 judgments *s.* before them
40:4 *s.* in order things to be *s.*
Lev. 24:8 ev. sabbath *s.* it in ord.
Num. 2:9 camp of J. first *s.* forth
8:13 *s.* the Levites bef. Aaron
27:16 let L. *s.* a man over cong.
Deut. 1:8 ha. *s.* land bef. you, 21
4:8 law which I *s.* bef. you, 44
7:7 L. did not *s.* his love on you
11:26 I *s.* before you blessing
14:24 cho. to *s.* name, *Neh.* 1:9
17:14 I will *s.* a king over me
28:1 L. G. will *s.* thee on high
30:15 I *s.* bef. you, life, death, 19
32:46 *s.* hearts to words I testify
Jos. 24:25 he *s.* a statute in Sh.
Jud. 6:18 *s.* my present bef. thee
7:19 had but newly *s.* watch
1 *Sam.* 2:8 rais. poor, to *s.* them
am. princes, *s.* world on th.
10:19 said, Nay, *s.* king over us
12:13 L. hath *s.* a king over you
2 *Sam.* 19:28 *s.* thy serv. at table
1 *K.* 2:15 Is. *s.* their faces on me
5:5 I will *s.* on throne sh. build
21:9 *s.* Naboth high am. peo. 12
2 *K.* 4:4 *s.* aside that wh. is full
20:1 *s.* house in order, *Is.* 38:1
1 *Chr.* 16:1 *s.* ark in mid. of tent
22:19 *s.* your heart to seek Lord
2 *Chr.* 11:16 *s.* th. hea. to seek L.
20:3 *s.* himself to seek Lord.
24:13 *s.* house of G. in his state
Neh. 2:6 king, I *s.* him a time
9:37 incre. to kings *s.* over us
13:11 gather. *s.* them in place
Job 6:4 terrors of God *s.* ag. me
Job 7:17 should *s.* his heart upon him
20 why *s.* me a mark ag. thee?
9:19 who *s.* me a time to plead?
30:18 *s.* forward my calamity
33:5 *s.* thy words in order
Ps. 2:2 kings of earth *s.* themsel.
6 have I *s.* king on holy hill
3:6 not afraid if 10,000 *s.* them.
4:3 L. *s.* apart him that is godly
16:8 I *s.* Lord always bef. me
31:8 *s.* my feet in large room
40:2 *s.* my feet upon a rock
50:21 I *s.* them bef. thine eyes
54:3 have not *s.* God bef. them
62:10 riches, *s.* not yo. hearts on
73:18 didst *s.* th. in slip. places
78:7 might *s.* their hope in God
8 genera. *s.* not heart aright
85:13 *s.* us in way of his steps
86:14 viol. men have not *s.* thee
91:14 he hath *s.* his love upon
me, theref. I *s.* him on high
101:3 *s.* no wicked thi. bef. eyes
104:9 *s.* bound th. may not pass
109:6 *s.* wicked man over him
113:8 may *s.* him with princes
118:5 *s.* me in a large place
141:3 *s.* a watch bef. my mouth
Prov. 1:25 *s.* at naught counsel
23:5 *s.* th. eyes on that is not ?
Ec. 3:11 *s.* world in their heart
7:14 G. *s.* one against the other
12:9 *s.* in order many proverbs
Is. 7:6 *s.* a king in midst of it
14:1 L. *s.* th. in their own land
19:2 I will *s.* Egypti. ag. Egypt.
22:7 *s.* themsel. in array at gate
42:4 have *s.* judgm. in the earth
44:7 shall *s.* it in order for me ?

46:7 and *s.* him in his place
66:19 I will *s.* a sign am. them
Jer. 1:10 I *s.* thee over nations
6:27 I have *s.* thee for a tower
7:12 place where I *s.* my name
9:13 forsaken law I *s.* bef. them
21:8 I *s.* before you way of life
24:6 *s.* eyes on them for good
26:4 walk in law I *s.* bef. you
34:16 serv. he had *s.* at liberty
38:22 friends have *s.* thee on
44:10 statutes wh. I *s.* bef. thee
Lam. 3:6 *s.* me in dark places
Ezek. 5:5 *s.* in midst of nations
7:20 theref. I *s.* it far from them
12:6 I *s.* thee for a sign unto Is.
17:22 highest branch, I will *s.* it
19:8 th. nations *s.* against him
22:7 *s.* light by fath. and moth.
24:2 king of Babylon *s.* ag. Jer.
7 she *s.* it upon top of a rock, 8
25 whereon they *s.* minds
26:20 *s.* glory in land of living
28:2 thou *s.* heart as heart of G.
40:4 *s.* heart upon all I sh. thee
44:8 *s.* keep. of charge in sanct.
Dan. 6:3 *s.* him over the realm
14 *s.* heart on Dan. to del. him
9:10 walk in laws he *s.* bef. us
10:12 *s.* thy heart to understand
Hos. 2:3 *s.* her as day was born
4:8 *s.* their heart on their iniq.
11:8 how sh. I *s.* th. as Zeboi. ?
Amos 9:4 *s.* eyes on them for ev.
Hab. 2:9 may *s.* his nest on high
Zec. 5:11 be *s.* on her own base
8:10 *s.* every man ag. neighbor
Mat. 10:35 to *s.* man at variance
25:33 *s.* sheep on right hand
Luke 4:18 *s.* at liberty bruised
10:34 *s.* him on his own beast
11:6 have nothing to *s.* bef. thee
23:11 Herod *s.* him at naught
John 2:10 *s.* forth good wine
3:33 *s.* to his seal that G. is true
Acts 7:5 so much as to *s.* foot on
13:9 Paul *s.* his eyes on him
18:10 no man *s.* on thee to hurt
Rom. 14:10 *s.* at naught brother?
1 *Cor.* 4:9 God *s.* forth apostles
6:4 *s.* to judge least esteemed
12:28 G. hath *s.* some in church
Eph. 1:20 *s.* him at right hand
Heb. 2:7 *s.* over work of hands
Rev. 3:8 *s.* bef. thee an open door

SET up.
Gen. 28:18 Jacob took stone,
and *s.* it *up*, 22 ; 31:45 ; 35:14
Lev. 26:1 nor *s.* *up* ima. of stone
Num. 10:21 other did *s.* it *up*
1 *Sam.* 15:11 repenteth I *s.* *up* S.
2 *Sam.* 3:10 to *s.* *up* throne of D.
7:12 I will *s.* *up* seed after thee
1 *K.* 15:4 to *s.* *up* son after him
2 *K.* 17:10 they *s.* th. *up* images
2 *Chr.* 25:14 Am. *s.* th. *up* gods
Ezr. 2:68 to *s.* *up* God's house
4:12 J. have *s.* *up* walls, 13, 16
Ezr. 5:11 house king of Is. *s.* *up*
Neh. 6:1 I had not *s.* *up* doors
Job. 5:11 *s.* *up* those that be low
16:12 and *s.* me *up* for his mark
Ps. 27:5 and *s.* me *up* upon rock
69:29 let thy salvation *s.* me *up*
89:42 *s.* *up* right hand of adver.
Prov. 8:23 was *s.* *up* everlasting
Jer. 11:13 *s.* *up* altars to thing?
Ezek. 14:3 men *s.* *up* their idols
31:4 the deep *s.* him *up* on high
Dan. 2:44 God sh. *s.* *up* a kingd.
5:19 whom he would he *s.* *up*
Hos. 8:4 they have *s.* *up* kings
Mal. 3:15 work wickedness *s.* *up*
Acts 6:13 *s.* *up* false witnesses
15:16 build ruins, and *s.* it *up*

SET, passive.
Gen. 24:33 th. was *s.* meat before

Ex. 32:22 th. are *s.* on mischief
1 *Sam.* 18:30 his name was *s.* by
26:24 thy life was much *s.* by
1 *K.* 14:4 for his eyes were *s.*
2 *K.* 12:4 money every man *s.* at
1 *Chr.* 19:10 J. saw battle was *s.*
2 *Chr.* 6:10 I am *s.* on thr. of Is.
29:35 house of Lord *s.* in order
31:15 in their *s.* office to give
Job 36:16 what sh. be *s.* on table
Ps. 10:8 privily *s.* against poor
141:2 let my prayer be *s.* forth
Ec. 8:11 heart is *s.* to do evil
10:6 folly is *s.* in great dignity
Is. 2:24 instead of well *s.* hair
Jer. 6:23 in *s.* array, *Joel* 2:5
31:29 teeth *s.* on edge, *Ezek.* 18:2
Dan. 7:10 judgment was *s.*
Mat. 5:14 a city *s.* on a hill
27:19 he was *s.* on judgm.-seat
Mark 1:32 when sun *s.* brought
9:12 things, he *s.* at naught
Luke 2:34 this child is *s.* for fall
7:8 a man *s.* under authority
10:8 eat such as are *s.* bef. you
Acts 4:11 the stone *s.* at naught
19:27 craft in danger to be *s.* at
26:32 man might ha. been *s.* at
1 *Cor.* 10:27 whatever is *s.* before
you
Gal. 3:1 Ch. had been *s.* forth
Heb. 6:18 lay hold on hope *s.* bef.
8:1 is *s.* on right hand, 12:2
12:1 run the race *s.* before us
2 joy that was *s.* before him
13:23 brother Tim. *s.* at liberty
Jude 7 cities *s.* forth for examp.
Rev. 3:21 *s.* down with Father
4:2 a throne was *s.* in heaven

SET day.

Acts 12:21 on *s.* day He. arrayed
See FACE, FACES, FEASTS.

SET time.

Gen. 17:21 Sa. shall bear at *s. t.*
Ex. 9:5 Lord appointed a *s. t.*
Job 14:13 wouldest appoint a *s. t.*
Ps. 102:13 *s. t.* to favor is come

SETH.

Gen. 5:3 and called him S.
6 S. begat Enos, 1 *Chr.* 1:1 ;
Luke 3:38

SETTER.

Acts 17:18 a *s.* forth of stra. gods

SETTEST.

Deut. 23:20 *s.* hand to, 28:8, 20
Job 7:12 that *s.* a watch over me?
Ps. 41:12 thou *s.* me before face

SETTETH.

Deut. 24:15 *s.* his heart on it
27:16 cursed that *s.* light by fa.
2 *Sam.* 22:34 *s.* me on hi. places,
Ps. 18:33
Job 28:3 he *s.* an end to darkness
Ps. 36:4 he *s.* himself in a way
65:6 by strength *s.* fast mount.
75:7 put. down one, *s.* up ano.
107:41 *s.* poor on high
Jer. 5:26 as he that *s.* snares
43:3 Baruch *s.* thee on ag. us
Ezek. 14:4 th. *s.* idols in heart, 7
Dan. 2:21 remov. kings and *s.* up
4:17 *s.* up over it basest of men

SETTING, S.

Ex. 28:17 set in it *s.* of stones
Ezek. 43:8 in *s.* of their threshold
Mat. 27:66 seal. stone, *s.* a watch
Luke 4:40 when sun was *s.* they

SETTLE.

Ezek. 43:14 fr. ground to lower *s.*
17 *s.* shall be 14 cubits long
20 blood on corners of *s.* 45:19

SETTLE, ST.

1 *Chr.* 17:14 will *s.* him in house
Ps. 65:10 thou *s.* furrows thereof
Ezek. 36:11 I will *s.* you af. your

Luke 21:14 *s.* it in your hearts
1 *Pet.* 5:10 G. strengthen, *s.* you

SETTLED.

1 *K.* 8:13 built a *s.* place for thee
2 *K.* 8:11 he *s.* his countenance
Ps. 119:89 word is *s.* in heaven
Prov. 8:25 before mount. were *s.*
Jer. 48:11 he hath *s.* on lees
Zep. 1:12 are *s.* on their lees
Col. 1:23 faith, grounded and *s.*

SEVEN.

Gen. 46:25 Bil. all souls were *s.*
Ex. 2:16 priest of M. had *s.* dau.
Lev. 23:15 *s.* sab. shall be com.
25:8 number *s.* sabbaths of yrs.
Num. 23:1 build here *s.* altars.
prep. *s.* oxen and *s.* rams, 29
Deut. 7:1 *s.* nations greater
16:9 *s.* weeks thou sh. number
28:7 L. cause ene. flee *s.* ways
25 shalt flee *s.* ways bef. them
Jos. 6:4 *s.* priests bearing *s.*
trumpets, 6, 8, 13
18:2 remained of Is. *s.* tribes
1 *Sam.* 2:5 barren hath born *s.*
16:10 Jesse made *s.* of his sons
2 *Sam.* 21:9 they fell all *s.* toge.
Ezr. 7:14 king and his *s.* couns.
Est. 1:14 the *s.* princes wh. saw
Job 5:19 in *s.* troubles no evil
Prov. 9:1 wisd. hath hewn *s.* pil.
26:25 th. are *s.* abominations
Ec. 11:2 portion to *s.* also to 8
Is. 4:1 *s.* women take hold of 1
11:15 L. shall smite in *s.* strea.
Ezek. 39:12 *s.* months be burying
Dan. 9:25 Mes. sh. be *s.* weeks
Mic. 5:5 against him *s.* sheph.
Zec. 3:9 upon one stone *s.* eyes
Mark 12:22 and *s.* had her, 23 ;
Luke 20:31, 33
Rev. 1:4 John to *s.* churches in A.
10:3 when he cried, *s.* thunders
12:3 dragon, having *s.* heads
and *s.* crowns, 13:1 ; 17:3, 7
15:1 I saw *s.* angels having the
s. last plagues, 6
7 to *s.* angels *s.* golden vials
17:1 one of the *s.* angels which
had the *s.* vials, 21:9
9 *s.* heads are *s.* mountains
11 beast is of the *s.* and goeth
See DAYS, HUNDRED.

SEVEN bullocks, *or* rams.

Num. 23:29 prepare *s. bul. s. r.*
29:32 seventh day *s. b.* two *r.*
1 *Chr.* 15:26 Lev. offered *s. b. s. r.*
2 *Chr.* 29:21 they brou. *s. b. s. r.*
Job 42:8 take you now *s. b. s. r.*
Ezek. 45:23 a burnt-offer. *s. bul.*

SEVENFOLD.

Gen. 4:15 venge. sh. be taken *s.*
24 if Cain shall be avenged *s.*
Lamech seventy and *s.*
Ps. 79:12 render *s.* into bosom
Prov. 6:31 he shall restore *s.*
Is. 30:26 light of sun shall be *s.*
See LAMBS, LAMPS.

SEVEN men.

2 *Sam.* 21:6 let *s. men* of his sons
Prov. 26:16 that *s. m.* that can
Jer. 52:25 *s. m.* that were near
Acts 6:3 look out *s. m.* of honest
SEVEN rams. *See* SEVEN *bul.*
See SEALS.

SEVEN sons.

Ruth 4:15 dau. better than *s. s.*
Job 1:2 were born unto him *s. s.*
42:13 had *s. s.* and three daugh.
Acts 19:14 *s. s.* of Sceva a Jew

SEVEN spirits.

Mat. 12:45 then goeth he, and
taketh *s. s. Luke* 11:26
Rev. 1:4 *s. s.* bef. throne of God

3:1 he that hath the *s. s.* of God
4:5 lamps, wh. are *s. s.* of God
5:6 seven eyes, are *s. s.* of God

SEVEN stars.

Amos 5:8 him that maketh *s. s.*
Rev. 1:16 in ri. hand *s. s.* 2:1 ; 3:1
20 myst. of *s. s.* thou sawest ;
s. s. are angels of *s.* churches
SEVEN and *Thirty. See* THIRTY.
See THOUSAND.

SEVEN times.

Gen. 33:3 Ja. bowed bef. Es. *s. t.*
Lev. 4:6 priests shall sprinkle of
the blood *s. t.* 17 ; 8:11 ; 14:7 ;
16:14, 19 ; *Num.* 19:4
14:16 sprink. oil wi. fin. *s. t.* 27
51 sprinkle house *s. t.*
25:8 number *s. t.* seven years
Lev. 26:18 pu. *s. t.* more, 21, 24, 28
Ps. 119:164 *s. t.* a day do I praise
Prov. 24:16 a just man fall, *s. t.*
Dan. 4:16 *s. t.* pass, 23, 25, 32
Mat. 18:21 sh. I forgive ? till *s. t.*
Luke 17:4 if brother tresp. *s. t. a*
day, and *s. times* a day turn
SEVEN and *Twenty. See*
TWENTY.

SEVEN years.

Gen. 29:18 serve *s. y.* for Rachel
20 Jac. served *s. y.* for Rachel
27 shalt serve me other *s. y.* 30
41:26 seven good kine are *s. y.*
the seven good ears are *s. y.*
29 *s. y.* of plenty, 34, 47, 48
53 the *s. y.* of plenteousness

SEVENS.

Gen. 7:2 clean bea. sh. take by *s.*

SEVENTEEN.

Gen. 37:2 Jos. being *s.* years old
Jer. 32:9 Jer. weighed *s.* shekels

SEVENTEENTH.

Gen. 7:11 on *s.* day the fountains
8:4 ark rested on *s.* day in the

SEVENTH.

Ex. 21:2 in *s.* he sh. go out free
31:15 the *s.* is sabbath of rest
Lev. 23:16 morrow after *s.* sab.
See DAY.

SEVENTH month.

Gen. 8:4 ark rested in *s. m.* on
Lev. 16:29 in *s. mon.* afflict your
souls, 23:27 ; 25:9
Num. 29:1 in *s. m.* holy conv. 12
1 *K.* 8:2 Isr. assembled at *s. m.*
Hag. 2:1 in *s. m.* the word came
Zec. 8:19 the fast of the *s. month*

SEVENTH year.

Ex. 23:11 *s. y.* thou sh. let it rest
Lev. 25:4 in *s. y.* shall be rest
Deut. 15:12 *s. y.* shalt let him go
2 *K.* 11:4 in *s. y.* Jehoiada sent
rulers and capt. 2 *Chr.* 23:1
Est. 2:16 Esther taken in *s. year*
Jer. 52:28 carried captive in *s. y.*
Ezek. 20:1 in the *s. y.* eld came

SEVENTY.

Gen. 4:24 truly Lam. *s.* and sev.
Ex. 1:5 of loins of Jacob were *s.*
24:1 and *s.* elders of Israel, 9
Num. 11:16 ga. to me *s.* men, 24
25 gave of spirit unto *s.* elders
36:9 slaying his *s.* brethren
2 *K.* 10:1 Ahab had *s.* sons in, 6
Is. 23:15 Tyre shall be forgot. *s.*
17 after end of *s.* years, the L.
Jer. 25:11 serve Babylon *s.* years
Ezek. 8:11 stood bef. them *s.* m.
Dan. 9:24 *s.* weeks are determin.
Zec. 7:5 even th. *s.* years did ye
Mat. 18:22 times, but until *s.* t.
Luke 10:1 L. appointed other *s.*
17 the *s.* returned ag. with joy

SEVER, ED.

Ex. 8:22 I will *s.* in that day
9:4 L. shall *s.* bet. cattle of Isr.
Lev. 20:26 I *s.* you fr. other peo.
Deut. 4:41 Moses *s.* three cities
Jud. 4:11 Heber *s.* from Kenites
Ezek. 39:14 *s.* out men of employ
Mat. 13:49 *s.* wicked fr. the just

SEVERAL, LY.

Num. 28:13 and a *s.* tenth deal,
21, 29 ; 29:10, 15
2 *K.* 15:5 Azariah dwelt in *s.*
house, 2 *Chr.* 26:21
2 *Chr.* 31:19 sons of A. in *s.* city
Mat. 25:15 accord. to *s.* ability
1 *Cor.* 12:11 to every man *s.*
Rev. 21:21 ev. *s.* ga. was of pearl

SEVERITY

Rom. 11:22 behold goodn. and *s.*

SEW.

Ec. 3:7 time to rend, time to *s.*
Ezek. 13:18 woe to women, *s.* pil.

SEWED, EST, ETH.

Gen. 3:7 *s.* fig-leaves together
Job 14:17 thou *s.* up mine iniq.
16:15 I have *s.* sackcloth upon
Mark 2:21 no man *s.* new cloth

SHAALBIM. *Jud.* 1:35
SHAASHGAZ. *Est.* 2:14

SHADE.

Ps. 121:5 L. is thy *s.* upon right

SHADOW.

Gen. 19:8 under *s.* of my roof
Jud. 9:15 put yo. trust in my *s.*
36 thou seest the *s.* of mount.
2 *K.* 20:9 sh. the *s.* go forward ?
10 light thing for *s.* to go down
1 *Chr.* 29:15 days as a *s.* *Job* 8:9
Job 7:2 as a serv. desireth the *s.*
14:2 he fleeth also as a *s.*
17:7 all my members are as a *s.*
40:22 trees cover him with th. *s.*
Ps. 17:8 hide me un. *s.* of wings
36:7 under *s.* of wings, 57:1
63:7 in *s.* of wings will I rejoice
80:10 hills were covered with *s.*
91:1 abide under *s.* of Almighty
102:11 my days are like a *s.*
109:23 I am gone like a *s.*
144:4 days are as a *s.* *Ec.* 8:13
Ec. 6:12 life he spendeth as a *s.*
Cant. 2:3 I sat under *s.* with del.
Is. 4:6 tabernacle for a *s.* in day
16:3 make thy *s.* as the night
25:4 hast been a *s.* from heat
5 bring heat with *s.* of a cloud
30:2 and trust in *s.* of Egypt
3 and the trust in *s.* of Egypt
32:2 as *s.* of a great rock
38:8 I will bring again *s.* of deg.
49:2 in *s.* of hand hid me, 51:16
Jer. 48:45 under *s.* of Heshbon
Lam. 4:20 und. his *s.* we sh. live
Ezek. 17:23 in *s.* thereof sh. they
31:6 und. his *s.* dw. all nations
12 peo. are gone down from *s.*
Dan. 4:12 beasts had *s.* under it
Hos. 4:13 bec. *s.* thereof is good
14:7 dwell under his *s.* sh. retu.
Jon. 4:5 and sat under in *s.*
8 it might be a *s.* over his head
Mark. 4:32 fowls lodge under *s.*
Acts 5:15 th. *s.* of P. might over.
Col. 2:17 a *s.* of things to come
Heb. 8:5 serve unto *s.* of heaven
10:1 having a *s.* of good things
Jam. 1:17 with whom no *s.* of tu.

See DEATH.

SHADOWS.

Cant. 2:17 *s.* flee away, 4:6
Jer. 6:4 for *s.* of the evening are

SHADOWING.

Is. 18:1 to land *s.* with wings
Ezek. 31:3 a cedar with *s.* shroud

Heb. 9:5 cherubim of gl. *s.* mer.

SHADRACH. *Dan.* 1:7 ; 2:49 ;
3:23–30

SHADY.

Job 40:21 he lieth under *s.* trees
22 the *s.* trees cover him with

SHAFT.

Ex. 25:31 his *s.* and branches,
his bowls, 37:17 ; *Num.* 8:4
Is. 49:2 made me a polished *s.*

SHAKE.

Jud. 16:20 I will go and *s.* mys.
Neh. 5:13 and said, So God *s.*
Job 4:14 made my bones to *s.*
15:33 shall *s.* off unripe grape
16:4 and *s.* my head at you
Ps. 46:3 tho' the mountains *s.*
69:23 make loins continu. to *s.*
72:16 fruit shall *s.* like Lebanon
Is. 2:19 he ariseth to *s.* earth, 21
10:15 as if rod should *s.* itself
32 he shall *s.* hand ag. mount
11:15 the Lord shall *s.* his hand
13:2 exalt the voice, *s.* the hand
13 I will *s.* heavens, *Joel* 3:16 ;
Hag. 2:6, 21
24:18 foundations of earth do *s.*
33:9 Bashan and Carmel *s.* off
52:2 *s.* thyself from dust, O Jer.
Jer. 23:9 broken, all my bones *s.*
Ezek. 26:10 walls sh. *s.* at noise
15 shall not isles *s.* at sound ?
27:28 suburbs shall *s.* at sound
31:16 I made nations *s.*
38:20 men shall *s.* at my pres.
Dan. 4:14 *s.* off his leaves
Amos 9:1 that the posts may *s.*
Hag. 2:7 I will *s.* all nations
Zec. 2:9 I will *s.* my hand on th.
Mat. 10:14 *s.* off dust of your feet,
Mark 6:11 ; *Luke* 9:5
28:4 for fear the keepers did *s.*
Luke 6:48 beat house, co. not *s.*
Heb. 12:26 I *s.* not earth only

SHAKED.

Ps. 109:25 look. on me, *s.* heads

SHAKEN.

Lev. 26:36 sound of a *s.* leaf shall
1 *K.* 14:15 as a reed in *s.* in wat.
2 *K.* 19:21 daugh. of Jerus. hath
s. head at thee, *Is.* 37:22
Neh. 5:13 even thus be he *s.* out
Job 16:12 neck, *s.* me to pieces
38:13 wicked mi. be *s.* out of it
Ps. 18:7 founda. of hills were *s.*
Nah. 2:3 fir-trees shall be ter. *s.*
3:12 if *s.* they fall into mouth
Mat. 11:7 *s.* with wind, *Lu.* 7:24
24:29 powers of heaven shall be
s. *Mark* 13:25 ; *Luke* 21:26
Luke 6:38 good meas. pressed, *s.*
Acts 4:31 prayed, place was *s.*
16:26 founda. of prison were *s.*
2 *Thes.* 2:2 not soon *s.* in mind
Heb. 12:27 remov. things that are
s. cannot be *s.* may remain
Rev. 6:13 fig-tree wh. *s.* of wind

SHAKETH.

Job 9:6 *s.* earth out of her place
Ps. 29:8 voice of L. *s.* wilderness
60:2 heal breaches, for it is *s.*
Is. 10:15 magnify ag. that *s.* ?
19:16 hand of Lord be *s.* over it
33:15 *s.* his hand from holding

SHAKING.

Job 41:29 laugh. at *s.* of a spear
Ps. 44:14 the *s.* of head among
Is. 17:6 *s.* of olive-tree, 24:13
19:16 because of the *s.* of hand
30:32 in bat. of *s.* shall he fight
Ezek. 37:7 beh. a *s.* bones came
38:19 th. shall be great *s.* in Is.

SHALIM.

1 *Sam.* 9:4 passed thro' land of S.

SHALISHA.

1 *Sam.* 9:4 passed thro' land of S.

SHALLUM.

2 *K.* 15:10 S. son of Jabesh
14 Menahem slew S. son of
22:14 Huld. the prophetess, the
wife of S. 2 *Chr.* 34:22
1 *Chr.* 2:40 of Judah, S. 4:25
6:12 of Levi, S. 7:13 S. the son
9:17 S. porter, 19 ; 31 S. the K.
2 *Chr.* 28:12 Jehizkiah son of S.
Ezr. 2:42 the child. of S. 10:24 ;
Neh. 7:45 ; *Jer.* 35:4
7:2 S. the son of Zadok
10:42 S. and Amariah had taken
Neh. 3:12 next repaired S.
Jer. 22:11 saith L. touching S.
32:7 Hanameel the son of S.

SHALMAN. *Hos.* 10:14

SHALMANESER.

2 *K.* 17:3 S. came against, 18:9

SHAMBLES.

1 *Cor.* 10:25 whatso. is sold in *s.*

SHAME.

Ex. 32:25 naked unto th. *s.*
Jud. 18:7 none to put them to *s.*
1 *Sam.* 20:34 father had done *s.*
2 *Sam.* 13:13 sh. I cause *s.* to go?
2 *Chr.* 32:21 return. with *s.* of fa.
Job 8:22 hate thee be clo. with *s.*
Ps. 4:2 how long turn gl. to *s.* ?
35:4 put them to *s.* that seek my
26 let them be clothed with *s.*
40:14 let th. be put to *s.* 83:17
15 deso. for a reward of their *s.*
44:7 hast put them to *s.* 53:5
9 hast cast off and put us to *s.*
15 *s.* of face covered me, 69:7
69:19 known my reproach and *s.*
70:3 turned back reward of *s.*
71:24 let them be bro. unto *s.*
83:16 fill their faces with *s.* O L.
89:45 hast covered him with *s.*
109:29 adversaries clo. with *s.*
119:31 O Lord put me not to *s.*
132:18 enem. will I clothe wi. *s.*
Prov. 3:35 *s.* sh. be the promot.
9:7 reproveth scorner, getteth *s.*
10:5 is a son that causeth *s.*
11:2 pride cometh, then com. *s.*
12:16 a prudent man cover. *s.*
13:5 loathsome and cometh to *s.*
18 *s.* shall be to him that refu.
14:35 wrath ag. him that caus. *s.*
17:2 a son that causeth *s.*
18:13 answer. bef. heareth, is *s.*
19:26 mother, is a son causeth *s.*
25:8 neigh. hath put thee to *s.*
10 that heareth it put thee to *s.*
29:15 child left br. mother to *s.*
Is. 30:4 uncover. to *s.* of Egypt
22:18 chariots shall be the *s.* of
30:3 stren. of Phar. your *s.* 5
47:3 yea, thy strength sh. be *s.*
50:6 I hid my face from *s.* and
54:4 thou shalt not be put to *s.*
for thou sh. forget *s.* of youth
61:7 *s.* you shall have double
Jer. 3:24 *s.* devoured the labor of
25 we lie down in *s.* and. conf.
13:26 discover. that thy *s.* ap.
20:18 days be consumed with *s.*
23:40 a perpetual *s.* not forgot.
46:12 the nations heard of thy *s.*
48:39 Moab turned back with *s.*
51:51 *s.* hath covered our faces
Ezek. 7:18 *s.* shall be on all faces
16:52 bear th. own *s.* for sins, 54
16:63 never open mouth
because of *s.*
32:24 have they borne their *s.* 25
30 bear their *s.* with them
34:29 nor bear the *s.* of heathen
36:6 ye have borne *s.* of heathen
7 they shall bear their *s.* 44:13
15 hear in thee *s.* of heathen
39:26 they have borne their *s.*

Dan. 12:2 awake, some to *s.*
Hos. 4:7 change their gl. into *s.*
  18 her rulers with *s.* do love
  9:10 separated themsel. unto *s.*
  10:6 Ephraim shall receive *s.* Isa.
Ob. 10 for violence *s.* sh. cover
Mic. 1:11 pass away, having *s.*
  2:6 prop. they shall not take *s.*
  7:10 *s.* sh. cover her which said
Nah. 3:5 I will show king. thy *s.*
Hab. 2:10 thou hast consulted *s.*
  16 thou art filled with *s.*
Zep. 3:5 unjust knoweth no *s.*
  19 they have been put to *s.*
Luke 14:9 begin with *s.* to take
Acts 5:41 worthy to suffer *s.*
1 *Cor.* 6:5 speak to your *s.* 15:34
  11:6 if it be a *s.* for a woman
  14 man have long hair, is a *s.*
  14:35 *s.* for wo. to sp. in church
Eph. 5:12 a *s.* to speak of things
Phil. 3:19 whose glory is their *s.*
Heb. 6:6 put him to an open *s.*
  12:2 endured cross, despising *s.*
Jude 13 foaming out their own *s.*
Rev. 3:18 *s.* of thy nakedness
  16:15 naked, and they see his *s.*

SHAME, ED, ETH.

2 *Sam.* 19:5 thou hast *s.* the faces
Ps. 14:6 have *s.* counsel of poor
Prov. 28:7 compan. of riotous *s.*
1 *Cor.* 4:14 I write not to *s.* you
  11:22 church of God, *s.* them ?

SHAMEFACEDNESS.

1 *Tim.* 2:9 women adorn with *s.*

SHAMEFUL, LY.

Jer. 11:13 set up altars to *s.* thi.
Hos. 2:5 conceived them, done *s.*
Hab. 2:16 *s.* spue. be on thy glo.
Mark 12:4 they sent him away *s.*
  handled, *Luke* 20:11
1 *Thes.* 2:2 and were *s.* entreated

SHAMELESSLY.

2 *Sam.* 6:20 fellows *s.* uncover.

SHAMGAR.

Jud. 3:31 after him was S. the
  5:6 in the days of S. highways

SHAMMAH.

Gen. 36:13 Re. S. 17 ; 1 *Chr.* 1:37
1 *Sam.* 16:9 S. the son of Jesse,
  13:13 ; 1 *Chr.* 2:13
2 *Sam.* 23:11 after him was S. 33
  25 S. the Harodite, 1 *Chr.* 7:37

SHAMMUAH.

Num. 13:4 to spy land, S. son
2 *Sam.* 5:14 S. s. of D. 1 *Chr.* 14:4
Neh. 11:17 Abda, son of S. dwelt

SHAPE, S.

Luke 3:22 descended in bodily *s.*
John 5:37 voice, nor seen his *s.*
Rev. 9:7 *s.* of locusts like horses

SHAPEN.

Ps. 51:5 behold, I was *s.* in iniq.

SHAPHAN.

2 *K.* 22:3 king Josiah sent S. the
  scribe, 2 *Chr.* 34:8
  8 gave book to S. 2 *Chr.* 34:15
  12 king commanded Ahikam
  son of S. and S. the scribe
  25:22 son of S. *Jer.* 39:14 ; 40:11
Jer. 26:24 the hand of son of S.
  29:3 sent by Elasah son of S.
  36:10 of Gemariah son of S.
Ezek. 8:11 Jaazaniah son of S.

SHAPHAT.

Num. 13:5 Sim. S. to spy land
1 *K.* 19:16 ano. Elisha, son of S.
2 *K.* 6:31 head of Elis. son of S.
1 *Chr.* 3:22 Shemaiah, Neari. S.
  5:12 of Gadites, S. in Bashan
  27:29 valleys was S. son of Ad.

SHARE.

1 *Sam.* 13:20 sharpen every man
  his *s.*

SHAREZER.

2 *K.* 19:37 S. his son, *Is.* 37:38

SHARON.

1 *Chr.* 5:16 in all suburbs of S.
  27:29 over herds that fed in S.
Cant. 2:1 the rose of S. the lily
Is. 33:9 S. is like a wilderness
  35:2 Carmel and S. given thee
  65:10 S. shall be a fold of flocks

SHARP.

Ex. 4:25 Zippor. took a *s.* stone
Jos. 5:2 make thee *s.* knives
1 *Sam.* 14:4 bet. passa. a *s.* rock
Job 41:30 *s.* stones are under him,
  he spread. *s.* pointed things
Ps. 45:5 arrow *s.* in the heart
  57:4 their tongue *s.* sword
Prov. 5:4 *s.* as two-edged sword
  25:18 man bears false witn. is *s.*
Is. 5:28 whose arrows are *s.*
  49:2 made my mouth like *s.* sw.
Acts 15:39 contention was so *s.*
Rev. 1:16 out of his mouth went
  a *s.* two-edged sword, 19:15
  14:14 in his hand a *s.* sickle, 17
  18 ang. cried to him had *s.* sic.

SHARPEN, ED, ETH.

1 *Sam.* 13:20 *s.* ev. man his share
  21 a file for axes, to *s.* goads
Ps. 140:3 they *s.* their tongues
Prov. 27:17 iron *s.* iron, man *s.*
Job 16:9 mine enemy *s.* his eyes
Ezek. 21:9 a sword is *s.* 10, 11

SHARPER.

Mic. 7:4 upr. *s.* than thorn-hedge
Heb. 4:12 word of G. *s.* than sw.

SHARPLY.

Jud. 8:1 did chide with Gid. *s.*
Tit. 1:13 rebuke them *s.* that

SHARPNESS.

2 *Cor.* 13:10 present I sho. use *s.*

SHAVE.

Lev. 13:33 scall shall he not *s.*
  14:8 unclean person sh. *s.* hair
  21:5 nor *s.* corner of th. beard
Num. 6:9 he shall *s.* his head
  18 Nazarite shall *s.* head of his
  8:7 let them *s.* flesh, wash clo.
Deut. 21:12 captive, *s.* her head
Jud. 16:19 caus. him to *s.* locks
Is. 7:20 L. shall *s.* with a razor
Ezek. 44:20 neither *s.* their heads
Acts 21:24 that they *s.* th. heads

SHAVED.

Gen. 41:14 Jos. *s.* changed raim.
2 *Sam.* 10:4 and *s.* off half their
  beards, 1 *Chr.* 19:4
Job 1:20 J. rent mantle, *s.* head

SHAVEH. *Gen.* 14:5

·SHAVEN.

Jud. 16:17 if I *s.* strength will
  22 hair began to grow after *s.*
Jer. 41:5 fourscore men, bear. *s.*
1 *Cor.* 11:5 as if she were *s.*
  6 if it be a shame to be *s.*

SHEAF.

Gen. 37:7 my *s.* arose, and stood
Lev. 23:11 wave *s.* bef. Lord, 12
Deut. 24:19 forgot *s.* not fetch it
Job 24:10 take away *s.* fr. hungry
Zec. 12:6 govern. like torch in *s.*

SHEAR, ING.

Gen. 31:19 La. went to *s.* sheep
  38:13 Ju. goeth to *s.* his sheep
Deut. 15:19 nor *s.* firstl. of sheep
1 *Sam.* 25:2 Nabal *s.* sheep in C.
  4 Da. heard Nabal did *s.* sheep

SHEARER, S.

Gen. 38:12 Ju. went to sheep-*s.*
1 *Sam.* 25:7 heard thou hast *s.*
  11 flesh I killed for my *s.*
2 *Sam.* 13:23 Ab. had *s.* in B. 24
Is. 53:7 sheep before *s.* is dumb
Acts 8:32 lamb dumb before *s.*

SHEARING-HOUSE.

2 *K.* 10:12 brethren of Ahaziah
  at *s.-h.* 14

SHEAR-JASHUB.

Is. 7:3 to meet Ah. thou and S.

SHEATH.

1 *Sam.* 17:51 Da. d. sword out *s.*
2 *Sam.* 20:8 sword fastened in *s.*
1 *Chr.* 21:27 angel put sw. in *s.*
Ezek. 21:3 draw sw. out of *s.* 4, 5
  30 cause it to return into *s.* ?
John 18:11 put up thy sw. into *s.*

SHEAVES.

Gen. 37:7 binding *s.* in the field
Ruth 2:7 let me glean am. *s.* 15
Neh. 13:15 on sab. bringing in *s.*
Ps. 126:6 bringing *s.* with him.
  129:7 that bindeth *s.* his bosom
Amos 2:13 as cart full of *s.*
Mic. 4:12 L. shall gather th. as *s.*

SHEBA, SHEBAH.

Gen. 10:7 son of Raamah S. 28
  25:3 Joksh. begat S. 1 *Chr.* 1:32
  26:33 Isaac called the well S.
Jos. 19:2 had S. in their inherit.
1 *K.* 10:1 when queen of S. heard
  of Solomon. 2 *Chr.* 9:1
1 *Chr.* 1:9 son of Raamah S. 22
1 *Chr.* 5:13 of the chil. of Gad, S.
Job 6:19 the companies of S.
Ps. 72:10 kings of S. and Seba
  15 given of gold of S. *Is.* 60:6
Jer. 6:20 purp. is incense fr. S. ?
Ezek. 27:22 merchants of S. 23
  38:13 S. sh. say, Art thou come

SHEBNA.

2 *K.* 18:18 came to Rabshakeh S.
  the scribe, 37 ; *Is.* 36:3
  19:2 sent S. to Isaiah, *Is.* 37:2
Is. 22:15 go to this treasurer, S.

SHECHEM.

Gen. 33:18 Ja. came to a ci. of S.
  19 hand of Hamor S. father
  34:2 S. lay with Di. 26 slew S.
  35:4 under an oak by S.
  37:12 feed father's flock in S.
  14 Jos. came from Hebr. to S.
Num. 26:31 of S. family of the
Jos. 17:2 lot for children of S.
  20:7 S. in mount Ephraim, a
  city, 21:21 ; 1 *Chr.* 6:67
  24:1 all the tribes of Israel to S.
  32 of Joseph buried they in S.
Jud. 8:31 Gid.'s concubine in S.
  9:1 son of Jerubbaal went to S.
  7 hearken to me, ye men of S.
  20 fire come out fr. men of S.
  28 who is S. 31 come to S.
  41 should not dwell in S.
  57 evil of men of S. did G. ren.
1 *K.* 12:1 went to S. 2 *Chr.* 10:1
  25 Jeroboam built S. in mount
1 *Chr.* 7:19 Shemida, Ahian, S.
Ps. 60:6 I will divide S. 108:7
Jer. 41:5 th. came certain fr. S.

SHED.

2 *Sam.* 20:10 Jo. *s.* Am.'s bowels
Mat. 26:28 is *s.* for remis. of sins
Acts 2:33 he hath *s.* forth this
Rom. 5:5 love of G. *s.* in hearts
Tit. 3:6 wh. he *s.* on us thro' J. C.

See BLOOD.

SHEDDER.

Ezek. 18:10 beget son *s.* of blood

SHEDDETH, ING.

Gen. 9:6 whoso *s.* man *s.* blood
Ezek. 22:3 city *s.* blood in midst
Heb. 9:22 without *s.* of blood

SHE-GOATS. *See* GOATS.

SHEEP.

Gen. 4:2 Abel was a keeper of *s.*
  29:6 Rachel cometh with *s.* 5
Ex. 9:3 hand of Lord is upon *s.*
  20:24 sh. sacrifice thereon thy *s.*

SHEEP

22:10 give to neighbor *s.* keep
Lev. 1:10 if his offering be of *s.*
22:19 ye sh. offer a male of *s.* 21
27:26 sanctify firstling of a *s.*
Num. 18:17 firstl. of *s.* not rede.
Deut. 7:13 bless flocks of thy *s.*
18:3 due fr. them that offer *s.* 4
22:1 not see broth.'s *s.* go astray
28:4 blessed be flocks of thy *s.*
Jos. 6:21 destroyed at Jericho *s.*
Jud. 6:4 Midianites left nei. *s.*
1 *Sam.* 8:17 king take tenth of
14:34 bring every man ox and *s.*
15:3 slay *s.* 9 Saul spread *s.*
14 what meaneth bleating of *s.*
16:11 behold, youngest keep. *s.*
17:15 David returned to feed *s.*
20 rose early, left *s.* wi. keeper
27:9 Da. took away *s.* the oxen
2 *Sam.* 7:8 took from follow. *s.*
24:17 but these *s.* what have
they done? 1 *Chr.* 21:17
1 *K.* 4:23 Sol.'s provision 100 *s.*
8:63 Solo. off. *s.* 2 *Chr.* 5:6 ; 7:5
2 *K.* 5:26 is it time to receive *s.?*
1 *Chr.* 5:21 took fr. H. 250,000 *s.*
2 *Chr.* 14:15 Asa carried fr. E. *s.*
15:11 offered of spoil 7,000 *s.*
18:2 A. killed *s.* for Jehoshaph.
30:24 Hezekiah did give 7,000 *s.*
31:6 brou. tithes of oxen and *s.*
Neh. 5:18 Nehem. one ox, six *s.*
Job 1:16 fire fallen, burnt up *s.*
31:20 not warm. wi. fleece of *s.*
42:12 had 14,000 *s.* 6,000 camels
Ps. 8:7 hast given him all *s.*
44:11 given us like *s.* for meat
49:14 like *s.* are laid in grave
74:1 why anger smo. ag. thy *s.?*
78:52 made peo. go forth like *s.*
95:7 we are *s.* of his hand, 100:3
119:176 astray like a lost *s.*
144:13 *s.* bring forth thousands
Is. 7:21 man sh. nourish two *s.*
22:13 joy and glad. killing of *s.*
53:6 we like *s.* are gone astray
Jer. 12:3 pull like *s.* for slaughter
50:6 my peo. hath been lost *s.*
17 Israel is as scattered *s.* lions

Ezek. 34:11 I will search my *s.* 12
Hos. 12:12 for a wife he kept *s.*
Joel 1:18 flock of *s.* made desol.
Mic. 5:8 a young lion among *s.*
Zec. 13:7 smite shepherd, and *s.*
scat. *Mat.* 26:31; *Mark* 14:27
Mat. 7:15 false proph. in *s.* cloth.
10:6 go to lost *s.* of house of Is.
12:12 how much man bet. th. *s.?*
15:24 sent but to lost *s.* of Israel
18:12 man ha. 100 *s.* one be gone
13 he rejoiceth more of that *s.*
Luke 15:4.
25:33 shall set *s.* on right hand
John 2:14 in tem. th. that sold *s.*
15 drove out of temple, and *s.*
10:2 entereth door sheph. of *s.*
3 *s.* hear voice, 27; 4 *s.* follow
7 said Jes. I am door of the *s.*
11 shepherd giv. life for his *s.*
12 a hireling leaveth the *s.* 13
14 I know *s.* 16 other *s.* I have
15 I lay down my life for the *s.*
26 ye are not of my *s.* as I said
21:16 saith to Peter, Feed my
s. 17
Heb. 13:20 L. Jes Shepherd of *s.*
Rev. 18:13 nine burth *s.* horses

As SHEEP.

Num. 27:17 *as s.* wh. ha. no shep.
1 *K.* 22:17 Israel *as s.* that have
no shepherd, 2 *Chr.* 18:16
Ps. 44:22 we are counted *as s.* for
the slaughter, *Rom.* 8:36
Is. 13:14 *as s.* that no man taketh
53:7 *as a s.* bef. shearers dumb
Mic. 2:12 put together *as s.* of B.

Mat. 9:36 scattered *as s.* having
no shepherd, *Mark* 6:34
10:16 send *as s.* midst of wolves
Acts 8:32 led *as s.* to slaughter
1 *Pet.* 2:25 *as s.* going astray

SHEEPCOTE, S.

1 *Sam.* 24:3 Saul came to *s.*
2 *Sam.* 7:8 took fr. *s.* 1 *Chr.* 17:7

SHEEPFOLD, S.

Num. 32:16 we will build *s.*
Jud. 5:16 why abodest amo. *s.?*
Ps. 78:70 Dav. took him from *s.*
John 10:1 entereth not *s.* by

SHEEP-GATE.

Neh. 3:1 Eliashib built the *s.-g.*
32 going up of corner to *s.-g.*
12:39 they went on to the *s.-g.*

SHEEP-MARKET.

John 5:2 at Jerusalem by *s.-m.*

SHEEP-MASTER.

2 *K.* 3:4 Mesha was a *s.-m.*

See SHEARERS.

SHEEPSKINS.

Heb. 11:37 they wandered in *s.*

SHEET.

Acts 10:11 descending as *s.* 11:5

SHEETS.

Jud. 14:12 I will give you 30 *s.*

SHEKEL.

Ex. 30:13 *s.* after the *s.* of the
sanctu. a *s.* 18 twenty gerahs.
Num. 3:47; *Ezek.* 45:12
15 not give less than half *s.*
1 *Sam.* 9:8 hath fourth part of *s.*
2 *K.* 7:1 mea. of flour for *s.* 16, 18
Neh. 10:32 charged wi. third of *s.*
Amos 8:5 ephah small, *s.* great

SHEKELS.

Gen. 23:15 land worth 400 *s.* 16
Ex. 21:32 give her master 30 *s.*
Lev. 5:15 estima. by *s.* 27:3-16
Deut. 22:29 damsel's father 50 *s.*
Jos. 7:21 spoils, 200 *s.* silver
Jud. 8:26 weight of rings 1,700 *s.*
17:2 1,100 *s.* I took ; 3 resto. *s.*
10 give thee ten *s.* silver
2 *Sam.* 14:26 Ab. wei. hair 200 *s.*
2 *K.* 15:20 exacted of each fifty *s.*
1 *Chr.* 21:25 David gave Ornan
600 *s.*
Neh. 5:15 gover. had taken 40 *s.*
Jer. 32:9 bou. field for 17 *s.* silver
Ezek. 4:10 be by weight 20 *s.*

See SANCTUARY.

SHELAH.

Gen. 38:5 Ju.'s son S. 11 till S.
26 I gave her not to S. my son
46:12 J. Er, Onan, and S. *Num.*
26:20; 1 *Chr.* 2:3; 4:21
1 *Chr.* 1:18 begat S. and S. E. 24

SHELEMIAH.

1 *Chr.* 26:14 lot eastw. fell to S.
Ezr. 10:39 S. and Nathan had
Neh. 13:13 I made S. treasurer
Jer. 36:14 S. son of Cushi, 26

SHELTER.

Job 24:8 emb. rock for want of *s.*
Ps. 61:3 hast been *s.* for me

SHELUMIEL.

Num. 1:6 S. son of Zurishaddai,
2:12; 7:36; 10:19

SHEM.

Gen. 5:32 Noah begat S. 6:10;
10:1; 1 *Chr.* 1:4
9:23 S. took a garm. and went
26 blessed be Lord God of S.
27 shall dwell in tents of S.
10:21 the children of S. 22, 31;
11:10; 1 *Chr.* 1:17
Luke 3:36 wh. was the son of S.

SHEMAIAH.

1 *K.* 12:22 word of the Lord came
to S. 2 *Chr.* 11:2; 12:7
1 *Chr.* 4:37 Shimri the son of S.
5:4 Reuben, S. the son of Joel
9:14 of the Levit. S. 16; 15:8, 11;
24:6; 26:4, 6, 7; 2 *Chr.* 17:8;
29:14; 31:15; 35:9; *Ezr.* 8:16;
10:21, 31
Ezr. 8:13 S. son of Adonikam
Neh. 3:29 S. keeper of the east
6:10 I came to the house of S.
10:8 S. a priest, 12:34, 42
11:15 of Lev. S. 12:6, 18, 35, 36
Jer. 26:20 Urijah the son of S.
29:24 S. the Nehelamite, 31, 32
36:12 Delaiah son of S. prince

SHEMINITH.

1 *Chr.* 15:21 with harps on the S.

SHENIR.

Deut. 3:9 the Amorites call S.
Cant. 4:8 look from the top of S.

SHEPHATIAH.

2 *Sam.* 3:4 S. son of D. 1 *Chr.* 3:3
1 *Chr.* 9:8 Meshullam son of S.
12:5 S. the Haruphite came to
27:16 ruler of Simeonit. was S.
Ezr. 2:4 child. of S. 372, *Neh.* 7:9
Jer. 38:1 S. heard the words of

SHEPHERD.

Gen. 46:34 *s.* is abomina. to Eg.
49:24 thence is *s.* stone of Israel
1 *Sam.* 17:40 stones into *s.* bag
Ps. 23:1 the Lord is my *s.*
80:1 give ear, O *s.* of Israel
Ec. 12:11 words given fr. one *s.*
Is. 38:12 age departed as *s.* tent
40:11 feed his flock like a *s.*
44:28 L. saith of Cy. he is my *s.*
63:11 bro. up with *s.* of his flock
Jer. 31:10 keep him as *s.* flock
43:12 array himself as a *s.*
49:19 who is *s.* will stand, 50:44
51:23 I will break *s.* his flock
Ezek. 34:5 scatter. because no *s.*
8 beca. prey bec. th. was no *s.*
12 *s.* seek. out flock am. sheep
23 I will set up one *s.* over th.
Da. feed them, be *s.* 37:24
Amos 3:12 as *s.* takes out mouth
Zec. 10:2 troubled, because no *s.*
11:15 instruments of a foolish *s.*
16 I will raise up a *s.* in land
17 woe to idle *s.* that leav. flo.
13:7 awake, O sword, ag. my *s.*
John 10:12 is hireling, not *s.*
14 a good *s.* know my sheep
16 shall be one fold, and one *s.*
Heb. 13:20 L. J. great *s.* of sheep
1 *Pet.* 2:25 now returned unto *s.*
5:4 when chief *s.* shall appear

See SHEEP.

SHEPHERDS.

Gen. 46:32 the men are *s.*
47:3 serv. are *s.* also our **fathers**
Ex. 2:17 *s.* came, dro. th. away
19 Eg. deliv. out of hand of *s.*
1 *Sam.* 25:7 now thy *s.* with us
Cant. 1:8 feed kids besi. *s.* tents
Is. 13:20 nor *s.* make folds there
31:4 multi. of *s.* called aga. him
56:11 *s.* that cannot understand
Jer. 6:3 *s.* shall come unto her
23:4 I will set up *s.* over them
25:34 howl, ye *s.* 35 *s.* no way
36 a voice of *s.* and a howling
33:12 cities be a habitation of *s.*
50:6 *s.* caused them to go astray
Ezek. 34:2 prophesy against *s.* of
Is. should not *s.* feed flocks?
8 nor did *s.* search for flock,
but the *s.* fed themselves
10 I am against *s.* neither shall
s. feed themselves any more
Amos 1:2 habitations of *s.* mourn
Mic. 5:5 raise agai. him seven *s.*

Nah. 3:18 thy *s.* slumber, O king
Zep. 2:6 coasts be cottages for *s.*
Zec. 10:3 anger kindled again. *s.*
11:3 a voice of the howling of *s.*
Zec. 11:5 th. own *s.* pity th. not
8 3 *s.* I cut off in one month
Luke 2:8 in same country *s.*
20 *s.* returned, glorifying God

SHERD, S.

Is. 30:14 th. sh. not be found a *s.*
Ezek. 23:34 thou sh. break the *s.*

SHERIFFS.

Dan. 3:2 Nebuchadnezzar sent
to gather the *s.* together, 3

SHESHACH.

Jer. 25:26 the king of S. shall
51:41 how is S. taken ! how is

SHESHBAZZAR.

Ezr. 1:8 numbered them to S.
11 all these did S. bring up
5:14 delivered to S. wh. he had
16 S. laid foundation of the

SHEW, *see* SHOW.

SHIBBOLETH.

Jud. 12:6 say now S. he said

SHIELD.

Gen. 15:1 thy *s.* and reward
Deut. 33:29 Lord, the *s.* of help
Jud. 5:8 *s.* or spear amo. 40,000
1 *Sam.* 17:7 one bearing a *s.* 41
2 *Sam.* 1:21 the *s.* of mighty., of
Saul as though not anoint.
22:3 he is my *s. Ps.* 3:3 ; 28:7 ;
119:114 ; 144:2
36 given me the *s.* of salvation, *Ps.* 18:35
1 *K.* 10:17 3 poun. of gold to 1 *s.*
2 *K.* 19:32 not come wi. *s. Is.* 37:33
1 *Chr.* 12:8 Gadites cou. handle *s.*
24 Jud. that bare *s.* and spear
34 Naph. wi. *s.* and spe. 37,000
2 *Chr.* 25:5 that could handle *s.*
Job 39:23 spear and *s.* rattleth
Ps. 5:12 compass him as with *s.*
33:20 Lord is our *s.* 59:11 ; 84:9
35:2 take hold of *s.* and buckler
76:3 brake arrows of bow. the *s.*
84:11 Lord God is sun and *s.*
91:4 his truth shall be thy *s.*
115:9 he is th. help and *s.* 10, 11
Prov. 30:5 *s.* to them that trust
Is. 21:5 arise, princes, anoint *s.*
22:6 Kir uncovered the *s.*
Jer. 46:3 order buckler and *s.*
9 come forth, that handle *s.*
Ezek. 23:24 ag. th. buckler and *s.*
27:10 hanged *s.* and helmet, 11
Nah. 2:3 *s.* of mighty made red
Eph. 6:16 taking *s.* of faith

SHIELDS.

2 *Sam.* 8:7 David took *s.* of gold,
1 *Chr.* 18:7
1 *K.* 10:17 Solomon made 300 *s.*
of beaten gold, 2 *Chr.* 9:16
14:26 Shishak took away all *s.*
of gold S. made, 2 *Chr.* 12:9
27 Rehoboam made in their
stead brazen *s.* 2 *Chr.* 12:10
2 *K.* 11:10 gave Da. *s.* 2 *Chr.* 23:9
2 *Chr.* 11:12 in city put *s.* and sp.
14:8 of Benja. that bare *s.* 17:17
26:14 Uzziah pre. *s.* and spears
32:5 Hez. made darts and *s.* 27.
Neh. 4:16 half held spears and *s.*
Ps. 47:9 *s.* of earth belong to G.
Jer. 51:11 bright arrows, gath. *s.*
Ezek. 38:4 with bucklers and *s.* 5
39:9 shall burn *s.* and weapons

SHIGGAION. *See* Psalm VII.

SHIGIONOTH.

Hab. 3:1 prayer of prophet on S

SHILOH.

Gen. 49:10 nor scep. dep. till S.

SHILOH.

Jos. 18:1 assemb. together at S.

---

8 cast lots for you in S. 10
22:9 departed from Isr. out of S.
Jud. 18:31 house of G. was in S.
21:12 brou. young virgins to S.
19 is a feast of the Lord in S.
21 if the daughters of S. dance
1 *Sam.* 1:3 up to worship in S.
24 Samuel to house of L. in S.
2:14 so did priests in S. to all
3:21 Lord appeared again in S.
4:3 the ark of the Lord out of S.
12 a man came to S. with his
14:3 Ahitub, Lord's priest in S.
1 *K.* 2:27 aga. house of Eli in S.
14:2 got thee to S. to Ahijah
4 Jeroboam's wife went to S.
Ps. 78:60 forsook taberna. of S.
Jer. 7:12 place which was in S.
14 th. house as I ha. done to S.
26:6 I make this house like S.
41:5 there came certain from S.

SHILOAH.

Is. 8:6 refuseth the waters of S.

SHIMEAH.

2 *Sam.* 13:3 Jonadab son of S.
32 ; 21:21 ; 1 *Chr.* 20:7
1 *Chr.* 3:5 S. was born to David
6:39 Berachiah, the son of S.

SHIMEI.

2 *Sam.* 16:5 S. son of Gera, 19:16
13 S. went along on hill's side
1 *K.* 2:8 thou hast with thee S.
39 two of the servants of S.
4:18 S. the son of Elah
1 *Chr.* 3:19 S. son of Pedaiah, 5:4
4:26 Mish. Hamuel, Zaccur, S.
27 S. had sixteen sons and six
6:17 S. son of Ge. 42 ; 23:7, 29
23:9 *s.* of S. 10 ; 25:17 tenth to S.
27:27 over vineyards was S.
2 *Chr.* 29:14 Heman, Jeh. and S.
31:12 over dedicated thi. S. 13
Ezr. 10:23 S. taken strange wife
Est. 2:5 son of Jair, son of S.
Zec. 12:13 family of S. shall

SHIMSHAI.

Ezr. 4:8 S. the scribe wrote. 9
17 king sent an answer to S.

SHINAR.

Gen. 10:10 Calneh in land of S.
11:2 found a plain in land of S.
14:1 Amraphel king of S.
Is. 11:11 recover remna. from S.
Dan. 1:2 carried into land of S.
Zec. 5:11 a house in land of S.

SHINE.

Num. 6:25 L. make his face *s.*
Job 3:4 neither let light *s.* on it
10:3 thou should. *s.* on counsel
11:17 thou shalt *s.* forth
18:5 spark of his fire sh. not *s.*
22:28 light sh. *s.* upon thy ways
36:32 commandeth it not to *s.*
37:15 caused light of cloud to *s.*
41:32 mak. path to *s.* after him
Ps. 31:16 make thy face *s.*
67:1 cause face to *s.* 80:3, 7, 19
80:1 dwellest betw. cherubim *s.*
104:15 oil to make his face to *s.*
119:135 make face *s.* upon serv.
Ec. 8:1 man's wisd. mak. face *s.*
Is. 13:10 not cause light to *s.*
60:1 arise, *s.* thy light is come
Jer. 5:28 are waxen fat, they *s.*
Dan. 9:17 cause thy face to *s.*
12:3 that be wise, sh. *s.* as stars
Mat. 5:16 let your light *s.*
13:43 righteous *s.* forth as sun
17:2 his face did *s.* as sun
2 G. commanded light to *s.*
Phil. 2:15 among whom ye *s.* as
Rev. 18:23 candle sh. *s.* no more
21:23 no need of sun or moon *s.*

SHINED.

Deut. 33:2 the L. *s.* forth fr. Par.
Job 29:3 candle *s.* upon my head
Ps. 50:2 perfect. of beauty G. *s.*
Is. 9:2 upon them hath light *s.*
Ezek. 43:2 the earth *s.* with glory
Acts 9:3 suddenly there *s.* about
12:7 and a light *s.* in the prison
2 *Cor.* 4:6 G. hath *s.* in our hearts

SHINETH.

Job 25:5 to the moon, it *s.* not
Ps. 139:12 night *s.* as the day
Prov. 4:18 shining light that *s.*
Mat. 24:27 lightning *s.* to west
John 1:5 the light *s.* in darkness
2 *Pet.* 1:19 light that *s.* in a dark
1 *John* 2:8 the true light now *s.*
Rev. 1:16 countenance as sun *s.*

SHINING.

2 *Sam.* 23:4 grass springing by *s.*
Prov. 4:18 the just is as *s.* light
Joel 2:10 stars sh. withd. *s.* 3:15
Mark 9:3 his raiment became *s.*
Luke 11:36 *s.* of a candle giveth
John 5:35 burning and *s.* light
Acts 26:13 above bright. of sun *s.*

SHIP.

Prov. 30:19 way of *s.* in the sea
Is. 33:21 no gallant *s.* shall pass
Jon. 1:3 Jonah found a *s.* going
Mat. 4:21 in a *s.* with Zebedee
8:24 *s.* was covered with waves
14:24 *s.* was tossed, *Mark* 4:37
Mark 1:19 in *s.* mending nets
4:38 in hinder part of *s.* asleep
8:14 had in the *s.* but one loaf
John 6:21 immediately the *s.* was
21:6 cast net on right side of *s.*
Acts 20:38 accompanied him to *s.*
21:2 a *s.* sailing over unto Phe.
27:2 entering a *s.* of Adramyt.

SHIPS.

Gen. 49:13 Zebul. a haven for *s.*
Num. 24:24 *s.* sh. come from Ch.
Deut. 28:68 L. sh. bring th. wi. *s.*
Jud. 5:17 did Dan remain in *s.* ?
1 *K.* 9:26 Solo. made a navy of *s.*
22:48 Jehoshaph. made *s.* of T.
s. were broken, 2 *Chr.* 20:37
2 *Chr.* 8:18 Hur. sent by serv. *s.*
9:21 king's ser. went to Tarshish
Job 9:26 they pass. as the swift *s.*
Ps. 48:7 breakest *s.* of Tarshish
104:26 go *s.* th. is that leviathan
107:23 that go down to sea in *s.*
Prov. 31:14 is like merchant *s.*
Is. 2:16 day of L. on *s.* of Tarsh.
23:1 howl, ye *s.* of Tarshish, 14
43:14 Chal. whose cry is in *s.*
60:9 the *s.* of Tarshish first
Ezek. 27:9 all *s.* of sea with mar.
25 *s.* of Tarsh. did sing of thee
30:9 messengers go forth in *s.*
Dan. 11:30 *s.* of Chittim shall
40 king sh. come with many *s.*
Luke 5:7 filled *s.* began to sink
Jam. 3:4 *s.* though they be great
Rev. 8:9 third part of *s.* destroy.
18:17 compa. in *s.* stood afar off

SHIP-BOARDS.

Ezek. 27:5 thy *s.-b.* of fir-trees

SHIPMASTER.

Jon. 1:6 *s.* said, Wh. mean. thou ?
Rev. 18:17 *s.* and sailors cried

SHIPMEN.

1 *K.* 9:27 Hiram sent *s.* that had
Acts 27:30 *s.* were about to flee

SHIPPING.

John 6:24 they took *s.* and came
SHIPHRAH. *Ex.* 1:15

SHIPWRECK.

2 *Cor.* 11:25 thrice suffered *s.*
1 *Tim.* 1:19 concer. faith made *s.*

SHISHAK.
1 *K.* 14:25 S. king of Egy. came
against Jeru-al. 2 *Chr.* 12:2
2 *Chr.* 12:5 gather. because of S.
I left you in hand of S.
7 not poured out on Jer. by S.
9 S. took away treasures of

SHITTAH-TREE.
Is. 41:19 I will plant the *s.-t.*

SHITTIM.
Num. 25:1 Israel abode in S.
Jos. 2:1 sent out of S. two men
3:1 they removed from S. and
Joel 3:18 shall water valley of S.
Mic. 6:5 answered him from S.

SHITTIM-WOOD.
Ex. 25:10 make ark of *s.-w.* 35:7;
37:1; *Deut.* 10:3
13 staves of *s.-w.* 28 ; 27:6;
37:4, 1?, 28 ; 38:6
23 make a table of *s.-w.* 37:10
26:15 tabernacle of *s.-w.* 36:20
32 pillows of *s.-w.* 37 ; 36:36
35:24 with wh. was found *s.-w.*

SHIVERS.
Rev. 2:27 ves. of potter bro. to *s.*

SHOBAB. 2 *Sam.* 5:14
SHOBACH. 2 *Sam.* 10:16

SHOCK, S.
Jud. 15:5 Samson burnt the *s.*
Job 5:26 like as *s.* of corn cometh

SHOD.
2 *Chr.* 28:15 took captives *s.* th.
Ezek. 16:10 I *s.* thee with badge.
Mark 6:9 be *s.* with sandals, put
Eph. 6:15 *s.* with prepar. of gos.

SHOE.
Deut. 25:9 bro.'s wife loose *s.* 10
29:5 thy *s.* is not waxen old
Jos. 5:15 put *s.* from off thy foot
Ruth 4:7 man plucked off his *s.*
Ps. 60:8 over Edom cast *s.* 108:9
Is. 20:2 put off thy *s.* fr. thy foot

SHOE-LATCHET.
Gen. 14:23 from thread to *s.-l.*
John 1:27 *s.-l.* not worthy to lo.

SHOES.
Ex. 3:5 put off thy *s.* *Acts* 7:33
12:11 eat it, with *s.* on your feet
Deut. 33:25 *s.* shall be iron and
brass
Jos. 9:5 old *s.* and clouted, 13
1 *K.* 2:5 put blood in *s.* on feet
Cant. 7:1 beautiful feet with *s.!*
Is. 5:27 nor latchet of *s.* be brok.
Ezek. 24:17 put on *s.* on feet, 23
Amos 2:6 th. sold the poor for *s.*
8:6 may buy needy for pair of *s.*
Mat. 3:11 *s.* not worthy to bear
10:10 carry neither *s.* *Luke* 10:4
Mark 1:7 latchet of whose *s.*
Luke 3:16 ; *Acts* 13:25
Luke 15:22 ring on ha. *s.* on feet
22:35 I sent you with, purse, *s.*

SHONE.
Ex. 34:29 wist not that face *s.*
30 skin of his face *s.* afraid, 35
2 *K.* 3:22 rose early, the sun *s.*
Luke 2:9 glory of Lord *s.* round
Acts 26:6 *s.* fr. heaven gre. light
Rev. 8:12 day *s.* not for 3d part

SHOOK.
2 *Sam.* 6:6 hold, for oxen *s.* ark
22:8 and the earth *s.* *Ps.* 18:7 ;
68:8 ; 77:18
Neh. 5:13 *s.* my lap, so G. shake
Is. 23:11 stretched, *s.* kingdoms
Acts 13:51 *s.* off dust of their feet
28:5 he *s.* off beast into the fire
Heb. 12:26 whose voice *s.* earth

SHOOT, ETH.
Ex. 36:33 nade middle bar to *s.*
1 *Sam.* 20:20 I will *s.* 3 arrows

2 *Sam.* 11:20 kn. ye not wo. *s. ?*
2 *K.* 13:17 Elisha said, *s.* he shot
19:32 but he shall not *s.* an
arrow there, *Is.* 37:33
1 *Chr.* 5:18 able to *s.* with bow
2 *Chr.* 26:15 engines to *s.* arrows
Job 8:16 branch *s.* in his garden
Ps. 11:2 privily *s.* at upright
22:7 they *s.* out lip, shake head
58:7 bendeth bow to *s.* arrows
64:3 to *s.* arrows, bitter words
7 God shall *s.* at them with ar.
144:6 *s.* out arrows, dest. them
Is. 27:8 measur. when it *s.* forth
Jer. 50:14 ye that bend bow, *s.*
Ezek. 31:14 nor *s.* among boughs
36:8 ye shall *s.* your branches
Mark 4:32 mustard-seed *s.* out
Luke 21:30 when they *s.* forth

SHOOTERS.
2 *Sam.* 11:24 *s.* shot on thy serv.

SHOOTING.
1 *Chr.* 12:2 ri. hand and left in *s.*
Amos 7:1 *s.* up of latter growth

SHORE.
Mat. 13:2 multitude stood on *s.*
48 when full, they drew to *s.*
John 21:4 morni. Je. stood on *s.*
Acts 21:5 kneeled on *s.* prayed
27:39 discove. a creek with a *s.*

See SEA.

SHORN.
Cant. 4:2 sheep that are even *s.*
Acts 18:18 havi. *s.* head in Cenc.
1 *Cor.* 11:6 wom. if not cov. be *s.*

SHOT.
Num. 11:23 L.'s hand waxen *s. ?*
Job 17:12 light *s.* beca. of darkn.
20:5 triumphing of wicked is *s.*
Ps. 89:47 remem. how *s.* time is
Rom. 3:23 come *s.* of glory
9:28 a *s.* work L. make on earth
1 *Cor.* 7:29 brethren, time is *s.*
1 *Thes.* 2:17 tak. fr. you *s.* time
Rev. 12:12 know. he hath *s.* time
17:10 must continue a *s.* space

See COME, CUT.

SHORTENED.
Ps. 89:45 days of youth thou *s.*
102:23 weak. strength, *s.* days
Prov. 10:27 years of wick. be *s.*
Is. 50:2 is my hand *s.* at all
59:1 behold, L.'s hand is not *s.*
Mat. 24:22 ex. those days should
be *s.* *Mark* 13:20

SHORTER.
Is. 28:20 bed *s.* th. a man stretch

SHORTLY.
Ezek. 7:8 now I *s.* pour out fury
1 *Cor.* 4:19 I will come to you *s.*
Phil. 2:19 trust to send Timo. *s.*
24 I trust I myself sh. come *s.*
Heb. 13:23 if he come *s.* I see
3 *John* 14 I trust I sh. *s.* see thee
Rev. 1:1 *s.* come to pass, 22:6

SHOT, Verb.
Gen. 49:23 the archers *s.* at him
Ex. 19:13 be stoned, or *s.* thro'
Num. 21:30 we have *s.* at them
2 *Sam.* 11:24 shooters *s.* fr. wall
2 *K.* 13:17 Elis. said, Shoot, he *s.*
2 *Chr.* 35:23 archers *s.* at Josiah
Ps. 18:14 *s.* out lightnings and
Jer. 9:8 tongue is an arrow *s.* out
Ezek. 17:6 beca. a vine, *s.* forth
31:10 *s.* up his top am. boughs

SHOULDER.
Gen. 21:14 putting bread H.'s *s.*
24:15 Reb. with pitcher on *s.* 45
49:15 Iss. bowed his *s.* to bear
Ex. 28:7 ephod ha. two *s.* pieces
29:27 sanctify *s.* of heave-offer.
Ex. 39:4 made *s.* pieces to coup.
Num. 6:19 *s.* of ram, *Deut.* 18:3

Jos. 4:5 take ev. man a st. on *s.*
Jud. 9:48 Abi. laid bow on his *s.*
1 *Sam.* 9:24 cook took up the *s.*
Neh. 9:29 withd. *s.* harden. neck
Job 31:36 I wou. take it on my *s.*
Ps. 81:6 I removed *s.* from burd.
Is. 9:4 hast broken staff of his *s.*
6 government sh. be on his *s.*
10:27 burden taken fr. off thy *s.*
22:22 key of D. will I lay on *s.*
46:7 they bear him upon the *s.*
Ezek. 12:7 I bare it on my *s.*
12 prince sh. bear upon his *s.*
24:4 gather pieces, thigh and *s.*
29:7 break and rent their *s.* 18
34:21 ye thrust with side and *s.*
Zec. 7:11 refused, pull. away *s.*
Luke 15:5 lay. it on *s.* rejoicing

SHOULDER-BLADE.
Job 31:22 arm fall from my *s.-b.*

Heave-SHOULDER.
Lev. 7:34 *h.-s* taken, *Num.* 6:20
10:14 *heave-s.* shall ye eat, 15

Right SHOULDER.
Ex. 29:22 take of ram *right s.*
Lev. 7:32 *r. s.* give unto priest
8:25 Moses took fat and *right s.*
9:21 *r. s.* waved is th. *Nu.* 18:18

SHOULDERS.
Gen. 9:23 laid garments upon *s.*
Ex. 12:34 troughs bound upon *s.*
Num. 7:9 sons of Ko. bear on *s.*
Deut. 33:12 shall dwell betw. *s.*
Jud. 16:3 Sam. took bar upon *s.*
1 *Sam.* 9:2 from *s.* upward, 10:23
17:6 had a target between his *s.*
2 *Chr.* 35:3 not be a bur. upon *s.*
Is. 11:14 sh. fly on *s.* of Philist.
14:25 burden depart fr. their *s.*
30:6 carry riches upon *s.* of ass.
49:22 daugh. be carried on th. *s.*
Ezek. 12:6 sight, bear it on thy *s.*
Mat. 23:4 bind burd. on men's *s.*

SHOUT, Substantive.
Num. 23:21 *s.* of king am. them
Jos. 6:5 shouted with great *s.* 20
1 *Sam.* 4:6 what mean. great *s. ?*
2 *Chr.* 13:15 men of Ju. gave a *s.*
Ezr. 3:13 could not discern *s.*
Ps. 47:5 G. is gone up with a *s.*
Jer. 25:30 Lord shall give a *s.*
51:14 shall lift a *s.* ag. Babylon
Acts 12:22 peo. gave a *s.* saying
1 *Thes.* 4:16 L. descend with a *s.*

SHOUT, ETH.
Ex. 32:18 not voice of them th. *s.*
Jos. 6:5 hear trumpet, people *s.*
10 not *s.* till bid *s.* th. sh. ye *s.*
Ps. 47:1 *s.* to God with triumph
78:65 like a mighty man that *s.*
Is. 12:6 *s.* thou inhabitant of Zi.
42:11 let them *s.* from mountain
44:23 *s.* ye lower parts of earth
Jer. 31:7 *s.* amo. chief of nations
50:15 Babyl. sinned, *s.* aga. her
Lam. 3:8 when I *s.* he shutteth
Zep. 3:14 *s.* O Israel, be glad
Zec. 9:9 *s.* O daughter of Jerusa.

SHOUTED.
Ex. 32:17 they *s.* he said, Noise
Lev. 9:24 fire consumed, they *s.*
Jos. 6:20 *s.* when priests blew
Jud. 15:14 P. *s.* against Samson
1 *Sam.* 4:5 Is. *s.* because of ark
10:24 peo. *s.* said, G. save king
17:20 host going, *s.* for battle
2 *Chr.* 13:15 Jud. G. smote Je.
Ezr. 3:11 praised Lord, they *s.*
12 many of people *s.* aloud, 13

See JOY.

SHOUTING, S.
2 *Sam.* 6:15 and brought up ark
with *s.* 1 *Chr.* 15:28
2 *Chr.* 15:14 sware to L. with *s.*
Job 39:25 smelleth battle, and *s.*

SHOUTING

Prov. 11:10 when wick. per. is *s.*
Is. 16:9 *s.* sum.-fruits fallen, 10
Jer. 20:16 let th. hear *s.* noontide
48:33 one shall tread with *s.* th.
8. shall be no *s.*
Ezek. 21:22 lift up voice with *s.*
Amos 1:14 a fire dev. Ra. with *s.*
2:2 M. shall die with tumult, *s.*
Zec. 4:7 forth head-stone with *s.*

SHOVEL.

Is. 30:24 been winnowed with *s.*

SHOVELS.

Ex. 27:3 shall make pans and *s.*
38:3 he made the pots and the *s.*
Num. 4:14 put on purple cloth *s.*
1 *K.* 7:40 Hiram made lavers, *s.*
45 ; 2 *Chr.* 4:11, 16
2 *K.* 25:14 *s.* took, and the
snuffers, *Jer.* 52:18

SHOW, Substantive.

Ps. 39:6 ev. man walk. in vain *s.*
Is. 3:9 the *s.* of th. countenance
Luke 20:47 for *s.* make long pra.
Gal. 6:12 make a fair *s.* in flesh
Col. 2:15 made *s.* of them openly
23 which things have *s.* of wi.

SHOW-BREAD.

Ex. 25:30 set upon a table *s.-b.*
1 *Sam.* 21:6 no bread but *s.-b.*
1 *K.* 7:48 table whereon *s.-b.* was
1 *Chr.* 23:29 service for the *s.-b.*
28:16 gave gold for tables of *s.-b.*
2 *Chr.* 2:4 a house for the *s.-b.*
29:18 have cleansed *s.-b.* table
Neh. 10:33 charge oursel. for *s.-b.*
Mat. 12:4 David entered and did
eat *s.-b. Mark* 2:26 ; *Luke* 6:4
Heb. 9:2 wherein was the *s.-b.*

SHOW.

Ex. 7:9 Ph. sh. speak, *s.* miracle
9:16 raised thee to *s.* my power
10:1 that I might *s.* my signs
14:13 see the salva. Lord will *s.*
18:20 shalt *s.* the way they must
walk, *Deut.* 1:33
25:9 accord. to all that I *s.* the
33:13 *s.* me now thy way
18 I beseech thee *s.* me thy
glory
Deut. 5:5 *s.* you word of the Lo.
7:2 nor *s.* mercy unto them
17:9 *s.* thee sentence of judgm.
28:50 old, nor *s.* favor to young
32:7 thy father, he will *s.* thee
1 *Sam.* 3:15 Sam. feared to *s.* Eli
8:9 *s.* them manner of the king
9:27 may *s.* thee the word of G.
14:12 and we will *s.* you a thing
25:8 ask, and they will *s.* thee
2 *Sam.* 15:25 he will *s.* me
1 *K.* 2:2 strong, *s.* thyself a man
18:1 go, *s.* thyself to Ahab, 2
2 *Chr.* 16:9 to *s.* himself strong
Ezr. 2:59 th. could not *s.* fathers'
house, *Neh.* 7:61
Est. 4:8 the writing to *s.* Esther
Job 10:16 he would *s.* these secrets
Ps. 4:6 who will *s.* us any good ?
9:14 *s.* forth all thy praise
16:11 wilt *s.* me the path of life
25:4 *s.* me thy ways, O Lord
14 L. will *s.* them his covenant
51:15 my mouth sh. *s.* thy praise
71:15 my mouth *s.* thy righte.
79:13 thy people *s.* thy praise
85:7 *s.* us mercy, O Lord
92:15 to *s.* that the L. is upright
106:2 who can *s.* all his praise
Prov. 18:24 must *s.* himself
Is. 27:11 form. them, *s.* no favor
30:30 L. sh. *s.* lightning of arm
41:22 *s.* us what shall happen,
let them *s.* the former th.
43:9 who can *s.* us former thi. ?
21 peo. shall *s.* forth my praise

44:7 things coming let them *s.*
46:8 remem. *s.* yourselves men
49:9 in darkness *s.* yourselves
60:6 *s.* forth praises of the Lord
Jer. 16:10 *s.* them all these words
42:3 thy God may *s.* us the way
51:31 to *s.* the king of Babylon
Ezek. 33:31 wi. mouth th. *s.* love
37:18 *s.* us what thou meanest?
43:10 *s.* the house to house of I.
Dan. 9:23 I am come to *s.* thee
Hab. 1:3 dost *s.* me iniquity ?
Mat. 8:4 *s.* thys. to priest, *Mark*
1:44 ; *Luke* 5:14 ; 17:14
11:4 *s.* John the things ye hear
14:2 mighty works *s. Mark* 6:14
16:1 desired he would *s.* a sign
24:24 and shall *s.* great signs
and wonders, *Mark* 13:22
Luke 1:19 sent to *s.* glad tidings
8:39 *s.* great thi. God hath done
John 5:20 will *s.* greater works
7:4 if thou do th. things *s.* thy.
11:57 if any kn. they shou. *s.* it
16:13 will *s.* you things to come
14 receive of mine, and *s.* it, 15
25 I sh. *s.* you plainly of Fath.
Acts 1:24 Lord *s.* whether of th.
7:3 come into land I sh. *s.* thee
12:17 *s.* these things to James
16:17 *s.* us way of salvation
26:23 should *s.* light to the peo.
Rom. 2:15 *s.* work of law written
9:17 that I might *s.* my power
22 if G. willing to *s.* his wrath
1 *Cor.* 11:26 ye do *s.* Lord's dea.
2 *Cor.* 8:24 *s.* proof of your love
1 *Thes.* 1:9 for they themselves *s.*
1 *Tim.* 6:15 in his times he sh. *s.*
2 *Tim.* 2:15 *s.* thyself appr. to G.
Heb. 6:11 that every one *s.* dilig.
Jam. 2:18 *s.* me thy faith witho.
3:13 *s.* works out of good conv.
1 *Pet.* 2:9 *s.* forth praises of him
1 *John* 1:2 *s.* unto you etern. life
Rev. 1:1 angel to *s.* servants, 22:6

I will SHOW.

Gen. 12:1 land that *I w. s.* thee
Ex. 33:19 *I w. s.* mercy on whom
I will s. mercy
Jud. 4:22 *I will s.* thee the man
1 *Sam.* 16:3 *I w. s.* what shalt do
20:13 then *I will s.* it thee
1 *K.* 18:15 *I w.* surely *s.* myself
2 *K.* 7:12 *I w. s.* you what Syria.
Job 15:17 *I w. s.* thee that which
Ps. 50:23 *I will s.* the salvation
of God, 91:16
Jer. 18:17 *I will s.* them the back
33:3 *I w. s.* thee mighty things
42:12 *I w. s.* mercies unto you
Dan. 11:2 *I w. s.* thee the truth
Joel 2:30 *I will s.* wonders in
heaven, *Acts* 2:19
Mic. 7:15 *I will s.* marvel. things
Zec. 1:9 *I will s.* thee what these
Luke 6:47 *I will s.* wh. he is like
Acts 9:16 *I will s.* how great thi.
Jam. 2:18 *I will s.* thee my faith
Rev. 4:1 *I will s.* the things wh.
See KINDNESS.

SHOWED.

Num. 13:26 *s.* them fruit of land
Deut. 34:12 Mo. *s.* in sight of Is.
Jud. 1:25 he *s.* them entrance
13:10 woman *s.* her husband
16:18 he hath *s.* me his heart
Ruth 2:11 *s.* me all th. hast done
1 *Sam.* 11:9 *s.* it to men of Jab.
24:18 Saul said, Thou hast *s.*
2 *Sam.* 11:22 messenger *s.* David
1 *K.* 1:27 not *s.* it to thy servant
16:27 his might that he *s.* 22:45
2 *K.* 6:6 he *s.* him the place
20:15 there is nothing I have
not *s.* them, *Is.* 39:4
Est. 1:4 *s.* riches of his kingdom

3:6 *s.* him the people of Morde.
Job 6:14 to afflicted pity sh. be *s.*
Ps. 71:18 until I ha. *s.* thy stren.
Prov. 26:26 wickedness sh. be *s.*
Ec. 2:19 I have *s.* myself wise
Is. 40:14 *s.* him way of understa.
Mat. 28:11 *s.* to chief priests
Luke 4:5 devil *s.* him all kingdo.
7:18 disciples of John *s.* him
14:21 serv. came and *s.* his lord
John 10:32 good works have I *s.*
21:1 Jesus *s.* himself again to
disciples, 14 ; *Acts* 1:3
Acts 7:26 Mo. *s.* himself to them
52 which *s.* bef. of the coming
20:20 *s.* taught you publicly
23:22 tell no man hast *s.* these
26:20 P. *s.* to them of Damascus
1 *Cor.* 10:28 for his sake that *s.*
Heb. 6:10 love which ye have *s.*

God, or Lord SHOWED.

Gen. 19:19 thy mercy *s.* to me
32:10 not worthy of mercies *s.*
39:21 the Lord *s.* Joseph mercy
41:25 God *s.* P. what he is about
39 foras. as God hath *s.* thee
48:11 G. ha. *s.* me also thy seed
Lev. 24:12 mind of L. might be *s.*
Num. 14:11 all signs I have *s.*
among them, *Deut.* 6:22
Deut. 4:36 upon earth he *s.* thee
5:24 L. our God *s.* us his glory
34:1 Lord *s.* him the land of G.
Jud. 13:23 nor would he have *s.*
2 *K.* 8:10 L. hath *s.* me, he shall
13 the L. *s.* me thou eh. be ki.
Ezr. 9:8 grace *s.* fr. L. our God
Ps. 60:3 thou hast *s.* thy people
71:20 hast *s.* me great troubles
111:6 *s.* the power of his works
118:27 God the L. *s.* us light
Is. 26:10 let favor be *s.* to wick.
43:12 *s.* when no strange God
48:3 I *s.* th. I did them sudden.
5 bef. it came to pass I *s.* thee
Jer. 38:21 word Lord hath *s.* me
Ezek. 11:25 thi. Lord hath *s.* me
Amos 7:1 Lord *s.* me, 4, 7 ; 8:1
Mic. 6:8 he hath *s.* thee, O man
Luke 1:58 Lord hath *s.* mercy
Acts 3:18 things which G. had *s.*
10:40 G. raised him and *s.* him
Rom. 1:19 G. hath *s.* it to them
2 *Pet.* 1:14 L. Jesus hath *s.* me

SHOWEDST, EST.

Neh. 9:10 *s.* signs upon Pharaoh
Jer. 11:18 thou *s.* me their doin.
Jer. 32:18 what *s.* loving-kind. to
John 2:18 what sign *s.* thou ? 6:30

SHOWETH.

Gen. 41:28 God is about to do, *s.*
Num. 23:3 whatsoever he *s.* me
Job 36:9 he *s.* their work
Ps. 19:2 night unto night *s.* kno.
112:5 good man *s.* favor
147:19 he *s.* his word unto Jac.
Prov. 12:17 speaks tru. *s.* right.
Is. 41:26 no. that *s.* your words
Mat. 4:8 *s.* him all kingdoms
John 5:20 Father *s.* Son all thin.

SHOWING.

Ex. 20:6 and *s.* mercy unto thousands, *Deut.* 5:10
Dan. 5:12 *s.* of hard sentences
Luke 1:80 in deserts till his *s.*
8:1 *s.* glad tidings of kingdom
2 *Thes.* 2:4 as G. *s.* himself
Tit. 2:7 in all things *s.* a pattern

SHOWER.

Ezek. 13:11 be overflowing *s.* 13
34:26 cause *s.* to come in season
Luke 12:54 say, There cometh *s.*

SHOWERS.

Deut. 32:2 my speech dist'l as *s.*
Job 24:8 the poor are wet with *s.*

SHOWERS

Ps. 65:10 mak. earth soft with *s.*
72:6 king shall come like *s.*
Jer. 3:3 *s.* have been withholden
14:22 can the heavens give *s.* ?
Ezek. 34:26 his season *s.* of bles.
Mic. 5:7 Jac. shall be as *s.* on gr.
Zec. 10:1 Lord shall give them *s.*

SHRANK.

Gen. 32:32 Is. not eat of sinew *s.*

SHRED.

2 *K.* 4:39 came and *s.* wild gour.

SHRINES.

Acts 19:24 Demet. made silver *s.*

SHROUD.

Ezek. 31:3 Assyr. a cedar with *s.*

SHRUBS.

Gen. 21:15 Ha. cast child und. *s.*

SHUAH.

Gen. 25:2 Ishbak, S. 1 *Chr.* 1:32
38:2 married daugh. of a Canaanite, nam. S. 12 ; 1 *Chr.* 2:3

SHUAL.

1 *Sam.* 13:17 turned to land of S.

SHULAMITE.

Cant. 6:13 O S. what see in S. ?

SHUN, NED.

Acts 20:27 not *s.* to decl. counsel
2 *Tim.* 2:16 *s.* profane babblings

SHUNAMMITE.

1 *K.* 1:3 they found Abishag a S.
2:17 he gave me Abishag the S.
22 why dost ask Abishag S.
2 *K.* 4:12 call this S. 36 ; 25

SHUNEM. 1 *Sam.* 28:4
SHUR. *Gen.* 16:7

SHUSHAN.

Neh. 1:1 I was in S. the palace
Est. 2:8 maidens gathered to S.
3:15 the city S. was perplexed
4:16 gather all the Jews in S.
8:15 the city of S. rejoiced and
9:11 number slain in S. was
15 Jews slew in S. three hund.

SHUT.

Gen. 7:16 the Lord *s.* him in
Ex. 14:3 wilderness *s.* them in
Num. 12:14 let her be *s.* out
15 Miriam was *s.* out fr. camp
Deut. 15:7 nor *s.* hand from poor
Jos. 2:7 they *s.* gate of Jericho
Jud. 9:51 they *s.* tower to them
1 *Sam.* 23:7 he is *s.* in, by enter.
Ps. 69:15 let not pit *s.* mouth
Is. 6:10 *s.* eyes lest they see
22:22 open and none shall *s.* he
shall *s.* none open
44:18 he hath *s.* their eyes
45:1 and gates shall not be *s.*
52:15 kings sh. *s.* their mouths
60:11 gates shall not be *s.* day
66:9 shall I *s.* womb, saith G. ?
Ezek. 3:24 go *s.* thys. with. hou.
44:2 G. hath entered, it sh. be *s.*
46:1 gate shall be *s.* six days
12 going forth, one sh. *s.* gate
Dan. 6:22 God hath *s.* lion's mo.
Acts 5:23 the prison found we *s.*
Rev. 11:6 have power to *s.* heav.
21:25 gates sh. not be *s.* by day
See DOOR.

SHUT up.

Lev. 13:11 shall not *s.* him *up*
14:38 priest shall *s.* *up* house
Deut. 11:17 and he *s.* *up* heaven
32:30 the Lord had *s.* them *up*
36 seeth there is none *s.* *up*
1 *Sam.* 1:5 L. *s.* *up* Han.'s womb
6 the Lord had *s.* *up* her womb
21 they *s.* their calves at home
1 *K.* 8:35 when heaven is *s.* *up*,
2 *Chr.* 6:26 ; 7:13
14:10 from Jeroboam him that
is *s.* *up*, 21:21 ; 2 *K.* 9:8

2 *K.* 14:26 th. was not any *s.* *up*
17:4 king of Assyria *s.* him *up*
2 *Chr.* 28:24 A. *s.* *up* doors, 29:7
Neh. 6:10 house of Sh. was *s.* *up*
Job 3:10 because it *s.* not *up*
11:10 *s.* *up*, who can hinder ?
38:8 who hath *s.* *up* the sea ?
Ps. 31:8 hast not *s.* me *up* into
77:9 ha. he *s.* *up* tender merc. ?
88:8 I am *s.* *up*, I cannot come
Is. 24:10 every house is *s.* *up*
22 they shall be *s.* *up* in prison
Jer. 13:19 cities of south be *s.* *up*
32:2 prophet was *s.* *up* by Z. 3
33:1 while he was *s.* *up*, 39:15
36:5 I am *s.* *up*, I cannot go
Dan. 8:26 *s.* thou *up* the vision
12:4 O Daniel, *s.* *up* the words
Mat. 23:13 *s.* *up* kingd. of heav.
Luke 3:20 *s.* *up* John in prison
4:25 heaven was *s.* *up* three yrs.
Acts 26:10 many did I *s.* *up*
Gal. 3:23 *s.* *up* to faith
Rev. 20:3 *s.* *up* devil, set a seal

SHUTTETH.

Job 12:14 he *s.* *up* a man
Prov. 17:28 that *s.* lips is a man
Is. 33:15 *s.* eyes from seeing
Lam. 3:8 when I cry he *s.* out
1 *John* 3:17 *s.* up bow. of compa.
Rev. 3:7 no m. *s.* and *s.* no m. op.

SHUTTING.

Jos. 2:5 about time of *s.* gate

SHUTTLE.

Job 7:6 swifter than a weaver's *s.*

SICK.

Gen. 48:1 behold, thy father is *s.*
Lev. 15:33 is *s.* of her flowers
1 *Sam.* 19:14 she said, He is *s.*
30:13 three days ago I fell *s.*
2 *Sam.* 12:15 L. strick ch. was *s.*
13:2 Amnon was vexed, fell *s.*
5 Jonadab said, Make thys. *s.*
6 Am. lay down made hims. *s.*
1 *K.* 14:1 the son of Jerob. fell *s.*
5 cometh to ask for son. is *s.*
17:17 son of the woman fell *s.*
2 *K.* 1:2 Ahaz. fell down, was *s.*
8:7 Benha. king of Syria was *s.*
29 Joram son of Ahab, bec. he
was *s.* 2 *Chr.* 22:6
13:14 Elisha was fallen *s.* died
20:1 Hezekiah *s.* unto death,
2 *Chr.* 32:24; *Is.* 38:1
Neh. 2:2 why sad, art not *s.* ?
Ps. 35:13 when they were *s.*
Prov. 13:12 hope deferred make.
the heart *s.*
23:35 stricken me, I was not *s.*
Cant. 5:8 I am *s.* of love
Is. 1:5 wh. head *s.* heart faint
33:24 inhab. not say, I am *s.*
38:9 Hezekiah had been *s.*
Jer. 14:18 art *s.* with famine
Ezek. 34:4 nor heal. that was *s.*
16 strengthen that wh. was *s.*
Hos. 7:5 princes made him *s.*
Mic. 6:13 I make thee *s.* in smi.
Mal. 1:8 offer *s.* is it not evil ?
Mat. 4:24 brou. to him *s.* people
8:14 Pet.'s wife's moth. *s.* of fe.
16 healed all th. were *s.* 14:14
9:12 but they that are *s.* *Mark*
2:17 ; *Luke* 5:31
10:8 heal the *s.* cleanse the lepers, *Luke* 9:2 ; 10:9
25:36 I was *s.* and ye visited me
Mark 6:5 laid hands on a few *s.*
13 anoint. many that were *s.*
56 laid *s.* in streets, *Acts* 5:15
16:18 lay hands on the *s.*
Luke 7:2 centurion's serv. was *s.*
10 serv. whole that had been *s.*
John 4:46 a nobleman's son *s.*
11:1 Laz. of Bethany was *s.*
3 L. he whom thou lovest is *s.*
Acts 9:37 Dorcas was *s.* and died

19:12 brou. the *s.* handkerchiefs
28:8 father of Publius lay *s.*
Phil. 2:26 heard he had been *s.*
2 *Tim.* 4:20 Tro. I left at Mil. *s.*
Jam. 5:14 *s.* let him call elders
See PALSY.

SICKLE.

Deut. 16:9 beg. to put *s.* to corn
23:25 not move *s.* unto neigh.'s
Jer. 50:16 cut off that handl. *s.*
Joel 3:13 put ye in *s.* harv. ripe
Mark 4:29 immedi. he put. in *s.*
Rev. 14:14 in his hand sharp *s.*
15 thrust in thy *s.* 16, 18, 19

SICKLY.

1 *Cor.* 11:30 for this cause ma. *s.*

SICKNESS.

Ex. 23:25 I will take *s.* away
Lev. 20:18 if lie wi. wom. hav. *s.*
Deut. 7:15 L. will take fr. thee *s.*
28:61 ev. *s.* not written in law
1 *K.* 8:37 whatsoever *s.* there be,
2 *Chr.* 6:28
17:17 his *s.* was so sore
2 *K.* 13:14 Elisha was sick of *s.*
2 *Chr.* 21:15 shalt have great *s.*
19 bow. fell out by rea. of *s.*
Ps. 41:3 wilt make his bed in *s.*
Ec. 5:17 sor. and wrath with *s.*
Is. 38:9 Hez. recovered of his *s.*
12 pining *s.* from day to night
Hos. 5:13 when Ephr. saw his *s.*
Mat. 4:23 Je. went healing all *s.*
9:35 Jesus went about heali. *s.*
10:1 to heal. *s.* *Mark* 3:15
John 11:4 *s.* is not unto death

SICKNESSES.

Deut. 28:59 sore *s.* of long conti.
29:22 when they see *s.* L. laid
Mat. 8:17 sa. Himself bare our *s.*

SIDE.

Gen. 6:16 do. of the ark in the *s.*
Ex. 12:7 stri. blood on *s.* pos. 22
17:12 stayed Moses' hands, one
on one *s.* the other on oth. *s.*
32:26 who is on the Lord's *s.* let
27 put ev. man his sword by *s.*
Lev. 1:15 blood wru. at *s.* of alt.
Num. 22:24 on this and that *s.*
32:19 not inh. yonder *s.* Jordan
Deut. 4:32 ask from one *s.* heav.
31:26 book of law in *s.* of ark
1 *Sam.* 4:18 fell by the *s.* of gate
20:25 and Abner sat by Saul's *s.*
2 *Sam.* 2:16 thrust sw. into his *s.*
13:34 king's sons came by hill *s.*
16:13 Shimei went on hill's *s.*
2 *K.* 9:32 who is on my *s.* who?
1 *Chr.* 12:18 David, and on thy *s.*
2 *Chr.* 11:12 Ju. and Benj. on *s.*
Job 18:12 destruc. ready at his *s.*
Ps. 91:7 thousand shall fall at *s.*
118:6 the Lord is on my *s.* I will
124:1 if it had not be. L. on *s.* 2
Is. 60:4 daughte. be nursed at *s.*
Ezek. 4:8 not turn from one *s.* to
9 days thou sh. lie upon thy *s.*
25:9 I will open the *s.* of Moab
34:21 thrust with *s.* and should.
Dan. 7:5 rais. up itself on one *s.*
11:17 she sh. not stand on his *s.*
John 19:34 wi. a spear pierced *s.*
20:20 showed his hands and *s.*
25 except I thrust hand into *s.*
27 hand, and thrust into my *s.*
Acts 16:13 on sab. went by riv. *s.*
Rev. 22:2 on either *s.* of river
See CHAMBERS.

Every SIDE.

1 *Sam.* 14:47 Saul fought on *e. s.*
1 *K.* 5:4 L. giv. rest on *e. s.*
1 *Chr.* 22:18 not giv. rest on *e. s.*
2 *Chr.* 14:7 hath giv. rest on *e. s.*
Ps. 12:8 the wicked walk on *e. s.*
31:13 fear was on *every s.*

Jer. 6:25 fear *e. s.* 20:10 ; 42:29
Ezek. 16:33 come to thee on *e. s.*
19:8 nations set ag. him on *e. s.*
23:22 bring th. ag. thee on *e. s.*
37:21 I will gather them on *e. s.*
2 *Cor.* 4:8 are troubled on *e. s.* 7:5

Farther SIDE.

Mark 10:1 J. came by *f. s.* Jord.
See LEFT.

On this SIDE.

Jos. 8:33 I. and jud. stood *on t. s.*
1 *Sam.* 23:26 Saul went *on this s.*
Ezr. 4:16 no portion *on this s.*
Ezek. 1:23 had two wings, *on t. s.*
40:39 were two tables *on this s.*
Dan. 12:5 stood two, one *on t. s.*

On other SIDE.

Jos. 24:2 fathers dwelt *on o. s.*
1 *Sam.* 14:40 I and Jona. *on o. s.*
Ob. 11 day thou stood. *on o. s.*
John 6:25 found him *on o. s.*

Right SIDE.

Ezek. 4:6 lie again on thy *r. s.*
47:1 from und. *r. s.* of house, 2
See SEA, SOUTH, WAY, WEST.

SIDES.

1 *Sam.* 24:3 David in *s.* of cave
1 *K.* 4:24 Sol. had peace on all *s.*
Ps. 48:2 Zion on *s.* of the north
Is. 14:13 I will sit on *s.* of north
15 brought down to *s.* of pit
Jer. 6:22 raised from *s.* of earth
49:32 bring calamity from all *s.*
Ezek. 1:17 went on four *s.* 10:11
48:1 th. are his *s.* east and west
Amos 6:10 say to him by *s.* of h.
Jon. 1:5 gone down to *s.* of ship

SIDON.

Gen. 10:5 Canaan begat S. his
19 border of Canaan. was fr. S.
Jud. 18:28 Laish was far fr. S.
Mat. 11:21 done in Tyre and S.
22 tolera. for S. *Luke* 10:13, 14
15:21 Jesus departed into coasts
of Tyre and S. *Mark* 7:24
Mark 3:8 they about Tyre and S.
came, *Luke* 6:17
7:31 from coasts of Tyre and S.
Luke 4:26 to Sarepta, a city of S.
Acts 12:20 displea. wi. them of S.
27:3 next day we touched at S.

SIEGE.

Deut. 20:19 to employ them in *s.*
28:53 sh. eat thy children in *s.*
2 *Chr.* 32:10 that ye abide in *s.?*
Is. 29:3 I will lay *s.* against thee
Jer. 19:9 eat flesh of friend in *s.*
Ezek. 4:2 lay *s.* ag. it, a fort, 3
Mic. 5:1 hath laid *s.* against us
Nah. 3:14 draw thee waters for *s.*
Zec. 12:2 cup of trembling in *s.*

SIEVE.

Is. 30:28 sift nations with the *s.*
Amos 9:9 as corn sifted in a *s.*

SIFT.

Is. 30:28 *s.* nations with sieve
Amos 9:9 I will *s.* Israel as corn
Luke 22:31 Sat. desired to *s.* you

SIGH.

Is. 24:7 all merry-hearted do *s.*
Lam. 1:4 priests *s.* 11 people *s.*
Ezek. 9:4 foreheads of men th. *s.*
21:6 *s.* with break. of thy loins

SIGHED, EST, ETH.

Ex. 2:23 Is. *s.* by reason of bon.
Lam. 1:8 she *s.* turneth backw.
Ezek. 21:7 say, Whereof *s.* thou ?
Mark 7:34 look. to heaven he *s.*
8:12 *s.* deeply in his spirit

SIGHING.

Job 3:24 my *s.* cometh bef. I eat
Ps. 12:5 *s.* of needy will I arise
31:10 spent with grief, years *s.*
79:11 let *s.* of the prisoner come

Is. 21:2 *s.* thereof I ma. to cease
35:10 sorrow and *s.* flee away
Jer. 45:3 I fainted in my *s.*

SIGHS.

Lam. 1:22 *s.* many, heart faint

SIGHT.

Gen. 2:9 every tree pleasant to *s.*
Ex. 3:3 turn and see th. great *s.*
24:17 *s.* of glory of L. like fire
Lev. 13:4 in *s.* not deep. th. skin
14:37 if plague in *s.* lower
Num. 13:33 in their *s.* as grassh.
27:19 give him charge in the *s.*
Deut. 28:34 mad for *s.* of eyes, 67
Jos. 23:5 G. drive them out of *s.*
24:17 did great signs in our *s.*
Job 18:3 why rep. vile in your *s.?*
21:8 seed established in their *s.*
34:26 striketh them in *s.* of oth.
41:9 not cast down at *s.* of him ?
Ps. 79:10 am. heathen in our *s.*
Ec. 6:9 better *s.* of eyes than
Is. 5:21 prudent in their own *s.*
11:3 not judge after *s.* of eyes
Jer. 51:24 evil in Zion in your *s.*
Ezek. 12:3 remo. by day in th. *s.*
20:9 in whose *s.* I made known
14 in who. *s.* I brought out, 22
43:11 show forms. write in th. *s.*
Dan. 4:11 *s.* thereof to end of, 20
Mat. 11:5 the blind receive their
s. 20:34 ; *Luke* 7:21
Luke 4:18 preach. *s.* to the blind
23:48 came to *s.* smote breasts
24:31 he vanished out of their *s.*
John 9:11 washed and I recei. *s.*
Acts 1:9 received him out of *s.*
7:31 Mo. saw, he wondered at *s.*
9:9 three days with. *s.* nor eat
18 he received *s.* forthwith
2 *Cor.* 5:7 we walk by fai. not *s.*

SIGHT of God.

Prov. 3:4 understand. in *s. of G.*
Acts 4:19 whe. right in *s. of G.*
8:21 heart not right in *s. of G.*
2 *Cor.* 2:17 in *s. of G.* speak we
7:12 care for you in *s. of God*
1 *Tim.* 2:3 acceptable in *s. of G.*

1 *Tim.* 6:13 I gi. th. ch. in *s. of G.*
1 *Pet.* 3:4 in *s. of G.* of great pri.

His SIGHT.

Ex. 15:26 wh. is right in *his s.*
Deut. 4:37 bro. thee out in *his s.*
Jud. 6:21 angel dep. out of *his s.*
2 *Sam.* 12:9 L. to do evil in *his s.*
2 *K.* 17:18 th. o. of *h. s.* 20, 23; 24:3
1 *Chr.* 19:13 L. do good in *his s.*
Job 25:5 stars not pure in *his s.*
Ps. 10:5 judgments out of *his s.*
72:14 preci. their blood in *his s.*
Ec. 2:26 giv. man good in *his s.*
8:3 not hasty to go out of *his s.*
Hos. 6:2 we shall live in *his s.*
Mark 10:52 Bartim. immediately
received *his s. Luke* 18:43
John 9:15 how he receiv. *his s.* 18
Acts 9:12 he might receive *his s.*
Col. 1:22 pres. you holy in *his s.*
Heb. 13:21 well-pleasing in *h. s.*
1 *John* 3:22 things pleas. in *h. s.*

In the SIGHT.

Gen. 47:18 left *in the s.* of lord
Ex. 4:30 signs *in the s.* of people
11:3 Mo. great *in the s.* of serv.
19:11 L. come down *in the s.* of
Lev. 20:17 cut off *in the s.* of peo.
26:45 out of Eg. *in the s.* of hea.
Num. 25:6 wom. *in the s.* of Mo.
33:3 *in the s.* of Egyptians
Deut. 31:7 M. said, *in the s.* of Is.
Jos. 10:12 *in the s.* of Israel
1 *Chr.* 28:8 *in the s.* of Is. keep
29:25 magni. Sol. *in the s.* of Is.
2 *Chr.* 32:23 Hez. magnifi. *in t. s.*
Ezr. 9:9 mercy *in the s.* of kings
Neh. 1:11 mercy *in the s.* of man

Ps. 78:12 thi. did he *in s.* of fath.
98:2 showed *in the s.* of heathen
Prov. 1:17 net spr. *in the s.* of b.
Ec. 11:9 walk *in the s.* of eyes
Jer. 43.9 hid stones *in t. s.* of Ju.
Ezek. 5:8 *in the s.* of nations
16:41 juagm. *in the s.* of women
28:25 as. in th. *in t. s.* of h. 39:27
Acts 7:10 wisdom *in the s.* of Ph.
Rom. 12:17 hon. *in the s.* of men
Rev. 13:14 *in the s.* of beast

See LORD.

My SIGHT.

Gen. 23:4 dead out of *my s.* 8
Ex. 33:12 found gra. in *my s.* 17
1 *Sam.* 29:6 coming good in *my s.*
9 I kn. thou art good in *my s.*
1 *K.* 8:25 not fail thee a man in
my s. 2 *Chr.* 6:16
11:38 that wh. is right in *my s.*
2 *K.* 21:15 done evil in *my s.*
23:27 remove Jud. out of *my s.*
Is. 43:4 wast precious in *my s.*
Jer. 7:15 cast you out of *my s.*
30 chil. of Ju. done ev. in *m. s.?*
15:1 cast them out of *my s.*
18:10 if it do evil in *my s.*
34:15 had done right in *my s.*
Ezek. 10:2 went in *my s.* to fill
Amos 9:3 hid from *my s.* in sea
Mark 10:51 L. that I might rec.
my s. Luke 18:41

Thy SIGHT.

Gen. 19:19 found grace in *thy s.*
21:12 let it not be griev. in *t. s.*
33:10 Ja. said, If I have found
grace in *thy s.* 47:29 ; *Ex.*
33:13, 16 ; 34:9 ; *Jud.* 6:17
1 *Sam.* 15:17 little in *th.* own *s.*
2 *Sam.* 7:9 enemies out of *thy s.*
19 a small thing in *thy s.*
14:22 I have found grace in *t. s.*
2 *K.* 1:13 life precious in *t. s.* 14
20:3 done good in *t. s. Is.* 38:3
Ps. 5:5 fool. not stand in *thy s.*
9:19 let heath. be judged in *t. s.*
51:4 I sinned, done evil in *t. s.*
76:7 who may stand in *thy s.?*
143:2 in *thy s.* no man justified
Is. 26:17 so ha. we been in *thy s.*
Jer. 18:23 blot out sin from *t. s.*
Jon. 2:4 I am cast out of *thy s.*
Mat. 11:26 so it seemed good in
thy s. Luke 10:21
Luke 15:21 sin. ag. heav. in *t. s.*
18:42 Jesus said, Receive *thy s.*
Acts 9:17 mightest receive *thy s.*
22:13 brother Saul, receive *t. s.*

See FAVOR, FIND.

SIGHTS.

Luke 21:11 fearful *s.* sh. there be

SIGN, Substantive.

Ex. 4:8 first *s.* believe latter *s.*
8:23 to-morrow shall this *s.* be
31:13 my sabbaths, a *s.* bet. me
and you, 17 ; *Ezek.* 20:12, 20
Num. 16:38 they sh. be a *s.* to
Deut. 6:8 for *s.* on hand, 11:18
13:1 arise a prophet, giveth a *s.*
28:46 on thee for *s.* and wonder
Jos. 4:6 this be a *s.* among you
Jud. 6:17 show me *s.* thou talk.
20:38 *s.* betw. Israel and liers in
1 *Sam.* 2:34 this shall be *s.* to
thee, 2 *K.* 19:29
14:10 this shall be a *s.* unto us
1 *K.* 13:3 *s.* Lord hath spoken
2 *K.* 20:8 what shall be the *s.*
9 this *s.* shall they have of the
Lord, *Is.* 37:30 ; 38:7, 22
2 *Chr.* 32:24 and he gave him a *s.*
Is. 7:11 ask thee a *s.* of the Lord
14 L. himself shall give you a *s.*
19:20 it shall be for a *s.* to Lord
20:3 Is. walked barefoot for a *s.*
55:13 for an everlasting *s.*

66:19 I will set a *s.* among them
Jer. 6:1 set up *s.* in Beth-haccer.
44:29 this be *s.* to you, *Lu.* 2:12
Ezek. 4:3 this be *s.* to house of I.
12:6 I set thee for a *s.* to Is. 11
14:8 make him a *s.* and a prov.
24:24 Ezek. is a *s.* 27 thou be *s.*
39:15 th. sh. he set up a *s.* by it
Mat. 12:38 Master, we wo. see a *s.*
16:1; *Mark* 8:11; *Luke* 11:16
39 seek. af. a *s.* no *s.* be given,
but *s.* of Jonas, 16:4; *Mark*
8:12; *Luke* 11:29, 30
24:3 what the *s.* of thy coming?
30 then appear *s.* of Son of man
26:48 betrayed him gave them *s.*
Mark 13:4 what *s.* when things
Luke 2:34 *s.* which be spoken
John 2:18 wh. *s.* show. th.? 6:30
Acts 28:11 whose *s.* was Castor
Rom. 4:11 received *s.* of circum.
1 *Cor.* 1:22 for Jews require a *s.*
14:22 wherefore tongues are *s.*
Rev. 15:1 I saw ano. *s.* in heaven

SIGN.
Dan. 6:8 establish decree, and *s.*

SIGNED.
Dan. 6:9 Darius *s.* the writing, 10

SIGNS.
Gen. 1:14 let them be for *s.*
Ex. 4:9 if they will not believe *s.*
17 with this rod th. shalt do *s.*
7:3 I will multiply my *s.* in Eg.
10:2 mayest tell thy son my *s.*
Num. 14:11 for all *s.* I showed
Deut. 4:34 take nation by *s.* 26:8
6:22 Lord showed *s.* on Egypt,
Neh. 9:10; *Ps.* 78:43
7:19 great *s.* thi. eyes saw, 29:3
34:11 in all *s.* L. sent him to do
1 *Sam.* 10:7 when th. *s.* are come
9 and all those *s.* came to pass
Ps. 74:4 th. set up ensigns for *s.*
9 we see not our *s.* there is no
105:27 showed his *s.* amo. them
Is. 8:18 I and children are for *s.*
Jer. 10:2 be not dismayed at *s.*
32:20 set *s.* and wonders in E.
Dan. 4:2 I thou. good to show *s.*
3 how great his *s.?* mighty
6:27 he worketh *s.* in heaven
Mat. 16:3 not discern *s.* of times?
24:24 th. shall arise false Christs
and show *s. Mark* 13:22
Mark 16:17 these *s.* follow them
20 confirming the word with *s.*
Luke 1:62 they made *s.* to Zacha.
21:11 and great *s.* shall there be
25 *s.* in sun, moon and stars
John 4:48 except ye see *s.* ye will
20:30 other *s.* truly did Jesus
Acts 2:19 I will show *s.* in earth
22 a man approved of G. by *s.*
43 *s.* were done by apost. 5:12
4:30 *s.* may be done by name
7:36 had showed *s.* and wonders
8:13 Simon wond. beholding *s.*
14:3 granted *s.* and wond. to be
Rom. 15:19 through mighty *s.*
and wonders, 2 *Cor.* 12:12
2 *Thes.* 2:9 work. of Satan, wi. *s.*
Heb. 2:4 G. bearing wit. with *s.*

SIGNET, S.
Gen. 38:18 thy *s.* and staff, 25
Ex. 28:11 like engravings of *s.*
21, 36; 39:14, 30
39:6 onyx-stones graven as *s.*
Jer. 22:24 though Coniah were *s.*
Dan. 6:17 king sealed it with *s.*
Hag. 2:23 I will make th. as a *s.*

SIGNIFICATION.
1 *Cor.* 14:10 none of th. with. *s.*

SIGNIFY.
Acts 21:26 to *s.* accomplishment
23:15 *s.* to capt. that he bring P.
25:27 not to *s.* the crimes laid

1 *Pet.* 1:11 search. what Sp. did *s.*

SIGNIFIED, ETH.
Acts 11:28 Agab. *s.* there should
Heb. 12:27 *s.* removing those thi.
Rev. 1:1 *s.* it by his angel to Jo.

SIGNIFYING.
John 12:33 *s.* by what death sho.
glorify God 18:32; 21:19
Heb. 9:8 H. Gh. *s.* that the way

SIHON.
Num. 21:23 S. would not suffer
Is. to pass, *Jud.* 11:20
27 let the city of S. be built
28 flame gone out fr. city of S.
34 as didst to S. *Deut.* 3:2, 6
Deut. 2:30 S. king of Heshbon
21 I have begun to give S. and
32 S. ca. out, 29:7; *Jud.* 11:20
31:4 do to them as he did to S.
Jos. 9:10 all that he did to S.
Jud. 11:21 God delivered S. into
Neh. 9:22 possessed land of S.
Jer. 48:45 flame com. fr. mi. of S.

SIHON, king of the Amorites.
Num. 21:21 messeng. to S. *k. of
A. Deut.* 2:26; *Jud.* 11:19
26 city of S. *k. of A. Jos.* 12:2
29 into captiv. to S. *k. of Am.*
34 to S. *ki. of A. Deut.* 3:2
Deut. 1:4 slain S. *k. of A.* king
of Bashan, *Ps.* 135:11 ; 136:19
Jos. 13:10 cities of S. *ki. of A.*

SIHOR.
Jos. 13:3 S. which is before
Jer. 2:18 to drink waters of S.

SILAS.
Acts 15:22 S. chief among, 27
34 it pleased S. to abide there
40 Pa. chose S. 16:19 caught S.
16:25 at midnight Paul and S.
29 fell down bef. Paul and S.
17:4 consorted with Paul and S.
10 sent away S. by night
15 commandm. to S. to come
18:5 S. and Timoth. were come

SILENCE.
Job 4:16 image before me, was *s.*
29:21 men gave ear, and kept *s.*
Ps. 31:18 lying lips be put to *s.*
39:2 I was dumb with *s.* I held
94:17 my soul almost dw. in *s.*
115:17 nei. any that go into *s.*
Is. 15:1 Moab bro. to *s.* Kir to *s.*
Jer. 8:14 our G. hath put us to *s.*
Lam. 3:28 sitteth alone, keep. *s.*
Amos 8:3 cast them forth with *s.*
Mat. 22:34 put Sadducees to *s.*
Acts 21:40 th. was made great *s.*
22:2 spake in Heb. they kept *s.*
1 *Tim.* 2:11 let wom. learn in *s.*
12 nor to usurp but to be in *s.*
1 *Pet.* 2:15 may put to *s.* ignor.
Rev. 8:1 there was *s.* in heaven

See KEEP, KEPT.

SILENT.
1 *Sam.* 2:9 wicked shall be *s.*
Ps. 22:2 I cry in night, not *s.*
28:1 not *s.* to me, if thou be *s.*
30:12 sing praise to th. not be *s.*
31:17 let wicked be *s.* in grave
Is. 47:5 sit thou *s.* and get thee
Jer. 8:14 defenced ci. let us be *s.*
Zec. 2:13 be *s.* O all flesh, bef. L.

SILK.
Prov. 31:22 her clothing is *s.*
Ezek. 16:10 I covered thee wi. *s.*
13 thy raiment was *s.*
Rev. 18:12 no man buyeth her *s.*

SILLY.
Job 5:2 envy slayeth the *s.* one
Hos. 7:11 Ephr. is like a *s.* dove
2 *Tim.* 3:6 lead captive *s.* wom.

SILOAH, SILOAM.
Neh. 3:15 repai. wall of pool of S.

Luke 13:4 on wh. tower in S. fell
John 9:7 wash in pool of S. 11

SILVANUS.
2 *Cor.* 1:19 preach. am. you by S.
1 *Thes.* 1:1 Paul, S. and Timoth.
to the church, 2 *Thes.* 1:1
1 *Pet.* 5:12 by S. a faithful broth.

SILVER.
Gen. 23:15 worth 400 shek. of *s.*
Ex. 20:23 not make gods of *s.*
26:19 sockets of *s.* 21, 25, 32 ;
36:24, 26, 30, 36
27:17 hooks shall be of *s.* 38:19
38:25 *s.* of th. that were numb.
Lev. 5:15 ram with estima. of *s.*
27:3 esti. of male 50 shek. of *s.*
6 of female three shekels of *s.*
16 hom. of bar. seed 50 shek. *s.*
Num. 7:13 offer. one *s.* charger,
b. bowl of 70 shekels, 19–79
Num. 7:84 12 cha. of *s.* 12 *s.* bowls
10:2 make two trumpets of *s.*
Deut. 22:19 amerce in 100 she. *s.*
29 give damsel's fa. 50 shek. *s.*
Jos. 7:21 I saw 200 shekels of *s.*
Jud. 17:2 1,100 shekels of *s.*
10 I will give ten shekels of *s.*
1 *Sam.* 9:8 fourth part of shek. *s.*
2 *Sam.* 18:11 I wo. given 10 sh. *s.*
12 should re. 1,000 shek. of *s.*
24:24 oxen for 50 shekels of *s.*
1 *K.* 10:21 none *s.* 2 *Chr.* 9:20
27 king made *s.* to be as stones
20:39 thou sh. pay a talent of *s.*
2 *K.* 5:22 give them a talent of *s.*
15:20 exacted of each 50 she. *s.*
18:15 Hezek. gave him all the *s.*
22:4 Hilk. may sum *s.* brought
1 *Chr.* 28:14 instruments of *s.*
29:2, 5
15 for the candlesticks of *s.*
17 by weight for ev. basin of *s.*
2 *Chr.* 17:11 Jehosha. presents *s.*
Neh. 5:15 gover. had 40 she. of *s.*
Job 3:15 filled houses with *s.*
22:25 thou sh. have plenty of *s.*
27:16 th. he heap up *s.* as dust
17 innocent shall divide the *s.*
28:15 nor shall *s.* be weighed for
Ps. 12:6 words of L. pure, as *s.*
66:10 hast tried us, as *s.* is tried
Prov. 2:4 if thou seekest her as *s.*
3:14 of wisd. is better than of *s.*
8:10 receive instruction, not *s.*
10:20 tongue of just is choice *s.*
16:16 get underst. rath. than *s.*
17:3 fining-pot is for *s.* and the
25:4 take away dross from the *s.*
Ec. 5:10 he that loveth *s.* shall
not be satisfied with *s.*
Cant. 8:9 will build a palace of *s.*
Is. 1:22 thy *s.* is become dross
30:22 sh. defile thy images of *s.*
48:10 I refined thee, not with *s.*
60:17 for iron I will bring *s.* and
Jer. 6:30 reproba. *s.* sh. men call
10:9 *s.* spr. in. plates is brought
32:9 I weighed him 17 she. of *s.,*
Ezek. 18:28 they are dross of *s.*
20 they gather. brass and iron
22 *s.* is melted in the furnace
27:12 with *s.* Tarshish traded in
Dan. 2:32 breast and arms were *s.*
Hos. 9:6 pleasant places for *s.*
13:2 made molten images of *s.*
Amos 2:6 they sold righte. for *s.*
8:6 that we may buy poor for *s.*
Zep. 1:11 howl, all that bear *s.*
Zec. 9:3 Tyrus heaped *s.* as dust
13:9 I will refine them as *s.*
Mal. 3:3 refiner and purifier of *s.*

See FILLETS, GOLD, PIECES.

SILVER, Adjective.
Gen. 44:2 put *s.* cup in sack's
Prov. 26:23 potsherd cov. with *s.*
Ec. 12:6 ever *s.* cord be loosed

Mat. 27:6 chief priests took *s.*
Acts 19:24 Dem. made *s.* shrines
See VESSELS.

SILVERLINGS.
Is. 7:23 thous. vines at thous. *s.*

SILVERSMITH.
Acts 19:24 Demetrius a *s.* made

Talents of SILVER.
1 *K.* 16:24 bought hill for 2 *t. o. s.*
2 *K.* 5:5 Naam. took ten *t. of s.*
23 two *tal. of s.* in two bags
15:19 M. gave Pul 1,000 *t. of s.*
1 *Chr.* 19:6 Ha. sent 1,000 *t. of s.*
22:14 a thous. thousand *t. of s.*
29:4 seven thou. *t. of* refined *s.*
2 *Chr.* 25:6 hir. men for 100 *t. of s.*
27:5 Am. gave Joth. 100 *t. of s.*
36:3 condem. land in 100 *t. of s.*
Ezr. 7:22 I decr. it to 100 *t. of s.*
8:26 I weigh. to hand 650 *t. of s.*
Est. 3:9 will pay 10,000 *t. of s.*

Vessels of SILVER.
Num. 7:85 *s. v.* weigh. 2,400 she.
2 *Sam.* 8:10 Jor. brought *v. of s.*
1 *K.* 10:25 man his pres. *ves. of s.*
2 *K.* 12:13 not made *ves. of s.*
1 *Chr.* 18:10 all manner of *v. of s.*
gold and brass, 2 *Chr.* 24:14
Ezr. 1:6 strength. with *v. of s.* 11
5:14 *v. of* gold and *s. of* house
8:26 I weighed *s. v.* hundred ta.
Dan. 5:2 bring golden and *s. v.*
11:8 carry their precious *v. of s.*

SIMEON.
Gen. 29:33 and called name S.
34:25 S. and Levi took each sw.
35:23 S. son of Leah, *Ex.* 1:2
42:24 Joseph took fr. them S. 36
43:23 he brought S. out unto
Gen. 46:10 sons of S. *Ex.* 6:15;
Num. 1:22; 26:12; 1 *Chr.*
4:24, 42; 12:25
48:5 Reuben and S. they shall
49:5 S. and Levi are brethren
Num. 1:6 prince of S. 2:12; 7:36
Deut. 27:12 S. Levi, and Judah
Jos. 19:1 second lot came to S. 9
Jud. 1:3 S. went with Judah, 17
2 *Chr.* 15:9 the strange. out of S.
34:6 so did Josiah in S.
Ezek. 48:24 S. have a portion, 33
Luke 2:25 whose name was S. 34
3:30 Levi, which was son of S.
Acts 13:1 at Antioch S. that was
15:14 S. hath declared how God

Tribe of SIMEON.
Num. 1:23 *t. of* S. numb. 59,300
2:12 *t. of* S. sh. pitch by Reuben
10:19 over the host of *tribe of* S.
13:5 *t. of* S. Shaph. to spy land
34:20 *t. of* S. Shemuel to divide
Jos. 19:1 second lot for *tr. of* S.
8 the inheritance of *tribe of* S.
21:4 of *tr.* of S. 9 ; 1 *Chr.* 6:65
Rev. 7:7 of *t. of* S. sealed 12,000

SIMILITUDE.
Num. 12:8 *s.* of the Lord shall
Deut. 4:12 but saw no *s.* 15, 16
2 *Chr.* 4:3 under it was *s.* of oxen
Ps. 106:20 changed glory into *s.*
144:12 stones polished after *s.*
Dan. 10:16 one like a. of sons of
Rom. 5:14 after *s.* of Ad.'s trans.
Heb. 7:15 after *s.* of Melchisedek
Jam. 3:9 men made after *s.* of G.

SIMILITUDES.
Hos. 12:10 I have used *s.*

SIMON.
Mat. 10:4 S. Canaan. *Mark* 3:18
13:55 James, Jos. S. *Mark* 6:3
16:17 blessed art th. S. Bar-jona
17:25 what thinkest thou S. ?
26:6 of S. the leper, *Mark* 14:3

27:32 man of Cyre. S. by name,
Mark 15:21 ; *Luke* 23:26
Mark 1:29 house of S. *Luke* 4:38
14:37 S. sleepest thou ? couldest
Luke 5:3 one of ships wh. was S.
4 he said unto S. Launch out
10 who were partners with S.
6:15 S. called Zelotes, *Acts* 1:13
7:40 S. I have somewhat to say
22:31 S. S. Satan hath desired to
24:34 risen, and appeared to S.
John 1:41 findeth his brother S.
42 Jesus said, Thou art S.
6:71 Ju. son of S. 12:4 ; 13:2, 26
21:15 S. son of Jo. lovest ? 16, 17
Acts 8:9 man S. who beforetime
13 then S. himself believed also
9:43 Peter tarried many days at
Joppa wi. one S. 10:6, 17, 32

See PETER.

SIMPLE.
Ps. 19:7 Lord maketh wise the *s.*
116:6 the Lord preserveth the *s.*
119:130 giv. understanding to *s.*
Prov. 1:4 to give subtilty to *s.*
22 how long, ye *s.* ones, will
32 turning away of *s.* shall slay
7:7 among *s.* ones a young man
8:5 O ye *s.* understand wisdom
9:4 whoso is *s.* let him turn, 16
13 a foolish woman is *s.*
14:15 *s.* believeth every word
18 *s.* inh. folly ; 19:25 *s.* beware
21:11 punished ; *s.* made wise
22:3 *s.* pass on are punish. 27:12
Ezek. 45:20 do for him that is *s.*
Rom. 16:18 fair speeches dec. *s.*
19 wise to good, *s.* concer. evil

SIMPLICITY.
2 *Sam.* 15:11 th. went in their *s.*
Prov. 1:22 how lo. wi. ye love *s.* ?
2 *Cor.* 1:12 in *s.* had conversation
11:3 corrupted from *s.* in Christ

SIN.
Ex. 16:1 I came to wildern. of S.
17:1 journey. fr. S. *Num.* 33:12
Ezek. 30:15 pour my fury up. S.
16 S. shall have great pain

SIN.
Gen. 4:7 not well, *s.* lie. at door
Ex. 34:7 forgiv. iniquity, and *s.*
Lev. 4:3 if priest *s.* accord. to *s.*
14 wh. *s.* is known, cong. offer
6:26 priest offereth it fr. *s.* 9:15
9:17 not suffer *s.* on neighbor
Num. 5:6 when man or wom. *s.*
12:11 I beseech, lay not *s.* upon
19:9 it is a purification for *s.* 17
27:3 father died in his own *s.*
Deut. 15:9 cry to L. it be *s.* 24:15
19:15 witness sh. not rise for *s.*
Deut. 21:22 if a man have com. *s.*
22:26 in damsel no *s.* wor. death
23:21 it would be *s.* in thee
24:16 put to death for his own *s.*
2 *K.* 14:6 ; 2 *Chr.* 25:4
1 *Sam.* 15:23 rebel. as *s.* of witch.
1 *K.* 8:34 forgive *s.* of thy people
36 forgive the *s.* of thy servants,
6:25, 27
12:30 this thing bec. a *s.* 13:34
2 *K.* 12:16 *s.* money was priests'
Job 20:11 his bones are full of *s.*
Ps. 32:1 blessed whose *s.* cover.
51:5 in *s.* did mother con. me
59:12 for *s.* of their mouth
109:7 let his prayer become *s.*
14 let not *s.* of mother be blot.
Prov. 10:16 wicked tendeth to *s.*
19 in words there want. not *s.*
14:9 fools make a mock at *s.*
34 *s.* is a reproach to any peo.
21:4 plowing of wicked is *s.*
24:9 thought of foolishness is *s.*
Is. 5:18 woe to th. who draw *s.*
30:1 that they may add *s.* to *s.*

31:7 idols your hands ma. for *s.*
53:10 make soul an offer. for *s.*
12 he bare *s.* of many
Jer. 17:1 *s.* of Ju. writ. with pen
3 I will give high place for *s.*
51:5 th. land was filled with *s.*
Lam. 4:6 punishm. of *s.* of Sod.
Hos. 4:8 eat up *s.* of people
10:8 *s.* of Is. shall be destroyed
12:8 no iniq. in me that were *s.*
Amos 8:14 sw. by *s.* of Samaria
Mic. 1:13 beginning of *s.* to Zion
6:7 fruit of body for *s.* of soul
Zec. 13:1 a fount. opened for *s.*
Mat. 12:31 all *s.* sh. be forgiven
John 1:29 tak. away *s.* of world
8:7 that is without *s.* am. you
34 whoso commit. *s.* serv. of *s.*
9:41 if blind, should have no *s.*
15:22 not come, had not *s.* 24
16:8 Comfor. will reprove of *s.* 9
9:11 deliv. me hath greater *s.*
Acts 7:60 lay not *s.* to th. charge
Rom. 3:9 J. and Gentil. under *s.*
20 by law is knowledge of *s.*
4:7 blessed whose *s.* is covered
5:12 *s.* ent. world, death by *s.*
13 till the law *s.* was in world
20 where *s.* abounded, grace
21 as *s.* reigned unto death
6:1 shall we continue in *s.* ?
2 sh. we th. are dead to *s.* live ?
7 he that is dead is freed fr. *s.*
10 he died, he died to *s.* once
11 reck. yourselves dead to *s.*
12 let not *s.* reign in yo. body
13 nor yield your memb. to *s.*
14 *s.* shall not have dominion
16 serv. ye are, whether of *s.*
17 G. thanked, were serv. of *s.*
18 being made free from *s.* 22
20 wh. ye were servants of *s.*
23 for the wages of *s.* is death
7:7 is law *s.* ? G. forbid ; kn. *s.*
8 *s.* tak. occasion wro. in me ;
without law *s.* is dead
9 commandm. came, *s.* revived
11 *s.* by commandm. slew me
17 *s.* that dwelleth in me, 20
23 bring. me into captiv. to *s.*
25 but with flesh, the law of *s.*
8:3 *s.* condemned *s.* in the flesh
10 body dead because of *s.*
14:23 whats. is not of faith is *s.*
1 *Cor.* 6:18 every *s.* a man doeth
15:56 the sting of death is *s.* and
the strength of *s.* is the law
2 *Cor.* 5:21 made him be *s.* for us
Gal. 2:17 Ch. the minister of *s.* ?
3:22 scrip. conclu. all under *s.*
2 *Thes.* 2:3 man of *s.* be revealed
Heb. 3:13 be hardened through *s.*
4:15 tempted, yet without *s.*
9:26 he appeared to put away *s.*
28 appear without *s.* to salvat.
10:6 in sacrifices for *s.* no pleas.
8 off. for *s.* thou wouldest not
18 remission, no offering for *s.*
11:25 enjoy the pleasures of *s.*
12:1 lay aside *s.* doth beset us
4 not resisted, striv. against *s.*
13:11 bod. of beasts for *s.* burnt
Jam. 1:15 it bring. forth *s.* and *s.*
when finished, bring. death
2:9 if have respect to per. ye *s.*
4:17 not good, to him it is *s.*
1 *Pet.* 2:22 did no *s.* nor guile
4:1 suff. in flesh, ceased from *s.*
2 *Pet.* 2:14 eyes can. cease fr. *s.*
1 *John* 1:7 the blood of Jesus
Christ his Son cleanseth us
from all *s.*
8 say, We have no *s.* we dece.
1 *John* 3:4 whoso comm. *s.* transgresseth ; *s.* is transgression
5 manifested, in him is no *s.*
8 committeth *s.* is of the devil
9 born of G. doth not commit *s.*

5:16 *s.* wh. is not to death, *s.*
17 all unrighteousn. is *s.* and
there is a *s.* not unto death
See BEAR.

Great SIN.
Gen. 20:9 brought on me *great s.*
Ex. 32:21 bro. *g. s.* on them
30 M. said, Ye sinned a *g. s.* 31
1 *Sam.* 2:17 *s.* of young men *g.*
2 *K.* 17:21 Jeroboam made them
a *great s.*

His SIN.
Lev. 4:3 bring for *his s.* a bullock
23 if *h. s.* come to knowl. 28
5:6 bring trespass-offer. for *h. s.*
1 *K.* 15:26 Nadab walked in *h. s.*
34 Baa. walked in way of *h. s.*
16:19 Zimri walked in *his s.*
26 Omri in *his s.*
2 *K.* 21:16 beside *h. s.* wherewith
made Judah
17 acts of Manasseh, and *h. s.*
2 *Chr.* 33:19 all *h. s.* bef. humbl.
Job 34:37 addeth rebellion to *h. s.*
Is. 27:9 fruit to take away *his s.*
Ezek. 3:20 shall die in *h. s.* 18:24
33:14 if he turn from *his s.*
Hos. 13:12 bound up, *h. s.* is hid
Mic. 3:8 full to declare to Is. *s.*

My SIN.
Gen. 31:36 what is *my s.* that th.
Ex. 10:17 forg. *my s.* this once
1 *Sam.* 15:25 I pray, pardon *my s.*
20:1 what *my s.* bef. thy father
1 *K.* 17:18 to call *my s.* to rem.
Job 10:6 thou search. after *my s.*
13:23 make me to know *my s.*
14:16 dost thou not watch *my s.*
35:3 if I be cleansed from *my s.*
Ps. 32:5 I acknowledged *my s.*
and thou forgavest *my s.*
38:3 nor rest because of *my s.*
18 iniqu. I be sorry for *my s.*
51:2 cleanse me from *my s.*
3 *my s.* bef. 59:3 not for *my s.*
Prov. 20:9 I am pure from *my s.*
Dan. 9:20 I was confessing *my s.*
See OFFERING.

Our SIN.
Ex. 34:9 pardon iniq. and *our s.*
Jer. 16:10 what *o. s.* we commit.

Their SIN.
Gen. 18:20 because *t. s.* is griev.
50:17 forgive *their s.* 2 *Chr.* 7:14
Ex. 32:32 if thou forgive *their s.*
34 when I visit, I will visit *t. s.*
Num. 5:7 they shall confess *t. s.*
Deut. 9:27 stubbornness, nor *t. s.*
1 *K.* 8:35 if they turn from *their
s.* 2 *Chr.* 6:26
Neh. 4:5 let not *t. s.* be blotted
Ps. 85:2 thou hast covered *t. s.*
Is. 3:9 they declare *t. s.* as Sod.
Jer. 16:18 recompense *t. s.* doub.
18:23 neither blot out *their s.*
31:34 rememb. *their s.* no more
36:3 that I may forgive *their s.*
John 15:22 have no cloak for *t. s.*

Thy SIN.
2 *Sam.* 12:13 Lord put away *t. s.*
Is. 6:7 taken away, *t. s.* purged

Your SIN.
Ex. 32:30 atonement for *your s.*
Num. 32:23 *y. s.* wi. find you out
Deut. 9:21 I took *y. s.* the calf
John 9:41 theref. *y. s.* remaineth

SIN, Verb.
Gen. 39:9 do this, and *s.* ag. G. ?
42:22 do not *s.* ag. the child
Ex. 20:20 fear, that thou *s.* not
23:33 lest make thee *s.* ag. me
Lev. 4:2 if soul *s.* thro' ignorance
3 if priest *s.* 13 if congregat.
27 if people *s.* thro' ignorance
5:1 if a soul *s.* and hear swear.

6:2 if a soul *s.* lie unto neighbor
Num. 16:22 *s.* wroth with all ?
Deut. 20:18 should you *s.* ag. L.
24:4 shalt not cause land to *s.*
1 *Sam.* 2:25 if one man *s.* against
another ; *s.* against the Lord
12:23 God forbid I should *s.*
14:33 people *s.* against Lord
34 *s.* not in eating with blood
19:4 let not king *s.* ag. servant
5 why *s.* ag. innocent blood ?
1 *K.* 8:46 if they shall *s.* against
thee, 2 *Chr.* 6:36
2 *K.* 21:11 Man. made Judah *s.*
2 *Chr.* 6:22 if man *s.* ag. neighbor
Neh. 6:13 and do so, and *s.*
13:26 did not Solo. *s.* by these
Job 2:10 did not J. *s.* wi. his lips
5:24 visit habitation, and not *s.*
10:14 if I *s.* thou markest me
31:30 nei. suffered mouth to *s.*
Ps. 4:4 stand in awe, and *s.* not
39:1 take heed I *s.* not
119:11 I might not *s.* ag. thee
Ec. 5:6 mouth cause flesh to *s.*
Jer. 32:35 do this to cau. J. to *s.*
Ezek. 3:21 rig. *s.* not, doth not *s.*
Hos. 8:11 Ephraim hath made
altars to *s.* altars to him to *s.*
13:2 now they *s.* more and more
Mat. 18:21 L. how oft brot. *s.* ?
John 5:14 *s.* no more, lest worse
8:11 nei. do I cond. *s.* no more
9:2 who did *s.* man or parents ?
Rom. 6:15 *s.* bec. not under law ?
1 *Cor.* 8:12 *s.* ag. breth. *s.* ag. C.
15:34 awake to righteous. *s.* not
Eph. 4:26 be ye angry and *s.* not
1 *Tim.* 5:20 them that *s.* rebuke
Heb. 10:26 if we *s.* wilfully after
1 *John* 2:1 I write unto you that
ye *s.* not, and if any man *s.*
3:9 can. *s.* bec. he is born of G.
5:16 any man see his brother *s.*
See ISRAEL.

SINAI.
Deut. 33:2 Lord came from S.
Jud. 5:5 melted, even that S.
Ps. 68:8 S. moved at presence
17 Lord is among us. as in S.
See MOUNT.

SINCERE.
Phil. 1:10 be *s.* till day of Ch.
1 *Pet.* 2:2 as babes desire *s.* milk

SINCERELY.
Jud. 9:16 if ye have done *s.* 19
Phil. 1:16 one preach Ch. not *s.*

SINCERITY.
Jos. 24:14 serve the Lord in *s.*
1 *Cor.* 5:8 unleavened bread of *s.*
2 *Cor.* 1:12 in godly *s.* we have
2:17 as of *s.* in the sight of God
8:8 to prove the *s.* of your love
Eph. 6:24 that love Lord J. in *s.*
Tit. 2:7 in doc. show. gravity, *s.*

SINEW.
Gen. 32:32 Israel eat not of the *s.*
touched J. in *s.* that shrank
Is. 48:4 thy neck is an iron *s.*

SINEWS.
Job 10:11 with bones and *s.*
30:17 bones are pierced, *s.* take
40:17 *s.* of his stones are wrap.
Ezek. 37:6 I will lay *s.* upon you
6 the *s.* and flesh came upon

SINFUL.
Num. 32:14 increase of *s.* men
Is. 1:4 ah *s.* nation, a peo. laden
Amos 9:8 eyes of L. on *s.* kingd.
Mark 8:38 ashamed in *s.* genera.
Luke 5:8 for I am a *s.* man, O L.
24:7 deliv. into hands of *s.* men
Rom. 7:13 sin bec. exceeding *s.*
8:3 send. S. in liken. of *s.* flesh

SING.
Ex. 15:21 *s.* to the Lord, 1 *Chr.*
16:23 ; *Ps.* 30:4 ; 95:1 ; 96:1, 2 ;
98:1 ; 147:7 ; 149:1 ; *Is.* 12:5
32:18 noise of them that *s.*
Num. 21:17 spring up, O well, *s.*
1 *Sam.* 21:11 did they not *s.* one
1 *Chr.* 16:9 *s.* unto him, *s.* psalms
33 the trees of the wood *s.* out
2 *Chr.* 20:22 they began to *s.* and
29:30 Hez. command. Lev. to *s.*
Job 29:13 I caused wid. heart *s.*
Ps. 21:13 so will we *s.* praise
33:2 praise the Lord, *s.* to him
3 *s.* to him a new so. *Is.* 42:10
51:14 *s.* of thy righteousn. 145:7
65:13 valleys shout, they also *s.*
66:2 *s.* forth honor of his name
4 earth *s.* to thee, they shall *s.*
67:4 let nations be glad and *s.*
68:32 *s.* to God, ye kingdoms
71:22 to thee will I *s.* 98:5
81:1 *s.* aloud to G. our strength
104:12 fowls *s.* among branches
105:2 *s.* to him, *s.* psal. unto him
137:3 *s.* us one of the songs of Z.
4 how shall we *s.* L. song in ?
138:5 they shall *s.* in ways of L.
149:5 *s.* aloud upon their beds
Prov. 29:6 righteous *s.* and rej.
Is. 23:15 after 70 years sh. T. *s.*
24:14 they shall *s.* for maj. of L.
26:19 *s.* ye that dwell in dust
27:2 in that day *s.* ye to her
35:6 then sk. tongue of dumb *s.*
Is. 38:20 we will *s.* my songs
42:11 let inhabitants of rock *s.*
44:23 *s.* O ye heav. for L. 49:13
52:8 with the voice shall they *s.*
9 *s.* to the L. ye waste places
54:1 *s.* O barren, didst not bear
65:14 my servants sh. *s.* for joy
Jer. 31:7 *s.* with gladness for Ja.
12 they shall *s.* in height of Z.
51:48 all that is therein shall *s.*
Ezek. 27:25 ships of Tarsh. did *s.*
Hos. 2:15 sh. *s.* in days of youth
Zep. 2:14 their voice shall *s.*
3:14 *s.* daugh. of Zion, *Zec.* 2:10
Jam. 5:13 any merry ? let him *s.*
Rev. 15:3 they *s.* song of Moses

I will SING.
Ex. 15:1 *I will s.* to the Lord,
Jud. 5:3 ; *Ps.* 13:6
Ps. 57:7 fixed, O God, *I will s.*
9 *I will s.* to thee am. nations
59:16 *I w. s.* of thy power, 89:1
17 unto thee, O my stror. *w. I s.*
101:1 *I will s.* of mercy and jud.
104:33 *I will s.* to the L. as long
144:9 *I will s.* a new song
Is. 5:1 now *will I s.* to well-belo.
Rom. 15:9 for this cause *will I s.*
1 *Cor.* 14:15 *I will s.* with the sp.
I will s. with understanding
See PRAISE, PRAISES.

SINGED.
Dan. 3:27 nor w. hair of head *s.*

SINGER.
1 *Chr.* 6:33 Heman a *s.* son of J.
Hab. 3:19 to chief *s.* on instrum.

SINGERS.
1 *K.* 10:12 made psalteries for *s.*
2 *Chr.* 9:11
1 *Chr.* 9:33 these are the *s.* 15:16
15:19 *s.* were appoint. to sound
27 Levites and *s.* had fine lin.
2 *Chr.* 5:13 trumpet. and *s.* were
20:21 Jehoshaphat appointed *s.*
23:13 peo. rejoiced also *s.* 29:28
35:15 the *s.* the sons of Asaph
Ezr. 2:41 *s.* childr. of Asaph 128
70 *s.* dwelt in cities, *Neh.* 7:73
7:7 some *s.* went up to Jerusa.

Neh. 7:1 the *s.* were appointed
10:29 the *s.* clave to their bret.
11:22 *s.* were over bus. of house
23 portion for *s.* 12:47 ; 13:5
12:28 sons of *s.* gathered thems.
29 the *s.* builded them villages
42 *s.* sang ; 45 *s.* kept ward of G.
46 in days of Da. there were *s.*
13:10 Levites and *s.* were fled
Ps. 68:25 *s.* went before
87:7 as well *s.* as players
Ezek. 40:44 chamb. of *s.* in court

Men-SINGERS, women-SINGERS.
Ec. 2:8 I gat *men-s.* and *wo.-s.*

SINGETH.
Prov. 25:20 so is he that *s.* songs

SINGING.
1 *Sam.* 18:6 wo. came out of Is. *s.*
1 *Chr.* 6:32 ministered with *s.*
13:8 Dav. and Is. played with *s.*
2 *Chr.* 23:18 offer burnt-off. wi. *s.*
30:21 *s.* with loud instru. to L.
Neh. 12:27 kept dedication wi. *s.*
Ps. 100:2 bef. presence with *s.*
126:2 our tongue filled with *s.*
Cant. 2:12 time of the *s.* of birds
Is. 14:7 they break forth into *s.*
16:10 in vineyards shall be no *s.*
35:2 sh. blossom with joy and *s.*
44:23 break into *s.* ye mount.
48:20 flee from Chaldeans wi. *s.*
49:13 break forth into *s.*
51:11 redeemed sh. come wi. *s.*
54:1 break forth into *s.* O bar.
55:12 mount. shall break into *s.*
Zep. 3:17 joy over thee with *s.*
Eph. 5:19 *s.* in y. heart, *Col.* 3:16

SINGING-MEN, SINGING-WOMEN.
2 *Sam.* 19:35 I hear *s.-m. s.-w.*
2 *Chr.* 35:25 the *s.-m.* spake of J.
Ezr. 2:65 200 *s.-m.* 200 *s.-women*
Neh. 7:67 245 *s.-m.* and *s.-women*

SINGLE.
Mat. 6:22 if eye *s.* whole body
full of light, *Luke* 11:34

SINGLENESS.
Acts 2:46 eat meat wi. *s.* of heart
Eph. 6:5 in *s.* of heart, *Col.* 3:22

SINGULAR.
Lev. 27:2 man shall make *s.* vow

SINK.
Ps. 69:2 I *s.* in deep mire where
Jer. 51:64 Baby. *s.* and not rise
Mat. 14:30 beginning to *s.* cried
Luke 5:7 so that they began to *s.*
9:44 sayings *s.* into your ears

SINNED.
Ex. 9:34 Pharaoh *s.* yet more
32:30 ye have *s.* a great sin, 31
33 whosoever hath *s.* him will
Lev. 4:3 for sin he hath *s.* a bul.
22 ruler *s.* 23 ; 28 one of peo.
5:5 confess he hath *s.*
6:4 bec. he hath *s.* shall restore
Num. 12:11 lay not *s.* wher. we *s.*
32:23 ye have *s.* against the L.
Deut. 9:16 behold, ye had *s.* ag. L.
18 your sins wh. ye *s.* in doing
Jos. 7:11 Isr. hath *s.* and trangr.
Jud. 11:27 I have not *s.* ag. thee
1 *Sam.* 19:4 he hath not *s.* ag th.
24:11 I have not *s.* against thee
1 *K.* 8:33 they have *s.* against
thee, 35 ; 2 *Chr.* 6:24, 26
50 forgive peo. th. *s.* 2 *Chr.* 6:39
15:30 Jer. which he *s.* 16:13, 19
18:9 what have I *s.* that thou
2 *K.* 17:7 Israel had *s.* against L.
21:17 sin th. Manas. *s.* is writ.
Neh. 9:29 *s.* against thy judgm.
Job 1:5 Job said, My sons ha. *s.*
22 in this J. *s.* not, nor charg.

8:4 if chil. have *s.* against him
24:19 so doth grave who have *s.*
Ps. 78:17 they *s.* yet more, 32
Is. 43:27 thy first father hath *s.*
Jer. 2:35 sayest, I have not *s.*
40:3 because ye have *s.* 44:23
50:14 Babylon hath *s.* ag. Lord
Lam. 1:8 Jer. hath grievously *s.*
5:7 fathers have *s.* and are not
Ezek. 18:24 sin he hath *s.* in th.
28:16 violence, and thou hast *s.*
37:23 dwelling-p. wherein th. *s.*
Hos. 4:7 as they increased they *s.*
10:9 thou hast *s.* fr. days of G.
Hab. 2:10 thou hast *s.* ag. soul
John 9:3 neither this man *s.* nor
Rom. 2:12 as have *s.* with. law,
s. in the law
3:23 all have *s.* and come. 5:12
5:14 death over them had not *s.*
16 not as it was by one that *s.*
1 *Cor.* 7:28 if marry, hast not *s.*
2 *Cor.* 12:21 I bewail many that *s.*
13:2 I write to them wh. have *s.*
Heb. 3:17 was it not wi. them *s.* ?
2 *Pet.* 2:4 G. spared not angels *s.*
1 *John* 1:10 if say, We have not *s.*

I have SINNED.
Ex. 9:27 Phar. said, *I h. s.* 10:16
Num. 22:34 Balaam said, *I h. s.*
Jos. 7:20 indeed, *I h. s.* ag. God
1 *Sam.* 15:24 Saul said, *I have s.*
30 ; 26:21
2 *Sam.* 12:13 Da. said to Na. *I h.
s.* 24:10, 17 ; 1 *Chr.* 21:8, 17
19:20 thy serv. doth know *I h. s.*
Job 7:20 *I h. s.* 33:27 say, *I h. s.*
Ps. 41:4 heal my soul, *I have s.*
51:4 against thee only *have I s.*
Mic. 7:9 *I have s.* against him
Mat. 27:4 Judas said, *I have s.*
Luke 15:18 prodi. said, *I h. s.* 21

We have SINNED.
Num. 12:11 sin, wherein *we h. s.*
14:40 for *we have s. Deut.* 1:41
21:7 *we h. s.* have spoken ag. L.
Jud. 10:10 *we h. s.* bec. we have
forsaken God, 1 *Sam.* 12:10
15 *we h. s.* do what seem. good
1 *Sam.* 7:6 and said, *we have s.*
1 *K.* 8:47 *we h. s.* done perversely
2 *Chr.* 6:37 *we h. s.* done amiss
Neh. 1:6 confess sins *we have s.*
Ps. 106:6 *we h. s.* with our fath.
Is. 42:24 L. ag. whom *we have s.*
64:5 thou art wroth, for *we h. s.*
Jer. 3:25 lie down in sh. *we h. s.*
8:14 given us gall, for *we h. s.*
14:20 acknow. wick. *we have s.*
Dan. 9:5 *we h. s.* committed ini.
15 *we have s.* done wickedly

SINNER.
Prov. 11:31 more wicked and *s.*
13:6 wickedn. overthroweth *s.*
22 wealth of *s.* laid up for just
Ec. 2:26 the *s.* he giveth travail
7:26 *s.* shall be taken by her
8:12 thro' *s.* do evil 100 times
9:2 so is *s.* and he that sweareth
18 one *s.* destroy. much good
Is. 65:20 *s.* being 100 years old
Lu. 7:37 wo. in city who was *s.*
15:7 joy in heaven over one *s.*
18:13 G. be merciful to me a *s.*
19:7 guest with man a *s.*
John 9:16 can *s.* do miracles ?
John 9:24 gi. G. praise, man is *s.*
25 whe. he be a *s.* I know not
Rom. 3:7 yet judged as a *s.* ?
Jam. 5:20 convert. *s.* save a soul
1 *Pet.* 4:18 where ungodly *s.* ap.

SINNERS.
Gen. 13:13 men of Sod. were *s.*
1 *Sam.* 15:18 utterly destroy *s.*
Ps. 1:1 stand. not in way of *s.*
5 nor *s.* in congre. of righteous

25:8 theref. will he teach *s.* way
26:9 gather not my soul with *s.*
51:13 *s.* sh. be converted to thee
104:35 let the *s.* be consumed
Prov. 1:10 if *s.* ent. consent not
13:21 evil pursueth *s.* to right.
23:17 let not thy heart envy *s.*
Is. 1:28 destr. of *s.* be together
13:9 destroy *s.* thereof out of it
33:14 the *s.* in Z. are afraid
Amos 9:10 *s.* shall die by sword
Mat. 9:10 many *s.* sat at meat
with Jesus, *Mark* 2:15
13 call right. but *s.* to repentance, *Mark* 2:17 ; *Luke* 5:32
11:19 fri. of pub. and *s. Lu.* 7:34
Luke 6:32 *s.* love those love them
33 what tha. ha. ye? *s.* do same
34 *s.* lend to *s.* to receive again
13:2 suppose th. these were *s.* 4
15:1 publicans and *s.* to hear
John 9:31 kn. G. heareth not *s.*
Rom. 5:8 wh. we were *s.* C. died
Gal. 2:15 Jews, not *s.* of Gentiles
17 if we ourselves are found *s.*
1 *Tim.* 1:9 the law is made for *s.*
15 Ch. Jesus came to save *s.*
Jam. 4:8 ye *s.* purify hearts
Jude 15 speeches *s.* have spoken

SINNEST.
Job 35:6 if thou *s.* what do. thou

SINNETH.
Num. 15:28 soul that *s.* ignoran.
29 law for him *s.* thro' ignor.
Deut. 19:15 not rise in sin he *s.*
1 *K.* 8:46 is no man that *s.* not
2 *Chr.* 6:36 ; *Ec.* 7:20
Prov. 8:36 he that *s.* wrong. soul
14:21 that despiseth neighbor *s.*
19:2 that hasteth with feet *s.*
20:2 whoso provoketh a king *s.*
Ezek. 14:13 wh. land *s.* I stretch
18:4 soul that *s.* it shall die, 20
33:12 for righteous. in day he *s.*
1 *Cor.* 6:18 fornicator *s.* ag. body
7:36 do what he will, *s.* not
Tit. 3:11 such is subverted and *s.*
1 *John* 3:6 whoso. abid. in him *s.*
not, whoso. *s.* hath not seen
8 devil *s.* from the beginning
5:18 whoso. is born of G. *s.* not

SINNING.
Gen. 20:6 I withheld thee fr. *s.*
Lev. 6:3 man does *s.* therein

SINS.
1 *K.* 14:16 give Is. up bec. of *s.*
15:3 Abij. walked in *s.* of Reho.
30 smote N. bec. of *s.* of Jero.
16:13 *s.* of Baasha, and *s.* of El.
31 light thing to wa. in *s.* of J.
2 *K.* 3:3 Jeho. cleaved to *s.* of J.
10:29 from *s.* of Jeroboam Jehu
13:6 Is. departed not fr. *s.* of J.
17:22 Is. walked in *s.* of Jerob.
24:3 remove Ju. for *s.* of Mana.
2 *Chr.* 28:10 are th. not wi. y. *s.* ?
Neh. 1:6 confess the *s.* of Israel
Job 13:23 how many are my *s.* ?
Ps. 19:13 keep thy servant fr. *s.*
25:7 remem. not *s.* of my youth
Prov. 5:22 hold. with cords of *s.*
10:12 strifes, love covereth all *s.*
28:13 that covereth *s.* not prosp.
Is. 40:2 received double for her *s.*
43:24 ma. me to serve wi. thy *s.*
25 blot out, not remem. thy *s.*
44:22 blot out as a cloud thy *s.*
Jer. 15:13 I give to spoil for *s.*
30:14 bec. thy *s.* increased, 15
50:20 *s.* of Judah sought
Lam. 3:39 for punishm. of his *s.*
4:13 *s.* of her proph. and priests
22 Edom, he will discov. thy *s.*
Ezek. 16:51 S. committed thy *s.*
52 bear thine own shame for *s.*
18:14 that seeth his father's *s.*
21 if wicked turn from his *s.*

23:49 shall bear *s.* of your idols
33:16 none of his *s.* be mention.
Dan. 9:24 make end of *s.*
Mic. 1:5 for *s.* of house of Israel
6:13 making desol. bec. of thy *s.*
Mat. 26:28 shed for remissi. of *s.*
Luke 24:47 remis. of *s.* preached
John 9:34 altogether born in *s.*
20:23 *s.* ye remit, whose *s.* reta.

Acts 22:16 wash away thy *s.*
Rom. 7:5 *s.* did work in members
Eph. 2:1 who were dead in *s.* 5
Col. 2:11 putti. off the body of *s.*
1 Tim. 5:22 partakers of men's *s.*
24 men's *s.* opened beforehand
Heb. 2:17 reconcilia. for *s.* of pe.
5:1 gifts and sacrifices for *s.*
7:27 for his own *s.* for people's
9:28 Ch. off. to bear *s.* of many
10:4 blood of goats take away *s.*
12 offered one sacrifice for *s.*
Jam. 5:20 and hide multit. of *s.*
1 Pet. 2:24 dead to *s.* live to righ.
3:18 Christ once suffered for *s.*
4:8 charity cover multitude of *s.*
2 Pet. 1:9 was purged from his *s.*
1 John 2:2 the *s.* of whole world
Rev. 18:4 be not partak. of her *s.*
5 her *s.* have reach. unto heav.

See FORGIVE, FORGIVEN.

My SINS.

Ps. 51:9 hide thy face from *my s.*
69:5 O G. *my s.* not hid fr. thee
Is. 38:17 cast *my s.* behind back

Our SINS.

1 Sam. 12:19 added to *our s.*
2 Chr. 28:13 int. to add to *our s.*
Neh. 9:37 ki. over us bec. of o. *s.*
Ps. 79:9 purge away *our s.*
90:8 *o.s.* in light of countenance
103:10 not dealt accord. to *o. s.*
Is. 59:12 *our s.* testify against us
Ezek. 33:10 if *our s.* be on us
Dan. 9:16 bec. of *o. s.* peo. beco.
1 Cor. 15:3 Christ died for *our s.*
Gal. 1:4 gave himself for *our s.*
Heb. 1:3 himself purged *our s.*
1 Pet. 2:24 his own self bare *o. s.*
1 John 1:9 if we confess *our s.*
3:5 manifest. to take away *o. s.*
Rev. 1:5 washed us from *our s.*

Their SINS.

Lev. 16:16 transgression in *th. s.*
Num. 16:26 consumed in all *t. s.*
1 K. 14:22 provoked with *their s.*
16:2 prov. me to anger with *t.s.*
Neh. 9:2 Israel confessed *their s.*
Is. 58:1 show house of Jacob *t. s.*
Jer. 14:10 vis. *t. s.* Hos. 8:13 ; 9:9
Mic. 7:19 cast all *t. s.* into sea
Mat. 1:21 save his peo. from *t. s.*
3:6 bapt. confes. *t. s.* Mark 1:5
Luke 1:77 salva. by remis. of *t. s.*
Rom. 11:27 shall take away *t. s.*
1 Thes. 2:16 to fill up *t. s.* alway
Heb. 8:12 I w. be merciful to *t. s.*
10:17 *th. s.* remember no more

Your SINS.

Lev. 16:30 may be clean fr. *y. s.*
26:18 punish you for *y. s.* 24, 28
Deut. 9:18 nor drink, bec. of *y. s.*
Jos. 24:19 G. will not forgi. *y. s.*
Is. 1:18 tho' *your s.* be as scarlet
59:2 *your s.* have hid his face
Jer. 5:25 *y. s.* withholden good
Ezek. 21:24 in doings *y. s.* appe.
Amos 5:12 know *y.* trans. and *s.*
John 8:21 seek me. die in *y. s.* 24
Acts 3:19 repent, that *y. s.* may
1 Cor. 15:17 raised, ye are in *y. s.*
Col. 2:13 you being dead in *y. s.*
1 John 2:12 *y. s.* are forgiven you

SION. Deut. 4:48

See ZION.

SIR, S.

Gen. 43:20 *s.* we ca. to buy food
Mat. 21:30 I go *s.* and went not
John 4:11 *s.* thou hast nothi. to
49 *s.* come ere my child die
5:7 I ha. no man to put me in
12:21 saying, *s.* we would see J.
Acts 7:26 *s.* ye are brethren, why
16:30 *s.* wh. mu. I do to be sa. ?
27:25 where. *s.* be of good cheer
Rev. 7:14 said to him, *s.* th. kno.

SIRION.

Deut. 3:9 which Sidonians call S.
Ps. 29:6 Lebanon and S. like a

SISERA.

Jud. 4:2 captain of host was S.
17 S. fled away on his feet, 22
5:20 the stars fought against S.
26 with hammer she smote S.
28 the mother of S. looked out
1 Sam. 12:9 sold into hand of S.
Ezr. 2:53 children of S. Nethinim went up, Neh. 7:55
Ps. 83:9 do unto them as to S.

SISTER.

Gen. 24:60 our *s.* be thou mother
34:13 defiled Dinah their *s.* 27
31 deal with our *s.* as a harlot ?

Ex. 2:4 his *s.* stood afar off
Lev. 18:9 shalt not uncover *s.*
11 thy *s.* 18 a wife to her *s.*
20:17 if a man take *s.* see nake.
21:3 his *s.* a virgin, be defiled
Num. 6:7 not defiled for his *s.*
Deut. 27:22 curs. that lieth wi. *s.*
Jud. 15:2 youn. *s.* fairer th. she ?
2 Sam. 13:1 Ab. had fair *s.* Tamar
22 had forced his *s.* Tamar, 32
Cant. 8:8 lit. *s.* hath no breasts
Jer. 3:7 treacherous *s.* Ju. saw it
8 *s.* feared not ; 10 *s.* not turn.
22:18 lament, saying, Ah, my *s.*
Ezek. 16:45 thou art *s.* of sisters
46 elder *s.* Samaria, youn. *s.* S.
48 So. thy *s.* not done as thou
22:11 ano. hath humbled his *s.*
23:4 Ah. elder, Aholibah her *s.*
18 mind was alienated from *s.*
31 thou walk. in way of thy *s.*
32 drink of thy *s.* cup deep, 33
44:25 *s.* that hath no hus. defile
Mat. 12:50 same is brother, *s.*
Luke 10:39 had a *s.* John 11:1, 5
John 19:25 stood by cross m.'s *s.*
Acts 23:16 Paul's *s.* son heard of
Rom. 16:1 Phebe our *s.* servant
1 Cor. 7:15 *s.* is not under bond.
9:5 we not power to lead a *s.* ?
Col. 4:10 Marcus *s.* son to Barna.
Jam. 2:15 if a bro. or *s.* be naked
2 John 13 children of thy elect *s.*

SISTER-IN-LAW.

Ruth 1:15 *s.-i.-l.* is gone back

My SISTER.

Gen. 12:13 say, thou art *my s.*
19 why saidst thou, She is *my*
s. 20:2, 5, 12 ; 26:7, 9
30:8 I have wrestled with *my s.*
2 Sam. 13:5 let *my s.* Ta. come, 6
20 hold thou thy peace, *my s.*
Job 17:14 said to worm, art *my s.*
Prov. 7:4 thou art *my s.*
Cant. 4:9 ravi. my heart, *my s.*
10 how fair is thy love, *my s.*
5:1 am come into my gar. *my s.*
2 open to me, *my s.* my love
Mark 3:35 same my bro. *my s.*
Luke 10:40 do. th. not care *my s.* ?

SISTERS.

Jos. 2:13 swe. ye will save my *s.*
Job 1:4 called for three *s.* to eat
42:11 came his brethren and *s.*
Ezek. 16:45 th. *s.* art sister of thy *s.*
51 thou hast justified thy *s.* 52
61 asha. when thou receive *s.*

Hos. 2:1 say unto your *s.* Ruha.
Mat. 13:56 *s.* with us ? Mark 6:3
1 Tim. 5:2 int. as *s.* with purity

SIT.

Num. 32:6 go to war ye *s.* here
Jud. 5:10 ye that *s.* in judgment
Ruth 4:1 ho, *s.* down here, 2
1 Sam. 9:22 *s.* in chiefest place
16:11 will not *s.* down till he co.
20:5 not fail to *s.* with king
2 Sam. 19:8 king doth *s.* in gate
1 K. 1:13 Solomon shall *s.* 17
8:25 not fail man to *s.* on thr. of
Is. 2 Chr. 6:16 ; Jer. 33:17
2 K. 7:3 *s.* here till we die ? 4
10:30 sons *s.* on throne, 15:12
18:27 to men who *s.* Is. 36:12
Ps. 26:5 will not *s.* with wicked
69:12 *s.* in gate speak aga. me
110:1 *s.* thou at my right hand
119:23 princes also did *s.*
127:2 vain for you to *s.* up late
Ec. 10:6 rich *s.* in low place
Is. 3:26 desolate *s.* on ground
16:5 *s.* upon the throne in truth
30:7 their strength is to *s.* still
42:7 bring them that *s.* in dark.
47:1 *s.* in dust, *s.* on grou. 52:2
5 *s.* thou silent, O daughter
14 not be a fire to *s.* before it
Jer. 8:14 why do we *s.* still ?
13:13 I will fill them that *s.*
18 say unto king, *s.* down 36:15
36:30 none to *s.* on throne of D.
48:18 come fr. glory, *s.* in thirst
Lam. 2:10 elders of Z. *s.* on gro.
Ezek. 26:16 *s.* upon the ground
28:2 said, I *s.* in seat of God
33:31 *s.* before thee as my peop.
44:3 prince shall *s.* in it to eat
Dan. 7:26 the judgment shall *s.*
Joel 3:12 *s.* to judge the heathen
Mic. 4:4 *s.* every man under vine
Zec. 3:8 thou and thy fellows *s.*
6:13 *s.* and rule upon his throne
Mat. 8:11 many sh. *s.* with Abr.
20:21 sons *s.* one on thy ri. hand
23 but to *s.* on my right hand,
Mark 10:37, 40
Mat. 23:2 Phar. *s.* in Moses' seat
26:36 *s.* ye here, Mark 14:32
Luke 9:14 *s.* by fifties in a comp.
12:37 make them to *s.* down
13:29 shall *s.* in kingdom of G.
14:8 *s.* not down in high. room
17:7 go, and *s.* down to meat
John 6:10 Je. said, Make men *s.*
Acts 2:30 Ch. to *s.* on his throne
8:31 come up and *s.* with him
1 Cor. 8:10 to see thee *s.* at meat
Jam. 2:3 *s.* th. here in good pla.
Rev. 3:21 *s.* with me in my thro.
21:7 for she saith, I *s.* a queen

SITTEST.

Ex. 18:14 why *s.* thou thyself ?
Deut. 6:7 talk of th. when thou *s.*
Ps. 50:20 thou *s.* and speakest
Prov. 23:1 *s.* to eat with a ruler
Jer. 22:2 that *s.* on the throne
Acts 23:3 *s.* thou to judge me ?

SITTETH.

Ex. 11:5 from first-born that *s.*
Lev. 15:4 ev. thing whereon he *s.*
Deut. 17:18 when he *s.* on throne
1 K. 1:46 Solomon *s.* on throne
Est. 6:10 Mordecai *s.* at gate
Ps. 1:1 nor *s.* in seat of scornful
10:8 he *s.* in the lurking places
29:10 *s.* on flood ; Lord *s.* king
47:8 G. *s.* on throne of holiness
99:1 L. *s.* betw. the cherubim
Prov. 9:14 for she *s.* at the door
20:8 king *s.* in throne of judgm.
Is. 28:6 to him that *s.* in judgm.
40:22 he that *s.* on the heavens
Jer. 29:16 saith of king that *s.*

Lam. 3:28 *s.* and keepeth silence
Zec. 2:11 behold, earth *s.* still
Mat. 23:22 swear by him that *s.*
Luke 14:28 *s.* not down first, 31
22:27 is not he that *s.* at meat ?
1 *Cor.* 14:30 if any thing be revealed to another that *s.* by
Col. 3:1 C. *s.* on right hand of G.
2 *Thes.* 2:4 G. *s.* in temp. of God
Rev. 5:13 power to him that *s.*
6:16 from face of him that *s.*
7:10 salva. to our God which *s.*

SITTING.

1 *K.* 10:5 *s.* of serv. 2 *Chr.* 9:4
13:14 man of God *s.* under oak
22:19 I saw L. *s.* upon his thro.
2 *Chr.* 18:18 ; *Is.* 6:1
2 *K.* 4:38 sons of proph. were *s.*
9:5 captains of the host were *s.*
Neh. 2:6 queen also *s.* by him
Est. 5:13 Mordecai the Jew *s.*
Ps. 139:2 knowest my down-*s.*
Jer. 17:25 king *s.* on thr. 22:4, 30
38:7 king *s.* in gate of Benjamin
Lam. 3:63 behold their *s.* down
Mat. 20:30 blind men *s.* by way
26:64 Son of man *s.* on right
hand of God, *Mark* 14:62
27:36 *s.* down, watched him
Mark 5:15 him that was poss. *s.*
16:5 they saw a young man *s.*
Lu{e} 2:46 s. in midst of doctors
8:35 and found him *s.* clothed
John 2:14 changers of money *s.*
Acts 2:2 house where th. were *s.*
Rev. 4:4 I saw twenty-four el-
ders *s.*

SITTING-PLACE.

2 *Chr.* 9:18 stays each side *s.-p.*

SITUATE.

Ezek. 27:3 art *s.* at entry of sea
Nah. 3:8 populous No th. was *s.*

SITUATION.

2 *K.* 2:19 *s.* of the city is pleasa.
Ps. 48:2 beauti. for *s.* joy of earth

SIVAN.

Est. 8:9 3d month, month of S.

SIX. *See* BRANCHES.

SIX cities.

Num. 35:6 be *s. c.* for ref. 13, 15

SIX cubits.

1 *Sam.* 17:4 Goliah's height *s. c.*
Ezek. 40:5 measuring-reed of *s. c.*
41:1 measured posts *s. c.* broad
8 foundations were *s.* great *c.*
Dan. 3:1 breadth of image *s. c.*

SIX months.

Luke 4:25 heav. was shut three
years and *s. m. Jam.* 5:17

SIX sheep.

Neh. 5:18 prep. daily *s.* choice *s.*

SIX sons.

Gen. 30:20 I have borne *s. s.*
1 *Chr.* 8:38 Azel had *s. s.* 9:44

SIX things.

Prov. 6:16 *s. t.* doth Lord hate

SIX times.

2 *K.* 13:19 ha. smitten five or *s. t.*

SIX troubles.

Job 5:19 sh. deliver thee in *s. tr.*

SIX water-pots.

John 2:6 were set there *s. wa.-p.*

SIX wings.

Is. 6:2 seraphim, each had *s. w.*
Rev. 4:8 4 beasts had each *s. w.*

SIX years.

Ex. 21:2 *s. y.* shall serve, seventh
go fr. *Deut.* 15:12 ; *Jer.* 34:14

SIXTH.

Lev. 25:21 bless. on you *s.* year
Ezr. 6:15 house finish. in *s.* year
Ezek. 4:11 drink water, *s.* part of

39:2 leave but the *s.* part of th.
Mat. 27:45 darkn. over land fr. *s.*
to ninth hour, *Mark* 15:33 ;
Luke 23:44
John 19:44 crucified about *s.* ho.
Rev. 21:20 *s.* founda. was sardius

SIXTY.

Gen. 5:15 Mahalal. lived *s.* years
21 Enoch lived *s.*-five years
Lev. 27:3 estimation fr. 20 to *s.*
Mat. 13:8 brought forth *s.* fold,
23 ; *Mark* 4:8, 20

SIZE.

Ex. 36:9 curtains were one *s.* 15
1 *K.* 7:37 bases one meas. and *s.*
1 *Chr.* 23:29 all manner of *s. Da.*

SKILL, Verb.

1 *K.* 5:6 *s.* to hew tim. 2 *Chr.* 2:8
2 *Chr.* 2:7 m. that can *s.* to grave
34:12 all that could *s.* of music

SKILL.

Ec. 9:11 nor favor to men of *s.*
Dan. 1:17 God gave them *s.*
9:22 come to give thee *s.* under.

SKILFUL.

1 *Chr.* 5:18 sons of Re. *s.* in war
15:22 instructed, bec. he was *s.*
28:21 be with thee every *s.* man
2 *Chr.* 2:14 a cunning man, *s.*
Ezek. 21:31 gi. you into ha. of *s.*
Dan. 1:4 children *s.* in all wisd.
Amos 5:16 *s.* of lamentation

SKILFULLY, NESS.

Ps. 33:3 sing new song, play *s.*
78:72 guided them by *s.* of hand

SKIN.

Ex. 22:27 his raiment for *s.*
29:14 bullock's flesh, *s. Lev.* 4:11
34:29 wist not that *s.* sho. 30, 35
Lev. 7:8 priest that offer. have *s.*
13:2 in *s.* a rising like plague
4 bright spot, white in the *s.*
11 old leprosy in *s.* of his flesh
56 sh. rend it out of gar. or *s.*
15:17 every *s.* whereon is seed
Num. 19:5 burn heifer, *s.* flesh
Job 2:4 *s.* for *s.* for all a man hath
7:5 *s.* broken, and loathsome
10:11 clo. me with *s.* and flesh
16:15 sewed sackcl. on *s.* defiled
18:13 it shall dev. strength of *s.*
19:20 bone cleaveth to my *s.* I
am esca. with *s.* of my teeth
26 after my *s.* worms des. body
30:30 *s.* black, bones are burnt
41:7 canst fill his *s.* with irons?
Ps. 102:5 my bones cleave to *s.*
Jer. 13:23 can Ethiop. change *s.* ?
Lam. 3:4 flesh and *s.* made old
4:8 *s.* cleaveth to their bones
5:10 our *s.* was black like oven
Ezek. 37:6 cover you with *s.* 8
Mic. 3:2 pluck off their *s.*
3 flay their *s.* from off them
Mark 1:6 John had a girdle of *s.*

SKINS.

Gen. 3:21 Lord made coats of *s.*
27:16 put *s.* of goats on hands
Ex. 35:23 *s.* of rams, badgers' *s.*
Lev. 13:59 law of plague of *s.*
16:27 burn in fire their *s.*
Num. 31:20 purify. rai. ma. of *s.*
Heb. 11:37 wandered in sheep *s.*

SKIP, PED, EDST.

Ps. 29:6 maketh them also to *s.*
114:4 mountains *s.* like rams, 6
Jer. 48:27 spakest, thou *s.* for joy

SKIPPING.

Cant. 2:8 cometh *s.* upon hills

SKIRT.

Deut. 22:30 not unco. father's *s.*
Ruth 3:9 spread *s.* over handma.
1 *Sam.* 15:27 he laid hold on *s.*

24:4 Da. cut off *s.* of Saul's robe
11 *s.* of thy robe in my hand
Ezek. 16:8 I sp. my *s.* over thee

Hag. 2:12 if one bear holy flesh
in *s.* and with *s.* touch bread
Zec. 8:23 10 men take hold of *s.*

SKIRTS.

Ps. 133:2 down to *s.* of garments
Jer. 2:34 in *s.* is found blood of
13:22 are thy *s.* discov. *Nah.* 3:5
Lam. 1:9 filthiness is in her *s.*
Ezek. 5:3 bind a few hairs in *s.*

SKULL.

Jud. 9:53 millsto. to break his *s.*
2 *K.* 9:35 no more of Jez. than *s.*
Mat. 27:33 Golgotha, place of a
s. Mark 15:22 ; *John* 19:17

SKY.

Deut. 33:26 rideth in excell. on *s.*
Job 37:18 hast th. spread out *s.* ?
Mat. 16:2 fair weather, *s.* red, 3
Luke 12:56 can discern face of *s.*
Heb. 11:12 many as stars of *s.*

SKIES.

2 *Sam.* 22:12 clou. of *s. Ps.* 18:11
Ps. 77:17 *s.* sent out a sound
Is. 45:8 let *s.* pour down righte.
Jer. 51:9 her judgm. lifted to *s.*

SLACK.

Deut. 7:10 he will be *s.* to him
Jos. 18:3 how long are ye *s.*
Prov. 10:4 poor deal. with *s.* ha.
Zep. 3:16 Z. let not hands be *s.*
2 *Pet.* 3:9 L. not *s.* concer. prom.

SLACK, ED.

Deut. 23:21 vow th. shalt not *s.*
Jos. 10:6 *s.* not hand from serva.
2 *K.* 4:24 *s.* not riding for me
Hab. 1:4 law *s.* judgm. never go.

SLACKNESS.

2 *Pet.* 3:9 as some men count *s.*

SLAIN, active.

Gen. 4:23 *s.* a man to my wound.
Num. 14:16 hath *s.* them in wil.
22:33 surely now I had *s.* thee
Deut. 21:1 not kno. who hath *s.*
Jud. 9:18 ha. *s.* sons upon stones
15:16 bone of an ass *s.* 1,000
1 *Sam.* 18:7 Saul *s.* thous, 21:11
22:21 Saul had *s.* Lord's priests
2 *Sam.* 1.16 I have *s.* Lord's ano.
4:11 wicked men have *s.* righte
13:30 A. hath *s.* all king's sons
21:12 Philist. had *s.* Saul in Gil.
1 *K.* 13:26 lion ha. to. and *s.* him
16:16 say, Zimri hath *s.* king
19:1 Ah. told he had *s.* prophets
10 Is. have *s.* thy prophets, 14
2 *K.* 14:5 servants who had *s.* ki.
2 *Chr.* 21:13 hast *s.* thy brethren
22:1 band of men had *s.* eldest
Est. 9:12 Jews have *s.* 500 men
Job 1:15 Sabeans have *s.* serv. 17
Prov. 7:26 strong men been *s.*
Is. 14:20 destroyed and *s.* people
Jer. 33:5 bod. of men *s.* in anger
41:4 had *s.* Gedaliah, 9, 16, 18
Lam. 2:21 *s.* th. in anger, 3:43
Ezek. 16:21 hast *s.* my children
23:39 *s.* their children to idols
Hos. 6:5 h. by words of mouth
Amos 4:10 young men have I *s.*
Acts 2:23 by wick. hands have *s.*
7:52 *s.* them th. showed coming
23:14 eat noth. till we have *s.* P.

SLAIN, passive.

Gen. 34:27 sons of Ja. came on *s.*
Lev. 26:17 be *s.* before your ene.
Num. 11:22 and the herds be *s.* ?
23:24 eat prey. drink blood of *s.*
25:14 Israelite that was *s.* Zimri
Deut. 21:1 if one be found *s.*
28:31 thine ox *s.* bef. thine eyes
Jos. 11:6 deli. them *s.* before Is.

13:22 Balaam also was among *s.*
Jud. 20:4 husband of the woman
   that was *s.*
1 *Sam.* 19:6 as L. liv. not be *s.*
  20:32 wherefore shall he be *s.*
  31:1 fell *s.* in Gilboa, 1 *Chr.* 10:1
2 *Sam.* 1:19 beauty of Israel is *s.*
  22 bl. of *s.* from fat of mighty
  25 O Jonathan, thou wast *s.* in
1 *K.* 11:15 Joab gone to bury *s.*
2 *K.* 3:23 the kings are surely *s.*
  11:8 cometh with. ranges, be *s.*
1 *Chr.* 5:22 fell down many *s.*
2 *Chr.* 13:17 fell *s.* of Isr. 500,000
Est. 7:4 for we are sold to be *s.*
Job 39:30 where *s.* are, th. is she
Ps. 62:3 ye shall be *s.* all of you
  88:5 like *s.* that lie in the grave
  89:10 hast broken Rah. as one *s.*
Prov. 22:13 sloth. sai. I shall be *s.*
  24:11 deliv. those ready to be *s.*
Is. 10:4 they shall fall under *s.*
  22:2 thy *s.* men not *s.* with sw.
Is. 26:21 earth no more cov. her *s.*
  27:7 *s.* accord. to slaughter of *s.*
  34:3 their *s.* also sh. be cast out
  66:16 *s.* of Lord shall be many
Jer. 9:1 might weep for *s.* of peo.
  14:18 go into field, beho. *s.* with
  18:21 let their young men be *s.*
  25:33 *s.* of L. be fr. end of earth
  41:9 Ishmael filled the pit wi. *s.*
  51:47 her *s.* shall fall in midst
  49 Bab. caused *s.* of Is. to fall
Lam. 2:21 priest and proph. be *s.*
  4:9 *s.* wi. sw. better than *s.* with
Ezek. 6:7 *s.* shall fall in midst
  9:7 fill courts with *s.*
  21:14 sw. of *s.* is of great men *s.*
  29 bring thee upon necks of *s.*
  26:6 her daugh. in field sh. be *s.*
  28:8 die deaths of th. that are *s.*
  30:11 shall fill land with the *s.*
  31:18 sh. lie with them *s.* 32:29
  32:20 fall in midst of the *s.* 25
  21 lie *s.* by sword, 22, 23, 24
  35:8 fill his mount. with *s.* men
  37:9 O breath. breathe on th. *s.*
Dan. 2:13 wise men should be *s.*
  5:30 in that night was Belsh. *s.*
  11:26 many shall fall down *s.*
Zep. 2:12 ye Ethiopi. shall be *s.*
Luke 9:22 Son of man must be *s.*
Acts 5:36 Theud. *s.* and as many
  7:42 ye offered to me *s.* beasts?
Eph. 2:16 cross, having *s.* enmity
Rev. 11:37 were *s.* with sword
  5:6 stood Lamb, as had been *s.*
  9 wast *s.* 12 Lamb *s.* 13:8
  6:9 souls of them that were *s.*

SLANDER, S.
Num. 14:36 by bring. a *s.* on land
Ps. 31:13 I ha. heard *s.* of many
Prov. 10:18 uttereth *s.* is a fool
Jer. 6:28 revolt. walking with *s.*
  9:4 every neighbor walk with *s.*

SLANDERED, EST, ETH.
2 *Sam.* 19:27 he hath *s.* thy serv.
Ps. 50:20 thou *s.* mother's son
  101:5 *s.* neighbor, him cut off

SLANDERERS.
1 *Tim.* 3:11 wives be grave, not *s.*

SLANDEROUSLY.
Rom. 3:8 not rather, as *s.* report.

SLANG.
1 *Sam.* 17:49 D. took sto. and *s.*

SLAUGHTER.
1 *Sam.* 14:14 first *s.* Jona. made
  30 had there not been great. *s.*
  17:57 D. returned fr. *s.* of Phili.
2 *Sam.* 17:9 is *s.* among people
Ps. 44:22 counted as sheep for *s.*
Prov. 7:22 after her, as ox to *s.*
Is. 10:26 accord. *s.* of Midian

14:21 prepare *s.* for his children
27:7 accord. to *s.* of them slain
34:2 delivered them to *s.*
53:7 bro. as lamb to *s. Jer.* 11:19
65:12 ye shall bow down to *s.*
Jer. 7:32 Toph. but val. of *s.* 19:6
  12:3 like sheep for *s.* prep. for *s.*
  25:34 days of *s.* are accomplish.
  48:15 young men are gone to *s.*
  50:27 let them go down to the *s.*
  51:40 bri. down like lambs to *s.*
Ezek. 9:2 every man a *s.* weapon
  21:10 sharpened to make sore *s.*
  28 sw. is drawn, for *s.* furbish.
  26:15 when *s.* is made in midst
Hos. 5:2 revolters profound to *s.*
Ob. 9 mount E. be cut off by *s.*
Zec. 11:4 sai. L. Feed flock of *s.*
  7 I will feed flock of *s.*
Acts 8:32 was led as a sheep to *s.*
  9:1 Saul yet breathing out *s.*
Rom. 8:36 counted as sheep for *s.*
Heb. 7:1 Abra. returning from *s.*
Jam. 5:5 hearts as in days of *s.*

See **GREAT.**

SLAVE, S.
Jer. 2:14 a serv. ? a home-born *s.* ?
Rev. 18:13 buy. merchandise of *s.*

SLAY.
Gen. 4:14 every one shall *s.* me
  20:4 wilt thou *s.* right. nation ?
  27:41 then will I *s.* brother Ja.
  34:30 gather ag. me and *s.* me
  37:20 come now, let us *s.* him
  42:37 *s.* my two sons if I bring
  43:16 bring men. *s.* make ready
Ex. 4:23 *s.* thy son first-born
  32:12 bring them out to *s.* them
Lev. 4:29 *s.* sin-off. 14:13 *s.* lamb
Num. 25:5 *s.* ye ev. one his men
Deut. 19:6 avenger pursue and *s.*
Jos. 13:22 Israel did *s.* Balaam
Jud. 8:20 said to J. Up, *s.* them
  9:54 *s.* me, that men say not
1 *Sam.* 2:25 Sec. L. would *s.* them
  14:34 bring ev. man ox, *s.* here
  19:15 bri. him that I may *s.* him
  20:8 if in me iniq. *s.* me thyself
  22:17 said, Turn and *s.* priests
2 *Sam.* 1:9 Sa. said, Stand and *s.*
1 *K.* 1:51 swear he will not *s.*
  18:12 cannot find thee, sh. *s.* me
  20:36 departed, lion *s.* thee
2 *K.* 8:12 young men wilt thou *s.*
  10:25 go in and *s.* them
  17:26 God sent lions, they *s.*
2 *Chr.* 23:14 *s.* her not in ho. of L.
Neh. 4:11 we will *s.* them, cause
Job 9:23 if scourge *s.* suddenly
  13:15 though he *s.* me yet will I
Ps. 34:21 evil shall *s.* wicked
  59:11 *s.* them not, lest my peop.
  94:6 they *s.* widow and stranger
  109:16 might *s.* broken in heart
  139:19 thou wilt *s.* wick. O God
Prov. 1:32 turn. of simple sh. *s.*
Is. 11:4 with breath shall he *s.*
  14:30 he shall *s.* thy remnant
  27:1 Lord shall *s.* the dragon
  65:15 for Lord God shall *s.* thee
Jer. 5:6 lion of forest sh. *s.* them
  20:4 carry Judah capti. *s.* them
  29:21 shall *s.* Ahab and Zedek.
  41:8 men fo. that said, *s.* us not
Ezek. 9:6 *s.* utter. old and young
  23:47 sh. *s.* sons and daughters
  26:8 he shall *s.* thy daughters
Hos. 2:3 *s.* her with thirst
  9:16 yet will I *s.* the fruit
Amos 2:3 I will *s.* the last of them
  9:1 I will *s.* all princes
Zec. 11:5 whose posses. *s.* them
Luke 11:49 some they shall *s.*
  19:27 bring hither, and *s.* them

To SLAY.
Gen. 18:25 far fr. thee *to s.* right.

22:10 Abra. stretched hand *to s.*
37:18 they conspired *to s.* him
Ex. 2:15 Ph. sought *to s.* Moses
  2:14 if come on neighbor *to s*
Deut. 9:28 brou. out *to s.* them
  27:25 taketh reward *to s.* inno.
1 *Sam.* 5:10 brou. the ark *to s.* us
  19:5 why then sin, *to s.* David ?
  11 S. went to watch and *s.* him
2 *Sam.* 3:37 not of king *to s.* Ab.
  21:2 Saul sought *to s.* them
1 *K.* 17:18 art come *to s.* my son ?
  18:9 deliv. me to Ahab *to s.* me
2 *Chr.* 20:23 utterly *to s.* and des.
Neh. 6:10 *to s.* th. in night *to s.*
Ps. 37:14 *to s.* such as be upright
  32 watcheth righte. seek. *to s.*
Jer. 15:3 appoint sw. *to s.* dogs
  18:23 know. their counsel *to s.*
Ezek. 13:19 *to s.* souls th. should
John 5:16 Jews, sou. *to s.* him
Acts 5:33 took counsel *to s.* apos.
  9:29 they went about *to s.* him
Rev. 9:15 prep. *to s.* third part

SLAYER.
Num. 35:11 cities of refuge th. *s.*
  Deut. 4:42 ; 19:3, 4 ; *Jos.* 20:3
  28 after death of high-priest *s.*
    shall return, *Jos.* 20:6
Deut. 19:6 lest avenger pursue *s.*
Jos. 20:5 shall not deliver the *s*
  21:13 Hebron city of ref. for *s.*
  21 Shech. 27 Golan a ref. for *s.*
  32 Kedesh in Galilee for the *s.*
  38 Ramoth in Gil. refuge for *s.*
Ezek. 21:11 sw. to be given to *s.*

SLAYETH.
Gen. 4:15 Lord said, Whoso. *s.* C.
Deut. 22:26 neighbor, and *s.* him
Job 5:2 wrath killeth, envy *s.*
Ezek. 28:9 bef. him that *s.* thee, I
  am G. ? in hand of him th. *s.*

SLAYING.
Jos. 8:24 Is. made end of *s.* 10:20
Jud. 9:56 G. rendered wick. in *s.*
1 *K.* 17:20 evil on wid. by *s.* son
Is. 57:5 *s.* children in the valleys
Ezek. 9:8 while th. were *s.* them

SLEEP, Substantive.
Gen. 2:21 God caused a *s.* on Ad.
  15:12 a deep *s.* fell on Abram
  28:16 Jacob awaked out of *s.*
  31:40 *s.* departed fr. mine eyes
Jud. 16:14 S. awaked out of *s.* 20
1 *Sam.* 26:12 a deep *s.* from God
Job 4:13 when deep *s.* fall. 33:15
  14:12 nor raised out of their *s.*
Ps. 13:3 lest I *s.* the *s.* of death
  76:5 stout-hearted slept their *s.*
  6 chari. and horse cast into *s.*
  78:65 Lord awaked us out of *s.*
Ps. 90:5 them away, th. are as a *s.*
  127:2 so he giveth his belov. *s.*
  132:4 I will not give *s.* to eyes
Prov. 3:24 lie down, *s.* be sweet
  4:16 their *s.* is taken away
  6:4 give not *s.* to thine eyes
  9 wh. wilt thou arise out of *s.* ?
  10 a little more *s.* 24:33
  19:15 slothfuln. casteth into *s.*
  20:13 love not *s.* lest co. to pov.
Ec. 5:12 the *s.* of laboring man
  8:16 nei. day nor night seeth *s.*
Is. 29:10 L. pour. on you deep *s.*
Jer. 31:26 my *s.* as sweet to me
  51:39 may sleep a perpet. *s.* 57
Dan. 2:1 his *s.* brake from him
  6:18 passed night his *s.* went fr.
  8:18 I was in deep *s.* 10:9
Zec. 4:1 man wakened out of *s.*
Mat. 1:24 J. being raised from *s.*
Luke 9:32 were heavy with *s.*
John 11:11 awake him out of *s.*
  13 spoken of taking rest in *s.*
Acts 16:27 keeper awak. out of *s.*
  20:9 Euty. being fallen into *s.*
Rom. 13:11 to awake out of *s.*

SLEEP, Verb.

Gen. 28:11 Jacob lay down to *s.*
Ex. 22:27 wherein shall he *s. ?*
Deut. 24:12 not *s.* with his pledge
31:16 *s.* with fath. 2 *Sam.* 7:12
Jud. 16:19 ma. him *s.* on her kn.
1 *Sam.* 3:3 Sam. laid down to *s.*
1 *K.* 1:21 lord the king shall *s.*
Est. 6:1 night could not king *s.*
Job 7:21 now sh. I *s.* in the dust
Ps. 4:8 will lay me down and *s.*
121:4 shall nei. slumber nor *s.*
Prov. 4:16 they *s.* not except
6:9 how long wilt th. *s.* O sing. ?
10 folding of hands to *s.* 24:33
Ec. 5:12 *s.* of lab. man is sweet,
abund. of rich not suffer *s.*
Cant. 5:2 I *s.* but my heart wak.
Is. 5:27 none sh. slumber nor *s.*
Jer. 51:39 may *s.* perp. sleep, 57
Ezek. 34:25 they shall *s.* in woods
Dan. 12:2 many that *s.* in dust
Mat. 26:45 on now, *Mark* 14:41
Mark 4:27 sho. *s.* and seed spri.
Luke 22:46 why *s.* ye ? rise
John 11:12 if he *s.* he sh. do well
1 *Cor.* 11:30 for th. cause many *s.*
15:51 we shall not all *s.*
1 *Thes.* 4:14 who *s.* in Je. will G.
5:6 let us not *s.* as do others
7 they that *s. s.* in the night
10 that whether we wake or *s.*

SLEEPER.

Jon. 1:6 what mean. thou, O *s.*

SLEEPEST.

Ps. 44:23 why *s.* thou, O Lord
Prov. 6:22 wh. thou *s.* it sh. keep
Mark 14:37 Simon, *s.* thou ?
Eph. 5:14 awake, thou that *s.*

SLEEPETH.

1 *K.* 18:27 said. Peradvent. he *s.*
Prov. 10:5 he that *s.* in harvest.
Hos. 7:6 their baker *s.* all night
Mat. 9:24 maid is not dead but
s. Mark 5:39; *Luke* 8:52
John 11:11 our friend Lazarus *s.*

SLEEPING.

1 *Sam.* 26:7 S. lay *s.* with trench
Is. 56:10 blind, *s.* loving slumber
Mark 13:36 lest com. find you *s.*
14:37 cometh and find. them *s.*
Acts 12:6 Peter was *s.* betw. two

SLEIGHT.

Eph. 4:14 carried by *s.* of men

SLEPT.

Gen. 2:21 Adam *s.* 41:5 Phara. *s.*
2 *Sam.* 11:9 Uriah *s.* at door of
1 *K.* 3:20 while thy handmaid *s.*
19:5 as he lay and *s.* an angel
Job 3:13 ha. been quiet and ha. *s.*
Ps. 3:5 I laid me down and *s.*
Mat. 13:25 while men *s.* his ene.
25:5 bridegroom tarried, they *s.*
27:52 bod. of saints wh. *s.* arose
28:13 disciples stole while we *s.*
1 *Cor.* 15:20 first-fruits of that *s.*

See FATHERS.

SLEW.

Gen. 34:25 *s.* males ; 26 *s.* Hamor
49:6 in their anger th. *s.* a man
Ex. 2:12 Moses *s.* the Egyptian
13:15 Lord *s.* all first-born in E.
Num. 31:7 they *s.* males of Mid.
8 *s.* kings of Mid. Bala. they *s.*
Jud. 1:4 they *s.* in Bezek 10,000
3:29 they *s.* of Moab 10,000 men
31 Shamgar *s.* of Phil. 600 men
7:25 they *s.* Oreb and Zeeb two
Jud. 9:5 Abim. *s.* breth. 70 pers.
14:19 Samson *s.* 30 men of As.
15:15 jaw-bone Samson *s.* 1,000
16:30 dead which he *s.* at death
1 *Sam.* 14:34 brou. his ox and *s.*
17:36 thy servant *s.* both lion

19:5 life in hand and *s.* Philist.
22:18 Doeg *s.* 85 persons that
29:5 sang. Saul *s.* thousands
2 *Sam.* 4:12 Da. *s.* them and cut
8:5 David *s.* of Syrians 22,000
21:1 because he *s.* Gibeonites
23:20 *s.* two lion-like men of
M. he *s.* a lion, 1 *Chr.* 11:22
1 *K.* 18:13 Jeze. *s.* prophets of L.
40 Elijah *s.* prophets of Baal
2 *K.* 9:31 peace, who *s.* master ?
10:9 I *s.* him, but who *s.* these ?
11:18 people *s.* Mat. priest of B.
14:6 chil. he *s.* not, 2 *Chr.* 25:4
7 he *s.* of Edom, 1 *Chr.* 18:12
17:25 L. sent lions wh. *s.* some
23:20 Jos. *s.* all the priests of
1 *Chr.* 7:21 men of Ga. in land *s.*
2 *Chr.* 21:4 Jehoram *s.* his breth.
Neh. 9:26 they *s.* thy prophets
Est. 9:16 Jews *s.* of foes 75,000
Ps. 78:31 God *s.* fattest of them
34 when he *s.* them, then they
105:29 into blood, *s.* their fish
135:10 *s.* great ; 136:18 *s.* kings
Is. 66:3 an ox as if he *s.* a man
Jer. 20:17 because he *s.* me not
41:3 Ishmael *s.* all the Jews
8 *s.* them not among brethren
Lam. 2:4 *s.* all that were pleas.
Dan. 3:22 fire *s.* men that took
5:19 whom he would he *s.*
Mat. 2:16 Herod sent, *s.* children
22:6 took his serv. and *s.* them
23:35 whom ye *s.* betw. temple
Luke 13:4 tower in Sil. fell and *s.*
Acts 5:30 Je. whom *s.* and hang.
10:39 Je. whom they *s.* and han.
Rom. 7:11 commandment *s.* me
1 *John* 3:12 C. who *s.* his brother

SLEW him.

Gen. 4:8 C. rose ag. Abel and *s. h.*
38:7 Er was wicked, Lord *s. h.*
Jud. 9:54 say not, A wom. *s. him*
12:6 took and *s. h.* at passages
1 *Sam.* 17:35 I can. him and *s. h.*
2 *Sam.* 1:10 stood upon and *s. h.*
4:7 smote Ish-bosheth and *s. h.*
18:15 compassed Absalom *s. h.*
1 *K.* 13:24 lion met and *s. h.* 20:36
2 *K.* 10:9 I conspired and *s. him*
15:10 Shall. conspired and *s. h.*
1 *Chr.* 10:14 therefore *s.* he *him*
2 *Chr.* 22:11 Athaliah *s. him* not
24:25 his own servants *s. him*
32:21 came of his bowels *s. h.*
33:24 his serv. *s. him* in house
Jer. 41:2 Ishm. *s. h.* whom king
Mat. 21:39 cast out of vine. *s. h.*
Acts 22:20 raim. of th. that *s. h.*

SLEWEST.

1 *Sam.* 21:9 sword of Goli. th. *s.*

SLIDE, ETH.

Deut. 32:35 foot sh. *s.* in due time
Ps. 26:1 trusted in L. I sh. not *s.*
37:31 none of nis steps shall *s.*
Hos. 4:16 Is. *s.* as backslid. heifer

SLIDDEN.

Jer. 8:5 why peo. of Jer. *s.* back

SLIGHTLY.

Jer. 6:14 healed my peo. *s.* 8:11

SLIME.

Gen. 11:3 brick for st. *s.* for mor.
Ex. 2:3 she daubed ark with *s.*

SLIME-PITS.

Gen. 14:10 Sid. was full of *s.-p.*

SLING, Verb.

Jud. 20:16 ev. one could *s.* stones
1 *Sam.* 25:29 them shall he *s.* out
Jer. 10:18 *s.* out inhabit. at once

SLING, S.

1 *Sam.* 17:40 Da. had *s.* in hand
50 David prevailed with a *s.*
25:29 sling enem. as out of a *s.*
2 *Chr.* 26:14 Uzziah prepared *s.*

Prov. 26:8 bindeth stone in a *s.*

SLINGERS.

2 *K.* 3:25 *s.* went about it, smote

SLING-STONES.

Job 41:28 *s.* turned into stubble

SLIP, PETH.

Deut. 19:5 head *s.* from helve
2 *Sam.* 22:37 feet not *s. Ps.* 18:36
Job 12:5 he that is ready to *s.*
Ps. 17:5 that my footst. *s.* nor
38:16 wh. foot *s.* they magnify
94:18 foot *s.* mercy held me up
Heb. 2:1 lest we sho. let them *s.*

SLIPPED.

1 *Sam.* 19:10 D. *s.* out of S.'s pre.
Ps. 73:2 steps had well nigh *s.*

SLIPPERY.

Ps. 35:6 let their way be dark, *s.*
73:18 didst set them in *s.* places
Jer. 23:12 th. way be to them *s.*

SLIPS.

Is. 17:10 thou shalt set it with *s.*

SLOTHFUL.

Jud. 18:9 be not *s.* to poss. land
Prov. 12:24 *s.* shall be under tri.
27 *s.* roast. not he took hunti.
15:19 way of *s.* is as a hedge
18:9 *s.* is broth. to great waster
19:24 *s.* hid. hand in bos. 26:15
21:25 desire of *s.* killeth him
22:13 *s.* saith, Th. is a lion, 26:13
24:30 went by field of *s.* viney.
Mat. 25:26 wicked and *s.* servant
Rom. 12:11 not *s.* in business
Heb. 6:12 ye be not *s.* but follow.

SLOTHFULNESS.

Prov. 19:15 *s.* cast. into deep sle.
Ec. 10:18 by *s.* building decayeth

SLOW.

Ex. 4:10 *s.* of speech, of *s.* tong.
Neh. 9:17 thou art G. *s.* to anger
Prov. 14:29 *s.* to wrath, of great
Luke 24:25 O fools, *s.* of heart
Tit. 1:12 Cretians liars, *s.* bellies
Jam. 1:19 *s.* to speak, *s.* to wrath

See ANGER.

SLOWLY.

Acts 27:7 had sailed *s.* many days

SLUGGARD.

Prov. 6:6 go to the ant, thou *s.*
9 how long wilt th. sleep, O *s.*
10:26 smoke to eyes, so *s.* to th.
13:4 the soul of *s.* desireth
20:4 the *s.* will not plough
26:16 *s.* wiser in own conceit

SLUICES.

Is. 19:10 th. make *s.* and ponds

SLUMBER, Substantive.

Ps. 132:4 not give *s.* to eyelids
Prov. 6:4 eyes, nor *s.* to eyelids
10 a little sleep, a little *s.* 24:33
Rom. 11:8 G. hath given them *s.*

SLUMBER, ED, ETH.

Ps. 121:3 that keep. will not *s.* 4
Is. 5:27 none shall *s.* nor sleep
56:10 watchm. lying, lov. to *s.*
Nah. 3:18 thy shepherds *s.* O
king
Mat. 25:5 bridegroom tar. th. *s.*
2 *Pet.* 2:3 their damnation *s.* not

SLUMBERINGS.

Job 33:15 God speak. in *s.* on bed

SMALL.

Gen. 30:15 is it *s.* matter that th.
Ex. 16:14 *s.* thi. *s.* as hoarfrost
Num. 16:13 is it *s.* thing th. hast
2 *Sam.* 7:19 a *s.* thing in thy
sight, O Lord, 1 *Chr.* 17.17
22:43 beat. *s.* as dust, *Ps.* 18:42
1 *K.* 19:12 after fire, still *s.* voice
Is. 7:13 is it *s.* th. to weary men?
60:22 a *s.* one sh. bec. a nation

Jer. 30:19 and they sh. not be *s.*
49:15 make thee *s.* am. heathen
Amos. 7:2 Ja. arise ? for he is *s.* 5
Ob. 2 made thee *s.* am. heathen
Zec. 4:10 desp. day of *s.* things ?

See GREAT.

SMALLEST.

1 *Sam.* 9:21 Benja. of *s.* tribes ?

SMART.

Prov. 11:15 surety for str. sh. *s.*

SMELL, Substantive.

Gen. 27:27 Is. smelled *s.* of raim.
  s. of my son is as *s.* of a field
Cant. 2:13 tender grape give *s.*
4:10 *s.* of oint. better th. spices
  11 *s.* of garm. like *s.* of Leban.
7:8 *s.* of thy nose like apples
Is. 3:24 instead of sweet *s.* stink
Dan. 3:27 nor *s.* of fire passed on
Hos. 14:6 his *s.* as Lebanon
Phil. 4:18 sent an od. of sweet *s.*

SMELL, Verb.

Ex. 30:38 make like to that to *s.*
Lev. 26:31 will not *s.* your odors
Deut. 4:28 wh. neither see nor *s.*
Ps. 45:8 garments *s.* of myrrh
115:6 noses have they, *s.* not
Amos 5:21 not *s.* in your assem.

SMELLED, ETH.

Gen. 8:21 Lord *s.* a sweet savor
27:27 Isaac *s.* raim. blessed him
Job 39:25 he *s.* the battle afar off

SMELLING.

Cant. 5:5 fing. with *s.* myrrh, 13
Eph. 5:2 sacrifi. to G. for *s.* sav.

SMELLING, Substantive

1 *Cor.* 12:17 hear. where were *s. ?*

SMITE.

Gen. 32:8 to one comp. and *s.* it
Ex. 7:17 I will *s.* upon waters
12:23 not suffer destroyer to *s.*
17:6 thou shalt *s.* rock in Horeb
21:18 if men strive, one *s.* ano.
  26 if a man *s.* eye of servant
Num. 22:6 prev. that we *s.* them
24:17 sceptre out of Is. *s.* them
25:17 vex Midianites, *s.* them
35:16 if he *s.* him with instrum.
  18 if he *s.* him wi. hand-weap.
Deut. 7:2 shalt *s.* Canaanites
13:15 shalt surely *s.* inhabitants
20:13 thou shalt *s.* every male
Jud. 6:16 thou sh. *s.* Midianites
20:31 then Benj. began to *s.* 39
1 *Sam.* 17:46 I will *s.* thee
18:11 Saul said, I will *s.* David
20:33 Saul cast javelin to *s.* him
23:2 *s.* Philistines ? Go, *s.* Phil.
26:8 let me *s.* him to earth
2 *Sam.* 2:22 why sho. I *s.* thee ?
13:28 when I say, *s.* Amnon
15:14 lest he *s.* city with sword
17:2 and I will *s.* the king only
18:11 said, Why not *s.* him th. ?
1 *K.* 20:35 in word of the L. *s.* me
2 *K.* 3:19 shall *s.* ev. fenced city
6:21 sh. I *s.* them ? sh. I *s.* th. ?
9:7 thou shalt *s.* house of Ahab
  27 Jehu said, *s.* him in the
13:17 sh. *s.* Syri. till consumed
  18 said to king, *s.* upon ground
Ps. 121:6 sun not *s.* thee by day
141:5 let righte. *s.* it be kindn.
Prov. 19:25 *s.* a scorner
Is. 10:24 shall *s.* thee with rod
49:10 nei. heat nor sun *s.* them
58:4 fast to *s.* with fist of wick.
Jer. 18:18 let us *s.* him wi. tong.
43:11 shall *s.* land of Eg. 46:13
Ezek. 5:2 part of hair, *s.* about
6:11 *s.* wi. hand. stamp wi. foot
21:12 son of man, *s.* on thy thi.
  14 prophesy, *s.* hands together
Amos 9:1 he said, *s.* lintel of do.

Mic. 5:1 they shall *s.* judge of Is.
Nah. 2:10 the knees *s.* together
Zec. 10:11 *s.* the waves in sea
11:6 deliv. men, they shall *s.* la.
Mat. 5:39 wh. sh. *s.* th. on cheek
24:49 begin to *s.* his fellow-serv.
Luke 22:49 Lord, shall we *s.* with
  the sword ?
Acts 23:2 commanded to *s.* Paul
2 *Cor.* 11:20 man *s.* you on face
Rev. 11:6 witne. hav. pow. to *s.*

SMITE, *referred* to God.

Gen. 8:21 nor will I *s.* any more
Ex. 3:20 stretch hand, and *s.* E.
9:15 I may *s.* thee and people
12:12 I will *s.* first-born in Eg.
Num. 14:12 *s.* them with pestil.
Deut. 28:35 L. *s.* thee in knees
33:11 *s.* through loins
1 *Sam.* 26:10 Da. said, L. shall *s.*
2 *Sam.* 5:24 shall Lord go to *s.*
  Philistines, 1 *Chr.* 14:15
1 *K.* 14:15 L. shall *s.* Is. as a reed
2 *K.* 6:18 *s.* this people wi. blin.
2 *Chr.* 21:14 wi. plague will L. *s.*
Is. 11:4 *s.* earth with rod of mou.
  15 the Lord shall *s.* Egypt in
  the seven streams, 19:22
Jer. 21:6 I will *s.* inhabit. of city
Ezek. 21:17 I will *s.* hands toge.
32:15 I *s.* th. that dwell in Egy.
39:3 *s.* thy bow out of hand
Amos 3:15 I will *s.* winter-house
6:11 Lord will *s.* great house
Zec. 9:4 L. will *s.* her power
12:4 I will *s.* ev. horse and rider
13:7 awake, O sword, *s.* Sheph.
  Mat. 26:31 ; *Mark* 14:27
14:12 plague wherewith L. *s.*
Mal. 4:6 lest I *s.* earth wi. a cur.
Rev. 19:15 with it sho. *s.* nations

SMITERS.

Is. 50:6 I gave my back to the *s.*

SMITEST, ETH.

Ex. 2:13 wheref. *s.* thy fellow ?
  21:12 *s.* man so he die
  15 *s.* fath. or moth. put to dea.
Deut. 25:11 wife to deliver husb.
  out of hand of him th. *s.* him
27:24 cursed that *s.* his neighb.
Job 26:12 by understanding he *s.*
Is. 9:13 turn not to him that *s.*
Lam. 3:30 cheek to him that *s.*
Ezek. 7:9 kn. that I am L. that *s.*

Luke 6:29 *s.* thee on one cheek
John 18:23 why *s.* thou me ?

SMITH.

1 *Sam.* 13:19 no *s.* found in Isra.
Is. 44:12 *s.* with tongs worketh
54:16 I created *s.* bloweth coals

SMITHS.

2 *K.* 24:14 Nebuchadnez. carried
  away *s.* 16 ; *Jer.* 24:1
Jer. 29:2 *s.* were departed fr. Jer.

SMITING.

Ex. 2:11 Egyptian *s.* a Hebrew
1 *K.* 20:37 so in *s.* wounded him
2 *K.* 3:24 went forward *s.* Moab
Mic. 6:13 make thee sick in *s.*

SMITTEN.

Ex. 7:25 after Lord had *s.* river
22:2 if thief be found, and be *s.*
Num. 14:42 go not up that ye be
  not *s. Deut.* 1:42
22:32 wherefore hast th. *s.* ass
33:4 buried first-born L. had *s.*
Deut. 28:7 cause enemies be *s.*
  25 L. cause th. be *s.* bef. enem.
Jud. 20:36 men *s.* 39 they are *s.*
1 *Sam.* 4:2 Is. *s.* bef. Philist. 10
3 why hath L. *s.* us bef. Phil. ?
6:19 lamented bec. L. *s.* many
30:1 Amalek had *s.* Ziklag
2 *Sam.* 2:31 had *s.* of Ab.'s men
11:15 that ye may be *s.*

1 *K.* 8:33 when people of Is. be *s.*
11:15 after he had *s.* ev. male
2 *K.* 2:14 when he had *s.* waters
3:23 kings have *s.* one another
14:10 hast *s.* Ed. 2 *Chr.* 25:19
2 *Chr.* 20:22 M. and Seir were *s.*
25:16 why should. thou be *s. ?*
26:20 because L. had *s.* him
Job 16:10 have *s.* me on cheek
Ps. 3:7 hast *s.* mine enemies
69:26 persec. him thou hast *s.*
102:4 my heart is *s.* withered
143:3 hath *s.* my life to ground
Is. 5:25 the L. hath *s.* his people
24:12 gate is *s.* with destruction
27:7 hath he *s.* him, as smo. th.
53:4 est. him stricken, *s.* of God
Jer. 2:30 in vain ha. I *s.* children
14:19 why hast thou *s.* us
Ezek. 22:13 I have *s.* my hand at
33:21 came, saying, City is *s.*
Hos. 6:1 he hath *s.* will bind up
9:16 Ephraim is *s.* root dried
Amos 4:9 *s.* you, ha. not return.
Acts 23:3 commanded me to be *s.*
Rev. 8:12 third part of sun was *s.*

SMOKE, Substantive.

Gen. 19:28 *s.* of co. went up as *s.*
Ex. 19:18 mount Sin. was on *s.*
Jos. 8:20 *s.* of Ai ascended up, 21
Jud. 20:38 ma. *s.* rise out of city
2 *Sam.* 22:9 there went up a *s.*
  out of his nostrils, *Ps.* 18:8
Job 41:20 out of his nostr. go. *s.*
Ps. 37:20 wicked consu. into *s.*
68:2 as *s.* is driven away
102:3 my days are consu. like *s.*
119:83 I am bec. like bottle in *s.*
Prov. 10·26 as *s.* to eyes, so slug.
Cant. 3 6 com. like pillars of *s.*
Is. 4:5 on her assemb. *s.* by day
6:4 the house was filled with *s.*
9:18 mount like lifting up of *s.*
14:31 shall come from north *s.*
34:10 *s.* thereof shall go up
51:6 heavens sh. vanish like *s.*
65:5 th. are as *s.* in my nose
Hos. 13.3 as *s.* out of chimney
Joel 2:30 fire, and pillars of *s.*
Nah. 2:13 burn her chariots in *s.*
Acts 2:19 fire, and vapor of *s.*
Rev. 8.4 *s.* of incense ascended
9:2 arose *s.* out of bottoml. pit
  3 came out of *s.* locu. on earth
17 out of mouth iss. fire and *s.*
18 3d part of men killed by *s.*
14:11 *s.* of their torment ascend.
15:8 temple was filled with *s.*
18:9 lament for her when see *s.*
18 they saw *s.* of her burning
19:3 and her *s.* rose up for ever

SMOKE.

Deut. 29:20 anger of Lord sh. *s.*
Ps. 74:1 G. why thine anger *s. ?*
104:32 toucheth hills, they *s.*
144:5 touch mountains, they *s.*

SMOKING.

Gen. 15:17 behold, a *s.* furnace
Ex. 20:18 peo. saw mountain *s.*
Is. 7:4 tails of th. *s.* firebrands
42:3 *s.* flax not que. *Mat.* 12:20

SMOOTH, ER.

Gen. 27:11 E. hairy, I am *s.* man
  16 skins of kids on *s.* of neck

1 *Sam.* 17:40 Da. chose 5 *s.* ston.
Ps. 55:21 words were *s.* th. butter
Prov. 5:3 her mouth is *s.* th. oil
Is. 30:10 speak unto us *s.* things
57:6 among *s.* stones of stream
Luke 3:5 rough ways be made *s.*

SMOOTHETH.

Is. 41:7 he that *s.* with hammer

SMOTE.

Gen. 19:11 *s.* men with blindness

Ex. 7:20 lift up rod, *s.* waters
12:27 when he *s.* the Egyptians
29 L. *s.* first-born in land of
Egypt, *Num.* 3:13 ; 8:17 ; *Ps.*
78:51 ; 105;36 ; 135:8
Num. 11:33 L. *s.* peo. wi. plague
20:11 Moses *s.* rock, *Ps.* 78:20
22:23 Balaam *s.* the ass, 25, 27
24:10 Balak *s.* his hands togeth.
32:4 the country the Lord *s.*
Jos. 9:18 *s.* th. not, bec. princes
11:12 *s.* all kings with sword, 17
20:5 *s.* his neighbor unwittingly
Jud. 4:21 *s.* nail into temples
5:26 *s.* Sisera, *s.* off his head
7:13 came and *s.* it that it fell
20:35 L. *s.* Benjamin before Isr.
1 Sam. 4:8 gods th. *s.* Egyptians
6:9 it is not his hand that *s.* us
17:49 Da. *s.* Philist. in forehead
25:38 Lord *s.* Nabal that he died
2 Sam. 14:7 him that *s.* his brot.
2 K. 2:8 Eli. *s.* waters ; 14 Elis. *s.*
6:18 he *s.* them with blindness
15:5 L. *s.* king, he was a leper
19:35 angel *s.* 185,000, *Is.* 37:36
2 Chr. 14:12 L. *s.* Ethiopians
Neh. 13:25 *s.* certain of them
Ps. 78:31 *s.* down chosen of Isra.
66 *s.* enemies in hinder parts
Cant. 5:7 watchmen, they *s.* me
Is. 10:20 no more stay on him *s.*
14:6 who *s.* people is persecut.
29 rod of him that *s.* thee is b.
30:31 Assyr. beaten down wh. *s.*
41:7 encoura. him that *s.* anvil
60:10 in my wrath I *s.* thee
Jer. 20:2 Pashur *s.* Jeremiah
31:19 after I was instructed I *s.*
Dan. 2:34 which *s.* the image, 35
5:6 Belshazzar's knees *s.* one a.
Hag. 2:17 I *s.* you with blasting
Mat. 26:51 Peter *s.* off his ear
68 who is he *s.* thee, *Lu.* 22:64
Luke 18:13 publican *s.* his breast
23:48 beholding Je. *s.* th. brea.
Acts 12:7 angel *s.* Peter on side

SMOTE him.
Ex. 21:19 he that *s. h.* be quit
Num. 35:21 he that *s. h.* sh. die
1 Sam. 24:5 David's heart *s. h.*
2 Sam. 2:23 *s. him* under fifth
rib, 3:27 ; 4:6
6:7 God *s. him* there for his error, 1 *Chr.* 13:10
1 K. 20:37 *s. h.* he wounded him
2 K. 19:37 his sons *s. him* with
sword, *Is.* 37:38
Is. 27:7 smote those that *s. h.* ?
57:17 for his coveteousn. I *s. h.*
Jer. 37:15 wroth with J. and *s. h.*
Mat. 26:67 *s. h.* with the hands
27:30 *s. h.* on head, *Mark* 15:19 ;
Luke 22:63 ; *John* 19:3
Acts 12:23 angel of Lord *s. him*

SMOTEST.
Ex. 17:5 wherew. thou *s.* river

SMYRNA.
Rev. 1:11 send to church in S.
2:8 to angel of church in S.

SNAIL.
Lev. 11:30 *s.* and mole unclean
Ps. 58:8 as a *s.* let ev. one pass

SNARE.
Ex. 10:7 how long th. man be *s.* ?
23:33 it will surely be *s.* unto
thee, *Deut.* 7:16 ; *Jud.* 2:3
34:12 no covenant, lest it be a *s.*
Jud. 8:27 bec. a *s.* unto Gideon
1 Sam. 18:21 that she may be a *s.*
28:9 layest thou a *s.* for my life ?
Job 18:8 a net, he walketh on a *s.*
10 the *s.* is laid for him in a tr.
Ps. 69:22 let their table become
a *s.* unto them, *Rom.* 11:9
91:3 deliver thee fr. *s.* of fowler

106:36 idols, wh. were *s.* to th.
119:110 wicked have laid *s.*
124:7 escaped as a bird out of *s.*
of fowler ; *s.* is broken
140:5 proud have hid a *s.* for me
141:9 keep me from the *s.* laid
142:3 they privily laid *s.* for me
Prov. 7:23 as a bird hasteth to *s.*
18:7 fool's lips are *s.* of his soul
Prov. 20:25 *s.* to man who devo.
22:25 and get a *s.* to thy soul
29:6 transgress. of evil man is *s.*
8 scorn. men br. a city into *s.*
25 fear of man bringeth a *s.*
Ec. 9:12 as birds caught in the *s.*
Is. 8:14 for a *s.* to inhabitants
24:17 pit, and the *s.* are upon
thee, 18 ; *Jer.* 48:43, 44
29:21 *s.* for him that reproveth
Jer. 50:24 I ha. laid a *s.* for thee
Lam. 3:47 a *s.* is come upon us
Ezek. 12:13 taken in my *s.* 17:20
Hos. 5:1 bec. ye have been a *s.*
9:8 the prophet is *s.* of fowler
Amos 3:5 can bird fall in a *s.* wh.
no gin is ? sh. one take up *s.* ?
Luke 21:35 as a *s.* shall it come
4 Cor. 7:35 not th. I may cast *s.*
1 Tim. 3:7 lest he fall in *s.*
6:8 rich, fall into a *s.* and lusts
2 Tim. 2:26 may recover out of *s.*

SNARED.
Deut. 7:25 not take idols, lest *s.*
12:30 take heed thou be not *s.*
Ps. 9:16 *s.* in work of hands
Prov. 6:2 *s.* with words, 12:13
Ec. 9:12 so are sons of men *s.*
Is. 8:15 many shall fall and be *s.*
28:13 they might fall, and be *s.*
42:22 they are all of them *s.*

SNARES.
Jos. 23:13 *s.* and traps unto you
2 Sam. 22:6 *s.* of death prevented
me, *Ps.* 18:5
Job 22:10 *s.* are round about thee
40:24 Behemoth's nose pierc. *s.*
Ps. 11:6 on wicked he sh. rain *s.*
38:12 seek my life, lay *s.* for me
64:5 commune of laying *s.* priv.
Prov. 13:14 *s.* of death, 14:27
22:5 thorns and *s.* are in way
Ec. 7:26 woman wh. heart is *s.*
Jer. 5:26 as he that setteth *s.*
18:22 for they hid *s.* for my feet

SNATCH.
Is. 9:20 he shall *s.* on right hand

SNEEZED.
2 K. 4:35 child *s.* seven times

SNORTING.
Jer. 8:16 *s.* of horses was heard

SNOUT.
Prov. 11:22 jewel in swine's *s.*

SNOW.
Ex. 4:6 hand was leprous as *s.*
Num. 12:10 Miriam became as *s.*
2 Sam. 23:20 sl. lion in time of *s.*
2 K. 5:27 Gehazi went whi. as *s.*
Job 6:16 and wherein the. is hid
9:30 if I wash myself in *s.* water
24:19 heat consumeth *s.* waters
37:6 saith to *s.* Be thou on earth
38:22 entered into treasures of *s.*
Ps. 51:7 I shall be whiter than *s.*
68:14 it was white as *s.* in Sal.
147:16 he giveth *s.* like wool
148:8 fire, hail, *s.* and vapor
Prov. 25:13 as cold of *s.* in harv.
26:1 as *s.* in summer, so honor
31:21 she is not afraid of the *s.*
Is. 1:18 sins as scar. white as *s.*
55:10 *s.* fr. heaven returneth not
Jer. 18:14 will a man leave *s.* ?
Lam. 4:7 her Nazar. purer th. *s.*
Dan. 7:9 garm. was white as *s.*
Mat. 28:3 raim. as *s. Mark* 9:3
Rev. 1:14 his hairs white as *s.*

SNOWY.
1 Chr. 11:22 slew a lion in *s.* day

SNUFFED.
Jer. 14:6 wild asses *s.* up wind
Mal. 1:13 ye have *s.* at it

SNUFF-DISHES.
Ex. 25:38 *s.-d.* of gold, 37:23
Num. 4:9 and cover his *s.-d.*

SNUFFERS.
Ex. 37:23 made his *s.* of pure
gold, 1 *K.* 7:50 ; *2 Chr.* 4:22
2 K. 12:13 *s.* made of money
25:14 *s.* took th. away, *Jer.* 52:18

SNUFFETH.
Jer. 2:24 a wild ass *s.* up wind

SO.
2 K. 17:4 sent messengers to S.

Not SO.
Job 9:35 but it is not *s.* with me
Mat. 20:26 it sh. *s.* be. am. you
John 14:2 if it were not *s.* I wou.
Acts 10:14 P. said, not *s.* L. 11:8
Jam. 3:10 these things ought
not *s.*

SOAKED.
Is. 34:7 land sh. be *s.* with blood

SOAP.
Jer. 2:22 wash, and take much *s.*
Mal. 3:2 for he is like fuller's *s.*

SOBER.
2 Cor. 5:13 whether we be *s.* it is
1 Thes. 5:6 let us watch and be *s.*
8 let us who are of day be *s.*
1 Tim. 3:2 bis. mu. be *s. Tit.* 1:8
11 deacons' wives must be *s.*
Tit. 2:2 that aged men be *s.*
4 teach young women to be *s.*
1 Pet. 1:13 gird loi. of mind, be *s.*
4:7 be ye *s.* watch unto prayer
5:8 be *s.* be vigilant, bec. your

SOBERLY.
Rom. 12:3 think *s.* acc. to faith
Tit. 2:12 teach. we should live *s.*

SOBER-MINDED.
Tit. 2:6 exh. yo. men to be *s.-m.*

SOBERNESS.
Acts 26:25 speak forth words of *s.*

SOBRIETY.
1 Tim. 2:9 adorn themse. with *s.*
15 continue in holiness with *s.*
SOCHO. *Jos.* 15:48

SOCKET.
Ex. 38:27 100 talents, talent for *s.*

SOCKETS.
Ex. 26:19 make forty *s.* of silver,
21 ; 36:24, 26
21 two *s.* 25 ; 36:24, 26
25 *s.* of silver, sixt. *s.* 36:30, 36
37 cast five *s.* of brass, 36:38
27:10 20 *s.* be of brass, 38:10, 11
12 west side pill. *s.* ten, 38:12
14 hangings on side, *s.* three
16 pillars sh. be 4. their *s.* four
17 hooks of sil. and *s.* brass, 18
35:11 pillars *s.* of tabernacle
38:27 *s.* of sanctu. *s.* veil, 100 *s.*
31 *s.* court, *s.* of court-gate
40:18 reared taberna. fastened *s.*
Num. 3:36 under custody sons of
Merari sh. be *s.* 37 ; 4:31, 32
Cant. 5:15 as pillars on *s.* of gold

SOD.
Gen. 25:29 Jacob *s.* pottage
2 Chr. 35:13 holy offerings *s.* they

SODDEN.
Ex. 12:9 raw, nor *s.* with water
Lev. 6:28 earthen ves. wherein is
s. be bro. if *s.* in brazen pot
Num. 6:19 priest sh. take *s.* sho.
1 Sam. 2:15 not have *s.* flesh
Lam. 4:10 women have *s.* child.

SODOM.

Gen. 13:10 bef. Lord destroy. S.
13 the men of S. were wicked
14:11 took all the goods of S.
12 took Lot who dwelt in S.
17 the king of S. went out to
18:20 because cry of S. is great
26 if I find in S. fifty righteous
19:24 Lord rained upon S. fire
Deut. 29:23 like overthrow of S.
Is. 13:19 ; *Jer* 49:18 ; 50:40
32:32 their vine is of vine of S.
Is. 1.9 should have been as S.
10 hear Lord, ye rulers of S.
3:9 shall declare their sin as S.
Jer. 23:14 are all unto me as S.
Lam. 4:6 punishm. of sin of S.
Ezek. 16:46 sister is S. 48, 49, 55
53 when I bring captivity of S.
Amos 4:11 as God overthrew S.
Zep. 2:9 surely M. shall be as S.
Mat. 10:15 for land of S. 11:24;
    Mark 6:11 ; *Luke* 10:12
Luke 17:29 Lot went out of S.
Rom. 9:29 we had been as S.
2 *Pet.* 2:6 turn. S. and Go. to as.
Jude 7 even as S. and Gomorrah
Rev. 11:8 spiritually called S.

SODOMITE.

Deut. 23:17 there shall be no S.

SODOMITES.

1 *K.* 14:24 there were also S. in
15:12 Asa took away S. 22:46
2 *K.* 23:7 bra. down houses of S.

SOFT.

Job 23:16 G. maketh my heart *s.*
41:3 will he speak *s.* words?
Ps. 65:10 thou makest it *s.*
Prov. 15:1 a *s.* answer turn. wra.
25:15 a *s.* tongue breaketh bone
Mat. 11:8 man clothed in *s.* rai.
    that wear *s.* cloth. *Luke* 7:25

SOFTER.

Ps. 55:21 words were *s.* than oil

SOFTLY.

Gen. 33:14 I will lead *s.* as cattle
Jud. 4:21 Jael went *s.* to him
Ruth 3:7 came *s.* and uncovered
1 *K.* 21:27 A. in sackcl. went *s.*
Is. 8:6 waters of Shil. that go *s.*
38:15 I shall go *s.* all my years
Acts 27:13 south wind blew *s.*

SOIL.

Ezek. 17:8 planted in good *s.*

SOJOURN.

Gen. 12:10 Ab. went to Eg. to *s.*
19:9 This fellow came in to *s.*
26:3 *s.* in this land, I will be
47:4 to *s.* in land are we come
Ex. 12:48 stran. wi. thee, *Lev.*
    19:33; *Num.* 9:14; 15:14
Lev. 17:8 strang. who *s.* th. offer
25:45 strangers that *s.* of them
Jud. 17:8 Levite went to *s.*
Ruth 1:1 Elimel. went to *s.* in M.
1 *K.* 17:20 widow wi. whom I *s.*
2 *K.* 8:1 *s.* where. thou canst *s.*
Ps. 120:5 woe is me, I *s.* in Mes.
Is. 23:7 her feet carry her to *s.*
52:4 my peo. went to Eg. to *s.*
Jer. 42:15 into Egypt, and go to
    s. there, 17 ; 44:12, 14, 28
42:22 die in place whither ye *s.*
Lam. 4:15 they shall no more *s.*
Ezek. 20:38 bring fr. where th. *s.*
47:22 you and strangers who *s.*
Acts 7:6 seed should *s.* in a stra.

SOJOURNED.

Gen. 20:1 Abraham *s.* in Gerar
21:34 and *s.* in Philistines' land
32:4 I *s.* with Laban, and stayed
35:27 where Abra. and Isaac *s.*
Deut. 18:6 Le. come fr. wh. he *s.*
26:5 *s.* in Egypt with a few
Jud. 17:7 a Lev. *s.* in Bethlehem

19:16 an old man *s.* in Gibeah
2 *K.* 8:2 she *s.* in land of Philist.
Ps. 105:23 Jac. *s.* in land of Ham
Heb. 11:9 by faith he *s.* in land

SOJOURNER.

Gen. 23:4 I am a *s.* with you
Lev. 22:10 *s.* of priest sh. not **eat**
25:35 *s.* fallen in decay
40 thy brother shall be as a *s.*
47 *s.* wax rich, brother sell to *s.*
Num. 35:15 six cities a ref. for *s.*
Ps. 39:12 stranger, *s.* as my f'th

SOJOURNERS.

Lev. 25:23 ye are strangers and *s*
2 *Sam.* 4:3 Beerothites were *s.*
1 *Chr.* 29:15 we are *s.* as our fat.

SOJOURNETH.

Ex. 3:22 woman borrow of th. *s.*
12:49 one law to stranger th. *s.*
    Lev. 16:29
Lev. 17:12 nor stranger that *s.*
18:26 that *s.* am. you shall keep
25:6 meat for stranger that *s.*
Num. 15:15 one ordi. for you **and**
    stranger that *s.* 16:29 ; 19:10
Jos. 20:9 cit. for strangers that *s.*
Ezr. 1:4 remaineth where he *s.*
Ezek. 14:7 every one that *s.* in Is.

SOJOURNING.

Ex. 12:40 the *s.* of Is. 430 years
Jud. 19:1 a Lev. *s.* on mount E.
1 *Pet.* 1:17 pass time of *s.* in fear

SOLACE.

Prov. 7:18 let us *s.* ourselves

SOLD.

Gen. 25:33 Esau *s.* his birthright
31:15 our father hath *s.* us
37:28 they *s.* Jos. to Ishmaelites
36 Midianites *s.* him into Eg.
41:56 Jos. *s.* corn to Egyptians
42:6 he it was that *s.* to people
45:4 I am Joseph whom ye *s.*
47:20 Egyptians *s.* every man
22 priests *s.* not their lands
Ex. 22:3 then shall he be *s.*
Lev. 25:23 land shall not be *s.*
33 house that was *s.* sh. go out
42 breth. sh. not be *s.* as bond
27:28 no devoted thing sh. be *s.*
Deut. 15:12 if thy brother be *s.*
32:30 except their Rock *s.* them
Jud. 2:14 he *s.* th. into enemies
10:7 *s.* them into hands of Phil.
1 *Sam.* 12:9 *s.* them into hand o'
1 *K.* 21:20 thou hast *s.* thyself to
2 *K.* 6:25 ass's head *s.* for 80 pie.
7:1 mea. of flour be *s.* for she. 16
17:17 Is. *s.* themselves to do ev.
Neh. 5:8 brethren who were *s.*
13:15 day wherein they *s.* vict.
16 bought and *s.* on sabbath
Est. 7:4 we are *s.* I and people
Ps. 105:17 Jos. was *s.* for serv.
Is. 50:1 which is it to whom I *s.*
    you ? have ye *s.* yourselves
52:3 ye *s.* yourselves for naught
Jer. 34:14 let go who hath been *s.*
Lam. 5:4 our wood is *s.* unto us
Ezek. 7:13 seller not retu. that *s.*
Joel 3:3 have *s.* a girl for wine
6 children of Judah have ye *s.*
7 out of place whit. ye *s.* them
Amos 2:6 they *s.* right. for silver
Mat. 10:29 not two sparrows *s.*
13:46 and *s.* all that he had
18:25 commanded him to be *s.*
'1:12 cast out th. that *s.* them
s. Mark 11:15; *Luke* 19:45
26:9 this ointm. might ha. been
    s. Mark 14:5; *John* 12:5
Luke 12:6 five sparrows *s.*
17:28 they *s.* they planted
John 2:14 in temple that *s.* oxen
16 said to them that *s.* doves
Acts 2:45 *s.* their possessi. 4:34
4:37 Joses having land *s.* it

5:1 Ananias *s.* 8 ye *s.* land for
4 after it was *s.* was it not in
Rom. 7:14 carnal, *s.* under sin
1 *Cor.* 10:25 whats. is *s.* in sham.
Heb. 12:16 for one morsel *s.* birt.

SOLDERING.

Is. 41:7 ready for *s.* he fastened

SOLDIER.

John 19:23 to every *s.* a part
Acts 10:7 Cornelius called a *s.*
28:16 suff. Paul to dwell with *s.*
2 *Tim.* 2:3 end. as a good *s.* of C.
4 hath chosen him to be a *s.*

SOLDIERS.

2 *Chr.* 25:13 *s.* fell upon cities
Ezr. 8:22 I ashamed to requ. *s.*
Is. 15:4 armed *s.* of Moab cry
Mat. 8:9 having *s.* und. *Luke* 7:8
27:27 the *s.* took J. and gathered
    to him *s.*
28:12 they gave money to *s.*
Luke 3:14 *s.* demanded, saying
John 19:23 the *s.* took his garm.
24 these things theref. *s.* did
32 then came *s.* and bra. legs
34 one of the *s.* with a spear
Acts 12:4 delivered Peter to *s.*
6 Pe. was sleeping bet. two *s.*
18 no small stir among the *s.*
21:35 he was borne of the *s.*
23:23 make ready 200 *s.*
27:31 P. said to the *s.* Except
32 then the *s.* cut off the ropes
42 *s.* counsel was to kill pris.

SOLE.

Gen. 8:9 dove found no rest for *s.*
Deut. 28:35 wi. botch from *s.* of
56 not set *s.* of foot upon gro.
65 nei. shall *s.* of thy foot **rest**
Jos. 1:3 place *s.* of foot to tread
2 *Sam.* 14:25 from *s.* of foot to cr.
Job 2:7 Satan smote Job fr. *s.* of
Is. 1:6 from *s.* of foot to head
Ezek. 1:7 *s.* of feet li. *s.* of calf's

See FEET.

SOLEMN.

Num. 10:10 in your *s.* days ye **sh.**
Ps. 92:3 praise with *s.* sound
Is. 1:13 iniq. even the *s.* meet.
Lam. 2:22 called as in a *s.* day
Hos. 9:5 will ye do in *s.* day ?

See ASSEMBLY, FEAST, FEASTS.

SOLEMNITY, IES.

Deut. 31:10 in the *s.* of the year
Is. 30:29 as wh. a holy *s.* is kept
33:20 upon Z. the city of our *s.*
Ezek. 45:17 burnt-offerings in *s.*
46:11 in *s.* meat-offering shall

SOLEMNLY.

Gen. 43:3 the man did *s.* protest
1 *Sam.* 8:9 yet protest *s.* to them

SOLITARY.

Job 3:7 let that night be *s.*
30:3 for famine they were *s.*
Ps. 68:6 G. setteth *s.* in families
107:4 wandered in a *s.* way
Is. 35:1 wilderness *s.* place
Lam. 1:1 how doth city sit *s.*
Mark 1:35 Je. departed to *s.* pl.

SOLITARILY.

Mic. 7:14 feed peo. which dw. *s.*

SOLOMON.

2 *Sam.* 5:14 there was born to
    David S. 1 *Chr.* 3:5 ; 14:4
12:24 he called his name S. and
1 *K.* 1:10 S. his brother, 19, 26
13 S. sh. reign after me, 17, 30
21 I and my son S. shall be
34 God save king S. 39, 43
37 wi. S. come so be he wi. S.
47 God make name of S. better
51 S. swear to me that he will
2:1 David charged S. his son, 23

3:1 S. made affinity with Phar.
3 S. loved Lord ; 10 S. asked
1 K. 3:5 Lord appear to S. 9:2 ;
  2 Chr. 1:7 ; 7:12
4:22 S. provision for one day
29 God gave S. wisdom, 5:12
34 hear wis. of S. from all the
  kings, Mat. 12:42 ; Luke 11:31
5:1 Hiram sent servants to S.
13 king S. raised a levy out of
6:14 S. built house and finished
  it, 2 Chr. 7:11 ; Acts 7:47
7:51 so ended the work S. made
8:1 S. assemb. elders, 2 Chr. 5:2
22 S. spread forth his hands to
54 S. made an end, 2 Chr. 7:1
65 S. held a feast ; 9:26 S. ma.
10:1 when queen of Sheba heard
  of fame of S. 2 Chr. 9:1
24 all sought to S. 2 Chr. 9:23
11:1 king S. loved many wom.
2 S. clave to these in love, 4
5 S. went after Ashtoreth and
6 S. did evil ; 7 S. built for C.
9 Lord was angry with S. 27
14 Hadad, an adversary to S.
14 S. sought therefore to kill
43 S. slept with his fathers
12:2 fled from the presence of S.
14:26 shields S. ma. 2 Chr. 12:9
2 K. 21:7 the Lord said to David
  and to S. 2 Chr. 33:7
1 Chr. 22:5 S. my son. is young
9 for his name shall be S. 17
28:6 S. thy son he shall build
9 thou S. my son, know the G.
11 David gave to S. pattern
29:1 S. my son, whom G. alone
19 give to S. my son a perfect
23 S. sat on the throne of the
25 L. magnified S. exceedingly
2 Chr. 2:17 S. number. strangers
3:3 things wherein S. was inst.
30:26 since time of S. not such
Ezr. 2:55 the children of S. serv.
  58 ; Neh. 7:57, 60 ; 11:3
Neh. 12:45 commandment of S.
13:26 did not king S. sin by th. ?
Prov. 1:1 prov. of S. 10:1 ; 25:1
Cant. 1:1 Song of songs wh. is S.
5 comely, as the curtains of S.
3:7 behold, his bed which is S.
11 behold king S. 8:12 S. must
8:11 S. had vineyard at Baal-h.
Jer. 52:20 sea S. ma. was carried
Mat. 1:6 Da. begat S. 7 S. begat
6:29 S. in all his gl. Luke 12:27
12:42 greater than S. Luke 11:31
John 10:23 Je. walked in S. por.
Acts 3:11 ran to them to S. porch
5:12 with one accord in S. por.

SOMEBODY.
Luke 8:46 Jesus said, s. touched
Acts 5:36 Theu. boasting to be s.

SOMETHING.
Mark 5:43 that s. should be giv.
Luke 11:54 seeking to catch s.
John 13:29 he sh. give s. to poor
Acts 3:5 expecting to receive s.
23:15 would inquire s. more per.
18 young man hath s. to say
Gal. 6:3 man think him. to be s.

SOMETIMES.
Eph. 2:13 ye who were s. afar off
Col. 3:7 in which ye walked s.

SOMEWHAT.
Lev. 4:22 wh. ruler hath done s.
1 K. 2:14 he said. I have s. to say
2 K. 5:20 I will run and take s.
Luke 7:40 have s. to say unto th.
Rom. 15:24 if first I be s. filled
2 Cor. 5:12 may have s. to answer
10:8 tho' I should boast s. more

Gal. 2:6 th. who seemed to be s.
Heb. 8:3 this man have s. to offer
Rev. 2:4 I have s. against thee

SON.
Gen. 17:16 I will give thee a s. of
  Sarah, 19 ; 18:10, 14
21:2 Sarah bare Abraham a s. 7
24:36 my master's wife bare a s.
  51 let her be master's s. wife
27:33 he hath given me this s.
30:6 G. heard me, given me s.
  24 Lord shall add to me ano. s.
35:17 thou shalt have this s.
37:3 bec. he was s. of old age
Ex. 1:16 if s. then ye kill him
  22 every s. born cast into river
2:10 child grew, and bec. her s.
Lev. 12:6 days of purify. for a s.
24:10 s. of an Israelitish woman
25:49 his uncle's s. may redeem
Num. 23:18 hearken, s. of Zip.
27:4 hath no s. 8 and have no s.

Deut. 13:6 if s. of mo. ent. thee.
21:16 not make s. of belov. first-
  born before s. of hated. 17
20 our s. is stubborn, rebellious
28:56 eye sh. be evil tow. her s.
Jos. 6:26 in young. s. set up gat.
Jud. 5:12 lead captive s. of Ab.
9:18 made s. of his servant king
11:2 thou art s. of strange wo.
34 he had nei. s. nor daughter
13:3 conceive and bear a s. 5, 7
Ruth 4:13 Ruth bare a s.
  17 a s. born to Naomi
1 Sam. 1:23 Hannah gave s. suck
4:20 fear not, th. hast borne a s.
10:11 wh. is come to s. of Kish ?
16:18 I have seen a s. of Jesse
17:55 whose s. ? 58 whose s. art
20:27 wheref. com. not s. of J. ?
  31 as long as s. of Jesse liveth
22:7 will s. of Jesse give fields?
9 I saw s. of Jesse com. to N.
12 hear, now, thou s. of Ahit.
25:10 who is the s. of Jesse?
17 he is such a s. of Belial
2 Sam. 1:13 I am s. of a stranger
9:9 give s. all that pertain. to S.
10:2 show kindness to s. of Na.
16:3 where is thy master's s.
18:12 put forth ha. ag. king's s.
18 have no s. to keep my name
20 because the king's s. is dead
1 K. 3:6 thou hast given him a s.
5:7 hath given David a wise s.
12:16 no inheritance in s. of
  Jesse, 2 Chr. 10:16
14:5 cometh to ask of thee for s.
22:26 Joa. king's s. 2 Chr. 18:25
2 K. 1:17 because he had no s.
4:16 season th. sh. embrace a s.
  28 did I desire a s. 37 took s.
6:29 give s. to eat him, hid s.
  32 s. of a murderer hath sent
8:1 whose s. he restored to life
11:1 s. was dead, 2 Chr. 22:9
4 Jehoiada sho. them king's s.
1 Chr. 12:18 side, thou s. of Jesse
22:9 behold, a s. shall be born
2 Chr. 21:17 never a s. left him
23:3 behold, king's s. shall rei.
Job 18:19 nei. have s. nor neph.
Ps. 2:12 kiss s. lest he be angry
72:1 righteous. unto king's s.
86:16 save s. of thy handmaid
89:22 nor s. of wicked. afflict h.
116:16 I am s. of thy hand-ma.
Prov. 3:12 s. in whom he deligh.
4:3 I was my father's s. belov.
10:1 a wise s. mak. glad fa. 15:20
5 gath. is wise s. sleep. in har.
  s. caus. shame, 17:2 ; 19:26
13:1 a wise s. heareth instruc.
17:25 foolish s. is a grief to fa.
19:13 foolish s. calamity of fath.
28:7 whoso keep. law is wise s.

31:2 s. of womb, s. of vows?
Ec. 5:14 begetteth a s. nothing
10:17 when king is s. of nobles
Is. 7:14 virgin conc. and bear s.
9:6 ch. born, unto us s. is given
14:12 O Lucifer, s. of morning
  22 I will cut off fr. Babylon s.
19:11 s. of wise, s. of kings
49:15 compassion on s. of womb
56:3 nei. s. of stranger speak
Jer. 6:26 mourn. as for only s.
33:21 sho. not have a s. to reign
Ezek. 14:20 deliv. nei. s. nor dau.
18:4 soul of s. is mine
  14 a s. that seeth his fa.'s sins
19 why doth not s. bear iniq.
20 s. not bear iniq. of father
44:25 for s. or daugh. they may
Hos. 13:13 he is an unwise s.
Amos 7:14 nor was I proph.'s s.
8:10 as mourning of an only s.
Mic. 7:6 s. dishonoreth father
Mal. 1:6 s. honoreth his father
Mat. 1:21 bring forth s. Luke 1:31
9:2 s. be of go. cheer, Mark 2:5
10:37 he that loveth s. or daug.
11:27 know. S. but Father, nor
  Father save S. Luke 10:22
13:55 the carpen.'s s. Mark 6:3 ;
  Luke 4:22
16:16 thou art Christ, S. of God
21:28 s. go work in my viney.
22:42 of Christ? whose s. is he?
Mark 12:6 having one s. beloved
13:32 hour knoweth not the S.
14:61 Christ, S. of the Blessed?
Luke 1:13 Elisab. shall bear a s.
  32 be called S. of the Highest
3:23 Jesus s. of Joseph, s. of H.
7:12 only s. of his mother
10:6 if s. of peace be there
11:11 if a s. ask bread of any
12:53 father divided against s.
Luke 15:13 younger s. gathered
16:25 s. remember, in thy lifet.
19:9 forasmuch as he is s. of A.
John 1:18 only S. in bosom of F.
3:35 Father loveth the S. 5:20
  36 beli. on S. believeth not S.
5:19 S. can do noth. of himself
  21 S. quicken. whom he will
  22 committed all judgm. to S.
  23 men should honor S. he th.
  honor. not S. honor. not F.
  26 given to S. to have life
6:40 ev. one who seeth the S.
  42 is not this Jes. s. of Joseph
8:35 s. abideth ; 9:19 is this s. ?
36 if S. shall make you free
9:20 we kn. that this is our s.
14:13 Fa. may be glorified in S.
17:12 none lost but s. of perdit.
Acts 4:36 Barnabas, s. of consol.
23:6 Pharisee, s. of a Pharisee
  16 Paul's sister's s. heard of
Rom. 9:9 Sarah shall have a s.
1 Cor. 15:28 then S. himself sub.
Gal. 4:7 no more serv. but s.
Phil. 2:22 as s. he serv. in gospel
Col. 4:10 Marcus sister's s. to B.
2 Thes. 2:3 man of sin, s. of per.
1 Tim. 1:18 commit to thee s. T.
Heb. 1:5 he shall be to me a s.
  8 to S. he saith, Thy throne
3:6 Christ as a s. over his own
5:8 tho' he were a s. yet learned
7:28 word of the oath maketh s.
11:24 refu. to be called s. of Ph.
12:6 scourg. every s. he receiv.
1 John 2:22 antic. deni. F. and S.
23 whosoever denieth the S.
  the same hath not the Fath.
24 continue in S. and in Fath.
4:14 Father sent S. to be Savi.
5:12 he that hath S. hath life
2 John 3 L. Je. Ch. S. of Father
9 hath both the Father and S.
See DAVID.

SON of God.

Dan. 3:25 fourth is like *s. of G.*
Mat. 8:29 thou S. *of G. Luke* 8:28
14:33 of a truth th. art *S. of G.*
26:63 whether be Ch. *S. of G.*
27:43 he said, I am the *S. of G.*
54 was *S. of G. Mark* 15:39
Mark 3:11 art *S. of G. John* 1:49
Luke 1:35 sh. be called *S. of G.*
3:38 *s.* of Adam, was *s. of G.*
4:41 crying, Thou art Christ th.
    S. of G. John 6:69 ; 11:27
22:70 art th. then the *S. of G.?*
John 1:34 this is the *S. of God*
3:18 the only begotten *S. of G.*
5:25 shall hear voice of *S. of G.?*
9:35 dost thou beli. on *S. of G.?*
10:36 I said, I am the *S. of God*
11:4 that *S. of G.* might be glo.
19:7 he made himself *S. of God*
20:31 beli. Je. is C. the *S. of G.*
Acts 8:37 J. Christ is the *S. of G.*
9:20 Christ, that he is *S. of G.*
Rom. 1:4 declared to be *S. of G.*
2 *Cor.* 1:19 the *S. of G.* was not
Gal. 2:20 by faith of *S. of God*
Eph. 4:13 knowledge of *S. of G*
Heb. 4:14 high-pr. J. the *S. of G*
6:6 crucify to themscl. *S. of G*
7:3 made like to the *S. of God*
10:29 trod. under foot *S. of God*
1 *John* 3:8 for this purp. *S. of G.*
4:15 shall confess Je. is *S. of God*
5:5 believeth Jesus is *S. of God*
10 that believeth on *S. of God*
13 believe on name of *S. of G.*
20 know that *S. of G.* is come
Rev. 2:18 write, saith *S. of God*

His SON.

Gen. 22:13 bu.-off. in stead of *h. s.*
25:11 Abraham, G. blessed *h. s.*
37:34 Jacob mourned for *his s.*
Ex. 32:29 every man upon *his s.*
Lev. 21:2 for *his s.* he may be
Num. 26:26 put on Elea. *h. s.* 28
Deut. 1:31 man doth bear *his s.*
7:3 thy daugh. not give to *his s.*
8:5 as a man chasteneth *his s.*
18:10 not any mak. *h. s.* to pass
2 *Sam.* 16:19 serve in pres. of *h. s.*
1 *K.* 11:36 and to *h. s.* will I give
2 *K.* 3:27 Moab took *his* eldest *s.*
16:3 A. made *his s.* to pass thro'
21:6 Manas. made *his s.* to pass
23:10 no man ml. make *h. s.* pass
2 *Chr.* 24:22 Jo. the ki. slew *h. s.*
Prov. 13:24 spareth rod, hat. *h. s.*
29:21 shall have him bec. *his s.*
30:4 what is *his s.* name?
Jer. 27:7 *his s.* and *his* son's *s.*
Mal. 3:17 as a man spareth *h. s.*
Mat. 21:37 last of all sent *his s.*
Mat. 22:2 made a marr. for *his s.*
45 how is he then *h. s.? Mark*
    12:37 ; *Luke* 20:44
John 3:16 gave *h.* only begot. *S.*
17 God sent not *his S.* to con.
Acts 3:13 God hath glori. *h. S.* J.
26 God having raised up *h. S.*
Rom. 1:9 serve in gospel of *h. S.*
8:3 God sending *his* own *S.* in
32 that spared not *his* own *S.*
Gal. 1:16 it pleas. G. to rev. *h. S.*
4:4 God sent forth *his S.*
1 *Thes.* 1:10 to wait for *his S.*
Heb. 1:2 spoken to us by *his S.*
Jam. 2:21 had offered Isaac *his s.*
1 *John* 1:3 fel. is with F. and *h. S.*
7 blood of Jes. Ch. *h. S.* clea.
3:23 believe on name of *h. S.*
5:9 he hath testified of *h. S.*
10 beli. not rec. G. gave of *h. S.*
11 this life is in *his S.*
20 we are in him, even *his S.*

SON-IN-LAW.

Gen. 19:12 hast thou any *s.-i.-l.?*
Jud. 15:6 Samson the *s.-i.-l.* of

19:5 damsel's fa. said to *s.-i.-l.*
1 *Sam.* 18:18 should be *s.-i.-l.* 23
22:14 faithful as king's *s.-i.-l.?*
2 *K.* 8:27 Jehoram was *s.-i.-l.*
Neh. 6:18 Tobiah was *s.-i.-l.* to
13:28 was *s.-i.-l.* to Sanballat

See BELOVED.

My SON.

Gen. 21:23 not deal fal. wi. *my s.*
22:7 he said, Here am I, *my s.*
24:3 not take wife to *my s.* 37
6 bring not *my s.* thither ag. 8
27:8 now theref. *my s.* obey, 43
18 am I, who art thou, *my s.?*
21 whe. thou be *my* very *s.* 24
37 what shall I do now, *my s.?*
37:33 and said, It is *my s.* coat
35 will go into grave to *my s.*
42:38 he said, *my s.* shall not go
45:28 Joseph is yet alive
Ex. 4:22 Is. is *my s.* even my
Jud. 8:23 neith. shall *my s.* rule
1 *Sam.* 3:6 I called not *my s.* lie
4:16 what is there done, *my s.?*
10:2 what shall I do for *my s.?*
24:16 voice, *my s.* David? 26:17
26:21 sinned, return, *my s.* Dav.
2 *Sam.* 7:14 he shall be *my s.*
13:25 *my s.* let us not all go
14:16 dest. me and *my s.* out of
16:11 *my s.* who came forth
18:33 king said, O *my s.* Absal.
    my s. my s. Absalom, 19:4
1 *K.* 3:20 took *my s.* from, 22, 23
17:12 dress it for me and *my s.*
2 *K.* 6:29 we boiled *my s.* and eat
14:9 dau. to *my s.* 2 *Chr.* 25:18
1 *Chr.* 17:13 shall be *my s.* 22:10
22:11 *my s.* Lord will be with
28:6 ha. chosen him to be *my s.*
29:1 Sol. *my s.* whom God hath
Ps. 2:7 thou art *my s. Acts* 13:33 ;
    Heb. 1:5 ; 5:5
Prov. 6:3 do this now, *my s.*
23:26 *my s.* give me thy heart
24:21 *my s.* fear thou the Lord
27:11 *my s.* be wise and make
31:2 what, *my s.* and what, son
Jer. 31:20 is Ephra. *my* dear *s.?*
Hos. 11:1 called *my s. Mat.* 2:15
Mat. 3:17 *my* beloved *S.* 17:5
Mark 9:17 I have brought *my s.*
Luke 9:38 Mast. look upon *my s.*
15:24 for this *my s.* was dead
1 *Tim.* 1:2 to Timothy *my* own *s.*
2 *Tim.* 2:1 *my s.* be stro. in grace
Tit. 1:4 to Titus *mine* own *s.*
Phile. 10 I beseech th. for *my s.*
Rev. 21:7 his *God*, he sh. be *my s.*

Thy SON.

Gen. 22:2 take t. *s.* thine only *s.*
24:5 must I needs bring *thy s.?*
37:32 know whe. it be *t. s.* coat
48:2 behold, *thy s.* Jos. cometh
Ex. 10:2 tell in the ears of *thy s.*
13:8 thou shalt show *thy s.*
14 wh. *t. s.* asketh, *Deut.* 6:20
Deut. 6:21 shalt say unto *thy s.*
7:3 nor daughter take unto *t. s.*
4 they will turn away *thy s.*
Jud. 6:30 bring out *t. s.* that he
8:22 rule over us, thou, *thy s.*
1 *Sam.* 16:19 send me David *t. s.*
1 *K.* 1:12 save life of *thy s.* Solo.
3:22 dead is *t. s.* 23 and *thy s.*
5:5 *thy s.* whom I will set upon
11:12 rend it out of hand of *t. s.*
17:13 for thee and for *thy s.*
19 give me *t. s.* 23 *t. s.* liveth
2 *K.* 4:36 he said, Take up *thy s.*
6:28 gi. *t. s.* that we may eat, 29
2 *K.* 16:7 I am thy ser. and *thy s.*
Prov. 19:18 chasten *thy s.* while
29:17 correct *thy s.* and he shall
Luke 9:41 Je. said, Bring *thy s.*
15:19 no more wor. to be *t. s.* 21
30 soon as this *t. s.* was come

John 4:50 *thy s.* liveth, 51, 53
17:1 glorify *t. S.* that *t. S.* may
19:26 saith, Woman, beh. *thy s.*

SON of man.

Ezekiel—above ninety times.

SONG.

Ex. 15:1 then sang Moses this *s.*
    unto the Lord, *Num.* 21:17
2 the Lord is my strength and
    s. Ps. 118:14 ; *Is.* 12:2
Deut. 31:19 wri. this *s.* th. th. *s.*
21 this *s.* sh. testify aga. them
22 Moses theref. wrote this *s.*
30 Mo. spake words of *s.* 32:44
Jud. 5:12 awake, Debor. utter *s.*
2 *Sam.* 22:1 Da. spa. words of *s.*
1 *Chr.* 6:31 D. set over serv. of *s.*
15:22 chief of Lev. was for *s.* 27
25:6 under their father for *s.*
2 *Chr.* 29:27 *s.* of the Lord began
Job 30:9 I am their *s.* by-word
Ps. 28:7 with *s.* will I praise
33:3 sing a new *s. Is.* 42:10
40:3 put a new *s.* in my mouth
42:8 in night his *s.* sh. be wi. me
69:12 I was *s.* of the drunkards
30 I will praise God with a *s.*
77:6 I call to remembra. my *s.*
96:1 O sing to the Lord a new *s.*
    98:1 ; 149:1
137:3 they required of us a *s.*
4 how sh. we sing Lord's *s.?*
144:9 I will sing a new *s.*
Ec. 7:5 man to hear *s.* of fools
Cant. 1:1 of songs which is S.
Is. 5:1 now will I sing a *s.*
24:9 sh. not drink wine wi. a *s.*
26:1 in th. day sh. th. *s.* be sung
30:29 shall have a *s.* as in night
Lam. 3:14 I was their *s.* all day
Ezek. 33:32 to them as a lovely *s.*
Rev. 5:9 they sung a new *s.* 14:3
14:3 no man could learn that *s.*
15:3 the *s.* of Moses and of L.

SONGS.

Gen. 31:27 sent thee away wi. *s.*
1 *K.* 4:32 *s.* a thousand and five
1 *Chr.* 25:7 were instructed in *s.*
Neh. 12:46 in days of D. were *s.*
Job 35:10 G. who giv. *s.* in night
Ps. 32:7 comp. wi. *s.* of deliver
119:54 have been my *s.* in house
187:3 sing us one of the *s.* of Z.
Prov. 25:20 singeth *s.* to heavy
Cant. 1:1 song of *s.* which is Sol.
Is. 23:16 melody, sing many *s.*
24:16 part of earth we heard *s.*
35:10 ranso. come to Z. with *s.*
38:20 we will sing my *s.*
Ezek. 26:13 noise of *s.* to cease
Amos 5:23 take away noise of *s.*
8:3 *s.* of temple shall be howli.
10 turn your *s.* into lamentati.
Eph. 5:19 in psalms, spiritual *s.*
Col. 3:16 hymns, and spiritual *s.*

SONS.

Gen. 9:19 the three *s.* of Noah
10:1 and to them were *s.* born
23:11 in pres. of *s.* of my people
27:29 let mother's *s.* bow down
42:5 *s.* of Is. came to buy corn
11 we are all one man's *s.* 32
46:5 *s.* of Israel carried Jacob
Lev. 26:29 eat flesh of your *s.*
Num. 27:3 father died, had no *s.*
36:3 married to *s.* of oth. tribes
Deut. 32:8 separated *s.* of Adam
Jud. 8:19 the *s.* of my mother
30 Gideon had 70 *s.* 10:4 Jair
12:14 Abdon had 40 *s.* 30 neph.
19:22 cert. *s.* of Bel. beset house
Ruth 1:11 are there any more *s.?*
1 *Sam.* 1:8 am not I bet. th. 10 *s.?*
2:12 *s.* of Eli were *s.* of Belial
8:11 take your *s.* appoint them

2 *Sam.* 2:18 three *s.* of Zeruiah
3:39 *s.* of Zeruiah be too hard
9:11 eat as one of king's *s.*
13:30 Absa. hath slain king's *s.*
16:10 what to do, *s.* of Z. ? 19:22
23:6 *s.* of Bel. shall be as thorns
1 *K.* 20:35 the *s.* of the prophets
21:10 set two men, *s.* of Belial
2 *K.* 10:8 heads of the king's *s.*
1 *Chr.* 21:20 Orn. and his four *s.*
28:4 among the *s.* of my fathers
2 *Chr.* 23:3 Lord said of *s.* of Da.
24:25 blood of the *s.* of Jehoiada
Est. 9:10 ten *s.* of Ha. slew they
13 Ha.'s ten *s.* be hanged, 14
Ps. 89:6 who amo. *s.* of mighty ?
144:12 our *s.* may be as plants
Is. 51:18 no. to guide her amo. *s.*
56:6 *s.* of strang. that join Lord
60:10 *s.* of stranger build walls
14 *s.* of them th. afflicted thee
Jer. 6:21 *s.* shall fall upon them
13:14 fathers and *s.* together
29:6 beget *s.* ta. wives for yo. *s.*
35:6 drink no wine, ye, nor *s.*
49:1 hath Israel no *s.* ? no heir ?
Lam. 4:2 precious *s.* of Zion
Ezek. 5:10 fathers eat *s. s.* fathers
20:31 your *s.* pass thro' the fire
23:37 caused *s.* to pass thro' fire
Hos. 1:10 ye are *s.* of living God
Amos 2:11 I raised up of your *s.*
Mal. 3:3 he shall purify *s.* of Le.
Mark 3:17 Boanerges, *s.* of thun.
Luke 11:19 your *s.* cast th. out ?
1 *Cor.* 4:14 but as my beloved *s.*
Gal. 4:5 receive the adopti. of *s.*
6 bec. ye are *s.* God hath sent
Heb. 2:10 bring. many *s.* to glory
11:21 Jacob blessed *s.* of Joseph
12:7 G. deal. with you as wi. *s.*

See AARON, DAUGHTER.

SONS of God.
Gen. 6:2 *s.* of *G.* saw daughters
Job 1:6 *s.* of *G.* came to pres. 2:1
38:7 *s.* of *G.* shouted for joy
Hos. 1:10 ye are *s.* of living God
John 1:12 power to bec. *s.* of *G.*
Rom. 8:14 8p. of God, are *s.* of *G.*
19 manifestation of *s. s.* of *God*
Phil. 2:15 be harmless. *s.* of *God*
1 *John* 3:1 we be called *s.* of *G.*
2 beloved, now are we *s.* of *G.*

His SONS.
Gen. 9:1 God blessed N. and *h. s.*
30:35 gave th. into hands of *h. s.*
50:12 *his s.* did unto him as he
Ex. 18:5 Jethro came with *h. s.*
28:1 take Aa. and *h. s.* to mini.
Lev. 6:22 priest of *his s.* is anoi.
Deut. 18:5 chosen him and *h. s.*
21:16 he maketh *h. s.* inherit
Jud. 9:18 slain *h. s.* 70 persons
17:11 Levite was as one of *his s.*
1 *Sam.* 2:22 heard all *his s.* did
8:1 S. when old made *h. s.* jud.
3 *his s.* walk. not in his ways
16:1 provided a king am. *his s.*
30:6 grieved, ev. man for *his s.*
2 *Sam.* 21:6 let 7 of *h. s.* be deli.
1 *K.* 13:11 *h. s.* came and to. him
12 *h. s.* seen way man of God
21:29 in *h. s.* days will I bring
2 *K.* 19:37 *his s.* smote him with
sword, *Is.* 37:38
2 *Chr.* 11:14 Jeroboam and *his s.*
21:7 give light to him and *h. s.*
17 carried away *his s.* save the
youngest of *his s.*
36:20 serv. to him and *his s.*
Ezr. 6:10 life of king and *his s.*
Est. 9:25 and *his s.* be hanged
Job 1:4 *his s.* went and feasted
14:21 *his s.* came to honor
38:32 canst guide A. with *h. s.* ?
42:16 J. saw *h. s.* and *h. s.* sons
Ezek. 46:16 a gift to any of *h. s.*

Dan. 11:10 *h. s.* sh. be stirred up
See MAN.

My SONS.
Gen. 48:9 J. said, They are *my s.*
1 *Sam.* 2:24 *my s.* it is no good
12:2 S. said, *my s.* are with you
1 *Chr.* 28:5 of all *my s.* chosen S.
Job 1:5 it may be *my s.* have sin.
Is. 45:11 to come concern. *my s.*
1 *Cor.* 4:14 but as *my beloved s.*
See SEVEN.

Thy SONS.
Ex. 12:24 th. and *t. s. Num.* 18:8
22:29 first-born of *thy s.* give
34:20 first-born of *t. s.* shalt red.
Lev. 10:14 thy due, and *t. s.* due
Num. 18:1 *t. s.* sh. bear iniquity
11 I have given them to *thy s.*
Deut. 4:9 teach *t. s.* and *t. s.* sons
1 *Sam.* 2:29 and honorest *thy s.*
8:5 *thy s.* walk not in thy ways
28:19 to-mor. *thy s.* be with me
2 *Sam.* 9:10 *t. s.* shall till land
2 *K.* 20:18 *thy s.* shall be eunuchs
in Babylon, *Is.* 39:7
Is. 49:22 they shall bring *thy s.*
51:20 *thy s.* have fainted
60:4 *thy s.* sh. come from far, 9
Jer. 48:46 *t. s.* are taken captives
Zec. 9:13 *t. s.* O Zi. against *t. s.*

Two SONS.
Gen. 10:25 to E. *t. s.* 1 *Chr.* 1:19
34:25 *two of s.* of Ja. slew males
Gen. 41:50 to Jos. were born *t. s.*
42:37 slay my *t. s.* if I bri. him
44:27 kn. my wife bare me *t. s.*
48:1 he took with him his *t. s.*
Ex. 18:3 Zipporah and her *t. s.*
Lev. 16:1 death of *t. s.* of Aaron
Ruth 1:1 *t. s.* Mahlon and Chil. 2
1 *Sam.* 2:34 come upon thy *t. s.*
4:4 the *two s.* of Eli were there
2 *Sam.* 14:6 handmaid had *two s.*
15:36 they had with them *t. s.*
21:8 king took *two s.* of Rizpah
Mat. 20:21 grant that th. my *t. s.*
21:28 a man had *t. s. Lu.* 15:11
26:37 Peter and *t. s.* of Zebedee
Acts 7:29 in Midi. he begat *t. s.*
Gal. 4:22 Abraham had *two s.*

SOON.
Ex. 2:18 ye are come so *s.* to-day ?
Deut. 4:26 ye shall *s.* utt. perish
Job 32:22 Maker *s.* take me away
Ps. 90:10 for it is *s.* cut off
106:13 they *s.* forgat his works
Tit. 1:7 not self-wil. not *s.* angry

SOONER.
Heb. 13:19 restored to you the *s.*
Jam. 1:11 the sun is no *s.* risen

SOOTHSAYER, S.
Jos. 13:22 Balaam son of Beor *s.*
Is. 2:6 peo. because they are *s.*
Dan. 2:27 secret cannot *s.* show
5:7 king cried aloud to bring *s.*
11 whom king made mas. of *s.*
Mic. 5:12 shalt have no more *s.*

SOOTHSAYING.
Acts 16:16 mast. much gain by *s.*

SOP.
John 13:26 to wh. I shall give a *s.*
27 after the *s.* Satan enter. 30

SOPATER. *Acts* 20:4

SORCERER, ESS.
Is. 57:3 draw hither, sons of *s.*
Acts 13:6 certain *s.* a false proph.
8 Elym. the *s.* withstood them

SORCERERS.
Ex. 7:11 called wise men and *s.*
Jer. 27:9 hearken not to your *s.*
Dan. 2:2 N. command. to call *s.*
Mal. 3:5 be a witn. against the *s.*
Rev. 21:8 *s.* sh. have part in lake

22:15 without are dogs and *s.*

SORCERY.
Acts 8:9 who beforetime used *s.*

SORCERIES.
Is. 47:9 come on thee for thy *s.*
12 stand with multi. of thy *s.*
Acts 8:11 long ti. bewitch. wi. *s.*
Rev. 9:21 nei. repented of th. *s.*
18:23 by *s.* were nations deceiv.

SORE, Adj. or Adv.
Gen. 19:9 pressed *s.* upon man
31:30 bec. thou *s.* longedst after
34:25 day, when they were *s.*
41:56 famine waxed *s.* in land
57 famine was so *s.* in all lands
43:1 famine *s.* in land, 47:4, 13
Deut. 6:22 Lord showed signs *s.*
Jud. 10:9 Israel was *s.* distress.
14:17 bec. she lay *s.* upon him
20:34 battle was *s.* 1 *Sam.* 31:3
2 *Sam.* 2:17 ; 2 *K.* 3:26
21:2 lifted their voices, wept *s.*
1 *Sam.* 1:10 Han. prayed, wept *s.*
5:7 his hand is *s.* on us, and on
14:52 *s.* war against Philistines
2 *Sam.* 13:36 and servant wept *s.*
1 *K.* 17:17 sickn. so *s.* no breath
2 *K.* 6:11 king of Syria *s.* troub.
20:3 Hezekiah wept *s. Is.* 38:3
2 *Chr.* 21:19 Jeho. died of *s.* dis.
28:19 Ahaz transgress. *s.* ag. L.
Ezr. 10:1 people wept very *s.*
Neh. 13:8 it grieved me *s.* theref.
Job 5:18 maketh *s.* bindeth up
Ps. 6:3 my soul is *s.* vexed
38:2 thy hand presseth me *s.*
44:19 thou hast *s.* broken us
55:4 my heart is *s.* pained
118:13 thou hast thrust *s.* at me
Is. 27:1 with *s.* and great sword
64:9 be not wroth very *s.* O Lo.
12 wilt thou afflict us very *s.* ?
Lam. 1:2 she weepeth *s.* in night
Ezek. 14:21 my four *s.* judgm.
Dan. 6:14 king was *s.* displeased
Mat. 21:15 th. were *s.* displeased
Mark 9:26 sp. cried. rent him *s.*
Acts 20:37 wept *s.* and kissed P.

See AFRAID.

SORE, Substantive.
Lev. 13:42 if a white reddish *s.*
2 *Chr.* 6:29 know his own *s.* grl.
Ps. 38:11 friends stand aloof fr. *s.*
Ps. 77:2 my *s.* ran in the night
Rev. 16:2 there fell a grievous *s.*

SOREK.
Jud. 16:4 a woman in vall. of S.

SORES.
Is. 1:6 bruises and putrefying *s.*
Luke 16:20 Lazarus full of *s.* 21
Rev. 16:11 blasphemed bec. of *s.*

SORELY.
Is. 23:5 *s.* pained at report of T.

SORER.
Heb. 10:29 how much *s.* punish.

SORROW.
Gen. 3:16 greatly multi. thy *s.* in
s. thou shalt bring forth ch.
17 in *s.* shalt thou eat of it
42:38 bring my gray hairs with
s. to the grave, 44:29, 31
Ex. 15:14 *s.* take hold of inhab.
Lev. 26:16 terror cause *s.* of heart
Deut. 28:65 L. sh. give *s.* of mind
1 *Chr.* 4:9 bec. I bare him wi. *s.*
Neh. 2:2 noth. else but *s.* of hea.
Est. 9:22 turned from *s.* to joy
Job 3:10 hid not *s.* fr. mine eyes
6:10 I would harden myself in *s.*
17:7 eye dim by reason of *s.*
41:22 *s.* is turned into joy
Ps. 13:2 having *s.* in my heart
38:17 my *s.* continually bef. me
39:2 help peace, my *s.* stirred
55:10 and *s.* in the midst of it

SORROW

90:10 their strength labor and *s.*
107:39 brought low through *s.*
116:3 I found trouble and *s.*
Prov. 10:10 that winketh caus. *s.*
22 L. mak. rich, addeth no *s.*
15:13 by *s.* of heart spirit is bro.
17:21 begetteth fool, doeth to *s.*
23:29 who ha. woe ? who hath *s.*
Ec. 1:18 knowledge, increaseth *s.*
5:17 hath much *s.* and wrath
7:3 *s.* is better than laughter
11:10 remove *s.* from thy heart
Is. 5:30 look to land, behold *s.*
14:3 L. shall give thee rest fr. *s.*
17:11 heap in day of desperate *s:*
29:2 distress Ariel, th. sh. be *s.*
35:10 *s.* and sighing shall flee
50:11 ye shall lie down in *s.*
51:11 *s.* and mourning flee away
65:14 sing, but ye sh. cry for *s.*
Jer. 8:18 comf. myself against *s.*
20:18 womb, see labor and *s. ?*
30:15 why criest thou ? *s.* incu.
31:13 make them rej. fr. their *s.*
45:3 L. hath add. grief to my *s.*
49:23 there is *s.* on the sea
Lam. 1:12 any *s.* like unto my *s.*
18 behold *s.* 3:65 give them *s.*
Ezek. 23:33 fill. wi. drunk. and *s.*
Luke 22:45 found th. sleep. for *s.*
John 16:6 *s.* ha. fill. your hearts
20 your *s.* shall be turn. to joy
21 wo. when in travail hath *s.*
22 and ye now therefore ha. *s.*
Rom. 9:2 I have *s.* in my heart
2 Cor. 2:3 I sho. have *s.* from th.
7 swallo. up with overmuch *s.*
7:10 godly *s.* work. repentance,
but *s.* of world worke. death
Phil. 2:27 lest I have *s.* upon *s.*
Rev. 18:7 *s.* give her, see no *s.*
21:4 be no more death, neith. *s.*

SORROW, Verb.

Jer. 31:12 shall not *s.* any more
51:29 land shall tremble and *s.*
Hos. 8:10 they shall *s.* for burden
1 Thes. 4:13 *s.* not as others

SORROWS.

Ex. 3:7 cry, for I know their *s.*
2 Sam. 22:6 *s.* of hell compassed
me about, Ps. 18:4, 5 ; 116:3
Job 9:28 I afraid of *s.*
21:17 God distribut. *s.* in anger
39:3 bow themselves, cast out *s.*
Ps. 16:4 *s.* shall be multiplied
32:10 many *s.* shall be to wick.
127:2 rise up, to eat bread of *s.*
Ec. 2:23 his days *s.* travail grief
Is. 13:8 and *s.* take hold of them
53:3 man of *s.* acquainted with
4 borne our griefs carri. our *s.*
Jer. 13:21 shall not *s.* take as wo.
49:24 *s.* taken her as a woman
Dan. 10:16 by visions *s.* turned
Hos. 13:13 *s.* of travailing wom.
Mat. 24:8 begin. of *s.* Mark 13:8
1 Tim. 6:10 pierced with many *s.*

SORROWED, ETH.

1 Sam. 10:2 thy father *s.* for you
2 Cor. 7:9 I rejoice ye *s.* to repe.
11 that ye *s.* after a godly sort

SORROWFUL.

1 Sam. 1:15 woman of a *s.* spirit
Job 6:7 refus. are as my *s.* meat
Ps. 69:29 I am poor and *s.* let
Prov. 14:13 in laugh. heart is *s.*
Jer. 31:25 replenis. every *s.* soul
Zep. 3:18 gather them that are *s.*
Zec. 9:5 Gaza see it, be very *s.*
Mat. 19:22 that saying, he went
away *s.* Luke 18:23, 24
26:22 were exc. *s.* Mark 14:19
31 began to be *s.* very heavy
38 soul exceed. *s.* Mark 14:34
John 16:20 shall be *s.* but sorrow
2 Cor. 6:10 *s.* yet always rejoici.
Phil. 2:28 I may be the less *s.*

SORROWING.

Luke 2:48 father and I so. thee *s.*
Acts 20:38 *s.* th. see face no more

SORRY.

1 Sam. 22:8 none of you that is *s.*
Neh. 8:10 holy to L. nei. be ye *s.*
Ps. 38:18 I will be *s.* for my sin
Is. 51:19 who shall be *s.* for thee
Mat. 14:9 king was *s.* Mark 6:26
17:23 and they were exceedi. *s.*
2 Cor. 2:2 if I ma. you *s.* sa. is *s.*
7:8 *s.* same epistle made you *s.*
9 rejoice not ye we. *s.* for ye *s.*

SORT.

Gen. 6:19 two of ev. *s.* in ark, 20
1 Chr. 24:5 divid. one *s.* wi. ano.
29:14 able to offer after this *s.*
Ezr. 4:8 wrote to Ar. after th. *s.*
Neh. 6:4 sent 4 times after this *s.*
Ezek. 23:42 men of the comm. *s.*
Dan. 1:10 worse th. chil. of yo. *s.*
3:29 no god can del. after this *s.*
Acts 17:5 lewd fellows of baser *s.*
Rom. 15:15 wri. boldly in some *s.*
1 Cor. 3:13 man's work of wh. *s.*
2 Cor. 7:11 sorrow. after godly *s.*
2 Tim. 3:6 of this *s.* who creep
3 John 6 journey after a godly *s.*

SORTS.

Deut. 22:11 garment of divers *s.*
Neh. 5:18 store of all *s.* of wine
Ps. 78:45 divers *s.* of flies, 105:31
Ezek. 27:24 merch. in all *s.* of th.
38:4 clothed with all *s.* of armor

SOSIPATER.

Rom. 16:21 Ja. and S. my kins.

SOSTHENES.

Acts 18:17 the Greeks took S.
1 Cor. 1:1 Paul and S. to church

SOTTISH.

Jer. 4:22 foolish. th. are *s.* child.

SOUGHT.

Gen. 43:30 he *s.* where to weep
Ex. 4:19 men dead wh. *s.* life
24 L. met him, *s.* to kill him
33:7 that *s.* L. went to taberna.
Num. 35:23 ene. nor *s.* his harm
Jud. 14:4 Samson *s.* occasion
1 Sam. 27:4 S. *s.* no more for him
2 Sam. 3:17 *s.* for Da. to be king
4:8 head of ene. that *s.* thy life
21:2 Saul *s.* to slay them in zeal
1 K. 10:24 earth *s.* to Sol. to hear
2 K. 2:17 *s.* three days for Elijah
1 Chr. 26:31 among Heb. were *s.*
Chr. 14:7 because we have *s.* L.
17:4 *s.* to Lord God of his father
25:15 *s.* after gods of Ed. ? 20
26:5 *s.* G. in days of Zechariah,
as long as he *s.* the Lord
Neh. 12:27 they *s.* the Levit. out
Est. 9:2 hand on such as *s.* hurt
Ps. 34:4 I *s.* Lord, he heard, 77:2
111:2 *s.* out of all that have ple.
119:10 with wh. heart I *s.* thee
94 I have *s.* thy precepts
Ec. 7:29 *s.* many inventions
12:9 preacher *s.* out many prov.
Is. 62:12 shalt be called *s.* out
65:1 *s.* of them asked not, found
of th. that *s.* not, Rom. 10:20
10 place for my peo. that *s.* me
Jer. 8:2 moon, whom they ha. *s.*
10:21 the pastors have not *s.* L.
26:21 king *s.* put him to death
50:20 iniquity of Israel sh. be *s.*
Lam. 1:19 they *s.* meat to relieve
Ezek. 22:30 I *s.* a man am. them
26:21 tho' *s.* yet never be found
34:4 nei. *s.* that which was lost
Dan. 8:15 I had *s.* for meaning
Ob. 6 Esau's hidden things *s.* up
Zep. 1:6 those that have not *s.*
Mat. 2:20 dead wh. *s.* child's life

SOUGHT him.

21:46 *s.* to lay hands upon him,
Mark 12:12 ; Luke 20:19
Luke 2:48 I *s.* thee sorrowing
49 how is it that ye *s.* me ?
11:16 others *s.* a sign fr. heaven
13:6 *s.* fru. thereon, found none
19:3 Zaccheus *s.* to see Jesus
John 7:11 J. *s.* him at feast, 11:56
30 they *s.* to take him, 10:39
Acts 12:19 when Herod *s.* for Pe.
17:5 they *s.* to bring them out
Rom. 9:32 bec. *s.* it not by faith
1 Thes. 2:6 nor of men *s.* we glo.
2 Tim. 1:17 in Rome he *s.* me
Heb. 8:7 place shou. have been *s.*
12:17 he *s.* carefully with tears

SOUGHT him.

1 Sam. 10:21 *s. h.* could not be f.
13:14 L. *s. h.* a man to be capt.
23:14 Saul *s. him* every day
1 Chr. 15:13 *s.* not after order
2 Chr. 14:7 *s. h.* he hath giv. rest
15:4 when th. *s. h.* he was found
15 they *s. h.* with their desire
Ps. 37:36 I *s. h.* could not be fou.
78:34 slew them then they *s. h.*
Cant. 3:1 by night I *s. h.* I *s. h.*
but I found him not, 2 ; 5:6
Luke 2:44 they *s. h.* among kins.
4:42 people *s. h.* came to him

SOUL.

Gen. 2:7 man became a living *s.*
34:8 *s.* of son longeth for daugh.
35:18 as her *s.* was in departing
Lev. 4:2 if a *s.* sin thro' ignoran.
5:1 if a *s.* sin, and hear sweari.
6:2 if *s.* lie ; 17:12 no *s.* eat blood
17:11 blood mak. atonem. for *s.*
22:11 if priest buy *s.*
23:30 whatso. *s.* doeth any work
Num. 21:4 *s.* of peo. discouraged
30:4 every bond she hath bound
her *s.* 5, 6, 7, 8, 9, 10, 11, 12, 13
31:28 one *s.* of five hund. for L.
Deut. 11:13 serve him with yo. *s.*
18 lay up th. words in your *s.*
13:3 which. you love L. with all
your *s.* Jos. 22:5 ; 1 K. 2:4
1 Sam. 18:1 *s.* of Jonathan knit
to *s.* of David
30:6 *s.* of the people was griev.
2 Sam. 5:8 blind hated of D.'s *s.*
13:39 *s.* of D. longed to go to A.
1 K. 8:48 return to thee with *s.*
17:21 let this child's *s.* come
2 K. 4:27 let alone, her *s.* is vex.
23:3 keep commandm. with *s.*
1 Chr. 22:19 set yo. *s.* to seek L.
2 Chr. 6:38 if they return with *s.*
15:12 seek the L. with their *s.*
Job 3:20 life giv. to bitter in *s. ?*
12:10 hand is *s.* of every thing
16:4 if yo. *s.* were in my soul's
24:12 *s.* of the wounded crieth
Ps. 19:7 law perfect converting *s.*
33:19 deliver their *s.* from death
34:22 L. redeem. *s.* of his serva.
49:8 redemption of *s.* precious
72:14 he shall redeem their *s.*
78:50 spared not th. *s.* fr. death
86:4 rejoice *s.* of thy serv. O L.
94:21 gather against *s.* of right.
105:15 sent leanness to their *s.*
107:18 their *s.* abhorreth all me.
26 th. *s.* melted bec. of trouble
Prov. 10:3 not suff. *s.* of righteo.
11:25 liberal *s.* shall be made fat
13:2 *s.* of transgressors sh. eat
19 desire accom. is sweet to *s.*
16:24 pleasant words sweet to *s.*
19:2 *s.* without knowl. not good
15 idle *s.* shall suffer hunger
21:10 *s.* of wicked desireth evil
22:23 Lord will spoil *s.* of those
25:13 he refresheth *s.* of masters
27:7 full *s.* loathe. honey-comb,
to hungry *s.* bitter is sweet

Is. 3:9 woe to their *s.* they have
32:6 make empty *s.* of hungry
55:2 let yo. *s.* delight in fatness
3 hear, and your *s.* shall live
58:10 if thou satisfy afflicted *s.*
66:3 th. *s.* delighteth in abomi.
Jer. 4:10 the swo. reacheth the *s.*
20:13 he delivered *s.* of the poor
31:12 their *s.* shall be as a gard.
38:16 L. liveth, made us this *s.*
Lam. 1:11 for meat to relieve *s.*
2:12 wh. their *s.* was poured out
3:25 the Lord is good to the *s.*
Ezek. 18:4 as *s.* of father, so *s.* of
son, the *s.* that sinneth, 20
24:21 what your *s.* pitieth shall
Hos. 9:4 *s.* shall not come into
Mat. 10:28 fear th. can destroy *s.*
Mark 12:33 lo. him wi. he. and *s.*
Acts 2:43 fear came on every *s.*
3:23 eve. *s.* which will not hear
4:32 multitude believ. of one *s.*
Rom. 13:1 let every *s.* be subject
1 *Thes.* 5:23 that your *s.* and bo.
Heb. 10:39 believe to saving of *s.*
Jam. 5:20 he sh. save a *s.* fr. dea.
1 *Pet.* 2:11 lusts war agai, the *s.*
2 *Pet.* 2:8 Lot vexed righteous *r.*
Rev. 16:3 ev. living *s.* died in sea

See AFFLICTED, BITTERNESS.

His SOUL.

Gen. 34:3 *his s.* clave to Dinah
Ex. 30:12 give ransom for *his s.*
Num. 30:2 sw. oath to bind *h. s*
Jud. 10:16 *his s.* was grieved for
16:16 so that *his s.* was vexed
2 *K.* 23:25 Josiah turned to Lord
with all *his s.* 2 *Chr.* 34:31
Job 14:22 *his s.* within him
21:25 dieth in bitterness of *h. s.*
23:13 what *his s.* desireth, even
27:8 when God tak. away *his s.*
31:30 sin, by wish. curse to *h. s.*
33:18 keepeth back *h. s.* fr. pit
22 *his s.* draw. near unto grave
28 will deliver *his s.* from, 30
Ps. 11:5 violence, *his s.* hateth
24:4 who had not lifted up *his s.*
25:13 *his s.* shall dwell at ease
49:18 wh. he lived he bless. *h. s.*
89:48 eh. he deliver *his s.* from?
109:31 save fr. th. condemn *h. s.*
Prov. 6:30 if steal to satisfy *h. s.*
16:17 his way, preserveth *h. s.*
21:23 his mouth, keepeth *his s.*
22:5 that doth keep *his s.* shall
23:14 shalt deliver *his s.* fr. hell
29:10 but the just seek *his s.*
Ec. 2:24 shou. make *his s.* enjoy
6:2 wanteth nothing for *his s.*
3 *his s.* be not filled with good
Is. 29:8 awak. and *his s.* empty
44:20 he cannot deliver *his s.*
53:10 ma. *his s.* an offer. for sin
11 see of travail of *his s.*
12 poured out *h. s.* unto death
Jer. 50:19 *his s.* shall be satisfied
51:6 deliver every man *his s.* 45
Ezek. 18:27 right. he sh. sa. *h. s.*
33:5 warning, shall deliver *h. s.*
Hab. 2:4 *his s.* that is lifted up
Mat. 16:26 lose *h.* own *s.* give in
exchange for *s.? Mark* 8:37
Acts 2:31 *his s.* not left in hell.

My SOUL.

Gen. 12:13 *my s.* sh. live because
19:20 let me escape, *my s.* shall
27:4 *my s.* may bless thee, 25
49:6 O *my s.* come not into their
Lev. 26:11 *my s.* sh. not abh. 30
1 *Sam.* 1:15 poured out *my s.* be.
24:11 thou huntest *my s.* to
26:21 beca. *my s.* was precious
2 *Sam.* 4:9 Lord who hath redeemed *my s.* 1 *K.* 1:29
Job 6:7 the things *my s.* refused

9:21 yet would I not kn. *my s.*
10:1 *my s.* is weary of life, I will
speak bitterness of *my s.*
19:2 how lo. will ye vex *my s.*
27:2 Alm. who hath vexed *my s.*
30:15 they pursue *my s.* as wind
16 *my s.* is poured out upon
25 was not *my s.* gri. for poor?
Ps. 3:2 who say of *my s.* There is
6:3 *my s.* is sore vex. but, O L.
4 deliver *my s.* 17:13; 22:20;
116:4; 120:2
13:2 sh. I take couns. in *my s.?*
16:10 not leave *my s. Acts* 2:27
23:3 he restoreth *my s.* he lead,
25:1 unto th. O L. do I lift *my s.*
20 O keep *my s.* and deliver me
26:9 gather not *my s.* with sin.
30:3 brought *my s.* from grave
31:7 hast known *my s.* in adver.
34:2 *my s.* sh. make boast in L.
35:3 say unto *my s.* I am thy sa.
4 put to shame that seek *my s.*
7 have digged a pit for *my s.*
9 *my s.* shall be joyful in Lord
13 I humbled *my s.* with fast.
41:4 heal *my s.* I have sinned
42:4 I pour out *my s.* in me
5 cast down O *my s.?* 11; **43:5**
6 O my G. *my s.* is cast down
54:4 L. is with that upho. *my s.*
55:18 delivered *my s.* in peace
56:6 when they wait for *my s.*
13 thou hast delivered *my s.*
57:1 be merciful, *my s.* trusteth
4 *my s.* is amo. lions and I lie
6 *my s.* is bowed down
59:3 they lie in wait for *my s.*
62:1 *my s.* waiteth upon God
5 *my s.* wait thou only upon G.
63:8 *my s.* followeth hard after
9 that seek *my s.* to destroy it
66:16 what G. ha. done for *my s.*
69:1 wa. are come in unto *my s.*
18 draw nigh to *my s.*
71:23 *my s.* shall rejoice
77:2 my sore ran, *my s.* refused
Ps. 84:2 *my s.* longeth for the L.
86:2 preserve *my s.* I am holy
4 O Lord, do I lift *my s.* 143:8
13 thou hast deliv. *my s.* from
88:3 *my s.* is full of troubles
14 why castest thou off *my s.?*
94:17 *my s.* had dwelt in silence
103:1 bless the Lord, O *my s.* 2,
22; 104:1, 35
109:20 them th. speak ag. *my s.*
116:7 ret. unto thy rest, O *my s.*
8 thou hast delivered *my s.*
119:20 *my s.* break. for longing
109 *my s.* is continu. in hand
129 therefore doth *my s.* keep
175 let *my s.* live and it shall
120:2 deliver *my s.* O Lord
6 *my s.* dw. wi. him that hate.
130:5 wait for the Lord, *my s.* 6
138:3 strengthen me in *my s.*
139:14 that *my s.* knoweth well
142:4 no man cared for *my s.*
7 bring *my s.* out of prison
143:11 bring *my s.* out of troub.
146:1 praise the Lord, O *my s.*
Ec. 7:28 which yet *my s.* seeketh
Cant. 1:7 wh. *my s.* lo. 3:1, 2, 3, 4
5:6 *my s.* failed when he spake
Is. 1:14 new moons *my s.* hateth
26:9 with *my s.* have I desired
38:17 in love to *my s.* deliv. it
61:10 *my s.* sh. be joyful in God
Jer. 4:19 hast heard, O *my s.*
5:9 *my s.* be avenged? 29; 9:9
6:8 instructed, lest *my s.* depart
12:7 beloved of *my s.* into hand
18:20 they dig. a pit for *my s.*
32:41 rej. over them *my whole s.*
Lam. 3:24 L. my por. saith *my s.*
58 pleased the causes of *my s.*
Mic. 6:7 body for sin of *my s.?*

7:1 *my s.* desired first ripe fruit
Mat. 12:18 in wh. *my s.* is pleas.
26:38 *my s.* is sor. *Mark* 14:34
Luke 1:46 *my s.* doth magnify L.
12:19 I will say to *my s.*
John 12:27 is *my s.* troubled
2 *Cor.* 1:23 for record upon *my s.*
Heb. 10:38 *my s.* sh. have no ple:

Our SOUL.

Num. 11:6 *our s.* is dried away
Ps. 33:20 *our s.* waiteth for Lord
44:25 *our s.* is bowed down
66:9 God who holdeth *our s.*
124:4 stre. had gone over *our s.*
Is. 26:8 the desire of *our s.* is

Own SOUL.

Deut. 13:6 friend as thine *o. s.*
Ps. 22:29 none can keep his *o. s.*
Prov. 6:32 destroyeth his *own s.*
8:36 sinneth, wrongeth his *o. s.*
19:16 commandm. keep. his *o. s.*
20:2 king, sinneth aga. his *o. s.*
29:24 partner with thief ha. *o. s.*
Mat. 16:26 if he shall gain world
and lose his *o. s.? Mark* 8:36
Luke 2:35 sword pierce thy *o. s.*

That SOUL.

Lev. 17:10 set face ag. *t. s.* 20:6
22:3 *that s.* shall be cut off from
23:30 *that s.* will I destroy from
Num. 15:31 *t. s.* sh. utter. be cut

Thy SOUL.

Gen. 26:19 *thy s.* may bless, 31
Deut. 4:9 keep *thy s.* diligently
29 if seek him with all *thy s.*
6:5 L. thy G. with all *t. s.* 30:6
10:12 serve Lord with all *t. s.*
12:15 whatso. *t. s.* lusteth, 14:26
26:16 do with *t. s.* 30:2 obey
with *thy s.*
30:2 obey wi. thy heart and *t. s.*
10 turn to Lord with all *thy s.*
1 *Sam.* 2:16 as much as *t. s.* desi.
20:4 whatsoever *t. s.* desireth
23:20 according to desire of *t. s.*
25:29 man risen to pursue *t. s.*
1 *K.* 11:37 reign according *t. s.*
Ps. 121:7 L. shall preserve *thy s.*
Prov. 2:10 know. is pleas. to *t. s.*
3:22 shall be life to *thy s.*
19:18 let not *thy s.* spare
22:25 and get a snare to *thy s.*
24:12 he that keepeth *t. s.* doth
14 knowl. of wisdom be to *t. s.*
29:17 he sh. give delight to *t. s.*
Is. 51:23 have said to *t. s.* Bow
58:10 draw out *thy s.* to hungry
11 Lord shall satisfy *thy s.*
Jer. 14:19 hath *thy s.* loathed Z.?
38:17 forth, *thy s.* shall live, 20
Ezek. 3:19 deliv. *thy s.* 21; 35:9
Hab. 2:10 hast sinned ag. *thy s.*
Mat. 22:37 love L. with all *thy s.*
Luke 12:30; *Luke* 10:27
Luke 12:20 *thy s.* be requ. of thee
3 *John* 2 even as *thy s.* prospere.
Rev. 18:14 fruits *t. s.* lust. after

See LIVETH.

SOULS.

Gen. 12:5 A. took *s.* th. had got
46:26 *s.* that came into Egypt
27 sons of Joseph in Egy. were
two *s.* all the *s.* of the house
of Jacob were 70 *s. Ex.* 1:5
Ex. 12:4 a lamb according to *s.*
30:15 atonement for your *s.* 16;
Lev. 17:11; *Num.* 31:50
Lev. 18:29 *s.* that commit them
20:25 not make your *s.* abomin.
Num. 16:38 sin. ag. their own *s.*
30:9 wherewith ha. bound th. *s.*
Jos. 23:14 know in all your *s.*
1 *Sam.* 25:29 *s.* of ene. shall sling
Ps. 72:13 shall save *s.* of needy
97:10 preserveth *s.* of his saints

Prov. 11:30 that win. *s.* is wise
14:25 a true witness deliver. *s.*
Is. 57:16 spi. should fail, and *s.*
Jer. 2:34 in thy skirts is bl. of *s.*
6:16 rest for your *s. Mat.* 11:29
26:19 procure evil against our *s.*
44:7 why com. evil ag. your *s. ?*
Lam. 1:19 sought meat to th. *s.*
Ezek. 7:19 sh. not satisfy their *s.*
13:18 hunt *s.* hunt *s.* of peo. 20
19 slay *s.* that should not die
14:14 should deliver their own *s.*
18:4 *s.* are mine; 22:25 devou. *s.*
Acts 2:41 added to them 3,000 *s.*
7:14 Jacob and his kindred 75 *s.*
14:22 confirming *s.* of disciples
15:24 troubled you, subvert. *s.*
27:37 we. in all in the ship 276 *s.*
1 *Thes.* 2:8 imparted our *s.* to you
Heb. 13:17 they watch for your *s.*
Jam. 1:21 word able to save yo. *s.*
1 *Pet.* 1:22 have purified your *s.*
3:20 that is, eight *s.* were saved
4:19 commit keep. of *s.* to him
Rev. 6:9 I saw *s.* of them slain
18:13 no man buyeth *s.* of men
20:4 I saw *s.* of them beheaded

See AFFLICT.

SOUND, Substantive.
Ex. 28:35 his *s.* shall be heard
Lev. 26:36 *s.* of a shaken leaf
Jos. 6:5 hear *s.* of trumpet, 20
2 *Sam.* 5:24 *s.* of going in tops of
mulberry-trees, 1 *Chr.* 14:15
1 *K.* 1:40 earth rent with the *s.*
14:6 Ahijah heard *s.* of her feet
18:41 *s.* of abundance of rain
2 *K.* 6:32 is not *s.* of mas.'s feet?
1 *Chr.* 16:42 with trum. make *s.*
2 *Chr* 5:13 one *s.* to be heard
Neh. 4:20 in wh. place ye hear *s.*
Job 15:21 dreadful *s.* in his ears
21:12 rejoice at *s.* of the organ
37:2 *s.* that go. out of his mouth
39:24 not believ. he it is the *s.*
Ps. 47:5 gone up with *s.* of trum.
77:17 water, skies sent out a *s.*
89:15 people that know joyful *s.*
92:3 sing upon harp with sol. *s.*
150:3 praise him wi. *s.* of trum.
Ec. 12:4 *s.* of grinding is low
Jer. 4:19 hast heard *s.* of trum.
6:17 hearken to *s.* of trumpet?
42:14 where we shall hear no *s.*
50:22 *s.* of battle is in the land
51:54 a *s.* of a cry from Babylon
Ezek. 10:5 *s.* of cherubim's wings
26:13 *s.* of thy harps be no more
15 sh. not the isles sha. at *s. ?*
27:28 suburbs shall shake at *s.*
31:16 made nati. to shake at *s.*
33:5 he heard *s.* of the trumpet
Dan. 3:5 ye hear the *s.* 7, 10, 15
Amos 2:2 Moab shall die with *s.*
Mat. 24:31 angels with great *s.*
John 3:8 hearest *s.* canst not tell
Acts 2:2 there came *s.* from hea.
Rom. 10:18 *s.* went into all earth
1 *Cor.* 14:7 thin. with. life giv. *s.* 8
Heb. 12:19 not come to *s.* of tru.
Rev. 1:15 as *s.* of many waters
9:9 *s.* of wings as *s.* of chariots

SOUND, Adjective.
Ps. 119:80 let my heart be *s.*
Prov. 2:7 he layeth up *s.* wisdom
8:14 counsel is mine and *s.* wis.
14:30 a *s.* heart is life of flesh
Luke 15:27 rec. him safe and *s.*
1 *Tim.* 1:10 contrary to *s.* doctri.
2 *Tim.* 1:7 G. hath giv. us *s.* mi.
13 hold fast form of *s.* words
4:3 will not endure *s.* doctrine
Tit. 1:9 be able by *s.* doctrine
13 that they may be *s.* in faith
2:1 things which become *s.*
doctrine

Tit. 2:2 th. aged men be *s.* in fa.
8 *s.* speech cannot be condem.

SOUND, Verb.
Num. 10:7 shall not *s.* an alarm
1 *Chr.* 15:19 were appointed to *s.*
Is. 16:11 my bowels sh. *s.* for M.
Jer. 48:36 my heart sh. *s.* for M.
Joel 2:1 *r.* alarm in holy mount.
Mat. 6:2 do not *s.* trumpet bef.
1 *Cor.* 15:52 the trumpet shall *s.*
Rev. 8:6 prep. themselves to *s.*
10:7 sev. angel shall begin to *s.*

SOUNDED.
Ex. 19:19 the trumpet *s.* long
1 *Sam.* 20:12 wh. I have *s.* father
Neh. 4:18 he that *s.* the trumpet
Luke 1:44 saluta. *s.* in my ears
Acts 27:28 *s.* found 20 fathoms
1 *Thes.* 1:8 fr. you *s.* word of L.
Rev. 8:7 first angel *s.* and there
8 second *s.* 10 third; 12 fourth
9:1 fifth *s.* 13 sixth; 11:15 sev.

SOUNDETH.
Ex. 19:13 when trumpet *s.* long

SOUNDING.
2 *Chr.* 5:12 with th. 120 priests *s.*
13:12 his priests with *s.* trum.
Is. 63:15 wh. is thy zeal and *s. ?*
Ezek. 7:7 not the *s.* of mountains
1 *Cor.* 13:1 not charity, as *s.* brass

SOUNDNESS.
Ps. 38:3 th. is no *s.* in my flesh, 7
Is. 1:6 no *s.* in it, but wounds
Acts 3:16 given him this perf. *s.*

SOUNDS.
1 *Cor.* 14:7 give a distinct. in *s.*

SOUR.
Is. 18:5 when *s.* grape is ripen.
Jer. 31:29 the fathers have eaten
a *s.* grape. *Ezek.* 18:2
30 ev. man that eateth *s.* grape
Hos. 4:18 their drink is *s.*

SOUTH.
Gen. 12:9 Abr. journeyed tow. *s.*
13:1 A. went into *s.* 3 went fr. *s.*
28:14 spr. abroad to north and *s.*
Num. 13:29 Amalekites dw. in *s.*
Deut. 33:23 pos. thou west and *s.*
1 *Sam.* 20:41 Dav. arose out of *s.*
1 *K.* 7:25 three looking towards
the *s.* 2 *Chr.* 4:4
Job 9:9 mak. chambers of the *s.*
39:26 stretch wings toward *s.*
Ps. 75:6 com. not fr. east nor *s.*
89:12 north and *s.* thou created
107:3 gathered fr. north and *s.*
Ec. 1:6 wind goeth toward *s.*
11:3 if the tree falleth toward *s.*
Is. 30:6 burden of beasts of *s.*
43:6 say to *s.* Keep not back
Jer. 13:19 cit. of *s.* shall be shut
32:44 buy fields in cities of *s.*
33:13 in cit. of *s.* shall flocks pa.
Ezek. 21:4 sword ag. all from *s.*
40:2 as the frame of a city on *s.*
Dan. 11:5 and the king of the *s.*
Ob. 19 they of *s.* sh. pos mount
20 captivity sh. poss. cit. of *s.*
Zec. 7:7 when men inhabited *s.*
14:4 mountain remove toward *s.*
Mat. 12:42 queen of *s.* shall rise
Luke 13:29 come fr. *s.* to sit do.
Acts 8:26 arise, and go toward *s.*
Rev. 21:13 on the *s.* three gates

SOUTH border.
Num. 34:3 *s. b.* the outmost coa.
Jos. 15:2 the *s. border* of Judah

SOUTH country.
Gen. 20:1 Abrah. sojourned *s. c.*
24:62 for Isaac dwelt in the *s. c.*

SOUTH land.
Jos. 15:19 given me *s. l. Jud.* 1:15

SOUTH quarter.
Num. 34:3 *s. q.* fr. Zin by coast

Jos. 18:15 *s. q.* fr. end of Kirjath.

SOUTH Ramoth.
1 *Sam.* 30:27 which were in *s. R.*

SOUTH side.
Ex. 26:18 boards on *s. s.* 36:23
Num. 2:10 on *s. s.* shall be stan.
Ezek. 48:16 *s. s.* 4,500 meas. 33

SOUTHWARD.
Gen. 13:14 L. said to A. Look *s*
Num. 13:17 get ye up this way *s.*

SOUTH-WEST.
Acts 27:12 lying toward *s.-w.*

SOUTH wind.
Job 37:17 quieteth earth by *s. w.*
Ps. 78:26 he brought in *s. w.*
Cant. 4:16 *s. w.* blow on my gar.
Luke 12:55 *s. w.* bl. will he heat
Acts 27:13 wh. *s. w.* blew softly

SOW, Substantive.
2 *Pet.* 2:22 the *s.* washed, to her

SOW, Verb.
Gen. 47:23 ye shall *s.* the land
Ex. 23:10 *s.* the land, *Lev.* 25:3
Lev. 19:19 sh. not *s.* wi. mingled
25:4 in sev. year shalt not *s.* 11
20 we shall not *s.* nor gather
26:16 shall *s.* your seed in vain
2 *K.* 19:29 in the third year *s.* ye.
Is. 37:30
Job 4:8 *s.* wickedness reap same
31:8 let me *s.* let another eat
Ps. 107:37 *s.* fields and vineyards
126:5 *s.* in tears sh. reap in joy
Ec. 11:4 observ. wind, sh. not *s.*
6 in the morning *s.* thy seed
Is. 28:24 ploughman pl. to *s. ?*
30:23 rain of seed thou shalt *s.*
32:20 blessed that *s.* beside wat.
Jer. 4:3 *s.* not among thorns
31:27 I will *s.* the house of Isr.
35:7 nei. build house nor *s.* seed
Hos. 2:23 I will *s.* her unto me
10:12 *s.* to yourselves in right.
Mic. 6:15 thou shalt *s.* not reap
Zec. 10:9 *s.* them among people
Mat. 6:26 fowls of the air *s.* not
13:3 a sower went forth to *s.*
Mark 4:3; *Luke* 8:5
27 didst thou *s.* good seed
Luke 12:24 ravens nei. *s.* nor reap
19:21 reap. thou didst not *s.* 22

SOWED, EDST.
Gen. 26:12 Is. *s.* in land sa. year
Deut. 11:10 wh. thou *s.* thy seed
Jud. 9:45 Abimelech *s.* Shechem
Mat. 13:24 man which *s.* good
seed; 25 *s.* tares, 39

SOWER.
Is. 55:10 it may give seed to *s.*
Jer. 50:16 cut off *s.* from Baby.
Mat. 13:18 hear ye parable of *s.*
Mark 4:14 *s.* soweth word
2 *Cor* 9:10 ministereth seed to *s.*

SOWEST.
1 *Cor.* 15:36 thou *s.* not quicken.
37 *s.* not body that shall be

SOWETH.
Prov. 6:14 *s.* discord; 19 *s.* disc.
11:18 that *s.* righteousn. a rew.
16:28 a froward man *s.* strife
22:8 *s.* iniquity, reap vanity
Amos 9:13 overtake him that *s.*
Mat. 13:37 that *s.* good seed is S.
Mark 4:14 sower *s.* the word
John 4:36 he that *s.* and reapeth
37 true, one *s.* another reapeth
2 *Cor.* 9:6 *s.* sparingly; *s.* bounti.
Gal. 6:7 whatsoever a man *s.*
8 that *s.* to flesh, reap corrup.

SOWING.
Lev. 11:37 if carc. fall on any *s.*
26:5 vint. shall reach to *s.* time

SOWN.

Deut. 21:4 val. nei. eared nor *s.*
22:9 lest fruit of seed *s.* be defi.
29:23 generation see land not *s.*
Jud. 6:3 Israel had *s.* Mid. came
Ps. 97:11 light is *s.* for righteous
Is. 19:7 thing *s.* by brook wither
40:24 plant. yea, shall not be *s.*
61:11 caus. things *s.* to spring
Jer. 2:2 after me in a land not *s.*
12:13 they have *s.* wheat, thorns
Ezek. 36:9 ye sh. be tilled and *s.*
Hos. 8:7 *s.* wind, reap whirlwind
Nah. 1:14 no more of thy name *s.*
Hag. 1:6 *s.* much, bring little
Mat. 13:19 catcheth away that
    which was *s. Mark* 4:15
25:24 reaping wh. th. hast not *s.*
Mark 4:16 wh. *s.* on stony grou.
18 *s.* am. thorns: 20 *s.* on gro.
31 wh. *s.* is less than all seeds
1 *Cor.* 9:11 *s.* to you spir. things
15:42 *s.* in cor. 43 *s.* in dishonor
44 it is *s.* a natural body. raised
2 *Cor.* 9:10 multiply your seed *s.*
Jam. 3:18 righteousn. *s.* in peace

SPACE.

Gen. 32:16 put a *s.* betwixt drove
Lev. 25:8 *s.* of 7 sabbaths of yea.
Jos. 3:4 a *s.* between you and it
1 *Sam.* 26:13 a. betw. D.'s comp.
Ezr. 9:8 *s.* grace sh. be showed
Luke 22:59 about *s.* of one hour
Acts 5:34 put apostles forth lit. *s.*
13:20 about *s.* of 450 years
19:8 spake boldly *s.* of 3 months
10 continued by *s.* of 2 years
34 about *s.* of two hours
20:21 *s.* of 3 years I ceased not
Rev. 2:21 I gave her *s.* to repent
8:1 silence about *s.* of half hour
Rev. 14:20 blood by *s.* of 1,600 fur.
17:10 must continue a short *s.*

SPAIN.

Rom. 15:24 whenso. I jour. to S.
28 I will come by you into S.

SPAKE.

Gen. 29:9 wh. he *s.* Rachel came
Deut. 1:43 I *s.* ye would not hear
28:68 L. br. thee by whereof I *s.*
1 *Sam.* 1:13 Han. *s.* in her heart
2 *K.* 9:12 and thus *s.* he to him
1 *Chr.* 18:19 one *s.* after manner
32:19 they *s.* ag. God of Jerusa.
Neh. 13:24 *s.* half in speech of A.
Job 2:13 sat down, none *s.* a word
19:18 I arose, they *s.* against me
29:22 after my words they *s.* not
32:16 they *s.* not, but stood still
Ps. 78:19 they *s.* against God
Prov. 30:1 the man *s.* unto Ithiel
    and Ucal
Jer. 20:8 for since I *s.* I cried out
Ezek. 24:18 so I *s.* to the people
Mat. 3:16 feared L. *s.* one to ano.
Mat. 9:33 devil cast out dumb *s.*
    29:22 *; Luke* 11:14
21:45 perceived he *s.* of them
Luke 1:55 as he *s.* to our fathers
2:50 understood not say. he *s.*
24:6 remember how he *s.* to you
36 as they thus *s.* Jesus stood
John 1:15 this was he of wh. I *s.*
7:13 no man *s.* openly of him
46 Never man *s.* like this man
8:27 understood not that he *s.*
10:6 wh. things they were *s.*
41 things John *s.* of this man
12:38 saying fulfil. he *s.* 18:9, 32
13:22 look. doubt. of who. he *s.*
24 who it sho. be of who. he *s.*
Acts 13:45 Jews *s.* ag. things sp.
22:9 heard not voice of him *s.*
26:24 as he *s.* for himself, Fest.
1 *Cor.* 13:11 wh. child *s.* as child
14:5 I would ye *s.* with tongues
Heb. 12:25 refus. him *s.* on earth

2 *Pet.* 1:21 men of G. *s.* as moved
Rev. 1:12 turn. to see voice th. *s.*

God SPAKE.

Gen. 35:15 place where *God s.*
Deut. 1:6 L. *God s.* to us in Hor.
Jos. 23:14 of good things *God s.*
John 9:29 we know *G. s.* to Mo.
Acts 7:6 and *God s.* on this wise
Heb. 1:1 *God* who *s.* in time past
See LORD, *expressly.*

Lord *or* God SPAKE, *implicitly.*

1 *Sam.* 9:17 which I *s.* to thee of
28:17 *Lord* hath done as he *s.*
1 *K.* 6:12 word I *s.* unto David
2 *Chr.* 6:4 who fulfilled that he *s.*
Ps. 33:9 he *s.* and it was done
Is. 65:12 I *s.* did not hear, 66:4
Jer. 7:13 I *s.* to you, rising up
22 I *s.* not to fathers, I broug.
14:14 I sent them not, neither *s.*
31:20 since I *s.* ag. him I rem.
Lam. 1:28 heard one that *s. 2:2*
Luke 24:44 these are words I *s.*
Heb. 4:4 he *s.* in a certain place

SPAKEST.

Jud. 13:11 man *s.* to woman ?
Neh. 9:13 *s.* with them fr. heaven
Jer. 48:27 since thou *s.* skippedst

SPAN.

Ex. 28:16 *s.* length, *s.* brea. 39:9
1 *Sam.* 17:4 G. height, 6 cu. a *s.*
Is. 40:12 meted heaven with *s.* ?
Lam. 2:20 wom. eat chil. *s.* long
Ezek. 43:13 bord. of altar be a *s.*

SPANNED.

Is. 48:13 right hand *s.* heavens

SPARE.

Gen. 18:24 not *s.* pl. for 50 right.
Deut. 13:8 sh. not *s.* nor conceal
29:20 Lord will not *s.* him
1 *Sam.* 15:3 destroy Amal. *s.* not
Neh. 13:22 *s.* me accor. to mercy
Job 6:10 let him not *s.* I have not
20:13 he *s.* and forsake it not
27:22 sh. cast upon him, not *s.*
30:10 *s.* not to spit in my face
Ps. 39:13 O *s.* that I may recover
72:13 he shall *s.* poor and needy
Prov. 6:34 not *s.* in day of veng.
19:18 let not soul *s.* for crying
Is. 9:19 no man shall *s.* brother
13:18 their eye shall not *s.* chil.
30:14 shall break it, shall not *s.*
54:2 *s.* lengthen cords
58:1 *s.* not, lift voice like trum.
Jer. 13:14 will not *s. Ezek.* 24:14
21:7 not *s.* th. 50:14 *s.* no arro.
51:3 *s.* ye not her young men
Ezek. 5:11 nor mine eyes *s.* 7:4,
    9 ; 8:18 ; 9:10
9:5 let not your eyes *s.*
Joel 2:17 say *s.* thy people, O L.
Jon. 4:11 should not I *s.* Nine. ?
Hab. 1:17 not *s.* to slay nations
Mal. 3:17 *s.* th. as man spar. son
Luke 15:17 bread enough to *s.*
Rom. 11:21 lest he also *s.* not
1 *Cor.* 7:28 have trouble, I *s.* you
2 *Cor.* 1:23 to *s.* you I came not
13:2 if I come again, will not *s.*

SPARED.

1 *Sam.* 15:9 Saul and people *s.*
24:10 kill thee, but mine eye *s.*
2 *Sam.* 12:4 *s.* to take of his flock
21:7 the king *s.* Mephibosheth
2 *K.* 5:20 master hath *s.* Naaman
Ps. 78:50 he *s.* not soul fr. death
Ezek. 20:17 mi. eye *s.* them from
Rom. 8:32 he that *s.* not his Son
11:21 if God *s.* not nat. branches
2 *Pet.* 2:4 if God *s.* not angels
5 *s.* not old world, saved Noah

SPARETH, ING.

Prov. 13:24 that *s.* rod, hat. son

17:27 hath knowledge *s.* words
21:26 righteous giveth, *s.* not
Mal. 3:17 as a man *s.* his son
Acts 20:29 wolves enter, not *s.*

SPARINGLY.

2 *Cor.* 9:6 he who sow. *s.* reap *s.*

SPARK.

Job 18:5 *s.* of his fire not shine
Is. 1:31 maker of it be as a *s.*

SPARKS.

Job 5:7 trouble as *s.* fly upward
41:19 burning lamps, *s.* of fire
Is. 50:11 comp. yourselves wi. *s.*

SPARKLED.

Ezek. 1:7 *s.* like color of brass

SPARROW.

Ps. 84:3 *s.* hath found a house
102:7 as a *s.* upon house-top

SPARROWS.

Mat. 10:29 two *s.* sold for farth. ?
31 more value th. *s. Luke* 12:7
Luke 12:6 5 *s.* sold for 2 farth. ?

SPAT.

John 9:6 spok. he *s.* on ground

SPEAK.

Gen. 18:27 ta. on me to *s.* to G. 31
24:50 we cannot *s.* bad or good
31:24 take heed thou *s.* not to J.
44:16 what shall we *s.* ?
Ex. 4:14 I kn. that he can *s.* well
29:42 wh. I will meet you to *s.*
34:35 he went in to *s.* with Lord
Num. 12:8 not afraid to *s.* ag. M.
22:35 word I *s.* that thou shalt *s.*
23:12 must I not *s.* which the L.
Deut. 18:19 words *s.* in my name
20 presume to *s.* in my name
2 *Sam.* 19:10 *s.* ye not a word
1 *K.* 12:7 *s.* go. words, 2 *Chr.* 10:7
22:24 spirit from me to *s.* to th.
    2 *Chr.* 18:23
Job 8:2 how long *s.* these thi. ?
11:5 oh that G. would *s.* ag. th.
13:7 will ye *s.* wickedly for G. ?
18:2 afterwards we will *s.*
36:2 ha. yet to *s.* on G.'s behalf
41:3 will he *s.* soft words ?
Ps. 2:5 them sh. he *s.* in wrath
28:3 which *s.* peace to neigh.
40:5 if I would declare and *s.* of
69:12 that sit in gate *s.* ag. me
71:10 mine enemies *s.* ag. me
85:8 I will hear what L. will *s.*
94:4 how long they *s.* hard thi. ?
119:172 my tongue shall *s.*
139:20 *s.* against thee wickedly
145:6 shall *s.* of might of thy
21 my mouth sh. *s.* praise of L.
Ec. 3:7 to be silent, time to *s.*
Is. 8:20 if they *s.* not accord. to
28:11 with ano. tongue sh. he *s.*
29:4 thou shalt *s.* out of ground
52:6 I am he that doth *s.*
Jer. 5:14 saith L. Bec. ye *s.* this
7:27 thou sh. *s.* all these words
13:12 thou shalt *s.* this word to
8:7 I shall *s.* about a nation, 9
20:9 I will not *s.* any more
26:2 *s.* words I command to *s.* 8
32:4 shall *s.* with him mouth to
    mouth
34:3 he shall *s.* with thee
Ezek. 2:7 thou shalt *s.* my words
24:27 shalt *s.* be no more dumb
Hab. 2:3 at the end it shall *s.*
Mat. 10:19 ye shall *s. Mark* 13:11
20 not ye that *s. Mark* 13:11
12:34 can ye being evil *s.* good ?
Mark 14:71 kn. not of wh. ye *s.*
Luke 1:19 I am sent to *s.* to thee
20 not able to *s.* till th. sh. be
22 wh. he came he could not *s.*
6:26 when men *s.* well of you
12:10 whosoever shall *s.* a word
John 3:11 verily we *s.* th. we kn.

9:21 of age, he shall s. for hims.
16:13 of. of himself, that shall he
Acts 2:11 hear them s. in tongu.
26:1 P. thou art permitted to s.
Rom. 15:18 I will not dare to s.
1 *Cor.* 3:1 I could not s. to you as
12:30 do all s. with ? 14:23 all s.
14:35 sha. for women to s. in ch.
2 *Cor.* 2:17 in sight of God s. we
4:13 we believe and therefore s.
12:19 we s. before God in Christ
Col. 4:4 manifest, as I ought to s.
1 *Thes.* 1:8 so that we need not s.
2:4 so we s. not as pleasing men
Tit. 3:2 put th. in mind to s. evil
Heb. 6:9 we thus s. 9:5 cannot s.
Jam. 1:19 let ev. man be sl. to s.
1 *John* 4:5 ?heref. s. they of world

SPEAK, *imperatively.*
Ex. 20:19 s. thou, we will hear
Deut. 3:26 Lord said, s. no more
5:27 s. to us that L. sh. s. to th.
1 *Sam.* 3:9 s. L. servant hear. 10
2 *Sam.* 17:6 his say. ? if not s.
1 *K.* 22:13 s. that which is good,
2 *Chr.* 18:12
Est. 5:14 to-morrow s. to king
Job 13:22 let me s. and answer
33:32 s. for I desire to justify th.
34:33 therof. s. what thou know.
Prov. 23:9 s. not in ears of a fool
Is. 8:10 s. word, it sh. not stand
30:10 who say. s. to us smooth
41:1 come near, then let them s.
Dan. 10:19 I said, Let my lord s.
Zec. 8:16 s. the truth, *Eph.* 4:25
Mark 13:11 given in that hour, s.
Acts 18:9 s. hold not thy peace
1 *Cor.* 14:28 let him s. to himself
29 let prophets s. two or three
Jam. 2:12 so s. ye and do, as th.

I SPEAK.
Ex. 19:9 peo. may hear, wh. *I s.*
Deut. 11:2 *I s.* not wi. your chil.
1 *K.* 22:14 L. saith, that *will I s.*
Job 9:35 then would *I s.* and not
13:3 *I would s.* to Almighty
16:4 *I* also could s. as ye do
37:20 shall it be told him *I s.?*
Ps. 45:1 *I s.* of things that I have
120:7 when *I s.* they are for war
Jer. 1:6 L. *I cannot s.* I am a ch.
6:10 sh. *I s.* and give warning ?
28:7 hear this word that *I s.* in
38:20 voice of the L. which *I s.*
Ezek. 3:27 when *I s.* with thee, I
John 4:26 Jesus saith, *I that s.*
6:63 the words that *I s.* to you
7:17 or whether *I s.* of myself
8:28 as Father taught me, *I s.*
38 *I s.* that which I have seen
12:49 gave com. what *I should s.*
50 *I s.* as Father said, so *I s.*
13:18 *I s.* not of all, I know
14:10 words *I s.* *I s.* not of mys.
17:13 these things *I s.* in world
Acts 21:37 P. said, May *I s.* to th.
26:26 bef. whom *I* also s. freely
Rom. 3:5 God unrighte. ? *I s.* as
6:19 *I s.* after manner, *Gal.* 3:15
1 *Cor.* 14:18 *I s.* with tongues
19 *I* had rather s. five words
2 *Cor.* 11:17 that wh. *I s.* *I s.* not
Eph. 6:20 that therein *I ma*? *s.*

I will SPEAK, *or* **will I.**
Gen. 18:30 L. angry, *I will s.* 32
Num. 12:8 with him *will I s.*
24:13 what L. sai. that *will I s.*
1 *K.* 22:14 ; 2 *Chr.* 18:13
Deut. 32:1 give ear, and *I will s.*
Jud. 6:39 Gideon said, *I will s.*
1 *K.* 2:18 well, *I will s.* for thee
Job 32:20 *I w. s.* th. I be refresh.
33:31 hold thy peace, *I will s.*
42:4 I beseech thee, and *I w. s.*
Ps. 50:7 hear, my peo. *I will s.*

73:15 if I say, *I will s.* thus
145:5 *I w. s.* of the honor of thy
Jer. 5:5 to great men, and *I w. s.*
Ezek. 2:1 stand on feet and *I w. s.*
12:25 *I will s.* and word I speak
1 *Cor.* 14:21 wi. other lips *w. I s.*

SPEAKER.
Ps. 140:11 let not evil s. be esta.
Acts 14:12 because he was chi. s.

SPEAKEST.
1 *Sam.* 9:21 wheref. then s. th. ?
Job 2:10 s. as one of foolish wom.
Is. 40:27 why s. thou, O Israel
Jer. 43:2 thou s. falsely, the Lord
Zec. 13:3 s. lies in name of Lord
John 16:29 now s. thou plainly
19:10 Pi. saith, s. thou not unto
Acts 17:19 know whereof th. s.?

SPEAKETH.
Gen. 45:12 it is my mouth that s.
Ex. 33:11 spa. to M. as man s.
Num. 23:26 all that Lord s.
Job 33:14 G. s. once, yea, twice
Prov. 6:13 he s. with his feet
16:13 they love him that s. right
26:25 wh. he s. fair, believe not
Jer. 10:1 word which L. s. to you
28:2 thus s. L. G. 29:25 ; 30:2 ;
Hag. 1:2 ; *Zec.* 6:12 ; 7:9
Ezek. 10:5 voice of G. when he s.
Mat. 10:20 S. of Father s. in you
John 3:31 of earth, s. of the earth
34 wh. God sent, s. words of G.
7:18 he that s. of himself, seek.
26 but lo, he s. boldly, they say
8:44 wh. he s. a lie, he s. of own
Acts 8:34 of wh. s. the pro. this?
Heb. 11:4 he being dead yet s.
12:24 that s. better things than
25 th. ye refuse not him that s.

SPEAKING.
Gen. 24:15 before he had done s.
45 before I had done s. in hea.
Deut. 11:19 s. of them when thou
Est. 10:3 s. peace to his seed
Job 1:16 wh. he was yet s. 17, 18
4:2 who can withhold from s. ?
32:15 no more, they left off s.
Is. 58:13 nor s. thine own words
65:24 while they are yet s. I
Jer. 7:13 early, s. 25:3 ; 34:14
Dan. 8:13 I heard one saint s.
Acts 14:3 they abode, s. boldly in
2 *Cor.* 13:3 a proof of Ch. s. in me
See END.

SPEAKING, S.
Mat. 6:7 th. be heard for much s.
Eph. 4:31 let evil s. be put away
1 *Pet.* 2:1 laying aside all evil s.

SPEAR.
Jos. 8:18 stretch out thy s. 26
Jud. 5:8 a s. seen among 40,000
1 *Sam.* 13:22 s. with any but wi.
17:7 staff of s. like weaver's bea.
2 *Sam.* 21:19 ; 1 *Chr.* 20:5
45 comest with a sword and s.
21:8 under thy hand a s.
26:7 S.'s s. stuck at bolster, 11
16 now see where king's s. is
2 *Sam.* 1:6 Saul lean. upon his s.
2:23 Abner with s. smote Asahel
23:7 with iron and staff of a s.
8 he lifted up his s. against 800
18 lifted up his s. against 300,
1 *Chr.* 11:11, 20
21 he slew the Egyptian with
his own s. 1 *Chr.* 11:23
Job 39:23 qui. rattleth, glitter. s.
41:26 s. of him that lay. at him
29 Leviathan laugheth at a s.
Ps. 35:3 draw out s. stop way
46:9 breake. bow and cutteth s.
Jer. 6:23 lay hold on bow and s.
Nah. 3:3 lifteth up sword and s.
Hab. 3:11 at shining of glitter. s.

John 19:34 one of the soldiers
with a s. pierced his side

SPEARS.
1 *Sam.* 13:19 Heb. make sw. or s.
2 *K.* 11:10 king David's s. that
were in temple, 2 *Chr.* 23:9
2 *Chr.* 11:12 in ev. city he put s.
26:14 Uzziah prep. for them s.
Neh. 4:13 I set the people with s.
16 the other half held the s. 21
Ps. 57:4 whose teeth are s. and
Is. 2:4 s. into hooks, *Mic.* 4:3
Jer. 46:4 furbish s. and put on
Ezek. 39:9 shall burn s. with fire
Joel 3:10 pruning-hooks into s.

SPEARMEN.
Ps. 68:30 rebuke company of s.
Acts 23:23 make ready 200 s.

SPECIAL.
Deut. 7:6 L. chosen thee, a s. pe.
Acts 19:11 s. miracles done by P.
See ESPECIALLY.

SPECKLED.
Gen. 30:32 removing the s. cattle
31:8 s. thy wages, cattle bare s.
Jer. 12:9 heritage is as s. bird
Zec. 1:8 red horses, s. and white

SPECTACLE.
1 *Cor.* 4:9 made a s. to the world

SPED.
Jud. 5:30 have they not s.?

SPEECH.
Gen. 4:23 hearken to my s.
11:1 whole earth was of one s.
Ex. 4:10 M. said, I am slow of s.
Deut. 22:14 give occas. of s. aga.
32:2 my s. shall distil as dew
2 *Sam.* 14:20 fetch ab. form of s.
19:11 the s. of Is. come to king
1 *K.* 3:10 Solomon's s. pleased L.
Neh. 13:24 chil. spake half in s.
Job 12:20 removeth s. of trusty
13:17 my s. and declara. 21:2 ;
Ps. 17:16 ; *Is.* 28:23 ; 32:9
24:25 make s. nothing worth ?
29:22 my s. dropped upon them
37:19 we cannot order our s. by
Ps. 19:2 day unto day uttereth s.
3 there is no s. wh. voice is not
Prov. 7:21 fair s. cau. him to yie.
17:7 excel. s. becom. not a fool
Cant. 4:3 lips like scarl. s. come.
Is. 29:4 thy s. sh. be low out of
the dust ; thy s. sh. whisper
33:19 deeper s. th. thou perceive
Jer. 31:23 shall use this s. in Ju.
Ezek. 1:24 voi. of s. as noise of h.
3:5 sent to a peo. of strange s. 6
Hab. 3:2 O L. I ha. heard thy s.
Mat. 26:73 thy s. bewrayeth th.
Mark 7:32 impediment in his s.
14:70 thy s. agreeth thereto
John 8:43 not underst. my s. ?
Acts 14:11 in s. of Lycaonia
20:7 continued his s. till midni.
1 *Cor.* 2:1 not with excelle. of s.
4 s. was not with entic. words
4:19 not the s. but the power
2 *Cor.* 3:12 great plainness of s.
7:4 great my boldness of s. tow.
10:10 his s. is contemptible
11:6 rude in s. not in knowled.
Col. 4:6 let s. be alw. with grace
Tit. 2:8 sound s. cannot be cond.

SPEECHES.
Num. 12:8 speak not in dark s.
Job 6:26 s. of one that is despe.
15:3 with s. he can do no good ?
32:14 nei. will I answer with s.
Rom. 16:18 by fair s. dec. hearts
Jude 15 convince them of hard s.

SPEECHLESS.
Mat. 22:12 garm. and he was s.
Luke 1:22 Zacharias remained s.
Acts 9:7 men with him stood s.

SPEED.

Gen. 24:12 O L. send me good *s.*
Ezr. 6:12 let it be done with *s.*
Is. 5:26 they shall come with *s.*
Acts 17:15 come to him wi. all *s.*
2 John 10 rec. not, nor bid G. *s.*
11 that biddeth him God *s.*

See MAKE, MADE.

SPEEDY.

Zep. 1:18 make a *s.* riddance

SPEEDILY.

2 Sam. 17:16 not in plains, *s.* pa.
Ezr. 6:13 king sent, they did *s.*
7:17 may. buy *s.* with this mon.
21 E. shall requi. it be done *s.*
26 let judgment be executed *s.*
Ps. 31:2 bow thine ear; deliv. *s.*
69:17 in trou. hear me *s.* 143:7
79:8 let thy mercies *s.* prev. us
102:2 in day when I call, ans. *s.*
Ec. 8:11 sent. not executed *s.*
Is. 58:8 health sh. spring forth *s.*
Zec. 8:21 let us go *s.* and pray

SPEND.

Deut. 32:23 I will *s.* mine arrows
Job 21:13 *s.* their days in wealth
36:11 *s.* their days in prosperity
Ps. 90:9 we *s.* our years as a tale
Is. 55:2 why *s.* money for that?
Acts 20:16 won. not *s.* time in A.
2 Cor. 12:15 I will very gladly *s.*

SPENDEST, ETH.

Prov. 21:20 a foolish man *s.* it up
29:3 with hariots, *s.* substance
Ec. 6:12 whi. he. as a shadow
Luke 10:35 whatsoever thou *s.*

SPENT.

Gen. 21:15 and the water was *s.*
47:18 not hide how money is *s.*
Lev. 26:20 strength be *s.* in vain
Jud. 19:11 by Jeb. day was far *s.*
1 Sam. 9:7 the bread is *s.* in our
Job 7:6 days are *s.* without hope
Ps. 31:10 my life is *s.* with grief
Is. 49:4 I have *s.* my strength
Jer. 37:21 the bread in city was *s.*
Mark 5:26 and had *s.* all that she
had, Luke 8:43
6:35 day was far *s.* Luke 24:29
Luke 15:14 prodigal had *s.* all
Acts 17:21 *s.* their time to tell
Rom. 13:12 the night is far *s.*
2 Cor. 12:15 I will gladly be *s.*
SPEW, SPEWING. *See* SPUE.

SPICE, Substantive.

Ex. 35:28 rulers brought *s.* and
Cant. 5:1 gath. myrrh wi. my *s.*

SPICES.

Gen. 43:11 carry a pres. balm, *s.*
Ex. 25:6 *s.* for anointing, 35:8
30:23 take thou *s.* of myrrh, 34
37:29 pure incense of sweet *s.*
1 K. 10:2 camels that bare *s.* 10;
2 Chr. 9:1
25 brought to Sol. *s.* 2 Chr. 9:24
2 K. 20:13 Hezekiah showed th.
s. ointment, Is. 39:2
1 Chr. 9:29 appoint. to oversee *s.*
30 sons of the priests made *s.*
2 Chr. 9:9 queen of Sh. gave S.
16:14 divers *s.* prep. for burial
32:27 He. made treasuries for *s.*
Cant. 4:10 thine ointments th. *s.*
14 myrrh and aloes, chief *s.*
16 blow upon my gard. that *s.*
5:13 his cheeks are as a bed of *s.*
3:2 my belo. is gone to bed of *s.*
8:14 to a hart upon mount. of *s.*
Ezek. 27:22 in fairs wi. chief of *s.*
Mark 16:1 M. had bought sweet
s. Luke 24:1
Luke 23:56 prepared *s.* and oint.
John 19:40 they wound it in *s.*

SPICE, Verb.

Ezek. 24:10 consume flesh and *s.*

SPICE-MERCHANTS.

1 K. 10:15 the traffic of the *s.-m.*

SPICED.

Cant. 8:2 cau. thee drink *s.* wine

SPICERY.

Gen. 37:25 Ishmael. bear. *s.* balm

SPIDER.

Job 8:14 wh. trust sh. be a *s.* web
Prov. 30:28 *s.* tak. hold wi. hands
Is. 59:5 eggs, and weave *s.* web

SPIKENARD.

Cant. 1:12 *s.* sendeth the smell
4:13 fruits, camphire with *s.* 14
Mark 14:3 alabaster box of ointment of *s.* John 12:3

SPILLED.

Gen. 38:9 On. *s.* seed on ground
Mark 2:22 wine is *s.* Luke 5:37

SPILT.

2 Sam. 14:14 water *s.* on ground

SPIN.

Ex. 35:25 wise-hearted, did *s.*
Mat. 6:28 neither *s.* Luke 12:27

SPINDLE.

Prov. 31:19 lay. her hands to *s.*

SPIRIT.

Gen. 41:8 Phar.'s *s.* was troubled
45:27 the *s.* of Jacob their fath.
Ex. 6:9 heark. not for angu. of *s.*
35:21 whom his *s.* made willing
Num. 11:17 I will take of *s.* 25
26 the *s.* rested on them
29 L. wo. put his *S.* upon them
14:24 he had ano. *s.* with him
27:18 Jos. a man in whom is *s.*
Deut. 2:30 L. hardened his *s.*
Jos. 5:1 nor was th. *s.* in them
Jud. 15:19 drunk his *s.* came
1 Sam. 30:12 eaten his *s.* came
1 K. 10:5 no *s.* in her, 2 Chr. 9:4
21:5 said, Why is thy *s.* so sad?
22:21 th. came a *s.* 2 Chr. 18:20
2 K. 2:9 double portion of *s.* on
15 *s.* of Elijah doth rest on El.
1 Chr. 5:26 Lord stirr. up *s.* of P.
12:18 *s.* came upon Amasai
28:12 pattern of all he had by *s.*
Ezr. 1:5 wh. *s.* G. raised to go up
Neh. 9:30 by *S.* in thy prophets
Job 4:15 a *s.* passed bef. my face
15:13 thou turnest thy *s.* ag. G.
20:3 *s.* of my understanding
26:4 whose *s.* came from thee?
13 by his *S.* he garnished hea.
32:8 there is a *s.* in man
18 *s.* within me constraineth
34:14 if he gather to hims. his *s.*
Ps. 32:2 in wh. *s.* there is no gu.
51:10 renew right *s.* within me
12 uphold me with thy free *S.*
73:12 shall cut off *s.* of princes
78:8 whose *s.* not stead. with G.
104:30 thou sendest forth thy *S.*
106:33 so they provoked his *S.*
139:7 whit. sh. I go fr. thy *S.?*
143:10 *S.* good, lead me to upr.
Prov. 14:29 he that is hasty of *s.*
15:4 perverseu. is a breach in *s.*
16:18 haughty *s.* goeth bef. a fall
Prov. 16:32 that rul. *s.* bet. th. he
18:14 *s.* of a man sust. infirmity
20:27 *s.* of a man is candle of L.
25:28 hath no rule over his *s.*
Ec. 3:21 *s.* of man, *s.* of beast
7:9 not hasty in *s.* to be angry
8:8 no power over *s.* to retain *s.*
10:4 if *s.* of ruler rise ag. thee
11:5 kno. not what is way of *s.*
12:7 the *s.* shall return to God
Is. 19:3 *s.* of Egypt shall fail
29:10 L. pour. on you *s.* of sleep
24 they th. erred in *s.* sh. come
31:3 their horses flesh and not *s.*
32:15 till *S.* be poured upon us

34:16 his *s.* it hath gathe. them
42:5 giveth *s.* to them that walk
48:16 L. G. and his *S.* hath sent
54:6 forsak. and grieved in *s.*
57:16 *s.* shall fail before me
61:1 *S.* of L. G. on me, Lu. 4:18
3 garment of praise for the *s.*
Jer. 51:11 L. raised *s.* of the king
Ezek. 1:12 whit. *S.* was to go, 20
2:2 the *s.* entered into me, 3:24
3:12 the *s.* took me up, 11:24
14 *s.* lifted me up, and I went
in heat of my *s.* 8:3; 11:1
13:3 proph. that follow own *s.*
21:7 every *s.* shall faint
Dan. 2:1 Nebuc. *s.* was troubled
4:8 in whom is *S.* of the holy
gods, 9, 18; 5:11, 14
5:12 excellent *s.* in Daniel, 6:3
Mic. 2:11 if man in *s.* and falseh.
Hag. 1:14 L. stirred *s.* of Zerub.
Zec. 7:12 sent his *S.* by prophets
12:1 form. *s.* of man within him
Mal. 2:15 had residue of *S.* 16
Mat. 4:1 Je. led up of *S.* Luke 4:1
14:26 say. It is a *s.* Mark 6:49
22:43 David in *s.* call him Lord?
26:41 *s.* is willing, Mark 14:38
Mark 1:10 *S.* descend. John 1:32
12 *S.* driveth him into wilder.
8:12 he sighed deeply in his *s.*
9:20 *s.* tare him; 26 *s.* cried
Luke 1:17 go before him in *s.*
80 child waxed str. in *s.* 2:40
2:27 he came by *S.* into temple
4:14 Je. returned in power of *S.*
8:55 her *s.* came ag. she arose
9:55 know not what *s.* ye are
10:21 in that hour J. rejoi. in *s.*
13:11 wom. had *s.* of infirmity
24:37 supp. they had seen a *s.*
39 *s.* ha. not flesh and bones
John 1:33 on wh. thou sh. see *S.*
3:34 G. giveth not *S.* by meas.
4:23 worship the Father in *s.*
24 G. is a *S.* worship him in *s.*
6:63 it is *s.* that quickeneth;
words I speak, they are *s.*
7:39 spake of *S.* 11:33 groan. in
13:21 he was troubled in *s.*
Acts 2:4 spake as *S.* gave them
6:10 were not able to resist *s.*
8:29 the *S.* said to Philip, Go
10:19 *S.* said unto Peter, 11:12
11:28 Agabus signified by *S.*
16:7 the *S.* suffered them not
17:16 his *s.* was stir. within him
18:5 Paul was pressed in *s.*
25 and being fervent in the *s.*
20:22 bound in the *S.* to Jerusa.
21:4 said to Saul through the *S.*
23:8 Sadducees say th. is no *s.*
9 if a *s.* hath spoken to him
Rom. 1:4 Son of God accord. to *s.*
2:29 circumcis. is of heart in *s.*
8:1 walk not aft. flesh, but *s.* 4
2 law of *s.* of life made me free
5 after the *S.* things of the *S.*
9 flesh but *s.* if so be that *S.*
10 *s.* is life bec. of righteousn.
11 quick. your bodies by his *S.*
13 if ye through the *S.* mortify
16 *S.* beareth witn. with our *s.*
23 ourse. who have fruits of *S.*
26 *S.* also help. our infirmities;
but the *S.* maketh interces.
27 kno. what is the mind of *S.*
1 Cor. 2:4 in demonstration of *S.*
10 G. hath revealed th. unto us
by *S.* for *S.* searcheth all th.
11 *s.* of man which is in him
12 not *s.* of world, but *s.* of G.
5:3 absent in body, present in *s.*
5 *s.* be saved in day of Lord J.
6:17 joined to the Lord is one *s.*
20 glori. G. in your body and *s.*
7:34 may be holy in body and *s.*
12:4 gifts, but same *S.* 8, 9, 11

8 given by *S.* word of wisdom
13 by one *S.* we are all baptiz.
   been made to drink into *S.*
14:2 in *s.* he speaketh mysteries
15 sing with *s.* 16 bless with *s.*
1 *Cor.* 15:45 A. was ma. a quick. *s.*
2 *Cor.* 3:6 but of the *s.* letter killeth, but the *s.* giveth life
8 ministrations of *s.* be glorio.
17 L. is that *S.* where *S.* of L.
4:13 we having same *s.* of faith
7:1 from filthiness of flesh and *s.*
13 because his *s.* was refreshed
11:4 *s.* which ye have not recei.
12:18 walk. we not in same *s. ?*
Gal. 3:2 receiv. ye *S.* by works ?
3 foolish, having begun in *s. ?*
5 he that ministereth to you *S.*
14 might receive promise of *S.*
4:6 G. sent forth *S.* of his Son
5:5 we thro' *S.* wait for hope
16 walk in *S.* 18 if led by *S.*
17 flesh lusteth against the *S.*
   and the *S.* against the flesh
25 if we live in *S.* walk in *S.*
6:8 soweth to *S.* shall of *S.* reap
18 grace of our Lord be with
   your *s. Phile.* 25
Eph. 2:2 *s.* that work. in child.
18 have access by one *S.* to F.
22 habitation of G. through *S.*
3:5 revealed to apostles by *S.*
16 strength. with might by *S.*
4:3 unity of *s.* in bond of peace
4 th. is one *S.* as ye are called
23 renewed in *s.* of your mind
5:18 not drunk, but filled wi. *s.*
6:17 sw. of *S.* is the word of God
18 praying with prayer in *S.*
Phil. 1:19 supply of *s.* of Je. Ch
27 that ye stand fast in one *s.*
2:1 any fellowship of the *S.*
3:3 which worship God in the *s.*
Col. 1:8 declared your love in *s.*
2:5 yet am I with you in the *s.*
1 *Thes.* 5:19 quench not *S.* despise
23 I pray G. your *s.* soul, body
2 *Thes.* 2:2 neith. by *s.* nor word
8 L. shall consume with the *s.*
13 chosen thro' sanctific. of *S.*
1 *Tim.* 3:16 God justified in *S.*
4:1 the *S.* speaketh expressly
12 be thou an example in *s.*
2 *Tim.* 4:22 L. J. C. be wi. thy *s.*
Heb. 4:12 dividing of soul and *s.*
9:14 who through the eternal *S.*
Jam. 2:26 body witho. *s.* is dead
4:5 the *s.* in us lusteth to envy
1 *Pet.* 1:2 thro' sanctification of *S.*
22 in obeying truth through *S.*
3:4 the ornament of a meek *s.*
18 but quickened by *S.*
4:6 live accord. to God in the *S.*
1 *John* 3:24 *s.* he hath given us
4:1 beloved, believe not every *s.*
2 ev. *s.* that confesseth Je. Ch.
3 ev. *s.* that confesseth not Je.
13 bec. hath given us of his *S.*
5:6 *S.* beareth witn. *S.* is truth
8 wit. in earth, *S.* water, blood
Jude 19 sensual, not having *S.*
Rev. 1:10 I was in *S.* on L.'s day
2:7 what *S.* saith to churches,
   11, 17, 29 ; 3:6, 13, 22
4:2 immediately I was in the *S.*
11:11 *S.* of life from *G.* entered
14:13 blessed are dead, saith *S.*
17:3 carried me in the *S.* 21:10
22:17 *S.* and bride say, Come

SPIRIT of adoption.
Rom. 8:15 ye have recei. *s.* of *a.*

SPIRIT of antichrist.
1 *John* 4:3 this is that *s.* of *anti.*

SPIRIT of bondage.
Rom. 8:15 have not recei. *s.* of *b.*
Born of the SPIRIT.
John 3:5 ex. man be *b.* of the *S.*

---

6 that which is *born of the S.*
8 so is ev. one that is *b.* of *S.*
Gal. 4:29 persec. him *b.* after *S.*
Broken SPIRIT.
Ps. 51:17 sacri. of G. are a *b. s.*
Prov. 15:13 sorrow of heart *s.* is *b.*
17:22 a *b. s.* drieth the bones
See CONTRITE.
SPIRIT of burning.
Is. 4:4 blood of Jer. by *s.* of *b.*
SPIRIT of Christ.
Rom. 8:9 if man ha. not *S.* of *C.*
1 *Pet.* 1:11 *S.* of *Ch.* did signify
SPIRIT of counsel.
Is. 11:2 *s.* of *c.* rest upon him
SPIRIT of divination.
Acts 16:16 possess. with *s.* of *di.*
Dumb SPIRIT.
Mark 9:17 son. who hath a *d. s.*
25 thou *dumb s.* I charge thee
Earnest of the SPIRIT.
2 *Cor.* 1:22 given us *e.* of *t. S.* 5:5
SPIRIT of error.
1 *John* 4:6 kn. we *s.* of tru. and *e.*
See EVIL.
Faithful SPIRIT.
Prov. 11:13 he that is of *faith. s.*
See FAMILIAR.
SPIRIT of fear.
2 *Tim.* 1:7 ha. not giv. us *s.* of *f.*
Foul SPIRIT.
Mark 9:25 he rebuked the *foul s.*
Rev. 18:2 become hold of ev. *f. s.*
Fruit of the SPIRIT.
Gal. 5:22 *f.* of the *S.* is love, joy
Eph. 5:9 *f.* of *t. S.* is in all good.
Good SPIRIT.
Neh. 9:20 th. gavest thy *good S.*
Ps. 143:10 thy *S.* is *g.* lead me
SPIRIT of God.
Gen. 1:2 *S.* of *G.* moved on wat.
41:38 a man in wh. *S.* of *God* is
Ex. 31:3 Bez. wi. *S.* of *G.* 35:31
Num. 24:2 *S.* of *G.* came on Bal.
1 *Sam.* 10:10 the *S.* of *God* came
   on Saul, 11:6 ; 19:23
19:20 *S.* of *G.* came on messen.
2 *Chr.* 15:1 *S.* of *G.* came on Aza.
Job 27:3 *S.* of *G.* is in my nost.
33:4 *S.* of *God* hath made me
Ezek. 11:24 in vision by *S.* of *G.*
Mat. 3:16 saw *S.* of *G.* descend.
12:28 cast out devils by *S.* of *G.*
Rom. 8:9 *S.* of *God* dwell in you
14 many as are led by *S.* of *G.*
15:19 by the power of *S.* of *G.*
1 *Cor.* 2:11 no man, but *S.* of *G.*
14 recei. not things of *S.* of *G.*
3:16 *S.* of *God* dwelleth in you
6:11 sanctified by the *S.* of *God*
7:40 I think I have *S.* of *God*
12:3 no man speak. by *S.* of *G.*
2 *Cor.* 3:3 written with *S.* of *G.*
Eph. 4:30 grie. not holy *S.* of *G.*
1 *Pet.* 4:14 *S.* of *God* rest. on you
1 *John* 4:2 hereby kn. ye *S.* of *G.*
SPIRIT of glory.
1 *Pet.* 4:14 *S.* of *g.* resteth on you
SPIRIT of grace.
Zec. 12:10 house of Da. *S.* of *g.*
Heb. 10:29 done desp. to *S.* of *g.*
See HOLY.
Humble SPIRIT.
Prov. 16:19 bet. to be of an *h. s.*
29:23 honor sh. uphold the *h. s.*
Is. 57:15 with him that is of *h. s.*
SPIRIT of jealousy.
Num. 5:14 *s.* of *j.* com. on him, 30
SPIRIT of judgment.
Is. 4:4 purged Jerusa. by *s.* of *j.*
28:6 L. shall be for a *s.* of *jud.*

SPIRIT of knowledge.
Is. 11:2 *s.* of *k.* sh. rest upon him
See LORD, LYING.
SPIRIT of meekness.
1 *Cor.* 4:21 come in *s.* of *m. ?*
Gal. 6:1 such a one in *s.* of *m.*
My SPIRIT.
Gen. 6:3 my *S.* sh. not always
Job 6:4 poison drinketh up my *s.*
7:11 speak in anguish of my *s.*
10:12 visita. hath preserv. m. *s.*
21:4 sho. not my *s.* be troubled
Ps. 31:5 into hand I com. my *s.*
77:3 my *s.* was overwhelmed
6 my *s.* made diligent search
142:3 my *s.* overwhelmed in me
143:4 theref. is my *s.* overwhel.
7 hear me, O L. my *s.* faileth
Prov. 1:23 I will pour out my *s.*
Is. 26:9 with my *s.* will I seek
30:1 covering, but not of my *s.*
38:16 in th. things is life of m. *s.*
42:1 I ha. put my *S.* upon him
44:3 pour my *S.* upon thy seed
59:21 my *S.* that is upon thee
Ezek. 3:14 went in heat of my *s.*
36:27 my *S.* within you, 37:14
39:29 pour. my *S.* on house of I.
Dan. 2:3 and my *s.* was troubled
7:15 I Dan. was griev. in my *s.*
Joel 2:28 I will pour out my *S.* on
   all flesh, 29 ; *Acts* 2:17, 18
Hag. 2:5 my *S.* remain. am. you
Zec. 4:6 by power, but by my *S.*
6:8 quiet. my *s.* in north count.
Mat. 12:18 I will put my *S.* on
Luke 1:47 my *s.* hate rejoi. in G.
23:46 in thy hands I com. my *s.*
Acts 7:59 Lord Je. receive my *s.*
Rom. 1:9 wh. I serve with my *s.*
1 *Cor.* 5:4 when gath. and my *s.*
14:14 my *s.* prayeth, but my
16:18 they have refresh. my *s.*
2 *Cor.* 2:13 had no rest in my *s.*
New SPIRIT.
Ezek. 11:19 a *n. s.* in you, 36:26
18:31 a new heart and *new s.*
Newness of SPIRIT.
Rom. 7:6 we sho. serve in *n.* of *s.*
Patient SPIRIT.
Ec. 7:8 *p.* in *s.* bet. than proud
Perverse SPIRIT.
Is. 19:14 L. hath mingled a *p. s.*
Poor SPIRIT.
Mat. 5:3 blessed are *poor* in *s.*
SPIRIT of promise.
Eph. 1:13 sealed with H. *S.* of *p.*
SPIRIT of prophecy.
Rev. 19:10 testim. of J. is *s.* of *p.*
SPIRIT of slumber.
Rom. 11:8 G. given them *s.* of *s.*
Sorrowful SPIRIT.
1 *Sam.* 1:15 a woman of a *s. s.*
SPIRIT of truth.
John 14:17 *S.* of *t.* whom world
15:26 *S.* of *t.* which proceedeth
16:13 when *S.* of *truth* is come
1 *John* 4:6 hereby kn. we *S.* of *t.*
See VEXATION.
Unclean SPIRIT.
Zec. 13:2 cause *uncl. s.* to pass
Mat. 12:43 when the *u. s.* is gone
   out of a man, *Luke* 11:24
Mark 1:23 synag. a man wi. *u. s.*
26 when *u. s.* had torn him
3:30 they said, He hath an *u. s.*
5:2 met him a man with *u. s.*
8 come out, th. *u. s. Luke* 8:29
7:25 whose daugh. had an *u. s.*
Luke 9:42 Jesus rebuked *u. s.*
SPIRIT of understanding.
Is. 11:2 the *s.* of *u.* sh. rest upon

SPIRIT of whoredoms.

Hos. 4:12 *s. of w.* caused to err
5:4 *s. of w.* is in midst of them

SPIRIT of wisdom.

Ex. 28:3 wh. I filled wi. *s. of w.*
Deut. 34:9 Joshua full of *s. of w.*
Is. 11:2 *s. of w.* sh. rest up. him
Eph. 1:17 G. may give *s. of w.*

Wounded SPIRIT.

Prov. 18:14 *w. s.* who can bear ?

SPIRITS.

Num. 16:22 O God, the God of *s.*
27:16
Ps. 104:4 mak. angels *s. Heb.* 1:7
Prov. 16:2 Lord weighed the *s.*
Zec. 6:5 th. are four *s.* of heaven
Mat. 8:16 cast out *s.* with word
10:1 power ag. uncl. *s. Mark* 6:7
Mark 1:27 commandeth he the
unclean *s. Luke* 4:36
3:11 uncl. *s.* fell down bef. him
5:13 unclean *s.* entered swine
Luke 10:20 rejoice not that *s.* are
8:7 *s.* crying, came out of many
1 *Cor.* 12:10 to ano. discern. of *s.*
14:32 *s.* of proph. are subject to
1 *Tim.* 4:1 giv. heed to seduc. *s.*
Heb. 1:14 not all ministering *s.*
12:9 in subjection to Fath. of *s.*
23 to *s.* of just men made per.
1 *Pet.* 3:19 preach. to *s.* in prison
1 *John* 4:1 try *s.* wheth. they are
Rev. 16:13 I saw 3 unclean *s.* like
14 they are the *s.* of devils

See EVIL, FAMILIAR, SEVEN.

SPIRITUAL.

Hos. 9:7 the *s.* man is mad
Rom. 1:11 impart to you *s.* gift
7:14 we know that the law is *s.*
15:27 partak. of their *s.* things
1 *Cor.* 2:13 comparing *s.* things
with *s.*
15 he that is *s.* judgeth all thi.
3:1 could not spe. to you as to *s.*
9:11 have sown unto you *s.*
10:3 did all eat same *s.* meat
4 same *s.* dri. drank of *s.* rock
12:1 concern. *s.* gifts, brethren
14:1 desire *s.* gifts ; 12 zeal. of *s.*
37 if any man think himself *s.*
15:44 *s.* body, there is a *s.* body
46 that was not first whi. is *s.*
afterwards that which is *s.*
Gal. 6:1 ye which are *s.* restore
Eph. 1:3 blessed us with *s.* bless.
5:19 speak. to yours. in *s.* songs
6:12 wrestle against *s.* wickedn.
Col. 1:9 filled with *s.* understand.
3:16 admon. in psa. and *s.* songs
1 *Pet.* 2:5 built up *s.* house, to
offer *s.* sacrifices

SPIRITUALLY.

Rom. 8:6 to be *s.* minded is life
1 *Cor.* 2:14 because are *s.* discer.
Rev. 11:8 whi. *s.* is called Sodom

SPIT, TED.

Lev. 15:8 *s.* on him that is clean
Num. 12:14 if fath. had *s.* in face
Deut. 25:9 she shall *s.* in his face
Job 30:10 sp. not to *s.* in my face
Mat. 26:67 they did *s.* in his face
27:30 and they *s.* upon him and
Mark 7:33 he *s.* touched tongue
8:23 when he had *s.* on his eyes
10:34 they shall *s.* upon him
14:65 began to *s.* on him, 15:19
Luke 18:32 spitef. entreated *s.* on

SPITE.

Ps. 10:14 for thou beholdest *s.* to

SPITEFULLY.

Mat. 22:6 they entreated them *s.*
Luke 18:32 shall be *s.* entreated

SPITTING.

Is. 50:6 I hid not my face from *s.*

SPITTLE.

1 *Sam.* 21:13 let his *s.* fall down
Job 7:19 alone, till I swallow *s.*
John 9:6 he made clay of *s.* and

SPOIL, Substantive.

Gen. 49:27 at night he divide *s.*
Ex. 15:9 enemy said, I divide *s.*
Num. 31:9 Is. took *s.* of cattle, 11
Deut. 2:35 *s.* of cities we took,
3:7 ; *Jos.* 8:27 ; 11:14
13:16 thou sh. gather all the *s.*
20:14 *s.* thou shalt take, *Jos.* 8:2
Jud. 5:30 necks of th. that take *s.*
14:19 Sam. slew 30 men, took *s.*
1 *Sam.* 14:30 eaten freely of *s.*
32 the people flew upon the *s.*
15:19 but didst fly upon the *s.*
30:16 because the great *s.* that
19 neither *s.* nor any thing was
20 and said, This is David's *s.*
22 we will not give them of *s.*
26 he sent of *s.* to elders of Ju.
2 *Sam.* 3:22 Joab bro. in great *s.*
12:30 he brought *s.* of Rabbah
2 *K.* 3:23 now, theref. M. to the *s.*
21:14 they sh. bec. *s.* to enemies
1 *Chr.* 20:2 fr. Rab. he brought *s.*
2 *Chr.* 14:13 carried away *s.* 14
15:11 they offered to Lord of *s.*
20:25 were 3 days gathering *s.*
24:23 Syri. sent *s.* to king of D.
28:8 took *s.* brou. *s.* to Samaria
14 armed men left capti. and *s.*
Ezr. 9:7 kings ha. been deli. to *s.*
Est. 3:13 take *s.* of them, 8:11
9:10 on *s.* laid they not th. hand
Job 29:17 I plucked *s.* out of teeth
Ps. 68:12 tarried at home divi. *s.*
119:162 rejoice, as one findeth *s.*
Prov. 1:13 sh. fill houses with *s.*
16:19 to divide *s.* with proud
31:11 he shall have no need of *s.*
Is. 3:14 *s.* of poor is in houses
8:4 *s.* of Samaria shall be taken
9:3 rejoice when they divide *s.*
10:6 give him charge to take *s.*
33:4 your *s.* shall be gathered
23 prey of a great *s.* divided
42:22 they are for a *s.* and none
24 who gave Jacob for a *s.* ?
53:12 he sh. divide *s.* wi. strong
Jer. 6:7 violence and *s.* is heard
15:13 thy subst. will I give to *s.*
17:3 I will give thy substa. to *s.*
20:8 I cried violence and *s.*
30:16 they that *s.* thee sh. be a *s.*
49:32 their cattle shall be a *s.*
50:10 Chaldea shall be a *s.*
Ezek. 7:21 I will give it for a *s.*
25:7 deliver Ammonite for a *s.*
26:5 Tyr. for a *s.* to nations, 12
29:19 Nebuch. take *s.* of Egypt
38:12 I will go up to take a *s.*
13 art thou come to take a *s.*
45:9 Is. remove violence and *s.*
Dan. 11:24 he shall scatter the *s.*
33 shall fall by *s.* many days
Nah. 2:9 *s.* of silver, *s.* of gold
Hab. 2:17 *s.* of beasts shall cover
Zec. 2:9 as *s.* to their servants
14:1 *s.* shall be divided in midst

SPOIL, Verb.

Ex. 3:22 ye shall *s.* Egyptians
1 *Sam.* 14:36 *s.* them until morn.
2 *Sam.* 23:10 people return. to *s.*
Ps. 44:10 they who hate us *s.*
89:41 all that pass by way *s.*
109:11 let strangers *s.* his labor
Prov. 22:23 will *s.* soul of those
24:15 O man, *s.* not resting-pla.
Cant. 2:15 foxes that *s.* vines
Is. 11:14 they sh. *s.* them of east
Is. 17:14 portion of th. that *s.* us
33:1 when shalt cease to *s.* thou
Jer. 5:6 wolf of even. sh. *s.* them
20:5 I will give Jerusal. to *s.* it
30:16 they that *s.* thee sh. be a *s.*

47:4 day cometh to *s.* Philistines
49:28 Kedar, *s.* men of the east
50:10 all that *s.* shall be satisfied
Ezek. 14:15 they *s.* it so that it be
32:12 they shall *s.* pomp of Egy.
39:10 they shall *s.* those that
Hos. 10:2 break altars, *s.* images
13:15 he shall *s.* treasure of all
Hab. 2:8 remn. of peo. sh. *s.* thee
Zep. 2:9 residue of people shall *s.*
Mat. 12:29 *s.* goods ? *Mark* 3:27
Col. 2:8 lest any man *s.* you

SPOILED.

Gen. 34:27 sons of Jacob *s.* city
Ex. 12:36 they *s.* the Egyptians
Deut. 28:29 sh. be oppress. and *s.*
Jud. 2:14 hand of spoilers that *s.*
1 *Sam.* 14:48 Is. fr. them that *s.*
2 *K.* 7:16 Is. *s.* tents of Syrians
2 *Chr.* 14:14 A. *s.* cities of Gerar
Job 12:17 leadeth coun. away *s.*
19 leads princes away *s.*
Ps. 76:5 the stout-hearted are *s.*
Prov. 22:23 spoil soul of th. that *s.*
Is. 13:16 their houses shall be *s.*
18:2 whose land rivers have *s.* 7
24:3 land shall be utterly *s.*
33:1 spoilest, and wast not *s.*
42:22 this is a people rob. and *s.*
Jer. 2:14 a serv. why is he *s.* ?
4:13 woe unto us, for we are *s.*
20 whole land is *s.* tents are *s.*
30 wh. thou art *s.* wh. wilt do ?
9:19 are we *s.* ! 10:20 taber. is *s.*
21:12 deliver him that is *s.* 22:3
25:36 L. hath *s.* their pasture
48:1 Nebo is *s.* 15 Moab is *s.* 20
49:3 Ai is *s.* 10 E. his seed is *s.*
51:55 Lord hath *s.* Babylon
Ezek. 18:7 *s.* none by violence, 16
12 hath oppressed, hath *s.* 18
23:46 I will give them to be *s.*
39:10 shall spoil those that *s.*
Hos. 10:14 fortresses shall be *s.*
Amos 3:11 thy palaces shall be *s.*
5:9 strengtheneth *s.* ag. strong
Mic. 2:4 say, We be utterly *s.*
Hab. 2:8 hast *s.* many nations
Zec. 2:8 sent to nations wh. *s.*
11:2 because mighty are *s.*
3 glory *s.* for pride of Jor. is *s.*
Col. 2:15 having *s.* principalities

SPOILER.

Is. 16:4 fr. face of *s.* the *s.* cease
21:2 *s.* spoileth, go up, O Elam
Jer. 6:26 *s.* suddenly come on us
15:8 I brought upon them a *s.*
48:8 *s.* sh. come upon every city
18 *s.* of M. shall come on thee
32 *s.* is fallen upon thy fruits
51:56 bec. *s.* is come on Babylon

SPOILERS.

Jud. 2:14 he delivered them into
hand of *s.* 2 *K.* 17:20
1 *Sam.* 13:17 *s.* out of camp of P.
14:15 the *s.* they also trembled
Jer. 12:12 *s.* are come upon high
51:48 *s.* come to her from north
53 from me sh. *s.* come to her

SPOILEST, ETH.

Ps. 35:10 needy from him that *s.*
Is. 21:2 spoiler *s. Hos.* 7:1 rob. *s.*
33:1 woe to thee that *s.*
Nah. 3:16 canker-worm *s.* flieth

SPOILING.

Ps. 35:12 good, to *s.* of my soul
Is. 22:4 *s.* of daught. of my peo.
Jer. 48:3 voice from Horonaim *s.*
Hab. 1:3 *s.* and violence bef. me
Heb. 10:34 joyf. *s.* of your goods

SPOILS.

Jos. 7:21 saw among *s.* a garment
1 *Chr.* 26:27 out of *s.* did dedic.
Is. 25:11 bri. down pride with *s.*
Luke 11:22 and divideth his *s.*
Heb. 7:4 Abrah. gave tenth of *s.*

SPOKEN.

Gen. 18:19 L. br. what he hath *s.*
Num. 14:28 as ye have *s.* so will
21:7 we have *s.* ag. L. and thee
23:19 he *s.* not make it good ?
Deut. 18:17 well *s.* that th. ha. *s.*
1 *Sam.* 25:30 L. done all he ha. *s.*
2 *Sam.* 2:27 *s.* people had gone up
1 *K.* 18:24 peo. said, It is well *s.*
2 *K.* 4:13 thou be *s.* for to king ?
Ps. 87:3 glorious things are *s.* of
Ec. 7:21 ta. heed to all words *s.*
Cant. 8:8 in the day wh. she be *s.*
Jer. 26:16 *s.* to us in name of L.
Mal. 3:13 wh. ha. we *s.* ag. thee ?
Luke 18:34 nor kn. they things *s.*
John 15:22 if I had not co. and *s.*
Acts 8:24 none of things *s.* come
13:46 word *s*ho. first ha. been *s.*
19:36 these things cannot be *s.*
Rom. 15:21 to wh. he was not *s.*
1 *Cor.* 10:30 why am I evil *s.* of
14:9 shall it be kno. what is *s.* ?
1 *Pet.* 4:14 on their part evil *s.* of
2 *Pet.* 2:2 way of truth evil *s.* of

SPOKEN, with God.

Gen. 21:2 time of wh. *God* had *s.*
Ps. 62:11 *G.* hath *s.* once, twice
Mat. 22:31 that wh. was *s.* by *G.*

See LORD.

I have, or have I SPOKEN.

Gen. 28:15 done what *I h.* *s.*
Ex. 32:13 land *I have s.* of
1 *Sam.* 20:23 matter wh. *I h.* *s.* of
Job 40:5 once *h.* *I. s.* will not ans.
Ps. 116:10 therefore *have I s.* 2
Cor. 4:13
Is. 45:19 *I h.* not *s.* in sec. 48:16
46:11 *I h.* *s.* it, bring it to pass
48:15 *I*, even *I h.* *s.* I called
Jer. 35:17 *I h.* *s.* have not heard
Ezek. 12:28 word *I h.* *s.* be done
13:7 L. saith, Albeit *I h.* not *s.*
26:5 *I h.* *s.* it, saith Lord, 28:10
38:17 art thou he of wh. *I h.* *s.*
John 12:49 *I h.* not *s.* of myself
14:25 *have I s.* 15:11 ; 16:1, 25, 33

SPOKEN, with prophet.

Mat. 2:23 fulfilled which was *s.*
by the *prophet*, 13:35 ; 27:35
3:3 that was *s.* of by the *p.* Es.
4:14 *s.* by *p.* 8:17 ; 12:17 ; 21:4

Thou hast SPOKEN.

Ex. 4:10 nor since *thou h. s.*
10:29 Moses said, *T. h. s.* well
33:17 I will do this thing *t. h. s.*
Deut. 1:14 thing which *t. h. s.*
2 *K.* 20:19 good is word of Lord
which *thou hast s. Is.* 39:8
Est. 6:10 let nothing fail *t. h. s.*
Jer. 3:5 *t. h. s.* done evil things
32:24 that *t. h. s.* is come to pass
44:16 as for word *t. h. s.* unto us
51:62 O L. *t. h. s.* ag. this place

SPOKES.

1 *K.* 7:33 felloes and *s.* all molten

SPOKESMAN.

Ex. 4:16 he sh. be thy *s.* to peo.

SPONGE.

Mat. 27:48 one of them took a *s.*
Mark 15:36 ; *John* 19:29

SPOON.

Num. 7:14 one *s.* of ten shekels,
20, 26, 32, 38, 44, 50, 56, 62

SPOONS.

Ex. 25:29 make dishes and *s.*
Num. 4:7 put there. dishes and *s.*
7:84 silver bowls, twelve *s.* 86
1 *K.* 7:50 *s.* we. gold, 2 *Chr.* 4:22
2 *K.* 25:14 *s.* took, *Jer.* 52:18, 19
2 *Chr.* 24:14 rest of money *s.* ma.

SPORT, Substantive.

Jud. 16:25 Sam. make *s.* made *s.*
27 beheld while Sams. made *s.*

Prov. 10:23 *s.* to fool to do misc.
26:19 saith, Am not I in *s.* ?

SPORT, ING.

Gen. 26:8 Isa. was *s.* wi. Rebek.
Is. 57:4 ag. whom *s.* yourselves ?
2 *Pet.* 2:13 *s.* themsel. with dec.

SPOT.

Num. 19:2 br. heifer without *s.*
28:3 two lambs without *s.* 9, 11 ;
29:17, 26
Deut. 32:5 *s.* is not *s.* of his chil.
Job 11:15 thy face without *s.*
Cant. 4:7 there is no *s.* in thee
Eph. 5:27 glori. church, not ha. *s.*
1 *Tim.* 6:14 keep com. without *s.*
Heb. 9:14 off. himself without *s.*
1 *Pet.* 1:19 as a lamb without *s.*
2 *Pet.* 3:14 be found without *s.*

See BRIGHT.

SPOTS.

Jer. 13:23 can leopard change *s.* ?
2 *Pet.* 2:13 *s.* they are and blemi.
Jude 12 the. are *s.* in your feasts

SPOTTED.

Gen. 30:32 removing *s.* cattle
39 brou. cattle, speckled and *s.*
Jude 23 hating garm. *s.* by flesh

SPOUSE, S.

Cant. 4:8 come from Leb. my *s.*
9 ravish. my heart, my sister, *s.*
10 fair thy love, my sister, *s.*
11 lips, O my *s.* drop as honey
Cant. 4:12 garden inc. is my sis. *s.*
5:1 into my garden, my sister, *s.*
Hos. 4:13 your *s.* commit adult.
14 I will not punish your *s.*

SPOUTS. *See* WATER-SPOUTS.

SPRANG.

Mark 4:8 fruit th. *s.* up, *Luke* 8:8
Acts 16:29 call. for light and *s.* in
Heb. 7:14 evident L. *s.* out of J.
11:12 there *s.* of one many

See SPRUNG.

SPREAD.

Gen. 33:19 wh. J. *s.* tent, 35:21
Lev. 13:5 plague *s.* not, 6, 23, 28
Num. 4:7 on table *s.* cloth, 11
Deut. 22:17 *s.* cloth before elders
Jud. 8:25 they *s.* a garment
15:9 Philistines *s.* thems. in L.
2 *Sam.* 5:18 Philist. also came and
s. thems. 22 ; 1 *Chr.* 14:9, 13
16:22 they *s.* Absal. tent on roof
17:19 wom. *s.* covering on well
21:10 Rizpah *s.* sackclo. for her
1 *K.* 8:54 with hands *s.* to heaven
2 *K.* 8:15 Hazael *s.* cloth on face
19:14 *s.* letter bef. L. *Is.* 37:14
Ps. 105:39 he *s.* a cloud for cov.
140:5 *s.* a net by the way-side
Prov. 1:17 net *s.* in sight of bird
Is. 14:11 worm is *s.* under thee
19:8 *s.* nets on water languish
33:23 they could not *s.* the sail
Jer. 8:2 they sh. *s.* them bef. sun
10:9 silv. *s.* into plates brought
Lam. 1:13 hath *s.* net for my feet
Ezek. 2:10 he *s.* the roll before me
12:13 my net al*s*o will I *s.* 17:20
26:14 be a place to *s.* nets upon
Hos. 5:1 have been a net *s.* on T.
7:12 when they go, I will *s.* net
14:6 branches sh. *s.* his beauty
Joel 2:2 as morn. *s.* upon mount
Mal. 2:3 I will *s.* dung on your fa.
Mat. 21:8 multit. *s.* garments in
way, *Mark* 11:8 ; *Luke* 19:36
Acts 4:17 but that it *s.* no further

SPREAD abroad.

Gen. 10:18 Cannanites were *s. a.*
28:14 thou shalt *s.* a. to west
Ex. 9:29 I will *s. a.* hand to L.
33 Moses *s. a.* his hands to L.
1 *Sam.* 30:16 th. were *s. a.* earth

---

2 *Sam.* 22:43 *s. a.* mine enemies
2 *Chr.* 26:8 Uzziah's name *s. a.* 15
Zec. 1:17 cities thro' prosp. *s. a.*
2:6 I *s.* you *a.* as the four winds
1 *Thes.* 1:8 faith to God-w. is *s. a.*

SPREAD forth.

Num. 24:6 as valleys are th. *s. f.*
1 *K.* 8:7 cherubim *s. f.* 2 wings
22 *S. s. f.* hands, 2 *Chr.* 6:12, 13
Is. 1:15 wh. ye *s. f.* your hands
25:11 he shall *s. f.* hands, swim.
42:5 saith G. he that *s. f.* earth
Ezek. 47:10 a place to *s. f.* nets

SPREAD over.

Num. 4:6 shall *s. o.* cloth of blue
Is. 25:7 that is *s. o.* all nations
Jer. 48:40 shall *s.* wings *o.* Moab
49:22 he sh. *s.* his wings *o.* Boz.
Ezek. 16:8 I *s.* my skirt *over* thee
19:8 nations *s.* their net *o.* him

SPREAD out.

Ex. 37:9 cherubim *s. o.* wings,
1 *Chr.* 28:18
Ezr. 9:5 *s. out* my hands to L.
Job 29:19 my root *s. o.* by water
37:18 hast th. wi, him *s. o.* sky ?
Is. 65:2 *s. o.* hands to a rebelli.
Lam. 1:10 advers. *s. o.* his hand
Ezek. 32:3 will *s. o.* net over thee

SPREADEST, ETH.

Lev. 13:8 if priest see that scab *s.*
Deut. 32:11 as eagle *s.* her wings
Job 9:8 G. who alone *s.* out heav.
26:9 and he *s.* his cloud upon it
36:30 he *s.* his light upon it
Prov. 29:5 flatter. neighb. *s.* a net
28:11 he that swim. *s.* hands
40:22 that *s.* heavens as a tent
44:24 I the L. that *s.* abroad
Jer. 4:31 daughter of Z. *s.* hands
17:8 a tree that *s.* out her roots
Ezek. 27:7 linen th. *s.* for thy sail
Lam. 1:17 Z. *s.* forth her hands

SPREADING.

Ps. 37:35 I have seen wicked *s.*
Ezek. 17:6 and became a *s.* vine

SPREADING, S.

Job 36:29 underst. *s.* of clouds ?
Ezek. 26:5 a place for *s.* of nets

SPRIGS.

Is. 18:5 afore harvest cut off *s.*
Ezek. 17:6 a vine, shot forth *s.*

SPRING, Substantive.

2 *K.* 2:21 he went forth to the *s.*
Prov. 25:26 troub. and corrupt *s.*
Cant. 4:12 spouse, is *s.* shut up
Is. 58:11 sh. be like *s.* of water
Hos. 13:15 his *s.* sh. become dry

SPRINGS.

Deut. 4:49 under *s.* of Pisgah
Jos. 10:40 smote country of *s.*
12:8 kings in plains and in *s.*
15:19 give me *s.* of water, gave
upper *s. Jud.* 1:15.
Job 38:16 hast entered into *s.* ?
Ps. 87:7 all my *s.* are in thee
104:10 he sendeth *s.* into valleys
107:33 turn. water *s.* into dry
35 turn. dry ground to water *s.*
Is. 35:7 land become *s.* of water
41:18 I will make dry land *s.*
49:10 by *s.* of water guide them
Jer. 51:36 I will make her *s.* dry

SPRING.

1 *Sam.* 9:26 about *s.* of day Sam.

See DAYSPRING.

SPRING.

Ezek. 17:9 in all leaves of her *s.*

SPRING, Verb.

Num. 21:17 Is. sang. *s.* up, O w.
Deut. 8:7 and depths that *s.* out
Jud. 19:25 when day began to *s.*
Job 5:6 nei. doth trouble *s.* out
38:27 bud of tender herb to *s.*

Ps. 85:11 truth sh. *s.* out of earth
92:7 wh. wicked *s.* as the grass
Is. 42:9 bef. they *s.* forth I tell
43:19 now it shall *s.* forth
44:4 they sh. *s.* up as am. grass
45:8 righteousness *s.* up togeth.
58:8 thy health shall *s.* forth
61:11 gard. causeth things to *s.*
Joel 2:22 for the pastures do *s.*
Mark 4:27 seed *s.* he kn. not how

SPRINGETH.
2 *K.* 19:29 eat in second year that
which *s.* of same, *Is.* 37:30
Hos. 10:4 thus judgment *s.* up

SPRINGING.
Gen. 26:19 found well of *s.* water
2 *Sam.* 23:4 as tender grass *s.* out
Ps. 65:10 thou blessedst the *s.*
John 4:14 a well of water *s.* up
Heb. 12:15 any root *s.* trouble you

SPRINKLE.
Ex. 9:8 let Moses *s.* the ashes
Lev. 14:7 *s.* on him to be cleansed
51 *s.* the house seven times
16:14 shall *s.* on mercy-seat, 15
Num. 8:7 *s.* water of purifying
19:18 shall *s.* it upon the tent
19 the clean person shall *s.* it
Is. 52:15 sh. he *s.* many nations
Ezek. 36:25 *s.* clean wa. upon you

SPRINKLED, ETH.
Ex. 9:10 *s.* ashes toward heaven
Lev. 7:14 priest's that *s.* blood
Num. 19:13 wa. not *s.* on him, 20
Job 2:12 *s.* dust on their heads
Heb. 9:19 he *s.* the book and peo.
10:22 hearts *s.* from evil conscie.
See BLOOD.

SPRINKLING.
Heb. 9:13 the ashes of a heifer *s.*
11:28 thro' faith kept *s.* of blood
12:24 we are come to blood of *s.*
1 *Pet.* 1:2 *s.* of blood of Jesus Ch.

SPROUT.
Job 14:7 tree that it will *s.* again

SPRUNG.
Mat. 4:16 shad. of death, light *s.*
13:5 and they *s.* up, *Mark* 4:5
26 but when blade was *s.* up
Luke 8:6 as soon as it was *s.* up

SPUE, ED.
Lev. 18:28 th. land *s.* you, 20:22
28 as it *s.* out nations th. were
Jer. 25:27 *s.* fall, rise no more
Rev. 3:16 then I will *s.* thee out

SPEWING.
Hab. 2:16 *s.* shall be on thy glory

SPUN.
Ex. 35:25 th. which they had *s.*

SPY.
Num. 13:16 M. sent to *s.* land, 17
21:32 Mo. sent to *s.* out Jaazer
Jos. 2:1 sent 2 men to *s.* 6:23, 25
Jud. 18:2 Dani. sent to *s.* 14, 17
2 *Sam.* 10:3 David sent serv. to *s.*
out the city, 1 *Chr.* 19:3
2 *K.* 6:13 go and *s.* where he is
Gal. 2:4 came in privily to *s.*

SPIED.
Ex. 2:11 *s.* Egyptian smiting
2 *K.* 9:17 a watchman *s.* company
13:21 they *s.* a band of men
23:16 he *s.* sepulchres that were
See ESPY, ESPIED.

SPIES.
Gen. 42:9 said, Ye are *s.* 14, 16
34 then sh. I know ye are no *s.*
Num. 21:1 Is. came by way of *s.*
Jos. 6:23 young men that were *s.*
1 *Sam.* 26:4 David sent out *s.*
2 *Sam.* 15:10 Absalom sent *s.*
Luke 20:20 they sent forth *s.*
Heb. 11:31 Rahab had received *s.*

SQUARE.
1 *K.* 7:5 doors and posts were *s.*
Ezek. 45:2 *s.* round about, 50 cub.
See FOUR-SQUARE.

SQUARED.
Ezek. 41:21 posts of temp. were *s.*

SQUARES.
Ezek. 43:16 square in 4 *s.* thereof

STABLE, Substantive.
Ezek. 25:5 I will make Rab. a *s.*

STABLE.
1 *Chr.* 16:30 world also sh. be *s.*

STABILITY.
Is. 33:6 knowl. *s.* of thy times
STABLISH. *See* ESTABLISH.

STACHYS.
Rom. 16:9 salute Urbane and S.

STACKS.
Ex. 22:6 *s.* of corn be consumed

STACTE.
Ex. 30:34 take to th. *s.* onycha

STAFF.
Gen. 32:10 with my *s.* I passed
38:18 give me thy sig. and *s.* 25
Ex. 12:11 with a *s.* in your hand
21:19 and walk abroad on his *s.*
Num. 13:23 between two on a *s.*
22:27 Balaam-sm. ass with a *s.*
Jud. 6:21 put forth end of *s.*
1 *Sam.* 17:7 *s.* of his spear like
weav.'s beam, 2 *Sam.* 21:19
40 Dav. took his *s.* in his hand
2 *Sam.* 3:29 one that leaneth
on a *s.*
23:7 fenced with *s.* of a spear
21 he went down to him with
a *s.* 1 *Chr.* 11:23
2 *K.* 4:29 take my *s.* lay my *s.* on
31 Geh. laid *s.* on face of child
18:21 thou trust. on *s.* *Is.* 36:6
Ps. 23:4 thy rod and *s.* comf. me
Is. 3:1 L. will take fr. Ju. the *s.*
9:4 hast brok. *s.* of his shoulder
10:5 and the *s.* in their hand is
15 or as if *s.* should lift itself
24 lift up his *s.* against thee
14:5 L. hath broken *s.* of wicked
28:27 fitches beaten out wi. a *s.*
30:32 wh. grounded *s.* shall pass
Jer. 48:17 how is strong *s.* broken
Ezek. 29:6 have been a *s.* to Isr.
Hos. 4:12 their *s.* declar. to them
Zec. 8:4 every man with his *s.*
11:10 I took my *s.* even beauty
14 I cut asunder my other *s.*
Mark 6:8 take nothing, save a *s.*
Heb. 11:21 lean. on top of his *s.*
See BREAD.

STAGGER.
Job 12:25 *s.* like a drunken man,
Ps. 107:27
Is. 29:9 they *s.* not with strong

STAGGERED, ETH.
Is. 19:14 as a drunken man *s.*
Rom. 4:20 *s.* not at promise of G.

STAIN.
Job 3:5 and shadow of death *s.* it
Is. 23:9 L. purposed to *s.* pride
63:3 sprinkled, I will *s.* my raim.

STAIRS.
1 *K.* 6:8 went up with winding *s.*
2 *K.* 9:13 under him on top of *s.*
Neh. 9:4 then stood on *s.* Jeshua
Cant. 2:14 in secret places of *s.*
Ezek. 43:17 *s.* look towards east
Acts 21:40 Paul stood on the *s.*

STALK.
Is. 33:20 not one of *s.* removed
54:2 cords and strengthen thy *s.*

STALK, S.
Gen. 41:5 seven ears on one *s.* 22

Jos. 2:6 hid them with *s.* of flax
Hos. 8:7 no *s.* bud yield no meal

STALL.
Amos 6:4 out of midst of the *s.*
Mal. 4:2 grow up as calves of *s.*
Luke 13:15 loose his ox from the *s.*

STALLS.
1 *K.* 4:26 Solomon had forty
thousand *s.* 2 *Chr.* 9:25
2 *Chr.* 32:28 Hezek. had *s.* for all
Hab. 3:17 there be no herd in *s.*

STALLED.
Prov. 15:17 th. a *s.* ox. and hatr.

STAMMERERS.
Is. 32:4 tongue of *s.* shall speak

STAMMERING.
Is. 28:11 *s.* lips and anoth. tongue
33:19 not see a peo. of *s.* tongue

STAMP.
2 *Sam.* 22:43 did *s.* them as mire
Ezek. 6:11 smite *s.* with thy foot

STAMPED.
Deut. 9:21 I *s.* calf and ground
2 *K.* 23:6 Josiah *s.* the grove
15 *s.* high pla. small to powder
2 *Chr.* 15:16 A. cut her idol and *s.*
Ezek. 25:6 thou hast *s.* with feet
Dan. 7:7 a fourth beast *s.* 19
8:7 he-goat cast down and *s.* 10

STAMPING.
Jer. 47:3 at noise of *s.* of hoofs

STANCHED.
Luke 8:44 wo.'s issue of blood *s.*

STAND.
Ezek. 29:7 their loins to be at a *s.*

STAND, Verb.
Lev. 27:14 priest, so shall it *s.* 17
Deut. 25:8 if he *s.* to it and say
Jos. 20:4 *s.* at enter. gate of city
1 *Sam.* 12:16 *s.* see this thing
19:3 *s.* beside my father in field
1 *K.* 17:1 as L. liveth bef. whom
I *s.* 18:15; 2 *K.* 3:14; 5:16
2 *K.* 5:11 I thought he will *s.*
10:4 not, how then shall we *s.* ?
1 *Chr.* 23:30 to *s.* every morning
2 *Chr.* 34:32 caused all pres. to *s.*
Ezr. 10:14 let rulers of congreg. *s.*
Est. 8:11 and to *s.* for their life
Job 8:15 lean on house, sh. not *s.*
19:25 *s.* at latter day on earth
Ps. 38:11 my kinsm. *s.* afar off
45:9 on right hand did *s.* queen
78:13 made waters to *s.* as heap
109:6 let Sa. *s.* at his right hand
31 shall *s.* at right hand of poor
122:2 our feet *s.* with. thy gates
130:3 mark iniqui. O L. who *s.* ?
Prov. 19:21 counsel of L. shall *s.*
25:6 *s.* not in pl. of great men
Ec. 8:3 *s.* not in an evil thing
Is. 7:7 saith L. It sh. not *s.* 8:10
14:24 as I purposed, so it sh. *s.*
40:8 word of our G. sh. *s.* for ever
46:10 counsel shall *s.* I do pleas.
61:5 strangers *s.* and feed flocks
Jer. 6:16 *s.* ye in the ways
44:28 know whose word shall *s.*
46:21 did not *s.* bec. day came
Ezek. 17:14 keeping cov. might *s.*
Dan. 2:44 kingd. shall *s.* for ever
11:6 king of the north sh. not *s.*
Mic. 5:4 *s.* and feed in strength
Nah. 2:8 *s.* shall they cry
Mal. 3:2 who *s.* when he appear.
Mark 11:25 when ye *s.* praying
Acts 1:11 why *s.* gaz. to heaven ?
5:20 go, *s.* and speak in temple
26:6 I *s.* and judged for hope
Rom. 14:4 G. able to ma. him. *s.*
2 *Cor.* 1:24 joy, for by faith ye *s.*
Eph. 6:13 having done all to *s.*
Pet. 5:12 grace of G. wherein *s.*

Rev. 3:20 I *s.* at door and knock
6:17 who shall be able to *s.* ?
18:15 merchants *s.* afar off

STAND abroad.

Deut. 24:11 *s. a.* man br. pledge

STAND against.

Lev. 19:16 nor *s. a.* blood of thy neighbor
Jer. 44:29 my words sh. *s. a.* you

STAND aloof.

Ps. 38:11 my friends *s. aloof*

STAND back.

Gen. 19:9 *s. b.* this fellow came

STAND before.

Ex. 8:20 *s. before* Pharaoh, 9:13
17:6 I will *s. before* thee on rock
Lev. 26:37 power to *s. b.* enem.
Jos. 7:12, 13; *Jud.* 2:14
Num. 27:21 he sh. *s. b.* Eleazar
35:12 till *s. b.* congre. *Jos.* 20:6
Deut. 7:24 no man able to *s. b.* th.
11:25; *Jos.* 1:5; 10:8; 23:9
9:2 who *s. b.* children of Anak?
19:17 both men shall *s. b.* Lord
29:10 *s.* this day all of you *b.* L.
1 *Sam.* 6:20 who able to *s. b.* L.?
1 *Sam.* 16:22 let David, I pray, *s. b.* me
1 *K.* 10:8 happy are thy servants who *s. b.* thee, 2 *Chr.* 9:7
2 *Chr.* 20:9 we *s. b.* house
Ezr. 9:15 we cannot *s. b.* thee
Job 41:10 who is able to *s. b.* me?
Prov. 22:29 a man diligent sh. *s.*
b. kings, shall not *s. b.* mean
27:4 who is able to *s. b.* envy?
Jer. 7:10 *s. b.* me in this house
15:19 if th. ret. th. shalt *s. b.* me
35:19 Jo. not want man to *s. b.*
49:19 shepherd *s. b.* me? 50:44
Dan. 1:5 at end might *s. b.* king
8:4 no beast might *s. b.* him
11:16 none shall *s. b.* him
Nah. 1:6 who can *s. b.* his indi. ?
Luke 21:36 worthy to *s. b.* Son
Rom. 14:10 all *s. b.* judgm.-seat
Rev. 20:12 small and gr. *s. b.* G.

STAND by.

Ex. 18:14 peo. *s. by* thee to even
Neh. 7:3 they *s. by* shut doors
Is. 65:5 *s. by,* I am ho. th. thou
Jer. 48:19 *s. by,* ask, What done
Zec. 3:7 walk am. th. that *s. by*
4:14 anointed ones that *s. by* L.
John 11:42 bec. of peo. wh. *s. by*

STAND fast.

Jer. 46:14 say ye, *s. f.* and prep.
1 *Cor.* 16:13 wat. ye, *s. f.* in faith
Gal. 5:1 *s. f.* in liberty Ch. made
Phil. 1:27 *s. f.* in sp. 4:1 *s. f.* in L.
1 *Thes.* 3:8 live, if ye *s. f.* in L.
2 *Thes.* 2:15 *s. f.* and hold trad.

STAND forth.

Mark 3:3 sa. to man, *s. f.* *Lu.* 6:8

STAND here.

Deut. 5:31 *s.* thou *here* by me
2 *Sam.* 18:30 turn aside, and *h.*
Mat. 20:6 why *s.* ye *h.* all day?
Acts 4:10 doth this man *s. here*

STAND in.

Ps. 4:4 *s.* in awe, and sin not
5:5 foolish sh. not *s. in* thy sig.
24:3 who sh. *s. in* his holy pl. ?
76:7 *s. in* thy sight wh. angry?
89:43 not made him to *s. in* bat.
134:1 by night *s. in* house, 135:2
Jer. 26:2 *s. in* court of L.'s house
Ezek. 13:5 not gone to *s. in* bat.
Dan. 12:13 *s. in* lot end of days
Zec. 14:4 feet *s. in* that day
Mat. 24:15 abomin. *s. in* holy pl.
Gal. 4:20 for I *s. in* doubt of you

STAND on.

Ex. 17:9 to-morrow I *s. on* hill

---

2 *K.* 6:31 if head of Eli. *s. on* him
Dan. 11:17 sh. not *s. on* his side

STAND out.

Ps. 73:7 eyes *s. out* with fatness

STAND perfect.

Col. 4:12 may *s. p.* and complete

STAND still.

Ex. 14:13 fear ye not, *s. s.* and see salv. of L. 2 *Chr.* 20:17
Num. 9:8 *s. s.* I will hear wh. L.
Jos. 3:8 ye shall *s. s.* in Jordan
10:12 sun *s. s.* upon Gibeon
1 *Sam.* 9:27 *s.* thou *s.* that I show
12:7 *s. s.* that I may reason
14:9 we will *s. s.* in our place
Job 37:14 *s. s.* consi. works of G.
Jer. 51:50 escaped sword *s.* not *s.*

STAND strong.

Ps. 30:7 made mountain to *s. s.*

STAND there.

Num. 11:16 may *s. t.* with thee
Deut. 18:7 Levites who *s. there*
Jam. 2:3 say to the poor, *s.* th. *t.*

STAND together.

Is. 50:8 let us *s. t.* who advers.

STAND up.

Neh. 9:5 *s. up,* bless L. your G.
Job 30:20 I *s. up,* thou regar. not
33:5 set words in order, *s. up*
Ps. 35:2 shield, *s. up* for my help
94:16 who will *s. up* for me ag.
Ec. 4:15 shall *s. up* in stead
Is. 27:9 images shall not *s. up*
44:11 let them *s. up,* yet they
48:13 call to th. they *s. up* tog.
51:17 awake, *s. up,* O Jerusa.
Dan. 8:22 4 kingd. *s. up* of nati.
11:2 sh. *s. up* 3 kings in Persia
3 a mighty king shall *s. up,* 4
14 many *s. up* ag. king of sou.
12:1 that time sh. Michael *s. up*
Acts 10:26 Peter said, *s. up,* I am

STAND upon.

Ex. 33:21 thou shalt *s. u.* rock
Deut. 27:12 shall *s. u.* mount Ge.
Jos. 3:13 shall *s. upon* a heap
2 *Sam.* 1:9 Saul said, *s. upon* me
1 *K.* 19:11 *s. u.* mount before L.
Ezek. 2:1 *s. u.* thy feet, *Acts* 26:16
33:26 *s. u.* sword, work abomi.
Dan. 7:4 made *s. upon* feet
Hab. 2:1 I will *s. u.* my watch
Zec. 14:12 while they *s. u.* feet

STAND upright.

Ps. 20:8 we are risen, and *s. u.*
Dan. 10:11 underst. words, *s. u.*
Acts 14:10 he said to cripple, *s. u.*

STAND with.

Num. 1:5 men that sh. *s. w.* you

STAND without.

Ezr. 10:13 are not able to *s. w.*
Mat. 12:47 *s. w.* to sp. *Luke* 8:20
Luke 13:25 ye begin to *s. with.*

STANDARD.

Num. 2:3 on east side sh. *s.* of J.
10 on south side be *s.* of Reu.
18 on west side be *s.* of Ephr.
25 on north side be the *s.* of D.
10:14 in first place went *s.* of J.
Is. 49:22 I will set up *s.* to peo.
59:19 L. sh. lift up a *s.* ag. him
62:10 lift up a *s.* for the people
Jer. 4:6 set up *s.* toward Zion
21 how long see *s.* hear trum.
50:2 set ye up *s.* 51:12, 27

STANDARD-BEARER.

Is. 10:18 as when *s.-b.* fainteth

STANDARDS.

Num. 2:31 Dan go hindm. wi. *s.*

STANDEST.

Gen. 24:31 wheref. *s.* thou with. ?

Ex. 3:5 place wher. th. *s.* is holy ground, *Jos.* 5:15; *Acts* 7:33
Ps. 10:1 why *s.* afar off, O Lord?
Rom. 11:20 bro. thou *s.* by faith

STANDETH.

Deut. 1:38 Jos. who *s.* bef. thee
29:15 with him that *s.* with us
Jud. 16:26 pillars wher. house *s.*
Ps. 1:1 nor *s.* in way of sinners
26:12 my feet *s.* in even place
33:11 counsel of Lord *s.* for ever
119:161 my heart *s.* in awe
Prov. 8:2 wisdom *s.* in high pl.
Cant. 2:9 behold, he *s.* beh. wall
Is. 3:13 to plead, *s.* to judge
46:7 set him in his place, he *s.*
Dan. 12:1 prince who *s.* for peo.
Zec. 11:16 nor feed that that *s.*
John 1:26 *s.* one among you
Rom. 14:4 to his own mas. he *s.*
1 *Cor.* 7:37 that *s.* steadf. in heart
8:13 eat no flesh while world *s.*
10:12 that thinketh he *s.* take heed lest he fall
Heb. 10:11 every priest *s.* daily
Jam. 5:9 judge *s.* before door
Rev. 10:8 angel who *s.* on sea

STANDING, Substantive.

Ps. 69:2 sink in mire whe. no *s.*
Mic. 1:11 shall rec. of you his *s.*

STANDING.

Lev. 26:1 nor rear ye up a *s.* im.
1 *Sam.* 19:20 S. *s.* appointed over
22:6 servants were *s.* about him
1 *K.* 22:19 h. of hea. *s.* 2 *Chr.* 18:18
Ps. 107:35 wildern. into *s.* water
Amos 9:1 I saw L. *s.* upon altar
Mic. 5:13 I will cut off thy *s.* im.
Zec. 3:1 Sa. *s.* at his right hand
6:5 go forth from *s.* before Lord
Mat. 6:5 love to pray *s.* in syna.
20:3 saw others *s.* idle in mark.
Luke 1:11 angel *s.* on side of alt.
John 8:9 and woman *s.* in midst
20:14 she saw Je. *s.* knew not
Acts 2:14 Peter *s.* up with eleven
5:25 men are *s.* in temple
7:55 J. *s.* on right hand of G. 56
22:20 I was *s.* by and consent.
Heb. 9:8 while taber. was yet *s.*
2 *Pet.* 3:5 earth *s.* out of water
Rev. 7:1 four angels *s.* on earth
18:10 *s.* off for fear of her torm.
19:17 an angel *s.* in the sun

See CORN.

STANK.

Ex. 7:21 the fish in the river *s.*
8:14 th. gathered frogs, land *s.*
16:20 manna bred worms and *s.*
2 *Sam.* 10:6 Ammon saw they *s.*

STARE.

Ps. 22:17 bones, Look and *s.*

STAR.

Num. 24:17 sh. co. a *s.* out of J.
Amos 5:26 ye have borne *s.*
Mat. 2:2 have seen his *s.* in east
9 lo, *s.* which they saw in east
Mat. 2:10 wh. they saw *s.* th. rej.
Acts 7:43 took up *s.* of your god
1 *Cor.* 15:41 *s.* differ. from ano. *s.*
Rev. 8:10 there fell a great *s.* 11
9:1 a *s.* fell from heaven to ear.

DAYSTAR. *See* DAY.

Morning STAR.

Rev. 2:28 I will give him *m. s.*
22:16 I am the bright and *m s.*

STAR-GAZERS.

Is. 47:13 let the *s.-g.* stand up

STARS.

Gen. 1:16 G. made lights, ma. *s.*
15:5 tell the *s.* if thou be able
37:9 sun, moon, and eleven *s.*
Deut. 4:19 when scest *s.* sho. be
Jud. 5:20 *s.* in their courses

Neh. 4:21 fr. morn. till *s.* appear.
Job 3:9 let *s.* of twilight be dark
9:7 sun, and sealeth up the *s.*
22:12 behold height of *s.*
25:5 *s.* are not pure in his sight
38:7 morning *s.* sang together
Ps. 8:3 moon and *s.* which thou
136:9 moon and *s.* to rule by ni.
147:4 telleth number of the *s.*
148:3 praise him, ye *s.* of light
Ec. 12:2 while sun or *s.* be not
Is. 14:13 ex. my throne above *s.*
Jer. 31:35 giveth *s.* for a light
Ezek. 32:7 I will make *s.* dark
Dan. 8:10 cast down some of *s.*
12:3 shall shine as *s.* for ever
Joel 2:10 *s.* withdraw shin. 3:15
Ob. 4 tho' set thy nest among *s.*
Luke 21:25 th. sh. be signs in *s.*
Acts 27:20 nei. sun nor *s.* appear
1 *Cor.* 15:41 another glory of *s.*
Heb. 11:12 so many as *s.* of sky
Jude 13 rag. waves, wandering *s.*
Rev. 8:12 third part of *s.* was
12:1 upon head a crown of 12 *s.*

See HEAVEN, SEVEN.

STATE.

Ps. 39:5 man at best *s.* is vanity
Mat. 12:45 last *s.* is worse than
the first, *Luke* 11:26

See ESTATE.

STATELY.

Ezek. 23:41 sattest upon a *s.* bed

STATION.

Is. 22:19 I will drive thee from *s*

STATURE.

Num. 13:32 saw, men of great *s.*
1 *Sam.* 16:7 look not on hei. of *s.*
2 *Sam.* 21:20 a man of great *s.*
1 *Chr.* 11:23; 20:6
Cant. 7:7 thy *s.* is like a pa.-tree
Is. 10:33 high one of *s.* be hewn
45:14 men of *s.* shall come over
Ezek. 13:18 kerchi. on head of *s.*
17:6 it became a vine of low *s.*
19:11 her *s.* was exalted among
31:3 Assy. was cedar of high *s.*
Mat. 6:27 not add one cubit to
his *s. Luke* 12:25
Luke 2:52 Jesus increased in *s.*
19:3 Zaccheus little of *s.* climb.
Eph. 4:13 measure of *s.* of Christ

STATUTE.

Ex. 15:25 he made a *s.* and ordi.
29:9 priests' office for perpet. *s.*
Lev. 3:17 a perpetual *s.* 16:34;
24:9; *Num.* 19:21
Num. 27:11 eh. be for a *s.* 35:29
Jos. 24:25 he set a *s.* in Shechem
1 *Sam.* 30:25 David made it a *s.*
Ps. 81:4 this was a *s.* for Israel
Dan. 6:7 consulted to estab. a *s.*
15 that no *s.* king establisheth

STATUTE for ever.

Ex. 27:21 it shall be a *s. for ever*,
28:43; 29:28; *Lev.* 6:18; 7:34;
10:9; 16:31; 23:21; *Num.* 18:23
Lev. 6:22 it is a *s. for e.* to the L.
Num. 19:10 to stran. for a *s. f. e.*

STATUTES.

Ex. 18:26 make them know *s.*
Lev. 10:11 teach Israel all the *s.*
Num. 30:16 these are *s.* the L.
Deut. 4:5 which shall hear th. *s.*
6:24 L. commanded to do th. *s.*
16:12 shall observe and do th. *s.*
17:19 may learn to keep these *s.*
1 *K.* 3:3 walking in *s.* of Da.
2 *K.* 17:8 walked in *s.* of hea. 19
34 neither do they after th. *s.*
37 *s.* he wrote, ye sh. observe
2 *Chr.* 33:8 take heed to do the *s.*
Neh. 9:14 commandedst them *s.*
Ps. 19:8 *s.* of Lord are right
Ezek. 20:25 I gave th. *s.* not good

33:15 if wicked walk in *s.* of life
Mic. 6:16 for *s.* of Omri are kept

His STATUTES.

Ex. 15:26 if thou wilt keep his *s.*
Deut. 6:17; 10:13; 11:1
Deut. 27:10 thou shalt do his *s.*
2 *Sam.* 22:23 *h. s.* I did not dep.
1 *K.* 8:61 perfect, to walk in *h. s.*
2 *K.* 17:15 they rejected *h. s.* and
23:3 made a covenant to keep
his s. 2 *Chr.* 34:31
Ezr. 7:11 Ezra a scribe of *his s.*
Ps. 18:22 did not put away *his s.*
105:45 they might observe *h. s.*
Jer. 44:23 in his law, nor in *h. s.*

See JUDGMENTS.

My STATUTES.

Gen. 26:5 Abraham kept *my s.*
Lev. 18:5 keep *my s.* 26; 19:19
25:18 wherefore ye sh. do *my s.*
26:3 if walk in *my s.* and keep
15 and if ye despise *my s.* or if
43 their soul abhorred *my s.*
1 *K.* 3:14 if thou wilt keep *my s.*
11:34 because he kept *my s.*
2 *K.* 17:13 keep my com. *my s.*
2 *Chr.* 7:19 if ye forsake *my s.*
Ps. 50:16 hast thou to decl. *my s.*
89:31 if they break *my s.*
Jer. 44:10 neither walk. in *my s.*
Ezek. 5:6 hath changed *my s.*
7 ye have not walked in *my s.*
11:20 they may walk in *my s.*
18:19 when son hath kept *my s.*
36:27 cau. you to walk in *my s.*
Zec. 1:6 *my s.* did take hold of

Thy STATUTES.

1 *Chr.* 29:19 heart to keep *thy s.*
Ps. 119:12 O Lord, teach me *t. s.*
26, 33, 64, 68, 124, 135
16 I will delight my. in *thy s.*
23 thy servant did med. in *t. s.*
48 and I will meditate in *thy s.*
54 *thy s.* have been my songs
71 that I might learn *thy s.*
80 let my heart be sou. in *t. s.*
83 yet do I not forget *thy s.*
112 inclined my heart to *t. s.*
117 I will have respect to *t. s.*
118 hast trod. that err fr. *t. s.*
155 the wicked seek not *t. s.*
171 thou hast taught *thy s.*

STAVES.

Ex. 25:13 makes *s.* of shittim-w.
28; 27:6; 30:5; 37:4
14 put *s.* into rings, 15; 27:7;
37:5; 38:7
40:20 he set *s.* on ark and put
Num. 4:6 put in *s.* ther. 8, 11, 14
21:18 nobles digged with their *s.*
1 *Sam.* 17:43 com. to me wi. *s.* ?
1 *Chr.* 15:15 L. carried ark wi. *s.*
Hab. 3:14 didst strike with his *s.*
Zec. 11:7 I took unto me two *s.*
Mat. 10:10 coats nor *s. Luke* 9:3
26:47 Judas, with him a multitude with *s. Mark* 14:43

STAY, Substantive.

Lev. 13:5 if plague in si. be at *s.*
2 *Sam.* 22:19 L. my *s. Ps.* 18:18
Is. 3:1 L. doth take away the *s.*
19:13 they that are *s.* of tribes

STAYS.

1 *K.* 10:19 *s.* on either side thro.
2 *Chr.* 9:18

STAY, Verb.

Gen. 19:17 nei. *s.* thou in plain
Ex. 9:28 ye shall *s.* no longer
Jos. 10:19 *s.* not, pursue after
Ruth 1:13 would ye *s.* for them ?
1 *Sam.* 15:16 I will tell thee
20:38 make speed, haste, *s.* not
2 *Sam.* 24:16 *s.* hand, 1 *Chr.* 21:15
Job 37:4 he will not *s.* them
38:37 can *s.* bottles of heaven

Prov. 28:17 let no man *s.* him
Cant. 2:5 *s.* me with flagons
Is. 10:20 sh. no more *s.* on him
29:9 *s.* yourselves and wonder
30:12 and *s.* on oppression
31:1 woe to th. that *s.* on hors.
48:2 *s.* themselves on God of Is.
50:10 trust in L. *s.* on his God
Jer. 4:6 *s.* not for I will bri. evil
20:9 I was weary, I could not *s.*
Dan. 4:35 none can *s.* his hand
Hos. 13:13 not *s.* in place

STAYED.

Gen. 8:10 Noah *s.* seven days, 12
32:4 I have *s.* there until now
Ex. 10:24 flocks and herds be *s.*
17:12 Aa. and Hur *s.* up Moses'
Num. 16:48 plague *s.* 50; 25:8;
2 *Sam.* 24:25; *Ps.* 106:30
Jos. 10:13 stood still, moon *s.*
1 *Sam.* 20:19 thou hast *s.* 3 days
24:7 Da. *s.* servants with words
1 *Sam.* 30:9 those that were left
behind *s.*
2 *Sam.* 17:17 Jon. *s.* by En-rogel
24:21 that plague may be *s.* fr.
people, 1 *Chr.* 21:22
1 *K.* 22:35 king was *s.* in chariot,
2 *Chr.* 18:34
2 *K.* 4:6 not a vessel more, oil *s.*
13:18 he smote thrice, and *s.*
15:20 king of Assyria *s.* not
Job 38:11 shall thy waves be *s.*
Is. 26:3 keep him wh. mind is *s.*
Lam. 4:6 overthro. no hands *s.*
Ezek. 31:15 great waters were *s.*
Hag. 1:10 heav. is *s.* earth is *s.*
Luke 4:42 peo. came and *s.* him
Acts 19:22 he himself *s.* in Asia

STAYETH.

Is. 27:8 he *s.* his rough wind

STEAD.

Gen. 30:2 Ja. said. Am I in G. *s.* ?
44:33 let serv. abide in *s.* of lad
Ex. 29:30 priest in *s. Lev.* 16:32
Num. 10:31 to us in *s.* of eyes
32:14 risen in your fathers' *s.*
Jos. 5:7 wh. he raised in their *s.*
Job 16:4 in my soul's *s.*
33:6 acc. to thy wish: in G.'s *s.*
34:24 sh. set others in their *s.*
2 *Cor.* 5:20 pray you in Ch.'s *s.*

See REIGNED.

STEADFAST.

Job 11:15 yea, thou shalt be *s.*
Ps. 78:8 spirit was not *s.* with G.
37 neither were *s.* in his covenant
Dan. 6:26 living God *s.* for ever
1 *Cor.* 7:37 stand. in his heart *s.*
15:58 beloved brethren, be *s.*
2 *Cor.* 1:7 our hope of you is *s.*
Heb. 2:2 spok. by angels was *s.*
3:14 if we hold our confid. *s.*
6:19 an anchor sure and *s.*
1 *Pet.* 5:9 whom resist *s.* in faith

STEADFASTLY.

2 *K.* 8:11 settled countenance *s.*
Luke 9:51 he *s.* set fa. to go to J.
Acts 1:10 while they looked *s.*
2:42 *s.* in the apostles' doctrine
6:15 they all looking *s.* on him
7:55 Step. looked *s.* into heav.
14:9 who *s.* beholding him, and
2 *Cor.* 3:7 Is. could not *s.* behold
13 could not *s.* look to the end

STEADFASTNESS.

Col. 2:5 *s.* of your faith in Christ
2 *Pet.* 3:17 lest ye fall fr. your *s.*

STEADS.

1 *Chr.* 5:22 they dwelt in their *s.*

STEADY.

Ex. 17:12 Moses' hands were *s.*

STEAL.

Gen. 31:27 wheref. didst *s.* away
44:8 how should we *s.* silver?
Ex. 20:15 shalt not *s. Lev.* 19:11;
Deut. 5:19; *Mat.* 19:18; *Rom.*
13:9
22:1 if a man *s.* an ox, he shall
2 *Sam.* 19:3 as people *s.* away
Prov. 6:30 if he *s.* to satisfy soul
30:9 or lest I be poor and *s.*
Jer. 7:9 will ye *s.* murder, and
23:30 I am ag. prophets that *s.*
Mat. 6:19 thi. break thro' and *s.*
20 thieves do not break nor *s.*
27:64 lest his disc. *s.* him away
Mark 10:19 do not *s. Luke* 18:20
John 10:10 thief com. but to *s.*
Rom. 2:21 sho. not *s.* dost thou *s.*
Eph. 4:28 that stole *s.* no more
STEALERS. See MENSTEALERS.

STEALETH.

Ex. 21:16 he that *s.* a man
Job 27:20 tempest *s.* him away
Zec. 5:3 for every one that *s.*

STEALING.

Deut. 24:7 if a man be found *s.*
Hos. 4:2 by swearing and *s.*

STEALTH.

2 *Sam.* 19:3 peo. gat them by *s.*

STEEL.

2 *Sam.* 22:35 *s.* is brok. *Ps.* 18:34
Job 20:24 bow of *s.* strike him
Jer. 15:12 shall iron break *s.?*

STEEP.

Ezek. 38:20 *s.* places shall fall
Mic. 1:4 poured down *s.* place
Mat. 8:32 the swine ran violent.
  down a *s.* place, *Mark* 5:13;
  Luke 8:33

STEM.

Is. 11:1 a rod out of *s.* of Jesse

STEP.

1 *Sam.* 20:3 th. is but *s.* between
Job 31:7 if my *s.* hath turned out

STEPHANAS.

1 *Cor.* 1:16 baptiz. housch. of S.
16:15 house of S. the first-fruits
17 I am glad of coming of S.

STEPHEN.

Acts 6:5 chose S. a man full, 8
7:59 they stoned S. calling on
8:2 devout men carried S. to his
11:19 abroad on perse. about S.
22:20 blood of thy martyr S.

STEPPED, ETH.

John 5:4 whosoev. first *s.* in was
7 another *s.* down before me

STEPS.

Ex. 20:26 neither go up by *s.*
2 *Sam.* 22:37 thou hast enlarged
  my *s. Ps.* 18:36
1 *K.* 10:19 the throne had six *s.*
  20 twelve lions on *s.* 2 *Chr.* 9:19
Job 14:16 thou numberest my *s.*
18:7 *s.* of his strength be strait.
23:11 my foot hath held his *s.*
29:6 I washed my *s.* with butter
31:4 see my ways and count *s.*
  37 decl. to him numb. of my *s.*
Ps. 17:11 compassed us in our *s.*
37:23 *s.* of a good man ordered
  31 none of his *s.* shall slide
44:18 nor have our *s.* declined
56:6 mark my *s.* when th. wait
57:6 prepared a net for my *s.*
73:2 my *s.* had well nigh slipped
85:13 set us in the way of his *s.*
119:133 order my *s.* in thy word
Prov. 4:12 thy *s.* not be straiten.
5:5 her *s.* take hold on hell
16:9 the Lord directeth his *s.*
16:26 *s.* of the needy sh. tread.
Jer. 10:23 not in man to dir. his *s.*
Lam. 4:18 they hunt our *s.* we

Ezek. 40:22 went to it by 7 *s.* 26
  49 brought me by *s.* whereby
Dan. 11:43 Ethiopi. be at his *s.*
Rom. 4:12 walk in *s.* of that faith
2 *Cor.* 12:18 walked we not in *s.?*
1 *Pet.* 2:21 that ye sho. fol. his *s.*

STERN.

Acts 27:29 cast 4 ancho. out of *s.*

STEWARD.

Gen. 15:2 and the *s.* of my house
43:19 they came near to the *s.*
1 *K.* 16:9 drunk in house of his *s.*
Mat. 20:8 L. of viney. saith to *s.*
Luke 8:3 wife of Chu. Herod's *s.*
12:42 who th. is that faithful *s.*
16:1 rich man who had a *s.*
  2 thou mayest be no longer *s.*
  8 L. commended the unjust *s.*
Tit. 1:7 bishop blameless *s.* of G.

STEWARDS.

1 *Chr.* 28:1 David assembled *s.*
1 *Cor.* 4:1 *s.* of mysteries of God
  2 required in *s.* that a man
1 *Pet.* 4:10 good *s.* of grace of G.

STEWARDSHIP.

Luke 16:2 give account of thy *s.*
  3 my lord taketh fr. me the *s.* 4

STICK, Verb.

Job 33:21 bones not seen, *s.* out
  41:17 scales are joined, they *s.*
Ps. 38:2 thi. arrows *s.* fast in me
Ezek. 29:4 cau. fish to *s.* to scales

STICKETH.

Prov. 18:24 friend *s.* closer than

STICK.

2 *K.* 6:6 cut down a *s.* and cast it
Lam. 4:8 skin withered like a *s.*
Ezek. 37:16 one *s.* another *s.* 17

STICKS.

Num. 15:32 gath. *s.* on sabbath
1 *K.* 17:10 woman was gather. *s.*
  12 behold, I am gather. two *s.*
Ezek. 37:20 *s.* whereon thou wri.
Acts 28:3 Paul gath. bundle of *s.*

STIFF.

Jer. 17:23 but made their neck *s.*

STIFF-HEARTED.

Ezek. 2:4 impud. child. and *s.-h.*

STIFF neck.

Deut. 31:27 I know thy *s. neck*
Ps. 75:5 speak not with a *s. neck*

STIFF-NECKED.

Ex. 32:9 this peo. is a *s.-n.* peo.
33:3 art a *s.-n.* people, *Deut.* 9:6
  5 say to Is. Ye are a *s.-n.* peo.
34:9 a *s.-n.* people, *Deut.* 9:13
Deut. 10:16 be no more *s.-n.*
2 *Chr.* 30:8 not *s.-n.* as your fath.
Acts 7:51 *s.-n.* ye resist H. Ghost

STIFFENED.

2 *Chr.* 36:13 *s.* his neck and har.

STILL, Adverb.

Ex. 9:2 and will hold them *s.*
Num. 14:38 Josh. and C. lived *s.*
2 *Sam.* 14:32 to have been th. *s.*
2 *K.* 7:4 and if we sit *s.* here
Job 2:9 dost *s.* retain th. integ.?
3:13 now should I have lain *s.*
20:13 tho' he keep it *s.* within
Ps. 49:9 that he should *s.* live
Jer. 8:14 why do we sit *s.,?*
Rev. 22:11 unj. *s.* filthy *s.* holy *s.*

See STAND, STOOD.

STILL, Adjective and Verb.

Ex. 15:16 sh. be as *s.* as a stone
Jud. 18:9 land good, are ye *s.?*
1 *K.* 19:12 after fire *s.* small voice
22:3 Ram. is ours, and we be *s.*
Ps. 4:4 commu. with heart, be *s.*
8:2 thou mightest *s.* the enemy
23:2 leadeth me beside *s.* waters
46:10 be *s.* and kn. that I am G.
76:8 the earth feared, and was *s.*

83:1 hold not, and be not *s.* O G.
107:29 so that waves ther. are *s.*
Is. 23:2 be *s.* ye inhabit. of isle
30:7 their strength is to sit *s.*
42:14 been *s.* and refrai. myself
Jer. 47:6 sw. of L. rest and be *s.*
Mark 4:39 to sea, Peace, be *s.*

STILLED.

Num. 13:30 Caleb *s.* the people
Neh. 8:11 the Levites *s.* the peo.

STILLEST, ETH.

Ps. 65:7 who *s.* noise of the seas
89:9 when waves ari. thou *s.* th.

STING, S.

1 *Cor.* 15:55 where is *s.?* 56 *s.* of
Rev. 9:19 were *s.* in their tails

STINGETH.

Prov. 23:32 it *s.* like an adder

STINK, Substantive.

Is. 3:24 instead smell, shall be *s.*
34:3 *s.* come out of their carcas.
Joel 2:20 his *s.* shall come up
Amos 4:10 made *s.* of your camps

STINK, Verb.

Gen. 34:30 ye have made me to *s.*
Ex. 7:18 and the river shall *s.*
16:24 manna laid up, did not *s.*
Ps. 38:5 wounds *s.* and corrupt

STINKETH, ING.

Ec. 10:1 send forth a *s.* savor
Is. 50:2 fish *s.* there is no water
John 11:39 L. by this time he *s.*

STIR, Verb.

Num. 24:9 who shall *s.* him up?
Job 17:8 innocent *s.* himself ag.
41:10 no. is so fierce th. dare *s.*
Ps. 35:23 *s.* up thyself, awake
78:38 did not *s.* up all his wrath
80:2 *s.* up thy strength, come
Prov. 15:1 griev. words *s.* anger
Cant. 2:7 that ye *s.* not up my
  love, 3:5; 8:4
Is. 10:26 L. shall *s.* up a scourge
13:17 behold, I will *s.* up Medes
42:13 he shall *s.* up jealousy
Dan. 11:2 shall *s.* up agai. realm
  25 *s.* up his power agai. king
2 *Tim.* 1:6 thou *s.* up gift of God
2 *Pet.* 1:13 meet to *s.* you up, 3:1

STIR, S.

Is. 22:2 full of *s.* a tumultu. city
Acts 12:18 *s.* among the soldiers
19:23 no small *s.* about way

STIRRED.

Ex. 35:21 *s.* him up, 26; 36:2
1 *Sam.* 22:8 my son hath *s.* up
26:19 L ha. *s.* thee up agai. me
1 *K.* 11:14 L. *s.* up an adversary
  23 G. *s.* him up ano. adversary
21:25 whom Jez. his wife *s.* up
1 *Chr.* 5:26 G. *s.* up spirit of Pul
2 *Chr.* 21:16 L. *s.* up Philistines
36:22 the Lord *s.* up the spirit
  of Cyrus, *Ezr.* 1:1
Ps. 39:2 and my sorrow was *s.*
Dan. 11:10 his sons shall be *s.* up
  25 king of south be *s.* up
Hag. 1:14 L. *s.* spirit of Zerubb.
Acts 6:12 they *s.* up the people,
  17:13; 21:27
13:50 Jews *s.* up devout women
14:2 unbelieving Jews *s.* Genti.
17:16 P. his spirit was *s.* in him

STIRRETH.

Deut. 32:11 as eagle *s.* her nest
Prov. 10:12 hatred *s.* up strifes
15:18 wrath. man *s.* strife, 29:22
28:25 he of proud heart *s.* strife
Is. 14:9 hell fr. ben. *s.* up dead
Is. 64:7 none *s.* up hims. to take
Luke 43:5 he *s.* up peo. teaching

STOCK.

Lev. 25:47 to the *s.* of stranger's
Job 14:8 though *s.* thereof die

Is. 40:24 their *s.* not take root
44:19 sh. I fall down to the *s.?*
Jer. 2:27 saying to a *s.* Thou art
10:8 *s.* is a doctrine of vanities
Acts 13:26 chil. of *s.* of Abraham
Phil. 3:5 of the *s.* of Is. a Hebr.

STOCKS.

Job 13:27 puttest my feet in *s.*
33:11 he putteth my feet in *s.*
Prov. 7:22 as fool to correct. of *s.*
Jer. 3:9 committed adul. with *s.*
20:2 Pashur put Jerem. in *s.* 3
29:26 put him in prison and *s.*
Hos. 4:12 peo. ask counsel at *s.*
Acts 16:24 their feet fast in *s.*

Gazing-STOCK.

Nah. 3:6 I will set th. as a *g.-s.*
Heb. 10:33 ye were made a *g.-s.?*

STOICS.

Acts 17:18 cer. philosophers of *s.*

STOLE.

Gen. 31:20 Ja. *s.* away unawares
2 Sam. 15:6 Absa. *s.* hearts of Is.
2 K. 11:2 Jehosheba *s.* Joash fr.
king's sons, *2 Chr.* 22:11
Mat. 28:13 disciples *s.* him while
Eph. 4:28 let him th. *s.* steal no

STOLEN.

Gen. 30:33 shall be counted *s.*
31:19 Rachel has *s.* images, 32
30 wherefore hast *s.* my gods?
40:15 ind. I was *s.* away out of
Ex. 22:7 if the stuff be *s.* out of
12 if it be *s.* from him, he shall
Jos. 7:11 they have *s.* and disse.
2 Sam. 19:41 have men of Jud. *s.*
21:12 men of Jab. had *s.* bones
Prov. 9:17 *s.* waters are sweet
Ob. 5 would they not have *s.?*

STOMACH.

1 Tim. 5:23 use wine for *s.* sake

STOMACHER.

Is. 3:24 inst. of *s.* gird. of sack.

STONE.

Gen. 11:3 they had brick for *s.*
28:18 Jacob set up a *s.* 22 ; 31:45
29:3 rolled *s.* from well's, 8, 10
35:14 Jacob set up a pillar of *s.*
49:24 the sheph. the *s.* of Israel
Ex. 4:25 Zippor. took a sharp *s.*
15:5 they sank to bottom as a *s.*
16 they shall be still as a *s.*
17:12 they took a *s.* and put it
21:18 if one smite ano. with a *s.*
28:10 six on 1 *s.* six on other *s.*
Lev. 26:1 nor set up image of *s.*
Num. 35:17 if smite with a *s.* 23
Jos. 4:5 take eve. man of you a *s.*
15:6 border went to *s.* of Bohan
18:17 border descend. to *s.* of B.
24:27 this *s.* shall be a witness
Jud. 9:5 slew 70 persons on *s.* 18
1 Sam. 6:18 *s.* remain. to this day
7:12 Samuel set up a *s.*
17:49 Da. took from his bag a *s.*
50 David prevailed with a *s.*
20:19 remain by the *s.* Ezel
25:37 Nab.'s hea. died, bec. as *s.*
2 Sam. 17:13 not one sm. *s.* found
1 K. 5:17 house was built of *s.*
18 cedar, there was no *s.* seen
2 K. 3:25 on land cast ev. man *s.*
1 Chr. 22:15 there are hew. of *s.*
2 Chr. 2:14 skilful to work in *s.*
Neh. 9:11 thou threwest as a *s.*
Job 28:2 brass is molten out of *s.*
38:30 waters are hid as with a *s.*
41:24 his heart is as firm as a *s.*
Ps. 91:12 lest thou dash foot ag.
s. Mat. 4:6 ; *Luke* 4:11
118:22 *s.* wh. build. ref. is head
s. Mat. 21:42 ; *Mark* 12:10
Prov. 26:8 as he that bindeth a *s.*
27 as he that rolleth a *s.* it will
27:3 a *s.* is heavy, a fool's wrath

Jer. 2:27 to a *s.* Th. hast brought
51:26 shall not take of thee a *s.*
Lam. 3:58 they cast a *s.* upon me
Dan. 2:34 a *s.* was cut out of, 45
6:17 a *s.* laid on mouth of den
Hab. 2:11 *s.* shall cry out of wall
19 woe to him saith to dumb *s.*
Hag. 2:15 *s.* was laid upon a *s.*
Zec. 3:9 upon one *s.* seven eyes
4:7 sh. bri. forth head *s.* thereof
7:12 made hearts as adamant *s.*
Mat. 7:9 will give *s.?* Luke 11:11
21:44 whoso. shall fall on this
s. shall be brok., *Luke* 20:18
Mat. 24:2 not be left one *s.* Mark
13:2 ; *Luke* 19:44 ; 21:6
27:66 sealing *s.* setting a watch
28:2 angel came and rol. back *s.*
Luke 4:3 command this *s.* th. it
20:17 *s.* which builders reject.
Acts 4:11 ; 1 Pet. 2:7
22:41 withdr. fr. them a *s.* cast
24:2 fou. *s.* rolled away, Mark
16:4 ; *John* 20:1
John 1:42 Cephas, by inter. a *s.*
2:6 were set six water-pots of *s.*
8:7 let him first cast *s.* at her
11:38 a cave, a *s.* lay upon it
39 take away *s.* 41 they took *s.*
Acts 17:29 Godhead is like *s.* gra.
Rev. 16:21 hail fell ev. *s.* wei. of
18:21 angel took up *s.*

Burdensome STONE.

Zec. 12:3 I will make Jer. a b. *s.*

See CORNER, GREAT, HEWED.

Hewn STONE.

Ex. 20:25 not build altar of h. *s.*
2 K. 22:6 timber and h. *s.* to re-
pair house, 2 Chr. 34:11
Lam. 3:9 encl. my ways wi. h. *s.*
Ezek. 40:42 four tables of h. *s.*
Amos 5:11 built houses of h. *s.*
Luke 23:53 sepulchre was h. in *s.*

Living STONE.

1 Pet. 2:4 coming as to l. *s.* chos.

Precious STONE.

Prov. 17:8 a gift is a p. *s.* to him
Is. 28:16 in Zion a p. *s.* 1 Pet. 2:6
Ezek. 28:13 p. *s.* was thy cover.
Rev. 17:4 with gold and p. *s.*
21:11 was like to a *s.* most p.

See STUMBLING.

STONE-SQUARERS.

1 K. 5:18 builders and *s.-s.* did

Tables of STONE.

Ex. 24:12 I give th. t. of *s.* 31:18
34:1 hew two t. of *s.* Deut. 10:1
Deut. 4:13 wrote on t. of *s.* 5:22
9:9 I was up to receive t. of *s.*
10 L. deliv. to me two t. of *s.*
1 K. 8:9 in ark save two t. of *s.*
2 Cor. 3:3 not in t. of *s.* in fleshly

Tried STONE.

Is. 28:16 I lay in Zion a tried *s.*

White STONE.

Rev. 2:17 I will give him a wh. *s.*

STONE, joined with wood.

Ex. 7:19 in vessels of w. and *s.*
Deut. 4:28 work of men's han. w.
and *s.* 28:36, 64 ; 29:17 ; 2 K.
19:18 ; Is. 37:19 ; Ezek. 20:32
Dan. 5:4 gods of wood and *s.* 23
Rev. 9:20 wor. idols of w. and *s.*

STONE of Zoheleth.

1 K. 1:9 Adonij. slew sheep by *s.*

See WALL.

STONE, Verb.

Ex. 8:26 will they not *s.* us?
17:4 almost ready to *s.* me
Lev. 20:2 people shall *s.* him
27 shall *s.* wizards with stones
24:14 let congreg. *s.* him, 16, 23
Num. 14:10 congre. bade *s.* them

15:35 sh. *s.* sabbath-breaker, 36
Deut. 13:10 *s.* with stones entic.
17:5 *s.* idolat. 21:21 *s.* rebellious
22:21 *s.* her that playeth whore
24 sh. *s.* adulterers with stones
1 K. 21:10 car. Nab. out, *s.* him
Ezek. 16:40 shall *s.* thee with st.
23:47 company shall *s.* them
Luke 20:6 the people will *s.* us
John 10:31 Jews took ston. to *s.*
32 for wh. of works do *s.* me?
11:8 Jews of late sou. to *s.* thee
Acts 14:5 assault made to *s.* th.

STONED.

Ex. 19:13 he shall be *s.* or shot
21:28 ox shall be surely *s.* 29, 32
Jos. 7:25 all Israel *s.* Achan
1 K. 12:18 all Israel *s.* Adoram,
2 Chr. 10:18
21:13 they *s.* Naboth, 14, 15
2 Chr. 24:21 they *s.* Zechariah in
Mat. 21:35 husband. beat one, *s.*
John 8:5 Moses com. such be *s.*
Acts 5:26 lest should have been *s.*
7:58 they *s.* Stephen, calling, 59
14:19 having *s.* Paul, drew him
2 Cor. 11:25 beaten, once was I *s.*
Heb. 11:37 they were *s.* th. were
12:20 touch mount it shall be *s.*

STONES.

Gen. 31:46 Jacob said, Gather *s.*
Ex. 28:11 engrave two *s.* 12
17 of *s.* even four rows of *s.*
Ex. 28:21 *s.* sh. be wi. names of Is.
39:7 that th. be *s.* for memorial
Lev. 14:42 *s.* in place of those *s.*
45 break down house, *s.* of it
21:20 or hath his *s.* broken
Deut. 8:9 a land wh. *s.* are iron
23:1 wound. in *s.* sh. not enter
27:4 set up these *s.* in mount E.
5 altar of *s.* 8 write on *s.*
Jos. 4:6 what mean these *s.?* 21
8 took twelve *s.* out of Jordan
8:32 wrote on *s.* a copy of law
Jud. 20:16 sli. *s.* at hair-breadth
1 Sam. 17:40 David chose five *s.*
2 Sam. 16:6 Shimei cast *s.* 13
1 K. 5:18 prepared timber and *s.*
10:27 king made silver to be as
s. 2 Chr. 1:15 ; 9:27
15:22 took away *s.* 2 Chr. 16:6
18:31 Elijah took twelve *s.*
2 K. 3:19 good piece land with *s.*
25 Kir-haraseth left th. the *s.*
1 Chr. 12:2 hurling *s.* shooting
2 Chr. 26:14 pre. slings to cast *s.*
Neh. 4:2 will they revive the *s.?*
Job 5:23 in league with *s.* of field
6:12 is strength the stren. of *s.?*
8:17 wrapped, seeth place of *s.*
14:19 the waters wear the *s.*
22:24 gold of O. as *s.* of brooks
28:6 the *s.* of it are place of
40:17 sinews of his *s.* are wrap.
Ps. 102:14 serv. take pleas. in *s.*
137:9 dasheth little ones aga. *s.*
Ec. 3:5 cast *s.* time to gather *s.*
10:9 whoso removeth *s.* be hurt
Is. 5:2 gathered out *s.* thereof
14:19 that go down to *s.* of pit
27:9 the *s.* of altar as chalk *s.*
54:11 I will lay *s.* with fair col.
12 I make bord. of pleasant *s.*
57:6 amo. smooth *s.* of stream
60:17 for *s.* iron ; 62:10 gather *s.*
Jer. 3:9 commit. adultery with *s.*
43:10 I will set his throne on *s.*
Lam. 4:1 *s.* of sanct. poured out
Ezek. 26:12 lay thy *s.* in water
28:14 walked in midst of *s.*
Mic. 1:6 pour down *s.* in valley
Zec. 5:4 consu. it with *s.* thereof
9:16 shall be as *s.* of a crown
Mat. 3:9 of these *s.* to raise up
children, *Luke* 3:8
4:3 command *s.* be made bread

STONES

Mark 12:4 at him they cast *s.*
13:1 see what manner of *s.* here
Luke 19:40 *s.* would immedi. cry
John 8:59 took *s.* to cast, 10:31
1 *Pet.* 2:5 as lively *s.* are built

See STONE, *Verb.*

Corner STONES.

Ps. 144:12 daughters be as *c. s.*

See COSTLY.

STONES of darkness.

Job 28:3 searcheth out *s. of d.*

STONES of emptiness.

Is. 34:11 stret. out upon *s. of e.*

Glistering STONES.

1 *Chr.* 29:2 I have prepared *g. s.*

Gravel STONES.

Lam. 3:16 bro. my teeth wi. *g. s.*

See GREAT.

Hea₂ of STONES.

Jos. 7:26 raised a *h. of s.* on Ac.
8:29 a *h. of s.* on king of Ai
2 *Sam.* 18:17 laid *h. of s.* on Abs.

Hewed STONES.

1 *K.* 5:17 brought *h. s.* foundati.
7:9 according to meas. of *h. s.* 11

Hewn STONES.

Is. 9:10 we will build with *h. s.*

Marble STONES.

1 *Chr.* 29:2 I have prepared *m. s.*

Precious STONES.

2 *Sam.* 12:30 tal. of gold wi. *p. s.*
1 *K.* 10:2 queen of S. ca. wi. *p. s.*
11 navy brou. *p. s.* 2 *Chr.* 9:10
1 *Chr.* 29:2 I prepared all *p. s.*
8 with whom *p. s.* were found
2 *Chr.* 3:6 garnis. house wi. *p. s.*
32:27 made treasuries for *p. s.*
Ezek. 27:22 occupied in fairs *p. s.*
Dan. 11:38 a god honor with *p. s.*
1 *Cor.* 3:12 build on founda. *p. s.*
Rev. 18:12 no man buyeth *p. s.*
21:19 founda. garnish. with *p. s.*

Whole STONES.

Deut. 27:6 al. of *w. s. Jos.* 8:31

Wrought STONES.

1 *Chr.* 22:2 masons to hew *w. s.*

STONEST, ING.

1 *Sam.* 30:6 people spake of *s.* D.
Mat. 23:37 *s.* th. sent, *Luke* 13:34

STONY.

Ps. 141:6 overthrown in *s.* places
Ezek. 11:19 I take *s.* heart, 36:26
Mat. 13:5 some fell on *s.* places,
20 ; *Mark* 4:5, 16

STOOD.

Gen. 18:22 Abraham *s.* before L.
Num. 16:48 *s.* bet. dead and liv.
Deut. 5:5 I *s.* bet. Lord and you
Jos. 3:16 waters *s.* and rose up
Est. 9:16 other Jews *s.* for lives
Ps. 33:9 command. and it *s.* fast
Jer. 46:15 they *s.* not because L.
Ezek. 1:21 those *s.* these *s.* 10:17
24 when they *s.* let down win.
Dan. 12:5 behold, there *s.* other
Mat. 12:46 brethren *s.* without
Acts 16:9 there *s.* man of Maced.
27:21 Paul *s.* forth in the midst

STOOD above.

Gen. 28:13 Lord *s. a.* the ladder
2 *Chr.* 24:20 Zechariah *s. a.* peo
Ps. 104:6 waters *s. a.* mountains

STOOD afar.

Ex. 20:18 people *s. afar* off, 21
Luke 17:12 ten lepers, *s. a.* off
Rev. 18:17 trade by sea *s. a.* off

STOOD before.

Gen. 19:27 place where he *s. b.* L.
43:15 went to Egy. *s. b.* Joseph
Lev. 9:5 congregation *s. b.* Lord
Jos. 20:9 until he *s. b.* congrega.
Jud. 20:28 Phinehas *s. b.* ark

---

1 *K.* 12:6 old men that *s. b.* Solo-
mon, 2 *Chr.* 10:6
8 young men *s. b.* 2 *Chr.* 10:8
22:21 spirit *s. b.* L. 2 *Chr.* 18:20
2 *K.* 10:4 two kings *s.* not *b.* him
Ps. 106:23 had not Mo. *s. b.* him
Jer. 18:20 I *s. b.* th. to spe. good
Ezek. 8:11 th. *s. b.* them 70 men
Dan. 1:19 th. *s. b.* the king. 2:2
Zec. 3:4 spake to those *s. b.* him

STOOD by.

Ex. 18:13 the people *s. by* Moses
Jud. 3:19 that *s. by* went fr. him
18:16 men *s. by* entering of gate
1 *Sam.* 1:26 wom. that *s. by* thee
1 *K.* 13:1 Jeroboam *s. by* altar
2 *K.* 2:7 they two *s. by* Jord. 13
Ezek. 43:6 man *s. by* me, and sa.
Dan. 7:16 near to one that *s. by*
Zec. 3:5 an angel of Lord *s. by*
Mark 14:37 one th. *s. by* drew sw.
15:35 some that *s. by,* wh. they
Luke 19:24 said to them th. *s. by*
Acts 23:11 night foll. L. *s. by* him
27:23 there *s. by* me angel of G.

STOOD in.

Ex. 5:20 Mo. and Aa. *s. in* way
Num. 12:5 L. *s. in* door of taber.
16:27 Dath. and Abir. *s. in* door
22:22 angel of L. *s. in* way. 24
Jos. 3:17 priest *s. in* Jordan, 4:10
2 *Sam.* 23:12 *s. in* midst ground
2 *Chr.* 30:16 th. *s. in* place, 35:10
34:31 king *s. in* his place
Neh. 8:7 people *s. in* their place
Jer. 23:18 who *s. in* counsel of L.
Ob. 14 nor *s. in* cross-way
Luke 24:36 Jesus *s. in* the midst
of them, *John* 20:19, 26
Rev. 5:6 *in* midst of elders *s.* a L.

STOOD on.

1 *Sam.* 17:3 Philist. *s. on* mountain, Israel *s. on* a mountain
26:13 David *s. on* top of a hill
1 *Chr.* 6:39 Asaph *s. on* ri. hand
Rev. 14:1 a Lamb *s. on* mount S.

STOOD over.

Deut. 31:15 pillar of cloud *s. o.*
Jos. 5:13 a man *s. o.* against him
Ezek. 10:4 glory of L. *s. o.* thres.
Mat. 2:9 star *s. o.* wh. child was
Luke 4:39 *s. o.* her, rebuked fever

STOOD round.

Acts 14:20 disciples *s. round* him
Rev. 7:11 angels *s. r.* about thro.

STOOD still.

Jos. 10:13 sun *s. s.* moon stayed
11:13 cities that *s. s.* in strength
2 *Sam.* 2:23 as many as came *s. s.*
20:12 when man saw people *s. s.*
Job 4:16 spirit *s. s.* I could not
discern.
32:16 they spake not, but *s. s.*
Hab. 3:11 sun and moon *s. still*
Mat. 20:32 Jesus *s. s.* called them
Mark 10:49 Je. *s. s.* commanded
Luke 7:14 th. that bare him *s. s.*

STOOD there.

Ex. 34:5 L. descended, and *s. t.*
Ezek. 3:23 behold, glo. of L. *s. t.*
Mat. 27:47 some *s. t. Mark* 11:5

STOOD up.

Gen. 23:3 Abr. *s. up* fr. bef. dead
Ex. 2:17 M. *s. up,* helped them
Num. 11:32 peo. *s. up* all night
1 *Chr.* 21:1 Sat. *s. up* against Is.
2 *Chr.* 13:4 Abijah *s. up* and said
20:19 Levites *s. up* to praise Lc.
Neh. 8:5 opened book, peo. *s. up*
9:3 they *s. up* in their place
Job 4:15 hair of my flesh *s. up*
29:8 yo. men saw me, aged *s. up*
30:28 I *s. up* and cried in cong.
Acts 4:26 kings of earth *s. up* ag.

STOOD upon.

Gen. 41:17 I *s. u.* bank of river
1 *Sam.* 17:51 David *s. u.* Philist.
2 *Sam.* 1:10 so I *s. u.* S. slew him
2 *K.* 13:21 and *s. upon* his feet
Amos 7:7 *s. u.* wall made by line
Rev. 11:11 two proph. *s. u.* feet

STOOD with.

Gen. 45:1 th. *s. with* him no man
Lam. 2:4 *s. with* right hand
Luke 9:32 two men th. *s. w.* him
John 18:18 Peter *s. with* them
2 *Tim.* 4:16 no man *s. with* me
17 L. *s. w.* me, strengthen. me

STOODEST.

Num. 22:34 kn. not thou *s.* in w.
Deut. 4:10 day that thou *s.* be. L.
Ob. 11 day thou *s.* on other side

STOOL, S.

Ex. 1:16 wh. ye see them on *s.*
2 *K.* 4:10 set for him bed, and *s.*

STOOP.

Job 9:13 proud hel. *s.* under him
Prov. 12:25 mak. heart of man *s.*
Is. 46:2 they *s.* they bow down
Mark 1:7 I am not worthy to *s.*

STOOPED.

Gen. 49:9 Jud. *s.* down, couched
1 *Sam.* 24:8 David *s.* 28:14 Saul *s.*
2 *Chr.* 36:17 no co. on him *s.*
John 8:6 Jesus *s.* down, wrote, 8
20:11 she *s.* down, and looked

STOOPETH, ING.

Is. 46:1 Nebo *s.* their idols
Luke 24:12 *s.* down, *John* 20:5

STOP.

1 *K.* 18:44 that rain *s.* thee not
2 *K.* 3:19 *s.* all wells of water, 25
2 *Chr.* 32:3 took coun. to *s.* wat.
Ps. 35:12 *s.* way ag. that persec.
107:42 iniquity sh. *s.* her mouth
Ezek. 39:11 *s.* noses of passengers.
2 *Cor.* 11:10 no man *s.* me

STOPPED.

Gen. 8:2 wind. of heaven were *s.*
26:15 Philistin. had *s.* wells, 18
Lev. 15:3 flesh be *s.* fr. his issue
2 *Chr.* 32:4 who *s.* all fountains
30 Hezekiah *s.* water-course
Neh. 4:7 breaches began to be *s.*
Ps. 63:11 that speake. lies, be *s.*
Jer. 51:32 passages are *s.* reeds
Zec. 7:11 refused, *s.* their ears
Acts 7:57 they *s.* their ears, ran
Rom. 3:19 ev. mouth may be *s.*
Tit. 1:11 wh. mouths must be *s.*
Heb. 11:33 *s.* mouths of lions

STOPPETH.

Job 5:16 iniquity *s.* her mouth
Ps. 58:4 like adder that *s.* ears
Prov. 21:13 whoso *s.* his ears
Is. 33:15 *s.* ears fr. hearing blood

STORE, Verb.

Amos 3:10 who *s.* up violence

STORE, Substantive.

Gen. 26:14 Isaac had *s.* of serva.
41:36 that food shall be for *s.*
Lev. 25:22 eat of old *s.* 26:10
Deut. 28:5 bles. be basket and *s.*
17 cursed sh. be basket and *s.*
32:34 is not this laid up in *s.*
1 *K.* 10:10 gave of spices great *s.*
2 *K.* 20:17 fathers laid up in *s.* to
1 *Chr.* 29:16 this *s.* com. of thine
2 *Chr.* 11:11 he put *s.* of victuals
31:10 that is left is this great *s.*
Neh. 5:18 *s.* of all sorts of wine
Ps. 144:13 our garners afford. *s.*
Is. 39:6 fathers laid up in *s.*
Nah. 2:9 there is none end of *s.*
1 *Cor.* 16:2 let ev. one lay by in *s.*
1 *Tim.* 6:19 laying in *s.* a good
2 *Pet.* 3:7 by word are kept in *s.*

STORE-CITIES.

1 *K.* 9:19 *cities* of *s.* Solomon had
2 *Chr.* 8:4 *s.*-*c* which he built, 6
16:4 th. smote *s.*-*c* of Naphtali
17:12 Jehosha. built *s.*-*c.* in Ju.

STOREHOUSE.

Mal. 3:10 bring tithes into the *s.*
Luke 12:24 the ravens have no *s.*
   nor barn

STOREHOUSES.

Gen. 41:56 Joseph opened the *s.*
Deut. 28:8 command bless. on *s.*
1 *Chr.* 27:25 over *s.* was Jehona.
2 *Chr.* 32:28 Hezekiah made *s.*
Ps. 33:7 layeth up depth in *s.*
Jer. 50:26 open her *s.* cast her

STORK.

Lev. 11:19 *s.* not eat, *Deut.* 14:18
Ps. 104:17 for *s.* the fir-trees
Jer. 8:7 *s.* knoweth her times
Zec. 5:9 had wings like a *s.*

STORM.

Job 21:18 as chaff that *s.* carrieth
   27:21 *s.* hurl. him out of place
Ps. 55:8 I hasten my escape fr. *s.*
   83:15 make them af. with thy *s.*
   107:29 he maketh the *s.* a calm
Is. 4:6 and for a covert from *s.*
   25:4 hast been a refuge from *s.*
   28:2 wh. as destroying *s.* shall
   29:6 shalt be visited with *s.*
Ezek. 38:9 shalt come like a *s.*
Nah. 1:3 Lord hath his way in *s.*
Mark 4:37 there arose a great *s.*
Luke 8:23 there came down a *s.*

STORMY.

Ps. 107:25 raiseth the *s.* wind
   148:8 *s.* wind fulfilling his word
Ezek. 13:11 *s.* wind shall rend, 13

STORY.

2 *Chr.* 13:22 acts of Abijah in *s.*
   24:27 in the *s.* of book of kings

STORIES.

Gen. 6:16 with sec. and third *s.*
Ezek. 41:16 galleries three *s.* over
   42:3 against gallery in three *s.* 5
Amos 9:6 build. his *s.* in heaven

STOUT.

Job 4:11 *s.* lion's whelps are sca.
Is. 10:12 I punish fruit of *s.* heart
Dan. 7:20 who. look was more *s.*
Mal. 3:13 your words ha. been *s.*

STOUT-HEARTED.

Ps. 76:5 *s.*-*h.* are spoiled, they
Is. 46:12 heark. unto me, ye *s.*-*h.*

STOUTNESS.

Is. 9:9 they say in the *s.* of heart

STRAIGHT.

Jos. 6:5 ascend *s.* before him, 20
Ps. 5:8 make thy way *s.* before
Ec. 1:15 crooked can. be made *s.*
   7:13 for who can make that *s.* ?
Is. 40:3 make *s.* in desert a high.
   4 the crooked shall be made *s.*
   42:16 ; 45:2 ; *Luke* 3:5
Jer. 31:9 cause to walk in *s.* way
Ezek. 1:7 their feet were *s.* feet
   9 they went *s.* forw. 12 ; 10:22
Mat. 3:3 make his paths *s.* *Mark*
   1:3 ; *Luke* 3:4 ; *John* 1:23
Luke 13:13 she was made *s.* and
Acts 9:11 go into street called S.
Heb. 12:13 made *s.* paths for feet

STRAIGHTWAY.

1 *Sam.* 9:13 ye shall *s.* find him
   28:20 Saul fell *s.* along on earth
Prov. 7:22 goeth after her *s.*
Mat. 4:20 *s.* left nets, *Mark* 1:18
   21:3 *s.* will send th. *Mark* 11:3
Mark 6:54 and *s.* they knew him
Luke 5:39 no man *s.* desire. new
John 13:32 God shall *s.* glorify
Acts 5:10 then fell she down *s.* at
   22:29 then *s.* they departed from

23:30 when told me, I sent *s.* to

STRAIN.

Mat. 23:24 guides *s.* at a gnat

STRAIT, S.

1 *Sam.* 13:6 saw they were in a *s.*
2 *Sam.* 24:14 in a *s.* 1 *Chr.* 21:13
Job 20:22 sufficiency sh. be in *s.*
   36:16 removed thee out of *s.*
Lam. 1:3 overtook her betwe. *s.*
Phil. 1:23 I am in *s.* betwixt two

STRAIT.

2 *K.* 6:1 place we dwell is two *s.*
Is. 49:20 place is too *s.* for me
Mat. 7:13 enter ye in at *s.* gate
   14 bec. *s.* is gate, *Luke* 13:24

STRAITEN, ETH.

Job 12:23 he enlar. nations and *s.*
Jer. 19:9 seek lives shall *s.* them

STRAITENED.

Job 18:7 steps of stre. shall be *s.*
   37:10 breadth of the waters is *s.*
Prov. 4:12 thy steps sh. not be *s.*
Ezek. 42:6 building was *s.* more
Mic. 2:7 is Spirit of Lord *s.* ?
Luke 12:50 how am I *s.* till it be
2 *Cor.* 6:12 not *s.* in us, *s.* in your

STRAITEST.

Acts 26:5 after most *s.* sect

STRAITLY.

Gen. 43:7 asked *s.* of our state
Jos. 6:1 Jericho was *s.* shut up.
Mark 1:43 he *s.* charged him and
Acts 4:17 let us *s.* threaten them
   5:28 did not we *s.* comma. you ?

STRAITNESS.

Deut. 28:53 eat child. in *s.* 55, 57
Job 36:16 place wh. there is no *s.*
Jer. 19:9 eat flesh of friend in *s.*

STRAKE.

Acts 27:17 they fearing *s.* sail
See STRUCK.

STRAKES. *See* STREAKS.

STRANGE.

Gen. 42:7 Joseph made himself *s.*
Ex. 2:22 stranger in *s.* land, 18:3
   21:8 sell her to a *s.* nation
   30:9 ye shall offer no *s.* incense
Lev. 10:1 Nadab and Abihu offered *s.* fire, *Num.* 3:4 ; 26:61
2 *K.* 19:24 I have drunk *s.* waters
Job 19:3 not asha. make your. *s.*
   17 my breath is *s.* to my wife
   31:3 a *s.* punishment to workers
Ps. 114:1 went fr. peo. of *s.* lang.
   137:4 sing L.'s song in *s.* land
Prov. 21:8 the way of man is *s.*
Is. 17:10 shalt set it with *s.* lips
   28:21 he may do his *s.* work,
   bring to pass his *s.* act
Jer. 2:21 how turned into *s.* vine
   8:19 provoked with *s.* vanities
Ezek. 3:5 sent to peo. of *s.* spee.
Hos. 8:12 counted a *s.* thing
Zep. 1:8 clothed with *s.* apparel
Luke 5:26 have seen *s.* things
Acts 7:6 sojourn in a *s.* land
   17:20 bringest *s.* things to ears
   26:11 I persecuted to *s.* cities
Heb. 11:9 sojou. as in *s.* country
   13:9 be not carried with *s.* doct.
1 *Pet.* 4:4 they think it *s.* ye run
   12 think it not *s.* concerning
   trial, as though *s.* thing
Jude 7 as So. going after *s.* flesh

See CHILDREN, GOD, GODS.

STRANGE wives.

1 *K.* 11:8 likewi. did he for *s.* w.
Ezr. 10:2 tak. *s.* w. 10, 14, 17, 44
   11 separ. yourselves from *s.* w.
   18 were found to have *s.* w.
Neh. 13:27 trans. in marry. *s.* w.

STRANGE woman.

Jud. 11:2 thou art son of a *s.* w.

Prov. 2:16 deliv. thee from *s.* w.
   5:3 lips of *s.* w. drop as honey-c.
   20 wilt th. be ravis. with *s.* w.
   6:24 from flattery of *s.* w. 7:5
   20:16 pledge for a *s.* w. 27:13
   23:27 and a *s.* w. is a narrow pit

STRANGE women.

1 *K.* 11:1 king loved many *s.* w.
Prov. 22:14 mouth of *s.* w. is pit
   23:33 th. eyes shall behold *s.* w.

STRANGELY.

Deut. 32:27 lest advers. behave *s.*

STRANGER.

Gen. 15:13 thy seed shall be a *s.*
   17:8 I will give thee land wherein thou art a *s.* 28:4 ; 37:1
   27 bought with money of the *s.*
   23:4 I am *s.* *Ps.* 39:12 ; 119:19
Ex. 2:22 I ha. been a *s.* in land
   12:19 cut off, whether a *s. Lev.*
   16:29 ; 17:15 ; *Num.* 15:30
   43 sh. no *s.* eat thereof, 29:33
   49 homeborn and *s. Lev.* 24:22 ;
   Num. 9:14 ; 15:15, 16, 29
   20:10 nor *s.* that is within thy
   gates, *Deut.* 5:14
   22:21 thou shalt not oppress a *s.*
   23:9 ye know heart of a *s.* seei.
   12 that the *s.* may be refreshed
   30:33 whoso. putteth it upon a *s.*
Lev. 17:12 neither sh. any *s.* eat
   19:10 sh. leave for *s.* 23:22 ; 25:6
   33 if a *s.* sojourn in the land
   22:10 no *s.* eat holy thing, 13
   22:25 neither from a *s.* hand
   24:16 as well *s.* when blasphem.
   25:35 tho' he be a *s.* thou shalt
   47 if a *s.* wax rich by thee
Num. 1:51 *s.* th. cometh nigh sh.
   be put to death, 3:10, 38
   15:14 if a *s.* sojo. will offer
   16:40 that no *s.* offer incense
   18:7 the *s.* that cometh nigh
   19:10 to Israel and *s.* a statute
   35:15 cit. of ref. for *s. Jos.* 20:9
Deut. 1:16 judge righte. betw. *s.*
   10:18 L. loveth the *s.* in giving
Deut. 10:19 love *s.* ye were stran.
   14:21 give that wh. dieth to *s.*
   17:15 not set a *s.* over thee
   23:20 unto a *s.* thou may. lend
   28:43 *s.* shall get above thee
   29:11 *s.* to enter in cove. wi. G.
   31:12 gather thy *s.* that he may
Jos. 8:33 *s.* stood to hear words
Jud. 19:12 not turn to city of *s.*
Ruth 2:10 seeing I am a *s.* ?
2 *Sam.* 1:13 I am the son of a *s.*
   15:19 thou art a *s.* and an exile
1 *K.* 3:18 there was no *s.* with us
   8:43 do all *s.* calleth, 2 *Chr.* 6:33
Job 15:19 no *s.* passed am. them
   19:15 maids count me for a *s.*
   31:32 *s.* did not lodge in street
Ps. 69:8 I am become a *s.* to my
   94:6 they slay the widow and *s.*
   109:11 let the *s.* spoil his labor
Prov. 2:16 to deliver thee from *s.*
   5:10 thy labors in house of a *s.*
   20 wilt thou emb. bosom of *s.* ?
   6:1 if hast stricken hand with *s.*
   7:5 they may keep thee from *s.*
   11:15 he that is surety for a *s.*
   14:10 a *s.* doth not intermeddle
   20:16 is surety for a *s.* 27:13
   27:2 let a *s.* praise thee
Ec. 6:2 not power to eat, a *s.*
Is. 56:3 neith. let son of *s.* speak
   6 the sons of *s.* that join them
   62:8 sons of *s.* not drink thy w.
Jer. 14:8 why be as a *s.* in land
Ezek. 14:7 ev. *s.* setteth up idols
   22:7 dealt by oppress. with *s.* 29
   44:9 no *s.* uncircumci. sh. enter
Ob. 12 in day he became a *s.*
Mal. 3:5 that turn aside fr. from
Mat. 25:35 was *s.* took me in, 43

38 when saw we thee a *s*. ? 44
Luke 17:18 not found save this *s*.
24:18 art thou only *s*. in Jeru. ?
John 10:5 *s*. will they not follow
Acts 7:29 Mo. was a *s*. in Midian
See FATHERLESS.

STRANGERS.

Gen. 31:15 are we not count. *s*. ?
36:7 land where. were *s*. *Ex*. 6:4
Ex. 22:21 in Egypt, 23:9 ; *Lev*.
19:34 ; 25:23 ; *Deut*. 10:19
Lev. 17:10 whatsoever of *s*. that
20:2 of *s*. that give seed to Mol.
25:45 children of *s*. shall ye buy
Jos. 8:35 *s*. that were conversing
2 *Sam*. 22:45 *s*. sh. submit them.
46 *s*. sh. fade away. *Ps*. 18:44,45
1 *Chr*. 16:19 ye were *s*. *Ps*. 105:12
22:2 D. commanded to gather *s*.
29:15 we are *s*. as were our fath.
2 *Chr*. 2:17 Solomon numbered *s*.
30:25 *s*. of Is. and Judah rejoic.
Neh. 9:2 seeds of Is. sepa. from *s*.
13:30 cleansed I them from all *s*.
Ps. 54:3 *s*. are risen up aga. me
146:9 the Lord preserveth the *s*.
Prov. 5:10 *s*. be filled wi. wealth
17 let be only thine own, not *s*.
Is. 1:7 your land *s*. devour it in
2:6 they please themselves in *s*.
5:17 places of fat ones sh. *s*. eat
14:1 *s*. sh. be joined with them
25:2 made a palace of *s*. no city
5 shalt bring down noise of *s*.
29:5 multitude of thy *s*. shall be
60:10 sons of *s*. sh. build walls
61:5 *s*. shall feed your flocks
Jer. 2:25 I have loved *s*. after th.
3:13 hast scatter. thy ways to *s*.
5:19 so sh. ye serve *s*. in a land
30:8 *s*. sh. no more serve thems.
35:7 live in land where ye be *s*.
51:51 *s*. are come into sanctuar.
Lam. 5:2 inher. is turn. to *s*. houses
Ezek. 7:21 I give it in. hand of *s*.
11:9 deliver you into hands of *s*.
16:32 wife taketh *s*. inst. of hus.
28:10 die deaths by hands of *s*.
30:12 make land waste by *s*.
31:12 *s*. have cut him off
44:7 brou. into my sanctuary *s*.
47:22 for an inheritance to the *s*.
Hos. 7:9 *s*. devoured his strength
8:7 the *s*. shall swallow it up
Joel 3:17 th. shall no *s*. pass thro'
Ob. 11 in the day that *s*. carried
Mat. 17:25 tribute? of chil. or *s*.
26 P. saith, Of *s*. 27:7 bury *s*.
John 10:5 they kn. not voice of *s*.
Acts 2:10 and *s*. of Rome, Jews
13:17 wh. th. dwelt as *s*. in Eg.
Eph. 2:12 were *s*. from the cove.
19 therefore ye are no more *s*.
1 *Tim*. 5:10 if she have lodged *s*.
Heb. 11:13 confessed they were *s*.
13:2 not forgetful to entertain *s*.
1 *Pet*. 1:1 to *s*. scat. thro' Pontus
1 *Pet*. 2:11 beseech you as *s*. pil.
3 *John* 5 whatso. thou doest to *s*.

Nah. 2:12 the lion did tear and *s*.
Acts 15:20 abst. from *s*. 29 ; 21:25

STRANGLING.

Job 7:15 my soul chooseth *s*. and

STRAW.

Gen. 24:25 we have *s*. and prove.
32 he gave *s*. and provender for
Ex. 5:7 no more give *s*. 10, 16, 18
11 get *s*. where you can find it
Jud. 19:19 there is *s*. and proven.
1 *K*. 4:28 barley, and *s*. for horses
Job 41:27 esteem. iron as *s*. brass
Is. 11:7 lion eat *s*. like ox, 65:25
25:10 Moab sh. be trodden as *s*.

STREAKS.

Gen. 30:37 Jacob pilled white *s*.

Lev. 14:37 if plague be wi. hol. *s*.

STREAM.

Num. 21:15 what he did at the *s*.
Job 6:15 as *s*. of brooks they pass
Ps. 124:4 the *s*. had gone over
Is. 27:12 L. shall beat off to the *s*.
30:28 breath as an overflowing *s*.
33 like a *s*. of brimstone
57:6 among smooth stones of *s*.
66:12 glory of G. like flowing *s*.
Dan. 7:10 fiery *s*. issu. and came
Amos 5:24 righteo. as mighty *s*.
Luke 6:48 *s*. beat vehemently, 49

STREAMS.

Ex. 7:19 stretch hand on *s*. 8:5
Ps. 46:4 *s*. make glad city of God
78:16 he brought *s*. out of rock
20 waters gushed, *s*. overflow.
126:4 turn ag. our captivi. as *s*.
Cant. 4:15 living waters, *s*. fr. L.
Is. 11:15 L. shall smite in sev. *s*.
30:25 on ev. high hill *s*. of wat.
33:21 place of broad rivers and *s*.
34:9 *s*. shall be turned into pitch
35:6 waters break out *s*. in desert

STREET.

Gen. 19:2 abide in *s*. all night
Deut. 13:16 gather spoil into *s*.
Jos. 2:19 go out of house into *s*.
Jud. 19:15 he sat down in a *s*. 17
2 *Sam*. 21:12 had stolen fr. the *s*.
22:43 stamp them as mire of *s*.
2 *Chr*. 29:4 gather. in east *s*. 32:6
Ezr. 10:9 peo. sat in *s*. of house
Neh. 8:1 people gathered into *s*.
8:3 he read therein before *s*.
Est. 6:9 on horseback thro. *s*. 11
Job 18:17 sh. have no name in *s*.
29:7 I prepared my seat in the *s*.
31:32 strang. did not lodge in *s*.
Prov. 7:8 pass. thro' the *s*. near
Is. 42:2 not hea. in *s*. *Mat*. 12:19
51:23 hast laid thy body as *s*.
59:14 truth is fallen in the *s*.
Jer. 37:21 bread out of bakers' *s*.
Lam. 2:19 faint for hun. is ev. *s*.
4:1 stones poured out in ev. *s*.
Ezek. 16:24 high place in *s*. 31
Dan. 9:25 the *s*. shall be built ag.
Acts 9:11 go into *s*. call. Straight
12:10 Peter pass. through one *s*.
Rev. 11:8 dead bodies sh. lie in *s*.
21:21 *s*. of city was pure gold
22:2 in midst of *s*. *s*. tree of life

STREETS.

2 *Sam*. 1:20 publish it not in *s*. of
1 *K*. 20:34 shalt make *s*. in Dam.
Ps. 18:42 I cast them as dirt in *s*.
55:11 guile depart not fr. her *s*.
144:13 sheep br. forth 10,000 in *s*.
14 be no complaining in our *s*.
Prov. 1:20 wisd. utter. voice in *s*.
5:16 rivers of waters in the *s*.
7:12 now is she in the *s*. lieth
22:13 lion, I shall be slain in *s*.
26:13 slothful said. A lion is in *s*.
Ec. 12:4 doors shall be shut in *s*.
5 the mourners go about the *s*.
Cant. 3:2 I will go about in the *s*.
Is. 5:25 carcasses were torn in *s*.
10:6 tread them like mire of *s*.
15:3 in th. *s*. they sh. gird them
24:11 a crying for wine in the *s*.
51:20 thy sons lie at head of *s*.
Jer. 5:1 run through *s*. of Jerus.
7:17 seest th. what they do in *s*.
34 cause to cease from *s*. of Je.
9:21 cut off young men from *s*.
11:6 proclaim words in *s*. of Je.
13 accord. to number of *s*. of J.
14:16 people be cast out in the *s*.
33:10 mirth shall be heard in *s*.
44:6 anger was kind. in *s*. of J.
9 wickedness they commi. in *s*.
48:38 shall be lamentation in *s*.
49:26 men shall fall in *s*. 50:30

Jer. 51:4 are thrust through in *s*.
Lam. 2:11 suckli. swoon in *s*. 12
21 young and old lie in the *s*.
4:5 delicately, are desolate in *s*.
8 Nazarit. are not known in *s*.
14 wandered as blind men in *s*.
18 th. hunt our steps in our *s*.
Ezek. 7:19 sh. cast silver in the *s*.
11:6 ye have filled *s*. with slain
26:11 hoofs of horses tread thy *s*.
28:23 will send blood into her *s*.
Amos 5:16 wailing in all *s*.
Mic. 7:10 trodden as mire of *s*.
Nah. 2:4 chariots shall rage in *s*.
3:10 dashed in pieces at top of *s*.
Zep. 3:6 I made their *s*. waste
Zec. 8:4 old women sh. dw. in *s*.
5 *s*. sh. be full of boys and gir.
9:3 heaped up gold as mire in *s*.
10:5 who tread down ene. in *s*.
Mat. 6:2 not sound a trum. in *s*.
5 pray standing in corners of *s*.
Mark 6:56 sick in *s*. *Acts* 5:15
Luke 10:10 go into the *s*. of same
13:26 thou hast taught in our *s*.
14:21 go into *s*. and lanes of city

STRENGTH.

Gen. 4:12 ground sh. not yield *s*.
Ex. 13:3 by *s*. L. brought, 14, 16
Num. 23:22 *s*. of unicorn, 24:8
Jud. 5:21 O my soul, hast trod. *s*.
1 *Sam*. 2:4 stumbl. are girt wi. *s*.
9 for by *s*. shall no man prevail
10 he shall give *s*. un. his king
15:29 the *S*. of Israel will not lie
28:22 that thou mayest have *s*.
2 *Sam*. 22:40 thou hast girded me
with *s*. *Ps*. 18:32, 39
2 *K*. 18:20 and *s*. for war, *Is*. 36:5
19:3 and there is no *s*. *Is*. 37:3
1 *Chr*. 16:27 *s*. and gladn. are in
28 give to the Lord glory and
s. *Ps*. 29:1 ; 96:7
26:8 their sons, able men for *s*.
29:12 in thy hand it is to give *s*.
2 *Chr*. 13:20 nei. did Jer. reco. *s*.
Neh. 4:10 *s*. of bearers of burdens
Job 9:19 if I speak of *s*. he is str.
12:13 wi. him is wisdom and *s*.
21 weakeneth *s*. of the mighty
18:13 it sh. devour *s*. of his skin
23:6 he would put *s*. in me
30:2 wher. might their *s*. profit
36:19 not esteem forces of *s*.
39:19 hast thou given horse *s*. ?
41:22 in his neck remaineth *s*.
Ps. 8:2 out of babes ordained *s*.
20:6 with saving *s*. of rig. hand
27:1 Lord is the *s*. of my life
28:8 he is saving *s*. of his anoi.
29:11 L. will give *s*. to his peo.
33:16 mighty is not deliv. by *s*.
39:13 that I may recover *s*.
46:1 God is our *s*. a very help, 81:1
60:7 Ephrai. is *s*. of head, 108:8
68:34 ascribe *s*. unto God, his
35 God of Israel that giveth *s*.
73:26 God is the *s*. of my heart
81:1 sing aloud unto God our *s*.
84:5 blessed is man whose *s*. is
7 they go from *s*. to *s*. ev. one
90:10 by rea. of *s*. be fourscore
93:1 thy Lord is clothed with *s*.
95:4 *s*. of the hills is his also
96:6 *s*. and beauty are in his sa.
99:4 the king's *s*. loveth judgm.
138:3 strengthenedst me with *s*.
140:7 O God, *s*. of my salvation
Prov. 8:14 I have *s*. 10:29 L. is *s*.
14:4 increase is by the *s*. of ox
21:22 a wise man cast. down *s*.
24:5 man of knowledge incr. *s*.
31:17 girdeth her loins with *s*.
25 *s*. and honor are her cloth.
Ec. 9:16 wisdom is better than *s*.
10:10 if iron blunt, put more *s*.
17 princes eat for *s*. not for dr.

Is. 5:22 men of *s.* to mingle dri.
10:13 by the *s.* of my hand
23:4 spoken, even the *s.* of sea
25:4 *s.* to the poor, *s.* to needy
26:4 L. JEHOVAH is everlast. *s.*
28:6 *s.* to them that turn battle
30:3 *s.* of Pharaoh sh. be shame
33:6 wisd. sh. be stability and *s.*
40:9 O Je. lift up voice with *s.*
29 no might, he increaseth *s.*
42:25 poured on him *s.* of battle
44:12 worketh it with *s.* of arms
45:24 in L. have I righte. and *s.*
51:9 awake, put on *s.* O Lord
Jer. 20:5 I will deli. all *s.* of city
51:53 tho' she fortify height of *s.*
Lam. 1:6 are gone without *s.*
Ezek. 30:15 fury on Sin, *s.* of Eg.
18 pomp of *s.* sh. cease, 33:28
Dan. 2:37 G. hath given thee *s.*

Dan. 2:41 th. sh. be in it *s.* of iron
11:15 neit. shall there be any *s.*
17 enter wi. *s.* of his kingdom
31 shall pollute sanctuary of *s.*
Joel 3:16 Lord the *s.* of Israel
Amos 6:13 not ta. horns by our *s.*
Nah. 3:9 E. and Eg were her *s.*
11 thou also shalt seek *s.*
Hag. 2:22 will destr. *s.* of kingd.
Luke 1:51 he showed *s.* with arm
Acts 3:7 his ancle bones recei. *s.*
Rom. 5:6 wh. without *s.* Ch. died
1 *Cor.* 15:56 *s.* of sin is the law
2 *Cor.* 1:8 we were pressed ab. *s.*
Heb. 11:11 Sarah herself recei. *s.*
Rev. 3:8 for thou hast a little *s.*
5:12 worthy is La. to receive *s.*
12:10 now is salvation and *s.*
17:13 these shall give *s.* to beast

His STRENGTH.

Ex. 14:27 sea returned to *his s.*
Deut. 21:17 he is begin. of *his s.*
Jud. 8:21 as man is, so is *his s.*
16:5 see wher. *his* great *s.* lieth
9 *his s.* not kn. 19 *his s.* went
2 *K.* 9:24 Jehu drew bow wi. *h. s.*
1 *Chr.* 16:11 seek the Lord and
  hi s. Ps. 105:4
Job 18:7 steps of *h. s.* sh. be stra.
12 *his s.* shall be hunger-bitten
13 first-born of death de. *his s.*
21:23 one dieth in *his* full *s.*
37:6 saith to great rain of *his s.*
39:11 trust *his. h. s.* is great?
21 rejoice. in *h. s.* 40:16 *h. s.* is
Ps. 33:17 nor deli. by *h.* great *s.*
52:7 this man made not G. *h. s.*
59:9 because of *h. s.* will I wait
65:6 by *h. s.* setteth fast mount.
68:34 ascribe *s.* to G. *his s.* is in
78:4 showing to generation *h. s.*
61 delive. *his s.* into captivity
Is. 44:12 he is hungry, *h. s.* fail.
62:8 the L. ha. sw. by arm of *h. s.*
63:1 travel. in greatness of *h. s.*
Dan. 11:2 by *h. s.* sh. stir up all
Hos. 7:9 strangers devoured *h. s.*
12:3 by *h. s.* he had power wi. G.
Rev. 1:16 count. as son in *his s.*

In STRENGTH.

Gen. 49:24 his bow abode *in s.*
1 *K.* 19:8 went *in the s.* of meat
Job 9:4 and mighty *in s.* 36:5
Ps. 71:16 I will go *in the s.* of L.
103:20 bless L. ye that excel *in s.*
147:10 delight not *in s.* of horse
Is. 30:2 strengthen *in s.* of Phar.
Mic. 5:4 he shall feed *in s.* of L.
Acts 9:22 S. increased more *in s.*

My STRENGTH.

Gen. 49:3 R. beginning of *my s.*
Ex. 15:2 the Lord is *my s.* 2 *Sam.*
22:33; *Ps.* 18:2; 28:7; 118:14;
  Is. 12:2
Jos. 14:11 as *my s.* was tnen, so
  is *my s.* now
Jud. 16:17 if I be shav. *my s.* will

Job 6:11 what is *my s.* that I sh.?
12 is *my s.* of stones?
Ps. 18:1 I love thee, O L. *my s.*
19:14 O L. *my s.* 22:15 *my s.* dr.
31:4 the net, for thou art *my s.*
10 *my s.* fails bec. 38:10; 71:9
43:2 thou art the God of *my s.*
59:17 to th. O *my s.* will I sing
62:7 art *my s.* 102:23 *my s.*
144:1 blessed be Lord, *my s.*
Is. 27:5 take hold of *my s.*
49:4 I have spent *my s.* for nau.
5 glorious, *my* G. sh. be *my s.*
Jer. 16:19 O L. *my s.* and fortress
Lam. 1:14 he made *my s.* to fall
3:18 *my s.* and hope perished
Hab. 3:19 the Lord God is *my s.*
Zec. 12:5 be *my s.* in L. of hosts
2 *Cor.* 12:9 *my s.* is made perfect

Their STRENGTH.

Jos. 11:13 cit. that stood in *t. s.*
Ps. 37:39 he is *their s.* in trouble
73:4 no ba. in death, *t. s.* is firm
78:51 he smote *their s.* 105:36
89:17 thou art the glory of *t. s.*
90:10 yet is *t. s.* labor and sor.
Prov. 20:29 glory of men is *t. s.*
Is. 30:7 I cried, *t. s.* is to sit still
40:31 that wait on L. renew *t. s.*
41:1 let the people renew *their s.*
63:6 I will bring down *their s.*
Ezek. 24:25 I take from them *t. s,*
Joel 2:22 fig-t. and vine yield *t. s.*

Thy STRENGTH.

Ex. 15:13 hast guid. them in *t. s.*
Deut. 33:25 as days, so sh. *t. s.* be
Jud. 16:6 tell wher. *t. s.* lieth, 15
2 *Chr.* 6:41 ark of *t. s. Ps.* 132:8
Ps. 21:1 king shall joy in *thy s.*
Ps. 21:13 be ex. O L. in . own *s.*
54:1 name, judge me by *thy s.*
68:28 G. hath commanded *thy s.*
71:18 until I have showed *thy s.*
74:13 didst divide sea by *thy s.*
77:14 hast declared *t. s.* am. pe.
80:2 stir up *thy s.* and save us
86:16 give *thy s.* to thy servant
110:2 L. shall send rod of *t. s.*
Prov. 24:10 faint, *thy s.* is small
31:3 give not *t. s.* unto women
Is. 17:10 not mind. of rock of *t. s.*
52:1 awake, put on *t. s.* O Zion
63:15 wh. is *thy* zeal and *thy s.*
Amos 3:11 he sh. bring down *t. s.*
Mark 12:30 love the Lord with all
  thy s. 33; *Luke* 10:27

Your STRENGTH.

Lev. 26:20 *y. s.* be spent in vain
Neh. 8:10 joy of the Lord is *y. s.*
Is. 23:14 ships, *your s.* is waste
30:15 in confidence shall be *y. s.*
Ezek. 24:21 my sanct. ex. of *y. s.*

STRENGTHEN.

Deut. 3:28 charge Joshua, *s.* him
Jud. 16:28 *s.* me, I pray thee
1 *K.* 20:22 *s.* thys. mark and see
Ezr. 6:22 *s.* their hands in work
Neh. 6:9 O God, *s.* my hands
Job 16:5 I wo. *s.* you with mouth
Ps. 20:2 Lord *s.* thee out of Zion
27:14 L. shall *s.* thy heart, 31:24
41:3 Lord will *s.* him on the bed
68:28 *s.* whi. thou hast wrought
89:21 mine arm also shall *s.* him
119:28 *s.* me accord. to thy word
30:2 to *s.* themselves in strength
33:23 they could not *s.* th. mast
35:3 *s.* we. hands; 41:10 I will *s.*
54:2 lengtb. cords, *s.* thy stakes
Jer. 23:14 *s.* hands of evil doers
Ezek. 7:13 nor sh. any *s.* himself
16:49 neither did she *s.* hand of
30:24 I will *s.* arms of king, 25
34:16 I will *s.* that wh. was sick
Dan. 11:1 stood to confirm and *s.*

Amos 2:14 strong sh. not *s.* force
Zec. 10:6 I will *s.* house of Judah
12 I will *s.* them in the Lord
Luke 22:32 when convert. *s.* bre.
1 *Pet.* 5:10 God stablish, *s.* you
Rev. 3:2 be watchful and *s.* thi.

STRENGTHENED.

Gen. 48:2 Israel *s.* himself
Jud. 3:12 Lord *s.* Eglon against
7:11 afterwards shall hands be *s.*
1 *Sam.* 23:16 Jona. *s.* hand in G.
2 *Sam.* 2:7 let your hands be *s.*
1 *Chr.* 11:10 who *s.* themselves
2 *Chr.* 1:1 Solom. was *s.* in king.
11:17 they *s.* kingdom of Judah
12:1 when Reho. had *s.* himself
24:13 set house of God and *s.* it
25:11 Amaziah *s.* himself
28:20 distressed Ahaz, but *s.* not
32:5 Hezek. *s.* himself, and built
Ezr. 1:6 that were about them *s.*
7:28 I was *s.* as hand of God was
Neh. 2:18 they *s.* their hands for
Job 4:3 thou hast *s.* weak hands
4 thou hast *s.* the feeble knees
Ps. 52:7 himself in wickedness
147:13 hath *s.* bars of thy gates
Prov. 8:28 when he *s.* fountains
Ezek. 13:22 ye *s.* hands of wicked
34:4 the diseased have ye not *s.*
Dan. 10:18 touched and *s.* me, 19
11:6 he that begat her and *s.* her
12 cast down many, not be *s.*
Hos. 7:15 ha. bound and *s.* arms
Acts 9:19 received meat, S. was *s.*
Eph. 3:16 to be *s.* with might
Col. 1:11 *s.* with all might accor.
2 *Tim.* 4:17 Lord stood and *s.* me

STRENGTHENEDST, ETH.

Job 15:25 he *s.* himself again. Al.
Ps. 104:15 which *s.* man's heart
138:3 and *s.* me with strength
Prov. 31:17 gird. loins, *s.* arms
Ec. 7:19 wisdom *s.* the wise
Is. 44:14 cypress and oak he *s.*
Amos 5:9 *s.* spoiled ag. strong
Phil. 4:13 all thro' C. who *s.* me

STRENGTHENING.

Luke 22:43 appe. an angel *s.* him
Acts 18:23 Paul *s.* all the discipl.

STRETCH

Ex. 7:19 *s.* out hand on waters
8:5 *s.* forth hand over streams
25:20 cherub. sh. *s.* their wings
Jos. 8:18 *s.* out the spear to Ai
2 *K.* 21:13 I will *s.* over Jerusal.
Job 11:13 if thou *s.* out tow. him
39:26 doth hawk *s.* her wings?
Ps. 68:31 soon *s.* her hands to G.
Is. 28:20 shorter th. a man can *s.*
34:11 *s.* upon it line of confusion
54:2 *s.* curtains of thy habitation
Jer. 10:20 none to *s.* forth tent
Ezek. 30:25 king of Bab. *s.* sword
Amos 6:4 *s.* themsel. on couches
Mat. 12:13 Je. said, *s.* thy hand
John 21:18 shalt *s.* forth hands
2 *Cor.* 10:14 *s.* not beyond meas.

STRETCHED

Gen. 22:10 A. *s.* hand to slay son
48:14 Israel *s.* out right hand
Ex. 8:6 Aa. *s.* out his hand, 17
9:23 Mo. *s.* forth his rod, 10:13
Jos. 8:18 Joshua *s.* out spear, 26
19 ran as he *s.* out his hand
1 *K.* 6:27 cherub. *s.* forth wings
17:21 and he *s.* himself on the
  child, 2 *K.* 4:34, 35
1 *Chr.* 21:16 angel with a swo. *s.*
Job 38:5 who hath *s.* line up. it?
Ps. 44:20 or *s.* to a strange god
88:9 I have *s.* my hands unto th.
136:6 to him that *s.* out earth
Prov. 1:24 bec. I *s.* out my hand
Is. 3:16 walk with *s.* forth necks

5:25 he *s.* forth hand ag. them,
  s. out still, 9:12, 17. 21 ; 10:4
14:26 this is hand that is *s.* out
  27 hand *s.* who sh. turn it back?
16:8 her branches are *s.* out
23:11 *s.* out his hand over sea
42:5 *s.* out heavens, 45:12 ; 51:13
Jer. 6:4 shadows of even. *s.* out
  10:12 *s.* out heavens by discreti.
  51:15 he *s.* heaven by understa.
Lam. 2:8 Lord hath *s.* out a line
Ezek. 1:11 wings were *s.* upward
  10:7 cherub *s.* forth his hand
  16:27 I have *s.* my hand over th.
Hos. 7:5 *s.* hand with scorners
Amos 6:7 that *s.* sh. be removed
Zec. 1:16 line be *s.* forth on Jer.
Mat. 12:13 *s.* hand, *Mark* 3:5
Luke 22:53 *s.* no hands aga. me
Acts 12:1 Her. *s.* hand to vex chu.
Rom. 10:21 all day I *s.* my hands

See ARM.

STRETCHEDST.

Ex. 15:12 thou *s.* thy right hand

STRETCHEST, ETH.

Job 15:25 *s.* his hand against God
  26:7 *s.* north over empty place
Ps. 104:2 who *s.* out the heavens
Prov. 31:20 *s.* her hand to poor
Is. 40:22 that *s.* out the heavens
  44:13 the carpen. *s.* out his rule
  24 *s.* forth heavens, *Zec.* 12:1

STRETCHING.

Is. 8:8 *s.* of his wings fill land
Acts 4:30 by *s.* forth hand to heal

STREWED.

Ex. 32:20 he ground calf, *s.* it
2 *Chr.* 34:4 he *s.* upon the graves
Mat. 21:8 cut do. branches and *s.*
  25:24 gath. where hast not *s.* 25

STRICKEN.

Gen. 18:11 well *s.* in age, 24:1
Jos. 13:1 J. was *s.* in yrs. 23:1, 2
Jud. 5:26 Jael had *s.* his temples
1 *K.* 1:1 David was *s.* in years
Prov. 6:1 *s.* thy hand with stran.
  23:35 they have *s.* me, I was
Is. 1:5 sho. ye be *s.* any more?
  16:7 they are *s.* 53:4 est. him *s.*
  53:8 for transgression was he *s.*
Jer. 5:3 thou hast *s.* them, they
Lam. 4:9 *s.* for want of fruits
Luke 1:7 Elizab. *s.* in years, 18

STRIFE.

Gen. 13:7 a *s.* bet. the herdmen
  8 Abra. said, Let there be no *s.*
Num. 27:14 rebell. in *s.* of cong.
Deut. 1:12 can I bear your *s.* ?
Jud. 12:2 I and peo. were at *s.*
2 *Sam.* 19:9 people were at *s.*
Ps. 31:20 keep fr. *s.* of tongues
  55:9 I have seen *s.* in the city
  80:6 makest us a *s.* to neighbors
  106:32 ang. him at waters of *s.*
Prov. 15:18 a wrathful man stir.
  s. slow to anger app. *s.* 29:22
  16:28 a froward man soweth *s.*
  17:1 house full of sacrifi. with *s.*
  14 begin. of *s.* one letteth out
  19 loveth transg. that loveth *s.*
  20:3 honor for man to cease fr. *s.*
  22:10 cast out scorner, *s.* cease
  26:17 he that meddleth with *s.*
  20 no talebearer, the *s.* ceaseth
  21 so is contentious to kind. *s.*
  28:25 proud heart stirreth up *s.*
  30:33 forcing of wrath bring. *s.*
Is. 58:4 ye fast for *s.* and debate
Jer. 15:10 borne me a man of *s.*
Ezek. 47:19 to waters of *s.* 48:28
Hab. 1:3 there are th. raise up *s.*
Luke 22:24 a *s.* among disciples
Rom. 13:13 honestly, not in *s.*
1 *Cor.* 3:3 there is among you *s.*
Gal. 5:20 works of the flesh are *s.*

Phil. 1:15 some preach Chr. of *s.*
  2:3 let nothing be done thro' *s.*
1 *Tim.* 6:4 wher. cometh envy *s.*
Heb. 6:16 an oath is end of all *s.*
Jam. 3:14 bitter envying and *s.*
  16 where *s.* is, there is confus.

STRIFES.

Prov. 10:12 hatred stirreth up *s.*
2 *Cor.* 12:20 envyings, wraths, *s.*
1 *Tim.* 6:4 quest. and *s.* of words
2 *Tim.* 2:23 knowing that they
  gender *s.*

STRIKE.

Deut. 21:4 *s.* off heifer's neck
2 *K.* 5:11 come and *s.* his hands
Job 17:3 who will *s.* ha. wi. me ?
  20:24 bow of steel *s.* him thro'
Ps. 110:5 *s.* thro' kings in wrath
Prov. 7:23 till a dart *s.* thro' liver
  17:26 it is not good to *s.* princes
  22:26 be not th. one th. *s.* hands
Hab. 3:14 *s.* thro' with his staves
Mark 14:65 did *s.* Je. with hands

STRIKER.

1 *Tim.* 3:3 bishop no *s.* *Tit.* 1:7

STRIKETH.

Job 34:26 he *s.* th. as wicked men
Prov. 17:18 void of understand. *s.*
Rev. 9:5 scorp. when he *s.* a man

STRING, S.

Ps. 11:2 make ready arrow on *s.*
  21:12 make thine arrows on *s.*
  33:2 instrum. of 10 *s.* 92:3 ; 144:9
Mark 7:35 *s.* of tongue loosed

STRINGED.

Ps. 150:4 praise him wi. *s.* instr.
Is. 38:20 sing songs to *s.* instru.
Hab. 3:19 singer on *s.* instrume.

STRIPE.

Ex. 21:25 for wound, *s.* for *s*

STRIPES.

Deut. 25:3 forty *s.* he may give
2 *Sam.* 7:14 with *s.* of children
Ps. 89:32 visit iniquity with *s.*
Prov. 17:10 hundred *s.* into a fool
  19:29 *s.* are prepared for fools
  20:30 so do *s.* the inward parts
Is. 53:5 with his *s.* we are healed,
  1 *Pet.* 2:24
Luke 12:47 beaten with many *s.*
  48 knew not, beaten wi. few *s.*
Acts 16:23 laid many *s.* upon th.
  33 same hour, washed their *s.*
2 *Cor.* 6:5 in *s.* in imprisonments
  11:23 in *s.* above measure
  24 of Jews received I forty *s.*

STRIP.

Num. 20:26 *s.* Aaron of garments
1 *Sam.* 31:8 Philistines came to
  s. slain, 1 *Chr.* 10:8
Is. 32:11 *s.* ye, make ye bare
Ezek. 16:39 they sh. *s.* thee, 23:26
Hos. 2:3 I *s.* her naked, set her

STRIPPED.

Gen. 37:23 they *s.* Joseph of coat
Ex. 33:6 Israel *s.* themselves
Num. 20:28 Moses *s.* Aa. of gar.
1 *Sam.* 18:4 Jonathan *s.* himself
  19:24 Saul *s.* off his clothes also
  31:9 Philist. *s.* Saul of his armor
2 *Chr.* 20:25 jewels wh. th. *s.* off
Job 19:9 *s.* me of glory and crown
  22:6 for thou hast *s.* of clothing
Mic. 1:8 therefore I will go *s.*
Mat. 27:28 they *s.* Jesus, put on
Luke 10:30 which *s.* him of raim.

STRIPLING.

1 *Sam.* 17:56 inq. whose son *s.* is

STRIVE.

Gen. 6:3 Spi. not always *s.* with
  26:20 herdmen of Gerar did *s.*
Ex. 21:18 if men *s.* together
  22 *s.* and hurt wo. *Deut.* 25:11
Deut. 33:3 with wh. thou didst *s.*

Jud. 11:25 did he ever *s.* aga. Is.
Job 33:13 why *s.* against him ?
Ps. 35:1 plead with them that *s.*
Prov. 3:30 *s.* not without cause
  25:8 go not forth hastily to *s.*
Is. 41:11 they that *s.* shall perish
  45:9 let potsherd *s.* wi. potsherd
Hos. 4:4 let no man *s.* thy peo-
  ple are as they that *s.*
Mat. 12:19 he shall not *s.*
Luke 13:24 *s.* to enter strait gate
Rom. 15:30 *s.* wi. me in prayers
2 *Tim.* 2:5 if a man *s.* for maste.
2 *Tim.* 2:14 th. th. *s.* not ab. wor.
  24 servant of Lord must not *s.*

STRIVED, ETH.

Is. 45:9 woe to him that *s.* wi. M.
Rom. 15:20 I *s.* to preach gospel
1 *Cor.* 9:25 *s.* for mastery is tem.

STRIVEN.

Jer. 50:24 bec. th. hast *s.* ag. L.

STRIVING.

Phil. 1:27 with mind *s.* for gospel
Col. 1:29 *s.* according to working
Heb. 12:4 not resisted, *s.* aga. sin

STRIVINGS.

2 *Sam.* 22:44 hast deliv. me from
  s. of the people, *Ps.* 18:43
Tit. 3:9 avoid contentions and *s.*

STROKE, S.

Deut. 17:8 hard betwe. *s.* and *s.*
  19:5 hand fetcheth a *s.* wi. axe
  21:5 by word every *s.* be tried
Est. 9:5 J. smote enem. with *s.*
Job 23:2 my *s.* is heavier th. my
  36:18 lest he take th. with his *s.*
Ps. 39:10 remove thy *s.* from me
Prov. 18:6 fool's mouth call. for *s.*
Is. 14:6 smote with a contin. *s.*
  30:26 the Lord healeth the *s.* of
Ezek. 24:16 desi. of eyes with a *s.*

STRONG.

Gen. 49:14 Issachar is a *s.* ass
  24 arms of hands were made *s.*
Ex. 6:1 with a *s.* hand shall, 13:9
Num. 20:20 Ed. came wi. *s.* hand
  21:24 border of Ammon was *s.*
  28:7 *s.* wine poured out to Lord
Deut. 2:36 not one city too *s.* for
Jos. 14:11 I am as *s.* this day
  17:13 Is. were wax. *s.* *Jud.* 1:28
  23:9 great nations and *s.*
Jud. 14:14 out of *s.* came sweet.
  18:26 Mic. saw they were too *s.*
1 *Sam.* 14:52 when S. saw *s.* man
2 *Sam.* 3:1 Abner made hims. *s.*
  10:11 if Syri. be too *s.* for me, if
  Am. be too *s.* 1 *Chr.* 19:12
1 *K.* 8:42 wh. hear of thy *s.* hand
2 *Chr.* 11:12 he made the cities *s.*
  17 made Rehoboam *s.* 3 years
  16:9 eyes run to show himself *s.*
  26:16 Uzziah was *s.* was lifted
Neh. 9:25 they took *s.* cities
Job 8:2 words be like a *s.* wind
  9:19 if I speak of stren. he is *s.*
  37:18 spread out sky that is *s.*
Ps. 19:5 rejoiceth as a *s.* man
  24:8 Lord *s.* and mighty
  30:7 made my mount. stand *s.*
  31:2 be thou my *s.* rock
  35:10 from him that is too *s.* for
  38:19 enemies are lively and *s.*
  60:9 who br. into *s.* city ? 108:10
  71:3 my *s.* habita. 7 my *s.* refuge
  80:15 branch thou madest *s.* 17
  89:8 who is a *s.* Lord like thee ?
  13 *s.* is thy hand, high is thy
  136:12 a *s.* hand, *Jer.* 32:21
Prov. 7:26 *s.* men have been
  11:16 wom. retai. honor, *s.* men
  18:19 harder to be won th. *s.* ci.
  24:5 wise *s.* 30:25 ants not *s.*
Ec. 9:11 battle is not to the *s.*
  12:3 *s.* men shall bow thems.
Cant. 8:6 for love is *s.* as death

Is. 8:7 L. bringeth waters, *s.* and
  11 L. spake to me with *s.* hand
17:9 *s.* cities sh. be as forsaken
25:3 theref. shall *s.* glorify thee
26:1 be sung, we have a *s.* city
28:2 hath a mighty and *s.* one
40:10 will come with a *s.* hand
  26 for that he is *s.* in power
53:12 shall divide spoil with *s.*
60:22 one shall bec. a *s.* nation
Jer. 21:5 will fight wi. a *s.* arm
48:14 mighty, *s.* men for war
49:19 come ag. habita. of the *s.*
50:34 th. Redeemer is *s.* the L.
  44 sh. come unto habita. of *s.*
Ezek. 3:14 hand of the L. was *s.*
26:17 city which wast *s.* in sea
30:21 make it *s.* to hold sword
  22 I will break *s.* arms of Pha.
32:21 *s.* shall speak to him
34:16 I will destroy fat and *s.*
Dan. 11:5 king and was *s.* 20
  22 thou, O king, art become *s.*
7:7 fourth beast terrible, *s.* exc.
11:23 he shall bec. *s.* wi. small
Joel 1:6 nation is come up, *s.* 2:2
2:11 he is *s.* that execut. word
3:10 let the weak say, I am *s.*
Amos 2:14 *s.* sh. not strengthen
5:9 strengtheneth spoiled ag. *s.*
Mic. 4:3 shall rebuke *s.* nations
  7 I will make her a *s.* nation
Nah. 2:1 make thy loins *s.*
Zec. 8:22 nations sh. seek L.
Mat. 12:29 how ent. *s.* man s ho.
  exc. bind *s.* man ? *Mark* 3:27
Luke 1:80 child waxed *s.* 2:40
11:21 a *s.* man armed keepeth
Acts 3:16 thro' faith made man *s.*
Rom. 4:20 was *s.* in faith
15:1 we th. are *s.* ought to bear
1 *Cor.* 4:10 are weak, ye are *s.*
2 *Cor.* 12:10 weak, then am I *s.*
13:9 we are weak, and ye are *s.*
Heb. 5:12 milk, not *s.* meat
11:34 out of weak. were made *s.*
1 *John* 2:14 ye are *s.* word of God
Rev. 5:2 I saw a *s.* angel proclai.
18:2 he cried with a *s.* voice
  8 *s.* is the Lord God who judg.

Be STRONG.

Num. 13:18 see whether, they *be s.*
  28 people *be s.* that dwell in
Deut. 11:18 keep co. that ye *be s.*
Jos. 17:18 drive Canaa. tho' *be s.*
1 *Sam.* 4:9 *be s.* quit yourselves
2 *Sam.* 16:21 han. of all shall *be s.*
1 *K.* 2:2 *be* thou *s.* show thyself a
1 *Chr.* 28:10 L. chosen thee, *be s.*
2 *Chr.* 15:7 *be s.* work sh. be re.
25:8 do it, *be s.* for the battle
Ezr. 9:12 that ye may *be s.*
Ps. 144:14 that oxen *be s.* to lab.
Is. 35:4 th. of fearful heart, *be s.*
Ezek. 22:14 can thy hands *be s.*
Dan. 2:42 kingd. sh. *be* partly *s.*
10:19 peace to th. *be s.* yea, *be s.*
11:5 king of the south shall *be s.*
  and he sh. *be s.* above him
  32 pe. that know G. shall *be s.*
Hag. 2:4 *be s.* O Zerubbabel, *be*
  O Joshua, *be s.* ye people
Zec. 8:19 let hands *be s.* ye that
  13 but let your hands *be s.*
1 *Cor.* 16:13 quit you li. m. *be s.*
Eph. 6:10 brethr. be *s.* in the L.
2 *Tim.* 2:1 my son, *be s.* in grace

See COURAGE, DRINK.

STRONG ones.

Ps. 10:10 may fall by his *s. ones*
Jer. 8:16 sound of neigh. of *s. on.*

STRONGER.

Gen. 25:23 one people shall be *s.*
30:42 feebler were L.'s *s.* Jac.'s
Num. 13:31 not able, they are *s.*
Jud. 14:18 what is *s.* th. a lion ?

---

2 *Sam.* 3:1 David waxed *s.* and *s.*
13:14 Amnon being *s.* than she
1 *K.* 20:23 *s.* we shall be *s.* 25
Job 17:9 cl. hands sh. be *s.* and *s.*
Ps. 105:24 he made them *s.* than
  142:6 deli. me, they are *s.* th. I
Jer. 20:7 thou art *s.* than I, and
Luke 11:22 wh. a *s.* th. he come
1 *Cor.* 1:25 weak. of G. is *s.* than
10:22 do we pro. L. ? are we *s.* ?

STRONGEST.

Prov. 30:30 wh. is *s.* am. beasts

STRONG-HOLD, S.

Num. 13:19 whe. in tents or *s.-h.*
Jud. 6:2 Is. ma. caves and *s.-h.*
1 *Sam.* 23:14 David abode in *s.-h.*
29 dwelt in *s.-h.* at En-gedi
2 *Sam.* 5:7 David took *s.-h.* of Z.
24:7 came to the *s.-h.* of Tyre
2 *K.* 8:12 their *s.-h.* set on fire
2 *Chr.* 11:11 Rehob. fortified *s.-h.*
Ps. 89:40 broug. his *s.-h.* to ruin
23:11 destroy *s.-h.* thereof
31:9 shall pass over to his *s.-h.*
Jer. 48:18 spoiler sh. destroy *s.-h.*
  41 the *s.-holds* are surprised
Lam. 2:2 he hath thr. down *s.-h.*
  5 Lord destroyed his *s.-holds*
Dan. 11:24 his devices aga. *s.-h.*
  39 thus sh. he go in most *s.-h.*
Mic. 4:8 *s.-h.* of the daugh. of Z.
Nah. 1:7 L. a *s.-h.* in day of trou.
3:12 thy *s.-h.* shall be like fig-t.
  14 draw waters, forti. thy *s.-h.*
Hab. 1:10 shall deride every *s.-h.*
Zec. 9:3 Tyrus did build a *s.-h.*
  12 turn to the *s.-h.* ye prisone.
2 *Cor.* 10:14 mig. to pull. do. *s.-h.*

STRONGLY.

Ezr. 6:3 let foundation be *s.* laid

STROVE.

Gen. 26:20 they *s.* with him, 21
  22 another well, and *s.* not
Ex. 2:13 two men of Hebrews *s.*
Lev. 24:10 man of Is. *s.* in camp
Num. 20:13 chil. of Is. *s.* with L.
26:9 Dathan, who *s.* against M.
2 *Sam.* 14:6 they two *s.* together
Dan. 7:2 four winds *s.* upon sea
John 6:52 the Jews *s.* am. them.
Acts 7:26 M. show. him. as th. *s.*
23:9 *s.* saying, We find no evil

STRUCK.

1 *Sam.* 2:14 he *s.* it into the pan
2 *Sam.* 12:15 the Lord *s.* the ch.
20:10 Jo. *s.* him not again, and
2 *Chr.* 13:20 the Lord *s.* Jerobo.
Mat. 26:51 one of them *s.* a serv.
Luke 22:64 they *s.* Jesus, *John*
  18:22

STRUGGLED.

Gen. 25:22 children *s.* together

STUBBLE.

Ex. 5:12 gath. *s.* instead of straw
15:7 wrath consumed them as *s.*
Job 13:25 wilt th. pursue dry *s.* ?
21:18 they are as *s.* before wind
41:28 stones are turned into *s.*
  29 darts are counted as *s.* he
Ps. 83:13 make them as *s.* before
Is. 5:24 as fire devoureth the *s.*
33:11 conceive chaff br. forth *s.*
40:24 whirlwind take away as *s.*
41:2 he gave them as driven *s.*
47:14 they shall be as *s.* the fire
Jer. 13:24 I will scatter th. as *s.*
Joel 2:5 flame, that devou. the *s.*
Ob. 18 house of E. sh. be for *s.*
Nah. 1:10 they sh. be devou. as *s.*
Mal. 4:1 wicked, and proud be *s.*
1 *Cor.* 3:12 on the found. hay, *s.*

STUBBORN.

Deut. 21:18 if a man ha. a *s.* son
  20 say to eld. This our son is *s.*
Jud. 2:19 ceased not from *s.* way

Ps. 78:8 not as fath. a *s.* gener.
Prov. 7:11 she is loud and *s.* her

STUBBORNNESS.

Deut. 9:27 look not to *s.* of peop.
1 *Sam.* 15:23 and *s.* is as iniquity

STUCK.

1 *Sam.* 26:7 spear *s.* in ground
Ps. 119:31 I ha. *s.* unto testimo.
Acts 27:41 part of the ship *s.* fast

STUDS.

Cant. 1:11 borders of gold wi. *s.*

STUDY.

Ec. 12:12 much *s.* is a weariness
1 *Thes.* 4:11 *s.* to be quiet
2 *Tim.* 2:15 *s.* to show thys. app.

STUDIETH.

Prov. 15:28 heart of righteous *s.*
24:2 their heart *s.* destruction

STUFF.

Gen. 31:37 th. hast search. my *s.*
45:20 regard not your *s.*
Ex. 22:7 if man deliv. *s.* to keep
36:7 the *s.* they had was suffici.
Jos. 7:11 they put it amo. their *s.*
1 *Sam.* 10:22 he hath hid amo. *s.*
25:13 two hund. abode by the *s.*
30:24 his part be that tarr. by *s.*
Ezek. 12:3 prepare *s.* for removal.
  4 bring forth thy *s.* by day, 7
Luke 17:31 house-top, *s.* in hou.

STUMBLE.

Prov. 3:23 walk, foot not *s.* 4:12
4:19 know not at what they *s.*
Is. 5:27 none sh. be weary nor *s.*
8:15 many among them shall *s.*
28:7 err in vision, *s.* in judgme.
59:10 we *s.* at noonday as night
63:13 led th. that th. sho. not *s.*
Jer. 13:16 before your feet *s.* on
18:15 caused them to *s.* in ways
20:11 therefore persecuto. sh. *s.*
31:9 in a way they shall not *s.*
46:6 they shall *s.* and fall
50:32 proud shall *s.* and fall
Dan. 11:19 he shall *s.* and fall
Nah. 2:5 shall *s.* in their walk
3:3 they shall *s.* on corpses
Mal. 2:8 have caused many to *s.*
1 *Pet.* 2:8 offence to them that *s.*

STUMBLED.

1 *Sam.* 2:4 that *s.* girt with stre.
1 *Chr.* 13:9 hold ark, for oxen *s.*
Ps. 27:2 came to eat flesh, th. *s.*
Jer. 46:12 mighty *s.* ag. mighty
Rom. 9:32 th. *s.* at stumb.-stone
11:11 have *s.* that they sho. fall

STUMBLETH.

Prov. 24:17 heart glad wh. he *s.*
John 11:9 walk in day, *s.* not
  10 if man walk in night he *s.*
Rom. 14:21 whereby thy bro. *s.*

STUMBLING.

John 2:10 is none occasion of *s.*

STUMBLING-BLOCK.

Lev. 19:14 nor put *s.-b.* bef. blind
Is. 57:14 take *s.-b.* out of way
Ezek. 3:20 I lay *s.-b.* before him
7:19 bec. it is *s.-b.* of their iniq.
14:3 they put *s.-b.* of iniqu. 4, 7
Rom. 11:9 made a trap, a *s.-b.*
Rom. 14:13 put *s.-b.* in br. way
1 *Cor.* 1:23 C. cruci. to Jews *s.-b.*
8:9 lest liber. of yours bec. *s.-b.*
Rev. 2:14 Bal. to cast *s.-b.* bef. Is.

STUMBLING-BLOCKS.

Jer. 6:21 I will lay *s.-b.* bef. peo.
Zep. 1:3 I will consume *s.-b.*

STUMBLING, with stone.

Is. 8:14 be for a *s.* of *s.* to Israel
Rom. 9:32 stumbled at th. *s.-s.*
  33 behold, I lay in Sion a *s.-st.*
1 *Pet.* 2:8 *s.* of *s.* to th. that stum.

STUMP.
1 *Sam.* 5:4 only *s.* of Da. was left
Dan. 4:15 leave *s.* in earth, 23, 26

SUBDUE.
Gen. 1:28 replenish earth, *s.* it
1 *Chr.* 17:10 I will *s.* thi. enemi.
Ps. 47:3 he shall *s.* peo. under
Is. 45:1 to *s.* nations before him
Dan. 7:24 he shall *s.* three kings
Mic. 7:19 will *s.* our iniquities
Zec. 9:15 *s.* with sling-stones
Phil. 3:21 he is able to *s.* all thi.

SUBDUED, EST.
Num. 32:22 land be *s.* before L.
29 land shall be *s.* before you
Deut. 20:20 bulwarks, until be *s.*
Jos. 18:1 land was *s.* before the
1 *Sam.* 7:13 Phili. were *s.* 2 *Sam.*
8:1 ; 1 *Chr.* 18:1 ; 20:4
2 *Sam.* 8:11 gold of nations he *s.*
22:40 th. *s.* under me, *Ps.* 18:39
1 *Chr.* 22:18 land is *s.* before Lord
Neh. 9:24 thou *s.* inhabi. of land
Ps. 81:14 soon have *s.* enemies
1 *Cor.* 15:28 all be *s.* unto him
Heb. 11:33 thro' faith *s.* kingdo.

SUBDUETH.
Ps. 18:47 it is G. *s.* peo. 144:2
Dan. 2:40 iron breaks and *s.* all

SUBJECT.
Luke 2:51 Jesus was *s.* to them
10:17 L. even devils are *s.* to us
20 rejo. not spirits are *s.* to you
Rom. 8:7 it is not *s.* to law of G.
20 creature was *s.* to vanity
13:1 let eve. soul be *s.* to powers
5 wherefo. ye must needs be *s.*
1 *Cor.* 14:32 spirits of prophets
15:28 then sh. Son hims. be *s.*
Eph. 5:24 as church is *s.* to Chr.
Col. 2:20 are ye *s.* to ordinances
Tit. 3:1 put in mind to *s.* to pow.
Heb. 2:15 lifetime *s.* to bondage
Jam. 5:17 Elias was *s.* to passio.
1 *Pet.* 2:18 serv. be *s.* to masters
3:22 pow. being made *s.* to him
5:5 all of you be *s.* one to ano.

SUBJECTED.
Rom. 8:20 who *s.* same in hope

SUBJECTION.
Ps. 106:42 enemies bron. into *s.*
Jer. 34:11 brought th. into *s.* 16
1 *Cor.* 9:27 br. my body into *s.*
2 *Cor.* 9:13 glorify G. for your *s.*
Gal. 2:5 we gave place by *s.* not
1 *Tim.* 2:11 wom. learn with all *s.*
3:4 having his children in *s.*
Heb. 2:5 put in *s.* world to come
8 put all things in *s.* under feet
12:9 rather be in *s.* to Father
1 *Pet.* 3:1 be in *s.* to husbands, 5

SUBMIT.
Gen. 16:9 *s.* thyself under her ha.
2 *Sam.* 22:45 strang. sh. *s.* themselves to me, *Ps.* 18:44
Ps. 66:3 enemies shall *s.* to thee
68:30 till every one *s.* with silv.
1 *Cor.* 16:16 that ye *s.* yourselves
Eph. 5:22 *s.* to husb. *Col.* 3:18
Heb. 13:17 *s.* th. watch for souls
Jas. 4:7 *s.* yourselves theref. to G.
1 *Pet.* 2:13 *s.* to every ordinance
5:5 younger *s.* yourself. to elder

SUBMITTED, ING.
1 *Chr.* 29:24 sons of Da. *s.* to Sol.
Ps. 81:15 haters of L. *s.* to him.
Rom. 10:3 not *s.* to righteousness
Eph. 5:21 *s.* yours. one to anoth.

SUBORNED.
Acts 6:11 then they *s.* men who

SUBSCRIBE, ED.
Is. 44:5 another shall *s.* unto L.
Jer. 32:10 I *s.* evidence, sealed it
12 in pres. of witnesses that *s.*
44 men shall *s.* evidences

SUBSTANCE.
Gen. 7:4 I will destroy ev. liv. *s.*
23 every living *s.* was destroyed
12:5 Abraham took *s.* they gath.
13:6 their *s.* was great, so they
15:14 shall come with great *s.*
Gen. 34:23 sh. not th. *s.* be ours ?
36:6 E. took his cattle and his *s.*
Deut. 11:6 swallow. them and *s.*
33:11 bless, L. his *s.* accept work
Jos. 14:4 gave Lev. cities for *s.*
1 *Chr.* 27:31 th. were rulers of *s.*
28:1 stewards over all *s.* of king
2 *Chr.* 21:17 carried away all *s.*
31:3 appoint. king's portion of *s.*
32:29 God had given Hez. *s.*
35:7 bullocks, th. were king's *s.*
Ezr. 8:21 seek ri. way for our *s.*
10:8 come, *s.* should be forfeited
Job 1:3 Job's *s.* was 7,000 sheep
10 his *s.* increased in the land
5:5 robber swallow. up their *s.*
6:22 Give a reward of your *s.* ?
15:29 nor shall his *s.* continue
20:18 according to *s.* restitution
22:20 whereas our *s.* is not cut
30:22 liftest, and dissolv. my *s.*
Ps. 17:14 leave their *s.* to babes
105:21 made Joseph ruler over *s.*
139:15 my *s.* was not hid fr. thee
16 thine eyes did see my *s.*
Prov. 1:13 sh. find all precious *s.*
3:9 honor L. with *s.* first fruits
6:31 he shall give *s.* of house
8:21 cause th. love me inherit *s.*
10:3 he casteth away *s.* of wick.
12:27 *s.* of a diligent man preci.
28:8 he that by usury increas. *s.*
29:3 with harlots, spend. his *s.*
Cant. 8:7 if a man give *s.* for love
Is. 6:13 as an oak wh. *s.* is in th.
so holy seed be *s.* thereof
Jer. 15:13 *s.* give to spoil, 17:3
Hos. 12:8 I have found me out *s.*
Ob. 13 nor laid hands on their *s.*
Mic. 4:13 I will consecrate th. *s.*
Luke 8:3 minister. to him th. *s.*
15:13 prodigal wasted his *s.*
Heb. 10:34 ye have in heaven a *s.*
11:1 faith is *s.* of thi. hoped for

SUBTILE.
Gen. 3:1 serpent more *s.* than any
2 *Sam.* 13:3 Jonadab was a *s.* man
Prov. 7:10 harlot. and *s.* of heart

SUBTILELY.
1 *Sam.* 23:22 told me, he deal. *s.*
Ps. 105:25 to deal *s.* with serv.
Acts 7:19 dealt *s.* with our kindr.

SUBTILTY.
Gen. 27:35 thy bro. came with *s.*
2 *K.* 10:19 Jehu did it in *s.* that
Prov. 1:4 to give *s.* to the simple
Mat. 26:4 might take Jesus by *s.*
Acts 13:10 O full of *s.* and mischi.
2 *Cor.* 11:3 beguiled Eve thro' *s.*

SUBURBS.
Lev. 25:34 field of *s.* not be sold
Num. 35:3 *s.* sh. be for th. cattle
7, 48 cit. sh. ye give wi. th. *s.*
Jos. 14:4 save cities wi. *s.* 21:2
2 *K.* 23:11 took by chamber in *s.*
2 *Chr.* 11:14 Levites left their *s.*
Ezek. 27:28 *s.* sh. shake at sound
48:15 place for dwelli. and for *s.*
See CITIES.

SUBVERT, ED, ING.
Lam. 3:36 to *s.* a man L. approv.
Acts 15:24 troubled you, *s.* souls
2 *Tim.* 2:14 to the *s.* of hearers
Tit. 1:11 who *s.* whole houses
3:11 th. is such is *s.* and sinneth

SUCCEED, EST.
Deut. 12:29 when thou *s.* 19:1
25:6 first-born *s.* his broth. dead

SUCCEEDED.
Deut. 2:12 children of Es. *s.* 22
21 Ammonites *s.* them

SUCCESS.
Jos. 1:8 prosper and have good *s.*

SUCCOTH.
Gen. 33:17 Jacob journeyed to S.
therefore it is called S.
Ex. 12:37 jour. fr. Rameses to S.
13:20 journ. fr. S. *Num.* 33:5, 6
Jos. 13:27 Gad had in valley S.
Jud. 8:5 Gid. said to men of S.
8 Penuel answ. as men of S.
16 he taught men of S.
1 *K.* 7:46 clay-ground between S.
and Zarthan, 2 *Cor.* 4:17
Ps. 60:6 mete valley of S. 108:7

SUCCOTH-BENOTH.
2 *K.* 17:30 men of Bab. made S.

SUCCOR, ED.
2 *Sam.* 8:5 Syri. came to S. Had.
18:3 better thou *s.* us out of city
21:17 Abishai *s.* him, smote Ph.
2 *Cor.* 6:2 day of salva. I *s.* thee
Heb. 2:18 able to *s.* them tempted

SUCCORER.
Rom. 16:2 she hath been *s.*

SUCH.
Ex. 34:10 *s.* as ha. not been done
Rev. 20:6 on *s.* death ha. no pow.

SUCH a one.
Gen. 41:38 can we find *s. a one*
Ruth 4:1 ho, *s. a one*, turn aside

SUCH things.
Neh. 6:8 no *s. t.* done as thou say.

SUCK, Substantive.
Gen. 21:7 Sarah given children *s.*
1 *Sam.* 1:23 Han. gave her son *s.*
1 *K.* 3:21 I rose to give child *s.*
Lam. 4:3 sea-monsters give *s.*
Mat. 24:19 them that gave *s.*
Mark 13:17 ; *Luke* 21:23
Luke 23:29 paps that never ga. *s.*

SUCK, Verb.
Deut. 32:13 made him to *s.* honey
33:19 they shall *s.* of abund. of
Job 3:12 or breast I should *s.* ?
20:16 he shall *s.* poison of asps
39:30 young ones *s.* up blood
Is. 60:16 thou shalt *s.* milk of G.
and shalt *s.* breast of kings
66:11 that ye may *s.* and be satis.
12 then shall ye *s.* sh. be borne
Ezek. 23:34 thou sh. even *s.* it out
Joel 2:16 gath. th. that *s.* breasts

SUCKED.
Cant. 8:1 *s.* breasts of mother
Luke 11:27 blessed are paps th. *s.*

SUCKING.
Num. 11:12 as fa. beareth *s.* child
1 *Sam.* 7:9 Samuel took a *s.* lamb
Is. 11:8 *s.* ch. play on hole of asp
49:15 can a wom. forget *s.* child
Lam. 4:4 tongue of *s.* child cleav.

SUCKLING, S.
Deut. 32:25 wi. man of gr. hairs
1 *Sam.* 15:3 slay man, inf. and *s.*
22:19 Doeg smo. children and *s.*
Ps. 8:2 out of mouth of babes
and *s.* *Mat.* 21:16
Jer. 44:7 cut off fr. you ch. and *s.*
Lam. 2:11 *s.* swoon in streets

SUDDEN.
Job 22:10 *s.* fear troubleth thee
Prov. 3:25 not afraid of *s.* fear
1 *Thes.* 5:3 then *s.* destruct. com.

SUDDENLY.
Num. 6:9 if any man die *s.*
12:4 the Lord spake *s.* unto Mo.
Jos. 10:9 Joshua came *s.* 11:7
2 *Sam.* 15:14 lest he overt. us *s.*
Job 5:3 *s.* I cursed his habitat.
9:23 if scourge by day slay *s.*

Ps. 6:10 let them be ashamed *s.*
64:4 *s.* do they shoot at him
Prov. 6:15 he shall be broken *s.*
24:22 their calamity sh. rise *s.*
29:1 shall *s.* be destroyed,
Ec. 9:12 it falleth *s.* upon them
Is. 29:5 it shall be at an inst. *s.*
47:11 desolation shall come *s.*
48:3 I did them *s.* they came
Jer. 6:26 spoiler shall *s.* come
15:8 have caused them to fall *s.*
49:19 will *s.* ma. him run, 50:44
51:8 Babylon is *s.* destroyed
Hab. 2:7 sh. they not rise up *s.*
Mal. 3:1 the Lord shall *s.* come
Mark 13:36 lest com. *s.* he find
Luke 9:39 and he *s.* crieth out
Acts 28:6 fallen down dead *s.*
1 *Tim.* 5:22 lay hands *s.* on no m.

SUE.
Mat. 5:40 if any man *s.* thee

SUFFER.
Ex. 22:18 sh. not *s.* witch to live
Lev. 19:17 not *s.* sin upon him
22:16 or *s.* th. to bear iniquity
Num. 21:23 Sih. would not *s.* Is.
Jos. 10:19 *s.* not to enter cities
Jud. 1:34 not *s.* th. to come down
Jer. hath. would not *s.* him.
1 *K.* 15:17 that might not *s.* any
Est. 3:8 not king's profit to *s.*
Job 9:18 not *s.* me to take breath
21:3 *s.* me that I may speak
36:2 *s.* me a little, I will show
Ps. 9:13 consider trouble I *s.* of
55:22 nev. *s.* right. to be moved
88:15 while I *s.* terrors, I am
89:33 nor will I *s.* faithful, fail
101:5 proud heart, will not I *s.*
121:3 not *s.* foot to be moved
Prov. 10:3 L. not *s.* righte. fam.
19:15 idle soul shall *s.* hunger
19 man of wrath sh. *s.* punish.
Ec. 5:6 *s.* not mouth to cause
12 abund. of rich not *s.* to sleep
Ezek. 44:20 nor *s.* locks to grow
Mat. 3:15 Jesus said, *s.* it to be
8:21 *s.* me to bury, *Luke* 9:59
16:21 he must *s.* many things
17:12; *Mark* 8:31; 9:12; *Lu.*
9:22; 17:25
17:17 how long shall I *s.* you?
Mark 9:19; *Luke* 9:41
19:14 *s.* little children, *Mark*
10:14; *Luke* 18:16
23:13 neither *s.* ye them th. are
Mark 7:12 *s.* him no more to do
11:16 Je. would not *s.* any man
Luke 22:51 *s.* ye thus far,
24:46 it behooved Christ to *s.*
Acts 3:18; 26:23
Acts 3:18 G. showed Ch. should *s.*
5:41 counted worthy to *s.* shame
7:24 seeing one *s.* wrong
9:16 must *s.* for my name's sake
21:39 *s.* me to speak to people
Rom. 8:17 if so be we *s.* wi. him
1 *Cor.* 3:15 if work be burnt sh. *s.*
9:12 used power but *s.* all thi.
10:13 will not *s.* to be tempted
12:36 if one mem. *s.* all mem. *s.*
2 *Cor.* 1:6 same suffer, wh. we *s.*
11:20 ye *s.* if a man bring you
Gal. 6:12 lest they sh. *s.* persec.
Phil. 1:29 given to believe and *s.*
1 *Thes.* 3:4 told you, we should *s.*
2 *Thes.* 1:5 kingd. of G. for wh. *s.*
1 *Tim.* 4:10 we both labor and *s.*
2 *Tim.* 1:12 for wh. cause I also *s.*
2:9 wherein I *s.* as an evil doer
12 if we *s.* we shall also reign
Heb. 11:25 choosing to *s.* afflicti.
13:22 *s.* the word of exhortation
1 *Pet.* 2:20 if ye do well, and *s.*
3:14 if ye *s.* for righteous. sake
17 it is bet. ye *s.* for well-doing
4:15 let none *s.* as a murderer

16 if any man *s.* as a Christian
19 let them that *s.* according to
Rev. 2:10 those things thou sh. *s.*
11:9 not *s.* dead bodies to be put

SUFFERED.
Gen. 20:6 therefore *s.* I thee not
31:7 God *s.* him not to hurt me
Deut. 8:3 he *s.* thee to hunger.
18:14 G. ha. not *s.* thee so to do
Jud. 3:28 *s.* not a man to pass
1 *Sam.* 24:7 D. *s.* them not to rise
1 *Chr.* 16:21 he *s.* no man to do
them wrong, *Ps.* 105:14
Job 31:30 neither have I *s.* mouth
Jer. 15:15 for thy sake I *s.* rebuke
Mat. 3:15 suf. it to be so, he *s.*
24:43 nor *s.* his hou. *Lu.* 12:39
27:19 I have *s.* many things this
Mark 1:34 he *s.* not dev. *Lu.* 4:41
5:19 Jesus *s.* him not, but said
26 *s.* many things of physici.
Luke 8:32 *s.* them to enter swine
51 he *s.* no man to go in,
13:2 because they *s.* such things
24:26 ought not Ch. to have *s.?*
Acts 13:18 about 40 years *s.* he
14:16 who *s.* all nations to walk
16:7 but the Spirit *s.* them not
19:30 discip. *s.* him not to enter
28:16 P. was *s.* to dwell by hims.
2 *Cor.* 7:12 not for his cau. th. *s.*
Gal. 3:4 have ye *s.* th. in vain?
Phil. 3:8 for whom I *s.* loss of all
1 *Thes.* 2:2 after that we had *s.*
14 have *s.* like things of your
Heb. 2:18 hath *s.* being tempted
5:8 learn. obed. by things he *s.*
7:23 they were not *s.* to continue
9:26 then must he often have *s.*
13:12 Jesus *s.* without the gate
1 *Pet.* 2:21 Christ *s.* for us, leav.
23 when he *s.* he threaten. not
3:18 Christ hath once *s.* for sins
4:1 Christ hath *s.* for us in flesh,
he that hath *s.* in the flesh
5:10 after ye have *s.* a while

SUFFEREST.
Rev. 2:20 bec. thou *s.* that wom.

SUFFERETH.
Ps. 66:9 bless G. who *s.* not our
107:38 *s.* not cattle to decrease
Acts 28:4 vengeance *s.* him not
1 *Cor.* 13:4 charity *s.* long, is kind

SUFFERING.
Acts 27:7 wind not *s.* us, we sail.
Jas. 5:10 an exam. of *s.* affliction
1 *Pet.* 2:19 if a man end. grief, *s.*
Jude 7 example, *s.* vengeance of

SUFFERING.
Heb. 2:9 for *s.* of death, crown.

SUFFERINGS.
Rom. 8:18 I reckon that the *s* of
2 *Cor.* 1:5 for as the *s.* of Christ
2 *Cor.* 1:6 endur. same *s.* wh. we
7 ye are partakers of the *s.*
Phil. 3:10 fellowship of his *s.*
Col. 1:24 now fill up. in my *s.*
Heb. 2:10 Captain perfect thro' *s.*
1 *Pet.* 1:11 it testified the *s.* of Ch.
4:13 ye are partakers of Ch.'s *s.*
5:1 I am a witn. of the *s.* of Ch.

SUFFICE.
Num. 11:22 sh. herds be sl. to *s.?*
Deut. 3:26 let it *s.* thee, speak no
1 *K.* 20:10 if dust of Samar. sh. *s.*
Ezek. 44:6 let it *s.* you of all, 45:9
1 *Pet.* 4:3 for the time past may *s.*

SUFFICED, ETH.
Jud. 21:14 wives, so they *s.*
Ruth 2:14 she did eat, and was *s.*
18 gave her, after she was *s.*
John 14:8 L. show Fath. it *s.* us

SUFFICIENCY.
Job 20:22 in fulness of his *s.*

2 *Cor.* 3:5 but our *s.* is of God
9:8 *s.* in all thi. ye may abound

SUFFICIENT.
Ex. 36:7 the stuff th. had was *s.*
Deut. 15:8 thou shalt lend him *s.*
33:7 let his hand be *s.* for him
Prov. 25:16 so much honey as *s.*
Is. 40:16 Leban. is not *s.* to burn
Mat. 6:34 *s.* to the day is the evil
Luke 14:28 whether he have *s.*
John 6:7 200 pennyworth is not *s.*
2 *Cor.* 2:6 *s.* to such a man is this
16 who is *s.* for these things?
3:5 not that we are *s.* of oursel.
12:9 he said, My grace is *s.*

SUFFICIENTLY.
Is. 23:18 bef. the Lord to eat *s.*

SUIT, S.
Jud. 17:10 I will give thee a *s.*
2 *Sam.* 15:4 man who ha. any *s.*
Job 11:19 many sh. make *s.* unto
Is. 3:22 changeable *s.* of apparel

SUM, Substantive.
Ex. 21:30 if laid on him a *s.* of
38:21 this is the *s.* of tabernacle
Num. 1:2 take *s.* of congre. 26:2
26:4 take the *s.* of the people
31:26 take the *s.* of the prey
2 *Sam.* 24:9 Joab gave up *s.* to
king, 1 *Chr.* 21:5
Est. 4:7 the *s.* of money Haman
Ps. 139:17 great is the *s.* of th.
Ezek. 28:12 thou sealest up the *s.*
Dan. 7:1 Daniel told *s.* of dream
Acts 7:16 Abraham bought for *s.*
22:28 with a great *s.* obtained I
Heb. 8:1 of the things th. is the *s.*

SUM.
2 *K.* 22:4 that he may *s.* the silver

SUMMER.
Gen. 8:22 *s.* and winter, day and
Ps. 32:4 turned into drought of *s.*
74:17 thou hast made *s.* and
Prov. 6:8 provid. meat in *s.* 30:25
10:5 gathereth in *s.* is wise son
26:1 snow in *s.* rain in harvest
Is. 28:4 as hasty fruit before *s.*
Jer. 8:20 harv. is past, *s.* is end.
Dan. 2:35 chaff of *s.* threshing-fl.
Zec. 14:8 in *s.* and winter
Mat. 24:32 ye kn. that *s.* is nigh,
Mark 13:28; *Luke* 21:30

SUMMER chamber.
Jud. 3:24 he cov. his feet in *s. c.*

SUMMER fruit.
2 *Sam.* 16:2 *s. f.* for young men
Amos 8:1 a basket of *s. fruit,* 2

SUMMER fruits.
2 *Sam.* 17:1 bro. 100 bun. of *s. f.*
Is. 16:9 shouting for *s. fruits*
Jer. 40:10 ga. wine and *s. f.* 12
48:32 spoiler is fallen on *s. f.*
Mic. 7:1 as wh. they gather *s. f.*

SUMMER-HOUSE.
Amos 3:15 smite winter-ho. *s.-h.*

SUMMER parlor.
Jud. 3:20 Eg. was sitting in *s. p.*

SUMMER.
Is. 18:6 fowls sh. *s.* upon them

SUMPTUOUSLY.
Luke 16:19 rich man fared *s.*

SUN.
Gen. 15:17 when *s.* went down
19:23 *s.* risen when Lot entered
28:11 Jacob tarried, bec. *s.* set
32:31 as he passed Pen. *s.* rose
37:9 *s.* moon, stars, made obeis.
Ex. 16:21 when *s.* waxed hot
22:3 if *s.* be risen, blood be shed
Lev. 22:7 when *s.* is down, he
shall be clean, *Deut.* 23:11
Num. 25:4 hang then ag. the *s.*
Deut. 4:19 lest wh. thou seest *s.*

17:3 hath worshipped either *s.*
24:15 nor eh. *s.* go down upon it
33:14 precious fruits brou. by *s.*
Jos. 1:4 tow. going down of *s.*
10:12 *s.* stand still upon Gibeon
13 *s.* stood still, moon stayed
Jud. 5:31 that love him be as *s.*
8:13 G. return. before *s.* was up
9:33 soon as *s.* is up, rise early
14:18 said, before *s.* went down
19:14 *s.* went down, they were
1 *Sam.* 11:9 *s.* be hot have help
2 *Sam.* 3:35 aught till *s.* be down
12:11 lie with wives in si. of *s.*
12 I will do this bef. Is. and *s.*
23:4 light of morn. when *s.* ris.
2 *K.* 3:22 and *s.* shone on water
23:5 them that burn ince. to *s.*
11 burnt chari. of *s.* with fire
Neh. 7:3 gates be ope. till *s.* hot
Job 8:16 hypocrite green bef. *s.*
9:7 commandeth *s.* riseth not
30:28 I went mourn. without *s.*
31:26 if I behold *s.* when it shi.
Ps. 19:4 set a tabernacle for *s.*
58:8 pass aw. th. they see not *s.*
72:5 fear thee as long as *s.* end.
17 name contin. as long as *s.*
74:16 prepared light and *s.*
84:11 L. God is a *s.* and shield
89:36 his throne sh. endure as *s.*
104:22 *s.* aris. they gath. thems.
121:6 *s.* shall not smite by day
136:8 him that made *s.* to rule
148:3 praise him, *s.* and moon
Ec. 1:5 *s.* riseth, *s.* goeth down
6:5 moreo. he hath not seen *s.*
11:7 pleas. for eyes to behold *s.*
12:2 wh. *s.* or stars be not dark.
Cant. 1:6 bec. *s.* looked on me
6:10 fair as moon, clear as *s.*
Is. 24:23 then *s.* sh. be ashamed
30:26 light of moon as *s.* light
49:10 nor heat nor *s.* smite th.
60:19 *s.* be no more li. by day
20 *s.* shall no more go down
Jer. 15:9 *s.* down while yet day
31:35 wh. giveth the *s.* for light
Ezek. 8:16 they worshipp. the *s.*
32:7 I will cover *s.* with cloud
Joel 2:10 *s.* be dark. 3:15; *Mat.*
24:29; *Mark* 13:24; *Luke* 23:45
31 *s.* sh. be turned to darkness
Amos 8:9 cause *s.* to go down
Jon. 4:8 wh. *s.* did arise, *s.* beat
Mic. 3:6 *s.* go down over proph.
Nah. 3:17 when *s.* aris. they flee
Hab. 3:11 *s.* and moon stood still
Mal. 4:2 to you *s.* of right. arise
Mat. 5:45 maketh his *s.* to rise
13:43 then sh. right. shine as *s.*
17:2 his face did shine as the *s.*
Rev. 1:16; 10:1
Mark 1:32 *s.* set, they bro. sick
Luke 4:40 when *s.* was setting
21:25 there shall be signs in *s.*
Acts 2:20 the *s.* into darkness
13:11 not seeing *s.* for a season
26:13 light above brightn. of *s.*
27:20 nei. *s.* nor stars appeared
1 *Cor.* 15:41 th. is one glory of *s.*
Eph. 4:26 let not *s.* go down
Jam. 1:11 *s.* is no sooner risen
Rev. 6:12 *s.* became as sackcloth
7:16 nor shall *s.* light on them
8:12 third part of *s.* was smit.
9:2 *s.* and the air were darken.
12:1 appeared wom. clo. with *s.*
16:8 angel poured out vial on *s.*
19:17 I saw angel standing on *s.*
21:23 city had no need of *s.* 22:5

See GOETH, GOING, RISING.

Under the SUN.
Ec. 1:3 what profit *under the s.?*
2:18, 19, 20, 22 ; 5:18 ; 9:9
9 there is no new thing *u. t. s.*

14 I have seen all works done
u. t. s. 2:17 : 4:3 ; 8:17 ; 9:3
2:11 there was no profit *u. t. s.*
3:16 I saw *u. t. s.* place of judg.
4:7 returned, I saw vanity *u. s.*
5:13 evil I seen *u. t. s.* 6:1 ; 10:5
6:12 tell what shall be *u. the s.*
8:9 ap. heart to every work *u. s.*
15 hath no better thing *u. t. s.*
9:6 portion in any thing *u. t. s.*
9 days he hath given th. *u. t. s.*
11 I saw *u. t. s.* race not to sw.
13 wisdom have I seen *u. t. s.*

SUNDER.
Ps. 46:9 cutteth the spear in *s.*
107:14 he brake their bands in *s.*
16 he hath cut bars of iron in *s.*
Is. 27:9 chalk stones beaten in *s.*

Is. 45:2 I will cut in *s.* bars of ir.
Nah. 1:13 I will burst bonds in *s.*
Luke 12:46 and cut him in *s.*

SUNDERED.
Job 41:17 stick, they cannot be *s.*

SUNDRY.
Heb. 1:1 God who at *s.* times

SUNG.
Ezr. 3:11 *s.* together by course
Is. 26:1 this song be *s.* in Judah
Mat. 26:30 *s.* hymn, *Mark* 14:26
Rev. 5:9 they *s.* a new song
14:3 *s.* as it were a new song

SUNK.
1 *Sam.* 17:49 stone *s.* into foreh.
2 *K.* 9:24 Jehoram *s.* in chariot
Ps. 9:15 heath. are *s.* in the pit
Jer. 38:6 down, so Jer. *s.* in mire
22 thy feet are *s.* in the mire
Lam. 2:9 her gates are *s.* in gro.
Acts 20:9 Eutychus *s.* down with

SUP, SUPPED.
Hab. 1:9 their faces shall *s.* up
Luke 17:8 make ready, I may *s.*
1 *Cor.* 11:25 took cup, when he
Rev. 3:20 I will *s.* with him, he

SUPERFLUITY.
Jam. 1:21 filthiness *s.* of naugh.

SUPERFLUOUS.
Lev. 21:18 man hath any thing *s.*
22:23 lamb, th. hath any thi. *s.*
2 *Cor.* 9:1 it is *s.* to write to you

SUPERSCRIPTION.
Mat. 22:20 wh. is image and *s.?*
Mark 12:16 ; *Luke* 20:24
Mark 15:26 *s.* of accu. *Luke* 23:38

SUPERSTITION.
Acts 25:19 questi. ag. him of *s.*

SUPERSTITIOUS.
Acts 17:22 in all thi. ye are too *s.*

SUPPER.
Mark 6:21 Herod made *s.* to lords
Luke 14:12 makest a dinner or *s.*
16 a cert. man made a great *s.*
24 none bid. shall taste of my *s.*
22:20 likewise also cup after *s.*
John 12:2 there they made Je. *s.*
13:2 *s.* ended ; 3 Je. ris. from *s.*
21:20 disc. lean. on breast at *s.*
1 *Cor.* 11:20 not to eat Lord's *s.*
21 taketh bef. other his own *s.*
Rev. 19:9 that are called to the *s.*
17 come to *s.* of the great God

SUPPLANT, ED.
Gen. 27:36 hath *s.* me two times
Jer. 9:4 every bro. will utterly *s.*

SUPPLE.
Ezek. 16:4 nei. washed to *s.* thee

SUPPLIANTS.
Zep. 3:10 my *s.* shall bring offer.

SUPPLICATION.
1 *Sam.* 13:12 I have not made *s.*
1 *K.* 8:28 respect to *s.* 2 *Chr.* 6:19
30 hearken thou to the *s.* 45, 49

52 eyes open to *s.* of thy serv.
54 made end of praying and *s.*
50 words wherewith I made *s.*
9:3 I heard thy *s.* th. hast made
2 *Chr.* 6:29 what *s.* shall be made
33:13 Lord heard Manasseh's *s.*
Est. 4:8 make *s.* for her people
Job 8:5 wouldest make *s.* to Al.
9:15 I wo. make my *s.* to judge
Ps. 6:9 Lord hath heard my *s.*
30:8 unto L. I made my *s.* 142:1
55:1 hide not thyself from my *s.*
119:170 let my *s.* come bef. thee
Is. 45:14 they sh. make *s.* to thee
Jer. 36:7 th. will present their *s.*
37:20 let my *s.* be accepted bef.
38:26 present. my *s.* bef. king
42:2 let our *s.* be accepted bef.
9 ye sent me to present your *s.*
Dan. 6:11 men and D. making *s.*
9:20 I was present. *s.* before G.
Hos. 12:4 and made *s.* to him
Acts 1:14 accord in prayer and *s.*
Eph. 6:18 with all prayer and *s.*
Phil. 4:6 but in every thing by *s.*

SUPPLICATIONS.
2 *Chr.* 6:21 hearken to *s.* of serv.
39 hear th. their prayer and *s.*
Job 41:3 will leviathan make *s.?*
Ps. 28:2 voice of my *s.* 140:6
6 he heard my *s.* 31:22 ; 116:1
86:6 attend to the voice of my *s.*
130:2 be attent. to my *s.* 143:1
Jer. 3:21 weeping and *s.* of Isr.
31:9 with *s.* will I lead them
Dan. 9:3 I set face to seek by *s.*
17 hear prayer of serv. and *s.*
18 we do not pres. *s.* for right.

Dan. 9:23 begin. of *s.* com. came
Zec. 12:10 pour out Spirit of *s.*
1 *Tim.* 2:1 *s.* be made for all men
5:5 continueth in *s.* and prayer
Heb. 5:7 he offered prayers and *s.*

SUPPLY, Substantive.
2 *Cor.* 8:14 abund. may be a *s.*
Phil. 1:19 through prayer and *s.*

SUPPLY, Verb.
Phil. 2:30 not regard. to *s.* lack
4:19 God shall *s.* all your need

SUPPLIED, ETH.
1 *Cor.* 16:17 what lack. they *s.*
2 *Cor.* 9:12 not only *s.* want of
11:9 what lacking, brethren *s.*
Eph. 4:16 that wh. every joint *s.*

SUPPORT.
Acts 20:35 ought to *s.* the weak,
1 *Thes.* 5:14

SUPPOSE.
2 *Sam.* 13:32 let not my lord *s.*
Luke 7:43 I *s.* that he to whom
12:51 *s.* I am co. to give peace
13:2 *s.* ye these Galileans were
John 21:25 I *s.* world could not
1 *Cor.* 7:26 I *s.* that this is good
2 *Cor.* 11:5 I *s.* I was not behind
1 *Pet.* 5:12 a faithful bro. as I *s.*

SUPPOSED.
Mat. 20:10 they *s.* they sho. have
Mark 6:49 *s.* it had been a spirit
Luke 3:23 Je. as was *s.* son of J.
Acts 7:25 *s.* his brethren would
25:18 none accus. of thi. as I *s.*
Phil. 2:25 I *s.* it neces. to send

SUPPOSING.
Luke 2:44 *s.* him to have been
Acts 14:19 drew P. out, *s.* he had
16:27 jailer *s.* prisoners had fled
27:13 *s.* they had obt. purpose
Phil. 1:16 *s.* to add affliction
1 *Tim.* 6:5 corrupt minds *s.* gain

SUPREME.
1 *Pet.* 2:13 whether to king as *s.*

SURE.
Ex. 3:19 I am *s.* king will not

Num. 32:23 be *s.* sin will find
1 *Sam.* 2:35 build a *s.* house
2 *Sam.* 23:5 cove. ordered and *s.*
1 *K.* 11:38 I build thee a *s.* house
Job 24:22 no man is *s.* of life
Ps. 111:7 his commandm. are *s.*
Prov. 6:3 make *s.* thy friend
Is. 33:16 bread given, waters *s.*
55:3 *s.* mercies of D. *Acts* 13:34
John 6:69 are *s.* thou art Christ
16:30 are we *s.* thou knowest
Rom. 15:29 I am *s.* when I come

SURELY.
Ec. 8:12 *s.* it sh. be well with th.
Is. 45:14 *s.* G. is in th. and there
Mat. 26:73 *s.* thou art one of th.
    Mark 14:70
Rev. 22:20 *s.* I come quickly
See DIE.

SURELY be put to death.
Gen. 26:11 man, *s. be put to d.*
Ex. 19:12 tou. mount, *s. p. to d.*
21:12 killeth, sh. *s. be put to d.*
  15 smiteth fa. sh. *s. be put to d.*
  16 steal. a man, sh. *s. be p. to d.*
  17 curseth his father, shall *s.*
    be put to death, Lev. 20:9
22:19 lieth with beast, sh. *s. be*
    put to death, Lev. 20:15, 16
31:14 defileth sab. *s. p. to d.* 15
Lev. 20:2 giveth to M. *s. p. to d.*
  10 adulteress sh. *s. be put to d.*
  11 lieth wi. fa. wife, bo..*s. p. d.*
  12 daughter-in-l. both *s. p. to d.*
  13 lie wi. mank. bo. *s. p. to d.*
24:16 blasphem. sh. *s. be p. to d.*
  17 killeth man, sh. *s. be put to*
    d. Num. 35:16, 17, 18, 21, 31
27:29 bad shall *s. be put to death*
Jud. 21:5 ca. not, *s. be put to d.*
Jer. 38:15 w. not *s. p. me to d. ?*

SURETY.
Gen. 43:9 I will be *s.* for him
  44:32 thy serv. bec. *s.* for lad
Job 17:3 put me in a *s.* with th.
Ps. 119:122 be *s.* for thy serv.
Prov. 6:1 if thou be *s.* for friend
11:15 he that is *s.* for stranger
17:18 becometh *s.* in presence
20:16 *s.* for stranger, 27:13
Heb. 7:22 Je. made *s.* of a better

SURETIES.
Prov. 22:26 not of th. that are *s.*

Of a SURETY.
Gen. 15:13 know *of a s.* thy seed
18:13 sh. I *of a s.* bear a child?
Gen. 26:9 *of a s.* she is thy wife
Acts 12:11 *of a s.* Lord sent ang.

SURETYSHIP.
Prov. 11:15 he that hateth *s.*

SURFEITING.
Luke 21:34 overcharged with *s.*

SURMISINGS.
1 *Tim.* 6:4 whereof com. evil *s.*

SURNAME, Substantive.
Mat. 10:3 Lebbeus, *s.* was Thad.
Acts 10:5 Sim. *s.* is P. 32; 11:13
12:12 John, *s.* was M. 25; 15:37

SURNAME, Verb.
Is. 44:5 *s.* hims. by name of Isr.

SURNAMED.
Is. 45:4 *s.* thee, tho' not kn. me
Mark 3:16 Si. he *s. P. Acts* 10:18
  17 he *s.* th. Boanerges, sons of
Acts 1:23 Barsabas, who was *s. J.*
  4:36 by apostles was *s.* Barnab.

SURPRISED.
Is. 33:14 fearfuln. *s.* hypocrites
Jer. 48:41 the strong-holds are *s.*
51:41 how is praise of earth *s. !*

SUSANNA.
Luke 8:3 Joanna and S. minist.

SUSTAIN, ED.
Gen. 27:37 wi. corn and wi. I *s.*
1 *K.* 17:9 comman. a widow to *s.*
Neh. 9:21 forty years didst *s.* th.
Ps. 3:5 I awaked, the Lord *s.* me
55:22 burden on L. he sh. *s.* th.
Prov. 18:14 spirit of man will *s.*
Is. 59:16 his righteous. it *s.* him

SUSTENANCE.
Jud. 6:4 Midian. left no *s.* for Is.
2 *Sam.* 19:32 Barzillai provid. *s.*
Acts 7:11 our fathers found no *s.*

SWADDLED.
Lam. 2:22 tho. I *s.* hath my ene.
Ezek. 16:4 not salt. not *s.* at all

SWADDLING.
Job 38:9 I made darkn. a *s.* band
Luke 2:7 wrap. him in *s.* clo. 12

SWALLOW.
Ps. 84:3 the *s.* hath found a nest
Prov. 26:2 as *s.* by flying, so the
Is. 38:14 like a crane or a *s.* did I
Jer. 8:7 crane and *s.* observe ti.

SWALLOW, Verb.
Num. 16:30 if earth open and *s.*
  34 lest the earth *s.* us up also
2 *Sam.* 20:19 why wilt thou *s.* up
  20 that I should *s.* up or destr.
Job 7:19 alone till I *s.* my spittle
20:18 shall restore, and not *s.* it
Ps. 21:9 the L. shall *s.* them up
56:1 O G. man would *s.* me up
  2 mine ene. would *s.* me up
57:3 repr. of him that would *s.*
69:15 nei. let the deep *s.* me up
Prov. 1:12 let us *s.* them up alive
Ec. 10:12 lips of fool *s.* up hims.
Is. 25:8 will *s.* up death in vict.
Hos. 8:7 strangers shall *s.* it up
Amos 8:4 ye that *s.* needy
Ob. 16 and they shall *s.* down
Jon. 1:17 Lord prep. a fish to *s.*
Mat. 23:24 stra. at gnat, *s.* camel

SWALLOWED.
Ex. 7:12 Aaron's rod *s.* th. rods
15:12 stretch. thy hand, earth *s.*
Num. 16:32 earth opened and *s.*
    26:10; *Deut.* 11:6
2 *Sam.* 17:16 lest king be *s.* up
Job 6:3 theref. my words are *s.*
20:15 he hath *s.* down riches
37:20 if speak, he sh. be *s.* up
Ps. 35:25 not say, we *s.* him up
106:17 the earth *s.* up Dathan
124:3 they had *s.* us up quick
Is. 28:7 priest and prophet are *s.*
49:19 they that *s.* thee up, shall
Jer. 51:34 *s.* me up like a dragon
  44 br. out mouth that he has. *s.*
Lam. 2:2 Lord hath *s.* up inhab.
  5 he hath *s.* up Israel, hath *s.*
  16 they say, We have *s.* her up
Ezek. 36:3 they have *s.* you up
Hos. 8:8 Israel is *s.* up am. Gent.
1 *Cor.* 15:54 death is *s.* up in vic.
2 *Cor.* 2:7 lest such a one be *s.* up
  5:4 that mortal. might be *s.* up
Rev. 12:16 earth *s.* up the flood

SWALLOWETH.
Job 5:5 robber *s.* their substance
39:24 he *s.* ground with fiercen.

SWAN.
Lev. 11:18 *s.* uncl. *Deut.* 14:16

SWARE.
Gen. 21:31 because th. *s.* both of
24:7 L. God of heaven *s.* to me
Gen. 24:9 servant *s.* to him conc.
25:33 Ja. said, Sw. to me. he *s.*
26:3 oath which I *s.* to Aurah.
  31 Abimel. and Isaac *s.* to one
31:53 Jacob *s.* by fear of Isaac
47:31 Jos. *s.* tc Jacob his father
50:24 G. will br. to land he *s.* to

SWEAR.
Ex. 13:5 land the Lord *s.* to thy
    fathers, 11; 33:1; *Num.* 14:16,
    30 ; 32:11 ; *Deut.* 1:8, 35 ; 6:10,
    18, 23 ; 7:13 ; 8:1 ; 11:9, 21 ;
    26:3 ; 28:11 ; 30:20 ; 31:21, 23 ;
    34:4 ; *Jos.* 1:6 ; 5:6 ; 21:43
Num. 32:10 ᵀ 's anger was kind.
    and he *s. Deut.* 1:34
Deut. 2:14 were wasted, as L. *s.*
  4:21 Lord *s.* that I should not
    31 not forget the coven. he *s.*
  7:12 wh. he *s.* to thy salvation
  8:18 covenant which he *s.* 9:5
Jos. 6:22 br. out Rahab as ye *s.*
  9:15 princes *s.* to Gibeonites
  20 because of oath we *s.* to th.
  14:9 M. *s.* on that day, saying
  21:44 according to all that he *s.*
Jud. 2:1 bro. to land which I *s.*
1 *Sam.* 19:6 Saul *s.* Da. shall not
  24:22 David *s.* to Saul
2 *Sam.* 3:35 Da. *s.* he would not
  19:23 D. *s.* to Shimei, 1 *K.* 2:8
1 *K.* 2:23 S. *s.* to A. he sho. die
2 *K.* 25:24 Gedaliah *s. Jer.* 40:9
2 *Chr.* 15:14 they *s.* to the Lord
Ezr. 10:5 they *s.* to put away
Ps. 95:11 I *s.* in wrath, *Heb.* 3:11
132:2 how he *s.* to L. and vowed
Jer. 38:16 king *s.* secretly to Jer.
Ezek. 16:8 I *s.* and entered cove.
Dan. 12:7 *s.* by him, *Rev.* 10:6
Mark 6:23 Herod *s.* to daughter
Luke 1:73 oath which he *s.* to A.
Heb. 3:18 to whom *s.* he that th.
  6:13 no greater, he *s.* by himself
  7:21 Lord *s.* and will not repent

See Their FATHERS.

SWAREST.
Ex. 32:13 to whom thou *s.* by
Num. 11:12 carry them to land *s.*
Deut. 26:15 as thou *s.* to our fat.
1 *K.* 1:17 thou *s.* that Solomon
Ps. 89:49 kindnesses th. *s.* to D.

SWARM, S.
Ex. 8:21 I will send *s.* of flies
  22 no *s.* of flies shall be in Go.
  24 there came a grie. *s.* of flies
  29 that *s.* of flies may depart
Jud. 14:8 a *s.* of bees and honey

SWEAR.
Gen. 21:23 Abim. said to Abr. *s.*
  24 and Abraham said, I will *s.*
  24:3 I will make thee *s.* by L.
  37 my master made me *s.*
  25:33 Jacob said, *s.* to me
  47:31 Jacob said to Joseph, *s.*
  50:5 father made me *s.* saying
Ex. 6:8 land concerning wh. I *s.*
Lev. 5:4 if a soul *s.* pronouncing
  19:12 ye shall not *s.* by name
Num. 30:2 if a man *s.* to bind
Deut. 6:13 *s.* by his name, 10:20
Jos. 2:12 Rahab said to spies, *s.*
  23:7 nor cause to *s.* by th. gods
Jud. 15:12 *s.* ye will not fall
1 *Sam.* 20:17 Jon. caused D. to *s.*
  24:21 *s.* th. wilt not cut off seed
  30:15 *s.* thou wilt nei. kill me
2 *Sam.* 19:7 *s.* by L. if th. go not
1 *K.* 1:13 didst thi. *s.* S. sh. reign
  51 let Solo. *s.* unto me to-day
  2:42 did I not ma. thee *s.* by L. ?
  8:31 oath laid on him to cause
    him to *s.* 2 *Chr.* 6:22
2 *Chr.* 36:13 Nebuc. made him *s.*
Ezr. 10:5 Ezra, Levi. and Isr. *s.*
Neh. 13:25 I made them *s.* by G.
Is. 3:7 in that day shall he *s.*
  19:18 five cities in Egypt sh. *s.*
  45:23 to me ev. tongue shall *s.*
  48:1 wh. *s.* by L. not in truth
  65:16 that swear. shall *s.* by G.
Jer. 4:2 thou shalt *s.* Lord liveth
  5:2 Lord liveth, they *s.* falsely
  7:9 murder, commit adultery, *s.*

SWEAR

12:16 s. by my name, as peo. s.
22:5 I s. saith Lord, this house
32:22 giv. them land th. didst s.
Hos. 4:15 not go to Beth-a. nor s.
Amos 8:14 s. by sin of Samaria
Zep. 1:5 that s. by L. s. by Mal.
Mat. 5:34 s. not : 36 s. not by h.
23:16 s. by temple, s. by gold
18 whoso shall s. by altar
20 whoso theref. sh. s. by altar
21 s. by temple ; 22 s. by heav.
26:74 be. to curse. s. *Mark* 14:71
Heb. 6:13 s. by no greater, he s.
Heb. 6:16 men verily s. by the gr.
Jam. 5:12 my brethren s. not

SWEARERS.

Mal. 3:5 a swift witness ag. s.

SWEARETH.

Lev. 6:3 was lost, and s. falsely
Ps. 15:4 that s. to his hurt
63:11 every one that s. by him
Ex. 9:2 he that s. as he feareth
Is. 65:16 he that s. swear by G.
Zec. 5:3 every one that s. cut off
4 enter house of him that s.
Mat. 23:18 whosoever s. by gift
20 s. by altar ; 21 s. by temple
22 s. by throne of God

SWEARING.

Lev. 5:1 soul sin, hear voice of s.
Jer. 23:10 bec. of s. land mourn.
Hos. 4:2 by s. lying, and steal.
10:4 s. falsely in making coven.

SWEAT.

Gen. 3:19 in s. of face eat bread
Ezek. 44:18 any thing causeth s.
Luke 22:44 s. as drops of blood

SWEEP.

Is. 14:23 s. it wi. besom of dest.
28:17 hail sh. s. refuge of lies
Luke 15:8 doth not s. house

SWEEPING.

Prov. 28:3 is like s. rain which

SWEET.

Ex. 15:25 tree into wat. made s.
30:23 s. cinna. and s. calamus
2 *Sam.* 23:1 D. s. psalmist of Isr.
Neh. 8:10 eat fat, drink the s.
Job 20:12 wickedness s. in mouth
21:33 clods of valley shall be s.
38:31 bind s. influ. of Pleiades ?
Ps. 55:14 we took s. counsel
104:34 medita. of him sh. be s.
119:103 s. thy words to taste
141:6 hear my words, they are s.
Prov. 3:24 thy sleep shall be s.
9:17 stolen waters are s. bread
13:19 desire accomplished is s.
16:24 pleasant words are s.
20:17 bread of dec. s. to a man
23:8 and lose thy s. words
24:13 eat honey-comb wh. is s.
27:7 to hun. soul bitter thing s.
Ec. 5:12 sleep of laboring man s.
11:7 truly light is s. a pl. thing
Cant. 2:3 fruit s. 14 s. is voice
5:5 fingers drop. with s. myrrh
13 as s. flowers, drop. s. myrrh
16 his mouth is most s. lovely
Is. 3:24 inst. of s. smell, stink
5:20 that put bitter for s. and s.
23:16 make s. melody, si. songs
Jer. 6:20 nor your sacri. s. to me
31:26 my sleep was s. to me
Jam. 3:11 pl. s. water and bitter ?
Rev. 10:9 in mouth s. as hon. 10

See INCENSE, ODORS, SAVOR.

SWEET cane.

Is. 43:24 thou brou. me no s. c.
Jer. 6:20 s. c. came fr. a far coun.

SWEET spices.

Ex. 30:34 take s. s. frankincense
37:29 he made pure inc. of s. s.
Mark 16:1 brou. s. s. anoint him

SWEET wine.

Is. 49:26 drun. wi. blood as s. w.
Amos 9:13 moun. shall drop s. w.
Mic. 6:15 s. w. not drink wine

SWEETER.

Jud. 14:18 what is s. th. honey ?
Ps. 19:12 thy word s. th. honey
119:103 words s. than honey

SWEETLY.

Job 24:20 worms shall feed s.
Cant. 7:9 best wi. goeth down s.

SWEETNESS.

Jud. 9:11 sho. I forsake my s. ?
14:14 out of strong came forth s.
Prov. 16:21 s. of lips incr. learn.
27:9 so doth s. of a man's friend
Ezek. 3:3 in mouth as hon. for s.

SWELL, ED.

Num. 5:21 th. rot, belly to s. 22
27 belly shall s. thigh shall rot
Deut. 8:4 nor thy foot s. 40 years
Neh. 9:21 forty years feet s. not

SWELLING, S.

Ps. 46:3 tho' mount. shake wi. s.
Is. 30:13 as a breach s. in a wall
Jer. 12:5 how do in s. of Jordan ?
49:19 lion from s. of Jord. 50:44
2 *Cor.* 12:20 lest there be s. tum.
2 *Pet.* 2:18 speak s. words of van.
Jude 16 their mouth speaketh s. words

SWEPT.

Jud. 5:21 riv. of Kishon s. them
Jer. 46:15 why valiant s. away ?
Mat. 12:44 find. it s. *Luke* 11:25

SWERVED.

1 *Tim.* 1:6 having s. turned aside

SWIFT.

Deut. 28:49 nation s. as eagle
1 *Chr.* 12:8 s. as roes on mount.
Job 9:26 passed away as s. ships
24:18 he is s. as waters, behold.
Prov. 6:18 feet s. run. to mischi.
Ec. 9:11 the race is not to s.
Is. 18:2 go, ye s. messengers
19:1 behold, L. rid. on s. cloud
30:16 ride on s. th. pursue be s.
Jer. 46:6 let not s. flee away, nor
Amos 2:14 flight sh. perish fr. s.
15 s. of foot sh. not deli. hims.
Mic. 1:13 bind chariot to s. beast
Mal. 3:5 a s. witn. ag. sorcerers
Rom. 3:15 feet s. to shed blood
Jam. 1:19 let every man be s.
2 *Pet.* 2:1 sh. bring s. destruction

SWIFTER.

2 *Sam.* 1:23 were s. than eagles
Job 7:6 days are s. than a shuttle
9:25 my days are s. than a post
Jer. 4:13 his horses s. than eagles
Lam. 4:19 persecut. s. th. eagles
Hab. 1:8 horses s. than leopards

SWIFTLY.

Ps. 147:15 his word runneth s.
Is. 5:26 behold, they sh. come s.
Dan. 9:21 Gabriel caused to fly s.
Joel 3:4 if ye recompense me s.

SWIM.

2 *K.* 6:6 and the iron did s.
Ps. 6:6 night ma. I my bed to s.
Is. 25:11 sprea. forth hands to s.
Ezek. 47:5 risen, waters to s.
Acts 27:42 lest any should s. out
43 comman. they that could s.

SWIMMEST, ETH.

Is. 25:11 as he that s. spreadeth
Ezek. 32:6 water land wher. th. s.

SWINE.

Lev. 11:7 s. is unclean, *Deut.* 14:8
Prov. 11:22 a jewel in a s. snout
Is. 65:4 which s. flesh and broth
66:3 as if he offered s. blood
17 eating s. flesh and abomin.

SWORD.

Mat. 7:6 nei. cast pearls befo. s.
8:30 herd of s. feeding, *Mark* 5:11 ; *Luke* 8:32
31 go into herd of s. *Mark* 5:12
32 went into s. the herd of s. ran, *Mark* 5:13 ; *Luke* 8:33
Mark 5:14 they that fed s. fled
Luke 15:15 he sent him to feed s.
16 filled belly with husks s. eat

SWOLLEN.

Acts 28:6 look. he should have s.

SWOON, ED.

Lam. 2:11 children s. in street
12 wh. they s. as the wounded

SWORD.

Gen. 3:24 cherubim and flam. s.
34:25 took each man his s.
Ex. 5:21 put a s. in their hand
32:27 put ev. man his s. by side
Lev. 26:6 nor s. go through land
25 br. s. upon you, *Ezek.* 5:17 ; 6:3 ; 14:17 ; 29:8 ; 33:2
33 I will draw out s. after you
37 they sh. fall as were fed s.
Num. 22:23 angel's s. drawn, 31
29 there was a s. in my hand
Deut. 32:25 s. without, terror
33:29 is s. of thy excellency
Jos. 5:13 stood with his s. drawn
24:12 not with thy s. nor bow
Jud. 7:18 s. of L. and Gideon, 20
8:20 youth drew not his s.
9:54 draw thy s. and slay me
20:35 destr. 25,100 that drew s.
46 fell were 25,000 that drew s.
1 *Sam.* 13:22 neither s. nor spear
15:33 s. as made wom. childless
17:39 David girded s. on, 25:13
50 th. was no s. in hand of Da.
51 D. took his s. and slew him
21:8 not und. hand spear or s. ?
9 s. of Goli. is wrapt in a cloth
22:10 he gave him s. of Goliath
13 given him bread and a s.
25:13 gird ye on ev. man his s.
31:4 Saul took a s. fell upon it
5 armor-bearer fell upon his s.
2 *Sam.* 1:22 s. of S. returned not
2:16 thrust s. into fellow's side
26 said, Sh. s. devour for ever ?
8:29 not fail one that fall. on s.
2 *Sam.* 11:25 s. devo. one as ano.
12:10 s. sh. never dep. fr. house
18:8 wood devour. more than s.
20:10 Amasa took no heed to s.
23:10 his hand clave unto s.
24:9 in Is. 800,000 men drew s.
1 *K.* 3:24 bring s. they broug. s.
19:17 that escapeth s. of Hazael
1 *Chr.* 5:18 men able to bear s.
10:4 Saul took a s. fell upon it
5 his armor-bear. fell on the s.
21:5 a 100,000 that drew s.
12 or 3 days the s. of the Lord
16 the angel having a s. drawn
27 he put up his s. again
30 he was afraid of s. of angel
2 *Chr.* 20:9 wh. s. of judgm. com.
Ezr. 9:7 kings are delivered to s.
Neh. 4:18 ev. one had his s. gird.
Est. 9:5 Jews smote ene. with s.
Job 5:20 deliver from power of s.
15:22 he is waited for of the s.
19:29 s. for wrath, punish. of s.
20:25 glittering s. cometh out
27:14 if he multiplied it is for s.
40:19 make his s. to approach
41:26 s. of him that layeth at
Ps. 7:12 if turn not will whet s.
17:13 deliv. from wicked, thy s.
17:14 wicked have drawn s.
15 s. shall enter their heart
43:3 gird thy s. on thy thigh
57:4 their tongue is a sharp s.
64:3 whet th. tongue like a s.
76:3 brake he the shield and s.
78:62 he gave his people to s.
149:6 a two-edged s. in th. hand

'rov. 5:4 her end as a two-edg. s.
12:18 speaketh like pierc. of s.
25:18 bear. false witness is a s.
Cant. 3:8 every man hath his s.
s. 2:4 nation not lift s. ag. nati.
31:8 the s. not of a mean man
34:6 s. of L. is filled with blood
41:2 he gave th. as dust to his s.
49:2 made mouth like sharp s.
51:19 famine and s. are come
65:12 I will number you to s.
66:16 by his s. will Lord plead
Jer. 2:30 your s. devoured proph.
4:10 s. reacheth unto the soul
5:12 neith. shall we see s. 14:13
6:25 s. of enemy is on ev. side
9:16 I will send a s. after them,
24:10; 25:27; 29:17; 49:37
12:12 s. of the L. shall devour
14:13 peo. say, Ye sh. not see s.
15 say s. and famine shall not
15:2 for the s. to the s. 43:11
3 I will appoint the s. to slay
9 residue will I deliver to s.
18:21 pour out th. blood by s.
25:16 they sh. be mad bec. of s.
29 call for a s. Ezek. 38:21
31 he will give wicked to s.
31:2 peo. left of s. found grace
32:24 city given because of s.
34:17 I proclaim a liberty to s.
42:16 s. ye feared sh. overtake
44:28 a small number esc. the s.
47:6 O thou s. of the Lord, how
48:2 O Madmen, s. shall pursue
10 curs. that keep. back his s.
50:16 fear of the oppressing s.
35 a s. is on Chaldea, saith L.
36 a s. on liars, s. on mighty
37 a s. on horses, s. on treasu.
51:50 ye that have escaped s.
Lam. 5:9 bre. by peril bec. of s.
Ezek. 5:2 I will draw out s. 12
17 I will bri. s. upon thee, 6:3
6:8 some that shall escape s.
7:15 s. is without, pestilence
11:8 ye feared s. I will bring a s.
14:17 if I bring a s. and say. s.
21 my four sore judgm. the s.
21:9 a s. a s. is sharpened, 11
12 terrors, by reason of the s.
13 what if s. contemn the rod ?
14 let s. be doubled, s. of great
15 set point of the s. against
19 appoint 2 ways, that s. may
20 appoint a way that s.
28 the s. the s. is drawn for the
30:4 s. shall come upon Egypt
21 to make it strong to hold s.
22 I will cause the s. to fall out
32:11 s. of the king of Babylon
33:3 when he seeth s. come on
4 if s. come and take him, 6
6 if watchmen see the s. come
26 ye stand upon your s.
35:5 thou hast shed blood by s.
Hos. 2:18 I will break bow and s.
11:6 s. shall abide on his cities
Amos 9:4 thence will I com. s.
Mic. 4:3 nation not lift s. ag. na.
6:14 delivereest, will I give to s.
Nah. 2:13 s. shall devour lions ·
3:3 horseman lift. up bright s.
15 there the s. sh. cut thee off
Zec. 9:13 made thee as s. of mi.
11:17 s. shall be upon his arm
13:7 awake, O s. ag. my sheph.
Mat. 10:34 not send peace, but s.
26:51 drew his s. struck serv.
Mark 14:47 ; John 18:10
52 put up ag. thy s. John 18:11
Luke 2:35 a s. sh. pierce thy soul
22:36 he that hath no s. let him
Acts 16:27 he drew his s. and wo.
Rom. 13:35 shall s. separate us
from the love of Christ ?
13:4 he beareth not s. in vain
Eph. 6:17 s. of Sp. which is word

Heb. 4:12 sharp. th. two-edged s.
Rev. 1:16 out of mouth went a s.
2:12 the sharp s. with two edges
6:4 was given to him a great s.
19:15 out of his mou. goeth s. 21

By the SWORD.

Gen. 27:40 by thy s. thou sh. live
Lev. 26:7 they sh. fall by the s. 8
2 Chr. 29:9 fath. ha. fallen b. t. s.
Job 33:18 from perish. by the s.
36:12 they shall perish by the s.
Ps. 44:3 got not land by their s.
78:64 their priests fell by the s.
Jer. 11:22 young men shall die
by the s. 18:21 ; Lam. 2:21
14:12 I will consu. them by t. s.
15 by s. and famine shall pro.
16:4 shall be consumed by the s.
44:12, 18, 27
19:7 cause them to fall by the s.
21:9 abideth, shall die by the s.
38:2 ; 42:17, 22
27:13 why will ye die by the s. ?
32:36 city sh. be deliver. by t. s.
33:4 houses thro. down by the s.
34:4 Zedek. sh. not die by the s.
44:13 I punished Jerusal. by t. s.
Ezek. 26:6 daugh. be slain by t. s.
11 he sh. slay thy peo. by t. s.
28:23 be judged in her by the s.
31:18 th. that be slain by the s.
32:20, 21; 22, 25, 30 ; 33:27
39:23 so they fell all by the s.
Hos. 1:7 will not save them by s.
Amos 7:11 Jerobo. sh. die by t. s.
9:10 my people sh. die by the s.
Hag. 2:22 ev. one by the s. of his
Rev. 13:14 had the wound by a s.

See EDGE, FALL.

From the SWORD.

Ex. 18:4 delivered me fr. the s.
Lev. 26:36 they sh. flee as f. a s.
1 K. 19:17 him that escap. f. t. s.
2 Chr. 36:20 escaped from the s.
Job 5:15 he saveth poor fr. the s.
39:22 neither turneth he f. t. s.
Ps. 22:20 deliver my soul fr. t. s.
144:10 delivereth David fr. t. s.
Is. 31:15 they fled f. t. drawn s.
31:8 but he shall flee from the s.
Jer. 21:7 such as are left fr. t. s.
46:16 let us go fr. the oppress. s.
Ezek. 12:16 I'll leave a few fr. s.
· 38:8 land that is brou. fr. the s.

My SWORD.

Gen. 48:22 I took fr. A. wi. m. s.
Ex. 15:9 I will draw my s. my
Deut. 32:41 whet my glit. s. 42
1 Sam. 21:8 neith. brought my s.
Ps. 44:6 neither shall my s. save
Is. 34:5 my s. shall be bathed in
Ezek. 21:3 I will draw my s.
5 I the Lord have drawn my s.
30:24 I have put my s. in ha. 25
32:10 when I sh. brandish my s.
Zec. 2:12 shall be slain by my s.

With the SWORD.

Gen. 31:26 as capti. taken w. t. s.
Ex. 5:3 lest he fall on us w. t. s.
22:24 I will kill you w. the s.
Num. 19:16 touch. slain w. t. s.
20:18 lest I come out w. the s.
31:8 Balaam they slew w. the s.
Deut. 28:22 L. sh. smi. th. w. t. s.
Jos. 10:11 Is. slew w. t. s. 13:22
11:10 smote king of Ha. w. t. s.
1 Sam. 17:45 thou comest w. t. s.
47 the Lord saveth not w. s.
2 Sam. 20:8 girdle w. a s. fasten.
1 K. 1:51 not slay serv. w. the s.
2:8 not put th. to death w. t. s.
19:1 had slain prophets w. t. s.
2 K. 8:12 wilt thou slay w. the s.
11:20 they slew Athaliah with
the s. 2 Chr. 23:21
2 Chr. 21:4 slew breth. w. the s.

36:17 slew young men w. the s.
Ps. 42:10 as w. a s. in my bones
Is. 1:20 sh. be devoured w. the s.
Is. 14:19 slain, ·hr. thro' w. a s.
22:2 thy men not slain w. the s.
27:1 Lord w. his strong s. shall
Jer. 5:17 impover. cities w. t. s.
14:18 behold the slain w. the s.
20:4 he sh. slay Judah w. the s.
27:8 nati. will I punish w. t. s.
29:18 I will persecute w. the s.
Lam. 4:9 that be slain w. the s.
Ezek. 7:15 in field sh. die w. t. s.
26:8 sh. slay daughters w. the s.
31:17 to hell with them that be
slain w. the s. 32:28, 32 ; 35:8
Amos 1:11 did pursue bro. w. s.
4:10 men have I slain w. the s.
9:1 I will slay last of th. w. t. s.
Mic. 5:6 waste Assyria w. the s.
Mat. 26:52 that take the s. shall
perish with the s.
Luke 22:49 sh. we smite w. t. s. ?
Acts 12:2 Her. killed Jas. w. t. s.
Heb. 11:37 tempt. slain w. the s.
Rev. 2:16 I will fight th. w. the s.
6:8 and power to kill w. s. and
13:10 killeth w. s. be kill. w. s.
19:21 remnant were slain with

SWORDS.

1 Sam. 13:19 lest Hebr. make s.
2 K. 3:26 took 700 men drew s.
Neh. 4:13 I set the people wi. s.
Ps. 55:21 words were drawn s.
59:7 belch out, s. are in th. lips
Prov. 30:14 gener. teeth are as s.
Cant. 3:8 hold s. expert in war
Is. 2:4 beat their s. into ploughshares, Mic. 4:3
21:15 they fled from the s.
Ezek. 16:40 thrust through wi. s.
23:47 dispatch them with th. s.
28:7 strangers sh. draw their s.
30:11 they shall draw their s.
32:12 by s. of the mighty will I
27 they have laid their s. und.
Joel 3:10 beat ploughsh. into s.
Mat. 26:47 with Ju. great multitude with s. Mark 14:43
Luke 22:38 beho. here are two s.

SWORN.

Gen. 22:16 by myself have I s.
saith L. Is. 45:23 ; Jer. 49:13;
51:14 ; Amos 6:8
Ex. 13:19 Joseph had straitly s.
17:16 Lord hath s. that he will
Lev. 6:5 about wh. had s. falsely
Deut. 7:8 keep oath s. Jer. 11:5
13:17 as he hath s. to thy fath
28:9 estab. sh. as he hath s. 29:13
31:7 bri. to land L. s. Neh. 9:15
Jos. 9:18 because princes had s.
19 we have s. to th. 2 Sam. 21:2
Jud. 21:1 men of Is. had s. to M.
7 have s. not to give wives, 18
1 Sam. 3:14 I ha. s. to hou. of E.
2 Sam. 21:2 Is. had s. to Gibeon.
2 Chr. 15:15 had s. with hearts
Neh. 9:15 land th. badst s. to give
Ps. 24:4 hath not s. deceitfully
89:3 I have s. to David my serv.
35 s. by my holiness, Amos 4:2
102:8 mad ag. me, are s. ag. me
110:4 L. hath s. will not repent
119:106 I have s. will perform
132:11 L. hath s. in truth to D.
Is. 14:24 Lord of hosts hath s.
45:23 I have s. by myself, word
54:9 I have s. wat. no more go
over earth, I have s.
62:8 L. hath s. by his ri. hand
Jer. 5:7 s. by th. that are no gods
44:26 I ha. s. by my great name
Ezek. 21:23 them that have s.
Amos 8:7 Lord hath s. by Jacob
Mic. 7:20 perf. mercy th. hast s.

Acts 2:30 know. God hath *s.* oath
7:17 pro. drew nigh God had *s.*
Heb. 4:3 I have *s.* in my wrath

SYCAMINE.
Luke 17:6 to a *s.* tr. Be plucked

SYCAMORE fruit.
Amos 7:14 and gather of *s. fruit*

SYCAMORE-TREE.
Luke 19:4 Zaccheus climbed *s.-t.*

SYCAMORE-TREES.
1 K. 10:27 Solomon made cedars
as *s.-trees*, *2 Chr.* 1:15; 9:27
1 Chr. 27:28 over *s.-t.* Baal-hanan
Ps. 78:47 he destroyed their *s.-t.*

SYCAMORES.
Is. 9:10 the *s.* are cut down

SYCHAR. *John* 4:5
SYENE. *Ezek.* 29:10

SYNAGOGUE.
Mat. 12:9 he went into their *s.*
13:54 tau. in their *s. Mark* 6:2
Mark 5:22 Jairus, one of the rul.
of the *s.* 36, 38; *Luke* 8:41, 49
Luke 4:16 custom, went into *s.*
20 eyes of all in *s.* fast. on him
7:5 loveth nation, built us a *s.*
John 9:22 he sho. be put out of *s.*
12:42 lest he be put out of *s.*
18:20 I ever taught in *s.* temple
Acts 6:9 then arose cert. of the *s.*
called *s.* of the Libertines
13:14 they went into *s.* on sab.
14:1 P. and Barna. went into *s.*
17:1 Thessalonica, wh. was a *s.*
17 he disputed in *s.* with Jews
18:4 reasoned in *s.* ev. sabbath
7 Justus, whose house join. *s.*
8 Crispus, chief ruler of the *s.*
17 Sosthenes, chief ruler of *s.*
26 Apollos began to speak in *s.*
22:19 beat. in *s.* such beli. 26:11
Rev. 2:9 but are the *s.* of Satan
3:9 I will make them of *s.* of Sa.

SYNAGOGUES.
Ps. 74:8 they burned all *s.* of G.

Mat. 4:23 Je. went teaching in *s.*
9:35; *Mark* 1:39; *Luke* 13:10
6:2 as hypocrites do in the *s.*
5 love to pray standing in *s.*
10:17 scourge you in *s.* 23:34
23:6 love chief seats in *s. Mark*
12:39; *Luke* 11:43; 20:46
Mark 13:9 in *s.* ye sh. be beaten
Luke 4:15 taught in *s.* glorified
44 he preached in *s.* of Galilee
12:11 they bring you unto *s.*
21:12 delivering you up to the *s.*
John 16:2 shall put you out *s.*
Acts 9:2 Saul desired letters to *s.*
20 he preached Christ in the *s.*
13:5 P. and Barn. preached in *s.*
15:21 being read in *s.* every sa.
24:12 neither raising people in *s.*

SYNTYCHE.
Phil. 4:2 I beseech Euod. and S.

SYRACUSE.
Acts 28:12 landing at S. tarried
three days

SYRIA.
Jud. 10:6 Is. served gods of S.
2 Sam. 8:6 David put garrisons
in S. 1 *Chr.* 18:6
15:8 I abode at Geshur in S.
1 K. 10:29 kings of S. did th. br.
11:25 Rezon reigned over S.
19:15 Haz. king of S. 2 *K.* 13:3
22:1 without war betw. S. and
2 K. 5:1 deliverance given to S.
6:23 bands of S. came no more
7:5 no man in the camp of S.
8:13 that thou sh. be king of S.
13:7 for the king of S. destroy.
17 arrow of deliveran. from S.
19 thou sh. smite S. but thrice
16:6 king of S. recove. El. to S.
2 Chr. 18:10 thou shalt push S.
24:23 host of S. came against
28:23 gods of kings of S. help
Is. 7:2 saying S. is confederate
8 for head of S. is Damascus
Ezek. 16:57 of the daughters of S.
27:16 S. was thy merchant
Hos. 12:12 fled into country of S.

Amos 1:5 S. shall go into captiv.
Mat. 4:24 went throughout all S.
Luke 2:2 Cyrenius governor of S.
Acts 15:23 to the brethren in S.
41 he went through S. and
18:18 sailed thence into S. 21:3;
Gal. 1:21

SYRIAC.
Dan. 2:4 spake to the king in S.

SYRIAN.
Gen. 25:20 daugh. of Bethuel S.
Lab. the S. 28:5; 31:20, 24
Deut. 26:5 a S. ready to perish
2 K. 5:20 spared Naaman this S.
18:26 speak in the S. *Is.* 36:11
Ezr. 4:7 written in S. tongue and
interpreted in S. tongue
Luke 4:27 saving Naaman the S.

SYRIANS.
2 Sam. 8:5 when S. of Da. came,
David slew of S. 22,000
6 the S. became David's servants, 1 *Chr.* 18:5, 6
13 returned from smiting of S.
10:6 Ammonites hired the S.
11 if S. be too str. 1 *Chr.* 19:12
19 the S. feared to help children of Ammon, 1 *Chr.* 19:19
1 K. 20:20 the S. fled, and Israel
27 flocks, but S. filled country
29 Israel slew of the S. 100,000
22:11 th. shalt thou push the S.
2 K. 5:2 the S. had taken a maid
2 K. 6:9 thith. S. are come down
7:4 let us fall unto host of S.
6 Lord made the host of the S.
10 we came to camp of the S.
8:28 S. wounded Joram, 29;
9:15; 2 *Chr.* 22:5
13:5 from under the hand of S.
17 for thou shalt smite the S.
16:6 the S. came to Elath and
Is. 9:12 S. bef. and Philistines
Jer. 35:11 for fear of army of S.
Amos 9:7 brou. the S. from Kir?

SYROPHENICIAN.
Mark 7:26 a Greek, a S. by. nat.

T

TABEAL.
Is. 7:6 a king. even the son of T.

TABERAH.
Num. 11:3 he called the place T.
Deut. 9:22 at T. he provoked L.

TAANACH 1 *K.* 4:12

TABERING.
Nah. 2:7 vo. of doves t. on brea.

TABERNACLE.
Ex. 25:9 make after pattern of *t.*
27:9 thou shalt make court of *t.*
19 vessels of *t.* of brass, 39:40
29:43 *t.* be sanctif. by my glory
33:7 Mo. pitch. *t.* without camp
11 Josh. departed not out of *t.*
36:8 them that wrou. work of *t.*
39:32 th. was work of *t.* finished
33 they brought the *t.* to Mo.
40:2 set up the *t.* 9 anoint *t.*
17 on first day the *t.* was reared
up, 18; *Num.* 7:1
33 reared court round about *t.*
34 glory of Lord filled the *t.* 35
36 cloud was taken from over
t. Num. 9:17; 10:11; 12:10
38 the cloud of Lord was on
the *t. Num.* 9:18, 19, 22
Lev. 8:10 Mo. anointed *t.* and all
15:31 die not when they defile *t.*
17:4 bringeth not offering bef. *t.*
26:11 will set my *t.* among you

Num. 1:50 appoint Levites over
t. bear *t.* sh. encamp ro. *t.* 53
51 when *t.* setteth forward,
and when *t.* is to be pitched
53 Levites sh. keep charge of *t.*
3:7, 25; 18:3; 31:30, 47
4:16 oversi. of *t.* pertain. to E.
5:17 priest sh. take of dust of *t.*
7:3 they brou. offering before *t.*
9:15 on day that *t.* was reared,
cloud cov. *t.* tent of testimo.
10:21 Kohathites did set up *t.*
11:24 Mos. set 70 elders round *t.*
26 they went not out unto *t.*
16:9 seem. small to do scr. of *t.*
24 get from about *t.* of Ko. 27
17:13 whos. com. near *t.* sh. die
Deut. 31:15 appeared in *t.* in clo.
Jos. 22:19 wherein L.'s *t.* dwell.
2 Sam. 6:17 set ark in midst of *t.*
7:6 ha. walked in tent and in *t.*
1 K. 2:28 Joab fled to *t.* of Lord
8:4 vessels in *t.* bro. 2 *Chr.* 5:5
1 Chr. 6:48 Levites for serv. of *t.*
9:23 they had oversight of the *t.*
16:39 priests before *t.* of Lord
17:5 ha. gone from one *t.* to ano.
21:29 *t.* M. made in wilderness
23:26 they sh. no more carry *t.*
2 Chr. 1:5 put brazen altar bef. *t.*
Job 5:24 kn. thy *t.* sh. be in pea.
18:6 light shall be dark in his *t.*
14 confidence be rooted out *t.*

15 destruc. shall dwell in his *t.*
19:12 his troops encamp rou. *t.*
20:26 ill with him th. is left in *t.*
29:4 wh. secret of G. was up. *t.*
31:31 if men of my *t.* said not
36:29 can any und. noise of *t.*?
Ps. 15:1 L. who sh. abide in *t.*?
19:4 in them he set a *t.* for sun
27:5 in secret of his *t.* hide me
6 I will offer in his *t.* sacrifices
61:4 I will abide in thy *t.*
76:2 in Salem is his *t.* dwell.-pl.
78:60 so he forsook *t.* of Shiloh
67 moreo. he refused *t.* of Jos.
132:3 I will not come into *t.* 7
Prov. 14:11 *t.* of upright flourish
Is. 4:6 *t.* for shadow from heat
16:5 he sh. sit on it in *t.* of Da.
33:20 *t.* th. sh. not be ta. down
Jer. 10:20 my *t.* is spoiled, cords
Lam. 2:4 slew all pleasant in *t.*
6 he hath violently ta. away *t.*
Ezek. 37:27 my *t.* sh. be with th.
41:1 which was breadth of *t.*
Amos 5:26 have borne *t.* of Mol.
9:11 will I raise up *t.* of D.
Acts 7:43 ye took up *t.* of Moloch
46 desired to find a *t.* for God
15:16 will build again *t.* of Dav.
2 *Cor.* 5:1 if house of *t.* be disso.
4 we th. are in th. *t.* do groan
Heb. 8:2 true *t.* which L. pitched
5 when Moses was to make *t.*

9:2 there was a *t*. made, sanctu.
3 *t*. which is called holiest
6 priests went alw. into first *t*.
8 while as first *t*. was yet stan.
11 priest by greater and per. *t*.
21 sprinkled with blood the *t*.
13:10 no right to eat wh. ser. *t*.
2 *Pet*. 1:13 as long as I am in *t*.
14 shortly I must put off my *t*.
Rev. 13:6 blasp. his name and *t*.
15:5 behold temple of *t*. opened

See CONGREGATION, DOOR.

TABERNACLE of witness.
Num. 17:7 M. la. rods in *t. of w*.
8 on mor. M. went into *t. of w*.
2 *Chr*. 24:6 br. colle. for *t. of w*.
Acts 7:44 our fathers had *t. of w*.

TABERNACLES.
Num. 24:5 how goodly thy *t*.
Job 11:14 let not wic. dwell in *t*.
12:6 *t*. of robbers prosper, they
15:34 fire sh. cons. *t*. of bribery
22:23 put away iniq. from thy *t*.
Ps. 43:3 let them bring me to *t*.
46:4 make glad holy place of *t*.
78:51 smote their strength in *t*.
83:6 *t*. of E. consulted together
84:1 how amiable are thy *t*.
118:15 salvation in *t*. of righte.
132:7 we will go into *t*. worship
Dan. 11:45 he sh. plant *t*. of pal.
Hos. 9:6 thorns sh. be in their *t*.
12:9 make thee to dwell in *t*.
Mal. 2:12 L. cut off man out of *t*.
Mat. 17:4 let us make here three
t. *Mark* 9:5; *Luke* 9:33
Heb. 11:9 Abrah. dwelling in *t*.

See FEAST.

TABITHA.
Acts 9:36 a disciple named T.
40 turn. to body said, T. arise

TABLE.
Ex. 25:23 thou sh. also make a *t*.
27 staves to bear *t*. 28 ; 37:14
31:8 Beza. sh. make *t*. and altar
37:10 made *t*. 16 vessels on *t*.
40:22 put *t*. in tent of congreg.
Lev. 24:6 six on a row on pure *t*.
Num. 3:31 Kohathites' charge *t*.
Jud. 1:7 gath. meat under my *t*.
1 *Sam*. 20:29 no. not to king's *t*.
34 Jona. arose from *t*. in anger
2 *Sam*. 9:7 Mephibosheth sh. eat
at my *t*. 10, 11, 13 ; 19:28
1 *K*. 2:7 be th. that eat at my *t*.
4:27 all that came to Solo.'s *t*.
10:5 queen of Sheba saw meat
of his *t*. 2 *Chr*. 9:4
13:20 as th. sat at *t*. word of L.
18:19 proph. eat at Jezebel's *t*.
2 *K*. 4:10 let us set for him a *t*.
Neh. 5:17 we. at my *t*. 150 Jews
Job 36:16 wh. should be set on *t*.
Ps. 23:5 thou preparest *t*. be. me
69:22 let th. *t*. become a snare
78:19 can G. furn. *t*. in wildern.
128:3 child. like plants about *t*.
Prov. 3:3 wri. on *t*. of heart, 7:3
9:2 wisd. hath furnished her *t*.
Cant. 1:12 wh. king sitteth at *t*.
Is. 21:5 prepare the *t*. eat
30:8 write before them in *t*.
65:11 prepare *t*. for that troop
Jer. 17:1 it is graven on *t*. of he.
Ezek. 23:41 preparc. a *t*. before it
39:20 ye shall be filled at my *t*.
41:22 this is *t*. that is bef. Lord
44:16 shall come near to my *t*.
Dan. 11:27 shall speak lies at *t*.
Mal. 1:7 *t*. of L. is contemptible
12 ye say, *t*. of Lord is pollut.
Mat. 15:27 dogs eat crumbs from
their master's *t*. *Mark* 7:28
Luke 16:21 crn. fr. rich man's *t*.
22:21 betrayeth, is wi. me on *t*.
30 may eat and drink at my *t*.

John 12:2 L. was one th. sat at *t*.
13:28 no man at *t*. knew wh. in.
Rom. 11:9 let their *t*. be a snare
1 *Cor*. 10:21 ye cannot be partakers of Lord's *t*. and *t*. of dev.

See SHOW-BREAD.

Writing TABLE.
Luke 1:63 Zacha. asked for *w*. *t*.

TABLES.
Ex. 32:15 *t*. were writ. on sides
16 *t*. were work of G. gra. on *t*.
Ex. 32:19 cast the *t*. out of his h.
34:1 write on *t*. words in first *t*.
Deut. 10:4 he wr. on *t*. acco. to *t*.
5 put *t*. in the ark, *Heb*. 9:4
1 *Chr*. 28:16 David ga. gold for *t*.
2 *Chr*. 4:8 Solo. also made ten *t*.
Is. 28:8 all *t*. are full of vomit
Ezek. 40:41 8 *t*. whereon sa.
42 four *t*. were of hewn stone
Hab. 2:2 write vision, plain on *t*.
Mat. 21:12 he overthrew *t*. of the
money-changers, *Mark* 11:15
Mark 7:4 wash. of cups, pots, *t*.
John 2:15 dro. out, overthrew *t*.
Acts 6:2 leave word of G. serve *t*.
2 *Chr*. 3:3 not in *t*. of st. fleshly *t*.

See STONE, TWO.

TABLETS.
Ex. 35:22 brought *t*. of jewels
Num. 31:50 brought *t*. atonement
Is. 3:20 I will take away the *t*.

TABOR.
Jud. 4:6 draw toward mount T.
12 Barak was gone to mount T.
8:18 they whom ye slew at T.?
1 *Sam*. 10:3 come to plain of T.
Ps. 89:12 T. and Hermon shall
Jer. 46:18 surely, as T. is among
Hos. 5:1 a net spread upon T.

TABRET.
Gen. 31:27 have sent thee with *t*.
1 *Sam*. 10:5 fr. high place with *t*.
Job 17:6 aforetime I was as a *t*.
Is. 5:12 *t*. and wine are in feasts

TABRETS.
1 *Sam*. 18:6 ca. to meet S. wi. *t*.
Is. 24:8 mirth of *t*. ceaseth, joy
30:32 it sh. be with *t*. and harps
Jer. 31:4 again be adorn. with *t*.
Ezek. 28:13 workmansh. of thy *t*.

TACHES.
Ex. 26:6 thou shalt make fifty *t*.
11 thou sh. make fifty *t*. 35:11
36:13 he made fifty *t*. of gold, 18
39:33 they brought his *t*. boards

TACKLING, S.
Is. 33:23 thy *t*. are loosed, could
Acts 27:19 third day cast out *t*.

TADMOR.
2 *Chr*. 8:4 Solomon built T.

**TAHAPANES, or TEHAPH-
NEHES.**
Jer. 2:16 the children of T. have
43:7 thus came they even to T.
46:14 punish in Noph and T.
Ezek. 30:18 at T. also the day sh.

TAHPENES.
1 *K*. 11:19 gave him sister of T.

TAIL.
Ex. 4:4 put out hand, ta. it by *t*.
Deut. 28:13 make head, not *t*. 44
Jud. 15:4 foxes, turned *t*. to *t*.
Job 40:17 behemoth mov. his *t*.
Is. 9:14 cut off fr. Is. head and *t*.
15 prophet teache. lies, he is *t*.
19:15 wo. wh. head or *t*. may do
Rev. 12:4 his *t*. dr. third of stars

TAILS.
Jud. 15:4 firebrand betw. two *t*.
Is. 7:4 two *t*. of these firebrands
Rev. 9:10 *t*. like scor. stings in *t*.
19 power in *t*. their *t*. like ser.

TAKE.
Gen. 13:9 if thou *t*. left hand
14:21 give me persons, *t*. goods
22:2 *t*. now thy son. th. only s.
24:3 shalt not *t*. wife to son, 37
31:32 discern what is thine, *t*. it
38:23 let her *t*. it to her, lest we
Ex. 6:7 I will *t*. you for a people
10:26 thereof must we *t*. serve L.
17:5 and thy rod *t*. in thy hand
20:7 not *t*. na. L. vain, *Deut*. 5:11
21:14 *t*. him from mine altar
23:8 sh. *t*. no gift, *Deut*. 16:19
34:9 *t*. us for inheritance
Lev. 25:46 ye sh. *t*. them for chil.
Num. 8:6 *t*. Levites from am. Is.
11:17 I will *t*. of spirit on thee
16:3 ye *t*. too much upon you, 7
Deut. 1:13 *t*. ye wise men
4:34 *t*. him a nation, fr. nation
25:8 if say, I like not to *t*. her
Jos. 10:42 their land did Josh. *t*.
20:4 they shall *t*. him into city
Jud. 14:15 called to *t*. th. we ha.
Ruth 2:10 should. *t*. knowledge
1 *Sam*. 2:16 then *t*. as soul desir.
17:46 and *t*. thy head from thee
19:14 S. sent messengers to *t*. D.
21:9 if thou wilt *t*. that, *t*. it
25:11 sh. I then *t*. bread and w.
2 *Sam*. 12:4 spared to *t*. his flock
2 *Sam*. 12:28 *t*. it, lest I *t*. city
16:9 go over, and *t*. off his head
19:19 king sh. *t*. to heart, 13:33
30 Mephibosh. said, Let him *t*.
1 *K*. 11:31 said to Jer. *t*. 10 piec.
14:3 *t*. ten loaves ; 18:40 *t*. prop.
20:18 war or peace, *t*. th. alive
22:26 *t*. Micaiah, car. him back
2 *K*. 5:16 urged to *t*. 20 I will *t*.
23 *t*. 2 talents ; 8:8 *t*. a present
10:14 *t*. th. alive ; 12:5 priests *t*.
19:30 *t*. root downward, *Is*. 37:31
1 *Chr*. 21:24 I will not *t*. that is
Ezr. 5:14 those did Cyrus *t*.
15 *t*. vessels, carry into temple
Job 23:10 he know. way that I *t*.
31:36 I wo. *t*. it on my shoulder
41:4 wilt thou *t*. him for serv. ?
Ps. 7:5 persecute my soul, and *t*.
51:11 *t*. not thy Holy Sp. fr. me
71:11 *t*. him, none to deliv. him
81:2 *t*. psalm ; 83:12 *t*. houses
89:33 kind. will I not *t*. fr. him
109:8 let another *t*. his office
119:43 *t*. not word of truth out
139:20 ene. *t*. thy name in vain
Prov. 6:25 neither let her *t*. thee
7:18 let us *t*. our fill of love
30:9 *t*. name of my God in vain
Ec. 5:15 shall *t*. nothing of labor
19 *t*. his portion, rejo. in labor
Is. 27:6 cause th. of J. to *t*. root
28:19 fr. time it goeth, sh. *t*. you
33:23 prey is divi. lame *t*. prey
40:24 their stock sh. not *t*. root
44:15 he will *t*. thereof
58:2 they *t*. deli. in approac. G.
66:21 I will *t*. of th. for priests
Jer. 2:22 *t*. soap ; 3:14 *t*. 1 of city
13:21 sh. not sorrows *t*. th. as ?
15:19 if thou *t*. precious fr. vile
18:22 have digged pit to *t*. me
19:1 *t*. of ancients of the people
25:9 I will *t*. families of north
10 will *t*. fr. th. voice of mirth
32:24 th. are come to city to *t*.
28 Nebu. king of Bab. sh. *t*. it
39:12 *t*. Jeremiah, look to him
50:15 *t*. vengeance upon her
51:26 shall not *t*. of thee stone
Lam. 2:13 wh. *t*. to wit. for th. ?
Ezek. 11:19 I will *t*. stony heart
24:5 *t*. choice of flock
25 when I *t*. fr. their strength
33:2 if peo. *t*. man of their coast
36:24 I will *t*. you from heathen
46:18 prince not *t*. peo.'s inher.

Dan. 7:18 saints shall *t.* kingd.
11:18 turn to isles, shall *t.* many
Hos. 14:2 *t.* with you words
Amos 5:12 afflict just, *t.* bribe
9:2 shall my hand *t.* them, 3
Jon. 4:3 *t.* I beseech th. my life
Mic. 2:2 covet fields, *t.* by viole.
Nah. 1:2 L. *t.* venge. on advers.
Hab. 1:10 th. sh. heap dust, *t.* it
Hag. 1:8 build house, I *t.* pleas.
2:23 will I *t.* thee, O Zerubbab.
Zec. 6:10 *t.* of them of captivity
Mat. 1:20 fear not to *t.* to th. M.
2:13 *t.* yo. child and its mother
6:25 *t.* no thought for your life,
    28, 31, 34 ; 10:19 ; *Mark* 13:11 ;
      Luke 12:11, 22, 26
15:26 it is not meet to *t.* chil-
    dren's bread, *Mark* 7:27
16:5 forg. to *t.* bread, *Mark* 8:14
18:16 *t.* with thee one or two
20:14 *t.* that thine is, go thy w.
24:17 let him on house-top not
    co. to *t.* any th., *Mark* 13:15
26:4 that they might *t.* Jesus by
    subtilty, *Mark* 14:1, 44
26 Je. took bread, said *t.* eat,
    Mark 14:22 ; 1 *Cor.* 11:24
52 they that *t.* sword sh. peri.
Mark 6:8 *t.* nothing for their
    journey, *Luke* 9:3
12:19 his br. *t.* wife, *Luke* 20:28
15:36 whether E. come to *t.* him
Luke 10:35 *t.* care of him ; 2:19 *t.*
    ease
14:9 begin with shame to *t.* low.
22:36 that hath purse let him *t.*
John 2:16 J. said, *t.* things hence
6:7 every one may *t.* a little
15 th. would come, *t.* by force
7:30 sou. to *t.* 32 ; 10:39 ; 11:57
10:17 lay down life, *t.* it aga. 18
16:15 sh. *t.* of mine and show it
17:15 shouldest *t.* th. out world
18:31 *t.* ye him, and judge him
19:6 *t.* him and crucify him
Acts 12:3 H. proceeded to *t.* Pet.
15:14 to *t.* of them a people
37 Barnab. determined to *t.* J.
38 P. thoug. not good to *t.* him
20:13 there intending to *t.* Paul

Acts 20:26 wherefore I *t.* you to
27:33 beson. them to *t.* meat, 34
1 *Cor.* 6:7 why not ra. *t.* wrong?
9:9 doth God *t.* care for oxen?
2 *Cor.* 11:20 if a man *t.* of you
1 *Tim.* 3:5 how *t.* care of church
2 *Tim.* 4:11 *t.* Mark, bring him
1 *Pet.* 2:20 if ye *t.* it patiently
Rev. 3:11 that no man *t.* thy cro.
5:9 thou art worthy to *t.* book
6:4 power to *t.* peace fr. earth
22:17 let him *t.* water of life

TAKE away.

Gen. 42:36 ye will *t.* Benjamin *a.*
Ex. 2:9 *t.* this child *a.* and nurse
10:17 may *t. a.* from me death
33:23 I will *t. away* my hand
Lev. 3:4 he *t. a.* 10, 15 ; 4:9 ; 7:4
4:31 *t. a.* all the fat thereof, 35
Num. 17:10 quite *t. a.* th. murm.
2 *Sam.* 4:11 shall I not *t.* you *a.*
5:6 except thou *t. a.* the blind
24:10 *t. a.* iniq. of thy servant
1 *K.* 2:31 *t. away* innocent blood
19:4 enough. O L. *t. a.* my life
10 seek my life to *t.* it *a.* 14
20:6 pleasant sh. servant *t. a.*
20:24 *t.* kings *a.* put captains
2 *K.* 2:3 Lord will *t. a.* master, 5
6:32 hath sent to *t. a.* my head
18:62 I come *t.* you *a. Is.* 36:17
1 *Chr.* 17:13 I wi. not *t.* mercy *a.*
Job 7:21 why dost not *t. a.* iniq.
24:2 they violently *t. a.* flocks
33:22 my Maker would *t.* me *a.*
36:18 beware, lest he *t.* thee *a.*

Ps. 31:13 devised to *t. a.* my life
52:5 he sh *t.* thee *a.* and pluck
58:9 he sh. *t.* them *a.* as with a
102:24 *t.* me not *a.* in midst of
Prov. 22:27 why should he *t. a.*
25:4 *t. a.* the dross from silver
5 *t. a.* wicked from behind king
Is. 1:25 will *t. away* all thy tin
10:2 to *t. a.* right from the poor
25:8 rebu. of his peo._sh. he *t. a.*
27:9 all fruit to *t. away* his sin
39:7 of thy sons shall they *t. a.*
58:9 if thou *t. away* from midst
Jer. 15:15 *t.* me not *a.* in long-s.
Ezek. 24:16 I *t. a.* desire of eyes
33:4 if sword come and *t. a.* 6
36:26 I will *t. a.* stony heart
Hos. 1:6 will utterly *t.* them *a.*
2:17 I will *t. a.* name of Baalim
5:14 *t. a.* none sh. rescue them
14:2 say unto him, *t. a.* iniquity
Amos 4:2 he will *t.* you *away*
Mic. 2:2 covet houses, *t.* them *a.*
Zep. 3:11 will *t. a.* out of midst
Zec. 9:7 *t. a.* blood out of mouth
Mal. 2:3 sh. *t.* you *a.* with dung
Mat. 5:40 *t. away* thy coat
Mark 14:36 Father, *t. a.* this cup
Luke 1:25 to *t. aw.* my reproach
17:31 not come down to *t.* it *a.*
John 11:39 Jesus said, *t. a.* stone
Rom. 11:27 when I sh. *t. a.* sins
1 *John* 3:5 manifest. to *t. a.* sins
Rev. 22:19 if any man *t. a.* from

See counsel.

TAKE heed.

Gen. 31:24 *t. h.* th. speak not, 29
Ex. 10:28 *t. h.* to thyself, 34:12 ;
    Deut. 4:9 ; 12:13, 19, 30 ;
    1 *Sam.* 19:2 ; 1 *Tim.* 4:16
19:12 *t. h.* to yourselves, *Deut.*
    2:4; 4:15, 23; 11:16; *Jos.* 23:11 ;
      Jer. 17:21
Num. 23:12 must I not *t. h.* to s.
Deut. 27:9 *t. h.* and heark. O Isr.
Jos. 22:5 *t. h.* to do commandm.
1 *K.* 2:4 if thy children *t. heed* to
    their way, 8:25 ; 2 *Chr.* 6:16
1 *Chr.* 28:10 *t. h.* for L. hath ch.
2 *Chr.* 19:6 *t. heed* what ye do
    7 let fear of L. be on you, *t. h.*
33:8 so that th. *t. h. Ezr.* 4:22
Job 36:21 *t. h.* reg. not iniquity
Ps. 39:1 I will *t. h.* to my ways
Ec. 7:21 *t.* no *h.* to words spoken
Is. 7:4 say unto him, *t. heed*
Jer. 9:4 *t. h.* every one of neigh.
Hos. 4:10 left off to *t. h.* to Lord
Mal. 2:15 *t. heed* to your spir. 16
Mat. 6:1 *t. h.* do not alms bef. m.
18:10 *t. h.* that ye despise not
24:4 *t. h.* lest any man deceive
    you, *Mark* 13:5
Mark 4:24 *t. h.* what you hear
13:9 *t. h.* to yourself, *Luke* 17:3 ;
      21:34 ; *Acts* 5:35 ; 20:28
23 *t. h.* I foretold. 33 *t. h.* watch
Luke 8:18 *t. h.* the. how ye hear
11:35 *t. h.* that lig. be not dark.
21:8 *t. h.* ye be not deceived
Acts 22:26 *t. heed* wh. thou doest
Rom. 11:21 *t. h.* lest he spare not
1 *Cor.* 3:10 man *t. h.* how he bui.
10:12 standeth *t. h.* lest he fall
Gal. 5:15 *t. h.* ye be not consum.
Heb. 3:12 *t. h.* lest heart of unbe.
2 *Pet.* 1:19 ye do well to *t. heed*

TAKE hold.

Ex. 15:14 sorrow *t. h.* of inhabi.
Deut. 32:41 if hand *t. h.* of judg.
Job 27:20 terrors *t. h.* on him as
36:17 justice *t. hold* on thee
38:13 mi. *t. h.* on ends of earth
Ps. 69:24 let anger *t. h.* of them
Prov. 2:19 nor *t. h.* of pa. of life
5:5 down, her steps *t. h.* on hell

Ec. 7:18 good that th. *t. h.* of
Is. 3:6 when a man *t. h.* of brot.
4:1 sev. wom. *t. h.* of one man
27:5 let him *t. h.* of my strength
6:4 stir. himself to *t. h.* of thee
Mic. 6:14 *t. h.* but sh. not deliver
Zec. 1:6 not *t. h.* of your fathe. ?
8:23 ten men *t. hold* of him
Luke 20:20 mi. *t. h.* of his words

TAKE up.

Gen. 41:34 *t. up* 5th part of land
Jos. 4:5 *t. up* every man a stone
2 *K.* 2:1 when L. would *t. up* El.
4:36 *t. up* son ; 6:7 *t. up* iron
9:25 *t. up* cast him into field
Ps. 16:4 nor *t. up* names
27:10 then the L. will *t.* me *up*
Jer. 9:10 mountains *t. up* weep.
18 *t. up* wail. 38:10 *t. up* Jer.
Ezek. 19:1 *t. up* lam. for princes
Amos 3:5 *t. up* snare from earth
5:1 hear word I *t. up* aga. you
Jon. 1:12 *t.* me *up* and cast me
Mat. 9:6 *t. up* bed, *Mark* 2:9, 11 ;
      Luke 5:24 ; *John* 5:8, 11, 12
16:24 *t. up* cross, *Mark* 8:34 ;
      10:21 ; *Luke* 9:23
17:27 *t. up* fish that first cometh

TAKEN.

Gen. 2:23 she was *t.* out of man
12:15 wo. was *t.* into P.'s house
19 I might have *t.* her to wife
14:14 Abr. heard brother was *t.*
18:27 I have *t.* upon me to speak
20:3 woman_thou hast *t.* is a w.
31:16 riches G. hath *t.* fr. father
Num. 3:12 L. hev. 8:16, 18 ; 18:6
5:13 nei. she be *t.* with manner
31:49 ha. *t.* sum of men of war
Deut. 20:7 wife, and hath not *t.*
24:1 when a man hath *t.* wife
Jos. 7:15 he that is *t.* be burnt
16 the tribe of Judah was *t.*
17 Zabdi was *t.* 18 Ac. was *t.*
Jud. 15:6 because he had *t.* wife
17:2 1,100 shekels that were *t.*
1 *Sam.* 4:11 ark *t.* 17, 19, 21, 22
7:14 cities wh. Philistines had *t.*
10:21 S. *t.* 12:3 ox have I *t. ?*
12:4 nor *t.* aught of man's hand
14:41 Saul and Jonathan were *t.*
42 cast lots, Jonathan was *t.*
30:19 noth. lacking they had *t.*
2 *Sam.* 12:9 hast *t.* his wife, 10
16:8 thou art *t.* in mischief
23:6 because they cannot be *t.*
1 *K.* 16:18 Zimri saw city was *t.*
2 *K.* 2:10 if thou see me when *t.*
18:10 ninth year of Ho. Sama. *t.*
Ezr. 9:2 they have *t.* of daught.
10:2 *t.* strange wives, 14, 17, 18
Neh. 5:15 hand *t.* of them bread
Est. 2:15 *t.* Esther for daughter
Job 16:12 hath *t.* me by my neck
24:24 they are *t.* out of the way
Ps. 9:15 in net hid is their foot *t.*
10:2 let them be *t.* in devices
59:12 let th. be *t.* in their pride
119:111 thy testimonies have I *t.*
Prov. 3:26 keep foot fr. being *t.*
6:2 art *t.* with words of mouth
11:6 transgressors shall be *t.*
Ec. 3:14 nor any thing *t.* front it
7:26 sinner shall be *t.* by her
Is. 7:5 have *t.* evil counsel agai.
8:15 many be broken, snared, *t.*
23:8 who hath *t.* coun. ag. T.'?
24:18 be *t.* in snare, *Jer.* 48:44
28:13 mi. be broken, snared, *t.*
33:20 tabernacle not be *t.* down
41:9 wh. I ha. *t.* fr. ends of earth
53:8 he was *t.* from prison and
Jer. 6:11 husband with wife be *t.*
12:2 planted, they have *t.* root
34:3 thon sh. surely be *t.* 38:23
38:28 till day that Jerus. was *t.*
39:5 when they had *t.* him

40:1 when he had *t.* him, being
48:1 Kiriath. is *t.* ? thou sh. be *t.*
41 Kerioth is *t.* 46 sons are *t.*
49:20 hear counsel *t.* against Ed.
50:2 Babylon is *t.* 24 ; 51:31, 41
Lam. 4:20 anointed of L. was *t.*
Ezek. 12:13 prince of Israel be *t.*
16:20 hast *t.* sons and daughte.
17:12 hath *t.* the king thereof
13 *t.* of king's seed, *t.* oath
20 he shall be *t.* in my snare
18:17 hath *t.* off his hand fr. po.
19:4 he was *t.* in their pit, 8
21:23 remembra. that they be *t.*
Dan. 5:2 whi. his father had *t.* 8
Amos 3:4 if ye have *t.* nothing, 5
12 so sh. I be *t.* that dw. in S.
Mat. 9:15 bridegroom be *t.* fr. th.
21:43 kingd. of God be *t.* fr. you
24:40 one *t.* *Luke* 17:34, 35, 36
28:12 had *t.* counsel
Mark 4:25 fr. him *t.* that which
9:36 he had *t.* him in arms
Luke 5:5 toiled, have *t.* nothing
19:8 if I have *t.* any thing from
John 7:44 some wo. have *t.* him
Acts 2:23 have *t.* by wick. hands
8:33 for his life is *t.* from earth
23:27 this man was *t.* of Jews
Rom. 9:6 word ha. *t.* none effect
1 *Thes.* 2:17 *t.* from you a sh. ti.
2 *Thes.* 2:7 until he be *t.*
2 *Tim.* 2:26 who are *t.* captive
2 *Pet.* 2:12 made to be destroyed
Rev. 11:17 th. hast *t.* great power
19:20 beast was *t.* and wi. him

TAKEN away.

Gen. 21:25 Abim.'s ser. had *t. a.*
27:36 he hath *t. a.* my blessing
31:1 J. hath *t. a.* all that is our
Ex. 14:11 hast *t.* us *away* to die
Lev. 14:43 he hath *t. a.* stones
Deut. 26:14 nor *t. away* aught
Jud. 18:24 have *t. a.* my gods
1 *Sam.* 21:6 day when it was *t. a.*
1 *K.* 22:43 high places were not
    t. away, 2 *K.* 12:3; 14:4;
    2 *Chr.* 15:17; 20:33
2 *K.* 2:9 bef. I be *t. a.* from thee
Job 1:21 L. gave, L. hath *t. aw.*
20:19 hath violently *t. a.* house
27:2 who hath *t. a.* my judgme.
34:5 God hath *t. a.* my judgm.
20 mighty be *t. a.* with. hand
Ps. 85:3 th. hast *t. a.* thy wrath
Prov. 4:16 their sleep is *t. away*
Is. 6:7 thine iniquity is *t. away*
8:4 spoil of Samaria sh. be *t. a.*
16:10 glad. *t. a.* 17:1 Da. *t. a.*
52:5 my peo. is *t. a.* for naught
57:1 merciful *t. a.* righteo. *t. a.*
64:6 our iniquities have *t.* us *a.*
Jer. 16:5 I have *t. aw.* my peace
Ezek. 33:6 he is *t. a.* in his iniq.
Amos 4:10 I ha. *t. a.* your horses
Mic. 2:9 ye have *t. aw.* my glory
Zep. 3:15 L. ha. *t. a.* thy judgm.
Mat. 13:12 fr. him *t. a.* that he
    hath, 25:29 ; *Luke* 8:18 ; 19:26
Luke 10:42 good part not be *t. a.*
John 19:31 that th. might be *t. a.*
Acts 27:20 sho. be saved was *t. a.*
1 *Cor.* 5:2 done th. might be *t. a.*

TAKEN hold.

1 *K.* 9:9 have *t. h.* on other gods
Job 30:16 days of afflic. have *t. h.*
Ps. 40:12 iniquities have *t. hold*
Is. 21:3 pangs have *t. h.* on me

TAKEN up.

Ex. 40:36 cloud was *t. up* from
Num. 9:17 w. cloud was *t. up,* 21
2 *Sam.* 18:9 Absalom was *t. up*
Jer. 29:22 of th. sh. be *t. up* curse
Ezek. 36:3 ye are *t. up* in the lips
Luke 9:17 *t. up* of fragments
Acts 1:9 he was *t. up,* a cloud
11 Jesus which is *t. up* fr. you

---

22 unto day he was *t. up* fr. us
20:9 Eutychus fell, *t. up* dead

TAKEST heed.

Ps. 144:3 that *t.* knowl. of him ?
Is. 58:3 thou *t.* no knowledge
Luke 19:21 *t. up* thou layedst not

TAKEST heed.

1 *Chr.* 22:13 if *t. h.* to fulfil statu.

TAKETH.

Ex. 20:7 that *t.* his name in vain,
    Deut. 5:11
32:11 an eagle *t.* them, beareth
Jos. 7:14 tribe L. *t.* shall come
Job 5:13 he *t.* wise in their crafti-
    ness, 1 *Cor.* 3:19
9:12 *t.* away, who can hinder ?
12:20 and *t.* away understand.
27:8 what is hope when God *t.* ?
Ps. 118:7 L. *t.* my part with th.
149:4 L. *t.* pleasure in his people
Prov. 1:19 which *t.* away life of
16:32 better than he that *t.* city
26:17 one that *t.* a dog by ears
Ec. 1:3 of his labor which he *t.*
Ec. 2:23 heart *t.* not rest in nig.
Is. 40:15 he *t.* up isles as a little
51:18 nor is there that *t.* her by
Ezek. 16:32 wh. *t.* strangers inst.
33:4 *t.* not warning ; 5 *t.* warn.
Mat. 4:5 devil *t.* him up into ho.
10:38 that *t.* not his cross, and
12:45 *t.* sev. spirits, *Luke* 11:26
Mark 4:15 Satan cometh, and *t.*
    away word, *Luke* 8:12
5:40 he *t.* father and mother of
9:18 wher. he *t.* him, he teareth
Luke 6:30 that *t.* goods, ask nor
9:39 a spirit *t.* him, he suddenly
John 1:29 Lamb of G. *t.* away sin
10:18 no man *t.* it from me
16:22 your joy no man *t.* fr. you
21:13 Je. then cometh, *t.* bread
1 *Cor.* 11:21 every one *t.* bef. an.
Heb. 10:9 he *t.* away the first

TAKETH hold.

Job 21:6 tremb. *t. h.* on my flesh
Prov. 30:28 spider *t. h.* wi. hands
Is. 56:6 that *t. h.* of my covenant

TAKING.

2 *Chr.* 19:7 with God no *t.* of gif.
Job 5:3 I have seen foolish *t.* root
Ps. 119:9 by *t.* heed thereto
Jer. 50:46 at noise of *t.* of Babyl.
Hos. 11:3 I taught Ephraim also
    to go, *t.* them by their arms
Mat. 6:27 by *t.* tho. *Luke* 12:25
Luke 19:22 *t.* up I laid not down
John 11:13 he had spok. of *t.* rest
2 *Cor.* 2:13 *t.* my leave of them, 1
3 *John* 7 th. went forth *t.* nothi.

TALE, s.

Ps. 90:9 we spend years as a *t.*
Ezek. 22:9 carry *t.* to shed blood
Luke 24:11 th. words seemed as *t.*

TALEBEARER.

Lev. 19:16 shalt not go as a *t.*
Prov. 11:13 *t.* rev. secrets, 20:19
18:8 words *t.* are wounds, 26:22
26:20 where is no *t.* strife

TALE, reckoning.

Ex. 5:8 the *t.* of bricks which
    18 yet shall he deliver the *t.* of
1 *Sam.* 18:27 foreski. in *t.* to king
1 *Chr.* 9:28 bring vessels in by *t.*

TALENT.

Ex. 25:39 *t.* of pure gold, 37:24
36:27 sockets, a *t.* for a socket
2 *Sam.* 12:30 weight of crown a *t.*
1 *K.* 20:39 shalt pay a *t.* of silver
2 *K.* 5:22 give them a *t.* of silver
23:33 of *t.* of gold, 2 *Chr.* 36:3
Zec. 5:7 th. was lifted a *t.* of lead
Mat. 25:25 I went and hid thy *t.*
28 take therefore the *t.* fr. him
Rev. 16:21 sto. about weight of *t.*

TALENTS.

Ex. 38:24 gold of off. was 29 *t.*
27 100 *t.* of silver were cast
1 *K.* 16:24 bought hill for two *t.*
2 *K.* 5:5 Naaman took ten *t.*
23 said, Be content, take two *t.*
15:19 Menahem gave P. 1,000 *t.*
18:14 appointed to Hezek. 300 *t.*
23:33 trib. of 100 *t.* 2 *Chr.* 36:3
1 *Chr.* 19:6 Ammon. sent 1,000 *t.*
29:4 David gave 3,000 *t.* of gold
    7 gold 5,000 *t.* of silver 10,000 *t.*
2 *Chr.* 25:9 what do for 100 *t.* ?
27:5 child. of Ammon gave 100 *t.*
Mat. 18:24 one ow. him 10,000 *t.*
25:15 to one he gave five *t.*

See GOLD, SILVER.

TALITHA cumi.

Mark 5:41 he said unto her, *t. c.*

TALK, Substantive.

Job 11:2 man full of *t.* be justi. ?
15:3 reason wi. unprofitable *t.* ?
Prov. 14:23 *t.* of lips tendeth to
Ec. 10:13 end of *t.* is mischievo.
Mat. 22:15 mi. entangle him in *t.*

TALK, Verb.

Num. 11:17 I will come and *t.*
Deut. 5:24 seen that God doth *t.*
6:7 shall *t.* of them when thou
1 *Sam.* 2:3 *t.* no more so proudly
2 *K.* 18:26 *t.* not with us in the
1 *Chr.* 16:9 *t.* ye of all his won-
    drous works, *Ps.* 105:2
Job 13:7 will ye *t.* deceitfully ?
Ps. 69:26 they *t.* to the grief of
71:24 my tongue shall *t.* of thy
77:12 I will *t.* of thy doings
119:27 so shall I *t.* of thy works
145:11 speak of thy king. and *t.*
Prov. 6:22 when th. awa. it sh. *t.*
24:2 and their lips *t.* of mischi.
Jer. 12:1 let me *t.* with th. of thy
Ezek. 3:22 arise, I will *t.* wi. thee
Dan. 10:17 how can thy serv. *t.*
John 14:30 I will not *t.* much

TALKED.

Gen. 45:15 his breth. *t.* with him
Ex. 20:22 I *t.* with you, *Deut.* 5:4
33:9 and the Lord *t.* with Moses
34:29 his face shone while he *t.*
1 *Sam.* 14:19 Saul *t.* unto priest
2 *Chr.* 25:16 it ca. to pass as he *t.*
Jer. 38:25 if princes hear I ha. *t.*
Luke 9:30 *t.* with him two mer
24:32 heart burn while he *t.*
John 4:27 marvelled that he *t.*
Acts 10:27 as P. *t.* with Cornelius
20:11 *t.* long, till break of day
26:31 th. *t.* between themselves
Rev. 21:15 he th. *t.* with me had

TALKERS.

Ezek. 36:3 taken up in lips of *t.*
Tit. 1:10 there are many vain *t.*

TALKEST, ETH.

Jud. 6:17 show me a sign thou *t.*
1 *K.* 1:14 while thou *t.* with king
Ps. 37:30 his tongue *t.* of judgm.
John 4:27 why *t.* thou with her ?
9:37 it is he that *t.* with thee

TALKING.

Gen. 17:22 he left off *t.* with him
1 *K.* 18:27 he is *t.* or pursuing
Est. 6:14 while they were *t.* wi.
Ezek. 33:30 people are *t.* ag. thee
Mat. 17:3 Mo. and Elias *t.* with
    him, *Mark* 9:4
Rev. 4:1 voice of a trumpet *t.*

TALKING.

Job 29:9 the princes refrained *t.*
Eph. 5:4 filthiness, nor foolish *t.*

TALL.

Deut. 2:10 *t.* as Anak. 21 ; 9:2
1 *K.* 19:23 will cut down *t.* cedar-
    trees, *Is.* 37:24

TALLER.
Deut. 1:28 people is *t.* than we

TAMAR.
Gen. 38:6 a wife, wh. na. was T.
24 was told Judah, T. hath
Ruth 4:12 Pharez, wh. T. bare to
　Judah, 1 *Chr.* 2:4; *Mat.* 1:3
2 *Sam.* 13:1 a fair sister, na. T.
2 *Amm.* fell sick for T. 22, 32
14:27 daugh. wh. name was T.
Ezek. 47:19 side southward fr. T.

TAME, ED.
Mark 5:4 neith. could man *t.* him
Jam. 3:7 of sea is *t.* hath been *t.*
　8 the tongue can no man *t.*

TAMMUZ.
Ezek. 8:14 wom. weeping for T.

TANNER.
Acts. 9:43 Pe. tarried wi. Si. a *t.*
10:6 lodged with Simon a *t.* 32

TAPESTRY. *See* COVERINGS.

TARE.
2 *Sam.* 13:31 king *t.* his garmen.
2 *K.* 2:24 two she-bears *t.* 42 chil.
Mark 9:20 spi. *t.* him, *Luke* 9:42

TARES.
Mat. 13:25 his enemy sowed *t.*
26 then appeared the *t.* also
29 lest while you gather up *t.*

TARGET, S.
1 *Sam.* 17:6 Gol. had a *t.* of brass
1 *K.* 10:16 Solom. made 200 *t.* 600
　shekels to one *t.* 2 *Chr.* 9:15
2 *Chr.* 14:8 army that bare *t.*

TARRY.
Gen. 19:2 *t.* all night, and wash
27:44 *t.* with Laban a few days
30:27 if I found favor in eyes *t.*
45:9 come down to me, *t.* not
Ex. 12:39 thrust out, cou. not *t.*
24:14 *t.* ye here till we come
Num. 22:19 I pray you, *t.* here
Jud. 5:28 why *t.* wheels of ch. ?
6:18 I will *t.* until thou come
Ruth 1:13 would ye *t.* for them
1 *Sam.* 1:23 *t.* until th. ha. wea.
10:8 seven days shalt thou *t.*
2 *Sam.* 10:5 at Jeri. till beards
　be grown, 1 *Chr.* 19:5
11:12 *t.* to-day ; 15:28 I will *t.*
18:14 Joab said, I may not *t.*
19:7 th. will not *t.* one with th.
2 *K.* 2:2 *t.* here, L. sent me, 4, 6
7:9 if we *t.* till morning light
14:10 gl. of this, and *t.* at home
Ps. 101:7 liar not *t.* in my sight
Prov. 23:30 that *t.* long at wine
Is. 46:13 my salvation sh. not *t.*
Jer. 14:8 turneth to *t.* for night
Hab. 2:3 though it *t.* wait for it,
　for it will not *t.*
Mat. 26:38 *t.* and wa. *Mark* 14:34
Luke 24:29 he went to *t.* with th.
　49 *t.* ye in city of Jerusalem
John 4:40 besought that he w. *t.*
21:22 if I will that he *t.* 23
Acts 10:48 th. prayed Peter to *t.*
18:20 they desired Paul to *t.*
28:14 were desired to *t.* 7 days
1 *Cor.* 11:33 wheref. *t.* one for a.
16:7 I tr. to *t.* a while with you
8 I will *t.* at Ephesus until P.
1 *Tim.* 3:15 if I *t.* long thou may.
Heb. 10:37 will come, and not *t.*

TARRIED.
Gen. 24:54 Abraham's servant *t.*
28:11 Jacob *t.* there all night
31:54 J. and Leb. *t.* all night
Num. 9:19 wh. cloud *t.* long, 22
Jud. 3:25 *t.* they were ashamed
19:8 they *t.* till the afternoon
Ruth 2:7 save that she *t.* a little
1 *Sam.* 13:8 he *t.* 7 days accord.
2 *Sam.* 15:17 king *t.* in place

20:5 he *t.* longer than set time
Ps. 68:12 she that *t.* divid. spoil
Mat. 25:5 bridegroom *t.* th. slept
Luke 1:21 people marvelled he *t.*
　2:43 child Jesus *t.* in Jerusalem
John 3:22 he *t.* and baptized
Acts 9:43 P. *t.* many days in Jop.
18:18 Paul *t.* a good while at C.
20:5 going befo. *t.* for us at Tr.
21:4 finding disci. we *t.* 7 days
　10 as we *t.* many days at Cesa.
25:6 Festus *t.* at Jerus. ten days
27:33 fourteenth day ye *t.* fast.
28:12 at Syracuse, we *t.* 3 days

TARRIEST, ETH.
1 *Sam.* 30:24 part that *t.* by stuff
Mic. 5:7 that *t.* not for a man,
Acts 22:16 and now why *t.* thou ?

TARRYING.
Ps. 40:17 make no *t.* O G. 70:5

TARSHISH.
Gen. 10:4 Elisha, T. 1 *Chr.* 1:7
1 *K.* 10:22 for the king had at sea
　a navy of T. 2 *Chr.* 9:21
2 *Chr.* 20:36 make ships go to T.
　37 broken, not able to go to T.
Ps. 48:7 th. breakest ships of T.
72:10 the kings of T. shall bring
Is. 2:16 Lord on all ships of T.
23:1 howl, ye ships of T. 14
　6 pass over to T. howl, ye
　10 thy land, O daughter of T.
60:9 the ships of T. shall wait
66:19 those that escape to T.
Jer. 10:9 silver is brought fr. T.
Ezek. 27:12 T. was thy merchant
　25 ships of T. did sing of thee
38:13 the merchants of T. shall
Jon. 1:3 rose up to flee unto T.
4:2 I fled before unto T. for I

TARSUS.
Acts 9:11 inq. for one Saul of T.
　30 the brethren sent him to T.
11:25 Barnabas departed to T.
21:39 who am a Jew of T. 22:3

TARTAK.
2 *K.* 17:31 made T. their god
TARTAN. 2 *K.* 18:17

TASK, S.
Ex. 5:13 fulfil works, daily *t.*
　14 why not fulfilled *t.* in mak.
　19 not minish fr. your daily *t.*

TASKMASTERS.
Ex. 1:11 they set over them *t.*
3:7 cry by reason of their *t.*
5:10 *t.* told people ; 13 *t.* hasted

TASTE, Substantive.
Ex. 16:31 *t.* of manna like wafers
Num. 11:8 *t.* was as *t.* of fresh oil
Job 6:6 any *t.* in white of an egg?
　30 my *t.* disc. perverse things
Ps. 119:103 sw. thy word to *t.* !
Prov. 24:13 honey-co. sweet to *t.*
Cant. 2:3 fruit sweet to my *t.*
Jer. 48:11 his *t.* remained in him

TASTE, Verb.
1 *Sam.* 14:43 but *t.* a little honey
2 *Sam.* 3:35 if I *t.* bread or aught
19:35 can servant *t.* what I eat?
Job 12:11 doth not mouth *t.* meat
Ps. 34:8 O *t.* and see L. is good
Jon. 3:7 nor flock *t.* any thing
Mat. 16:28 so. stand. here not *t.*
　of death, *Mark* 9:1 ; *Lu.* 9:27
Luke 14:24 none bidden *t.* of sup.
John 8:52 keep say. nev. *t.* death
Col. 2:21 touch not, *t.* not,
Heb. 2:9 sho. *t.* death for ev. man

TASTED, ETH.
1 *Sam.* 14:24 none *t.* 29 I *t.* hon.
Job 34:3 words as mouth *t.* meat
Dan. 5:2 Belshaz. while he *t.* wi.
Mat. 27:34 wh. he had *t.* thereof
John 2:9 ruler *t.* wat. made wine

Heb. 6:4 have *t.* of heavenly gift
1 *Pet.* 2:3 *t.* that L. is gracious

TATTLERS.
1 *Tim.* 5:13 not only idle, but *t.*

TATNAI. *Ezr.* 5:3, 6

TAUGHT.
Deut. 4:5 I have *t.* you statutes
31:22 Moses *t.* the children of Is.
Jud. 8:16 he *t.* men of Succoth
2 *K.* 17:28 *t.* them how to fear L.
2 *Chr.* 6:27 ha. *t.* them good way
17:9 Levites *t.* people in Judah
23:13 rejoiced, *t.* to sing praise
30:22 that *t.* knowledge of L.
35:3 Josiah said to L. that *t.* Is.
Neh. 8:9 Levites that *t.* people
Ps. 71:17 hast *t.* me, 119:102
119:171 hast *t.* me thy statutes
Prov. 4:4 he *t.* me also, and said
　11 I *t.* thee in way of wisdom
31:1 prophecy his moth. *t.* him
Ec. 12:9 he *t.* people knowledge
Is. 29:13 fear *t.* by prec. of men
40;13 being counsel. *t.* him, 14
54:13 thy child. shall be *t.* of G.
Jer. 2:33 theref. hast th. *t.* wick.
9:5 they *t.* tongues to speak lies
　14 after Baalim, whi. fathers *t.*
12:16 *t.* my peo. to swear by B.
13:21 *t.* them to be captains
28:16 *t.* them rebellion ag. Lord
29:32 he hath *t.* rebellion ag. L.
32:33 tho' I *t.* them, rising early
Ezek. 23:48 women *t.* not lewdn.
Hos. 10:11 Ephr. is as a heifer *t.*
11:3 I *t.* Ephraim to go, taking
Zec. 13:5 *t.* me to keep cattle
Mat. 7:29 he *t.* them as one hav-
　ing authority, *Mark* 1:22
28:15 th. took money, did as *t.*
Mark 6:30 told things done and *t.*
10:1 as he wont he *t.* th. again
Luke 11:1 as John *t.* his disciples
13:26 thou hast *t.* in our streets
John 6:45 they sh. be all *t.* of G.
7:14 Je. went into temple. *t.* 28 ;
　Mark 12:35 ; *Lu.* 19:47 ; 20:1
8:2 peo. came, he sat and *t.* th.
　28 as my Father hath *t.* me, I
18:20 I ever *t.* in the syn. gogue
Acts 4:2 grieved that they *t.* peo.
5:21 entered temple early and *t.*
11:26 P. and Barn. *t.* peo. 14:21
15:1 certain men *t.* the brethren
18:25 Apollos *t.* dilig. thi. of L.
20:20 I showed you and *t.* pub.
22:3 *t.* accord. to manner of law
Gal. 1:12 nor *t.* but by revelation
6:6 let him that is *t.* communi.
Eph. 4:21 if ye have been *t.*
Col. 2:7 faith, as ye have been *t.*
1 *Thes.* 4:9 ye are *t.* of G. to love
2 *Thes.* 2:15 hold tradi. ye have *t.*
Tit. 1:9 word, as he hath been *t.*
1 *John* 2:27 as anoint. ha. *t.* you
Rev. 2:14 *t.* Bal. to cast stum.-bl.

TAUNT, ING.
Jer. 24:9 I deliver them to be a *t.*
Ezek. 5:15 so it be repro. and *t.*
Hab. 2:6 these take up a *t.* prov.

TAXATION.
2 *K.* 23:35 exacted of every one *t.*

TAXED.
2 *K.* 23:35 Jehoiakim *t.* the land
Luke 2:1 a decree world sho. be *t.*
　3 all went to be *t.* 5 J. to be *t.*

TAXES, ING.
Dan. 11:20 stand up a raiser of *t.*
Luke 2:2 *t.* first made when Cy.
Acts 5:37 rose up J. in days of *t.*

TEACH.
Ex. 4:15 I will *t.* wh. ye sh. do
35:34 G. put in his heart he *t.*
Lev. 10:11 may *t.* Is. all statutes
14:57 to *t.* when uncl. and clean

TEACH

Deut. 4:1 hearken to judgm. I *t.*
10 that they may *t.* their child.
14 L. commanded me to *t.* 6:1
31:19 write and *t.* child. of Is.
33:10 they sh. *t.* Ja. judgments
Jud. 13:8 *t.* us what we shall do
1 Sam. 12:23 wi. *t.* you good way
2 Sam. 1:18 bade th. *t.* use of bow
2 Chr. 17:7 *t.* in cities of Judah.
Ezr. 7:10 to *t.* in Israel statutes
Job 21:22 shall any *t.* G. knowl.
27:11 will *t.* you by hand of G.
32:7 multitude of years *t.* wisd.
37:19 *t.* us what we shall say
Ps. 25:8 he will *t.* sinners
  9 meek will he guide and *t.*
Ps. 25:12 him the. fear. L. sh. he *t.*
34:11 I will *t.* you fear of the L.
51:13 I *t.* transgress. thy ways
90:12 *t.* us to number our days
105:22 and *t.* his senators wisd.
Prov. 9:9 *t.* a just man, he incre.
Is. 2:3 *t.* us his ways, Mic. 4:2
28:9 whom sh. he *t.* knowledge
  26 G. doth instruct and *t.* him
Jer. 9:20 *t.* your daught. wailing
31:34 *t.* no more nei. Heb. 8:11
Ezek. 44:23 *t.* my peo. difference
Dan. 1:4 whom they might *t.*
Mic. 3:11 priests ther. *t.* for hire
Hab. 2:19 saith to stone, it sh. *t.*
Mat. 5:19 *t.* men so; 28:19 *t.* na.
Luke 11:1 Lord, *t.* us to pray
12:12 Holy Gh. *t.* what to say
John 7:35 *t.* Gent. 9:34 dost *t.* ?
14:26 Holy Gh. *t.* you all things
Acts 1:1 Jesus began to do and *t.*
4:18 nor *t.* in name of Je. 5:28
5:42 ceased not to *t.* Jesus Chr.
16:21 *t.* customs wh. not lawful
1 Cor. 4:17 as I *t.* every where in
11:14 doth not nature itself *t.*
14:19 by voice I might *t.* others
1 Tim. 1:3 charge *t.* no oth. doc.
2:12 I suffer not a woman to *t.*
3:2 bish. apt to *t.* 2 Tim. 2:24
4:11 these thi. command and *t.*
6:2 these things *t.* and exhort
  3 if any *t.* otherw. he is proud
2 Tim. 2:2 men able to *t.* others
Tit. 2:4 *t.* yo. women to be sober
Heb. 5:12 need that one *t.* you
1 John 2:27 need not that any *t.*
Rev. 2:20 sufferest Jezebel to *t.*

See BEGAN.

TEACH me.

Job 6:24 *t. me,* will hold tongue
34:32 wh. I see not, *t.* thou *me*
Ps. 25:4 *t. me* paths ; 5 le. and *t.*
27:11 *t. me* thy way, O L. 86:11
119:12 *t. me* thy statutes, 26, 33, 64, 68, 124, 135
  66 *t. me* judgm. 108 *t. m.* thy j.
143:10 *t. me* to do thy will

TEACH thee.

Ex. 4:12 I *t. t.* what th. sh. say
Deut. 17:11 sentence they sh. *t. t.*
Job 8:10 fath. sh. they not *t. t.* ?
12:7 ask beasts, they shall *t. t.*
  8 speak to earth, it shall *t. t.*
33:33 hold peace, I sh. *t. t.* wisd.
Ps. 32:8 will *t. t.* in way sh. go.
45:4 ri. hand sh. *t. t.* ter. things

TEACH them.

Ex. 18:20 shalt *t. t.* ordinances
24:12 writ. th. thou mayest *t. t.*
Deut. 4:9 *t. them* thy son's sons
5:31 judgments thou shalt *t. t.*
6:7 *t. them* to thy children, 11:19
Jud. 3:2 Is. might know to *t. t.*
1 K. 8:36 thou *t. them* good way
2 K. 17:27 let him *t. t.* manner of
Ezr. 7:25 *t.* ye *t.* that know not
Ps. 132:12 keep testimony I *t. t.*
Mat. 5:19 whoso shall do and *t. t.*
Mark 6:34 began *t. t.* many thi.
8:31 to *t. t.* Son of man suffer

TEACHER.

1 Chr. 25:8 as well *t.* as scholar
Hab. 2:18 profit. image, *t.* of lies
John 3:2 thou art a *t.* come fr. G.
Rom. 2:20 confident thou art a *t.*
1 Tim. 2:7 of Gent. 2 Tim. 1:11

TEACHERS.

Ps. 119:99 more underst. than *t.*
Prov. 5:13 not obeyed voice of *t.*
Is. 30:20 yet sh. not *t.* be remov.
  but thine eyes sh. see thy *t.*
43:27 thy *t.* have transgressed
Acts 13:1 at Anti. were certain *t.*
1 Cor. 12:28 proph. *t.* 29 all *t.* ?
Eph. 4:11 evangelists, pastors, *t.*
1 Tim. 1:7 desir. to be *t.* of law
2 Tim. 4:3 heap to themselves *t.*
Tit. 2:3 women be *t.* of good thi.
Heb. 5:12 time ye ought to be *t.*
2 Pet. 2:1 sh. be false *t.* am. you

TEACHEST.

Ps. 94:12 blessed is man thou *t.*
Mat. 22:16 *t.* way of G. in truth, Mark 12:14 ; Luke 20:21
Acts 21:21 *t.* Jews to forsake M.
Rom. 2:21 *t.* ano. *t.* not thyself ?

TEACHETH.

2 Sam. 22:35 he *t.* my hands to war, Ps. 18:34
Job 35:11 who *t.* more th. beasts
36:22 G. exalt. who *t.* like him ?
Ps. 94:10 that *t.* man knowledge
144:1 which *t.* my hands to war
Prov. 6:13 wick. man *t.* wi. fing.
Prov. 16:23 hea. of wise *t.* his m.
Is. 9:15 the prophet that *t.* lies
48:17 I am thy G. which *t.* thee
Acts 21:28 man that *t.* all men
Rom. 12:7 he that *t.* on teaching
1 Cor. 2:13 wis. *t.* but wh. H. G. *t.*
Gal. 6:6 communi. to him th. *t.*
1 John 2:27 same anointing *t.* you

TEACHING.

2 Chr. 15:3 Is. without *t.* priest
Jer. 32:33 rising early and *t.* th.
Mat. 4:23 Jesus went about Galilee, *t.* 9:35 ; Luke 13:10
15:9 *t.* for doctrines commandments of men, Mark 7:7
26:55 I sat daily *t.* in temple
28:20 *t.* them to observe all thi.
Luke 23:5 *t.* throughout all Jewry
Acts 5:25 the apostles *t.* the peo.
15:35 Paul and B. in Antioch *t.*
Rom. 12:7 he that teacheth on *t.*
Col. 1:28 warning and *t.* ev. man
3:16 *t.* and admonish. one ano.
Tit. 1:11 *t.* things they ought not
2:12 *t.* us, denying ungodliness

TEAR, Verb.

Jud. 8:7 then will I *t.* your flesh
Ps. 7:2 lest *t.* my soul like lion
35:15 they did *t.* me, ceased not
50:22 consider this, lest I *t.* you
Jer. 15:3 I will appoint dogs to *t.*
16:7 nor shall men *t.* themselves
Ezek. 13:20 your pillows I will *t.*
Hos. 5:14 I will *t.* and go away
13:8 the wild beast shall *t.* them
Amos 1:11 his anger did *t.* perp.
Nah. 2:12 the lion did *t.* enough
Zec. 11:16 shepherd sh. *t.* claws

TEARETH.

Deut. 33:20 as a lion, and *t.* arm
Job 16:9 he *t.* me in his wrath
18:4 he *t.* himself in his anger
Mic. 5:8 young lion *t.* in pieces
Mark 9:18 he *t.* him, Luke 9:39

TEARS.

2 K. 20:5 I have seen *t.* Is. 38:5
Job 16:20 mine eye pour. out *t.*
Ps. 6:6 I water my couch with *t.*
39:12 hold not peace at my *t.*
42:3 my *t.* have been my meat
56:8 put th. my *t.* in thy bottle

80:5 wi. bread of *t.* giv. *t.* to dr.
116:8 hast delivered eyes from *t.*
126:5 th. sow in *t.* sh. reap in joy
Ec. 4:1 behold the *t.* of such as
Is. 16:9 I will water thee with *t.*
25:8 the Lord will wipe away *t.*
Jer. 9:1 O that mi. eyes were *t.* !
  18 our eyes run down with *t.*
13:17 eyes sh. run down with *t.*
14:17 let mine eyes run with *t.*
31:16 weeping, thine eyes fr. *t.*
Lam. 1:2 *t.* are on her cheeks
2:11 mine eyes do fail with *t.*
18 let *t.* run down like a river
Ezek. 24:16 neither sh. thy *t.* run
Mal. 2:13 cover. altar of L. wi. *t.*
Mark 9:24 father said with *t.* L.
Luke 7:38 to wash feet with *t.*
  44 she washed my feet with *t.*
Acts 20:19 serving the L. with *t.*
  31 cease not to warn with *t.*
2 Cor. 2:4 I wrote to you with *t.*
2 Tim. 1:4 mindful of thy *t.*
Heb. 5:7 offered supplica. with *t.*
12:17 he sought it caref. with *t.*
Rev. 7:17 G. sh. wipe away *t.* 21:4

TEATS.

Is. 32:12 they shall lament for *t.*
Ezek. 23:3 they bruised the *t.* 21

TEBETH.

Est. 2:16 tenth month, wh. is T.

TEDIOUS.

Acts 24:4 that I be not *t.* to thee

TEETH.

Gen. 49:12 his *t.* shall be white
Num. 11:33 wh. flesh was bet. *t.*
Deut. 32:24 will send *t.* of beasts
1 Sam. 2:13 flesh-hook of three *t.*
Job 4:10 *t.* of lions are broken
13:14 wherefore take flesh in *t.* ?
19:20 I escap. with skin of my *t.*
29:17 plucked spoil out of *t.* of
41:14 Leviathan's *t.* are terrible
Ps. 3:7 hast broken *t.* of ungodly
57:4 who, *t.* are spe. and arrows
58:6 break th. *t.* O G. in mouth
124:6 not given us as prey to *t.*
Prov. 10:26 as vinegar to the *t.*
30:14 wh. *t.* are swords. jaw-*t.*
Cant. 4:2 thy *t.* like a flock, 6:6
Is. 41:15 make instrum. hav. *t.*
Jer. 31:29 children's *t.* are set on edge, Ezek. 18:2
Lam. 3:16 hath broken my *t.*
Dan. 7:7 4th beast had iron *t.* 19
Joel 1:6 cheek *t.* of a great lion
Amos 4:6 have given clean. of *t.*
Mic. 3:5 bite with *t.* cry peace
Zec. 9:7 abominations from his *t.*
Mat. 27:44 cast the same in his *t.*
Rev. 9:8 their *t.* as the *t.* of lions

See GNASH.

TEIL-TREE.

Is. 6:13 as a *t.-t.* and as an oak

TEKEL.

Dan. 5:25 writ. Mene, Mene, T. 27 T. thou art weighed in the

TEKOAH, or TEKOA.

2 Sam. 14:2 Joab sent to T. to
  4 when the woman of T. spake
1 Chr. 2:24 Asher father of T.
4:5 Asher the father of T. had
2 Chr. 11:6 built Etam and T.
20:20 into the wilderness of T.
Jer. 6:1 blow the trumpet in T.
Amos 1:1 among herdmen of T.

TELL.

Gen. 15:5 *t.* stars if thou be able
32:5 I have sent to *t.* my lord
45:13 *t.* my father of my glory
Ex. 10:2 may. *t.* in ears of son
Num. 14:14 they will *t.* inhabita.
1 Sam. 6:2 *t.* us wherewith we
9:8 man of God, to *t.* us way
17:55 as liv. O king, I cannot *t.*

22:22 I knew he would *t.* Saul
27:11 lest they *t.* on us, saying
2 *Sam.* 1:20 *t.* it not in Gath
1 *K.* 1:20 that thou shouldest *t.*
18:12 when I come and *t.* Ahab
2 *K.* 7:9 th. we may *t.* the king's
9:12 said, It is false; *t.* us now
15 let none escape to go *t.* it
Ps. 22:17 I may *t.* my bones
26:7 *t.* of thy wondrous works
48:13 that ye may *t.* the genera.
Prov. 30:4 na. if thou canst *t.* ?
Ec. 6:12 who can *t.* what, 10:14
8:7 who can *t.* when it sh. be ?
10:20 that hath wings sh. *t.* mat.
Is. 6:11 this peo. ; 48:20 *t.* this
Jer. 15:2 *t.* such as are for death
23:27 dreams wh. they *t.* 28:32
36:16 we will *t.* king of th. words
17 *t.* us how thou didst write
Ezek. 24:19 not *t.* us what thi. ?
Dan. 2:4 O king, *t.* thy serv. 7
Joel 1:3 *t.* your child. let child.
Jon. 3:9 who can *t.* if God will
Mat. 8:4 see thou *t.* no man,
  Mark 8:26, 30 ; 9:9 ; *Lu.* 5:14 ;
  8:56 ; *Acts* 23:22
17:9 *t.* the vision to no man
18:15 *t.* him his fault alone
17 if he negl. to hear *t.* church
21:5 *t.* ye the daughter of Sion
24:3 *t.* us when shall these
  things be, *Mark,* 13:4
26:63 *t.* us whether thou be C.
  Luke 22:67 ; *John* 10:24
28:7 go and *t.* that he is risen
9 went to *t.* discip. *Mark* 16:7
Mark 1:30 they *t.* him of her
5:19 *t.* them how great things
11:33 we cannot *t.* *Mat.* 21:27 ;
  Luke 20:7
Luke 7:22 *t.* J. what ye have seen
John 3:8 canst not *t.* whence
4:25 wh. he is come, he will *t.*
8:14 cannot *t.* whence I come
16:18 a little while ? cannot *t.*
18:34 or did others *t.* it of me ?
Acts 15:27 shall *t.* same things
17:21 either to *t.* or hear some
2 *Cor.* 12:2 out of body I can. *t.* 3
Heb. 11:32 time would fail to *t.*

TELL me.

Gen. 12:18 why didst not *t. me* ?
24:49 *t. me,* if not, *t. me* that
31:27 steal aw. didst not *t. me*
32:29 Ja. said, *t. me* thy name
37:16 *t. me* wh. they feed flocks
Jos. 7:19 *t. me* what hast done
Ruth 4:4 if not redeem it, *t. me*
1 *Sam.* 14:43 S. said, *t. me* what
20:10 D. said, Who shall *t. me* ?
2 *Sam.* 1:4 how went mat. *t. me*
1 *K.* 22:16 *t. me* noth. but truth
2 *K.* 4:2 what do for thee, *t. me*
Job 34:34 men of underst. *t. me*
Cant. 1:7 *t. me,* O th. whom my
Mat. 21:24 th. which if you *t. me*
Luke 7:42 *t. me* wh. of them will
John 20:15 *t. me* wh. ha. laid him
Acts 23:19 what hast to *t. me* ?
Gal. 4:21 *t. me* ye that desire to

TELL thee.

Ex. 14:12 the word we did *t. t.*
Num. 23:3 showeth me, I will *t. t.*
Deut. 17:11 the judgm. they *t. t.*
Jud. 14:16 told it and sh. I *t. t.*
Ruth 3:4 he will *t. thee* what th.
1 *Sam.* 9:19 *t. t.* that is in heart
15:16 will *t. thee* what L. said
19:3 and what I see, I will *t. t.*
20:9 then would not I *t.* it *t.* ?
1 *Chr.* 17:10 I *t. thee* that the L.
Job 1:15 escap. to *t. t.* 16, 17, 19
Is. 19:12 let thy wise men *t. thee*
Luke 12:59 I *t. t.* sh. not depart
Acts 10:6 *t. t.* what to do, 11:14

I TELL you.

Gen. 49:1 that *I* may *t. you* what
Is. 42:9 forth *I t.* of them
Mat. 10:27 what *I t. you* in dark.
Mark 11:29 *I t.* y. by wh. author.
Luke 4:25 *I t.* y. of a truth, 9:27
13:27 *I t. you* I know you not
19:40 *I t.* y. if these hold peace
22:67 said, If *I t. you,* not belie.
John 3:12 beli. if *I t. you* of heav.
8:45 *I t.* y. the truth, *Gal.* 4:16
13:19 now *I t. you* befo. it come
16:7 *I t. you* truth, it is expedi.
Gal. 5:21 of which *I t. you* before
Phil. 3:18 of whom *I* now *t. you*

TELLEST.

Ps. 56:8 thou *t.* my wanderings

TELLETH.

2 *Sam.* 7:11 the L. *t.* thee that he
2 *K.* 6:12 Elisha *t.* the king of Is.
Ps. 41:6 when he goeth he *t.* it
101:7 he th. *t.* lies sh. not tarry
147:4 he *t.* number of the stars
Jer. 33:13 hands of him that *t.* th.
John 12:22 Philip cometh *t.* And.

TELLING.

Jud. 7:15 Gid. heard *t.* of dream
2 *Sam.* 11:19 made an end of *t.*
2 *K.* 8:5 as he was *t.* the king

TEMA.

Gen. 25:15 Hadar, T. 1 *Chr.* 1:30
Job 6:19 troops of T. looked for
Is. 21:14 the inhabitants of T.
Jer. 25:23 I made T. to drink the

TEMAN.

Gen. 36:11 sons of Eliphaz, T.
  15 duke T. 42 ; 1 *Chr.* 1:53
Jer. 49:7 is wisd. no more in T. ?
  20 hath purposed against T.
Ezek. 25:13 make desolate fr. T.
Amos 1:12 send a fire upon T.
Ob. 9 thy mighty men, O T.
Hab. 3:3 God came from T. Holy

TEMPERANCE.

Acts 24:25 as he reasoned of *t.*
Gal. 5:23 *t.* ag. such th. no law
2 *Pet.* 1:6 add to know. *t.* and to *t.*

TEMPERATE.

1 *Cor.* 9:25 striv. for mastery is *t.*
Tit. 1:8 bishop be *t.* 2:2 aged *t.*

TEMPER.

Ezek. 46:14 oil to *t.* wi. fine flour

TEMPERED.

Ex. 29:2 unleavened *t.* with oil
30:35 a perfume *t.* together
1 *Cor.* 12:24 God hath *t.* body

TEMPEST.

Job 9:17 breaketh me with a *t.*
27:20 a *t.* stealeth him away in
Ps. 11:6 on wicked sh. he rain *t.*
55:8 I hasten from storm and *t.*
83:15 so persecute them with *t.*
Is. 28:2 which as a *t.* of hail
29:6 visited with storm and *t.*
30:30 Assyr. be beaten with a *t.*
32:2 man shall be a covert fr. *t.*
54:11 O afflicted, tossed with *t.*
Amos 1:14 *t.* in day of whirlw.
Jon. 1:4 was a mighty *t.* in sea
  12 for my sake great *t.* is come
Mat. 8:24 there arose a *t.* in sea
Acts 27:18 exceed. tossed with *t.*
  20 no small *t.* lay on us, hope
Heb. 12:18 not co. to darkn. and *t.*
2 *Pet.* 2:17 clouds carried with a *t.*

TEMPESTUOUS.

Ps. 50:3 be very *t.* round him
Jon. 1:11 sea wrought and *t.* 13
Acts 27:14 arose ag. it *t.* wind

TEMPLE.

2 *Sam.* 22:7 he did hear my voice
  out of his *t. Ps.* 18:6
1 *K.* 6:17 *t.* before 40 cubits long
2 *Chr.* 36:7 put vessels in *t.* at B.

Ezr. 4:1 they builded *t.* unto L.
5:14 took out *t.* brought to *t.* 6:5
Neh. 6:10 hid in *t.* shut doors of *t.*
Ps. 27:4 beauty of L. inq. in *t.*
29:9 in *t.* ev. one speak of glory
48:9 kindness in midst of thy *t.*
68:29 because of thy *t.* at Jerus.
Is. 6:1 and his train filled the *t.*
Is. 44:28 to *t.* thy founda. be laid
66:6 a voice from *t.* voice of L.
Jer. 50:28 decl. veng. of *t.* 51:11
Ezek. 41:1 afterw. brou. me to *t.*
Dan. 5:2 vessels taken out of *t.* 3
Amos 8:3 songs of *t.* be howlings
Zec. 8:9 strong, that *t.* be built
Mal. 3:1 L. come sudd. to his *t.*
Mat. 4:5 set him on a pinnacle
  of *t. Luke* 4:9
12:6 place is one greater than *t.*
25:16 sw. by *t.* or gold of *t.* 17, 21
  35 wh. ye slew bet. *t.* and altar
24:1 show build. of *t. Luke* 21:5
26:61 I am able to dest. *t.* of G.
27:40 destroyest *t. Mark* 15:29
  51 veil of *t.* rent in twain, *Mark*
  15:38 ; *Luke* 23:45
Mark 11:16 carry vessels thro' *t.*
14:58 destroy *t.* ma. with hands
Luke 2:37 An. departed not fr. *t.*
John 2:15 he drove them out of *t.*
  19 destroy *t.* 21 spake of *t.* of
  20 forty and six years *t.* build.
Acts 3:2 laid daily at gate of *t.* to
  ask alms of them ent. *t.* 10
19:27 *t.* of Diana sho. be despis.
21:30 took Paul, drew him out *t.*
24:6 hath gone about to prof. *t.*
25:8 neither against *t.* nor Cesar
1 *Cor.* 3:16 that ye are *t.* of God
  17 if any man defile *t.* of G. him
  G. dest. *t.* holy, wh. *t.* ye are
6:19 your body is *t.* of H. Ghost
8:10 these sit at meat in idol's *t.*
9:13 they who minister live of *t.*
2 *Cor.* 6:16 hath *t.* of G. wi. idols
Rev. 7:15 serve day and ni. in *t.*
11:1 rise and measure *t.* of God
  19 *t.* of G. was open. in heaven
14:15 ano. angel came out of *t.*
15:5 *t.* of tabernacle was opened
  8 *t.* was filled with smoke from
16:1 I heard a voice out of *t.* 17
17:22 no *t.* Almig. and Lamb *t.*
See LORD, LORD.

In, or into the TEMPLE.

1 *Chr.* 6:10 priest's office in the *t.*
Ezr. 5:15 carry these ves. *i. t. t.*
Neh. 6:11 go *i. the t.* to save life
Mat. 12:5 priests in *t.* prof. sabb.
21:12 went *into the t.* to cast out
  them that sold in *t. t. Mark*
  11:15 ; *Luke* 19:45
  14 and lame came to him *i. t. t.*
  15 child. crying in *t.* Hosanna
26:55 teaching in *t. Luke* 21:37
27:5 cast down pieces of sil. *i. t.*
Mark 14:49 I was daily teaching
  in the *t. Luke* 22:53
Luke 1:21 tarried so long in *t. t.*
2:27 he came by Spirit into *t. t.*
  46 found him in the *t.* sitting
18:10 two men went into the *t.*
24:53 continu. in *t.* praising G.
Acts 2:46 with one accord in *t. t.*
5:21 Peter and John went *i. the t.*
  3 to go *into t.* 5:20 speak in *t.*
5:25 men are standing in *t.*
21:26 P. entered *t.* 27 saw in *t.*
  28 brought Greeks *t. t.* 29
24:12 neither found me in *the t.*
  18 J. found me purified in *t.*
26:21 cause J. caught me in *t.*
2 *Thes.* 2:4 as G. sitteth i. *t.* of G.
Rev. 3:12 I make a pillar in *t.*
15:8 no man able to enter *i. t. t.*

TEMPLES, of the head.

Jud. 4:21 sm. nail into his *t.* 22

5:26 she had stricken thro' his *t.*
Cant. 4:3 thy *t.* like pomegr. 6:7

TEMPLES.

Hos. 8:14 forgot Maker, build. *t.*
Joel 3:5 into *t.* my goodly things
Acts 7:48 the M. H. dwelleth not
     in *t.* made with hands, 17:24

TEMPORAL.

2 *Cor.* 4:18 for things seen are *t.*

TEMPT.

Gen. 22:1 God did *t.* Abraham
Ex. 17:2 wheref. do ye *t.* Lord ?
Deut. 6:16 ye shall not *t.* the L.
Is. 7:12 not ask, nor will I *t.* L.
Mal. 3:15 that *t.* God are deliv.
Mat. 4:7 shalt not *t.* the L. *Luke* 4:12
     22:18 why *t.* ye me ? *Mark* 12:15 ;
     Luke 20:23

Acts 5:9 ye have agreed to *t.* Sp.
     15:10 therefore why *t.* ye God ?
1 *Cor.* 7:5 Sa. *t.* you not for your
     10:9 neither let us *t.* Christ

TEMPTATION.

Ps. 95:8 as in *t.* in wild. *Heb.* 3:8
Mat. 6:13 and lead us not into *t.*
     Luke 11:4

Mat. 26:41 that ye enter not into
     t. Mark 14:38 ; *Luke* 22:40, 46
Luke 4:13 wh. devil ended his *t.*
     8:13 in a time of *t.* fall away
1 *Cor.* 10:13 no *t.* tak. you, wi. *t.*
Gal. 4:14 *t.* in flesh despised not
1 *Tim.* 6:9 that be rich fall into *t.*
Jam. 1:12 bless. that endureth *t.*
Rev. 3:10 keep thee fr. hour of *t.*

TEMPTATIONS.

Deut. 4:34 nati. out of nat. 'by *t.*
     7:19 great *t.* th. eyes saw, 29:3
Luke 22:28 contin. with me in *t.*
Acts 20:19 serv. G. with many *t.*
Jam. 1:2 joy when ye fall into *t.*
1 *Pet.* 1:6 are in heaviness thro' *t.*
2 *Pet.* 2:9 L. deli. godly out of *t.*

TEMPTED.

Ex. 17:7 because they *t.* Lord
Num. 14:22 ha. *t.* me ten times
Deut. 6:16 tempt G. ye *t.* in Ma.
Ps. 78:18 they *t.* G. in heart, 41
     56 *t.* and prov. most high God
95:9 when fath. *t.* me, *Heb.* 3:9
106:14 lusted, *t.* God in desert
Mal. 4:1 wildern. to be *t.* of the
     devil, *Mark* 1:13 ; *Luke* 4:2
Luke 10:25 a lawyer *t.* him
1 *Cor.* 10:9 some *t.* were destroy.
     13 not suffer you to be *t.* above
Gal. 6:1 lest thou also be *t.*
1 *Thes.* 3:5 by means tempter *t.*
Heb. 2:18 himself suff. being *t.*
     4:15 in all points *t.* like as we
     11:37 were sawn asun. were *t.*
Jam. 1:13 say wh. he is *t.* I am *t.*
     of God, for God cannot be *t.*
     14 ev. man *t.* wh. drawn of lust

TEMPTER.

Mat. 4:3 when *t.* came to him
1 *Thes.* 3:5 by means *t.* tempted

TEMPTETH.

Jam. 1:13 tempt. neither *t.* any

TEMPTING.

Mat. 16:1 the Pharisees *t.* Christ,
     Mark 8:11 ; *Luke* 11:16
     19:3 Pharis. came to him *t.* him
     22:35 lawyer asked quest. *t.* him
Mark 10:2 put away wife, *t.* him
John 8:6 this they said, *t.* him

TEN.

Gen. 16:3 Ab. dw. *t.* years in C.
     18:32 I will not dest. for *t.* sake
42:3 Jos.'s *t.* breth. went to buy
Ex. 34:28 wrote *t.* commandm.
     Deut. 4:13 ; 10:4

Lev. 26:26 *t.* women bake bread
Jos. 17:5 fell *t.* portions to Man.
Jud. 12:11 E. judged Is. *t.* years

20:10 take *t.* men of a hundred
Ruth 1:4 dwelt in Moab *t.* years
1 *Sam.* 1:8 not better th. *t.* sons?
2 *Sam.* 19:43 ha. *t.* parts in king
1 *K.* 11:31 *t.* piec. give *t.* trib. 35
     14:3 take *t.* loaves to Ahijah
2 *K.* 15:17 Mena. reigned *t.* years
Neh. 11:1 one of *t* to dw. at Jer.
Est. 9:10 *t.* sons of Ham. slew, 12
Ps. 33:2 instrument of *t.* strings,
     92:3 ; 144:9
Ec. 7:19 more than *t.* mighty men
Ezek. 45:14 homer of *t.* baths, *t.*
Amos 5:3 leave *t.* to house of Is.
     6:9 if *t.* remain in one house
Zec. 8:23 *t.* men take hold of Jew
Mat. 25:1 kingdom likened to *t.*
     virgins

Luke 15:8 wom. having *t.* pieces
     17:17 were th. not *t.* cleansed ?
     19:13 delivered them *t.* pounds
Rev. 12:3 a dragon hav. *t.* horns,
     13:1 ; 17:3
     17:12 the *t.* horns are *t.* kings

See CUBITS, DAYS, DEGREES,
     THOUSAND, THOUSANDS.

TEN times.

Gen. 31:7 changed wages *t. t.* 41
Num. 14:22 have tempt. me *t. t.*
Neh. 4:12 J. came, said to us *t. t.*
Job 19:3 *t.* reproached me
Dan. 1:20 found them *t. t.* better

TENS.

Ex. 18:21 over them rul. of *t.* 25
Deut. 1:15 heads, captains over *t.*

TENTH.

Gen. 28:22 surely give *t.* to thee
Lev. 27:32 *t.* shall be holy to L.
Num. 18:21 given child. of L. *t.*
1 *Sam.* 8:15 king take *t.* of seed
Is. 6:13 yet in it shall be a *t.*
John 1:39 it was about *t.* hour

See DAY, DEAL, MONTH, PART.

TEND.

Prov. 21:5 diligent *t.* to plente

TENDETH.

Prov. 10:16 labor of righteous *t.*
     11:19 as righteousness *t.* to life
     24 withholdeth, it *t.* to poverty
     14:23 talk of lips *t.* to penury
     19:23 fear of the Lord *t.* to life

TENDER.

Gen. 18:7 Abra. fetched a calf *t.*
     33:13 knd know. children are *t.*
Deut. 28:54 man that is *t.* among
     56 the *t.* and delicate woman
32:2 small rain on the *t.* herb
2 *Sam.* 23:4 as *t.* grass springing
2 *K.* 22:19 heart *t.* 2 *Chr.* 34:27
1 *Chr.* 22:5 Sol. young and *t.* 29:1
Job 14:7 *t.* branch will not cease
     38:27 cause the *t.* herb to spring
Prov. 4:3 *t.* and belov. in sight of
     27:25 the *t.* grass showeth itself
Cant. 2:13 the vines with *t.* grape
     7:12 see whether *t.* grape appear
Is. 47:1 no more be called *t.* and
     53:2 shall grow up as a *t.* plant
Ezek. 17:22 I will crop off a *t.* one
     4:15 in earth, in the *t.* grass, 23
Mat. 24:32 bra. is *t.* *Mark* 13:28
Luke 1:78 thro' *t.* mercy of God
Jam. 5:11 L. is pitiful, of *t.* mercy

TENDER-HEARTED.

2 *Chr.* 13:7 Reh. young and *t.-h.*
Eph. 4:32 be kind and *t.-h.*

See MERCIES.

TENDERNESS.

Deut. 28:56 set foot on gro. for *t.*

TENONS.

Ex. 26:17 two *t.* in one board, 19 ;
     36:22, 24

TENOR.

Gen. 43:7 according to *t.* of words
Ex. 34:27 after *t.* of these words

TENT.

Gen. 9:21 Noah was uncov. in *t.*
     12:8 Abra. pitched his *t.* 13:3
     13:12 Lot pitched his *t.* tow. S.
     18:1 sat in *t.* 6 hastened into *t.*
     9 where is Sa. he said, In the *t.*
     24:67 brought her to Sarah's *t.*
     26:17 Isaac pitched his *t.* in val.
     25 pitched his *t.* at Beer-sheba
     31:25 Jacob had pitched his *t.*
     33:18 Ja. pitched his *t.* before, 19
     35:21 Is. pitched his *t.* beyond
Ex. 18:7 M. and Jeth. came to *t.*
     33:8 stood every man at *t.* door
     10 they worshipped in *t.* door
     39:33 they brought the *t.* to Mo.
     40:19 he spread *t.* over taberna.
Lev. 14:8 tarry out of *t.* sev. days
Num. 9:15 cloud cov. *t.* of testi.
     11:10 heard people weep in *t.*
     19:14 when a man dieth in a *t.*
     18 a clean person sh. sprinkle *t.*
     25:8 went aft. man of Is. into *t.*
Jos. 7:21 hid in midst of my *t.*
     23 took them out of midst of *t.*
     24 Israel burnt his *t.* and all he
Jud. 4:17 Sisera fled to *t.* of Jael
     20 said, Stand in door of the *t.*
     21 Jael took a nail of the *t.* and
     5:24 blessed above women in *t.*
     7:8 he sent rest of Israel to his *t.*
     20:8 not any of us go to *t.*
1 *Sam.* 4:10 fled every man into
     his *t.* 2 *Sam.* 18:17 ; 19:8
     13:2 rest of people he sent to *t.*
     17:54 put Goliath's armor into *t.*
2 *Sam.* 7:6 walk. in a *t.* 1 *Chr.* 17:5
     16:22 they spread Absalom a *t.*
     20:22 retired every man to his *t.*
2 *K.* 7:8 lepers went into one *t.*
1 *Chr.* 15:1 Da. pitched a *t.* for ark
2 *Chr.* 25:22 fled ev. man to his *t.*
Ps. 78:60 the *t.* which he placed
Is. 13:20 nor Arabian pitch *t.* th.
     38:12 age removed as a shep.'s *t.*
     40:22 spreadeth them out as a *t.*
     54:2 enlarge the place of thy *t.*
Jer. 10:20 none to stretch forth *t.*
     37:10 rise up every man in his *t.*

TENT-MAKERS.

Acts 18:3 by occupation *t.-m.*

TENTS.

Gen. 4:20 such as dwell in *t.*
     9:27 Japheth shall dwell in *t.*
     13:5 Lot also had herds and *t.*
     25:27 a plain man, dwelling in *t.*
     31:33 L. went into maid-serv. *t.*
Ex. 16:16 gather for them in *t.*
Num. 1:52 Is. shall pitch their *t.*
     9:17 cloud abode, they pitched *t.*
     18 rested in their *t.* 20, 22, 23
     13:19 whether th. dwell in *t.* or
     16:26 depart from the *t.* of those
     27 stood in the door of their *t.*
Num. 24:2 Bal. saw Is. abid. in *t.*
     5 how goodly are thy *t.* O Jac.
Deut. 1:27 ye murmur. in your *t.*
     33 search a pla. to pitch your *t.*
     5:30 get you into your *t.* again
     11:6 earth swallowed up their *t.*
     33:18 rejoice, Issachar, in thy *t.*
Jos. 22:4 get you unto your *t.* 6.
     8 return wi. riches unto your *t.*
Jud. 6:5 Midianites came with *t.*
     8:11 way of them th. dwelt in *t.*
1 *Sam.* 17:53 spoil. Philistines' *t.*
2 *Sam.* 11:11 Is. and J. abide in *t.*
     20:1 every man to his *t.* 1 *K.*
     12:16 ; 2 *Chr.* 10:16
1 *K.* 8:66 I. we. to th. *t.* 2 *Chr.* 7:10
2 *K.* 7:7 Syrians left their *t.* 10
     8:21 peo. fled into their *t.* 14:12
13:5 children of Israel dwelt in *t.*
1 *Chr.* 4:41 they smote *t.* of Ham

5:10 they dwelt in Hagarites' *t.*
2 *Chr.* 14:15 smote *t.* of cattle
31:2 to praise in *t.* of the Lord
Ezr. 8:15 we abode in *t.* 3 days
Ps. 69:25 let none dw. in their *t.*
78:55 made Israel to dwell in *t.*
84:10 th. dwell in *t.* of wickedn.
106:25 murmured in their *t.* and
120:5 I dwell in the *t.* of Kedar
Cant. 1:5 comely as *t.* of Kedar
Jer. 4:20 sudd. are my *t.* spoiled
6:3 they shall pitch their *t.*
30:18 bring captiv. of Jacob's *t.*
35:7 days ye shall dwell in *t.*
10 but we have dwelt in *t.*
49:29 th. *t.* and flocks shall they
Hab. 3:7 I saw the *t.* of Cushan
Zec. 12:7 L. shall save *t.* of Jud.
14:15 plague of all in these *t.*

TERAH.
Gen. 11:24 begat T. 1 *Chr.* 1:26
26 T. begat Abr. 27; *Jos.* 24:2
31 T. took Abram his son, and

TERAPHIM.
Jud. 17:5 made an ephod and *t.*
18:14 in these houses is *t.* 20
Hos. 3:4 many days without *t.*

TERMED.
Is. 62:4 sh. no more be *t.* forsak.

TERRACES.
2 *Chr.* 9:11 ma. of algum-trees *t.*

TERRESTRIAL.
1 *Cor.* 15:40 bodies *t.* glory of *t.*

TERRIBLE.
Ex. 34:10 for it is a *t.* thing
Deut. 1:19 went thro' *t.* wild. 8:15
7:21 Lord is a mighty God and *t.*
10:17; *Neh.* 1:5; 4:14; 9:32
10:21 done *t.* thi. 2 *Sam.* 7:23
Jud. 13:6 angel of God, very *t.*
Job 37:22 with God is *t.* majesty
39:20 glory of his nostrils is *t.*
41:14 teeth are *t.* round about
Ps. 45:4 hand sh. teach *t.* things
47:2 the Lord most high is *t.* he
65:5 by *t.* things in righteousn.
66:3 *t.* art thou in thy works
5 *t.* in his doing towards men
68:35 thou art *t.* out of thy holy
76:12 he is *t.* to the kings of
99:3 prai. thy great and *t.* name
106:22 done *t.* things by R. sea
145:6 shall speak of thy *t.* acts
Cant. 6:4 art *t.* as an army, 10
Is. 13:11 lay low haughtin. of *t.*
18:2 to a peo. *t.* 7 fr. a people *t.*
21:1 from desert, from a *t.* land
25:3 the city of the *t.* nations
4 blast of *t.* ones is as a storm
5 branch of *t.* shall be bro. low
29:5 mult. of *t.* ones be as chaff
20 *t.* one is brought to naught
49:25 prey of *t.* sh. be delivered
64:3 when thou didst *t.* things
Jer. 15:21 red. out of hand of *t.*
20:11 L. as a mighty *t.* one
Lam. 5:10 because of *t.* famine
Ezek. 1:22 color of the *t.* crystal
28:7 will bring the *t.* of nations
upon thee, 30:11; 31:12
32:12 cause to fall *t.* of nations
Dan. 2:31 form of image was *t.*
7:7 fourth beast dreadf. and *t.*
Joel 2:11 L. is great and very *t.*
31 before the great and *t.* day
Hab. 1:7 Chaldeans are *t.* and
Zep. 2:11 L. will be *t.* unto M.
Heb. 12:21 so *t.* was sight that

TERRIBLENESS.
Deut. 26:8 L. brought us with *t.*
1 *Chr.* 17:21 make thee a name *t.*
Jer. 49:16 thy *t.* hath deceived th.

TERRIBLY.
Is. 2:19 to shake *t.* the earth, 21
Nah. 2:3 fir-trees sh. be *t.* shak.

TERRIFY.
Job 3:5 let blackness of day *t.* it
9:34 his rod. let not his fear *t.*
31:34 did countenance of famil. *t.*?
2 *Cor.* 10:9 seem as if I wo. *t.* you

TERRIFIED, EST.
Deut. 20:3 fear not nor be *t.*
Job 7:14 thou *t.* me thro' visions
Luke 21:9 hear of wars, be not *t.*
24:37 they were *t.* and affrighted
Phil. 1:28 in nothing *t.* by adv.

TERROR.
Gen. 35:5 the *t.* of God was upon
Lev. 26:16 will ap. over you *t.*
Deut. 32:25 sw. without, *t.* with.
34:12 in the *t.* which M. showed
Jos. 2:9 *t.* is fallen upon us
Job 31:23 destruc. fr. G. was a *t.*
33:7 my *t.* not make thee afraid
Ps. 91:5 not afr. for *t.* by night
Is. 10:33 L. will lop bough wi. *t.*
19:17 Ju. shall be a *t.* to Egypt
33:18 thy heart shall meditate *t.*
54:14 thou shalt be far from *t.*
Jer. 17:17 not a *t.* 20:4 *t.* to thys.
32:21 brought forth Isr. with *t.*
Ezek. 26:17 cause *t.* to be on all
21 I make th. a *t.* 27:36; 28:19
32:23 wh. caused *t.* 24, 25, 26, 27
30 with their *t.* they are asha.
32 I have caused my *t.* in land
Rom. 13:3 rulers not *t.* to good
2 *Cor.* 5:11 knowing the *t.* of L.
1 *Pet.* 3:14 be not afraid of th. *t.*

TERRORS.
Deut. 4:34 assa. to take nat. by *t.*
Job 6:4 *t.* of God set themselves
18:11 *t.* shall make him afraid
14 sh. bring him to king of *t.*
20:25 sword cometh, *t.* are upon
24:17 they are in the *t.* of death
27:20 *t.* take hold on him
30:15 *t.* are turned upon me
Ps. 55:4 *t.* of death are fallen on
73:19 utterly consumed with *t.*
88:15 while I suff. *t.* I am distr.
16 thy *t.* have cut me off
Jer. 15:8 caused *t.* to fall on city
Lam. 2:22 hast called my *t.*
Ezek. 21:12 *t.* by reason of sword

TERTIUS.
Rom. 16:22 I T. who wrote this

TERTULLUS.
Acts 24:1 certain orator nam. T.
2 T. began to accuse Paul

TESTAMENT.
Mat. 26:28 this is my blood in
new *t. Mark* 14:24
Luke 22:20 this cup is the new *t.*
1 *Cor.* 11:25
2 *Cor.* 3:6 made minis. of new *t.*
14 remains veil, in read. old *t.*
Heb. 7:22 surety of a better *t.*
9:15 he is mediator of new *t.* for
redemption under first *t.*
16 where a *t.* is, th. must death
17 *t.* is of force after men dead
20 this is blood of *t.* G. enjoin.
Rev. 11:19 in temple ark of *t.*

TESTATOR.
Heb. 9:16 of neces. be death of *t.*
17 no strength while *t.* liveth

TESTIFY.
Num. 35:30 one witness not *t.*
Deut. 8:19 I *t.* that ye sh. perish
19:16 if a false wit. *t.* against
31:21 song *t.* ag. them as witn.
32:46 set yo. hearts to wor. I *t.*
Neh. 9:34 wherew. thou didst *t.*
Job 15:6 thine own lips *t.* ag. th.
Ps. 50:7 O Is. I *t.* ag. thee, 81:8
Is. 59:12 our sins *t.* against us
Jer. 14:7 our iniquities *t.* ag. us
Hos. 5:5 pride of Israel doth *t.*
Amos 3:13 *t.* in house of Jacob

TESTIFIED.
Mic. 6:3 what have I done? *t.* ag.
Luke 16:28 send Laza. that he *t.*
John 2:25 that any sho. *t.* of man
3:11 *t.* have seen; 5:39 *t.* of me
7:7 bec. I *t.* of it; 15:26 *t.* of me
Acts 2:40 wi. oth. words did he *t.*
10:42 *t.* it is he was ordai. of G.
20:24 to *t.* gospel of grace of G.
26:5 know they, if th. would *t.*
Gal. 5:3 I *t.* to ev. man circum.
Eph. 4:17 this I say, and *t.* in L.
1 *John* 4:14 we ha. seen and do *t.*
Rev. 22:16 I Jesus sent ang. to *t.*
18 I *t.* to ev. man that heareth

TESTIFIED.
Ex. 21:29 it ha. been *t.* to owner
Deut. 19:18 *t.* falsely ag. brother
Ruth 1:21 see. L. hath *t.* ag. me
2 *Sam.* 1:16 thy mouth *t.* ag. th.
2 *K.* 17:13 yet L. *t.* against Israel
15 *t.* against them
2 *K.* 17:15 testim. he *t.* ag. them
2 *Chr.* 24:19 prophets *t.* against
them, *Neh.* 9:26
Neh. 13:15 I *t.* against them, 21
John 4:39 for saying wh. wo. *t.*
44 Je. himself *t.* a proph. 13:21
Acts 8:25 wh. they *t.* and preach
18:5 P. *t.* to Jews that J. was C.
23:11 as thou hast *t.* of me at J.
28:23 to whom he *t.* king. of G.
1 *Cor.* 15:15 bec. we ha. *t.* of G.
1 *Thes.* 4:6 we forewarned you, *t.*
1 *Tim.* 2:6 gave himself to be *t.*
Heb. 2:6 one in a certain place *t.*
1 *Pet.* 1:11 *t.* beforeh. sufferings
1 *John* 5:9 witness G. *t.* of his S.
3 *John* 3 *t.* of truth that is in th.

TESTIFIEDST, ETH.
Neh. 9:29 *t.* ag. them by Sp. 30
Hos. 7:10 pride of Is. *t.* his face
John 3:32 wh. he ha. seen, he *t.*
21:24 disciple wh. *t.* of these thi.
Heb. 7:17 he *t.* thou art a priest
Rev. 22:20 which *t.* these things

TESTIFYING.
Acts 20:21 *t.* both to Jews and G.
Heb. 11:4 witn. G. *t.* of his gifts
1 *Pet.* 5:12 *t.* this is grace of God

TESTIMONY.
Ex. 16:34 pot of manna bef. *t.*
25:16 sh. put into ark the *t.* 21
27:21 without vail before *t.*
30:6 mercy-s. over *t. Lev.* 16:13
31:18 gave M. two tables of *t.*
32:15 tables of *t.* in hand, 34:29
38:21 this is sum of tabern. of *t.*
Num. 1:50 Lev. over taber. of *t.*
53 Lev. pitch about taber. of *t.*
9:15 cloud covered the tent of *t.*
10:11 cloud taken off taber. of *t.*
17:4 thou sh. lay up rods bef. *t.*
10 bring Aa. rod again bef. *t.*
Ruth 4:7 and this was a *t.* in Is.
2 *K.* 11:12 gave the king the *t.*
2 *Chr.* 23:11
Ps. 78:5 he established a *t.* in J.
81:5 this he orda. in Jos. for *t.*
119:88 so sh. I keep *t.* of mouth
122:4 tribes go up to the *t.* of I.
132:12 if thy children keep my *t.*
Is. 8:16 bind up *t.* 20 law and *t.*
Mat. 8:4 gift M. commanded for
a *t. Mark* 1:44 ; *Luke* 5:44
10:18 *t.* against them, *Mark* 13:9
Mark 6:11 sh. dust for *t. Luke* 9:5
Luke 21:13 sh. turn to you for *t.*
John 3:32 no man receiv. his *t.*
33 that they receiv. *t.* set to seal
8:17 writ. *t.* of two men is true
21:24 know that his *t.* is true
Acts 13:22 to wh. also he gave *t.*
14:3 gave *t.* to word of his grace
22:18 they will not recei. thy *t.*
1 *Cor.* 1:6 as *t.* of C. was confir.
2:1 declaring unto you *t.* of God
2 *Cor.* 1:12 *t.* of our conscience

2 *Thes.* 1:10 bec. our *t.* was beli.
2 *Tim.* 1:8 not asham. of *t.* of L.
Heb. 3:5 *t.* of things which were
11:5 Enoch had *t.* he pleased G.
Rev. 1:2 bare record of *t.* of J. C.
9 I was in Patmos for *t.* of Je.
6:9 souls of th. were slain for *t.*
11:7 when they have finished *t.*
12:11 overca. by word of th. *t.*
17 war with them wh. have *t.*
15:5 tabernacle of *t.* in heaven
19:10 *t.* of J. is spirit of proph.

See ARK.

TESTIMONIES.

Deut. 4:45 these are *t.* M. spake
6:17 sh. diligently keep *t.* of G.
20 wh. mean *t.* G. commanded
1 *K.* 2:3 to keep his statutes and
his *t.* 2 *K.* 23:3 ; 1 *Chr.* 29:19 ;
2 *Chr.* 34:31
2 *K.* 17:15 rejected *t.* followed
Neh. 9:34 nor kings heark. to *t.*
Ps. 25:10 keep coven. and his *t.*
78:56 keep not *t.* 93:5 *t.* sure
99:7 th. kept *t.* and ordinances
119:2 bles. are they th. keep *t.*
14 I rejoiced in way of thy *t.*
22 I have kept thy *t.* 167, 168
24 thy *t.* deli. 31 I stuck to *t.*
36 incline my heart to thy *t.*
46 I will speak of *t.* bef. kings
59 I turned my feet to thy *t.*
79 have known *t.* turn to me
95 wick. waited, I consider *t.*
99 thy *t.* are my meditation
111 thy *t.* have I taken
119 I love thy *t.* 125 know *t.*
129 thy *t.* are wonderful
138 thy *t.* are righte. faithful
144 righteous. of *t.* everlasting
Ps. 119:146 save me, and I shall
keep *t.*
152 concerning *t.* I have kno.
157 yet do I not decline fr. *t.*
Jer. 44:23 have not walked in *t.*
THADDEUS. *Mark* 3:18

THANK.

Luke 6:32 those that love you
what *t.* have ye? 33:34

THANK, Verb.

1 *Chr.* 16:4 appoint. Lev. to *t.* L.
7 Da. delivered psalm to *t.* L.
23:30 stand ev. morning to *t.* L.
29:13 we *t.* thee, praise name
Dan. 2:23 I *t.* thee, praise thee
Mat. 11:25 Je. said, I *t.* thee, O
Fa. L. of heaven, *Luke* 10:21
Luke 17:9 doth he *t.* that serv. ?
18:11 G. I *t.* th. not as oth. men
John 11:41 Father, I *t.* thee
Rom. 1:8 I *t.* my God, 7:25
1 *Cor.* 1:4 I G. on your behalf
14 I *t.* G. I bapt. none of you
14:18 I *t.* G. I speak with tong.
Phil. 1:3 I *t.* G. on rem. of you
1 *Thes.* 2:13 for this cau. *t.* we G.
2 *Thes.* 1:3 are bound to *t.* God
1 *Tim.* 1:12 I *t.* Jesus Christ
2 *Tim.* 1:3 I *t.* G. whom I serve
Phile. 4 I *t.* God, mak. mention

See OFFERING.

THANKED.

2 *Sam.* 14:22 J. bowed, *t.* king
Acts 28:15 P. *t.* G. took courage
Rom. 6:17 G. be *t.* ye were serv.

THANKFUL.

Ps. 100:4 *t.* to him *Col.* 3:15
Rom. 1:21 glori. not, nor we. *t.*

THANKFULNESS.

Acts 24:3 we accept it with all *t.*

THANKING.

2 *Chr.* 5:13 singers were one *t.* L.

THANKWORTHY.

1 *Pet.* 2:19 *t.* if man endure grief

THANKS.

Neh. 12:31 companies th. gave *t.*
Dan. 6:10 he prayed, and gave *t.*
Mat. 26:27 he took the cup, and
gave *t. Luke* 22:17
Mark 8:6 seven loaves and ga. *t.*
14:23 when he had given *t.* he
Luke 2:38 Anna gave *t.* to Lord
22:19 and gave *t.* and brake it
John 6:11 when he had given *t.*
23 after Lord had given *t.*
Acts 27:35 bread, and ga. *t.* to G.
Rom. 14:6 for he giveth G. *t.* he
eateth not, and giveth G. *t.*
1 *Cor.* 11:24 had given *t.* he bra.
14:17 thou verily givest *t.* well
15:57 *t.* be to G. who giv. vict.
2 *Cor.* 1:11 *t.* may be given
2:14 *t.* to G. who caus. triumph
8:16 *t.* to G. who put care in T.
9:15 *t.* to G. for unspeak. gift
Eph. 5:20 giving *t.* always for all
1 *Thes.* 3:9 what *t.* can we render
Heb. 13:15 offer praise, giving *t.*
Rev. 4:9 give *t.* to him on throne

See GIVE, GIVING.

THANKSGIVING.

Lev. 7:12 if he offer it for a *t.*
13:15 ; 22:29
Neh. 11:17 to begin *t.* in prayer
12:8 which was over the *t.*
46 th. were songs of praise, *t.*
Ps. 26:7 publish with voice of *t.*
50:14 offer unto God *t.* pay vows
69:30 I will mag. him with *t.*
95:2 come before his face wi. *t.*
100:4 enter into his gates wi. *t.*
107:22 let sacrifice sacri. of *t.*
116:17 offer to thee sacri. of *t.*
147:7 sing to the L. with *t.* sing
Is. 51:3 *t.* and melo. found there
Jer. 30:19 out of them shall proceed *t.*
Amos 4:5 offer a sacrifice of *t.*
Jon. 2:9 sacrifice with voice of *t.*
2 *Cor.* 4:15 thro' *t.* grace redound
9:11 causeth thro' us *t.* to God
Phil. 4:6 wi. *t.* let your requests
Col. 2:7 abounding therein wi. *t.*
4:2 watch in the same with *t.*
1 *Tim.* 4:3 God to be rece. wi. *t.*
4 creature good if rece. with *t.*
Rev. 7:12 *t.* and hon. be to our G.

THANKSGIVINGS.

Neh. 12:27 keep dedication wi. *t.*
2 *Cor.* 9:12 abundant by many *t.*

THEATRE.

Acts 19:29 they rush. into the *t.*
31 would not adventure into *t.*

THEBEZ.

Jud. 9:50 went Abimelech to T.
2 *Sam.* 11:21 that he died in T.

THEFT, S.

Ex. 22:3 he be. sold for his *t.*
4 if the *t.* be found in his hand
Mat. 15:19 out of the heart proceed *t. Mark* 7:22
Rev. 9:21 nei. repented they of *t.*

THELASAR. 2 *K.* 19:12

THENCE.

Num. 23:13 curse me th. fr. *t.* 27
Deut. 4:29 if from *t.* thou seek L.
5:15 the Lord brought thee out
t. 6:23 ; 24:18
1 *K.* 2:36 go not forth from *t.*
2 *K.* 2:21 shall not be from *t.* any
Ezr. 6:6 theref. be ye far from *t.*
Is. 65:20 no more *t.* an infant of
Jer. 5:6 every one that goes *t.*
43:12 he shall go forth from *t.* in
Luke 16:26 that would come fr. *t.*

THEOPHILUS.

Luke 1:3 to write to thee, T.
Acts 1:1 treatise have I ma. O T.

THERE.

John 12:26 where I am. *t.* sh. my
14:3 where I am, *t.* ye may be

THEREAT.

Ex. 30:19 wash th. feet. 40:31
Mat. 7:13 many th. be wh. go in *t.*

THEREBY.

Gen. 24:14 *t.* I know thou
Job 22:21 with G. *t.* good will co.

THEREON.

Mat. 21:7 they set him *t. Luke*
19:35 ; *John* 12:14
19 found nothing *t.* but leaves,
Mark 11:13 ; *Luke* 13:6

THERETO.

Ps. 119:9 by taking heed *t.*

THEREUNTO.

1 *Pet.* 3:9 knowing ye are *t.* call.

THESSALONICA.

Acts 17:1 at T. was a synagogue
11 more noble than those of T.
27:2 one Aristarchus of T. being
Phil. 4:16 in T. ye sent once and
2 *Tim.* 4:10 Demas depart. to T.

THEUDAS.

Acts 5:36 bef. th. days rose up T.

THICK.

Deut. 32:15 waxen fat, grown *t.*
2 *Sam.* 18:9 mule we. unto *t.* bo.
2 *K.* 8:15 he took a *t.* cloth, and
Neh. 8:15 branches of *t.* trees
Job 15:26 runneth on *t.* bosses
Ps. 74:5 lift. up axes on *t.* trees
Ezek. 6:13 slain under ev. *t.* oak
19:11 stat. was am. *t.* branches
31:3 among *t.* boughs, 10, 14
Hab. 2:6 lad. himself with *t.* clay
Luke 11:29 peo. gathered *t.* tog.

See CLOUDS, DARKNESS.

THICKER.

1 *K.* 12:10 my little finger sh. be
t. than, 2 *Chr.* 10:10

THICKET, S.

Gen. 22:13 a ram caught in a *t.*
1 *Sam.* 13:6 Israel did hide in *t.*
Is. 9:18 wickedn. sh. kindle in *t.*
10:34 cut down *t.* of the forest
Jer. 4:7 lion is come up fr. his *t.*
29 city sh. flee and go into *t.*

THICKNESS.

2 *Chr.* 4:5 *t.* of sea a handbreadth
Jer. 52:21 *t.* of pillars four fingers
Ezek. 41:9 *t.* of wall five cubits
42:10 chamb. were in *t.* of wall

THIEF.

Ex. 22:2 if *t.* be found break. 7
Deut. 24:7 stealing, th. *t.* sh. die
Job 24:14 the murderer is as a *t.*
30:5 cried after them as after *t.*
Ps. 50:18 when thou sawest a *t.*
Prov. 6:30 not desp. *t.* if he steal
29:24 partner with *t.* hateth soul
Jer. 2:26 as a *t.* is ashamed when
Hos. 7:1 *t.* cometh in, robbers
Joel 2:9 enter at windows like *t.*
Zec. 5:4 shall enter house of *t.*
Mat. 24:43 *t.* wo. come, *Lu.* 12:39
26:55 are ye come as ag. a *t.* ?
Mark 14:48 ; *Luke* 22:52
Luke 12:33 wh. no *t.* approacheth
John 10:1 same is a *t.* and robber
10 *t.* cometh not but to steal
12:6 bec. he was a *t.* and had
1 *Thes.* 5:2 day of the L. cometh
as a *t.* 2 *Pet.* 3:10
4 day sho. overtake you as a *t.*
1 *Pet.* 4:15 let none suffer as a *t.*
Rev. 3:3 I will come as a *t.* 16:15

THIEVES.

Is. 1:23 princes are compan. of *t.*
Jer. 48:27 was not Is. among *t.* ?
49:9 if *t.* by night, *Ob.* 5

Mat. 6:19 where *t.* break through
20 wh. *t.* do not break through
21:13 made it a den of *t. Mark*
11:17; *Luke* 19:46
27:38 two *t.* cruci. *Mark* 15:27
44 the *t.* cast same in his teeth
Luke 10:30 went and fell am. *t.*
John 10:8 that ca. bef. me are *t.*
1 *Cor.* 6:10 nor *t.* inh. king. of G.

THIGH.

Gen. 24:2 hand under *t.* 9; 47:29
32:25 touched hollow of Ja.'s *t.*
Num. 5:21 L. mak. *t.* rot, 22, 27
Jud. 3:16 E. did gird dag. on *t.*
21 E. took dagger fr. right *t.*
15:8 Samson smote hip and *t.*
Ps. 45:3 gird sword on thy *t.*
Cant. 3:8 ev. man hath sw. on *t.*
Is. 47:2 uncover the *t.* pass over
Jer. 31:19 I smote upon my *t.*
Ezek. 21:12 smite theref. upon *t.*
24:4 gather the *t.* and shoulder
Rev. 19:16 hath on his *t.* a name

THIGHS.

Ex. 28:42 breeches reach to *t.*
Cant. 7:1 joints of *t.* like jewels
Dan. 2:32 belly and *t.* of brass

Gen. 41:6 7 *t.* ears, 7, 23, 24, 27
Ex. 39:3 beat gold into *t.* plates
Lev. 13:30 in it a yellow *t.* hair
1 *K.* 7:29 additi. made of *t.* work
Is. 17:4 glory of Ja. be made *t.*

THINE.

Gen. 14:23 any thing that is *t.*
Lev. 10:15 it sh. be *t.* thy sons,
Num. 18:9, 11, 13, 14, 15, 18
1 *K.* 3:26 let nei. be mine nor *t.*
20:4 O king, I am *t.* all I have
1 *Chr.* 12:18 *t.* are we, Dav. and
21:24 will not take that wh. is *t.*
Ps. 119:94 I am *t.* save me, I
John 17:6 *t.* they were; 9 are *t.*
10 all mine are *t.* and *t.* mine

Gen. 24:50 *t.* proceedeth from L.
34:7 *t.* ought not, 2 *Sam.* 13:12
41:32 *t.* is established by God
Ex. 18:11 *t.* wherein they dealt
17 *t.* that th. doest is not good
22:9 for any manner of lost *t.*
Lev. 4:13 the thing be hid fr. eyes
20:17 it is a wicked *t.* they sh.
Num. 16:30 if L. make a new *t.*
Deut. 1:14 *t.* thou hast spoken
12:32 what *t.* soever I command
13:14 truth, and *t.* certain, 17:4
18:22 if *t.* follow not, nor come
32:47 it is not a vain *t.* for you
Jud. 19:24 do not so vile a *t.*
Ruth 3:18 till he have finished *t.*
1 *Sam.* 3:11 I will do a *t.* in Isr.
17 what is the *t.* L. hath said?
4:7 not been such a *t.* heretof.
14:12 and we will show you a *t.*
18:20 told Saul, *t.* pleased him
2 *Sam.* 13:33 let not lord take *t.*
14:13 wheref. thought such *t.?*
18 hide not *t.* I shall ask thee
15:35 what *t.* shalt hear, tell Za.
1 *K.* 14:5 Jerob. cometh to ask *t.*
2 *K.* 20:9 the Lord will do the *t.*
1 *Chr.* 13:4 *t.* right in eyes of
17:23 let *t.* hast spok. be estab.
2 *Chr.* 29:36 *t.* done suddenly
Ezr. 7:27 a *t.* in king's heart
Est. 2:4 the *t.* pleased the king
Job 3:25 the *t.* I feared is come
6:8 th. G. wo. grant *t.* I long for
14:4 who can br. clean *t.* out of?
26:3 how hast decl. *t.* as it is?
42:7 not spo. *t.* that is right, 8
Ps. 2:1 why imagine a vain *t.?*
38:20 I follow *t.* that good is
89:34 nor alter *t.* that is gone
101:3 I set no wicked *t.* bef. eyes

Prov. 22:18 it is a pleasant *t.*
Ec. 7:8 better end of *t.* th. begin.
8:15 no better *t.* than to eat
11:7 pleas. *t.* for eyes to behold
Is. 29:16 sh. the *t.* framed say?
21 turn aside for *t.* of naught
40:15 isle. isles as a very little *t.*
43:19 I will do a new *t.* it shall
55:11 sh. prosper in *t.* where. I
66:8 who hath heard such a *t.*
Jer. 2:10 see if there be such a *t.*
18:13 Is. hath done a horrible *t.*
31:22 Lord hath created a new *t.*
Jer. 38:14 I will ask a *t.* hide not.
42:3 G. may show us *t.* we do
44:17 will do what *t.* goeth out
Lam. 2:13 what *t.* sh. I take to
witness? wh. *t.* liken to th.?
Ezek. 16:47 as if it were a little *t.*
Dan. 2:5 king said, *t.* is gone, 8
11 it is a rare *t.* king requireth
5:15 show interpreta. of the *t.*
6:12 *t.* is true, according to law
10:1 a *t.* was revealed to Daniel
Hos. 6:10 I ha. seen a horrible *t.*
Amos 5:11 rejoi. in a *t.* of naught
Mark 1:27 what *t.* is this? what
Luke 12:11 what *t.* ye sh. answ.
John 5:14 lest a worse *t.* come to
Acts 17:21 or hear some new *t.*
23:17 he hath a certain *t.* to tell
25:26 I have no cert. *t.* to write
Rom. 9:20 sh. *t.* form. say to him
1 *Cor.* 1:10 I beseech sp. same *t.*
2 *Cor.* 5:5 wro. us for self-same *t.*
Phil. 3:16 let us mind same *t.*
1 *Pet.* 4:12 as some stran. *t.* hap.
1 *John* 2:8 which *t.* is true in him

See ACCURSED.

Any THING.

Gen. 14:23 I will not take *any t.*
18:14 is *any t.* too hard for L.?
19:22 cannot do *any t.* till thou
be come
22:12 nei. do thou *any t.* to lad
30:31 Ja. said, Not give me *a. t.*
39:9 nei. hath he kept back *a. t.*
Ex. 20:17 nor *any t.* that is thy
neighbor's, *Deut.* 5:21
Lev. 15:6 sitteth on *a. t.* wher. 23
Num. 20:19 without doing *any t.*
22:38 have I power to say *a. t.?*
35:22 cast upon him *any t.*
Deut. 4:32 if hath been *a.* such *t.*
24:10 when dost lend bro. *a. t.*
31:13 who have known *any t.*
Jos. 21:45 failed not of *a. t.* spo.
Jud. 11:25 art *a. t.* better th. B.?
18:10 wh. no want of *a. t.* 19:19
1 *Sam.* 3:17 G. do so, if hide *a. t.*
20:26 S. spake not *a. t.* that day
21:2 let no man know *any t.* of
2 *Sam.* 13:2 tho. it hard to do *a. t.*
1 *K.* 10:3 was not *any t.* hid from
20:33 whether *a. t.* would come
2 *Chr.* 9:20 silv. not *a. t.* accoun.
Job 33:32 if thou hast *a. t.* to say
Ec. 1:10 *a. t.* whereof it may be
5:2 heart not hasty to utter *a. t.*
9:5 dead kn. not *a. t.* nor have
Jer. 32:27 *a. t.* too hard for me?
38:5 king not he th. can do *a. t.*
42:21 nor *a. t.* for wh. he sent me
Dan. 3:29 spe. *a. t.* amiss ag. G.
Mat. 18:19 agree touching *any t.*
24:17 take *any t.* out of his
house, *Mark* 13:15
Mark 4:22 *a. t.* secret, *Luke* 8:17
11:13 if he might find *any t.*
16:8 neither said they *any t.*
Luke 19:8 taken *a. t.* fr. any man
22:35 lacked ye *any t.?* nothing
John 1:3 with. him not *a. t.* ma.
7:4 no man doeth *a. t.* in secret
14:14 if ask *any t.* in my name
Acts 17:25 as tho' he needed *a. t.*

1 *Cor.* 10:19 that the idol is *a. t.*
2 *Cor.* 2:10 if I forgive *any t.*
1 *Thes.* 1:8 need not to spe. *a. t.*
1 *Tim.* 1:10 if th. be *a. t.* contra.
Rev. 21:27 *any t.* that defileth

Every THING.

Gen. 6:17 *ev. t.* in earth shall die
Lev. 22:37 offer *e. t.* upon his day
2 *Sam.* 15:36 send to me *every t.*

See CREEPETH, CREEPING, EVIL,
GOOD, GREAT, HOLY, LIGHT,
LIVING, ONE, SMALL.

That THING.

Gen. 18:17 hide fr. Abr. *t. t.* I do
Ex. 8:1 L. did *that t.* on morrow
Luke 9:21 to tell no man *that t.*
12:26 not able to do *t. t.* is least
Rom. 14:22 not himself in *that t.*

This THING.

Gen. 19:21 accep. th. concer. *t. t.*
20:10 that thou hast done *th. t.*
34:14 we cannot do *this t.*
41:28 *t.* is *t.* I have spoken to P.
44:7 we should do accor. to *t. t.*
Ex. 1:18 why have ye done *t. t.*
2:14 M. said, Surely *t. t.* is kno.
9:5 to-morrow L. shall do *t. t.*
16:16 *t.* is *t.* which Lord commanded. 32; 35:4; *Lev.* 8:5;
9:6; 17:2; *Num.* 30:1; 36:6;
Deut. 15:15; 24:18, 22
Ex. 18:14 wh. is *t. t.* doest to pe.?
29:1 *t.* is *t.* thou sh. do to them
33:17 I will do *t. t.* thou ha. spo.
Jos. 22:24 done it for fear of *t. t.*
Jud. 6:29 said, Who hath done *t.*
t.? Gideon hath done *this t.*
11:37 let *this t.* be done for me
20:9 *this* shall be *t.* we will do
21:11 *this* is *t.* ye shall do
1 *Sam.* 24:6 L. forbid I sh. do *t. t.*
26:16 *t.* is not good hast done
28:18 L. ha. done *t. t.* unto thee
2 *Sam.* 11:11 I do not *this t.*
12:5 man hath done *t. t.* sh. die
6 bec. he did *t. t.* had no pity
12 I will do *t. t.* before Israel
13:20 brother, regard not *this t.*
14:15 to speak of *this t.* to king
24:3 why doth lord del. in *t. t.?*
1 *K.* 1:27 is done by king?
3:10 pleased L. S. asked *t. t.* 11
12:24 return, for *t. t.* is from me
13:34 *t. t.* bec. sin to house of J.
20:9 tell king, *t. t.* I may not do
2 *K.* 5:18 in *t. t.* L. pardon serv.
11:5 *this* is *t.* that ye shall
do, 2 *Chr.* 23:4
17:12 L. said, Ye sh. not do *t. t.*
1 *Chr.* 11:19 G. forb. I sh. do *t. t.*
21:3 why doth my lord req. *t. t.*
8 sinned, bec. I have done *t. t.*
Ezr. 10:2 hope in Is. concer. *t. t.*
Neh. 2:19 wh. is *t. t.* that ye do.?
Is. 38:7 L. will do *t. t.* he ha. spo.
Jer. 22:4 if do *t. t.* enter in kings
40:3 theref. *t. t.* is come on you
Mark 5:32 her that done *this t.*
Luke 2:15 see *this t.* come to pass
22:23 which that should do *t. t.*
John 18:34 sayest *t. t.* of thyself?
2 *Cor.* 12:8 for *t. t.* I besought L.
Phil. 3:13 *t. t.* I do, press toward

Unclean THING.

Lev. 5:2 if a soul touch *u. t.* 7:21
7:19 flesh touch. *u. t.* not eaten
20:21 take bro.'s wife, it is *u. t.*
Deut. 23:14 see no *u. t.* in thee
Jud. 13:4 eat not any *u. t.* 7, 14
Is. 52:11 tou. no *u. t.* 2 *Cor.* 6:17
64:6 we are all as an *unclean t.*
Acts 10:14 never eaten any *t. u.*

THINGS.

Lev. 4:2 sin thro' ignor. conc. *t.*

Deut. 4:9 forget *t.* eyes have seen
29:29 secret *t.* belong unto Lord
32:35 *t.* th. come on them haste
1 *Sam.* 12:21 ye go after vain *t.*
2 *Sam.* 24:12 I offer thee three *t.*
    1 *Chr.* 21:10
1 *K.* 15:15 Asa brought in *t.* his
    father dedicated, 2 *Chr.* 15:18
1 *Chr.* 4:22 these are ancient *t.*
2 *Chr.* 12:12 in Jud. *t.* went well
Job 12:22 deep *t.* out of darkness
13:20 only do not two *t.* to me
41:34 behold. high *t.* king over
42:3 uttered *t.* too wonderful
Ps. 12:3 that speaketh proud *t.*
35:11 laid to charge *t.* I kn. not
45:1 I speak of *t.* I have made
60:3 showed thy people hard *t.*
65:5 by terrible *t.* wilt answer
72:18 G. who doeth wondrous *t.*
86:10 and doest wondrous *t.*
87:3 glorious *t.* are spo. of thee
94:4 how long utter hard *t.* ?
113:6 to behold *t.* in heaven
119:18 behold wondr. *t.* out law
131:1 or in *t.* too high for me
Prov. 8:6 speak of ex. *t.* right *t.*
22:20 written to th. excellent *t.*
23:33 thy heart utter perverse *t.*
30:7 two *t.* have I requ. of thee
    15 three *t.* that are never satis.
    18 three *t.* be too wonderful
21 for 3 *t.* earth is disquieted
24 four *t.* wh. are lit. on earth
29 there be three *t.* wh. go well
Ec. 7:25 wisdom and reason of *t.*
Is. 12:5 he hath done excellent *t.*
25:6 make to peo. feast of fat *t.*
41:23 show *t.* to come hereafter
42:9 *t.* come to pass, new *t.* dec.
44:7 *t.* that are com. shall come
45:11 ask me of *t.* to come
    19 I declare *t.* that are right
48:6 showed thee new *t.* hid. *t.*
64:3 thou didst terrible *t.* we
Jer. 2:8 *t.* do not profit, 16:19
8:13 I hav. giv. them sh. pass
Lam. 1:7 J. rememb. pleasant *t.*
2:14 proph. have seen foolish *t.*
Ezek. 11:5 I kn. *t.* come in mind
16:16 like *t.* shall not come
Joel 3:5 into temp. my goodly *t.*
Ob. 6 how are *t.* of Es. searched
Mic. 7:15 sh. unto him marv, *t.*
Zec. 4:10 desp. day of small *t.*
Mat. 6:34 thought for *t.* of itself
13:52 out of treas. *t.* new and old
22:21 render to Cesar *t.* that are
    C.'s, to God *t.* that are God's,
    Mark 12:17; *Luke* 20:25
Luke 5:26 seen strange *t.* to-day
6:46 and do not *t.* which I say
10:23 blessed eyes which see *t.*
18:27 *t.* impossible with men
19:42 known *t.* belong to peace
22:37 *t.* concer. me have an end
23:48 peo. behold *t.* were done
24:18 not kno. *t.* come to pass
John 1:50 greater *t.* than these
3:12 told earthly *t.* heavenly *t.*
16:13 will show you *t.* to come
Acts 4:20 cannot but spe. *t.* seen
    32 aught of *t.* he possessed
20:22 not know. *t.* sh. befall me
24:13 nei. can they prove the *t.*
Rom. 2:1 that judg. doest same *t.*
    14 by nat. *t.* contained in law
8:5 mind *t.* of flesh, mi. *t.* of S.
    38 nor *t.* present, nor *t.* to
    come, 1 *Cor.* 3:22
12:16 not high *t.* 17 *t.* honest
14:19 fol. *t.* that make for peace
1 *Cor.* 1:27 G. hath chosen fool. *t.*
    of world to confo. *t.* mighty
2:9 *t.* God hath prep. for them
    10 Spirit search. deep *t.* of G.
    11 what man know. *t.* of man
    12 might know *t.* freely given

---

    14 man receiveth not *t.* of Spi.
6:3 more *t.* that pert. to life, 4
10:20 *t.* which Gentiles sacrifice
14:37 acknowledge *t.* I write to
2 *Cor.* 1:13 write none other *t.* to
    17 or *t.* I purpose, do I purpo.
4:18 look not at *t.* wh. are seen
5:10 receive *t.* done in his body
    18 old *t.* passed, all *t.* bec. new
10:7 ye look on *t.* after outward
    13 boast of *t.* without meas. 15
    16 not boast in anoth. man's *t.*
11:30 glo. of *t.* wh. concern mine
Gal. 2:18 build ag. *t.* I destroyed
5:17 cannot do *t.* that ye would
Eph. 6:9 do same *t.* to them
Phil. 1:12 *t.* whi. happen. to me
2:4 lo. not ev. man on his own *t.*
    10 *t.* in hea. *t.* on earth, *t.* und.
    21 seek not *t.* which are J. C.'s
3:1 write same *t.* 19 earthly *t.*
4:8 whatso. *t.* are true, honest
    18 received *t.* sent from you
Col. 1:20 *t.* in earth, *t.* in heaven
2:23 which *t.* ha. show of wisd.
3:6 for wh. *t.* wrath of G. come.
1 *Thes.* 2:14 ye ha. suffer. like *t.*
2 *Thes.* 3:4 do *t.* wh. we commа.
1 *Tim.* 5:13 speak. *t.* ought not
2 *Tim.* 2:2 *t.* th. hast heard of me
3:14 continue in *t.* th. hast lear.
Tit. 2:1 spe. *t.* wh. become doc.
Heb. 2:1 heed to *t.* we have heard
6:9 we are persuaded better *t.*
11:1 faith substance of *t.* hoped,
    the evidence of *t.* not seen
    3 *t.* seen not made of *t.* wh. ap.
12:24 speak. better *t.* than Abel
1 *Pet.* 1:12 did minister *t.* report.
2 *Pet.* 2:12 evil of *t.* th. under. not
1 *John* 2:15 neither *t.* in the wor.
Rev. 1:19 write *t.* whi. thou hast
    seen, *t.* which are, *t.* sh. be
2:14 I have a few *t.* against thee
4:1 show thee *t.* must be hereaf.
21:4 former *t.* are passed away

See CREEPING, DEDICATE, DE-
    TESTABLE, EVIL, FORMER,
    HOLY, MANY, PRECIOUS,
    SUCH.

All THINGS.

Gen. 9:3 have I given you *all t.*
24:1 L. hath blessed Ab. in *all t.*
Ex. 29:35 do according to *all t.* I
    have commanded thee
Num. 1:50 Levites over *a. t.* that
Deut. 1:18 com. *a. t.* ye shou. do
4:7 our God is in *a. t.* we call for
12:8 not do after *a. t.* we do here
Jos. 1:17 hearken. to M. in *all t.*
Ruth 4:7 manner, to confirm *a. t.*
1 *Sam.* 3:17 hide any of *all t.*
19:7 Jonath. showed Dav. *all t.*
2 *Sam.* 11:18 Joab told Dav. *a. t.*
14:20 kn. *all t.* that are in earth
23:5 a covenant ordered in *all t.*
1 *K.* 21:26 he did *all t.* as Amori.
2 *K.* 20:15 they have seen *all t.*
1 *Chr.* 29:14 *all t.* come of thee
Neh. 9:6 thou, Lord, made *all t.*
    Acts 14:15; 17:24, 25; *Col.*
    1:16; *Rev.* 4:11
Job 41:34 he beholdeth *all* high *t.*
Ps. 8:6 hast put *all t.* under his
    feet, 1 *Cor.* 15:27; *Eph.* 1:22
57:2 God that performeth *all t.*
119:128 precepts concern. *all t.*
Prov. 3:15 more prec. th. *a. t.* 8:11
16:4 the Lord hath made *all t.*
28:5 seek L. understand *all t.*
Ec. 7:15 *all t.* have I seen
9:2 *all t.* come alike to all
10:19 but money answer. *all t.*
Is. 44:24 L. that mak. *all t.* 66:2
Jer. 10:16 is former of *all t.* 51:19
44:18 we wanted *all t.* and have
Ezek. 11:25 I spa. *a. t.* L. showed

Zep. 1:2 I will consume *all t.*
Mat. 7:12 *all t.* ye would men sh.
11:27 *a. t.* deli. to me, *Lu.* 10:22
19:26 with God *all t.* are pos-
    sible, *Mark* 10:27; 14:36
21:22 *all t.* whatsoever ye ask
28:20 teaching to observe *all t.*
Mark 6:30 they told him *all t.*
7:37 he hath done *all t.* well
13:23 I have foretold you *all t.*
Luke 2:20 praising God for *all t.*
9:43 wondered at *all t.* Jesus did
11:41 *all t.* are clean unto you
John 1:3 *all t.* were made by him
3:35 gi. *all t.* into his hand, 13:3
4:25 he will tell us *all t.*
    29 see a man who told me *a. t.*
5:20 Father showeth Son *all t.*
10:41 *a. t.* John spake were true
15:15 *all t.* I heard, I made kno.
16:15 *all t.* Fath. hath are mine
    30 we are sure thou know. *a. t.*
17:7 *all t.* thou hast given me
18:4 Jesus knowing *all t.* 19:28
21:17 P. said, L. thou know. *a. t.*
Acts 3:22 him sh. ye hear in *a. t.*
10:33 hear *all t.* command. of G.
    39 we are witnesses of *all t.* he
14:15 who made earth and *all t.*
20:35 I have showed you *all t.*
22:10 there it sh. be told th. *a. t.*
Rom. 8:28 we kn. *all t.* work for
    32 sh. he not free. gi. us *a. t.* ?
11:36 thro' him and to him *a. t.*
14:20 *all t.* indeed are pure
1 *Cor.* 2:10 Spirit searcheth *a. t.*
3:21 in men, for *all t.* are yours
6:12 *all t.* are not expedi. 10:23
8:6 one G. the F. of wh. are *a. t.*
    one L. J. C. by wh. are *all t.*
10:33 as I please men in *all t.*
11:12 *all t.* are of G. 2 *Cor.* 5:18
15:28 when *all t.* sh. be subdued
2 *Cor.* 4:15 *all t.* for your sakes
5:17 are away, *a. t.* become new
6:10 nothing, yet possess. *all t.*
7:14 spake *all t.* to you in truth
11:6 manifest to you in *all t.*
Eph. 1:10 gath. toge. in one *a. t.*
    22 to be head over *all t.*
3:9 in God, who created *all t.*
5:20 giv. thanks always for *a. t.*
6:21 make' known *all t.* *Col.* 4:9
Phil. 3:8 I count *all t.* but loss
4:12 and in *all t.* I am instruct.
    13 I can do *all t.* through Chr.
Col. 1:17 before *all t.* by him *a. t.*
1 *Thes.* 5:21 prove *all t.* hold fast
3 *John* 2 I wish above *all t.* that
Rev. 21:5 beh. I make *all t.* new
    7 that overcometh sh. inh. *a. t.*

These THINGS.

Gen. 42:36 J. said, *t. t.* are ag. me
Num. 15:13 all born shall do *t. t.*
Deut. 30:1 *t. t.* are come upon
Jos. 2:11 heard *t. t.* our hearts
2 *Sam.* 23:17 *t. t.* did these three
    mighty men, 1 *Chr.* 11:19
Neh. 13:26 did not So. sin by *t. t.*
Job 8:2 how long will speak *t. t.* ?
10:13 *t. t.* hast thou hid in heart
33:29 *t. t.* worketh G. with man
Ps. 15:5 he that doeth *t. t.* shall
50:21 *t. t.* hast thou done and I
Prov. 6:16 *t.* six *t.* doth L. hate
24:23 *t. t.* also belong to wise
Ec. 11:9 for *t. t.* will G. br. thee
Is. 38:16 O L. by *t. t.* men live,
    in *t. t.* is the life of my spir.
42:16 *t. t.* will I do, not forsake
51:19 *t.* two *t.* are come unto th.
Jer. 3:7 aft. she had done all *t. t.*
5:9 sh. I not vi. for *t. t.* ? 29 ; 9:9
9:24 for in *t. t.* do I delight
13:22 wheref. come *t. t.* on me?
14:22 thou hast made all *th. t.*
30:15 for thy sins ha. I done *t. t.*

Ezek. 16:30 doest all *t. t.* 17:18
17:12 kn. ye not what *t. t.* mean
23:30 I will do *th. t.* unto thee
24:19 wilt not tell wh. *t. t.* are?
Dan. 12:8 what be end of *t. t.* ?
Zec. 8:16 *t.* are the *t.* whi. ye sh.

Zec, 8:17 all *t.* are *t.* that I hate
Mat. 6:33 all *th. t.* shall be added
    unto you, *Luke* 12:31
13:56 whence then hath this
    man *these t. Mark* 6:2
19:20 all *t. t.* have I kept fr. my
23:36 *t. t.* sh. come on thee gen.
24:2 J. said, See ye not all *t. t.* ?
    3 tell us when shall *these t.*
    be? *Mark* 13:4 ; *Luke* 21:7
    34 till *t. t.* be fulfil. *Mark* 13:30
Luke 15:26 ask. wh. *t. t.* meant ?
24:21 third day since *th. t.* were
John 2:16 said, Take *t. t.* hence
    18 seeing that thou doest *t. t.*
3:9 Nic. said, How can *t. t.* be ?
13:17 if ye kn. *t. t.* happy are ye
15:21 all *t. t.* will they do, 16:3
Acts 7:1 are *these t.* so? 14:15 do
    ye *these t. ?*
15:17 the L. who doeth all *t. t.*
17:20 wo. know what *t. t.* mean
20:24 none of *these t.* move me
26:26 king knoweth of *these t.*
Rom. 8:31 what shall we say to
    these t. ?
    14:18 he that in *th. t.* serv. Chr.
Jam. 3:10 breth. *t. t.* ought not
2 *Pet.* 1:10 if ye do *these t.*
3:17 seeing ye know *t. t.* before

Those THINGS.

Lev. 22:2 in *t. t.* whi. they allow
Ps. 107:43 whoso will obser. *t. t.*
Is. 66:2 all *th. t.* hath my hand
Mat. 13:17 desired to see *t. t.* wh.
John 8:29 *t. t.* that please him
Acts 3:18 *t. t.* he hath fulfilled
13:45 spake ag. *those t.* which
26:16 of *t. t.* in wh. I will appe.
Col. 3:1 seek *t. t.* whi. are above
Jam. 2:16 give not *t. t.* wh. are

Unclean THINGS.

Hos. 9:3 they sh. eat *u. t.* in Assy.

What THINGS.

Ex. 10:2 tell son *w. t.* I wrought
Mat. 6:8 F. knows *w. t.* ye need
Mark 9:9 tell no man *w. t.* they
11:24 *w. t.* soever ye desire
Luke 7:22 tell J. *w. t.* have seen
24:35 they told *w. t.* were done
John 5:19 *what t.* he doeth
10:6 unders. not *w. t.* they were
11:46 told *w. t.* Jesus had done
Phil. 3:7 *w. t.* were gain to me

THINK.

Gen. 40:14 *t.* on me wh. it be well
Num. 36:6 marry to wh. *t.* best
2 *Sam.* 13:33 to *t.* king's sons are
2 *Chr.* 13:8 ye *t.* to withsta. king
Neh. 5:19 *t.* on me, my God
6:6 thou and Jews *t.* to rebel
    14 God *t.* on Tobiah and Sanb.
Est. 4:13 *t.* not thou shalt escape
Job 31:1 why should I *t.* upon a
    maid ?
41:32 would *t.* deep be hoary
Ec. 8:17 though a wise man *t.*
Is. 10:7 nor doth his heart *t.* so
Jer. 23:27 *t.* cause my peo. forget
29:11 thoughts I *t.* toward you
Ezek. 38:10 sh. *t.* an evil thought
Dan. 7:25 shall *t.* to change tim.
Jon. 1:6 if God will *t.* upon us
Zec. 11:12 if ye *t.* good give me
Mat. 3:9 and *t.* not to say within
5:17 *t.* not I am come to destroy
6:7 *t.* they sh. be heard for spe.
9:4 why *t.* ye evil in yo. hearts
10:34 *t.* not I co. to send peace
18:12 how *t.* ye? if ha. hundred

22:42 what *t.* ye of Chr. ? 26:66 ;
    Mark 14:64
24:44 as ye *t.* not, *Luke* 12:40
Luke 13:4 *t.* ye th. were sinners
John 5:39 ye *t.* ye have eter. life
    45 do not I. I will accuse you
11:56 wh. *t.* ye, th. he will not ?
16:2 will *t.* that he doth G. ser.
Acts 13:25 whom *t.* ye th. I am ?
17:29 not to *t.* that Godhead
26:2 I *t.* myself happy, king Ag.
Rom. 12:3 not to *t.* of hims. more
    than he ought to *t.* but to *t.*
1 *Cor.* 4:6 learn in us not to *t.* of
    9 I *t.* G. hath set forth us apo.
7:40 I *t.* also I have Spirit of G.
8:2 if any man *t.* he knoweth
12:23 we *t.* to be less honorable
14:37 if any *t.* himself a prophet
2 *Cor.* 3:5 to *t.* any thing of our.
10:2 I *t.* to be bold against some
    which *t.* of us
    7 Ch. let him *t.* this again, 11
11:16 let no man *t.* me a fool
12:6 lest any *t.* of me above wh.
Gal. 6:3 if a man *t.* himself to be
Eph. 3:20 above all we ask or *t.*
Phil. 4:8 if any praise, *t.* on these
Jam. 1:7 let not man *t.* he sh. re.
4:5 do ye *t.* that scripture saith
1 *Pet.* 4:4 wherein they *t.* strange
    12 *t.* it not strange concerning
2 *Pet.* 1:13 I *t.* it meet as long as

THINKEST.

2 *Sam.* 10:3 *t.* thou David doth
    honor thy fath. ? 1 *Chr.* 19:3
Job 35:2 *t.* thou this right, that
Mat. 17:25 What *t.* thou ? 22:17
26:53 *t.* th. I cannot pray to my
Luke 10:36 wh. *t.* th. was neigh.
Acts 28:22 de. to hear what th. *t.*
Rom. 2:3 *t.* thou this, O man

THINKETH.

2 *Sam.* 18:27 *t.* running of fore.
Ps. 40:17 poor, yet Lord *t.* on me
Prov. 23:7 as he *t.* in his heart
1 *Cor.* 10:12 let him that *t.* he st.
13:5 charity seek. not, *t.* no evil
Phil. 3:4 if any *t.* he hath where.

THINKING.

2 *Sam.* 4:10 *t.* to have bro. good
5:6 I. Da. cannot come in hither

THIRD.

Gen. 32:19 so commanded he *t.*
2 *K.* 1:13 he sent capt. of *t.* fifty
Is. 19:24 Is. sh. be *t.* with Egypt
Dan. 2:39 ano. *t.* kingd. of brass
5:7 *t.* ruler in kingdom, 16, 29
Zec. 6:3 in *t.* chariot white hors.
Mat. 20:3 went out about *t.* hour
22:26 likew. the *t.* died, *Mark*
    12:21 ; *Luke* 20:31
Luke 20:12 sent *t.* wounded him
Acts 2:15 seei. it is *t.* hour of day
23:23 ready at *t.* hour of night
2 *Cor.* 12:2 caught up to *t.* heav.
Rev. 4:7 *t.* beast h. face as a man
6:5 opened *t.* seal, heard *t.* beast
8:10 *t.* angel sounded, fell a star
11:14 be. *t.* woe cometh quickly
14:9 *t.* angel followed them
16:4 *t.* angel poured vial on riv.
See DAY, MONTH, PART.

THIRD time.

1 *Sam.* 3:8 L. called Samuel *t. t.*
19:21 Saul sent messenger *t. t.*
1 *K.* 18:34 do it *t. t.* th. did it *t. t.*
Ezek. 21:14 sword be doubled *t. t.*
Mat. 26:44 prayed *t. t. Ma.* 14:41
John 21:14 *t. t.* Je. showed hims.
    17 saith *t. t.* Lovest thou me ?
    P. grieved, bec. he said *t. t.*
2 *Cor.* 12:14 *t. t.* ready to co. 13:1

THIRD year.

Deut. 26:12 *t. y.* year of tithing
2 *K.* 19:29 in *t. y.* sow, *Is.* 37:30

THIRDLY.

1 *Cor.* 12:28 *t.* teachers, miracles

THIRST, Substantive.

Ex. 17:3 kill us and chil. with *t.*
Deut. 28:48 serve enemies in *t.*
29:19 to add drunkenness to *t.*
Jud. 15:18 now I shall die for *t.*
2 *Chr.* 32:11 persuade to die by *t.*
Neh. 9:15 brought. water for *t.* 20
Job 24:11 wine-presses and suf. *t.*
Ps. 69:21 in *t.* gave me vinegar
104:11 wild asses quench th. *t.*
Is. 5:13 multil . dried up with *t.*
41:17 when tongue faileth for *t.*
50:2 fish stinketh, dieth for *t.*
Jer. 2:25 withh. thy throat fr. *t.*
48:18 come fr. thy glory, sit in *t.*
Lam. 4:4 cleaveth to mou. for *t.*
Hos. 2:3 naked, slay her with *t.*
Amos 8:11 not *t.* for water
    13 young men shall faint for *t.*
2 *Cor.* 11:27 in hunger and *t.*

THIRST, Verb.

Is. 49:10 shall not hunger, nor *t.*
Mat. 5:6 hung. and *t.* after right.
John 4:13 drink. of this water *t.*
    14 drinketh, shall never *t.* 6:35
    15 give me this wa. th. I *t.* not
7:37 any *t.* let him come to me
19:28 after this, Jesus saith, I *t.*
Rom. 12:20 if enemy *t.* gi. drink
1 *Cor.* 4:11 to present hour we *t.*
Rev. 7:16 th. sh. not *t.* any more

THIRSTED, ETH.

Ex. 17:3 peo. *t.* there for water
Ps. 42:2 my soul *t.* for God, 63:1 ;
    143:6
Is. 48:21 they *t.* not when he led
55:1 ev. one that *t.* come to wa.

THIRSTY

Jud. 4:19 give me water, I am *t.*
2 *Sam.* 17:29 peo. is *t.* in wilder.
Ps. 63:1 longeth in *t.* land, 143:6
107:5 hungry and *t.* soul fainted
Prov. 25:21 if enemy *t.* gi. drink
    25 as cold waters to a *t.* soul,
    so good news
Is. 21:14 wat. to him that was *t.*
29:8 be as when *t.* man dream.
32:6 cause drink of the *t.* to fail
35:7 *t.* land bec. springs of wat.
44:3 pour wat. on him that is *t.*
65:13 serva. drink, but ye be *t.*
Ezek. 19:13 she is plan. in *t.* gro.
Mat. 25:35 I was *t.* ye gave drink
    37 when saw we thee *t. ?*
    42 I was *t.* ye gave no drink

THIRTEEN.

Gen. 17:25 Ish. was *t.* years old
Num. 29:13 offer *t.* bullocks, 14
1 *K.* 7:1 building house *t.* years

THIRTEENTH.

Gen. 14:4 in *t.* year they rebelled
See DAY.

THIRTIETH.

2 *K.* 15:13 reign in nine and *t. y.*
    17 nine and *t.* year of Azariah
25:27 seven and *t.* year of the
    captivity of Jehoi. *Jer.* 52:31
2 *Chr.* 15:19 five and *t.* year of A.
16:1 in six and *t.* year of Asa
Neh. 5:14 two and *t.* y. of A. 13:6

THIRTY.

Gen. 6:15 height of ark *t.* cubits
11:14 Salah lived *t.* years, begat
18:30 th. sh. be *t.* found, he sa.
    I will not do it if I find *t.*
41:46 Joseph was *t.* years old
Num. 4:23 from *t.* years old and
    up, 23, 47 ; 1 *Chr.* 23:3
Jud. 14:12 give you *t.* sheets
20:31 smite abo. *t.* men of Is. 39
1 *Sam.* 9:22 Saul sat amo. *t.* per.
2 *Sam.* 5:4 Dav. was *t.* years old
1 *K.* 4:22 provision was *t.* meas.

Jer. 38:10 take from hen. *t.* men
Ezek. 41:6 side chambers were *t.*
Zec. 11:12 weigh. for my price *t.*
  13 *t.* pieces of silver, *Mat.* 27:9
Mat. 13:8 brought forth some *t.*
  fold, 23 ; *Mark* 4:8, 20
  26:15 covenanted for *t.* pieces
  27:3 Judas brought ag. *t.* pieces
Luke 3:23 began to be *t.* yea. old
John 6:19 rowed 25 or *t.* furlongs
See DAYS.

THIRTY-ONE.
Jos. 12:24 kings J. subdu. *t.-one*
1 *K.* 16:23 in *t.* and o. year of A.

THIRTY-TWO.
Num. 31:40 L.'s tribu. *t.-t.* pers.

THIRTY-THREE.
Gen. 46:15 sons and daugh. *t.-t.*
Lev. 12:4 bl. of purify. *t.-t.* days

THIRTY-FOUR.
Gen. 11:16 Eber lived *t.-f* years

THIRTY-FIVE.
2 *Chr.* 3:15 pillars *t.-f.* cubits

THIRTY-SIX.
Jos. 7:5 men of Ai sm. *t.-s.* of Is.

THIRTY-SEVEN.
2 *Sam.* 23:39 Uriah, *t.-s.* in all

THIRTY-EIGHT.
Deut. 2:14 over Zered *t.-e.* years
John 5:5 had infirmity *t.-e.* years

THIRTY-NINE.
2 *Chr.* 16:12 A. in *t.-n.* year dis.
See THOUSAND.

THISTLE, S.
Gen. 3:18 *t.* shall it bring forth
2 *K.* 14:9 *t.* was in Leban. wild
  beast trod *t.* 2 *Chr.* 25:18
Job 31:40 let *t.* grow inst. wheat
Hos. 10:8 *t.* come up on th. altars
Mat. 7:16 do men ga. figs of *t.?*

THITHER.
Gen. 19:22 esca. *t.* tell be come *t.*
Num. 35:6 that the slayer may
  flee *t.* 11, 15 ; *Deut.* 4:42 ; 19:3,
  4 ; *Jos.* 20:3, 9
Deut. 1:37 sh. not go in *t.* 38, 39
2 *K.* 2:8 divided hither and *t.* 14
Luke 17:37 where carcass is, *t.*
  will the eagles be gathered
John 7:34 *t.* cannot come, 36
  11:8 and goeth thou *t.* again ?

THITHERWARD.
Jer. 50:5 to Z. with their faces *t.*

THOMAS.
Mat. 10:3 T. and Matthew, *Mark*
  3:18 ; *Luke* 6:15 ; *Acts* 1:13
John 11:16 T. said, Let us go
  20:24 T. was not with them
  26 T. with them, then came
    Jesus
John 20:27 to T. reach hith. fin.
  21:2 together Si Peter and T.

THONGS.
Acts 22:25 bound him with *t.*

THORN.
Job 41:2 canst bore jaw with *t. ?*
Prov. 26:9 as *t.* goeth into hand
Is. 55:13 instead of *t.* fir-tree
Ezek. 28:24 no more any grie. *t.*
Hos. 10:8 *t.* come up on th. alta.
Mic. 7:4 upri. sharper than *t.* he.
2 *Cor.* 12:7 gi. to me a *t.* in flesh

THORNS.
Gen. 3:18 *t.* and thistles br. forth
Ex. 22:6 break out, catch in *t.*
Num. 33:55 they sh. be *t.* in your
  sides, *Jud.* 2:3
Jos. 23:13 they shall be *t.* in eyes
2 *Sam.* 23:6 sons of Bel. be as *t.*
2 *Chr.* 33:11 took Man. among *t.*
Ps. 58:9 bef. pots feel *t.* take th.
  118:12 quenched as a fire of *t.*

Prov. 15:19 slothf. as hedge of *t.*
  22:5 *t.* are in way of froward
  24:31 it was grown over with *t.*
Ec. 7:6 as crackling of *t.* under
Cant. 2:2 lily am. *t.* so my love
Is. 7:19 they shall rest upon *t.*
  32:13 sh. come up *t.* and briers
  34:13 *t.* sh. come up in palaces
Jer. 4:3 and sow not among *t.*
  12:13 sown wheat, shall reap *t.*
Hos. 2:6 I will hedge way with *t.*
  9:6 *t.* sh. be in th. tabernacles
Nah. 1:10 be folden togeth. as *t.*
Mat. 7:16 do men gather grapes
  of *t. ? Luke* 6:44
  13:7 fell among *t.* 22 ; *Mark* 4:7,
  18 ; *Luke* 8:7, 14
  27:29 platted crown of *t.* put it
  on, *Mark* 15:17 ; *John* 19:2

THOROUGHLY. *See* THROUGH-
LY.

THOUGHT, Verb.
Gen. 20:11 I *t.* fear of God not in
  38:15 he *t.* her to be a harlot
  48:11 had not *t.* to see thy face
  50:20 ye *t.* evil against me
Ex. 32:14 repented of evil he *t.*
Num. 24:11 I *t.* to promote thee
  33:56 you, as I *t.* to do to them
Deut. 19:19 as he *t.* to have done
Jud. 15:2 I *t.* th. hadst hated her
1 *Sam.* 1:13 Eli *t.* she been drun.
  18:25 Saul *t.* to make David fall
2 *Sam.* 4:10 who *t.* I give reward
  13:2 Amnon *t.* it hard to do any
  21:16 Ishbi-be. *t.* to ha. slain D.
2 *K.* 5:11 I *t.* he will come out
2 *Chr.* 11:22 Reho. *t.* to make A.
  32:1 Sennacherib *t.* to win them
Neh. 6:2 th. *t.* to do me mischief
Est. 3:6 he *t.* scorn to lay hands
  6:6 Haman *t.* in his heart
Ps. 48:9 we *t.* of thy loving-kind.
  73:16 when I *t.* to know this it
  119:59 I *t.* on my ways, turned
Prov. 30:32 thou hast *t.* lay hand
Is. 14:24 *t.* so sh. it come to pass
Jer. 18:8 repent of evil I *t.* to do
Zec. 1:6 like as Lord of hosts *t.*
  8:14 *t.* to punish ; 15 *t.* do dwell
Mal. 3:16 for th. that *t.* on name
Mat. 1:20 while he *t.* on th. thin.
Mark 14:72 when he *t.* he wept
Luke 7:7 nor *t.* myself worthy to
  12:17 he *t.* within himself
  19:11 they *t.* kingd. of G. appear
John 11:13 *t.* he had spok. of rest
Acts 8:20 *t.* gift of G. be purcha.
  10:19 while Peter *t.* on vision
  12:9 but *t.* he saw a vision
  15:38 P. *t.* not good to take him
  26:8 why be *t.* a thi. incredible ?
  t. I ought to do many things
1 *Cor.* 13:11 child, I *t.* as a child
Phil. 2:6 *t.* it not robbery to eq.
Heb. 10:29 pun. he be *t.* worthy

THOUGHTEST.
Ps. 50:21 thou *t.* I was as thyself

THOUGHT.
Deut. 15:9 not a *t.* in thy heart
1 *Sam.* 9:5 lest my father take *t.*
Job 12:5 is despised in *t.* of him
  42:2 that no *t.* can be withhold.
Ps. 49:11 their *t.* is, their houses
  64:6 the inward *t.* of every one
  139:2 thou understandest my *t.*
Prov. 24:9 *t.* of foolishness is sin
Ec. 10:20 curse not king in *t.*
Ezek. 38:10 thou sh. think evil *t.*
Amos 4:13 declare. to man his *t.*
Mat. 6:25 take no *t.* for your life,
  31:34 ; 10:19 ; *Mark* 13:11 ;
    Luke 12:11. 22
Mat. 6:27 which of you by tak-
  ing *t.* can add unto stature?
  Luke 12:25

---

  28 take *t.* for rai. ? *Luke* 12:26
Acts 8:22 if *t.* of thy heart may
2 *Cor.* 10:5 bri. into captiv. ev. *t.*

THOUGHTS.
Gen. 6:5 imagination of *t.* of his
Jud. 5:15 for Reub. were great *t.*
1 *Chr.* 28:9 L. understandeth *t.*
  29:18 keep in imaginat. of the *t.*
Job 4:13 in *t.* fr. visions of night
  17:11 purpos. are broken, my *t.*
  20:2 my *t.* cause me to answer
  21:27 I know your *t.* and devic.
Ps. 10:4 God is not in all his *t.*
  33:11 the *t.* of his heart to all
  40:5 thy *t.* cannot be reckoned
  56:5 all their *t.* are against me
  92:5 how gre. thy works! thy *t.*
  94:11 L. knoweth the *t.* of man
  19 in multitude of *t.* within me
  119:113 I hate vain *t.* thy law
  139:17 how precious are thy *t.*
  23 O God, try me, know my *t.*
  146:4 in that very day his *t.* pe.
Prov. 12:5 the *t.* of the righteous
  15:26 the *t.* of wicked are abom.
  16:3 thy *t.* shall be established
  21:5 *t.* of the diligent tend to
Is. 55:7 let unrighteous forsake *t.*
  8 my *t.* are not your *t.* saith L.
  9 so are my *t.* higher th. yo. *t.*
  59:7 their *t.* are *t.* of iniquity
  65:2 peo. walketh after their *t.*
  66:18 I know their works and *t.*
Jer. 4:14 how long shall vain *t. ?*
  6:19 even the fruit of their *t.*
  23:20 till he have performed *t.*
  29:11 I know the *t.* I think to-
    wards you, *t.* of peace
Dan. 2:30 migh. know *t.* of heart
  4:5 Nebuchadnez.'s *t.* trou. him
  19 D. was astonish. *t.* troubled
  5:6 Belshazzar's *t.* troubled him
  10 Let not thy *t.* trouble thee
Mic. 4:12 they know not *t.* of L.
Mat. 9:4 J. knowi. their *t.* 12:25 ;
  Luke 5:22 ; 6:8 ; 9:47 ; 11:17
  15:19 out of heart proceed evil *t.*
  Mark 7:21
Luke 2:35 the *t.* of many hearts
  24:38 why do *t.* arise in hearts?
Rom. 2:15 their *t.* accusing
1 *Cor.* 3:20 the Lord knoweth *t.*
Heb. 4:12 God is a discerner of *t.*
Jam. 2:4 become judges of evil *t.*

THOUSAND.
Gen. 20:16 given bro. a *t.* pieces
Num. 31:4 of every tribe a *t.* 5, 6
  35:4 suburbs of cities are *t.* cub.
Deut. 1:11 L. ma. you a *t.* times
  7:9 G. keepeth cove. to *t.* gene.
  32:30 one chase a *t. ? Jos.* 23:10
Jud. 9:49 of Shec. died, about *t.*
  15:15 Samson slew a *t.* men, 16
  20:10 hundred of a *t.* a *t.* out of
1 *Sam.* 18:13 Dav. capt. over a *t.*
2 *Sam.* 19:17 there were a *t.* men
1 *Chr.* 12:14 great. was over a *t.*
  16:15 commanded to a *t.* gener.
Job 9:3 cannot answer one of a *t.*
  33:23 an interpreter, one of a *t.*
  42:12 Job had a *t.* yoke of oxen,
    a *t.* she-asses
Ps. 50:10 cattle on a *t.* hills are
  84:10 day in courts be. than a *t.*
  90:4 *t.* years in thy sight are but
  91:7 a *t.* shall fall at thy side
Ec. 6:6 though he live a *t.* years
  7:28 one man a among *t.* have I
Cant. 8:11 fruit was to bring a *t.*
Is. 7:23 a *t.* vines at a *t.* silverli.
  30:17 one *t.* shall flee at rebuke
  60:22 a little one shall beco. a *t.*
Ezek. 47:3 man measur. *t.* cubits
Amos 5:3 city went out by a *t.*
2 *Pet.* 3:8 one day wi. L. is as a *t.*
  years, a *t.* years as one day

Rev. 20:2 he bound Sa. a *t.* years
3 deceive no more, till *t.* years
4 they reigned with C. a *t.* yrs.
7 when the *t.* years are expired

One THOUSAND two hundred sixty.

Rev. 11:3 proph. *o. t. t. h. s.* days
12:6 feed her *o. t. t. h. s.* days

One THOUSAND two hundred ninety.

Dan. 12:11 shall be *o. t. t. h. n.*

THOUSAND three hundred thirty-five.

Dan. 12:12 co. to *t. t. h. t.-f.* days

One THOUSAND six hundred.

Rev. 14:20 space of *o. t. s. h.* fur.

Two THOUSAND.

Num. 35:5 mea. on east side *t. t.*
1 *K.* 7:26 sea contain. *t. t.* baths
2 *K.* 18:23 I will deliver thee *two t.* horses, *Is.* 36:8
Neh. 7:72 peo. gave *t. t.* pounds
Mark 5:13 about *two t.* swine

Two THOUSAND two hundred.

Neh. 7:71 *t. t. h.* pounds silver

Two THOUSAND three hundred.

Dan. 8:14 *t. t. t. h.* days, sanctu.

Two hundred THOUSAND.

2 *Chr.* 28:8 carried capt. *two h. t.*

Two hundred eighty THOUSAND.

2 *Chr.* 14:8 out of Benj. *t. h. e. t.*

Three THOUSAND.

Ex. 32:28 fell of people *three t.*
Jud. 15:11 *t. t.* went to bind S.
16:27 were upon roof *t. t.* men
1 *Sam.* 24:2 S. took *t. t.* men, 26:2
1 *K.* 4:32 So. spake *t. t.* proverbs
Job 1:3 substa. was *t. t.* camels
Jer. 52:28 carried capt. *t. t.* Jews
Acts 2:41 were added *t. t.* souls

Four THOUSAND.

1 *Sam.* 4:2 slew of Is. about *f. t.*
2 *Chr.* 9:25 Sol. had *f. t.* stalls
Mat. 15:38 th. that eat were *f. t.*
Mark 8:9
16:10 seven loaves among *four t.*
Mark 8:20
Acts 21:38 leddest into wild. *f. t.*

Five THOUSAND.

Jos. 8:12 he took about *f. t* men
Jud. 20:45 they gleaned *f. t.* men
Ezr. 2:69 they gave *f. t.* pounds
Mat. 14:21 had eat. were ab. *f. t.*
16:9 five loaves of *five t. Mark* 6:44; 8:19; *Luke* 9:14; *John* 6:10
Acts 4:4 that believed were *f. t.*

Six THOUSAND.

1 *Sam.* 13:5 against Is. with *s. t.*
2 *K.* 5:5 Naaman took *s. t.* piec.
1 *Chr.* 23:4 *six t.* were officers
Job 42:12 Job had *six t.* camels

Seven THOUSAND.

1 *K.* 19:8 I ha. left *s. t. Rom.* 11:4
1 *Chr.* 12:25 of Simeon, *seven t.*
29:4 I prep. *s. t.* talents of silver
2 *Chr.* 15:11 th. offer. *s. t.* sheep
30:24 Hezek. gave *seven t.* sheep
Job 1:3 his subst. was *s. t.* sheep
Rev. 11:13 were slain *s. t.* men

Ten THOUSAND.

Lev. 26:8 hundred sh. put *t. t.* to
Deut. 32:30 2 put *t. t.* to flight?
33:2 L. came with *t. t. Jude* 14
Jud. 1:4 they slew in Bezek *t. t.*
3:29 they slew of M. *t. t.* men
4:10 went up with *t. t.* men, 14
7:3 there remained to Gid. *t. t.*
2 *Sam.* 18:3 thou art worth *t. t.*
1 *K.* 5:14 sent to Lebanon *ten t.*

---

2 *K.* 14:7 Amaziah slew of E. *t. t.*
2 *Chr.* 25:11 smote of Seir *ten t.*
12 other *t. t.* left alive, did Ju.
30:24 Hezek. gave *ten t.* sheep
Est. 3:9 I will pay *t, t.* talents
Ps. 91:7 *t. t.* sh. fall at thy right
Cant. 5:10 is chiefest among *t. t.*
Dan. 7:10 *t. t.* times *t. t.* stood
Mat. 18:24 wh. owed *t. t.* talents
Luke 14:31 wheth. able with *t. t.*
1 *Cor.* 4:15 though you have *t. t.*
14:19 then *ten t.* words in an unknown tongue
Rev. 5:11 num. was *t. t.* time *t. t.*

Ten THOUSANDS.

Deut. 33:17 they are *t. t.* of Eph.
1 *Sam.* 18:7 Da. hath slain his *t. t.* 8; 21:11; 29:5
Ps. 3:6 I will not be afra. of *t. t.*
144:13 our sheep may bri. *t. t.*
Dan. 11:12 cast down many *t. t.*
Mic. 6:7 pleas. wi. *t. t.* riv. of oil

Twelve THOUSAND.

Jos. 8:25 th. fell of Ai were *t. t.*
Jud. 21:10 sent *t. t.* to Jabesh-g.
Rev. 7:5 tribe of Juda, Gad, *t. t.*
6 of Aser, Napht. Manas. *t. t.*
7 Simeon, Levi, Issachar, *t. t.*
8 Zabulon, Joseph, Benja. *t. t.*
21:16 measu. city *t. t.* furlongs

Fourteen THOUSAND.

Job 42:12 Job had *fourt. t.* sheep

Sixteen THOUSAND.

Num. 31:40 persons were *s. t.* 46

Eighteen THOUSAND.

Jud. 20:25 destroy. of Israel *e. t.*
1 *Chr.* 18:12 slew of Edom *e. e. t.*
29:7 gave of brass *e. t.* talents

Twenty THOUSAND.

1 *K.* 5:11 Solomon gave Hiram *t. t.* measures, 2 *Chr.* 2:10
Neh. 7:71 fath. gave *t. t.* dr. 72
Ps. 68:17 chariots of G. are *t. t.*
Luke 14:31 him that com. wi. *t. t.*

Twenty-two THOUSAND.

Num. 3:39 number of Lev. *t.-t. t.*
43 first-born males were *t.-t. t.*

Twenty-three THOUSAND.

1 *Cor.* 10:8 fell in one day *t.-t. t.*

Twenty-four THOUSAND.

Num. 25:9 died in plague *t.-f. t.*

Twenty-five THOUSAND.

Jud. 20:35 destroyed of B. *t.-f. t.*

Twenty-six THOUSAND.

Jud. 20:15 Benja. numb. *t.-s. t.*

Twenty-seven THOUSAND.

1 *K.* 20:30 wall fell on *t.-s. t.* men

Twenty-eight THOUSAND.

1 *Chr.* 12:35 expert in war, *t.-e. t.*

Thirty THOUSAND.

Num. 31:39 asses were *t. t.* 45
1 *K.* 5:13 the levy was *t. t.* men

Thirty-two THOUSAND.

Num. 31:35 *t.-t. t.* wo. tak. cap.

Thirty-three THOUSAND.

2 *Chr.* 35:7 gave *t.-t. t.* bullocks

Thirty-five THOUSAND.

Num. 1:37 of Benja. were *t.-f. t.*

Thirty-six THOUSAND.

Num. 31:38 beev. we. *t.* and *s. t.*

Thirty-seven THOUSAND.

1 *Chr.* 12:34 of Naph. *t.* and *s. t.*

Thirty-eight THOUSAND.

1 *Chr.* 23:3 Lev. fr. 30 years *t.-e. t.*

Forty THOUSAND.

Jos. 4:13 *f. t.* prepared for war
Jud. 5:8 shield seen am. *f. t.*?

Forty-two THOUSAND.

Ezr. 2:64 cong. *f.-t. t. Neh.* 7:66

Fifty THOUSAND.

1 *Sam.* 6:19 Lord smote *f. t.* men
1 *Chr.* 5:21 Hagarites sheep *f. t.*
12:33 of Zebulon *f. t.* keep rank
Acts 19:19 price of books *f. t.* pie.

Sixty THOUSAND.

2 *Chr.* 12:3 Shish. came with *s. t.*

Sixty-one THOUSAND.

Num. 31:34 booty was *s.-o. t.*
Ezr. 2:69 *s.-o. t.* drams of gold

Seventy THOUSAND.

2 *Sam.* 24:15 died of people *s. t.*
1 *K.* 5:15 Sol. had *seventy t.* that bare burdens, 2 *Chr.* 2:2, 18

Seventy-two THOUSAND.

Num. 31:33 of beeves *s.-t. t.*

Seventy-five THOUSAND.

Num. 31:32 booty was *s.-f. t.* sh.
Est. 9:16 J. slew of foes *s.-f. t.*

Seventy-six THOUSAND five hundred.

Num. 26:22 num. of J. *s.-s. t. f. h.*

Eighty THOUSAND.

1 *K.* 5:15 Solomon had *eighty t.* hewers, 2 *Chr.* 2:2, 18

Eighty-seven THOUSAND.

1 *Chr.* 7:5 Issachar reckon. *e.-s. t.*

THOUSAND THOUSAND.

1 *Chr.* 21:5 they of Is. were *t. t.*
22:14 I prepared a *t. t.* of talents
2 *Chr.* 14:9 Eth. came with *t. t.*

Two hundred THOUSAND THOUSAND.

Rev. 9:16 army of horse. *t. h. t. t.*

THOUSANDS.

Gen. 24:60 mcth. of *t.* of millions
Ex. 18:21 place ov. rul. of *t.* 25
20:6 sh. mercy to *t. Deut.* 5:10
34:7 keeping mercy for *t.* forgiv.
Num. 1:16 princes of trib. heads of *t.* 10:4; *Jos.* 22:14, 21, 30
10:36 return, O L. to *t.* of Israel
31:5 were deliver. out of *t.* of Is.
Deut. 1:15 I made captains ov. *t.*
33:17 they are *t.* of Manasseh
1 *Sam.* 8:12 appoint capt. over *t.*
10:19 present yourselves by *t.*
18:8 to me th. have ascri. but *t.*
22:7 son of J. make capt. of *t.?*
23:23 search throughout *t.* of J.
29:2 lords of Phil. passed by *t.*
2 *Sam.* 18:4 peo. came out by *t.*
Ps. 119:72 law better th. *t.* gold
Jer. 32:18 showest loving-k. to *t.*
Dan. 7:10 *t.* minister. unto him
Mic. 5:2 tho' little among *t.* of J.
6:7 will L. be plea. wi. *t.* rams?
Acts 21:20 *t.* of Jews which belie.
Rev. 5:11 number of them *t.* of *t.*

See CAPTAINS.

THREAD.

Jen. 14:23 not take fr. *t.* to latch.
38:28 bound on hand scarl. *t.* 30
Jos. 2:18 bind scar. *t.* in window
Jud. 16:9 bra. withs as *t.* of tow
12 he brake ropes fr. arms as *t.*
Cant. 4:3 lips like *t.* of scarlet

THREATEN, ED.

Acts 4:17 let us straitly *t.* th. 21
1 *Pet.* 2:23 wh. he suff. he *t.* not

THREATENING, S.

Acts 4:29 Lord, behold their *t.*
9:1 Saul yet breathing out *t.*
Eph. 6:9 same to them forbearing *t.*

THREE.

Gen. 18:2 and lo, *t.* men stood by
Ex. 21:11 do not th. *t.* unto her
Deut. 4:41 Moses served *t.* cities, 19:2, 3, 7, 9
17:6 mouth of *t.* witnes. 19:15
2 *Sam.* 24:12 I offer thee *t.* things, 1 *Chr.* 21:10

Prov. 30:15 *t.* things never satis.
18 *t.* thi. too wonderf. for me
21 for *t.* thi. earth is disquieted
29 *t.* things which go well,
Ezek. 14:14 *t.* men were in, 16, 18
Acts 10:19 *t.* men seek thee, 11:11
1 *Cor.* 13:13 now abideth these *t.*
14:27 by two, or at most by *t.*
29 let prophets speak two or *t.*
1 *Tim.* 5:19 before two or *t.* wit.
Heb. 10:28 died un. two or *t.* wit.
1 *John* 5:7 *t.* bear record in heaven, and these *t.* agree
See DAYS.

THREE months.
Gen. 38:24 about *t. m.* after it
Ex. 2:2 child, she hid him *t. m.*
2 *Sam.* 6:11 ark of L. continued
in ho. of O. *t. m.* 1 *Chr.* 13:14
24:13 wilt thou flee *t. m.* before
thine enemies? 1 *Chr.* 21:12
Amos 4:7 were yet *t. m.* to harv.
Acts 7:20 M. was nourished *t. m.*
19:8 P. spake the space of *t. m.*
23 Paul abode in Greece *t. m.*
Heb. 11:23 Mo. was hid *t. months*

THREE-TAVERNS. *Acts* 28:15

THREE times.
Ex. 23:14 *t. t.* keep a feast to me
17 *t. t.* in year all males shall
appear bef. L. *Deut.* 16:16
Num. 22:28 smitten me *t. t.* 32
1 *K.* 17:21 stretched on child *t. t.*
2 *K.* 13:25 *t. t.* did Joash beat H.
2 *Chr.* 8:13 offering *t. t.* in year
Dan. 6:10 he kneeled *t. t.* a day
13 D. maketh his petition *t. t.*
Acts 11:10 this was done *t. times*

THREE years.
Gen. 15:9 take heifer *t. y.* old
Lev. 25:21 br. forth fruits for *t. y.*
Deut. 14:28 end of *t. y.* br. tithe
1 *K.* 2:39 end of *t. y.* S.'s servant
10:22 once in *t. years* came navy
of Tarshish, 2 *Chr.* 9:21
2 *K.* 17:5 Assyr. besieged S. *t. y.*
18:10 at end of *t. y.* th. took it
1 *Chr.* 21:12 cho. either *t. y.* fam.
2 *Chr.* 11:17 made R. strong *t. y.*
t. y. th. walked in way of D.
31:16 fr. *t. y.* old and upwards
Is. 16:14 within *t. y.* as of hirel.
20:3 as Isa. walked barefoot *t. y.*
Jer. 48:34 as a heifer of *t. y.* old
Dan. 1:5 nourishing them *t. y.*
Amos 4:*r.* your tithes aft. *t. y.*
Luke 4:25 shut *t. y. Jam.* 5:17
13:7 th. *t. y.* I come seek. fruit
Acts 20:31 *t. y.* I ceased not to
Gal. 1:18 after *t. y.* I went to J.
See HUNDRED.

THREEFOLD.
Ec. 4:12 *t.* cord not quic. brok.

THREESCORE.
Gen. 25:26 Isaac *t.* wh. she bare
Deut. 3:4 took fr. them *t.* cities,
Jos. 13:30
2 *Sam.* 2:31 thr. hund. and *t.* died
1 *K.* 4:13 to him pertain. *t.* cities
6:2 length of L.'s house *t.* cub.
2 *K.* 25:19 he took *t.* men of peo.
1 *Chr.* 2:21 Hezron married *t.* old
2 *Chr.* 11:21 Rehob. took *t.* concu.
Ezr. 6:3 height of temple *t.* cub.
Cant. 3:7 *t.* vali. men are about
6:8 *t.* queens, fourscore concu.
Jer. 52:25 put to death *t.* men
Dan. 3:1 wh. height was *t.* cubits
Luke 24:13 fr. Jerus. *t.* furlongs
1 *Tim.* 5:9 widow be tak. und. *t.*
See SIXTY.

THREESCORE and one.
Num. 31:39 trib. of asses *t. a. o.*

THREESCORE and two.
Dan. 5:31 Dar. *t. a. t.* years old

9:25 in *t. a. t.* weeks street built
26 after *t. a. t.* weeks Messiah

THREESCORE and five.
Is. 7:8 within *t. a. f.* years Eph.

THREESCORE and six.
Gen. 46:26 came with Ja. *t. a. s.*

THREESCORE and ten.
Gen. 46:27 house of Ja. which ca.
into E. *t. a. t. Deut.* 10:22
50:3 mourned for Is. *t. a. t.* days
Ex. 15:27 *t. a. t.* tr. *Num.* 33:9
Jud. 1:7 *t. a. t.* kings, thum. cut
9:5 slew *t. and t.* persons, 18, 24
12:14 that rode on *t. and t.* asses
2 *Chr.* 29:32 bro. *t. a. t.* bullocks
36:21 to fulfil *t. and ten* years
Ps. 90:10 days of our y. *t. a. t.*
Zec. 1:12 indigna. *t. a. t.* years
Acts 23:23 ready *t. a. t.* horsem.
See SEVENTY.

THREESCORE and twelve.
Num. 31:38 trib. *t. and t.* beeves

THREESCORE and fifteen.
Acts 7:14 Jos.'s kindr. *t. and f.*

THRESH.
Is. 41:15 th. sh. *t.* mountains
Jer. 51:33 floor it is time to *t.* her
Mic. 4:13 and *t.* O daughter of Zi.
Hab. 3:12 didst *t.* heath. in anger

THRESHED, ETH.
Jud. 6:11 Gid. *t.* wheat by the
Is. 28:27 fitches not *t.* with inst.
Amos 1:3 because they *t.* Gilead
1 *Cor.* 9:10 *t.* in hope, be partaker

THRESHING.
Lev. 26:5 *t.* reach to vintage
2 *Sam.* 24:22 here be *t.* instruments, 1 *Cor.* 21:23
2 *K.* 13:7 made th. like dust by *t.*
1 *Chr.* 21:20 Ornan saw *t.* wheat
Is. 21:10 my *t.* and corn of floor
28:28 he will not ever be *t.* it
41:15 make sharp *t.* instrument
See FLOOR, FLOORS.

THRESHOLD.
Jud. 19:27 her hands were on *t.*
1 *Sam.* 5:4 hands cut off on the *t.*
5 tread not on *t.* of Dagon
1 *K.* 14:17 came to *t.* child died
Ezek. 9:3 glory of G. on *t.* 10:4
10:18 glory of G. departed fr. *t.*
43:8 in their sitting of their *t.*
46:2 prince shall worship at *t.*
47:1 waters issued from under *t.*
Zep. 1:9 pun. all that leap on *t.*

THRESHOLDS.
Neh. 12:25 keeping ward at the *t.*
Ezek. 43:8 setting threshold by *t.*
Zep. 2:14 desolation shall be *t.*

THREW.
2 *Sam.* 16:13 Shi. *t.* stones at Da.
2 *K.* 9:33 they *t.* Jezebel down
2 *Chr.* 31:1 *t.* down high places
Mark 12:42 she *t.* in two mites
Luke 9:42 the devil *t.* him down
Acts 22:23 cried, *t.* dust in air

THREWEST.
Neh. 9:11 persecu. *t.* into deeps

THRICE.
Ex. 34:23 *t.* in year sh. app. 24
2 *K.* 13:18 Joash smote *t.* stayed
19 shalt smite Syria but *t.*
Mat. 26:34 thou shalt deny me *t.*
75; *Mark* 14:30, 72; *Luke*
22:34, 61; *John* 13:38
Acts 10:16 this was done *t.* vessel
2 *Cor.* 11:25 *t.* was I beaten with
rods, *t.* I suffered shipwreck
12:8 for this I besought the L. *t.*

THROAT.
Ps. 5:9 *t.* is sepulch. *Rom.* 3:13
69:3 weary of crying, *t.* is dried

115:7 neither speak thro' their *t.*
Prov. 23:2 put a knife to *t.* if giv.
Jer. 2:25 withh. thy *t.* fr. thirst
Mat. 18:28 servant took him by *t.*

THRONE.
Gen. 41:40 in *t.* will I be greater
Deut. 17:18 sitteth on *t.* of king.
1 *Sam.* 2:8 make them inherit *t.*
2 *Sam.* 3:10 to set up *t.* of David
7:13 stablish *t.* of kingdom, 16
1 *K.* 1:13 Solomon shall sit on
my *t.* 17, 24, 30, 35
48 given one to sit on my *t.*
2:4 not fail thee a man on the *t.*
of Israel, 8:25; 9:5; 2 *Chr.*
6:16; *Jer.* 33:17
12 Sol. sat on *t.* of David, 24;
8:20; 10:9; 1 *Chr.* 29:23;
2 *Chr.* 6:10
10:18 king made a *t.* 2 *Chr.* 9:17
2 *K.* 10:3 set him on his fath. *t.*
30 fourth gener. sit on *t.* 15:12
11:19 Joa. sat on *t.* 2 *Chr.* 23:20
Neh. 3:7 repair. to *t.* of governor
Job 36:7 with kings are th. on *t.*
Ps. 9:4 thou satest in *t.* judging
11:4 the Lord's *t.* is in heaven
45:6 thy *t.* O God, is for ever,
Lam. 5:19; *Heb.* 1:8
47:8 G. sitteth on *t.* of his holi.
89:4 will build thy *t.* to all gen.
14 jus. and judgm. are of thy *t.*
94:20 sh. *t.* of iniq. ha. fellow.?
132:11 fr. of body will I set on *t.*
12 chil. shall sit on *t.* for ever
Prov. 20:8 king that sit. in *t.* of
Is. 6:1 I saw L. sitting upon a *t.*
9:7 on *t.* of Da. and his kingdom
14:13 I will exalt my *t.* ab. stars
22:23 Eliakim sh. be for glori. *t.*
47:1 there is no *t.* O daughter of
66:1 heaven is my *t. Acts* 7:49
Jer. 3:17 call Jerusalem *t.* of L.
13:13 kings th. sit on David's *t.*
14:21 do not disgrace *t.* of glory
17:12 a glori. high *t.* from begin.
25 sitting on *t.* of Da. 22:4, 30
22:2 sittest upon the *t.* 29:16
36:30 none to sit on *t.* of David
49:38 I will set my *t.* in Elam
Ezek. 1:26 likeness of a *t.* 10:1
43:7 place of my *t.* shall Is. no
Hag. 2:22 I will overthrow the *t.*
Mat. 5:34 heaven, G.'s *t.* 23:22
19:28 Son shall sit in *t.* 25:31
Luke 1:32 L. sh. give him *t.* of D.
Heb. 4:16 come boldly to *t.* of gr.
8:1 on ri. hand of *t.* of God, 12:2
Rev. 3:21 will I grant to sit in *t.*
4:2 a *t.* was set, one sat on the *t.*
3 was a rainbow round about *t.*
5 out of *t.* proceede. lightnings,
were seven lamps before *t.*
6 bef. *t.* was a sea of glass, in *t.*
and about *t.* were 4 beasts
10 bef. him that sat on *t.* 7:11
5:1 in hand of him that sat on *t.*
6 in the midst of the *t.* a Lamb
7 out of hand of him sat on *t.*
13 glory to him that sit. on *t.*
6:16 hide fr. him that sit. on *t.*
7:9 a multitude stood before *t.*
10 our God which sitteth on *t.*
15 they are bef. *t.* of God, that
sitteth on *t.* shall dwell
17 the Lamb in midst of *t.* shall
8:3 golden altar was before *t.*
14:3 sung a new song before *t.*
5 without fault before *t.* of G.
19:4 worshipped G. that sat on *t.*
20:11 I saw a great white *t.* and
21:5 he that sat on *t.* said, Beh.
22:1 a river proceeding out of *t.*
3 *t.* of God and of the Lamb

His THRONE.
Ex. 11:5 that sits on h. *t.* 12:29
2 *Sam.* 14:9 king and h. *t.* guiltl.

1 *K.* 1:37 L. make *h. t.* greater, 47
2:19 he bowed, and sat on *his t,*
   33 and on *his t.* shall be peace
16:11 as Zi. sat on *his t.* he slew
22:10 king of Is. and Jehoshaphat, king of Judah, sat each
   on *his t.* 2 *Chr.* 18:9
   19 L. sit. on *his t.* 2 *Chr.* 18:18
2 *K.* 13:13 Jerob. sat upon *his t.*
25:28 set *his t.* above the throne
   of kings, *Jer.* 52:32
Job 26:9 hold. back face of *his t.*
Ps. 9:7 prepared *h. t.* for judgm.
89:29 *his t.* to endure as days
   36 *his t.* shall endure as sun
   44 th. hast cast *his t.* to ground
97:2 judgment habita. of *his t.*
103:19 L. prep. *his t.* in heaven
Prov. 29:28 *h. t.* is upholden
Jer. 1:15 set each *his t.* at gates
33:21 D. not have a son on *h. t.*
43:10 I will set *his t.* on stones
Dan. 5:20 was deposed from *h. t.*
   7:9 *his t.* was like fiery flame
Jon. 3:6 king of N. rose fr. *h. t.*
Zec. 6:13 he shall rule upon *his
   t.* and be a priest on *his t.*
Acts 2:30 raise C. to sit on *his t.*
Rev. 1:4 from seven spi. bef. *h. t.*
3:21 set down wi. my F. in *h. t.*
Rev. 12:5 child was cau. up to *h. t.*

See ESTABLISH, ESTABLISHED.

THRONES.

Ps. 122:5 are set t. of judgment
Is. 14:9 raised up from their t.
Ezek. 26:16 princes sh. come fr. t.
Dan. 7:9 till t. were cast down
Mat. 19:28 sh. sit on 12 t. *Lu.* 22: 30
Col. 1:16 whether they be t.
Rev. 20:4 I saw t. and they sat

THRONG, ED, ING.

Mark 3:9 lest they should t. him
5:24 much peo. t. him, *Luke* 8:42
   31 thou seest multitude t. thee
Luke 8:45 the multitude t. thee

THROUGH.

Rom. 11:36 t. him, to him,
Eph. 4:6 one God who is t. all

THROUGHLY

Job 6:2 my grief were t. weighed
Ps. 51:2 wash me t. from iniq.
Jer. 7:5 if ye t. amend yo. ways
Ezek. 16:9 I t. wash. away blood
Mat. 3:12 t. purge, *Luke* 3:17

THROUGHOUT.

Mark 14:9 gosp. preach. t. world
John 19:23 woven from the top t.
Rom. 1:8 faith is spo. of t. world

See GENERATIONS.

THROW.

Jud. 2:2 sh. t. down their altars
6:25 t. down the altar of Baal
2 *K.* 9:33 t. her down, so they
Jer. 1:10 over nations t. down
31:28 I watched over them, to t.
Ezek. 16:39 th sh. t. down thine
Mic. 5:11 I will t. down thy stro.
Mal. 1:4 build, I will t. down

THROWING.

Num. 35:17 smite with t. stone

THROWN.

Ex. 15:1 horse and rider t. 21
Jud. 6:32 he hath t. down altar
2 *Sam.* 20:21 his head shall be t.
1 *K.* 19:10 Isr. have t. down, 14
Jer. 31:40 it shall not be t. down
50:15 her walls are t. down
Lam. 2:2 L. ha. t. down in wrath
   17 hath t. down, not pitied
Ezek. 29:5 I will leave th. t. into
38:20 mount. shall be t. down
Nah. 1:6 the rocks are t. down
Mat. 24:2 stone th. shall not be t.
   down, *Mark* 13:2; *Lu.* 21:6

Luke 4:35 when devil had t. him
Rev. 18:21 Babyl. sh. be t. down

THRUST.

Ex. 11:1 sh. surely t. you out
12:39 they were t. out of Egypt
Num. 22:25 Bala.'s ass t. herself
25:8 Phinehas t. them through
35:20 but if he t. him of hatred
   22 if he t. him suddenly with
Deut. 13:5 to t. thee out of way
   10 he sought to t. thee from L.
15:17 t. the awl through his ear
33:27 he shall t. out the enemy
Jud. 3:21 Eh. t. dagger into his
   6:38 he t. fleece together, and
9:41 Ze. t. out Gaal and breth.
   54 young man t. Ab. through
11:2 and they t. out Jephthah
1 *Sam.* 11:2 I may t. out yo. eyes
31:4 S. said, t. me through, lest
   uncircumcised t. 1 *Chr.* 10:4
2 *Sam.* 2:16 t. sw. in his fellow's
18:14 J. t. three darts thro' Abs.
23:6 Belial shall be as thorns t.
1 *K.* 2:27 Solom. t. out Abiathar
2 *K.* 4:27 Gehazi came to t. her
2 *Chr.* 26:20 they t. Uzziah out fr.
Ps. 118:13 thou hast t. at me
Is. 13:15 every one sh. be t. thro'
14:19 raiment of those th. are t.
Jer. 51:4 they that are t. through
Ezek. 16:40 they shall t. thee thro'
34:21 have t. wi. side and shoul.
46:18 t. them out of possessions
Joel 2:8 neither shall one t. ano.
Zec. 13:3 shall t. him through
Luke 4:29 rose and t. him out
   5:3 prayed he would t. out a lit
10:15 shall be t. down to hell
13:28 and you yourselves t. out
John 20:25 t. my ha. into his, 27
Acts 7:27 did wrong t. him away
   39 our fath. t. him from them
16:24 t. them into inner prison
   37 now do th. t. us out privily ?
27:39 if it were possi. to t. ship
Heb. 12:20 stoned or t. through
Rev. 14:15 t. in thy sickle, harv.
   16 t. in his sickle on the earth
   18 t. in thy sharp sickle

THRUSTETH.

Job 32:13 God t. him down

THUMB, S.

Ex. 29:20 put it on t. of right
   hand, *Lev.* 8:23; 14:14–28
Jud. 1:6 cau. him and cut off t.
   7 seventy kings hav. t. cut off

THUMMIM.

Ex. 28:30 put on breastplate, the
   urim and t. *Lev.* 8:8
Deut. 33:8 let thy t. and urim be
Ezr. 2:63 priest with urim and t.
   Neh. 7:65

THUNDER.

Ex. 9:23 the L. sent t. and hail
   29 the t. shall cease, nor shall
1 *Sam.* 7:10 L. thundered with t.
12:17 send t. 18 the Lord sent t.
Job 26:14 t. of power who und. ?
28:26 way for light. of t. 38;25
39:19 clothed neck with t. ?
   25 smelleth t. of captains afar
Ps. 77:18 voice of thy t. in heav.
81:7 I answ. thee in place of t.
104:7 at voice of thy t. th. hasted
Is. 29:6 sh. be visited of L. wi. t.
Mark 3:17 Boanerges, is sons of t.
Rev. 6:1 as it were the noise of t.
14:2 as the voice of a great t.

THUNDER, Verb.

1 *Sam.* 2:10 out of heav. sh. he t.
Job 40:9 canst thou t. like him ?

THUNDERS.

Ex. 9:33 t. and hail ceased, 34
19:16 t. and lightni. *Rev.* 16:18

See SEVEN.

THUNDERBOLTS.

Ps. 78:48 gave their flocks to t.

THUNDERED, ETH.

1 *Sam.* 7:10 Lord t. with thunder
2 *Sam.* 22:14 the L. t. *Ps.* 18:13
Job 37:4 he t. with his excellency
   5 G. t. marvellously with voice
Ps. 29:3 God of glory t. the Lord
John 12:29 heard it, said that it t.

THUNDERINGS.

Ex. 9:28 be no more mighty t.
20:18 all the people saw the t.
Rev. 4:5 out throne proc. t. 19:6
8:5 th. were voices and t. 11:19

THUS and THUS.

Jos. 7:20 t. and t. have I done
Jud. 18:4 t. and t. dealeth Micah
2 *Sam.* 17:15 t. a. t. did Ahithop.
   counsel A. and t. a. t. have I
1 *K.* 14:15 t. and t. say to Jero.'s
2 *K.* 5:4 t. and t. said maid of Is.
9:12 t. and t. spake he to me

THYATIRA.

Acts 16:14 of city of T. worship.
Rev. 1:11 wh. th. seest send to T.
2:18 to angel of church in T.
   24 to you and to the rest in T.

THYSELF.

Gen. 13:9 separate t. I pray thee
14:21 give persons, take goods t.
33:9 keep that thou hast unto t.
Ex. 10:3 refuse to humble t. ?
   28 take heed to t. see my face
   no more, 34:12; *Deut.* 4:9;
   12:13, 19:30; 1 *Sam.* 19:2
18:22 shall it be easier for t.
Est. 4:13 think not with t. thou
Ps. 49:18 thou doest well to t.
John 1:22 what sayest thou of t. ?
18:34 sayest thou this of t. ?
Rom. 14:22 hast faith ? have to t.

THYINE.

Rev. 18:12 merchant of t. wood

TIBERIAS.

John 6:1 Galilee, wh. is sea of T.
   23 came other boats from T.

TIBNI.

1 *K.* 16:21 half people followed T.
   22 ag. those that followed T.

TIDAL. *Gen.* 14:1, 9

TIDINGS.

Ex. 33:4 when peo. heard evil t.
1 *Sam.* 4:19 Phine. wife heard t.
11:4 told t. of men of Jabesh, 5
27:11 none alive to bring t. to G.
2 *Sam.* 4:4 when t. came of Saul
13:30 t. came, Absa. hath slain
18:19 run and bear king t.
   20 thou sh. not bear t. this day
   22 why run ? hast no t. ready
   31 C. said, t. my lord the king
1 *K.* 2:28 then t. came to Joab
14:6 I am sent to thee with t.
1 *Chr.* 10:9 to carry t. to idols
Ps. 142:7 not be afraid of evil t.
Jer. 20:15 cursed that brought t.
49:23 for they have heard evil t.
Ezek. 21:7 thou shalt answ. for t.
Dan. 11:44 t. out of east trouble
Luke 1:19 show thee glad t. 2:10
8:1 showing glad t. kingd. of G.
Acts 11:22 t. of th. things came
13:32 declare unto you glad t.
21:31 t. came to chief captain
Rom. 10:15 bring glad t. of good

See GOOD.

TIE.

1 *Sam.* 6:7 t. kine to the cart, 10
Prov. 6:21 and t. about thy neck

TIED.

Ex. 39:31 t. to it a lace of blue
2 *K.* 7:10 horses t. and asses t.
Mat. 21:2 ye shall find an ass t.
   Mark 11:2, 4; *Luke* 19:30

TIGLATH-PILESER.

2 *K.* 15:29 T. took Ij. and Kedesh
16:7 Ah. sent messengers to T.
1 *Chr.* 5:6 T. carried Bee. captive
26 God stirred up spirit of T.
2 *Chr.* 28:20 T. distressed Ahaz

TILE, ING.

Ezek. 4:1 son of man, take th. a *t.*
Luke 5:19 let him down thro' *t.*

TILL, Conjunctive.

Dan. 4:23 *t.* sev. times pass over
12:13 go thy way *t.* the end be
John 21:22 he tarry *t.* I come, 23
See CONSUMED, MORNING.

TILL, ED, EST, ETH.

Gen. 2:5 not a man to *t.* 3:23
4:12 when thou *t.* ground, it
2 *Sam.* 9:10 servants shall *t.* land
Prov. 12:11 that *t.* sh. be satisfied
28:19 th. *t.* land sh. have plenty
Jer. 27:11 they that *t.* it, and dw.
Ezek. 36:9 ye sh. be *t.* and sown
34 desolate land shall be *t.*

TILLAGE.

1 *Chr.* 27:26 them that were for *t.*
Neh. 10:37 Lev. have tithes of *t.*
Prov. 13:23 much food in *t.*

TILLER.

Gen. 4:2 Cain was *t.* of ground

TIMBER.

Lev. 14:45 sh. break down the *t.*
1 *K.* 5:18 so they prepared *t.*
1 *Chr.* 22:14 ; 2 *Chr.* 2:9
15:22 they took away *t.* of Ra.
Ezr. 5:8 *t.* is laid in walls
6:11 let *t.* be pulled fr. his house
Neh. 2:8 give me *t.* to ma. beams
Ezek. 26:12 lay thy *t.* in water
Hab. 2:11 beam out of *t.* answer
Zec. 5:4 shall consume it with *t.*

TIMBREL.

Ex. 15:20 Miri. took *t.* in hand
Job 21:12 they take *t.* and harp
Ps. 81:2 take psalm, bring *t.*
149:3 sing praises to him with *t.*
150:4 praise him with *t.*

TIMBRELS.

Ex. 15:20 wom. went out with *t.*
Jud. 11:34 daught. came with *t.*
2 *Sam.* 6:5 house of Is. played
before Lord on *t.* 1 *Chr.* 13:8
Ps. 68:25 damsels play. with *t.*

TIME.

Gen. 18:10 accord. to *t.* of life, 14
24:11 *t.* women go to draw wat.
39:5 fr. *t.* he made him overseer
47:29 *t.* drew nigh Is. must die
Ex. 21:19 shall pay for loss of *t.*
Lev. 15:25 beyond *t.* of separa.
18:18 besides other in her life-*t.*
Num. 13:20 *t.* was *t.* of ripe gra.
26:10 wh. *t.* fire devou. 250 men
Deut. 16:9 *t.* thou put sickle
Jos. 10:27 at *t.* of going down of
sun, 2 *Chr.* 18:31
42 land did Josh. take at one *t.*
Jud. 18:31 *t.* house of G. in Shi.
2 *Sam.* 7:11 since *t.* I command.
11:1 *t.* when kings go to battle
23:8 eight hund. slew at one *t.*
2 *K.* 5:26 is it *t.* to receive money
1 *Chr.* 2:23 *to* come from *t.* to *t.*
Ezr. 4:10 at such a *t.* 17 ; 7:12
10:13 and it is a *t.* of rain
Neh. 2:6 return? I set him a *t.*
Job 6:17 *t.* they wax warm
9:19 who shall set me a *t.*
15:32 accomplished before his *t.*
22:16 were cut down out of *t.*
38:23 preserved ag. *t.* of trouble
39:1 knoweth. th. *t.* br. forth? 2
Ps. 32:6 *t.* thou mayest be found
37:19 not be ashamed in evil *t.*
41:1 L. deli. him in *t.* of trouble

56:3 *t.* I am afraid, I trust in th.
69:13 prayer to thee in accept. *t.*
Ps. 81:15 their *t.* should have
endured
89:47 remember how short *t.* is
105:19 until *t.* his word came
Ec. 3:1 *t.* to ev. purpose, 17 ; 8:6
2 a *t.* to be born, a *t.* to die, a
t. to plant
7:17 why should thou die before
thy *t.* ?
8:5 wise man's heart discern. *t.*
9:11 *t.* and chance happen. to all
12 so are men snared in evil *t.*
Is. 26:17 near *t.* of her delivery
28:19 from *t.* it goeth forth
45:21 decla. this from ancient *t.*
48:16 from *t.* it was, there am I
49:8 in an acceptable *t.* I heard
60:22 L. will hasten it in his *t.*
Jer. 6:15 at *t.* I visit, cast down
8:7 swallow observe *t.* of com.
15 looked for *t.* of health
14:8 Saviour the. in *t.* of trouble
19 *t.* of healing, behold trouble
30:7 it is *t.* of Jacob's trouble
46:21 *t.* of their visitation 50:27
49:8 *t.* I will visit him, 50:31
19 who will app. me *t.* ? 50:44
51:33 floor, it is *t.* to thresh her
Ezek. 4:10 fr. *t.* to *t.* sh. thou eat
16:8 thy *t.* was the *t.* of love
57 as *t.* of thy reproach of dau.
30:3 it shall be the *t.* of heathen

Dan. 2:8 I know ye would gain *t.*
9 speak, till the *t.* be changed
16 desired he would give him *t.*
3:5 at wh. *t.* ye hear cornet, 15
7:12 lives were prolong. for a *t.*
22 *t.* came saints posses. kingd.
25 until *t.* and divid. of *t.* 12:7
8:17 at *t.* of end shall be vision
9:21 touched *t.* of evening obla.
11:24 forecast his devices for a *t.*
35 to make th. white, *t.* of end
40 at *t.* of end king of south
12:1 there shall be a *t.* of trouble
4 seal book, even to *t.* of end, 9
11 fr. *t.* sacrifice be taken away
Hos. 10:12 is it *t.* to seek the L.
Mic. 5:3 till *t.* she which travail.
Hag. 1:4 is it *t.* to dw. in houses?
Zec. 14:7 evening *t.* sh. be light
Mal. 3:11 cast her fruit before *t.*
Mat. 1:11 *t.* they were car. away
2:7 H. inquired *t.* star appeared
8:29 come to torment us bef. *t.* ?
21:34 when *t.* of fruit drew near
26:18 master saith, *t.* is at hand
Mark 1:15 *t.* is fulfilled, repent
4:17 and so endure but for a *t.*
6:35 now the *t.* is far passed
11:13 for *t.* of figs was not yet
13:33 ye know not wh. the *t.* is
Luke 1:57 Elisabeth's full *t.*
4:5 showed kingd. in mom. of *t.*
7:45 this woman, since *t.* I came
8:13 in *t.* of tempta. fall away
13:35 not see me till *t.* came
19:44 knew. not *t.* of visitation
John 7:6 my *t.* is not co. your *t.*
16:2 *t.* cometh, whosoev. killeth
25 *t.* com. I sh. no more speak
Acts 1:21 *t.* L. went in and out
7:17 when *t.* of prom. drew nigh
20 in what *t.* Moses was born
17:21 spent their *t.* in noth. else
Rom. 13:11 it is high *t.* to awake
1 *Cor.* 4:5 judge nothing before *t.*
7:5 except with consent for a *t.*
29 I say, brethren, *t.* is short
Eph. 5:16 redeeming *t.* *Col.* 4:5
1 *Thes.* 2:17 taken fr. you short *t.*
2 *Thes.* 2:6 might be revealed in *t.*
2 *Tim.* 4:3 *t.* come, will not end.
6 *t.* of my departure is at hand
Heb. 4:16 to help in *t.* of need

5:12 for *t.* ye ought to be teach.
9:9 figure for the *t.* then present
10 impos. till *t.* of reformation
11:32 *t.* would fail to tell of G.
Jam. 4:14 that appeareth little *t.*
1 *Pet.* 1:11 what manner of *t.* Sp.
17 pass *t.* of sojourning in fear
4:2 no longer live rest of his *t.*
Rev. 1:3 for *t.* is at hand, 22:10
10:3 there should be *t.* no longer
11:18 *t.* of dead, :ho. be judged
12:12 knoweth he hath a short *t.*
14 she is nourished for a *t.* and

Any TIME.

Lev. 25:32 Lev. redeem at *any t.*
Luke 21:34 a. *t.* hearts overchar.
John 1:18 no man seen G. at a. *t.*
5:37 nor heard his voice at *a. t.*
Heb. 2:1 lest at *any t.* we should
1 *John* 4:12 no man se. G. at *a. t.*

See APPOINTED, BEFORE, COME,
DAY, DUE.

In the TIME.

Gen. 38:27 came to pass in *the t.*
1 *K.* 15:23 in *the t.* of old age he
2 *Chr.* 28:22 in *the t.* of distress
Neh. 9:27 in *the t.* of trouble thou
Ps. 4:7 in *t. t.* when corn increa.
27:5 in *the t.* of trouble sh. hide
71:9 cast not off in *the t.* of age
Is. 33:2 salva. in *t. t.* of trouble
Jer. 2:27 in *the t.* of trouble they
28 save thee in *t. t.* of trouble
11:12 not save th. in *t. t.* of tro.
14 not hear th. in *t. t.* they cry
18:23 deal thus with th. in *t. t.*
Ezek. 27:34 in *t. t.* when thou sh.
Hos. 2:9 take corn in *the t.* ther.
Zec. 10:1 rain in *the t.* of rain
Mat. 13:30 in *the t.* of harvest
See LAST, LONG, MANY, OLD,
PAST, PROCESS, SET.

That TIME.

Neh. 4:16 from *t. t.* forth, 13:21
Is. 16:13 concern. M. since *t. t.*
18:7 in *that t.* shall the pres. be
45:21 who hath told it fr. *t. t.* ?
Mat. 4:17 from *t. t.* Je. began to
16:21 from *that t.* began to show
26:16 from *t. t.* J. sought oppor.

At that TIME.

Deut. 5:5 I stood between the
Lord and you *at that t.*
9:19 L. hearkened *at t. t.* 10:10
2 *Chr.* 30:3 not keep passo. *at t. t.*
35:17 Is. kept passover *at t. t.*
Zep. 3:20 *at that t.* will I br. you
Eph. 2:12 *at t. t.* we. without Ch.
See THIRD.

This TIME.

Ex. 9:14 *t. t.* send my plagues
18 to-morrow about *t. t.* I will
Num. 23:23 according to *t. t.*
Jud. 13:23 nor would at *t. t.* ha.
1 *Sam.* 9:13 ab. *t. t.* ye shall find
2 *Sam.* 17:7 coun. not good at *t. t.*
1 *K.* 2:26 not at *t. t.* put to death
19:2 to-morrow *t. t.* 20:6 ; 2 *K.*
7:1, 18 ; 10:6
Neh. 13:6 all *t. t.* was not I at J.
Est. 4:14 hold. thy peace at *t. t.*
Ps. 113:2 blessed be L. from *t. t.*
115:18 we will bless L. from *t. t.*
121:8 he will pres. thee from *t. t.*
Is. 48:6 showed new thi. fr. *t. t.*
Jer. 3:4 wilt thou not fr. *t. t.* cry?
Acts 1:6 wilt thou at *t. t.* restore?
24:25 answ. Go thy way for *t. t.*
Rom. 3:26 decl. at *t. t.* his right.
9:9 at *t. t.* will I come, S. shall
11:5 so at *t.* present *t.* there is a
1 *Cor.* 16:12 not to come at *t. t.*

TIMES.

Gen. 27:36 supplanted me two *t.*
Lev. 19:26 ye shall not observe *t.*
Deut. 18:10, 14

TIMES (cont.)

Deut. 4:42 hated not in *t.* past
Jud. 13:25 S. began to move at *t.*
16:20 I will go out as at other *t.*
20:31 began to kill as at other *t.*
1 *Sam.* 3:10 L. call. as at other *t.*
20:25 sat on seat as at other *t.*
2 *K.* 21:6 Manasseh observed *t.*
    2 *Chr.* 33:6
1 *Chr.* 12:32 had understand. of *t.*
29:30 the *t.* that went over him
2 *Chr.* 15:5 in those *t.* no peace
Est. 1:13 men which knew the *t.*
Job 24:1 *t.* are not hid. fr. Almi.
Ps. 9:9 L. a ref. in *t.* of trouble
10:1 why hid. in *t.* of trouble ?
31:15 my *t.* are in thy hand
44:1 works th. didst in *t.* of old
77:5 consider. years of ancient *t.*
Is. 33:6 knowledge stability of *t.*
46:10 from ancient *t.* things not
Ezek. 12:27 he prophesied of *t.*
Dan. 2:21 he changeth *t.*
7:25 think to change *t.* and laws
9:25 streets sh. be built in tro. *t.*
11:14 in th. *t.* shall many stand
12:7 for a time, *t. Rev.* 12:14
Mat. 16:3 not discern signs of *t.* ?
Luke 21:24 till *t.* of the Gentiles
Acts 1:7 not for you to kn. the *t*
3:19 *t.* of refreshing shall come
21 the *t.* of restitution of all
14:16 who in *t.* past suffered all
17:26 hath determined the *t.* be.
30 *t.* of ignorance God winked
Rom. 11:30 ye in *t.* past have not
2 *Cor.* 11:24 five *t.* rece. I stripes
Gal. 1:23 persecuted in *t.* past
4:10 days and months, *t.* years
Eph. 1:10 dispensa. of fuln. of *t.*
1 *Thes.* 5:1 of *t.* ye have no need
1 *Tim.* 4:1 in latter *t.* some shall
6:15 in his *t.* he sh. show who is
2 *Tim.* 3:1 in last days perilous *t.*
Tit. 1:3 in *t.* manifest, his word
Heb. 1:1 God who at sundry *t.*

All TIMES.

Lev. 16:2 come not at *all t.*
Ps. 34:1 I will bless Lord at *all t.*
62:8 trust in him at *all t.* ye peo.
119:20 to thy judgments at *all t.*
Prov. 5:19 breasts satisfy at *a. t.*
17:17 a friend loveth at *all t.*

See APPOINTED, MANY, SEVEN,
TEN, THREE.

TIMNATH.

Gen. 38:12 to his shearers in T.
Jud. 14:1 Samson went to T.

TIMON. *Acts* 6:5

TIMOTHEUS.

Acts 16:1 cert. disciple named T.
Rom. 16:21 T. my work-fellow
1 *Cor.* 16:10 if T. come, see that
2 *Cor.* 1:19 was preach. ev. by T.
Phil. 2:19 trust in L. to send T.
1 *Thes.* 3:2 we sent T. to comfort

TIMOTHY.

2 *Cor.* 1:1 and T. our brother
1 *Tim.* 1:2 T. my son, 2 *Tim.* 1:2
Heb. 13:23 bro. T. set at liberty

TIN.

Num. 31:22 *t.* that may abide fire
Is. 1:25 will take away all thy *t.*
Ezek. 22:18 they are brass, and *t.*
20 as they gather lead and *t.*
27:12 Tarshish was merch. in *t.*

TINGLE.

1 *Sam.* 3:11 cars of ev. one shall
t. 2 *K.* 21:12 ; *Jer.* 19:3

TINKLING.

Is. 3:16 mincing and making a *t.*
18 take away their *t.* ornam.
1 *Cor.* 13:1 I am bec. *t.* cymbal

TIP.

Luke 16:24 may dip *t.* of finger
See Right EAR.

TIPHSAH. 1 *K.* 4:24

TIRE, ED.

2 *K.* 9:30 Jezebel *t.* her head and
Ezek. 24:17 bind *t.* of thy head

TIRES.

Is. 3:18 L. will take away their *t.*
Ezek. 24:23 your *t.* sh. be on hea.

TIRHAKAH. 2 *K.* 19:9

TIRSHATHA.

Ezr. 2:63 T. said the. *Neh.* 7:65
Neh. 7:70 T. gave gold to the
10:1 sealed were Nehem. the T.

TIRZAH.

Num. 26:33 and T. daughters of
Zeloph. 36:11 ; *Jos.* 17:3
27:1 Hoglah, and Melc. and T.
Jos. 12:24 Joshua sm. king of T.
1 *K.* 14:17 Jeroboam's wife to T.
15:21 Baasha reigned in T. 33
16:8 Elah reigned in T. 15 Zi.
17 O. besieged in T. 23 reigned
2 *K.* 15:16 smote coasts from T.
Cant. 6:4 th. art beautiful as T.

TITHE.

Lev. 27:30 the *t.* of land is L.'s
Num. 18:26 off. a tenth part of *t.*
Deut. 12:17 not eat the *t.* of corn
14:23 eat *t.* in place the Lord
28 at end of three years bring *t.*
2 *Chr.* 31:5 they brought the *t.*
of all thin. 6, 12 ; *Neh.* 13:12
Neh. 10:38 Levites shall bring *t.*
Mat. 23:23 pay *t.* of mint, anise

TITHE, Verb.

Deut. 14:22 thou sh. *t.* increase.
Luke 11:42 ye *t.* mint and rue

TITHES.

Gen. 14:20 Abr. gave Melchi. *t.*
Lev. 27:31 man redeem of his *t.*
Num. 18:24 *t.* I have given to L.
28 heave-off. to Lord of your *t.*
Deut. 12:6 ye sh. bring your *t.* 11
26:12 made end of tithing the *t.*
Neh. 10:37 Levites might have *t.*
12:44 some were appointed for *t.*
13:5 aforetime they laid *t.* of
Amos 4:4 bring your *t. Mal.* 3:10
Mal. 3:8 ye have robbed me of *t.*
Luke 18:12 I give *t.* of all I poss.
Heb. 7:5 have command. to ta. *t.*
6 he received *t.* of Abraham
8 here men that die receive *t.*
9 Levi who received *t.* paid *t.*

TITHING.

Deut. 26:12 end of *t.* 3d year is *t.*

TITLE.

2 *K.* 23:17 wh. *t.* is that that I s.
John 19:19 P. wrote a *t.* and put
20 this *t.* read many of the Je.

TITLES.

Job 32:21 nor give flat. *t.* to man
22 I kn. not to give flattering *t.*

TITTLE.

Mat. 5:18 one *t.* shall in no wise
Luke 16:17 one *t.* of law to fail

TITUS.

2 *Cor.* 2:13 bec. I found not T.
7:6 comforted us by com. of T.
13 more joyed we for joy of T.
14 which I made before T.
8:6 desired T. *Gal.* 2:1 took T.
16 earnest care into heart of T.
23 whether any inquire of T.
12:18 T. made a gain of you ?
Gal. 2:3 nor was T. comp. to be
2 *Tim.* 4:10 T. is departed to D.

TO AND FRO. *See* FRO.
TOB. *Jud.* 11:3, 5

TOBIAH.

Ezr. 2:60 children of T. not sho.
Neh. 2:10 T. heard, 19 ; 4:7 ; 6:1
6:12 T. hired him ; 14 thi. of T.
19 T. sent let. put me in fear
13:4 Eliashib was allied to T.
8 cast forth house. stuff of T.

TOE.

Ex. 29:20 upon great *t.* of their
right foot, *Lev.* 8:23, 24 ;
14:14, 17, 25, 28

TOES.

Jud. 1:6 cut off thumbs and *t.*
7 seventy kings hav. *t.* cut off
1 *Chr.* 20:6 fingers and *t.* were 2
Dan. 2:41 thou sawest the *t.* 42

TOGARMAH.

Gen. 10:3 Riphath, T. 1 *Chr.* 1:6
Ezek. 27:14 of house of T. traded

TOGETHER.

Ezr. 4:3 ourselves *t.* will build
Prov. 22:2 rich and poor meet *t.*
Ec. 4:11 if two lie *t.* then they
Is. 65:25 wolf and lamb sh. feed *t.*
Mat. 18:20 two or three gath. *t.*
19:6 what God hath joined *t.* let
not man put, *Mark* 10:9

See DWELL.

TOI. 2 *Sam.* 8:9, 10

TOIL.

Gen. 5:29 conc. our work and *t.*
41:51 God made me forget my *t.*

TOIB, ED, ING.

Mat. 6:28 they *t.* not, neither do
they spin, *Luke* 12:27
Mark 6:48 saw them *t.* in rowing
Luke 5:5 Mast. we ha. *t.* all nig.

TOKEN.

Gen. 9:12 this is the *t.* of, 13, 17
Ex. 3:12 shall be a *t.* I sent thee
12:13 the blood shall be for a *t.*
13:16 for a *t.* upon thy hand
Num. 17:10 kept for *t.* ag. rebels
Jos. 2:12 and give me a true *t.*
Ps. 86:17 show me a *t.* for good
Mark 14:44 Ju. had given th. a *t.*
Phil. 1:28 evident *t.* of perdition
2 *Thes.* 1:5 *t.* of righteous judg.
3:17 which is the *t.* in ev. epist.

TOKENS.

Deut. 22:15 br. *t.* of virgin. 17, 20
Job 21:29 do ye not know th. *t.* ?
Ps. 65:8 they also are afraid at *t.*
135:9 sent *t.* in midst of thee
Is. 44:25 frustrateth *t.* of liars

TOLA.

Gen. 46:13 T. son of I. 1 *Chr.* 7:1
Jud. 10:1 T. son of Puah, arose

TOLD.

Gen. 37:10 he *t.* it to his father
Num. 23:26 *t.* not I thee, all that
Deut. 17:4 it be *t.* thee, behold
Jud. 6:13 his miracles fathers *t.*
13:6 neither *t.* he me his name
23 nor would have *t.* such thi.
14:2 he came up, *t.* his father
6 *t.* not fath. 9, 16 ; 1 *Sam.* 14:1
16:17 he *t.* her all his heart, 18
1 *K.* 8:5 and oxen could not be *t.*
13:11 they *t.* to their father
18:13 was it not *t.* my lord
2 *K.* 12:11 gave money, being *t.*
Est. 8:1 Est. had *t.* what he was
Job 15:18 which wise men have *t.*
Ps. 90:9 spend years as a tale *t.*
Is. 44:8 have not I *t.* thee from ?
45:21 who ha. *t.* it fr. that time ?
52:15 what had not been *t.* them
Dan. 8:26 vision which is *t.* true
Jon. 1:10 because he had *t.* them
Mat. 8:33 they went and *t.* every
Mat. 14:12 took the bo. and *t.* J.
Luke 1:45 performance of thin. *t.*
2:18 wondered at things *t.* by

John 5:15 man *t.* Jews it was J.
Acts 9:6 be *t.* thee what do, 22:10

TOLD him.

Gen. 22:3 place of wh. G. *t. h.* 9
1 *Sam.* 3:13 *t. h.* I will jud. hou.
25:36 she *t. h.* nothing till mor.
2 *K.* 6:10 place man of God *t. h.*
Job 37:20 it be *t. h.* that I speak
Mark 5:33 woman *t. h.* all truth

TOLD me.

2 *Sam.* 4:10 when one *t. me*
1 *K.* 10:7 the half was not *t. me,*
    2 *Chr.* 9:6
14:2 *t. me* I should be king over
2 *K.* 4:27 hid, and hath not *t. me*
8:14 he *t. me* th. should. recover
John 4:29 which *t. me* all thi. 39
Acts 27:25 sh. be as it was *t. me*

TOLD you.

Is. 40:21 *t. y.* from beginning?
Hab. 1:5 not beli. tho' it be *t. y.*
Mat. 24:25 behold, I *t. y.* before
28:7 ye shall see him, lo, I *t. y.*
John 3:12 If I *t. y.* earthly things
8:40 a man that hath *t. y.* truth
9:27 I have *t. y.* already, and ye
did not hear, 10:25
14:2 not so, I would have *t. y.*
29 I have *t. you* before it come
16:4 have I *t. you*, that wh. time
come, ye may remem. I *t. y.*
18:8 said, I have *t. you* I am he
Gal. 5:21 have I *t. y.* in time past
Phil. 3:18 walk of whom I *t. you*
1 *Thes.* 3:4 we *t. you* we sh. suff.
2 *Thes.* 2:5 I *t. you* these things

TOLERABLE.

Mat. 10:15 more *t.* for Sodo. and
Gomorrah, 11:24; *Mark* 6:11;
    Luke 10:12
11:22 more *t.* for Tyre, *Lu.* 10:14

TOLL.

Ezr. 4:13 th. will th. not pay *t.*
20 *t.* trib. and custom was paid
7:24 not be lawful to impose *t.*

TOMB.

Job 21:32 he shall remain in *t.*
Mat. 27:60 Joseph laid body in *t.*
Mark 6:29 laid John's corpse in *t.*

TOMBS.

Mat. 8:28 with devils com. out *t.*
    Mark 5:2, 3, 5 ; *Luke* 8:27
23:29 ye build *t.* of the prophets

TONGS.

Ex. 25:38 ma. *t.* thereof of gold
Num. 4:9 cov. *t.* wi. cloth of blue
1 *K.* 7:49 *t.* of gold, 2 *Chr.* 4:21
Is. 6:6 coal he had taken with *t.*
44:12 smith with *t.* work. coals

TONGUE.

Ex. 11:7 not a dog move his *t.*
Jos. 10:21 none moved *t.* ag. Isr.
Jud. 7:5 lappeth of water wi. *t.*
Job 5:21 he hid from scourge of *t.*
15:5 thou choosest *t.* of crafty
20:12 hide wickedn. under his *t.*
16 the viper's *t.* shall slay him
29:10 *t.* cleav. to roof of mouth
Ps. 5:9 they flatter with their *t.*
10:7 under his *t.* is mischief
12:3 cut off *t.* speak. proud thi.
4 with our *t.* will we prevail
15:3 backbiteth not with his *t.*
34:13 keep *t.* fr. evil, 1 *Pet.* 3:10
37:30 his *t.* talketh of judgment
50:19 and thy *t.* frameth deceit
52:2 thy *t.* deviseth mischiefs
57:4 their *t.* is a sharp sword
64:3 whet their *t.* like sword
8 make *t.* fall on themselves
68:23 *t.* of thy dogs may be dip.
73:9 their *t.* walketh thro' earth
109:2 spo. ag. me with lying *t.*
120:3 done to th. thou false *t. ?*
126:2 our *t.* filled with singing

Prov. 6:17 hateth proud, lying *t.*
24 flattery of *t.* of stra. woman
10:20 *t.* of just as choice silver
31 froward *t.* shall be cut out
12:18 *t.* of the wise is health
19 a lying *t.* is but for a mom.
15:2 *t.* of wise useth knowledge
4 a wholes. *t.* is a tree of life
16:1 answer of *t.* is from the L.
17:4 liar giv. ear to naughty *t.*
20 perv. *t.* falls into mischief
18:21 dea. and life in pow. of *t.*
21:6 treasu. by lying *t.* is vanity
23 whoso keepeth *t.* keep. soul
25:15 soft *t.* breaketh the bone
23 angry counten. a backbit. *t.*
26:28 lying *t.* hateth th. afflicted
Prov. 23:23 he that flat. with *t.*
31:26 in her *t.* is law of kindne.
Cant. 4:11 milk are under thy *t.*
Is. 3:8 because their *t.* is ag. L.
11:15 destroy *t.* of Egyptian sea
30:27 his *t.* is as a devour. fire
32:4 *t.* of stammer. speak plain.
33:19 not see peo. of stammer. *t.*
35:6 then shall *t.* of dumb sing
41:17 when th. *t.* fail. for thirst
45:23 unto me ev. *t.* shall swear
50:4 L. ha. giv. me *t.* of learned
54:17 every *t.* that shall rise
57:4 ag. whom draw ye out *t. ?*
59:3 your *t.* muttered perverse.
Jer. 9:3 bend their *t.* like bow
5 taught their *t.* to speak lies
8 *t.* is an arrow shot out
18:18 let us smite him with *t.*
Lam. 4:4 *t.* of sucking child cle.
Ezek. 3:26 make *t.* cleave to mo.
Hos. 7:16 princes fall for ra. of *t.*
Hab. 1:13 holdest *t.* when wicked
Zec. 14:12 *t.* consume in mouth
Mark 7:33 spit. and touch. his *t.*
35 his *t.* was loosed, *Luke* 1:64
Jam. 1:26 and bridleth not his *t.*
3:5 so the *t.* is a little member
6 *t.* is fire ; 8 *t.* no man tame
1 *John* 3:18 nor love in *t.* in tru.

See DECEITFUL, HOLD.

My TONGUE.

2 *Sam.* 23:2 his wo. was in *my t.*
Est. 7:4 if sold, I had held *my t.*
Job 6:30 is there iniqui. in *my t.*
27:4 nor shall *my t.* utter deceit
33:2 *my t.* hath spok. in mouth
Ps. 22:15 *my t.* cleaveth to jaws
35:28 *my t.* shall speak of thy
righteousness, 51:14 ; 71:24
39:1 heed th. I sin not wi. *my t.*
3 hot, then spake I with *my t.*
45:1 *my t.* is pen of ready writ.
66:17 G. was extolled with *my t.*
119:172 *my t.* speak of thy word
137:6 let *my t.* cleave to mouth
139:4 not a word in *my t.* but
Luke 16:24 dip finger, cool *my t.*
Acts 2:26 heart rejoice, *my t.* gl.

TONGUE, *for language, speech.*

Gen. 10:5 every one after his *t.*
Ex. 4:10 slow of speech, slow *t.*
Deut. 28:49 whose *t.* not unders.
Ezr. 4:7 letter written in Syr. *t.*
Is. 28:11 anoth. *t.* will he speak
Dan. 1:4 might teach *t.* of Chal.
John 5:2 call. in Hebrew *t.* Beth.
Acts 1:19 in proper *t.* Aceldama
2:8 how hear we in our own *t. ?*
26:14 saying in Hebrew *t.* Saul
Rom. 14:11 every *t.* confess to G.
1 *Cor.* 14:2 speak in unkn. *t.* 4:27
9 by *t.* words easy understood
26 every one hath a psalm, a *t.*
Phil. 2:11 ev. *t.* confess. J. is L.
Rev. 5:9 redeemed out of every *t.*
9:11 in Hebrew *t.* is Abaddon
14:6 gospel to preach unto ev. *t.*
16:16 in Hebrew *t.* Armageddon

TONGUED.

1 *Tim.* 3:8 be gra. not double-*t.*

TONGUES.

Gen. 10:20 sons of H. after th. *t.*
31 sons of Shem, after their *t.*
Ps. 31:20 keep th. fr. strife of *t.*
55:9 O Lord, and divide their *t.*
78:36 lied to him with their *t.*
140:3 sharpened *t.* like a serpe.
Is. 66:18 gath. all nations and *t.*
Jer. 23:31 use their *t.* and say
Mark 16:17 sh. speak wi. new *t.*
Acts 2:3 th. appeared cloven *t.* 4
11 hear in our *t.* works of God
10:46 heard them speak with *t.*
19:6 spake with *t.* prophesied
Rom. 3:13 with *t.* th. used dece.
1 *Cor.* 12:10 divers kinds of *t.* 28
30 do all speak with *t. ?* do all
13:1 tho' I speak with *t.* of men
8 whether *t.* they shall cease
14:5 I would ye all spake wi. *t.*
6 if I come to you speak. wi. *t.*
18 I speak with *t.* more than
21 with men of other *t.* I speak
22 *t.* for a sign ; 23 speak wi. *t.*
39 forbid not to speak with *t.*
Rev. 7:9 peo. and *t.* stood before
10:11 prophesy before natio. *t.*
11:9 *t.* and natio. see dead bod.
13:7 power given him over *t.*
16:10 gnawed their *t.* for pain
17:15 thou sawe. are nations, *t.*

TOOK.

Gen. 5:24 En. was not, G. *t.* him
Num. 11:25 L. *t.* of Spirit on him
1 *Sam.* 14:47 so Saul *t.* kingdom
2 *Sam.* 7:15 depart, as I *t.* fr. S.
Ps. 22:9 *t.* me out of womb, 71:6
48:6 fear *t.* hold on them there
55:14 *t.* sweet counsel together
Amos 7:15 L. *t.* me as I followed
Mat. 8:17 himself *t.* our infirmit.
25:43 stranger, ye *t.* me not in
Mark 12:20 the first *t.* a wife
21 second *t.* her, *Luke* 20:29, 30
14:49 teaching, and ye *t.* me not
John 19:27 *t.* her to his home
Acts 1:16 guide to th. who *t.* Je.
Phil. 2:7 *t.* on him form of serva.
Col. 2:14 *t.* it out of way

TOOK away.

Ps. 69:4 that which I *t.* not *aw.*
Cant. 5:7 keepers *t. aw.* my veil
Ezek. 16:50 I *t.* them *aw* as I saw
Hos. 13:11 *t.* king *a.* in my wra.
Mat. 24:39 flood came, *t.* them *a.*
John 11:41 they *t. aw.* the stone

He TOOK.

Gen. 34:2 Sh. saw her, *he t.* her
Ex. 4:6 when *he t.* it out, hand
2 *Sam.* 3:11 *he t.* hold of her
22:17 above *he t.* me, *Ps.* 18:16
1 *K.* 17:19 *he t.* her son out bos.
2 *K.* 5:24 *he t.* them fr. their ha.
Acts 16:33 *he t.* them same hour
21:11 *he t.* Paul's girdle, bound
Heb. 2:16 *he t.* not nat. of angels

They TOOK.

Gen. 6:2 *t.* wives they chose
14:11 *they t.* all goods of Sodom
12 *t.* Lot, Abram's brother's
Deut. 1:25 *t.* of the fruit of land
Jos. 6:20 peo. went, and *t.* city
11:19 all other *they t.* in battle
Jud. 3:6 *t.* their daught. to be
2 *K.* 10:14 *t.* them alive, and
Ezek. 23:13 I saw *th. t.* one way
Dan. 5:20 *t.* his glory from him
Mat. 21:46 *t.* him for a prophet
28:15 *t.* the money, and did as
Mark 12:8 *t.* him, killed him
Luke 22:54 *t.* him, *John* 19:16
Acts 13:29 *t.* him down fr. tree

TOOK up.

Num. 23:7 Balaam *t. up* his parable, 18 ; 24:3, 15, 20, 21, 23

Jos. 3:6 the priests *t. up* the ark,
  6:12 ; 1 *K.* 8:3
2 *K.* 2:13 he *t. up* mantle of Elij.
  10:15 *t.* him *up* into the chariot
Neh. 2:1 I *t. up* wine and gave
Ezek. 3:12 then the Spirit *t.* me
  up, 11:24 ; 43:5
Mat. 14:12 they *t. up* body of
  John, *Mark* 6:29
  16:9 many baskets ye *t. up*, 10
Mark 10:16 he *t.* them up in arms
Luke 2:28 *t.* him *up* in his arms
Acts 10:26 Pet. *t.* him *up*, saying
Rev. 18:21 mig. angel *t. up* stone

TOOKEST.

Ps. 99:8 tho. thou *t.* vengeance
Ezek. 16:18 *t.* thy broid. garmen.

TOOL.

Ex. 20:25 if l'ft up thy *t.* thou
  32:4 fashio:.ed it with a grav. *t.*
Deut. 27:5 . h. not lift any iron *t.*
1 *K.* 6:7 nor any *t.* of iron heard

TOOTH.

Ex. 21:24 give *t.* for *t. Lev.* 24:20 ;
  Deut. 19:21 ; *Mat.* 5:38
  27 if he smite man-servant's *t.*
  he shall go free for *t.* sake
Prov. 25:19 a broken *t.* a foot out

TOP

Gen. 11:4 tower wh. *t.* may reach
  28:12 *t.* of ladder reached heav.
  18 Ja. poured oil on *t.* of stone
Ex. 19:20 L. came on *t.* of Sinai
  24:17 like fire on *t.* of mount
  28:32 there shall be a hole in *t.*
  30:3 overlay *t.* with gold, 37:26
Num. 14:40 gat into *t.* of mount.
  20:28 Aaron died on *t.* of mount
  23:9 from *t.* of rocks I see him
Deut. 3:27 get into *t.* of Pis. 34:1
  28:35 fr. foot to *t.* of thy head
  33:16 on *t.* of him that was sep.
Jud. 6:26 build alt. on *t.* of rock
  9:51 peo. gat up to *t.* of tower
  15:8 Samson dwelt on *t.* of E.
1 *Sam.* 9:25 commun. on *t.* of, 26
2 *Sam.* 16:22 tent on *t.* of house
1 *K.* 10:19 the *t.* of throne round
2 *K.* 9:13 under him on *t.* of sta.
2 *Chr.* 25:12 cast from *t.* of rock
Est. 5:2 Esth. touch. *t.* of scept.
Ps. 72:16 corn on *t.* of mountains
  102:7 a sparrow on the house-*t.*
Prov. 8:2 she stand. in *t.* of high
21:9 in corner of house-*t.***, 25:24**
Prov. 23:34 lie. on the *t.* of a ma.
Cant. 4:8 the *t.* of Amana, fr. *t.*
Is. 2:2 L.'s house sh. be estabia.
  in *t.* of mountains, *Mic.* 4:1
  17:6 berries in *t.* of the bough
  30:17 a beacon on *t.* of mount.
  42:11 shout fr. the *t.* of mount.
Lam. 2:19 faint for hunger in *t.*
  4:1 stones poured in *t.* of street
Ezek. 17:4 he cropt off *t.* of twigs
  22 crop off *t.* of young twigs
  24:7 she set it on *t.* of a rock
  8 I set her blood on *t.* of rock
  26:4 ma. her like *t.* of rôck, 14
  31:3 *t.* was am. boughs, 10, 14
  43:12 house on *t.* of mountains
Nah. 3:10 dashed at *t.* of streets
Mat. 24:17 on house-*t. Mark*
  13:15 ; *Luke* 17:31
  27:51 veil rent fr. *t.* to bottom,
  Mark 15:38
Luke 5:19 they went on house-*t.*
John 19:23 woven fr. *t.* through.
Heb. 11:21 leaning on *t.* of staff

  See HILL.

TOPS.

Gen. 8:5 *t.* of mounta. were seen
2 *Sam.* 5:24 when hearest so. on
  t. of trees, 1 *Chr.* 14:15
2 *K.* 19:26 as grass upon house-*t.*
  Ps. 129:6 ; *Is.* 37:27

Job 24:24 cut off as the *t.* of ears
Is. 2:21 into *t.* of ragged rocks
  15:3 on *t.* of houses every one
  22:1 wholly gone up to house-*t.*
Jer. 48:38 lamenta. on house-*t.*
Ezek. 6:13 slain in *t.* of mounta.
Hos. 4:13 sacrifi. on *t.* of mount.
Zep. 1:5 worsh. host on house-*t.*
Mat. 10:27 preach upon house-*t.*
Luke 12:3 proclaim. on house-*t.*

TOPAZ.

Ex. 28:17 a sardius, a *t.* 39:10
Job 28:19 the *t.* of Ethiopia shall
Ezek. 28:13 *t.* was thy covering
Rev. 21:20 beryl, the ninth a *t.*

TOPHET.

2 *K.* 23:10 Josiah defiled T. in v.
Is. 30:33 for T. is ordained of old
Jer. 7:31 built high places of T.
  32 no more be called T. 19:6
  19:11 they shall bury in T.
  12 even make this city as T.
  13 Jerusa. shall be defiled as T.
  14 then came Jeremiah from T.

TORCH.

Zec. 12:6 make govern. like a *t.*

TORCHES.

Nah. 2:3 chariots sh. be with *t.*
  4 chariots shall seem like *t.*
John 18:3 Judas cometh with *t.*

TORMENT, S.

Mat. 4:24 tak. wi. disease and *t.*
Luke 16:23 lift up eyes bei. in *t.*
  28 lest th. come into place of *t.*
1 *John* 4:18 because fear hath *t.*
Rev. 9:5 was *t.* of a scorpion
  14:11 smoke of their *t.* ascend.
  18:7 so much *t.* and sorrow give
  10 afar off for fear of her *t.* 15

TORMENT, Verb.

Mat. 8:29 art thou come to *t.* us ?
Mark 5:7 *t.* me not, *Luke* 8:28

TORMENTED.

Mat. 8:6 serv. lieth grievously *t.*
Luke 16:24 I am *t.* in this flame
  25 he is comforted, thou art *t.*
Heb. 11:37 destitute, afflicted, *t.*
Rev. 9:5 should be *t.* five months
  11:10 two prophets *t.* them
  14:10 he sh. be *t.* with fire and
  20:10 shall be *t.* day and night

TORMENTORS.

Mat. 18:34 lord deliver. him to *t.*

TORN.

Gen. 31:39 which was *t.* of beasts
  44:28 Surely he is *t.* in pieces
Ex. 22:13 not make good what *t.*
  31 nor shall eat any flesh *t.* of
Lev. 7:24 fat of *t.* may be used
  17:15 if any eat that wh. was *t.*
  22:8 dieth itself. or *t.* of beasts
1 *K.* 13:26 lion, which hath *t.* him
  28 eaten carcass nor *t.* the ass
Is. 5:25 carcasses *t.* in streets
Jer. 5:6 that goeth out shall be *t.*
Ezek. 4:14 not eaten of that is *t.*
  44:31 priests sh. not eat th. is *t.*
Hos. 6:1 he hath *t.* he will heal
Mal. 1:13 bro. that which was *t.*
Mark 1:26 uncl. spirit had *t.* him

TORTOISE.

Lev. 11:29 the *t.* shall be unclean

TORTURED.

Heb. 11:35 oth. were *t.* not acce.

TOSS.

Is. 22:18 he will turn and *t.* thee
Jer. 5:22 tho' waves *t.* themselv.

TOSSED.

Ps. 109:23 I am *t.* up and down
Prov. 21:6 a vanity, *t.* to and fro
Is. 54:11 O thou afflicted, *t.* with
Mat. 14:24 ship was *t.* wi. waves
Acts 28:17 exceedi. *t.* with tem.

Eph. 4:14 children *t.* to and fro
Jam. 1:6 waver. is like wave *t.*

TOSSINGS.

Job 7:4 I am full of *t.* till dawn.

TOTTERING.

Ps. 62:3 ye shall be as a *t.* fence

TOUCH.

Gen. 3:3 nor shall ye *t.* it lest die
  20:6 suffered I thee not to *t.* her
Ex. 19:12 that ye *t.* not border
  13 shall not a hand *t.* it
Lev. 5:2 if a soul *t.* unclean thi.
  6:27 whatsoever sh. *t.* the flesh
  11:8 carcass sh. not *t. Deut.* 14:8
  31 whose. doth *t.* them when
  12:4 he sh. *t.* no hallowed thing
Num. 4:15 sh. not *t.* any holy th.
  16:26 and *t.* nothing of theirs
Jos. 9:19 theref. we may not *t.*
Ruth 2:9 they should not *t.* thee
2 *Sam.* 14:10 he shall not *t.* thee
  18:12 none *t.* the young man
  23:7 that shall *t.* them must be
1 *Chr.* 16:22 *t.* not mine anointed,
  Ps. 105:15
Job 1:11 *t.* all he hath, and he
  2:5 *t.* his bone and his flesh, he
  5:19 in seven sh. no evil *t.* thee
  6:7 that my soul refused to *t.*
Ps. 144:5 *t.* the mountains, and
Is. 52:11 *t.* no uncl. 2 *Cor.* 6:17
Jer. 12:14 that *t.* the inheritance
Lam. 4:14 men could not *t.* gar.
  15 it is unclean, depart, *t.* not
Hag. 2:12 if one with skirt *t.* br.
  13 if one that is unclean *t.*
Mat. 9:31 if I but *t. Mark* 5:28
  14:36 that they might *t.* the
  hem, *Mark* 6:56 ; 8:22
Mark 3:10 to *t.* him, *Luke* 6:19
  8:22 besou. him to *t.* blind man
Luke 11:46 ye *t.* not the burdens
  18:15 infants, that he would *t.*
John 20:17 Jesus saith, *t.* me not
1 *Cor.* 7:1 good not to *t.* a wom.
Col. 2:21 *t.* not, taste not, handle
Heb. 11:28 first-born, sho. *t.* th.
  12:20 if so much as beast *t.* mo.

TOUCHED.

Gen. 26:29 as we have not *t.* thee
  32:25 he *t.* Jacob's thigh, 82
Lev. 22:6 soul which hath *t.* any
Num. 31:19 whoso. hath *t.* any
Jud. 6:21 angel of L. *t.* the flesh
1 *Sam.* 10:26 wh. hearts G. ha. *t.*
1 *K.* 6:27 wings of cherubim *t.*
  19:5 an angel *t.* him, and said, 7
2 *K.* 13:21 when the man *t.* bon.
Est. 5:2 Esther *t.* top of sceptre
Job 19:21 hand of G. hath *t.* me
Is. 6:7 lo, this hath *t.* thy lips
Jer. 1:9 the Lord *t.* my mouth
Dan. 8:5 he-goat *t.* not ground
  18 *t.* me, and set me upright,
  9:21 ; 10:10, 16, 18
Mat. 8:3 and Jesus *t.* him, *Mark*
  1:41 ; *Luke* 5:13
  15 he *t.* her hand, the fever left
  9:20 diseased with an issue *t.*
  garm. *Mark* 5:27 ; *Luke* 5:13
  29 then *t.* he their eyes, 20:34
  14:36 many as *t.* him were made
  whole, *Mark* 6:56
Mark 5:30 *t.* clothes, *Lu.* 8:45, 47
  7:33 he spit, and *t.* his tongue
Luke 7:14 he came and *t.* the bier
  8:47 declared cause she *t.* him
  22:51 *t.* his ear, healed him
Acts 27:3 next day we *t.* at Zid.
Heb. 4:15 not priest wh. can. be *t.*
  12:18 to mount that might be *t.*

TOUCHETH.

Gen. 26:11 *t.* this man shall die
Ex. 19:12 whos. *t.* mount sh. die
  29:37 whatsoever *t.* altar be holy
  30:29 that *t.* them, *Lev.* 6:18

Lev. 7:19 flesh that *t.* uncl. thing
11:26 every one that *t.* be uncl.
15:5 whoso *t.* his bed, sh. wash
11 whomsoever he *t.* hath ies.
12 vessel of earth he *t.* broken
25 if on her bed wh. he *t.* it, be
uncl. 27 ; 22:4, 5 ; *Num.* 19:22
Num. 19:11 *t.* dead body, 13, 16

Num. 19:18 *t.* a bone ; 21 *t.* **water**
of separation
Jud. 16:9 broken when it *t.* fire
Job 4:5 it *t.* thee, th. art troubl.
Ps. 104:32 he *t.* hills, th. smoke
Prov. 6:29 whoso *t.* her, not inn.
Ezek. 17:10 when east wind *t.* it
Hos. 4:2 break, blood *t.* blood
Amos 9:5 L. of hosts that *t.* land
Zec. 2:8 *t.* you *t.* apple of eye
Luke 7:39 what wom. that *t.* him
1 *John* 5:18 wick. one *t.* him not

TOUCHING.

Lev. 5:13 as *t.* his sin he sinned
1 *Sam.* 20:23 *t.* matter thou and I
2 *K.* 22:18 *t.* words thou heard
Job 37:23 *t.* Almig. not find out
Ps. 45:1 things I made *t.* king
Ezek. 7:13 vision is *t.* multitude
Mat. 18:19 *t.* any thing they ask
Rom. 11:28 as *t.* elect. they are
1 *Cor.* 8:1 as *t.* things offer. idols
16:12 *t.* our brother Apollos
Col. 4:10 *t.* whom ye received
2 *Thes.* 3:4 confidence in L. *t.* you

TOW.

Jud. 16:9 as a thread of *t.* brok.
Is. 1:31 the strong shall be as *t.*
43:17 extinct, are quenched as *t.*

TOWARD, *or* TOWARDS.

Deut. 28:54 eye evil *t.* his broth.
56 shall be evil *t.* her husband
2 *Chr.* 24:16 bec. Jeho. had done
good in Is. *t.* G. *t.* his house
Ezr. 3:11 his mercy endur. *t.* Is.
Ps. 5:7 worship *t.* temple, 138:2
25:15 mine eyes are ever *t.* L.
28:2 I lift hands *t.* thy oracle
Is. 63:7 goodness *t.* house of Is.
Jer. 15:1 mind not be *t.* this peo.
Jon. 2:4 look *t.* thy holy temple
Luke 2:14 pea. good will *t.* men

See HEAVEN.

TOWEL.

John 13:4 he riseth, and took a *t.*

TOWER.

Gen. 11:4 let us build city and *t.*
5 Lord came to see city and *t.*
35:21 spread tent beyo. *t.* of E.
Jud. 8:9 I will break this *t.* 17
9:46 men of *t.* of Shech. entered
51 there was a strong *t.* in city
2 *Sam.* 22:51 he is *t.* of salvation
2 *K.* 5:24 came to *t.* he took th.
Ps. 61:3 a strong *t.* from enemy
Prov. 18:10 name of L. strong *t.*
Cant. 4:4 thy neck like *t.* of Da.
7:4 thy neck is as a *t.* of ivory
Is. 5:2 built *t.* in midst of viney.
Jer. 6:27 I have set thee for a *t.*
31:38 city built from *t.* of Han.
Ezek. 29:10 desolate fr. *t.* of Sy.
30:6 fr. *t.* of Syene sh. they fall
Mic. 4:8 O *t.* of flock
Hab. 2:1 I will set me upon *t.*
Zec. 14:10 inhabited fr. *t.* of H.
Mat. 21:33 built *t.* *Mark* 12:1
Luke 13:4 on whom *t.* of Sil. fell
14:28 you intending to build a *t.*

High TOWER.

2 *Sam.* 22:3 God is my *high t.* *Ps.*
18:2 ; 144:2
Is. 2:15 day of L. on every *h. t.*

TOWERS.

2 *Chr.* 14:7 build cit. and make *t.*
26:9 Uzziah built *t.* in Jerusa.
10 he built *t.* in desert

27:4 Jotham built castles and *t.*
32:5 Hezek. raised up wall to *t.*
Ps. 48:12 Zion, and tell her *t.*
Cant. 8:10 my breasts like *t.*
Is. 23:13 Assy. set up *t.* thereof
30:25 high hill riv. when *t.* fall
32:14 forts and *t.* sh. be for dens
33:18 wh. is he that counted *t. ?*
Ezek. 26:4 sh. break do. her *t.* 9
27:11 Gammad. were in thy *t.*
Zep. 3:6 their *t.* are desolate

TOWN.

Jos. 2:15 Ra.'s house on *t.* wall
1 *Sam.* 16:4 elders of *t.* trembled
23:7 by entering into a *t.* that
27:5 give me a place in some *t.*
Hab. 2:12 woe to him builds a *t.*
Mat. 10:11 whatso. *t.* ye enter
Mark 8:23 led bli. man out of *t.*
26 neither go into *t.* nor tell
any in *t.*
John 7:42 C. com. out of *t.* of B.
11:1 *t.* of Mary and sis. Martha
30 J. was not yet come into *t.*

TOWNS.

Est. 9:19 J. dwelt in unwalled *t.*
Jer. 19:15 bring on her *t.* the evil
Zec. 2:4 inhab. as *t.* with. walls
Luke 9:6 and went thro' the *t.*
12 that th. go into *t.* and lodge

TOWN-CLERK.

Acts 19:35 when *t.-c.* appeas. peo.

TRADE.

Gen. 46:32 *t.* about cattle, 34

TRADE, Verb.

Gen. 34:10 and *t.* you therein, 21
Rev. 18:17 as *t.* by sea stood afar

TRADED.

Ezek. 27:12 Tarsh. *t.* in thy fairs
13 Meshech *t.* persons of men
14 they of Togar. *t.* wi. horses
17 Ju. and Is. *t.* in thy market
Mat. 25:16 five tal. went and *t.*

TRADING.

Luke 19:15 ev. man gained by *t.*

TRADITION.

Mat. 15:2 why do disci. transgr.
t. of the elders? *Mark* 7:5
3 why do you transgr. comma.
of God by *t. ? Mark* 7:9
6 made commandment of G. of
none effect by *t. Mark* 7:13
Mark 7:3 hold. *t.* of elders, 8, 9
Col. 2:8 spoil you after *t.* of men
2 *Thes.* 3:6 *t.* wh. he recei. of us
1 *Pet.* 1:18 received by *t.* fr. fa.

TRADITIONS.

Gal. 1:14 zealous of *t.* of my fa.
2 *Thes.* 2:15 hold *t.* ye been tau.

TRAFFIC.

Gen. 42:34 and ye shall *t.* in land

TRAFFIC, Substantive.

1 *K.* 10:15 had of *t.* of merchants
Ezek. 17:4 car. it into land of *t.*
28:5 by *t.* hast thou increased
18 defiled sanct. by iniq. of *t.*

TRAFFICKERS.

Is. 23:8 whose *t.* are honorable

TRAIN.

1 *K.* 10:2 to Jerus. with great *t.*
Is. 6:1 his *t.* filled the temple

TRAIN, Verb.

Prov. 22:6 *t.* ch. in way he sh. go

TRAINED.

Gen. 14:14 Abram armed *t.* serv.

TRAITOR, S.

Luke 6:16 Iscariot which was *t.*
2 *Tim.* 3:4 in last days men be *t.*

TRAMPLE.

Ps. 91:13 dragon *t.* under foot
Is. 63:3 I will *t.* them in my fury
Mat. 7:6 lest th. *t.* th. und. foot

TRANCE.

Num. 24:4 falling into *t.* 16
Acts 10:10 he fell into a *t.*
11:5 and in a *t.* I saw a vision
22:17 in temple I was in a *t.*

TRANQUILLITY.

Dan. 4:27 be a length. of thy *t.*

TRANSFERRED.

1 *Cor.* 4:6 I ha. in figure *t.* to my

TRANSFIGURED.

Mat. 17:2 *t.* bef. them, *Mark* 9:2

TRANSFORMED, ING.

Rom. 12:2 be ye *t.* by renewing
2 *Cor.* 11:13 *t.* thems. into apost.
14 Sat. is *t.* into angel of light
15 no great thing if min. be *t.*

TRANSGRESS.

Num. 14:41 where. do ye *t.* com-
mandm. of L. ? 2 *Chr.* 24:20
1 *Sam.* 2:24 make L.'s peo. to *t.*
Neh. 1:8 if ye *t.* I will scat. you
13:27 heark. to you to *t.* ag. G. ?
Ps. 17:3 purp. mouth sh. not *t.*
25:3 ash. who *t.* without cause
Prov. 28:21 for bread that man *t.*
Jer. 2:20 thou saidst, I will not *t.*
Ezek. 20:38 purge out them th. *t.*
Amos 4:4 come to Beth-el and *t.*
Mat. 15:2 do disciples *t.* tradit. ?
3 why do ye *t.* comm. of God ?
Rom. 2:27 by circumcis. *t.* law

TRANSGRESSED.

Deut. 26:13 I have not *t.* com.
Jos. 7:11 they *t.* my covenant, 15
23:16 when ye have *t.* covenant
1 *Sam.* 14:33 have *t.* roll a stone
15:24 I have *t.* command. of L.
1 *K.* 8:50 wherein they have *t.*
1 *Chr.* 2:7 *t.* in thing accursed
5:25 they *t.* ag. G. of their fath.
2 *Chr.* 12:2 because they *t.* ag. L.
26:16 Uzziah *t.* against the L.
28:19 Ahaz *t.* sore against Lord
36:14 priests and peo. *t.* much
Ezr. 10:10 ye ha. *t.* taken wives
Ezr. 10:13 many th. *t.* in this th.
Is. 24:5 bec. they have *t.* laws
43:27 thy teachers ha. *t.* ag. me
66:24 look at men's carc. that *t.*
Jer. 2:8 the pastors *t.* against me
29 ye all have *t.* against me
3:13 acknowledge thou hast *t.*
33:8 iniquities whereby they *t.*
34:18 give men that *t.* covenant
Lam. 3:42 we ha. *t.* and rebelled
Ezek. 2:3 they and fath. *t.* ag. me
18:31 transgres, whereby ye *t.*
Dan. 9:11 all Is. have *t.* thy law
Hos. 7:13 destruction, bec. they *t.*
Zep. 3:11 doings wherein thou *t.*
Luke 15:29 nor *t.* thy command.

See COVENANT.

TRANSGRESSEST, ETH.

Est. 3:3 why *t.* king's com. ?
Prov. 16:10 mouth *t.* not in judg.
Hab. 2:5 because he *t.* by wine
1 *John* 3:4 committeth sin, *t.* law
2 *John* 9 whoso *t.* and abid. not

TRANSGRESSING.

Deut. 17:2 wickedn. in *t.*
Is. 59:13 in *t.* and lying ag. Lord

TRANSGRESSION.

Ex. 34:7 forgiving *t. Num.* 14:18
Jos. 22:22 if it be in *t.* ag. Lord
1 *Sam.* 24:11 no *t.* in my hand
1 *Chr.* 9:1 carried to Babyl. for *t.*
10:13 Saul died for *t.* committed
2 *Chr.* 29:19 Ahaz cast away in *t.*
Ezr. 9:4 bec. of *t.* of them
10:6 he mourned bec. of their *t.*
Job 7:21 why not pardon my *t.*
8:4 cast them away for their *t.*
13:23 make me to know my *t.*
14:17 my *t.* is sealed up in a bag

33:9 I am without *t*. I am inno.
34:6 wound is incurable with. *t*.
Ps. 19:13 innocent from great *t*.
32:1 blessed he wh. *t*. is forgiven
36:1 *t*. of wicked saith within
59:3 wait for soul, not for my *t*.
89:32 then will I visit their *t*.
107:17 fools bec. of *t*. are afflict.
Prov. 12:13 wick. is snared by *t*.
17:9 covereth *t*. seeketh love
19 loveth *t*. that loveth strife
19:11 his glory to pass over *t*.
28:2 for *t*. of land many princes
24 robbeth, saith, It is no *t*.
29:6 in *t*. of evil man is a snare
16 wicked multiplied, *t*. incre.
22 a furious man abound. in *t*.
Is. 24:20 *t*. thereof be heavy
53:8 for *t*. of peo. was he strick.
57:4 are ye not children of *t*. ?
58:1 show my people their *t*.
59:20 to them that turn from *t*.
Ezek. 33:12 deliver in day of his *t*.
Dan. 8:12 ag. sacri. by reas. of *t*.
13 sacrifice, and *t*. of desolat.
9:24 seventy weeks to finish *t*.
Amos 4:4 at Gilgal multiply *t*.
Mic. 1:5 for *t*. of Jacob is all this;
what is the *t*. of Jacob ?
3:8 full of power to dec. to J. *t*.
6:7 first-born for my *t*. and sin ?
7:18 passeth by *t*. of remnant
Acts 1:25 from which J. by *t*. fell
Rom. 4:15 wh. no law is, is no *t*.
5:14 after similit. of Adam's *t*.
1 *Tim.* 2:14 being dece. was in *t*.
Heb. 2:2 every *t*. receiv. recomp.
1 *John* 3:4 for sin is *t*. of the law

TRANSGRESSIONS.
Ex. 23:21 will not pard. your *t*.
Lev. 16:16 atonement bec. of *t*.
21 Aa. confess over goat th. *t*.
Jos. 24:19 will not forg. your *t*.
1 *K.* 8:50 forgive people their *t*.
Job 31:33 I covered my *t*. as Ad.
35:6 if thy *t*. be multiplied
36:9 showeth their work and *t*.
Ps. 5:10 cast them out in their *t*.
25:7 sins of my youth, my *t*.
32:5 I will confess my *t*. unto L.
39:8 deliver me from all my *t*.
51:1 mercy, blot out all my *t*.
3 for I acknowl. my *t*. my sin
65:3 as for our *t*. purge th. away
103:12 so far hath he removed *t*.
Is. 43:25 he that blotteth out *t*.
44:22 blot. as a thi. cloud thy *t*.
50:1 for your *t*. is your mother
53:5 he was wounded for our *t*.
59:12 our *t*. are multiplied bef.
thee, for our *t*. are with us
Jer. 5:6 because th. *t*. are many
Lam. 1:5 multitu. of her *t*. gone
14 yoke of my *t*. bound by his
22 do to th. as to me for my *t*.
Ezek. 14:11 nor polluted wi. th. *t*.
18:22 his *t*. not be mentioned
Ezek. 18:28 he turn. away from
all his *t*.
30 turn yourselves fr. your *t*.
31 cast away all your *t*.
21:24 your *t*. are discovered
33:10 if our *t*. be upon us
37:23 nor defile thems. with *t*.
39:24 according to their *t*. have
Amos 1:3 for three *t*. of Damas.
6 *t*. of Gaza ; 9 Tyrus ; 11 Ed.
13 *t*. of Am. 2:1 Moab ; 4 Ju.
2:6 Isr. 3:14 visit *t*. of Israel
5:12 I know your manifold *t*.
Mic. 1:13 *t*. of Is. found in thee
Gal. 3:19 law was add. bec. of *t*.
Heb. 9.15 for redemption of *t*.

TRANSGRESSOR.
Prov. 21:18 *t*. be ransom for upr.
22:12 he overthrow. words of *t*.
Is. 48:8 called a *t*. from womb

Gal. 2:18 I make myself a *t*.
Jam. 2:11 kill, th. art become *t*.

TRANSGRESSORS.
Ps. 37:38 *t*. be destroyed togeth.
51:13 will I teach *t*. thy ways
59:5 be not merciful to wick. *t*.
Prov. 2:22 *t*. shall be rooted out
11:3 perversen. of *t*. destr. them
6 *t*. be taken in their naughti.
13:2 soul of *t*. shall eat violence
15 favor, but way of *t*. is hard
23:28 she increaseth *t*. am. men
26:10 God rewardeth fool and *t*.
Is. 1:28 destruction of *t*. together
46:8 bring it ag. to mind, ye *t*.
53:12 he was numbered with *t*.
and made intercession for *t*.
Dan. 8:23 when *t*. are come
Hos. 14:9 but *t*. sh. fall therein
Mark 15:28 he was numbered
with *t*. *Luke* 22:37
Jam. 2:9 are convin. of law as *t*.

TRANSLATE, D.
2 *Sam.* 3:10 *t*. kingdom fr. Saul
Col. 1:13 *t*. us into kingd. of Son
Heb. 11:5 Enoch was *t*. that he

TRANSLATION.
Heb. 11:5 bef. *t*. he had testim.

TRANSPARENT.
Rev. 21:21 str. of city was *t*. glass

TRAP, S.
Jos. 23:13 shall be *t*. and snares
Job 18:10 and a *t*. is laid for him
Ps. 69:22 welfare, let become *t*.
Jer. 5:26 wait, set a *t*. catch men
Rom. 11:9 let their table be made
a snare, a *t*.

TRAVAIL.
Gen. 38:27 in time of her *t*.
Ex. 18:8 told Jethro *t*. by way
Num. 20:14 know. *t*. ha. befallen
Ps. 48:6 pain as woman in *t*.
Jer. 6:24 ; 13:21 ; 22:23 ; 49:24 ;
50:43 ; *Mic.* 4:9, 10
Ec. 1:13 sore *t*. G. given to men
2:23 days are sorrows, *t*. grief
26 to sinner he giveth *t*.
3:10 seen *t*. G. hath giv. to men
4:4 I considered all *t*. ev. work
6 than both hands full with *t*.
8 is vanity, yea, it is a sore *t*.
5:14 riches perish by evil *t*.
Is. 23:4 I *t*. not ; 53:11 *t*. of soul
54:1 that didst not *t*. with child
Jer. 4:31 voice as of woman in *t*.
30:6 see whether man doth *t*.
Lam. 3:5 compas. wi. gall and *t*.
John 16:21 woman in *t*. hath sor.
Gal. 4:19 my chil. of whom I *t*.
1 *Thes.* 2:9 for ye rememb. our *t*.
5:3 destruction cometh as *t*.
2 *Thes.* 3:8 wrought with *t*. night

TRAVAILED.
Gen. 35:16 Rach. *t*. 38:28 Tam. *t*.
1 *Sam.* 4:19 Phinehas' wife *t*.
Is. 66:7 bef. she *t*. brought forth
8 as soon as Zion *t*. brou. forth

TRAVAILEST, ETH.
Job 15:20 wick. man *t*. wi. pain
Ps. 7:14 behold, he *t*. with iniq.
Is. 13:8 in pain as a woman *t*.
21:3 pangs of a woman that *t*.
Jer. 31:8 her that *t*. with child
Mic. 5:3 till she who *t*. br. forth
Rom. 8:22 creation *t*. in pain
Gal. 4:27 break forth thou th. *t*.

TRAVAILING.
Is. 42:14 I cry like woman in *t*.
Hos. 13:13 sorrows of *t*. woman
Rev. 12:2 *t*. in birth, and pained

TRAVEL.
Acts 19:29 Paul's companion in *t*.
2 *Cor.* 8:19 chosen of churches
to *t*.

Prov. 6:11 as one that *t*. 24:34
Acts 11:19 *t*. as far as Phenice

TRAVELLER, S.
2 *Sam.* 12:4 came *t*. to rich man
Jud. 5:6 *t*. walk. thro' by-ways
Job 31:32 I open. my doors to *t*.

TRAVELLING.
Is. 21:13 O ye *t*. companies
63:1 who is this *t*. in his stren. ?
Mat. 25:14 heaven is as a man *t*.

TRAVERSING.
Jer. 2:23 dromedary *t*. her ways

TREACHEROUS.
Is. 21:2 *t*. dealeth treach. 24:16
Jer. 3:7 her *t*. sister Jud. saw it
8 her *t*. sister Jud. fear. not, 10
11 justi. herself more than *t*. J
9:2 an assembly of *t*. men
Zep. 3:4 proph. are light and *t*.

TREACHEROUSLY.
Jud. 9:23 dealt *t*. with Abimel.
Is. 33:1 deal. *t*. they dealt not *t*.
48:8 thou wouldest deal very *t*.
Jer. 3:20 as a wife *t*. departeth
5:11 of Judah dealt *t*. *Mal.* 2:11
12:1 why hap. th. deal very *t*. ?
6 they have dealt *t*. with thee
Lam. 1:2 her friends ha. dealt *t*.
Hos. 5:7 they dealt *t*. against L.
6:7 there they dealt *t*. agai. me
Mal. 2:10 why do we deal *t*. eve.
14 wife aga. whom th. dealt *t*.
15 let none deal *t*. against wife
16 take heed, th. ye deal not *t*.

TREACHERY.
2 *K.* 9:23 there is *t*. O Ahaziah

TREAD.
Deut. 11:24 whereon your feet *t*.
25 dre. of you on all land ye *t*.
33:29 thou sh. *t*. on high places
1 *Sam.* 5:5 none *t*. on thresho. of
Job 24:11 *t*. their wine-presses
40:12 *t*. down wick. in th. place
Ps. 7:5 let him *t*. down my life
44:5 thro' thy name we *t*. them
60:12 *t*. down our enemi. 108:13
91:13 thou shalt *t*. upon the lion
Is. 1:12 requir. to *t*. my courts?
10:6 to *t*. them down like mire
14:25 mountains *t*. him under
16:10 tread. shall *t*. out no wine
26:6 the foot shall *t*. it down
63:3 I will *t*. them in anger, 6
Jer. 25:30 as they that *t*. grapes
48:33 wine fail, none *t*. shout.
Ezek. 26:11 with horses sh. he *t*.
34:18 must *t*. residue with feet
Dan. 7:23 fourth beast *t*. it down
Hos. 10:11 Eph. loveth to *t*. corn
Mic. 1:3 L. will *t*. on high places
5:5 wh. Assyrian *t*. our palaces
6:15 thou shalt *t*. olives
Nah. 3:14 *t*. mortar, make brick.
Zec. 10:5 which *t*. their enemies
Mal. 4:3 ye shall *t*. down wicked
Luke 10:19 power to *t*. on scorp.
Rev. 11:2 city they *t*. under foot

TREADER, S.
Is. 16:10 *t*. shall tread no wine
Amos 9:13 *t*. of grapes sh. over.

TREADETH.
Deut. 25:4 not muz. ox wh. he *t*.
corn, 1 *Cor.* 9:9 ; 1 *Tim.* 5:18
Job 9:8 *t*. upon waves of the sea
Is. 41:25 come as potter *t*. clay
63:2 garme. like him th. *t*. wine
Amos 4:13 that *t*. on high places
Mic. 5:6 wh. he *t*. within borders
8 he both *t*. down and teareth
Rev. 19:15 he *t*. wine-press of wr.

TREADING.
Neh. 13:15 some *t*. wine-presses

Is. 7:25 be for *t.* of lesser cattle
22:5 a day of trou. and *t.* down
Amos 5:11 forasmuch as your *t.*

TREASON.
1 *K.* 16:20 acts of Zim. and his *t.*
2 *K.* 11:14 cried *t.* 2 *Chr.* 23:13 ,

TREASURE.
Gen. 43:23 God hath given you *t.*
Ex. 19:5 a peculiar *t. Ps.* 135:4
Deut. 28:12 L. shall open good *t.*
1 *Chr.* 29:8 the *t.* of house of L.
Ezr. 2:69 ability to *t.* of work
Neh. 7:70 Tirsh. gave to *t.* 1,000
71 fath. gave to the *t.* of work
Ps. 17:14 belly th. fillest with *t.*
135:4 chosen Is. for his pecu. *t.*
Prov. 15:6 in house of right. is *t.*
16 than great *t.* and trouble
21:20 there is a *t.* to be desired
Ec. 2:8 I gathered *t.* of kings
Is. 33:6 fear of the Lord is his *t.*
Ezek. 22:25 taken *t.* and precious
Hos. 13:15 spoil *t.* of pleas. ves.
Mat. 6:21 where *t.* is, *Lu.* 12:34
12:35 a good man out of good *t.*
evil man of evil *t. Luke* 6:45
13:44 kingd. of heav. is like a *t.*
52 bring. out of *t.* new and old
19:21 thou sh. have *t.* in heaven,
Mark 10:21 ; *Luke* 18:22
Luke 12:21 so is he that lay. up *t.*
33 provide *t.* in the heavens
Acts 8:27 eunu. had charge of *t.*
2 *Cor.* 4:7 t. in earthen vessels
Jam. 5:3 heaped *t.* for last days

TREASURE-CITIES.
Ex. 1:11 built for Pharaoh *t.-c.*

TREASURE-HOUSE.
Ezr. 5:17 search be made in *t.-h.*
7:20 bestow it out of king's *t.-h.*
Neh. 10:38 L. bring tithe to *t.-h.*
Dan. 1:2 brou. vessels into *t.-h.*

TREASURED, EST.
Is. 23:18 sh. not be *t.* nor laid up
Rom. 2:5 t. up wrath ag. day of

TREASURER, S.
Ezr. 1:8 Cyr. brou. vessels by *t.*
7:21 I Artax. make decree to *t.*
Neh. 13:13 I made *t.* over treas.
Is. 22:15 get thee unto this *t.*
Dan. 3:2 Nebuch. gathered *t.* 3

TREASURES.
Deut. 32:34 sealed up am. my *t.*
33:19 sh. suck of *t.* hid in sand
1 *K.* 7:51 put dedicated among *t.*
14:26 Shishak took away the *t.*
15:18 Asa took gold left in the
t. 2 *Chr.* 16:2
2 *K.* 12:18 Jehoa. took gold fou.
in *t.* 14:14 ; 16:8 Ahaz took
18:15 Hez. gave silv. found in *t.*
20:13 Hezek. showed silver and
gold in his *t.* 15 ; *Is.* 39:2, 4
24:13 Nebuchad. carried out the
t. of house of Lord and *t.* of
king's house, 2 *Chr.* 36:18
1 *Chr.* 26:26 brethr. were over *t.*
27:25 over king's *t.* was Azmav.
2 *Chr.* 8:15 command. concer. *t.*
Neh. 12:44 some appointed for *t.*
Job 3:21 dig more than for hid *t.*
38:22 *t.* of snow ? *t.* of hail ?
Prov. 2:4 if search. as for hid *t.*
8:21 I will fill *t.* of those that
10:2 t. of wickedn. profit noth.
21:6 get. of *t.* by lying tongue
Is. 2:7 neith. any end of their *t.*
10:13 I have robbed their *t.*
30:6 carry *t.* on bunches of cam.
45:3 I will give thee *t.* of dark.
Jer. 10:13 wind out of *t.* 51:16
15:13 *t.* to spoil, 17:3 ; 20:5
41:8 for we have *t.* in the field
48:7 bec. thou trusted in thy *t.*
49:4 daughter, trusted in her *t.*

50:37 a sword is on her *t.*
51:13 dwe. on waters abun. in *t.*
Ezek. 28:4 silver and gold in *t.*
Dan. 11:43 have power over *t.*
Mic. 6:10 are yet *t.* of wickedn. ?
Mat. 2:11 wh. th. had opened *t.*
6:19 lay not up for yourselves *t.*
20 lay up for yoursel. *t.* in hea.
Col. 2:3 in wh. are hid *t.* of wis.
Heb. 11:26 greater riches than *t.*

TREASURY.
Jos. 6:19 sil. sh. come into *t.* 24
Jer. 38:11 went into hou. und. *t.*
Mat. 27:6 not lawful to put in *t.*
Mark 12:41 Je. sat against *t.* and
beheld peo. cast mon. into *t.*
Luke 21:1 rich cast. gifts into *t.*
John 8:20 words spake Je. in *t.*

TREASURIES.
1 *Chr.* 9:26 Levites were over *t.*
28:11 gave Sol. pattern of *t.* 12
2 *Chr.* 32:27 Hez. made *t.* for sil.
Neh. 13:12 brought tithe into *t.*
Est. 3:9 bring it into king's *t.*
4:7 H. prom. to pay to king's *t.*
Ps. 135:7 bringeth wind out of *t.*

TREATISE.
Acts 1:1 former *t.* have I made

TREE.
Gen. 1:29 I have given you ev. *t.*
2:9 G. made ev. *t.* to grow, the *t.*
of life and *t.* of knowledge
16 of every *t.* of the garden
2:17 of *t.* of knowl. not eat, 3:3
3:6 woman saw the *t.* was good
11 hast thou eaten of *t.* ? 17
12 woman gave me of the *t.*
22 lest he take also of *t.* of life
24 to keep the way of *t.* of life
Gen. 18:4 rest yoursel. under *t.*
8 he stood by them und. the *t.*
40:19 Phara. sh. hang thee on *t.*
Ex. 9:25 the hail brake every *t.*
15:25 the Lord showed him a *t.*
Deut. 19:5 fetch. stroke to cut *t.*
20:19 *t.* of the field is man's life
21:23 body sh. not remain on *t.*
Jos. 8:29 take king of Ai from *t.*
1 *Sam.* 22:6 Saul abode under *t.*
31:13 they buried th. under a *t.*
2 *K.* 3:19 and shall fell ev. good *t.*
Est. 2:23 were hanged on a *t.*
Job 14:7 hope of a *t.* if cut down
19:10 hope hath he remo. like *t.*
24:20 wicked. sh. be brok. as *t.*
Ps. 1:3 like a *t.* plant by rivers
Prov. 3:18 she is a *t.* of life to th.
11:30 fr. of righte. is a *t.* of life
13:12 desire com. it is a *t.* of life
15:4 a wholes. tongue is a *t.* of
Ec. 11:3 if *t.* fall to the south or
north ; where the *t.* fall.
Isa. 40:20 chooseth a *t.* that will
44:19 sh. I fall d. to stock of *t.* ?
56:3 nei. eunu. say, I am dry *t.*
65:22 as days of a *t.* are days of
66:17 purify themsel. behind *t.*
Jer. 10:3 one cutteth a *t.*
11:19 let us destroy the *t.*
17:8 as a *t.* planted by waters
Ezek. 15:2 vine *t.* more th. any *t.*
17:24 brought down high *t.* exalted low *t.* dried up green *t.*
made dry *t.* to flourish
21:10 contemneth rod, as ev. *t.*
31:8 nor any *t.* in garden of G.
34:27 *t.* of field shall yield fruit
36:30 I will multiply fruit of *t.*
Dan. 4:10 beh. a *t.* 11, 14, 20, 23
Joel 2:22 fear not *t.* beareth fruit
Mat. 3:10 ev. *t.* that bringeth not
good fruit, 7:19 ; *Luke* 3:9
7:17 good *t.* bring. good fruit,
cor. *t.* evil fruit, *Luke* 6:43
18 good *t.* cannot bri. evil fruit
12:33 make *t.* good and fr. good,
t. is kno. by fruit, *Luke* 6:44

Luke 17:6 mi. say to sycamine *t.*
Acts 5:30 wh. ye hanged on a *t.*
10:39 Je. wh. they hanged on *t.*
Gal. 3:13 cursed is th. hang. on *t.*
1 *Pet.* 2:24 bare sins in body on *t.*
Rev. 2:7 I will give to eat of *t.*
7:1 wind sh. not blow on any *t.*
9:4 not hurt green thing, nor *t.*
22:2 in midst was the *t.* of life
14 may have right to *t.* of life

See GREEN.

TREES.
Gen. 3:8 hid amongst *t.* of gard.
23:17 *t.* were made sure to Abr.
Ex. 10:15 locusts did eat fr. of *t.*
Lev. 19:23 planted all man. of *t.*
23:40 take boughs of goodly *t.*
26:4 *t.* of the field shall yield
Num. 24:6 as *t.* of lign-aloes wh.
L. planted, and as cedar *t.*
Deut. 16:21 not plant grove of *t.*
20:19 sh. not destroy *t.* thereof
20 *t.* th. know. not *t.* for meat
Jos. 10:26 J. hang. them on 5 *t.*
Jud. 9:8 *t.* went to anoint king
9 to be promoted over *t.* 11, 13
10 *t.* said to the fig-tree reign
12 *t.* said to vine ; 14 *t.* to bra.
1 *K.* 4:33 he spake of *t.* fr. cedar
2 *K.* 3:25 they felled the good *t.*
1 *Chr.* 16:33 th. shall *t.* of wood
sing, *Ps.* 96:12
Neh. 10:35 bring first-fr. of *t.* 37
Job 40:21 lieth under shady *t.* 22
Ps. 74:5 lifted axes on thick *t.*
78:47 destroyed th. sycamore *t.*
104:16 *t.* of Lord are full of sap
105:33 brake *t.* of their coasts
148:9 fruitf. *t.* and cedars praise
Ec. 2:5 I planted *t.* of all kinds
Cant. 2:3 as apple-tree am. the *t.*
4:14 all *t.* of frankincense
Is. 7:2 moved as the *t.* of wood
10:19 the rest of the *t.* of forest
44:14 he strengthen. among *t.*
55:12 *t.* of the fields shall clap
61:3 be called *t.* of righteous.
Jer. 6:6 Lord said, Hew down *t.*
7:20 my fury sh. be poured on *t.*
Ezek. 17:24 the *t.* of field shall
know
20:28 they saw all the thick *t.*
31:5 height was exalted above *t.*
9 all the *t.* of Eden envied him
47:7 many *t.* on the one side and
12 by the riv. shall grow all *t.*
Joel 1:12 *t.* of field are withered
19 flame hath burnt all the *t.*
Mat. 3:10 axe laid to *t. Luke* 3:9
Mat. 21:8 others cut down bran.
of *t.* and strewed, *Mark* 11:8
Mark 8:24 I see men as *t.* walk.
Luke 21:29 beh. fig-tree and all *t.*
Jude 12 *t.* whose fruit withereth
Rev. 7:3 hurt not *t.* till we have
8:7 third part of *t.* was burnt up

See PALM.

TREMBLE.
Deut. 2:25 nations sh. *t.* because
20:3 do not *t.* because of them
Ezr. 10:3 that *t.* at commandm.
Job 9:6 the pillars thereof *t.*
26:11 the pillers of heaven *t.*
Ps. 60:2 hast made earth to *t.*
99:1 L. reigneth, let the peo. *t.*
114:7 *t.* earth, at presence of L.
Ec. 12:3 keepers of house sh. *t.*
Is. 5:25 hills did *t.* th. carcasses
14:16 man that made earth *t.*
32:11 *t.* ye wom. th. are at ease
64:2 natl. may *t.* at thy presence
66:5 hear word of L. ye that *t.*
Jer. 5:22 will ye not *t.* at my pre.
10:10 at his wrath earth shall *t.*
33:9 they sh. *t.* for the goodness
51:29 land of Babylon shall *t.*

Ezek. 26:16 I. at ev. mom. 32:10
18 now shall the isles *t.* in
Dan. 6:26 men *t.* bef. G. of Dan.
Hos. 11:10 chil. sh. *t.* from west
11 th. sh. *t.* as a bird out of E.
Joel 2:1 let inhabitants of land *t.*
10 qnake, the heavens shall *t.*
Amos 8:8 sh. not land *t.* for this?
Hab. 3:7 captains of Midi. did *t.*
Jan. 2:19 the devils beli. and *t.*

TREMBLED.

Gen. 27:33 I. *t.* very exceedingly
Ex. 19:16 peo. th. was in camp *t.*
Jud. 5:4 earth *t.* heavens drop-
ped, 2 *Sam.* 22:8; *Ps.* 18:7;
77:18; 97:4
1 *Sam.* 4:13 Eli's heart *t.* for ark
14:15 spoilers *t.* 16:4 elders *t.*
28:5 Saul was afraid, heart *t.*
Ezr. 9:4 assemb. ev. one that *t.*
Jer. 4:24 mountains *t. Hab.* 3:10
8:16 land *t.* at sound of neighl.
Dan. 5:19 all peo. and nations *t.*
Hab. 3:16 my belly *t.* and I *t.* in
Mark 16:8 fled fr. sepulch. th. *t.*
Acts 7:32 Moses *t.* 24:25 Felix *t.*

TREMBLETH.

Job 37:1 at this also my heart *t.*
Ps. 104:32 looketh on earth it *t.*
119:120 my flesh *t.* for fear
Is. 66:2 I will look to him that *t.*

TREMBLING.

Ex. 15:15 *t.* take hold on mighty
Deut. 28:65 L. sh. give *t.* heart
1 *Sam.* 13:7 people followed *t.*
14:15 in the host was a great *t.*
Ezr. 10:9 peo. sat *t.* because of
Job 4:14 fear ca. upon me and *t.*
21:6 *t.* taketh hold on my flesh
Ps. 2:11 serve L. rejoice with *t.*
55:5 fearfulness and *t.* are come
Is. 51:17 dregs of the cup of *t.* 22
Jer. 30:5 we heard a voice of *t.*
Ezek. 12:18 drink thy wat. wi. *t.*
26:16 clothe themselves with *t.*
Dan. 10:11 had spoken, I stood *t.*
Hos. 13:1 Eph. spake *t.* he exalt.
Zec. 12:2 make Jeru. a cup of *t.*
Mark 5:33 woman *t. Luke* 8:47
Acts 9:6 S. *t.* said, What wilt th.?
16:29 keeper came *t.* fell down
1 *Cor.* 2:3 with you in much *t.*
2 *Cor.* 7:15 wi. fear and *t.* ye rec.
Eph. 6:5 serv. be obed. with *t.*
Phil. 2:12 work out salva. with *t.*

TRENCH.

1 *Sam.* 17:20 Dav. came to the *t.*
26:5 S. lay sleeping in the *t.* 7
1 *K.* 18:32 Elijah made a *t.* about
35 filled the *t.* with water, 38
Luke 19:43 enemies sh. cast a *t.*

TRESPASS, Substantive.

Gen. 31:36 wh. is my *t.* that thou
50:17 forgive *t.* of thy servants
Ex. 22:9 manner of *t.* whether
Lev. 5:15 for his *t.* to L. a ram
26:40 conf. their *t.* th. trespass.
Num. 5:6 when any do *t.* ag. L.
7 he shall recompense his *t.*
27 if she *t.* against husband
1 *Sam.* 25:28 forg. *t.* of handm.
1 *Chr.* 21:3 be cause of *t.* to Is.?
2 *Chr.* 24:18 wr. come on J. for *t.*
28:13 ye intend to add to our *t.*
33:19 Manasseh's prayer and *t.*
Ezr. 9:2 rul. been chief in this *t.*
6 our *t.* is grown unto heavens
7 in great *t.* to this day, 13
Ezr. 10:10 wives, to incr. *t.* of Is.
19 th. offered a ram for their *t.*
Ezek. 17:20 I will plead for his *t.*
18:24 in his *t.* he hath trespass.
Dan. 9:7 bec. of *t.* they trespas.

TRESPASSES.

Ezr. 9:15 before thee in our *t.*

Ps. 68:21 one as goeth on in *t.*
Ezek. 39:26 they have borne th. *t.*
Mat. 6:14 if ye forg. men their *t.*
15 if forgive not *t.* neither will
your Fa. forgive yo. *t.* 18:35
Mark 11:25 Fath. may forgive *t.*
26 nei. will F. forgive your *t.*
2 *Cor.* 5:19 not imputing their *t.*
Eph. 2:1 who were dead in *t.*
Col. 2:13 having forg. you all *t.*

See COMMIT, COMMITTED, OFFER-
ING.

TRESPASS-MONEY.

2 *K.* 12:16 *t.-m.* was not brought

TRESPASS, Verb.

1 *K.* 8:31 man *t.* ag. his neighb.
2 *Chr.* 19:10 that they *t.* not
28:22 Ahaz did *t.* yet more
Mat. 18:15 if brother *t.* tell fault
Luke 17:3 if bro. *t.* rebuke him
4 if he *t.* ag. thee seven times

TRESPASSED.

Lev. 5:19 he hath *t.* against L.
26:40 if confess trespass they *t.*
Num. 5:7 recompensed ag. wh. *t.*
Deut. 32:51 bec. ye *t.* against me
2 *Chr.* 26:18 sanct. for th. hast *t.*
29:6 our fathers have *t.*
30:7 not like fath. who *t.* ag. L.
33:23 Amon *t.* more and more
Ezr. 10:2 we have *t.* ag. our God
Ezek. 17:20 trespass that he *t.*
39:23 they *t.* against me, 26
Dan. 9:7 trespass that they *t.*
Hos. 8:1 they *t.* against my law

TRESPASSING.

Lev. 6:7 any t. he hath done in *t.*
Ezek. 14:13 land sinneth by *t.*

TRIAL.

Job 9:23 laugh at *t.* of innocent
Ezek. 21:13 It is a *t.* what if swo.
2 *Cor.* 8:2 how in *t.* of affliction
Heb. 11:36 others had *t.* of mock.
1 *Pet.* 1:7 *t.* of your faith might
4:12 not strange concerning *t.*

TRIBE.

Num. 1:4 man of every *t.* 13:2;
34:18
4:18 cut not off *t.* of Kohathites
18:2 *t.* of thy father bring thou
31:4 of every *t.* a thousand, 5, 6
36:6 marry to the family of *t.* 8
9 inherit. from one *t.* to ano. *t.*
Deut. 1:23 I took twelve, one of
a *t. Jos.* 3:12; 4:2, 4
29:18 *t.* whose heart turneth
Jos. 7:14 *t.* which Lord taketh
18:4 give out 3 men for each *t.*
Jud. 21:3 one *t.* lacking in Is. 6
1 *K.* 11:13 one *t.* to son, 32, 36
1 *Chr.* 6:61 of family of that *t.*
Ezek. 47:23 in what *t.* the stran.
Heb. 7:13 he pertain. to anoth. *t.*
14 of wh. *t.* Mo. spake nothing

See REUBEN, SIMEON, *and the
rest.*

TRIBES.

Ex. 28:21 according to 12 *t.* 39:14
Num. 24:2 in tents accord. to *t.*
33:54 according to *t.* of fathers
34:13 give to the nine *t. Jos.*
13:7; 14:2
15 two *t.* and the half have received inheritance, *Jos.* 14:3
Deut. 1:13 wise men, am. your *t.*
18:5 G. hath cho. him out of *t.*
Jos. 7:14 brought according to *t.*
1 *Sam.* 10:19 present your. by *t.*
1 *K.* 11:31 I will give ten *t.* to
18:31 according to number of *t.*
Ps. 105:37 not one feeble amo. *t.*
122:4 the *t.* go up, *t.* of the Lord
Is. 19:13 that are stay of *t.*
49:6 to raise up the *t.* of Jacob
63:17 for *t.* of thine inheritance

Ezek. 45:8 to Isr. according to *t.*
Hab. 3:9 according to oaths of *t.*
Mat. 24:30 th. *t.* of earth mourn
Acts 26:7 promise our 12 *t.* hope
Jam. 1:1 the twelve *t.* scattered
Rev. 7:4 sealed 144,000 of all *t.*

See ISRAEL.

TRIBULATION.

Deut. 4:30 wh. in *t.* if thou turn
Jud. 10:14 let th. deliv. you in *t.*
1 *Sam.* 26:24 deli. me out of all *t.*
Mat. 13:21 when *t.* ariseth, he is
Mat. 24:21 then shall be great *t.*
29 immed. after *t. Mark* 13:24
John 16:33 ye shall have *t.*
Acts 14:22 we must thro' *t.* enter
Rom. 2:9 *t.* and ang. on eve. soul
5:3 know. *t.* worketh patience
8:35 shall *t.* separate us fr. Ch.?
12:12 rejo. in hope, patient in *t.*
2 *Cor.* 1:4 who comforte. us in *t.*
7:4 I am exceeding joyful in *t.*
1 *Thes.* 3:4 we should suffer *t.*
2 *Thes.* 1:6 recompense *t.* to th.
Rev. 1:9 John your compan. in *t.*
2:9 I know thy works, and *t.*
10 ye shall have *t.* ten days
22 I will cast th. into great *t.*
7:14 they which came of great *t.*

TRIBULATIONS.

1 *Sam.* 10:19 saved you out of *t.*
Rom. 5:3 but we glory in *t.* also
Eph. 3:13 faint not at *t.*
2 *Thes.* 1:4 for your faith in all *t.*

TRIBUTARY.

Lam. 1:1 how is she become *t.*

TRIBUTARIES.

Deut. 20:11 the people shall be *t.*
Jud. 1:30 Canaani. bec. *t.* 33, 35

TRIBUTE.

Gen. 49:15 Issa. bec. servant to *t.*
Num. 31:28 levy a *t.* to the Lord
37 Lord's *t.* of sheep was 675
38 L.'s *t.* of the beeves was 72
39 Lord's *t.* threescore and one
40 16,000 the Lord's *t.* 32 pers.
Deut. 16:10 with *t.* of a freewill
Jos. 16:10 Canaan. under *t.* 17:13
2 *Sam.* 20:24 Ad. was over *t.* 1 *K.*
4:6; 12:18; 2 *Chr.* 10:18
1 *K.* 9:21 on these did Sol. levy *t.*
2 *K.* 23:33 Pharaoh put land to *t.*
2 *Chr.* 8:8 did Solo. make pay *t.*
17:11 Philistines brou. *t.* silver
Ezr. 4:13 will they not pay *t.*
20 *t.* and custom paid to them
6:8 *t.* expenses be given to men
7:24 not lawful to imp. *t.* on Le.
Neh. 5:4 bor. money for king's *t.*
Prov. 12:24 slothful be under *t.*
Mat. 17:24 doth not mas. pay *t.?*
25 of whom do kings take *t.?*
22:17 is it lawf. to give *t.* to Ce.?
Mark 12:14; *Luke* 20:22
19 show me the *t.* money, they
Luke 23:2 forbidding *t.* to Cesar
Rom. 13:6 for this cau. pay ye *t.*
7 render *t.* to whom *t.* is due

TRICKLETH.

Lam. 3:49 mine eye *t.* down, and

TRIMMED, EST.

2 *Sam.* 19:24 M. had not *t.* beard
Jer. 2:33 *t.* way to seek love?
Mat. 25:7 arose, *t.* their lamps

TRIUMPH, ED, ING.

Ex. 15:1 he hath *t.* gloriously, 21
2 *Sam.* 1:20 lest uncircumcised *t.*
Ps. 25:2 let not enemies *t.* over
41:11 mine enemy doth not *t.*
60:8 Philistia, *t.* th. bec. of me
92:4 *t.* in works of thy hands
94:3 L. how long sh. wicked *t.?*
106:47 gi. thanks, *t.* in thy pra.
108:9 over Philistia will I *t.?*
2 *Cor.* 2:14 causeth us to *t.* in C.

Col. 2:15 show of them *t.* over

TRIUMPH, ING.

Job 20:5 that *t.* of wicked is short
Ps. 47:1 shout unto God with *t.*

Acts 16:8 by M. they came to T.
  11 loosing from T. 20:5 at T.
2 Cor. 2:12 when I came to T. to
2 Tim. 4:13 the cloak I left at T.

TRODE.

Jud. 9:27 *t.* grapes, cursed Abi.
  20:43 Is. *t.* Benjamites wi. ease
2 K. 7:17 people *t.* upon him, 20
  9:33 Jehu *t.* Jezebel under foot
  14:9 beast *t.* thist. 2 *Chr.* 25:18
Luke 12:1 they *t.* one on another

TRODDEN.

Deut. 1:36 land *t.* on, *Jos.* 14:9
Jud. 5:21 hast *t.* down strength
Job 22:15 old way wicked have *t.*
  28:8 lion's whelps have not *t.* it
Ps. 119:118 th. hast *t.* all that err
Is. 5:5 vineyard shall be *t.* down
  14:19 as a carcass *t.* under foot
  18:2 to nation meted, *t.* down
  25:10 M. *t.* under as straw is *t.*
  28:3 drunkards of Eph. sh. be *t.*
  18 scourge pass, then be *t.* do.
  63:3 I have *t.* wine-press alone
  18 adversaries have *t.* sanctua.
Jer. 12:10 th. have *t.* my portion
Lam. 1:15 L. hath *t.* under foot
  mighty men, hath *t.* virgin
Ezek. 34:19 flock eat ye have *t.*
Dan. 8:13 sanctu. and host be *t.*
Mic. 7:10 now shall she be *t.*
Mat. 5:13 salt unsavory to be *t.*
Luke 8:5 fell by way-side, was *t.*
  21:24 Jerus. sh. be *t.* of Gentil.
Heb. 10:29 *t.* under foot Son of G.
Rev. 14:20 wine-p. *t.* witho. city

TROGYLLIUM. *Acts* 20:15

TROOP.

Gen. 30:11 a *t.* cometh ; 49:19 a *t.*
  shall overcome him
1 Sam. 30:8 sh. I pursue this *t. ?*
2 Sam. 2:25 Benjamin bec. one *t.*
  3:22 Joab came from pursu. a *t.*
  22:30 I run through *t. Ps.* 18:29
  23:11 Phil. were gath. into a *t.*
  13 *t.* pitched in valley of Rep.
Is. 65:11 prep. a table for that *t.*
Jer. 18:22 sh. bring a *t.* suddenly
Hos. 7:1 *t.* of rob. spoileth with.
Amos 9:6 founded his *t.* in earth

TROOPS.

Job 6:19 the *t.* of Tema looked
  19:12 his *t.* come together, and
Jer. 5:7 they assembled by *t.* in
Hos. 6:9 as *t.* of robbers wait for
Mic. 5:1 gath. in *t.* O daug. of *t.*
Hab. 3:16 invade them wi. his *t.*

TROUBLE, Substantive.

1 Chr. 22:14 in my *t.* I prepared
2 Chr. 15:4 when they in *t.* did
  turn and sought L. *Neh.* 9:27
Neh. 9:32 let not all *t.* seem lit.
Job 3:26 nei. quiet, yet *t.* came
  5:6 neither doth *t.* spring out of
  7 man born to *t.* as sparks fly
  14:1 is of few days, full of *t.*
  15:24 *t.* shall make him afraid
  27:9 will G. hear wh. *t.* cometh ?
  30:25 I weep for him in *t.*
  34:29 quietn. who can make *t. ?*
  38:23 I reserved aga. time of *t.*
Ps. 9:9 L. will be a refuge in *t.*
  13 consider my *t.* wh. I suffer
  10:1 why hid. th. thyself in *t. ?*
  22:11 be not far fr. me, *t.* is near
  27:5 in time of *t.* he sh. hide me
  31:7 thou hast considered my *t.*
  9 mercy, O Lord, for I am in *t.*
  32:7 thou shalt pres. me from *t.*
  37:39 strength in time of *t.*

41:1 L. will deli. him in ti. of *t.*
46:1 God is our ref. a help in *t.*
54:7 he hath deliv. me out of *t.*
60:11 give us help from *t.*
66:14 my mouth hath spo. in *t.*
69:17 hide not face, I am in *t.*
73:5 they are not in *t.* as other
78:33 years did he consu. in *t.*
  49 cast on them indign. and *t.*
81:7 calledst in *t.* I deliv. thee
91:15 I will be with him in *t.*
102:2 hide not face fr. me in *t.*
107:6 cried to Lord in *t.* 13, 19
  26 soul is melted because of *t.*
  28 they cry to Lord in their *t.*
116:3 pains gat hold, I found *t.*
119:143 *t.* and angu. have taken
138:7 tho' I walk in midst of *t.*
142:2 I showed before him my *t.*
143:11 bring my soul out of *t.*
Prov. 11:8 right. del. out of *t.* 12:13
15:6 in revenues of wicked is *t.*
  16 than treas. and *t.* therewith
25:19 unfaithful man in *t.*
Is. 1:44 new-moons, they are a *t.*
8:22 look to earth and behold *t.*
17:14 behold at evening tide *t.*
26:16 L. in *t.* they visited thee
30:6 into land of *t.* carry riches
33:2 be our salvat. in time of *t.*
46:7 not save him out of *t.*
65:23 shall not bring forth for *t.*
Jer. 2:27 in *t.* will say, Save us
  28 if they can save th. in thy *t.*
8:15 looked for health, behold *t.*
11:12 shall not save them in *t.*
  14 in time th. cried for their *t.*
14:8 Saviour of Is. in time of *t.*
  19 looked for healing, beho. *t.*
30:7 it is time of Jacob's *t.*
Lam. 1:21 enem. heard of my *t.*
Dan. 12:1 there sh. be time of *t.*
1 Cor. 7:28 shall have *t.* in flesh
2 Cor. 1:4 able to com. them in *t.*
  8 not have you ignor. of our *t.*
2 Tim. 2:9 I suffer *t.* as evil-doer
See DAY.

TROUBLES.

Deut. 31:17 *t.* sh. befall them, 21
Job 5:19 he sh. del. thee in six *t.*
Ps. 25:17 *t.* of heart are enlarged
  22 redeem Is. O God, out of *t.*
Ps. 34:6 L. saved him out of *t.* 17
  71:20 wh. hast show. me sore *t.*
88:3 ear, for my soul is full of *t.*
Prov. 21:23 he keepeth soul fr. *t.*
Is. 65:16 former *t.* are forgotten
Mark 13:8 shall be famine and *t.*

TROUBLE, Verb.

Jos. 6:18 lest ye *t.* camp of Israel
  7:25 Lord shall *t.* thee this day
Jud. 11:35 one of th. that *t.* me
2 Chr. 32:18 they cried to *t.* th.
Ps. 3:1 how increas. that *t.* me ?
  13:4 those that *t.* me rejoice
Ezek. 32:13 nei. foot of man *t.* th.
  nor hoofs of beasts *t.* them
Dan. 4:19 let not interpr. *t.* thee
  5:10 let not thy thoughts *t.* thee
  11:44 tidings out of north *t.* him
Mat. 26:10 why *t.* ye the woman?
  Mark 14:6
Luke 7:6 Lord, *t.* not thyself
  11:7 say, *t.* me not, door is shut
Acts 15:19 *t.* not G. turned to G.
  16:20 th. do exceedingly *t.* city
  20:10 *t.* not yoursel. his life is
Gal. 1:7 there be some th. *t.* you
  5:12 th. were cut off who *t.* you
  6:17 hencefor. let no man *t.* me
2 Thes. 1:6 trib. to th. that *t.* you
Heb. 12:15 lest bitterness *t.* you

TROUBLED.

Gen. 34:30 ye ha. *t.* me, to make
41:8 in morn. Ph.'s spirit was *t.*
45:3 his brethren *t.* at his pres.
Ex. 14:24 L. *t.* host of Egyptians

Jos. 7:25 why hast thou *t.* us ?
1 Sam. 14:29 father hath *t.* land
  16:14 evil spirit fr. Lord *t.* him
  28:21 woman saw that S. was *t.*
2 Sam. 4:1 Abner dead, all Is. *t.*
1 K. 18:18 I have not *t.* Israel
2 K. 6:11 king of Syria was *t.*
Ezr. 4:4 peo. *t.* them in building
Job 4:5 toucheth thee, thou art *t.*
  21:4 why shou. not spirit be *t. ?*
  23:15 theref. am I *t.* at his pres.
  34:20 peo. sh. be *t.* at midnight
Ps. 30:7 hide thy face, I was *t.*
  38:6 I am *t.* 77:4 I am so *t.* I
  46:3 tho' waters roar and be *t.*
  48:5 kings were *t.* hasted away
  77:3 I remember. G. and was *t.*
  16 the depths also were *t.*
  83:17 let them be comfo. and *t.*
  90:7 by thy wrath are we *t.*
  104:29 hidest thy face, th. are *t.*
Prov. 25:26 is as a *t.* fountain
Is. 32:10 and years shall ye be *t.*
  11 wom. be *t.* ye careless ones
  57:20 wicked are like the *t.* sea
Jer. 31:20 my bowels are *t.*
Lam. 1:20 my bowels are *t.* 2:11
Ezek. 7:27 hands of peo. sh. be *t.*
  26:18 isles in sea shall be *t.*
  27:35 their kings be *t.* in count.
Dan. 2:1 Neb.'s spirit was *t.* 3
  4:5 visions of my head *t.* 7:15
  19 his thoughts *t.* him
  5:6 Belsha.'s thoughts *t.* him, 9
  7:28 my cogitations much *t.* me
Zec. 10:2 *t.* because no shepherd
Mat. 2:3 Herod was *t.* and Jerus.
  14:26 they were *t. Mark* 6:50
  24:6 not *t.* thi. must co. to pass,
  Mark 13:7 ; *John* 14:1, 27
Luke 1:12 Zac. was *t.* 29 Mary *t.*
  10:41 Martha *t.* about many thi.
  24:38 why are *t.* and why do
John 5:4 angel went and *t.* water
  7 no man wh. water is *t.* to put
  11:33 and was *t.* 12:27 ; 13:21
Acts 15:24 some fr. us have *t.* y.
  17:8 they *t.* people and rulers
2 Cor. 4:8 are *t.* on ev. side, 7:5
2 Thes. 1:7 to you that are *t.* rest
  2:2 that ye be not *t.* nei. by sp.
1 Pet. 3:14 not af. of terror, nor *t.*

TROUBLEDST.

Ezek. 32:2 thou *t.* waters wi. feet

TROUBLER.

1 Chr. 2:7 Achar, the *t.* of Israel

TROUBLEST, ETH.

1 Sam. 16:15 an evil spirit *t.* thee
1 K. 18:17 art thou he that *t.* Is. ?
Job 22:10 sudden fear *t.* thee
  23:16 heart soft, Almighty *t.* me
Prov. 11:17 that is cruel *t.* flesh
  29 that *t.* his house, inh. wind
  15:27 that is greedy of gain *t.*
Dan. 4:9 I know no secret *t.* thee
Mark 5:35 why *t.* thou Master ?
Luke 18:5 bec. this widow *t.* me
Gal. 5:10 he th. *t.* you shall bear

TROUBLING.

Job 3:17 there wicked cease fr. *t.*
John 5:4 step. in after *t.* of water

TROUBLOUS.

Dan. 9:25 sh. be built in *t.* times

TROUGH, S.

Gen. 24:20 empt. pitcher into *t.*
  30:38 J. set rods in watering *t.*
Ex. 2:16 they filled *t.* to water
  8:3 frogs sh. go into kneading-*t.*
  12:34 th. kneading *t.* bound up

TROW.

Luke 17:9 thank serva. ? I *t.* not

TRUCE-BREAKERS.

1 Tim. 3:3 last days shall be *t.-b.*

TRUE.

Gen. 42:11 we are *t.* men, 31
  19 if ye be *t.* men let one of y.

Deut. 17:4 if ye be *t.* and, 22:20
2 *Sam.* 7:28 God, thy words be *t.*
1 *K.* 10:6 it was a *t.* report I
  heard, 2 *Chr.* 9:5
22:16 tell me noth. but that is *t.*
Neh. 9:13 gavest them *t.* laws
Ps. 19:9 judgments of Lord are *t.*
119:160 thy word is *t.* fr. begin.
Jer. 42:5 the Lord be a *t.* witness
Dan. 3:14 is it *t.* O Shadrach, do
  24 *t.* O king ; 6:12 thing is *t.*
10:1 revealed and thing was *t.*
Mat. 22:16 thou art *t. Mark* 12:14
Luke 16:11 com. to trust *t.* riches
John 1:9 that was the *t.* light
4:37 herein is saying *t.* I soweth
5:31 of myself, my wit. is not *t.*
6:32 Father giveth the *t.* bread
7:18 same is *t.* 8:13 reco. not *t.*
  28 he that sent me is *t.* 8:26
8:14 record is *t.* 16 judgm. is *t.*
  17 testimony of two men is *t.*
10:41 all things J. spake were *t.*
9:35 and his record is *t.* 21:24
Acts 12:9 wist not that it was *t.*
2 *Cor.* 1:18 as God is *t.* our word
6:8 as deceivers, and yet *t.*
Phil. 4:8 whatsoev. things are *t.*
1 *Tim.* 3:1 this is a *t.* saying
Tit. 1:13 this witness is *t.* wher.
Heb. 8:2 *t.* tabernacle which L.
9:24 which are figures of the *t.*
10:22 draw near with a *t.* heart
1 *Pet.* 5:12 this is *t.* grace of God
2 *Pet.* 2:22 accordi. to *t.* proverb
1 *John* 2:8 which thing is *t.*
5:20 may kn. him that is *t.* and
  we are in him that is *t.*
3 *John* 12 we know our rec. is *t.*
Rev. 3:7 saith holy, he that is *t.*
  14 saith faithful and *t.* witness
6:10 long, O Lord, holy and *t. ?*
15:3 just and *t.* are thy ways
16:7 *t.* are thy judgments, 19:2
19:9 these are *t.* say. of G. 22:6
  11 he th. sat was Faith. and *T.*
21:5 write, for these words are *t.*

TRUE God.
2 *Chr.* 15:3 Is. ha. been wi. *t. G.*
Jer. 10:10 Lord is the *t. God*
John 17:3 eternal life to kn. *t. G.*
1 *Thes.* 1:9 turn fr. idols to *t. G.*
1 *John* 5:20 this is the *t. God*

TRULY.
Num. 14:21 *t.* as I live, saith L.
Ps. 116:16 *t.* I am thy servant
Prov. 12:22 deal *t.* are his delight
Mat. 27:54 *t.* this was Son of G.
Luke 20:21 teachest way of G. *t.*
John 4:18 no husb. saidst thou *t.*

TRUMP.
1 *Cor.* 15:52 at last *t.* dead shall
1 *Thes.* 4:16 L. shall des. with *t.*

TRUMPET.
Ex. 19:16 voice of *t.* excee. loud
20:18 people heard noise of *t.*
Num. 10:4 if th. blow wi. one *t.*
Jud. 7:16 put a *t.* in every man's
Ps. 81:3 blow *t.* in new moon
Is. 18:3 when he bloweth *t.* hear
27:13 great *t.* shall be blown
58:1 lift up thy voice like a *t.*
Jer. 4:5 blow ye the *t.* in land
6:1 blow the *t.* in Tekoah
51:27 blow *t.* among nations
Ezek. 7:14 they have blown *t.*
33:3 if ye blow *t.* and warn, 6
Hos. 5:8 blow ye the *t.* in Ramah
8:1 set the *t.* to thy mouth
Joel 2:1 blow the *t.* in Zion, 15
Amos 3:6 sh. *t.* be blo. not afra. ?
Zep. 1:16 day of *t.* ag. fenced cit.
Zec. 9:14 Lord God shall blow *t.*
Rev. 1:10 heard voice as of *t.* 4:1
9:14 sixth angel which had *t.*

See BLEW, SOUND, SOUNDED.

TRUMPETS.
Lev. 23:24 a memorial of blow. *t.*
Num. 10:2 make two *t.* of silver
Num. 10:8 sons of Aa. bl. with *t.*
  10 blow with *t.* over burnt-off.
29:1 day of blowing *t.* unto you
31:6 wi. *t.* to blow in his hand
Jos. 6:4 priests sh. blow with *t.*
  8 bearing seven *t.* of rams'
Jud. 7:8 300 men took *t.* 16
  19 they blew the *t.* 20, 22
2 *K.* 9:13 they blew with *t.* sayi.
11:14 trumpeters blew with *t.*
1 *Chr.* 13:8 with cymbals and *t.*
15:24 the priests did blow wi. *t.*
  before ark of God, 16:6, 42 ;
  2 *Chr.* 5:12 ; 7:6 ; 13:12, 14
  28 Israel brought up ark wi. *t.*
2 *Chr.* 5:13 they lift voice with *t.*
29:27 song of L. began with *t.*
Job 39:25 horse say. am. *t.* Ha, ha
Ps. 98:6 wi. *t.* make joyful noise

See SEVEN.

TRUMPETERS.
2 *K.* 11:14 and *t.* stood by king
2 *Chr.* 5:13 *t.* and singers were
29:28 singers sang, and *t.* sound.
Rev. 18:22 voi. of *t.* heard no mo.

TRUST.
Job 8:14 wh. *t.* sh. be a spider's
15:15 putteth no *t.* in his saints
Ps. 40:4 that maketh Lord his *t.*
71:5 O Lord God, thou art my *t.*
141:8 in thee is my *t.* leave not
Prov. 22:19 thy *t.* may be in Lord
28:25 that puts his *t.* in Lord
29:25 who putteth his *t.* in Lord
Is. 30:3 *t.* in Egypt shall be conf.
57:13 that putteth *t.* in me shall
Luke 16:11 com. to *t.* true riches
2 *Cor.* 3:4 such *t.* ha. we thro' C.
1 *Tim.* 1:11 gospel, com. to my *t.*
6:20 keep that commi. to thy *t.*

See PUT.

TRUST, Verb.
Ruth 2:12 thou art come to *t.*
2 *Sam.* 22:3 in him will I *t. Ps.*
  18:2 ; 91:2
  31 a buckler to all that *t.* in
  him, *Ps.* 18:30
1 *K.* 18:20 on whom dost thou *t. ?*
  2 *Chr.* 32:10 ; *Is.* 36:5
  21 so is Pharaoh to all that *t.*
  in him, *Is.* 36:6
  22 we *t.* in L. our God, *Is.* 36:7
  30 neither let Hezekiah make
  you *t.* in the Lord, *Is.* 36:15
Job 13:15 yet will I *t.* in him
15:31 let not him is. is decei. *t.*
35:14 judg. bef. him, *t.* in him
39:11 wilt *t.* him bec. strong ?
Ps. 20:7 some *t.* in chariots
25:2 I *t.* in thee, 31:6 ; 55:23 ;
  56:3 ; 143:8
31:19 hast wrou. for them th. *t.*
34:22 none th. *t.* in him sh. be
37:3 *t.* in the Lord, and do good,
  5 ; 40:3 ; 62:8 ; 115:9, 10, 11 ;
  Prov. 3:5 ; *Is.* 26:4
  40 he sh. save, because they *t.*
44:6 I will not *t.* in my bow
49:6 they that *t.* in their wealth
52:8 I *t.* in the mercy of God
61:4 I will *t.* in cov. of thy wings
62:10 *t.* not in oppression
64:10 righte. shall be glad, and *t.*
91:4 under his wings sh. thou *t.*
118:8 it is better to *t.* in Lord, 9
119:42 answer, I *t.* in thy word
125:1 that *t.* in the Lord sh. be
144:2 shield, and he in wh. I *t.*
Prov. 31:11 her husband doth *t.*
Is. 12:2 I will *t.* not be afraid
14:32 poor of his people shall *t.*
30:2 to *t.* in shadow of Egypt
  12 because ye *t.* in oppression

31:1 and *t.* in chariots because
42:17 ashamed th. *t.* in images
50:10 let him *t.* in name of L.
51:5 on mine arm shall they *t.*
59:4 they *t.* in vanity and speak
Jer. 7:4 *t.* ye not in lying words
  8 ye *t.* in lying words
  14 by name, wherein ye *t.*
9:4 and *t.* ye not in any brother
28:15 maketh peo. to *t.* in, 29:31
46:25 punish Ph. and all that *t.*
49:11 let thy widows *t.* in me
Ezek. 16:15 th. didst *t.* in beauty
33:13 if he *t.* to his own righte.
Hos. 10:13 thou didst *t.* in way
Amos 6:1 that *t.* in mount. of Sa.
Mic. 7:5 *t.* ye not in a friend
Nah. 1:7 L. knoweth them th. *t.*
Zep. 3:12 shall *t.* in name of L.
Mat. 12:21 in his name shall Gentiles *t. Rom.* 15:12
Mark 10:24 them that *t.* in riches
John 5:45 Moses in whom ye *t.*
Rom. 15:24 I *t.* to see you in my
1 *Cor.* 16:7 I *t.* to tarry a while
2 *Cor.* 1:9 sho. not *t.* in ourselves
  10 in whom we *t.* that he will
10:7 if any man *t.* to himself
Phil. 3:4 if any think. hath to *t.*
1 *Tim.* 4:10 we *t.* in living God
6:17 they *t.* not in uncertain
2 *John* 12 I *t.* to come unto you
3 *John* 14 I *t.* I shall shortly see
  thee

TRUSTED.
Deut. 32:37 rock in wh. they *t. ?*
Jud. 11:20 Sih. *t.* not Is. to pass
20:36 they *t.* to the liers in wait
2 *K.* 13:5 he *t.* in the Lord God
Ps. 13:5 I have *t.* in thy mercy
22:4 our fathers *t.* th. have *t.* 5
  8 he *t.* on Lord that he would
26:1 I have *t.* in L. 28:7 ; 31:14
33:21 have *t.* in his holy name
41:9 familiar friend in wh. I *t.*
52:7 I *t.* in abund. of his riches
78:22 *t.* not in his salvation
Is. 47:10 th. hast *t.* in thy wick.
Jer. 13:25 thou hast *t.* in falseh.
48:7 thou hast *t.* in thy works
49:4 daugh. that *t.* in her treas.
Dan. 3:28 God delivereth that *t.*
Zep. 3:2 she *t.* not in the Lord
Mat. 27:43 he *t.* in God, let him
Luke 11:22 armor wherein he *t.*
18:9 cer. which *t.* in themselves
24:21 we *t.* it had been he that
Eph. 1:12 who first *t.* in Christ
  13 in whom ye also *t.* after ye
1 *Pet.* 3:5 holy wom. who *t.* in G.

TRUSTEDST.
Deut. 28:52 walls down thou *t.*
Jer. 5:17 cities wherein thou *t.*
  12:5 land of peace wher. thou *t.*

TRUSTEST.
2 *K.* 18:19 what confidence is this
  wherein thou *t. ? Is.* 36:4
  21 *t.* on bruised reed, *Is.* 36:6
19:10 G. in wh. thou *t. Is.* 37:10

TRUSTETH.
Job 40:23 he *t.* that he can draw
Ps. 21:7 the king *t.* in the Lord
32:10 that *t.* in L. mercy shall
34:8 blessed is man th. *t.* 84:12 ;
  Prov. 16:20 ; *Jer.* 17:7
57:1 be merci. my soul *t.* in thee
86:2 save thy serv. that *t.* in thee
115:8 so is ev. one that *t.* 135:18
Prov. 11:28 he that *t.* in riches
28:26 that *t.* his heart is a fool
Is. 26:3 peace bec. he *t.* in thee
Jer. 17:5 cursed be man *t.* man
Hab. 2:18 maker of work *t.* ther.
1 *Tim.* 5:5 th. is a widow, *t.* in

TRUSTING.
Ps. 112:7 heart is fixed, *t.* in L.

TRUSTY.

Job 12:20 removeth speech of *t.*

TRUTH.

Gen. 24:27 not left dest. mas. of *t.*
32:10 not worthy of least of *t.*
42:16 be proved, whether any *t.*
Ex. 18:21 men of *t.* hating cov.
34:6 abundant in goodn. and *t.*
Deut. 13:14 if it be *t.* 32:4 G. of *t.*
2 *Sam.* 2:6 L. show kindn. and *t.*
15:20 mercy and *t.* be with thee
1 *K.* 17:24 word of the Lord is *t.*
2 *K.* 20:19 if *t.* be in my, *Is.* 39:8
2 *Chr.* 18:15 say nothing but *t.*
31:20 Hez. wrought that was *t.*
Est. 9:30 letters with words of *t.*
Ps. 15:2 speaketh *t.* in heart
25:10 paths of L. mercy and *t.*
31:5 redeemed me, O L. G. of *t.*
45:4 ride prosperously bec. of *t.*
51:6 thou desirest *t.* in inward
57:3 God shall send forth his *t.*
60:4 ban. be displayed bec. of *t.*
61:7 O prepare mercy and *t.*
85:10 mercy and *t.* met togeth.
11 *t.* shall spring out of earth
86:15 plenteous in mercy and *t.*
89:14 mercy and *t.* sh. go before
91:4 his *t.* shall be thy shield
96:13 he shall judge peo. with *t.*
98:3 he hath remembered his *t.*
100:5 his *t.* endur. to all, 117:2
119:30 I have chosen way of *t.*
142 and thy law is the *t.* 151
146:6 L. is God who keepeth *t.*
Prov. 3:3 let not *t.* forsake thee
8:7 for my mouth shall speak *t.*
12:17 he that speaks *t.* showeth
19 lip of *t.* shall be established
14:22 mercy and *t.* be to them
16:6 by mercy and *t.* iniquity is
20:28 mercy and *t.* preserve king

Prov. 22:21 kn. certain. of words
of *t.* answer the words of *t.*
23:23 buy the *t.* and sell it not
Ec. 12:10 writ. were words of *t.*
Is. 25:1 couns. are faithf. and *t.*
26:2 nation which keepeth *t.*
42:3 bring forth judgm. unto *t.*
43:9 let th. hear, and say, it is *t.*
59:4 nor any pleadeth for *t.*
14 for *t.* is fallen in the street
15 yea, *t.* faileth, and he
Jer. 5:1 if th. be that seeketh *t.*
3 O L. are not th. eyes upon *t. ?*
7:28 *t.* is perished and cut off
9:3 they are not valiant for *t.*
5 deceive and will not speak *t.*
33:6 revealed abundance of *t.*
Dan. 4:37 all whose works are *t.*
7:16 I asked him *t.* of this, 19
8:12 it cast down *t.* to ground
10:21 is noted in scriptures of *t.*
11:2 now will I show thee the *t.*
Hos. 4:1 no *t.* nor mercy in land
Mic. 7:20 wilt perform *t.* to Jac.
Zec. 8:3 Jer. be called city of *t.*
16 speak ye every man *t.* execute judgment of *t. Eph.* 4:25
19 theref. love the *t.* and peace
Mal. 2:6 law of *t.* in his mouth
Mat. 15:27 she said, *t.* Lord, yet
Mark 5:33 woman told him *t.*
12:32 Master, thou hast said *t.*
John 1:14 full of grace and *t.*
17 grace and *t.* came by J. C.
5:33 J. bare witness unto the *t.*
8:32 kn. *t.* and *t.* make you free
40 seek to kill me, that told *t.*
44 abode not in *t.* because no
t. in him.
45 I tell *t.* ye believe me not
46 if I say *t.* why not believe?
14:6 I am the way, *t.* the life
16:7 I tell you *t.* it is expedient
13 Sp. of *t.* guide you into all *t.*
17:19 be sanctified through *t.*

18:37 th. I should bear witness
to *t.* every one that is of *t.*
38 Pil. saith to him, what is *t. ?*
Acts 26:25 I spe. forth words of *t.*
Rom. 1:18 hold *t.* in unrighteous.
25 changed *t.* of God into a lie
2:2 judgm. of G. according to *t.*
8 to them that do not obey *t.*
20 whi. hast form of *t.* in law
3:7 if *t.* of G. ha. more abound.
9:1 I say *t.* in Christ, I lie not
15:8 minister of circumci. for *t.*
1 *Cor.* 5:8 unleavened bread of *t.*
2 *Cor.* 4:2 by manifestation of *t.*
7:14 boast. I made is found a *t.*
11:10 as *t.* of Ch. is in me none
12:6 for I will say the *t.*
13:8 we can do nothing ag. *t.*
Gal. 2:5 *t.* of gospel might conti.
14 walked not according to *t.*
3:1 ye should not obey *t.* 5:7
4:16 enemy bec. I tell you *t. ?*
Eph. 4:15 speak. the *t.* in love
21 taught by him as *t.* is in J.
5:9 fruit of Spirit is in all *t.*
6:14 hav. your loins girt with *t.*
2 *Thes.* 2:10 recei. not love of *t.*
12 damned who believe not *t.*
13 salvation thro' belief of *t.*
1 *Tim.* 2:4 come to knowl. of *t.*
7 I speak *t.* in Christ, lie not
3:15 the pillar and ground of *t.*
4:3 received of them wh. kn. *t.*
6:5 corrupt minds, destitu. of *t.*
2 *Tim.* 2:18 concern. *t.* ha. erred
25 repent. to acknowledg. of *t.*
3:7 to come to knowledge of *t.*
8 Jambres, so do these resist *t.*
4:4 turn away their ears from *t.*
Tit. 1:1 to acknowledging of *t.*
14 commandm. that turn fr. *t.*
Heb. 10:26 received knowl. of *t.*
Jam. 3:14 lie not against the *t.*
5:19 if any of you err fr. the *t.*
1 *Pet.* 1:22 purified in obeying *t.*
2 *Pet.* 2:2 way of *t.* evil spok. of
1 *John* 1:6 we lie, do not the *t.*
8 dec. ourselves, *t.* is not in us
2:4 *t.* not in him ; 27 *t.* is no lie
21 because ye know not *t.* and
no lie is of the *t.*
3:19 we know that we are of *t.*
5:6 witness, because Spirit is *t.*
2 *John* 1 they that have known *t.*
2 for *t.* sake that dwell. in us
3 *John* 3 tes. of *t.* that is in thee
8 might be fellow-helpers to *t.*
12 good report of men and of *t.*

In TRUTH.

Jos. 24:14 serve Lord in *t.* 1 *Sam.*
12:24
Jud. 9:15 if in *t.* ye anoint me
1 *K.* 2:4 if my children walk in *t.*
3:6 as Da. walked bef. thee in *t.*
2 *K.* 20:3 I have walked in *t.*
Ps. 33:4 works done in *t.* 111:8
132:11 L. hath sworn in *t.* to D.
145:18 L. nigh to all call in *t.*
Is. 10:20 stay on Holy One in *t.*
16:5 he shall sit upon it in *t.*
48:1 mention of G. but not in *t.*
61:8 I will direct th. work in *t.*
Jer. 4:2 swear, the L. liveth in *t.*
Zec. 8:8 I will be their God in *t.*
Mat. 22:16 teachest the way of
God in *t. Mark* 12:14
John 4:23 in spirit and in *t.* 24
2 *Cor.* 7:14 spake all things in *t.*
Phil. 1:18 whe. in *t.* C. preached
Col. 1:6 ye knew grace of G. in *t.*
1 *Thes.* 2:13 it is in *t.* word of G.
1 *John* 3:18 love in tongue, in *t.*
2 *John* 3 Son of the Father in *t.*
4 I found of thy children walking in *t.* 3 *John* 4

In the TRUTH.

Ps. 69:13 hear in *t. t.* of salva.

John 8:44 mur. abode not in *t. t.*
1 *Cor.* 13:6 charity rejoic. in *t. t.*
2 *Pet.* 1:12 be established in *t. t.*
2 *John* 1 I love in *t. t.* 3 *John* 1
3 *John* 3 as thou walkest in *t. t.*

Of a TRUTH.

Job 9:2 I know it is so *of a t.*
Jer. 26:15 *of a t.* Lord sent me
Dan. 2:47 *of a t.* it is, your G. is
Mat. 14:33 *of a t.* thou art Son
Luke 4:25 I tell you *of a t.* 9:27
12:44 *of a t.* I say unto, 21:3
John 6:14 *of a t.* th. proph. 7:40
Acts 4:27 *of a t.* ag. holy child J.
1 *Cor.* 14:25 God is in you *of a t.*

See SPIRIT.

Thy TRUTH.

Ps. 25:5 lead me in *thy t.* teach
26:3 and I have walked in *thy t.*
30:9 shall dust declare *thy t. ?*
40:10 *thy t.* from great congreg.
11 *thy t.* continu. preserve me
43:3 send out thy light and *t. t.*
54:5 enemies, cut th. off in *t. t.*
57:10 *thy t.* unto clouds, 108:4
71:22 praise *thy t.* 86:11 in *t. t.*
89:49 swarest to David in *thy t.*
115:1 glory for *t. t.* sake, 138:2
Is. 38:18 cannot hope for *thy t.*
19 chil. shall make known *t. t.*
Dan. 9:13 might understand *t. t.*
John 17:17 sanctify th. thro' *t. t.*

Word of TRUTH.

Ps. 119:43 take not *w. of t.* out
2 *Cor.* 6:7 appr. ours. by *w. of t.*
Eph. 1:13 that ye heard *w. of t.*
Col. 1:5 ye heard bef. in *w. of t.*
2 *Tim.* 2:15 dividing *word of t.*
Jam. 1:18 begat he us by *w. of t.*

TRY.

Jud. 7:4 I will *t.* them for thee
2 *Chr.* 32:31 G. left him to *t.* him
Job 7:18 that thou should. *t.* him
12:11 doth not the ear *t.* words
Ps. 11:4 eyelids *t.* chil. of men
26:2 *t.* my reins ; 139:23 *t.* me
Jer. 6:27 mayest kn. and *t.* way
9:7 melt and *t.* them, *Zec.* 13:9
17:10 Lord search heart, *t.* reins
Lam. 3:40 let us search and *t.*
Dan. 11:35 some fall to *t.* them
1 *Cor.* 3:13 fire *t.* ev. man's work
1 *Pet.* 4:12 trial wh. is to *t.* you
1 *John* 4:1 *t.* spirits whether of G.
Rev. 3:10 temptation to *t.* them

TRIED.

Deut. 21:5 by Lev. ev. stroke be *t.*
2 *Sam.* 22:31 the word of the
Lord is *t. Ps.* 18:30
Job 23:10 when he hath *t.* me
34:36 desire is that J. may be *t.*
Ps. 12:6 as silver is *t.* in furnace
17:3 th. hast *t.* me. find nothing
66:10 hast *t.* us as silver is *t.*
105:19 word of the Lord *t.* him
Is. 28:16 I lay in Z. a *t.* stone
Jer. 12:3 thou hast *t.* my heart
Dan. 12:10 many be puri. and *t.*
Zec. 13:9 try them as gold *t.*
Heb. 11:17 Abra. when he was *t.*
Jam. 1:12 when *t.* receive crown
1 *Pet.* 1:7 tho' it be *t.* with fire
Rev. 2:2 hast *t.* them which say
10 into prison, ye may be *t.*
3:18 buy of me gold *t.* in the fire

TRIEST, ETH.

1 *Chr.* 29:17 I know thou *t.* heart
Job 34:3 ear *t.* words as mouth
Ps. 7:9 righteous God *t.* hearts
11:5 the Lord *t.* the righteous
Prov. 17:3 but Lord *t.* the hearts
Jer. 11:20 O L. that *t.* the reins
20:12 L. of hosts that *t.* righte.
1 *Thes.* 2:4 but God who *t.* hearts

TRYING.

Jam. 1:3 *t.* of faith work. patien.

TRYPHENA, TRYPHOSA.
Rom. 16:12 salute T. and T. who

TUBAL.
Gen. 10:2 Ja. Javan, T. 1 *Ch.* 1:5
Is. 66:19 those that escape to T.
Ezek. 27:13 Javan T. thy merch.
32:26 Meshech, T. and multit.
38:2 of Meshech and T. 3 ; 39:1

TUMBLED.
Jud. 7:13 a cake *t.* into the host

TUMULT.
1 *Sam.* 4:14 wh. noise of this *t.?*
2 *Sam.* 18:29 I saw a *t.* but knew
2 *K.* 19:28 thy *t.* come unto mine ears, *Is.* 37:29
Ps. 65:7 stilleth *t.* of the people
74:23 *t.* of th. that rise ag. thee
83:2 lo, thine enemies make a *t.*
Is. 33:3 at noise of *t.* people fled
Jer. 11:16 with noise of a great *t.*
Hos. 10:14 *t.* rise among people
Amos 2:2 Moab shall die with *t.*
Zec. 14:13 a *t.* fr. Lord am. them
Mat. 27:24 rather a *t.* was made
Mark 5:38 he seeth *t.* and them
Acts 21:34 could not know for *t.*
24:18 with multitude, nor wi. *t.*

TUMULTS.
Amos 3:9 behold gre. *t.* in midst
2 *Cor.* 6:5 ourselves as min. in *t.*
12:20 whisperings, swellings, *t.*

TUMULTUOUS.
Is. 13:4 a *t.* noise of kingdoms
22:2 thou that art a *t.* city
Jer. 48:45 devour head of *t.* ones

TURN.
Est. 2:11 ev. maid's *t.* was come
15 when *t.* of Esther was come

TURN, Verb.
Gen. 24:49 that I may *t.* to right
Ex. 23:27 make thine enemies *t.*
32:12 *t.* from thy fierce wrath
Num. 14:25 to-morrow *t.* you
20:17 will not *t.* to right hand
22:23 he smote the ass to *t.* her
26 wh. was no way to *t.* right
Deut. 1:40 *t.* ye, take journey
30:3 Lord will *t.* their captivity
31:20 th. will th. *t.* to oth. gods
Jos. 1:7 *t.* not from it to right or
22:23 to *t.* from following L. 29
24:20 then he will *t.* and do
Jud. 20:8 nor any *t.* into house
1 *Sam.* 14:7 *t.* I am with thee
22:17 *t.* and slay priests of L. 18
2 *Sam.* 14:19 none can *t.* to ri. or
24 said, Let him *t.* to house
1 *K.* 8:35 *t.* from their sin, 2 *Chr.*
6:26, 37 ; 7:14
9:6 if you *t.* from following me
17:3 *t.* eastward, hide thyself
22:34 *t.* thy hand, 2 *Chr.* 18:33
2 *K.* 9:18 *t.* thee behind me, 19
17:13 *t.* ye from your evil ways, *Jer.* 18:8 ; 26:3 ; *Zec.* 1:3, 4
1 *Chr.* 12:23 to *t.* kingd. of Saul
2 *Chr.* 35:22 J. would not *t.* face
Neh. 1:9 *t.* and keep com. *Ezek.* 3:20 ; 18:21 ; 33:11, 14, 19
9:26 testified to *t.* them to thee
Job 5:1 wh. of saints wilt th. *t.?*
14:6 *t.* fr. him that he may rest
23:13 who can *t.* him?
24:4 they *t.* needy out of way
Ps. 4:2 how long will ye *t.* glory?
7:12 if he *t.* not,·will whet sw.
21:12 make them *t.* their back
25:16 *t.* unto me. 69:16 ; 86:16
85:4 *t.* us, O God of our salva.
119:79 let those th. fear thee *t.*
132:11 sworn to D. he will not *t.*
Prov. 1:23 *t.* you at my reproof
4:15 *t.* from it and pass away
27 *t.* not to right hand nor left
Ec. 3:20 and all *t.* to dust again

Cant. 2:17 *t.* my beloved, and
Is. 1:25 I will *t.* my hand on thee
13:14 every man *t.* to his people
19:6 shall *t.* rivers far away
22:18 he will *t.* and toss thee
23:17 she shall *t.* to her hire
28:6 strength to them *t.* battle
30:21 ye *t.* to right and left
31:6 *t.* ye to him fr. whom Is.
59:20 to them that *t.* fr. transg.
Jer. 2:35 his anger shall *t.* fr. me
8:7 and I said, *t.* unto me, 14
13:16 before he *t.* it into death
31:18 *t.* th. me, I sh. be turn.
44:5 hearken. not to *t.* fr. wick.
50:16 *t.* every one to his people
Lam. 5:21 *t.* us unto thee, O L.
Ezek. 3:19 he *t.* not fr. wick. 33:9
4:8 sh. not *t.* from one side to
7:22 my face will I *t.* fr. them
14:6 *t.* fr. idols, 18:30, 32 ; 33:9, 11 ; *Hos.* 12:6 ; *Joel* 2:12
36:9 I will *t.* unto you, and ye
38:12 to *t.* hand on desol. places
Dan. 9:13 might *t.* fr. iniquities
11:18 shall he *t.* face unto isles
19 shall *t.* his face toward fort
12:3 that *t.* many to righteous.
Hos. 5:4 frame their doings to *t.*
12:6 therefore *t.* thou to thy G.
Amos 1:8 *t.* my hand ag. Ekron
8:10 I will *t.* feasts into mourn.
Jon. 3:8 *t.* ev. one from evil way
Zep. 3:9 *t.* to people pure langu.
Zec. 9:12 *t.* you to strong-hold
13:7 *t.* my hand upon little ones
Mal. 4:6 he sh. *t.* heart of fathers
Mat. 5:39 cheek, *t.* to him other
Luke 1:17 to *t.* hearts of fathers
21:13 sh. *t.* to you for a testim.
Acts 13:46 we *t.* to the Gentiles
14:15 sho. *t.* from these vanities
26:18 to *t.* them from darkn. to
20 should repent and *t.* to God
Phil. 1:19 this sh. *t.* to my salva.
Tit. 1:14 comm. that *t.* fr. truth
Jam. 3:3 we *t.* about their body
2 *Pet.* 2:21 to *t.* from command.
Rev. 11:6 to *t.* waters to blood

TURN again.
Jud. 11:8 we *t. a.* to thee now
Ruth 1:11 *t. a.* my daughters, 12
1 *Sam.* 15:25 *t. a.* with me, 30
1 *K.* 8:33 when Israel shall *t. a.*
12:27 heart of people *t. again*
13:9 nor *t. a.* by same way, 17
2 *K.* 1:6 go *t. again* to the king
2 *Chr.* 30:6 *t. a.* to L. 9 if ye *t. a.*
Job 34:15 man sh. *t. a.* into dust
Ps. 18:37 nor did I *t. a.* till they
60:1 displeas. O *t.* thys. to us *a.*
80:3 *t.* us *a.* O L. of hosts, 7, 19
85:8 let them not *t. a.* to folly
104:9 th. *t.* not *a.* to cover earth
126:4 *t. again* our captivity
Jer. 25:5 *t.* ye *a.* from evil way
31:21 *t. a.* O virgin, *t. a.* to cit.
Lam. 3:40 try our ways, *t. again*
Ezek. 8:6 *t. a.* thou sh. see, 13, 15
Mic. 7:19 will *t. a.* have compas.
Zec. 10:9 live with child. *t. again*
Mat. 7:6 lest they *t. a.* and rend
Luke 10:6 it shall *t.* to you *again*
17:4 seven times in a day *t. a.*
Gal. 4:9 *t. a.* to weak elements

TURN aside.
Ex. 3:3 I will *t. a.* and see this
Deut. 5:32 not *t. a.* to right hand
17:20 *t.* not *a.* from command.
31:29 after my death ye will *t. a.*
Jos. 23:6 that ye *t.* not *a.* there-from, 1 *Sam.* 12:20, 21
Ruth 4:1 ho, such a one, *t. aside*
2 *Sam.* 2:21 *t. a.* and take armor
23 he refused to *t. aside*
18:30 king said, *t. a.* stand here
Ps. 40:4 respect. not such as *t. a.*

101:3 work of them that *t. a.*
125:5 for such as *t. a.* to crooked
Is. 10:2 *t. a.* needy from judgm.
29:21 *t. a.* just for thing of nau.
30:11 *t. aside* out of path
Lam. 3:35 to *t. a.* right of a man
Amos 2:7 that *t. a.* way of meek
5:12 they *t. a.* poor in the gate
Mal. 3:5 *t. a.* stranger from right

TURN away.
Gen. 27:44 till brother's fury *t. a.*
45 till thy broth.'s anger *t. a.*
Num. 32:15 if ye *t. a.* from after him, *Deut.* 30:17 ; *Jos.* 22:16 ; 2 *Chr.* 7:19
Deut. 7:4 they will *t. a.* thy son
13:5 he hath spoken to *t.* you *a.*
1 *K.* 11:2 th. will *t. a.* your heart
1 *Chr.* 14:14 go not *t. a.* fr. thence
2 *Chr.* 25:27 Amaziah did *t. a.*
29:10 that wrath may *t. a.* 30:8 ; *Ps.* 106:23 ; *Prov.* 24:18
30:9 L. will not *t. a.* his face
Ps. 119:37 *t. a.* mine eyes from
39 *t. a.* my reproach wh. I fear
Prov. 29:8 wise men *t. a.* wrath
Cant. 6:5 *t. a.* thine eyes fr. me
Is. 58:13 if *t. a.* foot from sabbath
Jer. 3:19 thou sh. not *t. a.* fr. me
8:4 sh. he *t. a.* and not return?
18:20 I stood to *t. a.* thy wrath
32:40 I will not *t. a.* from them
Ezek. 14:6 *t. a.* faces from abom.
Jon. 3:9 God will *t.·a.* from his
Mal. 2:6 did *t.* many *a.* from ini.
2 *Tim.* 3:5 traitors, fr. such *t. a.*
4:4 sh. *t. a.* their ears fr. truth
Heb. 12:25 how esca. if we *t. a.?*

TURN back.
Deut. 23:13 *t. b.* and cover that
Ps. 44:10 makest us to *t. b.* from
56:9 then sh. mine enemies *t. b.*
Is. 14:27 hand stretc. who *t. b.?*
Jer. 4:28 nei. will I *t. b.* from it
21:4 I will *t. b.* weapons of war
49:8 flee ye, *t. back.* dwell deep
Ezek. 38:4 I will *t.* thee *b.* 39:2
Mark 13:16 not *t. b.* to take gar.

TURN in.
Gen. 19:2 lords, *t. in*, I pray you
Jud. 4:18 *t. in*, my lord, *t. in*
19:11 let us *t. in* to this city of
2 *K.* 4:10 the man of God sh. *t. in*
Prov. 9:4 wh. is simple, *t. in*, 16

TURN to the Lord.
Deut. 4:30 if th. *t.* to the L. 30:10
2 *Sam.* 15:4 in trou. did *t.* to *t. L.*
Ps. 22:27 world shall *t.* to the L.
Lam. 3:40 try ways, *t.* to the L.
Hos. 14:2 take words, *t.* to the L.
Joel 2:13 rend heart, *t.* to the L.
Luke 1:16 many sh. he *t.* to the L.
2 *Cor.* 3:16 when it sh. *t.* to the L.

TURNED.
Gen. 3:24 a flaming sword wh. *t.*
42:24 Joseph *t.* about from them
Ex. 7:15 rod was *t.* to a serpent
14:5 heart of Pharaoh was *t.* ag.
Num. 21:33 *t.* and went by B.
Deut. 23:5 *t.* the curse, *Neh.* 13:2
31:18 are *t.* unto other gods
Jud. 2:17 they *t.* out of the way
15:4 S. took firebra. and *t.* tail
1 *Sam.* 10:6 sh. be *t.* to ano. man
14:21 they also *t.* to be with Is.
47 whithersoever he *t.* himself
15:27 Sam. *t.* about to go away
17:30 Dav. *t.* from him towards
2 *Sam.* 2:19 Asahel *t.* not fr. fol.
1 *K.* 2:15 the kingdom is *t.* about
28 Joab *t.* after Adonijah
8:14 the king *t.* his face about
11:9 his heart was *t.* fr. the L.

TURNED

2 *K.* 5:12 Naaman *t.* went away
20:2 *t.* his face to wall, *Is.* 38:2
23:25 no king *t.* to L. like him
26 L. *t.* not fierce. of his wrath
1 *Chr.* 10:14 *t.* kingd. unto David
2 *Chr.* 12:12 wrath of L. *t.* fr. him
20:10 *t.* fr. then destroyed not
29:6 fathers have *t.* their backs
Ezr. 6:22 *t.* heart of the king
Neh. 9:35 nei. *t.* fr. wick. works
Est. 9:1 tho' *t.* to the contrary
Job 16:11 G. *t.* me into hands of
19:19 wh. I loved are *t.* ag. me
28:5 it is *t.* up as it were fire
30:15 terrors are *t.* upon me
31:7 if my step *t.* out of the way
38:14 it is *t.* as clay to the seal
42:10 L. *t.* the captivity of Job
Ps. 9:17 wick. sh. be *t.* into hell
30:11 thou hast *t.* my mourning
81:14 *t.* my hand ag. adversary
105:25 he *t.* their heart to hate
119:59 I *t.* my feet unto testim.
Ec. 2:12 I *t.* mys. to behold wis.
Is. 21:4 pleasure he *t.* into fear
53:6 we have *t.* every one to his
63:10 was *t.* to be their enemy
Jer. 2:21 how *t.* into degenerate?
27 they ha. *t.* their back to me
3:10 Judah hath not *t.* to me
6:12 their houses sh. be *t.* unto
8:5 every one *t.* to his course
23:22 they should have *t.* fr. evil
31:18 I shall be *t.* 19 I was *t.*
32:33 they *t.* unto me the back
34:15 were now *t.* done right
16 ye *t.* and polluted my name
48:39 how hath M. *t.* thee back?
Lam. 1:20 heart is *t.* within me
3:3 surely against me is he *t.*
5:2 our inheri. is *t.* to strangers
21 turn us, O L. we sh. be *t.*
Ezek. 1:9 they *t.* not, 12; 10:11
17:6 a vine, whose branches *t.*
Dan. 10:16 my sorrows *t.* upon
Hos. 7:8 Ephraim is a cake not *t.*
11:8 my heart is *t.* within me
Joel 2:31 sun shall be *t. Acts* 2:20
Amos 6:12 ye have *t.* judg. into
Jon. 3:10 they *t.* from their evil
Hab. 2:16 cup of L.'s hand be *t.*
Zec. 14:10 land be *t.* into plain
Mark 5:30 Jes. *t.* about in press
Luke 22:61 L. *t.* looked upon Pe.
John 16:20 sor. shall *t.* into joy
Acts 7:42 God *t.* gave them up
9:35 all at Lyd. saw and *t.* to L.
11:21 a great number *t.* to Lord
15:19 the Gentiles are *t.* to God
17:6 ha. *t.* the world upside do.
1 *Thes.* 1:9 show how ye *t.* to G.
Heb. 11:34 *t.* to flight armies of
12:13 lest lame be *t.* out of way
Jam. 3:4 *t.* with a very sm. helm
2 *Pet.* 2:22 dog is *t.* to his vomit

TURNED again.

Ex. 4:7 it was *t. a.* as his flesh
Jud. 20:41 Is. *t. a.* Benjamites
1 *Sam.* 15:31 Samuel *t. a.* after S.
2 *Sam.* 22:38 I *t.* not *a.* till I had
Ps. 126:1 L. *t. a.* captivity of Zi.

TURNED aside.

Ex. 3:4 Lord saw that he *t. a.*
32:8 have *t. a. Deut.* 9:12, 16
1 *K.* 15:5 David *t.* not *aside* from
20:39 a man *t. a.* brought man
2 *K.* 22:2 Josiah *t.* not *a.* to right
Job 6:18 paths of their way *t. a.*
Cant. 6:1 is thy beloved *t. a.?*
Is. 44:20 deceived heart *t.* him *a.*
Lam. 3:11 hath *t. aside* my ways
1 *Tim.* 5:15 some already *t. aside*

TURNED away.

Num. 14:43 ye are *t. a.* from L.
20:21 Israel *t. away* from him
25:4 anger of Lord may be *t. a.*
11 Phine. hath *t.* my wrath *a.*

1 *K.* 11:3 wives *t. a.* his heart, 4
2 *Chr.* 29:6 our fathers *t. a.* faces
Ps. 66:20 not *t. away* my prayer
78:38 many time *t.* he anger *a.*
Is. 5:25 for all this his anger is
not *t. a.* 9:12, 17, 21 ; 10:4
12:1 anger *t. a.* 50:5 nor *t.* I *a.*
Jer. 5:25 your iniq. have *t. away*
46:5 have I seen th. *t. a.* back?
50:6 shepherds have *t.* them *a.*
Dan. 9:16 let thy fury be *t. a.*
Hos. 14:4 mine anger is *t. away*
Nah. 2:2 L. hath *t. a.* excellency
Acts 19:26 P. ha. *t. a.* much peo.
2 *Tim.* 1:15 they in Asia be *t. a.*

TURNED back.

Jos. 8:20 peo. *t. b.* upon pursuers
11:10 Joshua at that time *t. b.*
1 *Sam.* 15:11 Saul *t. b.* from foL
2 *Sam.* 1:22 bow of Jon. *t.* not *b.*
1 *K.* 18:37 hast *t.* their heart *b.*
22:33 not king of Is. they *t. b.*
2 *K.* 1:5 messengers *t. b.* why *t. b.*
2:24 *t. b.* and looked on them
15:20 king of Assyria *t. b.* stay.
1 *Chr.* 21:20 Orn. *t. b.* saw angel
Job 34:27 bec. they *t. b.* from him
Ps. 9:3 mine enemies are *t. back*
35:4 let them be *t. back*, 70:2, 3
44:18 our heart is not *t. b.* from
78:9 Ephr. *t. b.* in day of battle
41 *t. b.* and tempted God, 57
129:5 let th. be *t. b.* that hate Z.
Is. 42:17 *t. back* trust in images
Jer. 4:8 anger of Lord is not *t. b.*
11:10 they are *t. b.* to iniquities
46:21 they are *t. b.* fled away
Lam. 1:13 he hath *t.* me *b.* made
Zep. 1:6 that are *t. b.* from Lord
Luke 2:45 *t. b.* again to Jerusa.
John 20:14 she *t.* herself *b.* saw
Acts 7:39 in hea. *t. b.* ag. into E.

TURNED in.

Gen. 19:32 angels *t. in* unto Lot
38:1 Ju. *t. in* to Hirah the Adu.
Jud. 4:18 Sisera *t. in* unto Jael
18:3 the Danites *t. in* thither
2 *K.* 4:8 Elisha *t. in* thither
11 he *t. in* to the chamber

TURNEST.

1 *K.* 2:3 prosper whither. thou *t.*
Job 15:13 *t.* thy spirit ag. God
Ps. 90:3 thou *t.* man to destruct.

TURNETH.

Lev. 20:6 soul th. *t.* after wizards
Deut. 29:18 whose heart *t.* away
Jos. 7:8 when Is. *t.* their backs?
Job 39:22 the horse *t.* not back
Ps. 107:33 *t.* rivers into a wilder.
35 he *t.* wilderness into water
146:9 wicked he *t.* upside down
Prov. 15:1 soft ans. *t.* away wra.
21:1 *t.* king's heart whithersoe.
26:14 as door *t.* upon his hinges
28:9 *t.* away his ear fr. hearing
30:30 a lion *t.* not away for any
Ec. 1:6 wind *t.* about unto the
Cant. 1:7 sho. I be as one that *t.?*
Is. 9:13 the people *t.* not to him
24:1 Lord *t.* earth upside down
44:25 *t.* wise men backward
Jer. 14:8 that *t.* aside to tarry
49:24 Damascus *t.* herself to flee
Lam. 1:8 she sigheth and *t.* bac.
3:3 he *t.* his hand against me
Ezek. 18:24 righteous *t.* away fr.
his righteousness, 26 ; 33:18
27 wick. man *t.* aw. 28 ; 33:12
Amos 5:8 *t.* shadow of death into

TURNING.

2 *K.* 21:13 wipe Jer. as a dish, *t.*
2 *Chr.* 36:13 hardened heart fr. *t.*
Prov. 1:32 the *t.* away of simple
Is. 29:16 your *t.* of things upside
Mic. 2:4 *t.* away he hath divided
Acts 3:26 to bless you in *t.* you

Jam. 1:17 wi. wh. is no sha. of *t.*
Jude 4 *t.* grace of G. into lasciv.

TURTLE, 8.

Gen. 15:9 take a *t.* dove and a yo.
Lev. 5:7 he sh. bri. two *t.* doves,
12:8 : 14:22, 30 ; 15:14, 29
11 if not able to br. two *t.* dov.
12:6 she shall bring a *t.* dove
Num. 6:10 on 8th day sh. bri. 2 *t.*
Ps. 74:19 deliver not soul of *t.* d.
Cant. 2:12 voice of the *t.* is hea.
Jer. 8:7 *t.* and crane observe time
Luke 2:24 sacri. pair of *t.* doves

TUTORS.

Gal. 4:2 a child is under *t.* and

TWAIN.

1 *Sam.* 18:21 son-in-law one of *t.*
2 *K.* 4:33 shut the door on th. *t.*
Is. 6:2 with *t.* he cover. his face,
with *t.* he cover. feet, with *t.*
Jer. 34:18 they cut the calf in *t.*
Ezek. 21:19 both *t.* sh. come out
Mat. 5:41 a mile, go with him *t.*
19:5 they *t.* shall be one flesh
6 are no more *t. Mark* 10:8
21:31 whe. of *t.* did will of fath. ?
27:21 whe. of *t.* will I release ?
51 veil rent in *t. Mark* 15:38
Eph. 2:15 make in himself of *t.*

TWELFTH.

1 *K.* 19:19 oxen, he with the *t.*
Rev. 21:20 *t.* founda. was ameth.

See MONTH.

TWELVE.

Gen. 14:4 *t.* years they served C.
17:20 *t.* princes sh. Ishm. 25:16
35:22 the sons of Jacob were *t.*
42:13 thy serv. are *t.* breth. 32
49:28 these are *t.* tribes of Ier.
Ex. 15:27 Elim, where were *t.*
24:4 *t.* pillars acc. to *t.* tribes
28:21 *t.* precious stones, 39:14
Lev. 24:5 thou sh. bake *t.* cakes
Deut. 1:23 I took *t.* men of you
Jos. 3:12 take ye *t.* men, 4:2
4:3 *t.* stones out of Jor. 8, 9, 20
2 *Sam.* 2:15 arose *t.* of Benjamin, and *t.* servants of Dav.
1 *K.* 7:25 the sea stood on *t.* oxen,
44 ; 2 *Chr.* 4:15
10:20 *t.* lions on side, 2 *Chr.* 9:19
11:30 Ah. rent garm. in *t.* pieces
Neh. 5:14 *t.* years not eat. bread
Mat. 9:20 a wom. was diseabed *t.*
years, *Mark* 5:25 ; *Luke* 8:43
10:2 names of *t.* apos. *Luke* 6:13
26:20 he sat down with the *t.*
Mark 14:17 ; *Luke* 22:14
Mark 5:42 age of *t.* yrs. *Luke* 8:42
14:20 it is one of *t.* that dippeth
Luke 2:42 when Je. was *t.* years
John 6:70 have I not cho. you *t.?*
11:9 are th. not *t.* hours in day
1 *Cor.* 15:5 seen of Cep. th. of *t.*
Rev. 12:1 on head cro. of *t.* stars
21:12 city had *t.* gates, at gat. *t.*
14 wall of city had *t.* foundat.
in them names of *t.* apostles
21 the *t.* gates were *t.* pearls
22:2 tr. bare *t.* manner of fruits

See HUNDRED, THOUSAND.

TWENTY.

Gen. 18:31 be found *t.* there, I
will not destroy it for *t.* sake
31:38 *t.* ye. I have been with, 41
37:28 sold J. for *t.* pieces silver
Ex. 30:14 fr. *t.* old, 38:26 ; *Num.*
1:3, etc.
Lev. 27:3 estim. of males fr. *t.*
2 *K.* 4:42 brought man *t.* loaves
Ezr. 8:27 weighed *t.* bas. of gold
Zec. 5:2 length of roll *t.* cubits

TWENTY-TWO.

Jud. 10:3 Jair judged Is. *t.-t.* ye.

1 *Chr.* 12:28 house *t.-t.* captains
2 *Chr.* 13:21 Abi. begat *t.-t.* sons

TWENTY-THREE.

Jud. 10:2 T. judged Is. *t.-t.* yea.

TWENTY-FOUR.

2 *Sam.* 21:20 fing. and toes, *t.-f.*
Rev. 4:4 about throne were *t.-f.*
   seats, I saw *t.-f.* elders sit
5:8 *t.-f.* elders fell, 11:16; 19:4

TWENTY-FIVE.

Num. 8:24 from *t.-five* years old
Neh. 6:5 wall finished in *t.-f.* day

TWENTY-SIXTH.

1 *K.* 16:8 in *t.-s.* year of Asa Elah

TWENTY-SEVENTH.

Gen. 8:14 *t.-s.* day of sec. month

TWENTY-EIGHT.

Ex. 26:2 curtain *t.-e.* cubits, 36:9

TWENTY-NINE.

Gen. 11:24 Nahor lived *t.-n.* yea.

See THOUSAND.

TWICE.

Gen. 41:32 dream was doubled *t.*
Ex. 16:5 shall be *t.* as much, 22
1 *K.* 11:9 had appeared to him *t.*
2 *K.* 6:10 saved not once nor *t.*
Neh. 13:20 with. Jeru. once or *t.*
Job 33:14 God speak. once, yea *t.*
   40:5 yea *t.* but I will proceed no
42:10 Lord gave Job *t.* as much
Ps. 62:11 *t.* have I heard, power
Luke 18:12 I fast *t.* in the week
Jude 12 *t.* dead, pluck. up by ro.

TWIGS.

Ezek. 17:4 he cropped off top of *t.*
22 crop off fr. top of young *t.*

TWILIGHT.

1 *Sam.* 30:17 Da. smote th. fr. *t.*
2 *K.* 7:5 lepers rose in *t.* to go
7 Syrians arose and fled in *t.*
Job 3:9 let stars of the *t.* be dark
24:15 eye of adul. waiteth for *t.*
Prov. 7:9 in her house in *t.*
Ezek. 12:6 sh. carry it forth in *t.*
7 and brought it forth in the *t.*
12 prince shall bear it in the *t.*

TWINED. *See* FINE.

TWINKLING.

1 *Cor.* 15:52 changed in *t.* of eye

TWINS.

Gen. 25:24 Reb. had *t.* 38:27 Ta.
Cant. 4:2 every one bear *t.* 6:6
5 like two roes that are *t.* 7:3

TWO.

Gen. 4:19 Lamech took *t.* wives

6:19 *t.* of ev. sort bring into ark
7:2 beasts not clean by *t.* 9:15
25:23 *t.* nations are in thy womb
32:10 I am become *t.* bands
Ex. 21:21 if he continue day or *t.*
Lev. 5:7 shall bring *t.* doves or *t.*
   pigeons, 12:8; 14:22; 15:14,
   29; *Num.* 6:10
Deut. 21:15 if man have *t.* wives
32:30 *t.* put 10,000 to flight !
Jos. 14:3 *t.* tribes, 4; 21:16
21:25 wi. her suburbs, *t.* cities
Jud. 5:30 ev. man a damsel or *t.*
11:37 let me alone *t.* months
16:28 avenged for my *t.* eyes
1 *Sam.* 1:2 Elkanah had *t.* wives
27:3 D. *t.* wi. 30:5, 18; 2 *Sam.* 2:2
1 *K.* 3:18 none save *t.* in house '
18:21 halt ye bet. *t.* opinions ?
Job 13:20 do not *t.* thi. unto me
42:7 wra. is kind. ag. *t.* friends
Prov. 30:7 *t.* things I required
Ec. 4:9 *t.* are better than one
11 if *t.* lie toget. th. have heat
12 if one prevail, *t.* sh. withst.
Is. 47:9 these *t.* things sh. come
51:19 these two things are come
Jer. 2:13 peo. committed *t.* evils
3:14 one of a city, *t.* of a family
Amos 3:3 can *t.* walk together
Mat. 6:24 no man can serve *t.*
   masters, *Luke* 16:13
18:8 *t.* ha. or *t.* feet, *Mark* 9:43
9 having *t.* eyes, *Mark* 9:47
16 take wi. thee one or *t.* more
19 if *t.* of you agree on earth
20 wh. *t.* or three are gathered
24:40 then shall *t.* be in field
Mark 6:7 send them by *t.* and *t.*
Acts 1:24 whet. of these *t.* chos.
1 *Cor.* 6:16 *t.* be one fl. *Eph.* 5:31
14:27 by *t.* or at most by three
Phil. 1:23 in a strait betwixt *t.*

See DAUGHTERS, DAYS, KIDNEYS,
   LAMBS, SONS.

TWO men.

Ex. 2:13 *t. m.* of Hebrews strove
Num. 11:26 rema. *t. m.* in camp
Jos. 2:1 sent out *t. men* to spy
1 *Sam.* 10:2 find *t. men* by sepulc.
2 *Sam.* 12:1 *t. men* in one city
1 *K.* 2:32 fell on *t. men* righteous
21:10 set *t. men* before Nah. 13
Mat. 9:27 *t.* blind *men* followed
Luke 9:30 talked with him *t. m.*
17:34 *t. men* in bed; 36 *t. men*
   in field
18:10 *t. m.* went up to temple
John 8:17 testimony of *t. m.* true
Acts 9:38 they sent *t. m.* to Peter

TWO tables.

Ex. 31:18 gave to Moses *t. tables*
34:1 *t. t.* of stone, *Deut.* 10:1
4 hewed *t. tables, Deut.* 10:3
Deut. 4:13 wrote upon *t. t.* 5:22
9:10 Lord deliv. unto me *t. t.* 11
1 *K.* 8:9 nothing in ark save *t. t.*
   of stone, 2 *Chr.* 5:10
Ezek. 40:39 *t. t.* on side; 40 *t. t.*

TWO years.

Gen. 11:10 Arph. *t. y.* after flood
2 *Chr.* 21:19 aft. *t. y.* bowels fell
Jer. 28:3 in *t. y.* I'll bring ves. 11
Amos 1:1 *t. y.* before earthquake
Mal. 2:16 slew children fr. *t. y.*
Acts 19:10 *t. y.* in As. heard word
28:30 P. dwelt *t. y.* in his house

TWOFOLD.

Mat. 23:15 *t.* more child of hell

TYCHICUS.

Acts 20:4 T. accompanied Paul
Eph. 6:21 T. shall make known
Col. 4:7 sh. T. declare unto you
2 *Tim.* 4:12 T. sent to Ephesus
Tit. 3:12 I send T. unto thee

TYRANNUS.

Acts 19:9 disput. in school of T.

TYRE, or TYRUS.

Jos. 19:29 coast turn. to city T.
2 *Sam.* 24:7 to strong-hold of T.
1 *K.* 7:13 fetched Hira. out of T.
14 was a man of T. 2 *Chr.* 2:14
9:12 Hiram came out from T. to
Ezr. 3:7 meat and drink to them
   of T.
Neh. 13:16 dw. men of T. therein
Ps. 45:12 daughter of T. shall be
83:7 with the inhabitants of T.
87:4 Philistia and T. *Is.* 23:1
Is. 23:5 pain. at the report of T.
8 who ha. taken coun. ag. T. ?
15 T. shall be forgotten, 17
Jer. 25:22 made kings of T. drl.
27:3 send the yokes to kin. of T.
47:4 to cut off from T. and Zid.
Ezek. 26:2 T. said ag. Jerusalem
3 I am against thee, O T.
27:2 take up lamentation for T.
32 city like T. like destroyed ?
28:2 say to prince of T.
12 lamentation on king of T.
29:18 serve great service ag. T.
Hos. 9:13 Ephraim, as I saw T.
Joel 3:4 ye to do with me, O T. ?
Amos 1:9 three transgress. of T.
10 I will send fire on wall of T.
Zec. 9:2 T. and Zidon, though it
3 T. build herself a strong ho.
Mat. 11:21 if mighty works had
   been done in T. *Luke* 10:13
Acts 12:20 displeas. wi. th. of T.

U

UCAL.

Prov. 30:1 spoke to Ithiel and U.

UNACCUSTOMED.

Jer. 31:18 as a bullock *u.* to yoke

UNADVISEDLY.

Ps. 106:33 spake *u.* with his lips

UNAWARES.

Gen. 31:20 Jacob stole away *u.* 26
Num. 35:11 killeth any person *u.*
   15; *Deut.* 4:42; *Jos.* 20:3, 9
Ps. 35:8 destru. come on him *u.*
Luke 21:34 day come on you *u.*
Gal. 2:4 false breth. *u.* brought
Heb. 13:2 some enterta. angels *u.*
Jude 4 certain men crept in *u.*

UNBELIEF.

Mat. 13:58 works, because of *u.*
17:20 not cast out bec. of yo. *u.*

Mark 6:6 marvel. bec. of their *u.*
9:24 I believe, help th. mine *u.*
16:14 upbraid. them with th. *u.*
Rom. 3:3 sh. *u.* make faith with
4:20 he staggered not through *u.*
11:20 bec. of *u.* they were brok.
23 if they abide not still in *u.*
30 obtained mercy through *u.*
32 G. concluded them all in *u.*
1 *Tim.* 1:13 did it ignorant. in *u.*
Heb. 3:12 an evil heart of *u.*
19 could not enter bec. of *u.* 4:6
4:11 after same example of *u.*

UNBELIEVERS.

Luke 12:46 appoint por. wi. *u.*
1 *Cor.* 6:6 goeth to law before *u.*
   14:23 come in those that are *u.*
2 *Cor.* 6:14 unequal. yoked wi. *u.*

UNBELIEVING.

Acts 14:2 *u.* Jews stirr. Gentiles
1 *Cor.* 7:14 *u.* husband sanctified
15 *u.* if depart, let him depart
Tit. 1:15 unto *u.* is nothing pure
Rev. 21:8 *u.* have th. part in lake

UNBLAMABLE, Y.

Col. 1:22 to present you holy, *u.*
1 *Thes.* 2:10 how *u.* we behaved
3:13 may stablish your hearts *u.*

UNCERTAIN, LY.

1 *Cor.* 9:26 run. not as *u.* so fight
14:8 if trumpet give an *u.* sound
1 *Tim.* 6:17 nor trust in *u.* riches

UNCHANGEABLE.

Heb. 7:24 hath an *u.* priesthood

UNCIRCUMCISED.

Gen. 17:14 *u.* man-child shall be
   cut off

34:14 cannot give our sist. to *u.*
Ex. 6:12 who am of *u.* lips, 30
12:48 no *u.* person eat passover
Lev. 19:23 count fruit *u.* 3 years
26:41 if th. *u.* hearts be humbl.
Jos. 5:7 circumcised, th. were *u.*
Jud. 14:3 goest to take wife of *u.*
15:18 sh. I fall into hands of *u.*
1 *Sam.* 17:26 who is th. *u.* P. ? 36
31:4 lest th. *u.* come, 1 *Chr.* 10:4
2 *Sam.* 1:20 daugh. of *u.* triumph
Is. 52:1 no more come to thee *u.*
Jer. 6:10 their ear is *u.* th. cann.
9:25 punish circumcised with *u.*
26 nations *u.* house of Israel *u.*
Ezek. 28:10 shalt die death of *u.*
31:18 sh. lie in midst of *u.* 32:19,
21, 24, 25, 26, 27, 28, 29, 30, 32
44:7 strang. *u.* in heart, and *u.*
Acts 7:51 stiff-necked, *u.* in hea.
11:3 thou wentest in to men *u.*
Rom. 4:11 faith he had bei. *u.* 12
1 *Cor.* 7:18 let him not become *u.*

UNCIRCUMCISION.

Rom. 2:25 circumcis. is made *u.*
26 if *u.* keep righteous. of law
27 shall not *u.* judge thee ?
3:30 shall justify *u.* through fai.
4:9 bless. on circumcision or *u.*
10 wh. he was in circu. or *u. ?*
1 *Cor.* 7:18 any man called in *u.*
19 circumc. nothing, *u.* noth.
Gal. 2:7 gospel of *u.* committed
5:6 circum. avail. nor *u.* 6:15
Eph. 2:11 who are called *u.* by
Col. 2:13 dead in *u.* of flesh
3:11 circumcision nor *u.* but C.

UNCLE.

Lev. 10:4 Uzziel, the *u.* of Aaron
20:20 if a man lie with *u.* wife
25:49 *u.* or *u.* son may redeem
1 *Sam.* 10:14 Saul's *u.* said to, 15
14:50 Ab. son of Ner, Saul's *u.*
1 *Chr.* 27:32 Jonathan David's *u.*
Est. 2:7 brought *u.* daughter, 15
Jer. 32:7 son of Shallum thine *u.*
8 my *u.* son ca. unto me, 9, 12
Amos 6:10 a man's *u.* take him

UNCLEAN.

Lev. 5:2 if soul touch any *u.* thi.
carc. of *u.* cattle, bo *u.* 11:26
10:10 diff. betw. *u.* clean, 11:47
11:4 is *u.* 5, 6, 7, 29; *Deut.* 14:19
24 for these ye sh. be *u.* 25–40;
14:46 ; 15:5–27 ; 17:15 ; 22:6 ;
Num. 19:7–22
12:2 be *u.* seven days, 5 ; 15:25
13:45 in wh. plague is, cry *u. u.*
14:40 cast them into *u.* pl. 41, **45**
57 teach when *u.* and wh. clean
22:5 whereby may be made *u.*
Num. 6:7 sh. not make hims. *u.*
Deut. 12:15 *u.* and cle. 22 ; 15:22
Jos. 22:19 if your possessi. be *u.*
Ezr. 9:11 land ye go to pos. is *u.*
Job 36:14 hypocrites is among *u.*
Ec. 9:2 one event to clean and *u.*
Is. 6:5 I am a man of *u.* lips, in
midst of a people of *u.* lips
35:8 the *u.* shall not pass over it
52:1 no more come into the *u.*
Lam. 4:15 depart ye, it is *u.* de.
Ezek. 22:26 between clean and *u.*
44:23 discern betw. clean and *u.*
Hos. 9:3 they shall eat *u.* things
Hag. 2:13 one *u.* touch it, be *u.*
14 that wh. th. offer there is *u.*
Luke 4:33 had a spirit of *u.* devil
Acts 10:28 not call any man common or *u.* 11:8
Rom. 14:14 noth. is *u.* of itself,
thing be *u.* to him it is *u.*
1 *Cor.* 7:14 else children were *u.*
2 *Cor.* 6:17 touch not *u.* thing
Eph. 5:5 no *u.* person hath inhe.
Heb. 9:13 of heifer sprinkling *u.*

Rev. 18.2 bec. a cage of *u.* bird
See BEAST, SPIRIT, THING.

UNCLEAN Spirits.

Mat. 10:1 power against *u.*
spirits, *Mark* 6:7
Mark 1:27 com. *u. s. Luke* 4:36
3:11 *u. s.* when they saw him
5:13 *u. s.* went and ent. swine
Acts 5:16 were vexed with *u. s.*
8:7 *u. s.* came out of possessed
Rev. 16:13 saw 3 *u. s.* like frogs

UNCLEANNESS.

Lev. 5:3 whatsoever *u.* of man,
whatsoever *u.* 7:21 ; 22:5
7:20 having his *u.* on him, 22:3
15:31 separate Is. from their *u.*
18:19 as she is put apart for *u.*
Num. 5:19 not gone aside to *u.*
19:13 uncl. *u.* is yet upon him
Deut. 23:10 by reason of *u.* that
24:1 hath found some *u.* in her
2 *Sam.* 11:4 purified from her *u.*
2 *Chr.* 29:16 priests broug. out *u.*
Ezr. 9:11 filled the land with *u.*
Ezek. 36:17 as *u.* of removed wo.
39:24 according to their *u.*
Zec. 13:1 fountain opened for *u.*
Mat. 23:27 full of bones and *u.*
Rom. 1:24 G. also gave th. to *u.*
6:19 yielded members ser. to *u.*
2 *Cor.* 12:21 not repented of *u.*
Gal. 5:19 works of flesh are *u.*
Eph. 4:19 to work *u.* wi. greedi.
5:3 *u.* let it not once be named
Col. 3:5 mortify fornication, *u.*
1 *Thes.* 2:3 exhortation not of *u.*
4:7 God hath not called us to *u.*
2 *Pet.* 2:10 that walk in lust of *u.*

UNCLEANNESSES.

Ezek. 36:29 I will save you fr. *u.*

UNCLOTHED.

2 *Cor.* 5:4 not that we wo. be *u.*

UNCOMELY.

1 *Cor.* 7:36 beha. *u.* tow. virgin
12:23 *u.* parts have comeliness

UNCONDEMNED.

Acts 16:37 beaten us openly *u.*
22:25 that is a Roman and *u.*

UNCORRUPTNESS.

Tit. 2:7 in doctrine showing *u.*

UNCOVER.

Lev. 10:6 *u.* not your heads
18:6 not *u.* nakedn. of near kin
7 nakedness of fa. shalt not *u.*
8 not *u.* father's wife ; 9 sister
10 thy son's daug. shalt not *u.*
11 father's wife's dau. not *u.*
12 not *u.* nak. of fath.'s sister
13 not *u.* moth.'s sister, 20:19
14 not *u.* nakedn. of fath.'s br.
15 daug.-in-law ; 16 brother's
17 not *u.* a woman and daugh.
18 sh. not *u.* thy wife's sister
19 not *u.* wo. put apart, 20:18
21:10 high priest not *u.* head
Num. 5:18 priest *u.* wom.'s head
Ruth 3:4 sh. go in and *u.* his feet
Is. 47:2 *u.* thy locks, and *u.* thigh

UNCOVERED.

Gen. 9:21 Noah was *u.* in his te.
Lev. 20:11 *u.* his father's naked.
17 *u.* sister's ; 20 *u.* his uncle's
18 she hath *u.* founta. of blood
Ruth 3:7 came softly and *u.* feet
2 *Sam.* 6:20 *u.* hims. as vain fel.
Is. 20:4 led away with butto. *u.*
22:6 quiver, and Kir *u.* shield
47:3 thy nakedness shall be *u.*
Jer. 49:10 I *u.* his secret places
Ezek. 4:7 thine arm shall be *u.*
Hab. 2:16 let thy foreskin be *u.*
Mark 2:4 they *u.* roof wh. he was
1 *Cor.* 11:5 prophe. with head *u.*
13 is it comely th. wo. pray *u.?*

UNCOVERETH.

Lev. 20:19 for he *u.* his near kin
Deut. 27:20 *u.* his father's skirt
2 *Sam.* 6:20 vain fellows *u.* him.

UNCTION.

1 *John* 2:20 ye have *u.* fr. holy O.

UNDEFILED.

Ps. 119:1 blessed are *u.* in way
Cant. 5:2 love, my dove, my *u.*
6:9 my dove, my *u.* is one
Heb. 7:26 priest, holy, harml. *u.*
13:4 marriage honorable, bed *u.*
Jam. 1:27 pure religion and *u.*
1 *Pet.* 1:4 inher. incorruptible, *u.*

UNDER.

Mat. 2:16 fr. two yea. old and *u.*
Mat. 8:9 I am *u.* authority, hav.
Heb. 7:11 *u.* it peo. received law
See FEET.

UNDERGIRDING.

Acts 27:17 used helps, *u.* the ship

UNDERNEATH.

Deut. 33:27 *u.* are everlast. arms

UNDERSETTERS.

1 *K.* 7:30 four corners had *u.* 34

UNDERSTAND.

Gen. 11:7 not *u.* anoth.'s speech
41:15 I heard th. canst *u.* dream
Num. 16:30 *u.* these provoked L.
Deut. 28:49 tong. thou sh. not *u.*
2 *K.* 18:26 speak to servants in
Syr. langu. we *u.* it, *Is.* 36:11
1 *Chr.* 28:19 Lord made me *u.*
Neh. 8:3 before those th. could *u.*
7 people to *u.* law, 8, 13
Job 6:24 cause me to *u.* wherein
23:5 I would *u.* what he say
26:14 thunder of power who *u. ?*
32:9 neither do aged *u.* judgm.
36:29 can any *u.* spr. of clouds ?
Ps. 14:2 if any that did *u.* 53:2
19:12 who can *u.* his errors ?
82:5 not, neither will they *u.*
92:6 neither doth a fool *u.* this
94:8 *u.* ye brutish among peop.
107:43 sh. *u.* loving-kind. of L.
119:27 make me *u.* thy precepts
100 I *u.* more than ancients
Prov. 2:5 then *u.* fear of the Lord
9 shalt thou *u.* righteousness
8:5 O ye simple, *u.* wisdom
14:8 wisd. of prudent to *u.* way
19:25 and he will *u.* knowledge
20:24 how can man *u.* his way ?
28:5 evil men *u.* not judgment,
they that seek L. *u.* all thin.
29:19 tho' he *u.* will not answer
Is. 6:9 hear ye indeed, *u.* not
10 lest they *u.* with, *John* 12:40
28:9 whom make to *u.* doctri. ?
19 be vexation only to *u.* repo.
32:4 heart of rash *u.* knowledge
33:19 tongue thou canst not *u.*
41:20 *u.* together L. ha. done th.
43:10 may know and *u.* I am he
44:18 shut hearts. th. cannot *u.*
56:11 shepherds that cannot *u.*
Jer. 9:12 who wise that may *u. ?*
Ezek. 3:6 words th. canst not *u.*
Dan. 8:16 make this man *u.* vis.
17 said to me, *u.* O son of man
9:13 *u.* truth ; 23 *u.* matter, 25
10:12 didst set thy heart to *u.*
14 I am come to make thee *u.*
11:33 they that *u.* shall instruct
12:10 wicked not *u.* wise sh. *u.*
14:9 wise ? he shall *u.* these thi.
Mic. 4:12 neither *u.* counsel of L.
Mat. 13:13 not, neith. do they *u.*
14 and shall not *u.*
15:10 hear and *u.* *Mark* 7:14
17 do not ye yet *u. ?* 16:9, 11 ;
Mark 8:17, 21
24:15 let him *u.* *Mark* 13:14

Mark 4:12 hear. they may hear,
not u. *Luke* 8:10 ; *Acts* 28:26
14:68 nor u. I what thou sayest
Luke 24:45 might u. scriptures
John 8:43 why not u. my speech ?
Rom. 15:21 have not heard sh. u.
1 *Cor.* 13:2 tho' I u. all mysteries
Heb. 11:3 u. worlds were framed
2 *Pet.* 2:12 evil of thi. they u. not

UNDERSTANDEST.

Job 15:9 what u. thou, which is
Ps. 139:2 thou u. my thoughts
Jer. 5:15 neither u. what th. say
Acts 8:30 u. thou wh. th. readest ?

UNDERSTANDETH.

1 *Chr.* 28:9 Lord u. imaginations
Job 28:23 God u. the way thereof
Ps. 49:20 man in honor u. not
Prov. 8:9 all plain to him that u.
14:6 knowl. easy to him that u.
Jer. 9:24 glory in this, that he u.
Mat. 13:19 hear. word, u. it not
23 that heareth word, and u. it
Rom. 3:11 there is none that u.
1 *Cor.* 14:2 to men, for no man u.
16 he u. not what thou sayest

UNDERSTANDING.

Ex. 31:3 I have filled Bezaleel
with u. 35:31 ; 36:1
Deut. 4:6 this is your wis. and u.
32:28 neither is any u. in them
1 *K.* 3:11 hast asked u. to disce.
4:29 God gave Solomon u.
7:14 Hiram was filled with u.
1 *Chr.* 12:32 were men th. had u.
22:12 L. give thee wisd. and u.
2 *Chr.* 2:12 a wise son end. wi. u.
26:5 Zechari. had u. in visions
Ezr. 8:16 Joi. and El. men of u.
Neh. 8:2 that could hear with u.
10:28 ev. one hav. know. and u.
Job 12:3 I have u. as well as you
12 length of days u. 13 hath u.
20 he taketh away u. of aged
17:4 hast hid their heart from u.
20:3 my u. caus. me to answer
26:12 by his u. he smiteth thro'
28:12 where is place of u. ? 20
28 naid, To depart fr. evil is u.
32:8 Almighty giveth them u.
34:10 hearken to me, men of u.
16 if now th. hast u. hear this
34 let men of u. tell me
38:4 declare, if thou hast u.
36 who hath given u. to heart ?
39:17 neither imparted to her u.
Ps. 32:9 as mule that hath no u.
47:7 King, sing praises with u.
49:3 medita. of heart shall be u.
119:34 give u. 73, 125, 144, 169
99 I have u. 130 word giveth u.
104 thro' thy precepts I get u.
147:5 great our L. u. is infinite
Prov. 1:2 to perceive words of u.
2:2 thou apply th. heart to u.
3 if thou liftest up voice for u.
6 out of his mouth cometh u.
11 discretion pres. thee, u. sh.
3:5 lean not to thine own u.
13 happy is man th. getteth u.
19 by u. he establish. heavens
4:1 attend to kn. u. 5 get u. 7
5:1 bow thine ear to my u.
6:32 commit. adult. lacketh u.
7:4 and call u. thy kinswoman
8:1 doth not u. put forth voice ?
14 I am u. 9:6 in way of u.
9:4 him that wanteth u. 16
10 knowledge of the holy is u.
10:13 that hath u. wisd. is found
14:29 is slow to wrath is of u.
33 wisdom in him that hath u.
15:14 heart of him that hath u.
32 that heareth reproof get. u.
16:16 better to get u. than silv.
22 u. is a well-spring of life to
17:24 wisd. bef. him that ha. u.

18:2 fool hath no delight in u.
19:8 he that keepeth u. sh. find
25 reprove one that hath u.
21:16 wander. out of way of u.
30 there is no u. nor counsel
23:23 buy also instruct. and u.
24:3 by u. house is established
28:11 poor that hath u. search.
16 prince that wanteth u.
30:2 have not the u. of a matter
Ec. 9:11 nor rich. to men of u.
Is. 11:2 sp. of u. shall rest upon
3 make him of quick u.
27:11 for it is a people of no u.
29:14 u. of their prudent men
16 framed it, he had no u. ?
24 erred in spir. sh. come to u.
40:14 showed him way of u. ?
28 there is no search. of his u.
41:19 neither knowledge nor u.
Jer. 3:15 past. sh. feed you wi. u.
4:22 people foolish, have no u.
5:21 O foolish peo. without u.
51:15 stretched out heaven by u.
Ezek. 28:4 wi. thy u. thou hast
Dan. 1:17 Dan. had u. in visions
20 in matters of u. he found
2:21 giv. to them that know u.
4:34 mine u. returned to me
5:11 and u. was found, 12, 14
9:22 I am come to give thee u.
10:1 Daniel had u. of vision
11:35 some of th. of u. shall fall
Hos. 13:2 made idols ac. to th. u.
Ob. 7 there is no u. in him
8 sh. I not destroy u. out of E.?
Mat. 15:16 ye wi. u. ? *Mark* 7:18
Mark 12:33 to love him with u.
Luke 1:3 having had perfect u.
2:47 were astonished at his u.
24:45 then opened he their u.
Rom. 1:31 without u. coven.-br.
1 *Cor.* 1:19 bring to noth. the u.
14:14 sp. prayeth, u. is unfruit.
15 pray with u. sing with u.
19 ra. speak five words with u.
20 not child. in u. in u. be men
Eph. 1:18 eyes of u. being enlig.
4:18 having the u. darkened
Phil. 4:7 peace of G. pass. all u.
Col. 1:9 filled with all u. spiritu. u.
2:2 rich. of full assurance of u.
2 *Tim.* 2:7 the Lord give thee u.
1 *John* 5:20 G. hath giv. us an u.
Rev. 13:18 him that hath u.

See GOOD.

Man of UNDERSTANDING.

Ezr. 8:18 they broug. a m. of u.
Prov. 1:5 a m. of u. shall attain
10:23 a m. of u. hath wisdom
11:12 a m. of u. hold. his peace
15:21 a m. of u. walk. uprightly
17:27 a m. of u. is of an excell.
28 shutteth lips is d m. of u.
20:5 a m. of u. will dr. counsel
28:2 by a m. of u. state shall be

Void of UNDERSTANDING.

Prov. 7:7 a young man v. of u.
10:13 a rod for him th. is v. of u.
12:11 follow vain per. is v. of u.
17:18 a man v. of u. strik. han.
24:30 vineyard of man v. of u.

UNDERSTANDING, Adj.

Deut. 1:13 take wise men and u.
4:6 this nation is an u. people
1 *K.* 3:9 give servant an u. heart
12 lo, I have given thee an u.
Prov. 8:5 be of an u. heart
Dan. 1:4 u. science ; 8:23 u. dark
Eph. 5:17 u. what will of L. is
1 *Tim.* 1:7 u. neit. what they say

UNDERSTOOD.

Gen. 42:23 knew not Jos. u. th.
Deut. 32:29 were wise, they u.
1 *Sam.* 4:6 they u. ark of L. was
26:4 Da. u. that Saul was come

2 *Sam.* 3:37 u. it was not of D.
Neh. 8:12 had u. words that were
13:7 I u. of the evil Eliashib did
Job 13:1 mine ear heard and u. it
42:3 I uttered that I u. not
Ps. 73:17 then u. I their end
81:5 heard langu. that I u. not
106:7 our fath. u. not thy wond.
Is. 40:21 ha. ye not u. fr. founda.
44:18 nor u. for he shut th. eyes
Dan. 8:27 astonished, but none u.
9:2 Dan. u. by books ; 10:1 he u.
12:8 I heard, but I u. not, then
Mat. 13:51 have ye u. these thi. ?
16:12 then u. they how he bade
17:13 they u. that he spake of J.
Mark 9:32 u. not that sayi. *Luke*
2:50 ; 9:45 ; *John* 8:27 ; 10:6
Luke 18:34 they u. none of these
John 12:16 thi. u. not his discip.
Acts 7:25 he supposed they u. G.
would deliver th. they u. not
23:27 hav. u. he was a Roman
34 when I u. he was of Cilicia
Rom. 1:20 being u. by the things
1 *Cor.* 13:11 I u. as a child
14:9 ut. by tongue wor. to be u.
2 *Pet.* 3:16 some thi. hard to be u.

UNDERTAKE.

Is. 38:14 I am oppress. u. for me

UNDERTOOK.

Est. 9:23 Jews u. to do as they

UNDO.

Is. 58:6 the fast ? to u. burdens
Zep. 3:19 I will u. all that afflict

UNDONE.

Num. 21:29 thou art u. O people
Jos. 11:15 Joshua left nothing u.
Is. 6:5 woe is me, for I am u.
Mat. 23:23 lea. oth. u. *Lu.* 11:42

UNDRESSED.

Lev. 25:5 grapes of thy vine u. 11

UNEQUAL, LY.

Ezek. 18:25 are not y. ways u. ? 29
2 *Cor.* 6:14 be not u. yoked with

UNFAITHFUL, LY.

Ps. 78:57 they dealt u. like fath.
Prov. 25:19 confid. in an u. man

UNFEIGNED.

2 *Cor.* 6:6 by H. Ghost, by love u.
1 *Tim.* 1:5 pure heart, faith u.
2 *Tim.* 1:5 I call to remembr. u.
1 *Pet.* 1:22 thro' Spi. unto u. love

UNFRUITFUL.

Mat. 13:22 becom. u. *Mark* 4:19
1 *Cor.* 14:14 my understand. is u.
Eph. 5:11 no fellowship with u.
Tit. 3:14 that they be not u.
2 *Pet.* 1:8 neith. be barren nor u.

UNGIRDED.

Gen. 24:32 man u. the camels

UNGODLINESS.

Rom. 1:18 wrath of God agai. u.
11:26 he sh. turn away u. fr. Ja.
2 *Tim.* 2:16 will increase unto u.
Tit. 2:12 denying u. and worldly

UNGODLY.

2 *Sam.* 22:5 floods of u. men ma.
me afraid, *Ps.* 18:4
2 *Chr.* 19:2 shouldest thou help u.
Job 16:11 G. deliver. me to the u.
34:18 is it fit to say, Ye are u. ?
Ps. 1:1 walk. not in coun. of u.
1:4 u. are not so ; 5 u. not sta.
6 the way of the u. shall perish
3:7 hast broken the teeth of u.
43:1 pl. my cause ag. u. nation
73:12 these are u. who prosper
Prov. 16:27 u. man dig. up evil
19:28 u. witness scorneth judg.
Rom. 4:5 him that justifieth u.
5:6 in due time Chr. died for u.
1 *Tim.* 1:9 the law is for the u.
1 *Pet.* 4:18 where shall u. appear ?

2 *Pet.* 2:5 bringing the flood on *u.*
6 those who after should live *u.*
3:7 judgment and perdi. of *u.*
Jude 4 *u.* men turn. grace of God
15 convince *u.* of th. *u.* deeds
18 who walk after th. *u.* lusts

UNHOLY.

Lev. 10:10 differ. bet. holy and *u.*
1 *Tim.* 1:9 law was made for *u.*
2 *Tim.* 3:2 men be unthankful, *u.*
Heb. 10:29 counted blood of *u.*

UNICORN.

Num. 23:22 strength of *u.* 24:8
Job 39:9 will the *u.* serve thee?
10 canst bind *u.* in the furrow?
Ps. 29:6 Leb. and Sirion like *u.*
92:10 shall exalt like horn of *u.*

UNICORNS.

Deut. 33:17 horns like horns of *u.*
Ps. 22:21 heard from horns of *u.*
Is. 34:7 the *u.* shall come down

UNITE, D.

Gen. 49:6 mine honor be not *u.*
Ps. 86:11 *u.* my heart to fear

UNITY.

Ps. 133:1 for bre. to dwell in *u.*
Eph. 4:3 endeavoring to keep *u.*
13 till we come in the *u.* of

UNJUST.

Ps. 43:1 deliv. me from *u.* man
Prov. 11:7 hope of *u.* men peris.
28:8 who by *u.* gain increaseth
29:27 an *u.* man is an abomina.
Zep. 3:5 *u.* knoweth no shame
Mat. 5:45 sen. rai. on just and *u.*
Luke 16:8 L. commend. *u.* stew.
10 is *u.* in least, is *u.* in much
18:6 hear what *u.* judge saith
11 I am not as oth. men are, *u.*
Acts 24:15 resurrec. of just and *u.*
1 *Cor.* 6:1 any go to law bef. *u.*?
1 *Pet.* 3:18 Christ suf. just for *u.*
2 *Pet.* 2:9 res. *u.* to day of judg.
Rev. 22:11 th. is *u.* let him be *u.* st.

UNJUSTLY.

Ps. 82:2 how lo. will ye judge *u.*
Is. 26:10 in land of upri. deal *u.*

UNKNOWN.

Acts 17:23 inscript. To the *u.* G.
1 *Cor.* 14:2 sp. in *u.* tong. 4, 13, 27
14 if I pray in *u.* tongue
19 10,000 words in *u.* tongue
2 *Cor.* 6:9 as *u.* yet well known
Gal. 1:22 *u.* by face unto the

UNLADE.

Acts 21:3 ship was to *u.* burden

UNLAWFUL.

Acts 10:28 an *u.* thing for a man
2 *Pet.* 2:8 vexed his soul with *u.*

UNLEARNED.

Acts 4:13 perceived they were *u.*
1 *Cor.* 14:16 occupieth room of *u.*
23 come in those that are *u.* 24
2 *Tim.* 2:23 foolish and *u.* quest.
2 *Pet.* 3:16 they that are *u.* wrest

UNLEAVENED.

Ex. 12:39 they baked *u.* cakes
Lev. 2:4 an *u.* cake of fine flour
7:12 *u.* cakes mingled with oil
8:26 Moses took one *u.* cake
Num. 6:19 priest take one *u.* cake
Jos. 5:11 eat old corn of land *u.*
Jud. 6:19 Gid. made rea. *u.* cakes
20 take the flesh and *u.* cakes
21 ang. touc. flesh and *u.* cakes
1 *Chr.* 23:29 flour and *u.* cakes
1 *Cor.* 5:7 new lump, as ye are *u.*
See BREAD.

UNLOOSE.

Mark 1:7 shoes I am not worthy
to *u.* *Luke* 3:16; *John* 1:27

UNMARRIED.

1 *Cor.* 7:8 the *u.* 11 remain *u.*
32 he that is *u.* 34 *u.* woman

UNMERCIFUL.

Rom. 1:31 without affection, *u.*

UNMINDFUL.

Deut. 32:18 rock th. begat th. *u.*

UNMOVABLE.

Acts 27:41 forep. of ship rema. *v.*
1 *Cor.* 15:58 bret. be steadfast, *u.*

UNOCCUPIED.

Jud. 5:6 Sha. highways were *u.*

UNPERFECT.

Ps. 139:16 substan. yet being *u.*

UNPREPARED.

2 *Cor.* 9:4 if come and find you *u.*

UNPROFITABLE.

Job 15:3 sh. reason with *u.* talk
Mat. 25:30 cast *u.* ser. into dark.
Luke 17:10 say, We are *u.* serv.
Rom. 3:12 are altogether bec. *u.*
Tit. 3:9 genealogies, *u.* and vain
Phile. 11 in time past was *u.*
Heb. 13:17 wi. grief, th. is *u.*

UNPROFITABLENESS.

Heb. 7:18 the weakness and *u.*

UNPUNISHED.

Prov. 11:21 wicked sh. not be *u.*
16:5 the proud shall not be *u.*
17:5 glad at calamities not be *u.*
19:5 false witness not be *u.* 9
Jer. 25:29 utterly *u.* sh. not be *u.*
30:11 not leave thee altoget. *u.*
46:28 not leave thee wholly *u.*
49:12 sh. thou go *u.*? not go *u.*

UNQUENCHABLE.

Mat. 3:12 but burn the chaff with
u. fire, *Luke* 3:17

UNREASONABLE.

Acts 25:27 it seemeth *u.* to send
2 *Thes.* 3:2 delivered fr. *u.* men

UNREBUKABLE.

1 *Tim.* 6:14 keep this comm. *u.*

UNREPROVABLE.

Col. 1:22 to present you holy, *u.*

UNRIGHTEOUS.

Ex. 23:1 put not hand to be *u.*
Job 27:7 riseth ag. me be as *u.*
Ps. 71:4 deli. out of hand of *u.*
Is. 10:1 woe to th. that decree *u.*
55:7 *u.* man forsake thoughts
Luke 16:11 not faithful in *u.* ma.
Rom. 3:5 is G. *u.* who tak. ven.?
1 *Cor.* 6:9 the *u.* shall not inherit
Heb. 6:10 God is not *u.* to forget

UNRIGHTEOUSLY.

Deut. 25:16 all that do *u.* are ab.

UNRIGHTEOUSNESS.

Lev. 19:15 do no *u.* in judgm. 35
Ps. 92:15 there is no *u.* in him
Jer. 22:13 buildeth house by *u.*
Luke 16:19 friends of mam. of *u.*
John 7:18 true, no *u.* in him
Rom. 1:18 *u.* of men who hold
the truth in *u.*
29 filled with all *u.* fornication
2:8 them that obey *u.* indigna.
3:5 I our *u.* commend righte.
6:13 yield mem. as instru. of *u.*
9:14 is there *u.* with God?
2 *Cor.* 6:14 wh. fellow. with *u.*?
2 *Thes.* 2:10 wi. deceivab. of *u.*
12 beli. not, had pleasure in *u.*
Heb. 8:12 be merciful to their *u.*
2 *Pet.* 2:13 shall receive rew. of *u.*
15 Bal. who loved wages of *u.*
1 *John* 1:9 cleanse us from all *u.*
5:17 all *u.* is sin; th. is a sin not

UNRIPE.

Job 15:33 shall shake off *u.* grape

UNRULY.

1 *Thes.* 5:14 warn th. that are *u.*
Tit. 1:6 not accused of riot, or *u.*
10 there are many *u.* and vain
Jam. 3:8 the tongue is an *u.* evil

UNSATIABLE.

Ezek. 16:28 because thou wast *u.*

UNSAVORY.

Job 6:6 *u.* be eaten with. salt?

UNSEARCHABLE.

Job 5:9 G. doeth great th. and *u.*
Ps. 145:3 L. his greatness is *u.*
Prov. 25:3 heart of kings is *u.*
Rom. 11:33 how *u.* are his judg.
Eph. 3:8 preach *u.* riches of Ch.

UNSEEMLY.

Rom. 1:27 work. that which is *u.*
1 *Cor.* 13:5 doth not behave *u.*

UNSHOD.

Jer. 2:25 withhold from being *u.*

UNSKILFUL.

Heb. 5:13 babe is *u.* in the word

UNSPEAKABLE.

2 *Cor.* 9:15 thanks to G. for his *u.*
12:4 cau. up and heard *u.* words
1 *Pet.* 1:8 rejoice with joy *u.* full

UNSPOTTED.

Jam. 1:27 to keep himself *u.* from

UNSTABLE.

Gen. 49:4 *u.* as water, not excel
Jam. 1:8 doublemind. man is *u.*
2 *Pet.* 2:14 beguiling *u.* souls
3:16 unlearned and *u.* wrest

UNSTOPPED.

Is. 35:7 ears of the deaf sh. be *u.*

UNTAKEN.

2 *Cor.* 3:14 remain. veil *u.* away

UNTEMPERED.

Ezek. 13:10 others daubed it with
u. mortar, 11, 14, 15; 22:28

UNTHANKFUL.

Luke 6:35 he is kind to the *u.*
2 *Tim.* 3:2 blasphem. *u.* unholy

UNTIMELY.

Job 3:16 or as a hidden *u.* birth
Ps. 58:8 like *u.* birth of a woman
Ec. 6:3 an *u.* birth is better than
Rev. 6:13 as fig-trees cast. *u.* figs

UNTOWARD.

Acts 2:40 save from *u.* generation

UNWALLED.

Deut. 3:5 cities, beside *u.* towns
Est. 9:19 Jews dw. in *u.* towns
Ezek. 38:11 I will go to land of *u.*

UNWASHEN.

Mat. 15:20 to eat with *u.* hands,
Mark 7:2, 5

UNWEIGHED.

1 *K.* 7:47 Solomon left vessels *u.*

UNWISE.

Deut. 32:6 thus requi. L. *u.* peo.
Hos. 13:13 *u.* son, sh. not stay
Rom. 1:14 debtor to wise and *u.*
Eph. 5:17 be not *u.* but underst.

UNWITTINGLY.

Lev. 22:14 if eat of holy things *u.*
Jos. 20:3 that killeth person *u.* 5

UNWORTHY, ILY.

Acts 13:46 judge yourselves *u.* of
1 *Cor.* 6:2 are ye *u.* to judge the?
11:27 drink this cup of the L. *u.*
29 he that eateth and drink. *u.*

UP, *interjectional.*

Gen. 19:14 L. said, *u.* get ye out
44:4 Joseph said, *u.* follow after
Ex. 32:1 *u.* make us gods that
Jos. 7:13 *u.* sanctify the people
Jud. 4:14 *u.* for this is the day
8:20 to first-born, *u.* slay them
9:32 *u.* thou and the people that
19:28 *u.* and let us be going
1 *Sam.* 9:26 *u.* that I may send

UP.

Ps. 88:15 rea. to die fr. youth *u.*
Mat. 19:20 I kept fr. my youth *u.*

Luke 18:21 I kept fr. my youth *u.*
See DOWN.

UPBRAID, ED, ETH.

Jud. 8:15 with wh. ye did *u.* me
Mat. 11:20 then began he to *u.*
Mark 16:14 he *u.* th. with unbel.
Jam. 1:5 giveth liberally, *u.* not

UPHARSIN.

Dan. 5:25 Mene, Mene, Tekel, *U.*

UPHAZ.

Jer. 10:9 gold is brought from U.
Dan. 10:5 girded with gold of U.

UPHELD.

Is. 63:5 and my fury it *u.* me

UPHOLD.

Ps. 51:12 u. me with thy free Sp.
54:4 L. with th. that *u.* my soul
119:116 *u.* me according to word
Prov. 29:23 honor sh. *u.* humble
Is. 41:10 I will *u.* thee wi. right
42:1 my servant whom I *u.*
63:5 I wondered was none to *u.*
Ezek. 30:6 that *u.* Egypt sh. fall

UPHOLDEN.

Job 4:4 thy words have *u.* him
Prov. 20:28 throne is *u.* by mercy

UPHOLDEST, ETH.

Ps. 37:17 Lord *u.* the righteous
24 Lord *u.* him with his hand
41:12 thou *u.* me in mine integ.
63:8 follow, thy right hand *u.*
145:14 the Lord *u.* all that fall

UPHOLDING.

Heb. 1:3 *u.* all things by word of

UPPER.

Ex. 12:7 blood on *u.* door-posts
Lev. 13:45 put a cover. on *u.* lip
Deut. 24:6 no man take *u.* millst.
Jos. 15:19 gave *u.* spri. *Jud.* 1:15
Zep. 2:14 lodge in the *u.* lintels
Mark 14:15 will show you an *u.*
   room, *Luke* 22:12
Acts 1:13 went up into *u.* room
19:1 P. passed through *u.* coasts
See CHAMBER.

UPPERMOST.

Gen. 40:17 *u.* basket bakemeats
Is. 17:6 in top of the *u.* bough
9 cities sh. be as an *u.* branch
Mat. 23:6 they love the *u.* rooms,
   Mark 12:39 ; *Luke* 11:43

UPRIGHT.

Gen. 37:7 my sheaf. arose, sto. *u.*
Lev. 26:13 and made you go *u.*
1 *Sam.* 29:6 thou hast been *u.*
   with me, 2 *Chr.* 29:34
2 *Sam.* 22:24 I was also *u.* before
   him, *Ps.* 18:23
26 wi. *u.* show thy. *u. Ps.* 18:25
2 *Chr.* 29:34 Levites were more *u.*
Job 1:1 perf. and *u.* man, 8 ; 2:3
8:6 if *u.* he wou. awake for thee
12:4 *u.* man is laughed to scorn
17:8 *u.* men shall be astonished
Ps. 11:7 countenance behold *u.*
19:13 then sh. I be *u.* innocent
25:8 Lord is good and *u.* 92:15
33:1 for praise is comely for *u.*
37:14 as be of *u.* conversation
18 Lord knoweth days of the *u.*
37 perfect man, behold the *u.*
49:14 *u.* sh. have dominion over
111:1 praise L. in assemb. of *u.*
112:2 generation of *u.* be blesse.
4 to *u.* ariseth light in darkn.
119:137 *u.* are thy judgments
125:4 do good to the *u.* in heart
140:13 *u.* shall dwell in thy presence
Prov. 2:21 *u.* shall dwell in land
10:29 way of L. is strength to *u.*
11:3 integ. of *u.* guide them
6 righteousness of *u.* deli. them
11 by bless. of *u.* city exalted

20 *u.* in their way are his deli.
12:6 mouth of *u.* shall deli. them
13:6 righteousness keep. the *u.*
14:11 taberna. of *u.* sh. flourish
15:8 prayer of *u.* is his delight
16:17 way of *u.* to dep. fr. evil
21:18 transg. be ransom for *u.*
29 as for *u.* he direct his way
28:10 *u.* ha. good in possession
29:10 bloodthirsty hate the *u.*
27 *u.* is an abomina. to wicked
Ec. 7:29 found G. made man *u.*
12:10 written *u.* words of truth
Cant. 1:4 rememb. *u.* love thee
Is. 26:7 *u.* weigh path of just
Jer. 10:5 they are *u.* as palm-tr.
Dan. 8:18 touched and set me *u.*
11:17 enter and *u.* ones wi. him
Mic. 7:2 is none *u.* among men
4 *u.* sharper th. a thorn hedge
Hab. 2:4 lifted, not *u.* in him

See HEART, STAND, STOOD.

UPRIGHTLY.

Ps. 15:2 walketh *u.* shall abide
58:1 ye judge *u.* ? 75:2 judge *u.*
84:11 good fr. them that walk *u.*
Prov. 2:7 buckler to th. walk *u.*
10:9 walketh *u.* walketh surely
15:21 man of underst. walk. *u.*
28:18 whoso walk. *u.* be saved
Is. 33:15 speak. *u.* sh. dwell high
Amos 5:10 him that speaketh *u.*
Mic. 2:7 to him that walketh *u.*
Gal. 2:14 that th. walked not *u.*

UPRIGHTNESS.

1 *K.* 3:6 walked before thee in *u.*
1 *Chr.* 29:17 hast pleasure in *u.*
Job 4:6 and the *u.* of thy ways ?
33:23 to show unto man his *u.*
Ps. 9:8 judgment to people in *u.*
25:21 and *u.* preserve me
111:8 st. fast and are done in *u.*
143:10 lead me into land of *u.*
Prov. 2:13 who leave paths of *u.*
14:2 walketh in *u.* feareth Lord
28:6 better is poor walketh in *u.*
Is. 26:7 way of the just is *u.*
10 in land of *u.* deal unjustly
57:2 each one walking in his *u.*

See HEART.

UPRISING.

Ps. 139:2 my down-sitt. and *u.*

UPROAR.

1 *K.* 1:41 city being in an *u.*
Mat. 26:5 lest th. be *u. Mark* 14:2
Acts 17:5 Jews set city on an *u.*
19:40 question for this day's *u.*
20:1 after *u.* was ceased, Paul
21:31 Jerusalem in an *u.*
38 Egypt, who madest an *u.* ?

UPSIDE down.

2 *K.* 21:13 dish, turning it *u. d.*
Ps. 146:9 wicked he turn. *u. d.*
Is. 24:1 L. turneth earth *u. d.*
29:16 your turning of th. *u. d.*
Acts 17:6 have turn. world *u. d.*

UPWARD.

Num. 8:24 from 25 years old and
   u. 1 *Chr.* 23:3
1 *Sam.* 9:2 from should. *u.* 10:23
2 *K.* 19:30 bear fruit *u. Is.* 37:31
2 *Chr.* 31:16 fr. 3 years old and *u.*
Job 5:7 to trouble as sparks fly *u.*
Ec. 3:21 spirit of man goeth *u.*
Is. 8:21 curse God, and look *u.*
38:14 mine eyes fail looking *u.*
Ezek. 1:27 app. of loins *u.* 8:2
41:7 a winding about still *u.*
Hag. 2:15 fr. this day and *u.* 18

UR.

Gen. 11:28 before his father in U.
15:7 bro. thee out of U. *Neh.* 9:7
1 *Chr.* 11:35 Eliphal the son of U.

URGE, D.

Gen. 33:11 Jacob *u.* Esau, and he

Jud. 16:16 Delilah *u.* Samson
19:7 depart, his father-in-law *u.*
2 *K.* 2:17 *u.* him till ashamed
5:16 *u.* Elisha ; 23 he *u.* Gehazi
Luke 11:53 Pharisees began to *u.*

URGENT.

Ex. 12:33 Egypt. were *u.* on peo.
Dan. 3:22 king's conmmand. *u.*

URI.

Ex. 31:2 B. son of U. 35:30 ; 38:22;
   1 *Chr.* 2:20 ; 2 *Chr.* 1:5
1 *K.* 4:19 son of U. was in Gile.
Ezr. 10:24 Telem, and U. porters

URIAH, or URIJAH.

2 *Sam.* 11:3 Bath-sh. wife of U. ?
6 say, Send me U. the Hittite
14 sent it by U. 21 U. is dead
12:9 hast killed U. with sword
23:39 U. one of David's worthies
1 *K.* 15:5 only in matter of U.
1 *Chr.* 11:41 U. the Hittite
Ezr. 8:33 weighed by son of U.
Neh. 3:4 next repaired son of U.
21 Meremoth, son of U.
8:4 U. on his right hand
Is. 8:2 I took faithful witnes. U.
Mat. 1:6 Solomon of wife of U.

URIJAH.

2 *K.* 16:10 sent U. fashion of alt.
16 did U. as king A. comman.
Jer. 26:20 U. prophesied against
21 U. fled into Egypt

URIM.

Ex. 28:30 *u.* and thum. *Lev.* 8:8
Num. 27:21 coun. aft. judg. of *u.*
Deut. 33:8 let *u.* be with holy O.
1 *Sam.* 28:6 by *u.* nor prophets
Ezr. 2:63 prie. with *u. Neh.* 7:65

Against US.

Mark 9:40 he that is not *a. u.* is
   on our part, *Luke* 9:50
Rom. 8:31 G. for us, who *a. u.* ?

For US.

2 *Chr.* 13:10 as *f. u.* L. is our G.
Mat. 17:4 L. it is good *for u.* to
   be here, *Mark* 9:5 ; *Lu.* 9:33

From US.

1 *John* 2:19 they went out *fr. u.*

See DEPART.

Of US.

1 *John* 2:19 th. were not *of u.* for
   if they had been *of u.* they

To US-WARD.

Ps. 40:5 though. wh. are to *u.-w.*
Eph. 1:19 gre. of power to *u.-w.*
2 *Pet.* 3:9 long suffering to *u.-w.*

With US.

Mat. 1:23 interpret. is, G. *w. u.*

USE, Substantive.

Lev. 7:24 be used in any other *u.*
Deut. 26:14 aught for unclean *u.*
2 *Sam.* 1:18 teach Ju. *u.* of bow
1 *Chr.* 28:15 to *u.* of candlestick
Rom. 1:26 did change natural *u.*
Eph. 4:29 good to *u.* of edifying
2 *Tim.* 2:21 meet for master's *u.*
Heb. 5:14 by *u.* ha. senses exer.

USES.

Tit. 3:14 works for necessary *u.*

USE, Verb.

Lev. 19:26 neither *u.* enchantm.
Num. 10:2 *u.* trumpe. for calling
15:39 ye *u.* to go a whoring
1 *Chr.* 12:2 could *u.* right hand
Jer. 23:31 *u.* th. tongues and say
31:23 shall *u.* this speech in J.
46:11 vain *u.* many medicines
Ezek. 12:23 no more *u.* it a prov.
16:44 shall *u.* proverb ag. thee
18:2 that ye *u.* this proverb ?
3 not have occasion to use pro.
21:21 stood to *u.* divination
Mat. 6:7 *u.* not vain repetitions

Acts 14:5 to *u.* apostles despitef-
1 *Cor.* 7:21 made free, *u.* it rath-
    31 *u.* this world as not abus. it
2 *Cor.* 1:17 did I *u.* lightness
    3:12 we *u.* great plai. of speech
    13:10 present, I should *u.* sharp
Gal. 5:13 *u.* not liberty for occa.
1 *Tim.* 1:8 if a man *u.* it lawfully
    3:10 let th. *u.* office of a deacon
    5:23 *u.* wine for stomach's sake
1 *Pet.* 4:9 *u.* hospitality one to

USED.
Ex. 21:36 if ox hath *u.* to push
Lev. 7:24 may be *u.* in any use
Jud. 14:10 so *u.* you, men to do
    20 wh. Samson *u.* as his friend
2 *K.* 17:17 *u.* enchantments, 21:6
Jer. 2:24 ass *u.* to the wilderness
Ezek. 22:29 people *u.* oppression
    35:11 envy which thou hast *u.*
Hos. 12:10 *u.* similitude. by prop.
Mark 2:18 disc. of John *u.* to fa.
Acts 19:19 which *u.* curious arts
Rom. 3:13 with tongues *u.* deceit
1 *Cor.* 9:12 have not *u.* this pow.
    15 I ha. *u.* none of these things
1 *Thes.* 2:5 *u.* we flattering wor.
1 *Tim.* 3:13 ha. *u.* office of deac.
Heb. 10:33 companio. were so *u.*

USEST.
Ps. 119:132 *u.* to those that love

USETH.
Deut. 18:10 any th. *u.* divination
Est. 6:8 apparel king *u.* to wear
Prov. 15:2 the wise *u.* knowled.
    18:23 the poor *u.* entreati. rich
Jer. 22:13 *u.* service with. wages
Ezek. 16:44 that *u.* proverbs shall
Heb. 5:13 every one that *u.* milk

USING.
Col. 2:22 wh. are to perish wi. *u.*
1 *Pet.* 2:16 not *u.* liberty for clo.

USURP.
1 *Tim.* 2:12 wom. to *u.* authority

USURER.
Ex. 22:22 shalt not be as a *u.*

USURY.
Ex. 22:25 thou lay upon him *v.*
Lev. 25:36 take no *u.* of him, 37
Deut. 23:19 lend on *u.* to brother
    20 thou mayest lend upon *u.*
Neh. 5:7 exact *u.* 10 leave off *u.*
Ps. 15:5 putteth his money to *u.*
Prov. 28:8 *u.* increas. substance
Is. 24:2 tak. of *u.* so wi. gi. of *u.*
Jer. 15:10 neither lent on *u.* nor
    have men lent to me on *u.*
Ezek. 18:8 not giv. forth on *u.* 17
    13 given on *u.* 22:12 taken *u.*
Mat. 25:27 own wi. *u. Luke* 19:23

UTMOST OUTMOST.
Gen. 49:26 *u.* bound of the hills
Num. 22:41 see *u.* of peop. 23:13
Deut. 30:4 driven to *u.* parts
Jer. 9:26 *u.* corners, 25:23 ; 49:32

Luke 11:31 she came fr. *u.* parts

UTTER, Verb.
Lev. 5:1 if he do not *u.* it bear
Jos. 2:14 our life if ye *u.* not this
    20 if thou *u.* it we will be quit
Jud. 5:12 Debor. *u.* song. Arise
Job 8:10 shall th. not *u.* words ?
    15:2 wise man *u.* vain knowl. ?
    27:4 nor shall tongue *u.* deceit
    33:3 my lips shall *u.* knowledge
Ps. 78:2 I will *u.* dark sayings
    94:4 long shall *u.* hard things ?
    106:2 who can *u.* mighty acts ?
    119:171 my lips shall *u.* praise
    145:7 shall *u.* memory of goodn.
Prov. 14:5 false witn. will *u.* lies
    23:33 heart shall *u.* perv. things
Ec. 1:8 labor, man cannot *u.* it
    5:2 not hasty to *u.* before God
Is. 32:6 vile person will *u.* error
    48:20 *u.* it even to end of earth
Jer. 1:16 I will *u.* my judgments
    25:30 *u.* voice from holy habita.
Ezek. 24:3 *u.* a parab. unto rebel.
Joel 2:11 Lord shall *u.* his voice
    3:16 *u.* voice fr. Jeru. *Amos* 1:2
Mat. 13:35 I will *u.* things kept
1 *Cor.* 14:9 *u.* words easy under.
2 *Cor.* 12:4 not law. for man to *u.*

UTTER, Adjective.
1 *K.* 20:42 I appointed to *u.* des.
Nah. 1:8 make *u.* end of place
Zec. 14:11 no more *u.* destructi.

UTTERANCE.
Acts 2:4 spake as Spirit gave *u.*
1 *Cor.* 1:5 are enriched in all *u.*
2 *Cor.* 8:7 as ye abound in *u.* and
Eph. 6:19 pray. that *u.* be given
Col. 4:3 G. wo. open a door of *u.*

UTTERED.
Num. 30:6 husba. when she *u.* 8
Jud. 11:11 Jephthah *u.* his words
2 *Sam.* 22:14 Most High *u.* his
    voice, *Ps.* 46:6
Job 26:4 to whom hast *u.* words ?
    42:3 I *u.* that I understood not
Ps. 66:14 lips *u.* when in trouble
Hab. 3:10 deep *u.* his voice and
Rom. 8:26 groan. wh. can. be *u.*
Heb. 5:11 many th. hard to be *u.*
Rev. 10:3 seven thun. *u.* voices
    4 when seven thunders had *u.*

UTTERETH.
Job 15:5 thy mouth *u.* iniquities
Ps. 19:2 day unto day *u.* speech
Prov. 1:20 wisdom *u.* her voice
    21 she *u.* her words, saying
    10:18 that *u.* slander is a fool
    29:11 a fool *u.* all his mind, but
Jer. 10:13 wh. he *u.* voice, 51:16
Mic. 7:3 great man *u.* his desire

UTTERING.
Is. 59:13 *u.* from heart words

UTTERLY.
Ex. 17:14 *u.* put out remembra.

Jud. 15:2 I thou. hadst *u.* hated
    21:11 shall *u.* destroy eve. male
1 *Sam.* 15:3 *u.* dest. Amalekites
Is. 2:18 idols he shall *u.* abolish
    6:11 until land be *u.* desolate
    24:3 *u.* emptied ; 19 *u.* broken
Hos. 1:6 I will *u.* take th. away
    10:15 king of Israel *u.* cut off

See DESTROYED.

UTTERMOST.
2 *K.* 7:5 lep. came to *u.* part, 8
Neh. 1:9 were cast to *u.* part
Ps. 2:8 give *u.* parts for possess.
Mat. 5:26 till hast paid *u.* farth.
    12:42 ca. from *u.* parts to hear
Mark 13:27 gath. elect fr. *u.* part
Acts 24:22 I will kn. *u.* of your
1 *Thes.* 2:16 wrath is come to *u.*
Heb. 7:25 save them to *u.*

See UTMOST.

UZ.
Gen. 10:23 children of Aram ; U.
    36:28 of Dishan ; U. 1 *Chr.* 1:42
1 *Chr.* 1:17 Sh. Lud, Ara, and U.
Job 1:1 man in land of U. Job
Jer. 25:20 made king of U. drink
Lam. 4:21 O daught. of E. in U.

UZZA, UZZAH.
2 *Sam.* 6:3 U. drave, 1 *Chr.* 13:7, 9
    6 U. put forth his hand to ark
    8 L. had made breach upon U.
2 *K.* 21:18 buried in garden of U.
    26 Am. 1 *Chr.* 6:29 Mahli, U.
1 *Chr.* 8:7 remo. them, begat U.
Ezr. 2:49 childr. of U. *Neh.* 7:51

UZZIAH, *called* **AZARIAH, OZIAS.**
2 *K.* 15:13 in 39th year of U.
    34 Jotham did as his father U.
1 *Chr.* 6:24 a son of Kohath, U.
    11:44 U. the Ashterathite, vali.
    27:25 over storehouses son of U.
2 *Chr.* 26:1 all pe. made U. king
    8 Ammonites gave gifts to U.
    18 pertaineth not to thee, U. to
    21 U. a leper to day of death
Ezr. 10:21 U. son of Harim had
Neh. 11:4 dw. Athaiah son of U.
Is. 1:1 in the days of U. *Hos.* 1:1 ;
    Amos 1:1
    6:1 in year king U. died, I saw
Zec. 14:5 earthqu. in days of U.
Mat. 1:8 Joram begat O.
    9 O. begat Joatham

UZIEL.
Ex. 6:18 sons of Ko. Iz. U. *Num.*
    3:19 ; 1 *Chr.* 6:2, 18 ; 23:12
    22 and the sons of U. *Lev.* 10:4 ;
    Num. 3:30 ; 1 *Chr.* 15:10 ;
    23:20 ; 24:24
1 *Chr.* 4:42 of Simeon had U. for
    7:7 U. son of Bela ; 25:4 U. son
2 *Chr.* 29:14 Jeduthun ; She. U.
Neh. 3:8 U. of goldsmiths repair.

V

VAGABOND, S.
Gen. 4:12 a fugitive and *v.* shalt
    14 I shall be fugitive and *v.* in
Ps. 109:10 let his children be *v.*
Acts 19:13 certain *v.* Jews took

VAIN.
Ex. 5:9 let not regard *v.* words
Deut. 32:47 it is not a *v.* thing
Jud. 9:4 Abimelech hired *v.* per.
    11:3 gathered *v.* men to Jephth.
1 *Sam.* 12:21 shou. ye go after *v.*
2 *Sam.* 6:20 one of the *v.* fellows
2 *K.* 17:15 became *v.* and went
    18:20 are but *v.* words, *Is.* 36:5

---

2 *Chr.* 13:7 gath. to Jero. *v.* men
Job 11:11 he knoweth *v.* men
    12 for *v.* man would be wise
    15:2 wise man utter *v.* knowl.?
    16:3 sh. *v.* words have an end?
    27:12 are ye thus altogether *v.* ?
Ps. 2:1 imag. a *v.* thing, *Acts* 4:25
    26:4 I have not sat with *v.* per.
    33:17 horse *v.* thing for safety
    39:6 eve. man walk. in *v.* show
    60:11 *v.* is help of man, 108:12
    62:10 become not *v.* in robbery
    119:113 I hate *v.* thoughts
    127:2 *v.* for you to rise early

Prov. 12:11 followeth *v.* persons
    28:19 followeth *v.* persons shall
    31:30 favor deceitful, beauty *v.*
Ec. 6:12 all days of his *v.* life
Is. 1:13 br. no more *v.* oblations
    36:5 they are but *v.* words
Jer. 2:5 vanity, are become *v.*
    4:14 how long thy *v.* thoughts?
    10:3 customs of the peop. are *v.*
    23:16 prophets make you *v.* th.
Lam. 2:14 prophets have seen *v.*
    4:17 our eyes failed for *v.* help
Ezek. 12:24 no more any *v.* vision
    13:7 have ye not seen *v.* vision

Mal. 3:14 it is *v.* to serve God
Mat. 6:7 use not *v.* repetitions
Rom. 1:21 bec. *v.* in imaginatio.
1 *Cor.* 3:20 thoug. of wise are *v.*
15:14 is our preaching *v.* and
   your faith is also *v.* 17
Eph. 5:6 decei. you. wi. *v.* words
Col. 2:8 spoil you thro' *v.* deceit
1 *Tim.* 1:6 turn. aside to *v.* jang.
6:20 *v.* babblings, 2 *Tim.* 2:16
Tit. 1:10 unruly and *v.* talkers
Jos. 1:26 this man's religion is *v.*
2:20 know, O *v.* man, that faith
1 *Pet.* 1:18 redeemed fr. *v.* conv.

In VAIN.

Ex. 20:7 not take name of Lord
  in *v. Deut.* 5:11
Lev. 26:16 ye shall sow seed *in v.*
Job 9:29 why then labor I *in v. ?*
35:16 doth Job open mouth *in v.*
39:16 her labor is *in v.* without
41:9 behold, ho. of him is *in v.*
Ps. 89:47 hast th. m. men *in v. ?*
127:1 la. *in v.* watch. wak. *in v.*
Prov. 30:9 take name of G. *in. v.*
Is. 45:19 seed of Jac. seek *in v.*
49:4 I have labored *in v.* spent
  strength for naught *in v.*
Jer. 2:30 *in v.* have I smit. chil.
4:30 *in v.* sh. make thyself fair
8:8 are wise, lo, certainly *in v.*
46:11 *in v.* sh. thou use medici.
51:58 people shall labor *in v.*
Ezek. 6:10 kn. have not said *in v.*
Rom. 13:4 bear. not sword *in v.*
1 *Cor.* 15:2 unless ye belie. *in v.*
2 *Cor.* 6:1 not grace of G. *in v.*
Gal. 2:2 lest I should run *in v.*
  21 then Christ is dead *in v.*
1 *Thes.* 3:5 and our labor be *in v.*
Jam. 4:5 think scri. saith *in v. ?*

VAIN-GLORY.

Gal. 5:26 not be desirous of *v.-g.*
Phil. 2:3 noth. be done thro' *v.-g.*

VAINLY.

Col. 2:18 *v.* puffed up by fleshly

VALE.

Gen. 14:3 kings in *v.* of Sidd. 8
  10 *v.* of Siddim was full of pits
37:14 he sent Joseph out of *v.*
Deut. 1:7 in hills and in the *v.*
Jos. 10:40 J. smote country of *v.*
1 *K.* 10:27 cedars as sycamore-
  trees in *v.* 2 *Chr.* 1:15
Jer. 33:13 in cit. of *v.* sh. flocks

VALIANT.

1 *Sam.* 14:52 when S. saw *v.* man
16:18 son of J. a mighty *v.* man
18:17 be *v.* for me, and fight
26:15 Art not thou a *v.* man ?
31:12 the *v.* men took body of S.
2 *Sam.* 2:7 be *v.* 13:28; 17:10 is *v.*
11:16 he knew that *v.* men were
23:20 Benaiah, son of a *v.* man
  of Kabzeel, 1 *Chr.* 11:22
1 *K.* 1:42 for thou art a *v.* man
1 *Chr.* 7:2 sons of T. we. *v.* men
11:26 *v.* men of the armies were
Cant. 3:7 threescore *v.* men
  about it, of the *v.* of Israel
Is. 3:29 slew inhab. like *v.*
33:7 th. *v.* ones sh. cry without
Jer. 9:3 are not *v.* for the truth
46:15 are thy *v.* men. sw. away ?
Nah. 2:3 *v.* men are in scarlet
Heb. 11:34 through faith wax. *v.*

VALIANTEST.

Jud. 21:10 12,000 men of the *v.*

VALIANTLY.

Num. 24:18 and Israel shall do *v.*
1 *Chr.* 19:13 and let us behave *v.*
Ps. 60:12 we shall do *v.* 108:13
118:15 hand of Lord doeth *v.* 16

VALLEY.

Gen. 14:17 king of Sod. met at *v.*
Num. 32:9 went to *v.* of Eshcol
Deut. 1:24 came to *v.* of Eshcol
21:4 bring heifer to a rough *v.*
34:3 the plain of *v.* of Jericho
  6 he buried Moses in a *v.* in
Jos. 7:24 broug. them to *v.* of A.
10:12 moon, in *v.* of Aijalon
15:8 which is at end of the *v.*
Jud. 1:19 drive out inhabit. of *v.*
7:8 host of Midian was in *v.* 12
16:4 a woman in the *v.* of Sorek
1 *Sam.* 6:13 reap. wheat-ha. in *v.*
21:9 whom th. slewest in the *v.*
2 *Sam.* 5:18 spread themselves in
  v. of Rephaim, 22 ; 23:13
8:13 smi. Syrians in *v.* of salt
2 *K.* 2:16 Spirit cast him into *v.*
3:16 make this *v.* full of ditches
14:7 he slew of Edom in *v.* of
  salt, 1 *Chr.* 18:12
2 *Chr.* 35:22 fight in *v.* of Megid.
Job 21:33 clods of *v.* sh. be sweet
39:21 paweth in *v.* and rejoiceth
Ps. 23:4 I walk thro' *v.* of death
60:6 mete *v.* of Succoth, 108:7
84:6 passing through *v.* of Baca
Prov. 30:17 ravens of *v.* pick out
Cant. 6:11 went to see frui. of *v.*
Is. 17:5 gathereth in *v.* of Reph.
22:1 burden of *v.* of vision
  5 day of trouble in *v.* of vision
28:4 beauty on head of fat *v.*
  21 sh. be wroth as in *v.* of Gi.
40:4 every *v.* shall be exalted
65:10 *v.* of Ac. a place of herds
Jer. 2:23 see thy way in the *v.*
7:32 *v.* of H. *v.* of slaught. 19:6
21:13 ag. thee, O inhabita. of *v.*
48:8 *v.* perish, plain destroyed
49:4 why gloriest in flowi. *v. ?*
Ezek. 37:1 in *v.* full of bones
Hos. 1:5 bow of Is. in *v.* of Jezr.
2:15 give *v.* of A. door of hope
Joel 3:2 br. into *v.* of Jehoshap.
  14 multitudes in the *v.* of dec.
18 fountain shall water *v.* of S.
Zec. 12:11 mourning in *v.* of M.
14:4 there shall be a great *v.*
  5 shall flee to *v.* of mountains
Luke 3:5 every *v.* shall be filled
See GATE.

VALLEYS.

Num. 24:6 as *v.* are they spread
Deut. 8:7 depths spring out of *v.*
11:11 a land of hills and *v.*
1 *K.* 20:28 but he is not G. of *v.*
Job 30:6 to dwell in clifts of *v.*
39:10 he harrow *v.* after thee ?
Ps. 65:13 *v.* covered with corn
104:8 go down by *v.* unto place
  10 sendeth springs into the *v.*
Cant. 2:1 rose of Shar. lily of *v.*
Is. 22:7 thy *v.* full of chariots
28:1 which are on head of fat *v.*
41:18 open fount. in midst of *v.*
57:5 slaying the children in *v.*
Jer. 49:4 wheref. glori. thou in *v.*
Ezek. 6:3 hath L. to *v.* 36:4, 6
7:16 on mount. like doves of *v.*

VALOR.

Jud. 3:29 slew 10,000 men of *v.*
6:12 with th. mighty man of *v.*
11:1 Jephth. mighty man of *v.*
1 *K.* 11:28 Jeroboam, a man of *v.*
2 *K.* 5:1 Naa. mighty man in *v.*
1 *Chr.* 12:28 Zadok, a man of *v.*
2 *Chr.* 17:17 Eliada, a man of *v.*
See Mighty MEN.

VALUE.

Job 13:4 ye are physici. of no *v.*
Mat. 10:31 ye are of more *v.* than
  many sparrows, *Luke* 12:7

VALUE, ST.

Lev. 27:8 the priest shall *v.* him

  12 as thou *v.* it who art priest
Mat. 27:9 whom they of I. did *v.*

VALUED.

Lev. 27:16 barley *v.* at 50 shekels
Job 28:16 wisdom cannot be *v.*
  19 nei. shall it be *v.* with gold
Mat. 27:9 pri. of him that was *v.*

VANISH, ED, ETH.

Job 6:17 they wax warm, they *v.*

Job. 7:9 as cloud is consumed, *v.*
Is. 51:6 heavens shall *v.* away
Jer. 49:7 is their wisdom *v. ?*
Luke 24:31 *v.* out of their sight
1 *Cor.* 13:8 knowledge, it shall *v.*
Heb. 8:13 wax. old, ready to *v.*
Jam. 4:14 life is a vapor that *v.*

VANITY.

2 *K.* 17:15 followed fr. beca. vain
Job 7:3 ma. possess months of *v.*
  16 let me alone, days are *v.*
15:31 let not him that is deceiv.
  trust in *v.* sh. be recomp.
35 whschief, and bring forth *v.*
31:5 if I walked with *v.* or hast.
35:13 sure G. will not hear *v.*
Ps. 4:2 how long will ye love *v. ?*
10:7 under his tongue misc. *v.*
12:2 they speak *v.* every one to
24:4 hath not lifted up soul to *v.*
39:5 best estate is altogether *v.*
  11 man is *v.* 94:11 thoughts *v.*
41:6 he speaketh *v.* 144:8, 11
62:9 are *v.* and lighter than *v.*
78:33 days did he consume in *v.*
119:37 turn eyes from behold. *v.*
144:4 man is like to *v.* a shadow
Prov. 13:11 wealth gotten by *v.*
21:6 treas. by lying tong. is *v.*
22:8 soweth iniq. shall reap *v.*
30:8 remove from me *v.* and lies
Ec. 1:2 *v.* of vanities, saith the
  preacher, all is *v.* 14 ; 3:19 ;
  11:8 ; 12:8
2:1 this is also *v.* 15, 19, 21, 23 ;
  4:8, 16 ; 5:10 ; 6:2, 9 ; 7:6 ;
  8:10, 14
  11 beh. all was *v.* 17, 26 ; 4:4
4:7 I saw *v.* 6:4 cometh with *v.*
6:11 many things that incre. *v.*
7:15 thi. I ha. seen in days of *v.*
8:14 a *v.* that is done on earth
9:9 with wife all the days of *v.*
11:10 childhood and youth are *v.*
Is. 5:18 dr. iniq. with cords of *v.*
30:28 sift nations wi. sieve of *v.*
40:17 nations to him counted *v.*
  23 maketh judges of earth as *v.*
41:29 behold, they are all *v.* 44:9
57:13 wind carry, *v.* take them
58:9 take away *v.* 59:4 tru. in *v.*
Jer. 2:5 th. have walked after *v.*
10:15 they are *v.* errors, 51:18
16:19 fathers have inherited *v.*
18:15 people burnt incense to *v.*
Ezek. 13:6 th. have seen *v.* 22:28
  8 because ye have spoken *v.*
  9 prophets that see *v.* 21:29
  23 sh. see no more *v.* nor div.
Hos. 12:11 *v.* they sacri. bullocks
Hab. 2:13 weary themsel. for *v.*
Zec. 10:2 for idols have spok. *v.*
Rom. 8:20 creature subject to *v.*
Eph. 4:17 as Gentiles walk, in *v.*
2 *Pet.* 2:18 speak gre. words of *v.*

VANITIES.

Deut. 32:21 provo. me with their
  v. 1 *K.* 16:13,26 ; *Jer.* 8:19
Ps. 31:6 that regard lying *v.*
Ec. 1:2 vanity of *v.* saith, 12:8
5:7 in multi. of dreams are *v.*
Jer. 10:8 stock is doctrine of *v.*
14:22 any am. *v.* can cause rain ?
Jon. 2:8 that observe lying *v.*
Acts 14:15 ye should turn from *v.*

VAPOR, S.

Job 36:27 pour rain accord. to *v.*
  33 cattle also concerning the *v.*

VAPOR

Ps. 135:7 causeth *v.* to ascend
148:8 and *v.* fulfilling his word
Acts 2:19 signs in earth, *v.*
Jam. 4:14 what is your life? *a v.*

VARIABLENESS.

Jam. 1:17 lights, wi. wh. is no *v.*

VARIANCE.

Mat. 10:35 set a man at *v.* ag. fa.
Col. 5:20 works of flesh, hat. *v.*

VASHTI.

Est. 1:9 V. queen made a feast
12 queen V. refused to come at
19 V. come no more bef. king
2:17 made her queen inst. of V.

VAUNT, ETH.

Jud. 7:2 lest Isr. *v.* against me
1 *Cor.* 13:4 charity *v.* not itself

VEHEMENT.

Cant. 8:6 love, th. ha. a *v.* flame
Jon. 4:8 G. prepared a *v.* wind
2 *Cor.* 7:11 *v.* desire it wrought

VEHEMENTLY.

Mark 14:31 Peter spake more *v.*
Luke 6:48 beat *v.* on house, 49
11:53 Pha. began to urge him *v.*
23:10 stood and *v,* accused him

VEIL.

Gen. 24:65 Rebekah took a *v.*
38:14 Tam. covered hers. with *v.*
Ex. 26:31 sh. make a *v.* of blue
34:33 Moses put a *v.* on face, 35
36:35 *v.* of blue, 2 *Chr.* 3:14
Lev. 16:2 come not within the *v.*
15 bring his blood within *v.*
24:3 without *v.* sh. Aaron order
Ruth 3:15 bring *v.* th. hast upon
Cant. 5:7 keep. took away my *v.*
Is. 25:7 destroy *v.* spread over
Mat. 27:51 *v.* of temple was rent,
Mark 15:38 ; *Luke* 23:45
2 *Cor.* 3:13 M. put a *v.* over face
14 same *v.* untaken away, wh
v. is done away in Christ
15 to this day *v.* is upon heart
16 the *v.* shall be taken away
Heb. 6:19 wh. entereth within *v.*
9:3 aft. second *v.* the tabernacle
10:20 thro' the *v.* that is to say

Is. 3:23 L. will take away the *v.*

VEIN.

Job 28:1 there is a *v.* for silver

VENGEANCE.

Gen. 4:15 *v.* sh. be taken on him
Deut. 32:35 to me belongeth *v.*
and, *Ps.* 94:1 ; *Heb.* 10:30
41 render *v.* to mine enemies
43 will render *v.* to adversaries
Jud. 11:36 Lord hath taken *v.*
Ps. 58:10 rejoice wh. he seeth *v.*
99:8 took. *v.* of their inventions
149:7 execute *v.* upon heathen
Prov. 6:34 not spare in day of *v.*
Is. 34:8 day of *v.* 61:2 ; *Jer.* 51:6
35:4 your God will come with *v.*
47:3 I will take *v. Jer.* 51:36
59:17 he put on garments of *v.*
63:4 for day of *v.* is in my heart
Jer. 11:20 let see thy *v.* 20:12
46:10 day of *v.* 50:15 *v.* of the
Lord, 28
50:28 *v.* of L. *v.* of temp. 51:11
Lam. 3:60 hast seen all their *v.*
Ezek. 24:8 cause fury to take *v.*
25:12 by taking *v.* hath offended
14 *v.* on Edom by hand of Isr.
15 bec. Philistines have tak. *v.*
17 when I lay *v.* on Philistines
Mic. 5:15 execute *v.* 25:17
Nah. 1:2 Lord will take *v.* on his
adversaries
Luke 21:22 for these be days of *v.*
Acts 28:4 *v.* suffereth not to live
Rom. 3:5 unright. who tak. *v. ?*

12:19 *v.* is mine, saith the Lord
2 *Thes.* 1:8 flaming fire, taking *v.*
Jude 7 suffering *v.* of eternal fire

VENISON.

Gen. 25:28 because he eat of *v.*
27:3 go to field, take some *v.* 7
19 arise, and eat of my *v.* 31

VENOM.

Deut. 32:33 wine is *v.* of asps

VENOMOUS.

Acts 28:4 barbarians saw *v.* beast

VENT.

Job 32:19 as wine wh. hath no *v.*

VENTURE.

1 *K.* 22:34 a certain man drew a
bow at a *v.* 2 *Chr.* 18:33

VERIFIED.

Gen. 42:20 so sh. your words be *v.*
1 *K.* 8:26 and let thy word be *v.*
2 *Chr.* 6:17

VERILY.

Gen. 42:21 we are *v.* guilty
Mat. 5:88 *v.* I say unto you, 6:2,
5, 16 ; 8:10 ; 10:15, 23, 42 ;
11:11 ; 13:17 ; 16:28 ; 17:20 ;
18:3, 13, 18 ; 19:23, 28 ; 21:21,
31 ; 23:36 ; 24:2, 34, 47 ; 25:12,
40, 45 ; 26:13 ; *Mark* 3:28 ;
6:11 ; 8:12 ; 9:1, 41 ; 10:15, 29 ;
11:23 ; 12:43 ; 13:30 ; 14:9, 18,
25 ; *Luke* 4:24 ; 11:51 ; 12:37 ;
13:35 ; 18:17, 29 ; 21:32
26 *v.* I say unto thee, 26:34 ;
Mark 14:30 ; *Luke* 23:43
Acts 22:3 am *v.* a Jew born in T.
1 *Cor.* 5:3 I *v.* as absent in body
Heb. 2:16 *v.* he took not nature
1 *John* 2:5 in him *v.* is love of G.

VERILY, VERILY.

John 1:51 *v. v.* I say unto you,
5:19, 24, 25 ; 6:26, 32, 47, 53 ;
8:34, 51, 58 ; 10:1, 7 ; 12:24 ;
13:16, 20, 21 ; 14:12 ; 16:20, 23
John 3:3 *v. v.* I say unto thee,
5:11 ; 13:38 ; 21:18

VERITY.

Ps. 111:7 works of hands are *v.*
1 *Tim.* 2:7 teach. in faith and *v.*

VERMILION.

Jer. 22:14 and painted with *v.*
Ezek. 23:14 C. portrayed with *v.*

VERY.

Gen. 27:21 thou be my *v.* son E.
Ex. 9:16 in *v.* deed for this I
Deut. 30:14 word is *v.* nigh to th.
1 *Sam.* 25:34 in *v.* deed exc. thou
26:4 Saul was come in *v.* deed
Prov. 17:9 he separat. *v.* friends
John 7:26 this is *v.* Ch. *Acts* 9:22
8:4 taken in adultery, in *v.* act
1 *Thes.* 5:23 *v.* G. of peace sanc.

VESSEL.

Deut. 23:24 not put any in thy *v.*
1 *Sam.* 21:5 sancti. this day in *v.*
1 *K.* 17:10 fetch me water in *v.*
2 *K.* 4:6 bring *v.* not a *v.* more
Ps. 2:9 pieces like a potter's *v.*
31:12 I am like a broken *v.*
Prov. 25:4 come forth *v.* for finer
Is. 66:20 bring offer. in clean *v.*
Jer. 18:4 *v.* mar. in hand of pot.
22:28 *v.* wher. is no pleasure ?
25:34 ye sh. fall like a pleas. *v.*
48:11 M. not emptied fr. *v.* to *v.*
38 I have broken M. like a *v.*
51:34 Neb. made me empty *v.*
Ezek. 4:9 put them in one *v.* and
15:3 a pin of it to hang any *v. ?*
Hos. 8:8 *v.* wherein is no pleas.
Mark 11:16 carry *v.* thro' temple
Luke 8:16 covereth candle wi. *v.*
Acts 9:15 a chosen *v.* unto me
10:11 Pe. saw a certain *v.* 11:5

Rom. 9:21 make one *v.* to honor
1 *Thes.* 4:4 his *v.* in sanctificati.
2 *Tim.* 2:21 sh. be *v.* to honor
1 *Pet.* 3:7 to wife as to weaker *v.*

VESSELS.

Gen. 43:11 best fruits in your *v.*
Ex. 40:10 anoint *v. Lev.* 8:11
Num. 18:3 nigh *v.* of sanctuary
1 *Sam.* 9:7 bread spent in our *v.*
21:5 *v.* of young men are holy
2 *K.* 4:3 go, borrow *v.* abroad
2 *Chr.* 29:19 *v.* A. did cast away
Ezr. 1:7 Cyrus brought forth *v.*
5:15 take *v.* 7:19 *v.* given thee
Neh. 13:9 thither brought I *v.*
Is. 18:2 in *v.* of bulrushes
22:24 *v.* of small quantity, *v.* of
52:11 be clean that bear *v.* of L.
65:4 abominable things is in *v.*
Jer. 14:3 returned with *v.* empty
27:16 *v.* of L.'s house, 28:3
Dan. 5:23 brought *v.* of house
Hos. 13:15 treasure of pleas. *v.*
Hag. 2:16 dr. fifty *v.* out of press
Mat. 13:48 gathered good into *v.*
25:4 but wise took oil in their *v.*
Rom. 9:22 *v.* of wr. 23 *v.* of mercy
Rev. 2:27 as *v.* of potter be brok.

See BRASS, EARTHEN, GOLD, SIL-
VER.

VESTMENTS.

2 *K.* 10:22 *v.* for worshippers

VESTRY.

2 *K.* 10:22 said to him over *v.*

VESTURE, S.

Gen. 41:42 arrayed Joseph in *v.*
Deut. 22:12 ma. fringe on thy *v.*
Ps. 22:18 they cast lots upon my
v. Mat. 27:35 ; *John* 19:24
102:26 as a *v.* sh. thou change th.
Heb. 1:12 as a *v.* sh. thou fold th.
Rev. 19:13 clothed with *v.* dipt
16 on his *v.* and thigh a name

VEX.

Ex. 22:21 and thou shalt not *v.* a
stranger, *Lev.* 19:33
Lev. 18:18 wife to sister to *v.* her
Num. 25:17 *v.* the Midianites
18 they *v.* you with their wiles
33:55 ye let remain sh. *v.* you
2 *Sam.* 12:18 how will he *v.* him.
2 *Chr.* 15:6 God did *v.* them
Job 19:2 how long will ye *v.* soul
Ps. 2:5 *v.* th. in his displeasure
Is. 7:6 let us go ag. J. and *v.* it
11:13 Judah shall not *v.* Ephr.
Ezek. 32:9 I will *v.* hearts of peo.
Hab. 2:7 not awake that *v.* thee ?
Acts 12:1 Herod did *v.* the church

VEXATION, S.

Deut. 28:20 L. sh. send on thee *v.*
2 *Chr.* 15:5 *v.* were on inhabit.
Ec. 1:14 *v.* of spirit, 2:11, 17
17 *v.* of spi. 2:26 ; 4:4, 16 ; 6:9
2:22 ha. man of *v.* of his heart ?
4:6 hands full with *v.* of spirit
Is. 9:1 not such as was in her *v.*
28:19 a *v.* to understand report
65:14 ye sh. howl for *v.* of spirit

VEXED.

Num. 20:15 Egyptians *v.* us and
Jud. 2:18 of them that *v.* them
10:8 that year Ammonites *v.* Is.
16:16 his soul was *v.* unto death
1 *Sam.* 14:47 Saul *v.* his enemies
2 *Sam.* 13:2 Amnon *v.* fell sick
2 *K.* 4:27 alone, for his soul is *v.*
Neh. 9:27 enemies who *v.* them
Job 27:2 Almighty *v.* my soul
Ps. 6:2 my bones *v.* 3 soul *v.*
10 let enemies be asha. and *v.*
Is. 63:10 they rebelled and *v.* Sp.
Ezek. 22:5 infamous and much *v.*
7 *v.* fatherless ; 29 *v.* the poor

VIAL.

Mat. 15:22 daugh. is *v.* wi. devil
17:15 he is lunatic and sore *v.*
Luke 6:18 they that were *v.* with
unclean spirits. *Acts* 5:16
2 *Pet.* 2:7 Lot *v.* with conversat.
8 *v.* his righteous soul fr. day

VIAL.

1 *Sam.* 10:1 Sam. took a *v.* of oil
Rev. 16:2 first angel pour. his *v.*
3 second *v.* on sea ; 4 third *v.*
8 fourth *v.* 10 fifth *v.* on beast
12 sixth *v.* 17 sev. *v.* into air

VIALS.

Rev. 5:8 golden *v.* full of odors
15:7 gave seven angels seven *v.*
16:1 pour out *v.* of wrath of G.
17:1 angels wh. had 7 *v.* 21:9

VICTORY.

2 *Sam.* 19:2 *v.* th. day was turn.
22:10 L. wrought a great *v.* 12
1 *Chr.* 29:11 thine, O L., is the *v.*
Ps. 98:1 arm hath gotten him *v.*
Is. 25:8 will swallow up death in
v. 1 *Cor.* 15:54
Mat. 12:20 send judgm. unto *v.*
1 *Cor.* 15:55 O gra. where thy *v.* ?
57 to God, who giv. us the *v.*
1 *John* 5:4 this is the *v.* even fai.
Rev. 15:2 had got. *v.* over beast

VICTUAL, S.

Gen. 14:11 goods of Sod. and *v.*
Ex. 12:39 nei. had prepared *v.*
Lev. 25:37 nor lend him thy *v.*
Deut. 23:19 usury of *v.* of any th.
Jos. 1:11 prepare *v.* 9:11 take *v.*
9:14 the men took of their *v.*
Jud. 17:10 will gi. apparel and *v.*
1 *Sam.* 22:10 gave *v.* and sword
1 *K.* 4:7 provided *v.* for king, 27
11:18 Pharaoh appointed him *v.*
Neh. 10:31 peo. bring *v.* on sab.
13:15 ag. th. in day they sold *v.*
Jer. 40:5 capt. gave Jeremiah *v.*
44:17 then had we plenty of *v.*
Mat. 14:15 to buy *v. Luke* 9:12

VIEW, ED.

Jos. 2:7 *v.* land ; 7:2 *v.* country
7:2 *v.* Ai ; *Ezr.* 8:1 *v.* people
2 *K.* 2:7 prophets stood to *v.* 15
Neh. 2:13 *v.* walls of Jerus. 15

VIGILANT.

1 *Tim.* 3:2 a bishop must be *v.*
1 *Pet.* 5:8 be *v.* bec. your advers.

VILE.

Deut. 25:3 lest thy brot. seem *v.*
Jud. 19:24 do not so *v.* a thing
1 *Sam.* 3:13 sons made thems. *v.*
15:9 every thing that was *v.*
2 *Sam.* 6:22 I will yet be more *v.*
Job 18:3 why are we reputed *v.* ?
40:4 I am *v.* what shall I ans. ?
Ps. 15:4 *v.* person is contemned
Is. 32:5 *v.* person be no more
6 *v.* person will speak villany
Jer. 15:19 take prec. from the *v.*
29:17 I will make them *v.* figs
Lam. 1:11 O L. for I am bec. *v.*
Dan. 11:21 sh. stand a *v.* person
Nah. 1:14 make grave, th. art *v.*
3:6 cast filth on th. make thee *v.*
Rom. 1:26 G. gave them up to *v.*
Phil. 3:21 shall change *v.* body
Jam. 2:2 a poor man in *v.* raim.

2 *Sam.* 1:21 shield *v.* cast away

VILER, VILEST.

Job 30:8 they were *v.* than earth
Ps. 12:8 when *v.* men are exalted

VILLAGE.

Mat. 21:2 go into *v.* over ag. you,
Mark 11:2 ; *Luke* 19:30
Luke 24:13 two of th. went to *v.*

VILLAGES.

Lev. 25:31 houses of *v.* counted

Jud. 5:7 inhabitants of *v.* ceased
Neh. 6:2 meet in one of the *v.*
Est. 9:19 J. of *v.* made 14th day
Cant. 7:11 let us lodge in *v.*
Ezek. 38:11 to land of unwall. *v.*
Hab. 3:14 strike head of his *v.*
Mat. 14:15 they may go into the
the *v.* and buy, *Mark* 6:36

See CITIES.

VILLANY.

Is. 32:6 vile person will speak *v.*
Jer. 29:23 committed *v.* in Israel

VINE.

Gen. 40:9 a *v.* was before me
10 in *v.* were three branches
49:11 Judah binding his foal to
v. his ass's colt to choice *v.*
Lev. 25:5 nor ga. grapes of *v.* 11
Num. 6:4 eat nothing made of *v.*
Deut. 32:32 their *v.* is *v.* of Sod.
Jud. 9:12 trees said to *v.* reign
13:14 not eat that cometh of *v.*
1 *K.* 4:25 ev. man under his *v.*
2 *K.* 4:39 found a wild *v.* gather.
18:31 eat of own *v. Is.* 36:16
Job 15:33 sha. off grape as the *v.*
Ps. 80:8 hast bro. *v.* out of Eg.
14 look down, and visit this *v.*
128:3 wife sh. be as a fruitful *v.*
Cant. 6:11 whe. *v.* flourish. 7:12
7:8 breasts as clusters of the *v.*
Is. 5:2 plant. it with choicest *v.*
16:8 *v.* of Sibmah languisheth
9 bewail *v.* of Sib. *Jer.* 48:32
24:7 wine mourneth, *v.* languis.
32:12 sh. lament for fruitful *v.*
34:4 as leaf falleth from the *v.*
Jer. 2:21 I planted th. a noble *v.*
how turned into strange *v.* ?
6:9 glean remnant of Is. as a *v.*
8:13 no grapes on *v.* nor figs
Ezek. 15:2 *v.* more th. any tree ?
6 *v.* which I have given for fuel
17:6 it became a spreading *v.*
7 *v.* did bend roots towards
19:10 moth. is like *v.* in blood
Hos. 10:1 Israel is an empty *v.*
14:7 revive as corn, grow as *v.*
Joel 1:7 he laid my *v.* waste
12 *v.* is dried up, the fig-tree
2:22 fig-tree and *v.* yield stren.
Mic. 4:4 sit ev. man under his *v.*
Hag. 2:19 *v.* hath not bro. forth
Zec. 3:10 call ev. man under *v.*
8:12 the *v.* shall give her fruit
Mal. 3:11 nei. *v.* cast her fruit
Mat. 26:29 not drink of fruit of *v.*
Mark 14:25 ; *Luke* 22:18
John 15:1 I am the true *v.* 5
4 bear fruit, exc. it abide in *v.*
Jam. 3:12 can a *v.* bear figs?
Rev. 14:18 ga. clusters of *v.* 19

VINES.

Num. 20:5 no pl. of *v.* or pomeg.
Deut. 8:8 a land of wheat and *v.*
Ps. 78:47 he destroyed their *v.*
105:33 smote th. *v.* and fig-trees
Cant. 2:13 *v.* give a good smell
15 foxes, that spoil the *v.* our
v. have tender grapes
Is. 7:23 th. were a thousand *v.*
Jer. 5:17 they shall eat up thy *v.*
31:5 plant *v.* on mountains
Hos. 2:12 I will destroy her *v.*
Hab. 3:17 nei. fruit be in the *v.*

VINE-DRESSERS.

2 *K.* 25:12 left the poor of land to
be *v.-d. Jer.* 52:16
2 *Chr.* 26:10 Uzziah had *v.-d.*
Is. 61:5 sons of alien your *v.-d.*
Joel 1:11 be ashamed, O ye *v.-d.*

VINEGAR.

Num. 6:3 Naz. shall drink no *v.*
Ruth 2:14 dip thy morsel in *v.*
Ps. 69:21 gave *v. Mat.* 27:34
Prov. 10:26 as *v.* to the teeth

25:20 as *v.* upon nitre, so is he
Mat. 27:48 took a sponge and
filled it with *v. Mark* 15:36 ;
Luke 23:36 ; *John* 19:29, 30

VINEYARD.

Gen. 9:20 Noah planted a *v.* and
Ex. 22:5 if cause *v.* to be eaten
23:11 thou sh. deal with thy *v.*
Lev. 19:10 shalt not glean thy *v.*
25:3 six years sh. prune thy *v.*
4 nei. sow field, nor prune *v.*
Deut. 20:6 what man planted *v.* ?
22:9 not sow *v.* with div. seeds
23:24 comest into neighbor's *v.*
24:21 when gather. grapes of *v.*
28:30 plant *v.* not gath. grapes
1 *K.* 21:1 Nabo. had a *v.* hard by
2 give me thy *v.* I will give
thee a better *v.* 6
7 I will give thee *v.* of Naboth
Ps. 80:15 *v.* thy ri. hand planted
Prov. 24:30 I went by *v.* of man
31:16 hand she planteth a *v.*
Cant. 1:6 own *v.* have I not kept
8:11 Solomon had a *v.* he let *v.*
12 my *v.* is bef. me, O Solom.
Is. 1:8 Z. is left as cottage in *v.*
3:14 for ye have eaten up the *v.*
5:1 my beloved touching his *v.*
7 *v.* of L. of hosts is hou. of Is.
10 ten acres of *v.* yi. one bath
27:2 sing to her, *v.* of red wine
Jer. 12:10 pastors destroy. my *v.*
35:7 Rechab. sh. not plant *v.* 9
Mic. 1:6 Samaria as plant. of *v.*
Mat. 20:1 hire labor. into his *v.*
4 he said, Go ye also into *v.* 7
21:28 go work to-day in my *v.*
33 certain householder planted
v. Mark 12:1 ; *Luke* 20:9
Luke 13:6 fig-tree planted in *v.*
7 said unto dresser of *v.*
1 *Cor.* 9:7 planteth *v.* eat. not ?

VINEYARDS.

Num. 16:14 not giv. inher. of *v.*
20:17 not pass through *v.* 21:22
22:24 angel stood in path of *v.*
Deut. 6:11 he sware to give thee
v. Jos. 24:13 ; *Neh.* 9:25
28:39 shalt plant *v.* dress them
Jud. 15:5 the foxes burnt up *v.*
21:20 go and lie in wait in *v.*
1 *Sam.* 8:14 take yo. fields and *v.*
22:7 will son of J. give you *v.* ?
2 *K.* 5:26 is it time to receive *v.* ?
18:32 I take you to a land of *v.*
19:29 in the third year plant *v.*
1 *Chr.* 27:27 over *v.* was Shimei
Neh. 5:3 have mortgaged our *v.*
11 restore *v.* and olive-yards
Job 24:18 behold. not way of *v.*
Ps. 107:37 sow fields, plant *v.*
Ec. 2:4 houses, I planted me *v.*
Cant. 1:6 made me keeper of *v.*
14 as cluster of camphire in *v.*
7:12 let us get up early to the *v.*
Is. 16:10 in *v.* sh. be no singing
65:21 shall plant *v.* and eat the
fruit of them, *Amos* 9:14
Jer. 32:15 *v.* sh. be possessed ag.
39:10 Nebuzar-ad. gave poor *v.*
Ezek. 28:26 build hous. and pl. *v.*
Hos. 2:15 I will give her her *v.*
Amos 4:9 palmer-worm devo. *v.*
5:11 ye have planted *v.*
17 in all *v.* shall be wailing
Zep. 1:13 sh. plant *v.* not drink

VINTAGE.

Lev. 26:5 thresh. shall reach to
v. the *v.* reach to sowl. time
Jud. 8:2 better than *v.* of Abi. ?
Job 24:6 they gather *v.* of wick.
Is. 16:10 made *v.* shout. to cease
24:13 gleaning when *v.* is done
32:10 the *v.* shall fail, gathering
Jer. 48:32 spoiler is fallen up. *v.*
Mic. 7:1 as grape-gleanings of *v.*

Zec. 11:2 for. of *v.* is come down

VIOL, S.

Is. 5:12 harp and *v.* and wine
14:11 noise of *v.* brought down
Amos 5:23 not hear melody of *v.*
6:5 that chant to sound of *v.*

VIOLATED.

Ezek. 22:26 priests ha. *v.* my law

VIOLENCE.

Gen. 6:11 earth filled with *v.* 12
Lev. 6:2 if lie in thi. taken by *v.*
2 *Sam.* 22:3 savest me from *v.*
Ps. 11:5 loveth *v.* his soul hateth
55:9 I have seen *v.* and strife in
58:2 weigh the *v.* of your hands
72:14 shall redeem th. soul fr. *v.*
73:6 *v.* covereth them as a gar.
Prov. 4:17 they drink wine of *v.*
10:6 *v.* covereth the mouth, 11
13:2 transgressors shall eat *v.*
28:17 man that doeth *v.* to blood
Is. 53:9 he had done no *v.*
59:6 act of *v.* is in their hands
60:18 *v.* shall no more be heard
Jer. 6:7 *v.* and spoil heard in her
20:8 I spake, I cried *v.* and spoil
22:3 do no *v.* to the stranger
17 th. eyes, thy heart are for *v.*
51:35 *v.* done to me and flesh
46 *v.* in the land, ruler ag. rul.
Ezek. 7:11 *v.* risen up into a rod
23 for the city is full of *v.*
8:17 filled land with *v.* 28:16
12:19 because of the *v.* of them
18:7 spoiled none by *v.* 16, 18
45:9 Israel, remove *v.* and spoil
Joel 3:19 Edom a wildern. for *v.*
Amos 3:10 store *v.* in palaces
6:3 cause seat of *v.* to come
Ob. 10 for *v.* shame shall cover
Jon. 3:8 turn every one from *v.*
Mic. 2:2 covet fields, take by *v.*
6:12 the rich men are full of *v.*
Hab. 1:2 I cry out to thee of *v. ?*
3 *v.* bef. me ; 9 come all for *v.*
2:8 and for the *v.* of the laud
17 *v.* of Leba. cover thee, *v.* of
Zep. 1:9 fill mast. houses with *v.*
3:4 her priests have done *v.*
Mal. 2:16 covereth *v.* with garm.
Mat. 11:12 kingd. of hea. suff. *v.*
Luke 3:14 do *v.* to no man, nor
Acts 5:26 capt. bro. them with. *v.*
21:35 P. borne of soldiers for *v.*
27:41 was brok. for *v.* of waves
Heb. 11:34 quenched *v.* of fire
Rev. 18:21 with *v.* shall Babylon

VIOLENT.

2 *Sam.* 22:49 hast delivered me
from the *v.* man, *Ps.* 18:48
Ps. 7:16 his *v.* dealing come on
86:14 assemb. of *v.* men sought
140:1 preserve me fr. *v.* man, 4
11 evil shall hunt the *v.* man
Prov. 16:29 *v.* man enticeth
neighbor
Ec. 5:8 if thou seest *v.* pervert.
Mat. 11:12 the *v.* take it by force

VIOLENTLY.

Lev. 6:4 sh. rest. that he took *v.*
Deut. 28:31 ass shall be *v.* taken
Job 20:19 hath *v.* taken a house
24:2 they *v.* take away flocks
Is. 22:18 will *v.* turn and toss
Lam. 2:6 hath *v.* taken away tab.

VIPER.

Job 20:16 *v.* tongue sh. slay him
Is. 30:6 when. come *v.* and serp.
59:5 that is crushed br. into *v.*
Acts 28:3 *v.* fasten. on P.'s hand

VIPERS.

Mat. 3:7 O generation of *v.* 12:34 ;
23:33 ; *Luke* 3:7

VIRGIN.

Gen. 24:16 Rebekah was fair, *v.*

43 when the *v.* cometh to draw
Lev. 21:3 a *v.* he may be defiled
14 he shall take a *v.* to wife
Deut. 22:19 evil name upon a *v.*
23 *v.* betroth. 28 *v.* not betro.
32:25 destroy young man and *v.*
2 *Sam.* 13:2 sick for Ta. was a *v.*
2 *K.* 19:21 the *v.* the daughter of
Zi. laughed to scorn, *Is.* 37:22
Is. 7:14 *v.* sh. concei. *Mat.* 1:23
23:12 rejoice, O th. oppressed *v.*
47:1 sit in the dust, O *v.* of Ba.
62:5 as a yo. man marrieth a *v.*
Jer. 14:17 the *v.* dau. is broken
18:13 *v.* of Is. ha. done horrible
31:4 shalt be built, O *v.* of Israel
13 then sh. *v.* rejoice in dance
21 turn, O *v.* of Is. to thy citi.
46:11 O *v.* daughter of Egypt
Lam. 1:15 L. hath trod. *v.* of Ju.
2:13 comfort thee, O *v.* of Zion
Joel 1:8 lament like a *v.* girded
Amos 5:2 *v.* of Israel is fallen
Luke 1:27 angel was sent to a *v.*
1 *Cor.* 7:28 if a *v.* marry, not sin.
34 difference betw. wife and *v.*
37 that he will keep his *v.*
2 *Cor.* 11:2 pres. you as chaste *v.*

VIRGINS.

2 *Sam.* 13:18 were king's dau. *v.*
Ps. 45:14 *v.* her companions
Cant. 1:3 theref. do *v.* love thee
6:8 queens, *v.* without number
Is. 23:4 nor do I bring up *v.*
Lam. 1:4 her *v.* are afflicted
18 *v.* are gone into captivity
2:10 *v.* of Jer. hang their heads
21 *v.* and yo. men are fallen
Amos 8:13 that day shall *v.* faint
Mat. 25:1 heaven is lik. to ten *v.*
Acts 21:9 daugh. *v.* prophesied
1 *Cor.* 7:25 concern. *v.* I have not
Rev. 14:4 not defiled, they are *v.*

Young VIRGINS.

Jud. 21:12 were four hund. *y. v.*
1 *K.* 1:2 sought for king a *y. v.*
Est. 2:2 fair *y. v.* sou. for king
3 gather together the fair *y. v.*

VIRGINITY.

Lev. 21:13 take a wife in her *v.*
Deut. 22:15 bring tok. of *v.* 17, 20
Jud. 11:37 may bewail my *v.* 38
Ezek. 23:3 bruised teats of *v.* 8
Luke 2:36 A. lived 7 years fr. *v.*

VIRTUE.

Mark 5:30 *v.* had gone out of
him, *Luke* 6:19 ; 8:46
Phil. 4:8 if there be any *v.*
2 *Pet.* 1:3 called us to glo. and *v.*
5 add to faith *v.* to *v.* knowl.

VIRTUOUS, LY.

Ruth 3:11 thou art a *v.* woman
Prov. 12:4 a *v.* wom. is a crown
31:10 who can find a *v.* wom. ?
29 many daugh. have done *v.*

VISAGE.

Is. 52:14 his *v.* was marred
Lam. 4:8 *v.* is blacker th. a coal
Dan. 3:19 form of *v.* changed

VISIBLE.

Col. 1:16 all things created, *v.*

VISION.

Num. 24:4 *v.* of Almighty, 16
1 *Sam.* 3:1 there was no open *v.*
15 S. feared to show Eli the *v.*
2 *Sam.* 7:17 accord. to this *v.* did
Nathan speak, 1 *Chr.* 17:15
2 *Chr.* 32:32 written in *v.* of Isa.
Job 20:8 be chased away as a *v.*
Ps. 89:19 spakest in *v.* to II. O.
Prov. 29:18 wh. no *v.* peo. perish
Is. 1:1 the *v.* of Isa. son of Amoz
21:2 a grievous *v.* is declared
22:1 burden of valley of *v.* 5

28:7 they err in *v.* stumble in
29:7 be as a dream of a night *v.*
11 *v.* is become as a book seal.
Jer. 14:14 they proph. a false *v.*
23:16 sp. a *v.* of their own heart
Lam. 2:9 proph. find no *v.* fr. L.
Ezek. 7:13 *v.* is touching whole
26 they seek a *v.* of prophet
8:4 according to *v.* 11:24 ; 43:3
12:22 days are prolonged *v.* fail.
23 the effect of ev. *v.* is at hand
24 no more vain *v.* nor divina.
27 *v.* he seeth is for days
13:7 ha. ye not seen a vain *v. ?*
Dan. 2:19 revealed to D. in a *v.*
7:2 in my *v.* four winds strove
8:1 a *v.* appeared unto me
16 make this man understa. *v.*
26 shut up *v.* 27 astonish. at *v.*
9:21 whom I had seen in *v.* 23
10:1 he had understanding of *v.*
7 I saw *v.* men saw not *v.* 8
14 yet the *v.* is for many days
16 by *v.* my sorrows are turn.
11:14 exalt themsel. to estab. *v.*
Ob. 1 the *v.* of Obadiah
Mic. 3:6 ye shall not have a *v.*
Nah. 1:1 book of *v.* of Nahum
Hab. 2:2 write *v.* make it plain
3 *v.* is for an appointed time
Zec. 13:4 prophets asha. of his *v.*
Mat. 17:9 tell the *v.* to no man
Luke 1:22 perc. he had seen a *v.*
24:23 had seen a *v.* of angels
Acts 10:17 Peter doubted of *v.* 19
11:5 I saw a *v.* a vessel descend
12:9 but thought he saw a *v.*
16:9 *v.* appeared to Paul, 18:9
26:19 I was not disobedi. to *v.*
Rev. 9:17 I saw horses in the *v.*

In a VISION.

Gen. 15:1 L. came to Ab. *in a v.*
Num. 12:6 make myself kn. *in v.*
Ezek. 11:24 brought me *in a v.*
Dan. 8:2 I saw *in a v.* by river
Acts 9:10 to An. said L. *in a v.*
12 S. hath seen *in a v.* a man
10:3 Cor. saw *in a v.* an angel

VISIONS.

Gen. 46:2 God spake to Is. in *v.*
2 *Chr.* 9:29 written in *v.* of Iddo
26:5 Z. had understanding of *v.*
Job 4:13 thoughts fr. *v.* of night
7:14 thou terrifiest me thro' *v.*
Ezek. 1:1 I saw the *v.* of God
8:3 he bro. me in *v.* of G. to J.
13:16 which see *v.* of peace
40:2 in *v.* bro. he me to land of
Dan. 1:17 D. had underst. in *v.*
2:28 *v.* of thy head on thy bed
4:5 *v.* of my head troubled me
7:1 D. had *v.* of his head upon
7 I saw in night *v.* behold, 13
15 *v.* of my head troubled me
Hos. 12:10 I have multiplied *v.*
Joel 2:28 shall see *v.* *Acts* 2:17
2 *Cor.* 12:1 come to *v.* and revela.

VISIT.

Gen. 50:24 will *v.* 25 ; *Ex.* 13:19
Ex. 32:34 when I *v.* I will *v.* sin
Lev. 18:25 I do *v.* iniq. thereof
Job 5:24 shalt *v.* thy habitation
7:18 that thou shouldest *v.* him
Ps. 59:5 awake, to *v.* the heath.
80:14 look down and *v.* this vine
89:32 th. will I *v.* transgression
106:4 O *v.* me wi. thy salvation
Is. 23:17 the Lord will *v.* Tyre
Jer. 3:16 they shall *v.* ark of L.

Jer. 5:9 shall I not *v. ?* 29 ; 9:9
6:15 *v.* them, shall be cast down
14:10 rememb. iniq. and *v.* sins
15:15 thou kno. remem. and *v.*
23:2 *v.* on you evil of doings
27:22 there sh. they be till I *v.*
29:10 *v.* you and perf. my word

32:5 th. shall he be till I v. him
49:8 will v. Esau ; 50:31 v. Baby.
Lam. 4:22 he will v. thine iniq.
Hos. 2:13 v. on her days of Baal.
8:13 now will he v. th. sins, 9:9
Amos 3:14 I will v. alt. of Beth-el
Zep. 2:7 L. shall v. turn captiv.
Zec. 11:16 not v. th. that be cut
Acts 7:23 into heart to v. his br.
15:14 decla. how G. did v. Gent.
36 let us go and v. our breth.
Jam. 1:27 v. fatherl. and widows

VISITATION.
Num. 16:29 if visi. aft. v. of men
Job 10:12 thy v. preser. my spir.
Is. 10:3 what do in day of v. ?
Jer. 8:12 in time of v. cast down
10:15 in time of v. perish, 51:18
11:23 in year of v. 23:12 ; 48:44
46:21 time of th. v. come, 50:27
Hos. 9:7 the days of v. are come
Mic. 7:4 thy v. cometh, perplex.
Luke 19:44 knew. not time of v.
1 Pet. 2:12 glorify G. in day of v.

VISITED.
Gen. 21:1 Lord v. Sar. as he said
Ex. 3:16 I have surely v. you
4:31 heard that Lord had v. Is.
Num. 16:29 if th. be v. aft. visit.
Ruth 1:6 heard how L. v. people
1 Sam. 2:21 the Lord v. Hannah
Job 35:15 he hath v. in his anger
Ps. 17:3 thou hast v. me, thou
Prov. 19:23 sh. not be v. wi. evil
Is. 24:22 after many days be v.
26:14 theref. hast thou v. them
16 Lord in trouble have they v.
29:6 thou sh. be v. with thund.
Jer. 6:6 Jerusal. is city to be v.
23:2 scattered flock, not v. th.
Ezek. 38:8 after many days be v.
Zec. 10:3 L. of hosts v. his flock
Mat. 25:36 v. me ; 43 v. me not
Luke 1:68 v. and redeemed peop.
78 the day-spring hath v. us
7:16 God hath v. his people

VISITEST, ETH, ING.
Ex. 20:5 v. iniquity of fathers,
34:7 ; Num. 14:18 ; Deut. 5:9
Job 31:14 v. what sh. I answer ?
Ps. 8:4 thou v. him, Heb. 2:6
65:9 thou v. earth, waterest it

VOCATION.
Eph. 4:1 walk worthy of the v.

VOICE.
Gen. 4:10 v. of thy broth.'s blood
27:22 v. is Jacob's v. but hands
39:15 heard that I lift. up my v.
Ex. 4:8 believe v. of latter sign
19:19 God answered him by a v.
23:21 bewa. of him, obey his v.
24:3 people answer. with one v.
32:18 is not v. of th. that shout
Lev. 5:1 if soul hear v. of swear.
Num. 14:1 congr. lifted their v.
Deut. 4:30 if thou be obedi. to v.
8:20 would not be obedi. to v.
Jos. 6:10 nor make noise wi. v.
Jud. 18:3 they knew v. of Levite
1 Sam. 24:16 is this thy v. my
son David ? 26:17
2 Sam. 22:14 M. High uttered v.
1 K. 18:26 was no v. nor any, 29
19:12 after fire a still small v.
2 K. 4:31 neither v. nor hearing
7:10 there was no v. of man
19:22 ag. wh. exalt. v. ? Is. 37:23
1 Chr. 15:16 lifting up v. wi. joy
Job 2:12 Job's friends lift. up v.
3:7 let no joyful v. come there
30:31 the v. of them that weep
37:4 a v. roareth, he thundereth
5 God thundereth with his v.
40:9 thund. with a v. like him ?
26:7 publish with v. of thanksg.

31:22 heardest v. of supplicati.
42:4 went to house of G. wi. v.
44:16 v. of him th. reproacheth
46:6 uttered his v. earth melted
47:1 shout to G. wi. v. of trium.
66:19 attend. to v. of my prayer
68:33 send. out v. th. a mighty v.
74:23 forget not v. of enemies
77:1 cried unto L. with v. 142:1
18 v. of thy thunder in heaven
86:6 attend to v. of my suppli.
93:3 floods have lifted up th. v.
98:5 sing to L. with v. of psalm
Ps. 102:5 by reas. of v. of groan.
103:20 hearkening to v. of word
104:7 at v. of thund. th. hasted
118:15 v. of rejoic. in tabernac.
141:1 give ear to my v.
Prov. 1:20 uttereth v. in streets
2:3 if liftest up v. for understa.
5:13 not obeyed v. of my teach.
8:1 understand. put forth her v.
4 my v. is to sons of men
Ec. 5:3 a fool's v. is known by
6 sho. G. be angry at thy v. ?
10:20 bird of air sh. carry the v.
12:4 he shall rise at v. of bird
Cant. 2:8 the v. of my beloved
12 v. of turtle is heard in land
5:2 it is v. of beloved knocketh
Is. 6:4 posts moved at v. of him
13:2 exalt the v. shake the hand
29:4 v. as one that hath a spirit
30:19 graci. to thee at v. of cry
31:4 lion not afraid of their v.
40:3 v. th. crieth in wilder. Mat.
3:3 ; Mark 1:3 ; Luke 3:4.
6 v. said, Cry ; 48:20 v. of sing.
50:10 obeyeth v. of his servant
51:3 thanksgiving, v. of melody
52:8 wi. v. together sh. th. sing
65:19 v. of weeping shall be no
more heard, nor v. of crying
66:6 a v. of noise, a v. fr. temp.
Jer. 4:15 v. declareth from Dan
16 give their v. ag. cities of J.
6:23 v. roareth like sea, 50:42
7:34 v. of mirth, v. of gladness,
v. of the bridegroom, 16:9 ;
25:10 ; 33:11
8:19 v. of cry of dau. of people
10:13 when he uttereth v. 51:16
25:36 a v. of cry of shepherds
30:19 v. of th. that make merry
31:15 a v. was heard in Ram. 16
46:22 v. thereof go like a serp.
48:3 a v. of crying from Horon.
50:28 v. of them that flee
51:55 destro. out of her great v.
Ezek. 1:24 I heard v. of Almighty
10:5 as the v. of Almighty God
23:42 a v. of multitude at ease
33:32 one that hath a pleas. v.
43:2 v. li. noise of wat. Rev. 1:15
Dan. 4:31 there fell v. fr. heaven
6:20 cried with a lamentable v.
10:6 v. of words like v. of mult.
Joel 2:11 L. utter v. before army
3:16 utter v. from J. Amos 1:2
Jon. 2:9 with v. of thanksgiving
Nah. 2:7 lead as with v. of doves
Mat. 3:17 a v. fr. heaven, Mark
1:11 ; Luke 3:22
17:5 a v. out of cloud, this is
my S. Mark 9:7 ; Lu. 9:35, 36
Luke 1:44 v. of saluta. sounded
John 1:23 v. of one cry. in wild.
10:4 follow, for they kn. his v.
5 know not v. of strangers
12:28 then came a v. saying, I
30 v. came not because of me
18:37 that is of truth hear. my v.
Acts 9:7 hear. v. seeing no man
10:13 a v. say, Rise, 15 ; 11:9
12:14 when she knew Peter's v.
22 it is v. of a god. not of man
19:34 with v. cried, Great is Di.
24:21 exc. it be for this one v.

26:10 I gave my v. again. them
1 Cor. 14:11 know not mean of v.
19 by my v. I might teach oth.
Gal. 4:20 I des. to change my v.
1 Thes. 4:16 with v. of archangel
Heb. 12:26 whose v. shook earth
2 Pet. 1:17 v. fr. excellent glory
2:16 ass speaking with man's v.
Rev. 1:12 I turned to see the v.
16:17 there came a great v.

VOICE, with hear.
Gen. 4:23 hear my v. ye wives
Deut. 4:33 did people h. v. of G.
36 he made thee to hear his v.
5:25 if we h. v. of God, we die
33:7 hear, Lord, the v. of Judah
2 Sam. 19:35 I h. v. of singing ?
22:7 did h. my v. out of temple
Job 3:18 h. not v. of oppressor
37:2 h. attentive. noise of his v.
Ps. 5:3 my v. shalt thou hear
27:7 hear, O Lord, when I cry
wi. my v. 28:2 ; 64:1 ; 119:149 ;
130:2 ; 140:6
55:3 h. because of v. of enemy
17 cry aloud, he shall h. my v.
95:7 to-day if ye will hear his v.
Heb. 3:7, 15 ; 4:7
Cant. 2:14 let me h. v. sweet v.
Is. 32:9 h. my v. ye careless dau.
Jer. 9:10 can men h. v. of cattle
Mat. 12:19 neither any h. his v.
John 5:25 dead h. v. of Son, 28
10:3 sheep hear his v. 16, 27
Acts 22:14 should. h. v. of mouth
Rev. 3:29 if any man hear my v.

See HEARD.

VOICE, with hearken, ed.
Gen. 3:17 hast h. to v. of wife
16:2 Abram h. to v. of Sarai
Ex. 3:18 they shall h. to thy v.
4:8 nor h. to v. of the first sign
15:26 if diligently h. to v. of L.
18:19 h. to my v. I give counsel
24 and Moses h. to v. of Jethro
Num. 14:22 they have not h. to
my v. Deut. 9:23 ; 28:45
21:3 Lord h. to the v. of Israel
Deut. 1:45 L. would not h. to v.
15:5 if thou carefully h. to v. of
L. 26:17 ; 28:1, 2 ; 30:10
28:15 if th. wilt not h. to v. of L.
Jos. 10:14 L. h. to v. of a man
Jud. 2:20 people not h. to my v.
13:9 God h. to v. of Manoah
20:13 B. would not h. to v. of Is.
1 Sam. 2:25 h. not to v. of father
8:7 h. to the v. of people, 9:22
12:1 I have h. to your v. in all
25:35 go in peace, I h. to thy v.
28:22 h. thou to v. of thy hand.
2 Sam. 12:18 wo. not h. to our v.
2 K. 10:6 if ye will h. to my v.
Job 9:16 beli. he had h. to my v.
34:16 hearken to v. of my words
Ps. 5:2 h. to the v. of my cry
58:5 not h. to v. of charmers
81:11 peo. would not h. to my v.
Cant. 8:13 compan. h. to thy v.
Jer. 18:19 h. to v. of them that

See LIFT, LORD, LOUD, OBEY,
OBEYED.

VOICES.
Luke 17:13 lepers lifted up th. v.
23:23 the v. of priests prevailed
Acts 13:27 knew not v. of proph.
22:22 lift up their v. and said
1 Cor. 14:10 so many v. in world
Rev. 4:5 throne proceed. v. 16:18
8:5 into earth, and there were v.
13 by rea. of other v. of trump.
10:3 seven thunders uttered v. 4
11:15 there were v. in heaven
19 temple opened, th. were v.

VOID.

Gen. 1:2 earth with. form and *v.*
Num. 30:12 husb. made th. *v.* 15
Deut. 32:28 people *v.* of counsel
1 *K.* 22:10 in *v.* place. 2 *Chr.* 18:9
Ps. 89:39 made *v.* the covenant
119:126 have made *v.* thy law
Prov. 11:12 *v.* of wisd. despiseth
Is. 55:11 word not ret. to me *v.*
Jer. 4:23 earth. form and *v.*
19:7 I will make *v.* counsel of J.
Nah. 2:10 Nineveh is empty, *v.*
Acts 24:16 conscien. *v.* of offence
Rom. 3:31 do we make *v.* law ?
4:14 be heirs, faith is made *v.*
1 *Cor.* 9:15 make my glorying *v.*

See UNDERSTANDING.

VOLUME.

Ps. 40:7 in *v.* is writ. *Heb.* 10:7

VOLUNTARY.

Lev. 1:3 off. it of his own *v.* will
7:16 a *v.* offering shall be eaten
Ezek. 46:12 prepare *v.* burnt-off.
Col. 2:18 a *v.* humility, worship

VOLUNTARILY.

Ezek. 46:12 prepare offerings *v.*

VOMIT, ED, ETH.

Lev. 18:25 land *v.* inhabitants
Job 20:15 swallo. riches, *v.* them
Prov. 23:8 morsel eaten shalt *v.*
25:16 filled with honey and *v.* it
Jon. 2:10 the fish *v.* out Jonah

VOMIT, Substantive.

Prov. 26:11 dog return. to his *v.*

Is. 19:14 man stagger. in his *v.*
28:8 tables are full of *v.* filthin.
Jer. 48:26 Moab sh. wallow in *v.*
2 *Pet.* 2:22 dog is turned to his *v.*

VOW.

Gen. 28:20 Ja. vowed a *v.* 31:13
Lev. 7:16 sacri. be a *v.* 22:18, 21
27:2 wh. man make singular *v.*
Num. 6:2 when a man vow a *v.*
5 days of *v.* 21 according to *v.*
21:2 Israel vowed a *v.* to Lord
30:2 if man vow *v.* 3 wo. vow *a.*
9 every *v.* of widow shall stand
13 every *v.* her husband may
Deut. 23:18 br. price of dog for *v.*
21 when thou shalt vow a *v.*
Jud. 11:30 Jephthah vowed a *v.*
39 did wi. her according to *v.*
1 *Sam.* 1:11 Hannah vowed a *v.*
21 Elka. went to offer L. his *v.*
2 *Sam.* 15:7 let go and pay my *v.*
8 thy servant vowed a *v.* at G.
Ps. 65:1 to thee *v.* be performed
Ec. 5:4 when thou vowest a *v.*
Is. 19:21 they sh. vow a *v.* to L.
Acts 18:18 head, for he had a *v.*
21:23 which have a *v.* on them

VOWS.

Lev. 22:18 off. oblation for his *v.*
23:38 and beside all your *v.*
Num. 29:39 th. do beside your *v.*
30:5 not any of *v.* stand, 8, 12
Deut. 12:6 thi. bring *v.* 11, 17, 26
Job 22:27 thou shalt pay thy *v.*
Ps. 22:25 I will pay my *v.* 66:13 ;
116:14, 18

W

WAFER, S.

Ex. 16:31 the taste was like *w.*
29:2 *w.* unleav. anoint. with oil
23 *w.* out of basket, *Lev.* 8:26
Lev. 2:4 *w.* anointed with oil,
7:12 ; *Num.* 6:15
Num. 6:19 one *w.* on hands of N.

WAG.

Jer. 18:16 passeth sh. *w.* head
Lam. 2:15 *w.* heads at dau. of J.
Zep. 2:15 ev. one passeth sh. *w.*

WAGES.

Gen. 29:15 wh. shall thy *w.* be ?
30:28 app. thy *w.* I will give it
31:7 changed my *w.* ten tim. 41
8 the speckled shall be thy *w.*
Ex. 2:9 child, I will gi. thee *w.*
Lev. 19:13 *w.* of hired not abide
Jer. 22:13 neigh.'s serv. with. *w.*
Ezek. 29:18 had no *w.* nor army
19 her spoil sh. be *w.* for army
Hag. 1:6 earn. *w.* to put into bag
Mal. 3:5 oppress hireling in *w.*
Luke 3:14 be cont. with your *w.*
John 4:36 that reapeth receiv. *w.*
Rom. 6:23 the *w.* of sin is death
2 *Cor.* 11:8 taking *w.* of them
2 *Pet.* 2:15 B. lov. *w.* of unright.

WAGGING.

Mat. 27:39 th. passed by reviled
him, *w.* heads, *Mark* 15:29

WAGON, S.

Gen. 45:19 take *w.* out of Eg. 21
27 Jacob saw *w.* Jos. had sent
Num. 7:3 *w.* for two of princes
7 two *w.* 4 oxen to sons of G. 8
Ezek. 23:24 come ag. th. with *w.*

WAIL, ED.

Ezek. 32:18 *w.* for multit. of Eg.
Mic. 1:8 I will *w.* and howl
Mark 5:38 he seeth them th. *w.*
Rev. 1:7 kindr. of earth shall *w.*

WAILING.

Est. 4:3 whi. decree came was *w.*
Jer. 9:10 for mount. will I ta. *w.*
18 let them take up *w.* for us
19 a voice of *w.* heard out of Z.
20 teach your daughters *w.*
Ezek. 7:11 neither be *w.* for them
Ezek. 27:31 they sh. weep wi. *w.*
Amos 5:16 *w.* sh. be in all streets
17 in all vineyards shall be *w.*
Mic. 1:8 I will make wi. like dra.
Mat. 13:42 *w.* and gna. teeth, 50
Rev. 18:15 merchants stand *w.* 19

WAIT, Noun.

Num. 35:20 if hurl by lay. of *w.*
22 cast on him with. laying *w.*
Jer. 9:8 in his heart he lay. his *w.*

WAIT, Verb.

Num. 3:10 Aa. and sons shall *w.*
on priest's office, 8:24 ; 1 *Chr.*
23:28 ; 2 *Chr.* 5:11 ; 13:10
2 *K.* 6:33 sho. I *w.* for the L. ?
Job 14:14 I will *w.* till change
17:13 if I *w.* grave is my house
Ps. 25:3 let none that *w.* 69:6
5 on thee do I *w.* all the day
21 preserve me, for I *w.* on th.
27:14 *w.* on the Lord, 37:34 ;
Prov. 20:22
37:7 *w.* patiently ; 52:9 will *w.*
9 that *w.* on Lord shall inherit
39:7 *w.* I for ; 62:5 *w.* on God
56:6 when they *w.* for my soul
59:9 bec. of strength will I *w.*
69:3 mine eyes fail while I *w.*
104:27 th. *w.* upon thee, 145:15
123:2 our eyes *w.* on the L. God
130:5 I *w.* for Lord, soul doth *w.*
Is. 8:17 I will *w.* on the Lord
30:18 L. *w.* to be graci. blessed
are they that *w.* for him
40:31 th. *w.* on L. shall renew
42:4 isles shall *w.* for his law
49:23 not asham. that *w.* for me

50:14 pay *v.* 56:12 *v.* are on me
61:5 th. O G. hast heard my *v.*
8 that I may daily perf. my *v.*
Prov. 7:14 this day I paid my *v.*
20:25 snare after *v.* to make inq.
31:2 what the son of my *v.* ?
Jer. 44:25 will surely perf. our *v.*
Jon. 1:16 men fear. L. made *v.*
Nah. 1:15 keep feasts, perform *v.*

VOW, EST, ETH.

Num. 6:2 sepa. themselves to *v.*
Deut. 23:22 if forbear to *v.* no sin
Ps. 76:11 *v.* and pay to the Lord
Ec. 5:4 when thou *v.* a vow
5 better thou shouldest not *v.*
Mal. 1:14 *v.* to L. corrupt thing

VOWED.

Gen. 28:20 Jacob *v.* a vow, 31:13
Lev. 27:8 accord. to ability th. *v.*
Num. 6:21 law of N. who hath *v.*
21:2 Is. *v.* a vow to L. and said
30:6 a husband when she *v.* 10
Deut. 23:23 accord. as th. hast *v.*
Jud. 11:30 Jephthah *v.* a vow
Ps. 132:2 *v.* to the mighty God
Ec. 5:4 pay th. wh. thou hast *v.*
Jon. 2:9 I will pay that that I *v.*

VOYAGE.

Acts 27:10 *v.* will be with hurt

VULTURE.

Lev. 11:14 the *v.* and kite, *Deut.*
14:13
Job 28:7 path *v.* eye ha. not seen
Is. 34:15 there sh. *v.* be gathered

51:5 the isles shall *w.* upon me
59:9 we *w.* for light, but behold
60:9 the isles shall *w.* for me
Jer. 14:22 we will *w.* upon thee
Lam. 3:25 L. good to them th. *w.*
26 a man hope and quietly *w.*
Hos. 6:9 as troops of robbers *w.*
12:6 keep mercy and *w.* on God
Mic. 7:7 I will *w.* for God
Hab. 2:3 tarry, *w.* for it, it will
Zep. 3:8 *w.* upon me, saith Lord
Mark 3:9 small ship would *w.*
Luke 12:36 like men that *w.*
Acts 1:4 *w.* for promise of Father
Rom. 8:25 we with patience *w.*
12:7 let us *w.* on our ministeri.
1 *Cor.* 9:13 which *w.* at the altar
Gal. 5:5 we through the Sp. *w.*
1 *Thes.* 1:10 and to *w.* for his Son

See LAY, LAID, LYING.

WAITED.

Gen. 49:18 I ha. *w.* for thy salva.
1 *K.* 20:38 prophet *w.* for king
2 *K.* 5:2 maid *w.* on Naa.'s wife
1 *Chr.* 6:32 they *w.* on office, 33
Neh. 12:44 priests and L. that *w.*
Job 6:19 companies of Sheba *w.*
15:22 he is *w.* for of the sword
29:21 to me men gave ear, *w.*
23 *w.* for me as for the rain
30:26 I *w.* for light, dark. came
32:4 Elihu *w.* till J. had spoken
Ps. 40:1 I *w.* patiently for Lord
106:13 they *w.* not for counsel
119:95 wicked have *w.* for me
Is. 25:9 our God, we *w.* for him
26:8 in way of judg. have we *w.*
33:2 be gracious, we *w.* for thee
Ezek. 19:5 saw that she had *w.*
Mic. 1:12 inhabit. of Maroth *w.*
Zec. 11:11 poor of flock that *w.*
Luke 1:21 peo. *w.* for Zacharias
Acts 10:7 Corn. called sol. th. *w.*
17:16 while P. *w.* his spirit was

1 *Pet.* 3:20 long-suffer. of G. *w.*

WAITETH.

Job 24:15 eye of the adulterer *w.*
Ps. 33:20 our soul *w.* for Lord
62:1 my soul *w.* upon G. 130:6
65:1 praise *w.* for thee, O God
Prov. 27:18 he that *w.* on master
Is. 64:4 prepared for him that *w.*
Dan. 12:12 blessed is he that *w.*
Mic. 5:7 as showers that *w.* not
Rom. 8:19 *w.* for manifestation
Jam. 5:7 husbandman *w.* for fru.

WAITING.

Num. 8:25 fr. age of 50 cease *w.*
Prov. 8:34 *w.* at gates, *w.* posts
Luke 2:25 Simeon *w.* for consol.
John 5:3 *w.* for moving of water
Rom. 8:23 we ourselv. groan, *w.*
1 *Cor.* 1:7 *w.* for coming of our L.
2 *Thes.* 3:5 into patient *w.* for C.

WAKE, ED.

Ps. 139:18 when I *w.* I am still
Jer. 51:39 perp. sleep and not *w.*
Joel 3:9 *w.* up the mighty men
Zec. 4:1 angel came and *w.* me
1 *Thes.* 5:10 whether *w.* or sleep

WAKENED, ETH.

Is. 50:4 *w.* morning by morning,
he *w.* mine ear to hear
Joel 3:12 let heathen be *w.* and
Zec. 4:1 as a man that is *w.*

WAKETH, ING.

Ps. 77:4 th. holdest mine eyes *w.*
127:1 watchman *w.* in vain
Cant. 5:2 I sleep but my hea. *w.*

WALK, Verb.

Gen. 24:40 L. before whom I *w.*
48:15 bef. wh. my fathers did *w.*
Ex. 16:4 wheth. *w.* in law or no
18:20 way wherein th. must *w.*
21:19 if he *w.* abroad, that smote
Lev. 18:3 nor *w.* in ordin. 20:23
26:3 if ye *w.* in my statut. 1 *K.*
6:12; *Ezek.* 33:15; *Zec.* 3:7
12 I will *w.* am. you, be yo. G.
21 if *w.* contrary to me, 23, 27
24 I *w.* contrary to you, 28
Deut. 5:33 shall *w.* in ways of L.
13:4; 28:9; *Ezek.* 37:24
8:19 if ye *w.* after other gods ye
29:19 I *w.* in imagina. of heart
Jos. 22:5 take heed *w.* in ways
Jud. 5:10 ye that *w.* by the way
1 *Sam.* 2:30 house sh. *w.* bef. me
35 sh. *w.* before mine anointed
8:5 thy sons *w.* not in thy ways
1 *K.* 3:14 if wilt *w.* to keep my
comman. as Da. did *w.* 8.25 ;
9:4 ; 11:38 ; 2 *Chr.* 7:17
8:23 servants that *w.* before
thee, 2 *Chr.* 6:14
36 teach them way wherein
they should *w.* 2 *Chr.* 6:27
Ps. 12:8 wicked *w.* on every side
23:4 though I *w.* thro' the val.
26:11 will *w.* in mine integrity
55:13 may *w.* before G. in light
82:5 they *w.* on in darkness
84:11 no good fr. th. th. *w.* upr.
86:11 L. I will *w.* in thy truth
89:15 sh. *w.* in light of counten.
30 child. *w.* not in my judgm.
101:2 will *w.* in house with per.
115:7 feet have they, but *w.* not
116:9 I will *w.* before the Lord
119:3 do no iniquity, *w.* in ways
45 I will *w.* at liberty, I seek
138:7 I walk in midst of trouble
143:8 cause me kn. way I sh. *w.*
Prov. 2:7 buckler to th. that *w.*
20 may. *w.* in way of good men
3:23 then sh. thou *w.* in thy way
Is. 2:3 in his paths; *Mic.* 4:2
5 let us *w.* in light of the Lord
3:16 *w.* with stretched necks

8:11 not *w.* in way of this peo.
35:9 the redeemed sh. *w.* there
40:31 that wait on L. shall *w.*
42:5 giv. spirit to them that *w.*
24 would not *w.* in his ways
59:9 but we *w.* in darkness
Jer. 3:17 nor *w.* aft. imagination
18 Judah shall *w.* with Israel
6:16 said, We will not *w.* there.
7:6 if ye *w.* not after other gods
9 will ye *w.* after other gods ?
9:4 neighb. will *w.* wi. slanders
13:10 peo. which *w.* in imagina.
of heart, *w.* 16:12 ; 18:12
23:14 commit adult. *w.* in lies
42:3 G. may show wher. may *w.*
Lam. 5:8 Z. desolate, foxes *w.*
Ezek. 11:20 they *w.* in my statu.
37:24 they sh. *w.* in my judgm.
Dan. 4:37 *w.* in pride he is able
Hos. 11:10 shall *w.* after the Lord
14:9 the just shall *w.* in them
Joel 2:8 *w.* ev. one in his path
Amos 3:3 can two *w.* ex. agreed ?
Mic. 4:5 ev. one *w.* in name of G.
6:16 ye *w.* in counsels of Omri
Hab. 3:15 thou didst *w.* thro' sea
Zep. 1:17 they sh. *w.* like blind
Zec. 6:7 th. might *w.* to and fro
10:12 th. shall *w.* up and down
Mat. 11:5 the lame *w. Luke* 7:22
Mark 7:5 why *w.* not thy discip.
Luke 11:44 men that *w.* over th.
13:33 must *w.* to-day and to-mo.
24:17 commune as *w.* are sad ?
John 7:1 Je. wo. not *w.* in Jewry
8:12 not *w.* in darkness but lig.
11:9 if any *w.* in day, stum. not
10 man *w.* in night, stumbleth
Rom. 4:12. *w.* in steps of faith
6:4 also *w.* in newness of life
8:1 who *w.* not after the flesh, 4
2 *Cor.* 5:7 we *w.* by faith
6:16 dw. in them and *w.* in th.
10:3 tho' we *w.* in flesh, not war
Gal. 6:16 as many as *w.* accord.
Eph. 2:10 we should *w.* in them
4:1 *w.* worthy of the vocation
17 ye *w.* not as other Gentiles
5:15 see ye *w.* circumspectly
Phil. 3:17 mark them which *w.*
18 many *w.* of wh. I told you
Col. 1:10 that ye mi. *w.* worthy
of Lord, 1 *Thes.* 2:12
1 *Thes.* 4:12 ye may *w.* honestly
2 *Thes.* 3:11 which *w.* disorderly
2 *Pet.* 2:10 th. that *w.* after flesh
1 *John* 1:6 and *w.* in darkness
7 if *w.* in light as he in light
2 *John* 6 *w.* after his commandm.
3 *John* 4 children *w.* in the truth
Jude 18 mock. *w.* after their lus.
Rev. 3:4 they shall *w.* with me
9:20 cannot see, hear, nor *w.*
16:15 watch. lest he *w.* naked
21:24 nations *w.* in light of city

WALK, imperatively.

Gen. 13:17 w. thro. land, *Jos.* 18:8
17:1 *w.* before me, be perfect
Ps. 48:12 *w.* about Z. go round
Prov. 1:15 *w.* not in way wi. th.
Ec. 11:9 *w.* in ways of thy heart
Is. 2:5 let us *w.* in sight of Lord
30:21 this is the way, *w.* in it
50:11 *w.* in light of your fire
Jer. 6:16 good way, *w.* therein
25 go not into fields, nor *w.* by
7:23 *w.* in ways I command. you
Ezek. 20:18 *w.* ye not in stat. of
Zec. 6:7 might *w.* to and fro
Mat. 9:5 say, Rise, and *w. Mark*
2:9 ; *Luke* 5:23; *John* 5:8, 11,
12; *Acts* 3:6
John 12:35 *w.* wh. ye have light
Rom. 13:13 let us *w.* honestly
1 *Cor.* 7:17 ev. one, so let him *w.*
Gal. 5:16 *w.* in the Spirit, 25

Eph. 5:2 *w.* in love, C. loved us
8 *w.* as children of light
Phil. 3:16 let us *w.* by same rule
Col. 2:6 received C. so *w.* in him
4:5 *w.* in wisdom toward them

To WALK.

Lev. 18:4 *to w.* in my ordinances
Deut. 8:6 *to w.* in his ways, 10:12 ;
11:22; 13:5; 19:9; 26:17; 30:16;
Jos. 22:5; *Jud.* 2:22; 1 *K.*
2:3 ; 8:58 ; 2 *Chr.* 6:31
1 *K.* 2:4 take heed *to w.* in truth
8:61 *to w.* in statut. *Ezek.* 36:27
16:31 *to w.* in sins of Jeroboam
2 *K.* 10:31 no heed *to w.* in law
23:3 Josiah made a coven. *to w.*
after the Lord, 2 *Chr.* 34:31
2 *Chr.* 6:16 ta. heed *to w.* in law
Neh. 5:9 not *to w.* in fear of G. ?
10:29 an oath *to w.* in G.'s law
Ps. 78:10 refu. *to w.* in his law
Prov. 2:13 *to w.* in ways of dark.
Ec. 6:8 know. *to w.* bef. living
Jer. 18:15 *to w.* in paths
26:4 not hearken *to w.*
31:9 cause th. *to w.* in strai. way
Ezek. 36:12 men *to w.* upon you
Dan. 9:10 nor obeyed *to w.*
Mic. 6:8 *to w.* humb. with thy G.
Hab. 3:19 make me *to w.* on high
Zec. 1:10 sent *to w.* to and fro
3:7 *to w.* am. these th. stand by
Mat. 15:31 saw the lame *to w.*
Luke 20:46 desire *to w.* in robes
Acts 3:12 made this man *to w.*
14:16 nations *to w.* in th. ways
21:21 nor *to w.* after customs
1 *Thes.* 4:1 how you ought to *w.*
1 *John* 2:6 *to w.* as he walked

WALKED.

Gen. 5:22 Enoch *w.* wi. God, 24
6:9 a just man, and *w.* with N.
Ex. 14:29 Is. *w.* upon dry land
Lev. 26:40 th. *w.* contrary to me
Jos. 5:6 Is. *w.* 40 years in wild.
Jud. 2:17 way their fathers *w.*
5:6 travellers *w.* thro' by-paths
11:16 when Is. *w.* thro' wilder.
1 *Sam.* 8:3 *w.* not in his ways
2 *Sam.* 2:29 men *w.* all night
11:2 David *w.* on roof of house
1 *K.* 9:4 as David thy father *w.*
2 *Chr.* 6:16 ; 7:17
11:33 not *w.* in my ways, *Ezek.*
5:6, 7 ; 11:12 ; 20:13, 16, 21
15:26 *w.* in way of father, 22:52
34 Baasha *w.* in way of Jerob.
16:2 ; 2 *K.* 13:6 ; 17:22
2 *K.* 4:35 *w.* in house to and fro
17:8 H. *w.* in statutes of heath.
19 Judah *w.* in statutes of Isr.
which th. made, 2 *Chr.* 21:13
21:22 *w.* not in way of L. *Jer.*
9:13 ; 32:23 ; 44:10, 23
2 *K.* 22:2 Josiah *w.* in ways of
David, 2 *Chr.* 34:2
2 *Chr.* 11:17 *w.* in way of David
17:4 Je. *w.* in G.'s commandm.
21:12 not *w.* in ways of Jehosh.
Job 29:3 I *w.* through darkness
31:7 if my heart *w.* after eyes
Ps. 55:14 we *w.* to house of God
81:12 *w.* in their own counsels
13 O th. I had *w.* in my ways !
142:3 in way I *w.* th. laid snare
Is. 9:2 people th. *w.* i. darkness
20:3 Isaiah *w.* naked for a sign
Jer. 2:5 they *w.* after vanity, 8
7:24 *w.* in couns. of heart, 11:8
8:2 after wh. th. *w.* 9:14 ; 16:11
Ezek. 16:47 not *w.* after the ways
18:9 hath *w.* in my statutes, 17
23:31 *w.* in way of thy sister
28:14 hast *w.* in midst of stones
Amos 2:4 which their fathers *w.*
Nah. 2:11 even the old lion *w.*
Zec. 1:11 we *w.* to and fro, 6:7

Mal. 3:14 what profit we *w.*
   mournfully ?
Mark 16:12 J. appear. as they *w.*
John 6:66 disciples *w.* no more
  11:54 Jesus *w.* no more openly
Acts 3:8 leap. stood and *w.* 14:10
  14:8 cripple, who never had *w.*
2 *Cor.* 10:2 we *w.* accord. to flesh
  12:18 *w.* we not in same spirit ?
  w. we not in same steps?
Gal. 2:14 they *w.* not uprightly
Eph. 2:2 time past ye *w. Col.* 3:7
1 *Pet.* 4:3 we *w.* in lasciviousness

He WALKED.

1 *K.* 3:6 as *he w.* before thee
  15:3 Abijam *he w.* in all sins of his
    father, 2 *K.* 21:21
  16:26 *he w.* in ways of Jeroboam
  22:43 for *he w.* in all ways of Asa,
    2 *Chr.* 20:32
2 *K.* 8:18 *he w.* in ways of kings
    of Is. 16:3 ; 2 *Chr.* 21:6 ; 28:2
  27 *he w.* in way of kings, as
    did house of A. 2 *Chr.* 22:3, 5
2 *Chr.* 17:3 *he w.* in ways of Da.
Dan. 4:29 Nebuch. *he w.* in palace
Hos. 5:11 *he w.* aft. commandm.
Mal. 2:6 *he w.* with me in peace
Mat. 14:29 Peter *w.* on the water
1 *John* 2:6 ought to walk as *he w.*

I have WALKED.

Lev. 26:41 *I h. w.* contr. to them
1 *Sam.* 12:2 *I have w.* before you
2 *Sam.* 7:6 *I have w.* in a tent
  7 places wher. *I h. w.* with Is.
2 *K.* 20:3 how *I h. w.* befo. thee
Job 31:5 if *I have w.* with vanity
Ps. 26:1 for *I h. w.* in integrity
  3 *I h. w.* in thy truth, *Is.* 38:3

WALKEDST.

John 21:18 *w.* whit. th. wouldest

WALKEST.

Deut. 6:7 talk wh. thou *w.* 11:19
1 *K.* 2:42 day thou *w.* abroad
Is. 43:2 when thou *w.* thro' fire
Acts 21:24 thou thyself *w.* orderly
Rom. 14:15 *w.* not charitably
3 *John* 3 even as thou *w.* in truth

WALKETH.

Gen. 24:65 wh. man *w.* in field ?
Deut. 23:14 *w.* in midst of camp
1 *Sam.* 12:2 king *w.* before you
Job 18:8 and he *w.* on a snare
  22:14 he *w.* in circuit of heaven
34:8 and *w.* with wicked men
Ps. 1:1 *w.* not in couns. of ungo.
  15:2 he that *w.* uprightly shall
  39:6 ev. man *w.* in a vain show
  73:9 their tongue *w.* thro' earth
  91:6 pestilence that *w.* in dark.
  101:6 *w.* in perf. way serve me
  104:3 *w.* upon wings of wind
  128:1 bles. ev. one th. *w.* in ways
Prov. 6:12 *w.* with frow. mouth
  10:9 *w.* uprigh. *w.* surely, 28:18
  13:20 that *w.* with wise be wise
  14:2 *w.* in uprightn. feareth L.
  15:21 understand. *w.* uprightly
  19:1 poor *w.* in integrity, 28:6
  20:7 just man *w.* in his integr.
  28:26 whoso *w.* wisely be deliv.
Ec. 2:14 but fool *w.* in darkness
  10:3 he that is a fool *w.* by way
Is. 33:15 *w.* right. dw. on high
  50:10 *w.* in dark. hath no light
  65:2 which *w.* in way not good
Jer. 10:23 *w.* to direct his steps
  23:17 *w.* after imagina. of heart
Ezek. 11:21 heart *w.* after det. th.
Mic. 2:7 to him that *w.* upright.
Mat. 12:43 spirit is gone out, *w.*
  thro' dry places, *Luke* 11:24
John 12:35 that *w.* in darkness
2 *Thes.* 3:6 brother *w.* disorderly
1 *Pet.* 5:8 devil *w.* about seeking
1 *John* 2:11 hate. bro. *w.* in dark.

Rev. 2:1 *w.* in midst of candlest.

WALKING.

Gen. 3:8 voice of L. *w.* in garden
Deut. 2:7 Lord knoweth thy *w.*
1 *K.* 3:3 Sol. loved L. *w.* as Dav.
  16:19 Zimri *w.* in way of Jerob.
Job 1:7 fr. *w.* up and down, 2:2
  31:26 beheld moon *w.* in bright.
Ec. 10:7 princes *w.* as servants
Is. 3:16 *w.* and minc. as they go
  20:2 so, *w.* naked and barefoot
  57:2 each *w.* in his uprightness
Jer. 6:28 revolters, *w.* with sland.
Dan. 3:25 men loose, *w.* in fire
Mic. 2:11 if a man *w.* in spirit
Mat. 14:25 Jesus went *w.* on sea
  26 saw him *w. Mark* 6:48
Mark 8:24 I see men as trees *w.*
Luke 1:6 *w.* in all commandm.
Acts 3:8 lame man *w.* leaping, 9
  9:31 *w.* in the fear of the Lord
2 *Cor.* 4:2 not *w.* in craftiness
2 *Pet.* 3:3 *w.* after lusts, *Jude* 16
2 *John* 4 thy children *w.* in truth

WALL.

Gen. 49:6 they digged down a *w.*
  22 whose branches run over *w.*
Ex. 14:22 waters were a *w.* to
Lev. 14:37 if plague lower th. *w.*
Num. 22:24 *w.* on th. side, a *w.*
  25 ass crushed B.'s foot ag. *w.*
Jos. 2:15 Rah. dwelt on town-*w.*
  6:5 *w.* of city shall fall flat, 20
1 *Sam.* 18:11 smi. D. to *w.* 19:10
  20:25 king sat on seat by the *w.*
  25:16 they were a *w.* by night
  22 if I leave any th. pisseth ag.
    the *w.* 34 ; 1 *K.* 14:10 ; 16:11 ;
    21:21 ; 2 *K.* 9:8
  31:10 fastened Saul's body to *w.*
2 *Sam.* 11:20 they wo. shoot fr. *w.*
  21 fr. *w.* why went ye nigh *w. ?*
  20:15 the people battered the *w.*
  21 head sh. be thrown over *w.*
  22:30 I have leaped *w. Ps.* 18:29
1 *K.* 4:33 hyssop th. springs of *w.*
  20:30 a *w.* fell on 27,000 men
  21:23 dogs shall eat Jez. by *w.*
2 *K.* 3:27 for burnt-offering on *w.*
  4:10 a little chamber on *w.*
  6:26 king of Isr. pass. by on *w.*
  9:33 Jezebel's blood was on *w.*
  18:26 people on the *w. Is.* 36:11
  20:2 Hezekiah turned his face to
    the *w. Is.* 38:2
2 *Chr.* 25:23 Joash brake down *w.*
  36:19 Nebuchad. brake down *w.*
Ezr. 5:3 who com. to make *w. ?*
  9:9 give us a *w.* in Ju. and Jer.
Neh. 1:3 *w.* of J. is broken down
  2:15 I viewed *w.* 17 build *w.*
  4:3 fox sh. break their stone *w.*
  6 so built we *w.* all *w.* joined
  15 we returned all of us to *w.*
  6:6 for wh. cause th. build. *w.*
  15 *w.* was finished in month E.
  12:27 dedication of *w.* of Jerus.
  13:21 why lodge ye about *w. ?*
Ps. 62:3 a bowing *w.* shall ye be
Prov. 18:11 as high *w.* in conceit
  24:31 stone *w.* was broken down
Cant. 2:9 belov. stand. behind *w.*
  8:9 if she be a *w.* 10 I am a *w.*
Is. 2:15 day of L. on fenced *w.*
  5:5 I will break down the *w.*
  25:4 as a storm against the *w.*
  30:13 as a breach in a high *w.*
  59:10 grope for the *w.* like blind
Jer. 15:20 make thee a fenced *w.*
  49:27 I will kindle a fire in *w.*
  51:44 *w.* of Babylon shall fall
Lam. 2:8 to destroy *w.* of Zion
  18 O *w.* of daughter of Zion
Ezek. 4:3 for *w.* of iron between
  8:7 hole in *w.* 8 dig in *w.* 12:5
  10 idols of Is. portrayed on *w.*
  13:12 *w.* is fall. 15 ; 38:20 ev. *w.*

---

  15 accomplish my wrath on *w.*
  41:5 measured *w.* of the house
  43:8 setting *w.* betw. me and th.
Dan. 5:5 fingers wrote on the *w.*
  9:25 street sh. be built, and *w.*
Hos. 2:6 I will make a *w.*
Joel 2:7 they shall climb the *w.*
  9 they shall run upon the *w.*
Amos 1:7 I will send a fire on *w.*
  10 *w.* of Tyrus ; 14 *w.* of Rab.
  5:19 leaned his hand on the *w.*
  7:7 Lord stood upon a *w.* made
Nah. 2:5 shall make haste to *w.*
Hab. 2:11 stone sh. cry out of *w.*
Acts 9:25 let Saul down by the *w.*
  in a basket, 2 *Cor.* 11:33
23:3 G. sh. smite thee, whited *w.*

Eph. 2:14 Ch. ha. brok. down *w.*
Rev. 21:14 *w.* of city had 12 fou.
  18 the *w.* of it was of jasper

See BUILT.

WALLED.

Lev. 25:29 sell house in *w.* city
  30 *w.* city shall be established
Num. 13:28 *w.* great, *Deut.* 1:28

WALLOW, ED.

2 *Sam.* 20:12 Amasa *w.* in blood
Jer. 6:26 gird with sackcloth, *w.*
  25:34 *w.* yourselves in ashes
  48:26 M. shall *w.* in his vomit
Ezek. 27:30 they sh. *w.* in ashes
Mark 9:20 he fell on ground, *w.*

WALLOWING.

2 *Pet.* 2:22 sow washed to *w.*,

WALLS.

Lev. 14:37 if plague be in *w.* 39
  25:31 the villages having no *w.*
Deut. 3:5 cit. fenced with high *w.*
  28:52 till high *w.* come down
2 *K.* 25:4 men fled between 2 *w.*
  10 Chaldees brake down the *w.*
  of Jerusalem, *Jer.* 39:8
Ezr. 4:12 if city be built, *w.* 16
  5:8 timb. in *w.* work goeth fast
Neh. 4:7 *w.* of Jer. were made up
Job 24:11 make oil within th. *w.*
Ps. 51:18 build the *w.* of Jerus.
  55:10 they go about on *w.*
  122:7 peace be within thy *w.*
Prov. 25:28 city broken, with. *w.*
Cant. 5:7 keepers of *w.* took veil
Is. 22:5 a day of break. down *w.*
  25:12 thy *w.* sh. he bring down
  26:1 salvati. will G. app. for *w.*
  49:16 thy *w.* are continu. bef. me
  56:5 within my *w.* a place
  60:10 strang. shall build thy *w.*
  18 thou shalt call thy *w.* salva.
  62:6 I have set watchmen on *w.*
Jer. 1:15 set thrones ag. *w.* of J.
  5:10 go upon her *w.* destroy
  50:15 Bab.'s *w.* are down, 51:58
Ezek. 26:4 destroy *w.* Tyrus, **12**
  27:11 men of Arv. were upon *w.*
  33:30 talking against thee by *w.*
  38:11 all dwelling without *w.* or
Mic. 7:11 in day thy *w.* are built
Zec. 2:4 inhabit. towns with. *w.*
Heb. 11:30 *w.* of Jeri. fell down

WANDER.

Gen. 20:13 God caused me to *w.*
Num. 14:33 your chil. shall *w.* in
  wilderness 32:13 ; *Ps.* 107:40
Deut. 27:18 causeth blind to *w.*
Job 12:24 he causeth them to *w.*
  38:41 ravens *w.* for lack of meat
Ps. 55:7 then would I *w.* far off
  59:15 let them *w.* up and down
  119:10 let me not *w.* fr. comm.
Is. 47:15 they shall *w.* every one
Jer. 14:10 thus they loved to *w.*
  48:12 wanderers th. cause to *w.*
Amos 8:12 shall *w.* fr. sea to sea

WANDERERS.

Jer. 48:12 I will send to him *w.*

Hos. 9:17 be *w.* am. the nations

WANDERED.

Gen. 21:14 Hagar *w.* in wildern.
Ps. 107:4 w. in wildern. *Is.* 16:8
Lam. 4:14 have *w.* as blind men
Ezek. 34:6 my sheep *w.* through
Amos 4:8 three cities *w.* to 1 city
Heb. 11:37 *w.* about in sheep-sk.
    38 they *w.* in deserts, in moun.

WANDEREST, ETH.

Job 15:23 he *w.* abroad for bread
Prov. 21:16 *w.* out of way
    27:8 as a bird that *w.* from nest,
     so is a man that *w.*
Is. 16:3 bewray not him that *w.*
Jer. 2:20 under ev. green tree *w.*
    49:5 none sh. gather him that *w.*

WANDERING.

Gen. 37:15 he was *w.* in the field
Prov. 26:2 *w.* as swallow by fly.
Ec. 6:9 bet. sight of eyes th. *w.*
Is. 16:2 it shall be as a *w.* bird
1 *Tim.* 5:13 *w.* fr. house to house
Jude 13 *w.* stars to wh. is reser.

WANDERINGS.

Ps. 56:8 thou tellest my *w.* put

WANT, Substantive.

Deut. 28:48 serve thy ene. in *w.*
    57 she shall eat them for *w.*
Jud. 18:10 where is no *w.* 19:19
Job 24:8 they embrace rock for *w.*
    30:3 for *w.* they were solitary
    31:19 seen any perish for *w.*
Ps. 34:9 no *w.* to them that fear
Prov. 6:11 *w.* as arm. man, 24:34
    10:21 fools die for *w.* of wisdom
Prov. 13:23 destr. for *w.* of judg.
    14:28 in *w.* of people is destruc.
    21:5 that is hasty only to *w.*
    22:16 giv. to rich sh. come to *w.*
Lam. 4:9 stric. thro' *w.* of fruits
Amos 4:6 I have giv. *w.* of bread
Mark 12:44 of her *w.* cast in all
Luke 15:14 he began to be in *w.*
2 *Cor.* 8:14 abundance for th. *w.*
    9:12 supplieth *w.* of the saints
Phil. 4:11 not that I speak of *w.*

WANTS.

Jud. 19:20 all thy *w.* lie on me
Phil. 2:25 Ep. ministered to *w.*

WANT, Verb.

Ps. 23:1 shepherd, I shall not *w.*
    34:10 that seek Lord shall not *w.*
Prov. 13:25 belly of wicked sh. *w.*
Is. 34:16 none shall *w.* her mate
Jer. 33:17 D. not *w.* a man to sit
    18 Lev. not *w.* 35:19 J. not *w.*
Ezek. 4:17 th. they may *w.* bread

WANTED.

Jer. 44:18 we have *w.* all things
John 2:3 *w.* wine, mother of Je.
2 *Cor.* 11:9 wh. I *w.* I was charg.

Deut. 15:8 lend him in th. he *w.*
Prov. 9:4 th. *w.* understand. 16
    10:19 in words there *w.* not sin
    28:16 prince that *w.* understand.
Ec. 6:2 he *w.* noth. for his soul
Cant. 7:2 like goblet that *w.* not

WANTING.

2 *K.* 19:10 proph. of B. let none
    be *w.* whoso be *w.* not live
Prov. 19:7 pursu. wi. wor. yet *w.*
Ec. 1:15 *w.* cannot be numbered
Dan. 5:27 weighed and found *w.*
Tit. 1:5 set in order the things *w.*
    3:13 that noth. be *w.* unto them
Jam. 1:4 and entire, *w.* nothing

WANTON.

Is. 3:16 daught. walk wi. *w.* eyes
1 *Tim.* 5:11 wax *w.* ag. Christ
Jam. 5:5 have lived and been *w.*

WANTONNESS.

Rom. 13:13 not in chamb. and *w.*

---

2 *Pet.* 2:18 allure thro' much *w.*

WAR.

Ex. 1:10 when there is *w.* they
    13:17 lest peo. rep. when see *w.*
    17:16 L. will have *w.* with Ama.
    32:17 a noise of *w.* in the camp
Num. 1:3 all th. are able to go to
    w. 20:22 ; 26:2 ; *Deut.* 3:18
    10:9 if ye go to *w.* ye shall blow
    31:3 arm some of yoursel. to *w.*
    32:6 shall your breth. go to *w.* ?
    20 go before the Lord to *w.* 27
Deut. 4:34 G. assa. by *w.* to take
    21:10 wh. thou goest forth to *w.*
Jos. 11:23 land rest. fr. *w.* 14:15
    14:11 so is my strength for *w.*
Jud. 3:2 Is. might teach th. *w.*
    5:8 then was *w.* in the gates
    21:22 reserved not his wife in *w.*
1 *Sam.* 14:52 *w.* ag. Philist. 19:8
2 *Sam.* 3:1 *w.* bet. house of S. and
    11:7 Da. demand. how *w.* prosp.
1 *K.* 2:5 shed the blood of *w.* put
    the blood of *w.*
    14:30 *w.* bet. Re. and Jer. 15:6
    15:7 *w.* bet. Abijam and Jerob.
    16 *w.* bet. Asa and Baasha, 32
    20:18 come for *w.* take th. alive
    22:1 contin. 3 years without *w.*
2 *K.* 18:20 and strength for *w.*
1 *Chr.* 5:10 made *w.* with H. 19
    22 slain, bec. *w.* was of God
2 *Chr.* 15:19 no *w.* till 35th year
    35:21 house wherewith I ha. *w.*
Job 5:20 in *w.* redeem fr. sword
    10:17 changes and *w.* ag. me
    38:23 reserved against day of *w.*
Ps. 27:3 tho' *w.* rise against me
    55:21 but *w.* was in his heart
    68:30 scatter peo. th. deli. in *w.*
    120:7 wh. I speak th. are for *w.*
    140:2 continual. are gath. for *w.*
Prov. 20:18 with advice make *w.*
    24:6 by counsel th. sh. make *w.*
Ec. 3:8 time of *w.* time of peace
    8:8 th. is no discharge in th. *w.*
Is. 2:4 nor learn *w. Mic.* 4:3
    3:25 mighty shall fall in the *w.*
    21:15 fled fr. grievousness of *w.*
    36:5 counsel and strength for *w.*
Jer. 4:19 hast heard alarm of *w.*
    6:4 prepare ye *w.* against her
    23 as men for *w.* against thee
    21:2 Nebuch. maketh *w.* ag. us
    42:14 where we shall see no *w.*
    48:14 are mighty men for *w.* ?
Ezek. 17:17 nor Phar. make in *w.*
Dan. 7:21 made *w.* with saints
    9:26 to end of *w.* are desolation
Joel 3:9 prepare *w.* wake up men
Mic. 2:8 as men averse from *w.*
    3:5 even prepare *w.* against him
Luke 14:31 king going to ma. *w.* ?
Rev. 11:7 beast made *w.* ag. th.
    12:7 *w.* in heaven ag. dragon
    17 make *w.* with rem. of seed
    13:4 able to make *w.* wi. beast ?
    7 to make *w.* wi. saints, 17:14
    19:11 in righteousness make *w.*
    19 kings gathered to make *w.*

See EXPERT, MAN, MEN.

Weapons of WAR.

Deut. 1:41 ye girded on *w.* of *w.*
Jud. 18:11 600 wi. *w.* of *w.* 16, 17
2 *Sam.* 1:27 how are *w.* of *w.* per.
Ec. 9:18 wisd. bet. than *w.* of *w.*
Jer. 21:4 turn back *w.* of *w.*
    51:20 battle-axe and *w.* of *w.*
Ezek. 32:27 do. to hell wi. *w.* of *w.*

WAR, Verb.

2 *Sam.* 22:35 Lord teacheth my
    hands to *w. Ps.* 18:34 ; 144:1
2 *K.* 16:5 to *w.* against it, *Is.* 7:1
2 *Chr.* 6:34 if peo. *w.* ag. enemy
Is. 41:12 *w.* ag. thee be as noth.
2 *Cor.* 10:3 do not *w.* after flesh

---

1 *Tim.* 1:18 mightest *w.* a warf.
Jam. 4:1 lusts that *w.* in memb.
    2 fight and *w.* yet ye have not
1 *Pet.* 2:11 lusts wh. *w.* ag. soul

WARRED, ETH.

Num. 31:7 *w.* against Midianites
Jos. 24:9 Balak *w.* against Israel
1 *K.* 14:19 how he *w.* and reigned
    22:45 Jehosh. how he *w.* writ.
2 *K.* 6:8 king of Syria *w.* ag. Is.
2 *Chr.* 26:6 Uzziah *w.* ag. Philist.
2 *Tim.* 2:4 *w.* entangl. himself

WARRING.

2 *K.* 19:8 *w.* ag. Libnah, *Is.* 37:8
Rom. 7:23 a law in my memb. *w.*

WARRIOR, S.

1 *K.* 12:21 who were *w.* 2 *Ch.* 11:1
Is. 9:5 battle of *w.* is with noise

WARS.

Num. 21:14 in book of *w.* of Lord
Jud. 3:1 not known *w.* of Canaan
1 *Chr.* 22:8 great *w.* sh. not build
2 *Chr.* 16:9 hencef. shalt have *w.*
Ps. 46:9 he maketh *w.* to cease
Mat. 24:6 hear of *w.* and rumors
    of *w. Mark* 13:7 ; *Luke* 21:9
Jam. 4:1 from whence come *w.* ?

WARD.

Gen. 40:3 put in *w.* 4, 7 ; 41:10
    42:7 Joseph put brethren in *w.*
Lev. 24:12 put blasphemer in *w.*
Num. 15:34 gath. of sticks in *w.*
2 *Sam.* 20:3 ten concubin. in *w.*
1 *Chr.* 12:29 had kept *w.* of Saul
    25:8 cast lots, *w.* against *w.*
    26:16 by cause of *w.* goi. ag. *w.*
Neh. 12:24 thanks *w.* against *w.*
    25 porters keep. *w.* at gates, 45
Is. 21:8 I am set in my *w.*
Jer. 37:13 capt. of *w.* was there
Ezek. 19:9 they put Zedek. in *w.*
Acts 12:10 first and second *w.*

WARDS.

1 *Chr.* 9:23 house of taber. by *w.*
    26:12 hav. *w.* one ag. another
Neh. 13:30 appoint. *w.* of priests

WARDROBE.

2 *K.* 22:14 Shallum the keeper
    of the *w.* 2 *Chr.* 34:22

WARE.

Luke 8:27 man *w.* no clothes

WARE.

Acts 14:6 *w.* of it, fled to Lys.
2 *Tim.* 4:15 of coppersmith be *w.*

WARE, S.

Neh. 10:31 if peo. bri. *w.* on sab.
    13:16 men of Tyre brought *w.*
    20 merchants and sellers of *w.*
Jer. 10:17 gath. up *w.* out of land
Ezek. 27:16 by reas. of *w.* 18, 33
Jon. 1:5 mariners cast forth *w.*

WARFARE.

1 *Sam.* 28:1 gath. armies for *w.*
Is. 40:2 her *w.* is accomplished
1 *Cor.* 9:7 goeth a *w.* any time
2 *Cor.* 10:4 weap. of *w.* not carnal
1 *Tim.* 1:18 might. war a good *w.*

WARM.

2 *K.* 4:34 flesh of child waxed *w.*
Job 6:17 th. wax *w.* they vanish
    37:17 how garm. are *w.* when
Ec. 4:11 how can one be *w.* al. ?
Is. 44:15 take ther. and *w.* hims.
    47:14 sh. not be a coal to *w.*
Hag. 1:6 but there is none *w.*

WARMED, ETH, ING.

Job 31:20 were not *w.* wi. fleece
    39:14 ostrich *w.* eggs in dust
Is. 44:16 *w.* himself, and saith
Mark 14:54 and Pet. *w.* himself,
    John 18:18, 25
    67 when she saw P. *w.* himself
Jam. 2:16 depart in peace, be *w.*

WARN.

2 *Chr.* 19:10 sh. *w.* they tresp. not
Ezek. 3:18 to *w.* the wicked, 33:8
19 yet if thou *w.* wicked, 33:9
21 *w.* righteous; 33:3 *w.* peo. 7
Acts 20:31 I ceased not to *w.* ev.
1 *Cor.* 4:14 beloved sons I *w.* you
1 *Thes.* 5:14 *w.* that are unruly

WARNED.

2 *K.* 6:10 man of God *w.* him
Ps. 19:11 by them is servant *w.*
Ezek. 3:21 live, because he is *w.*
33:6 and the people be not *w.*
Mat. 2:12 Joseph being *w.* of G.
3:7 O generation of vipers, who
hath *w.* you? *Luke* 3:7
Acts 10:22 Cornelius *w.* from G.
Heb. 11:7 Noah *w.* prepared ark

WARNING.

Jer. 6:10 to whom sh. I give *w.?*
Ezek. 3:17.and give them *w.*
18 thou givest him not *w.* 20
33:4 tak. not *w.* 5 took not *w.*
Col. 1:28 *w.* every man, teaching

WARP.

Lev. 13:48 pla. in *w.* 49, 51, 57, 59
52 burn *w.* 56 rend *w.* 58 wash.

WAS.

Gen. 5:24 walked with G. *w.* not
Rev. 1:4 is and which *w.* 8; 4:8
17:8 beast th. saw. *w.* is not, 11

It WAS.

Ex. 16:15 wist not what *it w.*
Is. 48:16 from time that *it w.*
Ezek. 16:15 his *it w.* 19 thus *it w.*

WASH.

Gen. 18:4 *w.* y. feet, 19:2; 24:32
Ex. 2:5 daught. of P. came to *w.*
29:4 Aa. *w.* 30:19, 20, 21; 40:12
Lev. 6:27 shalt *w.* that whereon
13:54 *w.* thi. wherein plague is
14:8 *w.* himself, *Deut.* 23:11
9 *w.* his flesh in water, 15:16;
16:4, 24; 22:6
17:16 if he *w.* not sh. bear iniq.
Deut. 21:6 *w.* hands over heifer
Ruth 3:3 *w.* thyself, and anoint
1 *Sam.* 25:41 servant to *w.* feet
2 *Sam.* 11:8 go down and *w.* feet
2 *K.* 5:10 go *w.* in Jordan 7 times
12 may I not *w.* and be clean?
13 saith to thee, *w.* be clean?
2 *Chr.* 4:6 lavers to *w.* in, sea for
Job 9:30 if I *w.* myself wi. water
Ps. 26:6 I will *w.* my hands in
51:2 *w.* me from mine iniquity
7 *w.* me and I sh. be whiter th.
58:10 *w.* feet in blood of wicked
Is. 1:16 *w.* ye, make you clean
Jer. 2:22 tho' thou *w.* with nitre
4:14 *w.* thy heart from wickedn.
Ezek. 23:40 thou didst *w.* thyself
Mat. 6:17 when fastest, *w.* face
15:2 they *w.* not when they eat
Mark 7:3 exc. they *w.* eat not, 4
Luke 7:38 began to *w.* his feet
John 9:7 *w.* in pool of Siloam, 11
13:5 began to *w.* disciples' feet
6 Lord, dost thou *w.* my feet?
8 never *w.* me, feet, if I *w.* not
14 ought to *w.* one ano.'s feet
Acts 22:16 and *w.* away thy sins

See CLOTHES, FEET.

WASHED.

Gen. 43:24 water, they *w.* feet
31 Joseph *w.* face and went out
49:11 Ju. *w.* garments in wine
Ex. 40:32 *w.* as L. commanded
Lev. 13:55 plague aft. it is *w.* 58
Jud. 19:21 concub. *w.* their feet
2 *Sam.* 12:20 David arose and *w.*
1 *K.* 22:38 one *w.* chariot in pool
Job 29:6 I *w.* steps with butter
Ps. 73:13 I *w.* hands in innocen.
Prov. 30:12 not *w.* fr. filthiness

Cant. 5:3 I have *w.* my feet
12 his eyes are *w.* with milk
Is. 4:4 *w.* away filth of daughters
Ezek 16:4 nor wast *w.* in water
9 I thorou. *w.* away thy blood
Mat. 27:24 Pilate *w.* his hands
Luke 7:44 she hath *w.* my feet
11:38 marvelled he had not *w.*
John 9:7 he went and *w.* 11, 15
John 13:10 is *w.* need. not save to
14 Master have *w.* your feet
Acts 9:37 wh. when they had *w.*
16:33 he took them, *w.* stripes
1 *Cor.* 6:11 ye are *w.* sanctified
1 *Tim.* 5:10 if she *w.* saints' feet
Heb. 10:22 having our bodies *w.*
2 *Pet.* 2:22 sow *w.* to wallowing
Rev. 1:5 that *w.* us fr. our sins
7:14 have *w.* their robes white

See CLOTHES.

WASHEST, ING.

2 *Sam.* 11:2 Da. saw a woman *w.*
Job 14:19 *w.* away thi. wh. grow
Luke 5:2 fishermen were *w.* nets

WASHING, S.

Lev. 13:56 plague dark after *w.*
Neh. 4:23 ev. one put off for *w.*
Cant. 4:2 sheep came fr. *w.* 6:6
Mark 7:4 *w.* of cups and tables, 8
Eph. 5:26 cleanse wi. *w.* of wat.
Tit. 3:5 saved us by *w.* of regen.
Heb. 9:10 stood in meats and *w.*

WASHPOT.

Ps. 60:8 Moab is my *w.* 108:9

WAST.

Ob. 11 thou *w.* as one of them
Rev. 11:17 who art, and *w.* art

WASTE, Substantive.

Jer. 49:13 Bozrah shall bec. a *w.*
Mat. 26:8 to what purpose is this
w.? *Mark* 14:4

WASTE, Adjective.

Deut. 32:10 found him in *w.* wil.
Job 30:3 fleeing into the *w.* wil.
38:27 to satisfy desol. *w.* ground
Is. 24:1 Lord maketh earth *w.*
42:15 I will make *w.* mountains
49:17 that made *w.* sh. go forth
Jer. 2:15 lions made his land *w.*
46:19 Noph shall be *w.* and des.
Ezek. 5:14 I will make Jerusal. *w.*
29:9 Eg. shall be *w.* 10; 30:12
38:8 mountains been always *w.*
Nah. 2:10 Ninev. is void and *w.*
Zep. 3:6 I have made streets *w.*
Hag. 1:9 because my house is *w.*

See CITIES, LAY, LAID, PLACES.

WASTE, Verb.

1 *K.* 17:14 barrel of meal not *w.*
1 *Chr.* 17:9 no childr. of wick. *w.*
Ps. 80:13 boar of wood doth *w.*
Jer. 50:21 *w.* inhabitants of Pek.
Mic. 5:6 they sh. *w.* land of Assy.

WASTED.

Num. 14:33 till carcasses be *w.*
24:22 the Kenite shall be *w.*
Deut. 2:14 men of war were *w.*
1 *K.* 17:16 barrel of meal *w.* not
1 *Chr.* 20:1 J. *w.* country of Am.
Ps. 137:3 that *w.* required mirth
Is. 6:11 till cities be *w.* without
19:5 river sh. be *w.* dried up
60:12 nations sh. be utterly *w.*
Jer. 44:6 are *w.* and desolate as
Joel 1:10 field is *w.* corn is *w.*
Luke 15:13 prodig. *w.* substance
16:1 accused that he *w.* goods
Gal. 1:13 persecu. church and *w.*

WASTENESS.

Zep. 1:15 day of *w.* desolation

WASTER.

Prov. 18:9 brother to a great *w.*
Is. 54:16 created *w.* to destroy

WASTES.

Is. 61:4 they shall build old *w.*
Jer. 49:13 Boz. sh. be perpet. *w.*
Ezek. 33:24 that inhab. *w.* of Is.
27 they in the *w.* shall fall
36:4 thus saith L. to desolate *w.*
10 the *w.* shall be builded, 33

WASTETH.

Job 14:10 man dieth, *w.* away
Ps. 91:6 nor destruction that *w.*
Prov. 19:26 he that *w.* father

WASTING.

Is. 59:7 *w.* and destruction are in
60:18 not heard *w.* nor destruc.

WATCH, Substantive.

Ex. 14:24 in morn. *w.* L. looked
Jud. 7:19 middle *w.* had set *w.*
1 *Sam.* 11:11 S. came in morn. *w.*
2 *K.* 11:6 so shall ye keep the *w.*
of house, 7; 2 *Chr.* 23:6
Neh. 4:9 prayed to God set a *w.*
7:3 every one in his *w.* and
Job 7:12 am I a sea, that set. *w.?*
Ps. 90:4 a thous. years as a *w.*
141:3 set a *w.* before my mouth
Jer. 51:12 make the *w.* strong
Hab. 2:1 I will sta. upon my *w.*
Mat. 14:25 in 4th *w.* *Mark* 6:48
Mat. 24:43 wh. *w.* thief wo. come
27:65 ye have a *w.* go your way
66 seal. stone and setting a *w.*
28:11 some of *w.* came into city
Luke 2:8 shepherds keeping *w.*
12:38 if he come in second *w.*

WATCHES.

Neh. 12:9 over against th. in *w.*
Ps. 63:6 when I meditate in *w.*
119:148 mine eyes prev. night *w.*
Lam. 2:19 in beginning of the *w.*

WATCH, Verb.

Gen. 31:49 Lord *w.* between me
1 *Sam.* 19:11 Saul sent to *w.* Da.
Ezr. 8:29 *w.* ye, keep vessels till
Job 14:16 not *w.* over my sin?
Ps. 102:7 I *w.* am as sparrow
130:6 more than they that *w.*
Is. 21:5 *w.* in the watch-tower
29:20 all that *w.* for iniquity
Jer. 5:6 a leop. sh. *w.* over cities
31:28 so will I *w.* over them
44:27 I will *w.* over them
Nah. 2:1 keep munit. *w.* way
Hab. 2:1 I will *w.* to see what he
Mat. 24:42 *w.* therefore, 25:13;
Mark 13:35; *Luke* 21:36;
Acts 20:31
26:38 Jesus said, *w.* with me
40 could ye not *w.? Mark*
14:34, 37
41 *w.* and pray, *Mark* 13:33;
14:38; *Col.* 4:2
Mark 13:34 command. porter to
w. 37 I say unto all, *w.*
1 *Cor.* 16:13 *w.* stand in faith
1 *Thes.* 5:6 let us *w.* 1 *Pet.* 4:7
2 *Tim.* 4:5 *w.* th. in all things
Heb. 13:17 th. *w.* for your souls

WATCHED.

Jer. 20:10 familiars *w.* for halt.
31:28 as I have *w.* over them
Lam. 4:17 *w.* for a nation that
Dan. 9:14 Lord *w.* on evil
Mat. 24:43 man of house would
have *w.* *Luke* 12:39
27:36 sitting down they *w.* him
Mark 3:2 *w.* whether he would
heal on sab. *Luke* 6:7; 14:1
Luke 20:20 th. *w.* and sent spies
Acts 9:24 *w.* gates day and night

WATCHER, S.

Jer. 4:16 published that *w.* come
Dan. 4:13 *w.* and holy one came
17 degree of *w.* 23 king saw *w.*

WATCHETH.

Ps. 37:32 wicked *w.* righteous

Ezek. 7:6 it *w.* for th. it is come
Rev. 16:15 blessed is he that *w.*

WATCHFUL.
Rev. 3:2 be *w.* strengthen things

WATCHING, S.
1 Sam. 4:13 E. sat by way-si. *w.*
Prov. 8:34 heareth me, *w.* daily
Lam. 4:17 in *w.* we ha. watched
Mat. 27:54 centurion *w.* Jesus
Luke 12:37 L. when com. find *w.*
2 Cor. 6:5 in labors, in *w.* in fast.
11:27 in *w.* often, in hunger, thirst
Eph. 6:18 *w.* with perseverance

WATCHMAN.
2 Sam. 18:25 *w.* cried, told king
26 *w.* saw anoth. man running
2 K. 9:18 *w.* told, cometh not, 20
Ps. 127:1 *w.* waketh but in vain
Is. 21:6 set *w.* 11 *w.* what of the
   night?
Jer. 51:12 set up the *w.* prepare
Ezek. 3:17 made thee a *w.* 33:7
33:2 if peo. set him up for th. *w.*
Hos. 9:8 *w.* of Ephr. was with G.

WATCHMEN.
Cant. 3:3 *w.* go about city, 5:7
Is. 52:8 thy *w.* shall lift voice
56:10 his *w.* are blind, ignorant
62:6 I have set *w.* on thy walls
Jer. 6:17 set *w.* over you, saying
31:6 *w.* on mount Ephr. sh. cry
Mic. 7:4 day of thy *w.* cometh

WATCH-TOWER.
2 Chr. 20:24 Ju. came toward *w.*
Is. 21:5 watch in *w.* eat, drink
   8 I stand continually on the *w.*

WATER, Substantive.
Gen. 16:7 angel found Ha. by *w.*
18:4 let a little *w.* be fetched
21:14 Abra. took a bottle of *w.*
24:32 Laban gave the man *w.*
   43 give me *w.* to drink
26:20 *w.* is ours ; 32 found *w.*
43:24 the steward gave them *w.*
49:4 unstable as *w.* sh. not excel
Ex. 12:9 nor sodden with *w.*
17:6 shall come *w.* out of rock
Ex. 20:4 any likeness th. is in *w.*
23:25 L. bless thy bread and *w.*
29:4 Aaron and his sons shall
   wash them with *w.* 30:20;
   40:12 ; *Lev.* 8:6 ; 16:4, 24
Lev. 6:28 be scoured in *w.* 15:12
11:32 it must be put into *w.*
Num. 5:22 *w.* that causeth curse
8:7 sprinkle *w.* of purification
19:9 for a *w.* of separation, 13,
   20, 21 ; 31:23
20:8 *w.* out of the rock, 10, 11 ;
   Neh. 9:15 ; *Ps.* 114:8
13 *w.* of Meribah, 24 ; 27:14
21:5 th. is no bread, nor any *w.*
   16 gather peo. I will give th. *w.*
24:7 shall pour *w.* out of bucket
31:23 make go through the *w.*
Deut. 8:7 L. bri. to brooks of *w.*
11:11 land drinketh *w.* of rain
12:16 on earth as *w.* 24 ; 15:23
23:4 with *w.* in way, *Neh.* 13:2
Jos. 7:5 melted and became *w.*
Jud. 5:25 he asked *w.* gave milk
7:4 bring th. down to the *w.* 5
15:19 *w.* came out of the jaw
1 Sam. 7:6 gathered and drew *w.*
25:11 I take my bread and *w.*
26:11 take now the cruse of *w.*
30:12 nor drunk any *w.* 3 days
2 Sam. 14:14 are as *w.* on ground
17:21 arise and pass over the *w.*
21:10 till *w.* dropped on them
1 K. 13:19 did eat bread drank *w.*
   22 eaten bread and drunk *w.*
14:15 smite *w.* as a reed in *w.*
17:10 fetch, I pray, a little *w.*
18:4 fed them with bread and *w.*
   35 *w.* ran, filled trench wi. *w.*

38 fire of Lord licked up the *w.*
22:27 feed him with bread and
   w. of affliction, 2 *Chr.* 18:26
2 K. 2:19 the *w.* is naught, the
3:11 Eli. poured *w.* on Elijah's
17 valley shall be filled with *w.*
22 and the sun shone on the *w.*
6:5 the ax-head fell into *w.*
22 set bread and *w.* bef. them
8:15 dipped a thick cloth in *w.*
20:20 brought *w.* into the city
2 Chr. 32:4 king of Assy. find *w.*
Job 8:11 can flag grow with. *w.* ?
14:9 yet through the scent of *w.*
15:16 who drink. iniq. like *w.*
22:7 hast not given *w.* to weary
34:7 drinketh scorning like *w.*
Ps. 22:14 I am poured out like *w.*
65:9 river of God is full of *w.*
66:12 went through fire and *w.*
79:3 blood have th. shed like *w.*
88:17 came about me like *w.*
109:18 come into bowels like *w.*
Prov. 17:14 when one let. out *w.*
20:5 coun. of man like deep *w.*
27:19 as in *w.* face answereth
30:16 that is not filled with *w.*
Is. 1:22 thy wine mixed with *w.*
3:1 doth take away stay of *w.*
21:14 land of Tema brought *w.*
30:14 found a sherd to take *w.*
   20 L. gave you *w.* of affliction
41:17 when the poor seek *w.*
44:3 I will pour *w.* on thirsty
63:12 dividing *w.* before them
Jer. 13:1 girdle, put it not in *w.*
23:15 make th. drink *w.* of gall
Lam. 1:16 eyes ru... with *w.* 3:48
2:19 pour out thy heart like *w.*
5:4 we have drunken our *w.* for
Ezek. 4:17 want bread and *w.*
7:17 knees be weak as *w.* 21:7
16:4 nor wast thou washed in *w.*
   9 then washed I thee with *w.*
36:25 sprinkle cle. *w.* upon you
Hos. 2:5 lov. that gave me my *w.*
5:10 pour wrath on them like *w.*
10:7 king cut off as foam on *w.*
Amos 8:11 not fam. nor thi. of *w.*
Nah. 2:8 Nineveh like pool of *w.*
Hab. 3:10 overflow. of *w.* passed
Mat. 3:11 bapt. you wi. *w.* *Mark*
   1:8 ; *Luke* 3:16 ; *John* 1:26
16 J. went out of *w.* *Mark* 1:10
10:42 giv. cup of *w.* *Mark* 9:41
14:28 bid me come to thee on *w.*
17:15 falleth oft into fire and *w.*
27:24 Pilate took *w.* and washed
Mark 14:13 bearing pitcher of *w.*
   Luke 22:10
Luke 8:23 ship was filled with *w.*
   24 rebuked *w.* 25 *w.* obeyed
16:24 may dip his finger in *w.*
John 2:7 fill water-pots with *w.*
3:5 except a man be born of *w.*
   23 because there was much *w.*
4:10 living *w.* 11 ; 15 give me *w.*
   46 came wh. he made *w.* wine
5:3 waiting for moving of *w.*

John 5:4 ang. went down, tro. *w.*
7:38 out of his belly flow liv. *w.*
13:5 he poureth *w.* into a basin
19:34 came thereout blo. and *w.*
Acts 1:5 J. bapt. with *w.* 11:16
8:36 here is *w.* 38 went into *w.*
10:47 can any forbid *w.* th. be
Eph. 5:26 cle. it wi. wash. of *w.*
Heb. 9:19 blood of calves wi. *w.*
10:22 bod. washed with pure *w.*
Jam. 3:12 yield salt *w.* and fresh
1 Pet. 3:20 8 souls saved by *w.*
2 Pet. 2:17 th. are wells witho. *w.*
3:6 world bei. overflowed wi. *w.*
Jude 12 clouds they are with. *w.*
1 John 5:6 came by *w.* and blood
   8 three witn. Spirit, *w.* blood
Rev. 12:15 serpent cast out *w.*

16:12 Euphrates, *w.* dried up
21:6 give of fount. of *w.* of life
22:1 show. me a pure river of *w.*
17 let take *w.* of life freely

See BITTER, DRAW, DREW, DRINK,
   WELL.

No WATER.
Gen. 37:24 there was no *w.* in it
Ex. 15:22 fou. no *w.* 17:1 ; *Num.*
   20:2 ; 33:14 ; *Deut.* 8:15
1 K. 13:22 bread, and drink no *w.*
2 K. 3:9 there was no *w.* for host
Ps. 63:1 thirsty la. wh. no *w.* is
Is. 1:30 as garden that ha. no *w.*
44:12 smith drinketh no *w.*
50:2 stinketh bec. there is no *w.*
Jer. 2:13 cist. that can hold no *w.*
14:3 came to pits found no *w.*
38:6 in dungeon th. was no *w.*
Zec. 9:11 out of pit wher. no *w.*
Luke 7:44 thou gavest me no *w.*

WATER, Verb.
Gen. 2:10 out of E. to *w.* garden
29:7 *w.* sheep and feed them, 8
Ps. 6:6 I *w.* couch with my tears
72:6 as showers that *w.* earth
Ec. 2:6 pools of wa. to *w.* wood
Is. 16:9 I will *w.* thee with tears
27:3 I will *w.* it every moment
Ezek. 17:7 mi. *w.* it by furrows
32:6 I will *w.* with my blood
Joel 3:18 fountain *w.* valley of S.

WATERED, ST.
Gen. 2:6 mist th. *w.* face of gro.
13:10 Jord. that it was well *w.*
29:2 *w.* flocks, 3 ; 10 J. *w.* flocks
Ex. 2:17 and *w.* their flocks, 19
Deut. 11:10 it. it with thy foot
Prov. 11:25 water. be *w.* himself
Is. 58:11 sh. be like a *w.* garden
Jer. 31:12 soul sh. be a *w.* garden
1 Cor. 3:6 I planted, Apollos *w.*

WATEREST, ETH.
Ps. 65:9 visitest earth and *w.* it
10 thou *w.* the ridges thereof
104:13 *w.* hills from chambers
Prov. 11:25 th. *w.* sh. be watered
Is. 55:10 returneth not, *w.* earth
1 Cor. 3:7 nor *w.* any thing, 8

WATERING.
Gen. 30:38 rods in *w.* troughs
Job 37:11 by *w.* he weari. clouds
Luke 13:15 lead his ass to *w.* ?

WATER-BROOKS.
Ps. 42:1 hart panteth after *w.-b.*

WATER-COURSE, S.
2 Chr. 32:30 stopped upper *w.-c.*
Job 38:25 who hath divid. *w.-c.* ?
Is. 44:4 spri. as willows by *w.-c.*

WATER-FLOOD.
Ps. 69:15 let not *w.-f.* overfl. me

WATER-POT, S.
John 2:6 set there six *w.-p.* of st.
   7 J. saith, Fill *w.-p.* wi. water
4:28 wo. left *w.-p.* went to city

WATER-SPOUTS.
Ps. 42:7 deep at noise of *w.-s.*

WATER-SPRINGS.
Ps. 107:33 he turneth the *w.-s.*
   35 turneth dry grou. into *w.-s.*

WATERS.
Gen. 1:2 moved upon face of *w.*
6 divide the *w.* from the *w.* 7
9 let *w.* be gather. 20 *w.* bring
6:17 I br. a flood of *w.* on earth
7:17 *w.* increased, 18, 19, 20, 24
8:1 *w.* decrea. 3, 5 ; 13 *w.* dried
9:11 not cut off any more by *w.*
Ex. 7:17 smite *w.* 20 *w.* blood
8:6 stretched out hand over *w.*
14:21 by east wind the *w.* divid.
22 *w.* a wall, 29 ; 28 *w.* returned,
   15:19

15:8 *w.* were gathered together
23 could not drink of *w.* of M.
27 they encamped there by *w.*
Num. 24:6 cedar-trees beside *w.*
Deut. 10:7 to Jotbath, riv. of *w.*
32:51 trespass. at *w.* of Meribah
33:8 didst str. at *w.* of Meribah
Jos. 3:16 *w.* which came down
4:7 *w.* of Jordan were cut off
23 L. dried up *w.* of Jord. 5:1
11:5 pitched at *w.* of Merom
Jud. 5:19 kings by *w.* of Megid.
7:24 take the *w.* before them
2 *Sam.* 5:20 br. of *w.* 1 *Chr.* 14:11
12:27 I have tak. the city of *w.*
2 *K.* 2:8 smote *w.* 14 Elisha
21 went forth unto spring of *w.*
5:12 Damascus bet. th. *w.* of Is.
2 *Chr.* 32:3 took coun. to stop *w.*
Job 3:24 roarings poured like *w.*
5:10 who sendeth *w.* upon fields
11:16 remem. thy misery as *w.*
12:15 he withholdeth *w.* th. dry
14:11 as the *w.* fail from the sea
19 the *w.* wear the stones, thou
22:11 abunda. of *w.* cover, 38:34
24:18 he is swift as the *w.* thou
26:5 things formed fr. under *w.*
8 bindeth up *w.* in thick clou.
10 he compassed *w.* wi. clouds
27:20 ter. take ho. on him as *w.*
28:4 even *w.* forgotten of foot
25 he weigheth *w.* by measure
29:19 my root was spread by *w.*
80:14 came on me as brea. of *w.*
37:10 breadth of *w.* is straitened
38:30 *w.* are hid as with a stone
Ps. 23:2 lead. me beside still *w.*
33:7 he gathereth *w.* of the sea
46:3 though the *w.* thereof roar
58:7 let them melt away as *w.*
69:1 *w.* come in unto my soul
73:10 *w.* of a full cup are wrung
77:16 *w.* saw thee, O G. *w.* saw
78:13 made *w.* stand as a heap
20 smote rock that *w.* gushed,
    105:41; 114:8; *Is.* 48:21
81:7 I proved thee at *w.* 106:32
104:6 *w.* stood above mountains
105:29 he turned *w.* into blood
106:11 *w.* covered their enemies
119:136 rivers of *w.* run down
124:4 *w.* had overwhelmed us
5 proud *w.* gone over our soul
136:6 stretched earth above *w.*
147:18 wind to blow and *w.* flow
148:4 ye *w.* above the heavens
Prov. 5:15 drink *w.* out of cistern
16 let rivers of *w.* be dispersed
8:29 that the *w.* should not pass
9:17 stolen *w.* are sweet, bread
25:25 as cold *w.* to thirsty soul
30:4 who bound *w.* in a garment
Ec. 11:1 cast thy bread upon *w.*
Cant. 4:15 a well of *w.* streams
7 the Lord bringeth on th. *w.*
11:9 *w.* cover seas, *Hab.* 2:14
15:6 *w.* of Nimrim sh. be deso.
9 *w.* of Dimon be full of blood
17:12 like rushing of mighty *w.*
19:5 *w.* shall fail from the sea
22:9 gathered *w.* of lower pool
28:17 *w.* overflow hiding-place
32:20 bless th. sow beside all *w.*
33:16 bread given him, *w.* sure
35:6 in wildern. *w.* break forth
40:12 who hath measured *w.?*
43:2 thro' *w.* I will be with thee
16 maketh a path in mighty *w.*
10 I give *w.* in the wilderness
48:1 are come out of *w.* of Jud.
21 caused *w.* flow out of rock
51:10 which dri. *w.* of the deep
54:9 *w.* of Noah to me, *w.* not
55:1 th. thirsteth, come ye to *w.*
57:20 whose *w.* cast up mire

58:11 spring, whose *w.* fail not
Jer. 2:13 fountain of living *w.*
18 to do, to drink *w.* of Sihor?
6:7 as a fountain casteth out *w.*
8:14 G. hath given us *w.* of gall
9:1 O that my head were *w.?*
13 our eyelids gush out wi. *w.*
10:13 mult. of *w.* in heav. 51:16
14:3 nobles sent little ones to *w.*
15:18 as a liar, as *w.* that fail
17:8 as a tree planted by the *w.*
13 forsak. Lord, fountain of *w.*
18:14 shall cold *w.* be forsaken?
46:7 whose *w.* are moved, 8
47:2 *w.* rise up out of the north
48:34 *w.* of Nimrim be desolate
50:38 a drought is upon her *w.*
Lam. 3:54 *w.* flowed overhead
Ezek. 19:10 moth. like vine by *w.*
31:4 *w.* made him great
14 trees by *w.* exalt themselv.
32:2 troublest *w.* with thy feet
47:1 *w.* issu. fr. under threshold
Ezek. 47:3 brought me thro' *w.*
    the *w.* 4
5 *w.* were risen, *w.* to swim in
8 *w.* issued out toward east, 12
19 *w.* of strife in Kadesh, 48:28
Dan. 12:6 said to man upon *w.* 7
Amos 5:8 call. for *w.* of sea, 9:6
24 let judgm. run down as *w.*
Jon. 2:5 *w.* compassed me about
Mic. 1:4 as *w.* pour. down steep
Nah. 3:8 had *w.* round about it
14 draw *w.* for siege, fortify
Zec. 14:8 living *w.* sh. go fr. Jer.
2 *Cor.* 11:26 in perils of *w.*
Rev. 7:17 lead th. to fount. of *w.*
8:11 *w.* became wormwood and
11:6 have power over *w.* to turn
14:7 that made fountain of *w.*
16:4 angel poured his vial on *w.*
5 I heard ang. of *w.* say, Thou
17:15 the *w.* where whore sits

See DEEP, GREAT.

In, or **into WATERS.**
Ex. 15:10 th. sank as lead in *w.*
25 a tree when cast *into w.*
Lev. 11:9 shall eat what hath fins
    and scales *in w.* 10, 46;
    Deut. 14:9
Deut. 4:18 liken. of fish *in w.* 5:8
Jos. 3:13 feet of priests rest *in w.*
Neh. 9:11 threwest a stone *in w.*
Ps. 74:13 heads of dragons *in w.*
104:3 beams of his chamb. *in w.*
Mat. 8:32 sw. ran. perished *in w.*
Mark 9:22 cast into fire, *into w.*

Many WATERS.
Num. 24:7 seed shall be in *m. w.*
2 *Sam.* 22:17 drew me out of *m.
    w. Ps.* 18:16
Ps. 29:3 voice of L. upon *m. w.*
93:4 might. than noise of *m. w.*
Cant. 8:7 *m. w.* cannot qu. love
Is. 17:13 like rushing of *m. w.*
Jer. 51:13 dwellest upon *m. w.*
Ezek. 19:10 fruit. by rea. of *m. w.*
43:2 his voice was like noise of
    m. w. Rev. 1:15; 14:2; 19:6
Rev. 17:1 whore sitteth on *m. w.*

WAVE.
Jam. 1:6 waver. is like *w.* of sea

WAVE, Verb.
Ex. 29:24 *w.* them for wave-offer.
    Lev. 8:27; 23:20; *Num.* 6:20
26 shalt *w.* breast; 27 *w.* sho.
    Lev. 7:30; 8:29; 9:21; 10:15
Lev. 23:11 *w.* sheaf before L. 12
Num. 5:25 *w.* jealousy-offering

WAVED.
Lev. 14:21 take 1 lamb to be *w.*
See OFFERING.

WAVERETH.
Jam. 1:6 he that *w.* is like wave

WAVERING.
Heb. 10:23 hold faith without *w.*
Jam. 1:6 ask in faith, nothi. *w.*

WAVES.
Ps. 42:7 *w.* are gone over me
65:7 stilleth *w.* 89:9; 107:29
88:7 th. afflicted me with thy *w.*
93:3 floods lift up their *w.*
4 L. is mightier th. mighty *w.*
107:25 wind which lifteth up *w.*
Is. 48:18 righteous. as *w.* of sea
51:15 whose *w.* roared, *Jer.* 31:35
Jer. 5:22 tho' *w.* tossed, not pre.
51:42 Babyl. is covered with *w.*
55 Babylon where her *w.* roar
Ezek. 26:3 as sea causeth his *w.*
Jon. 2:3 thy *w.* passed over me
Zec. 10:11 shall smite *w.* in sea
Mat. 8:24 ship covered with *w.*
14:24 tossed with *w. Mark* 4:37
Luke 21:25 sea and *w.* roaring
Acts 27:41 part was bro. with *w.*
Jude 13 raging *w.* of sea, foami.

WAX.
Ps. 22:14 my heart is like *w.*
68:2 as *w.* melt. wicked perish
97:5 hills melted like *w.*
Mic. 1:4 cleft as *w.* before fire

WAX, Verb.
Ec. 22:24 wrath *w.* hot, 32:10
32:11 why doth thy wra. *w.* hot
22 let not anger of my lord *w.*
Lev. 25:47 or stranger *w.* rich
1 *Sam.* 3:2 eyes began to *w.* dim
Job 6:17 they *w.* warm, they van.
14:8 root thereof *w.* old in earth
Ps. 102:26 *w.* old as garment, *Is.*
    50:9; 51:6; *Heb.* 1:11
Is. 17:4 fatness of flesh *w.* lean
29:22 nei. shall his face *w.* pale
Jer. 6:24 our hands *w.* feeble
Mat. 24:12 love of many *w.* cold
Luke 12:33 bags wh. *w.* not old
1 *Tim.* 5:11 begun to *w.* wanton
2 *Tim.* 3:13 seduc. sh. *w.* worse

WAXED.
Gen. 26:13 Isaac *w.* great
41:56 famine *w.* sore in Egypt
Ex. 1:7 Israel *w.* mighty, 20
16:21 when sun *w.* hot
32:19 Moses' anger *w.* hot
Num. 11:23 L.'s hand *w.* short?
Deut. 8:4 their raiment *w.* not
    old, 29:5; *Neh.* 9:21
32:15 Jeshur. *w.* fat and kicked
Jos. 23:1 Joshua *w.* old, stricken
1 *Sam.* 2:5 had child. is *w.* feeble
2 *Sam.* 3:1 but Dav. *w.* stronger,
    1 *Chr.* 11:9
21:15 David fought, *w.* faint
2 *K.* 4:34 flesh of child *w.* warm
2 *Chr.* 13:21 Abijah *w.* mighty
17:12 Jehoshaphat *w.* great
24:15 Jehoi. *w.* old full of days
Est. 9:4 Mordecai *w.* greater
Ps. 32:3 silence my bones *w.* old
Jer. 49:24 Damascus *w.* feeble
50:43 king of Baby.'s hands *w.*
Dan. 8:8 he-goat *w.* very great
9 lit. horn *w.* exceed. great, 10
Mat. 13:15 this people's heart *w.*
    gross, *Acts* 28:27
Luke 1:80 child *w.* strong, 2:40
13:19 mustard seed *w.* great tree
Acts 13:46 P. and Barn. *w.* bold
Heb. 11:34 *w.* valiant in fight
Rev. 18:3 merchants *w.* rich

WAXEN, WAXED.
Gen. 18:12 after I am *w.* old
19:13 cry of Sod. was *w.* great
Lev. 25:25 bro. *w.* poor, 35, 39
Deut. 31:20 *w.* fat, turn to other
Jos. 17:13 child. of Is. *w.* strong
Jer. 5:27 bec. great and *w.* rich
28 they are *w.* fat, they shine
Ezek. 16:7 increased and *w.* great

WAXETH, ING.

Ps. 6:7 mine eye *w.* old because
Heb. 8:13 *w.* old, ready to vanish
Phil. 1:14 brethren *w.* confident

WAY.

Gen. 24:42 if thou prosper my *w.*
Ex. 13:17 through *w.* of Philist.
18 led people thro' *w.* of wild.
21 pillar of cloud to lead the *w.*
18:20 thou shalt show them the
   w. Neh. 9:19 ; *Ps.* 107:4
Num. 21:4 discouraged bec. *w.*
22:26 there was no *w.* to turn
Deut. 1:22 by what *w. Jos.* 3:4
8:2 remember *w.* Lord led you
14:24 if *w.* be too long for thee
17:16 return no more that *w.*
19:3 prepare a *w.* 6 *w.* is long
28:25 shalt go out one *w.* ag. th.
31:29 turn from *w.* I command
Jos. 23:14 I am going *w.* of earth
24:17 preser. us in *w.* we went
Jud. 2:19 ceased not fr. their *w.*
9:25 they rob. all came that *w.*
18:5 whether *w.* be prosperous
6 Lord is your *w.* wher. ye go
19:9 to-morrow get on your *w.*
1 *Sam.* 9:6 he can show us our *w.*
8 man of God to tell us *w.*
12:23 I will teach you good *w.*
15:20 have gone all L. sent me
2 *Sam.* 19:36 go little *w.* over J.
1 *K.* 2:2 I will go *w.* of all earth
8:36 teach th. good way to walk
13:9 turn ag. by *w.* thou camest
10 another *w.* 12 what *w. ?*
18:6 Ahab went one *w.* Obadi.
22:24 which *w.* went Spirit of
   Lord ? 2 *Chr.* 18:23
2 *K.* 3:8 which *w.* shall we go ?
5:19 departed fr. him a little *w.*
2 *Chr.* 6:27 taught them good *w.*
Ezr. 8:21 seek of him *w.* for us
Job 3:23 a man whose *w.* is hid
12:24 wander in a wilderness
   wh. there is no *w. Ps.* 107:40
16:22 go *w.* whence not return
22:15 hast thou marked old *w.*
23:10 he knoweth *w.* that I take
28:23 G. understands *w.* thereof
38:19 wh. is *w.* light dwelleth ?
Ps. 1:6 L. knoweth *w.* of righte
2:12 kiss Son, lest perish fr. *w.*
36:4 set. himself in *w.* not good
78:50 he made a *w.* to his anger
101:2 behave wisely in per. *w.* 6
119:27 underst. *w.* of precepts
29 remove from me *w.* of lying
30 I nave chosen *w.* of truth
32 I will run *w.* of thy comma.
33 teach me *w.* of statu. 143:8
104 I hate every false *w.* 128
Ps. 139:24 if there be wicked *w.*
146:9 *w.* of the wicked he turns
Prov. 2:8 preserveth *w.* of saints
12 deliv. thee fr. *w.* of evil man
4:19 *w.* of wicked is as darkness
6:23 *w.* of life, 15:24 ; *Jer.* 21:8
7:8 he went the *w.* to her house
27 her house is the *w.* to hell
12:15 *w.* of fool rig. in own eyes
26 *w.* of wick. seduceth them
13:15 *w.* of transgressors hard
14:12 *w.* whi. seem. right, 16:25
15:9 *w.* of wicked is abominati.
10 griev. to him th. forsak. *w.*
19 *w.* of slothf. man is a hedge
16:29 lead. him into *w.* not good
21:8 *w.* of man is froward and
30:19 *w.* of eagle, of serpent
20 such *w.* of adulterous wom.
Ec. 11:5 knowest not *w.* of Spirit
Is. 3:12 to err and destroy the *w.*
26:7 *w.* of just is uprightness
35:8 a *w.* called *w.* of holiness
40:14 who show. *w.* of unders. ?
43:16 L. mak. a *w.* in sea, 51:10

19 I will make *w.* in wildern.
49:11 make my mountains a *w.*
57:14 prepare *w.* 62:10 high *w.*
59:8 *w.* of peace they know not,
   Rom. 3:17
Jer. 6:16 where is the good *w.*
10:2 learn not *w.* of the heathen
23 *w.* of man is not in himself
12:1 doth *w.* of wicked prosp. ?
18:15 paths, in a *w.* not cast up
32:39 give th. one heart, one *w.*
42:3 L. thy G. may show us *w.*
50:5 they shall ask the *w.* to Z.
Ezek. 21:20 appoint *w.* swo. may
23:13 I saw th. both took one *w.*
43:2 glory came from *w.* of east
Amos 2:7 turn aside *w.* of meek
Mal. 3:1 prepare *w.* before me
Mat. 7:13 broad is *w.* to destruc.
14 narrow is *w.* lead. unto life
8:28 no man mi. pass by that *w.*
10:5 go not into *w.* of Gentiles
22:16 teach. *w.* of God in truth,
   Mark 12:14 ; *Luke* 20:21
Luke 5:19 by what *w.* bring him
10:31 there came a priest th. *w.*
15:20 wh. he was a great *w.* off
19:4 Z. to see him, pass that *w.*
John 10:1 climb. up some oth. *w.*
14:4 *w.* ye know ; 6 I am the *w.*
5 Lord, how can we know *w.?*
Acts 16:17 show us *w.* of salvati.
18:26 expound. to him *w.* of G.
19:9 but spake evil of that *w.*
23 arose no small stir about *w.*
24:14 after *w.* they call heresy
Rom. 14:13 to fall in brother's *w.*
1 *Cor.* 10:13 make a *w.* to escape
12:31 a more excellent *w.*
1 *Thes.* 3:11 L. Je. direct our *w.*
Heb. 9:8 the *w.* into the holiest
10:20 living *w.* he consecrated
Jam. 2:25 sent them out ano. *w.*
2 *Pet.* 2:2 *w.* of truth evil spo. of
15 have forsaken right *w.* and
   are following *w.* of Balaam
21 not known *w.* of righteous.
Rev. 16:12 *w.* of kings be prepar.

By the WAY.

Gen. 42:38 if misch. befall *by t. w.*
45:24 fall not out *by t. w.*
Num. 14:25 *by t. w.* of Red sea,
   21:4 ; *Deut.* 1:2, 40 ; 21:1
Deut. 6:7 walked *by t. w.* 11:19
25:18 met *by t. w.* 1 *Sam.* 15:2
28:68, L. sh. bring thee *by t. w.*
Jos. 5:7 not circum. them *by t. w.*
1 *K.* 13:9 not turn ag. *by t. w.* 17
20:38 prophet waited *by the w.*
2 *K.* 3:20 came water *by the w.*
19:28 I will turn th. back *by the
   w.* thou camest, *Is.* 37:29, 34
Ezr. 8:31 lay in wait *by the w.*
Job 21:29 not ask. th. go *by w. ?*
Ps. 80:12 th. who pass *by the w.*
89:41 that pass *by the w.* spoil
Ec. 10:3 fools walk *by the w.*
Is. 42:16 bring blind *by the w.*
48:17 God leadeth thee *by t. w.*
Jer. 2:17 he led thee *by the w.*
6:25 walk not *by t. w.* for sword
Ezek. 43:4 glory of L. came *by w.*
44:3 shall enter *by t. w.* 46:2, 8
46:9 he that entereth *by the w.*
Hos. 13:7 as a leopard *by the w.*
Mark 8:3 they faint *by the w.*
27 *by the w.* he asked his disc.
9:33 that ye disputed *by w. ?* 34
Luke 24:32 talked wi. us *by t. w.*
1 *Cor.* 16:7 not see you *by the w.*

Every WAY.

Ps. 119:101 refrain fr. e. evil *w.*
Ps. 119:104 I hate *e.*false *w.* 128
Prov. 21:2 *every w.* of man right
Ezek. 16:31 build. place in *e. w.*
Rom. 3:2 much *e. w.* bec. to th.

Phil. 1:18 *e w.* whe. in pretence
See EVIL.

His WAY.

Gen. 6:12 flesh had corrup. *h. w.*
2 *Sam.* 22:31 as for God, *his w.*
   is perfect, *Ps.* 18:30
1 *K.* 8:32 to bring *his w.* on his
   own head, 2 *Chr.* 6:23
Job 8:19 this is the joy of *his w.*
17:9 righte. shall hold on *his w.*
21:31 who shall declare *his w. ?*
23:11 *his w.* have I kept
36:23 who enjoined him *his w.?*
Ps. 25:9 meek will he teach *h. w.*
37:7 him who prosper. in *his w.*
23 and he delighteth in *his w.*
34 wait on L. and keep *his w.*
119:9 sh. young man clea. *h. w.*
Prov. 8:22 in beginning of *h. w.*
11:5 righ. of perfect direct *h. w.*
14:8 prudent is to unders. *h. w.*
16:9 a man's heart devis. *his w.*
17 that keepeth *his w.* preser.
19:3 foolish. of man perv. *h. w.*
20:14 when he is gone *his w.*
21:29 upright, directeth *his w.*
Is. 48:15 make *his w.* prospero.
55:7 let wicked forsake *his w.*
Jer. 4:7 destroyer of G. on *h. w.*
Ezek. 3:18 warn wicked fr. *h. w.*
19 turn not from *h. w.* 33:8, 9
13:22 sho. not return fr. *his w.*
Nah. 1:3 L. hath *h. w.* in whirl.
Jam. 1:24 beholdeth, goeth *h. w.*

In the WAY.

Gen. 24:27 I being *in the w.*
48 who led me *in the* right *w.*
35:3 L. was with me *in the w.*
Ex. 5:20 M. and A. stood *in t. w.*
23:20 to keep thee *in the w.*
Deut. 1:33 who went *in the w.*
1 *K.* 11:29 Ahijah found J. *in w.*
13:24 carc. was cast *in w.* 25:28
15:26 walked *in w.* of fath. 22:52
18:7 as Obadiah was *in the w.*
2 *K.* 8:18 he walked *in the w.* of
   the kings of Israel, 16:3 ;
   2 *Chr.* 21:6, 13
27 he walked *in the w.* of Aha.
2 *Chr.* 11:17 three years *in t. w.*
20:32 he walked *in the w.* of A.
Ezr. 8:22 the enemy *in the w.*
Neh. 9:12 to give th. light *in w.*
19 depart. not to lead *in t. w.*
Job 18:10 snare and trap *in t. w.*
Ps. 1:1 nor standeth *in the w.*
25:8 teach sinners *in the w.*
12 shall he teach *in the w.* 32:8
85:13 set us *in the w.* of steps
102:23 weak. strength *in the w.*
110:7 drink of brook *in the w.*
119:1 bless. are undefiled *in w.*
14 I have rejoiced *in the w.*
139:24 lead me *in the w.* everla.
142:3 *in the w.* they laid a snare
Prov. 1:15 walk not thou *in t. w.*
2:20 thou mayest walk *in t. w.*
4:11 I ha. taught thee *in the w.*
14 go not *in t. w.* of evil men
8:20 I lead *in t. w.* of righteous.
9:6 go *in the w.* of understand.
10:17 he is *in the w.* of life
12:28 *in the w.* of righteousness
13:6 him that is upright *in t. w.*
16:31 if it be found *in the w.* of
22:5 thorns and snares *in the w.*
6 train up a child *in the w.* he
23:19 guide thy heart *in the w.*
26:13 slothf. saith a lion *in t. w.*
29:27 upright *in the w.* is abom.
Ec. 12:5 fears shall be *in the w.*
Is. 8:11 not walk *in t. w.* of peo.
26:8 *in the w.* of thy judgments
57:17 went on *in the w.* of heart
65:2 walked *in the w.* not good
Jer. 2:18 wh. to do *in t. w.* of E. ?
   what to do *in t. w.* of Assy. ?

Ezek. 23:31 walk. *in t. w.* of sis.
Hos. 6:9 priests murder *in t. w.*
Mat. 5:25 agree whil. art *in t. w.*
  21:32 J. came *in the w.* of right.
Mark 11:8 spread garments *in t.
  w.* oth. strewed branches *in
  the w. Mat.* 21:8; *Lu.* 19:36
Luke 1:79 guide our feet *in t. w.*
  12:58 as thou art *in the w.* give
Acts 9:17 J. that appeared *in w.*
  27 he had seen the Lord *in w.*
Jude 11 have gone *in the w.* of C.
See LORD.

My WAY.

Gen. 24:56 Lord prospered *my w.*
2 Sam. 22:33 maketh *my w.* per-
  fect, *Ps.* 18:32
Job 19:8 fenced *my w.* that I can
Is. 40:27 sayest *my w.* is hid ?
Ezek. 18:25 is not *my w.* equal ?
John 8:21 I go *my w.* ye sh. seek
Rom. 15:24 brought on *my w.*
2 Cor. 1:16 be brought on *my w.*

Out of the WAY

Ex. 32:8 turned aside *o. of the w.
Deut.* 9:12, 16; *Jud.* 2:17
Deut. 11:28 if ye turn *o. of the w.*
  13:5 thrust thee *out of the w.*
  27:18 blind wander *out of the w.*
Job 24:4 turn needy *out of the w.*
  24 they are taken *out of the w.*
  31:7 if my step turned *o. of t. w.*
Prov. 21:16 wand. *out of the w.*
Is. 28:7 thro' drink are *o. of t. w.*
  30:11 get you *o. of the w.* turn
  57:14 take stumbling-bl. *o. of w.*
Mal. 2:8 departed *out of the w.*
Rom. 3:12 all gone *out of the w.*
Col. 2:14 took handwri. *o. of w.*
2 Thes. 2:7 be taken *out of the w.*
Heb. 5:2 comp. on them *o. of w.*
  12:13 lame be turned *o. of t. w.*

Own WAY.

Prov. 1:31 eat fruit of their *o. w.*
  20:24 can man unders. his *o w.* ?
Is. 53:6 turn. every one to *o. w.*
  56:11 they all look to their *o. w.*
Ezek. 22:31 *o. w.* have I recomp.
  36:17 defiled Isr. by their *o. w*

WAY-SIDE.

Gen. 38:21 har. th. was by *w.-s.* ?
1 Sam. 4:13 Eli sat by *w.-s.*
Ps. 140:5 proud spr. net by *w.-s.*
Mat. 13:4 seeds fell by *w.-s.* 19;
  Mark 4:4, 15 ; *Luke* 8:5, 12
  20:30 blind men sitting by *w.-s.*
Mark 10:46 blind Bartimeus sat
  by *w.-s.* begging, *Luke* 18:35

Their WAY.

1 K. 2:4 if children take heed to
  t. w. 8:25 ; *2 Chr.* 6:16
Job 6:18 paths of *t. w.* are turned
  19:12 troops raise up *t. w.* ag.
  29:25 I chose out *t. w.* sat chief
Ps. 35:6 let *their w.* be dark
  49:13 this *their w.* is their folly
Jer. 3:21 they have pervert. *t. w.*
  6:27 mayest know and try *t. w.*
Ezek. 7:27 I will do to them after
  their w. 9:10 ; 11:21
  14:22 ye sh. see *t. w.* and doings
  33:7 as for th. *t. w.* is not equal
  36:17 *t. w.* was bef. me as uncl.
  19 accord. to *t. w.* and doings
Acts 15:3 bro. on *t. w.* by church
See WENT.

This WAY.

Gen. 28:20 will keep me in *t. w.*
Ex. 2:12 Moses looked *t. w.* and
Jos. 8:20 no power to flee *t. w.*
2 K. 6:19 Elisha said, *t.* is not *w.*
Is. 30:21 *this* is *w.* walk ye in it
Acts 9:2 if he found any of *t. w.*
  22:4 I persecu. *t. w.* unto death

Thy WAY.

Gen. 24:40 L. will prosper *t. w.*
Ex. 33:13 I pray, show me *t. w.*
Num. 22:32 bec. *t. w.* is perverse
Jos. 1:8 eh. make *t. w.* prosper.
1 K. 19 15 return on *t. w.* to wil.
Ps. 5:8 make *t. w.* straight bef.
  27:11 teach me *t. w.* O L. 86:11
  37:5 commit *t. w.* unto the L.
  44:18 neit. declined from *t. w.*
  67:2 that *thy w.* may be known
  77:13 *t. w.* O G. is in sanctuary
  19 *t. w.* is in the sea, thy path
  119:37 and quicken me in *t. w.*
Prov. 3:23 eh. thou walk in *t. w.*
  5:8 remove *thy w.* far from her
Is. 57:10 in greatness of *thy w.*
Jer. 2:23 see *thy w.* in the valley
  33 why trim. thou *t. w.* to seek
  36 why gad. to change *thy w.* ?
  4:18 *thy w.* have procured these
Ezek. 16:43 I will recomp. *thy w.*
Hos. 2:6 I will hedge up *thy w.*
  10:13 bec. thou didst trust *t. w.*
Mat. 11:10 prepare *t. w.* before
  thee, *Mark* 1:2 ; *Luke* 7:27

WAYS.

Gen. 19:2 early, go on your *w.*
Deut. 5:33 walk in *w.* Lord com.
1 K. 22:43 he walked in *w.* of A.
2 K. 21:21 walked in *w.* of Man.
  22:2 he walked in *w.* of David,
    2 *Chr.* 17:3 ; 34:2
2 Chr. 21:12 walk. not in *w.* of J.
  22:3 he walked in *w.* of Ahab
  28:2 walked in *w.* of kings of Is.
Job 24:13 they kn. not *w.* of light
  30:12 raise up *w.* of destruction
  34:21 eyes are upon *w.* of man
  40:19 Behe. is chief of *w.* of G.
Ps. 84:5 in heart are *w.* of them
Prov. 1:19 so *w.* of ev. one greedy
  2:13 to walk in *w.* of darkness
  15 whose *w.* are crooked, fro.
  3:17 wisd.'s *w.* are *w.* of pleas.
  5:6 her *w.* are movable
  21 *w.* of man are bef. eyes of L.
  6:6 go to ant, consider her *w.*
  7:25 let not heart decl. to her *w.*
  14:12 end the *w.* of death, 16:25
  16:2 *w.* of a man cl. in his eyes
  7 when a man's *w.* please L.
  17:23 gift to perv. *w.* of judgm.
  31:27 looketh to *w.* of househ.
Ec. 11:9 walk in *w.* of thy heart
Is. 49:9 feed in *w.* and pastures
Jer. 2:23 dromedary travers. *w.*
  3:2 in *w.* hast thou sat as Arab.
  6:16 stand in *w.* and see, ask
  7:3 amend your *w.* 5 ; 26:13
  23 walk in *w.* I command, you
  12:16 diligently learn *w.* of peo.
  18:11 make *w.* and doings good
  32:19 eyes open on *w.* of men
Lam. 1:4 *w.* of Zion do mourn
  3:40 let us search and try our *w.*
Ezek. 18:25 are not *w.* uneq. ? 29
  20:43 remember your *w.* doings
  44 not acc. to your wicked *w.*
  21:19 son of man appoi. two *w.*
  21 stood at head of two *w.*
Hag. 1:5 consider your *w.* 7
Zec. 1:6 do according to our *w.*
Luke 3:5 rough *w.* made smooth
Acts 2:28 known to me *w.* of life

Any WAYS.

Lev. 20:4 do *â. w.* hide their eyes
Num. 30:15 *any w.* make void
2 Chr. 32:13 *â. w.* able to deliver
See BY-WAYS, EVIL, HIGH.

His WAYS.

Deut. 8:6 to walk in *h. w.* 26:17 ;
  28:9 ; 30:16 ; 1 *K.* 2:3
  10:12 walk in all *his w.* 11:22 ;
    Jos. 22:5 ; 1 *K.* 8:58
  19:9 love L. walk ever in *his w.*

  32:4 *h. w.* are judgm. *Dan.* 4:37
1 Sam. 8:3 walked not in *his w.*
  18:14 D. behav. wisely in *his w.*
1 K. 8:39 give every man according to his *w.* 2 *Chr.* 6:30
2 Chr. 13:22 *his w.* are written
  27:6 Jotham prepared *his w.*
  7 *h. w.* are writ. in book, 28:26
Job 26:14 these are parts of *h. w.*
  34:11 man find accord. to *h. w.*
  27 would not cons. any of *h. w.*
Ps. 10:5 *his w.* always grievous
  103:7 made known *h. w.* to Mo.
  119:3 iniq. they walk in *his w.*
  128:1 blessed that walk. in *h. w.*
  145:17 Lord is right. in all *h. w.*
Prov. 3:31 choose none of *his w.*
  10:9 perverteth *h. w.* be known
  14:2 perverse ir *h. w.* despi. L.
  19:16 despiseth *his w.* shall die
  22:25 lest thou learn *his w.*
  28:6 he that is perverse in *h. w.*
  18 perverse in *his w.* shall fall
Is. 2:3 teach us *his w. Mic.* 4:2
  42:24 would not walk in *his w.*
  45:13 I will direct *h. w.* saith L.
  57:18 I have seen *his w.*
Jer. 17:10 accord. to *his w.* 32:19
Ezek. 18:23 sho. return fr. *his w.*
  30 judge Is. acc. to *h. w.* 33:20
Hos. 9:8 snare of fowler in *h. w.*
  12:2 punish Jac. accord. to *h. w.*
Joel 2:7 march ev. one in *his w.*
Hab. 3:6 *his w.* are everlasting
Luke 1:76 bef. L. to prep. *his w.*
Rom. 11:33 *his w.* past finding
Jam. 1:8 is unstable in all *his w.*
  11 rich man fade aw. in *his w.*

See LORD.

My WAYS.

1 K. 3:14 if thou wilt walk in *my
  w.* 11:38 ; *Zec.* 3:7
Job 31:4 doth not he see *my w.*
Ps. 39:1 will take heed to *my w.*
  81:13 O th. Is. walk. in *my w.* !
  95:10 not kno. *my w. Heb.* 3:10
  119:5 O that *my w.* were direct.
  26 I have declared *my w.* and
  59 I thought on *my w.* turned
  168 all *my w.* are before thee
  139:3 acquainted wi. all *my w.*
Prov. 8:32 bles. that keep *my w.*
  23:26 let thine eyes obs. *my w.*
Is. 55:8 neit. your *ways my w.*
  9 *my w.* higher th. your *ways*
  58:2 delight to know *my w.*
Lam. 3:9 hath inclosed *my w.*
  11 he turned aside *my w.*
Ezek. 18:29 are not *my w.* equ. ?
Zec. 3:7 if wilt walk in *my w.*
Mal. 2:9 have not kept *my w.*
1 Cor. 4:17 remembr. of *my w.*

Own WAYS.

Job 13:15 I will maint. *my o. w.*
Prov. 14:14 filled with his *o. w.*
Is. 58:13 not doing thine *o. w.*
  66:3 th. have chosen their *o. w.*
Ezek. 36:31 remember your *o. w.*
  32 be ashamed for your *o. w.*
Acts 14:16 nati. to walk in *o. w.*

Their WAYS.

2 Chr. 7:14 turn fr. *t.* wicked *w.*
Job 24:23 his eyes are upon *t. w.*
Ps. 125:5 turn to *t.* crooked *w.*
Prov. 9:15 who go right on *t. w.*
Jer. 15:7 return not from *t. w.*
  16:17 mine eyes upon all *t. w.*
  18:15 caused to stumble in *t. w.*
Ezek. 14:23 when ye see *t. w.*
  16:47 hast not walk. after *t. w.*
Hos. 4:9 punish them for *t. w.*
Rom. 3:16 misery are in *t. w.*
2 Pet. 2:2 follow *t.* pernicious *w.*

Thy WAYS.

Deut. 28:29 not prosper in *thy w.*
1 Sam. 8:5 walk not in *thy w.*

2 *Chr.* 6:31 fear to walk in *thy w.*
Job 4:6 the uprightness of *thy w.*
21:14 not knowledge of *thy w.*
22:3 gain that mak. *t. w.* perf. ?
28 light sh. shine upon *thy w.*
Ps. 25:4 show me *thy w.* O Lord
51:13 teach transgressors *t. w.*
91:11 to keep thee in all *thy w.*
119:15 will ha. respect to *thy w.*
Prov. 3:6 in *t. w.* acknowl. him
4:26 let all *t. w.* be established
31:3 not *t. w.* to that wh. destr.
Is. 63:17 made us err from *t. w.*
64:5 that rememb. thee in *t. w.*
Jer. 2:33 hast taught wick. *t. w.*
3:13 thou hast scattered *thy w.*
Ezek. 7:3 accord. to *thy w.* 4, 8, 9
16:47 corrupted more in *thy w.*
61 remember *t. w.* be ashamed
24:14 according to *t. w.* judge
28:15 thou wast perfect in *t. w.*
Dan. 5:23 in wh. hand are *t. w.*
Rev. 15:3 just and true are *t. w.*

WAYFARING.

Jud. 19:17 a *w.* man in street
2 *Sam.* 12:4 flock to dress for *w.*
Is. 33:8 the *w.* man ceaseth
35:8 *w.* men sh. not err therein
Jer. 9:2 a lodg.-place of *w.* men
14:8 why should. be as *w.* man ?

WAY-MARKS.

Jer. 31:21 set thee up *w.-m.* make

WEAK.

Num. 13:18 whether strong or *w.*
Jud. 16:7 *w.* as oth. men, 11, 17
2 *Sam.* 3:39 I am *w.* tho' anoint.
2 *Chr.* 15:7 let not hands be *w.*
Job 4:3 strengthened *w.* hands
Ps. 6:2 I am *w.* 109:24 knees *w.*
Is. 14:10 art thou bec. *w.* as we?
35:3 strengthen ye the *w.* hands
Ezek. 7:17 knees *w.* as wat. 21:7
16:30 *w.* is thy heart, saith Lord
Joel 3:10 let *w.* say, I am strong
Mat. 26:41 flesh *w. Mark* 14:38
Acts 20:35 ye ought to supp. *w.*
Rom. 4:19 being not *w.* in faith
8:3 law was *w.* through flesh
14:1 that is *w.* in faith recei. ye
2 another who is *w.* eat. herbs
21 broth. stumb. or is made *w.*
15:1 ought to bear infirm. of *w.*
1 *Cor.* 1:27 *w.* things to confound
4:10 we are *w.* 8:7 being *w.* 10
8:12 wound their *w.* conscience
9:22 to the *w.* I became *w.* that
11:30 for this cause many are *w.*
2 *Cor.* 10:10 bodily presence is *w.*
11:21 I speak as we had been *w.*
29 who is *w.* and I am not *w.* ?
12:10 when I am *w.* then strong
13:3 wh. to you-ward in not *w.*
4 we are *w.* in him, but sh. live
9 wh. we are *w.* and ye strong
Gal. 4:9 turn ye to *w.* elements ?
1 *Thes.* 5:14 support *w.* be pati.

WEAK-HANDED.

2 *Sam.* 17:2 come wh. he is *w-h.*

WEAKEN.

Is. 14:12 wh. didst *w.* nations ?

WEAKENED, ETH.

Ezr. 4:4 people of land *w.* Judah
Neh. 6:9 their hands shall be *w.*
Job 12:21 he *w.* stren. of mighty
Ps. 102:23 *w.* my strength in way
Jer. 38:4 *w.* hands of men of war

WEAKER.

2 *Sam.* 3:1 S.'s house *w.* and *w.*
1 *Pet.* 3:7 honor wife as *w.* vessel

WEAKNESS.

1 *Cor.* 1:25 *w.* of God is stronger
2:3 I was with you in *w.*
15:43 sown in *w.* raised in pow.
2 *Cor.* 12:9 strength is perf. in *w.*
13:4 though crucified thro' *w.*

Heb. 7:18 going before for the *w.*
11:34 out of *w.* were made stro.

WEALTH.

Gen. 34:29 sons of Ja. took th. *w.*
Deut. 8:17 hand got me this *w.*
18 L. giv. thee power to get *w.*
Ruth 2:1 a kinsman, man of *w.*
1 *Sam.* 2:32 see enemy in all *w.*
2 *K.* 15:20 exacted of men of *w.*
2 *Chr.* 1:11 th. hast not asked *w.*
12 I will give th. riches and *w.*
Ezr. 9:12 nor seek peace or *w.*
Est. 10:3 M. seeking *w.* of peo.
Job 21:13 spend their days in *w.*
31:25 if I rejoiced bec. *w.* great
Ps. 44:12 dost not increase *w.*
49:6 trust in *w.* boast in riches
10 and leave their *w.* to others
112:3 *w.* and riches in his house
Prov. 5:19 lest stra. be fill. wi. *w.*
10:15 man's *w.* is his city, 18:11
13:11 *w.* gotten by vanity sh. be
22 *w.* of sinner is laid up
19:4 *w.* maketh many friends
Ec. 5:19 God hath given *w.* 6:2
Zec. 14:14 *w.* of heathen shall
Acts 19:25 by this craft have *w.*
1 *Cor.* 10:24 seek every man an-
    other's *w.*

WEALTHY.

Ps. 66:12 thou brou. us into *w.*
Jer. 49:31 get up unto *w.* nation

WEANED.

Gen. 21:8 Isaac grew and was *w.*
1 *Sam.* 1:22 not go till chi. be *w.*
1 *K.* 11:20 whom Taphenes *w.*
Ps. 131:2 *w.* of moth. soul as *w.*
Is. 11:8 *w.* child put his hand
28:9 them th. are *w.* from milk
Hos. 1:8 wh. she *w.* Lo-ruhama

WEAPON.

Deut. 23:13 a paddle upon *w.*
Neh. 4:17 other hand held a *w.*
Job 20:24 shall flee from iron *w.*
Is. 54:17 no *w.* form. sh. prosper
Ezek. 9:1 with his destroy. *w.* 2

WEAPONS.

Gen. 27:3 take, I pray, thy *w.*
1 *Sam.* 21:8 neither sword nor *w.*
2 *K.* 11:8 every man with his *w.*
    in hand, 11 ; 2 *Chr.* 23:7, 10
Is. 13:5 L. cometh and the *w.* of
    his indignation, *Jer.* 50:25
Jer. 22:7 prepare ev. one with *w.*
Ezek. 39:9 set on fire, burn *w.* 10
John 18:3 Judas cometh with *w.*
2 *Cor.* 10:4 *w.* of warf. not carnal

See WAR.

WEAR.

Ex. 18:18 wilt surely *w.* away
Deut. 22:5 woman not *w.* what
11 not *w.* garm. of divers sorts
1 *Sam.* 2:28 *w.* an ephod before
22:18 pers. that did *w.* an ephod
Job 14:19 waters *w.* the stones
Is. 4:1 eat our bread, *w.* apparel
Dan. 7:25 *w.* out saints of M. H.
Zec. 13:4 nor *w.* a rough garm.
Mat. 11:8 that *w.* soft clothing
Luke 9:12 day began to *w.* away

WEARETH, ING.

1 *Sam.* 14:3 priest *w.* an ephod
John 19:5 Jesus came *w.* purple
1 *Pet.* 3:3 let it not be *w.* of gold
Jam. 2:3 him that *w.* gay cloth.

WEARY.

Gen. 27:46 Rebek. said, I am *w.*
Deut. 25:18 Amalek sm. when *w.*
Jud. 4:21 J. smote Sis. when *w.*
8:15 bread to men that are *w.*
2 *Sam.* 16:14 and people came *w.*
17:2 come upon him while *w.*
23:10 smote Philist. till was *w.*
Job 3:17 wicked cease, *w.* at rest
10:1 my soul is *w.* of my life

16:7 he hath made me *w.* deso.
22:7 not given wat. to *w.* to dr.
Ps. 6:6 I am *w.* with groaning
68:9 confirm thine inh. when *w.*
69:3 I am *w.* of my crying
Prov. 3:11 be not *w.* of L.'s cor.
25:17 lest he be *w.* of thee
Is. 1:14 feasts are trouble, am *w.*
Is. 5:27 none sh. be *w.* nor stum.
7:13 is it small thing to *w.* men
16:12 when it is seen M. is *w.*
28:12 wherewi. cause *w.* to rest
32:2 shadow of rock in *w.* land
40:28 G. fainteth not, nei. is *w.*
30 youths shall faint and be *w.*
31 that wait on L. sh. not be *w.*
43:22 thou hast been *w.* of me
46:1 a burden to the *w.* beast
50:4 spe. a word to him th. is *w.*
Jer. 2:24 th. seek her will not *w.*
6:11 I am *w.* with holding in
9:5 they *w.* thems. to commit
15:6 I am *w.* with repenting
20:9 I was *w.* with forbearing
31:25 I have satiated *w.* soul
51:58 folk shall labor and be *w.*
64 B. sink and they shall be *w.*
Hab. 2:13 peo. sh. *w.* themselves
Luke 18:5 by contin. com. she *w.*
Gal. 6:9 let us not be *w.* in well-
    doing, 2 *Thes.* 3:13

WEARIED.

Gen. 19:11 *w.* themselves to find
Is. 43:23 nor have I *w.* thee
24 hast *w.* me with thine iniq.
47:13 art *w.* in multitude
57:10 *w.* in greatness of way
Jer. 4:31 soul is *w.* bec. of murd.
12:5 if run and they *w.* thee, if
    in land of peace they *w.* th.
Ezek. 24:12 *w.* herself with lies
Mic. 6:3 wherein have I *w.* thee
Mal. 2:17 *w.* Lord, wherein have
    we *w.* him ?
John 4:6 J. being *w.* sat on well
Heb. 12:3 lest ye be *w.* and faint

WEARIETH.

Job 37:11 he *w.* the thick cloud
Ec. 10:15 labor of foolish *w.*

WEARINESS.

Ec. 12:12 study his a *w.* of the flesh
Mal. 1:13 said, What a *w.* is it !
2 *Cor.* 11:27 *w.* and painfulness

WEARISOME.

Job 7:3 *w.* nights are appointed

WEASEL.

Lev. 11:29 *w.* and mouse, uncl.

WEATHER.

Job 37:22 fair *w.* com. out of nor.
Prov. 25:20 tak. a gar. in cold *w.*
Mat. 16:2 fair *w.* for sky is red
3 in morning it will be foul *w.*

WEAVE, EST.

Jud. 16:13 if th. *w.* seven locks
Is. 19:9 they that *w.* net-works
59:5 they *w.* a spider's web

WEAVER.

Ex. 35:35 work the work of *w.*
1 *Sam.* 17:7 staff of Goli.'s spear
    like a *w.* beam, 2 *Sam.* 21:19 ;
    1 *Chr.* 11:23 ; 20:5
Job 7:6 days swift. th. *w.* shuttle
Is. 38:12 I have cut off like a *w.*

WEB, S.

Jud. 16:13 if thou weavest **seven**
    locks with the *w.* 14
Job 8:14 shall be a spider's *w.*
Is. 59:5 they weave spider's *w.*
6 *w.* sh. not become garments

WEDDING.

Mat. 22:3 were bidden to *w.* 8, 10
11 man had not on a *w.* garm.
Luke 12:36 will return from *w.*
14:8 when th. art bidden to a *w.*

WEDGE.

Jos. 7:21 Achan saw a *w.* of gold
24 Joshua took Achan and *w.*
Is. 13:12 more precious than
golden *w.* of Ophir

WEDLOCK.

Ezek. 16:38 as women th. br. *w.*

WEEDS.

Jon. 2:5 *w.* were about my head

WEEK.

Gen. 29:27 fulfil her *w.* we will
28 Jacob did so, fulfill. her *w.*
Dan. 9:27 one *w.* in midst of *w.*
Mat. 28:1 1st day of *w. Mark* 16:2,
9; *Luke* 24:1; *John* 20:1, 19
Luke 18:12 I fast twice in the *w.*
Acts 20:7 first day of *w.* Paul
preached
1 *Cor.* 16:2 on first day of *w.* let

WEEKS.

Lev. 12:5 child, be unclean 2 *w.*
Num. 28:26 bri. offering after *w.*
Jer. 5:24 reserveth *w.* of harvest
Dan. 9:24 seventy *w.* are deter.
25 after threescore and 2 *w.* 26
10:2 I Dan. was mourning 3 *w.*
Dan. 10:3 nor ano. thys. till 3 *w.*

See FEAST, SEVEN.

WEEP.

Gen. 23:2 A. ca. to mourn and *w.*
43:30 Jos. sought where to *w.*
Num. 11:10 Moses heard peo. *w.*
13 they *w.* unto me, saying
1 *Sam.* 11:5 what ail. peo. th. *w. ?*
30:4 had no more power to *w.*
2 *Sam.* 1:24 daugh. of Is. *w.* over
12:21 thou didst *w.* for the child
2 *Chr.* 34:27 rend thy clothes, *w.*
Neh. 8:9 holy, mourn not, nor *w.*
Job 27:15 his widows sh. not *w.*
30:25 did I not *w.* for him
31 into voice of them that *w.*
Ec. 3:4 a time to *w.* a time to
Is. 15:2 gone to high places to *w.*
22:4 I will *w.* bitterly, labor not
30:19 thou shalt *w.* no more
33:7 ambassad. of peace sh. *w.*
Jer. 9:1 that I might *w.* day and
13:17 my soul shall *w.* in secret
places, mine eyes shall *w.*
22:10 *w.* not for the dead, nor
bemo. him, *w.* sore for him
48:32 O vine, I will *w.* for thee
Lam. 1:16 for these things I *w.*
Ezek. 24:16 thou mou. nor *w.* 23
27:31 sh. *w.* for thee with bitter.
Joel 1:5 drunkards, *w.* and howl
2:17 priests *w.* between porch
Mic. 1:10 declare it not, *w.* not
Zec. 7:3 sho. I *w.* in 5th month
Mark 5:39 why make ado and *w.*
Luke 6:21 blessed are ye that *w.*
25 woe to you th. laugh, sh. *w.*
7:13 *w.* not, 8:52; *Rev.* 5:5
23:28 *w.* not for me, *w.* for you.
John 11:31 goeth to grave to *w.*
16:20 ye sh. *w.* world sh. rejoice
Acts 21:13 what mean ye to *w.*
Rom. 12:15 *w.* wi. them that *w.*
1 *Cor.* 7:30 th. *w.* as though they
Jam. 4:9 afflicted, mourn, and *w.*
5:1 ye rich men, *w.* and howl
Rev. 18:11 merchants shall *w.*

WEEPEST.

1 *Sam.* 1:8 Han. why *w.* thou ?
John 20:13 wom. why *w.* th. ? 15

WEEPETH.

2 *Sam.* 19:1 behold the king *w.*
2 *K.* 8:12 Hazael said, Why *w. ?*
Ps. 126:6 goeth forth and *w.*
Lam. 1:2 she *w.* sore in the night

WEEPING.

Num. 25:6 *w.* bef. door of taber.
Deut. 34:8 days of *w.* for Moses

2 *Sam.* 3:16 husband with her *w.*
15:30 *w.* as they went up
Ezr. 3:13 not discern joy fr. *w.*
10:1 E. prayed and confess. *w.*
Est. 4:3 in ev. province was *w.*
Job 16:16 my face is foul with *w.*
Ps. 6:8 L. heard voice of my *w.*
30:5 *w.* may endure for a night
102:9 I mingl. my drink wi. *w.*
Is. 15:3 in their streets howl, *w.*
16:9 I will bewail with *w.* of Ja.
vine of Sibmah, *Jer.* 48:32
22:12 did L. of hosts call to *w.*
65:19 voice of *w.* no more heard
Jer. 3:21 *w.* of Is. heard on high
9:10 for mountains I take up *w.*
31:9 they shall come with *w.*
15 lamentation and *w.* Rachel
w. for her childr. *Mat.* 2:18
16 restrain thy voice from *w.*
41:6 Ish. went to meet them *w.*
48:5 continual *w.* shall go up
50:4 Judah going *w.* to seek L.
Ezek. 8:14 wom. *w.* for Tammuz
Joel 2:12 turn wi. fasting and *w.*
Mal. 2:13 covering altar with *w.*
Mat. 8:12 there *w.* be *w.* 22:13;
24:51 ; 25:30 ; *Luke* 13:28
Luke 7:38 wom. stood at feet *w.*
John 11:33 when Je. saw her *w.*
20:11 Mary stood without *w.*
Acts 9:39 wido. stood by him *w.*
Phil. 3:18 told you often, now *w.*
Rev. 18:15 merch. shall stand *w.*
19 shipmaster and sailors, *w.*

WEIGH.

1 *Chr.* 20:2 crown to *w.* a talent
Ezr. 8:29 keep until ye *w.* them
Ps. 58:2 *w.* violence of hands
Is. 26:7 thou dost *w.* path of just

WEIGHED.

Gen. 23:16 *w.* to Ephron silver
1 *Sam.* 2:3 by L. actions are *w.*
17:7 his spear's head *w.* 600
shekels, 2 *Sam.* 21:16
2 *Sam.* 14:26 Ab. *w.* hair of head
Ezr. 8:25 priests *w.* sil. and gold
Ezr. 8:26 *w.* into han. silver, 33
Job 6:2 oh that my grief were *w.*
28:15 nor shall silver be *w.* for
31:6 let me be *w.* in even bala.
Is. 40:12 who hath *w.* mount. ?
Jer. 32:9 Jeremi. *w.* him money
Dan. 5:27 thou art *w.* in balance
Zec. 11:12 they *w.* thirty pieces

WEIGHETH.

Job 28:25 he *w.* waters by meas.
Prov. 16:2 the Lord *w.* spirits

WEIGHING.

Num. 7:85 each *w.* 86 spoons *w.*

WEIGHT.

Gen. 43:21 money in sack full *w.*
Ex. 30:34 of each a like *w.*
Lev. 19:35 do no unright. in *w.*
26:26 deliver your bread by *w.*
Deut. 25:15 thou sh. have just *w.*
Jud. 8:26 *w.* of golden ear-rings
2 *Sam.* 12:30 *w.* of king's crown
1 *K.* 7:47 was *w.* of brass found
out, 2 *K.* 25:16
1 *Chr.* 28:14 he gave gold by *w.*
Job 28:25 make *w.* for the winds
Prov. 11:1 a just *w.* is his delight
16:11 a just *w.* and bal. are L.'s
Ezek. 4:10 thy meat sh. be by *w.*
16 they shall eat bread by *w.*
Zec. 5:8 *w.* of lead on mouth
2 *Cor.* 4:17 a more exceeding *w.*
Heb. 12:1 let us lay aside ev. *w.*
Rev. 16:21 stone of hail *w.* of tal.

WEIGHTS.

Lev. 19:36 just *w.* shall ye have
Deut. 25:13 sh. not ha. divers *w.*
Prov. 16:11 *w.* of bag his work
20:10 divers *w.* are abomina. 23
Mic. 6:11 wi. bag of deceitful *w.*

WEIGHTY.

Prov. 27:3 stone heavy, sand *w.*
2 *Cor.* 10:10 let. say they, are *w.*

WEIGHTIER.

Mat. 23:23 omitted *w.* matters

WELFARE.

Gen. 43:27 asked th. of their *w.*
Ex. 18:7 asked each other of *w.*
1 *Chr.* 18:10 sent to inq. of his *w.*
Neh. 2:10 man to seek *w.* of Is.
Job 30:15 my *w.* passeth away
Ps. 69:22 sho. have been for *w.*
Jer. 38:4 seeketh not *w.* of peo.

WELL, Substantive.

Gen. 21:19 she saw a *w.* of water
30 witness I have dig. this *w.*
24:13 I stand here by *w.* 43
Num. 21:16 *w.* whereof L. spake
17 spring up, O *w.* 18 dig. *w.*
2 *Sam.* 17:18 man that had *w.*
23:15 give me drink of water of
w. of Beth. 1 *Chr.* 11:17, 18
Ps. 84:6 passing Baca make it *w.*
Prov. 5:15 wat. of thine own cr.
10:11 a righte. man is *w.* of life
Cant. 4:15 a *w.* of waters fr. L.
John 4:6 Jacob's *w.* was there
11 *w.* is deep ; 12 J. gave us *w.*
14 sh. be in him a *w.* of water

WELLS.

Gen. 26:15 *w.* Abr.'s serv. digg.
18 Isaac digged ag. *w.* of water
Ex. 15:27 where were twelve *w.*
Num. 20:17 drink of water of *w.*
Deut. 6:11 *w.* thou diggedst not
2 *K.* 3:19 ye sh. stop *w.* of water
25 they stopped all *w.* of wat.
2 *Chr.* 26:10 towers and dig. *w.*
Is. 12:3 draw out of *w.* of salvat.
2 *Pet.* 2:17 are *w.* without water

WELL-SPRING.

Prov. 16:22 und. is a *w.-s.* of life
18:4 *w.-s.* of wisdom as a brook

WELL, Adverb.

Gen. 4:7 if thou dost not *w.* sin
12:13 that it may be *w.* wi. me
29:6 Ja. said, Is he *w. ?* he is *w.*
40:14 it shall be *w.* with thee
43:27 is your father *w. ?* is he
Ex. 4:14 I kn. he can speak *w.*
Num. 36:5 sons of Joseph said *w.*
Deut. 1:23 saying pleased me *w.*
3:20 rest to breth. as *w.* as you,
4:40 that it may go *w.* with th.
5:16 ; 6:3, 18 ; 12:25, 28 ; 19:13 ;
22:7 ; *Ruth* 3:1 ; *Eph.* 6:3
5:29 it might be *w.* with them
33 that it may be *w. Jer.* 7:23
15:16 because he is *w.* wi. thee
Jud. 14:3 she pleaseth me *w.* 7
1 *Sam.* 16:16 and thou sh. be *w.*
2 *Sam.* 18:28 and said. All is *w.*
1 *K.* 18:24 answered, *w.* spoken
2 *K.* 4:26 is it *w.* with thee ?
5:21 all *w.* 9:11 ; 7:9 do not *w.*
2 *Chr.* 12:12 in J. things went *w.*
Ps. 49:18 th. doest *w.* to thyself
Ec. 8:12 *w.* with them fear God
Is. 3:10 it shall be *w.* with him
Jer. 22:15 it was *w.* with him, 16
40:4 and I will look *w.* to thee
42:6 that it may be *w.* with us
Ezek. 33:32 one that can play *w.*
Mat. 25:21 *w.* done, th. good and
faithful serv. 23 ; *Luke* 19:17
Luke 20:39 Master, thou hast *w.*
said, *John* 4:17
1 *Tim.* 5:17 elders that rule *w.*
be counted worthy

See DO, FAVORED, PLEASED.

WELL-BELOVED.

Cant. 1:13 myrrh is my *w.-b.*
Is. 5:1 will I sing to my *w.-b.*
Mark 12:6 he sent his *w.-b.* son
Rom. 16:5 salute *w.-b.* Epenetus

3 *John* 1 elder to the *w.-b.* Gaius

Very WELL.
Acts 25:10 as thou *v. w.* knowest
2 *Tim.* 1:18 thou knowest *v. w.*

WELL-NIGH.
Ps. 73:2 steps had *w.-n.* slipped

WEN.
Lev. 22:22 having a *w.* or scurvy

WENCH.
2 *Sam.* 17:17 a *w.* told Jonathan

WENT.
Gen. 35:3 L. wi. me in way I *w.*
Deut. 1:31 bare th. in way ye *w.*
Jos. 24:*7 preser. in way we *w.*
Jud. 1:17 Judah *w.* wi. Simeon
1 *Sam.* 10:14 said, Whi. *w.* ye?
1 *K.* 13:12 said, What way *w.* he?
Mat. 21:30 I *,* o, sir, but *w.* not

WENT about.
Num. 11:8 people *w. a.* gath. it
2 *K.* 3:25 slinger *w. a.* smote it
2 *Chr.* 17:9 they *w. about,* taught
Ec. 2:20 I *w. a.* to cause my hea.
Cant. 5:7 watchmen that *w. a.*
Mat. 4:23 Jesus *w. about* teaching, 9:35 ; *Mark* 6:6
Acts 9:29 they *w. a.* to slay him, 21:31 ; 26:21
10:38 Jesus *w. about* doing good
13:11 he *w. about* seeking some to

WENT aside.
Luke 9:10 and *w. aside* privately
Acts 23:19 chief captain *w. aside*

WENT astray.
Ps. 119:67 before afflicted I *w. a.*
Ezek. 44:10 when Israel *w. a.* 15
48:11 priests wh. *w.* not *astray*
Mat. 18:13 which *w.* not *astray*

WENT away.
Mat. 19:22 he *w. away* sorrowful, *Mark* 10:22
26:42 he *w. away* second time
44 *w. a.* third time, *Mark* 14:39

WENT back.
1 *K.* 13:19 so he *w. back* and eat
John 6:66 many disciples *w. back*

WENT before.
Ex. 13:21 L. *w. b.* them in cloud
1 *Tim.* 1:18 prophecies wh. *w. b.*

WENT down.
Num. 16:33 *w. d.* alive into pit
Acts 8:38 th. both *w. d.* into wat.

WENT forth.
2 *Sam.* 20:8 as he *w. f.* it fell out

WENT out.
Gen. 44:28 one *w. out* from me
2 *Sam.* 13:9 they *w. o.* from him
John 13:30 received sop, *w. out*
1 *John* 2:19 they *w. out* from us

WENT over.
2 *K.* 2:14 smote waters, *w. over*

WENT their way.
Neh. 8:12 people *w. t. way* to eat
Zec. 10:2 *w. t. way* as a flock
Mat. 8:33 fled, and *w. their way*
20:4 you, and they *w. th. way*
22:5 light of it, and *w. th. way*
22 heard words they *w. t. way*

WENT up.
Gen. 17:22 God *w. up* from Abr.
49:4 *w. vp* to his father's bed
Ex. 19:3 Moses *w. up* to G. 20;
24:13, 15 ; 34:4 ; *Deut.* 10:3

WENT a whoring.
Jud. 2:17 Isr. *w. a whoring,* 8:33
Ps. 106:39 *w. a w.* with inventi.

WENTEST.
Jud. 5:4 when thou *w.* out of S.
2 *Sam.* 16:17 why *w.* thou not
19:25 wheref. *w.* thou not with

WEPT.
Gen. 21:16 Hag. *w.* 27:38 Es. *w.*
29:11 and Jacob *w.* 33:4 ; 37:35 ;
Hos. 12:4
42:24 Joseph *w.* 43:30 ; 45:2, 14,
15 ; 46:29 : 50:1, 17
Ex. 2:6 behold, the babe *w.*
Num. 11:4 child. of Is. *w.* 18, 20;
14:1 ; *Deut.* 1:45 ; 34:8 ; *Jud.*
2:4 : 20:23, 26 ; 21:2
Jud. 14:16 Samson's wife *w.*
Ruth 1:9 kissed daughters, *w.* 14
1 *Sam.* 1:7 Hannah *w.* not eat, 10
11:4 people *w.* 2 *Sam.* 3:32, 34
20:41 Jonathan and David *w.*
24:16 S. lifted up his v. and *w.*
30:4 and David *w.* 2 *Sam.* 1:12
2 *Sam.* 3:32 Da. *w.* at grave of A.
12:22 child alive, I fast. and *w.*
13:36 servants *w.* for Amnon
15:23 country *w.* 30 *w.* as he *w.*
18:33 moved, and *w.* for Absal.
2 *K.* 8:11 the man of God *w.*
13:14 Joash *w.* over Elisha
20:3 Hezekiah *w.* sore, *Is.* 38:3
22:19 king of Judah *w.* bef. me
Ezr. 3:12 priests seen 1st ho. *w.*
10:1 peo. *w.* very sore, *Neh.* 8:9
Neh. 1:4 wh. I heard words I *w.*
Job 2:12 friends lift. voice and *w.*
Ps. 69:10 when I *w.* and chasten.
137:1 by rivers of Babyl. we *w.*
Mat. 26:75 P. *w.* bitterly, *Mark*
14:72 ; *Luke* 22:62
Mark 5:38 them th. *w. Luke* 8:52
16:10 Mary told them as th. *w.*
Luke 7:32 mourned ye ha. not *w.*
19:41 beheld city and *w.* over it
John 11:35 Jesus *w.* 20:11 M. *w.*
Acts 20:37 *w.* fell on P.'s neck
1 *Cor.* 7:30 weep as tho' *w.* not
Rev. 5:4 *w.* because no man was

As It WERE.
Is. 53:3 we hid *as it w.* our faces
Luke 22:44 *as it w.* drops of blo.
John 7:10 but *as it w.* in secret
Rev. 10:1 his face *as it w.* sun
13:3 one of heads *as it w.* woun.
14:3 sung *as it w.* a new song
15:2 I saw *as it w.* a sea of glass

WEST.
Gen. 28:14 shalt spread abroad to *w.*
Deut. 33:23 possess *w.* and south
1 *K.* 7:25 three oxen towards *w.*
1 *Chr.* 9:24 porters tow. east, *w.*
north and south, 2 *Chr.* 4:4
12:15 to flight tow. east and *w.*
Ps. 75:6 promot. not from the *w.*
103:12 as far as east is from *w.*
107:3 gath. them fr. east and *w.*
Is. 11:14 fly on Philist. tow. *w.*
43:5 gather thee from the *w.*
45:6 that they may know fr. *w.*
49:12 come from north and *w.*
59:19 shall fear the L. from *w.*
Ezek. 48:1 his sides east and *w.*
Dan. 8:5 a he-goat came from *w.*
Hos. 11:10 children tremb. fr. *w.*
Zec. 8:7 I will save peo. from *w.*
14:4 mount of O. cleave tow. *w.*
Mat. 8:11 many shall come from east and *w. Luke* 13:29
24:27 as lightning shineth to *w.*
Luke 12:54 cloud rise out of *w.*
Rev. 21:13 and on *w.* three gates

WEST border.
Num. 34:6 this shall he *w. bord.*
Jos. 15:12 *w. b.* was to great sea
Ezek. 45:7 to the *w. b.* a portion

WESTERN.
Num. 34:6 as for the *w.* border

WEST quarter.
Jos. 18:14 this was *w. quarter*

WEST side.
Ex. 27:12 *w. s.* 50 cubits, 38:12

Num. 2:18 on *w. s.* stand. of Ep.
35:5 meas. on *w. s.* Lev.'s cities
Ezek. 48:3 to *w. s.* a portion for
Naphtali, 4, 5, 6, 7, 8, 23, 24

WESTWARD.
Gen. 13:14 A. looked east. and *w.*
Num. 3:23 behind tabernacle *w.*
Deut. 3:27 lift up thine eyes *w.*
Ezek. 48:18 resi. sh. be 10,000 *w.*
Dan. 8:4 I saw ram pushing *w.*

WEST wind.
Ex. 10:19 *w. w.* took away locu.

WET.
Job 24:8 th. are *w.* with showers
Dan. 4:15 let it he *w.* with dew of heaven, 23, 25, 33 ; 5:21

WHALE.
Job 7:12 am I a sea or a *w.* that
Ezek. 32:2 Phar. thou art as a *w.*
Mat. 12:40 Jo. was 3 days in *w.*

WHALES.
Gen. 1:21 God created great *w.*

WHAT.
Ex. 13:14 wh. son ask, *w.* this?
16:7 *w.* are we that ye murm. ?
15 they wist not *w.* it was
Deut. 20:5 *w.* man is th. ? 6, 7, 8
Jud. 18:8 *w.* say ye ? 18 *w.* do ?
24 *w.* have I more ? *w.* is this ?
w. aileth thee ?

WHATSOEVER.
Gen. 31:16 *w.* G. said unto thee
Num. 22:17 I will do *w.* thou say.
Deut. 12:32 *w.* I command, obs.
Jud. 10:15 do th. *w.* 1 *Sam.* 14:36
Ps. 115:3 God hath done *w.* he pleased, 135:6 ; *Ec.* 8:3
Ec. 3:14 *w.* God doeth, it sh. be
Mat. 5:37 *w.* is more than these
7:12 *w.* ye would men sho. do
17:12 done *w.* listed, *Mark* 9:13
20:4 *w.* right I will give you, 7
John 15:16 *w.* ye shall ask, 16:23

WHEAT.
Gen. 30:14 R. found mand. in *w.*
Ex. 9:32 *w.* and rye were not
34:22 first-fr. of *w. Num.* 18:12
Deut. 32:14 fat of kidneys of *w.*
Jud. 6:11 Gideon threshed *w.*
15:1 time of *w.* harvest Samson
Ruth 2:23 to end of *w.* harvest
1 *Sam.* 6:13 Beth-she. reaping *w.*
12:17 is it not *w.* harv. to-day ?
2 *Sam.* 4:6 they wo. ha. fetch. *w.*
1 *K.* 5:11 Solom. gave Hiram *w.*
1 *Chr.* 21:23 *w.* for meat-offering
Ezr. 6:9 need of, *w.* salt, wine
7:22 a hundred measures of *w.*
Job 31:40 thistles grow ins. of *w.*
Ps. 81:16 fed th. wi. finest of *w.*
147:14 fill. thee with finest of *w.*
Prov. 27:22 bray a fool among *w.*
Cant. 7:2 belly like a heap of *w.*
Jer. 12:13 they have sown *w.*
23:28 what is chaff to the *w.*
31:12 flow together for *w.*
Ezek. 27:17 Judah traded in *w.*
Joel 2:24 floors shall be full of *w.*
Amos 5:11 take fr. him bur. of *w.*
8:5 that we may set forth *w.*
6 buy poor, sell refuse of *w.*
Mat. 3:12 gath. his *w. Luke* 3:17
13:25 enemy sowed tares am. *w.*
29 lest ye root up *w.* wi. them
30 gather the *w.* into my barn
Luke 16:7 said 100 measu. of *w.*
22:31 Satan may sift you as *w.*
John 12:24 exc. *w.* fall to ground
Acts 27:38 cast *w.* into the sea
1 *Cor.* 15:37 it may chance of *w.*
Rev. 6:6 meas. of *w.* for a penny
18:13 merchand. of *w.* is depart.
See BARLEY.

WHEATEN.
Ex. 29:2 wafers make of *w.* flour

WHEEL.

Ps. 83:13 O G. make th. like *w.*
Prov. 20:26 king bringeth *w.* ov.
Ec. 12:6 or *w.* broken at cistern
Is. 28:28 nor break with *w.*
Ezek. 1:15 one *w.* upon the earth
  16 a *w.* in midst of a *w.* 10:10
  10:13 cried to the wheels, O *w.*

Ex. 14:25 took off th. chariot *w.*
Jud. 5:28 why tarry *w.* of chari.
Is. 5:28 their *w.* like a whirlwind
Jer. 18:3 he wrought work on *w.*
  47:3 at the rumbling of his *w.*
Ezek. 1:16 appearance of the *w.*
  3:13 at noise of *w.* over against
  10:19 *w.* were beside th. 11:22
  23:24 B. come ag. thee with *w.*
  26:10 walls shake at noise of *w.*
Dan. 7:9 his *w.* a burning fire
Nah. 3:2 noise of rattling of *w.*

WHELP, S.

2 Sam. 17:8 as bear robbed of *w.*
Prov. 17:12 a bear robbed of *w.*
Ezek. 19:2 nourish. *w.* am. lions
  3 she brought up one of her *w.*
Hos. 13:8 a bear bereaved of *w.*
Nah. 2:12 lion did tear for his *w.*

See LIONS.

WHEN.

Ps. 94:8 *w.* will ye be wise ?
Ec. 8:7 who can tell *w.* it be ?

WHENCE.

Gen. 42:7 *w.* come ye ? *Jos.* 9:8
Jud. 17:9 M. said, *w.* comest th. ?
  19:17 ; 2 *Sam.* 1:3 ; 2 *K.* 5:25 ;
  Job 1:7 ; 2:2 ; *Jon.* 1:8
Job 10:21 I go *w.* not ret. 16:22
John 7:28 and ye know *w.* I am
  8:14 ye cannot tell *w.* I come
  9:29 know not from *w.* he is, 30

WHENSOEVER.

Mark 14:7 *w.* ye may do th. good

WHERE.

Gen. 3:9 Lord said, *w.* art thou ?
Ex. 2:20 *w.* is he ? 2 *Sam.* 9:4
Job 9:24 if not, *w.* who is he ?
  14:10 the shod, and *w.* is he ?
  38:4 *w.* wast thou wh. I laid. ?
Luke 17:37 *w.* Lord ?
John 7:11 *w.* is he ? 9:12
  34 *w.* I am, 12:26 ; 14:3 ; 17:24

WHEREABOUT.

1 Sam. 21:2 let no man know *w.*

WHEREAS.

1 K. 8:18 *w.* it was in thy heart
Ezek. 13:7 *w.* ye say, L. saith it

WHEREFORE.

2 Sam. 16:10 say, *w.* done so ?
Mat. 26:50 *w.* art thou come ?

WHERETO.

Is. 55:11 sh. prosper *w.* I sent it

WHEREWITH.

Jud. 6:15 *w.* shall I save Israel ?
1 K. 22:22 Lord said, *w.* 2 *Chr.* 18:20
Mic. 6:6 *w.* come before Lord ?

WHEREWITHAL.

Mat. 6:31 *w.* shall we be clothed ?

WHET.

Deut. 32:41 I *w.* my glit. sword
Ps. 7:12 he will *w.* his sword
  64:3 who *w.* tongue like sword
Ec. 10:10 and he *w.* not edge

WHILE.

Ps. 49:18 *w.* he lived, he blessed
  63:4 bless thee *w.* I live, 146:2
Jer. 40:5 *w.* he was not go. back

A WHILE.

Gen. 46:29 Jos. wept a good *w.*
1 Sam. 9:27 S. said to S. st. a. *w.*
2 Sam. 7:19 hast spok. a great *w.*
Mat. 13:21 root, dureth for a. *w.*

Luke 8:13 which for a *w.* believe
  18:4 he would not for a *w.*
1 Pet. 5:10 after suffered a *w.*

All the WHILE.

1 Sam. 22:4 a. t. *w.* Da. was in
  25:7 none missing *all the w.* 16
  27:11 will be his man. *all the w.*
Job 27:3 *all t. w.* breath is in me

Long WHILE.

Acts 20:11 had talked a *long w.*

WHIP.

Prov. 26:3 a *w.* for the horse
Nah. 3:2 noise of a *w.* noise of

WHIPS.

1 K. 12:11 my fath. chastis. you
  with *w.* 14 ; 2 *Chr.* 10:11, 14

WHIRLETH.

Ec. 1:6 wind *w.* continually

WHIRLWIND.

2 K. 2:1 take up Elijah by a *w.* 11
Job 37:9 out of south cometh *w.*
  38:1 L. answ. Job out of *w.* 40:6
Ps. 58:9 take th. away as in a *w.*
  Prov. 10:25 ; *Hos.* 13:3
Prov. 1:27 destruction com. as *w.*
Is. 5:28 their wheels like a *w.*
  17:13 like a rolling thing bef. *w.*
  40:24 *w.* shall take them away
  41:16 the *w.* shall scatter them
  66:15 chariots like *w.* Jer. 4:13
Jer. 23:19 a *w.* of L. is gone forth
  25:32 a *w.* great *w.* sh. be raised
  30:23 a *w.* shall fall on wicked
Ezek. 1:4 a *w.* came out of north
Dan. 11:40 come aga. him like *w.*
Hos. 8:7 sown wind, shall reap *w.*
Amos 1:14 devour in day of *w.*
Nah. 1:3 L. hath his way in *w.*
Hab. 3:14 they came out as a *w.*
Zec. 7:14 I scattered th. with *w.*

WHIRLWINDS.

Is. 21:1 as *w.* in south pass thro'
Zec. 9:14 Lord go forth with *w.*

WHISPER, ED.

2 Sam. 12:19 Da. saw servants *w.*
Ps. 41:7 all that hate me *w.*
Is. 29:4 speech *w.* out of dust

WHISPERER, S.

Prov. 16:28 a *w.* separat. friends
Rom. 1:29 debate, deceit, *w.*

WHISPERINGS.

2 Cor. 12:20 lest there be *w.*

WHIT.

1 Sam. 3:18 S. told Eli every *w.*
John 7:23 man every *w.* whole
John 13:10 but is clean every *w.*
2 Cor. 11:5 not a *w.* behind apo.

WHITE.

Gen. 30:37 Jacob made *w.* appear
  49:12 his teeth be *w.* with milk
Ex. 16:31 like coriander-seed, *w.*
Lev. 13:3 turned *w.* 4, 20, 21, 25
Num. 12:10 leprous, *w.* as snow
Jud. 5:10 that ride on *w.* asses
2 K. 5:27 went out a leper, *w.*
2 Chr. 5:12 Levites arrayed in *w.*
Est. 8:15 Mord. went out in *w.*
Job 6:6 any taste in *w.* of egg ?
Ps. 68:14 it was *w.* as snow in
Ec. 9:8 let thy garments be *w.*
Cant. 5:10 beloved is *w.* ruddy
Is. 1:18 sins sh. be *w.* as snow
Ezek. 27:18 D. traded in *w.* wool
Dan. 7:9 garm. was *w.* as snow
  11:35 some fall to make them *w.*
  12:10 many purifi. and made *w.*
Joel 1:7 branches thereof are *w.*
Zec. 1:8 horses speckled and *w.*
Mat. 5:36 make hair *w.* or black
  17:2 his raim. was *w.* Luke 9:29
  28:3 raim. *w.* as snow, Acts 1:10
Mark 16:5 a man clothed in *w.*
John 4:35 fields are *w.* to harvest
Rev. 1:14 head and hairs were *w.*

  2:17 give him a *w.* stone, name
  3:4 shall walk with me in *w.*
  5 clothed in *w.* raiment, 4:4 ;
    7:9, 13 ; 15:6 ; 19:8, 14
  18 buy *w.* raiment, be clothed
  6:2 behold, a *w.* horse, 19:11
  7:14 made them *w.* in blood
  14:14 *w.* cloud ; 20:11 *w.* throne

WHITE, D.

Mat. 23:27 scribes like *w.* sepul.
Mark 9:3 no fuller can *w.* them
Acts 23:3 smite thee, thou *w.* wall

WHITER.

Ps. 51:7 I shall be *w.* than snow
Lam. 4:7 Nazarites *w.* th. milk

WHITHER.

1 Sam. 10:14 said, *w.* went ye ?
2 K. 5:25 thy servant went no *w.*
Heb. 11:8 went, not knowing *w.*

See GO, GOEST, GOETH.

WHITHERSOEVER.

Prov. 17:8 *w.* it turn. it prosper.
  21:1 king's heart *w.* he will
Mat 8:19 fol. *w.* goest, *Luke* 9:57
Rev. 14:4 follow L. *w.* he goeth

WHOLE.

2 Sam. 1:9 my life is yet *w.*
2 Chr. 15:15 sou. with *w.* desire
1 Cor. 12:17 if *w.* body were eye

See CONGREGATION, HEART.

WHOLE, *for* sound.

Jos. 5:8 abode in camp till *w.*
Job 5:18 and his hands make *w.*
Mat. 9:12 th. that be *w.* need not
  a physic. *Mark* 2:17 ; *Lu.* 5:31
  21 I shall be *w.* Mark 5:28
  12:13 and his hand was made *w.*
  Mark 3:5 ; *Luke* 6:10
  15:28 her daugh. was made *w.*
  31 wond. saw maimed to be *w.*
Mark 5:34 faith hath made th. *w.*
  go, be *w. Luke* 8:48 ; 17:19
Luke 7:10 found the servant *w.*
John 5:6 wilt th. be made *w. ?* 14
  7:23 made a man every whit *w.*
Acts 4:9 by what means he is *w.*
  9:34 J. Christ maketh thee *w.*

WHOLLY.

Num. 32:11 not *w.* followed me
Deut. 1:36 bec. Caleb *w.* followed
  Lord, *Jos.* 14:8, 9, 14
Jer. 46:28 leave thee *w.* unpunis.
1 Thes. 5:23 God sanctify you *w.*
1 Tim. 4:15 give thy. *w.* to them

WHOLESOME.

Prov. 15:4 *w.* tongue tree of life
1 Tim. 6:3 cons. not to *w.* words

WHOM.

1 K. 20:14 Ahab said, By *w. ?* 22:8
  Ezr. 10:44 ; *Rom.* 1:5 ; 5:2, 11
  Gal. 6:14

See BEFORE.

WHOMSOEVER.

Dan. 4:17 he giveth to *w.* he will,
  25:32 ; 5:21

WHORE.

Lev. 19:29 not cause to be a *w.*
  21:7 not take wife that is a *w.*
Deut. 22:21 play *w.* in father's
  23:17 there shall be no *w.* of Is.
  18 not bring hire of a *w.*
Jud. 19:2 concubine played *w.*
Prov. 23:27 a *w.* is a deep ditch
Is. 57:3 seed of adulterer and *w.*
Jer. 3:3 thou hast a *w.* forehead
Ezek. 16:28 thou hast played *w.*
Rev. 17:1 judgm. of great *w.* 19:2
  15 waters where *w.* sitteth, 16

WHORES.

Ezek. 16:33 they give gifts to *w.*
Hos. 4:14 are separated with *w.*

WHOREDOM.

Gen. 38:24 Ta. is wi. child by *w.*

Lev. 19:29 lest land fall to *w.*
Jer. 3:9 thro' lightness of her *w.*
13:27 seen lewdness of thy *w.*
Ezek. 16:33 may come for thy *w.*
23:8 they pour. their *w.* on her
17 Babylon defiled her with *w.*
43:7 not defile my holy n. by *w.*
9 let them put their *w.* fr. me
Hos. 4:11 *w.* and wine take heart
5:3 O Ephraim, th. commit. *w.*
6:10 there is the *w.* of Ephraim

WHOREDOMS.

Num. 14:33 wander and bear *w.*
2 *K.* 9:22 *w.* of thy mother Jezeb
2 *Chr.* 21:13 *w.* of house of Ahab
Jer. 3:2 polluted land with *w.*
Ezek. 16:20 is *w.* a small matter?
22 in *w.* not remember. youth
25 multiplied *w.* 26 increas. *w.*
34 contrary from women in *w.*
23:35 bear thy lewdness and *w.*
Hos. 1:2 wife and children of *w.*
2:2 let her put away her *w.*
4:12 *w.* caused them to err, 5:4
Nah. 3:4 *w.* selleth nat. thro' *w.*

See COMMIT.

WHOREMONGER, S.

Eph. 5:5 no *w.* hath any inherit.
1 *Tim.* 1:10 law made for *w.* liars
Heb. 13:4 *w.* and adulterers God
Rev. 21:8 *w.* have th. part in lake
22:15 without are *w.* murderers

WHORING. *See* GO, GONE, WENT.

WHORISH.

Prov. 6:26 by means of *w.* wom.
Ezek. 6:9 brok. with her *w.* heart
16:30 an imperious *w.* woman

WHOSE. *See* HEART.

WHOSESOEVER.

John 20:23 *w.* sin remit, *w.* sins

WHOSOEVER.

Mat. 11:6 bles. *w.* not be offend.
13:12 *w.* hath, to him be given
Gal. 5:10 bear judgm. *w.* he be
Rev. 22:17 *w.* will, let him take

WHY.

Jer. 25:13 turn ye, *w.* will ye
die? *Ezek.* 18:31; 33:11
Luke 2:48 *w.* thus dealt with us?
Acts 14:15 *w.* do ye these things?

WICKED.

Gen. 18:23 righteous wi. *w.* ? 25
38:7 Er was *w. Ex.* 9:27 people
are *w.*
Ex. 23:7 I will not justify *w.*
Lev. 20:17 it is a *w.* thing
Deut. 15:9 not thou. in *w.* heart
17:5 committed that *w.* thing
23:9 keep thee from ev. *w.* thing
25:1 condemn *w.* 1 *K.* 8:32
1 *Sam.* 2:9 *w.* be silent in darkn.
24:13 wick. proceedeth from *w.*
2 *K.* 17:11 Is. wrought *w.* things
2 *Chr.* 6:23 judge by requiti. *w.*
7:14 if my peo. turn fr. th. *w.*
ways, *Ezek.* 18:21; 33:11, 19
24:7 Athaliah that *w.* woman
Neh. 9:35 nor turned fr. *w.* ways,
Ezek. 3:19; 13:22
Est. 7:6 adversary is *w.* Haman
9:25 Haman's *w.* device sh. ret.
Job 3:17 *w.* cease from troubling
9:22 destroyeth perfect and *w.*
29 if I be *w.* why labor, 10:15
10:7 knowest that I am not *w.*
21:7 wherefore do the *w.* live?
30 *w.* reserv. to-day of destru.
27:7 let mine enemy be as *w.*
34:18 say to king, Thou art *w.* ?
38:13 *w.* might be shaken out of
15 from *w.* light is withholden
40:12 tread down *w.* in th. place
Ps. 7:11 God is angry with *w.*
9:5 thou hast destroyed the *w.*

16 *w.* snared in work of hands
17 *w.* shall be turned into hell
10:2 *w.* in pride persecute poor
3 *w.* boasteth; 4 *w.* not seek G.
13 wherefore doth *w.* cont. G. ?
11:2 *w.* bend their bow. make
5 but the *w.* his soul hateth
6 upon *w.* he shall rain snares
12:8 *w.* walk on every side
17:9 keep me fr. *w.* that oppress
Ps. 17:13 deli. my soul fr. the *w.*
26:5 I will not sit with the *w.*
27:2 when *w.* came upon me
28:3 draw me not away with *w.*
31:17 let the *w.* be ashamed
34:21 evil sh. slay *w.* hate right.
37:7 bringeth *w.* device to pass
10 *w.* shall not be, *Prov.* 10:25
12 *w.* plotteth; 20 *w.* sh. perish
14 *w.* have drawn out sword
16 better th. riches of many *w.*
21 *w.* borroweth, payeth not
32 *w.* watcheth the righteous
34 when *w.* are cut off, see it
35 I have seen *w.* in power
40 he sh. deliver them from *w.*
53:3 *w.* are estranged fr. womb
59:5 be not merciful to any *w.*
63:3 let *w.* perish at presence of
75:8 *w.* earth shall wring th. out
92:7 when *w.* spring as grass
94:3 how long sh. *w.* triumph ?
13 until pit be digged for *w.*
101:3 I will set no *w.* thing bef.
4 I will not know a *w.* person
8 I will destroy all *w.* of land
104:35 let the *w.* be no more
106:18 flame burnt up the *w.*
112:10 *w.* see it and be grieved
119:95 *w.* have waited to destroy
110 the *w.* laid a snare for me
119 thou puttest away all *w.*
155 salvation is far fr. the *w.*
139:19 surely thou wilt slay *w.*
21 if th. be any *w.* way in me
140:8 further not his *w.* device
141:4 to practice *w.* works with
10 let *w.* fall into th. own nets
145:20 all the *w.* will he destroy
147:6 casteth *w.* down to ground
Prov. 2:22 the *w.* shall be cut off
5:22 his iniquities shall take *w.*
6:18 heart that deviseth *w.* im.
10:30 *w.* shall not inhabit earth
11:5 *w.* shall fall by his wicked.
7 when a *w.* man dieth, expe.
8 the *w.* cometh in his stead
10 wh. *w.* perish th. is shouting
18 *w.* worketh a deceitful work
21 *w.* sh. not be unpunish. 31
12:2 *w.* devices will he condemn
7 the *w.* are overthrown, 21
12 *w.* desireth net of evil men
13 *w.* snared by transgression
21 *w.* sh. be filled wi. mischief
13:17 *w.* messenger falleth into
14:17 man of *w.* devices is hated
19 *w.* bow at gates of righteous
32 *w.* driven away in wickedn.
15:29 Lord is far from the *w.*
16:4 even *w.* for the day of evil
17:4 *w.* doer giv. heed to false
15 that. justifieth *w.* is abomin.
18:3 when *w.* cometh
20:26 a wise king scattereth *w.*
21:18 *w.* sh. be ransom for right.
27 bringeth it with a *w.* mind
24:16 *w.* shall fall into mischief
19 nei. be thou envious at *w.*
25:5 take *w.* from before king
26 righteous man fall. bef. *w.*
26:23 a *w.* heart like a potsherd
28:1 *w.* flee when no man purs.
4 th. that forsake law praise *w.*
12 wh. *w.* rise, 28; 15 *w.* ruler
29:2 when the *w.* beareth rule
7 *w.* regardeth not to know it

12 servants *w.* 16 *w.* multitude
Ec. 3:17 God shall judge the *w.*
7:17 be not overmuch *w.*
8:10 I saw the *w.* buried, they
13 it shall not be well with *w.*
Is. 5:23 justify *w.* for reward
11:4 with breath sh. he slay *w.*
13:11 I will punish *w.* for iniq.
32:7 he deviseth *w.* devices
53:9 he made his grave with *w.*
55:7 let the *w.* forsake his way
57:20 *w.* are like troubled sea
Jer. 2:33 taught *w.* thy ways
6:29 *w.* are not plucked away
17:9 heart deceitf. and desp. *w.*
25:31 he will give *w.* to sword
Ezek. 3:18 warn *w.* 19; 33:8, 9
8:9 behold the *w.* abominations
11:2 these men give *w.* counsel
18:23 have I pleas. that *w.* die ?
20:44 not according to *w.* ways
21:3 cut off from thee the *w.* 4
25 profane *w.* prince of Israel
33:15 if the *w.* restore pledge
Dan. 12:10 *w.* shall do wickedly
Mic. 6:11 shall I count them pure
with *w.* balances ?
Nah. 1:3 L. shall not acquit *w.*
11 there is come a *w.* counsel.
15 the *w.* shall no more pass
Hab. 1:4 *w.* doth compass right.
13 *w.* devour. man more right.
Zep. 1:3 consu. blocks with *w.*
Mal. 3:18 discern between righteous and *w.*
4:3 tread down *w.* as ashes
Mat. 12:45 more *w.* than himself,
so to this *w.* gen. *Luke* 11:26
13:49 angels sh. sever *w.* fr. just
16:4 *w.* generation seek. a sign
18:32 *w.* serv. 25:26 ; *Luke* 19:22
Acts 2:23 by *w.* hands ha. slain
18:14 if it were matter of *w.*
1 *Cor.* 5:13 put away *w.* person
Col. 1:21 enemies by *w.* works
2 *Thes.* 2:8 th. sh. *w.* be revealed

See MAN, MEN.

Of the WICKED.

Job 8:22 place of *w.* come to nau.
9:24 earth giv. into hand of *w.*
10:3 shine upon couns. of *t. w.*
11:20 eyes of the *w.* shall fail
16:11 into hands of the *w.*
18:5 light of the *w.* be put out
21 such are dwellings of *t. w.*
20:5 triumphing of the *w.* short
22 hand of *t. w.* sh. come upon
21:16 counsel of the *w.* 22:18
17 how oft is candle of the *w.*
put out ? *Prov.* 13:9 ; 24:20
28 where dwelling-pl. of *t. w.* ?
24:6 they gath. vintage of *t. w.*
29:17 I brake the jaws of *t. w.*
36:6 preserveth not life of *t. w.*
17 fulfilled judgment of the *w.*
Ps. 7:9 let wickedness of the *w.*
10:15 break arm of the *w.* man
22:16 assembly of the *w.*
36:1 transgression of the *w.*
11 let not hand of the *w.* rem.
37:17 arms of *t. w.* sh. be brok.
28 seed of the *w.* sh. be cut off
38 end of the *w.* sh. be cut off
55:3 bec. of oppression of *t. w.*
58:10 wash feet in bl. of the *w.*
64:2 hide me fr. counsel of *t. w.*
71:4 deliver me out of hand of
the *w.* 74:19; 82:4; 97:10
73:3 I saw prosperity of the *w.*
75:10 horns of *t. w.* will I cut off
82:2 will ye accept pers. of *w.* ?
91:8 see the reward of the *w.*
92:11 sh. hear my desire of *t. w.*
109:2 mouth of *t. w.* is opened
112:10 desi. of *t. w. Prov.* 10:28
119:53 bec. of the *w.* th. forsake
61 hands of *t. w.* have rob. me

125:3 rod of the w. sh. not rest
129:4 L. cut asun. cords of t. w.
140:4 keep me fr. hands of the w.
8 grant not, O L. desi. of t. w.
146:9 way of the w. turns
Prov. 2:14 in forwardn. of t. w.
3:25 not afra. of desola. of t. w.
33 curse of L. in house of t. w.
4:14 eat. not into path of t. w.
19 way of t. w. is as darkness
10:3 casteth away substa. of w.
6 viole. cover. mouth of w. 11
7 the name of the w. shall rot
16 fruit of t. w. tendeth to sin
20 heart of t. w. is little worth
24 fear of t. w. sh. come upon
27 years of the w. sh. be short.
32 mouth of t. w. speak. frow.
11:11 overthrew by mouth of w.
23 expecta. of the w. is wrath
12:5 counsels of t. w. are deceit
6 words of w. are to lie in wait
10 tender mercies of t. w. cruel
26 way of the w. seduceth
13:25 belly of the w. shall want
14:11 house of w. sh. be overth.
15:6 revenues of t. w. is trouble
8 sacrifi. of w. is abomin. 21:27
9 way of the w. is an abomina.
26 thou. of the w. are abomin.
28 mouth of w. pour. out evil
18:5 not good to acce. per. of w.
19:28 mouth of t. w. devoureth
21:4 plowing of the w. is sin
7 robbery of t. w. shall destroy
10 soul of the w. desireth evil
12 he consider. house of the w.
Is. 14:5 L. hath brok. staff of w.
Jer. 5:28 overpass deeds of t. w.
12:1 doth way of t. w. prosper ?
15:21 deliv. out of hand of t. w.
23:19 whirlw. on he. of w. 30:23
Ezek 13:22 strength. hands of w.
18:20 wickedness of the w.
21:29 br. thee upon necks of the w.
30:12 land into hand of the w.
33:11 no pleas. in death of t. w.
12 as for the wickedn. of t. w.
Dan. 12:10 none of w. sh. under.
Mic. 6:10 wicked. in house of w.
Hab. 3:13 wound. head of the w.
Eph. 6:16 qu. fiery darts of t. w.
2 *Pet.* 2:7 wi. conversation of w.
3:17 led away with error of t. w.

See one

To, or unto the WICKED.
Job 31:3 is not destr. to the w. ?
Ps. 32:10 many sorrows to t. w.
50:16 u. the w. God saith, What
Prov. 24:24 that saith u. the w.
29:27 upright is abomi. to t. w.
Ec. 9:2 event to right. and to w.
Is. 3:11 woe u. the w. sh. be ill
26:10 let favor be showed to w.
48:22 no peace, saith the Lord, *unto the w.* 57:21
Ezek. 3:18 I say *unto* w. 33:8, 14
7:21 give it to t. w. of the earth

WICKEDLY.
Gen. 19:7 not so w. *Jud.* 19:23
Deut. 9:18 ye sinned in doing w.
1 *Sam.* 12:25 if ye sh. still do w.
2 *Sam.* 22:22 I ha. not w. departed from my God, *Ps.* 18:21
24:17 I have sinned and done w.
2 *K.* 21:11 Manasseh done w.
2 *Chr.* 6:37 we have dealt w. *Neh.*
9:33 ; *Ps.* 106:6 ; *Dan.* 9:5, 15
20:35 Ahaziah did very w.
22:3 mother was couns. to do w.
Job 13:7 will you spe. w. for G. ?
34:12 surely God will not do w.
Ps. 73:8 they speak w. concern.
74:3 the enemy hath done w.
139:20 they speak ag. thee w.
Dan. 11:32 such as do w. against
12:10 but the wicked shall do w.

Mal. 4:1 that do w. be as stubble
WICKEDNESS.
Gen. 6:5 God saw w. was great
30:9 how can I do th. great w. ?
Lev. 18:17 not unco. it is w. 20:14
19:29 land become full of w.
20:14 that there be no w. among
Deut. 9:4 sv. of these nations, 5
13:11 Israel shall do no more w.
17:2 if any that hath wrou. w.
23:20 bec. of w. of thy doings
Jud. 9:56 G. rendered w. of Abi.
20:3 tell us, how was this w. ?
12 what w. is this th. is done ?
1 *Sam.* 12:17 see your w. is great
20 ye have done all this w.
24:13 w. proceed. from wicked
25:39 returned the w. of Nabal
2 *Sam.* 3:39 reward acc. to his w.
7:10 children of w. *Ps.* 89:22
1 *K.* 1:52 if w. be found in him
2:44 the w. thy heart is privy to
8:47 we have committed w.
21:25 Ahab sold him to work w.
2 *K.* 21:15 Manasseh wrought w.
1 *Chr.* 17:9 nor the children of w.
Job 4:8 that sow w. reap same
11:11 seeth w. 24:20 w. be brok.
14 let not w. dwell in taberna.
20:12 tho' w. be sweet in mouth
27:4 my lips shall not speak w.
34:10 far fr. G. he should do w.
Ps 5:4 that hath pleasure in w.
9 their inward part is very w.
7:9 let w. of wick. come to end
10:15 seek out w. 45:7 hatest w.
28:4 according to w. of endeav.
52:7 he strength. himself in w.
55:11 w. is in the midst thereof
15 w. is in their dwellings
58:2 yea, in heart yon work w.
84:10 th. to dwell in tents of w.
107:34 for w. them that dwell therein, *Jer.* 12:4
Prov. 4:17 they eat bread of w.
8:7 w. is abomina. to my lips
10:2 treasures of w. profit noth.
11:5 wicked shall fall by his w.
12:3 man not be establish. by w.
13:6 w. overthroweth the sinner
14:32 wicked is driven aw. in w.
16:12 abomination to commit w.
21:12 overthroweth wick. for w.
26:26 his w. shall be shown bef.
30:20 saith, I have done no w.
Ec. 3:16 judgment, w. was there
7:15 wicked prolong. life in w.
25 I applied to know w. of folly
8:8 nor w. deliver th. given to
Is. 9:18 for w. burneth as a fire
58:4 ye smite with the fist of w.
6 chosen, to loose bands of w.
Jer. 2:19 own w. sh. correct thee
4:14 wash thy heart from w.
6:7 casteth out w. continually
7:12 see wh. I did for w. of peo.
8:6 no man repented of his w.
14:20 we acknowledge, our w.
23:14 none doth ret. from his w.
33:5 whose w. I hid face fr. city
Jer. 44:9 ha. ye forg. w. of kings ?
Ezek. 3:19 if he turn not from w.
5:6 changed my judgm. into w.
7:11 violence risen into rod of w.
18:20 w. of wicked sh. be on him
27 turn. from w. he committed
31:11 driven him out for his w.
33:12 day he turneth from w. 19
Hos. 7:1 w. of S. was discovered
9:15 for w. of doings drive out
10:13 ploughed w. reaped iniq.
15 do to you beca. of your w.
Joel 3:13 overflow for w. is great
Mic. 6:10 trea sures of w. in house
Zec. 5:8 and he said, This is w.
Mal. 1:4 call them border of w.
3:15 th. that work w. are set up

Mark 7:22 out heart proceed. w.
Luke 11:39 iaw. part is full of w.
Acts 25:5 man, if any w. in him
Rom. 1:29 being filled wi. all w.
1 *Cor.* 5:3 leav. of malice and w.
Eph. 6:12 ag. w. in high places
1 *John* 5:19 wh. world lieth in w.

Their WICKEDNESS.
Deut. 9:27 look not to *their w.*
Ps. 94:23 cut them off in *their w.*
Prov. 21:12 overth. wick. for *t. w.*
Jer. 1:16 judgm. touching *t. w.*
14:16 pour *their w.* upon them
23:11 in house ha. I found *t. w.*
44:3 desolation because of *t. w.*
5 inclined ear to turn fr. *t. w.*
Lam. 1:22 let *t. w.* come before
Hos. 7:2 I remember all *their w.*
3 make king glad wi. *their w.*
9:15 *their w.* is in Gilgal
Jon. 1:2 *their w.* is come up
Mat. 22:18 Jesus perceived *t. w.*

Thy WICKEDNESS.
1 *K.* 2:44 L. return *thy w.* upon
Job 22:5 is not *thy w.* great ?
35:8 *thy w.* may hurt a man as
Is. 47:10 hast trusted in *thy w.*
Jer. 3:2 polluted land with *t. w.*
4:18 this is *t. w.* for it is bitter
22:22 be confounded for *thy w.*
Ezek. 16:23 ca. to pass after *t. w.*
57 bef. *thy w.* was discovered
Nah. 3:19 on whom hath not *thy w.* passed
Acts 8:22 repent of this *thy w.*

WIDE.
Deut. 15:8 shalt open hand w. 11
1 *Chr.* 4:40 land was w. quiet
Job 29:23 opened their mouth w.
30:14 came as w. breaking wat.
Ps. 35:21 opened their mouth w.
81:10 open thy mouth w.
104:25 this great and w. sea
Prov. 13:3 openeth w. his lips
21:9 wom. in a w. house, 25:24
Is. 57:4 make ye a w. mouth ?
Jer. 22:14 will build a w. house
Nah. 3:13 set w. op. to enemies
Mat. 7:13 w. gate to destruction

WIDENESS.
Ezek. 41:10 chambers w. 20 cub.

WIDOW.
Gen. 38:11 a w. in fath.'s house
14 put her w. garments off
Ex. 22:22 sh. not afflict any w.
Lev. 21:14 w. or harlot not take
22:13 if priest's daugh. be a w.
Num. 30:9 vow of w. stand ag.
Deut. 10:18 judgment of a w.
14:29 and w. shall come and eat, 16:11, 14 ; 26:12
24:17 nor take w. rai. to pledge
19 sheaf for w. 20, 21 ; 26:13
27:19 perverteth judgm. of w.
2 *Sam.* 14:5 I am a w. woman
1 *K.* 7:14 he was a w. son of
11:26 Zeruah was a w. woman
17:9 com. a w. to sustain thee
Job 24:3 take w. ox for a pledge
21 and doeth not good to w.
29:13 I caused w. heart to sing
31:16 caused eyes of w. to fail
Ps. 94:6 th. slay w. and stranger
109:9 child. be fatherl. wife a w.
146:9 reliev. fatherless and w.
Prov. 15:25 establ. border of w.
Is. 1:17 fatherless, plead for w.
23 nei. doth cause of w. come
47:3 I shall not sit as a w.
Jer. 7:6 if ye oppress not the w.
22:3 ; *Zec.* 7:10
Lam. 1:1 how is she bec. as a w.
Ezek. 22:7 have th. vexed the w.
44:22 take w. that had a priest
Mal. 3:5 those that oppress w.
Mark 12:42 w. threw in 2 mites

43 *w.* cast in more, *Lu.* 21:2, 3
Luke 2:37 Anna was a *w.* ab. 84
7:12 mother, and she was a *w.*
Luke 18:3 th. was a *w.* in th. city
  5 because this *w.* troubl. me
1 *Tim.* 5:4 if any *w.* have child.
  5 she is a *w.* ind. trust. in God
  9 let not *w.* be taken into num.
Rev. 18:7 I sit as a queen, no *w.*

WIDOWS.

Ex. 22:24 your wives shall be *w.*
Job 22:9 hast sent *w.* aw. empty
27:15 bur. in death, *w.* not weep
Ps. 68:5 judge of fatherl. and *w.*
78:64 their *w.* made no lament.
Is. 9:17 neither ha. mercy on *w.*
10:2 *w.* may be their prey, rob
Jer. 15:8 their *w.* are increased
18:21 let their wives be *w.* men
49:11 child. let *w.* trust in me
Lam. 5:3 our mothers are as *w.*
Ezek. 22:25 have made many *w.*
Mat. 23:14 ye devour *w.* houses
   Mark 12:40; *Luk.* 20:47
Luke 4:25 were many *w.* in Isr.
Acts 6:1 bec. *w.* were neglected
9:39 *w.* stood by him weeping
  41 he had called saints and *w.*
1 *Cor.* 7:8 I said to *w.* It is good
1 *Tim.* 5:3 honor *w.* that are *w.*
  11 but the younger *w.* refuse
  16 if any have *w.* relieve them
Jam. 1:27 religion is to visit *w.*

WIDOWHOOD.

Gen. 38:19 put on garments of *w.*
2 *Sam.* 20:3 shut up, living in *w.*
Is. 47:9 loss of children and *w.*
54:4 rememb. reproach of thy *w.*

WIFE.

Gen. 11:29 Abram's *w.* was Sarai,
  31; 12:17, 20; 20:18; 24:36
20:3 hast taken is a man's *w.*
21:21 Hag. took *w.* for Ishmael
25:1 Abraham took *w.* Keturah
27:46 Jac. take *w.* of daughters
38:6 Ju.lah took a *w.* for Er his
  8 go in unto thy brother's *w.*
Ex. 20:17 thou shalt not covet
  thy neighbor's *w. Deut.* 5:21
21:4 master ha. given him a *w.*
  10 if he take him another *w.*
Lev. 18:8 father's *w.* sh. thou not
  uncover, 20:11; *Deut.* 27:20
  15 son's *w.* 16 bro.'s *w.* 20:21
18 nei. take a *w.* to her sister
20:14 if man take a *w.* and her
21:7 priests not take *w.* a whore
13 high-priest take *w.* in virg.
Num. 5:12 if man's *w.* go asl. 29
36:8 be *w.* to one family of tribe
Deut. 13:6 if *w.* of bosom entice
20:7 betrothed *w.* not taken her
22:13 if a man take a *w.* hate her
  24 he humbleth neighbor's *w.*
30 a man not take his fa.'s *w.*
24:1 taken *w.* find uncleanness
  5 hath taken a new *w.* not war
25:5 *w.* of dead not marry stran.
  9 then sh. his bro.'s *w.* come
  11 or of one draweth near to
29:30 betroth *w.* another lie wi.
  54 his eye be evil toward *w.*
Jud. 4:4 Debor. *w.* of Lapidoth
17 Jael, *w.* of Heber, 21; 5:24
14:3 take a *w.* of uncircumcised
16 Samson's *w.* wept bef. him
20 *w.* was given to his compan.
21:18 that giveth a *w.* to Benj.
Ruth 4:5 buy it of R. *w.* of dead
2 *Sam.* 12:10 hast taken *w.* of U.
1 *K.* 14:2 known to be *w.* of Jer.
  6 come in, thou *w.* of Jerobo.
2 *K.* 5:2 waited on Naaman's *w.*
2 *Chr.* 22:11 *w.* of Jehoi. hid him
Prov. 5:18 rej. with *w.* of youth
6:29 goeth in to neighbor's *w.*

13:22 a *w.* findeth a good thing
19:13 contentions of *w.* dropp.
14 a prudent *w.* is from the L.
Ec. 9:9 joyfully live w. of youth
Is. 54:1 children of married *w.*
  6 called thee as a *w.* of youth
Jer. 3:20 surely as a *w.* departeth
5:8 neighed after neighbor's *w.*
6:11 husb. and *w.* sh. be taken
16:2 shalt not take thee a *w.*
Ezek. 16:32 as *w.* commit. adult.
18:11 and defiled his neighbor's
  w. 22:11; 33:26
Hos. 1:2 take a *w.* of whoredoms
12:12 Israel served for a *w.* kept
Mal. 2:14 witness bet. th. and *w.*
15 none deal treach. against *w.*
Mat. 1:6 that had been *w.* of U.
11:3 H. bound J. for Philip's *w.*
19:29 hath forsaken *w.* or child.
  Mark 10:29; *Luke* 18:29
22:25 seven breth. married a *w.*
  Mark 12:20; *Luke* 20:29
Luke 14:20 I have married a *w.*
17:32 remember Lot's *w.*
1 *Cor.* 5:1 should have fath.'s *w.*
7:3 husb. render to *w.* due benevolence, likew. *w.* to hus.
  4 *w.* hath not power over body
10 let not *w.* depart from hus.
14 *w.* is sanctified by husband
16 what knowest thou, O *w.*
27 loosed fr. *w.* seek not a *w.*
34 difference bet. *w.* and virgin
39 *w.* is bound as long as hus.
Eph. 5:23 husband is head of *w.*
33 let every one love his *w.*
  and *w.* see she rever. husb.
1 *Tim.* 3:2 has. of 1 *w.* 12; *Tit.* 1:6
5:9 the *w.* of one man
1 *Pet.* 3:7 giving honor to *w.* as
Rev. 21:9 bride, the Lamb's *w.*

His WIFE.

Gen. 2:24 a man sh. cleave to *his*
  w. Mat. 19:5; *Mark* 10:7
25 both naked, man and *his w.*
12:12 this is *his w.* will kill me
19:16 laid hold on hand of *his w.*
26 *his w.* look. back fr. behind
20:7 restore the man *his w.*
24:67 she bec. *h. w.* 1 *Sam.* 25:42
25:21 Isa. entreated L. for *h. w.*
26:7 men asked him of *his w.*
11 touch. man or *his w.* sh. die
39:9 kept back, thou art *his w.*
Ex. 21:3 *his w.* shall go wi. him
22:16 sh. endow her to be *h. w.*
Lev. 18:14 shalt not appro. *his w.*
Num. 5:14 if he be jealous of *his*
  w. 30
30:16 statu. bet. man and *his w.*
Deut. 22:19 she shall be *his w.* 29
24:5 he shall cheer up *his w.*
Jud. 13:11 Man. went after *h. w.*
15:1 Samson visited *his w.*
21:21 catch you ev. man *his w.*
1 *Sam.* 30:22 sa. to ev. man *h. w.*
2 *Sam.* 12:9 th. hast taken *h. w.*
2 *K.* 8:18 dau. of Ahab was *h. w.*
Est. 5:10 Haman called *his w.*
Ps. 109:9 let *his w.* be a widow
Jer. 3:1 if a man put away *his*
  w. Mat. 5:31, 32; 19:9; *Mark*
  10:11; *Luke* 16:18
Mat. 8:14 saw *his w.* mother sick
19:3 is it lawful for a man to
  put away *his w. ?* *Mark* 10:2
10 if the case of the man be so
  with *his w.*
22:25 left *his w.* to his brother,
  Mark 12:19; *Luke* 20:28
Luke 14:26 and hate not *his w.*
Acts 5:2 *his w.* also being privy
7 *h. w.* not knowing what was
18:2 Aquila with *his w.* Priscil.
24:24 Felix came with *his w.* D.
1 *Cor.* 7:2 let ev. man have *h. w.*

11 let not husb. put away *h. w.*
33 how he may please *his w.*
Eph. 5:28 loveth *h. w.* lov. hims.
31 join. to *h. w.* 33 love *his w.*
Rev. 19:7 his *w.* made hers. ready

My WIFE.

Gen. 20:11 will sl. me for *my w.*
12 bec. *my w.* 26:7 is *my w.*
29:21 Jacob said, Give me *my w.*
Ex. 21:5 I love *my w.* and chil.
Jud. 15:1 I will go in to *my w.*
2 *Sam.* 3:14 deliver me *my w.* M.
11:11 sh. I go to lie with *my w.*
Job 19:17 breath is stra. to *my w.*
31:10 let *my w.* grind unto ano.
Ezek. 24:18 at even *my w.* died
Hos. 2:2 she is not *my w.* nor
Luke 1:18 *my w.* is strick. in yrs.

Thy WIFE.

Gen. 3:17 heark. to voice of *t. w.*
12:18 why not tell me that she
  was *thy w. ?*
19 behold *thy w.* take her, go
17:19 *t. w.* sh. bear a son, 18:10
19:15 take *thy w.* and two dau.
26:9 of a surety she is *thy w.*
10 one mi. have lain with *t. w.*
Ex. 18:6 come unto th. and *t. w.*
Deut. 21:11 woul. ha. her to *t. w.*
13 go in to her, shall be *thy w.*
2 *Sam.* 12:10 wife of U. to be *t. w.*
Ps. 128:3 *t. w.* sh. be fruitf. vine
Amos 7:17 *t. w.* shall be a harlot
1 *Cor.* 7:16 thou sh. save *thy w.*

To WIFE.

Gen. 12:19 taken her to me *to w.*
34:4 get me this damsel *to w.*
  8 I pray, give her him *to w.* 12
Lev. 21:14 take a virgin *to w.*
Deut. 22:16 I gave my dau. *to w.*
Jos. 15:16 give Achsah my daug.
  to w. 17; *Jud.* 1:12, 13

Jud. 14:2 get her for me *to w.*
1 *Sam.* 18:17 her will I gi. th. *to w.*
1 *K.* 2:17 give me Abishag *to w.*
2 *K.* 14:9 thistle said, Give thy
  daughter, *to w.* 2 *Chr.* 25:18
2 *Chr.* 21:6 had daugh. of A. *to w.*
Mark 12:23 the seven had her *to*
  w. Luke 20:33

WILD.

Gen. 16:12 Ishm. will be *w.* man
Rom. 11:24 olive-tree, *w.* by nat.

See ASS, BEAST, BEASTS.

WILDERNESS.

Ex. 14:3 *w.* hath shut them in
Num. 14:2 wo. G. we died in *w.*
29 carcas. shall fall in *w.* 32:35
Deut. 1:19 went through *w.* 8:15
32:10 found him in howling *w.*
1 *K.* 19:15 retu. on thy way to *w.*
Job 24:5 *w.* yieldeth food for th.
Ps. 106:9 led through depths as
  thro' *w.* 136:16; *Amos* 2:10
107:35 turn. *w.* into stand. water
Cant. 3:6 cometh out of *w. ?* 8:5
Is. 14:17 that made world as *w. ?*
35:1 *w.* shall be glad for them
41:18 I will make the *w.* a pool
42:11 let *w.* and cities lift voice
50:2 at rebuke I make riv. a *w.*
51:3 he will make her *w.* like E.
64:10 cities are a *w.* Zion is *w.*
Jer. 2:31 ha. I been *w.* unto Is. ?
4:26 the fruitful place was a *w.*
12:10 made pleas. portion a *w.*
22:6 make thee a *w. Hos.* 2:3
Ezek. 6:14 laid more deso. th. *w.*
Joel 2:3 behind them a desol. *w.*
3:19 Edom sh. be a desolate *w.*
Zep. 2:13 make Ninev. like a *w.*

In the WILDERNESS.

Num. 14:22 mir. wh. I did *in t. w.*
32:15 he will yet ag. leave them
  in the w. Ezek. 29:5

Deut. 8:2 forty years *in the w.*
29:5 ; *Jos.* 5:6 ; 14:10
16 fed thee *in t. w.* manna ?
Neh. 9:21 didst aust. them *in t. w.*
Ps. 95:8 day of tempta. *in t. w.*
Prov. 21:19 better dwell *in t. w.*
Is. 32:16 judgm. sh. dwell *in w.*
35:6 *in w.* shall wat. break out
40:3 voice of him that crieth *in the w. Mat.* 3:3 ; *Mark* 1:3 ;
Luke 3:4 ; *John* 1:23
41:19 I will plant *in t. w.* cedar
43:19 will make a way *in the w.*
Jer. 2:2 went. after me *in the w.*
9:2 oh that I had *in t. w.* a lodg.
31:2 peo. found grace *in the w.*
48:6 be like the heath. *in the w.*
Lam. 4:19 laid wait for us *in t. w.*
Ezek. 19:13 she is planted *in w.*
20:13 Is. rebelled ag. me *in t. w.*
15 lifted my hand *in the w.* 23
34:25 shall dwell safely *in t. w.*
Hos. 9:10 I found Israel *in the w.*
13:5 I did know thee *in the w.*
Mat. 3:1 John preaching *in t. w.*
15:33 whe. so much bread *in w.*
to fill multitude ? *Mark* 8:4
Luke 15:4 leave 99 sheep *in t. w.*
Acts 7:30 angel appear. *in w.* 38
2 *Cor.* 11:26 in perils *in the w.*

Into the WILDERNESS.
Lev. 16:21 by a fit man *i. the w.*
22 sh. let go the goat *i. the w.*
Ezek. 20:10 I bro. them *i. the w.*
35 I will bring you *into the w.*
Hos. 2:14 I will bri. her *in the w.*
Mat. 11:7 what went ye out *in the w.* to see ? *Luke* 7:24
Luke 8:29 driven of devil *i. the w.*
Acts 21:38 led. *into w.* 4,000 men
Rev. 12:6 woman fled *i. t. w.* 14
17:3 so he carried me *into t. w.*

WILES.
Num. 25:18 th. vex you with *w.*
Eph. 6:11 able to stand ag. *w.*

WILILY.
Jos. 9:4 Gibeonites did work *w.*

WILL.
Deut. 33:16 for good *w.* of him
Ps. 27:12 deliver me not to *w.* of
41:2 not deliver to *w.* of enem.
Ezek. 16:27 delivered thee to *w.*
Mal. 2:13 recei. it with good *w.*
Mat. 7:21 doeth *w.* of Fath. 12:50
18:14 it is not *w.* of your Father
21:32 whether did *w.* of father ?
Luke 2:14 good *w.* toward men
23:25 delivered Jesus to their *w.*
John 1:13 not of *w.* of the flesh
4:34 my meat is to do *w.* of him
5:30 I seek the *w.* of my Father
6:39 this is the Father's *w.* 40
Acts 21:14 *w.* of the L. be done
Eph. 5:17 what the *w.* of Lord is
6:7 with good *w.* doing service
Phil. 1:15 preach C. of good *w.*
Heb. 10:10 by wh. *w.* are sancti.
1 *Pet.* 4:3 suffice to have wro. *w.*
2 *Pet.* 1:21 proph. came not by *w.*

WILL of God.
Ezr. 7:18 do after *w.* of your *G.*
Mark 3:35 whoso sh. do *w.* of *G.*
John 1:13 not of *w.* of man, *w. of G.*
Acts 13:36 generation by *w. of G.*
Rom. 1:10 pros. jour. by *w. of G.*
8:27 interces. accor. to *w. of G.*
12:2 accepta. and perf. *w. of G.*
15:32 come with joy by *w. of G.*
1 *Cor.* 1:1 Paul an apostle by *w. of G.* 2 *Cor.* 1:1 ; *Eph.* 1:1 ;
Col. 1:1 ; 2 *Tim.* 1:1
2 *Cor.* 8:5 ga. thems. by *w. of G.*
Gal. 1:4 deli. fr. evil by *w. of G.*
Eph. 6:6 doing the *w. of God*
Col. 4:12 complete in *w. of God*
1 *Thes.* 4:3 this is *w. of God,* 5:18

Heb. 10:36 have done *w.' of God*
1 *Pet.* 2:15 so is the *w. of God*
3:17 better if *w. of God* be so
4:2 live not to lusts, to *w. of G.*
19 suffer according to *w. of G.*
1 *John* 2:17 he that doeth *w. of G.*

His WILL.
Dan. 4:35 doeth accord. to *his w.*
8:4 he did according to *his w.*
11:3 do accord. to *his w.* 16, 36
Luke 12:47 nei. accord. to *his w.*
John 7:17 if any do *h. w.* sh. kn.
Acts 22:14 shouldest know *his w.*
Rom. 2:18 and knowest *his w. ?*
9:19 who hath resisted *his w. ?*
1 *Cor.* 7:37 hath power over *h. w.*
16:12 *his w.* not at all to come
Eph. 1:5 good pleasure of *his w.*
9 kn. to us mystery of *his w.*
Col. 1:9 with knowledge of *h. w.*
2 *Tim.* 2:26 taken capt. at *his w.*
Heb. 13:21 good work to do *h. w.*
1 *John* 5:14 ask accord. to *his w.*
Rev. 17:17 hearts to fulfil *his w.*

My WILL.
Luke 22:42 not *my w.* but thine
Acts 13:22 shall fulfil all *my w.*
1 *Cor.* 9:17 if I do this ag. *my w.*

Own WILL.
Lev. 1:3 shall offer it of his *o. w.*
19:5 as your *own w.* 22:19, 29
Dan. 11:16 according to his *o. w.*
John 5:30 I seek not mine *o. w.*
6:38 not to do mine *own w.*
Eph. 1:11 counsel of his *own w.*
Heb. 2:4 according to his *own w.*
Jam. 1:18 of his *o. w.* begat he us

Thy WILL.
Ps. 40:8 I delight to do *thy w.*
143:10 teach me to do *thy w.*
Mat. 6:10 *t. w.* be done, *Luke* 11:2
26:42 not pass, *thy w.* be done
Heb. 10:7 I come to do *thy w.* 9

WILL, Verb.
Job 13:13 let come on me what *w.*
Prov. 21:1 heart whither. he *w.*
Dan. 4:17 giveth it to whomsoever he *w.* 25, 32 ; 5:21
Mat. 8:3 and said, I *w.* be thou
clean, *Mark* 1:41 ; *Luke* 5:13
20:15 do wh. I *w.* wi. my own ?
26:39 not as I *w. Mark* 14:36
Mark 14:7 when. *w.* may do good
15:12 what *w.* ye I should do ?
Luke 4:6 to whomsoever I *w.*
12:49 what *w.* I, if it be kindl. ?
John 15:7 ask what ye *w.*
17:24 I *w.* that they be with me
21:22 if I *w.* that he tarry, 23
Rom. 7:18 to *w.* is pres. with me
Phil. 2:13 G. worketh both to *w.*
1 *Tim.* 5:14 I *w.* women marry
Jam. 4:15 if L. *w.* we sh. do this

WILL not.
Ezek. 20:3 I *w. n.* be inquired of
Amos 7:13 I *w. not* ag. pass, 8:2
Mat. 21:29 he answered, I *w. not*
John 5:40 ye *w. not* come to me

WILLETH.
Rom. 9:16 it is not of him th. *w.*

WILFULLY.
Heb. 10:26 if we sin *w.* after we

WILLING.
Gen. 24:5 wom. not *w.* to follow
Ex. 35:5 whosoever is of a *w.*
heart, 21, 22, 29
1 *Chr.* 28:9 serve G. wi. *w.* mind
29:5 who is *w.* to consecrate his
Ps. 110:3 thy people shall be *w.*
Is. 1:19 if *w.* sh. eat good of land
Mat. 1:19 not *w.* to make her a
26:41 spirit is *w.* flesh is weak
Luke 10:29 *w.* to justify himself
22:42 if thou be *w.* remove cup

John 5:35 ye were *w.* to rejoice
Rom. 9:22 if G. *w.* to show wrath
2 *Cor.* 5:8 *w.* rather to be absent
8:3 they were *w.* of themselves
12 if there be first a *w.* mind
1 *Thes.* 2:8 *w.* to have imparted
2 *Pet.* 3:9 not *w.* any sho. perish

WILLINGLY.
Ex. 25:2 ev. man that gives *w.*
Jud. 5:2 people *w.* offered, 9
1 *Chr.* 29:6 rulers off. *w.* 9, 14, 17 ;
2 *Chr.* 35:8 ; *Ezr.* 1:6 ; 3:5
2 *Chr.* 17:16 Amaziah *w.* himself
Neh. 11:2 that *w.* offered thems.
Prov. 31:13 work. *w.* with hands
Lam. 3:33 he doth not afflict *w.*
Hos. 5:11 Ephr. *w.* walked after
John 6:21 they *w.* received him
Rom. 8:20 subj. to vanity not *w.*
2 *Cor.* 9:17 if I do this *w.* a rew.
Phile. 14 not as of necessity, but
w. 1 *Pet.* 5:2
2 *Pet.* 3:5 they are *w.* ignorant

WILLOWS.
Lev. 23:40 shall take *w.* of brook
Job 40:22 *w.* of brook comp. him
Ps. 137:2 hanged harps on *w.*
Is. 15:7 car. riches to brook of *w.*
44:4 they shall spring up as *w.*

WILLOW-TREE
Ezek. 17:5 he has set it as a *w.-t.*

WILL-WORSHIP.
Col. 2:23 show of wisd. in *w.-w.*

WILT.
Jud. 1:14 wh. *w.* thou ? *Est.* 5:3 ;
Mat. 20:21 ; *Mark* 10:51 ; *Lu.*
18:41
Ps. 60:10 *w.* not thou, O God ?
108:11
Mat. 15:28 be it to th. as thou *w.*
17:4 if th. *w.* let us make taber.
26:39 not as I will, but as thou
w. Mark 14:36

WIMPLES.
Is. 3:22 take aw. mantles and *w.*

WIN, NETH.
2 *Chr.* 32:1 he thought to *w.* th.
Prov. 11:30 he that *w.* souls
Phil. 3:8 that I may *w.* Christ

WIND.
Gen. 8:1 God made a *w.* to pass
Ex. 15:10 didst blow with thy *w.*
Num. 11:31 *w.* brought quails
2 *Sam.* 22:11 was seen on wings
of *w. Ps.* 18:10 ; 104:3
1 *K.* 18:45 heaven black with *w.*
19:11 strong *w.* rent mountains
2 *K.* 3:17 shall not see *w.* nor rain
Job 1:19 came *w.* from wildern.
6:26 speeches which are as *w.*
7:7 O remem. that my life is *w.*
8:2 words of thy mouth like *w.*
21:18 they are as stubble bef. *w.*
30:15 ter. pursue my soul as *w.*
22 thou liftest me up to the *w.*
37:21 *w.* passeth, *Ps.* 103:16
Ps. 1:4 which *w.* driveth away
78:39 *w.* that passeth away
135:7 bringeth *w.* out of treas.
147:18 causeth his *w.* to blow
Prov. 11:29 he shall inherit *w.*
25:14 clouds and *w.* with rain
23 north *w.* driveth away rain
27:16 whoso hid. her, hideth *w.*
30:4 who gath. wind in his fists
Ec. 1:6 *w.* goeth toward south
5:16 what profit, labored for *w.*
11:4 he that observ. *w.* not sow
Cant. 4:16 awake, O north *w.*
Is. 7:2 trees are moved with *w.*
11:15 with *w.* shake his hand
26:18 as it were brou. forth *w.*
27:8 he stayeth his rough *w.*
32:2 as a hiding-place from *w.*

41:16 *w.* carry them away, 57:13
29 their molten images are *w.*
64:6 like *w.* have taken us away
Jer. 4:12 a *w.* from those places
5:13 prophets shall become *w.*
10:13 *w.* out of his treas. 51:16
22:22 *w.* shall eat up thy past.
Ezek. 5:2 thou shalt scatter in *w.*
12:14 scatter tow. *w.* about him
37:9 prophesy to *w.* say to *w.*
Dan. 2:35 *w.* carried them away
Hos. 4:19 *w.* hath bound her up
8:7 sown *w.* shall reap whirlw.
12:1 Ephraim feedeth on *w.*
Amos 4:13 he that createth *w.*
Jon. 1:4 L. sent a great *w.* to sea
Zec. 5:9 *w.* was in their wings
Mat. 11:7 a reed shaken with the *w. Luke* 7:24
14:24 *w.* was contrary, *Mark* 6:48; *Acts* 27:4
32 *w.* ceased, *Mark* 4:39; 6:51
John 3:8 *w.* blow. where it listeth
Acts 2:2 sound as of a mighty *w.*
Eph. 4:14 car. about with ev. *w.*
Jam. 1:6 like wave driven wi. *w.*
Rev. 6:13 wh. she is shaken of *w.*
7:1 *w.* should not blow on earth

WINDS.

Job 28:25 to make weight for *w.*
Ezek. 37:9 come from the four *w.*
Mat. 7:25 *w.* blew, beat house, 27
8:26 rebuked the *w. Luke* 8:24
27 even the *w.* and sea obey him? *Mark* 4:41; *Luke* 8:25
Jam. 3:4 ships driven of fierce *w.*
Jude 12 clouds carri. about of *w.*

See EAST, FOUR, SCATTER, STORMY.

WINDY.

Ps. 55:8 hasten from *w.* storm

WINDOW.

Gen. 6:16 a *w.* shalt thou make
8:6 Noah opened *w.* of the ark
26:8 king of Gerar looked out *w.*
Jos. 2:15 Rah. let spies thro' *w.*
21 she bound scarlet line in *w.*
Jud. 5:28 moth. looked out of *w.*
2 *Sam.* 6:16 Mi. looked thro' *w.*
2 *K.* 9:30 and look out at a *w.*
13:17 he said, Open *w.* eastward
Prov. 7:6 at *w.* I looked through
Acts 20:9 sat in *w.* a young man
2 *Cor.* 11:33 thro' a *w.* let down

WINDOWS.

Gen. 7:11 *w.* of heav. were open.
8:2 *w.* of heaven were stopped
2 *K.* 7:2 if L. make *w.* in hea. 19
Ec. 12:3 that look out of *w.*
Cant. 2:9 my beloved look. at *w.*
Is. 24:18 *w.* fr. on high are open
54:12 I will ma. thy *w.* of agates
60:8 flee as doves to their *w.*
Jer. 9:21 death is co. into our *w.*
22:14 that cutteth him out *w.*
Dan. 6:10 his *w.* being open
Joel 2:9 enter in at *w.* like thief
Zep. 2:14 voice shall sing in *w.*
Mal. 3:10 if I will not open *w.* of

WINE.

Gen. 9:24 Noah awoke fr. his *w.*
14:18 Melchisedek brought *w.*
49:11 washed his garments in *w.*
12 his eyes were red with *w.*
Ex. 29:40 fourth part of a hin of *w. Lev.* 23:13; *Num.* 15:5
Num. 6:3 separate himself fr. *w.*
28:7 cause strong *w.* to be pour.
Deut. 32:33 *w.* is poison of drag.
Jud. 9:13 leave *w.* wh. cheereth
19:19 th. is bread and *w.* for me
1 *Sam.* 1:14 put away *w.* fr. thee
25:37 when *w.* gone out of Nab.
2 *Sam.* 6:19 flesh, and a flagon of *w.* 1 *Chr.* 16:3

13:28 Am. heart merry with *w.*
16:2 *w.* such as faint may drink
Neh. 2:1 the *w.* was before him
5:15 gover. taken bread and *w.*
18 once in ten days st. of all *w.*
13:15 lad. asses with *w.* grapes
Est. 1:7 they gave them royal *w.*
10 heart of king merry with *w.*
5:6 king said to Esth. at *w.* 7:2
7:7 arising from banquet of *w.*
Job 1:13 *w.* in th. bro. house, 18
32:19 my belly is as *w.* no vent
Ps. 75:8 *w.* is red, full of mixture
78:65 shouteth by reason of *w.*
104:15 *w.* that mak. glad heart
Prov. 9:2 hath mingled her *w.*
20:1 *w.* is a mocker, str. drink
23:30 they that tarry long at *w.*
31 look not on *w.* wh. it is red
31:6 gi. *w.* to th. of heavy heart
Ec. 2:3 to give myself to *w.*
10:19 *w.* maketh merry, money
Cant. 1:2 love better th. *w.* 4:10
5:1 I have drunk my *w.*
7:9 roof of thy mou. like best *w.*
Is. 1:22 thy *w.* mixed with water
5:11 night, till *w.* inflame them
12 pipe and *w.* are in th. feasts
22:13 eating flesh and drink. *w.*
24:11 there is a crying for *w.*
27:2 red *w.* 55:1 come, buy *w.*
28:1 that are overcome with *w.*
7 they have also erred thro' *w.*
29:9 drunken, not wi. *w.* 51:21
56:12 come, say I will fetch *w.*
Jer. 23:9 man whom *w.* overcome
Jer. 25:15 take *w.* of fury at my hand
35:5 full of *w.* 40:12 gathered *w.*
48:33 I have caused *w.* to fail
51:7 nations drunken of her *w.*
Ezek. 27:18 Damascus trad. in *w.*
Dan. 1:5 king gave of *w.*
8 not to defile himself with *w.*
5:1 Belshazzar drank *w.* bef. 4
2 he tasted *w.* 23 drunk *w.*
10:3 neither came *w.* nor flesh
Hos. 2:9 take away my *w.* in sea.
3:1 gods, and love flagons of *w.*
14:7 scent be as *w.* of Lebanon
Joel 1:5 howl, ye drinkers of *w.*
Mic. 2:11 I will prophesy of *w.*
Hab. 2:5 he transgresseth by *w.*
Zec. 9:15 make noise, as thro' *w.*
10:7 hearts rejoice, as thro' *w.*
Luke 7:33 J. neither drinking *w.*
John 2:3 saith, They have no *w.*
9 tasted water made *w.* 4:46
10 at begin. set forth good *w.*
Eph. 5:18 be not drunk with *w.*
1 *Tim.* 3:3 not given to *w.* 8; *Tit.* 1:7; 2:3
5:23 use *w.* for stomach's sake
1 *Pet.* 4:3 walked in excess of *w.*
Rev. 16:19 give cup of *w.* of wrath
17:2 drunk with *w.* of forni. 18:3

See BOTTLE, CORN, DRINK, NEW, OFFERINGS, OIL, SWEET.

WINE-BIBBER, S.

Prov. 23:20 be not with *w.-b.*
Mat. 11:19 man a *w.-b. Luke* 7:34

WINE-BOTTLES.

Jos. 9:4 Gibeonites took *w.-bot.*
13 *b.* of *w.* which we filled

WINE-CELLARS.

1 *Chr.* 27:27 over *w.-c.* was Zabdi

WINE-FAT.

Is. 63:2 like him treadeth *w.-f.*
Mark 12:1 dig. a place for *w.-f.*

WINE-PRESS.

Num. 18:27 fulness of *w.-p.* 30
Deut. 15:14 furnish out of *w.-p.*
Jud. 6:11 thres. wheat by *w.-p.*
7:25 they slew at *w.-p.* of Zeeb
2 *K.* 6:27 help thee out of *w.-p.* ?
Is. 5:2 made a *w.-p.* therein

63:3 I have trodden *w.-p.* alone
Lam. 1:15 trodden Jud. as *w.-p.*
Hos. 9:2 *w.-p.* sh. not feed them
Mat. 21:33 digged a *w.-p.* in it
Rev. 14:19 cast it into gr. *w.-p.*
20 *w.-p.* trodden without city
19:15 he treadeth *w.-p.* of wrath

WINE-PRESSES.

Neh. 13:15 treading *w.-p.* on sab.
Job 24:11 tread their *w.-p.*
Jer. 48:33 wine to fail from *w.-p.*
Zec. 14:10 upon king's *w.-p.*

WINES.

Is. 25:6 make feast of *w.* on lees

WING.

2 *K.* 6:24 *w.* of cherub. 5 cubits other *w.* 27; 2 *Chr.* 3:11, 12
Is. 10:14 none that moved the *w.*
Ezek. 17:23 dw. fowl of every *w.*

WINGS.

Ex. 19:4 bare you on eagle's *w.*
25:20 covering mercy-seat with *w.* 37:9; 1 *K.* 8:7
Lev. 1:17 cleave it with *w.* ther.
Deut. 32:11 eagle spread. her *w.*
Ruth 2:12 under wh. *w.* thou art
2 *Sam.* 22:11 upon *w.* of wind
Job 39:13 gavest *w.* to peacock?
Ps. 17:8 hide me under thy *w.*
18:10 fly on *w.* of wind, 104:3
36:7 put th. trust under shadow of thy *w.* 57:1 ; 61:4 ; 91:4
55:6 O that I had *w.* like a dove
63:7 in shadow of *w.* will I rej.
68:13 sh. ye be as *w.* of a dove
139:9 if I take *w.* of morning
Prov. 23:5 riches make thems. *w.*
Ec. 10:20 whi. hath *w.* shall tell
Is. 6:2 each one had six *w.*
8:8 stretch. out his *w.* fill land
18:1 woe to land shadow. wi. *w.*
40:31 mount up with *w.* eagles
Jer. 48:9 give *w.* to M. may fly
40 he sh. spread his *w.* over M.
49:22 he sh. spread *w.* over Boz.
Ezek. 1:6 every one had four *w.*
9 *w.* were joined ; 10:12 *w.* full of eyes
24 I heard the noise of their *w.* 3:13 ; 10:5, 25
17:3 a great eagle with great *w.*
7 another great eagle with *w.*
Dan. 7:4 like lion, had eagles' *w.*
6 ano. having on back four *w.*
Hos. 4:19 bou. her up in her *w.*
Zec. 5:9 wind was in their *w.*
Mal. 4:2 with healing in his *w.*
Mat. 23:37 as a hen gathereth her chick. under *w. Luke* 13:34
Rev. 9:9 sound of th. *w.* as horses
12:14 to wom. were giv. two *w.*

WINGED.

Gen. 1:21 G. created ev. *w.* fowl
Deut. 4:17 liken. of any *w.* fowl
Ezek. 17:3 great eagle, long-*w.*

WINK, ED, ETH.

Job 15:12 wh. do thi. eyes *w.* at ?
Ps. 35:19 neither let them *w.*
Prov. 6:13 a wicked man *w.*
10:10 he th. *w.* causeth sorrow
Acts 17:30 ignorance God *w.* at

WINNOWED, ETH.

Ruth 3:2 Bo. *w.* barley to-night
Is. 30:24 hath been *w.* wi. shovel

WINTER.

Gen. 8:22 and *w.* shall not cease
Ps. 74:17 made summer and *w.*
Cant. 2:11 for lo, the *w.* is past
Zec. 14:8 in summer and *w.*
Mat. 24:20 pray that your flight be not in *w. Mark* 13:18
John 10:22 feast of dedicat. in *w.*
2 *Tim.* 4:21 to come before *w.*

WINTER-HOUSE.

Jer. 36:22 the king sat in *w.-h.*

Amos 3:15 I will smite *w.-h.*

WINTER, Verb.
Is. 18:6 beasts shall *w.* on them
Acts 27:12 not commod. to *w.* in
1 *Cor.* 16:6 abide, *w.* with you
Tit. 3:12 I determin. there to *w.*

WINTERED.
Acts 28:11 ship which *w.* in isle

WIPE.
2 *K.* 21:13 *w.* Jerusalem as a dish
Neh. 13:14 *w.* not out good deeds
Is. 25:8 Lord will *w.* away tears
fr. all faces, *Rev.* 7:17; 21:4
Luke 7:38 woman did *w.* th. with
hairs, 44 ; *John* 11:2 ; 12:3
John 13:5 began to *w.* them with

WIPED, ETH, ING.
2 *K.* 21:13 *w.* it as a man *w.* dish
Prov. 6:33 reproach not *w.* way
30:20 she eateth, *w.* her mouth

WIRES.
Ex. 39:3 cut gold plates into *w.*

WISDOM.
Ex. 31:3 I have filled him wi. Sp.
of God in *w.* 6 ; 35:31, 35
35:26 stirred them in *w.* 36:1, 2
Deut. 4:6 for this is your *w.* and
2 *Sam.* 14:20 acco. to *w.* of angel
20:22 woman went to peo. in *w.*
1 *K.* 3:28 saw *w.* of G. was in h.
4:29 God gave Solomon *w.* 5:12 ;
2 *Chr.* 1:12
30 Solomon's *w.* excelled *w.*
of Egypt, 34 ; 7:14 ; 10:4, 23,
24 ; 2 *Chr.* 9:3, 22, 23
1 *Chr.* 22:12 Lord give thee *w.*
2 *Chr.* 1:10 give *w.* 11 asked *w.*
Ezr. 7:25 after the *w.* of thy God
Job 4:21 die, even without *w.*
12:2 peo. *w.* shall die with you
13:5 and it should be your *w.*
15:8 dost thou restr. *w.* to thy. ?
26:3 coun. him th. hath no *w.* ?
28:12 where shall *w.* be found ?
20 whence cometh *w.* where
32:7 multitude of years teach *w.*
13 say, We have found out *w.*
33:33 and I shall teach thee *w.*
34:35 Job's words were with. *w.*
36:5 G. mighty in stren. and *w.*
38:37 who can num. clou. in *w.* ?
39:17 G. hath deprived her of *w.*
Ps. 37:30 mouth of righ. speak *w.*
51:6 shalt make me to know *w.*
90:12 apply our hearts to *w.*
104:24 in *w.* hast th. made wor.
105:22 and teach his senators *w.*
136:5 him th. by *w.* made heav.
Prov. 1:2 kn. *w.* 7 fools desp. *w.*
20 *w.* crieth, 8:1 ; 2:2 ear to *w.*
2:6 Lord giveth *w.* 3:21 keep *w.*
7 he layeth up *w.* for righteous
10 when *w.* entereth into heart
3:13 happy man that findeth *w.*
19 Lord by *w.* founded earth
4:5 get *w.* 7 ; 5:1 atte. to my *w.*
7:4 say to *w.* Thou art my sister
8:5 unders. *w.* 9:1 *w.* buildeth
12 I *w.* dwell with prudence
14 counsel is mine, sound *w.*
10:23 man of understan. hath *w.*
31 mouth of just brin. forth *w.*
12:8 commend. according to *w.*
Prov. 14:6 scorner seeketh *w.* fin.
8 *w.* of prudent is to understa.
33 *w.* resteth in heart of him
16:16 better to get *w.* than gold
17:16 in hand of fool to get *w.*
18:1 man intermeddleth with *w.*
19:8 that getteth *w.* loveth soul
21:30 there is no *w.* against L.
23:4 rich. cea. from thy own *w.*
9 a fool will despise *w.* of wor.
23 buy *w.* 24:3 thro' *w.* house
29:3 whoso loveth *w.* rejoiceth
15 the rod and reproof give *w.*

39:3 I nei. learned *w.* nor have
31:26 openeth her mouth wi. *w.*
Ec. 1:13 I gave my heart to *w.*
16 I have more *w.* than all
17 I gave my heart to know *w.*
18 for much *w.* is much grief
2:3 acquaint. my heart with *w.*
9 my *w.* remained with me
12 I turned myself to beho. *w.*
13 *w.* excel. folly ; 21 lab. in *w.*
26 G. give. *w.* 7:12 *w.* giv. life
7:19 *w.* strengtheneth the wise
23 all this I have proved by *w.*
25 I applied heart to seek *w.*
8:1 man's *w.* mak. face to shine
16 I appli. my heart to kn. *w.*
9:10 there is no *w.* in the grave
13 *w.* have I seen under sun
15 poor man by *w.* deliv. city
10:1 that is in reputation for *w.*
3 *w.* faileth him, he is a fool
Is. 10:13 by my *w.* I have done it
29:14 *w.* of their wise sh. perish
33:6 *w.* be stability of thy times
Jer. 9:23 let not wise glory in *w.*
10:12 establi. world by *w.* 51:15
Dan. 1:4 chil. skilful in all *w.*
2:14 answ. with counsel and *w.*
20 blessed be G. *w.* and might
21 he giveth *w.* to the wise
23 God, who hast given me *w.*
30 not revealed for any *w.*
5:11 *w.* of gods found in him
Mat. 12:42 came fr. utterm. parts
to hear *w.* of Sol. *Luke* 11:31
13:54 whence has this man *w.* ?
Luke 1:17 turn disobedient to *w.*
2:40 Jesus filled with *w.*
52 increased in *w.* and stature
11:49 also said the *w.* of God
21:15 give you a mouth and *w.*
Acts 6:3 seven men full of *w.*
10 we. not able to resist the *w.*
7:10 God gave Joseph *w.* in the
22 learned in *w.* of the Egypt.
1 *Cor.* 1:17 not with *w.* of words
19 destroy the *w.* of the wise
20 God made foolish the *w.* of
21 in the *w.* of God the world
by *w.* knew not G. it pleas.
22 and Greeks seek after *w.*
24 C. power of G. and *w.* of G.
30 God is made to us *w.*
2:4 not with words of man's *w.*
5 not stand in the *w.* of men
6 speak *w.* 7 speak *w.* of God
13 which man's *w.* teacheth
3:19 for the *w.* of this world is
2 *Cor.* 1:12 not with fleshly *w.*
Eph. 1:8 abour. toward us in *w.*
3:10 the manifold *w.* of God
Col. 1:9 mi. be filled with all *w.*
28 teaching eve. man in all *w.*
3:16 words dw. in you in all *w.*
4:5 walk in *w.* tow. them that
Jam. 1:5 any lack *w.* let him ask
3:15 this *w.* descendeth not from
2 *Pet.* 3:15 according to *w.* given
Rev. 5:12 the Lamb to receive *w.*
7:12 glory, and *w.* be to our God
17:9 the mind which hath *w.*

WISDOM, joined with is.
Job 6:13 and *is w.* driven quite
12:12 with ancient *is*, 13:16
28:18 *w. is* abo. rubi. *Prov.* 8:11
28 fear of the Lord that *is w.*
Prov. 4:7 *w. is* principal thing
10:13 with him that hath understanding *w. is* found
11:2 but with the lowly *is w.*
13:10 with well-advised *is w.*
14:8 the *w.* of the prudent *is* to
17:24 *w. is* before him that hath
24:7 *w. is* too high for a fool, he
Ec. 1:18 in much *w. is* much
7:11 *w. is* good with an inherit.
12 *w. is* a defence, and money

9:16 *w. is* better than strength;
the poor man's *w. is* despis.
18 *w. is* better than weapons
10:10 *w. is* profitable to direct
Jer. 8:9 lo, th. have rejected the
word, what *w. is* in them ?
49:7 *is w.* no more in Teman ?
Dan. 5:14 excellent *w. is* found
Mat. 11:19 but *w. is* justified of
her children, *Luke* 7:35
Mark 6:2 wh. *w. is* giv. to him ?
Jam. 3:17 *w.* from above *is* pure
Rev. 13:18 here *is w.* let him that

Of WISDOM.
Job 11:6 show thee secrets o^f *w.*
28:18 price of *w.* is above ru.bies
Ps. 49:3 speak of *w.* and m.edita.
111:10 fear of the Lord is the
beginning of *w.* *Prov.* 9:10
Prov. 1:3 instruct. of *w.* justice
4:11 in the way of *w.* have led
10:21 fools die for want of *w.*
11:12 he that is void of *w.* des.
15:21 to him that is desti. of *w.*
33 fear of L. is instruct. of *w.*
18:4 spring of *w.* as flow. brook
24:14 knowle. of *w.* to thy soul
Ec. 1:16 great experience of *w.*
Ezek. 28:12 the sum full of *w.*
Dan. 1:20 matters of *w.* be fou.
Mic. 6:9 the man of *w.* shall see
Rom. 11:33 depth of *w.* of God !
1 *Cor.* 2:1 of speech or of *w.*
12:8 by Spirit the word of *w.*
Col. 2:3 are hid all treasu. of *w.*
23 have indeed a show of *w.*
Jam. 3:13 show with meek. of *w.*
See SPIRIT.

Thy WISDOM.
1 *K.* 2:6 according to *thy w.*
10:6 true report I heard of *t. w.*
7 *thy w.* and prosperity exce.
8 hear *thy w.* 2 *Chr.* 9:5, 7
2 *Chr.* 9:6 *t. w.* was not told me
Job 39:26 th hawk fly by *t. w.*
Is. 47:10 *thy w.* perverted thee
Ezek. 28:4 *t. w.* and understanding hast got. thee riches, 5
17 corrupted *thy w.* by bright.

WISE.
Gen. 3:6 a tree to make one *w.*
41:39 none discreet and *w.* as
Ex. 23:8 the gift blindeth the
w. *Deut.* 16:19
Deut. 4:6 this nation is a *w.* peo.
32:29 O that they were *w.*
Jud. 5:29 her *w.* ladies answered
2 *Sam.* 14:20 my lord is *w.* accor.
1 *K.* 3:12 given thee a *w.* heart
5:7 blessed L. that hath given
David a *w.* son. 2 *Chr.* 2:12
1 *Chr.* 26:14 Zec. a *w.* counsellor
Job 5:13 taketh *w.* in own crafti.
9:4 he is *w.* in heart and stren.
11:12 vain man would be *w.*
22:2 he that is *w.* may be profi.
32:9 great men are not alw. *w.*
37:24 he respecteth not any that
are *w.* of heart
Ps. 2:10 be *w.* now, O ye kings
19:7 making *w.* the simple
36:3 left off to be *w.* do good
94:8 fools, when will ye be *w.* ?
107:43 whoso is *w.* and will ob.
Prov. 1:5 *w.* man at. *w.* counsel
6 understand *w.* and sayings
3:7 be not *w.* in thine own eyes
35 the *w.* shall inherit glory
6:6 be *w.* 8:33 ; 23:19 ; 27:11
9:12 be *w.* thou shall be *w.* for
10:1 a *w.* son maketh a glad father, 15:20
5 gathereth in summer is *w.*
8 *w.* receive commandments
19 he that refrai. his lips is *w.*
11:29 servant to the *w.* in heart
30 he that winneth souls is *w.*

12:15 hearken. to counsel is *w*.
18 tongue of the *w*. is health
13:1 a *w*. son heareth instruct.
14 law of *w*. is a founta. of life
20 walk. with *w*. men sh. be *w*.
14:3 lips of the *w*. preserve th.
24 crown of the *w*. is th. riches
35 favor is toward *w*. servant
15:2 the tongue of the *w*. useth knowledge aright.
7 lips of *w*. dispe. knowledge
12 a scorner will not go to *w*.
24 way of life is above to *w*.
31 reproof abideth among *w*.
16:21 *w*. in heart called prudent
23 heart of *w*. teach. his mouth
17:2 *w*. serv. shall rule over son
28 hol. his peace is counted *w*.
18:15 the *w*. seeketh knowledge
19:20 be *w*. in thy latter end
20:1 deceived thereby, is not *w*.
26 *w*. king scattereth wicked
21:11 simple is made *w*. when *w*. is instructed he rec. kno.
20 oil in the dwelling of the *w*.
22:17 hear the words of the *w*.

Prov. 23:15 be *w*. my hea. sh. rej.
24 begetteth a *w*. son have joy
24:6 by *w*. coun. make thy war
23 these things belong to *w*.
25:12 *w*. reprover on obedi. ear
26:5 answer a fool, lest he be *w*.
12 a man *w*. in his own conceit
28:7 whoso keep. law is *w*. son
11 rich is *w*. in his own conceit
30:24 be four things that are *w*.
Ec. 2:15 why was I more *w*. ?
16 th. is no remembrance of *w*.
19 wherein I show. myself *w*.
4:13 better *w*. child than foolish
6:8 wh. hath *w*. more th. fool ?
7:4 heart of *w*. house of mourn.
5 better to hear rebuke of *w*.
16 neither make thys. over *w*.
19 wisd. strengtheneth the *w*.
23 I will be *w*. far from me
9:1 *w*. are in the hand of God
11 I saw that bre. is not to *w*.
12:9 preacher was *w*. he taught
11 words of *w*. are as goads

Is. 5:21 woe to them that are *w*.
19:11 say ye, I am son of *w*. ?
31:2 yet he is also *w*. bring evil
Jer. 4:22 they are *w*. to do evil
8:8 how do ye say, We are *w*.
18:18 nor counsel perish fr. *w*.
Dan. 2:21 God giv. wisdom to *w*.
12:3 they that be *w*. shall shine
10 but the *w*. shall understand
Hos. 14:9 *w*. underst. th. things
Zec. 9:2 Tyrus and Zidon be *w*.
Mat. 10:16 be ye *w*. as serpents
11:25 because th. hast hid these things from *w*. *Luke* 10:21
24:45 who is faith. and *w*. ser. ?
25:2 five virgins *w*. five foolish
4 *w*. took oil in their vessels
Luke 12:42 who is that *w*. stew.
Rom. 1:14 I am debtor to the *w*.
22 profess. thems. *w*. be. fools
11:25 lest ye be *w*. in your conc.
12:16 be not *w*. in your conceits
16:19 *w*. to that which is good
27 to God only *w*. be glory, *1 Tim*. 1:17 ; *Jude* 25
1 Cor. 1:19 destroy wisdom of *w*.
20 where is the *w*. ?
27 chosen foolish th. to con. *w*.
3:10 as *w*. master-builder I lay
18 be *w*. let him become a fool
19 taketh *w*. in their craftiness
20 L. knows thoughts of the *w*.
4:10 but ye are *w*. in Christ
2 Cor. 10:12 compar. are not *w*.
Eph. 5:15 not as fools, but *w*.
2 Tim. 3:15 scrip. able to ma. *w*.

Any WISE.
Lev. 19:17 shall in a. *w*. rebuke
See MAN, MEN.

WISE-HEARTED.
Ex. 28:3 speak to all *w*.-*hearted*
31:6 I put wisdom in *w*.-*hearted*
35:10 every *w*.-*hearted* am. you
25 women *w*.-*hearted* did spin
36:1 wrought every *w*.-*h*. man
8 ev. *w*.-*h*. man made 10 curta.

WISE men.
Gen. 41:8 Phar. called for magicians and *w*. men, *Ex*. 7:11

In no WISE.
Mat. 5:18 shall in no *w*. pass
10:42 he shall in no *w*. lose rew.
Luke 18:17 he shall in no *w*. enter therein, *Rev*. 21:27
John 6:37 will in no *w*. cast out
Rom. 3:9 are we bet. ? in no *w*.

On this WISE.
Mat. 1:18 birth of C. was on t. *w*.
Acts 13:34 he said on t. *w*. I will
Heb. 4:4 spake of 7th day on t. *w*.

WISE woman.
2 Sam. 14:2 Joab fetched *w*. *w*.
20:16 cried a *w*. *w*. out of city
Prov. 14:1 ev. *w*. *w*. buil. house

WISELY.
Ex. 1:10 let us deal *w*. with them
1 Sam. 18:5 behav. *w*. 14, 15, 30
2 Chr. 11:23 Rehoboam dealt *w*.
Ps. 58:5 charming never so *w*.
64:9 shall *w*. cons. of his doings
101:2 I will behave myself *w*.
Prov. 16:20 handleth a matter *w*.
21:12 he *w*. considereth wicked
28:26 who walk. *w*. sh. be deliv.
Ec. 7:10 thou dost not inquire *w*.
Luke 16:8 becau. he had done *w*.

WISER.
1 K. 4:31 Sol. was *w*. th. all men
Job 35:11 mak. us *w*. than fowls
Ps. 119:98 made me *w*. th. enem.
Prov. 9:9 and he will be yet *w*.
26:16 slug. is *w*. in his conceit
Ezek. 28:3 thou art *w*. th. Daniel
Luke 16:8 in their generation *w*.
1 Cor. 1:25 fool. of G.-*w*. th. men

WISH.
Job 33:6 to thy *w*. in God's stead
Ps. 40:14 put to sha. that *w*. evil
73:7 more than heart could *w*.
Rom. 9:3 co. *w*. myself accursed
2 Cor. 13:9 we *w*. even your per.
3 John 2 I *w*. th. mayest prosper

WISHED.
Jon. 4:8 and *w*. himself to die
Acts 27:29 cast anch. *w*. for day

WISHING.
Job 31:30 *w*. a curse to his soul

WIST.
Ex. 16:15 th. *w*. not what it was
34:29 Mo. *w*. not his face shone
Jud. 16:20 *w*. not Lord departed
Mark 9:6 he *w*. not what to say
Luke 2:49 *w*. ye not I must be about my Father's business
Acts 12:9 *w*. it not true wh. was
23:5 *w*. not he was high-priest

To WIT.
Gen. 24:21 to *w*. wheth. L. made
Ex. 2:4 to *w*. what wou. be done
2 Cor. 5:19 to *w*. th. G. in C. rec.
8:1 we do you to *w*. of gr. of G.

WITCH.
Ex. 22:18 not suffer a *w*. to live
Deut. 18:10 not be am. you a *w*.

WITCHCRAFT.
1 Sam. 15:23 rebelli. as sin of *w*.
2 Chr. 33:6 Manasseh used *w*.
Gal. 5:20 works of flesh are *w*.

WITCHCRAFTS.
2 K. 9:22 Jezebel's *w*. are many
Mic. 5:12 cut off *w*. out of hand
Nah. 3:4 mist. of *w*. selleth nati.

WITHAL.
1 K. 19:1 *w*. Elij. slain prophets
Acts 25:27 not *w*. to signi. crimes

WITHDRAW.
1 Sam. 14:19 S. said to priest *w*.
Job 9:13 if God will not *w*. anger
13:21 *w*. thy hand far from me
33:17 that he may *w*. hand from
Prov. 25:17 *w*. fr. neigh.'s house
Ec. 7:18 fr. this *w*. not thy hand
Is. 60:20 neit. thy moon *w*. itself
Joel 2:10 stars *w*. shining, 3:15
2 Thes. 3:6 *w*. from every brother
1 Tim. 6:5 cor. minds *w*. thyself

WITHDRAWN.
Deut. 13:13 have *w*. inhabitants
Cant. 5:6 my beloved had *w*.
Lam. 2:8 hath not *w*. his hand
Ezek. 18:8 *w*. his hand from iniq.
Hos. 5:6 L. *w*. himself from them
Luke 22:41 was *w*. a stone's cast

WITHDRAWEST, ETH.
Ps. 74:11 why *w*. thy rig. hand ?
Job 36:7 *w*. not from righteous

WITHDREW.
Neh. 9:29 *w*. and would not hear
Ezek. 20:22 I *w*. my hand
Mat. 12:15 Je. knew, *w*. himself
Mark 3:7 J. *w*. fr. then. *Lu*. 5:16
Gal. 2:12 when they come, he *w*.

WITHER.
Ps. 1:3 his leaf also shall not *w*.
37:2 shall *w*. as the green herb
Is. 19:6 reeds and flags shall *w*.
7 thing sown by brooks sh. *w*.
40:24 blow upon them, shall *w*.
Jer. 12:4 shall herbs of field *w*. ?
Ezek. 17:9 cut off fruit that it *w*.
10 shall it not utterly *w*. ?
Amos 1:2 top of Carmel shall *w*.

WITHERED.
Gen. 41:23 seven ears *w*.
Ps. 102:4 heart is *w*. 11 I am *w*.
Is. 15:6 the hay is *w*. away
27:11 boughs are *w*. broken off
Lam. 4:8 Nazarite's skin is *w*.
Ezek. 19:12 rods *w*. and consum.
Joel 1:12 trees of the field are *w*.
17 barns broken down, corn *w*.
Amos 4:7 where it rained not *w*.
Jon. 4:7 smote gourd that it *w*.
Mat. 12:10 man wh. had his hand *w*. *Mark* 3:1, 3 ; *Luke* 6:6, 8
13:6 hav. no root, *w*. *Mark* 4:6
21:19 fig-tree *w*. 20 ; *Mark* 11:21
Luke 8:6 it *w*. bec. lacked moist.
John 5:3 *w*. folk wait. mov. wat.
15:6 cast fo. as a branch and *w*.

WITHERETH.
Job 8:12 flag *w*. before any herb
Ps. 90:6 even. cut down and *w*.
Ps. 129:6 gra. *w*. bef. groweth up
Is. 40:7 grass *w*. the flower fadeth, 8 ; *1 Pet*. 1:24
Jam. 1:11 the sun *w*. the grass
Jude 12 trees *w*. without fruit

WITHHELD, EST.
Gen. 20:6 I *w*. thee from sinning
22:12 thou hast not *w*. son
30:2 *w*. fr. thee, fruit of womb ?
Neh. 9:20 *w*. not manna
Job 31:16 have *w*. poor fr. desire
Ec. 2:10 I *w*. not my heart

WITHHOLD.
Gen. 23:6 none sh. *w*. his sepulc.
2 Sam. 13:13 he will not *w*. me
Job 4:2 who can *w*. himself from
Ps. 40:11 *w*. not thy mercies
84:11 no good thing will he *w*.
Prov. 3:27 *w*. not good
23:13 *w*. not correct. from child

Ec. 11:6 even. *w.* not thy hand
Jer. 2:25 *w.* foot fr. being unsh.

WITHHOLDEN.

1 *Sam.* 25:26 *w.* th. from reveng.
Job 22:7 *w.* bread from hungry
38:15 from wicked light is *w.*
42:2 no thought *w.* from thee
Ps. 21:2 hast not *w.* request
Jer. 3:3 showers have been *w.*
5:25 sins have *w.* good things
Ezek. 18:16 hath not *w.* pledge
Joel 1:13 drink-off. *w.* from God
Amos 4:7 I have *w.* rain from you

WITHHOLDETH.

Job 12:15 behold he *w.* waters
Prov. 11 24 *w.* more than meet
26 he that *w.* corn, peo. curse
2 *Thes.* 2:6 now ye kn. what *w.*

WITHIN.

Ec. 9:14 little city. few men *w.*
Luke 11:7 he from *w.* sh. answer

WITHOUT.

Gen. 24:31 wheref. stan. th. *w. ?*
Prov. 7:12 now she is *w.*
22:13 there is a lion *w.*
1 *Cor.* 5:13 but them that are *w.*

WITHOUT, *with* within.

Lev. 13:55 if garm. bare *w.* or *w.*
Ezek. 2:10 was written *w.* and *w.*

WITHS.

Jud. 16:7 bind with 7 green *w.*
8 brought *w.* 9 brake the *w.*

WITHSTAND.

Num. 22:32 angel went to *w.* Ba.
2 *Chr.* 13:7 R. could not *w.* them
8 ye think to *w.* kingdom of L.
20:6 none is able to *w.* thee
Est. 9:2 no man can co. *w.* Jews
Ec. 4:12 one prevail, two sh. *w.*
Dan. 11:15 his people sh. not *w.*
Acts 11:17 that I could *w.* God ?
Eph. 6:13 able to *w.* in evil day

WITHSTOOD.

2 *Chr.* 26:18 *w.* Uzziah the king
Dan. 10:13 prince of Pers. *w.* me
Acts 13:8 Elymas sorcerer *w.* th.
Gal. 2:11 I *w.* Peter to the face
2 *Tim.* 3:8 Jannes and J. *w.* Mo.
4:15 hath greatly *w.* our words

WITNESS.

Gen. 21:30 a *w.* that I dig. well
31:44 covenant be a *w.* betw. us
48 this heap a *w.* pillar a *w.* 52
50 God is *w.* between me and
thee, 1 *Thes.* 2:5
Ex. 22:13 if torn br. it for a *w.*
23:1 be not an unrighteous *w.*
Lev. 5:1 a soul sin and *w.* of sw.
Num. 5:13 if th. be no *w.* ag. her
35:30 one *w.* shall not testify,
Deut. 17:6 ; 19:15
Deut. 31:19 song be a *w.* 21, 26
Jos. 22:27 altar *w.* bet. us, 28, 34
24:27 this stone shall be a *w.*
Jud. 11:10 L. *w.* bet. us, *Jer.* 42:5
1 *Sam.* 12:5 L. *w.* against you
Job 16:8 my wrinkles *w.* ag. me
19 *w.* in heaven record on high
29:11 eye saw me it gave *w.*
Ps. 89:37 a faithful *w.* in heaven
Prov. 14:5 faithf. *w.* will not lie
25 a true *w.* delivereth souls
19:28 ungodly *w.* scorn. judgm.
24:28 be not *w.* ag. thy neighb.
Is. 19:20 a *w.* to the L. of hosts
55:4 given him for *w.* to people
Jer. 29:23 and am a *w.* saith L.
42:5 L. faithful *w.* between us
Mic. 1:2 let L. G. be *w.* ag. you
Mal. 2:14 L. *w.* bet. thee and wi.
3:5 swift *w.* against sorcerers
Mat. 24:14 preached for *w.* to na.
26 *w.* agreed not together, 59
Luke 22:71 need we further *w. ?*

John 1:7 came for a *w.* to bear *w.*
3:11 ye receive not our *w.*
26 whom bear. *w.* same bapti.
5:31 if bear *w.* mys. *w.* not true
32 *w.* he witness. of me is true
36 I have greater *w.* than John
37 Father hath borne *w.* of me
Acts 1:22 one ordained to be *w.*
4:33 gave *w.* of resurrect. of L.
10:43 all proph. *w.* whoso beli.
14:17 left not himself without *w.*
22:15 thou shalt be his *w.* to all
26:16 make thee minister and *w.*
Rom. 1:9 God is my *w.* I serve
2:15 conscience bearing *w.* 9:1
Tit. 1:13 this *w.* is true, rebuke
Heb. 2:4 God bear. *w.*,with signs
10:15 the Holy Ghost is *w.* to us
11:4 Abel obtained *w.* righteous
Jam. 5:3 rust shall be *w.* ag. you
1 *Pet.* 5:1 P. a *w.* of suffer. of C.
1 *John* 5:9 if we receive *w.* of m.
10 he th. beli. hath *w.* in him.
3 *John* 6 borne *w.* of thy charity
Rev. 1:5 Jesus Ch. the faithf. *w.*
3:14 write th. thi. saith true *w.*
20:4 were beheaded for *w.* of J.

See BARE, BEAR, BEARETH,
FALSE, TABERNACLE.

WITNESSES.

Num. 35:30 put to death by *w.*
Deut. 17:6 at mouth of two or
three *w.* shall he be put to
death, 19:15 ; 2 *Cor.* 13:1
7 hands of *w.* be first on him
Jos. 24:22 Josh. said, Ye are *w.*
Ruth 4:9 ye are *w.* I have bou. 10
Job 10:17 renew. thy *w.* ag. me
Is. 8:2 I took faithful *w.* to rec.
43:9 all nations bring their *w.*
10 my *w.* saith the L. 12 ; 44:8
44:9 they are their own *w.*
Jer. 32:10 I eval. evid. took *w.* 12
25 buy field, take *w.* 44
Mat. 18:16 mou. of two or th. *w.*
23:31 ye be *w.* to yourselves
26:65 need of *w. ? Mark* 14:63
Luke 24:48 ye are *w.* of th. thin.
Acts 1:8 ye sh. be *w.* in Jerusal.
2:32 Jesus G. raised up, whereof we are *w.* 3:15
5:32 *w.* of these things, 10:39
7:58 *w.* laid th. clothes at S.'s f.
10:41 unto *w.* chosen of G. to us
13:31 are his *w.* unto the people
1 *Thes.* 2:10 ye are *w.* God also
1 *Tim.* 5:19 no ac. but bef. 2 *w.*
6:12 good profes. bef. many *w.*
2 *Tim.* 2:2 thi. heard among *w.*
Heb. 10:28 died under 2 or 3 *w.*
12:1 compassed *w.* cloud of *w.*
Rev. 11:3 give power to my *w.*

See FALSE

WITNESS, Verb.

Deut. 4:26 I call heaven and earth
to *w.* against you
1 *Sam.* 12:3 here I am, *w.* ag. me
Is. 3:9 countenance *w.* ag. them
Lam. 2:13 what sh. I take to *w. ?*
Mat. 26:62 what is it wh. these
w. against thee ? *Mark* 14:60
27:13 how many things they *w.*
against thee ? *Mark* 15:4

WITNESSED, ETH, ING.

1 *K.* 21:13 men of B. *w.* ag. Nab.
John 5:32 witness *w.* of me
Acts 20:23 H. G. *w.* in every city
26:22 *w.* both to small and great
Rom. 3:21 being *w.* by law and
1 *Tim.* 6:13 bef. P. *w.* good conf.
Heb. 7:8 of whom it is *w.* he liv.

WITS.

Ps. 107:27 stag. at their *w.* end

WITTY.

Prov. 8:12 I find out *w.* inventi.

WITTINGLY.

Gen. 48:14 Is. guid. his hands *w.*

WIVES.

Gen. 4:19 Lamech took two *w.*
6:2 took them *w.* wh. they cho.
30:26 give me my *w.* and child.
31:50 if thou take other *w.*
Num. 14:3 *w.* and chil. be a prey
Deut. 17:17 nor multi. *w.* to him.
21:15 if a man have two *w.*
Jud. 8:30 Gideon had many *w.*
21:7 how do for *w.* for them ? 16
18 not give them *w.* of our da.
1 *Sam.* 25:43 they were Da.'s *w.*
2 *Sam.* 5:13 Da. took *w.* out of J.
12:8 gave master's *w.* into thy
1 *K.* 11:3 Solomon had 700 *w.*
4 his *w.* turn. his heart wh. old
20:7 sent for my *w.* and childr.

2 *Chr.* 11:21 Ma. above all his *w.*
23 he desired many *w.*
24:3 Jehoi. took for him two *w.*
29:9 our *w.* in captivity for this
Ezr. 10:3 a cov. to put aw. *w.* 44
Neh. 12:43 *w.* and chil. rejoiced
13:23 Jews married *w.* of Ashd.
Est. 1:20 *w.* give husbands hon.
Jer. 29:6 take *w.* and *w.* for sons
35:8 d. no wine, nor *w.* nor sons
Dan. 5:2 his *w.* drink therein, 3
Luke 17:27 eat, drank, marri. *w.*
Acts 21:5 on our way, with *w.*
1 *Cor.* 7:29 ha. *w.* be as had none
Eph. 5:22 *w.* submit to your husbands as unto the Lord, *Col.*
3:18 ; **1** *Pet.* 3:1
24 so let *w.* be to th. husbands
1 *Tim.* 4:7 refuse old *w.* fables
1 *Pet.* 2:1 won by conversa. of *w.*

See STRANGE.

Their WIVES.

Gen. 34:29 t. *w.* capt. **1** *Sam.* 30:3
Jud. 3:6 took daught. to be t. *w.*
2 *Chr.* 20:13 Ju. with t. *w.* stood
Ezr. 10:19 put away *their w.*
Neh. 5:1 cry of people and *th. w.*
10:28 t. *w.* entered into an oath
Is. 13:16 houses spoil. *w.* ravish.
Jer. 6:12 t. *w.* turned to oth. 8:10
14:16 none to bury *their w.*
18:21 t. *w.* be bereaved of child.
44:9 forgotten wicked. of t. *w.*
15 men knew t. *w.* burnt ince.
Ezek. 44:22 nor take for t. *w.* wi.
Dan. 6:24 cast t. *w.* into den of l.
Zec. 12:12 t. *w.* mourn, 13, 14
Eph. 5:28 love t. *w.* as th. bodies
1 *Tim.* 3:11 so must t. *w.* be gr.

Thy WIVES.

2 *Sam.* 12:11 take t. *w.* bef. eyes
19:5 who saved lives of t. *w.*
1 *K.* 20:3 gold is mine and t. *w.*
5 deliver me *thy w.* and child.
2 *Chr.* 21:14 L. will smite t. *w.*
Jer. 38:23 bring *thy w.* and chil.
Dan. 5:23 *thy w.* have dru. wine

Your WIVES.

Ex. 19:15 come not at *your w.*
22:24 *your w.* shall be widows
32:2 break ear-rings of *your w.*
Deut. 3:19 y. *w.* and little ones
remain in cities, *Jos.* 1:14
29:11 y. *w.* enter coven. with L.
Neh. 4:14 fight for y. *w.* and hou.
25 ye and *your w.* have spoken
Mat. 19:8 suff. to put away y. *w.*
Eph. 5:25 love *your w. Col.* 3:19

WIZARD, S.

Lev. 19:31 nor seek after *w.*
20:6 turns after *w.* I will cut off
27 a *w.* shall be put to death
Deut. 18:11 sh. not be am. you *w.*
1 *Sam.* 28:3 Saul put *w.* out, 9
2 *K.* 21:6 dealt with *w.* 2 *Chr.*
33:6

23:24 Josiah put *w*. out of land
Is. 8:19 *w*. that peep and mutter
19:3 shall seek to idols and *w*.

WOE.

Num. 21:29 *w*. to M. *Jer*. 48:46
1 *Sam*. 4:7 *w*. unto us, 8; *Jer*.
    4:13; 6:4; *Lam*. 5:16
Prov. 23:29 hath *w*. ? hath sor. ?
Ec. 4:10 *w*. to him that falls
10:16 *w*. to th. wh. king is a ch.
Is. 3:9 *w*. to their soul
    11 *w*. to wick. sh. be ill wi. h.
17:12 *w*. to multi. of many peo.
18:1 *w*. to the land with wings
28:1 *w*. to pride, to drunkards
29:1 *w*. to Ariel ; 33:1 *w*. to them
30:1 *w*. to rebellious children
45:9 *w*. to him striv. wi. Maker
    10 *w*. to him saith to father
Jer. 13:27 *w*. unto thee, O Jerus.
22:13 *w*. to him that builds
23:1 *w*. to pastors destroy sheep
48:1 *w*. to Nebo
Ezek. 2:10 written mour. and *w*.
13:3 *w*. to foolish prophets
    18 *w*. to wom. th. sew pillows
16:23 *w*. unto thee, saith L.
24:6 *w*. to bloody city, *Nah*. 3:1
30:2 howl, *w*. worth the day
34:2 *w*. be to the shepherds
Amos 5:18 *w*. to you de. day of L.
Hab. 2:6 *w*. to him that increas.
    9 *w*. to him that coveteth
    12 *w*. to him that build. a town
    15 *w*. to him giv. neigh. drink
    19 *w*. to him saith wood awake
Zep. 2:5 *w*. to inh. of sea-coasts
3:1 *w*. to her that is polluted
Zec. 11:17 *w*. to idol shepherd
Mat. 11:21 *w*. to thee, Chora. *w*.
    to thee, Bethsaida, *Luke* 10:13
18:7 *w*. to the world because of
    offences, *Luke* 17:1
23:13 *w*. unto you scribes and
    Pharisees, 14, 15, 23, 25, 27,
    29 ; *Luke* 11:44
    16 *w*. unto you, blind guides
26:24 *w*. to man by whom Son
    of man is betrayed, *Mark*
    14:21 ; *Luke* 22:22
Luke 6:24 *w*. unto you are rich
    25 *w*. to you that are full
    26 *w*. to you wh. all speak well
11:42 *w*. unto you, Pharisees, 43
    46 *w*. to you, ye lawyers, 47, 52
Rev. 8:13 *w*. w. *w*. to the inhabi-
    ters of the earth, 12:12
9:12 one *w*. past ; 11:14 sec. *w*.

WOE is me.

Ps. 120:5 *w*. *is me* th. I sojourn
Is. 6:5 *w*. *is me*, I am undone
Jer. 4:31 *w*. *is me*, soul wearied
10:19 *w*. *is me*, for my hurt
15:10 *w*. *is me*, moth. hast borne
45:3 *w*. *is me*, for L. added grief
Mic. 7:1 *w*. *is me*, I am as fruit

WOE unto me.

Job 10:15 if I be wicked, *w*. *u*. *me*
Is. 24:16 my leanness, *w*. *u*. *me*
1 *Cor*. 9:16 *w*. *u*. *me* if I preach

WOE to them.

Is. 5:8 *w*. *to them* that join house
    11 *w*. *to t*. that rise in morning
    18 *w*. *to them* that draw iniqu.
    20 *w*. *to t*. that call evil good
    21 *w*. *to them* wise in own eyes
    22 *w*. *to them* that drink wine
10:1 *w*. *to t*. decree unrigh. dec.
29:15 *w*. *to t*. that seek counsel
31:1 *w*. *to t*. th. go down to Eg.
Jer. 50:27 *w*. *to t*. their day come
Hos. 7:13 *w*. *to t*. have fled fr. me
9:12 *w*. *to t*. I depart from them
Amos 6:1 *w*. *to t*. at ease in Zion
Mic. 2:1 *w*. *to t*. devise iniquity
Mat. 24:19 *w*. *to t*. wh. are with
    chi. *Mark* 13:17 ; *Luke* 21:23

Jude 11 *w*. *to t*. gone way of Cain

WOES.

Rev. 9:12 two *w*. more hereafter

WOFUL.

Jer. 17:16 neither desired *w*. day

WOLF.

Gen.. 49:27 Benja. ravin as a *w*.
Is. 11:6 *w*. sh. dwell with lamb
65:25 *w*. and lamb feed together
Jer. 5:6 *w*. of evening spoil them
John 10:12 hirel. seeth *w*. coming

WOLVES.

Ezek. 22:27 her princ. are like *w*.
Hab. 1:8 horses fiercer than *w*.
Zep. 3:3 her judges evening *w*.
Mat. 7:15 inwardly they are *w*.
10:16 as sheep in midst of *w*.
Luke 10:3 send you forth am. *w*.
Acts 20:29 *w*. sh. ent. among you

WOMAN.

Gen. 2:22 rib of man made he *w*.
    23 she shall be called *w*.
    3:15 enmity between th. and *w*.
    24:5 peradven. *w*. not come, 39
    44 let same be *w*. L. appointed
Ex. 21:22 hurt a *w*. with child
Lev. 18:23 nor *w*. stand bef. beast
20:13 lie with mank. as with *w*.
Num. 5:18 set *w*. before Lord, 30
    27 *w*. be curse among her peo.
25:6 brought Midianitish *w*.
    8 Phineh. thrust *w*. thro' belly
31:17 kill ev. *w*. hath kno. man
Deut. 22:14 I took *w*. not a maid
Jos. 2:4 *w*. took men, hid them
    6:22 bring out thence *w*. Rahab
Jud. 4:9 Sisera into hand of *w*.
    9:53 *w*. cast millsto. on Abime-
    lech's head, 2 *Sam*. 11:21
    54 say not of me, *w*. slew him
14:3 never *w*. am. my people ?
19:26 came *w*. in dawni. of day
Ruth 1:5 *w*. was left of her sons
3:11 kn. thou art a virtuous *w*.
4:11 L. make *w*. like Rachel
1 *Sam*. 1:15 *w*. of sorrowful spi.
    26 I am *w*. stood by thee here
2:20 L. give thee seed of this *w*.
28:7 *w*. that hath a familiar spi.
2 *Sam*. 11:2 Da. saw *w*. washing
13:17 put this *w*. out, bolt door
17:19 *w*. spread cover. ov. well
20:22 then *w*. went to the peo.
1 *K*. 3:17 I and *w*. dwell in house
14:5 feign herself to be ano. *w*.
17:17 son of *w*. fell sick, died
2 *K*. 4:8 where was a great *w*.
2 *K*. 6:26 there cried a *w*. saying
    8:5 this is *w*. 9:34 see cursed *w*.
2 *Chr*. 24:7 Athal. that wick. *w*.
Job 31:9 if heart deceiv. by a *w*.
Ps. 48:6 pain as of a *w*. in travail,
      Is. 13:8 ; 21:3 ; 26:17 ; *Jer*.
      4:31 ; 6:24 ; 13:21 ; 22:23 ; 30:6 ;
      31:8 ; 48:41 ; 49:22, 24 ; 50:43
Prov. 6:24 keep thee fr. evil *w*.
    7:10 there met him a *w*. subtile
    9:13 a foolish *w*. is clamorous
12:4 virtu. *w*. is a crown, 31:10
14:1 ev. wise *w*. buildeth house
21:9 brawling *w*. in house, 19
31:10 who can find a virtu. *w*. ?
    30 *w*. that fears L. be praised
Ec. 7:26 *w*. wh. heart is snares
    28 *w*. am. th. I have not found
Is. 42:14 I cry like *w*. travailing
45:10 to *w*. what hast th. bro. ?
49:15 can *w*. forget suck. child ?
54:6 L. called thee as *w*. forsak.
Jer. 6:2 daughter of Zion to a *w*.
31:22 a *w*. compass a man
Lam. 1:17 J. is a menstruous *w*.
Ezek. 16:30 work of a whorish *w*.
23:44 went as they go in to *w*.
36:17 unclean. of a removed *w*.
Hos. 3:1 love *w*. beloved of friend

Is. 13:13 source of a travailing *w*.
    sh. come on him, *Mic*. 4:9, 10
Zec. 5:7 a *w*. that sit. in ephah
Mat. 5:28 whoso looketh on a *w*.
9:20 a *w*. whi. was diseased 12
    years, *Mark* 5:25 ; *Luke* 8:43
13:33 which a *w*. took and hid
15:28 O *w*. great is thy faith
22:27 last of all *w*. died also,
    Mark 12:22 ; *Luke* 20:32
26:10 said, Why trouble ye *w*.
    13 that *w*. hath done eth. be to.
Mark 10:12 if *w*. put away hush.
Luke 7:39 what man. of *w*. this ?
    44 Simon, seest thou this *w*. ?
13:16 ought not this *w*. daught.
John 2:4 *w*. wh. have I to do wi.
4:9 askest of me, a *w*. of Sama.
    39 many belie. for saying of *w*.
8:3 brought *w*. taken in adult. 4
    10 when Jesus saw none but *w*.
19:26 mother, *w*. behold thy son
Acts 9:36 *w*. was full of works
17:34 a *w*. named Damaris bell.
Rom. 1:27 men leaving use of *w*.
    7:2 *w*. that hath husb. is bound
1 *Cor*. 7:1 good not to touch a *w*.
    2 every *w*. have her own husb.
11:5 *w*. th. prayeth uncovered, 6
    7 *w*. is glory of the man, 8, 9
    10 *w*. ought to have power, 11
    12 as *w*. is of man, so m. by *w*.
    13 is it comely for *w*. to pray
    15 if a *w*. have long hair
Gal. 4:4 sent his S. made of a *w*.
1 *Thes*. 5:3 com. as travail on *w*.
1 *Tim*. 2:12 suff. not *w*. to teach
    14 *w*. being deceiv. in transgr.
Rev. 2:20 suff. *w*. Jezeb. to teach
12:1 appear. *w*. cloth. with sun
    6 *w*. fled ; 16 earth helped *w*.
    17 dragon was wroth with *w*.
17:3 I saw a *w*. sit on a beast
    6 *w*. drunken ; 7 mystery of *w*.

See BORN, MAN, STRANGE.

Young WOMAN.

Ruth 4:12 seed L. give th. of *y*. *w*.

WOMANKIND.

Lev. 18:22 not lie wi. man. as *w*.

WOMB.

Gen. 25:23 two nations in thy *w*.
    24 were twins in her *w*. 38:27
29:31 Leah's *w*. 30:22 Rach.'s *w*.
49:25 bless. of breasts and of *w*.
Ex. 13:2 whatso. open. *w*. mine
Num. 8:16 such as open ev. *w*.
Jud. 13:5 be a Nazarite fr. *w*. 7.
Ruth 1:11 any more sons in *w*. ?
1 *Sam*. 1:5 L. had shut up *w*. 6
Job 3:11 why died I not fr. *w*. ?
    10:18 why brou. me forth of *w*. ?
    24:20 the *w*. shall forget him
    31:15 made th. in *w*. make him ?
38:8 as if it had issu. out of *w*.
    29 out of whose *w*. came ice?
Ps. 22:9 who took me out of *w*.
    10 I was cast upon thee fr. *w*.
58:3 wick. are estranged fr. *w*.
71:6 been upholden from *w*.
110:3 willing, from *w*. of morn.
Prov. 30:16 barren *w*. says not
31:2 what, the son of my *w*. ?
Ec. 11:5 how bones grow in *w*.
Is. 44:2 Lord formed thee from
    the *w*. 24 ; 49:5
46:3 which are carried from *w*.
48:8 called a transgressor fr. *w*.
Is. 49:1 Lord called me from *w*.
    15 have compas. on son of *w*.
66:9 bring forth, and shut *w*. ?
Jer. 1:5 bef. th. camest out of *w*.
20:17 he slew me not from *w*.
    18 why ca. I forth out of *w*. ?
Ezek. 20:26 fire that openeth *w*.

WOMB (cont.)

Hos. 9:11 gl. flee fr. birth and *w.*
14 give them a miscarrying *w.*
12:3 took brother by heel in *w.*
Luke 1:31 sh. conceive in thy *w.*
41 babe leaped in her *w.* 44
2:21 bef. he was conceiv. in *w.*
23 male that open. *w.* be holy

See FRUIT, MOTHER.

WOMBS.

Gen. 20:18 L. had closed all *w.*
Luke 23:29 bless. *w.* never bare

WOMEN.

Gen. 24:11 *w.* go to draw water
Ex. 15:20 *w.* went after Miriam
35:25 *w.* wise-hearted spin. 26
Lev. 26:26 ten *w.* sh. bake bread
Num. 31:15 have saved *w.* alive
Jos. 8:35 Jo⁻. read law before *w.*
Jud. 5:24 blessed above *w.* Jael
21:14 saved *w.* of Jabesh-Gilead
1 *Sam.* 2:22 Eli heard lay wi. *w.*
15:33 thy sword made *w.* child.
18:7 *w.* answered one another
21:5 *w.* have been kept from us
three days
30:2 Amalek. had taken *w.* cap.
2 *Sam.* 1:26 passing love of *w.*
15:16 left ten *w.* to keep house
1 *K.* 3:16 came *w.* were harlots
2 *K.* 8:12 rip *w.* with child, 15:16
Neh. 13:26 outland. *w.* cause sin
Est. 1:9 made a feast for the *w.*
2:17 A. loved Esther above *w.*
3:13 little children and *w.* 8:11
Job 42:15 no *w.* fair as Job's dau.
Ps. 45:9 among thy honorable *w.*
Prov. 31:3 give not stren. to *w.*
Cant. 1:8 fair. among *w.* 5:9; 6:1
Is. 3:12 peo. *w.* rule over them
4:1 sev. *w.* ta. hold of one man
19:16 Egypt shall be like to *w.*
27:11 *w.* come, set them on fire
32:9 ye *w.* that are at ease
10 careless *w.* 11 *w.* be troub.
Jer. 7:18 *w.* knead their dough
9:17 mourning a.d cunning *w.*
20 yet hear word of L. O ye *w.*
38:22 *w.* left be brought to king
44:24 Jer. said to *w.* Hear word
50:37 they sh. become *w.* robbed
51:30 men of Ba. became as *w.*
Lam. 2:20 shall *w.* eat children?
4:10 *w.* have sodden th. children
5:11 they ravished *w.* in Zion
Ezek. 8:14 *w.* weeping for Tam.
9:6 slay maids, children, and *w.*
13:18 woe to *w.* that sew pillows
16:34 contrary from other *w.*
38 judge thee, as *w.* break
wedlock
23:2 two *w.* daughters of one
45 after man. of *w.* shed blood
48 *w.* tau. not to do after lewd.
Dan. 11:17 give him dau. of *w.*
37 nor sh. he regard des. of *w.*
Hos. 13:16 *w.* with child be rip.
Amos 1:13 ripped *w.* with child
Mic. 2:9 *w.* of people ye cast out
Nah. 3:13 people in midst are *w.*
Zec. 5:9 there came out two *w.*
8:4 old *w.* shall dwell in Jerus.
14:2 houses rifled, *w.* ravished
Mat. 11:11 th. are born of *w.* not
greater than Bapt. *Luke* 7:28
14:21 5,000 men, besi. *w.* 15:38
24:41 two *w.* grind. *Luke* 17:35
27:55 *w.* were beholding afar off
Luke 1:28 blessed among *w.* 42
24:22 *w.* made us astonish. 24
Acts 1:14 conti. in prayer wi. *w.*
13:50 Jews stirred up devout *w.*
16:13 speak to *w.* wh. resorted
17:4 of *w.* not a few believ. 12
Rom. 1:26 th. in *w.* did change use
1 *Cor.* 14:34 let *w.* keep silence
35 shame for *w.* to speak in ch.

Phil. 4:3 help *w.* which labored
1 *Tim.* 2:9 *w.* adorn in mod. ap.
10 becom. *w.* professing godli.
11 let *w.* learn with subjection
5:2 entreat elder *w.* as mothers
14 I will that young. *w.* marry
2 *Tim.* 3:6 captive *w.* laden with
sins
Tit. 2:3 aged *w.* behave as beco.
4 teach younger *w.* to be sober
Heb. 11:35 *w.* receiv. dead raised
1 *Pet.* 3:5 manner holy *w.* adorn.
Rev. 9:8 had hair as hair of *w.*
Rev. 14:4 that are not defil. wi. *w.*

See CHILDREN, MEN, STRANGE,
SINGING.

WOMEN-SERVANTS.

Gen. 20:14 Abimelech gave *w.-s.*
32:5 Jacob had men-serv. *w.-s.*

WON.

1 *Chr.* 26:27 spoils *w.* in battles
Prov. 18:19 offend. har. to be *w.*
1 *Pet.* 3:1 *w.* by conver. of wives

WONDER.

Deut. 13:1 give thee a sign or *w.*
2 sign of the *w.* come to pass
28:46 on thee fr a sign and *w.*
2 *Chr.* 32:31 sent to inquire of *w.*
Ps. 71:7 I am as a *w.* to many
Is. 20:3 walked barefoot for a *w.*
29:14 marvellous work and *w.*
Acts 3:10 they were filled wi. *w.*
Rev. 12:1 appear. a *w.* in heav. 3

WONDER, Verb.

Is. 29:9 stay yourselves and *w.*
Jer. 4:9 priests and proph. sh. *w.*
Hab. 1:5 regard, *w.* marvellously
Acts 13:41 despisers, *w.* and per.
Rev. 17:8 dwell on earth sh. *w.*

WONDERFUL.

Deut. 28:59 will ma. plagues *w.*
2 *Sam.* 1:26 love to me was *w.*
2 *Chr.* 2:9 house I am to build *w.*
Job 42:3 uttered things too *w.* for
Ps. 119:129 thy testimoni. are *w.*
139:6 knowledge too *w.* for me
Prov. 30:18 three thi. are too *w.*
Is. 9:6 his name sh. be called *W.*
25:1 thou hast done *w.* things
28:29 Lord, who is *w.* in coun.
Jer. 5:30 a *w.* thing is committed
Mat. 21:15 saw *w.* things he did

See WORKS.

WONDERFULLY.

1 *Sam.* 6:6 when he wrought *w.*
Ps. 139:14 for I am *w.* made
Lam. 1:9 Jerusal. came down *w.*
Dan. 8:24 he shall destroy *w.*

WONDERS.

Ex. 3:20 and smite Egypt with
my *w.* 7:3; 11:9; *Deut.* 6:22;
7:19; 26:8; 34:11
4:21 do those *w.* 11:10 did *w.*
5:11 fearf. in praises, doing *w.*
Deut. 4:34 to take a nation by *w.*
Jos. 3:5 to-morrow L. will do *w.*
1 *Chr.* 16:12 rem. his *w. Ps.* 105:5
Neh. 9:10 showedst *w.* on Phara.
17 nor were mindful of thy *w.*
Ps. 78:11, 43
Job 9:10 G. doeth *w.* with. num.
Ps. 77:11 I remember *w.* of old
14 thou art God that doest *w.*
88:10 wilt th. show *w.* to dead?
12 shall thy *w.* be kn. in dark?
89:5 heavens shall praise thy *w.*
96:3 declare his *w.* among peo.
105:27 showed his *w.* in land of
106:7 underst. not thy *w.* in Eg.
107:24 see works and *w.* in deep
135:9 sent *w.* in midst of Egypt
136:4 who alone doeth great *w.*
Is. 8:18 children are for *w.* in Is.
Jer. 32:20 set signs and *w.* in Eg.
21 brought forth people wi. *w.*

Dan. 4:2 to show signs and *w.*
3 great signs! mighty his *w.*!
6:27 he worketh *w.* in heaven
12:6 how long to end of th. *w.*?
Joel 2:30 I will sh. *w. Acts* 2:19
Mat. 24:24 show *w. Mark* 13:22
John 4:48 except ye see signs, *w.*
Acts 2:22 approved of God by *w.*
43 ma. signs and *w.* were done
4:30 *w.* done by name of Je. by
apostles, 5:12; 14:3; 15:12
6:8 Stephen did *w.* among peo.
7:36 after he had sh. *w.* in Eg.
Rom. 15:19 Gent. obed. thro' *w.*
2 *Cor.* 12:12 signs of apost. in *w.*
2 *Thes.* 2:9 com. in signs and *w.*
Heb. 2:4 witn. with signs and *w.*
Rev. 13:13 *w.* in sight of men

WONDERED.

Is. 59:16 *w.* was no intercessor
63:5 I *w.* th. was none to uphold
Zec. 3:8 hear, for they are *w.* at
Luke 2:18 they that heard it *w.*
4:22 they *w.* at gracious words
24:41 believed not for joy, *w.*
Acts 7:31 Mos. *w.* 8:13 Magus *w.*
Rev. 13:3 world *w.* after beast
17:6 I *w.* with great admiration

WONDERING.

Gen. 24:21 *w.* at her, held peace
Luke 24:12 Pe. *w.* at that which
Acts 3:11 people ran together *w.*

WONDROUS.

1 *Chr.* 16:9 talk of his *w.* wo. *Ps.*
26:7; 105:2; 119:27; 145:5
Job 37:14 consid. *w.* works of G.
16 dost kn. *w.* works of him?
Ps. 71:17 I declar. thy *w.* works
72:18 G. doeth *w.* things, 86:10
75:1 near, thy *w.* works declare
78:32 believed not for *w.* works
106:22 who had done *w.* works
119:18 behold *w.* thi. out of law
Jer. 21:2 accord. to his *w.* works

WONDROUSLY.

Jud. 13:19 the angel did *w.*
Joel 2:26 Lord dealt *w.* with you

WONT.

Num. 22:30 was I ever *w.* to do
so to thee?
2 *Sam.* 20:18 th. were *w.* to spe.
Mark 10:1 as he was *w.* he tau.
Luke 22:39 he was *w.* to mount

WOOD.

Gen. 22:6 Abraham took *w.*
7 Isa. said, Behold fire and *w.*
Num. 13:20 wheth. be *w.* or not
31:20 purify things made of *w.*
Deut. 10:1 make th. an ark of *w.*
19:5 when man goeth into *w.*
29:11 hewer of thy *w. Jos.* 9:21,
23, 27; *Jer.* 46:22
Jos. 17:18 mountain is a *w.*
1 *Sam.* 6:14 th. clave *w.* of cart
14:25 they of land came to a *w.*
23:16 Jonath. went to Da. in *w.*
2 *Sam.* 18:8 *w.* devoured people
1 *K.* 18:23 lay the bullock on *w.*
2 *K.* 2:24 two she-bears out of *w.*
1 *Chr.* 29:2 I have prepared *w.*
Ps. 80:13 boar of *w.* doth waste
132:6 found it in fields of *w.*
141:7 when one cleaveth *w.*
Prov. 26:20 no *w.* fire goeth out
21 as *w.* to fire, so is contenti.
Ec. 10:9 he that cleaveth *w.*
Is. 10:15 lift itself as if no *w.*
30:33 pile thereof is fire and *w.*
45:20 set up *w.* of their image
60:17 for iron silv. for *w.* brass
Jer. 5:14 make words fire, peo. *w.*
7:18 children gather *w.* the fa.
28:13 hast broken yokes of *w.*
Ezek. 15:3 sff. *w.* thereof be tak.
24:10 heap on *w.* 39:10 no *w.*

Mic. 7:14 flock whi. dwell in *w.*
Hab. 2:19 saith to *w.* Awake
Hag. 1:8 bring *w.* build house
Zec. 12:6 like a hearth among *w.*
1 *Cor.* 3:12 this founda. *w.* hay
2 *Tim.* 2:20 also vessels of *w.*

See OFFERING, STONE.

WOODS.
Ezek. 34:25 sleep safely in *w.*

WOOF.
Lev. 13:48 plague be in *w.* 51-59

WOOL.
Jud. 6:37 fleece of *w.* in floor
2 *K.* 3:4 100,000 rams with *w.*
Ps. 147:16 L. giveth snow like *w*
Prov. 31:13 seeketh *w.* and flax
Is. 1:18 sins like crim. be as *w.*
51:8 worm sh. eat them like *w.*
Ezek. 27:18 was merchant in *w.*
34:3 eat fat, clothe you with *w.*
44:17 no *w.* sh. come upon them
Dan. 7:9 hair like *w. Rev.* 1:14
Hos. 2:5 lovers that give me *w.*
9 I will recover my *w.* and flax

WOOLLEN.
Lev. 13:47 wheth. *w.* or linen, 59
48 in warp or woof of *w.* 52
19:19 a garment mingled of linen and *w. Deut.* 22:11

WORD.
Gen. 37:14 br. me *w.* ag. *Mat.* 2:8
44:18 let me sp. a *w.* 2 *Sam.* 14:12
Ex. 12:35 according to *w.* of Mo.
32:28 Levi did according to the *w. Lev.* 10:7
Num. 22:8 bri. you *w. Deut.* 1:22
20 the *w.* I say to thee, that do
35 *w.* I speak ; 38 *w.* God put.
23:5 L. put *w.* in Bala.'s mouth
Deut. 1:25 brought us *w.* again
4:2 not add to *w.* I comm. you
8:3 by *w.* that proceed. out of mouth of God, *Mat.* 4:4
18:20 prophet pres. to speak *w.*
21 how know the *w.* ? *Jer.* 28:9
21:5 by *w.* controversy be tried
30:14 *w.* is nigh thee, *Rom.* 10:8
Jos. 1:13 remember *w.* Moses
14:7 I brought *w.* 22:32 them *w.*
1 *Sam.* 4:1 *w.* of Sa. came to Is.
2 *Sam.* 3:11 not answer Ab. a *w.*
2 *Sam.* 7:7 and in all places spake I a *w.* 1 *Chr.* 17:6
25 *w.* thou hast spoken conce.
15:28 till there come *w.* fr. you
19:10 not a *w.* of bringing king
24:4 and the king's *w.* prevailed, 1 *Chr.* 21:4
1 *K.* 2:30 Ben. bro. king *w.* 2 *K.* 22:9, 20 ; 2 *Chr.* 34:16, 28
42 *w.* that I have heard is good
8:56 not failed one *w.* of prom.
18:21 answer. not a *w. Is.* 36:21
2 *K.* 18:28 hear *w.* of king of As.
1 *Chr.* 16:15 be ye mindful of *w.*
Ps. 105:8
21:12 advise *w.* I sh. bring him
Neh. 1:8 remember *w.* thou com.
Est. 1:21 according to *w.* of Me.
7:8 *w.* went out of king's mouth
Job 2:13 none spake a *w.* to Job
Ps. 17:4 by *w.* of thy lips I kept
68:11 L. gave *w.* many publish.
119:49 rememb. *w.* to thy serv.
123 eyes fail for *w.* of righteo.
139:4 there is not *w.* in tongue
Prov. 12:25 a good *w.* mak. glad
13:13 despiseth *w.* be destroyed
14:15 simple believeth every *w.*
15:23 *w.* spoken in season good
25:11 *w.* fitly spo. is like apples
Ec. 8:4 where *w.* of king, power
Is. 5:24 despised *w.* of Holy One
8:10 speak *w.* it shall not stand
9:8 the Lord sent a *w.* to Jacob
29:21 make man offend. for a *w.*

30:21 ears sh. hear *w.* behind th.
41:28 no counsel. could ans. *w.*
44:26 confirmeth *w.* of his serv.
45:23 *w.* is gone out of mouth
50:4 to speak a *w.* in season
Jer. 5:13 the *w.* is not in them
9:20 rec. *w.* of his mouth, 10:1
18:18 nor *w.* perish from proph.
23:36 every man's *w.* his burden
26:2 speak, diminish not a *w.*
34:5 I have pronounced the *w.*
37:17 king said, any *w.* fr. L. ?
44:16 for the *w.* spoken unto us
Ezek. 3:17 hear *w.* at mouth, 33:7
12:25 the *w.* shall come to pass
28 *w.* I have spok. sh. be done
13:6 they would confirm the *w.*
Dan. 3:28 ha. changed king's *w.*
4:17 demand by *w.* of holy ones
31 the *w.* in the king's mouth
Jon. 3:6 *w.* came to king of Nin.
Hag. 2:5 acco. to *w.* I covenant.
Mat. 8:8 speak the *w.* only
12:32 whoso speak. a *w.* against the Son of man, *Luke* 12:10
36 idle *w.* men sh. give accou.
13:21 because of the *w.* he is offended, *Mark* 4:17
15:23 Je. ans. woman not a *w.*
18:16 *w.* be establ. 2 *Cor.* 13:1
22:46 no man able to answ. a *w.*
27:14 Jesus answer. never a *w.*
28:8 run to bring disciples *w.*
Mark 4:14 sower soweth the *w.*
14:72 Pe. called to mind the *w.*
16:20 confirming *w.* with signs
Luke 4:36 amaz. what *w.* is this !
7:7 say in a *w.* my serv. healed
24:19 Je. mighty in *w.* and deed
John 1:1 in beginn. was the *W.*
14 the *W.* was made flesh
2:22 believed *w.* Jesus said, 4:50
12:48 *w.* I have spok. judge him
14:24 *w.* you hear is not mine
15:3 through *w.* I spake to you
20 rememb. *w.* I said unto you
25 that *w.* might be fulfilled
17:20 sh. believe me through *w.*
Acts 10:36 *w.* God sent to Israel
13:15 any *w.* of exhortation
26 to you is *w.* of salva. sent
15:7 th. Gentiles should hear *w.*
17:11 receiv. *w.* with readiness
20:32 I commend *w.* of his grace
28:25 Paul had spoken one *w.*
Rom. 10:8 that is the *w.* of faith
15:18 Gent. obe. by *w.* and deed
1 *Cor.* 4:20 not in *w.* but in power
12:8 *w.* of wisdom, *w.* of know.
2 *Cor.* 1:18 our *w.* to you was not
5:19 to us *w.* of reconciliation
10:11 as we are in *w.* by letters
Gal. 5:14 law is fulfill. in one *w.*
6:6 taught in *w.* communicate
Eph. 5:26 clea. with water by *w.*
Phil. 1:14 speak *w.* without fear
2:16 holding forth the *w.* of life
Col. 1:5 heard in *w.* of the truth
3:16 *w.* of C. dwell in you richly
17 do in *w.* or deed, do in name
1 *Thes.* 1:5 gospel came not in *w.*
6 received the *w.* in affliction
2:13 receive it not as *w.* of men
2 *Thes.* 2:2 not by Spi. nor by *w.*
15 wheth. by *w.* or our epistle
17 stablish you in ev. good *w.*
3:14 man obey not *w.* by epistle
1 *Tim.* 4:12 exam. of belie. in *w.*
5:17 labor in *w.* and doctrine
2 *Tim.* 2:17 *w.* eat as a canker
4:2 preach *w.* instant in season
Tit. 1:9 holding fast *w.* as taught
Heb. 1:3 all things by *w.* of pow.
2:2 if *w.* spoken by angels stea.
4:2 *w.* preached did not profit
5:13 unskilful in *w.* of righteo.
7:28 but the *w.* of the oath-
12:19 entreat. *w.* sh. not be spo.

13:22 suffer *w.* of exhortation
Jam. 1:21 receive the ingraft. *w.*
22 doers of *w.* not hearers only
23 if any be a hearer of the *w.*
3:2 if any man offend not in *w.*
1 *Pet.* 2:2 babes desire milk of *w.*
8 to them who stumble at *w.*
3:1 if any obey not *w.* they may
2 *Pet.* 1:19 more sure *w.* of pro.
3:7 heav. by *w.* are kept in store
1 *John* 1:1 handled *w.* of life
3:18 not love in *w.* but in deed
5:7 Father, *W.* and Holy G. one
Rev. 3:10 kept *w.* of my patience
12:11 overcome by *w.* of testi.

WORD of God.
1 *Sam.* 9:27 I show thee *w. of G.*
1 *K.* 12:22 *w. of G.* came to She.
1 *Chr.* 17:3 *w. of G.* came to Na.
Prov. 30:5 every *w. of G.* is pure
Is. 40:8 *w. of G.* stand for ever
Mark 7:13 *w. of God* of no effect
Luke 3:2 *w. of G.* came unto J.
4:4 not by bread but by *w. of G.*
5:1 pressed to hear *w. of God*
8:11 the seed is the *w. of God*
21 breth. th. wh. hear *w. of G.*
11:28 they that hear *w. of God*
John 10:35 gods to wh. *w. of G.*
Acts 4:31 sp. *w. of G.* wi. boldn.
6:2 not leave the *w. of God*
7 *w. of G.* increas. in Jer. 12:24
8:14 Samaria receiv. *w. of God*
11:1 Gentiles received *w. of G.*
13:7 desired to hear *w. of God*
44 city came to hear *w. of God*
46 *w. of G.* first spoken to you
19:20 mightily grew *w. of God*
Rom. 9:6 not as though *w. of God* hath taken none effect
10:17 hearing by the *w. of God*
1 *Cor.* 14:36 ca. *w. of G.* fr. you?
2 *Cor.* 2:17 many corr. *w. of God*
4:2 not handl. *w. of G.* deceitf.
Eph. 6:17 helmet of sal. *w. of G.*
Col. 1:25 given to fulfil *w. of G.*
1 *Thes.* 2:13 received *w. of God*
1 *Tim.* 4:5 sanctified by *w. of G.*
2 *Tim.* 2:9 *w. of G.* is not bound
Tit. 2:5 *w. of G.* be not blasph.
Heb. 4:12 *w. of G.* qui. and pow.
6:5 tasted the good *w. of God*
11:3 worlds framed by *w. of God*
13:7 spoken to you *w. of God*
1 *Pet.* 1:23 born ag. by *w. of God*
2 *Pet.* 3:5 by *w. of G.* heav. were
1 *John* 2:14 *w. of G.* abid. in you
Rev. 1:2 bare record of *w. of G.*
9 in isle of Patmos for *w. of G.*
6:9 were slain for *w. of God*
19:13 name is called *W. of God*
20:4 were beheaded for *w. of G.*

See HEARD.

His WORD.
Num. 27:21 at *his w.* they go out
30:2 a man vow not break *h. w.*
1 *Sam.* 1:23 the Lord estab. *h. w.*
2 *Sam.* 23:2 *h. w.* in my tongue
1 *K.* 2:4 the Lord continue *h. w.*
8:20 L. perfor. *h. w.* 2 *Chr.* 6:10
2 *K.* 1:16 no G. in Is. to inq. *h. w.*
2 *Chr.* 10:15 L. might perf. *h. w.*
Ps. 56:4 in G. I prai. *h. w.* 10
103:20 unto the voice of *his w.*
105:19 time that *his w.* came
28 rebelled not against *his w.*
106:24 believed not *his w.*
107:20 sent *his w.* healed them
130:5 L. and in *h. w.* do I hope
147:15 *his w.* run. very swiftly
18 sendeth *h. w.* melteth them
19 he showeth *his w.* unto Ja.
148:8 stormy wind fulfill. *h. w.*
Is. 66:5 ye that tremble at *h. w.*
Jer. 20:9 *his w.* was in my heart
Lam. 2:17 hath fulfilled *his w.*
Joel 2:11 strong th. execut. *h. w.*

Mat. 8:16 cast out spi. with *h. w.*
Luke 4:32 *his w.* was with power
John 4:41 many beli. *his* own *w.*
   5:38 not *his w.* abiding in you
Acts 2:41 that gladly rec. *his w.*

Tit. 1:3 hath manifested *his w.*
1 *John* 2:5 whoso keepeth *his w.*

See LORD.

My WORD.

Num. 11:23 *my w.* come to pass
20:24 rebelled against *my w.*
1 *K.* 6:12 perfor. *my w.* with th.
  17:1 but according to *my w.*
Is. 55:11 so sh. *my w.* that goeth
  66:2 to him that trem. at *my w.*
Jer. 1:12 hasten *my w.* to perf. it
  23:28 hath *my w.* speak *my w.*
  29 not *my w.* as a fire, sai. L. ?
  30 ag. proph. that steal *my w.*
  29:10 perf. *my good w.* to you
Mat. 24:35 *my w.* not pass away
John 5:24 he that heareth *my w.*
  8:31 continue in *my w.* dis. Ind.
  37 *my w.* hath no place in you
  43 bec. ye cannot hear *my w.*
Rev. 3:8 kept *my w.* not den. na.

This WORD.

Ex. 14:12 is not *t. w.* we tell th. ?
Jos. 14:10 L. spake *t. w.* to Mos.
2 *Sam.* 19:14 sent *this w.* to king
1 *K.* 2:23 not spok. *t. w.* against
   his own life
2 *K.* 19:21 *this* is the *w.* spoken
  of him, *Is.* 16:13 ; 24:3 ; 37:22
Ezr. 6:11 whoso. shall alter *t. w.*
  10:5 should do accord. to *this w.*
Is. 8:20 if speak not acc. to *t. w.*
  30:12 because ye despise *this w.*
Jer. 5:14 bec. ye spe. *t. w.* 23:38
  7:2 proclaim there *t. w.* and say
  13:12 speak unto them *this w.*
  14:17 therefore say *t. w.* to them
  22:1 L. said, Go and speak *t. w.*
  26:1 *t. w.* came from the Lord,
   saying, 27:1 ; 34:8 ; 36:1
  28:7 hear thou now *this w.* *Amos*
   3:1 ; 4:1 ; 5:1
Dan. 10:11 wh. he had spok. *t. w.*
Zec. 4:6 f. in *w.* of L. to Zernb.
Acts 22:22 gave audience to *t. w.*
Rom. 9:9 *this* is *w.* of promise
Heb. 12:27 *t. w.* once more signi.
1 *Pet.* 1:25 *t. w.* preached to you

Thy WORD.

Gen. 30:34 might be acc. to *t. w.*
  41:40 acc. to *t. w.* peo. be ruled
Ex. 8:10 be it according to *t. w.*
Num. 14:20 pardoned acc. to *t. w.*
Deut. 33:9 observed *t. w.* and cov.
1 *K.* 3:12 done accord. to *thy w.*
  8:26 let *thy w.* be verified
  18:36 done all th. things at *t. w.*
  22:13 let *thy w.* speak what is
   good, 2 *Chr.* 18:12
Ps. 119:9 by taking heed to *t. w.*
  11 *thy w.* ha. I hid in my heart
  16 I will not forget *thy w.*
  17 may live and keep *t. w.* 101
  25 quick. acco. to *t. w.* 107, 154
  28 strengthen me according to
   thy w. 116
  38 stablish *t. w.* 42 I tr. in *t. w.*
  41 salvation according to *t. w.*
  50 for *thy w.* quickened me
  58 be merciful ac. to *t. w.* 65, 76
  67 but now have I kept *thy w.*
  74 because I hoped in *t. w.* 147
  81 but I hope in *t. w.* 114 ; 140
  82 *thy w.* is very pure
  82 fail for *t. w.* 105 *t. w.* lamp
  89 O L. *t. w.* is settled in heav.
  133 order my steps in *thy w.*
  148 that I mi. meditate in *t. w.*
  158 bec. they kept not *thy w.*
  160 *t. w.* true ; 162 rej. at *t. w.*
  161 heart stand. in awe of *t. w.*

169 give me under. ac. to *t. w.*
170 deliver me accord. to *t. w.*
172 my tong. sh. speak of *t. w.*
138:2 thou hast magnified *t. w.*
Jer. 15:16 *t. w.* to me joy of heart
Ezek. 20:46 drop *t. w.* tow. south
  21:2 drop *t. w.* tow. holy places
Amos 7:16 drop not *t. w.* ag. Isa.
Hab. 3:9 bow naked, even *t. w.*
Luke 1:38 be it to me ac. to *t. w.*
  2:29 depart in peace, ac. to *t. w.*
  5:5 at *t. w.* I will let down net
John 17:6 they have kept *thy w.*
  14 given *thy w.* 17 *thy w.* truth
Acts 4:29 with boldn. speak *t. w.*

See TRUTH.

WORDS.

Ex. 4:15 shalt put *w.* in mouth
  5:9 let them not regard vain *w.*
  19:8 Moses returned *w.* of peo.
  23:8 gift perverteth *w.* of righteous, *Deut.* 16:19
  34:1 *w.* whi. were in first tables
  28 Moses wrote the *w.* of the
   covenant, *Deut.* 10:2
Deut. 2:26 Sihon wi. *w.* of peace
  28:14 not go aside fr. any of *w.*
  29:9 keep *w.* of this covenant,
   K. 23:3, 24 ; 2 *Chr.* 34:31
  32:1 hear, O earth, *w.* of my mo.
  Ps. 52:7 ; 78:1 ; *Prov.* 7:24
2 *Sam.* 19:43 *w.* of men fiercer
1 *K.* 22:13 behold, *w.* of proph.
   declare good, 2 *Chr.* 18:12
2 *K.* 6:13 Elisha telleth the *w.*
  18:20 they are vain *w.* *Is.* 36:5
2 *Chr.* 29:30 sing prais. wi. *w.* of
  32:8 people rested on *w.* of Hez.
Est. 9:30 letters with *w.* of peace
Job 6:26 ye imagine to reprove *w.*
  8:2 *w.* of mouth be like wind ?
  12:11 doth not ear try *w.* ? 34:3
  15:13 lettest *w.* go out of mouth
  16:3 shall vain *w.* have an end ?
  4 I could heap up *w.* ag. you
  18:2 how long ere make end *w.* ?
  19:2 how long bre. me wi. *w.* ?
  23:5 I would know *w.* he answ.
  12 I esteemed *w.* of his mouth
  35:16 multi. *w.* without knowl.
  38:2 who dark. counsel by *w.* ?
Ps. 19:14 let *w.* of my mouth be
  22:1 why far fr. *w.* of my roar. ?
  36:3 *w.* of his mouth are iniq.
  52:4 th. lovest all devouring *w.*
  55:21 *w.* of his mouth smoother
  59:12 *w.* of their lips let them
Prov. 1:6 understand *w.* of wise
  4:5 decline not from *w.* of, 5:7
  6:2 art snared with *w.* of mouth
  10:19 in *w.* wanteth not sin
  12:16 *w.* of wick. to lie in wait
  15:26 *w.* of pure are pleasant *w.*
  18:4 *w.* of mouth are as waters
  8 *w.* of talebea. wounds, 26:22
  19:7 he pursueth them with *w.*
  27 he causeth thee to err fr. *w.*
  22:12 overthrows *w.* of transg.
  17 bow ear, hear *w.* of the wise
  21 make thee know *w.* of truth
  23:8 thou sh. lose thy sweet *w.*
  29:19 serv. not be correct. by *w.*
Ec. 5:3 voice known by *w.* 10:14
  10:12 *w.* of wise are gracious
  12:10 sought out acceptable *w.*
  11 *w.* of wise as goads, nails
Is. 29:11 bec. *w.* of book seal.
  37:4 God will hear *w.* of Rabsh.
  59:13 uttering *w.* of falsehood
Jer. 11:2 hear *w.* of covenant, 6
  23:9 bec. of L. and *w.* of holin.
  44:28 remnant kn. wh. *w.* stand
Ezek. 3:6 *w.* th. canst not unders.
Dan. 7:25 speak *w.* ag. Most H.
12:4 shut up *w.* 9 *w.* are closed
Hos. 6:5 slain th. by *w.* of mouth
14:2 take with you *w.* and turn

Zec. 1:13 answered with good *w.*
  7:7 should ye not hear the *w. ?*
Mat. 26:44 prayed, saying same
   w. *Mark* 14:39
Luke 4:22 wondered at graci. *w.*
John 6:63 *w.* I speak to you
  68 thou hast *w.* of eternal life
  17:8 given them *w.* gavest me
Acts 2:40 with *w.* did he testify
  7:22 Moses was mighty in *w.*
  10:22 Cornel. warned to hear *w.*
  11:14 Peter, who sh. tell the *w.*
  15:15 to this agree *w.* of proph.
  24 certain troubled you wi. *w.*
  18:15 if it be a question of *w.*
  20:35 to remember *w.* of L. J.
  38 sorrowing for *w.* he spake
  26:25 I speak forth *w.* of truth
Rom. 16:18 by *w.* deceive hearts
1 *Cor.* 1:17 not wisd. of *w.* 2:4, 13
  14:9 except ye utter *w.* easy
  19 ra. speak 5 *w.* with underst.
Eph. 5:6 let no man dec. wi. *w.*
1 *Tim.* 4:6 nouri. in *w.* of faith
2 *Tim.* 2:14 strive not about *w.*
  4:15 he hath withstood our *w.*
2 *Pet.* 3:2 mindful of *w.* spoken
Rev. 1:3 hear *w.* of proph. 22:18
  22:19 take from *w.* of prophecy

All the WORDS.

Ex. 4:28 told Aar. a. *t. w.* of L.
24:3 Moses told people *all the w.*
   Num. 11:24
Deut. 9:10 on tables writ. *a. t. w.*
  17:19 keep *a. w.* 29:29 do *a. w.*
  27:3 write on stones *all t. w.* 8
  26 that confirmeth not *all t. w.*
  28:58 not observe to do *a. t. w.*
  31:12 observe to do *all the w.*
  32:44 Mo. spake *all t. w.* of song
  46 set hearts to *a. t. w.* I testi.
Jos. 8:34 read *all the w.* of law
1 *Sam.* 8:10 Samuel told *a. t. w.*
2 *K.* 23:2 Josiah read *all t. w.* of
   covenant, 2 *Chr.* 34:30
Prov. 8:8 *all the w.* of mouth
Ec. 7:21 no heed to *a. t. w.* spo.
Jer. 11:8 bring *all t. w.* of coven.
  26:2 speak *all t. w.* I command
  30:2 write *all t. w.* spoken, 36:2
  36:4 Ba. wrote *a. t. w.* of L. 32
  43:1 J. had ended *all t. w.* of L.
Acts 5:20 speak to peo. *all the w.*

WORDS of God.

Num. 24:4 wh. heard *w.* of *G.* 16
1 *Chr.* 25:5 ki.'s seer in *w.* of *G.*
Ezr. 9:4 trembleth at *w.* of *God*
Ps. 107:11 rebelled ag. *w.* of *God*
John 3:34 G. sent speak. *w.* of *G.*
  8:47 that is of *G.* hear. *w.* of *G.*
Rev. 17:17 until *w.* of *G.* be fulf.
See HEARD.

His WORDS.

Gen. 37:8 th. hated him for *h. w.*
Deut. 4:36 heard. *h. w.* out of fire
Jud. 11:11 Jephth. uttered *h. w.*
1 *Sam.* 3:19 let none of *h. w.* fall
2 *Chr.* 36:16 they despised *his w.*
Job 22:22 lay up *his w.* in heart
  32:14 not directed *h. w.* ag. me
  34:35 *his w.* were without wisd.
  37 he multiplieth *his w.* ag. G.
Ps. 55:21 *his w.* softer than oil
  106:12 then believed they *his w.*
Prov. 17:27 knowl. spareth *his w.*
  29:20 man th. is hasty in *h. w.* ?
  30:6 add thou not unto *his w.*
Is. 31:2 Lord not call back *his w.*
Jer. 18:18 not give heed to *h. w.*
Dan. 9:12 he hath confirm. *h. w.*
Amos 7:10 not able to bear *h. w.*
Mark 10:24 astonished at *his w.*
  12:13 to catch him in *his w.*
   Luke 20:20
Luke 20:26 not take hold of *h. w.*
24:8 they remembered *his w.*

See LORD.

My WORDS.

Num. 12:6 hear *my w.* *Job* 34:2
Deut. 4:10 make th. hear *my w.*
11:18 lay up *my w.* in yo. heart
18:18 I will put *my w.* in mouth
19 whoso. will not heark. to *my*
w. I requ. *Jer.* 29:19 ; 35:13
Neh. 6:19 uttered *my w.* to him
Job 6:3 *my w.* are swallowed up
19:23 O that *my w.* were written
29:22 *my w.* they spake not
33:1 hearken to all *my w.* 34:16
   Acts 2:14
3 *my w.* shall be of upri. 36:4
Ps. 5:1 give ear to *my w.* O Lord
50:17 casteth *my w.* behind th.
66:5 every day th. wrest *my w.*
141:6 they shall hear *my w.*
Prov. 1:23 make kn. *m. w.* to you
2:1 if thou wilt receive *my w.*
4:4 let thy heart retain *my w.*
20 my son, attend to *my w.*
7:1 my son, keep *my w.*
Is. 51:16 I have put *my w.* in thy
   mouth, *Jer.* 1:9
59:21 *my w.* wh. I put in mouth
Jer. 5:14 *my w.* in thy mouth
6:19 not hearkened to *my w.*
11:10 refused to hear *my w.*
18:2 cause thee to hear *my w.*
19:15 they mi. not hear *my w.*
23:22 caused peo. to hear *my w.*
25:8 ye have not heard *my w.*
13 bring upon that land *my w.*
39:16 bring *my w.* on this city
44:29 you may know *my w.*
Ezek. 2:7 speak *my w.* 3:4, 10.
12:28 none of *my w.* be prolon.
Mic. 2:7 do not *my w.* do good to
Zec. 1:6 *my w.* did they not take
Mark 8:38 ashamed of *my w.* of
   him Son be asha. *Luke* 9:26
13:31 *my w.* shall not pass away,
   Luke 21:33
Luke 1:20 thou believ. not *my w.*
John 5:47 how believe *my w.* ?
12:47 if any man hear *my w.*
48 he that receiveth not *my w.*
14:23 keep *my w.* 15:7 abide

Their WORDS.

Gen. 34:18 *t. w.* pleased Hamor
2 *Chr.* 9:6 I believed not *their w.*
Ps. 19:4 *their w.* to the end of the
   world, *Rom.* 10:18
Ezek. 2:6 be not afraid of *their w.*
Luke 24:11 *t. w.* seemed as tales

These WORDS.

Ex. 19:6 *t. w.* th. shalt speak, 7
20:1 God spake *t. w. Deut.* 5:22
34:27 write *these w. Jer.* 36:17
35:1 *these* are the w. which Lord
   commanded, *Deut.* 6:6 ; 29:1
Num. 16:31 end of *these w. Deut.*
   32:45 ; 1 *Sam.* 24:16
Deut. 12:28 all *these w. Zec.* 8:9
1 *Sam.* 21:12 David laid up *t. w.*
2 *K.* 23:16 man proclaimed *t. w.*
Jer. 3:12 procl. *t. w.* tow. north
7:27 speak *t. w.* unto th. 26:15
16:10 sh. *t. w.* 25:30 proph. *t. w.*
38:24 let no man know of *t. w.*
45:1 wh. he had writ. *t. w.* 51:60
51:61 when thou shalt read *t. w.*
Luke 24:44 *t.* are the w. I spake
John 9:22 *t. w.* spake his parents
10:21 *these* are not w. of a devil
Acts 2:22 men of Israel hear *t. w.*
10:44 while Pet. yet spake *t. w.*
13:42 *t. w.* might be preached
28:29 said *t. w.* Jews departed
1 *Thes.* 4:18 comfort one another
   with *these w.*
Rev. 21:5 *t. w.* true and faithful

Thy WORDS.

Deut. 33:3 ev. one sh. rec. of *t. w.*
Jos. 1:18 wh. not heark. to *t. w.*

Jud. 11:10 if do not acc. to *t. w.*
13:12 let *thy w.* come to pass
1 *Sam.* 15:24 I have transg. *t. w.*
28:21 I have hearkened to *t. w.*
2 *Sam.* 7:21 for *thy w.* sake
28 that God and *thy w.* be true
1 *K.* 1:14 come and confirm *t. w.*
Neh. 9:8 th. hast performed *t. w.*
Job 4:4 *t. w.* upheld him th. was
Ps. 119:57 said I wo. keep *t. w.*
103 sweet *t. w.* to my taste !
130 entrance of *t. w.* giv. light
139 enemies ha. forgotten *t. w.*
Prov. 23:8 shalt lose *t. w.* sweet w.
9 he will despise wisd. of *t. w.*
Ec. 5:2 not rash, let *t. w.* be few
Jer. 15:16 *thy w.* were found
Ezek. 33:31 hear *thy w.* 32
Dan. 10:12 Daniel, *thy w.* heard
Mat. 12:37 by *t. w.* shalt be justi.

Your WORDS.

Gen. 42:16 in prison *y. w.* be pro.
44:10 accord. to *y. w. Jos.* 2:21
Deut. 1:34 Lord heard *y. w.* 5:28
Job 32:11 I waited for *your w.*
Is. 41:26 none heareth *your w.*
Jer. 42:4 I will pray acc. to *y. w.*
Ezek. 35:13 have multiplied *y. w.*
Mal. 2:17 wearied L. with *y. w.*
3:13 *y. w.* been ag. me, saith L.
Mat. 10:14 not rec. nor hear *y. w.*

WORK.

Ex. 5:9 more *w.* laid on the men
12:16 no manner of *w.* shall be
   done, 20:10 ; *Lev.* 16:29, 23:3,
   28, 31 ; *Num.* 29:7
18:20 show the *w.* they must do
31:14 whoso doeth any *w.* ther.
   sh. be cut off. 15 ; *Lev.* 23:30
35:2 six days *w.* be done, 20:9
36:7 sufficient for all the *w.*
Lev. 23:7 do no servile *w.* therein,
   8, 21, 25, 35, 36 ; *Num.* 28:18,
   25, 26 ; 29:1, 12, 35
Deut. 4:28 *w.* of men's hands,
   27:15 ; 2 *K.* 19:18 ; 2 *Chr.*
   32:19 ; *Ps.* 115:4 ; 135:15
5:14 sabbath, in it thou shalt
   not *w.* 16:8 ; *Jer.* 17:22, 24
31:29 to provoke him thro' *w.*
   of hands, 1 *K.* 16:7 ; *Jer.* 32:30
33:11 bless L. acc. *w.* of his han.
1 *K.* 5:16 officers over *w.* 9:23
7:8 house had court of like *w.*
2 *K.* 12:11 into han. did *w.* 22:5, 9
1 *Chr.* 9:33 in that *w.* day and ni.
16:37 minister as day's *w.* requ.
29:1 the *w.* is great, *Neh.* 4:19
2 *Chr.* 31:21 ev. *w.* he began did it
34:12 men did the *w.* faithfully
Ezr. 4:24 then ceased the *w.*
5:8 this *w.* goeth fast on
6:7 let *w.* of house of G. alone
22 stren. hands in *w.* of house
10:13 nei. a *w.* of one day or two
Neh. 3:5 nob. put not necks to *w.*
4:11 slay th. cause *w.* to cease
6:3 why should the *w.* cease
16 they perc. this *w.* was of G.
7:70 the fathers gave to the *w.*
Job 1:10 blessed *w.* of his hands
10:3 despise *w.* of thy hands
14:15 desire to *w.* of thy hands
24:5 as asses go they to their *w.*
34:11 far *w.* of a man shall he
   render to him, 1 *Pet.* 1:17
19 they are all *w.* of his hands
36:9 he showeth *w.* and transg.
Ps. 8:3 I consi. *w.* of th. fingers
9:16 snared in *w.* of his hands
19:1 firmament show. handy *w.*
28:4 after the *w.* of their hands
44:1 heard what *w.* thou didst
90:17 establish *w.* of our hands
Ps. 95:9 fa. proved me, saw *my w.*
101:3 I hate the *w.* of them that
102:25 heav. are *w.* of thy hands

143:5 I muse on *w.* of thy hands
Prov. 11:18 worketh deceitful *w.*
Ec. 3:17 a time for every *w.*
5:6 sh. G. destroy *w.* of hands ?
8:9 I applied my heart to ev. *w.*
14 happen acc. to *w.* of wicked
9:10 there is no *w.* in grave
12:14 G. will bri. *w.* into judg.
Cant. 7:1 *w.* of a cun. workman
Is. 2:8 they worship *w.* of their
   own hands, 37:19 ; *Jer.* 1:16 ;
   10:3, 9, 15 ; 51:18
17:8 not look to *w.* of his hands
19:15 nei. be any *w.* for Egypt
25 Assyria the *w.* of my hands
28:21 that he may do his *w.*
29:16 sh. *w.* say of him made it
23 children, the *w.* of my hands
32:17 *w.* of righteousness, peace
45:11 concerni. *w.* of my hands
49:4 surely *my w.* is with my G.
60:21 inherit *w.* of my hands
61:8 I will direct th. *w.* in truth
64:8 we are the *w.* of thy hands
65:22 elect enjoy *w.* of thy hands
Jer. 32:19 great and mighty in *w.*
50:29 recompense her according
   to *w. Lam.* 3:64
Ezek. 15:3 shall wood do any *w.* ?
4 is it meet for *w.* ? 5 no *w.*
16:30 *w.* of a whorish woman
Hos. 13:2 the *w.* of craftsman
14:3 say no more to *w.* of hands
Mic. 5:13 no more *w. w.* of hands
Hab. 1:5 work a *w.* in your days
Hag. 2:14 so is ev. *w.* of hands
Mark 6:5 there do no mighty *w.*
John 7:21 done one *w.* ye marvel.
17:4 finished the *w.* thou gavest
Acts 5:38 if this *w.* be of men
13:2 *w.* whereunto I called them
41 I work a *w.* in your day
14:26 *w.* which they fulfilled
15:38 went not with them to *w.*
Rom. 2:15 show *w.* of law writ.
9:28 short *w.* L. make up. earth
11:6 otherwise *w.* is no more *w.*
1 *Cor.* 3:13 ev. man's *w.* be manif.
14 if *w.* abide ; 15 if *w.* burnt
9:1 are not ye my *w.* in Lord ?
Eph. 4:12 some for *w.* of minis.
Phil. 2:30 *w.* of C. was nigh death
2 *Thes.* 1:11 God fulfil *w.* of faith
2:17 stablish you in ev. good *w.*
2 *Tim.* 4:5 *w.* of an evangelist
Jam. 1:4 let patience ha. perf. *w.*
25 a doer of *w.* sh. be blessed

See EVIL.

WORK, S of God.

Ex. 32:16 tables were *w. of God*
Job 37:14 wondrous *w. of God*
Ps. 64:9 all declare the *w.* of G.
66:5 come and see *w. of God*
78:7 might not forget *w. of God*
Ec. 7:13 consider the *w. of God*
8:17 I beheld all the *w. of God*
11:5 thou knowest not *w. of God*
John 6:28 might work *w. of God*
29 this is *w. of God* that ye
9:3 that *w. of God* be manifest
Acts 2:11 hear th. speak *w. of G.*
Rom. 14:20 for meat destroy not
   the *w. of God*

See GOOD, GREAT.

His WORK.

Gen. 2:2 G. ended *h. w.* 3 rested
Ex. 36:4 every man from *his w.*
Deut. 32:4 *his w.* is perfect
Jud. 19:16 old man ca. fr. *his w.*
1 *Sam.* 8:16 take asses to *his w.*
1 *K.* 7:14 Hiram wrought *his w.*
1 *Chr.* 4:23 dw. wi. king for *h. w.*
2 *Chr.* 8:9 made no serv. for *h. w.*
16:5 Baasha let *his w.* cease
Neh. 4:15 return. ev. man to *h. w.*

Job 7:2 looketh for rew. of *h. w.*
36:24 rem. thou magnify *his w.*
37:7 all men may know *his w.*
Ps. 62:12 renderest to ev. man according to *h. w. Prov.* 24:29
104:23 man goeth to *his w.*
111:3 *h. w.* is honorable,glorious
Prov. 16:11 weights of bag *h. w.*
20:11 whether *his w.* be pure
21:8 for the pure *h. w.* is right
Is. 5:19 let him hasten *his w.*
10:12 L. performed *h.* whole *w.*
28:21 that he may do *his w.*
40:10 *his w.* is before him, 62:11
54:16 bring. an instru. for *h. w.*
Jer. 22:13 giveth not for *his w.*
Hab. 2:18 maker of *h. w.* trusteth
Mark 13:34 gave ev man *his w.*

John 4:34 my meat is to fin. *h. w.*
Gal. 6:4 every man prove *his w.*
Rev. 22:12 to every man as *h. w.*

See LORD, NEEDLE.

Our WORK.

Gen. 5:29 this sh. comfort *our w.*

Thy WORK.

Ex. 20:9 six days do all *thy w.*
23:12 ; *Deut.* 5:13
Ruth 2:12 L. recompense *thy w.*
Ps. 77:12 I will meditate *thy w.*
90:16 let *t. w.* ap. unto thy serv.
92:4 made me glad thro' *thy w.*
Prov. 24:27 prep. *thy w.* without
Is. 45:9 or *t. w.* hath no hands ?
Jer. 31:16 *thy w.* sh. be rewarded
Hab. 3:2 revive *thy w.* in years

Your WORK.

Ex. 5:11 not aught of *y. w.* dim.
2 *Chr.* 15:7 *y. w.* sh. be rewarded
Is. 41:24 *your w.* is of naught
1 *Thes.* 1:3 remember *y. w.* faith
Heb. 6:10 to forget *y. w.* of faith

WORK-FELLOW.

Rom. 16:21 my *w.-f.* salute you

WORK, Verb.

Ex. 5:18 go therefore now and *w.*
34:21 six days thou shalt *w.*
35:2 whoso *w.* ther. put to death
1 *Sam.* 14:6 may be Lord will *w.*
1 *K.* 21:20 sold thys. to *w.* evil, 25
Neh. 4:6 people had a mind to *w.*
Job 23:9 on left hand wh. he *w.*
Ps. 58:2 in heart you *w.* wicked.
119:126 it is time for Lord to *w.*
Prov. 11:18 wick. *w.* decei. work
Is. 19:9 they that *w.* in flax
43:13 I will *w.* who shall let it
Ezek. 33:26 ye *w.* abomination
Dan. 11:23 he sh. *w.* deceitfully
Mic. 2:1 woe to them that *w.* evil
Hab. 1:5 I will *w.* a work in your days, *Acts* 13:41
Hag. 2:4 *w.* for I am with you
Mal. 3:15 *w.* wicked. are set up
Mat. 21:28 go *w.* in my vineyard
Luke 13:14 wh. men ought to *w.*
John 5:17 Father worketh, I *w.*
6:28 might *w.* the works of God
30 said, What dost thou *w. ?*
9:4 I must *w.* the works of him
Rom. 7:5 sin did *w.* in our mem.
8:28 all thi. *w.* togeth. for good
Eph. 4:19 to *w.* uncleanness with
Phil. 2:12 *w.* out your salvation
1 *Thes.* 4:11 to *w.* with hands
2 *Thes.* 2:7 mys. of iniq. doth *w.*
3:10 not *w.* neit. should he eat
12 that with quietness they *w.*

See INIQUITY.

WORKER.

1 *K.* 7:14 was a *w.* in brass

WORKERS.

2 *K.* 23:24 *w.* wi. familiar spirits
2 *Cor.* 6:1 *w.* together with him
11:13 false apostles, deceitful *w.*

Phil. 3:2 dogs, beware of evil *w.*

See INIQUITY.

WORKS.

Ex. 5:13 fulfil your *w.* and tasks
Num. 16:28 sent me to do th. *w.*
Deut. 2:7 bles. thee in *w.* 16:15
Jud. 2:10 which knew not *w.*
1 *Sam.* 8:8 acc. to *w.* they done
1 *K.* 13:11 told *w.* man of G. did
2 *K.* 22:17 provoked me to anger with *w.* of hands, 2 *Chr.* 34:25
Neh. 9:35 nor turned fr. wick. *w.*
Ps. 14:1 done abominable *w.*
17:4 concerning the *w.* of men
92:4 triumph in *w.* of thy hands
111:2 *w.* of the Lord are great
7 *w.* of hands, verity and jud.
138:8 forsake not *w.* of own ha.
141:4 to practise wicked *w.*
Prov. 31:31 let her *w.* praise her
Ec. 1:14 I have seen *w.* done, 2:11
Is. 26:12 wrought our *w.* in us
Jer. 7:13 bec. ye have done th. *w.*
25:6 provo. not with *w.* ; 44:8
14 recompense them according to *w.* of hands, *Rev.* 2:23
Ezek. 6:6 your *w.* be abolished
Dan. 4:37 him wh. *w.* are truth
Mic. 6:16 *w.* of house of A. kept
Mat. 11:2 John heard *w.* of Chr.
John 5:20 show him greater *w.*
36 *w.* Father hath given me
7:3 may see the *w.* thou doest
7 I testify *w.* thereof are evil
8:39 would do *w.* of Abraham
9:4 I must work the *w.* of him
10:25 in *w.* I do in Father's name
32 for wh. of *w.* do ye sto. me ?
John 10:37 if I do not *w.* 38 believe *w.*
14:10 doeth *w.* 11 believe for *w.*
12 *w.* that I do, shall he do, gr.
15:24 if I had not done the *w.*
Acts 7:41 rejoiced in *w.* of hands
26:20 do *w.* meet for repentance
Rom. 3:27 by what law ? of *w. ?*
4:2 if Abr. were justified by *w.*
6 G. imputeth right. with. *w.*
9:11 not of *w.* but of him that
32 but as it were by *w.* of law
11:6 if by grace, no more of *w.*
13:12 cast off *w.* of darkness
Gal. 2:16 man is not justi. by *w.*
3:2 receiv. ye Sp. by *w.* of law ?
5 doeth he it by *w.* of the law
10 as many as are of *w.* of law
5:19 *w.* of the flesh are manifest
Eph. 2:9 not of *w.* lest any boast
5:11 wi. unfruitful *w.* of darkn.
Col. 1:21 enemies by wicked *w.*
1 *Thes.* 5:13 esteem for *w.* sake
2 *Tim.* 1:9 saved us, not according to our *w. Tit.* 3:5
Tit. 1:16 but in *w.* they deny G.
Heb. 1:10 heav. *w.* of thy hands
2:7 set him ov. *w.* of thy hands
3:9 your fathers saw my *w.*
4:3 although *w.* were finished
6:1 repentance from dead *w.*
9:14 purge consc. from dead *w.*
Jam. 2:14 not *w.* can faith save ?
17 faith with. *w.* is dead, 20:26
18 show me thy faith with. *w.*
21 was not Abr. justi. by *w. ?*
22 by *w.* was faith made perf.
24 by *w.* a man is justified
25 was not R. justified by *w.*
2 *Pet.* 3:10 *w.* therein burnt up
1 *John* 3:8 mi. destroy *w.* of devil
Rev. 2:26 that keepeth *w.* to end
9:20 repented not of *w.* of hands
18:6 double, according to her *w.*

See EVIL, GOOD, WORK *of* GOD.

His WORKS.

1 *Sam.* 19:4 *his w.* to thee good
2 *Chr.* 32:30 Hez. prosp. in *h. w.*
Ps. 33:4 *h. w.* are done in truth

78:11 forget *his w.* wond. 106:13
103:22 bless the Lord, all *his w.*
104:31 L. shall rejoice in *his w.*
107:22 declare *h. w.* with rejoic.
111:6 show. peo. power of *h. w.*
145:9 his mercies are over *h. w.*
17 Lord is holy in all *his w.*
Prov. 8:22 pos. me before *his w.*
24:12 render to ev. man ac. to *h. w. ?* Mat. 16:27 ; 2 *Tim.* 4:14
Ec. 3:22 man sh. rejoice in *h. w.*
Dan. 9:14 G. is right. in *his w.*
Acts 15:18 known to G. are *h. w.*
Heb. 4:4 rest. on 7th day fr. *h. w.*
10 hath ceased from *h.* own *w.*
Jam. 2:22 faith wro. with *h. w. ?*
3:13 of a good conversat. *his w.*

See LORD, MARVELLOUS, MIGHTY.

Their WORKS.

Ex. 5:4 let people from *their w.*
23:24 shalt not do after *their w.*
Neh. 6:14 accord. to these *t. w.*
Job 34:25 therof. he know. *t. w.*
Ps. 33:15 he considereth *their w.*
106:35 they learned *their w.*
39 thus defiled with *t.* own *w.*
Ec. 9:1 *t. w.* are in hand of God
Is. 29:15 *t. w.* are in the dark
41:29 vanity, *t. w.* are nothing
59:6 nor cover thems. wi. *t. w.*
66:18 I kn. *t. w.* and thoughts
Amos 8:7 nev. forg. any of *t. w.*
Jon. 3:10 G. saw *t. w.* th. turned
Mat. 23:3 do not ye after *t. w.*
5 *t. w.* do to be seen of men
2 *Cor.* 11:15 end accord. to *t. w.*
Rev. 14:13 *t. w.* do follow them
20:12 judged accord. to *t. w.* 13

Thy WORKS.

Deut. 3:24 according to *thy w. ?*
15:10 L. sh. bless thee in *t. w.*
2 *Chr.* 20:37 L. hath broken *t. w.*
Ps. 26:7 tell of *t.* wond. *w.* 145:4
66:3 how terri. art thou in *t. w.*
73:28 that I may declare *thy w.*
86:8 neither are any works like unto *thy w.*
92:5 O L. how great are *thy w.*
104:13 earth satisfied with the fruit of *thy w.*
24 how manifold are *thy w. !*
143:5 remem. I meditate on *t. w.*
145:10 *thy w.* shall praise thee
Prov. 16:3 commit *t. w.* to Lord
Ec. 9:7 God accepteth *thy w.*
Is. 57:12 I will declare *thy w.*
Jer. 48:7 thou trusted in *thy w.*

Jam. 2:18 sh. faith without *t. w.*
Rev. 2:2 I know *thy w.* 9, 13, 19 ; 3:1, 8, 15
3:2 I have not found *t. w.* perf.

Wonderful WORKS.

Ps. 40:5 many are thy *wond. w.*
78:4 showing his *wonderful w.*
107:8 praise L. for his *w. w.* to children of men, 15, 21, 31
111:4 made his *w. w.* remernb.
Mat. 7:22 in thy na. done *w. w.*
Acts 2:11 hear in tongues *w. w.*

See WONDROUS.

WORKETH.

Job 33:29 these *w.* God for man
Ps. 15:2 *w.* righteousness, dwell
101:7 *w.* deceit shall not dwell
Prov. 11:18 wicked *w.* deceitful
26:28 flattering mouth *w.* ruin
31:13 she *w.* with her hands
Ex. 3:9 what profit he that *w. ?*
Is. 44:12 the smith *w.* in coals
64:5 meetest him th. *w.* right.
Dan. 6:27 *w.* signs and wonders
John 5:17 my Fath. *w.* hitherto
Acts 10:35 he that *w.* righteous.
Rom. 2:10 to every one *w.* good
4:4 to him that *w.* is reward

5 him that *w*. not, but believ.
15 because the law *w*. wrath
5:3 tribulation *w*. patience
13:10 love *w*. no ill to neighbor
1 *Cor*. 12:6 it is same G. that *w*.
11 these *w*. that one and same
16:10 for he *w*. the work of L.
2 *Cor*. 4:12 then death *w*. in us
17 *w*. for us more weight of gl.
7:10 godly sor. *w*. repentance
Gal. 3:5 he that *w*. miracles
5:6 but faith which *w*. by love.
Eph. 1:11 who *w*. all things
2:2 spirit that *w*. in disobed.
3:20 according to power *w*. in us
Phil. 2:13 it is God *w*. in you
Col. 1:29 wh. *w*. in me mightily
1 *Thes*. 2:13 effectually *w*. in you
Jam. 1:3 try. of faith *w*. patience
20 wrath of man *w*. not right.
Rev. 21:27 whosoe. *w*. abomina.

WORKING, Participle.
Ps. 52:2 like a razor *w*. deceit.
74:12 *w*. salvation in the earth
Ezek. 46:1 gate shut six *w*. days
Mark 16:20 Lord *w*. with them
Rom. 1:27 *w*. that is unseemly
7:13 sin *w*. death in me by good
1 *Cor*. 4:12 *w*. with our hands
Eph. 4:28 *w*. thing that is good
2 *Thes*. 3:11 *w*. not, busybodies
Heb. 13:21 *w*. th. wh. is pleasing
Rev. 16:14 spir. of devils *w*. mira.

WORKING, Substantive.
Is. 28:29 Lord excellent in *w*.
1 *Cor*. 9:6 power to forbear *w*. ?
12:10 another the *w*. of miracles
Eph. 1:19 accord. to *w*. of power
3:7 giv. me by *w*. of his power
4:16 accord. to *w*. in measure
Phil. 3:21 accord. to *w*. thereby
Col. 1:29 his *w*. wh. work. in me
2 *Thes*. 2:9 after the *w*. of Satan

WORKMAN.
Ex. 35:35 work of cun. *w*. 38:23
Cant. 7:1 work of a cunning *w*.
Is. 40:19 *w*. melteth an image
20 seeketh to him a cun. *w*.
Jer. 10:3 work of *w*. with axe
Hos. 8:6 *w*. made it, not of God
Mat. 10:10 *w*. is worthy of meat
2 *Tim*. 2:15 a *w*. not to be asha.

WORKMANSHIP.
Ex. 31:3 and in all manner of *w*.
5; 35:31
2 *K*. 16:10 accord. to *w*. thereof
Ezek. 28:13 *w*. of tabrets prepar.
Eph. 2:10 we are his *w*. in C. Je.

WORKMEN.
2 *K*. 12:14 they gave that to the
w. 15; 2 *Chr*. 34:10, 17
1 *Chr*. 22:15 *w*. with th. in abun.
25:1 the number of the *w*.
2 *Chr*. 24:13 so the *w*. wrought
Ezr. 3:9 set *w*. in house of God
Is. 44:11 the *w*. they are of men
Acts 19:25 with *w*. of like occup.

WORLD.
1 *Sam*. 2:8 he set *w*. upon them
2 *Sam*. 22:16 the foundations of
the *w*. appeared, *Ps*. 18:15
1 *Chr*. 16:30 *w*. sh. not be moved
Job 18:18 sh. be chased out of *w*.
34:13 who hath disposed the *w*.
37:12 may do on the face of *w*.
Ps. 9:8 he shall judge the *w*. in
righteousness, 96:13; 98:9
Ps. 17:14 deliver from men of
the *w*.
19:4 to end of *w*. *Rom*. 10:18
22:27 ends of *w*. shall remember
24:1 the earth and the *w*. is the
Lord's, 98:7; *Nah*. 1:5
33:8 inhabit. of *w*. stand in awe
49:1 give ear, inhabitants of *w*.
50:12 for the *w*. is mine

77:18 lightnings light. *w*. 97:4
89:11 founded *w*. and its fulness
90:2 form. the earth and the *w*,
93:1 the *w*. also is established
96:10 *w*. also sh. be established
Prov. 8:26 not made dust of *w*.
Ec. 3:11 set *w*. in their heart
Is. 13:11 I will punish *w*. for evil
14:17 is this he made *w*. wild. ?
21 nor fill face of *w*. wi. cities
24:4 the *w*. languisheth away
27:6 Is. sh. fill the *w*. with fruit
34:1 let world hear, and all that
45:17 not confoun. *w*. with. end
Mat. 4:8 the devil showeth him
all kingd. of the *w*. *Luke* 4:5
5:14 ye are the light of the *w*.
13:38 field is *w*. good seed chil.
40 so shall it be in end of *w*. 49
16:26 what profit. gain *w*. lose
soul ? *Mark* 8:36; *Luke* 9:25
18:7 woe to *w*. bec. of offences
24:14 sh. be preached in all the
w. for witness, *Mark* 14:9
Luke 1:70 who ha. been since *w*.
began, *Acts* 3:21
2:1 decree that *w*. sh. be taxed
20:35 worthy to obtain that *w*.
John 1:10 he was in *w*. the *w*. was
made by him, *Acts* 17:24
29 L. of G. takes away sin of *w*.
3:16 God so loved the *w*. that
17 *w*. thro' him might be sav.
4:42 C. Savi. of *w*. 1 *John* 4:14
6:33 bread of G. giv. life to *w*.
51 my flesh, I give for life of *w*.
7:4 these th. show thyself to *w*.
7 *w*. cannot hate you
8:12 said, I am light of *w*. 9:5
12:19 the *w*. is gone after him
47 I co. not to jud. but save *w*.
14:17 Sp. wh. *w*. cannot receive
19 the *w*. seeth me no more
22 how manifest thyself unto
us and not unto the *w*. ?
27 I give, not as the *w*. giveth
31 the *w*. may know I love Fa'.
15:18 *w*. hate you, 1 *John* 3:13
19 of *w*. the *w*. love his own
16:20 but the *w*. shall rejoice
28 I leave *w*. and go to Father
33 I have overcome the *w*.
17:5 glory I had before *w*. was
6 name to men gav. out of *w*.
9 I pray not for *w*. but for them
14 *w*. hated th. bec. not of *w*.
15 not take them out of *w*.
16 not of *w*. as I am not of *w*.
21 that the *w*. may believe th.
hast sent me, 23
25 the *w*. hath not known me
18:20 I spake openly to *w*.
21:25 *w*. could not cont. books
Acts 17:6 turned *w*. upside down
19:27 Diana, Asia and *w*. worsh.
24:5 a mover of sedit. thro' *w*.
Rom. 1:8 faith is spo. of thro' *w*.
3:6 for how shall G. judge *w*. ?
18 *w*. may bec. guilty bef. G.
4:13 he should be heir of *w*.
11:12 fall of th. be riches of *w*.
15 if casting away of them be
reconciling of *w*.
1 *Cor*. 1:20 by wis. kn. not G.
2:7 wisdom G. ordained bef. *w*.
12 not received spirit of *w*.
3:22 *w*. or life, or death, yours
4:9 are made a spectacle to *w*.
13 we are made as filth of *w*.
5:10 then must ye go out of *w*.
6:2 kn. th. saints sh. judge *w*. ?
7:33 careth for things in *w*. 34
8:13 eat no flesh wh. *w*. stand.
11:32 not be condemned with *w*.
2 *Cor*. 5:19 C. reconc. *w*. to hims.
Gal. 6:14 by wh. *w*. is crucified
2 *Tim*. 1:9 in Christ before *w*.
began, *Tit*. 1:2

Heb. 2:5 in subjection *w*. to come
6:5 tasted powers of *w*. to come
11:38 of wh. *w*. was not worthy
Jam. 1:27 unspotted from the *w*.
3:6 tongue is a *w*. of iniquity
4:4 friend. of *w*. enmity with G.
2 *Pet*. 2:5 God spared not old *w*.
3:6 whereby *w*. that then was
1 *John* 2:2 propitia. for sins of *w*.
15 love not *w*. 16 is of the *w*.
17 the *w*. passeth away
1 *John* 3:1 the *w*. knoweth us not
4:5 they are of the *w*.
5:4 born of G. overcometh *w*.
19 whole *w*. lieth in wickedn.
Rev. 3:10 temptation come on *w*.
12:9 Satan, deceiveth whole *w*.
13:3 *w*. wondered after the beast

See FOUNDATION.

In, *or* into the WORLD.
Ps. 73:12 ungod. wh. pros. *i*. *t*. *w*.
Mat. 26:13 this gospel be preached *in the* whole *w*.
Mark 10:30 and *in the w*. to come
eternal life, *Luke* 18:30
John 1:9 man that comes *i*. *the w*.
10 he was *in the w*.
3:17 sent not his Son *into the w*.
19 light is come *into the w*.
6:14 should come *i*. *t*. *w*. 11:27
9:5 as long as I am *in the w*.
12:46 I am come a light *i*. *t*. *w*.
16:33 *in w*. ye sh. have tribula.
17:11 I am no more *in the w*.
12 while I was *in w*. I kept th.
18:37 for this came I *into the w*.
Rom. 5:12 sin entered *into the w*.
13 until law, sin was *in the w*.
1 *Cor*. 8:4 an idol is noth. *in t*. *w*.
Eph. 2:12 without God *in the w*.
Col. 1:6 as it is *in* all the *w*.
1 *Tim*. 1:15 Christ Jesus came
into the w. to save sinners
3:16 and believed on *in the w*.
Heb. 10:5 when he cometh *i*. *t*. *w*.
1 *Pet*. 5:9 afflict. that are *in t*. *w*.
1 *John* 2:15 love not thi. *in t*. *w*.
4:1 false prophets gone *i*. *t*. *w*.
3 now already is *it in the w*.
4 greater th. he that is *in t*. *w*.
5 sent his Son *into the w*. that
2 *John* 7 many deceivers *i*. *t*. *w*.

This WORLD.
Mat. 12:32 not forgi. him in *t*. *w*.
13:22 cares of *this w*. choke the
word, *Mark* 4:19
Luke 16:8 children of *this w*. are
20:34 children of *this w*. marry
John 8:23 ye are of *this w*.
9:39 for judg. I come into *t*. *w*.
12:25 that hateth life in *this w*.
31 now is judgment of *this w*.
13:1 should depart out of *t*. *w*.
14:30 prince of *this w*. cometh
16:11 prince of *this w*. is judged
18:36 kingdom is not of *this w*.
Rom. 12:2 not conformed to *t*. *w*.
1 *Cor*. 1:20 wh. is disp. of *t*. *w*.
2:6 speak not wisdom of *this w*.
3:18 if man seem. wise in *t*. *w*.
19 wisd. of *t*. *w*. foolish. wi. G.
5:10 not with fornicat. of *t*. *w*.
7:31 use *t*. *w*. as not abusing it
2 *Cor*. 4:4 god of *t*. *w*. blinded
Gal. 1:4 deli. us fr. *t*. present *w*.
Eph. 1:21 not only in *t*. *w*. but
2:2 according to course of *t*. *w*.
6:12 against rulers of *this w*.
1 *Tim*. 6:7 brou. nothing in *t*. *w*.
17 those that are rich in *t*. *w*.
2 *Tim*. 4:10 De. loved *t*. pres. *w*.
Tit. 2:12 live godly in *t*. pres. *w*.
Jam. 2:5 chosen poor of *this w*.
1 *John* 3:17 wh. hath *t*. *w*. good
4:17 as he is, so are we in *t*. *w*.

WORLDLY.
Tit. 2:12 ungodlin. and *w*. lusts

Heb. 9:1 first cov. had *w.* sanct.

WORLDS.

Heb. 1:2 by whom he made *w.*
11:3 *w.* were fram. by word of G.

WORM.

Ex. 16:24 neither any *w.* therein
Job 17:14 said to *w.* my mother
24:20 *w.* feed sweetly on him
25:6 man is a *w.* son of man
Ps. 22:6 I am a *w.* and no man
Is. 41:14 is spread under thee
41:14 fear not thou *w.* Jacob
51:8 *w.* sh. eat them like wool
66:24 their *w.* sh. not die. *Mark* 9:44, 46, 48
Jon. 4:7 a *w.* smote the gourd

WORMS.

Ex. 16:20 bred *w.* and stank
Deut. 28:39 the *w.* shall eat them
Job 7:5 clothed with *w.* and dust
19:26 tho' *w.* destroy this body
21:26 and *w.* shall cover them
Is. 14:11 and the *w.* cover thee
Mic. 7:17 out of holes like *w.*
Acts 12:23 Herod was eaten of *w.*

WORMWOOD.

Deut. 29:18 a root that beareth *w.*
Prov. 5:4 her end is bitter as *w.*
Jer. 9:15 feed them with *w.* 23:15
Lam. 3:15 made drunken with *w.*
19 my misery, the *w.* and gall
Amos 5:7 who turn judgm. to *w.*
Rev. 8:11 name of star called *W.*

WORSE.

Gen. 19:9 deal *w.* with thee than
2 *Sam.* 19:7 *w.* th. all that befell
K. 14:12 Judah was put to the *w.* 2 *Chr.* 25:22
1 *Chr.* 19:16 Syrians put to *w.* 19
2 *Chr.* 6:24 if people be put to *w.*
33:9 Manasseh made Jer. do *w.*
Jer. 7:26 *w.* th. their fath. 16:12
Dan. 1:10 see faces *w.* liking?
Mat. 12:45 last state of that man is *w.* than first, *Luke* 11:26
27:64 last error *w.* than the first
John 5:14 a *w.* thi. come unto th.
1 *Cor.* 8:8 if eat not are we *w.*
11:17 not for better but for *w.*
2 *Tim.* 3:13 seducers sh. wax *w.*
2 *Pet.* 2:20 latter end is *w.* with

WORSHIP.

Gen. 22:5 I and the lad will go and *w.*
Ex. 24:1 and *w.* ye afar off
34:14 thou shalt *w.* no other G.
Deut. 4:19 lest th. be driven to *w.*
8:19 if thou *w.* other gods, 11:16 ; 30:17
26:10 and *w.* before the L. thy God, *Ps.* 22:27, 29 ; 86:9
1 *Sam.* 3 man went up to *w.*
15:25 that I may *w.* Lord, 30
1 *K.* 12:30 the people went to *w.*
2 *K.* 5:18 *w.* in house of Rimmon
17:36 L. ye fear, him sh. ye *w.*
18:22 shall *w.* bef. this altar in Jeru. 2 *Chr.* 32:12 ; *Is.* 36:7
1 *Chr.* 16:29 *w.* L. in the beauty of holiness, *Ps.* 29:2 ; 66:4 ; 96:9 ; *Mat.* 4:10 ; *Luke* 4:8
Ps. 5:7 *w.* tow. thy temple 138:2
45:11 he is thy L. *w.* thou him
81:9 neither *w.* any strange god
95:6 let us *w.* and bow down
97:7 *w.* him all ye gods
99:5 *w.* at his footstool, 132:7
9 and *w.* at his holy hill
Is. 2:8 *w.* work of han. 20 ; 46:6
27:13 *w.* Lord in holy mount
49:7 princes also shall *w.*
66:23 all flesh *w.* before me
Jer. 7:2 enter th. gates to *w.* 26:2
13:10 *w.* other gods be as girdle
25:6 go not after oth. gods to *w.*

44:19 did we *w.* her with. men ?
Ezek. 46:2 he sh. *w.* at threshold
3 people of land sh. *w.* at door
9 entereth to *w.* by north gate
Dan. 3:5 *w.* golden image, 10, 15
12 not *w.* im. 18:23 ; 15 if ye *w.*
14 do not yet *w.* ima. I set up ?
Mic. 5:13 thou shalt no more *w.* work of thine hands
Zep. 1:5 that *w.* host of heaven
2:11 men sh. *w.* him, every one
Zec. 14:16 *w.* Lord of hosts, 17
Mat. 2:2 and come to *w.* him
8 that I may come and *w.* him
4:9 if thou wilt *w.* me, *Lu.* 4:7
15:9 but in vain they do *w.* me
John 4:20 in Jerusal. is the place wh. men oug. to *w. Mark* 7:7
22 ye *w.* ye know not what
23 *w.* the Father in spirit, 24
12:20 Greeks ca. to *w.* at feast
Acts 7:42 gave th. to *w.* host, 43
8:27 eunuch came to Jer. to *w.*
17:23 whom ye ignorantly *w.*
18:13 persuaded men to *w.* God
24:11 Paul came to Jerus. to *w.*
14 so *w.* I God of my fathers
1 *Cor.* 14:25 he will *w.* God
Phil. 3:3 which *w.* God in spirit
Heb. 1:6 let angels of G. *w.* him
Rev. 3:9 and *w.* before thy feet
4:10 *w.* him that liveth for ever
9:20 they should not *w.* devils
11:1 and them that *w.* therein
13:8 all that dwell on earth shall *w.* beast, 12
15 th. would not *w.* the image
14:7 *w.* him that made heaven
9 if any man *w.* beast and im.
11 who *w.* beast, have no rest
15:4 nations come, *w.* bef. him
19:10 I fell at his feet to *w.* 22:8 ; 22:9 *w.* God

WORSHIPPED.

Gen. 24:26 Abraham *w.* Lord, 48
52 Abraham's servant *w.* Lord
Ex. 32:1 Israel *w.* 12:27 ; 33:10
32:8 they made a calf, and *w.* it, *Ps.* 106:19
34:8 Mos. *w.* Jud. 7:15 Gid. *w.*
Deut. 17:3 served other gods, and *w.* 29:26 ; 1 *K.* 9:9 ; 2 *K.* 21:21 ; 2 *Chr.* 7:22 ; *Jer.* 1:16 ; 8:2 ; 16:11 ; 22:9
1 *Sam.* 1:19 Hannah *w.* before L.
28 Samuel *w.* 15:31 ; S. *w.* Lord
2 *Sam.* 12:20 D. arose *w.* 15:32
1 *K.* 11:33 forsaken me, *w.* Ash.
16:31 served Baal, *w.* him, 22:53
2 *K.* 17:16 they *w.* host of heaven, 21:3 , 2 *Chr.* 33:3
1 *Chr.* 29:20 cong. bowed, and *w.* L. 2 *Chr.* 7:3 ; 29:28, 29, 30
Neh. 8:6 all people *w.* Lord, 9:3
Job 1:20 Job *w. Ezek.* 8:16 so. sun
Dan. 2:46 king *w.* 3:7 *w.* image
Mat. 2:11 wise men fell, *w.* Christ
8:2 leper *w.* him, 9:18 a ruler *w.*
14:33 that were in ship *w.* him
15:25 woman of Canaan *w.* him
18:26 servant fell, *w.* his lord
28:9 held him by feet, *w.* him
17 disciples *w.* him, *Lu.* 24:52
Mark 5:6 ran out of tombs, *w.*
15:19 spit on him, bowing, *w.*
John 4:20 our fath. *w.* in mount.
9:38 man believed, and *w.* him
Acts 10:25 Cornelius *w.* Peter
16:14 Ly. *w.* God ; 18:7 Justus *w.*
17:25 neither is *w.* with hands
Rom. 1:25 *w.* creature more than
2 *Thes.* 2:4 exalteth above all *w.*
Heb. 11:21 Jacob *w. Rev.* 7:11
20 *w.* God
Rev. 5:14 twenty-four elders *w.* 11:16 ; 19:4
13:4 they *w.* dragon, *w.* beast

16:2 sore fell on them *w.* image
19:20 deceiv. that *w.* his image
20:4 souls that had not *w.* beast

WORSHIPPER, S.

2 *K.* 10:19 destroy *w.* of Baal
21 all *w.* of B. came, none left
23 none but the *w.* of Baal only
John 4:23 *w.* sh. worship in spirit
9:31 if any man be a *w.* of God
Acts 19:35 Ephesus is a *w.* of D.
Heb. 10:2 because *w.* once purged

WORSHIPPETH.

Neh. 9:6 host of heaven *w.* thee
Is. 44:15 maketh god, *w.* it, 17
Dan. 3:5 falleth not and *w.* 11
Acts 19:27 Asia and the world *w.*

WORSHIPPING.

2 *K.* 19:37 as he was *w.* in house of Nisroch, *Is.* 37:38
2 *Chr.* 20:18 Ju. fell down, *w.* L.
Mat. 20:20 Zeb's chil. came *w.*
Col. 2:18 begu. you in *w.* of ang.

WORST.

Ezek. 7:24 bri. *w.* of the heathen

WORTH.

Gen. 23:9 for as much money as it is *w.*
Job 24:25 make speech noth. *w.*
Prov. 10:20 heart of wick. lit. *w.*
Ezek. 30:2 say, howl, woe *w.* day

WORTHY.

Gen. 32:10 I am not *w.* of merci.
1 *Sam.* 1:5 he gave a *w.* portion
26:16 as L. liv. ye are *w.* to die
2 *Sam.* 22:4 who is *w.* to be praised, *Ps.* 18:3
1 *K.* 1:52 show himself a *w.* man
Jer. 26:11 *w.* to die ; 16 is not *w.*
Mat. 3:11 I am not *w.* to bear
8:8 Lord, I am not *w. Luke* 7:6
10:11 inquire who in it is *w.* 13
37 loveth more, he is not *w.* 38
22:8 which were bidden not *w.*
Mark 1:7 not *w.* to unloose, *Lu.* 3:16 ; *John* 1:27 ; *Acts* 13:25
Luke 3:8 fruits *w.* of repentance
7:4 *w.* for whom he sho. do this
7 nor thought I myself *w.*
10:7 laborer is *w.* of his hire
15:19 no more *w.* to be son, 21
Acts 24:2 *w.* deeds done to nati.
Rom. 8:18 not *w.* to be compared
Eph. 4:1 th. ye walk *w.* of voca.
Col. 1:10 ye might walk *w.* of L.
1 *Thes.* 2:12 ye would walk *w.*
1 *Tim.* 1:15 *w.* of acceptati. 4:9
5:18 laborer is *w.* of his reward
Heb. 11:38 world was not *w.*
Jam. 2:7 blasph. that *w.* name?
Rev. 3:4 walk in white, are *w.*
4:11 *w.* to receive glory, 5:12
5:2 who is *w.* to open the book
4 no man fo. *w.* to open book
9 thou art *w.* to take book
16:6 to drink, for they are *w.*

See COUNT, COUNTED, DEATH.

WORTHIES.

Nah. 2:5 he shall recount his *w.*

WORTHILY.

Ruth 4:11 do thou *w.* in Ephrat.

WOT, TETH.

Gen. 21:26 I *w.* not who done
39:8 *w.* not what is with me
44:15 *w.* ye not I can divine?
Ex. 32:1 we *w.* not what is become of him, 23 ; *Acts* 7:40
Num. 22:6 he *w.* thou bless.
Jos. 2:5 whither the men went I *w.* not
Acts 3:17 I *w.* thro' ignor. ye did
Rom. 11:2 *w.* ye not what scrip.
Phil. 1:22 what choose I *w.* not

WOVE.

2 *K.* 23:7 women wove hangings

WOVEN.

Ex. 28:32 bin. of *w.* work, 39:22
39:27 linen, *w.* work for Aaron
John 19:23 coat without seam, *w.*

WOULD.

Neh. 9:24 do with th. as they *w.*
Ps. 81:11 Israel *w.* none of me
Prov. 1:25 ye *w.* none of reproof
Mark 10:36 what *w.* ye I sho. do
Rom. 7:15 what *w.* that I do not
  19 the good that I *w.* I do not

WOULD God.

Ex. 16:3 *w. God* we had died in
  Egypt, *Num.* 14:2
Num. 11:29 *w. G.* people proph.
  20:3 *w. God* we died wh. breth.
Deut. 28:67 *w. God* it were even
Jos. 7:7 *w. God* we dw. on side
Jud. 9:29 *w. G.* peo. under hand
2 Sam. 18:33 *w. G.* I died for th.
2 K. 5:3 *w. G.* lord with prophet
Acts 26:29 *w. G.* all such as I am
1 Cor. 4:8 I *w. God* ye did reign
2 Cor. 11:1 *w.* to *G.* bear wi. me

WOULD not.

1 Sam. 20:9 *w. not* I tell thee?
Is. 30:15 and ye *w. not, Mat.*
  23:37 ; *Luke* 13:34
Rom. 7:16 do that whi. I *w. not*
  19 evil that I *w. not* that I do
2 Cor. 12:20 such as ye *w. not*

WOULDEST.

Jos. 15:18 and Caleb said, What
  w. thou? 1 *K.* 1:16

WOULDEST not.

John 21:18 carry whi. thou *w. n.*

WOUND.

Ex. 21:25 give *w.* for *w.* stripe
1 K. 22:35 blood ran out of *w.*
Job 34:6 my *w.* is incurable
Prov. 6:33 a *w.* and dishonor
  20:30 blueness of a *w.* cleanseth
Is. 30:26 heal. stroke of their *w.*
Jer. 10:19 for my *w.* is grievous
  15:18 why is my *w.* incurable?
  30:12 *w.* is grievous, *Nah.* 3:19
  14 I wounded thee with *w.*
Hos. 5:13 Jud. saw his *w.* could
Ob. 7 have laid a *w.* under thee
Mic. 1:9 her *w.* is incurable
Rev. 13:3 *w.* was healed, 12, 14

WOUNDS.

2 K. 8:29 king J. went to be heal.
  of the *w.* 9:15 ; *2 Chr.* 22:6
Job 9:17 he multiplied my *w.*
Ps. 38:5 my *w.* stink, corrupt
  147:3 and bindeth up their *w.*
Prov. 18:8 talebearer as *w.* 26:22
  23:29 hath *w.* without cause?
  27:6 faithful are *w.* of a friend
Is. 1:6 no soundness in it, but *w.*
Jer. 6:7 before me is grief and *w.*
  30:17 I will heal thee of thy *w.*
Zec. 13:6 are th. *w.* in thy hands?
Luke 10:34 Samari. bound up *w.*

WOUND, Verb.

Deut. 32:39 I *w.* and I heal
Ps. 68:21 God sh. *w.* his enemies
  110:6 *w.* heads ov. many countr.
1 Cor. 8:12 ye *w.* their conscience

WOUND.

John 19:40 th. *w.* body of Jesus
Acts 5:6 yo. men *w.* up Ananias

WOUNDED.

Deut. 23:1 he that is *w.* in stones
1 Sam. 17:52 *w.* of Philistines
2 Sam. 22:39 I have *w.* mine enemies, *Ps.* 18:38
1 K. 20:37 in smiting he *w.* him
  22:34 for I am *w. 2 Chr.* 18:33
2 Chr. 35:23 for I am sore *w.*
Job 24:12 soul of *w.* crieth out
Ps. 64:7 suddenly sh. they be *w.*
  69:26 grief of those th. hast *w.*

109:22 my heart is *w.* within me
Prov. 7:26 cast down many *w.*
  18:14 a *w.* spirit who can bear?
Cant. 5:7 found me, they *w.* me
Is. 51:9 art not it that *w.* drag.?
  53:5 he was *w.* for our transgr.
Jer. 30:14 I *w.* thee with wound
  37:10 th. remained but *w.* men
  51:52 thro' land *w.* shall groan
Lam. 2:12 they swooned as *w.*
Ezek. 26:15 when the *w.* cry
  28:23 *w.* be judged in the midst
  30:24 groanings of a *w.* man
Joel 2:8 fall on sword, not be *w.*
Zec. 13:6 *w.* in house of my frie.
Mark 12:4 *w.* him, *Luke* 20:12
Luke 10:30 am. thieves, *w.* him
Acts 19:16 fled out house nak. *w.*
Rev. 13:3 his heads as it were *w.*

WOUNDEDST, ETH.

Job 5:18 *w.* hands make whole
Hab. 3:13 thou *w.* head of wick.

WOUNDING.

Gen. 4:23 slain a man to my *w.*

WRAP.

Is. 28:20 he can *w.* himself in it
Mic. 7:3 reward, so they *w.* it up

WRAPPED, *or* WRAPT.

Gen. 38:14 Tamar *w.* herself
1 Sam. 21:9 sword is *w.* in cloth
1 K. 19:13 Elijah *w.* his face
2 K. 2:8 mantle, *w.* it together
Job 8:17 roots are *w.* about heap
  40:17 sinews of stones *w.* togeth.
Ezek. 21:15 swo. is *w.* for slaug.
Jon. 2:5 weeds *w.* about head
Mat. 27:59 Jos. *w.* body in linen,
  Mark 15:46 ; *Luke* 23:53
Luke 2:7 Mary *w.* him in clothes
  12 babe *w.* in swaddl. clothes
John 20:7 napkin *w.* together

WRATH.

(*Gen.* 49:7 cursed be their *w.*
Lev. 10:6 lest *w.* come upon peo.
Num. 1:53 no *w.* be on cong. 18:5
  16:46 there is *w.* gone out fr. L.
Deut. 9:7 provokedst L. to *w.* 22
  29:28 rooted them out in *w.*
  32:27 were it not I feared *w.*
Jos. 9:20 lest *w.* be upon us
  22:20 *w.* fell on all the congre.
2 Sam. 11:20 if king's *w.* arise
2 K. 23:26 L. turned not from *w*
1 Chr. 27:24 because th. fell *w.*
2 Chr. 19:2 theref. is *w.* on thee
  10 and so *w.* come upon you
  24:18 *w.* came on Ju. for tresp.
  28:13 there is fierce *w.* ag. Isr.
  29:10 his *w.* may turn away
  32:25 theref. th. was *w.* on him
Ezr. 5:12 had provoked G. to *w.*
  7:23 why sho. be *w.* ag. realm?
Neh. 13:18 bri. more *w.* upon Is.
Est. 1:18 th. arise too much *w.*
  2:1 *w.* of king was appeased
  3:5 bowed not, Ham. full of *w.*
  7:10 then was king's *w.* pacified
Job 5:2 for *w.* killeth foolish man
  19:29 for *w.* brings punishments
  21:20 drink of *w.* of Almighty
  36:13 hypocri. in heart heap *w.*
  18 because there is *w.* beware
Ps. 37:8 forsake *w.* 55:3 *w.* hate
  76:10 *w.* of man sh. praise thee
  138:7 stre. hand ag. *w.* of ene.
Prov. 11:23 exp. of wicked is *w*
  12:16 fool's *w.* presently known
  14:29 slow to *w.* of great under.
  15:1 soft answer turn. away *w.*
  16:14 *w.* of king as messeng. of
  19:12 king's *w.* as roar. of lion
  19 man of *w.* suffer punishm.
  21:14 rew. in bosom pacifieth *w.*
  24 scorner, who dealeth in *w.*
  27:3 fool's *w.* heavier than both
  4 *w.* is cruel, anger is outrage.

29:8 wise men turn away *w.*
  30:33 forcing of *w.* bring. strife
Ec. 5:17 much *w.* with sickness
Is. 13:9 day of L. cometh with *w.*
  14:6 who smote the people in *w.*
  54:8 in a little *w.* I hid my face
Jer. 21:5 fight against you in *w.*
  32:37 driven them in great *w.*
  44:8 provoke me to *w.* wi. idols
Ezek. 7:12 *w.* is on all multitude
Nah. 1:2 reserv. *w.* for enemies
Hab. 3:2 in *w.* remember mercy
Zep. 1:18 gold not deliver in *w.*
Zec. 7:12 a great *w.* from Lord
  8:14 fathers provoked me to *w.*
Mat. 3:7 flee from *w.* to come,
  Luke 3:7
Luke 4:28 fill. wi. *w. Acts* 19:28
  21:23 th. sh. be *w.* on this peo.
Rom. 2:5 treasurest up *w.* agai.
  8 to them th. obey unright. *w.*
  4:15 because law worketh *w.*
  5:9 be saved from *w.* thro' him
Rom. 9:22 ves. of *w.* fit. to destr.
  12:19 rather give place to *w.*
  13:4 minister of G. to execu. *w.*
  5 ye be subject, not only for *w.*
Gal. 5:20 works of flesh are *w.*
Eph. 2:3 by nature childr. of *w.*
  4:26 let not sun go do. upon *w.*
  31 let all *w.* anger, and clamor
  6:4 provoke not your chil. to *w.*
Col. 3:8 put off these, *w.* malice
1 Thes. 1:10 delivered us from *w.*
  2:16 for *w.* is come on them
  5:9 G. hath not appoi. us to *w.*
1 Tim. 2:8 lift. hands without *w.*
Heb. 11:27 not fearing *w.* of king
Jam. 1:19 slow to spe. slow to *w.*
  20 *w.* of man work. not right.
Rev. 6:16 hide us fr. *w.* of Lamb
  12:12 devil come, hav. great *w.*
  14:8 nations drink of *w.* 18:3

Day of WRATH.

Job 20:28 flow away in *d. of w.*
  21:30 wicked brou. to *day of w.*
Ps. 110:5 strike kings in *d. of w.*
Prov. 11:4 riches profit not in
  the *day of w.*
Zep. 1:15 that day is a *day of w.*
Rom. 2:5 treasu. w. ag. *d. of w.* ·
Rev. 6:17 great *d. of w.* is come

WRATH of God.

2 Chr. 28:11 *w. of God* upon you
Ezr. 10:14 *w. of God* be turned
Ps. 78:31 *w. of God* ca. on them
John 3:36 *w. of G.* abid. on him
Rom. 1:18 *w. of God* is revealed
Eph. 5:6 *w. of God* com. *Col.* 3:6
Rev. 14:10 dr. wine of *w. of God*
  19 into wine-press of *w. of G.*
  15:1 for th. is filled up *w. of G.*
  7 seven vials full of *w. of God*
Rev. 16:1 pour vial of *w. of God*
  19:15 tread. wine-pr. of *w. of G.*

His WRATH.

Deut. 29:23 L. overthr. in *his w.*
1 Sam. 28:18 execu. *h. w.* on A.
2 K. 23:26 L. turned not fr. *h. w.*
2 Chr. 29:10 *his* fierce *w.* may
  turn from us, 30:8
Ezr. 8:22 *his w.* is against them
Est. 7:7 from banquet in *his w.*
Job 16:9 he teareth me in *his w.*
  20:23 cast fury of *his w.* on him
Ps. 2:5 speak to them in *his w.*
  21:9 swallow them up in *his w.*
  58:9 take them away in *his w.*
  78:38 did not stir up all *his w.*
  49 cast on th. fierceness of *h. w.*
  106:23 Mo. stood to turn *his w.*
Prov. 14:35 *his w.* ag. him that
  24:18 lest L. turn *his w.* fr. him
Is. 16:6 Moab's pride and *his w.*
Jer. 7:29 L. forsak. gen. of *h. w.*
  10:10 at *his w.* earth sh. tremble
  48:30 I know *his w.* saith Lord

Lam. 2:2 thrown down in *his w.*
3:1 affliction by rod of *his w.*
Amos 1:11 kept *his w.* for ever
Rom. 9:22 G. will. to show *h. w.*
Rev. 16:19 cup of wine of *his w.*

See KINDLED, *Wrath of the* LORD.

My WRATH.

Ex. 22:24 *my w.* shall wax hot
32:10 that *my w.* may wax hot
Num. 25:11 hath turned *my w.*
2 *Chr.* 12:7 *my w.* shall not be
    poured out
Ps. 95:11 I sware in *my w.*
Is. 10:6 against people of *my w.*
60:10 for in *my w.* I smote thee
Ezek. 7:14 *my w.* is on multitude
13:15 thus will I accomp. *my w.*
21:31 in fire of *my w.* 22:21
22:31 I consu. them with *my w.*
38:19 in fire of *my w.* ha. I spo.
Hos. 5:10 I will pour *my w.* on
13:11 I took him away in *my w.*
Heb. 3:11 I sware in *my w.* they
4:3 as I have sworn in *my w.*

Thy WRATH.

Ex. 15:7 thou sentest *thy w.*
32:11 why doth *t. w.* wax hot ?
12 turn from *t. w.* and repent
Job 14:13 until *thy w.* be past
40:11 cast abroad rage of *thy w.*
Ps. 38:1 rebuke me not in *t. w.*
79:6 pour out *t. w.* on heathen
85:3 thou hast taken away *t. w.*
88:7 *thy w.* lieth hard on me
    16 *thy* fierce *w.* goeth over me
89:46 how long shall *thy w.*
    burn like fire ?
90:7 by *thy w.* are we troubled
9 days are passed away in *t. w.*
11 acc. to thy fear, so is *t. w.*
102:10 bec. of indigna. and *t. w.*
Jer. 18:20 to turn *thy w.* fr. them
Hab. 3:8 was *thy w.* ag. the sea
Rev. 11:18 *t. w.* is come, time of

WRATHFUL.

Ps. 69:24 let *w.* anger take hold
Prov. 15:18 a *w.* man stir. strife

WRATHS.

2 *Cor.* 12:20 envyings, *w.* strifes

WREATH, S.

1 *K.* 7:17 *w.* for the chapiters
2 *Chr.* 4:2 two *w.* to cover the
    two pommels
13 400 pomegranates on two *w.*
two rows of pomeg. on *w.*

WREATHED, EN.

Ex. 28:14 two chains at ends of
    w. work, 22, 24, 25 ; 39:15–18
2 *K.* 25:17 pillar of *w.* work he
Lam. 1:14 my transgres. are *w.*

WREST.

Ex. 23:2 many, to *w.* judgment
6 not *w.* judgment of thy poor
Deut. 16:19 shalt not *w.* judgm.
Ps. 56:5 ev. day th. *w.* my words
2 *Pet.* 3:16 that are unstable *w.*

WRESTLE.

Eph. 6:12 we *w.* not against flesh

WRESTLED.

Gen. 30:8 have I *w.* with sister
32:24 there *w.* a man with him
25 thigh out of joint as he *w.*

WRESTLINGS.

Gen. 30:8 wi. *w.* have I wrestled

WRETCHED.

Rom. 7:24 O *w.* man that I am
Rev. 3:17 know. not thou art *w.*

WRETCHEDNESS.

Num. 11:15 let me not see my *w.*

WRING, ED.

Lev. 1:15 priest *w.* off head, 5:8
Jud. 6:38 Gide. *w.* dew of fleece
Ps. 75:8 wicked sh. *w.* them out

WRINGING.

Prov. 30:33 *w.* of nose bri. blood

WRINKLE, S.

Job 16:8 hast filled me with *w.*
Eph. 5:27 not having spot or *w.*

WRITE.

Ex. 34:1 will *w.* on ta. *Deut.* 10:2
27 L. said to Mo. *w.* th. words
Num. 17:2 *w.* every man's name
3 *w.* Aaron's name on rod of L.
Deut. 6:9 *w.* them on posts, 11:20
24:1 let him *w.* her a bill of di-
    vorcement, 3 ; *Mark* 10:4
27:3 *w.* the words of this law, 8
31:19 *w.* ye this song for you
2 *Chr.* 26:22 acts of U. did Is. *w.*
Ezr. 5:10 *w.* the names of men
Neh. 9:38 sure coven. and *w.* it
Est. 8:8 *w.* ye also for the Jews
Prov. 3:3 *w.* on tab. of heart, 7:3
Is. 8:1 *w.* in great roll wi. a pen
10:1 *w.* grievousness prescribed
19 that a child may *w.* them
30:8 *w.* it before them in a table
Jer. 22:30 *w.* ye this man childl.
30:2 *w.* the words I have spok-
    en, 36:2, 17, 28
31:33 *w.* in th. hearts, *Heb.* 8:10
Ezek. 24:2 *w.* the na. of the day
37:16 *w.* for Judah and Israel
43:11 *w.* it in their sight
Hab. 2:2 *w.* the vision on tables
Luke 1:3 it seem. good to *w.* th.
16:6 *w.* fifty ; 7 *w.* fourscore
John 1:45 Mos. and prop. did *w.*
19:21 *w.* not, king of the Jews
Acts 15:20 *w.* that th. abstain fr.
25:26 no cert. thi. to *w.* my lord
1 *Cor.* 4:14 I *w.* not to sha. you
14:37 things I *w.* are command.
2 *Cor.* 1:13 we *w.* none other thi.
2:9 I *w.* that I might know
9:1 it is superfluous to *w.* you
13:2 I *w.* to th. wh. have sinned
10 I *w.* these thi. being absent
Gal. 1:20 things I *w.* unto you
Phil. 3:1 to *w.* the same things
1 *Thes.* 4:9 not that I *w.* 5:1
2 *Thes.* 3:17 is the token ; so I *w.*
1 *Tim.* 3:14 these *w.* I unto thee
Heb. 10:16 in minds will I *w.*
2 *Pet.* 3:1 I *w.* to you, **1** *John* 2:1
1 *John* 1:4 th. thi. *w.* we to you
2:7 I *w.* no new commandmn
    8 a new commandm. I *w.* you
12 I *w.* to you, lit. children, 13
13 I *w.* to you, fathers
2 *John* 12 many th. to *w.* to you
3 *John* 13 not wi. ink and pen *w.*
Jude 3 it was needful to *w.*
Rev. 1:11 what seest *w.* 19
Rev. 2:1 angel of ch. of Ephe. *w.*
8 angel of chur. of Smyrna *w.*
12 angel of chu. in Pergam. *w.*
18 angel of chu. in Thyatira *w.*
3:1 angel of church in Sardis *w.*
7 angel of chu. in Philadel. *w.*
12 I will *w.* on him new name
14 angel in ch. of Laodicea *w.*
10:4 abo. to *w.* voice said *w.* not
14:13 *w.* bles. are dead die in L.
19:9 *w.* bless. are called to sup.
21:5 *w.* words true and faithful

See BOOK.

WRITER.

Jud. 5:14 that handle pen of *w.*
Ps. 45:1 tong. is pen of ready *w.*
Ezek. 9:2 *w.* inkhorn by his si. 3

WRITEST, ETH.

Job 13:26 thou *w.* bitter things
Ps. 87:6 shall count wh. he *w.* up
Ezek. 37:20 sticks whereon th. *w.*

WRITING.

Ex. 32:16 the *w.* was *w.* of God
39:30 on plate of holy cro. a *w.*
Deut. 10:4 wrote acco. to first *w.*

31:24 wh. Mos. made end of *w.*
1 *Chr.* 28:19 L. made me und. *w.*
2 *Chr.* 2:11 Hur. answered in *w.*
21:12 a *w.* from Elij. to Jehoram
35:4 prepare accord. to *w.* of D.
36:22 Cyrus put the proclama-
    tion in *w. Ezr.* 1:1
Ezr. 4:7 *w.* of letter in Sy. tong.
Est. 1:22 sent letters accordi. to
    w. whereof, 3:12 : 8:9 ; 9:27
3:14 copy of *w.* published to all
4:8 Mord. gave Hata. copy of *w.*
8:8 the *w.* in the king's name
Is. 38:9 the *w.* of Hezekiah
Ezek. 13:9 not in *w.* of ho. of Is.
Dan. 5:7 whoso sh. read this *w.*
8 they could not read the *w.*
15 th. they should read this *w.*
16 if thou canst read the *w.*
17 I will read *w.* to the king
24 this is *w.* that was writ. 25
6:8 establ. decree, and sign *w.*
9 Darius signed *w.* and decree
10 Daniel knew *w.* was signed
Mat. 5:31 let him give her a *w.*
    of divorcement, 19:7
John 19:19 *w.* was, Jesus of Naz.

WRITING-TABLE.

Luke 1:63 Zacha. asked for *w.-t.*

WRITINGS.

John 5:47 if ye believe not his *w.*

WRITTEN.

Ex. 31:18 *w.* with the finger of
    God, *Deut.* 9:19
1 *K.* 21:11 elders did as it was *w.*
1 *Chr.* 4:41 *w.* by name sm. tents
2 *Chr.* 30:5 not kept passo. as *w.*
Ezr. 8:34 weight of ves. was *w.*
Nah. 6:6 sent letter wh. was *w.*
8:14 found *w.* in law to dwell
Est. 1:19 *w.* amo. laws of Medes
3:9 let it be *w.* that they may be
12 name of Ahasue. was it *w.*
8:5 *w.* to reverse Ham.'s letters
Ps. 69:28 not *w.* with righteous
102:18 *w.* for generati. to come
149:9 to execute judgment *w.*
Prov. 22:20 have not I *w.* to thee
Ec. 12:10 which was *w.* was up-
    right
Jer. 17:13 depart from me be *w.*
36:29 *w.* king of Baby. sh. come
Ezek. 2:10 *w.* within and witho.
13:9 *w.* in writ. of house of Ju.
Dan. 5:24 the writing was *w.* 25
Mat. 27:37 set up his accusat. *w.*
Mark 11:17 *w.* my hou. be called
15:26 his accusation was *w.* K.
    of J. *Luke* 23:38 ; *John* 19:20
Luke 4:17 place where it was *w.*
10:20 your names are *w.* in hea.
18:31 thi. *w.* be accompli. 21:22
John 3:17 remembered it was *w.*
10:34 is it not *w.* in your law
20:31 *w.* that ye might believe
21:25 if should be *w.* every one
Acts 13:29 fulfill. all that was *w.*
21:25 touching Ge. we have *w.*
Rom. 2:15 work of the law *w.*
4:23 not *w.* for his sake alone
1 *Cor.* 10:11 *w.* for our admonit.
2 *Cor.* 3:2 epistle *w.* in hearts
3 *w.* not with ink, but S. of G.
7 minis. of death *w.* in stones
Phile. 19 I Paul have *w.*
Heb. 12:23 church of first-born *w.*
Rev. 1:3 things wh. are *w.* ther.
2:17 in stone a new name *w.*
13:8 whose names are not *w.*
14:1 Fa.'s name *w.* in foreheads
Rev. 17:5 up. head was *w.* Myst.
19:12 name *w.* on his thigh, 16
21:12 names *w.* on the gates

Is WRITTEN.

Jos. 1:8 do all that *is w.* therein
2 *K.* 22:13 wh. *is w.* concern. us

Est. 8:8 *is w.* in king's name
Is. 4:3 that is *w.* among living
Jer. 17:1 sin of Judah *is w.*
Dan. 9:11 curse that *is w.* in law
Luke 10:26 what *is w.* in law ?
20:17 what is this that *is w. ?*
22:37 *is w.* must be accomplish.
John 15:25 be fulfilled that is *w.*
1 *Cor.* 4:6 to think ab. that *is w.*
9:10 for our sakes this *is w.*
15:54 he bro. to pass that *is w.*

It is WRITTEN.
Jos. 8:31 as *it is w.* in the law of
Moses, 1 *K.* 2:3; 2 *Chr.* 23:18;
25:4; 31:3; 35:12 *Ezr.* 3:2, 4;
6:18; *Neh.* 8:15; 10:34, 36;
Dan. 9:13
Ps. 40:7 in book *it is w.* of me,
Heb. 10:7
Is. 65:6 *it is w.* before me
Mat. 2:5 thus *it is w. Luke* 24:46
11:10 of whom *it is w. Luke* 7:27
26:24 as *it is w.* of him, *Mark*
9:13; 14:21, 27
31 *it is w. Luke* 4:8; *Acts* 23:5
Mark 9:12 *it is w.* of Son of man
Luke 2:23 *it is w.* in law of Lord
Rom. 11:8 according as *it is w*
1 *Cor.* 1:31; 2 *Cor.* 4:13
12:19 *it is w.* 14:11; *Gal.* 3:10
15:3 pleas. not himself, *it is w.*
1 *Cor.* 15:45 *it is w.* first man **A.**
1 *Pet.* 1:16 *it is w.* be ye holy

I have, or have I WRITTEN.
Hos. 8:12 *I have w.* of my law
John 19:22 what *I ha. w. I h. w.*
1 *John* 2:14 *I h. w.* to you fath.
26 these things *have I w.* 5:13

Were WRITTEN.
Num. 11:26 they were of them
that *were w.*
Job 19:23 O that my words *w. w.*
Luke 24:44 be fulfilled wh. *w. w.*
John 12:16 th. thi. *w. w.* of him
Rom. 15:4 whatsoever thi. *w. w.*
See BOOK.

WRONG.
Gen. 16:5 my *w.* be upon thee
Ex. 2:13 to him that did the *w.*
Deut. 19:16 to testify what is *w.*
Jud. 11:27 *w.* to war against me
1 *Chr.* 12:17 no *w.* in my hands
16:21 he suffered no man to do
them *w. Ps.* 105:14
Est. 1:16 not done *w.* to king
Job 19:7 cry out of *w.* not heard
Jer. 22:13 do no *w.* no violence
13 that buildeth chambers *w.*
Lam. 3:59 thou hast seen my *w.*
Hab. 1:4 *w.* judgment proceed.
Mat. 20:13 frie. I do thee no *w.*
Acts 7:24 see. one of th. suffer *w.*
26 why do ye *w.* one to anot. ?
27 he that did his neighbor *w.*
18:14 a matter of *w.* or lewdness
25:10 P. said, Have I done no *w.*
1 *Cor.* 6:7 why do ye not rather
take *w. ?*
8 ye do *w.* defraud brethren
2 *Cor.* 7:12 his cause th. done *w.*
12:13 burdensome, forg. this *w.*
Col. 3:25 doth *w.* receive for *w.*

WRONGED, ETH.
Prov. 8:36 sinneth *w.* own soul

2 *Cor.* 7:2 we have *w.* no man
Phile. 18 if he hath *w.* thee

WRONGFULLY.
Job 21:27 devices ye *w.* imagine
Ps. 35:19 let not enemi. *w.* rejoi.
38:19 that hate me *w.* multipli.
69:4 being mine enemies *w.*
119:86 they persecute me *w.*
Ezek. 22:29 oppressed strang. *w.*
1 *Pet.* 2:19 grief, suffering *w.*

WROTE.
Ex. 24:4 Moses *w.* all the words
of the Lord, *Deut.* 31:9
34:28 L. *w.* on tables words of
coven. *Deut.* 4:13; 5:22; 10:4
Num. 33:2 Moses *w.* their goings
Deut. 31:22 Moses *w.* this song
1 *Sam.* 10:25 Sam. *w.* manner of
2 *Sam.* 11:14 Dav. *w.* a letter, **15**
1 *K.* 21:8 Jezebel *w.* letters, **9**
2 *K.* 10:1 and Jehu *w.* letters, **6**
Chr. 24:6 Shemaiah *w.* bef. king
2 *Chr.* 30:1 Hezekiah *w.* to Eph.
Ezr. 4:6 *w.* accusation aga. Jud.
8 Rehum *w.* a letter ag. Jer. **9**
Est. 8:5 Haman *w.* to destroy J.
Jer. 51:60 Jerem. *w.* all the evil
Dan. 5:5 man's hand *w.* on wall
7:1 dream, and he *w.* the dream
Mark 10:5 Moses *w.* this precept
12:19 Moses *w.* to us, *Luke* 20:28
Luke 1:63 Zacharias *w.* saying
John 5:46 for Moses *w.* of me
8:6 wi. his fing. *w.* on ground, 8
19:19 Pilate *w.* title, and put it
21:24 John *w.* of these things
Acts 15:23 apostles *w.* let. by th.
18:27 brethren *w.* exhorting
23:25 Lysias *w.* after this man.
Rom. 16:22 I Terti. who *w.* this
1 *Cor.* 5:9 Paul *w.* in an epistle,
2 *Cor.* 2:3, 4 ; 7:12 ; *Eph.* 3:3 ;
Phile. 21
7:1 things whereof ye *w.* to me
2 *John* 5 not as th. I *w.* new com.
3 *John* 9 I *w.* to the church

WROTH.
Gen. 4:5 and Cain was very *w.*
6 L. sa. to C. Why art th. *w. ?*
31:26 Jacob was *w.* 34:7 sons *w.*
40:2 Pharaoh was *w.* 41:10
Ex. 16:20 and Moses was very *w.*
Num. 16:15; 31:14
16:22 wilt thou be *w.* with
Deut. 1:34 L. heard, was *w.* 3:26;
9:19 ; 2 *Sam.* 22:8 ; 2 *Chr.*
28:9 ; *Ps.* 18:7 ; 78:21, 59, 62
1 *Sam.* 18:8 S. was very *w.* 20:7
29:4 prince of Ph. *w.* with him
2 *Sam.* 3:8 Abner *w.* 13:21 D. *w.*
2 *K.* 5:11 but Naaman was *w.*
13:19 man of God *w.* with him
2 *Chr.* 16:10 Asa *w.* 26:19 Uz. *w.*
Neh. 4:1 Sanballat was *w.* took
Est. 1:12 theref. the king was *w.*
2:21 Bigthan and Teresh *w.*
Ps. 89:38 been *w.* with anointed
Is. 28:21 *w.* as in val. of Gibe.
47:6 I was *w.* with my people
54:9 I would not be *w.* with th.
57:16 nor will I be always *w.*
17 for iniquity of his covetousness was I *w.*
64:5 thou art *w.* we have sinned

9 be not *w.* very sore, O Lord
Jer. 37:15 the princes were *w.*
Lam. 5:22 th. art very *w.* ag. us
Mat. 2:16 Her. was exceeding *w.*
18:34 his lord was *w.* and deliv.
22:7 and the king was very *w.*
Rev. 12:17 the dragon was *w.*

WROUGHT, actively.
Gen. 34:7 Shechem *w.* folly in Is.
Ex. 10:2 what things I *w.* in E.
36:1 then *w.* Bezaleel and Ahol.
4 wise men *w.* work, 8 ; 39:6
Num. 23:23 what hath God *w. ?*
Deut. 17:2 hath *w.* wickedness
22:21 hath *w.* folly in Israel,
Jos. 20:10
31:18 for evils they sh. have *w.*
Ruth 2:19 show. with wh. she *w.*
1 *Sam.* 6:6 L. had *w.* wonderful.
11:13 hath *w.* salva. in Isr. 19:5
14:45 Jonathan hath *w.* with G.
2 *Sam.* 23:10 L. *w.* great vict. 12
1 *K.* 5:16 ev. people that *w.* 9:23
2 *K.* 17:11 Is. *w.* wick. *Neh.* 9:18
21:6 Manasseh *w.* much wickedness, 2 *Chr.* 33:6
2 *Chr.* 24:12 hir. such as *w.* iron
13 workmen *w.* work, 34:10, 13
Neh. 4:16 my serv. *w.* in work
17 every one with hand *w.*
Job 12:9 hand of L. hath *w.* this
36:23 say, thou hast *w.* iniqu. ?
Ps. . 31:19 hast *w.* for them that
68:28 strength. th. thou hast *w.*
78:43 had *w.* his signs in Egypt
Ec. 2:11 works my hands *w.*
Is. 26:12 th. hast *w.* works in us
18 ha. not *w.* any deliverance
41:4 who hath *w.* and done it ?
Jer. 18:3 he *w.* a work on wheels
Ezek. 20:9 I *w.* for my name's
sake, 14, 22, 44
29:20 because they *w.* for me
Dan. 4:2 won. that God hath *w.*
Jon. 1:11 sea *w.* tempestuous, 13
Zep. 2:3 who *w.* his judgment
Mat. 20:12 have *w.* but one hour
26:10 she hath *w.* a good work
Mark 14:6
Acts 15:12 wonders God *w.* 21:19
18:3 abode with Aquila and *w.*
Rom. 15:18 Ch. ha. not *w.* by me
2 *Cor.* 5:5 *w.* us for same thi. G.
Gal. 2:8 th. *w.* effectually in Pet.
Eph. 1:20 which he *w.* in Christ
Jam. 2:22 faith *w.* with works ?
1 *Pet.* 4:3 to have *w.* will of Gen.
2 *John* 8 lose not thi. we have *w.*

WROUGHT, passively.
Num. 31:51 took of them *w.* jew.
Deut. 21:3 heifer ha. not been *w.*
Neh. 6:16 this work was *w.* of G.
Ps. 45:13 her clothing of *w.* gold
139:15 in secret, curiously *w.*
Ec. 2:17 work *w.* under sun
John 3:21 manif. th. are *w.* in G.
Acts 5:12 wonders *w.* am. people

WROUGHTEST.
Ruth 2:19 sa. to her, wh. *w.* th. ?

WRUNG.
Lev. 1:15 blood sh. be *w.* out, 5:9
Ps. 73:10 wat. of cup *w.* to them
Is. 51:17 ha. *w.* out dregs of cup

Y

YARN.
1 *K.* 10:28 Solomo. had linen *y.*
out of Egypt, 2 *Chr.* 1:16

YEA.
Mat. 5:37 conve. be *y. Jam.* 5:12
2 *Cor.* 1:17 sho. be *y. y.* and nay
18 word toward you was not *y.*

19 for Son of God was not *y.*
20 promises of G. in him are *y.*

YEAR.
Gen. 17:21 Sar. shall bear next *y.*
Ex. 12:2 first month of the *y.*
23:14 keep feast in *y. Lev.* 23:41
29 not drive them out in one *y.*

Lev. 16:34 atonement once a *y.*
25:5 a *y.* of rest ; 29 within a *y.*
Num. 9:22 if *y.* that cloud tarried
14:34 for a *y.* sh. ye bear iniqu.
Jos. 5:12 eat fruit of Can. that *y.*
Jud. 10:8 that *y.* Am. vexed Isr.
11:40 to lament four days in *y.*

YEAR (continued)

17:10 give thee ten shek. by y.
1 Sam. 27:7 David dwelt y. and
1 K. 9:25 in a y. did Solom. offer
2 K. 19:29 eat this y. such things
    as grow of themsel. 1s. 37:30
Est. 9:27 keep two days every y.
Ps. 65:11 crowned y. with goodn.
Is. 6:1 in y. that Uzziah died
    21:16 in a y. glory of Kedar fail
    61:2 procl. acc. y. of L. Lu. 4:19
    63:4 y. of my redeemed is come
Jer. 11:23 y. of visit. 23:12 ; 48:44
    17:8 not careful in y. of drought
    28:16 saith L. th. y. th. shalt die
    51:46 rumor both come in one y.
Ezek. 4:6 appoin. each day for y.
    46:17 be his to the y. of liberty
Luke 2:41 went to Jerusal. ev. y.
    13:8 Lord, let it alone this y.
Acts 11:26 whole y. they assem.
2 Cor. 8:10 to be forward a y. ago
    9:2 Achaia was ready a y. ago
Heb. 9:7 pri. went in once a y. 25
    10:3 remembrance of sins ev. y.
Jam. 4:13 continue there a y.
Rev. 9:15 prepare for month, a y.

YEAR after YEAR.

2 Sam. 21:1 fam. 3 years y. a. y.

YEAR by YEAR.

Deut. 14:22 tithe inc. of thy seed
    field bringeth forth y. by y.
    15:20 eat before Lord y. by y.
1 Sam. 1:7 as he did so y. by y.
1 K. 10:25 they brought a rate y.
    by y. 2 Chr. 9:24
2 K. 17:4 as he had done y. by y.
Neh. 10:34 wood-offering. y. by y.
Heb. 10:1 they offered y. by y.

YEAR to YEAR.

Ex. 13:10 ordinance from y. to y.
1 Sam. 2:19 brou. coat fr. y. to y.
    7:16 Samuel went from y. to y.
2 Chr. 24:5 rep. house fr. y. to y.
Is. 29:1 add ye y. to y. let them
Zec. 14:16 fr. y. to y. to worship
See SECOND, THIRD, SEVENTH.

YEARLY.

Lev. 25:53 a y. serv. shall he be
Jud. 11:40 went y. to lament
    21:19 a feast of L. in Shiloh y.
1 Sam. 1:3 E. went y. to worship
    21 went to offer y. sacrifi. 2:19
    20:6 a y. sacrifice for family
Est. 9:21 keep 15th of same y.

YEARS.

Gen. 1:14 for seasons, days, y.
    25:7 days of the y. of Abraham
    8 Abraham died full of y.
    47:9 evil have y. of my life been
Ex. 34:22 feast at the y. end
Lev. 25:15 accord. to y. 16, 50, 52
    27:18 accord. to y. that remain
Deut. 32:7 y. of many generations
Jos. 13:1 Jos. was stricken in y.
1 Sam. 29:3 Da. been with th. y.
1 K. 1:1 David was stricken in y.
1 K. 17:1 not dew nor rain th. y.
2 Chr. 14:6 and Asa had no war
    in those y.
Job 10:5 thy y. as man's days
    15:20 num. of y. hid. to oppres.
    16:22 when a few y. are come
    32:7 multit. of y. teach wisdom
    36:11 spend their y. in pleasure
    26 nor can his y. be searched
Ps. 31:10 my y. spent with sigh.
    61:6 prol. y. as many generatio.
    77:5 the y. of ancient times
    10 the y. of the right hand
    78:33 their y. did he consume
    90:4 a thous. y. in thy sight are
    but as yesterday, 2 Pet. 3:8
    9 sp. our y. as a tale th. is told
    10 y. are threescore y. and ten
    15 y. wherein we ha. seen evil
    102:24 y. throughout all genera.

27 thy y. shall have no end
Prov. 4:10 y. of life many, 9:11
    5:9 lest thou give y. unto cruel
    10:27 y. of wicked sh. be short.
Ec. 12:1 nor y. draw nigh
Is. 21:16 accord. to y. of hireling
    38:10 I am deprived of my y.
    15 I shall go softly all my y.
Ezek. 4:5 on thee y. of th. iniq.
    22:4 thou art come unto thy y.
    38:8 latter y. th. come into land
Dan. 9:2 I underst. number of y.
    11:6 end of y. they join togeth.
    8 more y. than king of north
    13 king of north shall come
    after certain y.
Joel 2:2 y. of many generations
    25 restore y. locust hath eaten
Hab. 3:2 thy work in midst of y.
Mal. 3:4 offerings as in former y.
Luke 1:7 both were stri. in y. 18
Gal. 4:10 ye obse. months and y.
Heb. 1:12 thy u. shall not fail
    11:24 M. wh. come to y. refused
Rev. 20:2 bound Satan a thou. y.
    3 till thousand y. be fulfilled, 4
    7 when thousand y. are expir.

See Numeral words in their
    places, as HUNDRED, MANY,
    TWO, THREE, SIX, OLD.

YELL, ED

Jer. 51:38 like lions, they sh. y.
    2:15 lions roared and y. on him

YELLOW.

Lev. 13:30 if th. be in it a y. hair
    32 if th. be in it no y. hair, 36
Ps. 68:13 covered with y. gold

YEARN, ED.

Gen. 43:30 for his bowels did y.
1 K. 3:26 her bowels y. upon son

YESTERDAY.

Ex. 5:14 why not fulfill. task y. ?
1 Sam. 20:27 son of J. to meat y.
    15:20 thou camest but y.
2 K. 9:26 seen y. blood of Naboth
Job 8:9 we are of y. know noth.
Ps. 90:4 a thous. years, but as y.
John 4:52 y. the fever left him
Acts 7:28 kill me as Egyptian y.
Heb. 13:8 same y. and for ever

YESTERNIGHT.

Gen. 19:34 I lay y. with my fath.
    31:29 G. of your father spake y.
    42 affliction, rebuked thee y.

YIELD.

Gen. 4:12 earth not y. her stren.
    49:20 shall y. royal dainties
Lev. 19:25 y. to you the increase
    26:4 land shall y. her increase
    20 your land not y. her increa.
2 Chr. 30:8 y. yoursel. to the L.
Ps. 67:6 land y. her incre. 85:12
    107:37 may y. fruits of increase
Prov. 7:21 fair speech cau. him y.
Is. 5:10 ten acres sh. y. one bath
Hos. 8:7 the bud shall y. no meal
Joel 2:22 fig-tree y. strength
Hab. 3:17 altho' fields y. no meat
Acts 23:21 do not th. y. unto th.
Rom. 6:13 y. yourselves to God
    16 that to whom ye y. yoursel.
    19 y. members to righteous.
Jam. 3:12 no fount. y. salt water

YIELDED.

Gen. 49:33 Jacob y. up the ghost
Num. 17:8 rod of Aa. y. almonds
Dan. 3:28 y. th. bodies that they
Mat. 27:50 Jesus y. up the ghost
Rom. 6:19 ye have y. your mem.

YIELDETH.

Neh. 9:37 y. increase to kings
Job 24:5 wildern. y. food for th.
Heb. 12:11 y. fruit of righteous-
    ness

YIELDING.

Gen. 1:11 forth herb y. seed   12
    29 given you every tree y. seed
Ec. 10:4 y. pacifie. great offences
See FRUIT.

YOKE.

Gen. 27:40 break his y. Jer. 30:8
Lev. 26:13 I have broken the
    bands of your y. Ezek. 34:27
Num. 19:2 heif. on which never
    came y. Deut. 21:3 ; 1 Sa. 6:7
Deut. 28:48 he sh. put a y. of iron
    upon thy neck, Jer. 28:14
1 Sam. 11:7 S. took a y. of oxen
    14:14 wh. a y. of oxen mi. plow
1 K. 12:14 thy father made our y.
    griev. 10, 11, 14 ; 2 Chr. 10:4
    19:19 plowing wi. 12 y. of oxen
    21 took a y. of oxen, slew them
Job 1:3 Job had 500 y. of oxen
    42:12 had a thousand y. of oxen
Is. 9:4 thou hast broken the y. of
    his burden, 10:27 ; 14:25
    47:6 hast very heavi. laid thy y.
    58:6 and that ye break every y.
Jer. 2:20 of old time brok. thy y.
    5:5 these have broken thy y.
    27:8 will not put neck under y.
    11 bring their neck under y. 12
    28:2 broken y. of king of B. 4, 11
    12 H. had broken y. from Jer.
    31:18 bullock unaccustom. to y.
    51:23 break husband. and his y.
Lam. 1:14 y. of my transgres-
    sions is bound
    3:27 good for a man to bear y.
Hos. 11:4 as they that take off y.
Nah. 1:13 now will I break his y.
Mat. 11:29 take my y. upon you
    30 my y. is easy, burden light
Luke 14:19 I bought 5 y. of oxen
Acts 15:10 put y. on disciples'
    neck
Gal. 5:1 be not entangled with y.
1 Tim. 6:1 as many as under y.

YOKES.

Jer. 27:2 make bonds and y.
    28:13 hast broken y. of wood
Ezek. 30:18 when I break y. of E

YOKED.

2 Cor. 6:14 be not unequally y.

YOKE-FELLOW.

Phil. 4:3 I entreat thee, true y.-f.

YONDER.

Gen. 22:5 I and the lad will go y.
Num. 16:37 scatter th. the fire y.
    23:15 stand here, I meet Lord y.
Mat. 17:20 say, Rem. to y. place

YOUNG.

Gen. 31:38 she-goats not cast y.
    33:13 flocks with y. are with me
Ex. 23:26 nothing cast their y.
Lev. 22:28 shall not kill it and y.
Deut. 22:6 not take dam with y.
    7 let the dam go and take the y.
    28:50 not show favor to the y.
    32:11 as the eagle over her y.
1 Chr. 22:5 S. my son is y. 29:1
2 Chr. 13:6 when Rehob. was y.
    34:3 Josiah, while he was yet y.
Ps. 78:71 ewes great with y.
    84:3 where she may lay her y.
Is. 40:11 those that are with y.
Ezek. 17:4 cropped y. twigs, 22
Mark 7:25 y. dau. unclean spirit
John 21:18 y. thou gird. thyself
See OLD.

YOUNG ass, or asses.

Is. 30:6 carry riches on y. asses
    24 y. a. sh. eat clean provender
John 12:14 when he found a y. a.
See BULLOCK.

YOUNG bullocks.
Num. 28:11 offer two *y. b.* 19, 27
Ezr. 6:9 gi. what th. need, *y. b.*

YOUNG calf.
Lev. 9:2 take *y. c.* for sin-offering
See CHILD, CHILDREN

YOUNG cow.
Is. 7:21 man sh. nourish a *y. cow*

YOUNG dromedaries.
Est. 8:10 lett. by riders on *y. d.*

YOUNG eagles.
Prov. 30:17 *y. eagles* shall eat it

YOUNG hart.
Cant. 2:9 belo. like *y. h.* 17; 8:14
See LION, LIONS, MAN, MEN.

YOUNG one.
Deut. 28:57 evil toward her *y. o.*
Zec. 11:16 neither seek *y. one*

YOUNG ones.
Deut. 22:6 whether *y. o.* or eggs
Job 38:41 when his *y. o.* cry to G.
39:3 they bring forth their *y. o.*
4 their *y. o.* are in good liking
16 ostrich is harden. aga. *y. o.*
30 eagles' *y. o.* suck up blood
Is. 11:7 *y. o.* lie down together
Lam. 4:3 give suck to their *y. o.*

YOUNG pigeon.
Gen. 15:9 turtle-dove and *y. p.*
Lev. 12:6 bring *y. p.* for sin-offer.

YOUNG pigeons.
Lev. 1:14 bring his offer. of *y. p.*
5:7 he sh. bring two *y. pigeons*,
12:8 ; 14:22, 30 ; 15:14, 29 ;
Num. 6:10 ; *Luke* 2:24
11 if not able to bring 2 *y. p.*

YOUNG ravens.
Ps. 147:9 he giveth food to *y. r.*

YOUNG roes.
Cant. 4:5 breasts like *y. roes*, 7:3

YOUNG virgin.
1 K. 1:2 let there be sought a *y. v.*

YOUNG virgins.
Jud. 21:12 were found 400 *y. v.*
Est. 2:2 let *y. v.* be sou. for king
3 may gather together *y. v.*

YOUNG unicorn.
Ps. 29:6 and Sirion like a *y. u.*

YOUNG woman.
Ruth 4:12 L. give th. of this *y. w.*

YOUNG women.
Tit. 2:4 teach *y. w.* to be sober

YOUNGER.
Gen. 9:24 knew what *y.* son done
19:31 first-born said to the *y.* 34
38 the *y.* bare a son Ben-ammi
25:23 elder serve *y. Rom.* 9:12
29:18 I will serve 7 years for *y.*
26 it must not be so, to give *y.*
43:29 is this your *y.* brother of
48:14 Is. laid right ha. on the *y.*
19 *y.* brother be greater th. he
Jud. 1:13 *y.* brother took it, 3:9
15:2 is not her *y.* sister fairer ?
1 Sam. 14:49 Saul's *y.* daughter
1 Chr. 24:31 against *y.* brethren
Job 30:1 that are *y.* than I, have
Ezek. 16:46 thy *y.* sister is Sodom
Luke 15:12 *y.* said, Gi. me portion
13 *y.* gathered all, took journ.
22:26 greatest, let him be as *y.*
1 Tim. 5:1 entreat *y.* as brethren
2 the *y.* women as sisters, with
11 *y.* widows refuse, for when
14 I will that *y.* women marry
1 Pet. 5:5 *y.* submit to the elder

YOUNGEST.
Gen. 42:13 *y.* is with our fath. 32
15 except your *y.* brother com.
20, 34 ; 44:23, 26
43:33 *y.* according to his youth
44:2 cup in sack's mouth of *y.*
Jos. 6:26 in his *y.* son set up
gates, *1 K.* 16:34
Jud. 9:5 Jotham, *y.* son, was left
1 Sam. 16:11 there remains yet *y.*
17:14 David was *y.* the eldest
2 Chr. 21:17 none left save the *y.*
22:1 made Ahaz. his *y.* son king

YOURS.
2 Chr. 20:15 battle not *y.* God's
2 Cor. 12:14 I seek not *y.* but you

YOUTH.
Gen. 8:21 imagina. evil fr. his *y.*
43:33 youngest accord. to his *y.*
46:34 from our *y.* even till now
Lev. 22:13 in fa.'s house as in *y.*
Num. 30:3 in fa.'s house in *y.* 16
Jud. 8:20 the *y.* drew not sword
1 Sam. 17:33 a man of war fr. *y.*
42 a *y.* of fair countenance
55 said, Whose son is this *y. ?*
2 Sam. 19:7 evil befell thee fr. *y.*
1 K. 18:12 I fear Lord from *y.*
Job 13:26 possess iniqu. of my *y.*

20:11 bones full of sins of his *y.*
29:4 as I was in days of my *y.*
30:12 on my right hand rise *y.*
31:18 fr. *y.* he was brought up
33:25 shall return to days of *y.*
36:14 hypocrites die in *y.* and
Ps. 25:7 remember not sins of *y.*
71:5 art my trust from my *y.*
17 hast taught me from my *y.*
88:15 ready to die from my *y.*
89:45 days of his *y.* thou short.
103:5 thy *y.* renew. like eagle's
110:3 th. hast the dew of thy *y.*
127:4 so are children of thy *y.*
129:1 have afflicted me fr. my *y.*
144:12 as plants grown up in *y.*

Prov. 2:17 forsak. guide of her *y.*
5:18 rejoice with wife of thy *y.*
Ec. 11:9 rejoi. O man, in thy *y.*
10 childhood and *y.* are vanity
12:1 remember thy Creator in *y.*
Is. 47:12 has labored from *y.*
15 thy merchants fr. *y.* wander
54:4 sh. forget shame of thy *y.*
6 Lord called thee as wife of *y.*
Jer. 2:2 I remember kindn. of *y.*
3:4 thou art the guide of my *y.*
24 labor of our fathers from *y.*
25 our fathers from *y.* sinned
22:21 thy manner from thy *y.*
31:19 I did bear reproa. of my *y.*
32:30 only done evil fr. their *y.*
48:11 Moab been at ease from *y.*
Lam. 3:27 he bear yoke in his *y.*
Ezek. 4:14 not polluted fr. my *y.*
16:22 not remem. days of *y.* 43
60 rememb. my covenant in *y.*
23:3 committed whored. in *y.*
3 in *y.* they lay with her
19 call to remembra. her *y.* 21
Hos. 2:15 sing as in days of *y.*
Joel 1:8 as virgin for husb. of *y.*
Zec. 13:5 to keep cattle fr. my *y.*
Mal. 2:14 and the wife of thy *y.*
15 treach. again. wife of his *y.*
Mat. 19:20 th. have I kept fr. my
y. Mark 10:20 ; *Luke* 18:21
Acts 26:4 manner of life fr. my *y.*
1 Tim. 4:12 no man desp. thy *y.*

YOUTHS.
Prov. 7:7 among *y.* a young man
Is. 40:30 even the *y.* shall faint

YOUTHFUL.
2 Tim. 2:22 flee also *y.* lusts, but

Z

ZACCHEUS.
Luke 19:5 Z. haste, come down

ZACHARIAH, ZECHA-RIAH.
2 K. 14:29 Z. reigned, 15:8, 11
18:2 Abi dau. of Z. *2 Chr.* 29:1
1 Chr. 5:7 of Reubeni. Jeiel, Z.
9:21 Z. of Levit. 15:18, 24 ; 26:2
37 Geder, Ahio, Z. and Mickl.
16:5 to Asaph, Z. 24:25 Issh. Z.
26:11 Z. the 4th son of Hosah
14 Z. son of Shelemiah, wise
27:21 ruler was Iddo son of Z.
2 Chr. 17:7 Jehoshap. sent to Z.
20:14 Jahaziel son of Z. came
21:2 Jeiiel and Z. sons of Jeho.
24:20 Spirit of G. came upon Z.
26:5 sought G. in the days of Z.
29:13 Asaph, Z. sancti. himself
34:12 Z. of the Kohathites was
35:8 Hilkiah, Z. rulers of house
Ezr. 5:1 Z. son of Iddo prophes.
to J. in Jud. 6:14 ; *Neh.* 12:16
8:3 of Pharo. Z. 11 of Bebai, Z.
10:26 Elam, Z. *Neh.* 11:4 Z. son

Neh. 8:4 Ezra's left ha. stood Z.
11:5 Z. son of Shiloni ; 12 Pash.
12:35 Z. son of Jonathan, 41
Is. 8:2 Z. the son of Jeberechiah
Zec. 1:1 Z. son of Barachiah, 7 ;
Mat. 23:35 ; *Luke* 11:51
Luke 1:5 Z. a priest of the course
13 fear not, Z. 59 called him Z.

ZADOK.
2 Sam. 8:17 Z. and Abim. priests
15:29 Z. carried the ark of God
35 hast not with thee Z. ?
20:25 Z. and Abiathar, *1 K.* 4:4
1 K. 1:8 but Z. was not with, 26
45 Z. and Nathan have anoint.
2:35 Z. the priest, *1 Chr.* 29:22
4:2 Azariah son of Z. the priest
2 K. 15:33 dau. of Z. *2 Chr.* 27:1
1 Chr. 6:8 Ahitub begat Z. 12, 53
12:28 Z. a yo. man, mighty man
24:3 both Z. sons of El. and Ah.
27:17 of Aaronites Z. was capt.
2 Chr. 31:10 priest of house of Z.
Ezr. 7:2 son of Shall. son of Z.
Neh. 3:4 Z. repaired, 29 ; 10:21

11:11 the son of Z. Meshullam
13:13 I made Z. scribe treasurer
Ezek. 40:46 the sons of Z. 43:19 :
44:15
48:11 priests sanc. of sons of Z.

ZALMUNNA.
Jud. 8:5 pursu. aft. Zeba and Z.
6 hands of Zeba Z. in, 15
21 Gideon slew Zeba and Z.
Ps. 83:11 princes as Zeba and Z.

ZARAH.
Gen. 38:30 son called Z. 46:12
1 Chr. 2:4 Pharez and Z. *Mat.* 1:3
6 sons of Z. Zimri, and Ethan
See ZERAH.

ZAREPHATH.
1 K. 17:9 get thee to Z. 10
Ob. 20 of Israel sh. possess to Z.

ZEAL.
2 Sam. 21:2 slay them in his *z.*
2 K. 10:16 see my *z.* for the Lord
19:31 *z.* of L. do this, *Is.* 37:32
Ps. 69:9 the *z.* of thy house hath
eaten me up, *John* 2:17

119:139 my z. hath consum. me
Is. 9:7 z. of L. will perform this
59:17 was clad wi. z. as a cloak
63:15 wh. is thy z. and stren. ?
Ezek. 5:13 I have spoken it in z.
Rom. 10:2 they have a z. of God
2 *Cor.* 7:11 what z. ? 9:2 your z.
Phil. 3:6 concerning z. persecut.
Col. 4:13 hath a great z. for you

ZEALOUS.
Num. 25:11 was z. for my sake
13 he was z. for his God, made
Acts 21:20 they are all z. of law
22:3 z. towards God, *Gal.* 1:14
1 *Cor.* 14:12 z. of spiritual gifts
Tit. 2:14 people, z. of good works
Rev. 3:19 be z. theref. and repent

ZEALOUSLY.
Gal. 4:17 they z. affect you, not
18 it is good to be z. affected

ZEBAH. *See* ZALMUNNA.

ZEBEDEE.
Mat. 4:21 in ship with Z. father
10:2 James and John sons of Z.
26:37 ; *Mark* 1:19 ; 3:17 ; 10:35 ;
Luke 5:10 ; *John* 21:2
20:20 mother of Z. childr. 27:56
Mark 1:20 their father Z. in ship

ZEBOIM.
Gen. 14:2 king of Z. *Deut.* 29:23
1 *Sam.* 13:18 valley of Z. to the
Neh. 11:34 of Benja. dwelt at Z.
Hos. 11:8 shall I set thee as Z. ?

ZEBUL.
Jud. 9:28 Jerubba. Z. his officer
41 Z. thrust out Baal and bre.

ZEBULUN.
Gen. 30:20 L. called his name Z.
35:23 Reuben, Simeon, Jud. Z.
46:14 the sons of Z. *Num.* 1:30 ;
26:26
49:13 Z. shall dwell at haven
Num. 1:9 of Z. 2:7 ; 7:24 ; 10:16
Deut. 27:13 curse ; Reu. Gad, Z.
33:18 of Z. and Issac, Rejoice Z.
Jos. 19:10 lot came up for Z.
Jud. 1:30 Z. drive out inhabita.
4:10 Barak called Z. and Naphtali
5:14 out of Z. that handle pen
18 Z. and Naphtali jeoparded
6:35 he sent messengers to Z.
12:12 E. buried in country of Z.
Ps. 68:27 the princes of Z. and
Is. 9:1 lightly afflicted land of Z.
Ezek. 48:26 Z. a portion ; 33 gate
Mat. 4:13 in the borders of Z.
15 land of Z. and Nephthalim
Tribe of ZEBULUN.
Num. 1:31 numbered of t. of Z.
2:7 t. of Z. Eliab captain, 10:16
13:10 of t. of Z. Gaddiel to spy
34:25 prince of t. of Z. to divide
Jos. 21:7 t. of Z. 34 ; 1 *Chr.* 6:77
Rev. 7:8 of t. of Z. sealed 12,000

ZEDEKIAH.
1 *K.* 22:11 Z. made, 2 *Chr.* 18:10
24 Z. smote Mic. 2 *Chr.* 18:23
2 *K.* 24:17 changed name to Z.
25:7 of Z. *Jer.* 39:6, 7 ; 52:11
1 *Chr.* 3:15 son of Josiah, Z. 16
2 *Chr.* 36:10 made Z. his br. king
Jer. 21:7 deliver Z. and his peo.
29:22 Lord make thee like Z.
32:4 Z. shall not escape from
5 shall lead Z. to Babylon
Jer. 39:5 army overtook Z. 52:8

ZELOPHEHAD.
Num. 26:33 Z. had no sons, *Jos.*
17:3
27:7 daught. of Z. speak right
36:11 daughters of Z. married

ZELZAH.
1 *Sam.* 10:2 men by sepulc. at Z.

ZENAS.
Tit. 3:13 bring Z. on his journey

ZEPHANIAH.
2 *K.* 25:18 took Z. *Jer.* 52:24
1 *Chr.* 6:36 Z. of sons of Kohath.
Jer. 21:1 when Zedekiah sent Z.
29:25 letters in thy name to Z.
29 Z. read this letter in ears
37:3 Z. son of Maaseiah priest
Zep. 1:1 the word came to Z.
Zec. 6:10 house of Jos. son of Z.
14 sh. be to Hen the son of Z.

ZERAH.
Gen. 36:13 sons of Reuel, Z.
1 *Chr.* 1:37, 44
33 Jobab the son of Z. reigned
Num. 26:13 of Z. family of, 20
Jos. 7:1 son of Zabdi, son of Z.
22:20 son of Z. commit a tresp.
1 *Chr.* 4:24 sons of Sim. were Z.
6:21 Z. son of Iddo, 41 son of Z.
9:6 of sons of Z. Jeuel dwelt in
2 *Chr.* 14:9 Z. Ethiopian came
Neh. 11:24 Pethah. of chil. of Z.

ZERESH.
Est. 5:10 called for Z. his wife

ZERUBBABEL.
1 *Chr.* 3:19 son of Pedaiah, Z.
Ezr. 2:2 ca. up wi. Z. *Neh.* 12:1
3:2 Z. son of Shealtiel, 8 ; 5:2
Neh. 12:47 days of Z. gave port.
Hag. 1:1 word of the Lord to Z.
12 then Z. obeyed the voice of
14 Lord stirred up spirit of Z.
2:4 yet now be strong, O Z. 21
Zec. 4:6 word of Lord unto Z.
7 before Z. sh. become a plain
9 the hands of Z. have laid the

ZERUIAH.
2 *Sam.* 2:18 three sons of Z.
3:39 sons of Z. too hard for me
8:16 Joab son of Z. 1 *Chr.* 18:15
16:10 what have I to do with
you, ye sons of Z. ? 19:22
1 *Chr.* 2:16 whose sisters were Z.

ZIBA.
2 *Sam.* 9:2 art thou Z. ? 10 Z. had
16:4 Z. thine are all that pertain
19:29 thou and Z. divide land

ZIBEON.
Gen. 36:2 Anah daugh. of Z. 14
24 these are the children of Z.
1 *Chr.* 1:40 fed asses of Z. 29

ZIDON.
Gen. 49:13 border shall be to Z.
Jos. 11:8 chased th. to great Z.
19:28 Kanah, even unto great Z.
Jud. 10:6 and served gods of Z.
18:28 because it was far from Z.
1 *K.* 17:9 which belongeth to Z.
Ezr. 3:7 drink unto them of Z.
Is. 23:2 merch. of Z. replenished
4 O Z. the sea hath spoken
12 O thou virgin, daught. of Z.
Jer. 25:22 kings of Z. shall drink
27:3 and yokes to king of Z.
47:4 Tyre and Z. every helper
Ezek. 27:8 the inhabitants of Z.
28:21 set thy face against Z.
22 behold, I am ag. thee, O Z.
Joel 3:4 with me, O Tyre and Z.
Zec. 9:2 Tyrus and Z. though it

ZIDONIANS.
Jud. 10:12 Z. and Amalekites
18:7 careless, after manner of Z.
1 *K.* 11:1 Sol. loved women of Z.
33 Ashtoreth, goddess of Z.
Ezek. 32:30 Z. th. are gone down

ZIF.
1 *K.* 6:1 month of Z. is second
37 foundation laid in month Z.

ZIKLAG.
1 *Sam.* 27:6 Achish gave Z. to D.
30:14 we burnt Z. with fire

2 *Sam.* 1:1 D. abode 2 days in Z.
4:10 I slew them in Z.
1 *Chr.* 4:30 dw. at Z. *Neh.* 11:28
12:1 came to David to Z. 20

ZILPAH.
Gen. 29:24 Lab. gave to Leah Z.
30:9 Leah gaze Z. her maid to
10 Z. bare Jacob a son, 12
25:26 sons of Z. Gad, A. 46:18
37:2 lad was with the sons of Z.

ZIMRI.
Num. 25:14 th. was slain was Z.
1 *K.* 16:9 Z. conspired against, 16
15 Z. reigned 7 days in Tirzah
2 *K.* 9:31 had Z. peace, who ?
1 *Chr.* 2:6 sons of Zerah, Z. and
8:36 Z. son of Jehoadah, 9:42
Jer. 25:25 I made kings of Z. dr.

ZIN.
Num. 13:21 from wildern. of Z.
20:1 I came to desert of Z. 33:36
27:14 in desert of Z. *Deut.* 32:51

ZION.
2 *Sam.* 5:7 David took strong-
hold of Z. 1 *Chr.* 11:5
1 *K.* 8:1 which is Z. 2 *Chr.* 5:2
Ps. 2:6 on my holy hill of Z.
48:12 walk about Z. go round
about her

Ps. 51:18 thy good pleas. unto Z.
69:35 for God will save Z. and
87:2 the Lord loveth gates of Z.
5 said of Z. this and that man
97:8 Z. heard and was glad
102:13 and have mercy on Z.
16 when Lord shall build up Z.
126:1 L. turned captivity of Z.
129:5 be turned back th. hate Z.
132:13 the Lord hath chosen Z.
133:3 as dew on mountains of Z.
137:1 when we remembered Z.
3 sing us one of the son. of Z.
146:10 the Lord shall reign, O Z.
147:12 praise thy God, O Z.
149:2 let children of Z. be joyful
Is. 1:27 Z. shall be redeemed
12:6 shout, th. inhabitant of Z.
14:32 that Lord hath founded Z.
33:5 hath filled Z. with judgm.
20 look on Z. 35:10 come to Z.
34:8 for controversy of Z.
40:9 O Z. bringest good tidings
41:27 sh. say to Z. behold them
49:14 Z. said, L. hath forsaken
51:3 the Lord shall comfort Z.
11 sh. come with singing to Z.
16 say unto Z. Th. art my peo.
52:1 put on thy strength, O Z.
7 saith unto Z. Thy G. reigneth
8 Lord shall bring again Z.
59:20 Redeemer sh. come to Z.
60:14 Z. of the Holy One of Is.
62:1 for Z. sake will I not hold
64:10 Z. is a wilderness, Jerusa.
66:8 as soon as Z. travailed, she
Jer. 3:14 I will bring you to Z.
4:6 set up standard towards Z.
14:19 hath thy soul loathed Z.?
26:18 Z. shall be plow. *Mic.* 3:12

Jer. 30:17 Z. whom no man seek.
31:6 let us go up to Z. to the
12 and sing in height of Z.
50:5 they sh. ask the way to Z.
51:35 shall the inhabitant of Z.
Lam. 1:4 ways of Z. do mourn
17 Z. spreads forth her hands
4:2 sons of Z. compara. to gold
5:18 mountain of Z. is desolate
Joel 2:23 be glad, ye child. of Z.
Amos 1:2 Lord will roar from Z.
Mic. 3:10 th. build Z. with blood
4:2 for law shall go forth of Z.
11 let our eye look upon Z.

Zec. 1:14 I am jealous for Z. with
17 Lord shall yet comfort Z.
2:7 deliver thyself, O Z. 8:2
8:3 Lord, I am returned to Z.
9:13 raised up thy sons, O Z.

See DAUGHTER, DAUGHTERS.

In ZION.

Ps. 9:11 sing praises to L. who
dwell. *in* Z. 76:2 ; *Joel* 3:21
65:1 praise for thee, O G. *in* Z.
84:7 every one *in* Z. appeareth
99:2 L. is great *in* Z. he is high
102:21 decl. name of Lord *in* Z.
Is. 4:3 that is left *in* Z. shall be
10:24 O my peo. dwellest *in* Z.
28:16 beh. I lay *in* Z. for a foundation, a tried st. 1 *Pet.* 2:6
30:19 people shall dwell *in* Z.
31:9 the L. whose fire is *in* Z.
33:14 sinners *in* Z. are afraid
46:13 I will place salva. *in* Z.
61:3 them that mourn *in* Z.
Jer. 8:19 is not the Lord *in* Z. ?
50:28 declare *in* Z. vengeance
51:10 let us decl. *in* Z. the work
Jer. 51:24 evil that they have
done *in* Z.

Lam. 2:6 sabbaths forgot. *in* Z.
4:11 L. hath kindled fire *in* Z.
5:11 they ravished women *in* Z.
Joel 2:1 blow the trumpet *in* Z.
3:17 your God dwelling *in* Z.
Amos 6:1 that are at ease *in* Z.
Rom. 9:33 *in* Z. a stumbl. stone

Mount ZION.

2 *K.* 19:31 a remnant, they that
escape out of *mount* Z. *Is.*
37:32
Ps. 48:2 joy of earth is *mount* Z.
11 *m.* Z. rejoice ; 78:68 *m.* Z.
74:2 *m.* Z. wherein thou hast
125:1 as *m.* Z. cannot be remo.
Is. 4:5 dwelling-place of *m.* Z.
8:18 which dwell. in *mo.* Z. 18:7
10:12 perform. work upon *m.* Z.
24:23 Lord shall reign in *m.* Z.
29:8 fight aga. *m.* Z. 31:4 for
Joel 2:32 in *m.* Z. deliver. *Ob.* 17
Ob. 21 shall come up on *m.* Z.
Mic. 4:7 reign over th. in *m.* Z.
Heb. 12:22 are come unto *m.* Z.
Rev. 14:1 Lamb stood on *m.* Z.

Out of ZION.

Ps. 14:7 come *out of* Z. 53:6
20:2 streng. thee *o. of* Z. 110:2
128:5 bless thee *o. of* Z. 134:3
135:21 blessed be Lord *o. of* Z.
Is. 2:3 *out of* Z. shall go forth
Jer. 9:19 wail. is heard *out of* Z.
Joel 3:16 L. shall roar *out of* Z.
Rom. 11:26 come *out of* Z. deliv.

ZIPPORAH.

Ex. 2:21 Jethro gave Moses Z.
4:25 Z. took sharp stone, 18:2

ZOAN.

Num. 13:22 seven years bef. Z.
Ps. 78:12 things did he in Z. 43
Is. 19:11 princes of Z. fools, 13

30:4 for his princes were at Z.
Ezek. 30:14 I will set fire in Z.

ZOAR.

Gen. 14:2 of Bela, which is Z. 8
19:22 name of city was called Z.
Deut. 34:3 city of palm-tr. to Z.
Is. 15:5 fugitives sh. flee unto Z.
Jer. 48:34 uttered th. voice fr. Z.

ZOBAH.

1 *Sam.* 14:47 against kings of Z.
2 *Sam.* 8:3 Da. smote king of Z.
1 *K.* 11:24 ; 1 *Chr.* 18:3, 9
23:36 Igal son of Nathan of Z.
1 *K.* 11:23 fled from king of Z.

ZOPHAR.

Job 2:11 Z. Naamath. 11:1 ; 42:9

ZORAH.

Jos. 19:41 inheritance of Dan, Z.
Jud. 13:2 a certain man of Z.
25 Sams. bet Z. and Eshtaol
16:31 bur. Samson bet. Z. and
18:2 Danites sent from Z. to
8 came unto their breth. to Z.
2 *Chr.* 11:10 Rehoboam built Z.

ZOROBABEL.

Mat. 1:12 Salathiel begat Z. 13
Luke 3:27 Rhesa was son of Z.

ZUR.

Num. 25:15 daughter of Z. slain
31:8 Z. prince slain, *Jos.* 13:21
1 *Chr.* 8:30 Z. son of Gib. 9:36

ZUZIM.

Gen. 14:5 kings smote Z. in H.